The American Institute of Architects Legal Citator

STEVEN G.M. STEIN

THE AMERICAN INSTITUTE OF ARCHITECTS LEGAL CITATOR

STEVEN G.M. STEIN
Stein, Ray & Conway
Editor-in-Chief

1998 Edition

MATTHEW♦BENDER

QUESTIONS ABOUT THIS PUBLICATION?

For questions about the **Editorial Content** appearing in these volumes or reprint permission, please call:

Vincent F. Terrasi, J.D., at .... 1-800-252-9257 Ext. 2799
Internet Address: VTerrasi@bender.com
Thomas Backen, J.D., at .... 1-800-252-9257 Ext. 2591
Internet Address: TBacken@bender.com
Linda J. Folkman, J.D., at .... 1-800-252-9257 Ext. 2249
Internet Address: LFolkman.backen@bender.com

Outside the United States and Canada please call .... (212) 448-2000

For assistance with replacement pages, shipments, billing or other customer service matters, please call:

Customer Services Department at .... (800) 833-9844
Outside the United States and Canada, please call .... (518) 487-3000
Fax number .... (518) 487-3584

For information on other Matthew Bender publications, please call
Your account manager or .... (800) 223-1940
Outside the United States and Canada, please call .... (518) 487-3000

ISBN 0-8205-2482-4

This publication is designed to provide accurate and authoritative information in regard to the subject matter covered. It is sold with the understanding that the publisher is not engaged in rendering legal, accounting, or other professional services. If legal advice or other expert assistance is required, the services of a competent professional should be sought.

Copyright © 1998 By Matthew Bender & Company Incorporated
All Rights Reserved. Printed in United States of America.
No copyright is claimed in the text of statutes, regulations, and excerpts from court opinions quoted within this work. Permission to copy material exceeding fair use, 17 U.S.C. §107, may be licensed for a fee of $1 per page per copy from the Copyright Clearance Center, 222 Rosewood Drive, Danvers, MA. 01923, telephone (508) 750-8400.

MATTHEW BENDER

MATTHEW BENDER & CO., INC.
Editorial Offices
2 Park Avenue, New York, NY 10016-5675 (212) 448-2000
201 Mission St., San Francisco, CA 94105-1831 (415) 908-3200

1. AIA copyrighted material from AIA Documents A101, A111, A201, and B141 has been reproduced with the permission of The American Institute of Architects under permission number 96150. Further reproduction is prohibited.

2. Because AIA Documents are revised from time to time, users should ascertain from the AIA the current edition of these documents.

3. Copies of the current edition of these AIA documents may be purchased from The American Institute of Architects or its local distributors.

4. These AIA Documents and their various provisions contained in this Citator are not intended to be used as "model text." (Text taken from an existing document and incorporated, without attribution, into a newly created document is model text.) Rather, the AIA documents are intended to be used as standard forms which, in turn, are used as originals by the contracting parties with modifications being made by appending separated amendments or supplements or by filling in the blank spaces provided on the forms for user-specific information.

Material in this publication is also published in the fifth and sixth volume of *Construction Law* (Steven G.M. Stein, ed.).

The American Institute of Architects does not endorse and has not assisted in the preparation of Volumes 1 through 4 of *Construction Law*.

Table of Contents

How to Use the Citator (following this red divider card)

    A. Description H-1

    B. Organization H-1

    C. Research Example H-4

Document Reference Charts (following the second red divider card)

    A Series: Owner-Contractor Documents A-1

        Document Cross-Reference Charts A-5

        Document to Case Charts A-17

    B Series: Owner-Architect Documents B-1

        Document Cross-Reference Charts B-5

        Document to Case Charts B-7

    C Series: Architect-Consultant Documents C-1

        Document Cross-Reference Charts C-5

        Document to Case Charts C-7

Cases (following the third red divider card) 1

Table of Cases (following the last red divider card) TC-1

HOW TO USE THE CITATOR

A. Description

This edition of the *Citator* is a completely updated version of the *AIA Building Construction Legal Citator*, originally published by The American Institute of Architects in 1966. The *AIA Citator* is an important research tool that provides the user with the key cases that interpret the widely used AIA documents and AIA document language. The *Citator* includes charts that direct the user to cases interpreting particular AIA document provisions, as well as digests of those cases decided since 1974.

B. Organization

The *Citator* is divided into two main sections: document reference charts and cases.

Charts

The document reference charts are organized by document series as follows: A Series, Owner-Contractor Documents; B Series, Owner-Architect Documents, and C Series, Architect-Consultant Documents. For each document series, the *Citator* supplies two kinds of charts. The first type of chart, a "Document Cross-Reference Chart," lists comparable Articles in different editions of the same AIA document. Given the name or topic of an Article in one edition, the corresponding Article in other editions may be readily found from the chart. For example, under the Article title, "Work," in the "A101 Cross-Reference Chart" one can find the comparable Articles in the 1963, 1967, 1970, 1974, 1977 and 1987 editions. The listings in each chart are limited to Article titles (Paragraph titles are also supplied for A201, the General Conditions, and for the two latest editions of B141, the Standard Owner-Architect Agreement); the chart is not meant to be a comprehensive subject index.

The second type of chart, the "Document to Case Chart," is the key to using the *Citator*. The Document to Case Charts are organized chronologically by document number and edition. Each document is broken down by specific provisions (either by Articles or by Articles and Paragraphs), and under each provision is a list of the cases, by *Citator* Case Reference Number, which interpret that provision. (For the sake of convenience, the older cases included in the *Citator* are listed under editions of the documents that were not yet published when the cases were decided.)

Citator Case Reference Numbers are used to quickly find the cases on point in the "Cases" section of the *Citator*.

HOW TO USE THE CITATOR

The format of a typical Document to Case chart entry is:

A101-1963　STANDARD FORM OF AGREEMENT BETWEEN OWNER AND CONTRACTOR WHERE THE BASIS OF PAYMENT IS A STIPULATED SUM

Article 1 Scope of the Work

　　I
　　　　67002-IL
　　　　66001-MI
　　　　67001-MO
　　　　67003-TX

The primary heading is the number, edition, and title of the AIA document. Subheadings are the Articles (and sometimes Paragraphs) of the document, with their numbers and titles. Under each subheading, the cases that refer or are relevant to that document are divided into three categories:

　　I　cases involving an AIA document provision or identical language
　　II　cases probably involving an AIA document provision or similar language
　　III　cases that are analogous and helpful.

Each case has a five-digit *Citator* Case Reference Number and a suffix. The first two digits represent the year the case was decided and the other three identify the individual case. (The few cases in the *Citator* decided before 1900 omit these first two digits in order to avoid confusion with more recent cases.) The suffix is an abbreviation of the jurisdiction in which the case was decided. State courts, as well as courts for the District of Columbia and Puerto Rico, at all levels are indicated by the two-letter postal service abbreviation for the state:

HOW TO USE THE CITATOR

Abbreviations

Alabama	AL	Nebraska	NE
Alaska	AK	Nevada	NV
Arizona	AZ	New Hampshire	NH
Arkansas	AR	New Jersey	NJ
California	CA	New Mexico	NM
Colorado	CO	New York	NY
Connecticut	CT	North Carolina	NC
Delaware	DE	North Dakota	ND
District of Columbia	DC	Ohio	OH
Florida	FL	Oklahoma	OK
Georgia	GA	Oregon	OR
Hawaii	HI	Pennsylvania	PA
Idaho	ID	Puerto Rico	PR
Illinois	IL	Rhode Island	RI
Indiana	IN	South Carolina	SC
Iowa	IA	South Dakota	SD
Kansas	KS	Tennessee	TN
Kentucky	KY	Texas	TX
Louisiana	LA	Utah	UT
Maine	ME	Vermont	VT
Maryland	MD	Virginia	VA
Massachusetts	MA	Virgin Islands	VI
Michigan	MI	Washington	WA
Minnesota	MN	West Virginia	WV
Mississippi	MS	Wisconsin	WI
Missouri	MO	Wyoming	WY
Montana	MT		

Federal District Courts are indicated by district and state:

Northern District	ND (state abbreviation)
Southern District	SD
Eastern District	ED
Western District	WD
Middle District	MD
Central District	CD

Other federal court abbreviations are as follows:

Circuit Courts of Appeal	1CIR, 2CIR, DCCIR
Court of Claims or Claims Court	CC
Supreme Court	US

HOW TO USE THE CITATOR

This paperback version of the *AIA Citator* contains enhanced "Document to Case Charts" for the A101, A111, A201 and B141 documents. Preceding the case listings for the individual Articles or Paragraphs of these documents, you'll find the full text of the AIA provisions that the listed cases interpret.

Cases

In this section of the *Citator*, the cases are listed numerically by *Citator* Case Reference Number. Following the case citation is a list of AIA documents. If the case interprets the language of an AIA document or is otherwise helpful to an understanding of that document, the document will be included in this list. For cases decided from 1974 to the present, the user will also find a complete digest of the case.

A typical entry in the Cases section follows:

74002   Amelco Window Corp. v. Federal Ins. Co., 127 N.J. Super. 342, 317 A.2d 398 (App. Div. 1974)

    I: A201-1970, Art. 4, Para. 4.4

   II: A201-1970, Art. 7, Para. 7.5

  III: A311, Performance Bond

(A case digest appears here if the case was decided in 1974 or thereafter.)

C. Research Example

If you want to find out how the cases have interpreted Paragraph 7.4 of the 1976 edition of AIA Document A201, you would turn to the Document to Case chart for A201, 1976 Edition. You would then find the subheading in the chart to Paragraph 7.4. Under this subheading you will find several *Citator* Case Reference Numbers. The subheading for Paragraph 7.4 looks like this:

Paragraph 7.4 Claims for Damages

    I

        81028-NY

        78052-ND

   III

        77053-CA

Since cases 81028 and 78052 are listed under category I, you know that these two cases deal with this particular AIA provision or identical language. Since case 77053 is listed under category III, you know that this case is relevant to the point covered by this AIA provision, but does not specifically deal with this AIA provision or identical language.

The chart also tells you that case 81028 was decided in 1981 by a New York state court, case 78052 was decided in 1978 by a North Dakota court, and case 77053 was decided in 1977 by a California state court.

HOW TO USE THE CITATOR

By turning to the Cases section of the *Citator*, you will find the name of each of these three cases, as well as the citation and a digest for each case.

You should also use the Document Cross-Reference Chart to locate comparable provisions in different editions of the same AIA document, where additional cases on point may be found. (While it is usually possible to determine what AIA document is the source of the language interpreted in a case, it is not always possible to determine what edition of the document the language came from.) Since the Document Cross-Reference Chart is organized alphabetically by topic, you will also find this chart useful if you are not aware of which Article or Paragraph in the document covers the topic or contains the language for which you are looking.

Document Charts

A Series

Owner-Contractor Documents

---

1. AIA copyrighted material from AIA Documents A101, A111, A201, and B141 has been reproduced with the permission of The American Institute of Architects under permission number 96150. Further reproduction is prohibited.

2. Because AIA Documents are revised from time to time, users should ascertain from the AIA the current edition of these documents.

3. Copies of the current edition of these AIA documents may be purchased from The American Institute of Architects or its local distributors.

4. These AIA Documents and their various provisions contained in this Citator are not intended to be used as "model text." (Text taken from an existing document and incorporated, without attribution, into a newly created document is model text.) Rather, the AIA documents are intended to be used as standard forms which, in turn, are used as originals by the contracting parties with modifications being made by appending separated amendments or supplements or by filling in the blank spaces provided on the forms for user-specific information.

A SERIES DOCUMENT REFERENCE CHARTS

SYNOPSIS

Document Cross-Reference Charts

A101   Cross-Reference Chart
A107   Cross-Reference Chart
A111   Cross-Reference Chart
A201   Cross-Reference Chart
A401   Cross-Reference Chart

Document to Case Charts

A101-1963:   Standard Form of Agreement Between Owner and Contractor Where the Basis of Payment is a Stipulated Sum

A101-1967:   Standard Form of Agreement Between Owner and Contractor Where the Basis of Payment is a Stipulated Sum

A101-1974:   Standard Form of Agreement Between Owner and Contractor Where the Basis of Payment is a Stipulated Sum

A101-1977:   Standard Form of Agreement Between Owner and Contractor Where the Basis of Payment is a Stipulated Sum

A101-1987:   Standard Form of Agreement Between Owner and Contractor Where the Basis of Payment is a Stipulated Sum

A107-1963:   Standard Form of Agreement Between Owner and Contractor—The AIA Short Form Contract for Small Construction Contracts Where the Basis of Payment is a Stipulated Sum

A107-1966:   Standard Form of Agreement Between Owner and Contractor—Short Form Agreement for Small Construction Contracts Where the Basis of Payment is a Stipulated Sum

A107-1970:   Standard Form of Agreement Between Owner and Contractor—Short Form Agreement for Small Construction Contracts Where the Basis of Payment is a Stipulated Sum

A107-1974:   Standard Form of Agreement Between Owner and Contractor—Short Form Agreement for Small Construction Contracts Where the Basis of Payment is a Stipulated Sum

A107-1978:   Abbreviated Form of Agreement Between Owner and Contractor for Construction Projects of Limited Scope Where the Basis of Payment is a Stipulated Sum

A107-1987:   Abbreviated Form of Agreement Between Owner and Contractor for Construction Projects of Limited Scope Where the Basis of Payment is a Stipulated Sum

A DOCUMENT CROSS REFERENCE CHARTS

A111-1963: Standard Form of Agreement Between Owner and Contractor Where the Basis of Payment is the Cost of the Work Plus a Fee
A111-1967: Standard Form of Agreement Between Owner and Contractor Where the Basis of Payment is the Cost of the Work Plus a Fee
A111-1974: Standard Form of Agreement Between Owner and Contractor Where the Basis of Payment is the Cost of the Work Plus a Fee
A111-1978: Standard Form of Agreement Between Owner and Contractor Where the Basis of Payment is the Cost of the Work Plus a Fee
A111-1987: Standard Form of Agreement Between Owner and Contractor Where the Basis of Payment is the Cost of the Work Plus a Fee with or Without a Guaranteed Maximum Price
A117-1979: Abbreviated Form of Agreement Between Owner and Contractor for Construction Projects of Limited Scope Where the Basis of Payment is the Cost of the Work Plus a Fee
A117-1987: Abbreviated Form of Agreement Between Owner and Contractor for Construction Projects of Limited Scope Where the Basis of Payment is the Cost of the Work Plus a Fee
A201-1963: General Conditions of the Contract for the Construction of Buildings
A201-1967: General Conditions of the Contract for Construction
A201-1970: General Conditions of the Contract for Construction
A201-1976: General Conditions of the Contract for Construction
A201-1987: General Conditions of the Contract for Construction
A310-1963: Bid Bond
A310-1970: Bid Bond
A311-1963: Performance Bond and Labor and Material Payment Bond
A311-1970: Performance Bond and Labor and Material Payment Bond
A312-1984: Performance Bond and Payment Bond
A401-1963: Standard Form of Subcontract
A401-1967: Subcontract: Standard Form of Agreement Between Contractor and Subcontractor
A401-1972: Subcontract: Standard Form of Agreement Between Contractor and Subcontractor
A401-1978: Subcontract: Standard Form of Agreement Between Contractor and Subcontractor
A401-1987: Subcontract: Standard Form of Agreement Between Contractor and Subcontractor

DOCUMENT CROSS-REFERENCE CHARTS: A101

A101 CROSS-REFERENCE CHART

Article Title	1963	1967	1970	Article Number 1974	1977	1987	1997
Acceptance and final payment*	5	7*	6*	6*	6*	6	5.2
Architect (named)	1	3	p.1	p.1	p.1	p.1	p.1
Contract documents	6	1	1	1	1	1	1
Contract sum	3	5	4	4	4	4	4
Date of commencement and substantial completion	2	4	3	3	3	3	3
Enumeration of contract documents	—	—	—	—	—	9	8
Final payment	5	7	6	6	6	6	5.2
Miscellaneous	—	8	7	7	7	7	7
Progress payments	4	6	5	5	5	5	5.1
Scope of work	1	2	2	2	2	2	2
Termination or suspension	—	—	—	—	—	8	6
Time of commencement and (substantial) completion	2	4	3	3	3	3	3
Time of completion	2	4	3	3	3	3	3
Work	1	2	2	2	2	2	2

*See A201-1967 (Article 9.7), A201-1970 (Article 9.7) and A201-1976 (Article 9.9) for conditions of the certificate of final payment as included in A101-1963 (Article 5).

DOCUMENT CROSS-REFERENCE CHARTS: A107

A107 CROSS-REFERENCE CHART

Article Title	1963	1966	1970	1974	1978	1987	1997
Acceptance and final payment	5*	6	6	5	5	5	4.2
Arbitration	19	15	15	14	13	10.8	9.10
Architect	7, 18	9	9	8	8	10	9
Architect (identified)	1*	2	2	p.1	p.1	p.1	p.1
Changes in the work	8	22	22	21	18	13	12
Contract documents	1	8	8	7	7	7	6
Contractor	3, 5, 20	11	10	10	10	9	8
Contractor's liability insurance	13	19	19	18	17	17	16.1
Contract sum	3*	4	4	3	3	3	3
Correction of work	9	23	23	22	19	18	17
Enumeration of contract documents	6*	7	7	6	6	6	5
Final payment	5*	6	6	5	5	5	4.2
Insurance	13, 14, 15	19, 20, 21	19, 20, 21	18, 19, 20	17	17	16
Miscellaneous	—	—	—	25	13, 21	19	18
Other conditions	—	—	—	25	21	21	—
Owner	5	10	10	9	9	8	7
Owner's liability insurance	14	20	20	19	17	17	—
Payments	12, 16	17	17	16	15	15	14
Progress payments	4*	5	5	4	4	4	4.1
Property insurance	15	21	21	20	17	17	16.4
Protection of persons and property	6	18	18	17	16	16	15
Royalties and patents	4	14	14	13	10	9	8.11
Samples	2	11	11	10	10	9.8, 10.7	8.7
Separate contracts	17	13	13	12	12	12	11
Subcontracts	—	12	12	11	11	11	10
Termination by contractor	11	24	24	23	20	20	19.1
Termination by owner	10	25	25	24	20	20	19.2
Time	—	16	16	15	14	14	13

A107 CROSS-REFERENCE CHART (cont.)

Article Title	Article Number					
	1963	1966	1970	1974	1978	1987	1997
Time of commencement and completion	2*	3	3	2	2	2	2
Work	1*	1	1	1	1	1	1

* Indicates an Article of Agreement in the 1963 edition, where Articles of Agreement and Articles of General Conditions were numbered separately, each series beginning with an Article 1. In later editions, all Articles are numbered consecutively.

A111 CROSS-REFERENCE CHART

Article Number

Article Title	1963	1967	1974	1978	1987	1997
Accounting records	12	13	12	12	11	11
Architect	1	3	p.1	p.1	p.1	p.1
Applications for payment	13	14	13	13	12	12.1
Certificates for payment	14	15	14	14	12	12.1
Changes in the work	3	8	7	7	6	6
Contract documents	1	1	1	1	1	1
Contractor's duties and status	4	4	3	3	3	3
Contractor's fee	5	7	6	6	5	5
Contractor's fee for changes in the work	3	7	6	6	5	5
Contractor's financial responsibility	9	10	9	9	8	8
Cost of work and guaranteed maximum cost	—	6	5	5	5	5
Costs not to be reimbursed	7	10	9	9	8	8
Costs to be reimbursed	6	9	8	8	7	7
Disbursements	15	—	—	—	—	—
Discounts, rebates and refunds	8	11	10	10	9	9
Fee for services	5	7	6	6	5	5
Miscellaneous	(1)	17	16	16	14	14
Payments to contractor	14	15	14	14	12	12
Subcontracts and other agreements	10	12	11	11	10	10
Termination of contract	15	16	15	15	15	13
Time of commencement and completion	2	5	4	4	4	4
Title to work	11	—	—	—	—	—
Work	1	2	2	2	2	2

DOCUMENT CROSS-REFERENCE CHARTS: A201

A201 CROSS-REFERENCE CHART

Article Title	1963	1967	1970	1976	1987	1997
Acceptance of defective or non-conforming work	17	13.3	13.3	13.3	12.3	12.3
Access to work	13	7.8, 13.1	7.8, 13.1	7.8, 13.1	3.16	3.16
Administration of contract	13, 14, 31, 38, 39	2.2	2.2	2.2	4.2	4.2
Allowances	41	4.8	4.8	4.8	3.8	3.8
Arbitration	40	7.10	7.10	7.9	4.5	4.6
Architect	1	2	2	2	4	4
Architect, def.	1	2.1	2.1	2.2, 2.1	4.1	4.1
Architect's decisions	39	2.2	2.2	2.2	4.3.2	4.4.1
Architect's status; architect's supervision	38	2.2	2.2	2.2	4.1	4.2
Application for payments	24	9.2, 9.3	9.2, 9.3	9.2, 9.5	9.3	9.3
Assignment	33	7.2	7.2	7.2	13.2	13.2
Award of subcontracts and other contracts for portions of work	36	5.2	5.2	5.2	5.2	5.2
Cash allowances	41	4.8	4.8	4.8	3.8	3.8
Certificates for payment	25	9.4	9.4	9.4	9.4	9.4
Change orders	15, 16	12.1	12.1	12.1, 12.3	7.2	7.2
Claims for additional cost	16	12.2	12.2	12.3	4.3.7	4.3.5, 4.3.6
Claims for damages	31	7.4	7.4.	7.4	4.3, 4.4	4.3.8
Cleaning up	44	4.16	4.16	4.15	3.15	3.15
Communications	—	4.17	4.17	4.17	4.2.4	4.2.4
Concealed conditions	15	12.1	12.1	12.2	4.3.6	4.3.6
Construction procedures	14	4.3	4.3	4.3	3.3	3.3
Contract documents	1	1	1	1	1	1
Contract documents, def.	1	1.1	1.1	1.1	1.1.1	1.1.1
Contractor	1	4	4	4	3	3
Contractor, def.	1	4.1	4.1	4.1	3.1	3.1
Contractor's liability insurance	27	11.1	11.1	11.1	11.1	11.1
Contractor's right to stop work or terminate contract	23	9.6, 14.1	9.6, 14.1	9.6, 14.1	9.7, 14.1	9.7, 14.1
Contractor's superintendence and supervision	14	2.2, 4.2, 4.3, 4.9	2.2, 4.2, 4.3, 4.9	2.2, 4.2, 4.3	3.3, 3.9	3.3, 3.9
Contractor's warranty	9, 20	4.5	4.5	4.5	3.5	3.5
Contract sum	—	9.1	9.1	9.1	9.1	9.1
Copies of documents	4, 7	1.3	1.3	1.3, 3.2	1.3, 2.2	1.3, 2.2
Correction of work	19, 20	13.2	13.2	13.2	12.2	12.2

A201 CROSS-REFERENCE CHART (cont.)

Article Title	1963	1967	1970	1976	1987	1997
Cutting and patching of work	43	4.15	4.15	4.14	3.14	3.14
Cutting and patching under separate contracts	43	6.3	6.3	6.2, 4.14	6.2, 3.14	6.2, 3.14
Damages	31	2.2, 7.4	2.2, 7.4	2.2, 7.4	2.4, 4.3.9	2.4, 4.3.8, 4.3.10
Deductions for uncorrected work	17	13.3	13.3	13.3	12.3	12.3
Definitions	1	1.1, 2.1, 3.1, 4.1, 5.1, 7.1, 7.3, 8.1, 8.2	1.1, 2.1, 3.1, 4.1, 5.1, 7.1, 7.3, 8.1, 8.2	1.1, 2.1, 3.1, 4.1, 5.1, 7.1, 7.3, 8.1, 8.2	1.1, 2.1, 3.1, 4.1, 5.1, 7.2, 7.3, 8.1	1.1, 2.1, 3.1, 4.1, 5.1, 7.2, 7.3, 8.1
Delays and extensions of time	18	8.3	8.3	8.3	8.3	8.3
Detail drawings and instructions	3	1.2, 4.2, 4.11	1.2, 4.2, 4.11	1.2, 4.2, 4.11	1.2, 3.2, 3.11	1.2, 3.2, 3.11
Documents and samples at the site	6	4.12	4.12	4.11	3.11	3.11
Emergencies	12	10.3	10.3	10.3	10.3	10.6
Execution, correlation, intent and interpretation of documents	2, 3	1.2	1.2	1.2	1.2	1.2, 1.5
Failure of payment	23	9.6	9.6	9.7	9.7	9.7
Field orders (construction change directives)	—	12.4	12.4	—	7.3	7.3
Final completion and final payment	25, 32	9.7	9.7	9.9	9.10	9.10
Fire insurance with extended coverage	29	11.3, 11.4	11.3, 11.4	11.3, 11.4	11.3	11.3
Governing law	1	7.1	7.1	7.1	13.1	13.1
Guaranty bonds	30	7.5	7.5	7.5	11.4	11.5
Hazardous substances	—	—	—	—	10.1.2, 10.1.3, 10.1.4	10.3
Indemnification	—	4.18	4.18	4.18	3.18	3.18
Information and services required of owner	11	3.2	3.2	3.2	2.2	2.2
Insurance	27, 28, 29	11	11	11	11	11
Interest	25	7.9	7.9	7.8	13.6	13.6
Interpretation of documents	2.3	1.2	1.2	1.2	1.5	1.4
Labor and materials	9	4.4	4.4	4.4	3.4	3.4
Liens	32	9.7	9.7	9.3, 9.9	9.3.3, 9.10	9.3.3, 9.10
Loss of use insurance	29	11.4	11.4	11.4	11.3.3	11.4.3
Materials, appliances, employees	9	4.4, 4.5	4.4, 4.5	4.4, 4.5	3.3, 3.4, 3.5	3.3, 3.4, 3.5
Mediation	—	—	—	—	—	4.5
Minor changes in the work	15	12.3	12.3	12.4	7.4	7.4

DOCUMENT CROSS-REFERENCE CHARTS: A201

A201 CROSS-REFERENCE CHART (cont.)

Article Title	1963	1967	1970	1976	1987	1997
Mutual responsibility of contractors	34, 35	6.2	6.2	6.2	6.2	6.2
Owner	1	3	3	3	2	2
Owner, def.		3.1	3.1	3.1	2.1	2.1
Ownership and use of documents	4.7	1.3	1.3	1.3, 3.2	1.3	1.3
Ownership of drawings	7	1.3	1.3	1.3, 3.2	1.3	1.3
Owner's liability insurance	28	11.2	11.2	11.2	11.2	11.2
Owner's right to award separate contracts	35	6.1	6.1	6.1	6.1	6.1
Owner's right to carry out the work	21	7.6	3.4	3.4	2.4	2.4
Owner's right to clean up	44	6.4	6.4	6.4	6.3	6.3
Owner's right to perform work and to award separate contracts	35	6.1	6.1	6.1	6.1	6.1
Owner's right to stop work	—	—	3.3	3.3	2.3	2.3
Owner's right to suspend work	—	—	—	—	14.3	14.3
Owner's right to terminate	22	14.2	14.2	14.2	14.2	14.2, 14.4
Partial occupancy or use	23, 24, 25, 26, 32	9	9	9	9.9	9.9
Payments and completion	36, 37	9	9	9	9	9
Payments to subcontractors	26	5.4	5.4	9.5, 11.3	9.6	9.6
Payments withheld	30	9.5	9.5	9.6	9.5	9.5
Performance bond and labor and material payment bond	11	7.5	7.5	7.5	11.4	11.5
Permits, fees and notices	1	4.7	4.7	4.7	3.7	3.7
Progress and completion	24	8.2	8.2	8.2	8.2	8.2
Progress payments	3	9.3	9.3	9.5	9.6	9.6
Progress schedule	—	4.11	4.11	4.11	3.10	3.10
Project management protective liability insurance		—	—	—	—	11.3
Property insurance	29	11.3	11.3	11.3	11.3	11.4
Protection of persons and property	12, 42	10	10	10	10	10
Protection of work and property	12	10	10	10	10	10
Relations of contractor and subcontractor	37	5.3, 5.4	5.3, 5.4	5.3, 5.4	5.3	5.3
Responsibility for those performing the work	36	4.10	4.10	4.3	3.3	3.3
Review of contract documents	3, 14	4.2	4.2	4.2	3.2	3.2
Rights and remedies	—	—	7.6	7.6	13.4	13.4
Royalties and patents	10	7.7	7.7	4.17	3.17	3.17
Safety of persons and property	12, 42	10.2	10.2	10.2	10.2	10.2
Safety precautions and programs	12	10.1	10.1	10.1	10.1	10.1

DOCUMENT CROSS-REFERENCE CHARTS: A201

A201 CROSS-REFERENCE CHART (cont.)

Article Title	1963	1967	1970	1976	1987	1997
Separate contracts	35	6.1, 6.2	6.1, 6.2	6.1, 6.2	6.1, 6.2	6.1, 6.2
Samples	8	2.2, 4.13	2.2, 4.13	2.2, 4.13	3.11, 3.12, 4.2.7	3.11, 3.12, 4.2.7
Schedule of values	24	9.2	9.2	9.2	9.2	9.2
Shop drawings and samples	5, 8	2.2, 4.13	2.2, 4.13	2.2, 4.13	3.11, 3.12, 4.2.7	3.11, 3.12, 4.2.7
Shop drawings, product data and samples	5, 8	4.13	4.13	4.12	3.12	3.12
Statute of limitations	—	—	—	—	13.7	13.7
Subcontracts	36	4.10, 5	4.10, 5	4.10, 5	5	5
Subcontractors	1, 36	5.1	5.1	1.1, 5.1	5	5
Subcontractual relations, contingent assignment	37	5.3	5.3	5.3	5.3, 5.4	5.3, 5.4
Substantial completion and final payment	25, 32	9.7	9.7	9.8, 9.9	9.8, 9.10	9.8, 9.10
Successors and assigns	1, 33	7.2	7.2	7.2	13.2	13.2
Superintendent	14	4.9	4.9	4.9	3.9	3.9
Supervision and construction procedures	14	4.3	4.3	4.3	3.3	3.3
Surveys, permits, laws, taxes and regulations	11	3.2, 4.6, 4.7	3.2, 4.6, 4.7	3.2, 4.6, 4.7	2.2, 3.6, 3.7	2.2, 3.6, 3.7
Taxes	11	4.6	4.6	4.6	3.6	3.6
Termination by the contractor	23	14.1	14.1	14.1	14.1	14.1
Termination by the owner for cause	22	14.2	14.2	14.2	14.2	14.2
Termination by the owner for convenience	—	—	—	—	—	14.4
Tests	13	7.8	7.8	4.3, 7.7	3.3, 13.5	3.3, 13.5
Time	1, 18	8.1	8	8	8	8
Time, def.	1	8.1	8	8	8.1	8.1
Uncovering of work	13	13.1	13.1	13.1	12.1	12.1
Use of site	42	4.14	4.14	4.13	3.13	3.13
Use of premises	42	4.14, 10.2	4.14, 10.2	4.13, 10.2	3.13, 10.2	3.13, 10.2
Written notice	1	7.3	7.3	7.3	13.3	13.3

A401 CROSS-REFERENCE CHART

Article Title	1963	1967	1972	1978	1987	1997
Arbitration	5	13	14	13	6	6.2
Changes in the work	—	—	—	—	5	5
Contract documents	1	1	1	1	1	1
Contractor	5	11, 12	11, 12	12	3	3
Contractor's responsibilities	5	12	12	11, 12	3	3
Contract sum	4	4	4	4	10	10
Final payment	—	6	6	6	12	12
Insurance	—	9	9	9	13	13
Interest	—	—	13	5	15	15
Mediation	—	—	—	—	—	6.1
Miscellaneous	—	—	—	15	15	15
Mutual rights and responsibilities	—	—	—	—	2	2
Performance bond and labor and material payment bond	—	7	7	7	13	13
Progress payments	5	5	5	5	11	11
Subcontractor	5	11, 12	11, 12	11	4	4
Subcontractor's responsibilities	5	11	11	11, 12	4	4
Temporary site facilities	3	3	3	10	14	14
Time of commencement and completion	3	3	3	3	9	9
Work	1, 2	2	2	2	8	8
Working conditions	—	10	10	10	14	14

A–15   DOCUMENT TO CASE CHARTS: A101-1963

[The five-digit numbers in this chart are Citator Case Reference Numbers, which refer to the cases, in the Cases section. The suffixes indicate the state or, for federal cases, the court in which the case was decided.]

A101-1963—STANDARD FORM OF AGREEMENT BETWEEN OWNER AND CONTRACTOR WHERE THE BASIS OF PAYMENT IS A STIPULATED SUM

Text of Article 1—Scope of the Work

The Contractor shall furnish all of the materials and perform all of the work shown on the Drawings and described in the Specifications entitled: (*Here insert the caption descriptive of the work as used on other contract documents.*) _____ prepared by: _____ acting as and in these Contract Documents entitled the Architect; and shall do everything required by this Agreement, the General Conditions of the Contract, the Specifications and the Drawings.

Article 1   Scope of the Work

I

    67049-IL   67038-MO
    66007-MI   67052-TX

Text of Article 2—Time of Completion

The work to be performed under this Contract shall be commenced and completed as follows: (*Here insert stipulation as to liquidated damages, if any.*) _____

Article 2   Time of Completion

III

    40003-US
    66001-NJ

Text of Article 3—The Contract Sum

The Owner shall pay the Contractor for the performance of the Contract, subject to additions and deductions provided therein, in current funds as follows: (*State here the lump sum amount, unit prices, or both, as desired.*) _____ Where the quantities originally contemplated are so changed that application of the agreed unit price to the quantity of work performed is shown to create a hardship to the Owner or the Contractor, there shall be an equitable adjustment of the Contract to prevent such hardship.

DOCUMENT TO CASE CHARTS: A101-1963   A–16

[The five-digit numbers in this chart are Citator Case Reference Numbers, which refer to the cases, in the Cases section. The suffixes indicate the state or, for federal cases, the court in which the case was decided.]

Article 3   The Contract Sum

   I

      65029-MO
      67052-TX

Text of Article 4—Progress Payments

The Owner shall make payments on account of the Contract as provided therein, as follows: On or about the _____ day of each month _____ per cent of the value, based on the Contract prices of labor and materials incorporated in the work and _____ per cent of materials suitably stored at the site thereof or at some other location agreed upon in writing by the parties up to the _____ day of that month, as estimated by the Architect, less the aggregate of previous payments; and upon Substantial Completion of the entire work, a sum sufficient to increase the total payments to _____ per cent of the Contract price. (*Insert here any provision made for limiting or reducing the amount retained after the work reaches a certain stage of completion.*)

Article 4   Progress Payments

   I

      44001-KY

   II

      13005-TX
      28001-TX
      14003-WI

Text of Article 5—Acceptance and Final Payment

Final payment shall be due _____ days after Substantial Completion of the work provided the work be then fully completed and the contract fully performed.

Upon receipt of written notice that the work is ready for final inspection and acceptance, the Architect shall promptly make such inspection, and when he finds the work acceptable under the Contract and the Contract fully performed he shall promptly issue a final certificate, over his own signature, stating that the work provided for in this Contract has been completed and is accepted by him under the terms and conditions thereof, and that the entire balance found to be due the Contractor, and noted in said final certificate, is due and payable.

Before issuance of final payment the Contractor shall submit evidence satisfactory to the Architect that all payrolls, material bills, and other indebtedness connected with the work have been paid or otherwise satisfied.

If after the work has been Substantially Completed, full completion thereof is materially delayed through no fault of the Contractor, and the Architect so certifies, the Owner shall, upon certificate of the Architect, and without terminating the Contract, make payment of the balance due for that portion of the work fully

DOCUMENT TO CASE CHARTS: A101-1963

[The five-digit numbers in this chart are Citator Case Reference Numbers, which refer to the cases, in the Cases section. The suffixes indicate the state or, for federal cases, the court in which the case was decided.]

> completed and accepted. Such payment shall be made under the terms and conditions governing final payment, except that it shall not constitute a waiver of claims.

Article 5   Acceptance and Final Payment

    I

        66071-GA

   III

        65101-MO

> **Text of Article 6—The Contract Documents**
>
> The General Conditions of the Contract, the Supplementary General Conditions, the Specifications and the Drawings, together with this Agreement, form the Contract, and they are as fully a part of the Contract as if hereto attached or herein repeated. There follows an enumeration of the Contract Documents: _____

Article 6   The Contract Documents

    I

        67049-IL

   III

        66029-PA

DOCUMENT TO CASE CHARTS: A101-1967   A–18

[The five-digit numbers in this chart are Citator Case Reference Numbers, which refer to the cases, in the Cases section. The suffixes indicate the state or, for federal cases, the court in which the case was decided.]

A101-1967—STANDARD FORM OF AGREEMENT BETWEEN OWNER AND CONTRACTOR WHERE THE BASIS OF PAYMENT IS A STIPULATED SUM

Text of Article 1—The Contract Documents

The Contract Documents consist of this Agreement, Conditions of the Contract (General, Supplementary and other Conditions), Drawings, Specifications, all Addenda issued prior to execution of this Agreement and all Modifications issued subsequent thereto. These form the Contract, and all are as fully a part of the Contract as if attached to this Agreement or repeated herein. An enumeration of the Contract Documents appears in Article 8.

Article 1   The Contract Documents

    I

        71051-NDGA
        72087-TX

    III

        72112-MD

Article 2   The Work

Text of Article 3—Architect

The Architect for this Project is _____

Article 3   Architect

    I

        70091-IL

    III

        72055-NE

Text of Article 4—Time of Commencement and Completion

The Work to be performed under this Contract shall be commenced _____ and completed _____ *(Here insert any special provisions or liquidated damages relating to failure to complete on time.)*

DOCUMENT TO CASE CHARTS: A101-1967

[The five-digit numbers in this chart are Citator Case Reference Numbers, which refer to the cases, in the Cases section. The suffixes indicate the state or, for federal cases, the court in which the case was decided.]

Article 4 Time of Commencement and Completion

I

70029-CA

III

67019-MO
67024-TX

Text of Article 5—Contract Sum

The Owner shall pay the Contractor for the performance of the Work, subject to additions and deductions by Change Order as provided in the Conditions of the Contract, in current funds, the Contract Sum of _____ (*State here the lump sum amount. unit prices, or both, as desired.*)

Article 5 Contract Sum

I

73043-FL

Text of Article 6—Progress Payments

Based upon Applications for Payment submitted to the Architect by the Contractor and Certificates for Payment issued by the Architect, the Owner shall make progress payments on account of the Contract Sum to the Contractor as provided in the Conditions of the Contract as follows: On or about the _____ day of each month _____ per cent of the proportion of the Contract Sum properly allocable to labor, materials and equipment incorporated in the Work and _____ per cent of the portion of the Contract Sum properly allocable to materials and equipment suitably stored at the site or at some other location agreed upon in writing by the parties, up to the _____ day of that month, less the aggregate of previous payments in each case; and upon Substantial Completion of the entire Work, a sum sufficient to increase the total payments to _____ per cent of the Contract Sum, less such retainages as the Architect shall determine for all incomplete Work and unsettled claims. (*Here insert any provisions made for limiting or reducing the amount retained after the Work reaches a certain stage of completion.*) _____

Article 6 Progress Payments

I

71085-TN

Text of Article 7—Final Payment

Final payment, constituting the entire unpaid balance of the Contract Sum, shall be paid by the Owner to the Contractor _____ days after Substantial Completion of the Work unless otherwise stipulated in the Certificate of Substantial Completion,

DOCUMENT TO CASE CHARTS: A101-1967

[The five-digit numbers in this chart are Citator Case Reference Numbers, which refer to the cases, in the Cases section. The suffixes indicate the state or, for federal cases, the court in which the case was decided.]

> provided the Work has then been completed, the Contract fully performed, and a final Certificate for Payment has been issued by the Architect.

Article 7   Final Payment

    I

       72087-TX

Article 8   Miscellaneous Provisions

DOCUMENT TO CASE CHARTS: A101-1974

[The five-digit numbers in this chart are Citator Case Reference Numbers, which refer to the cases, in the Cases section. The suffixes indicate the state or, for federal cases, the court in which the case was decided.]

A101-1974—STANDARD FORM OF AGREEMENT BETWEEN OWNER AND CONTRACTOR WHERE THE BASIS OF PAYMENT IS A STIPULATED SUM

Article 1   The Contract Documents

Text of Article 2—The Work

The Contractor shall perform all the Work required by the Contract Documents for (*Here insert the caption descriptive of the Work as used on other contract Documents.*) _____

Article 2   The Work

    I

    75003-TX

Article 3   Time of Commencement and Completion

Article 4   Contract Sum

Article 5   Progress Payments

Text of Article 6—Final Payment

Final payment, constituting the entire unpaid balance of the Contract Sum, shall be paid by the Owner to the Contractor _____ days after Substantial Completion of the Work unless otherwise stipulated in the Certificate of Substantial Completion, provided the Work has then been completed, the Contract fully performed, and a final Certificate for Payment has been issued by the Architect.

Article 6   Final Payment

    I

    86056-MD

Article 7   Miscellaneous Provisions

DOCUMENT TO CASE CHARTS: A101-1977

[*The five-digit numbers in this chart are Citator Case Reference Numbers, which refer to the cases, in the Cases section. The suffixes indicate the state or, for federal cases, the court in which the case was decided.*]

A101-1977—STANDARD FORM OF AGREEMENT BETWEEN OWNER AND CONTRACTOR WHERE THE BASIS OF PAYMENT IS A STIPULATED SUM

> ### Text of Article 1—The Contract Documents
>
> The Contract Documents Consist of this Agreement, the Conditions of the Contract (General, Supplementary and other Conditions), the Drawings. the Specifications, all Addenda issued prior to and all Modifications issued after execution of this Agreement. These form the Contract, and all are as fully a part of the Contract as if attached to this Agreement or repeated herein. An enumeration of the Contract Documents appears in Article 7.

Article 1   The Contract Documents

    I

        82032-DKS   84038-MO
        79034-AZ   89026-MO
        90042-KS   94020-TX
        89049-MA   97003-WA
        82034-MS   79056-WY

    II

        82052-NV

> ### Text of Article 2—The Work
>
> The Contractor shall perform all the Work required by the Contract Documents for (*Here insert the caption descriptive of the Work as used on other Contract documents.*) _____

Article 2   The Work

    II

        82004-SDGA
        79067-NY

> ### Text of Article 3—Time of Commencement and Substantial Completion
>
> The Work to be performed under this Contract shall be commenced . . . and, subject to authorized adjustments, Substantial Completion shall be achieved not later than (*Here insert any special provisions for liquidated damages relating to failure to complete on time.*) _____

DOCUMENT TO CASE CHARTS: A101-1977

[The five-digit numbers in this chart are Citator Case Reference Numbers, which refer to the cases, in the Cases section. The suffixes indicate the state or, for federal cases, the court in which the case was decided.]

Article 3 Time of Commencement and Substantial Completion

I

79057-4CIR	83003-LA
85017-DDE	82045-NH
80032-NDIL	79032-OK
79034-AZ	80072-TN
78025-GA	79056-WY
79043-LA	81067-WY

II

82004-SDGA	80050-AR
80011-AR	80025-TX

III

79003-5CIR	79062-MO
81064-8CIR	78006-MT
79045-CA	75029-NJ
79046-CA	90010-NY
87027-IN	80009-SD
76062-LA	79036-VA
81065-LA	80039-WY

Text of Article 4—Contract Sum

The Owner shall pay the Contractor in current funds for the performance of the Work, subject to additions and deductions by Change Order as provided in the Contract Documents, the Contract Sum of _____ The Contract Sum is determined as follows: (*State here the base bid or other lump sum amount, accepted alternates, and unit prices, as applicable.*) _____

Article 4 Contract Sum

I

82045-NH

III

79052-LA	80044-WA
80065-MO	81045-WV
87040-SC	

Text of Article 5—Progress Payments

Based upon Applications for Payment submitted to the Architect by the Contractor and Certificates for Payment issued by the Architect, the Owner shall make progress payments on account of the Contract Sum to the Contractor as provided in the Contract Documents for the period ending the _____ day of the month as follows: Not later than _____ days following the end of the period covered by the Application for Payment . . . percent (_____ %) of the portion of the Contract Sum properly allocable to labor, materials and equipment incorporated in the Work and _____ percent (_____ %) of the portion of the Contract Sum

DOCUMENT TO CASE CHARTS: A101-1977   A–24

[The five-digit numbers in this chart are Citator Case Reference Numbers, which refer to the cases, in the Cases section. The suffixes indicate the state or, for federal cases, the court in which the case was decided.]

properly allocable to materials and equipment suitably stored at the site or at some other location agreed upon in writing, for the period covered by the Application for Payment, less the aggregate of previous payments made by the Owner; and upon Substantial Completion of the entire Work, a sum sufficient to increase the total payments to _____ percent (_____ %) of the Contract Sum, less such amounts as the Architect shall determine for all incomplete Work and unsettled claims as provided in the Contract Documents. (*If not covered elsewhere in the Contract Documents, here insert any provision for limiting or reducing the amount retained after the Work reaches a certain stage of completion.*) _____ Payments due and unpaid under the Contract Documents shall bear interest from the date payment is due at the rate entered below, or in the absence thereof, at the legal rate prevailing at the place of the Project. (*Here insert any rate of interest agreed upon.*) _____ (*Usury laws and requirements under the Federal Truth in Lending Act, similar state and local consumer credit laws and other regulations at the Owner's and Contractor's principal places of business, the location of the Project and elsewhere may affect the validity of this provision. Specific legal advice should be obtained with respect to deletion, modification, or other requirements such as written disclosure or waivers.*)

Article 5   **Progress Payments**

    I

        86014-AZ   84018-MO
        85020-IA   79032-OK

    II

        92001-7CIR   86070-IL
        84035-IL   81047-UT

    III

        81045-WV

Text of Article 6—Final Payment

Final payment, constituting the entire unpaid balance of the Contract Sum, shall be paid by the Owner to the Contractor when the Work has been completed, the Contract fully performed, and a final Certificate for Payment has been issued by the Architect.

DOCUMENT TO CASE CHARTS: A101-1977

[*The five-digit numbers in this chart are Citator Case Reference Numbers, which refer to the cases, in the Cases section. The suffixes indicate the state or, for federal cases, the court in which the case was decided.*]

Article 6   Final Payment

    I

        80002-AZ
        84018-MO

    II

        82004-SDGA

    III

        80026-GA
        83039-LA

Text of Article 7—Miscellaneous Provisions

7.1 Terms used in this Agreement which are defined in the Conditions of the Contract shall have the meanings designated in those Conditions.

7.2 The Contract Documents, which constitute the entire agreement between the Owner and the Contractor, are listed in Article 1 and, except for Modifications issued after execution of this Agreement, are enumerated as follows: (*List below the Agreement, the Conditions of the Contract (General, Supplementary, and other Conditions), the Drawings, the Specifications, and any Addenda and accepted alternates, showing page or sheet numbers in all cases and dates where applicable.*)

Article 7   Miscellaneous Provisions

    I

82032-DKS	84038-MO
79034-AZ	89026-MO
92008-DC	91035-SC
86061-FL	94020-TX
90042-KS	97003-WA
89049-MA	79056-WY
82034-MS	

    II

        82052-NV

DOCUMENT TO CASE CHARTS: A101-1987 A–26

[*The five-digit numbers in this chart are Citator Case Reference Numbers, which refer to the cases, in the Cases section. The suffixes indicate the state or, for federal cases, the court in which the case was decided.*]

A101-1987—STANDARD FORM OF AGREEMENT BETWEEN OWNER AND CONTRACTOR WHERE THE BASIS OF PAYMENT IS A STIPULATED SUM

Text of Article 1—The Contract Documents

The Contract Documents consist of this Agreement, Conditions of the Contract (General, Supplamantary and other Conditions), Drawings, Specifications, addenda issued prior to execution of this Agreement, other documents listed in this Agreement and Modifications issued after execution of this Agreement; these form the Contract, and are as fully a part of the Contract as if attached to this Agreement or repeated herein. The Contract represents the entire and integrated agreement between the parties hereto and supersedes prior negotiations, representations or agreements, either written or oral. An enumeration of the Contract Documents, other than Modifications, appears in Article 9.

Article 1 The Contract Documents

    I

        96001-7CIR

    II

        96001-7CIR
        97003-WA

Article 2 The Work

Text of Article 3—Date of Commencement and Substantial Completion

3.1 The date of commencement is the date from which the Contract Time of Paragraph 3.2 is measured, and shall be the date of this Agreement, as first written above, unless a different date is stated below or provision is made for the date to be fixed in a notice to proceed issued by the Owner. (*Insert the date of commencement, if it differs from the date of this Agreement or, if applicable, state that the date will be fixed in a notice to proceed.*) _____ Unless the date of commencement is established by a notice to proceed issued by the Owner, the Contractor shall notify the Owner in writing not less than five days before commencing the Work to permit the timely filing of mortgages, mechanic's liens and other security interests.

3.2 The Contractor shall achieve Substantial Completion of the entire Work not later than (*Insert the calendar date or number of calendar days after the date of commencement. Also insert any requirements for earlier Substantial Completion of certain portions of the Work, if not stated elsewhere in the Contract Documents.*) _____, subject to adjustments of this Contract Time as provided in the Contract Documents. (*Insert provisions, if any, for liquidated damages relating to failure to complete on time.*) _____

DOCUMENT TO CASE CHARTS: A101-1987

[The five-digit numbers in this chart are Citator Case Reference Numbers, which refer to the cases, in the Cases section. The suffixes indicate the state or, for federal cases, the court in which the case was decided.]

Article 3 Date of Commencement and Substantial Completion

I

91014-FL

Article 4 Contract Sum

Article 5 Progress Payments

Text of Article 6—Final Payment

Final payment, constituting the entire unpaid balance of the Contract Sum, shall be made by the Owner to the Contractor when (1) the Contract has been fully performed by the Contractor except for the Contractor's responsibility to correct nonconforming Work as provided in Subparagraph 12.2.2 of the General Conditions and to satisfy other requirements, if any, which necessarily survive final payment; and (2) a final Certificate for Payment has been issued by the Architect; such final payment shall be made by the Owner not more than 30 days after issuance of the Architect's final Certificate for Payment, or as follows: _____

Article 6 Final Payment

I

91035-SC

Text of Article 7—Miscellaneous Provisions

7.1 Where reference is made in this Agreement to a provision of the General Conditions or another Contract Document, the reference refers to that provision as amended or supplemented by othe provisions of the Contract Documents.

7.2 Payments due and unpaid under the Contract shall bear interest from the date payment is due at the rate stated below, or in the absence thereof, at the legal rate prevailing from time to time at the place where the Project is located.

(Insert rate of interest agreed upon, if any.)

(Usury laws and requirements under the Federal Truth in Lending Act, similar state and local consumer credit laws and other regulations at the Owner's and Contractor's principal places of business, the location of the Project and elsewhere may affect the validity of this provision. Legal advice should be obtained with respect to deletions or modifications, and also regarding requirements such as written disclosures or waivers.)

7.3 Other Provisions:

DOCUMENT TO CASE CHARTS: A101-1987 A–28

[The five-digit numbers in this chart are Citator Case Reference Numbers, which refer to the cases, in the Cases section. The suffixes indicate the state or, for federal cases, the court in which the case was decided.]

Article 7 Miscellaneous Provisions

I
96001-7CIR

Article 8 Termination or Suspension

Text of Article 9—Enumeration of Contract Documents

9.1 The Contract Documents, except for Modifications issued after execution of this Agreement, are enumerated as follows:

9.1.1 The Agreement is this executed Standard Form of Agreement Between Owner and Contractor, AIA Document A101, 1987 Edition.

9.1.2 The General Conditions are the General Conditions of the Contract for Construction, AIA Document A201, 1987 Edition.

9.1.3 The Supplementary and other Conditions of the Contract are those contained in the Project Manual dated   , and are as follows:

Document	Title	Pages

9.1.4 The Specifications are those contained in the Project Manual dated as in Subparagraph 9.1.3, and are as follows:

(Either list the Specifications here or refer to an exhibit attached to this Agreement)

Section	Title	Pages

9.1.5 The Drawings are as follows, and are dated   unless a different date is shown below:

(Either list the Drawings here or refer to an exhibit attached to this Agreement)

Number	Title	Pages

9.1.6 The addenda, if any, are as follows:

Number	Title	Pages

Portions of addenda relating to bidding requirements are not part of the Contract Documents unless the bidding requirements are also enumerated in this Article 9.

9.1.7 Other documents, if any, forming part of the Contract Documents are as follows:

(List here any additional documents which are intended to form part of the Contract Documents. The General Conditions provide that bidding requirements

DOCUMENT TO CASE CHARTS: A101-1987

[The five-digit numbers in this chart are Citator Case Reference Numbers, which refer to the cases, in the Cases section. The suffixes indicate the state or, for federal cases, the court in which the case was decided.]

> such as advertisement or invitation to bid, Instructions to Bidders, sample forms and the Contractor's bid are not part of the Contract Documents unless enumerated in this Agreement. They should be listed here only if intended to be part of the Contract Documents.)

Article 9 Enumeration of Contract Documents

    II

        96001-7CIR
        97003-WA

DOCUMENT TO CASE CHARTS: A107-1963

[The five-digit numbers in this chart are Citator Case Reference Numbers, which refer to the cases, in the Cases section. The suffixes indicate the state or, for federal cases, the court in which the case was decided.]

A107-1963—STANDARD FORM OF AGREEMENT BETWEEN OWNER AND CONTRACTOR—THE AIA SHORT FORM CONTRACT FOR SMALL CONSTRUCTION CONTRACTS WHERE THE BASIS OF PAYMENT IS A STIPULATED SUM

Article 1   Contract Documents

> II
>
>> 94020-TX
>
> III
>
>> 66029-PA
>> 66075-NY
>> 67069-IL

Article 2   Samples

> III
>
>> 66001-NJ

Article 3   Materials, Appliances, Employees

Article 4   Royalties and Patents

Article 5   Surveys, Permits and Regulations

Article 6   Protection of Work, Property and Persons

> III
>
>> 66084-MD

Article 7   Access to Work

> I
>
>> 66048-IL

Article 8   Changes in the Work

> I
>
>> 66031-ID
>> 66048-IL
>
> III
>
>> 67069-IL
>> 66047-NY

DOCUMENT TO CASE CHARTS: A107-1963

[The five-digit numbers in this chart are Citator Case Reference Numbers, which refer to the cases, in the Cases section. The suffixes indicate the state or, for federal cases, the court in which the case was decided.]

Article 9   Correction of Work

    I

        66048-IL

    II

        94020-TX

    III

        65115-PA

Article 10   Owner's Right to Terminate the Contract

    I

        66060-MD

    III

        56079-MD
        66021-TX

Article 11   Contractor's Right to Terminate Contract

    III

        66008-DC

Article 12   Payments

    III

        66068-CT
        66094-DE

Article 13   Contractor's Liability Insurance

Article 14   Owner's Liability Insurance

Article 15   Fire-Insurance with Extended Coverage

    I

        66059-OH

DOCUMENT TO CASE CHARTS: A107-1963

[The five-digit numbers in this chart are Citator Case Reference Numbers, which refer to the cases, in the Cases section. The suffixes indicate the state or, for federal cases, the court in which the case was decided.]

Article 16   Liens

Article 17   Separate Contracts

Article 18   The Architect's Status

      I

          66048-IL

Article 19   Arbitration

      I

          66091-MI

      II

          66058-FL

      III

          66019-CA
          66083-CA
          66075-NY

Article 20   Cleaning Up

DOCUMENT TO CASE CHARTS: A107-1966

[The five-digit numbers in this chart are Citator Case Reference Numbers, which refer to the cases, in the Cases section. The suffixes indicate the state or, for federal cases, the court in which the case was decided.]

A107-1966—STANDARD FORM OF AGREEMENT BETWEEN OWNER AND CONTRACTOR—SHORT FORM AGREEMENT FOR SMALL CONSTRUCTION CONTRACTS WHERE THE BASIS OF PAYMENT IS A STIPULATED SUM

Article 1   The Work

Article 2   Architect

Article 3   Time of Commencement and Completion

    I

        70091-IL
        70047-WA

Article 4   Contract Sum

Article 5   Progress Payments

Article 6   Final Payment

    II

        70023-AZ

Article 7   Enumeration of Contract Documents

Article 8   Contract Documents

    I

        70047-WA

    II

        70003-MD

Article 9   Architect

    I

        71066-NY

    II

        71056-KS   85035-MS
        71082-MI   82054-NC

    III

        70058-AZ
        67017-GA
        70016-MD

DOCUMENT TO CASE CHARTS: A107-1966

[The five-digit numbers in this chart are Citator Case Reference Numbers, which refer to the cases, in the Cases section. The suffixes indicate the state or, for federal cases, the court in which the case was decided.]

Article 10   Owner

Article 11   Contractor

    I

        70079-CO
        70092-FL

    II

        70075-FL   82037-PA
        71056-KS   70060-WA
        86025-MN   67045-WI
        82055-OR

    III

        71040-6CIR   70093-IL
        71023-EDLA   73108-IL
        71030-EDVA   70022-MO
        70048-AZ   71058-NC
        70065-AR   71063-NC
        70089-AR   71007-PA
        68003-CA   71027-PA
        70051-CA   70054-TX
        70057-CA   71012-TX
        70087-CT   72093-TX
        70081-DE   71010-VA
        69011-IL   70007-WA
        69031-IL   69015-WI

Article 12   Subcontracts

Article 13   Separate Contracts

Article 14   Royalties and Patents

Article 15   Arbitration

    I

        71016-5CIR   69029-MI
        70084-7CIR   71066-NY
        70074-SDNY   70072-OH
        68036-IL   82046-PA
        71026-IL   68028-TN

    II

        71057-CA   82025-IL
        70062-DC   82054-NC
        70012-FL   82055-OR

DOCUMENT TO CASE CHARTS: A107-1966

[The five-digit numbers in this chart are Citator Case Reference Numbers, which refer to the cases, in the Cases section. The suffixes indicate the state or, for federal cases, the court in which the case was decided.]

    III

        71045-7CIR   72024-IL
        70013-AZ   70040-NH
        70091-IL   70035-OH

Article 16   Time

Article 17   Payments

    I

        68036-IL
        71028-MI

    II

        68014-CA
        82054-NC
        82055-OR

    III

        71037-7CIR
        71019-IL
        68029-MN

Article 18   Protection of Persons and Property

    II

        82037-PA

    III

        67017-GA   70054-TX
        67061-IL   70049-VT
        71063-NC

Article 19   Contractor's Liability Insurance

Article 20   Owner's Liability Insurance

Article 21   Property Insurance

    II

        69010-IA

Article 22   Changes in the Work

    I

        71017-IL
        71021-MS

DOCUMENT TO CASE CHARTS: A107-1966

[The five-digit numbers in this chart are Citator Case Reference Numbers, which refer to the cases, in the Cases section. The suffixes indicate the state or, for federal cases, the court in which the case was decided.]

    II

        71031-CA   71083-WA
        82054-NC   67045-WI

    III

        68023-MN
        70019-TX

Article 23   Correction of Work

    I

        70079-CO   67033-MN
        68036-IL   70071-MS
        71028-MI

    II

        70030-MT

    III

        68003-CA   70009-MO
        70081-DE   71010-VA

Article 24   Termination by the Contractor

    III

        71025-IL

Article 25   Termination by the Owner

    I

        67026-MD

    II

        70067-MA

    III

        68003-CA
        70016-MD

DOCUMENT TO CASE CHARTS: A107-1970

[The five-digit numbers in this chart are Citator Case Reference Numbers, which refer to the cases, in the Cases section. The suffixes indicate the state or, for federal cases, the court in which the case was decided.]

A107-1970—STANDARD FORM OF AGREEMENT BETWEEN OWNER AND CONTRACTOR—SHORT FORM AGREEMENT FOR SMALL CONSTRUCTION CONTRACTS WHERE THE BASIS OF PAYMENT IS A STIPULATED SUM

Article 1   The Work

Article 2   Architect

Article 3   Time of Commencement and Completion

Article 4   Contract Sum

Article 5   Progress Payments

Article 6   Final Payment

Article 7   Enumeration of Contract Documents

Article 8   Contract Documents

Article 9   Architect

Article 10   Owner

Article 11   Contractor

      II

          72069-3CIR

      III

          74024-5CIR

Article 12   Subcontracts

Article 13   Separate Contracts

Article 14   Royalties and Patents

Article 15   Arbitration

Article 16   Time

Article 17   Payments

DOCUMENT TO CASE CHARTS: A107-1970

[The five-digit numbers in this chart are Citator Case Reference Numbers, which refer to the cases, in the Cases section. The suffixes indicate the state or, for federal cases, the court in which the case was decided.]

Article 18   Protection of Persons and Property

   III

      73092-9CIR

Article 19   Contractor's Liability Insurance

   III

      72041-NE

Article 20   Owner's Liability Insurance

Article 21   Property Insurance

Article 22   Changes in the Work

Article 23   Correction of Work

Article 24   Termination by the Contractor

Article 25   Termination by the Owner

DOCUMENT TO CASE CHARTS: A107-1974

[The five-digit numbers in this chart are Citator Case Reference Numbers, which refer to the cases, in the Cases section. The suffixes indicate the state or, for federal cases, the court in which the case was decided.]

A107-1974—STANDARD FORM OF AGREEMENT BETWEEN OWNER AND CONTRACTOR—SHORT FORM AGREEMENT FOR SMALL CONSTRUCTION CONTRACTS WHERE THE BASIS OF PAYMENT IS A STIPULATED SUM

Article 1   The Work

Article 2   Time of Commencement and Completion

Article 3   Contract Sum

Article 4   Progress Payments

      II

         84035-IL

Article 5   Final Payment

Article 6   Enumeration of Contract Documents

Article 7   Contract Documents

      I

         74019-KS

Article 8   Architect

Article 9   Owner

Article 10   Contractor

      II

         84006-TN

Article 11   Subcontracts

      II

         84039-CT

Article 12   Separate Contracts

Article 13   Royalties and Patents

Article 14   Arbitration

      I

         82003-PA

DOCUMENT TO CASE CHARTS: A107-1974

[The five-digit numbers in this chart are Citator Case Reference Numbers, which refer to the cases, in the Cases section. The suffixes indicate the state or, for federal cases, the court in which the case was decided.]

    II
        84039-CT

Article 15   Time

Article 16   Payments

    II
        84006-TN

Article 17   Protection of Persons and Property

Article 18   Contractor's Liability Insurance

Article 19   Owner's Liability Insurance

Article 20   Property Insurance

Article 21   Changes in the Work

Article 22   Correction of Work

    I
        74020-LA

    II
        84006-TN

Article 23   Termination by the Contractor

Article 24   Termination by the Owner

    I
        74019-KS
        74020-LA

Article 25   Miscellaneous Provisions

DOCUMENT TO CASE CHARTS: A107-1978

[The five-digit numbers in this chart are Citator Case Reference Numbers, which refer to the cases, in the Cases section. The suffixes indicate the state or, for federal cases, the court in which the case was decided.]

A107-1978—ABBREVIATED FORM OF AGREEMENT BETWEEN OWNER AND CONTRACTOR FOR CONSTRUCTION PROJECTS OF LIMITED SCOPE WHERE THE BASIS OF PAYMENT IS A STIPULATED SUM

Article 1 The Work

II

82004-SDGA
79067-NY

Article 2 Time of Commencement and Substantial Completion

I

88027-3CIR	79043-LA
79057-4CIR	83003-LA
80032-NDIL	80072-TN
79034-AZ	81067-WY

II

82004-SDGA	82045-NH
80011-AR	80025-TX
80050-AR	

III

79003-5CIR	79062-MO
81064-8CIR	78006-MT
79034-AZ	75029-NJ
79045-CA	91007-NM
79046-CA	90010-NY
80049-IN	80009-SD
87027-IN	79036-VA
76062-LA	80039-WY
83005-LA	

Article 3 Contract Sum

I

87040-SC

II

82045-NH

III

79052-LA	80065-MO
81065-LA	80044-WA

DOCUMENT TO CASE CHARTS: A107-1978

[The five-digit numbers in this chart are Citator Case Reference Numbers, which refer to the cases, in the Cases section. The suffixes indicate the state or, for federal cases, the court in which the case was decided.]

Article 4 Progress Payments

I

80032-NDIL 79032-OK
86014-AZ 87040-SC

II

92001-7CIR
86070-IL
81047-UT

III

89042-NDIL 86049-NH
90034-FL 81045-WV
83005-LA

Article 5 Final Payment

I

80002-AZ
89030-IL

II

82004-SDGA
86056-MD

III

90034-FL 83041-LA
80026-GA 86049-NH
83039-LA 81045-WV

Article 6 Enumeration of Contract Documents

I

92008-DC
89049-MA

II

82032-DKS 82034-MS
86061-FL 82052-NV
90042-KS

III

89026-MO

DOCUMENT TO CASE CHARTS: A107-1978

[The five-digit numbers in this chart are Citator Case Reference Numbers, which refer to the cases, in the Cases section. The suffixes indicate the state or, for federal cases, the court in which the case was decided.]

Article 7 Contract Documents

I

88027-3CIR	91006-FL
90050-7CIR	78024-GA
93010-SDNY	93022-ME
79034-AZ	89049-MA
90002-CO	91034-NM
92008-DC	86062-NY
89027-FL	90043-NY

II

85017-DDE	82034-MS
82004-SDGA	84038-MO
82032-DKS	82052-NV
91008-MDPA	88016-OH
86061-FL	90020-OH
91002-GA	85029-TN
90043-KS	87036-WA
86028-MA	

III

83013-1CIR	89026-MO
90048-10CIR	93001-NC
90039-WDNC	91007-NM
90008-CC	90016-NY
91019-AL	86018-NC
92014a-AL	86039-OK
83048-CA	83001-PA
86060-IL	91027-TN
89019-KS	87029-TX
84033-LA	87007-VA
81042-MA	

Article 8 Architect

I

82020-6CIR	78043-MD
81018-AR	80055-NY
83030-FL	81057-NY
78024-GA	83047-NY
79029-IL	88031-NC
92006-ME	80061-VT

II

89022-5CIR	82024-GA
83032-7CIR	91040-GA
83023-8CIR	93013-GA
82004-SDGA	90040-IL
91031-MDPA	91001-IN
87047-AL	91030-IA
90052-AL	83020-KS
92018-CT	89008-KS
89027-FL	86071-LA
94038-FL	88024-MA
73056-GA	89035-MD

DOCUMENT TO CASE CHARTS: A107-1978

[The five-digit numbers in this chart are Citator Case Reference Numbers, which refer to the cases, in the Cases section. The suffixes indicate the state or, for federal cases, the court in which the case was decided.]

86032-MN	84007-NY
89037-MN	84019-NY
89047-MS	89004-NY
86064-MO	89012-NY
87050-MO	90051-NY
88014-MO	90020-OH
91038-MO	82056-OK
95033-MO	84027-TX
90006-NE	87026-TX
93036-NE	91020-VT
83024-NY	85014-WY

III

82041-10CIR	83002-MA
90048-10CIR	86034-MA
91037-11CIR	90035-MA
82014-NDMS	89023-MI
82057-AL	92008d-MI
87037-AL	91024-MT
83006-AR	82007-NJ
86029-CT	85026-NY
92020a-CT	86047-NY
85037-FL	88035a-NY
81040-GA	89003-NY
85006-IL	89005-NC
87030-IL	87002-ND
92004-IL	79033-PA
82028-IN	86010-PA
86035-KS	90029-PA
80074-LA	87009-TN
88012-LA	90055-TX
88041-LA	88025-VA
90044-MD	89033-VA

Article 9 Owner

I

90032-IL
81067-WY

II

86006-IL	83042-MD
83020-KS	89016-NY

III

87037-AL
87009-TN

DOCUMENT TO CASE CHARTS: A107-1978

[*The five-digit numbers in this chart are Citator Case Reference Numbers, which refer to the cases, in the Cases section. The suffixes indicate the state or, for federal cases, the court in which the case was decided.*]

Article 10 Contractor

I

82020-6CIR	80048-MA
90050-7CIR	80071-MA
80007-8CIR	81072-MA
84017-8CIR	95011-MI
81012-AL	80054-MI
89021-CA	92003-MO
90002-CO	92003a-MO
92015-GA	85033-NE
79063-IN	83047-NY
81044-IL	89025-NC
93025-IL	92010b-OH
88033-IL	91010-TX
79043-LA	80061-VT
89036-LA	82038-WA

II

83010-5CIR	93018-MA
83023-8CIR	85008-MN
84014-8CIR	88026-MN
82004-SDGA	93058-MN
80042-DMD	91036a-MO
91013-SDMS	82001-NE
90013-AL	82048-NE
91036-AZ	85033-NE
84029-DC	90026-NE
87013-FL	86065-NJ
88005-FL	87048-NM
94038-FL	79067-NY
78056-GA	82021-NY
84032-GA	83024-NY
91040-GA	84001-NY
93013-GA	85023-NY
80056-IL	85038-NY
84028-IL	88001-NY
85019-IL	89015-NY
86013-IL	89016-NY
86068-IL	82056-OK
88033-IL	93043-PA
90040-IL	85013-TN
91025-IL	79040-TX
82018-IN	80035-TX
84015-IN	86058-TX
91001-IN	87019-TX
90042-KS	87026-TX
88042-KY	94009-TX
82009-LA	95036-TX
83038-LA	87011-VA
83040-LA	84005-WA
86072-LA	85016-WA
90056-LA	93040-WI
81013-MA	83050-WY
91016-MA	

DOCUMENT TO CASE CHARTS: A107-1978

[The five-digit numbers in this chart are Citator Case Reference Numbers, which refer to the cases, in the Cases section. The suffixes indicate the state or, for federal cases, the court in which the case was decided.]

III

89001-4CIR	86035-KS
83007-7CIR	83005-LA
87010-DME	83002-MA
82014-NDMS	86063-MA
90039-WDNC	89028-MA
80012-AL	85035-MI
85003-AL	87020-MI
87037-AL	84002-MN
91019-AL	93047-MN
92014a-AL	79072-MO
93004-AL	80010-MT
85011-AK	86043-MT
86022-AK	84031-NE
85025-CA	82007-NJ
85034-CA	91007-NM
86001-CT	81070-NY
87035-CA	87016-NY
93051-DC	92007-NY
80053-FL	93039-NY
79041-GA	87002-ND
81006-GA	91019-ND
81007-GA	86009-OH
88040-GA	93031-OH
90036-GA	76014-PA
85015-HI	90029-PA
79070-IL	91039-PA
80073-IL	82017-TN
85015a-IL	87009-TN
87008-IL	88002-TX
87042-IL	89033-VA
92004-IL	85028-WA
82028-IN	86057-WA
86052-IN	89041-WV
91023-IN	82023-WI
86050-IA	84013-WI

Article 11 Subcontracts

I

77049-CT
92015-GA

II

86037-3CIR	84016-KS
85027-4CIR	86072-LA
84014-8CIR	82034-MS
85005-AR	86067-MN
90002-CO	90017-NY
84032-GA	84036-OH
85003-GA	86026-OH
85021-GA	82058-PA
83028-IL	86002-TN
93025-IL	83050-WY
83020-KS	

DOCUMENT TO CASE CHARTS: A107-1978

[The five-digit numbers in this chart are Citator Case Reference Numbers, which refer to the cases, in the Cases section. The suffixes indicate the state or, for federal cases, the court in which the case was decided.]

III

82008-11CIR
93050-DPR
83045-SDNY
86055-AZ
90034-FL
80026-GA
86060-IL
80021-KS

83002-MA
92013-MA
84030-MI
86015-NY
89005-NC
89018-SC
82017-TN

Article 12 Work by Owner or by Separate Contractors

I

93025-IL
81001-MA

II

91008-MDPA
93025-IL

90005-IN
90047-IN

III

86017-CO
77048-DE
87028-IL

82007-NJ
86018-NC

Article 13 Miscellaneous Provisions

I

89048-US
84010-6CIR
91001-SDAL
86014-AZ
89002-AZ
76002-CO
81056-CO
82029-CO
89034-CT
93006-CT
92008-DC
81006-FL
81073-FL
82039-FL
83030-FL
91006-FL
91015-FL
90009-GA
80057-ID
81009-IL
81041-IL
84011-IL

89030-IL
90041-IN
90018-KS
93003-KY
81038-LA
90027-LA
92006-ME
78043-MD
90014-MD
92013-MA
82019-MI
87017-MN
80053-NY
80055-NY
81027-NY
81028-NY
81057-NY
80062-NY
92010-NC
93048-SC
93002-SD
89051-TX
92009a-TX

DOCUMENT TO CASE CHARTS: A107-1978

[The five-digit numbers in this chart are Citator Case Reference Numbers, which refer to the cases, in the Cases section. The suffixes indicate the state or, for federal cases, the court in which the case was decided.]

II

83033-US
86037-3CIR
85027-4CIR
87032-4CIR
83010-5CIR
86045-5CIR
87014-5CIR
90019-6CIR
84040-NDAL
87022-DDC
82032-DKS
88006-DME
85040-WDMO
88008-SDNY
90004-DSC
87005-NDTX
86021-AL
90038-AL
85005-AR
83008-CA
83016-CA
90046-CA
88029-CT
90001-CT
86023-DE
81054-FL
83018-FL
84004-FL
85004-FL
86020-FL
86031-FL
86041-FL
86061-FL
87001-FL
82024-GA
85003-GA
94003-GA
93008-IA
81014-IL
86070-IL

87015-IL
87018-IL
88039-IL
89011-IL
89044-IL
92021-IL
81023-KS
84016-KS
93052-LA
90022-ME
89035-MD
80076-MA
81013-MA
84003-MD
86036-MI
89023-MI
91012-MI
86067-MN
88009-MN
89010-MN
89046-MN
95033-MO
78060-MT
82049-NE
84007-NY
84019-NY
87039-NY
81010-NC
85002-NC
88031-NC
84036-OH
88016-OH
89018-SC
93048-SC
93024-TN
80025-TX
84027-TX
93054-TX
81047-UT
95023-VA

III

83009-6CIR
89050-6CIR
83011-8CIR
83026-8CIR
88044-NDGA
82042-DVI
93004-AL
84012-AZ
85041-AZ
90045-AZ
90003-CA
77023-CT
86029-CT
90053-CT
92020a-CT

79039-IL
83025-IL
89045-IL
79030-IA
80074-LA
83005-LA
82010-MD
89039-MD
79054-MA
92008d-MI
85042-MO
82015-NH
86054-NH
79023-NJ
77019-NY

DOCUMENT TO CASE CHARTS: A107-1978

[The five-digit numbers in this chart are Citator Case Reference Numbers, which refer to the cases, in the Cases section. The suffixes indicate the state or, for federal cases, the court in which the case was decided.]

    81005-NY   87045-PA
    85026-NY   87052-PA
    85043-NY   88013-PA
    86024-NY   91018-RI
    86047-NY   82012-SD
    88035a-NY   80008-TX
    86026-OH   86069-WI
    86010-PA

Article 14 Time

I

    80007-8CIR   89033-VA
    80002-AZ   80065-MO
    80049-IN   80010-MT
    89027-FL   81015-MT
    76008-MD   81016-MT
    83003-LA   79032-OK
    93020-NC   80022-OR
    92017-NJ   80009-SD
    83043-NY   80039-WY
    88031-NC   81067-WY

II

    84014-8CIR   87004-LA
    87033-8CIR   87017-MN
    82004-SDGA   86064-MO
    79058-CA   88020-NE
    85032-IN   82045-NH
    86070-IL   85029-TN

III

    84022-6CIR   83027-NY
    83007-7CIR   86005-NY
    85009-7CIR   86012-NY
    90048-10CIR   86053-NY
    89043-NDIL   86066-NY
    86029-CT   90007-NY
    85006-IL   85012-NC
    87030-IL   84025-OH
    87027-IN   86009-OH
    83005-LA   86004-PA
    90044-MD   86010-PA
    84030-MI   90015-PA
    91021-MO   83004-TX
    82007-NJ   88025-VA
    91007-NM   87025-WI

DOCUMENT TO CASE CHARTS: A107-1978

A–50

[The five-digit numbers in this chart are Citator Case Reference Numbers, which refer to the cases, in the Cases section. The suffixes indicate the state or, for federal cases, the court in which the case was decided.]

Article 15 Payments and Completion

I

90050-7CIR
95020-DPR
80002-AZ
76008-MD

79043-LA
83003-LA
81010-NC

II

81064-8CIR
84014-8CIR
91008-MDPA
84020-AK
84029-DC
89027-FL
91014-FL
82030-IL
83028-IL
88003-IL
90040-IL
90042-KS

82009-LA
83042-MD
86056-MD
89035-MD
79031-MN
89010-MN
82048-NE
90026-NE
84007-NY
81047-UT
82058-PA

III

83035-5CIR
82020-6CIR
83007-7CIR
82042-DVI
86029-CT
86051-CT
90034-FL
84016-KS
80040-LA
83005-LA
83039-LA
83041-LA

86008-LA
82050-MN
90030-MS
86049-NH
83029-NJ
83036-NY
85022-NY
84025-OH
88036-TX
88022-VA
87025-WI

Article 16 Protection of Persons and Property

I

81012-AL
92011-AZ

92021a-AZ
83047-NY

II

94038-FL
91040-GA
92010a-GA
84015-IN
91001-IN
83042-MD
81068-MT

92016a-MT
83014-NV
89016-NY
88016-OH
82056-OK
85029-TN

DOCUMENT TO CASE CHARTS: A107-1978

[The five-digit numbers in this chart are Citator Case Reference Numbers, which refer to the cases, in the Cases section. The suffixes indicate the state or, for federal cases, the court in which the case was decided.]

III

91037-11CIR
87037-AL
80029-AR
79071-DC
85037-FL
81058-GA
90036-GA
79070-IL
92004-IL
82028-IN

86052-IN
88035-IN
90035-MA
86038-MO
81036-NY
86018-NC
90029-PA
81016-TX
79015-VA

Article 17 Insurance

I

93010-SDNY
81056-CO
89040-CO
81041-IL
79063-IN
93022-ME

76008-MD
81072-MA
90043-NY
92010b-OH
92020-WA

II

88007-3CIR
87014-5CIR
91016-AL
88037-AZ
93056-AZ
85036-CO
90002-CO
85021-GA
93013-GA
86068-IL
91022-IL
83038-LA

83040-LA
91033-LA
86028-MA
94002-MO
79022-NY
85038-NY
88032-NC
88015-ND
88016-OH
90049-OK
92019a-TX
87036-WA

III

83015-11CIR
92014a-AL
83006-AR
78030-FL
81024-FL
79030-IA
80073-IL
87008-IL
87042-IL
80021-KS

94013-LA
86063-MA
83044-MN
78035-NJ
84026-NY
87002-ND
91029-ND
91027-TN
87007-VA
86046-WA

DOCUMENT TO CASE CHARTS: A107-1978

[The five-digit numbers in this chart are Citator Case Reference Numbers, which refer to the cases, in the Cases section. The suffixes indicate the state or, for federal cases, the court in which the case was decided.]

Article 18   Changes in the Work

I

80002-AZ	90009-GA
91005-FL	86003-NY

II

88008-SDNY	84038-MO
91031-MDPA	86030-MO
84029-DC	89032-MO
84032-GA	91038-MO
90009-GA	83034-NY
91005-IL	84019-NY
85032-IN	88020-ND
85020-IA	76019-PA
81023-KS	85029-TN
83020-KS	84027-TX
84018-MO	

III

89024-1CIR	85044-MN
82026-8CIR	88011-MS
90048-10CIR	91021-MO
82008-11CIR	81015-MT
89043-NDIL	82007-NJ
90008-CC	78077-NY
80070-AL	84026-NY
91004-AL	85022-NY
93004-AL	85030-NY
86055-AZ	86005-NY
86029-CT	86053-NY
79055-GA	90007-NY
90009-GA	85012-NC
80036-ID	84025-OH
81014-IL	86009-OH
87003-IL	86059-OH
87028-IL	80022-OR
84037-IN	83001-PA
89019-KS	86004-PA
79027-LA	86010-PA
84033-LA	86011-PA
90022-ME	83004-TX
90044-MD	87029-TX
84024-MA	88036-TX
86027-MA	88025-VA
86024-MA	85039-WV
84030-MI	

DOCUMENT TO CASE CHARTS: A107-1978

[The five-digit numbers in this chart are Citator Case Reference Numbers, which refer to the cases, in the Cases section. The suffixes indicate the state or, for federal cases, the court in which the case was decided.]

Article 19 Correction of Work

I

82020-6CIR
92015-GA
81057-NY

II

84029-DC
78056-GA
83028-IL
90040-IL
82009-LA

87024-MD
90026-NE
86065-NJ
83034-NY
85023-NY

III

81060-5CIR
82014-NDMS
80012-AL
93004-AL

87034-IL
84030-NE
82017-TN

Article 20 Termination of the Contract

II

91013-SDMS
80011-AR
88010-CO
90032-IL

94027-MN
84019-NY
88016-OH

III

82002-3CIR
83007-7CIR
86016-EDMO
92009-FL

83034-NY
90016-NY
85014a-OK
86042-WA

Article 21 Other Conditions or Provisions

Article 22 Correction of Work

II

83042-MD
83014-NV

DOCUMENT TO CASE CHARTS: A107-1987

[The five-digit numbers in this chart are Citator Case Reference Numbers, which refer to the cases, in the Cases section. The suffixes indicate the state or, for federal cases, the court in which the case was decided.]

A107-1987—ABBREVIATED FORM OF AGREEMENT BETWEEN OWNER AND CONTRACTOR FOR CONSTRUCTION PROJECTS OF LIMITED SCOPE WHERE THE BASIS OF PAYMENT IS A STIPULATED SUM

Article 1   The Work

Article 2   Date of Commencement and Substantial Completion

Article 3   Contract Sum

Article 4   Progress Payments

    II

        95034-VA

    III

        94050-AL
        95050-NY

Article 5   Final Payment

    II

        95034-VA

    III

        94050-AL
        95050-NY

Article 6   Enumeration of Contract Documents

    I

        95051-SDMS

    II

        94020-TX
        97003-WA
        97024-WV

Article 7   Contract Documents

    I

        95051-SDMS
        93019-NJ
        94004-MO

DOCUMENT TO CASE CHARTS: A107-1987

[The five-digit numbers in this chart are Citator Case Reference Numbers, which refer to the cases, in the Cases section. The suffixes indicate the state or, for federal cases, the court in which the case was decided.]

II

97025-CO
95031-MI
94020-TX

97003-WA
97024-WV

III

96025-NJ
93026-NY

Article 8 Owner

III

95044-MDAL
95040-GA
95008-VA

Article 9 Contractor

I

95051-SDMS
94043-NDNY
97009-CA
96009-LA
95011-MI
92003a-MO

93005-MO
93033-MO
95025-NJ
97025-NJ
92008a-PA

II

94044-MDGA
96015-DC
97002-DC
94038-FL
95006-GA
95040-GA
92008b-IA
92001a-ID
93025-IL
94036-IL
93018-MA
94047-MI
93053-MN
93014-MO
93033-MO

96018-MO
95004-NJ
95025-NJ
97014-NJ
93043-PA
97005-PA
92004f-TX
94009-TX
94033-TX
94045-TX
95036-TX
95049-TX
93028-UT
93035-UT
93040-WI
95045-WI

III

94039-5CIR
97020-10CIR
94040-11CIR
95044-MDAL
96019-DKS
96024-DKS
94023-SDMS
95035-SDNY
94022-DRI
95007-DRI
95019-AR

97008-CA
94032-DE
93051-DC
93009-FL
95032-FL
93034-GA
97019-ID
93015a-IL
94046-IL
95026-IL
96012-IL

DOCUMENT TO CASE CHARTS: A107-1987

[*The five-digit numbers in this chart are Citator Case Reference Numbers, which refer to the cases, in the Cases section. The suffixes indicate the state or, for federal cases, the court in which the case was decided.*]

96031-IL	95010-MN
94014-IN	96008-MN
92004d-LA	96043-MN
94013-LA	94005-MO
93038-LA	95004-NJ
95027-LA	96025-NJ
96003-LA	93039-NY
95015-ME	93030-OH
93041-MA	94042-OH
94029-MA	94048-OK
95028-MA	95012-OR
95030-MA	93031-PA
95041-MA	94024-PA
96021-MA	96027-TX
96026-MA	93042-UT
96029-MA	95013-UT
96035-MA	95008-VA
97006-MA	94035-WA
94016-MI	96007-WA
93047-MN	95048-WV
94037-MN	96041-WY

Article 10 Administration of the Contract

I

92012-DNJ	97018-MO
92014-AL	92007-NC
93006-CT	93019-NJ
93016-FL	97026-OH
93012-IL	92008a-PA
93003-KY	97023-PA
92019-LA	93002-SD
93011-MA	92005a-TX
93005-MO	97024-WV
94017-MO	

II

96020-8CIR	97007-NJ
94044-MDGA	96011-NY
95046-AL	95042-OH
93044-FL	95052-OH
94038-FL	93048-SC
92004b-GA	92002-TN
94003-GA	93024-TN
94026-GA	96023-TN
93008-IA	94045-TX
93052-LA	93054-TX
94006-MD	96027-TX
97011-MD	95023-VA
93046-MO	96014-VA
95033-MO	95001-WA
93036-NE	93049-WV
95004-NJ	94049-WY

DOCUMENT TO CASE CHARTS: A107-1987

[The five-digit numbers in this chart are Citator Case Reference Numbers, which refer to the cases, in the Cases section. The suffixes indicate the state or, for federal cases, the court in which the case was decided.]

III

95018-2CIR
96022-2CIR
97020-10CIR
96006-DCCIR
97001-MDGA
95014-AR
97016-AR
94018-CA
96038-CO
94041-CT
96002-DC
92004a-GA
93015a-IL
93027-IL
93045-IL

94021-LA
94005-MO
95016-NC
95022-NC
94001-NY
95024-NY
97022-NY
95009-PA
94030-TX
95022-TX
95008-VA
95001-WA
94019-WI
96039-WY

Article 11 Subcontracts

I

93025-IL
93019-NJ

II

97021-FL
93025-IL

III

97001-MDGA
96040-MO

Article 12 Construction by Owner or by Separate Contractors

I

93007-GA

II

94011-WDMI
92005b-AK
92004e-GA

93007-GA
93025-IL

III

95018-2CIR
96016-GA
96041-WY

DOCUMENT TO CASE CHARTS: A107-1987

[The five-digit numbers in this chart are Citator Case Reference Numbers, which refer to the cases, in the Cases section. The suffixes indicate the state or, for federal cases, the court in which the case was decided.]

Article 13   Changes in the Work

    I

        92012-DNJ

    II

        93015-OR
        95001-WA

    III

        93037-10CIR   93026-NY
        94040-11CIR   97010-OH
        92005b-AK   94031-RI
        92009b-ND   95001-WA

Article 14   Time

    I

        97018-MO

    II

        92004e-GA
        94036-IL

    III

        95018-2CIR   95047-LA
        94040-11CIR   96040-MO
        96036-FCIR   95008-VA
        97001-MDGA   95001-WA
        96016-GA   96039-WY
        97013-GA

Article 15   Payments and Completion

    II

        95001-WA

    III

        93009-FL   96040-MO
        93021-IL   94031-RI
        96004-LA

Article 16   Protection of Persons and Property

    I

        93005-MO

DOCUMENT TO CASE CHARTS: A107-1987

[The five-digit numbers in this chart are Citator Case Reference Numbers, which refer to the cases, in the Cases section. The suffixes indicate the state or, for federal cases, the court in which the case was decided.]

II

94044-MDGA
94038-FL
96009-LA
95004-NJ

97005-PA
94045-TX
96027-TX

III

95044-MDAL
96024-DKS
94032-DE
93034-GA
95040-GA
93015a-IL
93017-IL

94014-IN
92004d-LA
95030-MA
94005-MO
95003-OH
95038-OH

Article 17 Insurance

I

95051-SDMS

II

94011-WDMI
93056-AZ
94012-CA
97009-CA
97025-CO
96008-MN

94002-MO
94004-MO
93029-NH
95049-TX
95055-WI

III

93050-DPR
96012-IL
94013-LA
97004-MD

94037-MN
96043-MN
95004-NJ
95038-OH

Article 18 Correction of Work

II

96034-MO

III

94024-PA

Article 19 Miscellaneous Provisions

I

92012-DNJ
93011-MA
93048-SC

DOCUMENT TO CASE CHARTS: A107-1987

[The five-digit numbers in this chart are Citator Case Reference Numbers, which refer to the cases, in the Cases section. The suffixes indicate the state or, for federal cases, the court in which the case was decided.]

Article 20 Termination of the Contract

    I

        92012-DNJ

    II

        95020-DPR
        94027-MN

    III

        92021b-VA
        95008-VA

Article 21 Other Conditions or Provisions

DOCUMENT TO CASE CHARTS: A111-1963

[*The five-digit numbers in this chart are Citator Case Reference Numbers, which refer to the cases, in the Cases section. The suffixes indicate the state or, for federal cases, the court in which the case was decided.*]

A111-1963—STANDARD FORM OF AGREEMENT BETWEEN OWNER AND CONTRACTOR WHERE THE BASIS OF PAYMENT IS THE COST OF THE WORK PLUS A FEE

> **Text of Article 1—The Work to Be Done and the Documents Forming the Contract**
>
> The Contractor agrees to provide all the labor and materials and to do all things necessary for the proper construction and completion of the work shown and described in Drawings and in Specifications entitled: _____ and enumerated as follows: _____ The said Drawings and Specifications and the General Conditions of the Contract consisting of Articles numbered 1 to _____ and Supplementary General Conditions numbered: _____ together with this Agreement, constitute the Contract; the Drawings, Specifications, General Conditions and Supplementary General Conditions being as fully a part thereof and hereof as if hereto attached or herein repeated. If anything in the said General Conditions or Supplementary General Conditions is inconsistent with this Agreement, the Agreement shall govern. _____ The said documents have been prepared by: _____ therein and hereinafter called the architect.

Article 1   The Work to Be Done and the Documents Forming the Contract

    I

       65083-NC

Article 2   Time of Completion

Article 3   Changes in the Work

Article 4   The Contractor's Duties and Status

> **Text of Article 5—Fee for Services**
>
> In consideration of the performance of the contract, the Owner agrees to pay the Contractor, in current funds as compensation for his services hereunder as follows: _____

Article 5   Fee for Services

    I

       65083-NC

> **Text of Article 6—Costs to Be Reimbursed**
>
> The Owner agrees to reimburse the Contractor in current funds all costs necessarily incurred for the proper execution of the work and paid directly by the Contractor, such costs to include the following items, and to be at rates not higher

than the standard paid in the locality of the work except with prior consent of the Owner;

6.1 All labor directly on the Contractor's payroll, including social security and old age benefit taxes and other taxes related thereto.

6.2 Salaries of Contractor's employees stationed at the field office, in whatever capacity employed. Employees engaged, at shops or on the road, in expediting the production or transportation of material, shall be considered as stationed at the field office and their salaries paid for such part of their time as is employed on this work.

6.3 The proportion of transportation, traveling and hotel expenses of the Contractor or of his officers or employees incurred in discharge of duties connected with this work.

6.4 All expenses incurred for transportation to and from the work of the force required for its prosecution.

6.5 Permit fees, royalties, damages for infringement of patents, and costs of defending suits therefor and for deposits lost for causes other than the Contractor's negligence.

6.6 Losses and expenses, not compensated by insurance or otherwise, sustained by the Contractor in connection with the work, provided they have resulted from causes other than the fault or neglect of the Contractor. Such losses shall include settlements made with the written consent and approval of the Owner. No such losses and expenses shall be included in the cost of the work for the purpose of determining the Contractor's fee, but if, after a loss from fire, flood or similar cause not due to the fault or neglect of the Contractor, he be put in charge of reconstruction, he shall be paid for his services a fee proportionate to that named in Article 5 hereof.

6.7 Minor expenses, such as telegrams, telephone service, expressage, and similar petty cash items.

6.8 Cost of hand tools, not owned by the workmen, canvas and tarpaulins, consumed in the prosecution of the work, and depreciation on such tools, canvas and tarpaulins used but not consumed and which shall remain the property of the Contractor.

6.9 Materials, supplies, equipment and transportation required for the proper execution of the work, which shall include all temporary structures and their maintenance, including sales and other taxes related thereto.

6.10 The amounts of all subcontracts.

6.11 Premiums on all bonds and insurance policies called for under the Contract.

6.12 Rentals of all construction plant or parts thereof, whether rented from the Contractor or others, in accordance with rental agreements approved by the Architect. Transportation of said construction plant, costs of loading and unloading, cost of installation, dismantling and removal thereof and minor repairs and replacements during its use on the work—all in accordance with the terms of the said rental agreements.

DOCUMENT TO CASE CHARTS: A111-1963

[The five-digit numbers in this chart are Citator Case Reference Numbers, which refer to the cases, in the Cases section. The suffixes indicate the state or, for federal cases, the court in which the case was decided.]

Article 6 Costs to Be Reimbursed

I

65083-NC

II

94020-TX

III

66034-PA

Text of Article 7—Costs Not to Be Reimbursed

Reimbursement of expenses to the Contractor shall not include any of the following:

7.1 Salary of the Contractor, if an individual, or salary of any member of the Contractor, if a firm, or salary of any officer of the Contractor, if a corporation.

7.2 Salary of any person employed, during the execution of the work, in the main office or in any regularly established branch office of the Contractor.

7.3 Overhead or general expenses of any kind, except as these may be expressly included in Article 6.

7.4 Interest on capital employed either in plant or in expenditures on the work, except as may be expressly included in Article 6.

Article 7 Costs Not to Be Reimbursed

I

94004-MO

II

94020-TX
93026-NY

Text of Article 8—Discounts, Rebates, Refunds

All cash discounts shall accrue to the Contractor unless the Owner deposits funds with the Contractor with which to make payments, in which case the cash discounts shall accrue to the Owner. All trade discounts, rebates and refunds, and all returns from sale of surplus materials and equipment shall accrue to the Owner, and the Contractor shall make provisions so that they can be secured.

DOCUMENT TO CASE CHARTS: A111-1963 A–64

[The five-digit numbers in this chart are Citator Case Reference Numbers, which refer to the cases, in the Cases section. The suffixes indicate the state or, for federal cases, the court in which the case was decided.]

Article 8 Discounts, Rebates, Refunds

    III

        66034-PA

Text of Article 9—Contractor's Financial Responsibility

Any cost due to the negligence of the Contractor or anyone directly employed by him, either for the making good of defective work, disposal of material wrongly supplied, making good of damage to property, or excess costs or material or labor, or otherwise, shall be borne by the Contractor, and the Owner may withhold money due the Contractor to cover any such cost already paid by him as part of the cost of the work. This article supersedes the provisions of Articles 13, 19 and 20 of the General Conditions of the Contract so far as they are inconsistent herewith.

Article 9 Contractor's Financial Responsibility

    I

        65054-TX

    II

93025-IL	94009-TX
93053-MN	93028-UT
93033-MO	93035-UT
93043-PA	93040-WI

    III

93051-DC	93047-MN
93034-GA	94005-MO
94014-IN	93039-NY
93038-LA	93030-OH
94013-LA	93031-PA
93041-MA	93042-UT
94016-MI	

Article 10 Sub-Contracts

Article 11 Title to the Work

Article 12 Accounting, Inspection, Audit

Article 13 Applications for Payment

Article 14 Certificate for Payment

Article 15 Disbursements

Article 16 Termination of Contract

A–65 DOCUMENT TO CASE CHARTS: A111-1967

[*The five-digit numbers in this chart are Citator Case Reference Numbers, which refer to the cases, in the Cases section. The suffixes indicate the state or, for federal cases, the court in which the case was decided.*]

A111-1967—STANDARD FORM OF AGREEMENT BETWEEN OWNER AND CONTRACTOR WHERE THE BASIS OF PAYMENT IS THE COST OF THE WORK PLUS A FEE

Text of Article 1—The Contract Documents

The Contract Documents consist of this Agreement, Conditions of the Contract (General, Supplementary and other Conditions), Drawings, Specifications, all Addenda issued prior to execution of this Agreement and all Modifications issued subsequent thereto. These form the Contract, and all are as fully a part of the Contract as if attached to this Agreement or repeated herein. An enumeration of the Contract Documents appears in Article 17. If anything in the General Conditions is inconsistent with this Agreement, the Agreement shall govern.

Article 1   The Contract Documents

    I

        68007-10CIR
        71072-KY
        71008-MD

    III

        72112-MD

Text of Article 2—The Work

The Contractor shall perform all the Work required by the Contract Documents for (*Here insert the caption descriptive of the Work as used on other Contract Documents.*) _____

Article 2   The Work

    I

        68007-10CIR

Text of Article 3—Architect

The Architect for this Project is _____

Article 3   Architect

    I

        68007-10CIR

Text of Article 4—The Contractor's Duties and Status

The Contractor accepts the relationship of trust and confidence established between him and the Owner by this Agreement. He covenants with the Owner to furnish his best skill and judgment and to cooperate with the Architect in furthering

DOCUMENT TO CASE CHARTS: A111-1967

[The five-digit numbers in this chart are Citator Case Reference Numbers, which refer to the cases, in the Cases section. The suffixes indicate the state or, for federal cases, the court in which the case was decided.]

> the interests of the Owner. He agrees to furnish efficient business administration and superintendence and to use his best efforts to furnish at all times an adequate supply of workmen and materials, and to perform the Work in the best and soundest way and in the most expeditious and economical manner consistent with the interests of the Owner.

Article 4   **The Contractor's Duties and Status**

    I

        73057-MO

    III

        72108-IA

Article 5   **Time of Commencement and Completion**

Text of Article 6—Cost of the Work and Guaranteed Maximum Cost

6.1 The Owner agrees to reimburse the Contractor for the Cost of the Work as defined in Article 9. Such reimbursement shall be in addition to the Contractor's fee stipulated in Article 7.

6.2 The maximum cost to the Owner, including the Cost of the Work and the Contractor's Fee, is guaranteed not to exceed the sum of _____ dollars ($ _____); such Guaranteed Maximum Cost shall be increased or decreased for Changes in the Work as provided in Article 8. (*Here insert any provision for distribution of any savings. Delete Paragraph 6.2 if there is no Guaranteed Maximum Cost.*) _____

Article 6   **Cost of the Work and Guaranteed Maximum Cost**

    I

        73095-CA
        82027-PA

    II

        68011-CA   83014-NV
        70091-IL   67010-VT

    III

        71060-SC
        74039-NC

Text of Article 7—Contractor's Fee

7.1 In consideration of the performance of the Contract, the Owner agrees to pay the Contractor in current funds as compensation for his services a Contractor's Fee as follows: _____

DOCUMENT TO CASE CHARTS: A111-1967

[The five-digit numbers in this chart are Citator Case Reference Numbers, which refer to the cases, in the Cases section. The suffixes indicate the state or, for federal cases, the court in which the case was decided.]

> **7.2** For Changes in the Work, the Contractor's Fee shall be adjusted as follows: _____
>
> **7.3** The Contractor shall be paid _____ per cent (_____ %) of the proportionate amount of his Fee with each progress payment, and the balance of his Fee shall be paid at the time of final payment.

Article 7   Contractor's Fee

    I

        71072-KY
        73057-MO

    III

        73096-WA

> **Text of Article 8—Changes in the Work**
>
> **8.1** The Owner may make Changes in the Work in accordance with Article 12 of the General Conditions insofar as such Article is consistent with this Agreement. The Contractor shall be reimbursed for Changes in the Work on the basis of Cost of the Work as defined in Article 9.
>
> **8.2** The Contractor's Fee for Changes in the Work shall be as set forth in Paragraph 7.2, or in the absence of specific provisions therein, shall be adjusted by negotiation on the basis of the Fee established for the original Work.

Article 8   Changes in the Work

    I

        69032-CA   73057-MO
        69027-IA   82027-PA

> **Text of Article 9—Costs to Be Reimbursed**
>
> **9.1** The term Cost of the Work shall mean costs necessarily incurred in the proper performance of the Work and paid by the Contractor. Such costs shall be at rates not higher than the standard paid in the locality of the Work except with prior consent of the Owner, and shall include the items set forth below in this Article 9.
>
> **9.1.1** Wages paid for labor in the direct employ of the Contractor in the performance of the Work under applicable collective bargaining agreements, or under a salary or wage schedule agreed upon by the Owner and Contractor, and including such welfare or other benefits, if any, as may be payable with respect thereto.
>
> **9.1.2** Salaries of Contractor's employees when stationed at the field office, in whatever capacity employed. Employees engaged, at shops or on the road, in expediting the production or transportation of materials or equipment, shall be

considered as stationed at the field office and their salaries paid for that portion of their time spent on this Work.

9.1.3 Cost of contributions, assessments or taxes for such items as unemployment compensation and social security, insofar as such cost is based on wages, salaries, or other remuneration paid to employees of the Contractor and included in the Cost of the Work under Subparagraphs 9.1.1 and 9.1.2.

9.1.4 The proportion of reasonable transportation, traveling and hotel expenses of the Contractor or of his officers or employees incurred in discharge of duties connected with the Work.

9.1.5 Cost of all materials, supplies and equipment incorporated in the Work, including costs of transportation thereof.

9.1.6 Payments made by the Contractor to Subcontractors for Work performed pursuant to subcontracts under this Agreement.

9.1.7 Cost, including transportation and maintenance, of all materials, supplies, equipment, temporary facilities and hand tools not owned by the workmen, which are consumed in the performance of the Work, and cost less salvage value on such items used but not consumed which remain the property of the Contractor.

9.1.8 Rental charges of all necessary machinery and equipment, exclusive of hand tools, used at the site of the Work, whether rented from the Contractor or others, including installation, minor repairs and replacements, dismantling, removal, transportation and delivery costs thereof, at rental charges consistent with those prevailing in the area.

9.1.9 Cost of premiums for all bonds and insurance which the Contractor is required by the Contract Documents to purchase and maintain.

9.1.10 Sales, use or similar taxes related to the Work and for which the Contractor is liable imposed by any governmental authority.

9.1.11 Permit fees, royalties, damages for infringement of patents and costs of defending suits therefor, and deposits lost for causes other than the Contractor's negligence.

9.1.12 Losses and expenses, not compensated by insurance or otherwise, sustained by the Contractor in connection with the Work, provided they have resulted from causes other than the fault or neglect of the Contractor. Such losses shall include settlements made with the written consent and approval of the Owner. No such losses and expenses shall be included in the Cost of the Work for the purpose of determining the Contractor's Fee. If, however, such loss requires reconstruction and the Contractor is placed in charge thereof, he shall be paid for his services a Fee proportionate to that stated in Paragraph 7.1.

9.1.13 Minor expenses such as telegrams, long distance telephone calls, telephone service at the site, expressage, and similar petty cash items in connection with the Work.

9.1.14 Cost of removal of all debris.

[*The five-digit numbers in this chart are Citator Case Reference Numbers, which refer to the cases, in the Cases section. The suffixes indicate the state or, for federal cases, the court in which the case was decided.*]

> **9.1.15** Costs incurred due to an emergency affecting the safety of persons and property.
>
> **9.1.16** Other costs incurred in the performance of the Work if and to the extent approved in advance in writing by the Owner.

Article 9 Costs to Be Reimbursed

   I

      63007-10CIR
      73057-MO

   III

      73065-TX

> **Text of Article 10—Costs Not to Be Reimbursed**
>
> **10.1** The term Cost of the Work shall not include any of the items set forth below in this Article 10.
>
> **10.1.1** Salaries or other compensation of the Contractor's officers, executives, general managers, estimators, auditors, accountants, purchasing and contracting agents and other employees at the Contractor's principal office and branch offices, except employees of the Contractor when engaged at shops or on the road in expediting the production or transportation of materials or equipment for the Work.
>
> **10.1.2** Expenses of the Contractor's Principal and Branch Offices other than the Field Office.
>
> **10.1.3** Any part of the Contractor's capital expenses, including interest on the Contractor's capital employed for the Work.
>
> **10.1.4** Overhead or general expenses of any kind, except as may be expressly included in Article 9.
>
> **10.1.5** Costs due to the negligence of the Contractor, any Subcontractor, anyone directly or indirectly employed by any of them, or for whose acts any of them may be liable, including but not limited to the correction of defective Work, disposal of materials and equipment wrongly supplied, or making good any damage to property.
>
> **10.1.6** The cost of any item not specifically and expressly included in the items described in Article 9.
>
> **10.1.7** Costs in excess of the Guaranteed Maximum Cost, if any, as set forth in Article 6 and adjusted pursuant to Article 8.

DOCUMENT TO CASE CHARTS: A111-1967 — A-70

[The five-digit numbers in this chart are Citator Case Reference Numbers, which refer to the cases, in the Cases section. The suffixes indicate the state or, for federal cases, the court in which the case was decided.]

Article 10   Costs Not to Be Reimbursed

    I

        73057-MO

    II

        73029-5CIR

    III

        72041-NE
        72055-NE

Article 11   Discounts, Rebates and Refunds

Text of Article 12—Subcontracts

12.1 All portions of the Work that the Contractor's organization has not been accustomed to perform shall be performed under subcontracts. The Contractor shall request bids from subcontractors and shall deliver such bids to the Architect. The Architect will then determine, with the advice of the Contractor and subject to the approval of the Owner, which bids will be accepted.

12.2 All Subcontracts shall conform to the requirements of Paragraph 5.3 of the General Conditions. Subcontracts awarded on the basis of the cost of such work plus a fee shall also be subject to the provisions of this Agreement insofar as applicable.

Article 12   Subcontracts

    II

        73029-5CIR

Article 13   Accounting Records

Text of Article 14—Application for Payment

The Contractor shall, at least ten days before each progress payment falls due, deliver to the Architect a statement, sworn to if required, showing in complete detail all moneys paid out or costs incurred by him on account of the Cost of the Work during the previous month for which he is to be reimbursed under Article 6 and the amount of the Contractor's Fee due as provided in Article 7, together with payrolls for all labor and all receipted bills for which payment has been received.

Article 14   Application for Payment

    I

        68007-10CIR

Text of Article 15—Payments to the Contractor

15.1 The Architect will review the Contractor's statement of moneys due as provided in Article 14 and will promptly issue a Certificate for Payment to the Owner for such amount as he approves, which Certificate shall be payable on or about the _____ day of the month.

15.2 Final payment, constituting the unpaid balance of the Cost of the Work and of the Contractor's Fee, shall be paid by the Owner to the Contractor when the Work has been completed, the Contract fully performed and a final Certificate for Payment has been issued by the Architect. Final payment shall be due _____ days after the date of issuance of the final Certificate for Payment.

Article 15   Payments to the Contractor

    I

        68007-10CIR
        69032-CA

    II

        71070-GA

Text of Article 16—Termination of the Contract

16.1 The Contract may be terminated by the Contractor as provided in Article 14 of the General Conditions.

16.2 If the Owner terminates the Contract as provided in Article 14 of the General Conditions, he shall reimburse the Contractor for any unpaid Cost of the Work due him under Article 6, plus (1) the unpaid balance of the Fee computed upon the Cost of the Work to the date of termination at the rate of the percentage named in Article 7, or (2) if the Contractor's Fee be stated as a fixed sum, such an amount as will increase the payments on account of his Fee to a sum which bears the same ratio to the said fixed sum as the Cost of the Work at the time of termination bears to the adjusted Guaranteed Maximum Cost, if any, otherwise to a reasonable estimated Cost of the Work when completed. The Owner shall also pay to the Contractor fair compensation, either by purchase or rental at the election of the Owner, for any equipment retained. In case of such termination of the Contract the Owner shall further assume and become liable for obligations, commitments and unsettled claims that the Contractor has previously undertaken or incurred in good faith in connection with said Work. The Contractor shall, as a condition of receiving the payments referred to in this Article 16, execute and deliver all such papers and take all such steps, including the legal assignment of his contractual

DOCUMENT TO CASE CHARTS: A111-1967 A–72

> [*The five-digit numbers in this chart are Citator Case Reference Numbers, which refer to the cases, in the Cases section. The suffixes indicate the state or, for federal cases, the court in which the case was decided.*]

> rights, as the Owner may require for the purpose of fully vesting in him the rights and benefits of the Contractor under such obligations or commitments.

Article 16 Termination of the Contract

    I

        69032-CA
        71074-IL

    II

        72010-8CIR

> **Text of Article 17—Miscellaneous Provisions**
>
> **17.1** Terms used in this Agreement which are defined in the Conditions of the Contract shall have the meanings designated in those Conditions.
>
> **17.2** The Contract Documents, which constitute the entire agreement between the Owner and the Contractor, are listed in Article 1 and, except for Modifications issued after execution of this Agreement, are enumerated as follows: (*List below the Agreement, Conditions of the Contract, (General, Supplementary, other Conditions), Drawings, Specifications, Addenda and accepted Alternates, showing page or sheet numbers in all cases and dates where applicable.*) ———

Article 17 Miscellaneous Provisions

    I

        68007-10CIR

A-73 DOCUMENT TO CASE CHARTS: A111-1974

[*The five-digit numbers in this chart are Citator Case Reference Numbers, which refer to the cases, in the Cases section. The suffixes indicate the state or, for federal cases, the court in which the case was decided.*]

A111-1974—STANDARD FORM OF AGREEMENT BETWEEN OWNER AND CONTRACTOR WHERE THE BASIS OF PAYMENT IS THE COST OF THE WORK PLUS A FEE

Article 1 The Contract Documents

Article 2 The Work

Article 3 The Contractor's Duties and Status

Text of Article 4—Time of Commencement and Completion

The Work to be performed under this Contract shall be commenced _____ and completed (*Here insert any special provisions for liquidated damages relating to failure to complete on time.*) _____

Article 4 Time of Commencement and Completion

    I
        75004-PA

Text of Article 5—Cost of the Work and Guaranteed Maximum Cost

5.1 The Owner agrees to reimburse the Contractor for the Cost of the Work as defined in Article 8. Such reimbursement shall be in addition to the Contractor's Fee stipulated in Article 6.

5.2 The maximum cost to the Owner, including the Cost of the Work and the Contractor's Fee, is guaranteed not to exceed the sum of _____ dollars ($ _____); such Guaranteed Maximum Cost shall be increased or decreased for Changes in the Work as provided in Article 7. (*Here insert any provision for distribution of any savings. Delete Paragraph 5.2 if there is no Guaranteed Maximum Cost.*) _____

Article 5 Cost of the Work and Guaranteed Maximum Cost

    I
        75007-KS
        74014-OR

    III
        74021-NE

Article 6 Contractor's Fee

DOCUMENT TO CASE CHARTS: A111-1974 A–74

[The five-digit numbers in this chart are Citator Case Reference Numbers, which refer to the cases, in the Cases section. The suffixes indicate the state or, for federal cases, the court in which the case was decided.]

Text of Article 7—Changes in the Work

7.1 The Owner may make Changes in the Work in accordance with Article 12 of the General Conditions insofar as such Article is consistent with this Agreement. The Contractor shall be reimbursed for Changes in the Work on the basis of Cost of the Work as defined in Article 8.

7.2 The Contractor's Fee for Changes in the Work shall be as set forth in Paragraph 6.2, or in the absence of specific provisions therein, shall be adjusted by negotiation on the basis of the Fee established for the original Work.

Article 7   Changes in the Work

    I
        75007-KS

Text of Article 8—Costs to Be Reimbursed

8.1 The term Cost of the Work shall mean costs necessarily incurred in the proper performance of the Work and paid by the Contractor. Such costs shall be at rates not higher than the standard paid in the locality of the Work except with prior consent of the Owner, and shall include the items set forth below in this Article 8.

8.1.1 Wages paid for labor in the direct employ of the Contractor in the performance of the Work under applicable collective bargaining agreements, or under a salary or wage schedule agreed upon by the Owner and Contractor, and including such welfare or other benefits, if any, as may be payable with respect thereto.

8.1.2 Salaries of Contractor's Personnel when stationed at the field office, in whatever capacity employed. Personnel engaged, at shops or on the road, in expediting the production or transportation of materials or equipment, shall be considered as stationed at the field office and their salaries paid for that portion of their time spent on this Work.

8.1.3 Cost of contributions, assessments or taxes for such items as unemployment compensation and social security, insofar as such cost is based on wages, salaries, or other remuneration paid to employees of the Contractor and included in the Cost of the Work under Subparagraphs 8.1.1 and 8.1.2.

8.1.4 The proportion of reasonable transportation, traveling and hotel expenses of the Contractor or of his officers or employees incurred in discharge of duties connected with the Work.

8.1.5 Cost of all materials, supplies and equipment incorporated in the Work, including costs of transportation thereof.

8.1.6 Payments made by the Contractor to Subcontractors for Work performed pursuant to subcontracts under this Agreement.

DOCUMENT TO CASE CHARTS: A111-1974

[The five-digit numbers in this chart are Citator Case Reference Numbers, which refer to the cases, in the Cases section. The suffixes indicate the state or, for federal cases, the court in which the case was decided.]

8.1.7 Cost, including transportation and maintenance, of all materials, supplies, equipment, temporary facilities and hand tools not owned by the workmen, which are consumed in the performance of the Work, and cost less salvage value on such items used but not consumed which remain the property of the Contractor.

8.1.8 Rental charges of all necessary machinery and equipment, exclusive of hand tools, used at the site of the Work, whether rented from the Contractor or others, including installation, minor repairs and replacements, dismantling, removal, transportation and delivery costs thereof, at rental charges consistent with those prevailing in the area.

8.1.9 Cost of premiums for all bonds and insurance which the Contractor is required by the Contract Documents to purchase and maintain.

8.1.10 Sales, use or similar taxes related to the Work and for which the Contractor is liable imposed by any governmental authority.

8.1.11 Permit fees, royalties, damages for infringement of patents and costs of defending suits therefor, and deposits lost for causes other than the Contractor's negligence.

8.1.12 Losses and expenses, not compensated by insurance or otherwise, sustained by the Contractor in connection with the Work, provided they have resulted from causes other than the fault or neglect of the Contractor. Such losses shall include settlements made with the written consent and approval of the Owner. No such losses and expenses shall be included in the Cost of the Work for the purpose of determining the Contractor's Fee. If, however, such loss requires reconstruction and the Contractor is placed in charge thereof, he shall be paid for his services a Fee proportionate to that stated in Paragraph 6.1.

8.1.13 Minor expenses such as telegrams, long distance telephone calls, telephone service at the site, expressage, and similar petty cash items in connection with the Work.

8.1.14 Cost of removal of all debris.

8.1.15 Costs incurred due to an emergency affecting the safety of persons and property.

8.1.16 Other costs incurred in the performance of the Work if and to the extent approved in advance in writing by the Owner.

Article 8   Costs to Be Reimbursed

    III

        74021-NE

DOCUMENT TO CASE CHARTS: A111-1974   A–76

[The five-digit numbers in this chart are Citator Case Reference Numbers, which refer to the cases, in the Cases section. The suffixes indicate the state or, for federal cases, the court in which the case was decided.]

Text of Article 9—Costs Not to Be Reimbursed

9.1 The term Cost of the Work shall not include any of the items set forth below in this Article 9.

9.1.1 Salaries or other compensation of the Contractor's Personnel at the Contractor's principal office and branch offices.

9.1.2 Expenses of the Contractor's Principal and Branch Offices other than the Field Office.

9.1.3 Any part of the Contractor's capital expenses, including interest on the Contractor's capital employed for the Work.

9.1.4 Overhead or general expenses of any kind, except as may be expressly included in Article 8.

9.1.5 Costs due to the negligence of the Contractor, any Subcontractor, anyone directly or indirectly employed by any of them, or for whose acts any of them may be liable, including but not limited to the correction of defective or nonconforming Work, disposal of materials and equipment wrongly supplied, or making good any damage to property.

9.1.6 The cost of any item not specifically and expressly included in the items described in Article 8.

9.1.7 Costs in excess of the Guaranteed Maximum Cost, if any, as set forth in Article 5 and adjusted pursuant to Article 7.

Article 9   Costs Not to Be Reimbursed

    I

        75017-MD

    III

        74021-NE

Text of Article 10—Discounts, Rebates and Refunds

All cash discounts shall accrue to the Contractor unless the Owner deposits funds with the Contractor with which to make payments, in which case the cash discounts shall accrue to the Owner. All trade discounts, rebates and refunds, and all returns from sale of surplus materials and equipment shall accrue to the Owner, and the Contractor shall make provisions so that they can be secured. (*Here insert any provisions relating to deposits by the Owner to permit the Contractor to obtain cash discounts.*) ⎯⎯⎯⎯

DOCUMENT TO CASE CHARTS: A111-1974

[The five-digit numbers in this chart are Citator Case Reference Numbers, which refer to the cases, in the Cases section. The suffixes indicate the state or, for federal cases, the court in which the case was decided.]

Article 10   Discounts, Rebates and Refunds

> I
>
> 75017-MD

Article 11   Subcontracts

Article 12   Accounting Records

Text of Article 13—Applications for Payment

The Contractor shall, at least ten days before each progress payment falls due, deliver to the Architect a statement, sworn to if required, showing in complete detail all moneys paid out or costs incurred by him on account of the Cost of the Work during the previous month for which he is to be reimbursed under Article 5 and the amount of the Contractor's Fee due as provided in Article 6, together with payrolls for all labor and all receipted bills for which payment has been received.

Article 13   Applications for Payment

> I
>
> 78071-TX

Text of Article 14—Payments to the Contractor

14.1 The Architect will review the Contractor's statement of moneys due as provided in Article 13 and will promptly issue a Certificate for Payment to the Owner for such amount as he approves, which Certificate shall be payable on or about the _____ day of the month.

14.2 Final payment, constituting the unpaid balance of the Cost of the Work and of the Contractor's Fee, shall be paid by the Owner to the Contractor when the Work has been completed, the Contract fully performed and a final Certificate for Payment has been issued by the Architect. Final payment shall be due _____ days after the date of issuance of the final Certificate for Payment.

Article 14   Payments to the Contractor

> I
>
> 75017-MD
> 78071-TX

Text of Article 15—Termination of Contract

15.1 The Contract may be terminated by the Contractor as provided in Article 14 of the General Conditions.

15.2 If the Owner terminates the Contract as provided in Article 14 of the General Conditions, he shall reimburse the Contractor for any unpaid Cost of the Work due

DOCUMENT TO CASE CHARTS: A111-1974

[*The five-digit numbers in this chart are Citator Case Reference Numbers, which refer to the cases, in the Cases section. The suffixes indicate the state or, for federal cases, the court in which the case was decided.*]

> him under Article 5, plus (1) the unpaid balance of the Fee computed upon the Cost of the Work to the date of termination at the rate of the percentage named in Article 6, or (2) if the Contractor's Fee be stated as a fixed sum, such an amount as will increase the payments on account of his Fee to a sum which bears the same ratio to the said fixed sum as the Cost of the Work at the time of termination bears to the adjusted Guaranteed Maximum Cost, if any, otherwise to a reasonable estimated Cost of the Work when completed. The Owner shall also pay to the Contractor fair compensation, either by purchase or rental at the election of the Owner, for any equipment retained. In case of such termination of the Contract the Owner shall further assume and become liable for obligations, commitments and unsettled claims that the Contractor has previously undertaken or incurred in good faith in connection with said Work. The Contractor shall, as a condition of receiving the payments referred to in this Article 15, execute and deliver all such papers and take all such steps, including the legal assignment of his contractual rights, as the Owner may require for the purpose of fully vesting in him the rights and benefits of the Contractor under such obligations or commitments.

Article 15   Termination of Contract

    I

        78071-TX

Article 16   Miscellaneous Provisions

A–79   DOCUMENT TO CASE CHARTS: A111-1978

[The five-digit numbers in this chart are Citator Case Reference Numbers, which refer to the cases, in the Cases section. The suffixes indicate the state or, for federal cases, the court in which the case was decided.]

A111-1978—STANDARD FORM OF AGREEMENT BETWEEN OWNER AND CONTRACTOR WHERE THE BASIS OF PAYMENT IS THE COST OF THE WORK PLUS A FEE

Text of Article 1—The Contract Documents

1.1 The Contract Documents consist of this Agreement, the Conditions of the Contract (General, Supplementary and other Conditions), the Drawings, the Specifications, all Addenda issued prior to and all Modifications issued after execution of this Agreement. These form the Contract, and all are as fully a part of the Contract as if attached to this Agreement or repeated herein. An enumeration of the Contract Documents appears in Article 16. If anything in the Contract Documents is inconsistent with this Agreement, the Agreement shall govern.

Article 1   The Contract Documents

   I

      77055-FL   89026-MO
      80004-FL   93046-MO
      90042-KS   82052-NV
      82034-MS   95023-VA

   II

      76045-AK
      84038-MO

Text of Article 2—The Work

2.1 The Contractor shall perform all the Work required by the Contract Documents for (*Here insert the caption descriptive of the Work as used on other Contract Documents.*)

Article 2   The Work

   II

    79067-NY

Text of Article 3—The Contractor's Duties and Status

3.1 The Contractor accepts the relationship of trust and confidence established between him and the Owner by this Agreement. He covenants with the Owner to furnish his best skill and judgment and to cooperate with the Architect in furthering the interests of the Owner. He agrees to furnish efficient business administration and superintendence and to use his best efforts to furnish at all times an adequate supply of workmen and materials, and to perform the Work in the best way and in the most expeditious and economical manner consistent with the interests of the Owner.

DOCUMENT TO CASE CHARTS: A111-1978

[The five-digit numbers in this chart are Citator Case Reference Numbers, which refer to the cases, in the Cases section. The suffixes indicate the state or, for federal cases, the court in which the case was decided.]

Article 3 The Contractor's Duties and Status

I

    82020-6CIR   84023-MD
    90025-FL   77074-OR
    79043-LA

Text of Article 4—Time of Commencement and Substantial Completion

4.1 The Work to be performed under this Contract shall be commenced _____ and, subject to authorized adjustments, Substantial Completion shall be achieved not later than _____ (*Here insert any special provisions for liquidated damages relating to failure to complete on time.*)

Article 4 Time of Commencement and Substantial Completion

I

    79057-4CIR   91021-MO
    80032-NDIL   79032-OK
    87027-IN   80072-TN
    83003-LA   81067-WY

II

    85017-DDE
    80050-AR
    81047-UT

III

    79003-5CIR   78006-MT
    81064-8CIR   75029-NJ
    79045-CA   90010-NY
    79046-CA   80009-SD
    76062-LA   79036-VA
    81065-LA   80039-WY
    79062-MO

Text of Article 5—Cost of the Work and Guaranteed Maximum Cost

5.1 The Owner agrees to reimburse the Contractor for the Cost of the Work as defined in Article 8. Such reimbursement shall be in addition to the Contractor's Fee stipulated in Article 6.

5.2 The maximum cost to the Owner, including the Cost of the Work and the Contractor's Fee, is guaranteed not to exceed the sum of _____ dollars ($ _____); such Guaranteed Maximum Cost shall be increased or decreased for Changes in the Work as provided in Article 7. (*Here insert any provisions for distribution of any savings. Delete Paragraph 5.2 if there is no Guaranteed Maximum Cost.*) _____

DOCUMENT TO CASE CHARTS: A111-1978

[The five-digit numbers in this chart are Citator Case Reference Numbers, which refer to the cases, in the Cases section. The suffixes indicate the state or, for federal cases, the court in which the case was decided.]

Article 5 Cost of the Work and Guaranteed Maximum Cost

I

90034-FL
83017-GA
91021-MO

82031-NV
82027-PA
88019-SC

II

84023-MD

III

87053-GA
77036-TX
73018-TX

Text of Article 6—Contractor's Fee

6.1 In consideration of the performance of the Contract, the Owner agrees to pay the Contractor in current funds as compensation for his services a Contractor's Fee as follows: _____

6.2 For Changes in the Work, the Contractor's Fee shall be adjusted as follows: _____

6.3 The Contractor shall be paid _____ percent (_____ %) of the proportional amount of his Fee with each progress payment, and the balance of his Fee shall be paid at the time of final payment.

Article 6 Contractor's Fee

I

83017-GA
91021-MO
88019-SC

II

84023-MD

III

79052-LA

Text of Article 7—Changes in the Work

7.1 The Owner may make Changes in the Work as provided in the Contract Documents. The Contractor shall be reimbursed for Changes in the Work on the basis of Cost of the Work as defined in Article 8.

7.2 The Contractor's Fee for Changes in the Work shall be as set forth in Paragraph 6.2, or in the absence of specific provisions therein, shall be adjusted by negotiation on the basis of the Fee established for the original Work.

DOCUMENT TO CASE CHARTS: A111-1978

[The five-digit numbers in this chart are Citator Case Reference Numbers, which refer to the cases, in the Cases section. The suffixes indicate the state or, for federal cases, the court in which the case was decided.]

Article 7 Changes in the Work

I

      91021-MO

III

      78077-NY

Text of Article 8—Costs to Be Reimbursed

8.1 The term Cost of the Work shall mean costs necessarily incurred in the proper performance of the Work and paid by the Contractor. Such costs shall be at rates not higher than the standard paid in the locality of the Work except with prior consent of the Owner, and shall include the items set forth below in this Article 8.

8.1.1 Wages paid for labor in the direct employ of the Contractor in the performance of the Work under applicable collective bargaining agreements, or under a salary or wage schedule agreed upon by the Owner and Contractor, and including such welfare or other benefits, if any, as may be payable with respect thereto.

8.1.2 Salaries of Contractor's personnel when stationed at the field office, in whatever capacity employed. Personnel engaged, at shops or on the road, in expediting the production or transportation of materials or equipment, shall be considered as stationed at the field office and their salaries paid for that portion of their time spent on this Work.

8.1.3 Cost of contributions, assessments or taxes incurred during the performance of the Work for such items as unemployment compensation and social security, insofar as such cost is based on wages, salaries, or other remuneration paid to employees of the Contractor and included in the Cost of the Work under Subparagraphs 8.1.1 and 8.1.2.

8.1.4 The portion of reasonable travel and subsistence expenses of the Contractor or of his officers or employees incurred while traveling in discharge of duties connected with the Work.

8.1.5 Cost of all materials, supplies and equipment incorporated in the Work, including costs of transportation thereof.

8.1.6 Payments made by the Contractor to Subcontractors for Work performed pursuant to Subcontracts under this Agreement.

8.1.7 Cost, including transportation and maintenance, of all materials, supplies, equipment, temporary facilities and hand tools not owned by the workers, which are consumed in the performance of the Work, and cost less salvage value on such items used but not consumed which remain the property of the Contractor.

8.1.8 Rental charges of all necessary machinery and equipment, exclusive of hand tools, used at the site of the Work, whether rented from the Contractor or others, including installation, minor repairs and replacements, dismantling, removal,

DOCUMENT TO CASE CHARTS: A111-1978

[The five-digit numbers in this chart are Citator Case Reference Numbers, which refer to the cases, in the Cases section. The suffixes indicate the state or, for federal cases, the court in which the case was decided.]

transportation and delivery costs thereof, at rental charges consistent with those prevailing in the area.

8.1.9 Cost of premiums for all bonds and insurance which the Contractor is required by the Contract Documents to purchase and maintain.

8.1.10 Sales, use or similar taxes related to the Work and for which the Contractor is liable imposed by any governmental authority.

8.1.11 Permit fees, royalties, damages for infringement of patents and costs of defending suits therefor, and deposits lost for causes other than the Contractor's negligence.

8.1.12 Losses and expenses, not compensated by insurance or otherwise, sustained by the Contractor in connection with the Work, provided they have resulted from causes other than the fault or neglect of the Contractor. Such losses shall include settlements made with the written consent and approval of the Owner. No such losses and expenses shall be included in the Cost of the Work for the purpose of determining the Contractor's Fee. If, however, such loss requires reconstruction and the Contractor is placed in charge thereof, he shall be paid for his services a Fee proportionate to that stated in Paragraph 6.1.

8.1.13 Minor expenses such as telegrams, long distance telephone calls, telephone service at the site, expressage and similar petty cash items in connection with the Work.

8.1.14 Cost of removal of all debris.

8.1.15 Costs incurred due to an emergency affecting the safety of persons and property.

8.1.16 Other costs incurred in the performance of the Work if and to the extent approved in advance in writing by the Owner. (*Here insert modifications or limitations to any of the above Subparagraphs, such as equipment rental charges and small tool charges applicable to the Work.*) _____

Article 8 Costs to Be Reimbursed

    I

        90034-FL   82031-NV
        91021-MO   77074-OR

    II

        84023-MD

III

    79052-LA
    80065-MO

Text of Article 9—Costs Not to Be Reimbursed

9.1 The term Cost of the Work shall not include any of the items set forth below in this Article 9.

9.1.1 Salaries or other compensation of the Contractor's personnel at the Contractor's principal office and branch offices.

9.1.2 Expenses of the Contractor's principal and branch offices other than the field office.

9.1.3 Any part of the Contractor's capital expenses, including interest on the Contractor's capital employed for the Work.

9.1.4 Except as specifically provided for in Subparagraph 8.1.8 or in modifications thereto, rental costs of machinery and equipment.

9.1.5 Overhead or general expenses of any kind, except as may be expressly included in Article 8.

9.1.6 Costs due to the negligence of the Contractor, any Subcontractor, anyone directly or indirectly employed by any of them, or for whose acts any of them may be liable, including but not limited to the correction of defective or nonconforming Work, disposal of materials and equipment wrongly supplied, or making good any damage to property.

9.1.7 The cost of any item not specifically and expressly included in the items described in Article 8.

9.1.8 Costs in excess of the Guaranteed Maximum Cost, if any, as set forth in Article 5 and adjusted pursuant to Article 7.

Article 9   Costs Not to Be Reimbursed

    I

        82027-PA

    II

        84023-MD

    III

        82020-6CIR

Article 10   Discounts, Rebates and Refunds

DOCUMENT TO CASE CHARTS: A111-1978

[The five-digit numbers in this chart are Citator Case Reference Numbers, which refer to the cases, in the Cases section. The suffixes indicate the state or, for federal cases, the court in which the case was decided.]

Text of Article 11—Subcontracts and Other Agreements

11.1 All portions of the Work that the Contractor's organization does not perform shall be performed under Subcontracts or by other appropriate agreement with the Contractor. The Contractor shall request bids from Subcontractors and shall deliver such bids to the Architect. The Owner will then determine, with the advice of the Contractor and subject to the reasonable objection of the Architect, which bids will be accepted.

11.2 All Subcontracts shall conform to the requirements of the Contract Documents. Subcontracts awarded on the basis of the cost of such work plus a fee shall also be subject to the provisions of this Agreement insofar as applicable.

Article 11   Subcontracts and Other Agreements

I

77074-OR
80004-FL

Text of Article 12—Accounting Records

12.1 The Contractor shall check all materials, equipment and labor entering into the Work and shall keep such full and detailed accounts as may be necessary for proper financial management under this Agreement, and the system shall be satisfactory to the Owner. The Owner shall be afforded access to all the Contractor's records, books, correspondence, instructions, drawings, receipts, vouchers, memoranda and similar data relating to this Contract, and the Contractor shall preserve all such records for a period of three years, or for such longer period as may be required by law, after the final payment.

Article 12   Accounting Records

III

79052-LA

Text of Article 13—Applications for Payment

13.1 The Contractor shall, at least ten days before each payment falls due, deliver to the Architect an itemized statement, notarized if required, showing in complete detail all moneys paid out or costs incurred by him on account of the Cost of the Work during the previous month for which he is to be reimbursed under Article 5 and the amount of the Contractor's Fee due as provided in Article 6, together with payrolls for all labor and such other data supporting the Contractor's right to payment for Subcontracts or materials as the Owner or the Architect may require.

DOCUMENT TO CASE CHARTS: A111-1978

A–86

[The five-digit numbers in this chart are Citator Case Reference Numbers, which refer to the cases, in the Cases section. The suffixes indicate the state or, for federal cases, the court in which the case was decided.]

Article 13   Applications for Payment

   III

      79052-LA

Text of Article 14—Payments to the Contractor

14.1 The Architect will review the Contractor's Applications for Payment and will promptly take appropriate action thereon as provided in the Contract Documents. Such amount as he may recommend for payment shall be payable by the Owner not later than the _____ day of the month.

14.1.1 In taking action on the Contractor's Applications for Payment, the Architect shall be entitled to rely on the accuracy and completeness of the information furnished by the Contractor and shall not be deemed to represent that he has made audits of the supporting data, exhaustive or continuous on-site inspections or that he has made any examination to ascertain how or for what purposes the Contractor has used the moneys previously paid on account of the Contract.

14.2 Final payment, constituting the entire unpaid balance of the Cost of the Work and of the Contractor's Fee, shall be paid by the Owner to the Contractor _____ days after Substantial Completion of the Work unless otherwise stipulated in the Certificate of Substantial Completion, provided the Work has been completed, the Contract fully performed, and final payment has been recommended by the Architect.

14.3 Payments due and unpaid under the Contract Documents shall bear interest from the date payment is due at the rate entered below, or in the absence thereof, at the legal rate prevailing at the place of the Project. *(Here insert any rate of interest agreed upon.)* _____ *(Usuary laws and requirements under the Federal Truth in Lending Act, similar state and local consumer credit laws and other regulations at the Owner's and Contractor's principal places of business, the location of the Project and elsewhere may affect the validity of this provision. Specific legal advice should be obtained with respect to deletion, modification or other requirements such as written disclosures or waivers.)*

Article 14   Payments to the Contractor

   I

      82020-6CIR   86014-AZ
      92001-7CIR   82031-NV
      80002-AZ   79032-OK

A-87 DOCUMENT TO CASE CHARTS: A111-1978

[The five-digit numbers in this chart are Citator Case Reference Numbers, which refer to the cases, in the Cases section. The suffixes indicate the state or, for federal cases, the court in which the case was decided.]

    II

        85020-IA
        86056-MD

    III

        77055-FL

Article 15 Termination of Contract

Text of Article 16—Miscellaneous Provisions

16.1 Terms used in this Agreement which are defined in the Contract Documents shall have the meanings designated in those Contract Documents.

16.2 The Contract Documents, which constitute the entire agreement between the Owner and the Contractor, are listed in Article 1 and, except for Modifications issued after execution of this Agreement, are enumerated as follows: (*List below the Agreement the Conditions of the Contract, [General, Suppplementary, and other Conditions], the Drawings, the Specifications, and any Addenda and accepted alternates, showing page or sheet numbers in all cases and dates where applicable.*)

Article 16 Miscellaneous Provisions

    I

        92008-DC   89026-MO
        77012-IL   82052-NV
        90042-KS   91035-SC
        89049-MA   95023-VA
        82034-MS

    II

        76045-AK
        84023-MD

    III

        87053-GA

DOCUMENT TO CASE CHARTS: A111-1987 A–88

[The five-digit numbers in this chart are Citator Case Reference Numbers, which refer to the cases, in the Cases section. The suffixes indicate the state or, for federal cases, the court in which the case was decided.]

A111-1987—STANDARD FORM OF AGREEMENT BETWEEN OWNER AND CONTRACTOR WHERE THE BASIS OF PAYMENT IS THE COST OF WORK PLUS A FEE WITH OR WITHOUT A GUARANTEED MAXIMUM PRICE

Text of Article 1—The Contract Documents

1.1 The Contract Documents consist of this Agreement, Conditions of the Contract (General, Supplementary and other Conditions), Drawings, Specifications, Addenda issued prior to execution of this Agreement, other documents listed in this Agreement and Modifications issued after execution of this Agreement; these form the Contract, and are as fully a part of the Contract as if attached to this Agreement or repeated herein. The Contract represents the entire and integrated agreement between the parties hereto and supersedes prior negotiations, representations or agreements, either written or oral. An enumeration of the Contract Documents, other than Modifications, appears in Article 16. If anything in the other Contract Documents is inconsistent with this Agreement, this Agreement shall govern.

Article 1   The Contract Documents

              I
              95023-VA

Article 2   The Work of this Contract

Article 3   Relationship of the Parties

Article 4   Date of Commencement and Substantial Completion

Text of Article 5—Contract Sum

5.1 The Owner shall pay the Contractor in current funds for the Contractor's performance of the Contract the Contract Sum consisting of the Cost of the Work as defined in Article 7 and the Contractor's Fee determined as follows: *(State a lump sum, percentage of Cost of the Work or other provision for determining the Contractor's Fee, and explain how the Contractor's Fee is to be adjusted for changes in the Work.)* _____

5.2 GUARANTEED MAXIMUM PRICE (IF APPLICABLE)

5.2.1 The sum of the Cost of the Work and the Contractor's Fee is guaranteed by the Contractor not to exceed _____ Dollars ($ _____), subject to additions and deductions by Change Order as provided in the Contract Documents. Such maximum sum is referred to in the Contract Documents as the Guaranteed Maximum Price. Costs which would cause the Guaranteed Maximum Price to be exceeded shall be paid by the Contractor without reimbursement by the Owner.

DOCUMENT TO CASE CHARTS: A111-1987

[*The five-digit numbers in this chart are Citator Case Reference Numbers, which refer to the cases, in the Cases section. The suffixes indicate the state or, for federal cases, the court in which the case was decided.*]

(Insert specific provisions if the Contractor is to participate in any savings.)
_____

5.2.2 The Guaranteed Maximum Price is based upon the following alternates, if any, which are described in the Contract Documents and are hereby accepted by the Owner: (*State the numbers or other identification of accepted alternates, but only if a Guaranteed Maximum Price is inserted in Subparagraph 5.2.1. If decisions on other alternates are to be made by the Owner subsequent to the execution of this Agreement, attach a schedule of such other alternates showing the amount for each and the date until which that amount is valid.*) _____

5.2.3 The amounts agreed to for unit prices, if any, are as follows: (*State unit prices only if a Guaranteed Maximum Price is inserted in Subparagraph 5.2.1.*)
_____

Article 5   Contract Sum

            I
            94028-ID

Article 6   Changes in the Work

Article 7   Costs to Be Reimbursed

Text of Article 8—Costs Not to Be Reimbursed

8.1 The Cost of the Work shall not include:

8.1.1 Salaries and other compensation of the Contractor's personnel stationed at the Contractor's principal office or offices other than the site office, except as specifically provided in Clauses 7.1.1.2 and 7.1.1.3 or as may be provided in Article 14.

8.1.2 Expenses of the Contractor's principal office and offices other than the site office.

8.1.3 Overhead and general expenses, except as may be expressly included in Article 7.

8.1.4 The Contractor's capital expenses, including interest on the Contractor's capital employed for the Work.

8.1.5 Rental costs of machinery and equipment, except as specifically provided in Clause 7.1.4.2.

8.1.6 Except as provided in Subparagraphs 7.2.2 through 7.2.4 and Paragraph 13.5 of this Agreement, costs due to the fault or negligence of the Contractor, Subcontractors, anyone directly or indirectly employed by any of them, or for whose acts any of them may be liable, including but not limited to costs for the correction of damaged, defective or nonconforming Work, disposal and replacement of

DOCUMENT TO CASE CHARTS: A111-1987   A–90

[The five-digit numbers in this chart are Citator Case Reference Numbers, which refer to the cases, in the Cases section. The suffixes indicate the state or, for federal cases, the court in which the case was decided.]

> materials and equipment incorrectly ordered or supplied, and making good damage to property not forming part of the Work.
>
> **8.1.7** Any cost not specifically and expressly described in Article 7.
>
> **8.1.8** Costs which would cause the Guaranteed Maximum Price, if any, to be exceeded.

Article 8   Costs Not to Be Reimbursed

I

94028-ID

Article 9   Discounts, Rebates and Refunds

Article 10   Subcontracts and Other Agreements

Article 11   Accounting Records

Article 12   Progress Payments

Article 13   Final Payment

Article 14   Miscellaneous Provisions

Article 15   Termination or Suspension

> **Text of Article 16—Enumeration of Contract Documents**
>
> **16.1** The Contract Documents, except for Modifications issued after execution of this Agreement, are enumerated as follows:
>
> **16.1.1** The Agreement is this executed Standard Form of Agreement Between Owner and Contractor, AIA Document A111, 1987 Edition.
>
> **16.1.2** The General Conditions are the General Conditions of the Contract for Construction, AIA Document A201, 1987 Edition.
>
> **16.1.3** The Supplementary and other Conditions of the Contract are those contained In the Project Manual dated _____, and are as follows:
> Document _____ Title _____ Pages _____
>
> **16.1.4** The Specifications are those contained in the Project Manual dated as in Paragraph 16.1.3. and are as follows: (*Either list the Specifications here or refer to an exhibit attached to this Agreement.*)
> Section _____ Title _____ Pages _____
>
> **16.1.5** The Drawings are as follows, and are dated _____ unless a different date is shown below: (*Either list the Drawings here or refer to an exhibit attached to this Agreement.*)
> Number _____ Title _____ Pages _____

DOCUMENT TO CASE CHARTS: A111-1987

[The five-digit numbers in this chart are Citator Case Reference Numbers, which refer to the cases, in the Cases section. The suffixes indicate the state or, for federal cases, the court in which the case was decided.]

16.1.6 The Addenda, if any, are as follows:
Number _____ **Date** _____ **Pages** _____

Portions of Addenda relating to bidding requirements are not part of the Contract Documents unless the bidding requirements are also enumerated in this Article 16.

16.1.7 Other Documents, if any, forming part of the Contract Documents are as follows: (*List here any additional documents which are intended to form part of the Contract Documents. The General Conditions provide that bidding requirements such as advertisement or invitation to bid, Instructions to Bidders, sample forms and the Contractor's bid are not part of the Contract Documents unless enumerated in this Agreement. They should be listed here only if intended to be part of the Contract Documents.*) _____

Article 16 Enumeration of Contract Documents

I

94028-ID

DOCUMENT TO CASE CHARTS: A117-1979

[The five-digit numbers in this chart are Citator Case Reference Numbers, which refer to the cases, in the Cases section. The suffixes indicate the state or, for federal cases, the court in which the case was decided.]

A117-1979—ABBREVIATED FORM OF AGREEMENT BETWEEN OWNER AND CONTRACTOR FOR CONSTRUCTION PROJECTS OF LIMITED SCOPE WHERE THE BASIS OF PAYMENT IS THE COST OF THE WORK PLUS A FEE

Article 1   The Work

    II

        82004-SDGA
        93036-NE
        79067-NY

Article 2   The Contractor's Duties and Status

    I

        82020-6CIR
        84023-MD

    II

        79067-NY

Article 3   Time of Commencement and Substantial Completion

    I

        88027-3CIR   83003-LA
        79057-4CIR   80072-TN
        80032-NDIL   81067-WY
        79043-LA

    II

        82004-SDGA
        80011-AR
        80050-AR

    III

        81064-8CIR   79062-MO
        79045-CA   90010-NY
        79046-CA   80009-SD
        80049-IN   79036-VA
        87027-IN   80039-WY
        81065-LA

Article 4   Cost of the Work and Guaranteed Maximum Cost

    I

        79043-LA   82031-NV
        83017-GA   88019-SC

DOCUMENT TO CASE CHARTS: A117-1979

[The five-digit numbers in this chart are Citator Case Reference Numbers, which refer to the cases, in the Cases section. The suffixes indicate the state or, for federal cases, the court in which the case was decided.]

    II

        79052-LA
        84023-MD

    III

        91007-NM

Article 5   Contractor's Fee

    I

        83017-GA
        88019-SC

    II

        84023-MD

    III

        79052-LA

Article 6   Costs to Be Reimbursed

    I

        82031-NV

    II

        84023-MD

    III

        79052-LA
        80065-MO

Article 7   Costs Not to Be Reimbursed

    II

        84023-MD

    III

        82004-6CIR

Article 8   Accounting Records

    II

        86070-IL

DOCUMENT TO CASE CHARTS: A117-1979

[The five-digit numbers in this chart are Citator Case Reference Numbers, which refer to the cases, in the Cases section. The suffixes indicate the state or, for federal cases, the court in which the case was decided.]

    III

        79052-LA
        86049-NH

Article 9   Payments to the Contractor

    I

80002-AZ	82031-NV
86014-AZ	79032-OK

    II

92001-7CIR	86056-MD
82004-SDGA	81047-UT
89030-IL	

    III

89042-NDIL	83039-LA
90034-FL	83041-LA
83005-LA	86049-NH

Article 10   Other Conditions and Provisions

    I

92008-DC	82052-NV
89049-MA	91035-SC
82034-MS	

    II

        86061-FL
        90042-KS

    III

        93004-AL
        89026-MO

Article 11   Contract Documents

    I

88027-3CIR	91006-FL
90050-7CIR	93022-ME
93010-SDNY	89049-MA
90002-CO	91034-NM
92008-DC	90043-NY
89027-FL	

    II

85017-DDE	86028-MA
82004-SDGA	82034-MS
91008-MDPA	84038-MO
84020-AK	82052-NV
86061-FL	88016-OH
91002-GA	90020-OH
90042-KS	85029-TN

DOCUMENT TO CASE CHARTS: A117-1979

[The five-digit numbers in this chart are Citator Case Reference Numbers, which refer to the cases, in the Cases section. The suffixes indicate the state or, for federal cases, the court in which the case was decided.]

III

83013-1CIR	81042-MA
90048-10CIR	89026-MO
90039-WDNC	91007-NM
90008-CC	90016-NY
91019-AL	86018-NC
92014a-AL	86039-OK
83048-CA	83001-PA
86060-IL	87029-TX
89019-KS	87007-VA
84033-LA	

Article 12 Architect

I

82020-6CIR	92006-ME
91031-MDPA	91038-MO
81018-AR	80055-NY
83030-FL	81057-NY
91040-GA	83047-NY
79029-IL	88031-NC
91001-IN	80061-VT
91030-IA	91024-VT

II

89022-5CIR	86032-MO
83032-7CIR	87050-MO
83023-8CIR	88014-MO
82004-SDGA	86064-MO
90052-AL	95033-MO
92018-CT	90006-NE
89027-FL	83024-NY
94038-FL	84019-NY
93013-GA	89004-NY
82020-GA	89012-NY
90040-IL	90051-NY
89008-KS	90020-OH
86071-LA	82056-OK
89035-MD	84027-TX
88024-MA	87026-TX
89037-MN	85014-WY
89047-MS	

III

82041-10CIR	92004-IL
90048-10CIR	82028-IN
91037-11CIR	86035-KS
82014-NDMS	80074-LA
82057-AL	88012-LA
87037-AL	88041-LA
83006-AR	83002-MA
86029-CT	86034-MA
92020a-CT	90035-MA
85037-FL	89023-MI
81040-GA	92008d-MI
85006-IL	91024-MT
87030-IL	82007-NJ

DOCUMENT TO CASE CHARTS: A117-1979

[The five-digit numbers in this chart are Citator Case Reference Numbers, which refer to the cases, in the Cases section. The suffixes indicate the state or, for federal cases, the court in which the case was decided.]

85026-NY
86047-NY
88035a-NY
89003-NY
89005-NC
87002-ND
79033-PA

86010-PA
90029-PA
88025-VA
89033-VA
87009-TN
90055-TX

Article 13 Owner

I

90032-IL
81067-WY

II

86006-IL
84007-NY

89016-NY
79040-TX

III

87037-AL
87009-TN

Article 14 Contractor

I

82020-6CIR
90050-7CIR
80007-8CIR
84017-8CIR
81012-AL
89021-CA
90002-CO
81004-IL
88033-IL
93025-IL
79063-IN
89036-LA
80071-MA

81072-MA
80054-MI
95011-MI
92003-MO
92003a-MO
85033-NE
83047-NY
89025-NC
92010b-OH
92008a-PA
91010-TX
80061-VT
82038-WA

II

83010-5CIR
83023-8CIR
82004-SDGA
80042-DMD
91013-SDMS
90013-AL
91036-AZ
84029-DC
87013-FL
88005-FL
94038-FL
84032-GA
91040-GA
93013-GA
80056-IL
84028-IL

85019-IL
86013-IL
86068-IL
88033-IL
90040-IL
91025-IL
93025-IL
82018-IN
84015-IN
91001-IN
90042-KS
88042-KY
82009-LA
83038-LA
83040-LA
86072-LA

DOCUMENT TO CASE CHARTS: A117-1979

[The five-digit numbers in this chart are Citator Case Reference Numbers, which refer to the cases, in the Cases section. The suffixes indicate the state or, for federal cases, the court in which the case was decided.]

90056-LA
81013-MA
91017-MA
93018-MA
85008-MN
88026-MN
93053-MN
91036a-MO
82001-NE
82048-NE
85033-NE
90026-NE
86065-NJ
87048-NM
79067-NY
82021-NY
83024-NY
84001-NY
85023-NY

85038-NY
88001-NY
89015-NY
82056-OK
93043-PA
85013-TN
79040-TX
80035-TX
86058-TX
87019-TX
87026-TX
94009-TX
95036-TX
87011-VA
84005-WA
85016-WA
93040-WI
83050-WY

III

89001-4CIR
83007-7CIR
87010-DME
82014-NDMS
90039-WDNC
80012-AL
85003a-AL
87037-AL
91019-AL
92014a-AL
85011-AK
86022-AK
85025-CA
85034-CA
87035-CA
86001-CT
93051-DC
80053-FL
79041-GA
81007-GA
88040-GA
90036-GA
85015-HI
79070-IL
80073-IL
85015a-IL
87008-IL
87042-IL
92004-IL
82028-IN
86052-IN
91001-IN
91023-IN
86050-IA
86035-KS

83005-LA
94013-LA
83002-MA
86063-MA
89028-MA
85035-MI
87020-MI
84002-MN
93047-MN
79072-MO
80010-MT
86043-MT
84031-NE
82007-NJ
91007-NM
81070-NY
87016-NY
89016-NY
92007-NY
93039-NY
87002-ND
91029-ND
86009-OH
90029-PA
91039-PA
93031-PA
82017-TN
87009-TN
88002-TX
89033-VA
85028-WA
86057-WA
89041-WV
82023-WI
84013-WI

DOCUMENT TO CASE CHARTS: A117-1979

[The five-digit numbers in this chart are Citator Case Reference Numbers, which refer to the cases, in the Cases section. The suffixes indicate the state or, for federal cases, the court in which the case was decided.]

Article 15 Subcontracts

I

92015-GA
939025-IL

II

86037-3CIR
85027-4CIR
85005-AR
90002-CO
85003-GA
85021-GA
93025-IL
84016-KS

86072-LA
86067-MN
82034-MS
84036-OH
86026-OH
82058-PA
86002-TN
83050-WY

III

82008-11CIR
83045-SDNY
86055-AZ
90034-FL
86060-IL
80021-KS

84030-MI
86015-NY
90016-NY
89005-NC
89015-SC
82017-TN

Article 16 Work by Owner or by Separate Contractors

I

93025-IL

II

91008-MDPA
93025-IL

90005-IN
90047-IN

III

86017-CO
87028-IL
82007-NJ

86018-NC
89005-NC

Article 17 Miscellaneous Provisions

I

89048-US
84010-6CIR
91009-SDAL
86014-AZ
81056-CO
82029-CO
89034-CT
93006-CT
92008-DC
81006-FL
81073-FL
83030-FL
91006-FL
91015-FL

90009-GA
80057-ID
81009-IL
81041-IL
84011-IL
90041-IN
90018-KS
93003-KY
81038-LA
90027-LA
92006-ME
90014-MD
92013-MA
82011-MI

DOCUMENT TO CASE CHARTS: A117-1979

[The five-digit numbers in this chart are Citator Case Reference Numbers, which refer to the cases, in the Cases section. The suffixes indicate the state or, for federal cases, the court in which the case was decided.]

87017-MN
80055-NY
81028-NY
81057-NY
92010-NC

93048-SC
93002-SD
91018-RI
89051-TX
92009a-TX

II

83033-US
89048-US
86037-3CIR
87032-4CIR
83010-5CIR
86045-5CIR
90019-6CIR
84040-NDAL
87022-DDC
82032-DKS
88006-DME
85040-WDMO
88008-SDNY
90004-DSC
87005-NDTX
86021-AL
90038-AL
85005-AR
83008-CA
83016-CA
90046-CA
88029-CT
90001-CT
86023-DE
81054-FL
82039-FL
83018-FL
84004-FL
85004-FL
86041-FL
86061-FL
86061-FL
87001-FL
82024-GA
94003-GA
93008-IA
81014-IL
87015-IL
87018-IL

88039-IL
89011-IL
89030-IL
89044-IL
92021-IL
93025-IL
81023-KS
84016-KS
93052-LA
90022-ME
84003-MD
89034-MD
80076-MA
81013-MA
86036-MI
91012-MI
82049-MN
86067-MN
88009-MN
89010-MN
89046-MN
95033-MO
84007-NY
84019-NY
86062-NY
87039-NY
81010-NC
85002-NC
88031-NC
84036-OH
88016-OH
89018-SC
93048-SC
93024-TN
80025-TX
84027-TX
93054-TX
81047-UT
95023-VA

III

83008-6CIR
89050-6CIR
83011-8CIR
83026-8CIR
88044-NDGA
82042-DVI
93004-AL
84012-AZ
85041-AZ
90045-AZ

90003-CA
86029-CT
90053-CT
92020a-CT
79039-IL
83025-IL
89045-IL
79030-IA
80073-LA
80074-LA

DOCUMENT TO CASE CHARTS: A117-1979

[The five-digit numbers in this chart are Citator Case Reference Numbers, which refer to the cases, in the Cases section. The suffixes indicate the state or, for federal cases, the court in which the case was decided.]

83005-LA
79054-MA
82010-MD
89037-MD
89023-MI
92008d-MI
85042-MO
82015-NH
86054-NH
79023-NJ
81005-NY
85026-NY

85043-NY
86024-NY
86047-NY
88035a-NY
86026-OH
86010-PA
87045-PA
88013-PA
82012-SD
80008-TX
87052-WA
86069-WI

Article 18 Time

I

80002-AZ
92021a-AZ
89027-FL
92010a-GA
83003-LA
91012-MI
92016a-MT

93020-NC
92017-NJ
91007-NM
88031-NC
79032-OK
81067-WY

II

87033-8CIR
82004-SDGA
79058-CA
85032-IN
87004-LA

87017-MN
88020-NE
86064-MO
85029-TN

III

84022-6CIR
83007-7CIR
85009-7CIR
90048-10CIR
89043-NDIL
86029-CT
85006-IL
87030-IL
80049-IN
87027-IN
83005-LA
80022-OK
90044-MD
84030-MI
81015-MT
82007-NJ
83027-NY

86005-NY
86012-NY
86066-NY
90007-NY
85012-NC
84025-OH
86009-OH
86004-PA
86010-PA
90015-PA
80009-SD
83004-TX
88025-VA
89033-VA
87025-WI
80039-WY

DOCUMENT TO CASE CHARTS: A117-1979

[The five-digit numbers in this chart are Citator Case Reference Numbers, which refer to the cases, in the Cases section. The suffixes indicate the state or, for federal cases, the court in which the case was decided.]

Article 19 Payments and Completion

I

82020-6CIR	79043-LA
90050-7CIR	83003-LA
80002-AZ	81010-NC

II

81064-8CIR	86056-MD
91008-MDPA	89035-MD
95020-DPR	79031-MN
84029-DC	89010-MN
91014-FL	82048-NE
88003-IL	90026-NE
90040-IL	84007-NY
90042-KS	82058-PA
82009-LA	81047-UT

III

83035-5CIR	83041-LA
83007-7CIR	86008-LA
82042-DVI	90030-MS
86029-CT	86049-NH
86051-CT	83036-NY
90034-FL	85022-NY
84016-KS	84025-OH
80040-LA	88036-TX
83005-LA	88022-VA
83039-LA	87025-WI

Article 20 Protection of Persons and Property

I

81012-AL
92011-AZ
83047-NY

II

91040-GA	88016-OH
93013-GA	81068-MT
84015-IN	89016-NY
90005-IN	82056-OK
91001-IN	85029-TN

III

91037-11CIR	82028-IN
87037-AL	86052-IN
80029-AR	88035-IN
79071-DC	90035-MA
85037-FL	86038-MO
94038-FL	81036-NY
81058-GA	86018-NC
90036-GA	90029-PA
79070-IL	81016-TX
92004-IL	

DOCUMENT TO CASE CHARTS: A117-1979

[The five-digit numbers in this chart are Citator Case Reference Numbers, which refer to the cases, in the Cases section. The suffixes indicate the state or, for federal cases, the court in which the case was decided.]

Article 21 Insurance

I

93010-SDNY
89040-CO
79063-IN
93022-ME

81072-MA
92010b-OH
90043-NY
92020-WA

II

88007-3CIR
91016-AL
88037-AZ
93056-AZ
85036-CO
90002-CO
85021-GA
86068-IL
91022-IL
83038-LA
83040-LA

91033-LA
86028-MA
94002-MO
79022-NY
85038-NY
88032-NC
88015-ND
88016-OH
90049-OK
92019a-TX
87036-WA

III

83015-11CIR
93050-DPR
92014a-AL
83006-AR
81024-FL
80026-GA
80073-IL
87008-IL
87042-IL
80021-KS

94013-LA
86063-MA
83044-MN
84026-NY
87002-ND
91029-ND
91027-TN
87007-VA
86046-WA

Article 22 Changes in the Work

I

80002-AZ
91006-FL
90009-GA

81001-MA
86003-NY

II

88008-SDNY
91031-MDPA
91005-AL
84029-DC
84032-GA
90012-GA
85032-IN
85022-IA
81023-KS

84018-MO
84038-MO
86030-MO
89032-MO
91021-MO
88020-NE
84019-NY
85029-TN
84027-TX

DOCUMENT TO CASE CHARTS: A117-1979

[The five-digit numbers in this chart are Citator Case Reference Numbers, which refer to the cases, in the Cases section. The suffixes indicate the state or, for federal cases, the court in which the case was decided.]

III

90008-CC	86034-MA
89024-1CIR	84030-MI
82026-8CIR	85044-MN
90048-10CIR	88011-MS
82008-11CIR	82007-NJ
89043-NDIL	84026-NY
80070-AL	85022-NY
93004-AL	85030-NY
86055-AZ	86005-NY
86029-CT	90007-NY
79055-GA	85012-NC
90009-GA	84025-OH
80036-ID	86009-OH
84037-IN	86059-OH
81014-IL	80022-OR
87003-IL	83001-PA
87028-IL	86004-PA
89019-KS	86010-PA
79027-LA	86011-PA
84033-LA	83004-TX
90022-ME	87029-TX
90044-MD	88036-TX
84024-MA	88025-VA
86027-MA	85039-WV

Article 23   Correction of Work

I

82020-6CIR
92015-GA
81057-NY

II

84029-DC	90026-NE
90040-IL	86065-NJ
82009-LA	85023-NY
87024-MD	

III

81060-5CIR	87034-IL
82014-NDMS	82017-TN
80012-AL	84031-NE
93004-AL	

Article 24   Termination of the Contract

II

91013-SDMS	90032-IL
80011-AR	84019-NY
88010-CO	88016-OH

DOCUMENT TO CASE CHARTS: A117-1979

[The five-digit numbers in this chart are Citator Case Reference Numbers, which refer to the cases, in the Cases section. The suffixes indicate the state or, for federal cases, the court in which the case was decided.]

II

    94027-MN

III

82002-3CIR	90016-NY
83007-7CIR	87002-ND
86016-EDMO	85014a-OK
92009-FL	86042-WA

Article 25   Other Conditions or Provisions

DOCUMENT TO CASE CHARTS: A117-1987

[*The five-digit numbers in this chart are Citator Case Reference Numbers, which refer to the cases, in the Cases section. The suffixes indicate the state or, for federal cases, the court in which the case was decided.*]

A117-1987—ABBREVIATED FORM OF AGREEMENT BETWEEN OWNER AND CONTRACTOR FOR CONSTRUCTION PROJECTS OF LIMITED SCOPE WHERE THE BASIS OF PAYMENT IS THE COST OF THE WORK PLUS A FEE

Article 1 The Work

Article 2 Relationship of the Parties

Article 3 Date of Commencement and Substantial Completion

Article 4 Contract Sum

Article 5 Costs to be Reimbursed

Article 6 Costs Not to be Reimbursed

Article 7 Discounts, Rebates and Refunds

Article 8 Accounting Records

Article 9 Progress Payments

    II

        95034-VA

    III

        94050-AL
        95050-NY

Article 10 Final Payment

    II

        95034-VA

    III

        94050-AL
        95050-NY

Article 11 Enumeration of Contract Documents

    I

        95051-SDMS

    II

        94020-TX
        97003-WA
        97024-WV

DOCUMENT TO CASE CHARTS: A117-1987

[The five-digit numbers in this chart are Citator Case Reference Numbers, which refer to the cases, in the Cases section. The suffixes indicate the state or, for federal cases, the court in which the case was decided.]

Article 12 Contract Documents

I

95051-SDMS
93019-NJ
94004-MO

II

97025-CO
94020-TX

97003-WA
97024-WV

III

93001-NC
96025-NJ
93026-NY

Article 13 Owner

III

95044-MDAL
95040-GA
95008-VA

Article 14 Contractor

I

95051-SDMS
94043-NDNY
97009-CA
96009-LA
95011-MI
92003a-MO

93005-MO
93033-MO
95025-NJ
97017-NJ
92008a-PA

II

94044-MDGA
96015-DC
97002-DC
94038-FL
95006-GA
95040-GA
92008b-IA
92001a-ID
93025-IL
93018-MA
94047-MI
93053-MN
93014-MO
93033-MO
96018-MO
95004-NJ

95025-NJ
97014-NJ
97005-PA
92004f-TX
94009-TX
94033-TX
94045-TX
95036-TX
95049-TX
96027-TX
93028-UT
93035-UT
93043-UT
93040-WI
95045-WI

DOCUMENT TO CASE CHARTS: A117-1987

[The five-digit numbers in this chart are Citator Case Reference Numbers, which refer to the cases, in the Cases section. The suffixes indicate the state or, for federal cases, the court in which the case was decided.]

III

94038-5CIR	95028-MA
97020-10CIR	95030-MA
94040-11CIR	95041-MA
95044-MDAL	96021-MA
96019-DKS	96026-MA
96024-DKS	96029-MA
94023-SDMS	96035-MA
95035-SDNY	97006-MA
94022-DRI	94016-MI
95007-DRI	93047-MN
95019-AR	94037-MN
97008-CA	95010-MN
94032-DE	96008-MN
93051-DC	96043-MN
93009-FL	94005-MO
95032-FL	95004-NJ
93034-GA	96025-NJ
97019-ID	93039-NY
93015a-IL	93030-OH
94046-IL	94042-OH
95026-IL	94048-OK
96012-IL	95012-OR
96031-IL	96010-OR
94014-IN	93031-PA
92004d-LA	94024-PA
93038-LA	93042-UT
94013-LA	95013-UT
95027-LA	95008-VA
96003-LA	94035-WA
95015-ME	96007-WA
93041-MA	95048-WV
94029-MA	96041-WY

Article 15   Administration of the Contract

I

92012-DNJ	94017-MO
92014-AL	97018-MO
93006-CT	92016-NC
93016-FL	93019-NJ
93012-IL	97026-OH
93003-KY	97023-PA
92019-LA	93002-SD
93011-MA	92005a-TX
93005-MO	97024-WV

II

96020-8CIR	93008-IA
94044-MDGA	93052-LA
95020-DPR	94006-MD
95046-AL	97011-MD
93044-FL	93046-MO
94038-FL	95033-MO
92004b-GA	93036-NE
94003-GA	95004-NJ
94026-GA	97007-NJ

DOCUMENT TO CASE CHARTS: A117-1987

[The five-digit numbers in this chart are Citator Case Reference Numbers, which refer to the cases, in the Cases section. The suffixes indicate the state or, for federal cases, the court in which the case was decided.]

96011-NY
95042-OH
95052-OH
93048-SC
92002-TN
93024-TN
96023-TN
93054-TX

94045-TX
96027-TX
95023-VA
96014-VA
95001-WA
93049-WV
94049-WY

III

95018-2CIR
96022-2CIR
97020-10CIR
96006-DCCIR
97001-MDGA
95014-AR
97016-AR
94018-CA
96038-CO
94041-CT
96002-DC
92004a-GA
93015a-IL
93027-IL
93045-IL

94021-LA
94005-MO
95022-NC
95016-NC
94001-NY
95024-NY
97022-NY
95009-PA
94030-TX
95002-TX
95008-VA
95001-WA
94019-WI
96039-WY

Article 16 Subcontracts

I

93025-IL
93019-NJ
95023-VA

II

97021-FL
93025-IL

III

95018-2CIR
97001-MDGA
96040-MO

Article 17 Construction by Owner or by Separate Contractors

I

93007-GA

II

94011-WDMI
92004e-GA

93007-GA
93025-IL

DOCUMENT TO CASE CHARTS: A117-1987

[The five-digit numbers in this chart are Citator Case Reference Numbers, which refer to the cases, in the Cases section. The suffixes indicate the state or, for federal cases, the court in which the case was decided.]

   III

      92005b-AK
      96016-GA
      96041-WY

Article 18 Changes in the Work

   I

      92012-DNJ

   II

      93015-OR
      95001-WA

   III

93037-10CIR	93026-NY
94040-11CIR	97010-OH
92005b-AK	94031-RI
92009b-ND	95001-WA

Article 19 Time

   I

      97018-MO

   II

      92004e-GA
      95047-LA

   III

95018-2CIR	97013-GA
94040-11CIR	96040-MO
96036-FCIR	95008-VA
97001-MDGA	95001-WA
96016-GA	96039-WY

Article 20 Payments and Completion

   II

      95001-WA

   III

93009-FL	96040-MO
93021-IL	94031-RI
96004-LA	

DOCUMENT TO CASE CHARTS: A117-1987

[The five-digit numbers in this chart are Citator Case Reference Numbers, which refer to the cases, in the Cases section. The suffixes indicate the state or, for federal cases, the court in which the case was decided.]

Article 21 Protection of Persons and Property

I

93005-MO
92016a-MT

II

94044-MDGA
94038-FL
96009-LA
96008-MN

95004-NJ
97005-PA
94045-TX
96027-TX

III

95044-MDAL
96024-DKS
94032-DE
93034-GA
95040-GA
93015a-IL
93017-IL

94014-IN
92004d-LA
95030-MA
94005-MO
95003-OH
95038-OH

Article 22 Insurance

I

95051-SDMS

II

94011-WDMI
93056-AZ
94012-CA
97009-CA
97025-CO

94002-MO
94004-MO
93029-NH
95049-TX
93055-WI

III

93050-DPR
96012-IL
94013-LA
97004-MD

94037-MN
96043-MN
95004-NJ
95038-OH

Article 23 Correction of Work

II

96034-MO

III

94024-PA

DOCUMENT TO CASE CHARTS: A117-1987

[*The five-digit numbers in this chart are Citator Case Reference Numbers, which refer to the cases, in the Cases section. The suffixes indicate the state or, for federal cases, the court in which the case was decided.*]

Article 24   Miscellaneous Provisions

    I

        92012-DNJ
        93011-MA
        93048-SC

Article 25   Termination of the Contract

    I

        92012-DNJ

    II

        94027-MN

    III

        92021b-VA
        95008-VA

Article 26   Other Conditions or Provisions

DOCUMENT TO CASE CHARTS: A201-1963 — A–112

[The five-digit numbers in this chart are Citator Case Reference Numbers, which refer to the cases, in the Cases section. The suffixes indicate the state or, for federal cases, the court in which the case was decided.]

A201-1963—GENERAL CONDITIONS OF THE CONTRACT FOR THE CONSTRUCTION OF BUILDINGS

Text of Article 1—Definitions

a) The Contract Documents consist of the Agreement, the General Conditions of the Contract, the Supplementary General Conditions, the Drawings and Specifications, including all modifications thereof incorporated in the documents before their execution. These form the Contract.

b) The Owner, the Contractor and the Architect are those mentioned as such in the Agreement. They are treated throughout the Contract Documents as if each were of the singular number and masculine gender.

c) The term Subcontractor, as employed herein, includes only those having a direct contract with the Contractor and it includes one who furnishes material worked to a special design according to the Drawings or Specifications of this work, but does not include one who merely furnishes material not so worked.

d) Written notice shall be deemed to have been duly served if delivered in person to the individual or to a member of the firm or to an officer of the corporation for whom it is intended, or if delivered at or sent by registered mail to the last business address known to him who gives the notice.

e) The term "work" of the Contractor or Subcontractor includes labor or materials or both.

f) All time limits stated in the Contract Documents are of the essence of the Contract.

g) The law of the place of building shall govern the construction of the Contract.

h) The date of substantial completion of a project or specified area of a project is the date when construction is sufficiently completed, in accordance with Contract Documents, as modified by any change orders agreed by the parties, so that the Owner can occupy the project or specified area of the project for the use it was intended.

Article 1   Definitions

I

    59004-8CIR   33001-MO
    15002-CA   67052-TX
    36001-KY

A–113 DOCUMENT TO CASE CHARTS: A201-1963

[*The five-digit numbers in this chart are Citator Case Reference Numbers, which refer to the cases, in the Cases section. The suffixes indicate the state or, for federal cases, the court in which the case was decided.*]

    II

        12001-CT
        42002-GA
        15003-NY

    III

66096-SDNY	21001-GA
56005-CA	65048-MO

Text of Article 2—Execution, Correlation and Intent of Documents

The Contract Documents shall be signed in duplicate by the Owner and the Contractor. In case either the Owner or the Contractor or both fail to sign the General Conditions, Supplementary General Conditions, Drawings or Specifications, the Architect shall identify them.

The Contract Documents are complementary, and what is called for by any one shall be as binding as if called for by all. The intention of the documents is to include all labor and materials, equipment and transportation necessary for the proper execution of the work. Materials or work described in words which so applied have a well-known technical or trade meaning shall be held to refer to such recognized standards.

It is not intended, that work not covered under any heading, section, branch, class or trade of the Specifications, shall be supplied unless it is shown on Drawings or is reasonably inferable therefrom as being necessary to produce the intended results.

Article 2   Execution, Correlation and Intent of Documents

    I

        60011-CA
        37002-NH

    II

        33001-MO

    III

        67069-IL

Text of Article 3—Detail Drawings and Instructions

The Architect shall furnish with reasonable promptness, additional instructions by means of drawings or otherwise, necessary for the proper execution of the work. All such drawings and instructions shall be consistent with the Contract Documents, true developments thereof, and reasonably inferable therefrom.

The work shall be executed in conformity therewith and the Contractor shall do no work without proper drawings and instructions.

Immediately after being awarded the Contract the Contractor shall prepare an

DOCUMENT TO CASE CHARTS: A201-1963 A–114

[The five-digit numbers in this chart are Citator Case Reference Numbers, which refer to the cases, in the Cases section. The suffixes indicate the state or, for federal cases, the court in which the case was decided.]

> estimated Progress Schedule and submit it for Architect's approval. It shall indicate the dates for the starting and completion of the various stages of construction.

Article 3 Detail Drawings and Instructions

    I

        44002-MA

Article 4 Copies Furnished

> ### Text of Article 5—Shop Drawings
>
> The Contractor shall check and verify all field measurements and shall submit with such promptness as to cause no delay in his own work or in that of any other Contractor, three copies, checked and approved by him, of all shop or setting drawings and schedules required for the work of the various trades. The Architect shall check and approve, with reasonable promptness, such schedules and drawings only for conformance with the design concept of the Project and compliance with the information given in the Contract Documents. The Contractor shall make any corrections required by the Architect, file with him two corrected copies and furnish such other copies as may be needed. The Architect's approval of such drawings or schedules shall not relieve the Contractor from responsibility for deviations from Drawings or Specifications, unless he has in writing called the Architect's attention to such deviations at the time of submission, and secured his written approval, nor shall it relieve him from responsibility for errors in shop drawings or schedules.

Article 5 Shop Drawings

    III

        61006-LA

Article 6 Drawings and Specifications on the Work

Article 7 Ownership of Drawings

A-115　　　**DOCUMENT TO CASE CHARTS: A201-1963**

[The five-digit numbers in this chart are Citator Case Reference Numbers, which refer to the cases, in the Cases section. The suffixes indicate the state or, for federal cases, the court in which the case was decided.]

Article 8　Samples

Text of Article 9—Materials, Appliances, Employees

Unless otherwise stipulated, the Contractor shall provide and pay for all materials, labor, water, tools, equipment, light, power, transportation and other facilities necessary for the execution and completion of the work.

Unless otherwise specified all materials shall be new and both workmanship and materials shall be of good quality. The Contractor shall, if required, furnish satisfactory evidence as to the kind and quality of materials.

The Contractor shall at all times enforce strict discipline and good order among his employees, and shall not employ on the work any unfit person or anyone not skilled in the work assigned to him.

Article 9　Materials, Appliances, Employees

　　　I

　　　　　65002-DC
　　　　　65091-NJ

　　　II

　　　　　65016-MDGA
　　　　　51003-NJ

Article 10　Royalties and Patents

Text of Article 11—Surveys, Permits, Laws, Taxes and Regulations

The Owner shall furnish all surveys unless otherwise specified.

Permits and licenses necessary for the prosecution of the work shall be secured and paid for by the Contractor. Easements for permanent structures or permanent changes in existing facilities shall be secured and paid for by the Owner, unless otherwise specified.

The Contractor shall give all notices and comply with all laws, ordinances, rules and regulations bearing on the conduct of the work as drawn and specified. If the Contractor observes that the Drawings and Specifications are at variance therewith, he shall promptly notify the Architect in writing and any necessary changes shall be adjusted as provided in the Contract for changes in the work. If the Contractor performs any work knowing it to be contrary to such laws, ordinances, rules and regulations, and without such notice to the Architect, he shall bear all costs arising therefrom.

Wherever the law of the place of building requires a sales, consumer, use, or other similar tax, the Contractor shall pay such tax.

DOCUMENT TO CASE CHARTS: A201-1963

[The five-digit numbers in this chart are Citator Case Reference Numbers, which refer to the cases, in the Cases section. The suffixes indicate the state or, for federal cases, the court in which the case was decided.]

Article 11   Surveys, Permits, Laws, Taxes and Regulations

    I

        60008-CA

    II

        16003-NY

    III

        20001-WA

Text of Article 12—Protection of Work and Property

The Contractor shall continuously maintain adequate protection of all his work from damage and shall protect the Owner's property from injury or loss arising in connection with the Contract. He shall make good any such damage, injury or loss, except such as may be directly due to errors in the Contract Documents or caused by agents or employees of the Owner, or due to causes beyond the Contractor's control and not to his fault or negligence. He shall adequately protect adjacent property as provided by law and the Contract Documents.

The Contractor shall take all necessary precautions for the safety of employees on the work, and shall comply with all applicable provisions of Federal, State, and Municipal safety laws and building codes to prevent accidents or injury to persons on, about or adjacent to the premises where the work is being performed. He shall erect and properly maintain at all times, as required by the conditions and progress of the work, all necessary safeguards for the protection of workmen and the public and shall post danger signs warning against the hazards created by such features of construction as protruding nails, hoists, well holes, elevator hatchways, scaffolding, window openings, stairways and falling materials; and he shall designate a responsible member of his organization on the work, whose duty shall be the prevention of accidents. The name and position of any person so designated shall be reported to the Architect by the Contractor.

In an emergency affecting the safety of life or of the work or of adjoining property, the Contractor, without special instruction or authorization from the Architect or Owner, is hereby permitted to act, at his discretion, to prevent such threatened loss or injury; and he shall so act, without appeal, if so authorized or instructed. Any compensation, claimed by the Contractor on account of emergency work, shall be determined by agreement or arbitration.

DOCUMENT TO CASE CHARTS: A201-1963

[The five-digit numbers in this chart are Citator Case Reference Numbers, which refer to the cases, in the Cases section. The suffixes indicate the state or, for federal cases, the court in which the case was decided.]

Article 12 Protection of Work and Property

I

67067-AR	67027-IA
14001-CA	44001-KY
67049-IL	67057-MN

II

66112-NC
67040-TX

III

63001-8CIR	65013-IL
65111-8CIR	65019-IL
67066-AK	66084-MD
67044-CA	66009-NY
65051-DE	67054-UT
67020-ID	

Text of Article 13—Access to Work

The Architect and his representatives shall at all times have access to the work wherever it is in preparation or progress and the Contractor shall provide proper facilities for such access and so that the Architect may perform his functions under the Contract Documents.

If the Specifications, the Architect's instructions, laws, ordinances or any public authority require any work to be specially tested or approved, the Contractor shall give the Architect timely notice of its readiness for observation by the Architect or inspection by another authority, and if the inspection is by another authority, of the date fixed for such inspection, required certificates of inspection being secured by the Contractor. Observations by the Architect shall be promptly made, and where practicable at the source of supply. If any work should be covered up without approval or consent of the Architect, it must, if required by the Architect, be uncovered for examination at the Contractor's expense.

Re-examination of questioned work may be ordered by the Architect and if so ordered the work must be uncovered by the Contractor. If such work be found in accordance with the Contract Documents the Owner shall pay the cost of reexamination and replacement. If such work be found not in accordance with the Contract Documents the Contractor shall pay such cost, unless it be found that the defect in the work was caused by a Contractor employed as provided in Article 35, and in that event the Owner shall pay such cost.

DOCUMENT TO CASE CHARTS: A201-1963 A–118

[The five-digit numbers in this chart are Citator Case Reference Numbers, which refer to the cases, in the Cases section. The suffixes indicate the state or, for federal cases, the court in which the case was decided.]

Article 13 Access to Work

    I

        67049-IL

Text of Article 14—Contractor's Superintendence and Supervision

The Contractor shall keep on his work, during its progress, a competent superintendent and any necessary assistants, all satisfactory to the Architect. The superintendent shall not be changed except with the consent of the Architect, unless the superintendent proves to be unsatisfactory to the Contractor and ceases to be in his employ. The superintendent shall represent the Contractor in his absence and all directions given to him shall be as binding as if given to the Contractor. Important directions shall be confirmed in writing to the Contractor. Other directions shall be so confirmed on written request in each case. The Architect shall not be responsible for the acts or omissions of the superintendent or his assistants.

The Contractor shall give efficient supervision to the work, using his best skill and attention. He shall carefully study and compare all Drawings, Specifications and other instructions and shall at once report to the Architect any error, inconsistency or omission which he may discover, but he shall not be liable to the Owner for any damage resulting from any errors or deficiencies in the Contract Documents or other instructions by the Architect.

Article 14 Contractor's Superintendence and Supervision

    I

        52004-ID
        67049-IL

    II

        57004-CA
        52005-NM
        62007-TX

    III

        63001-8CIR   29003-MD
        58004-10CIR   61011-NY
        65019-IL   38001-RI

Text of Article 15—Changes in the Work

The Owner, without invalidating the Contract, may order extra work or make changes by altering, adding to or deducting from the work, the Contract Sum being adjusted accordingly. All such work shall be executed under the conditions of the original Contract except that any claim for extension of time caused thereby shall be adjusted at the time of ordering such change.

A–119 DOCUMENT TO CASE CHARTS: A201-1963

[The five-digit numbers in this chart are Citator Case Reference Numbers, which refer to the cases, in the Cases section. The suffixes indicate the state or, for federal cases, the court in which the case was decided.]

> In giving instructions, the Architect shall have authority to make minor changes in the work, not involving extra cost, and not inconsistent with the purposes of the building, but otherwise, except in an emergency endangering life or property, no extra work or change shall be made unless in pursuance of a written order from the Owner signed or countersigned by the Architect, or a written order from the Architect stating that the Owner has authorized the extra work or charge, and no claim for an addition to the Contract Sum shall be valid unless so ordered.
>
> The value of any such extra work or change shall be determined in one or more of the following ways:
>
> a) By estimate and acceptance in a lump sum.
>
> b) By unit prices named in the Contract or subsequently agreed upon.
>
> c) By cost and percentage or by cost and a fixed fee.
>
> If none of the above methods is agreed upon, the Contractor, provided he receives an order as above, shall proceed with the work. In such case and also under case (c), he shall keep and present in such form as the Architect may direct, a correct account of the cost, together with vouchers. In any case, the Architect shall certify to the amount, including reasonable allowance for overhead and profit, due to the Contractor. Pending final determination of value, payments on account of changes shall be made on the Architect's certificate.
>
> Should conditions encountered below the surface of the ground be at variance with the conditions indicated by the Drawings and Specifications the Contract Sum shall be equitably adjusted upon claim by either party made within a reasonable time after the first observance of the conditions.

Article 15   Changes in the Work

I

29005-AZ	20002-MO
60008-CA	65029-MO
67049-IL	37002-NH
44001-KY	31005-TX
44002-MA	65063-VA

II

65049-NDMS	33001-MO
27001-CA	15004-MT
57004-CA	16001-NY
46001-IA	28001-TX
16002-MA	

DOCUMENT TO CASE CHARTS: A201-1963

[The five-digit numbers in this chart are Citator Case Reference Numbers, which refer to the cases, in the Cases section. The suffixes indicate the state or, for federal cases, the court in which the case was decided.]

III

001-US	62004-LA
66110-US	11001-MA
66042-5CIR	17001-MA
41001-6CIR	35002-MA
66055-9CIR	54003-MA
58004-10CIR	59003-MA
65118-EDVA	61005-MA
58005-SDWV	62008-MA
65057-CC	64004-MA
65081-CC	65079-MA
65092-CC	59002-MN
65123-CC	65048-MO
66037-CC	002-NE
66099-CC	66081-NH
66102-CC	66020-NY
66092-AK	66039-NY
65008-CA	66047-NY
67013-CA	67016-NC
67022-CA	60010-OK
67030-CA	65033-PA
67043-CA	60002-TX
67074-CA	65108-TX
23002-HI	66080-UT
67007-IL	65073-VA
67069-IL	58006-WA

Text of Article 16—Claims for Extra Cost

If the Contractor claims that any instructions by drawings or otherwise involve extra cost under the Contract, he shall give the Architect written notice thereof within a reasonable time after the receipt of such instructions, and in any event before proceeding to execute the work, except in emergency endangering life or property, and the procedure shall then be as provided for changes in the work. No such claim shall be valid unless so made.

Article 16   Claims for Extra Cost

I

67012-MA
65029-MO

II

65034-FL
61004-OR

DOCUMENT TO CASE CHARTS: A201-1963

[The five-digit numbers in this chart are Citator Case Reference Numbers, which refer to the cases, in the Cases section. The suffixes indicate the state or, for federal cases, the court in which the case was decided.]

III

66110-US	66099-CC
65043-2CIR	66118-CC
65056-4CIR	54001-CA
66042-5CIR	65008-CA
66055-9CIR	67043-CA
65016-MDGA	65078-GA
65049-NDMS	66093-GA
66056-MDPA	67007-IL
65036-CC	67069-IL
65041-CC	65030-MA
65050-CC	65079-MA
65053-CC	65048-MO
65057-CC	67016-NC
65080-CC	66020-NY
65081-CC	66039-NY
65096-CC	66047-NY
65123-CC	66082-SC
66016-CC	65108-TX
66037-CC	66080-UT
66044-CC	65073-VA

Article 17   Deductions for Uncorrected Work

Text of Article 18—Delays and Extension of Time

If the Contractor be delayed at any time in the progress of the work by any act or neglect of the Owner or the Architect, or of any employee of either, or by any separate Contractor employed by the Owner, or by changes ordered in the work, or by labor disputes, fire, unusual delay in transportation, unavoidable casualties or any causes beyond the Contractor's control, or by delay authorized by the Architect pending arbitration, or by any cause which the Architect shall decide to justify the delay, then the time of completion shall be extended for such reasonable time as the Architect may decide.

No such extension shall be made for delay occurring more than seven days before claim therefor is made in writing to the Architect. In the case of a continuing cause of delay, only one claim is necessary.

If no schedule or agreement stating the dates upon which drawings shall be furnished is made, then no claim for delay shall be allowed on account of failure to furnish drawings until two weeks after demand for such drawings and not then unless such claim be reasonable.

This article does not exclude the recovery of damages for delay by either party under other provisions in the Contract Documents.

DOCUMENT TO CASE CHARTS: A201-1963

[The five-digit numbers in this chart are Citator Case Reference Numbers, which refer to the cases, in the Cases section. The suffixes indicate the state or, for federal cases, the court in which the case was decided.]

Article 18 Delays and Extension of Time

I

61009-WDPA	66013-MD
25002-CA	60001-MO
60008-CA	53001-SC

II

27001-CA	46001-IA
31003-IL	67006-MA

III

66110-US	66114-DE
65014-7CIR	64003-GA
65022-EDNC	67062-LA
65072-9CIR	67070-MA
66086-9CIR	64002-MA
65053-CC	66001-NJ
65057-CC	63006-NY
65092-CC	67056-NY
65123-CC	20004-UT
65062-CA	

Text of Article 19—Correction of Work Before Substantial Completion

The Contractor shall promptly remove from the premises all work condemned by the Architect as failing to conform to the Contract, whether incorporated or not, and the Contractor shall promptly replace and reexecute his own work in accordance with the Contract and without expense to the Owner and shall bear the expense of making good all work of other contractors destroyed or damaged by such removal or replacement.

If the Contractor does not remove such condemned work within a reasonable time, fixed by written notice, the Owner may remove it and may store the material at the expense of the Contractor. If the Contractor does not pay the expenses of such removal within ten days' time thereafter, the Owner may, upon ten days' written notice, sell such materials at auction or at private sale and shall account for the net proceeds thereof, after deducting all the costs and expenses that should have been borne by the Contractor.

Article 19 Correction of Work Before Substantial Completion

I

67049-IL

DOCUMENT TO CASE CHARTS: A201-1963

[The five-digit numbers in this chart are Citator Case Reference Numbers, which refer to the cases, in the Cases section. The suffixes indicate the state or, for federal cases, the court in which the case was decided.]

III

    65072-9CIR

> **Text of Article 20—Correction of Work After Substantial Completion**
>
> The Contractor shall remedy any defects due to faulty materials or workmanship and pay for any damage to other work resulting therefrom, which shall appear within a period of one year from the date of Substantial Completion as defined in these General Conditions, and in accordance with the terms of any special guarantees provided in the Contract. The Owner shall give notice of observed defects with reasonable promptness. All questions arising under this Article shall be decided by the Architect subject to arbitration, notwithstanding final payment.

Article 20   Correction of Work After Substantial Completion

  I

    65099-LA   65007-NY
    43002-MN   61001-WA
    67033-MN   66098-WA

  II

    60009-HI   21002-NY
    54002-MS   67040-TX
    65094-NE

  III

    65012-5CIR   66052-NC
    67005-KY   65115-PA

> **Text of Article 21—Owner's Right to Do Work**
>
> If the Contractor should neglect to prosecute the work properly or fail to perform any provision of the Contract, the Owner, after three days' written notice to the Contractor may, without prejudice to any other remedy he may have, make good such deficiencies and may deduct the cost thereof from the payment then or thereafter due the Contractor, provided, however, that the Architect shall approve both such action and the amount charged to the Contractor.

Article 21   Owner's Right to Do Work

  I

    17004-CT
    39003-UT

DOCUMENT TO CASE CHARTS: A201-1963

[*The five-digit numbers in this chart are Citator Case Reference Numbers, which refer to the cases, in the Cases section. The suffixes indicate the state or, for federal cases, the court in which the case was decided.*]

II

    53001-SC
    13005-TX

III

    65105-NY

Text of Article 22—Owner's Right to Terminate Contract

If the Contractor should be adjudged a bankrupt, or if he should make a general assignment for the benefit of his creditors, or if a receiver should be appointed on account of his insolvency, or if he should persistently or repeatedly refuse or should fail, except in cases for which extension of time is provided, to supply enough properly skilled workmen or proper materials, or if he should fail to make prompt payment to subcontractors or for material or labor, or persistently disregard laws, ordinances or the instructions of the Architect, or otherwise be guilty of a substantial violation of any provision of the Contract, then the Owner, upon the certificate of the Architect that sufficient cause exists to justify such action, may, without prejudice to any other right or remedy and after giving the Contractor, and his surety if any, seven days' written notice, terminate the employment of the Contractor and take possession of the premises and of all materials, tools and appliances thereon and finish the work by whatever method he may deem expedient. In such case the Contractor shall not be entitled to receive any further payment until the work is finished. If the unpaid balance of the Contract Sum shall exceed the expense of finishing the work including compensation for additional architectural, managerial and administrative services, such excess shall be paid to the Contractor. If such expense shall exceed such unpaid balance, the Contractor shall pay the difference to the Owner. The expense incurred by the Owner as herein provided, and the damage incurred through the Contractor's default, shall be certified by the Architect.

Article 22 Owner's Right to Terminate Contract

I

13001-CA	51002-MD
15002-CA	53004-MS
17004-CT	60001-MO
66074-FL	39003-UT
66119-FL	

II

30001-MA	35003-TX
51003-NJ	17003-VA

A–125　　　**DOCUMENT TO CASE CHARTS: A201-1963**

[The five-digit numbers in this chart are Citator Case Reference Numbers, which refer to the cases, in the Cases section. The suffixes indicate the state or, for federal cases, the court in which the case was decided.]

III

66076-CC　　　　　　　　　　　　66079-MD
41002-CA　　　　　　　　　　　　65105-NY
67009-CA　　　　　　　　　　　　66012-NY

Text of Article 23—Contractor's Right to Stop Work or Terminate Contract

If the work should be stopped under an order of any court, or other public authority, for a period of thirty days, through no act or fault of the Contractor or of anyone employed by him, then the Contractor may, upon seven days' written notice to the Owner and the Architect, terminate the Contract and recover from the Owner payment for all work executed and any proven loss sustained upon any plant or materials and reasonable profit and damages.

Should the Architect fail to issue any Certificate for Payment, through no fault of the Contractor, within seven days after the Contractor's formal request for payment or if the Owner should fail to pay to the Contractor within seven days of its maturity and presentation, any sum certified by the Architect or awarded by arbitrators, then the Contractor may, upon seven days' written notice to the Owner and the Architect, stop the work or terminate the Contract as set out in the preceding paragraph.

Article 23　Contractor's Right to Stop Work or Terminate Contract

I

27003-IL

III

66053-SDCA
66008-DC

Text of Article 24—Applications for Payments

At least ten days before each payment falls due, the Contractor shall submit to the Architect an itemized application for payment, supported to the extent required by the Architect by receipts or other vouchers, showing payments for materials and labor, payments to subcontractors and such other evidence of the Contractor's right to payment as the Architect may direct.

If payments are made on valuation of work done, the Contractor shall, before the first application, submit to the Architect a schedule of values of the various parts of the work, including quantities, aggregating the total sum of the Contract, divided so as to facilitate payments to subcontractors in accordance with Article 37(e) made out in such form as the Architect and the Contractor may agree upon, and, if required, supported by such evidence as to its correctness as the Architect may direct. This schedule, when approved by the Architect, shall be used as a basis

DOCUMENT TO CASE CHARTS: A201-1963 A–126

[The five-digit numbers in this chart are Citator Case Reference Numbers, which refer to the cases, in the Cases section. The suffixes indicate the state or, for federal cases, the court in which the case was decided.]

for Certificates for Payment, unless it be found to be in error. In applying for payments, the Contractor shall submit a statement based upon this schedule.

If payments are made on account of materials not incorporated in the work but delivered and suitably stored at the site, or at some other location agreed upon in writing, such payments shall be conditioned upon submission by the Contractor of bills of sale or such other procedure as will establish the Owner's title to such material or otherwise adequately protect the Owner's interest including applicable insurance.

Article 24   Applications for Payments

    I

        13001-CA

    II

        51003-NJ

    III

        65009-5CIR   65117-6CIR
        65100-5CIR   57002-NE

Text of Article 25—Certificates for Payments

If the Contractor has made application for payment as above, the Architect shall, not later than the date when each payment falls due, issue a Certificate for Payment to the Contractor for such amount as he decides to be properly due, or state in writing his reasons for withholding a certificate.

No certificate issued nor payment made to the Contractor, nor partial or entire use or occupancy of the work by the Owner, shall be an acceptance of any work or materials not in accordance with the Contract. When advised by the Contractor that the work is substantially completed, the Architect and the Contractor shall within a reasonable time make a joint inspection of the work and if the Architect shall determine that the work is substantially completed, he shall then prepare a Certificate of Substantial Completion, which shall be submitted to the Owner and the Contractor for their execution. The making and acceptance of the final payment shall constitute a waiver of all claims by the Owner, other than those arising from unsettled liens, from faulty work appearing after Substantial Completion or from failure to comply with Drawings and Specifications and the terms of any special guarantees specified in the Contract and of all claims by the Contractor, except those previously made and still unsettled.

Should the Owner fail to pay the sum named in any Certificate for Payment issued by the Architect or in any award by arbitration, upon demand when due, the Contractor shall receive, in addition to the sum named in the Certificate for Payment. interest thereon at the legal rate in force at the place of building.

DOCUMENT TO CASE CHARTS: A201-1963

[The five-digit numbers in this chart are Citator Case Reference Numbers, which refer to the cases, in the Cases section. The suffixes indicate the state or, for federal cases, the court in which the case was decided.]

Article 25 Certificates for Payments

I

13001-CA	65083-NC
54004-CA	06001-NY
37003-IL	14002-NY
39002-FL	14004-NY
62011-MI	16003-NY
49003-MS	34003-NY
67033-MN	34001-TX
43002-MN	65063-VA
20002-MO	23001-WA
60001-MO	

II

62001-5CIR	65094-NE
17005-CO	50003-OR
42002-GA	13005-TX
31003-IL	36002-WI
18001-MA	53002-WA

III

07001-US	004-MA
65009-5CIR	43001-MI
32001-8CIR	57002-NE
66035-CC	66009-NY
65015-AZ	66097-NY
21003-CA	67002-NY
65077-ID	61003-NC
62005-IN	66082-SC
66108-MD	60003-TX

Text of Article 26—Payments Withheld

The Architect may withhold or, on account of subsequently discovered evidence, nullify the whole or a part of any certificate to such extent as may be necessary in his reasonable opinion to protect the Owner from loss on account of:

a) Defective work not remedied.

b) Claims filed or reasonable evidence indicating probable filing of claims.

c) Failure of the Contractor to make payments properly to subcontractors or for material or labor.

d) A reasonable doubt that the Contract can be completed for the balance then unpaid.

e) Damage to another Contractor.

When the above grounds are removed payment shall be made for amounts withheld because of them.

DOCUMENT TO CASE CHARTS: A201-1963   A–128

[The five-digit numbers in this chart are Citator Case Reference Numbers, which refer to the cases, in the Cases section. The suffixes indicate the state or, for federal cases, the court in which the case was decided.]

Article 26 Payments Withheld

    I

        41003-NM
        53001-SC

    III

65009-5CIR	65015-AZ
65072-9CIR	65077-ID
66068-DCT	65076-NY

Text of Article 27—Contractor's Liability Insurance

The Contractor shall maintain such insurance as will protect him from claims under workmen's compensation acts and other employee benefits acts; from claims for damages because of bodily injury, including death, to his employees and all others; and from claims for damages to property—any or all of which may arise out of or result from the Contractor's operations under the Contract, whether such operations be by himself or by any subcontractor or anyone directly or indirectly employed by either of them. This insurance shall be written for not less than any limits of liability specified as part of the Contract. Certificates of such insurance shall be filed with the Owner and Architect.

Article 27 Contractor's Liability Insurance

    III

65005-6CIR	67044-CA
65039-6CIR	65013-IL
63001-8CIR	66046-IL
65095-8CIR	66070-IL
66101-9CIR	66087-IL
65024-DCCIR	66026-IN
65010-CA	65122-KY
66045-CA	

Article 28 Owner's Liability Insurance

Text of Article 29—Fire Insurance with Extended Coverage

Unless otherwise provided, the Owner shall effect and maintain fire insurance with extended coverage upon the entire structure on which the work of the Contract is to be done to one hundred per cent of the insurable value thereof, including items of labor and materials connected therewith whether in or adjacent to the structure insured, materials in place or to be used as part of the permanent construction including surplus materials, shanties, protective fences, bridges, temporary structures, miscellaneous materials and supplies incident to the work, and such scaffolds, stagings, towers, forms, and equipment as are not owned or rented by the Contractor, the cost of which is included in the cost of the work. EXCLUSIONS: This insurance does not cover any tools owned by mechanics, any tools, equipment, scaffolding,

DOCUMENT TO CASE CHARTS: A201-1963

[The five-digit numbers in this chart are Citator Case Reference Numbers, which refer to the cases, in the Cases section. The suffixes indicate the state or, for federal cases, the court in which the case was decided.]

staging, towers, and forms owned or rented by the Contractor, the capital value of which is not included in the cost of the work, or any cook shanties, bunk houses or other structures erected for housing the workmen. The loss, if any, is to be made adjustable with and payable to the Owner as Trustee for the insureds and Contractors and subcontractors as their interests may appear, except in such cases as may require payment of all or a proportion of said insurance to be made to a mortgagee as his interests may appear.

Certificates of such insurance shall be filed with the Contractor if he so requires. If the Owner fails to effect or maintain insurance as above and so notifies the Contractor, the Contractor may insure his own interests and that of the subcontractors and charge the cost thereof to the Owner. If the Contractor is damaged by failure of the Owner to maintain such insurance or to so notify the Contractor he may recover as stipulated in the Contract for recovery of damages. If other special insurance not herein provided for is required by the Contractor, the Owner shall effect such insurance at the Contractor's expense by appropriate riders to his fire insurance policy. The Owner, Contractor, and all subcontractors waive all rights, each against the others, for damages caused by fire or other perils covered by insurance provided under the terms of this article, except such rights as they may have to the proceeds of insurance held by the Owner as Trustee.

The Owner shall be responsible for and at his option may insure against loss of use of his existing property, due to fire or otherwise, however caused. If required in writing by any party in interest, the Owner as Trustee shall, upon the occurrence of loss, give bond for the proper performance of his duties. He shall deposit any money received from insurance in an account separate from all his other funds and he shall distribute it in accordance with such agreement as the parties in interest may reach, or under an award of arbitrators appointed, one by the Owner, another by joint action of the other parties in interest, all other procedure being as provided elsewhere in the Contract for arbitration. If after loss no special agreement is made, replacement of injured work shall be ordered and executed as provided for changes in the work.

The Trustee shall have power to adjust and settle any loss with the insurers unless one of the Contractors Interested shall object in writing within three working days of the occurrence of loss, and thereupon arbitrators shall be chosen as above. The Trustee shall in that case make settlement with the insurers in accordance with the directions of such arbitrators, who shall also, if distribution by arbitration is required, direct such distribution.

DOCUMENT TO CASE CHARTS: A201-1963

[The five-digit numbers in this chart are Citator Case Reference Numbers, which refer to the cases, in the Cases section. The suffixes indicate the state or, for federal cases, the court in which the case was decided.]

Article 29 Fire Insurance with Extended Coverage

I

    62009-FL
    62006-ND

III

    66066-IL
    63003-MN

Text of Article 30—Guaranty Bonds

The Owner shall have the right, prior to the signing of the Contract, to require the Contractor to furnish bond covering the faithful performance of the Contract and the payment of all obligations arising thereunder, in such form as the Owner may prescribe and with such sureties as he may approve. If such bond is required by instructions given previous to the submission of bids, the premium shall be paid by the Contractor; if subsequent thereto, it shall be paid by the Owner.

Article 30 Guaranty Bonds

I

    65091-NJ

III

    65068-8CIR

Text of Article 31—Damages

Should either party to the Contract suffer damages because of any wrongful act or neglect of the other party or of anyone employed by him, claim shall be made in writing to the party liable within a reasonable time of the first observance of such damage and not later than the final payment, except as expressly stipulated otherwise in the case of faulty work or materials, and shall be adjusted by agreement or arbitration.

Article 31 Damages

I

    65124-SDIA   44002-MA
    61009-WDPA   43002-MN
    41002-CA   67033-MN
    62009-FL   14005-NY
    66119-FL

DOCUMENT TO CASE CHARTS: A201-1963

[The five-digit numbers in this chart are Citator Case Reference Numbers, which refer to the cases, in the Cases section. The suffixes indicate the state or, for federal cases, the court in which the case was decided.]

III

41001-6CIR	66045-CA
66086-9CIR	66008-DC
65001-10CIR	29003-MD
65123-CC	

Text of Article 32—Liens

Neither the final payment nor any part of the retained percentage shall become due until the Contractor, if required, shall deliver to the Owner a complete release of all liens arising out of the Contract, or receipts in full in lieu thereof and, if required in either case, an affidavit that so far as he has knowledge or information the releases and receipts include all the labor and material for which a lien could be filed; but the Contractor may, if any subcontractor refuses to furnish a release or receipt in full, furnish a bond satisfactory to the Owner, to indemnify him against any lien. If any lien remains unsatisfied after all payments are made, the Contractor shall refund to the Owner all moneys that the latter may be compelled to pay in discharging such a lien, including all costs and a reasonable attorney's fee.

Article 32   Liens

I

52006-CC
13001-CA

II

06001-NY
69016-PA

III

65117-6CIR	65040-NJ
12002-AR	65075-PA
13003-CO	

Text of Article 33—Assignment

Neither party to the Contract shall assign the Contract or sublet it as a whole without the written consent of the other, nor shall the Contractor assign any moneys due or to become due to him hereunder, without the previous written consent of the Owner.

DOCUMENT TO CASE CHARTS: A201-1963 A–132

[The five-digit numbers in this chart are Citator Case Reference Numbers, which refer to the cases, in the Cases section. The suffixes indicate the state or, for federal cases, the court in which the case was decided.]

Article 33 Assignment

    II

        56004-CT
        17002-GA

    III

        16004-US   52001-NY
        65018-10CIR   35001-PA
        66063-10CIR   56002-PA
        62002-CA

Text of Article 34—Mutual Responsibility of Contractors

Should the Contractor cause damage to any separate contractor on the work the Contractor agrees, upon due notice, to settle with such contractor by agreement or arbitration, if he will so settle. If such separate contractor sues the Owner on account of any damage alleged to have been so sustained, the Owner shall notify the Contractor, who shall defend such proceedings at the Owner's expense and, if any judgment against the Owner arise therefrom, the Contractor shall pay or satisfy it and pay all costs incurred by the Owner.

Article 34 Mutual Responsibility of Contractors

    I

        39003-UT

    II

        67040-TX

Text of Article 35—Separate Contracts

The Owner reserves the right to let other contracts in connection with this work under similar General Conditions. The Contractor shall afford other contractors reasonable opportunity for the introduction and storage of their materials and the execution of their work, and shall properly connect and coordinate his work with theirs.

If any part of the Contractor's work depends for proper execution or results upon the work of any other contractor, the Contractor shall inspect and promptly report to the Architect any defects in such work that render it unsuitable for such proper execution and results. Failure of the Contractor so to inspect and report shall constitute an acceptance of the other contractor's work as fit and proper for the reception of his work, except as to defects which may develop in the other contractor's work after the execution of his work.

To insure the proper execution of his subsequent work the Contractor shall measure work already in place and shall at once report to the Architect any discrepancy between the executed work and the Drawings.

DOCUMENT TO CASE CHARTS: A201-1963

[*The five-digit numbers in this chart are Citator Case Reference Numbers, which refer to the cases, in the Cases section. The suffixes indicate the state or, for federal cases, the court in which the case was decided.*]

Article 35 Separate Contracts

I
   44003-LA

III
   66023-NY

Text of Article 36—Subcontracts

As soon as practicable and before awarding any subcontracts, the Contractor shall notify the Architect in writing of the names of the subcontractors proposed for the principal parts of the work, and for such other parts as the Architect may direct, and shall not employ any to whom the Architect or the Owner may have a reasonable objection.

If before or after the execution of the Contract a change of any subcontractor on such list is required by the Architect or by the Owner prior to the award of the relevant contract, the Contract Sum shall be increased or decreased by the difference in cost occasioned by such change.

The Contractor shall not be required to employ any subcontractor against whom he has a reasonable objection.

The Architect shall, on request, furnish to any subcontractor, wherever practicable, evidence of the amounts certified on his account.

The Contractor agrees that he is as fully responsible to the Owner for the acts and omissions of his subcontractors and of persons either directly or indirectly employed by them, as he is for the acts and omissions of persons directly employed by him.

Nothing contained in the Contract Documents shall create any contractual relation between any subcontractor and the Owner.

Article 36 Subcontracts

I
   44003-LA
   39004-MI
   67052-TX

II
   58002-4CIR
   67031-VA

DOCUMENT TO CASE CHARTS: A201-1963 A–134

[The five-digit numbers in this chart are Citator Case Reference Numbers, which refer to the cases, in the Cases section. The suffixes indicate the state or, for federal cases, the court in which the case was decided.]

III

  65045-1CIR   65106-IA
  65082-8CIR   65038-MA
  65010-CA   65087-OR

Text of Article 37—Relations of Contractor and Subcontractor

The Contractor agrees to bind every Subcontractor and every Subcontractor agrees to be bound by the terms of the Agreement, the General Conditions of the Contract, the Supplementary General Conditions, the Drawings and Specifications as far as applicable to his work, including the following provisions of this article, unless specifically noted to the contrary in a subcontract approved in writing as adequate by the Owner or Architect.

The Subcontractor agrees—

a) To be bound to the Contractor by the terms of the Agreement, General Conditions of the Contract, the Supplementary General Conditions, the Drawings and Specifications, and to assume toward him all the obligations and responsibilities that he, by those documents, assumes toward the Owner.

b) To submit to the Contractor applications for payment in such reasonable time as to enable the Contractor to apply for payment under Article 24 of the General Conditions.

c) To make all claims for extras, for extensions of time and for damages for delays or otherwise, to the Contractor in the manner provided in the General Conditions of the Contract and the Supplementary General Conditions for like claims by the Contractor upon the Owner, except that the time for making claims for extra cost is one week.

The Contractor agrees—

d) To be bound to the Subcontractor by all the obligations that the Owner assumes to the Contractor under the Agreement, General Conditions of the Contract, the Supplementary General Conditions, the Drawings and Specifications, and by all the provisions thereof affording remedies and redress to the Contractor from the Owner.

e) To pay the Subcontractor, upon the payment of certificates, if issued under the schedule of values described in Article 24 of the General Conditions, the amount allowed to the Contractor on account of the Subcontractor's work to the extent of the Subcontractor's interest therein.

f) To pay the Subcontractor, upon the payment of certificates, if issued otherwise than as in (e), so that at all times his total payments shall be as large in proportion to the value of the work done by him as the total amount certified to the Contractor is to the value of the work done by him.

g) To pay the Subcontractor to such extent as may be provided by the Contract Documents or the subcontract, if either of these provides for earlier or larger payments than the above.

DOCUMENT TO CASE CHARTS: A201-1963

[*The five-digit numbers in this chart are Citator Case Reference Numbers, which refer to the cases, in the Cases section. The suffixes indicate the state or, for federal cases, the court in which the case was decided.*]

h) To pay the Subcontractor on demand for his work or materials as far as executed and fixed in place, less the retained percentage, at the time the Certificate for Payment should issue, even though the Architect fails to issue it for any cause not the fault of the Subcontractor.

j) To pay the Subcontractor a just share of any fire insurance money received by him, the Contractor, under Article 29 of the General Conditions.

k) To make no demand for liquidated damages or penalty for delay in any sum in excess of such amount as may be specifically named in the subcontract.

l) That no claim for services rendered or materials furnished by the Contractor to the Subcontractor shall be valid unless written notice thereof is given by the Contractor to the Subcontractor during the first ten days of the calendar month following that in which the claim originated.

m) To give the Subcontractor an opportunity to be present and to submit evidence in any arbitration involving his rights.

n) To name as arbitrator under arbitration proceedings as provided in the General Conditions the person nominated by the Subcontractor, if the sole cause of dispute is the work, materials, rights or responsibilities of the Subcontractor; or, if of the Subcontractor and any other subcontractor jointly, to name as such arbitrator the person upon whom they agree.

The Contractor and the Subcontractor agree that—

o) In the matter of arbitration, their rights and obligations and all procedure, shall be analogous to those set forth in this Contract: provided, however, that a decision by the Architect shall not be a condition precedent to arbitration.

Nothing in this article shall create any obligation on the part of the Owner to pay or to see to the payment of any sums to any subcontractor.

Article 37 Relations of Contractor and Subcontractor

I

42001-5CIR
61009-WDPA
52004-ID
67027-LA
65037-MD

67012-MA
34001-MO
61004-OR
67052-TX
39003-UT

II

67053-CO

DOCUMENT TO CASE CHARTS: A201-1963   A–136

[The five-digit numbers in this chart are Citator Case Reference Numbers, which refer to the cases, in the Cases section. The suffixes indicate the state or, for federal cases, the court in which the case was decided.]

III

65045-1CIR	65118-EDVA
65100-5CIR	65088-IN
66042-5CIR	65020-ME
65072-9CIR	65079-MA
66015-9CIR	65087-OR
66104-DMT	65042-WI

Text of Article 38—Architect's Status: Architect's Supervision

The Architect shall be the Owner's representative during the construction period. The Architect will make periodic visits to the site to familiarize himself generally with the progress and quality of the work and to determine in general if the work is proceeding in accordance with the Contract Documents. He will not be required to make exhaustive or continuous on-site inspections to check the quality or quantity of the work and he will not be responsible for the Contractor's failure to carry out the construction work in accordance with the Contract Documents. During such visits and on the basis of his observations while at the site, he will keep the Owner informed of the progress of the work, will endeavor to guard the Owner against defects and deficiencies in the work of Contractors, and he may condemn work as failing to conform to the Contract Documents. He shall have authority to act on behalf of the Owner only to the extent expressly provided in the Contract Documents or otherwise in writing, which shall be shown to the Contractor. He shall have authority to stop the work whenever such stoppage may be necessary in his reasonable opinion to insure the proper execution of the Contract.

The Architect shall be, in the first instance, the interpreter of the conditions of the Contract and the judge of its performance. He shall side neither with the Owner nor with the Contractor, but shall use his powers under the Contract to enforce its faithful performance by both.

In case of the termination of the employment of the Architect, the Owner shall appoint a capable and reputable Architect against whom the Contractor makes no reasonable, objection, whose status under the contract shall be that of the former Architect; any dispute in connection with such appointment shall be subject to arbitration.

Article 38   Architect's Status: Architect's Supervision

I

67067-AR	31005-TX
54004-CA	34001-TX
67049-IL	37001-TX
65099-LA	23001-WA
44002-MA	65063-VA
39004-MI	

DOCUMENT TO CASE CHARTS: A201-1963

[The five-digit numbers in this chart are Citator Case Reference Numbers, which refer to the cases, in the Cases section. The suffixes indicate the state or, for federal cases, the court in which the case was decided.]

II

    58003-GA   65094-NE
    66041-IL   66112-NC

III

    66036-1CIR   61006-LA
    63001-8CIR   63007-LA
    59005-DRI   66069-MI
    66023-CC   15003-MN
    65015-AZ   54006-MS
    60006-AR   003-NY
    53005-CA   38001-RI
    64003-GA   66090-TX
    65019-IL   67054-UT

Text of Article 39—Architect's Decisions

The Architect shall, within a reasonable time, make decisions on all claims of the Owner or Contractor and on all other matters relating to the execution and progress of the work or the interpretation of the Contract Documents.

The Architect's decision, in matters relating to artistic effect, shall be final, if within the terms of the Contract Documents.

Except as above or as otherwise expressly provided in the Contract Documents, all the Architect's decisions are subject to arbitration.

If, however, the Architect fails to render a decision within ten days after the parties have presented their evidence, either party may then demand arbitration. If the Architect renders a decision after arbitration proceedings have been initiated, such decision may be entered as evidence but shall not disturb or interrupt such proceedings except where such decision is acceptable to the parties concerned.

Article 39 Architect's Decisions

I

    65124-SDIA   43002-MN
    13001-CA   37002-NH
    67049-IL   65007-NY
    65067-LA   60007-SC
    65099-LA   37001-TX
    44002-MA

II

    28003-IA   50003-OR
    31002-NY   60005-TX
    66112-NC   13004-WA

DOCUMENT TO CASE CHARTS: A201-1963   A–138

[*The five-digit numbers in this chart are Citator Case Reference Numbers, which refer to the cases, in the Cases section. The suffixes indicate the state or, for federal cases, the court in which the case was decided.*]

III

65012-5CIR	67043-CA
65120-5CIR	66114-DE
66092-AK	64003-GA
60004-AZ	29004-NM
65015-AZ	67036-NY
56006-CA	67008-PA

Text of Article 40—Arbitration

All disputes, claims or questions subject to arbitration under the Contract shall be submitted to arbitration in accordance with the provisions, then obtaining, of the Standard Form of Arbitration Procedure of The American Institute of Architects, and the Agreement shall be specifically enforceable under the prevailing arbitration law, and judgment upon the award rendered may be entered in the court of the forum, state or federal, having jurisdiction. It is mutually agreed that the decision of the arbitrators shall be a condition precedent to any right of legal action that either party may have against the other.

The Contractor shall not cause a delay of the work during any arbitration proceedings, except by agreement with the Owner.

Notice of the demand for arbitration of a dispute shall be filed in writing with the other party to the Contract, and a copy filed with the Architect. The demand for arbitration shall be made within a reasonable time after the dispute has arisen; in no case, however, shall the demand be made later than the time of final payment, except as otherwise expressly stipulated in the Contract.

The arbitrators, if they deem that the case requires it, are authorized to award to the party whose contention is sustained, such sums as they or a majority of them shall deem proper to compensate him for the time and expense incident to the proceeding and, if the arbitration was demanded without reasonable cause, they may also award damages for delay. The arbitrators shall fix their own compensation, unless otherwise provided by agreement, and shall assess the costs and charges of the proceedings upon either or both parties.

Article 40   Arbitration

I

56003-DCCIR	37002-NH
25002-CA	52003-NY
66116-DE	66050-NY
66119-FL	65007-NY
65099-LA	65059-PA
66013-MD	67065-WA
49003-MS	65103-WI
43002-MN	

DOCUMENT TO CASE CHARTS: A201-1963

[The five-digit numbers in this chart are Citator Case Reference Numbers, which refer to the cases, in the Cases section. The suffixes indicate the state or, for federal cases, the court in which the case was decided.]

II

65027-CT	66113-PA
65067-LA	24002-SC
66065-ND	60007-SC

III

66110-US	29004-NM
61010-2CIR	66004-NY
65120-5CIR	66022-NY
65111-8CIR	66024-NY
66096-SDNY	66027-NY
66056-MDPA	66039-NY
65081-CC	66054-NY
60004-AZ	67060-NY
66019-CA	63004-OH
66083-CA	65033-PA
65093-CO	65121-PA
65026-CT	67008-PA
67011-MD	

Article 41   Cash Allowances

Article 42   Uses of Premises

Article 43   Cutting, Patching

Article 44   Cleaning Up

DOCUMENT TO CASE CHARTS: A201-1967 A–140

[*The five-digit numbers in this chart are Citator Case Reference Numbers, which refer to the cases, in the Cases section. The suffixes indicate the state or, for federal cases, the court in which the case was decided.*]

A201-1967—GENERAL CONDITIONS OF THE CONTRACT FOR CONSTRUCTION

Article 1   Contract Documents

Text of Paragraph 1.1—Definitions

1.1.1 THE CONTRACT DOCUMENTS

The Contract Documents consist of the Agreement, the Conditions of the Contract (General, Supplementary and other Conditions), the Drawings, the Specifications, all Addenda issued prior to execution of the Agreement, and all Modifications thereto. A Modification is (1) a written amendment to the Contract signed by both parties, (2) a Change Order, (3) a written interpretation issued by the Architect pursuant to Subparagraph 1.2.5, or (4) a written order for a minor change in the Work issued by the Architect pursuant to Paragraph 12.3. A Modification may be made only after execution of the Contract.

1.1.2 THE CONTRACT

The Contract Documents form the Contract. The Contract represents the entire and integrated agreement between the parties hereto and supersedes all prior negotiations, representations, or agreements, either written or oral, including the bidding documents. The Contract may be amended or modified only by a Modification as defined in Subparagraph 1.1.1.

1.1.3 THE WORK

The term Work includes all labor necessary to produce the construction required by the Contract Documents and all materials and equipment incorporated or to be incorporated in such construction.

1.1.4 THE PROJECT

The Project is the total construction designed by the Architect of which the Work performed under the Contract Documents may be the whole or a part.

Paragraph 1.1   Definitions

    I

        71036-MI
        70047-WA

    II

        70003-MD
        72112-MD

Text of Paragraph 1.2—Execution, Correlation, Intent and Interpretations

1.2.1 The Contract Documents shall be signed in not less than triplicate by the Owner and Contractor. If either the Owner or the Contractor or both do not sign

DOCUMENT TO CASE CHARTS: A201-1967

[*The five-digit numbers in this chart are Citator Case Reference Numbers, which refer to the cases, in the Cases section. The suffixes indicate the state or, for federal cases, the court in which the case was decided.*]

the Conditions of the Contract, Drawings, Specifications, or any of the other Contract Documents, the Architect shall identify them.

1.2.2 By executing the Contract, the Contractor represents that he has visited the site, familiarized himself with the local conditions under which the Work is to be performed, and correlated his observations with the requirements of the Contract Documents.

1.2.3 The Contract Documents are complementary, and what is required by any one shall be as binding as if required by all. The intention of the Documents is to include all labor, materials, equipment and other items as provided in Subparagraph 4.4.1 necessary for the proper execution and completion of the Work. It is not intended that Work not covered under any heading, section, branch, class or trade of the Specifications shall be supplied unless it is required elsewhere in the Contract Documents or is reasonably inferable therefrom as being necessary to produce the intended results. Words which have well-known technical or trade meanings are used herein in accordance with such recognized meanings.

1.2.4 The organization of the Specifications into divisions, sections and articles, and the arrangement of Drawings shall not control the Contractor in dividing the Work among Subcontractors or in establishing the extent of Work to be performed by any trade.

1.2.5 Written interpretations necessary for the proper execution or progress of the Work, in the form of drawings or otherwise, will be issued with reasonable promptness by the Architect and in accordance with any schedule agreed upon. Such interpretations shall be consistent with and reasonably inferable from the Contract Documents, and may be effected by Field Order.

Paragraph 1.2   Execution, Correlation, Intent and Interpretations

   I

       67051-SDTX

  III

       71032-TX

Text of Paragraph 1.3—Copies Furnished and Ownership

1.3.1 Unless otherwise provided in the Contract Documents, the Contractor will be furnished, free of charge, all copies of Drawings and Specifications reasonably necessary for the execution of the Work.

1.3.2 All Drawings, Specifications and copies thereof furnished by the Architect are and shall remain his property. They are not to be used on any other project, and, the exception of one contract set for each party to the Contract, are to be returned to the Architect on request at the completion of the Work.

DOCUMENT TO CASE CHARTS: A201-1967 A–142

[The five-digit numbers in this chart are Citator Case Reference Numbers, which refer to the cases, in the Cases section. The suffixes indicate the state or, for federal cases, the court in which the case was decided.]

Paragraph 1.3   Copies Furnished and Ownership

    I

        67004-UT

Article 2   Architect

Text of Paragraph 2.1—Definition

2.1.1 The Architect is the person or organization identified as such in the Agreement and is referred to throughout the Contract Documents as if singular in number and masculine in gender. The term Architect means the Architect or his authorized representative.

2.1.2 Nothing contained in the Contract Documents shall create any contractual relationship between the Architect and the Contractor.

Paragraph 2.1   Definition

    I

        71020-EDLA

Text of Paragraph 2.2—Administration of the Contract

2.2.1 The Architect will provide general Administration of the Construction Contract, including performance of the functions hereinafter described.

2.2.2 The Architect will be the Owner's representative during construction and until final payment. The Architect will have authority to act on behalf of the Owner to the extent provided in the Contract Documents, unless otherwise modified by written instrument which will be shown to the Contractor. The Architect will advise and consult with the Owner, and all of the Owner's instructions to the Contractor shall be issued through the Architect.

2.2.3 The Architect shall at all times have access to the Work wherever it is in preparation and progress. The Contractor shall provide facilities for such access so the Architect may perform his functions under the Contract Documents.

2.2.4 The Architect will make periodic visits to the site to familiarize himself generally with the progress and quality of the Work and to determine in general if the Work is proceeding in accordance with the Contract Documents. On the basis of hid on-site observations as an architect, he will keep the Owner informed of the progress of the Work, and will endeavor to guard the Owner against defects and deficiencies in the Work of the Contractor. The Architect will not be required to make exhaustive or continuous on-site inspections to check the quality or quantity of the Work. The Architect will not be responsible for construction means, methods, techniques, sequences or procedures, or for safety precautions and programs in connection with the Work, and he will not be responsible for the Contractor's failure to carry out the Work in accordance with the Contract Documents.

(Matthew Bender & Co., Inc.)   (Pub.435)

DOCUMENT TO CASE CHARTS: A201-1967

[The five-digit numbers in this chart are Citator Case Reference Numbers, which refer to the cases, in the Cases section. The suffixes indicate the state or, for federal cases, the court in which the case was decided.]

2.2.5 Based on such observations and the Contractor's Applications for Payment, the Architect will determine the amounts owing to the Contractor and will issue Certificates for Payment in such amounts, as provided in Paragraph 9.4.

2.2.6 The Architect will be, in the first instance, the interpreter of the requirements of the Contract Documents and the judge of the performance thereunder by both the Owner and Contractor. The Architect will, within a reasonable time, render such interpretations as he may deem necessary for the proper execution or progress of the Work.

2.2.7 Claims, disputes and other matters in question between the Contractor and the Owner relating to the execution or progress of the Work or the interpretation of the Contract Documents shall be referred initially to the Architect for decision which he will render in writing within a reasonable time.

2.2.8 All interpretations and decisions of the Architect shall be consistent with the intent of the Contract Documents. In his capacity as interpreter and judge, he will exercise his best efforts to insure faithful performance by both the Owner and the Contractor and will not show partiality to either.

2.2.9 The Architect's decisions in matters relating to artistic effect will be final if consistent with the intent of the Contract Documents.

2.2.10 Any claim, dispute or other matter that has been referred to the Architect, except those relating to artistic effect as provided in Subparagraph 2.2.9 and except any which have been waived by the making or acceptance of final payment as provided in Subparagraphs 9.7.5 and 9.7.6, shall be subject to arbitration upon the written demand of either party. However, no demand for arbitration of any such claim, dispute or other matter may be made until the earlier of:

.1   the date on which the Architect has rendered his decision, or

.2   the tenth day after the parties have presented their evidence to the Architect or have been given a reasonable opportunity to do so, if the Architect has not rendered his written decision by that date.

2.2.11 If a decision of the Architect's made in writing and states that it is final but subject to appeal, no demand for arbitration of a claim, dispute or other matter covered by such decision may be made later than thirty days after the date on which the party making the demand received the decision. The failure to demand arbitration within said thirty days' period will result in the Architect's decision becoming final and binding upon the Owner and the Contractor. If the Architect renders a decision after arbitration proceedings have been initiated, such decision may be entered as evidence but will not supersede any arbitration proceedings except where the decision is acceptable to the parties concerned.

2.2.12 The Architect will have authority to reject Work which does not conform to the Contract Documents. Whenever, in his reasonable opinion, he considers it necessary or advisable to insure the proper implementation of the intent of the Contract Documents, he will have authority to require the Contractor to stop the

DOCUMENT TO CASE CHARTS: A201-1967

[The five-digit numbers in this chart are Citator Case Reference Numbers, which refer to the cases, in the Cases section. The suffixes indicate the state or, for federal cases, the court in which the case was decided.]

Work or any portion thereof, or to require special inspection or testing of the Work as provided in Subparagraph 7.8.2 whether or not such Work be then fabricated, installed or completed. However, neither the Architect's authority to act under this Subparagraph 2.2.12, nor any decision made by him in good faith either to exercise or not to exercise such authority, shall give rise to any duty or responsibility of the Architect to the Contractor, any Subcontractor, any of their agents or employees, or any other person performing any of the Work.

2.2.13 The Architect will review Shop Drawings and Samples as provided in Subparagraphs 4.13.1 through 4.13.8 inclusive.

2.2.14 The Architect will prepare Change Orders in accordance with Article 12, and will have authority to order minor changes in the Work as provided in Subparagraph 12.3.1.

2.2.15 The Architect will conduct inspections to determine the dates of Substantial Completion and final completion, will receive written guarantees and related documents required by the Contract and assembled by the Contractor, and will issue a final Certificate for Payment.

2.2.16 If the Owner and Architect agree, the Architect will provide one or more Full-time Project Representatives to assist the Architect in carrying out his responsibilities at the site. The duties, responsibilities and limitations of authority of any such Project Representative shall be as set forth in an exhibit to be incorporated in the Contract Documents.

2.2.17 The duties, responsibilities and limitations of authority of the Architect as the Owner's representative during construction as set forth in Articles 1 through 14 inclusive of these General Conditions will not be modified or extended without written consent of the Owner and the Architect which will be shown to the Contractor.

2.2.18 The Architect will not be responsible for the acts or omissions of the Contractor, any Subcontractors, or any of their agents or employees, or any other persons performing any of the Work.

2.2.19 In case of the termination of the employment of the Architect, the Owner shall appoint an architect against whom the Contractor makes no reasonable objection, whose status under the Contract Documents shall be that of the former architect. Any dispute in connection with such appointment shall be subject to arbitration.

DOCUMENT TO CASE CHARTS: A201-1967

[The five-digit numbers in this chart are Citator Case Reference Numbers, which refer to the cases, in the Cases section. The suffixes indicate the state or, for federal cases, the court in which the case was decided.]

Paragraph 2.2   Administration of the Contract

I

69046-AZ	71021-MS
70069-AZ	82035-MS
68018-AR	71014-NY
69032-CA	71066-NY
71079-CO	69019-OK
69006-LA	68010-TX
70020-MD	69034-WA

II

69007-4CIR	71056-KS
68001-8CIR	71082-MI
68051-CA	68019-NV
71002-CA	71015-NY
70017-GA	

III

70008-6CIR	70016-MD
70041-DCCIR	71064-MD
70058-AZ	68002-MA
67017-GA	70034-MA
69025-IL	68055-MS
71025-IL	67071-MO
70061-KS	67047-PA
68021-LA	71010-VA

Article 3   Owner

Paragraph 3.1   Definition

Text of Paragraph 3.2—Information and Services Required of the Owner

3.2.1 The Owner shall furnish all surveys describing, the physical characteristics, legal limits and utility locations for the site of the Project.

3.2.2 The Owner shall secure and pay for easements for permanent structures or permanent changes in existing facilities.

3.2.3 Information or services under the Owner's control shall be furnished by the Owner with reasonable promptness to avoid delay in the orderly progress of the Work.

3.2.4 The Owner shall issue all instructions to the Contractor through the Architect.

3.2.5 The foregoing are in addition to other duties and responsibilities of the Owner enumerated herein and especially those in respect to Payment and Insurance in Articles 9 and 11 respectively.

DOCUMENT TO CASE CHARTS: A201-1967

[The five-digit numbers in this chart are Citator Case Reference Numbers, which refer to the cases, in the Cases section. The suffixes indicate the state or, for federal cases, the court in which the case was decided.]

Paragraph 3.2 Information and Services Required of the Owner

    I

        69047-MO

    II

        70094-CA
        70017-GA

    III

        71064-MD

Article 4   Contractor

Paragraph 4.1 Definition

Text of Paragraph 4.2—Review of Contract Documents

4.2.1 The Contractor shall carefully study and compare the Agreement, Conditions of the Contract, Drawings, Specifications, Addenda and Modifications and shall at once report to the Architect any error, inconsistency or omission he may discover; but the Contractor shall not be liable to the Owner or the Architect for any damage resulting from any such errors, inconsistencies or omissions. The Contractor shall do no Work without Drawings, Specifications or interpretations.

Paragraph 4.2 Review of Contract Documents

    I

        67051-SDTX
        69032-CA
        69034-WA

    II

        68019-NV

Text of Paragraph 4.3—Supervision and Construction Procedures

4.3.1 The Contractor shall supervise and direct the Work, using his best skill and attention. He shall be solely responsible for all construction means, methods, techniques, sequences and procedures and for coordinating all portions of the Work under the Contract.

DOCUMENT TO CASE CHARTS: A201-1967

[The five-digit numbers in this chart are Citator Case Reference Numbers, which refer to the cases, in the Cases section. The suffixes indicate the state or, for federal cases, the court in which the case was decided.]

Paragraph 4.3   Supervision and Construction Procedures

   I

      69034-WA

   II

      68019-NV

   III

      70008-6CIR   69047-MO
      70081-DE   71027-PA

Text of Paragraph 4.4—Labor and Materials

4.4.1 Unless otherwise specifically noted, the Contractor shall provide and pay for all labor, materials, equipment, tools, construction equipment and machinery, water, heat, utilities, transportation, and other facilities and services necessary for the proper execution and completion of the Work.

4.4.2 The Contractor shall at all times enforce strict discipline and good order among his employees and shall not employ on the Work any unfit person or anyone not skilled in the task assigned to him.

Paragraph 4.4   Labor and Materials

   I

      70027-SDFL
      68008-MT
      71086-NC

   II

      67021-IL
      69002-TX

   III

      71030-EDVA
      70016-MD
      68049-TX

Text of Paragraph 4.5—Warranty

4.5.1 The Contractor warrants to the Owner and the Architect that all materials and equipment furnished under this Contract will be new unless otherwise specified, and that all Work will be of good quality, free from faults and defects and in conformance with the Contract Documents. All Work not so conforming to these standards may be considered defective. If required by the Architect, the Contractor shall furnish satisfactory evidence as to the kind and quality of materials and equipment.

4.5.2 The warranty provided in this Paragraph 4.5 shall be in addition to and

DOCUMENT TO CASE CHARTS: A201-1967   A–148

[The five-digit numbers in this chart are Citator Case Reference Numbers, which refer to the cases, in the Cases section. The suffixes indicate the state or, for federal cases, the court in which the case was decided.]

> not in limitation of any other warranty or remedy required by law or by the Contract Documents.

Paragraph 4.5   Warranty

    I

        70079-CO   67033-MN
        70092-FL   68008-MT

    III

        70048-AZ   70006-MA
        70089-AR   71058-NC
        70081-DE   71010-VA

Paragraph 4.6   Taxes

> **Text of Paragraph 4.7—Permits, Fees and Notices**
>
> **4.7.1** The Contractor shall secure and pay for all permits, governmental fees and licenses necessary for the proper execution and completion of the Work.
>
> **4.7.2** The Contractor shall give all notices and comply with all laws, ordinances, rules, regulations and orders of any public authority bearing on the performance of the Work. If the Contractor observes that any of the Contract Documents are at variance therewith in any respect, he shall promptly notify the Architect in writing, and any necessary changes shall be adjusted by appropriate Modification. If the Contractor performs any Work knowing it to be contrary to such laws, ordinances, rules and regulations, and without such notice to the Architect, he shall assume full responsibility therefor and shall bear all costs attributable thereto.

Paragraph 4.7   Permits, Fees and Notices

    I

        69047-MO

    II

        67045-WI

    III

        70051-CA   70007-WA
        70057-CA   69015-WI
        69031-IL

Paragraph 4.8   Cash Allowances

DOCUMENT TO CASE CHARTS: A201-1967

[The five-digit numbers in this chart are Citator Case Reference Numbers, which refer to the cases, in the Cases section. The suffixes indicate the state or, for federal cases, the court in which the case was decided.]

Text of Paragraph 4.9—Superintendent

4.9.1 The Contractor shall employ a competent superintendent and necessary assistants who shall be in attendance at the Project site during the progress of the Work. The superintendent shall be satisfactory to the Architect, and shall not be changed except with the consent of the Architect, unless the superintendent proves to be unsatisfactory to the Contractor and ceases to be in his employ. The superintendent shall represent the Contractor and all communications given to the superintendent shall be as binding as if given to the Contractor. Important communications will be confirmed in writing. Other communications will be so confirmed on written request in each case.

Paragraph 4.9 Superintendent

    I

        69034-WA

    II

        68019-NV

    III

        71069-OK

Text of Paragraph 4.10—Responsibility For Those Performing the Work

4.10.1 The Contractor shall be responsible to the Owner for the acts and omissions of all his employees and all Subcontractors, their agents and employees, and all other persons performing any of the Work under a contract with the Contractor.

Paragraph 4.10 Responsibility For Those Performing the Work

    I

        69021-DMA
        69054-LA

    III

        70054-TX

Text of Paragraph 4.11—Progress Schedule

4.11.1 The Contractor, immediately after being awarded the Contract, shall prepare and submit for the Architect's approval an estimated progress schedule for the Work. The progress schedule shall be related to the entire Project to the extent required by the Contract Documents. This schedule shall indicate the dates for the starting and completion of the various stages of construction and shall be revised as required by the conditions of the Work, subject to the Architect's approval.

DOCUMENT TO CASE CHARTS: A201-1967

[The five-digit numbers in this chart are Citator Case Reference Numbers, which refer to the cases, in the Cases section. The suffixes indicate the state or, for federal cases, the court in which the case was decided.]

Paragraph 4.11 Progress Schedule

    I

        67051-SDTX

Paragraph 4.12 Drawings and Specifications at the Site

Text of Paragraph 4.13—Shop Drawings and Samples

4.13.1 Shop Drawings are drawings, diagrams, illustrations, schedules, performance charts, brochures and other data which are prepared by the Contractor or any Subcontractor, manufacturer, supplier or distributor, and which illustrate some portion of the Work.

4.13.2 Samples are physical examples furnished by the Contractor to illustrate materials, equipment or workmanship, and to establish standards by which the Work will be judged.

4.13.3 The Contractor shall review, stamp with his approval and submit, with reasonable promptness and in orderly sequence so as to cause no delay in the Work or in the work of any other contractor, all Shop Drawings and Samples required by the Contract Documents subsequently by the Architect as covered by Modifications. Shop Drawings and Samples shall be properly identified as specified, or as the Architect may require. At the time of submission the Contractor shall inform the Architect in writing of any deviation in the Shop Drawings or Samples from the requirements of the Contract Documents.

4.13.4 By approving and submitting Shop Drawings and Samples, the Contractor thereby represents that he has determined and verified all field measurements, field construction criteria, materials, catalog numbers and similar data, or will do so, and that he has checked and coordinated each Shop Drawing and Sample with the requirements of the Work and of the Contract Documents.

4.13.5 The Architect will review and approve Shop Drawings and Samples with reasonable promptness so as to cause no delay, but only for conformance with the design concept of the Project and with the information given in the Contract Documents. The Architect's approval of a Separate item shall not indicate approval of an assembly in which the item functions.

4.13.6 The Contractor shall make any corrections required by the Architect and shall resubmit the required number of corrected copies of Shop Drawings or new Samples until approved. The Contractor shall direct specific attention in writing or on resubmitted Shop Drawings to revisions other than the corrections requested by the Architect on previous submissions.

4.13.7 The Architect's approval of Shop Drawings or Samples shall not relieve the Contractor of responsibility for any deviation from the requirements of the Contract Documents unless the Contractor has informed the Architect in writing of such deviation at the time of submission and the Architect has given written

DOCUMENT TO CASE CHARTS: A201-1967

[The five-digit numbers in this chart are Citator Case Reference Numbers, which refer to the cases, in the Cases section. The suffixes indicate the state or, for federal cases, the court in which the case was decided.]

> approval to the specific deviation, nor shall the Architect's approval relieve the Contractor from responsibility for errors or omissions in the Shop Drawings or Samples.
>
> **4.13.8** No portion of the Work requiring a Shop Drawing or Sample submission shall be commenced until the submission has been approved by the Architect. All such portions of the Work shall be in accordance with approved Shop Drawings and Samples.

Paragraph 4.13 Shop Drawings and Samples

    I

        69021-DMA

    II

        68009-FL

    III

        71029-3CIR
        68053-LA

Paragraph 4.14 Use of Site

Paragraph 4.15 Cutting and Patching of Work

> ## Text of Paragraph 4.16—Cleaning Up
>
> **4.16.1** The Contractor at all times shall keep the premises free from accumulation of waste materials or rubbish caused by his operations. At the completion of the Work he shall remove all his waste materials and rubbish from and about the Project as well as all his tools, construction equipment, machinery and surplus materials, and shall clean all glass surfaces and leave the Work "broom-clean" or its equivalent, except as otherwise specified.
>
> **4.16.2** If the Contractor fails to clean up, the Owner may do so and the cost thereof shall be charged to the Contractor as provided in Paragraph 7.6.

Paragraph 4.16 Cleaning Up

    III

        68055-MS

Paragraph 4.17 Communications

> ## Text of Paragraph 4.18—Indemnification
>
> **4.18.1** The Contractor shall indemnify and hold harmless the Owner and the Architect and their agents and employees from and against all claims, damages,

DOCUMENT TO CASE CHARTS: A201-1967

[The five-digit numbers in this chart are Citator Case Reference Numbers, which refer to the cases, in the Cases section. The suffixes indicate the state or, for federal cases, the court in which the case was decided.]

losses and expenses including attorneys' fees arising out of or resulting from the performance of the Work, provided that any such claim, damage, loss or expense **(a)** is attributable to bodily injury, sickness, disease or death, or to injury to or destruction of tangible property (other than the Work itself) including the loss of use resulting therefrom, and **(b)** is caused in whole or in part by any negligent act or omission of the Contractor, any Subcontractor, anyone directly or indirectly employed by any of them or anyone for whose acts any of them may be liable, regardless of whether or not it is caused in part by a party indemnified hereunder.

4.18.2 In any and all claims against the Owner or the Architect or any of their agents or employees by any employee of the Contractor, any Subcontractor, anyone directly or indirectly employed by any of them or anyone for whose acts any of them may be liable, the indemnification obligation under this Paragraph 4.18 shall not be limited in any way by any limitation on the amount or type of damages, compensation or benefits payable by or for the Contractor or any Subcontractor under workmen's compensation acts, disability benefit acts or other employee benefit acts.

4.18.3 The obligations of the Contractor under this Paragraph 4.18 shall not extend to the liability of the Architect, his agents or employees arising out of (1) the preparation or approval of maps, drawings, opinions, reports, surveys, Change Orders, designs or specifications, or (2) the giving of or the failure to give directions or instructions by the Architect, his agents or employees provided such giving or failure to give is the primary cause of the injury or damage.

Paragraph 4.18   Indemnification

    II

        71046-7CIR   71056-KS
        70075-FL   69035-LA
        69014-IL   67048-MO
        69018-IL   69002-TX
        73108-IL   70060-WA

    III

        71040-6CIR   70038-IL
        70064-10CIR   70093-IL
        71023-EDLA   69036-LA
        70065-AR   69042-LA
        69051-CA   70022-MO
        70031-CA   71007-PA
        68024-IL   70054-TX
        69011-IL   71012-TX
        69031-IL   72093-TX
        69048-IL

A–153   **DOCUMENT TO CASE CHARTS: A201-1967**

[The five-digit numbers in this chart are Citator Case Reference Numbers, which refer to the cases, in the Cases section. The suffixes indicate the state or, for federal cases, the court in which the case was decided.]

Article 5   Subcontractors

Text of Paragraph 5.1—Definition

5.1.1 A Subcontractor is a person or organization who has a direct contract with the Contractor to perform any of the Work at the site. The term Subcontractor is referred to throughout the Contract Documents as if singular in number and masculine in gender and means a Subcontractor or his authorized representative.

5.1.2 A Sub-subcontractor is a person or organization who has a direct or indirect contract with a Subcontractor to perform any of the Work at the site. The term Sub-subcontractor is referred to throughout the Contract Documents as if singular in number and masculine in gender and means a Sub-subcontractor or an authorized representative thereof.

5.1.3 Nothing contained in the Contract Documents shall create any contractual relation between the Owner or the Architect and any Subcontractor or Sub-subcontractor.

Paragraph 5.1   Definition

    I

        70027-SDFL   67021-IL
        69021-DMA   69054-LA

    II

        70070-MI

    III

        70018-CT

Text of Paragraph 5.2—Award of Subcontracts and Other Contracts for Portions of the Work

5.2.1 As soon as practicable after bids are received and prior to the award of the Contract, the successful bidder shall furnish to the Architect in writing for acceptance by the Owner and the Architect a list of the names of the subcontractors or other persons or organizations (including those who are to furnish materials or equipment fabricated to a special design) proposed for such portions of the Work as may be designated in the bidding requirements, or, if none is so designated, the names of the Subcontractors proposed for the principal portions of the Work. Prior to the award of the Contract, the Architect shall notify the successful bidder in writing if either the Owner or the Architect, after due investigation, has reasonable objection to any person or organization on such list. Failure of the Owner or Architect to make an objection to any person or organization on the list prior to the award shall Constitute acceptance of such person or organization.

DOCUMENT TO CASE CHARTS: A201-1967   A–154

[The five-digit numbers in this chart are Citator Case Reference Numbers, which refer to the cases, in the Cases section. The suffixes indicate the state or, for federal cases, the court in which the case was decided.]

5.2.2 If, prior to the award of the Contract, the Owner or Architect has a reasonable and substantial objection to any person or Organization on such list, and refuses in writing to accept such person or organization, the successful bidder may, prior to the award, withdraw his bid without forfeiture of bid security. If the successful bidder submits an acceptable substitute with an increase in his bid price to cover the difference in cost occasioned by such substitution, the Owner may, at his discretion, accept the increased bid price or he may disqualify the bid. If, after the award, the Owner or Architect refuses to accept any person or organization on such list, the Contractor shall submit an acceptable substitute and the Contract Sum shall be increased or decreased by the difference in cost occasioned by such substitution and an appropriate Change Order shall be issued; however, no increase in the Contract Sum shall be allowed for any such substitution unless the Contractor has acted promptly and responsively in submitting a name with respect there to prior to the award.

5.2.3 The Contractor shall not contract with any Subcontractor or any person or organization proposed for portions of the Work designated in the bidding requirements or, if none is so designated, with any Subcontractor proposed for the principal portions of the Work who has not been accepted by the Owner and the Architect. The Contractor will not be required to contract with any subcontractor or person or organization against whom he has a reasonable objection.

5.2.4 If the Owner or the Architect requires a change of any proposed Subcontractor or person or organization previously accepted by them, the Contract Sum shall be increased or decreased by the difference in cost occasioned by such change and an appropriate Change Order shall be issued.

5.2.5 The Contractor shall not make any substitution for any Subcontractor or person or organization who has been accepted by the Owner and the Architect, unless the substitution is acceptable to the Owner and the Architect.

Paragraph 5.2   Award of Subcontracts and Other Contracts for Portions of the Work

    I

        69021-DMA
        67021-IL
        69054-LA

Text of Paragraph 5.3—Subcontractual Relations

5.3.1 All work performed for the Contractor by a Subcontractor shall be pursuant to an appropriate agreement between the Contractor and the Subcontractor (and where appropriate between Subcontractors and Sub-subcontractors) which shall contain provisions that:

.1   preserve and protect the rights of the Owner and the Architect under the Contract with respect to the Work to be performed under the subcontract so that the subcontracting thereof will not prejudice such rights;

DOCUMENT TO CASE CHARTS: A201-1967

[The five-digit numbers in this chart are Citator Case Reference Numbers, which refer to the cases, in the Cases section. The suffixes indicate the state or, for federal cases, the court in which the case was decided.]

.2 require that such Work be performed in accordance with the requirements of the Contract Documents;

.3 require submission to the Contractor of applications for payment under each subcontract to which the Contractor is a party, in reasonable time to enable the Contractor to apply for payment in accordance with Article 9;

.4 require that all claims for additional costs, extensions of time, damages for delays or otherwise with respect to subcontracted portions of the Work shall be submitted to the Contractor (via any Subcontractor or Sub-subcontractor where appropriate) in the manner provided in the Contract Documents for like claims by the Contractor upon the Owner;

.5 waive all rights the Contracting parties may have against one another for damages caused by fire or other perils covered by the property insurance described in Paragraph 11.3, except such rights as they may have to the proceeds of such insurance held by the Owner as trustee under Paragraph 11.3; and

.6 obligate each Subcontractor specifically to consent to the provisions of this Paragraph 5.3.

Paragraph 5.3 Subcontractual Relations

I

69021-DMA 69038-MS
69022-FL 68008-MT
67021-IL 68031-NY

II

69017-NY

III

70028-DC
70052-MA

Text of Paragraph 5.4—Payments to Subcontractors

5.4.1 The Contractor shall pay each Subcontractor, upon receipt of payment from the Owner, an amount equal to the percentage of completion allowed to the Contractor on account of such Subcontractor's Work. The Contractor shall also require each Subcontractor to make similar payments to his subcontractors.

5.4.2 If the Architect fails to issue a Certificate for Payment for any cause which is the fault of the Contractor and not the fault of a particular Subcontractor, the Contractor shall pay that Subcontractor on demand, made at any time after the Certificate for Payment should otherwise have been issued, for his Work to the extent completed, less the retained percentage.

DOCUMENT TO CASE CHARTS: A201-1967   A–156

[The five-digit numbers in this chart are Citator Case Reference Numbers, which refer to the cases, in the Cases section. The suffixes indicate the state or, for federal cases, the court in which the case was decided.]

> **5.4.3** The Contractor shall pay each Subcontractor a just share of any insurance moneys received by the Contractor under Article 11, and he shall require each Subcontractor to make similar payments to his subcontractors.
>
> **5.4.4** The Architect may, on request and at his discretion, furnish to any Subcontractor, if practicable, information regarding percentages of completion certified to the Contractor on account of Work done by such Subcontractors.
>
> **5.4.5** Neither the Owner nor the Architect shall have any obligation to pay or to see to the payment of any moneys to any Subcontractor except as may otherwise be required by law.

Paragraph 5.4   Payments to Subcontractors

    I

        69021-DMA   69054-LA
        69022-FL   69038-MS
        67021-IL

    II

        69017-NY

Article 6   **Separate Contracts**

Paragraph 6.1   Owner's Right to Award Separate Contracts

Paragraph 6.2   Mutual Responsibility of Contractors

> **Text of Paragraph 6.3—Cutting and Patching Under Separate Contracts**
>
> **6.3.1** The Contractor shall do all cutting, fitting or patching of his Work that may be required to fit it to receive or be received by the work of other contractors shown in the Contract Documents. The Contractor shall not endanger any work of any other contractors by cutting, excavating or otherwise altering any work and shall not cut or alter the work of any other contractor except with the written consent of the Architect.
>
> **6.3.2** Any costs caused by defective or ill-timed work shall be borne by the party responsible therefor.

Paragraph 6.3   Cutting and Patching Under Separate Contracts

    II

        71002-CA

> **Text of Paragraph 6.4—Owner's Right to Clean Up**
>
> **6.4.1** If a dispute arises between the separate contractors as to their responsibility for cleaning up as required by Paragraph 4.16, the Owner may clean up and charge

DOCUMENT TO CASE CHARTS: A201-1967

[*The five-digit numbers in this chart are Citator Case Reference Numbers, which refer to the cases, in the Cases section. The suffixes indicate the state or, for federal cases, the court in which the case was decided.*]

> the cost thereof to the several contractors as the Architect shall determine to be just.

Paragraph 6.4 Owner's Right to Clean Up

    III

        68055-MS

Article 7 Miscellaneous Provisions

> ### Text of Paragraph 7.1—Law of the Place
>
> 7.1.1 The Contract shall be governed by the law of the place where the Project is located.

Paragraph 7.1 Law of the Place

    I

        55001-VA

> ### Text of Paragraph 7.2—Successors and Assigns
>
> 7.2.1 The Owner and the Contractor each binds himself, his partners, successors, assigns and legal representatives to the other party hereto and to the partners, successors, assigns and legal. representatives of such other party in respect to all covenants, agreements and obligations contained in the Contract Documents. Neither party to the Contract shall assign the Contract or sublet it as a whole without the written consent of the other, nor shall the Contractor assign any moneys due or to become due to him hereunder, without the previous written consent of the Owner.

Paragraph 7.2 Successors and Assigns

    I

        68017-DE
        69038-MS

    III

        69048-IL

Paragraph 7.3 Written Notice

> ### Text of Paragraph 7.4—Claims for Damages
>
> 7.4.1 Should either party to the Contract suffer injury or damage to person or property because of any act or omission of the other party or of any of his employees, agents or others for whose acts he is legally liable, claim shall be made in writing

DOCUMENT TO CASE CHARTS: A201-1967   A–158

[The five-digit numbers in this chart are Citator Case Reference Numbers, which refer to the cases, in the Cases section. The suffixes indicate the state or, for federal cases, the court in which the case was decided.]

> to such other party within a reasonable time after the first observance of such injury or damage.

Paragraph 7.4   Claims for Damages

    I

        68018-AR   67033-MN
        69032-CA   71014-NY

    III

        70087-CT
        70028-DC

> **Text of Paragraph 7.5—Performance Bond and Labor and Material Payment Bond**
>
> 7.5.1 The Owner shall have the right, prior to signing the Contract, to require the Contractor to furnish bonds covering the faithful performance of the Contract and the payment of all obligations arising thereunder in such form and amount as the Owner may prescribe and with such sureties as may be agreeable to the parties. If such bonds are stipulated in the bidding requirements, the premiums shall be paid by the Contractor; if required subsequent to the submission of quotations or bids, the cost shall be reimbursed by the Owner. The Contractor shall deliver the required bonds to the Owner not later than the date of execution of the Contract, or if the Work is commenced prior thereto in response to a notice to proceed, the Contractor shall, prior to commencement of the Work, submit evidence satisfactory to the Owner that such bonds will be issued.

Paragraph 7.5   Performance Bond and Labor and Material Payment Bond

    I

        70011-2CIR   68008-MT
        68034-AL   71086-NC

    II

        70070-MI

Paragraph 7.6   Owner's Right to Carry Out the Work

Paragraph 7.7   Royalties and Patents

> **Text of Paragraph 7.8—Tests**
>
> 7.8.1 If the Contract Documents, laws, ordinances, rules, regulations or orders of any public authority having jurisdiction require any Work to be inspected, tested or approved, the Contractor shall give the Architect timely notice of its readiness and of the date arranged so the Architect may observe such inspection, testing or

approval. The Contractor shall bear all costs of such inspections, tests and approvals unless otherwise provided.

7.8.2 If after the commencement of the Work the Architect determines that any Work requires special inspection, testing or approval which Subparagraph 7.8.1 does not include, he will, upon written authorization from the Owner, instruct the Contractor to order such special inspection, testing or approval, and the Contractor shall give notice as in Subparagraph 7.8.1. If such special inspection or testing reveals a failure of the Work to comply (1) with the requirements of the Contract Documents or (2), with respect to the performance of the Work, with laws, ordinances, rules, regulations or orders of any public authority having jurisdiction, the Contractor shall bear all costs thereof, including the Architect's additional services made necessary by such failure; otherwise the Owner shall bear such costs, and an appropriate Change Order shall be issued.

7.8.3 Required certificates of inspection, testing or approval shall be secured by the Contractor and promptly delivered by him to the Architect.

7.8.4 If the Architect wishes to observe the inspections, tests or approvals required by this Paragraph 7.8, he will do so promptly and, where practicable, at the source of supply.

7.8.5 Neither the observations of the Architect in his administration of the Contract, nor inspections, tests or approvals by persons other than the Contractor shall relieve the Contractor from his obligations to perform the Work in accordance with the Contract Documents.

Paragraph 7.8 Tests

    I

        70020-MD

    II

        68019-NV

Text of Paragraph 7.9—Interest

7.9.1 Any moneys not paid when due to either party under this Contract shall bear interest at the legal rate in force at the place of the Project.

Paragraph 7.9 Interest

    I

        69021-DMA

DOCUMENT TO CASE CHARTS: A201-1967

A–160

[The five-digit numbers in this chart are Citator Case Reference Numbers, which refer to the cases, in the Cases section. The suffixes indicate the state or, for federal cases, the court in which the case was decided.]

III

    69005-CT
    69041-CT
    69037-NY

Text of Paragraph 7.10—Arbitration

7.10.1 All claims, disputes and other matters in question arising out of, or relating to, this Contract or the breach thereof, except as set forth in Subparagraph 2.2.9 with respect to the Architect's decisions on matters relating to artistic effect, and except for claims which have been waived by the making or acceptance of final payment as provided by Subparagraphs 9.7.5 and 9.7.6, shall be decided by arbitration in accordance with the Construction Industry Arbitration Rules of the American Arbitration Association then obtaining unless the parties mutually agree otherwise. This agreement so to arbitrate shall be specifically enforceable under the prevailing arbitration law. The award rendered by the arbitrators shall be final, and judgment may be entered upon it in accordance with applicable law in any court having jurisdiction thereof.

7.10.2 Notice of the demand for arbitration shall be filed in writing with the other party to the Contract and with the American Arbitration Association, and a copy shall be filed with the Architect. The demand for arbitration shall be made within the time limits specified in Sub-paragraphs 2.2.10 and 2.2.11 where applicable, and in all other cases within a reasonable time after the claim, dispute or other matter in question has arisen, and in no event shall it be made after institution of legal or equitable proceedings based on such claim, dispute or other matter in question would be barred by the applicable statute of limitations.

7.10.3 The Contractor shall carry on the Work and maintain the progress schedule during any arbitration proceedings, unless otherwise agreed by him and the Owner in writing.

Paragraph 7.10   Arbitration

I

67039-3CIR	71026-IL
71016-5CIR	68026-MA
70084-7CIR	69029-MI
70074-SDNY	68031-NY
69046-AZ	71014-NY
71006-AZ	71055-NY
68018-AR	71066-NY
69032-CA	70072-OH
71079-CO	68028-TN
67073-GA	

DOCUMENT TO CASE CHARTS: A201-1967

[The five-digit numbers in this chart are Citator Case Reference Numbers, which refer to the cases, in the Cases section. The suffixes indicate the state or, for federal cases, the court in which the case was decided.]

II

69004-CA	72018-IL
71057-CA	83029-NJ
68043-CO	70004-NY
70062-DC	70037-NY
70012-FL	72008-NY
70091-IL	70080-WA

III

71045-7CIR	70040-NH
70013-AZ	69039-NY
71054-CA	71018-NY
59005-CT	71076-NY
68039-DE	71080-NY
71044-HI	70035-OH
69025-IL	70045-WA
72024-IL	

Article 8 Time

Text of Paragraph 8.1—Definitions

8.1.1 The Contract Time is the period of time allotted in the Contract Documents for completion of the Work.

8.1.2 The date of commencement of the Work is the date established in a notice to proceed. If there is no notice to proceed, it shall be the date of the Agreement or such other date as may be established therein.

8.1.3 The Date of Substantial Completion of the Work or designated portion thereof is the Date certified by the Architect when construction is sufficiently complete, in accordance with the Contract Documents, so the Owner may occupy the Work or designated portion thereof for the use for which it is intended.

Paragraph 8.1 Definitions

I

70047-WA

Text of Paragraph 8.2—Progress and Completion

8.2.1 All time limits stated in the Contract Documents are of the essence of the Contract.

8.2.2 The Contractor shall begin the Work on the date of commencement as defined in Subparagraph 8.1.2. He shall carry the Work forward expeditiously with adequate forces and shall complete it within the Contract Time.

DOCUMENT TO CASE CHARTS: A201-1967   A–162

[*The five-digit numbers in this chart are Citator Case Reference Numbers, which refer to the cases, in the Cases section. The suffixes indicate the state or, for federal cases, the court in which the case was decided.*]

Paragraph 8.2   Progress and Completion

    III

        71025-IL

Text of Paragraph 8.3—Delays and Extensions of Time

8.3.1 If the Contractor is delayed at any time in the progress of the Work by any act or neglect of the Owner or the Architect, or by any employee of either, or by any separate contractor employed by the Owner, or by changes ordered in the Work, or by labor disputes, fire, unusual delay in transportation, unavoidable casualties or any causes beyond the Contractor's control, or by delay authorized by the Owner pending arbitration, or by any cause which the Architect determines may justify the delay, then the Contract Time shall be extended by Change Order for such reasonable time as the Architect may determine.

8.3.2 All claims for extension of time shall be made in writing to the Architect no more than fifteen days after the occurrence of the delay; otherwise they shall be waived. In the case of a continuing cause of delay only one claim is necessary.

8.3.3 If no schedule or agreement is made stating the dates upon which written interpretations as set forth in Subparagraph 1.2.5 shall be furnished, then no claim for delay shall be allowed on account of failure to furnish such interpretations until fifteen days after demand is made for them, and not then unless such claim is reasonable.

8.3.4 This Paragraph 8.3 does not exclude the recovery of damages for delay by either party under other provisions of the Contract Documents.

Paragraph 8.3   Delays and Extensions of Time

    I

        67051-SDTX   68046-MO
        69032-CA   69019-OK
        70029-CA   68050-PA

    II

        71071-NY

    III

        70001-CA   69025-IL
        71075-CO   69053-NY

Article 9   Payments and Completion

A–163 **DOCUMENT TO CASE CHARTS: A201-1967**

[The five-digit numbers in this chart are Citator Case Reference Numbers, which refer to the cases, in the Cases section. The suffixes indicate the state or, for federal cases, the court in which the case was decided.]

Paragraph 9.1 Contract Sum

Text of Paragraph 9.2—Schedule of Values

9.2.1 Before the first Application for Payment, the Contractor shall submit to the Architect a schedule of values of the various portions of the Work, including quantities if required by the Architect, aggregating the total Contract Sum, divided so as to facilitate payments to Sub-contractors in accordance with Paragraph 5.4, prepared in such form as specified or as the Architect and the Contractor may agree upon, and supported by such data to substantiate its correctness as the Architect may require. Each item in the schedule of values shall include its proper share of overhead and profit. This schedule, when approved by the Architect, shall be used only as a basis for the Contractor's Applications for Payment.

Paragraph 9.2 Schedule of Values

    I

        69021-DMA

    III

        68038-IL

Text of Paragraph 9.3—Progress Payments

9.3.1 At least ten days before each progress payment falls due, the Contractor shall submit to the Architect an itemized Application for Payment, supported by such data substantiating the Contractor's right to payment as the Owner or the Architect may require.

9.3.2 If payments are to be made on account of materials or equipment not incorporated in the Work but delivered and suitably stored at the site, or at some other location agreed upon in writing, such payments shall be conditioned upon submission by the Contractor of bills of sale or such other procedures satisfactory to the Owner to establish the Owner's title to such materials or equipment or otherwise protect the Owner's interest including applicable insurance and transportation to the site.

9.3.3 The Contractor warrants and guarantees that title to all Work, materials and equipment covered by an Application for Payment, whether incorporated in the Project or not, will pass to the Owner upon the receipt of such payment by the Contractor, free and clear of all liens, claims, security interests or encumbrances, hereinafter referred to in this Article 9 as "liens"; and that no Work, materials or equipment covered by an Application for Payment will have been acquired by the Contractor, or by any other person performing the Work at the site or furnishing

DOCUMENT TO CASE CHARTS: A201-1967   A–164

[The five-digit numbers in this chart are Citator Case Reference Numbers, which refer to the cases, in the Cases section. The suffixes indicate the state or, for federal cases, the court in which the case was decided.]

> materials and equipment for the Project, subject to an agreement under which an interest therein or an encumbrance thereon is retained by the seller or otherwise imposed by the Contractor or such other person.

Paragraph 9.3   Progress Payments

    I

        70027-SDFL
        69021-DMA

    III

        71059-2CIR   71019-IL
        68038-IL   67023-MO

> **Text of Paragraph 9.4—Certificates for Payment**
>
> **9.4.1** If the Contractor has made Application for Payment as above, the Architect will, with reasonable promptness but not more than seven days after the receipt of the Application, issue a Certificate for Payment to the Owner, with a copy to the Contractor, for such amount as he determines to be properly due, or state in writing his reasons for withholding a Certificate as provided in Subparagraph 9.5.1.
>
> **9.4.2** The issuance of a Certificate for Payment will constitute a representation by the Architect to the Owner, based on his observations at the site as provided in Subparagraph 2.2.4 and the data comprising the Application for Payment, that the Work has progressed to the point indicated; that, to the best of his knowledge, information and belief, the quality of the Work is in accordance with the Contract Documents (subject to an evaluation of the Work as a functioning whole upon Substantial Completion, to the results of any subsequent tests required by the Contract Documents, to minor deviations from the Contract Documents correctable prior to completion, and to any specific qualifications stated in his Certificate); and that the Contractor is entitled to payment in the amount certified. In addition, the Architect's final Certificate for Payment will constitute a further representation that the conditions precedent to the Contractor's being entitled to final payment as set forth in Subparagraph 9.7.2 have been fulfilled. However, by issuing a Certificate for Payment, the Architect shall not thereby be deemed to represent that he has made exhaustive or continuous on-site inspections to check the quality or quantity of the Work or that he has reviewed the construction means, methods, techniques, sequences or procedures, or that he has made any examination to ascertain how or for what purpose the Contractor has used the moneys previously paid on account of the Contract Sum.
>
> **9.4.3** After the Architect has issued a Certificate for Payment, the Owner shall make payment in the manner provided in the Agreement.
>
> **9.4.4** No Certificate for a progress payment, nor any progress payment, nor any partial or entire use or occupancy of the Project by the Owner, shall constitute an acceptance of any Work not in accordance with the Contract Documents.

DOCUMENT TO CASE CHARTS: A201-1967

[*The five-digit numbers in this chart are Citator Case Reference Numbers, which refer to the cases, in the Cases section. The suffixes indicate the state or, for federal cases, the court in which the case was decided.*]

Paragraph 9.4 Certificates for Payment

    I

        69021-DMA   69019-OK
        67033-MN   68010-TX

    II

        67018-5CIR
        70012-FL

Text of Paragraph 9.5—Payments Withheld

9.5.1 The Architect may decline to approve an Application for Payment and may withhold his Certificate in whole or in part if in his opinion he is unable to make representations to the Owner as provided in Subparagraph 9.4.2. The Architect may also decline to approve any Applications for Payment or, because of subsequently discovered evidence or subsequent inspections, he may nullify the whole or any part of any Certificate for Payment previously issued to such extent as may be necessary in his opinion to protect the Owner from loss because of:

.1   defective work not remedied,

.2   claims filed or reasonable evidence indicating probable filing of claims,

.3   failure of the Contractor to make payments properly to Subcontractors or for labor, materials or equipment,

.4   reasonable doubt that the Work can be completed for the unpaid balance of the Contract Sum,

.5   damage to another contractor,

.6   reasonable indication that the Work will not be completed within the Contract Time, or

.7   unsatisfactory prosecution of the Work by the Contractor.

    9.5.2 When the above grounds in, Subparagraph 9.5.1 are removed, payment shall be made for amounts withheld because of them.

Paragraph 9.5 Payments Withheld

    I

        69021-DMA
        69032-CA
        69019-OK

Paragraph 9.6 Failure of Payment

DOCUMENT TO CASE CHARTS: A201-1967 A–166

[The five-digit numbers in this chart are Citator Case Reference Numbers, which refer to the cases, in the Cases section. The suffixes indicate the state or, for federal cases, the court in which the case was decided.]

Text of Paragraph 9.7—Substantial Completion and Final Payment

9.7.1 When the Contractor determines that the Work or a designated portion thereof acceptable to the Owner is substantially complete, the Contractor shall prepare for submission to the Architect a list of items to be completed or corrected. The failure to include any items on such list does not alter the responsibility of the Contractor to complete all Work in accordance with the Contract Documents. When the Architect on the basis of an inspection determines that the Work is substantially complete, he will then prepare a Certificate of Substantial Completion which shall establish the Date of Substantial Completion, shall state the responsibilities of the Owner and the Contractor for maintenance, heat, utilities, and insurance, and shall fix the time within which the Contractor shall complete the items listed therein, said time to be within the Contract Time unless extended pursuant to Paragraph 8.3. The Certificate of Substantial Completion shall be submitted to the Owner and the Contractor for their written acceptance of the responsibilities assigned to them in such Certificate.

9.7.2 Upon receipt of written notice that the Work is ready for final inspection and acceptance and upon receipt of a final Application for Payment, the Architect will promptly make such inspection and, when he finds the Work acceptable under the Contract Documents and the Contract fully performed, he will promptly issue a final Certificate for Payment stating that to the best of his knowledge, information and belief, and on the basis of his observations and inspections, the Work has been completed in accordance with the terms and conditions of the Contract Documents and that the entire balance found to be due the Contractor, and noted in said final Certificate. is due and payable.

9.7.3 Neither the final payment nor the remaining retained percentage shall become due until the Contractor submits to the Architect (1) an Affidavit that all payrolls, bills for materials and equipment, and other indebtedness connected with the Work for which the Owner or his property might in any way be responsible, have been paid or otherwise satisfied, (2) consent of surety, if any, to final payment and (3), if required by the Owner, other data establishing payment or satisfaction of all such obligations, such as receipts, releases and waivers of liens arising out of the Contract, to the extent and in such form as may be designated by the Owner. If any Subcontractor refuses to furnish a release or waiver required by the Owner, the Contractor may furnish a bond satisfactory to the Owner to indemnify him against any such lien. If any such lien remains unsatisfied after all payments are made, the Contractor shall refund to the Owner all moneys that the latter may be compelled to pay in discharging such lien, including all costs and reasonable attorneys' fees.

9.7.4 If after Substantial Completion of the Work final completion thereof is materially delayed through no fault of the Contractor, and the Architect so confirms, the Owner shall, upon certification by the Architect, and without terminating the Contract, make payment of the balance due for that portion of the Work fully completed and accepted. If the remaining balance for Work not fully completed or corrected is less than the retainage stipulated in the Agreement, and if bonds have been furnished as required in Subparagraph 7.5.1, the written consent of the surety to the payment of the balance due for that portion of the Work fully completed and accepted shall be submitted by the Contractor to the Architect prior to certification of such payment. Such payment shall be made under the terms and conditions governing final payment, except that it shall not constitute a waiver of claims.

9.7.5 The making of final payment shall constitute a waiver of all claims by the Owner except those arising from:

.1   unsettled liens,

.2   faulty or defective Work appearing after Substantial Completion,

.3   failure of the Work to comply with the requirements of the Contract Documents. or

.4   terms of any special guarantees required by the Contract Documents.

9.7.6 The acceptance of final payment shall constitute a waiver of all claims by the Contractor except those previously made in writing and still unsettled.

Paragraph 9.7   Substantial Completion and Final Payment

    I

        69021-DMA   71028-MI
        69019-OK   68010-TX
        70061-KS

    II

        67018-5CIR
        71068-AK

    III

        71037-7CIR   68029-MN
        70053-CO   71084-KY
        70016-MD   70032-TX

Article 10 Protection of Persons and Property

Text of Paragraph 10.1—Safety Precautions and Programs

10.1.1 The Contractor shall be responsible for initiating, maintaining and supervising all safety precautions and programs in connection with the Work.

DOCUMENT TO CASE CHARTS: A201-1967   A–168

[The five-digit numbers in this chart are Citator Case Reference Numbers, which refer to the cases, in the Cases section. The suffixes indicate the state or, for federal cases, the court in which the case was decided.]

Paragraph 10.1   Safety Precautions and Programs

   I

       67021-IL   68012-NC
       69054-LA   71063-NC

   III

       68047-IL

Text of Paragraph 10.2—Safety of Persons and Property

10.2.1 The Contractor shall take all reasonable precautions for the safety of, and shall provide all reasonable protection to prevent damage, injury or loss to:

.1   all employees on the Work and all other persons who may be affected thereby;

.2   all the Work and all materials and equipment to be incorporated therein, whether in storage on or off the site, under the care, custody or control of the Contractor or any of his Subcontractors or Sub-subcontractors; and

.3   other property at the site or adjacent thereto, including trees, shrubs, lawns, walks, pavements, roadways, structures and utilities not designated for removal, relocation or replacement in the course of construction.

10.2.2 The Contractor shall comply with all applicable laws, ordinances, rules, regulations and orders of any public authority having jurisdiction for the safety of persons or property or to protect them from damage, injury or loss. He shall erect and maintain, as required by existing conditions and progress of the Work, all reasonable safeguards for safety and protection, including posting danger signs and other warnings against hazards, promulgating safety regulations and notifying owners and users of adjacent utilities.

10.2.3 When the use or storage of explosives or other hazardous materials or equipment is necessary for the execution of the Work, the Contractor shall exercise the utmost care and shall carry on such activities under the supervision of properly qualified personnel.

10.2.4 All damage or loss to any property referred to in Clauses 10.2.1.2 and 10.2.1.3 caused in whole or in part by the Contractor, any Subcontractor, any Sub-subcontractor, or anyone directly or indirectly employed by any of them, or by anyone for whose acts any of them may be liable, shall be remedied by the Contractor, except damage or loss attributable to faulty Drawings or Specifications or to the acts or omissions of the Owner or Architect or anyone employed by either of them or for whose acts either of them may be liable, and not attributable to the fault or negligence of the Contractor.

10.2.5 The Contractor shall designate a responsible member of his organization at the site whose duty shall be the prevention of accidents. This person shall be the Contractor's superintendent unless otherwise designated in writing by the Contractor to the Owner and the Architect.

A–169   DOCUMENT TO CASE CHARTS: A201-1967

[The five-digit numbers in this chart are Citator Case Reference Numbers, which refer to the cases, in the Cases section. The suffixes indicate the state or, for federal cases, the court in which the case was decided.]

> **10.2.6** The Contractor shall not load or permit any part of the Work to be loaded so as to endanger its safety.

Paragraph 10.2 Safety of Persons and Property

    I

        68018-AR   69054-LA
        67021-IL   68012-NC
        69044-IL

    III

        71029-3CIR   69047-MO
        67061-IL   71063-NC
        68047-IL   69049-TX
        69031-IL   70049-VT
        71038-IL

> **Text of Paragraph 10.3—Emergencies**
>
> **10.3.1** In any emergency affecting the safety of persons or property, the Contractor shall act, at his discretion, to prevent threatened damage, injury or loss. Any additional compensation or extension of time claimed by the Contractor on account of emergency work shall be determined as provided in Article 12 for Changes in the Work.

Paragraph 10.3 Emergencies

    I

        67021-IL
        69054-LA
        68012-NC

    III

        71029-3CIR
        68047-IL

Article 11 Insurance

> **Text of Paragraph 11.1—Contractor's Liability Insurance**
>
> **11.1.1** The Contractor shall purchase and maintain such insurance as will protect him from claims set forth below which may arise out of or result from the Contractor's operations under the Contract, whether such operations be by himself or by any Subcontractor or by anyone directly or indirectly employed by any of them, or by anyone for whose acts any of them may be liable:
>
> **.1**   claims under workmen's compensation, disability benefit and other similar employee benefit acts;

DOCUMENT TO CASE CHARTS: A201-1967 A–170

[The five-digit numbers in this chart are Citator Case Reference Numbers, which refer to the cases, in the Cases section. The suffixes indicate the state or, for federal cases, the court in which the case was decided.]

.2 claims for damages because of bodily injury, occupational sickness or disease, or death of his employees, and claims insured by usual personal injury liability coverage;

.3 claims for damages because of bodily injury, sickness or disease, or death of any person other than his employees, and claims insured by usual personal injury liability coverage; and

.4 claims for damages because of injury to or destruction of tangible property, including loss of use resulting therefrom.

11.1.2 The insurance required by Subparagraph 11.1.1 shall be written for not less than any limits of liability specified in the Contract Documents, or required by law, whichever is greater, and shall include contractual liability insurance as applicable to the Contractor's obligations under Paragraph 4.18.

11.1.3 Certificates of Insurance acceptable to the Owner shall be filed with the Owner prior to commencement of the Work. These Certificates shall contain a provision that coverages afforded under the policies will not be cancelled until at least fifteen days' prior written notice has been given to the Owner.

Paragraph 11.1   Contractor's Liability Insurance

    III

        69013-NY

Paragraph 11.2   Owner's Liability Insurance

Text of Paragraph 11.3—Property Insurance

11.3.1 Unless otherwise provided, the Owner shall purchase and maintain property insurance upon the entire Work at the site to the full insurable value thereof. This insurance shall include the interests of the Owner, the Contractor, Subcontractors and Sub-subcontractors in the Work and shall insure against the perils of Fire, Extended Coverage, Vandalism and Malicious Mischief.

11.3.2 The Owner shall purchase and maintain such steam boiler and machinery insurance as may be required by the Contract Documents or by law. This insurance shall include the interests of the Owner, the Contractor, Subcontractors and Sub-subcontractors in the Work.

11.3.3 Any insured loss is to be adjusted with the Owner and made payable to the Owner as trustee for the insureds, as their interests may appear, subject to the requirements of any applicable mortgagee clause and of Subparagraph 11.3.8.

11.3.4 The Owner shall file a copy of all policies with the Contractor before an exposure to loss may occur. If the Owner does not intend to purchase such insurance, he shall inform the Contractor in writing prior to commencement of the Work. The Contractor may then effect insurance which will protect the interests of himself, his Subcontractors and the Sub-subcontractors in the Work, and by appropriate

A-171 **DOCUMENT TO CASE CHARTS: A201-1967**

[The five-digit numbers in this chart are Citator Case Reference Numbers, which refer to the cases, in the Cases section. The suffixes indicate the state or, for federal cases, the court in which the case was decided.]

Change Order the cost thereof shall be charged to the Owner. If the Contractor is damaged by failure of the Owner to purchase or maintain such insurance and so to notify the Contractor, then the Owner shall bear all reasonable costs properly attributable thereto.

11.3.5 If the Contractor requests in writing that other special insurance be included in the property insurance policy, the Owner shall, if possible, include such insurance, and the cost thereof shall be charged to the Contractor by appropriate Change Order.

11.3.6 The Owner and Contractor waive all rights against each other for damages caused by fire or other perils to the extent covered by insurance provided under this Paragraph 11.3, except such rights as they may have to the proceeds of such insurance held by the Owner as trustee. The Contractor shall require similar waivers by Subcontractors and Sub-subcontractors in accordance with Clause 5.3.1.5.

11.3.7 If required in writing by any party in interest, the Owner as trustee shall, upon the occurrence of an insured loss, give bond for the proper performance of his duties. He shall deposit in a separate account any money so received, and he shall distribute it in accordance with such agreement as the parties in interest may reach, or in accordance with an award by arbitration in which case the procedure shall be as provided in Paragraph 7.10. If after such loss no other special agreement is made, replacement of damaged work shall be covered by an appropriate Change Order.

11.3.8 The Owner as trustee shall have power to adjust and settle any loss with the insurers unless one of the parties in interest shall object in writing within five days after the occurrence of loss to the Owner's exercise of this power, and if such objection be made, arbitrators shall be chosen as provided in Paragraph 7.10. The Owner as trustee shall, in that case, make settlement with the insurers in accordance with the directions of such arbitrators. If distribution of the insurance proceeds by arbitration is required, the arbitrators will direct such distribution.

Paragraph 11.3 Property Insurance

    II

        69010-IA

    III

        70066-MD

Paragraph 11.4 Loss of Use Insurance

DOCUMENT TO CASE CHARTS: A201-1967

[The five-digit numbers in this chart are Citator Case Reference Numbers, which refer to the cases, in the Cases section. The suffixes indicate the state or, for federal cases, the court in which the case was decided.]

Article 12 Changes in the Work

Text of Paragraph 12.1—Change Orders

12.1.1 The Owner, without invalidating the Contract, may order Changes in the Work within the general scope of the Contract consisting of additions, deletions or other revisions, the Contract Sum and the Contract Time being adjusted accordingly. All such Changes in the Work shall be authorized by Change Order, and shall be executed under the applicable conditions of the Contract Documents.

12.1.2 A Change Order is a written order to the Contractor signed by the Owner and the Architect, issued after the execution of the Contract, authorizing a Change in the Work or an adjustment in the Contract Sum or the Contract Time. Alternatively, the Change Order may be signed by the Architect alone, provided he has written authority from the Owner for such procedure and that a copy of such written authority is furnished to the Contractor upon request. The Contract Sum and the Contract Time may be changed only by Change Order.

12.1.3 The cost or credit to the Owner resulting from a Change in the Work shall be determined in one or more of the following ways:

.1   by mutual acceptance of a lump sum properly itemized;

.2   by unit prices stated in the Contract Documents or subsequently agreed upon; or

.3   by cost and a mutually acceptable fixed or percentage fee.

12.1.4 If none of the methods set forth in Subparagraph 12.1.3 is agreed upon, the Contractor, provided he receives a Change Order, shall promptly proceed with the Work involved. The cost of such Work shall then be determined by the Architect on the basis of the Contractor's reasonable expenditures and savings, including, in the case of an increase in the Contract Sum, a reasonable allowance for overhead and profit. In such case, and also under Clause 12.1.3.3 above, the Contractor shall keep and present, in such form as the Architect may prescribe, an itemized accounting together with appropriate supporting data. Pending final determination of cost to the Owner, payments on account shall be made on the Architect's Certificate for Payment. The amount of credit to be allowed by the Contractor to the Owner for any deletion or change which results in a net decrease in cost will be the amount of the actual net decrease as confirmed by the Architect. When both additions and credits are involved in any one change, the allowance for overhead and profit shall be figured on the basis of net increase, if any.

12.1.5 If unit prices are stated in the Contract Documents or subsequently agreed upon, and if the quantities originally contemplated are so changed in a proposed Change Order that application of the agreed unit prices to the quantities of Work proposed will create a hardship on the Owner or the Contractor, the applicable unit prices shall be equitably adjusted to prevent such hardship.

DOCUMENT TO CASE CHARTS: A201-1967

[The five-digit numbers in this chart are Citator Case Reference Numbers, which refer to the cases, in the Cases section. The suffixes indicate the state or, for federal cases, the court in which the case was decided.]

12.1.6 Should concealed conditions encountered in the performance of the Work below the surface of the ground be at variance with the conditions indicated by the Contract Documents or should unknown physical conditions below the surface of the ground of an unusual nature, differing materially from those ordinarily encountered and generally recognized as inherent in work of the character provided for in this Contract, be encountered, the Contract Sum shall be equitably adjusted by Change Order upon claim by either party made within a reasonable time after the first observance of the conditions.

12.1.7 If the Contractor claims that additional cost or time is involved because of (1) any written interpretation issued pursuant to Subparagraph 1.2.5, (2) any order by the Architect to stop the Work pursuant to Subparagraph 2.2.12 where the Contractor was not at fault, or (3) any written order for a minor change in the Work issued pursuant to Paragraph 12.3, the Contractor shall make such claim as provided in Paragraph 12.2.

Paragraph 12.1   Change Orders

    I

71051-NDGA	71066-NY
68018-AR	69019-OK
71017-IL	69034-WA
71021-MS	67072-WI
67029-MO	

    II

70094-CA	69037-NY
71002-CA	82027-PA
71031-CA	71083-WA
68043-CO	67045-WI

    III

70041-DCCIR	68023-MN
67063-IL	68055-MS
72054-IL	68037-NY
70039-HI	68006-PA
68054-LA	70019-TX
70016-MD	

Text of Paragraph 12.2—Claims for Additional Cost or Time

12.2.1 If the Contractor wishes to make a claim for an increase in the Contract Sum or an extension in the Contract Time, he shall give the Architect written notice thereof within a reasonable time after the occurrence of the event giving rise to such claim. This notice shall be given by the Contractor before proceeding to execute the Work, except in an emergency endangering life or property in which case the Contractor shall proceed in accordance with Subparagraph 10.3.1. No such claim shall be valid unless so made. If the Owner and the Contractor cannot agree on the amount of the adjustment in the Contract Sum or the Contract Time, it shall

DOCUMENT TO CASE CHARTS: A201-1967   A–174

[The five-digit numbers in this chart are Citator Case Reference Numbers, which refer to the cases, in the Cases section. The suffixes indicate the state or, for federal cases, the court in which the case was decided.]

> be determined by the Architect. Any change in the Contract Sum or Contract Time resulting from such claim shall be authorized by Change Order.

Paragraph 12.2   Claims for Additional Cost or Time

    I

        71051-NDGA   71066-NY
        68018-AR   69019-OK
        70029-CA   70014-TX
        71021-MS   69034-WA

    II

        68040-CO   71003-NY
        70003-MD   82027-PA
        69037-NY   67045-WI

    III

        70041-DCCIR   72054-IL
        69008-NDMS   68054-LA
        67063-IL   68055-MS
        71017-IL   68037-NY

> **Text of Paragraph 12.3—Minor Changes in the Work**
>
> **12.3.1** The Architect shall have authority to order minor changes in the Work not involving an adjustment in the Contract Sum or an extension of the Contract Time and not inconsistent with the intent of the Contract Documents. Such changes may be effected by Field Order or by other written order. Such changes shall be binding on the Owner and the Contractor.

Paragraph 12.3   Minor Changes in the Work

    I

        68018-AR   67029-MO
        71021-MS   67072-WI

    II

        69037-NY

    III

        70041-DCCIR   68054-LA
        67063-IL   68023-MN

Paragraph 12.4   Field Orders

A–175　　DOCUMENT TO CASE CHARTS: A201-1967

[*The five-digit numbers in this chart are Citator Case Reference Numbers, which refer to the cases, in the Cases section. The suffixes indicate the state or, for federal cases, the court in which the case was decided.*]

Article 13　Uncovering and Correction of Work

Text of Paragraph 13.1—Uncovering of Work

13.1.1 If any Work should be covered contrary to the request of the Architect, it must, if required by the Architect, be uncovered for his observation and replaced, at the Contractor's expense.

13.1.2 If any other Work has been covered which the Architect has not specifically requested to observe prior to being covered, the Architect may request to see such Work and it shall be uncovered by the Contractor. If such Work be found in accordance with the Contract Documents, the cost of uncovering and replacement shall, by appropriate Change Order, be charged to the Owner. If such Work be found not in accordance with the Contract Documents, the Contractor shall pay such costs unless it be found that this condition was caused by a separate contractor employed as provided in Article 6, and in that event the Owner shall be responsible for the payment of such costs.

Paragraph 13.1　Uncovering of Work

　　I
　　　　70020-MD

Text of Paragraph 13.2—Correction of Work

13.2.1 The Contractor shall promptly correct all Work rejected by the Architect as defective or as failing to conform to the Contract Documents whether observed before or after Substantial Completion and whether or not fabricated, installed or completed. The Contractor shall bear all costs of correcting such rejected Work, including the cost of the Architect's additional services thereby made necessary.

13.2.2 If, within one year after the Date of Substantial Completion or within such longer period of time as may be prescribed by law or by the terms of any applicable special guarantee required by the Contract Documents, any of the Work is found to be defective or not in accordance with the Contract Documents, the Contractor shall correct it promptly after receipt of a written notice from the Owner to do so unless the Owner has previously given the Contractor a written acceptance of such condition. The Owner shall give such notice promptly after discovery of the condition.

13.2.3 All such defective or non-conforming Work under Subparagraphs 13.2.1 and 13.2.2 shall be removed from the site where necessary, and the Work shall be corrected to comply with the Contract Documents without cost to the Owner.

13.2.4 The Contractor shall bear the cost of making good all work of separate contractors destroyed or damaged by such removal or correction.

13.2.5 If the Contractor does not remove such defective or non-conforming Work within a reasonable time fixed by written notice from the Architect, the Owner may

DOCUMENT TO CASE CHARTS: A201-1967

A–176

[The five-digit numbers in this chart are Citator Case Reference Numbers, which refer to the cases, in the Cases section. The suffixes indicate the state or, for federal cases, the court in which the case was decided.]

> remove it and may store the materials or equipment at the expense of the Contractor. If the Contractor does not pay the cost of such removal and storage within ten days thereafter, the Owner may upon ten additional days' written notice sell such Work at auction or at private sale and shall account for the net proceeds thereof, after deducting all the costs that should have been borne by the Contractor including compensation for additional architectural services. If such proceeds of sale do not cover all costs which the Contractor should have borne, the difference shall be charged to the Contractor and an appropriate Change Order shall be issued. If the payments then or thereafter due the Contractor are not sufficient to cover such amount, the Contractor shall pay the difference to the Owner.
>
> **13.2.6** If the Contractor fails to correct such defective or non-conforming Work, the Owner may correct it in accordance with Paragraph 7.6.
>
> **13.2.7** The obligations of the Contractor under this Paragraph 13.2 shall be in addition to and not in limitation of any obligations imposed upon him by special guarantees required by the Contract Documents or otherwise prescribed by law.

Paragraph 13.2   Correction of Work

   I

       68018-AR   70071-MS
       70079-CO   71066-NY
       71028-MI   69019-OK
       67033-MN   68010-TX

   II

       70030-MT
       68052-TX

   III

       70081-DE   71010-VA
       70016-MD   71043-WA
       70009-MO

> **Text of Paragraph 13.3—Acceptance of Defective or Non-Conforming Work**
>
> **13.3.1** If the Owner prefers to accept defective or non-conforming Work, he may do so instead of requiring its removal and correction, in which case a Change Order will be issued to reflect an appropriate reduction in the Contract Sum, or, if the amount is determined after final payment, it shall be paid by the Contractor.

DOCUMENT TO CASE CHARTS: A201-1967

[The five-digit numbers in this chart are Citator Case Reference Numbers, which refer to the cases, in the Cases section. The suffixes indicate the state or, for federal cases, the court in which the case was decided.]

Paragraph 13.3 Acceptance of Defective or Non-Conforming Work

    I

        71051-NDGA
        82035-MS

    III

        70087-CT
        70081-DE

Article 14 Termination of the Contract

Paragraph 14.1 Termination by the Contractor

Text of Paragraph 14.2—Termination by the Owner

14.2.1 If the Contractor is adjudged a bankrupt, or if he makes a general assignment for the benefit of his creditors, or if a receiver is appointed on account of his insolvency, or if he persistently or repeatedly refuses or fails, except in cases for which extension of time is provided, to supply enough properly skilled workmen or proper materials, or if he fails to make prompt payment to Subcontractors or for materials or labor, or persistently disregards laws, ordinances, rules, regulations or orders of any public authority having jurisdiction, or otherwise is guilty of a substantial violation of a provision of the Contract Documents, then the Owner, upon certification by the Architect that sufficient cause exists to justify such action, may, without prejudice to any right or remedy and after giving the Contractor and his surety, if any, seven days' written notice, terminate the employment of the Contractor and take possession of the site and of all materials, equipment, tools, construction equipment and machinery thereon owned by the Contractor and may finish the Work by whatever method he may deem expedient. In such case the Contractor shall not be entitled to receive any further payment until the Work is finished.

14.2.2 If the unpaid balance of the Contract Sum exceeds the costs of finishing the Work, including compensation for the Architect's additional services, such excess shall be paid to the Contractor. If such costs exceed such unpaid balance, the Contractor shall pay the difference to the Owner. The costs incurred by the Owner as herein provided shall be certified by the Architect.

Paragraph 14.2 Termination by the Owner

    I

        69021-DMA
        69032-CA
        71074-IL

DOCUMENT TO CASE CHARTS: A201-1967

[The five-digit numbers in this chart are Citator Case Reference Numbers, which refer to the cases, in the Cases section. The suffixes indicate the state or, for federal cases, the court in which the case was decided.]

II

    70067-MA
    68045-NY

III

    68033-MA
    67025-NY

DOCUMENT TO CASE CHARTS: A201-1970

[The five-digit numbers in this chart are Citator Case Reference Numbers, which refer to the cases, in the Cases section. The suffixes indicate the state or, for federal cases, the court in which the case was decided.]

A201-1970—GENERAL CONDITIONS OF THE CONTRACT FOR CONSTRUCTION

Article 1 Contract Documents

Text of Paragraph 1.1—Definitions

1.1.1 THE CONTRACT DOCUMENTS

The Contract Documents consist of the Agreement, the Conditions of the Contract (General, Supplementary and other Conditions), the Drawings, the Specifications, all Addenda issued prior to execution of the Contract, and all Modifications thereto. A Modification is (1) a written amendment to the Contract signed by both parties, (2) a Change Order, (3) a written interpretation issued by the Architect pursuant to Subparagraph 1.2.5, or (4) a written order for a minor change in the Work issued by the Architect pursuant to Paragraph 12.3. A Modification may be made only after execution of the Contract.

1.1.2 THE CONTRACT

The Contract Documents form the Contract. The Contract represents the entire and integrated agreement between the parties hereto and supersedes all prior negotiations, representations, or agreements, either written or oral, including the bidding documents. The Contract may be amended or modified only by a Modification as defined in Subparagraph 1.1.1.

1.1.3 THE WORK

The term Work includes all labor necessary to produce the construction required by the Contract Documents, and all materials and equipment incorporated or to be incorporated in such construction.

1.1.4 THE PROJECT

The Project is the total construction designed by the Architect of which the Work performed under the Contract Documents may be the whole or a part.

Paragraph 1.1   Definitions

    I

        72097-IL

    II

        72038-KS
        72113-MD

DOCUMENT TO CASE CHARTS: A201-1970 A–180

[The five-digit numbers in this chart are Citator Case Reference Numbers, which refer to the cases, in the Cases section. The suffixes indicate the state or, for federal cases, the court in which the case was decided.]

III

72066-7CIR
72109-GA
73006-GA
73087-LA

74017-MD
73022-MO
73063-NE

Text of Paragraph 1.2—Execution, Correlation, Intent and Interpretations

1.2.1 The Contract Documents shall be signed in not less than triplicate by the Owner and Contractor. If either the Owner or the Contractor or both do not sign the Conditions of the Contract, Drawings, Specifications, or any of the other Contract Documents, the Architect shall identify them.

1.2.2 By executing the Contract, the Contractor represents that he has visited the site, familiarized himself with the local conditions under which the Work is to be performed, and correlated his observations with the requirements of the Contract Documents.

1.2.3 The Contract Documents are complementary, and what is required by any one shall be as binding as if required by all. The intention of the Documents is to include all labor, materials, equipment and other items as provided in Subparagraph 4.4.1 necessary for the proper execution and completion of the Work. It is not intended that Work not covered under any heading, section, branch, class or trade of the Specifications shall be supplied unless it is required elsewhere in the Contract Documents or is reasonably inferable therefrom as being necessary to produce the intended results. Words which have well-known technical or trade meanings are used herein in accordance with such recognized meanings.

1.2.4 The organization of the Specifications into divisions, sections and articles, and the arrangement of Drawings shall not control the Contractor in dividing the Work among Subcontractors or in establishing the extent of Work to be performed by any trade.

1.2.5 Written interpretations necessary for the proper execution or progress of the Work, in the form of drawings or otherwise, will be issued with reasonable promptness by the Architect and in accordance with any schedule agreed upon. Either party to the Contract may make written request to the Architect for such interpretations. Such interpretations shall be consistent with and reasonably inferable from the Contract Documents, and may be effected by Field Order.

Paragraph 1.2   Execution, Correlation, Intent and Interpretations

III

72048-MT

DOCUMENT TO CASE CHARTS: A201-1970

[The five-digit numbers in this chart are Citator Case Reference Numbers, which refer to the cases, in the Cases section. The suffixes indicate the state or, for federal cases, the court in which the case was decided.]

Text of Paragraph 1.3—Copies Furnished and Ownership

1.3.1 Unless otherwise provided in the Contract Documents, the Contractor will be furnished, free of charge, all copies of Drawings and Specifications reasonably necessary for the execution of the Work.

1.3.2 All Drawings, Specifications and copies thereof furnished by the Architect are and shall remain his property. They are not to be used on any other project, and, with the exception of one contract set for each party to the Contract, are to be returned to the Architect on request at the completion of the Work.

Paragraph 1.3 Copies Furnished and Ownership

    III

        73084-8CIR   73060-GA
        72074-CA   72012-OH

Article 2   Architect

Text of Paragraph 2.1—Definition

2.1.1 The Architect is the person or organization licensed to practice architecture and identified as such in the Agreement and is referred to throughout the Contract Documents as if singular in number and masculine in gender. The term Architect means the Architect or his authorized representative.

2.1.2 Nothing contained in the Contract Documents shall create any contractual relationship between the Architect and the Contractor.

Paragraph 2.1 Definition

    II

        73050-9CIR
        73097-CT

    III

        72106-DCO

Text of Paragraph 2.2—Administration of the Contract

2.2.1 The Architect will provide general Administration of the Construction Contract, including performance of the functions hereinafter described.

2.2.2 The Architect will be the Owner's representative during construction and until final payment. The Architect will have authority to act on behalf of the Owner to the extent provided in the Contract Documents, unless otherwise modified by written instrument which will be shown to the Contractor. The Architect will advise and consult with the Owner, and all of the Owner's instructions to the Contractor shall be issued through the Architect.

DOCUMENT TO CASE CHARTS: A201-1970

[The five-digit numbers in this chart are Citator Case Reference Numbers, which refer to the cases, in the Cases section. The suffixes indicate the state or, for federal cases, the court in which the case was decided.]

2.2.3 The Architect shall at all times have access to the Work wherever it is in preparation and progress. The Contractor shall provide facilities for such access so the Architect may perform his functions under the Contract Documents.

2.2.4 The Architect will make periodic visits to the site to familiarize himself generally with the progress and quality of the Work and to determine in general if the Work is proceeding in accordance with the Contract Documents. On the basis of his on-site observations as an architect, he will keep the Owner informed of the progress of the Work, and will endeavor to guard the Owner against defects and deficiencies in the Work of the Contractor. The Architect will not be required to make exhaustive or continuous on-site inspections to check the quality or quantity of the Work. The Architect will not be responsible for construction means, methods, techniques, sequences or procedures, or for safety precautions and programs in connection with the Work, and he will not be responsible for the Contractor's failure to carry out the Work in accordance with the Contract Documents.

2.2.5 Based on such observations and the Contractor's Applications for Payment, the Architect will determine the amounts owing to the Contractor and will issue Certificates for Payment in such amounts, as provided in Paragraph 9.4.

2.2.6 The Architect will be, in the first instance, the interpreter of the requirements of the Contract Documents and the judge of the performance thereunder by both the Owner and Contractor. The Architect will within a reasonable time, render such interpretations as he may deem necessary for the proper execution or progress of the Work.

2.2.7 Claims, disputes and other matters in question between the Contractor and the Owner relating to the execution or progress of the Work or the interpretation of the Contract Documents shall be referred initially to the Architect for decision which he will render in writing within a reasonable time.

2.2.8 All interpretations and decisions of the Architect shall be consistent with the intent of the Contract Documents. In his capacity as interpreter and judge, he will exercise his best efforts to insure faithful performance by both the Owner and the Contractor and will not show partiality to either.

2.2.9 The Architect's decisions in matters relating to artistic effect will be final if consistent with the intent of the Contract Documents.

2.2.10 Any claim, dispute or other matter that has been referred to the Architect, except those relating to artistic effect as provided in Subparagraph 2.2.9 and except any which have been waived by the making or acceptance of final payment as provided in Subparagraphs 9.7.5 and 9.7.6, shall be subject to arbitration upon the written demand of either party. However, no demand for arbitration of any such claim, dispute or other matter may be made until the earlier of:

.1   The date on which the Architect has rendered his written decision, or

.2   the tenth day after the parties have presented their evidence to the Architect or have been given a reasonable opportunity to do so, if the Architect has not rendered his written decision by that date.

DOCUMENT TO CASE CHARTS: A201-1970

[The five-digit numbers in this chart are Citator Case Reference Numbers, which refer to the cases, in the Cases section. The suffixes indicate the state or, for federal cases, the court in which the case was decided.]

2.2.11 If a decision of the Architect is made in writing and states that it is final but subject to appeal, no demand for arbitration of a claim, dispute or other matter covered by such decision may be made later than thirty days after the date on which the party making the demand received the decision. The failure to demand arbitration within said thirty days' period will result in the Architect's decision becoming final and binding upon the Owner and the Contractor. If the Architect renders a decision after arbitration proceedings have been initiated, such decision may be entered as evidence but will not supersede any arbitration proceedings unless the decision is acceptable to the parties concerned.

2.2.12 The Architect will have authority to reject Work which does not conform to the Contract Documents. Whenever, in his reasonable opinion, he considers it necessary or advisable to insure the proper implementation of the intent of the Contract Documents, he will have authority to require special inspection or testing of the Work in accordance with Subparagraph 7.8.2 whether or not such Work be then fabricated, installed or completed. However, neither the Architect's authority to act under this Subparagraph 2.2.12, nor any decision made by him in good faith either to exercise or not to exercise such authority, shall give rise to any duty or responsibility of the Architect to the Contractor, any Subcontractor, any of their agents or employees, or any other person performing any of the Work.

2.2.13 The Architect will review Shop Drawings and Samples as provided in Subparagraphs 4.13.1 through 4.13.8 inclusive.

2.2.14 The Architect will prepare Change Orders in accordance with Article 12, and will have authority to order minor changes in the Work as provided in Subparagraph 12.3.1.

2.2.15 The Architect will conduct inspections to determine the dates of Substantial Completion and final completion, will receive and review written guarantees and related documents required by the Contract and assembled by the Contractor and will issue a final Certificate for Payment.

2.2.16 If the Owner and Architect agree, the Architect will provide one or more Full-Time Project Representatives to assist the Architect in carrying out his responsibilities at the site. The duties, responsibilities and limitations of authority of any such Project Representative shall be as set forth in an exhibit to be incorporated in the Contract Documents.

2.2.17 The duties, responsibilities and limitations of authority of the Architect as the Owner's representative during construction as set forth in Articles 1 through 14 inclusive of these General Conditions will not be modified or extended without written consent of the Owner, the Contractor and the Architect.

2.2.18 The Architect will not be responsible for the acts or omissions of the Contractor, any Subcontractors, or any of their agents or employees, or any other persons performing any of the Work.

2.2.19 In case of the termination of the employment of the Architect, the Owner shall appoint an architect against whom the Contractor makes no reasonable

DOCUMENT TO CASE CHARTS: A201-1970   A–184

[The five-digit numbers in this chart are Citator Case Reference Numbers, which refer to the cases, in the Cases section. The suffixes indicate the state or, for federal cases, the court in which the case was decided.]

> objection whose status under the Contract Documents shall be that of the former architect. Any dispute in connection with such appointment shall be subject to arbitration.

Paragraph 2.2   Administration of the Contract

    I

        73058-EDVA   72063-MD
        75027-DVI   74005-MD
        74040-AK   82054-NC
        75021-IL   74014-OR
        73104-KS   75001-WV
        74003-LA

    II

        72006-IL   75015-NY
        72027-MA   73042-PA
        73019-NY   73109-RI

    III

        73001-MDPA   71078-NY
        73129-CA   73067-NC
        73007-FL   73114-ND
        73027-FL   73069-WA

Article 3   Owner

Paragraph 3.1   Definition

> **Text of Paragraph 3.2—Information and Services Required of the Owner**
>
> **3.2.1** The Owner shall furnish all surveys describing, the physical characteristics, legal limits and utility locations for the site of the Project.
>
> **3.2.2** The Owner shall secure and pay for easements for permanent structures or permanent changes in existing facilities.
>
> **3.2.3** Information or services under the Owner's control shall be furnished by the Owner with reasonable promptness to avoid delay in the orderly progress of the Work.
>
> **3.2.4** The Owner shall issue all instructions to the Contractor through the Architect.
>
> **3.2.5** The foregoing are in addition to other duties and responsibilities of the Owner enumerated herein and especially those in respect to Payment and Insurance in Articles 9 and 11 respectively.

A–185 DOCUMENT TO CASE CHARTS: A201-1970

[*The five-digit numbers in this chart are Citator Case Reference Numbers, which refer to the cases, in the Cases section. The suffixes indicate the state or, for federal cases, the court in which the case was decided.*]

Paragraph 3.2   Information and Services Required of the Owner

    II

        84006-TN

Paragraph 3.3   Owner's Right to Stop the Work

Text of Paragraph 3.4—Owner's Right to Carry Out the Work

3.4.1 If the Contractor defaults or neglects to carry out the Work in accordance with the Contract Documents or fails to perform any provision of the Contract, the Owner may, after seven days' written notice to the Contractor and without prejudice to any other remedy he may have, make good such deficiencies. In such case an appropriate Change Order shall be issued deducting from the payments then or thereafter due the Contractor the cost of correcting such deficiencies, including the cost of the Architect's additional services made necessary by such default, neglect or failure. The Architect must approve both such action and the amount charged to the Contractor. If the payments then or thereafter due the Contractor are not sufficient to cover such amount, the Contractor shall pay the difference to the Owner.

Paragraph 3.4   Owner's Right to Carry Out the Work

    I

        73066-TX

    III

        75024-NY

Article 4   Contractor

Text of Paragraph 4.1—Definition

4.1.1 The Contractor is the person or organization identified as such in the Agreement and is referred to throughout the Contract Documents as if singular in number and masculine in gender. The term Contractor means the Contractor or his authorized representative.

Paragraph 4.1   Definition

    I

        82037-PA

Text of Paragraph 4.2—Review of Contract Documents

4.2.1 The Contractor shall carefully study and compare the Contract Documents and shall at once report to the Architect any error, inconsistency or omission he may discover. The Contractor shall not be liable to the Owner or the Architect for

> [The five-digit numbers in this chart are Citator Case Reference Numbers, which refer to the cases, in the Cases section. The suffixes indicate the state or, for federal cases, the court in which the case was decided.]

> any damage resulting from any such errors, inconsistencies or omissions in the Contract Documents. The Contractor shall do no Work without Drawings, Specifications or Modifications.

Paragraph 4.2   Review of Contract Documents

    III

        72059-LA

> **Text of Paragraph 4.3—Supervision and Construction Procedures**
>
> **4.3.1** The Contractor shall supervise and direct the Work, using his best skill and attention. He shall be solely responsible for all construction means, methods, techniques, sequences and procedures and for coordinating all portions of the Work under the Contract.

Paragraph 4.3   Supervision and Construction Procedures

    I

        75027-DVI

    III

        71078-NY
        72084-NY

> **Text of Paragraph 4.4—Labor and Materials**
>
> **4.4.1** Unless otherwise specifically noted, the Contractor shall provide and pay for all labor, materials, equipment, tools, construction equipment and machinery, water, heat, utilities, transportation, and other facilities and services necessary for the proper execution and completion of the Work.
>
> **4.4.2** The Contractor shall at all times enforce strict discipline and good order among his employees and shall not employ on the Work any unfit person or anyone not skilled in the task assigned to him.

Paragraph 4.4   Labor and Materials

    I

        74002-NJ

    II

        71001-NJ

> **Text of Paragraph 4.5—Warranty**
>
> **4.5.1** The Contractor warrants to the Owner and the Architect that all materials and equipment furnished under this Contract will be new unless otherwise specified, and that all Work will be of good quality, free from faults and defects and in

DOCUMENT TO CASE CHARTS: A201-1970

[The five-digit numbers in this chart are Citator Case Reference Numbers, which refer to the cases, in the Cases section. The suffixes indicate the state or, for federal cases, the court in which the case was decided.]

> conformance with the Contract Documents. All Work not so conforming to these standards may be considered defective. If required by the Architect, the Contractor shall furnish satisfactory evidence as to the kind and quality of materials and equipment.

Paragraph 4.5   Warranty

    I

        75002-IL
        73052-MO
        73066-TX

    II

        72022-AR
        84006-TN

    III

        72044-4CIR   74034-IL
        72094-DE   72108-IA
        74018-DE

Paragraph 4.6   Taxes

Text of Paragraph 4.7—Permits, Fees and Notices

4.7.1 The Contractor shall secure and pay for all permits, governmental fees and licenses necessary for the proper execution and completion of the Work, which are applicable at the time the bids are received. It is not the responsibility of the Contractor to make certain that the Drawings and Specifications are in accordance with applicable laws, statutes, building codes and regulations.

4.7.2 The Contractor shall give all notices and comply with all laws, ordinances, rules, regulations and orders of any public authority bearing on the performance of the Work. If the Contractor observes that any of the Contract Documents are at variance therewith in any respect, he shall promptly notify the Architect in writing, and any necessary changes shall be adjusted by appropriate Modification. If the Contractor performs any Work knowing it to be contrary to such laws, ordinances, rules and regulations, and without such notice to the Architect, he shall assume full responsibility therefor and shall bear all costs attributable thereto.

DOCUMENT TO CASE CHARTS: A201-1970

[*The five-digit numbers in this chart are Citator Case Reference Numbers, which refer to the cases, in the Cases section. The suffixes indicate the state or, for federal cases, the court in which the case was decided.*]

Paragraph 4.7   Permits, Fees and Notices

    III

        74024-5CIR
        73118-CA
        72036-IN

Paragraph 4.8   Cash Allowances

Paragraph 4.9   Superintendent

Text of Paragraph 4.10—Responsibility for Those Performing the Work

4.10.1 The Contractor shall be responsible to the Owner for the acts and omissions of all his employees and all Subcontractors, their agents and employees, and all other persons performing any of the Work under a contract with the Contractor.

Paragraph 4.10   Responsibility for Those Performing the Work

    II

        72022-AR

Paragraph 4.11   Progress Schedule

Paragraph 4.12   Drawings and Specifications at the Site

Paragraph 4.13   Shop Drawings and Samples

Paragraph 4.14   Use of Site

Paragraph 4.15   Cutting and Patching of Work

Text of Paragraph 4.16—Cleaning Up

4.16.1 The Contractor at all times shall keep the premises free from accumulation of waste materials or rubbish caused by his operations. At the completion of the Work he shall remove all his waste materials and rubbish from and about the Project as well as all his tools, construction equipment, machinery and surplus materials, and shall clean all glass surfaces and leave the Work "broom-clean" or its equivalent, except as otherwise specified.

4.16.2 If the Contractor fails to clean up, the Owner may do so and the cost thereof shall be charged to the Contractor as provided in Paragraph 3.4.

A-189 DOCUMENT TO CASE CHARTS: A201-1970

[The five-digit numbers in this chart are Citator Case Reference Numbers, which refer to the cases, in the Cases section. The suffixes indicate the state or, for federal cases, the court in which the case was decided.]

Paragraph 4.16 Cleaning Up

   II

      73015-GA

Paragraph 4.17 Communications

Text of Paragraph 4.18—Indemnification

4.18.1 The Contractor shall indemnify and hold harmless the Owner and the Architect and their agents and employees from and against all claims, damages, losses and expenses including attorneys' fees arising out of or resulting from the performance of the Work, provided that any such claim, damage, loss or expense (1) is attributable to bodily injury, sickness, disease or death, or to injury to or destruction of tangible property (other than the Work itself) including the loss of use resulting there from, and (2) is caused in whole or in part by any negligent act or omission of the Contractor, any Subcontractor, anyone directly or indirectly employed by any of them or anyone for whose acts any of them may be liable, regardless of whether or not it is caused in part by a party indemnified hereunder.

4.18.2 In any and all claims against the Owner or the Architect or any of their agents or employees by any employee of the Contractor, any Subcontractor, anyone directly or indirectly employed by any of them or anyone for whose acts any of them may be liable, the indemnification obligation under this Paragraph 4.18 shall not be limited in any way by any limitation on the amount or type of damages, compensation or benefits payable by or for the Contractor or any Subcontractor under workmens compensation acts, disability benefit acts or other employee benefit acts.

4.18.3 The obligations of the Contractor under this Paragraph 4.18 shall not extend to the liability of the Architect, his agents or employees arising out of (1) the preparation or approval of maps, drawings, opinions, reports, surveys, Change Orders, designs or specifications, or (2) the giving of or the failure to give directions or instructions by the Architect, his agents or employees provided such giving or failure to give is the primary cause of the injury or damage.

Paragraph 4.18 Indemnification

   I

      72067-IA   82055-OR
      82051-LA   73056-WA
      86025-MN

DOCUMENT TO CASE CHARTS: A201-1970   A–190

[The five-digit numbers in this chart are Citator Case Reference Numbers, which refer to the cases, in the Cases section. The suffixes indicate the state or, for federal cases, the court in which the case was decided.]

II

    71040-6CIR

III

    70086-US   73055-DE
    74038-5CIR   73017-LA
    74037-7CIR   73072-MI
    74004-8CIR   72048-MT
    73013-SDSD   74026-NC
    73004-EDTN   73099-TX
    72062-CA   73062-WA

Article 5   Subcontractors

Text of Paragraph 5.1—Definition

5.1.1 A Subcontractor is a person or organization who has a direct contract with the Contractor to perform any of the Work at the site. The term Subcontractor is referred to throughout the Contract Documents as if singular in number and masculine in gender and means a Subcontractor or his authorized representative.

5.1.2 A Sub-subcontractor is a person or organization who has a direct or indirect contract with a Subcontractor to perform any of the Work at the site. The term Sub-subcontractor is referred to throughout the Contract Documents as if singular in number and masculine in gender and means a Sub-subcontractor or an authorized representative thereof.

5.1.3 Nothing contained in the Contract Documents shall create any contractual relation between the Owner or the Architect and any Subcontractor or Sub-subcontractor.

Paragraph 5.1   Definition

I

    73122-NDMS
    84039-CT

III

    73089-SDIA
    73090-MO

Text of Paragraph 5.2—Award of Subcontracts and Other Contracts for Portions of the Work

5.2.1 Unless otherwise specified in the Contract Documents or in the Instructions to Bidders, the Contractor, as soon as practicable after the award of the Contract, shall furnish to the Architect in writing for acceptance by the Owner and the Architect a list of the names of the Subcontractors proposed for the principal portions of the Work. The Architect shall promptly notify the Contractor in writing if either

DOCUMENT TO CASE CHARTS: A201-1970

[The five-digit numbers in this chart are Citator Case Reference Numbers, which refer to the cases, in the Cases section. The suffixes indicate the state or, for federal cases, the court in which the case was decided.]

the Owner or the Architect, after due investigation, has reasonable objection to any Subcontractor on such list and does not accept him. Failure of the Owner or Architect to make objection promptly to any Subcontractor on the list shall constitute acceptance of such Subcontractor.

5.2.2 The Contractor shall not contract with any Subcontractor or any person or organization (including those who are to furnish materials or equipment fabricated to a special design) proposed for portions of the Work designated in the Contract Documents or in the Instructions to Bidders or, if none is so designated, with any Subcontractor proposed for the principal portions of the Work who has been rejected by the Owner and the Architect. The Contractor will not be required to contract with any Subcontractor or person or organization against whom he has a reasonable objection.

5.2.3 If the Owner or Architect refuses to accept any Subcontractor or person or organization on a list submitted by the Contractor in response to the requirements of the Contract Documents or the Instructions to Bidders, the Contractor shall submit an acceptable substitute and the Contract Sum shall be increased or decreased by the difference in cost occasioned by such substitution and an appropriate Change Order shall be issued; however, no increase in the Contract Sum shall be allowed for any such substitution unless the Contractor has acted promptly and responsively in submitting for acceptance any list or lists of names as required by the Contract Documents or the Instructions to Bidders.

5.2.4 If the Owner or the Architect requires a change of any proposed Subcontractor or person or organization previously accepted by them, the Contract Sum shall be increased or decreased by the difference in cost occasioned by such change and an appropriate Change Order shall be issued.

5.2.5 The Contractor shall not make any substitution for any Subcontractor or person or organization who has been accepted by the Owner and the Architect, unless the substitution is acceptable to the Owner and the Architect.

Paragraph 5.2 Award of Subcontracts and Other Contracts for Portions of the Work

I

    73122-NDMS

III

    73029-5CIR
    72058-NY
    74030-NC

Text of Paragraph 5.3—Subcontractual Relations

5.3.1 All work performed for the Contractor by a Subcontractor shall be pursuant to an appropriate agreement between the Contractor and the Subcontractor (and where appropriate between Subcontractors and Sub-subcontractors) which shall contain provisions that:

DOCUMENT TO CASE CHARTS: A201-1970 A–192

[The five-digit numbers in this chart are Citator Case Reference Numbers, which refer to the cases, in the Cases section. The suffixes indicate the state or, for federal cases, the court in which the case was decided.]

.1 preserve and protect the rights of the Owner and the Architect under the Contract with respect to the Work to be performed under the subcontract so that the subcontracting thereof will not prejudice such rights;

.2 require that such Work be performed in accordance with the requirements of the Contract Documents;

.3 require submission to the Contractor of applications for payment under each subcontract to which the Contractor is a party, in reasonable time to enable the Contractor to apply for payment in accordance with Article 9;

.4 require that all claims for additional costs, extensions of time, damages for delays or otherwise with respect to subcontracted portions of the Work shall be submitted to the Contractor (via any Subcontractor or Sub-subcontractor where appropriate) in sufficient time so that the Contractor may comply in the manner provided in the Contract Documents for like claims by the Contractor upon the Owner;

.5 waive all rights the contracting parties may have against one another for damages caused by fire or other perils covered by the property insurance described in Paragraph 11.3, except such rights as they may have to the proceeds of such insurance held by the Owner as trustee under Paragraph 11.3; and

.6 obligate each Subcontractor specifically to consent to the provisions of this Paragraph 5.3.

Paragraph 5.3   Subcontractual Relations

   I

      75026-EDPA
      73058-EDVA

   II

      73039-5CIR

   III

      73049-OR

Text of Paragraph 5.4—Payments to Subcontractors

5.4.1 The Contractor shall pay each Subcontractor, upon receipt of payment from the Owner, an amount equal to the percentage of completion allowed to the Contractor on account of such Subcontractor's Work, less the percentage retained from payments to the Contractor. The Contractor shall also require each Subcontractor to make similar payments to his subcontractors.

5.4.2 If the Architect fails to issue a Certificate for Payment for any cause which is the fault of the Contractor and not the fault of a particular Subcontractor, the Contractor shall pay that Subcontractor on demand, made at any time after the

> Certificate for Payment should otherwise have been issued, for his Work to the extent completed, less the retained percentage.
>
> **5.4.3** The Contractor shall pay each Subcontractor a just share of any insurance moneys received by the Contractor under Article 11, and he shall require each Subcontractor to make similar payments to his subcontractors.
>
> **5.4.4** The Architect may, on request and at his discretion, furnish to any Subcontractor, if practicable, information regarding percentages of completion certified to the Contractor on account of Work done by such Subcontractors.
>
> **5.4.5** Neither the Owner nor the Architect shall have any obligation to pay or to see to the payment of any moneys to any Subcontractor except as may otherwise be required by law.

Paragraph 5.4   Payments to Subcontractors

    II

        71070-GA

    III

        72114-CA   73090-MO
        74035-GA   75022-NY

Article 6   Separate Contracts

> **Text of Paragraph 6.1—Owner's Right to Award Separate Contracts**
>
> **6.1.1** The Owner reserves the right to award other contracts in connection with other portions of the Project under these or similar Conditions of the Contract.
>
> **6.1.2** When separate contracts are awarded for different portions of the Project, "the Contractor" in the contract documents in each case shall be the contractor who signs each separate contract.

Paragraph 6.1   Owner's Right to Award Separate Contracts

    III

        72047-NC

> **Text of Paragraph 6.2—Mutual Responsibility of Contractors**
>
> **6.2.1** The Contractor shall afford other contractors reasonable opportunity for the introduction and storage of their materials and equipment and the execution of their work, and shall properly connect and coordinate his Work with theirs.
>
> **6.2.2** If any part of the Contractor's Work depends for proper execution or results upon the work of any other separate contractor, the Contractor shall inspect and promptly report to the Architect any apparent discrepancies or defects in such work that render it unsuitable for such proper execution and results. Failure of the

DOCUMENT TO CASE CHARTS: A201-1970 A–194

[The five-digit numbers in this chart are Citator Case Reference Numbers, which refer to the cases, in the Cases section. The suffixes indicate the state or, for federal cases, the court in which the case was decided.]

> Contractor so to inspect and report shall constitute an acceptance of the other contractor's work as fit and proper to receive his Work, except as to defects which may develop in the other separate contractor's work after the execution of the Contractor's Work.
>
> **6.2.3** Should the Contractor cause damage to the work or property of any separate contractor on the Project, the Contractor shall, upon due notice, settle with such other contractor by agreement or arbitration, if he will so settle. If such separate contractor sues the Owner or initiates an arbitration proceeding on account of any damage alleged to have been so sustained, the Owner shall notify the Contractor who shall defend such proceedings at the Owner's expense, and if any judgment or award against the Owner arises therefrom the Contractor shall pay or satisfy it and shall reimburse the Owner for all attorneys' fees and court or arbitration costs which the Owner has incurred.

Paragraph 6.2   Mutual Responsibility of Contractors

    I

        87012-MS

Paragraph 6.3   Cutting and Patching under Separate Contracts

Paragraph 6.4   Owner's Right to Clean Up

Article 7   Miscellaneous Provisions

> **Text of Paragraph 7.1—Governing Law**
>
> **7.1.1** The Contract shall be governed by the law of the place where the Project is located.

Paragraph 7.1   Governing Law

    II

        82050-TN

    III

        73118-CA   74006-IL
        71053-CT   72088-NJ
        72032-CO   72050-NY
        72107-DE   72080-NY
        73100-GA   72002-RI

DOCUMENT TO CASE CHARTS: A201-1970

A–195

[The five-digit numbers in this chart are Citator Case Reference Numbers, which refer to the cases, in the Cases section. The suffixes indicate the state or, for federal cases, the court in which the case was decided.]

Paragraph 7.2 Successors and Assigns

Text of Paragraph 7.2

7.2.1 The Owner and the Contractor each binds himself, his partners, successors, assigns and legal representatives to the other party hereto and to the partners, successors, assigns and legal representatives of such other party in respect to all covenants, agreements and obligations contained in the Contract Documents. Neither party to the Contract shall assign the Contract or sublet it as a whole without the written consent of the other, nor shall the Contractor assign any moneys due or to become due to him hereunder, without the previous written consent of the Owner.

Paragraph 7.2 Successors and Assigns

    I

        75028-6CIR

    II

        74023-GA

Paragraph 7.3 Written Notice

Text of Paragraph 7.4—Claims for Damages

7.4.1 Should either party to the Contract suffer injury or damage to person or property because of any act or omission of the other party or of any of his employees, agents or others for whose acts he is legally liable, claim shall be made in writing to such other party within a reasonable time after the first observance of such injury or damage.

Paragraph 7.4 Claims for Damages

    I

        75002-IL

Text of Paragraph 7.5—Performance Bond and Labor and Material Payment Bond

7.5.1 The Owner shall have the right to require the Contractor to furnish bonds covering the faithful performance of the Contract and the payment of all obligations arising thereunder if and as required in the Instructions to Bidders or elsewhere in the Contract Documents.

DOCUMENT TO CASE CHARTS: A201-1970   A–196

[The five-digit numbers in this chart are Citator Case Reference Numbers, which refer to the cases, in the Cases section. The suffixes indicate the state or, for federal cases, the court in which the case was decided.]

Paragraph 7.5 Performance Bond and Labor and Material Payment Bond

    I

        74031-GA
        74002-NJ

    III

        71013-2CIR
        72039-5CIR
        72049-5CIR

Text of Paragraph 7.6—Rights and Remedies

7.6.1 The duties and obligations imposed by the Contract Documents and the rights and remedies available thereunder shall be in addition to and not a limitation of any duties, obligations, rights and remedies otherwise imposed or available by law.

Paragraph 7.6 Rights and Remedies

    I

        82025-IL
        74014-OR

    III

        73126-1CIR
        72077-3CIR
        74030-NC

Paragraph 7.7 Royalties and Patents

Paragraph 7.8 Tests

Text of Paragraph 7.9—Interest

7.9.1 Any moneys not paid when due to either party under this Contract shall bear interest at the legal rate in force at the place of the Project.

Paragraph 7.9 Interest

    III

        72056-7CIR
        74034-IL
        74021-NE

Text of Paragraph 7.10—Arbitration

7.10.1 All claims, disputes and other matters in question arising out of, or relating to, this Contract or the breach thereof, except as set forth in Subparagraph 2.2.9 with respect to the Architect's decisions on matters relating to artistic effect, and

DOCUMENT TO CASE CHARTS: A201-1970

[The five-digit numbers in this chart are Citator Case Reference Numbers, which refer to the cases, in the Cases section. The suffixes indicate the state or, for federal cases, the court in which the case was decided.]

except for claims which have been waived by the making or acceptance of final payment as provided by Subparagraphs 9.7.5 and 9.7.6, shall be decided by arbitration in accordance with the Construction Industry Arbitration Rules of the American Arbitration Association then obtaining unless the parties mutually agree otherwise. This agreement to arbitrate shall be specifically enforceable under the prevailing arbitration law. The award rendered by the arbitrators shall be final, and judgment may be entered upon it in accordance with applicable law in any court having jurisdiction thereof.

7.10.2 Notice of the demand for arbitration shall be filed in writing with the other party to the Contract and with the American Arbitration Association, and a copy shall be filed with the Architect. The demand for arbitration shall be made within the time limits specified in Sub-paragraphs 2.2.10 and 2.2.11 where applicable, and in all other cases within a reasonable time after the claim, dispute or other matter in question has arisen, and in no event shall it be made after the date when institution of legal or equitable proceedings based on such claim, dispute or other matter in question would be barred by the applicable statute of limitations.

7.10.3 The Contractor shall carry on the Work and maintain the progress schedule during any arbitration proceedings, unless otherwise agreed by him and the Owner in writing.

Paragraph 7.10   Arbitration

I

74022-DDE	83042-MD
75026-EDPA	73033-MI
84039-CT	73071-MI
74040-AK	72111-NJ
72033-IL	82054-NC
75018-IL	82055-OR
75021-IL	74009-PA
82025-IL	75004-PA
74003-LA	75005-PA
72063-MD	82046-PA
74005-MD	75001-WV

II

82030-IL	73094-PA
72027-MA	82003-PA
82050-MN	73011-VA
83043-NY	73034-VA
73042-PA	

DOCUMENT TO CASE CHARTS: A201-1970

[The five-digit numbers in this chart are Citator Case Reference Numbers, which refer to the cases, in the Cases section. The suffixes indicate the state or, for federal cases, the court in which the case was decided.]

III

72078-1CIR	71062-GA
71013-2CIR	74035-GA
75010-3CIR	73088-IL
73054-5CIR	72001-NY
74043-5CIR	73091-NY
74010-DDC	73105-NY
73001-MDPA	73083-ND
73116-AZ	73102-OR
75023-CA	72002-RI
73073-FL	73128-WI
73075-FL	

Article 8   Time

Text of Paragraph 8.1—Definitions

8.1.1 The Contract Time is the period of time allotted in the Contract Documents for completion of the Work.

8.1.2 The date of commencement of the Work is the date established in a notice to proceed. If there is no notice to proceed, it shall be the date of the Agreement or such other date as may be established therein.

8.1.3 The Date of Substantial Completion of the Work or designated portion thereof is the Date certified by the Architect when construction is sufficiently complete, in accordance with the Contract Documents, so the Owner may occupy the Work or designated portion thereof for the use for which it is intended.

8.1.4 The term day as used in the Contract Documents shall mean calendar day.

Paragraph 8.1   Definitions

I

75013-NC
75004-PA

III

73089-SDIA
72020-CO

Text of Paragraph 8.2—Progress and Completion

8.2.1 All time limits stated in the Contract Documents are of the essence of the Contract.

8.2.2 The Contractor shall begin the Work on the date of commencement as defined in Subparagraph 8.1.2. He shall carry the Work forward expeditiously with adequate forces and shall complete it within the Contract Time.

8.2.3 If a date or time of completion is included in the Contract, it shall be the

DOCUMENT TO CASE CHARTS: A201-1970

[The five-digit numbers in this chart are Citator Case Reference Numbers, which refer to the cases, in the Cases section. The suffixes indicate the state or, for federal cases, the court in which the case was decided.]

> Date of Substantial Completion as defined in Subparagraph 8.1.3, including authorized extensions thereto, unless otherwise provided.

Paragraph 8.2 Progress and Completion

    I

        75013-NC

   III

        72043-NC
        72096-GA

> **Text of Paragraph 8.3—Delays and Extensions of Time**
>
> **8.3.1** If the Contractor is delayed at any time in the progress of the Work by any act or neglect of the Owner or the Architect, or by any employee of either, or by any Separate contractor employed by the Owner, or by changes ordered in the Work, or by labor disputes, fire, unusual delay in transportation, unavoidable casualties or any causes beyond the Contractor's control, or by delay authorized by the Owner pending arbitration, or by any cause which the Architect determines may justify the delay, then the Contract Time shall be extended by Change Order for such reasonable time as the Architect may determine.
>
> **8.3.2** All claims for extension of time shall be made in writing to the Architect no more than twenty days after the occurrence of the delay; otherwise they shall be waived. In the case of a continuing cause of delay only one claim is necessary.
>
> **8.3.3** If no schedule or agreement is made stating the dates upon which written interpretations as set forth in Subparagraph 1.2.5 shall be furnished, then no claim for delay shall be allowed on account of failure to furnish such interpretations until fifteen days after demand is made for them, and not then unless such claim is reasonable.
>
> **8.3.4** This Paragraph 8.3 does not exclude the recovery of damages for delay by either party under other provisions of the Contract Documents.

Paragraph 8.3 Delays and Extensions of Time

    I

        74040-AK   75013-NC
        73104-KS   75004-PA
        73052-MO

DOCUMENT TO CASE CHARTS: A201-1970

[The five-digit numbers in this chart are Citator Case Reference Numbers, which refer to the cases, in the Cases section. The suffixes indicate the state or, for federal cases, the court in which the case was decided.]

    II

        73039-5CIR
        72019-10CIR
        73034-VA

    III

74024-5CIR	73030-NY
72096-GA	74025-NY
73053-FL	72043-NC
74012-IL	73115-WA
73020-NY	71033-WA

Article 9 Payments and Completion

Text of Paragraph 9.1—Contract Sum

9.1.1 The Contract Sum is stated in the Agreement and is the total amount payable by the Owner to the Contractor for the performance of the Work under the Contract Documents.

Paragraph 9.1   Contract Sum

    I

        73043-FL
        75013-NC

Text of Paragraph 9.2—Schedule of Values

9.2.1 Before the first Application for Payment, the Contractor shall submit to the Architect a schedule of values of the various portions of the Work, including quantities if required by the Architect, aggregating the total Contract Sum, divided so as to facilitate payments to Subcontractors in accordance with Paragraph 5.4, prepared in such form as specified or as the Architect and the Contractor may agree upon, and supported by such data to substantiate its correctness as the Architect may require. Each item in the schedule of values shall include its proper share of overhead and profit. This schedule, when approved by the Architect, shall be used only as a basis for the Contractor's Applications for Payment.

Paragraph 9.2   Schedule of Values

    I

        75013-NC

DOCUMENT TO CASE CHARTS: A201-1970

[The five-digit numbers in this chart are Citator Case Reference Numbers, which refer to the cases, in the Cases section. The suffixes indicate the state or, for federal cases, the court in which the case was decided.]

II

    71070-GA

Text of Paragraph 9.3—Progress Payments

9.3.1 At least ten days before each progress payment falls due, the Contractor shall submit to the Architect an itemized Application for Payment, supported by such data substantiating the Contractor's right to payment as the Owner or the Architect may require.

9.3.2 If payments are to be made on account of materials or equipment not incorporated in the Work but delivered and suitably stored at the site, or at some other location agreed upon in writing, such payments shall be conditioned upon submission by the Contractor of bills of sale or such other procedures satisfactory to the Owner to establish the Owner's title to such materials or equipment or otherwise protect the Owner's interest including applicable insurance and transportation to the site.

9.3.3 The Contractor warrants and guarantees that title to all Work, materials and equipment covered by an Application for Payment, whether incorporated in the Project or not, will pass to the Owner upon the receipt of such payment by the Contractor, free and clear of all liens, claims, security interests or encumbrances, hereinafter referred to in this Article 9 as "liens"; and that no Work, materials or equipment covered by an Application for Payment will have been acquired by the Contractor; or by any other person performing the Work at the site or furnishing materials and equipment for the Project, subject to an agreement under which an interest therein or an encumbrance thereon is retained by the seller or otherwise imposed by the Contractor or such other person.

Paragraph 9.3   Progress Payments

    I

        75013-NC
        74014-OR

Text of Paragraph 9.4—Certificates for Payment

9.4.1 If the Contractor has made Application for Payment as above, the Architect will, with reasonable promptness but not more than seven days after the receipt of the Application, issue a Certificate for Payment to the Owner, with a copy to the Contractor, for such amount as he determines to be properly due, or state in writing his reasons for withholding a Certificate as provided in Subparagraph 9.5.1.

9.4.2 The issuance of a Certificate for Payment will constitute a representation by the Architect to the Owner, based on his observations at the site as provided in Subparagraph 2.2.4 and the data comprising the Application for Payment, that the Work has progressed to the point indicated; that, to the best of his knowledge, information and belief, the quality of the Work is in accordance with the Contract

DOCUMENT TO CASE CHARTS: A201-1970

[The five-digit numbers in this chart are Citator Case Reference Numbers, which refer to the cases, in the Cases section. The suffixes indicate the state or, for federal cases, the court in which the case was decided.]

Documents (subject to an evaluation of the Work for conformance with the Contract Documents upon Substantial Completion, to the results of any subsequent tests required by the Contract Documents, to minor deviations from the Contract Documents correctable prior to completion, and to any specific qualifications stated in his Certificate); and that the Contractor is entitled to payment in the amount certified. In addition, the Architect's final Certificate for Payment will constitute a further representation that the conditions precedent to the Contractor's being entitled to final payment as set forth in Subparagraph 9.7.2 have been fulfilled. However, by issuing a Certificate for Payment, the Architect shall not thereby be deemed to represent that he has made exhaustive or continuous on-site inspections to check the quality or quantity of the Work or that he has reviewed the construction means, methods, techniques, sequences or procedures, or that he has made any examination to ascertain how or for what purpose the Contractor has used the moneys previously paid on account of the Contract Sum.

9.4.3 After the Architect has issued a Certificate for Payment, the Owner shall make payment in the manner provided in the Agreement.

9.4.4 No certificate for a progress payment, nor any progress payment, nor any partial or entire use or occupancy of the Project by the Owner, shall constitute an acceptance of any Work not in accordance with the Contract Documents.

Paragraph 9.4 Certificates for Payment

   I

       75002-IL   75013-NC
       73104-KS   74014-OR

   III

       73068-ME
       72023-NM

Text of Paragraph 9.5—Payments Withheld

9.5.1 The Architect may decline to approve an Application for Payment and may withhold his Certificate in whole or in part, to the extent necessary reasonably to protect the Owner, if in his opinion he is unable to make representations to the Owner as provided in Subparagraph 9.4.2. The Architect may also decline to approve any Applications for Payment or, because of subsequently discovered evidence or subsequent inspections, he may nullify the whole or any part of any Certificate for Payment previously issued, to such extent as may be necessary in his opinion to protect the Owner from loss because of:

.1   defective work not remedied,

.2   third party claims filed or reasonable evidence indicating probable filing of such claims,

A–203 DOCUMENT TO CASE CHARTS: A201-1970

[The five-digit numbers in this chart are Citator Case Reference Numbers, which refer to the cases, in the Cases section. The suffixes indicate the state or, for federal cases, the court in which the case was decided.]

> .3 failure of the Contractor to make payments properly to Subcontractors or for labor, materials or equipment,
>
> .4 reasonable doubt that the Work can be completed for the unpaid balance of the Contract Sum,
>
> .5 damage to another contractor,
>
> .6 reasonable indication that the Work will not be completed within the Contract Time, or
>
> .7 unsatisfactory prosecution of the Work by the Contractor.
>
> 9.5.2 When the above grounds in Subparagraph 9.5.1 are removed, payment shall be made for amounts withheld because of them.

Paragraph 9.5   Payments Withheld

    I

        75013-NC
        74014-OR

    III

        73010-7CIR
        74034-IL

> **Text of Paragraph 9.6—Failure of Payment**
>
> 9.6.1 If the Architect should fail to issue any Certificate for Payment, through no fault of the Contractor, within seven days after receipt of the Contractor's Application for Payment, or if the Owner should fail to pay the Contractor within seven days after the date of payment established in the Agreement any amount certified by the Architect or awarded by arbitration, then the Contractor may, upon seven additional days' written notice to the Owner and the Architect, stop the Work until payment of the amount owing has been received.

Paragraph 9.6   Failure of Payment

    I

        75013-NC

    II

        72040-EDPA

    III

        73003-MA

[The five-digit numbers in this chart are Citator Case Reference Numbers, which refer to the cases, in the Cases section. The suffixes indicate the state or, for federal cases, the court in which the case was decided.]

Text of Paragraph 9.7—Substantial Completion and Final Payment

9.7.1 When the Contractor determines that the Work or a designated portion thereof acceptable to the Owner is substantially complete, the Contractor shall prepare for submission to the Architect a list of items to be completed or corrected. The failure to include any items on such list does not alter the responsibility of the Contractor to complete all Work in accordance with the Contract Documents. When the Architect on the basis of an inspection determines that the Work is substantially complete, he will then prepare a Certificate of Substantial Completion which shall establish the Date of Substantial Completion, shall state the responsibilities of the Owner and the Contractor for maintenance, heat, utilities, and insurance, and shall fix the time within which the Contractor shall complete the items listed therein. The Certificate of Substantial Completion shall be submitted to the Owner and the Contractor for their written acceptance of the responsibilities assigned to them in such Certificate.

9.7.2 Upon receipt of written notice that the Work is ready for final inspection and acceptance and upon receipt of a final Application for Payment, the Architect will promptly make such inspection and, when he finds the Work acceptable under the Contract Documents and the Contract fully performed, he will promptly issue a final Certificate for Payment stating that to the best of his knowledge, information and belief, and on the basis of his observations and inspections, the Work has been completed in accordance with the terms and conditions of the Contract Documents and that the entire balance found to be due the Contractor, and noted in said final Certificate, is due and payable.

9.7.3 Neither the final payment nor the remaining retained percentage shall become due until the Contractor submits to the Architect (1) an Affidavit that all payrolls, bills for materials and equipment, and other indebtedness connected with the Work for which the Owner or his property might in any way be responsible, have been paid or otherwise satisfied, (2) consent of surety, if any, to final payment and (3), if required by the Owner, other data establishing payment or satisfaction of all such obligations, such as receipts, releases and waivers of liens arising out of the Contract, to the extent and in such form as may be designated by the Owner. If any Subcontractor refuses to furnish a release or waiver required by the Owner, the Contractor may furnish a bond satisfactory to the Owner to indemnify him against any such lien. If any such lien remains unsatisfied after all payments are made, the Contractor shall refund to the Owner all moneys that the latter may be compelled to pay in discharging such lien, including all costs and reasonable attorneys' fees.

9.7.4 If after Substantial Completion of the Work final completion thereof is materially delayed through no fault of the Contractor, and the Architect so confirms, the Owner shall, upon certification by the Architect, and without terminating the Contract, make payment of the balance due for that portion of the Work fully completed and accepted. If the remaining balance for Work not fully completed

DOCUMENT TO CASE CHARTS: A201-1970

[The five-digit numbers in this chart are Citator Case Reference Numbers, which refer to the cases, in the Cases section. The suffixes indicate the state or, for federal cases, the court in which the case was decided.]

> or corrected is less than the retainage stipulated in the Agreement, and if bonds have been furnished as required in Subparagraph 7.5.1, the written consent of the surety to the payment of the balance due for that portion of the Work fully completed and accepted shall be submitted by the Contractor to the Architect prior to certification of such payment. Such payment shall be made under the terms and conditions governing final payment, except that it shall not constitute a waiver of claims.
>
> **9.7.5** The making of final payment shall constitute a waiver of all claims by the Owner except those arising from:
>
> .1   unsettled liens,
>
> .2   faulty or defective Work appearing after Substantial Completion,
>
> .3   failure of the Work to comply with the requirements of the Contract Documents, or
>
> .4   terms of any special guarantees required by the Contract Documents.
>
> **9.7.6** The acceptance of final payment shall constitute a waiver of all claims by the Contractor except those previously made in writing and still unsettled.

Paragraph 9.7   Substantial Completion and Final Payment

    I

        75002-IL   82054-NC
        73033-MI   82055-OR
        74007-NC   72087-TX
        75013-NC   71088-UT

    II

        72019-10CIR   72006-IL
        72040-EDPA   72038-KS
        73077-ID   84006-TN

    III

        72044-4CIR   72112-MD
        73010-7CIR   72081-MO
        72083-DCCIR   73022-MO
        74008-DDE   72015-ND
        73089-SDIA   73102-OR
        73079-WDOK   72085-SC
        72045-MA

Article 10   Protection of Persons and Property

> ## Text of Paragraph 10.1—Safety Precautions and Programs
>
> **10.1.1** The Contractor shall be responsible for initiating, maintaining and supervising all safety precautions and programs in connection with the Work.

DOCUMENT TO CASE CHARTS: A201-1970 A–206

[The five-digit numbers in this chart are Citator Case Reference Numbers, which refer to the cases, in the Cases section. The suffixes indicate the state or, for federal cases, the court in which the case was decided.]

Paragraph 10.1   Safety Precautions and Programs

 I

  72067-IA
  74009-PA

 III

  73014-AR   71078-NY
  73027-FL   72080-NY
  74027-GA

Text of Paragraph 10.2—Safety of Persons and Property

10.2.1 The Contractor shall take all reasonable precautions for the safety of, and shall provide all reasonable protection to prevent damage, injury or loss to:

.1 all employees on the Work and all other persons who may be affected thereby;

.2 all the Work and all materials and equipment to be incorporated therein, whether in storage on or off the site, under the care, custody or control of the Contractor or any of his Subcontractors of Sub-subcontractors; and

.3 other property at the site or adjacent thereto, including trees, shrubs, lawns, walks, pavements, roadways, structures and utilities not designated for removal, relocation or replacement in the course of construction.

10.2.2 The Contractor shall comply with all applicable laws, ordinances, rules, regulations and lawful orders of any public authority having jurisdiction for the safety of persons or property or to protect them from damage, injury or loss. He shall erect and maintain, as required by existing conditions and progress of the Work, all reasonable safeguards for safety and protection, including posting danger signs and other warnings against hazards, promulgating safety regulations and notifying owners and users of adjacent utilities.

10.2.3 When the use or storage of explosives or other hazardous materials or equipment is necessary for the execution of the Work, the Contractor shall exercise the utmost care and shall carry on such activities under the Supervision of properly qualified personnel.

10.2.4 All damage or loss to any property referred to in Clauses 10.2.1.2 and 10.2.1.3 caused in whole or in part by the Contractor, any Subcontractor, any Sub-subcontractor, or anyone directly or indirectly employed by any of them, or by anyone for whose acts any of them may be liable, shall be remedied by the Contractor, except damage or loss attributable to faulty Drawings or Specifications or to the acts or omissions of the Owner or Architect or anyone employed by either of them or for whose acts either of them may be liable, and not attributable to the fault or negligence of the Contractor.

10.2.5 The Contractor shall designate a responsible member of his organization at the site whose duty shall be the prevention of accidents. This person shall be

DOCUMENT TO CASE CHARTS: A201-1970

[The five-digit numbers in this chart are Citator Case Reference Numbers, which refer to the cases, in the Cases section. The suffixes indicate the state or, for federal cases, the court in which the case was decided.]

> the Contractor's superintendent unless otherwise designated in writing by the Contractor to the Owner and the Architect.
>
> **10.2.6** The Contractor shall not load or permit any part of the Work to be loaded so as to endanger its safety.

Paragraph 10.2   Safety of Persons and Property

    I

        75020-AR   82037-PA
        72067-IA   71088-UT
        73046-NE

    II

        73015-GA

    III

        73106-5CIR   73028-IA
        73092-9CIR   72082-ME
        73047-NDMS   73030-MD
        72065-WDPA   73024-MI
        73014-AR   72051-MN
        72072-CA   72009-MO
        72031-CT   72092-NE
        73027-FL   71078-NY
        74027-GA   73018-NY
        73076-IL   72086-NC
        73123-IL   73099-TX
        74006-IL   72061-UT
        74034-IL   73069-WA

Paragraph 10.3   Emergencies

Article 11   Insurance

> ### Text of Paragraph 11.1—Contractor's Liability Insurance
>
> **11.1.1** The Contractor shall purchase and maintain such insurance as will protect him from claims set forth below which may arise out of or result from the Contractor's operations under the Contract, whether such operations be by himself or by any Subcontractor or by anyone directly or indirectly employed by any of them, or by anyone for whose acts any of them may be liable:
>
> .1   claims under workmen's compensation, disability benefit and other similar employee benefit acts;
>
> .2   claims for damages because of bodily injury, occupational sickness or disease, or death of his employees;
>
> .3   claims for damages because of bodily injury, sickness or disease, or death of any person other than his employees;

DOCUMENT TO CASE CHARTS: A201-1970   A–208

[The five-digit numbers in this chart are Citator Case Reference Numbers, which refer to the cases, in the Cases section. The suffixes indicate the state or, for federal cases, the court in which the case was decided.]

.4 claims for damages insured by usual personal injury liability coverage which are sustained (1) by any person as a result of an offense directly or indirectly related to the employment of such person by the Contractor, or (2) by any other person; and

.5 claims for damages because of injury to or destruction of tangible property, including loss of use resulting therefrom.

11.1.2 The insurance required by Subparagraph 11.1.1 shall be written for not less than any limits of liability specified in the Contract Documents, or required by law, whichever is greater, and shall include contractual liability insurance as applicable to the Contractor's obligations under Paragraph 4.18.

11.1.3 Certificates of Insurance acceptable to the Owner shall be filed with the Owner prior to commencement of the Work. These Certificates shall contain a provision that coverages afforded under the policies will not be canceled until at least fifteen days' prior written notice has been given to the Owner.

Paragraph 11.1   Contractor's Liability Insurance

   III

      73082-EDPA   73059-NJ
      72003-WDTN   73036-NC

Paragraph 11.2   Owner's Liability Insurance

Text of Paragraph 11.3—Property Insurance

11.3.1 Unless otherwise provided, the Owner shall purchase and maintain property insurance upon the entire Work at the site to the full insurable value thereof. This insurance shall include the interests of the Owner, the Contractor, Subcontractors and Sub-subcontractors in the Work and shall insure against the perils of Fire, Extended Coverage, Vandalism and Malicious Mischief.

11.3.2 The Owner shall purchase and maintain such steam boiler and machinery insurance as may be required by the Contract Documents or by law. This insurance shall include the interests of the Owner, the Contractor, Subcontractors and Sub-subcontractors in the Work.

11.3.3 Any insured loss is to be adjusted with the Owner and made payable to the Owner as trustee for the insureds, as their interests may appear, subject to the requirements of any applicable mortgagee clause and of Subparagraph 11.3.8.

11.3.4 The Owner shall file a copy of all policies with the Contractor before an exposure to loss may occur. If the Owner does not intend to purchase such insurance, he shall inform the Contractor in writing prior to commencement of the Work. The Contractor may then effect insurance which will protect the interests of himself, his Subcontractors and the Sub-subcontractors in the Work and by appropriate Change Order the cost thereof shall be charged to the Owner. If the Contractor is

[The five-digit numbers in this chart are Citator Case Reference Numbers, which refer to the cases, in the Cases section. The suffixes indicate the state or, for federal cases, the court in which the case was decided.]

damaged by failure of the Owner to purchase or maintain such insurance and so to notify the Contractor, then the Owner shall bear all reasonable costs properly attributable thereto.

11.3.5 If the Contractor requests in writing that insurance for special hazards be included in the property insurance policy, the Owner shall, if possible, include such insurance, and the cost thereof shall be charged to the Contractor by appropriate Change Order.

11.3.6 The Owner and Contractor waive all rights against each other for damages caused by fire or other perils to the extent covered by insurance provided under this Paragraph 11.3, except such rights as they may have to the proceeds of such insurance held by the Owner as trustee. The Contractor shall require similar waivers by Subcontractors and Sub-subcontractors in accordance with Clause 5.3.1.5.

11.3.7 If required in writing by any party in interest, the Owner as trustee shall, upon the occurrence of an insured loss, give bond for the proper performance of his duties. He shall deposit in a separate account any money so received, and he shall distribute it in accordance with such agreement as the parties in interest may reach, or in accordance with an award by arbitration in which case the procedure shall be as provided in Paragraph 7.10. If after such loss no other special agreement is made, replacement of damaged work shall be covered by an appropriate Change Order.

11.3.8 The Owner as trustee shall have power to adjust and settle any loss with the insurers unless one of the parties in interest shall object in writing within five days after the occurrence of loss to the Owner's exercise of this power, and if such objection be made, arbitrators shall be chosen as provided in Paragraph 7.10. The Owner as trustee shall, in that case, make settlement with the insurers in accordance with the directions of such arbitrators. If distribution of the insurance proceeds by arbitration is required, the arbitrators will direct such distribution.

Paragraph 11.3   Property Insurance

    III

        72003-WDTN
        71004-GA

Paragraph 11.4   Loss of Use Insurance

Article 12   Changes in the Work

Text of Paragraph 12.1—Change Orders

12.1.1 The Owner, without invalidating the Contract, may order Changes in the Work within the general scope of the Contract consisting of additions, deletions or other revisions, the Contract Sum and the Contract Time being adjusted

DOCUMENT TO CASE CHARTS: A201-1970

[*The five-digit numbers in this chart are Citator Case Reference Numbers, which refer to the cases, in the Cases section. The suffixes indicate the state or, for federal cases, the court in which the case was decided.*]

accordingly. All such Changes in the Work shall be authorized by Change Order, and shall be executed under the applicable conditions of the Contract Documents.

12.1.2 A Change Order is a written order to the Contractor signed by the Owner and the Architect, issued after the execution of the Contract, authorizing a Change in the Work or an adjustment in the Contract Sum or the Contract Time. Alternatively, the Change Order may be signed by the Architect alone, provided he has written authority from the Owner for such procedure and that a copy of such written authority is furnished to the Contractor upon request. A Change Order may also be signed by the Contractor if he agrees to the adjustment in the Contract Sum or the Contract Time. The Contract Sum and the Contract Time may be changed only by Change Order.

12.1.3 The cost or credit to the Owner resulting from a Change in the Work shall be determined in one or more of the following ways:

.1   by mutual acceptance of a lump sum properly itemized;

.2   by unit prices stated in the Contract Documents or subsequently agreed upon; or

.3   by cost and a mutually acceptable fixed or percentage fee.

12.1.4 If none of the methods set forth in Subparagraph 12.1.3 is agreed upon, the Contractor, provided he receives a Change Order, shall promptly proceed with the Work involved. The cost of such Work shall then be determined by the Architect on the basis of the Contractor's reasonable expenditures and savings, including, in the case of an increase in the Contract Sum, a reasonable allowance for overhead and profit. In such case, and also under Clause 12.1.3.3 above, the Contractor shall keep and present, in such form as the Architect may prescribe, an itemized accounting together with appropriate supporting data. Pending final determination of cost to the Owner, payments on account shall be made on the Architect's Certificate for Payment. The amount of credit to be allowed by the Contractor to the Owner for any deletion or change which results in a net decrease in cost will be the amount of the actual net decrease as confirmed by the Architect. When both additions and credits are involved in any one change, the allowance for overhead and profit shall be figured on the basis of net increase, if any.

12.1.5 If unit prices are stated in the Contract Documents or subsequently agreed upon, and if the quantities originally contemplated are so changed in a proposed Change Order that application of the agreed unit prices to the quantities of Work proposed will create a hardship on the Owner or the Contractor, the applicable unit prices shall be equitably adjusted to prevent such hardship.

12.1.6 Should concealed conditions encountered in the performance of the Work below the surface of the ground be at variance with the conditions indicated by the Contract Documents or should unknown physical conditions below the surface of the ground of an unusual nature, differing materially from those ordinarily encountered and generally recognized as inherent in work of the character provided for in this Contract, be encountered, the Contract Sum shall be equitably adjusted

DOCUMENT TO CASE CHARTS: A201-1970

[The five-digit numbers in this chart are Citator Case Reference Numbers, which refer to the cases, in the Cases section. The suffixes indicate the state or, for federal cases, the court in which the case was decided.]

by Change Order upon claim by either party made within twenty days after the first observance of the conditions.

12.1.7 If the Contractor claims that additional cost is involved because of (1) any written interpretation issued pursuant to Subparagraph 1.2.5, (2) any order by the Owner to stop the Work pursuant to Paragraph 3.3 where the Contractor was not at fault, or (3) any written order for a minor change in the Work issued pursuant to Paragraph 12.3, the Contractor shall make such claim as provided in Paragraph 12.2.

Paragraph 12.1   Change Orders

   I

         73043-FL   75013-NC
         72097-IL   82054-NC
         73104-KS   74036-WI
         75007-KS

   II

         71037-7CIR   72025-FL
         75014-8CIR   72064-NY
         72019-10CIR   84006-TN

   III

         73040-5CIR   72035-MD
         72026-FL   74017-MD
         72054-IL   72014-NY
         73009-IL   73016-NY
         74044-IL   73105-NY
         74028-KS

Text of Paragraph 12.2—Claims for Additional Cost

12.2.1 If the Contractor wishes to make a claim for an increase in the Contract Sum, he shall give the Architect written notice thereof within twenty days after the occurrence of the event giving rise to such claim. This notice shall be given by the Contractor before proceeding to execute the Work, except in an emergency endangering life or property in which case the Contractor shall proceed in accordance with Subparagraph 10.3.1. No such claim shall be valid unless so made. If the Owner and the Contractor cannot agree on the amount of the adjustment in the Contract Sum, it shall be determined by the Architect. Any change in the Contract Sum resulting from such claim shall be authorized by Change Order.

DOCUMENT TO CASE CHARTS: A201-1970 A–212

[The five-digit numbers in this chart are Citator Case Reference Numbers, which refer to the cases, in the Cases section. The suffixes indicate the state or, for federal cases, the court in which the case was decided.]

Paragraph 12.2   Claims for Additional Cost

   I

   73043-FL   75013-NC
   73012-GA   82054-NC
   74007-NC

   II

   73039-5CIR   73042-PA
   75014-8CIR   73034-VA

   III

   72026-FL   72089-NM
   73009-IL   73016-NY
   74013-IL   73105-NY
   73086-IN   73023-SC
   74028-KS   72099-SD
   73074-MA   73044-WI
   65095-NM

Text of Paragraph 12.3—Minor Changes in the Work

12.3.1 The Architect shall have authority to order minor changes in the Work not involving an adjustment in the Contract Sum or an extension of the Contract Time and not inconsistent with the intent of the Contract Documents. Such changes may be effected by Field Order or by other written order. Such changes shall be binding on the Owner and the Contractor.

Paragraph 12.3   Minor Changes in the Work

   I

   75027-DVI
   75013-NC

Text of Paragraph 12.4—Field Orders

12.4.1 The Architect may issue written Field Orders which interpret the Contract Documents in accordance with Subparagraph 1.2.5 or which order minor changes in the Work in accordance with Paragraph 12.3 without change in Contract Sum or Contract Time. The Contractor shall carry out such Field Orders promptly.

Paragraph 12.4   Field Orders

   I

   75013-NC

Article 13   Uncovering and Correction of Work

A–213   DOCUMENT TO CASE CHARTS: A201-1970

[The five-digit numbers in this chart are Citator Case Reference Numbers, which refer to the cases, in the Cases section. The suffixes indicate the state or, for federal cases, the court in which the case was decided.]

Paragraph 13.1   Uncovering of Work

Text of Paragraph 13.2—Correction of Work

13.2.1 The Contractor shall promptly correct all Work rejected by the Architect as defective or as failing to conform to the Contract Documents whether observed before or after Substantial Completion and whether or not fabricated, installed or completed. The Contractor shall bear all cost of correcting such rejected Work, including the cost of the Architect's additional services thereby made necessary.

13.2.2 If, within one year after the Date of Substantial Completion or within such longer period of time as may be prescribed by law or by the terms of any applicable special guarantee required by the Contract Documents, any of the Work is found to be defective or not in accordance with the Contract Documents, the Contractor shall correct it promptly after receipt of a written notice from the Owner to do so unless the Owner has previously given the Contractor a written acceptance of such condition. The Owner shall give such notice promptly after discovery of the condition.

13.2.3 All such defective or non-conforming Work under Subparagraphs 13.2.1 and 13.2.2 shall be removed from the site if necessary, and the Work shall be corrected to comply with the Contract Documents without cost to the Owner.

13.2.4 The Contractor shall bear the cost of making good all work of separate contractors destroyed or damaged by such removal or correction.

13.2.5 If the Contractor does not remove such defective or non-conforming Work within a reasonable time fixed by written notice from the Architect, the Owner may remove it and may store the materials or equipment at the expense of the Contractor. If the Contractor does not pay the cost of such removal and storage within ten days thereafter, the Owner may upon ten additional days' written notice sell such Work at auction or at private sale and shall account for the net proceeds thereof, after deducting all the costs that should have been borne by the Contractor including compensation for additional architectural services. If such proceeds of sale do not cover all costs which the Contractor should have borne, the difference shall be charged to the Contractor and an appropriate Change Order shall be issued. If the payments then or thereafter due the Contractor are not sufficient to cover such amount, the Contractor shall pay the difference to the Owner.

13.2.6 If the Contractor fails to correct such defective or non-conforming Work, the Owner may correct it in accordance with Paragraph 3.4.

DOCUMENT TO CASE CHARTS: A201-1970

A–214

[*The five-digit numbers in this chart are Citator Case Reference Numbers, which refer to the cases, in the Cases section. The suffixes indicate the state or, for federal cases, the court in which the case was decided.*]

Paragraph 13.2   Correction of Work

> I
>
> > 75002-IL
> > 73104-KS
> > 73066-TX
>
> II
>
> > 84006-TN
>
> III
>
> > 72105-NDIA
> > 72030-AZ
> > 75024-NY

Text of Paragraph 13.3—Acceptance of Defective or Non-Conforming Work

13.3.1 If the Owner prefers to accept defective or nonconforming Work, he may do so instead of requiring its removal and correction, in which case a Change Order will be issued to reflect an appropriate reduction in the Contract Sum, or, if the amount is determined after final payment, it shall be paid by the Contractor.

Paragraph 13.3   Acceptance of Defective or Non-Conforming Work

> III
>
> > 72011-1CIR
> > 74024-5CIR

Article 14   Termination of the Contract

Text of Paragraph 14.1—Termination by the Contractor

14.1.1 If the Work is stopped for a period of thirty days under an order of any court or other public authority having jurisdiction, or as a result of an act of government, such as a declaration of a national emergency making materials unavailable, through no act or fault of the Contractor or a Subcontractor or their agents or employees or any other persons performing any of the Work under a contract with the Contractor, or if the Work should be stopped for a period of thirty days by the Contractor for the Architect's failure to issue a Certificate for Payment as provided in Paragraph 9.6 or for the Owner's failure to make payment thereon as provided in Paragraph 9.6, then the Contractor may, upon seven days' written notice to the Owner and the Architect, terminate the Contract and recover from the Owner payment for all Work executed and for any proven loss sustained upon any materials, equipment, tools, construction equipment and machinery, including reasonable profit and damages.

A–215 **DOCUMENT TO CASE CHARTS: A201-1970**

[The five-digit numbers in this chart are Citator Case Reference Numbers, which refer to the cases, in the Cases section. The suffixes indicate the state or, for federal cases, the court in which the case was decided.]

Paragraph 14.1 Termination by the Contractor

    III

        73032-TX
        71033-WA

Text of Paragraph 14.2—Termination by the Owner

14.2.1 If the Contractor is adjudged a bankrupt, or if he makes a general assignment for the benefit of his creditors, or if a receiver is appointed on account of his insolvency, or if he persistently or repeatedly refuses or fails, except in cases for which extension of time is provided, to supply enough properly skilled workmen or proper materials, or if he fails to make prompt payment to Subcontractors or for materials or labor, or persistently disregards laws, ordinances, rules, regulations or orders of any public authority having jurisdiction, or otherwise is guilty of a substantial violation of a provision of the Contract Documents, then the Owner, upon certification by the Architect that sufficient cause exists to justify such action, may, without prejudice to any right or remedy and after giving the Contractor and his surety, if any, seven days' written notice, terminate the employment of the Contractor and take possession of the site and of all materials, equipment, tools, construction equipment and machinery thereon owned by the Contractor and may finish the Work by whatever method he may deem expedient. In such case the Contractor shall not be entitled to receive any further payment until the Work is finished.

14.2.2 If the unpaid balance of the Contract Sum exceeds the Costs of finishing the Work, including compensation for the Architect's additional services, such excess shall be paid to the Contractor. If such costs exceed such unpaid balance, the Contractor shall pay the difference to the Owner. The Costs incurred by the Owner as herein provided shall be certified by the Architect.

Paragraph 14.2 Termination by the Owner

    I

        75028-6CIR
        74011-SDWV
        73095-CA

    III

        74015-IL

DOCUMENT TO CASE CHARTS: A201-1976 A–216

[The five-digit numbers in this chart are Citator Case Reference Numbers, which refer to the cases, in the Cases section. The suffixes indicate the state or, for federal cases, the court in which the case was decided.]

A201-1976—GENERAL CONDITIONS OF THE CONTRACT FOR CONSTRUCTION

Article 1   Contract Documents

Text of Paragraph 1.1—Definitions

1.1.1 THE CONTRACT DOCUMENTS

The Contract Documents consist of the Owner-Contractor Agreement, the Conditions of the Contract (General, Supplementary and other Conditions), the Drawings, the Specifications, and all Addenda issued prior to and all Modifications issued after execution of the Contract. A Modification is (1) a written amendment to the Contract signed by both parties, (2) a Change Order, (3) a written interpretation issued by the Architect pursuant to Sub-paragraph 2.2.8, or (4) a written order for a minor change in the Work issued by the Architect pursuant to Paragraph 12.4. The Contract Documents do not include Bidding Documents such as the Advertisement or Invitation to Bid, the Instructions to Bidders, sample forms, the Contractor's Bid or portions of Addenda relating to any of these, or any other documents, unless specifically enumerated in the Owner-Contractor Agreement.

1.1.2 THE CONTRACT

The Contract Documents form the Contract for Construction. This Contract represents the entire and integrated agreement between the parties hereto and supersedes all prior negotiations, representations, or agreements, either written or oral. The Contract may be amended or modified only by a Modification as defined in Subparagraph 1.1.1. The Contract Documents shall not be construed to create any contractual relationship of any kind between the Architect and the Contractor, but the Architect shall be entitled to performance of obligations intended for his benefit, and to enforcement thereof. Nothing contained in the Contract Documents shall create any contractual relationship between the Owner or the Architect and any Subcontractor or Sub-subcontractor.

1.1.3 THE WORK

The Work comprises the completed construction required by the Contract Documents and includes all labor necessary to produce such construction, and all materials and equipment incorporated or to be incorporated in such construction.

1.1.4 THE PROJECT

The Project is the total construction of which the Work performed under the Contract Documents may be the whole or a part.

DOCUMENT TO CASE CHARTS: A201-1976

[The five-digit numbers in this chart are Citator Case Reference Numbers, which refer to the cases, in the Cases section. The suffixes indicate the state or, for federal cases, the court in which the case was decided.]

Paragraph 1.1   Definitions

    I

        88027-3CIR   82034-MS
        90050-7CIR   84038-MO
        85017-DDE   82052-NV
        91008-MDPA   76032-NJ
        93010-SDNY   91034-NM
        90002-CO   78004-NY
        92008-DC   90043-NY
        89027-FL   79004-NC
        91006-FL   88016-OH
        79005-GA   77030-SC
        91002-GA   87046-SC
        76030-ID   85029-TN
        77012-IL   87029-TX
        83020-KS   87007-VA
        93022-ME   87036-WA
        86028-MA

    II

        88017-DDE   90042-KS
        76017-EDWA   89049-MA
        77028-AZ   90020-OH
        86061-FL   91017-TN

    III

        81052-NDAL   77060-MT
        90039-WDNC   79011-MT
        91019-AL   91007-NM
        92014a-AL   76016-NY
        77044-CA   77076-NY
        78032-CA   78062-NY
        83048-CA   79001-NY
        76049-IL   90016-NY
        77073-IL   79061-NC
        81030-LA   86018-NC
        81031-LA   82047-OH
        84033-LA   86039-OK
        77010-MD   76066-PA
        89026-MO   90021-SC

Paragraph 1.1.1   The Contract Documents

    I

        95023-VA

Text of Paragraph 1.2—Execution, Correlation and Intent

1.2.1 The Contract Documents shall be signed in not less than triplicate by the Owner and Contractor. If either the Owner or the Contractor or both do not sign the Conditions of the Contract, Drawings, Specifications, or any of the other Contract Documents, the Architect shall identify such Documents.

DOCUMENT TO CASE CHARTS: A201-1976   A–218

[The five-digit numbers in this chart are Citator Case Reference Numbers, which refer to the cases, in the Cases section. The suffixes indicate the state or, for federal cases, the court in which the case was decided.]

1.2.2 By executing the Contract, the Contractor represents that he has visited the site, familiarized himself with the local conditions under which the Work is to be performed, and correlated his observations with the requirements of the Contract Documents.

1.2.3 The intent of the Contract Documents is to include all items necessary for the proper execution and completion of the Work. The Contract Documents are complementary, and what is required by any one shall be as binding as if required by all. Work not covered in the Contract Documents will not be required unless it is consistent therewith and is reasonably inferable therefrom as being necessary to produce the intended results. Words and abbreviations which have well-known technical or trade meanings are used in the Contract Documents in accordance with such recognized meanings.

1.2.4 The organization of the Specifications into divisions, sections and articles, and the arrangement of Drawings shall not control the Contractor in dividing the Work among Subcontractors or in establishing the extent of Work to be performed by any trade.

Paragraph 1.2   Execution, Correlation and Intent

    I

        82004-SDGA   84038-MO
        82032-DKS   91034-NM
        79034-AZ   77030-SC

    II

        90039-WDNC
        76045-AK

    III

        83013-1CIR   89019-KS
        90048-10CIR   77010-MD
        90008-CC   83041-PA
        83048-CA   77020-WA

Text of Paragraph 1.3—Ownership and Use of Documents

1.3.1 All Drawings, Specifications and copies thereof furnished by the Architect are and shall remain his property. They are to be used only with respect to this Project and are not to be used on any other project. With the exception of one contract set for each party to the Contract, such documents are to be returned or suitably accounted for to the Architect on request at the completion of the Work. Submission or distribution to meet official regulatory requirements or for other purposes in connection with the Project is not to be construed as publication in derogation of the Architect's common law copyright or other reserved rights.

DOCUMENT TO CASE CHARTS: A201-1976

[The five-digit numbers in this chart are Citator Case Reference Numbers, which refer to the cases, in the Cases section. The suffixes indicate the state or, for federal cases, the court in which the case was decided.]

Paragraph 1.3 Ownership and Use of Documents

    I

        85024-NDIL

Article 2 Architect

Text of Paragraph 2.1—Definition

2.1.1 The Architect is the person lawfully licensed to practice architecture, or an entity lawfully practicing architecture identified as such in the Owner-Contractor Agreement, and is referred to throughout the Contract Documents as if singular in number and masculine in gender. The term Architect means the Architect or his authorized representative.

Paragraph 2.1 Definition

    I

        78024-GA
        83020-KS
        88012-LA

    III

        88004-NY

Text of Paragraph 2.2—Administration of the Contract

2.2.1 The Architect will provide administration of the Contract as hereinafter described.

2.2.2 The Architect will be the Owner's representative during construction and until final payment is due. The Architect will advise and consult with the Owner. The Owner's instructions to the Contractor shall be forwarded through the Architect. The Architect will have authority to act on behalf of the Owner only to the extent provided in the Contract Documents, unless otherwise modified by written instrument in accordance with Subparagraph 2.2.18.

2.2.3 The Architect will visit the site at intervals appropriate to the stage of construction to familiarize himself generally with the progress and quality of the Work and to determine in general if the Work is proceeding in accordance with the Contract Documents. However, the Architect will not be required to make exhaustive or continuous on-site inspections to check the quality or quantity of the Work. On the basis of his on-site observations as an architect, he will keep the Owner informed of the progress of the Work, and will endeavor to guard the Owner against defects and deficiencies in the Work of the Contractor.

2.2.4 The Architect will not be responsible for and will not have control or charge of construction means, methods, techniques, sequences or procedures, or for safety precautions and programs in connection with the Work, and he will not be

DOCUMENT TO CASE CHARTS: A201-1976 A–220

[*The five-digit numbers in this chart are Citator Case Reference Numbers, which refer to the cases, in the Cases section. The suffixes indicate the state or, for federal cases, the court in which the case was decided.*]

responsible for the Contractor's failure to carry out the Work in accordance with the Contract Documents. The Architect will not be responsible for or have control or charge over the acts or omissions of the Contractor, Subcontractors, or any of their agents or employees, or any other persons performing any of the Work.

2.2.5 The Architect shall at all times have access to the Work wherever it is in preparation and progress. The Contractor shall provide facilities for such access so the Architect may perform his functions under the Contract Documents.

2.2.6 Based on the Architect's observations and an evaluation of the Contractor's Applications for Payment, the Architect will determine the amounts owing to the Contractor and will issue Certificates for Payment in such amounts, as provided in Paragraph 9.4.

2.2.7 The Architect will be the interpreter of the requirements of the Contract Documents and the judge of the performance thereunder by both the Owner and Contractor.

2.2.8 The Architect will render interpretations necessary for the proper execution or progress of the Work, with reasonable promptness and in accordance with any time limit agreed upon. Either party to the Contract may make written request to the Architect for such interpretations.

2.2.9 Claims, disputes and other matters in question between the Contractor and the Owner relating to the execution or progress of the Work or the interpretation of the Contract Documents shall be referred initially to the Architect for decision which he will render in writing within a reasonable time.

2.2.10 All interpretations and decisions of the Architect shall be consistent with the intent of and reasonably inferable from the Contract Documents and will be in writing or in the form of drawings. In his capacity as interpreter and judge, he will endeavor to secure faithful performance by both the Owner and the Contractor, will not show partiality to either, and will not be liable for the result of any interpretation or decision rendered in good faith in such capacity.

2.2.11 The Architect's decisions in matters relating to artistic effect will be final if consistent with the intent of the Contract Documents.

2.2.12 Any claim, dispute or other matter in question between the Contractor and the Owner referred to the Architect, except those relating to artistic effect as provided in Subparagraph 2.2.11 and except those which have been waived by the making or acceptance of final payment as provided in Subparagraphs 9.9.4 and 9.9.5, shall be subject to arbitration upon the written demand of either party. However, no demand for arbitration of any such claim, dispute or other matter may be made until the earlier of (1) the date on which the Architect has rendered a written decision, or (2) the tenth day after the parties have presented their evidence to the Architect or have been given a reasonable opportunity to do so, if the Architect has not rendered his written decision by that date. When such a written decision of the Architect states (1) that the decision is final but subject to appeal, and (2) that any demand for arbitration of a claim, dispute or other matter covered by such decision must be made within thirty days after the date on which the party making the demand receives the written decision, failure to demand arbitration within said thirty days' period will result in the Architect's decision becoming final and binding upon the Owner and the Contractor. If the Architect renders a decision after arbitration proceedings have been initiated, such decision may be entered as evidence but will not supersede any arbitration proceedings unless the decision is acceptable to all parties concerned.

2.2.13 The Architect will have authority to reject Work which does not conform to the Contract Documents. Whenever, in his opinion, he considers it necessary or advisable for the implementation of the intent of the Contract Documents, he will have authority to require special inspection or testing of the Work in accordance with Subparagraph 7.7.2 whether or not such Work be then fabricated, installed or completed. However, neither the Architect's authority to act under this Subparagraph 2.2.13, nor any decision made by him in good faith either to exercise or not to exercise such authority, shall give rise to any duty or responsibility of the Architect to the Contractor, any Subcontractor, any of their agents or employees, or any other person performing any of the Work.

2.2.14 The Architect will review and approve or take other appropriate action upon Contractor's submittals such as Shop Drawings, Product Data and Samples, but only for conformance with the design concept of the Work and with the information given in the Contract Documents. Such action shall be taken with reasonable promptness so as to cause no delay. The Architect's approval of a specific item shall not indicate approval of an assembly of which the item is a component.

2.2.15 The Architect will prepare Change Orders in accordance with Article 12, and will have authority to order minor changes in the Work as provided in Subparagraph 12.4.1.

2.2.16 The Architect will conduct inspections to determine the dates of Substantial Completion and final completion, will receive and forward to the Owner for the Owner's review written warranties and related documents required by the Contract and assembled by the Contractor, and will issue a final Certificate for Payment upon compliance with the requirements of Paragraph 9.9.

2.2.17 If the Owner and Architect agree, the Architect will provide one or more Project Representatives to assist the Architect in carrying out his responsibilities at the site. The duties, responsibilities and limitations of authority of any such Project Representative shall be as set forth in an exhibit to be incorporated in the Contract Documents.

2.2.18 The duties, responsibilities and limitations of authority of the Architect as the Owner's representative during construction as set forth in the Contract Documents will not be modified or extended without written consent of the Owner, the Contractor and the Architect.

2.2.19 In case of the termination of the employment of the Architect, the Owner shall appoint an architect against whom the Contractor makes no reasonable

DOCUMENT TO CASE CHARTS: A201-1976

[The five-digit numbers in this chart are Citator Case Reference Numbers, which refer to the cases, in the Cases section. The suffixes indicate the state or, for federal cases, the court in which the case was decided.]

> objection whose status under the Contract Documents shall be that of the former architect. Any dispute in connection with such appointment shall be subject to arbitration.

Paragraph 2.2 Administration of the Contract

    I

81061-3CIR	92006-ME
89022-5CIR	83042-MD
82020-6CIR	89035-MD
81037-7CIR	89037-MD
83023-8CIR	88024-MA
82004-SDGA	77027-MS
81018-AR	86064-MO
78076-CO	91038-MO
76051-CT	77032-NE
79051-DE	76021-NV
79012-FL	77083-NJ
83030-FL	76048-NY
78024-GA	76053-NY
82024-GA	77003-NY
91040-GA	77064-NY
93013-GA	81057-NY
77012-IL	83047-NY
77029-IL	84007-NY
78045-IL	84019-NY
79029-IL	89003-NY
80020-IL	89012-NY
84034-IL	91028-NY
90040-IL	88031-NC
83020-KS	78052-ND
89008-KS	82056-OK
83003-LA	84027-TX
86071-LA	87026-TX
88012-LA	80061-VT
	85014-WY

    II

89022-5CIR	89023-MI
83032-7CIR	77061-MN
90048-10CIR	89047-MS
91031-MDPA	86032-MO
76017-EDWA	87050-MO
87047-AL	88014-MO
90052-AL	90006-NE
77028-AZ	76028-NY
92018-CT	77037-NY
77002-DC	77047-NY
81029-FL	83024-NY
78056-GA	89004-NY
81014-IL	90051-NY
89030-IL	89005-NC
91001-IN	87002-ND
91030-IA	90020-OH
76010-LA	91020-VT
	89033-VA

DOCUMENT TO CASE CHARTS: A201-1976

[The five-digit numbers in this chart are Citator Case Reference Numbers, which refer to the cases, in the Cases section. The suffixes indicate the state or, for federal cases, the court in which the case was decided.]

III

82041-10CIR	88041-LA
90048-10CIR	91032-LA
91037-11CIR	78047-MD
82014-NDMS	82010-MD
82057-AL	83002-MA
87037-AL	86034-MA
83006-AR	90035-MA
77044-CA	92008d-MI
77086-CA	90030-MS
75032-CT	91024-MT
86029-CT	82015-NH
92020a-CT	82007-NJ
85037-FL	81005-NY
90031-FL	85026-NY
81040-GA	86047-NY
76049-IL	88035a-NY
77058-IL	79008-OR
78019-IL	79033-PA
79010-IL	86010-PA
85006-IL	90029-PA
87030-IL	80009-SD
92004-IL	87009-TN
82028-IN	90055-TX
91001-IN	77022-VA
76063-IA	88025-VA
86035-KS	87025-WI
80074-LA	

Paragraph 2.2.2

III

90056-LA

Paragraph 2.2.3

I

93036-NE

III

90056-LA

Paragraph 2.2.4

I

94038-FL

III

90056-LA

DOCUMENT TO CASE CHARTS: A201-1976

[*The five-digit numbers in this chart are Citator Case Reference Numbers, which refer to the cases, in the Cases section. The suffixes indicate the state or, for federal cases, the court in which the case was decided.*]

Paragraph 2.2.7

I

95033-MO

Paragraph 2.2.9

I

95033-MO

Paragraph 2.2.12

I

95033-MO

Article 3 Owner

Paragraph 3.1 Definition

Text of Paragraph 3.2—Information and Services Required of the Owner

3.2.1 The Owner shall, at the request of the Contractor, at the time of execution of the Owner-Contractor Agreement, furnish to the Contractor reasonable evidence that he has made financial arrangements to fulfill his obligations under the Contract. Unless such reasonable evidence is furnished, the Contractor is not required to execute the Owner-Contractor Agreement or to commence the Work.

3.2.2 The Owner shall furnish all surveys describing the physical characteristics, legal limitations and utility locations for the site of the Project, and a legal description of the site.

3.2.3 Except as provided in Subparagraph 4.7.1, the Owner shall secure and pay for necessary approvals, easements, assessments and charges required for the construction, use or occupancy of permanent structures or for permanent changes in existing facilities.

3.2.4 Information or services under the Owner's control shall be furnished by the Owner with reasonable promptness to avoid delay in the orderly progress of the Work.

3.2.5 Unless otherwise provided in the Contract Documents, the Contractor will be furnished, free of charge, all Copies of Drawings and Specifications reasonably necessary for the execution of the Work.

3.2.6 The Owner shall forward all instructions to the Contractor through the Architect.

3.2.7 The foregoing are in addition to other duties and responsibilities of the Owner enumerated herein and especially those in respect to Work by Owner or by Separate Contractors, Payments and Completion, and Insurance in Articles 6, 9 and 11 respectively.

DOCUMENT TO CASE CHARTS: A201-1976

[The five-digit numbers in this chart are Citator Case Reference Numbers, which refer to the cases, in the Cases section. The suffixes indicate the state or, for federal cases, the court in which the case was decided.]

Paragraph 3.2   Information and Services Required of the Owner

   I

      85032-IN
      79004-NC
      85029-TN

   II

      76001-EDAR
      86006-IL

   III

76061-NDGA	77039-NY
83048-CA	78029-NY
83019-CO	78079-NY
78039-FL	85014a-OK
77007-HI	76011-PA
79009-MD	76009-TX
76023-NJ	77040-TX

Text of Paragraph 3.3—Owner's Right to Stop the Work

3.3.1 If the Contractor fails to correct defective Work as required by Paragraph 13.2 or persistently fails to carry out the Work in accordance with the Contract Documents, the Owner, by a written order signed personally or by an agent specifically so empowered by the Owner in writing, may order the Contractor to stop the Work, or any portion thereof, until the cause for such order has been eliminated; however, this right of the Owner to stop the Work shall not give rise to any duty on the part of the Owner to exercise this right for the benefit of the Contractor or any other person or entity, except to the extent required by Subparagraph 6.1.3.

Paragraph 3.3   Owner's Right to Stop the Work

   I

      90032-IL
      83020-KS
      89016-NY

   III

      87037-AL
      78055-IL

Text of Paragraph 3.4—Owner's Right to Carry Out the Work

3.4.1 If the Contractor defaults or neglects to carry out the Work in accordance with the Contract Documents and fails within seven days after receipt of written notice from the Owner to commence and continue correction of such default or neglect with diligence and promptness, the Owner may, after seven days following receipt by the Contractor of an additional written notice and without prejudice to any other remedy he may have, make good such deficiencies. In such case an

DOCUMENT TO CASE CHARTS: A201-1976

A–226

[*The five-digit numbers in this chart are Citator Case Reference Numbers, which refer to the cases, in the Cases section. The suffixes indicate the state or, for federal cases, the court in which the case was decided.*]

> appropriate Change Order shall be issued deducting from the payments then or thereafter due the Contractor the cost of correcting such deficiencies, including compensation for the Architect's additional services made necessary by such default, neglect or failure. Such action by the Owner and the amount charged to the Contractor are both subject to the prior approval of the Architect. If the payments then or thereafter due the Contractor are not sufficient to cover such amount, the Contractor shall pay the difference to the Owner.

Paragraph 3.4   Owner's Right to Carry Out the Work

    I

        89016-NY
        78052-ND
        81067-WY

    II

        88010-CO

    III

        87037-AL
        78055-IL
        87009-TN

Article 4   **Contractor**

Paragraph 4.1   Definition

> ### Text of Paragraph 4.2—Review of the Contract Documents
>
> **4.2.1** Tile Contractor shall carefully study and compare the Contract Documents and shall at once report to the Architect any error, inconsistency or omission he may discover. The Contractor shall not be liable to the Owner or the Architect for any damage resulting from any such errors, inconsistencies or omissions in the Contract Documents. The Contractor shall perform no portion of the Work at any time without Contract Documents or, where required, approved Shop Drawings, Product Data or Samples for such portion of the Work.

Paragraph 4.2   Review of the Contract Documents

    I

        82004-SDGA
        82032-DKS
        77063-WA

A-227   DOCUMENT TO CASE CHARTS: A201-1976

[The five-digit numbers in this chart are Citator Case Reference Numbers, which refer to the cases, in the Cases section. The suffixes indicate the state or, for federal cases, the court in which the case was decided.]

 II

  90039-WDNC
  90020-OH
  84027-TX

 III

  78037-AR   79001-NY
  76025-IL   79008-OR
  84002-MN   86010-PA
  78015-NY

Text of Paragraph 4.3—Supervision and Construction Procedures

4.3.1 The Contractor shall supervise and direct the Work, using his best skill and attention. He shall be solely responsible for all construction means, methods, techniques, sequences and procedures and for coordinating all portions of the Work under the Contract.

4.3.2 The Contractor shall be responsible to the Owner for the acts and omissions of his employees, Subcontractors and their agents and employees, and other persons performing any of the Work under a contract with the Contractor.

4.3.3 The Contractor shall not be relieved from his obligations to perform the Work in accordance with the Contract Documents either by the activities or duties of the Architect in his administration of the Contract, or by inspections, tests or approvals required or performed under Paragraph 7.7 by persons other than the Contractor.

Paragraph 4.3 Supervision and Construction Procedures

 I

  82020-6CIR   78038-NY
  82004-SDGA   83047-NY
  95020-DPR   89016-NY
  78074-AL   78052-ND
  84029-DC   87002-ND
  91040-GA   82056-OK
  93013-GA   87026-TX
  81044-IL   80061-VT
  88033-IL   87011-VA
  83020-KS

 II

  83010-5CIR   82001-NE
  78056-GA   88028-NJ
  82018-IN   83024-NY
  84015-IN   84019-NY
  91001-IN   80035-TX

DOCUMENT TO CASE CHARTS: A201-1976

[The five-digit numbers in this chart are Citator Case Reference Numbers, which refer to the cases, in the Cases section. The suffixes indicate the state or, for federal cases, the court in which the case was decided.]

III

83007-7CIR	78047-MD
82014-NDMS	83002-MA
85003a-AL	82007-NJ
87037-AL	76024-NY
77073-IL	90029-PA
78019-IL	82017-TN
79070-IL	87009-TN
92004-IL	79002-VT
82028-IN	77020-WA
86035-KS	

Paragraph 4.3.1

I

94038-FL
93025-IL

Paragraph 4.3.2

I

93025-IL

Text of Paragraph 4.4—Labor and Materials

4.4.1 Unless otherwise provided in the Contract documents, the Contractor shall provide and pay for all labor, materials, equipment, tools, construction equipment and machinery, water, heat, utilities, transportation, and other facilities and services necessary for the proper execution and completion of the Work, whether temporary or permanent and whether or not incorporated or to be incorporated in the Work.

4.4.2 The Contractor shall at all times enforce strict discipline and good order among his employees and shall not employ on the Work any unfit person or anyone not skilled in the task assigned to him.

Paragraph 4.4   Labor and Materials

I

88042-KY
80048-MA
85033-NE

II

90039-WDNC	82021-NY
78056-GA	83024-NY
84032-GA	

DOCUMENT TO CASE CHARTS: A201-1976

[The five-digit numbers in this chart are Citator Case Reference Numbers, which refer to the cases, in the Cases section. The suffixes indicate the state or, for federal cases, the court in which the case was decided.]

III

85003a-AL 91007-NM
78061-IL 78057-MO

Text of Paragraph 4.5—Warranty

4.5.1 The Contractor warrants to the Owner and the Architect that all materials and equipment furnished under this Contract will be new unless otherwise specified, and that all Work will be of good quality, free from faults and defects and in conformance with the Contract Documents. All Work not conforming to these requirements, including substitutions not properly approved and authorized, may be considered defective. If required by the Architect, the Contractor shall furnish satisfactory evidence as to the kind and quality of materials and equipment. This warranty is not limited by the provisions of Paragraph 13.2.

Paragraph 4.5 Warranty

I

79057-4CIR 93025-IL
82020-6CIR 79043-LA
90050-7CIR 82009-LA
84029-DC 82048-NE
88005-FL 90026-NE
92015-GA 85023-NY
90040-IL 78052-ND
91025-IL

II

91013-SDMS 79021-NM
88033-IL 79067-NY
86065-NJ 83024-NY

III

89001-4CIR 76050-MD
82014-NDMS 79072-MO
80012-AL 80010-MT
93004-AL 84031-NE
81007-GA 76027-NY
80024-IN 77051-NY
86052-IN 77001-ND
86035-KS 77038-PA
83005-LA 87009-TN
81050-ME

Text of Paragraph 4.6—Taxes

4.6.1 The Contractor shall pay all sales, consumer, use and other similar taxes for the Work or portions thereof provided by the Contractor which are legally enacted at the time bids are received, whether or not yet effective.

DOCUMENT TO CASE CHARTS: A201-1976

[The five-digit numbers in this chart are Citator Case Reference Numbers, which refer to the cases, in the Cases section. The suffixes indicate the state or, for federal cases, the court in which the case was decided.]

Paragraph 4.6 Taxes

    II

        82038-WA

Text of Paragraph 4.7—Permits, Fees and Notices

4.7.1 Unless otherwise provided in the Contract Documents, the Contractor shall secure and pay for the building permit and for all other permits and governmental fees, licenses and inspections necessary for the proper execution and completion of the Work which are customarily secured after execution of the Contract and which are legally required at the time the bids are received.

4.7.2 The Contractor shall give all notices and comply with all laws, ordinances, rules, regulations and lawful orders of any public authority bearing on the performance of the Work.

4.7.3 It is not the responsibility of the Contractor to make certain that the Contract Documents are in accordance with applicable laws, statutes, building codes and regulations. If the Contractor observes that any of the Contract Documents are at variance therewith in any respect, he shall promptly notify the Architect in writing, and any necessary changes shall be accomplished by appropriate Modification.

4.7.4 If the Contractor performs any Work knowing it to be contrary to such laws, ordinances, rules and regulations, and without such notice to the Architect, he shall assume full responsibility therefor and shall bear all costs attributable thereto.

Paragraph 4.7 Permits, Fees and Notices

    I

        78007-FL   85033-NE
        86072-LA   77063-WA

    II

        82018-IN
        79067-NY
        82021-NY

    III

        86009-OH
        76014-PA
        89033-VA

Paragraph 4.8 Allowances

Paragraph 4.9 Superintendent

DOCUMENT TO CASE CHARTS: A201-1976

[The five-digit numbers in this chart are Citator Case Reference Numbers, which refer to the cases, in the Cases section. The suffixes indicate the state or, for federal cases, the court in which the case was decided.]

Text of Paragraph 4.10—Progress Schedule

4.10.1 The Contractor, immediately after being awarded the Contract, shall prepare and submit for the Owner's and Architect's information an estimated progress schedule or the Work. The progress schedule shall be related to the entire Project to the extent required by the Contract Documents, and shall provide for expeditious and practicable execution of the Work.

Paragraph 4.10 Progress Schedule

    I

        85029-TN

    III

        83007-7CIR

Paragraph 4.11 Documents and Samples at the Site

Text of Paragraph 4.12—Shop Drawings, Product Data and Samples

4.12.1 Shop Drawings are drawings, diagrams, schedules and other data specially prepared for the Work by the Contractor or any Subcontractor, manufacturer, supplier or distributor to illustrate some portion of the Work.

4.12.2 Product Data are illustrations, standard schedules, performance charts, instructions, brochures, diagrams and other information furnished by the Contractor to illustrate a material, product or system for some portion of the Work.

4.12.3 Samples are physical examples which illustrate materials, equipment or workmanship and establish standards by which the Work will be judged.

4.12.4 The Contractor shall review, approve and submit, with reasonable promptness and in such sequence as to cause no delay in the Work or in the work of the Owner or any separate contractor, all Shop Drawings, Product Data and Samples required by the Contract Documents.

4.12.5 By approving and submitting Shop Drawings, Product Data and Samples, the Contractor represents that he has determined and verified all materials, field measurements, and field construction criteria related thereto, or will do so, and that he has checked and coordinated the information contained within such submittals with the requirements of the Work and of the Contract Documents.

4.12.6 The Contractor shall not be relieved of responsibility for any deviation from the requirements of the Contract Documents by the Architect's approval of Shop Drawings, Product Data or Samples under Subparagraph 2.2.14 unless the Contractor has specifically informed the Architect in writing of such deviation at the time of submission and the Architect has given written approval to the specific deviation. The Contractor shall not be relieved from responsibility for errors or

DOCUMENT TO CASE CHARTS: A201-1976

A-232

[The five-digit numbers in this chart are Citator Case Reference Numbers, which refer to the cases, in the Cases section. The suffixes indicate the state or, for federal cases, the court in which the case was decided.]

omissions in the Shop Drawings, Product Data or Samples by the Architect's approval thereof.

4.12.7 The Contractor shall direct specific attention, in writing or on resubmitted Shop Drawings, Product Data or Samples, to revisions other than those requested by the Architect on previous submittals.

4.12.8 No portion of the Work requiring submission of a Shop Drawing, Product Data or Sample shall be commenced until the submittal has been approved by the Architect as provided in Subparagraph 2.2.14. All such portions of the Work shall be in accordance with approved submittals.

Paragraph 4.12 Shop Drawings, Product Data and Samples

    I

        82020-6CIR   77032-NE
        83023-8CIR   82056-OK

    II

        76010-LA
        76028-NY

    III

        83002-MA
        78029-NY
        89033-VA

Text of Paragraph 4.13—Use of Site

4.13.1 The Contractor shall confine operations at the site to areas permitted by law, ordinances, permits and the Contract Documents and shall not unreasonably encumber the site with any materials or equipment.

Paragraph 4.13 Use of Site

    I

        83022-MO
        85029-TN

    III

        86018-NC

Text of Paragraph 4.14—Cutting and Patching of Work

4.14.1 The Contractor shall be responsible for all cutting, fitting or patching that may be required to complete the Work or to make its several parts fit together properly.

4.14.2 The Contractor shall not damage or endanger any portion of the Work or the work of the Owner or any separate contractors by cutting, patching or otherwise altering any work, or by excavation. The Contractor shall not cut or

DOCUMENT TO CASE CHARTS: A201-1976

[The five-digit numbers in this chart are Citator Case Reference Numbers, which refer to the cases, in the Cases section. The suffixes indicate the state or, for federal cases, the court in which the case was decided.]

> otherwise alter the work of the Owner or any separate contractor except with the written consent of the Owner and of such separate contractor. The Contractor shall not unreasonably withhold from the Owner or any separate contractor his consent to cutting or otherwise altering the Work.

Paragraph 4.14 Cutting and Patching of Work

    I

        85029-TN

   III

        86018-NC

Text of Paragraph 4.15—Cleaning Up

4.15.1 The Contractor at all times shall keep the premises free from accumulation of waste materials or rubbish caused by his operations. At the completion of the Work he shall remove all his waste materials and rubbish from and about the Project as well as all his tools, construction equipment, machinery and surplus materials.

4.15.2 If the Contractor fails to clean up at the completion of the Work, the Owner may do so as provided in Paragraph 3.4 and the cost thereof shall be charged to the Contractor.

Paragraph 4.15 Cleaning Up

    II

        79067-NY

Paragraph 4.16 Communications

Paragraph 4.17 Royalties and Patents

Text of Paragraph 4.18—Indemnification

4.18.1 To the fullest extent permitted by law, the Contractor shall indemnify and hold harmless the Owner and the Architect and their agents and employees from and against all claims, damages, losses and expenses, including but not limited to attorneys' fees, arising out of or resulting from the performance of the Work, provided that any such claim, damage, loss or expense (1) is attributable to bodily injury, sickness, disease or death, or to injury to or destruction of tangible property (other than the Work itself) including the loss of use resulting therefrom, and (2) is caused in whole or in part by any negligent act or omission of the Contractor, any Subcontractor, anyone directly or indirectly employed by any of them or anyone for whose acts any of them may be liable, regardless of whether or not it is caused in part by a party indemnified hereunder. Such obligation shall not be construed to negate, abridge, or otherwise reduce any other right or obligation of indemnity

DOCUMENT TO CASE CHARTS: A201-1976

[The five-digit numbers in this chart are Citator Case Reference Numbers, which refer to the cases, in the Cases section. The suffixes indicate the state or, for federal cases, the court in which the case was decided.]

which would otherwise exist as to any party or person described in this Paragraph 4.18.

4.18.2 In any and all claims against the Owner or the Architect or any of their agents or employees by any employee of the Contractor, any Subcontractor, anyone directly or indirectly employed by any of them or anyone for whose acts any of them may be liable, the indemnification obligation under this Paragraph 4.18 shall not be limited in any way by any limitation on the amount or type of damages, compensation or benefits payable by or for the Contractor or any Subcontractor under workers' or workmen's compensation acts, disability benefit acts or other employee benefit acts.

4.18.3 The obligations of the Contractor under this Paragraph 4.18 shall not extend to the liability of the Architect, his agents or employees, arising out of (1) the preparation or approval of maps, drawings, opinions, reports, surveys, change orders, designs or specifications, or (2) the giving of or the failure to give directions or instructions by the Architect, his agents or employees provided such giving or failure to give is the primary cause of the injury or damage.

Paragraph 4.18   Indemnification

I
```
        80007-8CIR              80071-MA
        84014-8CIR              81072-MA
        84017-8CIR              80054-MI
        81012-AL                88026-MN
        91036-AZ                92003-MO
        90002-CO                92003a-MO
        87013-FL                88001-NY
        77013-GA                79042-NC
        81046-GA                89025-NC
        76030-ID                92010b-OH
        86068-IL                92008a-PA
        79063-IN                87026-TX
        83040-LA                91010-TX
        89036-LA                87011-VA
        90056-LA                83050-WY
```

II
```
        80042-DMD               85008-MN
        90013-AL                91036a-MO
        89021-CA                78020-NV
        80056-IL                79021-NM
        84028-IL                87048-NM
        85019-IL                77017-NY
        86013-IL                85038-NY
        82018-IN                89015-NY
        91001-IN                85013-TN
        90042-KS                79040-TX
        83038-LA                86058-TX
        81013-MA                87019-TX
        91017-MA                84005-WA
        93018-MA                85016-WA
```

DOCUMENT TO CASE CHARTS: A201-1976

[The five-digit numbers in this chart are Citator Case Reference Numbers, which refer to the cases, in the Cases section. The suffixes indicate the state or, for federal cases, the court in which the case was decided.]

III

89001-4CIR	85015a-IL
81051-5CIR	87008-IL
83007-7CIR	87042-IL
87010-DME	76031-IN
85011-AK	91023-IN
86022-AK	86050-IA
91009-AL	76036-LA
92014a-AL	86063-MA
76029-CA	89028-MA
77056-CA	85035-MI
78028-CA	87020-MI
79016-CA	76067-MO
85025-CA	86043-MT
85034-CA	76056-NY
87035-CA	77043-NY
86001-CT	78062-NY
80053-FL	81070-NY
79041-GA	87016-NY
88040-GA	92007-NY
90036-GA	91029-ND
85015-HI	91039-PA
77016-IL	88002-TX
77024-IL	85028-WA
77062-IL	86057-WA
77071-IL	89041-WV
78055-IL	82023-WI
78061-IL	84013-WI
80073-IL	

Paragraph 4.18.1

I

95011-MI
93043-PA

II

93053-MN	95036-TX
94009-TX	93040-WI

III

93051-DC	93039-NY
94013-LA	93031-PA
93047-MN	

Article 5 Subcontractors

Text of Paragraph 5.1—Definition

5.1.1 A Subcontractor is a person or entity who has a direct contract with the Contractor to perform any of the Work at the site. The term Subcontractor is referred to throughout the Contract Documents as if singular in number and masculine in gender and means a Subcontractor or his authorized representative. The term Subcontractor does not include any separate contractor or his subcontractors.

DOCUMENT TO CASE CHARTS: A201-1976

[*The five-digit numbers in this chart are Citator Case Reference Numbers, which refer to the cases, in the Cases section. The suffixes indicate the state or, for federal cases, the court in which the case was decided.*]

5.1.2 A Sub-subcontractor is a person or entity who has a direct or indirect contract with a Subcontractor to perform any of the Work at the site. The term Sub-subcontractor is referred to throughout the Contract Documents as if singular in number and masculine in gender and means a Sub-subcontractor or an authorized representative thereof.

Paragraph 5.1   Definition

    I

       90002-CO

Paragraph 5.1.1

    I

       93025-IL

Text of Paragraph 5.2—Award of Subcontracts and Other Contracts for Portions of the Work

5.2.1 Unless otherwise required by the Contract Documents or the Bidding Documents, the Contractor, as soon as practicable after the award of the Contract, shall furnish to the Owner and the Architect in writing the names of the persons or entities (including those who are to furnish materials or equipment fabricated to a special design) proposed for each of the principal portions of the Work. The Architect will promptly reply to the Contractor in writing stating whether or not the Owner or the Architect, after due investigation, has reasonable objection to any such proposed person or entity. Failure of the Owner or Architect to reply promptly shall constitute notice of no reasonable objection.

5.2.2 The Contractor shall not contract with any such proposed person or entity to whom the Owner or the Architect has made reasonable objection under the provisions of Subparagraph 5.2.1. The Contractor shall not be required to contract with anyone to whom he has a reasonable objection.

5.2.3 If the Owner or the Architect has reasonable objection to any such proposed person or entity, the Contractor shall submit a substitute to whom the Owner or the Architect has no reasonable objection, and the Contract Sum shall be increased or decreased by the difference in cost occasioned by such substitution and an appropriate Change Order shall be issued; however, no increase in the Contract Sum shall be allowed for any such substitution unless the Contractor has acted promptly and responsively in submitting names as required by Subparagraph 5.2.1.

5.2.4 The Contractor shall make no substitution for any Subcontractor, person or entity previously selected if the Owner or Architect makes reasonable objection to such substitution.

DOCUMENT TO CASE CHARTS: A201-1976

[The five-digit numbers in this chart are Citator Case Reference Numbers, which refer to the cases, in the Cases section. The suffixes indicate the state or, for federal cases, the court in which the case was decided.]

Paragraph 5.2 Award of Subcontracts and Other Contracts for Portions of the Work

    I

        77049-CT

    II

        82058-PA

    III

        77040-TX
        83007-7CIR

Paragraph 5.2.1

    II

        93025-IL

Paragraph 5.2.2

    II

        93025-IL

Text of Parargraph 5.3—Subcontractual Relations

5.3.1 By an appropriate agreement, written where legally required for validity, the Contractor shall require each Subcontractor, to the extent of the Work to be performed by the Subcontractor, to be bound to the Contractor by the terms of the Contract Documents, and to assume toward the Contractor all the obligations and responsibilities which the Contractor, by these Documents, assumes toward the Owner and the Architect. Said agreement shall preserve and protect the rights of the Owner and the Architect under the Contract Documents with respect to the Work to be performed by the Subcontractor so that the subcontracting thereof will not prejudice such rights, and shall allow to the Subcontractor, unless specifically provided otherwise in the Contractor-Subcontractor agreement, the benefit of all rights, remedies and redress against the Contractor that the Contractor, by these Documents, has against the Owner. Where appropriate, the Contractor shall require each Subcontractor to enter into similar agreements with his Sub-subcontractors. The Contractor shall make available to each proposed Subcontractor, prior to the execution of the Subcontract, copies of the Contract Documents to which the Subcontractor will be bound by this Paragraph 5.3, and identify to the Subcontractor any terms and conditions of the proposed Subcontract which may be at variance with the Contract Documents. Each Subcontractor shall similarly make copies of such Documents available to his Sub-subcontractors.

DOCUMENT TO CASE CHARTS: A201-1976   A–238

[The five-digit numbers in this chart are Citator Case Reference Numbers, which refer to the cases, in the Cases section. The suffixes indicate the state or, for federal cases, the court in which the case was decided.]

Paragraph 5.3   Subcontractual Relations

   I

85027-4CIR	92015-GA
84014-8CIR	89045-IL
83045-SDNY	86072-LA
86055-AZ	83002-MA
85005-AR	82034-MS
80023-CT	77081-NJ
86023-DE	93019-NJ
90034-FL	84036-OH
85003-GA	

   II

86037-3CIR	88028-NJ
84020-AK	86026-OH
93025-IL	86002-TN
79063-IN	84005-WA
86067-MN	

   III

82008-11CIR	84030-MI
81052-NDAL	86015-NY
88040-GA	90016-NY
86060-IL	89005-NC
80021-KS	89018-SC
87006-MA	82017-TN

Article 6   Work by Owner or by Separate Contractors

> ### Text of Paragraph 6.1—Owner's Right to Perform Work and to Award Separate Contracts
>
> **6.1.1** The Owner reserves the right to perform work related to the Project with his own forces, and to award separate contracts in connection with other portions of the Project or other work on the site under these or similar Conditions of the Contract. If the Contractor claims that delay or additional Cost is involved because of such action by the Owner, he shall make such claim as provided elsewhere in the Contract Documents.
>
> **6.1.2** When separate contracts are awarded for different portions of the Project or other work on the site, the term Contractor in the Contract Documents in each case shall mean the Contractor who executes each separate Owner-Contractor Agreement.
>
> **6.1.3** The Owner will provide for the coordination of the work of his own forces and of each separate contractor with the work of the Contractor, who shall cooperate therewith as provided in Paragraph 6.2.

DOCUMENT TO CASE CHARTS: A201-1976

[The five-digit numbers in this chart are Citator Case Reference Numbers, which refer to the cases, in the Cases section. The suffixes indicate the state or, for federal cases, the court in which the case was decided.]

Paragraph 6.1   Owner's Right to Perform Work and to Award Separate Contracts

   I

      90047-IN
      85029-TN

   III

86017-CO	82007-NJ
77048-DE	76052-NY
88035-IN	89005-NC

Paragraph 6.1.1

   II

      93025-IL

Text of Paragraph 6.2—Mutual Responsibility

6.2.1 The Contractor shall afford the Owner and separate contractors reasonable opportunity for the introduction and storage of their materials and equipment and the execution of their work, and shall connect and coordinate his Work with theirs as required by the Contract Documents.

6.2.2 If any part of the Contractor's Work depends for proper execution or results upon the work of the Owner or any separate contractor, the Contractor shall, prior to proceeding with the Work, promptly report to the Architect any apparent discrepancies or defects in such other work that render it unsuitable for such proper execution and results. Failure of the Contractor so to report shall constitute an acceptance of the Owner's or separate contractors' work as fit and proper to receive his Work, except as to defects which may subsequently become apparent in such work by others.

6.2.3 Any costs caused by defective or ill-timed work shall be borne by the party responsible therefor.

6.2.4 Should the Contractor wrongfully cause damage to the work or property of the Owner, or to other work on the site, the Contractor shall promptly remedy such damage as provided in Subparagraph 10.2.5.

6.2.5 Should the Contractor wrongfully cause damage to the work or property of any separate contractor, the Contractor shall upon due notice promptly attempt to settle with such other contractor by agreement, or otherwise to resolve the dispute. If such separate contractor sues or initiates an arbitration proceeding against the Owner on account of any damage alleged to have been caused by the Contractor, the Owner shall notify the Contractor who shall defend such proceedings at the Owner's expense, and if any judgment or award against the Owner arises therefrom the Contractor shall pay or satisfy it and shall reimburse the Owner for all attorneys' fees and court or arbitration costs which the Owner has incurred.

DOCUMENT TO CASE CHARTS: A201-1976

[The five-digit numbers in this chart are Citator Case Reference Numbers, which refer to the cases, in the Cases section. The suffixes indicate the state or, for federal cases, the court in which the case was decided.]

Paragraph 6.2   Mutual Responsibility

    I

        85017-DDE   90047-IN
        91008-MDPA   85029-TN
        90005-IN

    II

        93007-GA

    III

        86017-CO   88035-IN
        93007-GA   82007-NJ
        77046-IL   86018-NC
        87028-IL   89005-NC

Paragraph 6.2.1

    II

        93025-IL

Paragraph 6.2.3

    I

        93025-IL

Text of Paragraph 6.3—Owner's Right to Clean Up

6.3.1 If a dispute arises between the Contractor and separate contractors as to their responsibility for cleaning up as required by Paragraph 4.15, the Owner may clean up and charge the cost thereof to the contractors responsible therefor as the Architect shall determine to be just.

Paragraph 6.3   Owner's Right to Clean Up

    III

        86029-CT

Article 7   Miscellaneous Provisions

Text of Paragraph 7.1—Governing Law

7.1.1 The Contract shall be governed by the law of the place where the Project is located.

A–241   **DOCUMENT TO CASE CHARTS: A201-1976**

[The five-digit numbers in this chart are Citator Case Reference Numbers, which refer to the cases, in the Cases section. The suffixes indicate the state or, for federal cases, the court in which the case was decided.]

Paragraph 7.1   Governing Law

    I

        89048-US   77030-SC
        78066-LA   93048-SC

    II

        88008-SDNY

    III

        77072-AR
        78005-NY
        91018-RI

Text of Parargraph 7.2—Successors and Assigns

7.2.1 The Owner and the Contractor each binds himself, his partners, successors, assigns and legal representatives to the other party hereto and to the partners, successors, assigns and legal representatives of such other party in respect to all covenants, agreements and obligations contained in the Contract Documents. Neither party to the Contract shall assign the Contract or sublet it as a whole without the written consent of the other, nor shall the Contractor assign any moneys due or to become due to him hereunder, without the previous written consent of the Owner.

Paragraph 7.2   Successors and Assigns

    I

        90040-IL
        90014-MD
        82034-MS

    II

        84015-IN

    III

        88039-IL
        77045-NY
        78001-SC

Paragraph 7.3   Written Notice

Text of Parargraph 7.4—Claims for Damages

7.4.1 Should either party to the Contract suffer injury or damage to person or property because of any act or omission of the other party or of any of his employees, agents or others for whose acts he is legally liable, claim shall be made in writing to such other party within a reasonable time after the first observance of such injury or damage.

DOCUMENT TO CASE CHARTS: A201-1976

[The five-digit numbers in this chart are Citator Case Reference Numbers, which refer to the cases, in the Cases section. The suffixes indicate the state or, for federal cases, the court in which the case was decided.]

Paragraph 7.4   Claims for Damages

    I

        90040-IL   78052-ND
        81028-NY   88016-OH

    II

        84035-IL

    III

        77053-CA

Text of Paragraph 7.5—Performance Bond and Labor and Material Payment Bond

7.5.1 The Owner shall have the right to require the Contractor to furnish bonds covering the faithful performance of the Contract and the payment of all obligations arising thereunder if and as required in the Bidding Documents or in the Contract Documents.

Paragraph 7.5   Performance Bond and Labor and Material Payment Bond

    I

        89013-LA
        80063-MA

    II

        79025-NC

    III

        83006-AR   80060-NY
        80053-FL   79042-NC
        81042-MA

Text of Paragraph 7.6—Rights and Remedies

7.6.1 The duties and obligations imposed by the Contract Documents and the rights and remedies available thereunder shall be in addition to and not a limitation of any duties, obligations, rights and remedies otherwise imposed or available by law.

7.6.2 No action or failure to act by the Owner, Architect or Contractor shall constitute a waiver of any right or duty afforded any of them under the Contract, nor shall any such action or failure to act constitute an approval of or acquiescence in any breach thereunder, except as may be specifically agreed in writing.

A–243   **DOCUMENT TO CASE CHARTS: A201-1976**

[The five-digit numbers in this chart are Citator Case Reference Numbers, which refer to the cases, in the Cases section. The suffixes indicate the state or, for federal cases, the court in which the case was decided.]

Paragraph 7.6   Rights and Remedies

   I

95020-DPR	81028-NY
76002-CO	84007-NY
87034-IL	81034-OR
88003-IL	87011-VA
89008-KS	79056-WY

   II

90048-10CIR

   III

77004-AK	82036-NY
80041-AK	77009-OK
77048-DE	88025-VA
77001-ND	78051-WA

Text of Paragraph 7.7—Tests

7.7.1 If the Contract Documents, laws, ordinances, rules, regulations or orders of any public authority having jurisdiction require any portion of the Work to be inspected, tested or approved, the Contractor shall give the Architect timely notice of its readiness so the Architect may observe such inspection, testing or approval. The Contractor shall bear all costs of such inspections, tests or approvals conducted by public authorities. Unless otherwise provided, the Owner shall bear all costs of other inspections, tests or approvals.

7.7.2 If the Architect determines that any Work requires special inspection, testing, or approval which Subparagraph 7.7.1 does not include, he will, upon written authorization from the Owner, instruct the Contractor to order such special inspection, testing or approval, and the Contractor shall give notice as provided in Subparagraph 7.7.1. If such special inspection or testing reveals a failure of the Work to comply with the requirements of the Contract Documents, the Contractor shall bear all costs thereof, including compensation for the Architect's additional services made necessary by such failure; otherwise the Owner shall bear such costs, and an appropriate Change Order shall be issued.

7.7.3 Required certificates of inspection, testing or approval shall be secured by the Contractor and promptly delivered by him to the Architect.

7.7.4 If the Architect is to observe the inspections, tests or approvals required by the Contract Documents, he will do so promptly and, where practicable, at the source of supply.

DOCUMENT TO CASE CHARTS: A201-1976   A–244

[The five-digit numbers in this chart are Citator Case Reference Numbers, which refer to the cases, in the Cases section. The suffixes indicate the state or, for federal cases, the court in which the case was decided.]

Paragraph 7.7   Tests

    I

        76069-CO
        84034-IL
        90040-IL

    III

        86029-CT   76011-PA
        79013-NY   76013-PA

Paragraph 7.7.1

    I

        93036-NE

Paragraph 7.7.4

    I

        93036-NE

Text of Paragraph 7.8—Interest

7.8.1 Payments due and unpaid under the Contract Documents shall bear interest from the date payment is due at such rate as the parties may agree upon in writing or, in the absence thereof, at the legal rate prevailing at the place of the Project.

Paragraph 7.8   Interest

    I

        85020-IA
        82031-NV
        77085-RI

    II

        81047-UT

Text of Paragraph 7.9—Arbitration

7.9.1 All claims, disputes and other matters in question between the Contractor and the Owner arising out of, or relating to, the Contract Documents or the breach thereof, except as provided in Subparagraph 2.2.11 with respect to the Architect's decisions on matters relating to artistic effect, and except for claims which have been waived by the making or acceptance of final payment as provided by Subparagraphs 9.9.4 and 9.9.5, shall be decided by arbitration in accordance with the Construction Industry Arbitration Rules of the American Arbitration Association then obtaining unless the parties mutually agree otherwise. No arbitration arising out of or relating to the Contract Documents shall include, by consolidation, joinder or in any other manner, the Architect, his employees or consultants except by written consent containing a specific reference to the Owner-Contractor Agreement and

DOCUMENT TO CASE CHARTS: A201-1976

[The five-digit numbers in this chart are Citator Case Reference Numbers, which refer to the cases, in the Cases section. The suffixes indicate the state or, for federal cases, the court in which the case was decided.]

signed by the Architect, the Owner, the Contractor and any other person sought to be joined. No arbitration shall include by consolidation, joinder or in any other manner, parties other than the Owner, the Contractor and any other persons substantially involved in a common question of fact or law, whose presence is required if complete relief is to be accorded in the arbitration. No person other than the Owner or Contractor shall be included as an original third party or additional third party to an arbitration whose interest or responsibility is insubstantial. Any consent to arbitration involving an additional person or persons shall not constitute consent to arbitration of any dispute not described therein or with any person not named or described therein. The foregoing agreement to arbitrate and any other agreement to arbitrate with an additional person or persons duly consented to by the parties to the Owner-Contractor Agreement shall be specifically enforceable under the prevailing arbitration law. The award rendered by the arbitrators shall be final, and judgment may be entered upon it in accordance with applicable law in any court having jurisdiction thereof.

7.9.2 Notice of the demand for arbitration shall be filed in writing with the other party to the Owner-Contractor Agreement and with the American Arbitration Association, and a copy shall be filed with the Architect. The demand for arbitration shall be made within the time limits specified in Subparagraph 2.2.12 where applicable, and in all other cases within a reasonable time after the claim, dispute or other matter in question has arisen, and in no event shall it be made after the date when institution of legal or equitable proceedings based on such claim, dispute or other matter in question would be barred by the applicable statute of limitations.

7.9.3 Unless otherwise agreed in writing, the Contractor shall carry on the Work and maintain its progress during any arbitration proceedings, and the Owner shall continue to make payments to the Contractor in accordance with the Contract Documents.

Paragraph 7.9 Arbitration

I

89048-US	76051-CT
85040-4CIR	80023-CT
87032-4CIR	80046-CT
87014-5CIR	89034-CT
81039-6CIR	90001-CT
84010-6CIR	93006-CT
81037-7CIR	79051-DE
91009-SDAL	92008-DC
87022-DDC	76005-FL
82032-DKS	79012-FL
88008-SDNY	81006-FL
77083a-EDPA	81073-FL
86014-AZ	83030-FL
89002-AZ	86031-FL
85005-AR	86061-FL
81056-CO	91006-FL
82029-CO	91015-FL

DOCUMENT TO CASE CHARTS: A201-1976

[The five-digit numbers in this chart are Citator Case Reference Numbers, which refer to the cases, in the Cases section. The suffixes indicate the state or, for federal cases, the court in which the case was decided.]

82024-GA	89010-MN
85003-GA	89046-MN
90009-GA	76021-NV
80057-ID	76032-NJ
78031-IL	77081-NJ
78059-IL	78044-NM
81009-IL	76053-NY
81041-IL	77003-NY
84011-IL	77064-NY
89011-IL	78038-NY
89044-IL	78073-NY
89045-IL	80055-NY
92021-IL	81028-NY
90041-IN	81057-NY
90018-KS	84007-NY
77034-KY	84019-NY
93003-KY	89014-NY
78049-LA	88031-NC
78067-LA	92010-NC
81038-LA	81074-OH
90027-LA	84036-OH
92006-ME	81034-OR
76041-MD	78023-PA
81049-MD	78078-PA
81066-MD	77085-RI
84003-MD	77030-SC
89035-MD	87046-SC
90014-MD	89018-SC
76054-MA	93002-SD
92013-MA	84027-TX
82011-MI	89051-TX
87017-MN	92009a-TX

II

83033-US	93008-IA
86037-3CIR	81014-IL
83010-5CIR	87015-IL
86045-5CIR	87018-IL
90019-6CIR	88039-IL
84040-NDAL	89030-IL
88006-DME	81023-KS
85040-WDMO	90022-ME
90004-DSC	78043-MD
87005-NDTX	80076-MA
86021-AL	81013-MA
83008-CA	86036-MI
83016-CA	89023-MI
90046-CA	91012-MI
88029-CT	82049-MN
86023-DE	86067-MN
81054-FL	88009-MN
82039-FL	78060-MT
83018-FL	77037-NY
84004-FL	77047-NY
85004-FL	86062-NY
86020-FL	87039-NY
86041-FL	81010-NC
87001-FL	85002-NC

DOCUMENT TO CASE CHARTS: A201-1976

[The five-digit numbers in this chart are Citator Case Reference Numbers, which refer to the cases, in the Cases section. The suffixes indicate the state or, for federal cases, the court in which the case was decided.]

    81047-UT

III

89024-1CIR	76058-MI
83008-6CIR	77031-MI
89050-6CIR	92008d-MI
83026-8CIR	76057-MN
88044-NDGA	85042-MO
82042-DVI	82015-NH
93004-AL	86054-NH
75030-AZ	76037-NJ
84012-AZ	79023-NJ
85041-AZ	77019-NY
90045-AZ	77025-NY
77072-AR	77084-NY
76039-CA	81005-NY
79024-CA	85026-NY
90003-CA	85043-NY
77023-CT	86024-NY
86029-CT	86047-NY
90053-CT	88035a-NY
92020a-CT	86004-PA
79039-IL	86010-PA
83025-IL	87045-PA
78017-LA	87052-PA
79030-LA	88013-PA
80062-LA	91018-RI
80074-LA	79006-SC
83005-LA	82012-SD
82010-MD	76035-TX
89039-MD	77050-TX
79038-MA	80008-TX
79054-MA	86069-WI

Paragraph 7.9.1

I

92001b-CA	93048-SC
93052-LA	93054-TX
95033-MO	95023-VA

II

94003-GA
93024-TN

Paragraph 7.9.3

I

95033-MO

DOCUMENT TO CASE CHARTS: A201-1976 A–248

[The five-digit numbers in this chart are Citator Case Reference Numbers, which refer to the cases, in the Cases section. The suffixes indicate the state or, for federal cases, the court in which the case was decided.]

Article 8 Time

Text of Paragraph 8.1—Definitions

8.1.1 Unless otherwise provided, the Contract Time is the period of time allotted in the Contract Documents for Substantial Completion of the Work as defined in Subparagraph 8.1.3, including authorized adjustments thereto.

8.1.2 The date of commencement of the Work is the date established in a notice to proceed. If there is no notice to proceed, it shall be the date of the Owner-Contractor Agreement or such other date as may be established therein.

8.1.3 The Date of Substantial Completion of the Work or designated portion thereof is the Date certified by the Architect when construction is sufficiently complete, in accordance with the Contract Documents, so the Owner can occupy or utilize the Work or designated portion thereof for the use for which it is intended.

8.1.4 The term day as used in the Contract Documents shall mean calendar day unless otherwise specifically designated.

Paragraph 8.1   Definitions

    I

        82004-SDGA   76008-MD
        89027-FL   82045-NH
        83003-LA   92017-NJ

    II

        87004-LA
        83029-NJ

    III

        81060-5CIR   90030-MS
        85031-AK   84031-NE
        80049-IN   82007-NJ
        87027-IN   87025-WI
        83005-LA

Text of Paragraph 8.2—Progress and Completion

8.2.1 All time limits stated in the Contract Documents are of the essence of the Contract.

8.2.2 The Contractor shall begin the Work on the date of commencement as defined in Subparagraph 8.1.2. He shall carry the Work forward expeditiously with adequate forces and shall achieve Substantial Completion within the Contract Time.

DOCUMENT TO CASE CHARTS: A201-1976

[The five-digit numbers in this chart are Citator Case Reference Numbers, which refer to the cases, in the Cases section. The suffixes indicate the state or, for federal cases, the court in which the case was decided.]

Paragraph 8.2 Progress and Completion

    I

        82004-SDGA   77063-WA
        82045-NH   81067-WY

    III

        83007-7CIR   81015-MT
        87027-IN   86004-PA

Text of Paragraph 8.3—Delays and Extensions of Time

8.3.1 If the Contractor is delayed at any time in the progress of the Work by any act or neglect of the Owner or the Architect, or by any employee of either, or by any separate contractor employed by the Owner, or by changes ordered in the Work, or by labor disputes, fire, unusual delay in transportation, adverse weather conditions not reasonably anticipatable, unavoidable casualties, or any causes beyond the Contractor's control, or by delay authorized by the Owner pending arbitration, or by any other cause which the Architect determines may justify the delay, then the Contract Time shall be extended by Change Order for such reasonable time as the Architect may determine.

8.3.2 Any claim for extension of time shall be made in writing to the Architect not more than twenty days after the commencement of the delay; otherwise it shall be waived. In the case of a continuing delay only one claim is necessary. The Contractor shall provide an estimate of the probable effect of such delay on the progress of the Work.

8.3.3 If no agreement is made stating the dates upon which interpretations as provided in Subparagraph 2.2.8 shall be furnished, then no claim for delay shall be allowed on account of failure to furnish such interpretations until fifteen days after written request is made for them, and not then unless such claim is reasonable.

8.3.4 This Paragraph 8.3 does not exclude the recovery of damages for delay by either party under other provisions of the Contract Documents.

Paragraph 8.3 Delays and Extensions of Time

    I

        87033-8CIR   88020-NE
        80002-AZ   79032-OK
        85032-IN   85029-TN
        83042-MD   78040-UT
        80065-MO   77063-WA
        86064-MO   79056-WY
        91021-MO   81067-WY
        93020-NC

DOCUMENT TO CASE CHARTS: A201-1976 A–250

[The five-digit numbers in this chart are Citator Case Reference Numbers, which refer to the cases, in the Cases section. The suffixes indicate the state or, for federal cases, the court in which the case was decided.]

II

    80033-8CIR   79058-CA
    80011-AR   83014-NV

III

88027-3CIR	91007-NM
76020-5CIR	77039-NY
84022-6CIR	77084-NY
83007-7CIR	78029-NY
85009-7CIR	78077-NY
90048-10CIR	82036-NY
89043-NDIL	83027-NY
81071-CT	86005-NY
86029-CT	86012-NY
77048-DE	86053-NY
77007-HI	86066-NY
85006-IL	90007-NY
87030-IL	84025-OH
87027-IN	86009-OH
76062-LA	80022-OR
90044-MD	86010-PA
87006-MA	90015-PA
84030-MI	80009-SD
78006-MT	83004-TX
75029-NJ	88025-VA
76015-NJ	89033-VA
76023-NJ	77020-WA
82007-NJ	80039-WY

Article 9 Payments and Completion

Text of Paragraph 9.1—Contract Sum

9.1.1 The Contract Sum is stated in the Owner-Contractor Agreement and, including authorized adjustments thereto, is the total amount payable by the Owner to the Contractor for the performance of the Work under the Contract documents.

Paragraph 9.1 Contract Sum

    I

        83017-GA

    III

        81052-NDAL

Text of Paragraph 9.2—Schedule of Values

9.2.1 Before the first Application for Payment, the Contractor shall submit to the Architect a schedule of values allocated to the various portions of the Work, prepared in such form and supported by such data to substantiate its accuracy as

DOCUMENT TO CASE CHARTS: A201-1976

[The five-digit numbers in this chart are Citator Case Reference Numbers, which refer to the cases, in the Cases section. The suffixes indicate the state or, for federal cases, the court in which the case was decided.]

> the Architect may require. This schedule, unless objected to by the Architect, shall be used only as a basis for the Contractors's Applications for Payment.

Paragraph 9.2 Schedule of Values

    II

        83014-NV

    III

        86029-CT

Text of Paragraph 9.3—Applications for Payment

9.3.1 At least ten days before the date for each progress payment established in the Owner-Contractor Agreement, the Contractor shall submit to the Architect an itemized Application for Payment, notarized if required, supported by such data substantiating the Contractor's right to payment as the Owner or the Architect may require, and reflecting retainage, if any, as provided elsewhere in the Contract Documents.

9.3.2 Unless otherwise provided in the Contract Documents, payments will be made on account of materials or equipment not incorporated in the Work but delivered and suitably stored at the site and, if approved in advance by the Owner, payments may similarly be made for materials or equipment suitably stored at some other location agreed upon in writing. Payments for materials or equipment stored on or off the site shall be conditioned upon submission by the Contractor of bills of sale or such other procedures satisfactory to the Owner to establish the Owner's title to such materials or equipment or otherwise protect the Owner's interest, including applicable insurance and transportation to the site for those materials and equipment stored off the site.

9.3.3 The Contractor warrants that title to all Work, materials and equipment covered by an Application for Payment will pass to the Owner either by incorporation in the construction or upon the receipt of payment by the Contractor, whichever occurs first, free and clear of all liens, claims, security interests or encumbrances, hereinafter referred to in this Article 9 as "liens"; and that no Work, materials or equipment covered by an Application for Payment will have been acquired by the Contractor, or by any other person performing Work at the site or furnishing materials and equipment for the Project, subject to an agreement under which an interest therein or an encumbrance thereon is retained by the seller or otherwise imposed by the Contractor or such other person.

DOCUMENT TO CASE CHARTS: A201-1976 A–252

[The five-digit numbers in this chart are Citator Case Reference Numbers, which refer to the cases, in the Cases section. The suffixes indicate the state or, for federal cases, the court in which the case was decided.]

Paragraph 9.3   Applications for Payment

I

    83028-IL
    78071-TX
    80027-VA

II

    91027-TN

III

89042-NDIL	86008-LA
83019-CO	86049-NH
86051-CT	77040-TX
86070-IL	88022-VA

Text of Paragraph 9.4—Certificates for Payment

9.4.1 The Architect will, within seven days after the receipt of the Contractor's Application for Payment, either issue a Certificate for Payment to the Owner, with a copy to the Contractor, for such amount as the Architect determines is properly due, or notify the Contractor in writing his reasons for withholding a Certificate as provided in Subparagraph 9.6.1.

9.4.2 The issuance of a Certificate for Payment will constitute a representation by the Architect to the Owner, based on his observations at the site as provided in Subparagraph 2.2.3 and the data comprising the Application for Payment, that the Work has progressed to the point indicated; that, to the best of his knowledge, information and belief, the quality of the Work is in accordance with the Contract Documents (subject to an evaluation of the Work for conformance with the Contract Documents upon Substantial Completion, to the results of any subsequent tests required by or performed under the Contract Documents, to minor deviations from the Contract Documents correctable prior to completion, and to any specific qualifications stated in his Certificate); and that the Contractor is entitled to payment in the amount certified. However, by issuing a Certificate for Payment, the Architect shall not thereby be deemed to represent that he has made exhaustive or continuous on-site inspections to check the quality or quantity of the Work or that he has reviewed the construction means, methods, techniques, sequences or procedures, or that he has made any examination to ascertain how or for what purpose the Contractor has used the moneys previously paid on account of the Contract Sum.

A–253   **DOCUMENT TO CASE CHARTS: A201-1976**

[*The five-digit numbers in this chart are Citator Case Reference Numbers, which refer to the cases, in the Cases section. The suffixes indicate the state or, for federal cases, the court in which the case was decided.*]

Paragraph 9.4   Certificates for Payment

    I

        82020-6CIR   89012-NY
        95020-DPR   77085-RI
        84029-DC   85029-TN
        77027-MS   78071-TX

    II

        89022-5CIR   89047-MS
        87047-AL   88014-MO

    III

        89042-NDIL   86029-CT
        77004-AK   86008-CT

Paragraph 9.4.2

    II

        93036-NE

Text of Paragraph 9.5—Progress Payments

9.5.1 After the Architect has issued a Certificate for Payment, the Owner shall make payment in the manner and within the time provided in the Contract Documents.

9.5.2 The Contractor shall promptly pay each Subcontractor, upon receipt of payment from the Owner, out of the amount paid to the Contractor on account of such Subcontractor's Work, the amount to which said Subcontractor is entitled, reflecting the percentage actually retained, if any, from payments to the Contractor on account of such Subcontractor's Work. The Contractor shall, by an appropriate agreement with each Subcontractor, require each Subcontractor to make payments to his Sub-subcontractors in similar manner.

9.5.3 The Architect may, on request and at his discretion, furnish to any Subcontractor, if practicable, information regarding the percentages of completion or the amounts applied for by the Contractor and the action taken thereon by the Architect on account of Work done by such Subcontractor.

9.5.4 Neither the Owner nor the Architect shall have any obligation to pay or to see to the payment of any moneys to any Subcontractor except as may otherwise be required by law.

9.5.5 No Certificate for a progress payment, nor any progress payment, nor any partial or entire use or occupancy of the Project by the Owner, shall constitute an acceptance of any Work not in accordance with the Contract Documents.

DOCUMENT TO CASE CHARTS: A201-1976

[The five-digit numbers in this chart are Citator Case Reference Numbers, which refer to the cases, in the Cases section. The suffixes indicate the state or, for federal cases, the court in which the case was decided.]

Paragraph 9.5   Progress Payments

I

    95020-DPR   77054-NC
    84029-DC   79032-OK
    90034-FL   78071-TX

II

    77070-CA
    84035-IL
    88028-NJ

III

    83035-5CIR   76063-IA
    83007-7CIR   83005-LA
    89042-NDIL   83039-LA
    83019-CO   86008-LA
    81071-CT   91003-MD
    79014-FL   91011-MD
    88005-FL   84021-MA
    88030-FL   90033-MN
    86048-GA   79011-MT
    86070-IL   86049-NH

Text of Paragraph 9.6—Payments Withheld

9.6.1 The Architect may decline to certify payment and may withhold his Certificate in whole or in part, to the extent necessary reasonably to protect the Owner, if in his opinion he is unable to make representations to the Owner as provided in Subparagraph 9.4.2. If the Architect is unable to make representations to the Owner as provided in Subparagraph 9.4.2 and to certify payment in the amount of the Application, he will notify the Contractor as provided in Subparagraph 9.4.1. If the Contractor and the Architect cannot agree on a revised amount, the Architect will promptly issue a Certificate for Payment for the amount for which he is able to make such representations to the Owner. The Architect may also decline to certify payment or, because of subsequently discovered evidence or subsequent observations, he may nullify the whole or any part of any Certificate for Payment previously issued, to such extent as may be necessary in his opinion to protect the Owner from loss because of:

.1   defective Work not remedied,

.2   third party claims filed or reasonable evidence indicating probable filing of such claims,

.3   failure of the Contractor to make payments properly to Subcontractors or for labor, materials or equipment,

.4   reasonable evidence that the Work cannot be completed for the unpaid balance of the Contract Sum,

.5   damage to the Owner or another contractor,

DOCUMENT TO CASE CHARTS: A201-1976

[*The five-digit numbers in this chart are Citator Case Reference Numbers, which refer to the cases, in the Cases section. The suffixes indicate the state or, for federal cases, the court in which the case was decided.*]

.6 reasonable evidence that the Work will not be completed within the Contract Time, or

.7 persistent failure to carry out the Work in accordance with the Contract Documents.

9.6.2 When the above grounds in Subparagraph 9.6.1 are removed, payment shall be made for amounts withheld because of them.

Paragraph 9.6 Payments Withheld

   I

      84029-DC   77054-NC
      88003-IL   79056-WY
      89035-MD   81067-WY

   II

      81064-8CIR

   III

      83007-7CIR   83005-LA
      77004-AK   83041-LA
      76070-CA   86008-LA
      86029-CT

Text of Paragraph 9.7—Failure of Payment

9.7.1 If the Architect does not issue a Certificate for Payment, through no fault of the Contractor, within seven days after receipt of the Contractor's Application for Payment, or if the Owner does not pay the Contractor within seven days after the date established in the Contract Documents any amount certified by the Architect or awarded by arbitration, then the Contractor may, upon seven additional days' written notice to the Owner and the Architect, stop the Work until payment of the amount owing has been received. The Contract Sum shall be increased by the amount of the Contractor's reasonable costs of shut-down, delay and start-up, which shall be effected by appropriate Change Order in accordance with Paragraph 12.3.

Paragraph 9.7 Failure of Payment

   I

      79043-LA
      78071-TX

   III

      90023-2CIR   77045-NY
      86008-LA   90015-PA
      84021-MA   93054-TX

DOCUMENT TO CASE CHARTS: A201-1976

[The five-digit numbers in this chart are Citator Case Reference Numbers, which refer to the cases, in the Cases section. The suffixes indicate the state or, for federal cases, the court in which the case was decided.]

Text of Paragraph 9.8—Substantial Completion

9.8.1 When the Contractor considers that the Work, or a designated portion thereof which is acceptable to the Owner, is substantially complete as defined in Subparagraph 8.1.3, the Contractor shall prepare for submission to the Architect a list of items to be completed or corrected. The failure to include any items on such list does not alter the responsibility of the Contractor to complete all Work in accordance with the Contract Documents. When the Architect on the basis of an inspection determines that the Work or designated portion thereof is substantially complete, he will then prepare a Certificate of Substantial Completion which shall establish the Date of Substantial Completion, shall state the responsibilities of the Owner and the Contractor for security, maintenance, heat, utilities, damage to the Work, and insurance, and shall fix the time within which the Contractor shall complete the items listed therein. Warranties required by the Contract Documents shall commence on the Date of Substantial Completion of the Work or designated portion thereof unless otherwise provided in the Certificate of Substantial Completion. The Certificate of Substantial Completion shall be submitted to the Owner and the Contractor for their written acceptance of the responsibilities assigned to them in such Certificate.

9.8.2 Upon Substantial Completion of the Work or designated portion thereof and upon application by the Contractor and certification by the Architect, the Owner shall make payment, reflecting adjustment in retainage, if any, for such Work or portion thereof, as provided in the Contract Documents.

Paragraph 9.8   Substantial Completion

    I

        80002-AZ   83003-LA
        89027-FL   76008-MD
        79043-LA   78052-ND

    III

        85031-AK   83041-LA
        86029-CT   90030-MS
        83005-LA   78035-NJ
        83039-LA   87025-WI

Paragraph 9.8.1

    I

        95020-DPR

Text of Paragraph 9.9—Final Completion and Final Payment

9.9.1 Upon receipt of written notice that the Work is ready for final inspection and acceptance and upon receipt of a final Application for Payment, the Architect will promptly make such inspection and, when he finds the Work acceptable under the Contract Documents and the Contract fully performed, he will promptly issue a final Certificate for Payment stating that to the best of his knowledge, information and belief, and on the basis of his observations and inspections, the Work has been completed in accordance with the terms and conditions of the Contract Documents and that the entire balance found to be due the Contractor, and noted in said final Certificate, is due and payable. The Architect's final Certificate for Payment will constitute a further representation that the conditions precedent to the Contractor's being entitled to final payment as set forth in Subparagraph 9.9.2 have been fulfilled.

9.9.2 Neither the final payment nor the remaining retained percentage shall become due until the Contractor submits to the Architect (1) an affidavit that all payrolls, bills for materials and equipment, and other indebtedness connected with the Work for which the Owner or his property might in any way be responsible, have been paid or otherwise satisfied, (2) consent of surety, if any, to final payment and (3), if required by the Owner, other data establishing payment or satisfaction of all such obligations, such as receipts, releases and waivers of liens arising out of the Contract, to the extent and in such form as may be designated by the Owner. If any Subcontractor refuses to furnish a release or waiver required by the Owner, the Contractor may furnish a bond satisfactory to the Owner to indemnify him against any such lien. If any such lien remains unsatisfied after all payments are made, the Contractor shall refund to the Owner all moneys that the latter may be compelled to pay in discharging such lien, including all costs and reasonable attorneys' fees.

9.9.3 If, after Substantial Completion of the Work, final completion thereof is materially delayed through no fault of the Contractor or by the issuance of Change Orders affecting final completion, and the Architect so confirms, the Owner shall, upon application by the Contractor and certification by the Architect, and without terminating the Contract, make payment of the balance due for that portion of the Work fully completed and accepted. If the remaining balance for Work not fully completed or corrected is less than the retainage stipulated in the Contract Documents, and if bonds have been furnished as provided in Paragraph 7.5, the written consent of the surety to the payment of the balance due for that portion of the Work fully completed and accepted shall be submitted by the Contractor to the Architect prior to certification of such payment. Such payment shall be made under the terms and conditions governing final payment, except that it shall not constitute a waiver of claims.

9.9.4 The making of final payment shall constitute a waiver of all claims by the Owner except those arising from:

.1   unsettled liens,

.2   faulty or defective Work appearing after Substantial Completion,

.3   failure of the Work to comply with the requirements of the Contract Documents, or

.4   terms of any special warranties required by the Contract Documents.

DOCUMENT TO CASE CHARTS: A201-1976 A–258

[The five-digit numbers in this chart are Citator Case Reference Numbers, which refer to the cases, in the Cases section. The suffixes indicate the state or, for federal cases, the court in which the case was decided.]

> **9.9.5** The acceptance of final payment shall constitute a waiver of all claims by the Contractor except those previously made in writing and identified by the Contractor as unsettled at the time of the final Application for Payment.

Paragraph 9.9 Final Completion and Final Payment

    I

        81061-3CIR   89035-MD
        82020-6CIR   89010-MN
        91008-MDPA   77083-NJ
        80002-AZ   90026-NJ
        84029-DC   92017-NJ
        90034-FL   81010-NC
        91014-FL   84007-NY
        88003-IL   79032-OK
        90040-IL   78040-UT
        82009-LA   80027-VA
        86056-MD   81035-VA

    II

        78022-7CIR   77037-NY
        89030-IL   82058-PA
        79031-MN   81047-UT
        82048-NE

    III

        83035-5CIR   86008-LA
        90050-7CIR   90030-MS
        77011-WDMO   86049-NH
        82042-DVI   79013-NY
        86051-CT   83036-NY
        80040-LA   85022-NY
        83039-LA   84025-OH
        83041-LA   88036-TX

Article 10 Protection of Persons and Property

Text of Paragraph 10.1—Safety Precautions and Programs

> **10.1.1** The Contractor shall be responsible for initiating, maintaining and supervising all safety precautions and programs in connection with the Work.

Paragraph 10.1 Safety Precautions and Programs

    I

        92011-AZ   82028-IN
        92021a-AZ   83020-KS
        78076-CO   92016a-MT
        91040-GA   83047-NY
        92010a-GA   89016-NY
        93013-GA   82056-OK

DOCUMENT TO CASE CHARTS: A201-1976

[*The five-digit numbers in this chart are Citator Case Reference Numbers, which refer to the cases, in the Cases section. The suffixes indicate the state or, for federal cases, the court in which the case was decided.*]

II

94038-FL	91001-IN
84015-IN	81068-MT

III

91037-11CIR	90035-MA
87037-AL	86038-MO
92004-IL	76024-NY
88035-IN	81036-NY
85037-NY	90029-PA
90036-GA	

Text of Paragraph 10.2—Safety of Persons and Property

10.2.1 The Contractor shall take all reasonable precautions for the safety of, and shall provide all reasonable protection to prevent damage, injury or loss to:

.1 all employees on the Work and all other persons who may be affected thereby;

.2 all the Work and all materials and equipment to be incorporated therein, whether in storage on or off the site, under the care, custody or control of the Contractor or any of his Subcontractors or Sub-subcontractors; and

.3 other property at the site or adjacent thereto, including trees, shrubs, lawns, walks, pavements, roadways, structures and utilities not designated for removal, relocation or replacement in the course of construction.

10.2.2 The Contractor shall give all notices and comply with all applicable laws, ordinances, rules, regulations and lawful orders of any public authority bearing on the safety of persons or property or their protection from damage, injury or loss.

10.2.3 The Contractor shall erect and maintain, as required by existing conditions and progress of the Work, all reasonable safeguards for safety and protection, including posting danger signs and other warnings against hazards, promulgating safety regulations and notifying owners and users of adjacent utilities.

10.2.4 When the use or storage of explosives or other hazardous materials or equipment is necessary for the execution of the Work, the Contractor shall exercise the utmost care and shall carry on such activities under the supervision of properly qualified personnel.

10.2.5 The Contractor shall promptly remedy all damage or loss (other than damage or loss insured under Paragraph 11.3) to any property referred to in Clauses 10.2.1.2 and 10.2.1.3 caused in whole or in part by the Contractor, any Subcontractor, any Sub-subcontractor, or anyone directly or indirectly employed by any of them, or by anyone for whose acts any of them may be liable and for which the Contractor is responsible under Clauses 10.2.1.2 and 10.2.1.3, except damage or loss attributable to the acts or omissions of the Owner or Architect or anyone directly or indirectly employed by either of them, or by anyone for whose acts either of them may be liable, and not attributable to the fault or negligence of the Contractor.

DOCUMENT TO CASE CHARTS: A201-1976

[The five-digit numbers in this chart are Citator Case Reference Numbers, which refer to the cases, in the Cases section. The suffixes indicate the state or, for federal cases, the court in which the case was decided.]

> The foregoing obligations of the Contractor are in addition to his obligations under Paragraph 4.18.
>
> **10.2.6** The Contractor shall designate a responsible member of his organization at the site whose duty shall be the prevention of accidents. This person shall be the Contractor's superintendent unless otherwise designated by the Contractor in writing to the Owner and the Architect.
>
> **10.2.7** The Contractor shall not load or permit any part of the Work to be loaded so as to endanger its safety.

Paragraph 10.2 Safety of Persons and Property

   I

81012-AL	79060-KS
92011-AZ	83020-KS
92021a-AZ	92016a-MT
78076-CO	83047-NY
91040-GA	89016-NY
92010a-GA	88016-OH
93013-GA	82056-OK
78045-IL	85029-TN
90005-IN	

   II

84015-IN
83034-NY

   III

87037-AL	86052-IN
80030-AK	88035-IN
80029-AR	81027-LA
79071-DC	86038-MO
85037-FL	76024-NY
81058-GA	86018-NC
79070-IL	81036-NY
92004-IL	81016-TX
82028-IN	79015-VA

Paragraph 10.2.1

   II

94038-FL

> ### Text of Paragraph 10.3—Emergencies
>
> **10.3.1** In any emergency affecting the safety of persons or property, the Contractor shall act, at his discretion, to prevent threatened damage, injury or loss. Any additional compensation or extension of time claimed by the Contractor on account of emergency work shall be determined as provided in Article 12 for Changes in the Work.

DOCUMENT TO CASE CHARTS: A201-1976

[The five-digit numbers in this chart are Citator Case Reference Numbers, which refer to the cases, in the Cases section. The suffixes indicate the state or, for federal cases, the court in which the case was decided.]

Paragraph 10.3 Emergencies

    I

        86055-AZ
        89016-NY
        79033-PA

    III

        86038-MO

Article 11 Insurance

Text of Paragraph 11.1—Contractor's Liability Insurance

11.1.1 The Contractor shall purchase and maintain such insurance as will protect him from claims set forth below which may arise out of or result from the Contractor's operations under the Contract, whether such operations be by himself or by any Subcontractor or by anyone directly or indirectly employed by any of them, or by anyone for whose acts any of them may be liable:

.1   claims under workers' or workmen's compensation, disability benefit and other similar employee benefit acts;

.2   claims for damages because of bodily injury, occupational sickness or disease, or death of his employees;

.3   claims for damages because of bodily injury, sickness or disease, or death of any person other than his employees;

.4   claims for damages insured by usual personal injury liability coverage which are sustained (1) by any person as a result of an offense directly or indirectly related to the employment of such person by the Contractor, or (2) by any other person;

.5   claims for damages, other than to the Work itself, because of injury to or destruction of tangible property, including loss of use resulting therefrom; and

.6   claims for damages because of bodily injury or death of any person or property damage arising out of the ownership, maintenance or use of any motor vehicle.

11.1.2 The insurance required by Subparagraph 11.1.1 shall be written for not less than any limits of liability specified in the Contract Documents, or required by law, whichever is greater.

11.1.3 The insurance required by Subparagraph 11.1.1 shall include contractual liability insurance applicable to the Contractor's obligations under Paragraph 4.18.

11.1.4 Certificates of Insurance acceptable to the Owner shall be filed with the Owner prior to commencement of the Work. These Certificates shall contain a provision that coverages afforded under the policies will not be cancelled until at least thirty days' prior written notice has been given to the Owner.

DOCUMENT TO CASE CHARTS: A201-1976

[The five-digit numbers in this chart are Citator Case Reference Numbers, which refer to the cases, in the Cases section. The suffixes indicate the state or, for federal cases, the court in which the case was decided.]

Paragraph 11.1   Contractor's Liability Insurance

   I

      91022-IL   84036-OH
      81072-MA   88016-OH
      85038-NY   87036-WA
      79042-NC

   II

      89040-CO   79021-NM
      80056-IL   83034-NY
      83038-LA   90043-NY
      83040-LA   90049-OK

   III

      83015-11CIR   86063-MA
      83006-AR   84030-MI
      80073-IL   83044-MN
      87008-IL   84026-NY
      87042-IL   91029-ND
      78046-IA   86046-WA
      80021-KS

Paragraph 11.1.1

   I

      93010-SDNY
      94004-MO
      92010b-OH

   III

      92014a-AL
      94013-LA

Paragraph 11.1.2

   III

      94013-LA

Paragraph 11.1.3

   III

      94013-LA

Paragraph 11.1.4

   III

      94013-LA

Text of Paragraph 11.2—Owner's Liability Insurance

11.2.1 The Owner shall be responsible for purchasing and maintaining his own liability insurance and, at his option, may purchase and maintain such insurance as will protect him against claims which may arise from operations under the Contract.

Paragraph 11.2 Owner's Liability Insurance

  II

    89040-CO
    90049-OK

Text of Paragraph 11.3—Property Insurance

11.3.1 Unless otherwise provided, the Owner shall purchase and maintain property insurance upon the entire Work at the site to the full insurable value thereof. This insurance shall include the interests of the Owner, the Contractor, Subcontractors and Sub-subcontractors in the Work and shall insure against the perils of fire and extended coverage and shall include "all risk" insurance for physical loss or damage including, without duplication of coverage, theft, vandalism and malicious mischief. If the Owner does not intend to purchase such insurance for the full insurable value of the entire Work, he shall inform the Contractor in Writing prior to commencement of the Work. The Contractor may then effect insurance which will protect the interests of himself, his Subcontractors and the Sub-subcontractors in the Work, and by appropriate Change Order the cost thereof shall be charged to the Owner. If the Contractor is damaged by failure of the Owner to purchase or maintain such insurance and to so notify the Contractor, then the Owner shall bear all reasonable costs properly attributable thereto. If not covered under the all risk insurance or otherwise provided in the Contract Documents, the Contractor shall effect and maintain similar property insurance on portions of the Work stored off the site or in transit when such portions of the Work are to be included in an Application for Payment under Subparagraph 9.3.2.

11.3.2 The Owner shall purchase and maintain such boiler and machinery insurance as may be required by the Contract Documents or by law. This insurance shall include the interests of the Owner, the Contractor, Subcontractors and Sub-subcontractors in the Work.

11.3.3 Any loss insured under Subparagraph 11.3.1 is to be adjusted with the Owner and made payable to the Owner as trustee for the insureds, as their interests may appear, subject to the requirements of any applicable mortgagee clause and of Subparagraph 11.3.8. The Contractor shall pay each Subcontractor a just share of any insurance moneys received by the Contractor, and by appropriate agreement, written where legally required for validity, shall require each Subcontractor to make payments to his Sub-subcontractors in similar manner.

11.3.4 The Owner shall file a copy of all policies with the Contractor before an exposure to loss may occur.

11.3.5 If the Contractor requests in writing that insurance for risks other than those described in Subparagraphs 11.3.1 and 11.3.2 or other special hazards be

[*The five-digit numbers in this chart are Citator Case Reference Numbers, which refer to the cases, in the Cases section. The suffixes indicate the state or, for federal cases, the court in which the case was decided.*]

included in the property insurance policy, the Owner shall, if possible, include such insurance, and the cost thereof shall be charged to the Contractor by appropriate Change Order.

11.3.6 The Owner and Contractor waive all rights against (1) each other and the Subcontractors, Sub-subcontractors. agents and employees each of the other, and (2) the Architect and separate contractors, if any, and their subcontractors, sub-subcontractors, agents and employees, for damages caused by fire or other perils to the extent covered by Insurance obtained pursuant to this Paragraph 11.3 or any other property insurance applicable to the Work, except such rights as they may have to the proceeds of such insurance held by the Owner as trustee. The foregoing waiver afforded the Architect, his agents and employees shall not extend to the liability imposed by Subparagraph 4.18.3. The Owner or the Contractor, as appropriate, shall require of the Architect, separate contractors, Subcontractors and Sub-subcontractors by appropriate agreements, written where legally required for validity, similar waivers each in favor of all other parties enumerated in this Subparagraph 11.3.6.

11.3.7 If required in writing by any party in interest, the Owner as trustee shall, upon the occurrence of an insured loss, give bond for the proper performance of his duties. He shall deposit in a separate account any money so received, and he shall distribute it in accordance with such agreement as the parties in interest may reach, or in accordance with an award by arbitration in which case the procedure shall be as provided in Paragraph 7.9. If after such loss no other special agreement is made, replacement of damaged work shall be covered by an appropriate Change Order.

11.3.8 The Owner as trustee shall have power to adjust and settle any loss with the insurers unless one of the parties in interest shall object in writing within five days after the occurrence of loss to the Owner's exercise of this power, and if such objection be made, arbitrators shall be chosen as provided in Paragraph 7.9. The Owner as trustee shall, in that case, make settlement with the insurers in accordance with the directions of such arbitrators. If distribution of the insurance proceeds by arbitration is required, the arbitrators will direct such distribution.

11.3.9 If the Owner finds it necessary to occupy or use a portion or portions of the Work prior to Substantial Completion thereof, such occupancy or use shall not commence prior to a time mutually agreed to by the Owner and Contractor and to which the insurance company or companies providing the property insurance have consented by endorsement to the policy or policies. This insurance shall not be cancelled or lapsed on account of such partial occupancy or use. Consent of the Contractor and of the insurance company or companies to such occupancy or use shall not be unreasonably withheld.

DOCUMENT TO CASE CHARTS: A201-1976

[The five-digit numbers in this chart are Citator Case Reference Numbers, which refer to the cases, in the Cases section. The suffixes indicate the state or, for federal cases, the court in which the case was decided.]

Paragraph 11.3   Property Insurance

    I

88006-3CIR	76008-MD
93010-SDNY	81026-MA
91016-AL	86028-MA
88037-AZ	85038-NY
85036-CO	88032-NC
79005-GA	88015-ND
85021-GA	92010b-OH
86068-IL	77021-SD
91022-IL	92019a-TX
79063-IN	87007-VA
91033-LA	87036-WA
93022-ME	92020-WA

    II

93010-SDNY	90043-NY
79021-NM	91027-TN
79022-NY	

    III

76065-CA	78035-NJ
78030-FL	84026-NY
81024-FL	81045-WV
77075-IL	

Paragraph 11.3.1

    I

        93056-AZ
        94002-MO

Paragraph 11.3.6

    I

        93056-AZ
        94002-MO

    II

        93050-DPR

Text of Paragraph 11.4—Loss of Use Insurance

11.4.1 The Owner, at his option, may purchase and maintain such insurance as will insure him against loss of use of his property due to fire or other hazards, however caused. The Owner waives all rights of action against the Contractor for loss of use of his property, including consequential losses due to fire or other hazards however caused, to the extent covered by insurance under this Paragraph 11.4.

DOCUMENT TO CASE CHARTS: A201-1976

[The five-digit numbers in this chart are Citator Case Reference Numbers, which refer to the cases, in the Cases section. The suffixes indicate the state or, for federal cases, the court in which the case was decided.]

Paragraph 11.4 Loss of Use Insurance

   I

   86068-IL
   87007-VA
   87036-WA

   II

   79022-NY
   90049-OK

Article 12   Changes in the Work

Text of Paragraph 12.1—Change Orders

12.1.1 A Change Order is a written order to the Contractor signed by the Owner and the Architect, issued after execution of the Contract, authorizing a change in the Work or an adjustment in the Contract Sum or the Contract Time. The Contract Sum and the Contract Time may be changed only by Change Order. A Change Order signed by the Contractor indicates his agreement therewith, including the adjustment in the Contract Sum or the Contract Time.

12.1.2 The Owner, without invalidating the Contract, may order changes in the Work within the general scope of the Contract consisting of additions, deletions or other revisions, the Contract Sum and the Contract Time being adjusted accordingly. All such changes in the Work shall be authorized by Change Order, and shall be performed under the applicable conditions of the Contract Documents.

12.1.3 The cost or credit to the Owner resulting from a change in the Work shall be determined in one or more of the following ways:

.1   by mutual acceptance of a lump sum properly itemized and supported by sufficient substantiating data to permit evaluation;

.2   by unit prices stated in the Contract Documents or subsequently agreed upon;

.3   by cost to be determined in a manner agreed upon by the parties and a mutually acceptable fixed or percentage fee; or

.4   by the method provided in Subparagraph 12.1.4.

12.1.4 If none of the methods set forth in Clauses 12.1.3.1, 12.1.3.2 or 12.1.3.3 is agreed upon, the Contractor, provided he receives a written order signed by the Owner, shall promptly proceed with the Work involved. The cost of such Work shall then be determined by the Architect on the basis of the reasonable expenditures and savings of those performing the Work attributable to the change, including, in the case of an increase in the Contract Sum, a reasonable allowance for overhead and profit. In such case, and also under Clauses 12.1.3.3 and 12.1.3.4 above, the Contractor shall keep and present, in such form as the Architect may prescribe, an itemized accounting together with appropriate supporting data for inclusion in

DOCUMENT TO CASE CHARTS: A201-1976

[The five-digit numbers in this chart are Citator Case Reference Numbers, which refer to the cases, in the Cases section. The suffixes indicate the state or, for federal cases, the court in which the case was decided.]

a Change Order. Unless otherwise provided in the Contract Documents, cost shall be limited to the following: cost of materials, including sales tax and cost of delivery; cost of labor, including social security, old age and unemployment insurance, and fringe benefits required by agreement or custom; workers' or workmen's compensation insurance; bond premiums; rental value of equipment and machinery; and the additional costs of supervision and field office personnel directly attributable to the change. Pending final determination of cost to the Owner, payments on account shall be made on the Architect's Certificate for Payment. The amount of credit to be allowed by the Contractor to the Owner for any deletion or change which results in a net decrease in the Contract Sum will be the amount of the actual net cost as confirmed by the Architect. When both additions and credits covering related Work or substitutions are involved in any one change, the allowance for overhead and profit shall be figured on the basis of the net increase, if any, with respect to that change.

12.1.5 If unit prices are stated in the Contract Documents or subsequently agreed upon, and if the quantities originally contemplated are so changed in a proposed Change Order that application of the agreed unit prices to the quantities of Work proposed will cause substantial inequity to the Owner or the Contractor, the applicable unit prices shall be equitably adjusted.

Paragraph 12.1   Change Orders

    I

80002-AZ	91021-MO
84029-DC	91038-MO
90009-GA	93020-NC
91005-IL	77032-NE
81066-MD	88020-NE
83042-MD	84019-NY
84018-MO	85029-TN
84038-MO	77063-WA
86030-MO	78040-UT

    II

80033-8CIR	90022-ME
88008-SDNY	88011-MS
91031-MDPA	89032-MO
76017-EDWA	83014-NV
91006-FL	77018-NY
90012-GA	76019-PA
77057-IL	79017-TX
81023-KS	87029-TX

DOCUMENT TO CASE CHARTS: A201-1976

[*The five-digit numbers in this chart are Citator Case Reference Numbers, which refer to the cases, in the Cases section. The suffixes indicate the state or, for federal cases, the court in which the case was decided.*]

III

89024-1CIR	84024-MA
82026-8CIR	86027-MA
90048-10CIR	84030-MI
80070-AL	77041-MN
91004-AL	85044-MN
93004-AL	80018-NE
79066-AZ	75029-NJ
78037-AR	77014-NY
79018-CA	77084-NY
86029-CT	78072-NY
79055-GA	78077-NY
77065-ID	85022-NY
80036-ID	90007-NY
77026-IL	84025-OH
77073-IL	79008-OR
78026-IL	80022-OR
78042-IL	83001-PA
81014-IL	86004-PA
87003-IL	86011-PA
87028-IL	83004-TX
76064-LA	76006-TX
77077-LA	88036-TX
79027-LA	76018-VT
84033-LA	79002-VT
78013-MD	88025-VA

Paragraph 12.1.1

I

95023-VA

Text of Paragraph 12.2—Concealed Conditions

12.2.1 Should concealed conditions encountered in the performance of the Work below the surface of the ground or should concealed or unknown conditions in an existing structure be at variance with the conditions indicated by the Contract Documents, or should unknown physical conditions below the surface of the ground or should concealed or unknown conditions in an existing structure of an unusual nature, differing materially from those ordinarily encountered and generally recognized as inherent in work of the character provided for in this Contract, be encountered, the Contract Sum shall be equitably adjusted by Change Order upon claim by either party made within twenty days after the first observance of the conditions.

DOCUMENT TO CASE CHARTS: A201-1976

[The five-digit numbers in this chart are Citator Case Reference Numbers, which refer to the cases, in the Cases section. The suffixes indicate the state or, for federal cases, the court in which the case was decided.]

Paragraph 12.2 Concealed Conditions

I

95017-5CIR	77032-NE
91002-GA	79033-PA
83042-MD	84027-TX
81001-MA	

II

76001-EDAR	83014-NV
90039-WDNC	76043-WI
84035-IL	

III

83013-1CIR	78015-NY
76061-NDGA	78072-NY
91004-AL	78079-NY
78039-FL	85030-NY
85018-ID	86005-NY
77073-IL	82047-OH
86033-IL	84025-OH
86060-IL	86059-OH
89019-KS	76011-PA
76022-MD	76013-PA
79009-MD	86004-PA
86027-MA	86010-PA
85044-MN	90015-PA
77039-NY	76009-TX
77052-NY	89033-VA

Text of Paragraph 12.3—Claims for Additional Cost

12.3.1 If the Contractor wishes to make a claim for an increase in the Contract Sum, he shall give the Architect written notice thereof within twenty days after the occurrence of the event giving rise to such claim. This notice shall be given by the Contractor before proceeding to execute the Work, except in an emergency endangering life or property in which case the Contractor shall proceed in accordance with Paragraph 10.3. No such claim shall be valid unless so made. If the Owner and the Contractor cannot agree on the amount of the adjustment in the Contract Sum, it shall be determined by the Architect. Any change in the Contract Sum resulting from such claim shall be authorized by Change Order.

12.3.2 If the Contractor claims that additional cost is involved because of, but not limited to, (1) any written interpretation pursuant to Subparagraph 2.2.8, (2) any order by the Owner to stop the Work pursuant to Paragraph 3.3 where the Contractor was not at fault, (3) any written order for a minor change in the Work issued pursuant to Paragraph 12.4, or (4) failure of payment by the Owner pursuant to Paragraph 9.7, the Contractor shall make such claim as provided in Subparagraph 12.3.1.

DOCUMENT TO CASE CHARTS: A201-1976

[The five-digit numbers in this chart are Citator Case Reference Numbers, which refer to the cases, in the Cases section. The suffixes indicate the state or, for federal cases, the court in which the case was decided.]

Paragraph 12.3 Claims for Additional Cost

I

82004-SDGA	86030-MO
86055-AZ	91021-MO
90009-GA	77081-NJ
91005-IL	86003-NY
85032-IN	81022a-NC
85020-IA	85029-TN
81066-MD	84037-TX
84038-MO	77063-WA

II

80033-8CIR	88011-MS
91006-FL	84026-NY
84032-GA	86062-NY

III

88027-3CIR	85044-MN
76020-5CIR	75029-NJ
85009-7CIR	82007-NJ
90048-10CIR	91007-NM
82008-11CIR	85030-NY
89043-NDIL	86005-NY
90008-CC	86053-NY
91004-AL	90007-NY
81071-CT	85012-NC
86029-CT	84025-OH
84030-DC	86009-OH
77073-IL	86059-OH
81014-IL	76066-PA
85006-IL	86004-PA
87003-IL	86010-PA
84037-IN	86011-PA
89019-KS	90015-PA
84033-LA	83004-TX
84024-MA	88025-VA
86027-MA	89029-VA
86034-MA	89033-VA
87006-MA	85039-WV
84030-MI	

Text of Paragraph 12.4—Minor Changes in the Work

12.4.1 The Architect will have authority to order minor changes in the Work not involving an adjustment in the Contract Sum or an extension of the Contract Time and not inconsistent with the intent of the Contract Documents. Such changes shall be effected by written order, and shall be binding on the Owner and the Contractor. The Contractor shall carry out such written orders promptly.

DOCUMENT TO CASE CHARTS: A201-1976

[The five-digit numbers in this chart are Citator Case Reference Numbers, which refer to the cases, in the Cases section. The suffixes indicate the state or, for federal cases, the court in which the case was decided.]

Paragraph 12.4 Minor Changes in the Work

    II

        91031-MDPA

    III

        82026-8CIR
        86011-PA

Article 13 Uncovering and Correction of Work

Text of Paragraph 13.1—Uncovering of Work

13.1.1 If any portion of the Work should be covered contrary to the request of the Architect or to requirements specifically expressed in the Contract Documents, it must, if required in writing by the Architect, be uncovered for his observation and shall be replaced at the Contractor's expense.

13.1.2 If any other portion of the Work has been covered which the Architect has not specifically requested to observe prior to being covered, the Architect may request to see such Work and it shall be uncovered by the Contractor. If such Work be found in accordance with the Contract Documents, the cost of uncovering and replacement shall, by appropriate Change Order, be charged to the Owner. If such Work be found not in accordance with the Contract Documents, the Contractor shall pay such costs unless it be found that this condition was caused by the Owner or a separate contractor as provided in Article 6, in which event the Owner shall be responsible for the payment of such costs.

Paragraph 13.1 Uncovering of Work

    I

        88024-MA
        84036-OH

    II

        87002-ND

    III

        91026-IL

Text of Paragraph 13.2—Correction of Work

13.2.1 The Contractor shall promptly correct all Work rejected by the Architect as defective or as failing to conform to the Contract Documents whether observed before or after Substantial Completion and whether or not fabricated, installed or completed. The Contractor shall bear all costs of correcting such rejected Work, including compensation for the Architect's additional services made necessary thereby.

[The five-digit numbers in this chart are Citator Case Reference Numbers, which refer to the cases, in the Cases section. The suffixes indicate the state or, for federal cases, the court in which the case was decided.]

13.2.2 If, within one year after the Date of Substantial Completion of the Work or designated portion thereof or within one year after acceptance by the Owner of designated equipment or within such longer period of time as may be prescribed by law or by the terms of any applicable special warranty required by the Contract Documents, any of the Work is found to be defective or not in accordance with the Contract Documents, the Contractor shall correct it promptly after receipt of a written notice from the Owner to do so unless the Owner has previously given the Contractor a written acceptance of such condition. This obligation shall survive termination of the Contract. The Owner shall give such notice promptly after discovery of the condition.

13.2.3 The Contractor shall remove from the site all portions of the Work which are defective or non-conforming and which have not been corrected under Subparagraphs 4.5.1, 13.2.1 and 13.2.2, unless removal is waived by the Owner.

13.2.4 If the Contractor fails to correct defective or nonconforming Work as provided in Subparagraphs 4.5.1, 13.2.1 and 13.2.2, the Owner may correct it in accordance with Paragraph 3.4.

13.2.5 If the Contractor does not proceed with the correction of such defective or non-conforming Work within a reasonable time fixed by written notice from the Architect, the Owner may remove it and may store the materials or equipment at the expense of the Contractor. If the Contractor does not pay the cost of such removal and storage within ten days thereafter, the Owner may upon ten additional days' written notice sell such Work at auction or at private sale and shall account for the net proceeds thereof, after deducting all the costs that should have been borne by the Contractor, including compensation for the Architect's additional services made necessary thereby. If such proceeds of sale do not cover all costs which the Contractor should have borne, the difference shall be charged to the Contractor and an appropriate Change Order shall be issued. If the payments then or thereafter due the Contractor are not sufficient to cover such amount, the Contractor shall pay the difference to the Owner.

13.2.6 The Contractor shall bear the cost of making good all work of the Owner or separate contractors destroyed or damaged by such correction or removal.

13.2.7 Nothing contained in this Paragraph 13.2 shall be construed to establish a period of limitation with respect to any other obligation which the Contractor might have under the Contract Documents, including Paragraph 4.5 hereof. The establishment of the time period of one year after the Date of Substantial Completion or such longer period of time as may be prescribed by law or by the terms of any warranty required by the Contract Documents relates only to the specific obligation of the Contractor to correct the Work, and has no relationship to the time within which his obligation to comply with the Contract Documents may be sought to be enforced, nor to the time within which proceedings may be commenced to establish the Contractor's liability with respect to his obligations other than specifically to correct the Work.

DOCUMENT TO CASE CHARTS: A201-1976

[The five-digit numbers in this chart are Citator Case Reference Numbers, which refer to the cases, in the Cases section. The suffixes indicate the state or, for federal cases, the court in which the case was decided.]

Paragraph 13.2   Correction of Work

    I

79057-4CIR	91025-IL
82020-6CIR	82009-LA
84029-DC	87024-MD
78007-FL	90026-NE
80004-FL	86065-NJ
92015-GA	81057-NY
76030-ID	85023-NY
87034-IL	78052-ND
90040-IL	

    II

78056-GA	77018-NY
79021-NM	87002-ND
76028-NY	

    III

81060-5CIR	78054-IL
82014-NDMS	87034-IL
80012-AL	80049-IN
93004-AL	81050-ME
85031-AK	84031-NE
78032-CA	77009-OK
75032-CT	76013-PA
78010-GA	77038-PA
77046-IL	82017-TN

Text of Paragraph 13.3—Acceptance of Defective or Non-Conforming Work

13.3.1 If the Owner prefers to accept defective or non-conforming Work, he may do so instead of requiring its removal and correction. in which case a Change Order will be issued to reflect a reduction in the Contract Sum where appropriate and equitable. Such adjustment shall be effected whether or not final payment has been made.

Paragraph 13.3   Acceptance of Defective or Non-Conforming Work

    I

        84029-DC

Article 14   Termination of the Contract

Text of Paragraph 14.1—Termination by the Contractor

14.1.1 If the Work is stopped for a period of thirty days under an order of any court or other public authority having jurisdiction, or as a result of an act of government, such as a declaration of a national emergency making materials unavailable, through no act or fault of the Contractor or a Subcontractor or their agents or employees or any other persons performing any of the Work under a

DOCUMENT TO CASE CHARTS: A201-1976 A–274

[The five-digit numbers in this chart are Citator Case Reference Numbers, which refer to the cases, in the Cases section. The suffixes indicate the state or, for federal cases, the court in which the case was decided.]

> contract with the Contractor, or if the Work should be stopped for a period of thirty days by the Contractor because the Architect has not issued a Certificate for Payment as provided in Paragraph 9.7 or because the Owner has not made payment thereon as provided in Paragraph 9.7, then the Contractor may, upon seven additional days' written notice to the Owner and the Architect, terminate the Contract and recover from the Owner payment for all Work executed and for any proven loss sustained upon any materials, equipment, tools, construction equipment and machinery, including reasonable profit and damages.

Paragraph 14.1 Termination by the Contractor

    II

        91013-SDMS

    III

        78041-CO
        92009-FL
        77040-TX

> **Text of Paragraph 14.2—Termination by the Owner**
>
> **14.2.1** If the Contractor is adjudged a bankrupt, or if he makes a general assignment for the benefit of his creditors, or if a receiver is appointed on account of his solvency, or if he persistently or repeatedly refuses or fails, except in cases for which extension of time is provided, to supply enough properly skilled workmen or proper materials, or if he fails to make prompt payment to Subcontractors or for materials or labor, or persistently disregards laws, ordinances, rules, regulations or orders of any public authority having jurisdiction, or otherwise is guilty of a substantial violation of a provision of the Contract Documents, then the Owner, upon certification by the Architect that sufficient cause exists to justify such action, may, without prejudice to any right or remedy and after giving the Contractor and his surety, if any, seven days' written notice, terminate the employment of the Contractor and take possession of the site and of all materials, equipment, tools, construction equipment and machinery thereon owned by the Contractor and may finish the Work by whatever method he may deem expedient. In such case the Contractor shall not be entitled to receive any further payment until the Work is finished.
>
> **14.2.2** If the unpaid balance of the Contract Sum exceeds the costs of finishing the Work, including compensation for the Architect's additional services made necessary thereby, such excess shall be paid to the Contractor. If such costs exceed the unpaid balance, the Contractor shall pay the difference to the Owner. The amount to be paid to the Contractor or to the Owner, as the case may be, shall be certified by the Architect, upon application, in the manner provided in Paragraph 9.4, and his obligation for payment shall survive the termination of the Contract.

DOCUMENT TO CASE CHARTS: A201-1976

[The five-digit numbers in this chart are Citator Case Reference Numbers, which refer to the cases, in the Cases section. The suffixes indicate the state or, for federal cases, the court in which the case was decided.]

Paragraph 14.2   Termination by the Owner

   I

      79057-4CIR   88016-OH
      78031-IL   79032-OK
      84019-NY   78021-TN

   II

      91013-SDMS   87002-ND
      80011-AR   82058-PA
      88010-CO   80025-TX
      90032-IL

   III

      82002-3CIR   86024-NY
      83007-7CIR   90016-NY
      86016-EDMO   85014a-OK
      77004-AK   76006-TX
      92009-FL   78001-SC
      78055-IL   86042-WA

Paragraph 14.2.1

   II

      94027-MN

DOCUMENT TO CASE CHARTS: A201-1987

[The five-digit numbers in this chart are Citator Case Reference Numbers, which refer to the cases, in the Cases section. The suffixes indicate the state or, for federal cases, the court in which the case was decided.]

A201-1987—GENERAL CONDITIONS OF THE CONTRACT FOR CONSTRUCTION

Article 1 General Provisions

Paragraph 1.1 Basic Definitions

Text of Paragraph 1.1.1—The Contract Documents

The Contract Documents consist of the Agreement between Owner and Contractor (hereinafter the Agreement). Conditions of the Contract (General, Supplementary and other Conditions), Drawings, Specifications, addenda issued prior to execution of the Contract, other documents listed in the Agreement and Modifications issued after execution of the Contract. A Modification is (1) a written amendment to the Contract signed by both parties, (2) a Change Order, (3) a Construction Change Directive or (4) a written order for a minor change in the Work issued by the Architect. Unless specifically enumerated in the Agreement, the Contract Documents do not include other documents such as bidding requirements (advertisement or invitation to bid, Instructions to Bidders, sample forms, the Contractor's bid or portions of addenda relating to bidding requirements).

Paragraph 1.1.1 The Contract Documents

    I

        95023-VA

    II

        97003-WA
        97024-WV

Text of Paragraph 1.1.2—The Contract

The Contract Documents form the Contract for Construction. The Contract represents the entire and integrated agreement between the parties hereto and supersedes prior negotiations, representations or agreements, either written or oral. The Contract may be amended or modified only by a Modification. The Contract Documents shall not be construed to create a contractual relationship of any kind (1) between the Architect and Contractor, (2) between the Owner and a Subcontractor or Sub-subcontractor or (3) between any persons or entities other than the Owner and Contractor. The Architect shall, however, be entitled to performance and enforcement of obligations under the Contract intended to facilitate performance of the Architect's duties.

A–277   **DOCUMENT TO CASE CHARTS: A201-1987**

[*The five-digit numbers in this chart are Citator Case Reference Numbers, which refer to the cases, in the Cases section. The suffixes indicate the state or, for federal cases, the court in which the case was decided.*]

Paragraph 1.1.2   The Contract

    I

        93019-NJ

    II

        95031-MI
        97024-WV

Text of Paragraph 1.1.3—The Work

The term "Work" means the construction and services required by the Contract Documents, whether completed or partially completed, and includes all other labor, materials, equipment and services provided or to be provided by the Contractor to fulfill the Contractor's obligations. The Work may constitute the whole or a part of the Project.

Paragraph 1.1.3   The Work

    I

        95051-SDMS
        97025-CO
        94004-MO

    III

        96025-NJ

Paragraph 1.1.4   The Project

Paragraph 1.1.5   The Drawings

Paragraph 1.1.6   The Specifications

Paragraph 1.1.7   The Project Manual

Paragraph 1.2   Execution, Correlation and Intent

Paragraph 1.3   Ownership and Use of Architect's Drawings, Specifications and Other Documents

---

Text of Paragraph 1.3.1

The Drawings, Specifications and other documents prepared by the Architect are instruments of the Architect's service through which the Work to be executed by the Contractor is described. The Contractor may retain one contract record set. Neither the Contractor nor any Subcontractor, Sub-subcontractor or material or equipment supplier shall own or claim a copyright in the Drawings. Specifications and other documents prepared by the Architect, and unless otherwise indicated the Architect shall be deemed the author of them and will retain all common law, statutory and other reserved rights, in addition to the copyright. All copies of them, except the Contractor's record set, shall be returned or suitably accounted for to

DOCUMENT TO CASE CHARTS: A201-1987 A–278

[The five-digit numbers in this chart are Citator Case Reference Numbers, which refer to the cases, in the Cases section. The suffixes indicate the state or, for federal cases, the court in which the case was decided.]

> the Architect, on request, upon completion of the Work. The Drawings, Specifications and other documents prepared by the Architect, and copies thereof furnished to the Contractor, are for use solely with respect to this Project. They are not to be used by the Contractor or any Subcontractor, Sub-subcontractor or material or equipment supplier on other projects or for additions to this Project outside the scope of the Work without the specific written consent of the Owner and Architect. The Contractor, Subcontractors, Sub-subcontractors and material or equipment suppliers are granted a limited license to use and reproduce applicable portions of the Drawings, Specifications and other documents prepared by the Architect appropriate to and for use in the execution of their Work under the Contract Documents. All copies made under this license shall bear the statutory copyright notice, if any, shown on the Drawings, Specifications and other documents prepared by the Architect. Submittal or distribution to meet official regulatory requirements or for other purposes in connection with this Project is not to be construed as publication in derogation of the Architect's copyright or other reserved rights.

Paragraph 1.3.1

    III

        94010-EDLA

Paragraph 1.4   Capitalization

Paragraph 1.5   Interpretation

Article 2   Owner

Paragraph 2.1   Definition

> **Text of Paragraph 2.1.1**
>
> The Owner is the person or entity identified as such in the Agreement and is referred to throughout the Contract Documents as if singular in number. The term "Owner" means the Owner or the Owner's authorized representative.

Paragraph 2.1.1

    I

        96004-LA

Paragraph 2.2   Information and Services Required of the Owner

> **Text of Paragraph 2.2.1**
>
> The Owner shall, at the request of the Contractor, prior to execution of the Agreement and promptly from time to time thereafter, furnish to the Contractor reasonable evidence that financial arrangements have been made to fulfill the Owner's obligations under the Contract. *[Note: Unless such reasonable evidence*

DOCUMENT TO CASE CHARTS: A201-1987

[*The five-digit numbers in this chart are Citator Case Reference Numbers, which refer to the cases, in the Cases section. The suffixes indicate the state or, for federal cases, the court in which the case was decided.*]

> were furnished on request prior to the execution of the Agreement, the prospective contractor would not be required to execute the Agreement or to commence the Work.]

Paragraph 2.2.1

    III

        93026-NY
        95008-VA

Text of Paragraph 2.2.3

2.2.3 Except for permits and fees which are the responsibility of the Contractor under the Contract Documents, the Owner shall secure and pay for necessary approvals, easements, assessments and charges required for construction, use or occupancy of permanent structures or for permanent changes in existing facilities.

Paragraph 2.2.3

    III

        95008-VA

Paragraph 2.3   Owner's Right to Stop the Work

    III

        95040-GA

Paragraph 2.3.1

Text of Paragraph 2.3.1

2.3.1 If the Contractor fails to correct Work which is not in accordance with the requirements of the Contract Documents as required by Paragraph 12.2 or persistently fails to carry out Work in accordance with the Contract Documents, the Owner, by written order signed personally or by an agent specifically so empowered by the Owner in writing, may order the Contractor to stop the Work, or any portion thereof, until the cause for such order has been eliminated; however, the right of the Owner to stop the Work shall not give rise to a duty on the part of the Owner to exercise this right for the benefit of the Contractor or any other person or entity, except to the extent required by Subparagraph 6.1.3.

DOCUMENT TO CASE CHARTS: A201-1987 A–280

[The five-digit numbers in this chart are Citator Case Reference Numbers, which refer to the cases, in the Cases section. The suffixes indicate the state or, for federal cases, the court in which the case was decided.]

Paragraph 2.3.1

    III

        95044-MDAL

Text of Paragraph 2.4—Owner's Right to Carry Out the Work

2.4.1 If the Contractor defaults or neglects to carry out the Work in accordance with the Contract Documents and fails within a seven-day period after receipt of written notice from the Owner to commence and continue correction of such default or neglect with diligence and promptness, the Owner may after such seven-day period give the Contractor a second written notice to correct such deficiencies within a second seven-day period. If the Contractor within such second seven-day period after receipt of such second notice fails to commence and continue to correct any deficiencies, the Owner may, without prejudice to other remedies the Owner may have, correct such deficiencies. In such case an appropriate Change Order shall be issued deducting from payments then or thereafter due the Contractor the cost of correcting such deficiencies, including compensation for the Architect's additional services and expenses made necessary by such default, neglect or failure. Such action by the Owner and amounts charged to the Contractor are both subject to prior approval of the Architect. If payments then or thereafter due the Contractor are not sufficient to cover such amounts, the Contractor shall pay the difference to the Owner.

Paragraph 2.4   Owner's Right to Carry Out the Work

    III

        95040-GA

Article 3   Contractor

Paragraph 3.1   Definition

Paragraph 3.2   Review of Contract Documents and Field Conditions by Contractor

---

Text of Paragraph 3.2.1

The Contractor shall carefully study and compare the Contract Documents with each other and with information furnished by the Owner pursuant to Subparagraph 2.2.2 and shall at once report to the Architect errors, inconsistencies or omissions discovered. The Contractor shall not be liable to the Owner or Architect for damage resulting from errors, inconsistencies or omissions in the Contract Documents unless the Contractor recognized such error, inconsistency or omission and knowingly failed to report it to the Architect. If the Contractor performs any construction activity knowing it involves a recognized error, inconsistency or omission in the Contract Documents without such notice to the Architect, the Contractor shall

DOCUMENT TO CASE CHARTS: A201-1987

[The five-digit numbers in this chart are Citator Case Reference Numbers, which refer to the cases, in the Cases section. The suffixes indicate the state or, for federal cases, the court in which the case was decided.]

> assume appropriate responsibility for such performance and shall bear an appropriate amount of the attributable costs for correction.

Paragraph 3.2.1

    III

        93026-NY   95008-VA
        93001-NC   96039-WY

> **Text of Paragraph 3.2.2**
>
> The Contractor shall take field measurements and verify field conditions and shall carefully compare such field measurements and conditions and other information known to the Contractor with the Contract Documents before commencing activities. Errors, inconsistencies or omissions discovered shall be reported to the Architect at once.

Paragraph 3.2.2

    III

        93026-NY
        93001-NC
        95008-VA

> **Text of Paragraph 3.2.3**
>
> 3.2.3 The Contractor shall perform the Work in accordance with the Contract Documents and submittals approved pursuant to Paragraph 3.12.

Paragraph 3.2.3

    III

        95008-VA

Paragraph 3.3   Supervision and Construction Procedures

    II

        95004-NJ

    III

        94040-11CIR
        92004d-LA
        95030-MA

> **Text of Paragraph 3.3.1**
>
> The Contractor shall supervise and direct the Work using the Contractor's best skill and attention. The Contractor shall be solely responsible for and have control over construction means, methods, techniques, sequences and procedures and for

DOCUMENT TO CASE CHARTS: A201-1987 A–282

[The five-digit numbers in this chart are Citator Case Reference Numbers, which refer to the cases, in the Cases section. The suffixes indicate the state or, for federal cases, the court in which the case was decided.]

coordinating all portions of the Work under the Contract, unless Contract Documents give other specific instructions concerning these matters.

Paragraph 3.3.1

    I

        94038-FL   93033-MO
        96009-LA   97005-PA
        93005-MO

    II

        94044-MDGA   94045-TX
        95040-GA   96027-TX
        93025-IL

    III

        97020-10CIR   94005-MO
        95044-MDAL   96025-NJ
        93034-GA   95008-VA
        93015a-IL   96041-WY

Text of Paragraph 3.3.2

The Contractor shall be responsible to the Owner for acts and omissions of the Contractor's employees, Subcontractors and their agents and employees, and other persons performing portions of the Work under a contract with the Contractor.

Paragraph 3.3.2

    I

        95051-SDMS
        96009-LA
        93033-MO

    II

        93025-IL

    III

        95044-MDAL   93015a-IL
        93034-GA   96025-NJ

Text of Paragraph 3.3.3

3.3.3 The Contractor shall not be relieved of obligations to perform the Work in accordance with the Contract Documents either by activities or duties of the Architect in the Architect's administration of the Contract, or by tests, inspections or approvals required or performed by persons other than the Contractor.

DOCUMENT TO CASE CHARTS: A201-1987

[The five-digit numbers in this chart are Citator Case Reference Numbers, which refer to the cases, in the Cases section. The suffixes indicate the state or, for federal cases, the court in which the case was decided.]

Paragraph 3.3.3

    I

        95020-DPR

    III

        95044-MDAL
        95029-EDVA

Text of Paragraph 3.3.4

The Contractor shall be responsible for inspection of portions of Work already performed under this Contract to determine that such portions are in proper condition to receive subsequent Work.

Paragraph 3.3.4

    I

        93033-MO

Paragraph 3.4   Labor and Materials

    III

        95030-MA

Text of Paragraph 3.4.1

Unless otherwise provided in the Contract Documents, the Contractor shall provide and pay for labor, materials, equipment, tools, construction equipment and machinery, water, heat, utilities, transportation, and other facilities and services necessary for proper execution and completion of the Work, whether temporary or permanent and whether or not incorporated or to be incorporated in the Work.

Paragraph 3.4.1

    I

        95051-SDMS

    III

        95044-MDAL
        93034-GA

Text of Paragraph 3.4.2

3.4.2 The Contractor shall enforce strict discipline and good order among the Contractor's employees and other persons carrying out the Contract. The Contractor shall not permit employment of unfit persons or persons not skilled in tasks assigned to them.

DOCUMENT TO CASE CHARTS: A201-1987   A–284

[The five-digit numbers in this chart are Citator Case Reference Numbers, which refer to the cases, in the Cases section. The suffixes indicate the state or, for federal cases, the court in which the case was decided.]

Paragraph 3.4.2

    II

        93015a-IL

    III

        95044-MDAL

Paragraph 3.5   Warranty

Text of Paragraph 3.5.1

The Contractor warrants to the Owner and Architect that materials and equipment furnished under the Contract will be of good quality and new unless otherwise required or permitted by the Contract Documents, that the Work will be free from defects not inherent in the quality required or permitted, and that the Work will conform with the requirements of the Contract Documents. Work not conforming to these requirements, including substitutions not properly approved and authorized, may be considered defective. The Contractor's warranty excludes remedy for damage or defect caused by abuse, modifications not executed by the Contractor, improper or insufficient maintenance, improper operation, or normal wear and tear under normal usage. If required by the Architect, the Contractor shall furnish satisfactory evidence as to the kind and quality of materials and equipment.

Paragraph 3.5.1

    II

        93025-IL

    III

        94024-PA
        95008-VA

Paragraph 3.6   Taxes

Paragraph 3.7   Permits, Fees and Notices

Text of Paragraph 3.7.1

3.7.1 Unless otherwise provided in the Contract Documents, the Contractor shall secure and pay for the building permit and other permits and governmental fees, licenses and inspections necessary for proper execution and completion of the Work which are customarily secured after execution of the Contract and which are legally required when bids are received or negotiations concluded.

DOCUMENT TO CASE CHARTS: A201-1987

[The five-digit numbers in this chart are Citator Case Reference Numbers, which refer to the cases, in the Cases section. The suffixes indicate the state or, for federal cases, the court in which the case was decided.]

Paragraph 3.7.1

    III

        95008-VA

Text of Paragraph 3.7.2

The Contractor shall comply with and give notices required by laws, ordinances, rules, regulations and lawful orders of public authorities bearing on performance of the Work.

Paragraph 3.7.2

    III

        97020-10CIR
        94032-DE
        94014-IN

Text of Paragraph 3.7.3

3.7.3 It is not the Contractor's responsibility to ascertain that the Contract Documents are in accordance with applicable laws, statutes, ordinances, building codes, and rules and regulations. However, if the Contractor observes that portions of the Contract Documents are at variance therewith, the Contractor shall promptly notify the Architect and Owner in writing, and necessary changes shall be accomplished by appropriate Modification.

Paragraph 3.7.3

    III

        95008-VA

Paragraph 3.8   Allowances

Paragraph 3.9   Superintendent

    III

        95030-MA

Text of Paragraph 3.9.1

3.9.1 The Contractor shall employ a competent superintendent and necessary assistants who shall be in attendance at the Project site during performance of the Work. The superintendent shall represent the Contractor, and communications given to the superintendent shall be as binding as if given to the Contractor. Important communications shall be confirmed in writing. Other communications shall be similarly confirmed on written request in each case.

DOCUMENT TO CASE CHARTS: A201-1987

A–286

[The five-digit numbers in this chart are Citator Case Reference Numbers, which refer to the cases, in the Cases section. The suffixes indicate the state or, for federal cases, the court in which the case was decided.]

Paragraph 3.9.1

    III

        95044-MDAL

Paragraph 3.10   Contractor's Construction Schedules

Text of Paragraph 3.10.1

3.10.1 The Contractor, promptly after being awarded the Contract, shall prepare and submit for the Owner's and Architect's information a Contractor's construction schedule for the Work. The schedule shall not exceed time limits current under the Contract Documents, shall be revised at appropriate intervals as required by the conditions of the Work and Project, shall be related to the entire Project to the extent required by the Contract Documents, and shall provide for expeditious and practicable execution of the Work.

Paragraph 3.10.1

    III

        94040-11CIR

Text of Paragraph 3.10.3

3.10.3 The Contractor shall conform to the most recent schedules.

Paragraph 3.10.3

    III

        94040-11CIR

Paragraph 3.11   Documents and Samples at the Site

Paragraph 3.12   Shop Drawings, Product Data and Samples

Paragraph 3.13   Use of Site

Paragraph 3.14   Cutting and Patching

Paragraph 3.15   Cleaning Up

Paragraph 3.16   Access to Work

Paragraph 3.17   Royalties and Patents

Paragraph 3.18   Indemnification

Text of Paragraph 3.18.1

To the fullest extent permitted by law, the Contractor shall indemnify and hold harmless the Owner, Architect, Architect's consultants, and agents and employees of any of them from and against claims, damages, losses and expenses, including

DOCUMENT TO CASE CHARTS: A201-1987

[The five-digit numbers in this chart are Citator Case Reference Numbers, which refer to the cases, in the Cases section. The suffixes indicate the state or, for federal cases, the court in which the case was decided.]

> but not limited to attorneys' fees, arising out of or resulting from performance of the Work, provided that such claim, damage, loss or expense is attributable to bodily injury, sickness, disease or death, or to injury to or destruction of tangible property (other than the Work itself) including loss of use resulting therefrom, but only to the extent caused in whole or in part by negligent acts or omissions of the Contractor, a Subcontractor, anyone directly or indirectly employed by them or anyone for whose acts they may be liable, regardless of whether or not such claim, damage, loss or expense is caused in part by a party indemnified hereunder. Such obligation shall not be construed to negate, abridge, or reduce other rights or obligations of indemnity which would otherwise exist as to a party or person described in this Paragraph 3.18.

Paragraph 3.18.1

I

95051-SDMS	93033-MO
94043-NDNY	97017-NJ
97009-CA	92008a-PA
95011-MN	97005-PA
92003a-MO	93028-UT

II

96015-DC	95025-NJ
97002-DC	97014-NJ
95006-GA	93043-PA
92001a-ID	92004f-TX
94036-IL	94009-TX
92008b-IA	94033-TX
93018-MA	95036-TX
94047-MI	95049-TX
93053-MN	93035-UT
96008-MN	93040-WA
93014-MO	95045-WI
96018-MO	

III

94039-5CIR	92004d-LA
96019-DKS	93038-LA
96024-DKS	94013-LA
94023-SDMS	95027-LA
95035-SDNY	96003-LA
94022-DRI	95015-ME
95007-DRI	93041-MA
95009-AR	94029-MA
97008-CA	95028-MA
93051-DC	95041-MA
93009-FL	96021-MA
95032-FL	96026-MA
97019-ID	96029-MA
94046-IL	96035-MA
95026-IL	97006-MA
96012-IL	94016-MI
96031-IL	93047-MN

DOCUMENT TO CASE CHARTS: A201-1987

[*The five-digit numbers in this chart are Citator Case Reference Numbers, which refer to the cases, in the Cases section. The suffixes indicate the state or, for federal cases, the court in which the case was decided.*]

94037-MN	95012-OR
95010-MN	96010-OR
96043-MN	93031-PA
95004-NJ	93042-UT
93039-NY	95013-UT
93030-OH	94035-WA
94042-OH	96007-WA
94048-OK	95048-WV

Text of Paragraph 3.18.2

In claims against any person or entity indemnified under this Paragraph 3.18 by an employee of the Contractor, a Subcontractor, anyone directly or indirectly employed by them or anyone for whose acts they may be liable, the indemnification obligation under this Paragraph 3.18 shall not be limited by a limitation on amount or type of damages, compensation or benefits payable by or for the Contractor or a Subcontractor under workers' or workmen's compensation acts, disability benefit acts or other employee benefit acts.

Paragraph 3.18.2

    I

        95025-NJ
        97005-PA

    II

        97002-DC
        97014-NJ

    III

        96007-WA

Article 4 Administration of the Contract

Paragraph 4.1 Architect

Paragraph 4.2 Architect's Administration of the Contract

Text of Paragraph 4.2.1

4.2.1 The Architect will provide administration of the Contract as described in the Contract Documents, and will be the Owner's representative (1) during construction, (2) until final payment is due and (3) with the Owner's concurrence, from time to time during the correction period described in Paragraph 12.2. The Architect will advise and consult with the Owner. The Architect will have authority to act on behalf of the Owner only to the extent provided in the Contract Documents, unless otherwise modified by written instrument in accordance with other provisions of the Contract.

DOCUMENT TO CASE CHARTS: A201-1987

[The five-digit numbers in this chart are Citator Case Reference Numbers, which refer to the cases, in the Cases section. The suffixes indicate the state or, for federal cases, the court in which the case was decided.]

Paragraph 4.2.1

    I

        95001-WA

    II

        94044-MDGA
        92004b-GA
        94045-TX

Text of Paragraph 4.2.2

The Architect will visit the site at intervals appropriate to the stage of construction to become generally familiar with the progress and quality of the completed Work and to determine in general if the Work is being performed in a manner indicating that the Work, when completed, will be in accordance with the Contract Documents. However, the Architect will not be required to make exhaustive or continuous on-site inspections to check quality or quantity of the Work. On the basis of on-site observations as an architect, the Architect will keep the Owner informed of progress of the Work, and will endeavor to guard the Owner against defects and deficiencies in the Work.

Paragraph 4.2.2

    I

        93005-MO

    II

        96020-8CIR   95042-OH
        94044-MDGA   95052-OH
        93036-NE   94045-TX
        95004-NJ

    III

        95018-2CIR
        97020-10CIR
        93015a-IL

Text of Paragraph 4.2.3

4.2.3 The Architect will not have control over or charge of and will not be responsible for construction means, methods, techniques, sequences or procedures, or for safety precautions and programs in connection with the Work, since these are solely the Contractor's responsibility as provided in Paragraph 3.3. The Architect will not be responsible for the Contractor's failure to carry out the Work in accordance with the Contract Documents. The Architect will not have control over or charge of and will not be responsible for acts or omissions of the Contractor, Subcontractors, or their agents or employees, or of any other persons performing portions of the Work.

DOCUMENT TO CASE CHARTS: A201-1987

[The five-digit numbers in this chart are Citator Case Reference Numbers, which refer to the cases, in the Cases section. The suffixes indicate the state or, for federal cases, the court in which the case was decided.]

Paragraph 4.2.3

    I

        93005-MO

    II

96020-8CIR	95042-OH
94044-MDGA	95052-OH
95004-NJ	94045-TX

    III

        95018-2CIR
        97020-10CIR
        93015a-IL

Paragraph 4.2.4 Communications Facilitating Contract Administration

---

Text of Paragraph 4.2.5

4.2.5 Based on the Architect's observations and evaluations of the Contractor's Applications for Payment, the Architect will review and certify the amounts due the Contractor and will issue Certificates for Payment in such amounts.

Paragraph 4.2.5

    II

        92002-TN

Text of Paragraph 4.2.6

The Architect will have authority to reject Work which does not conform to the Contract Documents. Whenever the Architect considers it necessary or advisable for implementation of the intent of the Contract Documents, the Architect will have authority to require additional inspection or testing of the Work in accordance with Subparagraphs 13.5.2 and 13.5.3, whether or not such Work is fabricated, installed or completed. However, neither this authority of the Architect nor a decision made in good faith either to exercise or not to exercise such authority shall give rise to a duty or responsibility of the Architect to the Contractor, Subcontractors, material and equipment suppliers, their agents or employees, or other persons performing portions of the Work.

DOCUMENT TO CASE CHARTS: A201-1987

[*The five-digit numbers in this chart are Citator Case Reference Numbers, which refer to the cases, in the Cases section. The suffixes indicate the state or, for federal cases, the court in which the case was decided.*]

Paragraph 4.2.6

    II

        95004-NJ

    III

        95018-2CIR   93045-IL
        95029-EDVA   95022-NC

Text of Paragraph 4.2.7

4.2.7 The Architect will review and approve or take other appropriate action upon the Contractor's submittals such as Shop Drawings, Product Data and Samples, but only for the limited purpose of checking for conformance with information given and the design concept expressed in the Contract Documents. The Architect's action will be taken with such reasonable promptness as to cause no delay in the Work or in the activities of the Owner, Contractor or separate contractors, while allowing sufficient time in the Architect's professional judgment to permit adequate review. Review of such submittals is not conducted for the purpose of determining the accuracy and completeness of other details such as dimensions and quantities, or for substantiating instructions for installation or performance of equipment or systems, all of which remain the responsibility of the Contractor as required by the Contract Documents. The Architect's review of the Contractor's submittals shall not relieve the Contractor of the obligations under Paragraphs 3.3, 3.5 and 3.12. The Architect's review shall not constitute approval of safety precautions or, unless otherwise specifically stated by the Architect, of any construction means, methods, techniques, sequences or procedures. The Architect's approval of a specific item shall not indicate approval of an assembly of which the item is a component.

Paragraph 4.2.7

    III

        95008-VA

Text of Paragraph 4.2.8

4.2.8 The Architect will prepare Change Orders and Construction Change Directives, and may authorize minor changes in the Work as provided in Paragraph 7.4.

DOCUMENT TO CASE CHARTS: A201-1987

[The five-digit numbers in this chart are Citator Case Reference Numbers, which refer to the cases, in the Cases section. The suffixes indicate the state or, for federal cases, the court in which the case was decided.]

Paragraph 4.2.8

    I

        97018-MO

    III

        95001-WA

Text of Paragraph 4.2.9

4.2.9 The Architect will conduct inspections to determine the date or dates of Substantial Completion and the date of final completion, will receive and forward to the Owner for the Owner's review and records written warranties and related documents required by the Contract and assembled by the Contractor, and will issue a final Certificate for Payment upon compliance with the requirements of the Contract Documents.

Paragraph 4.2.9

    II

        92002-TN

    III

        95029-EDVA
        94045-TX

Text of Paragraph 4.2.11

The Architect will interpret and decide matters concerning performance under and requirements of the Contract Documents on written request of either the Owner or Contractor. The Architect's response to such requests will be made with reasonable promptness and within any time limits agreed upon. If no agreement is made concerning the time within which interpretations required of the Architect shall be furnished in compliance with this Paragraph 4.2, then delay shall not be recognized on account of failure by the Architect to furnish such interpretations until 15 days after written request is made for them.

Paragraph 4.2.11

    I

        97018-MO

DOCUMENT TO CASE CHARTS: A201-1987

[The five-digit numbers in this chart are Citator Case Reference Numbers, which refer to the cases, in the Cases section. The suffixes indicate the state or, for federal cases, the court in which the case was decided.]

    II

        92004b-GA
        94017-MO
        95033-MO

    III

        95018-2CIR
        94041-CT

Text of Paragraph 4.2.12

4.2.12 Interpretations and decisions of the Architect will be consistent with the intent of and reasonably inferable from the Contract Documents and will be in writing or in the form of drawings. When making such interpretations and decisions, the Architect will endeavor to secure faithful performance by both Owner and Contractor, will not show partiality to either and will not be liable for results of interpretations or decisions so rendered in good faith.

Paragraph 4.2.12

    I

        97018-MO

    II

        92004b-GA

    III

        95018-2CIR
        94041-CT

Text of Paragraph 4.2.13

4.2.13 The Architect's decisions on matters relating to aesthetic effect will be final if consistent with the intent expressed in the Contract Documents.

Paragraph 4.2.13

    I

        97018-MO

    II

        92004b-GA

DOCUMENT TO CASE CHARTS: A201-1987

[The five-digit numbers in this chart are Citator Case Reference Numbers, which refer to the cases, in the Cases section. The suffixes indicate the state or, for federal cases, the court in which the case was decided.]

    III

        94041-CT

Paragraph 4.3   Claims and Disputes

    II

        95033-MO

    III

        97001-MDGA
        96016-GA

Text of Paragraph 4.3.1—Definition

A Claim is a demand or assertion by one of the parties seeking, as a matter of right, adjustment or interpretation of Contract terms, payment of money, extension of time or other relief with respect to the terms of the Contract. The term "Claim" also includes other disputes and matters in question between the Owner and Contractor arising out of or relating to the Contract. Claims must be made by written notice. The responsibility to substantiate Claims shall rest with the party making the Claim.

Paragraph 4.3.1   Definition

    I

        93046-MO

    III

        92004a-GA

Text of Paragraph 4.3.2—Decision of the Architect

Claims, including those alleging an error or omission by the Architect, shall be referred initially to the Architect for action as provided in Paragraph 4.4. A decision by the Architect, as provided in Subparagraph 4.4.4, shall be required as a condition precedent to arbitration or litigation of a Claim between the Contractor and Owner as to all such matters arising prior to the date final payment is due, regardless of (1) whether such matters relate to execution and progress of the Work or (2) the extent to which the Work has been completed. The decision by the Architect in response to a Claim shall not be a condition precedent to arbitration or litigation in the event (1) the position of Architect is vacant, (2) the Architect has not received evidence or has failed to render a decision within agreed time limits, (3) the Architect has failed to take action required under Subparagraph 4.4.4 within 30 days after the Claim is made, (4) 45 days have passed after the Claim has been referred to the Architect or (5) the Claim relates to a mechanic's lien.

DOCUMENT TO CASE CHARTS: A201-1987

[The five-digit numbers in this chart are Citator Case Reference Numbers, which refer to the cases, in the Cases section. The suffixes indicate the state or, for federal cases, the court in which the case was decided.]

Paragraph 4.3.2   Decision of Architect

   I

      94038-FL
      97018-MO

   II

      92004b-GA
      93045-IL
      96027-TX

   III

      94041-CT   995024-NY
      92004a-GA   97002-NY
      94005-MO   96039-WY
      95022-NC

Text of Paragraph 4.3.3—Time Limits on Claims

4.3.3 Time Limits on Claims. Claims by either party must be made within 21 days after occurrence of the event giving rise to such Claim or within 21 days after the claimant first recognizes the condition giving rise to the Claim, whichever is later. Claims must be made by written notice. An additional Claim made after the initial Claim has been implemented by Change Order will not be considered unless submitted in a timely manner.

Paragraph 4.3.3   Time Limits on Claims

   I

      97018-MO

   III

      97022-NY
      95001-WA
      96039-WY

Text of Paragraph 4.3.4—Continuing Contract Performance

4.3.4 Continuing Contract Performance. Pending final resolution of a Claim including arbitration, unless otherwise agreed in writing the Contractor shall proceed diligently with performance of the Contract and the Owner shall continue to make payments in accordance with the Contract Documents.

DOCUMENT TO CASE CHARTS: A201-1987

[The five-digit numbers in this chart are Citator Case Reference Numbers, which refer to the cases, in the Cases section. The suffixes indicate the state or, for federal cases, the court in which the case was decided.]

Paragraph 4.3.4 Continuing Contract Performance

    III

        92018a-MT

Text of Paragraph 4.3.5—Waiver of Claims: Final Payment

4.3.5 Waiver of Claims: Final Payment. The making of final payment shall constitute a waiver of Claims by the Owner except those arising from:

.1   liens, Claims, security interests or encumbrances arising out of the Contract and unsettled;

.2   failure of the Work to comply with the requirements of the Contract Documents; or

.3   terms of special warranties required by the Contract Documents.

Paragraph 4.3.5 Waiver of Claims: Final Payment

    I

        95001-WA

    III

        94031-RI

Text of Paragraph 4.3.6—Claims for Concealed or Unknown Conditions

If conditions are encountered at the site which are (1) subsurface or otherwise concealed physical conditions which differ materially from those indicated in the Contract Documents or (2) unknown physical conditions of an unusual nature, which differ materially from those ordinarily found to exist and generally recognized as inherent in construction activities of the character provided for in the Contract Documents, then notice by the observing party shall be given to the other party promptly before conditions are disturbed and in no event later than 21 days after first observance of the conditions. The Architect will promptly investigate such conditions and if they differ materially and cause an increase or decrease in the Contractor's cost of, or time required for, performance of any part of the Work, will recommend an equitable adjustment in the Contract Sum or Contract Time, or both. If the Architect determines that the conditions at the site are not materially different from those indicated in the Contract Documents and that no change in the terms of the Contract is justified, the Architect shall so notify the Owner and Contractor in writing, stating the reasons. Claims by either party in opposition to such determination must be made within 21 days after the Architect has given notice of the decision. If the Owner and Contractor cannot agree on an adjustment in the Contract Sum or Contract Time, the adjustment shall be referred to the Architect for initial determination, subject to further proceedings pursuant to Paragraph 4.4.

DOCUMENT TO CASE CHARTS: A201-1987

[The five-digit numbers in this chart are Citator Case Reference Numbers, which refer to the cases, in the Cases section. The suffixes indicate the state or, for federal cases, the court in which the case was decided.]

Paragraph 4.3.6 Claims for Concealed or Unknown Conditions

    II

        95017-5CIR

    III

        94008-5CIR
        96036-FCIR
        93026-NY

Text of Paragraph 4.3.7—Claims for Additional Cost

If the Contractor wishes to make Claim for an increase in the Contract Sum, written notice as provided herein shall be given before proceeding to execute the Work. Prior notice is not required for Claims relating to an emergency endangering life or property arising under Paragraph 10.3. If the Contractor believes additional cost is involved for reasons including but not limited to (1) a written interpretation from the Architect, (2) an order by the Owner to stop the Work where the Contractor was not at fault, (3) a written order for a minor change in the Work issued by the Architect, (4) failure of payment by the Owner, (5) termination of the Contract by the Owner, (6) Owner's suspension or (7) other reasonable grounds, Claim shall be filed in accordance with the procedure established herein.

Paragraph 4.3.7 Claims for Additional Cost

    I

        93019-NJ

    II

        92004b-GA

    III

        96036-FCIR   95001-WA
        93026-NY   96039-WY
        92009b-ND

Text of Paragraph 4.3.8—Claims for Additional Time

4.3.8 Claims for Additional Time

4.3.8.1 If the Contractor wishes to make Claim for an increase in the Contract Time, written notice as provided herein shall be given. The Contractor's Claim shall include an estimate of cost and of probable effect of delay on progress of the Work. In the case of a continuing delay only one Claim is necessary.

4.3.8.2 If adverse weather conditions are the basis for a Claim for additional time, such Claim shall be documented by data substantiating that weather conditions were abnormal for the period of time and could not have been reasonably anticipated, and that weather conditions had an adverse effect on the scheduled construction.

DOCUMENT TO CASE CHARTS: A201-1987

[The five-digit numbers in this chart are Citator Case Reference Numbers, which refer to the cases, in the Cases section. The suffixes indicate the state or, for federal cases, the court in which the case was decided.]

Paragraph 4.3.8 Claims for Additional Time

    II

        92004b-GA
        92004e-GA

    III

        95018-2CIR   95001-WA
        96036-FCIR   96039-WY

Paragraph 4.3.8.1 Claims for Additional Time

    I

        97018-MO

Paragraph 4.3.8.2 Claims for Additional Time

    I

        97018-MO

Paragraph 4.3.9 Injury or Damage to Person or Property

Paragraph 4.4 Resolution of Claims and Disputes

    II

        95033-MO

Text of Paragraph 4.4.1

4.4.1 The Architect will review Claims and take one or more of the following preliminary actions within ten days of receipt of a Claim: (1) request additional supporting data from the claimant, (2) submit a schedule to the parties indicating when the Architect expects to take action, (3) reject the Claim in whole or in part, stating reasons for rejection, (4) recommend approval of the Claim by the other party or (5) suggest a compromise. The Architect may also, but is not obligated to, notify the surety, if any, of the nature and amount of the Claim.

Paragraph 4.4.1

    III

        94041-CT
        92004a-GA
        95024-NY

Text of Paragraph 4.4.2

4.4.2 If a Claim has been resolved, the Architect will prepare or obtain appropriate documentation.

DOCUMENT TO CASE CHARTS: A201-1987

[The five-digit numbers in this chart are Citator Case Reference Numbers, which refer to the cases, in the Cases section. The suffixes indicate the state or, for federal cases, the court in which the case was decided.]

Paragraph 4.4.2

    III

        94041-CT

Text of Paragraph 4.4.3

4.4.3 If a Claim has not been resolved, the party making the Claim shall, within ten days after the Architect's preliminary response, take one or more of the following actions: (1) submit additional supporting data requested by the Architect, (2) modify the initial Claim or (3) notify the Architect that the initial Claim stands.

Paragraph 4.4.3

    I

        97018-MO

    III

        94041-CT
        95024-NY
        97022-NY

Text of Paragraph 4.4.4

4.4.4 If a Claim has not been resolved after consideration of the foregoing and of further evidence presented by the parties or requested by the Architect, the Architect will notify the parties in writing that the Architect's decision will be made within seven days, which decision shall be final and binding on the parties but subject to arbitration. Upon expiration of such time period, the Architect will render to the parties the Architect's written decision relative to the Claim, including any change in the Contract Sum or Contract Time or both. If there is a surety and there appears to be a possibility of a Contractor's default, the Architect may, but is not obligated to, notify the surety and request the surety's assistance in resolving the controversy.

Paragraph 4.4.4

    I

        97018-MO

    III

        94041-CT   95024-NY
        92004a-GA   97022-NY

Paragraph 4.5   Arbitration

Text of Paragraph 4.5.1—Controversies and Claims Subject to Arbitration

Any controversy or Claim arising out of or related to the Contract, or the breach

DOCUMENT TO CASE CHARTS: A201-1987 A–300

[The five-digit numbers in this chart are Citator Case Reference Numbers, which refer to the cases, in the Cases section. The suffixes indicate the state or, for federal cases, the court in which the case was decided.]

thereof, shall be settled by arbitration in accordance with the Construction Industry Arbitration Rules of the American Arbitration Association, and judgment upon the award rendered by the arbitrator or arbitrators may be entered in any court having jurisdiction thereof, except controversies or Claims relating to aesthetic effect and except those waived as provided for in Subparagraph 4.3.5. Such controversies or Claims upon which the Architect has given notice and rendered a decision as provided in Subparagraph 4.4.4 shall be subject to arbitration upon written demand of either party. Arbitration may be commenced when 45 days have passed after a Claim has been referred to the Architect as provided in Paragraph 4.3 and no decision has been rendered.

Paragraph 4.5.1 Controversies and Claims Subject to Arbitration

I

92012-DNJ	93019-NJ
92014-AL	97007-NJ
95046-AL	89014-NY
95014-AR	92016-NC
93006-CT	97026-OH
93016-FL	97023-PA
93044-FL	93002-SD
93012-IL	96023-TN
93003-KY	92005a-TX
92019-LA	95023-VA
94005-MD	93049-WV
93011-MA	97024-WV
93046-MO	

II

94003-GA	96011-NY
94026-GA	93048-SC
93008-IA	93024-TN
93052-LA	93054-TX
97011-MD	96014-VA
94017-MO	94049-WY
95033-MO	

III

96022-2CIR	94021-LA
96006-DCCIR	95016-NC
97016-AR	95024-NY
94018-CA	97022-NY
96038-CO	95009-PA
94041-CT	94030-TX
96002-DC	95002-TX
92004a-GA	94019-WI
93027-IL	

Text of Paragraph 4.5.2—Rules and Notices for Arbitration

Claims between the Owner and Contractor not resolved under Paragraph 4.4, shall if subject to arbitration under Subparagraph 4.5.1, be decided by arbitration in accordance with the Construction Industry Arbitration Rules of the American

A–301   **DOCUMENT TO CASE CHARTS: A201-1987**

[The five-digit numbers in this chart are Citator Case Reference Numbers, which refer to the cases, in the Cases section. The suffixes indicate the state or, for federal cases, the court in which the case was decided.]

> Arbitration Association currently in effect, unless the parties mutually agree otherwise. Notice of demand for arbitration shall be filed in writing with the other party to the Agreement between the Owner and Contractor and with the American Arbitration Association, and a copy shall be filed with the Architect.

Paragraph 4.5.2   Rules and Notices for Arbitration

   I

      95046-AL   93046-MO
      93006-CT   93019-NJ
      93016-FL   97007-NJ
      93044-FL   97026-OH
      93012-IL   97023-PA
      93003-KY   93002-SD
      94006-MD   93049-WV
      93011-MA   97024-WV

   II

      94003-GA   93048-SC
      93008-IA   93024-TN
      93052-LA   96023-TN
      97011-MD   93054-TX
      94017-MO   96014-VA
      95033-MO   94049-WY
      96011-NY

   III

      96022-2CIR   94021-LA
      96006-DCCIR   94001-NY
      97016-AR   97022-NY
      94018-CA   95009-PA
      96038-CO   94030-TX
      94041-CT   95002-TX
      96002-DC   94019-WI
      93027-IL

> **Text of Paragraph 4.5.3—Contract Performance During Arbitration**
>
> During arbitration proceedings, the Owner and Contractor shall comply with Subparagraph 4.3.4.

Paragraph 4.5.3   Contract Performance During Arbitration

   I

      95046-AL   93046-MO
      93006-CT   93019-NJ
      93016-FL   97007-NJ
      93044-FL   97026-OH
      93012-IL   97023-PA
      93003-KY   93002-SD
      94006-MD   93049-WV
      93011-MA   97024-WV

DOCUMENT TO CASE CHARTS: A201-1987

[The five-digit numbers in this chart are Citator Case Reference Numbers, which refer to the cases, in the Cases section. The suffixes indicate the state or, for federal cases, the court in which the case was decided.]

   II

       94003-GA   93048-SC
       93008-IA   93024-TN
       93052-LA   96023-TN
       97011-MD   93054-TX
       94017-MO   96014-VA
       95033-MO   94049-WY
       96011-NY

   III

       96022-2CIR   93027-IL
       96006-DCCIR   94021-LA
       97016-AR   97022-NY
       94018-CA   95009-PA
       96038-CO   94030-TX
       94041-CT   95002-TX
       96002-DC   94019-WI

Text of Paragraph 4.5.4—When Arbitration May Be Demanded

Demand for arbitration of any Claim may not be made until the earlier of (1) the date on which the Architect has rendered a final written decision on the Claim, (2) the tenth day after the parties have presented evidence to the Architect or have been given reasonable opportunity to do so, if the Architect has not rendered a final written decision by that date, or (3) any of the five events described in Subparagraph 4.3.2.

Paragraph 4.5.4   When Arbitration May Be Demanded

   I

       95046-AL   93046-MO
       93006-CT   93019-NJ
       93016-FL   97007-NJ
       93044-FL   97026-OH
       93012-IL   97023-PA
       93003-KY   93002-SD
       94006-MD   93049-WV
       93011-MA   97024-WV

   II

       94003-GA   93048-SC
       93008-IA   93024-TN
       93052-LA   96023-TN
       97011-MD   93054-TX
       94017-MO   96014-VA
       95033-MO   94049-WY
       96011-NY

A-303   DOCUMENT TO CASE CHARTS: A201-1987

[The five-digit numbers in this chart are Citator Case Reference Numbers, which refer to the cases, in the Cases section. The suffixes indicate the state or, for federal cases, the court in which the case was decided.]

   III

      96022-2CIR   94021-LA
      96006-DCCIR   94001-NY
      97016-AR   97022-NY
      94018-CA   94019-WI
      96038-CO   95009-PA
      94041-CT   94030-TX
      96002-DC   95002-TX
      93027-IL

Text of Paragraph 4.5.4.1

4.5.4.1 When a written decision of the Architect states that (1) the decision is final but subject to arbitration and (2) a demand for arbitration of a Claim corrected by such decision must be made within 30 days after the date on which the party making the demand receives the final written decision then failure to demand arbitration within said 30 days period shall result in the Architect's decision becoming final and binding upon the Owner and Contractor. If the Architect renders a decision after arbitration proceedings have been initiated, such decision may be entered as evidence, but shall not supersede arbitration proceedings unless the decision is acceptable to all parties concerned.

Paragraph 4.5.4.1

   I

      95046-AL   93019-NJ
      93006-CT   97007-NJ
      93016-FL   97026-OH
      93012-IL   97023-PA
      93003-KY   93002-SD
      93011-MA   97024-WV

   II

      93008-IA   96023-TN
      97011-MD   96014-VA
      95033-MO   94049-WY
      96011-NY

   III

      96022-2CIR   96002-DC
      96006-DCCIR   97022-NY
      97016-AR   95009-PA
      96038-CO   94030-TX
      94041-CT   95002-TX

Text of Paragraph 4.5.4.2

4.5.4.2 A demand for arbitration shall be made within the time limits specified in Subparagraphs 4.5.1 and 4.5.4 and Clause 4.5.4.1 as applicable, and in other cases within a reasonable time after the Claim has arisen, and in no event shall it be made after the date when institution of legal or equitable proceedings based on such Claim

DOCUMENT TO CASE CHARTS: A201-1987

A–304

[The five-digit numbers in this chart are Citator Case Reference Numbers, which refer to the cases, in the Cases section. The suffixes indicate the state or, for federal cases, the court in which the case was decided.]

> would be barred by the applicable statute of limitations as determined pursuant to Paragraph 13.7.

Paragraph 4.5.4.2

    I

95046-AL	97007-NJ
93006-CT	92016-NC
93016-FL	97026-OH
93012-IL	97023-PA
93003-KY	93002-SD
93011-MA	97024-WV
93019-NJ	

    II

93008-IA	96023-TN
97011-MD	96014-VA
95033-MO	94049-WY
96011-NY	

    III

96022-2CIR	96002-DC
96006-DCCIR	97022-NY
97016-AR	95009-PA
96038-CO	94030-TX
94041-CT	95002-TX

Text of Paragraph 4.5.5—Limitation on Consolidation or Joinder

No arbitration arising out of or relating to the Contract Documents shall include, by consolidation or joinder or in any other manner, the Architect, the Architect's employees or consultants, except by written consent containing specific reference to the Agreement and signed by the Architect, Owner, Contractor and any other person or entity sought to be joined. No arbitration shall include, by consolidation or joinder or in any other manner, parties other than the Owner, Contractor, a separate contractor as described in Article 6 and other persons substantially involved in a common question of fact or law whose presence is required if complete relief is to be accorded in arbitration. No person or entity other than the Owner, Contractor or a separate contractor as described in Article 6 shall be included as an original third party or additional third party to an arbitration whose interest or responsibility is insubstantial. Consent to arbitration involving an additional person or entity shall not constitute consent to arbitration of a dispute not described therein or with a person or entity not named or described therein. The foregoing agreement to arbitrate and other agreements to arbitrate with an additional person or entity duly consented to by parties to the Agreement shall be specifically enforceable under applicable law in any court having jurisdiction thereof.

DOCUMENT TO CASE CHARTS: A201-1987

[The five-digit numbers in this chart are Citator Case Reference Numbers, which refer to the cases, in the Cases section. The suffixes indicate the state or, for federal cases, the court in which the case was decided.]

Paragraph 4.5.5   Limitation on Consolidation or Joinder

I

95046-AL	93046-MO
93006-CT	93019-NJ
93016-FL	97007-NJ
93044-FL	97026-OH
93012-IL	97023-PA
93003-KY	93002-SD
94006-MD	93049-WV
93011-MA	97024-WV

II

94003-GA	93048-SC
93008-IA	93024-TN
93052-LA	96023-TN
97011-MD	93054-TX
94017-MO	96014-VA
95033-MO	94049-WY
96011-NY	

III

96022-2CIR	93027-IL
96006-DCCIR	94021-LA
97016-AR	97022-NY
94018-CA	95009-PA
96038-CO	94030-TX
94041-CT	95002-TX
96002-DC	94019-WI

Text of Paragraph 4.5.6—Claims and Timely Assertion of Claims

A party who files a notice of demand for arbitration must assert in the demand all Claims then known to that party on which arbitration is permitted to be demanded. When a party fails to include a Claim through oversight, inadvertence or excusable neglect, or when a Claim has matured or been acquired subsequently, the arbitrator or arbitrators may permit amendment.

Paragraph 4.5.6   Claims and Timely Assertion of Claims

I

95046-AL	93046-MO
93006-CT	93019-NJ
93016-FL	97007-NJ
93044-FL	97026-OH
93012-IL	97023-PA
93003-KY	93002-SD
94006-MD	93049-WV
93011-MA	97024-WV

DOCUMENT TO CASE CHARTS: A201-1987 A–306

[The five-digit numbers in this chart are Citator Case Reference Numbers, which refer to the cases, in the Cases section. The suffixes indicate the state or, for federal cases, the court in which the case was decided.]

 II

   94003-GA   93048-SC
   93008-IA   93024-TN
   93052-LA   96023-TN
   97011-MD   93054-TX
   94017-MO   96014-VA
   95033-MO   94049-WY
   96011-NY

 III

   96022-2CIR   93027-IL
   96006-DCCIR   94021-LA
   97016-AR   97022-NY
   94018-CA   95009-PA
   96038-CO   94030-TX
   94041-CT   95002-TX
   96002-DC   94019-WI

Text of Paragraph 4.5.7—Judgment on Final Award

The award rendered by the arbitrator or arbitrators shall be final, and judgment may be entered upon it in accordance with applicable law in any court having jurisdiction thereof.

Paragraph 4.5.7 Judgment on Final Award

 I

   95046-AL   93019-NJ
   93006-CT   97007-NJ
   93016-FL   95016-NC
   93044-FL   97026-OH
   93012-IL   97023-PA
   93003-KY   93002-SD
   94006-MD   93049-WV
   93011-MA   97024-WV
   93046-MO

 II

   94003-GA   96011-NY
   94026-GA   93048-SC
   93008-IA   93024-TN
   93052-LA   96023-TN
   97011-MD   93024-TX
   94017-MO   96014-VA
   95033-MO   94049-WY

 III

   96022-2CIR   93027-IL
   96006-DCCIR   94021-LA
   97016-AR   97022-NY
   94018-CA   95009-PA
   96038-CO   94030-TX
   94041-CT   95002-TX
   96002-DC   94019-WI

A–307

DOCUMENT TO CASE CHARTS: A201-1987

[The five-digit numbers in this chart are Citator Case Reference Numbers, which refer to the cases, in the Cases section. The suffixes indicate the state or, for federal cases, the court in which the case was decided.]

Article 5 Subcontractors

Paragraph 5.1 Definitions

Paragraph 5.2 Award of Subcontracts and Other Contracts for Portions of the Work

Paragraph 5.3 Subcontractual Relations

Text of Paragraph 5.3.1

5.3.1 By appropriate agreement, written where legally required for validity, the Contractor shall require each Subcontractor, to the extent of the Work to be performed by the Subcontractor, to be bound to the Contractor by terms of the Contract Documents, and to assume toward the Contractor all the obligations and responsibilities which the Contractor, by these Documents, assumes toward the Owner and Architect. Each subcontract agreement shall preserve and protect the rights of the Owner and Architect under the Contract Documents with respect to Work to be performed by the Subcontractor so that subcontracting thereof will not prejudice such rights, and shall allow to the Subcontractor, unless specifically provided otherwise in the subcontract agreement, the benefit of all rights, remedies and redress against the Contractor that the Contractor, by the Contract Documents, has against the Owner. Where appropriate, the Contractor shall require each Subcontractor to enter into similar agreements with Sub-subcontractors. The Contractor shall make available to each proposed Subcontractor, prior to the execution of the subcontract agreement, copies of the Contract Documents to which the Subcontractor will be bound, and, upon written request of the Subcontractor, identify to the Subcontractor terms and conditions of the proposed subcontract agreement which may be at variance with the Contract Documents. Subcontractors shall similarly make copies of applicable portions of such documents available to their respective proposed Sub-subcontractors.

Paragraph 5.3.1

    I

        97021-FL

  III

        96040-MO

DOCUMENT TO CASE CHARTS: A201-1987

[The five-digit numbers in this chart are Citator Case Reference Numbers, which refer to the cases, in the Cases section. The suffixes indicate the state or, for federal cases, the court in which the case was decided.]

Paragraph 5.4 Contingent Assignment of Subcontracts

Article 6 Construction by Owner or by Separate Contractors

Paragraph 6.1 Owner's Right to Perform Construction and to Award Separate Contracts

    III

        92005b-AK

Text of Paragraph 6.1.1

The Owner reserves the right to perform construction or operations related to the Project with the Owner's own forces, and to award separate contracts in connection with other portions of the Project or other construction or operations on the site under Conditions of the Contract identical or substantially similar to these including those portions related to insurance and waiver of subrogation. If the Contractor claims that delay or additional cost is involved because of such action by the Owner, the Contractor shall make such Claim as provided elsewhere in the Contract Documents.

Paragraph 6.1.1

    I

        94011-WDMI

    III

        95037-GA

Text of Paragraph 6.1.3

The Owner shall provide for coordination of the activities of the Owner's own forces and of each separate contractor with the Work of the Contractor, who shall cooperate with them. The Contractor shall participate with other separate contractors and the Owner in reviewing their construction schedules when directed to do so. The Contractor shall make any revisions to the construction schedule and Contract Sum deemed necessary after a joint review and mutual agreement. The construction schedules shall then constitute the schedules to be used by the Contractor, separate contractors and the Owner until subsequently revised.

Paragraph 6.1.3

    III

        95037-GA
        96016-GA

DOCUMENT TO CASE CHARTS: A201-1987

[*The five-digit numbers in this chart are Citator Case Reference Numbers, which refer to the cases, in the Cases section. The suffixes indicate the state or, for federal cases, the court in which the case was decided.*]

Paragraph 6.2 Mutual Responsibility

    II

        92004e-GA

Text of Paragraph 6.2.1

6.2.1 The Contractor shall afford the Owner and separate contractors reasonable opportunity for introduction and storage of their materials and equipment and performance of their activities and shall connect and coordinate the Contractor's construction and operations with theirs as required by the Contract Documents.

Paragraph 6.2.1

    I

        93007-GA

Text of Paragraph 6.2.2

6.2.2 If part of the Contractor's Work depends for proper execution or results upon construction or operations by the Owner or a separate contractor, the Contractor shall, prior to proceeding with that portion of the Work, promptly report to the Architect apparent discrepancies or defects in such other construction that would render it unsuitable for such proper execution and results. Failure of the Contractor so to report shall constitute an acknowledgment that the Owner's or separate contractor's complete or partially completed construction is fit and proper to receive the Contractor's Work, except as to defects not then reasonably discoverable.

Paragraph 6.2.2

    III

        93007-GA

Text of Paragraph 6.2.3

6.2.3 Costs caused by delays or by improperly timed activities or defective construction shall be borne by the party responsible therefor.

Paragraph 6.2.3

    I

        95018-2CIR

DOCUMENT TO CASE CHARTS: A201-1987

[The five-digit numbers in this chart are Citator Case Reference Numbers, which refer to the cases, in the Cases section. The suffixes indicate the state or, for federal cases, the court in which the case was decided.]

    III

        93007-GA

Text of Paragraph 6.2.4

6.2.4 The Contractor shall promptly remedy damage wrongfully caused by the Contractor to completed or partially completed construction or to property of the Owner or separate contractors as provided in Subparagraph 10.2.5.

Paragraph 6.2.4

    III

        93007-GA

Paragraph 6.3   Owner's Right to Clean Up

Article 7   Changes in the Work

Paragraph 7.1   Changes

    III

        92009b-ND
        97010-OH

Text of Paragraph 7.1.1

Changes in the Work may be accomplished after execution of the Contract, and without invalidating the Contract, by Change Order, Construction Change Directive or order for a minor change in the Work, subject to the limitations stated in this Article 7 and elsewhere in the Contract Documents.

Paragraph 7.1.1

    III

        93037-10CIR
        94040-11CIR

Text of Paragraph 7.1.2

A Change Order shall be based upon agreement among the Owner, Contractor and Architect; a Construction Change Directive requires agreement by the Owner and Architect and may or may not be agreed to by the Contractor; an order for a minor change in the Work may be issued by the Architect alone.

DOCUMENT TO CASE CHARTS: A201-1987

[The five-digit numbers in this chart are Citator Case Reference Numbers, which refer to the cases, in the Cases section. The suffixes indicate the state or, for federal cases, the court in which the case was decided.]

Paragraph 7.1.2

    III

        93037-10CIR

Text of Paragraph 7.1.4

7.1.4 If unit prices are stated in the Contract Documents or subsequently agreed upon, and if quantities originally contemplated are so changed in a proposed Change Order or Construction Change Directive that application of such unit prices to quantities of Work proposed will cause substantial inequity to the Owner or Contractor, the applicable unit prices shall be equitably adjusted.

Paragraph 7.1.4

    II

        93015-OR

Paragraph 7.2   Change Orders

    III

        92005b-AK
        92009b-ND
        97010-OH

Text of Paragraph 7.2.1

A Change Order is a written instrument prepared by the Architect and signed by the Owner, Contractor and Architect, stating their agreement upon all of the following:

.1   a change in the Work;

.2   the amount of the adjustments in the Contract Sum, if any; and

.3   the extent of the adjustment in the Contract Time, if any.

Paragraph 7.2.1

    I

        92012-DNJ
        95023-VA

    III

        93037-10CIR
        94040-11CIR
        95001-WA

DOCUMENT TO CASE CHARTS: A201-1987 A–312

[The five-digit numbers in this chart are Citator Case Reference Numbers, which refer to the cases, in the Cases section. The suffixes indicate the state or, for federal cases, the court in which the case was decided.]

Paragraph 7.3 Construction Change Directives

    III

        92005b-AK
        92009b-ND
        97010-OH

Text of Paragraph 7.3.1

A Construction Change Directive is a written order prepared by the Architect and signed by the Owner and Architect, directing a change in the Work and stating a proposed basis for adjustment, if any, in the Contract Sum or Contract Time, or both. The Owner may by Construction Change Directive, without invalidating the Contract, order changes in the Work within the general scope of the Contract consisting of additions, deletions or other revisions, the Contract Sum and Contract Time being adjusted accordingly.

Paragraph 7.3.1

    I

        92012-DNJ

    III

        93037-10CIR
        94040-11CIR

Text of Paragraph 7.3.3

7.3.3 If the Construction Change Directive provides for an adjustment to the Contract Sum, the adjustment shall be based on one of the following methods:

.1   mutual acceptance of a lump sum properly itemized and supported by sufficient substantiating data to permit evaluation;

.2   unit prices stated in the Contract Documents or subsequently agreed upon;

.3   cost to be determined in a manner agreed upon by the parties and a mutually acceptable fixed or percentage fee; or

.4   as provided in Subparagraph 7.3.6.

Paragraph 7.3.3

    III

        94040-11CIR

Text of Paragraph 7.3.4

7.3.4 Upon receipt of a Construction Change Directive, the Contractor shall promptly proceed with the change in the Work involved and advise the Architect of the Contractor's agreement or disagreement with the method, if any, provided in the Construction Change Directive for determining the proposed adjustment in the Contract Sum or Contract Time.

Paragraph 7.3.4

    III

        94031-RI

Text of Paragraph 7.3.5

7.3.5 A Construction Change Directive signed by the Contractor indicates the agreement of the Contractor therewith, including adjustment in Contract Sum and Contract Time or the method for determining them. Such agreement shall be effective immediately and shall be recorded as a Change Order.

Paragraph 7.3.5

    III

        94031-RI

Text of Paragraph 7.3.6

7.3.6 If the Contractor does not respond promptly or disagrees with the method for adjustment in the Contract Sum, the method and the adjustment shall be determined by the Architect on the basis of reasonable expenditures and savings of those performing the Work attributable to the change, including, in case of an increase in the Contract Sum, a reasonable allowance for overhead and profit. In such case, and also under Clause 7.3.3.3, the Contractor shall keep and present, in such form as the Architect may prescribe, an itemized accounting together with appropriate supporting data. Unless otherwise provided in the Contract Documents, costs for the purposes of this Subparagraph 7.3.6 shall be limited to the following:

.1   costs of labor, including social security, old age and unemployment insurance, fringe benefits required by agreement or custom, and workers' or workmen's compensation insurance;

.2   costs of materials, supplies and equipment, including cost of transportation, whether incorporated or consumed;

.3   rental costs of machinery and equipment, exclusive of hand tools, whether rented from the Contractor or others;

.4   costs of premiums for all bonds and insurance, permit fees, and sales, use or similar taxes related to the Work; and

.5   additional costs of supervision and field office personnel directly attributable to the change.

DOCUMENT TO CASE CHARTS: A201-1987 A–314

[The five-digit numbers in this chart are Citator Case Reference Numbers, which refer to the cases, in the Cases section. The suffixes indicate the state or, for federal cases, the court in which the case was decided.]

Paragraph 7.3.6

    III

        94040-11CIR
        94031-RI
        95001-WA

Text of Paragraph 7.3.7

7.3.7 Pending final determination of cost to the Owner, amounts not in dispute may be included in Applications for Payment. The amount of credit to be allowed by the Contractor to the Owner for a deletion or change which results in a net decrease in the Contract Sum shall be actual net cost as confirmed by the Architect. When both additions and credits covering related Work or substitutions are involved in a change, the allowance for overhead and profit shall be figured on the basis of net increase, if any, with respect to that change.

Paragraph 7.3.7

    III

        94031-RI

Text of Paragraph 7.3.8

7.3.8 If the Owner and Contractor do not agree with the adjustment in Contract Time or the method for determining it, the adjustment or the method shall be referred to the Architect for determination.

Paragraph 7.3.8

    III

        94040-11CIR
        94031-RI

Text of Paragraph 7.3.9

7.3.9 When the Owner and Contractor agree with the determination made by the Architect concerning the adjustments in the Contract Sum and Contract Time, or otherwise reach agreement upon the adjustments, such agreement shall be effective immediately and shall be recorded by preparation and execution of an appropriate Change Order.

DOCUMENT TO CASE CHARTS: A201-1987

[The five-digit numbers in this chart are Citator Case Reference Numbers, which refer to the cases, in the Cases section. The suffixes indicate the state or, for federal cases, the court in which the case was decided.]

Paragraph 7.3.9

    III

        94031-RI

Paragraph 7.4 Minor Changes in the Work

Article 8 Time

Paragraph 8.1 Definitions

Text of Paragraph 8.1.1

8.1.1 Unless provided, Contract Time is the period of time, including authorized adjustments, allotted in the Contract Documents for Substantial Completion of the Work.

Paragraph 8.1.1

    I

        97018-MO

Text of Paragraph 8.2—Progress and Completion

8.2.1 Time limits stated in the Contract Documents are of the essence of the Contract. By executing the Agreement the Contractor confirms that the Contract Time is a reasonable period for performing the Work.

8.2.2 The Contractor shall not knowingly, except by agreement or instruction of the Owner in writing, prematurely commence operations on the site or elsewhere prior to the effective date of insurance required by Article 11 to be furnished by the Contractor. The date of commencement of the Work shall not be changed by the effective date of such insurance. Unless the date of commencement is established by a notice to proceed given by the Owner, the Contractor shall notify the Owner in writing not less than five days or other agreed period before commencing the Work to permit the timely filing of mortgages, mechanic's liens and other security interests.

8.2.3 The Contractor shall proceed expeditiously with adequate forces and shall achieve Substantial Completion within the Contract Time.

DOCUMENT TO CASE CHARTS: A201-1987   A–316

[*The five-digit numbers in this chart are Citator Case Reference Numbers, which refer to the cases, in the Cases section. The suffixes indicate the state or, for federal cases, the court in which the case was decided.*]

Paragraph 8.2   Progress and Completion

    III

        94040-11CIR
        95008-VA

Paragraph 8.2.1

    II

        95047-LA

Text of Paragraph 8.3—Delays and Extensions of Time

8.3.1 If the Contractor is delayed at any time in progress of the Work by an act or neglect of the Owner or Architect, or of an employee of either, or of a separate contractor employed by the Owner, or by changes ordered in the Work, or by labor disputes, fire, unusual delay in deliveries unavoidable casualties or other causes beyond the Contractor's control, or by delay authorized by the Owner pending arbitration, or by other causes which the Architect determines may justify delay, then the Contract Time shall be extended by Change Order for such reasonable time as the Architect may determine.

8.3.2 Claims relating to time shall be made in accordance with applicable provisions of Paragraph 4.3.

8.3.3 This Paragraph 8.3 does not preclude recovery of damages for delay by either party under other provisions of the Contract Documents.

Paragraph 8.3   Delays and Extensions of Time

    III

        95018-2CIR   97013-GA
        94040-11CIR   97040-MO
        97001-MDGA   95008-VA
        96016-GA

Paragraph 8.3.1

    I

        97018-MO

Article 9   Payments and Completion

Paragraph 9.1   Contract Sum

Paragraph 9.2   Schedule of Values

Paragraph 9.3   Applications for Payment

Paragraph 9.4   Certificates for Payment

DOCUMENT TO CASE CHARTS: A201-1987

[The five-digit numbers in this chart are Citator Case Reference Numbers, which refer to the cases, in the Cases section. The suffixes indicate the state or, for federal cases, the court in which the case was decided.]

Text of Paragraph 9.4.2

The issuance of a Certificate for Payment will constitute a representation by the Architect to the Owner, based on the Architect's observations at the site and the data comprising the Application for Payment, that the Work has progressed to the point indicated and that, to the best of the Architect's knowledge, information and belief, quality of the Work is in accordance with the Contract Documents. The foregoing representations are subject to an evaluation of the Work for conformance with the Contract Documents upon Substantial Completion, to results of subsequent tests and inspections, to minor deviations from the Contract Documents correctable prior to completion and to specific qualifications expressed by the Architect. The issuance of a Certificate for Payment will further constitute a representation that the Contractor is entitled to payment in the amount certified. However, the issuance of a Certificate for Payment will not be a representation that the Architect has (1) made exhaustive or continuous on-site inspections to check the quality or quantity of the Work, (2) reviewed construction means, methods, techniques, sequences or procedures, (3) reviewed copies of requisitions received from Subcontractors and material suppliers and other data requested by the Owner to substantiate the Contractor's right to payment or (4) made examination to ascertain how or for what purpose the Contractor has used money previously paid on account of the Contract Sum.

Paragraph 9.4.2

    II

        95040-DPR
        93036-NE

    III

        95029-EDVA

Paragraph 9.5   Decisions to Withhold Certification

Paragraph 9.6   Progress Payments

    III

        94050-AL
        95050-NY

Text of Paragraph 9.6.2

The Contractor shall promptly pay each Subcontractor, upon receipt of payment from the Owner, out of the amount paid to the Contractor on account of such Subcontractor's portion of the Work, the amount to which said Subcontractor is entitled, reflecting percentages actually retained from payments to the Contractor on account of such Subcontractor's portion of the Work. The Contractor shall, by

DOCUMENT TO CASE CHARTS: A201-1987 A–318

[The five-digit numbers in this chart are Citator Case Reference Numbers, which refer to the cases, in the Cases section. The suffixes indicate the state or, for federal cases, the court in which the case was decided.]

> appropriate agreement with each Subcontractor, require each Subcontractor to make payments to Sub-subcontractors in similar manner.

Paragraph 9.6.2

    I

        95034-VA

> **Text of Paragraph 9.6.6**
>
> **9.6.6** A Certificate for Payment, a progress payment, or partial or entire use or occupancy of the Project by the Owner shall not constitute acceptance of Work not in accordance with the Contract Documents.

Paragraph 9.6.6

    I

        95020-DPR

Paragraph 9.7   Failure of Payment

> **Text of Paragraph 9.7.1**
>
> If the Architect does not issue a Certificate for Payment, through no fault of the Contractor, within seven days after receipt of the Contractor's Application for Payment, or if the Owner does not pay the Contractor within seven days after the date established in the Contract Documents the amount certified by the Architect or awarded by arbitration, then the Contractor may, upon seven additional days' written notice to the Owner and Architect, stop the Work until payment of the amount owing has been received. The Contract Time shall be extended appropriately and the Contract Sum shall be increased by the amount of the Contractor's reasonable costs of shut-down, delay and start-up, which shall be accomplished as provided in Article 7.

Paragraph 9.7.1

    II

        93054-TX

Paragraph 9.8   Substantial Completion

> **Text of Paragraph 9.8.1**
>
> **9.8.1** Substantial Completion is the stage in the progress of the Work when the Work or designated portion thereof is sufficiently complete in accordance with the Contract Documents so the Owner can occupy or utilize the Work for its intended use.

A–319 DOCUMENT TO CASE CHARTS: A201-1987

[The five-digit numbers in this chart are Citator Case Reference Numbers, which refer to the cases, in the Cases section. The suffixes indicate the state or, for federal cases, the court in which the case was decided.]

Paragraph 9.8.1

    III

        93021-IL

Text of Paragraph 9.8.2

9.8.2 When the Contractor considers that the Work, or a portion thereof which the Owner agrees to accept separately, is substantially complete, the Contractor shall prepare and submit to the Architect a comprehensive list of items to be completed or corrected. The Contractor shall proceed promptly to complete and correct items on the list. Failure to include an item on such list does not alter the responsibility of the Contractor to complete all Work in accordance with the Contract Documents. Upon receipt of the Contractor's list, the Architect will make an inspection to determine whether the Work or designated portion thereof is substantially complete. If the Architect's inspection discloses any item, whether or not included on the Contractor's list, which is not in accordance with the requirements of the Contract Documents, the Contractor shall, before issuance of the Certificate of Substantial Completion, complete or correct such item upon notification by the Architect. The Contractor shall then submit a request for another inspection by the Architect to determine Substantial Completion. When the Work or designated portion thereof is substantially complete, the Architect will prepare a Certificate of Substantial Completion which shall establish the date of Substantial Completion, shall establish responsibilities of the Owner and Contractor for security, maintenance, heat, utilities, damage to the Work and insurance, and shall fix the time within which the Contractor shall finish all items on the list accompanying the Certificate Warranties required by the Contract Documents shall commence on the date of Substantial Completion of the Work or designated portion thereof unless otherwise provided in the Certificate of Substantial Completion. The Certificate of Substantial Completion shall be submitted to the Owner and Contractor for their written acceptance of responsibilities assigned to them in such Certificate.

Paragraph 9.8.2

    I

        95020-DPR

Text of Paragraph 9.8.3

9.8.3 Upon Substantial Completion of the Work or designated portion thereof and upon application by the Contractor and certification by the Architect, the Owner shall make payment, reflecting adjustment in retainage, if any, for such Work or portion thereof as provided in the Contract Documents.

DOCUMENT TO CASE CHARTS: A201-1987

[The five-digit numbers in this chart are Citator Case Reference Numbers, which refer to the cases, in the Cases section. The suffixes indicate the state or, for federal cases, the court in which the case was decided.]

Paragraph 9.8.3

    Ill

        93021-IL

Paragraph 9.9   Partial Occupancy or Use

Text of Paragraph 9.9.1

9.9.1 The Owner may occupy or use any completed or partially completed portion of the Work at any stage when such portion is designated by separate agreement with the Contractor, provided such occupancy or use is consented to by the insurer as required under Subparagraph 11.3.11 and authorized by public authorities having jurisdiction over the Work. Such partial occupancy or use may commence whether or not the portion is substantially complete, provided the Owner and Contractor have accepted in writing the responsibilities assigned to each of them for payments, retainage if any, security, maintenance, heat, utilities, damage to the Work and insurance, and have agreed in writing concerning the period for correction of the Work and commencement of warranties required by the Contract Documents. When the Contractor considers a portion substantially complete, the Contractor shall prepare and submit a list to the Architect as provided under Subparagraph 9.8.2. Consent of the Contractor to partial occupancy or use shall not be unreasonably withheld. The stage of the progress of the Work shall be determined by written agreement between the Owner and Contractor or, if no agreement is reached, by decision of the Architect.

Paragraph 9.9.1

    Ill

        93021-IL

Paragraph 9.10   Final Completion and Final Payment

    Ill

        94050-AL
        95050-NY

Text of Paragraph 9.10.1

9.10.1 Upon receipt of written notice that the Work is ready for final inspection and acceptance and upon receipt of a final Application for Payment, the Architect will promptly make such inspection and, when the Architect finds the Work acceptable under the Contract Documents and the Contract fully performed, the Architect will promptly issue a final Certificate for Payment stating that to the best of the Architect's knowledge, information and belief, and on the basis of the Architect's observations and inspections, the Work has been completed in accordance with terms and conditions of the Contract Documents and that the entire balance found to be due the Contractor and noted in said final Certificate is due and payable.

A–321 DOCUMENT TO CASE CHARTS: A201-1987

[*The five-digit numbers in this chart are Citator Case Reference Numbers, which refer to the cases, in the Cases section. The suffixes indicate the state or, for federal cases, the court in which the case was decided.*]

> The Architect's final Certificate for Payment will constitute a further representation that conditions listed in Subparagraph 9.10.2 as precedent to the Contractor's being entitled to final payment have been fulfilled.

Paragraph 9.10.1

    III

        93021-IL
        96004-LA

Text of Paragraph 9.10.2

9.10.2 Neither final payment nor any remaining retained percentage shall become due until the Contractor submits to the Architect (1) an affidavit that payrolls, bills for materials and equipment, and other indebtedness connected with the Work for which the Owner or the Owner's property might be responsible or encumbered (less amounts withheld by Owner) have been paid or otherwise satisfied, (2) a certificate evidencing that insurance required by the Contract Documents to remain in force after final payment is currently in effect and will not be cancelled or allowed to expire until at least 30 days' prior written notice has been given to the Owner, (3) a written statement that the Contractor knows of no substantial reason that the insurance will not be renewable to cover the period required by the Contract Documents, (4) consent of surety, if any, to final payment and (5), if required by the Owner, other data establishing payment or satisfaction of obligations, such as receipts, releases and waivers of liens, claims, security interests or encumberances arising out of the Contract, to the extent and in such form is may be designated by the Owner. If a Subcontractor refuses to furnish a release or waiver required by the Owner, the Contractor may furnish a bond satisfactory to the Owner to indemnify the Owner against such lien. If such lien remains unsatisfied after payments are made, the Contractor shall refund to the Owner all money that the Owner may be compelled to pay in discharging such lien, including all costs and reasonable attorneys' fees.

Paragraph 9.10.2

    II

        95001-WA

    III

        93009-FL
        93021-IL
        96040-MO

Text of Paragraph 9.10.3

9.10.3 If, after Substantial Completion of the Work, final completion thereof is materially delayed through no fault of the Contractor or by issuance of Change Orders affecting final completion, and the Architect so confirms, the Owner shall,

DOCUMENT TO CASE CHARTS: A201-1987

[The five-digit numbers in this chart are Citator Case Reference Numbers, which refer to the cases, in the Cases section. The suffixes indicate the state or, for federal cases, the court in which the case was decided.]

> upon application by the Contractor and certification by the Architect, and without terminating the Contract, make payment of the balance due for that portion of the Work fully completed and accepted. If the remaining balance for Work not fully completed or corrected is less than retainage stipulated in the Contract Documents, and if bonds have been furnished, the written consent of surety to payment of the balance due for that portion of the Work fully completed and accepted shall be submitted by the Contractor to the Architect prior to certification of such payment. Such payment shall be made under terms and conditions governing final payment, except that it shall not constitute a waiver of claims. The making of final payment shall constitute a waiver of claims by the Owner as provided in Subparagraph 4.3.5.

Paragraph 9.10.3

    III

        93021-IL
        96004-LA

> **Text of Paragraph 9.10.4**
>
> **9.10.4** Acceptance of final payment by the Contractor, a Sub-contractor or material supplier shall constitute a waiver of claims by that payee except those previously made in writing and identified by that payee as unsettled at the time of final Application for Payment. Such waivers shall be in addition to the waiver described in Subparagraph 4.3.5.

Paragraph 9.10.4

    II

        95001-WA

    III

        93021-IL
        94031-RI

Article 10 Protection of Persons and Property

Paragraph 10.1 Safety Precautions and Programs

    I

        92016a-MT

    II

        95004-NJ

DOCUMENT TO CASE CHARTS: A201-1987

[The five-digit numbers in this chart are Citator Case Reference Numbers, which refer to the cases, in the Cases section. The suffixes indicate the state or, for federal cases, the court in which the case was decided.]

III

    95044-MDAL   95030-MA
    93034-GA   94005-MO
    95040-GA   95003-OH
    92004d-LA   95038-OH

Text of Paragraph 10.1.1

10.1.1 The Contractor shall be responsible for initiating, maintaining and supervising all safety precautions and programs in connection with the performance of the Contract.

Paragraph 10.1.1

  I

    96009-LA
    93033-MO

  II

    94044-MDGA
    94038-FL
    94045-TX

  III

    93015a-IL

Text of Paragraph 10.1.4

10.1.4 To the fullest extent permitted by law, the Owner shall indemnify and hold harmless the Contractor, Architect, Architect's consultants and agents and employees of any of them from and against claims, damages, losses and expenses including but not limited to attorneys' fees, arising out of or resulting from performance of the Work in the affected area if in fact the material is asbestos or polychlorinated biphenyl (PCB) and has not been rendered harmless, provided that such claim, damage, loss or expense is attributable to bodily injury, sickness, disease or death, or to injury to or destruction of tangible property (other than the Work itself) including loss of use resulting therefrom, but only to the extent caused in whole or in part by negligent acts or omissions of the Owner, anyone directly or indirectly employed by the Owner or anyone for whose acts the Owner may be liable, regardless of whether or not such claim, damage, loss or expense is caused in part by a party indemnified hereunder. Such obligation shall not be construed to negate, abridge, or reduce other rights or obligations of indemnity which would otherwise exist as to a party or person described in this Subparagraph 10.1.4.

DOCUMENT TO CASE CHARTS: A201-1987

[The five-digit numbers in this chart are Citator Case Reference Numbers, which refer to the cases, in the Cases section. The suffixes indicate the state or, for federal cases, the court in which the case was decided.]

Paragraph 10.1.4

I

94043-NDNY	93005-MO
97009-CA	97017-NJ
95011-MI	92008a-PA
92003a-MO	

II

96015-DC	97014-NJ
95006-GA	93043-PA
92001a-ID	97005-PA
94036-IL	92004f-TX
92008b-IA	94009-TX
93018-MA	94033-TX
94047-MI	95036-TX
93053-MN	95049-TX
96008-MN	93028-UT
93014-MO	93035-UT
96018-MO	93040-WV
95025-NJ	95045-WI

III

94039-5CIR	95028-MA
96019-DKS	95041-MA
96024-DKS	96021-MA
94023-SDMS	96026-MA
95035-SDNY	96029-MA
94022-DRI	96035-MA
95007-DRI	97006-MA
95019-AR	94016-MI
97008-CA	93047-MN
93051-DC	94037-MN
93009-FL	95010-MN
95032-FL	96043-MN
97019-ID	93039-NY
94046-IL	93030-OH
95026-IL	94042-OH
96012-IL	94048-OK
96031-IL	95012-OR
92004d-LA	96010-OR
93038-LA	93031-PA
94013-LA	93042-UT
95027-LA	95013-UT
96003-LA	94035-WA
95015-ME	96007-WA
93041-MA	95048-WV
94029-MA	

A–325 **DOCUMENT TO CASE CHARTS: A201-1987**

[*The five-digit numbers in this chart are Citator Case Reference Numbers, which refer to the cases, in the Cases section. The suffixes indicate the state or, for federal cases, the court in which the case was decided.*]

Paragraph 10.2   Safety of Persons and Property

    I

        92016a-MT

    II

        95004-NJ

    III

95044-MDAL	95030-MA
93034-GA	94005-MO
95040-GA	95003-OH
92004d-LA	95038-OH

Text of Paragraph 10.2.1

10.2.1 The Contractor shall take reasonable precautions for safety of, and shall provide reasonable protection to prevent damage, injury or loss to:

.1   employees on the Work and other persons who may be affected thereby;

.2   the Work and materials and equipment to be incorporated therein, whether in storage on or off the site, under care, custody or control of the Contractor or the Contractor's Subcontractors or Sub-subcontractors; and

.3   other property at the site or adjacent thereto, such as trees, shrubs, lawns, walks, pavements, roadways, structures and utilities not designated for removal, relocation or replacement in the course of construction.

Paragraph 10.2.1

    I

        96009-LA
        93005-MO
        97005-PA

    II

94044-MDGA	94045-TX
94038-FL	96027-TX

    III

96019-DKS	93015a-IL
96024-DKS	93017-IL

Text of Paragraph 10.2.2

10.2.2 The Contractor shall give notices and comply with applicable laws, ordinances, rules, regulations and lawful orders of public authorities bearing on safety of persons or property or their protection from damage, injury or loss.

DOCUMENT TO CASE CHARTS: A201-1987

[The five-digit numbers in this chart are Citator Case Reference Numbers, which refer to the cases, in the Cases section. The suffixes indicate the state or, for federal cases, the court in which the case was decided.]

Paragraph 10.2.2

   I

      96009-LA

   III

      96019-DKS   93017-IL
      94032-DE   94014-IN

Text of Paragraph 10.2.3

10.2.3 The Contractor shall erect and maintain, as required by existing conditions and performance of the Contract, reasonable safeguards for safety and protection, including posting danger signs and other warnings against hazards, promulgating safety regulations and notifying owners and users of adjacent sites and utilities.

Paragraph 10.2.3

   I

      96009-LA

   II

      94044-MDGA
      94045-TX

   III

      93015a-IL
      93017-IL

Text of Paragraph 10.2.5

10.2.5 The Contractor shall promptly remedy damage and loss (other than damage or loss insured under property insurance required by the Contract Documents) to property referred to in Clauses 10.2.1.2 and 10.2.1.3 caused in whole or in part by the Contractor, a Subcontractor, a Sub-subcontractor, or anyone directly or indirectly employed by any of them, or by anyone for whose acts they may be liable and for which the Contractor is responsible under Clauses 10.2.1.2 and 10.2.1.3, except damage or loss attributable to acts or omissions of the Owner or Architect or anyone directly or indirectly employed by either of them, or by anyone for whose acts either of them may be liable, and not attributable to the fault or negligence of the Contractor. The foregoing obligations of the Contractor are in addition to the Contractor's obligations under Paragraph 3.18.

DOCUMENT TO CASE CHARTS: A201-1987

[The five-digit numbers in this chart are Citator Case Reference Numbers, which refer to the cases, in the Cases section. The suffixes indicate the state or, for federal cases, the court in which the case was decided.]

Paragraph 10.2.5

    III

        93017-IL

Text of Paragraph 10.2.6

10.2.6 The Contractor shall designate a responsible member of the Contractor's organization at the site whose duty shall be the prevention of accidents. This person shall be the Contractor's superintendent unless otherwise designated by the Contractor in writing to the Owner and Architect.

Paragraph 10.2.6

    III

        93015a-IL
        93017-IL

Paragraph 10.3   Emergencies

Text of Paragraph 10.3.1

10.3.1 In an emergency affecting safety of persons or property, the Contractor shall act, at the Contractor's discretion, to prevent threatened damage, injury or loss. Additional compensation or extension of time claimed by the Contractor on account of an emergency shall be determined as provided in Paragraph 4.3 and Article 7.

Paragraph 10.3.1

    III

        94005-MO

Article 11   Insurance and Bonds

Paragraph 11.1   Contractor's Liability Insurance

    I

        97009-CA

    II

        95049-TX

    III

        97004-MD
        96043-MN
        95004-NJ

DOCUMENT TO CASE CHARTS: A201-1987

[The five-digit numbers in this chart are Citator Case Reference Numbers, which refer to the cases, in the Cases section. The suffixes indicate the state or, for federal cases, the court in which the case was decided.]

Text of Paragraph 11.1.1

The Contractor shall purchase from and maintain in a company or companies lawfully authorized to do business in the jurisdiction in which the Project is located such insurance as will protect the Contractor from claims set forth below which may arise out of or result from the Contractor's operations under the Contract and for which the Contractor may be legally liable, whether such operations be by the Contractor or by a Subcontractor or by anyone directly or indirectly employed by any of them, or by anyone for whose acts any of them may be liable:

.1 claims under workers' or workmen's compensation, disability benefit and other similar employee benefit acts which are applicable to the Work to be performed;

.2 claims for damages because of bodily injury, occupational sickness or disease, or death of the Contractor's employees;

.3 claims for damages because of bodily injury, sickness or disease, or death of any person other than the Contractor's employees;

.4 claims for damages insured by usual personal injury liability coverage which are sustained (1) by a person as a result of an offense directly or indirectly related to employment of such person by the Contractor, or (2) by another person;

.5 claims for damages, other than to the Work itself, because of injury to or destruction of tangible property, including loss of use resulting therefrom;

.6 claims for damages because of bodily injury, death of a person or property damages arising out of ownership, maintenance or use of a motor vehicle; and

.7 claims involving contractual liability insurance applicable to the Contractor's obligations under Paragraph 3.18.

Paragraph 11.1.1

    I

        94004-MO

    II

        95051-SDMS
        96008-MN

DOCUMENT TO CASE CHARTS: A201-1987

[The five-digit numbers in this chart are Citator Case Reference Numbers, which refer to the cases, in the Cases section. The suffixes indicate the state or, for federal cases, the court in which the case was decided.]

III

  96012-IL   94037-MN
  94013-LA   95038-OH

Text of Paragraph 11.1.2

The insurance required by Subparagraph 11.1.1 shall be written for not less than limits of liability specified in the Contract Documents or required by law whichever coverage is greater. Coverages, whether written on an occurrence or claims-made basis, shall be maintained without interruption from date of commencement of the Work until date of final payment and termination of any coverage required to be maintained after final payment.

Paragraph 11.1.2

 II

   96008-MN

 III

   94013-LA
   94037-MN

Text of Paragraph 11.1.3

Certificates of Insurance acceptable to the Owner shall be filed with the Owner prior to commencement of the Work. These Certificates and the insurance policies required by this Paragraph 11.1 shall contain a provision that coverages afforded under the policies will not be cancelled or allowed to expire until at least 30 days' prior written notice has been given to the Owner. If any of the foregoing insurance coverages are required to remain in force after final payment and are reasonably available, an additional certificate evidencing continuation of such coverage shall be submitted with the final Application for Payment as required by Subparagraph 9.10.2. Information concerning reduction of coverage shall be furnished by the Contractor with reasonable promptness in accordance with the Contractor's information and belief.

Paragraph 11.1.3

 III

  96019-DKS   94013-LA
  96012-IL   94037-MN

Paragraph 11.2 Owner's Liability Insurance

Paragraph 11.3 Property Insurance

Text of Paragraph 11.3.1

Unless otherwise provided, the Owner shall purchase and maintain, in a company

DOCUMENT TO CASE CHARTS: A201-1987 A–330

[The five-digit numbers in this chart are Citator Case Reference Numbers, which refer to the cases, in the Cases section. The suffixes indicate the state or, for federal cases, the court in which the case was decided.]

> or companies lawfully authorized to do business in the jurisdiction in which the Project is located, property insurance in the amount of the initial Contract Sum as well as subsequent modifications thereto for the entire Work at the site on a rplacement cost basis without voluntary deductibles. Such property insurance shall be maintained, unless otherwise provided in the Contract Documents or otherwise agreed in writing by all persons and entities who are beneficiaries of such insurance, until final payment has been made as provided in Paragraph 9.10 or until no person or entity other than the Owner has an insurable interest in the property required by this Paragraph 11.3 to be covered, whichever is earlier. This insurance shall include interests of the Owner, the Contractor, Subcontractors and Sub-subcontractors in the Work.

Paragraph 11.3.1

I

    93056-AZ   97025-CO
    94012-CA   94004-MO

II

    95051-SDMS
    94004-MO

> **Text of Paragraph 11.3.1.1**
>
> Property insurance shall be on an all-risk policy from and shall insure against the perils of fire and extended coverage and physical loss or damage including, without duplication of coverage, theft, vandalism, malicious mischief, collapse, false-work, temporary buildings and debris removal including demolition occasioned by enforcement of any applicable legal requirements, and shall cover reasonable compensation for Architect's services and expenses required as a result of such insured loss. Coverage for other perils shall not be required unless otherwise provided in the Contract Documents.

Paragraph 11.3.1.1

III

    95038-OH

Paragraph 11.3.2   Boiler and Machinery Insurance

> **Text of Paragraph 11.3.3—Loss of Use Insurance**
>
> The Owner, at the Owner's option, may purchase and maintain such insurance as will insure the Owner against loss of use of the Owner's property due to fire or other hazards, however caused. The Owner waives all rights of action against the Contractor for loss of use of the Owner's property, including consequential losses due to fire or other hazards however caused.

A–331   DOCUMENT TO CASE CHARTS: A201-1987

[The five-digit numbers in this chart are Citator Case Reference Numbers, which refer to the cases, in the Cases section. The suffixes indicate the state or, for federal cases, the court in which the case was decided.]

Paragraph 11.3.3   Loss of Use Insurance

    I

        93029-NH

Text of Paragraph 11.3.5

If during the Project construction period the Owner insures properties, real or personal or both, adjoining or adjacent to the site by property insurance under policies separate from those insuring the Project, or if after final payment property insurance is to be provided on the completed Project through a policy or policies other than those insuring the Project during the construction period, the Owner shall waive all rights in accordance with the terms of Subparagraph 11.3.7 for damages caused by fire or other perils covered by this separate property insurance. All separate policies shall provide this waiver of subrogation by endorsement or otherwise.

Paragraph 11.3.5

    I

        97025-CO
        93029-NH

Text of Paragraph 11.3.7—Waivers of Subrogation

The Owner and Contractor waive all rights against (1) each other and any of their subcontractors, sub-subcontractors, agents and employees, each of the other, and (2) the Architect, Architect's consultants, separate contractors described in Article 6, if any, and any of their subcontractors, sub-subcontractors, agents and employees, for damages caused by fire or other perils to the extent covered by property insurance obtained pursuant to this Paragraph 11.3 for other property insurance applicable to the Work, except such rights as they have to proceeds of such insurance held by the Owner as fiduciary. The Owner or Contractor, as appropriate, shall require of the Architect, Architect's consultants, separate contractors described in Article 6, if any, and the subcontractors, sub-subcontractors, agents and employees of any of them, by appropriate agreements, written where legally required for validity, similar waivers each in favor of other parties enumerated herein. The policies shall provide such waivers of subrogation by endorsement or otherwise. A waiver of subrogation shall be effective as to a person or entity even though that person or entity would otherwise have a duty of indemnification, contractual or otherwise, did not pay the insurance premium directly or indirectly, and whether or not the person or entity had an insurable interest in the property damaged.

DOCUMENT TO CASE CHARTS: A201-1987   A–332

[The five-digit numbers in this chart are Citator Case Reference Numbers, which refer to the cases, in the Cases section. The suffixes indicate the state or, for federal cases, the court in which the case was decided.]

Paragraph 11.3.7   Waivers of Subrogation

    I

        94012-CA   94004-MO
        97009-CA   93029-NH
        97025-CO   94011-WDMI

    II

        95051-SDMS   94002-MO
        93050-DPR   93055-WI
        93056-AZ

    III

        95038-OH

Paragraph 11.4   Performance Bond and Payment Bond

Article 12   Uncovering and Correction of Work

Paragraph 12.1   Uncovering of Work

Paragraph 12.2   Correction of Work

Text of Paragraph 12.2.2

12.2.2 If, within one year after the date of Substantial Completion of the Work or designated portion thereof, or after the date for commencement of warranties established under Sub-paragraph 9.9.1, or by terms of an applicable special warranty required by the Contract Documents, any of the Work is found to be not in accordance with the requirements of the Contract Documents, the Contractor shall correct it promptly after receipt of written notice from the Owner to do so unless the Owner has previously given the Contractor a written acceptance of such condition. This period of one year shall be extended with respect to portions of Work first performed after Substantial Completion by the period of time between Substantial Completion and the actual performance of the Work. This obligation under this Subparagraph 12.2.2 shall survive acceptance of the Work under the Contract and termination of the Contract. The Owner shall give such notice promptly after discovery of the condition.

Paragraph 12.2.2

    II

        96034-MO

A–333 DOCUMENT TO CASE CHARTS: A201-1987

[*The five-digit numbers in this chart are Citator Case Reference Numbers, which refer to the cases, in the Cases section. The suffixes indicate the state or, for federal cases, the court in which the case was decided.*]

    III

        94024-PA

Text of Paragraph 12.2.4

12.2.4 If the Contractor fails to correct nonconforming Work within a reasonable time, the Owner may correct it in accordance with Paragraph 2.4. If the Contractor does not proceed with correction of such nonconforming Work within a reasonable time fixed by written notice from the Architect, the Owner may remove it and store the salvable materials or equipment at the Contractor's expense. If the Contractor does not pay costs of such removal and storage within ten days after written notice, the Owner may upon ten additional days' written notice sell such materials and equipment at auction or at private sale and shall account for the proceeds thereof, after deducting costs and damages that should have been borne by the Contractor, including compensation for the Architect's services and expenses made necessary thereby. If such proceeds of sale do not cover costs which the Contractor should have borne, the Contract Sum shall be reduced by the deficiency. If payments then or thereafter due the Contractor are not sufficient to cover such amount, the Contractor shall pay the difference to the Owner.

Paragraph 12.2.4

    III

        94024-PA

Paragraph 12.3   Acceptance of Nonconforming Work

Article 13   Miscellaneous Provisions

Paragraph 13.1   Governing Law

Text of Paragraph 13.1.1

The Contract shall be governed by the law of the place where the Project is located.

Paragraph 13.1.1

    I

        92012-DNJ   93011-MA
        93016-FL   93019-NJ
        93012-IL   93048-SC

Paragraph 13.2   Successors and Assigns

Text of Paragraph 13.2.1

The Owner and Contractor respectively bind themselves, their partners,

DOCUMENT TO CASE CHARTS: A201-1987   A–334

[The five-digit numbers in this chart are Citator Case Reference Numbers, which refer to the cases, in the Cases section. The suffixes indicate the state or, for federal cases, the court in which the case was decided.]

successors, assigns and legal representatives to the other party hereto and to partners, successors, assigns and legal representatives of such other party in respect to covenants, agreements and obligations contained in the Contract Documents. Neither party to the Contract shall assign the Contract as a whole without written consent of the other. If either party attempts to make such an assignment without such consent, that party shall nevertheless remain legally responsible for all obligations under the Contract.

Paragraph 13.2.1

    I

        96013-GA

    II

        96034-MO
        93015-OR
        94025-WA

Paragraph 13.3   Written Notice

Paragraph 13.4   Rights and Remedies

Text of Paragraph 13.4.1

13.4.1 Duties and obligations imposed by the Contract Documents and rights and remedies available thereunder shall be in addition to and not a limitation of duties, obligations, rights and remedies otherwise imposed or available by law.

Paragraph 13.4.1

    I

        96023-TN

    II

        92004c-GA

Text of Paragraph 13.4.2

13.4.2 No action or failure to act by the Owner, Architect or Contractor shall constitute a waiver of a right or duty afforded them under the Contract, nor shall such action or failure to act constitute approval of or acquiescence in a breach thereunder, except as may be specifically agreed in writing.

DOCUMENT TO CASE CHARTS: A201-1987

[The five-digit numbers in this chart are Citator Case Reference Numbers, which refer to the cases, in the Cases section. The suffixes indicate the state or, for federal cases, the court in which the case was decided.]

Paragraph 13.4.2

    I

        95020-DPR

Paragraph 13.5   Tests and Inspections

    III

        95044-MDAL
        95029-EDVA

Text of Paragraph 13.5.1

Tests, inspections and approvals of portions of the Work required by the Contract Documents or by laws, ordinances, rules, regulations or orders of public authorities having jurisdiction shall be made at an appropriate time. Unless otherwise provided, the Contractor shall make arrangements for such tests, inspections and approvals with an independent testing laboratory or entity acceptable to the Owner, or with the appropriate pubic authority, and shall bear all related costs of tests, inspections and approvals. The Contractor shall give the Architect timely notice of when and where tests and inspections are to be made so the Architect may observe such procedures. The Owner shall bear costs of tests, inspections or approvals which do not become requirements until after bids are received or negotiations concluded.

Paragraph 13.5.1

    II

        93036-NE

Text of Paragraph 13.5.5

If the Architect is to observe tests, inspections or approvals required by the Contract Documents, the Architect will do so promptly and, where practicable, at the normal place of testing.

Paragraph 13.5.5

    II

        93036-NE

Paragraph 13.6   Interest

Paragraph 13.7   Commencement of Statutory Limitation Period

Article 14   Termination or Suspension of the Contract

Paragraph 14.1   Termination by the Contractor

DOCUMENT TO CASE CHARTS: A201-1987 — A-336

[The five-digit numbers in this chart are Citator Case Reference Numbers, which refer to the cases, in the Cases section. The suffixes indicate the state or, for federal cases, the court in which the case was decided.]

Text of Paragraph 14.1.1

14.1.1 The Contractor may terminate the Contract if the Work is stopped for a period of 30 days through no act or fault of the Contractor or a Subcontractor, Sub-subcontractor or their agents or employees or any other persons performing portions of the Work under contract with the Contractor, for any of the following reasons:

.1 issuance of an order of a court or other public authority having jurisdiction;

.2 an act of government, such as a declaration of national emergency, making material unavailable;

.3 because the Architect has not issued a Certificate for Payment and has not notified the Contractor of the reason for withholding certification as provided in Subparagraph 9.4.1, or because the Owner has not made payment on a Certificate for Payment within the time stated in the Contract Documents;

.4 if repeated suspensions, delays or interruptions by the Owner as described in Paragraph 14.3 constitute in the aggregate more than 100 percent of the total number of days scheduled for completion, or 120 days in any 365-day period, whichever is less; or

.5 the Owner has failed to furnish to the Contractor promptly, upon the Contractor's request, reasonable evidence as required by Subparagraph 2.2.1.

Paragraph 14.1.1

    I

        92012-DNJ

Text of Paragraph 14.1.2

14.1.2 If one of the above reasons exists, the Contractor may upon seven additional days' written notice to the Owner and Architect, terminate the Contract and recover from the Owner payment for Work executed and for proven loss with respect to materials equipment, tools, and construction equipment and machinery including reasonable overhead, profit and damages.

Paragraph 14.1.2

    I

        92012-DNJ

Text of Paragraph 14.1.3

14.1.3 If the Work is stopped for a period of 60 days through no act or fault of the Contractor or a Subcontractor or their agents or employees or any other persons performing portions of the Work under contract with the Contractor because the Owner has persistently failed to fulfill the Owner's obligations under the Contract Documents with respect to matters important to the progress of the Work,

DOCUMENT TO CASE CHARTS: A201-1987

[The five-digit numbers in this chart are Citator Case Reference Numbers, which refer to the cases, in the Cases section. The suffixes indicate the state or, for federal cases, the court in which the case was decided.]

> the Contractor may, upon seven additional days' written notice to the Owner and the Architect, terminate the Contract and recover from the Owner as provided in Subparagraph 14.1.2.

Paragraph 14.1.3

    I

        92012-DNJ

Paragraph 14.2   Termination by Owner for Cause

    III

        92021b-VA

Text of Paragraph 14.2.1

14.2.1 The Owner may terminate the Contract if the Contractor:

.1   persistently or repeatedly refuses or fails to supply enough properly skilled workers or proper materials;

.2   fails to make payment to Subcontractors for materials or labor in accordance with the respective agreements between the Contractor and the Subcontractors;

.3   persistently disregards laws, ordinances, or rules, regulations or orders of a public authority having jurisdiction; or

.4   otherwise is guilty of substantial breach of a provision of the Contract Documents.

Paragraph 14.2.1

    II

        94027-MN

    III

        95008-VA

Text of Paragraph 14.2.2

14.2.2 When any of the above reasons exist, the Owner, upon certification by the Architect that sufficient cause exists to justify such action, may without prejudice to any other rights or remedies of the Owner and after giving the Contractor and the Contractor's surety, if any, seven days' written notice, terminate employment of the Contractor and may, subject to any prior rights of the surety:

.1   take possession of the site and of all materials, equipment, tools, and construction equipment and machinery thereon owned by the Contractor.

.2   accept assignment of subcontracts pursuant to Paragraph 5.4; and

DOCUMENT TO CASE CHARTS: A201-1987 A–338

[The five-digit numbers in this chart are Citator Case Reference Numbers, which refer to the cases, in the Cases section. The suffixes indicate the state or, for federal cases, the court in which the case was decided.]

> .3 finish the Work by whatever reasonable method the Owner may deem expedient.

Paragraph 14.2.2

    II

        94027-MN

   III

        95008-VA

> **Text of Paragraph 14.2.3**
>
> **14.2.3** When the Owner terminates the Contract for one of the reasons stated in Subparagraph 14.2.1, the Contractor shall not be entitled to receive further payment until the Work is finished.

Paragraph 14.2.3

    III

        95008-VA

> **Text of Paragraph 14.2.4**
>
> **14.2.4** If the unpaid balance of the Contract Sum exceeds costs of finishing the Work, including compensation for the Architect's services and expenses made necessary thereby, such excess shall be paid to the Contractor. If such costs exceed the unpaid balance, the Contractor shall pay the difference to the Owner. The amount to be paid to the Contractor or Owner, as the case may be, shall be certified by the Architect, upon application, and this obligation for payment shall survive termination of the Contract.

Paragraph 14.2.4

    III

        95008-VA

Paragraph 14.3   Suspension by the Owner for Convenience

DOCUMENT TO CASE CHARTS: A201-1987

[The five-digit numbers in this chart are Citator Case Reference Numbers, which refer to the cases, in the Cases section. The suffixes indicate the state or, for federal cases, the court in which the case was decided.]

> ### Text of Paragraph 14.3.3
> **14.3.3** Adjustments made in the cost of performance may have a mutually agreed fixed or percentage fee.

Paragraph 14.3.3

    II

        94027-MN

DOCUMENT TO CASE CHARTS: A310-1963

[*The five-digit numbers in this chart are Citator Case Reference Numbers, which refer to the cases, in the Cases section. The suffixes indicate the state or, for federal cases, the court in which the case was decided.*]

A310-1963—BID BOND
III
    65061-NH

DOCUMENT TO CASE CHARTS: A310-1970

[The five-digit numbers in this chart are Citator Case Reference Numbers, which refer to the cases, in the Cases section. The suffixes indicate the state or, for federal cases, the court in which the case was decided.]

A310-1970—BID BOND

I

    69009-NY

II

    77010-MD
    76044-MS

III

    73051-IL
    69033-MA
    72060-NY

DOCUMENT TO CASE CHARTS: A311-1963

[The five-digit numbers in this chart are Citator Case Reference Numbers, which refer to the cases, in the Cases section. The suffixes indicate the state or, for federal cases, the court in which the case was decided.]

A311-1963—PERFORMANCE BOND AND LABOR AND MATERIAL PAYMENT BOND

Performance Bond

III

    66077-DCCIR   67035-CA
    66030-CA   66100-NY
    66111-CA

Labor and Material Payment Bond

I

29002-AL	66067-MS
25002-CA	67028-MS
28002-CA	32002-TX
29001-CT	65047-TX
65002-DC	66062-TX
31004-FL	39003-UT
66025-FL	66064-VA
26001-MD	66038-WA
67050-MD	

II

66057-5CIR	33002-KY
67053-CO	65037-MD
66011-DCO	31006-MO
13006-KS	

III

65110-2CIR	65069-WDOK
65009-5CIR	65021-WDPA
65100-5CIR	66010-WDPA
66017-5CIR	66003-DPR
65023-7CIR	66018-CA
65044-8CIR	66030-CA
65068-8CIR	66078-CA
65082-8CIR	65089-DE
65107-8CIR	65003-FL
65113-8CIR	65119-FL
65065-9CIR	67032-HI
65072-9CIR	65077-ID
66015-9CIR	65017-IL
66086-9CIR	65025-IL
65035-10CIR	66005-IL
65058-10CIR	65020-ME
65116-10CIR	66108-MD
66063-10CIR	65011-MA
66103-NDCA	66049-MO
65109-EDLA	65094-NE
66106-DMA	64005-NJ
65090-WDMO	66061-ND
65104-DMT	64001-OH
66104-DMT	56002-PA
65052-DNJ	65055-PA
65112-NDNY	65114-PA
66105-EDNY	65108-TX

DOCUMENT TO CASE CHARTS: A311-1963

[The five-digit numbers in this chart are Citator Case Reference Numbers, which refer to the cases, in the Cases section. The suffixes indicate the state or, for federal cases, the court in which the case was decided.]

€7055-TX
€6051-WA

DOCUMENT TO CASE CHARTS: A311-1970

[The five-digit numbers in this chart are Citator Case Reference Numbers, which refer to the cases, in the Cases section. The suffixes indicate the state or, for federal cases, the court in which the case was decided.]

A311-1970—PERFORMANCE BOND AND LABOR AND MATERIAL PAYMENT BOND

Performance Bond

I

79057-4CIR
75033-DE
80003-FL
80005-FL
81032-LA

80063-MA
79068-MN
81074-OH
80069-TX

II

71013-2CIR
75028-6CIR
74011-SDWV
80011-AR
79058-CA
77002-DC
68027-FL

69024-IL
76058-MI
72095-NY
77018-NY
79007-NY
79042-NC
80017-OR

III

72044-4CIR
72039-5CIR
72049-5CIR
71011-SDWV
71062-AZ
68041-CA
70063-CA
70078-CA
70090-CA
71024-CA
76070-CA
69026-FL
78002-FL
78027-FL
79047-FL
80001-FL
70005-GA
80068-GA
80013-IL
71084-KY
73008-LA
76055-LA
76068-MD
78013-MD
72034-MI
70043-MO
73041-MO
77080-MT

74002-NJ
76012-NJ
78035-NJ
67068-NY
70025-NY
70033-NY
70050-NY
70059-NY
70083-NY
70085-NY
72004-NY
75022-NY
76052-NY
77045-NY
79037-NY
79053-NY
80034-NY
80060-NY
71067-OK
72079-OK
68048-SD
73032-TX
78071-TX
70002-UT
79015-VA
77066-WA
71042-WY

DOCUMENT TO CASE CHARTS: A311-1970

[The five-digit numbers in this chart are Citator Case Reference Numbers, which refer to the cases, in the Cases section. The suffixes indicate the state or, for federal cases, the court in which the case was decided.]

Labor and Material Payment Bond

I

81019-3CIR	76047-NY
80014-DCCIR	80066-NY
69028-AL	71050-NC
75033-DE	76060-NC
81068a-FL	80031-NC
74031-GA	70056-SC
79020-MI	55001-VA
80075-MS	70042-VA
77015-NE	80043-WV
68005-NY	79056-WY
75002-NY	81067-WY

II

75028-6CIR	76058-MI
78022-7CIR	77083-NJ
30052-CA	76003-NY
69052-CA	77004-NY
77070-CA	79007-NY
71005-CT	70077-OR
57003-FL	80017-OR
58027-FL	79019-TX
81025-FL	80058-TX
71022-ID	

III

81061-3CIR	80016-LA
76059-4CIR	79064-MD
72049-5CIR	80059-MA
73061-5CIR	81042-MA
72046-10CIR	81011-MI
75012-EDMI	77041-MN
71011-SDWV	71001-NJ
79049-AZ	68015-NY
77053-CA	76038-NY
78069-CA	78005-NY
78027-FL	81043-NY
79047-FL	78050-PA
80001-FL	78075-PA
80068-GA	75016-SC
69024-IL	66043-TN
76007-IL	68049-TX
77016-IL	77078-TX
80028-IL	72076-WI
77082-KY	

DOCUMENT TO CASE CHARTS: A312-1984

[The five-digit numbers in this chart are Citator Case Reference Numbers, which refer to the cases, in the Cases section. The suffixes indicate the state or, for federal cases, the court in which the case was decided.]

A312-1984—PERFORMANCE BOND AND PAYMENT BOND
Performance Bond

Article 1

    III

        97016-AR
        97011-MD

Article 2

    II

        96005-PA

Article 3

Paragraph 3.1

    I

        95035-SDNY

Paragraph 3.2

    I

        95035-SDNY

Paragraph 3.3

    I

        95035-SDNY

Article 4

    III

        96017-NDIL

Paragraph 4.1

    II

        96005-PA

Paragraph 4.2

    II

        96005-PA

DOCUMENT TO CASE CHARTS: A312-1984

[The five-digit numbers in this chart are Citator Case Reference Numbers, which refer to the cases, in the Cases section. The suffixes indicate the state or, for federal cases, the court in which the case was decided.]

Paragraph 4.3
    II
        96005-PA

Article 5
    III
        96017-NDIL

Article 6
    III
        96005-PA

Paragraph 6.1
    III
        96005-PA

Paragraph 6.2
    III
        96005-PA

Paragraph 6.3
    III
        96005-PA

Article 8
    II
        96005-PA

DOCUMENT TO CASE CHARTS: A401-1963   A–348

[The five-digit numbers in this chart are Citator Case Reference Numbers, which refer to the cases, in the Cases section. The suffixes indicate the state or, for federal cases, the court in which the case was decided.]

A401-1963—STANDARD FORM OF SUBCONTRACT

Article 1

   III

      66055-9CIR
      66032-NDTX
      67014-MD

Article 2

Article 3

   III

      65045-1CIR   65066-WA
      65071-PA   65084-WA

Article 4

   I

      66095-FL

   III

      66002-GA

Article 5

   I

      66116-DE
      66095-FL

   II

      65037-MD
      66065-ND
      67040-TX

   III

      65045-1CIR   66014-GA
      66107-4CIR   65020-ME
      66006-9CIR   66108-MD
      66055-9CIR   67014-MD
      66073-10CIR   65048-MO
      66109-EDLA   65004-NY
      65031-AZ   65064-NY
      67001-CA   66072-NY
      67030-CA   66100-NY
      67034-CA   65087-OR
      66115-CT   65108-TX
      65051-DE   66080-UT
      65078-GA

A-349 DOCUMENT TO CASE CHARTS: A401-1967

[The five-digit numbers in this chart are Citator Case Reference Numbers, which refer to the cases, in the Cases section. The suffixes indicate the state or, for federal cases, the court in which the case was decided.]

A401-1967—SUBCONTRACT: THE STANDARD FORM OF AGREEMENT BETWEEN CONTRACTOR AND SUBCONTRACTOR

Article 1 The Contract Documents

    I

        69044-IL

Article 2 The Work

    I

        68013-GA
        71036-MI
        68008-MT

    III

        68020-5CIR

Article 3 Time of Commencement and Completion

    III

        68020-5CIR

Article 4 The Contract Sum

Article 5 Progress Payments

    III

        71019-IL
        69001-MA

Article 6 Final Payment

    I

        70061-KS

    III

        69003-NY
        71050-NC

Article 7 Performance and Labor and Material Payment Bonds

    I

        68044-AZ
        69022-FL

(Matthew Bender & Co., Inc.)

DOCUMENT TO CASE CHARTS: A401-1967 A–350

[The five-digit numbers in this chart are Citator Case Reference Numbers, which refer to the cases, in the Cases section. The suffixes indicate the state or, for federal cases, the court in which the case was decided.]

Article 8   Temporary Site Facilities

Article 9   Insurance

   II

       71035-AZ

Article 10   Working Conditions

Article 11   Subcontractor's Responsibilities

   I

       70092-FL
       68008-MT

   II

       71046-7CIR   86025-MN
       67044-CA   82037-PA
       68051-CA   70082-WA
       68016-IL   68025-WI

   III

       68020-5CIR   73108-IL
       71040-6CIR   70036-KS
       70064-10CIR   70061-KS
       70041-DCCIR   69020-KY
       71030-EDVA   70066-MD
       70065-AR   70052-MA
       71049-GA   70044-MO
       69048-IL   70055-NC
       70038-IL   71047-TN
       70068-IL   69043-TX
       70093-IL   70054-TX
       71019-IL   72093-TX
       71038-IL

Article 12   Contractor's Responsibilities

   I

       69017-NY

   III

       68004-MD
       69003-NY

DOCUMENT TO CASE CHARTS: A401-1967

[The five-digit numbers in this chart are Citator Case Reference Numbers, which refer to the cases, in the Cases section. The suffixes indicate the state or, for federal cases, the court in which the case was decided.]

Article 13 Arbitration

I

    68031-NY

II

    67037-DC
    82030-IL

[The five-digit numbers in this chart are Citator Case Reference Numbers, which refer to the cases, in the Cases section. The suffixes indicate the state or, for federal cases, the court in which the case was decided.]

A401-1972—SUBCONTRACT: STANDARD FORM OF AGREEMENT BETWEEN CONTRACTOR AND SUBCONTRACTOR

Article 1 The Contract Documents

    III

        73023-SC

Article 2 The Work

    I

        71085-TN

Article 3 Time of Commencement and Completion

    II

        73035-VA

    III

        73021-5CIR   72013-KS
        73026-GA   72110-ND

Article 4 The Contract Sum

Article 5 Progress Payments

    III

        73119-DE
        72017-NY
        74041-WI

Article 6 Final Payment

    III

        73078-WDOK
        72021-NY

Article 7 Performance and Labor and Material Payment Bonds

    III

        72046-10CIR

Article 8 Temporary Facilities and Services

Article 9 Insurance

    I

        73098-AR
        75009-GA
        71085-TN

DOCUMENT TO CASE CHARTS: A401-1972

[The five-digit numbers in this chart are Citator Case Reference Numbers, which refer to the cases, in the Cases section. The suffixes indicate the state or, for federal cases, the court in which the case was decided.]

    III

        73037-DCCIR

Article 10   **Working Conditions**

Article 11   **Subcontractor's Responsibilities**

    I

72100-3CIR	74003-LA
73058-EDVA	73112-NY
73098-AR	73056-WA
75009-GA	

    II

72077-3CIR	73015-GA
72102-9CIR	74023-GA
84020-AK	

    III

75010-3CIR	72013-KS
74038-5CIR	72070-IL
72098-4CIR	73108-IL
72104-5CIR	72068-LA
73061-5CIR	73017-LA
74037-7CIR	73107-LA
72016-DCCIR	72112-MD
72083-DCCIR	73025-MN
72105-NDIA	74029-NE
73079-WDOK	72014-NY
75012-EDMI	72053-NY
73047-NDMS	72080-NY
71073-DSC	73018-NY
73120-AL	73125-NY
73002-AZ	72103-NC
73117-AZ	73049-OR
72073-AR	73038-RI
72062-CA	71052-TX
72072-CA	72093-TX
73110-CO	73031-TX
72007-DE	73099-TX
72107-DE	72037-WA
71009-GA	72052-WA
73006-GA	72101-WA
73026-GA	72090-WV
73093-GA	

Article 12   **Contractor's Responsibilities**

    I

        73058-EDVA

DOCUMENT TO CASE CHARTS: A401-1972

[The five-digit numbers in this chart are Citator Case Reference Numbers, which refer to the cases, in the Cases section. The suffixes indicate the state or, for federal cases, the court in which the case was decided.]

III

    73010-7CIR   75022-NY
    73006-GA   74041-WI
    73113-NE

Article 13 Interest

II

    72063-MD
    72111-NJ

III

    73121-1CIR

Article 14 Arbitration

I

    73058-EDVA

II

    75026-EDPA

III

    72078-1CIR   74010-DDC
    73054-5CIR   73116-AZ
    73061-5CIR   72001-NY

DOCUMENT TO CASE CHARTS: A401-1978

[The five-digit numbers in this chart are Citator Case Reference Numbers, which refer to the cases, in the Cases section. The suffixes indicate the state or, for federal cases, the court in which the case was decided.]

A401-1978—SUBCONTRACT: STANDARD FORM OF AGREEMENT BETWEEN CONTRACTOR AND SUBCONTRACTOR

Article 1   The Contract Documents

I

80023-CT	95039-MO
91006-FL	81022a-NC
85003-GA	78023-PA
89049-MA	81055-SD
82034-MS	86002-TN

II

76045-AK	89026-MO
79051-DE	83031-NC
86061-FL	86026-OH
78043-MD	79065-UT
84038-MO	80051-UT

III

81052-NDAL	81031-LA
83045-SDNY	77076-NY
86023-DE	78038-NY
90034-FL	78068-NY
79041-GA	86047-NY
81040-GA	90011-NY
82040-IL	78063-TX

Article 2   The Work

I

85003-GA
95039-MO
86002-TN

III

91019-AL	80047-MO
92014a-AL	90016-NY
81040-GA	

Article 3   Time of Commencement and Substantial Completion

I

80061-VT

II

80033-8CIR
81069-DDC
82001-NE

DOCUMENT TO CASE CHARTS: A401-1978

[*The five-digit numbers in this chart are Citator Case Reference Numbers, which refer to the cases, in the Cases section. The suffixes indicate the state or, for federal cases, the court in which the case was decided.*]

III

    88027-3CIR
    75032-CT
    80006-CA

Article 4 The Contract Sum

I

    81001-MA
    86040-MN
    86002-TN

II

    81052-NDAL

Article 5 Progress Payments

I

    78003-LA

II

92001-7CIR	86008-LA
85007-AR	81017-NH
85001-IL	80019-TX

III

    83035-5CIR
    91014-FL
    78068-NY

Article 6 Final Payment

I

    87038-TX

II

78022-7CIR	90033-MN
86008-LA	87051-PA

III

79026-CA	91014-FL
77067-FL	90017-GA
78002-FL	86049-NH
88005-FL	76033-NY
90034-FL	86075-NY

DOCUMENT TO CASE CHARTS: A401-1978

[The five-digit numbers in this chart are Citator Case Reference Numbers, which refer to the cases, in the Cases section. The suffixes indicate the state or, for federal cases, the court in which the case was decided.]

Article 7 Performance Bond and Labor and Material Payment Bond

    III

        81042-MA

Article 8 Temporary Facilities and Services

Article 9 Insurance

    I

        30070-AL   81026-MA
        93056-AZ   81072-MA

    II

        85021-GA   86046-WA
        83038-LA   83050-WY

    III

        79050-AZ   91003-MD
        76065-CA   86063-MA
        86029-CT   79035-MN
        78030-FL   83044-MN
        85015-HI   90028-NY
        77075-IL   91029-ND
        88043-IL

Article 10 Working Conditions

Article 11 Subcontractor

    I

        89031-9CIR   83022-MO
        84009-EDLA   92003-MO
        80070-AL   97017-NJ
        76051-CT   78004-NY
        78070-DE   88018-NY
        88005-FL   79004-NC
        85003-GA   83031-NC
        93013-GA   89025-NC
        83028-IL   92008a-PA
        78003-LA   86002-TN
        86072-LA   86058-TX
        89036-LA   88002-TX
        81072-MA   91010-TX
        95011-MI   94009-TX
        85008-MN   95036-TX
        86067-MN   77063-WA
        82034-MS   92005-WA

DOCUMENT TO CASE CHARTS: A401-1978

[The five-digit numbers in this chart are Citator Case Reference Numbers, which refer to the cases, in the Cases section. The suffixes indicate the state or, for federal cases, the court in which the case was decided.]

II

86037-3CIR	83038-LA
88027-3CIR	83040-LA
85027-4CIR	86008-LA
83021-7CIR	90056-LA
83032-7CIR	78043-MD
80033-8CIR	81013-MA
84014-8CIR	89028-MA
89031-9CIR	91017-MA
81069-DDC	93018-MA
80042-DMD	88026-MN
90013-AL	93053-MN
86055-AZ	86030-MO
91036-AZ	91036a-MO
85007-AR	82033-MT
89021-CA	82001-NE
76042-CO	81017-NH
84039-CT	87048-NM
79051-DE	86015-NY
79048-FL	88001-NY
87013-FL	89015-NY
91006-FL	79025-NC
78008-GA	86026-OH
84032-GA	93043-PA
85021-GA	83012-RI
77057-IL	85013-TN
84028-IL	87019-TX
85001-IL	80051-UT
85019-IL	87011-VA
86013-IL	80067-WA
91001-IN	84005-WA
86050-IA	85016-WA
84016-KS	93040-WI
90042-KS	83050-WY

III

90023-2CIR	79050-AZ
80022a-3CIR	76029-CA
89001-4CIR	76065-CA
76020-5CIR	76070-CA
82005-5CIR	76071-CA
83035-5CIR	77056-CA
85009-7CIR	78032-CA
82008-11CIR	78033-CA
83015-11CIR	79016-CA
88038-11CIR	85025-CA
81048-NDAL	85034-CA
81021-NDFL	87035-CA
89043-NDIL	90002-CO
87010-DME	81071-CT
83045-SDNY	86001-CT
75031-WDPA	86023-DE
81053-AL	93051-DC
82019-AL	78002-FL
91019-AL	81022-FL
92014a-AL	88005-FL
85011-AK	88030-FL
86022-AK	90034-FL

DOCUMENT TO CASE CHARTS: A401-1978

[The five-digit numbers in this chart are Citator Case Reference Numbers, which refer to the cases, in the Cases section. The suffixes indicate the state or, for federal cases, the court in which the case was decided.]

91014-FL	86043-MT
79041-GA	80018-NE
81040-GA	77081-NJ
86048-GA	76024-NY
88040-GA	76027-NY
90036-GA	76056-NY
92015-GA	77014-NY
81033-HI	77043-NY
85015-HI	77076-NY
77016-IL	78005-NY
77024-IL	78068-NY
77046-IL	81003-NY
77062-IL	81070-NY
77071-IL	86075-NY
77079-IL	87016-NY
81075-IL	90011-NY
82040-IL	90016-NY
85006-IL	92007-NY
85015a-IL	93039-NY
86060-IL	89005-NC
88043-IL	91029-ND
89045-IL	77009-OK
91025-IL	80038-OK
91023-IN	91039-PA
80041-KS	93031-PA
78065-LA	91018-RI
94013-LA	89018-SC
83002-MA	82017-TN
86063-MA	77078-TX
87006-MA	78063-TX
80054-MI	87029-TX
85035-MI	89029-VA
87020-MI	83049-WA
77041-MN	85028-WA
79035-MN	86057-WA
81059-MN	85039-WV
83044-MN	89041-WV
93047-MN	82023-WI
77060-MT	87044-WY

Article 12   Contractor

I

88010-CO	87051-PA
83028-IL	86002-TN
81072-MA	87038-TX

II

84010-6CIR	86072-LA
81063-10CIR	91011-MD
85007-AR	81002-MO
79051-DE	90033-MN
87041-FL	77015-NE
85001-IL	81017-NH
84016-KS	80051-UT
86008-LA	86046-WA

DOCUMENT TO CASE CHARTS: A401-1978

[The five-digit numbers in this chart are Citator Case Reference Numbers, which refer to the cases, in the Cases section. The suffixes indicate the state or, for federal cases, the court in which the case was decided.]

III

88027-3CIR
82005-5CIR
83035-5CIR
81048-NDAL
89042-NDIL
88034-WDNC
82019-AL
79069-AZ
80041-AK
75032-CT
81071-CT
77067-FL
88030-FL
90034-FL
91014-FL

77013-GA
86048-GA
90036-GA
77046-IL
84021-MA
87006-MA
84030-MI
79011-MT
80018-NE
86049-NH
76033-NY
77014-NY
86075-NY
86007-OH
82017-TN

Article 13 Arbitration

I

86045-5CIR
81037-7CIR
91009-SDAL
87005-NDTX
86014-AZ
89002-AZ
80023-CT
89034-CT
93006-CT
81006-FL
86041-FL
87001-FL
91015-FL
85003-GA
90009-GA
94003-GA
79039-IL
83028-IL
89011-IL

90041-IN
90018-KS
93003-KY
90027-LA
76041-MD
92013-MA
87017-MN
76021-NV
76034-NY
76053-NY
77064-NY
88018-NY
92010-NC
81074-OH
78023-PA
77085-RI
93002-SD
87038-TX
89051-TX
92009a-TX

II

89048-US
86037-3CIR
85027-4CIR
87032-4CIR
87014-5CIR
90019-6CIR
84040-NDAL
87022-DDC
88006-DME
85040-WDMO
88008-SDNY
79059-WDPA
90004-DSC
86021-AL
90038-AL
90046-CA

88029-CT
90001-CT
79051-DE
85004-FL
86020-FL
86031-FL
86061-FL
91006-FL
93008-IA
87015-IL
87018-IL
88039-IL
89044-IL
92021-IL
84016-KS
93052-LA

DOCUMENT TO CASE CHARTS: A401-1978

[*The five-digit numbers in this chart are Citator Case Reference Numbers, which refer to the cases, in the Cases section. The suffixes indicate the state or, for federal cases, the court in which the case was decided.*]

90022-ME
90014-MD
81013-MA
86036-MI
91012-MI
86067-MN
88009-MN
89010-MN
89046-MN

95033-MO
86062-NY
87039-NY
85002-NC
88016-OH
93048-SC
93024-TN
93054-TX
5023-VA

III

89050-6CIR
88038-11CIR
81008-NDAL
88044-NDGA
75030-AZ
84012-AZ
85041-AZ
90035-AZ
77072-AR
77008-CA
79024-CA
90003-CA
90053-CT
86023-DE
82040-IL
89030-IL
89045-IL
89039-MD
79038-MA

85042-MO
86054-NH
76037-NJ
77081-NJ
78038-NY
78068-NY
79037-NY
85043-NY
86024-NY
88021-NY
88031-NC
86026-OH
87045-PA
87052-PA
88013-PA
91018-RI
89018-SC
86069-WI

Article 14 Termination

I

88010-CO
78021-TN

II

89031-9CIR
76042-CO

76010-LA
77015-NE

III

92009-FL
92015-GA
76004-MO
78068-NY

86024-NY
90016-NY
76040-OK

DOCUMENT TO CASE CHARTS: A401-1978

[The five-digit numbers in this chart are Citator Case Reference Numbers, which refer to the cases, in the Cases section. The suffixes indicate the state or, for federal cases, the court in which the case was decided.]

Article 15 Miscellaneous Provisions

 I

   80023-CT   95039-MO
   89049-MA   91035-SC

 II

   79065-UT

 III

   79041-GA
   76055-LA
   78038-NY

DOCUMENT TO CASE CHARTS: A401-1987

[The five-digit numbers in this chart are Citator Case Reference Numbers, which refer to the cases, in the Cases section. The suffixes indicate the state or, for federal cases, the court in which the case was decided.]

A401-1987—STANDARD FORM OF AGREEMENT BETWEEN CONTRACTOR AND SUBCONTRACTOR

Article 1 The Subcontract Documents

II

93014-MO
95039-MO

III

97009-CA
96040-MO
96032-MS

Article 2 Mutual Rights and Responsibilities

II

97021-FL
93014-MO

III

97001-MDGA   95030-MA
93051-DC   96032-MS
97013-GA   93028-UT
96037-IL

Article 3 Contractor

II

95018-2CIR
95022-NC

III

97001-MDGA
96041-WY

Article 4 Subcontractor

I

94043-NDNY   95025-NJ
97009-CA   97014-NJ
95011-MI   92008a-PA
92003a-MO   95036-TX
93033-MO

II

96015-DC   93053-MN
97002-DC   96008-MN
95006-GA   93014-MO
92008b-IA   96018-MO
92001a-ID   95025-NJ
94036-IL   97014-NJ
93018-MA   93043-PA
94047-MI   97005-PA

DOCUMENT TO CASE CHARTS: A401-1987   A–364

[The five-digit numbers in this chart are Citator Case Reference Numbers, which refer to the cases, in the Cases section. The suffixes indicate the state or, for federal cases, the court in which the case was decided.]

        92004f-TX   93035-UT
        94009-TX   93040-WI
        94033-TX   95045-WI
        95049-TX

   III

        95018-2CIR   96021-MA
        94039-5CIR   96026-MA
        96019-DKS   96029-MA
        96024-DKS   96035-MA
        94023-SDMS   97006-MA
        95034-SDNY   94016-MI
        94022-DRI   95005-MI
        95007-DRI   93047-MN
        95019-AR   94037-MN
        97008-CA   95010-MN
        94032-DE   96043-MN
        93051-DC   95022-NC
        95032-FL   95021-NE
        97019-ID   95044-NJ
        94046-IL   93039-NY
        95026-IL   93030-OH
        96012-IL   94042-OH
        96031-IL   95003-OH
        92004d-LA   94048-OK
        93038-LA   95012-OR
        94013-LA   96010-OR
        95027-LA   93031-PA
        96003-LA   93028-UT
        95015-ME   93042-UT
        93041-MA   95013-UT
        94029-MA   94035-WA
        95028-MA   96007-WA
        95032-MA   95048-WV
        95041-MA

Article 5   **Changes in the Work**

   I

        94026-GA

   III

        995018-2CIR   97013-GA
        97001-MDGA   96040-MO

Article 6   **Arbitration**

   I

        92014-AL   95016-NC
        93006-CT   93019-NJ
        93016-FL   96011-NY
        94026-GA   97026-OH
        93012-IL   97023-PA
        93003-KY   93002-SD
        93011-MA   92005a-TX
        92016-NC   97024-WV

DOCUMENT TO CASE CHARTS: A401-1987

[*The five-digit numbers in this chart are Citator Case Reference Numbers, which refer to the cases, in the Cases section. The suffixes indicate the state or, for federal cases, the court in which the case was decided.*]

II

95046-AL	95033-MO
93044-FL	97007-NJ
92004c-GA	93048-SC
94003-GA	93024-TN
93008-IA	96023-TN
93052-LA	93054-TX
94006-MD	95023-VA
97011-MD	96014-VA
93046-MO	93049-WV
94017-MO	94049-WY

III

96022-2CIR	94021-LA
96006-DCCIR	95016-NC
95014-AR	94001-NY
97016-AR	95024-NY
94018-CA	97022-NY
96038-CO	95009-PA
94041-CT	94030-TX
96002-DC	95002-TX
93027-IL	94019-WI

Article 7 Termination, Suspension or Assignment of the Subcontract

III

95022-NC	94015-NJ
95021-NE	94025-WA

Article 8 The Work

II

95039-MO

Article 9 Date of Commencement and Substantial Completion

III

95018-2CIR

Article 10 Subcontract Sum

Article 11 Progress Payments

I

95034-VA

III

94050-AL	95005-MI
97015-AZ	95050-NY
97027-CA	96033-TN
95043-IL	

DOCUMENT TO CASE CHARTS: A401-1987

[The five-digit numbers in this chart are Citator Case Reference Numbers, which refer to the cases, in the Cases section. The suffixes indicate the state or, for federal cases, the court in which the case was decided.]

Article 12 Final Payment

 I

  95034-VA

 II

  96017-NDIL

 III

  94050-AL   95005-MI
  97015-AZ   93032-NY
  97027-CA   95050-NY
  95043-IL

Article 13 Insurance and Bonds

 I

  93056-AZ

 II

  93014-MO
  95049-TX
  93055-WI

 III

  96012-IL
  97004-MD
  94037-MN

Article 14 Temporary Facilities and Working Conditions

Article 15 Miscellaneous Provisions

Article 16 Enumeration of Subcontract Documents

 II

  95039-MO

 III

  96040-MO

B Series

Owner-Architect Documents

1. AIA copyrighted material from AIA Documents A101, A111, A201, and B141 has been reproduced with the permission of The American Institute of Architects under permission number 96150. Further reproduction is prohibited.

2. Because AIA Documents are revised from time to time, users should ascertain from the AIA the current edition of these documents.

3. Copies of the current edition of these AIA documents may be purchased from The American Institute of Architects or its local distributors.

4. These AIA Documents and their various provisions contained in this Citator are not intended to be used as "model text." (Text taken from an existing document and incorporated, without attribution, into a newly created document is model text.) Rather, the AIA documents are intended to be used as standard forms which, in turn, are used as originals by the contracting parties with modifications being made by appending separated amendments or supplements or by filling in the blank spaces provided on the forms for user-specific information.

B Series

Owner-Architect Documents

1. AIA Document B141 Standard Form of Agreement Between Owner and Architect has been reproduced with the permission of The American Institute of Architects under permission number 91051. Further reproduction is prohibited.

2. Because AIA Documents are revised from time to time, users should ascertain from the AIA the current editions of their Documents.

3. Copies of the current edition of these AIA documents may be purchased from The American Institute of Architects or its local distributors.

4. The AIA Documents and their various provisions engrossed herein are not intended to be used as models. They substitute for the existing documents and internal and willing manuals used; moreover, the documents is modified by the user, the AIA documents are intended to serve as standard forms which, if further discussed or agreed to by the contracting parties, with modifications being made by appending, deleting, striking out, or supplementing as may fitting in the final document, but not on the owner-architect information.

B SERIES DOCUMENT REFERENCE CHARTS

SYNOPSIS

Document Cross-Reference Charts

B131 & B141 Cross-Reference Charts

Document to Case Charts

B131-1963: Standard Form of Agreement Between Owner and Architect on a Basis of Percentage of Construction Cost
B131-1967: Standard Form of Agreement Between Owner and Architect on a Basis of Percentage of Construction Cost
B131-1970: Standard Form of Agreement Between Owner and Architect on a Basis of Percentage of Construction Cost
B141-1974: Standard Form of Agreement Between Owner and Architect
B141-1977: Standard Form of Agreement Between Owner and Architect
B141-1987: Standard Form of Agreement Between Owner and Architect

B131 & B141 CROSS-REFERENCE CHARTS

Article Number

Article Title	B131 1963	B131 1967	B131 1970	B141 1974	B141 1977	B141 1987	B141 1997
Applicable law	—	13	13	13	11	9	1.3.7
Arbitration	13	11	11	11	9	7	1.3.5
Architect agrees to provide professional services	1	1	1	1	—	1	1.2.3
Architect's accounting records	9	7	7	7	7	10.6	1.3.9
							1.3.3, 2.8.2,
Architect's additional services	4	1	1	1	1	3	2.8.3
Architect's basic services	3	1	1	1	1	2	2
Architect's services	3	1	1	1	1	1	1.2.3
Construction cost	6	3	3	3	3	5	1.3, 2.1.7
Direct & reimbursable expense	7	4, 5	4, 5	4, 5	4, 5	10.2	1.3.9.2
Direct personnel expense	7	4	4	4	4	10.1	1.3.9.4
Extent of agreement	—	12	12	12	13	9	1.4.1
Governing law	6	13	13	13	11	9	1.3.7
Mediation	—	—	—	—	—	—	1.3.4
Miscellaneous	—	—	—	—	11	9	1.3.7
Owner agrees to compensate architect	2	11	11	11	14	11	—
Owner and architect agree to renegotiate under certain conditions	—	—	—	III	—	—	—
Owner's responsibilities	5	2	2	2	2	4	1.22, 2.2
Ownership of documents	11	9	9	9	9	6	1.3.2
Payments to the architect	8	6	6	6	6	10	1.3.9
Project construction cost	6	3	3	3	3	5	1.3
Reimbursable expense	7	5	5	5	5	10.2	1.3.9.2
Successors and assigns	12	10	10	10	12	9	1.3.7.9
Termination of agreement	10	8	8	8	10	8	1.3.8

DOCUMENT TO CASE CHARTS: B131-1963

[The five-digit numbers in this chart are Citator Case Reference Numbers, which refer to the cases, in the Cases section. The suffixes indicate the state or, for federal cases, the court in which the case was decided.]

B131-1963—STANDARD FORM OF AGREEMENT BETWEEN OWNER AND ARCHITECT ON A BASIS OF A PERCENTAGE OF CONSTRUCTION COST

Article 1 The Architect Agrees to Provide Professional Services for the Project as Hereinafter Set Forth

    III

        65006-TX

Article 2 The Owner Agrees to Pay the Architect as Compensation for His Services

    II

        65074-IL
        66033-MO

    III

        65097-9CIR   34004-OK
        45002-CA   65098-MI
        66040-LA

Article 3 Architect's Basic Services

    I

        39001-CA   33003-NY
        50002-CA   53003-NY
        51001-CA   34002-PA
        23003-MA   40002-PA
        52002-MA   40001-VA

    II

        65060-CO

    III

        65032-AZ   67049-IL
        66088-AZ   66040-LA
        65070-CA   61011-NY
        65086-CA   67054-UT

Article 4 Architect's Additional Services

    I

        24001-NY

DOCUMENT TO CASE CHARTS: B131-1963

[The five-digit numbers in this chart are Citator Case Reference Numbers, which refer to the cases, in the Cases section. The suffixes indicate the state or, for federal cases, the court in which the case was decided.]

Article 5   **The Owner's Responsibilities**

Article 6   **Project Construction Cost**

    I

49002-CA	41004-MI
50001-LA	50004-MI
53006-LA	52007-MI
63002-LA	61002-OH
63008-LA	44004-WI
54005-IL	57003-TX
59001-IL	57001-UT
65102-IL	

    II

61008-CO	15001-KS
65102-IL	58001-TX

    III

65086-CA	26002-NC
19001-LA	20003-ND
56001-LA	22001-PA
25001-NY	31001-TX

Article 7   **Direct & Reimbursable Expense**

    I

        60011-CA

Article 8   **Payments to the Architect**

    I

48001-AR	41004-MI
49002-CA	50004-MI
50001-LA	52007-MI
53006-LA	61002-OH
63002-LA	47001-OK
63008-LA	49001-TX
54005-IL	57001-UT
59001-IL	44004-WI
23003-MA	

    II

62010-CT	15001-KS
13006-KS	58001-TX

    III

66088-AZ	56001-LA
65046-CA	25001-NY
65070-CA	26002-NC
65086-CA	20003-ND
19002-KY	13002-WA
19001-LA	13007-WA

DOCUMENT TO CASE CHARTS: B131-1963

[The five-digit numbers in this chart are Citator Case Reference Numbers, which refer to the cases, in the Cases section. The suffixes indicate the state or, for federal cases, the court in which the case was decided.]

Article 9   Architect's Accounting Records

Article 10   Termination of Agreement

    I

        59001-IL

   III

        65032-AZ   19002-KY
        65070-CA   13002-WA

Article 11   Ownership of Documents

    I

        38002-MO

Article 12   Successors and Assigns

    I

        45001-CO
        66117-TX

Article 13   Arbitration

    I

        66085-IL
        66117-TX

   III

        63005-CT

DOCUMENT TO CASE CHARTS: B131-1967

[The five-digit numbers in this chart are Citator Case Reference Numbers, which refer to the cases, in the Cases section. The suffixes indicate the state or, for federal cases, the court in which the case was decided.]

B131-1967—STANDARD FORM OF AGREEMENT BETWEEN OWNER AND ARCHITECT ON A BASIS OF A PERCENTAGE OF CONSTRUCTION COST

Article 1 Architect's Services

   I

      70069-AZ   68042-NH
      70076-DC   70014-TX
      67058-GA

   II

      65028-GA
      71082-MI
      82035-MS

   III

      70017-GA
      71065-TX
      70010-WY

Article 2 The Owner's Responsibilities

   I

      68035-DVI

   III

      70017-GA

Article 3 Construction Cost

   I

      70021-DCCIR
      70076-DC

   III

      70073-AZ

Article 4 Direct Personnel Expense

Article 5 Reimbursable Expenses

   I

      68035-DVI

   II

      67046-CA

DOCUMENT TO CASE CHARTS: B131-1967

[The five-digit numbers in this chart are Citator Case Reference Numbers, which refer to the cases, in the Cases section. The suffixes indicate the state or, for federal cases, the court in which the case was decided.]

Article 6   Payments to the Architect

    I

        70076-DC   70026-NC
        67058-GA   70014-TX
        67064-IA   69045-WA

    II

        71087-GA
        69040-IL

Article 7   Architect's Accounting Records

Article 8   Termination of Agreement

    I

        70076-DC

    II

        67046-CA

    III

        70088-CA

Article 9   Ownership of Documents

Article 10   Successors and Assigns

    I

        69030-LA

Article 11   Arbitration

    I

        71026-IL   70035-OH
        68042-NH   71055-NY
        67059-OH

    II

        67015-CO
        69050-MA
        71081-NY

    III

        71045-7CIR
        70091-IL

DOCUMENT TO CASE CHARTS: B131-1967   B–12

[The five-digit numbers in this chart are Citator Case Reference Numbers, which refer to the cases, in the Cases section. The suffixes indicate the state or, for federal cases, the court in which the case was decided.]

Article 12   Extent of Agreement

1

    70026-NC
    70015-OK

Article 13   Applicable Law

DOCUMENT TO CASE CHARTS: B131-1970

[The five-digit numbers in this chart are Citator Case Reference Numbers, which refer to the cases, in the Cases section. The suffixes indicate the state or, for federal cases, the court in which the case was decided.]

B131-1970—STANDARD FORM OF AGREEMENT BETWEEN OWNER AND ARCHITECT ON A BASIS OF A PERCENTAGE OF CONSTRUCTION COST

Article 1 Architect's Services

    I

        72056-IL   73124-NC
        73081-MA   73048-TX
        73064-MN   73056-WA

    II

        72115-IL
        73005-NH
        73109-RI

    III

        73007-FL
        73101-NM
        74001-WI

Article 2 The Owner's Responsibilities

    I

        73048-TX

Article 3 Construction Cost

    I   72056-IL

        73064-MN
        73111-TX

    III

        72005-4CIR

Article 4 Direct Personnel Expense

Article 5 Reimbursable Expenses

Article 6 Payments to the Architect

    I

        72056-IL
        73080-LA
        73081-MA

DOCUMENT TO CASE CHARTS: B131-1970

[The five-digit numbers in this chart are Citator Case Reference Numbers, which refer to the cases, in the Cases section. The suffixes indicate the state or, for federal cases, the court in which the case was decided.]

II

    73050-9CIR
    73005-NH

III

    72028-AR   73085-IL
    71034-CT   72071-TX
    72042-GA

Article 7   Architect's Accounting Records

Article 8   Termination of Agreement

I

    73080-LA

Article 9   Ownership of Documents

III

    73084-8CIR

Article 10   Successors and Assigns

Article 11   Arbitration

I

    72091-3CIR   73071-MI
    74022-DDE   73045-MN
    72033-IL

III

    73001-MDPA

Article 12   Extent of Agreement

Article 13   Governing Law

III

    74033-WI

B–15

DOCUMENT TO CASE CHARTS: B141-1974

[The five-digit numbers in this chart are Citator Case Reference Numbers, which refer to the cases, in the Cases section. The suffixes indicate the state or, for federal cases, the court in which the case was decided.]

B141-1974—STANDARD FORM OF AGREEMENT BETWEEN OWNER AND ARCHITECT

Text of Article 1—Architect's Services

BASIC SERVICES

1.1 The Architect's Basic Services consist of the five phases described below and include normal structural, mechanical and electrical engineering services and any other services included in Article 14 as Basic Services.

SCHEMATIC DESIGN PHASE

1.1.1 The Architect shall review the program furnished by the Owner to ascertain the requirements of the Project and shall confirm such requirements to the Owner.

1.1.2 Based on the mutually agreed upon program, the Architect shall prepare Schematic Design Studies consisting of drawings and other documents illustrating the sale and relationship of Project components for approval by the Owner.

1.1.3 The Architect shall submit to the Owner a Statement of Probable Construction Cost based on current area, volume or other unit costs.

DESIGN DEVELOPMENT PHASE

1.1.4 The Architect shall prepare from the approved schematic Design Studies, for approval by the Owner, the Design Development Documents consisting of drawings and other documents to fix and describe the size and character of the entire Project as to structural, mechanical and electrical systems, materials and such other essentials as may be appropriate.

1.1.5 The Architect shall submit to the Owner a further Statement of Probable Construction Cost.

CONSTRUCTION DOCUMENTS PHASE

1.1.6 The Architect shall prepare from the approved Design Development Documents, for approval by the Owner, Drawings and Specifications setting forth in detail the requirements for the construction of the entire Project including the necessary bidding information, and shall assist in the preparation of bidding forms, the Conditions of the Contract, and the form of Agreement between the Owner and the Contractor.

1.1.7 The Architect shall advise the Owner of any adjustments to previous Statements of Probable Construction Cost indicated by changes in requirements or general market conditions.

1.1.8 The Architect shall assist the Owner in filing the required documents for the approval of governmental authorities having jurisdiction over the Project.

BIDDING OR NEGOTIATION PHASE

1.1.9 The Architect, following the Owner's approval of the Construction Documents and of the latest Statement of probable Construction Cost, shall assist the Owner in obtaining bids or negotiated proposals and in awarding and preparing construction contracts.

CONSTRUCTION PHASE—ADMINISTRATION OF THE CONSTRUCTION CONTRACT

1.1.10 The Construction Phase will commence with the award of the Construction Contract and will terminate when the final Certificate for Payment is issued to the Owner,

1.1.11 The Architect shall provide Administration of the Construction Contract as set forth in AIA Document A201, General Conditions of the Contract for Construction, and the extent of his duties and responsibilities and the limitations of his authority as assigned thereunder shall not be modified without his written consent.

1.1.12 The Architect, as the representative of the Owner during the Construction Phase, shall advise and consult with the Owner and all of the Owner's instructions to the Contractor shall be issued through the Architect. The Architect shall have authority to act on behalf of the Owner to the extent provided in the General Conditions unless otherwise modified in writing.

1.1.13 The Architect shall at all times have access to the Work wherever it is in preparation or progress.

1.1.14 The Architect shall make periodic visits to the site to familiarize himself generally with the progress and quality of the Work and to determine in general if the Work is proceeding in accordance with the Contract Documents. On the basis of his on-site observations as an architect, he shall endeavor to guard the Owner against defects and deficiencies in the Work of the Contractor. The Architect shall not be required to make exhaustive or continuous on-site inspections to check the quality or quantity of the Work. The Architect shall not be responsible for construction means, methods, techniques, sequences or procedures, or for safety precautions and programs in connection with the Work, and he shall not be responsible for the Contractor's failure to carry out the Work in accordance with the Contract Documents.

1.1.15 Based on such observations at the site and on the Contractor's Applications for Payment, the Architect shall determine the amount owing to the Contractor and shall issue Certificates for Payment in such amounts. The issuance of a Certificate for Payment shall constitute a representation by the Architect to the Owner, based on the Architect's observations at the site as provided in Subparagraph 1.1.14 and the data comprising the Application for Payment, that the Work has progressed to the point indicated; that to the best of the Architect's knowledge, information and belief, the quality of the Work is in accordance with the Contract Documents (subject to an evaluation of the Work for conformance with the Contract Documents upon Substantial Completion, to the results of any subsequent tests required by the Contract Documents, to minor deviations from the Contract Documents correctable prior to completion, and to any specific qualifications stated in the Certificate for

DOCUMENT TO CASE CHARTS: B141-1974

[The five-digit numbers in this chart are Citator Case Reference Numbers, which refer to the cases, in the Cases section. The suffixes indicate the state or, for federal cases, the court in which the case was decided.]

Payment); and that the Contractor is entitled to payment in the amount certified. By issuing a Certificate for Payment, the Architect shall not be deemed to represent that he has made any examination to ascertain how and for what purpose the Contractor has used the moneys paid on account of the Contract Sum.

1.1.16 The Architect shall be, in the first instance, the interpreter of the requirements of the Contract Documents and the impartial judge of the performance there-under by both the Owner and Contractor. The Architect shall make decisions on all claims of the Owner or Contractor relating to the execution and progress of the Work and on all other matters or questions related thereto. The Architect's decisions in matters relating to artistic effect shall be final if consistent with the intent of the Contract Documents.

1.1.17 The Architect shall have authority to reject Work which does not conform to the Contract Documents. Whenever, in his reasonable opinion, he considers it necessary or advisable to insure the proper implementation of the intent of the Contract Documents, he will have authority to require special inspection or testing of any Work in accordance with the provisions of the Contract Documents whether or not such Work be then fabricated, installed or completed.

1.1.18 The Architect shall review and approve shop drawings, samples, and other submissions of the Contractor only for conformance with the design concept of the Project and for compliance with the information given in the Contract Documents.

1.1.19 The Architect shall prepare Change Orders.

1.1.20 The Architect shall conduct inspections to determine the Dates of Substantial Completion and final completion, shall receive and review written guarantees and related documents assembled by the Contractor, and shall issue a final Certificate for Payment.

1.1.21 The Architect shall not be responsible for the acts or omissions of the Contractor, or any Subcontractors, or any of the Contractor's or Subcontractors' agents or employees, or any other persons performing any of the Work.

1.2 PROJECT REPRESENTATION BEYOND BASIC SERVICES

1.2.1 If more extensive representation at the site than is described under Subparagraphs 1.1.10 through 1.1.21 inclusive is required, and if the Owner and Architect agree, the Architect shall provide one or more Full-Time Project Representatives to assist the Architect.

1.2.2 Such Full-Time Project Representatives shall be selected, employed and directed by the Architect, and the Architect shall be compensated therefor as mutually agreed between the Owner and the Architect as set forth in an exhibit appended to this Agreement.

1.2.3 The duties, responsibilities and limitations of authority of such Full-Time Project Representatives shall be set forth in an exhibit appended to this Agreement.

1.2.4 Through the on-site observations by Full-Time Project Representatives of the Work in progress, the Architect shall endeavor to provide further protection

[*The five-digit numbers in this chart are Citator Case Reference Numbers, which refer to the cases, in the Cases section. The suffixes indicate the state or, for federal cases, the court in which the case was decided.*]

for the Owner against defects in the Work, but the furnishing of such project representation shall not make the Architect responsible for construction means, methods, techniques, sequences or procedures, or for safety precautions and programs, or for the Contractor's failure to perform the Work in accordance with the Contract Documents.

1.3 ADDITIONAL SERVICES

The following Services shall be provided when authorized in writing by the Owner, and they shall be paid for by the Owner as hereinbefore provided.

1.3.1 Providing analyses of the Owner's needs, and programming the requirements of the Project.

1.3.2 Providing financial feasibility or other special studies.

1.3.3 Providing planning surveys, site evaluations, environmental studies or comparative studies of prospective sites.

1.3.4 Providing design services relative to future facilities, systems and equipment which are not intended to be constructed as part of the Project.

1.3.5 Providing services to investigate existing conditions or facilities or to make measured drawings thereof, or to verify the accuracy of drawings or other information furnished by the Owner.

1.3.6 Preparing documents for alternate bids or out-of-sequence services requested by the Owner.

1.3.7 Providing Detailed Estimates of Construction Cost or detailed quantity surveys or inventories of material, equipment and labor.

1.3.8 Providing interior design and other services required for or in connection with the selection of furniture and furnishings.

1.3.9 Providing services for planning tenant or rental spaces.

1.3.10 Making revisions in Drawings, Specifications or other documents when such revisions are inconsistent with written approvals or instructions previously given and are due to causes beyond the control of the Architect.

1.3.11 Preparing supporting data and other services in connection with Change Orders if the change in the Basic Compensation resulting from the adjusted Contract Sum is not commensurate with the services required of the Architect.

1.3.12 Making investigations involving detailed appraisals and valuations of existing facilities, and surveys or inventories required in connection with construction performed by the Owner.

1.3.13 Providing consultation concerning replacement of any Work damaged by fire or other cause during construction, and furnishing professional services of the type set forth in Paragraph 1.1 as may be required in connection with the replacement of such Work.

DOCUMENT TO CASE CHARTS: B141-1974

[The five-digit numbers in this chart are Citator Case Reference Numbers, which refer to the cases, in the Cases section. The suffixes indicate the state or, for federal cases, the court in which the case was decided.]

1.3.14 Providing professional services made necessary by the default of the Contractor or by major defects in the Work of the Contractor in the performance of the Construction Contract.

1.3.15 Preparing a set of reproducible record prints of drawings showing significant changes in the Work made during the construction process, based on marked-up prints, drawings and other data furnished by the Contractor to the Architect.

1.3.16 Providing extensive assistance in the utilization of any equipment or system such as initial start-up or testing, adjusting and balancing, preparation of operation and maintenance manuals, training personnel for operation and maintenance, and consultation during operation.

1.3.17 Providing services after issuance to the Owner of the final Certificate for Payment.

1.3.18 Preparing to serve or serving as an expert witness in connection with any public hearing, arbitration proceeding or legal proceeding.

1.3.19 Providing services of professional consultants for other than the normal structural, mechanical and electrical engineering services for the Project.

1.3.20 Providing any other services not otherwise included in this Agreement or not customarily furnished in accordance with generally accepted architectural practice.

Article 1   Architect's Services

    I

        75011-IL   84006-TN
        74016-MN   74042-WI
        75006-NE

    II

        75015-NY

Text of Article 2—The Owner's Responsibilities

2.1 The Owner shall provide full information, including a complete program, regarding his requirements for the Project.

2.2 The Owner shall designate, when necessary, a representative authorized to act in his behalf with respect to the Project. The Owner shall examine documents submitted by the Architect and shall render decisions pertaining thereto promptly, to avoid unreasonable delay in the progress of the Architect's services.

2.3 The Owner shall furnish a certified land survey of the site giving, as applicable, grades and lines of streets, alleys, pavements and adjoining property; rights-of-way, restrictions, easements, encroachments, zoning, deed restrictions, boundaries and contours of the site; locations, dimensions and complete data

DOCUMENT TO CASE CHARTS: B141-1974

[The five-digit numbers in this chart are Citator Case Reference Numbers, which refer to the cases, in the Cases section. The suffixes indicate the state or, for federal cases, the court in which the case was decided.]

pertaining to existing buildings, other improvements and trees; and full information concerning available service and utility lines both public and private, above and below grade, including inverts and depths.

2.4 The Owner shall furnish the services of a soils engineer or other consultant when such services are deemed necessary by the Architect, including reports, test borings, test pits, soil bearing values, percolation tests, air and water pollution tests, ground corrosion and resistivity tests and other necessary operations for determining sub-soil, air and water conditions, with appropriate professional recommendations.

2.5 The Owner shall furnish structural, mechanical, chemical and other laboratory tests, inspections and reports as required by law or the Contract Documents.

2.6 The Owner shall furnish such legal, accounting, and insurance counseling services as may be necessary for the Project, and such auditing services as he may require to ascertain how or for what purposes the Contractor has used the moneys paid to him under the Construction Contract.

2.7 The services, information, surveys and reports required by Paragraphs 2.3 through 2.6 inclusive shall be furnished at the Owner's expense, and the Architect shall be entitled to rely upon the accuracy and completeness thereof.

2.8 If the Owner becomes aware of any fault or defect in the Project or nonconformance with the Contract Documents, he shall give prompt written notice thereof to the Architect.

2.9 The Owner shall furnish information required of him as expeditiously as necessary for the orderly progress of the Work.

Article 2   The Owner's Responsibilities

I

75027-DVI
74016-MN
84006-TN

Text of Article 3—Construction Cost

3.1 If the Construction Cost is to be used as the basis for determining the Architect's Compensation for Basic Services, it shall be the total cost or estimated cost to the Owner of all Work designed or specified by the Architect. The Construction Cost shall be determined as follows, with precedence in the order listed:

3.1.1 For completed construction, the cost of all such Work, including costs of managing construction;

3.1.2 For Work not constructed, (1) the lowest bona fide bid received from a qualified bidder for any or all of such Work, or (2) if the Work is not bid, the bona fide negotiated proposal submitted for any or all of such Work; or

[*The five-digit numbers in this chart are Citator Case Reference Numbers, which refer to the cases, in the Cases section. The suffixes indicate the state or, for federal cases, the court in which the case was decided.*]

3.1.3 For Work for which no such bid or proposal is received, (1) the latest Detailed Estimate of Construction Cost if one is available, or (2) the latest Statement of Probable Construction Cost.

3.2 Construction Cost does not include the compensation of the Architect and his consultants, the cost of the land, rights-of-way, or other costs which are the responsibility of the Owner as provided in Paragraphs 2.3 through 2.6 inclusive.

3.3 The cost of labor, materials and equipment furnished by the Owner for the Project shall be included in the Construction Cost at current market rates including a reasonable allowance for overhead and profit.

3.4 Statements of Probable Construction Cost and Detailed Cost Estimates prepared by the Architect represent his best judgment as a design professional familiar with the construction industry. It is recognized, however, that neither the Architect nor the Owner has any control over the cost of labor, materials or equipment, over the contractors' methods of determining bid prices, or over competitive bidding or market conditions. Accordingly, the Architect cannot and does not guarantee that bids will not vary from any Statement of Probable Construction Cost or other cost estimate prepared by him.

3.5 When a fixed limit of Construction Cost is established as a condition of this Agreement, it shall be in writing signed by the parties and shall include a bidding contingency of ten percent unless another amount is agreed upon in writing. When such a fixed limit is established, the Architect shall be permitted to determine what materials, equipment, component systems and types of construction are to be included in the Contract Documents, and to make reasonable adjustments in the scope of the Project to bring it within the fixed limit. The architect may also include in the Contract Documents alternate bids to adjust the Construction Cost to the fixed limit.

3.5.1 If the Bidding or Negotiating Phase has not commenced within six months after the Architect submits the Construction Documents to the Owner, any fixed limit of Construction Cost established as a condition of this Agreement shall be adjusted to reflect any change in the general level of prices which may have occurred in the construction industry for the area in which the Project is located. The adjustment shall reflect changes between the date of submission of the Construction Documents to the Owner and the date on which proposals are sought.

3.5.2 When a fixed limit of Construction Cost, including the Bidding contingency (adjusted as provided in Subparagraph 3.5.1, if applicable), is established as a condition of this Agreement and is exceeded by the lowest bona fide bid or negotiated proposal, the Detailed Estimate of Construction Cost or the Statement of Probable Construction cost, the Owner shall (1) give written approval of an increase in such fixed limit, (2) authorize rebidding the Project within a reasonable time, or (3) cooperate in revising the Project scope and quality as required to reduce the Probable Construction Cost. In the case of (3) the Architect, without additional charge, shall modify the Drawings and Specifications as necessary to bring the

DOCUMENT TO CASE CHARTS: B141-1974

[The five-digit numbers in this chart are Citator Case Reference Numbers, which refer to the cases, in the Cases section. The suffixes indicate the state or, for federal cases, the court in which the case was decided.]

> Construction Cost within the fixed limit. The providing of such service shall be the limit of the Architect's responsibility in this regard, and having done so, the Architect shall be entitled to compensation in accordance with this Agreement.

Article 3   Construction Cost

I

74032-FL
74016-MN

Article 4   Direct Personnel Expense

Article 5   Reimbursable Expenses

Text of Article 6—Payments to the Architect

6.1 Payments on account of the Architect's Basic Services shall be made as follows:

6.1.1 An initial payment as set forth in Paragraph II is the minimum payment under this Agreement.

6.1.2 Subsequent payments for Basic Services shall be made monthly in proportion to services performed so that the compensation at the completion of each Phase, except when the compensation is on the basis of a Multiple of Direct Personnel Expense, shall equal the following percentages of the total Basic Compensation:

Phase	Percentage
Schematic Design Phase	15%
Design Development Phase	35%
Construction Documents Phase	75%
Bidding or Negotiation Phase	80%
Construction Phase	100%

6.1.3 If the Contract Time initially established in the Construction Contract is exceeded by more than thirty days through no fault of the Architect, compensation for Basic Services performed by Principals, employees and professional consultants required to complete the Administration of the Construction Contract beyond the thirtieth day shall be computed as set forth in Paragraph II for Additional Services.

6.2 Payments for Additional Services of the Architect as defined in Paragraph 1.3, and for Reimbursable Expenses as defined in Article 5, shall be made monthly upon presentation of the Architect's statement of services rendered.

6.3 No deductions shall be made from the Architect's compensation on account of penalty, liquidated damages, or other sums withheld from payments to contractors.

DOCUMENT TO CASE CHARTS: B141-1974

[The five-digit numbers in this chart are Citator Case Reference Numbers, which refer to the cases, in the Cases section. The suffixes indicate the state or, for federal cases, the court in which the case was decided.]

> **6.4** If the Project is suspended for more than three months or abandoned in whole or in part, the Architect shall be paid his compensation for services performed prior to receipt of written notice from the Owner of such suspension or abandonment, together with Reimbursable Expenses then due and all termination expenses as defined in Paragraph 8.3 resulting from such suspension or abandonment. If the Project is resumed after being suspended for more than three months, the Architect's compensation shall be subject to renegotiation.
>
> **6.5** Payments due the Architect under this Agreement shall bear interest at the legal rate commencing sixty days after the date of billing.

Article 6   Payments to the Architect

    I

        74016-MN

    II

        75025-IL

Article 7   Architect's Accounting Records

Article 8   Termination of Agreement

Article 9   Ownership of Documents

Article 10   Successors and Assigns

Text of Article 11—Arbitration

11.1 All claims, disputes and other matters in question between the parties to this Agreement, arising out of, or relating to this Agreement or the breach thereof, shall be decided by arbitration in accordance with the Construction Industry Arbitration Rules of the American Arbitration Association then obtaining unless the parties mutually agree otherwise. No arbitration, arising out of, or relating to this Agreement, shall include, by consolidation, joinder or in any other manner, any additional party not a party to this Agreement except by written consent containing a specific reference to this Agreement and signed by all the parties hereto. Any consent to arbitration involving an additional party or parties shall not constitute consent to arbitration of any dispute not described therein or with any party not named or described therein. This Agreement to arbitrate and any agreement to arbitrate with an additional party or parties duly consented to by the parties hereto shall be specifically enforceable under the prevailing arbitration law.

11.2 Notice of the demand for arbitration shall be filed in writing with the other party to this Agreement and with the American Arbitration Association. The demand shall be made within a reasonable time after the claim, dispute or other matter in question has arisen. In no event shall the demand for arbitration be made after the

DOCUMENT TO CASE CHARTS: B141-1974

[*The five-digit numbers in this chart are Citator Case Reference Numbers, which refer to the cases, in the Cases section. The suffixes indicate the state or, for federal cases, the court in which the case was decided.*]

date when institution of legal or equitable proceedings based on such claim, dispute or other matter in question would be barred by the applicable statute of limitations.

11.3 The award rendered by the arbitrators shall be final, and judgment may be entered upon it in accordance with applicable law in any court having jurisdiction thereof.

Article 11   Arbitration

   I

      75008-FL

   II

      75015-NY

Text of Article 12—Extent of Agreement

This Agreement represents the entire and integrated agreement between the Owner and the Architect and supersedes all prior negotiations. representations or agreements, either written or oral. This Agreement may be amended only by written instrument signed by both Owner and Architect.

Article 12   Extent of Agreement

      I   74032-FL

Article 13   Governing Law

Article 14   Other Conditions or Services

DOCUMENT TO CASE CHARTS: B141-1977

[The five-digit numbers in this chart are Citator Case Reference Numbers, which refer to the cases, in the Cases section. The suffixes indicate the state or, for federal cases, the court in which the case was decided.]

B141-1977—STANDARD FORM OF AGREEMENT BETWEEN OWNER AND ARCHITECT

Text of Article 1—Architect's Services and Responsibilities

BASIC SERVICES

The Architect's Basic Services consist of the five phases described in Paragraphs 1.1 through 1.5 and include normal structural, mechanical and electrical engineering services and any other services included in Article 15 as part of Basic Services.

1.1 SCHEMATIC DESIGN PHASE

1.1.1 The Architect shall review the program furnished by the Owner to ascertain the requirements of the Project and shall review the understanding of such requirements with the Owner.

1.1.2 The Architect shall provide a preliminary evaluation of the program and the Project budget requirements, each in terms of the other, subject to the limitations set forth in Subparagraph 3.2.1.

1.1.3 The Architect shall review with the Owner alternative approaches to design and construction of the Project.

1.1.4 Based on the mutually agreed upon program and Project budget requirements, the Architect shall prepare, for approval by the Owner, Schematic Design Documents consisting of drawings and other documents illustrating the scale and relationship of Project components.

1.1.5 The Architect shall submit to the Owner a Statement of Probable Construction Cost based on current area, volume or other unit costs.

1.2 DESIGN DEVELOPMENT PHASE

1.2.1 Based on the approved Schematic Design Documents and any adjustments authorized by the Owner in the program or Project budget, the Architect shall prepare, for approval by the Owner, Design Development Documents consisting of drawings and other documents to fix and describe the size and character of the entire Project as to architectural, structural, mechanical and electrical systems, materials and such other elements as may be appropriate.

1.2.2 The Architect shall submit to the Owner a further Statement of Probable Construction Cost.

1.3 CONSTRUCTION DOCUMENTS PHASE

1.3.1 Based on the approved Design Development Documents and any further adjustments in the scope or quality of the Project or in the Project budget authorized by the Owner, the Architect shall prepare, for approval by the Owner, Construction Documents consisting of Drawings and Specifications setting forth in detail the requirements for the construction of the Project.

[The five-digit numbers in this chart are Citator Case Reference Numbers, which refer to the cases, in the Cases section. The suffixes indicate the state or, for federal cases, the court in which the case was decided.]

1.3.2 The Architect shall assist the Owner in the preparation of the necessary bidding information, bidding forms, the Conditions of the Contract, and the form of Agreement between the Owner and the Contractor.

1.3.3 The Architect shall advise the Owner of any adjustments to previous Statements of Probable Construction Cost indicated by changes in requirements or general market conditions.

1.3.4 The Architect shall assist the Owner in connection with the Owner's responsibility for filing documents required for the approval of governmental authorities having jurisdiction over the Project.

1.4 BIDDING OR NEGOTIATION PHASE

1.4.1 The Architect, following the Owner's approval of the Construction Documents and of the latest Statement of Probable Construction Cost, shall assist the Owner in obtaining bids or negotiated proposals, and assist in awarding and preparing contracts for construction.

1.5 CONSTRUCTION PHASE—ADMINISTRATION OF THE CONSTRUCTION CONTRACT

1.5.1 The Construction Phase will commence with the award of the Contract for Construction and, together with the Architect's obligation to provide Basic Services under this Agreement, will terminate when final payment to the Contractor is due, or in the absence of a final Certificate for Payment or of such due date, sixty days after the Date of Substantial Completion of the Work, whichever occurs first.

1.5.2 Unless otherwise provided in this Agreement and incorporated in the Contract Documents, the Architect shall provide administration of the Contract for Construction as set forth below and in the edition of AIA Document A201, General Conditions of the Contract for Construction, current as of the date of this Agreement.

1.5.3 The Architect shall be a representative of the Owner during the Construction Phase, and shall advise and consult with the Owner. Instructions to the Contractor shall be forwarded through the Architect. The Architect shall have authority to act on behalf of the Owner only to the extent provided in the Contract Documents unless otherwise modified by written instrument in accordance with Subparagraph 1.5.16.

1.5.4 The Architect shall visit the site at intervals appropriate to the stage of construction or as otherwise agreed by the Architect in writing to become generally familiar with the progress and quality of the Work and to determine in general if the Work is proceeding in accordance with the Contract Documents. However, the Architect shall not be required to make exhaustive or continuous on-site inspections to check the quality or quantity of the Work. On the basis of such on-site observations as an architect, the Architect shall keep the Owner informed of the progress and quality of the Work, and shall endeavor to guard the Owner against defects and deficiencies in the Work of the Contractor.

1.5.5 The Architect shall not have control or charge of and shall not be responsible for construction means, methods, techniques, sequences or procedures, or for safety

DOCUMENT TO CASE CHARTS: B141-1977

[The five-digit numbers in this chart are Citator Case Reference Numbers, which refer to the cases, in the Cases section. The suffixes indicate the state or, for federal cases, the court in which the case was decided.]

precautions and programs in connection with the Work, for the acts or omissions of the Contractor, Sub-contractors or any other persons performing any of the Work, or for the failure of any of them to carry out the Work in accordance with the Contract Documents.

1.5.6 The Architect shall at all times have access to the Work wherever it is in preparation or progress.

1.5.7 The Architect shall determine the amounts owing to the Contractor based on observations at the site and on evaluations of the Contractor's Applications for Payment, and shall issue Certificates for Payment in such amounts, as provided in the Contract Documents.

1.5.8 The issuance of a Certificate for Payment shall constitute a representation by the Architect to the Owner, based on the Architect's observations at the site as provided in Subparagraph 1.5.4 and on the data comprising the Contractor's Application for Payment, that the Work has progressed to the point indicated; that, to the best of the Architect's knowledge, information and belief, the quality of the Work is in accordance with the Contract Documents (subject to an evaluation of the Work for conformance with the Contract Documents upon Substantial Completion, to the results of any subsequent tests required by or performed under the Contract Documents, to minor deviations from the Contract Documents correctable prior to completion, and to any specific qualifications stated in the Certificate for Payment); and that the Contractor is entitled to payment in the amount certified. However, the issuance of a Certificate for Payment shall not be a representation that the Architect has made any examination to ascertain how and for what purpose the Contractor has used the moneys paid on account of the Contract Sum.

1.5.9 The Architect shall be the interpreter of the requirements of the Contract Documents and the judge of the performance thereunder by both the Owner and Contractor. The Architect shall render interpretations necessary for the proper execution or progress of the Work with reasonable promptness on written request of either the Owner or the Contractor, and shall render written decisions, within a reasonable time, on all claims, disputes and other matters in question between the Owner and the Contractor relating to the execution or progress of the Work or the interpretation of the Contract Documents.

1.5.10 Interpretations and decisions of the Architect shall be consistent with the intent of and reasonably inferable from the Contract Documents and shall be in written or graphic form. In the capacity of interpreter and judge, the Architect shall endeavor to secure faithful performance by both the Owner and the Contractor, shall not show partiality to either, and shall not be liable for the result of any interpretation or decision rendered in good faith in such capacity.

1.5.11 The Architect's decisions in matters relating to artistic effect shall be final if consistent with the intent of the Contract Documents. The Architect's decisions on any other claims, disputes or other matters, including those in question between the Owner and the Contractor, shall be subject to arbitration as provided in this Agreement and in the Contract Documents.

[*The five-digit numbers in this chart are Citator Case Reference Numbers, which refer to the cases, in the Cases section. The suffixes indicate the state or, for federal cases, the court in which the case was decided.*]

1.5.12 The Architect shall have authority to reject Work which does not conform to the Contract Documents. Whenever, in the Architect's reasonable opinion, it is necessary or advisable for the implementation of the intent of the Contract Documents, the Architect will have authority to require special inspection or testing of the Work in accordance with the provisions of the Contract Documents, whether or not such Work be then fabricated, installed or completed.

1.5.13 The Architect shall review and approve or take other appropriate action upon the Contractor's submittals such as Shop Drawings, Product Data and Samples, but only for conformance with the design concept of the Work and with the information given in the Contract Documents. Such action shall be taken with reasonable promptness so as to cause no delay. The Architect's approval of a specific item shall not indicate approval of an assembly of which the item is a component.

1.5.14 The Architect shall prepare Change Orders for the Owner's approval and execution in accordance with the Contract Documents, and shall have authority to order minor changes in the Work not involving an adjustment in the Contract Sum or an extension of the Contract Time which are not inconsistent with the intent of the Contract Documents.

1.5.15 The Architect shall conduct inspections to determine the Dates of Substantial Completion and final completion, shall receive and forward to the Owner for the Owner's review written warranties and related documents required by the Contract Documents and assembled by the Contractor, and shall issue a final Certificate for Payment.

1.5.16 The extent of the duties, responsibilities and limitations of authority of the Architect as the Owner's representative during construction shall not be modified or extended without written consent of the Owner, the Contractor and the Architect.

1.6 PROJECT REPRESENTATION BEYOND BASIC SERVICES

1.6.1 If the Owner and Architect agree that more extensive representation at the site than is described in Paragraph 1.5 shall be provided, the Architect shall provide one or more Project Representatives to assist the Architect in carrying out such responsibilities at the site.

1.6.2 Such Project Representatives shall be selected, employed and directed by the Architect, and the Architect shall be compensated therefor as mutually agreed between the Owner and the Architect as set forth in an exhibit appended to this Agreement, which shall describe the duties, responsibilities and limitations of authority of such Project Representatives.

1.6.3 Through the observations by such Project Representatives, the Architect shall endeavor to provide further protection for the Owner against defects and deficiencies in the Work, but the furnishing of such project representation shall not modify the rights, responsibilities or obligations of the Architect as described in Paragraph 1.5.

[The five-digit numbers in this chart are Citator Case Reference Numbers, which refer to the cases, in the Cases section. The suffixes indicate the state or, for federal cases, the court in which the case was decided.]

1.7 ADDITIONAL SERVICES

The following Services are not included in Basic Services unless so identified in Article 15. They shall be provided if authorized or confirmed in writing by the Owner, and they shall be paid for by the Owner as provided in this Agreement, in addition to the compensation for Basic Services.

1.7.1 Providing analyses of the Owner's needs, and programming the requirements of the Project.

1.7.2 Providing financial feasibility or other special studies.

1.7.3 Providing planning surveys, site evaluations, environmental studies or comparative studies of prospective sites, and preparing special surveys, studies and submissions required for approvals of governmental authorities or others having jurisdiction over the Project.

1.7.4 Providing services relative to future facilities, systems and equipment which are not intended to be constructed during the Construction Phase.

1.7.5 Providing services to investigate existing conditions or facilities or to make measured drawings thereof, or to verify the accuracy of drawings or other information furnished by the Owner.

1.7.6 Preparing documents of alternate, separate or sequential bids or providing extra services in connection with bidding, negotiation or construction prior to the completion of the Construction Documents Phase, when requested by the Owner.

1.7.7 Providing coordination of Work performed by separate contractors or by the Owner's own forces.

1.7.8 Providing services in connection with the work of a construction manager or separate consultants retained by the Owner.

1.7.9 Providing Detailed Estimates of Construction Cost, analyses of owning and operating costs, or detailed quantity surveys or inventories of material, equipment and labor.

1.7.10 Providing interior design and other similar services required for or in connection with the selection, procurement or installation of furniture, furnishings and related equipment.

1.7.11 Providing services for planning tenant or rental spaces.

1.7.12 Making revisions in Drawings, Specifications or other documents when such revisions are inconsistent with written approvals or instructions previously given, are required by the enactment or revision of codes, laws or regulations subsequent to the preparation of such documents or are due to other causes not solely within the control of the Architect.

1.7.13 Preparing Drawings, Specifications and supporting data and providing other services in connection with Change Orders to the extent that the adjustment in the Basic Compensation resulting from the adjusted Construction Cost is not

DOCUMENT TO CASE CHARTS: B141-1977

[*The five-digit numbers in this chart are Citator Case Reference Numbers, which refer to the cases, in the Cases section. The suffixes indicate the state or, for federal cases, the court in which the case was decided.*]

commensurate with the services required of the Architect, provided such Change Orders are required by causes not solely within the control of the Architect.

1.7.14 Making investigations, surveys, valuations, inventories or detailed appraisals of existing facilities, and services required in connection with construction performed by the Owner.

1.7.15 Providing consultation concerning replacement of any Work damaged by fire or other cause during construction, and furnishing services as may be required in connection with the replacement of such Work.

1.7.16 Providing services made necessary by the default of the Contractor, or by major defects or deficiencies in the Work of the Contractor, or by failure of performance of either the Owner or Contractor under the Contract for Construction.

1.7.17 Preparing a set of reproducible record drawings showing significant changes in the Work made during construction based on marked-up prints, drawings and other data furnished by the Contractor to the Architect.

1.7.18 Providing extensive assistance in the utilization of any equipment or system such as initial start-up or testing, adjusting and balancing, preparation of operation and maintenance manuals, training personnel for operation and maintenance, and consultation during operation.

1.7.19 Providing services after issuance to the Owner of the final Certificate for Payment, or in the absence of a final Certificate for Payment, more than sixty days after the Date of Substantial Completion of the Work.

1.7.20 Preparing to serve or serving as an expert witness in connection with any public hearing, arbitration proceeding or legal proceeding.

1.7.21 Providing services of consultants for other than the normal architectural, structural, mechanical and electrical engineering services for the Project.

1.7.22 Providing any other services not otherwise included in this Agreement or not customarily furnished in accordance with generally accepted architectural practice.

1.8 TIME

1.8.1 The Architect shall perform Basic and Additional Services as expeditiously as is consistent with professional skill and care and the orderly progress of the Work. Upon request of the Owner, the Architect shall submit for the Owner's approval a schedule for the performance of the Architect's services which shall be adjusted as required as the Project proceeds, and shall include allowances for periods of time required for the Owner's review and approval of submissions and for approvals of authorities having jurisdiction over the Project. This schedule, when approved by the Owner, shall not, except for reasonable cause, be exceeded by the Architect.

DOCUMENT TO CASE CHARTS: B141-1977

[The five-digit numbers in this chart are Citator Case Reference Numbers, which refer to the cases, in the Cases section. The suffixes indicate the state or, for federal cases, the court in which the case was decided.]

Article 1 Architect's Services and Responsibilities

    I

        82020-6CIR   79029-IL
        76051-CT   77061-MN
        77029-IL   78064-MT
        78012-IL   78009-TX
        78019-IL   78018-TX
        78045-IL   80061-VT

    II

        77028-AZ   78036-TX
        77002-DC   80037-TX
        77027-MS   79044-WI

    III

        78076-CO   78047-MD
        77042-IL   78057-MO
        77058-IL   77035-NY
        79010-IL   77022-VA

Paragraph 1.1 Schematic Design Phase

Paragraph 1.1.5

    I

        89020-TX

    II

        86073-LA
        83024-NY
        89006-UT

    III

        87049-SD
        88025-VA

Paragraph 1.2 Design Development Phase

Paragraph 1.2.2

    I

        89020-TX

    II

        86073-LA
        89006-UT

DOCUMENT TO CASE CHARTS: B141-1977

[The five-digit numbers in this chart are Citator Case Reference Numbers, which refer to the cases, in the Cases section. The suffixes indicate the state or, for federal cases, the court in which the case was decided.]

III

82044-NH
87049-SD
88025-VA

Paragraph 1.3 Construction Documents Phase

Paragraph 1.3.4

I

83023-8CIR
89020-TX

II

86073-LA
89006-UT

III

76026-FL	87049-SD
88041-LA	88025-VA
82044-NH	

Paragraph 1.4 Bidding or Negotiation Phase

Paragraph 1.4.1

I

89020-TX

II

86073-LA
89006-UT

Paragraph 1.5 Construction Phase—Administration of the Construction Contract

I

89022-5CIR	90030-MS
83023-8CIR	88014-MO
78024-GA	90006-NE
91040-GA	83047-NY
93013-GA	84007-NY
84034-IL	89004-NY
89007-KS	89012-NY
83003-LA	89020-TX
86071-LA	85014-WY

II

89022-5CIR	91001-IN
82004-SDGA	91030-IA
91031-MDPA	88012-LA
87047-AL	89035-MD
90052-AL	89037-MN
82024-GA	89047-MS
80020-IL	86032-MO
90040-IL	86064-MO

DOCUMENT TO CASE CHARTS: B141-1977

[The five-digit numbers in this chart are Citator Case Reference Numbers, which refer to the cases, in the Cases section. The suffixes indicate the state or, for federal cases, the court in which the case was decided.]

    87050-MO   87026-TX
    90051-NY   89006-UT
    90020-OH

   III

    82041-10CIR   92008d-MI
    82014-NDMS   91024-MT
    82057-AL   89017-NE
    86074-AR   82007-NJ
    86029-CT   86047-NY
    85037-FL   88035a-NY
    89027-FL   89003-NY
    90031-FL   89005-NC
    92004-IL   87002-ND
    82028-IN   91018-RI
    88041-LA   90055-TX
    83002-MA   88025-VA
    90035-MA

Paragraph 1.5.3

   III

    90056-LA

Paragraph 1.5.4

   III

    90056-LA

Paragraph 1.5.5

   II

    94038-FL

   III

    90056-LA

Paragraph 1.6   Project Representation Beyond Basic Services

Paragraph 1.6.3

   II

    82004-SDGA
    88012-LA

   III

    89022-5CIR   91001-IN
    90031-FL   89047-MS

DOCUMENT TO CASE CHARTS: B141-1977

[The five-digit numbers in this chart are Citator Case Reference Numbers, which refer to the cases, in the Cases section. The suffixes indicate the state or, for federal cases, the court in which the case was decided.]

Paragraph 1.7 Additional Services

Paragraph 1.7.22

    I

        90037-FL
        89006-UT

    III

        88025-VA

Text of Article 2—The Owner's Responsibilities

2.1 The Owner shall provide full information regarding requirements for the Project including a program, which shall set forth the Owner's design objectives, constraints and criteria, including space requirements and relationships, flexibility and expandability, special equipment and systems and site requirements.

2.2 If the Owner provides a budget for the Project it shall include contingencies for bidding, changes in the Work during construction, and other costs which are the responsibility of the Owner, including those described in this Article 2 and in Subparagraph 3.1.2. The Owner shall, at the request of the Architect, provide a statement of funds available for the Project, and their source.

2.3 The Owner shall designate, when necessary, a representative authorized to act in the Owner's behalf with respect to the Project. The Owner or such authorized representative shall examine the documents submitted by the Architect and shall render decisions pertaining thereto promptly, to avoid unreasonable delay in the progress of the Architect's services.

2.4 The Owner shall furnish a legal description and a certified land survey of the site, giving, as applicable, grades and lines of streets, alleys, pavements and adjoining property; rights-of-way, restrictions, easements, encroachments, zoning, deed restrictions, boundaries and contours of the site; locations, dimensions and complete data pertaining to existing buildings, other improvements and trees; and full information concerning available service and utility lines both public and private, above and below grade, including inverts and depths.

2.5 The Owner shall furnish the services of soil engineers or other consultants when such services are deemed necessary by the Architect. Such services shall include test borings, test pits, soil bearing values, percolation tests, air and water pollution tests, ground corrosion and resistivity tests, including necessary operations for determining sub-soil, air and water conditions, with reports and appropriate professional recommendations.

2.6 The Owner shall furnish structural, mechanical, chemical and other laboratory tests, inspections and reports as required by law or the Contract Documents.

2.7 The Owner shall furnish all legal, accounting and insurance counseling services as may be necessary at any time for the Project, including such auditing

DOCUMENT TO CASE CHARTS: B141-1977

[The five-digit numbers in this chart are Citator Case Reference Numbers, which refer to the cases, in the Cases section. The suffixes indicate the state or, for federal cases, the court in which the case was decided.]

> services as the Owner may require to verify the Contractor's Applications for Payment or to ascertain how or for what purposes the Contractor uses the moneys paid by or on behalf of the Owner.
>
> **2.8** The services, information, surveys and reports required by Paragraphs 2.4 through 2.7 inclusive shall be furnished at the Owner's expense, and the Architect shall be entitled to rely upon the accuracy and completeness thereof.
>
> **2.9** If the Owner observes or otherwise becomes aware of any fault or defect in the Project or nonconformance with the Contract Documents, prompt written notice thereof shall be given by the Owner to the Architect.
>
> **2.10** The Owner shall furnish required information and services and shall render approvals and decisions as expeditiously as necessary for the orderly progress of the Architect's services and of the Work.

Article 2   The Owner's Responsibilities

Paragraph 2.1

    I

        86006-IL

Paragraph 2.3

    I

        86006-IL

Paragraph 2.4

    III

        76026-FL

Paragraph 2.6

    II

        83024-NY

Paragraph 2.7

    I

        86006-IL

Paragraph 2.8

    I

        86006-IL

DOCUMENT TO CASE CHARTS: B141-1977   B–36

[The five-digit numbers in this chart are Citator Case Reference Numbers, which refer to the cases, in the Cases section. The suffixes indicate the state or, for federal cases, the court in which the case was decided.]

Paragraph 2.9

    I

      89006-UT

Text of Article 3—Construction Cost

3.1 DEFINITION

3.1.1 The Construction Cost shall be the total cost or estimated cost to the Owner of all elements of the Project designed or specified by the Architect.

3.1.2 The Construction Cost shall include at current market rates, including a reasonable allowance for overhead and profit, the cost of labor and materials furnished by the Owner and any equipment which has been designed, specified, selected or specially provided for by the Architect.

3.1.3 Construction Cost does not include the compensation of the Architect and the Architect's consultants, the cost of the land, rights-of-way, or other costs which are the responsibility of the Owner as provided in Article 2.

3.2 RESPONSIBILITY FOR CONSTRUCTION COST

3.2.1 Evaluations of the Owner's Project budget, Statements of Probable Construction Cost and Detailed Estimates of Construction Cost, if any, prepared by the Architect, represent the Architect's best judgment as a design professional familiar with the construction industry. It is recognized, however, that neither the Architect nor the Owner has control over the cost of labor, materials or equipment, over the Contractor's methods of determining bid prices, or over competitive bidding, market or negotiating conditions. Accordingly, the Architect cannot and does not warrant or represent that bids or negotiated prices will not vary from the Project budget proposed, established or approved by the Owner, if any, or from any Statement of Probable Construction Cost or other cost estimate or evaluation prepared by the Architect.

3.2.2 No fixed limit of Construction Cost shall be established as a condition of this Agreement by the furnishing, proposal or establishment of a Project budget under Sub-paragraph 1.1.2 or Paragraph 2.2 or otherwise, unless such fixed limit has been agreed upon in writing and signed by the parties hereto. If such a fixed limit has been established, the Architect shall be permitted to include contingencies for design, bidding and price escalation, to determine what materials, equipment, component systems and types of construction are to be included in the Contract Documents, to make reasonable adjustments in the scope of the Project and to include in the Contract Documents alternate bids to adjust the Construction Cost to the fixed limit. Any such fixed limit shall be increased in the amount of any increase in the Contract Sum occurring after execution of the Contract for Construction.

3.2.3 If the Bidding or Negotiation Phase has not commenced within three months after the Architect submits the Construction Documents to the Owner, any Project

[*The five-digit numbers in this chart are Citator Case Reference Numbers, which refer to the cases, in the Cases section. The suffixes indicate the state or, for federal cases, the court in which the case was decided.*]

> budget or fixed limit of Construction Cost shall be adjusted to reflect any change in the general level of prices in the construction industry between the date of submission of the Construction Documents to the Owner and the date on which proposals are sought.
>
> **3.2.4** If a Project budget or fixed limit of Construction Cost (adjusted as provided in Subparagraph 3.2.3) is exceeded by the lowest bona fide bid or negotiated proposal, the Owner shall (1) give written approval of an increase in such fixed limit, (2) authorize rebidding or renegotiating of the Project within a reasonable time, (3) if the Project is abandoned, terminate in accordance with Paragraph 10.2, or (4) cooperate in revising the Project scope and quality as required to reduce the Construction Cost. In the case of (4), provided a fixed limit of Construction Cost has been established as a condition of this Agreement, the Architect, without additional charge, shall modify the Drawings and Specifications as necessary to comply with the fixed limit. The providing of such service shall be the limit of the Architect's responsibility arising from the establishment of such fixed limit, and having done so, the Architect shall be entitled to compensation for all services performed, in accordance with this Agreement, whether or not the Construction Phase is commenced.

Article 3   Construction Cost

    I

        78064-MT
        78018-TX

    II

        78011-IL

    III

        78014-IL
        78053-NY
        80064-PA

Paragraph 3.1   Definition

Paragraph 3.1.3

    I

        83037-NY

DOCUMENT TO CASE CHARTS: B141-1977

[The five-digit numbers in this chart are Citator Case Reference Numbers, which refer to the cases, in the Cases section. The suffixes indicate the state or, for federal cases, the court in which the case was decided.]

Paragraph 3.2   Responsibility for Construction Cost

Paragraph 3.2.4

    I

        83037-NY

    II

        86073-LA

    III

        89017-NE

Article 4   Direct Personnel Expense

Article 5   Reimbursable Expenses

Text of Article 6—Payments to the Architect

6.1 PAYMENTS ON ACCOUNT OF BASIC SERVICES

6.1.1 An initial payment as set forth in Paragraph 14.1 is the minimum payment under this Agreement.

6.1.2 Subsequent payments for Basic Services shall be made monthly and shall be in proportion to services performed within each Phase of services, on the basis set forth in Article 14.

6.1.3 If and to the extent that the Contract Time initially established in the Contract for Construction is exceeded or extended through no fault of the Architect, compensation for any Basic Services required for such extended period of Administration of the Construction Contract shall be computed as set forth in Paragraph 14.4 for Additional Services.

6.1.4 When compensation is based on a percentage of Construction Cost, and any portions of the Project are deleted or otherwise not constructed, compensation for such portions of the Project shall be payable to the extent services are performed on such portions, in accordance with the schedule set forth in Subparagraph 14.2.2, based on (1) the lowest bona fide bid or negotiated proposal or, (2) if no such bid or proposal is received, the most recent Statement of Probable Construction Cost or Detailed Estimate of Construction Cost for such portions of the Project.

DOCUMENT TO CASE CHARTS: B141-1977

[The five-digit numbers in this chart are Citator Case Reference Numbers, which refer to the cases, in the Cases section. The suffixes indicate the state or, for federal cases, the court in which the case was decided.]

Article 6 Payments to the Architect

    II

        78036-TX

    III

        78053-NY

Paragraph 6.1   Payments on Account of Basic Services

Paragraph 6.1.4

    I

        87023-NY

    III

        89017-NE
        88025-VA

Article 7 Architect's Accounting Records

Text of Article 8—Ownership and Use of Documents

8.1 Drawings and Specifications as instruments of service are and shall remain the property of the Architect whether the Project for which they are made is executed or not. The Owner shall be permitted to retain copies, including reproducible copies, of Drawings and Specifications for information and reference in connection with the Owner's use and occupancy of the Project. The Drawings and Specifications shall not be used by the Owner on other projects, for additions to this Project, or for completion of this Project by others provided the Architect is not in default under this Agreement, except by agreement in writing and with appropriate compensation to the Architect.

8.2 Submission or distribution to meet official regulatory requirements or for other purposes in connection with the Project is not to be construed as publication in derogation of the Architect's rights.

Article 8 Ownership and Use of Documents

Paragraph 8.1

    I

        85024-NDIL
        93023-GA
        89038-NE

DOCUMENT TO CASE CHARTS: B141-1977

[The five-digit numbers in this chart are Citator Case Reference Numbers, which refer to the cases, in the Cases section. The suffixes indicate the state or, for federal cases, the court in which the case was decided.]

Paragraph 8.2

    I

        93023-GA

Text of Article 9—Arbitration

9.1 All claims, disputes and other matters in question between the parties to this Agreement, arising out of or relating to this Agreement or the breach thereof, shall be decided by arbitration in accordance with the Construction Industry Arbitration Rules of the American Arbitration Association then obtaining unless the parties mutually agree otherwise. No arbitration, arising out of or relating to this Agreement, shall include, by consolidation, joinder or in any other manner, any additional person not a party to this Agreement except by written consent containing a specific reference to this Agreement and signed by the Architect, the Owner, and any other person sought to be joined. Any consent to arbitration involving an additional person or persons shall not constitute consent to arbitration of any dispute not described therein or with any person not named or described therein. This Agreement to arbitrate and any agreement to arbitrate with an additional person or persons duly consented to by the parties to this Agreement shall be specifically enforceable under the prevailing arbitration law.

9.2 Notice of the demand for arbitration shall be filed in writing with the other party to this Agreement and with the American Arbitration Association. The demand shall be made within a reasonable time after the claim, dispute or other matter in question has arisen. In no event shall the demand for arbitration be made after the date when institution of legal or equitable proceedings based on such claim, dispute or other matter in question would be barred by the applicable statute of limitations.

9.3 The award rendered by the arbitrators shall be final, and judgment may be entered upon it in accordance with applicable law in any court having jurisdiction thereof.

Article 9   Arbitration

    I

75034-CO	81049-MD
76069-CO	76032-NJ
77059-CT	79028-NY
78058-IL	78023-PA

    II

        76046-FL
        77033-LA

DOCUMENT TO CASE CHARTS: B141-1977

[The five-digit numbers in this chart are Citator Case Reference Numbers, which refer to the cases, in the Cases section. The suffixes indicate the state or, for federal cases, the court in which the case was decided.]

III

77025-NY
79006-SC

Paragraph 9.1

I

91009-SDAL	93003-KY
90038-AL	90027-LA
36014-AZ	92013-MA
89002-AZ	87017-MN
89034-CT	89046-MN
93006-CT	84007-NY
85004-FL	85002-NC
91015-FL	92010-NC
90009-GA	93002-SD
92021-IL	93024-TN
90041-IN	89051-TX
90018-KS	

II

89048-US	82024-GA
86037-3CIR	94003-GA
87032-4CIR	87015-IL
86045-5CIR	87018-IL
87014-5CIR	88039-IL
90019-6CIR	89011-IL
87022-DDC	93008-IA
88006-DME	93052-LA
85040-WDMO	90022-ME
88008-SDNY	90014-MD
90004-DSC	86036-MI
87005-NDTX	86067-MI
86021-AL	91012-MI
83016-CA	86067-MN
90046-CA	88009-MN
88029-CT	89010-MN
90001-CT	95033-MO
86020-FL	86062-NY
86031-FL	87039-NY
86041-FL	88016-OH
86061-FL	89018-SC
87001-FL	93048-SC
91006-FL	93054-TX
	95023-VA

III

89050-6CIR	85042-MO
88044-NDGA	86054-NH
85041-AZ	85043-NY
90045-AZ	86024-NY
90003-CA	86047-NY
86029-CT	88031-NC
90053-CT	86026-OH
86023-DE	87045-PA
89030-IL	87052-PA
89045-IL	88013-PA
89039-MD	91018-RI

DOCUMENT TO CASE CHARTS: B141-1977

[The five-digit numbers in this chart are Citator Case Reference Numbers, which refer to the cases, in the Cases section. The suffixes indicate the state or, for federal cases, the court in which the case was decided.]

86069-WI

Paragraph 9.2

I

90038-AL	84007-NY
93006-CT	85002-NC
93003-KY	93002-SD
89046-MN	93024-TN

II

87032-4CIR	89044-IL
87014-5CIR	93008-IA
87022-DDC	93052-LA
90004-DSC	95033-MO
90001-CT	86062-NY
86031-FL	93048-SC
94003-GA	93054-TX
87018-IL	

III

86029-CT	86047-NY
86024-NY	87045-PA

Paragraph 9.3

I

93006-CT	93002-SD
90038-IL	93024-TN
93003-KY	

II

87032-4CIR	87018-IL
87014-5CIR	93008-IA
87022-DDC	93052-LA
90004-DSC	95033-MO
90001-CT	86062-NY
86031-FL	93048-SC
94003-GA	93054-TX

III

86029-CT	86047-NY
86024-NY	87045-PA

Text of Article 10—Termination of Agreement

10.1 This Agreement may be terminated by either party upon seven days' written notice should the other party fail substantially to perform in accordance with its terms through no fault of the party initiating the termination.

10.2 This Agreement may be terminated by the Owner upon at least seven days' written notice to the Architect in the event that the Project is permanently abandoned.

DOCUMENT TO CASE CHARTS: B141-1977

[The five-digit numbers in this chart are Citator Case Reference Numbers, which refer to the cases, in the Cases section. The suffixes indicate the state or, for federal cases, the court in which the case was decided.]

> **10.3** In the event of termination not the fault of the Architect, the Architect shall be compensated for all services performed to termination date, together with Reimbursable Expenses then due and all Termination Expenses as defined in Paragraph 10.4.
>
> **10.4** Termination Expenses include expenses directly attributable to termination for which the Architect is not otherwise compensated, plus an amount computed as a percentage of the total Basic and Additional Compensation earned to the time of termination, as follows:
>
> **.1** 20 percent if termination occurs during the Schematic Design Phase; or
>
> **.2** 10 percent if termination occurs during the Design Development Phase; or
>
> **.3** 5 percent if termination occurs during any subsequent phase.

Article 10 Termination of Agreement

    I

        81062-NE
        79073-TN
        78009-TX

Paragraph 10.1

    I

        92009-FL
        89017-NE
        89020-TX

    III

        82006-TX

Paragraph 10.2

    I

        92009-FL

    III

        82006-TX

Paragraph 10.3

    II

        92009-FL

DOCUMENT TO CASE CHARTS: B141-1977

[The five-digit numbers in this chart are Citator Case Reference Numbers, which refer to the cases, in the Cases section. The suffixes indicate the state or, for federal cases, the court in which the case was decided.]

    III

        90024-MO

Paragraph 10.4

    II

        92009-FL

Text of Article 11—Miscellaneous Provisions

11.1 Unless otherwise specified, this Agreement shall be governed by the law of the principal place of business of the Architect.

11.2 Terms in this Agreement shall have the same meaning as those in AIA Document A201, General Conditions of the Contract for Construction, current as of the date of this Agreement.

11.3 As between the parties to this Agreement: as to all acts or failures to act by either party to this Agreement, any applicable statute of limitations shall commence to run and any alleged cause of action shall be deemed to have accrued in any and all events not later than the relevant Date of Substantial Completion of the Work, and as to any acts or failures to act occurring after the relevant Date of Substantial Completion, not later than the date of issuance of the final Certificate for Payment.

11.4 The Owner and the Architect waive all rights against each other and against the contractors, consultants, agents and employees of the other for damages covered by any property insurance during construction as set forth in the edition of AIA Document A201, General Conditions, current as of the date of this Agreement. The Owner and the Architect each shall require appropriate similar waivers from their contractors, consultants and agents.

Article 11   Miscellaneous Provisions

    I

        77059-CT

    III

        77022-VA
        79002-VT

Paragraph 11.1

    II

        89048-US

DOCUMENT TO CASE CHARTS: B141-1977

[The five-digit numbers in this chart are Citator Case Reference Numbers, which refer to the cases, in the Cases section. The suffixes indicate the state or, for federal cases, the court in which the case was decided.]

    III

        91018-RI

Paragraph 11.2

    I

        93036-NE

Paragraph 11.3

    I

        84007-NY

Paragraph 11.4

    I

        94011-WDMI
        88032-NC

    III

        87031-SDNY
        86074-AR

Text of Article 12—Successors and Assigns

12.1 The Owner and the Architect, respectively, bind themselves, their partners, successors, assigns and legal representatives to the other party to this Agreement and to the partners, successors, assigns and legal representatives of such other party with respect to all covenants of this Agreement. Neither the Owner nor the Architect shall assign, sublet or transfer any interest in this Agreement without the written consent of the other.

Article 12 Successors and Assigns

Paragraph 12.1

    I

        75034-CO
        88023-MN
        87021-TN

    II

        90014-MD

Text of Article 13—Extent of Agreement

13.1 This Agreement represents the entire and integrated agreement between the Owner and the Architect and supersedes all prior negotiations, representations or agreements, either written or oral. This Agreement may be amended only by written instrument signed by both Owner and Architect.

DOCUMENT TO CASE CHARTS: B141-1977 B–46

[The five-digit numbers in this chart are Citator Case Reference Numbers, which refer to the cases, in the Cases section. The suffixes indicate the state or, for federal cases, the court in which the case was decided.]

Article 13 Extent of Agreement

Paragraph 13.1

    I

        78058-IL
        78016-MN

    II

        77028-AZ
        78011-IL
        84038-MO

    III

        86061-FL
        90021-SC

Text of Article 14—Basis of Compensation

The Owner shall compensate the Architect for the Scope of Services provided, in accordance with Article 6, Payments to the Architect, and the other Terms and Conditions of this Agreement, as follows:

14.1 AN INITIAL PAYMENT of _____ dollars ($ _____) shall be made upon execution of this Agreement and credited to the Owner's account as follows:

14.2 BASIC COMPENSATION

14.2.1 FOR BASIC SERVICES, as described in Paragraphs 1.1 through 1.5, and any other services included in Article 15 as part of Basic Services, Basic Compensation shall be computed as follows: *(Here insert basis of compensation, including fixed amounts, multiples or percentages, and identify Phases to which particular methods of compensation apply, if necessary.)*

14.2.2 Where compensation is based on a Stipulated Sum or Percentage of Construction Cost, payments for Basic Services shall be made as provided in Subparagraph 6.1.2, so that Basic Compensation for each Phase shall equal the following percentages of the total Basic Compensation payable: *(Include any additional Phases as appropriate.)*

    Schematic Design Phase: . . . . percent (____%)

    Design Development Phase: . . . . percent (____%)

    Construction Documents Phase: . . . . percent (____%)

    Bidding or Negotiation Phase: . . . . percent (____%)

    Construction Phase: . . . . percent (____%)

14.3 FOR PROJECT REPRESENTATION BEYOND BASIC SERVICES, as described in Paragraph 1.6, Compensation shall be computed separately in accordance with Subparagraph 1.6.2.

DOCUMENT TO CASE CHARTS: B141-1977

[The five-digit numbers in this chart are Citator Case Reference Numbers, which refer to the cases, in the Cases section. The suffixes indicate the state or, for federal cases, the court in which the case was decided.]

14.4 COMPENSATION FOR ADDITIONAL SERVICES

14.4.1 FOR ADDITIONAL SERVICES OF THE ARCHITECT, as described in Paragraph 1.7, and any other services included in Article 15 as part of Additional Services, but excluding Additional Services of consultants, Compensation shall be computed as follows: *(Here insert basis of compensation, including rates and/or multiples of Direct Personnel Expense for Principals and employees, and identify Principals and classify employees, if required. Identify specific services to which particular methods of compensation apply, if necessary.)*

14.4.2 FOR ADDITIONAL SERVICES OF CONSULTANTS, including additional structural, mechanical and electrical engineering services and those provided under Subparagraph 1.7.21 or identified in Article 15 as part of Additional Services, a multiple of _____ (_____) times the amount billed to the Architect for such services. *(Identify specific types of consultants in Article 15, if required.)*

14.5 FOR REIMBURSABLE EXPENSES, as described in Article 5, and any other items included in Article 15 as Reimbursable Expenses, a multiple of _____ (_____) times the amounts expended by the Architect, the Architect's employees and consultants in the interest of the Project.

14.6 Payments due the Architect and unpaid under this Agreement shall bear interest from the date payment is due at the rate entered below, or in the absence thereof, at the legal rate prevailing at the principal place of business of the Architect. *(Here insert any rate of interest agreed upon.)* _____ *(Usury laws and requirements under the Federal Truth in Lending Act, similar state and local consumer credit laws and other regulations at the Owner's and Architect's principal places of business, the location of the Project and elsewhere may affect the validity of this provision. Specific legal advice should be obtained with respect to deletion, modification, or other requirements such as written disclosures or waivers.)*

14.7 The Owner and the Architect agree in accordance with the Terms and Conditions of this Agreement that:

14.7.1 IF THE SCOPE of the Project or of the Architect's Services is changed materially, the amounts of compensation shall be equitably adjusted.

14.7.2 IF THE SERVICES covered by this Agreement have not been completed within (_____) months of the date hereof, through no fault of the Architect, the amounts of compensation, rates and multiples set forth herein shall be equitably adjusted.

DOCUMENT TO CASE CHARTS: B141-1977

[The five-digit numbers in this chart are Citator Case Reference Numbers, which refer to the cases, in the Cases section. The suffixes indicate the state or, for federal cases, the court in which the case was decided.]

Article 14 Basis of Compensation

    I

        80045-10CIR   79073-TN
        78064-MT   78009-TX

    II

        77033-LA
        78036-TX
        80037-TX

    III

        78053-NY

Paragraph 14.1 Basic Compensation

    III

        90054-LA

Paragraph 14.2 Basic compensation

    II

        89017-NE

    III

        86073-LA
        90054-LA
        88025-VA

Paragraph 14.3

    III

        90054-LA

Paragraph 14.4 Compensation for Additional Services

    III

        90054-LA
        88025-VA

Paragraph 14.5

    III

        90054-LA

DOCUMENT TO CASE CHARTS: B141-1977

[The five-digit numbers in this chart are Citator Case Reference Numbers, which refer to the cases, in the Cases section. The suffixes indicate the state or, for federal cases, the court in which the case was decided.]

Paragraph 14.6

    I

        89009-TX

    II

        92001-7CIR
        89017-NE

    III

        90054-LA

Article 15   Other Conditions or Services

    I

        78058-IL

    III

        80064-PA

DOCUMENT TO CASE CHARTS: B141-1987

[The five-digit numbers in this chart are Citator Case Reference Numbers, which refer to the cases, in the Cases section. The suffixes indicate the state or, for federal cases, the court in which the case was decided.]

B141-1987—STANDARD FORM OF AGREEMENT BETWEEN OWNER AND ARCHITECT

Article 1 Architect's Responsibilities

Text of Article 2—Scope of Architect's Basic Services

2.1 DEFINITION

2.1.1 The Architect's Basic Services consist of those described in Paragraphs 2.2 through 2.6 and any other services identified in Article 12 as part of Basic Services, and include normal structural, mechanical and electrical engineering services.

2.2 SCHEMATIC DESIGN PHASE

2.2.1 The Architect shall review the program furnished by the Owner to ascertain the requirements of the Project and shall arrive at a mutual understanding of such requirements with the Owner.

2.2.2 The Architect shall provide a preliminary evaluation of the Owner's program, schedule and construction budget requirements, each in terms of the other, subject to the limitations set forth in Subparagraph 5.2.1.

2.2.3 The Architect shall review with the Owner alternative approaches to design and construction of the Project.

2.2.4 Based on the mutually agreed-upon program, schedule and construction budget requirements, the Architect shall prepare, for approval by the Owner, Schematic Design Documents consisting of drawings and other documents illustrating the scale and relationship of Project components.

2.2.5 The Architect shall submit to the Owner a preliminary estimate of Construction Cost based on current area, volume or other unit costs.

2.3 DESIGN DEVELOPMENT PHASE

2.3.1 Based on the approved Schematic Design Documents and any adjustments authorized by the Owner in the program, schedule or construction budget, the Architect shall prepare, for approval by the Owner, Design Development Documents consisting of drawings and other documents to fix and describe the size and character of the Project as to architectural, structural, mechanical and electrical systems, materials and such other elements as may be appropriate.

2.3.2 The Architect shall advise the Owner of any adjustments to the preliminary estimate of Construction Cost.

DOCUMENT TO CASE CHARTS: B141-1987

[The five-digit numbers in this chart are Citator Case Reference Numbers, which refer to the cases, in the Cases section. The suffixes indicate the state or, for federal cases, the court in which the case was decided.]

2.4 CONSTRUCTION DOCUMENTS PHASE

2.4.1 Based on the approved Design Development Documents and any further adjustments in the scope or quality of the Project or in the construction budget authorized by the Owner, the Architect shall prepare, for approval by the Owner, Construction Documents consisting of Drawings and Specifications setting forth in detail the requirements for the construction of the Project.

2.4.2 The Architect shall assist the Owner in the preparation of the necessary bidding information, bidding forms, the Conditions of the Contract, and the form of Agreement between the Owner and Contractor.

2.4.3 The Architect shall advise the Owner of any adjustments to previous preliminary estimates of Construction Cost indicated by changes in requirements or general market conditions.

2.4.4 The Architect shall assist the Owner in connection with the Owner's responsibility for filing documents required for the approval of governmental authorities having jurisdiction over the Project.

2.5 BIDDING OR NEGOTIATION PHASE

2.5.1 The Architect, following the Owner's approval of the Construction Documents and of the latest preliminary estimate of Construction Cost, shall assist the Owner in obtaining bids or negotiated proposals and assist in awarding and preparing contracts for construction.

2.6 CONSTRUCTION PHASE—ADMINISTRATION OF THE CONSTRUCTION CONTRACT

2.6.1 The Architect's responsibility to provide Basic Services for the Construction Phase under this Agreement commences with the award of the Contract for Construction and terminates at the earlier of the issuance to the Owner of the final Certificate for Payment or 60 days after the date of Substantial Completion of the Work, unless extended under the terms of Subparagraph 10.3.3.

2.6.2 The Architect shall provide administration of the Contract for Construction as set forth below and in the edition of AIA Document A201, General Conditions of the Contract for Construction, current as of the date of this Agreement, unless otherwise provided in this Agreement.

2.6.3 Duties, responsibilities and limitations of authority of the Architect shall not be restricted, modified or extended without written agreement of the Owner and Architect with consent of the Contractor, which consent shall not be unreasonably withheld.

2.6.4 The Architect shall be a representative of and shall advise and consult with the Owner (1) during construction until final payment to the Contractor is due, and (2) as an Additional Service at the Owner's direction from time to time during the correction period described in the Contract for Construction. The Architect shall have authority to act on behalf of the Owner only to the extent provided in this Agreement unless otherwise modified by written instrument.

DOCUMENT TO CASE CHARTS: B141-1987

[The five-digit numbers in this chart are Citator Case Reference Numbers, which refer to the cases, in the Cases section. The suffixes indicate the state or, for federal cases, the court in which the case was decided.]

2.6.5 The Architect shall visit the site at intervals appropriate to the stage of construction or as otherwise agreed by the Owner and Architect in writing to become generally familiar with the progress and quality of the Work completed and to determine in general if the Work is being performed in a manner indicating that the Work when completed will be in accordance with the Contract Documents. However, the Architect shall not be required to make exhaustive or continuous on-site inspections to check the quality or quantity of the Work. On the basis of on-site observations as an architect, the Architect shall keep the Owner informed of the progress and quality of the Work, and shall endeavor to guard the Owner against defects and deficiencies in the Work. (*More extensive site representation may be agreed to as an Additional Service, as described in Paragraph 3.2.*)

2.6.6 The Architect shall not have control over or charge of and shall not be responsible for construction means, methods, techniques, sequences or procedures, or for safety precautions and programs in connection with the Work, since these are solely the Contractor's responsibility under the Contract for Construction. The Architect shall not be responsible for the Contractor's schedules or failure to carry out the Work in accordance with the Contract Documents. The Architect shall not have control over or charge of acts or omissions of the Contractor, Subcontractors, or their agents or employees, or of any other persons performing portions of the Work.

2.6.7 The Architect shall at all times have access to the Work wherever it is in preparation or progress.

2.6.8 Except as may otherwise be provided in the Contract Documents or when direct communications have been specially authorized, the Owner and Contractor shall communicate through the Architect. Communications by and with the Architect's consultants shall be through the Architect.

2.6.9 Based on the Architect's observations and evaluations of the Contractor's Applications for Payment, the Architect shall review and certify the amounts due the Contractor.

2.6.10 The Architect's certification for payment shall constitute a representation to the Owner, based on the Architect's observations at the site as provided in Subparagraph 2.6.5 and on the data comprising the Contractor's Application for Payment, that the Work has progressed to the point indicated and that, to the best of the Architect's knowledge, information and belief, quality of the Work is in accordance with the Contract Documents. The foregoing representations are subject to an evaluation of the Work for conformance with the Contract Documents upon Substantial Completion, to results of subsequent tests and inspections, to minor deviations from the Contract Documents correctable prior to completion and to specific qualifications expressed by the Architect. The issuance of a Certificate for Payment shall further constitute a representation that the Contractor is entitled to payment in the amount certified. However, the issuance of a Certificate for Payment shall not be a representation that the Architect has (1) made exhaustive or continuous on-site inspections to check the quality or quantity of the Work, (2) reviewed construction means, methods, techniques, sequences or procedures, (3) reviewed copies of requisitions received from Subcontractors and material suppliers and other data requested by the Owner to substantiate the Contractor's right to payment or (4) ascertained how or for what purpose the Contractor has used money previously paid on account of the Contract Sum.

2.6.11 The Architect shall have authority to reject Work which does not conform to the Contract Documents. Whenever the Architect considers it necessary or advisable for implementation of the intent of the Contract Documents, the Architect will have authority to require additional inspection or testing of the Work in accordance with the provisions of the Contract Documents, whether or not such Work is fabricated, installed or completed. However, neither this authority of the Architect nor a decision made in good faith either to exercise or not to exercise such authority shall give rise to a duty or responsibility of the Architect to the Contractor, Subcontractors, material and equipment suppliers, their agents or employees or other persons performing portions of the Work.

2.6.12 The Architect shall review and approve or take other appropriate action upon Contractor's submittals such as Shop Drawings. Product Data and Samples, but only for the limited purpose of checking for conformance with information given and the design concept expressed in the Contract Documents. The Architect's action shall be taken with such reasonable promptness as to cause no delay in the Work or in the construction of the Owner or of separate contractors, while allowing sufficient time in the Architect's professional judgment to permit adequate review. Review of such submittals is not conducted for the purpose of determining the accuracy and completeness of other details such as dimensions and quantities or for substantiating instructions for installation or performance of equipment of systems designed by the Contractor, all of which remain the responsibility of the Contractor to the extent required by the Contract Documents. The Architect's review shall not constitute approval of safety precautions or, unless otherwise specifically stated by the Architect, of construction means, methods, techniques, sequences or procedures. The Architect's approval of a specific item shall not indicate approval of an assembly of which the item is a component. When professional certification of performance characteristics of materials, systems or equipment is required by the Contract Documents, the Architect shall be entitled to rely upon such certification to establish that the materials, systems or equipment will meet the performance criteria required by the Contract Documents.

2.6.13 The Architect shall prepare Change Orders and Construction Change Directives, with supporting documentation and data if deemed necessary by the Architect as provided in Subparagraphs 3.1.1 and 3.3.3, for the Owner's approval and execution in accordance with the Contract Documents, and may authorize minor changes in the Work not involving an adjustment in the Contract Sum or an extension of the Contract Time which are not inconsistent with the intent of the Contract Documents.

2.6.14 The Architect shall conduct inspections to determine the date or dates of Substantial Completion and the date of final completion, shall receive and forward

[*The five-digit numbers in this chart are Citator Case Reference Numbers, which refer to the cases, in the Cases section. The suffixes indicate the state or, for federal cases, the court in which the case was decided.*]

to the Owner for the Owner's review and records written warranties and related documents required by the Contract Documents and assembled by the Contractor, and shall issue a final Certificate for Payment upon compliance with the requirements of the Contract Documents.

2.6.15 The Architect shall interpret and decide matters concerning performance of the Owner and Contractor under the requirements of the Contract Documents on written request of either the Owner or Contractor. The Architect's response to such requests shall be made with reasonable promptness and within any time limits agreed upon.

2.6.16 Interpretations and decisions of the Architect shall be consistent with the intent of and reasonably inferable from the Contract Documents and shall be in writing or in the form of drawings. When making such interpretations and initial decisions, the Architect shall endeavor to secure faithful performance by both Owner and Contractor, shall not show partiality to either, and shall not be liable for results of interpretations or decisions so rendered in good faith.

2.6.17 The Architect's decisions on matters relating to aesthetic effect shall be final if consistent with the intent expressed in the Contract Documents.

2.6.18 The Architect shall render written decisions within a reasonable time on all claims, disputes or other matters in question between the Owner and Contractor relating to the execution or progress of the Work as provided in the Contract Documents.

2.6.19 The Architect's decisions on claims, disputes or other matters, including those in question between the Owner and Contractor, except for those relating to aesthetic effect as provided in Subparagraph 2.6.17, shall be subject to arbitration as provided in this Agreement and in the Contract Documents.

Article 2   Scope of Architect's Basic Services

Paragraph 2.4   Construction Documents Phase
    I
        94004-MO

Paragraph 2.6   Construction Phase—Administration of the Construction Contract
    I
        93005-MO

DOCUMENT TO CASE CHARTS: B141-1987

[The five-digit numbers in this chart are Citator Case Reference Numbers, which refer to the cases, in the Cases section. The suffixes indicate the state or, for federal cases, the court in which the case was decided.]

    II

        92004b-GA
        92002-TN

    III

        92004a-GA

Paragraph 2.6.2

    III

        94005-MO
        95001-WA

Paragraph 2.6.4

    II

        94044-MDGA
        94045-TX

    III

        93015a-IL
        95001-TX

Paragraph 2.6.5

    I

        93003-MO

    II

96020-8CIR	95052-OH
94044-MDGA	94045-TX
95004-NJ	96027-TX
95042-OH	

    III

        95018-2CIR
        97020-10CIR

Paragraph 2.6.6

    I

        93033-MO

    II

96020-8CIR	95042-OH
94044-MDGA	95052-OH
94038-FL	94045-TX
93045-IL	96027-TX
95004-NJ	

DOCUMENT TO CASE CHARTS: B141-1987

[The five-digit numbers in this chart are Citator Case Reference Numbers, which refer to the cases, in the Cases section. The suffixes indicate the state or, for federal cases, the court in which the case was decided.]

    III

        95018-2CIR
        97020-10CIR
        93015a-IL

Paragraph 2.6.11

    II

        95004-NJ

    III

        95018-2CIR
        93045-IL
        95022-NC

Paragraph 2.6.12

    III

        95008-VA

Paragraph 2.6.13

    I

        97018-MO

    III

        95001-WA

Paragraph 2.6.14

    II

        94045-TX

Paragraph 2.6.15

    I

        97018-MO

    II

        94017-MO

    III

        95018-2CIR
        94041-CT
        95024-NY

DOCUMENT TO CASE CHARTS: B141-1987

[*The five-digit numbers in this chart are Citator Case Reference Numbers, which refer to the cases, in the Cases section. The suffixes indicate the state or, for federal cases, the court in which the case was decided.*]

Paragraph 2.6.16

I

    95001-WA

III

    95018-2CIR   95024-NY
    94041-CT   97022-NY

Paragraph 2.6.17

I

    97018-MO

III

    95024-NY

Paragraph 2.6.18

I

    97018-MO

III

    95024-NY
    97022-NY

Paragraph 2.6.19

I

    97018-MO

III

    94041-CT   97022-NY
    95024-NY   95022-NC

Article 3   Additional Services

Article 4   Owner's Responsibilities

Article 5   Construction Cost

Paragraph 5.2   Responsibility for Construction Cost

Text of Paragraph 5.2.1

5.2.1 Evaluations of the Owner's Project budget, preliminary estimates of Constructor Cost and detailed estimates of Construction Cost, if any, prepared by the Architect, represent the Architect's best judgment as a design professional familiar with the construction industry. It is recognized however, that neither the Architect nor the Owner has control over the cost of labor, materials or equipment, over the Contractors methods of determining bid prices, or over competitive bidding, market or negotiating conditions. Accordingly, the Architect cannot and does not

DOCUMENT TO CASE CHARTS: B141-1987

[*The five-digit numbers in this chart are Citator Case Reference Numbers, which refer to the cases, in the Cases section. The suffixes indicate the state or, for federal cases, the court in which the case was decided.*]

warrant or represent that bids or negotiated prices will not vary from the Owner's Project budget or from any estimate of Construction Cost or evaluation prepared or agreed to by the Architect.

Paragraph 5.2.1

I

96030-VT

Text of Paragraph 5.2.2

5.2.2 No fixed limit of Construction Cost shall be established as a condition of this Agreement by the furnishing, proposal or establishment of a Project budget, unless such fixed limit has been agreed upon in writing and signed by the parties hereto. If such a fixed limit has been established, the Architect shall be permitted to include contingencies for design, bidding and price escalation, to determine what materials, equipment, component systems and types of construction are to be included in the Contract Documents, to make reasonable adjustments in the scope of the Project and to include in the Contract Documents alternate bids to adjust the Construction Cost to the fixed limit. Fixed limits, if any, shall be increased in the amount of an increase in the Contract Sum occurring after execution of the Contract for Construction.

Paragraph 5.2.2

I

96030-VT

DOCUMENT TO CASE CHARTS: B141-1987

[The five-digit numbers in this chart are Citator Case Reference Numbers, which refer to the cases, in the Cases section. The suffixes indicate the state or, for federal cases, the court in which the case was decided.]

Text of Article 6—Use of Architect's Drawings, Specifications and Other Documents

6.1 The Drawings, Specifications and other documents prepared by the Architect for this Project are instruments of the Architect's service for use solely with respect to this Project and, unless otherwise provided, the Architect shall be deemed the author of these documents and shall retain all common law, statutory and other reserved rights, including the copyright. The Owner shall be permitted to retain copies, including reproducible copies, of the Architect's Drawings, Specifications and other documents for information and reference in connection with the Owner's use and occupancy of the Project. The Architect's Drawings, Specifications or other documents shall not be used by the Owner or others on other projects, for additions to this Project or for completion of this Project by others, unless the Architect is adjudged to be in default under this Agreement, except by agreement in writing and with appropriate compensation to the Architect.

6.2 Submission or distribution of documents to meet official regulatory requirements or for similar purposes in connection with the Project is not to be construed as publication in derogation of the Architect's reserved rights.

Article 6   Use of Architect's Drawings, Specifications and Other Documents

Paragraph 6.1

    I

        93023-GA

    III

        94010-EDLA

Paragraph 6.2

    I

        93023-GA

Text of Article 7—Arbitration

7.1 Claims, disputes or other matters in question between the parties to this Agreement arising out of or relating to this Agreement or breach thereof shall be subject to and decided by arbitration in accordance with the Construction Industry Arbitration Rules of the American Arbitration Association currently in effect unless the parties mutually agree otherwise.

7.2 Demand for arbitration shall be filed in writing with the other party to this Agreement and with the American Arbitration Association. A demand for arbitration shall be made within a reasonable time after the claim, dispute or other matter in question has arisen. In no event shall the demand for arbitration be made after the

DOCUMENT TO CASE CHARTS: B141-1987

[The five-digit numbers in this chart are Citator Case Reference Numbers, which refer to the cases, in the Cases section. The suffixes indicate the state or, for federal cases, the court in which the case was decided.]

date when institution of legal or equitable proceedings based on such claim, dispute or other matter in question would be barred by the applicable statutes of limitations.

7.3 No arbitration arising out of or relating to this Agreement shall include, by consolidation, joinder or in any other manner, an additional person or entity not a party to this Agreement, except by written consent containing a specific reference to this Agreement signed by the Owner, Architect, and any other person or entity sought to be joined. Consent to arbitration involving an additional person or entity shall not constitute consent to arbitration of any claim, dispute or other matter in question not described in the written consent or with a person or entity not named or described therein. The foregoing agreement to arbitrate and other agreements to arbitrate with an additional person or entity duly consented to by the parties to this Agreement shall be specifically enforceable in accordance with applicable law in any court having jurisdiction thereof.

7.4 The award rendered by the arbitrator or arbitrators shall be final, and judgment may be entered upon it in accordance with applicable law in any court having jurisdiction thereof.

Article 7 Arbitration

Paragraph 7.1

I

92012-DNJ	93019-NJ
92014-AL	92016-NC
93006-CT	97026-OH
93016-FL	97023-PA
93012-IL	93002-SD
93003-KY	92005a-TX
93011-MA	97024-WV
93046-MO	94049-WY
97018-MO	

II

95046-AL	97007-NJ
93044-FL	96011-NY
94003-GA	93048-SC
94026-GA	93024-TN
93008-IA	96023-TN
93052-LA	93054-TX
94006-MD	95023-VA
97011-MD	96014-VA
94017-MO	93049-WV
95033-MO	

DOCUMENT TO CASE CHARTS: B141-1987

[The five-digit numbers in this chart are Citator Case Reference Numbers, which refer to the cases, in the Cases section. The suffixes indicate the state or, for federal cases, the court in which the case was decided.]

III

96022-2CIR	93027-IL
96006-DCCIR	94021-LA
95014-AR	97022-NY
97016-AR	95016-NC
94018-CA	95009-PA
96038-CO	94030-TX
94041-CT	95002-TX
96002-DC	94019-WI

Paragraph 7.2

I

93006-CT	92016-NC
93016-FL	97026-OH
93012-IL	97023-PA
93003-KY	93002-SD
93011-MA	92005a-TX
93046-MO	97024-WV
93019-NJ	94049-WY

II

95046-AL	97007-NJ
93044-FL	96011-NY
94003-GA	93048-SC
93008-IA	93024-TN
93052-LA	96023-TN
94006-MD	93054-TX
97011-MD	96014-VA
94017-MO	93049-WV
95033-MO	

III

96022-2CIR	93027-IL
96006-DCCIR	94021-LA
97016-AR	97022-NY
94018-CA	95009-PA
96038-CO	94030-TX
94041-CT	95002-TX
96002-DC	94019-WI

Paragraph 7.3

I

92012-DNJ	93019-NJ
93006-CT	97026-OH
93016-FL	97023-PA
93012-IL	93002-SD
93003-KY	92005a-TX
93011-MA	97024-WV
93046-MO	94049-WY

DOCUMENT TO CASE CHARTS: B141-1987

[The five-digit numbers in this chart are Citator Case Reference Numbers, which refer to the cases, in the Cases section. The suffixes indicate the state or, for federal cases, the court in which the case was decided.]

II

95046-AL
93044-FL
94003-GA
93008-IA
93052-LA
94006-MD
97011-MD
94017-MO
95033-MO

97007-NJ
96011-NY
93048-SC
93024-TN
96023-TN
93054-TX
96014-VA
93049-WV

III

96022-2CIR
96006-DCCIR
97016-AR
94018-CA
96038-CO
94041-CT
96002-DC

93027-IL
94021-LA
97022-NY
95009-PA
94030-TX
95002-TX
94019-WI

Paragraph 7.4

I

93006-CT
93016-FL
93012-IL
93003-KY
93011-MA
93046-MO
97018-MO
93019-NJ

95016-NC
97026-OH
97023-PA
93002-SD
92005a-TX
97024-WV
94049-WY

II

95046-AL
93044-FL
94003-GA
94026-GA
93008-IA
93052-LA
94006-MD
97011-MD
94017-MO

95033-MO
97007-NJ
96011-NY
93048-SC
93024-TN
96023-TN
93054-TX
96014-VA
93049-WV

III

96022-2CIR
96006-DCCIR
97016-AR
94018-CA
96038-CO
94041-CT
96002-DC
93027-IL

94021-LA
95033-MO
97022-NY
95009-PA
94030-TX
95002-TX
94019-WI

B-63   DOCUMENT TO CASE CHARTS: B141-1987

[The five-digit numbers in this chart are Citator Case Reference Numbers, which refer to the cases, in the Cases section. The suffixes indicate the state or, for federal cases, the court in which the case was decided.]

Article 8   Termination, Suspension or Abandonment

Text of Paragraph 8.6

8.6 In the event of termination not the fault of the Architect, the Architect shall be compensated for services performed prior to termination, together with Reimbursable Expenses then due and all Termination Expenses as defined in Paragraph 8.7.

Paragraph 8.6

    III

        96042-PA

Text of Paragraph 8.7

8.7 Termination Expenses are in addition to compensation for Basic and Additional Services, and include expenses which are directly attributable to termination. Termination Expenses shall be computed as a percentage of the total compensation for Basic Services and Additional Services earned to the time of termination, as follows:

.1   Twenty percent of the total compensation for Basic and Additional Services earned to date if termination occurs before or during the predesign, site analysis, or Schematic Design Phases; or

.2   Ten percent of the total compensation for Basic and Additional Services earned to date if termination occurs during the Design Development Phase; or

.3   Five percent of the total compensation for Basic and Additional Services earned to date if termination occurs during any subsequent phase.

Paragraph 8.7

    III

        96042-PA

Text of Article 9—Miscellaneous Provisions

9.1 Unless otherwise provided, this Agreement shall be governed by the law of the principal place of business of the Architect.

9.2 Terms in this Agreement shall have the same meaning as those in AIA Document A201, General Conditions of the Contract for Construction, current as of the date of this Agreement.

9.3 Causes of action between the parties to this Agreement pertaining to acts or failures to act shall be deemed to have accrued and the applicable statutes of limitations shall commence to run not later than either the date of Substantial Completion for acts or failures to act occurring prior to Substantial Completion,

DOCUMENT TO CASE CHARTS: B141-1987

[*The five-digit numbers in this chart are Citator Case Reference Numbers, which refer to the cases, in the Cases section. The suffixes indicate the state or, for federal cases, the court in which the case was decided.*]

or the date of issuance of the final Certificate for Payment for acts or failures to act occurring after Substantial Completion.

9.4 The Owner and Architect waive all rights against each other and against the contractors, consultants, agents and employees of the other for damages, but only to the extent covered by property insurance during construction, except such rights as they may have to the proceeds of such insurance as set forth in the edition of AIA Document A201, General Conditions of the Contract for Construction, current as of the date of this Agreement. The Owner and Architect each shall require similar waivers from their contractors, consultants and agents.

9.5 The Owner and Architect, respectively, bind themselves, their partners, successors, assigns and legal representatives to the other party to this Agreement and to the partners, successors, assigns and legal representatives of such other party with respect to all covenants of this Agreement. Neither Owner nor Architect shall assign this Agreement without the written consent of the other.

9.6 This Agreement represents the entire and integrated agreement between the Owner and Architect and supersedes all prior negotiations, representations or agreements, either written or oral. This Agreement may be amended only by written instrument signed by both Owner and Architect.

9.7 Nothing contained in this Agreement shall create a contractual relationship with or a cause of action in favor of a third party against either the Owner or Architect.

9.8 Unless otherwise provided in this Agreement, the Architect and Architect's consultants shall have no responsibility for the discovery, presence, handling, removal or disposal of or exposure of persons to hazardous materials in any form at the Project site, including but not limited to asbestos, asbestos products, polychlorinated biphenyl (PCB) or other toxic substances.

9.9 The Architect shall have the right to include representations of the design of the Project, including photographs of the exterior and interior, among the Architect's promotional and professional materials. The Architect's materials shall not include the Owner's confidential or proprietary information if the Owner has previously advised the Architect in writing of the specific information considered by the Owner to be confidential or proprietary. The Owner shall provide professional credit for the Architect on the construction sign and in the promotional materials for the Project.

DOCUMENT TO CASE CHARTS: B141-1987

[The five-digit numbers in this chart are Citator Case Reference Numbers, which refer to the cases, in the Cases section. The suffixes indicate the state or, for federal cases, the court in which the case was decided.]

Article 9 Miscellaneous Provisions

Paragraph 9.1

    I

        93011-MA
        92009a-TX

Paragraph 9.2

    I

        93036-NE

Paragraph 9.4

    I

        94004-MO

    II

        94011-WDMI

    III

        95004-NJ

Paragraph 9.5

    I

        94025-WA

Article 10 Payments to the Architect

Article 11 Basis of Compensation

Article 12 Other Conditions or Services

C Series

Architect-Consultant Documents

C SERIES DOCUMENT REFERENCE CHARTS

SYNOPSIS

Document Cross-Reference Charts

C101, C131 & C141   Cross-Reference Charts

Document to Case Charts

C131-1967: Standard Form of Agreement Between Architect and Engineer of a Basis of a Percentage of Construction Cost
C131-1970: Standard Form of Agreement Between Architect and Engineer of a Basis of a Percentage of Construction Cost
C141-1974: Standard Form of Agreement Between Architect and Engineer
C141-1979: Standard Form of Agreement Between Architect and Engineer
C141-1987: Standard Form of Agreement Between Architect and Consultant

DOCUMENT CROSS-REF. CHARTS: C101, C131 & C141

C101, C131 & C141 CROSS-REFERENCE CHARTS

Article Title	C101 1963	C131 1967	C131 1970	C141 1974	C141 1979	C141 1997
Applicable law	—	13	13	13	12	11.1
Arbitration	13	11	11	11	9	9.2
Architect agrees to pay engineer	2	II	II	II	15	13
Architect's responsibilities	5	2	2	2	2	6
Construction cost	6	3	3	3	3	3.2, 7
Direct and reimbursable expense	7	4, 5	4, 5	4, 5	4, 5	12.6, 12.7
Direct personnel expense	7	4	4	4	4	12.7
Engineer agrees to provide services	1	1	1	1	1	4
Engineer's additional services	4	1	1	1	1	5
Engineer's basic services	3	1	1	1	1	4
Engineer's records	9	7	7	7	7	8
Engineer's services	3, 4	1	1	1	1	4
Extent of agreement	—	12	12	12	14	11.6
Insurance	11	9	9	9	11	12.8
Mediation	—	—	—	—	—	9.1
Payments to engineer	8	6	6	6	6	13
Reimbursable expenses	7	5	5	5	5	12.6
Relationship of architect and engineer	3	III	III	IV	I, II	2, 3
Successors and assigns	12	10	10	10	13	11.5
Termination of agreement	10	8	8	8	10	10

[*The five-digit numbers in this chart are Citator Case Reference Numbers, which refer to the cases, in the Cases section. The suffixes indicate the state or, for federal cases, the court in which the case was decided.*]

C131-1967—STANDARD FORM OF AGREEMENT BETWEEN ARCHITECT AND ENGINEER ON A BASIS OF A PERCENTAGE OF CONSTRUCTION COST

Article 1   Engineer's Services

    II

        68032-MD

    III

        61007-MI

Article 2   The Architect's Responsibilities

Article 3   Construction Cost

    III

        31007-1CIR

Article 4   Direct Personnel Expense

Article 5   Reimbursable Expenses

Article 6   Payments to the Engineer

Article 7   Engineer's Records

Article 8   Termination of Agreement

Article 9   Insurance

Article 10   Successors and Assigns

Article 11   Arbitration

Article 12   Extent of Agreement

Article 13   Applicable Law

DOCUMENT TO CASE CHARTS: C131-1970

[The five-digit numbers in this chart are Citator Case Reference Numbers, which refer to the cases, in the Cases section. The suffixes indicate the state or, for federal cases, the court in which the case was decided.]

C131-1970—STANDARD FORM OF AGREEMENT BETWEEN ARCHITECT AND ENGINEER ON A BASIS OF A PERCENTAGE OF CONSTRUCTION COST

Article 1   Engineer's Services

    II

        72075-OR

    III

        73089-SDIA
        72089-NM

Article 2   The Architect's Responsibilities

    III

        73069-WA

Article 3   Construction Cost

Article 4   Direct Personnel Expense

Article 5   Reimbursable Expenses

Article 6   Payments to the Engineer

Article 7   Engineer's Records

Article 8   Termination of Agreement

Article 9   Ownership of Documents

Article 10   Insurance

    III

        72029-9CIR

Article 11   Successors and Assigns

Article 12   Arbitration

Article 13   Extent of Agreement

Article 14   Governing Law

    III

        73069-WA

DOCUMENT TO CASE CHARTS: C141-1974

[The five-digit numbers in this chart are Citator Case Reference Numbers, which refer to the cases, in the Cases section. The suffixes indicate the state or, for federal cases, the court in which the case was decided.]

C141-1974—STANDARD FORM OF AGREEMENT BETWEEN ARCHITECT AND ENGINEER

Article 1   Engineer's Services

Article 2   The Architect's Responsibilities

Article 3   Construction Cost

Article 4   Direct Personnel Expense

Article 5   Reimbursable Expenses

Article 6   Payment to the Engineer

Article 7   Engineer's Records

Article 8   Termination of Agreement

Article 9   Ownership of Documents

Article 10   Insurance

Article 11   Successors and Assigns

Article 12   Arbitration

III

75019-NY

Article 13   Extent of Agreement

Article 14   Governing Law

Article 15   Other Conditions or Services

DOCUMENT TO CASE CHARTS: C141-1979

[The five-digit numbers in this chart are Citator Case Reference Numbers, which refer to the cases, in the Cases section. The suffixes indicate the state or, for federal cases, the court in which the case was decided.]

C141-1979—STANDARD FORM OF AGREEMENT BETWEEN ARCHITECT AND ENGINEER

Article 1 Engineer's Services and Responsibilities

    III

        78047-MD

Article 2 The Architect's Responsibilities

Article 3 Construction Cost

Article 4 Direct Personnel Expense

Article 5 Reimbursable Expenses

Article 6 Payments to the Engineer

Article 7 Engineer's Accounting Records

Article 8 Ownership and Use of Documents

Article 9 Arbitration

    III

        77068-NY

Article 10 Termination of Agreement

Article 11 Insurance

Article 12 Miscellaneous Provisions

Article 13 Successors and Assigns

Article 14 Extent of Agreement

DOCUMENT TO CASE CHARTS: C141-1987

[*The five-digit numbers in this chart are Citator Case Reference Numbers, which refer to the cases, in the Cases section. The suffixes indicate the state or, for federal cases, the court in which the case was decided.*]

C141-1987—STANDARD FORM OF AGREEMENT BETWEEN ARCHITECT AND CONSULTANT

Article 1   Consultant's Responsibilities

Article 2   Scope of Consultant's Basic Services

Article 3   Additional Services

Article 4   Architect's Responsibilities

Article 5   Construction Cost

Article 6   Use of Consultant's Drawings, Specifications and Other Documents

Article 7   Arbitration

Article 8   Termination, Suspension or Abandonment

Article 9   Miscellaneous Provisions

Article 10   Payments to the Consultant

Article 11   Basis of Compensation

Article 12   Other Conditions or Services

Cases

> **PLEASE NOTE:**
>
> Case digests are provided for all cases decided since 1974.

001 Wood v. Fort Wayne, 119 U.S. 312 (1886)

    III: A201-1963, Art. 15

002 Erskine v. Johnson, 23 Neb. 261, 36 N.W. 510 (1888)

    III: A201-1963, Art. 15

003 Hubert v. Aitken, 15 Daly 237, 5 N.Y.S. 839 (Sup. Ct. 1889)

    III: A201-1963, Art. 38

004 Corey v. Eastman, 166 Mass. 279, 44 N.E. 217 (1896)

    III: A201-1963, Art. 25

06001 Thompson-Starrett Co. v. Brooklyn Heights Reality Co., 111 A.D. 358, 98 N.Y.S. 128 (1906)

    I: A201-1963, Art. 25
    III: A201-1963, Art. 32

07001 Mercantile Trust Co. v. Hensey, 205 U.S. 298, 27 S. Ct. 535, 51 L. Ed. 811 (1907)

    III: A201-1963, Art. 25

11001 Johnson v. Norcross Bros., 209 Mass. 445, 95 N.E. 833 (1911)

    III: A201-1963, Art. 15

12001 Cruthers v. Donahoe, 85 Conn. 629, 84 A. 322 (1912)

    II: A201-1963, Art. 1

12002 Roland v. Lindsey, 104 Ark. 49, 146 S.W. 115 (1912)

    III: A201-1963, Art. 32

13001 American-Hawaiian Engineering & Construction Co. v. Butler, 165 Cal. 497, 133 P. 280 (1913)

    I: A201-1963, Art. 22
    I: A201-1963, Art. 24
    I: A201-1963, Art. 25
    I: A201-1963, Art. 32
    I: A201-1963, Art. 39

13002 Gould v. McCormick, 75 Wash. 61, 134 P. 676 (1913)

    III: B131-1963, Art. 8
    III: B131-1963, Art. 10

13003 Noonan v. Stein, 56 Colo. 64, 136 P. 1181 (1913)

    III: A201-1963, Art. 32

13004 Northwestern Marble & Tile Co. v. Megrath, 72 Wash. 441, 130 P. 484 (1913)

    II: A201-1963, Art. 39

13005 Welsh v. Warren, 159 S.W. 106 (Tex. Civ. App. 1913)

    II: A101-1963, Art. 4
    II: A201-1963, Art. 21
    II: A201-1963, Art. 25

13006 YMCA v. United States Fidelity & Guar. Corp., 90 Kan. 332, 133 P. 894 (1913)

    II: A311-1963, Labor & Material Payment Bond
    II: B131-1963, Art. 8

13007 Gauntt v. Chehalis County, 72 Wash. 106, 129 P. 888 (1913)

    III: B131-1963, Art. 8

14001 Alta Planing Mill Co. v. Garland, 167 Cal. 179, 138 P. 738 (1914)

    I: A201-1963, Art. 12

14002 Borup v. Von Kokeritz, 162 A.D. 394, 147 N.Y.S. 832 (1914)

    I: A201-1963, Art. 25

14003 Burroughs v. School District No. 2, Town of Richland, 155 Wis. 426, 144 N.W. 977 (1914)

    II: A101-1963, Art. 4

14004 Merrill-Ruckgaber Co. v. City of New York, 160 A.D. 513, 145 N.Y.S. 577 (1914)

    I: A201-1963, Art. 25

14005 Mohawk Overall Co. v. Brown, 163 A.D. 157, 148 N.Y.S. 369 (1914)

      I: A201-1963, Art. 31

15001 Bair v. School District No. 141, 94 Kan. 144, 146 P. 347 (1915)

      II: B131-1963, Art. 6
      II: B131-1963, Art. 8

15002 Connell v. Higgens, 170 Cal. 541, 150 P. 769 (1915)

      I: A201-1963, Art. 1
      I: A201-1963, Art. 22

15004 Interstate Lumber Co. v. Western Mortgage & Warranty Title Co., 51 Mont. 190. 149 P. 975 (1915)

      II: A201-1963, Art. 15

16001 Fetterolf v. S & L Construction Co., 175 A.D. 177, 161 N.Y.S. 549 (1916)

      II A201-1963, Art. 15

16002 Howard v. Harvard Congregational Soc., 223 Mass. 562, 112 N.E. 233 (1916)

      II: A201-1963, Art. 15

16003 Meulenbergh v. Coe, 160 N.Y.S. 581 (Sup. Ct. 1916)

      I: A201-1963, Art. 25
      II: A201-1963, Art. 1
      II: A201-1963, Art. 11

16004 Portuguese-American Bank v. Welles, 242 U.S. 7, 37 S. Ct. 3, 60 L. Ed. 116 (1916)

      III: A201-1963, Art. 33

17001 Burns v. Thorndike, 228 Mass. 552, 117 N.E. 799 (1917)

      III: A201-1963, Art. 15

17002 Citizens Bank v. Timmons, 19 Ga. App. 480, 91 S.E. 1050 (1917)

      II: A201-1963, Art. 33

17003	Maddux v. Buchanan, 121 Va. 102, 92 S.E. 830 (1917)	
	II:	A201-1963, Art. 22
17004	M.J. Daly & Sons v. New Haven Hotel Co., 91 Conn. 280, 99 A. 853 (1917)	
	I:	A201-1963, Art. 21
	I:	A201-1963, Art. 22
17005	Stewart v. Breckenridge, 69 Colo. 108, 169 P. 543 (1917)	
	II:	A201-1963, Art. 25
18001	Hennebique Construction Co. v. Boston Cold Storage & Terminal Co., 230 Mass. 456, 119 N.E. 948 (1918)	
	II:	A201-1963, Art. 25
19001	MacDonnell v. Dreyfous, 144 La. 891, 81 So. 383 (1919)	
	III:	B131-1963, Art. 6
	III:	B131-1963, Art. 8
19002	O'Kain v. Davis, 186 Ky. 184, 216 S.W. 354 (1919)	
	III:	B131-1963, Art. 8
	III:	B131-1963, Art. 10
20001	Bebb v. Jordan, 111 Wash. 73, 189 P. 553 (1920)	
	III:	A201-1963, Art. 11
20002	Hunt v. Owen Building & Investment Co., 219 S.W. 138 (Mo. Ct. App. 1920)	
	I:	A201-1963, Art. 15
	I:	A201-1963, Art. 25
20003	Keck v. Kavanaugh, 45 N.D. 81, 177 N.W. 99 (1920)	
	III:	B131-1963, Art. 6
	III:	B131-1963, Art. 8
20004	Russell v. Bothwell & Swaner Co., 57 Utah 362, 194 P. 1109 (1920)	
	III:	A201-1963, Art. 18

21001 Brown-Randolph Co. v. Gude, 151 Ga. 281, 106 S.E. 161 (1921)

    II: A201-1963, Art. 1

21002 Jacob & Youngs v. Kent, 230 N.Y. 239, 129 N.E. 889 (1921)

    II: A201-1963, Art. 20

21003 Thomas Haverty Co. v. Jones, 185 Cal. 285, 197 P. 105 (1921)

    III: A201-1963, Art. 25

22001 Orth v. Board of Public Education, 272 Pa. 411, 166 A. 366 (1922)

    III: B131-1963, Art. 6

23001 Hurley v. Kiona-Benton School District No. 27, 124 Wash. 537, 215 P. 21 (1923)

    I: A201-1963, Art. 25
    I: A201-1963, Art. 38

23002 Saiki v. Lee Sing, 27 Haw. 399 (1923)

    III: A201-1963, Art. 15

23003 Schwender v. Schrafft, 246 Mass. 543, 141 N.E. 511 (1923)

    I: B131-1963, Art. 3
    I: B131-1963, Art. 8

24001 Kinney v. Massachusetts Bonding & Insurance Co., 210 A.D. 285, 206 N.Y.S. 163 (1924)

    I: B131-1963, Art. 4

24002 Leonard v. People's Tobacco Warehouse Co., 128 S.C. 155, 122 S.E. 678 (1924)

    II: A201-1963, Art. 40

25001 Pierce v. Board of Educ., 125 Misc. 589, 211 N.Y.S. 788 (Sup. Ct. 1925)

    III: B131-1963, Art. 6
    III: B131-1963, Art. 8

25002 Roberts v. Security Trust & Savings Bank, 196 Cal. 557, 238 P. 673 (1925)

    I: A201-1963, Art. 18

I:	A201-1963, Art. 40
I:	A311-1963, Labor & Material Payment Bond

26001 Hartford Accident & Indemnity Co. v. W. & J. Knox Net & Twine Co., 150 Md. 40, 132 A. 261 (1926)

I:	A311-1963, Labor & Material Payment Bond

26002 Hite v. Aydlett, 192 N.C. 166, 134 S.E. 419 (1926)

III:	B131-1963, Art. 6
III:	B131-1963, Art. 8

27001 Bavin & Burch Co. v. Bard, 81 Cal. App. 722, 255 P. 200 (1927)

II:	A201-1963, Art. 15
II:	A201-1963, Art. 18

28001 Aetna Casualty & Sur. Co. v. Robertson Lumber Co., 3 S.W.2d 895 (Tex. Civ. App. 1928)

II:	A101-1963, Art. 4
II:	A201-1963, Art. 15

28002 Bowman v. Maryland Casualty Co., 88 Cal. App. 481, 263 P. 826 (1928)

III:	A311-1963, Labor & Material Payment Bond

28003 Granette Products Co. v. Arthur H. Neumann & Co., 208 Iowa 24, 221 N.W. 197 (1928)

II:	A201-1963, Art. 39

29001 Byram Lumber & Supply Co. v. Page, 109 Conn. 256, 146 A. 293 (1929)

I:	A311-1963, Labor & Material Payment Bond

29002 Fidelity & Deposit Co. v. Rainer, 220 Ala. 262, 125 So. 55 (1929)

I:	A311-1963, Labor & Material Payment Bond

29003 Hammaker v. Schleigh, 157 Md. 652, 147 A. 790 (1929)

III:	A201-1963, Art. 14
III:	A201-1963, Art. 31

29004 Odell v. Colmor Irrigation & Land Co., 34 N.M. 277, 280 P. 398 (1929)

    III: A201-1963, Art. 39
    III: A201-1963, Art. 40

29005 Sitkin v. Smith, 35 Ariz. 226 P. 521 (1929)

    I: A201-1963, Art. 15

30001 Walsh v. Cornwell, 272 Mass. 555, 172 N.E. 855 (1930)

    II: A201-1963, Art. 22

31001 Capitol Hotel Co. v. Rittenberry, 41 S.W.2d 697 (Tex. Civ. App. 1931)

    III: B131-1963, Art. 6

31002 Charles S. Wood & Co. v. Alvord & Swift, 232 A.D. 603, 251 N.Y.S. 35 (1931)

    II: A201-1963, Art. 39

31003 Edward Edinger Co. v. Willis, 260 Ill. App. 106 (1931)

    II: A201-1963, Art. 18
    II: A201-1963, Art. 25

31004 Johnson Electric Co. v. Columbia Casualty Co., 101 Fla. 186, 133 So. 850 (1931)

    I: A311-1963, Labor & Material Payment Bond

31005 Manett, Seastrunk & Buckner v. Terminal Building Corp., 120 Tex. 374, 39 S.W.2d 1 (1931)

    I: A201-1963, Art. 15
    I: A201-1963, Art. 38

31006 Noonan v. Independence Indemnity Co., 328 Mo. 706, 41 S.W.2d 162 (1931)

    II: A311-1963, Labor & Material Payment Bond

31007 Pettee v. City of Nashua, 50 F.2d 50 (1st Cir. 1931)

    II: C131-1967, Art. 3

32001 Hall v. Union Indemnity Co., 61 F.2d 85 (8th Cir. 1932)

    III: A201-1963, Art. 25

32002 William Cameron & Co. v. American Sur. Co., 55 S.W.2d 1032 (Comm'n App. Tex. 1932)

    I: A311-1963, Labor & Material Payment Bond

33001 Bowman v. C. O. Jones Building Co., 332 Mo. 520, 58 S.W.2d 718 (1933)

    I: A201-1963, Art. 1
    II: A201-1963, Art. 2
    II: A201-1963, Art. 15

33002 New York Indemnity Co. v. Hurst, 252 Ky. 59, 66 S.W.2d 8 (1933)

    II: A311-1963, Labor & Material Payment Bond

33003 Nieman-Irving & Co. v. Lazenby, 263 N.Y. 91, 188 N.E. 265 (1933)

    I: B131-1963, Art. 3

34001 American Sur. Co. v. Shaw, 69 S.W.2d 47 (Comm'n App. Tex. 1934)

    I: A201-1963, Art. 25
    I: A201-1963, Art. 37
    I: A201-1963, Art. 38

34002 Childs v. Smeltzer, 315 Pa. 91, 171 A. 883 (1934)

    I: B131-1963, Art. 3

34003 Elizabeth Sash, Door & Supply Co., v. St. Vincent's Hospital, 241 A.D. 751, 270 N.Y.S. 195 (1934)

    I: A201-1963, Art. 25

34004 Raitman v. McCune, 167 Okla. 511, 30 P.2d 878 (1934)

    III: B131-1963, Art. 2

35001 Concrete Form Co. v. W.T. Grange Construction Co., 320 Pa. 205, 181 A. 589 (1935)

    III: A201-1963, Art. 33

35002 Crane Construction Co. v. Commonwealth, 290 Mass. 249, 195 N.E. 110 (1935)

    III: A201-1963, Art. 15

35003 Standard Accident Insurance Co. v. Laird, 81 S.W.2d 271 (Tex. Civ. App. 1935)

    II: A201-1963, Art. 22

36001 Foster v. Sellards, 263 Ky. 752, 93 S.W.2d 834 (1936)

    I: A201-1963, Art. 1

36002 Nees v. Weaver, 222 Wis. 492, 269 N.W. 266 (1936)

    II: A201-1963, Art. 25

37001 Croft v. H. M. Cohen Lumber & Building Co., 107 S.W.2d 1040 (Tex. Civ. App. 1937)

    I: A201-1963, Art. 38
    I: A201-1963, Art. 39

37002 N.E. Redlon Co. v. Franklin Square Corp., 91 N.H. 502, 195 A. 348 (1937)

    I: A201-1963, Art. 2
    I: A201-1963, Art. 15
    I: A201-1963, Art. 39
    I: A201-1963, Art. 40

37003 Underground Construction Co. v. Sanitary District, 367 Ill. 360, 11 N.E.2d 361 (1937)

    I: A201-1963, Art. 23
    I: A201-1963, Art. 25

38001 Chiaverini v. Vail, 67 R.I. 111, 200 A. 462 (1938)

    III: A201-1963, Art. 14
    III: A201-1963, Art. 38

38002 Kurfiss v. Cowherd, 233 Mo. App. 397, 121 S.W.2d 282 (1938)

    I: B131-1963, Art. 11

39001 Baer v. Tippett, 34 Cal. App. 2d 33, 92 P.2d 1028 (1939)

    I: B131-1963, Art. 3

39002 Clement v. Pensacola Builders Supply Co., 138 Fla. 629, 189 So. 852 (1939)

    I: A201-1963, Art. 25

39003   Corporation of President of Jesus Chirst of Latter Day Saints v. Hartford Accident & Indemnity Co., 98 Utah 297, 95 P.2d 736 (1939)

    I: A201-1963, Art. 21
    I: A201-1963, Art. 22
    I: A201-1963, Art. 34
    I: A201-1963, Art. 37
    I: A311-1963, Labor & Material Payment Bond

39004   Harrigan & Reid Co. v. Hudson, 291 Mich. 478, 289 N.W. 222 (1939)

    I: A201-1963, Art. 36
    I: A201-1963, Art. 38

40001   Bott v. Moser, 175 Va. 11, 7 S.E.2d 217 (1940)

    I: B131-1963, Art. 3

40002   F.F. Bolinger Co. v. Wildmann Brewing Corp., 339 Pa. 289, 14 A.2d 81 (1940)

    I: B131-1963, Art. 3

40003   Six Companies of California v. Joint Highway Dist. No 13, 311 U.S. 180, 61 S. Ct. 186, 85 L. Ed. 114 (1940)

    III: A101-1963, Art. 2

41001   Grand Trunk Western Railroad v. H.W. Nelson Co., 116 F.2d 823 (6th Cir. 1941)

    III: A201-1963, Art. 15
    III: A201-1963, Art. 31

41002   Henderson v. Oakes-Waterman Builders, 44 Cal. App. 2d 615, 112 P.2d 662 (1941)

    I: A201-1963, Art. 31
    III: A201-1963, Art. 22

41003   Montgomery v. Karavas, 45 N.M. 287, 114 P.2d 776 (1941)

    I: A201-1963, Art. 26

41004   Wetzel v. Roberts, 296 Mich. 114, 295 N.W. 580 (1941)

    I: B131-1963, Art. 6

	I:	B131-1963, Art. 8

42001   Knutson v. Metallic Slab Form Co., 128 F.2d 408 (5th Cir. 1942)

        I: A201-1963, Art. 37

42002   Pittsburgh Plate Glass Co. v. American Sur. Co., 66 Ga. App. 805, 19 S.E.2d 357 (1942)

        II: A201-1963, Art. 1
        II: A201-1963, Art. 25

43001   Hersey Gravel Co. v. State, 305 Mich. 333, 9 N.W.2d 567 (1943)

        III: A201-1963, Art. 25

43002   Independent School District No. 35 v. A. Hedenberg & Co., 214 Minn. 82, 7 N.W.2d 511 (1943)

        I: A201-1963, Art. 20
        I: A201-1963, Art. 25
        I: A201-1963, Art. 31
        I: A201-1963, Art. 39
        I: A201-1963, Art. 40

44001   Goin v. Board of Educ., 298 Ky. 645, 183 S.W.2d 819 (1944)

        I: A101-1963, Art. 4
        I: A201-1963, Art. 12
        I: A201-1963, Art. 15

44002   Morgan v. Town of Burlington, 316 Mass. 413, 55 N.E.2d 758 (1944)

        I: A201-1963, Art. 3
        I: A201-1963, Art. 15
        I: A201-1963, Art. 31
        I: A201-1963, Art. 38
        I: A201-1963, Art. 39

44003   Schultz v. Gund, 19 So. 2d 682 (La. Ct. App. 1944)

        I: A201-1963, Art. 35
        I: A201-1963, Art. 36

44004 Mitterhausen v. South Wisconsin Conference Association of Seventh Day Adventists, 245 Wis. 353, 14 N.W.2d 19 (1944)

    I: B131-1963, Art. 6
    I: B131-1963, Art. 8

45001 School District No. 3 v. Central Savings Bank & Trust Co., 113 Colo. 487, 159 P.2d 361 (1945)

    I: B131-1963, Art. 12

45002 Stevenson v. San Diego County, 26 Cal. 2d 842, 161 P.2d 553 (1945)

    III: B131-1963, Art. 2

46001 Berg v. Kucharo Construction Co., 237 Iowa 478, 21 N.W.2d 561 (1946)

    II: A201-1963, Art. 15
    II: A201-1963, Art. 18

47001 Board of Comm'rs v. Vahlberg, 198 Okla. 527, 180 P.2d 144 (1947)

    I: B131-1963, Art. 8

48001 Doup v. Almand, 212 Ark. 687, 207 S.W.2d 601 (1948)

    I: B131-1963, Art. 8

49001 Bueche v. Eikenroht, 220 S.W.2d 911 (Tex. Civ. App. 1949)

    I: B131-1963, Art. 8

49002 Rowell v. Crow, 93 Cal. App. 2d 500, 209 P.2d 149 (1949)

    I: B131-1963, Art. 6
    I: B131-1963, Art. 8

49003 Standard Millwork & Supply Co. v. Mississippi Steel & Iron Co., 205 Miss. 96, 38 So. 2d 448 (1949)

    I: A201-1963, Art. 25
    I: A201-1963, Art. 40

50001 Fuhrmann v. Catanese, 44 So. 2d 230 (La. Ct. App. 1950)

    I: B131-1963, Art. 6
    I: B131-1963, Art. 8

50002 Goldberg v. Underhill, 95 Cal. App. 2d 700, 213 P.2d 516 (1950)

    I: B131-1963, Art. 3

50003 Halvorson v. Blue Mountain Prune Growers Co-op., 188 Or. 661, 214 P.2d 986 (1950)

    II: A201-1963, Art. 25
    II: A201-1963, Art. 39

50004 Loyal Order of Moose, Adrian Lodge 1034 v. Faulhaber, 327 Mich. 244, 41 N.W.2d 535 (1950)

    I: B131-1963, Art. 6
    I: B131-1963, Art. 8

51001 Alexander v. Hammarberg, 103 Cal. App. 2d 872, 230 P.2d 399 (1951)

    I: B131-1963, Art. 3

51002 Keystone Engineering Corp. v. Sutter, 196 Md. 620, 78 A.2d 191 (1951)

    I: A201-1963, Art. 22

51003 Washington Construction Co. v. Spinella, 8 N.J. 212, 84 A.2d 617 (1951)

    II: A201-1963, Art. 9
    II: A201-1963, Art. 22
    II: A201-1963, Art. 24

52001 Allhusen v. Caristo Construction Corp., 303 N.Y. 446, 103 N.E.2d 891 (1952)

    III: A201-1963, Art. 33

52002 Gifford v. Commissioner of Public Health, 328 Mass. 608, 105 N.E.2d 476 (1952)

    I: B131-1963, Art. 3

52003 Hatzel & Buehler v. George A. Fuller Co., 303 N.Y. 836, 104 N.E.2d 376 (1952)

    I: A201-1963, Art. 40

52004 Puget Sound National Bank v. C.B. Lauch Construction Co., 73 Idaho 68, 245 P.2d 800 (1952)

    I: A201-1963, Art. 14

	I:	A201-1963, Art. 37

52005 Staley v. New, 56 N.M. 756, 250 P.2d 893 (1952)

      II: A201-1963, Art. 14

52006 Warren Brothers Roads Co. v. United States, 105 F. Supp. 826 (Ct. Cl. 1952)

      I: A201-1963, Art. 32

52007 Zannoth v. Booth Radio Stations, Inc., 333 Mich. 233, 52 N.W.2d 678 (1952)

      I: B131-1963, Art. 6
      I: B131-1963, Art. 8

53001 Austin-Griffith, Inc. v. Goldberg, 224 S.C. 372, 79 S.E.2d 447 (1953)

      I: A201-1963, Art. 18
      I: A201-1963, Art. 26
      II: A201-1963, Art. 21

53002 Haugen v. Raupach, 43 Wash. 2d 147, 269 P.2d 340 (1953)

      II: A201-1963, Art. 25

53003 *In re* Kaelber, 281 A.D. 980, 120 N.Y.S.2d 566 (1953)

      I: B131-1963, Art. 3

53004 Oden Construction Co. v. Helton, 218 Miss. 41, 65 So. 2d 442 (1953)

      I: A201-1963, Art. 22

53005 Paxton v. Alameda County, 119 Cal. App. 2d 393, 259 P.2d 934 (1953)

      III: A201-1963, Art. 38

53006 Rosenthal v. Gauthier, 224 La. 341, 69 So. 2d 367 (1953)

      I: B131-1963, Art. 6
      I: B131-1963, Art. 8

54001 Frank T. Hickey, Inc. v. Los Angeles Jewish Community Council, 128 Cal. App. 2d 676, 276 P.2d 52 (1954)

      III: A201-1963, Art. 16

54002 Havard v. Board of Supervisors, 220 Miss. 359, 70 So. 2d 875 (1954)

    II: A201-1963, Art. 20

54003 Lewis v. Commonwealth, 332 Mass. 4, 122 N.E.2d 888 (1954)

    III: A201-1963, Art. 15

54004 Palmer v. Brown, 127 Cal. App. 2d 44, 273 P.2d 306 (1954)

    I: A201-1963, Art. 25
    I: A201-1963, Art. 38

54005 Spitz v. Brickhouse, 3 Ill. App. 2d 536, 123 N.E.2d 117 (1954)

    I: B131-1963, Art. 6
    I: B131-1963, Art. 8

54006 State v. Malvaney 221 Miss. 190, 72 So. 2d 424 (1954)

    III: A201-1963, Art. 38

55001 Cohen v. Mayflower Corp., 196 Va. 1153, 86 S.E.2d 860 (1955)

    I: A201-1967, Art. 7, Para. 7.1
    I: A311-1970, Labor & Material Payment Bond

56001 Allison v. Pick, 229 La. 524, 86 So. 2d 179 (1956)

    III: B131-1963, Art. 6
    III: B131-1963, Art. 8

56002 *In re* Stormer's Estate, 385 Pa. 382, 123 A.2d 627 (1956)

    III: A201-1963, Art. 33
    III: A311-1963, Labor & Material Payment Bond

56003 John W. Johnson, Inc., v. 2500 Wisconsin Avenue, 231 F.2d 761 (D.C. Cir. 1956)

    I: A201-1963, Art. 40

56004 Lewin & Sons v. Herman, 143 Conn. 146, 120 A.2d 423 (1956)

    I: A201-1963, Art. 33

56005 Martin v. Karsh, 142 Cal. App. 2d 468, 298 P.2d 635 (1956)

    III: A201-1963, Art. 1

56006 Pacific Coast Builders v. Antioch Live Oak Unified School District, 144 Cal. App. 2d 125, 300 P.2d 309 (1956)

    III: A201-1963, Art. 39

57001 Parrish v. Tahtaras, 7 Utah 2d 87, 318 P.2d 642 (1957)

    I: B131-1963, Art. 6
    I: B131-1963, Art. 8

57002 Stillinger & Napier v. Central States Grain Co., 164 Neb. 458, 82 N.W.2d 637 (1957)

    III: A201-1963, Art. 24
    III: A201-1963, Art. 25

57003 Texas Delta Upsilon Foundation v. Fehr, 307 S.W.2d 124 (Tex. Civ. App. 1957)

    I: B131-1963, Art. 6

57004 Wilson v. Keefe, 150 Cal. App. 2d 178, 309 P.2d 516 (1957)

    II: A201-1963, Art. 14
    II: A201-1963, Art. 15

58001 Baylor University v. Carlander, 316 S.W.2d 277 (Tex. Civ. App. 1958)

    II: B131-1963, Art. 6
    II: B131-1963, Art. 8

58002 Davies v. Kahn, 251 F.2d 324 (4th Cir. 1958)

    II: A201-1963, Art. 36

58003 Huggins v. Atlanta Tile & Marble Co., 98 Ga. App. 597, 106 S.E.2d 191 (1958)

    II: A201-1963, Art. 38

58004 J. T. Majors & Son v. Lippert Bros., 263 F.2d 650 (10th Cir. 1958)

    III: A201-1963, Art. 14

	III: A201-1963, Art. 15

58005 S. J. Groves & Sons v. West Virginia Turnpike Commission, 164 F. Supp. 816 (S.D. W. Va. 1958)

III: A201-1963, Art. 15

58006 Wenzler & Ward Plumbing & Heating Co. v. Sellen, 53 Wash. 2d 96, 330 P.2d 1068 (1958)

III: A201-1963, Art. 15

59001 Furst v. Board of Educ., 20 Ill. App. 2d 205, 155 N.E.2d 654 (1959)

I: B131-1963, Art. 6
I: B131-1963, Art. 8
I: B131-1963, Art. 10

59002 Lundstrom Construction Co. v. Dygert, 254 Minn. 224, 94 N.W.2d 527 (1959)

III: A201-1963, Art. 15

59003 M. DeMatteo Construction Co. v. Commonwealth, 338 Mass. 568, 156 N.E.2d 659 (1959)

III: A201-1963, Art. 15

59004 National Sur. Corp. v. Curators of University of Missouri, 268 F.2d 525 (8th Cir. 1959)

I: A201-1963, Art. 1

59005 Pastorelli v. Associated Engineers, 176 F. Supp. 159 (D.R.I. 1959)

III: A201-1963, Art. 38

60001 Bloomfield Reorganized School District No. R-14 v. Stites, 336 S.W.2d 95 (Mo. 1960)

I: A201-1963, Art. 18
I: A201-1963, Art. 22
I: A201-1963, Art. 25

60002 Chambless v. J. J. Fritch, General Contractor, Inc., 336 S.W.2d 200 (Tex. Civ. App. 1960)

III: A201-1963, Art. 15

60003   C.H. Leavell & Co., v. Vilbig Bros., 160 Tex. 600, 335 S.W.2d 211 (1960)

       III: A201-1963, Art. 25

60004   Craviolini v. Scholer & Fuller Assoicated Architects, 89 Ariz. 24, 357 P.2d 611 (1960)

       II: A201-1963, Art. 39
       II: A201-1963, Art. 40

60005   Eckert-Fair Construction Co. v. Flabiano, 342 S.W.2d 629 (Tex. Civ. App. 1960)

       II: A201-1963, Art. 39

60006   Erhart v. Hummonds, 232 Ark. 133, 334 S.W.2d 869 (1960)

       III: A201-1963, Art. 38

60007   Hines v. Farr, 235 S.C. 436, 112 S.E.2d 33 (1960)

       I: A201-1963, Art. 39
       II: A201-1963, Art. 40

60008   Howard J. White, Inc. v. Varian Associates, 178 Cal. App. 2d 348, 2 Cal. Rptr. 871 (1960)

       I: A201-1963, Art. 11
       I: A201-1963, Art. 15
       I: A201-1963, Art. 18

60009   Izumi v. Kwan Doo Park, 44 Haw. 123, 351 P.2d 1083 (1960)

       II: A201-1963, Art. 20

60010   Kenison v. Baldwin, 351 P.2d 307 (Okla. 1960)

       III: A201-1963, Art. 15

60011   Pedersen v. Fiksdal, 185 Cal. App. 2d 30, 7 Cal. Rptr. 874 (1960)

       I: A201-1963, Art. 2
       I: B131-1963, Art. 7

61001   Baldwin v. Alberti, 58 Wash. 2d 243, 362 P.2d 258 (1961)

       I: A201-1963, Art. 20

61002 Caldwell v. United Presbyterian Church, 20 Ohio Op. 2d 364, 180 N.E.2d 638 (Ct. Common Pleas 1961)

    I: B131-1963, Art. 6
    I: B131-1963, Art. 8

61003 City of Durham v. Reidsville Engineering Co., 255 N.C. 98, 120 S.E.2d 564 (1961)

    III: A201-1963, Art. 25

61004 Collins v. Post, 227 Or. 299, 362 P.2d 325 (1961)

    I: A201-1963, Art. 37
    II: A201-1963, Art. 16

61005 Costonis v. Medford Housing Auth., 343 Mass. 108, 176 N.E.2d 25 (1961)

    III: A201-1963, Art. 15

61006 Day v. National U.S. Radiator Corp., 241 La. 288, 128 So. 2d 660 (1961)

    III: A201-1963, Art. 5
    III: A201-1963, Art. 38

61007 George Wagschal Associates, Inc. v. West, 362 Mich. 676, 107 N.W.2d 874 (1961)

    III: C131-1967, Art. 1

61008 Kovacheff v. Langhart, 147 Colo. 339, 363 P.2d 702 (1961)

    II: B131-1963, Art. 6

61009 Lichter v. Mellon-Stuart Co., 193 F. Supp. 216 (W.D. Pa. 1961), *reh'g denied,* 196 F. Supp. 149 (1961)

    I: A201-1963, Art. 18
    I: A201-1963, Art. 31
    I: A201-1963, Art. 37

61010 Metro Industrial Painting Corp. v. Terminal Construction Co., 287 F.2d 382 (2d Cir. 1961)

    III: A201-1963, Art. 40

61011 Olsen v. Chase Manhatten Bank, 9 N.Y.2d 829, 175 N.E.2d 350, 215 N.Y.S.2d 773 (1961)

    III: A201-1963, Art. 14
    III: B131-1963, Art. 3

62001 Arkin Construction Co. v. Reynolds Metal Co. 310 F.2d 11, (5th Cir. 1962)

    II: A201-1963, Art. 25

62002 Benton v. Hoffman Plastering Co., 207 Cal. App. 2d 61, 24 Cal. Rptr. 268 (1962)

    III: A201-1963, Art. 33

62003 (UNASSIGNED)

62004 Gross v. Breaux, 144 So. 2d 763 (La. Ct. App. 1962)

    III: A201-1963, Art. 15

62005 James I. Barnes Construction Co. v. Washington Township, 134 Ind. App. 461, 184 N.E.2d 763 (1962)

    III: A201-1963, Art. 2

62006 Reishus v. Implement Dealers Mutual Insurance Co., 118 N.W.2d 673 (N.D. 1962)

    I: A201-1963, Art. 29

62007 Sands Motel v. Hargrave, 358 S.W.2d 670 (Tex. Civ. App. 1962)

    II: A201-1963, Art. 14

62008 Savignano v. Gloucester Housing Auth., 344 Mass. 668, 183 N.E.2d 862 (1962)

    III: A201-1963, Art. 15

62009 Smith v. Ryan, 142 So. 2d 139 (Fla. Dist. Ct. App. 1962)

    I: A201-1963, Art. 29
    I: A201-1963, Art. 31

62010 Vece v. Medical Center, Inc., 149 Conn. 518, 182 A.2d 407 (1962)

    II: B131-1963, Art. 8

62011 W. J. Howard & Sons v. Meyer, 367 Mich. 300, 116 N.W.2d 752 (1962)

    I: A201-1963, Art. 25

63001 Fidelity & Casualty Co. v. J.A. Jones Constr. Co., 200 F. Supp. 264 (E.D. Ark. 1961), *aff'd,* 325 F.2d 605 (8th Cir. 1963)

    III: A201-1963, Art. 12
    III: A201-1963, Art. 14
    III: A201-1963, Art. 27
    III: A201-1963, Art. 38

63002 Hirsch v. Kuhne, 149 So. 2d 630 (La. Ct. App. 1963)

    I: B131-1963, Art. 6
    I: B131-1963, Art. 8

63003 Independent School District No. 877 v. Loberg Plumbing & Heating Co., 266 Minn. 426, 123 N.W.2d 793 (1963)

    III: A201-1963, Art. 29

63004 Ken Carver & Sons v. Lenahan, 8 Ohio App. 2d 13, 220 N.E.2d 373 (1963)

    III: A201-1963, Art. 40

63005 Skidmore, Owings & Merrill v. Connecticut General Life Insurance Co., 25 Conn. Supp. 76, 197 A.2d 83 (Super. Ct. 1963)

    III: B131-1963, Art. 1

63006 Tappets-Abbott-McCarthy-Stratton v. New York State Thruway Authority, 18 A.D.2d 402, 239 N.Y.S.2d 732 (1963), *modifying* 38 Misc. 2d 30, 237 N.Y.S.2d 167 (Ct. Cl. 1963), *aff'd,* 13 N.Y.2d 1091, 196 N.E.2d 64, 246 N.Y.S.2d 409 (1963)

    III: A201-1963, Art. 18

63007 Thomas v. Fromherz Engineers, 159 So. 2d 612 (La. Ct. App. 1963)

    III: A201-1963, Art. 38

63008 Tsoi v. Ebenezer Baptist Church, 153 So. 2d 592 (La. Ct. App. 1963)

    I: B131-1963, Art. 6
    I: B131-1963, Art. 8

64001	Ben-Tom Corp. v. Buckeye Union Casualty Co., 2 Ohio Misc. 125, 207 N.E.2d 582 (1964)	

        III: A311-1963, Labor & Material Payment Bond

64002   Charles T. Main, Inc. v. Massachusetts Turnpike Authority, 347 Mass. 154, 196 N.E.2d 821 (1964)

        III: A201-1963, Art. 18

64003   City of Atlanta v. J.J. Black & Co., 110 Ga. App. 667, 139 S.E.2d 515 (1964)

        III: A201-1963, Art. 18
        III: A201-1963, Art. 38
        III: A201-1963, Art. 39

64004   Clarkeson Engineering Co. v. Massachusetts Turnpike Authority, 347 Mass. 173, 196 N.E.2d 834 (1964)

        III: A201-1963, Art. 15

64005   Ferrante v. McGinnis, 92 N.J. Super. 87, 222 A.2d 190 (1964)

        III: A311-1963, Labor & Material Payment Bond

65001   Ace Construction Co. v. W.H. Nichols & Co., 353 F.2d 110 (10th Cir. 1965)

        III: A201-1963, Art. 31

65002   Aetna Casualty & Sur. Co. v. Kemp Smith Co., 208 A.2d 737 (D.C. 1965)

        I: A201-1963, Art. 9
        I: A311-1963, Labor & Material Payment Bon

65003   Aetna Insurance Co. v. Estero Manufacturing & Builders Supply, Inc., 174 So. 2d 747 (Fla. Dist. Ct. App. 1965)

        III: A311-1963, Labor & Material Payment Bond

65004   A.J. Eckert Co. v. M.S. Kelliher Co., 23 A.D.2d 591, 255 N.Y.S.2d 727 (1965)

        III: A401-1963, Art. 5

65005   American Casualty Co. v. Timmons, 352 F.2d 563 (6th Cir. 1965)

        III: A201-1963, Art. 27

65006 Anderson v. Smith, 398 S.W.2d 635 (Tex. Civ. App. 1965)

    III: B131-1963, Art. 1

65007 A-1 Camp Chair Service Co. v. William L. Crow Construction Co., 24 A.D.2d 623, 262 N.Y.S.2d 166 (1965)

    I: A201-1963, Art. 20
    I: A201-1963, Art. 39
    I: A201-1963, Art. 40

65008 A. Teichert & Son v. State, 238 Cal. App. 2d 736, 48 Cal. Rptr. 225 (1965)

    III: A201-1963, Art. 15
    III: A201-1963, Art. 16

65009 Autrey v. Williams & Dunlap, 343 F.2d 730 (5th Cir. 1965)

    III: A201-1963, Art. 24
    III: A201-1963, Art. 25
    III: A201-1963, Art. 26
    III: A311-1963, Labor & Material Payment Bond

65010 Baldwin Contracting Co. v. Winston Steel Works, 236 Cal. App. 2d 565, 46 Cal. Rptr. 421 (1965)

    III: A201-1963, Art. 27
    III: A201-1963, Art. 36

65011 Bayer & Mingolla Construction Co. v. Deschenes, 348 Mass. 594, 205 N.E.2d 208 (1965)

    III: A311-1963, Labor & Material Payment Bond

65012 Beaufort Concrete Co. v. Atlantic States Construction Co., 352 F.2d 460 (5th Cir. 1965)

    III: A201-1963, Art. 20
    III: A201-1963, Art. 39

65013 Bella Kay Building Corp. v. City of Chicago, 58 Ill. App. 2d 230, 208 N.E.2d 60 (1965)

    III: A201-1963, Art. 12
    III: A201-1963, Art. 27

1965 CASES

65014   Bethlehem Steel Corp. v. City of Chicago, 350 F.2d 649 (7th Cir. 1965)

         III: A201-1963, Art. 18

65015   Blecick v. School District No. 18, 2 Ariz. App. 115, 406 P.2d 750 (1965)

         III: A201-1963, Art. 25
         III: A201-1963, Art. 26
         III: A201-1963, Art. 38
         III: A201-1963, Art. 39

65016   Blount Construction Co. v. Housing Auth., 253 F. Supp. 188 (M.D. Ga. 1965)

         II: A201-1963, Art. 9
         III: A201-1963, Art. 16

65017   Board of Educ. v. Hartford Accident & Indemnity Co., 60 Ill. App. 2d 320, 208 N.E.2d 51 (1965)

         III: A311-1963, Labor & Material Payment Bond

65018   Bushman Construction Co. v. Conner, 351 F.2d 681 (10th Cir. 1965)

         III: A201-1963, Art. 33

65019   Carlson v. Metropolitan Sanitary District, 64 Ill. App. 2d 331, 213 N.E.2d 129 (1965)

         III: A201-1963, Art. 12
         III: A201-1963, Art. 14
         III: A201-1963, Art. 38

65020   Carpenter v. Massachusetts Bonding & Insurance Co., 161 Me. 1, 206 A.2d 225 (1965)

         III: A201-1963, Art. 37
         III: A311-1963, Labor & Material Payment Bond
         III: A401-1963, Art. 5

65021   Central Contracting Co. v. Maryland Casualty Co., 242 F. Supp. 858 (W.D. Pa. 1965)

         III: A311-1963, Labor & Material Payment Bond

65022   Chicora Construction Co. v. United States, 252 F. Supp. 910 (E.D.N.C. 1965)

         III: A201-1963, Art. 18

65023 Chrysler Corp. v. Hanover Insurance Co., 350 F.2d 652 (7th Cir. 1965)

    III: A311-1963, Labor & Material Payment Bond

65024 Ciejek v. Crane Service Co., 351 F.2d 788 (D.C. Cir., 1965)

    III: A201-1963, Art. 27

65025 City of DeKalb v. Sornsin, 32 Ill. App. 2d 284, 205 N.E.2d 254 (1965)

    III: A311-1963, Labor & Material Payment Bond

65026 College Plaza, Inc. v. Harlaco, Inc., 152 Conn. 327, 206 A.2d 832 (1965)

    III: A201-1963, Art. 40

65027 Conte v. Town of Weston, 26 Conn. Supp. 41, 211 A.2d 706 (Ct. C.P. 1965)

    II: A201-1963, Art. 40

65028 Covil v. Rober & Co. Associates, 112 Ga. App. 163, 144 S.E.2d 450 (1965)

    II: B131-1967, Art. 1

65029 Cure v. City of Jefferson, 396 S.W.2d 727 (Mo. 1965)

    I: A101-1963, Art. 3
    I: A201-1963, Art. 15
    I: A201-1963, Art. 16

65030 Daniel O'Connell's Sons v. Commonwealth, 349 Mass. 642, 212 N.E.2d 219 (1965)

    III: A201-1963, Art. 16

65031 Darrell T. Stuart Contractor v. J.A. Bridges & Rustproofing, Inc., 2 Ariz. App. 63, 406 P.2d 413 (1965)

    III: A401-1963, Art. 5

65032 Deuel v. McCollum, 1 Ariz. App. 188, 400 P.2d 859 (1965)

    III: B131-1963, Art. 3
    III: B131-1963, Art. 10

65033 Donovan v. R.W. Rexford Co., 418 Pa. 376, 211 A.2d 459 (1965)

    III: A201-1963, Art. 15

III: A201-1963, Art. 40

65034   Doral Country Club v. Curcie Bros., 174 So. 2d 749 (Dist. Ct. App. Fla. 1965)

III: A201-1963, Art. 16

65035   Equitable Fire & Marine Insurance Co. v. Allied Steel Construction Co., 351 F.2d 275 (10th Cir. 1965)

III: A311-1963, Labor & Material Payment Bond

65036   Farnsworth & Chambers Co. v. United States, 346 F.2d 577 (Ct. Cl. 1965)

III: A201-1963, Art. 16

65037   Fishman Construction Co. v. Hansen, 238 Md. 418, 209 A.2d 605 (1965)

I: A201-1963, Art. 37
II: A311-1963, Labor & Material Payment Bond
II: A401-1963, Art. 5

65038   Fred. J. McClean Heating Supplies v. M. J. Walsh & Sons, 349 Mass. 489, 209 N.E.2d 340 (1965)

III: A201-1963, Art. 36

65039   General Accident Fire & Life Assurance Corp. v. Finegan & Burgess, Inc., 351 F.2d 168 (6th Cir. 1965)

III: A201-1963, Art. 27

65040   General Elec. Co. v. E. Fred Sulzer & Co., 86 N.J. Super. 520, 207 A.2d 346 (Law Div. 1965)

III: A201-1963, Art. 32

65041   Gholson, Byars & Holmes Construction Co. v. United States, 351 F.2d 987 (Ct. Cl. 1965)

III: A201-1963, Art. 16

65042   Goebel v. General Building Service Co., 26 Wis. 2d 129, 131 N.W.2d 852 (1965)

III: A201-1963, Art. 37

65043   Gottlieb Contracting, Inc. v. United States, 353 F.2d 777 (2d Cir. 1965)

III: A201-1963, Art. 16

CASES

65044 Great American Insurance Co. v. Louis Lesser Enterprises, Inc., 353 F.2d 997 (8th Cir. 1965)

    III: A311-1963, Labor & Material Payment Bond

65045 Green Manor Construction Co. v. Highland Painting Service, 345 F.2d 657 (1st Cir. 1965)

    III: A201-1963, Art. 36
    III: A201-1963, Art. 37
    III: A401-1963, Art. 3
    III: A401-1963, Art. 5

65046 Haines v. Bechdolt, 231 Cal. App. 2d 239, 42 Cal. Rptr. 53 (1965)

    III: B131-1963, Art. 8

65047 Hass v. Aetna Insurance Co., 391 S.W.2d 756 (Tex. Civ. App. 1965)

    I: A311-1963, Labor & Material Payment Bond

65048 Haughton Elevator Co. v. C. Rallo Contracting Co., 395 S.W.2d 238 (Mo. Ct. App. 1965)

    III: A201-1963, Art. 1
    III: A201-1963, Art. 15
    III: A201-1963, Art. 16
    III: A401-1963, Art. 5

65049 Henry v. United States, 250 F. Supp. 526 (N.D. Miss. 1965)

    II: A201-1963, Art. 15
    III: A201-1963, Art. 16

65050 Hol-Gar Manufacturing Corp. v. United States, 351 F.2d 972 (Ct. Cl. 1965)

    III: A201-1963, Art. 16

65051 Hollingsworth v. Chrysler Corp., 208 A.2d 61 (Del. Super. Ct. 1965)

    III: A201-1963, Art. 12
    III: A401-1963, Art. 5

65052 United States *ex rel.* Wellman Engineering Co. v. M.S.I. Corp., 246 F. Supp. 337 (D.N.J. 1965)

    III: A311-1963, Labor & Material Payment Bond

65053 Hunt & Willett, Inc. v. United States, 351 F.2d 980 (Ct. Cl. 1965)

    III: A201-1963, Art. 16
    III: A201-1963, Art. 18

65054 Inwood Construction Co. v. Huntington Corp., 400 S.W.2d 372 (Tex. Civ. App. 1965)

    I: A111-1963, Art. 9

65055 Jacobs v. Northeastern Corp., 416 Pa. 417, 206 A.2d 49 (1965)

    III: A311-1963, Labor & Material Payment Bond

65056 James Julian, Inc. v. President of Elkton, 341 F.2d 205 (4th Cir. 1965)

    III: A201-1963, Art. 16

65057 J.D. Hedin Construction Co. v. United States, 347 F.2d 235 (Ct. Cl. 1965)

    III: A201-1963, Art. 15
    III: A201-1963, Art. 16
    III: A201-1963, Art. 18

65058 J.F. White Engineering Corp. v. General Insurance Co., 351 F.2d 231 (10th Cir. 1965)

    III: A311-1963, Labor & Material Payment Bond

65059 John A. Robbins Co. v. Airportels, Inc., 418 Pa. 257, 210 A.2d 896 (1965)

    I: A201-1963, Art. 40

65060 Kellogg v. Pizza Oven, Inc., 157 Colo. 295, 402 P.2d 633 (1965)

    II: B131-1963, Art. 3

65061 Kenneth E. Curran, Inc. v. State, 215 A.2d 702 (N.H. 1965)

    III: A310-1963, Bid Bond

65062 Kenworthy v. State, 236 Cal. App. 2d 378, 46 Cal. Rptr. 396 (1965)

    III: A201-1963, Art. 18

65063 Kirk Reid Co. v. Fine, 205 Va. 778, 139 S.E.2d 829 (1965)

    I: A201-1963, Art. 15

I: A201-1963, Art. 25
I: A201-1963, Art. 38

65064 Lafayette Iron Works v. Wilaka Constructon Co., 23 A.D.2d 487, 255 N.Y.S.2d 693 (1965)

III: A401-1963, Art. 5

65065 L & E Co. v. United States, 351 F.2d 880 (9th Cir. 1965)

III: A311-1963, Labor & Material Payment Bond

65066 Lano v. Osberg Construction Co., 67 Wash. 2d 659, 409 P.2d 466 (1965)

III: A401-1963, Art. 3

65067 Lawton v. Cain, 172 So. 2d 734 (La. Ct. App. 1965)

I: A201-1963, Art. 39
II: A201-1963, Art. 40

65068 Lesser v. William Holliday Cord Associates, 349 F.2d 490 (8th Cir. 1965)

III: A201-1963, Art. 30
III: A311-1963, Labor & Material Payment Bond

65069 Lippert Brothers v. National Union Fire Insurance Co., 247 F. Supp. 874 (W.D. Okla. 1965)

III: A311-1963, Labor & Material Payment Bond

65070 Lunden v. County of Los Angeles, 233 Cal. App. 2d 811, 43 Cal. Rptr. 849 (1965)

III: B131-1963, Art. 3
III: B131-1963, Art. 8
III: B131-1963, Art. 10

65071 Luria Engineering Co. v. Aetna Casualty & Sur. Co., 206 Pa. Super. 333, 213 A.2d 151 (1965)

III: A401-1963, Art. 3

65072 Macri v. United States, 353 F.2d 804 (9th Cir. 1965)

III: A201-1963, Art. 18

	III: A201-1963, Art. 19
	III: A201-1963, Art. 26
	III: A201-1963, Art. 37
	III: A311-1963, Labor & Material Payment Bond
65073	Main v. Department of Highways, 206 Va. 143, 142 S.E.2d 524 (1965)
	III: A201-1963, Art. 15
	III: A201-1963, Art. 16
65074	Mandel v. Jordan, 57 Ill. App. 2d 276, 207 N.E.2d 12 (1965)
	II: B131-1963, Art. 2
65075	McCarthy v. Reese, 419 Pa. 489, 215 A.2d 257 (1965)
	III: A201-1963, Art. 32
65076	M.F. Hickey Co. v. Port of New York Authority, 23 A.D.2d 739, 258 N.Y.S.2d 129 (1965)
	III: A201-1963, Art. 26
65077	Minidoka County v. Krieger, 88 Idaho 395, 399 P.2d 962 (1965)
	III: A201-1963, Art. 25
	III: A201-1963, Art. 26
	III: A311-1963, Labor & Material Payment Bond
65078	Mion Chemical Brick Corp. v. Daniel Construction Co., 111 Ga. 369, 141 S.E.2d 839 (1965)
	III: A201-1963, Art. 16
	III: A401-1963, Art. 5
65079	M.L. Shalloo, Inc. v. Ricciardi & Sons Construction, 348 Mass. 682, 205 N.E.2d 239 (1965)
	III: A201-1963, Art. 15
	III: A201-1963, Art. 16
	III: A201-1963, Art. 37
65080	Morrison-Knudsen Co. v. United States, 345 F.2d 535 (Ct. Cl. 1965)
	III: A201-1963, Art. 16

65081 Morrison-Knudsen Co. v. United States, 345 F.2d 833 (Ct. Cl. 1965)

    III: A201-1963, Art. 15
    III: A201-1963, Art. 16
    III: A201-1963, Art. 40

65082 National Union Fire Insurance Co. v. D & L Construction Co., 353 F.2d 169 (8th Cir. 1965)

    III: A201-1963, Art. 36
    III: A311-1963, Labor & Material Payment Bond

65083 Oldham & Worth, Inc. v. Bratton, 263 N.C. 307, 139 S.E.2d 653 (1965)

    I: A111-1963, Art. 1
    I: A111-1963, Art. 5
    I: A111-1963, Art. 6
    I: A111-1963, Art. 13
    I: A201-1963, Art. 25

65084 Paduano v. J.C. Boespflug Construction Co., 66 Wash. 2d 527, 403 P.2d 841 (1965)

    III: A401-1963, Art. 3

65085 (UNASSIGNED)

65086 Parsons v. Bristol Development Co., 42 Cal. Rptr. 378 (1965), *vacated*, 62 Cal. 2d 861, 402 P.2d 839, 44 Cal. Rptr. 767 (1965)

    III: B131-1963, Art. 3
    III: B131-1963, Art. 6
    III: B131-1963, Art.

65087 Paul B. Emerick Co. v. William Bohnenkamp & Associates, 242 Or. 253, 409 P.2d 332 (1965)

    III: A201-1963, Art. 36
    III: A201-1963, Art. 37
    III: A401-1963, Art. 5

65088 Peyronnin Construction Co. v. Weiss, 137 Ind. App. 417, 208 N.E.2d 489 (1965)

    III: A201-1963, Art. 37

65089	Royal Indemnity Co. v. Alexander Industries, Inc., 58 Del. 548, 211 A.2d 919 (1965)	
	III:	A311-1963, Labor & Material Payment Bond
65090	Russell v. Travelers Indem. Co., 244 F. Supp. 419 (W.D. Mo. 1965)	
	III:	A311-1963, Labor & Material Payment Bond
65091	Schlanger v. Federal Insurance Co., 44 N.J. 17, 206 A.2d 874 (1965)	
	I:	A201-1963, Art. 9
	I:	A201-1963, Art. 30
65092	Schmid v. United States, 351 F.2d 651 (Ct. Cl. 1965)	
	III:	A201-1963, Art. 15
	III:	A201-1963, Art. 18
65093	School District No. Six v. Alfred Watts Grant & Associates, 156 Colo. 328, 399 P.2d 101 (1965)	
	III:	A201-1963, Art. 40
65094	School District No. 65 R v. Universal Sur. Co., 178 Neb. 746, 135 N.W.2d 232 (1965)	
	II:	A201-1963, Art. 20
	II:	A201-1963, Art. 25
	II:	A201-1963, Art. 38
	III:	A311-1963, Labor & Material Payment Bond
65095	Schultz & Lindsay Construction Co. v. Erickson, 352 F.2d 425 (8th Cir. 1965)	
	III:	A201-1963, Art. 27
65096	Schutt Construction Co. v. United States, 353 F.2d 1018 (Ct. Cl. 1965)	
	III:	A201-1963, Art. 16
65097	1700 Ocean Avenue Corp. v. G B R Associates, 354 F.2d 993 (9th Cir. 1965)	
	III:	B131-1963, Art. 2
65098	Smith, Hinchman & Grylls Associates v. River Rouge Public Building Authority, 374 Mich. 514, 132 N.W.2d 682 (1965)	
	III:	B131-1963, Art. 2

65099 Southern Motels Investment Corp. v. Tower Contracting Co., 174 So. 2d 852 (La. Ct. App. 1965)

    I: A201-1963, Art. 20
    I: A201-1963, Art. 38
    I: A201-1963, Art. 39
    I: A201-1963, Art. 40

65100 S.S. Silberblatt, Inc. v. United States, 353 F.2d 545 (5th Cir. 1965)

    III: A201-1963, Art. 24
    III: A201-1963, Art. 37
    III: A311-1963, Labor & Material Payment Bond

65101 State v. Bob Eldridge Construction Co., 397 S.W.2d 7 (Mo. Ct. App. 1965)

    III: A101-1963, Art. 5

65102 Stevens v. Fanning, 59 Ill. App. 2d 285, 207 N.E.2d 136 (1965)

    II: B131-1963, Art. 6

65103 Strudell Asphalt, Inc. v. Bernstein, 29 Wis. 2d 184, 138 N.W.2d 209 (1965)

    I: A201-1963, Art. 40

65104 Sun Insurance Co. v. Diversified Engineers, Inc., 240 F. Supp. 606 (D. Mont. 1965)

    III: A311-1963, Labor & Material Payment Bond

65105 Tibbetts Contracting Corp. v. O & E Contracting Co., 15 N.Y.2d 324, 206 N.E.2d 340, 258 N.Y.S.2d 400 (1965)

    III: A201-1963, Art. 21
    III: A201-1963, Art. 22

65106 Trapani v. Parish of Jefferson, 180 So. 2d 850 (La. Ct. App. 1965)

    III: A201-1963, Art. 36

65107 Tri State Insurance Co. v. United States, 340 F.2d 542 (8th Cir. 1965)

    III: A311-1963, Labor & Material Payment Bond

65108 Uhlhorn v. Reid, 398 S.W.2d 169 (Tex. Civ. App. 1965)

    III: A201-1963, Art. 15

III:	A201-1963, Art. 16
III:	A311-1963, Labor & Material Payment Bond
III:	A401-1963, Art. 5

65109 United States v. Continental Casualty Co., 245 F. Supp. 871 (E.D. La. 1965)

    III: A311-1963, Labor & Material Payment Bond

65110 United States *ex rel.* A. & J. Freidman Supply Co. v. M.S.I. Corp., 350 F.2d 285 (2d Cir. 1965)

    III: A311-1963, Labor & Material Payment Bond

65111 United States v. Peter Kiewit Sons' Co., 345 F.2d 879 (8th Cir. 1965)

    III: A201-1963, Art. 12
    III: A201-1963, Art. 40

65112 United States v. Walsh, 240 F. Supp. 1019 (N.D.N.Y. 1965)

    III: A311-1963, Labor & Material Payment Bond

65113 United States v. Western Contracting Corp. 341 F.2d 383 (8th Cir. 1965)

    III: A311-1963, Labor & Material Payment Bond

65114 Van Cor, Inc. v. American Casualty Co., 417 Pa. 408, 208 A.2d 267 (1965)

    III: A311-1963, Labor & Material Payment Bond

65115 Verzella v. Caste Bros., Inc., 207 Pa. Super. 74, 215 A.2d 264 (1965)

    III: A107-1963, Art. 9
    III: A201-1963, Art. 20

65116 Wagner v. Fireman's Fund Ins. Co., 352 F.2d 410 (10th Cir. 1965)

    III: A311-1963, Labor & Material Payment Bond

65117 Walker v. Paramount Engineering Co., 353 F.2d 445 (6th Cir. 1965)

    III: A201-1963, Art. 24
    III: A201-1963, Art. 32

65118 Wallace Process Piping Co. v. Martin-Marietta Corp., 251 F. Supp. 411 (E.D. Va. 1965)

    III: A201-1963, Art. 15

III: A201-1963, Art. 37

65119 W.F. Thompson Construction Co. v. Southeastern Palm Beach County Hospital District, 174 So. 2d 410 (Fla. Dist. Ct. App. 1965)

III: A311-1963, Labor & Material Payment Bond

65120 William A. Smith Contracting Co. v. West Central Texas Municipal Water District, 344 F.2d 470 (5th Cir. 1965)

III: A201-1963, Art. 39
III: A201-1963, Art. 40

65121 Wingate Construction Co. v. Schweizer Dipple, Inc., 419 Pa. 74, 213 A.2d 275 (1965)

III: A201-1963, Art. 40

65122 Wittenberg Engineering & Construction Co. v. Liberty Mutual Insurance Co., 390 S.W.2d 877 (Ky. 1965)

III: A201-1963, Art. 27

65123 Wunderlich Contracting Co. v. United States, 351 F.2d 956 (Ct. Cl. 1965)

III: A201-1963, Art. 15
III: A201-1963, Art. 16
III: A201-1963, Art. 18
III: A201-1963, Art. 31

65124 Younker Brothers v. Standard Construction Co., 241 F. Supp. 17 (S.D. Iowa 1965)

I: A201-1963, Art. 31
I: A201-1963, Art. 39

66001 Ace Stone, Inc. v. Township of Wayne, 89 N.J. Super. 482, 215 A.2d 560 (App. Div. 1965), *rev'd,* 47 N.J. 431, 221 A.2d 515 (1966)

III: A101-1963, Art. 2
III: A107-1963, Art. 2
III: A201-1963, Art. 18

66002 Algernon Blair, Inc. v. National Sur. Corp., 222 Ga. 672, 151 S.E.2d 724 (1966)

III: A401-1963, Art. 4

66003 American Radiator & Standard Sanitary Corp. v. Maryland Casualty Co., 258 F. Supp. 6 (D.P.R. 1966)

    III: A311-1963, Labor & Material Payment Bond

66004 Anthony Muratore Contracting Co. v. Frouge Construction Co., 26 A.D.2d 832, 273 N.Y.S.2d 933 (1966)

    III: A201-1963, Art. 40

66005 Arrow Contractors Equipment Co. v. Siegel, 68 Ill. App. 2d 447, 216 N.E.2d 181 (1966)

    III: A311-1963, Labor & Material Payment Bond

66006 Baker & Ford Co. v. United States *ex rel.* Urban Plumbing & Heating Co., 363 F.2d 605 (9th Cir. 1966)

    III: A401-1963, Art. 5

66007 Beacon Plaza Shopping Center, Inc. v. Tri-Cities Construction & Supply Co., 2 Mich. App. 415, 140 N.W.2d 531 (1966)

    I: A101-1963, Art. 1

66008 Bergman v. Parker, 216 A.2d 581 (D.C. 1966)

    III: A107-1963, Art. 11
    III: A201-1963, Art. 23
    III: A201-1963, Art. 31

66009 Board of Educ. v. A. Barbaresi & Son, 25 A.D.2d 855, 269 N.Y.S.2d 823 (1966)

    III: A201-1963, Art. 12
    III: A201-1963, Art. 25

66010 Borough of Nanty-Glo v. Fireman's Fund Ins. Co., 250 F. Supp. 329 (W.D. Pa. 1966)

    III: A311-1963, Labor & Material Payment Bond

66011 Bushman Construction Co. v. Conner, 260 F. Supp. 779 (D. Colo. 1966)

    II: A311-1963, Labor & Material Payment Bond

66012 Casale v. August Bohl Contracting Co., 26 A.D.2d 974, 275 N.Y.S.2d 140 (1966)

    III: A201-1963, Art. 22

66013 Chillum-Adelphi Volunteer Fire Department, Inc. v. Button & Goode, Inc., 242 Md. 509, 219 A.2d 801 (1966)

    I: A201-1963, Art. 18
    I: A201-1963, Art. 40

66014 City of Albany v. Oxford Construction Co., 221 Ga. 872, 148 S.E.2d 324 (1966)

    III: A401-1963, Art. 5

66015 Consolidated Electric Co. v. United States, 355 F.2d 437 (9th Cir. 1966)

    III: A201-1963, Art. 37
    III: A311-1963, Labor & Material Payment Bond

66016 Construction Service Co. v. United States, 357 F.2d 973 (Ct. Cl. 1966)

    III: A201-1963, Art. 16

66017 Continental Casualty Co. v. C. O. Brand, Inc., 355 F.2d 969 (5th Cir. 1966)

    III: A311-1963, Labor & Material Payment Bond

66018 Continental Casualty Co. v. Hartford Accident & Indemnity Co., 243 Cal. App. 2d 445, 52 Cal. Rptr. 438 (1966)

    III: A311-1963, Labor & Material Payment Bond

66019 Cook v. Superior Court, 240 Cal. App. 2d 880, 50 Cal. Rptr. 81 (1966)

    III: A107-1963, Art. 19
    III: A201-1963, Art. 40

66020 Davis Acoustical Corp. v. National Sur. Corp., 27 A.D.2d 624, 275 N.Y.S.2d 925 (1966)

    III: A201-1963, Art. 15
    III: A201-1963, Art. 16

66021 Delhi Pipeline Corp. v. Lewis, Inc., 408 S.W.2d 295 (Tex. Civ. App. 1966)

    III: A107-1963, Art. 10

1966   **CASES**

66022   Dormitory Authority v. Span Electric Corp., 18 N.Y.2d 114, 218 N.E.2d 693, 271 N.Y.S.2d 983 (1966)

          III: A201-1963, Art. 40

66023   Forest Electric Corp. v. State, 52 Misc. 2d 215, 275 N.Y.S.2d 917 (Ct. Cl. 1966)

          III: A201-1963, Art. 35
          III: A201-1963, Art. 38

66024   Frouge Corp. v. New York Housing Auth., 26 A.D.2d 269, 273 N.Y.S.2d 657 (1966)

          III: A201-1963, Art. 40

66025   Fuller Industries, Inc. v. R. Terry Blazier & Son, 188 So. 2d 2 (Fla. Dist Ct. App. 1966)

          I: A311-1963, Labor & Material Payment Bond

66026   General Accident & Fire Assurance Corp. v. New Era Corp., 138 Ind. App. 349, 213 N.E.2d 329 (1966)

          III: A201-1963, Art. 27

66027   G.H. & J.T. Kelly, Inc. v. Torson Electric Co., 51 Misc. 2d 655, 273 N.Y.S.2d 694 (1966)

          III: A201-1963, Art. 40

66028   (UNASSIGNED)

66029   Giuliani Construction Co. v. School District, 207 Pa. Super. 498, 217 A.2d 793 (1966)

          III: A101-1963, Art. 6
          III: A107-1963, Art. 1

66030   Gordy v. United Pacific Insurance Group, 243 Cal. App. 2d 445, 52 Cal. Rptr. 438 (1966)

          III: A311-1963, Performance Bond
          III: A311-1963, Labor & Material Payment Bond

66031   Harrington v. McCarthy, 420 P.2d 790 (Idaho 1966)

          I: A107-1963, Art. 8

66032 H.B. Zachry Co. v. Travelers Indem. Co., 262 F. Supp. 237 (N.D. Tex. 1966)

    III: A401-1963, Art. 1

66033 Henger Co. v. Doctors' North Roads Building, Inc., 409 S.W.2d 489 (Mo. Ct. App. 1966)

    II: B131-1963, Art. 2

66034 Herre Bros. v. Rhoads, 208 Pa. Super. 357, 223 A.2d 486 (1966)

    III: A111-1963, Art. 6
    III: A111-1963, Art. 8

66035 H.L.C. & Associates Construction Co. v. United States, 367 F.2d 586 (Ct. Cl. 1966)

    III: A201-1963, Art. 25

66036 Holdam v. Middlesex Supply, Inc., 355 F.2d 122 (1st Cir. 1966)

    III: A201-1963, Art. 38

66037 Hol-Gar Manufacturing Corp. v. United States, 360 F.2d 634 (Ct. Cl. 1966)

    III: A201-1963, Art. 15
    III: A201-1963, Art. 16

66038 Honewell, Inc. v. Babcock, 68 Wash. 2d 239, 412 P.2d 511 (1966)

    I: A311-1963, Labor & Material Payment Bond

66039 *In re* Wilaka Construction Co., 17 N.Y.2d 195, 216 N.E.2d 696, 269 N.Y.S.2d 697 (1966)

    III: A201-1963, Art. 15
    III: A201-1963, Art. 16
    III: A201-1963, Art. 40

66040 Jacka v. Ouachita Parish School Board, 249 La. 223, 186 So. 2d 571 (1966)

    III: B131-1963, Art. 2
    III: B131-1963, Art. 3

66041 Jackson v. John F. Beasley Construction Co., 76 Ill. App. 2d 282, 222 N.E.2d 209 (1966)

    II: A201-1963, Art. 38

66042   Jackson v. Sam Finley, Inc., 366 F.2d 148 (5th Cir. 1966)

    III: A201-1963, Art. 15
    III: A201-1963, Art. 16
    III: A201-1963, Art. 37

66043   J.A. Jones Constr. Co. v. Lawrence Bros. 57 Tenn. App. 415, 419 S.W.2d 186 (1966)

    III: A311-1970, Labor & Material Payment Bond

66044   J.G. Watts Construction Co. v. United States, 355 F.2d 573 (Ct. Cl. 1966)

    III: A201-1963, Art. 16

66045   John E. Branagh & Sons v. Witcosky, 242 Cal. App. 2d 835, 51 Cal. Rptr. 844 (1966)

    III: A201-1963, Art. 27
    III: A201-1963, Art. 31

66046   Johnson v. Darin & Armstrong, Inc., 68 Ill. App. 2d 420, 216 N.E.2d 231 (1966)

    III: A201-1963, Art. 27

66047   Joseph F. Egan, Inc. v. City of New York, 17 N.Y.2d 90, 268 N.Y.S.2d 301, 215 N.E.2d 490 (1966)

    III: A107-1963, Art. 8
    III: A201-1963, Art. 15
    III: A201-1963, Art. 16

66048   Kobus v. Formfit Co., 35 Ill.2d 533, 221 N.E.2d 633 (1966)

    I: A107-1963, Art. 7
    I: A107-1963, Art. 8
    I: A107-1963, Art. 9
    I: A107-1963, Art. 18

66049   La Salle Iron Works, Inc. v. Largen, 410 S.W.2d 87 (Mo. 1966)

    III: A311-1963, Labor & Material Payment Bond

66050 L.A. Wenger Contracting Co. v. Temple Emanu-El, 49 Misc. 2d 189, 267 N.Y.S.2d 21 (Sup. Ct. 1966)

    I: A201-1963, Art. 40

66051 Layrite Concrete Products, Inc. v. H. Halvorsen, Inc., 68 Wash. 2d 70, 411 P.2d 405 (1966)

    III: A311-1963, Labor & Material Payment Bond

66052 Legette v. Pittman, 268 N.C. 292, 150 S.E.2d 420 (1966)

    III: A201-1963, Art. 20

66053 Main Cornice Works, Inc. v. National Union Fire Insurance Co., 258 F. Supp. 377 (S.D. Cal. 1966)

    III: A201-1963, Art. 23

66054 Manitt Construction Corp. v. J.S. Plumbing & Heating Corp., 50 Misc. 2d 502, 270 N.Y.S.2d 716 (Sup. Ct. 1966)

    III: A201-1963, Art. 40

66055 McDaniel v. Ashton-Mardian Co., 357 F.2d 511 (9th Cir. 1966)

    III: A201-1963, Art. 15
    III: A201-1963, Art. 16
    III: A401-1963, Art. 1
    III: A401-1963, Art. 5

66056 Merritt-Chapman & Scott Corp. v. Pennsylvania Turnpike Commission, 261 F. Supp. 1 (M.D. Pa. 1966)

    III: A201-1963, Art. 16
    III: A201-1963, Art. 40

66057 Midtown Bank v. Travelers Indem. Co., 366 F.2d 459 (5th Cir. 1966)

    II: A311-1963, Labor & Material Payment Bond

66058 Mike Bradford & Co. v. Gulf States Steel Co., 184 So. 2d 911 (Fla. Dist. Ct. App. 1966)

    II: A107-1963, Art. 19

66059 Motorists Mutual Insurance Co. v. Jones, 9 Ohio Misc. 113, 223 N.E.2d 381 (C.P. Lake County 1966)

    I: A107-1963, Art. 15

66060 Murray v. Fishman Construction Co., 241 Md. 538, 217 A.2d 357 (1966)

    I: A107-1963, Art. 10

66061 Nelson v. Hagen, 146 N.W.2d 873 (N.D. 1966)

    III: A311-1963, Labor & Material Payment Bond

66062 New Amsterdam Casualty Co. v. Bettes, 407 S.W.2d 301 (Tex. Civ. App. 1966)

    I: A311-1963, Labor & Material Payment Bond

66063 Nickell v. United States, 355 F.2d 73 (10th Cir. 1966)

    III: A201-1963, Art. 33
    III: A311-1963, Labor & Material Payment Bond

66064 Noland Co. v. West End Realty Corp., 206 Va. 938, 147 S.E.2d 105 (1966)

    I: A311-1963, Labor & Material Payment Bond

66065 Nordenstrom v. Swedberg, 143 N.W.2d 848 (N.D. 1966)

    II: A201-1963, Art. 40
    II: A401-1963, Art. 5

66066 Olin Mathieson Chemical Corp. v. J.J. Wuellner & Sons, 72 Ill. App. 2d 488, 218 N.E.2d 823 (1966)

    III: A201-1963, Art. 29

66067 O'Neal Steel Co. v. Leon C. Miles, Inc., 187 So. 2d 19 (Miss. 1966)

    I: A311-1963, Labor & Material Payment Bond

66068 Pacella Brothers v. Metropolitan Dist., 259 F. Supp. 715 (D. Conn. 1966)

    III: A107-1963, Art. 12
    III: A201-1963, Art. 26

66069 P & M Construction Co. v. Hammond Ventures, Inc., 3 Mich App. 306, 142 N.W.2d 468 (1966)

    III: A201-1963, Art. 38

66070 Patent Scaffolding Co. v. Standard Oil Co., 68 Ill. App. 2d 29, 215 N.E.2d 1 (1966)

    III: A201-1963, Art. 27

66071 Perlis & Sons v. Peacock Construction Co., 222 Ga. 723, 152 S.E.2d 390 (1966)

    I: A101-1963, Art. 5

66072 Pettinelli Electric Co. v. William A. Berbusse, Jr., Inc., 25 A.D.2d 736, 268 N.Y.S.2d 951 (1966)

    III: A401-1963, Art. 5

66073 Pittsburgh Des Moines Steel Co. v. American Sur. Co., 365 F.2d 412 (10th Cir. 1966)

    III: A401-1963, Art. 5

66074 Plowden & Roberts, Inc. v. Conway, 192 So. 2d 528 (Fla. Dist. Ct. App. 1966)

    I: A201-1963, Art. 22

66075 Race Co. v. Oxford Hall Contracting Corp., 25 A.D.2d 665, 268 N.Y.S.2d 175 (1966)

    III: A107-1963, Art. 1
    III: A107-1963, Art. 19

66076 Radiation Technology, Inc. v. United States, 366 F.2d 1003 (Ct. Cl. 1966)

    III: A201-1963, Art. 22

66077 Reliance Insurance Co. v. Colbert, 365 F.2d 530 (D.C. Cir. 1966)

    III: A311-1963, Performance Bond

66078 Rexroth & Rexroth, Inc. v. General Gas Co., 242 Cal. App. 2d 363, 52 Cal. Rptr. 505 (1966)

    III: A311-1963, Labor & Material Payment Bond

66079 Rhoads v. Nasco, 242 Md. 723, 219 A.2d 387 (1966)

      III: A107-1963, Art. 10
      III: A201-1963, Art. 22

66080 Richards Contracting Co. v. Fullmer Bros., 18 Utah 2d 177, 417 P.2d 755 (1966)

      III: A201-1963, Art. 15
      III: A201-1963, Art. 16
      III: A401-1963, Art. 5

66081 Robbins v. Perini Corp., 220 A.2d 737 (N.H. 1966)

      III: A201-1963, Art. 15

66082 Robert E. Lee & Co. v. Commission of Public Works, 284 S.C. 84, 149 S.E.2d 55 (1966)

      III: A201-1963, Art. 16
      III: A201-1963, Art. 25

66083 Roberts v. Fortune Homes, Inc., 240 Cal. App. 2d 238, 49 Cal. Rptr. 429 (1966)

      III: A107-1963, Art. 19
      III: A201-1963, Art. 40

66084 Rockland Bleach & Dye Works Co. v. H.J. Williams Corp., 242 Md. 375, 219 A.2d 48 (1966)

      III: A107-1963, Art. 6
      III: A201-1963, Art. 12

66085 School District No. 46 v. Del Bianco, 68 Ill. App. 2d 145, 215 N.E.2d 25 (1966)

      I: B131-1963, Art. 13

66086 Seaboard Sur. Co. v. United States, 355 F.2d 139 (9th Cir. 1966)

      III: A201-1963, Art. 18
      III: A201-1963, Art. 31
      III: A311-1963, Labor & Material Payment Bond

66087 Shell Oil Co. v. Hercules Constr. Co., 74 Ill. App. 2d 166, 219 N.E.2d 392 (1966)

    III: A201-1963, Art. 27

66088 Siegel v. Haver, 4 Ariz. 119, 417 P.2d 928 (1966)

    III: B131-1963, Art. 3
    III: B131-1963, Art. 8

66089 (UNASSIGNED)

66090 South Texas Building Co. v. Ideal Engineering, Inc., 402 S.W.2d 292 (Tex. Civ. App. 1966)

    III: A201-1963, Art. 38

66091 Stadel v. Granger Brothers, 4 Mich. App. 250, 144 N.W.2d 609 (1966)

    I: A107-1963, Art. 1

66092 State Department of Highways v. A & G Excavating Co., 421 P.2d 309 (Alaska 1966)

    III: A201-1963, Art. 15
    III: A201-1963, Art. 39

66093 State Highway Dept. v. Hewitt Contracting Co., 221 Ga. 621, 146 S.E.2d 632 (1966)

    III: A201-1963, Art. 16

66094 State v. Dabson, 217 A.2d 497 (Del. 1966)

    III: A107-1963, Art. 12

66095 Tassinari v. Chaney, 187 So. 2d 376 (Fla. Dist. Ct. App. 1966)

    I: A401-1963, Art. 4
    I: A401-1963, Art. 5

66096 Tepper Realty Co. v. Mosaic Tile Co., 259 F. Supp. 688 (S.D.N.Y. 1966)

    III: A201-1963, Art. 1
    III: A201-1963, Art. 40

66097 Terry Contracting Inc. v. State, 51 Misc. 2d 545, 273 N.Y.S.2d (Ct. Cl. 1966)

    III: A201-1963, Art. 25

66098 Teufel v. Wienir, 68 Wash. 2d 31, 411 P.2d 151 (1966)

    I: A201-1963, Art. 20

66099 T.F. Scholes, Inc. v. United States, 357 F.2d 963 (Ct. Cl. 1966)

    III: A201-1963, Art. 15
    III: A201-1963, Art. 16

66100 Transamerica Insurance Co. v. Yonkers Contracting Co., 49 Misc. 2d 512, 267 N.Y.S.2d 669 (Sup. Ct. 1966)

    III: A311-1963, Performance Bond
    III: A401-1963, Art. 5

66101 Unitec Corp. v. Beatty Safeway Scaffold Co., 358 F.2d 470 (9th Cir. 1966)

    III: A201-1963, Art. 27

66102 United Contractors v. United States, 368 F.2d 585 (Ct. Cl. 1966)

    III: A201-1963, Art. 15

66103 United States *ex rel.* A. Teichert & Son v. Anchor Contractors, Inc., 257 F. Supp. 474 (N.D. Cal. 1966)

    III: A311-1963, Labor & Material Payment Bon

66104 United States *ex rel.* Chemetron Corp. v. George A. Fuller Co., 250 F. Supp. 649 (D. Mont. 1966)

    III: A201-1963, Art. 37
    III: A311-1963, Labor & Material Payment Bond

66105 United States *ex rel.* Lincoln Electric Products Co. v. Greene Electrical Service, Inc., 252 F. Supp. 324 (E.D.N.Y. 1966)

    III: A311-1963, Labor & Material Payment Bond

66106 United States *ex rel.* Powers Regulator Co. v. Farina Construction Corp., 261 F. Supp. 278 (D. Mass. 1966)

    III: A311-1963, Labor & Material Payment Bond

66107 United States *ex rel.* Shields, Inc. v. Citizens & Southern National Bank, 367 F.2d 473 (4th Cir. 1966)

    III: A401-1963, Art. 5

66108 United States Fidelity & Guar. Co. v. Hamilton & Spiegel, Inc., 241 Md. 133, 215 A.2d 735 (1966)

    III: A201-1963, Art. 25
    III: A311-1963, Labor & Material Payment Bond
    III: A401-1963, Art. 5

66109 United States Fidelity & Guar. Co. v. James F. O'Neil Co., 254 F. Supp. 140 (E.D. La. 1966)

    III: A401-1963, Art. 5

66110 United States v. Utah Construction & Mining Co., 384 U.S. 394, 86 S. Ct. 1545, 16 L. Ed. 2d 642 (1966)

    III: A201-1963, Art. 15
    III: A201-1963, Art. 16
    III: A201-1963, Art. 18
    III: A201-1963, Art. 40

66111 Vendrigo Highlands, Inc. v. Security Insurance Co., 240 Cal. App. 2d 527, 49 Cal. Rptr. 736 (1966)

    III: A311-1963, Performance Bond

66112 Wellborn Plumbing & Heating Co. v. Randolph County Board of Education, 268 N.C. 85, 150 S.E.2d 65 (1966)

    II: A201-1963, Art. 12
    II: A201-1963, Art. 38
    II: A201-1963, Art. 39

66113 Westmoreland Hospital Ass'n v. Westmoreland Construction Co., 423 Pa. 255, 223 A.2d 681 (1966)

    II: A201-1963, Art. 40

66114 Wilson Contracting Co. v. State, 224 A.2d 396 (Del. 1966)

    III: A201-1963, Art. 18

III: A201-1963, Art. 39

66115   W.L. Walker Co. v. Green Manor Construction Co., 3 Conn. Cir. Ct. 637, 222 A.2d 813 (1966)

III: A401-1963, Art. 5

66116   W.R. Ferguson, Inc. v. William A. Berbusse, Jr., Inc., 216 A.2d 876 (Super. Ct. Del. 1966)

I: A201-1963, Art. 40
I: A401-1963, Art. 5

66117   Yarber v. Morey, 403 S.W.2d 166 (Tex. Civ. App. 1966)

I: B131-1963, Art. 12
I: B131-1963, Art. 13

66118   Merritt-Chapman & Scott Corp. v. United States, 355 F.2d 622 (Ct. Cl. 1966)

III: A201-1963, Art. 16

66119   G & N Construction Co. v. Kirpatovsky, 181 So. 2d 664 (Fla. 1966)

I: A201-1963, Art. 22
I: A201-1963, Art. 31
I: A201-1963, Art. 40

67001   A.D. Hoppe Co. v. Fred Katz Construction Co., 249 Cal. App. 2d 154, 57 Cal. Rptr. 95 (1967)

III: A401-1963, Art. 5

67002   A.E. Ottaviano, Inc. v. State, 52 Misc. 2d 998, 227 N.Y.S.2d 538 (Ct. Cl. 1967)

III: A201-1963, Art. 25

67003   American Fire & Casualty Co. v. Charles Sales Corp., 203 So. 2d 670 (Fla. Dist. Ct. App. 1967)

II: A311-1970, Labor & Material Payment Bond

67004   Ashworth v. Glover, 20 Utah 2d 85, 433 P.2d 315 (1967)

I: A201-1967, Art. 1, Para. 1.3

67005 Baker Pool Co. v. Bennett, 411 S.W.2d 335 (Ct. App. Ky. 1967)

    III: A201-1963, Art. 20

67006 Baltimore Contractors, Inc. v. Dupree, 352 Mass. 83, 223 N.E.2d 702 (1967)

    II: A201-1963, Art. 18

67007 Bank of Broadway v. General Aluminum Door & Entrance Co., 80 Ill. App. 2d 15, 225 N.E.2d 134 (1967)

    III: A201-1963, Art. 15
    III: A201-1963, Art. 16

67008 Ben Contruction Co. v. Sanitary Authority, 424 Pa. 40, 225 A.2d 886 (1967)

    III: A201-1963, Art. 39
    III: A201-1963, Art. 40

67009 Call v. Alcan Pacific Co., 251 Cal. App. 2d 442, 59 Cal. Rptr. 763 (1967)

    III: A201-1963, Art. 22

67010 Cass-Warner Corp. v. Brickman, 126 Vt. 329, 229 A.2d 309 (1967)

    II: A111-1967, Art. 6

67011 Caton Ridge, Inc. v. Bonnett, 245 Md. 268, 225 A.2d 853 (1967)

    III: A201-1963, Art. 40

67012 Chiappisi v. Granger Contracting Co., 352 Mass. 174, 223 N.E.2d 924 (1967)

    I: A201-1963, Art. 16
    I: A201-1963, Art. 37

67013 City of Salinas v. Souza & McCue Construction Co., 66 Cal. 2d 217, 424 P.2d 921, 57 Cal. Rptr. 337 (1967)

    III: A201-1963, Art. 15

67014 Clifton D. Mayhew, Inc. v. George A. Fuller Co., 248 Md. 1, 234 A.2d 509 (1967)

    III: A401-1963, Art. 1
    III: A401-1963, Art. 5

67015 Colorado Real Estate Development, Inc. v. Sternberg, 164 Colo. 63, 433 P.2d 341 (1967)

    II: B131-1963, Art. 11

67016 Connolly v. Asheville Contract Co., 269 N.C. 423, 152 S.E.2d 433 (1967)

    III: A201-1963, Art. 15
    III: A201-1963, Art. 16

67017 Continental Casualty Co. v. Wilson-Avery, Inc., 115 Ga. App. 793, 156 S.E.2d 152 (1967)

    III: A107-1966, Art. 9
    III: A107-1966, Art. 18
    III: A201-1967, Art. 2, Para. 2.2

67018 Continental Casualty Co. v. Public Building Authority, 381 F.2d 10 (5th Cir. 1967)

    II: A201-1967, Art. 9, Para. 9.4
    II: A201-1967, Art. 9, Para. 9.7

67019 Corrigan Co. Mechanical Contractors v. Fleischer, 423 S.W.2d 2209 (Mo. 1967)

    III: A101-1967, Art. 4

67020 Davis v. Nelson-Deppe, Inc., 424 P.2d 733 (Idaho 1967)

    III: A201-1963, Art. 12

67021 Dinschel v. United States Gypsum Co., 83 Ill. App. 2d 466, 288 N.E.2d 106 (1967)

    I: A201-1967, Art. 5, Para. 5.1
    I: A201-1967, Art. 5, Para. 5.2
    I: A201-1967, Art. 5, Para. 5.3
    I: A201-1967, Art. 5, Para. 5.4
    I: A201-1967, Art. 10, Para. 10.1
    I: A201-1967, Art. 10, Para. 10.2
    I: A201-1967, Art. 10, Para. 10.3
    II: A201-1967, Art. 4, Para. 4.4

67022   E. H. Morrill Co. v. State, 51 Cal. Rptr. 205 (1966), *vacated,* 65 Cal. 2d 787, 423 P.2d 551, 56 Cal. Rptr. 479 (1967)

    III: A201-1963, Art. 15

67023   E. O. Dorsch Electric Co. v. Knickerbocker Construction Co., 417 S.W.2d 936 (Mo. 1967)

    III: A201-1967, Art. 9, Para. 9.3

67024   Ezon v. Faulkner Construction Co., 422 S.W.2d 568 (Tex. 1967)

    III: A101-1967, Art. 4

67025   Fair Pavillions, Inc., v. First National City Bank 19 N.Y.2d 512, 281 N.Y.S.2d 23 (1967)

    III: A201-1967, Art. 14, Para. 14.2

67026   First National Realty Corp. v. Warren-Ehret Co., 247 Md. 652, 233 A.2d 811 (1967)

    I: A107-1966, Art. 25

67027   Giarratano v. Weitz Co., 259 Iowa 1292, 147 N.W.2d 824 (1967)

    I: A201-1963, Art. 12
    I: A201-1963, Art. 37

67028   Graybar Electric Co. v. St. Paul Fire & Marine Ins. Co., 195 So. 2d 82 (Miss. 1967)

    I: A311-1963, Labor & Material Payment Bond

67029   H.B. Deal Construction Co. v. Labor Discount Center, Inc., 418 S.W.2d 940 (Mo. 1967)

    I: A201-1967, Art. 12, Para. 12.1
    I: A201-1967, Art. 12, Para. 12.3

67030   Healy v. Brewster, 251 Cal. App. 2d 541, 59 Cal. Rptr. 752 (1967)

    III: A201-1963, Art. 15
    III: A401-1963, Art. 5

67031 Hendrick Construction Co. v. C.E. Thurston & Sons, Inc., 207 Va. 803, 153 S.E.2d 204 (1967)

    II: A201-1963, Art. 36

67032 Honolulu Roofing Co. v. Felix, 49 Haw. 578, 426 P.2d 298 (1967)

    III: A311-1963, Labor & Material Payment Bond

67033 Independent Consolidated School District No. 24 v. Carlstrom, 277 Minn. 117, 151 N.W.2d 784 (1967)

    I: A107-1966, Art. 23
    I: A201-1963, Art. 20
    I: A201-1963, Art. 25
    I: A201-1963, Art. 31
    I: A201-1967, Art. 4, Para. 4.5
    I: A201-1967, Art. 7, Para. 7.4
    I: A201-1967, Art. 9, Para. 9.4
    I: A201-1967, Art. 13, Para. 13.2

67034 Integrated, Inc. v. Alex Fergusson Electrical Contractors, 250 Cal. App. 2d 287, 58 Cal. Rptr. 503 (1967)

    III: A401-1963, Art. 5

67035 Jen-Mar Construction Co. v. Brown, 247 Cal. App. 2d 564, 55 Cal. Rptr. 832 (1967)

    III: A311-1963, Performance Bond

67036 Joseph Davis, Inc. v. Merritt-Chapman & Scott Corp., 27 A.D.2d 114, 276 N.Y.S.2d 479 (1967)

    III: A201-1963, Art. 39

67037 J.P. Greathouse Steel Erectors, Inc. v. Blount Brothers Construction Co., 374 F.2d 324 (D.C. Cir. 1967)

    II: A401-1967, Art. 13

67038 Kahn v. Prahl, 414 S.W.2d 269 (Mo. 1967)

    I: A101-1963, Art. 1

67039 La Vale Plaza, Inc. v. R. S. Noonan, 378 F.2d 569 (3d Cir. 1967)

    I: A201-1967, Art. 7, Para. 7.10

67040 Le Blanc, Inc. v. Gulf Bitulithic Co., 412 S.W.2d 86 (Tex. Civ. App. 1967)

    II: A201-1963, Art. 12
    II: A201-1963, Art. 20
    II: A201-1963, Art. 34
    II: A401-1963, Art. 5

67041 (UNASSIGNED)

67042 (UNASSIGNED)

67043 Macomber v. State, 250 Cal. App. 2d 391, 58 Cal. Rptr. 393 (1967)

    III: A201-1963, Art. 15
    III: A201-1963, Art. 16
    III: A201-1963, Art. 39

67044 Markley v. Beagle, 59 Cal. Rptr. 809, 429 P.2d 129 (1967)

    II: A401-1967, Art. 11
    III: A201-1963, Art. 12
    III: A201-1963, Art. 27

67045 Martinson v. Brooks Equipment Leasing Inc., 36 Wis. 2d 209, 152 N.W.2d 849 (1967)

    II: A107-1966, Art. 11
    II: A107-1966, Art. 22
    II: A201-1967, Art. 4, Para. 4.7
    II: A201-1967, Art. 12, Para. 12.1
    II: A201-1967, Art. 12, Para. 12.2

67046 McDonald v. Filice, 252 Cal. App. 2d 613, 60 Cal. Rptr. 832 (1967)

    II: B131-1967, Art. 5
    II: B131-1967, Art. 8

67047 Mesker Brothers Iron Co. v. Burke Brothers, 425 Pa. 130, 228 A.2d 773 (1967)

    III: A201-1967, Art. 2, Para. 2.2

67048	\multicolumn{2}{l}{Midwestern Realty Corp. v. City of Grandview, 416 S.W.2d 35 (Mo. 1967)}
	II:	A201-1967, Art. 4, Para. 4.18
67049	\multicolumn{2}{l}{Miller v. DeWitt, 37 Ill. 2d 273, 226 N.E.2d 630 (1967)}

- **67048** Midwestern Realty Corp. v. City of Grandview, 416 S.W.2d 35 (Mo. 1967)

  II: A201-1967, Art. 4, Para. 4.18

- **67049** Miller v. DeWitt, 37 Ill. 2d 273, 226 N.E.2d 630 (1967)

  I: A101-1963, Art. 1
  I: A101-1963, Art. 6
  I: A201-1963, Art. 12
  I: A201-1963, Art. 13
  I: A201-1963, Art. 14
  I: A201-1963, Art. 15
  I: A201-1963, Art. 19
  I: A201-1963, Art. 38
  I: A201-1963, Art. 39
  III: B131-1963, Art. 3

- **67050** Montgomery County Bd. of Educ. *ex rel.* Carrier Corp. v. Glassman Construction Co., 225 A.2d 448 (Md. 1967)

  I: A311-1963, Labor & Material Payment Bond

- **67051** Montgomery Ward & Co. v. Robert Cagle Building Co., 265 F. Supp. 469 (S.D. Tex. 1967)

  I: A201-1967, Art. 1, Para. 1.2
  I: A201-1967, Art. 4, Para. 4.2
  I: A201-1967, Art. 4, Para. 4.11
  I: A201-1967, Art. 8, Para. 8.3

- **67052** Morrison Supply Co. v. M.W. Hamilton & Co., 411 S.W.2d 790 (Tex. Civ. App. 1967)

  I: A101-1963, Art. 1
  I: A101-1963, Art. 3
  I: A201-1963, Art. 1
  I: A201-1963, Art. 36
  I: A201-1963, Art. 37

- **67053** National Union Fire Insurance Co. v. Denver Brick & Pipe Co., 162 Colo. 519, 427 P.2d 861 (1967)

  II: A201-1963, Art. 37

| | II: | A311-1963, Labor & Material Payment Bond |

67054 Nauman v. Harold K. Beecher & Associates, 19 Utah 2d 101, 426 P.2d 621 (1967)

	III:	A201-1963, Art. 12
	III:	A201-1963, Art. 38
	III:	B131-1963, Art. 3

67055 New Amsterdam Casualty Co. v. Texas Industries, Inc., 414 S.W.2d 914 (Tex. 1967)

| | III: | A311-1963, Labor & Material Payment Bond |

67056 Norman Co. v. County of Nassau, 27 A.D.2d 936, 278 N.Y.S.2d 719 (1967)

| | III: | A201-1963, Art. 18 |

67057 Rausch v. Julius B. Nelson & Sons, 149 N.W.2d 1 (Minn. 1967)

| | I: | A201-1963, Art. 12 |

67058 Reynolds v. Long, 115 Ga. App. 182, 154 S.E.2d 299 (1967)

| | I: | B131-1967, Art. 1 |
| | I: | B131-1967, Art. 6 |

67059 Rosser v. Hochwalt, 12 Ohio App. 2d 129, 231 N.E.2d 334 (1967)

| | I: | B131-1967, Art. 11 |

67060 Sherwood Village Cooperative A v. Had-Ten Estates Corp., 53 Misc. 2d 27, 277 N.Y.S.2d 877 (Sup. Ct. 1967)

| | III: | A201-1963, Art. 40 |

67061 Skezas v. Safeway Steel Products, Inc., 85 Ill. App. 2d 295, 229 N.E.2d 718 (1967)

| | III: | A107-1966, Art. 18 |
| | III: | A201-1967, Art. 10, Para. 10.2 |

67062 Southern Construction Co. v. Housing Auth., 189 So. 2d 454 (La. Ct. App. 1966), *modified,* 250 La. 569, 197 So. 2d 628 (1967)

| | III: | A201-1963, Art. 18 |

67063 Stahelin v. Board of Educ., 87 Ill. App. 2d 28, 230 N.E.2d 465 (1967)

    III: A201-1967, Art. 12, Para. 12.1
    III: A201-1967, Art. 12, Para. 12.2
    III: A201-1967, Art. 12, Para. 12.3

67064 Teig & Johnson v. Speelmon, 261 Iowa 210, 153 N.W.2d 818 (1967)

    I: B131-1967, Art. 6

67065 Thorgaard Plumbing & Heating Co. v. County of King, 71 Wash. 2d 126, 426 P.2d 828 (1967)

    I: A201-1963, Art. 40

67066 United States v. Henry, 427 P.2d 584 (Alaska 1967)

    III: A201-1963, Art. 12

67067 Walker v. Wittenberg, Delony & Davidson, Inc., 242 Ark. 97, 412 S.W.2d 621 (1967)

    I: A201-1963, Art. 12
    I: A201-1963, Art. 38

67068 Walsh v. International Fidelity Insurance Co., 55 Misc. 2d 565, 285 N.Y.S.2d 327 (1967)

    III: A311-1970, Performance Bond

67069 Watson Lumber Co. v. Guennewig, 79 Ill. App. 2d 377, 226 N.W.2d 270 (1967)

    III: A107-1963, Art. 1
    III: A107-1963, Art. 8
    III: A201-1963, Art. 2
    III: A201-1963, Art. 15
    III: A201-1963, Art. 16

67070 Wes-Julian Construction Corp. v. Commonwealth, 351 Mass. 588, 223 N.E.2d 72 (1967)

    III: A201-1963, Art. 18

67071 Westerhold v. Carroll, 419 S.W.2d 73 (Mo. 1967)

    III: A201-1963, Art. 2, Para. 2.2

67072 Wiggens Construction Co. v. Joint School District No. 3, 35 Wis. 2d 632, 151 N.W.2d 642 (1967)

    I: A201-1967, Art. 12, Para. 12.1
    I: A201-1967, Art. 12, Para. 12.3

67073 Wright v. Cecil A. Mason Construction Co., 15 Ga. App. 729, 155 S.E.2d 725 (1967)

    I: A201-1963, Art. 7, Para. 7.10

67074 Wunderlich v. State, 50 Cal. Rptr. 151 (1966), *vacated,* 65 Cal. 2d 777, 423 P.2d 545, 56 Cal. Rptr. 473 (1967)

    III: A201-1963, Art. 15

68001 Aetna Insurance Co. v. Hellmuth, Obata & Kassabaum, Inc., 392 F.2d 472 (8th Cir. 1968)

    II: A201-1967, Art. 2, Para. 2.2

68002 Albre Marble & Tile Co. v. Goverman, 353 Mass. 546, 233 N.E.2d 533 (1968)

    III: A201-1967, Art. 2, Para. 2.2

68003 Amerson v. Christman, 261 Cal App. 2d 811, 68 Cal. Rptr. 378 (1968)

    III: A107-1966, Art. 11
    III: A107-1966, Art. 23
    III: A107-1966, Art. 25

68004 Atlantic States Construction Co. v. Drummond, 251 Md. 77, 246 A.2d 251 (1968)

    III: A401-1967, Art. 12

68005 Begner-Seitel Lumber Co. v. Insurance Co. of N. Am., 31 A.D. 2d 575, 294 N.Y.S.2d 931 (1968)

    I: A311-1970, Labor & Material Payment Bond

68006 Branna Construction Co. v. West Allegheny School Authority, 430 Pa. 214, 242 A.2d 244 (1968)

    III: A201-1967, Art. 12, Para. 12.1

CASES

68007 Byler v. Great American Insurance Co., 395 F.2d 273 (10th Cir. 1968)

    I: A111-1967, Art. 1
    I: A111-1967, Art. 2
    I: A111-1967, Art. 3
    I: A111-1967, Art. 9
    I: A111-1967, Art. 14
    I: A111-1967, Art. 15
    I: A111-1967, Art. 17

68008 Carl Weissman & Sons v. St. Paul Fire & Marine Ins. Co., 152 Mont. 310, 448 P.2d 740 (1968)

    I: A201-1967, Art. 4, Para. 4.4
    I: A201-1967, Art. 4, Para. 4.5
    I: A201-1967, Art. 5, Para. 5.3
    I: A201-1967, Art. 7, Para. 7.5
    I: A401-1967, Art. 2
    I: A401-1967, Art. 11

68009 City National Bank v. Chitwood Construction Co., 210 So. 2d 235 (Fla. Dist. Ct. App. 1968)

    II: A201-1967, Art. 4, Para. 4.13

68010 City of Midland v. Waller, 430 S.W.2d 473 (Tex. 1968)

    I: A201-1967, Art. 2, Para. 2.2
    I: A201-1967, Art. 9, Para. 9.4
    I: A201-1967, Art. 9, Para. 9.7
    I: A201-1967, Art. 13, Para. 13.2

68011 Distefano v. Hall, 263 Cal. App. 2d 380, 69 Cal. Rptr. 691 (1968)

    I: A111-1967, Art. 6

68012 Dixie Container Corp. v. Dale, 273 N.C. 624, 160 S.E.2d 708 (1968)

    I: A201-1967, Art. 10, Para. 10.1
    I: A201-1967, Art. 10, Para. 10.2
    I: A201-1967, Art. 10, Para. 10.3

68013 Eller & Heyward, Inc. v. Jackson, 117 Ga. App. 753, 162 S.E.2d 238 (1968)

    I: A401-1967, Art. 2

68014 Famous Builders, Inc. v. Bolin, 264 Cal. App. 2d 37, 70 Cal. Rptr. 17 (1968)

    II: A107-1966, Art. 17

68015 Ferrante Equipment Co. v. Charles Simkin & Sons, 30 A.D.2d 525, 290 N.Y.S.2d 246 (1968)

    III: A311-1970, Labor & Material Payment Bond

68016 Fresco v. Anthony R. Delisi, General Contractor, Inc., 103 Ill. App. 2d 457, 243 N.E.2d 871 (1968)

    II: A401-1967, Art. 11

68017 Hartford Accident & Indemnity Co. v. Long, 245 A.2d 800 (Del. Ch. 1968)

    I: A201-1967, Art. 7, Para. 7.2

68018 Heiskell v. H.C. Enterprise, Inc., 244 Ark. 857, 429 S.W.2d 71 (1968)

    I: A201-1967, Art. 2, Para. 2.2
    I: A201-1967, Art. 7, Para. 7.4
    I: A201-1967, Art. 7, Para. 7.10
    I: A201-1967, Art. 10, Para. 10.2
    I: A201-1967, Art. 12, Para. 12.1
    I: A201-1967, Art. 12, Para. 12.2
    I: A201-1967, Art. 12, Para. 12.3
    I: A201-1967, Art. 13, Para. 13.2

68019 Home Furniture, Inc. v. Brunzell Construction Co., 84 Nev. 309, 440 P.2d 398 (1968)

    II: A201-1967, Art. 2, Para. 2.2
    II: A201-1967, Art. 4, Para. 4.2
    II: A201-1967, Art. 4, Para. 4.3
    II: A201-1967, Art. 4, Para. 4.9
    II: A201-1967, Art. 7, Para. 7.8

68020 International Erectors v. Wilhoit Steel Erectors & Rental Service, 400 F.2d 465 (5th Cir. 1968)

    III: A401-1967, Art. 2
    III: A401-1967, Art. 3
    III: A401-1967, Art. 11

1968 CASES

68021 J.H. Jenkins Contractor, Inc. v. City of Denham Springs, 216 So. 2d 549 (La. Ct. App. 1968)

    III: A201-1967, Art. 2, Para. 2.2

68022 (UNASSIGNED)

68023 Klar v. Park Construction Co., 281 Minn. 323, 161 N.W.2d 839 (1968)

    III: A107-1966, Art. 22
    III: A201-1967, Art. 12, Para. 12.1
    III: A201-1967, Art. 12, Para. 12.

68024 Knickerbocker Roofing & Paving Co. v. Mendius Associates, 95 Ill. App. 2d 96, 237 N.E.2d 813 (1968)

    III: A201-1967, Art. 4, Para. 4.18

68025 Larsen v. J. I. Case Co., 37 Wis. 2d 516, 155 N.W.2d 666 (1968)

    II: A401-1967, Art. 11

68026 Lincoln-Sudbury Regional School District v. Frasca Construction Corp., 354 Mass. 22, 234 N.E.2d 759 (1968)

    I: A201-1967, Art. 7, Para. 7.10

68027 Logan v. Aetna Casualty & Sur. Co., 208 So. 2d 131 (Fla. Dist. Ct. App. 1968)

    II: A311-1970, Performance Bond
    II: A311-1970, Labor & Material Payment Bond

68028 Meirowsky v. Phipps, 222 Tenn. 112, 432 S.W.2d 885 (1968)

    I: A107-1966, Art. 15
    I: A201-1967, Art. 7, Para. 7.10

68029 M.E. Kraft Excavating & Grading Co. v. Barac Construction Co., 279 Minn. 278, 156 N.W.2d 748 (1968)

    III: A107-1966, Art. 17
    III: A201-1967, Art. 9, Para. 9.7

68030 (UNASSIGNED)

68031 Mid-Atlantic Construction Corp. v. Guido, 30 A.D.2d 232, 291 N.Y.S.2d 501 (1968)

        I: A201-1967, Art. 5, Para. 5.3
        I: A201-1967, Art. 7, Para. 7.10
        I: A401-1967, Art. 1

68032 Morris J. Liebergott & Associate v. Investment Building Corp., 249 Md. 584, 241 A.2d 138 (1968)

        III: C131-1967, Art. 1

68033 New England Structures, Inc. v. Loranger, 354 Mass. 62, 234 N.E.2d 888 (1968)

        III: A201-1967, Art. 14, Para. 14.2

68034 Pacific Insurance Co. v. Wilbanks, 283 Ala. 1, 214 So. 2d 279 (1968)

        I: A201-1967, Art. 7, Para. 7.5

68035 Pan American Realty Trust v. Twenty One Kings, Inc., 297 F. Supp. 143 (D.V.I 1968)

        I: B131-1967, Art. 2
        I: B131-1967, Art. 5

68036 Ramonas v. Kerelis, 102 Ill. App. 2d 468, 243 N.E.2d 711 (1968)

        I: A107-1966, Art. 15
        I: A107-1966, Art. 17
        I: A107-1966, Art. 23

68037 Robert Chuckrow Construction Co. v. Horowitz Bros., 30 A.D 2d 789, 291 N.Y.S.2d 921 (1968)

        III: A201-1967, Art. 12, Para. 12.1
        III: A201-1967, Art. 12, Para. 12.2

68038 Ross v. Danter Associates, 102 Ill. App. 2d 354 (1968)

        III: A201-1967, Art. 9, Para. 9.2
        III: A201-1967, Art. 9, Para. 9.3

68039	Ruckman & Hansen, Inc. v. Delaware River & Bay Authority, 244 A.2d 277 (Del. 1968)	
	III:	A201-1967, Art. 7, Para. 7.10
68040	R. W. Mier Construction Co. v. Concrete Contractors, Inc., 165 Colo. 563, 440 P.2d 788 (1968)	
	II:	A201-1967, Art. 12, Para. 12.2
68041	St. Paul Fire & Marine Ins. Co. v. James I. Barnes Construction Co., 267 Cal. App. 2d 931, 73 Cal. Rptr. 618 (1968)	
	III:	A311-1970, Performance Bond
68042	Second Congregation Society v. Hugh Stubbins & Associates, 108 N.H. 446, 237 A.2d 673 (1968)	
	I:	B131-1967, Art. 1
	I:	B131-1967, Art. 11
68043	Sisters of Mercy v. Mead & Mount Construction Co., 165 Colo. 447, 439 P.2d 733 (1968)	
	II:	A201-1967, Art. 7, Para. 7.10
	II:	A201-1967, Art. 12, Para. 12.1
68044	Sorensen v. Robert N. Ewing, General Contractor, 8 Ariz. App. 540, 448 P.2d 110 (1968)	
	I:	A401-1963, Art. 7
68045	Soundwall Construction Corp. v. Moncarol Construction Corp., 56 Misc. 2d 892, 290 N.Y.S.2d 363 (Sup. Ct. 1968)	
	II:	A201-1967, Art. 14, Para. 14.2
68046	Southwest Engineering Co. v. Reorganized School District R-9, 434 S.W.2d 743 (Mo. 1968)	
	I:	A201-1967, Art. 8, Para. 8.3
68047	Spiezio v. Commonwealth Edison Co., 91 Ill. App. 2d 392, 235 N.E.2d 323 (1968)	
	III:	A201-1967, Art. 10, Para. 10.1
	III:	A201-1967, Art. 10, Para. 10.2

III: A201-1967, Art. 10, Para. 10.3

68048 State v. Johnson, 83 S.D. 444, 160 N.W.2d 637 (1968)

III: A311-1970, Performance Bond

68049 Trinity Universal Insurance Co. v. Barlite, Inc., 424 S.W.2d 303 (Tex. 1968)

III: A201-1967, Art. 4, Para. 4.4
III: A311-1970, Labor & Material Payment Bond

68050 Universal Builders, Inc. v. Moon Motor Lodge, 430 Pa. 550, 244 A.2d 10 (1968)

I: A201-1967, Art. 8, Para. 8.3

68051 Walnut Creek Electric v. Reynolds Construction Co., 263 Cal. App. 2d 511, 69 Cal. Rptr. 667 (1968)

II: A201-1967, Art. 2, Para. 2.2
II: A401-1967, Art. 11

68052 Warner Construction Co. v. Blue Diamond Co., 429 S.W.2d 912 (Tex. 1968)

II: A201-1967, Art. 13, Para. 13.2

68053 Washington Parish Police Jury v. Belcher & Sons, Inc., 215 So. 2d 849 (La. Ct. App. 1968)

III: A201-1967, Art. 4, Para. 413

68054 Welch-Eckman Construction Co. v. Vancouver Plywood Co., 213 So. 2d 134 (La. Ct. App. 1968)

III: A201-1967, Art. 12, Para. 12.1
III: A201-1967, Art. 12, Para. 12.2
III: A201-1967, Art. 12, Para. 12.3

68055 Williams v. Sullivan, Long & Haggarty, Inc., 209 So. 2d 618 (Miss. 1968)

III: A201-1967, Art. 2, Para. 2.2
III: A201-1967, Art. 4, Para. 4.16
III: A201-1967, Art. 6, Para. 6.4
III: A201-1967, Art. 12, Para. 12.1
III: A201-1967, Art. 12, Para. 12.2

69001	A. J. Wolfe Co. v. Baltimore Contractors, Inc., 355 Mass. 361, 244 N.E.2d 717 (1969)	
	III:	A401-1967, Art. 5
69002	Aluminum Co. of America v. Commercial Contracting Co., 438 S.W.2d 853 (Tex. 1969)	
	II:	A201-1967, Art. 4, Para. 4.4
	II:	A201-1967, Art. 4, Para. 4.18
69003	A R C Electrical Construction Co. v. George A. Fuller Co., 24 N.Y.2d 99, 247 N.E.2d 111 (1969)	
	III:	A401-1967, Art. 6
	III:	A401-1967, Art. 12
69004	Argo Construction Co. v. County of Los Angeles, 271 Cal. App. 2d 54, 76 Cal. Rptr. 361 (1969)	
	II:	A201-1967, Art. 7, Para. 7.10
69005	A. Sangivanni & Sons v. F. M. Floryan & Co., 158 Conn. 467, 262 A.2d 159 (1969)	
	III:	A201-1967, Art. 7, Para. 7.9
	III:	A201-1967, Art. 7, Para. 7.10
69006	Baker v. Keller Construction Co., 219 So. 2d 569 (La. Ct. App. 1969)	
	I:	A201-1967, Art. 2, Para. 2.2
69007	Ballou v. Basic Construction Co, 407 F.2d 1137 (4th Cir. 1969)	
	II:	A201-1967, Art. 2, Para. 2.2
69008	Baton Rouge Contracting Co. v. West Hatchie Drainage District, 304 F. Supp. 580 (N.D. Miss. 1969)	
	III:	A201-1967, Art. 12, Para. 12.2
69009	Brook-Lea Country Club v. Hanover Insurance Co., 61 Misc. 2d 896, 306 N.Y.S.2d 780 (1969)	
	I:	A311-1970, Bid Bond

69010 Connor v. Thompson Construction & Development Co., 166 N.W.2d 109 (Iowa 1969)

    II: A107-1966, Art. 21
    II: A201-1967, Art.11, Para. 11.3

69011 Consumers Construction Co. v. American Motorists Insurance Co., 118 Ill. App. 2d 441, 254 N.E.2d 265 (1969)

    III: A107-1966, Art. 11
    III: A201-1967, Art. 4, Para. 4.18

69012 (UNASSIGNED)

69013 Corbett v. Brown, 32 A.D.2d 27, 299 N.Y.S.2d 219 (1969)

    III: A201-1967, Art. 11, Para. 11.1

69014 Deel v. United States Steel Corp., 105 Ill. App. 2d 170, 245 N.E.2d 109 (1969)

    II: A201-1967, Art. 4, Para. 4.1

69015 Diamond Homes, Inc. v. Bodovinac, 42 Wis. 2d 683, 168 N.W.2d 75 (1969)

    III: A107-1966, Art. 11
    III: A201-1967, Art. 4, Para. 4.7

69016 Duff v. Hoffman, 63 Pa. 191 (1969)

    II: A201-1967, Art. 32

69017 Fehlhaber Corp. v. Unicorn Management Corp., 32 A.D.2d 367, 302 N.Y.S.2d 98 (1969)

    II: A201-1967, Art. 5, Para. 5.3
    II: A201-1967, Art. 5, Para. 5.4
    II: A401-1967, Art. 1

69018 Fields v. Lawter Chemicals, Inc., 113 Ill. App. 2d 320, 252 N.E.2d 120 (1969)

    II: A201-1967, Art. 4, Para. 4.18

69019 Flour Mills of America Inc. v. American Steel Building Co., 449 P.2d 861 (Okla. 1969)

    I: A201-1967, Art. 2, Para.2.2

	I:	A201-1967, Art. 8, Para. 8.3
	I:	A201-1967, Art. 9, Para. 9.4
	I:	A201-1967, Art. 9, Para. 9.5
	I:	A201-1967, Art. 9, Para. 9.7
	I:	A201-1967, Art. 12, Para. 12.1
	I:	A201-1967, Art. 12, Para. 12.2
	I:	A201-1967, Art. 13, Para. 13.2

69020 Forcum-Lannon, Inc. v. Wells, 438 S.W.2d 508 (Ky. 1969)

    III: A401-1963, Art. 11

69021 Framingham Trust Co. v. Gould-National Batteries, Inc., 307 F. Supp. 1008 (D. Mass. 1969)

	I:	A201-1967, Art. 4, Para. 4.10
	I:	A201-1967, Art. 4, Para. 4.13
	I:	A201-1967, Art. 5, Para. 5.1
	I:	A201-1967, Art. 5, Para. 5.2
	I:	A201-1967, Art. 5, Para. 5.3
	I:	A201-1967, Art. 5, Para. 5.4
	I:	A201-1967, Art. 7, Para. 7.9
	I:	A201-1967, Art. 9, Para. 9.2
	I:	A201-1967, Art. 9, Para. 9.3
	I:	A201-1967, Art. 9, Para. 9.4
	I:	A201-1967, Art. 9, Para. 9.5
	I:	A201-1967, Art. 9, Para. 9.7
	I:	A201-1967, Art. 14, Para. 14.2

69022 Frank J. Rooney, Inc. v. Charles W. Ackerman, Inc., 219 So. 2d 110 (Fla. Dist. Ct. App. 1969)

	I:	A201-1967, Art. 5, Para. 5.3
	I:	A201-1967, Art. 5, Para. 5.4
	I:	A401-1967, Art. 7

69023 (UNASSIGNED)

69024 Hammen v. Hansen & Werhane, Inc., 105 Ill. App. 2d 428, 244 N.E.2d 841 (1969), *rev'd,* 44 Ill. 2d 76, 254 N.E.2d 464 (1969)

    III: A311-1970, Performance Bond

	III:	A311-1970, Labor & Material Payment Bon

69025 Harrison F. Blades, Inc. v. Jarman Memorial Hospital Building Fund, 109 Ill. App. 2d 224, 248 N.E.2d 289 (1969)

      III: A201-1967, Art. 2, Para. 2.2
      III: A201-1967, Art. 7, Para. 7.10
      III: A201-1967, Art. 8, Para. 8.3

69026 Harrison v. American Fire & Casualty Co., 266 So. 2d 28 (Fla. Dist. Ct. App. 1969)

      III: A311-1970, Performance Bond

69027 Hetherington Letter Co. v. O.F. Paulson Construction Co., 171 N.W.2d 264 (Iowa 1969)

      I: A111-1967, Art. 8

69028 Home Indemnity Co. v. Daniels Construction Co., 285 Ala. 68, 228 So. 2d 824 (1969)

      I: A311-1970, Labor & Material Payment Bond

69029 J. Brodie & Son v. George A. Fuller Co., 16 Mich. App. 137, 167 N.W.2d 886 (1969)

      I: A107-1966, Art. 15
      I: A201-1967, Art. 7, Para. 7.10

69030 Johson v. Iowa Rice Dryer Inc., 226 So. 2d 194 (La. Ct. App. 1969)

      I: B131-1967, Art. 10

69031 Kaspar v. Clinton-Jackson Corp., 118 Ill. App. 2d 364, 254 N.E.2d 826 (1969)

      III: A107-1966, Art. 11
      III: A201-1967, Art. 4, Para. 4.7
      III: A201-1967, Art. 4, Para. 4.18
      III: A201-1967, Art. 10, Para. 10.2

69032 Lesser Towers, Inc. v. Roscoe-Ajax Construction Co., 271 Cal. App. 2d 675, 77 Cal. Rptr. 100 (1969)

      I: A111-1967, Art. 8
      I: A111-1967, Art. 15

I:	A111-1967, Art. 16
I:	A201-1967, Art. 2, Para. 2.2
I:	A201-1967, Art. 4, Para. 4.2
I:	A201-1967, Art. 7, Para. 7.4
I:	A201-1967, Art. 7, Para. 7.10
I:	A201-1967, Art. 8, Para. 8.3
I:	A201-1967, Art. 9, Para. 9.5
I:	A201-1967, Art. 14, Para. 14.2

69033 Lincoln-Sudbury Regional School District v. Brandt-Jordan Corp., 356 Mass. 114, 248 N.E.2d 477 (1969)

    III: A311-1970, Bid Bond

69034 Lindbrook Construction, Inc. v. Mukilteo School District No. 6, 76 Wash. 2d 710, 458 P.2d 1 (1969)

I:	A201-1967, Art. 2, Para. 2.2
I:	A201-1967, Art. 4, Para. 4.2
I:	A201-1967, Art. 4, Para. 4.3
I:	A201-1967, Art. 4, Para. 4.9
I:	A201-1967, Art. 12, Para. 12.1
I:	A201-1967, Art. 12, Para. 12.2

69035 Maloney v. Oak Builders, Inc., 224 So. 2d 161 (La. Ct. App. 1969)

    II: A201-1967, Art. 4, Para. 4.18

69036 Mayeux v. J.B. Talley Construction Co., 228 So. 2d 536 (La. Ct. App. 1969)

    III: A201-1967, Art. 4, Para. 4.18

69037 McKay Construction Co. v. Board of Educ., 33 A.D.2d 862, 306 N.Y.S.2d 52 (1969)

II:	A201-1967, Art. 12, Para. 12.1
II:	A201-1967, Art. 12, Para. 12.2
II:	A201-1967, Art. 12, Para. 12.3
III:	A201-1967, Art. 7, Para. 7.9

69038 Merchants & Farmers Bank v. McClendon, 220 So. 2d 815 (Miss. 1969)

I:	A201-1967, Art. 5, Para. 5.3
I:	A201-1967, Art. 5, Para. 5.4

             I: A201-1967, Art. 7, Para. 7.2

69039   Met Food Corp. v. M. Eisenberg & Bros., 59 Misc. 2d 498, 299 N.Y.S.2d 696 (1969)

             III: A201-1967, Art. 7, Para. 7.10

69040   Michalowski v. Richter Spring Corp., 112 Ill. App. 2d 451, 251 N.E.2d 299 (1969)

             II: B131-1967, Art. 6

69041   Namerow v. Colangelo, 6 Conn. Cir. Ct. 9, 262 A.2d 187 (1969)

             III: A201-1967, Art. 7, Para. 7.9

69042   New Orleans Unity Society v. Standard Roofing Co., 224 So. 2d 60 (La. Ct. App. 1969)

             III: A201-1967, Art. 4, Para. 4.18

69043   Nixon Construction Co. v. Downs, 441 S.W.2d 284 (Tex. 1969)

             III: A401-1963, Art. 11

69044   Pantaleo v. Gamm, 106 Ill. App. 2d 116, 245 N.E.2d 618 (1969)

             I: A201-1967, Art. 10, Para. 10.2
             I: A401-1967, Art. 1

69045   Parker v. Theubet, 1 Wash. App. 285, 461 P.2d 9 (1969)

             I: B131-1967, Art. 6

69046   Park Imperial, Inc. v. E. L. Farmer Construction Co., 9 Ariz. App. 511, 454 P.2d 181 (1969)

             I: A201-1967, Art. 2, Para. 2.2
             I: A201-1967, Art. 7, Para. 7.10

69047   Paulus v. City of St. Louis, 446 S.W.2d 144 (Mo. 1969)

             I: A201-1967, Art. 3, Para. 3.2
             I: A201-1967, Art. 4, Para. 4.7
             III: A201-1967, Art. 4, Para. 4.3
             III: A201-1967, Art. 10, Para. 10.2

69048 Perschke v. Westinghouse Electric Corp., 111 Ill. App. 2d 33, 249, N.E.2d 698 (1969)

    III: A201-1967, Art. 4, Para. 4.18
    III: A201-1967, Art. 7, Para. 7.2
    III: A401-1967, Art. 11

69049 Pit Construction Co. v. Holman, 438 S.W.2d 662 (Tex. 1969)

    III: A201-1967, Art. 10, Para. 10.2

69050 Pittsfield, General Hospital v. Markus, 355 Mass. 519, 246 N.E.2d 444 (1969)

    II: B131-1967, Art. 11

69051 Pylon, Inc. v. Olympic Insurance Co., 271 Cal. App. 2d 643, 77 Cal. Rptr. 72 (1969)

    III: A201-1967, Art. 4, Para. 4.18

69052 Sanders v. American Casualty Co., 269 Cal. App. 2d 306, 74 Cal. Rptr. 634 (1969)

    II: A311-1970, Labor & Material Payment Bond

69053 Shalman v. Board of Educ., 31 A.D.2d 338, 297 N.Y.S.2d 1000 (1969)

    III: A201-1967, Art. 8, Para. 8.3

69054 Sisters of the Good Shepherd v. Quinn Construction Co., 225 So. 2d 225 (La. Ct. App. 1969)

    I: A201-1967, Art. 4, Para. 4.10
    I: A201-1967, Art. 5, Para. 5.1
    I: A201-1967, Art. 5, Para. 5.2
    I: A201-1967, Art. 5, Para. 5.4
    I: A201-1967, Art. 10, Para. 10.1
    I: A201-1967, Art. 10, Para. 10.2
    I: A201-1967, Art. 10, Para. 10.3

70001 A. A. Baxter Corp. v. Colt Industries, Inc., 10 Cal. App. 3d 144, 88 Cal. Rptr. 842 (1970)

    III: A201-1967, Art. 8, Para. 8.3

70002   A. A. Maycock, Inc. v. General Insurance Co., 24 Utah 2d 369, 472 P.2d 424 (1970)

    III: A311-1970, Performance Bond

70003   A & A Masonry Contractors, Inc. v. Howard Polinger, 259 Md. 199, 269 A.2d 566 (1970)

    II: A107-1966, Art. 8
    II: A201-1967, Art. 1, Para. 1.1
    II: A201-1967, Art. 12, Para. 12.2

70004   Adelphi Enterprises, Inc. v. Mirpa, Inc., 33 A.D.2d 1019, 307 N.Y.S.2d 978 (1970)

    II: A201-1967, Art. 7, Para. 7.10

70005   Aetna Casualty & Sur. Co. v. Aluminum Co. of America, 122 Ga. App. 324, 176 S.E.2d 654 (1970)

    III: A311-1970, Performance Bond

70006   Albano v. Western Construction Corp., 357 Mass. 647, 260 N.E.2d 212 (1970)

    III: A201-1967, Art. 4, Para. 4.5

70007   Andrews Fixture Co. v. Olin, 2 Wash. App. 774, 472 P.2d 420 (1970)

    III: A107-1966, Art. 11
    III: A201-1967, Art. 4, Para. 4.7

70008   Baker v. Pidgeon Thomas Co., 422 F.2d 744 (6th Cir. 1970)

    III: A201-1967, Art. 2, Para. 2.2
    III: A201-1967, Art. 4, Para. 4.3

70009   Ballwin Plaza Corp. v. H.B. Deal Construction Co., 462 S.W.2d 687 (Mo. 1970)

    III: A107-1966, Art. 23
    III: A201-1967, Art. 13, Para. 13.2

70010   Banner v. Town of Dayton, 474 P.2d 300 (Wyo. 1970)

    III: B131-1967, Art. 1

70011 Bethlehem Fabricators, Inc. v. British Overseas Airways Corp., 434 F.2d 840 (2d Cir. 1970)

    I: A201-1967, Art. 7, Para. 7.5

70012 Bickerstaff v. Frazier, 232 So. 2d 191 (Fla. 1970)

    II: A107-1966, Art. 15
    II: A201-1967, Art. 7, Para. 7.10
    II: A201-1967, Art. 9, Para. 9.4

70013 Bolo Corp. v. Homes & Son Construction Co., 105 Ariz. 343, 464 P.2d 788 (1970)

    III: A107-1966, Art. 15
    III: A201-1967, Art. 7, Para. 7.10

70014 Brown v. Cox, 459 S.W.2d 471 (Tex. Civ. App. 1970)

    I: A201-1967, Art. 12, Para. 12.2
    I: B131-1967, Art. 1
    I: B131-1967, Art. 6

70015 Carmichael v. Board of County Commissioners, 475 P.2d 387 (Okla. 1970)

    I: B131-1967, Art. 12

70016 Charles Burton Builders, Inc. v. L & S Construction Co., 260 Md. 66, 271 A.2d 534 (1970)

    III: A107-1966, Art. 9
    III: A107-1966, Art. 25
    III: A201-1967, Art. 2, Para. 2.2
    III: A201-1967, Art. 4, Para. 4.4
    III: A201-1967, Art. 9, Para. 9.7
    III: A201-1967, Art. 12, Para. 12.1
    III: A201-1967, Art. 13, Para. 13.2

70017 Chastain v. Atlanta Gas Light Co., 122 Ga. App. 90, 176 S.E.2d 487 (1970)

    II: A201-1967, Art. 2, Para. 2.2
    II: A201-1967, Art. 3, Para. 3.2
    III: B131-1967, Art. 1
    III: B131-1967, Art. 2

70018   Cianelli v. Levy, 6 Conn. Cir. Ct. 507, 276 A.2d 912 (1970)

        III: A201-1967, Art. 5, Para. 5.1

70019   D. H. Overmyer Co. v. Harbinson, 453 S.W.2d 368 (Tex. Civ. App. 1970)

        III: A107-1966, Art. 22
        III: A201-1967, Art. 12, Para. 12.1

70020   Dillon Properties, Inc. v. Minmar Builders, Inc., 257 Md. 274, 262 A.2d 740 (1970)

        I: A201-1967, Art. 2, Para. 2.2
        I: A201-1967, Art. 7, Para. 7.8
        I: A201-1967, Art. 13, Para. 13.1

70021   Douglas v. First National Realty Corp., 437 F 2d 666 (D.C. Cir 1970)

        I: B131-1967, Art. 3

70022   Drake, O'Mera & Associates v. American Testing & Engineering Corp., 459 S.W.2d 363 (Mo. 1970)

        III: A107-1966, Art. 11
        III: A201-1967, Art. 4, Para. 4.18

70023   Economy v. Frohme, 13 Ariz. App. 177, 474 P.2d 836 (1970)

        II: A107-1966, Art. 6

70024   (UNASSIGNED)

70025   Ferrante Equipment Co. v. Lasker-Goldman Corp., 26 A.D.2d 280, 309 N.Y.S.2d 913 (1970)

        III: A311-1970, Performance Bond

70026   Fischel & Taylor v. Grifton United Methodist Church, 9 N.C. App. 224, 175 S.E.2d 785 (1970)

        I: B131-1967, Art. 6
        I: B131-1967, Art. 12

70027   Florida v. Wesley Construction Co., 316 F. Supp. 490 (S.D. Fla. 1970)

        I: A201-1967, Art. 4, Para. 4.4

I:	A201-1967, Art. 5, Para. 5.1
I:	A201-1967, Art. 9, Para. 9.3

70028 Fowler v. A & A Co., 262 A.2d 344 (D.C. 1970)

III:	A201-1967, Art. 5, Para. 5.3
III:	A201-1967, Art. 7, Para. 7.4

70029 General Insurance Co. of America v. Commerce Hyatt House, 5 Cal. App. 3d 460, 85 Cal. Rptr. 317 (1970)

I:	A101-1967, Art. 4
I:	A201-1967, Art. 8, Para. 8.3
I:	A201-1967, Art. 12, Para. 12.2

70030 Grass Range High School District No. 27 v. Wallace Diteman, Inc., 155 Mont. 10, 465 P.2d 814 (1970)

II:	A107-1966, Art. 23
II:	A201-1967, Art. 13, Para. 13.2

70031 Gribaldo, Jacobs, Jones & Associates. v. Agrippina Versicherunges A.G., 91 Cal. Rptr. 6, 476 P.2d 406 (Cal. 1970)

III:	A201-1967, Art. 4, Para. 4.18

70032 Griffin v. Holiday Inns of America, 452 S.W.2d 517 (Tex. Civ. App. 1970)

III:	A201-1967, Art. 9, Para. 9.7

70033 Hall & Co. v. Continental Casualty Co., 34 A.D.2d 1028, 310 N.Y.S 2d 950 (Sup. Ct. 1970)

III:	A311-1970, Performance Bond

70034 Henry B. Byors & Sons, Inc. v. Board of Water Commissioners, 264 N.E.2d 657 (Mass. 1970)

III:	A201-1967, Art. 2, Para. 2.2

70035 Hochwalt v. Rosser, 26 Ohio Misc. 267, 271 N.E.2d 325 (1970)

I:	B131-1967, Art. 11
III:	A107-1966, Art. 15
III:	A201-1967, Art. 7, Para. 7.10

70036 Huxol v. Nickell, 206 Kan. 102, 476 P.2d 606 (1970)

    III: A401-1967, Art. 11

70037 In re National Equipment Rental, Ltd., 35 A.D.2d 132 314 N.Y.S.2d 838 (1970)

    II: A201-1967, Art. 7, Para. 7.10

70038 In re University of Chicago, 129 Ill. App. 2d 157, 262 N.E.2d 806 (1970)

    III: A201-1967, Art. 4, Para. 4.18
    III: A401-1967, Art. 11

70039 J.A. Thompson & Son v. Hawaii, 465 P.2d 148 (Haw. 1970)

    III: A201-1967, Art. 12, Para. 12.1

70040 J. Dunn & Sons v. Paragon Homes, 110 N.H. 215, 265 A.2d 5 (1970)

    III: A107-1966, Art. 15
    III: A201-1967, Art. 7, Para. 7.10

70041 John W. Johnson, Inc. v. Basic Construction Co., 292 F. Supp. 300 (D.D.C. 1968), aff'd, 429 F.2d 764 (D.C. Cir. 1970)

    III: A201-1967, Art. 2, Para. 2.2
    III: A201-1967, Art. 12, Para. 12.1
    III: A201-1967, Art. 12, Para. 12.2
    III: A201-1967, Art. 12, Para. 12.3
    III: A401-1967, Art. 11

70042 Joseph F. Hughes & Co., v. George H. Robinson Corp., 211 Va. 4, 175 S.E.2d 413 (1970)

    I: A311-1970, Labor & Material Payment Bond

70043 J. R. Meade & Co. v. Barrett & Co., 453 S.W.2d 632 (Mo. Ct. App. 1970)

    III: A311-1970, Performance Bond

70044 Kaiser v. Cyon Metal Products, Inc., 461 S.W.2d 893 (Mo. Ct. App. 1970)

    III: A401-1967, Art. 11

70045 Keith Adams & Associates v. Edwards, 3 Wash. App. 623, 477 P.2d 36 (1970)

    III: A201-1967, Art. 7, Para. 7.10

70046 (UNASSIGNED)

70047 Kenworth Northwest Sales & Service, Inc. v. Batts, 2 Wash. App. 424, 468 P.2d 469 (1970)

    I: A107-1966, Art. 3
    I: A107-1966, Art. 8
    I: A201-1967, Art. 1, Para. 1.1
    I: A201-1967, Art. 8, Para. 8.

70048 Kubby v. Crescent Steel, 105 Ariz 459, 466 P.2d 753 (1970)

    III: A107-1966, Art. 11
    III: A201-1967, Art. 4, Para. 4.5

70049 Lane Construction Corp. v. Vermont, 128 Vt. 421, 265 A.2d 441 (1970)

    III: A107-1966, Art. 18
    III: A201-1967, Art. 10, Para. 102

70050 L.B. Foster Co. v. Melbras-Manco, Inc., 34 A.D.2d 638, 310 N.Y.S.2d 76 (1970)

    III: A311-1970, Performance Bond

70051 Lewis v. Arboles Development Co., 8 Cal. App. 3d 812, 87 Cal. Rptr. 539 (1970)

    III: A107-1966, Art. 11
    III: A201-1967, Art. 4, Para. 4.7

70052 Limbach Co. v. George B. H. Macomber Co., 357 Mass. 475, 258 N.E.2d 548 (1970)

    III: A201-1967, Art. 5, Para. 5.3
    III: A401-1967, Art. 11

70053 Malott & Peterson Grundy, Inc. v. Reynolds Construction Co., 427 P.2d 701 (Colo. App. 1970)

    III: A201-1967, Art. 9, Para. 9.7

70054 McCann Construction Co. v. Joe Adams & Son, 458 S.W.2d 477 (Tex. Civ. App. 1970), *rev'd*, 475 S.W.2d 721 (Tex. 1971)

    III: A107-1966, Art. 11

III: A107-1966, Art. 18
III: A201-1967, Art. 4, Para. 4.10
III: A201-1967, Art. 4, Para. 4.18
III: A401-1967, Art. 11

[*Editor's Note:* For reversal by the Supreme Court of Texas, *see* case number 71052 *infra.*]

70055 Meares v. Nixon Constructon Co. 7 N.C. App. 614, 173 S.E.2d 593 (1970)

III: A401-1967, Art. 11

70056 Metal Service Corp. v. Industrial Electric Co., 253 S.C. 507, 171 S.E.2d 703 (1970)

I: A311-1970, Labor & Material Payment Bond

70057 Muth v. Leineke, 9 Cal. App. 3d 433, 88 Cal. Rptr. 1 (1970)

III: A107-1966, Art. 11
III: A201-1967, Art. 4, Para. 4.7

70058 New Pueblo Constructors, Inc. v. Lake Patagonia Recreation Association, 12 Ariz. App. 12, 467 P.2d 88 (1970)

III: A107-1966, Art. 9
III: A201-1967, Art. 2, Para. 2.2

70059 Nimke v. Intra-State, Inc., 34 A.D.2d 675, 301 N.Y.S.2d 462 (1970)

III: A311-1970, Performance Bond

70060 Northern Pacific Railway Co. v. Chemetron Corp., 2 Wash. App. 338, 467 P.2d 884 (1970)

II: A107-1966, Art. 11
II: A201-1967, Art. 4, Para. 4.18

70061 O. K. Johnson Electric, Inc., v. Hess-Martin Corp., 204 Kan. 478, 464 P.2d 206 (1970)

I: A201-1967, Art. 9, Para. 9.7
I: A401-1963, Art. 6
III: A201-1967, Art. 2, Para. 2.2
III: A401-1963, Art. 11

70062 Overby v. Barnett, 262 A.2d 604 (D.C. 1970)

    II: A107-1966, Art. 15
    II: A201-1967, Art. 7, Para. 7.10

70063 Pacific Employers Insurance Co. v. State, 91 Cal. Rptr. 273, 477 P.2d 129 (Cal. 1970)

    III: A311-1970, Performance Bond

70064 Parsons v. Amerada Hess Corp., 422 F.2d 610 (10th Cir. 1970)

    III: A201-1967, Art. 4, Para. 4.18
    III: A401-1967, Art. 11

70065 Pickens-Bond Construction Co. v. North Little Rock Electric Co., 249 Ark. 389, 459 S.W.2d 549 (1970)

    III: A107-1966, Art. 11
    III: A201-1967, Art. 4, Para. 4.18
    III: A401-1967, Art. 11

[*Editor's Note:* For subsequent appeal after remand, *see* case number 72073 *infra.*]

70066 Port City Construction Co. v. Adams & Douglas, Inc., 260 Md. 585, 73 A.2d 121 (1970)

    III: A201-1967, Art. 11, Para. 11.3
    III: A401-1967, Art. 11

70067 Providence Washington Insurance Co. v. Beck, 356 Mass. 741, 255 N.E.2d 601 (1970)

    II: A107-1966, Art. 25
    II: A201-1967, Art. 14, Para. 14.2

70068 Rao Electrical Equipment Co. v. MacDonald Engineering Co., 124 Ill. App. 2d 158, 260 N.E.2d 294 (1970)

    III: A401-1967, Art. 11

70069 Reber v. Chandler High School District No. 202, 13 Ariz. App. 133, 474 P.2d 852 (1970)

    I: A201-1967, Art. 2, Para. 2.2
    I: B131-1967, Art. 1

70070 Roulo v. Automobile Club of Michigan, 24 Mich. App. 32, 179 N.W.2d 712 (1970)

    II: A201-1967, Art. 5, Para. 5.1
    II: A201-1967, Art. 7, Para. 7.5

70071 St. Andrews Episcopal Day School v. Walsh Plumbing Co., 234 So. 2d 922 (Miss. 1970)

    I: A107-1966, Art. 23
    I: A201-1967, Art. 13, Para. 13.2

70072 Sanford Construction Co. v. Rosenblatt, 25 Ohio Misc. 99, 266 N.E.2d 267 (Ohio Mun. Ct. 1970)

    I: A107-1966, Art. 15
    I: A201-1967, Art. 7, Para. 7.10

70073 School District No. One v. Hastings, 11 Ariz. App. 522, 466 P.2d 395 (1970), *rev'd,* 106 Ariz. 175, 472 P.2d 44 (1970)

    III: B131-1967, Art. 3

70074 Sears, Roebuck & Co. v. Glenwall Co., 325 F. Supp. 86 (S.D.N.Y. 1970)

    I: A107-1966, Art. 15
    I: A201-1967, Art. 7, Para. 7.10

70075 Shafer & Miller v. Miami Heart Institute, 237 So. 2d 310 (Fla. 1970)

    II: A107-1966, Art. 11
    II: A201-1967, Art. 4, Para. 4.18

70076 Standley v. Egbert, 267 A.2d 365 (D.C. 1970)

    I: B131-1967, Art. 1
    I: B131-1967, Art. 3
    I: B131-1967, Art. 6
    I: B131-1967, Art. 8

70077 State *ex rel.* Nilsen v. Hoff, 3 Or. App. 398, 474 P.2d 11 (1970)

    II: A311-1970, Labor & Material Payment Bond

70078	State v. General Insurance Co. of America, 13 Cal. App. 3d 853, 96 Cal. Rptr. 744 (1970)	
	III:	A311-1970, Performance Bond
70079	Summit Construction Co. v. Yeager Garden Acres, Inc. 28 Colo. App. 110, 470 P.2d 870 (1970)	
	I:	A107-1966, Art. 11
	I:	A107-1966, Art. 23
	I:	A201-1967, Art. 4, Para. 4.5
	I:	A201-1967, Art. 13, Para. 13.2
70080	Teufel Construction Co. v. American Arbitration Ass'n, 3 Wash. App. 24, 472 P.2d 572 (1970)	
	II:	A201-1967, Art. 7, Para. 7.10
70081	Trader v. Grampp Builders, Inc., 263 A.2d 304 (Del. Super. Ct. 1970)	
	III:	A107-1966, Art. 11
	III:	A107-1966, Art. 23
	III:	A201-1967, Art. 4, Para. 4.3
	III:	A201-1967, Art. 4, Para. 4.5
	III:	A201-1967, Art. 13, Para. 13.2
	III:	A201-1967, Art. 13, Para. 13.3
70082	Tucci & Sons v. Carl T. Madsen, Inc., 1 Wash App. 1035, 467 P.2d 386 (1970)	
	II:	A401-1967, Art. 11
70083	Ulster Electric Supply Co. v. Maryland Casualty Co., 35 A.D.2d 309, 316 N.Y.S.2d 159 (1970)	
	III:	A311-1970, Performance Bond
70084	Uniroyal, Inc. v. A. Epstein & Sons, 428 F.2d 523 (7th Cir. 1970)	
	I:	A107-1966, Art. 15
	I:	A201-1967, Art. 7, Para. 7.10
70085	United States Fidelity & Guar. Co. v. Green, 34 A.D 2d 935, 311 N.Y.S.2d 779 (1970)	
	III:	A311-1970, Performance Bond

70086   United States v. Seckinger, 397 U.S. 203, 90 S. Ct. 880, 25 L. Ed. 2d 224 (1970)

        III: A201-1967, Art. 4, Para. 4.18

United States brought action against contractor for indemnity for judgment obtained against U.S. by subcontractor's employee for personal injuries.

The Supreme Court reversed the dismissal of the United States' complaint which had been affirmed in the Court of Appeals, and it remanded the case. In the construction contract between Seckinger Co. and the United States, an indemnification provision stated that the contractor "shall be responsible for all damages to persons or property that occur as a result of his fault or negligence." The Supreme Court agreed with the Court of Appeals that an indemnification provision could not be construed to allow a party to recover for its own negligence unless the court is firmly convinced that such an interpretation reflects the intention of the parties. The Supreme Court stated that the traditional reluctance of courts to allow indemnification for one's own negligence was particularly applicable to a situation in which there is a vast disparity in bargaining power and economic resources, as between the United States and government contractors.

The Court found that the most reasonable construction of the clause wa that Seckinger should indemnify the United States only to the extent of its own negligence.

In a footnote, the Court referred to the indemnification clause in A201 as an example of an indemnification clause that specifically describes the effect of the negligence of the indemnitee. The court declined to decide whether a clause designed to encompass indemnification for the indemnitee's negligence must include a "hold harmless" clause or must explicitly extend indemnification to injuries occasioned by the indemnitee's negligence.

70087   Vernali v. Centrella, 28 Conn. Supp. 476, 266 A.2d 200 (Super. Ct. 1970)

        III: A107-1966, Art. 11
        III: A201-1967, Art. 7, Para. 7.4
        III: A201-1967, Art. 13, Para. 13.3

70088   Walker v. Lytton Savings & Loan Ass'n, 2 Cal. App. 3d 152, 465 P.2d 497 (1970)

        III: B131-1967, Art. 8

70089   Wawak v. Stewart, 247 Ark. 1093, 449 S.W.2d 922 (1970)

        III: A107-1966, Art. 11
        III: A201-1967, Art. 4, Para. 4.5

70090	Weisz Trucking Co. v. Emil R. Wohl Construction, 13 Cal. App. 3d 256, 91 Cal. Rptr. 489 (1970)	
	III:	A311-1970, Performance Bond
70091	William B. Lucke, Inc. v. Spiegel, 131 Ill. App. 2d 532, 266 N.E.2d 504 (1970)	
	I:	A101-1967, Art. 3
	I:	A107-1966, Art. 3
	II:	A111-1967, Art. 6
	II:	A201-1967, Art. 7, Para. 7.10
	III:	A107-1966, Art. 15
	III:	B131-1967, Art. 11
70092	Wood-Hopkins Contracting Co. v. Masonry Contractors, Inc., 235 So. 2d 548 (Fla. 1970)	
	I:	A107-1966, Art. 11
	I:	A201-1967, Art. 4, Para. 4.5
	I:	A401-1967, Art. 11
70093	Wrobel v. Trapani, 129 Ill. App. 2d 306, 264 N.E.2d 240 (1970)	
	III:	A107-1966, Art. 11
	III:	A201-1967, Art. 4, Para. 4.18
	III:	A401-1967, Art. 11
70094	Warner Construction Corp. v. City of Los Angeles, 270 Cal. App. 2d 517, 76 Cal. Rptr. 60 (1969), *vacated,* 466 P.2d 996, 85 Cal. Rptr. 996 (Cal. 1970)	
	II:	A201-1967, Art. 3, Para. 3.2
	II:	A201-1967, Art. 12, Para. 12.1
71001	Acoustics, Inc. v. Hanover Insurance Co., 118 N.J. Super. 361, 287 A.2d 482 (1971)	
	II:	A201-1967, Art. 4, Para. 4.4
	III:	A311-1970, Labor & Material Payment Bond
71002	Acoustics, Inc. v. Trepte Construction Co., 14 Cal. App. 3d 887, 92 Cal. Rptr. 723 (1971)	
	II:	A201-1967, Art. 2, Para. 2.2
	II:	A201-1967, Art. 6, Para. 6.3

II:	A201-1967, Art. 12, Para. 12.1

71003 Amadens, Inc. v. State, 36 A.D 2d 873, 320 N.Y.S.2d 677 (1971)

II:	A201-1967, Art. 12, Para. 12.2

71004 American Insurance Co. v. Bateman, 125 Ga. App. 189, 186 S.E.2d 547 (1971)

III:	A201-1970, Art. 11, Para. 11.3

71005 American Mason's Supply Co. v. F. W. Brown Co., 29 Conn. Supp. 203, 280 A.2d 366 (1971)

II:	A311-1970, Labor & Material Payment Bond

71006 A. P. Brown Co. v. Superior Court, 16 Ariz. App. 38, 490 P.2d 867 (1971)

I:	A201-1967, Art. 7, Para. 7.10

71007 Babcock & Wilcox Co. v. Fischbach & Moore, Inc., 218 Pa. Super. 324, 280 A.2d 582 (1971)

III:	A107-1966, Art. 11
III:	A201-1967, Art. 4, Para. 4.18

71008 Baldi Construction Engineers Inc. v. Wheel Awhile, Inc., 263 Md. 670, 284 A.2d 248 (1971)

I:	A111-1967, Art. 1

71009 Batson-Cook Co. v. R. C. Pierce Roofing Co., 124 Ga. App. 835, 186 S.E.2d 358 (1971)

III:	A401-1972, Art. 11

71010 Bender-Miller Co. v. Thomwood Farms, Inc., 211 Va. 585, 179 S.E.2d 636 (1971)

III:	A107-1966, Art. 11
III:	A107-1966, Art. 23
III:	A201-1967, Art. 2, Para. 2.2
III:	A201-1967, Art. 4, Para. 4.5
III:	A201-1967, Art. 13, Para. 13.2

71011 Ben-Tom Supply Co. v. v. N. Green & Co., 338 F. Supp. 59 (S.D. W. Va. 1971)

III:	A311-1970, Performance Bond

	III: A311-1970, Labor & Material Payment Bond
71012	Bluebonnet Electrical Corp. v. Universal Electrical Construction Co., 467 S.W.2d 567 (Tex. Civ. App. 1971)

       III: A107-1966, Art. 11
       III: A201-1967, Art. 4, Para. 4.18

71013   Board of Educ. v. Aetna Casualty & Sur. Co., 453 F.2d 264 (2d Cir. 1971)

       II: A311-1970, Performance Bond
       III: A201-1970, Art. 7, Para. 7.5
       III: A201-1970, Art. 7, Para. 7.10

71014   Board of Educ. v. Delle Cese, 65 Misc. 2d 473, 318 N.Y.S.2d 773 (Sup. Ct. 1971)

       I: A201-1967, Art. 2, Para. 2.2
       I: A201-1967, Art. 7, Para. 7.4
       I: A201-1967, Art. 7, Para. 7.10

71015   Board of Educ. v. Dobson Construction Co., 67 Misc 2d 1094, 325 N.Y.S.2d 826 (Sup. Ct. 1971)

       II: A201-1967, Art. 2, Para. 2.2

71016   Burton-Dixie Corp. v. Timothy McCarthy Construction Co., 436 F.2d 405 (5th Cir. 1971)

       I: A107-1966, Art. 15
       I: A201-1967, Art. 7, Para. 7.10

71017   Castle Concrete v. Fleetwood Associates, 131 Ill. App. 2d 286, 268 N.E.2d 474 (1971)

       I: A107-1966, Art. 22
       I: A201-1967, Art. 12, Para. 12.1
       III: A201-1967, Art. 12, Para. 12.2

71018   Chasin v. Chasin, 37 A.D.2d 839, 326 N.Y.S.2d 151 (1971)

       III: A201-1967, Art. 7, Para. 7.10

71019   Chicago Bridge & Iron Co. v. Reliance Insurance Co., 46 Ill. 2d 522, 264 N.E.2d 134 (1971)

       III: A107-1966, Art. 17

	III:	A201-1967, Art. 9, Para. 9.3
	III:	A401-1967, Art. 5
	III:	A401-1967, Art. 11

71020 C.H. Leavell & Co. v. Glantz Contracting Corp., 322 F. Supp. 779 (E.D. La. 1971)

    I: A201-1967, Art. 2, Para. 2.1

71021 Citizens National Bank v. L. L. Glascock, Inc., 243 So. 2d 67 (Miss. 1971)

    I: A107-1966, Art. 22
    I: A201-1967, Art. 2, Para. 2.2
    I: A201-1967, Art. 12, Para. 12.1
    I: A201-1967, Art. 12, Para. 12.2
    I: A201-1967, Art. 12, Para. 12.3

71022 City of Weippe v. Yarno, 94 Idaho 257, 486 P.2d 268 (1971)

    II: A311-1970, Labor & Material Payment Bond

71023 Cole v. Chevron Chemical Co., 334 F. Supp. 263 (E.D. La. 1971)

    III: A107-1966, Art. 11
    III: A201-1967, Art. 4, Para. 4.18

71024 Consolidated Electrical Distributors, Inc. v. Kirkham, Chaon & Kirkham, Inc., 18 Cal. App. 3d 54, 95 Cal. Rptr. 673 (1971)

    III: A311-1970, Performance Bond

71025 Consumers Construction Co. v. County of Cook, 1 Ill. App. 3d 1087, 275 N.E.2d 696 (1971)

    III: A107-1966, Art. 24
    III: A201-1967, Art. 2, Para. 2.2
    III: A201-1967, Art. 8, Para. 8.2

71026 County of Stephenson v. Bradley & Bradley, Inc., 2 Ill. App. 3d 421, 275 N.E.2d 675 (1971)

    I: A107-1966, Art. 15
    I: A201-1967, Art. 7, Para., 7.10
    I: B131-1967, Art. 11

71027 Crane v. I. T. E. Circuit Breaker Co., 443 Pa. 442, 278 A.2d 362 (1971)

    III: A107-1966, Art. 11
    III: A201-1967, Art. 4, Para. 4.3

71028 Cree Coaches, Inc. v. Panel Suppliers, Inc., 384 Mich. 646, 186 N.W.2d 335 (1971)

    I: A107-1966, Art. 17
    I: A107-1966, Art. 23
    I: A201-1967, Art. 9, Para. 9.7
    I: A201-1967, Art. 13, Para. 13.2

71029 Creswell v. Housing Auth., 449 F.2d 557 (3d Cir. 1971)

    III: A201-1967, Art. 4, Para. 4.13
    III: A201-1967, Art. 10, Para. 10.2
    III: A201-1967, Art. 10, Para. 10.3

71030 Daniel Construction Co. v. Welch Contracting Corp. 335 F. Supp. 303 (E.D. Va. 1971)

    III: A107-1966, Art. 11
    III: A201-1967, Art. 4, Para. 4.4
    III: A401-1967, Art. 11

71031 Daugherty Co. v. Kimberly-Clark Corp., 14 Cal. App. 3d 151, 92 Cal. Rptr. 120 (1971)

    II: A107-1966, Art. 22
    II: A201-1967, Art. 12, Para. 12.1

71032 Dill v. Helms, 468 S.W.2d 608 (Tex. Civ. App. 1971)

    III: A201-1967, Art. 1, Para. 1.2

71033 Dravo Corp. v. L. W. Moses Co., 6 Wash. App. 74, 492 P.2d 1058 (1971)

    III: A201-1967, Art. 8, Para. 8.3
    III: A201-1967, Art. 14, Para. 14.1

71034 DuBose v. Carabetta, 161 Conn. 254, 287 A.2d 357 (1971)

    III: B131-1967, Art. 6

71035 Employers Mutual Liability Insurance Co. v. Robert E. McKee General Contractors, Inc., 16 Ariz. App. 77, 491 P.2d 27 (1971)

    II: A401-1967, Art.

71036 Ensign Painting Co. v. Alfred A. Smith, Inc., 21 Mich. App. 494, 175 N.W.2d 789 (1970) *rev'd on other grounds,* 385 Mich. 268, 188 N.W.2d 534 (1971)

    I: A201-1967, Art. 1, Para. 1.1
    I: A401-1967, Art. 2

71037 Fattore v. Metropolitan Sewerage Commission, 313 F. Supp. 208 (E.D. Wis. 1970), *rev'd,* 454 F.2d 537 (7th Cir. 1971)

    II: A201-1970, Art. 12, Para. 12.1
    III: A107-1966, Art. 17
    III: A201-1967, Art. 9, Para. 9.7

71038 Fifteenth Avenue Christian Church v. Moline Heat & Contracting Co. 13 Ill. App. 3d 766, 265 N.E.2d 405 (1971)

    III: A201-1967, Art. 10, Para. 10.2
    III: A401-1967, Art. 11

71039 (UNASSIGNED)

71040 Ford Motor Co. v. W. F. Holt & Sons, 335 F. Supp. 775 (M.D. Tenn 1971), *modified,* 453 F.2d 116 (6th Cir. 1971)

    II: A201-1970, Art. 4, Para. 4.18
    III: A107-1966, Art. 11
    III: A201-1967, Art. 4, Para. 4.18
    III: A401-1967, Art. 11

71041 (UNASSIGNED)

71042 Frontier Plumbing & Heating Co. v. Fitch, 480 P.2d 398 (Wyo. 1971)

    III: A311-1970, Performance Bond

71043 Fuller v. Rosinski, 79 Wash. 2d 719, 488 P.2d 1061 (1971)

    III: A201-1967, Art. 13, Para. 13.

71044 Gregg Kendall & Associates v. Kauhi, 53 Haw. 88, 488 P.2d 136 (1971)

    III: A201-1967, Art. 7, Para. 7.10

71045 Halcon International, Inc. v. Monsanto Australia, Ltd., 446 F.2d 156 (7th Cir. 1971)

    III: A107-1966, Art. 15
    III: A201-1967, Art. 7, Para. 7.10
    III: B131-1967, Art. 11

71046 Hanley v. James McHugh Construction Co., 444 F.2d 1006 (7th Cir. 1971)

    II: A201-1967, Art. 4, Para. 4.18
    II: A401-1967, Art. 11

71047 Harpeth Valley Utilities District v. Due, 225 Tenn. 181, 465 S.W.2d 353 (1971)

    III: A401-1967, Art. 11

71048 Hart v. Dominion Insurance Co., 29 Colo. App. 404, 487 P.2d 826 (1971)

    III: A201-1967, Art. 7, Para. 7.10

71049 Holder Construction Co. v. Ed Smith & Sons, 124 Ga. App. 89, 182 S.E.2d 919 (1971)

    III: A401-1967, Art. 11

71050 Howard-Green Electrical Co. v. Chaney & James Construction Co., 12 N.C. App. 63, 182 S.E.2d 601 (1971)

    I: A311-1970, Labor & Material Payment Bond
    II: A401-1967, Art. 6

71051 J.A. Jones Constr. Co. v. Greenbriar Shopping Center, 332 F. Supp. 1336 (N.D. Ga. 1971)

    I: A101-1967, Art. 1
    I: A201-1967, Art. 12, Para. 12.1
    I: A201-1967, Art. 12, Para. 12.2
    I: A201-1967, Art. 13, Para. 13.3

71052 Joe Adams & Son v. McCann Construction Co., 475 S.W.2d 721 (Tex. 1971)

    III: A401-1967, Art. 11

71053 Johnson Acoustics, Inc. v. P.J. Carlin Construction Co., 29 Conn. Supp. 457, 292 A.2d 273 (Super. Ct. 1971)

    III: A201-1970, Art. 7, Para. 7.1

71054 Jones v. Kvistad, 19 Cal. App. 3d 836, 97 Cal. Rptr. 100 (1971)

    III: A201-1967, Art. 7, Para. 7.10

71055 Kingsbrook Jewish Medical Center v. Katz, 37 A.D.2d 518, 321 N.Y.S.2d 773 (1971)

    I: A201-1967, Art. 7, Para. 7.10
    I: B131-1967, Art. 11

71056 Kirsch v. Dondlinger & Sons Construction Co., 206 Kan. 701, 482 P.2d 10 (1971)

    II: A107-1966, Art. 9
    II: A107-1966, Art. 11
    II: A201-1967, Art. 2, Para. 2.2
    II: A201-1967, Art. 4, Para. 4.18

71057 Kustom Kraft Homes v. Leivenstein, 14 Cal. App. 3d 805, 92 Cal. Rptr. 650 (1971)

    II: A107-1966, Art. 15
    II: A201-1967, Art. 7, Para. 7.10

71058 Langley v. Helms, 12 N.C. App. 620, 184 S.E.2d 393 (1971)

    III: A107-1966, Art. 11
    III: A201-1967, Art. 4, Para. 4.5

71059 Leo Spear Construction Co. v. Fidelity & Casualty Co., 446 F.2d 439 (2d Cir. 1971)

    III: A201-1967, Art. 9, Para. 9.3

71060 Lewis v. Carnaggio, 257 S.C. 54, 183 S.E.2d 899 (1971)

    III: A111-1967, Art. 6

71061 L. M. White Contructing Co. v. St. Joseph Structural Steel Co., 15 Ariz. App. 260, 488 P.2d 196 (1971)

    III: A311-1970, Performance Bond

71062   Locklear v. Payne, 124 Ga. App. 845, 186 S.E.2d 439 (1971)

        III: A201-1970, Art. 7, Para. 7.10

71063   Maness v. Fowler-Jones Construction Co., 10 N.C. App. 592, 179 S.E.2d 816 (1971)

        I: A201-1967, Art. 10, Para. 10.1
        III: A107-1966, Art. 11
        III: A107-1966, Art. 18
        III: A201-1967, Art. 10, Para. 10.2

70164   Mann v. Philip Vizzini & Son, 263 Md. 471, 283 A.2d 577 (1971)

        III: A201-1967, Art. 2, Para. 2.2
        III: A201-1967, Art. 3, Para. 3.2

71065   Marble Falls Housing Auth. v. McKinley, 474 S.W.2d 292 (Tex. Civ. App. 1971)

        III: B131-1967, Art. 1

71066   Methodist Church v. Glen-Rich Construction Corp., 29 A.D.2d 773, 287 N.Y.S.2d 728 (1968), *aff'd*, 27 N.Y.2d 357, 267 N.E.2d 88 (1971)

        I: A107-1966, Art. 9
        I: A107-1966, Art. 15
        I: A201-1967, Art. 2, Para. 2.2
        I: A201-1967, Art. 7, Para. 7.10
        I: A201-1967, Art. 12, Para. 12.1
        I: A201-1967, Art. 12, Para. 12.2
        I: A201-1967, Art. 13, Para. 13.2

71067   Mid-Continent Casualty Co. v. P & H Supply, Inc., 490 P.2d 1358 (Okla. 1971)

        III: A311-1970, Performance Bond

71068   Nordin Construction Co. v. City of Nome, 489 P.2d 455 (Alaska 1971)

        II: A201-1967, Art. 9, Para. 9.7

71069   Paul Hardman, Inc. v. Bradley, 486 P.2d 731 (Okla. 1971)

        III: A201-1967, Art. 4, Para. 4.9

71070 Pickett v. Chamblee Construction Co., 124 Ga. App. 769, 186 S.E.2d 123 (1971)

    II: A111-1967, Art. 15
    II: A201-1967, Art. 5, Para. 5.4
    II: A201-1970, Art. 9, Para. 9.2

71071 Rao Electrical Equipment Co. v. State, 36 A.D.2d 1019, 321 N.Y.S.2d 670 (1971)

    II: A201-1967, Art. 8, Para. 8.3

71072 R C R Leasing, Inc. v. Harping Sales & Erectors, Inc., 474 S.W.2d 870 (Ky. 1971)

    I: A111-1967, Art. 1
    I: A111-1967, Art. 7

71073 Reamer Industries, Inc. v. McQuay, Inc., 344 F. Supp. 540 (D.S.C. 1971)

    III: A401-1967, Art. 11

71074 Robinhorne Construction Corp. v. Snyder, 47 Ill. 2d 349, 265 N.E.2d 670 (1971)

    I: A111-1967, Art. 16
    I: A201-1967, Art. 14, Para. 14.2

71075 Rocky Mountain Plastics Corp. v. Seder Plastics Corp., 488 P.2d 99 (Colo. 1971)

    III: A201-1967, Art. 8, Para. 8.3

71076 Royal Globe Insurance Co. v. Spain, 36 A.D.2d 632, 319 N.Y.S.2d 115 (1971)

    III: A201-1967, Art. 7, Para. 7.10

71077 (UNASSIGNED)

71078 Smullen v. City of New York, 28 N.Y.2d 66, 268 N.E.2d 763 (1971)

    III: A201-1970, Art. 2, Para. 2.2
    III: A201-1970, Art. 4, Para. 4.3
    III: A201-1970, Art. 10, Para. 10.1
    III: A201-1970, Art. 10, Para. 10.

71079 Sollenberger v. A. A. Construction Co., 481 P.2d 428 (Colo. 1971)

    I: A201-1967, Art. 2, Para. 2.2
    I: A201-1967, Art. 7, Para. 7.10

71080 Stewart M. Muller Construction Co. v. Clement Ferdinand & Co., 36 A.D. 2d 814, 320 N.Y.S.2d 277 (1971)

    III: A201-1967, Art. 7, Para. 7.10

71081 Sullivan & Cromwell v. Hudson & Manhatten Corp., 29 N.Y.2d 523, 324 N.Y.S.2d 79 (1971)

    II: B131-1967, Art. 11

71082 Swarthout v. Beard, 33 Mich. App. 395, 190 N.W.2d 373 (1971)

    II: A107-1966, Art. 9
    II: A201-1967, Art. 2, Para. 2.2
    II: B131-1967, Art. 1

71083 Swenson v. Lowe, 5 Wash. App. 186, 486 P.2d 1120 (1971)

    II: A107-1966, Art. 22
    II: A201-1967, Art. 12, Para. 12.1

71084 United Bonding Insurance Co. v. Sperry & Hutchinson Co., 465 S.W.2d 291 (Ky. 1971)

    III: A201-1967, Art. 9, Para. 9.7
    III: A311-1970, Performance Bond

71085 Vinsant Plumbing & Heating Co. v. Rudder Construction Co., 486 S.W.2d 540 (Tenn. Ct. App. 1971)

    I: A101-1972, Art. 6
    I: A401-1972, Art. 2
    I: A401-1972, Art. 9

71086 West Durham Lumber Co. v. Aetna Casualty & Sur. Co., 12 N.C. App. 641, 184 S.E.2d 399 (1971)

    I: A201-1967, Art. 4, Para. 4.4
    I: A201-1967, Art. 7, Para. 7.5

71087 Willner & Millkey v. Shure, 124 Ga. App. 268, 183 S.E.2d 479 (1971)

    II: B131-1967, Art. 6

71088 Zion's Cooperative Mercantile Institute v. Jacobson Construction Co., 27 Utah 2d 6, 492 P.2d 135 (1971)

    I: A201-1970, Art. 9, Para. 9.7
    I: A201-1970, Art. 10, Para. 10.2

72001 A. Burgart, Inc. v. Foster-Lipkins Corp., 30 N.Y.2d 901, 335 N.Y.S.2d 562 (1972)

    III: A201-1970, Art. 7, Para. 7.10
    III: A401-1972, Art. 14

72002 A.C. Beals Co. v. Rhode Island Hospital, 110 R.I. 275, 292 A.2d 865 (1972)

    III: A201-1970, Art. 7, Para. 7.1
    III: A201-1970, Art. 7, Para. 7.10

72003 Adamsville Lumber Co. v. Rainey, 348 F. Supp. 373 (W.D. Tenn. 1972)

    III: A201-1970, Art. 11, Para. 11.1
    III: A201-1970, Art. 11, Para. 11.3

72004 Aetna Casualty & Sur. Co. v. Lafayette, 30 N.Y.2d 638, 282 N.E.2d 621 (1972)

    III: A311-1970, Performance Bond

72005 Aghnides v. Marmon Group, Inc., 463 F.2d 384 (4th Cir. 1972)

    III: B131-1970, Art. 3

72006 A. H. Sollinger Construction Co. v. Illinois Building Authority, 5 Ill. App. 3d 554, 283 N.E.2d 508 (1972)

    II: A201-1970, Art. 2, Para. 2.2
    II: A201-1970, Art. 9, Para. 9.7

72007 All-State Investigation & Security Agency v. Turner Constr. Co., 301 A.2d 273 (Del. 1972)

    III: A401-1972, Art. 11

72008   Amco Steel Corp. v. Renago Construction Inc., 34 A.D.2d 887, 312 N.Y.S.2d 161 (1972)

    II: A201-1967, Art. 7, Para. 7.10

72009   Anderson v. Cahill, 485 S.W.2d 76 (Mo. 1972)

    III: A201-1970, Art. 10, Para. 10.2

72010   Armour & Co. v. Nord, 463 F.2d 8 (8th Cir. 1972)

    II: A111-1967, Art. 16

72011   A. W. Therrien Co. v. H. K. Ferguson Co., 470 F.2d 912 (1st Cir. 1972)

    III: A201-1970, Art. 13, Para. 13.3

72012   Ballard, H. T. Kirk & Associates v. Poston, 33 Ohio App. 2d 117, 293 N.E.2d 102 (1972)

    III: A201-1970, Art. 1, Para. 1.3

72013   Berthot v. Stroble, 208 Kan. 839, 494 P.2d 1133 (1972)

    III: A401-1972, Art. 3
    III: A401-1972, Art. 11

72014   Bibeau Construction Co. v. Hauser Bros, 329 A.D.2d 955, 333 N.Y.S.2d 459 (1972)

    III: A201-1970, Art. 12, Para. 12.1
    III: A401-1972, Art. 11

72015   Bismark Baptist Church v. Wiedemann Industries, Inc., 201 N.W.2d 434 (N.D. 1972)

    III: A201-1970, Art. 9, Para. 9.7

72016   Bland v. L'Enfant Plaza North, Inc., 473 F.2d 156 (D.C. Cir. 1972)

    III: A401-1972, Art. 11

72017   Borden Co. v. Foster-Lipkins Corp., 39 A.D.2d 633, 331 N.Y.S.2d 138 (1972)

    III: A201-1970, Art. 7, Para. 7.10

72018   Borg, Inc. v. Morris Middle School District No. 54, 3 Ill. App. 3d 913 (1972)

    III: A201-1967, Art. 7, Para. 7.10

72019 Brooks Towers Corp. v. Hunkin-Conkey Construction Co., 454 F.2d 120 (10th Cir. 1972)

    II: A201-1970, Art. 8, Para. 8.3
    II: A201-1970, Art. 9, Para. 9.7
    II: A201-1970, Art. 12, Para. 12.1

72020 Buehner Schokbeton Co. v. Horne's Crane Service Co., 500 P.2d 140 (Colo. Ct. App. 1972)

    III: A201-1970, Art. 8, Para. 8.1

72021 Cable-Wiedemer, Inc. v. A. Freiderich & Sons, 71 Misc. 2d 443, 336 N.Y.S.2d 139 (County Ct. 1972)

    III: A401-1972, Art. 6

72022 C & B Construction Co. v. Nashville School District No. 1, 253 Ark. 73, 484 S.W.2d 519 (1972)

    II: A201-1970, Art. 4, Para. 4.5
    II: A201-1970, Art. 4, Para. 4.10

72023 Chavez v. Gribble, 83 N.M. 688, 496 P.2d 1084 (1972)

    III: A201-1970, Art. 9, Para. 9.4

72024 City of Joliet v. Fennewald, 3 Ill. App. 3d 913, 278 N.E.2d 818 (1972)

    III: A107-1966, Art. 15
    III: A201-1967, Art. 7, Para. 7.10

72025 City of Miami Beach v. Fein, 263 So. 2d 258 (Fla. Dist. Ct. App. 1972)

    II: A201-1970, Art. 12, Para. 12.1

72026 City of Miami Beach v. Fryd Construction Corp., 264 So. 2d 13 (Fla. Dist. Ct. App. 1972)

    III: A201-1970, Art. 12, Para. 12.1
    III: A201-1970, Art. 12, Para. 12.2

72027 City of Worcester v. Park Construction Co., 361 Mass. 879, 281 N.E.2d 600 (1972)

    II: A201-1970, Art. 2, Para. 2.2

	II: A201-1970, Art. 7, Para. 7.10
72028	Clark v. Madeira, 252 Ark. 157, 477 S.W.2d 817 (1972)
	III: B131-1970, Art. 6
72029	Cornell, Howland, Hayes & Merryfield, Inc., v. Continental Casualty Co., 465 F.2d 22 (9th Cir. 1972)
	III: C141-1974, Art. 10
72030	County of Maricopa v. Walsh & Oberg Architects, Inc., 16 Ariz. App. 439, 494 P.2d 44 (1972)
	III: A201-1970, Art. 13, Para. 13.2
72031	Darling v. Burrone Brothers, 162 Conn. 187, 292 A.2d 912 (1972)
	III: A201-1970, Art. 10, Para. 10.2
72032	Davidson v. Prime Homes, Inc., 506 P.2d 1238 (Colo. 1972)
	III: A201-1970, Art. 7, Para. 7.1
72033	Del Bianco & Associates v. Adam, 6 Ill. App. 3d 286, 285 N.E.2d 480 (1972)
	I: A201-1970, Art. 7, Para. 7.10
	I: B131-1970, Art. 11
72034	Dover & Co. v. United Pacific Insurance Co., 38 Mich. App. 727, 197 N.W.2d 126 (1972)
	III: A311-1970, Performance Bond
72035	Dowling v. Bruffey, 266 Md. 77, 291 A.2d 471 (1972)
	III: A201-1970, Art. 12, Para. 12.1
72036	Drost v. Professional Building Service Corp., 153 Ind. App. 273, 286 N.E.2d 846 (1972)
	III: A201-1970, Art. 4, Para. 4.7
72037	Erickson Paving Co. v. Yardley Drilling Co., 7 Wash. App. 681, 502 P.2d 334 (1972)
	III: A401-1972, Art. 11

72038   Farmers & Merchants State Bank v. Snodgrass & Sons Construction Co., 209 Kan. 119, 495 P.2d 985 (1972)

      II: A201-1970, Art. 1, Para. 1.1
      II: A201-1970, Art. 9, Para. 9.7

72039   Fidelity & Deposit Co. v. Scott Brothers Construction Co., 461 F.2d 640 (5th Cir 1972)

      III: A201-1970, Art. 7, Para. 7.5
      III: A311-1970, Performance Bond

72040   Formigli Corp. v. Fox, 348 F. Supp. 629 (E.D. Pa. 1972)

      II: A201-1970, Art. 9, Para. 9.6
      II: A201-1970, Art. 9, Para. 9.7

72041   Frazier, Inc. v. 20th Century Home Builders, Inc., 188 Neb. 618, 198 N.W.2d 478 (1972)

      III: A107-1970, Art. 19
      III: A111-1967, Art. 10

72042   G. E. C. Corp. v. Levy, 126 Ga. App. 604, 191 S.E.2d 461 (1972)

      III: B131-1970, Art. 6

72043   Gelder & Associates v. Continental Ins. Co., 15 N.C. App. 686, 190 S.E.2d 674 (1972)

      III: A201-1970, Art. 8, Para. 8.2
      III: A201-1970, Art. 8, Para. 8.3

72044   Gurney Industries, Inc. v. St. Paul Fire & Marine Ins. Co., 467 F.2d 588 (4th Cir. 1972)

      III: A201-1970, Art. 4, Para. 4.5
      III: A201-1970, Art. 9, Para. 9.7
      III: A311-1970, Performance Bond

72045   Hayeck Building & Realty Co. v. Turcotte, 361 Mass. 785, 282 N.E.2d 907 (1972)

      III: A201-1970, Art. 9, Para. 9.7

72046 Hensel Phelps Construction Co. v. General Signal Corp., 460 F.2d 109 (10th Cir. 1972)

    III: A311-1970, Labor & Material Payment Bond
    III: A401-1972, Art. 7

72047 Hobson Construction Co. v. Holiday Inns, Inc., 14 N.C. App. 475, 188 S.E.2d 617 (1972)

    III: A201-1970, Art. 6, Para. 6.1

72048 Hoerner Woldorf Corp. v. Bumstead-Woolford Co., 158 Mont. 472, 494 P.2d 293 (1972)

    II: A201-1970, Art. 1, Para. 1.1
    III: A201-1970, Art. 4, Para. 4.18

72049 Houdaille Industries v. United Bonding Insurance Co. 453 F.2d 1048 (5th Cir. 1972)

    III: A201-1970, Art. 7, Para. 7.5
    III: A311-1970, Performance Bond
    III: A311-1970, Labor & Material Payment Bond

72050 Hunkin-Conkey Construction Co. v. City of Dunkirk, 69 Misc. 2d 1042, 332 N.Y.S.2d 689 (Sup. Ct. 1972)

    III: A201-1970, Art. 7, Para. 7.1

72051 Ismil v. L.H. Sowles Co., 295 Minn. 120, 203 N.W.2d 354 (1972)

    III: A201-1970, Art. 10, Para. 10.2

72052 Karnatz v. Murphy Pacific Corp., 8 Wash. App. 76, 503 P.2d 1145 (1972)

    III: A401-1972, Art. 11

72053 Keefe v. Balling Construction, Inc., 39 A.D.2d 638, 331 N.Y.S.2d 293 (1972)

    III: A401-1972, Art. 1

72054 Kenney Construction Co. v. Metropolitan Sanitary District, 128 Ill. App. 2d 104, 262 N.E.2d 842 (1970), *rev'd and remanded*, 52 Ill. 2d 187, 288 N.E.2d 1 (1972)

    III: A201-1967, Art. 12, Para. 12.1

III: A201-1967, Art. 12, Para. 12.2
III: A201-1970, Art. 12, Para. 12.1

[*Editor's Note:* For subsequent appeal after remand, *see* case number 74044 *infra.*]

72055 Knight Brothers v. State, 189 Neb. 64, 199 N.W.2d 720 (1972)

III: A101-1967, Art. 3
III: A111-1967, Art. 10

72056 Kurz v. Quincy Post No. 37, American Legion, 5 Ill. App. 3d 412, 283 N.E.2d 8 (1972)

I: B131-1970, Art. 1
I: B131-1970, Art. 3
I: B131-1970, Art. 6

72057 (UNASSIGNED)

72058 L.A. Wenger Contracting Co. v. State University Construction Fund, 40 A.D.2d 569, 334 N.Y.S.2d 704 (1972)

III: A201-1970, Art. 5, Para. 5.2

72059 Lebreton v. Brown, 260 So. 2d 767 (La. Ct. App. 1972)

III: A201-1970, Art. 4, Para. 4.2

72060 Le Chase Construction Corp. v. City of Rochester, 74 Misc. 2d 825, 346 N.Y.S.2d 20 (1972)

III: A310-1970, Bid Bond

72061 Lindsay v. Gibbons & Reed, 27 Utah 2d 419, 497 P.2d 28 (1972)

III: A201-1970, Art. 10, Para. 10.2

72062 MacDonald & Kruse, Inc. v. San Jose Steel Co., 20 Cal. App. 3d 413, 105 Cal. Rptr. 725 (1972)

III: A201-1970, Art. 4, Para. 4.18
III: A401-1972, Art. 11

72063 Maietta v. Greenvield, 267 Md. 287, 297 A.2d 244 (1972)

I: A201-1970, Art. 2, Para. 2.2

>   I: A201-1970, Art. 7. Para. 7.10
>   II: A401-1972, Art. 13

72064 Mardan Construction Corp. v. Village of Nyack Housing Auth., 37 A.D.2d 994, 327 N.Y.S.2d 518 (1972)

>   II: A201-1970, Art. 12, Para. 12.1

72065 Mazzoleni v. Shenango Steel Erectors, Inc., 344 F. Supp. 589 (W.D.Pa. 1972)

>   III: A201-1970, Art. 10, Para. 10.2

72066 M. Bender & Son v. West 16th Street Realty Corp., 458 F.2d 1316 (7th Cir. 1972)

>   III: A201-1970, Art. 1, Para. 1.1
>   III: A201-1970, Art. 7, Para. 7.9

72067 McCarthy v. J. P. Cullen & Son, 199 N.W.2d 362 (Iowa 1972)

>   I: A201-1970, Art. 4, Para. 4.18
>   I: A201-1970, Art. 10, Para. 10.1
>   I: A201-1970, Art. 10, Para. 10.2

72068 McGowan-Rigsby Supply, Inc. v. Charles Carta & Co., 268 So. 2d 716 (La. Ct. App. 1972)

>   III: A401-1972, Art. 11

72069 McMaster, Inc. v. Pennsbury Village Co., 460 F.2d 520 (3d Cir. 1972)

>   III: A107-1970, Art. 11

72070 Mesker Brothers Iron Co. v. Des Lauriers Column Mould Co., 8 Ill. App. 3d 113, 289 N.E.2d 223 (1972)

>   III: A401-1972, Art. 11

72071 Moore v. Bolton, 480 S.W.2d 805 (Tex. Civ. App. 1972)

>   III: B131-1970, Art. 6

72072 Morgan v. Stubblefield, 6 Cal. 3d 606, 100 Cal Rptr. 1, 493 P.2d 465 (1972)

>   III: A201-1970, Art. 10, Para. 10.2
>   III: A401-1972, Art. 11

72073 North Little Rock Electric Co. v. Pickens-Bond Construction Co., 253 Ark. 172, 485 S.W.2d 197 (1972)

    III: A401-1972, Art. 11

72074 Oakes v. Suelynn Corp., 24 Cal. App. 3d 271, 100 Cal. Rptr. 838 (1972)

    III: A201-1970, Art. 1, Para. 1.3

72075 Owings v. Rose, 626 Or. 247, 497 P.2d 1183 (1972)

    II: C131-1970, Art. 1

72076 Peabody Seating Co. v. Jim Cullen, Inc., 56 Wis. 2d 119, 201 N.W.2d 546 (1972)

    III: A311-1970, Labor & Material Payment Bond

72077 Pickering v. Daniel J. Keating Co., 460 F.2d 820 (3d Cir. 1973)

    II: A401-1972, Art. 11
    III: A201-1970, Art. 7, Para. 7.6

72078 Pioneer Industries v. Gevyn Construction Corp., 458 F.2d 582 (1st Cir. 1972)

    III: A201-1970, Art. 7, Para. 7.10
    III: A401-1972, Art. 14

72079 Pipeline Industry Benefit Fund v. Aetna Casualty & Sur. Co., 503 P.2d 1286 (Okla. Ct. App. 1972)

    III: A311-1970, Performance Bond

72080 Polatschek v. City of New York, 39 A.D.2d 584, 331 N.Y.S.2d 966 (1972)

    III: A201-1970, Art. 7, Para. 7.1
    III: A201-1970, Art. 10, Para. 10.1
    III: A401-1972, Art. 11

72081 Public Water Supply District No. 8 v. Maryland Casualty Co., 478 S.W.2d 293 (Mo. 1972)

    III: A201-1970, Art. 9, Para. 9.7

72082 Quinn v. Moore, 292 A.2d 846 (Me. 1972)

    III: A201-1970, Art. 10, Para. 10.2

72083 Redding & Co. v. Russwine Construction Corp., 463 F.2d 929 (D.C. Cir. 1972)

    III: A201-1970, Art. 9, Para. 9.7
    III: A401-1972, Art. 11

72084 Rosoff Brothers v. State, 29 A.D.2d 974, 332 N.Y.S.2d 798 (1972)

    III: A201-1970, Art. 4, Para. 4.3

72085 Ruscon Construction Co. v. Beaufort-Jasper Water Authority, 259 S.C. 314, 191 S.E.2d 715 (1972)

    III: A201-1970, Art. 9, Para. 9.7

72086 Rwenbark v. Atlantic States Construction Co., 14 N.C. App. 609, 188 S.E.2d 747 (1972)

    III: A201-1970, Art. 10, Para. 10.2

72087 Ryan v. Thurmond, 481 S.W.2d 199 (Tex. 1972)

    I: A101-1967, Art. 1
    I: A101-1967, Art. 7
    I: A201-1970, Art. 9, Para. 9.7

72088 Salesian Society v. Formigli Corp., 120 N.J. Super. 493, 295 A.2d 19 (1972)

    III: A201-1970, Art. 7, Para. 7.1

72089 Schultz & Lindsay Construction Co. v. State, 83 N.M. 534, 494 P.2d 612 (1972)

    III: A201-1970, Art. 12, Para. 12.2
    III: C131-1970, Art. 1

72090 Sellers v. Owens-Illinois Glass Co., 156 W. Va. 87, 191 S.E.2d 166 (1972)

    III: A401-1972, Art. 11

72091 Sigal v. Three K's, Ltd, 456 F.2d 1242 (3d Cir. 1972)

    I: B131-1970, Art. 11

72092 Simon v. Omaha Public Power District, 189 Neb. 183, 202 N.W.2d 157 (1972)

    III: A201-1970, Art. 10, Para. 10.2

72093 Sira & Payne, Inc. v. Wallace & Riddle, 470 S.W.2d 793 (Tex. Civ. App. 1971), *rev'd,* 484 S.W.2d 559 (Tex. 1972)

    III: A107-1966, Art. 11
    III: A201-1967, Art. 4, Para. 4.18
    III: A401-1967, Art. 11
    III: A401-1972, Art. 11

72094 Smith v. Berwin Builders, 287 A.2d 693 (Del. Super. Ct. 1972)

    III: A201-1970, Art. 4, Para. 4.5

72095 Stanley R. Benjamin, Inc. v. Fidelity & Casualty Co., 72 Misc. 2d 742, 340 N.Y.S.2d 578 (1972)

    II: A311-1970, Performance Bond

72096 State Highway Dept. v. Hall Paving Co., 127 Ga. App. 625, 194 S.E.2d 493 (1972)

    III: A201-1970, Art. 8, Para. 8.2
    III: A201-1970, Art. 8, Para. 8.3

72097 Strom v. Lipschultz, 5 Ill. App. 3d 308, 282 N.E.2d 257 (1972)

    I: A201-1970, Art. 1, Para. 1.1
    I: A201-1970, Art. 12, Para. 12.1

72098 Summers v. Crown Construction Co., 453 F.2d 998 (4th Cir. 1972)

    III: A401-1972, Art. 11

72099 G.H. Lindekugel & Sons v. South Dakota Highway Commission, 87 S.D. 32, 202 N.W.2d 125 (1972)

    III: A201-1970, Art. 12, Para. 12.2

72100 Thompson-Starrett International, Inc. v. Tropic Plumbing, Inc., 457 F.2d 1349 (3d Cir. 1972)

    I: A401-1972, Art. 11

72101 Transamerica Insurance Co. v. Parker Henry Glass Co., 7 Wash. App. 208, 499 P.2d 21 (1972)

    III: A401-1972, Art. 11

72102	Transpac Construction Co. v. Clark & Groff Engineers, Inc., 466 F.2d 823 (9th cir. 1972)	
	II:	A401-1972, Art. 11
72103	United States Fidelity & Guar. Co. v. Davis Mechanical Contractors, Inc., 15 N.C. App. 127, 189 S.E.2d 553 (1972)	
	III:	A401-1972, Art. 11
72104	United States v. Foster Construction, 456 F.2d 250 (5th Cir. 1972)	
	III:	A401-1972, Art. 11
72105	Walker Manufacturing Co. v. Henkel Construction Co., 346 F. Supp. 621 (N.D. Iowa 1972)	
	III:	A201-1970, Art. 13, Para. 13.2
	III:	A401-1972, Art. 11
72106	Warde v. Davis, 351 F. Supp. 519 (D. Colo. 1972)	
	III:	A201-1970, Art. 2, Para. 2.1
72107	Wenke v. Amoco Chemicals Corp., 290 A.2d 670 (Del. Super. Ct. 1972)	
	III:	A201-1970, Art. 7, Para. 7.1
	II:	A401-1972, Art. 11
72108	Busker v. Sokolowski, 203 N.W.2d 301 (Iowa 1972)	
	III:	A111-1967, Art. 4
	III:	A201-1970, Art. 4, Para. 4.5
72109	Western Contracting Corp. v. State Highway Dept., 125 Ga. App. 376, 187 S.E.2d 690 (1972)	
	III:	A201-1970, Art. 1, Para. 1.1
72110	Wieman-Slechta Co. v. Pascoe Steel Corp., 351 F. Supp. 840 (N.D. 1972)	
	III:	A401-1972, Art. 3
72111	William C. Blanchard Co. v. Beach Concrete Co., 121 N.J. Super. 418, 297 A.2d 587 (Ch. Div. 1972)	
	I:	A201-1970, Art. 7, Para. 7.10

II: A401-1972, Art. 13

72112   William F. Klingensmith, Inc. v. David H. Snell Landscape Contractor, Inc., 265 Md. 654, 291 A.2d 56 (1972)

II: A201-1967, Art. 1, Para. 1.1
III: A101-1967, Art. 1
III: A111-1967, Art. 1
III: A201-1970, Art. 9, Para. 9.7
III: A401-1972, Art. 11

72113   Wolfe v. Warfield, 266 Md. 621, 296 A.2d 158 (1972)

II: A201-1970, Art. 1, Para. 1.1

72114   Yamanishi v. Breily & Corrishaw, Inc., 29 Cal. App. 3d 457, 105 Cal. Rptr. 580 (1972)

III: A201-1970, Art. 5, Para. 5.4

72115   Comm v. Goodman, 6 Ill. App. 3d 847, 286 N.E.2d 758 (1972)

II: B131-1970, Art. 1

73001   Aberthaw Construction Co. v. Centre County Hospital, 366 F. Supp. 513 (M.D. Pa. 1973)

III: A201-1970, Art. 2, Para. 2.2
III: A201-1970, Art. 7, Para. 7.10
III: B131-1970, Art. 11

73002   Adams Tree Service, Inc. v. Transamerica Title Insurance Co., 20 Ariz. App. 214, 511 P.2d 658 (1973)

III: A401-1972, Art. 11

73003   Aerostatic Engineering Corp. v. Szczawinski, 1 Mass. App. Ct. 141, 294 N.E.2d 521 (1973)

III: A201-1970, Art. 9, Para. 9.6

73004   Agus v. Future Chattanooga Development Corp., 358 F. Supp. 246 (E.D. Tenn. 1973)

III: A201-1970, Art. 4, Para. 4.18

73005 Anderson-Nichols & Co. v. Page, 113 N.H. 445, 309 A.2d 148 (1973)

  II: B131-1970, Art. 1
  II: B131-1970, Art. 6

73006 Anken Construction Co. v. Artistic Ornamental Iron, Inc., 129 Ga. App. 32, 198 S.E.2d 389 (1973)

  III: A201-1970, Art. 1, Para. 1.1
  III: A401-1972, Art. 11
  III: A401-1972, Art. 12

73007 A.R. Moyer, Inc. v. Graham, 285 So. 2d 397 (Fla. 1973)

  III: A201-1970, Art. 2, Para. 2.2
  III: B131-1970, Art. 1

73008 Arrow Construction Co. v. American Employers Insurance Co., 273 So. 2d 582 (La. Ct. App. 1973)

  III: A311-1970, Performance Bond

73009 Atlee Electric Co. v. Johnson Constr. Co., 14 Ill. App. 3d 716, 303 N.E.2d 192 (1973)

  III: A201-1970, Art. 12, Para. 12.1
  III: A201-1970, Art. 12, Para. 12.2

73010 Avco Delta Corp. Canada v. United States, 484 F.2d 692 (7th Cir. 1973)

  III: A201-1970, Art. 9, Para. 9.5
  III: A201-1970, Art. 9, Para. 9.7
  III: A401-1972, Art. 12

73011 Basic Construction Co. v. Community Hospital, 213 Va. 587, 194 S.E.2d 895 (1973)

  II: A201-1970, Art. 7, Para. 7.10

73012 Batson-Cook Co. v. Loden & Co., 129 Ga. App. 376, 199 S.E.2d 591 (1973)

  I: A201-1970, Art. 12, Para. 12.2

73013 Beeker v. Central Telephone & Utility Corp., 365 F. Supp. 984 (S.D.S.D. 1973)

  III: A201-1970, Art. 4, Para. 4.18

73014 Ben M. Hogan Co. v. Nichols, 254 Ark. 771, 496 S.W.2d 404 (1973)

    III: A201-1970, Art. 10, Para. 10.1
    III: A201-1970, Art. 10, Para. 10.2

73015 Benson Paint Co. v. Williams Construction Co., 128 Ga. App. 47, 195 S.E.2d 671 (1973)

    II: A201-1970, Art. 4, Para. 4.16
    II: A201-1970, Art. 10, Para. 10.2
    II: A401-1972, Art. 11

73016 Bero Construction Corp. v. New York State Thruway Authority, 41 A.D.2d 691, 342 N.Y.S.2d 503 (1973)

    III: A201-1970, Art. 12, Para. 12.1
    III: A201-1970, Art. 12, Para. 12.2

73017 Bewley Furniture Co. v. Maryland Casualty Co., 285 So. 2d 216 (La. 1973)

    III: A201-1970, Art. 4, Para. 4.18
    III: A401-1972, Art. 11

73018 Bignami v. Caristo Construction Corp., 42 A.D.2d 600, 345 N.Y.S.2d 103 (1973)

    III: A201-1970, Art. 10, Para. 10.2
    III: A401-1972, Art. 11

73019 Board of Educ. v. Wager Construction Corp., 74 Misc. 2d 864, 346 N.Y.S.2d 24 (Sup. Ct. 1973)

    II: A201-1970, Art. 2, Para. 2.2

73020 Bone Contracting Co. v. Depot Construction Corp., 42 A.D.2d 812, 346 N.Y.S.2d 435 (1973)

    III: A201-1970, Art. 8, Para. 8.3

73021 Boyd Construction Co. v. T.L. James & Co., 477 F.2d 34 (5th Cir. 1973)

    III: A401-1972, Art. 3

73022 Bullock Co. v. Allen, 493 S.W.2d 5 (Mo. Ct. App. 1973)

    III: A201-1970, Art. 1, Para. 1.1

  III: A201-1970, Art. 9, Para. 9.7

73023 Carolina Mechanical Contractors, Inc. v. Yeargin Constr. Co., 261 S.C. 1 198, S.E.2d 224 (1973)

  III: A201-1970, Art. 12, Para. 12.2
  III: A401-1972, Art. 1

73024 Carr v. Detroit Edison Co., 49 Mich. App. 332, 212 N.W.2d 70 (1973)

  III: A201-1970, Art. 10, Para. 10.2

73025 Christy v. Menasha Corp., 297 Minn. 334, 211 NW.2d 773 (1973)

  III: A401-1972, Art. 11

73026 Concrete Materials of Georgia, Inc. v. Smith & Plaster Co., 127 Ga. App. 817, 195 S.E.2d 219 (1973)

  III: A401-1972, Art. 3
  III: A401-1972, Art. 11

73027 Conklin v. Cohen, 262 So. 2d 717 (Fla. Dist. Ct. App. 1972), *vacated,* 287 So. 2d 56 (Fla. 1973)

  III: A201-1970, Art. 2, Para. 2.2
  III: A201-1970, Art. 10, Para. 10.1
  III: A201-1970, Art. 10, Para. 10.2

73028 Craven v. Oggero, 213 N.W.2d 678 (Iowa 1973)

  III: A201-1970, Art. 10, Para. 10.2

73029 Crown Construction Co. v. Opelika Manufacturing Corp. 343 F. Supp. 1266 (N.D. Ga. 1972), *modified,* 480 F.2d 149 (5th Cir. 1973)

  II: A111-1967, Art. 10
  II: A111-1967, Art. 12
  III: A201-1970, Art. 5, Para. 5.2

73030 D'Angelo v. State, 41 A.D.2d 77, 341 N.Y.S.2d 84 (1973)

  III: A201-1970, Art. 8, Para. 8.3

73031 Davis v. Anderson, 501 S.W.2d 459 (Tex. Civ. App. 1973)

  III: A401-1972, Art. 11

73032 Deer Park Bank v. Aetna Insurance Co., 493 S.W.2d 305 (Tex. Civ. App. 1973)

    III: A201-1970, Art. 14, Para. 14.1
    III: A311-1970, Performance Bond

73033 Detroit Demolition Corp. v. Burroughs Corp., 45 Mich. App. 72, 205 N.W.2d 856 (1973)

    I: A201-1970, Art. 7, Para. 7.10
    I: A201-1970, Art. 9, Para. 9.7

73034 Doyle & Russell, Inc. v. Roanoke Hospital Association, 213 Va. 489, 193 S.E.2d 662 (1973)

    II: A201-1970, Art. 7, Para. 7.10
    II: A201-1970, Art. 8, Para. 8.3
    II: A201-1970, Art. 12, Para. 12.2

73035 Doyle & Russell, Inc. v. Welch Pile Driving Corp., 213 Va. 698, 194 S.E.2d 719 (1973)

    II: A401-1972, Art. 3

73036 Dunton v. Daniel Construction Co., 19 N.C. App. 51, 198 S.E.2d 8 (1973)

    III: A201-1970, Art. 11, Para. 11.1

73037 Eastern Foundation Co. v. Creswell, 475 F.2d 351 (D.C. Cir. 1973)

    III: A401-1972, Art. 9

73038 Edward R. Marden Corp. v. S & R Construction Co., 112 R. I. 332, 309 A.2d 675 (1973)

    III: A401-1972, Art. 11

73039 Ernst v. General Motors Corp., 482 F.2d 1047 (5th Cir. 1973)

    II: A201-1970, Art. 5, Para. 5.3
    II: A201-1970, Art. 8, Para. 8.3
    II: A201-1970, Art. 12, Para. 12.2

73040 Excavators & Erectors, Inc. v. Bullard Engineers, Inc. 489 F.2d 318 (5th Cir. 1973)

    III: A201-1970, Art. 12, Para. 12.1

73041 First State Bank v. Reorganized School District R-3, 495 S.W.2d 471 (Mo. Ct. App. 1973)

    III: A311-1970, Performance Bond

73042 Fischer v. Borsher, 226 Pa. Super. 463, 313 A.2d 311 (1973)

    II: A201-1970, Art. 2, Para. 2.2
    II: A201-1970, Art. 7, Para. 7.10
    II: A201-1970, Art. 12, Para. 12.2

73043 Fletcher v. Laguna Vista Corp., 275 So. 2d 579 (Fla. Dist. Ct. App. 1973)

    I: A101-1967, Art. 5
    I: A201-1970, Art. 9, Para. 9.1
    I: A201-1970, Art. 12, Para. 12.1
    I: A201-1970, Art. 12, Para. 12.2

73044 Gottschalk Brothers v. City of Wasau, 56 Wis. 2d 848, 203 N.W.2d 140 (1973)

    III: A201-1970, Art. 12, Para. 12.2

73045 Grover-Diamond Assoc. v. American Arbitration Ass'n, 297 Minn. 324, 211 N.W. 2d 787 (1973)

    I: B131-1970, Art. 11

73046 Hand v. Roriek Construction Co., 190 Neb. 191, 206 N.W.2d 835 (1973)

    I: A201-1970, Art. 10, Para. 10.2

73047 Hare v. Federal Compress & Warehouse Co., 359 F. Supp. 214 (N.D. Miss. 1973)

    III: A201-1970, Art. 10, Para. 10.2
    III: A401-1972, Art. 11

73048 Harris County v. Howard, 494 S.W.2d 250 (Tex. Civ. App. 1973)

    I: B131-1970, Art. 1
    I: B131-1970, Art. 2

73049 Hawkins v. Teeples & Thatcher, Inc., 515 P.2d 927 (Or. 1973)

    III: A201-1970, Art. 5, Para. 5.3
    III: A401-1972, Art. 11

73050 Hedla v. McCool, 476 F.2d 1223 (9th Cir. 1973)

    II: A201-1970, Art. 2, Para. 2.1
    II: B131-1970, Art. 6

73051 Hennepin Public Water District v. Petersen Construction Co., 54 Ill. 2d 327, 297 N.E.2d 131 (1973)

    III: A310-1970, Bid Bond

73052 Herbert & Brooner Construction Co. v. Golden 499 S.W.2d 541 (Mo. Ct. App. 1973)

    I: A201-1970, Art. 4, Para. 4.5
    I: A201-1970, Art. 8, Para. 8.3

73053 Hillsborough County Aviation Authority v. Cone Brothers Contracting Co., 285 So. 2d 619 (Fla. Dist. Ct. App. 1973)

    III: A201-1970, Art. 8, Para. 8.3

73054 Hill v. George A. Fuller Co., 473 F.2d 217 (5th Cir. 1973)

    III: A201-1970, Art. 7, Para. 7.10
    III: A401-1972, Art. 14

73055 Howard, Needles, Tammen & Bergendoff v. Steers, Perini & Pomeroy, 312 A.2d 621 (Del. 1973)

    III: A201-1970, Art. 4, Para. 4.18

73056 J. & J. Electric, Inc. v. Gilbert H. Moen Co., 9 Wash. App. 954, 516 P.2d 217 (1973)

    I: A201-1970, Art. 4, Para. 4.18
    I: A401-1972, Art. 11
    I: B131-1970, Art. 1

73057 J.E. Hathman, Inc. v. Alpha Epsilon Club, 491 S.W.2d 261 (Mo. 1973)

    I: A111-1967, Art. 4
    I: A111-1967, Art. 7
    I: A111-1967, Art. 8
    I: A111-1967, Art. 9
    I: A111-1967, Art. 10

73058 John W. Johnson, Inc. v. J.A. Jones Constr. Co., 369 F. Supp. 484 (E.D. Va. 1973)

    I: A201-1970, Art. 2, Para. 2.2
    I: A201-1970, Art. 5, Para. 5.3
    I: A401-1972, Art. 11
    I: A401-1972, Art. 12
    I: A401-1972, Art. 14

73059 Jones v. Continental Casualty Co., 123 N.J. Super. 353, 303 A.2d 91 (Ch. Div. 1973)

    III: A201-1970, Art. 11, Para. 11.1

73060 Jones v. Spindel, 128 Ga. App. 88, 196 S.E.2d 22 (1973)

    III: A201-1970, Art. 1, Para. 1.3

73061 J. S. & H. Construction Co. v. Richmond County Hospital Authority, 473 F.2d 212 (5th Cir. 1973)

    III: A311-1970, Labor & Material Payment Bond
    III: A401-1972, Art. 11
    III: A401-1972, Art. 14

73062 Kaiser Aluminum & Chemical Co. v. Finrow Painting Co., 10 Wash. App. 178, 516 P.2d 798 (1973)

    III: A201-1970, Art. 4, Para. 4.18

73063 Kingery Construction Co., v. Board of Regents, 189 Neb. 453, 203 N.W.2d 150 (1973)

    III: A201-1970, Art. 1, Para. 1.1

73064 Kostohryz v. McGuire, 298 Minn. 513, 212 N.W.2d 850 (1973)

    I: B131-1970, Art. 1
    I: B131-1970, Art. 3

73065 Kubela v. Schuessler Lumber Co. 492 S.W.2d 92 (Tex Civ. App. 1973)

    III: A111-1967, Art. 9

CASES

73066 Lebco, Inc. v. MacGregor Park National Bank, 500 S.W.2d 698 (Tex. Civ. App. 1973)

    I: A201-1970, Art. 3, Para. 3.4
    I: A201-1970, Art. 4, Para. 4.5
    I: A201-1970, Art. 13, Para. 13.2

73067 Lincoln County v. Skinner, 19 N.C. App. 127, 198 S.E.2d 40 (1973)

    III: A201-1970, Art. 2, Para. 2.2

73068 Loyal Erectors, Inc. v. Hamilton & Son, 312 A.2d 748 (Me. 1973)

    III: A201-1970, Art. 9, Para. 9.4

73069 Loyland v. Stone & Webster Eng'g Corp., 9 Wash. App. 682, 514 P.2d 184 (1973)

    III: A201-1970, Art. 2, Para. 2.2
    III: A201-1970, Art. 10, Para. 10.2
    III: C131-1970, Art. 2
    III: C131-1970, Art. 14

73070 Maryland Sales & Service Corp. v. Howell, 19 Md. App. 352, 311 A.2d 432 (1973)

    III: A201-1970, Art. 10, Para. 10.2

73071 McCandliss v. Ward W. Ross, Inc., 45 Mich. App. 342, 206 N.W.2d 455 (1973)

    I: A201-1970, Art. 7, Para. 7.10
    I: B131-1970, Art. 11

73072 McLouth Steel Corp. v. A. E. Anderson Construction Corp., 48 Mich. App. 424, 210 N.W.2d 448 (1973)

    III: A201-1970, Art. 4, Para. 4.18

73073 Merkle v. Rice Construction Co., 271 So. 2d 220 (Fla. Dist. Ct. App. 1973)

    III: A201-1970, Art. 7, Para. 7.10

73074 Metro Insulation Corp. v. Leventhal, 294 N.E.2d 508 (Mass. App. Ct. 1973)

    III: A201-1970, Art. 12, Para. 12.2

73075	Mills v. Robert W. Gottfried, Inc., 272 So. 2d 837 (Fla. Dist. Ct. App. 1973)	
	III:	A201-1970, Art. 7, Para. 7.10
73076	Mississippi Meadows, Inc. v. Hodson, 13 Ill. App. 3d 24, 299 N.E.2d 359 (1973)	
	III:	A201-1970, Art. 10, Para. 10.2
73077	Mitchell v. Flandor, 95 Idaho 228, 506 P.2d 455 (1973)	
	II:	A201-1970, Art. 9, Para. 9.7
73078	Moore v. Continental Casualty Co., 353 F. Supp. 105 (W.D. Okla. 1973)	
	III:	A401-1972, Art. 6
73079	Moore v. Continental Casualty Co., 366 F. Supp. 954 (W.D. Okla. 1973)	
	III:	A201-1970, Art. 9, Para. 9.7
	III:	A401-1972, Art. 11
73080	Moossy v. Huckabay Hospital, Inc., 283 So. 2d 699 (La. 1973)	
	I:	B131-1970, Art. 6
	I:	B131-1970, Art. 8
73081	Murphy v. City of Brockton, 364 Mass. 377, 305 N.E.2d 103 (1973)	
	I:	B131-1970, Art. 1
	I:	B131-1970, Art. 6
73082	Nuzzo v. Commercial Concrete Co., 366 F. Supp. 1333 (E.D. Pa. 1973)	
	III:	A201-1970, Art. 11, Para. 11.1
73083	Nelson Paving Co. v. Hjelle, 207 N.W.2d 225 (N.D. 1973)	
	III:	A201-1970, Art. 7, Para. 7.10
73084	Nucor Corp. v. Tennessee Forging Steel Service, 476 F.2d 386 (8th Cir. 1973)	
	III:	A201-1970, Art. 1, Para. 1.3
	III:	B131-1970, Art. 9

73085 Orput-Orput & Assoc., Inc. v. McCarthy, 12 Ill. App. 3d 88, 298 N.E.2d 225 (1973)

    III: B131-1970, Art. 6

73086 Oxford Development Corp. v. Rausauer Builders, Inc., 158 Ind. App. 622, 304 N.E.2d 211 (1973)

    III: A201-1970, Art. 12, Para. 12.2

73087 Page v. H. B. White & Son, 277 So. 2d 725 (La. 1973)

    III: A201-1970, Art. 1, Para. 1.1

73088 Paschen Contractors, Inc. v. John J. Calnan Co., 13 Ill. App. 3d 485, 300 N.E.2d 795 (1973)

    III: A201-1970, Art. 7, Para. 7.10

73089 Peter Kiewit Sons' Co. v. Iowa Southern Utilities Co., 355 F. Supp. 376 (S.D. Iowa 1973)

    III: A201-1970, Art. 5, Para. 5.1
    III: A201-1970, Art. 8, Para. 8.1
    III: A201-1970, Art. 9, Para. 9.7
    III: C131-1970, Art. 1

73090 Rackers & Backlesse, Inc. v. Kinstler, 497 S.W.2d 549 (Mo. Ct. App. 1973)

    III: A201-1970, Art. 5, Para. 5.1
    III: A201-1970, Art. 5, Para. 5.4

73091 Raisur Corp. v. New York City Hous. Auth., 32 N.Y.2d 279, 344 N.Y.S.2d 917 (1973)

    III: A201-1970, Art. 7, Para. 7.10

73092 Ray v. Monsanto Co., 473 F.2d 219 (9th Cir. 1973)

    III: A107-1970, Art. 18
    III: A201-1970, Art. 10, Para. 10.2

73093 Redman Development Corp. v. Piedmont Heating & Air Conditioning, Inc., 128 Ga. App. 477, 197 S.E.2d 167 (1973)

    III: A401-1972, Art. 11

73094	Reisman v. Ranoel Realty Co., 224 Pa. Super. 220, 303 A.2d 511 (1973)	
	II:	A201-1970, Art. 7, Para. 7.10
73095	Robinson & Wilson, Inc. v. Stone, 35 Cal. App. 3d 396, 110 Cal. Rptr. 675 (1973)	
	I:	A111-1967, Art. 6
	I:	A201-1970, Art. 14, Para. 14.2
73096	Rosellini v. Banchero, 8 Wash. App. 383, 506 P.2d 866 (1973)	
	III:	A111-1967, Art. 7
73097	Rossetti v. City of New Britain, 163 Conn. 283, 303 A.2d 714 (1973)	
	II:	A201-1970, Art. 2, Para. 2.1
73098	Royal Service Co. v. Whitehead Construction Co., 254 Ark. 234, 492 S.W.2d 423 (1973)	
	I:	A401-1972, Art. 9
	I:	A401-1972, Art. 11
73099	Shell Chemical Co. v. Lamb, 493 S.W.2d 742 (Tex. 1973)	
	III:	A201-1970, Art. 4, Para. 4.18
	III:	A201-1970, Art. 10, Para. 10.2
	III:	A401-1972, Art. 11
73100	Southwire Co. v. Metal Equipment Co., 129 Ga. App. 49, 198 S.E.2d 687 (1973)	
	III:	A201-1970, Art. 7, Para. 7.1
73101	Standhardt v. Flintcote Co., 84 N.M. 796, 508 P.2d 1283 (1973)	
	III:	B131-1970, Art. 1
73102	State Department of Human Resources v. Williams, 12 Or. App. 133, 505 P.2d 936 (1973)	
	III:	A201-1970, Art. 7, Para. 7.10
	III:	A201-1970, Art. 9, Para. 9.7

73103 (UNASSIGNED)

73104 Steffek v. Wichers, 211 Kan. 342, 507 P.2d 274 (1973)

        I: A201-1970, Art. 2, Para. 2.2
        I: A201-1970, Art. 8, Para. 8.3
        I: A201-1970, Art. 9, Para. 9.4
        I: A201-1970, Art. 12, Para. 12.1
        I: A201-1970, Art. 13, Para. 13.2

73105 Stewart-Scott Construction Corp. v. F. & M. Schaefer Co., 41 A.D.2d 788, 341 N.Y.S.2d 269 (1973)

        III: A201-1970, Art. 7, Para. 7.10
        III: A201-1970, Art. 12, Para. 12.1
        III: A201-1970, Art. 12, Para. 12.2

73106 Strickland v. Transamerica Co., 481 F.2d 138 (5th Cir. 1973)

        III: A201-1970, Art. 10, Para. 10.2

73107 Super Construction Co. v. New Orleans Levee Board, 286 So. 2d 134 (La. Ct. App. 1973)

        III: A401-1972, Art. 11

73108 Tatar v. Maxon Construction Co., 3 Ill. App. 3d 352, 277 N.E.2d 715 (1973), *aff'd*, 54 Ill. 2d 64, 294 N.E.2d 272 (1973)

        II: A201-1967, Art. 4, Para. 4.18
        III: A107-1966, Art. 11
        III: A401-1967, Art. 11
        III: A401-1972, Art. 11

73109 Temple Sinai-Suburban Reform Temple v. Richmond, 112 R.I. 234, 308 A.2d 508 (1973)

        II: A201-1970, Art. 2, Para. 2.2
        II: B131-1970, Art. 1

73110 Titan Construction Co. v. Nolf, 31 Colo. App. 21, 500 P.2d 377 (1972), *rev'd*, 3 Colo. 188, 515 P.2d 1123 (1973)

        III: A401-1972, Art. 11

73111 Torres v. Jarmon, 501 S.W.2d 369 (Tex. Civ. App. 1973)

       I: B131-1970, Art. 3

73112 Triple M. Roofing Co. v. Greater Jericho Corp., 43 A.D.2d 594, 349 N.Y.S.2d 771 (1973)

       I: A401-1972, Art. 11

73113 Universal Terrazzo & Tile Co. v. Parsons Corp., 189 Neb. 634, 204 N.W.2d 149 (1973)

       III: A401-1972, Art. 12

73114 Van Ornum v. Otter Tail Power Co., 210 N.W.2d 188 (ND. 1973)

       III: A201-1970, Art. 2, Para. 2.2

73115 V. C. Edwards Contracting Co. v. Port of Tacoma, 83 Wash. 2d 7, 514 P.2d 1381 (1973)

       III: A201-1970, Art. 8, Para. 8.3

73116 Verdex Steel & Construction Co. v. Board of Supervisors, 19 Ariz. App. 547, 509 P.2d 240 (1973)

       III: A201-1970, Art. 7, Para. 7.10
       III: A401-1972, Art. 14

73117 Vinnell Corp. v. State, 109 Ariz 87, 505 P.2d 547 (1973)

       III: A401-1972, Art. 11

73118 Vitek, Inc. v. Alvarado Ice Palace, 34 Cal. App. 3d 586, 110 Cal. Rptr. 86 (1973)

       III: A201-1970, Art. 4, Para. 4.7
       III: A201-1970, Art. 7, Para. 7.1

73119 Waller v. J. E. Brenneman Co., 307 A.2d 550 (Del. Super. Ct. 1973)

       III: A401—1972, Art.5

73120 Walter L. Couse & Co. v. Hardy Corp., 49 Ala. App. 522, 274 So. 2d 316 (Civ. App. 1972), *cert. denied,* 290 Ala. 134, 274 So. 2d 322 (1973)

       III: A401-1972, Art. 11

73121 Warren Brothers v. Cardi Corp. 471 F.2d 1304 (1st Cir. 1973)

    III: A401-1972, Art. 13

73122 Warren G. Kleban Engineering Corp. v. Caldwell, 361 F. Supp. 805 (N.D. Miss. 1973)

    I: A201-1970, Art. 5, Para. 5.1
    I: A201-1970, Art. 5, Para. 5.2

73123 Wheeler v. Aetna Casualty & Sur. Co., 11 Ill. App. 3d 841, 298 N.E.2d 329 (1973)

    III: A201-1970, Art. 10, Para. 10.2

73124 Williams & Associates v. Ramsey Products Corp., 19 N.C. App. 9, 198 S.E.2d 67 (1973)

    I: B131-1970, Art. 1

73125 Williams v. D. A. H. Construction Corp., 42 A.D.2d 877, 346 N.Y.S.2d 862 (1973)

    III: A401-1972, Art. 11

73126 Wilson v. Nooter Corp. 475 F.2d 487 (1st Cir. 1973)

    III: A201-1970, Art. 7, Para. 7.6

73127 (UNASSIGNED)

73128 Gallagher v. Schernecker, 60 Wis. 2d 143, 208 N.W.2d 437 (1973)

    III: A201-1970, Art. 7, Para. 7.10

73129 Titan Enterprises, Inc. v. Armo Construction, Inc., 32 Cal. App. 3d 828, 108 Cal. Rptr. 456 (1973)

    III: A201-1970, Art. 2, Para. 2.2

74001 A.E. Investment Corp. v. Link Builders, Inc. 62 Wis. 2d 479, 214 N.W.2d 764 (1974)

      III: B131-1970, Art. 1

74002 Amelco Window Corp. v. Federal Insurance Co. 127 N.J. Super. 342, 317 A.2d 398 (App. Div. 1974)

      I: A201-1970, Art. 4, Para. 4.4
      I: A201-1970, Art. 7, Para. 7.5
      III: A311-1970, Performance Bond

Subcontractor sued general contractor's surety to recover balance of payment due on a construction contract after general contractor defaulted because of its bankruptcy. Subcontractor's suit was based on a third-party beneficiary theory because of a performance bond between the owner and the surety and because of a contract between the owner and general contractor which required payment for all labor and materials. Although a labor and material payment bond was never executed, the Superior Court, Appellate Division, reversed the trial court and held that the subcontractor was a third-party beneficiary under the performance bond.

74003 Bartley, Inc. v. Jefferson Parish School Board, 302 So. 2d 280 (La. 1974)

      I: A201-1970, Art. 2, Para. 2.2
      I: A201-1970, Art. 7, Para. 7.10
      I: A401-1972, Art. 11

Contractor sued subcontractor and owner to compel arbitration. The owner and subcontractor claimed the demand for arbitration was premature because the contracts stated that disputes were to be first submitted to the architect and claimed waiver of the right to arbitrate. They also claimed that the subcontract did not require arbitration.

The Supreme Court of Louisiana, applying the state arbitration statute, reversed the decision of the Court of Appeals and found that the questions of procedural arbitrability should be decided by arbitration and not by the courts. The claim that the subcontract did not require arbitration was also said to be without merit since the prime contract, which required arbitration of all disputes, was incorporated by reference.

74004   Becker v. Black & Veatch Consulting Engineers, 509 F.2d 42 (8th Cir. 1974)

         III: A201-1970, Art. 4, Para. 4.18

Persons injured in gas pipeline explosion sued utility which owned it, contractor, and consulting engineer. Owner, contractor, and engineer sued each other for indemnification.

The indemnity clause in the construction contract between the utility owner and the contractor provided that the latter would indemnify the owner "from loss and damage and from claims made on account of work done under this contract." Interpreting this provision, the Court of Appeals found it was broad enough to cover claims founded in part upon the owner's negligence in connection with the work. The contract read as a whole placed no express time limitation on the contractor's duty to indemnify the owner, so that its obligation was not limited to claims arising prior to completion of the contract. The court held that the phrase "work done under this contract" entitled the owner to indemnification to the extent that its own negligence related to work done under the contract but did not protect the owner from its own independent negligent conduct. The utility was to recover for its failure to inspect and discover the defective crossover which caused the explosion, since this negligence related to work done under the contract, but it could not recover for its independent negligence occurring after receiving notification of the gas leak.

74005   Bel Pre Medical Center, Inc. v. Frederick Contractors, Inc., 21 Md. App. 307, 320 A.2d 558 (1974)

         I: A201-1970, Art. 2, Para. 2.2
         I: A201-1970, Art. 7, Para. 7.10

Owner filed suit against contractor to compel arbitration concerning balance allegedly due the contractor after contractor had filed mechanic's lien. Contractor requested an injunction to stay arbitration on the ground that the demand for arbitration was not made within thirty days of the receipt of the architect's letter denying the claim for payment as required by the construction contract.

The Court of Special Appeals reversed the Circuit Court's granting of the injunction and held that once it is determined that the parties are obligated to submit to binding arbitration, procedural questions that bear on the final disposition of the dispute should be left to the arbitrator and not the court.

74006   Bitner v. Lester B. Knight & Associates, 16 Ill. App. 3d 857, 307 N.E.2d 136 (1974)

         III: A201-1970, Art. 7, Para. 7.1
         III: A201-1970, Art. 10, Para. 10.2

74007 Cape Fear Electric Co. v. Star News Newspapers, 22 N.C. App. 519, 207 S.E.2d 323 (1974)

  I: A201-1970, Art. 9, Para. 9.7
  I: A201-1970, Art. 12, Para. 12.2

Contractor sued owner for increased cost of installing more expensive electrical materials allegedly pursuant to instructions from owner's engineer. Contractor requested a formal change order from architects but none was ever issued. The final billing certified by architects did not include the higher cost of the installed materials.

The Court of Appeals affirmed the District Court's dismissal of the contractor's action. Even though final payment was made on the certified billing, the court found no waiver of the claim, since the contract provision excepted "claims made in writing and still unsettled." The court also held, however, that the contract stated that "the contract sum may be changed only by change order."

74008 Carpenter International, Inc. v. Kaiser Jamaica Corp., 369 F. Supp. 1138 (D. Del. 1974)

  III: A201-1970, Art. 9, Para. 9.7

74009 Children's Hospital v. American Arbitration Ass'n, 231 Pa. Super. 230, 331 A.2d. 848 (1974)

  I: A201-1970, Art. 7, Para. 7.1
  I: A201-1970, Art. 10, Para. 10.1

Dispute arose between general contractor and three prime contractors over allocation of responsibility for safety precautions since each construction contract stated the "contractor" was responsible. Pursuant to a joint request for an interpretation of the contract provision, the architect determined that the general contractor was responsible for the safety precautions.

The general contractor disputed this information and filed a demand for arbitration against the owner with the American Arbitration Association as arbitrator, alleging the other contractors were responsible for a portion of the costs. The owner then filed for arbitration against the three prime contractors and filed a motion for consolidation of the arbitration disputes. The Court of Common Pleas issued the order of consolidation, which the three prime contractors appealed.

Superior Court affirmed the Circuit Court's ruling and held that since all disputes arose out of the architect's decision which the four contractors had jointly requested and since all four contracts contained identical arbitration and safety provisions, not to consolidate the arbitration would injure the owner and force it to forego a contract benefit to which it was entitled.

74010 Clifton D. Mayhew, Inc. v. Mabro Construction Inc., 383 F. Supp. 192 (D.D.C. 1974)

       II: A201-1970, Art. 7, Para. 7.10

       III: A401-1972, Art. 14

Subcontractor sued contractor for payment for labor and materials; contractor moved to stay proceedings pending arbitration and to compel arbitration.

The contract provided that: "Any dispute arising under this contract shall be submitted to arbitration. The Subcontractor agrees that he will not take any legal action or institute proceedings of any kind . . . until the contractor either shall have refused to submit the same to arbitration or . . . shall have rejected . . . the decision of the Arbitrators." The subcontractor, as a defense to the contractor's motion, claimed they had agreed to cancel the contract.

The District Court interpreted the federal arbitration act and construed the U.S. Supreme Court's decision in *Prima Paint Corp. v. Flood & Conklin Mfg. Co.,* 388 U.S. 395, 87 S. Ct. 1801, 18 L. Ed. 2d 1270 (1967), and held that when a party alleges that the entire contract was canceled, the issue of arbitrability is for the arbitrators and not the courts to decide. The court may only decide issues relating to the arbitration agreement. The parties are also entitled to agree in their contract that one of the questions referable to arbitration is the issue of whether the contract has been terminated, abandoned, or canceled. In the contract clause specifying that the subcontractor would "not take any legal action or institute proceedings of any kind" until he tried arbitration, the court found such an agreement.

74011 Continental Realty Corp. v. Andrew J. Crevolin Co., 380 F. Supp. 246 (S.D. W. Va. 1974)

       I: A201-1970, Art. 14, Para. 14.2

       II: A311-1970, Performance Bond

Owner sued contractor and surety for breach of building contract.

The contractor was certified by the architect as in default of its contractual obligations. The owner in turn called upon the surety to fulfill its obligations under the performance bond. The surety let bids for completion of the project, but failed to arrange for further construction work. Damages to the owner were augmented due to the surety's breach.

The District Court found that the surety's liability to the owner was for the amount of damages sustained by its breach. The rule that a surety's liability is limited to the penal sum of the bond does not apply when the contractual duty to the owner is breached. Increased construction costs and lost profits as a result of delays in completion were clearly foreseeable, and thus could properly be included in the damages.

74012 Contracting & Material Co. v. City of Chicago, 20 Ill. App. 3d 684, 314 N.E.2d 598 (1974)

   III: A201-1970, Art. 8, Para. 8.3

Contractor sued city for increased costs when city demanded completion at original date despite delays due to labor dispute and work stoppage ordered by city.

The Appellate Court reversed the Circuit Court's judgment for the city. The city had repeatedly refused the contractor's request for extension of the completion date to offset time lost due to a city-ordered suspension of work and a strike, although contract language permitted extensions for these reasons. The City of Chicago Provisions allowed extensions only pursuant to work suspensions ordered by the city. Since these were ambiguous and conflicting provisions, the court construed them so as to avoid finding any part of the contract as a nullity and found that the City Provisions did not supersede or negate the delays clause in the contract. Both circumstances of excusable delay gave the contractor a right to an extension. The court also found that the city's action in holding the contractor to the original completion date, denying it the extensions to which it was entitled, amounted to an acceleration of the performance under contract, so as to give the contractor a right to its increased costs.

74013 Decatur Construction Co. v. Central Illinois Public Services Co., 16 Ill. App. 3d 1056, 307 N.E.2d 431 (1974)

   III: A201-1970, Art. 12, Para. 12.2

74014 Devlin v. Milwaukie Covenant Church, 269 Or. 596, 525 P.2d 998 (1974)

   I: A111-1974, Art. 5
   I: A201-1970, Art. 2, Para. 2.2
   I: A201-1970, Art. 7, Para. 7.6
   I: A201-1970, Art. 9, Para. 9.3
   I: A201-1970, Art. 9, Para. 9.4
   I: A201-1970, Art. 9, Para. 9.5

Contractor filed suit to foreclose mechanic's lien against owner. Owner counterclaimed for damages for breach of contract.

The Supreme Court reversed the decision of the Circuit Court, which had held in favor of the contractor, and stated that the contract was a cost plus fee contract with a guaranteed maximum cost, which had been breached by the contractor when he stopped work. The architect had refused to certify monthly payments when it became apparent that costs would exceed the guaranteed maximum. The contractor's notice under the contract that it would stop the work in seven days, if a periodic payment was not received, was not proper unless he was then entitled to the payment. Under the contract provisions, the applications for payment by the contractor had to be submitted to and approved by the architect, based on his judgment of the work and the application had to be itemized and supported by data. Any disputes had to be decided first by the architect and then either party was entitled to arbitration. Since the contractor had not complied with the contract terms his work stoppage was a contract breach for which the owner was entitled to damages.

74015   Fandrich v. Allstate Insurance Co., 25 Ill. App. 3d 301, 322 N.E.2d 843 (1974)

         III: A201-1970, Art. 14, Para. 14.2

Employee sued owner for personal injuries on basis of Illinois Structural Work Act and common law negligence. Circuit Court entered judgment for owner and employee appealed.

The Appellate court affirmed the Circuit Court and stated that there was sufficient evidence to support the jury's determination that the contractor was not an agent of the owner but rather was an independent contractor, which status meant that the owner was not responsible for his negligent acts. The court stated that the contract provision which authorized the owner to terminate the contract under specific conditions did not give the owner the right to terminate the contract at any time without cause because of the addition of the language "or for any other reason." The contract documents read as a whole gave the owner the right to terminate only for good cause and after the architect certified that there was such good cause.

74016   Griswold & Rauma, Architects, Inc. v. Aesculapius Corp., 301 Minn. 121, 221 N.W.2d 556 (1974)

         I: B141-1974, Art. 1
         I: B141-1974, Art. 2
         I: B141-1974, Art. 3
         I: B141-1974, Art. 6

Architect filed suit to foreclose on lien for architectural services rendered to owner. Owner counterclaimed to recover fees already paid alleging architect breached contract by grossly underestimating the probable cost of construction. District Court granted judgment for owner and architect appealed.

The Supreme Court reversed, stating that the four relevant factors were whether the figure is guaranteed or merely an approximation, whether the excess of actual or probable cost resulted by change orders of the owner, whether owner has waived right to object to architect's performance by not objecting or not objecting in timely fashion and whether architect has made reasonable cost revisions on an excessive bid.

The Court concluded that the architect did not guarantee the maximum cost figure, the provable cost did not substantially exceed the cost figure, the owner approved substantial changes in the original plan, and the architect suggested reasonable revisions in plans to reduce costs.

74017   Hoffman v. Glock, 20 Md. App. 284, 315 A.2d 551 (1974)

        III: A201-1970, Art. 1, Para. 1.1

        III: A201-1970, Art. 12, Para. 12.1

Owners sued contractor for damages, and contractor counterclaimed. The Court of Special Appeals affirmed the Circuit Court's denial of owners' claim and the contractor's counterclaim. The court denied the owners' claim because they were stopped from enforcing the requirement that all changes to the work be in writing because of their acceptance of a series of oral modifications. The court noted that the contract did not contain a clause stating that the contract contained the entire agreement of the parties. The contractor's counterclaim was also denied because he failed to prove damages for the changes in the work.

74018   ICI America, Inc. v. Martin-Marietta Corp., 368 F.Supp. 1148 (Del. 1974)

        III: A201-1970, Art. 4, Para. 4.5

74019   Jim Mahoney, Inc. v. Galokee Corp., 214 Kan. 754, 522 P.2d 428 (1974)

        I: A107-1974, Art.

        I: A107-1974, Art. 24

Contractor sued owner for balance owed on project and owner counterclaimed for cost of completion for alleged breach of contract.

The Supreme Court affirmed the District Court's judgment for the owner as to the award of damages based on repair costs, since the building had been completed so that it was occupied and used by the owner for the purposes contemplated by the parties, and since correction or completion would not unreasonably modify or destroy work done by the contractor. The standard of diminution of value was improper under these circumstances. The court also pointed out that the parties had reasonably contemplated this rule by including a contract provision that if the contractor defaults or neglects to carry out the work in accordance with the contract, the owner could terminate the contract, take possession of the site, and finish the work at the expense of the contractor.

The court also held that where there is a conflict between the provisions of a building contract and the provisions of plans and specifications incorporated into the contract by reference in the contract, the language of the contract itself should prevail.

74020   Keating v. Miller, 292 So. 2d 759 (La. Ct. App. 1974)

        I: A107-1974, Art. 22

        I: A107-1974, Art. 24

Contractor sued owner for balance due after owner terminated contract and owner counterclaimed for cost of completion due to defective workmanship.

The Court of Appeals reversed the Judicial District court, finding that the sections of the contract entitled "Correction of Work" and "Termination by Owner" gave the owner the right to terminate the contract and complete the work himself when the contractor reduced the length of the house by two feet without the owner's permission and constructed a brick veneer wall so poorly that it collapsed twice. Although the owner waived the breach of non-compliance with specifications by permitting construction to continue after he learned that the house had been reduced in length, he had a right to terminate when the contractor failed to correct the deficient brickwork after due notice.

74021   LaPuzza v. Prom Town House Motor Inn, Inc., 191 Neb. 687, 217 N.W.2d 472 (1974)

    III: A111-1974, Art. 5
    III: A111-1974, Art. 8
    III: A111-1974, Art. 9
    III: A201-1970, Art. 7, Para. 7.9

Contractor filed suit to foreclose a mechanic's lien. Trial court determined that the lien was valid and owner appealed.

The Supreme Court affirmed the trial court's decision as to an alleged oral agreement for a guaranteed maximum cost in cost plus fee contract, since the parol evidence rule would exclude testimony concerning such agreement. It also affirmed as to trial court's allowance of subcontractor's overhead as a proper cost of contractor to be reimbursed by owner, citing the general rule enunciated in a similar case. It also affirmed the trial court's allowance of interest from the date due rather than from date of the judgment, since the contract specifically so stated.

74022   Milton Schwartz & Associates v. Magness Corp., 368 F. Supp. 749 (D. Del. 1974)

    I: A201-1970, Art. 7, Para. 7.10
    I: B131-1970, Art. 11

74023   Mingledorff's, Inc. v. Hicks, 133 Ga. App. 27, 209 S.E.2d 661 (1974)

    II: A201-1970, Art. 7, Para. 7.
    II: A401-1970, Art. 11

The assignee of a subcontractor sued the contractor to recover money owed subcontractor. The contractor assigned a portion of money due without written consent of the subcontractor although the contract contained a clause prohibiting assignment of the contract "or any part thereof" without written consent of the other party to the contract.

The Court of Appeals affirmed the trial court's decision upholding the validity of the anti-assignment clause. The phrase "or any part thereof" precluded limited assignment of the right under the contract to the money due the subcontractor.

74024 Nat Harrison Associates v. Gulf State Utils. Co., 491 F.2d 578 (5th Cir. 1974)

    III: A107-1970, Art. 11
    III: A201-1970, Art. 4, Para. 4.7
    III: A201-1970, Art. 8, Para. 8.3
    III: A201-1970, Art. 13, Para. 13.3

74025 New Again Construction Co. v. City of New York, 76 Misc. 2d 943, 351 N.Y.S.2d 895 (Sup. Ct. 1974)

    III: A201-1970, Art. 8, Para. 8.3

74026 Norfolk and Western Ry. Co. v. Werner Industries, 21 N.C. App. 116, 203 S.E.2d 321 (1974)

    III: A201-1970, Art. 4, Para. 4.18

Owner sued contractor for repayment of an employee's personal injury claim pursuant to indemnity provision in contract which provided that contractor would indemnify owner for injury to persons "caused by or resulting from any acts or omissions, negligent or otherwise, of Contractor." Owner claimed this wording would protect it against loss caused by the negligence of owner, contractor, both, or neither.

The Court of Appeals affirmed the trial court's grant of summary judgment to the contractor and strictly construed the provisions to only require contractor to indemnify owner for contractor's negligence.

74027 Otto v. Hendry, 132 Ga. App. 598, 208 S.E.2d 611 (1974)

    III: A201-1970, Art. 10, Para. 10.1
    III: A201-1970, Art. 10, Para. 10.2

An employee of subcontractor sued contractor for personal injuries sustained in repair of fire-damaged house while descending dangerous stairwell.

The court of Appeals affirmed the lower court's denial of summary judgment and stated that a contractor in possession and control of a building is bound to take reasonable measures to protect business invitees on the premises from injuries due to hidden defects or places of unusual danger.

74028 Owens v. City of Bartlett, Labette County, 215 Kan. 840, 528 P.2d 1235 (1974)

    III: A201-1970, Art. 12, Para. 12.1
    III: A201-1970, Art. 12, Para. 12.2

Contractor sued city for extra cost of rock removal in construction of water distribution system.

The Supreme Court of Kansas affirmed the District Court's award of the extra amount claimed. The court held that the city council and the mayor waived the change order provision of the contract by furnishing the contractor with special rock removal equipment and by paying 71.5 percent of the cost of the extra work even though there was never a written change order. The contract provided: "no claims for any extra work or materials shall be allowed unless it is ordered in writing by the Owner or its authorized representative."

74029   Peter Kiewit Sons' Co. v. Okeeke Elevator Co., 191 Neb. 50, 213 N.W.2d 731 (1974)

        III: A401-1972, Art. 11

74030   Poole & Kent Corp. v. C.E. Thurston & Sons, Inc., 286 N.C. 121, 209 S.E.2d 450 (1974)

        III: A201-1970, Art. 5, Para. 5.
        III: A201-1970, Art. 7, Para. 7.5

Subcontractor sued second-tier subcontractor for beach of contract provision that second-tier subcontractor was to provide an acceptable work force; latter counterclaimed for wrongful contract termination. Second-tier subcontractors were union members at time of contract with subcontractor; later the collective bargaining agreement expired and was never renegotiated. Union members picketed the work site and other subcontractors' employees refused to work. The Court of Appeals affirmed the trial court and held that the public policy of North Carolina, as found in its statues, prohibited membership or non-membership in a labor union as a condition of employment. Since valid laws existing at the time and place a contract is entered into become a part of the contract unless expressly excluded, these statutes governed the issue of employees' union membership under the contract. The subcontractor's cancellation of the second-tier subcontractor was held to be unwarranted.

74031   Robinson Explosives, Inc. v. Dalon Contracting Co., 132 Ga. App. 849, 209 S.E.2d 264 (1974)

        I: A201-1970, Art. 7, Para. 7.5
        I: A311-1970, Labor & Material Payment Bond

Supplier of subcontractor sued contractor and its surety on labor and material payment bond, and trial court dismissed the complaint.

The Court of Appeals reversed the trial court and held that the language of the bond clearly indicated that a supplier of a subcontractor could recover as a "claimant," which was defined as "one having a direct contract with the Principal or with a Subcontractor of the Principal for labor, material, or both, used or reasonably required for use in the performance of the Contract." The Court also stated that although the bond declared that the obligee "may sue on the bond for the use of such claimant," the supplier had properly brought suit in its own name because of a statute allowing the beneficiary of a contract between other parties to bring suit against the promisor.

74032 Roll v. Spero, 293 So. 2d 270 (Fla. Dist. Ct. App. 1974)

   I: B141-1974, Art. 3
   I: B141-1974, Art. 12

Architects sued owner for balance due for plans and specifications prepared for project never completed because of high bids received by owner.

The District Court of Appeals reversed the Circuit Court and found evidence could not support the parties' establishment of $250,000 as a fixed limit of construction cost, which would have resulted in a lower architect's fee. The contract provided that any modifications to the contract must be in writing.

74033 Rosenthal v. Kurz, 62 Wis. 2d 1, 213 N.W.2d 741 (1974)

   III: B131-1970, Art. 13

74034 St. Joseph Hospital v. Corbetta Construction Co., 21 Ill. App. 3d 925, 316 N.E.2d 51 (1974)

   III: A201-1970, Art. 4, Para. 4.5
   III: A201-1970, Art. 7, Para. 7.9
   III: A201-1970, Art. 9, Para. 9.5
   III: A201-1970, Art. 10, Para. 10.2

Hospital brought suit against architect, contractor and manufacturer of paneling for damages for installation of paneling which did not comply with city code.

The Appellate Court affirmed in part and reversed in part the decision of the Cook County Circuit Court. The hospital was granted recovery from the architect for the cost of removal and reconstruction of the paneling to comply with the city code. The court also held that the architect could not escape liability for these damages by his refusal to issue a final certificate for payment, which had permitted the hospital to withhold from the contractor a sufficient sum of money to cover its loss, since the error was that of the architect. The court held that the specification of wall paneling by the architect was a warranty made by the hospital and architect to the contractor that the material was suitable, and therefore the contractor was not liable to the hospital on its written guarantee in the contract. The court did not require the contractor to indemnify the hospital or architect for the results of what they ordered the contractor to do, since under Illinois law an indemnification clause must clearly state that a party can be indemnified for its own negligence or omission.

The contract provision that stated that the contractor would comply with all codes and would be responsible to the hospital for all damages for the violation of codes, also did not make the contractor liable to the hospital because the court believed this was another version of the hospital's contention that the contractor should indemnify the hospital for what it had ordered the contractor to do. The hospital was required to pay the contractor the amount wrongfully withheld by the hospital when the architect refused to issue a final certificate for payment. The hospital was required, however, to pay interest only from the date of the judgment to be determined later by remand to the trial court. Interest did not run from an earlier date since the amount was not due under the contract until the architect issued the final certificate for payment for that amount.

74035   Sasser & Co. v. Griffin, 133 Ga. App. 83, 210 S.E.2d 34 (1974)

       III: A201-1970, Art. 5, Para. 5.4
       III: A201-1970, Art. 7, Para. 7.10

Subcontractor sued contractor for payment for plumbing, heating and air conditioning work.

The subcontract provided for progress payments to be made "from money received from the owner only" and called for payment "within 10 days of receiving money from the owner—approximately the 20th of the month."

The Court of Appeals found that payment by the owner may be a condition precedent to a subcontractor's right of payment, if the contract contains an express provision clearly indicating that to be the intent of the parties. This language clearly expressed such an intention, the court stated.

A contract provision for arbitration of "any question" concerning the work was void and unenforceable, the court found, since it would deprive the parties of access to the judicial system. The Court of Appeals held that an arbitration clause may not be a condition precedent to the right to sue on the contract if it concerns "all questions" arising thereunder.

74036   Scherrer Construction Co. v. Burlington Memorial Hospital, 64 Wis. 2d 720, 221 N.W.2d 855 (1974)

       I: A201-1970, Art. 12, Para. 12.1

Owner requested Circuit Court to vacate an arbitration award which granted to contractor additional compensation for unexpected sub-soil conditions. Circuit Court confirmed the arbitration award and owner appealed.

The Supreme Court affirmed and held that the arbitrators did not exceed their powers, although one arbitrator stated he would be guided by an AIA contract provision, which conflicted with a Projected Requirements provision, because the AIA provision was national in scope. The court stated that using the AIA provision could be supported by a "conflicts clause" in the Supplementary Conditions and the award also could be supported by the doctrine of impossibility of performance.

74037 Schroeder v. C. F. Braun Co., 502 F.2d 235 (7th Cir. 1974)

      III: A201-1970, Art. 4, Para. 4.18

      III: A401-1972, Art. 11

Employee of sub-subcontractor sued his employer, subcontractor, contractor, and two owners for injuries sustained in a fall from a cooling tower under construction where scaffolding required by state law was not provided.

The contract between the owners and the contractor provided that the contractor would indemnify the owners for injuries to any person "arising out of any act or omission of Contractor or its Subcontractors" in connection with the work. The Court of Appeals sustained the judgments for the plaintiff and for contractual indemnity. The term "subcontractor" included those who take a portion of a contract from a subcontractor, so that indemnification was required for the negligence of the sub-subcontractor, the court held.

The contract between the contractor and subcontractor contained a similar provision requiring the subcontractor to indemnify the contractor and owner. The owner and contractor were entitled to indemnity under the contract provision regardless of the sub-subcontractor's obligation.

The indemnity clause in the contract between the subcontractor and sub-subcontractor provided that "injury" was to be construed to include injury resulting from among other things, failure to use scaffolding where necessary. The court found that the sub-subcontractor's active misconduct in failing to provide scaffolding caused the employee's injuries, so that the liability of the subcontractor and owner clearly arose "in connection with" or "out of performance of" the work by the sub-subcontractor. The sub-subcontractor's active negligence caused the accident. The court suggested that a party may be indemnified against its own passive negligence, although indemnification against one's own active negligence would be impermissible.

74038 Smith v. United States, 497 F.2d 500 (5th Cir. 1974)

      III: A201-1970, Art. 4, Para. 4.18

      III: A401-1972, Art. 11

Employees of subcontractor sued their employer, other subcontractors, contractor and the United States for injuries sustained in a blasting accident.

The Court of Appeals reversed and remanded to the District Court. The Court of Appeals stated that the contract between the United States and the prime contractor contained an indemnification clause similar to the AIA provision, which was "drafted so as to allow the indemnitee immunity from its own negligence (assuming the contractor is himself negligent)." This contract had "hold harmless" language but did not explicitly state whether indemnification should obtain regardless of the indemnitee's negligence.

The Court of Appeals found that if either "hold harmless" language or an express disclaimer was used, then there is a strong indication to provide indemnification regardless of the indemnitee's negligence. The court also stated that each of the subcontracts incorporated the terms of the prime contract and therefore each respective subcontractor was entitled to indemnity, until the final sub-contractor.

74039   T.A. Loving Co. v. Latham, 20 N.C. App. 318, 201 S.E.2d 516 (1974)

        III: A111-1967, Art. 6

74040   University of Alaska v. Modern Construction, Inc., 522 P.2d 1132 (Alaska 1974)

        I: A201-1970, Art. 2, Para. 2.2
        I: A201-1970, Art. 7, Para. 7.1
        I: A201-1970, Art. 8, Para. 8.3

University filed motions to vacate arbitrators' award to general contractor for delay damages attributed to owner and for clarification of award. Superior Court denied motion to vacate and confirmed award, and university appealed.

Supreme Court affirmed the judgment and stated that the arbitrators had not exceeded their powers by deciding that the issue of delay damages was arbitrable under the contract provision which mandated arbitration of "all claims, disputes and other matters in question arising out of this contract or the breach thereof. . . ." Another contract section expressed the parties' intent that "any claim, dispute or other matter that has been referred to the Architect . . . shall be subject to arbitration upon the written demand of either party." A third contract section, which specifically addressed the issue of delays, stated that "This Paragraph . . . does not exclude the recovery of damages for delay by either party under other provisions of the Contract Documents."

74041   Voight v. Nanz, 61 Wis. 2d 710, 213 N.W.2d 749 (1974)

        III: A401-1972, Art. 5
        III: A401-1972, Art. 12

74042   Vonasek v. Hirsch & Stevens, Inc., 65 Wis. 2d 1, 221 N.W. 2d 815 (1974)

        I: B141-1974, Art. 1

Contractor sued architect to recover cost of a roof collapse and alleged that architect provided an inadequate level of supervision and defective plans and specifications. The Circuit Court dismissed the complaint finding the cause of damage to be a deficiency in the construction procedure adopted by the contractor and not a defect in the design plans or lack of architect's supervision.

The Supreme Court affirmed and held that the contract provision controlling the construction phase of the agreement did not require the architect to specify procedures or supervise work in order to see if proper procedures were being followed and that although architect had been continuously represented at construction site, this did not increase architect's responsibility or alter architect's lack of duty to interfere with contractor's judgment as to construction procedures.

74043 Wickes Corp. v. Industrial Financial Corp., 493 F.2d 1173 (5th Cir. 1974)

III: A201-1970, Art. 7, Para. 7.10

Owner filed demand for arbitration with the American Arbitration Association pursuant to arbitration clause of contract. Contractor filed a suit in court together with a motion to stay the arbitration proceedings.

The contract provided for final and binding arbitration and stipulated that the Florida statute on arbitration would not apply. The court interpreted the plain meaning of this statute as permitting the parties to a contract to expressly agree that Chapter 682 would not apply, and that the contract provision effectively precluded application of the Florida statute. The Court of Appeals then applied the common law of Florida and interpreted this portion of the contract to mean that the parties intended voluntarily to used arbitration to settle any controversies but that, notwithstanding the stated intention, either party could refuse to arbitrate. Therefore, the contractor's demand for a stay of arbitration should have been granted, since it manifested the contractor's unwillingness to arbitrate.

74044 Kenney Construction Co. v. Metropolitan Sanitary District, 56 Ill. 2d 516, 309 N.E.2d 221 (1974)

III: A201-1970, Art. 12, Para. 12.1

Contractor sued Sanitary District for increased cost of work resulting from unexpected soil conditions.

The Supreme Court affirmed the Circuit Court's award of additional compensation to the contractor under the "Changed Conditions" provision. Due to subsoil conditions which could not have been anticipated by either the contractor or the Sanitary District, the contractor had to employ a different, more costly construction method and was entitled to recover the actual cost of the changed-conditions work plus percentage mark-ups, less the amount already paid for such work. The court held that the actual cost must be determined without regard to profit or loss on other portions of the work not affected by the soil conditions.

75001   Board of Educ. v. W. Harley Miller, Inc., 221 S.E. 2d 882 (W. Va. 1975)

   I: A201-1970, Art. 2, Para. 2.2
   I: A201-1970, Art. 7, Para. 7.10

Owner obtained an injunction to restrain the contractor from proceeding with arbitration.

The parties disputed the amount of an unanticipated quantity of rock to be removed. The contractor filed a timely demand for arbitration. The Supreme Court of Appeals reversed the Circuit Court and held that the parties had a contractual obligation to submit the dispute to arbitration before either may resort to court action. The court found that the language of the arbitration clause created a condition precedent which rendered proceeding by arbitration mandatory and precluded any right to bring civil action in court until the arbitration had been completed. The phrases "shall be decided by arbitration" and "shall be specifically enforceable" were crucial in creating the condition precedent. The common law rule that an agreement to submit to arbitration was voidable at any time before award was greatly diminished by the broad rule that an agreement was not voidable if a condition precedent of arbitration arose either from express language or by necessary implication in the arbitration provision.

75002   Board of Regents v. Wilson, 27 Ill. App. 3d 26, 326 N.E.2d 216 (1975)

   I: A201-1970, Art. 4, Para. 4.5
   I: A201-1970, Art. 7, Para. 7.4
   I: A201-1970, Art. 9, Para. 9.4
   I: A201-1970, Art. 9, Para. 9.7
   I: A201-1970, Art. 13, Para. 13.2

University Board of Regents brought action against the contractor for breach of contractual duty to correct defects.

The Appellate Court reversed and remanded the Circuit Court's decision. After construing contract provisions concerning warranty and guarantee, claims for damages, certificates for payment, substantial completion and final payment, and correction of work, the court held that the owner had a claim for damages due to defects in the work even when the defect appeared more than one year after final payment.

75003   Bruce Campbell & Son Construction Co. v. Britton Drive, Inc., 527 S.W.2d 852 (Tex. 1975)

   I: A101-1974, Art. 2

Owner of apartment complex sued builder and builder's surety to recover damages arising from builder's failure to comply with certain contractual provisions to repair construction defects. The District Court overruled builder's petition requesting the suit be brought in a county other than the county where the construction site was located and the builder appealed.

The Court of Civil Appeals affirmed the District Court and held that although the contract provision describing the work did not specify the county of performance of the work, extraneous proof was admissible to identify that county, since such evidence did not vary, modify or enlarge the terms of the contract. Suit was held to be proper in the county identified by that proof.

75004   Campbell-Ellsworth, Inc. v. Holy Trinity Serbian Orthodox Church-School Congregation, 233 Pa. Super. 126, 336 A.2d 346 (1975)

I: A111-1974, Art. 4
I: A201-1970, Art. 7, Para. 7.10
I: A201-1970, Art. 8, Para. 8.1
I: A201-1970, Art. 8, Para. 8.3

Contractor and owner submitted to arbitration. Arbitrators made an award in favor of contractor, who filed a court petition to confirm the arbitration award.

The Superior Court first decided that the enforcement of the award was controlled by common law standards rather than the Pennsylvania Arbitration Act, since the agreement was silent. Although the contractor had failed to make a written claim for an extension of time and had failed to complete the work within the stated period, the Superior Court stated that it was an error for the lower court to vacate the arbitrators' award of damages since the arbitrators could have held that the owner had waived these contract conditions.

75005   Chester City School Authority, v. Aberthaw Construction Co., 460 Pa. 342, 333 A.2d 758 (1975)

I: A201-1970, Art. 7, Para. 7.10

Owner sued contractor for breach of construction contract when flooding waters caused severe damage to school building grounds. Pursuant to contract provision, contractor demanded arbitration of dispute. School authority filed an action to enjoin the arbitration proceedings. The Supreme Court reversed and remanded to the Court of Common Pleas for arbitration. The Court found that the arbitration clause survived the termination of the contract whether by performance, breach, or otherwise, since the arbitration provisions clearly called for arbitration of all claims and disputes, whether arising from the contract or its breach, and in the factors listed which affect the obligation to arbitrate, no mention is made of termination. The Court also stated although the arbitration clause required the parties to carry on the work during arbitration, this clause did not indicate that the arbitration procedure was only to be utilized during the life of the contract, but rather was meant for the work to be carried on for items not in dispute.

75006 Clark & Enersen, Hamersky, Schlaebitz, Burroughs & Thomsen, Inc. v. Schimmel Hotels Corp., 194 Neb. 810, 235 N.W.2d 870 (1975)

   I: B141-1974, Art. 1

Architect sued hotel owner to recover cost of preliminary architectural and engineering services for a hotel addition which was never begun. Architect's claim to recovery was based on a theory of quantum meruit and also on allegations that the owner made representations sufficient to make architect expect compensation for architectural services and referred to an unexecuted AIA agreement. District Court rejected the latter claim and the architect appealed.

The Supreme Court affirmed the District Court's decision, and held that where pleadings fail to allege facts constituting the making of a promise or the manifesting of assent to be bound by terms of a written but unexecuted agreement, a separate recovery distinct from the cause of action in quantum meruit will not be granted.

75007 Coonrod & Walz Construction Co. v. Motel Enterprises, Inc. 217 Kan. 63, 535 P.2d 971 (1975)

   I: A111-1974, Art. 5
   I: A111-1974, Art. 7
   I: A201-1970, Art. 12, Para. 12.1

Contractor and subcontractors sued each other and owner for payments in excess of guaranteed maximum cost.

The Supreme Court affirmed the District Court's holding that the owner did not waive the guaranteed maximum cost provision of the contract and convert the contract to only a cost plus fee agreement. By the issuance of numerous changes that were not in writing as required by the contract, the owner did waive the requirement that any changes be in writing, so that the total amount due was the guaranteed maximum plus the amount for the changes.

75008 Damora v. Stresscon International, Inc., 324 So. 2d 80 (Fla. 1975)

   I: B141-1974, Art. 11

Architect filed suit against owners to compel arbitration and owners filed a complaint for damages for architect's negligence in preparing plans and supervising construction.

The Supreme Court of Florida affirmed the denial of an order to arbitrate. It held that an addendum to the standard AIA contract arbitration clause, which provided for arbitration in New York City, rendered the agreement to arbitrate outside the authority of the Florida Arbitration Code. The court said it had no jurisdiction to compel arbitration in another state. Because of this contract provision, the agreement to arbitrate was voidable at the insistence of either party.

75009 Executive Development Properties, Inc. v. Andrews Plumbing Co., 134 Ga. App. 618, 215 S.E.2d 318 (1975)

    I: A401-1972, Art. 9
    I: A401-1972, Art. 11

Contractor sued subcontractor for fire damage to building caused by subcontractor's alleged negligence. Contractor appealed grant of summary judgment to subcontractor.

The Court of Appeals, construing a contract provision concerning insurance, together with provisions concerning the subcontractor's responsibilities, found a contractual obligation that the subcontractor maintain insurance against losses from its negligence and indemnify the contractor for any such losses.

The contractor did not waive its rights for indemnification by the subcontractor because the contractor had been indemnified by its own insurer. However, because the contractor's insurance company had sued in the name of the contractor by a loan receipt or subrogation contract, the Court of Appeals reversed the grant of summary judgment since there was a genuine issue as to whether there was a proper party plaintiff.

75010 Gavlik Construction Co. v. H.F. Campbell Co., 526 F.2d 777 (3d Cir. 1975)

    III: A201-1970, Art. 7, Para. 7.10
    III: A401-1972, Art. 11

Subcontractor sued contractor and appealed stay of arbitration between them.

The Court of Appeals found that the contractor's third-party complaint against the owner did not constitute a waiver of its contractual right to arbitration, since under Pennsylvania law, arbitration is a favored method for resolution of disputes. It also found that a claim for payment due after complete performance was a proper subject for arbitration, since arbitration was not limited to disputes arising during performance. The arbitration clause in the contract between the owner and the contractor bound them to arbitrate all disputes without limitation upon the parties that might be involved; when this clause was read together with one in the subcontract which bound the subcontractor to the contractor by the terms and provisions of all the contract documents, the court concluded that the owner, contractor and subcontractor had agreed to consolidate arbitration of their disputes. Since the claim for payment raised questions concerning the obligations of the owner, contractor and subcontractor, only three-party arbitration could solve the dispute.

75011 Hattis Associates, Inc. v. Metro Sports, Inc., 34 Ill. App. 3d 125, 339 N.E.2d 270 (1975)

    I: B141-1974, Art. 1

Corporate architectural firm brought action to foreclose mechanic's lien; owner counterclaimed for recovery of fees paid to architects.

The Appellate Court affirmed the Circuit Court's holding that the contract for services by the architectural corporation was valid under the Illinois Architectural Act. The corporation's vice president and managing agent, a licensed architect, met the requirements of the Act for planning and supervision of the work by a licensed architect although he was an officer of both the owner-corporation and the architectural corporation. The court said the contract provision on fees stating that Hattis would perform the basic architectural services would not be construed as calling for the personal services of the head of the corporation, who was licensed as an engineer but not as an architect, but rather for services of licensed architects.

75012   Hub Electric Co. v. Aetna Casualty & Sur. Co., 400 F. Supp. 77 (E.D. Mich. 1975)

> III: A311-1970, Labor & Material Payment Bond
> III: A401-1972, Art. 11

Materialman sued contractor and surety for payment for supplies.

The District Court examined the requirements of both the bond and the Michigan statute for the time of giving notice to the contractor that the supplier has furnished materials. Although the statute required a "claimant not having a direct contractual relationship with the contractor" to notify the contractor within thirty days of first supplying materials to him, the bond required notice only within six days after furnishing the lost material. The court found that the supplier could not recover on the bond even though it met the notice requirements therein. The statutory notice requirement could not be waived, since the provisions of the statute are to be read into the bond and given full force and effect.

However, the court sustained the materialman's claim that it was a subcontractor, and thus not subject to the statutory notice requirements, since it met the test of a subcontractor that it take under and agree to perform in accordance with the original contract.

75013   J.R. Graham & Son, Inc. v. Randolph County Board of Education, 25 N.C. App. 163, 212 S.E.2d 542 (1975)

> I: A201-1970, Art. 8, Para. 8.1
> I: A201-1970, Art. 8, Para. 8.2
> I: A201-1970, Art. 8, Para. 8.3
> I: A201-1970, Art. 9, Para. 9.1
> I: A201-1970, Art. 9, Para. 9.2
> I: A201-1970, Art. 9, Para. 9.3
> I: A201-1970, Art. 9, Para. 9.4
> I: A201-1970, Art. 9, Para. 9.5
> I: A201-1970, Art. 9, Para. 9.6
> I: A201-1970, Art. 9, Para. 9.7
> I: A201-1970, Art. 12, Para. 12.1

I: A201-1970, Art. 12, Para. 12.2
I: A201-1970, Art. 12, Para. 12.3
I: A201-1970, Art. 12, Para. 12.4

Contractor sued school board to recover liquidated damages withheld for delay in completion of school.

The Court of Appeals affirmed the Superior Court's holding that the school board was not entitled to liquidated damages and held that the delay was due to the fault of the school board and the ineptness of the architect. The court held that the contractor's failure to request an extension of time did not amount to a waiver of grounds for delay. Since the school board had ignored an original request for extension, the contractor was not required to submit further requests. The architect's arbitrary and capricious refusal to certify installment payments to the contractor supported the award of interest on late payments. The court also found that the contractor could not recover the cost of additional work not required under the contract without a written change order, since the architect orally instructed the contractor to do the work.

75014   Moorhead Construction Co. v. City of Grand Forks, 508 F.2d 1008 (8th Cir. 1975)

II: A201-1970, Art. 12, Para. 12.1
II: A201-1970, Art. 12, Para. 12.2

Contractor sued owner for equitable adjustment to contract sum. The contractor in preparing its bid on work for a sewage treatment plant, necessarily relied upon the city's implied warranty that the soil and the plant site would meet the composition specifications. After the work had begun, the contractor discovered unstable, moist soil which did not meet specifications and was forced to work by different, more expensive methods. The contractor promptly gave the city notice and demanded an equitable adjustment of the contract sum.

The Court of Appeals affirmed the District Court's finding of contract liability based on the "changed conditions" clause and the city's breach of implied warranty. The city's failure to correct the difficult soil conditions, after it had notice and before the contractor started work, inequitably shifted the increased cost of the work to the contractor. Nonetheless, the difficult soil conditions did constitute "changed conditions" and "unknown physical conditions of an unusual nature."

75015   Naetzker v. Brocton Central School District, 50 A.D.2d 142, 376 N.Y.S.2d 300 (1975)

II: A201-1970, Art. 2, Para. 2.2
II: B141-1974, Art. 1
II: B141-1974, Art. 11

School district demanded arbitration of claim against contractor and architects for roof leakage; architects moved for a stay of arbitration on ground that claim was time barred.

The Supreme Court, Appellate Division, Fourth Department, affirmed the finding of the Chautauqua Supreme Court that the claim was time barred. It found that the limitation period for professional malpractice applied rather than the longer period for breach of contract since the tenor of the contract indicated the intent that the architects be bound by a standard of due care generally followed by members of their profession. The longer period for fraud also did not apply since the architects' issuance of a final certificate for payment was not the proximate cause of the damage. The professional malpractice accrued upon the substantial completion of the building and application of the "continuing treatment" doctrine would not qualify the claim as timely.

75016   O & M Manufacturing Co. v. Southern Generator & Engine Sales, Inc. 265 S.C. 302, 217 S.E.2d 723 (1975)

         III: A311-1970, Labor & Material Payment Bond

Supplier sued subcontractor and its surety under a labor and material payment bond for balance due on materials.

The Supreme Court found that, under the language of the bond, the liability of the subcontractor and its surety to the supplier was dependent upon whether the contractor or the owner was liable for the materials used in the performance of the subcontract. Supplier was denied recovery because it failed to prove liability of either the owner or the general contractor.

75017   O-S Corp. v. Samuel A. Kroll, Inc., 29 Md. App. 406, 348 A.2d 870 (1975)

         I: A111-1974, Art. 9
         I: A111-1974, Art. 10
         I: A111-1974, Art. 14

Owner moved to vacate arbitration award favorable to contractor. Court of Special Appeals reversed the Circuit Court and remanded.

The court held that under the Maryland Uniform Arbitration Act it could vacate only those portions of the arbitration award "tainted by improbity" or based on a "completely irrational" interpretation of the contract. Arbitrators had awarded the contractor the amount billed to the owner for wages, although it was much greater than the actual wages paid, plus 15 percent of the billings as reimbursement for insurance costs such as Social Security and worker's compensation. The court found that this award was completely unjustified under any rational interpretation of the contract section entitled "Costs To Be Reimbursed," since that section stipulates that wages *paid* for labor under a schedule agreed upon are to be reimbursed. The portion of the award in excess of the amount actually paid to the employees was vacated.

The contractor was also awarded a sum for field overhead caused by changes made at the owner's request. The owner's contention that the section "Costs Not To Be

Reimbursed" excludes overhead from reimbursable costs was rejected and this award was affirmed, since the section on Costs To Be Reimbursed allows repayment of the costs of a field office.

Although the contractor failed to submit to the architect timely statements of expenses as required under the section entitled "Applications for Payment," the court permitted the arbitrators' award of expenses for equipment rental to stand since the award was not "completely irrational."

75018   People *ex rel.* Delisi Construction v. Board of Educ., 26 Ill. App. 3d 893, 326 N.E.2d 55 (1975)

I: A201-1970, Art. 7, Para. 7.10

Board of Education filed a petition to stay further judicial proceedings and to compel arbitration of the issue of damages after the Circuit Court held that there existed a valid contract and that the contractor had breached that contract. The Circuit Court denied the stay and a judgment for damages was awarded to the Board.

The Appellate Court reversed the judgment for damages and remanded with directions to grant the stay. The court stated that the contractor had not waived arbitration of the issue of damages by participation in the judicial proceeding concerning the existence of a contract, since under the Uniform Arbitration Act and the arbitration clause of the contract, the contractor could not invoke the arbitration clause until there was a determination of a valid contract. The court also pointed out the arbitration clause stated that the arbitrable questions should be decided by the Construction Industry Arbitration Rules, and these rules provided that no judicial proceedings should be deemed a waiver of the right to arbitrate.

75019   Perkins & Will v. Syska & Hennessy & Garfinkel, Marenberg & Assoc., 50 A.D.2d 226, 376 N.Y.S.2d 533 (1975)

III: C141-1974, Art. 12

Pursuant to demand for arbitration initiated by contractor against owner, the latter commenced arbitration proceedings against architect seeking to recover amount of damage claimed by contractor. Architect served a demand for arbitration on both the mechanical and structural engineers. There was no time limitation in the agreement between the engineers and the architect which would afford the engineers an opportunity to participate in the arbitration against the architect, and the engineers counterclaimed that arbitration be permanently stayed on the ground that the demand was untimely. The Supreme Court, Special Term, denied the applications by the engineers to stay arbitration and on appeal, the Supreme Court, Appellate Division, affirmed the Special Term's ruling. The court held that while there was no time limitation set forth in the agreement between architect and engineers, the implied covenant of good faith warrants reading into the contractual procedure a requirement that notice be given within a reasonable time so as to afford a meaningful opportunity for participation in the arbitration against the architect.

The court further stated that the notice of the engineers was timely under the circumstances.

75020   Pete Smith Co. v. City of El Dorado, 258 Ark. 862, 529 S.W.2d 147 (1975)

        I: A201-1970, Art. 10, Para. 10.2

Contractor filed action for declaratory judgment for relief from fixed contract amount under doctrine of commercial frustration after torrential rainfall eroded golf course project. Trial court denied relief and contractor appealed.

Supreme Court affirmed the judgment and stated that the trial court did not err whether the decision was based on the theory that the doctrine was not applicable in the event of a partial frustration that only increased the cost of performance, or whether the decision was based on the intent of the contract provisions that the contractor bear the risk of unfavorable weather.

75021   Roosevelt University v. Mayfair Construction Co., 28 Ill. App. 3d 1045, 331 N.E.2d 835 (1975)

        I: A201-1970, Art. 2, Para. 2.2
        I: A201-1970, Art. 7. Para. 7.10

Owner asked stay of arbitration and declaratory judgment that none of the controversies in question was arbitrable. Contractor claimed damages from delays caused by owner.

The Appellate Court affirmed the Circuit Court's decision that the contractor's claim for damages due to owner-caused delay was arbitrable. The court found that the contractor's obligation to demand arbitration within thirty days after the architect has rendered a written decision or lose the right to arbitrate arises only if the architect characterizes his decision as final but subject to appeal. The Court of Appeals also found that the contractor's claim for liquidated damages was subject to arbitration, since the decisions of the owner as to the contractor's liability for liquidated damages was not made final or conclusive under the contract. The decision of the Circuit Court as to the arbitrability of the owner's claims on the punch list was reversed. These claims were not arbitrable, since the architect is the judge of performance under the "Administration" provision of the contract, even though another contract provision identical to the section entitled "Arbitration" provides for arbitration of "initial" decisions of the architect.

75022   Schuler-Haas Electrical Corp. v. Aetna Casualty & Sur. Co., 49 A.D.2d 60, 371 N.Y.S.2d 107 (1975)

        I: A311-1970, Labor & Material Payment Bond
        III: A201-1970, Art. 5, Para. 5.4
        III: A311-1970, Performance Bond
        III: A401-1972, Art. 12

Subcontractors sued surety on labor and material payment bond for money due for work performed.

The Supreme Court, Appellate Division, reversed the lower court. The contracts between the contractor and subcontractors stated that their rights were subject to the terms of the contract between the owner and contractor and both contracts provided that subcontractors were to be paid when the contractor had received payment from the owner. The performance bond provided that the surety was not liable unless the owner made payments to the contractor in accordance with the contract, although the labor and material bond did not include such a provision. The court held that the performance bond and the two contracts would not read together with the payment bond so as to defeat the claims of the subcontractors.

75023 Spence v. Omnibus Industries, Inc., 44 Cal. App. 3d 970, 119 Cal. Rptr. 171 (1975)

   III: A201-1970, Art. 7, Para. 7.10

Homeowners filed suit against contractors for breach of remodeling contract and for fraud, thereby waiving arbitration.

The Court of Appeals reversed, as error, the Superior Court's grant of the contractors' petition and it ordered that the contractors, not the owners, pay the arbitration filing fee, which was substantially greater than the court filing fee. The court found that the printed form contract that stated that the parties shall settle their disputes by arbitration according to the rules of the American Arbitration Association may not be so interpreted as to force a claimant into the position of one initiating arbitration when the claimant has in fact chosen to waive arbitration by filing suit in court. The rules of the American Arbitration Association provide that the party initiating arbitration shall pay the filing fee. The court stated that since the homeowners did not desire arbitration and had waived it by filing the court action, if the contractors wished to choose arbitration, then they, as initiators, must pay for the arbitration fee.

75024 Stage v. Village of Oswego, 48 A.D.2d 985, 369 N.Y.S.2d 883 (1975)

   III: A201-1970, Art. 3, Para. 3.4
   III: A201-1970, Art. 13, Para. 13.2

Contractor sued owner-village for additional costs. Village counterclaimed for cost of street repair.

The Supreme Court, Appellate Division, reversed the judgment of the lower court and held that the village could not recover the repair costs under the contractor's guarantee, which entitled the owner only to indemnity if the contractor failed to repair defective materials or workmanship promptly. Since there was no notice given to the contractor of defects unrepaired prior to the expiration of the guarantee, the village could not recover the cost of these repairs.

75025   Stark v. Ralph F. Roussey & Associates, Inc., 25 Ill. App. 3d 659, 323 N.E.2d 826 (1975)

    II: B141-1974, Art. 6

Architect sued to foreclose mechanic's lien filed against owner-builder for his fees after owner-builder declined to proceed with construction of building designed by architect.

The Appellate Court reversed the decision of the Circuit Court, which had granted damages on a quantum meruit basis since the contract under which an architect is employed is to govern his compensation. The court held that the architect should recover the stated percentage of the cost as determined by the bid, notwithstanding the abandonment of the project by the owner-builder since the architect had completed that portion of the work.

75026   Vespe Contracting Co. v. Anvan Corp., 399 F. Supp. 516 (E.D. Pa. 1975)

    I: A201-1970, Art. 5, Para. 5.3
    I: A201-1970, Art. 7, Para. 7.10
    II: A401-1972, Art. 14

Subcontractor sued contractor; contractor moved to stay the suit pending arbitration.

The court addressed the issues of whether the parties had agreed to arbitrate, whether they had arbitrable claims, and whether there was a waiver of the right to arbitration. It found that, despite some ambiguities of language, there was a binding agreement to arbitrate. Although there was no specific clause in the subcontract requiring arbitration, the subcontract documents alone were not determinative of this issue. Since the subcontractor had agreed to perform the work in accordance with the General Conditions, these Conditions were intended by the parties to be a part of their agreement. Although they contain no express provision requiring the arbitration of disputes between a contractor and subcontractor, the court found in the section entitled "Subcontractors" a duty of the subcontractor to submit its claim for damages to the contractor in sufficient time for him to comply in the manner provided by the contract document for like claims by the contractor upon the owner. The court related this provision to the arbitration clause, finding an indication that these parties intended to settle their disputes in the same manner as the owner and contractor, *i.e.*, through arbitration. Furthermore, the subcontractor was bound even though he did not sign the General Conditions.

[*Editor's Note:* For subsequent rehearing, *see* case number 77083a *infra.*]

75027   Whitfield Construction Co. Inc. v. Commercial Development Corp., 392 F. Supp. 982 (D.V.I. 1975)

    I: A201-1970, Art. 2, Para. 2.2
    I: A201-1970, Art. 4, Para. 4.3

I: A201-1970, Art. 12, Para. 12.3
I: B141-1974, Art. 2

Contractor sued owner for money due and owing; owner counterclaimed for damages caused by poor workmanship.

In resolving one of the disputes concerning unworkmanlike procedures, the District Court resolved conflicting testimony on proper pile driving methods by citing the contract section that gave the contractor full responsibility for the choice of method.

The owner retained a civil engineer as his representative on the project, although there was no written contract between them. His duties were to assure the owner of compliance with the contract, report any deviations to him, and advise him as to the reasonableness of requests for payment. The court stated that his duties were not those contemplated for his position under B141 which gave the owner's representative authority to render decisions but he was clearly the owner's agent so that his errors and omissions were imputable to the owner.

After the contractor deviated from specifications for construction of the walls when the owner refused to pay for certain strengthening devices, the architect, contractor and owner's representative orally agreed upon a substitution of less costly materials. The court found that this change required a written field order under the construction contract. It further held that the contractor was not relieved from liability for this action despite the consent, oral or written, of the architect. The court found that the architect had no power to waive the contractual stipulation requiring a written order for alterations. When the owner's representative discovered that the change had been made, he and the owner were within their rights when they called a halt to the project, since the owner never authorized the change.

75028 Winston Corp. v. Continental Casualty Co., 508 F.2d 1298 (6th Cir. 1975)

I: A201-1970, Art. 7, Para. 7.2
I: A201-1970, Art. 14, Para. 14.2
II: A311-1970, Performance Bond
II: A311-1970, Labor & Material Payment Bond

Owner sued contractor's surety to recover on performance and payment bond.

When construction of a nursing home was still unfinished five months after the scheduled completion date, the owner and contractor agreed to assign the construction contracts and subcontracts permitting the owner to take possession of the premises and assume construction itself but with the contractor's continuing participation. The owner gave the surety oral notice on the day of the execution of the assignment and mailed the surety a copy of it.

The Court of Appeals reversed the District Court and found that the terms of the contract gave the owner absolute rights to terminate employment of the contractor and to assume construction itself. The court held that the agreement, even if it was considered a termination, could not be a novation so as to discharge the surety, since this action was contemplated by the terms of the contract. The court also found that since the owner's failure to notify the surety seven days prior to dismissal of the contractor, as required by the termination clause of the contract, was an insubstantial breach and did not prejudice the surety, its obligation remained in effect. The performance and payment bonds had been executed for a substantial consideration and stated that they would remain in full force and effect until the contractor's performance and payment under the contract. The surety also had known that the contractor was a poor risk prior to execution of bonds and knew of the difficulties prior to the assignment.

75029   Buckley & Co. v. State, 140 N.J. Super. 289, 356 A.2d 56 (Law Div. 1975)

> III: A111-1977, Art. 3
> III: A107-1978, Art. 2
> III: A111-1978, Art. 4
> III: A201-1976, Art. 8, Para. 8.3
> III: A201-1976, Art. 12, Para. 12.1
> III: A201-1976, Art. 12, Para. 12.3

Contractor, for itself and subcontractors, sued the state, claiming damages resulting from various delays were not barred by a "no damages for delay" clause and that liquidated damages against the contractor were inappropriate.

The Superior Court granted relief for the contractor only when the delay was not contemplated by the parties in the contract, nor dealt with by no-damages clauses, and was not concurrent with other delays associated with problems which were contemplated and dealt with by such clauses. Delays caused by defects in the state's plans were compensable as a breach of contract since no facts or contractual provisions existed to show such defects had been contemplated when the parties signed the contract. Liquidated damages were denied as to deals which resulted either from acts of omission or commission by both sides, or "acts and conditions over which neither had control" or for delays for which no causal relation could be shown.

75030   EFC Development Corp. v. F. F. Baugh Plumbing & Heating, Inc., 24 Ariz. App. 566, 540 P.2d 185 (1975)

> III: A201-1976, Art. 7, Para. 7.9
> III: A401-1978, Art. 13

The Superior Court confirmed an arbitration award for a subcontractor against the contractor, and the Court of Appeals affirmed in part and reversed in part.

The subcontractor's reduction of its work force as a response to lack of progress payments was not an implied abandonment and repudiation of its arbitration right since "the very purpose of arbitration provisions would be defeated and their effectiveness severely limited if a party were held to have abandoned his arbitration merely because his action might be construed to constitute a breach of the contract prior to the time he seeks a clarification of those rights through arbitration."

Although the subcontractor had requested a state administrative body to revoke the contractor's license, such action was not a waiver of arbitration since it had continually pressed for arbitration. The subcontractor's filing of a mechanics' and materialmen's lien was after the initiation of arbitration and its foreclosure suit was after the arbitration award; therefore, there was no waiver of arbitration. The subcontractor's lawsuit to compel arbitration, which also requested other relief, was not a waiver, since the injunction requested was intended to aid the motion to compel arbitration and the damages requested were for a separate contract.

75031   G.C.S., Inc. v. Foster Wheeler Corp., 437 F. Supp. 757 (W.D. Pa. 1975)

      III: A401-1978, Art. 11

Contractor and subcontractor filed cross suits against each other seeking damages for delay in completion. The District Court granted summary judgment for the contractor.

The subcontractor contended that the change orders, extra work and drawing revisions were of such a scope as to amount to active interference by the contractor. The contract allowed the contractor to make changes in the work, although the subcontractor never requested extra time as allowed by the contract. The District Court held that no evidence had been produced of affirmative or positive interference that would survive the purchase order clause that stated that the contractor was not responsible for damages due to delay.

75032   Hartford Electric Applicators of Thermalux, Inc., v. Alden, 169 Conn. 177, 363 A.2d 135 (1975)

      III: A201-1976, Art. 2, Para. 2.2
      III: A201-1976, Art. 13, Para. 13.2
      III: A401-1978, Art. 3
      III: A401-1978, Art. 12

Subcontractor sued the owner-contractors, one of whom was also the architect, for payment of balance due under the contract. Owner-contractor counterclaimed alleging breach of contract because the work was not approved by the architect and was unworkmanlike and late. The trial court granted judgment for the subcontractor on the counterclaim.

The Supreme Court held that the work had been performed properly, and that the failure of the owner-contractors' architect to inspect pursuant to an architect's duties under the contract did not excuse it from payment.

The Court held for the subcontractor on the counterclaim for lateness, reversing the lower court. The Court held that because there were delays in starting caused by the owner-contractors, the proper measure of time was the number of days thereafter, which were "bargained for by the parties and assigned by the contract for performance. . . ."

Where delays were attributable to both parties, the liquidated damages clause was abrogated.

75033 Rumsey Electric Co. v. University of Delaware, 358 A.2d 712 (Del. 1976), *aff'g* 334 A.2d 226 (Del. Super. Ct. 1975)

        I: A311-1970, Performance Bond
        I: A311-1970, Labor & Material Payment Bond

Materialman to defunct subcontractor sought to recover as a third party beneficiary on the performance bond from the contractor, its surety and owner. The Superior Court denied relief.

The Supreme Court affirmed the holding that the material supplier and the owner were protected by the performance bond. However, the supplier failed to file suit within one year from the date of the project's completion as required by the bond. Absent "express statutory provision to the contrary" a statutory period of limitations does not prevent a shorter period from being agreed to contractually. The owner-University was acting in its private capacity, and thus the statue of limitations appropriate for state agencies did not apply.

75034 Thomas Wells & Associates v. Cardinal Properties, Inc., 37 Colo. App. 1, 543 P.2d 1275 (1975)

        I: B141-1974, Art. 9
        I: B141-1974, Art. 12

Architect sued the owners to recover its fees. The 20 percent owner who had not been a party to the contract moved for a dismissal as there had been no arbitration. The District Court granted the motion to dismiss.

The Court of Appeals affirmed. The 20 percent owner had not waived its right to arbitration by its successful motions to dismiss for other reasons on four previous complaints by the architect. The 20 percent owner had the right to insist on arbitration since a contract provision stated that the owners bound themselves and its partners.

[*Editor's Note:* For subsequent review by the Supreme Court of Colorado, *see* case number 76069 *infra.*]

76001   Al Johnson Construction Co. v. Missouri Pacific Railroad Co., 426 F. Supp. 639 (E.D. Ark. 1976)

    II: A201-1976, Art. 3, Para. 3.2
    II: A201-1976, Art. 12, Para. 12.2

Contractor sued railroad-owner for increased compensation for concealed subsurface conditions inconsistent with test borings supplied by the railroad-owner under disclaimer as to their accuracy. The District Court entered judgments for the contractor. Because of the site conditions and the short time interval before the bids were closed, the contractor had been unable to develop its own data. "Under such circumstances, the disclaimers could only be binding against the contractor on variations in conditions that were of a minor or nonsubstantial nature and which a contractor could reasonably have expected to foresee and allow for in the preparation of its bid."

76002   Alspaugh v. District Court in and for the County of Boulder, 190 Colo. 282, 545 P.2d 1362 (1976)

    I: A107-1978, Art. 13
    I: A201-1976, Art. 7, Para. 7.6

Homeowners sought a writ of prohibition from the Supreme Court against the District Court hearing its suit with the contractor because the court had not compelled arbitration. The contractor had responded to the arbitration demand, but reserved its right to arbitrate "only as a condition precedent to a possible court action." The owners sued to compel arbitration and for other counts of negligence and breach of contract. The contractor countered with a suit to foreclose on its mechanic's lien. The District Court held that these suits constituted a waiver by implication of the right to arbitration.

The Supreme Court declined to issue a writ to force the lower court to compel arbitration since any such error should be corrected on appeal.

76003   American Industrial Contracting Co. v. Travelers Indem. Co., 54 A.D.2d 679, 387 N.Y.S.2d 260 (1976)

    II: A311-1970, Labor & Material Payment Bond

Sub-sub-subcontractor sued the surety on the contractor's payment bond. The Supreme Court ordered payment to the sub-sub-subcontractor.

The Appellate Division reversed. The bond defined a claimant as "one having a direct contract with either the Principal or with a subcontractor of the Principal," and thus it was not within the ambit of the bond. Since the notice requirements of the bond were not met, the court did not deal with the issue of whether a "change work order" from the contractor to the sub-sub-subcontractor constituted "a direct contract with . . . a subcontractor of the Principal."

76004 Artcraft Cabinet, Inc. v. Watajo, Inc., 540 S.W.2d 918 (Mo. Ct. App. 1976)

        III: A401-1978, Art. 14

Subcontractor sued contractor for mechanic's lien and contract damages, and the contractor counterclaimed for breach of contract for delay in performance. The Circuit Court rendered judgment for the subcontractor and dismissed the counterclaim.

The Court of Appeals affirmed. The subcontractor had not breached the contract provision concerning the time of installation of materials, since the contractor had hindered its performance.

76005 Beach Resorts International, Inc. v. Clarmac Marine Construction Co., 339 So. 2d 689 (Fla. Dist. Ct. App. 1976)

        I: A201-1976, Art. 7, Para. 7.9

A contractor filed suit to foreclose its mechanic's lien. The owner filed an answer to the suit that the contract provided for arbitration. The contractor voluntarily proceeded with the arbitration. The arbitrators made an award for the contractor, who petitioned the court for entry of judgment on the award and also to award attorney's fees. The Circuit Court entered judgment and attorney's fees pursuant to a mechanic's lien statute.

The Court of Appeals reversed as to the award of attorney's fees. The parties were bound by the arbitration clause which had as its purpose the resolution of disputes outside of the court. The arbitrators' award contained no attorney's fees; none were allowed under the Florida arbitration statute, nor was there any special agreement for attorney's fees. The mechanic's lien statute, which allowed attorney's fees, did not apply, since enforcement of the arbitration award was not necessary by resort to the mechanic's lien statute.

76006 Black Lake Pipe Line Co. v. Union Construction Co., 538 S.W.2d 80 (Tex. 1976)

        III: A201-1976, Art. 12, Para. 12.1
        III: A201-1976, Art. 14, Para. 14.2

Contractor and subcontractor sued the pipeline company-owner for extra work performed without a written change order. The District Court held for the contractor and the subcontractor and the Court of Civil Appeals affirmed.

The Supreme Court reversed. The extra work performed was not outside the scope of the contract so the contractor and subcontractor could not recover in quantum meruit. The failure of the owner to supply pipe and its insistence on a second shift of workers were breach of contract items and not claims for extras. As to other work ordered by the owner's inspectors, the contractor and subcontractor were entitled to recover only if they proved bad faith or that the "requirements imposed by the inspectors were not reasonably within the scope of the technical specifications."

The owner had the contractual right to terminate the contract if an insufficient number of workers were employed. Accordingly, the owner's pressure on the contractor to add a second shift of workers was needed to meet the contract schedule, and the threat by the owner to withhold payment or terminate unless a second shift was added, did not constitute economic duress. There was no basis for a claim of tortious interference with the second shift. The owner's "interference" was privileged and was not "without right or justification," since it resulted from the exercise of the owner's superior interest in the contract.

76007   Board of Local Improvements v. St. Paul Fire & Marine Ins., 39 Ill. App. 3d 255, 350 N.E.2d 36 (1976)

III: A311-1970, Labor & Material Payment Bond

Equipment supplier to a contractor under a rental agreement sued the surety on a payment bond. The Circuit Court found for the equipment supplier.

The Appellate Court reversed. Although the contractor and surety were free to contract in the payment bond for more liability than required by the statute, the phrase "repairs on machinery, equipment and tools" did not include rental payments.

76008   Brodsky v. Princemont Construction Co., 30 Md. 569, 354 A.2d 440 (1976)

I: A107-1978, Art. 14
I: A107-1978, Art. 15
I: A107-1978, Art. 17
I: A201-1976, Art. 8, Para. 8.1
I: A201-1976, Art. 9, Para. 9.8
I: A201-1976, Art. 11, Para. 11.3

Owner (and insurer as subrogee) sued the contractor for damages from the contractor's negligence. Contractor's motion for summary judgment was granted by the Circuit Court, and the owner and insurer appealed.

The Court of Special Appeals affirmed, holding that the insurer as subrogee was bound by the contract provisions of the owner-subrogor which waived "all rights against the contractor to the extent covered by insurance." Since the owner-subrogor had contractually waived his rights, the insurer-subrogee was bound by this waiver. The subrogee obtained no rights greater than the rights of the subrogor.

The fact that part of one of the contracted-for buildings could have been occupied, did not constitute "substantial completion" sufficient to relieve the contractor from his responsibility. The completed portion was still part of "the work under the contract" and therefore, was still subject to the insurance requirements of the contract.

76009   Brown-McKee, Inc. v. Western Beef, Inc., 538 S.W.2d 840 (Tex. Civ. App. 1976)

      III: A201-1976, Art. 3, Para. 3.2
      III: A201-1976, Art. 12, Para. 12.2

Contractor sued the owner over unexpected subsurface conditions, alleging that the owner had misrepresented the conditions, and sought payment for extra work. The District Court held for the owner.

The Court of Civil Appeals affirmed. The owner's representation that a survey had been made which showed no rock underlying the land did not constitute fraud in the inducement to the contract or mutual mistake of fact.

76010   Cast-Crete Corp. v. West Baro Corp., 339 So. 2d 413 (La. Ct. App. 1976)

      II: A201-1976, Art. 2, Para. 2.2
      II: A201-1976, Art. 4, Para. 4.12
      II: A401-1978, Art. 14

Subcontractor sued the contractor over contractor's breach, after the subcontractor produced concrete joists which matched contractor approved show drawings but lacked plumbing holes the contractor had expected from the plans and specifications. The Judicial District Court held for the subcontractor.

The Court of Appeals affirmed, holding that the contractor's superintendent had apparent authority to sign the subcontractor's shop drawings. These shop drawings were the basis of the subcontract formed by the contractor's purchase order. The contractor breached this contract by stopping payment and billing the subcontractor for the cost of cutting plumbing holes. This breach entitled the subcontractor to cease performance.

76011   Central Penn Industries, Inc. v. Commonwealth of Pennsylvania, 25 Pa. Commw. 25, 358 A.2d 445 (1976)

      III: A201-1976, Art. 3, Para. 3.2
      III: A201-1976, Art. 7, Para. 7.7
      III: A201-1976, Art. 12, Para. 12.2

The state-owner appealed from a Board of Arbitration award for extra work resulting from unforseen subsurface conditions. The Commonwealth Court affirmed the Board's denial of the contractor's claim for additional compensation for subsoil excavation and reversed the Board's award of additional compensation to the contractor for borrow excavation. The contract provided that subsurface profiles supplied by the state for the bidding were not to be relied on and that the contractor was to develop his own data for such conditions. The fact that only a month was allowed for investigation before the bids were closed did not constitute constructive fraud by the state. Although the state failed to notify the contractor of later tests as to the necessity for borrow excavation, so as to possibly constitute constructive fraud on its part, the contractor had not given the written notice required by the contract as a condition to its claim.

76012   Clearwater Associates, Inc. v. F. H. Bridge & Son, Contractors, 144 N.J. Super. 223, 365 A.2d 200 (App. Div. 1976)

         III: A311-1970, Performance Bond

The assignee of the obligee of the performance bond sued the surety, after the contractor defaulted and the surety refused to fulfill the terms of the bond. The original obligee, the municipality of Clearwater, had allowed the assignee to complete the project. The Superior Court, Law Division, dismissed the suit on the theory that the obligee could not assign its rights.

The Superior Court, Appellate Division, reversed, holding that the rights of the obligee were sometimes assignable. The assignee in the contract of assignment expressly undertook to complete the work covered by the performance bond. The Court held that an obligee may assign its rights under a bond "where the assignment is the for the purpose of obtaining the performance guaranteed by the bond and upon a showing that the improvements have been made." The Court noted that the surety had been compensated when it issued the bond earlier, and that the surety had a clear liability which should not be exonerated "simply because the bargained-for improvements were completed by an assignee of the claim by agreement with the municipality."

76013   Commonwealth of Pennsylvania v. Osage Co., 24 Pa. Commw. 276, 355 A.2d 845 (1976)

         III: A201-1976, Art. 7, Para. 7.7
         III: A201-1976, Art. 12, Para. 12.2
         III: A201-1976, Art. 13, Para. 13.2

The contractor appealed the decision of the state Board of Arbitration of Claims, which denied the contractor's request for increased compensation for unforseen subsurface conditions and for the wrongful rejection and subsequent replacement of pavement.

The Commonwealth Court affirmed the award denying the claims for additional costs for the unforseen dredging required. Relying on the express terms of the contract, the Court held that the risk for the accuracy of the date given by the state in seeking bids was a risk placed on the contractor. The Court held that the same legal analysis applied to unforseen underwater bottom elevations to be dredged as would apply to unforseen subsurface conditions on land.

As to the rejection of the first soil-cement pavement, the Court vacated the Board of Arbitration Claims order denying relief, since the state's misrepresentation that the cement had passed the required tests could be the basis for constructive fraud and interference with the contract.

76014 Contractor Industries and Acceptance Corp. v. Zerr, 241 Pa. Super. 92, 359 A.2d 803 (1976)

    III: A107-1978, Art. 10
    III: A201-1976, Art. 4, Para. 4.7

Contractor sued owner for contract price and was awarded his costs for labor and materials. Owner appealed the award.

The Superior Court reversed the Court of Common Pleas and remanded. The Court found that the contract to erect an above-ground pool required the owner to obtain the needed permits. The contract was not illegal even though the pool was installed in violation of local ordinance. The court held that, since neither the subject matter of the contract nor its performance were illegal, it was enforceable.

The contractor's practice of not getting permits or even inquiring about them "amounted to a deliberate refusal to know and to do what a reasonable business engaged in the construction industry should know and do." The contractor did not mitigate the damages and was awarded only his transportation costs less the owner's expenses in taking down the pool, for a total recovery of $20.

76015 Curtis Elevator Co. v. Hampshire House, Inc., 142 N.J. Super. 537, 362 A.2d 73 (Law Div. 1976)

    III: A201-1976, Art. 8, Para. 8.3

Contractor sued owner for balance due on contract and for extras requested by the owner. Contractor had been unable to complete the installation of the elevators due to a strike. Owner then hired a nonunion contractor to be supplied material and supervised by the original contractor.

The Court held that the contract was valid and awarded the original contractor the balance of the contract price. The lack of a completion date did not make the contract illusory, since the law implies that it be done in a reasonable time. The presence of a "strike clause" disclaiming the contractor's liability for damage or delay did not make the contract unconscionable since both parties were experienced and skilled in the area, and the contract had been "thoroughly negotiated at arms' length as to both terms and price." The contractor's claim for supervising the nonunion contractor was denied since the "supervisory role was incorporated in the price of the total contractor [*sic*]," and thus, was not extra work outside of the contract.

76016 Data Electric Co. v. NAB Construction Corp., 52 A.D.2d 779, 383 N.Y.S.2d 14 (1976)

    III: A201-1976, Art. 1, Para. 1.1

Subcontractor sued the owner and the contractor for damages due to delay and interferences. The owner filed a motion for summary judgment which the Supreme Court denied.

The Appellate Division reversed, holding that the subcontractor had no right to sue for a breach of the owner-contractor contract since there was no privity of contract. The contract deemed the subcontractors to be agents of the contractor, and denied the creation of any owner-subcontractor contractual relationship unless by a separate writing signed by all the parties. The Court denied that this provision had been waived, thus keeping the court from finding an owner-subcontractor contractual relationship.

76017   Detweiler Bros., Inc. v. John Graham & Co., 412 F. Supp. 416 (E.D. Wash. 1976)

II:	A201-1976, Art. 1, Para. 1.1
II:	A201-1976, Art. 2, Para. 2.2
II:	A201-1976, Art. 12, Para. 12.1

Subcontractor sued the architect for alleged misrepresentations. The architect had initially approved the subcontractor's request to substitute "grooved" pipe for welded pipe, but later required the removal and replacement of the grooved pipe. The subcontractor sued on the initial representation that grooved pipe would meet the contract specifications.

The District Court denied the architect's motion for summary judgment. The subcontractor could not sue as a third-party beneficiary on the owner-architect contract but could maintain an action based on negligence if it could prove a duty owed by the architect and a breach of that duty. Since these constituted issues of material fact, summary judgment was inappropriate.

76018   Devenow v. St. Peter, 134 Vt. 245, 356 A.2d 502 (1976)

III:	A201-1976, Art. 12, Para. 12.1

Contractor sued owner to recover for work done under a separate oral contract which the owner considered to be a verbal modification of the written contract.

The Supreme Court affirmed the Superior Court's finding that there was a second oral contract and not a change order. This second verbal contract was for additional work, and thus the contractor was not bound by the first contract's requirement that all change orders be in writing.

Since the second contract was silent on the price term, the owner was ordered to pay on the basis of a quantum meruit theory of recovery.

76019   Dick Corp. v. State Public School Building Authority, 27 Pa. Commw. 498, 365 A.2d 663 (1976)

II:	A107-1978, Art. 18
II:	A201-1976, Art. 12, Para. 12.1

Contractor appealed to the Commonwealth Court from an arbitrator's award of partial relief.

The Court held that where the contract specifically required written change orders, the contractor was not required to accept a verbal change order and could temporarily halt performance as to that portion of the work. The contractor also could recover damages for the owner's delay in preparing the written change order.

76020 E.C. Ernst, Inc. v. General Motors Corp., 537 F.2d 105 (5th Cir. 1976), *aff'g after remand* 482 F.2d 1047 (5th Cir. 1973)

> III: A201-1976, Art. 8, Para. 8.3
> III: A201-1976, Art. 12, Para. 12.3
> III: A401-1978, Art. 11

In an appeal following remand, the Fifth Circuit affirmed that the jury could have reasonably concluded that the written notice of a claim by the electrical subcontractor for an act or omission causing damage or loss may have been contractually inadequate, since there had been a period of almost 20 months between a general notice of a claim and its specific details and after the building was fully operational.

76021 Exber, Inc. v. Sletten Construction Co., 92 Nev. 721, 558 P.2d 517 (1976)

> I: A201-1976, Art. 2, Para. 2.2
> I: A201-1976, Art. 7, Para. 7.9
> I: A401-1978, Art. 13

The contractor demanded arbitration with the owner, and the owner declined to participate in the arbitration because the demand was not timely and subcontractors were to be included pursuant to arbitration clauses in their subcontracts. The owner sought to stay the arbitration, and the District Court ordered a consolidated arbitration.

The Supreme Court affirmed. There had been a timely demand for arbitration, which was a condition precedent to the right to arbitrate. The architect's denial of the claims had not stated that it was "final but subject to appeal" as required by the owner-contractor contract. Although the issue of timeliness of a demand for arbitration was to be settled by the arbitrators, the Court held it was unnecessary to remand and further delay the resolution of the issue. The District court's decision as to the timeliness of demand was upheld. The Court also held that under the Uniform Arbitration Act the courts had power to order consolidation where as here a single arbitration would avoid the possibility of inconsistent results, would save time and expense, and would not prejudice any of the parties.

76022 Fran Realty, Inc. v. Thomas, 30 Md. App. 362, 354 A.2d 196 (1976)

> III: A201-1976, Art. 12, Para. 12.2

Owners sued contractor-developer for specific performance of the contract after the developer declined to go forward with construction because of a high water table.

The Court of Special Appeals affirmed the chancellor's award of monetary damages. The court held that the subsurface conditions "should have been known" to the developer and that "construction could have proceeded without extraordinary cost."

76023   Franklin Contracting Co. v. State, 144 N.J. Super. 402, 365 A.2d 952 (App. Div. 1976)

    III: A201-1976, Art. 3, Para. 3.2
    III: A201-1976, Art. 8, Para. 8.3

Contractor sued state claiming that the state's misrepresentations and its failure to timely furnish right of ways negated the "no damages for delay" clause. The Superior Court upheld the "no damages" clause and denied relief for the contractor.

The Superior Court, Appellate Division, reversed, holding that the contractor could recover overhead and profit loss resulting from the delay, as the contractor had met its contractual obligations and had relied on the state's assurances that the right of ways were available. The Court construed the "no damages for delay" clause as not including delays caused by the state's failing to perform its contractual duties and misrepresenting to the contractor that their duties were complete.

76024   Freeo v. Victor A. Perosi, Inc., 54 A.D.2d 684, 387 N.Y.S.2d 268 (1976)

    III: A201-1976, Art. 4, Para. 4.3
    III: A201-1976, Art. 10, Para. 10.1
    III: A201-1976, Art. 10, Para. 10.2
    III: A401-1978, Art. 11

Injured excavation contractor's employee sued the owner-contractor and plumbing subcontractor. The Supreme Court held for the owner-contractor and the subcontractor.

The Appellate Division reversed only as to the owner-contractor. Owners and contractors are responsible for the conditions of the common areas of the worksite. The court stated that "subcontractors are responsible for suppling safety devices in the areas created by, and intimately connected with, their work." The owner-contractor did not actively control, direct or supervise the work. Whether the plumbing subcontractor, whose employees were working together with those of the excavation subcontractor, was legally responsible was to be determined by the jury upon retrial.

76025   Georgetown Township High School District No. 218 v. Hardy, 38 Ill. App. 3d 722, 349 N.E.2d 88 (1976)

    III: A201-1976, Art. 4, Para. 4.2

School district-owner sued the contractor after the roof blew off. The Circuit Court dismissed the complaint.

The Appellate Court affirmed the dismissal of the portion of the complaint that alleged that the contractor had failed to build so as to withstand certain wind pressures. The contractor was not liable for damages if he followed the plans and specifications even if they were defective. However, the Court remanded for trial on the further issue as to whether the contractor had deviated from certain of the plans and specifications.

76026 Graulich v. Frederic H. Berlowe & Associates, Inc., 338 So. 2d 1109 (Fla. Dist. Ct. App. 1976)

    III: B141-1977, Art. 1, Para. 1.3

    III: B141-1977, Art. 2, Para. 2.4

Engineers retained by the architect sought to foreclose mechanic's liens against the owners who brought a third-party action against the architects. The District Court held for the engineers against the owners and for the owners against the architects.

The District Court of Appeals affirmed. The failure of the architect to investigate the zoning laws and submit plans to the county for approval and the consequent necessity for a variance entitled the owners to cease payments. The contractual duty of the architect was determined by "normal common practices of architects of the community." The owners had not bargained for this substandard performance and were entitled to withhold payments.

76027 Guidetti v. Pratt Plumbing & Heating, Inc., 55 A.D.2d 720, 389 N.Y.S.2d 170 (1976)

    III: A201-1976, Art. 4, Para. 4.5

    III: A401-1978, Art. 11

Contractor sued the plumbing subcontractor for damages for breach of contract. The Supreme Court, Trial Term, held for the contractor and the Supreme Court, Appellate Division, affirmed. The subcontractor's work violated the local plumbing code in that the sewage pipes sloped away from the sewer and back through the apartment building. This error violated contract provisions that the plumbing would be installed in a compliance with the code and that all work was to be completed in a workmanlike manner according to standard practices.

76028 Helmer-Cronin Construction, Inc. v. Central School District No. 1, 51 A.D.2d 1085, 381 N.Y.S.2d 347 (1976)

    II: A201-1976, Art. 2, Para. 2.2

    II: A201-1976, Art. 4, Para. 4.12

    II: A201-1976, Art. 13, Para. 13.2

Contractor sued the school district-owner for the cost of using backfill which the architect had disapproved. The Supreme Court denied the owner's motion to dismiss.

The Appellate Division affirmed. Under contract provisions the architect had the power to approve or disapprove the backfill, but the material also had to meet certain compaction standards. A testing company selected by the architect stated that the material did not meet those standards. When materials were supplied by the contractor, according to a contract provision it had to guarantee them against defects for one year following the issuance of a final certificate by the architect. Under these circumstances the architect's disapproval may have been bad faith or palpable mistake, and the denial of the owner's motion to dismiss was proper.

76029   Herman Christensen & Sons, Inc. v. Paris Plastering Co., 61 Cal. App. 3d 237, 132 Cal. Rptr. 86 (1976)

> III: A201-1976, Art. 4, Para. 4.18
> III: A401-1978, Art. 11

Subcontractor's employee fell off a defective scaffolding and sued the contractor, who sought indemnity from the subcontractor. The Superior Court ordered the subcontractor to indemnify the contractor.

The Court of Appeals affirmed. The indemnity clause required indemnity even for the contractor-indemnitee's own negligence. The indemnity clause was specific enough to include the concurrent passive negligence of the contractor and subcontractor. Only the contractor's concurrent active negligence would have relieved the subcontractor of his duty to indemnify. Mere nonfeasance or a failure to perform a duty will not give rise to active negligence.

76030   Idaho State University v. Mitchell, 97 Idaho 724, 522 P.2d 776 (1976)

> I: A201-1976, Art. 1, Para. 1.1
> I: A201-1976, Art. 4, Para. 4.18
> I: A201-1976, Art. 13, Para. 13.2

State university-owner sued the architect and contractor concerning a water pipe failure and consequent flooding. The contractor filed a third party action against its subcontractor for contractual indemnity. The District Court entered summary judgment against the contractor and subcontractor.

The Supreme Court reversed and remanded. Under a contract provision for warranty of defective work, the contractor and subcontractor were responsible for correction of the defective work itself and not for the other damages resulting from the flood, since the portions of the complete project damaged by flooding were not part of the work, as defined by the contract.

The indemnity provision did not require the contractor to pay for the flood damage unless the areas flooded were "other than the work itself," and required that the owner prove the damage occurred due to the negligent act or omission of the contractor. The Supreme Court remanded to the trial court for resolution of this issue.

76031   Indian State Highway Comm'n v. Thomas, 169 Ind. App. 13, 346 N.E.2d 252 (1976)

III: A201-1976, Art. 4, Para. 4.18

Contractor's injured employee sued the state-owner who sought indemnity from the contractor. The Circuit Court held that the contractor need not indemnify the owner.

The Court of Appeals affirmed. Unless expressly and unequivocally stated and entered into "knowingly and willingly," the contractor-indemnitor does not have a contractual duty to indemnify for the owner-indemnitee's own negligence.

The contractor had breached his contractual duty to abide by state worker safety laws, and the state was also negligent because of the on-site inaction of its engineer and safety inspector. The negligence of the contractor was irrelevant in construing the question of whether or not the contractor is required to "indemnify the state against an expense which the state would not in this case be required to bear but for its own negligence."

76032   James Stewart Polshek & Associates v. Bergen County Iron Works, 142 N.J. Super. 516, 362 A.2d 63 (Ch. Div. 1976)

I: A201-1976, Art. 1, Para. 1.1
I: A201-1976, Art. 7, Para. 7.9
I: B141-1974, Art. 9

Architect sought an injunction to prevent its being made a party to the arbitration proceeding between the owner and the contractor.

The Superior Court, Chancery Division, held that the unwilling architect could not be made a party to arbitration by the contractor's demand. In the absence of consent or a contractor-architect contractual relationship, the architect could not be forced into arbitration. The architect's participation in choosing the arbitrators was subject to its objections and was "proper as a contingent measure. . . ." Such participation did not constitute a waiver of the architect's objections. The crossclaim of the owner against the architect was treated as the demand for arbitration required by the contract.

However, the owner-architect and the owner-contractor arbitrations were held to be so interrelated that the "resolving of either controversy will certainly affect the other. . .," and so it would have been within the court's jurisdiction to order the arbitration proceedings consolidated. The court found that consolidation was justified, despite the lack of statutory authority, by the "common thread of facts," and the judicial goals of fairness in administration, elimination of unjustifiable expense and delay, simplicity in procedure and "securing a just determination."

76033 Kalwall Corp. v. D. Capolino Design & Renovation, 54 A.D.2d 941, 388 N.Y.S.2d 346 (1976)

    III: A401-1978, Art. 6
    III: A401-1978, Art. 12

Subcontractor sued the contractor and its surety seeking the balance due in the subcontract. The Supreme Court refused to grant summary judgment.

The Appellate Division reversed. The subcontract provided for progress payments of 85 percent of the value of the work, and the balance was to be retained until 30 days after the subcontract work was completed, accepted and approved by the owner. The court interpreted the contract provisions as meaning that the owner's acceptance merely fixed the time when payment was due, but was not a condition precedent to payment to the subcontractor.

Payment by the owner to the contractor was not the exclusive method to determine the owner's acceptance and approval, and since the owner had expressed its acceptance and approval in a letter, the subcontractor was entitled to summary judgment for the agreed contract price.

76034 L. A. Swyer Co. v. John W. Cowper Co., 55 A.D.2d 774, 389 N.Y.S.2d 197 (1976)

    I: A401-1978, Art. 13

The subcontract provided that arbitration would be in the same manner as provided in the owner-contractor agreement, but that contract was totally silent on arbitration. The subcontractor demanded arbitration and the contractor sought a court-ordered stay. The Supreme Court declined to stay the arbitration.

The Appellate Division affirmed. The subcontract's provision was "broad, clear and unambiguous." "The absence of any provision in the main contract, to which reference was to be had for the manner and method of procedure, does not alter the clear and dominant purpose of these parties, as evidenced by their written agreement, to submit *all* disputes to arbitration."

76035 L.H. Lacy Co. v. City of Lubbock, 546 S.W.2d 373 (Tex. Civ. App. 1976)

    III: A201-1976, Art. 7, Para. 7.9

The contractor sued the City of Lubbock to enforce an arbitration award. The District Court affirmed the award. The Court of Civil Appeals reversed. The contract provided for arbitration but the clause was unenforceable because under a Texas arbitration statute, construction contracts were excluded and under Texas common law an agreement to arbitrate future disputes was not binding upon the parties. Since the city did not consent to jurisdiction of the arbitrators, its participation in the proceedings did not constitute ratification of an agreement to arbitrate.

[*Editor's Note:* For reversal by the Supreme Court of Texas, *see* case number 77050 *infra.*]

76036   Lee v. Allied Chemical Corp., 331 So. 2d 608 (La. Ct. App. 1976)

        III: A201-1976, Art. 4, Para. 4.18

Contractor's employee was injured on the job and sued the owner and several of its employees, who in turn filed third party claims for indemnity against the contractor and its insurer. The Judicial District Court held that the insurer was not required to defend the owner's employees but was required to defend the owner.

The Court of Appeals reversed, holding that under the clause at issue the contractor-indemnitor's duty to the corporation included a duty to the employees. The intent of the clause was that the contractor-indemnitor was bound to indemnify against even the indemnitee's own negligence despite the absence of the words "negligence of the indemnitees."

76037   Long Branch Sewerage Authority v. Molnar Electrical Contractors, Inc., 143 N.J. Super. 492, 363 A.2d 917 (Ch. Div. 1976)

        III: A201-1976, Art. 7, Para. 7.9
        III: A401-1978, Art. 13

Owner sued five contractors seeking a joint arbitration, after the arbitrator declined to bring four other contractors into the original owner-contractor arbitration.

The Superior Court held that the common arbitration clause in each of the five owner-contractor contracts could be enforced in a joint proceeding. The contractors all knew of the identical arbitration clauses in each others' contracts. "Where there are conflicting claims, a common contract term, and knowledge by all the parties of the common term, enforcement of a one-unit arbitration may be required to avoid conflicting and inconsistent results." The court ordered a single arbitration panel to hear each of the five owner-contractor arbitrations. The joint proceeding ordered was not a consolidation of all five arbitrations into one.

Since there was neither consent nor contractual relations between the contractors, contractor-contractor claims could not be heard.

76038   Lyell Excavating Corp. v. International Fidelity Insurance Co, 54 A.D.2d 606, 387 N.Y.S.2d 496 (1976)

        III: A311-1970, Labor and Material Payment Bond

Subcontractor sued the surety on the labor and material payment bond. The Supreme Court granted summary judgment for the subcontractor.

The Appellate Division affirmed. The subcontractor had proven the existence of the bond and its participants, had fully performed its contractual obligations, had not been paid, and had given proper notice under the bond. The surety's defenses were that its coverage of the bond was for only part of the project's time span and that there had been no showing that the contractor was the principal of the surety. The court found that both defenses were bereft of any factual basis and that summary judgment for the subcontractor was appropriate.

76039   Maddy v. Castle, 58 Cal. App. 3d 716, 130 Cal. Rptr. 160 (1976)

III: A201-1976, Art. 7, Para. 7.9

Contractor filed suit in small claims court for the balance due under the contract. The owner filed a suit in the municipal court for damages and declaratory relief and asked that the small claims court action be transferred to the municipal court. In the municipal court, the contractor demanded arbitration, and the owner responded that the contractor had waived his right to arbitration. The contractor filed a petition to compel arbitration in the Superior Court which found no waiver and ordered arbitration. The owner moved in the Superior Court to vacate the award, but the Court confirmed the award.

The Court of Appeals reversed. The owner had not raised the issue of arbitrability and waiver before the arbitrator, and so was not precluded from raising it before the Court of Appeals. The contractor had waived his right to arbitration by filing the initial claim in small claims court. The owner's later suit in the municipal court did not affect the contractor's waiver, since he had already chosen the judicial system as his forum. By waiving his right to arbitrate his small claims court action for damages, the contractor had also waived his right to arbitrate the owner's counterclaims, since those counterclaims were raised as defenses to the contractor's claim and were part of the same basic issue.

76040   M & W Masonry Construction, Inc. v. Head, 562 P.2d 957 (Okla. Ct. App. 1976)

III: A401-1978, Art. 14

Subcontractor sued the contractor over the balance due and the contractor counterclaimed for wrongful termination and for completion of the work. The District Court held for the contractor on both claims.

The Court of Appeals reversed. The contractor committed a material breach of the contract when it ceased making the contractually required progress payments since there was no justification for this action. Accordingly, the subcontractor correctly terminated the contract.

76041   McKinney Drilling Co. v. Mach I Limited Partnership, 32 Md. App. 205, 359 A.2d 100 (1976)

I: A201-1976, Art. 7, Para. 7.9
I: A401-1978, Art. 13

Contractor filed a motion to vacate an arbitration award for the subcontractor. The arbitrator failed to consider a counterclaim of the contractor because he believed it was outside the scope of the arbitration.

The Court of Special Appeals affirmed the Circuit Court's vacating of the award, in part because under the Maryland Code provision for the standard for vacating an arbitration award, the arbitrator had exceeded his authority by not considering the counterclaim. The court noted that the claim and counterclaim arose from the same factual dispute, that the arbitration award purported to settle all claims and that the contract provision for arbitration stated that all claims should be decided by arbitration.

76042   McStain Corp. v. Elfline Plumbing & Heating, Inc., 38 Colo. App. 473, 558 P.2d 588 (1976)

        II: A401-1978, Art. 11
        II: A401-1978, Art. 14

Subcontractor sued the contractor for retainage of payments and the owner counterclaimed. The District Court granted summary judgment for the subcontractor and dismissed the counterclaim.

The Court of Appeals reversed and remanded. The contract clause which stated that written notice to the subcontractor was necessary before the contractor could complete the performance of the subcontractor was not applicable, since the dispute concerned damage to adjacent property and not work under the contract. Since the contract clause concerning indemnification of the contractor for damage to third parties did not require written notice prior to repairs made by the contractor, the contractor was entitled to be reimbursed, assuming that the subcontractor was liable for the damage.

76043   Metropolitan Sewerage Commission v. R.W. Construction, Inc., 72 Wis. 2d 365, 241 N.W.2d 371 (1976)

        II: A201-1976, Art. 12, Para. 12.2

A contractor for an underground sewer encountered unexpected artesian ground water and sought equitable adjustment under the changed circumstances clause of its contract with the county-owner. The owner refused to make an adjustment and the contractor ceased work. The owner terminated the contract and brought suit against the contractor for the increased costs charged by the completion contractor. The Circuit Court entered judgment for the owner and dismissed the counterclaim of the contractor.

The Supreme Court reversed. The artesian water was a changed condition materially different from specifications and drawings. The contract clause also only required the owner's representative to know of the problem and did not require a formal notice of the claim. The contractor was justified in its refusal to continue performance, since the owner's persistent refusal to adjust the contract sum was a material breach of the contract.

76044 Mississippi State Bldg. Comm'n v. Becknell Construction, Inc., 329 So. 2d 57 (Miss. 1976)

    II: A310-1970, Bid Bond

The state sued for bond forfeiture against the contractor and its surety. The Chancery Court granted judgment for the contractor and surety, holding that equitable relief should be granted for their erroneous bid.

The Supreme Court affirmed, holding that the bidder's transposition of numbers on a form completed while en route, just before the deadline, constituted suitable grounds for equitable relief. In this case the mistake was not due to the contractor's gross negligence, and the state was notified of the mistake before any serious harm was caused by it.

76045   Modern Construction, Inc. v. Barce, Inc., 556 P.2d 528 (Alaska 1976)

    II: A111-1978, Art. 1
    II: A111-1978, Art. 16
    II: A201-1976, Art. 1, Para. 1.2
    II: A401-1978, Art. 1

The contractor sued the subcontractor for breach of contract. The subcontractor demanded arbitration in accordance with the general conditions. The subcontract had attempted incorporation by the following provision:

> The general conditions consisting of Paragraph 1 through . . . , attached hereto are part of this Subcontract and by this reference are incorporated in this Subcontract and made a part hereof as fully as though set forth herein.

The blank was not filled in. Because the general conditions were held not to be attached, the Superior Court held that the contract was ambiguous and ruled against the subcontractor that had provided the form contract, and thus, had created the ambiguity.

The Supreme Court reversed and remanded for a full hearing on whether the general conditions had been attached. If the general conditions had been attached, then there would be no ambiguity and arbitration. If they had not been attached, then there would have been an ambiguity to be resolved against the subcontractor who had supplied the form.

76046   Morton Z. Levine and Associates v. Van Deree, 334 So. 2d 287 (Fla. Dist. Ct. App. 1976)

    II: B141-1977, Art. 9

Homeowners sued the architect for negligence, misrepresentation, breach of fiduciary duties and breach of contract. The Circuit Court ordered arbitration only on the breach of contract counts and denied arbitration on the counts of negligence, misrepresentation and breach of fiduciary duties.

The District Court of Appeals reversed, holding that arbitration was proper on all the counts. Since there were no allegations of fraud or other factors which could be a basis for nullifying the arbitration clause, it should be enforced. The purpose of the clause was to avoid litigation such as contained in that lawsuit.

76047 New York Plumber's Specialties Co. v. W. J. Barney Corp., 52 A.D.2d 832, 384 N.Y.S.2d 1 (1976)

I: A311-1970, Labor and Material Payment Bond

Supplier to subcontractor sued the contractor's surety for payment based on a labor and material payment bond. The Supreme Court granted summary judgment for the supplier.

The Appellate Division modified the decision. In order to be a claimant under the terms of the bond there had to be a direct contract between the supplier and the subcontractor. The running account constituted a series of contractual relationships with the subcontractor. However, since the 90 day notice required under the terms of the bond was not given for one delivery of materials, the claim for that amount was disallowed.

76048 Niagara Mohawk Power Corp. v. Perfetto & Whalen Construction Corp., 52 A.D.2d 1081, 384 N.Y.S.2d 299 (1976)

I: A201-1976, Art. 2, Para. 2.2

Power company-owner filed a motion to stay arbitration demanded by the contractor. The Supreme Court granted the stay.

The Appellate Division reversed. Since the contract required that the architect's decisions state that it was "final but subject to appeal," the 30-day period of the contract during which to appeal the architect's decisions did not start to run. Therefore, the contractor's request for arbitration was timely as to the entire two year series of architect's decisions.

76049 Normoyle-Berg & Associates, Inc. v. Village of Deer Creek, 39 Ill. App. 3d 744, 350 N.E.2d 559 (1976)

III: A201-1976, Art. 1, Para. 1.1
III: A201-1976, Art. 2, Para. 2.2

A general contractor sued the engineer for its negligent supervision and acts. The contractor and the engineer had separate contracts with the owner. The trial court granted a motion to dismiss.

The Appellate Court reversed. The two engineers had a duty to the contractor to avoid causing extra expenses despite the lack of privity. A supervising engineer was held to know that the contractor would be directly affected by its conduct.

76050 North County School District R-1 v. Fidelity & Deposit Co. of Maryland, 539 S.W.2d 469 (Mo. Ct. App. 1976)

  III: A201-1976, Art. 4, Para. 4.5

School district-owner sued the contractor and its surety regarding a leaky roof. The contractor counterclaimed for the balance due under the contract, and the surety cross-claimed against the contractor. The Circuit Court held for the school district-owner.

The Court of Appeals reversed. The fact that the roof leaked did not justify the conclusion that it failed to conform to the plans and specifications or was built in an unworkmanlike manner. The Court held that this principal was particularly true where the plans and specifications are provided to the contractor by the owner, and the contractor did not become an insurer that the plans and specifications were sufficient to provide an adequate roof.

76051 Norton Heights Fire Dept. v. Vuono-Lione, Inc., 168 Conn. 276, 362 A.2d 982 (1976)

  I: A201-1976, Art. 2, Para. 2.2
  I: A201-1976, Art. 7, Para. 7.9
  I: A401-1978, Art. 11
  I: B141-1977, Art. 1

The owner sought to stay the arbitration proceedings, but the Superior Court allowed the arbitration to proceed.

The Supreme Court per curiam affirmed the holding that a contract clause made "matters relating to artistic effect" an area where the architect's decision was final; but that disputes over the floor color and blemishes from defective workmanship were subject to arbitration as a question of contract compliance.

76052 Novak & Co. v. Travelers Indem. Co., 56 A.D.2d 418, 392 N.Y.S.2d 901 (1977), *aff'g* 85 Misc. 2d 957, 381 N.Y.S.2d 646 (Sup. Ct. 1976)

  III: A201-1976, Art. 6, Para. 6.1
  III: A311-1970, Performance Bond

Plumbing contractor obtained an uncollected court judgment against the foundation contractor. The plumbing contractor sued the surety of the foundation contractor. The Supreme Court granted summary judgment for the surety.

The Appellate Division affirmed. Under the terms of the owner-plumbing contractor and owner-foundation contractor contract, neither contractor could sue the owner for damages from the other contractor's delay. While the contractors were liable to each other, the language of the performance bond did not make each contractor's surety liable to the other contractor. The purpose of the performance bond was to ensure construction of the project for the owner, and fellow contractors were not third-party beneficiaries of the owner's performance bond.

76053 Pearl Street Development Corp. v. Conduit & Foundation Corp., 41 N.Y.2d 167, 359 N.E.2d 693 (1976)

    I: A201-1976, Art. 2, Para. 2.2
    I: A201-1976, Art. 7, Para. 7.9
    I: A401-1978, Art. 13

Contractor sought to stay arbitration demanded by the subcontractor. The Supreme Court, New York County, denied the stay, and the Supreme Court, Appellate Division, affirmed.

The Court of Appeals affirmed. The owner-contractor contract, which was incorporated by reference into the subcontract, provided that disputes relating to the progress of the work or the interpretation of the contract documents, should be referred initially to the architect for his decision. The owner-contractor contract also provided that a demand for arbitration should be made within a reasonable time after the claim arose. The arbitration provision of the subcontract did not contain these conditions precedent to arbitration. The Court held that the interpretation of the relationship of the two contracts should be determined by the arbitrators and not by the courts.

76054 Pioneer Acceptance Corp. v. Irving Coven Construction, Inc., 4 Mass. App. Ct. 433, 350 N.E.2d 466 (1976)

    I: A201-1976, Art. 7, Para. 7.9

Owner sued the contractor seeking judgment that the demand for arbitration was untimely. The Superior Court held for the contractor.

The Appeals Court reversed. The demand for arbitration was not timely, since it was made six years after the date of final payment specified in the contract. A contract provision stated that the demand should be made no later than final payment, and the court had been presented with no other contract provisions or facts which may have extended the time for demand after the date of final payment.

76055 Pittman Construction Co. v. Meadows, 337 So. 2d 892 (La. Ct. App. 1976)

    III: A311-1970, Performance Bond
    III: A401-1978, Art. 15

In order to avoid delays and accommodate the subcontractor, the contractor put the subcontractor's employees on its own payroll and paid for much of the subcontractor's materials. After being unable to arrange reimbursement for the costs above the subcontract price, the contractor sued the subcontractor and its surety under the subcontractor's performance bond. The District Court granted judgment for the contractor.

The Court of Appeals affirmed, holding that the agreement of the contractor to take over the subcontractor's expenses and settle accounts after completion was a modification supplementing the contract.

The surety was also bound, since the takeover of expenses agreement was a modification of the subcontract which it guaranteed under the performance bond. Notice to the surety was not required before a modification was effective, and the bond also stated that no alterations of the contract would release the surety.

76056   Porter v. Avlis Contracting Corp., 86 Misc. 2d 235, 381 N.Y.S.2d 595 (Sup. Ct. 1976)

    III: A201-1976, Art. 4, Para. 4.18
    III: A401-1978, Art. 11

Administratrix of subcontractor's employee, who was killed when the building he was working on collapsed, brought wrongful death actions against the contractor and the subcontractors, who cross-claimed against each other and the contractor. The Supreme Court held that one of the subcontractors had assumed the risk of accidents when it agreed to a broad indemnity agreement. The language of the indemnity clause was clear and unambiguous that the contractor was to be indemnified, even for its own negligence, and therefore the subcontractor assumed the entire risk of any liability in completing the project (*Affirmed* on other grounds at 57 A.D.2d 222, 394 N.Y.S.2d 226 (1977)).

76057   Prestressed Concrete, Inc. v. Adolfson & Peterson, Inc. 308 Minn. 20, 240 N.W.2d 551 (1976)

    III: A201-1976, Art. 7, Para. 7.9

Subcontractor sued the contractor and the owner for damages. The owner filed a third-party claim for indemnity against the architect and the architect's engineers. Only, the owner-architect contract contained an arbitration clause, and the architect filed a motion to compel arbitration. The District Court denied the architect's motion.

The Supreme Court affirmed. Since only two of five parties would be bound by the arbitration, the basis of the favored status that arbitration usually enjoyed in the courts was not present. Instead of expediting the settlement of disputes simply, clearly and inexpensively, the arbitration would increase delay, complexity and costs. Litigation with joinder of all parties and claims was a better remedy than arbitration between only two parties.

76058   P.R. Post Corp. v. Maryland Casualty Co., 68 Mich. App. 182, 242 N.W. 2d 62 (1976)

    II: A311-1970, Labor and Material Payment Bond
    II: A311-1970, Performance Bond

III: A201-1976, Art. 7, Para. 7.9

Owner was granted an arbitration award against the contractor, and the owner then brought suit against the surety of the contractor's performance and labor and material payment bonds. The surety filed a motion to strike any reference to the arbitration proceedings in the owner's complaint, and the owner filed a motion for summary judgment. The Circuit Court granted the surety's motion and denied the owner's motion.

The Court of Appeals reversed. Since the surety had supplied the bond forms, the Court construed the bond provisions against the surety. The bond provision that the "contract is by reference made a part hereof" was construed as the surety's agreement to be bound by the arbitration clause in the owner-contractor contract. Notwithstanding the surety's claim that it had no notice of the arbitration hearing, the arbitration award was *prima facie* evidence. There was no fraud or collusion to cause an exception to that rule, since there was no duty of the owner to take any steps to inform the surety of problems.

76059   R.C. Stanhope, Inc. v. Roanoke Construction Co., 539 F.2d 992 (4th Cir. 1976)

III: A311-1970, Labor and Material Payment Bond

Equipment lessor to subcontractor sought to recover for rental charges and the value of missing rental equipment by suit filed against the contractor and its surety on the contractor's labor and material payment bond. The District Court awarded summary judgment for the lessor.

The Fifth Circuit Court of Appeals affirmed. The language "materials furnished" in the Virginia statute was interpreted to include rental charges and the value of missing rental equipment. The Court based this holding on a prior Supreme Court of Virginia case which interpreted the language "materials furnished" in a payment bond.

76060   RGK, Inc. v. United States Fidelity & Guar. Co., 292 N.C. 668, 235 S.E.2d 234 (1977), *aff'g* 31 N.C. App. 708, 230 S.E.2d 600 (1976)

I: A311-1970, Labor & Material Payment Bond

Subcontractor sued the contractor, its surety and the owner seeking to recover on the labor and material payment bond. The Superior Court dismissed the complaint, and the Court of Appeals reversed.

The Supreme Court affirmed the Court of Appeals. The surety was not liable only if the contractor properly failed to apply the money it received from the owner, since this would create a fidelity bond instead of a surety bond. The surety received a premium for payment of materialmen if the contractor did not pay them, and the real purpose of that bond was to enable the general contractor to purchase upon credit.

76061   Robert E. McKee, Inc. v. City of Atlanta, 414 F. Supp. 957 (N.D. Ga. 1976)

III: A201-1976, Art. 3, Para. 3.2

III: A201-1976, Art. 12, Para. 12.2

Contractor sued the city for compensation for extra work done due to unforseen subsurface conditions. The District Court denied the city's motion for summary judgment.

The contract put the risk of unexpected subsurface conditions clearly on the contractor. The contractor had failed to prove that the city's providing such subsurface information as it had was equivalent to misrepresentation. Summary judgment was inappropriate since whether the contractor could have discovered the conditions through reasonable investigation, and whether the city's data was inaccurate, were questions of fact for the jury.

76062   Roger Johnson Construction Co. v. Bossier City, 330 So. 2d 338 (La. Ct. App. 1976)

III: A101-1977, Art. 3
III: A107-1978, Art. 2
III: A111-1978, Art. 4
III: A201-1976, Art. 8, Para. 8.3

Contractor sued the city-owner to recover amounts withheld as liquidated damages for delay. The Judicial District Court rejected the contractor's contention that the contract provision relating to "severe weather" relieved it of the responsibility for delay.

The Court of Appeals affirmed. The contract could have been timely completed had the contractor used sufficient crews and worked on all the work sites during good weather periods.

76063   Roland A. Wilson & Associates v. Forty-O-Four Grand Corp., 246 N.W.2d 922 (Iowa 1976)

III: A201-1976, Art. 2, Para. 2.2
III: A201-1976, Art. 9, Para. 9.5

Architect sued the owner to recover the balance of his fee. The District Court denied his claim.

The Supreme Court affirmed. The architect had failed to use reasonable care in carrying out his contractual duty of approving payments to the contractor, since he did not retest windows after the contractor alleged that they were repaired.

76064   S.A. Stephenson v. Smith, 337 So. 2d 570 (La. Ct. App. 1976)

III: A201-1976, Art. 12, Para. 12.1

A materialman sued a homeowner and contractor for unpaid building supplies. The homeowner and contractor filed cross-claims against each other, and the Judicial District Court held for the homeowner.

The Court of Appeals affirmed. The contractor had rebuilt substantial portions of the roof following the homeowner's complaint. The extra work was done with the homeowner's knowledge but since the homeowner had not agreed to pay for it, the burden of proving the value of the extra work was on the contractor. The contractor produced no evidence of the value, and therefore, could not recover for it. The homeowner was entitled to judgment for the cost of completing the building.

76065   St. Paul Fire & Marine Ins. Co. v. Murray Plumbing & Heating Corp., 65 Cal. App. 3d 66, 135 Cal. Rptr. 120 (1976)

> III: A201-1976, Art. 11, Para. 11.3
> III: A401-1978, Art. 9
> III: A401-1978, Art. 11

Insurer of contractor brought suit against subcontractors for reimbursement for payment to contractor under a builders' risk policy. The Superior court held for the subcontractors.

The Court of Appeals affirmed. Since the contractor's builder risk policy insured the contractor for "its account and/or the account of its subcontractors," the subcontractors were co-insureds. The insurer had no right of subrogation as a result of an indemnity clause in the subcontract, since the insurer could not be subrogated against a coinsured. Furthermore, when the insured paid the contractor, it recognized the rights of the subcontractors as co-insureds, since it had not made payment under a reservation of rights.

76066   Security Painting Co. v. Commonwealth of Pennsylvania, 24 Pa. Commw. 507, 357 A.2d 251 (1976)

> III: A201-1976, Art. 1, Para. 1.1
> III: A201-1976, Art. 12, Para. 12.3

The contractor filed an arbitration demand alleging that it had performed extra work for which a written change order was not needed.

The Commonwealth Court reversed the decision of the Board of Arbitration of Claims awarding compensation for the alleged extra work. The contractor was merely meeting the contract specifications and not performing extra work. The verbal assurances and misrepresentations of the state's jobsite officials could not be the basis for a recovery as it did not comply with the contract's requirement that change orders be in writing. All relief was denied the contractor.

76067   Southwestern Bell Telephone Co. v. J.A. Tobin Constr. Co., 536 S.W.2d 881 (Mo. Ct. App. 1976)

> III: A201-1976, Art. 4, Para. 4.18

Telephone company sued the contractor as a third-party beneficiary of the owner-contractor agreement. The Circuit Court held for the telephone company.

The Court of Appeals reversed. The telephone company had negligently relocated its buried cable so that the contractor severed it while building a drainage ditch in conformity with the specifications. The telephone company was a third-party beneficiary of the owner-contractor agreement, including its indemnity provisions. The contractor had clearly assumed responsibility for its own negligence. While it is possible to require indemnity for a third-party beneficiary even for its own negligence, the contract was not sufficiently clear, unambiguous and unequivocal so as to require it. "Broad, indefinite or general terms are not sufficient to impose contractual indemnification."

76068 State Highway Admin. v. Transamerica Ins. Co., 278 Md. 690, 367 A.2d 509 (1976)

        III: A311-1970, Performance Bond

Under a performance bond, the state sued defaulting contractor and the surety which had completed the contract for damages resulting from the contractor's handling of waste fill. The Circuit Court awarded damages against the contractor and in favor of the state for a landslide of improperly disposed of fill on state ground. The surety was awarded damages against the state for the unpaid contract balance.

The Court of Appeals affirmed the decision holding that the duty of the surety and the principal were coextensive. Since the bond incorporated the terms of the contract, both must be construed together. The surety was liable for the negligence of the contractor only if the negligence occurred in the performance of the contract. The performance bond was only to ensure the completion of the contracted-for items, and the state could not seek to recover on the contractor's negligence on waste-disposal operations not part of the contract. Damages from such noncontractual activities would be more appropriately claimed from the contractor's insurance company rather than the surety.

76069 Thomas Wells & Associates v. Cardinal Properties, Inc., 192 Colo. 197, 557 P.2d 396 (1976)

        I: A201-1976, Art. 7, Para. 7.7
        I: B141-1977, Art. 9

Architect sued owner to recover its fee. Owner asserted, as a defense, the architect's failure to arbitrate the issue and the District Court granted owner's motion for summary judgment. The Appellate Court affirmed.

The Supreme Court reversed, finding that the architect had made a sufficient offer of proof to substantiate its claim that the owner had agreed to waive the arbitration requirement. In view of the factual issues in dispute, the granting of the owner's motion was improper.

76070 Votaw Precision Tool Co. v. Air Canada, 60 Cal. App. 3d 52, 131 Cal. Rptr. 335 (1976)

        III: A201-1976, Art. 9, Para. 9.6

III: A311-1970, Performance Bond
III: A401-1978, Art. 11

Subcontractor sought declaratory relief against the owner, and the Superior Court entered judgment for the owner.

The Court of Appeals affirmed. Even if the subcontractor was a third-party beneficiary of the owner-contractor contract, it could not assert greater rights than the contractor. The fact that the subcontractor fully performed as to the contractor was irrelevant. The architect did not approve further payment to the contractor, pursuant to a contract provision for retainage for proper completion of the work. Since the contractor was not entitled to payment, the subcontractor also was not entitled to further payment. The owner had no duty to seek to collect from the contractor's surety in order to pay off the subcontractor. The subcontractor's remedy was to sue that surety as a third-party beneficiary of the bond.

76071 Western Contracting Corp. v. Southwest Steel Rolling Mills, Inc., 58 Cal. App. 3d 532, 129 Cal. Rptr. 782 (1976)

III: A401-1978, Art. 11

A widow of an employee of a subcontractor sued the contractor and subcontractor for damages for wrongful death. The contractor cross-claimed against the subcontractor for indemnity, but the Superior Court granted the subcontractor's motion for summary judgment.

The Court of Appeals reversed. Under a subcontract clause, any negligence by the contractor would eliminate the subcontractor's obligation to indemnify irrespective of whether the subcontractor might also have been the cause of the contractor's liability. The particular work of the subcontractor involved such a "high degree of risk in relation to the particular surroundings" that the contractor might have been negligent only vicariously for the employee's death. Under this circumstance the contractor could be indemnified, and the court remanded for trial on the issue of negligence.

77001 Air Heaters, Inc. v. Johnson Electric, Inc. 258 N.W.2d 649 (N.D. 1977)

    III: A201-1976, Art. 4, Para. 4.5
    III: A201-1976, Art. 7, Para. 7.6

Owner sued the contractor for a fire caused by the contractor's faulty installation of the electrical system. The District Court held for the owners.

The Supreme Court affirmed. The installation of the electrical wiring was not a sale of goods, and therefore, the Uniform Commercial Code warranties did not apply. However, an implied warranty of fitness for the intended purpose was breached by the contractor, which warranty existed under certain limited circumstances.

77002 Alfred A. Altimont, Inc. v. Chatelain, Samperton & Nolan, 374 A.2d 284 (D.C. Ct. App. 1977)

    II: A201-1976, Art. 2, Para. 2.2
    II: A311-1970, Performance Bond
    II: B141-1977, Art. 1

Contractor sued architect for libel, slander and tortious interference with a contractual relationship. The architect had, by letter, told the contractor's performance bond surety of a possible default, blamed the contractor for the delays and accused the contractor of "extreme negligence." The Superior Court granted the architect's motion for a directed verdict.

The Court of Appeals affirmed, holding that there was no showing of intent to procure the owner's breach. To recover for interference with a prospective advantage both intent and damages must be shown. As to the slander and libel charges, the architect had a qualified privilege when it wrote to the surety. Such a privilege is lost if the possessor acts with malice, but the architect was found not to have such malice. The architect had a duty to protect the interest of the owner, since he was designated in the contract as the owner's representative.

77003 American Airlines, Inc. v. Licon Associates, Inc. 56 A.D.2d 774, 392 N.Y.S.2d 451 (1977)

    I: A201-1976, Art. 2, Para. 2.2
    I: A201-1976, Art. 7, Para. 7.9

Contractor demanded arbitration, and the owner sought a stay on the grounds that the architect had not rendered a decision on the merits of the dispute. The Supreme Court denied the requested stay.

The Appellate Division affirmed. The contractor had sent a claim letter to the architect, which contained all the evidence that it would present, and the architect sent the contractor a letter stating that not enough evidence had been presented. The court stated that this constituted a ruling of rejection of the claim and satisfied the condition precedent to a demand for arbitration. The contractor's claim for injury to reputation was arbitrable since the contract provided for arbitration of "all claims, disputes and other matters in question arising out of, or relating to, this contract or the breach thereof."

77004   Arctic Contractors, Inc. v. State, 564 P.2d 30 (Alaska 1977)

> III: A201-1976, Art. 7, Para. 7.6
> III: A201-1976, Art. 9, Para. 9.4
> III: A201-1976, Art. 9, Para. 9.6
> III: A201-1976, Art. 14, Para. 14.2

The state sued the contractor for failing to provide proper payment and performance bonds. The contractor counterclaimed over the termination of the contract. The Superior Court entered a judgment favorable in part to both sides, but both appealed.

The Supreme Court reversed and remanded the case on several points. The bonds tendered by the contractor had been accepted by the state without any investigation or confirmation. While the contractor had the duty to execute the bonds, it was the obligation of the state to approve and accept the bonds. The contractor's duty to supply the bonds was continuous, and so, it should have supplied new bonds when the state noticed their defects during construction. The state's allowing the contractor to continue, after a demand for new complying bonds, was not a waiver or estoppel of its rights. The state was justified in withholding a progress payment in order to compel the production of new and proper bonds. The right to withhold progress payments is limited to "circumstances which clearly warrant it." However, the state should have supplied proper and complete notice before it withheld the progress payment, and thus, the state also breached the contract.

The state did have the right to terminate the contract and seek a completion contractor, but it could not then also seek to collect liquidated damages for delay in completion of the project. In such circumstances the liquidated damage clause would operate as a penalty, and thus, be unenforceable under Alaska law.

77005   Area Masonry, Ltd. v. Dormitory Authority, 64 A.D.2d 810, 407 N.Y.S.2d 279 (1978), *aff'g* 91 Misc. 2d 396, 398 N.Y.S.2d 119 (Sup. Ct. 1977)

> II: A311-1970, Labor and Material Payment Bond

Subcontractor brought suit against the owner after the subcontractor's action against the contractor's sureties was defended by sureties on the theory that the sureties had been discharged by the owner's changes to the contract. The Supreme Court dismissed the subcontractor's complaint.

The Appellate Division affirmed. There was no discharge of the sureties by reason of the owner's changes in the contract. The subcontractor had an "independent and enforceable right as a beneficiary upon the bond," and the owner was powerless to alter the subcontractor's potential claims upon the bond against the surety. At most, the contract changes might have relieved the surety of its duties to the owner, but not to the subcontractor, unless the changes had been so great that they amounted to abandonment of the contract to which the subcontractor would be charged with notice.

77006 (UNASSIGNED)

77007 Associated Engineers & Contractors, Inc. v. State, 58 Haw. 187, 567 P.2d 397 (1977)

        III: A201-1976, Art. 3, Para. 3.
        III: A201-1976, Art. 8, Para. 8.3

Contractor sued the State of Haw., alleging failure to supply complete weather information. The state counterclaimed, alleging delay and resulting expenses. The Circuit Court held for the contractor on its claim and for the state on its counterclaims.

The Supreme Court affirmed the award for the state on the counterclaim and reversed the judgment for the contractor on its claim. The risk of abnormal weather conditions is borne by the contractor. The state had indicated that more comprehensive weather information was available, and the inclusion of partial weather data and omission of "cold weather specifications" did not amount to a representation by the state of weather conditions which would be encountered on the job site. Since the contract clearly stated that no extensions of time would be granted, the state was under no obligation to grant an extension even for unanticipated snow and ice on a mountaintop site in Haw..

77008 Atlas Plastering, Inc. v. Superior Court, County of Alameda, 72 Cal. App. 3d 63, 140 Cal. Rptr. 59 (1977)

        III: A401-1978, Art. 13

Subcontractors sought a writ in the Court of Appeals to reverse the Superior Court's granting of the contractor's request for consolidation of several contractor-subcontractor arbitrations. The Court of Appeals granted the writ, thus preventing consolidation. Each of the subcontracts contained an identically worded arbitration clause.

Each arbitration clause called for each party to appoint one arbitrator with those two arbitrators to select a third arbitrator. The court did not have the power to force consolidation because it would require the arbitration to be conducted in a different manner than that which had been consented to by agreement.

77009 Baker-Crow Construction Co. v. Hames Electric, Inc. 566 P.2d 153 (Okla. Ct. App. 1977)

        III: A201-1976, Art. 7, Para. 7.6
        III: A201-1976, Art. 13, Para. 13.2

III: A401-1978, Art. 11

Contractor sued the subcontractor for its work that did not meet local ordinances. The District Court held for the subcontractor.

The Court of Appeals reversed and remanded. The lapsed one-year warranty was not the contractor's exclusive remedy for the subcontractor's breach, since warranty clauses are not generally intended to limit the remedy to defects occurring within the warranty period. In addition, a contract provision stated that the remedy was cumulative.

77010   Baltimore County v. John K. Ruff, Inc., 281 Md. 62, 375 A.2d 237 (1977)

II: A310-1970, Bid Bond
III: A201-1976, Art. 1, Para. 1.1
III: A201-1976, Art. 1, Para. 1.2

Contractor sought to rescind its bid on a public construction contract on which it had omitted the labor costs in a "simple mathematical mistake." The owner counterclaimed against the contractor and its surety.

The Court of Appeals affirmed the decision of the Circuit Court to allow recission and dismissed the claims against the surety on the bid bond. The courts may find a contract unconscionable from the "various circumstances surrounding each case." It held that the mistake was material and substantial and further stated that whether the mistake would render the bidder insolvent was only one element to be considered but was not controlling.

77011   Bennett Construction Co. v. Allen Gardens, Inc., 433 F. Supp. 825 (W.D. Mo. 1977).

III: A201-1976, Art. 9, Para. 9.9

Contractor sued the Secretary of HUD as mortgage insurer and present mortgagee for unpaid progress payments, retainage and compensation for extra work. The District Court held that the construction contractor was a third-party creditor beneficiary of the building loan agreement. The fact that there had been no formal closing of the HUD mortgage to the now defunct owner was not a valid defense to paying the retainage, progress payments and other compensation owed to the contractor. The contractor had "fully and satisfactorily completed construction . . . a result which was the ultimate purpose of the various agreements executed by the parties."

77012   Bert C. Young & Sons Corp. v. Association of Franciscan Sisters of the Sacred Heart, 47 Ill. App. 3d 336, 361 N.E.2d 1162 (1977)

I: A111-1978, Art. 16
I: A201-1976, Art. 1, Para. 1.1
I: A201-1976, Art. 2, Para. 2.2

The contractor on a hospital construction project sought a declaratory judgment as to whether it was required to place in the present floor the ductwork and pipes for a future addition. The Circuit Court dismissed the suit.

Since one of the conflicting proposals was expressed in the contract and the other was incorporated by reference into the contract, the architect was properly within his authority under the contract to decide which proposal should be used.

The contractor's failure to demand arbitration of the architect's decision acted as a waiver by the contractor of his right to arbitrate and rendered the architect's decision final.

77013 Binswanger Glass Co. v. Beers Construction Co., 141 Ga. App. 715, 234 S.E.2d 363 (1977)

    I: A201-1976, Art. 4, Para. 4.18
    III: A401-1978, Art. 12

General contractor sued subcontractor claiming the subcontractor was liable under an indemnification clause for the death of subcontractor's employee.

The Court of Appeals affirmed the Superior Court's decision for the general contractor. The contractor-subcontractor contract incorporated the indemnification clause of the general conditions. That clause would not require indemnification for the contractor's negligence unless it concurred with the subcontractor's negligence.

77014 Burmar Electrical Corp. v. Starrett Bros., 60 A.D.2d 561, 400 N.Y.S.2d 346 (1977)

    III: A201-1976, Art. 12, Para. 12.1
    III: A401-1978, Art. 11
    III: A401-1978, Art. 12

Subcontractor sued the contractor to recover for extras. The Supreme Court granted summary judgment for the subcontractor.

The Appellate Division reversed. According to a contract provision, payment for extras to the subcontractor was conditioned on the owner's payment to the contractor. Since the owner had not yet reached a conclusion with respect to the claims for extras, summary judgment was inappropriate.

77015 Cagle, Inc. v. Sammons, 198 Neb. 595, 254 N.W.2d 398 (1977)

    I: A311-1970, Labor and Material Payment Bond
    II: A401-1978, Art. 12
    III: A401-1978, Art. 14

Contractor sued the subcontractor and its surety on a labor and material payment bond for work finished by the contractor after the subcontractor defaulted. The District Court sustained a demurrer for the surety.

The Supreme Court reversed and remanded for trial. The bond listed the owner of the project as the obligee. The contract provision which allowed the contractor to take over and complete the work on default did not make the contractor a claimant since that clause did not constitute a "direct contract with the Principal." However, since the contractor paid claims of laborers and materialmen after the default for work performed before the default, the contractor was subrogated to the rights of the laborers and materialmen. Subrogation was a proper legal theory since the contractor acted to protect his own position and was not a volunteer.

77016   Capua v. W. E. O'Neil Construction Co., 67 Ill. 2d 255, 367 N.E.2d 669 (1977)

> III: A201-1976, Art. 4, Para. 4.18
> III: A311-1970, Labor and Material Payment Bond
> III: A401-1978, Art. 11

Subcontractor's injured worker sued the contractor and the city-owner. The city-owner sought indemnity from the contractor and its sureties under the terms of the construction bond. The Circuit Court dismissed the indemnity actions as being contrary to a state law forbidding certain types of indemnity between contractor and owner.

The Supreme Court reversed. The statute applied only to construction contracts, not to the terms of the construction bond. The court construed the statute to mean that the legislature intended that a surety would provide a relatively certain payment to an injured worker if the owner were in default.

77017   Carollo v. Consolidated Edison Co. of New York, Inc., 57 A.D.2d 853, 394 N.Y.S.2d 267 (1977)

> II: A201-1976, Art. 4, Para. 4.18

Excavation contractor's injured employee sued the utility for whom the contractor was working. The utility sought indemnity from the contractor. The Supreme Court ordered the contractor to pay for any liability the utility might have to the worker.

The Appellate Division affirmed. The contractor had been negligent and owed indemnity to the utility notwithstanding the utility's own active negligence. The fact that liability arose only in part from the contractor's actions did not excuse it from its contracted for duty to indemnify the utility.

77018   Carrols Equities Crop. v. Villnave, 57 A.D.2d 1044, 395 N.Y.S.2d 800 (1977)

> II: A201-1976, Art. 12, Para. 12.1
> II: A201-1976, Art. 13, Para. 13.2

II: A311-1970, Performance Bond

Owner sued the contractor and its surety for breach of contract due to uneven settling of the building. The surety cross-claimed against the contractor for indemnity under the bond. The Supreme Court held for both the owner and the surety against the contractor.

The Appellate Division modified the decision. The contractor had breached the contract by not placing the foundation in the "one foot of virgin soil" as required by the contract. The one-year warranty provision of the contract applied only to the contractor's duty to correct defects through its supplemental performance, and the one-year warranty was not an exclusive remedy.

The change orders and alterations to the plans did not invalidate the performance bond. The surety was deemed to have assented to the contract's provisions allowing such changes and was bound by the amended plans. The cross-claim of the surety was proper but not on the principle of indemnity since the contractor had never signed the bond, nor impliedly consented to it. After paying the owner, the surety would be subrogated to its rights against the contractor.

77019   City of Elmira v. Larry Walter, Inc., 60 A.D.2d 669, 400 N.Y.S.2d 204 (1977)

III: A107-1978, Art. 13
III: A201-1976, Art. 7, Para. 7.9

Contractor brought suit to stay the arbitration demanded by the owner. The Supreme Court, Special Term, Chemung County, granted a stay as to all the issues except the contractor's allegations of nonpayment.

The Supreme Court, Appellate Division, affirmed, holding that the question of fulfillment of conditions precedent to arbitration was for the courts and not the arbitrators. Under the contract the owner was the only party entitled to demand arbitration, but arbitration would also result if the owner failed to settle a claim or dispute. Accordingly, the arbitration clause was not entirely one-sided so as to be invalid. The court also stated that the condition precedent of the owner's decisions as to the contractor's claims had been met as to the issue of nonpayment but not as to the other issues.

77020   City of Seattle v. Dyad Construction, Inc., 17 Wash. App. 501, 565 P.2d 423 (1977)

III: A201-1976, Art. 1, Para. 1.2
III: A201-1976, Art. 4, Para. 4.3
III: A201-1976, Art. 8, Para. 8.3

The city-owner sued to recover money erroneously paid to the contractor, who counterclaimed for damages based on owner-caused delays. The Superior Court awarded the owner the amount of the overpayment less an amount to compensate the contractor for extra work performed at the owner's request. The contractor's counterclaim for delay damages was denied.

The Court of Appeals upheld the contractor's award for extra work performed and reversed the denial of the contractor's counterclaim for delay damages. The owner did not have the right to insist on certain measures, since the contractor had been proceeding in "workmanlike fashion and was utilizing normal contemplated construction procedures." The owner was also responsible for its faulty plans and specifications and the resulting delays despite the contractor's inspection of the area prior to bidding. The contract provided for an extension of time for conditions beyond the contractor's control. This normally would have precluded damages for delay. However, the owner "arbitrarily and without justification directed the manner and method of the contractor's performance" and produced faulty specifications and caused delays. "These findings demonstrate changed conditions that could not have been anticipated, brought about by active interference and unforeseeable delays that transcend the contract."

77021 City Sioux Falls v. Henry Carlson Co., 258 N.W.2d 676 (S.D. 1977)

I: A201-1976, Art. 11, Para. 11.3

The city-owner sued remodeling contractors to recover its progress payments after a fire destroyed the building when the project was substantially completed. The contractors counterclaimed for the balance of the contract price. The Circuit Court denied relief to both on the basis that the contract stated that the risk of loss remained on the contractors until completion, and the city had been compensated by insurance, thus waiving its rights against the contractors.

The Supreme Court affirmed. The court noted that if the city-owner had not modified the property insurance provisions of the AIA standard form contract, the city-owner would have had to provide insurance coverage for the loss of the contractors. Since the city-owner had drafted the contract, the ambiguity was resolved against it.

77022 Comptroller of Virginia *ex rel.* Virginia Military Institute v. King, 217 Va. 751, 232 S.E.2d 895 (1977)

III: A201-1976, Art. 2, Para. 2.2
III: B141-1977, Art. 1
III: B141-1977, Art. 11

Owner sued architects for damages to a building. The Circuit Court held the suit barred by the statute of limitations.

The Supreme Court reversed. The breach of contract action for defective design was barred since the statute of limitations began to run upon final approval of the plans and specifications. However, the architects by contract had a duty to supervise the construction and the breach of contract action for negligent supervision was not barred by the statute of limitations.

77023 Conte v. City of Norwalk, 173 Conn. 77, 376 A.2d 412 (1977)

III: A107-1978, Art. 13

III: A201-1976, Art. 7, Para. 7.9

Contractor submitted a claim for arbitration and objected when the owner submitted a counterclaim. The contractor then sought an injunction against the arbitrators' hearing the counterclaim.

The Superior Court denied the injunction and the Supreme Court affirmed. Since the contract clearly made arbitrability a matter for the arbitrators to decide, the courts should not issue injunctions. When arbitrability is for the arbitrators, the proper way to dispute it is to object in the arbitration proceeding to the arbitrator. After the arbitrator's award the objecting part may ask the courts to vacate on the grounds of arbitrability.

77024   Cotter v. Consolidated Constr. Co., 50 Ill. App. 3d 332, 365 N.E.2d 636 (1977)

III: A201-1976, Art. 4, Para. 4.18
III: A401-1978, Art. 11

Subcontractor's injured employee sued the contractor, who sought indemnity from the subcontractor. The Circuit Court held for the injured employee and required the subcontractor to indemnify the contractor.

The Appellate Court reversed as to the indemnity. The language of the contract provision was not so clear or explicit that the subcontractor-indemnitor should be required to indemnify the contractor-indemnitee for its own negligence.

77025   County of Sullivan v. Edward L. Nezelek, Inc., 42 N.Y.2d 123, 397 N.Y.S.2d 371, 366 N.E.2d 72 (1977)

III: A201-1976, Art. 7, Para. 7.9
III: B141-1977, Art. 9

The architect's motion for a stay of arbitration was denied, and the Supreme Court ordered consolidation of the architect-owner and owner-contractor arbitration. The Appellate Division affirmed.

The Court of Appeals upheld the authority and propriety of the court to order consolidation. Both the owner-architect and the owner-contractor agreements had contained broad arbitration clauses. Because of the pattern of New York decisions, "parties signing an agreement to arbitrate must be held to do so in contemplation of the announced authority of the courts in proper cases to direct consolidation." Parties that wished to avoid consolidation should include in their contracts appropriate provisions to preclude or limit consolidation and be extremely specific in drafting the arbitration clauses. Because of the similarity of facts and the risk of inconsistent awards, the order for consolidation was proper.

77026   Custom Builders, Inc. v. Clemons, 52 Ill. App. 3d 399, 367 N.E.2d 537 (1977)

III: A201-1976, Art. 12, Para. 12.1

TABLE OF CASES

[The five-digit numbers in this table are *Citator* Case Reference Numbers, which refer to the cases in the Cases section]

Wright v. Tidmore 93023
Wrobel v. Trapani 70093
W.T. Grange Construction Co.; Concrete Form Co. v. 35001
W.T. Rich Co.; Dilaveris v. 95030
Wunderlich v. State 67074
Wunderlich Contracting Co. v. United States 65123
WVP Corp.; Fabe v. 88014
Wylie Indep. School Dist. v. TMC Found., Inc. 89051
Wyoming Johnson, Inc. v. Stagg Indus., Inc. 83050

X

Y

Yamanishi v. Breily & Cornshaw, Inc. ... 72114
Yamnitz v. Polytech, Inc. 79072
Yarber v. Morey 66117
Yardley Drilling Co.; Erickson Paving Co. v. 72037
Yarno; Weippe, City of v. 71022
Yeager Garden Acres, Inc.; Summit Construction Co. v. 70079
Yeargin Constr. Co.; Carolina Mechanical Contractors, Inc. v. 73023
Yeargin Constr. Co.; Procter & Gamble Paper Prod. Co. v. 90036
Yeargin Enter., Inc.; Traynham v. 91035
Yearwood and Johnson Architects, Inc. v. Langford 79073
Yeshiva Univ. v. Fidelity & Deposit Co. of Maryland 86075
YMCA v. U.S. Fidelity & Guaranty Corp. 13006
Yocum v. Minden 90056
Yoder; Post Bros. Construction Co. v. 77070
Yonkers Contracting Co. v. Port Auth. Trans-Hudson Corp. 95024
Yonkers Contracting Co.; Transamerica Insurance Co. v. 66100
York City Sewer Auth.; Shook of West Virginia, Inc. v. 91031
Younker Brothers v. Standard Construction Co. 65124
Yow v. Hussey, Gay, Bell & DeYoung Int'l, Inc. 91040

Z

Zab Dev. Co.; Laughlin Recreational Enters., Inc. v. 82031
Zannoth v. Booth Radio Stations, Inc. 52007
Zerr; Contractor Industries and Acceptance Corp. v. 76014
Zettel v. Paschen Contractors, Inc. 81075
Zeus Dev. Corp.; Kelso-Burnett Co. v. 82030
Zion's Cooperative Mercantile Institute v. Jacobson Construction Co. 71088
Zontelli & Sons, Inc. v. Nashwauk, City of 85044
Zoological Soc'y of Buffalo, Inc.; Hess v. 87023
Zurn Engineers v. State 77086

TABLE OF CASES

[The five-digit numbers in this table are *Citator* Case Reference Numbers, which refer to the cases in the Cases section]

Wiggens Construction Co. v. Joint School District No. 3 67072
Wilaka Construction Co., In re 66039
Wilaka Constructon Co.; Lafayette Iron Works v. 65064
Wilbanks; Pacific Insurance Co. v. 68034
Wild West Trading Co. v. gbs & h Architects, Landscape Architects, Planners, Inc. 94049
Wildmann Brewing Corp.; F.F. Bolinger Co. v. 40002
Wiley N. Jackson Co.; Richmond Shopping Center, Inc. v. 79015
Wilharm v. M.J. Constr. Co. 97025
Wilhoit Steel Erectors & Rental Service; International Erectors v. 68020
Willard, Inc. v. Powertherm Corp. 82058
William A. Berbusse, Jr., Inc.; Pettinelli Electric Co. v. 66072
William A. Berbusse, Jr., Inc.; W.R. Ferguson, Inc. v. 66116
William A. Smith Contracting Co. v. West Central Texas Municipal Water District 65120
William B. Lucke, Inc. v. Spiegel 70091
William Bayley Co.; Beckham v. 87005
William Bohnenkamp & Associates; Paul B. Emerick Co. v. 65087
William C. Blanchard Co. v. Beach Concrete Co. 72111
William Cameron & Co. v. American Surety Co. 32002
William F. Klingensmith, Inc. v. David H. Snell Landscape Contractor, Inc. 72112
William Holliday Cord Associates; Lesser v. 65068
William L. Crow Construction Co.; A-1 Camp Chair Service Co. v. 65007
William Passalacqua Builders, Inc. v. Mayfair House Association, Inc. 81073
Williams v. D. A. H. Construction Corp. . . 73125
Williams v. Gervais F. Favrot Co. 86072
Williams; State Department of Human Resources v. 73102
Williams v. Sullivan, Long & Haggarty, Inc. 68055
Williams & Associates v. Ramsey Products Corp. 73124
Williams Construction Co.; Benson Paint Co. v. 73015
Williams & Dunlap; Autrey v. 65009
Williams Eng'g, Inc. v. Goodyear 86073
Willis; Edward Edinger Co. v. 31003
Willis Realty Assocs. v. Cimino Constr. Co. 93022
Willner & Millkey v. Shure 71087
Willoughby Roofing & Supply Co. v. Kajima Int'l, Inc. 84040
Wilson; Board of Regents v. 75002
Wilson v. Keefe 57004
Wilson v. Nooter Corp. 73126
Wilson-Avery, Inc.; Continental Casualty Co. v. 67017
Wilson Contracting Co. v. State 66114
Wilson Elec. Contractors, Inc. v. Minnotte Contracting Corp. 89050
Windowmaster Corp. v. B. G. Danis Co. . . 81174
Wingate Construction Co. v. Schweizer Dipple, Inc. 65121
Winn-Senter Constr. v. Katie Franks, Inc. 91038
Winston Corp. v. Continental Casualty Co. 75028
Winston-Salem, City of; Watson Elec. Constr. Co. v. 93020
Winston Steel Works; Baldwin Contracting Co. v. 65010
Witcosky; John E. Branagh & Sons v. . . . 66045
Wittenberg, Delony & Davidson, Inc.; Walker v. 67067
Wittenberg Engineering & Construction Co. v. Liberty Mutual Insurance Co. 65122
W.L. Jorden & Co. v. Blythe Indus., Inc. 88044
W.L. Walker Co. v. Green Manor Construction Co. 66115
Wm. R. Clarke Corp. v. Safeco Ins. Co. of Am. 97027
W.M. Schlosser Co. v. Maryland Drywall Co. 96015
Wolf; C & M Ventures, Inc. v. 91006
Wolfe v. Warfield 72113
Wood v. Fort Wayne 001
Wood-Hopkins Contracting Co. v. Masonry Contractors, Inc. 70092
Woodburn v. Consolidation Coal Co. . . . 91039
Woodrow Wilson Constr. Co. v. MMR-Radon Constructors, Inc. 94021
Woodward Heating & Air Conditioning Co. v. American Arbitration Association 78078
Worcester, City of v. Park Construction Co. 72027
Worthy Bros. Pipeline Corp.; St. Lawrence Explosives Corp. v. 96011
W.R. Ferguson, Inc. v. William A. Berbusse, Jr., Inc. 66116
Wrecking Corp. of America v. Memorial Hospital for Cancer and Allied Diseases 78079
Wright v. Cecil A. Mason Construction Co. 67073

TABLE OF CASES

[The five-digit numbers in this table are *Citator* Case Reference Numbers, which refer to the cases in the Cases section]

Werner Industries; Norfolk and Western Ry. Co. v. 74026
Wesco Elec., Inc.; 71 Construction v. ... 96041
Wes-Julian Construction Corp. v. Commonwealth 67070
Wesley Construction Co.; Florida v. 70027
Wesleyan Univ. v. Rissil Constr. Assocs., Inc. ... 84039
West; George Wagschal Associates, Inc. v. 61007
West Allegheny School Authority; Branna Construction Co. v. 68006
West Baro Corp.; Cast-Crete Corp. v. ... 76010
West Bend Mut.; Schaub v. 95045
West Central Texas Municipal Water District; William A. Smith Contracting Co. v. 65120
West Durham Lumber Co. v. Aetna Casualty & Surety Co. 71086
West End Realty Corp.; Noland Co. v. ... 66064
West Hatchie Drainage District; Baton Rouge Contracting Co. v. 69008
West Manchester Township Sewer Auth.; Brady Contracting Co. v. 86004
West Plains Bridge and Grading Co.; N.B. Harty General Contractors, Inc. v. 80047
West Point Constr. Co.; United States Fidelity & Guar. Co. v. 88038
West 16th Street Realty Corp.; M. Bender & Son v. 72066
West Virginia ex rel Center Designs v. Henning 97024
West Virginia Turnpike Commission; S. J. Groves & Sons v. 58005
Westech, Inc.; Palmer Steel Structures v. ... 78060
Westerfield v. Arjack, Co. 79070
Westerhold v. Carroll 67071
Westmoreland Hospital Ass'n v. Westmoreland Construction Co. 66113
Western Beef, Inc.; Brown-McKee, Inc. v. 76009
Western Casualty and Surety Co. v. Honeywell, Inc. 80075
Western Construction Corp.; Albano v. ... 70006
Western Contracting Corp. v. Southwest Steel Rolling Mills, Inc. 76071
Western Contracting Corp. v. State Highway Dept. 72109
Western Contracting Corp.; United States v. 65113
Western Mortgage & Warranty Title Co.; Interstate Lumber Co. v. 15004
Western Stress, Inc.; H.E. Wiese, Inc. v. ... 81031
Western Union Telegraph Company v. Massman Construction Co. 79071

Westinghouse Electric Corp.; Perschke v. 69048
Westminster Construction Corp. v. PPG Industries, Inc. 77085
Westmoreland Construction Co.; Westmoreland Hospital Ass'n v. 66113
Weston, Town of; Conte v. 65027
Westville, Village of v. Loitz Bros. Constr. Co. ... 83039
Wetzel v. Roberts 41004
Weyland Mach. Shop, Inc.; Baldwin Co. v. 85005
Weyland Mach. Shop, Inc.; Gurtler, Hebert & Co. v. 81030
W.F. Thompson Construction Co. v. Southeastern Palm Beach County Hospital District .. 65119
W.G. Mills, Inc.; Balboa Insurance Co. v. 81006
W.H. Nichols & Co.; Ace Construction Co. v. ... 65001
Whalen v. K-Mart Corp. 88043
Wheel Awhile, Inc.; Baldi Construction Engineers Inc. v. 71008
Wheeler v. Aetna Casualty & Surety Co. 73123
Wheeler & Lewis v. Slifer 78076
White; H.C. Jessee, Estate of v. 82017
White Budd Van Ness Partnership v. Major-Gladys Drive Joint Venture 90055
Whitehall, City of v. Southern Mechanical Contracting, Inc. 80011
Whitehead Construction Co.; Royal Service Co. v. 73098
Whitehurst Bros., Inc.; Prepakt Concrete Co. v. ... 77072
Whitfield Construction Co. Inc. v. Commercial Development Corp. 75027
Whitmyer Bros., Inc. v. New York, State of 78077
Whittle v. Pagani Brothers Construction Co. 81072
Wichers; Steffek v. 73104
Wick Constr. Co.; Industrial Indem. Co. v. 84020
Wick Constr. Co.; Lull v. 80041
Wickes Corp. v. Industrial Financial Corp. 74043
Wicklund v. Gus J. Bouten Constr. Co. ... 83049
Wiedemann Industries, Inc.; Bismark Baptist Church v. 72015
Wieman-Slechta Co. v. Pascoe Steel Corp. 72110
Wienir; Teufel v. 66098

TABLE OF CASES

TC–65

[The five-digit numbers in this table are *Citator* Case Reference Numbers, which refer to the cases in the Cases section]

Walsh v. Cornwell	30001
Walsh v. International Fidelity Insurance Co.	67068
Walsh; United States v.	65112
Walsh & Oberg Architects, Inc.; Maricopa, County of v.	72030
Walsh Plumbing Co.; St. Andrews Episcopal Day School v.	70071
Walter A. Stanley & Son, Inc. v. Trustees of Hackley School	77084
Walter C. Carlson Associates; Fruzyna v.	79029
Walter Kidde Constructors, Inc. v. State	81071
Walter L. Couse & Co. v. Hardy Corp.	73120
Walters v. Landis Constr. Co.	88041
Walton v. Datry	87053
Wangler Constr. Co.; Ure v.	92021
Ward W. Ross, Inc.; McCandliss v.	73071
Warde v. Davis	72106
Warfield; Wolfe v.	72113
Warner Construction Co. v. Blue Diamond Co.	68052
Warner Construction Corp. v. Los Angeles, City of	70094
Warren; Welsh v.	13005
Warren Brothers v. Cardi Corp.	73121
Warren Brothers Co.; Aetna Casualty & Surety Co. v.	78002
Warren Brothers Roads Co. v. United States	52006
Warren-Ehret Co.; First National Realty Corp. v.	67026
Warren G. Kleban Engineering Corp. v. Caldwell	73122
Wasau, City of; Gottschalk Brothers v.	73044
Washington Construction Co. v. Spinella	51003
Washington Elementary School Dist. No. 6 v. Baglino Corp.	91036
Washington Parish Police Jury v. Belcher & Sons, Inc.	68053
Washington Pub. Power Supply Sys.; Lampson Universal Rigging, Inc. v.	86042
Washington Township; James I. Barnes Construction Co. v.	62005
Wasserstein v. Kovatch	93019
Watajo, Inc.; Artcraft Cabinet, Inc. v.	76004
Waterwiese v. KBA Constr. Managers, Inc.	91036a
Waterworks District No. 1 v. Babin	80074
Watkins; Reeves v.	81062
Watson Construction Co. v. Reppel Steel & Supply Co.	79069
Watson Elec. Constr. Co. v. Winston-Salem, City of	93020
Watson-Forsberg Co.; Holmes v.	92008c
Watson Lumber Co. v. Guennewig	67069
Watson, Watson, Rutland/Architects, Inc. v. Montgomery County Bd. of Educ.	90052
Wawak v. Stewart	70089
W.B. Lloyd Construction Co.; Shoffner Industries, Inc. v.	79061
W.C. English, Inc. v. Commonwealth, Dept. of Transp.	92021b
W.E. Erickson Constr., Inc. v. Congress-Kenilworth Corp.	86070
W.E. Koehler Constr. Co. v. Medical Center of Blue Springs	84038
Weaver; Nees v.	36002
Webb v. Lawson-Avila Constr.	95049
Weber Eng'g Co.; Falcon Steel Co. v.	86023
Weeks v. Alabama Elec. Coop., Inc.	82057
Weeshoff Construction Co. v. Los Angeles County Flood Control District	79018
Wehr Constructors, Inc. v. Steel Fabricators, Inc.	88042
Weidner v. Szostek	93021
Weill Constr. Co. v. Thibodeaux	86071
Weippe, City of v. Yarno	71022
Weiss; Peyronnin Construction Co. v.	65088
Weisz Trucking Co. v. Emil R. Wohl Construction	70090
Weitz Co.; Giarratano v.	67027
Welch v. California, State of	83048
Welch v. Grant Dev. Co.	83047
Welch v. McDougal	94020
Welch; Treasure State Industries, Inc. v.	77080
Welch Constr. Co.; Parem Contracting Corp. v.	86049
Welch Contracting Corp.; Daniel Construction Co. v.	71030
Welch-Eckman Construction Co. v. Vancouver Plywood Co.	68054
Welch Group, Inc. v. Creative Drywall, Inc.	90053
Welch Pile Driving Corp.; Doyle & Russell, Inc. v.	73035
Wellborn Plumbing & Heating Co. v. Randolph County Board of Education	66112
Welles; Portuguese-American Bank v.	16004
Wells; Forcum-Lannon, Inc. v.	69020
Wells & Parker Architects, Inc. v. Monroe-McKeen Plaza Hous. Dev. Corp.	90054
Welsh v. Warren	13005
Wendling; Kleb v.	79010
Wenke v. Amoco Chemicals Corp.	72107
Wenzel v. Boyles Galvanizing Co.	91037
Wenzler & Ward Plumbing & Heating Co. v. Sellen	58006

(Matthew Bender & Co., Inc.) (Pub.435)

TABLE OF CASES

[The five-digit numbers in this table are *Citator* Case Reference Numbers, which refer to the cases in the Cases section]

Van Deree; Morton Z. Levine and Associates v. . . 76046
Van Ornum v. Otter Tail Power Co. 73114
Van Vickle v. C.W. Scheurer 96043
Vancouver Plywood Co.; Welch-Eckman Construction Co. v. 68054
Vandygriff v. Commonwealth Edison Co. 80073
VanKirk v. Green Constr. Co. 95048
Vappi Co.; Jones v. 89028
Varian Associates; Howard J. White, Inc. v. 60008
Vece v. Medical Center, Inc. 62010
Vega v. Griffiths Constr., Inc. 92021a
Vendrigo Highlands, Inc. v. Security Insurance Co. 66111
Verdex Steel & Construction Co. v. Board of Supervisors 73116
Vermont; Lane Construction Corp. v. . . . 70049
Vermont Marble Co. v. Baltimore Contractors, Inc. 81069
Vernali v. Centrella 70087
Vernon, Town of; Multi-Service Contractors, Inc. v. 80046
Verzella v. Caste Bros., Inc. 65115
Vespe Contracting Co. v. Anvan Corp. . . 75026; 77083a
Vey v. Port Authority of New York & New Jersey 81070
Vicik; J.F. Inc. v. 81041
Victor A. Perosi, Inc.; Freeo v. 76024
Vilbig Bros.; C.H. Leavell & Co. v. 60003
Village Construction Co.; Gateway Drywall & Decorating, Inc. v. 79039
Village Dev. Co.; Midwest Materials Co. v. 91021
Village of River Grove; Jandrisits v. 96031
Villnave; Carrols Equities Crop. v. 77018
Vincennes Community School Corp.; Slutsky-Peltz Plumbing & Heating Co. v. 90041
Vinnell Corp. v. State 73117
Vinsant Plumbing & Heating Co. v. Rudder Construction Co. 71085
Vitek, Inc. v. Alvarado Ice Palace 73118
V.L. Nicholson Co. v. Transcon Investment & Financial Ltd. 80072
Voight v. Nanz 74041
Volt Information Sciences, Inc. v. Board of Trustees 89048
Von Kokeritz, Borup v. 14002
Vonasek v. Hirsch & Stevens, Inc. 74042
Votaw Precision Tool Co. v. Air Canada . . 76070
Vuono-Lione, Inc.; Norton Heights Fire Dept. v. 76051

W

W. C. B. Assoc.; Balboa Insurance Co. v. 80005
W. E. O'Neil Construction Co.; Capua v. 77016
W. F. Holt & Sons; Ford Motor Co. v. . . . 71040
W. Harley Miller, Inc.; Board of Education v. 75001
W. J. Barney Corp.; New York Plumber's Specialties Co. v. 76047
W. J. Howard & Sons v. Meyer 62011
W. & J. Knox Net & Twine Co.; Hartford Accident & Indemnity Co. v. 26001
W. L. Cobb Construction Co.; Jones v. . . 79047
W. O. Taylor Commercial Refrigeration & Electric Co.; Fairchild v. 81024
W & W Steel Co.; Waggoner v. 82056
W. William Graham, Inc. v. Cave City . . 86074
W.A. Botting Plumbing & Heating Co. v. Constructors-Pamco 87052
Wade Lupe Constr. Co.; Riggi v. 91028
Wager Construction Corp.; Board of Education v. 73019
Wager Construction Corp.; Schuler-Haas Electric Corp. v. 77076
Waggoner v. W & W Steel Co. 82056
Wagner v. Fireman's Fund Insurance Co. 65116
Walbridge Aldinger Co. v. Walcon Corp. 94047
Walcon Corp.; Walbridge Aldinger Co. v. 94047
Waldinger Corp.; John F. Harkins Co. v. . . 86037
Walijarvi; Mounds View, City of v. 78016
Walker; Fauntleroy v. 79036
Walker v. Lytton Savings & Loan Ass'n . . 70088
Walker v. Paramount Engineering Co. . . . 65117
Walker v. V & V Constr. Co. 89049
Walker v. Wittenberg, Delony & Davidson, Inc. 67067
Walker Manufacturing Co. v. Henkel Construction Co. 72105
Wallace v. Sherwood Constr. Co. 94048
Wallace Diteman, Inc.; Grass Range High School District No. 27 v. 70030
Wallace Process Piping Co. v. Martin-Marietta Corp. 65118
Wallace & Riddle; Sira & Payne, Inc. v. . . 72093
Waller v. J. E. Brenneman Co. 73119
Waller; Midland, City of v. 68010
Walls, Inc. v. Atlantic Realty Co. 88040
Walnut Associates; The Foley Co. v. 80065
Walnut Creek Electric v. Reynolds Construction Co. 68051

(Matthew Bender & Co., Inc.) (Pub.435)

TABLE OF CASES

[The five-digit numbers in this table are Citator *Case Reference Numbers, which refer to the cases in the Cases section]*

United States ex rel. A. Teichert & Son v. Anchor Contractors, Inc. 66103
United States ex rel. Chemetron Corp. v. George A. Fuller Co. 66104
United States ex rel. Lincoln Electric Products Co. v. Greene Electrical Service, Inc. 66105
United States ex rel. Powers Regulator Co. v. Farina Construction Corp. 66106
United States ex rel. Shields, Inc. v. Citizens & Southern National Bank 66107
United States ex rel. Urban Plumbing & Heating Co.; Baker & Ford Co. v. 66006
United States ex rel. Wellman Engineering Co. v. M.S.I. Corp. 65052
United States Fidelity & Guar. Co. v. Blankenship Plumbing Co. 80068
United States Fidelity & Guar. Co. v. Davis Mechanical Contractors, Inc. 72103
United States Fidelity & Guar. Co. v. Eastern Hills Methodist Church 80069
United States Fidelity & Guar. Co. v. Escambia Electric and Appliance Co. 80070
United States Fidelity & Guar. Co. v. Farrar's Plumbing & Heating Co. 88037, 93056
United States Fidelity & Guar. Co. v. Green 70085
United States Fidelity & Guar. Co. v. Hamilton & Spiegel, Inc. 66108
United States Fidelity & Guar. Co.; Haywood County Consolidated School System v. 79042
United States Fidelity & Guar. Co. v. Jacksonville State University 78074
United States Fidelity & Guar. Co. v. James F. O'Neil Co. 66109
United States Fidelity & Guar. Co. v. Miller 77082
United States Fidelity & Guar. Co.; RGK, Inc. v. .,.......... 76060
United States Fidelity & Guar. Co.; State v. 91033
United States Fidelity & Guar. Co.; Tony and Leo, Inc. v. 79068
United States Fidelity & Guar. Co. v. West Point Constr. Co. 88038
United States Fidelity & Guar. Corp.; YMCA v. 13006
United States Fire Ins. Co. v. Ammala ... 83044
United States Fire Ins. Co.; Gerdmann v. 84013
United States Gypsum Co.; Dinschel v. .. 67021
United States Steel Corp.; Deel v. 69014
United States Steel Corp. v. Turner Constr. Co. .. 83045

Universal Builders, Inc. v. Moon Motor Lodge .. 68050
Universal Constructors, Inc.; Brookridge Apartments, Ltd. v. 92002
Universal Electrical Construction Co.; Bluebonnet Electrical Corp. v. 71012
Universal Surety Co.; School District No. 65 R v. 65094
Universal Tavern Corp.; Shanahan v. 78064
Universal Terrazzo & Tile Co. v. Parsons Corp. ... 73113
University of Alaska v. Modern Construction, Inc. 74040
University of Connecticut Educ. Properties; Conntech Dev. Co. v. 96022
University of Chicago, In re 70038
University of Delaware; Rumsey Electric Co. v. ... 75033
University of Kansas Medical Center; Evans Electrical Construction Co. v. 81023
Urban Inv. & Dev. Co. v. Turner Constr. Co. 93018
Urbinati v. Simplex Wire & Cable Co. ... 80071
Ure v. Wangler Constr. Co. 92021
U.R.S. Co. v. Gulfport-Biloxi Regional Airport Auth. 89047
URS Co.-Kansas City v. Titus County Hosp. Dist. 85040
U.S. Insulation, Inc. v. Hilro Constr. Co. ... 85041
Utah Construction & Mining Co.; United States v. 66110
Utah Power & Light Co.; Freund v. 95013

V

V. C. Edwards Contracting Co. v. Port of Tacoma 73115
V. Petrillo & Son, Inc. v. American Construction Co. 77083
V & V Constr. Co.; Walker v. 89049
Va. Beach, City of; Continental Ins. Co. v. 95029
Vacanti & Randazzo Constr. Co.; Able Elec. Co. v. 82001
Vahlberg; Board of Commissioners v. ... 47001
Vail; Chiaverini v. 38001
Valden Associates; Board of Education, Union Free School District No. 3, Town o v. 79022
Valley Corp.; Thompson v. 95021
Valley Force Industries, Inc. v. Armand Corporation, Inc. 78075
Valley Inland Pacific Constructors, Inc.; Union County School Dist. v. 82055
Van Cor, Inc. v. American Casualty Co. .. 65114

TABLE OF CASES

[The five-digit numbers in this table are *Citator* Case Reference Numbers, which refer to the cases in the Cases section]

Troup Brothers, Inc.; Genstar Southern Development Corp. v. 81029
Trumbull Corp.; Commonwealth of Pennsylvania, Dept. of Transp. v. 86011
Trump-Equitable Fifth Ave. Co. v. H.R.H. Constr. Corp. 85038
Trust Estate of (see name of party)
Trustees of Asbury United Methodist Church v. Taylor & Parrish, Inc. 95023
Trustees of Boston University; John D. Ahern Co. v. 81042
Trustees of Hackley School; Walter A. Stanley & Son, Inc. v. 77084
Trustees of Indiana Univ. v. Aetna Casualty & Surety Co. 90050
Tsoi v. Ebenezer Baptist Church 63008
Tsombikos v. Brager 90051
Tucci & Sons v. Carl T. Madsen, Inc. . . . 70082
Tull; Gundersons, Inc. v. 83019
Turcotte; Hayeck Building & Realty Co. v. 72045
Turner/Cargile; Nicholson v. 95052
Turner Constr. Co.; All-State Investigation & Security Agency v. 72007
Turner Constr. Co.; Cafferkey v. 86007
Turner Constr. Co. v. Eppoliti, Inc. 92020a
Turner Constr. Co. v. Midwest Curtainwalls, Inc. 89045
Turner Constr. Co.; United States Steel Corp. v. . . 83045
Turner Constr. Co.; Urban Inv. & Dev. Co. v. . . . 93018
Turtle Lake, Village of v. Orvedahl Constr., Inc. 86069
Tustin, City of; Leatherby Insurance Co. v. . . . 77053
TWC Holdings, Inc. v. John F. Harkins Co. 86037
Twenty One Kings, Inc.; Pan American Realty Trust v. 68035
Twin City Constr. Co.; Bethesda Lutheran Church v. 84002
Twin Village Construction Corp. v. New York, State of 78072
Two Exch. Plaza Partners; Brown v. 89006
2500 Wisconsin Avenue; John W. Johnson, Inc. v. 56003
Two State Constr. Co.; Miller v. 95016
20th Century Home Builders, Inc.; Frazier, Inc. v. 72041
200 Levee Drive Assocs., Ltd. v. Bor-Son Bldg. Corp. 89046
Tyee Elec., Inc.; Mountain States Constr. Co. v. . . . 86046
Tyler Constr. Corp.; Andy Floors Inc. v. . . . 94001

U

Uhlhorn v. Reid 65108
Uhlir v. Golden Triangle Dev. Corp. 88036
Ukrainian National Urban Renewal Corp. v. Joseph L. Muscarelle, Inc. 77081
Ulster Electric Supply Co. v. Maryland Casualty Co. 70083
Underground Construction Co. v. Sanitary District 37003
Underhill; Goldberg v. 50002
Unger v. Eichleay Corp. 93017
Unger; 530 East 89 Corp. v. 77035
Unicorn Management Corp.; Fehlhaber Corp. v. . . . 69017
Union Building Corp. v. J. & J. Building & Maintenance Contractors, Inc. 79017
Union Carbide Corp.; Rovnak v. 78062
Union Construction Co.; Black Lake Pipe Line Co. v. 76006
Union County School Dist. v. Valley Inland Pacific Constructors, Inc. 82055
Union Indemnity Co.; Hall v. 32001
Union Oil Co. of California; Quilico v. . . 78061
Uniroyal, Inc. v. A. Epstein & Sons 70084
Unitec Corp. v. Beatty Safeway Scaffold Co. . . . 66101
United Bonding Insurance Co.; Houdaille Industries v. 72049
United Bonding Insurance Co. v. Sperry & Hutchinson Co. 71084
United Contractors v. United States 66102
United Eng'g & Constructors, Inc.; L.K. Comstock & Co. v. 89031
United Eng'r & Constructors, Inc.; Phillips v. . . . 86052
United H.R.B. Gen. Contractors, Inc.; Automobile Ins. Co. v. 94002
United Nations Development Corp. v. Norkin Plumbing Co. 78073
United Pacific Insurance Co.; Dover & Co. v . . . 72034
United Pacific Insurance Group; Gordy v. 66030
United Plate Glass Co., Div. of Chromalloy Am. Corp. v. Metal Trims Indus., Inc. . . . 87051
United Presbyterian Church; Caldwell v. . . 61002
United States v. (see name of defendant)
United States Dev. Corp.; Joseph J. Legat Architects, P.C. v. 85024
United States ex rel. A. & J. Freidman Supply Co. v. M.S.I. Corp. 65110

TABLE OF CASES

TC–61

[The five-digit numbers in this table are *Citator* Case Reference Numbers, which refer to the cases in the Cases section]

Ting-Wan Liang v. Malawista 79067
Tippett; Baer v. 39001
Tirante v. Gulf State Utils. Co. 82051
Titan Constr. Corp.; Keel v. 86039
Titan Construction Co. v. Nolf 73110
Titan Enterprises, Inc. v. Armo Construction, Inc. 73129
Titus County Hosp. Dist.; URS Co.-Kansas City v. 85040
T.L. James & Co.; Boyd Construction Co. v. . . . 73021
TMC Found., Inc.; Wylie Indep. School Dist. v. . . 89051
Todd; Carroccia v. 80010
Toll Bros. & Developers; Carvalho v. . . . 95004
Tomlinson v. Dartmoor Constr. Corp. . . . 94046
Tonn & Blank, Inc. v. Board of Comm'rs 90047
Tony and Leo, Inc. v. United States Fidelity & Guaranty Co. 79068
Top Line Constr. Co. v. J.W. Cook & Sons 95022
Torcon, Inc. v. Alexian Bros. Hosp. 86065
Torres v. Jarmon 73111
Torson Constr. Co.; Burns & McDonnell Eng'g Co. v. 92003a
Torson Electric Co.; G.H. & J.T. Kelly, Inc. v. . . . 66027
Touchet Valley Grain Growers, Inc. v. Opp & Seibold Gen. Constr., Inc. 92020
Tower Contracting Co.; Southern Motels Investment Corp. v. 65099
Town & Country Bank of Springfield v. James M. Canfield Contracting Co. 77079
Town of Silverton v. Phoenix Heat Source Sys. . . . 97025
Township of Wayne; Ace Stone, Inc. v. . . 66001
Tracy Trombley Constr. Co.; Board of Educ. Salmon River Cent. School Dist. v. 86003
Trader v. Grampp Builders, Inc. 70081
Trans Pacific Industries, Inc.; Sacramento v. 79058
Trans Urban Constr. Co.; New York Bd. of Fire Underwriters v. 83034
Trans Western Leasing Corp. v. Corrao Constr. Co. 82052
Transamerica Co.; Strickland v. 73106
Transamerica Insurance; State Highway Administration v. 76068
Transamerica Insurance Co.; Culligan Corp. v. . . 78022
Transamerica Insurance Co. v. Parker Henry Glass Co. 72101

Transamerica Insurance Co. v. Yonkers Contracting Co. 66100
Transamerica Title Insurance Co.; Adams Tree Service, Inc. v. 73002
Transcon Investment & Financial Ltd.; V.L. Nicholson Co. v. 80072
Transcontinental Ins. Co. v. National Union Fire Ins. Co. 96012
Transcontinental Ins. Co. v. Pepper Constr. Co. . . . 96037
Transpac Construction Co. v. Clark & Groff Engineers, Inc. 72102
Transpower Constructors, Div. of Harrison Int'l Corp. v. Grand River Dam Auth. 90048
Trapani v. Parish of Jefferson 65106
Trapani; Wrobel v. 70093
Travelers Indem. Co.; Alwinseal, Inc. v. . . 78005
Travelers Indem. Co.; American Industrial Contracting Co. v. 76003
Travelers Indem. Co.; Granite Computer Leasing Corp. v. 90023
Travelers Indem. Co. v. Hayes Contractors, Inc. . . . 86067
Travelers Indem. Co.; H.B. Zachry Co. v. 66032
Travelers Indem. Co.; Midtown Bank v. . . 66057
Travelers Indem. Co. v. National Gypsum Co. . . . 81068a
Travelers Indem. Co.; Novak & Co. v. . . . 76052
Travelers Indem. Co.; Russell v. 65090
Travelers Ins. Co. v. Dickey 90049
Traylor Bros., Inc.; Barth Elec. Co. v. . . . 90005
Traynham v. Yeargin Enter., Inc. 91035
Treasure State Industries, Inc. v. Welch . . 77080
Trepte Construction Co.; Acoustics, Inc. v. . . . 71002
Tri-Cities Construction & Supply Co.; Beacon Plaza Shopping Center, Inc. v. 66007
Tri-City Constr. Co. v. A.C. Kirkwood & Assocs. 87050
Tri-M. Erectors, Inc. v. Donald M. Drake Co. . . . 80067
Tri State Insurance Co. v. United States . . 65107
Triangle Air Conditioning, Inc. v. Caswell County Bd. of Educ. 82054
Trinity Indus., Inc.; Morse/Diesel, Inc. v. 95018
Trinity Universal Insurance Co. v. Barlite, Inc. . . . 68049
Triple M. Roofing Co. v. Greater Jericho Corp. . . . 73112
Tropic Plumbing, Inc.; Thompson-Starrett International, Inc. v. 72100

(Matthew Bender & Co., Inc.)

(Pub.435)

TABLE OF CASES

[The five-digit numbers in this table are *Citator* Case Reference Numbers, which refer to the cases in the Cases section]

Szostek; Weidner v. 93021

T

T.A. Loving Co.; Bolton Corp. v. 89005
T.A. Loving Co. v. Latham 74039
Taber Partners I v. Insurance Co. of N. Am. 95020
Tahtaras; Parrish v. 57001
Tallahassee; E.C. Ernst, Inc. v. 81021
Tassinari v. Chaney 66095
Tatar v. Maxon Construction Co. 73108
Tate Engineering, Inc.; Stouffer Construction Co. v. 79064
Tayco Constr. Co. v. LaCuisine Restaurant, Inc. . . . 92019
Taylor v. Allegretto 91034
Taylor & Parrish, Inc.; Trustees of Asbury United Methodist Church v. 95023
TDE, Ltd. v. Israel 89044
T.E. Cuttino Constr. Co.; Osteen v. 93048
T.E. Driskell Grading Co.; Pro Metal Bldg. Sys., Inc. v. 84032
Technical School Authority v. Bogar & Bink . . . 78023
Teeples & Thatcher, Inc.; Hawkins v. . . . 73049
Teig & Johnson v. Speelmon 67064
Teitge v. Remy Constr. Co. 88035
Temple Eastex, Inc. v. Old Orchard Creek Partners, Ltd. 92019a
Temple Emanu-El; L.A. Wenger Contracting Co. v. 66050
Temple Sinai-Suburban Reform Temple v. Richmond 73109
Tenneco Oil Co.; Griffin v. 93038
Tennessee Forging Steel Service; Nucor Corp. v. 73084
Tennessee River Pulp & Paper Co. v. Eichleay Corp. 82050
Tennessee Tile, Inc.; Robert H. Smith, Inc. v. 86058
Tepper Realty Co. v. Mosaic Tile Co. . . . 66096
Terminal Building Corp ; Manett, Seastrunk & Buckner v. 31005
Terminal Construction Co.; Metro Industrial Painting Corp. v. 61010
Terre Haute Indus., Inc.; Indiana & Michigan Elec. Co. v. 87027
Terrebonne Parish School Bd.; D & O Contractors, Inc. v. 89013
Territorial Construction Inc.; Armand v. . . 79020
Terry Contracting Inc. v. State 66097
Teufel v. Wienir 66098
Teufel Construction Co. v. American Arbitration Ass'n. 70080

Texas Bank & Trust Co. v. Campbell Bros., Inc. 78071
Texas Construction Associates, Inc. v. Balli 77078
Texas Delta Upsilon Foundation v. Fehr . . 57003
Texas Industries, Inc.; New Amsterdam Casualty Co. v. 67055
T.F. Scholes, Inc. v. United States 66099
Theubet; Parker v. 69045
Thibodeaux; Weill Constr. Co. v. 86071
Third and Catalina Construction Partnership; Sullins v. 79066
Thomas; Cobb v. 78018
Thomas; Fran Realty, Inc. v. 76022
Thomas v. Fromherz Engineers 63007
Thomas; Indian State Highway Commission v. . . . 76031
Thomas Crimmins Contracting Co. v. New York 88035a
Thomas Haverty Co. v. Jones 21003
Thomas Wells & Associates v. Cardinal Properties, Inc. 75034; 76069
Thompson v. Jespersen 90046
Thompson v. Valley Corp. 95021
Thompson Construction & Development Co.; Connor v. 69010
Thompson-Starrett Co. v. Brooklyn Heights Reality Co. 05001
Thompson-Starrett International, Inc. v. Tropic Plumbing, Inc. 72100
Thomwood Farms, Inc.; Bender-Miller Co. v. . . . 71010
Thorgaard Plumbing & Heating Co. v. King, County of 67065
Thorleif Larsen & Son, Inc.; Osolo School Bldgs., Inc. v. 85032
Thorndike; Burns v. 17001
3-D Excavators, Inc.; Plantation Pipe Line Co. v. 81058
Three K's, Ltd; Sigal v. 72091
Thunderbird Masonry; Exch. v. 93056
Thunderbolt Enterprises, Inc.; Northwestern Engineering Co. v. 81055
Thurmond; Ryan v. 72087
Tibbetts Contracting Corp. v. O & E Contracting Co. 65105
Tidmore; Wright v. 93023
Tilley Steel, Inc.; Marathon Steel Co. v. . . 77056
Timberline Electric Supply Corp. v. Insurance Company of North America 80066
Timmons; American Casualty Co. v. 65005
Timmons; Citizens Bank v. 17002
Timothy McCarthy Construction Co.; Burton-Dixie Corp. v. 71016

TABLE OF CASES TC–59

[The five-digit numbers in this table are *Citator* Case Reference Numbers, which refer to the cases in the Cases section]

Stevens/Leinweber/Sullens, Inc. v. Holm Dev. & Management, Inc. 90045
Stevenson v. San Diego County 45002
Stewart v. Breckenridge 17005
Stewart; Wawak v. 70089
Stewart M. Muller Construction Co.; Alvord and Swift v. 78004
Stewart M. Muller Construction Co. v. Clement Ferdinand & Co. 71080
Stewart-Scott Construction Corp. v. F. & M. Schaefer Co. 73105
Stillinger & Napier v. Central States Grain Co. . . 57002
Stillwater Leased Housing Assocs. v. Kraus-Anderson Constr. Co. 82049
Stites; Bloomfield Reorganized School District No. R-14 v. 60001
Stone; Robinson & Wilson, Inc. v. 73095
Stone & Webster Eng'g Corp.; Loyland v. 73069
Stone & Webster Eng'g Corp.; Parent v. . . 90035
Stool; Fidelity and Deposit Co. of Maryland v. . . 80025
Storm Lake, City of; Ida Grove Roofing & Improvements, Inc. v. 85020
Stormer's Estate, In re 56002
Stouffer Construction Co. v. Tate Engineering, Inc. 79064
Stratton; Gay v. 77036
Stratton v. New York State Thruway Authority . . 63006
Strauss; Ben Trovato Properties, Inc. v. . . 81007
Strauss Construction Co.; Central Industrial Engineering Co. v. 79026
Streator Township High School Dist. #40; Busick v. 92004
Strescon Industries, Inc.; Sweetman v. . . . 78070
Stresscon International, Inc.; Damora v. . . 75008
Strickland v. Transamerica Co. 73106
Strober Bros., Inc.; Port Liberte Partners v. 88028
Stroble; Berthot v. 72013
Strom v. Lipschultz 72097
Strudell Asphalt, Inc. v. Bernstein 65103
Stuart Constr. Co.; Mississippi Coast Coliseum Comm'n v. 82035
Stubblefield; Morgan v. 72072
Stubenrauch Assoc., Inc.; Holy Family Catholic Congregation v. 87025
Stucki-Miller, Inc. v. Santa Fe Engineers, Inc. . . . 79065
Sturdy Concrete Corp. v. NAB Construction Corp. 78068
Suelynn Corp.; Oakes v. 72074

Suffolk Construction Co.; Bjorkman v. . . . 97006
Suffolk, County of; Babylon Assocs. v. . . . 84001
Sugar Beach Condominium Ass'n; Dunn Constr. Co. v. 91009, 95046
Sukut-Coulson, Inc. v. Allied Canon Co. . . 78069
Sullins v. Third and Catalina Construction Partnership 79066
Sullivan; E. E. Dean Snavely, Inc. v. . . . 78027
Sullivan v. Kisly 83043
Sullivan, County of v. Edward L. Nezelek, Inc. . . 77025
Sullivan & Cromwell v. Hudson & Manhatten Corp. 71081
Sullivan, Long & Haggarty, Inc.; Williams v. . . . 68055
Sulzbach Construction Co.; Klinger-Holtz v. 78046
Summers v. Crown Construction Co. 72098
Summit Construction Co. v. Yeager Garden Acres, Inc. 70079
Sun Insurance Co. v. Diversified Engineers, Inc. 65104
Sun Oil Co.; McClane v. 81051
Super Construction Co. v. New Orleans Levee Board 73107
Superior; Forest City Dillon, Inc. v. 84012
Superior Court; A. P. Brown Co. v. 71006
Superior Court; Cook v. 66019
Superior Court, County of Alameda; Atlas Plastering, Inc. v. 77008
Superior Court; Davlar Corp. v. 97009
Superior Glass Co. v. First Bristol County National Bank 80063
Supermarkets Gen. Corp.; Mahony-Troast Constr. Co. v. 83029
Sussex Assoc. Ltd. Partnership; J.A. Moore Constr. Co. v. 88017
Sutter; Keystone Engineering Corp. v. . . . 51002
Swarthout v. Beard 71082
Swartz v. Ford, Bacon & Davis Constr. Corp. . . . 85037
Swedberg; Nordenstrom v. 66065
Sweetman v. Strescon Industries, Inc. . . . 78070
Swenson v. Lowe 71083
Swift Bros. Constr. Co.; Henningson, Durham & Richardson, Inc. v. 84017
Swindell Dressler Co. v. Commonwealth Department of Transportation 80064
Syska & Hennessy; Perkins & Will Partnership v. 77068
Syska & Hennessy & Garfinkel, Marenberg & Assoc.; Perkins & Will v. 75019
Szczawinski; Aerostatic Engineering Corp. v. . . . 73003

(Matthew Bender & Co., Inc.) (Pub.435)

TABLE OF CASES

[The five-digit numbers in this table are *Citator* Case Reference Numbers, which refer to the cases in the Cases section]

St. Paul Fire & Marine Ins. Co.; Carl Weissman & Sons v. 68008
St. Paul Fire & Marine Ins. Co. v. Freeman-White Assocs., Inc. 88032
St. Paul Fire & Marine Ins. Co. v. Gilpatrick Constr. Co. 87044
St. Paul Fire & Marine Ins. Co.; Graybar Electric Co. v. 67028
St. Paul Fire & Marine Ins. Co.; Gurney Industries, Inc. v. 72044
St. Paul Fire & Marine Ins. Co. v. James I. Barnes Construction Co. 68041
St. Paul Fire & Marine Ins. Co. v. Murray Plumbing and Heating Corp. 76065
St. Peter; Devenow v. 76018
St. Petersburg Beach, City of; Anderson-Parrish Assoc., Inc. v. 85004
St. Regis Corp.; Dudley v. 86016
St. Vincent's Hospital; Elizabeth Sash, Door & Supply Co. v. 34003
Stade; Himmel Corp. v. 77042
Stadel v. Granger Brothers 66091
Stage v. Oswego, Village of 75024
Stagg Indus., Inc.; Wyoming Johnson, Inc. v. 83050
Stahelin v. Board of Education 67063
Staley v. New 52005
Stallings & Sons, Ex parte 95046
Standard Accident Insurance Co. v. Laird 35003
Standard Co. of New Orleans, Inc. v. Elliott Construction Co. 78067
Standard Construction Co.; Younker Brothers v. 65124
Standard Millwork & Supply Co. v. Mississippi Steel & Iron Co. 49003
Standard Oil Co.; Patent Scaffolding Co. v. 66070
Standard Roofing Co.; New Orleans Unity Society v. 69042
Standhardt v. Flintcote Co. 73101
Standley v. Egbert 70076
Stanley R. Benjamin, Inc. v. Fidelity & Casualty Co. 72095
Stanley Smith & Sons; Godwin v. ... 89018
Star News Newspapers; Cape Fear Electric Co. v. 74007
Stark v. Ralph F. Roussey & Associates, Inc. 75025
Starrett Bros.; Burmar Electrical Corp. v. 77014
State v. (see name of defendant)
State Department of Highways v. A & G Excavating Co. 66092
State Department of Human Resources v. Williams 73102
State Dept. of Transp. & Pub. Facilities; Earth Movers of Fairbanks, Inc. v. 92005b
State ex (see name of state)
State ex rel. (see name of state)
State Farm Ins. Co.; Monical v. 91022
State Farm Mutual Automobile Insurance Co.; Emberton v. 77029
State Highway Admin. v. Greiner Eng'g Sciences, Inc. 90044
State Highway Admin. v. Transamerica Insurance 76068
State Highway Commission of the State of Mississippi; Dahlstrom Corp. v. 79003
State Highway Dept. v. Hall Paving Co. ... 72096
State Highway Dept. v. Hewitt Contracting Co. 66093
State Highway Dept.; Western Contracting Corp. v. 72109
State of (see name of state)
State Public School Building Authority; Dick Corp. v. 75019
State Surety Co. v. Lamb Construction Co. 81067
State University Construction Fund; Meathe v. 78053
State University Construction Fund; L.A. Wenger Contracting Co. v. 72058
Statesville Roofing & Heating Co. v. Duncan 88034
Stauffer Constr. Co. v. Board of Educ. of Montgomery County 83042
Steamboat Dev. Corp. v. Bacjac Indus., Inc. 85036
Steel Fabricators, Inc.; Wehr Constructors, Inc. v. 88042
Steele & Sons, Inc.; Financial Indemnity Co. v. 81025
Steelform Contracting Co.; Gilbert Financial Corp. v. 78032
Steers, Perini & Pomeroy; Howard, Needles, Tammen & Bergendoff v. 73055
Steffek v. Wichers 73104
Stein; Noonan v. 13003
Steinberg v. Fleischer 86064
Stepanek v. Kober Construction 81068
Stephanich; Bleck v. 78011
Stephenson, County of v. Bradley & Bradley, Inc. 71026
Sternberg; Colorado Real Estate Development, Inc. v. 67015
Stevens v. Fanning 65102

TABLE OF CASES

TC–57

[The five-digit numbers in this table are *Citator* Case Reference Numbers, which refer to the cases in the Cases section]

Sollenberger v. A. A. Construction Co.	71079
Solomon, Cordwell, Buenz & Assocs.; Cadral Corp. v.	86006
Somerset Community Hosp. V. Allan B. Mitchell & Assocs. Inc.	96042
Sorensen v. Robert N. Ewing, General Contractor	68044
Sornsin; DeKalb, City of v.	65025
Soundwall Construction Corp. v. Moncarol Construction Corp.	68045
South Burlington School District v. Calcagni	80061
South Dakota Bldg. Auth. v. Geiger-Berger Assocs., P.C.	87049
South Dakota Dept. of Transportation; Brezina Construction Co. v.	80009
South Dakota Highway Commission; G.H. Lindekugel & Sons v.	72099
South Texas Building Co. v. Ideal Engineering, Inc.	66090
South Tippecanoe School Building Corp. v. Shambaugh & Son	79063
South Wisconsin Conference Association of Seventh Day Advent; Mitterhausen v.	44004
Southbend Contractors, Inc. v. Parrish of Jefferson	81065
Southeast Roofing & Sheet Metal, Inc.; School Bd. of Orange County v.	86061
Southeastern Palm Beach County Hospital District; W.F. Thompson Construction Co. v.	65119
Southern Construction Co. v. Housing Authority	67062
Southern Generator & Engine Sales, Inc.; O & M Manufacturing Co. v.	75016
Southern Maryland Hospital Center v. Edward M. Crough, Inc.	81066
Southern Mechanical Contracting, Inc.; Whitehall, City of v.	80011
Southern Mechanical Inc.; R.C. Small & Assocs., Inc. v.	87038
Southern Motels Investment Corp. v. Tower Contracting Co.	65099
Southern Roof Deck Applicators, Inc.; Campbell v.	81012
Southport Marine, Inc.; Misener Marine Construction Co. v.	79048
Southwest Engineering Co. v. Reorganized School District R-9	68046
Southwest Nat'l Bank v. Simpson & Son, Inc.	90042
Southwest Steel Rolling Mills, Inc.; Western Contracting Corp. v.	76071
Southwestern Bell Telephone Co. v. J.A. Tobin Construction Co.	76067
Southwire Co. v. Metal Equipment Co.	73100
Souza & McCue Construction Co.; Salinas, City of v.	67013
Sovereign Construction Co.; April v.	81003
Spain; Royal Globe Insurance Co. v.	71076
Span Electric Corp.; Dormitory Authority v.	66022
Spann, Hall, Ritchie, Inc.; Sheetz, Aiken & Aiken, Inc. v.	87047
Speelmon; Teig & Johnson v.	67064
Speers v. H.P. Hood, Inc.	86063
Spence v. Omnibus Industries, Inc.	75023
Spence Bros., Inc.; Gordon Sel-Way, Inc. v.	91012
Spencer v. Hoffman	80062
Spero; Roll v.	74032
Sperry & Hutchinson Co.; United Bonding Insurance Co. v.	71084
Spiegel; William B. Lucke, Inc. v.	70091
Spiezio v. Commonwealth Edison Co.	68047
Spindel; Jones v.	73060
Spinella; Washington Construction Co. v.	51003
Spinney, Coady and Parker Architects, Inc.; Meek v.	77058
Spitz v. Brickhouse	54005
Spokane, City of; Lester N. Johnson Co. v.	78051
Springfield, City of; American Drilling Service Co. v.	81002
Springfield, City of; Fontaine Bros., Inc. v.	93011
Springfield Mechanical Co.; Ralph Korte Construction Co. v.	77075
S.S. Silberblatt, Inc. v. United States	65100
S.S.D.W. Co. v. Brisk Waterproofing Co.	90043
St. Andrews Episcopal Day School v. Walsh Plumbing Co.	70071
St. Bernard Linen Serv., Inc.; Rudy Brown Bldrs., Inc. v.	83039
St. John v. Naperville, City of	87042
St. Joseph Hospital v. Corbetta Construction Co.	74034
St. Joseph Structural Steel Co.; L. M. White Contracting Co. v.	71061
St. Lawrence Explosives Corp. v. Worthy Bros. Pipeline Corp.	96011
St. Louis, City of; Paulus v.	69047
St. Paul Fire & Marine Ins.; Board of Local Improvements v.	76007
St. Paul Fire & Marine Ins. Co.; Camelot Excavating Co. v.	81011

TABLE OF CASES

[The five-digit numbers in this table are *Citator* Case Reference Numbers, which refer to the cases in the Cases section]

Shambaugh & Son; South Tippecanoe School Building Corp. v. 79063
Shamokin Area School Auth. v. Farfield Co. ... 82046
Shamrock Constr. Co.; Sears, Roebuck & Co. v. 83040
Shanahan v. Universal Tavern Corp. 78064
Shaughnessy, Fickel & Scott, Architects; Dillard v. 93033
Shaw; American Surety Co. v. 34001
Shaw v. Bridges-Gallagher, Inc. 88033
Shaw v. East Coast Builders, Inc. 87046
Sheetz, Aiken & Aiken, Inc v. Spann, Hall, Ritchie, Inc. 87047
Shelbyville, City of; Alexander v. 91001
Shell Chemical Co. v. Lamb 73099
Shell Oil Co. v. Hercules Construction Co. 66087
Shelter Mut.; Couvillion v. 96003
Shenango Steel Erectors, Inc.; Mazzoleni v. 72065
Shepherd Components, Inc. v. Brice Petrides-Donohue & Assocs., Inc. 91030
Sheridan Area Water Supply Joint Powers Bd; Rissler & McMurry Co. v. 96039
Sherman v. Demaria Bldg. Co. 94016
Sherwood Constr. Co.; Wallace v. 94048
Sherwood Pacific, Inc.; Pacific County v. 77066
Sherwood Village Cooperative A v. Had-Ten Estates Corp. 67060
Shoffner Industries, Inc. v. W.B. Lloyd Construction Co. 79061
Shook of West Virginia, Inc. v. York City Sewer Auth. 91031
Shure; Willner & Millkey v. 71087
Sibille v. Meyer 78065
Sides Construction Co. v. Scott City, City of ... 79062
Siegel; Arrow Contractors Equipment Co. v. 66005
Siegel v. Haver 66088
Sierra v. Garcia 87048
Sigal v. Three K's, Ltd 72091
Silver Dollar City, Inc. v. Kitsmiller Constr. Co. 94017
Simon v. Omaha Public Power District .. 72092
Simplex Wire & Cable Co.; Urbinati v. .. 80071
Simpson & Son, Inc.; Scuthwest Nat'l Bank v. .. 90042
Sira & Payne, Inc. v. Wallace & Riddle .. 72093
Sisson & Ryan, Inc.; Chesapeake & Potomac Telephone Co. of Virginia v. 87011

Sisters of Mercy v. Mead & Mount Construction Co. 68043
Sisters of Saint John the Baptist, Providence Rest Convent v. Phillips R. Geraghty Constructor, Inc. 86062
Sisters of the Good Shepherd v. Quinn Construction Co. 69054
Sitkin v. Smith 29005
Six Companies of California v. Joint Highway Dist. No 13 40003
S.K. Whitty & Co. v. Laurence L. Lambert & Assocs. 91032
Skezas v. Safeway Steel Products, Inc. ... 67061
Skidmore, Owings & Merrill v. Connecticut General Life Insurance Co. 63005
Skinner; Lincoln County v. 73067
Slaught v. Bencomo Roofing Co. 94018
Slaysman; Norman S. Wright & Co., S.W. v. ... 79049
Sletten Construction Co.; Exber, Inc. v. ... 76021
Slifer; Wheeler & Lewis v. 78076
Slutsky-Peltz Plumbing & Heating Co. v. Vincennes Community School Corp. 90041
S.M. Wilson & Co.; J.F., Inc. v. 87028
Smallwood; Campagna v. 83005
Smelley; Medical Clinic Board v. 31053
Smeltzer; Childs v. 34002
S.M.G. Corp.; John Goffredo & Sons, Inc. v. ... 82027
Smith; Anderson v. 65006
Smith v. Berwin Builders 72094
Smith v. Cumberland Group 97023
Smith v. Dugan & Meyers Constr. Co. ... 84036
Smith v. Erftmier 82048
Smith; Henry Roy Portwood, Inc. v. 93013
Smith; Javernick v. 80036
Smith; Pero Bldg. Co. v. 86051
Smith v. Ryan 62009
Smith; S.A. Stephenson v. 76064
Smith v. Scott 77077
Smith; Sitkin v. 29005
Smith v. United States 74038
Smith, Hinchman & Grylls Associates v. River Rouge Public Building Authority 65098
Smith & Plaster Co.; Concrete Materials of Georgia, Inc. v. 73026
Smullen v. New York, City of 71078
Snodgrass & Sons Construction Co.; Farmers & Merchants State Bank v. 72038
Snyder v. Eanes Indep. Sch. Dist. 93054
Snyder; Robinhorne Construction Corp. v. 71074
Sokol; Barbera v. 80006
Sokolowski; Busker v. 72108

(Matthew Bender & Co., Inc.) (Pub.435)

TABLE OF CASES

[The five-digit numbers in this table are *Citator* Case Reference Numbers, which refer to the cases in the Cases section]

Sartori; J.M. Beeson Co. v. 89027
Sasser & Co. v. Griffin 74035
Savignano v. Gloucester Housing Authority 62008
Saxon Constr. & Management Corp. v. Masterclean of North Carolina, Inc. 94015
Scarlett Harbor Assocs. Ltd. Partnership; Hartford Accident & Indem. Co. v. 97011
Schaub v. West Bend Mut. 95045
Schenck Constr. Co.; Rashid v. 93049
Schernecker; Gallagher v. 73128
Scherrer Construction Co. v. Burlington Memorial Hospital 74036
Schimmel Hotels Corp.; Clark & Enersen, Hamersky, Schlaebitz, Burroughs & T v. 75006
Schlanger v. Federal Insurance Co. 65091
Schleigh; Hammaker v. 29003
Schmid v. United States 65092
Schneider, Inc. v. Research-Cottrell, Inc. .. 79059
Scholer & Fuller Assoicated Architects; Craviolini v. 60004
School Bd. of Orange County v. Southeast Roofing & Sheet Metal, Inc. 86061
School District; Giuliani Construction Co. v. ... 66029
School District No. 46 v. Del Bianco ... 66085
School District No. One v. Hastings 70073
School District No. 18; Blecick v. 65015
School District No. 141; Bair v. 15001
School District No. Six v. Alfred Watts Grant & Associates 65093
School District No. 65 R v. Universal Surety Co. 65094
School District No. 3 v. Central Savings Bank & Trust Co. 45001
School District No. 2, Town of Richland; Burroughs v. 14003
Schopke Constr. & Eng'g, Inc.; Indian River Colony Club v. 92009
Schrafft; Schwender v. 23003
Schroeder v. C. F. Braun Co. 74037
Schuessler Lumber Co.; Kubela v. 73065
Schuler-Haas Electric Corp. v. Wager Construction Corp. 77076
Schuler-Haas Electrical Corp. v. Aetna Casualty & Surety Co. 75022
Schultz v. Gund 44003
Schultz & Lindsay Construction Co. v. Erickson 65095
Schultz & Lindsay Construction Co. v. State ... 72089
Schumacher & Forelle, Inc.; New York Telephone Co. v. 77064
Schutt Construction Co. v. United States .. 65096

Schwarz-Jordan, Inc. of Houston v. Delisle Construction Co. 78063
Schweizer Dipple, Inc.; Wingate Construction Co. v. 65121
Schwender v. Schrafft 23003
Sciacca; Maxus, Inc. v. 92014
Scorse; Hobbs v. 77043
Scott; Smith v. 77077
Scott Brothers Construction Co.; Fidelity & Deposit Co. v. 72039
Scott City, City of; Sides Construction Co. v. 79062
Scruggs; DeKalb County v. 78025
S.D. Warren Co.; McGraw v. 95015
Sea Crest Constr. Co.; North Hempstead, Town of v. 86066
Seaboard Surety Co. v. United States ... 66086
Seabreeze Constr. Corp.; Lake Plumbing, Inc. v. 86041
Seaman Unified School District v. Casson Construction Co. 79060
Sears, Roebuck & Co. v. Glenwall Co. ... 70074
Sears, Roebuck & Co. v. Shamrock Constr. Co. ... 83040
Seattle, City of v. Dyad Construction, Inc. .. 77020
Seattle Sch. Dist. No. 1; Berschauer/Phillips Constr. Co. v. 94025
Seckinger; United States v. 70086
Second Congregation Society v. Hugh Stubbins & Associates 68042
Security Insurance Co.; Vendrigo Highlands, Inc. v. 66111
Security Painting Co. v. Commonwealth of Pennsylvania 76066
Security Trust & Savings Bank; Roberts v. ... 25002
Seder Plastics Corp.; Rocky Mountain Plastics Corp. v. 71075
Sehlbert Mechanical Corp. v. Kessel/Duff Construction Corp. 80060
Seifert v. Regents of Univ. of Minn. 93053
Sellards; Foster v. 36001
Sellen; Wenzler & Ward Plumbing & Heating Co. v. 58006
Sellen Constr. Co.; Public Employees Mutual Ins. Co. v. 87036
Sellers v. Owens-Illinois Glass Co. 72090
71 Construction v. Wesco Elec., Inc. 96041
Shafer & Miller v. Miami Heart Institute 70075
Shalman v. Board of Education 69053
Shama Restaurant Co.; Hercules & Co. v. 92008

(Matthew Bender & Co., Inc.)
(Pub.435)

[The five-digit numbers in this table are *Citator* Case Reference Numbers, which refer to the cases in the Cases section]

Royal Inv. & Dev. Corp. v. Monty's Air Conditioning Serv., Inc. 87041
Royal Service Co. v. Whitehead Construction Co. 73098
Ruby-Collins, Inc. v. Charlotte, City of .. 90039
Ruckman & Hansen, Inc. v. Delaware River & Bay Authority 68039
Rudder Construction Co.; Vinsant Plumbing & Heating Co. v. 71085
Rudy Brown Bldrs., Inc. v. St. Bernard Linen Serv., Inc. 83039
Ruffin Woody & Assocs., Inc. v. Person County 88031
Rugby Mun. Airport Auth.; Johnson Constr., Inc. v. 92009b
Rumsey Electric Co. v. University of Delaware .. 75033
Rupp v. American Crystal Sugar Co. 91029
Ruscon Construction Co. v. Beaufort-Jasper Water Authority 72085
Rush Presbyterian St. Luke's Medical Center v. Safeco Ins. Co. 89042; 89043
Russell v. Bothwell & Swaner Co. 20004
Russell v. Travelers Indemnity Co. 65090
Russellville Steel Co. v. A & R Excavating, Inc. 93052
Russwine Construction Corp.; Redding & Co. v. 72083
Rutgers State Univ.; Broadway Maintenance Corp. v. 82007
Rutter v. McLaughlin 80057
R.W. Construction, Inc.; Metropolitan Sewerage Commission v. 76043
R.W. Granger & Sons, Inc.; Massachusetts Elec. Sys., Inc. v. 92013
R.W. Rexford Co.; Donovan v. 65033
Rwenbark v. Atlantic States Construction Co. 72086
Ryan; Smith v. 62009
Ryan v. Thurmond 72087

S

S & H Erectors, Inc.; Davison Specialty Chem. Co. v. 85013
S. J. Groves & Sons v. West Virginia Turnpike Commission 58005
S & L Construction Co.; Fetterolf v. 16001
S & M Constructors v. Columbus, City of 82047
S & R Construction Co.; Edward R. Marden Corp. v. 73038
S.A. Stephenson v. Smith 76064
Sacramento v. Trans Pacific Industries, Inc. 79058

Safeco Ins. Co.; Rush Presbyterian St. Luke's Medical Center v. 89042; 89043
Safeco Ins. Co. of Am. v. J. L. Henson, Inc. ... 80058
Safeco Ins. Co. of Am.; Wm. R. Clarke Corp. ... 97027
Safeway Steel Products, Inc.; Skezas v. .. 67061
Safeway Stores; Havens v. 84016
Safeway Stores, Inc.; Arrowhead, Inc. v. . 78006
Sagamore Group, Inc. v. Commissioner of Transp. 92018
Saiki v. Lee Sing 23002
Saint Augustine Pools, Inc. v. James M. Barker Inc. 97021
Saint Joseph's Hospital, Inc.; Norair Engineering Corp. v. 73056
St. Paul Fire & Marine Ins. Co.; Brown & Kerr v. 96017
Salem Building Supply Co. v. J.B.L. Construction Co. 80059
Salem Eng'g & Constr. Corp. v. Londonderry School Dist. 82045
Salesian Society v. Formigli Corp. 72088
Salinas, City of v. Souza & McCue Construction Co. 67013
Salt Lake City Corp.; Ericksen v. 93035
Salus Corp.; Maxum Found., Inc. v. 85027; 87032
Sam Finley, Inc.; Jackson v. 66042
Sammons; Cagle, Inc. v. 77015
Samuel A. Kroll, Inc.; O-S Corp. v. 75017
San Diego County; Stevenson v. 45002
San Jose Steel Co.; MacDonald & Kruse, Inc. v. 72062
San Ore-Gardner v. Missouri Pacific Railroad Co. 81064
Sanders v. American Casualty Co. 69052
Sandock; F.D. Borkholder Co. v. 80024
Sands Motel v. Hargrave 62007
Sanford Construction Co. v. Rosenblatt .. 70072
Sanitary Authority; Ben Contruction Co. v. 67008
Sanitary District; Underground Construction Co. v. 37003
Sanitary Sewer Auth. of Borough of Shickshinny v. Dial Assocs. Constr. Group, Inc. 87045
Santa Fe Engineers, Inc.; Stucki-Miller, Inc. v. ... 79065
Santucci Constr. Co. v. Danville, City of .. 84035
In re Saranac Cent. Shc. Dist. (Sweet Assocs., Inc.) 97022
Sargent, Webster, Crenshaw & Folley; Board of Educ. of Hudson City School Dist. v. 89004
Sarnoff v. De Graf Bros., Inc. 90040

TABLE OF CASES

[The five-digit numbers in this table are *Citator* Case Reference Numbers, which refer to the cases in the Cases section]

Roanoke Construction Co.; R.C. Stanhope, Inc. v. 76059
Roanoke Hospital Association; Doyle & Russell, Inc. v. 73034
Robbins v. Perini Corp. 66081
Rober & Co. Associates; Covil v. 65028
Robert Cagle Building Co.; Montgomery Ward & Co. v. 67051
Robert Chuckrow Construction Co. v. Horowitz Bros. 68037
Robert E. Lee & Co. v. Commission of Public Works 66082
Robert E. McKee General Contractors, Inc.; Employers Mutual Liability Insurance Co. v. ... 71035
Robert E. McKee, Inc. v. Atlanta, City of 76061
Robert E. McKee, Inc.; Cahn Elec. Co. v. 86008
Robert F. Ackermann & Associates, Inc.; R.E.M. IV, Inc. v. 81059
Robert F. Wilson, Inc. v. Post-Tensioned Structures, Inc. 88030
Robert H. Smith, Inc. v. Tennessee Tile, Inc. ... 86058
Robert Kerris, Inc.; Dravo Corp. v. 81019
Robert M. Swedroe, Architects/Planners, A.I.A., P.A. v. First American Inv. Corp. 90037
Robert N. Ewing, General Contractor; Sorensen v. 68044
Robert Reid Engineers, Inc.; Linton Co. v. 81048
Robert W. Gottfried, Inc.; Mills v. 73075
Roberts v. Fortune Homes, Inc. 66083
Roberts v. Security Trust & Savings Bank 25002
Roberts; Wetzel v. 41004
Roberts Cabinet Co.; J.O. Hooker & Sons Inc. v. 96032
Roberts Elec. Contractors, Inc.; Lord & Son Constr., Inc. v. 93044
Robertson; Ford v. 87021
Robertson Lumber Co.; Aetna Casualty & Surety Co. v. 28001
Robinhorne Construction Corp. v. Snyder 71074
Robinson v. A.Z. Shmina & Sons Co. ... 80054
Robinson Explosives, Inc. v. Dalon Contracting Co. 74031
Robinson & Wilson, Inc. v. Stone 73095
Rochester, City of; Le Chase Construction Corp. v. 72060
Rochester Institute of Technology; Pignott Construction International, Ltd. v. 81057

Rockingham National Bank; Graves Construction Co. v. 80027
Rockland v. Primiano Construction Co. ... 80055
Rockland Bleach & Dye Works Co. v. H.J. Williams Corp. 66084
Rocky Mountain Plastics Corp. v. Seder Plastics Corp. 71075
Rodriguez v. McDonnell Douglas Corp. ... 79016
Roen Design Assocs., Inc.; Fairbanks North Star Borough v. 86022
Roger J. Au & Son, Inc. v. Northeast Ohio Regional Sewer Dist. 86059
Roger Johnson Construction Co. v. Bossier City 76062
Roland v. Lindsey 12002
Roland A. Wilson & Associates v. Forty-O-Four Grand Corp. 76063
Roll v. Spero 74032
Rome v. Commonwealth Edison Co. 80056
Romero v. Parkhill, Smith & Cooper, Inc. 94045
Ronald Adams, Contractor, Inc. v. State .. 84033
Roosevelt University v. Mayfair Construction Co. 75021
Roriek Construction Co.; Hand v. 73046
Roscoe v. Jones 90038
Roscoe-Ajax Construction Co.; Lesser Towers, Inc. v. 69032
Rose; Owings v. 72075
Rosellini v. Banchero 73096
Rosemont, Village of v. Lentin Lumber Co. 86068
Rosenblatt; Sanford Construction Co. v. .. 70072
Rosenthal v. Gauthier 53006
Rosenthal v. Kurz 74033
Rosinski; Fuller v. 71043
Rosoff Brothers v. State 72084
Rosos Litho Supply Corp. v. Hansen 84034
Ross v. Danter Associates 68038
Rosser v. Hochwalt 67059
Rosser; Hochwalt v. 70035
Rossetti v. New Britain, City of 73097
Roulo v. Automobile Club of Michigan .. 70070
Rovnak v. Union Carbide Corp. 78062
Rowell v. Crow 49002
Roy A. Elam Masonry, Inc. v. Fru-Con Constr. Corp 96040
Roy Strom Excavating & Grading Co. v. Miller-Davis Co. 86060
Royal Elec. Co.; Blaine Economic Dev. Auth. v. 94027
Royal Globe Insurance Co. v. Spain 71076
Royal Indemnity Co. v. Alexander Industries, Inc. 65089

[The five-digit numbers in this table are *Citator* Case Reference Numbers, which refer to the cases in the Cases section]

Redding & Co. v. Russwine Construction Corp. . . . 72083
Redevelopment Authority v. Fidelity & Deposit Co. 81061
Redfern v. R.E. Dailey & Co. 85035
Redman Development Corp. v. Piedmont Heating & Air Conditioning, Inc. 73093
Reed, Wible & Brown, Inc. v. Mahogany Run Dev. Corp. 82042
Reese; McCarthy v. 65075
Reeves v. Hill Aero, Inc. 89038
Reeves v. Watkins 81062
Regents of Univ. of Minn.; Seifert v. . . . 93053
Regina Constr. Corp. v. Envirmech Contracting Corp. 89039
Rego Park Garden Assocs., Inc. v. Elite Gen. Contracting Corp. 87039
Reid; Uhlhorn v. 65108
Reidsville Engineering Co.; Durham, City of v. . . 61003
Reishus v. Implement Dealers Mutual Insurance Co. 62006
Reisman v. Ranoel Realty Co. 73094
Reliance Insurance Co.; Chicago Bridge & Iron Co. v. 71019
Reliance Insurance Co. v. Colbert 66077
Relying on Larsen v. J.I. Case Co., A.I.A. Citator 95045
R.E.M. IV, Inc. v. Robert F. Ackermann & Associates, Inc. 81059
Remy Constr. Co.; Teitge v. 88035
Renago Construction Inc.; Amco Steel Corp. v. . . 72008
Rentenbach Constuctors, Inc.; Buchanan v. . . . 96018
Reorganized School District R-9; Southwest Engineering Co. v. 68046
Reorganized School District R-3; First State Bank v. 73041
Reppel Steel & Supply Co.; Watson Construction Co. v. 79069
Research-Cottrell, Inc.; Schneider, Inc. v. 79059
Rexroth & Rexroth, Inc. v. General Gas Co. 66078
Reynolds v. Long 67058
Reynolds Construction Co.; Malott & Peterson Grundy, Inc. v. 70053
Reynolds Construction Co.; Walnut Creek Electric v. 68051
Reynolds Metal Co.; Arkin Construction Co. v. . . 62001
RGK, Inc. v. United States Fidelity & Guaranty Co. 76060

Rhoads; Herre Bros. v. 66034
Rhoads v. Nasco 66079
Rhode Island Hospital; A.C. Beals Co. v. 72002
Ricciardi & Sons Construction; M.L. Shalloo, Inc. v. 65079
Rice Construction Co.; Merkle v. 73073
Richards Contracting Co. v. Fullmer Bros. 66080
Richardson Hosp. Auth.; Del E. Webb Constr. v. 87014
Richmond v. Grabowski 89040
Richmond; Temple Sinai-Suburban Reform Temple v. 73109
Richmond County Hospital Authority; J. S. & H. Construction Co. v. 73061
Richmond Shopping Center, Inc. v. Wiley N. Jackson Co. 79015
Richmond Steel, Inc. v. Legal & Gen. Assurance Soc'y, Ltd. 93050
Richter Spring Corp.; Michalowski v. . . . 69040
Ridge Sheet Metal Co. v. Morrell 85056
Riefolo Construction Co.; Hartford Fire Insurance Co. v. 78035
Riggi v. Wade Lupe Constr. Co. 91028
Riggins v. Bechtel Power Corp. 86057
Riggle v. Allied Chem. Corp. 89041
Rinaldi Constr., Inc.; Eis Group Cornwall Hill Dev. Corp. v. 89014
Ringer v. Graham 87040
Ringland; Herter v. 92008b
Ringwelski v. Pederson 96038
Rio Rancho Estates v. Beyerlein 31063
Rissil Constr. Assocs., Inc.; E & F Construction Co. v. 80023
Rissil Constr. Assocs., Inc.; Wesleyan Univ. v. . . . 84039
Rissler & McMurry Co. v. Sheridan Area Water Supply Joint Powers Bd. 96039
Rittenberry; Capitol Hotel Co. v. 31001
River Crest, Inc.; Al Smith's Plumbing & Heating Service, Inc. v. 78003
River Rouge Public Building Authority; Smith, Hinchman & Grylls Associates v. 65098
River Valley, Inc. v. American States Ins. Co. . . . 85007
Rivergate Corp.; Mario & DiBono Plastering Co. v. 88021
Rivers & Bryan, Inc. v. HBE Corp. 93051
R.J. Novick Construction Co.; Gonzales v. 78033
R.K. Stewart & Son, Inc.; Martin County v. . . . 83031
R.N. Rouse & Co.; Johnson County v. . . . 92010

TABLE OF CASES

[The five-digit numbers in this table are *Citator* Case Reference Numbers, which refer to the cases in the Cases section]

Puritan Mills, Inc. v. Pickering Construction Co. 79055
Pylon, Inc. v. Olympic Insurance Co. . . . 69051

Q

Qazi; A.W. Wendell & Sons, Inc. v. 93025
Quail Bluff Assocs.; Eke Bldrs., Inc. v. . . 85014a
Quannapowitt Dev., Inc.; Harnois v. 93041
Quilico v. Union Oil Co. of California . . . 78061
Quin Blair Enterprises, Inc. v. Julien Construction Co. 79056
Quincy Post No. 37, American Legion; Kurz v. 72056
Quinn v. Moore 72082
Quinn Assoc., Inc. v. Borkowski 88029
Quinn Construction Co.; Sisters of the Good Shepherd v. 69054
Quintana-Howell Joint Venture; Aztec Servs., Inc. v. 82006

R

R. C. Pierce Roofing Co.; Batson-Cook Co. v. . . 71009
R C R Leasing, Inc. v. Harping Sales & Erectors, Inc. 71072
R-Monde Contractors, Inc.; Diocese of Rochester v. 89012
R & R Construction Co. v. Junior College District No. 529 77073
R. S. Noonan; La Vale Plaza, Inc. v. 67039
R. Terry Blazier & Son; Fuller Industries, Inc. v. 66025
R. W. King Construction Co. v. Melbourne, City of 80053
R. W. Mier Construction Co. v. Concrete Contractors, Inc. 68040
R. Zoppo Co. v. Manchester, City of 82044
Race Co. v. Oxford Hall Contracting Corp. . . . 66075
Racine Trust; Miller v. 78054
Rackers & Backlesse, Inc. v. Kinstler . . . 73090
Radford Petroleum Equip. Co.; B.G. Coney Co. v. 85007
Radiation Technology, Inc. v. United States 66076
Raffa Assocs. v. Boca Raton Resort & Club 93016
Ragan Enter., Inc.; L & B Constr. Co. v. 97013
Ragnar Benson, Inc.; Premier Elec. Constr. Co. v. 82040
Rainer; Fidelity & Deposit Co. v. 29002

Rainey; Adamsville Lumber Co. v. 72003
Raisur Corp. v. New York City Housing Authority 73091
Raitman v. McCune 34004
Rakstag Assocs.; Maniscav. 93045
Ralph Allen, Inc. v. Lumpkin 77074
Ralph F. Roussey & Associates, Inc.; Stark v. . . . 75025
Ralph Korte Construction Co. v. Springfield Mechanical Co. 77075
Ralph L. Dickerson Constr. Co.; May v. . . 90030
Ralph M. Parsons Co. v. Combustion Equip. Assoc., Inc. 85034
Ramada Development Co. v. Rauch 81060
Ramey Constr. Co. v. Apache Tribe of Mescalero Reservation 82041
Ramirez v. Alabama Power Co. 95044
Ramonas v. Kerelis 68036
Ramsey Products Corp.; Williams & Associates v. 73124
Randolph County Board of Education; J.R. Graham & Son, Inc. v. 75013
Randolph County Board of Education; Wellborn Plumbing & Heating Co. v. 66112
Ranger Construction Co. v. Prince William County School Board 79057
Ranier Construction Co.; American Continental Life Insurance Co. v. 80002
Ranoel Realty Co.; Reisman v. 73094
Rao Electrical Equipment Co. v. MacDonald Engineering Co. 70068
Rao Electrical Equipment Co. v. State . . . 71071
Rapp Constr. Co. v. Jay Realty Co. 91027
Rashid v. Schenck Constr. Co. 93049
Rauch; Ramada Development Co. v. 81060
Raupach; Haugen v. 53002
Rausauer Builders, Inc.; Oxford Development Corp. v. 73086
Rausch v. Julius B. Nelson & Sons 67057
Ray v. Monsanto Co. 73092
R.C. Foss & Sons, Inc.; Demers Nursing Home Inc. v. 82015
R.C. Mahon Co.; N.E. Finch Co. v. 77062
R.C. Small & Assocs., Inc. v. Southern Mechanical Inc. 87038
R.C. Stanhope, Inc. v. Roanoke Construction Co. 76059
R.C. Tolman Construction Co.; Prince v. . . 80051
R.E. Dailey & Co.; Redfern v. 85035
Reamer Industries, Inc. v. McQuay, Inc. . . 71073
Reaves; Guerin Contractors, Inc. v. 80029
Reber v. Chandler High School District No. 202 70069

TABLE OF CASES

[The five-digit numbers in this table are *Citator* Case Reference Numbers, which refer to the cases in the Cases section]

Plaquemine, City of; Diamond B Constr. Co. v. . . . 96004
Plowden & Roberts, Inc. v. Conway 66074
PMS Construction Co.; DeKalb County v. 78024
Polakov; Concourse Beauty School, Inc. v. 88008
Polatschek v. New York, City of 72080
Polytech, Inc.; Yamnitz v. 79072
Pomeroy v. Anderson 82038
Poole v. Ocean Drilling & Exploration Co. 83038
Poole & Kent Corp. v. C.E. Thurston & Sons, Inc. 74030
Port Auth.; Ardsley Construction Co. v. . . 81005
Port Auth. of Allegheny County; Marshall v. . . . 90029
Port Auth. of New York; Nasser, Estate of v. . . . 89015
Port Auth. of New York & New Jersey; Vey v. . . 81070
Port Auth. Trans-Hudson Corp.; Yonkers Contracting Co. v. 95024
Port City Construction Co. v. Adams & Douglas, Inc. 70066
Port Liberte Partners v. Strober Bros., Inc. 88028
Port of New York Authority; M.F. Hickey Co. v. 65076
Port of Tacoma; V. C. Edwards Contracting Co. v. 73115
Porter v. Avlis Contracting Corp. 76056
Portuguese-American Bank v. Welles . . . 16004
Post; Collins v. 61004
Post Bros. Construction Co. v. Yoder . . . 77070
Post Tensioned Eng'g Corp. v. Fairways Plaza Assocs. 82038
Post-Tensioned Structures, Inc.; Robert F. Wilson, Inc. v. 88030
Poston; Ballard, H. T. Kirk & Associates v. 72012
Poteat; Batson-Cook Company v. 78008
Poughkeepsie v. Holden Construction Co. 79053
Powell; Gilbert v. 83017
Powell's General Contracting Co. v. Marshfield Housing Authority 79054
Power Process Piping, Inc.; Fischbach-Natkin Co. v. 87020
Power Technology Ctr. Ltd. Partnership; Contract Constr. Inc. v. 94006
Powertherm Corp.; Willard, Inc. v. 82058
PPG Industries, Inc. v. Continental Heller Corp. . . 79050

PPG Industries, Inc.; Westminster Construction Corp. v. 77085
P.R. Post Corp. v. Maryland Casualty Co. 76058
Prahl; Kahn v. 67038
Prairie Land Constr., Inc. v. Modesto . . . 91026
Prater v. Luhr Bros. 77071
Pratt Plumbing & Heating, Inc.; Guidetti v. 76027
PRC Eng'g, Inc.; Moore v. 90031
Premier Elec. Constr. Co. v. Ragnar Benson, Inc. 82040
Prepakt Concrete Co. v. Whitehurst Bros., Inc. 77072
President of Elkton; James Julian, Inc. v. 65056
Prestressed Concrete, Inc. v. Adolfson & Peterson, Inc. 76057
Prichard Bros. v. Grady Co. 89037
Priesmeyer; Holmquest v. 78037
Prima Paint Corp. v. Flood & Conklin Mfg. Co. 74010
Prime Constr. Co.; Brown v. 84005
Prime Homes, Inc.; Davidson v. 72032
Primiano Construction Co.; Rockland v. . . 80055
Prince v. R.C. Tolman Construction Co. . . 80051
Prince William County School Board; Ranger Construction Co. v. 79057
Princemont Construction Co.; Brodsky v. 76008
Pro Metal Bldg. Sys., Inc. v. T.E. Driskell Grading Co. 84032
Process Design Assocs.; Ivanov v. 93015a
Process Engineering Co.; Dickerson Construction Co. v. 77027
Procter & Gamble Paper Prod. Co. v. Yeargin Constr. Co. 90036
Professional Building Service Corp.; Drost v. 72036
Progress Glass Co. v. American Insurance Co. . . . 80052
Prom Town House Motor Inn, Inc.; LaPuzza v. . . 74021
Providence Washington Insurance Co. v. Beck . . 70067
Public Building Authority; Continental Casualty Co. v. 67018
Public Employees Mutual Ins. Co. v. Sellen Constr. Co. 87036
Public Water Supply District No. 8 v. Maryland Casualty Co. 72081
Puget Sound National Bank v. C.B. Lauch Construction Co. 52004
Pugh v. Butler Tel. Co. 87037

TABLE OF CASES

[The five-digit numbers in this table are *Citator* Case Reference Numbers, which refer to the cases in the Cases section]

Pensacola Builders Supply Co.; Clement v. 39002
People v. (see name of defendant)
People ex (see name of defendant)
People ex rel. (see name of defendant)
People's Tobacco Warehouse Co.; Leonard v. ... 24002
Pepper Constr. Co. v. Transcontinental Ins. Co. ... 96037
Perfetto & Whalen Construction Corp.; Geneseo Central School v. 81028
Perfetto & Whalen Construction Corp.; Niagara Mohawk Power Corp. v. 76048
Perini Corp. v. Greate Bay Hotel & Casino, Inc. ... 92017
Perini Corp.; Robbins v. 66081
Perkins & Will v. Syska & Hennessy & Garfinkel, Marenberg & Assoc. 75019
Perkins & Will Partnership v. Syska and Hennessy 77068
Perlis & Sons v. Peacock Construction Co. 66071
Pero Bldg. Co. v. Smith 86051
Perritt v. Bernhard Mechanical 96009
Perryman v. Huber, Hunt & Nichols, Inc. 94014
Perschke v. Westinghouse Electric Corp. ... 69048
Person County; Ruffin Woody & Assocs., Inc. v. 88031
Pete Smith Co. v. El Dorado, City of ... 75020
Peter Kiewit Sons' Co. v. Iowa Southern Utilities Co. 73089
Peter Kiewit Sons' Co. v. Okeeke Elevator Co. ... 74029
Peter Kiewit Sons' Co.; United States v. ... 65111
Petersen Construction Co.; Hennepin Public Water District v. 73051
Petition of (see name of party)
Pettee v. Nashua, City of 31007
Pettinaro Construction Co. v. Harry Partridge, Jr., & Sons 79051
Pettinelli Electric Co. v. William A. Berbusse, Jr., Inc. 66072
Peyronnin Construction Co. v. Weiss 65088
P.G. Miron Constr. Co.; State v. 94019
Phenix-Georgetown, Inc. v. Chas. H. Tompkins Co. 84029
Philip Vizzini & Son; Mann v. 70164
Phillips v. Ben M. Hogan Co. 80050
Phillips v. United Eng'r & Constructors, Inc. 86052
Phillips R. Geraghty Constructor, Inc.; Sisters of Saint John the Baptist, Providence Rest Convent v. 86062

Phipps; Meirowsky v. 68028
Phoenix Contracting Corp. v. New York Health & Hosp. Corp. 86053
Phoenix Contractors, Inc. v. General Motors Corp. 84030
Phoenix Heat Source Sys.; Town of Silverton v. 97025
Pick; Allison v. 56001
Pickens-Bond Construction Co. v. North Little Rock Electric Co. 70065
Pickens-Bond Construction Co.; North Little Rock Electric Co. v. 72073
Pickering v. Daniel J. Keating Co. 72077
Pickering Construction Co.; Puritan Mills, Inc. v. 79055
Pickett v. Chamblee Construction Co. 71070
Pidgeon Thomas Co.; Baker v. 70008
Piedmont Heating & Air Conditioning, Inc.; Redman Development Corp. v. 73093
Pierce v. Board of Education 25001
Pierce; McCarthy Bros. Constr. Co. v. ... 87033
Pierce Assoc., Inc. v. Nemours Found. ... 88027
Pignott Construction International, Ltd. v. Rochester Institute of Technology 81057
Pine Gravel, Inc. v. Cianchette 86054
Pioneer Acceptance Corp. v. Irving Coven Construction, Inc. 76054
Pioneer Enters., Inc. v. Edens 84031
Pioneer Industries v. Gevyn Construction Corp. ... 72078
Pioneer Roofing Co. v. Mardian Constr. Co. 86055
Pipe Welding Supply Co. v. Haskell, Conner & Frost 83037
Pipeline Industry Benefit Fund v. Aetna Casualty & Surety Co. 72079
Pit Construction Co. v. Holman 69049
Pittman; Legette v. 66052
Pittman Construction Co. v. Meadows ... 76055
Pittsburgh, City of v. American Asbestos Control Co. 93031
Pittsburgh Des Moines Steel Co. v. American Surety Co. 66073
Pittsburgh-Des Moines Steel Co.; Garden Grove Community Church v. 83016
Pittsburgh Plate Glass Co. v. American Surety Co. 42002
Pittsfield, General Hospital v. Markus ... 69050
Pizza Oven, Inc.; Kellogg v. 65060
P.J. Carlin Construction Co.; Johnson Acoustics, Inc. v. 71053
Planning Systems Corp. v. Murrell 79052
Plantation Pipe Line Co. v. 3-D Excavators, Inc. 81058

TABLE OF CASES

[The five-digit numbers in this table are *Citator* Case Reference Numbers, which refer to the cases in the Cases section]

P

P & H Supply, Inc.; Mid-Continent Casualty Co. v. 71067
Ozinga Transp. Sys. Inc. v. Michigan Ash Sales, Inc. 97019
P & M Construction Co. v. Hammond Ventures, Inc. 66069
Pace Constr. Corp.; OBS Co v. 90034
Pacella Brothers v. Metropolitan Dist. ... 66068
Pacific Coast Builders v. Antioch Live Oak Unified School District 56006
Pacific County v. Sherwood Pacific, Inc. ... 77066
Pacific Employers Insurance Co. v. State ... 70063
Pacific Insurance Co. v. Wilbanks 68034
Padgett v. CH2M Hill Southeast, Inc. ... 94044
Paduano v. J.C. Boespflug Construction Co. 65084
Pagani Brothers Construction Co.; Whittle v. ... 81072
Page; Anderson-Nichols & Co. v. 73005
Page; Byram Lumber & Supply Co. v. 29001
Page v. H. B. White & Son 73087
Palmer v. Brown 54004
Palmer v. General Health, Inc. 89036
Palmer Steel Structures v. Westech, Inc. .. 78060
Pan American Realty Trust v. Twenty One Kings, Inc. 68035
Panel Suppliers, Inc.; Cree Coaches, Inc. v. 71028
Pantaleo v. Gamm 69044
Paragon Homes; J. Dunn & Sons v. 70040
Paramount Engineering Co.; Walker v. ... 65117
Parem Contracting Corp. v. Welch Constr. Co. ... 86049
Parent v. Stone & Webster Eng'g Corp. ... 90035
Paris Plastering Co.; Herman Christensen & Sons, Inc. v. 76029
Parish of Jefferson; Trapani v. 65106
Park Construction Co.; Klar v. 68023
Park Construction Co.; Worcester, City of v. ... 72027
Park Imperial, Inc. v. E. L. Farmer Construction Co. 69046
Park Shore Dev. Co.; Higley South, Inc. v. 86031
Park Steel Corp.; Erland Constr. Co. v. .. 96026
Parker; Austin v. 82005
Parker; Bergman v. 66008
Parker v. Theubet 69045
Parker Henry Glass Co.; Transamerica Insurance Co. v. 72101
Parkhill-Goodloe Co.; Jacksonville Port Authority v. 78039

Parkhill, Smith & Cooper, Inc.; Romero v. 94045
Parma Community Gen. Hosp. Ass'n; Floor Craft Floor Covering, Inc. v. 90020
Parrish v. Tahtaras 57001
Parrish of Jefferson; Southbend Contractors, Inc. v. 81065
Parsons v. Amerada Hess Corp. 70064
Parsons v. Bristol Development Co. 65086
Parsons Corp.; Universal Terrazzo & Tile Co. v. 73113
Parsons & Whittemore Contractors Corp.; Fidelity and Deposit Co. of Maryland v. 79037
Paschen Contractors, Inc. v. John J. Calnan Co. 73088
Paschen Contractors, Inc.; Zettel v. 81075
Pascoe Steel Corp.; Wieman-Slechta Co. v. 72110
Pastorelli v. Associated Engineers 59005
Patent Scaffolding Co. v. Standard Oil Co. 66070
Paul B. Emerick Co. v. William Bohnenkamp & Associates 65087
Paul Hardman, Inc. v. Bradley 71069
Paul Mullins Construction Co. v. Alspaugh ... 81056
Paulus v. St. Louis, City of 69047
Paxton v. Alameda County 53005
Payne; Locklear v. 71062
Payne Plumbing & Heating Co. v. Bob McKiness Excavating & Grading, Inc. 86050
Peabody Seating Co. v. Jim Cullen, Inc. .. 72076
Peacock Construction Co. v. Modern Air Conditioning, Inc. 77067
Peacock Construction Co.; Perlis & Sons v. 66071
Pearl Street Development Corp. v. Conduit & Foundation Corp. 76053
Peck v. Horrocks Eng'rs 97020
Pedersen v. Fiksdal 60011
Pendleton, City of; Humbert Excavating, Inc. v. 93015
Pederson; Ringwelski v. 96038
Pennsbury Village Co.; McMaster, Inc. v. 72069
Pennsylvania Dept. of Gen. Servs. v. G. Weinberger Co. 82037
Pennsylvania National Mutual Casualty Insurance Co.; Lehigh Electric Products Co. v. ... 78050
Pennsylvania Roofing Co.; DiLucente Corp. v. 95009
Pennsylvania Turnpike Commission; Merritt-Chapman & Scott Corp. v. 66056

TABLE OF CASES

[The five-digit numbers in this table are *Citator* Case Reference Numbers, which refer to the cases in the Cases section]

Novak v. BASF Corp.	94043
Novak & Co. v. New York City Hous. Auth.	84026
Novak & Co. v. Travelers Indemnity Co.	76052
NRS Constr. Corp. v. Board of Educ.	83036
NSC Contractors, Inc. v. Borders	89035
Nucor Corp. v. Tennessee Forging Steel Service	73084
Nuzzo v. Commercial Concrete Co.	73082
Nyack Housing Authority, Village of; Mardan Construction Corp. v.	72064

O

O & E Contracting Co.; Tibbetts Contracting Corp. v.	65105
O. K. Johnson Electric, Inc. v. Hess-Martin Corp.	70061
O & M Manufacturing Co. v. Southern Generator & Engine Sales, Inc.	75016
O-S Corp. v. Samuel A. Kroll, Inc.	75017
Oak Builders, Inc.; Maloney v.	69035
Oakes v. Suelynn Corp.	72074
Oakes-Waterman Builders; Henderson v.	41002
Obray v. Mitchell	77065
OBS Co. v. Pace Constr. Corp.	90034
Ocean Drilling & Exploration Co.; Poole v.	83038
Ockerlund Constr. Co.; Hibbler v.	85019
Odell v. Colmor Irrigation & Land Co.	29004
O'Dell v. Custom Builders Corp.	78057
Oden Construction Co. v. Helton	53004
Odom; Cocke v.	80012
O.F. Paulson Construction Co.; Hetherington Letter Co. v.	69027
Oggero; Craven v.	73028
O'Kain v. Davis	19002
Okeeke Elevator Co.; Peter Kiewit Sons' Co. v.	74029
OKI Am., Inc.; Englehart v.	93034
Old Orchard Creek Partners, Ltd.; Temple Eastex, Inc. v.	92019a
Oldham & Worth, Inc. v. Bratton	65083
Olin; Andrews Fixture Co. v.	70007
Olin Mathieson Chemical Corp. v. J.J. Wuellner & Sons	66066
Olsen v. Chase Manhatten Bank	61011
Olshan Demolishing Co. v. Angleton Indep. School Dist.	84027
Olympic Constr., Inc. v. Drywall Interiors, Inc.	86048
Olympic Insurance Co.; Pylon, Inc. v.	69051
Olympus Corp. v. United States	96036
Omaha Public Power District; Simon v.	72092
Omega Painting, Inc.; State v.	84037
Omnibus Industries, Inc.; Spence v.	75023
155 Harbor Drive Condominium Ass'n v. Harbor Point	91025
1700 Ocean Avenue Corp. v. G B R Associates	65097
O'Neal Steel Co. v. Leon C. Miles, Inc.	66067
Onondaga, Town of; John E. Fisher Constr. Co. v.	85022
Opelika Manufacturing Corp.; Crown Construction Co. v.	73029
Open Kitchens, Inc. v. Gullo Int'l Dev. Corp.	84028
Opp & Seibold Gen. Constr., Inc.; Touchet Valley Grain Growers, Inc. v.	92020
Orput-Orput & Assoc., Inc. v. McCarthy	73085
Orth v. Board of Public Education	22001
Orto v. Jackson	80049
Orvedahl Constr., Inc.; Turtle Lake, Village of v.	86069
Osage Co.; Commonwealth of Pennsylvania v.	76013
Osberg Construction Co.; Lano v.	65066
Osolo School Bldgs., Inc. v. Thorleif Larsen & Son, Inc.	85032
Osteen v. T.E. Cuttino Constr. Co.	93048
Oster v. Medtronic, Inc.	88026
Oswego, Village of; Stage v.	75024
Van Ornum v. Otter Tail Power Co.	73114
Otis Erecting Co.; Hortman v.	82023
Otter Tail Power Co.; Van Ornum v.	73114
Ottinger; Mor-Wood Contractors, Inc. v.	90032
Otto v. Hendry	74027
Ouachita Parish School Board; Jacka v.	66040
Overby v. Barnett	70062
Overland Constructors, Inc. v. Millard School Dist.	85033
Owen Building & Investment Co.; Hunt v.	20002
Owens v. Bartlett, Labette County, City of	74028
Owens-Illinois Glass Co.; Sellers v.	72090
Owens & Woods Partnership; Castle Constr. Co./Tuskegee Lumber Co. v.	91004
Owings v. Rose	72075
Oxford Construction Co.; Albany, City of v.	66014
Oxford Development Corp. v. Rausauer Builders, Inc.	73086
Oxford Hall Contracting Corp.; Race Co. v.	66075
Ozdeger v. Altay	78058; 78059

TABLE OF CASES

[The five-digit numbers in this table are *Citator* Case Reference Numbers, which refer to the cases in the Cases section]

New York, City of; Nab-Tern Constructors v. . . . 86012
New York, City of; Naclerio Contracting Co. v. . . 86047
New York, City of; New Again Construction Co. v. 74025
New York, City of; Polatschek v. 72080
New York, City of; Smullen v. 71078
New York Health & Hosp. Corp.; Phoenix Contracting Corp. v. 86053
New York Housing Authority; Frouge Corp. v. . . 66024
New York Indemnity Co. v. Hurst 33002
New York Plumber's Specialties Co. v. W. J. Barney Corp. 76047
New York, State of; Chemical Bank v. . . 78015
New York, State of; Fehlhaber Corp. v. . . 78029
New York, State of; Fireman's Insurance Co. of Newark, New Jersey v. 79007
New York, State of; Grow Construction Co. v. . . 77039
New York, State of; Twin Village Construction Corp. v. 78072
New York, State of; Whitmyer Bros., Inc. v. . . . 78077
New York State Thruway Authority; Bero Construction Corp. v. 73016
New York State Thruway Authority; Stratton v. . . 63006
New York Telephone Co. v. Schumacher & Forelle, Inc. 77064
Newkirk Construction Corp. v. Gulf County 79014
Niagara Mohawk Power Corp. v. Perfetto & Whalen Construction Corp. 76048
Nicholas Acoustics & Specialty Co. v. H & M Constr. Co. 83035
Nichols; Ben. M. Hogan Co. v. 73014
Nicholson v Turner/Cargile 95052
Nickell; Huxol v. 70036
Nickell v. United States 66063
Nickles & Wells Constr. Co.; Mississippi Bank v. 82034
Nieman-Irving & Co. v. Lazenby 33003
Nilsen, State ex rel. v. Hoff 70077
Nimke v. Intra-State, Inc. 70059
Nixon Construction Co. v. Downs 69043
Nixon Constructon Co.; Meares v. 70055
N.J. Riebe Enters., Inc.; Lewis v. 92011
Noland Co. v. West End Realty Corp. . . . 66064
Nolf; Titan Construction Co. v. 73110
Nome, City of; Nordin Construction Co. v. 71068
Noonan v. Independence Indemnity Co. . . 31006

Noonan v. Stein 13003
Nooter Corp.; Wilson v. 73126
Norair Engineering Corp. v. Saint Joseph's Hospital, Inc. 73056
Norcross Bros.; Johnson v. 11001
Nord; Armour & Co. v. 72010
Nordenstrom v. Swedberg 66065
Nordin Construction Co. v. Nome, City of 71068
Norfolk Air Conditioning Corp.; J.W. Creech, Inc. v. 89029
Norfolk and Western Ry. Co. v. Werner Industries 74026
Norkin Plumbing Co.; United Nations Development Corp. v. 78073
Norman Co. v. Nassau, County of 67056
Norman S. Wright & Co., S.W. v. Slaysman 79049
Normoyle-Berg & Associates, Inc. v. Deer Creek, Village of 76049
North Carolina Dept. of Admin.; Davidson & Jones, Inc. v. 85012
North Carolina, State of; E.L. Scott Roofing Co. v. 86018
North County School District R-1 v. Fidelity & Deposit Co. of Maryland 76050
North End Health Center, Inc.; E.D.S. Constr. v. 87017
North Hempstead, Town of v. Sea Crest Constr. Co. 86066
North Little Rock Electric Co. v. Pickens-Bond Construction Co. 72073
North Little Rock Electric Co.; Pickens-Bond Construction Co. v. 70065
Northeast Ohio Regional Sewer Dist.; Mon-Rite Constr. Co. v. 84025
Northeast Ohio Regional Sewer Dist.; Roger J. Au & Son, Inc. v. 86059
Northeastern Corp.; Jacobs v. 65055
Northern Improvements Co.; All Seasons Water Users Ass'n, Inc. v. 87002
Northern Montana Hosp. v. Knight 91024
Northern Pacific Railway Co. v. Chemetron Corp. 70060
Northern States Power Co.; Hurlburt v. . . 94037
Northwest Community Hospital; Kelly v. 78045
Northwestern Engineering Co. v. Thunderbolt Enterprises, Inc. 81055
Northwestern Marble & Tile Co. v. Megrath 13004
Norton Heights Fire Dept. v. Vuono-Lione, Inc. 76051
Norwalk, City of; Conte v. 77023

TABLE OF CASES

[The five-digit numbers in this table are *Citator* Case Reference Numbers, which refer to the cases in the Cases section]

Nashua, City of; Pettee v. 31007
Nashville School District No. 1; C & B Construction Co. v. 72022
Nashwauk, City of; Zontelli & Sons, Inc. v. 85044
Nassau, County of; Norman Co. v. 67056
Nasser, Estate of v. Port Auth. of New York . . . 89015
Nat Harrison Associates v. Gulf State Utilities Co. 74024
National Equipment Rental, Ltd., In re . . . 70037
National Gypsum Co.; Travelers Indem. Co. v. . . 81068a
National Hydro Sys. v. M.A. Mortenson Co. 93047
National Surety Corp.; Algernon Blair, Inc. v. 66002
National Surety Corp. v. Curators of University of Missouri 59004
National Surety Corp.; Davis Acoustical Corp. v. 66020
National Union Fire Insurance Co. v. D & L Construction Co. 65082
National Union Fire Insurance Co. v. Denver Brick & Pipe Co. 67053
National Union Fire Insurance Co.; Lippert Brothers v. 65069
National Union Fire Insurance Co.; Main Cornice Works, Inc. v. 66053
National Union Fire Insurance Co.; Transcontinental Ins. Co. v. 96012
National U.S. Radiator Corp.; Day v. . . . 61006
Nauman v. Harold K. Beecher & Associates 67054
Nave v. Harlan Jones Drilling 92016a
N.B. Harty General Contractors, Inc. v. West Plains Bridge and Grading Co. 80047
N.D. Judds Co.; Hillcrest Country Club v. 90026
N.E. Finch Co. v. R.C. Mahon Co. 77062
N.E. Redlon Co. v. Franklin Square Corp. 37002
Nearing, Staats, Prelogar & Jones; McCarney v. . . . 93046
Nebel Heating Corp.; Fortin v. 81026
Nees v. Weaver 36002
Nelse Mortensen & Co. v. Group Health Cooperative of Puget Sound 77063
Nelsen; Adams v. 85002
Nelson v. Commonwealth of Virginia . . . 88025
Nelson v. Hagen 66061
Nelson-Deppe, Inc.; Davis v. 67020
Nelson Paving Co. v. Hjelle 73083
Nemours Found.; Gilbane Bldg. Co. v. . . . 85017

Nemours Found.; Pierce Assoc., Inc. v. . . . 88027
Neshobe Dev., Inc.; McGee Constr. Co. v. 91020
New; Staley v. 52005
New Again Construction Co. v. New York, City of 74025
New Amsterdam Casualty Co. v. Bettes . . 66062
New Amsterdam Casualty Co. v. Texas Industries, Inc. 67055
New Bedford Redevelopment Auth.; D. Federico Co. v. 83013
New Britain, City of; Rossetti v. 73097
New Boston Garden Corp.; Herson v. . . . 96029
New England Concrete Pipe Corp. v. D/C Systems of New England 80048
New England Structures, Inc. v. Loranger 68033
New Era Corp.; General Accident & Fire Assurance Corp. v. 66026
New Hampshire Ins. Co.; Melrose Hous. Auth. v. 88024
New Hanover, County of; Davidson and Jones, Inc. v. 79004
New Haven Hotel Co.; M.J. Daly & Sons v. . . . 17004
New Orleans Levee Board; Super Construction Co. v. 73107
New Orleans Unity Society v. Standard Roofing Co. 69042
New Pueblo Constructors, Inc. v. Lake Patagonia Recreation Association 70058
New York; Himbele v. 81036
New York; Thomas Crimmins Contracting Co. v. 88035a
New York Bd. of Fire Underwriters v. Trans Urban Constr. Co. 83034
New York City Hous. Auth.; Novak & Co. v. . . . 84026
New York City Hous. Auth.; Raisur Corp. v. . . . 73091
New York, City of; Blau Mechanical Corp. v. . . . 90007
New York, City of; Buckley & Co. v. . . . 86005
New York, City of; Corinno Civetta Constr. Corp. v. 86012
New York, City of; Joseph F. Egan, Inc. v. 66047
New York, City of; Kalich-Jarchq, Inc. v. 83027
New York, City of v. Kalish-Jarcho, Inc. 90011
New York, City of; Merrill-Ruckgaber Co. v. . . . 14004

TABLE OF CASES

[The five-digit numbers in this table are *Citator* Case Reference Numbers, which refer to the cases in the Cases section]

Moore v. Clearing Industrial District, Inc. 78055
Moore v. Continental Casualty Co. . 73078; 73079
Moore v. Dayton Power & Light Co. . . . 94042
Moore; Huber, Hunt & Nichols, Inc. v. . . 77044
Moore v. PRC Eng'g, Inc. 90031
Moore; Quinn v. 72082
Moore Constr. Co. v. Clarksville Dept. of Elec. . . 85029
Moore Heating & Plumbing, Inc. v. Huber, Hunt & Nichols 91023
Moorhead Construction Co. v. Grand Forks, City of 75014
Moossy v. Huckabay Hospital, Inc. 73080
Mor-Wood Contractors, Inc. v. Ottinger . . 90032
Morey; Yarber v. 66117
Morgan v. Burlington, Town of 44002
Morgan v. Stubblefield 72072
Morganti, Inc. v. Boehringer Ingelheim Pharmaceuticals, Inc. 89034
Morin Bldg. Prod. Co. v. Baystone Constr. 83032
Morrell; Ridge Sheet Metal Co. v. 86056
Morris J. Liebergott & Associate v. Investment Building Corp. 68032
Morris Middle School District No. 54; Borg, Inc. v. 72018
Morrison-Knudsen Co. v. United States . . 65080; 65081
Morrison Supply Co. v. M.W. Hamilton & Co. . . 67052
Morse/Diesel, Inc.; Mears Park Holding Corp. v. 88023
Morse/Diesel, Inc. v. Trinity Indus., Inc. . . 95018
Morse/UBM Joint Venture; L.K. Comstock & Co. v. 87030
Morton Thiokol, Inc. v. Metal Bldg. Alteration Co. 87035
Morton Z. Levine and Associates v. Van Deree . . 76046
Mosaic Tile Co.; Tepper Realty Co. v. . . . 66096
Moser; Bott v. 40001
Moses H. Cone Memorial Hosp. v. Mercury Constr. 83033
Mosher Steel Co.; McDevitt & Street Co. v. 91019
Motel Enterprises, Inc.; Coonrod & Walz Construction Co. v. 75007
Motorists Mutual Insurance Co. v. Jones . . . 66059
Mounds View, City of v. Walijarvi 78016
Moundsview Independent School District No. 621 v. Buetow & Associates, Inc. 77061
Mountain States Constr. Co. v. Tyee Elec., Inc. . . 86046
Moweaqua, Village of; Horton Indus., Inc. v. . . 86033
Moyers Corners Fire Dept. Inc.; Chase Architectural Assocs. v. 84007
Moyers Corners Fire Dept., Inc.; J.R. Gallagher Constr. Co. v. 84007
Mrozik Constr. Inc. v. Lovering Assoc., Inc. 90033
M.S. Kelliher Co.; A.J. Eckert Co. v. . . . 65004
MSI Constr. Managers, Inc.; Frank v. . . . 95011
M.S.I. Corp.; United States ex rel. A. & J. Freidman Supply Co. v. 65110
M.S.I. Corp.; United States ex rel. Wellman Engineering Co. v. 65052
Mueller; B & M Constr., Inc. v. 89002
Mukilteo School District No. 6; Lindbrook Construction, Inc. v. 69034
Mularz v. Greater Park City Co. 30045
Multi-Service Contractors, Inc. v. Vernon, Town of 80046
Municipal & Indus. Pipe Serv., Inc.; Houma, L.A. v. 89022
Murphy v. Brockton, City of 73081
Murphy Pacific Corp.; Karnatz v. 72052
Murray v. Fishman Construction Co. . . . 66060
Murray Plumbing and Heating Corp.; St. Paul Fire & Marine Insurance Co. v. 76065
Murrell; Planning Systems Corp. v. 79052
Muth v. Leineke 70057
M.W. Hamilton & Co.; Morrison Supply Co. v. . . 67052
Myers v. Burger King Corp. 94013
MYS Corp.; Fite and Warmath Construction Co. v. 77034

N

NAB Construction Corp.; Data Electric Co. v. . . . 76016
NAB Construction Corp.; Sturdy Concrete Corp. v. 78068
Nab-Tern Constructors v. New York, City of . . . 86012
Nabholz Constr. Corp. v. Graham 95019
Naclerio Contracting Co. v. EPA . . 82036; 85030
Naclerio Contracting Co. v. New York, City of . . 86047
Naetzker v. Brocton Central School District 75015
Nagar Constr. Co.; Francavilla v. 89016
Namerow v. Colangelo 69041
Nanz; Voight v. 74041
Naperville, City of; St. John v. 87042
Nasco; Rhoads v. 66079

TABLE OF CASES
TC-43

[The five-digit numbers in this table are *Citator* Case Reference Numbers, which refer to the cases in the Cases section]

Miller v. Melany	77060
Miller v. Racine Trust	78054
Miller v. Two State Constr. Co.	95016
Miller; United States Fidelity & Guaranty Co. v.	77082
Miller Bldg. Corp. v. Coastline Assocs. Ltd. Partnership	92016
Miller Chem. Co.; Getzschman v.	89017
Miller Construction Co. v. First Baptist Church	81054
Miller-Davis Co.; Roy Strom Excavating & Grading Co. v.	86060
Millgard Corp. v. McKee/Mays	95017
Mills v. Robert W. Gottfried, Inc.	73075
Milton Schwartz & Associates v. Magness Corp.	74022
Milwaukie Covenant Church; Devlin v.	74014
Minden; Yocum v.	90056
Mingledorff's, Inc. v. Hicks	74023
Minidoka County v. Krieger	65077
Minmar Builders, Inc.; Dillon Properties, Inc. v.	70020
Minnotte Contracting Corp.; Wilson Elec. Contractors, Inc. v.	89050
Mion Chemical Brick Corp. v. Daniel Construction Co.	65078
Mirpa, Inc.; Adelphi Enterprises, Inc. v.	70004
Misener Marine Construction Co. v. Southport Marine, Inc.	79048
Mississippi Bank v. Nickles & Wells Constr. Co.	82034
Mississippi Coast Coliseum Comm'n v. Stuart Constr. Co.	82035
Mississippi Meadows, Inc. v. Hodson	73076
Mississippi State Bldg. Comm'n v. Becknell Construction, Inc.	76044
Mississippi State Bldg. Comm'n; CIG Contractors, Inc. v.	87012
Mississippi Steel & Iron Co.; Standard Millwork & Supply Co. v.	49003
Missouri Pacific Railroad Co.; Al Johnson Construction Co. v.	76001
Missouri Pacific Railroad Co.; San Ore-Gardner v.	81064
Mitchell v. Flandor	73077
Mitchell; Idaho State University v.	76030
Mitchell; Obray v.	77065
Mitchell-Hughback, Inc.; Butler v.	94004
Mitsuo Kawamota & Assocs., Inc.; Belgum v.	90006
Mitterhausen v. South Wisconsin Conference Association of Seventh Day Advent	44004
M.J. Constr. Co.; Wilharm v.	97026
M.J. Daly & Sons v. New Haven Hotel Co.	17004
M.L. Shalloo, Inc. v. Ricciardi & Sons Construction	65079
MMR-Radon Constructors, Inc.; Woodrow Wilson Constr. Co. v.	94021
Mobil Oil Corp.; Gulf Offshore Co. v.	79040
Modern Air Conditioning, Inc.; Peacock Construction Co. v.	77067
Modern Builders, Inc. of Tacoma v. Manke	80044
Modern Construction, Inc. v. Barce, Inc.	76045
Modern Construction, Inc.; University of Alaska v.	74040
Modesto; Prairie Land Constr., Inc. v.	91026
Modular Age, Inc.; Atlantic National Bank of Jacksonville v.	78007
Mohawk Overall Co. v. Brown	14005
Moline Heat & Contracting Co.; Fifteenth Avenue Christian Church v.	71038
Molnar Electrical Contractors, Inc.; Long Branch Sewerage Authority v.	76037
Mon-Rite Constr. Co. v. Northeast Ohio Regional Sewer Dist.	84025
Moncarol Construction Corp.; Soundwall Construction Corp. v.	68045
Monical v. State Farm Ins. Co.	91022
Monmouth Pub. Schools Dist. 38 v. D.H. Rouse Co.	87034
Monroe County Drain Comm'r; Joba Constr. Co. v.	86036
Monroe-McKeen Plaza Hous. Dev. Corp.; Wells & Parker Architects, Inc. v.	90054
Monroe, Town of; Kecko Piping Co. v.	77049
Monsanto Australia, Ltd.; Halcon International, Inc. v.	71045
Monsanto Co.; Ray v.	73092
Montalbano Bldrs.; J & K Cement Constr. v.	83025
Montana Sixth Judicial Dist. Ct.; State ex rel. Park County v.	92018a
Montgomery v. Karavas	41003
Montgomery County Bd. of Educ.; Watson, Watson, Rutland/Architects, Inc. v.	90052
Montgomery County Bd. of Educ. ex rel. Carrier Corp. v. Glassman Construction Co.	67050
Montgomery Ward & Co. v. Robert Cagle Building Co.	67051
Monty's Air Conditioning Serv., Inc.; Royal Inv. & Dev. Corp. v.	87041
Moon Motor Lodge; Universal Builders, Inc. v.	68050
Moore v. Bolton	72071

TABLE OF CASES

[The five-digit numbers in this table are *Citator* Case Reference Numbers, which refer to the cases in the Cases section]

Melbras-Manco, Inc.; L.B. Foster Co. v. . . . 70050
Mellon-Stuart Co.; Lichter v. 61009
Melrose Hous. Auth. v. New Hampshire Ins. Co. 88024
Memorial Hospital for Cancer and Allied Diseases; Wrecking Corp. of America v. 78079
Memphis Constr. Co.; Jordan, Village of v. 85043
Menasha Corp.; Christy v. 73025
Mendius Associates; Knickerbocker Roofing & Paving Co. v. 68024
Meneley Construction Co.; Community Consolidated School District v. 80013
Mercantile Trust Co. v. Hensey 07001
Merchants & Farmers Bank v. McClendon 69038
Mercury Constr.; Moses H. Cone Memorial Hosp. v. 83033
Meridian, City of v. Algernon Blair, Inc. . . 83010
Merkle v. Rice Construction Co. 73073
Merrill-Ruckgaber Co. v. New York, City of . . . 14004
Merritt-Chapman & Scott Corp.; Joseph Davis, Inc. v. 67036
Merritt-Chapman & Scott Corp. v. Pennsylvania Turnpike Commission 66056
Merritt-Chapman & Scott Corp. v. United States 66118
Mesker Brothers Iron Co. v. Burke Brothers 67047
Mesker Brothers Iron Co. v. Des Lauriers Column Mould Co. 72070
Met Food Corp. v. M. Eisenberg & Bros. 69039
Metal Bldg. Alteration Co.; Morton Thiokol, Inc. v. 87035
Metal Equipment Co.; Southwire Co. v. . . . 73100
Metal Service Corp. v. Industrial Electric Co. . . . 70056
Metal Trims Indus., Inc.; United Plate Glass Co., Div. of Chromalloy Am. Corp. v. 87051
Metallic Slab Form Co.; Knutson v. 42001
Methodist Church v. Glen-Rich Construction Corp. 71066
Metro Industrial Painting Corp. v. Terminal Construction Co. 61010
Metro Insulation Corp. v. Leventhal 73074
Metro Sports, Inc.; Hattis Associates, Inc. v. 75011
Metron Eng'g & Constr. Co.; Atlantic Mut. Ins. Co. v. 96001
Metropolitan Dist.; Pacella Brothers v. . . . 66068
Metropolitan Sanitary District; Carlson v. 65019
Metropolitan Sanitary District; Kenney Construction Co. v. 72054; 74044
Metropolitan Sewerage Commission; Fattore v. . . . 71037
Metropolitan Sewerage Commission v. R.W. Construction, Inc. 76043
Metz, Train, Olson & Youngren; Butler v. 78014
Meulenbergh v. Coe 16003
Meyer; Sibille v. 78065
Meyer; W. J. Howard & Sons v. 62011
Meyers v. Lakeridge Development Co. . . . 77059
M.F. Hickey Co. v. Port of New York Authority . . . 65076
Miami Beach, City of v. Fein 72025
Miami Beach, City of v. Fryd Construction Corp. 72026
Miami Heart Institute; Shafer & Miller v. 70075
Michalowski v. Richter Spring Corp. . . . 69040
Michigan Ash Sales, Inc.; Ozinga Transp. Sys. Inc. v. 97019
Mid-Atlantic Construction Corp. v. Guido . . . 68031
Mid-Continent Casualty Co. v. P & H Supply, Inc. 71067
Midas Realty Corp.; King v. 92010a
Middle-West Concrete Forming and Equipment Co. v. General Insurance Co. of America 80043
Middlesex Supply, Inc.; Holdam v. 66036
Midland, City of v. Waller 68010
Midstate Constructors, Inc.; Blanks v. . . . 80008
Midtown Bank v. Travelers Indemnity Co. . . . 66057
Midwest Curtainwalls, Inc.; Turner Constr Co. v. 89045
Midwest Materials Co. v. Village Dev. Co. 91021
Midwest Mechanical Contractors, Inc.; Case v. . . 94005
Midwest Mechanical Contractors, Inc. v. Commonwealth Constr. Co. 86045
Midwestern Realty Corp. v. Grandview, City of . . 67048
Mike Bradford & Co. v. Gulf States Steel Co. . . . 66058
Miles; Emlenton Area Mun. Auth. v. 88013
Miley v. Johnson & Johnson Orthopaedics, Inc. . . . 96035
Millard School Dist.; Overland Constructors, Inc. v. 85033
Miller v. DeWitt 67049
Miller; Keating v. 74020

TABLE OF CASES

TC–41

[The five-digit numbers in this table are *Citator* Case Reference Numbers, which refer to the cases in the Cases section]

Mayflower Corp.; Cohen v.	55001
Mazal American Partners; Harvey v.	92007
Mazzoleni v. Shenango Steel Erectors, Inc.	72065
McAllen Indep. School Dist.; D. Wilson Constr. Co. v.	92005a
McBro, Inc. v. M & M Glass Co.	92014a
McCain-Winkler Partnership; I.D.C., Inc. v.	81038
McCandliss v. Ward W. Ross, Inc.	73071
McCann Construction Co. v. Joe Adams & Son	70054
McCann Construction Co.; Joe Adams & Son v.	71052
McCann Steel Co.; Centex-Rodgers Constr. Co. v.	92004c
McCarney v. Nearing, Staats, Prelogar & Jones	93046
McCarthy; Harrington v.	66031
McCarthy v. J. P. Cullen & Son	72067
McCarthy; Orput-Orput & Assoc., Inc. v.	73085
McCarthy v. Reese	65075
McCarthy Bros. Constr. Co. v. Pierce	87033
McClane v. Sun Oil Co.	81051
McClendon; Merchants & Farmers Bank v.	69038
McCollum; Deuel v.	65032
McConnell; Construction Contracting & Management, Inc. v.	91007
McCool; Hedla v.	73050
McCormick; Gould v.	13002
McCullen; King Brothers Building Contractors, Inc. v.	80040
McCune; Raitman v.	34004
McDaniel v. Ashton-Mardian Co.	66055
McDaniel Grading, Inc.; ADC Constr. Co. v.	85003
McDermott; Burns v.	95027
McDevitt & Street Co.; Blue Cross of Southwestern Virginia v.	87007
McDevitt & Street Co. v. K-C Air Conditioning Serv., Inc.	92015
McDevitt & Street Co. v. Marriott Corp.	89032
McDevitt & Street Co. v. Mosher Steel Co.	91019
McDonald v. Filice	67046
McDonnell Douglas Corp.; Rodriguez v.	79016
McDougal; Welch v.	94020
McDowell v. Austin Co.	85028
McGee Constr. Co. v. Neshobe Dev., Inc.	91020
McGinnis; Ferrante v.	64005
McGowan-Rigsby Supply, Inc. v. Charles Carta & Co.	72068
McGraw v. S.D. Warren Co.	95015
McGuire; Kostohryz v.	73064
MCI Telecommunications Corp.; Galin Corp. v.	94008
McKay Construction Co. v. Board of Education	69037
McKee/Mays; Millgard Corp. v.	95017
McKinley; Marble Falls Housing Authority v.	71065
McKinney Drilling Co. v. Collins Co.	81052
McKinney Drilling Co. v. Mach I Limited Partnership	76041
McLaughlin; Rutter v.	80057
McLouth Steel Corp. v. A. E. Anderson Construction Corp.	73072
McMaster, Inc. v. Pennsbury Village Co.	72069
McMerit Constr. Co. v. Knightsbridge Dev. Co.	88022
McQuay, Inc.; Reamer Industries, Inc. v.	71073
McStain Corp. v. Elfline Plumbing & Heating, Inc.	76042
M.D. Hardy, Inc.; Marine Colloids, Inc. v.	81050
M.E. Kraft Excavating & Grading Co. v. Barac Construction Co.	68029
Mead & Mount Construction Co.; Sisters of Mercy v.	68043
Meadows; Pittman Construction Co. v.	76055
Meares v. Nixon Constructon Co.	70055
Mears Park Holding Corp. v. Morse/Diesel, Inc.	88023
Meathe v. State University Construction Fund	78053
Mechanical Constr. Corp.; Desco Vitro Glaze, Inc. v.	90016
Meco Sys. v. Dancing Bear Entertainment Inc.	97018
Medford Housing Authority; Costonis v.	61005
Medical Center, Inc.; Vece v.	62010
Medical Center of Blue Springs; W.E. Koehler Constr. Co. v.	84038
Medical Clinic Board v. Smelley	81053
Medtronic, Inc.; Oster v.	88026
Meek v. Spinney, Coady and Parker Architects, Inc.	77058
Megrath; Northwestern Marble & Tile Co. v.	13004
Meirowsky v. Phipps	68028
Melany; Miller v.	77060
Melbourne, City of; R. W. King Construction Co. v.	80053

(Matthew Bender & Co., Inc.) (Pub.435)

TABLE OF CASES

Manett, Seastrunk & Buckner v. Terminal Building Corp. 31005
Manisca v. Rakstag Assocs. 93045
Manitt Construction Corp. v. J.S. Plumbing & Heating Corp. 66054
Manke; Modern Builders, Inc. of Tacoma v. 80044
Mann v. Philip Vizzini & Son 70164
Many, Town of; Freeman v. 81027
Marathon Steel Co. v. Tilley Steel, Inc. . . 77056
Marble Falls Housing Authority v. McKinley . . . 71065
Mardan Construction Corp. v. Nyack Housing Authority, Village of 72064
Mardian Constr. Co.; Pioneer Roofing Co. v. 86055
Maricopa, County of v. Walsh & Oberg Architects, Inc. 72030
Marine Colloids, Inc. v. M.D. Hardy, Inc. . . . 81050
Mario & DiBono Plastering Co. v. Rivergate Corp. 88021
Marion Apartments, Ltd.; Eastline Corp. v. 88011
Markley v. Beagle 67044
Markus; Pittsfield, General Hospital v. . . . 69050
Markway Constr. Co. v. Kirchenbauer . . . 89032
Marmon Group, Inc.; Aghnides v. 72005
Maross Constr., Inc. v. Central N.Y. Regional Transp. Auth. 85026
Marriage of (see name of party)
Marriott Corp. v. Dasta Constr. Co. 94040
Marriott Corp.; McDevitt & Street Co. v. 89032
Marshall v. Port Auth. of Allegheny County 90029
Marshfield Housing Authority; Powell's General Contracting Co. v. 79054
Martin; Atlantic Shores Resort Joint Venture v. . . 90004
Martin v. Karsh 56005
Martin County v. R.K. Stewart & Son, Inc. 83031
Martin K. Eby; Constr. Co.; Allgood Elec. Co. v. 97001
Martin Marietta Aluminum; Action Eng'g v. 82002
Martin-Marietta Corp.; ICI America, Inc. v. 74018
Martin-Marietta Corp.; Wallace Process Piping Co. v. 65118
Martinson v. Brooks Equipment Leasing Inc. . . . 67045

Maryland Casualty Co.; American Radiator & Standard Sanitary Corp. v. 66003
Maryland Casualty Co.; Bewley Furniture Co. v. 73017
Maryland Casualty Co.; Bowman v. 28002
Maryland Casualty Co.; Central Contracting Co. v. 65021
Maryland Casualty Co.; P.R. Post Corp. v. 76058
Maryland Casualty Co.; Public Water Supply District No. 8 v. 72081
Maryland Casualty Co.; Ulster Electric Supply Co. v. 70083
Maryland Drywall Co.; W.M. Schlosser Co. v. . . . 96015
Maryland Sales & Service Corp. v. Howell 73070
Mason v. Callas Contractors, Inc. 80042
Masonry Contractors, Inc.; Wood-Hopkins Contracting Co. v. 70092
Massachusetts Bonding & Insurance Co.; Carpenter v. 65020
Massachusetts Bonding & Insurance Co.; Kinney v. 24001
Massachusetts Elec. Sys., Inc. v. R.W. Granger & Sons, Inc. 92013
Massachusetts Turnpike Authority; Charles T. Main, Inc. v. 64002
Massachusetts Turnpike Authority; Clarkeson Engineering Co. v. 64004
Massman Construction Co.; Western Union Telegraph Company v. 79071
Masterclean of North Carolina, Inc.; Saxon Constr. & Management Corp. v. 94015
Mathis v. Daines 82033
Matson, Inc. v. Lamb & Assocs. Packaging Inc. . . 97016
Matter of (see name of party)
Mautz v. J.P. Patti Co. 97017
Maxon Construction Co.; Tatar v. 73108
Maxum Found., Inc. v. Salus Corp. 85027; 87032
Maxus, Inc. v. Sciacca 92014
May v. Ralph L. Dickerson Constr. Co. . . 90030
May Constr. Co. v. Benton Sch. Dist. No. 8 95014
Mayer Paving and Asphalt Co. v. Carl A. Morse, Inc. 77057
Mayeux v. J.B. Talley Construction Co. . . 69036
Mayfair Construction Co.; Carpentersville v. . . . 81014
Mayfair Construction Co.; Roosevelt University v. 75021
Mayfair House Association, Inc.; William Passalacqua Builders, Inc. v. 81073

TABLE OF CASES

[The five-digit numbers in this table are *Citator* Case Reference Numbers, which refer to the cases in the Cases section]

Louis Lesser Enterprises, Inc.; Great American Insurance Co. v. 65044
Lovering Assoc., Inc.; Mrozik Constr. Inc. v. ... 90033
Lowe; Swenson v. 71083
Lowry Hill Constr. Co.; Kenko, Inc. v. ... 86040
Loyal Erectors, Inc. v. Hamilton & Son ... 73068
Loyal Order of Moose, Adrian Lodge 1034 v. Faulhaber 50004
Loyland v. Stone & Webster Engineering Corp. ... 73069
L.R. Foy Constr. Co. v. Dean L. Dauley & Waldrof Assocs. 82032
LSSC Corp.; Elzinga & Volkers, Inc. v. ... 94007
Lubbock, City of; L.H. Lacy Co. v. 76035; 77050
Luczak Bros., Inc. v. Generes 83028
Lueder Constr. Co. v. Lincoln Elec. Sys. ... 88020
Luhr Bros.; Prater v. 77071
Lull v. Wick Construction Co. 80041
Lumberman's Mut. Casualty Co.; Aetna Casualty & Sur. Co. v. 88001
Lumpkin; Ralph Allen, Inc. v. 77074
Lunden v. Los Angeles, County of 65070
Lundstrom Construction Co. v. Dygert ... 59002
Lurgi Corp.; Coverdill v. 86013
Luria Engineering Co. v. Aetna Casualty & Surety Co. 65071
Lutz Eng'g Co. v. Industrial Louvers, Inc. 91018
Lyell Excavating Corp. v. International Fidelity Insurance Co 76038
Lyondell Petrochemical Co.; Belmont Constructors, Inc. v. 95002
Lyons v. Krathen 79012
Lytton Savings & Loan Ass'n; Walker v. 70088

M

M. Bender & Son v. West 16th Street Realty Corp. 72066
M. DeMatteo Construction Co. v. Commonwealth 59003
M. Eisenberg & Bros.; Met Food Corp. v. 69039
M. J. Walsh & Sons; Fred. J. McClean Heating Supplies v. 65038
M. K. Steel, Inc.; Blount Brothers Corp. v. 81008
M & L Bldg. Corp. v. Housing Auth. ... 94041
M & L Land Co.; Bouten Constr. Co. v. ... 94028
M & M Glass Co.; McBro, Inc. v. ... 92014a
M & P Equip. Co.; Carroll-Boone Water Dist. v. 83006

M & W Ltd. Partnership; Frank A. Scibetta Plumbing & Heating Corp. v. 82021
M & W Masonry Construction, Inc. v. Head ... 76040
M.A. Mortenson Co.; National Hydro Sys. v. ... 93047
Mabro Construction Inc.; Clifton D. Mayhew, Inc. v. 74010
Macchia v. Liggett 79013
MacDonald Engineering Co.; Rao Electrical Equipment Co. v. 70068
MacDonald & Kruse, Inc. v. San Jose Steel Co. ... 72062
MacDonnell v. Dreyfous 19001
MacGregor Park National Bank; Lebco, Inc. v. ... 73066
Mach I Limited Partnership; McKinney Drilling Co. v. 76041
MacIntyre v. Green's Pool Service, Inc. ... 77055
Macomber v. State 67043
Macon Bibb County Water & Sewerage Auth.; C.B.I. Na-Con, Inc. v. 92004b
Macri v. United States 65072
Maddux v. Buchanan 17003
Maddy v. Castle 76039
Madeira; Clark v. 72028
Magness Corp.; Milton Schwartz & Associates v. 74022
Mahogany Run Dev. Corp.; Reed, Wible & Brown, Inc. v. 82042
Mahony-Troast Constr. Co. v. Supermarkets Gen. Corp. 83029
Maietta v. Greenvield 72063
Main v. Department of Highways 65073
Main Cornice Works, Inc. v. National Union Fire Insurance Co. 66053
Major-Gladys Drive Joint Venture; White Budd Van Ness Partnership v. 90055
Malawista; Ting-Wan Liang v. 79067
Maloney v. Oak Builders, Inc. 69035
Malott & Peterson Grundy, Inc. v. Reynolds Construction Co. 70053
Malouf Towers Rental Co.; Fairway Builders, Inc. v. 79034
Malvaney; State v. 54006
Mamaroneck, Village of; Bilotta Constr. Corp. v. 93026
Manalili v. Commercial Mowing & Grading 83030
Manchester, City of; R. Zoppo Co. v. ... 82044
Mandel v. Jordan 65074
Maness v. Fowler-Jones Construction Co. 71063

TABLE OF CASES

[The five-digit numbers in this table are *Citator* Case Reference Numbers, which refer to the cases in the Cases section]

Lenexa, City of v. C.L. Fairley Constr. Co. 89008
L'Enfant Plaza North, Inc.; Bland v. 72016
Lentin Lumber Co.; Rosemont, Village of v. ... 86068
Leo Spear Construction Co. v. Fidelity & Casualty Co. 71059
Leon C. Miles, Inc.; O'Neal Steel Co. v. ... 66067
Leonard v. People's Tobacco Warehouse Co. ... 24002
Leroy Prod., Inc.; Gordon-Maizel Constr. Co. v. 87022
Lesser v. William Holliday Cord Associates 65068
Lesser Towers, Inc. v. Roscoe-Ajax Construction Co. 69032
Lester B. Knight & Associates; Bitner v. .. 74006
Lester N. Johnson Co. v. Spokane, City of 78051
Leventhal; Metro Insulation Corp. v. 73074
Lever Bros. Co.; Howe v. 93014
Levy; Cianelli v. 70018
Levy; G. E. C. Corp. v. 72042
Lewin & Sons v. Herman 56004
Lewis v. Arboles Development Co. 70051
Lewis v. Carnaggio 71060
Lewis v. Commonwealth 54003
Lewis v. N.J. Riebe Enters., Inc. 92011
Lewis-Brady Builders Supply, Inc. v. Bedros ... 77054
Lewis, Inc.; Delhi Pipeline Corp. v. 66021
L.H. Lacy Co. v. Lubbock, City of . 76035; 77050
L. Harvey Concrete, Inc. v. Agro Constr. & Supply Co. 97015
Liberty Mutual Insurance Co.; Wittenberg Engineering & Construction Co. v. 65122
License of (see name of party)
Lichter v. Mellon-Stuart Co. 61009
Licon Associates, Inc.; American Airlines, Inc. v. 77003
Liggett; Macchia v. 79013
Limbach Co. v. George B. H. Macomber Co. ... 70052
Lincoln County v. Skinner 73067
Lincoln Elec. Sys.; Lueder Constr. Co. v. 88020
Lincoln-Sudbury Regional School District v. Brandt-Jordan Corp. 69033
Lincoln-Sudbury Regional School District v. Frasca Construction Corp. 68026
Lindbrook Construction, Inc. v. Mukilteo School District No. 6 69034
Lindon City v. Engineers Construction Co. 81047

Lindsay v. Gibbons & Reed 72061
Lindsey; Roland v. 12002
Link Builders, Inc.; A.E. Investment Corp. v. ... 74001
Linton Co. v. Robert Reid Engineers, Inc. 81048
Lippert Bros.; J. T. Majors & Son v. 58004
Lippert Brothers v. National Union Fire Insurance Co. 65069
Lipschultz; Strom v. 72097
Lisbon; A. Dubreuil & Sons, Inc. v. 90001
Litton Bionetics, Inc. v. Glen Construction Co. ... 81049
L.K. Comstock & Co. v. Morse/UBM Joint Venture 87030
L.K. Comstock & Co. v. United Eng'g & Constructors, Inc. 89031
Lloyd's Underwriters v. Craig & Rush, Inc. 94012
Loberg Plumbing & Heating Co.; Independent School District No. 877 v. 63003
Locklear v. Payne 71062
Loden & Co.; Batson-Cook Co. v. 73012
Logan v. Aetna Casualty & Surety Co. ... 68027
Logansport, City of; Jones v. 82028
Loitz Bros. Constr. Co.; Westville, Village of v. 88039
Lombard Co.; Illinois ex rel. Skinner v. ... 82025
Londonderry School Dist.; Salem Eng'g & Constr. Corp. v. 82045
Long; Hartford Accident & Indemnity Co. v. ... 68017
Long; Lazer Constr. Co. v. 88019
Long; Reynolds v. 67058
Long Branch Sewerage Authority v. Molnar Electrical Contractors, Inc. 76037
Long Island Lighting Co. v. IMO Delaval, Inc. .. 87031
Loranger; New England Structures, Inc. v. 68033
Lord & Son Constr., Inc. v. Roberts Elec. Contractors, Inc. 93044
Los Angeles, City of; Warner Construction Corp. v. 70094
Los Angeles County Flood Control District; Weeshoff Construction Co. v. 79018
Los Angeles, County of; Argo Construction Co. v. 69004
Los Angeles, County of; Lunden v. ... 65070
Los Angeles Jewish Community Council; Frank T. Hickey, Inc. v. 54001
Lott Constructors, Inc. v. Jackson Township Bd. of Educ. 92012

TABLE OF CASES

[The five-digit numbers in this table are Citator *Case Reference Numbers, which refer to the cases in the Cases section]*

L & S Construction Co.; Charles Burton Builders, Inc. v. 70016
L. W. Moses Co.; Dravo Corp. v. 71033
La Salle Iron Works, Inc. v. Largen 66049
La Salle National Bank; Illinois Valley Asphalt, Inc. v. 77046
La Vale Plaza, Inc. v. R. S. Noonan 67039
L.A. Wenger Contracting Co. v. State University Construction Fund 72058
L.A. Wenger Contracting Co. v. Temple Emanu-El 66050
Labor Discount Center, Inc.; H.B. Deal Construction Co. v. 67029
Laconco, Inc.; State v. 83041
LaCuisine Restaurant, Inc.; Tayco Constr. Co. v. 92019
Lafayette; Aetna Casualty & Surety Co. v. 72004
Lafayette Iron Works v. Wilaka Constructon Co. 65064
Lagerstrom v. Beers Construction Co. ... 81046
Laguna Vista Corp.; Fletcher v. 73043
Laird; Standard Accident Insurance Co. v. 35003
Lake County Public Building Commission; Corbetta Construction Co. of Illinois v. 78019
Lake Patagonia Recreation Association; New Pueblo Constructors, Inc. v. 70058
Lake Plumbing, Inc. v. Seabreeze Constr. Corp. ... 86041
Lakeridge Development Co.; Meyers v. ... 77059
Lakeshore Plaza Enterprises, Inc.; Benning Construction Co. v. 78010
Lamb; Shell Chemical Co. v. 73099
Lamb & Assocs. Packaging Inc.; Matson, Inc. v. 97016
Lamb Construction Co.; State Surety Co. v. 81067
Lampson Universal Rigging, Inc. v. Washington Pub. Power Supply·Sys. 86042
Landis Constr. Co.; Walters v. 88041
Landis Construction Co. v. Health Education Authority 78049
Landmark Associates; Diomar v. 80020
Land's End Hous. Co.; Groves v. 93039
Lane Construction Corp. v. Vermont 70049
Lange v. Blake 77051
Langford; Yearwood and Johnson Architects, Inc. v. 79073
Langhart; Kovacheff v. 61008
Langley v. Helms 71058
Lano v. Osberg Construction Co. 65066
LaPuzza v. Prom Town House Motor Inn, Inc. ... 74021

Largen; La Salle Iron Works, Inc. v. 66049
Larry Walter, Inc.; Elmira, City of v. ... 77019; 90010
Larsen v. J. I. Case Co. 68025
Lasar v. Bechtel Power Corp. 86043
Lascola; Burdette v. 78013
Lasker-Goldman Corp.; Ferrante Equipment Co. v. 70025
Latham; T.A. Loving Co. v. 74039
Laughlin Recreational Enters., Inc. v. Zab Dev. Co. 82031
Laura Roofing & Renovating Co. v. Board of Education of the City of New York 77052
Laurence L. Lambert & Assocs.; S.K. Whitty & Co. v. 91032
Lavastone Industries of Central Texas, Inc.; Denta Rama, Inc. v. 80019
Lawrence Bros.; J.A. Jones Construction Co. v. ... 66043
Lawrence, City of v. Flazarano 80076
Lawrence-Lynch Corp. v. Department of Environmental Management 84024
Lawson-Avila Constr.; Webb v. 95049
Lawter Chemicals, Inc.; Fields v. 69018
Lawton v. Cain 65067
Layrite Concrete Products, Inc. v. H. Halvorsen, Inc. 66051
Lazenby; Nieman-Irving & Co. v. 33003
Lazer Constr. Co. v. Long 88019
L.B. Foster Co. v. Melbras-Manco, Inc. .. 70050
L.D.A., Inc. v. Cross 81045
Le Blanc, Inc. v. Gulf Bitulithic Co. 67040
Le Chase Construction Corp. v. Rochester, City of 72060
Leatherby Insurance Co. v. Tustin, City of 77053
Lebco, Inc. v. MacGregor Park National Bank ... 73066
Lebreton v. Brown 72059
Ledgewood, Inc.; F.O. Bailey Co. v. 92006
Lee v. Allied Chemical Corp. 76036
Lee Sing; Saiki v. 23002
Legal & Gen. Assurance Soc'y, Ltd.; Richmond Steel, Inc. v. 93050
Legette v. Pittman 66052
Lehigh Electric Products Co. v. Pennsylvania National Mutual Casualty Insurance Co. 78050
Leineke; Muth v. 70057
Leitao v. Damon G. Douglas Co. 97014
Leivenstein; Kustom Kraft Homes v. 71057
Leland E. Burns, Inc.; Hillman v. 89021
Len Immke Buick, Inc. v. Architectural Alliance 92010b
Lenahan; Ken Carver & Sons v. 63004

TABLE OF CASES

[The five-digit numbers in this table are *Citator* Case Reference Numbers, which refer to the cases in the Cases section]

Kent; Jacob & Youngs v. 21002
Kent Sch. Dist. No. 415; Absher Constr. Co. v. . . 95001
Kenwick; Brennan v. 81009
Kenworth Northwest Sales & Service, Inc. v. Batts 70047
Kenworthy v. State 65062
Kerelis; Ramonas v. 68036
Kessel/Duff Construction Corp.; Sehlbert Mechanical Corp. v. 80060
Kettelhut Constr., Inc.; Harris v. 84015
Keystone Engineering Corp. v. Sutter . . . 51002
Kiewit v. Constr. Co.; Collins v. 96021
Kilianek v. Kim 89030
Kim; Kilianek v. 89030
Kimberly-Clark Corp.; Daugherty Co. v. . . 71031
King; Comptroller of Virginia ex rel. Virginia Military Institute v. 77022
King v. Midas Realty Corp. 92010a
King Brothers Building Contractors, Inc. v. McCullen 80040
King, County of; Thorgaard Plumbing & Heating Co. v. 67065
King Enters., In re 82026
Kingery Construction Co. v. Board of Regents 73063
Kingsbrook Jewish Medical Center v. Katz 71055
Kinney v. G.W. Lisk Co. 90028
Kinney v. Massachusetts Bonding & Insurance Co. 24001
Kinsey v. Farmland Indus. Inc. 94039
Kinstler; Rackers & Backlesse, Inc. v. . . . 73090
Kiona; Hurley v. 23001
Kirchenbauer; Markway Constr. Co. v. . . . 89032
Kirk Reid Co. v. Fine 65063
Kirkham, Chaon & Kirkham, Inc.; Consolidated Electrical Distributors, Inc. v. 71024
Kirpatovsky; G & N Construction Co. v. . . 66119
Kirsch v. Dondlinger & Sons Construction Co. . . 71056
Kisly; Sullivan v. 83043
Kitsmiller Constr. Co.; Silver Dollar City, Inc. v. 94017
Kittyhawk Landing Apartments III v. Anglin Constr. Co. 87029
K.L. House Construction Co. v. Albuquerque, City of 78044
Klar v. Park Construction Co. 68023
Kleb v. Wendling 79010
Kleeman v. Fragman Construction Co. . . . 81044
Kline; General State Authority v. 77038
Klinger-Holtz v. Sulzbach Construction Co. 78046

Knickerbocker Construction Co.; E. O. Dorsch Electric Co. v. 67023
Knickerbocker Roofing & Paving Co. v. Mendius Associates 68024
Knight; Northern Montana Hosp. v. 91024
Knight Brothers v. State 72055
Knightsbridge Dev. Co.; McMerit Constr. Co. v. 88022
Knutson v. Metallic Slab Form Co. 42001
Kober Construction; Stepanek v. 81068
Kobus v. Formfit Co. 66048
Koch v. Construction Technology, Inc. . . . 96033
Kolea; Barrack v. 94024
Koppers Co.; E.C. Ernst, Inc. v. 80022a
Korte Constr. Co. v. Deaconess Manor Ass'n. . . . 95034
Kosmerl v. Barbor 79011
Kostohryz v. McGuire 73064
Kovacheff v. Langhart 61008
Kovatch; Wasserstein v. 93019
Krass Plus Clothiers, Inc. v. Church's Fried Chicken 93043
Krathen; Lyons v. 79012
Kraus-Anderson Constr. Co.; Stillwater Leased Housing Assocs. v. 82049
Krieger v. J. E. Greiner Co. 78047
Krieger; Minidoka County v. 65077
Krohn; Fireman's Fund Ins. Co. v. 93010
Krupp Asset Management Corp.; Haden v. 91013
Kubby v. Crescent Steel 70048
Kubela v. Schuessler Lumber Co. 73065
Kucharo Construction Co.; Berg v. 46001
Kuhne; Hirsch v. 63002
Kupper Assocs.; Bradford v. 95025
Kurfiss v. Cowherd 38002
Kurz v. Quincy Post No. 37, American Legion . . 72056
Kurz; Rosenthal v. 74033
Kustom Kraft Homes v. Leivenstein 71057
Kvistad; Jones v. 71054
Kwan Doo Park; Izumi v. 60009

L

L. A. Swyer Co. v. John W. Cowper Co. 76034
L & B Constr. Co. v. Ragan Enter., Inc. . . 97013
L & E Co. v. United States 65065
L. H. Sowles Co.; Ismil v. 72051
L. L. Glascock, Inc.; Citizens National Bank v. . . 71021
L. M. White Contructing Co. v. St. Joseph Structural Steel Co. 71061

TABLE OF CASES

[The five-digit numbers in this table are *Citator* Case Reference Numbers, which refer to the cases in the Cases section]

Joseph F. Egan, Inc. v. New York, City of 66047
Joseph F. Hughes & Co. v. George H. Robinson Corp. 70042
Joseph F. Trionfo & Sons, Inc. v. Board of Education 79009
Joseph F. Trionfo & Sons, Inc. v. Ernest B. LaRosa & Sons, Inc. 78043
Joseph J. Legat Architects, P.C. v. United States Dev. Corp. 85024
Joseph L. Muscarelle, Inc.; Ukrainian National Urban Renewal Corp. v. 77081
J.P. Greathouse Steel Erectors, Inc. v. Blount Brothers Construction Co. 67037
J.P. Patti Co.; Mautz v. 97017
J.R. Gallagher Constr. Co. v. Moyers Corners Fire Dept., Inc. 84007
J.R. Graham & Son, Inc. v. Randolph County Board of Education 75013
J.S. Alberici Constr. Co.; Herington v. . . . 94036, 95026
J.S. Plumbing & Heating Corp.; Manitt Construction Corp. v. 66054
J.T. Constr. Co.; Foster, Henry, Henry & Thorpe, Inc. v. 91010
Judd Constr. Co. v. Evans Joint Venture . . 82029
Julien Construction Co.; Quin Blair Enterprises, Inc. v. 79056
Julius B. Nelson & Sons; Rausch v. 67057
Junior College District No. 529; R & R Construction Co. v. 77073
Juno Construction Corp.; Burke County Public Schools Board of Education v. 81010
Juno Indus., Inc. v. Heery Int'l 94038
J.V.B. Indus., Inc.; Federated Dept. Stores, Inc. v. 90019
J.W. Cook & Sons; Top Line Constr. Co. v. 95022
J.W. Creech, Inc. v. Norfolk Air Conditioning Corp. 89029

K

K-C Air Conditioning Serv., Inc.; McDevitt & St. Co. v. 92015
K-Mart Corp.; Whalen v. 88043
Kaelber, In re 53003
Kahn; Davies v. 58002
Kahn v. Prahl 67038
Kaiser v. Cyon Metal Products, Inc. 70044
Kaiser Aluminum & Chemical Co. v. Finrow Painting Co. 73062
Kaiser Eng'rs, Inc. v. Grinnell Fire Protection Sys. Co. 85025
Kaiser Jamaica Corp.; Carpenter International, Inc. v. 74008
Kajima Int'l, Inc.; Willoughby Roofing & Supply Co. v. 84040
Kalich-Jarcho, Inc. v. New York, City of 83027
Kalish-Jarcho, Inc.; New York, City of v. 90011
Kalwall Corp. v. D. Capolino Design & Renovation 76033
Kandik Constr., Inc.; Fairbanks North Star Borough v. 86022
Kansas Power & Light Co.; Green Constr. Co. v. 89019; 93037
Karavas; Montgomery v. 41003
Karnatz v. Murphy Pacific Corp. 72052
Karsh; Martin v. 56005
Kaspar v. Clinton-Jackson Corp. 69031
Katie Franks, Inc.; Winn-Senter Constr. v. 91038
Katz; Kingsbrook Jewish Medical Center v. 71055
Katzner v. Kelleher Constr. 96008
Kauhi; Gregg Kendall & Associates v. . . . 71044
Kavanaugh; Keck v. 20003
Kay-Locke, Inc.; Jeremiah Sullivan & Sons v. 84021
KBA Constr. Managers, Inc.; Waterwiese v. 91036a
Keating; Aronson v. 80004
Keating v. Miller 74020
Keck v. Kavanaugh 20003
Kecko Piping Co. v. Monroe, Town of . . 77049
Keefe v. Balling Construction, Inc. 72053
Keefe; Wilson v. 57004
Keel v. Titan Constr. Corp. 86039
Keith v. Burzynski 80039
Keith Adams & Associates v. Edwards . . 70045
Kelleher Constr.; Katzner v. 96008
Keller Construction Co.; Baker v. 69006
Kellogg v. Pizza Oven, Inc. 65060
Kelly v. Dimeo, Inc. 91017
Kelly v. Northwest Community Hospital . . 78045
Kelso-Burnett Co. v. Zeus Dev. Corp. . . . 82030
Kemp v. Bechtel Constr. Co. 86038
Kemp; J.A. Tobin Constr. Co. v. 86035
Kemp Smith Co.; Aetna Casualty & Surety Co. v. 65002
Ken Carver & Sons v. Lenahan 63004
Kenison v. Baldwin 60010
Kenko, Inc. v. Lowry Hill Constr. Co. . . . 86040
Kenneth E. Curran, Inc. v. State 65061
Kenney Construction Co. v. Metropolitan Sanitary District 72054; 74044

TABLE OF CASES

[The five-digit numbers in this table are *Citator* Case Reference Numbers, which refer to the cases in the Cases section]

J.F. Inc. v. Vicik 81041
J.F. White Engineering Corp. v. General Insurance Co. 65058
J.G. Watts Construction Co. v. United States . . . 66044
JGA Constr. Corp. v. Burns Elec. Co. . . . 88018
J.H. Hiser Constr. Co.; Jones v. 84023
J.H. Jenkins Contractor, Inc. v. Denham Springs, City of 68021
Jim Carlson Constr., Inc. v. Bailey 89026
Jim Cullen, Inc.; Peabody Seating Co. v. . . 72076
Jim Mahoney, Inc. v. Galokee Corp. 74019
Jim W. Miller Constr., Inc.; David Co. v. 88009; 89010
J.J. Black & Co.; Atlanta, City of v. 64003
J.J. Wuellner & Sons; Olin Mathieson Chemical Corp. v. 66066
J.L. Williams & Co.; Howard P. Foley Co. v. . . . 80033
J.M. Beeson Co. v. Sartori 89027
J.M. Humphries Constr. Co.; APAC-Tennessee, Inc. v. 86002
J.M. Weller Assocs., Inc.; Charlebois v. . . 88004
J.O. Hooker & Sons, Inc. v. Roberts Cabinet Co. 96032
Joba Constr. Co. v. Monroe County Drain Comm'r 86036
Joe Adams & Son v. McCann Construction Co. . . . 71052
Joe Adams & Son; McCann Construction Co. v. 70054
Joe Kleim Bldrs., Inc.; Diersen v. 87015
John v. Bovee 78041
John A. Robbins Co. v. Airportels, Inc. . . 65059
John D. Ahern Co. v. Trustees of Boston University 81042
John E. Branagh & Sons v. Witcosky . . . 66045
John E. Fisher Constr. Co. v. Onondaga, Town of 85022
John F. Beasley Construction Co.; Jackson v. . . . 66041
John F. Harkins Co.; TWC Holdings, Inc. v. . . . 86037
John F. Harkins Co. v. Waldinger Corp. . . 86037
John Goffredo & Sons, Inc. v. S.M.G. Corp. . . . 82027
John Graham & Co.; Detweiler Bros., Inc. v. . . . 76017
John J. Calnan Co.; Paschen Contractors, Inc. v. 73088
John Johnson Concrete Gutter Co. v. American Empire Insurance Co. 81043
John K. Ruff, Inc.; Baltimore County v. . . 77010
John Price Associates v. Davis 78040
John W. Cowper Co. v. Buffalo Hotel Dev. Venture 85023
John W. Cowper Co.; L. A. Swyer Co. v. 76034
John W. Johnson, Inc. v. Basic Construction Co. 70041
John W. Johnson, Inc. v. J.A. Jones Construction Co. 73058
John W. Johnson, Inc. v. 2500 Wisconsin Avenue 56003
Johnson v. Darin & Armstrong, Inc. 66046
Johnson; Erskine v. 002
Johnson v. E.V. Cox Construction Co. . . . 80038
Johnson v. Norcross Bros. 11001
Johnson; State v. 68048
Johnson Acoustics, Inc. v. P.J. Carlin Construction Co. 71053
Johnson Constr. Co.; Atlee Electric Co. v. 73009
Johnson Constr., Inc. v. Rugby Mun. Airport Auth. 92009b
Johnson Controls, Inc. v. Cedar Rapids, Iowa, City of 83026
Johnson County v. R.N. Rouse & Co. . . . 92010
Johnson Electric Co. v. Columbia Casualty Co. 31004
Johnson Electric, Inc.; Air Heaters, Inc. v. 77001
Johnson & Johnson; Miley v. 96035
Johson v. Iowa Rice Dryer Inc. 69030
Joint Highway Dist. No 13; Six Companies of California v. 40003
Joint School District No. 3; Wiggens Construction Co. v. 67072
Joliet, City of v. Fennewald 72024
Jones v. Continental Casualty Co. 73059
Jones v. J.H. Hiser Constr. Co. 84023
Jones v. Kvistad 71054
Jones v. Logansport, City of 82028
Jones; Motorists Mutual Insurance Co. v. 66059
Jones; Roscoe v. 90038
Jones v. Spindel 73060
Jones; Thomas Haverty Co. v. 21003
Jones v. Vappi Co. 89028
Jones v. W. L. Cobb Construction Co. . . 79047
Joray Mason Contractors, Inc. v. Four J's Construction Corp. 78042
Jordan; Bebb v. 20001
Jordan; Mandel v. 65074
Jordan, Village of v. Memphis Constr. Co. 85043
Joseph Davis, Inc. v. Merritt-Chapman & Scott Corp. 67036

TABLE OF CASES

TC–33

[The five-digit numbers in this table are *Citator* Case Reference Numbers, which refer to the cases in the Cases section]

J. & J. Building & Maintenance Contractors, Inc.; Union Building Corp. v. 79017
J. & J. Electric, Inc. v. Gilbert H. Moen Co. ... 73056
J. J. Fritch, General Contractor, Inc.; Chambless v. 60002
J & K Cement Constr. v. Montalbano Bldrs. 83025
J. L. Henson, Inc.; Safeco Insurance Co. of America v. 80058
J. P. Cullen & Son; McCarthy v. 72067
J. R. Meade & Co. v. Barrett & Co. 70043
J. S. & H. Construction Co. v. Richmond County Hospital Authority 73061
J. T. Majors & Son v. Lippert Bros. 58004
J.A. Jones Constr. Co. v. Dover, City of .. 77048
J.A. Jones Constr. Co.; Dozier v. 84009
J.A. Jones Constr. Co.; Fidelity & Casualty Co. v. 63001
J.A. Jones Constr. Co. v. Greenbriar Shopping Center 71051
J.A. Jones Construction Co.; John W. Johnson, Inc. v. 73058
J.A. Jones Construction Co. v. Lawrence Bros. ... 66043
J.A. Moore Constr. Co. v. Sussex Assoc. Ltd. Partnership 88017
J.A. Sullivan Corp. v. Commonwealth ... 86034
J.A. Tobin Constr. Co. v. Kemp 86035
J.A. Tobin Constr. Co.; Southwestern Bell Telephone Co. v. 76067
Jacka v. Ouachita Parish School Board .. 66040
Jackson; Eller & Heyward, Inc. v. 68013
Jackson v. John F. Beasley Construction Co. ... 66041
Jackson; Orto v. 80049
Jackson v. Sam Finley, Inc. 66042
Jackson Township Bd. of Educ.; Lott Constructors, Inc. v. 92012
Jacksonville Port Authority v. Parkhill-Goodloe Co. 78039
Jacksonville State University; United States Fidelity & Guaranty Co. v. 78074
Jacob & Youngs v. Kent 21002
Jacobs v. Northeastern Corp. 65055
Jacobsen Constr. Co. v. Blaine Constr. Co. ... 93042
Jacobson Construction Co.; Zion's Cooperative Mercantile Institute v. 71088
Jacques; City School District v. 79028
Jaeger v. Henningson, Durham & Richardson, Inc. 83023
J'Aire Corp. v. Gregory 79045

James F. O'Neil Co.; United States Fidelity & Guaranty Co. v. 66109
James I. Barnes Construction Co.; St. Paul Fire & Marine Insurance Co. v. 68041
James I. Barnes Construction Co. v. Washington Township 62005
James Julian, Inc. v. President of Elkton .. 65056
James M. Barker Co.; Henson v. 90025
James M. Barker, Inc.; Saint Augustine Pools Inc. v. 97021
James M. Canfield Contracting Co.; Town & Country Bank of Springfield v. 77079
James McHugh Construction Co.; Hanley v. 71046
James River-Pennington, Inc.; Blout Int'l, Ltd. v. 93004
James Stewart Polshek & Associates v. Bergen County Iron Works 75032
Jandrisits v. Village of River Grove 96031
Jarman Memorial Hospital Building Fund; Harrison F. Blades, Inc. v. 69025
Jarmon; Torres v. 73111
Jasper Construction, Inc. v. Foothill Junior College 79046
Javernick v. Smith 80036
Jay Realty Co.; Rapp Constr. Co. v. 91027
J.B. Sheet Metal, Inc.; Healey v. 95013
J.B. Talley Construction Co.; Mayeux v. .. 69036
J.B.L. Construction Co.; Salem Building Supply Co. v. 80059
J.C. Boespflug Construction Co.; Paduano v. ... 65084
J.C. Penney Co. v. Davis & Davis, Inc. .. 81040
J.D. Hedin Construction Co. v. United States ... 65057
J.E. Hathman, Inc. v. Alpha Epsilon Club 73057
Jefferson, City of; Cure v. 65029
Jefferson, County of v. Barton-Douglas Contractors, Inc. 79030
Jefferson Parish School Board; Bartley, Inc. v. .. 74003
Jelac Corp.; Aetna Casualty & Surety Co. v. ... 87001
Jen-Mar Construction Co. v. Brown 67035
Jeremiah Sullivan & Sons v. Kay-Locke, Inc. ... 84021
Jespersen; Thompson v. 90046
Jetty, Inc. v. Hall-McGuff Architects 80037
Jewish Bd. of Guardians v. Grumman Allied Indus., Inc. 83024
J.F. Barton Contracting Co.; Brookhaven Landscape & Grading Co. v. 82008
J.F., Inc. v. S.M. Wilson & Co. 87028

(Matthew Bender & Co., Inc.) (Pub.435)

TABLE OF CASES

[The five-digit numbers in this table are *Citator* Case Reference Numbers, which refer to the cases in the Cases section]

Ida Grove Roofing & Improvements, Inc. v. Storm Lake, City of 85020
Idaho State University v. Mitchell 76030
I.D.C., Inc. v. McCain-Winkler Partnership 81038
Ideal Engineering, Inc.; South Texas Building Co. v. 66090
Illinois Building Authority; A. H. Sollinger Construction Co. v. 72006
Illinois ex rel. Skinner v. Lombard Co. .. 82025
Illinois Valley Asphalt, Inc. v. La Salle National Bank 77046
IMO Delaval, Inc.; Long Island Lighting Co. v. .. 87031
Implement Dealers Mutual Insurance Co.; Reishus v. 62006
In re (see name of party)
Independence Bank v. Erin Mechanical .. 88016
Independence Indemnity Co.; Noonan v. .. 31006
Independent Consolidated School District No. 24 v. Carlstrom 67033
Independent School District No. 877 v. Loberg Plumbing & Heating Co 63003
Independent School District No. 35 v. A. Hedenberg & Co. 43002
Indian River Colony Club v. Schopke Constr. & Eng'g, Inc. 92009
Indian State Highway Commission v. Thomas 76031
Indiana Ins. Co. v. Erlich 94011
Indiana & Michigan Elec. Co. v. Terre Haute Indus., Inc. 87027
Industrial Electric Co.; Metal Service Corp. v. 70056
Industrial Financial Corp.; Wickes Corp. v. 74043
Industrial Indem. Co. v. Wick Constr. Co. 84020
Industrial Louvers, Inc.; Lutz Eng'g Co. v. 91018
Industrial Risk Insurers v Garlock Equip. Co. 91016
Ingram & Greene, Inc.; Delta Elec., Inc. v. 86015
Insurance Co. of North America; Bogner-Seitel Lumber Co. v. 68005
Insurance Co. of North America; Copeland Sand and Gravel, Inc. v. 80017
Insurance Co. of North America; Fowler v. 80026
Insurance Co. of North America; Taber Partners I v. 95020
Insurance Co. of North America; Timberline Electric Supply Corp. v. 80066

Insurance Guaranty Assoc.; H & H Sewer Systems, Inc. v. 81032
Integrated, Inc. v. Alex Fergusson Electrical Contractors 67034
International Builders of Florida, Inc.; Fred McGilvray, Inc. v. 78030
International Erectors v. Wilhoit Steel Erectors & Rental Service 68020
International Fidelity Ins. Co.; Henderson Inv. Corp. v. 91015
International Fidelity Ins. Co; Lyell Excavating Corp. v. 76038
International Fidelity Ins. Co.; Walsh v. .. 67068
International Paper Co. v. Corporex Constructors, Inc. 89025
Interstate Contractors Supply Co.; Department of Transp. v. 90015
Interstate Lumber Co. v. Western Mortgage & Warranty Title Co. 15004
Intra-State, Inc.; Nimke v. 70059
Investment Building Corp.; Morris J. Liebergott & Associate v. 68032
Inwood Construction Co. v. Huntington Corp. ... 65054
Iowa Rice Dryer Inc.; Johson v. 69030
Iowa Southern Utilities Co.; Peter Kiewit Sons' Co. v. 73089
Ironbound Fin. Servs. v. Certified Contracting, Inc. 97012
Irving Coven Construction, Inc.; Pioneer Acceptance Corp. v. 76054
Island on Lake Travis, Ltd. v. Hayman Co. Gen. Contractors, Inc. 92009a
Island Steel Erectors, Inc.; Gilbert H. Moen Co. v. 96007
Island Villa Developers, Inc. v. Bonner Roofing & Sheet Metal Co. 85021
Ismil v. L. H. Sowles Co. 72051
Israel; TDE, Ltd. v. 89044
Ivanov v. Process Design Assocs. 93015a
Izumi v. Kwan Doo Park 60009

J

J. A. Bridges & Rustproofing, Inc.; Darrell T. Stuart Contractor v. 65031
J. A. Thompson & Son v. Hawaii 70039
J. Brodie & Son v. George A. Fuller Co. 69029
J. Dunn & Sons v. Paragon Homes 70040
J. E. Brenneman Co.; Waller v. 73119
J. E. Greiner Co.; Krieger v. 78047
J. I. Case Co.; Larsen v. 68025
J.I. Case Co., A.I.A. Citator; Relying on Larsen v. 95045

TABLE OF CASES

TC-31

[The five-digit numbers in this table are *Citator* Case Reference Numbers, which refer to the cases in the Cases section]

Horowitz Bros.; Robert Chuckrow Construction Co. v. 68037
Horrocks Eng'rs, Inc.; Peck v. 97020
Hortman v. Becker Construction Co. 79044
Hortman v. Otis Erecting Co. 82023
Horton Indus., Inc. v. Moweaqua, Village of ... 86033
Hot Springs, City of v. Gunderson's Inc. ... 82012
Hotz Corp.; Carabetta Builders, Inc. v. ... 93006
Houdaille Industries v. United Bonding Insurance Co. 72049
Houma, L.A. v. Municipal & Indus. Pipe Serv., Inc. 89022
Housing Authority; Blount Construction Co. v. ... 65016
Housing Authority; Creswell v. 71029
Housing Autority; M & L Bldg. Corp. v. ... 94041
Housing Authority; Southern Construction Co. v. 67062
Housing Authority of the City of Texarkana v. E. W. Johnson Construction Co. 78038
Housing Vermont v. Goldsmith & Morris 96030
Houston, City of; Derr Constr. Co. v. ... 92004f
Howard; Harris County v. 73048
Howard v. Harvard Congregational Soc. ... 16002
Howard Corp.; Bond v. 95003
Howard-Green Electrical Co. v. Chaney & James Construction Co. 71050
Howard J. White, Inc. v. Varian Associates 60008
Howard, Needles, Tammen & Bergendoff v. Steers, Perini & Pomeroy 73055
Howard P. Foley Co. v. J.L. Williams & Co. ... 80033
Howard Polinger; A & A Masonry Contractors, Inc. v. 70003
Howe v. Lever Bros. Co. 93014
Howell; Maryland Sales & Service Corp. v. ... 73070
H.P. Hood, Inc.; Speers v. 86063
H.R.H. Constr. Corp.; Trump-Equitable Fifth Ave. Co. v. 85038
HRH Construction Corp. v. Bethlehem Steel Corp. 78035
H.R.H. Prince Ltc. Faisal M. Saud v. Batson-Cook Co. 82024
Hub Electric Co. v. Aetna Casualty & Surety Co. 75012
Huber Constr. Co.; Cuhaci & Peterson Architects, Inc. v. 87013
Huber, Hunt & Nichols; Moore Heating & Plumbing, Inc. v. 91023

Huber, Hunt & Nichols, Inc. v. Moore ... 77044
Huber, Hunt & Nichols, Inc.; Perryman v. 94014
Hubert v. Aitken 003
Huckabay Hospital, Inc.; Moossy v. 73080
Hudson; Harrigan & Reid Co. v. 39004
Hudson & Manhatten Corp.; Sullivan & Cromwell v. 71081
Huer, Johns, Neel, Rivers & Webb; Hanna v. ... 83020
Huggins v. Atlanta Tile & Marble Co. ... 58003
Hugh Stubbins & Associates; Second Congregation Society v. 68042
Hughes Masonry Co. v. Greater Clark County School Building Corp. 81037
Humbert Excavating, Inc. v. Pendleton, City of .. 93015
Hummonds; Erhart v. 60006
Hunkin-Conkey Construction Co.; Brooks Towers Corp. v. 72019
Hunkin-Conkey Construction Co. v. Dunkirk, City of 72050
Hunt v. Bankers & Shippers Insurance Co. of New York 77045; 80034
Hunt v. Ellisor & Tanner, Inc. 87026
Hunt v. Owen Building & Investment Co. 20002
Hunt & Willett, Inc. v. United States ... 65053
Huntington Beach, City of; E. L. White, Inc. v. .. 78028
Huntington Corp.; Inwood Construction Co. v. .. 65054
Huntington Woods v. Ajax Paving Indus., Inc. .. 89023; 92008d
Hurlburt v. Northern States Power Co. ... 94037
Hurlen Constr.; Gall Landau Young Constr. Co. v. 85016
Hurley v. Fox 90027
Hurley v. Kiona 23001
Hurst; New York Indemnity Co. v. 33002
Husar Indus., Inc. v. A.L. Huber & Sons, Inc. ... 84018
Hussey, Gay, Bell & DeYoung Int'l, Inc.; Yow v. ... 91040
Huxol v. Nickell 70036
H.W. Nelson Co.; Grand Trunk Western Railroad v. 41001
Hyatt Cheek Builders-Engineers Co. v. Board of Regents of University of Texas 80035

I

I. T. E.; Crane v. 71027
ICI America, Inc. v. Martin-Marietta Corp. 74018

TABLE OF CASES

[The five-digit numbers in this table are *Citator* Case Reference Numbers, which refer to the cases in the Cases section]

Hercules Constr. Co.; Shell Oil Co. v. . . . 66087
Herington v. J.S. Alberici Constr. Co. . . . 94036, 95026
Herman; Lewin & Sons v. 56004
Herman Christensen & Sons, Inc. v. Paris Plastering Co. 76029
Herre Bros. v. Rhoads 66034
Hersey Gravel Co. v. State 43001
Hershey Foods Corp. v. General Elec. Serv. Co. 92008a
Herson v. New Boston Garden Corp. . . . 96029
Herter v. Ringland 92008b
Hess v. Zoological Soc'y of Buffalo, Inc. 87023
Hess-Martin Corp.; O. K. Johnson Electric, Inc. v. 70061
Hetherington Letter Co. v. O.F. Paulson Construction Co. 69027
Hewitt Contracting Co.; State Highway Department v. 66093
Heyman; Harry Skolnick & Sons v. 86029
H.F. Campbell Co.; Gavlik Construction Co. v. . . 75010
Hibbler v. Ockerlund Constr. Co. 85019
Hicks; Mingledorff's, Inc. v. 74023
Higgens; Connell v. 15002
Highland Painting Service; Green Manor Construction Co. v. 65045
Higley South, Inc. v. Park Shore Dev. Co. 86031
Hill v. George A. Fuller Co. 73054
Hill Aero, Inc.; Reeves v. 89038
Hillcrest Country Club v. N.D. Judds Co. 90026
Hilliard & Bartko Joint Venture v. Fedco Sys., Inc. 87024
Hillman v. Leland E. Burns, Inc. 89021
Hillsborough County Aviation Authority v. Cone Brothers Contracting Co. 73053
Hilro Constr. Co.; U.S. Insulation, Inc. v. 85041
Himbele v. New York 81036
Himmel Corp. v. Stade 77042
Hines v. Farr 60007
Hirsch v. Kuhne 63002
Hirsch & Stevens, Inc.; Vonasek v. 74042
Hite v. Aydlett 26002
H.J. Williams Corp.; Rockland Bleach & Dye Works Co. v. 66084
Hjelle; Nelson Paving Co. v. 73083
H.L.C. & Associates Construction Co. v. United States 66035
Hobbs v. Scorse 77043

Hobson Construction Co. v. Holiday Inns, Inc. . . . 72047
Hochwalt v. Rosser 70035
Hochwalt; Rosser v. 67059
Hodson; Mississippi Meadows, Inc. v. 73076
Hoerner Woldorf Corp. v. Bumstead-Woolford Co. 72048
Hoff; Nilsen, State ex rel. v. 70077
Hoffman; Duff v. 69016
Hoffman v. Glock 74017
Hoffman; Spencer v. 80062
Hoffman Plastering Co.; Benton v. 62002
Hol-Gar Manufacturing Corp. v. United States . . . 65050; 66037
Holdam v. Middlesex Supply, Inc. 66036
Holden Construction Co.; Poughkeepsie v. 79053
Holder Construction Co. v. Ed Smith & Sons . . . 71049
Holewinski; Borck v. 84004
Holiday Inns, Inc.; Hobson Construction Co. v . . . 72047
Holiday Inns of America; Griffin v. 70032
Hollingsworth v. Chrysler Corp. 65051
Holly & Smith; Guillot-Vogt Assocs., Inc. v. . . . 94010
Holm Dev. & Management, Inc.; Stevens/Leinweber/Sullens, Inc. v. 90045
Holman; Pit Construction Co. v. 69049
Holmes v. Watson-Forsberg Co. 92008c
Holmquest v. Priesmeyer 78037
Holy Family Catholic Congregation v. Stuberrauch Assoc., Inc. 37025
Holy Trinity Serbian Orthodox Church-School Congregation; Campbell-Ellsworth, Inc. v. 75004
Home Furniture, Inc. v. Brunzell Construction Co. 68019
Home Indemnity Co. v. Daniels Construction Co. 69028
Homeco, Inc. v. Belford 79008
Homes & Son Construction Co.; Bolo Corp. v. . . . 70013
Homontowski; Continental Cas. Co. v. . . . 93055
Honewell, Inc. v. Babcock 66038
Honey v. Barnes Hosp. 86032
Honeywell, Inc.; Western Casualty and Surety Co. v. 80075
Honolulu Roofing Co. v. Felix 67032
Hooper, City of; Fauss Construction, Inc. v. 77032
Horizon Dev. Co.; Braegelmann v. 85008
Horne's Crane Service Co.; Buehner Schokbeton Co. v. 72020

(Matthew Bender & Co., Inc.)

TABLE OF CASES

[The five-digit numbers in this table are *Citator* Case Reference Numbers, which refer to the cases in the Cases section]

Haskell Co.; Exchange Mut. Ins. Co. v. . . . 84010
Haskell, Conner & Frost; Pipe Welding Supply Co. v. 83037
Hass v. Aetna Insurance Co. 65047
Hastings; School District No. One v. 70073
Hastings & Chivetta Architects v. Burch . . 90024
Hattis Associates, Inc. v. Metro Sports, Inc. 75011
Hatzel & Buehler v. George A. Fuller Co. 52003
Hatzel & Buehler, Inc.; Board of Educ., Longwood Cent. School Dist. v. 89003
Haugen v. Raupach 53002
Haughton Elevator Co. v. C. Rallo Contracting Co. 65048
Hauser Bros; Bibeau Construction Co. v. 72014
Havard v. Board of Supervisors 54002
Havens v. Safeway Stores 84016
Haver; Siegel v. 66088
Hawaii; J. A. Thompson & Son v. 70039
Hawkins v. Teeples & Thatcher, Inc. 73049
Hayeck Building & Realty Co. v. Turcotte 72045
Hayes Contractors, Inc.; Travelers Indem. Co. v. 86067
Hayes Drilling, Inc. v. Curtiss-Manes Constr. Co. 86030
Hayle Floor Covering, Inc. v. First Minnesota Construction Co. 77041
Hayman Co. Gen. Contractors, Inc.; Island on Lake Travis, Ltd. v. 92009a
Hays v. Centennial Floors, Inc. 95012
Haywood County Consolidated School System v. United States Fidelity & Guaranty Co. 79042
H.B. Deal Construction Co.; Ballwin Plaza Corp. v. 70009
H.B. Deal Construction Co. v. Labor Discount Center, Inc. 67029
H.B. Zachry Co. v. Travelers Indemnity Co. 66032
HBE Corp.; Rivers & Bryan, Inc. v. 93051
H.C. Enterprise, Inc.; Heiskell v. 68018
H.C. Jessee, Estate of v. White 82017
H.E. Wiese, Inc. v. Western Stress, Inc. . . 81031
Head; M & W Masonry Construction, Inc. v. 76040
Healey v. J.B. Sheet Metal, Inc. 95013
Health Education Authority; Landis Construction Co. v. 78049
Healy v. Brewster 67030
Hedla v. McCool 73050
Heery Int'l; Juno Indus., Inc. v. 94038

Heiskell v. H.C. Enterprise, Inc. 68018
Hellmuth, Obata & Kassabaum, Inc.; Aetna Insurance Co. v. 68001
Helmer-Cronin Construction, Inc. v. Central School District No. 1 76028
Helms; Dill v. 71032
Helms; Langley v. 71058
Helton; Oden Construction Co. v. 53004
Hemenway Co. v. Bartex, Inc. of Texas . . 79043
Henderson v. Oakes-Waterman Builders . . 41002
Henderson Inv. Corp. v. International Fidelity Ins. Co. 91015
Hendrick Construction Co. v. C.E. Thurston & Sons, Inc. 67031
Hendrix; A. E. Finley & Associates, Inc. v. 78001
Hendrix; Craig Constr Co. v. 90013
Hendry; Otto v. 74027
Henger Co. v. Doctors' North Roads Building, Inc. 66033
Henkel Construction Co.; Walker Manufacturing Co. v. 72105
Hennebique Construction Co. v. Boston Cold Storage & Terminal Co. 18001
Hennepin Public Water District v. Petersen Construction Co. 73051
Henning; State ex rel Center Designs v. . . 97024
Henningson, Durham & Richardson, Inc.; Jaeger v. 83023
Henningson, Durham & Richardson, Inc. v. Swift Bros. Constr. Co. 84017
Henrico Doctor's Hospital and Diagnostic Clinic, Inc. v. Doyle & Russell, Inc. 81035
Henry v. United States 65049
Henry; United States v. 67066
Henry B. Byors & Sons, Inc. v. Board of Water Commissioners 70034
Henry C. Beck Co. v. Ft. Wayne Structural Steel Co. 83021
Henry Carlson Co.; City Sioux Falls v. . . 77021
Henry Contracting, Inc.; American Druggists Ins. Co. v. 87004
Henry Ross Constr. Co.; D.E. Wright Elec., Inc. v. 89011
Henry Roy Portwood, Inc. v. Smith 93013
Hensel Phelps Construction Co. v. General Signal Corp. 72046
Hensey; Mercantile Trust Co. v. 07001
Henson v. James M. Barker Co. 90025
Herbert & Brooner Construction Co. v. Golden . . 73052
Hercules & Co. v. Shama Restaurant Co. 92008
Hercules Constr. Co. v. C.J. Moritz Co. . . 83022

TABLE OF CASES

[The five-digit numbers in this table are *Citator* Case Reference Numbers, which refer to the cases in the Cases section]

Had-Ten Estates Corp.; Sherwood Village Cooperative A v. 67060
Haden v. Krupp Asset Management Corp. 91013
Haemonetics Corp. v. Brophy & Phillips Co. 86028
Haener v. Ada County Highway Dist. 85018
Hagen; Nelson v. 66061
Haines v. Bechdolt 65046
Halcon International, Inc. v. Monsanto Australia, Ltd. 71045
Hall v. Andow 81033
Hall; Distefano v. 68011
Hall v. Union Indemnity Co. 32001
Hall & Co. v. Continental Casualty Co. 70033
Hall-McGuff Architects; Jetty, Inc. v. 80037
Hall Paving Co.; State Highway Dept. v. 72096
Halvorson v. Blue Mountain Prune Growers Co-op. 50003
Hames Electric, Inc.; Baker-Crow Construction Co. v. 77009
Hamilton & Son; Loyal Erectors, Inc. v. 73068
Hamilton & Spiegel, Inc.; United States Fidelity & Guaranty Co. v. 66108
Hammaker v. Schleigh 29003
Hammarberg; Alexander v. 51001
Hammen v. Hansen & Werhane, Inc. 69024
Hammond v. Bechtel, Inc. 80030
Hammond Ventures, Inc.; P & M Construction Co. v. 66069
Hampshire House, Inc.; Curtis Elevator Co. v. 76015
Hand v. Roriek Construction Co. 73046
Hanley v. James McHugh Construction Co. 71046
Hanna v. Huer, Johns, Neel, Rivers & Webb 83020
Hanover Insurance Co.; Acoustics, Inc. v. 71001
Hanover Insurance Co.; Brook-Lea Country Club v. 69009
Hanover Insurance Co.; Chrysler Corp. v. 65023
Hansen; Fishman Construction Co. v. 65037
Hansen; Rosos Litho Supply Corp. v. 84034
Hansen & Werhane, Inc.; Hammen v. 69024
Hanson Southwest Corp. v. Dal-Mac Construction Co. 77040
Hapeville Hotel, Ltd. Partnership; American Demolition, Inc. v. 91002
Harbor Point; 155 Harbor Drive Condominium Ass'n v. 91025

Hardy; Georgetown Township High School District No. 218 v. 76025
Hardy Corp.; Walter L. Couse & Co. v. 73120
Hare v. Federal Compress & Warehouse Co. 73047
Hargrave; Sands Motel v. 62007
Harlaco, Inc.; College Plaza, Inc. v. 65026
Harlan Jones Drilling; Nave v. 92016a
Harnois v. Quannapowitt Dev., Inc. 93041
Harold K. Beecher & Associates; Nauman v. 67054
Harpeth Valley Utilities District v. Due 71047
Harping Sales & Erectors, Inc.; R C R Leasing, Inc. v. 71072
Harrigan & Reid Co. v. Hudson 39004
Harrington v. McCarthy 66031
Harris v. Dyer 81034
Harris v. Kettelhut Constr., Inc. 84015
Harris Air Sys., Inc. v. Gentrac, Inc. 91014
Harris County v. Howard 73048
Harrison v. American Fire & Casualty Co. 69026
Harrison F. Blades, Inc. v. Jarman Memorial Hospital Building Fund 69025
Harry Partridge, Jr., & Sons; Pettinaro Construction Co. v. 79051
Harry Skolnick & Sons v. Heyman 86029
Harsco Corp. v. Cisne & Associates, Inc. 80031
Hart v. Dominion Insurance Co. 71048
Hart, City of; F.J. Siller & Co. v. 77031
Hartford Accident & Indemnity Co. v. Boise Cascade Corp. 80032
Hartford Accident & Indemnity Co.; Board of Education v. 65017
Hartford Accident & Indemnity Co.; Continental Casualty Co. v. 56018
Hartford Accident & Indemnity Co.; Corporation of President of Jesus Chirst of Latter Day Saint v. 39003
Hartford Accident & Indemnity Co. v. Long 68017
Hartford Accident & Indemnity Co. v. Scarlett Harbor Assocs. Ltd. Partnership 97011
Hartford Accident & Indemnity Co. v. W. & J. Knox Net & Twine Co. 26001
Hartford Electric Applicators of Thermalux, Inc. v. Alden 75032
Hartford Fire Insurance Co. v. Riefolo Construction Co. 78035
Hartline-Thomas, Inc. v. Arthur Pew Construction Co. 79041
Harvard Congregational Soc.; Howard v. 16002
Harvey v. Mazal American Partners 92007

TABLE OF CASES

TC–27

[The five-digit numbers in this table are *Citator* Case Reference Numbers, which refer to the cases in the Cases section]

Greate Bay Hotel & Casino, Inc.; Perini Corp. v. 92017
Greater Clark County School Building Corp.; Hughes Masonry Co. v. 81037
Greater Jericho Corp.; Triple M. Roofing Co. v. ... 73112
Greater Park City Co.; Mularz v. 80045
Greeley & Hansen; Bates & Rogers Constr. Corp. v. 85006
Green; United States Fidelity & Guaranty Co. v. 70085
Green Constr. Co. v. Kansas Power & Light Co. 89019; 93037
Green Constr. Co.; VanKirk v. 95048
Green Manor Construction Co. v. Highland Painting Service 65045
Green Manor Construction Co.; W.L. Walker Co. v. 66115
Greenbriar Shopping Center; J. A. Jones Construction Co. v. 71051
Greene Electrical Service, Inc.; United States ex rel. Lincoln Electric Products Co. v. 66105
Green's Pool Service, Inc.; MacIntyre v. ... 77055
Greensboro-High Point Airport Auth.; APAC-Carolina, Inc. v. 93001
Greenvield; Maietta v. 72063
Gregg Kendall & Associates v. Kauhi ... 71044
Gregory; J'Aire Corp. v. 79045
Greiner Eng'g Sciences, Inc.; State Highway Admin. v. 90044
Gribaldo, Jacobs, Jones & Associates. v. Agrippina Versicherunges A.G. 70031
Gribble; Chavez v. 72023
Griffin v. Holiday Inns of America 70032
Griffin; Sasser & Co. v. 74035
Griffin v. Tenneco Oil Co. 93038
Griffin Wellpoint Corp. v. Englehardt, Inc. 80028
Griffiths Constr., Inc.; Vega v. 92021a
Grifton United Methodist Church; Fischel & Taylor v. 70026
Grinnell Fire Protection Sys. Co.; Kaiser Eng'rs, Inc. v. 85025
Griswold & Rauma, Architects, Inc. v. Aesculapius Corp. 74016
Gross v. Breaux 62004
Group Health Cooperative of Puget Sound; Nelse Mortensen & Co. v. 77063
Grover-Diamond Assoc. v. American Arbitration Ass'n. 73045
Groves v. Land's End Hous. Co. 93039
Grow Construction Co. v. New York, State of ... 77039

Grumman Allied Indus., Inc.; Jewish Bd. of Guardians v. 83024
Grunley Constr. Co. v. Conway Corp. ... 96028
Guardianship of (see name of party)
Gude; Brown-Randolph Co. v. 21001
Guennewig; Watson Lumber Co. v. 67069
Guerin Contractors, Inc. v. Reaves 80029
Guidetti v. Pratt Plumbing & Heating, Inc. 76027
Guido; Mid-Atlantic Construction Corp. v. 68031
Guillot-Vogt Assocs., Inc. v. Holly & Smith 94010
Guiterrez; Clearwater Constructors, Inc. v. 81016
Gulf Bitulithic Co.; Le Blanc, Inc. v. ... 67040
Gulf County; Newkirk Construction Corp. v. ... 79014
Gulf Offshore Co. v. Mobil Oil Corp. ... 79040
Gulf State Utils. Co.; Nat Harrison Associates v. 74024
Gulf State Utils. Co.; Tirante v. 82051
Gulf States Steel Co.; Mike Bradford & Co. v. ... 66058
Gulfport-Biloxi Regional Airport Auth.; U.R.S. Co. v. 89047
Gullo Int'l Dev. Corp.; Open Kitchens, Inc. v. ... 84028
Gund; Schultz v. 44003
Gunderson's Inc.; Hot Springs, City of v. 82012
Gundersons, Inc. v. Tull 83019
Gunka v. Consolidated Papers, Inc. 93040
Gunter Hotel of San Antonio, Inc. v. Buck 89020
Gurney Industries, Inc. v. St. Paul Fire & Marine Insurance Co. 72044
Gurtler, Hebert & Co. v. Weyland Machine Shop, Inc. 81030
Gus J. Bouten Constr. Co.; Wicklund v. ... 83049
G.W. Lisk Co.; Kinney v. 90028

H

H. B. White & Son; Page v. 73087
H & H Sewer Systems, Inc. v. Insurance Guaranty Assoc. 81032
H. Halvorsen, Inc.; Layrite Concrete Products, Inc. v. 66051
H. K. Ferguson Co.; A. W. Therrien Co. v. 72011
H. M. Cohen Lumber & Building Co.; Croft v. 37001
H & M Constr. Co.; Nicholas Acoustics & Specialty Co. v. 83035

TABLE OF CASES

[The five-digit numbers in this table are *Citator* Case Reference Numbers, which refer to the cases in the Cases section]

Gilbane Bldg. Co. v. Nemours Found. . . . 85017
Gilbert v. Powell 83017
Gilbert Financial Corp. v. Steelform Contracting Co.
. . . . 78032
Gilbert H. Moen Co. v. Island Steel Erectors, Inc.
. . . . 96007
Gilbert H. Moen Co.; J. & J. Electric, Inc. v. . . .
73056
Gill; Clark-Fitzpatrick, Inc./Franki Found. Co. v.
. . . . 94031
Gilliland v. Elmwood Properties 90021
Gilpatrick Constr. Co.; St. Paul Fire & Marine Ins. Co. v. 87044
Giuliani Construction Co. v. School District . . . .
66029
Glantz Contracting Corp.; C.H. Leavell & Co. v.
. . . . 71020
Glassman Construction Co.; Montgomery County Board of Education ex rel. Carrier Corp. v. . . .
67050
Glen Constr. Co.; Crown Oil & Wax Co. v. . . .
90014
Glen Constr. Co.; Litton Bionetics, Inc. v. . . .
81049
Glen-Rich Construction Corp.; Methodist Church v.
. . . . 71066
Glendale Constr. Serv., Inc. v. Accurate Air Sys., Inc.
. . . . 94009
Glenn H. Johnson Constr. Co. v. Board of Educ., Community Consol. Sch. Dist. No. 15 . . . . .
93012
Glenwall Co.; Sears, Roebuck & Co. v. . . 70074
Glock; Hoffman v. 74017
Gloucester, City of; Glynn v. 86027
Gloucester Housing Authority; Savignano v. . . . .
62008
Glover; Ashworth v. 67004
Glynn v. Gloucester, City of 86027
Godwin v. Stanley Smith & Sons 89018
Goebel v. General Building Service Co. . . 65042
Goin v. Board of Education 44001
Goldberg; Austin-Griffith, Inc. v. 53001
Goldberg v. Underhill 50002
Golden; Anderson v. 82004
Golden; Herbert & Brooner Construction Co. v. . . .
73052
Golden Hills Resort, Inc.; Azcon Constr. Co. v. . . .
93002
Golden Triangle Dev. Corp.; Uhlir v. . . . 88036
Goldsmith & Morris; Housing Vermont v. . . . . .
96030
Gonzales v. R.J. Novick Construction Co. . . . .
78033
Goodman; Comm v. 72115

Goodyear; Williams Eng'g, Inc. v. 86073
Gordon-Maizel Constr. Co. v. Leroy Prod., Inc. . .
87022
Gordon Sel-Way, Inc. v. Spence Bros., Inc. . . . .
91012
Gordy v. United Pacific Insurance Group . . . . .
66030
Gottlieb Contracting, Inc. v. United States . . . . .
65043
Gottschalk Brothers v. Wasau, City of . . . 73044
Gould v. McCormick 13002
Gould-National Batteries, Inc.; Framingham Trust Co. v. 69021
Goverman; Albre Marble & Tile Co. v. . . . 68002
Grabowski; Richmond v. 89040
Grady Co.; Prichard Bros. v. 89037
Graham; A.R. Moyer, Inc. v. 73007
Graham v. Freese & Nichols, Inc. 96027
Graham; Nabholz Constr. Corp. v. 95019
Graham; Ringer v. 87040
Graham Contracting, Inc. v. Flagler County . . . .
83018
Grampp Builders, Inc.; Trader v. 70081
Grand Forks, City of; Moorhead Construction Co. v.
. . . . 75014
Grand River Dam Auth.; Transpower Constructors, Div. of Harrison Int'l Corp. v. 90048
Grand Trunk Western Railroad v. H.W. Nelson Co.
. . . . 41001
Grandview, City of; Midwestern Realty Corp. v.
. . . . 67048
Granette Products Co. v. Arthur H. Neumann & Co.
. . . . 28003
Granger Bros., Inc.; B.J. Harland Elec. Co. v. . . .
87006
Granger Brothers; Stadel v. 66091
Granger Contracting Co.; Chiappisi v. . . . 67012
Granger Northern, Inc. v. Cianchette 90022
Grani Installation, Inc.; CBCO, Inc. v. . . . 79024
Granite Computer Leasing Corp. v. Travelers Indem. Co. 90023
Grant Dev. Co.; Welch v. 83047
Grass Range High School District No. 27 v. Wallace Diteman, Inc. 70030
Graulich v. Frederic H. Berlowe & Associates, Inc.
. . . . 76026
Graves Constr. Co.; Gibbons v. 84014
Graves Constr. Co. v. Rockingham National Bank
. . . . 80027
Graybar Electric Co. v. St. Paul Fire & Marine Insurance Co. 67028
Great American Insurance Co.; Byler v. . . 68007
Great American Insurance Co. v. Louis Lesser Enterprises, Inc. 65044

(Matthew Bender & Co., Inc.) (Pub.435)

TABLE OF CASES

[The five-digit numbers in this table are *Citator* Case Reference Numbers, which refer to the cases in the Cases section]

Gavlik Construction Co. v. H.F. Campbell Co. . . . 75010
Gay v. Stratton 77036
gbs & h Architects, Landscape Architects, Planners, Inc.; Wild West Trading Co. v. 94049
G.C.S., Inc. v. Foster Wheeler Corp. 75031
Geiger-Berger Assocs., P.C.; South Dakota Bldg. Auth. v. 87049
Gelder & Associates v. Continental Insurance Co. 72043
General Accident & Fire Assurance Corp. v. New Era Corp. 66026
General Accident Fire & Life Assurance Corp. v. Finegan & Burgess, Inc. 65039
General Aluminum Door & Entrance Co.; Bank of Broadway v. 67007
General Builders, Inc.; Atlas Assurance Co. v. 79021
General Building Service Co.; Goebel v. . . 65042
General Elec. Co. v. E. Fred Sulzer & Co. 65040
General Elec. Serv. Co.; Hershey Foods Corp. v. 92008a
General Gas Co.; Rexroth & Rexroth, Inc. v. . . . 66078
General Health, Inc.; Palmer v. 89036
General Insurance Co.; A. A. Maycock, Inc. v. . . 70002
General Insurance Co.; J.F. White Engineering Corp. v. 65058
General Insurance Co. of America v. Commerce Hyatt House 70029
General Insurance Co. of America; Middle-West Concrete Forming and Equipment Co. v. 80043
General Insurance Co. of America; State v. 70078
General Motors Corp.; E.C. Ernst, Inc. v. 76020
General Motors Corp.; Ernst v. 73039
General Motors Corp.; Phoenix Contractors, Inc. v. 84030
General Signal Corp.; Hensel Phelps Construction Co. v. 72046
General State Authority v. Kline 77038
Generes; Luczak Bros., Inc. v. 83028
Geneseo Central School v. Perfetto & Whalen Construction Corp. 81028
Genstar Southern Development Corp. v. Troup Brothers, Inc. 81029
Gentrac, Inc.; Harris Air Sys., Inc. v. . . . 91014
George A. Fuller Co.; A R C Electrical Construction Co. v. 69003

George A. Fuller Co. v. Albin Gustafson Co. . . . 77037
George A. Fuller Co.; Chicago College of Osteopathic Medicine v. 83007; 85009
George A. Fuller Co.; Clifton D. Mayhew, Inc. v. 67014
George A. Fuller Co.; Hatzel & Buehler v. 52003
George A. Fuller Co.; Hill v. 73054
George A. Fuller Co.; J. Brodie & Son v. 69029
George A. Fuller Co.; United States ex rel. Chemetron Corp. v. 66104
George B. H. Macomber Co.; Limbach Co. v. . . . 70052
George H. Robinson Corp.; Joseph F. Hughes & Co. v. 70042
George Hyman Constr. Co.; Capitol Place I Assocs. L.P. v. 96002
George Wagschal Associates, Inc. v. West 61007
Georgetown Township High School District No. 218 v. Hardy 76025
Georgia Sprinkler Co.; Frank Briscoe Co. v. . . . 83015
Gerald E. Morrisey, Inc.; Alexander v. . . . 79002
Gerdmann v. United States Fire Ins. Co. . . 84013
Gervais F. Favrot Co.; City Stores Co. v. 78017
Gervais F. Favrot Co.; Williams v. 86072
Getzschman v. Miller Chem. Co. 89017
Gevyn Construction Corp.; Pioneer Industries v. 72078
G.H. & J.T. Kelly, Inc. v. Torson Electic Co. . . . 66027
G.H. Lindekugel & Sons v. South Dakota Highway Commission 72099
Gholson, Byars & Holmes Construction Co. v. United States 65041
Giant Enterprises, Inc.; Central Louisiana Electric Co. v. 79027
Giarratano v. Weitz Co. 67027
Gibbons v. Graves Constr. Co. 84014
Gibbons-Grable Co. v. Gilbane Bldg. Co. 86026
Gibbons & Reed; Lindsay v. 72061
Gifford v. Commissioner of Public Health 52002
Gilbane Bldg. Co.; Architectural Sys., Inc. v. . . . 91003
Gilbane Bldg. Co. v. Brisk Waterproofing Co. . . . 91011
Gilbane Bldg. Co.; Gibbons-Grable Co. v. 86026

(Matthew Bender & Co., Inc.) (Pub.435)

TABLE OF CASES

[The five-digit numbers in this table are *Citator* Case Reference Numbers, which refer to the cases in the Cases section]

Francavilla v. Nagar Constr. Co. 89016
Frank v. MSI Constr. Managers, Inc. 95011
Frank A. Scibetta Plumbing & Heating Corp. v. M & W Ltd. Partnership 82021
Frank Briscoe Co. v. Georgia Sprinkler Co. 83015
Frank J. Rooney, Inc. v. Charles W. Ackerman, Inc. 69022
Frank T. Hickey, Inc. v. Los Angeles Jewish Community Council 54001
Franklin; Allegheny Home Improvement Corp. v. 82003
Franklin Contracting Co. v. State 76023
Franklin County Convention Facilities Auth.; Foster Wheeler Envirersponse, Inc. v. 97010
Franklin Square Corp.; N.E Redlon Co. v. 37002
Frasca Construction Corp.; Lincoln-Sudbury Regional School District v. 68026
Frazier; Bickerstaff v. 70012
Frazier, Inc. v. 20th Century Home Builders, Inc. 72041
Fred. J. McClean Heating Supplies v. M. J. Walsh & Sons 65038
Fred Katz Construction Co.. A.D. Hoppe Co. v. .. 67001
Fred McGilvray, Inc. v. International Builders of Florida, Inc. 78030
Frederic H. Berlowe & Associates, Inc.; Graulich v. 76026
Frederick Contractors, Inc.: Bel Pre Medical Center, Inc. v. 74005
Fredericksburg, City of; Contracting Northwest, Inc. v. 83011
Frederickson v. Alton M. Johnson Co. ... 86025
Freeman v. Many, Town of 81027
Freeman-Darling, Inc.; Dearborn, City of v. 82011
Freeman-White Assocs., Inc.; St. Paul Fire & Marine Ins. Co. v. 88032
Freeo v. Victor A. Perosi, Inc. 76024
Freese & Nichols, Inc.; Graham v. 96027
Fresco v. Anthony R. Delisi, General Contractor, Inc. 68016
Freund v. Utah Power & Light Co. 95013
Friedman, Altschuler & Sincere v. Arlington Structural Steel Co. 85015a
Frohme; Economy v. 70023
Fromherz Engineers; Thomas v. 63007
Frontier Plumbing & Heating Co. v. Fitch 71042
Frouge Construction Co.; Anthony Muratore Contracting Co. v. 66004

Frouge Corp. v. New York Housing Authority .. 66024
Fru-Con Constr. Corp.; Department of Transp. v. 92004e; 93007
Fru-Con Constr. Corp.; Roy A. Elam Masonry Inc. v. 96040
Fruzyna v. Walter C. Carlson Associates .. 79029
Fryd Construction Corp.; Miami Beach, City of v. 72026
Ft. Wayne Structural Steel Co.; Henry C. Beck Co. v. 83021
Fuhrmann v. Catanese 50001
Fuller v. Rosinski 71043
Fuller Industries, Inc. v. R. Terry Blazier & Son 66025
Fullmer Bros.; Richards Contracting Co. v. 65080
Furst v. Board of Education 59001
Future Chattanooga Development Corp.; Agus v. 73004

G

G B R Associates; 1700 Ocean Avenue Corp. v. 65097
G. E. C. Corp. v. Levy 72042
G. E. Drywall, Inc.; Edward L. Nezelek, Inc. v. ... 81022
G & N Construction Co. v. Kirpatovsky .. 66119
G. Weinberger Co.; Pennsylvania Dept. of Gen. Servs. v. 82037
Gables CVF, Inc. v. Bahr, Vermeer & Haecker Architect, Ltd. 93036
Galin Corp. v. MCI Telecommunications Corp. ... 94008
Gall Landau Young Constr. Co. v. Hurlen Constr. 85016
Gallagher v. Schernecker 73128
Galokee Corp.; Jim Mahoney, Inc. v. 74019
Gamm; Pantaleo v. 69044
Garber; Firmin v. 77033
Garcia; Sierra v. 87048
Garcia Lopez; Constructora Bauza v. 95020
Garden Grove Community Church v. Pittsburgh-Des Moines Steel Co. 83016
Garland; Alta Planing Mill Co. v. 14001
Garlock Equip. Co.; Industrial Risk Insurers v. ... 91016
Garver v. Ferguson 78031
Garza; B-F-W Constr. Co. v. 88002
Gateway Drywall & Decorating, Inc. v. Village Construction Co. 79039
Gauntt v. Chehalis County 13007
Gauthier; Rosenthal v. 53006

TABLE OF CASES

[The five-digit numbers in this table are *Citator* Case Reference Numbers, which refer to the cases in the Cases section]

First Baptist Church; Miller Construction Co. v. . . . 81054
First Bristol County National Bank; Superior Glass Co. v. 80063
First Condominium Dev. Co. v. Apex Constr. & Eng'g Corp. 84011
First Indem. of Am. Ins. Co.; Eagle Fire Protection Corp. v. 96025
First Minnesota Construction Co.; Hayle Floor Covering, Inc. v. 77041
First National Bank of Akron v. Cann . . . 82020
First National City Bank; Fair Pavillions, Inc. v. 67025
First National Realty Corp.; Douglas v. . . 70021
First National Realty Corp. v. Warren-Ehret Co. 67026
First State Bank v. Reorganized School District R-3 73041
Fischbach & Moore, Inc.; Babcock & Wilcox Co. v. 71007
Fischbach-Natkin Co. v. Power Process Piping, Inc. 87020
Fischel & Taylor v. Grifton United Methodist Church 70026
Fischer v. Borsher 73042
Fischer Sand & Aggregate, Inc.; Farmington Plumbing & Heating Co. v. 79035
Fishman Construction Co. v. Hansen 65037
Fishman Construction Co.; Murray v. . . . 66060
Fisk Elec. Co. v. Constructors & Assocs. 94033
Fitch; Frontier Plumbing & Heating Co. v. 71042
Fite and Warmath Construction Co. v. MYS Corp. 77034
530 East 89 Corp. v. Unger 77035
F.J. Busse, Inc. v. Department of General Services 79033
F.J. Siller & Co. v. Hart, City of 77031
Flabiano; Eckert-Fair Construction Co. v. 60005
Flagler County; Graham Contracting, Inc. v. . . . 83018
Flandor; Mitchell v. 73077
Flazarano; Lawrence, City of v. 80076
Fleetwood Associates; Castle Concrete v. 71017
Fleischer; Corrigan Co. Mechanical Contractors v. 67019
Fleischer; Steinberg v. 86064
Fletcher v. Laguna Vista Corp. 73043
Flintcote Co.; Standhardt v. 73101
Flood & Conklin Mfg. Co.; Prima Paint Corp. v. 74010

Floor Craft Floor Covering, Inc. v. Parma Community Gen. Hosp. Ass'n 90020
Floors, Inc. v. B.G. Danis of New England, Inc. 79038
Florida v. Wesley Construction Co. 70027
Flour Mills of America Inc. v. American Steel Building Co. 69019
F.O. Bailey Co. v. Ledgewood, Inc. 92006
The Foley Co. v. Walnut Associates 80065
Fontaine Bros., Inc. v. Springfield, City of 93011
Foothill Junior College; Jasper Construction, Inc. v. 79046
Forcum-Lannom Assocs., Inc.; Ethyl Corp. v. . . . 82018
Forcum-Lannon, Inc. v. Wells 69020
Ford v. Robertson 87021
Ford, Bacon & Davis Constr. Corp.; Swartz v. . . . 85037
Ford Motor Co. v. W. F. Holt & Sons . . . 71040
Forest City Dillon, Inc. v. Superior 84012
Forest Electric Corp. v. State 66023
Formfit Co.; Kobus v. 66048
Formigli Corp. v. Fox 72040
Formigli Corp.; Salesian Society v. 72088
Fort Wayne; Wood v. 001
Fortin v. Nebel Heating Corp. 81026
Fortune Homes, Inc.; Roberts v. 66083
Forty-O-Four Grand Corp.; Roland A. Wilson & Associates v. 76063
Foster v. Sellards 36001
Foster Construction; United States v. . . . 72104
Foster, Henry, Henry & Thorpe, Inc. v. J.T. Constr. Co. 91010
Foster-Lipkins Corp.; A. Burgart, Inc. v. . . 72001
Foster-Lipkins Corp.; Borden Co. v. 72017
Foster Wheeler Envirespouse, Inc. v. Franklin County Convention Facilities Auth. 97010
Foster Wheeler Corp.; G.C.S., Inc. v. . . . 75031
Four J's Construction Corp.; Joray Mason Contractors, Inc. v. 78042
Fowler v. A & A Co. 70028
Fowler v. Insurance Co. of North America 80026
Fowler-Jones Construction Co.; Maness v. 71063
Fox; Formigli Corp. v. 72040
Fox; Hurley v. 90027
Fragman Construction Co.; Kleeman v. . . 81044
Framingham Trust Co. v. Gould-National Batteries, Inc. 69021
Frampton v. Dauphin Distribution Servs. Co. 94034
Fran Realty, Inc. v. Thomas 76022

[The five-digit numbers in this table are *Citator* Case Reference Numbers, which refer to the cases in the Cases section]

Fanning; Stevens v. 65102
Farfield Co.; Shamokin Area School Auth. v. ... 82046
Farina Construction Corp.; United States ex rel. Powers Regulator Co. v. 66106
Farm Bldrs., Inc.; Farmer's Elevator & Mercantile Co. v. 88015
Farmer's Elevator & Mercantile Co. v. Farm Bldrs., Inc. 88015
Farmers & Merchants State Bank v. Snodgrass & Sons Construction Co. 72038
Farmington Plumbing & Heating Co. v. Fischer Sand & Aggregate, Inc. 79035
Farmland Indus., Inc.; Kinsey v. 94039
Farnsworth & Chambers Co. v. United States ... 65036
Farr; Hines v. 60007
Farrar's Plumbing & Heating Co.; United States Fidelity & Guar. Co. v. 88037, 93056
Fattore v. Metropolitan Sewerage Commission .. 71037
Faulhaber; Loyal Order of Moose, Adrian Lodge 1034 v. 50004
Faulkner Construction Co.; Ezon v. 67024
Fauntleroy v. Walker 79036
Fauss Construction, Inc. v. Hooper, City of 77032
F.D. Borkholder Co. v. Sandock 80024
Fedco Sys., Inc.; Hilliard & Bartko Joint Venture v. 87024
Federal Compress & Warehouse Co.; Hare v. .. 73047
Federal Insurance Co.; Amelco Window Corp. v. 74002
Federal Insurance Co.; Episcopal Housing Corp. v. 77030; 79006
Federal Insurance Co.; Schlanger v. 65091
Federated Dept. Stores, Inc. v. J.V.B. Indus., Inc. 90019
Fehlhaber Corp. v. New York, State of .. 78029
Fehlhaber Corp. v. Unicorn Management Corp. .. 69017
Fehr; Texas Delta Upsilon Foundation v. 57003
Fein; Miami Beach, City of v. 72025
Felix; Honolulu Roofing Co. v. 67032
Fennewald; Joliet, City of v. 72024
Ferguson; Garver v. 78031
Ferran Concrete Co. v. Commerce Elec., Inc. 86024
Ferrante v. McGinnis 64005
Ferrante Equipment Co. v. Charles Simkin & Sons 68015
Ferrante Equipment Co. v. Lasker-Goldman Corp. 70025
Fetterolf v. S & L Construction Co. 16001
F.F. Bolinger Co. v. Wildmann Brewing Corp. ... 40002
Fidelity & Casualty Co. v. J. A. Jones Construction Co. 63001
Fidelity & Casualty Co.; Leo Spear Construction Co. v. 71059
Fidelity & Casualty Co.; Stanley R. Benjamin, Inc. v. 72095
Fidelity & Casualty Co. of N.Y. v. Central Bank of Birmingham 82019
Fidelity & Deposit Co. v. Rainer 29002
Fidelity & Deposit Co.; Redevelopment Authority v. 81061
Fidelity & Deposit Co. v. Scott Brothers Construction Co. 72039
Fidelity & Deposit Co. of Maryland; Boys Club of San Fernando Valley, Inc. v. 92001b
Fidelity & Deposit Co. of Maryland; North County School District R-1 v. 76050
Fidelity & Deposit Co. of Maryland v. Parsons & Whittemore Contractors Corp. 79037
Fidelity & Deposit Co. of Maryland v. Stool ... 30025
Fidelity & Deposit Co. of Maryland; Yeshiva Univ. v. 86075
Fidelity & Guar. Ins. Co. v. Craig Wilkinson, Inc., ... 95051
Fidelity Deposit Co.; Dauphin, County of v. 91008
Fields v. Lawter Chemicals, Inc. 69018
Fifteenth Avenue Christian Church v. Moline Heat & Contracting Co. 71038
Figgs v. Bellevue Holding Co. 94032
Fiksdal; Pedersen v. 60011
Filice; McDonald v. 67046
Financial Indemnity Co. v. Steele & Sons, Inc. ... 81025
Fine; Kirk Reid Co. v. 65063
Finegan & Burgess, Inc.; General Accident Fire & Life Assurance Corp. v. 65039
Finrow Painting Co.; Kaiser Aluminum & Chemical Co. v. 73062
Fireman's Fund Ins. Co.; Borough of Nanty-Glo v. 66010
Fireman's Fund Ins. Co. v. Krohn 93010
Fireman's Fund Ins. Co.; Wagner v. 65116
Fireman's Ins. Co. of Newark, New Jersey v. New York, State of 79007
Firmin v. Garber 77033
First American Inv. Corp.; Robert M. Swedroe, Architects/Planners, A.I.A., P.A. v. 90037

TABLE OF CASES

[The five-digit numbers in this table are Citator *Case Reference Numbers, which refer to the cases in the Cases section]*

Emcco, Inc.; Donlinger & Sons' Construction Co. v. 80021
Emil R. Wohl Construction; Weisz Trucking Co. v. 70090
Emlenton Area Mun. Auth. v. Miles 88013
Employers Ins. of Wausau; Certain Teed Corp. v. 96019
Employers Mutual Liability Insurance Co. v. Robert E. McKee General Contractors, Inc. .. 71035
Empresa Nacional De Ingenieria; Cianbro Corp. v. 88006
Engineers Construction Co.; Lindon City v. 81047
Englehardt, Inc.; Griffin Wellpoint Corp. v. 80028
Englehart v. OKI Am., Inc. 93034
Ensign Painting Co. v. Alfred A. Smith, Inc. ... 71036
Entropic Landscapes, Inc. v. Brown 93009
Envirmech Contracting Corp.; Regina Constr. Corp. v. 89039
EPA; Naclerio Contracting Co. v. . 82036; 85030
Episcopal Housing Corp. v. Federal Insurance Co. 77030; 79006
Eppoliti, Inc.; Turner Constr. Co. v. ... 92020a
Equitable Fire & Marine Insurance Co. v. Allied Steel Construction Co. 65035
Erftmier; Smith v. 82048
Erhart v. Hummonds 60006
Ericksen v. Salt Lake City Corp. 93035
Erickson; Schultz & Lindsay Construction Co. v. 65095
Erickson Paving Co. v. Yardley Drilling Co. ... 72037
Erin Mechanical; Independence Bank v. ... 88016
Erlich; Indiana Ins. Co. v. 94011
Ernest B. LaRosa & Sons, Inc.; Joseph F. Trionfo & Sons, Inc. v. 78043
Erland Constr. Co. v. Park Steel Corp. ... 96026
Ernst v. General Motors Corp. 73039
Erskine v. Johnson 002
Escambia Electric and Appliance Co.; United States Fidelity & Guaranty Co. v. 80070
Espaniola v. Cawdrey Mars Joint Venture 85015
Est. of (see name of party)
Estate of (see name of party)
Estero Manufacturing & Builders Supply, Inc.; Aetna Insurance Co. v. 65003
Ethyl Corp. v. Daniel Constr. Co. . 87019; 94033
Ethyl Corp. v. Forcum-Lannom Assocs., Inc. ... 82018
Eugene W. Kelsey & Son, Inc. v. Architectural Openings, Inc. 86020

E.V. Cox Construction Co. v. Brookline Associates 79032
E.V. Cox Construction Co.; Johnson v. .. 80038
E.V. Love v. Double "AA" Constructors, Inc. ... 77028
Evans Electrical Construction Co. v. University of Kansas Medical Center 81023
Evans Joint Venture; Judd Constr. Co. v. 82029
Ex parte (see name of applicant)
Ex rel. (see name of relator)
Exber, Inc. v. Sletten Construction Co. ... 76021
Excavators & Erectors, Inc. v. Bullard Engineers, Inc. 73040
Exch. v. Thunderbird Masonry 93056
Exchange Mut. Ins. Co. v. Haskell Co. .. 84010
Executive Development Properties, Inc. v. Andrews Plumbing Co. 75009
Exxon Corp., U.S.A.; Crane v. 92004d
Ezon v. Faulkner Construction Co. 67024

F

F. F. Baugh Plumbing & Heating, Inc.; EFC Development Corp. v. 75030
F. H. Bridge & Son, Contractors; Clearwater Associates, Inc. v. 76012
F. M. Floryan & Co.; A. Sangivanni & Sons v. ... 69005
F. & M. Schaefer Co.; Stewart-Scott Construction Corp. v. 73105
F & T Contractors, Inc., In re 81038
F. W. Brown Co.; American Mason's Supply Co. v. 71005
Fabe v. WVP Corp. 88014
Facilities Development Corp.; Acme Builders, Inc. v. 79001
Fair Pavillions, Inc. v. First National City Bank 67025
Fairbanks North Star Borough v. Kandik Constr., Inc. 86022
Fairbanks North Star Borough v. Roen Design Assocs., Inc. 86022
Fairchild v. W. O. Taylor Commercial Refrigeration & Electric Co. 81024
Fairway Builders, Inc. v. Malouf Towers Rental Co. 79034
Fairways Plaza Assocs. v. Commercial Constr. Corp. 82038
Fairways Plaza Assocs.; Post Tensioned Eng'g Corp. v. 82038
Falcon Steel Co. v. Weber Eng'g Co. ... 86023
Famous Builders, Inc. v. Bolin 68014
Fandrich v. Allstate Insurance Co. 74015

TABLE OF CASES

[The five-digit numbers in this table are *Citator* Case Reference Numbers, which refer to the cases in the Cases section]

Dunn Constr. Co. v. Sugar Beach Condominium Ass'n 91009, 95046
Dunton v. Daniel Construction Co. 73036
Dupree; Baltimore Contractors, Inc. v. ... 67006
Durham, City of v. Reidsville Engineering Co. ... 61003
Dutchess Community College, In the Matter of ... 77047
D.W. Hutt Consultants, Inc. v. Construction Maintenance Sys., Inc. 95010
Dyad Construction, Inc.; Seattle, City of v. ... 77020
Dyer; Harris v. 81034
Dygert; Lundstrom Construction Co. v. ... 59002

E

E. Carl Schiewe, Inc. v. Brady 80022
E. E. Dean Snavely, Inc. v. Sullivan 78027
E & F Construction Co. v. Rissil Construction Associates, Inc. 80023
E. Fred Sulzer & Co.; General Electric Co. v. ... 65040
E. H. Morrill Co. v. State 67022
E. L. Farmer Construction Co.; Park Imperial, Inc. v. 69046
E. L. White, Inc. v. Huntington Beach, City of ... 78028
E. O. Dorsch Electric Co. v. Knickerbocker Construction Co. 67023
E. W. Johnson Construction Co.; Housing Authority of the City of Texarkana v. 78038
Eagle Fire Protection Corp. v. First Indem. of Am Ins. Co. 96025
Eagle's Nest Ltd. Partnership v. Brunzell 83014
Eanes Indep. Sch. Dist.; Snyder v. 93054
Earth Movers of Fairbanks, Inc. v. State Dept. of Transp. & Pub. Facilities 92005b
East Coast Builders, Inc.; Shaw v. 87046
Eastern Foundation Co. v. Creswell 73037
Eastern Hills Methodist Church; United States Fidelity and Guaranty Co. v. 80069
Eastline Corp. v. Marion Apartments, Ltd. 88011
Eastman; Corey v. 004
E.B. Jones Constr. Co. v. City & County of Denver 86017
E.B. Ludwig Steel Corp. v. C.J. Waddell Contractors, Inc. 88012
Ebenezer Baptist Church; Tsoi v. 63008
E.C. Ernst, Inc. v. General Motors Corp. ... 76020
E.C. Ernst, Inc. v. Koppers Co. 80022a
E.C. Ernst, Inc. v. Tallahassee 81021

E.C. Long, Inc. v. Brennan's of Atlanta .. 79005
Eckert-Fair Construction Co. v. Flabiano .. 60005
Economy v. Frohme 70023
Ed Smith & Sons; Holder Construction Co. v. ... 71049
Edens; Pioneer Enters., Inc. v. 84031
E.D.S. Constr. v. North End Health Center, Inc. ... 87017
Edward Edinger Co. v. Willis 31003
Edward Elec. Co. v. Automation, Inc. ... 87018
Edward L. Nezelek, Inc. v. G. E. Drywall, Inc. ... 81022
Edward L. Nezelek, Inc.; Sullivan, County of v. ... 77025
Edward M. Crough, Inc.; Southern Maryland Hospital Center v. 81066
Edward R. Marden Corp. v. S & R Construction Co. 73038
Edwards; Keith Adams & Associates v. .. 70045
EFC Development Corp. v. F. F. Baugh Plumbing & Heating, Inc. 75030
Egbert; Standley v. 70076
Eichleay Corp.; Tennessee River Pulp & Paper Co. v. 82050
Eichleay Corp.; Unger v. 93017
Eikenroht; Bueche v. 49001
Eis Group Cornwall Hill Dev. Corp. v. Rinaldi Constr., Inc. 89014
Eke Bldrs., Inc. v. Quail Bluff Assocs. ... 85014a
El Dorado, City of; Pete Smith Co. v. 75020
E.L. Scott Roofing Co. v. North Carolina, State of 86018
Elec-trol, Inc. v. C.J. Kern Contractors, Inc. 81022a
Electric Corp. of Kansas City; D.M. Ward Constr. Co. v. 90018
Elfline Plumbing & Heating, Inc.; McStain Corp. v. 76042
Elite Gen. Contracting Corp.; Rego Park Garden Assocs., Inc. v. 87039
Elizabeth Sash, Door & Supply Co. v. St. Vincent's Hospital 34003
Eller & Heyward, Inc. v. Jackson 68013
Elliott Construction Co.; Standard Co. of New Orleans, Inc. v. 78067
Ellisor & Tanner, Inc.; Hunt v. 87026
Elmira, City of v. Larry Walter, Inc. 77019; 90010
Elmwood Properties; Gilliland v. 90021
Elton; Brixen & Christopher, Architects v. 89006
Elzinga & Volkers, Inc. v. LSSC Corp. ... 94007
Emberton v. State Farm Mutual Automobile Insurance Co. 77029

TABLE OF CASES

TC–19

[The five-digit numbers in this table are *Citator* Case Reference Numbers, which refer to the cases in the Cases section]

Dial Assocs. Constr. Group, Inc.; Sanitary Sewer Auth. of Borough of Shickshinny v. . . .	87045
Diamond B Constr. Co. v. Plaquemine, City of	96004
Diamond Homes, Inc. v. Bodovinac	69015
Dick Corp. v. State Public School Building Authority	76019
Dickerson Construction Co. v. Process Engineering Co.	77027
Dickey; Travelers Ins. Co. v.	90049
Dickson County v. Bomar Constr. Co.	96023
Diersen v. Joe Kleim Bldrs., Inc.	87015
Dilaveris v. W.T. Rich Co.	95030
Dill v. Helms	71032
Dillard v. Shaughnessy, Fickel & Scott, Architects	93033
Dillon Properties, Inc. v. Minmar Builders, Inc.	70020
DiLucente Corp. v. Pennsylvania Roofing Co.	95009
DiMaria Constr. Inc.; Commerce Bank N.A. v.	97007
Dimeo, Inc.; Kelly v.	91017
Dinschel v. United States Gypsum Co.	67021
Diocese of Rochester v. R-Monde Contractors, Inc.	89012
Diomar v. Landmark Associates	80020
Distefano v. Hall	68011
District; Alspaugh v.	76002
Diversified Engineers, Inc.; Sun Insurance Co. v.	65104
Diversified R. B. & T. Construction Co.; Brick Township Municipal Utilities Authority v.	79023
Dixie Container Corp. v. Dale	68012
Dixie Roof Decks, Inc. v. Borggren/Dickson Constr., Inc.	90017
Dixon v. Certain Teed	96024
D.K. Meyer Corp. v. Bevco, Inc.	80017
D.M. Holden v. Contractor's Crane Service	81017
D.M. Ward Constr. Co. v. Electric Corp. of Kansas City	90018
Dobson Construction Co.; Board of Education v.	71015
Doctors' North Roads Building, Inc.; Henger Co. v.	66033
Dominion Insurance Co.; Hart v.	71048
Donahoe; Cruthers v.	12001
Donald M. Drake Co.; Tri-M. Erectors, Inc. v.	80067
Donaldson, Lufkin & Jenrette Futures, Inc. v. Barr	83025
Dondlinger & Sons Construction Co. v. Emcco, Inc.	80021
Dondlinger & Sons Construction Co.; Kirsch v.	71056
Donovan v. R.W. Rexford Co.	65033
Doral Country Club v. Curcie Bros.	65034
Dormitory Authority; Area Masonry, Ltd. v.	77005
Dormitory Authority v. Span Electric Corp.	66022
Double "AA" Constructors, Inc.; E.V. Love v.	77028
Douglas v. First National Realty Corp.	70021
Douglas Northwest, Inc. v. Bill O'Brien & Sons Constr., Inc.	92005
Doup v. Almand	48001
Dover, City of; J.A. Jones Construction Co. v.	77048
Dover & Co. v. United Pacific Insurance Co.	72034
Dowling v. Bruffey	72035
Downs; Nixon Construction Co. v.	69043
Doyle & Russell, Inc.; Henrico Doctor's Hospital and Diagnostic Clinic, Inc. v.	81035
Doyle & Russell, Inc. v. Roanoke Hospital Association	73034
Doyle & Russell, Inc. v. Welch Pile Driving Corp.	73035
Dozier v. J.A. Jones Constr. Co.	84009
Drake, O'Mera & Associates v. American Testing & Engineering Corp.	70022
Dravo Corp. v. L. W. Moses Co.	71033
Dravo Corp. v. Robert Kerris, Inc.	81019
Dressler; Delta Construction, Inc. v.	78026
Dreyfous; MacDonnell v.	19001
Drost v. Professional Building Service Corp.	72036
Drummond; Atlantic States Construction Co. v.	68004
Drywall Interiors, Inc.; Olympic Constr., Inc. v.	86048
Drzewinski v. Atlantic Scaffold & Ladder Co.	87016
DSK Constr., Inc.; Commerce, Crowdus & Canton, Ltd. v.	89009
DuBose v. Carabetta	71034
Dudley v. St. Regis Corp.	86016
Due; Harpeth Valley Utilities District v.	71047
Duff v. Hoffman	69016
Dugan & Meyers Constr. Co.; Smith v.	84036
Duluth Lumber and Plywood Co. v. Delta Development, Inc.	79031
Duncan; Statesville Roofing & Heating Co. v.	88034
Dunkirk, City of; Hunkin-Conkey Construction Co. v.	72050

TABLE OF CASES

[The five-digit numbers in this table are *Citator* Case Reference Numbers, which refer to the cases in the Cases section]

Davis v. Anderson 73031
Davis; John Price Associates v. 78040
Davis v. Nelson-Deppe, Inc. 67020
Davis; O'Kain v. 19002
Davis; Warde v. 72106
Davis Acoustical Corp. v. National Surety Corp.
.... 66020
Davis & Davis, Inc.; J.C. Penney Co. v. .. 81040
Davis Mechanical Contractors, Inc.; United States Fidelity & Guaranty Co. v. 72103
Davison Specialty Chem. Co. v. S & H Erectors, Inc.
.... 85013
Davlar Corp. v. Superior Court 97009
Day v. National U.S. Radiator Corp. 61006
Dayton Power & Light Co.; Moore v. ... 94042
Dayton, Town of; Banner v. 70010
D.C. McClain, Inc. v. Arlington County .. 95008
De Graf Bros., Inc.; Sarnoff v. 90040
D.E. Wright Elec., Inc. v. Henry Ross Constr. Co.
.... 89011
Deaconess Manor Ass'n; Korte Constr. Co. v. ...
.... 96034
Dean L. Dauley & Waldrof Assocs.; L.R. Foy Constr. Co. v. 82032
Dearborn, City of v. Freeman-Darling, Inc. ....
.... 82011
Decatur Construction Co. v. Central Illinois Public Services Co. 74013
Deel v. United States Steel Corp. 69014
Deer Creek, Village of; Normoyle-Berg & Associates, Inc. v. 76049
Deer Park Bank v. Aetna Insurance Co. .. 73032
Dehnert v. Arrow Sprinklers, Inc. 85014
DeKalb, City of v. Sornsin 65025
DeKalb County v. PMS Construction Co. ....
.... 78024
DeKalb County v. Scruggs 78025
Del Bianco; School District No. 46 v. ... 66085
Del Bianco & Associates v. Adam 72033
Del Bianco & Associates, Inc.; Board of Education of Community Consolidated School District v. ...
.... 78012
Del E. Webb Constr. v. Richardson Hosp. Auth.
.... 87014
DeLara; Beller v. 78009
Delaware River & Bay Authority; Ruckman & Hansen, Inc. v. 68039
Delhi Pipeline Corp. v. Lewis, Inc. 66021
Delisi Construction, People ex rel. v. Board of Education 75018
Delisle Construction Co.; Schwarz-Jordan, Inc. of Houston v. 78063
Delle Cese; Board of Education v. 71014
Delta Construction, Inc. v. Dressler 78026

Delta Development, Inc.; Duluth Lumber and Plywood Co. v. 79031
Delta Elec., Inc. v. Ingram & Greene, Inc. .....
.... 86015
Demaria Bldg. Co.; Sherman v. 94016
Dember Constr. Corp.; David Fanarof, Inc. v. ...
.... 93032
Demers Nursing Home Inc. v. R.C. Foss & Sons, Inc.
.... 82015
Denham Springs, City of; J.H. Jenkins Contractor, Inc. v. 68021
Denta Rama, Inc. v. Lavastone Industries of Central Texas, Inc. 80019
Denton Constr. Co.; Board of Regents of North Texas State Univ. v. 83004
Denver Brick & Pipe Co.; National Union Fire Insurance Co. v. 67053
Denver Ventures, Inc. v. Arlington Lane Corp. ...
.... 88010
Department of Environmental Management; Lawrence-Lynch Corp. v. 84024
Department of General Services; F.J. Busse, Inc. v.
.... 79033
Department of Highways; Main v. 65073
Department of Transp.; APAC-Georgia, Inc. v. ...
.... 96016
Department of Transp. v. Fru-Con Constr. Corp.
.... 92004e; 93007
Department of Transp. v. Interstate Contractors Supply Co. 90015
Depot Construction Corp.; Bone Contracting Co. v.
.... 73020
Derr Constr. Co. v. Houston, City of ... 92004f
Des Lauriers Column Mould Co.; Mesker Brothers Iron Co. v. 72070
Des Moines Asphalt & Paving Co. v. Colcon Indus. Corp. 93008
Deschenes; Bayer & Mingolla Construction Co. v.
.... 65011
Desco Vitro Glaze, Inc. v. Mechanical Constr. Corp.
.... 90016
Detroit Demolition Corp. v. Burroughs Corp. ...
.... 73033
Detroit Edison Co.; Carr v. 73024
Detweiler Bros., Inc. v. John Graham & Co. ....
.... 76017
Deuel v. McCollum 65032
Devenow v. St. Peter 76018
Devlin v. Milwaukie Covenant Church ... 74014
DeWitt; Miller v. 67049
DeWitt & Assocs., Inc.; Burns v. 92003
Dewor Dev.; Christensen v. 83008
D.H. Rouse Co.; Monmouth Pub. Schools Dist. 38 v.
.... 87034

TABLE OF CASES
TC–17

[The five-digit numbers in this table are *Citator* Case Reference Numbers, which refer to the cases in the Cases section]

Cree Coaches, Inc. v. Panel Suppliers, Inc. 71028
Crescent Steel; Kubby v. 70048
Creswell; Eastern Foundation Co. v. 73037
Creswell v. Housing Authority 71029
Croft v. H. M. Cohen Lumber & Building Co. . . . 37001
Cross; L.D.A., Inc. v. 81045
Crow; Rowell v. 49002
Crown Construction Co. v. Opelika Manufacturing Corp. 73029
Crown Construction Co.; Summers v. . . . 72098
Crown Oil & Wax Co. v. Glen Constr. Co. 90014
Cruthers v. Donahoe 12001
CSI, Ltd.; Chadwick v. 93029
Cuhaci & Peterson Architects, Inc. v. Huber Constr. Co. 87013
Culligan Corp. v. Transamerica Insurance Co. . . . 78022
Cumberland Group; Smith v. 97023
Curators of University of Missouri; National Surety Corp. v. 59004
Curcie Bros.; Doral Country Club v. 65034
Cure v. Jefferson, City of 65029
Curtis; Corrao Construction Co. v. 78020
Curtis Elevator Co. v. Hampshire House, Inc. . . . 76015
Curtiss-Manes Constr. Co.; Hayes Drilling, Inc. v. 86030
Custody of (see name of party)
Custom Builders Corp.; O'Dell v. 78057
Custom Builders, Inc. v. Clemons 77026
Cyon Metal Products, Inc.; Kaiser v. 70044

D

D. A. H. Construction Corp.; Williams v. 73125
D/C Systems of New England; New England Concrete Pipe Corp. v. 80048
D. Capolino Design & Renovation; Kalwall Corp. v. 76033
D. Federico Co. v. New Bedford Redevelopment Auth. 83013
D & L Construction Co.; National Union Fire Insurance Co. v. 65082
D & O Contractors, Inc. v. Terrebonne Parish School Bd. 89013
D. Wilson Constr. Co. v. McAllen Indep. School Dist. 92005a
Dabson; State v. 66094
Dahlstrom Corp. v. State Highway Commission of the State of Mississippi 79003

Daines; Mathis v. 82033
Dal-Mac Construction Co.; Hanson Southwest Corp. v. 77040
Dale; Dixie Container Corp. v. 68012
Dalon Contracting Co.; Robinson Explosives, Inc. v. 74031
Damon G. Douglas Co.; Leitao v. 97014
Damora v. Stresscon International, Inc. . . . 75008
Dancing Bear Entertainment, Inc.; Meco Sys. v. 97018
Dan Cowling & Associates, Inc. v. Board of Educ. of Clinton School Dist. 81018
D'Angelo v. State 73030
Daniel Constr. Co.; Ethyl Corp. v. . 87019; 94033
Daniel Construction Co.; Dunton v. 73036
Daniel Construction Co.; Mion Chemical Brick Corp. v. 65078
Daniel Construction Co. v. Welch Contracting Corp. 71030
Daniel J. Keating Co.; Pickering v. 72077
Daniel O'Connell's Sons v. Commonwealth 65030
Daniel O'Connell's Sons, Inc.; Acmat v. . . 83002
Daniels Construction Co.; Home Indemnity Co. v. 69028
Danter Associates; Ross v. 68038
Danville, City of; Santucci Constr. Co. v. 84035
Darin & Armstrong, Inc.; Johnson v. 66046
Darling v. Burrone Brothers 72031
Darrell T. Stuart Contractor v. J. A. Bridges & Rustproofing, Inc. 65031
Dartmoor Constr. Corp.; Tomlinson v. . . . 94046
Dasta Constr. Co.; Marriott Corp. v. 94040
Data Electric Co. v. NAB Construction Corp. 76016
Datry; Walton v. 87053
Daugherty Co. v. Kimberly-Clark Corp. . . 71031
Dauphin, County of v. Fidelity Deposit Co. 91008
Dauphin Distribution Servs. Co.; Frampton v. . . . 94034
David Co. v. Jim W. Miller Constr., Inc. 88009; 89010
David Fanarof, Inc. v. Dember Constr. Corp. . . . 93032
David H. Snell Landscape Contractor, Inc.; William F. Klingensmith, Inc. v. 72112
Davidson v. Prime Homes, Inc. 72032
Davidson & Jones, Inc. v. New Hanover, County of 79004
Davidson & Jones, Inc. v. North Carolina Dept. of Admin. 85012
Davies v. Kahn 58002

TABLE OF CASES

[The five-digit numbers in this table are *Citator* Case Reference Numbers, which refer to the cases in the Cases section]

Conte v. Weston, Town of 65027
Continental Casualty Co. v. C. O. Brand, Inc. ... 66017
Continental Casualty Co.; Cornell, Howland, Hayes & Merryfield, Inc. v. 72029
Continental Casualty Co.; Hall & Co. v. ... 70033
Continental Casualty Co. v. Hartford Accident & Indemnity Co. 66018
Continental Casualty Co. v. Homontowski 93055
Continental Casualty Co.; Jones v. 73059
Continental Casualty Co.; Moore v. 73078; 73079
Continental Casualty Co. v. Public Building Authority 67018
Continental Casualty Co.; United States v. 65109
Continental Casualty Co. v. Wilson-Avery, Inc. ... 67017
Continental Casualty Co.; Winston Corp. v. 75028
Continental Heller Corp. v. Amtech Mechanical Servs. 97008
Continental Heller Corp.; PPG Industries, Inc. v. 79050
Continental Ins. Co.; Centerre Trust Co. v. 88003
Continental Ins. Co.; Gelder & Associates v. ... 72043
Continental Ins. Co. v. Va. Beach, City of 95029
Continental Realty Corp. v. Andrew J. Crevolin Co. 74011
Contract Constr. Inc. v. Power Technology Ctr. Ltd. Partnership 94006
Contracting & Material Co. v. Chicago, City of .. 74012
Contracting Northwest, Inc. v. Fredericksburg, City of 83011
Contractor Industries and Acceptance Corp. v. Zerr 76014
Contractor's Crane Service; D.M. Holden v. 81017
Conway; Plowden & Roberts, Inc. v. 66074
Cook v. Superior Ct. 66019
Cook, County of; Consumers Construction Co. v. 71025
Coonrod & Walz Construction Co. v. Motel Enterprises, Inc. 75007
Copeland Sand and Gravel, Inc. v. Insurance Company of North America 80017
Corbett v. Brown 69013
Corbetta Construction Co.; St. Joseph Hospital v. 74034

Corbetta Construction Co. of Illinois v. Lake County Public Building Commission 78019
Corey v. Eastman 004
Corinno Civetta Constr. Corp. v. New York, City of 86012
Cornell, Howland, Hayes & Merryfield, Inc. v. Continental Casualty Co. 72029
Cornwell; Walsh v. 30001
Corporation of President of Jesus Chrst of Latter Day Saint v. Hartford Accident and Indemnity Co. 39003
Corporex Constructors, Inc.; International Paper Co. v. 89025
Corrao Constr. Co. v. Curtis 78020
Corrao Constr. Co.; Trans Western Leasing Corp. v. 82052
Corrente v. Conforti & Eisele Co. 83012
Corrigan Co. Mechanical Contractors v. Fleischer 67019
Cosentino v. A.F. Lusi Constr. Co. 84008
Cosimini v. Atkinson-Kiewit Joint Venture 95007
Costa & Head (Atrium), Ltd., Ex parte .. 86021
Costonis v. Medford Housing Authority .. 61005
Cotter v. Consolidated Construction Co. ... 77024
County v. (see name of defendant)
County of (see name of county)
Couvillion v. Shelter Mut. 96003
Coverdill v. Lurgi Corp. 86013
Covil v. Rober & Co. Associates 65028
Cowherd; Kurfiss v. 38002
Cox; Brown v. 70014
Crabtree; Aetna Casualty & Surety Co. v. 80001
Crabtree Masonry Co. v. C & R Construction, Inc. 78021
Craig Constr Co. v. Hendrix 90013
Craig & Rush, Inc.; Lloyd's Underwriters v. 94012
Craig-Wilkinson, Inc.;Fidelity & Guar. Ins. Co. v. 95051
Crane v. Exxon Corp., U.S.A. 92004d
Crane v. I. T. E. 71027
Crane Construction Co. v. Commonwealth 35002
Crane Service Co.; Ciejek v. 65024
Craven v. Oggero 73028
Craviolini v. Scholer & Fuller Associated Architects 60004
Creative Builders, Inc. v. Avenue Dev., Inc. 86014
Creative Drywall, Inc.; Welch Group, Inc. v. ... 90053

TABLE OF CASES

[The five-digit numbers in this table are *Citator* Case Reference Numbers, which refer to the cases in the Cases section]

Commercial Standard Insurance Co.; Argonaut Insurance Co. v. 80003
Commercial Union Ins. Co. v. Baltimore Gas & Elec. Co. 97004
Commercial Union Ins. Co. v. Bituminous Casualty Corp. 88007
Commission v. (see name of opposing party)
Commission of Public Works; Robert E. Lee & Co. v. 66082
Commissioner v. (see name of opposing party)
Commissioner of Internal Revenue (see name of defendant)
Commissioner of Public Health; Gifford v. 52002
Commissioner of Transp.; Sagamore Group, Inc. v. 92018
Commonwealth v. (see name of defendant)
Commonwealth Constr. Co.; Midwest Mechanical Contractors, Inc. v. 86045
Commonwealth Dept. of Transp.; Acchione & Canuso, Inc. v. 83001
Commonwealth Dept. of Transp.; Swindell Dressler Co. v. 80064
Commonwealth, Dept. of Transp.; W.C. English, Inc. v. 92021b
Commonwealth Edison Co.; Rome v. . . . 80056
Commonwealth Edison Co.; Spiezio v. . . . 68047
Commonwealth Edison Co.; Vandygriff v. 80073
Commonwealth ex rel. (see name of relator)
Commonwealth of Pennsylvania; Central Penn Industries, Inc. v. 76011
Commonwealth of Pennsylvania v. Osage Co. 76013
Commonwealth of Pennsylvania; Security Painting Co. v. 76066
Commonwealth of Pennsylvania, Dept. of Transp. v. Trumbull Corp. 86011
Commonwealth of Virginia; Nelson v. . . . 88025
Community Consolidated School District v. Meneley Construction Co. 80013
Community Hospital; Basic Construction Co. v. . . . 73011
Comptroller of Virginia ex rel. Virginia Military Institute v. King 77022
Concourse Beauty School, Inc. v. Polakov 88008
Concrete Contractors, Inc.; R. W. Mier Construction Co. v. 68040
Concrete Form Co. v. W.T. Grange Construction Co. 35001
Concrete Materials of Georgia, Inc. v. Smith & Plaster Co. 73026

Conduit & Foundation Corp.; Pearl Street Development Corp. v. 76053
Cone Brothers Contracting Co.; Hillsborough County Aviation Authority v. 73053
Conesco Industries, Ltd. v. Conforti & Eisele, Inc. 80014
Conforti & Eisele Co.; Corrente v. 83012
Conforti & Eisele, Inc.; Conesco Industries, Ltd. v. 80014
Congress-Kenilworth Corp.; W.E. Erickson Constr., Inc. v. 86070
Conklin v. Cohen 73027
Conway Corp.; Grunley Constr. Co. v. . . . 96028
Connecticut General Life Insurance Co.; Skidmore, Owings & Merrill v. 63005
Connell v. Higgens 15002
Conner; Bushman Construction Co. v. . . . 65018; 66011
Connolly v. Asheville Contract Co. 67016
Connor v. Thompson Construction & Development Co. 69010
Conntech Dev. Co. v. University of Connecticut Educ. Properties Inc. 96022
Conservatorship of (see name of party)
Consolidated Constr. Co.; Brouillette v. . . 82009
Consolidated Constr. Co.; Cotter v. . . . 77024
Consolidated Edison Co. of New York, Inc.; Carollo v. 77017
Consolidated Electric Co. v. United States 66015
Consolidated Electrical Distributors, Inc. v. Kirkham, Chaon & Kirkham, Inc. 71024
Consolidated Fed. Corp. v. Cain 90012
Consolidated Papers, Inc.; Gunka v. 93040
Consolidation Coal Co.; Woodburn v. . . . 91039
Construction Contracting & Management, Inc. v. McConnell 91007
Construction Maintenance Sys., Inc.; D.W. Hutt Consultants, Inc. v. 95010
Construction Materials, Inc. v. American Fidelity Fire Insurance Co. 80016
Construction Service Co. v. United States 66016
Construction Technology, Inc.; Koch v. . . 96033
Constructora Bauza v. Garcia\Lopez 95020
Constructors & Assocs.; Fisk Elec. Co. v. 94033
Constructors-Pamco; W.A. Botting Plumbing & Heating Co. v. 87052
Consumers Construction Co. v. American Motorists Insurance Co. 69011
Consumers Construction Co. v. Cook, County of 71025
Conte v. Norwalk, City of 77023

TABLE OF CASES

[The five-digit numbers in this table are *Citator* Case Reference Numbers, which refer to the cases in the Cases section]

City v. (see name of defendant)
City and County of (see name of city and county)
City & County of Denver; E.B. Jones Constr. Co. v. 86017
City National Bank v. Chitwood Construction Co. 68009
City School District v. Jacques 79028
City Sioux Falls v. Henry Carlson Co. 77021
City Stores Co. v. Gervais F. Favrot Co. ... 78017
C.J. Kern Contractors, Inc.: Elec-trol, Inc. v. 81022a
C.J. Moritz Co.; Hercules Constr. Co. v. ... 83022
C.J. Waddell Contractors, Inc.; E.B. Ludwig Steel Corp. v. 88012
C.J.M. Constr., Inc. v. Chandler Plumbing & Heating, Inc. 85011
C.L. Fairley Constr. Co.; Lenexa, City of v. 89008
C.L. Maddox, Inc. V Benham Group Inc. 96020
C.L. Winter, Inc.; Baytown, City of v. ... 94030
Clark v. Madeira 72028
Clark-Dietz & Assocs.-Eng'rs, Inc.; Columbus v. 82014
Clark & Enersen, Hamersky, Schlaebitz, Burroughs & T v. Schimmel Hotels Corp. 75006
Clark-Fitzpatrick, Inc./Franki Found. Co. v. Gill ... 94031
Clark & Groff Engineers, Inc.; Transpac Construction Co. v. 72102
Clarkeson Engineering Co. v. Massachusetts Turnpike Authority 64004
Clarksville Dept. of Elec.; Moore Constr. Co. v. 85029
Clarmac Marine Construction Co.; Beach Resorts International, Inc. v. 76005
Clearing Industrial District, Inc.; Moore v. 78055
Clearwater Associates, Inc. v. F. H. Bridge & Son, Contractors 76012
Clearwater Constructors, Inc. v. Guiterrez 81016
Clement v. Pensacola Builders Supply Co. 39002
Clement Ferdinand & Co.; Stewart M. Muller Construction Co. v. 71080
Clemons; Custom Builders, Inc. v. 77026
Cleveland Wrecking Co. v. Central Nat'l Bank .. 91005
Clifton D. Mayhew, Inc. v. George A. Fuller Co. 67014
Clifton D. Mayhew, Inc. v. Mabro Construction Inc. 74010
Clinton-Jackson Corp.; Kaspar v. 69031

Coastline Assocs. Ltd. Partnership; Miller Bldg. Corp. v. 92016
Coatsville Contractors & Eng'rs, Inc. v. Borough of Ridley Park 86010
Cobb v. Thomas 78018
Cocke v. Odom 80012
Coe; Meulenbergh v. 16003
Coeur d'Alene, City of; Beitzel v. 92001a
Cohen; Conklin v. 73027
Cohen v. Mayflower Corp. 55001
Colangelo; Namerow v. 69041
Colbert; Reliance Insurance Co. v. 66077
Colcon Indus. Corp.; Des Moines Asphalt & Paving Co. v. 93008
Cole v. Chevron Chemical Co. 71023
College Park, City of v. Batson-Cook Co. 90009
College Plaza, Inc. v. Harlaco, Inc. 55026
Collins v. Kiewit Constr. Co. 96021
Collins v. Post 61004
Collins Co.; McKinney Drilling Co. v. 81052
Colmor Irrigation & Land Co.; Odell v. .. 29004
Colorado Real Estate Development, Inc. v. Sternberg 67015
It Industries, Inc.; A. A. Baxter Corp. v. .. 70001
Columbia Casualty Co.; Johnson Electric Co. v. 31004
Columbus v. Clark-Dietz & Assocs.-Eng'rs, Inc. 82014
Columbus, City of v. Alden E. Stilson & Assocs. 93030
Columbus, City of; S & M Constructors v. 82047
Combustion Equip. Assoc., Inc.; Ralph M. Parsons Co. v. 85034
Comm v. Goodman 72115
Commerce Bank, N.A. v. DiMaria Constr. 97007
Commerce, Crowdus & Canton, Ltd. v. DSK Constr., Inc. 89009
Commerce Elec., Inc.; Ferran Concrete Co. v. 86024
Commerce Hyatt House; General Insurance Co. of America v. 70029
Commercial Concrete Co.; Nuzzo v. 73082
Commercial Constr. Corp.; Fairways Plaza Assocs. v. 82038
Commercial Contracting Co.; Aluminum Co. of America v. 69002
Commercial Development Corp.; Whitfield Construction Co. Inc. v. 75027
Commercial Mowing & Grading; Manalili v. 83030

TABLE OF CASES

[The five-digit numbers in this table are *Citator* Case Reference Numbers, which refer to the cases in the Cases section]

C.H. Leavell & Co. v. Vilbig Bros.	60003
Chadwick v. CSI, Ltd.	93029
Chamblee Construction Co.; Pickett v.	71070
Chambless v. J. J. Fritch, General Contractor, Inc.	60002
Chandler High School District No. 202; Reber v.	70069
Chandler Plumbing & Heating, Inc.; C.J.M. Constr., Inc. v.	85011
Chaney; Tassinari v.	66095
Chaney & James Construction Co.; Howard-Green Electrical Co. v.	71050
Charlebois v. J.M. Weller Assocs., Inc.	88004
Charles Burton Builders, Inc. v. L & S Construction Co.	70016
Charles Carta & Co.; McGowan-Rigsby Supply, Inc. v.	72068
Charles J. Frank, Inc. v. Associated Jewish Charities Inc.	82010
Charles R. Perry Constr., Inc. v. C. Barry Gibson & Assocs., Inc.	88005
Charles S. Wood & Co. v. Alvord & Swift	31002
Charles Sales Corp.; American Fire & Casualty Co. v.	67003
Charles Simkin & Sons; Ferrante Equipment Co. v.	68015
Charles T. Main, Inc. v. Massachusetts Turnpike Authority	64002
Charles W. Ackerman, Inc.; Frank J. Rooney, Inc. v.	69022
Charlotte, City of; Ruby-Collins, Inc. v.	90039
Chas. H. Tompkins Co.; Phenix-Georgetown, Inc. v.	84029
Chase Architectural Assocs. v. Moyers Corners Fire Dept. Inc.	84007
Chase Manhattan Bank; Olsen v.	61011
Chasin v. Chasin	71018
Chasin; Chasin v.	71018
Chastain v. Atlanta Gas Light Co.	70017
Chatelain, Samperton & Nolan; Alfred A. Altimont, Inc. v.	77002
Chavez v. Gribble	72023
Chehalis County; Gauntt v.	13007
Chemetron Corp.; Northern Pacific Railway Co. v.	70060
Chemical Bank v. New York, State of	78015
Chesapeake & Potomac Telephone Co. of Virginia v. Sisson & Ryan, Inc.	87011
Cheschi v. Boston Edison Co.	95028
Chester City School Authority v. Aberthaw Construction Co.	75005
Chevron Chemical Co.; Cole v.	71023
Chiappisi v. Granger Contracting Co.	67012
Chiaverini v. Vail	38001
Chicago Bridge & Iron Co. v. Reliance Insurance Co.	71019
Chicago, City of; Bella Kay Building Corp. v.	65013
Chicago, City of; Bethlehem Steel Corp. v.	65014
Chicago, City of; Contracting & Material Co. v.	74012
Chicago College of Osteopathic Medicine v. George A. Fuller Co.	83007; 85009
Chicora Construction Co. v. United States	65022
Children's Hospital v. American Arbitration Association	74009
Childs v. Smeltzer	34002
Chillum-Adelphi Volunteer Fire Department, Inc. v. Button & Goode, Inc.	66013
Chitwood Construction Co.; City National Bank v.	68009
Christensen v. Dewor Dev.	83008
Christman; Amerson v.	68003
Christman Co. v. Anthony S. Brown Dev. Co.	95005
Christy v. Menasha Corp.	73025
Chrysler Corp. v. Hanover Insurance Co.	65023
Chrysler Corp.; Hollingsworth v.	65051
Chrysler Realty Corp.; Carrabine Constr. Co. v.	86009
CH2M Hill Southeast, Inc.; Padgett v.	94044
Church's Fried Chicken; Krass Plus Clothiers, Inc. v.	93043
Cianbro Corp. v. Empresa Nacional De Ingenieria	88006
Cianchette; Granger Northern, Inc. v.	90022
Cianchette; Pine Gravel, Inc. v.	86054
Cianelli v. Levy	70018
Ciejek v. Crane Service Co.	65024
CIG Contractors, Inc. v. Mississippi State Bldg. Comm'n	87012
Cimino Constr. Co.; Willis Realty Assocs. v.	93022
Cincinnati Gas & Elec. Co. v. Benjamin F. Shaw Co.	83009
Cisne & Associates, Inc.; Harsco Corp. v.	80031
Citadel Corp. v. All-South Subcontractors, Inc.	95006
Citizens Bank v. Timmons	17002
Citizens National Bank v. L. L. Glascock, Inc.	71021
Citizens & Southern National Bank; United States ex rel. Shields, Inc. v.	66107

TABLE OF CASES

[The five-digit numbers in this table are *Citator* Case Reference Numbers, which refer to the cases in the Cases section]

Carlander; Baylor University v. 58001
Carlson v. Metropolitan Sanitary District . . 65019
Carlstrom; Independent Consolidated School District No. 24 v. 67033
Carmichael v. Board of County Commissioners . . 70015
Carnaggio; Lewis v. 71060
Carolina Builders Corp. v. AAA Dry Wall, Inc. . . 79025
Carolina Mechanical Contractors, Inc. v. Yeargin Construction Co. 73023
Carollo v. Consolidated Edison Co. of New York, Inc. 77017
Caron v. Barkan Construction Co. 81013
Carpenter v. Massachusetts Bonding & Insurance Co. 65020
Carpenter International, Inc. v. Kaiser Jamaica Corp. 74008
Carpentersville v. Mayfair Construction Co. 81014
Carr v. Detroit Edison Co. 73024
Carrabine Constr. Co. v. Chrysler Realty Corp. . . 86009
Carriger v. Ballenger 81015
Carroccia v. Todd 80010
Carroll; Westerhold v. 67071
Carroll-Boone Water Dist. v. M & P Equip. Co. 83006
Carrols Equities Crop. v. Villnave 77018
Carvalho v. Toll Bros. & Developers . . . 95004
Casale v. August Bohl Contracting Co. . . . 66012
Case v. Midwest Mechanical Contractors, Inc. . . . 94005
Cass-Warner Corp. v. Brickman 67010
Casson Construction Co.; Seaman Unified School District v. 79060
Cast-Crete Corp. v. West Baro Corp. 76010
Caste Bros., Inc.; Verzella v. 65115
Castle; Maddy v. 76039
Castle Concrete v. Fleetwood Associates . . 71017
Castle Constr. Co./Tuskegee Lumber Co. v. Owens & Woods Partnership 91004
Caswell County Bd. of Educ.; Triangle Air Conditioning, Inc. v. 82054
Catanese; Fuhrmann v. 50001
Caton Ridge, Inc. v. Bonnett 67011
Cave City; W. William Graham, Inc. v. . . 86074
Cawdrey Mars Joint Venture; Espaniola v. 85015
C.B. Lauch Construction Co.; Puget Sound National Bank v. 52004
CBCO, Inc. v. Grani Installation, Inc. . . . 79024
C.B.I. Na-Con, Inc. v. Macon Bibb County Water & Sewerage Auth. 92004b

CCM Corp. v. United States 90008
C.E. Thurston & Sons, Inc.; Hendrick Construction Co. v. 67031
C.E. Thurston & Sons, Inc.; Poole & Kent Corp. v. 74030
Cecil A. Mason Construction Co.; Wright v. 67073
Cedar Rapids, Iowa, City of; Johnson Controls, Inc. v. 33026
Centennial Floors, Inc.; Hays v. 95012
Center Bros.; Bishop Contracting Co. v. . . 94003; 94026
Center Designs v. Henning, State ex rel . . 97024
Centerre Trust Co. v. Continental Ins. Co. 88003
Centex Constr. Co.; United States v. 85039
Centex-Rodgers Constr. Co. v. McCann Steel Co. 92004c
Central Bank of Birmingham; Fidelity & Casualty Co. of N.Y. v. 82019
Central Contracting Co. v. Maryland Casualty Co. 65021
Central Illinois Public Services Co.; Decatur Construction Co. v. 74013
Central Industrial Engineering Co. v. Strauss Construction Co. 79026
Central Louisiana Electric Co. v. Giant Enterprises, Inc. 79027
Central Marine Power Co.; Burns & Roe, Inc. v. 87010
Central Nat'l Bank; Cleveland Wrecking Co. v. 91005
Central N.Y. Regional Transp. Auth.; Maross Constr., Inc. v. 85026
Central Penn Industries, Inc. v. Commonwealth of Pennsylvania 76011
Central Savings Bank & Trust Co.; School District No. 3 v. 45001
Central School District No. 1; Helmer-Cronin Construction, Inc. v. 76028
Central States Grain Co.; Stillinger & Napier v. 57002
Central Telephone & Utility Corp.; Beeker v. 73013
Centre County Hospital; Aberthaw Construction Co. v. 73001
Centrella; Vernali v. 70087
Certain Teed; Dixon v. 96024
Certain Teed Corp. v. Employers Ins. of Wausau 96019
Certified Contracting Inc.; Ironbound Fin. Servs. v. 97012
C.H. Leavell & Co. v. Glantz Contracting Corp. 71020

TABLE OF CASES

[The five-digit numbers in this table are *Citator* Case Reference Numbers, which refer to the cases in the Cases section]

Burns v. Thorndike 17001
Burns Elec. Co.; JGA Constr. Corp. v. ... 88018
Burns & McDonnell Eng'g Co. v. Torson Constr. Co. 92003a
Burns & Roe, Inc. v. Central Marine Power Co. 87010
Burrone Brothers; Darling v. 72031
Burroughs v. School District No. 2, Town of Richland 14003
Burroughs Corp.; Detroit Demolition Corp. v. ... 73033
Burton-Dixie Corp. v. Timothy McCarthy Construction Co. 71016
Burzynski; Keith v. 80039
Bushman Construction Co. v. Conner ... 65018; 66011
Busick v. Streator Township High School Dist. #40 92004
Busker v. Sokolowski 72108
Butler; American-Hawaiian Engineering & Construction Co. v. 13001
Butler v. Metz, Train, Olson & Youngren 78014
Butler v. Mitchell-Hughback, Inc. 94004
Butler Tel. Co.; Pugh v. 87037
Button & Goode, Inc.; Chillum-Adelphi Volunteer Fire Department, Inc. v. 66013
Byler v. Great American Insurance Co. .. 68007
Byram Lumber & Supply Co. v. Page ... 29001

C

C & B Construction Co. v. Nashville School District No. 1 72022
C. Barry Gibson & Assocs., Inc.; Charles R. Perry Constr., Inc. v. 88005
C. F. Braun Co.; Schroeder v. 74037
C & M Ventures, Inc. v. Wolf 91006
C. O. Brand, Inc.; Continental Casualty Co. v. .. 66017
C. O. Jones Building Co.; Bowman v. .. 33001
C & R Construction, Inc.; Crabtree Masonry Co. v. 78021
C. Rallo Contracting Co.; Haughton Elevator Co. v. 65048
C.W. Scheurer; Van Vickle v. 96043
Cable-Wiedemer, Inc. v. A. Freiderich & Sons .. 72021
Cadral Corp. v. Solomon, Cordwell, Buenz & Assocs. 86006
Cafferkey v. Turner Constr. Co. 86007
Cagle, Inc. v. Sammons 77015
Cahill; Anderson v. 72009
Cahn Elec. Co. v. Robert E. McKee, Inc. 86008

Cain; Consolidated Fed. Corp. v. 90012
Cain; Lawton v. 65067
Cairo, Village of v. Bodine Contracting Co. 85042
Calcagni; South Burlington School District v. ... 80061
Caldwell v. United Presbyterian Church .. 61002
Caldwell; Warren G. Kleban Engineering Corp. v. 73122
California, State of; Welch v. 83048
Call v. Alcan Pacific Co. 67009
Callahan v. A.J. Welch Equip. Corp. 94029
Callas Contractors, Inc.; Mason v. 80042
Cam Constr. Co.; Board of County Comm'rs of Frederick County v. 84003
Camelot Excavating Co. v. St. Paul Fire and Marine Insurance Co. 81011
Campagna v. Smallwood 83005
Campbell; A.A. Conte, Inc. v. 85001
Campbell v. Southern Roof Deck Applicators, Inc. 81012
Campbell Bros., Inc.; Texas Bank & Trust Co. v. 78071
Campbell Constr. Co.; American Cyanamid Co. v. 94023
Campbell County Bd. of Educ. v. Brownlee-Kesterson, Inc. 84006
Campbell-Ellsworth, Inc. v. Holy Trinity Serbian Orthodox Church-School Congregation 75004
Canam Steel Corp.; Aetna Casualty & Sur. Co. v. 90002
Cann; First Nat'l Bank of Akron v. 82020
Cape Fear Electric Co. v. Star News Newspapers 74007
Capitol Crane Co.; Alpha Crane Serv., Inc. v. .. 86001
Capitol Hotel Co. v. Rittenberry 31001
Capitol Place I Assocs. L.P. v. George Hyman Constr. Co. 96002
Capua v. W. E. O'Neil Construction Co. .. 77016
Carabetta; DuBose v. 71034
Carabetta Builders, Inc. v. Hotz Corp. ... 93006
Cardi Corp.; Warren Brothers v. 73121
Cardinal Properties, Inc.; Thomas Wells & Associates v. 75034; 76069
Caribbean Lumber Co. v. Anderson 92004a
Caristo Construction Corp.; Allhusen v. .. 52001
Caristo Construction Corp.; Bignami v. .. 73018
Carl A. Morse, Inc.; Mayer Paving and Asphalt Co. v. 77057
Carl T. Madsen, Inc.; Tucci & Sons v. ... 70082
Carl Weissman & Sons v. St. Paul Fire & Marine Insurance Co. 68008

TABLE OF CASES

[The five-digit numbers in this table are *Citator* Case Reference Numbers, which refer to the cases in the Cases section]

Brice Petrides-Donohue & Assocs., Inc.; Shepherd Components, Inc. v. 91030
Brick Township Municipal Utilities Authority v. Diversified R. B. & T. Construction Co. 79023
Brickhouse; Spitz v. 54005
Brickman; Cass-Warner Corp. v. 67010
Bridges-Gallagher, Inc.; Shaw v. 88033
Brisk Waterproofing Co.; Gilbane Bldg. Co. v. ... 91011
Brisk Waterproofing Co.; S.S.D.W. Co. v. 90043
Bristol Development Co.; Parsons v. 65086
British Overseas Airways Corp.; Bethlehem Fabricators, Inc. v. 70011
Britton Drive, Inc.; Bruce Campbell & Son Construction Co. v. 75003
Brixen & Christopher, Architects v. Elton 89006
Broadway Maintenance Corp. v. Rutgers State Univ. 82007
Brockton, City of; Murphy v. 73081
Brocton Central School District; Naetzker v. ... 75015
Brodsky v. Princemont Construction Co. ... 76008
Brook-Lea Country Club v. Hanover Insurance Co. 69009
Brookfield-North Riverside Water Comm'n v. Abbott Contractors, Inc. 93027
Brookhaven Landscape & Grading Co. v. J.F. Barton Contracting Co. 82008
Brookline Associates; E V. Cox Construction Co. v. 79032
Brooklyn Heights Reality Co.; Thompson-Starrett Co. v. 06001
Brookridge Apartments, Ltd. v. Universal Constructors, Inc. 92002
Brooks Equipment Leasing Inc.; Martinson v. ... 67045
Brooks Towers Corp. v. Hunkin-Conkey Construction Co. 72019
Brophy & Phillips Co. Haemonetics Corp. v. ... 86028
Brouillette v. Consolidated Constr. Co. ... 82009
Brown v. Boyer-Washington Boulevard Assocs. .. 93028
Brown; Corbett v. 69013
Brown v. Cox 70014
Brown & Kerr Inc. v. St. Paul Fire & Marine Ins. Co., ... 96017
Brown; Entropic Landscapes, Inc. v. 93009
Brown; Jen-Mar Construction Co. v. 67035
Brown; Lebreton v. 72059
Brown; Mohawk Overall Co. v. 14005
Brown; Palmer v. 54004
Brown v. Prime Constr. Co. 84005
Brown v. Two Exch. Plaza Partners 89006
Brown-McKee, Inc. v. Western Beef, Inc. 76009
Brown-Randolph Co. v. Gude 21001
Brownlee-Kesterson, Inc.; Campbell County Bd. of Educ. v. 84006
Bruce Campbell & Son Construction Co. v. Britton Drive, Inc. 75003
Bruffey; Dowling v. 72035
Brunzell; Eagle's Nest Ltd. Partnership v. 33014
Brunzell Construction Co.; Home Furniture, Inc. v. 68019
BSP Div. of Envirotech Corp.; Aiken County v. ... 89001
Buchanan; Maddux v. 17003
Buck; Gunter Hotel of San Antonio, Inc. v. 89020
Buchanan v. Rentenbach Constructors Inc. 96018
Union Casualty Co.; Ben-Tom Corp. v. .. 64001
Buckley & Co. v. New York, City of ... 86005
Buckley & Co. v. State 75029
Bueche v. Eikenroht 49001
Buehner Schokbeton Co. v. Horne's Crane Service Co. 72020
Buetow & Associates, Inc.; Moundsview Independent School District No. 621 v. 77061
Buffalo Hotel Dev. Venture; John W. Cowper Co. v. 85023
Bullard Engineers, Inc.; Excavators & Erectors, Inc. v. 73040
Bullock Co. v. Allen 73022
Bumstead-Woolford Co.; Hoerner Woldorf Corp. v. 72048
Burch; Hastings & Chivetta Architects v. 90024
Burdette v. Lascola 78013
Burger King Corp.; Myers v. 94013
Burke Brothers; Mesker Brothers Iron Co. v. 67047
Burke County Public Schools Board of Education v. Juno Construction Corp. 81010
Burlington v. Arnold Constr. Co. 87009
Burlington Memorial Hospital; Scherrer Construction Co. v. 74036
Burlington, Town of; Morgan v. 44002
Burmar Electrical Corp. v. Starrett Bros. ... 77014
Burns v. Black & Veatch Architects, Inc. 93005
Burns v. DeWitt & Assocs., Inc. 92003
Burns v. McDermott 95027

TABLE OF CASES

[The five-digit numbers in this table are *Citator* Case Reference Numbers, which refer to the cases in the Cases section]

Board of Local Improvements v. St. Paul Fire and Marine Insurance 76007
Board of Public Education; Orth v. 22001
Board of Regents; Kingery Construction Co. v. . . . 73063
Board of Regents v. Wilson 75002
Board of Regents of North Texas State Univ. v. Denton Constr. Co. 83004
Board of Regents of University of Texas; Hyatt Cheek Builders-Engineers Co. v. 80035
Board of Supervisors; Havard v. 54002
Board of Supervisors; Verdex Steel & Construction Co. v. 73116
Board of Trustees; Volt Information Sciences, Inc. v. 89048
Board of Water Commissioners; Henry B. Byors & Sons, Inc. v. 70034
Bob Eldridge Construction Co.; State v. . . 65101
Bob McKiness Excavating & Grading, Inc.; Payne Plumbing & Heating Co. v. 86050
Boca Raton Resort & Club; Raffa Assocs. v. . . . 93016
Bodine Contracting Co.; Cairo, Village of v. . . . 85042
Bodovinac; Diamond Homes, Inc. v. 69015
Boehringer Ingelheim Pharmaceuticals, Inc.; Morganti, Inc. v. 89034
Bogar & Bink; Technical School Authority v. . . . 78023
Bogner-Seitel Lumber Co. v. Insurance Co. of North America 68005
Boise Cascade Corp.; Hartford Accident and Indemnity Co. v. 80032
Bolin; Famous Builders, Inc. v. 68014
Bolo Corp. v. Homes & Son Construction Co. . . . 70013
Bolton; Moore v. 72071
Bolton Corp. v. T.A. Loving Co. 89005
Bomar Constr. Co.; Dickson County v. . . 96023
Bond v. Howard Corp. 95003
Bone Contracting Co. v. Depot Construction Corp. 73020
Bonner Roofing & Sheet Metal Co.; Island Villa Developers, Inc. v. 85021
Bonnett; Caton Ridge, Inc. v. 67011
Booth Radio Stations, Inc.; Zannoth v. . . . 52007
Bor-Son Bldg. Corp.; 200 Levee Drive Assocs., Ltd. v. 89046
Borck v. Holewinski 84004
Borden Co. v. Foster-Lipkins Corp. 72017
Borders; NSC Contractors, Inc. v. 89035
Borg, Inc. v. Morris Middle School District No. 54 72018

Borggren/Dickson Constr., Inc.; Dixie Roof Decks, Inc. v. 90017
Borkowski; Quinn Assoc., Inc. v. 88029
Borough of Nanty-Glo v. Fireman's Fund Insurance Co. 66010
Borough of Ridley Park; Coatsville Contractors & Eng'rs, Inc. v. 86010
Borsher; Fischer v. 73042
Borup v. Von Kokeritz 14002
Bosio v. Branigar Org., Inc. 87008
Bossier City; Roger Johnson Construction Co. v. 76062
Boston Cold Storage & Terminal Co.; Hennebique Construction Co. v. 18001
Boston Edison Co.; Cheschi v. 95028
Boston Shipyard Corp., In re 89024
Bothwell & Swaner Co.; Russell v. 20004
Bott v. Moser 40001
Bouten Constr. Co. v. M & L Land Co. . . 94028
Bovee; John v. 78041
Bowman v. C. O. Jones Building Co. 33001
Bowman v. Maryland Casualty Co. 28002
Boyd Construction Co. v. T.L. James & Co. 73021
Boyer-Washington Boulevard Assocs.; Brown v. 93028
Boyles Galvanizing Co.; Wenzel v. 91037
Boys Club of San Fernando Valley, Inc. v. Fidelity & Deposit Co. of Maryland 92001b
Bradford v. Kupper Assocs. 95025
Bradley; Paul Hardman, Inc. v. 71069
Bradley & Bradley, Inc.; Stephenson, County of v. 71026
Brady; E. Carl Schiewe, Inc. v. 80022
Brady Contracting Co. v. West Manchester Township Sewer Auth. 86004
Braegelmann v. Horizon Dev. Co. 85008
Brager; Tsombikos v. 90051
Brandt-Jordan Corp.; Lincoln-Sudbury Regional School District v. 69033
Branigar Org., Inc.; Bosio v. 87008
Branna Construction Co. v. West Allegheny School Authority 68006
Bratton; Oldham & Worth, Inc. v. 65083
Braye v. Archer 95026
Breaux; Gross v. 62004
Breckenridge; Stewart v. 17005
Breily & Corrishaw, Inc.; Yamanishi v. . . 72114
Brennan v. Kenwick 81009
Brennan's of Atlanta; E.C. Long, Inc. v. . . 79005
Brewster; Healy v. 67030
Brezina Construction Co. v. South Dakota Dept. of Transportation 80009

TABLE OF CASES

[The five-digit numbers in this table are *Citator* Case Reference Numbers, which refer to the cases in the Cases section]

Biggs; Ambrose v. 87003
Bignami v. Caristo Construction Corp. ... 73018
Bill O'Brien & Sons Constr., Inc.; Douglas Northwest, Inc. v. 92005
Bilotta Constr. Corp. v. Mamaroneck, Village of 93026
Binswanger Glass Co. v. Beers Construction Co. 77013
Bishop Contracting Co. v. Center Bros. ... 94003; 94026
Bismark Baptist Church v. Wiedemann Industries, Inc. 72015
Bitner v. Lester B. Knight & Associates .. 74006
Bituminous Casualty Corp.; Commercial Union Ins. Co. v. 88007
B.J. Harland Elec. Co. v. Granger Bros., Inc. ... 87006
Bjorkman v. Suffolk Constr. Co. 97006
Black Lake Pipe Line Co. v. Union Construction Co. 76006
Black & Veatch Architects, Inc.; Burns v. 93005
Black & Veatch Consulting Engineers; Becker v. 74004
Blaine Constr. Co.; Jacobsen Constr. Co. v. 93042
Blaine Economic Dev. Auth. v. Royal Elec. Co. .. 94027
Blake; Lange v. 77051
Bland v. L'Enfant Plaza North, Inc. 72016
Blankenship Plumbing Co.; United States Fidelity & Guaranty Co. v. 80068
Blanks v. Midstate Constructors, Inc. ... 80008
Blau Mechanical Corp. v. New York, City of ... 90007
Blecick v. School District No. 18 65015
Bleck v. Stephanich 78011
Bloomfield Reorganized School District No. R-14 v. Stites 60001
Blount Brothers Construction Co.; J.P. Greathouse Steel Erectors, Inc. v. 67037
Blount Brothers Corp. v. M. K. Steel, Inc. 81008
Blount Construction Co. v. Housing Authority ... 65016
Blout Int'l, Ltd. v. James River-Pennington, Inc. 93004
Blue Cross of Southwestern Virginia v. McDevitt & Street Co. 87007
Blue Diamond Co.; Warner Construction Co. v. ... 68052
Blue Mountain Prune Growers Co-op.; Halvorson v. 50003
Bluebonnet Electrical Corp. v. Universal Electrical Construction Co. 71012
Blythe Indus., Inc.; W.L. Jorden & Co. v. 88044
Board of Comm'rs; Tonn & Blank, Inc. v. 90047
Board of Comm'rs v. Vahlberg 47001
Board of County Comm'rs; Carmichael v. 70015
Board of County Comm'rs of Frederick County v. Cam Constr. Co. 84003
Board of Educ. v. A. Barbaresi & Son ... 66009
Board of Educ. v. Aetna Casualty & Surety Co. ... 71013
Board of Educ.; Delisi Construction, People ex rel. v. 75018
Board of Educ. v. Delle Cese 71014
Board of Educ. v. Dobson Construction Co. 71015
Board of Educ.; Furst v. 59001
Board of Educ.; Goin v. 44001
Board of Educ. v. Hartford Accident & Indemnity Co. 65017
Board of Educ.; Joseph F. Trionfo & Sons, Inc. v. 79009
Board of Educ.; McKay Construction Co. v. 69037
Board of Educ.; NRS Constr. Corp. v. ... 83036
Board of Educ.; Pierce v. 25001
Board of Educ.; Shalman v. 69053
Board of Educ.; Stahelin v. 67063
Board of Educ. v. W. Harley Miller, Inc. 75001
Board of Educ. v. Wager Construction Corp. ... 73019
Board of Educ., Community Consol. Sch. Dist. No. 15; Glenn H. Johnson Constr. Co. v. ... 93012
Board of Educ., Longwood Cent. School Dist. v. Hatzel & Buehler, Inc. 89003
Board of Educ. of Clinton School Dist.; Dan Cowling & Associates, Inc. v. 81018
Board of Educ. of Community Consolidated School District v. Del Bianco & Associates, Inc. 78012
Board of Educ. of Hudson City School Dist. v. Sargent, Webster, Crenshaw & Folley ... 89004
Board of Educ. of Montgomery County; Stauffer Constr. Co. v. 83042
Board of Educ. of the City of New York; Laura Roofing & Renovating Co. v. 77052
Board of Educ. Salmon River Cent. School Dist. v. Tracy Trombley Constr. Co. 86003
Board of Educ., Union Free School District No. 3, Town o v. Valden Associates 79022

TABLE OF CASES

[The five-digit numbers in this table are *Citator* Case Reference Numbers, which refer to the cases in the Cases section]

Beacon Plaza Shopping Center, Inc. v. Tri-Cities Construction & Supply Co. 66007
Beagle; Markley v. 67044
Beam; Alabama Power Co. v. 85003a
Beard; Swarthout v. 71082
Beatty Safeway Scaffold Co.; Unitec Corp. v. . . . 66101
Beaufort Concrete Co. v. Atlantic States Construction Co. 65012
Beaufort-Jasper Water Authority; Ruscon Construction Co. v. 72085
Bebb v. Jordan 20001
Bechdolt; Haines v. 65046
Bechtel Constr. Co.; Kemp v. 86038
Bechtel, Inc.; Hammond v. 80030
Bechtel Power Corp.; Lasar v. 86043
Bechtel Power Corp.; Riggins v. 86057
Beck; Providence Washington Insurance Co. v. . . . 70067
Becker v. Black & Veatch Consulting Engineers 74004
Becker Construction Co.; Hortman v. . . . 79044
Beckham v. William Bayley Co. 87005
Becknell Construction, Inc.; Mississippi State Building Commission v. 76044
Bedros; Lewis-Brady Builders Supply, Inc. v. . . . 77054
Beeker v. Central Telephone & Utility Corp. 73013
Beers Construction Co.; Binswanger Glass Co. v. 77013
Beers Construction Co.; Lagerstrom v. . . . 81046
Beitzel v. Coeur d'Alene, City of 92001a
Bel Pre Medical Center, Inc. v. Frederick Contractors, Inc. 74005
Belcher & Sons, Inc.; Washington Parish Police Jury v. 68053
Belford; Homeco, Inc. v. 79008
Belgum v. Mitsuo Kawamota & Assocs., Inc. . . . 90006
Bell-Gallyardt & Wells, Inc.; Bartak v. . . . 80007
Bella Kay Building Corp. v. Chicago, City of . . . 65013
Beller v. DeLara 78009
Bellevue Holding Co.; Figgs v. 94032
Belmont Constructors, Inc. v. Lyondell Petrochemical Co. 95002
Ben Contruction Co. v. Sanitary Authority 67008
Ben M. Hogan Co. v. Nichols 73014
Ben M. Hogan Co.; Phillips v. 80050
Ben-Tom Corp. v. Buckeye Union Casualty Co. . . . 64001
Ben Trovato Properties, Inc. v. Strauss . . . 81007

Bencomo Roofing Co.; Slaught v. 94018
Bender-Miller Co. v. Thomwood Farms, Inc. . . . 71010
Benjamin F. Shaw Co.; Cincinnati Gas & Elec. Co. v. 83009
Bennett; Baker Pool Co. v. 67005
Bennett Construction Co. v. Allen Gardens, Inc. . . . 77011
Benning Construction Co. v. Lakeshore Plaza Enterprises, Inc. 78010
Benson Paint Co. v. Williams Construction Co. . . . 73015
Bentham Group Inc.; C.L. Maddox, Inc. v. 96020
Benton v. Hoffman Plastering Co. 62002
Benton Sch. Dist. No. 8; May Constr. Co. v. . . . 95014
Berg v. Kucharo Construction Co. 46001
Bergen County Iron Works; James Stewart Polshek & Associates v. 75032
Bergman v. Parker 66008
Bernhard Mechanical; Perritt v. 96009
Bernstein; Strudell Asphalt, Inc. v. 65103
Bero Construction Corp. v. New York State Thruway Authority 73016
Berschauer/Phillips Constr. Co. v. Seattle Sch. Dist. No. 1 94025
Bert C. Young & Sons Corp. v. Association of Franciscan Sisters of the Sacred Heart 77012
Berthot v. Stroble 72013
Berwin Builders; Smith v. 72094
Best Prods. Co. v. A.F. Callan & Co. . . . 97005
Bethesda Lutheran Church v. Twin City Constr. Co. 84002
Bethlehem Fabricators, Inc. v. British Overseas Airways Corp. 70011
Bethlehem Steel Corp. v. Chicago, City of 65014
Bethlehem Steel Corp.; HRH Construction Corp. v. 78035
Bettes; New Amsterdam Casualty Co. v. . . 66062
Bevco, Inc.; D.K. Meyer Corp. v. 80018
Bewley Furniture Co. v. Maryland Casualty Co. . . . 73017
Beyerlein; Rio Rancho Estates v. 81063
Beyt, Rish, Robbins Group, Architects, Inc. v. Appalachian Regional Healthcare, Inc. 93003
B-F-W Constr. Co. v. Garza 88002
B.G. Coney Co. v. Radford Petroleum Equip. Co. 85007
B.G. Danis of New England, Inc.; Floors, Inc. v. 79038
Bibeau Construction Co. v. Hauser Bros . . 72014
Bickerstaff v. Frazier 70012

TABLE OF CASES

[The five-digit numbers in this table are *Citator* Case Reference Numbers, which refer to the cases in the Cases section]

Bahr, Vermeer & Haecker Architect, Ltd.; Gables CVF, Inc. v. 93036
Bailey; Jim Carlson Constr., Inc. v. 89026
Bair v. School District No. 141 15001
Baker v. Keller Construction Co. 69006
Baker v. Pidgeon Thomas Co. 70008
Baker-Crow Construction Co. v. Hames Electric, Inc. 77009
Baker & Ford Co. v. United States ex rel. Urban Plumbing & Heating Co. 66006
Baker Pool Co. v. Bennett 67005
Balboa Insurance Co. v. W. C. B. Assoc. 80005
Balboa Insurance Co. v. W.G. Mills, Inc. 81006
Baldi Construction Engineers Inc. v. Wheel Awhile, Inc. 71008
Baldwin v. Alberti 61001
Baldwin; Kenison v. 60010
Baldwin Co. v. Weyland Mach. Shop, Inc. 85005
Baldwin Contracting Co. v. Winston Steel Works 65010
Ballard, H. T. Kirk & Associates v. Poston 72012
Ballenger; Carriger v. 81015
Balli; Texas Construction Associates, Inc. v. 77078
Balling Construction, Inc.; Keefe v. 72053
Ballou v. Basic Construction Co 69007
Ballwin Plaza Corp. v. H.B. Deal Construction Co. 70009
Baltimore Contractors, Inc.; A. J. Wolfe Co. v. .. 69001
Baltimore Contractors, Inc. v. Dupree ... 67006
Baltimore Contractors, Inc.; Vermont Marble Co. v. 81069
Baltimore County v. John K. Ruff, Inc. .. 77010
Baltimore Gas & Elect. Co. v. Commercial Union Ins. Co. 97004
Banchero; Rosellini v. 73096
Bank of Broadway v. General Aluminum Door & Entrance Co. 67007
Bankers & Shippers Insurance Co. of New York; Hunt v. 77045; 80034
Banner v. Dayton, Town of 70010
Barac Construction Co.; M.E. Kraft Excavating & Grading Co. v. 68029
Barbera v. Sokol 80006
Barbor; Kosmerl v. 79011
Barce, Inc.; Modern Construction, Inc. v. 76045
Bard; Bavin & Burch Co. v. 27001
Barkan Construction Co.; Caron v. 81013

Barlite, Inc.; Trinity Universal Insurance Co. v. .. 68049
Barnes Hosp.; Honey v. 86032
Barnett; Overby v. 70062
Barr; Donaldson, Lufkin & Jenrette Futures, Inc. v. 83025
Barrack v. Kolea 94024
Barrett & Co.; J. R. Meade & Co. v. 70043
Bartak v. Bell-Gallyardt & Wells, Inc. ... 80007
Bartex, Inc. of Texas; Hemenway Co. v. .. 79043
Barth Elec. Co. v. Traylor Bros., Inc. ... 90005
Bartlett, Labette County, City of; Owens v. 74028
Bartlett Wrecking, Inc.; Allen & O'Hara, Inc. v. 92001
Bartley, Inc. v. Jefferson Parish School Board 74003
Barton-Douglas Contractors, Inc.; Jefferson, County of v. 79030
BASF Corp.; Novak v. 94043
Basic Construction Co.; Ballou v. 69007
Basic Construction Co. v. Community Hospital .. 73011
Basic Construction Co.; John W. Johnson, Inc. v. 70041
Bateman; American Insurance Co. v. 71004
Bates & Rogers Constr. Corp. v. Greeley & Hansen 85006
Baton Rouge Contracting Co. v. West Hatchie Drainage District 69008
Batson-Cook Co.; College Park, City of v. 90009
Batson-Cook Co.; H.R.H. Prince Ltc. Faisal M. Saud v. 82024
Batson-Cook Co. v. Loden & Co. 73012
Batson-Cook Co. v. Poteat 78008
Batson-Cook Co. v. R. C. Pierce Roofing Co. ... 71009
Batts; Kenworth Northwest Sales & Service, Inc. v. 70047
Bavin & Burch Co. v. Bard 27001
Bayer & Mingolla Construction Co. v. Deschenes 65011
Baylor University v. Carlander 58001
Baystone Constr.; Morin Bldg. Prod. Co. v. 83032
Baytown, City of v. C.L. Winter, Inc. ... 94030
Beach Concrete Co.; William C. Blanchard Co. v. 72111
Beach Resorts International, Inc. v. Clarmac Marine Construction Co. 76005
Beacon Construction Co.; A. Amorello & Sons v. 81001

TABLE OF CASES

TC-5

[The five-digit numbers in this table are *Citator* Case Reference Numbers, which refer to the cases in the Cases section]

Arlington Structural Steel Co.; Friedman, Altschuler & Sincere v. 85015a
Armand v. Territorial Construction Inc. ... 79020
Armand Corporation, Inc.; Valley Force Industries, Inc. v. 78075
Armo Construction, Inc.; Titan Enterprises, Inc. v. 73129
Armour & Co. v. Nord 72010
Arnold Constr. Co.; Burlington v. 87009
Aronson v. Keating 80004
Arrow Construction Co. v. American Employers Insurance Co. 73008
Arrow Contractors Equipment Co. v. Siegel 66005
Arrow Sprinklers, Inc.; Dehnert v. 85014
Arrowhead, Inc. v. Safeway Stores, Inc. .. 78006
Artcraft Cabinet, Inc. v. Watajo, Inc. 76004
Arthur H. Neumann & Co.; Granette Products Co. v. 28003
Arthur Pew Construction Co. v. Hartline-Thomas, Inc. v. 79041
Artistic Ornamental Iron, Inc.; Anken Construction Co. v. 73006
A.S. Johnson Co. v. Atlantic Masonry Co. 97002
Asheville Contract Co.; Connolly v. 67016
Ashton-Mardian Co.; McDaniel v. 66055
Ashworth v. Glover 67004
Associated Engineers; Pastorelli v. 59005
Associated Engineers & Contractors, Inc. v. State 77007
Associated Jewish Charities Inc.; Charles J. Frank, Inc. v. 82010
Association of Franciscan Sisters of the Sacred Heart; Bert C. Young & Sons Corp. v. 77012
Atkinson-Kiewit Joint Venture; Cosimini v. 95007
Atlanta, City of v. J.J. Black & Co. 64003
Atlanta, City of; Robert E. McKee, Inc. v. 76061
Atlanta Gas Light Co.; Chastain v. 70017
Atlanta Tile & Marble Co.; Huggins v. .. 58003
Atlantic Masonry Co.; A.S. Johnson Co. v. 97002
Atlantic Mutual Ins. Co. v. Metron Eng'g & Constr. Co. 96001
Atlantic National Bank of Jacksonville v. Modular Age, Inc. 78007
Atlantic Realty Co.; Walls, Inc. v. 88040
Atlantic Scaffold & Ladder Co.; Drzewinski v. .. 87016
Atlantic Shores Resort Joint Venture v. Martin .. 90004

Atlantic States Construction Co.; Beaufort Concrete Co. v. 65012
Atlantic States Construction Co. v. Drummond .. 68004
Atlantic States Construction Co.; Rwenbark v. ... 72086
Atlas Assurance Co. v. General Builders, Inc. ... 79021
Atlas Plastering, Inc. v. Superior Court, County of Alameda 77008
Atlas Roofing & Skylight Co.; A & B Constr., Inc. v. 94022
Atlee Electric Co. v. Johnson Construction Co. .. 73009
Au-Yang; American Builder's Ass'n v. ... 90003
August Bohl Contracting Co.; Casale v. .. 66012
Austin v. Parker 82005
Austin Co.; McDowell v. 85028
Austin-Griffith, Inc. v. Goldberg 53001
Automation, Inc.; Edward Elec. Co. v. 87018
Automobile Club of Michigan; Roulo v. .. 70070
Automobile Ins. Co. v. United H.R.B. Gen. Contractors, Inc. 94002
Autrey v. Williams & Dunlap 65009
Avco Delta Corp. Canada v. United States 73010
Avenue Dev., Inc.; Creative Builders, Inc. v. ... 86014
Avlis Contracting Corp.; Porter v. 76056
A.W. Wendell & Sons, Inc. v. Qazi 93025
Axthelm & Swett Constr., Inc. v. Caudill 97003
Aydlett; Hite v. 26002
A.Z. Shmina & Sons Co.; Robinson v. ... 80054
Azcon Constr. Co. v. Golden Hills Resort, Inc. .. 93002
Aztec Servs., Inc. v. Quintana-Howell Joint Venture 82006

B

B. G. Danis Co.; Windowmaster Corp. v. 81174
B & M Constr., Inc. v. Mueller 89002
Babcock; Honeywell, Inc. v. 66038
Babcock & Wilcox Co. v. Fischbach & Moore, Inc. 71007
Babin; Waterworks District No. 1 v. 80074
Babylon Assocs. v. Suffolk, County of ... 84001
Bacjac Indus., Inc.; Steamboat Dev. Corp. v. ... 85036
Baer v. Tippett 39001
Baglino Corp.; Washington Elementary No. 6 v. ....

TABLE OF CASES

[The five-digit numbers in this table are *Citator* Case Reference Numbers, which refer to the cases in the Cases section]

American Insurance Co.; Progress Glass Co. v. . . . 80052
American Mason's Supply Co. v. F. W. Brown Co. 71005
American Motorists Insurance Co.; Consumers Construction Co. v. 69011
American Radiator & Standard Sanitary Corp. v. Maryland Casualty Co. 66003
American States Ins. Co.; River Valley, Inc. v. . . 85007
American Steel Building Co.; Flour Mills of America Inc. v. 69019
American Surety Co.; Pittsburgh Des Moines Steel Co. v. 66073
American Surety Co.; Pittsburgh Plate Glass Co. v. 42002
American Surety Co. v. Shaw 34001
American Surety Co.; William Cameron & Co. v. 32002
American Testing & Engineering Corp.; Drake, O'Mera & Associates v. 70022
Amerson v. Christman 68003
Ammala; United States Fire Ins. Co. v. . . 83044
Amoco Chemicals Corp.; Wenke v. 72107
Amtech Mechanical Servs.; Continental Heller Corp. v. 97008
Anchor Contractors, Inc.. United States ex rel. A. Teichert & Son v. 66103
Anderson v. Cahill 72009
Anderson; Caribbean Lumber Co. v. . . . 92004a
Anderson; Davis v. 73031
Anderson v. Golden 82004
Anderson; Pomeroy v. 82038
Anderson v. Smith 65006
Anderson County v. Architectural Techniques Corp. 93024
Anderson-Nichols & Co. v. Page 73005
Anderson-Parrish Assoc., Inc. v. St. Petersburg Beach, City of 85004
Andow; Hall v. 81033
Andrew J. Crevolin Co.; Continental Realty Corp. v. 74011
Andrews Fixture Co. v. Olin 70007
Andrews Plumbing Co.; Executive Development Properties, Inc. v. 75009
Andy Floors Inc. v. Tyler Constr. Corp. . . 94001
Angleton Indep. School Dist.; Olshan Demolishing Co. v. 84027
Anglin Constr. Co.; Kittyhawk Landing Apartments III v. 87029
Anken Construction Co. v. Artistic Ornamental Iron, Inc. 73006
Anthony Muratore Contracting Co. v. Frouge Construction Co. 66004

Anthony R. Delisi, General Contractor, Inc.; Fresco v. 68016
Anthony S. Brown Dev. Co.; Christman Co. v. 95005
Antioch Live Oak Unified School District; Pacific Coast Builders v. 56006
Anvan Corp.; Vespe Contracting Co. v. . . 75026; 77083a
APAC-Carolina, Inc. v. Greensboro-High Point Airport Auth. 93001
APAC-Georgia, Inc. v. Department of Transport., ... 96016
APAC-Tennessee, Inc. v. J.M. Humphries Constr. Co. 86002
Apache Tribe of Mescalero Reservation; Ramey Constr. Co. v. 82041
Apex Constr. & Eng'g Corp.; First Condominium Dev. Co. v. 84011
Appalachian Regional Healthcare, Inc.; Beyt, Rish, Robbins Group, Architects, Inc. v. . . . 93003
Appeal of (see name of party)
Appeal of Estate of (see name of party)
Application of (see name of applicant)
April v. Sovereign Construction Co. 81003
A.R. Moyer, Inc. v. Graham 73007
Arbitration Between Liebhafsky & Comstruct Assocs., Inc. 84019
Arboles Development Co.; Lewis v. 70051
Archer; Braye v. 95026
Architectural Alliance; Len Immke Buick, Inc. v. 92010b
Architectural Openings, Inc.; Eugene W. Kelsey & Son, Inc. v. 86020
Architectural Sys., Inc. v. Gilbane Bldg. Co. 91003
Architectural Techniques Corp.; Anderson County v. 93024
Arctic Contractors, Inc. v. State 77004
Ardsley Construction Co. v. Port Authority 81005
Area Masonry, Ltd. v. Dormitory Authority 77005
Argo Construction Co. v. Los Angeles, County of 69004
Argonaut Insurance Co. v. ABC Steel Products Co. 79019
Argonaut Insurance Co. v. Commercial Standard Insurance Co. 80003
Arjack, Co.; Westerfield v. 79070
Arkin Construction Co. v. Reynolds Metal Co. 62001
Arlington County; D.C. McClain, Inc. v. . . 95008
Arlington Lane Corp.; Denver Ventures, Inc. v. 88010

TABLE OF CASES
TC-3

[The five-digit numbers in this table are *Citator* Case Reference Numbers, which refer to the cases in the Cases section]

Algernon Blair, Inc.; Meridian, City of v. 83010
Algernon Blair, Inc. v. National Surety Corp. 66002
Allan B. Mitchell & Assocs. Inc.; Somerset Community Hosp. 96042
Allgood Elec. Co. v. Martin K. Eby Constr. Co. 97001
All Seasons Water Users Ass'n, Inc. v. Northern Improvements Co. 87002
All-South Subcontractors, Inc.; Citadel Corp. v. . . . 95006
All-State Investigation & Security Agency v. Turner Construction Co. 72007
Alleged Contempt of (see name of party)
Allegheny Home Improvement Corp. v. Franklin 82003
Allegretto; Taylor v. 91034
Allen v. A & W Contractors, Inc. 83003
Allen; Bullock Co. v. 73022
Allen Gardens, Inc.; Bennett Construction Co. v. 77011
Allen & O'Hara, Inc. v. Bartlett Wrecking, Inc. . . . 92001
Allhusen v. Caristo Construction Corp. . . . 52001
Allied Canon Co.; Sukut-Coulson, Inc. v. 78069
Allied Chemical Corp.; Lee v. 76036
Allied Chemical Corp.; Riggle v. 89041
Allied Steel Construction Co.; Equitable Fire & Marine Insurance Co. v. 65035
Allison v. Pick 56001
Allstate Insurance Co.; Fandrich v. 74015
Almand; Doup v. 48001
Alpha Crane Serv., Inc. v. Capitol Crane Co. . . . 86001
Alpha Epsilon Club; J.E. Hathman, Inc. v. 73057
Alspaugh v. District 76002
Alspaugh; Paul Mullins Construction Co. v. 81056
Alta Planing Mill Co. v. Garland 14001
Altay; Ozdeger v. 78058; 78059
Alton M. Johnson Co.; Frederickson v. . . . 86025
Aluminum Co. of America; Aetna Casualty & Surety Co. v. 70005
Aluminum Co. of America v. Commercial Contracting Co. 69002
Alvarado Ice Palace; Vitek, Inc. v. 73118
Alvord & Swift; Charles S. Wood & Co. v. 31002
Alvord & Swift v. Stewart M. Muller Construction Co. 78004

Alwinseal, Inc. v. Travelers Indemnity Co. 78005
Amadens, Inc. v. State 71003
Ambrose v. Biggs 87003
Amco Steel Corp. v. Renago Construction Inc. . . . 72008
Amelco Window Corp. v. Federal Insurance Co. 74002
Amerada Hess Corp.; Parsons v. 70064
American Airlines, Inc. v. Licon Associates, Inc. 77003
American Arbitration Ass'n; Children's Hospital v. 74009
American Arbitration Ass'n; Grover-Diamond Assoc. v. 73045
American Arbitration Ass'n; Teufel Construction Co. v. 70080
American Arbitration Ass'n; Woodward Heating & Air Conditioning Co. v. 78078
American Asbestos Control Co.; Pittsburgh, City of v. 93031
American Builder's Ass'n v. Au-Yang . . . 90003
American Casualty Co.; Sanders v. 69052
American Casualty Co. v. Timmons 65005
American Casualty Co.; Van Cor, Inc. v. 65114
American Construction Co.; V. Petrillo & Son, Inc. v. 77083
American Continental Life Insurance Co. v. Ranier Construction Co. 80002
American Crystal Sugar Co.; Rupp v. . . . 91029
American Cyanamid Co. v. Campbell Constr. Co. 94023
American Demolition, Inc. v. Hapeville Hotel, Ltd. Partnership 91002
American Drilling Service Co. v. Springfield, City of 81002
American Druggists Ins. Co. v. Henry Contracting, Inc. 87004
American Empire Insurance Co.; John Johnson Concrete Gutter Co. v. 81043
American Employers Insurance Co.; Arrow Construction Co. v. 73008
American Fidelity Fire Insurance Co.; Construction Materials, Inc. v. 80016
American Fire & Casualty Co. v. Charles Sales Corp. 67003
American Fire & Casualty Co.; Harrison v. 69026
American-Hawaiian Engineering & Construction Co. v. Butler 13001
American Industrial Contracting Co. v. Travelers Indemnity Co. 76003
American Insurance Co. v. Bateman 71004

TABLE OF CASES

[The five-digit numbers in this table are *Citator* Case Reference Numbers, which refer to the cases in the Cases section]

Adoption of (see name of party)
A.E. Investment Corp. v. Link Builders, Inc. . . . 74001
A.E. Ottaviano, Inc. v. State 67002
Aerostatic Engineering Corp. v. Szczawinski . . . 73003
Aesculapius Corp.; Griswold & Rauma, Architects, Inc. v. 74016
Aetna Casualty & Surety Co. v. Aluminum Co. of America 70005
Aetna Casualty & Surety Co.; Board of Education v. 71013
Aetna Casualty & Surety Co. v. Canam Steel Corp. 90002
Aetna Casualty & Surety Co. v. Crabtree 80001
Aetna Casualty & Surety Co.; Hub Electric Co. v. 75012
Aetna Casualty & Surety Co. v. Jelac Corp. 87001
Aetna Casualty & Surety Co. v. Kemp Smith Co. 65002
Aetna Casualty & Surety Co. v. Lafayette 72004
Aetna Casualty & Surety Co.; Logan v. . . 68027
Aetna Casualty & Surety Co. v. Lumberman's Mut. Casualty Co. 88001
Aetna Casualty & Surety Co.; Luria Engineering Co. v. 65071
Aetna Casualty & Surety Co.; Pipeline Industry Benefit Fund v. 72079
Aetna Casualty & Surety Co. v. Robertson Lumber Co. 28001
Aetna Casualty & Surety Co.; Schuler-Haas Electrical Corp. v. 75022
Aetna Casualty & Surety Co.; Trustees of Indiana Univ. v. 90050
Aetna Casualty & Surety Co. v. Warren Brothers Co. 78002
Aetna Casualty & Surety Co.; West Durham Lumber Co. v. 71086
Aetna Casualty & Surety Co.; Wheeler v. 73123
Aetna Insurance Co.; Deer Park Bank v. . . 73032
Aetna Insurance Co. v. Estero Manufacturing & Builders Supply, Inc. 65003
Aetna Insurance Co.; Hass v. 65047
Aetna Insurance Co. v. Hellmuth, Obata & Kassabaum, Inc. 68001
A.F. Lusi Constr. Co.; Cosentino v. 84008
Aghnides v. Marmon Group, Inc. 72005
Agrippina Versicherunges A.G.; Gribaldo, Jacobs, Jones & Associates. v. 70031

Agro Constr. & Supply Co.; L. Harvey Concrete 97015
Agus v. Future Chattanooga Development Corp. 73004
Aiken County v. BSP Div. of Envirotech Corp. 89001
Air Canada; Votaw Precision Tool Co. v. 76070
Air Heaters, Inc. v. Johnson Electric, Inc. 77001
Airportels, Inc.; John A. Robbins Co. v. . . 65059
Aitken; Hubert v. 003
A.J. Eckert Co. v. M.S. Kelliher Co. 65004
A.J. Welch Equip. Corp.; Callahan v. . . . 94029
Ajax Paving Indus., Inc.; Huntington Woods v. . . 89023; 92008d
A.L. Huber & Sons, Inc.; Husar Indus., Inc. v. . . 84018
Al Johnson Construction Co. v. Missouri Pacific Railroad Co. 76001
Al Smith's Plumbing & Heating Service, Inc. v. River Crest, Inc. 78003
Alabama Elec. Coop., Inc.; Weeks v. . . . 82057
Alabama Power Co. v. Beam 85003a
Alabama Power Co.; Ramirez v. 95044
Alameda County; Paxton v. 53005
Albano v. Western Construction Corp. . . . 70006
Albany, City of v. Oxford Construction Co. 66014
Alberti; Baldwin v. 61001
Albin Gustafson Co.; George A. Fuller Co. v. 77037
Albre Marble & Tile Co. v. Goverman . . 68002
Albuquerque, City of; K.L. House Construction Co. v. 78044
Alcan Pacific Co.; Call v. 67009
Alden; Hartford Electric Applicators of Thermalux, Inc. v. 75032
Alden E. Stilson & Assocs.; Columbus, City of v. 93030
Alex Fergusson Electrical Contractors; Integrated, Inc. v. 67034
Alexander v. Gerald E. Morrisey, Inc. . . . 79002
Alexander v. Hammarberg 51001
Alexander v. Shelbyville, City of 91001
Alexander Industries, Inc.; Royal Indemnity Co. v. 65089
Alexian Bros. Hosp.; Torcon, Inc. v. . . . 86065
Alfred A. Altimont, Inc. v. Chatelain, Samperton & Nolan 77002
Alfred A. Smith, Inc.; Ensign Painting Co. v. 71036
Alfred Watts Grant & Associates; School District No. Six v. 65093

TABLE OF CASES

[The five-digit numbers in this table are *Citator* Case Reference Numbers, which refer to the cases in the Cases section]

A

A. A. Baxter Corp. v. Colt Industries, Inc. 70001
A & A Co.; Fowler v. 70028
A. A. Construction Co.; Sollenberger v. . . . 71079
A & A Masonry Contractors, Inc. v. Howard Polinger 70003
A. A. Maycock, Inc. v. General Insurance Co. 70002
A. Amorello & Sons v. Beacon Construction Co. 81001
A & B Constr., Inc. v. Atlas Roofing & Skylight Co. 94022
A. Barbaresi & Son; Board of Education v. 66009
A. Burgart, Inc. v. Foster-Lipkins Corp. . . . 72001
A. Dubreuil & Sons, Inc. v. Lisbon 90001
A. E. Anderson Construction Corp.; McLouth Steel Corp. v. 73072
A. E. Finley & Associates, Inc. v. Hendrix 78001
A. Epstein & Sons; Uniroyal, Inc. v. 70084
A.F. Callan & Co.; Best Prods. Co. v. . . . 97005
A. Freiderich & Sons; Cable-Wiedemer, Inc. v. 72021
A & G Excavating Co.; State Department of Highways v. 66092
A. H. Sollinger Construction Co. v. Illinois Building Authority 72006
A. Hedenberg & Co.; Independent School District No. 35 v. 43002
A. J. Wolfe Co. v. Baltimore Contractors, Inc. 69001
A-1 Camp Chair Service Co. v. William L. Crow Construction Co. 65007
A. P. Brown Co. v. Superior Court 71006
A R C Electrical Construction Co. v. George A. Fuller Co. 69003
A & R Excavating, Inc.; Russellville Steel Co. v. 93052
A. Sangivanni & Sons v. F. M. Floryan & Co. 69005
A. Teichert & Son v. State 65008
A & W Contractors, Inc.; Allen v. 83003
A. W. Therrien Co. v. H. K. Ferguson Co. 72011
A.A. Conte, Inc. v. Campbell 85001

AAA Dry Wall, Inc.; Carolina Builders Corp. v. 79025
Abbott Contractors, Inc.; Brookfield-North Riverside Water Comm'n v. 93027
ABC Steel Products Co.; Argonaut Insurance Co. v. 79019
Aberthaw Construction Co. v. Centre County Hospital 73001
Aberthaw Construction Co.; Chester City School Authority v. 75005
Able Elec. Co. v. Vacanti & Randazzo Constr. Co. 82001
Absher Constr. Co. v. Kent Sch. Dist. No. 415 95001
A.C. Beals Co. v. Rhode Island Hospital . . 72002
A.C. Kirkwood & Assocs.; Tri-City Constr. Co. v. 87050
Acchione & Canuso, Inc. v. Commonwealth Dept. of Transp. 83001
Accurate Air Sys., Inc.; Glendale Constr. Serv., Inc. v. 94009
Ace Construction Co. v. W.H. Nichols & Co. 65001
Ace Stone, Inc. v. Township of Wayne . . 66001
Acmat v. Daniel O'Connell's Sons, Inc. . . 83002
Acme Builders, Inc. v. Facilities Development Corp. 79001
Acoustics, Inc. v. Hanover Insurance Co. 71001
Acoustics, Inc. v. Trepte Construction Co. 71002
Action Eng'g v. Martin Marietta Aluminum 82002
A.D. Hoppe Co. v. Fred Katz Construction Co. 67001
Ada County Highway Dist.; Haener v. . . . 85018
Adam; Del Bianco & Associates v. 72033
Adams v. Nelsen 85002
Adams & Douglas, Inc.; Port City Construction Co. v. 70066
Adams Tree Service, Inc. v. Transamerica Title Insurance Co. 73002
Adamsville Lumber Co. v. Rainey 72003
ADC Constr. Co. v. McDaniel Grading, Inc. 85003
Adelphi Enterprises, Inc. v. Mirpa, Inc. . . 70004
Adolfson & Peterson, Inc.; Prestressed Concrete, Inc. v. 76057

Table of Cases

court concluded that the provision was contrary to the state's public policy and was unenforceable because it effected an impermissible indirect waiver or forfeiture of the subcontractor's mechanic's lien rights in the event of nonpayment by the owner. The court held further that because they were unenforceable, pay-when-paid provisions in subcontracts did not insulate either contractors or their payment bond sureties from their contractual obligations to pay subcontractors for work performed.

The pay-when-paid clause at issue provided that:

Receipt of funds by Contractor from Owner is a condition precedent to the Contractor's obligation to pay Subcontractor under this Agreement, regardless of the reason for Owner's nonpayment, whether attributable to the fault of the Owner, Contractor, Subcontractor, or due to any other cause . . . .

1. Contractor shall have no obligation, legal, equitable or otherwise, to pay Subcontractor for Work performed by Subcontractor unless and until Contractor is paid by the Owner for the Work performed by Subcontractor. Furthermore, in the event Contractor is never paid by Owner for Subcontractor's Work, then Subcontractor shall forever be barred from making, and hereby waives, in perpetuity, any claim against Contractor therefor. * * *

4. Nothing in this Addendum shall be interpreted as limiting Subcontractor's right to enforce its statutory mechanic's lien rights or remedies, if any, against Project property and Subcontractor expressly agrees that such mechanic's lien rights, if any, shall be its sole remedy and mean for payment (regardless of whether the value [of] Project property is sufficient or insufficient, for any reason, to satisfy Subcontractor's claim) on account of Work performed by Subcontractor for which Contractor has not been paid by Owner.

I:	A201-1987, Art. 4, Para. 4.5.2
I:	A201-1987, Art. 4, Para. 4.5.3
I:	A201-1987, Art. 4, Para. 4.5.4
I:	A201-1987, Art. 4, Para. 4.5.4.1
I:	A201-1987, Art. 4, Para. 4.5.4.2
I:	A201-1987, Art. 4, Para. 4.5.5
I:	A201-1987, Art. 4, Para. 4.5.6
I:	A201-1987, Art. 4, Para. 4.5.7
I:	A401-1987, Art. 6, Para. 6.1
I:	A401-1987, Art. 6, Para. 6.2
I:	A401-1987, Art. 6, Para. 6.3
I:	A401-1987, Art. 6, Para. 6.4
I:	A401-1987, Art. 6, Para. 6.5
I:	B141-1987, Art. 7, Para. 7.1
I:	B141-1987, Art. 7, Para. 7.2
I:	B141-1987, Art. 7, Para. 7.3
I:	B141-1987, Art. 7, Para. 7.4

At issue on appeal was whether the court in equity or an arbitrator should resolve a claim for rescission based on the theory of frustration of purpose under a contract containing a broadly worded arbitration clause when there was no challenge to the validity of the clause itself. Relying on the general rule of law that in the face of a valid arbitration clause, questions regarding the validity of the entire contract must be decided by arbitration, the court held that when there was no challenge to the validity of the clause itself, and the clause was broadly worded, the arbitrator, and not the trial court sitting in equity, should resolve the claim for rescission.

The owner and contractor had entered into an American Institute of Architects Standard Form of Agreement Between Owner and Contractor which contained an arbitration clause that provided in pertinent part that "All claims or disputes between the Contractor and the Owner arising out [of] or relating to the Contract, or the breach thereof, shall be decided by arbitration. . . ."

97027 Wm. R. Clarke Corp. v. Safeco Ins. Co. of Am., 15 Cal. 4th 882, 64 Cal. Rptr. 2d 578, 938 P.2d 372 (1997)

III:	A401-1987, Art. 11, Para. 11.3
III:	A401-1987, Art. 12, Para. 12.1

The Supreme Court of California decided, as a matter of first impression, the validity of a pay-when-paid provision. At issue before the court was whether a subcontractor could collect on a contractor's payment bond for work it had performed under a contract containing a pay-when-paid provision when the owner had not paid the contractor. The

incurred during the period of construction; (2) damages to the work performed under the contract; and (3) damages occurring as a result of the conduct of a subcontractor and not a provider of materials. The trial court granted summary judgment for contractor and subcontractors. Owner appealed. The appellate court affirmed the judgment with respect to the owner's claim for damages to the "work" and reversed with respect to all other damages.

The owner-contractor agreement included the American Institute of Architects General Conditions of the Contract for Construction, Document No. A201, 1987 edition, specifically Paragraphs 11.3.5 and 11.3.7.

The appellate court, reading the provisions together, held that Paragraph 11.3.7 waived the subrogation rights of both the owner and the contractor for damages caused by fire to the extent covered by the owner's property insurance obtained pursuant to Paragraph 11.3 or other property insurance applicable to the "work." The agreement defined "work" as "the construction and services required by the Contract Documents, whether completed or partially completed, and includes all other labor, materials, equipment and services provided or to be provided by the Contractor to fulfill the Contractor's obligations." The scope of the waiver of subrogation was limited to the value of the work performed under the contract and was inapplicable to other fire damages.

The court then turned to the issue of whether the waiver of subrogation clause applied to damage occurring after construction and final payment. The court noted that Paragraph 11.3.7 referred to two types of insurance, property insurance procured by the owner covering "the entire Work at the site," and "other property insurance applicable to the Work . . . ." The court rejected the owner's argument that this language referred only to builder's risk insurance, because the provision contained no reference to builder's risk insurance, nor did it reflect any intent to limit the waiver of subrogation rights to damages occurring before final payment. The phrase, "other property insurance applicable to the Work," referred to any property insurance applicable to the work other than that procured under Paragraph 11.3.1. In addition, the waiver provision further extended to persons or entities whether or not such persons or entities had an insurable interest in the damaged property. Therefore, the fact that a contractor had finished its work and had no remaining insurable interest in the property did not terminate the waiver of subrogation rights.

The court concluded that because property insurance applicable to the work, other than that obtained pursuant to Paragraph 11.3.1, may remain in effect after the final completion date, so too may a waiver of subrogation under Paragraph 11.3.7 remain in effect. Therefore, the waiver of subrogation clause barred subrogation for insured losses to the work occurring after the final completion date and the date final payment was made.

97026   Wilharm v. M.J. Constr. Co., 1997 Ohio App. LEXIS 591 (Ohio Ct. App. Feb. 20, 1997)

I: A107-1987, Art. 10, Para. 10.8
I: A117-1987, Art. 15, Para. 15.8
I: A201-1987, Art. 4, Para. 4.5.1

I:	A401-1987, Art. 6, Para. 6.4
I:	A401-1987, Art. 6, Para. 6.5
I:	B141-1987, Art. 7, Para. 7.1
I:	B141-1987, Art. 7, Para. 7.2
I:	B141-1987, Art. 7, Para. 7.3
I:	B141-1987, Art. 7, Para. 7.4

Owner submitted its payment dispute to arbitration after receiving contractor's notice of mechanic's lien. Contractor brought an action to enforce its lien and to stay arbitration. The court stayed the arbitration on the grounds that there was no agreement to arbitrate. Owner appealed, and the appellate court ordered arbitration.

The parties entered into the American Institute of Architects Standard Form of Agreement Between Owner and Contractor, Document No. A101/CMa, 1992 edition, which included the American Institute of Architects General Conditions of the Contract for Construction, Document No. A201/CMa, 1992 edition.

The appellate court held that the parties intended that arbitration be a condition precedent to the bringing of an action in a court of law because the clause provided that any controversy or claim arising out of or related to the contract or the breach thereof shall be settled by arbitration. Although the arbitration clause did not provide that it was specifically enforceable under prevailing arbitration law, it did provide that "judgment upon the award rendered by the arbitrator or arbitrators may be entered in any court having jurisdiction thereof" except as to specific enumerated controversies.

97025 Town of Silverton v. Phoenix Heat Source Sys., 1997 Colo. App. LEXIS 8 (Ct. App. 1997)

II:	A107-1987, Art. 7, Para. 7.4
II:	A107-1987, Art. 17, Para. 17.3
II:	A107-1987, Art. 17, Para. 17.6
II:	A117-1987, Art. 12, Para. 12.4
II:	A117-1987, Art. 22, Para. 22.3
II:	A117-1987, Art. 22, Para. 22.6
I:	A201-1987, Art. 1, Para. 1.1.3
I:	A201-1987, Art. 11, Para. 11.3.1
I:	A201-1987, Art. 11, Para. 11.3.5
I:	A201-1987, Art. 11, Para. 11.3.7

Owner appealed from summary judgment entered in favor of contractor and subcontractors on owner's action for fire damages allegedly resulting from faulty installation of a snow melting system. The contractor and subcontractors moved for summary judgment on the grounds that owner had waived its right to subrogation. The owner argued that the waiver provisions were inapplicable because they were limited to (1) damages

The owner and contractor entered into the American Institute of Architects Abbreviated Form of Agreement Between Owner and Contractor, Document No. A117, 1987 edition, specifically Paragraph 15.8.

On appeal, the owner argued that the agreement to arbitrate was not assignable without owner's consent, which owner would not have given considering that performance under the contract was already in default when the contract was assigned.

The court found that contractor's assignment of its rights and duties under the contract to assignee was valid and effective. Moreover, the court found that owner's on-site construction progress meetings, correspondence addressed directly to the assignee, and progress payments made payable to assignee constituted sufficient evidence to support a finding that owner ratified the contract assignment to contractor's assignee.

Moreover, there was no limitation as to assignment or arbitration placed on the parties by the broad language of Paragraph 15.8 which provided for mandatory arbitration of all contractually related disputes.

The court held that a valid arbitration agreement existed between the parties and that the assignee's claim was within the scope of the agreement.

97024   State ex rel. Center Designs, Inc. v. Henning, 1997 W. Va. LEXIS 149 (W. Va. July 10, 1997)

II:	A107-1987, Art. 6, Para. 6.1	
II:	A107-1987, Art. 7, Para. 7.1	
I:	A107-1987, Art. 10, Para. 10.8	
II:	A117-1987, Art. 11, Para. 11.1	
II:	A117-1987, Art. 12, Para. 12.1	
I:	A117-1987, Art. 15, Para. 15.8	
II:	A201-1987, Art. 1, Para. 1.1.1	
II:	A201-1987, Art. 1, Para. 1.1.2	
I:	A201-1987, Art. 4, Para. 4.5.1	
I:	A201-1987, Art. 4, Para. 4.5.2	
I:	A201-1987, Art. 4, Para. 4.5.3	
I:	A201-1987, Art. 4, Para. 4.5.4	
I:	A201-1987, Art. 4, Para. 4.5.4.1	
I:	A201-1987, Art. 4, Para. 4.5.4.2	
I:	A201-1987, Art. 4, Para. 4.5.5	
I:	A201-1987, Art. 4, Para. 4.5.6	
I:	A201-1987, Art. 4, Para. 4.5.7	
I:	A401-1987, Art. 6, Para. 6.1	
I:	A401-1987, Art. 6, Para. 6.2	
I:	A401-1987, Art. 6, Para. 6.3	

The owner-contractor agreement provided that all disputes be initially referred to the architect for resolution and that they were subject to arbitration upon written demand of either party. The court held that under the explicit terms of the agreement, the thirty day time limitation within which a demand for arbitration had to be made only applied in the event that the architect issued a written decision on a disputed matter and such decision stated that (1) it was final but subject to appeal; and (2) any demand for arbitration be made within thirty days after its receipt. The evidence established that none of the letters sent to contractor contained the required language; therefore, the thirty day time restriction was never triggered. Rather, contractor only had to demand arbitration "within a reasonable time after the claim."

97023   Smith v. Cumberland Group, 455 Pa. Super. 276, 687 A.2d 1167 (1997)

I:	A107-1987, Art. 10, Para. 10.8	
I:	A117-1987, Art. 15, Para. 15.8	
I:	A201-1987, Art. 4, Para. 4.5.1	
I:	A201-1987, Art. 4, Para. 4.5.2	
I:	A201-1987, Art. 4, Para. 4.5.3	
I:	A201-1987, Art. 4, Para. 4.5.4	
I:	A201-1987, Art. 4, Para. 4.5.4.1	
I:	A201-1987, Art. 4, Para. 4.5.4.2	
I:	A201-1987, Art. 4, Para. 4.5.5	
I:	A201-1987, Art. 4, Para. 4.5.6	
I:	A201-1987, Art. 4, Para. 4.5.7	
I:	A401-1987, Art. 6, Para. 6.1	
I:	A401-1987, Art. 6, Para. 6.2	
I:	A401-1987, Art. 6, Para. 6.3	
I:	A401-1987, Art. 6, Para. 6.4	
I:	A401-1987, Art. 6, Para. 6.5	
I:	B141-1987, Art. 7, Para. 7.1	
I:	B141-1987, Art. 7, Para. 7.2	
I:	B141-1987, Art. 7, Para. 7.3	
I:	B141-1987, Art. 7, Para. 7.4	

Assignee contractor filed a demand for arbitration of a dispute against owner for the balance of the payment due the original contractor. Owner filed an action against assignee-contractor and the original contractor alleging that contractor failed to substantially complete the work by the agreed to completion date. Owner filed an application to stay arbitration, claiming that assignee-contractor was not a party to the subcontract and that owner never agreed to arbitrate any dispute with contractor's assignee. The trial court granted owner's application to stay arbitration. Contractor and contractor's assignee appealed, and the appellate court reversed.

Paragraph 5.3.1 of the owner-contractor agreement did not confer the right to arbitrate on the subcontractor, because paragraph 15 of the subcontract provided that any dispute be brought in court.

97022 In re Saranac Cent. Sch. Dist. (Sweet Assocs., Inc.), 651 N.Y.S.2d 759 (App. Div. 1997)

III:	A107-1987, Art. 10, Para. 10.5	
III:	A107-1987, Art. 10, Para. 10.8	
III:	A117-1987, Art. 15, Para. 15.5	
III:	A117-1987, Art. 15, Para. 15.8	
III:	A201-1987, Art. 4, Para. 4.3.2	
III:	A201-1987, Art. 4, Para. 4.3.3	
III:	A201-1987, Art. 4, Para. 4.4.3	
III:	A201-1987, Art. 4, Para. 4.4.4	
III:	A201-1987, Art. 4, Para. 4.5.1	
III:	A201-1987, Art. 4, Para. 4.5.2	
III:	A201-1987, Art. 4, Para. 4.5.3	
III:	A201-1987, Art. 4, Para. 4.5.4	
III:	A201-1987, Art. 4, Para. 4.5.4.1	
III:	A201-1987, Art. 4, Para. 4.5.4.2	
III:	A201-1987, Art. 4, Para. 4.5.5	
III:	A201-1987, Art. 4, Para. 4.5.6	
III:	A201-1987, Art. 4, Para. 4.5.7	
III:	A401-1987, Art. 6, Para. 6.1	
III:	A401-1987, Art. 6, Para. 6.2	
III:	A401-1987, Art. 6, Para. 6.3	
III:	A401-1987, Art. 6, Para. 6.4	
III:	A401-1987, Art. 6, Para. 6.5	
III:	B141-1987, Art. 2, Para. 2.6.16	
III:	B141-1987, Art. 2, Para. 2.6.18	
III:	B141-1987, Art. 2, Para. 2.6.19	
III:	B141-1987, Art. 7, Para. 7.1	
III:	B141-1987, Art. 7, Para. 7.2	
III:	B141-1987, Art. 7, Para. 7.3	
III:	B141-1987, Art. 7, Para. 7.4	

Owner moved to stay arbitration of contractor's claim for additional compensation, arguing that contractor's demand for arbitration was not timely. The trial court denied the motion to stay, and owner appealed. The appellate court upheld the conclusion of the trial court and ordered arbitration of the dispute.

97021 St. Augustine Pools, Inc. v. James M. Barker, Inc., 687 So. 2d 957 (Fla. Dist. Ct. App. 1997)

II: A107-1987, Art. 11, Para. 11.2
II: A117-1987, Art. 16, Para. 16.2
I: A201-1987, Art. 5, Para. 5.3.1
II: A401-1987, Art. 2, Para. 2.1

On appeal of contractor's third-party action against subcontractor for defective construction, the appellate court held that the subcontract did not incorporate the arbitration agreement in the owner-contractor agreement. Furthermore, the owner-contractor agreement did not confer on subcontractor the right to arbitration.

The subcontract provided that:

[Paragraph] 15. . . . any claim or cause of action against the Contractor or Owner arising out of, in connection with, or by virtue of the relationship created by this Agreement, shall be brought and filed in . . . and shall be heard by a judge of the appropriate court therein.

[Paragraph] 16. This Agreement is subject to the General Contract between the Owner and General Contractor. Subcontractor acknowledges that he is familiar with the General Contract and the General Conditions thereof and agrees to comply with all applicable provisions thereof.

The owner-contractor agreement contained a flow-down provision which stated in Paragraph 5.3.1 that:

By an appropriate agreement, written where legally required for validity, the Contractor shall require each Subcontractor, to the extent of the Work to be performed by the Subcontractor, to be bound to the Contractor by the terms of the Contract Documents, and to assume toward the Contractor all the obligations and responsibilities which the Contractor, by these Documents, assumes toward the Owner and the Architect. Said agreement shall preserve and protect the rights of the Owner and the Architect under the Contract Documents with respect to the Work to be performed by the Subcontractor so that the subcontracting thereof will not prejudice such rights, and shall allow to the Subcontractor, unless specifically provided otherwise in the Contractor-Subcontractor agreement, the benefit of all rights, remedies, and redress against the contractor that the Contractor, by these Documents, has against the Owner.

As to whether the subcontract incorporated the arbitration agreement contained in the owner-contractor agreement, the court held that the phrase "subject to" contained in paragraph 16 meant "liable, subordinate, subservient, inferior, obedient to; governed or affected by; provided that; provided; answerable." Further, the words "subject to" usually indicated a condition to one party's duty of performance and not a promise by the other. Applying these definitions to the subcontract, the intent of the parties was to not incorporate the arbitration language of the owner-contractor agreement into the subcontract. Read as a whole, paragraph 16 indicated that the owner-contractor agreement was referenced solely to make the subcontractor aware of its duties and requirements.

III: A201-1987, Art. 4, Para. 4.2.3
III: B141-1987, Art. 2, Para. 2.6.5
III: B141-1987, Art. 2, Para. 2.6.6

Decedent's estate brought a wrongful death action, and the trial court granted summary judgment to defendant/engineer. On appeal, the Tenth Circuit determined that, as a matter of law, engineer owed no duty of care to decedent with regard to safety at the site. Decedent's estate argued that (1) engineer assumed a contractual duty to maintain worker safety; (2) engineer had assumed a duty to maintain safety precautions on the day of the accident because it was consulted about how to proceed with the work; and (3) engineer's liability could be predicated on the fact that engineer had actual knowledge of the safety problem.

The owner-engineer agreement provided that engineer agreed to:

physically oversee . . . the work . . . to determine that the work performed [was] in accordance with the plans and specifications . . . [and] will comply with and assist the owner to require all contractors . . . employed in the completion of the project to comply with all applicable Federal, State and Local laws. In addition, [engineer] will conform to the requirements of the Utah State Division of Health . . . [however, engineer] shall not be responsible for construction means, methods, techniques, sequences or procedures, or for safety precautions and programs in connection with the work.

The owner-contractor agreement expressly allocated responsibility for safety to the contractor by providing that the contractor:

[W]ill be responsible for initiating, maintaining and supervising all safety precautions and programs in connection with the Work. He will take all necessary precautions for the safety of, and will provide the necessary protection to prevent damage, injury or loss to all employees on the work . . .

Turning first to the issue of engineer's contractual assumption of duty to decedent, the court held that under state law engineer's contractual supervisory duties did not include an assumption of duty to maintain safety at the site when the contract clearly provided that engineer would not be "responsible . . . for construction safety."

As to engineer's implied assumption of duty, engineer owed no duty to decedent because engineer played no role in the actual construction. A supervising engineer's participation in a construction decision did not obligate the engineer to ensure that all safety precautions were complied with in the implementation of that decision.

The court rejected the estate's argument that engineer had actual knowledge of the safety problem as the engineer contractually declined to accept responsibility for worker safety and did not, in fact, exercise control of worker safety at the site.

The court concluded that the estate presented no evidence from which a reasonable jury could infer that engineer either contractually or impliedly assumed a duty of care to decedent. Engineer contractually disavowed any responsibility for safety, and there was no evidence that engineer acted unreasonably in its duties as supervising engineer.

Michigan's obligations to indemnify Northern Indiana under this provision shall not apply to any liabilities arising from Northern Indiana's sole negligence or that portion of any liabilities that arise out of Northern Indiana's or any other third parties contributing negligent acts or omissions.

The subcontract provided:

Ozinga shall defend and indemnify and save NIPSCO and MAC and all of NIPSCO's and MAC's employees harmless from any and all claims, losses, damages, demands, suits, actions, payments, judgements [sic], costs and expenses, including attorneys' fees, arising or alleged to arise from personal injuries, including death, or damage to property, including the loss of use thereof, and resulting from, arising out of or in connection with this Agreement, including, without limitation, all liability imposed by virtue of any law designed to protect persons employed at the work sites.

Ozinga's obligations to indemnify NIPSCO and MAC under this provision shall not apply to any liabilities arising from NIPSCO's or MAC's sole negligence or that portion of any liabilities that arise out of NIPSCO's or MAC's contributing negligent acts or omissions.

The court determined that the indemnification clause in the subcontract contemplated claims, damages, losses, suits, and actions arising from personal injuries. These words were also the language of negligence. Taken in context, the court concluded that the words clearly, unequivocally and expressly provided that the indemnification clause applied to subcontractor's negligence.

The court rejected the subcontractor's argument that the indemnification provision was unenforceable because it purported to create an exception not only in the event of owner and/or contractor's sole negligence, but also for their contributory negligence. The omission of the words "third parties" directly preceding the contributory negligence language was a scrivener's error because the clause contained in the owner-contractor agreement was identical to the indemnification clause in the subcontract but for the last sentence referring to "contributing negligence."

97020   Peck v. Horrocks Eng'rs, Inc., 106 F.3d 949 (10th Cir. 1997)

	III:	A107-1987, Art. 9, Para. 9.1
	III:	A107-1987, Art. 9, Para. 9.6
	III:	A107-1987, Art. 10, Para. 10.2
	III:	A107-1987, Art. 10, Para. 10.3
	III:	A117-1987, Art. 14, Para. 14.1
	III:	A117-1987, Art. 14, Para. 14.6
	III:	A117-1987, Art. 15, Para. 15.2
	III:	A117-1987, Art. 15, Para. 15.3
	III:	A201-1987, Art. 3, Para. 3.3.1
	III:	A201-1987, Art. 3, Para. 3.7.2
	III:	A201-1987, Art. 4, Para. 4.2.2

The court concluded that contractor had failed to demonstrate, as a matter of law, that architect's decision granting the time extension was intended to be final and binding.

The court then addressed the issue of whether summary judgment for architect was inappropriate when a material fact existed as to whether architect breached its contractual duty to act impartially and in good faith.

Specifically, the agreements provided that architect had to act impartially and in good faith in resolving owner/contractor disputes. The court found that Paragraphs 2.6.15 and 2.6.18 of the owner-architect agreement placed a contractual duty on the architect to make decisions regarding claims. The term "claim" was defined as including a request for extension of time in Paragraph 4.3.1. Paragraph 4.3.1 placed responsibility for substantiating a claim on the party making the claim. Additionally, Paragraphs 4.3.3, 4.4.1, 4.4.3, 4.4.4 and 4.3.8.1 of the general conditions prescribed time limits for the presentation of claims, set time frames in which architect was to act, and established procedures for asserting claims. Paragraph 4.3.8.2 provided that if adverse weather conditions were the basis for an extension of time, the claim "shall be documented by data substantiating that weather conditions were abnormal for the period of time and could not have been reasonably anticipated . . . ."

Architect had failed to prove that it had complied with Paragraph 4.4.1 by taking one or more of the "preliminary actions" listed in that Paragraph within ten days of receipt of the claim, nor did the record reflect that architect required contractor to substantiate its claim for a time extension. Architect's actions and other evidence raised genuine issues of fact regarding architect's partiality and good faith.

97019 Ozinga Transp. Sys., Inc. v. Michigan Ash Sales, Inc., 676 N.E.2d 379 (Ind. Ct. App. 1997)

III:	A107-1987, Art. 9, Para. 9.12	
III:	A117-1987, Art. 14, Para. 14.12	
III:	A201-1987, Art. 3, Para. 3.18.1	
III:	A201-1987, Art. 10, Para. 10.1.4	
III:	A401-1987, Art. 4, Para. 4.6.1	

On appeal of a grant of summary judgment to owner and contractor on cross-claims for indemnification, the appellate court held that the indemnity clause in the subcontract was valid and enforceable.

The owner-contractor agreement provided:

Michigan shall defend and indemnify and save Northern Indiana and all of Northern Indiana's employees harmless from any and all claims, losses, damages, demands, suits, actions, payments, judgments, costs and expenses, including attorneys' fees, arising or alleged to arise from personal injuries, including death, or damage to property, including the loss of use thereof, and resulting from, arising out of or in connection with this Agreement, including, without limitation, all liability imposed by virtue of any law designed to protect persons employed at the work sites.

[if] the date of commencement is later than September 1, 1993, the substantial completion date shall be extended by an equal number of days corresponding to the delay in the date of commencement, provided, however, that such delay in the date of commencement is not due to any failure by Contractor to timely apply for and provide all information and perform all acts necessary to be performed by Contractor for the issuance of the building permit. Said paragraph is further amended to provide that if the Contractor shall fail to complete the work by April 1, 1994, except for delays caused by Contractor's failure to receive plans and specifications in a timely manner from Architect, delays occurring because of the failure of the City of Branson or any . . . agency thereof to timely approve plans, specifications or perform inspections, or delays resulting from inclement weather . . . , the Contractor shall pay or allow to Owner the sum of Five Thousand Dollars ($5,000) per day as liquidated . . . damages for every day the work shall remain uncompleted beyond the said completion date. In the event of such delays, the Architect shall establish a new date by which the work should reasonably be completed . . .

The general conditions were altered further when contractor and owner deleted the arbitration provision from the form. As a consequence, they removed from the construction documents all references to arbitration procedure, process, and time frames, as well as the language stating that the arbitration award would be final. However, they left intact numerous other references to arbitration in other parts of the construction documents.

The owner and architect entered into the American Institute of Architects Standard Form of Agreement Between Owner and Architect, Document No. B141, 1987 edition.

First, the court addressed the issue of whether the contractor was bound by the architect's decision extending the completion date. The court held that the pertinent sections in the owner-architect agreement and the owner-contractor agreement were susceptible to differing interpretations.

Specifically, Paragraph 4.2.13 indicated that architect's decisions regarding aesthetic effect was final. The language in Paragraph 4.3.2, which provided that architect make a decision as a condition precedent to arbitration or litigation, suggested that architect's decision on time extensions was not intended to be binding and final. However, the language in Paragraph 4.4.4, which stated that architect's decision "shall be final and binding on the parties subject to arbitration," was deleted by the parties. The court questioned the intent of the parties as expressed by their deletion of the arbitration provision. One interpretation was that they intended no arbitration; however, they could have intended that there be arbitration but without the Paragraph 4.5 language. The court reasoned that if the parties intended no arbitration, then one plausible interpretation of Paragraph 4.4.4 was that the parties intended architect's decisions to be final. But such an interpretation conflicted with the language in Paragraphs 4.2.13 and 4.3.2 which indicated that only decisions relating to aesthetics were intended to be final and binding.

Furthermore, such an interpretation raised questions about what the parties intended in Paragraph 4.3.2 which provided that architect make a decision "as a condition precedent to arbitration or litigation." On the other hand, if the parties intended that arbitration of disputes occur but without the procedure of Paragraph 4.5, then it would be clear that the architect's decisions were not final and binding.

I: A107-1987, Art. 10, Para. 10.8
I: A107-1987, Art. 14, Para. 14.3
I: A117-1987, Art. 15, Para. 15.5
I: A117-1987, Art. 15, Para. 15.8
I: A117-1987, Art. 19, Para. 19.3
I: A201-1987, Art. 4, Para. 4.2.8
I: A201-1987, Art. 4, Para. 4.2.11
I: A201-1987, Art. 4, Para. 4.2.12
I: A201-1987, Art. 4, Para. 4.2.13
I: A201-1987, Art. 4, Para. 4.3.2
I: A201-1987, Art. 4, Para. 4.3.3
I: A201-1987, Art. 4, Para. 4.3.8.1
I: A201-1987, Art. 4, Para. 4.3.8.2
I: A201-1987, Art. 4, Para. 4.4.3
I: A201-1987, Art. 4, Para. 4.4.4
I: A201-1987, Art. 8, Para. 8.1.1
I: A201-1987, Art. 8, Para. 8.3.1
I: B141-1987, Art. 2, Para. 2.6.13
I: B141-1987, Art. 2, Para. 2.6.15
I: B141-1987, Art. 2, Para. 2.6.17
I: B141-1987, Art. 2, Para. 2.6.18
I: B141-1987, Art. 2, Para. 2.6.19
I: B141-1987, Art. 7, Para. 7.1
I: B141-1987, Art. 7, Para. 7.4

Contractor filed a lien action against owner. Owner counterclaimed for liquidated damages resulting from contractor's failure to substantially complete its work by the completion date set forth in the owner-contractor agreement. Contractor filed a response alleging that architect authorized additional time for completion of the project and that the project was substantially completed by the extended date. Owner then filed a cross-claim against architect alleging that if owner was bound by architect's extension of the completion date, such action was in breach of architect's contract and architect was liable to owner in an amount equal to any amount that owner was unable to recover from contractor because of the extension of time. Contractor and architect filed motions for summary judgment. The trial court entered summary judgment in favor of contractor and in favor of architect on owner's cross-claim for breach of contract. The appellate court reversed summary judgment for contractor and architect.

The owner and contractor entered into an agreement which included the American Institute of Architects General Conditions of the Contract for Construction, Document No. A201-1987 edition. However, Paragraph 4.2 was modified to add that:

III: B141-1987, Art. 7, Para. 7.4

The Supreme Court of Arkansas held that when an arbitration provision was incorporated by reference into the performance bond, the owner had to arbitrate its claim against the surety.

The performance bond stated that "Contractor [Matson] has by written agreement dated October 31, 1991, entered into a contract with Owner [Lamb] for a new manufacturing building . . . which contract is by reference made a part hereof, and is hereinafter referred to as the Contract." The bond further provided that "Any suit under this bond must be instituted before the expiration of two (2) years from the date on which final payment under the Contract falls due." The owner-contractor agreement contained a clause requiring arbitration of disputes relating to performance or breach of contract.

Since owner was relying on the owner-contractor agreement to prove its breach of contract claims against contractor, owner could not avoid the arbitration provision by arguing that it was not incorporated by reference into the performance bond.

97017   Mautz v. J.P. Patti Co., 298 N.J. Super. 13, 688 A.2d 1088 (1997)

I: A107-1987, Art. 9, Para. 9.12
I: A117-1987, Art. 14, Para. 14.12
I: A201-1987, Art. 3, Para. 3.18.1
I: A201-1987, Art. 10, Para. 10.1.4
I: A401-1987, Art. 4, Para. 4.6.1
I: A401-1987, Art. 4, Para. 4.6.2
I: A401-1978, Art. 11, Para. 11.11.1
I: A401-1978, Art. 11, Para. 11.11.2

On appeal of the trial court's dismissal of contractor's claim for indemnity from subcontractor for personal injury damages paid to subcontractor's employee, the appellate court held that the indemnity agreement expressly and unambiguously provided for partial indemnity, to the extent the subcontractor's negligent acts or omissions contributed to its employee's injury.

The parties had entered into the American Institute of Architects Standard Form of Agreement Between Contractor and Subcontractor, Document No. A401, 1978 edition, specifically Paragraphs 11.11.1 and 11.11.2.

The clause was clear and unambiguous, stating that subcontractor was obligated to indemnify contractor but only to the extent that the claim was caused by subcontractor's own negligence. Furthermore, the indemnity was available "regardless of whether [the claim] is caused in part by a party indemnified hereunder."

97018   Meco Sys. v. Dancing Bear Entertainment, Inc., 948 S.W.2d 185 (Mo. Ct. App. 1997)

I: A107-1987, Art. 10, Para. 10.5

The appellate court, relying on its decision in Watson Constr. Co. v. Reppel Steel & Supply Co., Digest No. 79069, restated the rule that in order to create a condition precedent limiting recovery to a specific fund, there must be contractual language demonstrating the parties' unequivocal intent that the obligation is to be paid out of that fund and not otherwise. The court found that the language of the instant provision clearly stated an intent to limit recovery to the payments received from the owner. The subcontract expressly stated that receipt of payment from the owner was a "condition precedent" to recovery. It further stated that "payment for either progress payments or final payment is not due and owing . . . until the owner has made such payment to the contractor." Finally, the contract identified as the source of funding for the subcontract the "progress and final payments that are to be made by the owner to the contractor." The language sufficiently demonstrated that the parties clearly and unequivocally intended to create a valid and enforceable condition precedent shifting the risk of nonpayment from contractor to subcontractor.

The court concluded that the pay-when-paid provision was effective as a condition precedent to excuse the contractor from paying the subcontractor when a corresponding payment was not received by the contractor from the owner.

97016 Matson, Inc. v. Lamb & Assocs. Packaging, Inc., 328 Ark. 705, 947 S.W.2d 324 (1997)

III:	A107-1987, Art. 10, Para. 10.8	
III:	A117-1987, Art. 15, Para. 15.8	
III:	A201-1987, Art. 4, Para. 4.5.1	
III:	A201-1987, Art. 4, Para. 4.5.2	
III:	A201-1987, Art. 4, Para. 4.5.3	
III:	A201-1987, Art. 4, Para. 4.5.4	
III:	A201-1987, Art. 4, Para. 4.5.4.1	
III:	A201-1987, Art. 4, Para. 4.5.4.2	
III:	A201-1987, Art. 4, Para. 4.5.5	
III:	A201-1987, Art. 4, Para. 4.5.6	
III:	A201-1987, Art. 4, Para. 4.5.7	
III:	A312-1984, Performance Bond, Para. 1	
III:	A401-1987, Art. 6, Para. 6.1	
III:	A401-1987, Art. 6, Para. 6.2	
III:	A401-1987, Art. 6, Para. 6.3	
III:	A401-1987, Art. 6, Para. 6.4	
III:	A401-1987, Art. 6, Para. 6.5	
III:	B141-1987, Art. 7, Para. 7.1	
III:	B141-1987, Art. 7, Para. 7.2	
III:	B141-1987, Art. 7, Para. 7.3	

subcontractor/vendor under workers' compensation acts, disability benefit acts, or other employee benefits acts.

The appellate court held that worker's claim arose out of or resulted from "the performance of the subcontractor's work" within the meaning of the indemnity provision. The words "arising out of" referred to a claim "growing out of" or having its "origin in" the subject matter of the subcontractor's work. Although the words "resulting from" could imply a causal relationship between the subcontractor's work and the claim. the court did not interpret the clause as requiring fault on the subcontractor's part as a prerequisite to indemnification. Instead, the court held that the words required only a substantial nexus between the claim and the subject matter of the subcontractor's work.

In addition, the jury's finding that worker was contributorily negligent brought contractor's claim within the scope of the indemnity provision which clearly required that subcontractor hold contractor harmless for any claim "attributable to bodily injury . . . caused in whole or in part by any negligent act or omission of the subcontractor . . . or anyone directly or indirectly employed by [subcontractor] . . . regardless of whether it is caused in part by a party indemnified . . . ."

Relying on Collins v. Kiewit Constr. Co., Digest No. 96021, and the contract language which provided that "regardless of whether it is caused in part by a party indemnified," the court concluded that the worker's own negligence did not limit the subcontractor's indemnification obligation to the share of damages caused by worker's negligence.

97015   L. Harvey Concrete, Inc. v. Agro Constr. & Supply Co., 939 P.2d 811 (Ariz. Ct. App. 1997)

         III: A401-1987, Art. 11, Para. 11.3
         III: A401-1987, Art. 12, Para. 12.1

Subcontractor brought an action for additional compensation against contractor and the payment bond surety. The contractor and surety moved for summary judgment on the grounds that payment was excused pursuant to the terms of the pay-when-paid provision in the subcontract. The trial court entered summary judgment in favor of contractor and surety. The subcontractor appealed. Among other issues on appeal was whether the pay-when-paid clause was an enforceable condition precedent to contractor's liability to subcontractor. The appellate court upheld the judgment of the trial court on this issue.

The subcontract provided that:

Notwithstanding anything to the contrary in the preceding paragraphs of this agreement, subcontractor agrees as a condition precedent to payment, of either progress or final payment, that the owner shall have first paid the payment applied for to the contractor, and that payment for either progress payments or final payment is not due and owing to the subcontractor as provided for herein until the owner has made such payment to the contractor. The subcontractor recognizes that the source of funding for this subcontract agreement are [sic] the progress and final payments that are to be made by the owner to contractor.

remedy was an extension of time for completion of its work, equal to the amount of the delay. The word "only," according to its usual signification, meant "solely" or "exclusively." Since in this clause the word "only" directly preceded the phrase "an extension of time," it was evident that contractor and subcontractor agreed that an extension of time would be subcontractor's exclusive remedy in the event of delay caused by contractor.

Under the unambiguous terms of the owner-contractor agreement and the subcontract, the flow-down clause incorporated the no-damage-for-delay provision into the subcontract, barring the subcontractor's action against the contractor for delay damages.

97014   Leitao v. Damon G. Douglas Co., 301 N.J. Super. 187, 693 A.2d 1209 (1997)

	II:	A107-1987, Art. 9, Para. 9.12
	II:	A107-1987, Art. 9, Para. 9.12.1
	II:	A117-1987, Art. 14, Para. 14.12
	II:	A117-1987, Art. 14, Para. 14.12.1
	II:	A201-1987, Art. 3, Para. 3.18.1
	II:	A201-1987, Art. 3, Para. 3.18.2
	II:	A201-1987, Art. 10, Para. 10.1.4
	II:	A401-1987, Art. 4, Para. 4.6.1
	II:	A401-1987, Art. 4, Para. 4.6.2

Contractor brought a third-party indemnification action against subcontractor for personal injury damages paid to subcontractor's injured employee. The trial court granted contractor's indemnity claim on the grounds that the claim arose out of the performance of subcontractor's work and was in part caused by worker's negligence. The subcontractor appealed. The appellate court affirmed.

The subcontract provided:

The subcontractor/vendor shall indemnify and hold harmless Damon G. Douglas Company and all of its agents and employees from and against all claims, damages, losses, and expenses, including attorney's fees arising out of or resulting from the performance of the subcontractor/vendor's work under this purchase order, provided that any such claim,damage, loss or expense a) is attributable to bodily injury, sickness, disease, or death, or to injury to or destruction of tangible property (other than work itself), including the loss of use resulting therefrom, and b) is caused in whole or in part by any negligent act or omission of the subcontractor/vendor or anyone directly or indirectly employed by them or anyone for whose acts they may be liable, regardless of whether it is caused in part by a party indemnified hereunder.

In any and all claims against Damon G. Douglas Company or any of its agents or employees by any employees of the subcontractor/vendor, anyone directly or indirectly employed by them or anyone for whose acts they may be liable, the indemnification obligation under this Agreement shall not be limited in any way by any limitation on the amount or type of damages, compensation, or benefits payable by or for the

and to determine whether the flow-down clause barred the action for delay damages when the subcontract also provided that "only an extension of time" would be accorded the subcontractor in the event of contractor-caused delay.

The owner-contractor agreement provided that:

The contractor [L & B] expressly agrees that the contractor's sole remedy for . . . delay shall be an extension of contract time and that the contractor shall make no demand for damages or extended overhead. The Contractor shall not be entitled to payment or compensation of any kind from the Owner for direct, indirect, or impact damages . . . arising because of any hindrance or delay from any cause whatsoever [except those involving fraud and bad faith].

The subcontract provided that:

Should subcontractor be delayed in his work by contractor then contractor shall owe subcontractor therefor only an extension of time for completion equal to the delay caused and then only if a written claim for delay is made to the contractor within forty-eight hours from the time of the beginning of the delay.

The contractor [L & B] has heretofore entered into a General Contract with [the Owner] . . . and which is now made a part of this Sub-contract insofar as [it] appl[ies].

Contractor shall have the same rights and privileges as against the Sub-contractor herein as the Owner in the General Contract has against the Contractor. Sub-contractor acknowledges that he has read the General Contract and all plans and specifications and is familiar therewith and agrees to comply with and perform all provisions thereof applicable to Sub-contractor.

The Sub-contractor agrees to be bound to the contractor by the terms of the contract documents and assume toward the contractor all of the obligations and responsibilities that the contractor by aforesaid document assumes toward the Owner.

Turning first to the flow-down clause, the court held that as the clause stated that "contractor shall have the same rights and privileges as against the Sub-contractor . . . as the Owner in the General Contract has against the Contractor," the clause meant that the contractor may invoke against the subcontractor all of the rights and defenses that the owner would be able to invoke against the contractor under the owner-contractor agreement. Therefore, the rights and defenses available to the owner against the contractor clearly and unambiguously barred the recovery of delay damages.

The court held further that the second clause which read "the Sub-contractor agrees to . . . assume . . . toward the contractor all of the obligations and responsibilities that the contractor by [the general contract] assumes toward the [project] Owner," removed any conceivable doubt that the subcontractor was bound to the contractor in the same manner as the contractor was bound to the owner. Because the owner-contractor agreement accorded the owner protection from an action brought by the contractor for delay damages, it necessarily followed that the subcontract accorded the same protection to the contractor vis a vis the subcontractor.

Turning to the issue of delay damages, the court held that the clause "contractor shall owe subcontractor therefor only an extension of time for completion equal to the delay," clearly and unambiguously meant that in the event of delay the subcontractor's exclusive

The parties had entered into an agreement which included an arbitration provision similar to Paragraph 4.5.1 of the American Institute of Architects General Conditions of the Contract for Construction, Document No. A201, 1987 edition. The bond provided that:

> Whereas, Principal has by written agreement . . . entered into a subcontract with Obligee for Renovation and addition to Scarlett Seed Building . . . which subcontract is by reference made a part hereof, and is hereinafter referred to as the subcontract.

97012   Ironbound Fin. Servs. v. Certified Contracting, Inc., 1997 U.S. Dist. LEXIS 2574 (S.D.N.Y. Mar. 10, 1997)

II:	A107-1987, Art. 20, Para. 20.2
II:	A117-1987, Art. 25, Para. 25.2
I:	A201-1987, Art. 14, Para. 14.2.3
I:	A201-1987, Art. 14, Para. 14.2.4

Contractor's assignee brought an action against owner for payment after owner terminated the contractor. At issue before the district court was whether contractor was entitled to additional payments when contractor had defaulted on the contract and surety had completed the work at a loss.

The owner and contractor entered into the American Institute of Architects Standard Form of Agreement Between Owner and Contractor, Document No. A101, which included Paragraphs 14.2.3 and 14.2.4 of the American Institute of Architects General Conditions of the Contract for Construction, Document No. A201, 1987 edition.

The district court held that because contractor missed the completion date and defaulted on its contract with the owner, the contractor's right to payment was extinguished, even for work that had been completed. The contract terms clearly provided that: (1) if owner terminated contractor for cause, then owner was entitled to use the remaining contract funds to complete the Project; (2) contractor and its assignee's right to receive any further payments was stayed; and (3) the right was extinguished if the completion costs exceeded the remaining contract funds.

97013   L & B Constr. Co. v. Ragan Enter., Inc., 267 Ga. 809, 482 S.E.2d 279 (1997)

III:	A107-1987, Art. 14, Para. 14.3
III:	A117-1987, Art. 19, Para. 19.3
III:	A201-1987, Art. 8, Para. 8.3
III:	A401-1987, Art. 2, Para. 2.1
III:	A401-1987, Art. 5, Para. 5.3

The Supreme Court of Georgia granted certiorari in subcontractor's action for delay damages to review the construction of a flow-down clause purported to incorporate a no-damage-for-delay provision from the owner-contractor agreement into a subcontract, clearly provided that "[n]o alterations shall be made in the work shown or described by the plans and specifications, except upon the written order of the Owner." Whatever legal significance there was in defining "scope of work," and regardless of whether the removal of excess contaminated waste fell within that definition, the work constituted an "alteration," for which a written order was required.

The court concluded that contractor could not recover damages absent a written change order.

97011   Hartford Accident & Indem. Co. v. Scarlett Harbor Assocs. Ltd. Partnership, 346 Md. 122, 695 A.2d 153 (1997)

II:	A107-1987, Art. 10, Para. 10.8	
II:	A117-1987, Art. 15, Para. 15.8	
II:	A201-1987, Art. 4, Para. 4.5.1	
II:	A201-1987, Art. 4, Para. 4.5.2	
II:	A201-1987, Art. 4, Para. 4.5.3	
II:	A201-1987, Art. 4, Para. 4.5.4	
II:	A201-1987, Art. 4, Para. 4.5.4.1	
II:	A201-1987, Art. 4, Para. 4.5.4.2	
II:	A201-1987, Art. 4, Para. 4.5.5	
II:	A201-1987, Art. 4, Para. 4.5.6	
II:	A201-1987, Art. 4, Para. 4.5.7	
III:	A312-1984, Performance Bond, Para. 1	
II:	A401-1987, Art. 6, Para. 6.1	
II:	A401-1987, Art. 6, Para. 6.2	
II:	A401-1987, Art. 6, Para. 6.3	
II:	A401-1987, Art. 6, Para. 6.4	
II:	A401-1987, Art. 6, Para. 6.5	
II:	B141-1987, Art. 7, Para. 7.1	
II:	B141-1987, Art. 7, Para. 7.2	
II:	B141-1987, Art. 7, Para. 7.3	
II:	B141-1987, Art. 7, Para. 7.4	

The appellate court held that the owner had not agreed to arbitrate its claim against the bond when an arbitration provision was incorporated by reference into the performance bond.

By incorporating into the bond the contract that contained owner's promise to arbitrate with contractor, the bond literally had incorporated only owner's promise to arbitrate with contractor. The bond did not, by its terms, express any enlargement of the obligations of contractor, and, even if surety, acting unilaterally, or surety and contractor, acting by agreement, undertook to enlarge the obligations of the owner, that attempted enlargement would be ineffective.

on the grounds that contractor's insurer had waived its subrogation rights. Subcontractor filed a petition for a writ of mandate requesting that the appellate court compel the entry of summary judgment. The appellate court issued the writ.

The owner-contractor agreement included the American Institute of Architects General Conditions of the Contract for Construction, Document No. A201, 1987 edition, Paragraph 11.3.7. The subcontract incorporated the owner-contractor agreement by reference and provided that any conflicts between the two would be controlled by the subcontract. The subcontract was silent on the subject of subrogation but it did obligate subcontractor to indemnify contractor and owner for any damage caused by subcontractor's negligence.

The appellate court held that the waiver of subrogation defeated all of insurer's claims against subcontractor. The language was plain and unambiguous and covered all claims that contractor might have had against subcontractor for breach of contract or negligence. With language requiring owner and contractor to "waive all rights against . . . each other and any of their subcontractors . . . each of the other, . . . " all parties waived their rights against all other parties.

The court rejected insurer's argument that it was not bound by the subrogation waiver because subcontractor was not a party to the owner-contractor agreement. Rather, subcontractor was a party to the subcontract which incorporated the owner-contractor agreement by reference.

The court also rejected insurer's contention that there was an inconsistency between the subrogation waiver and the subcontract's indemnity provision. The subrogation waiver applied to claims covered by insurance, while the indemnity provision applied to claims that were not covered by insurance.

The court concluded that subrogation waivers and indemnity provisions were "horses of different colors," and, as such, were not inconsistent.

97010   Foster Wheeler Envirespsonse, Inc. v. Franklin County Convention Facilities Auth., 78 Ohio St. 3d 353, 678 N.E.2d 519 (1997)

III:	A107-1987, Art. 13, Para. 13.1
III:	A107-1987, Art. 13, Para. 13.2
III:	A117-1987, Art. 18, Para. 18.1
III:	A117-1987, Art. 18, Para. 18.2
III:	A201-1987, Art. 7, Para. 7.1
III:	A201-1987, Art. 7, Para. 7.2
III:	A201-1987, Art. 7, Para. 7.3

The Supreme Court of Ohio rejected the lower appellate court's interpretation of the phrase "scope of the work" contained in the written change order provision of a unit price contract for the disposal of hazardous waste. The appellate court interpreted the provision as requiring a written authorization only for changes in the "scope of work." The court held that a written change order was required for "alterations," because the agreement

III:	A201-1987, Art. 3, Para. 3.18.1
III:	A201-1987, Art. 10, Para. 10.1.4
III:	A401-1987, Art. 4, Para. 4.6.1

In contractor's third-party indemnification action against subcontractor for personal injury and property damages paid to owner and owner's employees, the appellate court held that the plain language of the indemnity provision required subcontractor to indemnify contractor for losses arising out of "any act" of subcontractor, which included the installation of a defective valve manufactured by a supplier but properly installed by the subcontractor. Under the indemnity agreement contractor was not required to prove fault or a causal connection between the work performed by subcontractor and the injury in order to establish a duty on the part of subcontractor to defend and indemnify contractor.

The indemnity clause provided in pertinent part that subcontractor indemnify contractor for loss:

> [which] arises out of or is in any way connected with the performance of work under this Subcontract. [Further, indemnity] shall apply to any acts or omissions, willful misconduct or negligent conduct, whether active or passive, on the part of Subcontractor . . . including attorney's fees[, which] arises out of or is in any way connected with the performance of work under this Subcontract.

Furthermore, the plain language of the clause also required the subcontractor to indemnify contractor for attorney fees resulting from a breach of any contract provision including, but not limited to, breach of the indemnity provision.

97009 Davlar Corp. v. Superior Court, 53 Cal. App. 4th 1121, 62 Cal. Rptr. 2d 199 (1997)

I:	A107-1987, Art. 9, Para. 9.12
II:	A107-1987, Art. 17, Para. 17.1
II:	A107-1987, Art. 17, Para. 17.6
I:	A117-1987, Art. 14, Para. 14.12
II:	A117-1987, Art. 22, Para. 22.1
II:	A117-1987, Art. 22, Para. 22.6
I:	A201-1987, Art. 3, Para. 3.18.1
I:	A201-1987, Art. 10, Para. 10.1.4
I:	A201-1987, Art. 11, Para. 11.1
I:	A201-1987, Art. 11, Para. 11.3.7
III:	A401-1987, Art. 1, Para. 1.1
I:	A401-1987, Art. 4, Para. 4.6.1

Contractor's insurer brought a subrogation action against subcontractor and its insurer for fire damage to contractor's property. Subcontractor moved for summary judgment

II:	A401-1987, Art. 6, Para. 6.3
II:	A401-1987, Art. 6, Para. 6.4
II:	A401-1987, Art. 6, Para. 6.5
II:	B141-1987, Art. 7, Para. 7.1
II:	B141-1987, Art. 7, Para. 7.2
II:	B141-1987, Art. 7, Para. 7.3
II:	B141-1987, Art. 7, Para. 7.4

Contractor filed a demand for arbitration of its claim for damages resulting from owner's termination of the contract for failure to complete construction in a timely manner. Owner filed an action to enjoin arbitration on the grounds that contractor had failed to satisfy two conditions precedent to the right to arbitrate, namely, filing a claim within twenty-one days of the "occurrence" giving rise to its claim and obtaining a decision from the architect. Contractor filed a motion to dismiss and a cross-motion for attorney fees. The trial court denied owner's motions and the parties arbitrated the dispute. Contractor was awarded damages. Owner moved to vacate the award. The trial court confirmed the arbitration award. Both parties appealed. The appellate court consolidated the appeals and affirmed.

The owner-contractor agreement included the American Institute of Architects General Conditions of the Contract for Construction, Document No. A201, 1987 edition, specifically Paragraphs 4.3.2, 4.3.3 and 4.5.1.

The appellate court held that the arbitration clause required the submission to arbitration of not only "any claim" but also "[a]ny Controversy . . . arising out of or related to the Contract, or the breach thereof." The term "any controversy" has a broader meaning than simply "any claim" and includes any dispute between the parties relating to the contract. The court's interpretation of the meaning of "any controversy" was reinforced by the fact that the arbitration clause applied to any controversy "related to" the contract or any alleged breach. The court found that its reading of the arbitration clause furthered the state's policy of minimizing the role of courts in the arbitration process.

The court concluded that the parties' dispute as to whether contractor satisfied the procedural preconditions of arbitration of its claim arising out of owner's alleged breach constituted a "controversy . . . related to the Contract, or the breach thereof." Therefore, the trial court correctly construed the arbitration clause as requiring that the arbitrator decide whether contractor was foreclosed from arbitrating because it did not file a claim with the architect or demand arbitration within twenty-one days of termination of the contract.

97008 Continental Heller Corp. v. Amtech Mechanical Servs., Inc., 53 Cal. App. 4th 500, 61 Cal. Rptr. 2d 668, *review denied*, 1997 Cal. LEXIS 2609 (Cal. May 14, 1997)

III:	A107-1987, Art. 9, Para. 9.12
III:	A117-1987, Art. 14, Para. 14.12

person . . . received or sustained by or from the contractor and his employees . . . in doing the work or in consequence of any improper materials, implements or labor used or employed therein," as not requiring that the injury be caused, either in whole or in part, by the subcontractor. Rather, the subcontractor could be required to indemnify the contractor for personal injuries exclusively caused by the contractor's own negligence, in contravention of the state statute.

Referring to Callahan v. A.J. Welch Equip. Corp., Digest No. 94029, andHarnois v. Quannapowitt Dev., Inc., Digest No. 93041, the court concluded that the indemnification clause violated the state statute and was unenforceable because the subcontractor's obligation to indemnify contractor was not limited to injuries resulting from subcontractor's own negligence, acts, or omissions, but rather extended to injuries which may have resulted exclusively from the acts of the contractor.

The court rejected the contractor's argument that the flow-down provision in the subcontract, which contained the words "except to the extent that provisions contained [in the contract documents] are by their terms or by law applicable only to the Contractor," required that any language violative of the state statute be construed as limited to contractor, and, therefore, not incorporated into the subcontract. The purported saving language [in the subcontract] was not located directly within the indemnity provision of the owner-contractor agreement, making it questionable whether the parties intended the language to serve as saving language for the indemnity clause.

97007   Commerce Bank, N.A. v. DiMaria Constr., Inc., 300 N.J. Super. 9, 692 A.2d 54 (1997)

II:	A107-1987, Art. 10, Para. 10.5	
II:	A107-1987, Art. 10, Para. 10.8	
II:	A117-1987, Art. 15, Para. 15.5	
II:	A117-1987, Art. 15, Para. 15.8	
I:	A201-1987, Art. 4, Para. 4.3.2	
I:	A201-1987, Art. 4, Para. 4.3.3	
I:	A201-1987, Art. 4, Para. 4.5.1	
I:	A201-1987, Art. 4, Para. 4.5.2	
I:	A201-1987, Art. 4, Para. 4.5.3	
I:	A201-1987, Art. 4, Para. 4.5.4	
I:	A201-1987, Art. 4, Para. 4.5.4.1	
I:	A201-1987, Art. 4, Para. 4.5.4.2	
I:	A201-1987, Art. 4, Para. 4.5.5	
I:	A201-1987, Art. 4, Para. 4.5.6	
I:	A201-1987, Art. 4, Para. 4.5.7	
II:	A401-1987, Art. 6, Para. 6.1	
II:	A401-1987, Art. 6, Para. 6.2	

contractor was responsible for insuring that workers' used adequate safety procedures while working on a deteriorated roof, neither owner or its agent, by contract or conduct, undertook to enforce or supervise safety procedures such as would incur a duty to decedent to exercise reasonable care for his safety.

Pursuant to the state's statute which required that settlement payments had to be attributable to the indemnitee's legal liability for the claim, the court rejected the owner's argument that the "regardless" clause in the indemnity agreement extended the right to indemnification beyond the state's common law actual liability rule.

The court concluded that since the owner and its agent were not liable to decedent, the settlement payments were voluntary, and, as such, precluded indemnification.

97006 Bjorkman v. Suffolk Constr. Co., 42 Mass. App. Ct. 591, 679 N.E.2d 559 (1997)

III:	A107-1987, Art. 9, Para. 9.12
III:	A117-1987, Art. 14, Para. 14.12
III:	A201-1987, Art. 3, Para. 3.18.1
III:	A201-1987, Art. 10, Para. 10.1.4
III:	A401-1987, Art. 4, Para. 4.6.1

Subcontractor's injured employee brought an action for personal injury damages against contractor, and contractor impleaded subcontractor, claiming a right to indemnification. The trial court declared the indemnity clause void as against public policy. Contractor appealed. The appellate court affirmed.

The owner-contractor agreement contained the following indemnification provision which was made applicable to subcontractor by the subcontract:

The contractor shall assume the defense of, and indemnify and save harmless, the Commonwealth . . . from all claims relating to labor performed or furnished and materials used or employed for the work; . . . to injuries to any person or corporation received or sustained by or from the contractor and his employees, and subcontractors and employees, in doing the work, or in consequence of any improper materials, implements or labor used or employed therein; and to any act, omission or neglect of the contractor and his employees therein.

The subcontract provided that:

The Subcontractor agrees to be bound to the Contractor by the terms of the hereinbefore described plans, specifications (including all general conditions stated therein) and Addenda No. 1, 2 and 3, and to assume to the Contractor all the obligations and responsibilities that the Contractor by those documents assumes to the Commonwealth of Massachusetts Division of Capital Planning & Operations, hereinafter called the 'Awarding Authority,' except to the extent that provisions contained therein are by their terms or by law applicable to the Contractor.

The appellate court interpreted the owner-contractor agreement, which required the subcontractor to indemnify the contractor for "claims relating . . . to injuries to any

97005   Best Prods. Co. v. A.F. Callan & Co., 1997 U.S. Dist. LEXIS 1914 (E.D. Pa. Feb. 26, 1997)

II:	A107-1987, Art. 9, Para. 9.1
II:	A107-1987, Art. 9, Para. 9.12
II:	A107-1987, Art. 9, Para. 9.12.1
II:	A107-1987, Art. 16, Para. 16.1
II:	A117-1987, Art. 14, Para. 14.1
II:	A117-1987, Art. 14, Para. 14.12
II:	A117-1987, Art. 14, Para. 14.12.1
II:	A117-1987, Art. 21, Para. 21.1
I:	A201-1987, Art. 3, Para. 3.3.1
I:	A201-1987, Art. 3, Para. 3.18.1
I:	A201-1987, Art. 3, Para. 3.18.2
II:	A201-1987, Art. 10, Para. 10.1.4
I:	A201-1987, Art. 10, Para. 10.2.1
II:	A401-1987, Art. 4, Para. 4.6.1

Decedent's estate brought a wrongful death action against owner and owner's agent. Owner and its agent settled with decedent's estate. Owner filed a third-party indemnification action against contractor.

The owner and contractor entered into an American Institute of Architects agreement which contained provisions similar to Paragraphs 3.3.1, 3.18.1, 3.18.2 and 10.2.1 of the American Institute of Architects General Conditions of the Contract for Construction, Document No. A201, 1987 edition. The specifications provided that:

Section 1.1.2.17. It is the responsibility of the Contractor to ascertain all existing conditions and verify all dimensions of areas included in the Scope of Work during the time of site inspection. Representations herein are of general existing conditions, but neither the Owner or the Consultant assumes any responsibility for assessment of existing conditions for bidding purposes or that representations of existing conditions stated hereon are accurate.

Section 2.1.2.3. The Owner will have a quality assurance representative on the job during the time of all construction . . . . All field decisions regarding conditions encountered during construction, verification of areas of work covered by unit prices and field change orders will be made by the owner's field QA representative.

Section 4.1.2.1. Check all deck surfaces for deterioration and repair/replace decking as required to provide a structurally sound substrate for installation of the new roofing assembly.

Section 2.1.6.2. The Contractor and the Owner's representative shall check all surfaces over which the roofing materials are to be installed.

The facts disclosed that contractor was causally negligent. Furthermore, the facts did not support a finding of negligence on the part of owner or owner's agent. Because

III:	A117-1987, Art. 22, Para. 22.1
III:	A201-1987, Art. 11, Para. 11.1
III:	A401-1987, Art. 13, Para. 13.1
III:	A401-1987, Art. 13, Para. 13.2
III:	A401-1987, Art. 13, Para. 13.3

This case presented numerous issues arising from multi-party litigation of a personal injury action. Contractor argued on appeal that subcontractor's insurer had a duty to defend and indemnify contractor from damages arising from a personal injury action brought by a third-party. Subcontractor argued that it had not breached its contact to provide insurance for contractor when the injury arose from contractor's own negligence in not backfilling a pit after subcontractor had excavated the pit, and the subcontract did not require it to obtain insurance to cover contractor's own negligence.

The agreement provided that the policy be endorsed as follows:

Such insurance as afforded by this policy for the benefit of BGE shall be primary as respects any claims, losses, damages, expenses, or liabilities arising out of work or services for BGE, and insured hereunder, and any insurance carried by BGE shall be excess of and noncontributing with insurance afforded by this policy.

The appellate court held that the subcontractor did not breach the agreement when it procured a policy that did not cover contractor for contractor's own negligence. The agreement required subcontractor to provide contractor with coverage for potential claims by third parties that were based on subcontractor's work. It was plain that, through the contract, contractor sought to insulate itself from claims grounded on the actions of its subcontractor, over which it would have only supervisory control, but for which contractor could potentially be found derivatively liable. Contractor apparently recognized that by contracting with subcontractor to perform work on contractor's behalf it was assuming the risk of liability if subcontractor's work resulted in legal action against it. Therefore, according to the court, contractor sought to shift that risk back to subcontractor by requiring subcontractor to provide appropriate insurance coverage.

The court held that the subcontract did not require subcontractor to provide contractor with insurance coverage for claims brought against contractor based on contractor's own negligence. The contract expressly required subcontractor to carry coverage for itself, with an endorsement to also cover contractor. While the agreement provided that the coverage was to protect contractor from "claims, losses, damages, expenses, or liabilities arising out of work or services for BGE," it did not apply to liabilities arising from work performed by contractor.

As required by the subcontract, the policy provided contractor with coverage for claims brought against it based on subcontractor's work. The policy also provided contractor with coverage for claims based on contractor's acts or omissions in supervising subcontractor.

The court concluded that subcontractor was not required to insure contractor for contractor's own negligence.

II:	A101-1987, Art. 1
II:	A101-1987, Art. 9
II:	A107-1987, Art. 6
II:	A107-1987, Art. 7, Para. 7.1
II:	A117-1987, Art. 11
II:	A117-1987, Art. 12, Para. 12.1
II:	A201-1987, Art. 1, Para. 1.1.1

On appeal of the trial court's award of lien damages to contractor and delay damages to owner, the owner argued that the American Institute of Architects General Conditions of the Contract for Construction, Document No. A201, was part of the owner-contractor agreement.

The owner-contractor agreement provided that:

The Contract Documents consists of this Agreement, the Conditions of the Contract (General, Supplementary and other Conditions), the Drawings, the Specifications, all Addenda issued prior to and all Modifications issued after execution of the Agreement. These form the Contract, and all are as fully a part of the Contract as if attached to this Agreement of [sic] repeated herein. An enumeration of the Contract Documents appears in Article 7.

7.2 The Contract Documents, which constitute the entire Agreement between the Owner and the Contractor, are listed in Article 1 and, except for Modifications issued after execution of this Agreement, are enumerated as follows:

1. LEGRO & ASSOCIATES SITE PLANS & ENGINEERING PAGE 1 & 2 DATED FEB 14, 1992.

The appellate court held that (1) Article 7 did not enumerate the American Institute of Architects General Conditions, Document No. A201 or any other general conditions documents; (2) the language in Paragraph 7.2 was confusing in that it both referred back to the documents named in Article I and purported to enumerate the documents; (3) Article I named general categories of documents which should have been more specifically identified; and (4) the American Institute of Architects materials, which were part of the bid information, suggested that the American Institute of Architects had more than one general conditions form. Even if it was clear that the general conditions document referred to an American Institute of Architects form, further specification would be necessary to determine which form was a part of the owner-contractor agreement.

The court concluded that there was substantial evidence in the record to support the trial court's determination that the American Institute of Architects General Conditions of the Contract for Construction, Document No. A201, was not incorporated into the owner-contractor agreement.

97004 Baltimore Gas & Elec. Co. v. Commercial Union Ins. Co., 113 Md. App. 540, 688 A.2d 496 (1997)

III:	A107-1987, Art. 17, Para. 17.1

motion to compel arbitration and dismissed its arbitration demand against masonry subcontractor. Subcontractor then filed the present action against masonry subcontractor seeking indemnification or contribution for the amount paid in settlement to worker, and for any amount subcontractor was required to pay to indemnify contractor. The trial court found that subcontractor was not a third-party beneficiary of the masonry subcontractor's agreement with contractor and dismissed subcontractor's complaint. Subcontractor appealed, and the appellate court reversed.

The indemnity agreement provided that masonry subcontractor indemnify: "the Owner, SIGAL . . . and other contractors and subcontractor" against all claims "arising out of or resulting from the performance of [Atlantic's] work . . . to the extent caused or alleged to be caused in whole or in any part by any negligent act or omission of [Atlantic] . . . regardless of whether it is caused in part by a party indemnified hereunder."

The agreement also provided for waiver of worker's compensation exclusivity:

> In any and all claims against the Owner, SIGAL . . . and other contractors or subcontractors . . . by any employees of the Subcontractor . . . the indemnification obligation under this Section 18 shall not be limited in any way by any limitation on the amount or type of damages, compensation or benefits payable by or for the Subcontractor under Worker's or Workmen's Compensation Acts, disability benefit acts or other employee benefit acts.

The appellate court held that from the plain language of the indemnity agreement, subcontractor was an intended beneficiary with the right to enforce the clause. The agreement required masonry subcontractor to indemnify not only the owner and contractor, but also "other contractors and subcontractors." This additional language would be meaningless unless it was interpreted as manifesting an intention to benefit subcontractor and those in similar situations who were required to pay damages as a result of the masonry subcontractor's negligence. Furthermore, the duty to indemnify was expressed in terms that made the duty run directly to the indemnitee, including the other subcontractors.

The waiver of the worker's compensation clause did not apply since subcontractor did not rely on the implied waiver of masonry subcontractor's right not to be sued by its own employees, but instead sought recovery under the contractual provision in which masonry subcontractor expressly waived its immunity from such claims.

The court limited its ruling to a finding that for purposes of dismissal of the claim, subcontractor was considered an intended beneficiary entitled to whatever indemnification was intended by the parties to flow to subcontractors under that clause, leaving to the trial court to determine, on the basis of the full trial record, what the contract language meant under the facts of the case.

97003   Axthelm & Swett Constr., Inc. v. Caudill, 1997 Wash. App. LEXIS 735 (Wash. Ct. App. May 12, 1997)

        I: A101-1977, Art. 1
        I: A101-1977, Art. 7, Para. 7.2

Section E-16(c) of the owner-contractor agreement provided that any decision of the architect regarding claims for extra work was final and binding unless there was written notice of protest within twelve days.

The district court rejected the subcontractor's argument that letters written to contractor by or on behalf of subcontractor constituted sufficient notice under Section 11 of subcontractor's intention to assert delay claims. The owner-contractor agreement required subcontractor to provide notice of a claim within fifteen days "after occurrence of the event on which the claim is based," and Section 11 required subcontractor to timely file any delay claim "within ten (10) days from the commencement of the alleged damage . . . ." Subcontractor's first written notice of any claim for delays was not submitted until six months had elapsed, rather than within the period of time set forth in Section 11.

There was insufficient evidence that contractor's affirmative acts could have caused subcontractor to believe it was not necessary to provide notice of its claim for delay damages.

The court held further that it was undisputed that subcontractor had failed to appeal the architect's decision regarding its claim for damages resulting from extra work. The court concluded that since Section E-16(c) was incorporated into the subcontract, it was subcontractor's responsibility to appeal from any decision it believed was adverse to its interests.

97002 A.S. Johnson Co. v. Atlantic Masonry Co., 693 A.2d 1117 (D.C. 1997)

II:	A107-1987, Art. 9, Para. 9.12
II:	A107-1987, Art. 9, Para. 9.12.1
II:	A117-1987, Art. 14, Para. 14.12
II:	A117-1987, Art. 14, Para. 14.12.1
II:	A201-1987, Art. 3, Para. 3.18.1
II:	A201-1987, Art. 3, Para. 3.18.2
II:	A401-1987, Art. 4, Para. 4.6.1
II:	A401-1987, Art. 4, Para. 4.6.2

Masonry subcontractor's injured employee brought a negligence action against another subcontractor and contractor. Contractor then filed an arbitration claim against subcontractor seeking indemnification for the amounts contractor paid to worker. Contractor then filed the present action against masonry subcontractor for indemnification or contribution as a third-party beneficiary of the subcontract between contractor and masonry subcontractor that required masonry subcontractor to indemnify the contractor, but also "other contractors or subcontractors" for amounts paid as a result of masonry subcontractor's negligence. Subcontractor then filed a demand for arbitration against masonry subcontractor seeking indemnity or contribution. Masonry subcontractor filed a complaint to stay the arbitration proceeding, arguing that there was no agreement to arbitrate between the subcontractors, and that subcontractor had no agreement with masonry subcontractor providing for indemnification. The court denied subcontractor's

97001 Allgood Elec. Co. v. Martin K. Eby Constr. Co., 959 F. Supp. 1573 (M.D. Ga. 1997)

III:	A107-1987, Art. 10, Para. 10.5
III:	A107-1987, Art. 11, Para. 11.2
III:	A107-1987, Art. 14, Para. 14.3
III:	A117-1987, Art. 15, Para. 15.
III:	A117-1987, Art. 16, Para. 16.2
III:	A117-1987, Art. 19, Para. 19.3
III:	A201-1987, Art. 4, Para. 4.3
III:	A201-1987, Art. 8, Para. 8.3
III:	A401-1987, Art. 2, Para. 2.1
III:	A401-1987, Art. 3, Para. 3.3
III:	A401-1987, Art. 5, Para. 5.3

Subcontractor brought an action against contractor and its sureties to recover damages resulting from contractor's delays. The district court entered summary judgment in favor of contractor and sureties. Subcontractor appealed, and the court of appeals reversed and remanded. On remand, the district court held that the notice requirements in Section 11 of the subcontract were determinative as to subcontractor's claims for delay damages; contractor did not waive its right to timely notice; and it was subcontractor's responsibility to appeal from any decision by architect that it believed was adverse to its interests.

Section 11 provided that:

SECTION 11. DELAYS. Subcontractor shall not be entitled to an adjustment in time or Subcontract price for delays or damages caused by the Owner and/or Architect-Engineer, inclement weather, strikes or other delays or damages unless such price change or time extension is approved in writing by the Owner or its authorized representative. Any damages which Subcontractor alleges that the Owner, Architect-Engineer, Contractor, other Subcontractor, or any other party for whom Contractor may be liable has caused him or is causing him must be filed in writing with the Contractor within ten (10) days from the commencement of the alleged damage and a full accounting filed within ten (10) days after the extent of damage is known or the cause of damage ceases, whichever is the sooner; otherwise, any such claims will be considered void.

The owner-contractor agreement provided that subcontractor agreed:

[t]o be bound to the contractor by the terms of the contract documents and to assume toward the contractor all the obligations and responsibilities that the contractor by the aforesaid documents assumes toward the owner . . .

No claim of the contractor for damage shall be valid unless written notice thereof shall have been received by the owner by registered mail within 15 days after occurrence of the event on which the claim is based . . .

In addition, the subcontractor had agreed to provide the contractor with insurance coverage for "all damages" to "all persons, whether employees or otherwise," "in any manner connected" to the work under the subcontract. The agreement to provide insurance converted the indemnity provision from an unenforceable indemnification agreement to an enforceable insurance agreement permitted by state statute. Furthermore, this agreement to provide insurance was clear and unequivocal. Subcontractor's failure to include contractor as an additional insured as required by the subcontract did not limit contractor's ability to recover from subcontractor.

The indemnification agreement authorized the recovery of attorney fees when contractor was required to defend its right to indemnification on appeal in a complex case. The court concluded that pursuant to the terms of the agreement contractor was entitled to recovery attorney fees on appeal. The court remanded the issue to the trial court for recalculation of the amount of the fees.

96043 Van Vickle v. C.W. Scheurer & Sons, Inc., 556 N.W.2d 238 (Minn. Ct. App. 1996), *review denied,* 1997 Minn. LEXIS 196 (Minn. Mar. 18, 1997)

III:	A107-1987, Art. 9, Para. 9.12
III:	A107-1987, Art. 17, Para. 17.1
III:	A117-1987, Art. 14, Para. 14.12
III:	A117-1987, Art. 22, Para. 22.1
III:	A201-1987, Art. 3, Para. 3.18.1
III:	A201-1987, Art. 10, Para. 10.1.4
III:	A201-1987, Art. 11, Para. 11.1
III:	A401-1987, Art. 4, Para. 4.6.1

Subcontractor's injured employee brought a negligence action against contractor and excavation subcontractor. The subcontractor who employed worker did not have a written agreement with the contractor. Contractor and subcontractor cross-claimed for indemnity. Contractor tendered its defense to subcontractor and subcontractor refused the tender. Injured worker then settled with contractor and subcontractor, each contributing an equal amount to the settlement. The trial court granted contractor summary judgment, finding that because worker was injured on the site it was proper for contractor to seek indemnity from subcontractor. Contractor was awarded its requested damages, attorney fees, and prejudgment interest. Subcontractor appealed. Contractor also appealed the amount of the award of attorney fees.

The subcontract provided in pertinent part that the subcontractor agreed to:

obtain, maintain and pay for such insurance as may be required by the General Contract . . . and to furnish the Contractor satisfactory evidence that it has complied with this paragraph; . . . The Subcontractor agrees to assume entire responsibility and liability, to the fullest extent permitted by law, for all damages or injury to all persons, whether employees or otherwise, . . . arising out of [the contract work], resulting from or in any manner connected with, the execution of the work provided for in this Subcontract and the Subcontractor, to the fullest extent permitted by law, agrees to indemnify and save harmless the Contractor, . . . from all such claims including, . . . claims for which the Contractor may be or may be claimed to be, liable and legal fees and disbursements paid or incurred to enforce the provisions of this paragraph and the Subcontractor further agrees to obtain, maintain and pay for such general liability insurance coverage and endorsements as will insure the provisions of this paragraph.

Subcontractor did not obtain the insurance and did not name contractor as an additional insured.

The appellate court held that the subcontract did provide indemnification to contractor for the personal injury claims of an employee of a different subcontractor. The court reasoned that subcontractor agreed to indemnify contractor for any claims which contractor "may be or may be claimed to be" liable. While there was no evidence that contractor was negligent, the worker "claimed" contractor was negligent.

III: A107-1987, Art. 12, Para. 12.2
III: A117-1987, Art. 14, Para. 14.1
III: A117-1987, Art. 17, Para. 17.2
III: A201-1987, Art. 3, Para. 3.3.1
III: A401-1987, Art. 3, Para. 3.1.1

When the subcontract required the subcontractor to "perform and coordinate his work with that of the Contractor and other sub-contractors to the best interest of the project as a whole as directed by the Contractor . . . " the contractor was required by this language to provide the subcontractor with sufficient notice of an equipment start-up to enable the subcontractor to "perform and coordinate his work." The contractor had failed to notify the subcontractor of a start-up test which resulted in damage to the project.

96042 Somerset Community Hosp. v. Allan B. Mitchell & Assocs., Inc., 454 Pa. Super. 188, 685 A.2d 141 (1996)

III: B141-1987, Art. 8, Para. 8.6
III: B141-1987, Art. 8, Para. 8.7

On owner's appeal of judgment entered for architect, the appellate court held that on the issue of damages architect was entitled to prejudgment interest.

The owner-architect agreement provided:

6.2.1 Owner may withhold all or any portions of payments otherwise claimed by the Architect [DRS] pursuant to this agreement which are in dispute between the parties until a final court determination is made of the Owner's [Hospital] liability to Architect or Architect's liability to Owner which can be set off or deducted from any amount which may otherwise be due from Owner to Architect or until such dispute is mutually resolved by agreement between Owner and Architect.

Section 9.1 of the agreement provided:

If . . . termination is because of a breach of or non-performance by Architect, Architect shall receive no compensation other than compensation already paid and shall be subject to liability for damages for breach or nonperformance. If the termination [of this contract] is not based upon a breach of the agreement or nonperformance by Architect, then Architect shall be entitled to full compensation for all phases of the Project which have been completed at the time written notice of termination is received.

The appellate court held that Section 9.1 provided that if the architect breached the agreement the owner would be entitled to damages which would include prejudgment interest as a right under basic contract law. Similarly, the converse should be true for the architect as the injured party. When Section 9.1 was read in light of the entire contract, and specifically Section 6.2.1, the court concluded that the architect was properly awarded prejudgment interest.

8.3.4, and the final payment provision in Section 9.9.2. The subcontract also provided that:

IN THE EVENT OF CONFLICT BETWEEN THE CONTRACT DOCUMENTS AND THIS SUBCONTRACT, THE PROVISIONS OF THIS SUBCONTRACT SHALL GOVERN.

Article 3.C stated in part:

Should Subcontractor be delayed by any act or omission of Contractor, Engineer or Owner, or by any other cause beyond Subcontractor's control and if the cause of delay is not due to any act or omission of Subcontractor, Subcontractor shall be entitled to request a reasonable extension of time for completion of the Subcontract work . . . No payment of any kind, for compensation, or for damages, or otherwise, shall be made to Subcontractor because of any such delay even though Subcontractor's extension of time request be granted, unless Owner is obligated to pay Contractor compensation or damages because of such delay, and then, as and when Owner pays such compensation or damages to Contractor, Subcontractor shall receive that share of such compensation or damages which can be agreed to or proven to have been directly attributable to such delay.

The appellate court held that Article 3.C barred subcontractor's claim for delay damages against contractor if the damages were solely attributable to the fourteen-month delay of its performance. Under the unambiguous language of Article 3.C, subcontractor was precluded from seeking such damages unless owner was obligated to contractor for the same. The record showed that contractor had included subcontractor's claim for delay damages in its own claim against the owner, which was still pending. The court concluded that subcontractor's action was, at best, premature.

Further, Article 3.C was not a no-damage-for-delay clause. Subcontractor was not absolutely barred from seeking damages for delay but could recover through contractor its share of delay damages for which owner was liable. Subcontractor's right to recover delay damages was contingent upon the success of contractor's pending action against the owner.

As to the owner-contractor agreement, the court held that Article 3.C was not ambiguous when read in conjunction with the sections of the agreement incorporated into the subcontract. Specifically, the court found that Article 3.C did not conflict with Section 8.3.4, which permitted the recovery of damages for delay by either of the parties to the owner-contractor agreement, or with Section 5.3, which allowed subcontractors the benefit of all rights, remedies and redress against contractor that contractor had against owner, as Section 5.3 included the qualifier, "unless specifically provided otherwise in the Contractor-Subcontractor agreement[.]" Section 5.3 expressly deferred to contrary provisions in the subcontract, such as Article 3.C. Also, there was no conflict between Article 3.C and Section 9.9.2 because the provisions addressed entirely different matters.

96041 71 Constr. v. Wesco Elec., Inc., 924 P.2d 991 (Wyo. 1996)

III:A107-1987, Art. 9, Para. 9.1

statement that the adjustment claimed is the entire adjustment to which the Claimant has reason to believe it is entitled as a result of the occurrence of said event. All Claims for adjustments in the Contract Time shall be determined by Engineer in accordance with paragraph 9.11 if Owner and Contractor cannot otherwise agree. No Claim for an adjustment in the Contract Price will be valid if not submitted in accordance with this paragraph 12.1."

The appellate court held that the above terms were clear and unambiguous, specifically setting forth a mandatory procedure to establish the claims of the contractor. The procedure required the contractor to give written notice when it discovered any error or discrepancy in the contract documents or when it anticipated a change in the contract price or time. The court rejected contractor's argument that because change orders were regularly provided after the start or completion of work arranged through oral requests, the owner had waived the requirement for timely written claims. The undisputed evidence demonstrated that during construction, written field orders were regularly issued and were eventually incorporated into change orders. The court concluded that contractor failed to comply with the written claims procedure specifically set forth in the contract.

96040   Roy A. Elam Masonry, Inc. v. Fru-Con Constr. Corp., 922 S.W.2d 783 (Mo. Ct. App. 1996)

III:	A107-1987, Art. 11, Para. 11.2
III:	A107-1987, Art. 14, Para. 14.3
III:	A107-1987, Art. 15, Para. 15.4
III:	A117-1987, Art. 16, Para. 16.2
III:	A117-1987, Art. 19, Para. 19.3
III:	A117-1987, Art. 20, Para. 20.4
III:	A201-1987, Art. 5, Para. 5.3.1
III:	A201-1987, Art. 8, Para. 8.3
III:	A201-1987, Art. 9, Para. 9.10.2
III:	A401-1987, Art. 1, Para. 1.1
III:	A401-1987, Art. 5, Para. 5.3
III:	A401-1987, Art. 16, Para. 16.1

Subcontractor brought an action against contractor for damages resulting from a fourteen-month delay in the start date of subcontractor's work. Contractor then brought an action against owner for delay damages. Contractor moved to stay subcontractor's action, arguing that contractor would not be liable to subcontractor for delay damages unless and until contractor received payment for same from the owner. The trial court denied contractor's motion. Subcontractor's claim was tried and the jury returned a verdict for subcontractor. The trial court denied contractor's post-trial motions, and Contractor appealed.

The terms of the owner-contractor agreement were incorporated into the subcontract, specifically the flow-down provision in Section 5.3, the delay damage provision in Section

III: A201-1987, Art. 4, Para. 4.3.3
III: A201-1987, Art. 4, Para. 4.3.7
III: A201-1987, Art. 4, Para. 4.3.8

Contractor brought an action against owner alleging breach of duty not to interfere, breach of implied warranty of plans, and breach of contract. Owner filed a motion for summary judgment on the grounds that contractor's failure to follow the contract's written claim procedures barred its claims. Contractor then amended its complaint to include numerous actions against the engineer. The engineer filed a motion for summary judgment. The trial court granted owner's and engineer's motions for summary judgment, and Contractor appealed. The appellate court affirmed.

The owner-contractor agreement provided that:

3.2 If, during the performance of the Work, Contractor finds a conflict, error or discrepancy in the Contract Documents, Contractor shall so report to Engineer in writing at once and before proceeding with the Work affected thereby shall obtain a written interpretation or clarification from Engineer; however, Contractor shall not be liable to Owner or Engineer for failure to report any conflict, error or discrepancy in the Contract Documents unless Contractor had actual knowledge thereof or should reasonably have known thereof.

9.12 . . . The rendering of a decision by Engineer . . . with respect to any such Claim, dispute or other matter . . . will be a condition precedent to any exercise by Owner or Contractor of such rights or remedies as either may otherwise have under the Contract Documents or by Laws or Regulations in respect of any such Claim, dispute or other matter.

11.2 The Contract Price may only be changed by a Change Order or by a Written Amendment. Any Claim for an increase or decrease in the Contract Price shall be based on written notice delivered by the party making the Claim to the other party and to the Engineer promptly (but in no event later than thirty days) after the occurrence of the event giving rise to the Claim and stating the general nature of the claim. Notice of the amount of the Claim with the supporting data shall be delivered within sixty days after such occurrence . . . and shall be accompanied by Claimant's written statement that the amount claimed covers all known amounts (direct, indirect and consequential) to which the Claimant is entitled as a result of the occurrence of said event. All Claims for adjustment in the Contract Price shall be determined by Engineer in accordance with paragraph 9.11 if Owner and Contractor cannot otherwise agree on the amount involved. No Claim for an adjustment in the Contract Price will be valid if not submitted in accordance with this paragraph 11.2.

12.1 The Contract Time may only be changed by a Change Order or a Written Amendment. Any Claim for an extension or shortening of the Contract Time shall be based on written notice delivered by the party making the Claim to the other party and to the Engineer promptly (but in no event later than thirty days) after the occurrence of the event giving rise to the Claim and stating the general nature of the Claim. Notice of the extent of the Claim with supporting data shall be delivered within sixty days after such occurrence . . . and shall be accompanied by the Claimant's written

III:	A401-1987, Art. 6, Para. 6.3
III:	A401-1987, Art. 6, Para. 6.4
III:	A401-1987, Art. 6, Para. 6.5
III:	B141-1987, Art. 7, Para. 7.1
III:	B141-1987, Art. 7, Para. 7.2
III:	B141-1987, Art. 7, Para. 7.3
III:	B141-1987, Art. 7, Para. 7.4

In contractor's appeal of the trial court's order denying its motion to confirm an arbitration award in its favor, the appellate court held that the trial court erred in interpreting the arbitration clause as reflecting the parties' intent that the award be non-binding.

The arbitration clause provided that:

Any disagreement arising out of this contract or from the breach thereof shall be submitted to arbitration, and judgment upon the award rendered may be entered in the court of the forum, state or federal, having jurisdiction. It is mutually agreed that the decision of the arbitrators shall be a condition precedent to any right of legal action that either party may have against the other. The arbitration shall be held under the Standard Form of Arbitration Procedure of the American Institute of Architects or under the Rules of the American Arbitration Association.

The appellate court held that the trial court's interpretation of the provision severely limited application of the language which provided that "judgment upon the award rendered may be entered in the court of the forum, state or federal, having jurisdiction." In addition, the court disagreed with the trial court's conclusion that the use of the word "may" in the sentence authorizing a judgment to be entered on the award evidenced an intent that the award be non-binding. The appellate court construed this language merely to reflect an intent that the prevailing party in the arbitration be allowed the option of obtaining a judgment on the award for purposes of enforcement or collection should that prove necessary or desirable.

The court concluded that the arbitration clause called for a binding arbitration award and that such award was a condition to any further "legal action" either to modify, correct, or vacate the award.

96039   Rissler & McMurry Co. v. Sheridan Area Water Supply Joint Powers Bd., 929 P.2d 1228 (Wyo. 1996)

III:	A107-1987, Art. 10, Para. 10.5
III:	A107-1987, Art. 14, Para. 14.3
III:	A117-1987, Art. 15, Para. 15.5
III:	A117-1987, Art. 19, Para. 19.3
III:	A201-1987, Art. 3, Para. 3.2.1
III:	A201-1987, Art. 4, Para. 4.3.2

Contractor filed a declaratory judgment action against sub-subcontractor's insurer alleging that sub-subcontractor was required to insure contractor for personal injury damages paid to sub-subcontractor's employee pursuant to a flow-down provision in the agreement between the subcontractor and the sub-subcontractor. The parties filed cross-motions for summary judgment. The trial court granted summary judgment for contractor on the issue of coverage because the agreement was unambiguous. Both parties appealed. The insurer argued that its insured did not contract with subcontractor to provide insurance. Furthermore, the clause in the agreement upon which owner relied referred only to "work performed" requirements and had nothing to do with insurance obligations. Contractor argued that sub-subcontractor was required to provide insurance pursuant to the flow-down clause in the sub-subcontract. The appellate court reversed the grant of summary judgment to contractor.

The sub-subcontract provided in pertinent part that:

Work performed by [Climatemp] shall be in strict accordance with all applicable plans, general conditions, specifications, and addenda thereto, and [Climatemp] is bound by all provisions of these documents and also all other documents to which [Advance] is bound, and to the same extent.

The contract language upon which insurer relied was susceptible to more than one reasonable interpretation. It was reasonable to interpret the language, "all other documents to which [Advance] is bound," to mean that the parties intended that sub-subcontractor was bound to provide insurance for contractor because subcontractor contracted to provide insurance for contractor. On the other hand, it was also reasonable to infer that the language was modified by the language preceding it and was confined only to work performed pursuant to the sub-subcontract. Read together, the language "work performed" and "all other documents to which Advance is bound," created an ambiguity. The issue was thus improperly resolved by the trial court on a motion for summary judgment.

96038   Ringwelski v. Pederson, 919 P.2d 957 (Colo. Ct. App. 1996)

III:	A107-1987, Art. 10, Para. 10.8	
III:	A117-1987, Art. 15, Para. 15.8	
III:	A201-1987, Art. 4, Para. 4.5.1	
III:	A201-1987, Art. 4, Para. 4.5.2	
III:	A201-1987, Art. 4, Para. 4.5.3	
III:	A201-1987, Art. 4, Para. 4.5.4	
III:	A201-1987, Art. 4, Para. 4.5.4.1	
III:	A201-1987, Art. 4, Para. 4.5.4.2	
III:	A201-1987, Art. 4, Para. 4.5.5	
III:	A201-1987, Art. 4, Para. 4.5.6	
III:	A201-1987, Art. 4, Para. 4.5.7	
III:	A401-1987, Art. 6, Para. 6.1	
III:	A401-1987, Art. 6, Para. 6.2	

96036 Olympus Corp. v. United States, 98 F.3d 1314 (Fed. Cir. 1996)

    III: A107-1987, Art. 14, Para. 14.3
    III: A117-1987, Art. 19, Para. 19.3
    III: A201-1987, Art. 4, Para. 4.3.6
    III: A201-1987, Art. 4, Para. 4.3.7
    III: A201-1987, Art. 4, Para. 4.3.8

Contractor brought an action against the government for an equitable adjustment to the contract sum pursuant to the differing site conditions clause in the agreement. The Court of Appeals for the Federal Circuit affirmed the grant of summary judgment to the government.

The government and contractor entered into a fixed-price contract which provided in relevant part that:

(a) The Contractor [Olympus] shall promptly, and before the conditions are disturbed, give a written notice to the Contracting Officer of (1) subsurface or latent physical conditions at the site which differ materially from those indicated in this contract, or (2) unknown physical conditions at the site, of an unusual nature, which differ materially from those ordinarily encountered and generally recognized as inherent in the work of the character provided for in the contract; (b) The Contracting Officer shall investigate the site conditions promptly after receiving the notice. If the conditions do materially so differ and cause an increase or decrease in the Contractor's cost of, or the time required for, performing any part of the work under this contract, whether or not changed as a result of the conditions, an equitable adjustment shall be made under this clause and the contract modified in writing accordingly.

The appellate court held that the differing site condition clause did not apply to the contractor's claim of an equitable adjustment for strike delays and soil contaminant delays. Neither event existed at the time the contract was executed, and the clause applied only to conditions existing at the time of contracting.

The purpose of this clause was to shift the risk of adverse subsurface or latent physical conditions from the contractor, who normally bore such risk under a fixed-price contract, to the government. Furthermore, the clause was a risk-shifting device which did not, as contractor argued, shift the risk of all unanticipated adverse conditions from the contractor to the government.

In addition to the temporal limitation, the differing site conditions clause applied only to the "physical" conditions at the work site, not to actions of third-parties that denied the contractor access to the work site.

96037 Pepper Constr. Co. v. Transcontinental Ins. Co., 285 Ill. App. 3d 573, 220 Ill. Dec. 707, 673 N.E.2d 1128 (1996)

    III: A401-1987, Art. 2, Para. 2.1
    III: A401-1987, Art. 2, Para. 2.2

executory on the date of the assignment and, therefore, the assignment of contract rights, including the right to have disputes settled by arbitration, was valid.

96035 Miley v. Johnson & Johnson Orthopaedics, Inc., 41 Mass. App. Ct. 30, 668 N.E.2d 369, *review denied*, 423 Mass. 1111, 672 N.E.2d 539 (1996)

> III: A107-1987, Art. 9, Para. 9.12
> III: A117-1987, Art. 14, Para. 14.12
> III: A201-1987, Art. 3, Para. 3.18.1
> III: A201-1987, Art. 10, Para. 10.1.4
> III: A401-1987, Art. 4, Para. 4.6.1

Injured third party brought a negligence action against owner, contractor, and subcontractors. Contractor brought a third-party indemnification action against subcontractors. The trial court granted summary judgment to contractor and subcontractors on the issue of liability and dismissed contractor's cross-complaint as moot. The injured third party then settled with contractor and subcontractors. All parties appealed. The remaining issue on appeal was whether the indemnity clause in the subcontracts extended to owner and contractor's legal expenses after it had been established by final judgment that the owner and contractor owed nothing to the injured third party. The appellate court affirmed, holding that the subcontractors were not bound to indemnify contractor and owner for legal expenses.

The indemnity clause in the subcontracts provided that:

Subcontractor shall, to the fullest extent permitted by law and to the extent that any such claims, losses, liabilities or expenses are caused in whole or in part by any act or omission of Subcontractor, anyone directly or indirectly employed by Subcontractor or anyone for whose acts Subcontractor may be liable, regardless of whether or not any such claims, losses, liabilities or expenses are caused in part by a party indemnified hereunder, indemnify and hold harmless Contractor, Architect, Engineer and Owner and the agents and employees of Contractor, Architect, Engineer and Owner from and against any and all claims, losses, liabilities and expenses, including attorney's fees, arising out of or in any manner caused by, connected with or resulting from Subcontractor's performance of this Subcontract or the presence of Subcontractor or Subcontractor's employees and/or agents at the Project site.

The appellate court rejected the owner's and contractor's argument that implicit in the indemnity provision was a duty to defend against job related claims, a duty which included the payment of legal expenses. The owner and contractor relied on the language which called upon the subcontractors to "indemnify and hold harmless . . . from . . . all claims, losses, liabilities and expenses, including attorney's fees . . . ." This language was not enough to impose a duty to defend because such a duty was independent of the obligation to indemnify. Furthermore, the inclusion of attorney's fees as an indemnifiable expense did not automatically impose a duty to defend.

causes of action which the Assignor may have in connection with the development, use or operation of the [Project] prior to the date hereof.

The assignment clause in Paragraph 7.2.1 of the owner-contractor agreement provided that:

> The Owner [OHP] and the Contractor [Korte] each binds himself, his partners, successors, assigns, and legal representatives to the other party herewith and to the partners, successors, assigns and legal representatives of such other party in respect to all covenants, agreements and obligations contained in the Contract Documents. Neither party to the Contract shall assign the Contract or sublet it as a whole without the consent of the other, nor shall the Contractor assign any money due or to become due to him hereunder, without the previous written consent of the Owner.

Paragraph 13.2.2 provided that:

> If, within one year after the Date of Substantial Completion of the Work or a designated portion thereof or within one year after acceptance by the Owner of designated equipment or within such longer period of time as may be prescribed by law or by the terms of any applicable special warranty required by the contract documents, any of the work is found to be defective or not in accordance with the Contract Documents, the Contractor shall correct it promptly.

The owner did not obtain the contractor's consent before assigning the contract.

The appellate court rejected the trial court's interpretation of Paragraph 7.2.1 as prohibiting only the assignment of the whole contract without the consent of the non-assigning contractual party, and its interpretation of the phrase "as a whole" as modifying both the assignment and the subletting of the contract. This interpretation ascribed an extraordinary degree of carelessness to the drafting of the language and was insupportable. Further, it was far more reasonable to conclude that if the parties had intended to permit partial assignments and subletting and to prohibit only unconsented assignment and subletting which transferred the contract as a whole, the relevant sentence in Article 7.2.1 would read: "Neither party to the contract shall assign or sublet the contract as a whole . . . ." As the sentence actually read, subletting the contract as a whole without the consent of the other party was prohibited, but unconsented to assignment of the contract was prohibited whether in whole or in part.

Turning to the issue of the validity of the assignment, the court held that its construction of Paragraph 7.2.1 did not necessarily require a finding of invalidity. To be a valid assignment, the court had to find that the contract was fully executed at the time of the assignment.

The court rejected the contractor's argument that it was obligated under Paragraph 13.2.2 at the time of the assignment, making the contract executory. Relying on McDevitt and St. Co. v. K-C Air Conditioning Serv., Inc., Digest No. 92015, contractor argued that the phrase "such longer period as may be prescribed by law" was a reference to the statute of limitations applicable to breach of contract claims. The more reasonable interpretation was that the "longer period of time" that "may be prescribed by law" was a warranty period imposed on construction contracts by statute in some states. Because there was no state statute on construction warranty periods, the contract was no longer

the issue of the validity of the payment clause, and a related bond issue, to the Tennessee Supreme Court.

The subcontract included a payment clause which provided in pertinent part that:

Partial payments subject to all applicable provisions of the Contract shall be made when and as payments are received by the Contractor. The Subcontractor may be required as a condition precedent to any payment to furnish evidence satisfactory to the Contractor that all payrolls, materials bills, and other indebtedness applicable to the work have been paid.

Addressing the issue of whether the payment clause established owner's payment to contractor as a condition precedent to contractor's obligation to pay subcontractor, the court held that the language of the clause did not evidence the parties' intention to shift the risk of the owner's nonperformance from the contractor to the subcontractor with sufficient clarity to qualify as a condition precedent.

The court reasoned that the first sentence, "payments . . . shall be made when and as they are received by the Contractor . . .", could be interpreted as a timing provision and was not necessarily indicative of the parties' intent to make contractor's obligation to pay subcontractor dependent upon contractor being paid by owner. Moreover, the second sentence in the clause, which provided that the "Subcontractor may be required as a condition precedent to any payment to furnish evidence satisfactory to the Contractor that all payrolls, material bills, and other indebtedness applicable to the work have been paid," illustrated that the parties knew how to create a condition precedent if they so desired. That they did not use such unambiguous language in the first sentence prevented the court from construing the provision as a condition precedent to subcontractor's right to payment.

96034   Korte Constr. Co. v. Deaconess Manor Ass'n, 927 S.W.2d 395 (Mo. Ct. App. 1996)

  II: A107-1987, Art. 18, Para. 18.1
  II: A117-1987, Art. 23, Para. 23.1
  II: A201-1987, Art. 12, Para. 12.2.2
  II: A201-1987, Art. 13, Para. 13.2.1

Contractor filed a petition to enjoin arbitration on the grounds that owner's assignment of the right to arbitration was invalid. The trial court denied contractor's petition, and contractor appealed. The appellate court affirmed.

The assignment stated that:

1. Assignor [OHP] hereby sells, assigns and transfers unto Assignee [DMA], all of Assignor's right, title and interest, if any, in the following: . . . B. All existing warranties and guaranties covering the [Project] Improvements of which Assignor is the beneficiary (if any), to the extent such warranties and guaranties are assignable; C. All contracts and agreements affecting the [Project] Improvements (if any), to the extent such contracts or agreements are assignable; . . . G. Any and all claims or

96032   J.O. Hooker & Sons, Inc. v. Roberts Cabinet Co., 683 So. 2d 396 (Miss. 1996)

       III: A401-1987, Art. 1, Para. 1.1
       III: A401-1987, Art. 2, Para. 2.1
       III: A401-1987, Art. 2, Para. 2.2

Subcontractor brought a breach of contract action against contractor for additional compensation. The trial court granted subcontractor summary judgment, finding that the contractor's duty to dispose of cabinets as required by the owner-contractor agreement did not flow-down to the subcontractor. The jury awarded subcontractor's requested damages. Contractor appealed, arguing that the "as per specs and plans" language in the subcontract served to incorporate by reference the contractor's duty to dispose of the cabinets as set forth in the contractor's agreement with the owner. The appellate court upheld the judgment of the trial court.

The subcontract provided that subcontractor: "furnish cabinets, tops, plastic laminates on walls and furr down materials and fronts for hot water heaters as per plans and specs for the price listed below."

The agreement also provided that: "the price includes the cost of tear-out (sic) old cabinets and installation of new cabinets."

The agreement was silent as to any duty on the part of the subcontractor to dispose of the old cabinets.

The specifications of the owner-contractor agreement provided that the scope of the job included removing all existing kitchen cabinets and shelves and disposing of them in accordance with local laws and ordinances.

The appellate court held that although the subcontract referred to the "plans and specs" of the owner-contractor agreement, the language did not in any way indicate an intent by subcontractor to assume additional and expensive duties which were not set forth in the subcontract. The court interpreted the phrase "as per specs and plans" as applying to the "furnish[ing]" of cabinets and not to their "removal". Furthermore, if contractor had desired that subcontractor be obligated to assume the specific contractual obligations set forth in the owner-contractor agreement such language should have been included in the subcontract.

The court concluded that, as a matter of law, subcontractor did not assume the specific contractual duties relating to the disposal of the cabinets.

96033   Koch v. Construction Technology, Inc., 924 S.W.2d 68 (Tenn. 1996)

       III: A401-1987, Art. 11, Para. 11.3

Subcontractor brought a breach of contract action against contractor for additional compensation. The trial court upheld the validity of the pay-when-paid clause and entered judgment for subcontractor in the amount paid by owner to contractor. Both parties moved to amend the judgment. The trial court denied both motions, and the subcontractor appealed. The appellate court affirmed. Subcontractor was granted permission to appeal

96030   Housing Vermont v. Goldsmith & Morris, 685 A.2d 1086 (Vt. 1996)

        I: B141-1987, Art. 5, Para. 5.2.1
        I: B141-1987, Art. 5, Para. 5.2.2

The appellate court, after upholding judgment for owner in owner's malpractice action against architect, addressed the issue of whether architect was responsible for cost overruns resulting from architect's failure to produce a final grading plan in addition to the grading information contained in the site plan.

The court held that Paragraph 5.2.1 and 5.2.2 of the American Institute of Architects Standard Form of Agreement Between Owner and Architect, Document No. B141, 1987 edition, contained a broadly worded disclaimer that did not clearly express the intention of the parties to relieve the architect of liability for its own negligence. The disclaimer did not contain a reference to negligence or wrongful conduct of any kind.

96031   Jandrisits v. Village of River Grove, 283 Ill. App. 3d 152, 218 Ill. Dec. 640, 669 N.E.2d 1166 (1996)

        III: A107-1987, Art. 9, Para. 9.12
        III: A117-1987, Art. 14, Para. 14.12
        III: A201-1987, Art. 3, Para. 3.18.1
        III: A201-1987, Art. 10, Para. 10.1.4
        III: A401-1987, Art. 4, Para. 4.6.1

Third party brought a negligence action for personal injury damages against owner and others. The trial court denied owner's motion for summary judgment. Owner, as an additional insured, then tendered its defense to contractor's insurer. The insurer denied the tender. Owner then filed a third-party action against contractor for indemnification and contribution. Owner moved for summary judgment on the issue of indemnification. Contractor and owner settled with the third party. The trial court denied owner's motion on the grounds that the indemnification agreement violated the state's anti-indemnification statute, which prohibited indemnification for one's own negligence. The appellate court agreed, although it vacated the judgment on other grounds.

The owner-contractor agreement required contractor to defend and indemnify the owner for losses "caused or resulting or claimed to be caused or resulting from the work or services of the Contractor or those for whom he is responsible."

The appellate court held that the indemnity agreement was not the type of agreement the state statute prohibited. It was clear from the unambiguous language of the clause that contractor had agreed to indemnify the owner for contractor's negligence and did not agree to indemnify the owner for the owner's own negligence. The court affirmed the judgment of the trial court on the grounds that the evidence established that the owner was liable to the injured third-party for owner's own negligence.

against owner's causal negligence; and (c) the provision was void because it did not limit subcontractor's indemnification responsibility only to accidents caused by subcontractor. The appellate court affirmed.

The subcontract provided that:

Subcontractor [Mass Electric] hereby releases and shall indemnify, defend and hold harmless Owner [NBG] and Contractor [Bechtel] and their subsidiaries and affiliates and the officers, agents, employees, successors and assigns and authorized representatives of all of the foregoing from and against any and all suits, actions, legal or administrative proceedings, claims, demands, damages, liabilities, interest, attorney's fees, costs and expenses of whatsoever kind or nature including those arising out of injury or death of Subcontractor's employees whether arising before or after completion of the work hereunder and in any manner directly or indirectly caused, occasioned or contributed to in whole or in part, or claimed to be caused, occasioned or contributed to in whole or in part, by reason of any act, omission, fault or negligence whether active or passive of Subcontractor, its subcontractors or of anyone acting under its direction or control or on its behalf in connection with or incidental to the performance of this contract. Subcontractor's aforesaid release, indemnity and hold harmless obligations, or portions or applications thereof, shall apply even in the event of the fault or negligence, whether active or passive, or strict liability of the parties released, indemnified or held harmless to [the] fullest extent permitted by law, but in no event shall they apply to liability caused by the sole negligence or willful misconduct of the parties released, indemnified or held harmless.

Addressing the subcontractor's first argument, the appellate court held that the subcontract placed no temporal limits upon subcontractor's indemnification obligation. The agreement provided subcontractor "shall indemnify, defend and hold harmless [NBG] . . . from and against any and all suits, actions . . . damages, liabilities . . . whether arising before or after completion of the work hereunder." The language of the clause encompassed the temporal lag.

Addressing the subcontractor's second argument, the appellate court held that the plain language of the indemnity provision placed no limitation upon subcontractor's obligation even if there was separate and intervening negligence by owner. So long as the injury was not caused by owner's "sole negligence or willful misconduct," the contract required indemnification even "in the event of the fault or negligence" of owner. Furthermore, the agreement did not in any way qualify subcontractor's indemnity obligation by limiting it to instances when owner's negligence was indivisible and concurrent with that of subcontractor.

As to the subcontractor's third argument, the appellate court interpreted the indemnity language as limiting subcontractor's obligation to instances in which there was a causal connection between the subcontractor's work and the injury. Notwithstanding subcontractor's attempt to differentiate the statutory language of "caused by" from the indemnity language, "occasioned . . . by reason of any act, omission, fault or negligence whether active or passive of Subcontractor," the language of the clause avoided the nullifying effect of the state statute because the language in context was the functional equivalent of "caused by."

The appellate court held that neither concerns expressed by the engineer at weekly safety meetings, or the stoppage of the work by the engineer, supported a finding that the engineer exercised control over the premises or the safety at the site. The contract authorized the engineer to stop the work when it observed defective workmanship, and nothing in the record indicated that the stoppage dealt with safety rather than the quality of the work.

96028   Grunley Constr. Co. v. Conway Corp., 676 A.2d 477 (D.C. 1996)

        II: A107-1987, Art. 9, Para. 9.12

        II: A117-1987, Art. 14, Para. 14.12

        II: A201-1987, Art. 3, Para. 3.18.1

        II: A201-1987, Art. 10, Para. 10.1.4

        II: A401-1987, Art. 4, Para. 4.6.1

Contractor appealed the trial court's grant of summary judgment to subcontractor on the grounds that subcontractor was not required to indemnify contractor for contractor's own negligence. The appellate court reversed the judgment.

The subcontract provided that:

The Subcontractor shall indemnify and save harmless Contractor and Owner from any and all claims and liabilities for property damage and personal injury, including death, arising out of or resulting from or in connection with the execution of the work.

Relying on the decision in W.M. Schlosser Co. v. Maryland Drywall Co., Digest No. 96015, the appellate court was compelled to conclude that the indemnification provision was sufficiently broad to include indemnification for damages resulting from contractor's own negligence.

96029   Herson v. New Boston Garden Corp., 40 Mass. App. Ct. 779, 667 N.E.2d 907 (1996), *review denied,* 423 Mass. 1108, 671 N.E.2d 951 (1996)

        III: A107-1987, Art. 9, Para. 9.12

        III: A117-1987, Art. 14, Para. 14.12

        III: A201-1987, Art. 3, Para. 3.18.1

        III: A201-1987, Art. 10, Para. 10.1.4

        III: A401-1987, Art. 4, Para. 4.6.1

Owner brought a third-party indemnification action against subcontractor for personal injury damages paid to another subcontractor's employee. The trial court entered judgment for owner and subcontractor appealed. Among numerous other issues on appeal, the subcontractor argued that (a) the trial court erred in interpreting the indemnity clause as applying to owner's independent liability for an accident occurring three years after the subcontractor had performed its work; (b) to the extent the provision applied, it applied only in proportion to the percentage of subcontractor's causal negligence as measured

limited to counsel fees which the CONTRACTOR or OWNER may sustain or become liable for on account of any claim, suit or action resulting from or arising out of the negligence of the SUBCONTRACTOR, his Agents, Employees or Sub[-]Subcontractors.

Article XIV provided for the protection of the construction work and the project site against mechanics' and materialmen's liens, attachments, restraining orders, and the like.

In interpreting Article XIV the appellate court agreed with the trial court that the provision lacked language providing for a causal link between the subcontractor's action or failure to act and the cause of injury as required by the state statute. However, the court went on to hold that when the subject of the clause was not bodily injury or property damage, it was not the operative provision. The operative provision, Article IV, dealt with job safety and insurance against liability for bodily injury and property damage.

The court concluded that when the subcontractor was not negligent but its sub-subcontractor was negligent due to the negligence of its employee, Article IV expressly bound the subcontractor to indemnify the owner and the contractor for damages resulting from the worker's injury.

96027   Graham v. Freese & Nichols, Inc., 927 S.W.2d 294 (Tex. Ct. App. 1996)

II:	A107-1987, Art. 9, Para. 9.1	
II:	A107-1987, Art. 10, Para. 10.5	
II:	A107-1987, Art. 16, Para. 16.1	
II:	A117-1987, Art. 14, Para. 14.1	
II:	A117-1987, Art. 15, Para. 15.5	
II:	A117-1987, Art. 15, Para. 21.1	
II:	A201-1987, Art. 3, Para. 3.3.1	
II:	A201-1987, Art. 4, Para. 4.3.2	
II:	A201-1987, Art. 10, Para. 10.2.1	
II:	B141-1987, Art. 2, Para. 2.6.5	
II:	B141-1987, Art. 2, Para. 2.6.6	

Contractor's injured employee brought a negligence action against engineer. The trial court granted engineer's motion for summary judgment. On appeal, injured worker argued that engineer retained sufficient control over safety and over the premises to owe worker a duty of care. The appellate court affirmed.

The owner-engineer agreement contained a safety provision similar to Paragraphs 2.6.6 and an on-site observation provision similar to Paragraph 2.6.5 of the American Institute of Architects Standard Form of Agreement Between Owner and Architect, Document No. B141, 1987 edition. The owner-contractor agreement provided that contractor retained exclusive control over the construction procedures and safety at the work site. The agreement also expressly stated that the engineer was not responsible for the means of construction or for safety at the site.

III:	A117-1987, Art. 14, Para. 14.1
III:	A117-1987, Art. 14, Para. 14.7
III:	A201-1987, Art. 1, Para. 1.1.3
III:	A201-1987, Art. 3, Para. 3.3.1
III:	A201-1987, Art. 3, Para. 3.3.2

The Supreme Court of New Jersey, in interpreting a claim limitation period in a surety bond, determined that the "work" of the subcontractors constituted the "work" of the contractor.

The owner-contractor agreement provided:

The terms and conditions stated in this Agreement are applicable to the procurement by the Company of asbestos removal services and certain construction work, which shall include Contractor's obligation to furnish the supervision, engineering, tradesmen, equipment, vehicles, tools, materials, identification, packaging, labeling, transportation and disposal as required to perform the asbestos removal services and construction work as further defined in the applicable drawings and specifications (the "Work") attached hereto or referenced in the orders placed pursuant to this Agreement.

The court held that the term "work" was defined in the "drawings and specifications" attached to the contract and in the "Orders placed pursuant to" the contract. The contractor's "work" included "furnish[ing] the supervision" of the construction. In addition, other sections of the contract discussed the "work" performed by the subcontractors and the contractor's duty to supervise their work. The court thus concluded that the "work" of the subcontractors constituted the "work" of the contractor.

96026   Erland Constr. Co. v. Park Steel Corp., 41 Mass. App. Ct. 919, 671 N.E.2d 953, *review denied,* 423 Mass. 1113, 674 N.E.2d 246 (1996)

III:	A107-1987, Art. 9, Para. 9.12
III:	A117-1987, Art. 14, Para. 14.12
III:	A201-1987, Art. 3, Para. 3.18.1
III:	A201-1987, Art. 10, Para. 10.1.4
III:	A401-1987, Art. 4, Para. 4.6.1

Sub-subcontractor's employee brought a negligence action against owner and contractor. Contractor brought a third-party indemnification action against subcontractor. The jury found that both worker and contractor were negligent and subcontractor was not negligent. The trial court determined that the indemnity provision in the contract was unlawful pursuant to state statute because it imposed indemnity obligations in the absence of a causal link. Judgment was entered for subcontractor. Contractor appealed, and the appellate court reversed.

The subcontract provided in Article IV that:

The SUBCONTRACTOR agrees to indemnify and hold the CONTRACTOR and OWNER harmless from any and all loss, damage, cost or expense, including but not

96024 Dixon v. CertainTeed Corp., 944 F. Supp. 1501 (D. Kan. 1996)

III:	A107-1987, Art. 9, Para. 9.12	
III:	A107-1987, Art. 16, Para. 16.1	
III:	A117-1987, Art. 14, Para. 14.12	
III:	A117-1987, Art. 21, Para. 21.1	
III:	A201-1987, Art. 3, Para. 3.18.1	
III:	A201-1987, Art. 10, Para. 10.1.4	
III:	A201-1987, Art. 10, Para. 10.2.1	
III:	A401-1987, Art. 4, Para. 4.6.1	

Contractor's injured employee brought a negligence action against owner, construction manager, and their insurers. Owner and construction manager brought a third-party indemnification action against contractor. At issue was whether two of the indemnification provisions in the agreement were in conflict or whether they established a duty on the part of contractor to indemnify owner for owner's own acts of negligence. The district court entered judgment for owner and construction manager.

The owner-contractor agreement contained five indemnification clauses, two of which were relevant to the dispute. Article 10 required contractor to hold harmless owner and its agents from any claims or losses arising out of contractor's work at owner's facility regardless of whether owner's negligence caused the losses or claims. Article 5.10, the health and safety clause of the agreement, required contractor to take all necessary precautions not to jeopardize the health and/or safety of personnel or property involved in the construction project at owner's facility. It also required contractor to indemnify owner in the event contractor violated the section's requirements and caused owner a loss. The article was silent as to indemnification for owner's negligence.

The district court found that the indemnification provisions in the construction contract were not ambiguous; that Article 5.10 omitted the requirement for indemnification for owner's negligence did not render the provision ambiguous.

The court interpreted Article 10 as requiring the contractor to indemnify the owner or its agents for any claims or losses arising out of contractor's operations at owner's facility. The unequivocal language of this section indicated the parties' intention for the contractor to indemnify not only the owner, but also owner's agent, the construction manager, for their own negligence, but not for their sole negligence.

96025 Eagle Fire Protection Corp. v. First Indem. of Am. Ins. Co., 145 N.J. 345, 678 A.2d 699 (1996)

III:	A107-1987, Art. 7, Para. 7.4	
III:	A107-1987, Art. 9, Para. 9.1	
III:	A107-1987, Art. 9, Para. 9.7	
III:	A117-1987, Art. 12, Para. 12.4	

enforcement or application" of the agreement, and, as such, was a matter within the authority of the arbitrators to resolve pursuant to Section 26.01.

96023 Dickson County v. Bomar Constr. Co., 935 S.W.2d 413 (Tenn. Ct. App. 1996)

II:	A107-1987, Art. 10, Para. 10.8	
II:	A117-1987, Art. 15, Para. 15.8	
I:	A201-1987, Art. 4, Para. 4.5.1	
II:	A201-1987, Art. 4, Para. 4.5.2	
II:	A201-1987, Art. 4, Para. 4.5.3	
II:	A201-1987, Art. 4, Para. 4.5.4	
II:	A201-1987, Art. 4, Para. 4.5.4.1	
II:	A201-1987, Art. 4, Para. 4.5.4.2	
II:	A201-1987, Art. 4, Para. 4.5.5	
II:	A201-1987, Art. 4, Para. 4.5.6	
II:	A201-1987, Art. 4, Para. 4.5.7	
I:	A201-1987, Art. 13, Para. 13.4.1	
II:	A401-1987, Art. 6, Para. 6.1	
II:	A401-1987, Art. 6, Para. 6.2	
II:	A401-1987, Art. 6, Para. 6.3	
II:	A401-1987, Art. 6, Para. 6.4	
II:	A401-1987, Art. 6, Para. 6.5	
II:	B141-1987, Art. 7, Para. 7.1	
II:	B141-1987, Art. 7, Para. 7.2	
II:	B141-1987, Art. 7, Para. 7.3	
II:	B141-1987, Art. 7, Para. 7.4	

Contractor appealed the trial court's order dismissing its demand for arbitration on the grounds that the rights and remedies provision of the owner-contractor agreement gave the parties an option to proceed under the contract or by remedies available under law. The appellate court reversed and ordered arbitration of the dispute.

The owner-contractor agreement contained provisions identical to Paragraphs 4.5.1 and Paragraph 13.4.1 of the American Institute of Architects General Conditions of the Contract for Construction, Document No. A201, 1987 edition.

The appellate court interpreted the provisions so as to produce the "harmony and effectiveness of both," holding that the arbitration provision meant that the parties were obligated to submit to arbitration all disputes arising under the contract. While the rights and remedies provision meant that the parties did not waive other unspecified rights or remedies, it did not nullify their obligation to arbitrate.

III:	A401-1987, Art. 6, Para. 6.4
III:	A401-1987, Art. 6, Para. 6.5
III:	B141-1987, Art. 7, Para. 7.1
III:	B141-1987, Art. 7, Para. 7.2
III:	B141-1987, Art. 7, Para. 7.3
III:	B141-1987, Art. 7, Para. 7.4

Owner appealed from a judgment granting contractor's motion to confirm an arbitration award. The Second Circuit Court of Appeals affirmed.

The agreement provided for arbitration in Section 26.01, "[i]n the event a controversy or breach by either party under this Agreement shall arise as to the construction, enforcement or application thereof, the parties hereby agree to submit such issue to arbitration."

Section 26.02 required the parties to continue performance during arbitration:

> [u]nless otherwise agreed to in writing, throughout such arbitration proceedings the parties shall continue to perform their respective duties and obligations . . . under the Agreement and all actions by the parties to otherwise enforce their rights hereunder with respect to such disputed item shall be stayed.

Section 25.01, the default clause, provided that a party shall be considered in default if it (i) abandons the project; (ii) becomes insolvent or bankrupt, or (iii) fails to timely cure noncompliance with the terms and condition of the agreement after receiving notice of default.

Section 25.02 provided "[i]n the event of a default by UCEPI or [ConnTech], the non-defaulting party shall be entitled to (i) terminate this Agreement upon fifteen (15) days prior written notice to the other, and (ii) such other remedies available at law or equity."

Addressing the owner's argument that if contractor's default and termination claims were found to be arbitrable, the default provision would be rendered meaningless, the appellate court held that the contract sections were not mutually exclusive.

If the disputes between the parties arose in regard to interpretation of their respective responsibilities under the agreement, neither party was in default under the terms of Section 25.02.

The court construed the arbitration provision in Section 26.01 as providing arbitration as the means of resolving the contractor's claims, reasoning that by accusing the other party of failure to comply with the terms of the agreement, the parties had disputed the "construction, enforcement or application" of the agreement. The district court properly found the issues arbitrable in light of the plain language of the agreement and the federal policy strongly favoring arbitration.

As to whether the contractor forfeited its right to arbitrate by failing to perform during the arbitration as required by Section 26.02, the court interpreted the provision as a status quo clause which did not expressly provide that continued performance was a condition precedent to arbitration. Furthermore, the dispute over the meaning of Section 26.02 involved a "controversy or breach by either party [that has arisen] as to the construction,

was ordered to indemnify contractor, and Subcontractor appealed. The appellate court affirmed.

The indemnity provision in the subcontract provided that:

The Subcontractor further specifically obligates itself to the Contractor, Owner and any other party required to be indemnified under the Prime Contract, jointly and separately, in the following respects, to wit: . . . (b) to defend and indemnify them against and save them harmless from any and all claims, suits or liability for damages to property including loss of use thereof, injuries to persons, including death, and from any other claims, suits or liability on account of acts or omissions of Subcontractor, or any of its subcontractors, suppliers, officers, agents, employees or servants, whether or not caused in part by the active or passive negligence or other fault of a party indemnified hereunder; provided, however, Subcontractor's duty hereunder shall not arise if such claims, suits or liability, injuries or death or other claims or suits, are caused by the sole negligence of a party indemnified hereunder unless otherwise provided in the Prime Contract. Subcontractor's obligation hereunder shall not be limited by the provisions of any Workers' Compensation act or similar statute . . .

The indemnity clause plainly stated that subcontractor had a duty to indemnify for "injur[y] . . . on account of acts or omissions of . . . any of its . . . employees." Accordingly, any finding of negligence on the part of the worker brought subcontractor within the terms of the provision. Furthermore, on its face, the clause did not limit indemnification when the negligence of the indemnified party was also a cause of that injury. The only contractual limitation was for an injury caused by the sole negligence of the indemnitee, and, although the contractor's apportioned negligence was substantial, it was not entire.

96022 Conntech Dev. Co. v. University of Connecticut Educ. Properties, Inc., 102 F.3d 677 (2nd Cir. 1996)

III:	A107-1987, Art. 10, Para. 10.8	
III:	A117-1987, Art. 15, Para. 15.8	
III:	A201-1987, Art. 4, Para. 4.5.1	
III:	A201-1987, Art. 4, Para. 4.5.2	
III:	A201-1987, Art. 4, Para. 4.5.3	
III:	A201-1987, Art. 4, Para. 4.5.4	
III:	A201-1987, Art. 4, Para. 4.5.4.1	
III:	A201-1987, Art. 4, Para. 4.5.4.2	
III:	A201-1987, Art. 4, Para. 4.5.5	
III:	A201-1987, Art. 4, Para. 4.5.6	
III:	A201-1987, Art. 4, Para. 4.5.7	
III:	A401-1987, Art. 6, Para. 6.1	
III:	A401-1987, Art. 6, Para. 6.2	
III:	A401-1987, Art. 6, Para. 6.3	

Insurer was liable under the additional insured endorsement to indemnify owner in worker's action for personal injury damages.

96020   C.L. Maddox, Inc. v. Benham Group, Inc., 88 F.3d 592 (8th Cir. 1996)

II:	A107-1987, Art. 10, Para. 10.2
II:	A107-1987, Art. 10, Para. 10.3
II:	A117-1987, Art. 15, Para. 15.2
II:	A117-1987, Art. 15, Para. 15.3
II:	A201-1987, Art. 4, Para. 4.2.2
II:	A201-1987, Art. 4, Para. 4.2.3
II:	B141-1987, Art. 2, Para. 2.6.5
II:	B141-1987, Art. 2, Para. 2.6.6

The Eighth Circuit Court of Appeals held that since engineer was not contractually responsible for the acts or omissions of contractor, or for the failure of contractor to carry out its work in accordance with the contract documents, the engineer was not liable to contractor for damages resulting from contractor's own negligence.

The engineering subcontract contained provisions similar to Paragraphs 2.6.5 and 2.6.6 of the American Institute of Architects Standard Form of Agreement Between Owner and Architect, Document No. B141, 1987 edition.

The court held that the provision similar to Paragraph 2.6.6 provided that the engineer was not responsible for the acts or omissions of contractor, nor was engineer responsible for the failure of contractor to carry out its work in accordance with the plans and specifications.

The provision similar to Paragraph 2.6.5 placed a duty on engineer to visit the work site and make recommendations to contractor; however, this duty did not make the engineer a guarantor of contractor's work.

The court concluded that engineer had no contractual duty to act as insurer against contractor's own negligence.

96021   Collins v. Kiewit Constr. Co., 40 Mass. App. Ct. 796, 667 N.E.2d 904 (1996)

III:	A107-1987, Art. 9, Para. 9.12
III:	A117-1987, Art. 14, Para. 14.12
III:	A201-1987, Art. 3, Para. 3.18.1
III:	A201-1987, Art. 10, Para. 10.1.4
III:	A401-1987, Art. 4, Para. 4.6.1

Subcontractor's injured employee brought a negligence action against contractor. Contractor brought a third-party indemnification action against subcontractor. The jury found that worker was 3% negligent and contractor was 97% negligent. Subcontractor policies obligated contractor's insurer to defend and indemnify owner in worker's negligence action. The district court found that the additional insured endorsement covered owner's potential liability for its own negligence.

The additional insured endorsement provided coverage for liability "arising out of" the operations of the insured, but only to the extent that the coverage was required by the owner-contractor agreement. The owner-contractor agreement, in Article 9.5, required the contractor to provide the owner with a certificate of insurance which verified that contractor had secured insurance coverage for all of the liability that it assumed under the construction contract. Article 10 of the agreement provided that:

> To the fullest extent permitted by law, [contractor] agrees to indemnify, defend and hold harmless [owner] . . . from and against all claims, demands, causes of action, losses, costs and expenses . . . arising out of or incident to the performance of the Work or the presence of [contractor] . . . on the premises of [owner] . . . provided that such Losses are attributable to bodily injury, sickness, disease or death . . . regardless of whether or not such Losses were caused in part by the negligence or other fault of [owner] . . . and provided further that [contractor] shall not be liable for Losses caused by the sole negligence of [owner] . . .

Article 5.10 provided that contractor:

> shall take all necessary precautions required in order not to jeopardize the health and/or safety of [contractor's] personnel or property, [owner's] or other contractors' personnel or property, or members of the general public or their property. [Contractor] and its subcontractor shall perform the Work in accordance with all applicable laws, ordinances, rules, regulations, and orders, of any public authority . . . [contractor] further agrees to indemnify, defend, and hold [owner] . . . harmless from and against all claims, demands, causes of action, losses . . . costs and expenses . . . arising out of or incident to [contractor's] or any Subcontractor's failure to perform the Work, or any part thereof, in accordance with the requirements of this section.

The court reasoned that to ascertain the scope of insurance coverage owned to owner under the additional insured endorsement, the court would first have to determine what liability contractor had assumed under the owner-contractor agreement.

The court found that the two indemnification provisions were not in conflict because they were unrelated. Section 5.10, although silent on the issue of owner's negligence, covered liability that the contractor would incur for its own failure to protect the health and safety of persons or property associated with the project. On the other hand, Article 10, which required indemnification for owner's negligence, established contractor's duty to indemnify owner in the event that a cause of action was brought against contractor that could be unrelated to health and safety issues but arose from contractor's work.

The court concluded that pursuant to Article 10, contractor had to indemnify owner even if the loss resulted from owner's own negligence.

Furthermore, the express language in Section 9.5 (not cited by the court) required contractor to provide owner with insurance coverage that would indemnify owner for its own negligence, but not for its sole negligence, in a cause of action arising from contractor's work.

96018   Buchanan v. Rentenbach Constructors, Inc., 922 S.W.2d 467 (Mo. Ct. App. 1996)

II:	A107-1987, Art. 9, Para. 9.12
II:	A117-1987, Art. 14, Para. 14.12
II:	A201-1987, Art. 3, Para. 3.18.1
II:	A201-1987, Art. 10, Para. 10.1.4
II:	A401-1987, Art. 4, Para. 4.6.1

Subcontractor's injured employee brought a negligence action against contractor. Contractor filed its answer and asserted an affirmative defense of contributory negligence. The contractor also brought a third-party action for indemnification against subcontractor. Subcontractor moved to dismiss the third-party petition, arguing that the subcontract did not contain a clear and unequivocal provision requiring subcontractor to indemnify contractor against claims based solely upon contractor's negligence. The motion further asserted that the third-party petition failed to state a cause of action upon which relief could be granted. The trial court granted subcontractor's motion to dismiss. Contractor appealed. The appellate court reversed and remanded the dismissal of contractor's petition.

The subcontract contained an indemnity provision similar to Paragraph 4.6.1 of the American Institute of Architects Standard Form of Agreement Between Contractor and Subcontractor, Document No. A401, 1987.

Addressing the issue of whether the agreement contained a clear and unequivocal duty for subcontractor to indemnify contractor for claims based on contractor's own negligence, the court held that because the provision specifically stated that subcontractor shall indemnify contractor for any claims or damages "regardless of whether it is caused in part by a party indemnified . . .", the language was sufficiently clear to survive a motion to dismiss.

96019   CertainTeed Corp. v. Employers Ins. of Wausau, 939 F. Supp. 826 (D. Kan. 1996)

III:	A107-1987, Art. 9, Para. 9.12
III:	A117-1987, Art. 14, Para. 14.12
III:	A201-1987, Art. 3, Para. 3.18.1
III:	A201-1987, Art. 10, Para. 10.1.4
III:	A201-1987, Art. 10, Para. 10.2.1
III:	A201-1987, Art. 10, Para. 10.2.2
III:	A201-1987, Art. 11, Para. 11.1.3
III:	A401-1987, Art. 4, Para. 4.6.1

Contractor's injured employee brought a negligence action against owner. Owner sought a declaration that the additional insured endorsement in contractor's insurance

granting of his request . . . If the Engineer finds that The Work was delayed because of conditions beyond the control and without the fault of the Contractor, he may extend the time for completion in such amount as the conditions justify.

Provision 105.13 did not apply to damages for delay but was specifically intended to address compensation for unforeseen change orders in highway contracts.

As for Provision 108.07, the court held that numerous letters from the contractor indicating that specific delays would cause "domino-effect" delays in the entire project were "in the spirit" of Provision 108.07 and raised a triable issue of whether contractor's notice was sufficient to comply with notice of delay clause.

The court held further that contractor was entitled to delay damages from Department of Transportation's failure to coordinate if the contractor could show that its delays resulted from Department's failure to use reasonable efforts to compel timely resolution of problems associated with design changes.

96017 Brown & Kerr Inc. v. St. Paul Fire & Marine Ins. Co., 940 F. Supp. 1245 (N.D. Ill. 1996)

   Ill: A312-1984, Performance Bond, Art. 4

   Ill: A312-1984, Performance Bond, Art. 5

   Ill: A401-1987, Art. 12, Para. 12.1

Subcontractor brought an action against contractor's surety for payment of completed work under the subcontract and for extras. Subcontractor moved for partial summary judgment on the unpaid balance due under the subcontract. The contractor was not paid by the owner for the work performed by the subcontractor. Among other issues on appeal, the surety argued that because the contractor had not been paid by the owner, the surety had no obligation to pay subcontractor pursuant to the pay-when-paid clause in Paragraph 12.1 of the subcontract. The appellate court granted subcontractor partial summary judgment.

The subcontract contained a final payment provision similar to Paragraph 12.1 of the American Institute of Architects Standard Form of Agreement Between Contractor and Subcontractor, Document No. A401, 1987 edition. The payment bond authorized any subcontractor who had not been paid within ninety days after completing its work to sue under the bond. The bond did not incorporate the payment terms of the subcontract.

The court found that the pay-when-paid provision did not preclude payment under the bond because (a) the bond did not incorporate the payment terms of the subcontract; (b) the subcontractor was suing under the bond and not the subcontract; and (c) the subcontractor had satisfactorily performed its obligations under the subcontract.

The court refused to construe the pay-when-paid provision as a condition precedent to payment absent evidence that the subcontractor had assumed the risk of forfeiture in the event of a dispute between the owner and contractor. Rather, the court construed the clause as establishing the timing of the payment.

The subcontractor shall promptly indemnify and save and hold harmless the General Contractor and the Owner from any and all claims, liabilities and expenses for property damage or personal injury; including death, arising out of or resulting from or in connection with the execution of the work provided for in this Agreement.

The appellate court found that the language used was sufficiently comprehensive to include indemnification for damages resulting from the contractor's negligence. The court found that the language used in the subcontract "indemnify . . . from any and all claims" was no different from the language "indemnify against any loss" and "assume all liability for any and all loss," both of which were held in other cases to include indemnification for negligence. The court found that the provision was clear and certain in its terms, and concluded that the trial court erred in granting judgment in favor of the subcontractor.

96016 APAC-Georgia, Inc. v. Department of Transp., 221 Ga. App. 604, 472 S.E.2d 97 (1996), *cert. denied,* 1996 Ga. LEXIS 1025 (Ga. Sept. 20, 1996)

III:	A107-1987, Art. 12, Para. 12.1	
III:	A107-1987, Art. 12, Para. 12.2	
III:	A107-1987, Art. 12, Para. 12.3	
III:	A107-1987, Art. 14, Para. 14.3	
III:	A117-1987, Art. 17, Para. 17.1	
III:	A117-1987, Art. 17, Para. 17.2	
III:	A117-1987, Art. 17, Para. 17.3	
III:	A117-1987, Art. 19, Para. 19.3	
III:	A201-1987, Art. 4, Para. 4.3	
III:	A201-1987, Art. 6, Para. 6.1.3	
III:	A201-1987, Art. 8, Para. 8.3	

The appellate court reversed and remanded the trial court's rulings on the issue of notice required by contractor to claim delay damages.

The contract stated in Provision 105.13, Claims for Adjustments and Disputes, that:

In any case where the Contractor believes that extra compensation is due him, the Contractor shall notify the Engineer in writing of his intention to claim such extra compensation before beginning The Work on which said claim is based. If such notification is not given, in writing, before such work is begun, then the Contractor hereby agrees that no extra compensation is due and waives all rights to claim extra compensation for said Work . . . If the claim . . . is found to be just, it will be paid as Extra Work, as provided in 109.05 for Force Account Work.

Provision 108.07, Extension of Contract Time, stated that:

If the normal progress of The Work is delayed for reasons beyond his control, the Contractor shall, with (sic) fifteen days after the start of such a delay, file a written request to the Engineer for an extension of time setting forth therein the reasons and providing complete documentation for the delay which he believes will justify the

II:	A201-1987, Art. 4, Para. 4.5.6
II:	A201-1987, Art. 4, Para. 4.5.7
II:	A401-1987, Art. 6, Para. 6.1
II:	A401-1987, Art. 6, Para. 6.2
II:	A401-1987, Art. 6, Para. 6.3
II:	A401-1987, Art. 6, Para. 6.4
II:	A401-1987, Art. 6, Para. 6.5
II:	B141-1987, Art. 7, Para. 7.1
II:	B141-1987, Art. 7, Para. 7.2
II:	B141-1987, Art. 7, Para. 7.3
II:	B141-1987, Art. 7, Para. 7.4

This appeal presents numerous issues arising from awards in two arbitration proceedings resulting from the defective construction of a bulkhead. An issue of first impression before the Supreme Court of Virginia was whether the absence of specific language addressing who decides arbitrability reflected the parties' intent to include or exclude arbitrability determinations from the arbitrator's authority. The construction contract included a broad arbitration clause which provided for arbitration of any controversy or claim "arising out of or relating to the Contract or the breach thereof." The court held that, in the absence of a clear agreement showing that the parties intended that the arbitrator decide questions of arbitrability, that question was to be resolved by the court. The court also found that where the contract clearly stated that the award was to be "final" and that judgment "may be entered" on the award by a court, the contract reflected the parties' understanding that the arbitration process would end with the award and that any further consideration of the award or action regarding compliance with it would be undertaken in a different forum.

96015   W.M. Schlosser Co. v. Maryland Drywall Co., Inc., 673 A.2d 647 (D.C. 1996)

II:	A107-1987, Art. 9, Para. 9.12
II:	A117-1987, Art. 14, Para. 14.12
II:	A201-1987, Art. 3, Para. 3.18.1
II:	A201-1987, Art. 10, Para. 10.1.4
II:	A401-1987, Art. 4, Para. 4.6.1

These consolidated appeals arose from an injury sustained by subcontractor's injured employee. The owner appealed the trial court's denial of its motion for judgment as a matter of law after the jury returned a verdict for employee. The contractor appealed the entry of judgment in favor of the subcontractor, denying contractor's indemnification claim, where the court found that both parties were negligent. The appellate court reversed the judgment of the trial court in both appeals.

The subcontract provided that:

96013 TRST Atlanta, Inc. v. 1815 The Exch., Inc., 220 Ga. App. 184, 469 S.E.2d 238, *cert. denied,* 1996 Ga. LEXIS 634 (Ga. May 10, 1996)

    I: A201-1987, Art. 13, Para. 13.2.1

Owner's assignor brought a breach of contract action against contractor. Contractor and its performance bond surety moved for summary judgment on the grounds that (a) owner's claims against contractor were barred by the anti-assignment provision in the owner-contractor agreement; (b) contractor had been released by the owner; (c) the owner's assignor was not a successor of the original obligee on the performance bond; (d) the action was barred by the period of limitation contained in the bond; and (e) surety had been released by the owner. The trial court granted surety's motion, finding that owner's assignor was an assignee of owner and not its successor, and, as a consequence, was not authorized to recover on the performance bond. The court denied the contractor's motion. The owner appealed from the grant of summary judgment to surety and contractor cross-appealed from the denial of its motion for summary judgment. The appellate court affirmed the judgment of the trial court.

The parties entered into the American Institute of Architects Standard Form of Agreement Between Owner and Contractor, Document No. A101, 1987 edition, which incorporated by reference the American Institute of Architects General Conditions of the Contract for Construction, Document No. A201, 1987 edition, specifically Paragraph 13.2.1.

The appellate court upheld the finding of the trial court that owner's assignor was not a successor to the owner and was not authorized to recover against surety on the performance bond. The court then found that neither the assignment of personalty nor the conveyance of ownership interest by general warranty deed from owner, as debtor in default, to owner's assignor, was an assignment of the construction contract as a whole pursuant to Paragraph 13.2.1. Furthermore, the court found that Paragraph 13.2.1 did not expressly operate to release the non-consenting party but rather anticipated assignments and provided that an unconsented-to assignment did not release the assignor.

96014 Waterfront Marine Constr., Inc. v. North End 49ers Sandbridge Bulkhead Groups A, B & C, 251 Va. 417, 468 S.E.2d 894 (1996)

    II: A107-1987, Art. 10, Para. 10.8
    II: A117-1987, Art. 15, Para. 15.8
    II: A201-1987, Art. 4, Para. 4.5.1
    II: A201-1987, Art. 4, Para. 4.5.2
    II: A201-1987, Art. 4, Para. 4.5.3
    II: A201-1987, Art. 4, Para. 4.5.4
    II: A201-1987, Art. 4, Para. 4.5.4.1
    II: A201-1987, Art. 4, Para. 4.5.4.2
    II: A201-1987, Art. 4, Para. 4.5.5

4. Insurance Requirements

A. Subcontractor shall furnish, at Subcontractor's expense, prior to commencing upon the performance of the Work and keep in full force and effect during Subcontractor's performance thereof, the following insurance: . . .

B. Subcontractor shall obtain and furnish at Subcontractor's expense so-called Contractual Liability Endorsements to all policies described above, except Workmen's Compensation Insurance, whereby the insurer shall insure Subcontractor's obligations under Paragraph 17 and 18 herein . . .

Section 18:

Subcontractor hereby assumes entire responsibility and liability for any and all damage or injury of any kind or nature whatever (including death resulting therefrom) to all persons, whether employees of the Subcontractor or otherwise, and to all property caused by, resulting from, arising out of or occurring in connection with the execution of the Work; and if any claims for such damage or injury (including death resulting therefrom) be made or asserted, whether or not such claims are based upon Contractor's alleged active or passive negligence or participation in the wrong or upon any alleged breach of any statutory duty or obligation on the part of Contractor, Subcontractor agrees to indemnify and save harmless Contractor and the Owner * * * from and against any and all such claims, and further from and against any and all loss, costs, expense, liability, damage or injury, including legal fees and disbursements, that any of them * * * may directly or indirectly sustain, suffer or incur as a result thereof and Subcontractor does * * * hereby assume, on behalf of Contractor * * * the defense of any action at law or in equity which may be brought against any of them upon * * * or by reason of such claims and to pay on behalf of Contractor * * * in any such action(s).

The appellate court found that before addressing the issue of whether the contractor was an additional insured under the general liability policy, the court had to determine whether any of the insurance provisions of the subcontract were void under the Illinois statute. That statute provided that agreements in construction contracts to insure one's own obligations to indemnify another person for his negligence are void, but agreements to procure insurance for that other person are not void. Therefore, the first issue before the court was whether the subcontract contained an indemnity agreement or an agreement to obtain insurance.

The court found that (a) the indemnification provision in Section 18 was void under the Indemnification Act as an agreement by subcontractor to personally indemnify contractor for its own negligence; (b) the portion of the contract in which subcontractor agreed to purchase insurance to insure its obligations under Section 18 was void because it was tied to a void indemnity provision; and (c) there was no agreement to obtain insurance other than the void agreement and no express requirement in the subcontract that contractor be named an insured under subcontractor's policies or that the insurance subcontractor furnished would cover contractor's liability. The court held that contractor was not an additional insured under the subcontractor's policy and thus subcontractor's insurer had no duty to defend or indemnify the contractor.

specifically Paragraph 6.1. The parties crossed out the language in Paragraph 6.4 which provided that the award rendered by the arbitrators was final.

The district court addressed the subcontractor's argument that where Paragraph 6.4 was crossed out but the words remained in the document, the paragraph was effectively "redacted" and should be ignored by the court. This would leave Paragraph 6.1 which referred to the AAA Rules which made the arbitration binding. The court found that in this case, where the stricken language was left legible on the same paper as the subcontract, but was crossed out, the court could not refer to Paragraph 6.4 because the language of Paragraph 6.1 was not ambiguous. The court rejected the contractor's argument that even if Paragraph 6.4 was not considered, Paragraph 6.1 was ambiguous because, as distinguished from relevant caselaw which stated that the arbitration shall be "pursuant" to the AAA Rules or "governed" by them, it referred to the AAA Rules as setting forth "the manner and procedure" of the arbitration. The district court confirmed and entered judgment on the award to subcontractor.

96012 Transcontinental Ins. Co. v. National Union Fire Ins. Co., 278 Ill. App. 3d 357, 214 Ill. Dec. 934, 662 N.E.2d 500 (1996)

Ill:	A107-1987, Art. 9, Para. 9.12	
Ill:	A107-1987, Art. 17, Para. 17.1	
Ill:	A117-1987, Art. 14, Para. 14.12	
Ill:	A117-1987, Art. 22, Para. 22.1	
Ill:	A201-1987, Art. 3, Para. 3.18.1	
Ill:	A201-1987, Art. 10, Para. 10.1.4	
Ill:	A201-1987, Art. 11, Para. 11.1.1	
Ill:	A201-1987, Art. 1, Para. 11.1.3	
Ill:	A401-1987, Art. 4, Para. 4.6.1	
Ill:	A401-1987, Art. 13, Para. 13.1	
Ill:	A401-1987, Art. 13, Para. 13.2	

Subcontractor's injured employee brought an action against contractor and others alleging violation of the Illinois Structural Work Act. Subcontractor's insurer refused tender of contractor's defense, claiming that contractor was not an additional insured under the commercial general liability policy. Contractor and its surety filed a declaratory judgment action in which they sought a declaration that subcontractor's surety had wrongfully refused to defend contractor and had to reimburse contractor for sums expended in its defense. Subcontractor's insurer filed a counterclaim in which it sought a declaration that it had no duty to defend or indemnify. The parties filed cross motions for summary judgment which the trial court granted in part and denied in part, finding that the subcontractor's insurer had no duty to indemnify the contractor but it had a duty to defend contractor. Both parties appealed. The appellate court affirmed in part and reversed in part, ruling that there was no duty to defend or indemnify.

The subcontract provided that:

discretionary. The court found that the use of the word "shall" rather than "may" in the clause "the court shall award costs, expenses including attorneys' fees to the party justly entitled to them," implied an intent to make the award of attorneys' fees mandatory, not discretionary. Furthermore, the court inferred from the provision which referred to "the party justly entitled," rather than "a party justly entitled," that the parties intended that someone would recover attorneys' fees. The court held that the "party justly entitled" to attorneys' fees is the "prevailing party," and therefore the state statute made the award of attorneys' fees mandatory to that party. The court upheld the finding of the trial court that the contractor was the "prevailing party" and remanded for a determination of the attorneys' fees to which it was entitled.

96011 St. Lawrence Explosives Corp. v. Worthy Bros. Pipeline Corp., 916 F. Supp. 187 (N.D.N.Y. 1996)

II:	A107-1987, Art. 10, Para. 10.8
II:	A117-1987, Art. 15, Para. 15.8
II:	A201-1987, Art. 4, Para. 4.5.1
II:	A201-1987, Art. 4, Para. 4.5.2
II:	A201-1987, Art. 4, Para. 4.5.3
II:	A201-1987, Art. 4, Para. 4.5.4
II:	A201-1987, Art. 4, Para. 4.5.4.1
II:	A201-1987, Art. 4, Para. 4.5.4.2
II:	A201-1987, Art. 4, Para. 4.5.5
II:	A201-1987, Art. 4, Para. 4.5.6
II:	A201-1987, Art. 4, Para. 4.5.7
I:	A401-1987, Art. 6, Para. 6.1
I:	A401-1987, Art. 6, Para. 6.2
I:	A401-1987, Art. 6, Para. 6.3
I:	A401-1987, Art. 6, Para. 6.4
I:	A401-1987, Art. 6, Para. 6.5
II:	B141-1987, Art. 7, Para. 7.1
II:	B141-1987, Art. 7, Para. 7.2
II:	B141-1987, Art. 7, Para. 7.3
II:	B141-1987, Art. 7, Para. 7.4

Subcontractor petitioned the district court to confirm and enter judgment upon an award granted by an arbitrator in its favor pursuant to the terms of the subcontract. The primary issue before the district court was whether the arbitration provided for in the subcontract was binding or nonbinding upon the parties.

The parties entered into the American Institute of Architects Standard Form of Agreement Between Contractor and Subcontractor, Document No. A401, 1987 edition,

I:	A117-1987, Art. 14, Para. 14.7
II:	A117-1987, Art. 21, Para. 21.1
I:	A201-1987, Art. 3, Para. 3.3.1
I:	A201-1987, Art. 3, Para. 3.3.2
I:	A201-1987, Art. 10, Para. 10.1.1
I:	A201-1987, Art. 10, Para. 10.2.1
I:	A201-1987, Art. 10, Para. 10.2.2
I:	A201-1987, Art. 10, Para. 10.2.3

Subcontractor's injured employee brought an action for personal injury damages against contractor and owner. The trial court granted owner summary judgment and employee appealed. Among numerous other issues on appeal, the employee argued that the owner voluntarily assumed a duty to protect the employee. The appellate court affirmed the judgment of the trial court.

The owner-contractor agreement included the American Institute of Architects General Conditions of the Contract for Construction, Document Number A201, 1987 edition, specifically Paragraphs 3.3.1, 3.3.2, 10.1.1, 10.2.1, 10.2.2 and 10.2.3.

The appellate court found that the contract clearly placed the responsibility for all safety aspects of the project on the contractor, and nowhere in the contract was any of the responsibility or the right to control or supervise the work placed on the owner. Furthermore, the evidence also established that the contractor retained the sole responsibility for the safety of its employees and negated the employee's argument that the owner voluntarily assumed such a duty.

96010 Quality Contractors, Inc. v. Jacobsen, 139 Or. App. 366, 911 P.2d 1268, *review denied*, 323 Or. 691 (1996)

III:	A107-1987, Art. 9, Para. 9.12
III:	A117-1987, Art. 14, Para. 14.12
III:	A201-1987, Art. 3, Para. 3.18.1
III:	A201-1987, Art. 10, Para. 10.1.4
III:	A401-1987, Art. 4, Para. 4.6.1

Among numerous other issues on appeal was whether the trial court erred in refusing to award contractor attorneys' fees under the owner-contractor agreement. The appellate court reversed the decision of the trial court on the issue of attorneys' fees.

The contract provided that "[i]f either party becomes involved in litigation arising out of this Agreement, the court shall award costs, expenses including attorney fees to the party justly entitled to them."

The appellate court found that the phrase "party justly entitled" was ambiguous because the provision could be read as either "prevailing party," thus invoking the mandatory award of attorneys' fees language of the state statute, or the phase could mean that the award of attorneys' fees was subject to equitable considerations making the award

1. Claims under Worker's Compensation, disability benefit and other similar employee benefit acts,

2. Claims for damages because of bodily injury, occupational sickness or disease, or death of its employees, and claims insured by usual personal injury liability coverage with employment related Exclusion Removed,

* * *

5. Claims for damages insured by usual personal injury liability coverage which are sustained (a) by any person as a result of an offense directly or indirectly related to the employment of such person by the Contractor, or (b) by any other person . . .

* * *

10.1.3 The insurance required by subparagraph 10.1.1 shall be written for not less than any limits of liability specified below or required by law, whichever is greater, *and shall include contractual liability insurance as applicable to the Contractor's obligations under paragraphs 2.10, 2.17 and 7.2.7.*

(Italics in original.)

The supreme court found that Paragraph 2.17 was ambiguous as to whether the parties intended to indemnify design-builder from claims arising out of its own negligence where the provision could be read as either an agreement to indemnify the design-builder from all claims regardless of who was at fault or as an agreement to only indemnify design-builder from claims caused "in whole or in part by any negligent act or omission of the Contractor . . . ." Furthermore, even if the language was clearly and unequivocally intended to indemnify design-builder from its own negligence, it could not be enforced under Minnesota law.

Turning to the insurance provisions in Paragraphs 10.1.1 and 10.1.3, the court found that under these provisions the contractors had to procure insurance only against claims arising from their own operations. The language of the provisions did not require the contractors to purchase insurance for claims arising out of design-builder's operations, acts or omissions. The language was clearly intended to protect the design-builder from claims arising out of the activities of contractor, subcontractor, and others.

The court concluded that because there was no agreement to procure insurance coverage for claims arising out of design-builder's own negligence, any attempt by the parties in their construction contract to relieve design-builder from liability for its own acts and operations could not be enforced.

96009 Perritt v. Bernhard Mechanical Contractors, Inc., 669 So. 2d 599 (La. App. 1996)

I:	A107-1987, Art. 9, Para. 9.1
I:	A107-1987, Art. 9, Para. 9.7
II:	A107-1987, Art. 16, Para. 16.1
I:	A117-1987, Art. 14, Para. 14.1

II: A401-1987, Art. 4, Para. 4.6.1

Subcontractor's injured employee brought a negligence action against the concrete/masonry contractor and the design-builder. The concrete/masonry contractor and design-builder cross-claimed against each other and brought a third-party action for indemnification against concrete contractor and subcontractor. Design-builder moved for summary judgment, arguing that both contractors were required to defend and indemnify it from all claims, including claims arising out of its own negligence. The two contractors moved for summary judgment, contending that their responsibility to design-builder was limited to indemnification from claims arising only from their own actions. The trial court granted contractors' motions for summary judgment, finding that the contract only required the contractors to purchase general liability insurance for claims "which may arise out of or result from the Contractor's operations under the Contract," and not for claims arising out of design-builder's own operations. The jury returned a verdict finding that the parties, with the exception of the concrete/masonry contractor, were jointly responsible for employee's injuries. The design-builder appealed the court's summary judgment order to the appellate court. The court affirmed, concluding that under the contracts neither contractor had a duty to defend or indemnify design-builder for its own negligence where neither contractor had agreed to procure insurance which covered such negligence claims. The design-builder appealed to the Supreme Court of Minnesota. The court affirmed the judgment of the appellate court.

The design-builder/contractor agreements incorporated by reference the General Conditions of the agreement between the owner and the design-builder which contained the following indemnity and insurance provisions:

2.17 Indemnification Against Injury or Damage. The Contractor shall indemnify and hold harmless the Owner, the Design/Builder, the Design/Builder's Architect and Consultants, and their agents and employees from and against all claims, damages, losses and expenses (including Attorneys' fees) *arising out of or resulting from the performance of the Work*, provided that any such claim, damage, loss or expense (a) is attributable to bodily injury, sickness, disease or death, or to injury to or destruction of tangible property * * *, and (b) *is caused in whole or in part by any negligent act or omission of the Contractor, any Subcontractors or Sub-subcontractors, anyone directly or indirectly employed by any of them or anyone for whose acts any of them may be liable, regardless of whether or not it is caused in part by a party indemnified hereunder.*

10.1 Contractor's Liability Insurance. The Contractor shall provide liability insurance as follows:

10.1.1 The Contractor shall purchase and maintain comprehensive general liability insurance as will protect himself, the Design/Builder, the Design/Builder's Architect and Consultants, and the Owner from claims set forth *below which may arise out of or result from the Contractor's operations under the Contract*, whether such claims arise during contract performance or subsequent to completion of operations under the Contract and whether such operations be by himself or by any Subcontractor or by anyone directly or indirectly employed by any of them or by anyone for whose acts any of them may be liable.

[Subcontractor's] duty to indemnify [contractor] shall not apply to liability for damages arising out of bodily injury to persons or damages to property caused by or resulting from the sole negligence of [contractor] or its agent or employees.

[Subcontractor's] duty to indemnify [contractor] for liability for damages arising out of bodily injury to persons or damage to property caused by or resulting from the concurrent negligence of (a) [contractor] or its agents or employees, and (b) [subcontractor] or its agents or employees, shall apply only to the extent of negligence of [subcontractor] or its agents or employees.

[Subcontractor] specifically and expressly waives any immunity that may be granted it under the Washington State Industrial Insurance Act, Title 51 RCW. Further, the indemnification obligation under this Subcontract shall not be limited in any way by any limitation on . . . benefits payable to or for any third party under the workers' compensation acts . . . .

[Subcontractor's] duty to defend, indemnify and hold [contractor] harmless shall include . . . [contractor's] personnel-related costs, reasonable attorneys' fees, court costs and all other claim-related expenses.

THE UNDERSIGNED HEREBY CERTIFY THAT THIS ADDENDUM HAS BEEN MUTUALLY NEGOTIATED.

The supreme court, after reviewing the state statute, found that the addendum was valid and enforceable, but only to the extent subcontractor's negligence caused injured employee's injuries. The court, after reviewing the addendum, found that it created a duty to defend and indemnify where subcontractor's negligence contributed to the injury giving rise to liability. The addendum imposed upon the subcontractor a duty to indemnify the contractor "for liability for damages arising out of bodily injury . . . caused by or resulting from the concurrent negligence" of contractor and subcontractor. Both contractor and subcontractor were concurrently responsible for safety at the site. The court concluded that there remained a question of fact as to the negligence of contractor and subcontractor, particularly where the subcontractor was cited for workplace safety violations. The court found that summary judgment was improper where there was evidence that injured employee's injuries were the result of violations of safety regulations and the injuries resulted from the concurrent negligence of subcontractor and contractor.

96008   Katzner v. Kelleher Constr., 545 N.W.2d 378 (Minn. 1996)

II: A107-1987, Art. 9, Para. 9.12
II: A107-1987, Art. 17, Para. 17.1
II: A117-1987, Art. 14, Para. 14.12
II: A117-1987, Art. 21, Para. 21.1
II: A201-1987, Art. 3, Para. 3.18.1
II: A201-1987, Art. 10, Para. 10.1.4
II: A201-1987, Art. 11, Para. 11.1.1
II: A201-1987, Art. 11, Para. 11.1.2

The appellate court found that there was no indication that the parties intended to preclude arbitration of the claims advanced by the subcontractor and ordered arbitration of all claims. The court adopted the subcontractor's interpretation of Article 9(c) that the dispute, to be arbitrable, could not be one "involving the Government or the terms of the Prime Contract" unless relief was sought from the government or pursuant to the terms of the owner-contractor agreement. The court concluded that this interpretation applied to require arbitration where the government ordered the work and agreed to pay the contractor for the extra work, and the contractor had directed the subcontractor to perform the work.

96007 Gilbert H. Moen Co. v. Island Steel Erectors, Inc., 128 Wash. 2d 745, 912 P.2d 472 (1996), *rev'g* 75 Wash. App. 480, 878 P.2d 1246 (1994)

III:	A107-1987, Art. 9, Para. 9.12	
III:	A107-1987, Art. 9, Para. 9.12.1	
III:	A117-1987, Art. 14, Para. 14.12	
III:	A117-1987, Art. 14, Para. 14.12.1	
III:	A201-1987, Art. 3, Para. 3.18.1	
III:	A201-1987, Art. 3, Para. 3.18.2	
III:	A201-1987, Art. 10, Para. 10.1.4	
III:	A401-1987, Art. 4, Para. 4.6.1	
III:	A401-1987, Art. 4, Para. 4.6.2	

Contractor settled a personal injury action brought by subcontractor's injured employee. At a statutory hearing, the trial court found the agreed upon amount to be reasonable and stated that the settlement was based on the contractor's share of the fault, and was not a measure of damages in any future claim against the subcontractor. Contractor then sought indemnity from subcontractor. Contractor appealed from a summary judgment ruling which denied its indemnity claim, and subcontractor cross-appealed from a ruling that it had a duty to defend contractor against injured employee's claim. The appellate court reversed in part, holding that the subcontractor had no duty to defend or indemnify the contractor where contractor had been liable only for its own independent negligence and could not have been jointly liable with subcontractor. The parties appealed to the Supreme Court of Washington to determine the validity of the indemnification agreement pursuant to the state statute which permitted enforcement of indemnification agreements involving concurrent negligence of parties in the construction setting. The supreme court reversed the decision of the appellate court.

The parties executed a typewritten Indemnification Addendum to the subcontract which provided that:

[Subcontractor] agrees to defend, indemnify, and hold [contractor] harmless from any and all claims, demands, losses and liabilities to or by third parties . . . connected with, services performed . . . by [subcontractor's] employees to the fullest extent permitted by law and subject to the limitations provided below.

III:	A117-1987, Art. 15, Para. 15.8
III:	A201-1987, Art. 4, Para. 4.5.1
III:	A201-1987, Art. 4, Para. 4.5.2
III:	A201-1987, Art. 4, Para. 4.5.3
III:	A201-1987, Art. 4, Para. 4.5.4
III:	A201-1987, Art. 4, Para. 4.5.4.1
III:	A201-1987, Art. 4, Para. 4.5.4.2
III:	A201-1987, Art. 4, Para. 4.5.5
III:	A201-1987, Art. 4, Para. 4.5.6
III:	A201-1987, Art. 4, Para. 4.5.7
III:	A401-1987, Art. 6, Para. 6.1
III:	A401-1987, Art. 6, Para. 6.2
III:	A401-1987, Art. 6, Para. 6.3
III:	A401-1987, Art. 6, Para. 6.4
III:	A401-1987, Art. 6, Para. 6.5
III:	B141-1987, Art. 7, Para. 7.1
III:	B141-1987, Art. 7, Para. 7.2
III:	B141-1987, Art. 7, Para. 7.3
III:	B141-1987, Art. 7, Para. 7.4

Subcontractor filed a demand for arbitration of its breach of contract claim against contractor for additional compensation resulting from extra work required by changes made by the government, arguing that contractor (a) failed to provide timely and accurate information; (b) failed to present subcontractor's request for equitable adjustment to government; and (c) failed to distribute to subcontractor an equitable share of the additional compensation it had received from the government. Contractor moved to stay the proceedings. The district court found that most of subcontractor's claims were not arbitrable because Article 9(c) precluded arbitration of claims that required either an interpretation of the prime contract or an evaluation of the government's behavior for their resolution. The Court of Appeals for the District of Columbia reversed the judgment of the district court.

The subcontract provided in Article 9(c) that:

> "any dispute or any controversy between [contractor] and [subcontractor] *not* involving the Government or the terms of the Prime Contract" had to be resolved through binding arbitration.

(Italics in original.)

In the interim, before the dispute was resolved, the subcontractor was bound to follow the instructions of the contractor "without interruption, deficiency, or delay." The subcontract also permitted subcontractor to pursue a claim against the government in contractor's name so long as contractor had "a reasonable opportunity to monitor and participate in any such claim or dispute."

into the bond, provided for delay damages. Surety appealed. The issue on appeal was whether owner, as a matter of law, could recover delay damages, liquidated damages, and attorneys' fees against surety under a performance bond issued pursuant to Section 3 of the Bond Law, 8 P.S. § 193(a)(1), which did not provide specifically for such remedies, but did incorporate the terms and conditions of the owner-contractor agreement providing for those damages. The appellate court affirmed the judgment of the trial court.

The performance bond stated:

WHEREAS, Contractor has by written agreement dated February 8, 1989, entered into a contract with Owner . . . which contract is by reference made a part hereof, and is hereinafter referred to as the Contract.

NOW, THEREFORE, THE CONDITION OF THIS OBLIGATION is such that, if Contractor shall promptly and faithfully perform said Contract, then this obligation shall be null and void; otherwise it shall remain in full force and effect.

The Surety hereby waives notice of any alteration or extension of time made by the Owner.

Whenever Contractor shall be, and is declared by Owner to be in default under the Contract, the Owner having performed Owner's obligations thereunder, the Surety may promptly remedy the default, or shall promptly

(1) Complete the Contract *in accordance with its terms and conditions*, or

(2) Obtain a bid or bids for completing the Contract *in accordance with its terms and conditions*, and . . . arrange for a contract between [the lowest responsible] bidder and Owner, and make available as Work progresses . . . sufficient funds to pay the cost of completion less the balance of the contract price; but not exceeding, *including other costs and damages for which the Surety may be liable hereunder, the amount set forth in the first paragraph hereof*. The term "balance of the contract price," as used in this paragraph, shall mean the total amount payable by Owner to Contractor under the Contract and any amendments thereto, less the amount properly paid by Owner to Contractor.

(Italics in original.)

The appellate court found that although the bond did not specifically enumerate the "other costs and damages," to limit surety's obligation merely to the cost of completion would render the clause referring to the "other costs and damages" meaningless. The court agreed with the surety's argument that the "whereas" clause incorporating the owner-contractor agreement only set out the condition of surety's liability rather than the scope of the liability. However, the court disagreed with surety that its liability was limited to completion costs. After examining the language of the bond and the state statute, the court concluded that the terms of the bond could be sufficiently broad to extend coverage to damages beyond completion costs.

96006 Finegold, Alexander & Assocs., Inc. v. Setty & Assocs., Ltd., 81 F.3d 206 (D.C. Cir. 1996)

III: A107-1987, Art. 10, Para. 10.8

I:	A201-1987, Art. 2, Para. 2.1.1
III:	A201-1987, Art. 9, Para. 9.10.1
III:	A201-1987, Art. 9, Para. 9.10.3

Contractor brought an action against owner for payment of retainage. The trial court granted contractor's motion for summary judgment and ordered the owner to pay the retainage with interest and attorneys' fees. The owner appealed. Among numerous other specifications of error, the owner argued that the trial court erred in deciding that the actions of the engineer, as owner's agent, were binding on the owner and constituted an acceptance of contractor's work. The appellate court upheld the decision of the trial court.

The owner-contractor agreement provided in Section 9.10.5 that:

If upon final inspection of the work it shall be found by the Owner that the plans, specifications, contract, or change orders for the work shall not have been fully complied with, the Owner shall, until such compliance shall have been effected or adjustments satisfactory to it shall have been made, refuse to direct final payment.

The contract defined "owner" as "the person or entity identified as such in the agreement and is referred to throughout the contract documents as if singular in number. The term 'Owner' means the Owner or the Owner's authorized representative."

The appellate court concluded that the term "owner" in Section 9.10.5 was equivalent to "owner's representative" and entitled the owner or the owner's representative to make final inspection and withhold payment if the plans and specifications were not followed by the contractor.

96005 Dowington Area Sch. Dist. v. Int'l Fidelity Ins. Co., 671 A.2d 782 (Pa. Commw. 1996)

II:	A312-1984, Art. 2
II:	A312-1984, Art. 4, Para. 4.1
II:	A312-1984, Art. 4, Para. 4.2
II:	A312-1984, Art. 4, Para. 4.3
III:	A312-1984, Art. 6
III:	A312-1984, Art. 6, Para. 6.1
III:	A312-1984, Art. 6, Para. 6.2
III:	A312-1984, Art. 6, Para. 6.3
II:	A312-1984, Art. 8

Owner brought an action against performance bond surety for completion damages, delay damages, liquidated damages, and attorneys' fees after contractor's default. The surety moved for partial summary judgment on the grounds that it was not liable for the delay damages, liquidated damages and attorneys' fees under the express language of the performance bond and pursuant to Pennsylvania bond law. The trial court denied surety's motion because the construction contract, which was incorporated by reference

Under the contract the parties agreed to arbitrate claims arising from the contract, and also agreed that "in no event" shall a demand for arbitration "be made after the date when institution of legal or equitable proceedings based on such claim, dispute, or other matter in question would be barred by the applicable statute of limitations."

The appellate court held that whether the statute of limitations had run was for the court to decide in the absence of an unambiguous contractual provision to the contrary. Reviewing the contract, the court found that the owner and contractor clearly intended for the duty to arbitrate to end once the limitations period had expired.

96003   Couvillion v. Shelter Mut. Ins. Co., 672 So. 2d 277 (La. App. 1996)

   III: A107-1987, Art. 9, Para. 9.12
   III: A117-1987, Art. 14, Para. 14.12
   III: A201-1987, Art. 3, Para. 3.18.1
   III: A201-1987, Art. 10, Para. 10.1.4
   III: A401-1987, Art. 4, Para. 4.6.1

This appeal presents numerous issues arising from multi-party personal injury litigation which was generated by the construction of a turnaround at a chemical plant. At issue on appeal was whether the trial court erred in holding on owner's third-party demand that contractor had to indemnify owner for any amounts owner was held liable to injured worker. The appellate court upheld the decision of the trial court.

The owner-contractor agreement provided that:

[Contractor] agrees to indemnify and save [owner] . . . harmless from and against any and all claims, suits and liabilities based upon . . . injury to any person (including death) arising out of or attributable to the presence of [contractor], its employees, subcontractor or agents . . . upon the premises of [owner] or the performance or non-performance by [contractor] . . . of the work to be performed . . . including but not limited to injuries or damages caused solely or in part by the negligence of [owner].

The appellate court found that under the clear language of the provision, if the personal injury arose out of the performance or non-performance of the contract work, indemnification was owed by contractor even if the injury did not occur on owner's premises. The court then found that but for the performance of the contract work by the contractor, the worker would not have been injured. Under these circumstances, and in view of the fact that the agreement unequivocally indicated the intention that owner should be indemnified even against its own negligence, the court found no error in the ruling of the trial court.

96004   Diamond B Constr. Co. v. City of Plaquemine, 673 So. 2d 636 (La. App. 1996)

   III: A107-1987, Art. 15, Para. 15.4
   III: A117-1987, Art. 20, Para. 20.4

to Article 7 for clarification. The court turned to Paragraph 7.2 which expressly provided that all contract documents be listed and noted that the General Conditions were not listed. The court reasoned that where Article 7 expressly referred to definitions contained in the "Conditions of the Contract" and referred to Article 1, and where Article 1 expressly referred to "General" conditions, a fact finder could reasonably conclude that the parties intended to incorporate "General" conditions and that A201/CM provided those conditions. On the other hand, a fact finder could also conclude that the parties' failure to enumerate either A201/CM or other "General" conditions under Paragraph 7.2 evinced an intent not to include A201/CM. The court concluded as a matter of law that the contract was ambiguous regarding whether it incorporated by reference A201/CM, and the resolution of that ambiguity was a question of fact for a jury.

Applying general contract interpretation principles, the court also rejected the district court's reasoning that reading the agreement without A201/CM would not be reasonable because without the general conditions the parties would not have a complete agreement.

96002   Capitol Place I Assocs. L.P. v. George Hyman Constr. Co., 673 A.2d 194 (D.C. 1996)

III:	A107-1987, Art. 10, Para. 10.8	
III:	A117-1987, Art. 15, Para. 15.8	
III:	A201-1987, Art. 4, Para. 4.5.1	
III:	A201-1987, Art. 4, Para. 4.5.2	
III:	A201-1987, Art. 4, Para. 4.5.3	
III:	A201-1987, Art. 4, Para. 4.5.4	
III:	A201-1987, Art. 4, Para. 4.5.4.1	
III:	A201-1987, Art. 4, Para. 4.5.4.2	
III:	A201-1987, Art. 4, Para. 4.5.5	
III:	A201-1987, Art. 4, Para. 4.5.6	
III:	A201-1987, Art. 4, Para. 4.5.7	
III:	A401-1987, Art. 6, Para. 6.1	
III:	A401-1987, Art. 6, Para. 6.2	
III:	A401-1987, Art. 6, Para. 6.3	
III:	A401-1987, Art. 6, Para. 6.4	
III:	A401-1987, Art. 6, Para. 6.5	
III:	B141-1987, Art. 7, Para. 7.1	
III:	B141-1987, Art. 7, Para. 7.2	
III:	B141-1987, Art. 7, Para. 7.3	
III:	B141-1987, Art. 7, Para. 7.4	

The appellate court upheld the trial court's grant of a preliminary injunction to contractor, finding that the owner's demand for arbitration was barred by the statute of limitations.

96001 Atlantic Mut. Ins. Co. v. Metron Eng'g & Constr. Co., 83 F.3d 897 (7th Cir. 1996)

> I: A101-1977, Art. 1
> I: A101-1977, Art. 7, Para. 7.1
> I: A101-1977, Art. 7, Para. 7.2
> II: A101-1987, Art. 1
> II: A101-1987, Art. 9, Para. 9.1

Surety brought an action, under theories of negligence, breach of contract, and breach of express and implied warranties, against construction manager for fire-related damages paid to owner. Construction Manager moved for summary judgment. The district court granted construction manager's motion, finding that the surety's action was precluded by the waiver of subrogation clause contained in Paragraph 11.3.6 of the American Institute of Architects General Conditions, Document No. A201/CM, 1980 edition. Surety appealed, claiming that the General Conditions were not part of the parties' agreement because they were not attached to the agreement, they were not expressly enumerated as a contract document as required under Article 7, and surety never provided owner with a copy of the General Conditions. The Seventh Circuit Court of Appeals reversed the decision of the district court.

The parties entered into the American Institute of Architects Standard Form of Agreement Between Owner and Contractor, Document Number A101/CM, 1980 edition, specifically the instructional language below the heading, and Articles 1 and 7, enumerating and defining the contract documents. The General Conditions were not listed under Article 7.

The court of appeals noted that, because the parties merely filled-in the blanks on a form document, the agreement contained instructional language and boilerplate provisions that complicated t]heir analysis. After reviewing the contract provisions listed above, the court concluded that (a) the instructional language was merely an instruction to persons using the form that the American Institute of Architects had created other documents that could be used in conjunction with the owner-contractor agreement to provide general conditions; (b) Article 1 referred only to "Conditions of the Contract" with no requirement that the parties use A201/CM; and (c) where Article 1 stated that "An enumeration of the Contract Documents appears in Article 7," the court analysis must center on Article 7.

Turning first to Paragraph 7.1, the court found that the provision made clear that the terms contained in the agreement were defined in the "Conditions of the Contract." This reference strongly suggested to the court that, in fact, the parties did rely on an extraneous document entitled "Conditions of the Contract." However, where Paragraph 7.1 made no mention of either "General" conditions or A201/CM, the court would not find that the document referred to was in fact A201/CM.

Paragraph 7.2, however, presented a "conundrum." The court read Paragraph 7.2 as referring the court back to Article 1 for enumeration, which in turn directed the court

II:	A107-1987, Art. 10, Para. 10.3
II:	A117-1987, Art. 15, Para. 15.2
II:	A117-1987, Art. 15, Para. 15.3
II:	A201-1987, Art. 4, Para. 4.2.2
II:	A201-1987, Art. 4, Para. 4.2.3
II:	B141-1987, Art. 2, Para. 2.6.5
II:	B141-1987, Art. 2, Para. 2.6.6

Decedents' estates appealed a grant of summary judgment to architect and structural engineer, alleging defendants owed contractual, tort, and statutory duties to decedents to stop or prevent unsafe practices.

The agreements between the owner-architect and the architect-engineer provided that the architect/engineer visit the site to insure that the work was proceeding in accordance with the contract documents. The agreements also contained language similar to Paragraph 4.3.2 of the American Institute of Architects General Conditions of the Contract for Construction, Document No. A201, 1987 edition, and Paragraph 2.6.6 of the American Institute of Architects Standard Form of Agreement Between Owner and Architect, Document No. B141, 1987 edition.

The provisions regarding safety and construction means and techniques expressly provided that the architect/engineer had no contractual duties to advise the contractor of hazardous construction procedures or to make the site safe. Furthermore, because the contract provided that the architect/engineer's on-site inspections were for the purpose of insuring that the construction met with the architect's design specifications, there was no contractual duty to make the construction site safe for the workers. The contract terms were unambiguous and controlling.

II: A201-1987, Art. 11, Para. 11.3.1
II: A201-1987, Art. 11, Para. 11.3.7

Homeowner's insurer brought a subrogation action against contractor for damages resulting from a fire that started while contractor was constructing an addition to owner's residence. The fire destroyed the existing residence, its contents, and the addition. Owner's residence insurer and contractor moved for summary judgment. The insurer argued that the fire was caused by the negligence of contractor's employees. Contractor argued that Paragraph 17.6 of the owner-contractor agreement barred insurer's negligence action for damage outside the scope of the "work." The appellate court denied contractor's motion.

The owner and contractor entered into the American Institute of Architects Abbreviated Form of Agreement Between Owner and Contractor, Document Number A107, 1987 edition, specifically Articles 6 and 21, and Paragraphs 7.4, 9.2, 9.7, 9.12, 17.1, 17.3 and 17.6. The parties amended Paragraph 17.3 to require the contractor to obtain builder's risk insurance covering the loss of the addition. The homeowner's insurance covered the loss of the residence and its contents.

The district court, relying on the Missouri court's interpretation of "work" in Butler v. Mitchell Huqeback. Inc., Digest No. 94004, found that owner's residence and its contents were not "materials" or "equipment" provided by the contractor, nor were they "construction and services required by the Contract."

Having concluded that the damages to the residence and its contents were not damage to the "work," the court rejected the contractor's argument that its Paragraph 9.9 duty to keep "the premises and surrounding area" clean, and other requirements set forth in the specifications, made the existing residence a part of the "work" as defined by the contract. The court also rejected the contractor's argument that the new construction, which was connected to the existing residence, transformed the entire residence and all of its contents into "work" as defined by the contract.

Furthermore, the court found that relieving contractor of liability for its own negligence was not supported by a complete reading of the agreement. The court reasoned that if the contractor was to be relieved of liability for the negligence of its employees, there would be no reason for requiring the contractor to acquire liability insurance as required by Paragraph 17.1. In addition, there would be no reason for including Paragraphs 9.12 and 9.7, which imposed liability on the contractor for negligent damage to non-work property.

Turning to the waiver of subrogation clause, the court concluded that Paragraph 17.6 did not constitute a waiver of insurer's claim for fire damages caused by contractor's negligence because the waiver related solely to damages to the "work," and the damages claimed by insurer did not relate to the "work" but to other property of owner which was also damaged by the fire.

95052   Nicholson v. Turner/Cargile, 107 Ohio App. 3d 797, 669 N.E.2d 529 (1995)

II: A107-1987, Art. 10, Para. 10.2

The court rejected the subcontractor's argument that the pay-when-paid provision merely fixed a time for payment where the subcontract, unambiguously and explicitly, made payment from the owner to the contractor a "condition precedent" to any payment to subcontractor.

The court, after reviewing the intent and remedial nature of New York's lien law, held that a pay-when-paid provision which forces a subcontractor to assume the risk that the owner will fail to pay the contractor is void and unenforceable as contrary to public policy set forth in the New York Lien Law § 34. The court found, however, that a pay-when-paid provision which merely fixed a time for payment did not indefinitely suspend a subcontractor's right to payment, and did not violate public policy as stated in the Lien Law.

Under the facts of this case, the court found that where the owner had become insolvent and never made another payment to the contractor, subcontractor's right to receive payment was indefinitely postponed and subcontractor had effectively waived its right to enforce its mechanic's lien. The waiver occurred by operation of the pay-when-paid provision because liens cannot be enforced until a debt becomes due and payable.

95051 Fidelity & Guar. Ins. Co. v. Craig-Wilkinson, Inc., 948 F. Supp. 608 (S.D. Miss. 1995), *aff'd without opinion,* 101 F.3d 699 (5th Cir. 1996)

I:	A107-1987, Art. 6
I:	A107-1987, Art. 7, Para. 7.4
I:	A107-1987, Art. 9, Para. 9.2
I:	A107-1987, Art. 9, Para. 9.7
I:	A107-1987, Art. 9, Para. 9.12
I:	A107-1987, Art. 17, Para. 17.1
I:	A107-1987, Art. 17, Para. 17.3
I:	A107-1987, Art. 17, Para. 17.6
I:	A117-1987, Art. 11
I:	A117-1987, Art. 12, Para. 12.4
I:	A117-1987, Art. 14, Para. 14.2
I:	A117-1987, Art. 14, Para. 14.7
I:	A117-1987, Art. 14, Para. 14.12
I:	A117-1987, Art. 22, Para. 22.1
I:	A117-1987, Art. 22, Para. 22.3
I:	A117-1987, Art. 22, Para. 22.6
I:	A201-1987, Art. 1, Para. 1.1.3
I:	A201-1987, Art. 3, Para. 3.3.2
I:	A201-1987, Art. 3, Para. 3.4.1
I:	A201-1987, Art. 3, Para. 3.18.1
II:	A201-1987, Art. 11, Para. 11.1.1

95050 West-Fair Elec. Contractors v. Aetna Cas. & Sur. Co., 87 N.Y.2d 148, 638 N.Y.S.2d 394, 661 N.E.2d 967 (1995), *answer conformed to*, 78 F.3d 61 (2d Cir. 1996)

III:	A107-1987, Art. 4, Para. 4.1
III:	A107-1987, Art. 5, Para. 5.1
III:	A117-1987, Art. 9, Para. 9.1
III:	A117-1987, Art. 10, Para. 10.1
III:	A201-1987, Art. 9, Para. 9.6
III:	A201-1987, Art. 9, Para. 9.10
III:	A401-1987, Art. 11, Para. 11.1
III:	A401-1987, Art. 11, Para. 11.3
III:	A401-1987, Art. 12, Para. 12.1

Subcontractor brought actions against contractor and the payment bond surety seeking the balance due under the subcontract. Contractor and surety moved for summary judgment, arguing that because the subcontract contained a pay-when-paid provision which limited the contractor's liability to the sums the contractor received from the owner, and because the owner had failed to pay, the contractor, and in turn the surety, had no obligation to pay the subcontractor. The subcontractor moved for summary judgment, arguing that the pay-when-paid provision merely fixed a time for payment, and that the surety was required under the terms of the payment bond to pay the subcontractor after 90 days if the contractor failed to pay within that time. The district court granted the subcontractor summary judgment, explaining that the pay-when-paid provisions indefinitely suspended subcontractors' enforcement rights under the state's lien law because the subcontractor could obtain payment only after the owner paid the contractor. If the owner failed to pay the contractor, payment to the subcontractor would never be due and the subcontractor would never be able to enforce its mechanic's lien. The district court voided the pay-when-paid provision as against the state's public policy. The court also held the surety liable under the bond because the surety had assumed a direct obligation to the subcontractor under the plain language of the bond. The Second Circuit Court of Appeals certified, to the New York court, the question of whether a pay-when-paid provision in a subcontract, which transferred the risk of an owner's default from the contractor to a subcontractor, violated New York public policy as set forth in the Lien Law. The New York court answered this question in the affirmative and did not reach the second certified question.

The subcontract provided in pertinent part that:

IT IS SPECIFICALLY UNDERSTOOD AND AGREED THAT THE PAYMENT TO THE TRADE CONTRACTOR [plaintiff] IS DEPENDENT, AS A CONDITION PRECEDENT, UPON THE CONSTRUCTION MANAGER [the general contractor] RECEIVING CONTRACT PAYMENTS, INCLUDING RETAINER FROM THE OWNER.

II:	A201-1987, Art. 10, Para. 10.1.4
II:	A201-1987, Art. 11, Para. 11.1
II:	A401-1987, Art. 4, Para. 4.6.1
II:	A401-1987, Art. 13, Para. 13.1
II:	A401-1987, Art. 13, Para. 13.2
II:	A401-1987, Art. 13, Para. 13.3

Contractor brought a declaratory judgment action claiming indemnification from subcontractor. All parties moved for summary judgment. The trial court entered partial summary judgment for contractor on its breach of contract action and subcontractor appealed. Among numerous other issues on appeal was whether the contractor was entitled to indemnification from subcontractor for exemplary damages resulting from its own gross negligence where the indemnity agreement in the subcontract specifically expressed an obligation to indemnify the contractor for its own negligence but was silent as to gross negligence. The appellate court held that the indemnification clause obligated the subcontractor to indemnify the contractor for damages arising from contractor's own gross negligence.

The subcontract provided in pertinent part that:

12. The Subcontractor shall carry and pay for . . . (2) public liability insurance consisting of both bodily injury and property damage coverage and including contractual liability coverage. All of the said policies shall be in a sum and with limits and companies acceptable to Contractor. The Subcontractor shall furnish Contractor with copies of said policies or with certificates showing names of carriers, numbers of the policies and expirations dates. Upon request Subcontractor agrees to defend at its own cost and *to indemnify and hold harmless the Contractor and its agents and employees from any and all liability, damages*, losses, claims and expenses howsoever caused resulting directly or indirectly from or connected with the performance of this agreement, *irrespective of whether such liability, damages, losses, claims and/or expenses are actually or allegedly, caused wholly or in part through the negligence of Contractor or any of its agents, employees or other Subcontractors.*

(Italics in original.)

The appellate court found that under the terms of this agreement the subcontractor expressly agreed to indemnify contractor for its own negligence. The court then noted that the rules of contract construction require that indemnity agreements be strictly construed in favor of the indemnitor. However, the subcontract specifically provided that in the event of a dispute over the meaning or application of the contract, the contract should be construed "fairly and reasonably and neither more strongly for nor against either party." Applying a fair and reasonable meaning to the terms of the contract, the court determined that when the parties used the term "negligence" they indicated their intent to indemnify contractor from the consequences of all degrees of its own negligence, including gross negligence.

III:	A201-1987, Art. 3, Para. 3.18.1	
III:	A201-1987, Art. 10, Para. 10.1.4	
III:	A401-1987, Art. 4, Para. 4.6.1	

Owner filed a declaratory judgment action contending that contractor and its surety were required to indemnify owner for delay damages awarded to a second contractor. The court granted owner summary judgment and contractor and surety appealed. The appellate court affirmed the judgment of the trial court.

The owner-contractor agreement contained several provisions that contained indemnification language. Paragraph 4 provided that:

CONTRACTOR agrees . . . to save the DEPARTMENT harmless from all liability or damage to persons or property that may accrue during and by reason of acts of negligence of the CONTRACTOR, his agents, employees, or subcontractors if there be such.

General Provision 107.14 provided that:

The Contractor shall indemnify and save harmless the Department, its officers and employees, from all suits, actions, or claims of any character brought because of any injuries or damage received or sustained by any person, persons, or property on account of the operations of the Contractor; . . . or because of any act or omission, neglect, or misconduct of the Contractor.

The bond required contractor and surety to comply with the terms and conditions "of the road contract" and to "save harmless [owner] from any expense incurred through the failure of said contractor . . . to complete the work as specified, and for any damages growing out of the carelessness or negligence of said contractor . . . [and] from all losses to it . . . from any cause whatever . . . in the manner of constructing said Road."

The appellate court rejected several of contractor's and surety's arguments for limited liability before turning to contractor's argument that the indemnity language cited above only covered liability arising from damages or losses through injury to persons or property. The court found that the language was plain, unambiguous and broad enough to cover the losses incurred by the second contractor as a result of the delay, neglect, and omissions of contractor. The court reasoned that where the broad indemnity language in General Provision 107.14 covered "all suits, actions, or claims of any character" arising "on account of the operations of the Contractor," and where the bond indemnity language was even broader, covering losses to owner from any cause whatsoever from the construction of the road, the language required contractor and surety to indemnify owner.

95049 Webb v. Lawson-Avila Constr., Inc., 911 S.W.2d 457 (Tex. App. 1995)

II:	A107-1987, Art. 9, Para. 9.12	
II:	A107-1987, Art. 17, Para. 17.1	
II:	A117-1987, Art. 14, Para. 14.12	
II:	A117-1987, Art. 22, Para. 22.1	
II:	A201-1987, Art. 3, Para. 3.18.1	

The owner-contractor agreement included the American Institute of Architects General Conditions of the Contract for Construction, Document No. A201, 1987 edition, specifically Paragraphs 4.5.1 and 4.5.5. There was no arbitration clause in the owner-architect agreement, which was not an A.I.A. document, or in any documents incorporated into that agreement.

The supreme court, relying on *Dunn Constr. Co. v. Sugar Beach Condominium Ass'n*, digest number 91009, found that a party whose contract does not contain an arbitration clause can be forced to arbitrate claims under a theory of equitable estoppel where there is a close relationship between the nonsignatory and the other parties as well as a relationship of the alleged wrongs to the nonsignatory's contractual obligations and duties. However, the court refused to adopt the doctrine of equitable estoppel to the architect because the General Conditions contained Paragraph 4.5.5 which specifically prohibited arbitration with the architect, and there was no written consent to arbitration containing a specific reference to an agreement signed by the architect, owner, and contractor.

95047 Utley-James of La., Inc. v. State of La., Div. of Adm., Dep't of Facility Planning & Control, 671 So. 2d 473 (La. App. 1995)

> II: A107-1987, Art. 14, Para. 14.1
> II: A117-1987, Art. 19, Para. 19.1
> II: A201-1987, Art. 8, Para. 8.2.1

Contractor brought an action against owner to recover sums withheld from the final payment as liquidated delay damages. Surety joined in the action, alleging that contractor assigned its rights to the proceeds to it under an assignment of accounts receivable. In dismissing the action, the trial court found, among numerous other findings, that the owner did not have to put the contractor in default where the owner-contractor agreement contained the phrase "time is of the essence." The contractor appealed on numerous alleged errors of the trial court, including its interpretation of the clause "time is of the essence." The appellate court upheld the finding of the trial court.

The owner-contractor agreement contained the following language in Section 8.2.1 of the supplementary conditions:

> Time is of the essence and completion of the work must be within the time stated in the contract. . . . The Owner will suffer financial loss if the Project is not substantially complete in the time set forth in the Contract Documents.

The appellate court found that Section 8.2.1 was a clear agreement that time was of the essence, which eliminated the necessity of putting the contractor in default.

95048 VanKirk v. Green Constr. Co., 195 W. Va. 714, 466 S.E.2d 782 (1995), *cert. denied*, 116 S. Ct. 2571 (1996)

> III: A107-1987, Art. 9, Para. 9.12
> III: A117-1987, Art. 14, Para. 14.12

or liability incurred by Owner and Contractor . . . for personal injury . . . arising or alleged to have arisen, whether directly or indirectly, *on account of or in connection with any work done* by Subcontractor *under this Subcontract* . . . .

c. Subcontractor shall submit to Contractor, within three (3) calendar days of the occurrence of any accident, copies of all reports arising out of any *injuries to its employees* . . . arising or alleged to have arisen on account of any work done by Subcontractor under the Contract Documents.

(Italics in original.)

Relying on *Larsen v. J.I. Case Co., A.I.A. Citator* case number 68025, the appellate court found that the Wisconsin Worker's Compensation Act did not require that the indemnification agreement contain specific phrases such as "liable to one's own employees" or "waive workers' compensation" as a condition precedent to waiver of workers' compensation immunity by an employer.

95046   Ex parte Stallings & Sons, Inc., 670 So. 2d 861 (Ala. 1995)

II:	A107-1987, Art. 10, Para. 10.8	
II:	A117-1987, Art. 15, Para. 15.8	
I:	A201-1987, Art. 4, Para. 4.5.1	
I:	A201-1987, Art. 4, Para. 4.5.2	
I:	A201-1987, Art. 4, Para. 4.5.3	
I:	A201-1987, Art. 4, Para. 4.5.4	
I:	A201-1987, Art. 4, Para. 4.5.4.1	
I:	A201-1987, Art. 4, Para. 4.5.4.2	
I:	A201-1987, Art. 4, Para. 4.5.5	
I:	A201-1987, Art. 4, Para. 4.5.6	
I:	A201-1987, Art. 4, Para. 4.5.7	
II:	A401-1987, Art. 6, Para. 6.1	
II:	A401-1987, Art. 6, Para. 6.2	
II:	A401-1987, Art. 6, Para. 6.3	
II:	A401-1987, Art. 6, Para. 6.4	
II:	A401-1987, Art. 6, Para. 6.5	
II:	B141-1987, Art. 7, Para. 7.1	
II:	B141-1987, Art. 7, Para. 7.2	
II:	B141-1987, Art. 7, Para. 7.3	
II:	B141-1987, Art. 7, Para. 7.4	

Contractors sought a writ of mandamus ordering the trial court to vacate its order staying their action against the architect pending arbitration and ordering the parties to arbitrate. The Supreme Court of Alabama granted the writ.

The Company reserves the right, but shall not be obligated, to appoint inspectors to follow the progress of the work with authority to suspend work not in accordance with the Contract. Acceptance or approval by the inspector shall in no event be deemed to constitute final acceptance of the same by the Company. The inspection by the Company's inspector shall not relieve the Contractor of any responsibility for the proper performance of the work. Inspection . . . shall not be deemed to be supervision by the Company of the Contractor, its agents, servants or employees, but shall be only for the purpose of assuring that the work complies with the Contract . . . .

The owner relinquished "any right to control the methods or manner of performance of the work by the Contractor."

The court first addressed the issue of whether the owner owed a legal duty to the worker, an employee of an independent contractor, to provide a safe work environment. The court reviewed the terms of the owner-contractor agreement and found that it unambiguously established that the owner did not retain or reserve the right to control the "manner" in which the contractor performed the work. The owner merely reserved the right to supervise and inspect the work to assure that contractor complied with the terms of the contract. In addition, the owner had no contractual obligation to perform safety inspections. Finally, the court found that the owner fulfilled any duty it had to warn the worker that the electrical lines were energized by giving notice to the contractor's supervisory personnel.

The court concluded that neither the terms of the contract nor owner's actions raised a disputed factual issue as to whether the owner delegated the duty regarding safety at the job site to the contractor or whether the owner retained sufficient control over the work to give rise to liability.

95045   Schaub v. West Bend Mut., 195 Wis. 2d 181, 536 N.W.2d 123 (1995)

II:	A107-1987, Art. 9, Para. 9.12
II:	A117-1987, Art. 14, Para. 14.12
II:	A201-1987, Art. 3, Para. 3.18.1
II:	A201-1987, Art. 10, Para. 10.1.4
II:	A401-1987, Art. 4, Para. 4.6.1

Subcontractor's injured employee brought a negligence action against contractor. Contractor brought a third-party indemnification action against subcontractor based upon the indemnification paragraph of their subcontract. The trial court held that where the indemnification agreement did not specifically waive subcontractor's immunity from suit under the state's worker's compensation act the agreement was unenforceable. The appellate court reversed the decision of the trial court.

The subcontract provided in pertinent part that:

a. Subcontractor agrees to save harmless and defend Owner and Contractor from *any and all claims*, demands, judgments and costs of suit or defense, including attorneys' fees, and *indemnify* and reimburse Owner and Contractor *for any expense, damage*

III: A107-1987, Art. 9, Para. 9.1
III: A107-1987, Art. 9, Para. 9.2
III: A107-1987, Art. 9, Para. 9.3
III: A107-1987, Art. 9, Para. 9.7
III: A107-1987, Art. 16, Para. 16.1
III: A117-1987, Art. 13, Para. 13.3
III: A117-1987, Art. 14, Para. 14.1
III: A117-1987, Art. 14, Para. 14.2
III: A117-1987, Art. 14, Para. 14.3
III: A117-1987, Art. 14, Para. 14.7
III: A117-1987, Art. 21, Para. 21.1
III: A201-1987, Art. 2, Para. 2.3.1
III: A201-1987, Art. 3, Para. 3.3.1
III: A201-1987, Art. 3, Para. 3.3.2
III: A201-1987, Art. 3, Para. 3.3.3
III: A201-1987, Art. 3, Para. 3.4.1
III: A201-1987, Art. 3, Para. 3.4.2
III: A201-1987, Art. 3, Para. 3.9.1
III: A201-1987, Art. 10, Para. 10.1
III: A201-1987, Art. 10, Para. 10.2
III: A201-1987, Art. 13, Para. 13.5

Contractor's injured employee brought a negligence and wanton misconduct action against owner. The worker argued that owner (1) breached its duty to provide him a safe work place, (2) failed to perform safety inspections at the work site, and (3) failed to warn the worker of the danger of working around energized wires. The District Court granted owner's motion for summary judgment.

The owner-contractor agreement provided in pertinent part that:

The Contractor will furnish adequate numbers of trained, qualified and experienced personnel . . . to perform the work requested by the Company. Such personnel shall be skilled and properly trained to work on and in the vicinity of energized electrical equipment, structures, and lines, and who are fully cognizant of the hazards involved . . . .

The Contractor shall accept all equipment and structures of the Company as found, and will make its own inspections for the purpose of determining the hazards incident to working thereon or thereabout and will adopt suitable precautions and methods for the protection and safety of its employees . . . .

The Contractor, in doing the work herein called for, shall not act as an agent or employee of the Company, but shall be and act as an independent contractor . . . , having supervision over and responsibility for the safety and actions of his employees . . . .

If the Subcontractor is making satisfactory progress with the Work (in the General Contractor's reasonable opinion), is not in default under this Agreement, and complies with all the documentation requirements of this Agreement, and if (but only to the extent that) the General Contractor or his approved Agent, i.e., Chicago Title & Trust has received payment from the Owner for such Work, the General Contractor will make monthly payments to the Subcontractor of ninety percent of the value of Work performed during the month until the total of monthly payments equals fifty percent (50%) of the total amount to be paid to the subcontractor for the Work by the General Contractor.* From and after the date such fifty percent amount is reached, the General Contractor shall not retain any further amounts from subsequent monthly payments to the Subcontractor. The amount retained * by the General Contractor shall be disbursed to the Subcontractor upon the last to occur of (a) Three (3) months after final completion of the Work and acceptance by the Owner; (b) the Owner has paid the General Contractor the entire balance related to the Work due to the General Contractor under the Principal Contract; and (c) the Subcontractor has delivered to the General Contractor waivers of all liens, as-built drawings (if requested) and guaranties. At such time, the General Contractor shall pay such retainage to the Subcontractor, less any amounts the General Contractor has applied to cure any default under this Agreement.**

*Subcontractor will provide trade payment breakdowns for General Contractor's approval by phases . . . . Retention shall be disbursed by phase, three (3) months after satisfying the conditions set forth in the subcontract and acceptance by both the Architect and the Owner.

**The default is to be adjudged by the Architect and the Subcontractor has ample opportunity to correct any such default.

The following language was added to Article 3:

If a conflict arises between Owner and General Contractor . . . this subcontractor will receive payment in a timely manner just as if the conflict did not exist.

Final payment shall be held no more than the stated three months in the event that other subcontractor's [sic] or the General Contractor has [sic] not completed their work.

The appellate court upheld the trial court's finding that the language added to Article 3 rendered the pay-when-paid provision inoperable where owner's failure to pay the contractor created a "conflict" within the meaning of the clause. Here, the ensuing claims and lawsuits emanating from the owner's non-payment due to its insolvency were conflicts. The court then found that the added language regarding final payment was clear and unambiguous and overruled any condition precedent. The bargained for modifications, which the court found were unambiguous and unequivocal, were timing provisions for interim and final payment. Subcontractor's timely completion of its work triggered its right to final payment.

95044   Ramirez v. Alabama Power Co., 898 F. Supp. 1537 (M.D. Ala. 1995), *aff'd without opinion*, 86 F.3d 1170 (11th Cir. 1996)

         III: A107-1987, Art. 8, Para. 8.3

Shall not be responsible for the acts or omissions of the Contractors, their subcontractors or material suppliers, or any of the Contractors or subcontractor's agents or employees or any other persons performing any of the work.

The agreement between the architect/engineer and structural engineer required the structural engineer to visit the site to:

[B]ecome generally familiar with the progress and quality of the Work . . . and to determine in general if the Work is being performed in a manner indicating that the Work, when complete, will be in accordance with the Contract Documents.

According to the contract, on making these on-site observations the structural engineer was to inform the architect/engineer of the "progress of the Work . . . and shall endeavor to guard [owner] against defects and deficiencies in such Work."

The contract contained more specific provisions which not only held the contractor responsible for building processes, but also dictated that the architect/engineer was not responsible for the contractor "in the building process." The agreement provided that architect/engineer:

Shall not be responsible for construction means, methods, techniques, sequences or procedures, or for safety precautions and programs in connection with the work and * * * shall not be responsible for the Contractor's failure to carry out the work in accordance with the Construction Drawings and Specifications.

The appellate court found that the above provisions clearly indicated that the architect/engineer and the structural engineer had no contractual duties to advise the contractor of hazardous construction procedures or to make the site safe. The court concluded that where the on-site inspections were for the purpose of insuring that the construction met the design specifications, the architect/engineer and structural engineer did not have a contractual duty to make the construction site safe for the decedents. The court also overruled the estates' assignments of error based on tort and statute.

95043 Premier Elec. Constr. Co. v. American Nat'l Bank of Chicago, 276 Ill. App. 3d 816, 212 Ill. Dec. 4, 656 N.E.2d 157, *modified*, 213 Ill. Dec. 128, 658 N.E.2d 877 (App. Ct. 1995)

Ill:	A401-1987, Art. 11, Para. 11.1	
Ill:	A401-1987, Art. 11, Para. 11.3	
Ill:	A401-1987, Art. 11, Para. 11.7	
Ill:	A401-1987, Art. 12, Para. 12.1	

This case presents numerous issues arising from complex, multi-party litigation which was generated by the renovation of a condominium building. Among numerous other findings of the trial court, subcontractor appealed from a grant of partial summary judgment on its breach of contract action against contractor for failure to pay the subcontractor for all completed work. At issue was whether the subcontract's pay-when-paid clause barred subcontractor's claim.

The payment clause in Article 3 provided that:

(Italics in original.)

The appellate court interpreted this language as limiting the subcontractor's obligation to indemnify to cases in which there was a causal connection between the subcontractor's work and the injury. The court found that the provision was not null and void under the state statute which provided that a general contractor may require indemnification by the subcontractor only in connection with harm "caused by" the subcontractor, its employees, agents, or subcontractors. The court rejected the roofing subcontractor's reliance on the court's reasoning in *Harnois v. Quannapowitt Dev., Inc.*, digest number 93041, to differentiate the statutory language "caused by" from the language "arising out of or in consequence of" used in the subcontract. The clause in the subcontract, according to the court, tied indemnity to "the performance of the Subcontractor's work under this Contract" and to "the performance . . . of the work performed," an equivalent of the statutory "caused by." In addition, the state statute did not require a finding of negligence in order to trigger the indemnity provision.

95042   Nicholson v. Turner/Cargile, 107 Ohio App. 3d 797, 669 N.E.2d 529 (1995)

II:	A107-1987, Art. 10, Para. 10.2
II:	A107-1987, Art. 10, Para. 10.3
II:	A117-1987, Art. 15, Para. 15.2
II:	A117-1987, Art. 15, Para. 15.3
II:	A201-1987, Art. 4, Para. 4.2.2
II:	A201-1987, Art. 4, Para. 4.2.3
II:	B141-1987, Art. 2, Para. 2.6.5
II:	B141-1987, Art. 2, Para. 2.6.6

The subcontractor's employees' estates brought wrongful death actions against numerous parties, including the architect/engineer and the structural engineer. The trial court entered summary judgment for architect/engineer and structural engineer, finding that they did not owe a legal duty to decedents. The decedents' estates argued on appeal that the architect/engineer and structural engineer had contractual, tort, and statutory duties to stop or prevent the decedents' unsafe practices. As to contractual duties, the appellate court upheld the trial court's grant of summary judgment.

The owner-architect/engineer agreement required the architect/engineer to visit the site to "become generally familiar with the progress and quality of the work and to determine in general if it is proceeding in accordance with Construction Drawings and Specifications."

According to the contract, on making these on-site observations the architect/engineer was to inform the owner of the "progress and quality of the work and shall endeavor to guard the [owner] against defects and deficiencies in the work of the Contractor."

Architect/engineer was further insulated from responsibility for the acts of the contractor because the agreement provided that architect/engineer:

executing the work. The appellate court reversed the trial court's denial of owner's motion for summary judgment.

The owner-contractor agreement specifically provided that the contractor was not the agent of owner and that contractor had "the sole and entire responsibility for all . . . construction methods, . . . and for supervising, directing, coordinating, phasing, and scheduling the work."

Furthermore, the agreement provided that contractor was responsible for safety at the site. The contract gave the owner the right to ensure that contractor's work conformed to the contract drawings and specifications and the right to order the work stopped or resumed, inspect its progress, or prescribe alterations and deviations. It also allowed the owner to dismiss any person who was unfit or unskilled and restricted the contractor's right to terminate the job-site supervisor without owner's consent.

The appellate court found that these contract provisions did not give the owner control over contractor's work. The owner merely had a general right to order the work stopped or resumed, to inspect its progress, to make suggestions or recommendations which need not necessarily be followed, or to prescribe alterations and deviations. These general rights did not give the owner control over the contractor's methods of work. The contractor remained solely and entirely responsible for all construction methods.

95041   M. DeMatteo Constr. Co. v. A.C. Dellovade, Inc., 39 Mass. App. Ct. 1, 652 N.E.2d 635, *review denied*, 421 Mass. 1103, 655 N.E.2d 1277 (1995)

> III: A107-1987, Art. 9, Para. 9.12
> III: A117-1987, Art. 14, Para. 14.12
> III: A201-1987, Art. 3, Para. 3.18.1
> III: A201-1987, Art. 10, Para. 10.1.4
> III: A401-1987, Art. 4, Para. 4.6.1

Injured employee of roofing subcontractor brought an action for personal injury damages against contractor and another subcontractor for negligent maintenance of the work site. The contractor brought a third-party action for indemnification against the roofing subcontractor. The trial court granted contractor's motion for summary judgment and subcontractor appealed. At issue on appeal was the enforceability of the indemnification provision in the subcontract. The appellate court upheld the judgment of the trial court.

The subcontract provided in pertinent part that:

The Subcontractor shall fully indemnify and hold harmless the Contractor and any of its agents and employees from all claims, liabilities, liens, demands, damages, expenses, including attorneys' fees, and causes of action for or on account of any injury to persons or damage to property *arising out of or in consequence of the performance of the Subcontractor's work under this Contract*. Subcontractor further indemnifies and holds harmless the Contractor from any and all claims . . . which relates [*sic*] to the *performance*, quality, acceptability or fitness of the work performed . . . by the Subcontractor.

I:	A401-1978, Art. 15, Para. 15.2
II:	A401-1987, Art. 1, Para. 1.1
II:	A401-1987, Art. 8, Para. 8.1
II:	A401-1987, Art. 16, Para. 16.1

Subcontractors brought mechanic's lien actions against owner and contractor. Among numerous issues on appeal was whether the electrical subcontractor was obligated under the subcontract to complete the parking lot lighting system. The appellate court upheld the trial court's holding that the parking lot lighting system was not within subcontractor's scope of work under the subcontract.

The contractor and subcontractor entered into the American Institute of Architects Standard Form of Agreement Between Contractor and Subcontractor, Document No. A401, 1978 edition, specifically Paragraph 1.1, 2.1 and 15.2.

The appellate court found that the subcontract contained contradictory provisions and was ambiguous on its face where Paragraph 2.1 included "16530 -Site Lighting" [the parking lot lighting], while the parking lot lighting system was not enumerated in Paragraph 15.2. The court upheld the trial court's finding as supported by substantial evidence because the subcontractor did not receive a copy of 16530 before signing the subcontract and the contractor asked the subcontractor to bid the parking lot lighting after the subcontract was signed.

95040   Kraft Gen. Foods, Inc. v. Maxwell, 219 Ga. App. 211, 464 S.E.2d 639 (1995)

III:	A107-1987, Art. 8, Para. 8.3
II:	A107-1987, Art. 9, Para. 9.1
III:	A107-1987, Art. 16, Para. 16.1
III:	A117-1987, Art. 13, Para. 13.3
II:	A117-1987, Art. 14, Para. 14.1
III:	A117-1987, Art. 21, Para. 21.1
III:	A201-1987, Art. 2, Para. 2.3
III:	A201-1987, Art. 2, Para. 2.4
II:	A201-1987, Art. 3, Para. 3.3.1
III:	A201-1987, Art. 10, Para. 10.1
III:	A201-1987, Art. 10, Para. 10.2

An injured laborer employed by the subcontractor brought an action for personal injury damages against the owner, owner's lessee, and another party. The trial court denied the parties' motions for summary judgment. The appellate court granted their applications for interlocutory appeal. Among numerous other issues on appeal, the owner argued that it was not liable to laborer where it had relinquished full possession and control of the property to the contractor. The injured laborer argued that the owner did not completely surrender control where the owner retained the right to direct or control the manner of

claims because contractor was not an insured under the builder's risk policy. Contractor appealed. The appellate court reversed, holding that the owner contractually waived its right to pursue the contractor for the loss sustained by a windstorm because it agreed to shift the risk of that loss onto the insurer. The insurer, as the owner's subrogee, could not succeed to rights greater than those possessed by the owner.

The owner-contractor agreement provided that the contractor "was responsible for * * * [t]he safety and good condition of all work and materials embraced in or affected by [its] contract, until the completion of [its] contract as an entirety." The contractor was also to "be responsible for all precautions as may be necessary to fully protect [its] work both during its execution and until its final acceptance, in default of such [contractor would] be held responsible for all damage incurred."

The insurance provisions required both the owner and the contractor to obtain insurance for the project. The contractor agreed to:

[M]aintain insurance to protect [it] and the Owner from claims for personal injury, direct or derivative, including death, or claims for property damage, resulting from operations under this contract, by itself, [its] subcontractor, or anyone directly or indirectly employed by them.

The owner agreed to procure a builder's risk policy to protect, among others, the contractor from "loss incurred by theft, fire, lightning, extended coverage, vandalism, and malicious mischief in the full amount of the contract."

The appellate court found that under the insurance provisions of the owner-contractor agreement, the owner agreed to insure the contractor against loss "incurred by theft, fire, lightning, extended coverage, vandalism, and malicious mischief in the full amount of the contract." The court, after reviewing case law, concluded that "extended coverage" was a term that embraced the risk of loss by windstorm. Furthermore, the owner and contractor mutually agreed to shift the described risk from contractor, on which it had been placed by the provision requiring contractor to obtain certain insurance, to the insurer, although contractor would continue to guarantee the "safety and good condition" of the work in all other respects. After reviewing the contract and other evidence, the court concluded that both the contractor and the owner intended for both of them to be fully protected by the builder's risk policy against windstorm loss, without reference to who was to be named as the insured on the policy, or who was to pay the premium. If they did not so intend, there was no reason for them to include an agreement to insure in their contract, which was clearly meant to vitiate the need for each of them to purchase builder's risk insurance separately. Further, the court was persuaded that the parties intended to be protected against covered losses even if the loss was facilitated by their own negligence.

95039 Kingston Elec., Inc. v. Wal-Mart Properties, Inc., 901 S.W.2d 260 (Mo. App. 1995)

I: A401-1978, Art. 1, Para. 1.1
I: A401-1978, Art. 2, Para. 2.1

because none of the contract provisions cited by contractor expressly delegated to owner a duty to coordinate or sequence the work of its contractors to avoid delay.

The court then found that the language of paragraph 108.04 which provided that "rights of the [prime contractors] will be established by the [DOT] in order to secure the completion of the various parts of [the project] in harmony" failed to expressly impose a duty upon owner to coordinate and sequence the work of the prime contractors. Furthermore, in interpreting the contract as a whole, the court found that paragraph 108.04 did not purport to do anything but allow owner to secure completion of any particular part of the project to minimize inconvenience to the public. The court upheld the trial court's grant of summary judgment on these issues.

The court then addressed the owner's argument that the claim was barred because contractor failed to request a written extension of time to complete its work as required by Paragraph 108.07 of the contract. That provision stated that "[i]f the normal progress of the Work is delayed for reasons beyond his control, the Contractor, shall within fifteen days after the start of such a delay, file a written request to [owner] for an extension of time setting forth therein the reasons for the delay which he believes will justify the granting of his request." The court found that the grading contractor was required to give written notice as a condition precedent to recovery. The court reversed the trial court's denial of summary judgment to owner on this issue.

95038 Indiana Ins. Co. v. Carnegie Constr., Inc., 104 Ohio App. 3d 219, 661 N.E.2d 776, *discretionary appeal denied*, 74 Ohio St. 3d 1444, 656 N.E.2d 344 (1995)

III:	A107-1987, Art. 16, Para. 16.1	
III:	A107-1987, Art. 17, Para. 17.1	
III:	A107-1987, Art. 17, Para. 17.3	
III:	A107-1987, Art. 17, Para. 17.6	
III:	A117-1987, Art. 21, Para. 21.1	
III:	A117-1987, Art. 22, Para. 22.1	
III:	A117-1987, Art. 22, Para. 22.3	
III:	A117-1987, Art. 22, Para. 22.6	
III:	A201-1987, Art. 10, Para. 10.1	
III:	A201-1987, Art. 10, Para. 10.2	
III:	A201-1987, Art. 11, Para. 11.1.1	
III:	A201-1987, Art. 11, Para. 11.3.3.1	
III:	A201-1987, Art. 11, Para. 11.3.7	

Insurer brought a subrogation action against contractor alleging negligence and breach of contract. Contractor moved for a declaration that the insurer could not bring a subrogated claim against an insured, or in the alternative, that the owner and contractor agreed to make contractor an insured. The trial court denied contractor's motion, holding that neither the insurance policy nor the owner-contractor agreement barred insurer's

II:	A201-1987, Art. 10, Para. 10.1.4
I:	A401-1978, Art. 11, Para. 11.11.1
I:	A401-1978, Art. 11, Para. 11.11.2
I:	A401-1987, Art. 4, Para. 4.6.1
I:	A401-1987, Art. 4, Para. 4.6.2

The estate of subcontractor's employee brought a negligence action against owner, contractor and numerous subcontractors. Contractor brought a third-party action against decedent's employer for contribution, indemnity and attorneys' fees. The trial court entered summary judgment for decedent's employer on the grounds that the subcontract did not indemnify the contractor for its own negligence. The contractor appealed. At issue on appeal was whether the indemnity agreement met the express negligence test as a matter of law. The appellate court affirmed the judgment of the trial court.

The parties entered into the American Institute of Architects Standard Form of Agreement between Contractor and Subcontractor, Document No. A401, 1978 edition, specifically Paragraphs 11.11.1 and 11.11.2.

Applying the analysis set forth in *Robert H. Smith, Inc. v. Tennessee Tile, Inc.*, digest number 86058, the appellate court found that the agreement did not expressly indemnify contractor for its own negligence.

95037 Holloway Constr. Co. v. Department of Transp., 218 Ga. App. 243, 461 S.E.2d 257, *cert. denied*, 1995 Ga. LEXIS 1196 (Nov. 9, 1995)

III:	A201-1987, Art. 6, Para. 6.1.1
III:	A201-1987, Art. 6, Para. 6.1.3

This is the third case resulting from a highway construction project, see *Department of Transp. v. Fru-Con Constr. Corp.*, digest numbers 92004e and 93007. In the instant case, owner moved for summary judgment on the grounds that the damages the prime grading contractor sought for extended overhead and equipment costs were attributable solely to delays caused by other contractors and that owner was not liable for the damages by virtue of the contract's no-damage-for-delay provision. Grading contractor argued that paragraph 105.07 did not bar recovery where owner breached its express contractual duty to coordinate and sequence the work of its contractors. The trial court granted owner partial summary judgment and both owner and grading contractor appealed. Among numerous other findings, the appellate court affirmed in part and reversed in part the trial court's grant of summary judgment to owner.

The court previously held that paragraph 105.07 of the contract was a valid no-damage-for-delay clause causing any claim made by the grading contractor for delay due to an implied duty to coordinate or sequence to fail. The grading contractor now argued that because the owner also breached express contractual obligations to coordinate contractors, its claim for damages was not barred by paragraph 105.07 as that provision did not address damages caused by a breach of the contract. The appellate court rejected this argument

Surety and contractor delivered to owner, as obligee, the American Institute of Architects Performance Bond, Document A312, 1984 edition, specifically Paragraphs 3.1, 3.2 and 3.3, and the American Institute of Architects Payment Bond, Document No. A312, 1984 edition, for the projects.

The court held that the indemnity agreement provided that, on demand, the contractor would pay to the surety:

[A]ll losses and expenses, including attorney's fees, incurred by [surety] "by reason of having executed any Bond" on [contractor's] behalf . . . . In the event of default by [contractor] the agreement states that [surety] has the right, at its sole discretion, to take possession of the work for which a bond was executed and to arrange for the project's completion. The agreement further provides that [contractor] is deemed to be in default if the obligee of a bond declares it to be in default . . . . [S]urety . . . has the exclusive right to determine in good faith whether any claims made on the bond shall be paid, compromised or defended.

Except for the contract prices and completion dates, the pertinent terms of the contracts and bonds were identical.

The district court found that surety could not recover from contractor unless, under the terms of the performance bonds, surety was obligated to complete the projects. Surety argued that under the plain language of the performance bonds its obligation to complete the projects arose when the owner declared the contractor in default for failure to perform and gave written notice that it was terminating the contracts. The contractor argued that the surety was not entitled to indemnification because the surety completed the projects as a volunteer because its obligations under the performance bonds did not arise due to the fact that the owner withheld progress payments.

The district court denied surety's motion for summary judgment on the issue of owner default because an issue of fact existed regarding the owner default. The court found that the performance bonds clearly stated that the surety's obligation arose only "if there is no Owner Default." The court rejected the surety's interpretation of the clause as providing that its obligation arose when it was "satisfied" that there was no owner default. The court concluded that the surety was obligated to complete the contracts only if the owner was actually not in default, and the bonds specifically provided that failure to make required payments to the contractor constituted owner default. The court denied the parties' cross-motions for summary judgment on other grounds.

95036   Glendale Constr. Serv., Inc. v. Accurate Air Sys., Inc., 902 S.W.2d 536 (Tex. App. 1995)

II:	A107-1978, Art. 10, Para. 10.11
II:	A107-1987, Art. 9, Para. 9.12
II:	A117-1979, Art. 14, Para. 14.11
II:	A117-1987, Art. 14, Para. 14.12
II:	A201-1976, Art. 4, Para. 4.18.1
II:	A201-1987, Art. 3, Para. 3.18.1

No. A201, 1987 edition, specifically Paragraph 9.6.2. The contractor and subcontractors entered into the American Institute of Architects Standard Form of Agreement Between Contractor and Subcontractor, Document No. A401, 1987 edition, specifically Paragraphs 11.3 and 12.1. In each subcontract the contractor struck out the language following the word "owner" in both paragraphs.

The supreme court, as a matter of first impression, addressed the issue of a contractor's absolute defense under a pay-when-paid clause.

The court first considered whether the contracts were clear on their face as to the parties' intent that the pay-when-paid clause was a condition precedent to payment. In construing Paragraphs 11.3 and 12.1 of the subcontracts, the court noted the absence of language which would permit a finding that the parties contemplated payment "within a reasonable time." Likewise, there was nothing in the subcontracts to allow the court to find that the parties clearly understood that this clause asserted a condition precedent to payment. Moreover, the subcontracts did not contain unequivocal language dealing with the possible insolvency of the owner sufficient to show that the subcontractors assumed that risk of loss. Based on this analysis, the court concluded that the phrases "after the Contractor receives payment from the Owner" and "has received payment from the Owner" constituted latent ambiguities in the contracts permitting the use of parol and other extrinsic evidence to determine the intent of the parties.

The court then considered each individual contract to determine whether negotiations and prior dealings of the parties manifested their intent with respect to the ambiguous provisions. The court found that the record of the case clearly demonstrated that the contractor intended an absolute "pay-when-paid defense," however, only where the subcontractor manifested the same intent would the absolute defense be available to the contractor.

95035 General Ins. Co. of America v. K. Capolino Constr. Corp., 903 F. Supp. 623, *reh'g denied*, 908 F. Supp. 197 (S.D.N.Y. 1995)

III:	A107-1987, Art. 9, Para. 9.12
III:	A117-1987, Art. 14, Para. 14.12
III:	A201-1987, Art. 3, Para. 3.18.1
III:	A201-1987, Art. 10, Para. 10.1.4
I:	A312-1984, Para. 3.1
I:	A312-1984, Para. 3.2
I:	A312-1984, Para. 3.3
III:	A401-1987, Art. 4, Para. 4.6.1

Contractor's surety brought an indemnification action against contractor for costs incurred in completing construction contracts for which surety had issued performance bonds. Contractor filed numerous counterclaims. Both parties moved for summary judgment.

[I]f the total amount of damages arising from the claim or dispute, as estimated by the Architect, are less than $200,000. Any claim, dispute or other matter in question for which the amount of damages is estimated by the Architect to be greater than $200,000, is not subject to arbitration unless the parties mutually agree otherwise."

The appellate court was unable to conclude that the clause clearly excluded arbitration of contractor's claim. The court reasoned that where the parties vested the architect with the obligation to determine initially "claims, disputes and other matters in question," the word "claims" indicated the parties' belief that more than one claim would be involved. Furthermore, the arbitration provision required that "all claims, disputes, and other matters" be arbitrated. However, the amendment to the arbitration provision establishing the $200,000 floor referred singularly to a "claim or dispute" and placed on the architect the obligation to determine the total amount of damages arising from the claim or dispute. "Total amount of damages," according to the court, could mean different types or items of damage arising from a single dispute.

Pursuant to the terms of the contract, the court adopted the architect's interpretation that the word "claim" meant each single incident or issue for which contractor's claim of damage was made. In addition, the court found that the various items which made up the claim were each fact intensive and required application of different legal concepts. On these grounds, the court concluded that the strong presumption in favor of arbitration was not overcome by contractor combining a series of claims into one claim based on allegations of bad plans, poor supervision and administration.

95034 Galloway Corp. v. S.B. Ballard Constr. Co., 250 Va. 493, 464 S.E.2d 349 (1995)

II:	A107-1987, Art. 4, Para. 4.1
II:	A107-1987, Art. 5, Para. 5.1
II:	A117-1987, Art. 9, Para. 9.1
II:	A117-1987, Art. 10, Para. 10.1
I:	A201-1987, Art. 9, Para. 9.6.2
I:	A401-1987, Art. 11, Para. 11.3
I:	A401-1987, Art. 12, Para. 12.1

Contractor brought an action against owner to enforce its mechanic's lien claims after owner failed to make progress payments to contractor. Numerous subcontractors filed actions against owner and contractor to enforce their mechanic's lien claims and against contractor for failure to make progress payments as required by the subcontracts. On the subcontractors' breach of contract action against the contractor the trial court found that contractor did not have an absolute pay-when-paid defense where the phrases "after the Contractor receives payment from the Owner" and "has received payment from the Owner" only permitted the contractor to delay payments. Contractor appealed. The Supreme Court of Virginia affirmed in part and reversed in part.

The owner and contractor entered into an agreement which included the American Institute of Architects General Conditions of the Contract for Construction, Document

I:	A201-1976, Art. 2, Para. 2.2.7
I:	A201-1976, Art. 2, Para. 2.2.9
I:	A201-1976, Art. 2, Para. 2.2.12
I:	A201-1976, Art. 7, Para. 7.9.1
I:	A201-1976, Art. 7, Para. 7.9.3
II:	A201-1987, Art. 4, Para. 4.2.11
II:	A201-1987, Art. 4, Para. 4.3
II:	A201-1987, Art. 4, Para. 4.4
II:	A201-1987, Art. 4, Para. 4.5.1
II:	A201-1987, Art. 4, Para. 4.5.2
II:	A201-1987, Art. 4, Para. 4.5.3
II:	A201-1987, Art. 4, Para. 4.5.4
II:	A201-1987, Art. 4, Para. 4.5.4.1
II:	A201-1987, Art. 4, Para. 4.5.4.2
II:	A201-1987, Art. 4, Para. 4.5.5
II:	A201-1987, Art. 4, Para. 4.5.6
II:	A201-1987, Art. 4, Para. 4.5.7
II:	A401-1978, Art. 13, Para. 13.1
II:	A401-1987, Art. 6, Para. 6.1
II:	A401-1987, Art. 6, Para. 6.2
II:	A401-1987, Art. 6, Para. 6.3
II:	A401-1987, Art. 6, Para. 6.4
II:	A401-1987, Art. 6, Para. 6.5
II:	B141-1977, Art. 9, Para. 9.1
II:	B141-1977, Art. 9, Para. 9.2
II:	B141-1977, Art. 9, Para. 9.3
II:	B141-1987, Art. 7, Para. 7.1
II:	B141-1987, Art. 7, Para. 7.2
II:	B141-1987, Art. 7, Para. 7.3
II:	B141-1987, Art. 7, Para. 7.4

Contractor brought an action against owner claiming breach of contract, quantum meruit and misrepresentation. Owner demanded arbitration and filed a motion to stay proceedings. The trial court denied owner's motion on the grounds that the "claim" asserted by the contractor was not arbitrable under the terms of the owner-contractor agreement. The appellate court reversed the judgment of the trial court.

The parties entered into an owner-contractor agreement which included the American Institute of Architects General Conditions of the Contract for Construction, Document No. A201, 1976 edition, specifically Paragraphs 2.2.7, 2.2.9, 2.2.12, 7.9.1 and 7.9.3. By amendment the parties added the following clause to the first line of Paragraph 7.9.1:

any claim or right of action against the Owner or the Construction Manager which does not otherwise exist without regard to this Agreement.

(Italics in original.)

The appellate court interpreted the above language as exacting no express promises to act to benefit the contractor, and, in fact, expressly stating that the agreement did not give rise to any third-party beneficiary status on behalf of any contractor. Furthermore, the construction manager's promises to manage the project ran to the owner rather than to the contractor. The court concluded that where the construction manager's duties to supervise and manage the project would affect, and possibly benefit, the contractor, they were incidental and did not confer third-party beneficiary status on the contractor.

95032   First Union Nat'l Bank of Fla. v. 2800 S.E. Dune Drive Condominium Ass'n, Inc., 661 So. 2d 955 (Fla. Dist. Ct. App. 1995)

	III:	A107-1987, Art. 9, Para. 9.12
	III:	A117-1987, Art. 14, Para. 14.12
	III:	A201-1987, Art. 3, Para. 3.18.1
	III:	A201-1987, Art. 10, Para. 10.1.4
	III:	A401-1987, Art. 4, Para. 4.6.1

Contractor appealed the trial court's grant of attorneys' fees to owner in owner's action for an injunction and declaratory relief under a letter of credit.

The owner-contractor agreement provided that:

Contractor shall reimburse Association for reasonable attorneys' fees and costs including such fees and costs for any proceeding, trial or appeal, incurred by reason of Contractor's failure to perform under this Contract or any part thereof.

The appellate court reversed the decision of the trial court, holding that the language of the provision did not authorize the award of attorneys' fees for the letter of credit litigation until after the conclusion of pending litigation involving the contractor's performance under the contract.

95033   Fru-Con Constr. Co. v. Southwestern Redevelopment Corp. II, 908 S.W.2d 741 (Mo. App. 1995)

	II:	A107-1978, Art. 8, Para. 8.5
	II:	A107-1978, Art. 13, Para. 13.2
	II:	A107-1987, Art. 10, Para. 10.5
	II:	A107-1987, Art. 10, Para. 10.8
	II:	A117-1979, Art. 12, Para. 12.5
	II:	A117-1979, Art. 17, Para. 17.2
	II:	A117-1987, Art. 15, Para. 15.5
	II:	A117-1987, Art. 15, Para. 15.8

[T]ake all proper precautions to protect persons from injury, unnecessary interference or inconvenience, and be responsible for the results of any failure in doing so . . .

[H]ave on the job site a superintendent "who shall have *general* charge of the project operation."

(Italics in original.)

Under these provisions, the court concluded, contractor merely retained a general right to control the work. The provisions did not confer "sole" responsibility over "all" safety aspects of the work. The clause which required contractor to "take all proper precautions to protect . . . and be responsible for the results of any failure in doing so" made the contractor liable, under general principles of negligence, for its own acts and omissions, but was not, by itself, evidence of a duty owed to the employee of a subcontractor. The provision which required contractor to have a superintendent at the site merely recognized contractor's general right to oversee the project, leaving undisturbed subcontractor's right to control the safety aspects of its own work.

The court held that contractor's contractual relationships with the owner and with the subcontractor did not confer "a sufficient right of control over the work as to create a duty of reasonable care" toward the injured employee.

95031 Dynamic Constr. Co. v. Barton Malow Co., 214 Mich. App. 425, 543 N.W.2d 31 (1995)

II:	A107-1987, Art. 7, Para. 7.1	
II:	A107-1987, Art. 7, Para. 7.2	
II:	A117-1987, Art. 12, Para. 12.1	
II:	A117-1987, Art. 12, Para. 12.2	
II:	A201-1987, Art. 1, Para. 1.1.2	

Contractor brought a breach of contract action against construction manager. The construction manager moved for summary judgment claiming that contractor failed to state a cause of action because there was no contract between the parties. The trial court denied the construction manager's motion on the grounds that contractor was a third-party beneficiary of the construction manager's agreement with the owner. The construction manager appealed. The appellate court reversed the decision of the trial court.

The owner-construction manager agreement provided in pertinent part that:

15.1 This agreement represents the entire and integrated Agreement between the Owner and Construction Manager . . . . This Agreement shall not be superseded by provisions of contracts for construction and may be amended only by written instrument signed by both Owner and Construction Manager.

15.2 Nothing contained herein shall be deemed to create any contractual relationship between the Construction Manager and the Architect or any of the contractors . . . on the Project; *nor shall anything contained herein be deemed to give any third party*

III: A117-1987, Art. 21, Para. 21.1
III: A201-1987, Art. 3, Para. 3.3
III: A201-1987, Art. 3, Para. 3.4
III: A201-1987, Art. 3, Para. 3.9
III: A201-1987, Art. 10, Para. 10.1
III: A201-1987, Art. 10, Para. 10.2
III: A401-1987, Art. 2, Para. 2.1
III: A401-1987, Art. 4, Para. 4.1
III: A401-1987, Art. 4, Para. 4.3

An injured employee of subcontractor brought an action against contractor to recover personal injury damages. The trial court entered judgment against the injured employee allocating fifty-five percent of the fault to him and forty-five percent to the contractor. Contractor was ordered to pay damages to injured employee and loss of consortium damages. The injured employee appealed. Contractor cross-appealed the denial of its motion for judgment notwithstanding the verdict in which it claimed that its contractual relationships with the owner and subcontractor did not confer upon the contractor a sufficient right of control over the safety aspects of the job to create a duty of reasonable care toward injured employee. The appellate court upheld the damages judgment but reversed the judgment entered against the contractor for loss of consortium damages.

The subcontract provided in pertinent part that contractor shall:

[A]ssume to the Subcontractor all the obligations and responsibilities that the Awarding Authority by the terms of the hereinbefore described documents assumes to the Contractor.

The subcontract also provided that:

[C]ontractor is obligated "to prosecute and complete" its portion of the work under the general contract "so that [subcontractor] will be able to begin, prosecute and complete" its work upon notice from contractor . . . [the] section goes on to obligate [subcontractor] to complete its work "with due consideration" to the general contract's stated completion date.

The appellate court interpreted these provisions as merely allowing contractor and subcontractor jointly to engage in all aspects of the work, including safety, but not to confer on the contractor the degree of control required to conclude that the subcontractor was not free to execute the work as it saw fit. Furthermore, the subcontract did not contain a provision directing contractor to oversee or direct subcontractor's work.

The owner-contractor agreement required the contractor to:

[S]upervise and direct the work. He shall be solely responsible for all construction means, methods, techniques, sequences, and procedures and for coordinating all portions of the work of the Contract.

. . . .

The Contractor shall be responsible for the entire project operations and shall properly coordinate the work of all trades and give all customary and proper assistance to all Subcontractors.

the city at any time prior to the expiration of the guarantee period from recovering damages for work actually defective.

If the contract documents, owner's instructions, laws, ordinances, or any public authority require any work to be specifically tested or approved, the contractor shall give the owner timely notice of its readiness for inspection and, if the inspection is by another authority than the owner, of the date fixed for such inspection, inspections by the owner shall be promptly made. . . .

Article 39 required the engineer or owner to make reasonable inspections to ensure that the project was completed in accordance with the contract documents.

The district court found that:

1. Section 1.03 clearly provided that it was the owner who decided how much was to be paid to the contractor, and that this determination was dependent upon the items being satisfactorily installed and in accordance with the contract terms; and

2. the language "satisfactorily installed" and "completed in accordance with the contract" clearly included testing and inspection, as these requirements were all part of the measurement to fix the amount owed the contractor; and

3. the payment terms "total amount due" did not necessarily mean the entire amount due as claimed to be satisfactorily completed by the contractor without checking, testing, or inspecting to determine if any of it actually functioned correctly, but could be read to denote the amount "properly" due, in other words, the amount due for all work meeting all contract requirements and specifications; and

4. Article 13 reasserted the owner's responsibility to inspect and test, therefore, to reconcile the terms in Article 13 with Article 39, Article 13 could not be read to be a complete disclaimer of the owner's duty to inspect.

The court interpreted the above provisions as clearly stating that where the inspector and the engineer, and through them the owner, did not perform reasonable inspections and tests which were required under the contract prior to making complete payment to the contractor, the payments to the contractor were premature and not in accordance with the contract. Therefore, the premature payments to the contractor were a material variation from the contract discharging surety from its obligations to the extent that it was prejudiced by the owner's actions.

95030 Dilaveris v. W.T. Rich Co., 39 Mass. App. Ct. 115, 653 N.E.2d 1134, *review granted*, 421 Mass. 1105, 656 N.E.2d 1259 (1995)

III:	A107-1987, Art. 9, Para. 9.1	
III:	A107-1987, Art. 9, Para. 9.3	
III:	A107-1987, Art. 9, Para. 9.7	
III:	A107-1987, Art. 16, Para. 16.1	
III:	A117-1987, Art. 14, Para. 14.1	
III:	A117-1987, Art. 14, Para. 14.3	
III:	A117-1987, Art. 14, Para. 14.7	

95029   Continental Ins. Co. v. City of Va. Beach, 908 F. Supp. 341 (E.D. Va. 1995)

III:	A201-1987, Art. 3, Para. 3.3.3
III:	A201-1987, Art. 4, Para. 4.2.6
III:	A201-1987, Art. 4, Para. 4.2.9
III:	A201-1987, Art. 9, Para. 9.4.2
III:	A201-1987, Art. 13, Para. 13.5

Contractor's surety filed an action against owner alleging that its duty as surety under a performance bond was discharged when the owner materially deviated from the terms of the owner-contractor agreement. Surety sought damages in the amount it paid to its completion contractor to correct or complete the work performed by the original contractor, plus prejudgment interest, consulting fees and court costs. The district court entered judgment for surety, ruling that where the contract required the owner to make reasonable and prompt inspections before paying the contractor and the owner failed to make such inspections before paying the contractor substantial sums, the owner materially deviated from the contract, resulting in surety's discharge from its obligations to the extent that it was prejudiced by the owner's actions.

The owner-contractor agreement set forth the payment and inspection procedures. The Specifications detailed the procedures and requirements for specific components of the project. The agreement provided in Section 1.03 that "measurement of the various pay items will be made by the owner . . . the measurement of all items is based upon their satisfactorily being installed and completed in accordance with the terms of the contract documents." Section 1.03 also listed the specific elements which were included as part of the cost of each component of the project.

The payment procedures stated that "each application for payment by the contractor shall be submitted on the forms provided by the Department of Public Utilities."

The form itself stated that "the work as indicated on attached estimate has been inspected and is deemed acceptable as per specifications. Quantities and type of materials are in accordance with the contract and any subsequent change orders."

The language in Section G did not provide for a specific retainage percentage, however, Article 27 allowed the owner to withhold payment for work improperly performed.

Article 13 provided that:

The owner will appoint such person or persons as he may deem necessary to properly inspect the materials furnished and work done under the contract, and to see that the same strictly correspond with the drawings and specifications and bid documents. Work and materials will be inspected promptly, but if, for any reason delay should occur, the contractor shall have no claim for damages or extra compensation.

The failure of the inspector to reject or condemn improper materials and workmanship shall not prevent the owner from rejecting materials and workmanship found defective at any time prior to the final acceptance of the completed work, nor shall it be considered a waiver of any defects which may be discovered later, or as preventing

shall survive even the termination of this Blanket Subcontractor's Agreement, regardless of how such termination be effected.

The appellate court found that while the indemnity agreement did not specifically refer to attorneys' fees, the language "bear the expense of the investigations and defenses of all claims or demands or causes of action" could reasonably be interpreted to include attorneys' fees as part of the "expense of . . . defenses."

95028   Cheschi v. Boston Edison Co., 39 Mass. App. Ct. 133, 654 N.E.2d 48, *review denied*, 421 Mass. 1105, 656 N.E.2d 1258 (1995), *review denied*, 665 N.E.2d 1277 (1996)

III:	A107-1987, Art. 9, Para. 9.12
III:	A117-1987, Art. 14, Para. 14.12
III:	A201-1987, Art. 3, Para. 3.18.1
III:	A201-1987, Art. 10, Para. 10.1.4
III:	A401-1987, Art. 4, Para. 4.6.1

Contractor's injured employee brought a negligence action against owner. Owner filed a third-party indemnification action against contractor. The jury found that owner was not negligent. The trial court granted owner's motion for entry of judgment on its claim for indemnification seeking legal fees and costs. Among other issues on appeal, contractor argued that it was not liable to owner for attorneys' fees and costs under the indemnification agreement because owner failed to promptly notify contractor of worker's claim as the contract required. The appellate court reversed the judgment entered for owner.

The indemnity agreement contained in the Maintenance Services Agreement provided in pertinent part that:

Bechtel will indemnify Owner from and against liability to third parties imposed by law upon Owner for injury to or death of persons and for loss of or damage to property, caused by Bechtel's negligence in the performance of Services. Bechtel agrees to defend any claim or suit brought against Owner based upon any such injury, death, loss or damage arising out of such negligence, and shall pay all costs and expenses, including legal fees, in connection with such claim or suit, provided Owner gives Bechtel prompt notice of such claim or suit and provides such reasonable assistance in connection therewith as Bechtel may request.

The appellate court found that owner's notice to contractor two and one-half years after the negligence action was filed was not "prompt" as required by the indemnification agreement. The court reasoned that the use of the term "provided" should be construed as the parties' intention that prompt notification be a condition precedent to contractor's obligation to indemnify owner. The court concluded that owner's failure to give contractor prompt notice of worker's lawsuit relieved contractor of its obligation to reimburse owner its costs of defending the action. Furthermore, the court found that the contractor was not required to show prejudice as a result of the delayed notice where the agreement did not require proof of prejudice as a condition of its enforcement.

III: A401-1987, Art. 4, Para. 4.6.1

Contractor's injured employee brought a workers' compensation action against contractor and an action under the Illinois Structural Work Act against owner. Owner moved to amend its third-party action against contractor for unlimited contribution based on a boiler construction contract and on the court's decision in *Herington v. J.S. Alberici Construction Co.*, case digest number 94036. The trial court denied owner's motion, finding that the contract was unenforceable under the state's anti-indemnification statute. The owner then moved to amend its third-party complaint based on a purchase order. The trial court found that the purchase order did not violate the state statute and should be applied under *Herington*. Contractor brought this interlocutory appeal. The appellate court reversed the judgment of the trial court on this issue.

The purchase order provided that:

[E]xcept to the extent that any such injury or damage is due solely and directly to [owner's] negligence, * * * [contractor] shall pay [owner] for all loss which may result in any way from any act or omission of [contractor].

On interlocutory appeal, the Illinois Supreme Court reversed the judgment of the appellate court and held that the purchase order was an enforceable contract for contribution.

95027   Burns v. McDermott, Inc., 665 So. 2d 76 (La. Ct. App. 1995)

III: A107-1987, Art. 9, Para. 9.12
III: A117-1987, Art. 14, Para. 14.12
III: A201-1987, Art. 3, Para. 3.18.1
III: A201-1987, Art. 10, Para. 10.1.4
III: A401-1987, Art. 4, Para. 4.6.1

Contractor's injured employee brought an action for personal injury damages against owner. Owner filed a third-party indemnification action against contractor and its surety and moved for summary judgment. The district court denied owner's motion on the grounds that the indemnity provision violated the state anti-indemnity statute. The court also denied owner's alternative claim for defense costs and attorneys' fees on the grounds that the subcontract did not allow recovery of defense costs and attorneys' fees. The owner appealed. The appellate court reversed the district court's denial of attorneys' fees and defense costs.

The subcontract provided in pertinent part that:

Subcontractor shall be obligated to bear the expense of the investigations and defenses of all claims or demands or causes of action against which McDermott is indemnified herein, and all lawsuits and administrative proceedings arising therefrom, and to pay the full amounts of and bear all loss from any judgment or fine or penalty or other sanctions rendered against or imposed upon McDermott, its employees, officers or agents, when such lawsuits or proceedings are finally determined, it being stipulated that all obligations of indemnity assumed herein by either Subcontractor or McDermott

I: A107-1987, Art. 9, Para. 9.12.1
II: A117-1987, Art. 14, Para. 14.12
I: A117-1987, Art. 14, Para. 14.12.1
II: A201-1987, Art. 3, Para. 3.18.1
I: A201-1987, Art. 3, Para. 3.18.2
II: A201-1987, Art. 10, Para. 10.1.4
II: A401-1987, Art. 4, Para. 4.6.1
I: A401-1987, Art. 4, Para. 4.6.2

This action presents numerous issues arising from multi-party personal injury litigation generated by the rehabilitation of sewer lines. At issue on appeal was whether the contractor was required to indemnify the owner and engineer for attorneys' fees and costs. The appellate court reversed the decision of the trial court that the owner and engineer were not entitled to indemnity.

The owner-contractor agreement contained an indemnification provision in Paragraph 24.2 identical to the indemnification provision in Paragraph 3.18.2 of the American Institute of Architects General Conditions of the Contract for Construction, Document Number A201, 1987 edition. Paragraph 24.1 stated that:

24.1 The CONTRACTOR will indemnify and hold harmless the OWNER and the ENGINEER and their agents and employees from and against all claims, damages, losses and expenses including attorney's fees arising out of or resulting from the performance of the WORK, provided that any such claims, damage, loss or expense is attributable to bodily injury, sickness, disease or death, or to injury to or destruction of tangible property including the loss of use resulting therefrom; *and is caused in whole or in part by any negligent or willful act or omission of the CONTRACTOR, AND SUBCONTRACTOR*, anyone directly or indirectly employed by any of them or anyone for whose acts any of them may be liable.

(Italics in original.)

The appellate court found that where the claims clearly arose or resulted from "the performance of the WORK," and where the provision expressly included indemnification from "expenses including attorneys' fees arising out of or resulting from the performance of the WORK," the owner and engineer were entitled to indemnification.

95026 Braye v. Archer-Daniels-Midland Co., 276 Ill. App. 3d 1066, 213 Ill. Dec. 514, 659 N.E.2d 430 (1995), *appeal granted*, 166 Ill. 2d 536, 216 Ill. Dec. 1, 664 N.E.2d 638 (1996), *aff'd in part and rev'd in part, remanded*, 175 Ill. 2d 201, 222 Ill. Dec. 91, 676 N.E.2d 1295 (1997)

III: A107-1987, Art. 9, Para. 9.12
III: A117-1987, Art. 14, Para. 14.12
III: A201-1987, Art. 3, Para. 3.18.1
III: A201-1987, Art. 10, Para. 10.1.4

The appellate court dismissed contractor's action against owner under a public works contract. The court reasoned that contractor failed to state a cause of action because contractor was deliberately seeking to escape the bargained-for dispute resolution clause, and to avoid any challenge to engineer's decision by invoking a public policy argument. The contractor had alleged that owner misrepresented site conditions and furnished contractor with incomplete information and a defective design. The lower court entered judgment for contractor and added that contractor was free to litigate its action at law *de novo*, as there was a question as to whether the contract violated public policy by providing for resolution of the dispute by owner's engineer.

The owner/contractor agreement provided as follows:

To resolve all disputes and to prevent litigation the parties to this Contract authorize the Chief Engineer to decide all questions of any nature whatsoever arising out of, under, or in connection with, or in any way related to or on account of, this Contract (including claims in the nature of breach of Contract or fraud or misrepresentation before or subsequent to acceptance of the Contractor's Proposal and claims of a type which are barred by the provisions of this Contract) and his decision shall be conclusive, final and binding on the parties. His decision may be based on such assistance as he may find desirable. The effect of his decision shall not be impaired or waived by any negotiations or settlement offers in connection with the question decided . . . .

All such questions shall be submitted in writing by the Contractor to the Chief Engineer for his decision, together with all evidence and other pertinent information in regard to such questions, in order that a fair and impartial decision may be made. In any action against [owner] relating to any such question the Contractor must allege in his complaint and prove such submission, which shall be a condition precedent to any such action. No evidence or information shall be introduced or relied upon in such an action that has not been so presented to the Chief Engineer . . . .

Owner argued that contractor ignored the dispute resolution clause by couching its complaint so as to litigate the underlying dispute, *de novo*, for damages in an action at law. Furthermore, owner argued that the complaint did not even mention the actions and determination of the engineer, who, in accordance with the contract, issued a final and binding report.

The appellate court found that the purpose of the clause was to prevent the very type of litigation that the contractor initiated, namely, a *de novo* action at law. The clause clearly made submission of the issue to the engineer the basis upon which judicial review was to be conducted, and a condition precedent to any action at law. The court concluded that contractor had failed to state a cause of action because the complaint did not refer to the dispute resolution clause and the decision made by engineer under its authority.

95025 Bradford v. Kupper Assocs., 283 N.J. Super. 556, 662 A.2d 1004 (1995), *cert. denied*, 677 A.2d 759 (N.J. 1996).

II: A107-1987, Art. 9, Para. 9.12

contract between the parties. The Supreme Court of Virginia reversed the judgment of the trial court.

The owner and contractor entered into the American Institute of Architects Standard Form of Agreement Between Owner and Contractor, Document No. A111, 1978 edition, specifically Paragraphs 1.1 and 16.2, which incorporated the American Institute of Architects General Conditions of the Contract for Construction, 1976 edition, specifically Paragraphs 1.1.1, 7.9.1 and 12.1.1.

The supreme court found that, based on the court's review of the record, the change order had not been "signed by the Owner" as required by Paragraph 12.1.1, because the individuals signing it had no authority to bind the owner. The court reasoned that because the change order was not executed by the owner as required by Paragraph 12.1.1 of the General Conditions, it was not a "Contract Document" as defined in Paragraph 1.1 of the owner/contractor agreement and Paragraph 1.1.1 of the General Conditions. Therefore, contractor's claim for quantum meruit recovery for the work performed under the invalid change order was not a claim "relating to the Contract Documents." By the parties' agreement, claims not relating to the Contract Documents were not within the arbitrator's scope of authority. The court concluded that the arbitrator exceeded the scope of the authority granted by Paragraph 7.9.1 of the owner/contractor agreement by addressing whether contractor was entitled to payment for work that had not been performed in accordance with the contract documents.

95024 Yonkers Contracting Co. v. Port Auth. Trans-Hudson Corp., 208 A.D.2d 63, 621 N.Y.S.2d 642 (1995), *aff'd*, 87 N.Y.2d 927, 640 N.Y.S.2d 866, 663 N.E.2d 907 (1996), *reh'g denied*, 88 N.Y.2d 875, 645 N.Y.S. 2d 449, 668 N.E.2d 420 (1996)

III:	A107-1987, Art. 10, Para. 10.5	
III:	A107-1987, Art. 10, Para. 10.8	
III:	A117-1987, Art. 15, Para. 15.5	
III:	A117-1987, Art. 15, Para. 15.8	
III:	A201-1987, Art. 4, Para. 4.3.2	
III:	A201-1987, Art. 4, Para. 4.4.1	
III:	A201-1987, Art. 4, Para. 4.4.3	
III:	A201-1987, Art. 4, Para. 4.4.4	
III:	A201-1987, Art. 4, Para. 4.5.1	
III:	A401-1987, Art. 6, Para. 6.1	
III:	B141-1987, Art. 2, Para. 2.6.15	
III:	B141-1987, Art. 2, Para. 2.6.16	
III:	B141-1987, Art. 2, Para. 2.6.17	
III:	B141-1987, Art. 2, Para. 2.6.18	
III:	B141-1987, Art. 2, Para. 2.6.19	

I:	A111-1978, Art. 16, Para. 16.2
I:	A111-1987, Art. 1, Para. 1.1
I:	A111-1987, Art. 16, Para. 16.1
II:	A117-1979, Art. 17, Para. 17.2
II:	A117-1987, Art. 15, Para. 15.8
I:	A201-1976, Art. 1, Para. 1.1.1
I:	A201-1976, Art. 7, Para. 7.9.1
I:	A201-1976, Art. 12, Para. 12.1.1
I:	A201-1987, Art. 1, Para. 1.1.1
I:	A201-1987, Art. 4, Para. 4.5.1
I:	A201-1987, Art. 7, Para. 7.2.1
II:	A401-1978, Art. 13, Para. 13.1
II:	A401-1987, Art. 6, Para. 6.1
II:	B141-1977, Art. 9, Para. 9.1
II:	B141-1987, Art. 7, Para. 7.1

Contractor demanded arbitration of its claim that a change order increased the guaranteed maximum cost to build a new sanctuary and education building. Owner filed a motion for a declaratory judgment as to the amount due contractor under the "guaranteed maximum cost" contract, arguing that the change order claiming additional compensation was invalid because it had been executed by two trustees of the church who were not authorized to bind the owner to the change orders. In response to owner's action for a declaratory judgment, contractor moved to compel arbitration. The arbitrator found that although the change order was executed by individuals without the authority to bind the owner, the contractor could recover in quantum meruit. The owner requested that the trial court confirm the arbitrator's ruling that the change order was invalid, but vacate that portion of the arbitrator's decision holding that contractor could assert a request for quantum meruit relief. Owner contended that this ruling exceeded the arbitrator's powers because it was outside the scope of the matters submitted to him by the trial court's order compelling arbitration. The trial court granted the owner's request confirming in part and vacating in part the arbitrator's decision. Contractor filed an amended demand for arbitration, asserting claims based on breach of contract and quantum meruit. Contractor again moved to compel arbitration. The court granted contractor's motion and ordered a second arbitration proceeding. The contractor's quantum meruit claim was arbitrated, resulting in an award to contractor in full settlement of all claims submitted to arbitration. The trial court then entered a modified order in favor of contractor against the owner, and ruled that the arbitration clause in the contract was broad enough to encompass the issue of quantum meruit relief because the claim arose "out of, or relates to, the contract." Both owner and contractor appealed. The owner argued on appeal that the arbitrator exceeded his power in allowing recovery in quantum meruit when there was an express

III:	A401-1987, Art. 3, Para. 3.4.1
III:	A401-1987, Art. 4, Para. 4.1.5
III:	A401-1987, Art. 4, Para. 4.5.1
III:	A401-1987, Art. 7, Para. 7.2.1
III:	B141-1987, Art. 2, Para. 2.6.11
III:	B141-1987, Art. 2, Para. 2.6.19

Subcontractor brought an action against contractor to recover retainage and contractor counterclaimed. Contractor based its counterclaim on the fact that subcontractor did not perform its work as required by the subcontract, necessitating contractor to incur expenses in order to complete the work. Contractor then backcharged its costs against the retainage. The trial court granted contractor summary judgment and awarded damages. Subcontractor appealed.

The subcontract provided in pertinent part as follows:

[S]hould the Subcontractor, at any time . . . refuse to follow plans and specifications, or fail in any respect to prosecute the covenant on its part to be performed, the Contractor shall have the right . . . to terminate this contract in whole or in part. The Architect/Engineer and/or Owner's Representative shall be the judge of the acceptable work and settlement shall be made to this point on this basis. In that event, Contractor shall provide the necessary material, labor, etc. to complete the contract in whole or in part and charge the cost thereof to the Subcontractor crediting or debiting his account as the case may be when the work under this contract is fully completed and accepted. The Subcontractor expressly agrees to accept and to abide by the above clause in this connection and further agrees that . . . nothing herein shall affect the right of the Contractor to recover damages from the Subcontractor for delay or malperformance or nonperformance of this contract.

The appellate court found that because the subcontract designated architect as the judge of acceptable work, the architect's decision was final and binding absent evidence of fraud or gross mistake. The court found that subcontractor did not prove fraud or gross mistake in the architect's rejection of contractor's work. Moreover, the court rejected the subcontractor's contention that contractor's weekly inspections and approval of the work prior to making payment negated architect's rejection. The architect's judgment as to the substandard quality of subcontractor's work was, therefore, final and contractor was entitled to backcharge the subcontractor for the costs incurred in completing the work.

95023   Trustees of Asbury United Methodist Church v. Taylor & Parrish, Inc., 452 S.E.2d 847 (Va. 1995)

II:	A107-1978, Art. 13, Para. 13.2
II:	A107-1987, Art. 10, Para. 10.8
I:	A111-1978, Art. 1, Para. 1.1

On September 4, when subcontractor failed to show up to work, contractor informed subcontractor in writing that it was exercising its right to terminate the subcontract.

The subcontract provided in Article III as follows:

[T]he work called for in this contract shall be performed promptly as requested by the contractor. The subcontractor agrees to complete his work in sufficient time and in such a manner to enable the contractor to complete the work in its contract with the Owner no later than November 21, 1991.

The Agreement further provided in paragraph XV:

[I]n case the Sub-Contractor shall fail to correct, replace and/or re-execute faulty or defective work done and/or materials furnished under this contract, when and as required by the Contractor, or shall fail to complete or diligently proceed with this contract within the time herein provided for, the Contractor upon three days' written notice to the Sub-Contractor shall have the right to correct, replace and/or re-execute such faulty or defective work, or to take over this contract and complete same, and to charge the cost thereof to the Sub-Contractor, together with any liquidated damages caused by a delay in the performance of this contract.

The appellate court found that the two clauses of Article III were not inconsistent. The court's understanding of the plain language of both clauses of Article III, when read together, was that subcontractor agreed to complete its work at contractor's request, and to permit contractor to meet its contract requirements with the owner, no later than November 21, 1991, absent a request for earlier performance. The court found Article III to be unambiguous, and, for this reason, ignored the various interpretations of Article III which the parties suggested.

Moreover, the court found that the first clause of Article III, which gave the contractor the right to request that the subcontractor perform its work promptly notwithstanding the November 21 completion date, was in the nature of an acceleration clause. However, the court found from its review of the facts that what contractor was seeking was adequate assurance from the subcontractor that its work would be completed in a timely and satisfactory manner, not accelerated performance. Based on this finding, the court concluded that the subcontractor's erratic work schedule, the quality of its work, and the fact that its work was on the critical path, provided the contractor with just cause to enforce the termination provision of the subcontract.

95022 Top Line Constr. Co. v. J.W. Cook & Sons, 118 N.C. App. 429, 455 S.E.2d 463 (1995)

III:	A107-1987, Art. 10, Para. 10.5
III:	A107-1987, Art. 10, Para. 10.6
III:	A117-1987, Art. 15, Para. 15.5
III:	A117-1987, Art. 15, Para. 15.6
III:	A201-1987, Art. 4, Para. 4.2.6
III:	A201-1987, Art. 4, Para. 4.3.2

facilitate completion of the project, the owner and contractor entered into an Interim Agreement. Under the terms of this agreement owner paid Applications Nos. 15 and 16, the completion date was extended, and owner and contractor filed a joint stipulation to stay the arbitration until the project was substantially completed.

The district court found that the legal precedents established by *Constructora Bauza* were inapplicable where the construction contracts were the law between the parties.

Turning to the contract issues, the court found that the owner/contractor agreements included very specific language in Paragraphs 4.3.3, 7.6.2 and 9.4.2 dealing with the acceptance of work performed by the contractor and the legal consequences of making progress payments under the contract. Most important, the contract expressly provided in Paragraph 9.5.5 that neither certificate for progress payment nor the use or occupancy of the project by the owner constituted an acceptance of any work not in accordance with the contract. The court concluded that under the contract provisions the fact that the owner paid for work performed by contractor and certified by the architect did not preclude owner from presenting its claims for apparent defects.

A related case involving this contractor against a subcontractor for indemnification on the above claim was denied summary judgment because the contractor did not have an opportunity to fully litigate the issue of indemnity. The district court denied subcontractor's motion for summary judgment, finding that giving effect to *res judicata* would create an inequitable result. See *Taber Partners I v. Insurance Co. of N. Am.*, 875 F. Supp. 88 (D.P.R. 1995).

95021 Thompson v. Valley Corp., 3 Neb. App. 459, 528 N.W.2d 352 (1995)

III: A401-1987, Art. 4, Para. 4.1.1
III: A401-1987, Art. 7, Para. 7.2.1

Contractor appealed a lower court judgment that contractor had unilaterally terminated the subcontract without just cause. The lower court awarded subcontractor damages. The appellate court reversed the decision of the lower court because the subcontract expressly provided contractor with the right to request that subcontractor promptly and satisfactorily perform its work, and, if subcontractor failed to do so, to terminate the agreement.

The subcontractor commenced work on the project and continued to work in a sporadic fashion. As of August 12, 1991, the subcontractor's work was on the critical path. The subcontractor worked on August 22, 23, and 24 but failed to show up to work on August 26. The contractor's project manager called the subcontractor and informed him that he was not performing the work in a timely and satisfactory manner and that he had three days to complete the work and remedy the defects. If subcontractor failed to complete the work and remedy all deficiencies in the quality of the work, the contractor intended to exercise its right to take over the subcontract as provided for in paragraph XV of the subcontract. Although the contractor ostensibly gave subcontractor three days to complete its work, contractor allowed subcontractor to work on the project for an additional week.

95020   Taber Partners I v. Insurance Co. of N. Am., 875 F. Supp. 81 (D.P.R. 1995), *motion for new trial denied*, 917 F. Supp. 112 (D.P.R. 1996)

II:	A107-1978, Art. 15, Para. 15.3
II:	A107-1987, Art. 20, Para. 20.3
II:	A117-1979, Art. 19, Para. 19.3
II:	A117-1987, Art. 15, Para. 15.3
I:	A201-1976, Art. 4, Para. 4.3.3
I:	A201-1976, Art. 7, Para. 7.6.2
I:	A201-1976, Art. 9, Para. 9.4.2
I:	A201-1976, Art. 9, Para. 9.5.5
I:	A201-1976, Art. 9, Para. 9.8.1
I:	A201-1987, Art. 3, Para. 3.3.3
I:	A201-1987, Art. 9, Para. 9.4.2
I:	A201-1987, Art. 9, Para. 9.6.6
I:	A201-1987, Art. 9, Para. 9.8.2
I:	A201-1987, Art. 13, Para. 13.4.2

Owner brought an action against contractor for breach of three construction contracts and for damages resulting from delay and defective construction. Contractor moved for summary judgment on the grounds that (1) owner could not claim damages for defective construction where neither architect nor owner complained of the defects before payments were made; (2) where the Interim Agreement novated one of the contracts pursuant to *Constructora Bauza, infra,* the owner had accepted all work performed before the effective date of the Interim Agreement "as is"; and (3) pursuant to *Constructora Bauza, infra,* if contractor received over 90% of the contract price its work was "substantially completed." At issue before the district court was whether the Puerto Rico Supreme Court's decision in *Constructora Bauza v. Garcia Lopez,* 91 J.T.S. 99 (1991), mandated judgment for contractor. The district court denied contractor's motion.

The owner and contractor entered into three construction contracts, two of which, the Tower contract and the Specialty contract, were the American Institute of Architects Standard Form of Agreement Between Owner and Contractor, Document No. A101, which incorporated by reference the American Institute of Architects General Conditions of the Contract for Construction, Document No. A201, 1976 edition, specifically Paragraphs 4.3.3, 7.6.2, 9.4.2, 9.5.5 and 9.8.1. The contracts also included two sets of specially tailored conditions, specifications, and plans.

After owner refused to pay contractors Applications for Payment Nos. 15 and 16 on the grounds that contractor had failed to conduct its work in a workmanlike manner and failed to achieve timely substantial completion, contractor filed a demand for arbitration of the payment dispute and for a declaration that would allow it to suspend performance until owner paid Applications Nos. 15 and 16. To resolve these differences and to

permitted substantial compliance with the notice requirement in instances when strict compliance would have been extremely difficult.

95019 Nabholz Constr. Corp. v. Graham, 319 Ark. 396, 892 S.W.2d 456 (1995)

III:	A107-1987, Art. 9, Para. 9.12	
III:	A117-1987, Art. 14, Para. 14.12	
III:	A201-1987, Art. 3, Para. 3.18.1	
III:	A201-1987, Art. 10, Para. 10.1.4	
III:	A401-1987, Art. 4, Para. 4.6.1.	

Contractor appealed the trial court's failure to enforce agreements indemnifying contractor against damages for injuries to an employee of subcontractor. The jury found contractor solely at fault for injuries caused when employee fell through a hole in the floor cut and covered at the direction of contractor. The jury awarded damages against contractor and determined that subcontractors were not obligated to indemnify because contractor's fault established the defense of "acquiescence." The appellate court reversed and remanded.

The standard subcontract's indemnity clause provided:

Article X. In addition to the foregoing provisions, the parties also agree that Subcontractor shall:

. . . .

9.(b) Indemnify, hold harmless and defend Contractor, its agents and employees from any lawsuits, cause of action, claims, liabilities and damages, of any kind and nature, including, but not limited to, attorney's fees and costs arising out of the performance of this Contract whether attributable in whole or in part to any act, omission or negligence of Contractor, its agents or employees, and including, but not limited to, any and all lawsuits, causes of action, claims, liabilities and damages, as provided above which Contractor, its agents or employees may sustain by reason of any failure by Subcontractor to indemnify as provided herein, or any failure by Subcontractor to otherwise perform its obligations pursuant to this Contract, or by reason of the injury to perform its obligations pursuant to this Contract, or by reason of the injury to or death of any person or persons or the damage to, loss of use of or destruction of any property resulting from Work undertaken herein.

The appellate court concluded that the indemnity agreement was unequivocal in its stated intent to absolve contractor of its own liability. The court found that the phrase "attributable in whole or in part to any act, omission or negligence of Contractor," related back to the phrase "lawsuits, causes of action, claims, liabilities and damages." The court declined to void the indemnity provision as against public policy and deferred to the state legislature. Additionally, the court held that the trial court's jury instruction that acquiescence was a complete defense was erroneous. The court declined to expand a tort defense to a contract action.

The Subcontractor shall undertake and complete the Work under the direction and supervision of the Contractor, and to the entire satisfaction of the Contractor, the Owner and the Architect.

Paragraph 1C-6(e) of the Specifications provided:

The Architect will be the sole judge of conformity. No materials shall be installed except in accordance with the plans and specifications or the Architect's written amendments thereto.

Article 3-N of the General Conditions provided:

The Architect, the Owner and the Contractor each will have the authority to reject subcontractor's work which does not conform to the Contract Documents.

Other contract provisions and the specifications provided detailed descriptions of the subcontractor's work.

The appellate court upheld the district court's interpretation of the above-cited provisions to mean that, while subcontractor may choose its means and methods, its choices were subject to approval by the architect. The court rejected subcontractor's contention that architect's role was "advisory only," and determined that architect could, at its discretion, reject means and methods as inconsistent with the contract documents. The court added that the "advisory only" language was in contemplation of a dispute arising over interpretation of the plans and specifications, which was not an issue in this case. The court concluded that the architect acted within the scope of its authority as delegated by the subcontract.

Subcontractor argued that its proposed methods of erecting the trusses and bracing should not have been rejected by the architect because they satisfied industry standards. The appellate court disagreed, and stated that the architect's discretionary authority was not unbounded, but absent a showing by the subcontractor of bad faith, fraud, or palpable mistake equivalent to bad faith, architect's decision had to be accepted as final and valid.

Subcontractor also defended against the charge of late performance by contending that much of its delay was attributable to inclement weather. The district court ruled that the term "inclement weather," as provided for in the subcontract, was ambiguous, and allowed contractor to introduce parol evidence to show that performance would be excused only in cases of unusually severe weather. The court charged the jury to decide what interpretation was intended by the contracting parties, and subcontractor argued that ascertaining whether a writing is ambiguous is a matter of law, and that the district court erred in allowing the jury to decide. The appellate court disagreed, and found that reasonable people familiar with both the subcontract and the construction industry might well differ in their understanding of the term "inclement weather," which was supported by contractor's evidence of industry usage of the term as indefinite and imprecise. The appellate court found that it was properly left for a jury determination.

The appellate court also rejected subcontractor's argument that the jury should have been instructed on waiver because subcontractor did not provide sufficient evidence to warrant such an instruction. Subcontractor alleged that the contractor waived the provision of the subcontract that required written notice of damages and delay claims, but the appellate court found that the evidence demonstrated, at best, that contractor might have

Schedule B, of paragraph 53, of the subcontract which provided that "[s]ubcontractor shall be entitled to include as cost the cost of labor, materials, equipment, supplies and other resultant costs occasioned by such delays and changes notwithstanding any other provision contained in this agreement." The court relieved the tension that existed among the three contract provisions by virtue of the "notwithstanding" clause, which essentially overrides, in part, the two "no-damages-for-delay" provisions found elsewhere in the subcontract. The court rejected the contractor's assertion that Article 2.1 of the subcontract should apply. That provision stated that "in the event of any inconsistency between the terms and conditions" of the subcontract and the General Conditions "the more restrictive provision, as applied to the Subcontractor, shall govern." The court concluded that once the "notwithstanding" clause was applied, there was no inconsistency. Moreover, the court concluded that the district court should have construed the contract according to its unambiguous terms, and should have clearly instructed the jury that subcontractor had the right, under Paragraph 53, to recover any costs occasioned by delays in "the commencement, prosecution or completion of the work" that were not its own fault.

Subcontractor then sought to defend against the claim of late performance, and to establish its counterclaim, by introducing evidence that its proposed methods for erecting the trusses and for temporarily bracing the structure were adequate, and that the architect's directives to use alternative methods were unreasonable, unnecessary, and the cause of substantial delay. The district court ruled prior to trial that the architect's decisions as to the methods used were final and valid absent a showing of bad faith, fraud or palpable mistakes equivalent to bad faith. Furthermore, subcontractor could only present evidence on the architect's decision if the evidence allowed a reasonable jury to conclude that the claims of bad faith were correct. The testimony of subcontractor's expert was limited at trial. On appeal the subcontractor argued that the contract provisions, when read together, circumscribed the architect's control over the methods of construction and thereby limited the architect's authority to reject subcontractor's plans.

Article 3-A of the subcontract's General Provisions stated the following:

The Architect shall, on behalf of the Owner, periodically make on-site inspections of the work to check the quality and progress of the work and to monitor construction activities. Notwithstanding the foregoing, the Architect will not be responsible for, and will not have control or charge of construction means, methods, techniques, sequences or procedures or for safety precautions and programs in connection with the work and he will not be responsible for any subcontractor's failure to carry out the work in accordance with the Contract Documents.

Article 3-B of the General Conditions provided:

The architect shall be the interpreter of the plans and specifications. In the event of dispute, the Architect shall side with none of Owner, the Contractor or the subcontractor, and the Architect shall also render a decision as to the items to be included within the scope of the work, which decision is advisory only.

Other broad provisions in the subcontract reposed approval authority in the architect. Article 2.2 stated in part:

argued that the district court erred in refusing to allow subcontractor's expert to challenge contractor's evidence of damages. The appellate court reversed the judgment of the district court. The appellate court held that the subcontractor was deprived of a fair trial on its counterclaim.

The subcontract provided in Paragraph 53 as follows:

Should the Subcontractor be obstructed or delayed in the commencement, prosecution or completion of the work, without fault on his part, by action or inaction on the part of the Owner, Architect, Engineer or Contractor, or by changes in the work, the Subcontractor shall be entitled to include as cost the cost of labor, materials, equipment, supplies and other resultant costs occasioned by such delays and changes notwithstanding any other provision contained in this agreement.

Article 16-G of the General Conditions provided:

Should the subcontractor be obstructed or delayed in the commencement, prosecution or completion of the work, without fault on his part, . . . then he shall be entitled to an extension of time for a period equivalent to the time lost by reason of any or all of the causes aforesaid but no claim for extension of time on account of delay shall be allowable unless a claim in writing therefor is presented to the Contractor with reasonable diligence but in any event not later than within four (4) days after the commencement of such claimed delay. The mere presentation of such claim shall not establish the validity of the cause of delay or of the extension of time for completion. The subcontractor expressly agrees not to make, and hereby waives, any claim for damages, including those resulting from increased supervision, labor or material costs, on account of any delay, obstruction or hindrance for any cause whatsoever, including but not limited to the aforesaid causes, and agrees that the sole right and remedy therefor shall be an extension of time.

Article 3.4 of the subcontract provided:

All loss or damage arising from any of the Work through unforeseen or unusual obstructions, difficulties or delays which may be encountered in the prosecution of same or through the action of the elements shall be borne by the Subcontractor.

The trial judge explained to the jury that subcontractor's "claim for damages on account of delays allegedly caused by [contractor] and its subcontractors" was an "area of ambiguity" in the subcontract. The jury's attention was directed to Article 16-G of the General Conditions and Article 3.4 of the subcontract. The pertinent provisions were read to the jury. The judge noted subcontractor's contention that "these provisions of the subcontract have been negated by paragraph 53 of schedule B," and in turn the paragraph was read to the jury. The jury was instructed as follows:

Once again, it is your job to construe the subcontract in light of all the evidence, to ascertain what the parties intended with respect to [subcontractor's] ability to assert claims for damages on account of delay. Whatever understanding you reach you must then apply in evaluating [subcontractor's] delay claims.

The appellate court found that the fatal flaw in these instructions was that the subcontract, in fact, contained no ambiguity as to subcontractor's right to seek damages for delays caused by others. Subcontractor's counterclaim for damages was based on

95018   Morse/Diesel, Inc. v. Trinity Indus., Inc., 67 F.3d 435 (2d Cir. 1995)

III:	A107-1987, Art. 10, Para. 10.2
III:	A107-1987, Art. 10, Para. 10.3
III:	A107-1987, Art. 10, Para. 10.5
III:	A107-1987, Art. 10, Para. 10.6
III:	A107-1987, Art. 12, Para. 12.3
III:	A107-1987, Art. 14, Para. 14.3
III:	A117-1987, Art. 15, Para. 15.2
III:	A117-1987, Art. 15, Para. 15.3
III:	A117-1987, Art. 15, Para. 15.5
III:	A117-1987, Art. 17, Para. 17.3
III:	A117-1987, Art. 19, Para. 19.3
III:	A201-1987, Art. 4, Para. 4.2.2
III:	A201-1987, Art. 4, Para. 4.2.3
III:	A201-1987, Art. 4, Para. 4.2.6
III:	A201-1987, Art. 4, Para. 4.2.11
III:	A201-1987, Art. 4, Para. 4.2.12
III:	A201-1987, Art. 4, Para. 4.3.8
III:	A201-1987, Art. 6, Para. 6.2.3
III:	A201-1987, Art. 8, Para. 8.3
III:	A401-1987, Art. 3, Para. 3.3.1
III:	A401-1987, Art. 4, Para. 4.1.1
III:	A401-1987, Art. 4, Para. 4.1.5
III:	A401-1987, Art. 5, Para. 5.3
III:	A401-1987, Art. 9, Para. 9.3
III:	B141-1987, Art. 2, Para. 2.6.5
III:	B141-1987, Art. 2, Para. 2.6.6
III:	B141-1987, Art. 2, Para. 2.6.11
III:	B141-1987, Art. 2, Para. 2.6.15
III:	B141-1987, Art. 2, Para. 2.6.16

Contractor brought an action against structural steel subcontractor and its surety for damages arising from delayed performance of the subcontract. Subcontractor counterclaimed and alleged that its delay resulted from the architect's and structural engineer's demands regarding the installation of certain special steel trusses. Subcontractor also argued that inclement weather caused substantial delay. The district court entered judgment for contractor. Subcontractor and its surety appealed. On appeal, subcontractor

Subcontractor brought an action against contractor to recover additional costs resulting from unanticipated subsurface soil conditions. The district court had redacted Section 1.21(b)(3) of the instructions to bidders in the version of the contract that was introduced into evidence. The deleted language read: "nor is [the soil report] a part of the Contract Documents." The court also excised Section 1.21(c)(2), which stated that the owner, architect, and contractor "disclaim any responsibility for the accuracy . . . of the soils investigation [and] interpretation of that data." The court forbade owner and contractor to mention this language or to elicit it at trial. The jury returned a verdict for subcontractor on the ground that subcontractor reasonably relied on the subsurface information furnished in the preparation of its bid. The contractor appealed and the appellate court reversed the judgment of the district court. The court found that the subcontract provided for a price adjustment in only two circumstances, where the subcontractor encountered conditions at variance with those indicated in the subcontract or at variance with those ordinarily encountered, neither of which was present.

In addition to the instructions to bidders cited above, the subcontract contained a concealed conditions provision identical to Paragraph 12.2.1 of the American Institute of Architects General Conditions of the Contract for Construction, Document No. A201, 1976 edition.

The appellate court found that the subcontractor's sole theory of recovery was a breach of contract claim based on the first half of Paragraph 12.2.1, which permitted a price adjustment if conditions were "at variance with the conditions indicated by the Contract Documents." The court rejected this theory because it ignored the disclaimer language in the invitation to bidders which provided that "[t]he [soil] report is not a warranty of subsurface conditions, nor is it a part of the Contract Documents." The court found that, because the soil report was not a part of the contract documents, it could not form the basis of a claim that conditions were "at variance with the conditions indicated by the Contract Documents." Furthermore, subcontractor ignored the second half of Paragraph 12.2.1 which dealt with conditions "not ordinarily encountered."

The court rejected the subcontractor's argument that courts have held that the phrase, "conditions indicated by the Contract Documents," could embrace soil reports that were not part of the contract documents. The court found that the plain language of Section 1.21 of the invitation to bidders "disclaimed any responsibility" and excluded the soil report from the contract documents.

The court also rejected subcontractor's argument that Paragraph 12.2.1 would lack meaning if the disclaimers were given effect. The court found that Paragraph 12.2.1 would still allow for equitable adjustment based on conditions that were not "ordinarily encountered." It would also allow for equitable adjustment based on variances from any contract documents. The court stated that it was enforcing the disclaimers over Paragraph 12.2.1 because they specifically mentioned the soil report while the concealed conditions clause did not.

The court concluded that subcontractor risked the presence of underground water by not boring its own hole instead of relying on the soil report.

95016 Miller v. Two State Constr. Co., 118 N.C. App. 412, 455 S.E.2d 678 (1995)

    III: A107-1987, Art. 10, Para. 10.8
    III: A117-1987, Art. 15, Para. 15.8
    III: A201-1987, Art. 4, Para. 4.5.1
    I: A201-1987, Art. 4, Para. 4.5.7
    III: A401-1987, Art. 6, Para. 6.1
    I: A401-1987, Art. 6, Para. 6.4
    III: B141-1987, Art. 7, Para. 7.1
    I: B141-1987, Art. 7, Para. 7.4

Contractor appealed from an order staying arbitration of a dispute with subcontractor. The trial court determined that the mandatory arbitration provision was unconscionable and unenforceable both under the state constitution, and state statute, because it required waiver of the right to a jury trial. The trial court relied on North Carolina's constitutional guaranty of a right to jury trial and on N.C. Gen. Stat. § 22B-10. The appellate court reversed.

The arbitration clause in the subcontract provided:

All claims, disputes and other matters in questions arising out of, or relating to, this Subcontract or the breach thereof shall be decided by arbitration in accordance with the Construction Industry Arbitration Rules of the American Arbitration Association. This agreement to arbitrate shall be specifically enforceable under the prevailing arbitration law. The award rendered by the arbitrators shall be final, and judgment may be entered upon in accordance with applicable law in any court having jurisdiction thereof.

The appellate court noted the strong public policy in favor of arbitration. According to the court, arbitration did not cut off access to courts because arbitration awards required confirmation by courts. Thus, the court concluded that a mandatory arbitration agreement was not an unenforceable contract requiring waiver of a jury trial.

The court rejected subcontractor's argument that contractor waived arbitration by withholding payments, seizing subcontractor's property, barring subcontractor from the project, seeking to have subcontractor arrested for stealing, and delaying its demand for arbitration. According to the court, contractor's actions were not sufficient to establish prejudice in view of contractor's timely demand for arbitration prior to filing its answer in the instant action.

95017 Millgard Corp. v. McKee/Mays, 49 F.3d 1070 (5th Cir. 1995)

    II: A201-1987, Art. 4, Para. 4.3.6
    I: A201-1976, Art. 12, Para. 12.2.1

General Conditions of the Contract for Construction, Document No. A201, 1987 edition. Owner responded that Paragraph 4.5.1 provided an exception for "claims relating to aesthetic effect . . . ." The trial court denied contractor's motion to compel arbitration and contractor appealed. The Supreme Court of Arkansas affirmed the judgment of the trial court.

The supreme court held that the owner's complaint was based on a question concerning "aesthetic effect" where "aesthetic" was defined as "pertaining to a sense of the beautiful . . . ." Pursuant to the unambiguous language of Paragraph 4.5.1 the court found that owner's "aesthetic effect" claims were not arbitrable.

95015   McGraw v. S.D. Warren Co., 656 A.2d 1222 (Me. 1995)

III:	A107-1987, Art. 9, Para. 9.12
III:	A117-1987, Art. 14, Para. 14.12
III:	A201-1987, Art. 3, Para. 3.18.1
III:	A201-1987, Art. 10, Para. 10.1.4
III:	A401-1987, Art. 4, Para. 4.6.1.

Owner appealed from a judgment in favor of contractor on owner's claims for indemnification for contractor's worker's injuries from smoke stack emissions at a paper mill site. The trial court determined that the owner was negligent and the contractor was not negligent. Having interpreted the indemnification clause as excluding indemnification of owner's own negligence, the trial court entered judgment against owner. The appellate court affirmed.

The indemnity clause of the owner/contractor agreement provided the following:

(a) The contractor is responsible for and shall continuously maintain protection of all the work and property in the vicinity of the work from damage or loss from any cause arising in connection with the contract and any work performed thereunder. [Contractor] shall indemnify and hold owner harmless for any claims, suits, losses or expenses including attorneys' fees suffered by [owner] arising out of injury to any person including [owner's] or [contractor's] employees or damage to any property, including [owner's] property if the injury or damage is caused in whole or in part by [contractor] or any of [contractor's] subcontractors, material men or anyone directly or indirectly employed or otherwise controlled by any of them while engaged in the performance of any work hereunder.

Relying on a rule of interpretation requiring strict construction against extending indemnification to include recovery by the indemnitee for its own negligence, the court interpreted the indemnity clause to exclude owner's own negligence. According to the court, no clear and unequivocal language reflected a mutual intention to indemnify owner against its own negligence. The court also concluded that ample evidence supported the trial court's determination of liability.

Contractor appealed from summary judgment in favor of subcontractor and sub-subcontractor on its claim for indemnification for worker's injuries. The appellate court voided the indemnification clause of the subcontract where it provided for indemnification of contractor's own sole negligence in violation of state statute.

The indemnity clause of the subcontract provided as follows:

(a) General Liability: Sub-Contractor shall indemnify and save General Contractor, its officers or agents harmless from and against any and all loss, damage, injury, liability, and claims thereof for injuries to or death of persons, and all loss of or damage to property of others, resulting directly or indirectly from Sub-Contractor's performance of this contract.

The applicable state statute was Utah Code Ann. § 13-8-1.

The appellate court interpreted the broad language of the indemnity clause, "any and all" in conjunction with "liability," as clearly encompassing liability arising out of the contractor's sole negligence. The court rejected contractor's argument that "resulting directly or indirectly from Sub-Contractor's performance of this contract" limited indemnification to those claims arising out of subcontractor's own negligence. The court relied on the Utah Supreme Court's interpretation of a similar indemnity clause in *Freund v. Utah Power & Light Co.*, 793 P.2d 362 (Utah 1990).

The court granted summary judgment against contractor and found that the indemnity clause was void as against public policy. The court noted that it would have been a "simple matter" for the parties to limit the indemnification provision so that it did not run contrary to statute by excepting those situations in which the contractor's sole negligence resulted in contractor's liability. The sub-subcontractor claims were also dismissed because they were derivative of subcontractor's obligation to indemnify.

95014 May Constr. Co. v. Benton Sch. Dist. No. 8, 320 Ark. 147, 895 S.W.2d 521 (1995)

III:	A107-1987, Art. 10, Para. 10.8	
III:	A117-1987, Art. 15, Para. 15.8	
I:	A201-1987, Art. 5, Para. 4.5.1	
III:	A401-1987, Art. 6, Para. 6.1	
III:	B141-1987, Art. 7, Para. 7.1	

Owner brought an action against contractor which alleged, in part, that contractor failed to comply with the plans and specifications. Owner claimed that applying a substituted curing material caused the finish on the concrete floors of a school building to experience gross and unsightly scuff marks from student traffic to the extent that the appearance of the floors became totally unacceptable. Contractor moved to stay the proceedings and compel arbitration pursuant to Paragraph 4.5.1 of the American Institute of Architects

Owner appealed judgment in favor of contractor on its indemnification cross-claim in a personal injury action. Owner engaged contractor to replace tub wraps in its housing units. One of owner's tenants brought a personal injury action based on injuries received from inhaling the adhesive used to apply the tub wrap in her unit. Although most of the claims were against both owner and contractor, one claim solely against the owner alleged that it failed to properly design the unit to provide adequate ventilation. Tenant settled with owner. However, the settlement agreement did not specify which claims were discharged. The trial court entered judgment against owner on its indemnity claim, because the court concluded that the indemnity clause was void pursuant to state statute to the extent it sought to indemnify owner for its sole negligence where owner failed to prove which amounts of the settlement pertained to claims other the one based on its sole negligence. The appellate court affirmed.

The indemnity clause in the owner/contractor agreement provided as follows:

CONTRACTOR agrees that the performance under this contract is at CONTRACTOR'S sole risk and that the CONTRACTOR shall indemnify the [owner], its commissioners, agents, officers and employees, against, and hold them harmless from, any and all liability for damages, costs, losses and expenses resulting from, arising out of, or in any way connected with this contract, or from CONTRACTOR'S failure to perform fully hereunder, and CONTRACTOR further agrees to defend the [owner], its commissioners, agents, officers and employees, against all suits, actions or proceedings brought by any third party against them for which CONTRACTOR would be liable hereunder.

The applicable state statute was Or. Rev. Stat. § 30.140(2).

The appellate court concluded that the indemnity clause fell within the proscription of the state statute because the language, "any and all liability . . . arising out of, or in any way connected with this contract," had or could have had the effect of indemnifying owner for its sole negligence. Accordingly, the court voided the clause to the extent its application required indemnification for owner's sole negligence.

Although owner argued on appeal that the settlement pertained only to claims on which contractor could have been held at least partially liable, it made no effort to show at trial which claims were settled at what cost. Since the owner did not prove that the settlement did not pertain to tenant's claim solely against owner for negligent design of ventilation, the court concluded that owner failed to prove entitlement to indemnification from contractor.

95013   Healey v. J.B. Sheet Metal, Inc., 892 P.2d 1047 (Utah Ct. App. 1995)

        III: A107-1987, Art. 9, Para. 9.12
        III: A117-1987, Art. 14, Para. 14.12
        III: A201-1987, Art. 3, Para. 3.18.1
        III: A201-1987, Art. 10, Para. 10.1.4
        III: A401-1987, Art. 4, Para. 4.6.1.

Contractor sought indemnification from subcontractor, based on a contract provision which required subcontractor to indemnify contractor and to obtain insurance. The court concluded, based on a state statute requiring every employer to obtain workers' compensation insurance, that allowing a contractor to shift its workers' compensation expenses through indemnification would contravene public policy that requires employers to bear the burden of their employees' work-related injuries. Accordingly, the indemnification provision was unenforceable because contractor had failed to carry its own workers' compensation insurance.

95011 Frank v. MSI Constr. Managers, Inc., 208 Mich. App. 340, 527 N.W.2d 79 (1995), *appeal denied*, 451 Mich. 851, 546 N.W.2d 254 (1996)

> I: A107-1978, Art. 10, Para. 10.11
> I: A107-1987, Art. 9, Para. 9.12
> I: A117-1979, Art. 14, Para. 14.11
> I: A117-1987, Art. 14, Para. 14.12
> I: A201-1976, Art. 4, Para. 4.18.1
> I: A201-1987, Art. 3, Para. 3.18.1
> I: A201-1987, Art. 10, Para. 10.1.4
> I: A401-1978, Art. 11, Para. 11.11.1
> I: A401-1987, Art. 4, Para. 4.6.1.

Subcontractor, who supplied steel beams that were involved in the worker's accident, appealed judgment in favor of contractor requiring subcontractor to fully indemnify contractor for contractor's liability to injured worker. The appellate court vacated the judgment in part, instructing the trial court to require indemnification only to the extent of subcontractor's negligence but not for contractor's negligence.

The parties entered into the American Institute of Architects Standard Form of Agreement Between Contractor and Subcontractor, Document No. A401, 1978 edition, which provided for indemnification in Paragraph 11.11.1.

The appellate court construed that portion that read "to the extent caused in whole or in part by any negligent act or omission of the subcontractor" as limiting indemnification to the extent of subcontractor's negligence.

95012 Hays v. Centennial Floors, Inc., 133 Or. App. 689, 893 P.2d 564 (1995)

> III: A107-1987, Art. 9, Para. 9.12
> III: A117-1987, Art. 14, Para. 14.12
> III: A201-1987, Art. 3, Para. 3.18.1
> III: A201-1987, Art. 10, Para. 10.1.4
> III: A401-1987, Art. 4, Para. 4.6.1.

contract with him shall then be limited to an action at law initiated in either Allegheny County or the site where the project is to be constructed, at the election of the contractor. In any event, regardless of any election, Contractor may at any time demand that Subcontractor be limited to the type of action to which the Contractor is limited, whether legal or by arbitration, if the contractor avers that another party is liable over to him for claims by this Subcontractor. Contractor may initiate an action against the Subcontractor in arbitration, law, or equity, at its option, and Subcontractor agrees that the various courts located in Allegheny County, Pennsylvania, or the site where the project is located, at the election of the Contractor, shall have jurisdiction of both the person and matter alleged in any complaint, and any arbitration shall be within the Pittsburgh district, unless Contractor desires to file elsewhere. The Subcontractor shall carry on the work and maintain the progress scheduled during any arbitration proceedings, unless otherwise agreed by Subcontractor and Contractor in writing.

The appellate court interpreted this clause to require that subcontractor submit its claim to arbitration unless it notified and received contractor's approval to pursue the claim in court. Subcontractor did not choose the option of filing a lawsuit in court. Rather, it notified contractor of its intent to file a demand for arbitration, and according to the terms of the contract, contractor could not object to this choice. Only when subcontractor sought to file a suit in court could contractor overrule its decision and force subcontractor into arbitration. The court concluded that the trial court was correct in declining to enjoin the arbitration because contractor was clearly not entitled to an injunction.

95010 D.W. Hutt Consultants, Inc. v. Construction Maintenance Sys., Inc., 526 N.W.2d 62 (Minn. Ct. App. 1995)

III: A107-1987, Art. 9, Para. 9.12
III: A117-1987, Art. 14, Para. 14.12
III: A201-1987, Art. 3, Para. 3.18.1
III: A201-1987, Art. 10, Para. 10.1.4
III: A401-1987, Art. 4, Para. 4.6.1.

Subcontractor appealed summary judgment ordering it to indemnify contractor for workers' compensation paid to injured worker. The appellate court reversed.

The injured worker was originally hired by the sub-subcontractor to install vinyl siding. After a payment dispute, sub-subcontractor quit the job, but the contractor agreed to keep employee on the job. Employee fell from a ladder, injuring his knee and ankle. Contractor had no workers' compensation insurance, so employee recovered benefits from a state workers' compensation fund and initiated a workers' compensation proceeding against contractor, subcontractor, and sub-subcontractor. The worker's compensation judge found that the injured worker was contractor's employee at the time of his injury. The judge ordered contractor to reimburse the state fund and pay employee's attorneys' fees.

III: A201-1987, Art. 4, Para. 4.5.1
III: A201-1987, Art. 4, Para. 4.5.2
III: A201-1987, Art. 4, Para. 4.5.3
III: A201-1987, Art. 4, Para. 4.5.4
III: A201-1987, Art. 4, Para. 4.5.4.1
III: A201-1987, Art. 4, Para. 4.5.4.2
III: A201-1987, Art. 4, Para. 4.5.5
III: A201-1987, Art. 4, Para. 4.5.6
III: A201-1987, Art. 4, Para. 4.5.7
III: A401-1987, Art. 6, Para. 6.1
III: A401-1987, Art. 6, Para. 6.2
III: A401-1987, Art. 6, Para. 6.3
III: A401-1987, Art. 6, Para. 6.4
III: A401-1987, Art. 6, Para. 6.5
III: B141-1987, Art. 7, Para. 7.1
III: B141-1987, Art. 7, Para. 7.2
III: B141-1987, Art. 7, Para. 7.3
III: B141-1987, Art. 7, Para. 7.4

Contractor appealed denial of its motion for a preliminary injunction enjoining arbitration proceedings initiated by subcontractor. The trial court declined to enjoin the arbitration, and the appellate court affirmed. The appellate court held that the plain language of the arbitration clause indicated that subcontractor could submit its claim to arbitration.

The arbitration clause provided:

30. In case of any dispute or disagreement under this agreement, or with respect to any other work performed on the job site, it is agreed that such dispute shall be submitted to the American Arbitration Association under the rules then pertaining to contractors or construction disputes. No law suit or any other action at law may be substituted without first complying with the terms of this arbitration provision.

Should any dispute or controversy whatsoever arise between the Contractor and Subcontractor, . . . then Subcontractor shall follow all of the provisions of the contract documents with respect to conditions precedent to the making of claims and shall give twenty (20) days written notice to Contractor of Subcontractor's intent to resort to legal action; in which case Contractor, by mailing a notice within said twenty (20) day period, may elect to require the said Subcontractor or parties who contract with him to proceed pursuant to the American Arbitration Association Construction Industry Rules, in which case the judgment and award rendered by the arbitrators may be entered in any court having jurisdiction thereof; and should Contractor not elect to proceed through American Arbitration Rules, the Subcontractor and parties who

The supreme court found that, although the contract plainly required that contractor verify the measurements and dimensions shown on the drawings before commencing construction, the contractor failed to do so. The evidence revealed that contractor did not discover any discrepancies until after it had begun to execute the work. The court concluded that, had contractor complied with the contract, the county would have had the opportunity to make the necessary revisions before contractor commenced its work.

The fourth issue on appeal was whether the county wrongfully terminated the contract. Contractor and its surety claimed that it was entitled to substantial time extensions because of the post-tensioning design errors, and that it had not failed to comply with the applicable contractual deadlines and, therefore, was not in default at the time of county's termination. The county asserted that, as a matter of law, the county was entitled to terminate because contractor had failed to perform the work as required by the contract. The owner/contractor agreement provided as follows:

a. It is hereby understood and mutually agreed by and between the Contractor and the Owner that the date of beginning, the rate of progress, and the time for completion of the work to be done hereunder are essential conditions of the Contract. The Contractor agrees that the work shall be started promptly upon receipt of any communication authorizing the Contractor to proceed and shall be prosecuted regularly, diligently, and uninterruptedly at a rate of progress that will ensure full completion thereof in the shortest length of time consistent with good workmanship.

b. It is further agreed that time is of the essence of each and every portion of this Contract and of the Specifications wherein a definite and certain length of time is fixed for the performance of any act whatsoever.

c. It is further agreed that where an additional time is allowed for the performance of any act by the Contractor according to the new time limit fixed by such extension shall be of the essence of this Contract.

The supreme court found that the plain and unambiguous contract language, including Change Order No. 4, required contractor to prosecute the work "regularly, diligently, and uninterruptedly" and to complete the bridge by the date set forth in Change Order No. 4. The court found that contractor failed to complete the bridge because of its belief that the county was required to provide the easement, and that without the easement, the bridge could not be constructed in accordance with the contract documents. Based on its previous finding that contractor was required to obtain the easement, the court held that, as a matter of law, the county was justified in terminating the contract because contractor failed to meet the contractual requirement of constructing the bridge in a diligent and timely manner.

95009   DiLucente Corp. v. Pennsylvania Roofing Co., 440 Pa. Super. 450, 655 A.2d 1035 (1995), *appeal denied*, 666 A.2d 1056, 1995 Pa. LEXIS 797 (Oct. 2, 1995)

    III: A107-1987, Art. 10, Para. 10.8
    III: A117-1987, Art. 15, Para. 15.8

The supreme court held that the language of the above provisions did not require the county to obtain the easement. The court read Paragraph 8 as clearly requiring the county to only provide the lands shown on the contract drawings. The parties agreed that the land needed to post-tension the bridge was not shown on the drawings. In addition, Paragraph 9 clearly required the contractor to obtain the necessary easement at its expense where the additional land needed to perform the post-tensioning was not an area "available on the [construction] site or right-of-way."

The second issue on appeal was whether the owner's approval of shop drawings proposing an alternate method to post-tension the bridge relieved the contractor of its contractual obligation to build the bridge in compliance with the contract documents. After reviewing the shop drawings the engineer affixed a stamp which contained the following language:

> Review of this document is for conformance with the design concept of the project only. Contractor is responsible for confirming field dimensions, for information that pertains solely to the fabrication processes or to techniques of construction, and for coordination of the work of all trades. This review does not relieve the contractor from complying with all requirements of the contract documents.

The county's employees reviewed the drawings and affixed a stamp on the drawings which stated, "Accepted as noted" and was signed by a county employee. The owner/contractor agreement provided the following:

> The Engineer shall pass upon the shop drawings with reasonable promptness. Checking and/or approval of shop drawings will be general, for conformance with the design concept of the Project and compliance with the information given in the Contract Documents, and will not include quantities, detailed dimensions, nor adjustments of dimensions to actual field conditions. Approval shall not be construed as permitting any departure from contract requirements . . . nor as relieving the Contractor of the responsibility for any error in details, dimensions or otherwise that may exist.

The supreme court found that the contract documents clearly stated that contractor remained responsible for any errors in the shop drawings. The court found that the uncontroverted evidence revealed that the shop drawings were defective. Applying the plain language in the contract, the supreme court held that the county's approval of the shop drawing did not relieve contractor of its obligation to properly construct the bridge.

The third issue on appeal was whether contractor was entitled to recover damages for alleged design errors after failing to verify dimensions as required by the contract. The owner/contractor agreement provided as follows:

> A. The Contractor shall carry out the Work in accordance with the Drawings and Specifications. The measurements and dimensions shown on these drawings shall be verified at the site by the Contractor. The Contractor shall be responsible for all dimensions and coordinated execution of the Work. The Contractor shall verify that bridge components will fit as specified, or notify the Engineer sufficiently in advance if components do not fit so that modifications can be made without holding up the work . . . . Where there are discrepancies in the contract documents [the Contractor shall] notify the Engineer before proceeding with the Work.

III:	A201-1987, Art. 14, Para. 14.2.2
III:	A201-1987, Art. 14, Para. 14.2.3
III:	A201-1987, Art. 14, Para. 14.2.4
III:	B141-1987, Art. 2, Para. 2.6.12

Contractor brought an action against county for damages it incurred resulting from county's wrongful termination of a contract to construct a bridge and for defective design of the bridge. County counterclaimed for breach of contract and breach of certain express and implied warranties. County filed a third-party action against contractor's surety and against the engineer. The jury returned a verdict for contractor and contractor's surety and a verdict against the engineer. The trial court granted county's motion to set aside the verdict, and the court set aside the verdict against the engineer as well. Contractor and its surety appealed. The Supreme Court of Virginia affirmed.

Contractor was unable to provide the means and methods necessary to post-tension the bridge without obtaining an easement from a third-party property owner. As a result of contractor's failure, the county and contractor executed Change Order No. 4, which required the county to pay contractor an additional sum in return for contractor's agreement to complete the bridge by a date certain. The change order provided that the additional payment would constitute "full compensation" to complete all remaining work on the bridge, including minor revisions. Several months later, contractor informed the county that it would not complete construction of the bridge unless the county agreed to pay an additional sum and provide the easement for the post-tension construction process. The county refused and sent the contractor a notice of intent to terminate the contract, which it subsequently terminated.

The first issue on appeal was whether the contract required the county or the contractor to provide the easement. The owner/contractor agreement provided as follows:

8. The Owner shall provide the lands shown on the Drawings upon which the work under the Contract is to be performed and to be used for rights of way and for access. In case all of the lands, rights-of-way or easements have not been obtained as herein contemplated before construction begins, the Contractor shall begin his work on such lands and rights-of-way as the Owner may have previously acquired. If by reason of tardy acquisition of all of the lands, rights-of-way or easements, the Contractor is unduly delayed in his prosecution of the work, as determined by the Engineer, then the Contractor shall be entitled to make claim and act as stipulated hereinafter for extension of time and other provisions of these Contract Documents.

9. Should the Contractor require additional land for temporary construction facilities and for storage of materials and equipment other than the areas available on the site or right-of-way, or as otherwise furnished by the Owner, he shall provide such other lands and access thereto entirely at his own expense and without liability to the Owner. The Contractor shall not enter upon private property for any purpose without written permission.

its duty to indemnify contractor. The court narrowed subcontractor's performance obligation under the indemnity clause, so the insurance obligation became equally limited. The contract, as modified, extends the subcontractor's indemnity and insurance obligations only to those damages attributable to subcontractor's negligence; thus, contractor was not entitled to damages.

95008   D.C. McClain, Inc. v. Arlington County, 249 Va. 131, 452 S.E.2d 659 (1995)

	III:	A107-1987, Art. 8, Para. 8.2
	III:	A107-1987, Art. 9, Para. 9.1
	III:	A107-1987, Art. 9, Para. 9.4
	III:	A107-1987, Art. 9, Para. 9.5
	III:	A107-1987, Art. 9, Para. 9.6
	III:	A107-1987, Art. 10, Para. 10.7
	III:	A107-1987, Art. 14, Para. 14.1
	III:	A107-1987, Art. 14, Para. 14.3
	III:	A107-1987, Art. 20, Para. 20.2
	III:	A117-1987, Art. 13, Para. 13.2
	III:	A117-1987, Art. 14, Para. 14.1
	III:	A117-1987, Art. 14, Para. 14.4
	III:	A117-1987, Art. 14, Para. 14.5
	III:	A117-1987, Art. 14, Para. 14.6
	III:	A117-1987, Art. 15, Para. 15.7
	III:	A117-1987, Art. 19, Para. 19.1
	III:	A117-1987, Art. 19, Para. 19.3
	III:	A117-1987, Art. 25, Para. 25.2
	III:	A201-1987, Art. 2, Para. 2.2.2
	III:	A201-1987, Art. 2, Para. 2.2.3
	III:	A201-1987, Art. 3, Para. 3.2.1
	III:	A201-1987, Art. 3, Para. 3.2.2
	III:	A201-1987, Art. 3, Para. 3.2.3
	III:	A201-1987, Art. 3, Para. 3.3.1
	III:	A201-1987, Art. 3, Para. 3.5.1
	III:	A201-1987, Art. 3, Para. 3.7.1
	III:	A201-1987, Art. 3, Para. 3.7.3
	III:	A201-1987, Art. 4, Para. 4.2.7
	III:	A201-1987, Art. 8, Para. 8.2
	III:	A201-1987, Art. 8, Para. 8.3
	III:	A201-1987, Art. 14, Para. 14.2.1

recoverable versus nonrecoverable fees, the court concluded that the jury verdict awarding zero damages for attorneys' fees was not in error.

95007   Cosimini v. Atkinson-Kiewit Joint Venture, 877 F. Supp. 68 (D.R.I. 1995)

> III: A107-1987, Art. 9, Para. 9.12
> III: A117-1987, Art. 14, Para. 14.12
> III: A201-1987, Art. 3, Para. 3.18.1
> III: A201-1987, Art. 10, Para. 10.1.4
> III: A401-1987, Art. 4, Para. 4.6.1.

Subcontractor's employee brought a negligence action against contractor after collecting workers' compensation from subcontractor. Based upon a Rhode Island statute, the district court modified an indemnity provision of the subcontract by voiding as against public policy that portion purporting to obligate the subcontractor to pay for the contractor's own negligence.

The indemnity clause in the subcontract provided in pertinent part as follows:

[1] Subcontractor shall indemnify contractor against any claim, loss, damage, expense, or liability arising out of acts or omissions of Subcontractor in any way connected with the performance of this Subcontract unless due solely to Contractor's negligence. . . .

[2] Subcontractor shall, at his own expense, maintain in effect at all times during the performance hereof with insurers and under forms of policies satisfactory to Contractor: [workers' compensation and employer's liability insurance of 1 million dollars naming the Contractor as an additional insured, comprehensive general and automobile liability insurance of 1 million dollars naming the Contractor as an additional insured, and hull and machinery and protection and indemnity insurance of 2 million dollars].

Such insurance shall cover performance of the above indemnity obligation. . . .

On appeal, subcontractor argued, based on R.I. Gen. Laws § 6–34–1, that the indemnity clause was void as against public policy, and subcontractor was not required to indemnify contractor. Alternatively, contractor argued that even though the statute precluded indemnification for its own negligence, the state law did not preclude indemnification for that portion of liability attributable to subcontractor's negligence. The district court interpreted the indemnity provision as covering all damages recovered against contractor unless contractor was found solely responsible. The clause was judicially modified to comply with the state statute which requires that a contractor cannot indemnify itself through its subcontractor for its own negligence.

Contractor also argued that since subcontractor was contractually required to procure insurance, then subcontractor's policy should cover damages attributable to contractor's negligence. The court rejected this argument, stating that without express language to the contrary, subcontractor did not intend to incur a duty to procure insurance beyond

found that the contract contained an unambiguous pay-when-paid provision which provided in pertinent part that "the receipt of such payments by the [Contractor] being a condition precedent to payments to the subcontractor." The final payment provisions of the contract also clearly conditioned payment to subcontractor upon the payment by the owners to contractor.

Next, subcontractor argued that even if the pay-when-paid clause were enforced it should be interpreted as postponing payment for a reasonable amount of time, not indefinitely. The court found that the contract contained no language limiting the condition precedent to any "reasonable time."

The court found it unnecessary to decide whether the failure of a contractor to inform a subcontractor about a lack of financing before entering into a subcontract results in a breach of contract. The court relied on the trial court's determination that subcontractor had knowledge of the lack of financing and, therefore, had no cause of action with respect to this issue.

95006 Citadel Corp. v. All-South Subcontractors, Inc., 217 Ga. App. 736, 458 S.E.2d 711 (1995), *cert. denied*, 1995 Ga. LEXIS 1082 (Oct. 2, 1995)

II: A107-1987, Art. 9, Para. 9.12
II: A117-1987, Art. 14, Para. 14.12
II: A201-1987, Art. 3, Para. 3.18.1
II: A201-1987, Art. 10, Para. 10.1.4
II: A401-1987, Art. 4, Para. 4.6.1.

Contractor appealed jury's failure to award attorneys' fees, incurred in defending a claim for damages resulting from defective roofing. Contractor sought to enforce the indemnity clause of the roofing subcontract related to attorneys' fees. At trial, no evidence was presented to the jury which apportioned the attorneys' fees between recoverable expenses from defending the roofing damages claim and the nonrecoverable expenses from enforcing the indemnity agreement. The trial court entered judgment on the jury's special verdict, finding that contractor was entitled to zero damages from its indemnification claim against subcontractor. The appellate court affirmed.

The indemnity clause in the subcontract provided:

[Subcontractor] shall indemnify, hold harmless and defend [contractor] against all claims, damages, losses and expenses, including attorney fees, arising out of [subcontractor's] Work under [the] Subcontract. . . .

The appellate court found that the contractor was required to prove attorneys' fees "with sufficient particularity to permit the [jury] to distinguish between time and expenses attributable to [recoverable fees for the roofing damages counterclaim] and time and expenses attributable to [nonrecoverable fees incurred in enforcing the indemnity agreement.]" Because no evidence was presented from which the jury could determine what portion of the total amount of attorney time and expenses were attributable to

The trial court had determined that a reading of subparagraphs b and c together, required contractor to indemnify engineer "by insurance, and having failed to do that, it must provide the relief itself," and granted summary judgment to engineer on the issue of indemnification. The appellate court found, however, that by the very terms of the clause, contractor agreed to indemnify the owner, not the engineer. Moreover, the clause was sufficiently ambiguous to permit a reading that contractor was agreeing to indemnify the owner only for contractor's own negligence in carrying out its contractual construction duties. The court refused to construe the clause as requiring contractor to indemnify engineer against losses resulting from engineer's own conduct because that was neither expressed in unequivocal terms, nor was it reasonably implied, even when subparagraphs b and c were read together.

The court then found that contractor also agreed under subparagraph c to name the owner "and Engineer as additional insured" under contractor's general liability policy. Contractor failed to have engineer named as an additional insured under its policy, and engineer was therefore entitled to recover its loss sustained as a result of contractor's failure to do so. However, after reviewing the record, the court concluded that engineer suffered no loss and awarded no damages.

95005 Christman Co. v. Anthony S. Brown Dev. Co., 210 Mich. App. 416, 533 N.W.2d 838 (1995), *appeal denied*, 450 Mich. 1015, 549 N.W.2d 562 (1996)

III:	A201-1987, Art. 9, Para. 9.6.2	
III:	A401-1987, Art. 4, Para. 4.7.1	
III:	A401-1987, Art. 11, Para. 11.3	
III:	A401-1987, Art. 11, Para. 11.8.1	
III:	A401-1987, Art. 12, Para. 12.1	

Construction manager brought an action against owner for payment for work performed based on owner's assurance that financing for the project was forthcoming. Construction manager's suit alleged intentional or negligent misrepresentation, deceit, breach of contract, and breach of a third-party beneficiary contract by the owner, and sought foreclosure of liens and a guarantee of payment. The claim seeking foreclosure of the liens was made on behalf of both contractor and numerous subcontractors. Construction manager settled with owner, and, as part of the settlement, all subcontractors, with the exception of the defendant/cross-plaintiff, agreed to accept a pro-rata portion of the installment payments made by owner over time, dependent upon when the contractor received them. The subcontractor cross-claimed against contractor and owner seeking immediate payment. The trial court entered summary judgment for owner and contractor, finding that the subcontract clearly provided that payments to subcontractor would not be made until contractor was paid for the work by the owner. Subcontractor appealed. The appellate court affirmed the judgment of the trial court.

On appeal, subcontractor claimed that the payment provisions of the subcontract were ambiguous and, therefore, had to be construed against contractor. The appellate court

in connection with the work. Furthermore, contractor assumed sole responsibility for the construction means, methods and techniques, and for the "acts and omissions of its employees." It also agreed to "cause its employees, agent and subcontractor to cease the performance of the work at the direction of the Engineer." Engineer's site representative was present when the accident occurred and acknowledged that he knew that the unshored trench could have been dangerous. Approximately one week before the accident, the engineer noted that the trench was unstable because water had pooled in the bottom and the walls caved or slid onto the trench floor.

Paragraph 15 of the owner/contractor agreement contained the following pertinent indemnity clauses:

b. Subject to the provisions of Section 14(d)(2) hereof, [Contractor] agrees to indemnify and hold [Owner] harmless from any and all responsibility or damages, either of personal injury or property or to the Work, arising out of the construction of the Work and against any judgments obtained against [Owner] with respect thereto and [Contractor] agrees to provide a defense, at its cost, for [Owner] in any action filed against it with respect thereto.

c. Prior to commencement of the Work, [Contractor] shall submit the required insurance certificates to Engineer and [Owner's] attorney for review and transmittal to [Owner]. All such certifications shall name [Owner] and Engineer as additional insureds, and shall provide that [Contractor's] insurance carrier shall give [Owner] at least thirty (30) days written notice prior to any change or cancellation of coverage.

The appellate court found no New Jersey precedent on the issue of whether an engineer, contractually obligated to supervise a construction site on behalf of the owner, owed a duty to job-site workers to protect them from injuries resulting from unsafe conditions. However, in other jurisdictions the court found a split of authority as to whether an engineer or architect owed such a duty. In the case law of other jurisdictions generally, the inquiries focused on the extent to which the professional assumed a supervisory role under relevant provisions of the contract. In particular, in *Hanna v. Huer, Johns, Neel, Rivers & Webb*, 233 Kan. 206, 662 P.2d 243 (1983) (see case digest number 83020), the court observed that "we agree with plaintiffs' contentions that if [the architect] had actual knowledge of unsafe practices they should have taken some action." The *Hanna* court reasoned that "as a professional, an architect cannot stand idly by with actual knowledge of unsafe safety practices on the job site and take no steps to advise or warn the owner or contractor."

The court applied this reasoning to the estate's action and concluded that engineer owned a duty to "take some reasonable action to prevent injury" to workers exposed to the trench. The court noted that the provisions of the owner/contractor agreement did not specifically place the responsibility for the safety of the workers upon engineer. However, the court found that the absence of such a provision only meant that the engineer needed to exercise reasonable care to take some action when unique circumstances present at the job site demanded such action. Relying on *Hanna*, the court found that fairness and policy dictated imposition of a duty upon the engineer because, as a professional, he should not "stand idly by with actual knowledge of unsafe practices on the job site and take no steps" to prevent injury to workers at risk.

II:	A201-1987, Art. 4, Para. 4.2.2
II:	A201-1987, Art. 4, Para. 4.2.3
II:	A201-1987, Art. 4, Para. 4.2.6
II:	A201-1987, Art. 10, Para. 10.1
II:	A201-1987, Art. 10, Para. 10.2
III:	A201-1987, Art. 11, Para. 11.1
III:	A401-1987, Art. 4, Para. 4.6.1
II:	B141-1987, Art. 2, Para. 2.6.5
II:	B141-1987, Art. 2, Para. 2.6.6
II:	B141-1987, Art. 2, Para. 2.6.11
III:	B141-1987, Art. 9, Para. 9.4

An employee of subcontractor was crushed to death when a trench collapsed at a sewer installation site. The decedent's estate brought a wrongful death action against contractor, engineer and owner. Engineer cross-claimed against contractor for indemnity and contractor brought a third-party action against subcontractor. The estate settled with contractor and subcontractor. The trial court granted engineer summary judgment, ruling that the engineer's duty was defined and limited by the contract terms under which contractor, not engineer, had the sole responsibility to make safety inspections and to provide the necessary safeguards to protect workers from dangerous conditions at the site. Even though the engineer may have had actual knowledge of the dangerous nature of the trench, the court also granted summary judgment to engineer on its indemnity action against contractor. The estate and contractor appealed, and the appellate court reversed the judgment of the lower court.

The owner and contractor entered into a facility agreement which provided that the sewer facilities were to be constructed by contractor in accordance with the plans prepared by engineer. Under the agreement, engineer would have a full-time representative at the site to ensure that the contractor's work was performed in accordance with the plans, specifications and contract documents. Engineer's supervisory role at the site was defined in the agreement, including its right to demand improvement in "the contractor's work or rate of progress." However, the agreement also provided the following:

> [N]either compliance with such order nor failure of [the engineer] to issue such orders shall relieve the Contractor from his obligation to secure the degree of safety . . . required by the contract. The Contractor alone shall be responsible for the safety, adequacy and efficiency of his plant, equipment and methods.

Engineer reserved the right, under the agreement, to inspect contractor's work and had the authority to reject it when it did not comply with the facility documents or plans and specifications. The documents also incorporated by reference specifications of the New Jersey Construction Safety Code, and regulations promulgated under OHSA. However, the agreement also provided that the engineer "shall not have control" over the construction means, methods, techniques, or "safety precautions" used by contractor

Furthermore, the court rejected worker's assertions that the contract created a duty of care extending from contractor to the employees of the subcontractor. The court found that the contractor's retention of the authority to monitor and coordinate activities of subcontractors and the contractor's retention of control over safety policies and procedures did not rise to the level of active participation, as required by *Cafferkey*, necessary to impose a duty of care on the contractor regarding the subcontractor's employees.

With respect to worker's argument that the contractor gave "directives" to the worker, the court found that contractor's actions also did not demonstrate active participation, but rather confirmed contractor's general supervisory role in the project and its general concern for site safety.

The court held that, for purposes of establishing liability to an injured employee of an independent subcontractor, the phrase "actively participated" meant that the contractor directed the activity which resulted in the injury and/or gave or denied permission for the critical acts that led to the employee's injury, rather than merely exercising a general supervisory role over the project.

95004   Carvalho v. Toll Bros. & Developers, 278 N.J. Super. 451, 651 A.2d 492 (App. Div. 1995), *cert. granted,* 658 A.2d 726 (N.J. 1995); *aff'd and remanded*, 143 N.J. 565, 675 A.2d 209 (1996)

II:	A107-1987, Art. 9, Para. 9.1	
II:	A107-1987, Art. 9, Para. 9.3	
II:	A107-1987, Art. 9, Para. 9.7	
III:	A107-1987, Art. 9, Para. 9.12	
II:	A107-1987, Art. 10, Para. 10.2	
II:	A107-1987, Art. 10, Para. 10.3	
II:	A107-1987, Art. 10, Para. 10.6	
II:	A107-1987, Art. 16, Para. 16.1	
III:	A107-1987, Art. 17, Para. 17.1	
II:	A117-1987, Art. 14, Para. 14.1	
II:	A117-1987, Art. 14, Para. 14.3	
II:	A117-1987, Art. 14, Para. 14.7	
III:	A117-1987, Art. 14, Para. 14.12	
II:	A117-1987, Art. 15, Para. 15.2	
II:	A117-1987, Art. 15, Para. 15.3	
II:	A117-1987, Art. 15, Para. 15.6	
II:	A117-1987, Art. 21, Para. 21.1	
III:	A117-1987, Art. 22, Para. 22.1	
II:	A201-1987, Art. 3, Para. 3.3	
III:	A201-1987, Art. 3, Para. 3.18.1	

encouraging bad faith participation in alternative dispute resolution to avoid mandatory arbitration. According to the court, the apparent intent of the clause, read as a whole, was to employ some type of alternative dispute resolution before resorting to litigation. The court concluded that reading the provision as meaning arbitration was a default resolution method when the parties are unable to agree to another method did not create an absurd result.

95003   Bond v. Howard Corp., 72 Ohio St. 3d 332, 650 N.E.2d 416 (1995)

> III: A107-1987, Art. 16, Para. 16.1
> III: A117-1987, Art. 21, Para. 21.1
> III: A201-1987, Art. 10, Para. 10.1
> III: A201-1987, Art. 10, Para. 10.2
> III: A401-1987, Art. 4, Para. 4.3.1

Subcontractor's injured employee brought a negligence action against contractor and subcontractor and an intentional tort action against subcontractor. The trial court granted contractor and subcontractor summary judgment. The appellate court affirmed the judgment of the trial court. The Supreme Court of Ohio affirmed the judgment of the appellate court.

The owner/contractor agreement required contractor to comply with and enforce any applicable safety laws, rules or regulations. The subcontract required subcontractor to obtain permission and special instructions from contractor prior to beginning work in any area on the job site. The subcontract further provided that contractor had the right to remove any equipment and personnel that created an unsafe condition at the site.

On appeal the injured worker argued that ample evidence existed for the court to find that the contractor had retained sufficient control over the site and had "actually participated" in the subcontractor's work by making daily inspections of the site and, on one occasion, by giving "directives" to the injured worker. On another occasion the contractor required the subcontractor to repair a scaffolding that had been improperly erected by subcontractor. Finally, the contractor had admitted that it was responsible for providing guarding and fall protection for the opening through which worker fell.

To determine whether the contractor owed a duty to protect worker from injuries, the court examined prior decisions where it discussed the duties and responsibilities of a contractor, including *Cafferkey v. Turner Constr. Co.*, 21 Ohio St. 3d 110, 488 N.E.2d 189 (1986) (see case digest number 86007). The court found that a mere concern for safety was not enough to establish a contractor's active participation in subcontractor's work under *Cafferkey*. The court concluded that the lower courts had properly held that contractor was entitled to summary judgment because it neither gave nor denied permission for the critical acts that led to workers injuries, and because the critical acts were performed by another of subcontractor's employees.

III: A201-1987, Art. 4, Para. 4.5.4
III: A201-1987, Art. 4, Para. 4.5.4.1
III: A201-1987, Art. 4, Para. 4.5.4.2
III: A201-1987, Art. 4, Para. 4.5.5
III: A201-1987, Art. 4, Para. 4.5.6
III: A201-1987, Art. 4, Para. 4.5.7
III: A401-1987, Art. 6, Para. 6.1
III: A401-1987, Art. 6, Para. 6.2
III: A401-1987, Art. 6, Para. 6.3
III: A401-1987, Art. 6, Para. 6.4
III: A401-1987, Art. 6, Para. 6.5
III: B141-1987, Art. 7, Para. 7.1
III: B141-1987, Art. 7, Para. 7.2
III: B141-1987, Art. 7, Para. 7.3
III: B141-1987, Art. 7, Para. 7.4

Contractor appealed the denial of its motion to compel arbitration on a completion dispute over a new chemical plant. The trial court concluded that, pursuant to the alternative dispute resolution clause, arbitration was not mandatory unless there was no timely agreement to an alternative dispute resolution method. Accordingly, arbitration was not required because the parties had agreed to try mediation. The appellate court affirmed the judgment of the trial court.

The owner/contractor agreement provided in pertinent part as follows:

In the event that there is any claim, dispute or other matter, arising out of or related to this Contract . . . or from the breach or alleged breach thereof, the parties shall initially cooperate in good faith to resolve the same between executives of the parties who do not have direct responsibility for administration of this contract, and will explore whether techniques such as mediation, mini-trials, mock trial or other techniques of alternative dispute resolution might be useful in resolving the matter in question. If the parties cannot agree within 10 days on a different method of resolving the matter, the matter shall be submitted by the parties to and be decided by binding arbitration . . . . The demand for arbitration shall be made within a reasonable time after the time period stated above for the parties to agree on an alternate means of resolving the matter has expired . . . .

The appellate court construed the clause, "if the parties cannot agree within 10 days on a different method of resolving the matter," to constitute a condition precedent to mandatory arbitration. The condition was satisfied because the parties submitted their dispute to mediation, notwithstanding its unsuccessful conclusion.

The court rejected contractor's argument that the clause should be read as a covenant rather than as a condition because it would otherwise impose the "absurd result" of

Contractor claimed that it was not timely notified of sub-subcontractor's claim and admitted that it did not provide written notice of the claim to owner within the 14-day period as required by the contract. Contractor argued that owner's attendance at project meetings and engineer's input as to the problems encountered by sub-subcontractor constituted notice to the owner. After review of the record, the appellate court concluded that no claim was made and owner had no actual knowledge of sub-subcontractor's concerns.

Addressing the issues of agency and waiver of notice, the court found that the owner had made no written waiver of the notice requirement nor did the contractor offer proof of specific conduct by the owner evidencing an intent to waive the contract provisions. The agreement explicitly denied the authority of the architect and its engineering consultant to act as owner's agent. The owner/contractor agreement deleted from the AIA standard form contract the phrase that the architect "will be the Owner's representative." In addition, the owner/architect agreement expressly provided that notice by third parties to the architect would not be deemed notice to the owner. The court concluded that where the owner did not waive the notice requirement, or designate the architect or engineer as its agent with authority to waive the notice requirement, the contractor was required to comply with the notice requirements in the contract.

Contractor next argued that the provisions of the contract that required contractor to give notice of claims and enter into the dispute resolution process were void pursuant to a Washington state statute which makes unenforceable any contract provision waiving a contractor's right to recover damages for delay. However, the owner/contractor agreement did not "waive, release, or extinguish" any rights to delay damages. In addition, the contractor admitted that it failed to follow the contractual dispute resolution process it had followed for numerous other claims. The court rejected all of contractor's excuses for its failure and found that the dispute resolution procedures in the contract were clearly mandatory and contractor had waived the sub-subcontractor's claim by failing to follow those procedures. Furthermore, the court found that contractor had explicitly waived the sub-subcontractor's claim by failing to identify the claim in its affidavit and by accepting final payment pursuant to the terms of the owner/contractor agreement.

Addressing whether the claim limitation period set forth in the supplemental general conditions of the owner/contractor agreement precluded contractor's claim, the court ruled that the contractor did not bring suit in a timely manner after the date of substantial completion.

95002   Belmont Constructors, Inc. v. Lyondell Petrochemical Co., 896 S.W.2d 352 (Tex. Ct. App. 1995)

III:	A107-1987, Art. 10, Para. 10.8
III:	A117-1987, Art. 15, Para. 15.8
III:	A201-1987, Art. 4, Para. 4.5.1
III:	A201-1987, Art. 4, Para. 4.5.2
III:	A201-1987, Art. 4, Para. 4.5.3

subcontractor and sub-subcontractor appealed. The appellate court affirmed the judgment of the trial court.

The contractor was contractually required (1) to give the owner prompt and detailed written notice of any claim 14 days after events gave rise to the claim; (2) to enter into structured dispute resolution procedures; and (3) to mediate any remaining disputes before a lawsuit could be commenced. These requirements could not be waived by the owner except by an explicit written waiver. Failure to provide the written notification was an absolute waiver of any claims. Acceptance of final payment also constituted waiver of all unidentified claims. As a condition to receiving final payment the contractor was required to certify to the owner that it had paid in full all known claims for which the owner might in any way be held responsible. Two days before making this certification, the contractor received a copy of a letter written by the sub-subcontractor to the subcontractor indicating that the sub-subcontractor anticipated making a claim for equitable adjustment. The contractor did not amend its certification to include the claim. Contractor then sent a copy of the sub-subcontractor's letter to the owner, stating in the transmittal letter that it was not notified of the claim prior to its certification. Contractor then received and accepted final payment.

The owner/contractor agreement included General and Supplemental Conditions. Certain provisions were identical to the American Institute of Architects General Conditions of the Contract for Construction, Document No. A201, 1987 edition, Paragraphs 4.2.1, 4.3.5 and 9.10.4. The supplemental conditions required the contractor to notify the owner and architect within 7 days of any proposed change in the schedule and provided further that:

> [A]ll claims for additional cost must be made according to Paragraph 4.4, or they will be waived . . . .
>
> . . . .
>
> [T]he Contractor shall give written notice to the Owner and the Architect of all claims within fourteen days of the event giving rise to them . . . .
>
> . . . .
>
> [A]ny claim . . . for damages, additional payment for any reason, or extension of time, whether under the Contract or otherwise, shall be conclusively deemed to have been waived by the Contractor unless a timely written claim therefor is made pursuant to and in strict accordance with the applicable provisions of the Contract; or, if (and only if) no such provision is applicable, unless such claim is set forth in detail in writing and received by the Owner within 7 calendar days after the facts . . . .

The supplemental conditions also required that contractor bring suit within 120 days after the date of substantial completion.

The owner/architect agreement contained a provision identical to Paragraph 2.6.16 of the American Institute of Architects Standard Form of Agreement Between Owner and Architect, Document No. B141, 1987 edition. Paragraph 7.3.4 of the supplemental conditions authorized the architect to determine the reasonable value of a change ordered by the owner through a formal contract change. It did not authorize approval of changes or claims.

95001 Absher Constr. Co. v. Kent Sch. Dist. No. 415, 77 Wash. App. 137, 890 P.2d 1071 (1995), *modified*, 917 P.2d 1086, 1996 Wash. App. LEXIS 158 (May 3, 1996)

II:	A107-1987, Art. 10, Para. 10.1
III:	A107-1987, Art. 10, Para. 10.5
II:	A107-1987, Art. 13, Para. 13.1
III:	A107-1987, Art. 13, Para. 13.2
III:	A107-1987, Art. 14, Para. 14.3
II:	A107-1987, Art. 15, Para. 15.4
II:	A107-1987, Art. 15, Para. 15.5
II:	A117-1987, Art. 15, Para. 15.1
III:	A117-1987, Art. 15, Para. 15.5
II:	A117-1987, Art. 18, Para. 18.1
III:	A117-1987, Art. 18, Para. 18.2
III:	A117-1987, Art. 19, Para. 19.3
II:	A117-1987, Art. 20, Para. 20.4
II:	A117-1987, Art. 20, Para. 20.5
I:	A201-1987, Art. 4, Para. 4.2.1
III:	A201-1987, Art. 4, Para. 4.2.8
I:	A201-1987, Art. 4, Para. 4.2.12
III:	A201-1987, Art. 4, Para. 4.3.3
I:	A201-1987, Art. 4, Para. 4.3.5
III:	A201-1987, Art. 4, Para. 4.3.7
III:	A201-1987, Art. 4, Para. 4.3.8
III:	A201-1987, Art. 7, Para. 7.2.1
III:	A201-1987, Art. 7, Para. 7.3.6
II:	A201-1987, Art. 9, Para. 9.10.2
II:	A201-1987, Art. 9, Para. 9.10.4
III:	B141-1987, Art. 2, Para. 2.6.2
III:	B141-1987, Art. 2, Para. 2.6.4
III:	B141-1987, Art. 2, Para. 2.6.13
I:	B141-1987, Art. 2, Para. 2.6.16

Sub-subcontractor filed a lien against the statutory retainage and payment bond. Contractor, subcontractor and sub-subcontractor filed a breach of contract action against owner for failure to pay sub-subcontractor's equitable adjustment claim. The trial court entered summary judgment for owner and awarded owner attorneys' fees. The contractor,

Claims for extra work will be allowed only where written authorization has been given prior to execution of such extra work.

The appellate court found that where the change order expressly provided that contractor would pay the subcontractor for the extra work without requiring the owner to first pay the contractor for the work, contractor had waived the condition precedent in the subcontract's pay-when-paid provision.

a clear arbitration clause. Furthermore, the architect's claims for services which it performed pursuant to the letter agreement were also subject to arbitration because the letter agreement clearly incorporated "all terms and conditions of the existing Phase I contract," which included the arbitration clause. The court concluded that the arbitrators did not exceed their authority when they considered the claims for services that architects had performed under the Phase I agreement and the letter agreement.

However, the architect's remaining claims were based upon unsigned proposed agreements, which the court found expressly incorporated neither the Phase I agreement nor its arbitration clause. The court concluded that the unsigned proposed agreements did not "arise out of or relate to" the signed Phase I agreement, as was required by Paragraph 7.1, and were therefore not arbitrable.

94050   Valley Steel Constr., Inc. v. Addison Fabricators, Inc., 658 So. 2d 352 (Ala. 1994)

III:	A107-1987, Art. 4, Para. 4.1
III:	A107-1987, Art. 5, Para. 5.1
III:	A117-1987, Art. 9, Para. 9.1
III:	A117-1987, Art. 10, Para. 10.1
III:	A201-1987, Art. 9, Para. 9.6
III:	A201-1987, Art. 9, Para. 9.10
III:	A401-1987, Art. 11, Para. 11.3
III:	A401-1987, Art. 12, Para. 12.1

Subcontractor brought a breach of contract action against contractor. The trial court entered judgment for subcontractor, finding that the contractor, by issuing the change order, authorized the extra work performed by the subcontractor and expressly agreed to pay subcontractor for the extra work even though contractor knew that the owner objected to the additional charges. The contractor appealed. On appeal the contractor argued that (a) it did not owe subcontractor for the additional work because it was not, in fact, extra work, but rather was work that subcontractor contracted to perform; (b) there was no consideration to support the change order; and (c) because owner paid contractor only the original contract price, under the terms of the pay-when-paid clause contractor had no duty to pay subcontractor.

The subcontract provided that:

It shall be an express condition precedent to the obligation of the contractor to pay the Subcontractor that the Owner make payments to the contractor covering the Subcontractor's portion of the work . . . Final payment to the Subcontractor will be made upon receipt [of] final payment from the Owner, it being expressly understood and agreed that receipt by the Contractor of final payments covering the Subcontractor's portion of the work shall be an express condition precedent to final payment to the Subcontractor by the Contractor.

II:	A401-1987, Art. 6, Para. 6.1	
II:	A401-1987, Art. 6, Para. 6.2	
II:	A401-1987, Art. 6, Para. 6.3	
II:	A401-1987, Art. 6, Para. 6.4	
II:	A401-1987, Art. 6, Para. 6.5	
I:	B141-1987, Art. 7, Para. 7.1	
I:	B141-1987, Art. 7, Para. 7.2	
I:	B141-1987, Art. 7, Para. 7.3	
I:	B141-1987, Art. 7, Para. 7.4	

Architect filed liens against owner's property and subsequently filed an action to foreclose the liens as well as for damages for breach of contract based on owner's failure to pay architect for services rendered. The parties then filed a joint stipulation to arbitrate pursuant to Paragraph 7.1 of the owner/architect agreement. The lower court ordered the parties to "submit all appropriate claims" to arbitration. Before the arbitration began, owner filed an answer and counterclaim against architect, claiming that architect had breached the Phase I agreement and that architect had been negligent in administering the Phase I agreement. In its answer to the counterclaim, architect argued that owner's claims were subject to arbitration. At the beginning of the arbitration hearing, owner contended, among other issues, that the arbitrators did not have authority to consider architect's claims that had been made on the basis of the unsigned proposed Phase II agreement. The parties proceeded to arbitration. The arbitrators entered an award which, in pertinent part, awarded architect damages and required owner to pay all administrative fees, expenses and costs and to reimburse the architect for fees and costs paid to the American Arbitration Association. Owner moved to vacate or modify the award. The lower court denied owner's motion, confirmed the award, and entered judgment against owner. The Supreme Court of Wyoming affirmed in part and reversed in part.

The parties had entered into the American Institute of Architects Standard Form of Agreement Between Owner and Architect, Document No. B141, 1987 edition, which provided for arbitration of disputes pursuant to Paragraph 7.1. This agreement was revised by a letter agreement providing for additional services and incorporating "all terms and conditions of the existing [Phase I] contract." The architect then sent the owner a letter containing revisions for Phase I which were never executed by the owner. The architect also prepared an identical AIA agreement for Phase II which was not executed by the owner. The architect had performed services which were beyond the scope of the Phase I agreement.

Among numerous other claims made by the owner, the supreme court first addressed the issue of whether the lower court erred when it held that the arbitrators had authority to consider all of architect's claims. Owner argued that the scope of the arbitration proceeding was limited to the Phase I agreement.

The court found that the architect's claims for services which it performed under the Phase I agreement were subject to arbitration because the Phase I agreement contained

Subcontractor agrees to indemnify and hold harmless the owner and/or the contractor and their agents and employees, from and against any and all demands, claims, suits, causes of action, damages, losses, penalties, and/or expenses, including attorneys fees, arising out of or resulting from subcontractor's performance of the work required by the subcontract, regardless of whether such demand, claim, suit, cause of action, loss, penalty, or expense is incident to or arises out of conditions or omissions permitted or acts performed by an indemnitee unless said demand, claim suit, cause of action, damage, loss, penalty or expense is caused by the sole negligence of the indemnitee.

In response to subcontractor's argument that contractor was required to show that some negligence by subcontractor caused worker's injuries, the appellate court found that subcontractor's performance of the subcontract was a "cause in fact" of worker's injury because (1) the worker was on the job site as subcontractor's agent, performing duties required of subcontractor under the subcontract; and (2) but for this performance of work under the subcontract, worker would not have been injured. The court concluded that worker's injuries arose out of the performance of the subcontract.

In response to subcontractor's argument that contractor should not recover for losses caused by its own negligence, the court found that by the express language of the subcontract, subcontractor agreed to indemnify contractor from all losses arising out of its performance of the subcontract "regardless of whether such . . . loss is incident to or arises out of conditions or omissions permitted or acts performed by an indemnitee." This language clearly contemplated indemnification even if the loss resulted from contractor's negligence.

Moreover, the subcontract language provided the indemnity will apply "unless said . . . loss is caused by the sole negligence of the indemnitee." Considered as a whole, the court found that the subcontract unequivocally and clearly required subcontractor to indemnify contractor for losses attributable to its own negligence, unless contractor's negligence was the sole cause of the loss.

94049   Wild West Trading Co. v. gbs & h Architects, Landscape Architects, Planners, Inc., 881 P.2d 1070 (Wyo. 1994)

II:	A107-1987, Art. 10, Para. 10.8
II:	A117-1987, Art. 15, Para. 15.8
II:	A201-1987, Art. 4, Para. 4.5.1
II:	A201-1987, Art. 4, Para. 4.5.2
II:	A201-1987, Art. 4, Para. 4.5.3
II:	A201-1987, Art. 4, Para. 4.5.4
II:	A201-1987, Art. 4, Para. 4.5.4.1
II:	A201-1987, Art. 4, Para. 4.5.4.2
II:	A201-1987, Art. 4, Para. 4.5.5
II:	A201-1987, Art. 4, Para. 4.5.6
II:	A201-1987, Art. 4, Para. 4.5.7

II: A117-1987, Art. 14, Para. 14.12
II: A201-1987, Art. 3, Para. 3.18.1
II: A201-1987, Art. 10, Para. 10.1.4
II: A401-1987, Art. 4, Para. 4.6.1

Contractor appealed from dismissal of its motion for summary judgment for contractual indemnity from subcontractor. The appellate court reversed the decision of the lower court.

The subcontract contained two indemnity provisions. Article X broadly required subcontractor to indemnify contractor for:

> [A]ny claim, injury damage . . . arising out of, resulting from or occurring in connection with the performance of the Work by the Subcontractor or its agents or employees. . . .

Attachment G provided that:

> The subcontractor shall not indemnify the contractor against the contractor's breach of warranty or duty.

The appellate court found that the subcontract, as changed by Attachment G, unambiguously provided that subcontractor was under no duty to indemnify contractor for contractor's breach of duty. However, no such breach of duty was established by the subcontractor. Therefore, without the establishment of a breach of duty by the contractor, the broad provision of Article X, by which subcontractor agreed to indemnify contractor against any claim arising out of subcontractor's employees' actions, entitled contractor to be indemnified by subcontractor.

94048 Wallace v. Sherwood Constr. Co., 877 P.2d 632 (Okla. Ct. App. 1994)

III: A107-1987, Art. 9, Para. 9.12
III: A117-1987, Art. 14, Para. 14.12
III: A201-1987, Art. 3, Para. 3.18.1
III: A201-1987, Art. 10, Para. 10.1.4
III: A401-1987, Art. 4, Para. 4.6.1

In an action by subcontractor's injured employee for damages, the jury determined that both worker and contractor were equally negligent. Contractor brought a third party action for indemnity against subcontractor. The subcontractor moved for summary judgment on the grounds that the subcontractor was not liable to contractor because contractor failed to show that subcontractor's negligence caused worker's injuries. The trial court entered judgment for contractor on the indemnification action and subcontractor appealed. The appellate court affirmed the judgment of the trial court.

The subcontract provided in pertinent part that:

The following language from the General Conditions of the owner/contractor agreement further defined the engineer's status, duties and responsibilities during construction:

> Neither the Engineer's authority to act under this paragraph nor any decision made by him in good faith either to exercise or not exercise such authority shall give rise to any duty or responsibility of the Engineer to the Contractor, any Subcontractor, any of their agents or employees or any other person performing any of the Work[.]

The appellate court found that no provision of the owner/engineer agreement gave engineer, expressly or impliedly, any control over the manner in which the contractor, the subcontractors or their respective employees did their work. Moreover, the quoted provisions of the contracts specifically excluded any duty or responsibility on the part of the engineer. The court concluded that where no provision of the owner/engineer agreement gave engineer the kind of control that would impose on it a duty to keep the premises safe for an employee of a subcontractor, engineer was entitled to summary judgment.

94046 Tomlinson v. Dartmoor Constr. Corp., 268 Ill. App. 3d 677, 206 Ill. Dec. 371, 645 N.E.2d 376 (1994)

Ill: A107-1987, Art. 9, Para. 9.12
Ill: A117-1987, Art. 14, Para. 14.12
Ill: A201-1987, Art. 3, Para. 3.18.1
Ill: A201-1987, Art. 10, Para. 10.1.4
Ill: A401-1987, Art. 4, Para. 4.6.1

Owner brought an action against contractor to recover for construction defects under a warranty and for attorney fees pursuant to the contract. The trial court entered judgment for owner under the warranty and awarded attorney fees. On appeal the contractor argued that because the trial court did not award owner damages for all of the defects it alleged in the complaint, owner can only recover attorney fees for those issues upon which it prevailed. The appellate court affirmed the judgment of the trial court.

The fee-shifting provision in the owner-contractor agreement provided the following:

> In the event that a dispute arises hereunder, the prevailing party shall be entitled to receive from the other party any and all costs and expenses, including reasonable attorneys' fees, incurred by the prevailing party in connection with such dispute.

The appellate court ruled that the owner was the sole "prevailing party" within the meaning of the fee-shifting provision and that the trial court correctly ordered contractor to pay the amount of the judgment entered in favor of owner.

94047 Walbridge Aldinger Co. v. Walcon Corp., 207 Mich. App. 566, 525 N.W.2d 489 (1994)

II: A107-1987, Art. 9, Para. 9.12

II:	A201-1987, Art. 10, Para. 10.2.3
II:	B141-1987, Art. 2, Para. 2.6.4
II:	B141-1987, Art. 2, Para. 2.6.5
II:	B141-1987, Art. 2, Para. 2.6.6
II:	B141-1987, Art. 2, Para. 2.6.14

Subcontractor's injured employee brought a negligence action against contractor and subcontractor and a suit against owner and engineer, which were consolidated for trial. Injured worker argued in pertinent part that the engineer was negligent in its supervision, control, and inspection of the construction site and that such negligence was a proximate cause of the injuries sustained by worker. The engineer moved for summary judgment, arguing that it owed no duty to worker and that it was not part of a joint enterprise because it had no control over the work on the site. The trial court entered summary judgment for engineer and worker appealed. Among numerous issues on appeal was whether an engineering firm employed by owner to provide engineering services in connection with the construction of a sewage treatment plant owed a duty to an employee of a subcontractor. The appellate court affirmed the judgment of the trial court.

The owner/engineer agreement provided the following:

[T]he Engineer shall serve as the Owner's professional representative in all the phases of the Project, and shall give consultation and advice to the Owner during the performance of his services.

It then provided for engineer's duties and responsibilities during the construction phase, including the following:

2. Make periodic visits to each construction site to observe the progress of the executed work and to determine in general if such work meets the essential performance and design features and the technical and functional requirements of the contract documents; the Engineer will not be required to make exhaustive or continuous on-site inspections to check the quality or quantity of the work; he will not be responsible for the construction means, methods, techniques, sequences or procedures or the safety precautions incident thereto; his efforts will be directed toward providing assurance for the Owner that each completed construction contract will conform to the engineering requirements of the contract documents. . . .

. . . .

6. Conduct an inspection on each construction contract, to determine if it is substantially complete and a final inspection to determine if it has been completed in accordance with the contract documents and the contractor has fulfilled all of his obligations thereunder so that the Engineer may approve, in writing, final payment to the Contractor.

7. The Engineer shall not be responsible for the acts or omissions of the contractor, any subcontractor or any of the contractor's subcontractor's agents or employees or any other person performing any of the work under a construction contract.

incident thereto, and Engineer will not be responsible for Contractor's failure to perform or furnish the work in accordance with the Contract Documents. . . .

The agreement further provided:

The Contractor shall be solely and completely responsible for conditions of the job site, including safety and all persons (including employees) and property during performance of the work. This requirement shall apply continuously and not be limited to normal working hours. . . .

The Contractor shall develop and maintain for the duration of this Contract, a safety program that will effectively incorporate and implement all required safety provisions. . . .

The duty of the Engineer to conduct construction review oaf the work does not include review or approval of the adequacy of the Contractor's safety program, safety supervisor, or any safety measures taken in, on or near the construction site. . . .

Relying on the decision in *Yow v. Hussey, Gay, Bell & DeYoung Int'l, Inc.*, 201 Ga. App. 857, 412 S.E.2d 565 (1991), *cert. denied*, 1992 Ga. LEXIS 116 (Ga. 1992) (see case digest number 91040), the district court found that absent a contractual right or responsibility to supervise and control the construction work, including site safety, the engineer should incur no liability for injuries to workers proximately caused by ordinary negligence at the site. The court found that the contract provisions clearly placed the obligation for site safety on the contractor.

94045 Romero v. Parkhill, Smith & Cooper, Inc., 881 S.W.2d 522 (Tex. Ct. App. 1994)

	II:	A107-1987, Art. 9, Para. 9.1
	II:	A107-1987, Art. 10, Para. 10.1
	II:	A107-1987, Art. 10, Para. 10.2
	II:	A107-1987, Art. 10, Para. 10.3
	II:	A107-1987, Art. 16, Para. 16.1
	II:	A117-1987, Art. 14, Para. 14.1
	II:	A117-1987, Art. 15, Para. 15.1
	II:	A117-1987, Art. 15, Para. 15.2
	II:	A117-1987, Art. 15, Para. 15.3
	II:	A117-1987, Art. 21, Para. 21.1
	II:	A201-1987, Art. 3, Para. 3.3.1
	II:	A201-1987, Art. 4, Para. 4.2.1
	II:	A201-1987, Art. 4, Para. 4.2.2
	II:	A201-1987, Art. 4, Para. 4.2.3
	III:	A201-1987, Art. 4, Para. 4.2.9
	II:	A201-1987, Art. 10, Para. 10.1.1
	II:	A201-1987, Art. 10, Para. 10.2.1

II:	A107-1987, Art. 10, Para. 10.3
II:	A107-1987, Art. 16, Para. 16.1
II:	A117-1987, Art. 14, Para. 14.1
II:	A117-1987, Art. 15, Para. 15.1
II:	A117-1987, Art. 15, Para. 15.2
II:	A117-1987, Art. 15, Para. 15.3
II:	A117-1987, Art. 21, Para. 21.1
II:	A201-1987, Art. 3, Para. 3.3.1
II:	A201-1987, Art. 4, Para. 4.2.1
II:	A201-1987, Art. 4, Para. 4.2.2
II:	A201-1987, Art. 4, Para. 4.2.3
II:	A201-1987, Art. 10, Para. 10.1.1
II:	A201-1987, Art. 10, Para. 10.2.1
II:	A201-1987, Art. 10, Para. 10.2.3
II:	B141-1987, Art. 2, Para. 2.6.4
II:	B141-1987, Art. 2, Para. 2.6.5
II:	B141-1987, Art. 2, Para. 2.6.6

Injured worker brought a negligence action against engineer and others. Engineer moved for summary judgment on the ground that because it did not have responsibility for safety at the site, it could not be held liable for negligence regarding site safety. The district court granted engineer's motion for summary judgment.

The owner-contractor agreement provided in pertinent part that:

The Engineer will be the Owner's representative during the construction period. His authority and responsibility will be limited to the provisions set forth in these Contract Documents. . . . However, neither Engineer's authority to act under this provision, nor any decision made by him in good faith either to exercise or not to exercise such authority, shall give rise to any duty or responsibility of the Engineer to the Contractor, any Subcontractor, their respective Sureties, any of their agents or employees, or any other person performing any of the work.

The Engineer will make visits to the site at intervals appropriate to the various stages of construction to observe the progress and quality of the work and to determine, n general if the work is proceeding in accordance with the intent of the Contract Documents. . . . Visits and observations made by the Engineer shall not relieve the Contractor of his obligation to conduct comprehensive inspections of the work and to furnish material and perform acceptable work, and provide adequate safety precautions, in conformance with the intent of the Contract. . . .

Engineer will not be responsible for Contractor's means, methods, techniques, sequences or procedures of construction, or the safety precautions and programs

incident of or related to any such possible damages. The court found that these two areas of indemnification were severable and different.

94043   Novak v. BASF Corp., 869 F. Supp. 113 (N.D.N.Y. 1994)

        I: A107-1987, Art. 9, Para. 9.12
        I: A117-1987, Art. 14, Para. 14.12
        I: A201-1987, Art. 3, Para. 3.18.1
        I: A201-1987, Art. 10, Para. 10.1.4
        I: A401-1987, Art. 4, Para. 4.6.1

Among numerous issues on appeal, the appellate court upheld the trial court's grant of summary judgment to owner on owner's action against contractor and subcontractor for contractual indemnification. The court found that both the owner-contractor agreement and the subcontract contained broad-based indemnification clauses that expressly protected owner from liability for damage or injury resulting on the site, as well as for costs and attorney fees.

The owner-contractor agreement provided that:

Contractor shall be responsible for and shall indemnify and hold harmless Owner, its officers, agents and employees, from and against: . . . (b) any and all liability, damage, loss, cost, expense, claim, demand, suit, action, judgment, recovery for or on account of any injury or death of person . . . injury, death, or damage to property of Owners or Contractors, representatives arising out of, or in any way occurring directly or indirectly with the Work, including, without limitation, delegable or nondelegable duties imposed on Contractor or Owner by law, except for such injury, death or damage as is caused by the sole negligence of Owner; and Contractor shall, at its sole expense, defend any and all actions based thereon.

The contractor and subcontractor had entered into the American Institute of Architects Standard Form of Agreement Between Contractor and Subcontractor, Document No. A401, 1987 edition, specifically Paragraph 4.6.1.

The appellate court found that the language of both provisions manifested a clear intent to indemnify.

Based on it reading of Paragraph 4.6.1, the court granted contractor summary judgment on contractor's action against subcontractor for contractual indemnity where subcontractor failed to prove contractor's negligence.

94044   Padgett v. CH2M Hill Southeast, Inc., 866 F. Supp. 563 (M.D. Ga. 1994)

        II: A107-1987, Art. 9, Para. 9.1
        II: A107-1987, Art. 10, Para. 10.1
        II: A107-1987, Art. 10, Para. 10.2

The court concluded that the contract had to be given effect according to its clear and unambiguous terms.

94042   Moore v. Dayton Power & Light Co., 99 Ohio App. 3d 138, 650 N.E.2d 127 (1994), *review pending*, 71 Ohio St. 3d 1478, 645 N.E.2d 1258, *and motion overruled*, 71 Ohio St. 3d 1481, 645 N.E.2d 1260, *and dismissed*, 72 Ohio St. 3d 1417, 648 N.E.2d 510 (1995)

III:	A107-1987, Art. 9, Para. 9.12
III:	A117-1987, Art. 14, Para. 14.12
III:	A201-1987, Art. 3, Para. 3.18.1
III:	A201-1987, Art. 10, Para. 10.1.4
III:	A401-1987, Art. 4, Para. 4.6.1

Contractor's injured employee brought a negligence action against owner for injuries sustained during the painting of towers and equipment at an electrical substation. Owner moved for summary judgment. Owner then filed a third-party indemnity action against contractor and both parties moved for summary judgment. The lower court granted owner summary judgment in the negligence action on the grounds that owner did not possess superior knowledge of the danger and there was no question of material fact that owner was negligent in not deenergizing the power lines. The court awarded owner fees and costs. At issue in the earlier unreported action and on appeal was whether subcontractor was contractually obligated to reimburse owner for legal fees and costs incurred in defending a tort action brought by contractor's employee. The appellate court affirmed the judgment of the lower court based on a different interpretation of the hold harmless provision.

The indemnity agreement provided as follows:

[Contractor] shall indemnify and save harmless [Owner] from any and all costs and expenses, including but not restricted to attorney's fees and court costs, arising from, caused by or incident or related to injuries or damages to property . . . or persons, . . . including, but not restricted to employees and agents of [Contractor] in the performance of their duties or otherwise which may arise or be incident or related in any way to any of the work . . . to be performed or provided hereunder.

The applicable state statutes were Ohio Rev. Code Ann. §§ 2305.31 and 4123.74.

In the earlier unreported action the court construed the indemnification language in the owner/contractor agreement and concluded that the indemnity provision was void as against public policy. Thus, contractor could not be required to indemnify owner for owner's sole or concurrent negligence. Although agreeing with the trial court's conclusion, the appellate court interpreted the contract language as not extending to indemnification for damages arising out of injuries as contemplated by the Ohio statutes, but as limited to indemnification for all costs and expenses, including attorney fees, which are an

III:	A201-1987, Art. 4, Para. 4.5.6
III:	A201-1987, Art. 4, Para. 4.5.7
III:	A401-1987, Art. 6, Para. 6.1
III:	A401-1987, Art. 6, Para. 6.2
III:	A401-1987, Art. 6, Para. 6.3
III:	A401-1987, Art. 6, Para. 6.4
III:	A401-1987, Art. 6, Para. 6.5
III:	B141-1987, Art. 2, Para. 2.6.15
III:	B141-1987, Art. 2, Para. 2.6.16
III:	B141-1987, Art. 2, Para. 2.6.19
III:	B141-1987, Art. 7, Para. 7.1
III:	B141-1987, Art. 7, Para. 7.2
III:	B141-1987, Art. 7, Para. 7.3
III:	B141-1987, Art. 7, Para. 7.4

Owner appealed the trial court's entry of summary judgment for contractor, contending that the trial court had erred in failing to enforce the parties' agreement that decisions of the project architect and the owner concerning the interpretation of the contract documents were final, binding and conclusive. The appellate court reversed the decision of the trial court.

The owner-contractor agreement provided in Paragraph 2(b) as follows:

[A]ll drawings are a working part of these specifications and any questions or disagreements arising as to the true intent of this specification or the drawing, or the kind and quality of the work required thereby, shall be decided by the Architect, local Authority and Department of Housing, whose interpretations thereof shall be final, conclusive and bind to all parties.

In response to contractor's argument on appeal that the applicable case law would give effect to a clause such as Paragraph 2(b) only if the architect were the sole arbiter of disputes, the appellate court found that the parties freely conferred dispute resolution authority on a tripartite panel rather than solely on the architect. Moreover, the court found that Paragraph 2(b) clearly provided that the interpretation of the panel would be final and conclusive. The court found that although words such as "final," "binding," and "conclusive" had a "terminal and unconditional tone," the decision of the panel could be challenged upon proof of fraud bad faith, arbitrariness or gross misconduct.

In response to contractor's argument that the panel's decision was not binding because it was not an interpretation of the contract but rather an expansion of it, the court found that the plain language of the agreement permitted the panel to resolve any dispute regarding the scope of the contractor's obligations under the contract. The panel was given the authority to resolve all disagreements regarding the "true intent of this specification or the drawing or the kind and quality of work required thereby. . . ."

The court rejected all of contractor's arguments that it orally complied with the contract provisions. The court found that contractor waived application of the provisions by failing to make a proper request for an extension of time as required by the contract.

Finally, the court found that contractor agreed not to permit its subcontractors and suppliers to lien the project. The contract provided that:

[I]n the event that any such lien shall be filed, [Contractor] agrees to take all steps necessary and proper for the release and discharge of such lien . . . and in default of performing such obligation, agrees to reimburse the Owner, on demand, for all monies paid by Owner in releasing, satisfying, and discharging of such liens.

The court ruled that since the contractor failed to abide by this provision, then the owner was entitled to set off the amount of the outstanding contract balances due contractor for amounts owner paid to contractor's suppliers and subcontractors.

The court concluded that under the terms of the contracts, the owner had absolute authority to modify the construction schedule, while contractor was obligated to abide by owner's instructions. Although these terms may seem "one-sided," the court found that contractor was aware of the provisions at the time it bid the contract, and had the opportunity to increase its proposed contract prices to account for the risks it would be assuming.

94041 M & L Bldg. Corp. v. Housing Auth., 35 Conn. App. 379, 646 A.2d 244, *appeal denied*, 231 Conn. 925, 648 A.2d 164 (1994)

III:	A107-1987, Art. 10, Para. 10.5	
III:	A107-1987, Art. 10, Para. 10.8	
III:	A117-1987, Art. 15, Para. 15.5	
III:	A117-1987, Art. 15, Para. 15.8	
III:	A201-1987, Art. 4, Para. 4.2.11	
III:	A201-1987, Art. 4, Para. 4.2.12	
III:	A201-1987, Art. 4, Para. 4.2.13	
III:	A201-1987, Art. 4, Para. 4.3.2	
III:	A201-1987, Art. 4, Para. 4.4.1	
III:	A201-1987, Art. 4, Para. 4.4.2	
III:	A201-1987, Art. 4, Para. 4.4.3	
III:	A201-1987, Art. 4, Para. 4.4.4	
III:	A201-1987, Art. 4, Para. 4.5.1	
III:	A201-1987, Art. 4, Para. 4.5.2	
III:	A201-1987, Art. 4, Para. 4.5.3	
III:	A201-1987, Art. 4, Para. 4.5.4	
III:	A201-1987, Art. 4, Para. 4.5.4.1	
III:	A201-1987, Art. 4, Para. 4.5.4.2	
III:	A201-1987, Art. 4, Para. 4.5.5	

or unforeseen, including . . . labor and materials" and that "all loss or damage arising from any of the work through unforeseen or unusual obstructions, difficulties or delays which may be encountered in prosecution of the work, or through the action of the elements shall be borne by Contractor." The court concluded that under this pricing arrangement the contractor bore the risks associated with underestimating its price or failing to account for unexpected additional costs. However, contractor would reap all of the benefits of any cost savings in the event the project was completed at an earlier date, or in a more efficient manner than originally anticipated.

The court, in discussing the issue of delay, found that contractor was also aware of both the potential for delay in this project and the fact that it would not be entitled to demand additional compensation for delay from owner upon completion. Despite this knowledge, contractor priced its contracts under the unrealistic expectation that there would be no modifications to the progress schedule and that the work would be prosecuted "in an efficient production-type manner, working normal hours with optimum crew sizes." The court found, however, that contractor did protect itself from unforeseen delays beyond its control, including those caused by the "act or neglect" of owner or owner's subcontractors or from "changes ordered in the scope of the work."

Additionally, the court found that the no-damage-for-delay clause gave the contractor the right to seek a time extension for performing in the event of delay, and in consideration of this right, contractor agreed not to seek delay damages. The agreement provided the following:

> If the Contractor is delayed at any time in the progress of the Work by any act or neglect of Owner or by any contractor employed by Owner, or by changes ordered in the scope of the Work, or by fire, adverse weather conditions not reasonably anticipated, or any other causes beyond the control of the Contractor, then the required completion date or duration set forth in the progress schedule shall be extended by the amount of time that the Contractor shall have been delayed thereby. However, to the fullest extent permitted by law, Owner . . . and [its] agents and employees shall not be held responsible for any loss or damage sustained by Contractor, or additional costs incurred by Contractor, through delay caused by Owner, . . . or [its] agents or employees, or any other Contractor or Subcontractor, or by abnormal weather conditions, or by any other cause, and Contractor agrees that the sole right and remedy therefor shall be an extension of time.

The agreement also contained a provision requiring contractor to submit a written request detailing the cause and length of the delay, as well as the length of the requested extension. The condition also required that the request be submitted within seven days of the commencement of the delay. Specifically, the agreement provided that:

> Any claim for extension of time shall be made in writing by the Contractor to Owner, for approval by Owner, within seven (7) days after commencement of the delay. Contractor's failure to give such written notice to Owner shall deprive the Contractor of his right to claim an extension of time and any damages or additional costs incurred by Contractor resulting from such delay. In the case of a continuing cause of delay, only one claim shall be necessary. The giving of such notice shall not of itself establish the validity of the cause of delay or of the extension of time for completion.

merits, and limited owner's award to its costs of action. Contractor appealed. Among numerous issues on appeal was whether the contract documents precluded contractor's claims for additional and unanticipated expenses incurred in performing its work. In affirming the judgment of the trial court, the appellate court held that contractor's failure to comply with the contractually provided measures for relief barred contractor from recovering for its delay, impact, and inefficiency damages. Furthermore, the court found that contractor was not entitled to recover its outstanding contract balances because those amounts were offset by payments made by the owner on contractor's behalf. The appellate court concluded, through analysis of the contract documents, that the various recovery theories advanced by the contractor were invalid.

Pursuant to the terms of the progress schedule provision of the General Conditions, the court found that the owner "specifically reserved the right to modify the progress schedule as required by conditions of the work," while contractor, for its part, "agreed to comply with the progress schedule established by the owner, or any revision thereof." The relevant portion of he General Conditions provided as follows:

> The Contractor agrees to comply with the progress schedule established by the Owner, or any revision thereof, and agrees that the Work shall be prosecuted regularly, diligently and uninterrupted, within the time specified. Owner specifically reserves the right to modify the progress schedule as required by the conditions of work.
>
> Should the Contractor fail to comply with the progress schedule or, in the Owner's opinion, otherwise fail, refuse or neglect to supply sufficient labor and/or material in the prosecution of the Work, Owner shall have the right to (1) direct Contractor to furnish such additional labor and/or material as may, in the Owner's opinion, be required to comply with the progress schedule or otherwise diligently prosecute the Work. . . . Any costs incurred by Owner pursuant to the exercise of its rights under this paragraph shall be borne by the Contractor and shall not increase the Contract Sum.

In addition to the foregoing, Section 3.1 of the two contracts reiterated owner's right to modify the progress schedule:

> TIME IS OF THE ESSENCE OF THIS AGREEMENT. The Owner may sustain financial loss if the project or any part thereof is delayed because the Contractor fails to perform any part of the work in accordance with the contract documents, including, without limitation, a failure to comply with the schedule for this project, or any revision thereof, established by Owner. The Contractor shall begin the work at the time directed by the Owner and perform its obligations under this agreement with diligence and sufficient manpower to maintain the progress of the work as scheduled by Owner, without delaying other contractors or areas of work. At the request of the Owner, the Contractor shall perform certain parts of the work before other parts . . . all without any increase in the contract sum.

The court concluded that the owner had complete discretion to adjust the schedule as well as to demand that contractor comply with such adjustments without additional compensation.

Pursuant to the terms of the lump-sum pricing arrangement, the contractor should have known that its "Contract Sum" should have included "all increases in costs, foreseen

The court concluded that the provision was not meant to apply to "any contract, construction, or maintenance work" but rather to "any contract construction or maintenance work being done" for the earlier project.

94040 Marriott Corp. v. Dasta Constr. Co., 26 F. 3d 1057, *reh'g denied*, 37 F.3d 639 (11th Cir. 1994) (en banc)

III:	A107-1987, Art. 9, Para. 9.1	
III:	A107-1987, Art. 9, Para. 9.7	
III:	A107-1987, Art. 13, Para. 13.1	
III:	A107-1987, Art. 13, Para. 13.2	
III:	A107-1987, Art. 13, Para. 13.3	
III:	A107-1987, Art. 14, Para. 14.1	
III:	A107-1987, Art. 14, Para. 14.3	
III:	A117-1987, Art. 14, Para. 14.1	
III:	A117-1987, Art. 14, Para. 14.7	
III:	A117-1987, Art. 18, Para. 18.1	
III:	A117-1987, Art. 18, Para. 18.2	
III:	A117-1987, Art. 18, Para. 18.3	
III:	A117-1987, Art. 19, Para. 19.1	
III:	A117-1987, Art. 19, Para. 19.3	
III:	A201-1987, Art. 3, Para. 3.3	
III:	A201-1987, Art. 3, Para. 3.10.1	
III:	A201-1987, Art. 3, Para. 3.10.3	
III:	A201-1987, Art. 7, Para. 7.1.1	
III:	A201-1987, Art. 7, Para. 7.2.1	
III:	A201-1987, Art. 7, Para. 7.3.1	
III:	A201-1987, Art. 7, Para. 7.3.3	
III:	A201-1987, Art. 7, Para. 7.3.6	
III:	A201-1987, Art. 7, Para. 7.3.8	
III:	A201-1987, Art. 8, Para. 8.2	
III:	A201-1987, Art. 8, Para. 8.3	

Owner, acting also as general manager, brought an action against contractor to recover payment made to subcontractors and suppliers on behalf of contractor. Contractor counterclaimed against owner for interference and breach of contract. After a jury trial, owner was awarded the sums it had paid to the subcontractors and suppliers. Contractor was awarded damages on its counterclaim. The district court then granted owner's motion for judgment notwithstanding the verdict, dismissed contractor's counterclaim on the

94039 Kinsey v. Farmland Indus., Inc., 853 F. Supp. 231 (W.D. La. 1994), *aff'd without opinion*, 43 F.3d 669 (5th Cir. 1994)

III:	A107-1987, Art. 9, Para. 9.12
III:	A117-1987, Art. 14, Para. 14.12
III:	A201-1987, Art. 3, Para. 3.18.1
III:	A201-1987, Art. 10, Para. 10.1.4
III:	A401-1987, Art. 4, Para. 4.6.1

Contractor's injured worker brought a negligence action against owner. The district court granted owner's motion for summary judgment on injured employee's claim, concluding that owner was injured worker's "statutory employer." Owner then moved for summary judgment on its claim against contractor for indemnification for attorneys' fees incurred in defending worker's claim. In response to owner's motion, contractor argued that it was not obligated to indemnify owner under an agreement entered into for an earlier project where its successful bid for the project in question was the entire agreement of the parties. The district court denied owner's motion.

The indemnity agreement, contained in owner's standard form agreement, which was executed by the contractor for an earlier project, was applicable to "any contract construction or maintenance work being done in [owner's] plant as designated by [owner's] employees." It provided in pertinent part that:

In the event you or any of your employees . . . suffer injury or death, or [property damage] . . . on or about our premises while so engaged or present on our premises in connection therewith, you agree to indemnify and hold harmless [owner], its officers, agents, and employees, and any other corporation on its behalf, liable from any loss, cost, or damage, including reasonable attorneys' fees incurred on account of such injury, death or property damage, whether or not such casualty results from or is contributed to by negligence of [owner], or its employees.

The court found that the indemnification provision was clear and unambiguous. The provision required that contractor indemnify owner for "any loss, cost, or damage, including reasonable attorneys' fees incurred" and applied to "any contract construction or maintenance work being done in [owner's] plant." However, the clause stated that the indemnification provision applied to "any contract construction or maintenance work being done." It did not state, as the owner argued, that the indemnification provision applied to "any contract, construction, or maintenance work." In reaching this construction of the indemnity language, the court reasoned that the gerund "being done" imposed a sense of present activity upon the nouns "construction" and "maintenance work." The court concluded that this evidenced the parties' intention that the provision apply only to the "contract construction or maintenance work" being performed at the time the provision was executed, *i.e.*, the earlier project. The absence of commas evidenced the parties' intention that "contract" serve as an adjective, modifying "construction" and "maintenance work" and not, as owner suggests, a noun with independent significance.

The court also rejected the worker's argument that owner was vicariously liable because it participated in the construction through its agent, the construction manager. The court found that the construction manager contracted with owner (1) to provide an on-site management team responsible for contract administration; (2) to establish and implement coordination procedures between the owner, design consultant, and all prime contractors and suppliers; (3) to establish submittal procedures; (4) to maintain records on the project; and (5) to establish and maintain a testing program. The court found that the construction manager had no contractual obligation to supervise, control or give advice regarding the construction, nor did the record show that owner gave construction manager such authority outside of the contract.

In upholding summary judgment for construction manager, the court found that the agreement between the parties did not contain a provision that imposed a duty upon the construction manager to provide for worker safety. The court found that although the construction manager was contractually charged with conducting inspections of the contractor's work, the contract clearly provided that the construction manager "shall not . . . have control or charge of or advise on or issue directions concerning aspects of the construction means, methods, techniques, sequences; or for the procedures or safety procedures or programs in connection with the work."

Furthermore, the court found that although the construction manager was charged with conducting inspections and recording tests to ensure compliance with the contract, construction manager had no contractual authority to control the construction "means, methods or procedures" used by the contractor. The court found that there was no factual basis in the record to support worker's argument that the construction manager assumed a duty to supervise the construction by its supervision and control over the means and methods used by the contractor.

Additionally, in reversing summary judgment for the engineer, the court found that a review of the provisions of the owner/engineer agreement raised the issue of whether a contractual duty to review "submittals" or "other contractor-provided information" to determine compliance with the contract documents included within its scope a duty to review contractor's proposal to pressure test the pipe with air rather than water. The court stated that, if the contract obligated the engineer to perform that duty, then it was required to exercise such reasonable care, technical skill and ability, and diligence as are ordinarily required of engineers in the course of providing such services in order to avoid unreasonable risks to foreseeable plaintiffs. Furthermore, if engineer's contract required that it approve submittals for changes in the method of testing the pipe, then engineer owed owner, and the workers affected by those changes, its professional expertise to determine that the changes met engineering standards. In addition, the court found that testimony in the record raised a question of fact as to whether engineer assumed a duty to review the change in the testing method by not objecting to the change.

The court reversed summary judgment for engineer's parent company, stating that the parent company failed to meet its burden as the moving party to show that its contractual obligations had been assigned. Absent proof on the record, the court found that vicarious liability was an issue for the jury to decide and remanded.

II:	A117-1979, Art. 20, Para. 20.1
II:	A117-1987, Art. 14, Para. 14.1
II:	A117-1987, Art. 15, Para. 15.3
II:	A117-1987, Art. 21, Para. 21.1
I:	A201-1976, Art. 2, Para. 2.2.4
I:	A201-1976, Art. 4, Para. 4.3.1
II:	A201-1976, Art. 10, Para. 10.1.1
II:	A201-1976, Art. 10, Para. 10.2.1
I:	A201-1987, Art. 3, Para. 3.3.1
I:	A201-1987, Art. 4, Para. 4.3.2
II:	A201-1987, Art. 10, Para. 10.1.1
II:	A201-1987, Art. 10, Para. 10.2.1
II:	B141-1977, Art. 1, Para. 1.5.5
II:	B141-1987, Art. 2, Para. 2.6.6

Contractor's injured employee and the estate of contractor's deceased employee brought a strict liability negligence action against distributor and manufacturer, as well as a negligence action against owner, construction manager and engineer. The trial court granted owner, construction manager, engineer and engineer's parent company summary judgment on the issue of liability. The appellate court affirmed in part and reversed in part the judgment of the trial court.

The owner/contractor agreement included provisions identical to Paragraphs 2.2.4 and 4.3.1 of the American Institute of Architects General Conditions of the Contract for Construction, Document No. A201, 1976 edition. The agreement also contained a provision, similar to Paragraph 10.1.1, which provided in pertinent part that:

> The Contractor shall be responsible for initiating, maintaining and supervising all safety precautions and programs in connection with the Work. The Contractor shall take all precautions and follow all procedures for the safety of, and shall provide all protection to prevent injury to, all persons involved in any way in the Work and all other persons, including without limitation the employees, agents, guests, visitors, invitees and licensees of the Owner who may be affected thereby. These precautions shall include, but in no event be limited to: the posting of danger signs and personal notification to affected persons of the existence of a hazard of whatever nature . . . .

The appellate court upheld the decision of the trial court granting summary judgment to owner because the owner/contractor agreement clearly provided that the contractor was responsible for safety at the site. The record did not support the worker's and estate's contention that owner had assumed a supervisory role at the site. The court found that although the owner had the right to inspect work for conformance with the contract, that right did not change the owner from a passive nonparticipant to an active participant in the construction with the right to supervise or control the work.

agents and employees from all such claims including, without limiting the generality of the foregoing, claims for which the Contractor may be or may be claimed to be, liable and legal fees and disbursements paid or incurred to enforce the provisions of this paragraph and the Subcontractor further agrees to obtain, maintain and pay for such general liability insurance coverage and endorsements as will insure the provisions of this paragraph.

The agreement further provided in Attachment B that:

Notwithstanding the provisions of paragraph 7 of this Subcontract Agreement, the indemnity set forth therein shall apply only to the extent that the underlying injury or damage attributable to the negligence or otherwise wrongful act or omission, including breach of a specific contractual duty, of Subcontractor. Subcontractor further agrees to indemnify, defend and save harmless Contractor from and against all claims arising within the scope of the types and limits of insurance Subcontractor has agreed to obtain pursuant to this Subcontract Agreement (a) to the same extent as said insurance if Subcontractor fails to obtain and keep in force said insurance and (b) to the full extent of the deductible amount of self-insured retention of said insurance.

The applicable state statutes were Minn. Stat. §§ 337.02 and 337.05, subd. 1.

In construing Paragraph 7 the appellate court, relying on *Holmes v. Watson-Forsberg Co.*, 488 N.W.2d 473 (Minn. 1992) (see case digest number 92008c), found that the provision was not a contract to indemnify but rather was a risk-shifting mechanism often used in the construction industry, requiring the subcontractor to provide insurance benefits to the contractor even for claims based on the contractor's own negligence.

Subcontractor argued that Attachment B had to be construed in light of the state statutory provision that its insurance obligation could apply only to damages attributable to its own negligence. The court found, however, that limitations on an indemnification obligation did not prevent the parties from agreeing that one party was to obtain insurance to cover harm beyond that attributable to its own negligence. The court concluded that where the subcontractor had obtained the coverage contemplated in Paragraph 7 of the subcontract, and where the subcontractor was contractually required to provide the insurance benefits to the contractor, the contractor was entitled to judgment as a matter of law.

94038   Juno Indus., Inc. v. Heery Int'l, 646 So. 2d 818 (Fla. Dist. Ct. App. 1994)

II:	A107-1978, Art. 8, Para. 8.3	
II:	A107-1978, Art. 10, Para. 10.1	
II:	A107-1978, Art. 16, Para. 16.1	
II:	A107-1987, Art. 9, Para. 9.1	
II:	A107-1987, Art. 10, Para. 10.3	
II:	A107-1987, Art. 16, Para. 16.1	
II:	A117-1979, Art. 12, Para. 12.3	
II:	A117-1979, Art. 14, Para. 14.1	

from any damages contractor would be required to pay because of negligence on subcontractor's part or a violation of the Structural Work Act by subcontractor. Based on its holding that the agreement was in truth an agreement to make contribution, the court found that when subcontractor entered into the agreement it waived the workers' compensation limit defense, as between it and contractor.

94037 Hurlburt v. Northern States Power Co., 524 N.W.2d 546 (Minn. Ct. App. 1994)

III:	A107-1987, Art. 9, Para. 9.12	
III:	A107-1987, Art. 17, Para. 17.1	
III:	A117-1987, Art. 14, Para. 14.12	
III:	A117-1987, Art. 22, Para. 22.1	
III:	A201-1987, Art. 3, Para. 3.18.1	
III:	A201-1987, Art. 10, Para. 10.1.4	
III:	A201-1987, Art. 11, Para. 11.1.1	
III:	A201-1987, Art. 11, Para. 11.1.2	
III:	A201-1987, Art. 11, Para. 11.1.3	
III:	A401-1987, Art. 4, Para. 4.6.1	
III:	A401-1987, Art. 13, Para. 13.1	
III:	A401-1987, Art. 13, Para. 13.2	
III:	A401-1987, Art. 13, Para. 13.3	

Subcontractor's injured employee brought a negligence action against contractor and owner. The contractor filed a third-party complaint against the subcontractor, claiming that subcontractor was contractually obligated to pay all sums for which contractor was liable. The contractor moved for partial summary judgment against the subcontractor. The trial court granted contractor's motion and ordered the subcontractor to provide the contractor with its insurance benefits. The case was then tried to a jury which found the contractor was negligent and assessed damages. Subcontractor appealed. Among numerous issues on appeal was whether a subcontractor could contract to procure insurance for a contractor's negligence. The appellate court affirmed the judgment of the trial court.

Paragraph 7 of the subcontract provided that:

[Subcontractor shall] assume entire responsibility and liability, to the fullest extent permitted by law, for all damages or injury to all persons, whether employees or otherwise, and to all property, arising out of it, resulting from or in any manner connected with, the execution of the work provided for in this Subcontract or occurring or resulting from the use by the Subcontractor, his agents or employees, of materials, equipment, instrumentalities or other property, whether the same be owned by the Contractor, the Subcontractor or third parties, and the Subcontractor, to the fullest extent permitted by law, agrees to indemnify and save harmless the Contractor, his

An injured employee of subcontractor brought a negligence action and an action under the Illinois Structural Work Act against contractor. In response, contractor filed a third-party complaint against subcontractor for contribution and for indemnification from subcontractor. The trial court granted subcontractor's motion to dismiss the indemnity counts, and contractor appealed. The appellate court affirmed the trial court's decision on other grounds.

The subcontract provided that:

(c) For all Subcontract work performed in Illinois or performed by Illinois Subcontractors, the following term is in effect:

Subcontractor hereby assumes the entire liability for its own negligence and the negligence of its own employees; in addition, Subcontractor hereby assumes the entire liability arising from any alleged violation of the Structural Work Act . . . that Subcontractor knew of or by the exercise of ordinary care should have known of; Subcontractor agrees to indemnify and save harmless Contractor and its agents, . . . from and against all loss, expense, damage or injury, including legal fees, that Contractor may sustain as a result of any claims predicated or [sic] said allegations of Subcontractor's own negligence or on Subcontractor's alleged violation of the Structural Work Act as above set forth. This provision shall specifically not require Subcontractor to indemnify Contractor from Contractor's own alleged negligence in violation of Chapter 29, Section 61 of the Illinois Revised Statutes. In the event claim of any such loss, expense, damage, or injury, as above defined and limited, is made against Contractor [or] its agents . . . Contractor may: (1) withhold from any payment due or hereafter becoming due to Subcontractor under the terms of this contract, an amount sufficient in Contractor's judgment to protect and indemnify Contractor from all such claims, expenses, legal fees, loss, damage or injury as above defined and limited; or (2) require Subcontractor to furnish a surety bond in such amount so determined; or (3) require Subcontractor to provide suitable indemnity acceptable to Contractor.

Contractor first argued that the agreement did not contravene the Illinois anti-indemnity statute because contractor was not seeking indemnity for its own negligence. Rather, contractor sought indemnity only for the portion of the liability attributable to subcontractor's violation of the Illinois Structural Work Act and subcontractor's own negligence. The appellate court held that under the indemnity provision of the subcontract, contractor sought contribution, not "partial indemnity," and there was no violation of the anti-indemnity statute. However, the appellate court upheld the trial court's decision, concluding that if Paragraph 8(c) were construed to create a cause of action for contractual contribution, independent of the Contribution Act, such a construction would contravene the public policy of Illinois as it would run afoul of the good-faith-settlement and dismissal provisions of the Act.

Next, the court addressed subcontractor's argument that allowing a cause of action to flow from the indemnity provision would circumvent Illinois decisions that limit an employer's contribution liability to the amount of workers' compensation. The court found that pursuant to the indemnity provision subcontractor assumed "the entire liability" for its own negligence and the "entire liability" arising from any violation of the Structural Work Act on its part. Subcontractor agreed to "indemnify and save harmless" contractor

III: B141-1987, Art. 2, Para. 2.6.4

III: B141-1987, Art. 2, Para. 2.6.6

The estate of Subcontractor's deceased employee brought an action against, owner, contractor, architect and electric power company. The estate alleged that architect had been negligent in failing to warn workers of the hazards involved in working next to a power line and in failing to take any steps to minimize the danger. The trial court granted architect's motion for summary judgment and the estate appealed. The appellate court affirmed the judgment of the trial court.

Pursuant to the terms of the owner/architect agreement the contractor was responsible for supervising all construction activity, and was also charged with initiating, maintaining and supervising safety precautions at the site. According to the express terms of the agreement, the architect was not to be responsible for and was not to have control over construction activities or safety measures. By separate agreement, contractor contracted with architect for the preparation of the project's construction drawings and foundation design. Pursuant to the terms of that agreement, architect's responsibility was limited to the preparation of documents.

The appellate court found that architect was not hired to supervise construction or to act as the owner's representative on the construction site. Architect was employed by the contractor to do design work and to prepare certain drawings. The court found that neither architect's contract with contractor nor contractor's contract with owner could be construed as imposing upon architect a duty to supervise the construction work or be responsible for the safety of workers. Furthermore, the architect, in the absence of a duty imposed by contract or course of conduct, had no duty to take affirmative action to protect workers from hazards on the site which were either known or readily visible.

94035   (UNASSIGNED)

94036   Herington v. J.S. Alberici Constr. Co., 266 Ill. App. 3d 489, 203 Ill. Dec. 348, 639 N.E.2d 907 (1994), *appeal granted sub nom.,* Braye v. Archer-Daniels-Midland Co., 166 Ill. 2d 536, 216 Ill. Dec. 1, 664 N.E.2d 638 (1996), *and reversed in part,* 175 Ill. 2d 201, 222 Ill. Dec. 91, 676 N.E.2d 1295 (1997), See Digest No. 95026

II: A107-1987, Art. 9, Para. 9.12

II: A117-1987, Art. 14, Para. 14.12

II: A201-1987, Art. 3, Para. 3.18.1

II: A201-1987, Art. 10, Para. 10.1.4

II: A401-1987, Art. 4, Para. 4.6.1

94033   Fisk Elec. Co. v. Constructors & Assocs., 888 S.W.2d 813 (Tex. 1994)

II:	A107-1987, Art. 9, Para. 9.12
II:	A117-1987, Art. 14, Para. 14.12
II:	A201-1987, Art. 3, Para. 3.18.1
II:	A201-1987, Art. 10, Para. 10.1.4
II:	A401-1987, Art. 4, Para. 4.6.1

The Texas Supreme Court relied on *Ethyl Corp. v. Daniel Constr. Co.*, 725 S.W.2d 705 (Tex. 1987) (see case digest number 87019), in adopting the "express negligence test" to require that parties seeking to indemnify themselves for their own negligence must express that intent in specific terms. The high court found that the following indemnity clause did not fulfill the *Ethyl Corp.* test:

> [T]o the fullest extent permitted by law, [Subcontractor] shall indemnify, hold harmless, and defend [Contractor] . . . from and against all claims, damages, losses, and expenses, including but not limited to attorney's fees . . . [arising out of or resulting from the performance of Subcontractor's work.]

The court stated that the express negligence requirement was a rule of contract interpretation, and found no duty to indemnify within the four corners of the subcontract. Moreover, the contractor, as the negligent party, was not entitled to indemnity and not entitled to recover costs of defending a negligence action brought by subcontractor's employee.

94034   Frampton v. Dauphin Distribution Servs. Co., 436 Pa. Super. 486, 648 A.2d 326 (1994), *appeal denied*, 657 A.2d 491, 540 Pa. 620 (1995)

III:	A107-1987, Art. 9, Para. 9.1
III:	A107-1987, Art. 10, Para. 10.1
III:	A107-1987, Art. 10, Para. 10.3
III:	A107-1987, Art. 16, Para. 16.1
III:	A117-1987, Art. 14, Para. 14.1
III:	A117-1987, Art. 15, Para. 15.1
III:	A117-1987, Art. 15, Para. 15.3
III:	A117-1987, Art. 21, Para. 21.1
III:	A201-1987, Art. 3, Para. 3.3.1
III:	A201-1987, Art. 4, Para. 4.2.1
III:	A201-1987, Art. 4, Para. 4.2.3
III:	A201-1987, Art. 10, Para. 10.1.1
III:	A201-1987, Art. 10, Para. 10.2.1
III:	A201-1987, Art. 10, Para. 10.2.3

concluded that the owner had received actual notice of the claim because the contractor had notified the owner by letter of a possible claim and owner had had the opportunity to account for the costs. Additionally, the contractor gave notice prior to beginning of repairs, which were approved by the owner.

94032   Figgs v. Bellevue Holding Co., 652 A.2d 1084 (Del. Super. Ct. 1994)

III:	A107-1987, Art. 9, Para. 9.6	
III:	A107-1987, Art. 16, Para. 16.1	
III:	A117-1987, Art. 14, Para. 14.6	
III:	A117-1987, Art. 21, Para. 21.1	
III:	A201-1987, Art. 3, Para. 3.7.2	
III:	A201-1987, Art. 10, Para. 10.2.2	
III:	A401-1987, Art. 4, Para. 4.3.1	

Subcontractor's injured employee brought a negligence action against contractor and steel subcontractor. The trial court granted subcontractor summary judgment because subcontractor was no longer on the job site at the time of the accident, did not have control over the area, and, therefore, did not owe a duty to the employee of another subcontractor. Injured worker then moved for reargument, contending among other issues that subcontractor owed worker a duty pursuant to the subcontract and a duty to abide by OSHA regulations pursuant to the general conditions provided in the bid documents. The trial court granted subcontractor summary judgment on the breach of contract claim. The appellate court vacated the oral judgment of the trial court, and on the claim of breach of contract granted subcontractor summary judgment.

The subcontract provided in pertinent part that:

[Subcontractor shall] comply with all applicable laws, building codes, ordinances, regulations and orders of any public authority bearing on the design and construction of the Work under this Agreement.

Paragraph 7.1 of the general conditions of the bid documents provided that:

[Contractor and all subcontractors] shall comply with, and cooperate with other Contractors, Architect/Engineer, and/or Owner in complying with legal Requirements, including but not limited to OSHA requirements.

The appellate court found that OSHA imposed a duty upon a subcontractor to protect only its own employees. The court found that subcontractor's agreement to abide by OSHA regulations did not result in a change of subcontractor's duty to the employee of another subcontractor. The court construed the subcontract and bid instructions as requiring the subcontractor to comply with all OSHA requirements imposed upon any subcontractor at a construction site but the subcontract did not require the subcontractor to assume additional responsibility or liability. The court reasoned that if the parties intended subcontractor to assume additional duties, that intent would have been stated in the language of the subcontract.

contract. The court concluded that by rendering an award the arbiters presumably found that contractor had timely made its request for arbitration.

The court then found that the arbiters did not exceed their authority by awarding expert, claim preparation and attorneys' fees, where the contract authorized the arbiters "to award the party whose contention is sustained, such sums as they deem proper for the time, expense and trouble" incident to the arbitration.

94031   Clark-Fitzpatrick, Inc./Franki Found. Co. v. Gill, 652 A.2d 440 (R.I. 1994)

        III: A107-1987, Art. 13, Para. 13.2
        III: A107-1987, Art. 15, Para. 15.5
        III: A117-1987, Art. 18, Para. 18.2
        III: A117-1987, Art. 20, Para. 20.5
        III: A201-1987, Art. 4, Para. 4.3.5
        III: A201-1987, Art. 7, Para. 7.3.4
        III: A201-1987, Art. 7, Para. 7.3.5
        III: A201-1987, Art. 7, Para. 7.3.6
        III: A201-1987, Art. 7, Para. 7.3.7
        III: A201-1987, Art. 7, Para. 7.3.8
        III: A201-1987, Art. 7, Para. 7.3.9
        III: A201-1987, Art. 9, Para. 9.10.4

DOT appealed and contractor and subcontractor cross-appealed from judgments entered against DOT for damages arising from the construction of a bridge. Among numerous issues on appeal and cross-appeal, owner argued that, because the contractor had failed to file a formal claim letter as required by the contract, the trial court erred in awarding damages to the contractor for remedial work it performed. The Supreme Court of Rhode Island affirmed the judgment of the trial court.

The contract documents applicable to the project included the Standard Specifications for Road and Bridge Construction (the blue book), supplemental specifications, plans, and special provisions. The claims provision stated that:

If, in any case, the Contractor deems that additional compensation is due him for work or material not clearly covered in the contract or not ordered by the Engineer as extra work, as defined herein, the Contractor shall notify the Engineer in writing of his intention to make a claim for such additional compensation before he begins the work on which he bases the claim. If such notification is not given, and the Engineer is not afforded proper facilities by the Contractor for keeping strict account of actual cost as required, then the Contractor hereby agrees to waive any claim for such additional compensation.

The supreme court affirmed the trial court's finding that contractor's failure to give formal notice as required by the claims provision was not a waiver of claim. The court

III: A401-1987, Art. 6, Para. 6.5
III: B141-1987, Art. 7, Para. 7.1
III: B141-1987, Art. 7, Para. 7.2
III: B141-1987, Art. 7, Para. 7.3
III: B141-1987, Art. 7, Para. 7.4

Contractor demanded arbitration of its dispute against owner for additional costs resulting from unanticipated site conditions. Owner refused to arbitrate, asserting that contractor's demand for arbitration was untimely. Contractor filed suit and obtained an order compelling arbitration. The arbiters entered an award in favor of contractor for damages resulting from changed conditions, its claim preparation costs, expert fees and attorney fees. Contractor was ordered to pay owner for damages resulting from contractor's failure to complete its contract. The arbiters' award was confirmed by the trial court and owner appealed. The appellate court affirmed the judgment of the trial court.

The owner/contractor agreement provided that: "[a]ll questions of dispute under this Agreement shall be submitted to arbitration at the request of either party to the dispute." On appeal, among numerous other points of error, owner argued that the arbiters' award of damages "incurred by contractor as a result of changed conditions" was erroneous because the conditions of the construction site never changed and contractor never complained about "changed conditions" in its original or amended specification of claims; therefore, the arbiters exceeded their powers. The appellate court found that (1) the arbitration provision in the contract provided that "all questions of dispute" arising under the contract were to be arbitrated; (2) the court order compelling arbitration directed the parties to arbitrate "all disputes between them"; and (3) a dispute existed regarding whether there were "changed conditions." The court found that, in light of these findings and the broad arbitration clause in the contract, the arbiters did not exceed their authority in rendering an award based on changed conditions.

Owner then argued that the arbiters exceeded their powers by disregarding the express terms of the owner/contractor agreement, which made contractor responsible for conditions at the site. The court found that the express written terms of the contract, however, also made the owner responsible for the adequacy of the design and the sufficiency of the contract documents. Based on the court's finding that the arbiters were empowered to resolve all disputes between the parties which arose under the contract, the court found that "all disputes" included a determination of owner's obligations under the contract to disclose site conditions, as well as contractor's responsibility under the contract as a bidder to examine the site and the plans.

The owner then argued that the arbitration proceedings exceeded the arbiters' authority because contractor failed to timely demand arbitration. The court found that the arbiters' power to resolve all issues between the parties arising under the contract contemplated a determination by the arbiters of the timeliness of the demand under the terms of the

permitted by law." The court did not consider the indemnity clause void under the state statute because of this limitation.

The next issue before the court was whether "cause," as used in the state statute, required a finding of negligence. The court ruled that the subcontractor waived this issue by failing to raise it at trial.

Additionally, subcontractor argued that the judge erroneously determined that indemnification of the contractor for its own negligence was required, absent express language in the indemnity clause. The court found that the absence of specific language does not preclude the right to indemnity if the intent sufficiently appears in the language of the contract and circumstances attending its execution. Based on the scope of the language which provided for indemnification "from and against any and all claims for bodily injury and death and for property damage or any other loss or damage suffered or incurred by the . . . Contractor . . . to the fullest extent permitted by law," the court concluded that the trial judge did not err in ruling that subcontractor's contractual obligation covered claims resulting from the concurrent fault of both subcontractor and contractor.

Subcontractor then argued that the trial judge erred in failing to find second subcontractor liable to contractor where the indemnity clause in both subcontracts was identical. The trial judge's decision was based on his conclusion that it would have been inequitable to do so because it would have resulted in a "windfall" for the contractor. The appellate court disagreed because there was no evidence in the record to distinguish one subcontractor's liability for indemnity to the contractor from the other's. In light of the previous holding that the excavation subcontractor could not obtain contribution from the contractor, there had been no loss suffered by contractor and, consequently, no entitlement to indemnification from either subcontractor.

94030   City of Baytown v. C.L. Winter, Inc., 886 S.W.2d 515 (Tex. Ct. App. 1994)

	III:	A107-1987, Art. 10, Para. 10.8
	III:	A117-1987, Art. 15, Para. 15.8
	III:	A201-1987, Art. 4, Para. 4.5.1
	III:	A201-1987, Art. 4, Para. 4.5.2
	III:	A201-1987, Art. 4, Para. 4.5.3
	III:	A201-1987, Art. 4, Para. 4.5.4
	III:	A201-1987, Art. 4, Para. 4.5.4.1
	III:	A201-1987, Art. 4, Para. 4.5.4.2
	III:	A201-1987, Art. 4, Para. 4.5.5
	III:	A201-1987, Art. 4, Para. 4.5.6
	III:	A201-1987, Art. 4, Para. 4.5.7
	III:	A401-1987, Art. 6, Para. 6.1
	III:	A401-1987, Art. 6, Para. 6.2
	III:	A401-1987, Art. 6, Para. 6.3
	III:	A401-1987, Art. 6, Para. 6.4

94029 Callahan v. A.J. Welch Equip. Corp., 36 Mass. App. Ct. 608, 634 N.E.2d 134 (1994)

    III: A107-1987, Art. 9, Para. 9.12
    III: A117-1987, Art. 14, Para. 14.12
    III: A201-1987, Art. 3, Para. 3.18.1
    III: A201-1987, Art. 10, Para. 10.1.4
    III: A401-1987, Art. 4, Para. 4.6.1

An injured employee of an earth support systems subcontractor brought a negligence action against contractor and excavation subcontractor. Contractor brought an indemnity action against both subcontractors. In response, excavation subcontractor filed claims for contribution against contractor and the earth subcontractor. Prior to trial, the excavation subcontractor entered into a settlement agreement with injured worker. Injured worker then dismissed its claims against excavation subcontractor and contractor. The cross-claims and third-party complaints for indemnification and contribution went to trial. The parties agreed that the case would be submitted to the jury on special verdict questions, which asked whether contractor was negligent, whether contractor proximately caused the injury, and whether the subcontractors caused the accident. The jury found that contractor was negligent and both subcontractors "caused" the accident. The judge made numerous rulings, among them that contractor was not entitled to indemnification from excavation subcontractor but was entitled to indemnification from earth subcontractor for the amount excavation subcontractor was awarded as contribution from contractor. Earth support systems subcontractor appealed, contending, among numerous other issues regarding contribution, that the trial court erred in finding subcontractor liable to contractor because the indemnification clauses in both subcontracts were identical. Furthermore, under state statute, subcontractor could not be held liable unless the subcontractor was negligent. Subcontractor claimed that the jury's finding that it was a "cause" of the accident was not a finding of negligence.

Both subcontracts contained identical indemnification clauses, which provided that:

> To the fullest extent permitted by law, Subcontractor shall defend and save the Owner and Contractor harmless and indemnified from and against any and all claims for bodily injury and death and for property damage or any other loss or damage suffered or incurred by the Owner, any separate contractors employed by the Owner, or by Contractor or any Subcontractor employed by the Owner or Contractor, resulting from the negligence or any act or omission of Subcontractor or his agents, or arising out of or in any way connected with the performance, attempted performance, or failure to perform the Work by Subcontractor.

The applicable Massachusetts state statute was Mass. Gen. L. ch. 149, § 29C.

The appellate court found that subcontractor's obligation to indemnify was limited to an injury resulting from its own negligence or that of its agents "to the fullest extent

Contractor brought a breach of contract action and a lien foreclosure action against owners. The trial court granted judgment in favor of contractor but only for a portion of its claims and awarded owners costs and fees for defense of the lien claim. Both contractor and owner appealed. Among numerous other issues, contractor argued that the trial court erred (1) in finding that the parties' contract contained a guaranteed maximum price which limited the amount of construction costs recoverable by contractor; (2) in construing the contract language dealing with establishment of a "Guaranteed Maximum Price" ("GMP"); (3) by ignoring other language that was critical to carrying out the intent of the parties; and (4) in failing to read the contract language in the context of the circumstances existing when the contract was executed and the circumstances which both parties contemplated would follow in the course of events. The appellate court affirmed in part and vacated in part the judgment of the trial court.

The parties entered into the American Institute of Architects Standard Form of Agreement Between Owner and Contractor, Document No. A111, 1987 edition. Specifically at issue, were Paragraphs 5.2.1, 5.2.2, 8.1, 8.1.8, and 16.1.3 through 16.1.6 which incorporated the American Institute of Architects General Conditions of the Contract for Construction, Document No. A201, 1987 edition. The contractor added the following to Paragraph 5.2.2.:

A Guaranteed Maximum Price will be provided by the Contractor after completion of the design and development documents and then become a part of this Agreement. The Contractor's fee will be included in the Guaranteed Maximum Price. If the Owner and Contractor do not agree upon a Guaranteed Maximum Price, this entire Agreement becomes null and void. If a contingency amount is included in the Guaranteed Maximum Price, it will be used for changes approved by the Owner. Any unused amount of the contingency will be returned in full to the Owner.

The contractor added the following to Paragraph 8.1.8: "except where changes required by the Owner occur that add to the Guaranteed Maximum Price and any costs necessitated by City, State, or Federal requirements not incorporated in the working drawings and specifications at the time the Guaranteed Maximum Price is established."

Paragraphs 16.1.3 through 16.1.6 provided that the working drawings and project manual from which the GMP was to be established would be added by an amendment to the agreement after they were finalized. The contract documents also included a letter written by contractor to owner stating the amount of contractor's GMP pursuant to Paragraph 5.2.1.

Contractor issued a letter establishing a GMP before the construction drawings were complete but contended that the letter did not constitute a final GMP limiting its "cost plus agreement." Although the court agreed that the contractor had prematurely issued the letter, it held that the letter was an offer accepted by the owner. Moreover, the court decided that the language of Article 16, which provided that "[t]he final working drawings and project manual from which the Guaranteed Maximum Price is established will be added by an Amendment to the Agreement when they are finalized," was not so inconsistent with Paragraph 5.2.1 as to create an ambiguity concerning the establishment of the GMP.

providing contractor with written notice to cure seven (7) days prior to the stop-work order, and granted contractor partial summary judgment. As a result, contractor was awarded damages and lost profits and owner appealed. The appellate court affirmed the judgment of the trial court.

After the parties' repeated failure to resolve numerous "contract/scheduling delays," owner issued a stop-work order and a notice of intent to terminate the contract. Pursuant to the stop-work order, contractor left the site and owner hired another contractor to complete the work. The owner/contractor agreement contained a termination provision which stated that:

[I]f the Contractor persistently or repeatedly refuses or fails, except in cases for which extension of time is provided, to supply enough properly skilled workers or proper materials, . . . or otherwise is guilty of a substantial violation of a provision of the Contract Documents, and fails within seven days after receipt of written notice to commence and continue correction of such default, neglect or violation with diligence and promptness, the Owner . . . may, after seven days following receipt by the Contractor of an additional written notice . . . terminate the employment of the Contractor and take possession of the site and of all materials, equipment, tools, construction equipment and machinery thereon owned by the Contractor and may finish the Work by whatever methods the Owner may deem expedient.

Contractor's duty was to "commence and continue correction" of its inadequate performance only "after receipt of written notice." The appellate court held that, since providing written notice of termination was an express condition of the contract, owner had no right to terminate until contractor was given seven days to correct its performance. The court found, however, that the termination provision did not describe what had to be included in the written notice. The court, therefore, interpreted the termination provision to include the condition that owner's written notice to cure needed to describe the inadequate performance and had to fairly advise contractor that owner considered the inadequate performance serious enough that, without prompt correction, the contract would be terminated.

94028   Bouten Constr. Co. v. M & L Land Co., 125 Idaho 957, 877 P.2d 928 (1994)

I:	A111-1987, Art. 5, Para. 5.2.1
I:	A111-1987, Art. 5, Para. 5.2.2
I:	A111-1987, Art. 8, Para. 8.1
I:	A111-1987, Art. 8, Para. 8.1.8
I:	A111-1987, Art. 16, Para. 16.1.3
I:	A111-1987, Art. 16, Para. 16.1.4
I:	A111-1987, Art. 16, Para. 16.1.5
I:	A111-1987, Art. 16, Para. 16.1.6

Contractor appealed a jury verdict in favor of subcontractor in an action to collect on extra-work orders. Contractor argued that the trial court erred by denying its motion to enforce the arbitration clause in the subcontract because the contractor failed to establish it was an aggrieved party, as was required by state law. The appellate court reversed the judgment of the trial court.

The parties entered into the American Institute of Architect Standard Form of Agreement Between Contractor and Subcontractor, Document No. 401, 1987 edition, specifically Paragraph 5.2, which required subcontractor to submit written copies of any claim for adjustment to the contract sum or time to owner, and Paragraphs 6.1 and 6.4, which provided for the arbitration of disputes.

The Georgia statute governing arbitration provided in pertinent part that "upon motion by an aggrieved party, the court shall compel arbitration of an issue upon its determination that the agreement to arbitrate was valid and that the claim was not barred by time limitations. . . ."

The appellate court found that contractor was clearly an aggrieved party under the state statute because subcontractor was attempting to recover attorney fees in the litigation which were not available to it in arbitration pursuant to the terms of the subcontract. The court found that (1) there was no dispute that the subject matter of the litigation was governed by the AIA contract because the extra-work orders reflected work that subcontractor had agreed to perform in the subcontract; (2) in addition to containing an arbitration clause, the subcontract provided for extra-work or changes in the work required of the subcontractor; and (3) arbitration was not barred by any contractual time limitation. The court remanded for an order compelling the parties to submit their dispute to arbitration.

94027 Blaine Economic Dev. Auth. v. Royal Elec. Co., 520 N.W.2d 473 (Minn. Ct. App. 1994)

II:	A107-1978, Art. 20, Para. 20.2
II:	A107-1987, Art. 20, Para. 20.2
II:	A117-1979, Art. 24, Para. 24.2
II:	A117-1987, Art. 25, Para. 25.2
II:	A201-1976, Art. 14, Para. 14.2.1
II:	A201-1987, Art. 14, Para. 14.2.1
II:	A201-1987, Art. 14, Para. 14.2.2
II:	A201-1987, Art. 14, Para. 14.3.3

Owner brought a breach of contract action against contractor. Contractor counterclaimed for wrongful termination of the contract and for damages. The trial court found, on the issue of liability, that the owner wrongfully terminated the contract by not

I: B141-1987, Art. 9, Para. 9.5

Contractor brought a breach of contract action against owner alleging that owner's incomplete and defective plans, together with owner's failure to manage or participate in construction inspections, breached express and implied contractual obligations to contractor. Contractor sought purely economic damages. In its amended complaint, contractor alleged that the architect's plans were inaccurate and incomplete. Contractor and owner entered into a settlement agreement that provided in pertinent part that the owner assign to contractor "any and all claims relating to this project" against architect and others. Contractor filed a second amended complaint to assert the assigned claims for economic loss. Architect filed a motion for summary judgment requesting dismissal of contractor's claims on the ground that the anti-assignment clause in the owner/architect agreement prohibited the owner from assigning its breach of contract claim to contractor. The trial court granted architect's motion, and contractor appealed. The pertinent issue before the court was whether contractor's assigned action against the architect was barred by the economic loss rule. The Supreme Court of Washington reversed the judgment of the lower court and held that the anti-assignment clause in the owner/architect agreement did not prohibit the owner's assignment of its breach of contract claim against architect.

The owner and architect entered into an agreement which contained an anti-assignment clause identical to Paragraph 9.5 of the American Institute of Architects Standard Form of Agreement Between Owner and Architect, Document No. B141, 1987 edition.

The supreme court found that a general anti-assignment clause, such as Paragraph 9.5, aimed at prohibiting the assignment of a contractual performance, does not, absent specific language to the contrary, prohibit the assignment of a breach of contract action. Paragraph 9.5, as construed by the court, was intended to prohibit the exchange of contractual performances. The court held that a general assignment clause (that is, one directed at the performance of the contract) did not prohibit the assignment of a breach of contract action if the architect completed the terms of its contract prior to assignment.

94026   Bishop Contracting Co. v. Center Bros., 213 Ga. App. 804, 445 S.E.2d 780 (1994), *cert. denied*, 1994 Ga. LEXIS 1119 (Ga. Oct. 17, 1994)

II: A107-1987, Art. 10, Para. 10.8
II: A117-1987, Art. 15, Para. 15.8
II: A201-1987, Art. 4, Para. 4.5.1
II: A201-1987, Art. 4, Para. 4.5.7
I: A401-1987, Art. 5, Para. 5.2
I: A401-1987, Art. 6, Para. 6.1
I: A401-1987, Art. 6, Para. 6.4
II: B141-1987, Art. 7, Para. 7.1
II: B141-1987, Art. 7, Para. 7.4

III: A117-1987, Art. 23, Para. 23.2
III: A201-1987, Art. 3, Para. 3.5.1
III: A201-1987, Art. 12, Para. 12.2.2
III: A201-1987, Art. 12, Para. 12.2.4

Builder appealed from a judgment awarding owner damages for breach of contract. After numerous problems arose during the construction of the owner's home, the owner requested that the builder make "acceptable arrangements" to cure the defects and complete the home. The parties were unable to resolve their differences and the owner filed an action for breach of contract. The complaint alleged that the house was not constructed in a workmanlike manner and that builder was uncooperative, arrogant, and nonresponsive to owner's written complaints. Builder argued, *inter alia,* that the trial court erred in awarding owner money damages despite an express agreement between the parties that limited builder's obligation, if the work was incomplete or substandard, to the repair and replacement of any defective materials, equipment or workmanship. The Appellate court affirmed the judgment of the trial court.

The agreement stated in pertinent part that:

(b). Said dwelling unit and appurtenances shall be constructed in a first class, workmanlike manner . . . .

. . . .

(e). Seller warrants to Buyer that all materials and equipment incorporated into the alterations and construction of the dwelling unit and appurtenances will be new, good quality, free from liens and defects. . . . The foregoing warranties shall run to buyer only, shall be exclusive and in lieu of any and all other warranties. . . . These warranties shall continue for a period of twelve (12) months from the date of the settlement, and any claim made by Buyer pursuant to these warranties must be in writing to Seller and received by Seller within said twelve (12) month period from the date of the settlement. Seller's obligation under these warranties is limited to the repair or replacement of any defective materials, equipment or workmanship.

The appellate court found that the clause was enforceable, but that it did not limit owner's remedy by allowing builder unlimited attempts to cure the defects. Rather, the exclusive-remedy clause only required owner to give builder a reasonable time to cure defective materials and workmanship. The court read the clause so as to limit the damage award to actual, as opposed to consequential and incidental, damages. Therefore, the court held that the clause did not preclude an award of money damages for builders' breach of contract.

94025   Berschauer/Phillips Constr. Co. v. Seattle Sch. Dist. No. 1, 124 Wash. 2d 816, 881 P.2d 986 (1994)

II: A201-1987, Art. 13, Para. 13.2.1
III: A401-1987, Art. 7, Para. 7.3

III: A401-1987, Art. 4, Para. 4.6.1

Contractor's injured employee brought a negligence action against owner. Owner demanded that contractor assume the defense of owner in that action based upon the indemnity provision in the owner/contractor agreement. Contractor claimed that worker's injury resulted from the sole negligence of owner, and, therefore, refused to defend owner in that action. After a jury trial and subsequent appeal determined that owner was negligent in some unspecified manner but that owner's negligence was not a proximate cause of worker's injuries, the owner sought enforcement of the indemnity clause in the owner/contractor agreement for the costs in defending the previous suit. Owner filed this action for damages and for a declaratory judgment that contractor was required to indemnify owner against all costs and expenses, including reasonable attorneys' fees, incurred by owner.

The indemnity clause in the owner/contractor agreement provided as follows:

[Contractor shall indemnify Owner against] any and all claims, losses, demands, causes of action and any and all related costs and expense, of every kind and character including, without limitation, reasonable attorneys' fees . . . on account of personal injuries or death . . . growing out of, incident to, or resulting directly or indirectly from the performance by [Contractor] hereunder, whether such loss, damage, injury or liability is contributed to by the negligence of [Owner] . . . or by premises themselves or any equipment thereon . . . or from other causes whatsoever; except that [Contractor] shall have no liability for damages or the costs incident thereto caused by the sole negligence of [Owner].

The district court determined that since owner was absolved of any liability to injured worker, and owner incurred costs and expenses as a result of defending itself in the previous suit, contractor's agreement to indemnify owner was enforceable. Contractor was, therefore, obligated to pay for owner's costs and expenses that arose out of contractor's performance of the contract.

Contractor further attacked the enforceability of the indemnity provision as a "hold harmless" provision and void as against public policy pursuant to Mississippi's anti-indemnity statute. The court disagreed, reasoning that the thrust of the owner/contractor agreement fell outside the scope of the statute, which only bars indemnity for one's own negligence. Since the owner was cleared of liability to the injured worker, the statute was inapplicable. Thus, the district court granted recovery to the owner.

94024 Barrack v. Kolea, 438 Pa. Super. 11, 651 A.2d 149 (1994)

III: A107-1987, Art. 9, Para. 9.4
III: A107-1987, Art. 18, Para. 18.1
III: A107-1987, Art. 18, Para. 18.2
III: A117-1987, Art. 14, Para. 14.4
III: A117-1987, Art. 23, Para. 23.1

III:	A117-1987, Art. 14, Para. 14.12	
III:	A201-1987, Art. 3, Para. 3.18.1	
III:	A201-1987, Art. 10, Para. 10.1.4	
III:	A401-1987, Art. 4, Para. 4.6.1	

Contractor brought an indemnity action against subcontractor for damages paid in settlement to subcontractor's injured employee. Both parties moved for summary judgment. Contractor alleged that subcontractor was obligated to indemnify contractor under an express, implied-in-fact or implied-in-law contract for contractor's liability to injured worker which resulted from subcontractor's negligence. Contractor argued that subcontractor assumed responsibility for its employees when it signed the subcontract, including safety obligations, and that the court should infer from the subcontract's language that subcontractor agreed to indemnify contractor should any accidents arise due to subcontractor's failure to adhere to safety regulations. Where it had not been judicially determined whether either party was negligent, the district court assumed, in deciding the issue of indemnity, that both parties were guilty of some negligence in causing worker's injury.

The subcontract provided in pertinent part that:

The above-specified project is to be completed in strict conformance with all specifications and conditions relating to this agreement. In addition, the project is to be performed in compliance with OSHA Regulations and local, state and national building codes. Although the contractor has control over the quality of all work relating to this project, the subcontractor is an independent contractor in all respects. The subcontractor is responsible for his employees, his subcontractors, materials, equipment and all applicable taxes, benefits and insurances. The subcontractor is responsible for coordinating his activity with other trades and promptly cleaning up any surplus or refuse which was created by his work. . . .

The district court held that there was no express promise by subcontractor to indemnify contractor for contractor's settlement with injured worker. The contractor maintained that the following contractual language constituted a save-and-hold-harmless provision: "[t]he subcontractor is responsible for his employees, his subcontractors, materials, equipment and all applicable taxes, benefits and insurances. . . ." The court found that when this language was strictly construed, contractor's argument was without merit.

94023 American Cyanamid Co. v. Campbell Constr. Co., 864 F. Supp. 580 (S.D. Miss. 1994)

III:	A107-1987, Art. 9, Para. 9.12	
III:	A117-1987, Art. 14, Para. 14.12	
III:	A201-1987, Art. 3, Para. 3.18.1	
III:	A201-1987, Art. 10, Para. 10.1.4	

III:	A401–1987, Art. 6, Para. 6.2
III:	A401–1987, Art. 6, Para. 6.3
III:	A401–1987, Art. 6, Para. 6.4
III:	A401–1987, Art. 6, Para. 6.5
III:	B141–1987, Art. 7, Para. 7.1
III:	B141–1987, Art. 7, Para. 7.2
III:	B141–1987, Art. 7, Para. 7.3
III:	B141–1987, Art. 7, Para. 7.4

Contractor sought a stay of its pending arbitration with subcontractor, arguing that the dispute was not subject to arbitration pursuant to an exception provision in the subcontract. The trial court denied the petition for stay, and the appellate court affirmed.

The subcontract provided that disputes were subject to arbitration with the following specified exception:

This agreement to arbitrate shall not apply to any claim . . . (b) asserted by the Subcontractor against the Contractor if the Contractor asserts said claim, either in whole or part, against the Owner and the contract between the Contractor and Owner does not provide for binding arbitration, or does so provide but the two arbitration proceedings are not consolidated, or the Contractor and Owner have not subsequently agreed to arbitrate said claim, in either case of which the parties hereto shall so notify each other either before or after demand for arbitration is made.

Subcontractor demanded arbitration with contractor, claiming nonpayment for performed work. The contractor sent a letter to owner, submitting a claim for the subcontractor's requested amount. The contractor contested the arbitrability of the subcontractor's claim against it, arguing that the dispute fell within the subcontract's exception "(b)" because the contractor asserted the claim against the owner and the owner-contractor agreement did not provide for arbitration.

The appellate court rejected contractor's argument that it had asserted the claim against the owner. The court looked to the owner-contractor agreement, which provided that "a written demand . . . is not a claim . . . until certified." The contractor was required to submit, among other things, a certification that the claim was made in good faith. The court determined that the contractor did not make a claim because the contractor had failed to submit a certification to the owner. The court concluded that, because the contractor had not asserted a claim against the owner, exception "(b)" to arbitration contained in the subcontract was inapplicable. Thus, the subcontractor's claim against contractor was subject to arbitration.

94022   A & B Constr., Inc. v. Atlas Roofing & Skylight Co., 867 F. Supp. 100 (D.R.I. 1994)

III:	A107–1987, Art. 9, Para. 9.12

II:	A117–1987, Art. 11, Para. 11.1	
II:	A117–1987, Art. 12, Para. 12.1	

Subcontractor's injured employee's appealed from the lower court's grant of summary judgment in favor of contractor and owner. The appellate court construed the provisions of the owner-contractor agreement to determine the propriety of summary judgment as to worker's negligence claim. The court concluded that, where the summary judgment record did not indicate that the American Institute of Architects General Conditions of the Contract for Construction, Document No. A201, 1976 edition, was part of the owner-contractor agreement, worker was not entitled to recover damages. Worker had claimed damages based on contractor's duty to provide a safe workplace under Paragraphs 4.3, 4.7.2, 4.7.4, 4.9, 10.2 and 10.2 of the General Conditions.

The court examined the American Institute of Architects Standard Form of Agreement Between Owner and Contractor, Document No. 101, 1977 edition, and the General Conditions. The court rejected the worker's argument that the General Conditions, which were not executed by the parties or attached to the owner-contractor agreement, was incorporated by reference by the sentence set forth on the cover page of the owner-contractor agreement that stated "Use only with the 1976 Edition of AIA Document A201, General Conditions of the Contract for Construction." The court construed this language as precatory, merely cautioning users not to use the owner-contractor agreement with another set of general conditions. Relying on Article 1 of A101 which defined "Contract Documents" and required that they be enumerated in Paragraph 7.2, which was left blank, the court concluded that the provisions of A201 were not made part of the owner-contractor agreement and could not be relied on by worker to establish its negligence claim.

94021 Woodrow Wilson Constr. Co. v. MMR-Radon Constructors, Inc., 635 So. 2d 758 (La. Ct. App.), *cert. denied*, 639 So. 2d 1167 (La. 1994)

III:	A107–1987, Art. 10, Para. 10.8	
III:	A117–1987, Art. 15, Para. 15.8	
III:	A201–1987, Art. 4, Para. 4.5.1	
III:	A201–1987, Art. 4, Para. 4.5.2	
III:	A201–1987, Art. 4, Para. 4.5.3	
III:	A201–1987, Art. 4, Para. 4.5.4	
III:	A201–1987, Art. 4, Para. 4.5.4.1	
III:	A201–1987, Art. 4, Para. 4.5.4.2	
III:	A201–1987, Art. 4, Para. 4.5.5	
III:	A201–1987, Art. 4, Para. 4.5.6	
III:	A201–1987, Art. 4, Para. 4.5.7	
III:	A401–1987, Art. 6, Para. 6.1	

III:	A201–1987, Art. 4, Para. 4.5.5
III:	A201–1987, Art. 4, Para. 4.5.6
III:	A201–1987, Art. 4, Para. 4.5.7
III:	A401–1987, Art. 6, Para. 6.1
III:	A401–1987, Art. 6, Para. 6.2
III:	A401–1987, Art. 6, Para. 6.3
III:	A401–1987, Art. 6, Para. 6.4
III:	A401–1987, Art. 6, Para. 6.5
III:	B141–1987, Art. 7, Para. 7.1
III:	B141–1987, Art. 7, Para. 7.2
III:	B141–1987, Art. 7, Para. 7.3
III:	B141–1987, Art. 7, Para. 7.4

Contractor appealed the grant of summary judgment denying arbitration of its claim against the state for extra costs incurred in constructing a state university building. The Wisconsin Supreme Court enforced the arbitration provision notwithstanding the state's sovereign immunity defense.

The arbitration clause provided in pertinent part that "[t]he agreement to arbitrate shall be strictly enforceable in accordance with [state statute]." The referenced Wisconsin statute provided in pertinent part that "an agreement . . . to submit to arbitration . . . shall be valid, irrevocable and enforceable." Another Wisconsin statute provided that the contracting state agency was authorized to enter into building contracts.

The Wisconsin Supreme Court noted that the agency's power to agree to arbitrate was based on its right to contract. Thus, the state by implication authorized the agency to agree to arbitration of disputes and waived sovereign immunity. The court rejected the state's argument that enforcing the arbitration clause would deny the state the prerogative of determining claim resolution procedures, conflicting with a statutory scheme for filing claims. The court saw no conflict because it viewed the statutory claim procedures and potential resultant litigation as distinct from the arbitration process. The court stated that contractor would be required to follow the statutory claim procedures if an award were granted at the conclusion of arbitration.

94020 Welch v. McDougal, 876 S.W.2d 218 (Tex. Ct. App. 1994)

I:	A101–1977, Art. 1
I:	A101–1977, Art. 7, Para. 7.2
II:	A101–1987, Art. 1
II:	A101–1987, Art. 9, Para. 9.1
II:	A107–1987, Art. 6, Para. 6.1
II:	A107–1987, Art. 7, Para. 7.1

clause of the subcontracts provided in pertinent part that "[i]n case of any dispute between the parties as to the interpretation of this agreement or the performance of the same, either party may demand that the dispute be submitted to arbitration. . . ." The subcontracts also contained an assumption provision, which stated in pertinent part as follows:

> The work to be done hereunder is a portion of the work required of Contractor under the General Contract referred to in the Special Conditions hereof. Insofar as applicable, Subcontractor shall be bound by all of the terms and conditions of the Contract Documents, and shall strictly comply therewith. All rights and remedies reserved to Owner under the Contract Documents shall apply to and be possessed by Contractor in its dealings with Subcontractor.

The owner-contractor agreement contained an arbitration clause which provided in pertinent part that "[a]ny dispute arising out of the work agreed on herein must be raised and settled in an arbitration proceeding held in accordance with the Construction Industry Rules of the American Arbitration Association then in effect or, if not then in effect, in accordance with [state statute]."

The appellate court found that the terms of the owner-contractor agreement, including the arbitration provision, was incorporated by reference into the subcontracts. The assumption provision accorded the contractor the same rights and remedies against the subcontractors as those accorded the owner against the contractor. According to the court, the subcontractors were required by the assumption clause to submit their disputes to arbitration since the contractor was required by the owner-contractor agreement to submit any disputes with the owner to arbitration.

Subcontractors argued that construing the assumption clause as incorporating the arbitration provisions contained in the owner-contractor agreement into the subcontracts resulted in an ambiguity because the agreements contained different arbitration procedures. The subcontractors maintained that such ambiguity should be resolved in their favor. The court found no such ambiguity. According to the court, the arbitration provision in the subcontracts governed disputes arising only between contractor and subcontractors and the arbitration provision in the owner-contractor agreement governed disputes between the owner and contractor.

94019   State v. P.G. Miron Constr. Co., 181 Wis. 2d 1045, 512 N.W.2d 499 (1994)

III:	A107–1987, Art. 10, Para. 10.8	
III:	A117–1987, Art. 15, Para. 15.8	
III:	A201–1987, Art. 4, Para. 4.5.1	
III:	A201–1987, Art. 4, Para. 4.5.2	
III:	A201–1987, Art. 4, Para. 4.5.3	
III:	A201–1987, Art. 4, Para. 4.5.4	
III:	A201–1987, Art. 4, Para. 4.5.4.1	
III:	A201–1987, Art. 4, Para. 4.5.4.2	

According to the court, because owner also served as architect, evidence indicating that contractor presented change orders to the owner, who then delayed action on the orders, was sufficient to support an inference that contractor's claim was presented to the "architect."

94018 Slaught v. Bencomo Roofing Co., 25 Cal. App. 4th 744, 30 Cal. Rptr. 2d 618 (1994)

III:	A107–1987, Art. 10, Para. 10.8
III:	A117–1987, Art. 15, Para. 15.8
III:	A201–1987, Art. 4, Para. 4.5.1
III:	A201–1987, Art. 4, Para. 4.5.2
III:	A201–1987, Art. 4, Para. 4.5.3
III:	A201–1987, Art. 4, Para. 4.5.4
III:	A201–1987, Art. 4, Para. 4.5.4.1
III:	A201–1987, Art. 4, Para. 4.5.4.2
III:	A201–1987, Art. 4, Para. 4.5.5
III:	A201–1987, Art. 4, Para. 4.5.6
III:	A201–1987, Art. 4, Para. 4.5.7
III:	A401–1987, Art. 6, Para. 6.1
III:	A401–1987, Art. 6, Para. 6.2
III:	A401–1987, Art. 6, Para. 6.3
III:	A401–1987, Art. 6, Para. 6.4
III:	A401–1987, Art. 6, Para. 6.5
III:	B141–1987, Art. 7, Para. 7.1
III:	B141–1987, Art. 7, Para. 7.2
III:	B141–1987, Art. 7, Para. 7.3
III:	B141–1987, Art. 7, Para. 7.4

Contractor appealed denial of its petition to compel arbitration with subcontractors and to consolidate subcontractor arbitration proceedings with ongoing arbitration between contractor and owner. The trial court offered no statement of decision with its denial of the petition. The appellate court reversed.

Contractor first demanded arbitration with owner, seeking out-of-pocket expenses and costs. Owner counterclaimed, seeking damages based on contractor's failure to properly supervise subcontractors and based on subcontractors' defective construction of the project. Contractor demanded that subcontractors join in the arbitration, and each declined.

At issue was the construction of the arbitration clauses of the owner-contractor agreement and the subcontracts, together with an assumption clause. The arbitration

II:	A201–1987, Art. 4, Para. 4.2.11
II:	A201–1987, Art. 4, Para. 4.5.1
II:	A201–1987, Art. 4, Para. 4.5.2
II:	A201–1987, Art. 4, Para. 4.5.3
II:	A201–1987, Art. 4, Para. 4.5.4
II:	A201–1987, Art. 4, Para. 4.5.4.1
II:	A201–1987, Art. 4, Para. 4.5.4.2
II:	A201–1987, Art. 4, Para. 4.5.5
II:	A201–1987, Art. 4, Para. 4.5.6
II:	A201–1987, Art. 4, Para. 4.5.7
II:	A401–1987, Art. 6, Para. 6.1
II:	A401–1987, Art. 6, Para. 6.2
II:	A401–1987, Art. 6, Para. 6.3
II:	A401–1987, Art. 6, Para. 6.4
II:	A401–1987, Art. 6, Para. 6.5
II:	B141–1987, Art. 2, Para. 2.6.15
II:	B141–1987, Art. 7, Para. 7.1
II:	B141–1987, Art. 7, Para. 7.2
II:	B141–1987, Art. 7, Para. 7.3
II:	B141–1987, Art. 7, Para. 7.4

Contractor appealed denial of its motion to compel arbitration with owner over disputed nonpayments and withheld change orders. The trial court concluded that contractor had waived its right to arbitration by pursuing a mechanics' lien action. The appellate court reversed and remanded.

The arbitration provision contained in the owner-contractor agreement was identical to Paragraph 10.8 of the American Institute of Architects Abbreviated Form of Agreement Between Owner and Contractor, Document No. A107, 1987 edition. The court also relied on Paragraph 10.5, which required that claims first be submitted to the architect.

The appellate court rejected owner's argument that under state law a mechanics' lien action was the sole remedy for multi-party disputes. Owner also argued that state law precluded application of the Federal Arbitration Act (FAA). The court determined that the FAA was not preempted by the procedures prescribed for mechanics' liens by state statute where there was sufficient evidence to support a finding of interstate commerce. Relying on precedent to the effect that the filing of a mechanic's lien did not preclude the enforcement of an arbitration clause, the court concluded that contractor's participation in a mechanics' lien process initiated by a subcontractor was not sufficient to waive its right to arbitration.

The court also rejected owner's argument that contractor waived the arbitration provision by failing to submit its claim to architect as required by the arbitration provision.

negligence of "any other person or persons" was ambiguous with respect to whether the parties intended to indemnify construction manager for its own negligence. The appellate court affirmed the judgment of the trial court.

The indemnification provision in the agreement (in which the subcontractor is referred to as the "Contractor") stated the following:

> The Contractor . . . shall secure, defend, protect, hold harmless and indemnify the owner . . . , the Construction Manager . . . and the Architect . . . and any of their respective agents, servants and employees against any liability, loss, claims, demands, suits, costs, fees and expenses whatsoever arising from bodily injury, sickness, disease, (including death resulting therefrom), of any persons, or the damage or destruction of any property, including loss of use, arising out of or in connection with the performance of any work relating to this contract including extras [sic] work assigned to the Contractor, based upon any act or omission, negligent or otherwise, of (a) the Contractor or any of its agents, employees or servants, (b) any Sub/Subcontractor supplier or materialman of the Contractor or any agents, employees or servants thereof, (c) any other person or persons. The obligations of indemnification contained herein shall exclude only those matters in which the claim arises out of allegations of the sole negligence of the Owner, the Architect, the Construction Manager or any of their respective agents, servants and employees. The obligations herein shall apply to claims which sound in either tort or contract.

The appellate court rejected the subcontractor's argument that the indemnity provision was ambiguous because it required indemnification for damages caused by the acts of "any other person or persons" without referring to construction manager by name or title while the exclusionary clause referred to construction manager by title. Subcontractor argued that the use of one term in one portion of the provision and the omission of that term in another related portion of the provision evidenced an intent to exclude the term where it did not appear. The court found that, although the indemnity provision employed broad language in the indemnity clause and specific language in the exclusionary clause, this did not create an ambiguity regarding the parties' intent to indemnify construction manager against damages caused by its own negligence but not for damages caused by its sole negligence.

The court found that subcontractor's indemnification of construction manager for construction manager's own negligence did not violate the state's anti-indemnification statute where construction manager was not seeking indemnification from damages or injures caused by its sole negligence.

94017   Silver Dollar City, Inc. v. Kitsmiller Constr. Co., 874 S.W.2d 526 (Mo. Ct. App. 1994)

I:	A107–1987, Art. 10, Para. 10.5
I:	A107–1987, Art. 10, Para. 10.8
I:	A117–1987, Art. 15, Para. 15.5
I:	A117–1987, Art. 15, Para. 15.8

all supervision, equipment, and work items not provided by subcontractors, and for reviewing the safety programs of subcontractors and making recommendations.

The appellate court found that the construction manager clearly had a contractual duty to require the subcontractors to install safety nets or to install the nets itself. The court concluded that the construction manager was potentially liable to the estate on the grounds that the construction manager had assumed a contractual duty to enforce all state and federal employment safety regulations on a project-wide basis during the course of construction and was obligated to require the subcontractors to comply with all safety regulations.

94015 Saxon Constr. & Management Corp. v. Masterclean of North Carolina, Inc., 273 N.J. Super. 231, 641 A.2d 1056 (App. Div.), *cert. denied*, 645 A.2d 142 (N.J. 1994)

III: A401–1987, Art. 7, Para. 7.2.1

In contractor's breach-of-contract action against subcontractor, the appellate court upheld the trial court's finding that the termination clause in the subcontract was void as against public policy. The express language of the termination provision sanctioned the subcontractor's termination for "repeated failure . . . to carry out [its contractual duty]. . . ." The court found that the clause served as an incentive for the subcontractor to breach the contract upon learning that its services could be purchased at an amount less than the contract price and, in that event, the contract provided "if the unpaid balance of the Contract Sum exceeds the expense of finishing the Work, such excess shall be paid to the Subcontractor. . . ."

94016 Sherman v. Demaria Bldg. Co., 203 Mich. App. 593, 513 N.W.2d 187 (1994)

III: A107–1987, Art. 9, Para. 9.12
III: A117–1987, Art. 14, Para. 14.12
III: A201–1987, Art. 3, Para. 3.18.1
III: A201–1987, Art. 10, Para. 10.1.4
III: A401–1987, Art. 4, Para. 4.6.1

Subcontractor's injured employee brought a negligence action against owner, construction manager and architect. Construction manager brought a third-party indemnification action against subcontractor. The trial court found that the indemnity agreement was unambiguous and ruled that subcontractor was required to indemnify construction manager for any damages assessed against construction manager in connection with the injury. Subcontractor appealed on the grounds that the broad language which provided that subcontractor would indemnify construction manager for damages caused by the

Among numerous other issues on appeal, the contractor argued that the trial court erred in failing to limited owner's indemnification to the stated amount of insurance. The indemnity clause referred specifically to the insurance clause. The relevant contract provisions stated that "[t]he contractor shall indemnify, defend and save and hold harmless the Owner from those claims set forth in the above paragraph captioned Insurance, including reasonable attorneys' fees." The insurance provision stated the following:

The contractor shall maintain insurance to protect the Owner and [h]imself from claims which may arise from the Contractor's operations, whether such operations be by himself, any sub-contractor, anyone directly or indirectly employed by any of them, or by whose acts they may be liable. . . . This insurance shall be written for not less than limits of liability required by law, or $1,000,000 aggregate (single limit applicable to bodily injury and property damages combined) [,] whichever is greater.

The appellate court found that the indemnity clause was not limited to the minimum amount of insurance coverage provided in the insurance clause. Contractor was free to and did maintain higher insurance limits to protect itself against its indemnity requirements. The court found that the trial court had not erred in holding that the indemnity provision required contractor to fully indemnify owner for all damages.

94014   Perryman v. Huber, Hunt & Nichols, Inc., 628 N.E.2d 1240 (Ind. Ct. App. 1994)

	III:	A107–1987, Art. 9, Para. 9.6
	III:	A107–1987, Art. 16, Para. 16.1
	III:	A117–1987, Art. 14, Para. 14.6
	III:	A117–1987, Art. 21, Para. 21.1
	III:	A201–1987, Art. 3, Para. 3.7.2
	III:	A201–1987, Art. 10, Para. 10.2.2

Subcontractor's deceased employee's estate brought an action against construction manager. The trial court granted construction manager's motion for summary judgment. The court reasoned that construction manager had not assumed a duty, either by conduct or contract, to require all workers to comply with safety regulations, and that construction manager was not responsible for installing safety nets around the building under construction. The estate appealed. The appellate court reversed the judgment of the trial court.

The owner-construction manager agreement provided in Article 12.13 that "[t]he Construction Manager . . . hereby agrees that it will comply with all applicable state and federal statutes and other governmental regulations pertaining to employment, and that it will require like compliance therewith from all Trade Contractors. . . ." The agreement also provided that construction manager was responsible for maintaining a competent full-time staff at the job site to direct and monitor subcontractors, for determining the adequacy of the personnel and equipment of subcontractors, for providing

construction and caused by rain and intrusion. The trial court granted contractor summary judgment on the basis of a waiver-of-subrogation clause contained in the contract. The appellate court affirmed.

The owner-contractor agreement included the American Institute of Architects General Conditions of the Contract for Construction, Document No. A201, 1987 edition, specifically Paragraphs 11.3.1 and 11.3.7 renumbered as paragraph 17.3.1 and 17.3.3 respectively. At issue was the provision of the contract whereby "the owner and contractor waive all rights against each other . . . for damages caused by fire or other perils to the extent covered by property insurance obtained pursuant to this Paragraph 17.3 or other property insurance applicable to the work."

Citing numerous jurisdictions that had reached a similar conclusion, the appellate court ruled that, under the plain language of the agreement, the waiver applied.

94013   Myers v. Burger King Corp., 638 So. 2d 369 (La. Ct. App. 1994)

	III:	A107–1978, Art. 10, Para. 10.11
	III:	A107–1978, Art. 17, Para. 17.1
	III:	A107–1987, Art. 9, Para. 9.12
	III:	A107–1987, Art. 17, Para. 17.1
	III:	A117–1979, Art. 14, Para. 14.11
	III:	A117–1979, Art. 21, Para. 21.1
	III:	A117–1987, Art. 14, Para. 14.12
	III:	A117–1987, Art. 22, Para. 22.1
	III:	A201–1976, Art. 4, Para. 4.18.1
	III:	A201–1976, Art. 11, Para. 11.1.1
	III:	A201–1976, Art. 11, Para. 11.1.2
	III:	A201–1976, Art. 11, Para. 11.1.3
	III:	A201–1976, Art. 11, Para. 11.1.4
	III:	A201–1987, Art. 3, Para. 3.18.1
	III:	A201–1987, Art. 10, Para. 10.1.4
	III:	A201–1987, Art. 11, Para. 11.1.1
	III:	A201–1987, Art. 11, Para. 11.1.2
	III:	A201–1987, Art. 11, Para. 11.1.3
	III:	A401–1978, Art. 11, Para. 11.11.1
	III:	A401–1987, Art. 4, Para. 4.6.1

Contractor's injured employee brought a negligence action against owner and others. Owner filed a third-party indemnity action against contractor. The trial court entered judgment in favor of owner and contractor appealed. The appellate court affirmed.

agreement effectively precluded carrier's action. The district court granted defendants' motions for summary judgment, except with respect to that part of the complaint alleging gross negligence.

The owner-contractor agreement contained the American Institute of Architects General Conditions of the Contract for Construction, Document No. A201, 1987 edition, specifically Paragraphs 6.1.1 and 11.3.7. The owner and architect entered into the American Institute of Architects Standard Form of Agreement Between Owner and Architect, Document No. B141, 1977 edition, specifically Paragraph 11.4.

Noting that the subrogee's claims against the defendants were subject to any defenses that the defendants might have had against the owner, the court held that, under New York law, the owner's waiver of subrogation in the architect's agreement constituted an effective waiver and release of the claims. It further held that, under Michigan law, the claims against the contractors were also barred by the waiver. Furthermore, the court held that Michigan's statute voiding promises to indemnify another party against that other party's sole negligence was inapplicable because the provisions at issue did not call for indemnification. The court applied these same findings to the defendant subcontractors.

Paragraph 6.1.1 of the General Conditions stated that, if the owner performed construction or operations related to the project with the owner's own forces, the contracts with such separate contractors would include "conditions of the contract identical or substantially similar to these including those portions related to insurance and waiver of subrogation. . . ." The court held that owner breached its contract by hiring an outside contractor without complying with the terms of Paragraph 6.1.1 and therefore the insurance carrier, as subrogee of the owner, was not in a position to contend that the waiver of subrogation clause that should have been in place pursuant to that provision was not part of the owner's contract.

Finally, the court deemed that, with respect to claims of gross negligence, the waivers and releases would be ineffective as a defense and permitted the counts alleging such negligence to stand.

94012   Lloyd's Underwriters v. Craig & Rush, Inc., 26 Cal. App. 4th 1194, 32 Cal. Rptr. 2d 144 (1994)

II:	A107–1987, Art. 17, Para. 17.3
II:	A107–1987, Art. 17, Para. 17.6
II:	A117–1987, Art. 22, Para. 22.3
II:	A117–1987, Art. 22, Para. 22.6
I:	A201–1987, Art. 11, Para. 11.3.1
I:	A201–1987, Art. 11, Para. 11.3.7

Owner's property insurer brought a claim against contractor for amounts the insurer had paid to the owner for damages sustained in the interior of a facility undergoing

the plans without the approval of the initial engineer. The initial engineer had received a copyright certificate for the plans. The initial engineer filed an infringement of copyright action against the state and the completing architect.

Owner and completing architect moved to dismiss the engineer's complaint for infringement of copyright, or in the alternative, for summary judgment. The owner argued that engineer had no claim for infringement where the owner-architect agreement, as well as state law, provided that the drawings prepared by engineer became the property of the owner. The district court denied the motions.

The owner-architect agreement provided in pertinent part as follows:

Drawings and Specifications are, and shall remain, the property of the Owner whether the Project for which they are made is executed or not. Such documents may be used by the Owner to construct one or more like projects without the approval of, or additional compensation to, the Designer. The Designer shall not be liable for injury or damage resulting from re-use of drawings and specifications if the Designer is not involved in the re-use project. Prior to re-use of construction documents for a project in which the Designer is not also involved, the Owner will remove and obliterate from such documents all identification of the original designer, including name, address and professional seal or stamp.

The district court found that the owner could not bind the engineer to the terms of the owner-architect agreement without fulfilling the original project architect's payment obligations to the engineer. Furthermore, the court rejected the owner's argument that it owned the drawings where the owner failed to demonstrate as a matter of law that engineer was bound by the owner-architect agreement and that engineer had voluntarily transferred the drawings.

94011   Indiana Ins. Co. v. Erlich, 880 F. Supp. 513 (W.D. Mich. 1994)

II:	A107–1987,	Art. 12, Para. 12.1
II:	A107–1987,	Art. 17, Para. 17.6
II:	A117–1987,	Art. 17, Para. 17.1
II:	A117–1987,	Art. 22, Para. 22.6
I:	A201–1987,	Art. 6, Para. 6.1.1
I:	A201–1987,	Art. 11, Para. 11.3.7
I:	B141–1977,	Art. 11, Para. 11.4
II:	B141–1987,	Art. 9, Para. 9.4

Property insurance carrier, subrogated to the rights of owner, instituted an action against architect, the architect's structural engineer, the contractor, its subcontractor and a sub-subcontractor for monies it paid to repair and replace the wall in an old library that allegedly had collapsed as a result of work performed during a renovation project. Defendants all brought motions for summary judgment on the ground that the waiver-of-subrogation clause contained in the owner-contractor agreement and in the architect's

action against the decedent's employer for contribution, indemnity and attorneys' fees. The trial court granted subcontractor's motion for summary judgment on the ground that the subcontractor had not agreed to indemnify contractor for its own negligence. Contractor appealed. The appellate court upheld the judgment of the trial court.

The indemnity provisions in the subcontract were identical to Paragraphs 11.11.1 and 11.11.2 of the American Institute of Architects Standard Form of Agreement Between Contractor and Subcontractor, Document No. A401, 1978 edition.

Among numerous other points of error, the appellate court rejected the contractor's argument that the language of the indemnity provision clearly and specifically provided that the subcontractor would indemnify the contractor for its own negligence. The court found that the indemnity provision in Paragraph 11.11.1 was almost identical to a provision in an earlier case. That provision required a subcontractor to indemnify the contractor for "any negligent act or omission of the Subcontractor . . . arising out of or resulting from the performance of the Subcontractor's Work . . . regardless of whether it is caused in part by a party indemnified hereunder. . . ." The court, in that case, held that the subcontractor did not, by this language, indemnify the contractor for contractor's own negligence. Applying the same analysis to Paragraph 11.11.1, the court held that contractor was not entitled to indemnity for its own negligence.

The court rejected the contractor's argument that it was entitled to attorney fees because its cause of action for fees was separate from its claim for indemnification. The court held that Paragraph 11.11.1 only provided for contractor to recover attorney fees where subcontractor was negligent. Contractor was not entitled to fees where contractor was claiming indemnification for its own negligence.

94010 Guillot-Vogt Assocs., Inc. v. Holly & Smith, 848 F. Supp. 682 (E.D. La. 1994)

        III: A201–1987, Art. 1, Para. 1.3.1
        III: B141–1987, Art. 6, Para. 6.1

The State of Louisiana entered into an agreement with the initial architect for the design of a roof and for other repairs to a technical institute building. The architect and engineer orally agreed that engineer would design the mechanical/electrical portions of the project. Engineer submitted its plans, which bore the title blocks of the architect and engineer and were stamped by engineer. After engineer's submission, the initial architect informed the state that it could not complete the project and requested that the state assign the project's completion to another architect. The state assigned the project to the completing architect. At the time of the assignment, the initial architect had been paid by the owner but the architect had not paid the engineer. Engineer refused to complete the engineering drawings as requested by the completing architect on the grounds that engineer had not been paid the balance of its fee. At the request of the state, the completing architect removed the initial architect's and the engineer's title blocks and stamps, stamped the plans with its title block, and hired a consulting engineer to review, revise and complete

Contractor filed an action against owner for breach of contract, in quantum meruit, and in tort. The district court dismissed the action. Contractor appealed. The court of appeals construed the district court's dismissal of the case as a grant of summary judgment to owner. The court of appeals upheld the judgment of the district court.

The owner-contractor agreement set a time frame for claims arising from unanticipated conditions. The provision required contractor to notify owner within five days of an event that could give rise to a claim or that might extend the period of time to complete the contract. It then provided that contractor submit to owner within fourteen days a statement substantiating the change in circumstances and estimating its impact. Upon request, contractor would have to document any claims submitted for extra compensation or for an extension of time.

The appellate court rejected the contractor's argument that the notice-of-claims provision applied to work to complete the contract but did not apply to extra work that was unanticipated and beyond the scope of the contract. Contractor failed to submit its claim to owner within the time frame set forth in the contract. The court defined extra work as work required in the performance of the contract arising from conditions that could not be anticipated. The court construed the notice provision as setting the time frame for reporting "the happening of any event" which contractor believed might have given rise to a claim "for an increase in contract price" or "the period of performance." Furthermore, the clause addressed precisely the sort of unanticipated event that resulted in extra work and required the contractor to report the events in a timely fashion. The court concluded that contractor did not comply with the notice provision and did not submit an estimate of the impact within the time frame. Without such notice, owner could not respond to contractor's concerns in a timely manner. Because of contractor's delay, contractor was precluded from recovering for any extra work contractor performed.

94009 Glendale Constr. Serv., Inc. v. Accurate Air Sys., Inc., 1994 Tex. App. LEXIS 2105 (Tex. Ct. App. Aug. 25, 1994)

II:	A107–1978,	Art. 10, Para. 10.11
II:	A107–1987,	Art. 9, Para. 9.12
II:	A117–1979,	Art. 14, Para. 14.11
II:	A117–1987,	Art. 14, Para. 14.12
II:	A201–1976,	Art. 4, Para. 4.18.1
II:	A201–1987,	Art. 3, Para. 3.18.1
II:	A201–1987,	Art. 10, Para. 10.1.4
I:	A401–1978,	Art. 11, Para. 11.11.1
I:	A401–1978,	Art. 11, Para. 11.11.2
II:	A401–1987,	Art. 4, Para. 4.6.1

Subcontractor's deceased employee's estate brought a negligence action against owner, contractor, subcontractor, and others. Contractor brought a third-party indemnification

II:	A401–1987, Art. 6, Para. 6.3
II:	A401–1987, Art. 6, Para. 6.4
II:	A401–1987, Art. 6, Para. 6.5
II:	B141–1987, Art. 7, Para. 7.1
II:	B141–1987, Art. 7, Para. 7.2
II:	B141–1987, Art. 7, Para. 7.3
II:	B141–1987, Art. 7, Para. 7.4

Subcontractor's deceased employee's estate brought an action against owner. Owner brought a third-party action against contractor for indemnity. Contractor moved to compel arbitration. The contractor appealed denial of its motion to compel arbitration and to stay owner's third-party complaint seeking indemnity. The appellate court reversed and remanded with directions to order arbitration.

The arbitration provisions contained in the general conditions of the owner-contractor agreement were identical to Paragraph 4.5.1 of the American Institute of Architects General Conditions of the Contract for Construction, Document No. A201, 1987 edition.

The appellate court interpreted the "controversy or Claim arising out of or related to the Contract, or breach thereof" language of the arbitration clause to include owner's third-party claims for indemnification and breach of contract. The court found that, even if the owner's claim for indemnification was tort-based rather than contract-based, it would still be based on contractor's failure to keep the site safe, and would thus have arisen from the owner's contractual relationship with the contractor. The court declined to follow the rule adopted by the court of another state. According to that rule, indemnification claims based on third-party tort allegations are not intended to be covered by an arbitration agreement between owner and contractor. The court viewed the rule as flawed because it failed to recognize the distinction between the underlying tort action and the indemnification action that was grounded on and arose out of the owner/contractor agreement.

The court also rejected owner's argument that contractor waived its right to arbitration by failing to submit the third-party claim first to architect. According to the court, the agreement did not require a party responding to a claim (as opposed to a party asserting a claim) to first submit it to the architect.

94007   (UNASSIGNED)

94008   Galin Corp. v. MCI Telecommunications Corp., 12 F.3d 465 (5th Cir.), *cert. denied*, __U.S.__, 114 S. Ct. 2743, 129 L. Ed. 2d 862 (1994)

III: A201–1987, Art. 4, Para. 4.3.6

never agreed to supervise the construction or to be responsible for safety on the project. Injured worker appealed. The appellate court affirmed the judgment of the trial court.

The owner-architect agreement provided the following:

The consultant . . . shall review the safety programs of each of the general contractors and their trade contractors and make appropriate recommendations. In making such recommendations and carrying out such review, the consultant shall not be required to make exhaustive or continuous inspections to check safety precautions and programs in connection with the project. The performance of such services by the consultant shall not relieve the general contractors and trade contractors of their responsibilities for the safety of persons and property.

The owner-contractor agreement specifically provided that the contractor was responsible for providing and maintaining guard rails. The contract further provided that contractor could only remove safety devices with the approval of the architect. In addition, the contractor was required to designate a member of its organization to be available at the site to prevent accidents.

The appellate court found that the owner-contractor agreement clearly provided that the contractor was responsible for safety at the site. Furthermore, the architect's contractual responsibility to "review the safety programs . . . and make appropriate recommendations . . ." did not relieve the contractor of its contractual duty to provide a safe workplace.

The court also found that the engineer was not responsible for site safety because the agreement between the architect and engineer specifically provided that the engineer was not responsible for "construction means, methods, techniques, sequences or procedures, for safety precautions and programs in connection with the work, for the acts or omissions of the contractor, subcontractors or any other persons performing any of the work. . . ."

94006   Contract Constr. Inc. v. Power Technology Ctr. Ltd. Partnership, 100 Md. App. 173, 640 A.2d 251 (1994)

	II:	A107–1987, Art. 10, Para. 10.8
	II:	A117–1987, Art. 15, Para. 15.8
	I:	A201–1987, Art. 4, Para. 4.5.1
	I:	A201–1987, Art. 4, Para. 4.5.2
	I:	A201–1987, Art. 4, Para. 4.5.3
	I:	A201–1987, Art. 4, Para. 4.5.4
	I:	A201–1987, Art. 4, Para. 4.5.4.1
	I:	A201–1987, Art. 4, Para. 4.5.4.2
	I:	A201–1987, Art. 4, Para. 4.5.5
	I:	A201–1987, Art. 4, Para. 4.5.6
	I:	A201–1987, Art. 4, Para. 4.5.7
	II:	A401–1987, Art. 6, Para. 6.1
	II:	A401–1987, Art. 6, Para. 6.2

contained in Paragraph 9.4 of the owner-architect agreement should have been considered in determining the rights and obligations of the parties because the architect was not a party to the owner-contractor agreement. The court found that the architect had the right to enforce the waiver-of-subrogation clause as a third-party beneficiary because the architect's name appeared adjacent to the term "Architect" on the title page of the agreement and because the agreement incorporated by reference the General Conditions.

The court found, however, that owner's waiver of subrogation was limited to the value of the "Work." The court construed Paragraph 11.3.1 as requiring the owner to maintain property insurance limited to the amount of the agreed-to contract sum as well as the amount of subsequent modifications; however, owner was not required to maintain insurance in excess of the contract sum and modifications or for the value of the entire buildings and its contents. Furthermore, pursuant to Paragraph 11.3.7 the owner waived all rights against the architect to the extent owner obtained insurance applicable to the "Work." The court allowed the action against the retrofit architect only to the extent its negligence caused damages in excess of the value of the work.

The court also rejected the owner's argument that work performed by the architect after the architect had been paid its fee was not subject to the waiver-of-subrogation clause in Paragraph 11.3.7. The court held, however, that the retrofit architect's contract was still in force pursuant to Paragraph 2.4.1, because the architect's services were not fully rendered at the date of loss.

94005 Case v. Midwest Mechanical Contractors, Inc., 876 S.W.2d 51 (Mo. Ct. App. 1994)

III:	A107–1987, Art. 9, Para. 9.1	
III:	A107–1987, Art. 10, Para. 10.5	
III:	A107–1987, Art. 16, Para. 16.1	
III:	A117–1987, Art. 14, Para. 14.1	
III:	A117–1987, Art. 15, Para. 15.5	
III:	A117–1987, Art. 21, Para. 21.1	
III:	A201–1987, Art. 3, Para. 3.3.1	
III:	A201–1987, Art. 4, Para. 4.3.2	
III:	A201–1987, Art. 10, Para. 10.1	
III:	A201–1987, Art. 10, Para. 10.2	
III:	A201–1987, Art. 10, Para. 10.3	
III:	B141–1987, Art. 2, Para. 2.2.6	

Subcontractor's injured employee brought a negligence action against the architect and mechanical/electrical engineer for failing to provide a railing or barrier along the roof edge of a correctional center under construction. The trial court granted architect's and engineer's motions for summary judgment on the ground that the architect and engineer

I:	A117–1987, Art. 12, Para. 12.4
II:	A117–1987, Art. 22, Para. 22.1
II:	A117–1987, Art. 22, Para. 22.3
II:	A117–1987, Art. 22, Para. 22.6
I:	A201–1987, Art. 1, Para. 1.1.3
I:	A201–1987, Art. 11, Para. 11.1.1
I:	A201–1987, Art. 11, Para. 11.3.1
I:	A201–1987, Art. 11, Para. 11.3.7
I:	B141–1987, Art. 2, Para. 2.4.1
I:	B141–1987, Art. 9, Para. 9.4

Owner purchased an office/warehouse building and contracted with architect, engineer and contractor to retrofit the building. Retrofit architect entered into a contract with engineer to perform engineering services for the building's retrofit. A portion of the roof collapsed after contractor had substantially completed the retrofit but before final payment. An investigation by owner and engineer after the collapse revealed original construction defects that allegedly caused the collapse and were in violation of local building codes. Owner's property insurance carrier paid owner for its loss and claimed a right to subrogation with respect to the amount paid to owner.

Owner brought a breach of contract action against the retrofit architect and a negligence action against retrofit architect, engineer and the original contractor. Third- and fourth-party actions were filed by the original contractor and subcontractors. The trial court sustained the retrofit architect's motion for summary judgment on the ground that owner contractually waived all claims against the architect. On appeal, the owner argued that the trial court erred in sustaining the architect's motion for summary judgment. The appellate court affirmed in part the judgment of the trial court and modified the judgment to hold that owner waived its rights to recover against architect in the amount of the value of the "Work."

The owner and retrofit architect had entered into the American Institute of Architects Standard Form of Agreement Between Owner and Architect, Document No. B141, 1987 edition, specifically Paragraph 9.4. The owner and retrofit contractor had entered into a Standard Form of Agreement Between Owner and Contractor that incorporated the American Institute of Architects General Conditions of the Contract for Construction, Document No. A201, 1987 edition, specifically Paragraphs 1.1.3, 11.1.1, 11.3.1 and 11.3.7.

In addressing one of the owner's points on appeal (namely, that the trial court erred in sustaining architect's motion for summary judgment on the ground that the owner waived all claims against the architect), the court, relying on Paragraph 11.3.7 of the General Conditions, found that the owner waived all claims against the architect where the owner agreed to "waive all rights against . . . (2) the Architect, Architect's consultants, . . . for damages caused by fire to the extent covered by property insurance. . . ." The court rejected the owner's argument that only the waiver clause

II:	A201–1987, Art. 4, Para. 4.5.5
II:	A201–1987, Art. 4, Para. 4.5.6
II:	A201–1987, Art. 4, Para. 4.5.7
I:	A401–1978, Art. 13, Para. 13.1
II:	A401–1987, Art. 6, Para. 6.1
II:	A401–1987, Art. 6, Para. 6.2
II:	A401–1987, Art. 6, Para. 6.3
II:	A401–1987, Art. 6, Para. 6.4
II:	A401–1987, Art. 6, Para. 6.5
II:	B141–1977, Art. 9, Para. 9.1
II:	B141–1977, Art. 9, Para. 9.2
II:	B141–1977, Art. 9, Para. 9.3
II:	B141–1987, Art. 7, Para. 7.1
II:	B141–1987, Art. 7, Para. 7.2
II:	B141–1987, Art. 7, Para. 7.3
II:	B141–1987, Art. 7, Para. 7.4

Subcontractor brought an action against contractor for extras. After the jury entered a verdict in favor of subcontractor, contractor appealed denial of its motion to enforce the arbitration clause of the agreement. The trial court denied contractor's motion to stay the court action pending arbitration. The trial court reasoned that contractor had failed to satisfy a state statute requiring a party seeking arbitration to establish that it was an aggrieved party, that the controversy was governed by a valid agreement to arbitrate, and that arbitration was not time-barred. The appellate court reversed and remanded.

The parties had entered into the American Institute of Architects Standard Form of Agreement Between Contractor and Subcontractor, Document No. A401, 1978 edition, specifically Paragraph 13.1.

The appellate court concluded that contractor was an aggrieved party because subcontractor was attempting to recover attorney fees in litigation that were not available in arbitration. The court further concluded that the subcontract provided for arbitration, and no time limitation barred arbitration. Accordingly, the court reversed the judgment and remanded with directions to compel arbitration.

94004 Butler v. Mitchell-Hughback, Inc., 1994 Mo. App. LEXIS 1329 (Mo. Ct. App. Aug. 16, 1994), *aff'd in part and rev'd in part*, 895 S.W.2d 15 (Mo. 1995)

I:	A107–1987, Art. 7, Para. 7.4
II:	A107–1987, Art. 17, Para. 17.1
II:	A107–1987, Art. 17, Para. 17.3
II:	A107–1987, Art. 17, Para. 17.6

II:	A107–1987, Art. 17, Para. 17.3
II:	A107–1987, Art. 17, Para. 17.6
II:	A117–1979, Art. 21, Para. 21.3
II:	A117–1979, Art. 21, Para. 21.6
II:	A117–1987, Art. 22, Para. 22.3
II:	A117–1987, Art. 22, Para. 22.6
I:	A201–1976, Art. 11, Para. 11.3.1
I:	A201–1976, Art. 11, Para. 11.3.6
II:	A201–1987, Art. 11, Para. 11.3.1
II:	A201–1987, Art. 11, Para. 11.3.7

Owner's property insurance carrier brought an action against the contractor and subcontractor. The carrier alleged faulty installation of the electrical system that led to a fire loss. The trial court granted contractor's motion for summary judgment on the basis of the waiver-of-subrogation clause in the owner-contractor agreement. The appellate court reversed the judgment of the trial court.

The owner-contractor agreement included the American Institute of Architects General Conditions of the Contract for Construction, Document No. A201, 1976 edition, specifically Paragraphs 11.3.1 and 11.3.6.

At issue before the appellate court was whether the waiver of subrogation survived completion of the project. The court determined summary judgment was inappropriate because the waiver of subrogation did not survive that portion of the contractor's agreement which made final payment a waiver of all claims by the owners, except those arising from defective work. The court determined that the preservation of such rights after final payment rendered the waiver-of-subrogation clause inapplicable.

94003 Bishop Contracting Co. v. Center Bros., 213 Ga. App. 804, 445 S.E.2d 780 (1994)

II:	A107–1978, Art. 13, Para. 13.2
II:	A107–1987, Art. 10, Para. 10.8
II:	A117–1979, Art. 17, Para. 17.2
II:	A117–1987, Art. 15, Para. 15.8
II:	A201–1976, Art. 7, Para. 7.9.1
II:	A201–1987, Art. 4, Para. 4.5.1
II:	A201–1987, Art. 4, Para. 4.5.2
II:	A201–1987, Art. 4, Para. 4.5.3
II:	A201–1987, Art. 4, Para. 4.5.4
II:	A201–1987, Art. 4, Para. 4.5.4.1
II:	A201–1987, Art. 4, Para. 4.5.4.2

94001   Andy Floors Inc. v. Tyler Constr. Corp., 202 A.D.2d 938, 609 N.Y.S.2d 692 (1994)

    III: A107–1987, Art. 10, Para. 10.8
    III: A117–1987, Art. 15, Para. 15.8
    III: A201–1987, Art. 4, Para. 4.5.2
    III: A201–1987, Art. 4, Para. 4.5.4
    III: A201–1987, Art. 4, Para. 4.5.4.1
    III: A201–1987, Art. 4, Para. 4.5.4.2
    III: A401–1987, Art. 6, Para. 6.1
    III: A401–1987, Art. 6, Para. 6.3

Subcontractor appealed denial of its application to stay arbitration. Subcontractor had argued that contractor's demand was not timely filed within the requisite six-month period. The trial court concluded that contractor's notice was timely served, and the appellate court affirmed.

Contractor served a demand for arbitration six months after a dispute arose regarding subcontractor's installation of the floor in the project under construction. The demand was served by certified mail, return receipt requested, and was received two days after the expiration of the six-month period.

The subcontract agreement incorporated the arbitration provisions of the general contract, which provided in pertinent part as follows:

Notice of the demand for arbitration shall be filed in writing with the other parties to the dispute who have agreed to arbitrate, and with the American Arbitration Association. The demand for arbitration shall be made within a reasonable time after the claim, dispute or other matter in question has arisen, and in no event shall it be made more than six months after the claim has arisen.

The appellate court relied on a state statute that expressly prescribed the method of service for a demand for arbitration as "in the same manner as a summons or by registered or certified mail, return receipt requested." The appellate court found that the trial court's reliance on the statute was proper where the parties failed to prescribe a method of service other than that set forth in the statute and where the agreement did not evidence an unambiguous intent to impose a method of service more restrictive than the statute. Having determined that the method of service was proper, the court concluded that the demand was timely because mail is deemed served when posted.

94002   Automobile Ins. Co. v. United H.R.B. Gen. Contractors, Inc., 876 S.W.2d 791 (Mo. Ct. App. 1994)

    II: A107–1978, Art. 17, Para. 17.3
    II: A107–1978, Art. 17, Para. 17.6

agreement, prior to any loss caused by the contractor's negligence. Furthermore, the insurance contract, which prohibited the owner from taking action to impair the surety's rights "after loss," did not prohibit owner from impairing its subrogation rights at any time. Because the insurance contract did not prohibit the waiver of subrogation rights except "after loss," surety had no right to recovery from the contractor.

93056   Fire Ins. Exch. v. Thunderbird Masonry, 177 Ariz. 365, 868 P.2d 948 (1993)

II:	A107-1978, Art. 17, Para. 17.3	
II:	A107-1978, Art. 17, Para. 17.6	
II:	A107-1987, Art. 17, Para. 17.3	
II:	A107-1987, Art. 17, Para. 17.6	
II:	A117-1979, Art. 21, Para. 21.3	
II:	A117-1979, Art. 21, Para. 21.6	
II:	A117-1987, Art. 22, Para. 22.3	
II:	A117-1987, Art. 22, Para. 22.6	
I:	A201-1976, Art. 11, Para. 11.3.1	
I:	A201-1976, Art. 11, Para. 11.3.6	
I:	A201-1987, Art. 11, Para. 11.3.1	
II:	A201-1987, Art. 11, Para. 11.3.7	
I:	A401-1978, Art. 9, Para. 9.2	
I:	A401-1987, Art. 13, Para. 13.2	

  This appeal presents numerous issues arising from litigation resulting from the development of a condominium complex. The owner-contractor agreement included the American Institute of Architects General Conditions of the Contract for Construction, Document No. A201, 1976 edition, specifically Paragraphs 11.3.1 and 11.3.6. The contractor and subcontractor entered into the American Institute of Architects Standard Form of Agreement Between Contractor and Subcontractor, Document No. A401, 1978 edition, specifically Paragraph 9.2.

  In subcontractor's appeal from summary judgment entered for the builder's risk insurer, the appellate court reversed, reasoning that where construction lender, as loss payee, stepped into the owner's position, and where owner had executed enforceable American Institute of Architect form waivers, the loss payee had no rights against subcontractor to which the builder's risk insurer could be subrogated. The court relied on *United States Fidelity & Guar. Co. v. Farrar's Plumbing & Heating Co.*, digest number 88037, in which the court held that identical American Institute of Architect form waivers negated any claim by owner against subcontractor.

it provided the contractor a right to stop work if payment was not made. The court further concluded that Paragraph 9.7.1 did not apply because it stated that owner must pay an award within seven days after the date established in the Contract Documents and the contract failed to provide a payment schedule for arbitration awards.

The court interpreted Paragraph 7.9.1 as providing that arbitration awards were subject to applicable law. Looking to a state statute which provided ninety days to apply for vacation or modification of arbitration awards, the court concluded that, as a matter of law, any implied reasonable payment period could be no less than the ninety-day appeal period allowed. Accordingly, owner did not breach any contract term in timing its payment.

93055 Continental Cas. Co. v. Homontowski, 181 Wis. 2d 129, 510 N.W.2d 743 (1993)

II: A107-1987, Art. 17, Para. 17.6
II: A117-1987, Art. 22, Para. 22.6
II: A201-1987, Art. 11, Para. 11.3.7
II: A401-1987, Art. 13, Para. 13.5

Owner's surety brought an action against contractor to recover the amount paid to owner as fire damages resulting from contractor's negligence. The trial court denied contractor's motion for summary judgment, finding that the subrogation waiver between the contractor and owner was void and unenforceable against surety because the owner did not notify surety that it had waived the right to pursue damages from the contractor. The trial court entered judgment for surety. Contractor argued on appeal that the owner's waiver of subrogation precluded the surety from pursuing a subrogation claim against contractor. The appellate court reversed the judgment of the trial court.

The owner-contractor agreement provided in pertinent part that:

The owner and contractor waive all rights against . . . each other and any of their subcontractors, sub-subcontractors, agents and employees, each of the other . . . for damages caused by fire or other perils to the extent covered by property insurance . . . waiver of subrogation shall be effective as to a person or entity even though that person or entity would otherwise have a duty of indemnification, contractual or otherwise, did not pay the insurance premium directly or indirectly, and whether or not the person or entity had an insurable interest in the property damage.

The insurance contract provided that if surety made a payment to owner and owner had the right to recover damages from another, the rights transferred to surety. The provision prohibited owner from taking action to impair surety's subrogation rights "after loss." The clause also indicated that surety succeeded to its insured's right to recover damages only after it made payment to the insured.

The appellate court found that the terms of the insurance contract and the owner-contractor agreement were plain and unambiguous. Owner had waived its right to pursue contractor for negligence damages at the time it entered into the owner-contractor

I:	A201–1976, Art. 7, Para. 7.9.1
I:	A201–1976, Art. 9, Para. 9.7.1
II:	A201–1987, Art. 4, Para. 4.5.1
II:	A201–1987, Art. 4, Para. 4.5.2
II:	A201–1987, Art. 4, Para. 4.5.3
II:	A201–1987, Art. 4, Para. 4.5.4
II:	A201–1987, Art. 4, Para. 4.5.4.1
II:	A201–1987, Art. 4, Para. 4.5.4.2
II:	A201–1987, Art. 4, Para. 4.5.5
II:	A201–1987, Art. 4, Para. 4.5.6
II:	A201–1987, Art. 4, Para. 4.5.7
II:	A201–1987, Art. 9, Para. 9.7.1
II:	A401–1978, Art. 13, Para. 13.1
II:	A401–1987, Art. 6, Para. 6.1
II:	A401–1987, Art. 6, Para. 6.2
II:	A401–1987, Art. 6, Para. 6.3
II:	A401–1987, Art. 6, Para. 6.4
II:	A401–1987, Art. 6, Para. 6.5
II:	B141–1977, Art. 9, Para. 9.1
II:	B141–1977, Art. 9, Para. 9.2
II:	B141–1977, Art. 9, Para. 9.3
II:	B141–1987, Art. 7, Para. 7.1
II:	B141–1987, Art. 7, Para. 7.2
II:	B141–1987, Art. 7, Para. 7.3
II:	B141–1987, Art. 7, Para. 7.4

Contractor appealed summary judgment in favor of owner on contractor's breach of contract claim. Contractor had sought damages resulting from owner's delay in paying the arbitration award. The appellate court affirmed.

The parties arbitrated contractor's claim for monthly progress payments that the owner had withheld because of architect's failure to certify masonry work. Sixty–four days after an arbitration award in contractor's favor, owner paid. Contractor filed suit for breach of contract, claiming payment within seven days was required by the agreement.

The owner-contractor agreement included the American Institute of Architects General Conditions of the Contract for Construction, Document No. A201, 1976 edition, specifically Paragraphs 7.9.1 and 9.7.1.

The appellate court rejected contractor's argument that Paragraph 9.7.1 provided a seven–day period for payment of arbitrations awards. According to the court, the provision did not include a covenant to pay an award within a specified time; rather,

93053 Seifert v. Regents of Univ. of Minn., 505 N.W.2d 83 (Minn. Ct. App. 1993), *review denied*, 1993 Minn. LEXIS 758 (Minn. Oct. 28, 1993)

II:	A107–1978, Art. 10, Para. 10.11
II:	A107–1987, Art. 9, Para. 9.12
II:	A117–1979, Art. 14, Para. 14.11
II:	A117–1987, Art. 14, Para. 14.12
II:	A201–1976, Art. 4, Para. 4.18.1
II:	A201–1987, Art. 3, Para. 3.18.1
II:	A201–1987, Art. 10, Para. 10.1.4
II:	A401–1978, Art. 11, Para. 11.11.1
II:	A401–1987, Art. 4, Para. 4.6.1

Owner and contractor brought cross-motions for summary judgment with respect to the applicability of an indemnity provision by which the contractor was required to indemnify the owner. The contractor defended against the purported indemnity on the basis of Minnesota's statute invalidating certain indemnity provisions contained in construction contracts. The trial court granted the owner summary judgment. The appellate court upheld the trial court's determination but reversed with respect to other issues.

The indemnity agreement provided as follows:

To the fullest extent permitted by law, [contractor] shall indemnify and hold harmless [owner] . . . and their agents and employees from and against all claims, damages, losses and expenses including attorney's fees arising out of or resulting from the performance, or lack of performance of the Work, provided that any such claim, damage, loss or expense (1) is attributable to bodily injury . . . and, (2) is caused in whole or in part by any negligent act or omission of [contractor], any Subcontractor, anyone directly or indirectly employed by any of them or anyone for whose acts any of them may be liable, regardless of whether or not it is caused in part by a party indemnified hereunder.

The appellate court held that the Minnesota statute, which provides that indemnification agreements in construction contracts are unenforceable "except to the extent" they provide indemnification for the promisor's own negligence, was inapplicable because no evidence was submitted that supported a finding of negligence on the owner's part.

93054 Snyder v. Eanes Indep. Sch. Dist., 860 S.W.2d 692 (Tex. Ct. App. 1993)

II:	A107–1978, Art. 13, Para. 13.2
II:	A107–1987, Art. 10, Para. 10.8
II:	A117–1979, Art. 17, Para. 17.2
II:	A117–1987, Art. 15, Para. 15.8

II:	A201–1987, Art. 4, Para. 4.5.1
II:	A201–1987, Art. 4, Para. 4.5.2
II:	A201–1987, Art. 4, Para. 4.5.3
II:	A201–1987, Art. 4, Para. 4.5.4
II:	A201–1987, Art. 4, Para. 4.5.4.1
II:	A201–1987, Art. 4, Para. 4.5.4.2
II:	A201–1987, Art. 4, Para. 4.5.5
II:	A201–1987, Art. 4, Para. 4.5.6
II:	A201–1987, Art. 4, Para. 4.5.7
II:	A401–1978, Art. 13, Para. 13.1
II:	A401–1987, Art. 6, Para. 6.1
II:	A401–1987, Art. 6, Para. 6.2
II:	A401–1987, Art. 6, Para. 6.3
II:	A401–1987, Art. 6, Para. 6.4
II:	A401–1987, Art. 6, Para. 6.5
II:	B141–1977, Art. 9, Para. 9.1
II:	B141–1977, Art. 9, Para. 9.2
II:	B141–1977, Art. 9, Para. 9.3
II:	B141–1987, Art. 7, Para. 7.1
II:	B141–1987, Art. 7, Para. 7.2
II:	B141–1987, Art. 7, Para. 7.3
II:	B141–1987, Art. 7, Para. 7.4

Subcontractor appealed the trial court's lifting of its stay of arbitration. The appellate court affirmed.

The dispute arose concerning the scope of sub-subcontractor's work pursuant to a purchase order for steel infrastructure equipment and erection. The purchase order provided in part as follows: "Furnish all required labor, supervision, equipment . . . to perform the erection work as called for in the attached subcontract." A copy of the subcontract, which incorporated the owner-contractor agreement by reference, was attached. The owner-contractor agreement included an arbitration provision identical to that found in the American Institute of Architects General Conditions of the Contract for Construction, Document No. A201, 1976 edition, Paragraph 7.9.1.

The appellate court concluded that the language of the purchase order was not ambiguous and that it incorporated, both by reference and attachment, the subcontract in its entirety (which in turn incorporated the owner-contractor agreement, including its arbitration provision). Accordingly, the court enforced the arbitration provision incorporated by reference.

III: A401–1987, Art. 4, Para. 4.6.1

Masonry subcontractor's deceased employee's estate brought a negligence action against owner, contractor, and roofing subcontractor. Contractor brought a third-party action against masonry subcontractor for indemnity pursuant to the terms of the subcontract. The trial court entered judgment for contractor on the ground that the agreement required the subcontractor to indemnify the contractor for contractor's own negligence. Subcontractor appealed. The appellate court reversed the judgment of the trial court.

The indemnification provision provided as follows:

Subcontractor agrees to observe and comply with all federal, state and local statutes and/or ordinances relating to the performance of this subcontract (including the Occupational Safety and Health Act of 1970, as amended),* to assume all responsibilities of the Contractor thereto, and to indemnify and hold harmless Contractor from all penalties, damages or other loss resulting from subcontractor's failure to do so. Subcontractor shall pay the cost of permits and licenses required to perform this subcontract.

*Subcontractor is not responsible for others who are not in conformance with OSHA.

The appellate court interpreted the agreement as requiring the subcontractor to indemnify contractor only for losses resulting from subcontractor's failure to comply with OSHA and other safety statutes. The court found that the phrase "Subcontractor is not responsible for others who are not in conformance with OSHA" was ambiguous where "others" could be read to encompass other subcontractors or also to include the contractor. Furthermore, the court found that indemnification was limited (1) to "all penalties, damages or other loss . . . ," (2) to liability for subcontractor's failure to comply with "statutes and ordinances", and (3) by the provision "Subcontractor is not responsible for others who are not in conformance with OSHA." The indemnification did not extend to liability for negligence in connection with performance of the contract or to injury or loss resulting from performance of the contract.

The court concluded that the indemnification clause could not be invoked to require subcontractor to indemnify contractor for contractor's own negligence or for the negligence of others.

93052 Russellville Steel Co. v. A & R Excavating, Inc., 624 So. 2d 11 (La. Ct. App. 1993)

II: A107–1978, Art. 13, Para. 13.2
II: A107–1987, Art. 10, Para. 10.8
II: A117–1979, Art. 17, Para. 17.2
II: A117–1987, Art. 15, Para. 15.8
I: A201–1976, Art. 7, Para. 7.9.1

III: A117–1979, Art. 21, Para. 21.6
III: A117–1987, Art. 22, Para. 22.6
II: A201–1976, Art. 11, Para. 11.3.6
II: A201–1987, Art. 11, Para. 11.3.7

Subcontractor contracted to install certain steel components for a composing facility. Subcontractor was made counter-defendant by the contractor's builder's-risk carrier, who had paid contractor for damages arising from a collapse of a portion of the project's steel structure. The builder's-risk carrier claimed that it was entitled to be subrogated to the contractor's right to recover the damages from the subcontractor because the subcontractor was allegedly the party responsible for the collapse. On subcontractor's motion for summary judgment, the court held that the builder's-risk carrier was precluded from bringing an action against the subcontractor.

The subcontract included a waiver of subrogation whereby the contractor and subcontractor waived "all rights against (1) each other and each of their subcontractors, sub-subcontractor, agents, employees, each of the other . . . for damages caused by fire or other perils to the extent covered by property insurance provided under the prime contract or other property insurance applicable to the work. . . ."

The court determined that the contractor had waived its rights against the subcontractor to the extent that the general contractor's losses were covered by insurance. Since the builder's-risk carrier could only exercise the same rights as (and no more than) the contractor had, the builder's-risk carrier was also prevented by the waiver of subrogation from bringing an action against the subcontractor for damages.

93051   Rivers & Bryan, Inc. v. HBE Corp., 628 A.2d 631 (D.C. 1993)

III: A107–1978, Art. 10, Para. 10.11
III: A107–1987, Art. 9, Para. 9.12
III: A117–1979, Art. 14, Para. 14.11
III: A117–1987, Art. 14, Para. 14.12
III: A201–1976, Art. 4, Para. 4.18.1
III: A201–1987, Art. 3, Para. 3.18.1
III: A201–1987, Art. 10, Para. 10.1.4
III: A401–1978, Art. 11, Para. 11.1.1
III: A401–1978, Art. 11, Para. 11.3.1
III: A401–1978, Art. 11, Para. 11.3.2
III: A401–1978, Art. 11, Para. 11.11.1
III: A401–1987, Art. 2, Para. 2.1
III: A401–1987, Art. 4, Para. 4.2.1
III: A401–1987, Art. 4, Para. 4.2.2

I:	A201–1987, Art. 4, Para. 4.5.2
I:	A201–1987, Art. 4, Para. 4.5.3
I:	A201–1987, Art. 4, Para. 4.5.4
I:	A201–1987, Art. 4, Para. 4.5.4.1
I:	A201–1987, Art. 4, Para. 4.5.4.2
I:	A201–1987, Art. 4, Para. 4.5.5
I:	A201–1987, Art. 4, Para. 4.5.6
I:	A201–1987, Art. 4, Para. 4.5.7
II:	A401–1987, Art. 6, Para. 6.1
II:	A401–1987, Art. 6, Para. 6.2
II:	A401–1987, Art. 6, Para. 6.3
II:	A401–1987, Art. 6, Para. 6.4
II:	A401–1987, Art. 6, Para. 6.5
II:	B141–1987, Art. 7, Para. 7.1
II:	B141–1987, Art. 7, Para. 7.2
II:	B141–1987, Art. 7, Para. 7.3
II:	B141–1987, Art. 7, Para. 7.4

Owner appealed the dismissal of its action against contractor's performance bond surety to collect an arbitration award. The appellate court reversed and remanded with directions to reinstate the action.

The performance bond at issue incorporated by reference the owner/contractor agreement, which included arbitration provisions identical to Paragraphs 4.5.1, 4.5.5 and 4.5.7 of the American Institute of Architects General Conditions of the Contract for Construction, Document No. A201, 1987 edition. The bond provided that surety was jointly and severally liable with contractor against losses resulting from contractor's default. After contractor terminated the contract, owner notified surety of default and proceeded to arbitration, where an award was made in owner's favor. Owner filed a civil action to enforce the award against contractor and surety. Surety acknowledged that contractor was incapable of making payment on the judgment. The trial court dismissed the action against surety.

In concluding that the arbitration award was binding on surety, the appellate court reasoned that the surety had agreed to arbitrate by incorporating into the performance bond the contract containing the arbitration provision.

93050 Richmond Steel, Inc. v. Legal & Gen. Assurance Soc'y, Ltd., 821 F. Supp. 793 (D.P.R. 1993)

III:	A107–1978, Art. 11, Para. 11.6
III:	A107–1987, Art. 17, Para. 17.6

II:	A201–1987, Art. 4, Para. 4.5.6
II:	A201–1987, Art. 4, Para. 4.5.7
I:	A201–1987, Art. 13, Para. 13.1.1
II:	A401–1978, Art. 13, Para. 13.1
II:	A401–1987, Art. 6, Para. 6.1
II:	A401–1987, Art. 6, Para. 6.2
II:	A401–1987, Art. 6, Para. 6.3
II:	A401–1987, Art. 6, Para. 6.4
II:	A401–1987, Art. 6, Para. 6.5
II:	B141–1977, Art. 9, Para. 9.1
II:	B141–1977, Art. 9, Para. 9.2
II:	B141–1977, Art. 9, Para. 9.3
II:	B141–1987, Art. 7, Para. 7.1
II:	B141–1987, Art. 7, Para. 7.2
II:	B141–1987, Art. 7, Para. 7.3
II:	B141–1987, Art. 7, Para. 7.4

Contractor appealed the denial of its motion to dismiss owner's breach of contract action, based on an enforceable agreement to arbitrate. The appellate court reversed.

The owner and contractor had entered into the American Institute of Architects Standard Form of Agreement Between Owner and Contractor, Document No. A101, 1977 edition, which incorporated by reference the American Institute of Architects General Conditions of the Contract for Construction, Document No. A201, 1976 edition, specifically Paragraphs 7.1.1 and 7.9.1. A state statute required that notice should be printed on the contract's front page if it included an arbitration clause. Although an arbitration clause was included, the agreement did not provide on its front page notice that arbitration was required.

The appellate court determined that the choice-of-law and arbitration provisions created an ambiguity when read together. Relying on the rule of construction requiring an interpretation that gives effect to all provisions, the court concluded that the arbitration provision was enforceable and that the choice-of-law provision had to be interpreted as indicating the parties' intent to have validity and construction of the contract determined by arbitrators according to state law.

93049   Rashid v. Schenck Constr. Co., 190 W. Va. 363, 438 S.E.2d 543, *remanded*, 843 F. Supp. 1081 (S.D. W. Va. 1993)

II:	A107–1987, Art. 10, Para. 10.8
II:	A117–1987, Art. 15, Para. 15.8
I:	A201–1987, Art. 4, Para. 4.5.1

(according to the trial court) required contractor to indemnify engineer for subcontractor's claim against engineer; and the second, in the settlement agreement, which required subcontractor to indemnify contractor for engineer's claim against contractor. Subcontractor appealed. The appellate court reversed the judgment of the trial court on the grounds that the court erred in interpreting the indemnity provision in the owner-contractor agreement.

The indemnity clause in the owner-contractor agreement provided that contractor "shall indemnify and hold harmless and defend the COMMISSION and the ENGINEER . . . from and against all claims . . . which arise out of or result from performance of the WORK by CONTRACTOR and its employees, its Subcontractors, suppliers, material people, and other agents or consultants."

The appellate court found that this provision did not require contractor to indemnify engineer for subcontractor's claims against engineer because engineer was not one of contractor's "employees, its Subcontractors, suppliers, material people, and other agents or consultants." Furthermore, the clause did not expressly provide that contractor would indemnify engineer for its own negligence.

The court concluded that because the provision did not require contractor to indemnify engineer for subcontractor's claim against engineer, subcontractor could not be obligated by the settlement agreement to indemnify engineer based on a claim by engineer for indemnity from contractor. The claim against contractor would fail. Accordingly, subcontractor's claim against engineer was not void.

93048   Osteen v. T.E. Cuttino Constr. Co., 434 S.E.2d 281 (S.C. 1993)

I:	A107–1978, Art. 13, Para. 13.1
II:	A107–1978, Art. 13, Para. 13.2
II:	A107–1987, Art. 10, Para. 10.8
I:	A107–1987, Art. 19, Para. 19.1
I:	A117–1979, Art. 17, Para. 17.1
II:	A117–1979, Art. 17, Para. 17.2
II:	A117–1987, Art. 15, Para. 15.8
I:	A117–1987, Art. 24, Para. 24.1
I:	A201–1976, Art. 7, Para. 7.1.1
I:	A201–1976, Art. 7, Para. 7.9.1
II:	A201–1987, Art. 4, Para. 4.5.1
II:	A201–1987, Art. 4, Para. 4.5.2
II:	A201–1987, Art. 4, Para. 4.5.3
II:	A201–1987, Art. 4, Para. 4.5.4
II:	A201–1987, Art. 4, Para. 4.5.4.1
II:	A201–1987, Art. 4, Para. 4.5.4.2
II:	A201–1987, Art. 4, Para. 4.5.5

The dispute arose after owner fired architect. Owner and contractor executed an escrow agreement requiring owner to deposit funds in the account and allocating payment to contractor upon completion of its work. In related proceedings, both architect and contractor sought arbitration with the owner, which the trial court declined to compel.

As a preliminary matter, the appellate court ruled that the case involved interstate commerce, requiring application of the Federal Arbitration Act (FAA).

On the question of whether the owner/architect agreement was unenforceable because it failed to include notice of the arbitration provision as required by state statute, the court concluded that the state statute could not be applied to defeat arbitration where the contract was governed by the FAA. Accordingly, the arbitration agreement between architect and owner was enforceable notwithstanding failure to include the notice provision.

The court also concluded that the arbitration provision of the owner/contractor general conditions was enforceable and was not superseded by the later escrow agreement, which failed to provide for arbitration. According to the court, the original contract made its terms applicable to subsequent modifications. As a result, the arbitration provision extended to the dispute arising from the contract that eventually led to execution of the escrow agreement.

93047 National Hydro Sys. v. M.A. Mortenson Co., 507 N.W.2d 27 (Minn. Ct. App. 1993), *review granted*, 1994 Minn. LEXIS 40 (Minn. Jan. 21, 1994), *and aff'd*, 529 N.W. 2d 690 (Minn. 1995)

> III: A107–1978, Art. 10, Para. 10.11
> III: A107–1987, Art. 9, Para. 9.12
> III: A117–1979, Art. 14, Para. 14.11
> III: A117–1987, Art. 14, Para. 14.12
> III: A201–1976, Art. 4, Para. 4.18.1
> III: A201–1987, Art. 3, Para. 3.18.1
> III: A201–1987, Art. 10, Para. 10.1.4
> III: A401–1978, Art. 11, Para. 11.1.1
> III: A401–1987, Art. 4, Para. 4.6.1

Subcontractor brought an action against engineer for additional costs incurred as a result of engineer's negligent preparation of specifications and an action against contractor for nonpayment. Subcontractor and contractor entered into a settlement agreement that required subcontractor to defend and indemnify contractor in the event engineer claimed indemnity from contractor. Engineer then filed a motion for summary judgment against subcontractor. The trial court granted engineer summary judgment on the ground that the following two indemnity provisions created a circuity of obligation that voided subcontractor's claim against engineer: the first, in the owner-contractor agreement, which

issue as to whether the architect-engineer was a person "in charge of the work" within the meaning of the Illinois Structural Work Act.

93046   McCarney v. Nearing, Staats, Prelogar & Jones, 866 S.W.2d 881 (Mo. Ct. App. 1993)

II:	A107–1987, Art. 10, Para. 10.8
I:	A111–1987, Art. 1, Para. 1.1
II:	A117–1987, Art. 15, Para. 15.8
I:	A201–1987, Art. 4, Para. 4.3.1
I:	A201–1987, Art. 4, Para. 4.5.1
I:	A201–1987, Art. 4, Para. 4.5.2
I:	A201–1987, Art. 4, Para. 4.5.3
I:	A201–1987, Art. 4, Para. 4.5.4
I:	A201–1987, Art. 4, Para. 4.5.4.1
I:	A201–1987, Art. 4, Para. 4.5.4.2
I:	A201–1987, Art. 4, Para. 4.5.5
I:	A201–1987, Art. 4, Para. 4.5.6
I:	A201–1987, Art. 4, Para. 4.5.7
II:	A401–1987, Art. 6, Para. 6.1
II:	A401–1987, Art. 6, Para. 6.2
II:	A401–1987, Art. 6, Para. 6.3
II:	A401–1987, Art. 6, Para. 6.4
II:	A401–1987, Art. 6, Para. 6.5
I:	B141–1987, Art. 7, Para. 7.1
I:	B141–1987, Art. 7, Para. 7.2
I:	B141–1987, Art. 7, Para. 7.3
I:	B141–1987, Art. 7, Para. 7.4

In consolidated cases on appeal, architect appealed denial of its petition to compel owner to arbitrate and owner sought a writ of prohibition to require the trial court to stay arbitration. The appellate court remanded with directions to compel arbitration, reversing the trial court's order staying arbitration and dismissing the writ proceeding.

The owner and architect had entered into the American Institute of Architects Standard Form of Agreement Between Owner and Architect, Document No. B141, 1987 edition. The owner and contractor had entered into the American Institute of Architects Standard Form of Agreement Between Owner and Contractor, Document No. A111, 1987 edition, which incorporated the American Institute of Architects General Conditions of the Contract for Construction, Document No. A201, 1987 edition.

Architects General Conditions of the Contract for Construction, Document No. A201, 1987 edition, specifically Paragraph 4.5.1.

The court concluded that interpretation of the subcontract, including the incorporated specification, was governed by the incorporated arbitration provision.

93045   Manisca v. Rakstag Assocs., 256 Ill. App. 3d 756, 194 Ill. Dec. 911, 628 N.E.2d 408 (1993)

III:	A107–1987, Art. 10, Para. 10.3
III:	A107–1987, Art. 10, Para. 10.6
III:	A117–1987, Art. 15, Para. 15.3
III:	A117–1987, Art. 15, Para. 15.6
III:	A201–1987, Art. 4, Para. 4.2.6
II:	A201–1987, Art. 4, Para. 4.3.2
II:	B141–1987, Art. 2, Para. 2.6.6
III:	B141–1987, Art. 2, Para. 2.6.11

Roofing contractor's deceased employee's estate brought an action against architect-engineer under the Illinois Structural Work Act. The trial court granted architect-engineer's motion for summary judgment on the ground that the architect-engineer was not in charge of the work performed by the decedent. The appellate court reversed the judgment of the trial court.

The agreement between the owner and architect-engineer provided that the architect-engineer would not be responsible for the construction means, methods, techniques, sequences, procedures, or supervision or for the safety precautions and programs in connection with the project. The architect-engineer had been designated by the owner at its "Authorized Representative" pursuant to the terms of Paragraph 3.01, and, as such, architect-engineer had the right to reject or stop the work. However, the contract provided that the contractor "shall retain exclusive control over all duties and responsibilities imposed by the Structural Work Act."

The appellate court found that the agreement was insufficient to create a triable issue of fact as to whether architect-engineer was in charge of the work where the agreement created an obligation on architect-engineer's part to prepare and approve documents and to observe the project on a periodic basis to ensure that the work was completed according to the specifications. Moreover, the agreement did not obligate architect-engineer to perform continuous on–site inspections nor did it grant architect-engineer the authority to stop the work or to control the methods and techniques of construction. However, the architect-engineer, acting as the owner's authorized representative under Paragraph 3.01, was granted all of the authority of the owner and this authority did include the right to stop the work. The court concluded that the authority granted to the architect-engineer by Paragraph 3.01, together with other evidence on the record, created a triable

The owner-contractor agreement included the American Institute of Architects General Conditions of the Contract for Construction, Document No. A201, 1976 edition, specifically the indemnification clause in Paragraph 4.18.1.

The court held that the indemnification clause was valid and enforceable despite an additional indemnity of lesser inclusiveness also provided for in the contractor agreement. The court determined that the existence of two indemnity clauses inconsistent with one another did not create an ambiguity, but rather the more detailed indemnification clause in the General Conditions resolved the ambiguity by amplifying the provisions of the more limited indemnity.

93044 Lord & Son Constr., Inc. v. Roberts Elec. Contractors, Inc., 624 So. 2d 376 (Fla. Dist. Ct. App. 1993)

II:	A107–1987, Art. 10, Para. 10.8
II:	A117–1987, Art. 15, Para. 15.8
I:	A201–1987, Art. 4, Para. 4.5.1
I:	A201–1987, Art. 4, Para. 4.5.2
I:	A201–1987, Art. 4, Para. 4.5.3
I:	A201–1987, Art. 4, Para. 4.5.4
I:	A201–1987, Art. 4, Para. 4.5.4.1
I:	A201–1987, Art. 4, Para. 4.5.4.2
I:	A201–1987, Art. 4, Para. 4.5.5
I:	A201–1987, Art. 4, Para. 4.5.6
I:	A201–1987, Art. 4, Para. 4.5.7
II:	A401–1987, Art. 6, Para. 6.1
II:	A401–1987, Art. 6, Para. 6.2
II:	A401–1987, Art. 6, Para. 6.3
II:	A401–1987, Art. 6, Para. 6.4
II:	A401–1987, Art. 6, Para. 6.5
II:	B141–1987, Art. 7, Para. 7.1
II:	B141–1987, Art. 7, Para. 7.2
II:	B141–1987, Art. 7, Para. 7.3
II:	B141–1987, Art. 7, Para. 7.4

Owner appealed from final judgment on a jury verdict in subcontractor's favor in a contract dispute. The trial court had denied contractor's motion to compel arbitration. The appellate court reversed and remanded with directions to compel arbitration.

The parties' dispute related to subcontractor's claim that it lost money as a result of contractor's delays. The contractor/subcontractor agreement incorporated specifications by reference. One specification incorporated by reference the American Institute of

Subcontractor shall indemnify contractor and/or owner against, and save each harmless from . . . (2) any and all loss, damage, injury, liability and claims thereof for injuries to or death to persons and loss of or damages to property resulting directly or indirectly from subcontractor's performance of this agreement, regardless of the negligence of owner, the contractor, or their agents or employees; provided that where such loss, damage, injury, liability or claims are the result of active negligence on the part of owner or contractor or their respective agents or employees, and is [sic] not caused or contributed to by an omission to perform some duty also imposed on subcontractor, its agents or employees, such indemnity shall not apply to such party guilty of such active negligence unless the prime contract otherwise provides. . . .

The appellate court found that, in the construction industry, an indemnity agreement violated public policy if it required indemnification of the indemnitee for its sole negligence. The court construed the agreement as providing that, if owner or contractor were solely and actively negligent, they would not be indemnified by subcontractor. However, if owner or contractor were solely and passively negligent, subcontractor would be required to indemnify them. By requiring indemnity in the event of such sole and passive negligence, the agreement was found to violate Utah public policy.

93043   Krass Plus Clothiers, Inc. v. Church's Fried Chicken, 26 Phila. 434, 1993 Phila. Cty. Rptr. LEXIS 63 (Pa. C.P. Nov. 17, 1993)

II:	A107–1978, Art. 10, Para. 10.11	
II:	A107–1987, Art. 9, Para. 9.12	
II:	A117–1979, Art. 14, Para. 14.11	
II:	A117–1987, Art. 14, Para. 14.12	
I:	A201–1976, Art. 4, Para. 4.18.1	
II:	A201–1987, Art. 3, Para. 3.18.1	
II:	A201–1987, Art. 10, Para. 10.1.4	
II:	A401–1978, Art. 11, Para. 11.11.1	
II:	A401–1987, Art. 4, Para. 4.6.1	

The plaintiff maintained an action for damage incurred from a fire at defendant's premises. The fire had damaged the plaintiff's structure because of improperly permitted holes in the party wall between plaintiff's and defendant's structures. The trial court determined that both the contractor who constructed the building and the owner were negligent in permitting damages to occur to the neighbor's property and allocated 80% of the cause of negligence to the contractor and 20% to the owner. At issue was whether the indemnification clause provided for full indemnity of the defendant owner, relieving the owner of liability and requiring the defendant contractor to make payment to the plaintiff in full.

Subcontractor's injured employee brought a third-party negligence action against contractor for failure to provide a safe work environment. Contractor impleaded subcontractor to enforce the indemnification provision in the subcontract. The court dismissed contractor's action before trial. The jury returned a verdict apportioning negligence between contractor and worker and the court entered final judgment for subcontractor. Contractor appealed. The appellate court affirmed the judgment of the trial court.

The indemnification clause provided in pertinent part as follows:

Subcontractor further agrees that he will, during the performance of this work comply with all safety requirements and programs of the Contractor, place proper guards around the same for the prevention of accidents, and shall indemnify the Owner, the Contractor, its or their officers, agents and employees, and save them harmless from any and all liability, suits, actions, demands (just or unjust), any and all damages and any and all costs or fees on account of injuries to person or property, including accidental death, arising out of or in connection with the work, or by reason of the operations under this contract, whether such liability be the result of the alleged active or passive negligence of the Owner or Contractor, their agents, servants, employees or by reason of any participation in the wrong or upon any breach of any statutory duty or obligation on the part of the Owner or Contractor. . . .

The appellate court found that the clause was void under Massachusetts statute because it contained a provision requiring the subcontractor to indemnify the contractor for an injury that may not have been caused by the subcontractor or its employees, agents or subcontractors.

93042 Jacobsen Constr. Co. v. Blaine Constr. Co., 863 P.2d 1329 (Utah Ct. App. 1993), *cert. granted*, 878 P.2d 1154 (Utah), *and appeal dismissed*, 878 P.2d 1151 (Utah 1994)

III:	A107–1987, Art. 9, Para. 9.12
III:	A117–1987, Art. 14, Para. 14.12
III:	A201–1987, Art. 3, Para. 3.18.1
III:	A201–1987, Art. 10, Para. 10.1.4
III:	A401–1987, Art. 4, Para. 4.6.1

Subcontractor's injured employee brought an action against owner and contractor alleging failure to provide a hazard-free work environment. Owner and contractor filed a third-party indemnity action against subcontractor. The trial court granted owner and contractor summary judgment on the ground that subcontractor agreed to indemnify owner and contractor regardless of their negligence. Subcontractor appealed. The appellate court vacated the grant of summary judgment on the ground that the indemnity provision was void as against public policy.

The indemnity provision stated in pertinent part as follows:

II:	A107–1987, Art. 9, Para. 9.12
II:	A117–1979, Art. 14, Para. 14.11
II:	A117–1987, Art. 14, Para. 14.12
II:	A201–1976, Art. 4, Para. 4.18.1
II:	A201–1987, Art. 3, Para. 3.18.1
II:	A201–1987, Art. 10, Para. 10.1.4
II:	A401–1978, Art. 11, Para. 11.1.1
II:	A401–1987, Art. 4, Para. 4.6.1

Contractor's injured employee brought an action against owner alleging violation of the Wisconsin safe–place statute. Owner impleaded contractor, alleging that, if owner were found liable, contractor would be required to indemnify owner pursuant to the indemnity agreement. The trial court entered an order requiring contractor to indemnify owner for any liability to worker even if the liability resulted from owner's own negligence. Contractor appealed. The appellate court affirmed the judgment of the trial court.

The indemnity agreement between owner and contractor provided in pertinent part as follows:

The Contractor shall indemnify and hold harmless [owner] from . . . all claims, damages, losses and expenses . . . arising out of or resulting from the performance of the work or services, provided that . . . [such claim, damage, loss or expense] is caused in whole or in part by any negligent act or omission of the Contractor . . . regardless of whether or not it is caused in part by a party indemnified hereunder.

The appellate court concluded that contractor was obligated to indemnify owner for any amount owner was liable to worker irrespective of owner's negligence. The court construed the language which required contractor to indemnify owner "regardless of whether or not . . . [such claim, damage, loss or expense] is caused in part by a party indemnified hereunder" as unambiguous language obligating the contractor to indemnify the owner for injury or damage arising out of the contractor's work under the contract regardless of whether it was caused in part by owner's negligence.

93041 Harnois v. Quannapowitt Dev., Inc., 35 Mass. App. Ct. 286, 619 N.E.2d 351, *review denied*, 416 Mass. 1106, 622 N.E.2d 1364 (1993)

III:	A107–1987, Art. 9, Para. 9.12
III:	A117–1987, Art. 14, Para. 14.12
III:	A201–1987, Art. 3, Para. 3.18.1
III:	A201–1987, Art. 10, Para. 10.1.4
III:	A401–1987, Art. 4, Para. 4.3.1
III:	A401–1987, Art. 4, Para. 4.6.1

The court reasoned that Paragraph 17.1 provided that owner would be indemnified by contractor for all claims brought as a result of contractor's work, including claims based on negligence and gross negligence. The reciprocal indemnity provision in Paragraph 4 specifically included claims based on negligence or gross negligence. Therefore, where all forms of negligence were subject to indemnification, it logically followed that, to give the exclusionary clause a sensible meaning, it had to be interpreted as excluding intentional acts by the employees of either party.

The court concluded that where worker's claim was for punitive damages for conduct falling somewhere between negligence and intentional wrongdoing, the claim was included in the indemnity provisions. Based on the interpretation of Paragraph 17.1 as providing indemnity for any and all claims and causes of action except for a claim resulting from an intentional act, the court also rejected the contractor's argument that, because a claim for exemplary damages was not specifically described in the indemnity provisions, there could be no implied intent to include the claim.

93039   Groves v. Land's End Hous. Co., 196 A.D.2d 406, 601 N.Y.S.2d 3 (1993)

III:	A107–1978, Art. 10, Para. 10.11	
III:	A107–1987, Art. 9, Para. 9.12	
III:	A117–1979, Art. 14, Para. 14.11	
III:	A117–1987, Art. 14, Para. 14.12	
III:	A201–1976, Art. 4, Para. 4.18.1	
III:	A201–1987, Art. 3, Para. 3.18.1	
III:	A201–1987, Art. 10, Para. 10.1.4	
III:	A401–1978, Art. 11, Para. 11.1.1	
III:	A401–1987, Art. 4, Para. 4.6.1	

Contractor's injured employee brought an action against owner and others pursuant to New York Labor Law § 240(1). The owner brought a third-party indemnification action against contractor. The trial court granted owner's motion for summary judgment. Contractor appealed. The appellate court reversed the judgment of the trial court.

The indemnity provision provided that contractor "agrees to indemnify and hold [owner] harmless provided [owner] is free from fault from all claims for bodily injury and property damage . . . that may arise as a direct result from [contractor's] operations under this Agreement."

The appellate court denied the owner the benefit of the indemnity clause where owner was not "free from fault" and where the owner failed to demonstrate that the worker's injury arose as a "direct result" of contractor's operations under the agreement.

93040   Gunka v. Consolidated Papers, Inc., 179 Wis. 2d 525, 508 N.W.2d 426 (1993)

II: A107–1978, Art. 10, Para. 10.11

III: A201–1987, Art. 3, Para. 3.18.1
III: A201–1987, Art. 10, Para. 10.1.4
III: A401–1987, Art. 4, Para. 4.6.1

Contractor's injured employee brought an action against owner for exemplary damages resulting from owner's wanton and reckless disregard for public safety in the handling, transportation, or storage of hazardous substances pursuant to state statute. Owner filed a third-party indemnity action against contractor. Owner and contractor filed cross-motions for summary judgment. The trial court entered judgment for contractor on the ground that contractor was not liable to owner for the costs and expenses incurred in defending the injured worker's damage action. Owner appealed. The appellate court affirmed the judgment of the trial court.

The indemnification agreement provided in pertinent part as follows:

OWNER and CONTRACTOR agree to the following indemnification obligations for all losses, costs, and expenses (including but not limited to all defense costs and attorney's fees) of alleged or actual legal liabilities and negotiated settlements for personal injuries, illnesses, or deaths sustained by employees, including liabilities and settlements based on occurrences caused or alleged to be caused by the other party's sole negligence or gross negligence, or involving the concurrent negligence of the other party. . . . PROVIDED, HOWEVER, that these indemnity obligations shall not apply in cases of injuries, illnesses, or deaths intentionally caused by willful misconduct of employees of either party to this Agreement. . . . Each party to this Agreement agrees to investigate, handle, respond to, provide defense for, and defend any claim or other potential legal liability for which it is responsible under this Agreement's indemnification provisions at its sole expense, and agrees to bear all other related costs and expenses, even if such claim, etc., is groundless, false or fraudulent.

Paragraph 17.1 found in Exhibit "A" to the contract stated the following:

[Contractor agrees] to protect, indemnify and hold the OWNER free and harmless from and against any and all claims, liens, demands, and causes of action of every kind and character, including the amounts of judgments, penalties, interest, court costs and legal fees incurred by the OWNER in defense of same arising in favor of governmental agencies or third parties (including employees of the CONTRACTOR or subcontractor) on account of taxes, claims, liens, debts, personal injuries, death, or damages to rented equipment or other property, and without limitation by enumeration, all other claims or demands of every character occurring or in anywise incident to, in connection with or arising out of the work to be performed by the CONTRACTOR hereunder, except insofar as responsibility may be expressly assumed by the OWNER under the provisions of this Contract.

The appellate court found that the agreement did not provide for indemnification in situations in which the injuries were "intentionally caused by the willful misconduct of employees" of either party. The court considered all of the provisions together to reach the conclusion that intentional acts were meant to be excluded from the duty to indemnify.

Conditions of the Contract for Construction. . . ." The court then referred to Paragraphs 2.2.3, 7.7.1, 7.7.4, and 9.4.2 to define the architect's duty to observe.

After considering Paragraph 2.2.3 and other evidence, the court found that the contract was ambiguous as to what the parties meant by "observation of construction." The court concluded that factual questions existed as to the scope of the architect's duty to observe and as to whether the architect exercised the requisite skill and care in meeting its obligation, precluding summary judgment.

93037   Green Constr. Co. v. Kansas Power & Light Co., 1 F.3d 1005 (10th Cir. 1993)

III:	A107–1987, Art. 13, Para. 13.1
III:	A107–1987, Art. 13, Para. 13.2
III:	A107–1987, Art. 13, Para. 13.3
III:	A117–1987, Art. 18, Para. 18.1
III:	A117–1987, Art. 18, Para. 18.2
III:	A117–1987, Art. 18, Para. 18.3
III:	A201–1987, Art. 7, Para. 7.1.1
III:	A201–1987, Art. 7, Para. 7.1.2
III:	A201–1987, Art. 7, Para. 7.2.1
III:	A201–1987, Art. 7, Para. 7.3.1

Contractor appealed the district court's order limiting its recovery to contract damages and disallowing additional expenses. Among numerous other points on appeal, the contractor argued that extra work caused by wet soil resulted in a material change in the scope of the project, entitling contractor to additional compensation. The appellate court upheld the judgment of the district court.

The owner-contractor agreement provided in pertinent part that "[t]he COMPANY, without invalidating the Contract, may order any extra work or make any changes by altering, adding to or reducing the work, provided the Contract price be adjusted as provided herein and evidenced by written agreement. . . ."

The court found that the contractor was not entitled to additional compensation where the work it contracted for was more expensive than anticipated due to wet soil. The court upheld the trial court's finding that the changes clause applied only to changes in the scope of the work caused by amendments to the project design and not to difficulties in performance due to unforeseen conditions.

93038   Griffin v. Tenneco Oil Co., 625 So. 2d 1090 (La. Ct. App. 1993), *cert. denied*, 631 So. 2d 449 (La. 1994)

III:	A107–1987, Art. 9, Para. 9.12
III:	A117–1987, Art. 14, Para. 14.2

II:	A201–1987, Art. 9, Para. 9.4.2
II:	A201–1987, Art. 13, Para. 13.5.1
II:	A201–1987, Art. 13, Para. 13.5.5
I:	B141–1977, Art. 11, Para. 11.2
I:	B141–1987, Art. 9, Para. 9.2

Joint venture filed a third-party action against the architect and others seeking contribution and/or indemnification for claims arising from a condominium association's action against the joint venture and others for repair damages resulting from defective construction of individual units. The trial court entered summary judgment in favor of the architect and others, and the joint venture appealed. On appeal, the architect argued that its contractual duty to observe the construction merely obligated it to determine the degree of completion of the project, but did not require it to discover and report deviations from the plans. The architect relied on Paragraph 1.5.5 of the owner-architect agreement. The joint venture argued on appeal that the contract did require the architect to report deviations from the plans. The Supreme Court of Nebraska reversed the judgment of the trial court.

The joint venture and architect had entered into the American Institute of Architects Standard Form of Agreement Between Owner and Architect, Document No. B141, 1977 edition, which was modified to exclude many services, the fees for such services, and the provisions for the architect's inspection and oversight of the project. The parties added a provision requiring the architect to observe the project and report to the joint venture on the percentage of completion, for which the architect would be compensated at a set amount per site visit. Under the modified agreement the architect provided abbreviated design drawings and other documents to be used in the construction. The record indicated that the contractor had deviated from the plans; however, the architect reported to the joint venture that the project was substantially completed and generally in accordance with the plans and specifications.

The supreme court rejected the architect's argument that Paragraph 1.5.5 absolved it from liability for its breach of the duty to inform the joint venture of deviations from the plans and specifications where the architect had agreed to make periodic observations. Relying on *Hunt v. Ellisor & Tanner, Inc.*, 739 S.W.2d 933 (Tex. Ct. App. 1987) (see case digest number 87026), the court concluded that the language of Paragraph 1.5.5 was exculpatory language that constituted nothing other than an agreement that the architect was not the insurer or guarantor of the contractor's work.

In addressing the issue of whether the architect had a duty to report deviations from the plans and specifications, the court noted that the observation provisions contained in Paragraph 1.5 of the standard form AIA owner-architect agreement was deleted by the parties. The parties did provide that the architect would be compensated at a fixed amount per trip for "observation of construction" and the court relied on Paragraph 11.2 to define "observation of construction." Paragraph 11.2 stated that "[t]erms in this Agreement shall have the same meaning as those in AIA Document A201, General

93035   Ericksen v. Salt Lake City Corp., 858 P.2d 995 (Utah 1993)

        II: A107–1987, Art. 9, Para. 9.12
        II: A117–1987, Art. 14, Para. 14.2
        II: A201–1987, Art. 3, Para. 3.18.1
        II: A201–1987, Art. 10, Para. 10.1.4
        II: A401–1987, Art. 4, Para. 4.6.1

Contractor's injured employee brought a negligence action against owner. Owner brought a third-party indemnity action against contractor. The trial court granted contractor summary judgment on the ground that contractor had no duty to indemnify owner for owner's employee's negligence. Owner appealed. The Utah Supreme Court affirmed the judgment of the trial court.

The owner-contractor agreement provided the following:

[Contractor will] at all times protect, indemnify, save harmless and defend the City, its agents and employees from any and all claims, demands, judgments, expenses, including reasonable attorney's fees, and all other damages of every kind and nature made, rendered or incurred by or in behalf of any person or persons whomsoever, including the parties hereto and their employees, which may arise out of any act or failure to act, work or other activity related in any way to the project, by the said Contractor, its agents, subcontractors, materialmen or employees in the performance and execution of this Agreement.

The supreme court found that the indemnity clause clearly entitled the city to indemnification only when the claim arose out of an act of the "contractor, its agents, subcontractors, materialmen, or employees in the performance and execution of the agreement." Owner's employee was not an agent, subcontractor, materialman, or employee of city.

93036   Gables CVF, Inc. v. Bahr, Vermeer & Haecker Architect, Ltd., 244 Neb. 346, 506 N.W.2d 706, *modified*, 244 Neb. 613 (1993)

        II: A107–1978, Art. 8, Para. 8.3
        II: A107–1987, Art. 10, Para. 10.2
        II: A117–1979, Art. 12, Para. 12.3
        II: A117–1987, Art. 15, Para. 15.2
        I: A201–1976, Art. 2, Para. 2.2.3
        I: A201–1976, Art. 7, Para. 7.7.1
        I: A201–1976, Art. 7, Para. 7.7.4
        I: A201–1976, Art. 9, Para. 9.4.2
        II: A201–1987, Art. 4, Para. 4.2.2

it was required to pay the owner as reimbursement for the attorneys' fees it incurred by defending the worker's claim. The court reversed the judgment of the trial court on this issue.

93034   Englehart v. OKI Am., Inc., 209 Ga. App. 151, 433 S.E.2d 331 (1993), *cert. denied*, 1993 Ga. LEXIS 1065 (Ga. Nov. 5, 1993)

        III: A107–1987, Art. 9, Para. 9.1
        III: A107–1987, Art. 9, Para. 9.2
        III: A107–1987, Art. 16, Para. 16.1
        III: A117–1987, Art. 14, Para. 14.1
        III: A117–1987, Art. 14, Para. 14.2
        III: A117–1987, Art. 21, Para. 21.1
        III: A201–1987, Art. 3, Para. 3.3.1
        III: A201–1987, Art. 3, Para. 3.3.2
        III: A201–1987, Art. 3, Para. 3.4.1
        III: A201–1987, Art. 10, Para. 10.1
        III: A201–1987, Art. 10, Para. 10.2

Subcontractor's injured employee brought a negligence action against owner seeking personal injury damages. The trial court granted summary judgment to owner. Injured worker appealed. The appellate court upheld the judgment of the trial court.

The owner-contractor agreement provided that the contractor "shall be responsible for furnishing the design and for the construction of the Project . . . . The Contractor will provide all construction supervision, inspection, labor, materials, tools, construction equipment and subcontracted items necessary for the execution and completion of the Project . . . ." The contract also provided the following:

> The Contractor shall take necessary precautions for the safety of its employees on the Work, and shall comply with all applicable provisions of federal, state and municipal safety laws to prevent accidents or injury to persons on, about or adjacent to the Project site . . . . The Owner . . . shall have no contractual obligation to the Contractor's subcontractors and shall communicate with such Subcontractors only through the Contractor.

The appellate court found that the contract gave complete control of the site to the contractor and made the contractor solely responsible for the safety of its employees. The owner's retention of the right to ensure that contractor's work conformed to the contract did not support a finding that owner exercised control over the manner in which the contractor performed the work. Furthermore, the evidence indicated that the owner had surrendered the premises to contractor and did not interfere with contractor's status as an independent contractor.

or engineer had assumed responsibility for site safety beyond the terms of their contracts. The terms of the General Conditions made the contractor responsible for site safety.

After the trial court's award of summary judgment, architect and engineer filed cross-claims for contractual indemnity against contractor. In a separate appeal, they challenged the trial court's order dismissing these claims. The trial court had ruled that the indemnification provision of the owner/contractor agreement did not apply to claims based on architect's and engineer's own alleged negligence. The appellate court reversed the judgment of the trial court, 884 S.W.2d 722.

The owner/contractor agreement included the American Institute of Architects General Conditions of the Contract for Construction, Document No. A201, 1987 edition, specifically Paragraph 3.18.

Architects and engineers argued on appeal that Paragraph 3.18.1 satisfied Kansas state law, which does not allow for indemnity for one's own negligence, unless the agreement specifically and expressly so provides.

The appellate court found that Paragraph 3.18.1 specifically and unambiguously stated that the contractor would indemnify the architect and engineer for that portion of damage caused by the contractor or its subcontractors regardless of any claimed liability on the part of the architect or engineer.

The court remanded the action for a determination as to whether the negligent acts or omissions of the subcontractors and/or the contractor were the whole cause of the worker's injuries, or if not, the court had to decide what portion of fault should be ascribed to the subcontractors and/or the contractor. If the appellate court determined that the contractor's or subcontractor's negligence was the "whole cause" of the accident, the contractor would be required to reimburse the architects and engineers for all their reasonable legal expenses, including attorney fees incurred defending this matter. If a percentage of fault was ascribed to the contractor and/or the subcontractor, the contractor would be required to reimburse the same percentage of the expenses and legal fees to architects and engineers.

On remand, contractor settled with the architect and engineer.

Contractor then appealed the trial court's ruling on its motion for summary judgment (943 S.W.2d 711) that the indemnity provision in the subcontract did not require subcontractor to indemnify contractor for attorneys' fees it expended in defending the action brought by the worker. The appellate court affirmed the trial court's determination that under the state statute, contractor's own attorneys' fees were not included in the provision requiring subcontractor to indemnify contractor for "any liability, loss, cost or expenses . . . caused by either the General Contractor or the Sub-Contractor or by their work" absent an express contractual provision.

The court found, however, that the provision was broad enough to require subcontractor to indemnify contractor where the sums paid by contractor to the architect and engineer in settlement of their claims constituted a liability of contractor which came within the indemnity provision of the subcontract. The subcontract required subcontractor to indemnify contractor for "any liability, loss, cost or expense" resulting from worker's injury. Similarly, the subcontract required that subcontractor reimburse contractor for the sum

Subcontractor brought an action against contractor to recover the balance due under the subcontract. The trial court entered judgment for subcontractor and contractor appealed. The appellate court reversed the judgment of the trial court.

Paragraph 14 of the subcontract provided in pertinent part that "[p]ayment of purchaser by owner shall be a condition precedent to Vendor's right to payment hereunder."

The appellate court found that the contract language clearly provided that owner's payment to the contractor was a condition precedent to subcontractor's right to receive payment under the subcontract. The court concluded that, where the condition precedent to subcontractor's right to receive payment had not been satisfied, without fault on the part of the contractor, subcontractor was not entitled to summary judgment.

93033   Dillard v. Shaughnessy, Fickel & Scott, Architects, 864 S.W.2d 368 (Mo. Ct. App. 1993), *remanded* 884 S.W.2d 722 (Mo. Ct. App. 1994), *appeal after remand*, 943 S.W.2d 711 (Mo. Ct. App. 1997)

II:	A107–1987, Art. 9, Para. 9.1	
II:	A107–1987, Art. 9, Para. 9.7	
II:	A117–1987, Art. 14, Para. 14.1	
II:	A117–1987, Art. 14, Para. 14.7	
I:	A201–1987, Art. 3, Para. 3.3.1	
I:	A201–1987, Art. 3, Para. 3.3.2	
I:	A201–1987, Art. 3, Para. 3.3.4	
I:	B141–1987, Art. 2, Para. 2.6.5	
I:	B141–1987, Art. 2, Para. 2.6.6	

Subcontractor's employee, injured at a job site in Kansas, brought a negligence action against architect, engineer and others. The worker argued that the architect and engineer had a duty to see that the wall in question was properly reinforced or braced during construction, that proper site safety precautions were followed, and that safety inspections were conducted. The trial court granted architect, and engineer's motions for summary judgment on the ground that neither architect nor engineer owed worker a duty to maintain a safe site or to conduct inspections. Furthermore, a Kansas statute provided immunity to architect and engineer. Injured worker appealed. The appellate court affirmed the judgment of the trial court, 864 S.W.2d 368.

The owner and architect had entered into the American Institute of Architects Standard Form of Agreement Between Owner and Architect, Document No. B141, 1987 edition, specifically Paragraphs 2.6.5 and 2.6.6. The owner-contractor agreement included the American Institute of Architects General Conditions of the Contract for Construction, Document No. A201, 1987 edition, specifically Paragraphs 3.3.1, 3.3.2 and 3.3.4.

The appellate court found no contractual provisions making architect or engineer responsible for site safety and no evidence in the record to show that either architect

III: A117–1987, Art. 14, Para. 14.12
III: A201–1976, Art. 4, Para. 4.18.1
III: A201–1987, Art. 3, Para. 3.18.1
III: A201–1987, Art. 10, Para. 10.1.4
III: A401–1978, Art. 11, Para. 11.1.1
III: A401–1987, Art. 4, Para. 4.6.1

City brought a declaratory judgment action against contractor invoking the indemnity, insurance and other liability provisions in an asbestos-removal contract. The trial court granted contractor's motion for summary judgment and the appellate court affirmed the judgment of the trial court.

The indemnity clause stated the following:

Contractor agrees to indemnify, save and hold harmless and defend City, its officers and employees, from any and all liens, charges, claims [sic] demands, losses, costs including but not limited to legal fees and court costs, causes of action or suits of any kind or nature whatsoever, in law or in equity, judgments, liabilities and damages of any and every kind and nature whatsoever, from any causes whatsoever, whether known or unknown, foreseen or unforeseen, arising by reason of or during the performance of any work of any kind or nature covered by this contract.

The contractor further agreed that:

[Contractor will] indemnify and save harmless the City of Pittsburgh, its officers, employees an [d] agents from all suits, actions and proceedings of every kind which may be brought against the City or her officers, employees or agents for or on account of any injuries or damages to persons or property, received or sustained by any person or persons, firm or corporation by or from [American Asbestos], or his employees or agents while engaged in the prosecution of the work under this agreement . . . or by or on account of any accident that may occur during the performance of the work. . . .

The court found that the indemnity and the liability-for-damages provisions did not contain clear and unequivocal language by which contractor agreed to indemnify the City for its own negligence. In order for the City to be indemnified for its own negligence, the contract would have had to clearly state that there was an obligation to indemnify for losses occasioned by the indemnitee's own negligence.

The court rejected the Pennsylvania Supreme Court's ruling in an earlier case that, where the indemnitee's negligence was "merely" passive, words indemnifying the indemnitee against its own negligence were unnecessary.

93032 David Fanarof, Inc. v. Dember Constr. Corp., 195 A.D.2d 346, 600 N.Y.S.2d 226 (1993)

III: A401–1987, Art. 12, Para. 12.1

by Paragraph 11.3.1), the court determined that the provisions of Paragraph 11.3.5 with respect to the insurance of adjoining or adjacent property under a policy "separate" from that insuring the Work were applicable because the insurance was intended to protect the interest of the owner, contractor, subcontractor, sub-subcontractors and the Work as described in Paragraph 11.3.1.

93030 City of Columbus v. Alden E. Stilson & Assocs., 90 Ohio App. 3d 608, 630 N.E.2d 59 (1993)

> III: A107–1987, Art. 9, Para. 9.12
> III: A117–1987, Art. 14, Para. 14.2
> III: A201–1987, Art. 3, Para. 3.18.1
> III: A201–1987, Art. 10, Para. 10.1.4
> III: A401–1987, Art. 4, Para. 4.6.1

Contractor brought an action against owner for delay damages and additional compensation resulting from inadequate drawings, plans and data furnished by the owner. Owner made numerous demands that engineer defend the owner as provided in the owner-engineer agreement. After engineer declined to do so, owner brought an indemnification action against engineer. The trial court entered a declaratory judgment finding that engineer was required by the indemnity clause to assume owner's defense. Engineer appealed. Among numerous issues on appeal, the engineer argued that the indemnification clause was ambiguous and should be interpreted to require engineer to indemnify owner only for losses due to engineer's negligence. The appellate court upheld the declaratory judgment of the trial court.

The indemnification agreement provided the following:

> The Engineers shall assume the defense of and indemnify and save harmless the City from any claims or liabilities of any type or nature to any person, firm or corporation, arising in any manner from the Engineers' performance of the work covered by the engineering contract, and [they] shall pay any judgment obtained or growing out of said claims or liabilities of any of them.

The appellate court found that the clear and unambiguous language of the indemnification agreement was enforceable despite its broad scope. The court declined to read the prerequisite of negligence into the clause.

93031 City of Pittsburgh v. American Asbestos Control Co., 157 Pa. Commw. 235, 629 A.2d 265 (1993)

> III: A107–1978, Art. 10, Para. 10.11
> III: A107–1987, Art. 9, Para. 9.12
> III: A117–1979, Art. 14, Para. 14.11

are not caused or contributed to by omission to perform some duty also imposed on the subcontractor, his agents or employees, such indemnity will not apply to such party guilty of such active negligence unless the prime contract documents otherwise provide.

The supreme court found that, because the subcontract's indemnity provision contained the phrase "unless the prime contract documents otherwise provide," the indemnity provision in the owner-contractor agreement governed. The court then found that subcontractor was bound to indemnify contractor from and against all damages arising out of or resulting from the performance of subcontractor's work but only to the extent they were caused in whole or in part by negligent acts or omissions of subcontractor or its sub-subcontractor.

93029   Chadwick v. CSI, Ltd., 137 N.H. 515, 629 A.2d 820 (1993)

II:	A107–1987, Art. 17, Para. 17.6	
II:	A117–1987, Art. 22, Para. 22.6	
I:	A201–1987, Art. 11, Para. 11.3.3	
I:	A201–1987, Art. 11, Para. 11.3.5	
I:	A201–1987, Art. 11, Para. 11.3.7	

Subcontractor brought an action against contractor and owner for failure to pay for materials and services provided with respect to a subcontract to install floors in the auditorium of the owner's school. The owner counterclaimed against the subcontractor alleging that subcontractor's negligence had caused a fire that destroyed the auditorium and adjoining portions of the school. The jury rendered a verdict in favor of the subcontractor and contractor against the owner. The court interpreted a waiver-of-subrogation provision in the owner/contractor agreement as precluding the owner's claim against the subcontractor to the extent the damages caused by the fire were covered by the owner's own insurance. On appeal, the Supreme Court of New Hampshire affirmed.

The owner and contractor had entered into an American Institute of Architects Standard Form of Agreement Between Owner and Contractor, which incorporated by reference the American Institute of Architects General Conditions of the Contract for Construction, Doc. No. A201, 1987 edition, specifically Paragraph 11.3.3 "Loss of Use Insurance," Paragraph 11.3.5, which provides for waiver of the owner's rights to make a claim against the contractor to the extent the owner insures properties adjoining or adjacent to the site, and Paragraph 11.3.7, the waiver-of-subrogation provision.

The supreme court held that these provisions did not constitute exculpatory provisions prohibited by New Hampshire law and that the trial court correctly applied the waiver-of-subrogation provisions to the Work in light of the duty of the contractor to indemnify the owner because of injury or destruction of tangible property pursuant to the indemnity provision. Finally, even though the owner had insured the work by raising limits on its preexisting property insurance (and not by procuring a separate policy as contemplated

further conference could be scheduled. If it could be shown that there were addition data to justify review of the decision, a time extension could be granted to allow the data to be submitted. Contractor wrote to engineer that it questioned engineer's authority to review the dispute. Contractor asked that the authority issue be resolved first and reserved the right to submit additional data. Contractor never submitted additional data.

The appellate court rejected contractor's argument that engineer's decision was not final. According to the court, the contract specifically limited the time period in which arbitration might be demanded. Contractor's failure to submit additional data and to timely submit the dispute to the American Arbitration Association indicated a waiver based on conduct inconsistent with the arbitration provision.

93028   Brown v. Boyer-Washington Boulevard Assocs., 856 P.2d 352 (Utah 1993)

II:	A107–1987, Art. 9, Para. 9.12
II:	A117–1987, Art. 14, Para. 14.12
I:	A201–1987 Art. 3, Para. 3.18.1
II:	A201–1987, Art. 10, Para. 10.1.4
III:	A401–1987, Art. 2, Para. 2.1
III:	A401–1987, Art. 4, Para. 4.6.1

Sub-subcontractor's injured employee brought an action against contractor and owner, alleging contractor's failure to install safety cables as required by the owner-contractor agreement. Contractor filed a third-party action against sub-subcontractor for the purpose of determining sub-subcontractor's portion of fault and a cross-claim against subcontractor for indemnification under the terms of both the owner-contractor agreement and the subcontract. The trial court dismissed contractor's third-party action against sub-subcontractor. The trial court granted subcontractor's motion for summary judgment on contractor's cross-claim for indemnity. Contractor appealed. The Utah Supreme Court reversed the trial court's dismissal of the third-party complaint and affirmed the judgment on the cross-claim for indemnity.

The owner-contractor agreement contained an indemnity provision identical to Paragraph 3.18.1 of the American Institute of Architects General Conditions of the Contract for Construction Document No. A201, 1987 edition. In the subcontract, the subcontractor agreed to be bound to contractor "by all obligations of the prime contract as they may apply to the work herein described as if the contractor were in the place of the owner, and subcontractor were in place of the contractor." The indemnity clause in the subcontract provided as follows:

> [Subcontractor] shall indemnify contractor against and save harmless from any and all loss, damage, injury, liability, and claims thereof for injuries to persons resulting directly or indirectly from subcontractors' performance of this agreement, regardless of the negligence of the contractor, provided that where such loss, damage, injury, liability or claims are the result of active negligence on the part of the contractor and

III: A117–1987, Art. 15, Para. 15.8
III: A201–1987, Art. 4, Para. 4.5.1
III: A201–1987, Art. 4, Para. 4.5.2
III: A201–1987, Art. 4, Para. 4.5.3
III: A201–1987, Art. 4, Para. 4.5.4
III: A201–1987, Art. 4, Para. 4.5.4.1
III: A201–1987, Art. 4, Para. 4.5.4.2
III: A201–1987, Art. 4, Para. 4.5.5
III: A201–1987, Art. 4, Para. 4.5.6
III: A201–1987, Art. 4, Para. 4.5.7
III: A401–1987, Art. 6, Para. 6.1
III: A401–1987, Art. 6, Para. 6.2
III: A401–1987, Art. 6, Para. 6.3
III: A401–1987, Art. 6, Para. 6.4
III: A401–1987, Art. 6, Para. 6.5
III: B141–1987, Art. 7, Para. 7.1
III: B141–1987, Art. 7, Para. 7.2
III: B141–1987, Art. 7, Para. 7.3
III: B141–1987, Art. 7, Para. 7.4

Owner appealed the grant of contractor's motion to compel arbitration and judgment in favor of contractor on cross-motions for summary judgment on owner's claim seeking enforcement of engineer's decision in favor of owner. The appellate court reversed.

The parties' dispute related to owner's claim of defective work based on contaminants in the water pipes installed pursuant to a water–supply construction contract. The arbitration provision stated that all claims, disputes and other matters in question were to be decided by the American Arbitration Association, subject to a limitation which stated the following:

No demand for arbitration of any such claim, dispute or other matter will be made later than thirty days after the date on which ENGINEER has rendered a written decision in respect thereof in accordance with paragraph 9.11. and the failure to demand arbitration within said thirty day period shall result in ENGINEER'S decision being final and binding upon the parties.

Owner submitted the dispute to engineer within the thirty–day period required by the contract. The engineer concluded that the work was defective and that contractor was liable for the cost of repair. Owner filed suit to enforce the engineer's decision. Contractor thereafter demanded arbitration, almost two years after engineer's decision was rendered.

Contractor argued on appeal that the engineer's decision was not final because the engineer by subsequent letter provided that, after the parties reviewed its findings, a

reviewing that evidence, the court determined that the trial court had erred in finding no liability on the part of the contractor for the acts of the subcontractor hired by owner.

93026   Bilotta Constr. Corp. v. Village of Mamaroneck, 199 A.D.2d 230, 604 N.Y.S.2d 966 (1993)

        Ill: A107–1987, Art. 7, Para. 7.3
        Ill: A107–1987, Art. 13, Para. 13.3
        Ill: A117–1987, Art. 12, Para. 12.3
        Ill: A117–1987, Art. 18, Para. 18.3
        Ill: A201–1987, Art. 2, Para. 2.2.2
        Ill: A201–1987, Art. 3, Para. 3.2.1
        Ill: A201–1987, Art. 3, Para. 3.2.2
        Ill: A201–1987, Art. 4, Para. 4.3.6
        Ill: A201–1987, Art. 4, Para. 4.3.7

Contractor brought an action against owner and engineer for costs incurred for unanticipated work resulting from engineer's negligent preparation of bid documents and fraudulent misrepresentation of the nature and scope of the work. The trial court dismissed the contractor's complaint. The appellate court affirmed the dismissal.

The contract documents contained numerous clauses relieving the owner and engineer of liability and requiring the contractor to personally inspect the site. The contract stated that the "Contractor agrees that he shall neither have nor assert against the Owner or Engineer any claim for damages for extra work or otherwise or for relief from any obligation of this Contract based upon the failure by the Owner or Engineer to obtain or to furnish additional subsurface information or to furnish all subsurface information in the Owner's or Engineer's possession or based upon any inadequacy or inaccuracy of the information furnished." In addition, the contract provide that "at the time of the opening of Bids, each Bidder will be presumed to have inspected the site of the proposed work" and that "the Contractor shall . . . make all detail surveys needed for construction." The elevation data was to be regarded as approximate, with no guarantee of accuracy.

The appellate court found that the contractor failed to establish that the engineer had acted negligently or that the owner and engineer had acted fraudulently where the contract documents clearly provided that the elevations were approximate, that the contractor should not rely on the approximations, and that the contractor was obligated to conduct its own investigation of the site. Furthermore the contractor failed to produce evidence to establish that the engineer's approximations were not reasonably correct.

93027   Brookfield-North Riverside Water Comm'n v. Abbott Contractors, Inc., 250 Ill. App. 3d 588, 190 Ill. Dec. 284, 621 N.E.2d 153, *appeal denied*, 153 Ill. 2d 557, 191 Ill. Dec. 616, 624 N.E.2d 804 (1993)

        Ill: A107–1987, Art. 10, Para. 10.8

II:	A201–1976, Art. 6, Para. 6.2.1
I:	A201–1976, Art. 6, Para. 6.2.3
II:	A201–1987, Art. 3, Para. 3.3.1
II:	A201–1987, Art. 3, Para. 3.3.2
II:	A201–1987, Art. 3, Para. 3.5.1
II:	A201–1987, Art. 5, Para. 5.1.1
II:	A201–1987, Art. 5, Para. 5.2.1
II:	A201–1987, Art. 5, Para. 5.2.2
II:	A201–1987, Art. 5, Para. 5.2.3
II:	A201–1987, Art. 5, Para. 5.3.1
II:	A201–1987, Art. 6, Para. 6.1.1
II:	A201–1987, Art. 6, Para. 6.2.1
II:	A201–1987, Art. 6, Para. 6.2.3

Contractor brought a breach of contract action against owner for nonpayment of extras. The owner asserted affirmative defenses alleging that contractor failed to substantially perform under the contract and failed to supervise and direct all work on the project. After a bench trial, the court found that the owner had failed to sustain the burden of proving its affirmative defenses. The trial court entered judgment for contractor on the ground that contractor substantially performed all of the work required under the contract in a good and workmanlike manner. Owner appealed. Among numerous other issues on appeal, the owner argued that contractor had a duty to supervise all subcontractors, including a subcontractor selected and hired by the owner under a separate contract, and the contractor's failure to supervise caused the owner's damages. The appellate court reversed in part the judgment of the trial court.

The owner and contractor had entered into an agreement similar to the American Institute of Architects Abbreviated Form of Agreement Between Owner and Contractor, Document No. A107, 1978 edition, specifically Paragraphs 10.1, 10.4, 10.7, 11.1, 11.2, 12.1, 12.2 and 12.3.

The appellate court found that the clear language of the contract provided that the contractor "shall supervise and direct the work" and "shall be solely responsible for all means, methods, techniques, sequences and procedures and for coordinating all portions of the Work under the Contract." Contractor also warranted that "all Work will be of good quality, free from faults and defects and in conformance with the Contract Documents" and would be considered defective if not so conforming. Furthermore, even though the contract stated that contractor assumed liability for "all" work, it specifically exculpated liability for subcontractors operating under a separate contract. Based on the foregoing, the appellate court found that the language concerning contractor's liability for the work of all subcontractors was ambiguous and, therefore, extrinsic evidence as to the conduct of the contractor towards the subcontractor in question was admissible. After

I:	A107–1978, Art. 10, Para. 10.7
I:	A107–1978, Art. 11, Para. 11.1
II:	A107–1978, Art. 11, Para. 11.2
II:	A107–1978, Art. 12, Para. 12.1
I:	A107–1978, Art. 12, Para. 12.2
I:	A107–1978, Art. 12, Para. 12.3
II:	A107–1987, Art. 9, Para. 9.1
II:	A107–1987, Art. 9, Para. 9.4
II:	A107–1987, Art. 9, Para. 9.7
I:	A107–1987, Art. 11, Para. 11.1
II:	A107–1987, Art. 11, Para. 11.2
II:	A107–1987, Art. 12, Para. 12.1
II:	A107–1987, Art. 12, Para. 12.2
II:	A107–1987, Art. 12, Para. 12.3
I:	A117–1979, Art. 14, Para. 14.1
II:	A117–1979, Art. 14, Para. 14.4
II:	A117–1979, Art. 14, Para. 14.7
I:	A117–1979, Art. 15, Para. 15.1
II:	A117–1979, Art. 15, Para. 15.2
II:	A117–1979, Art. 16, Para. 16.1
II:	A117–1979, Art. 16, Para. 16.2
I:	A117–1979, Art. 16, Para. 16.3
II:	A117–1987, Art. 14, Para. 14.1
II:	A117–1987, Art. 14, Para. 14.4
II:	A117–1987, Art. 14, Para. 14.7
I:	A117–1987, Art. 16, Para. 16.1
II:	A117–1987, Art. 16, Para. 16.2
II:	A117–1987, Art. 17, Para. 17.1
II:	A117–1987, Art. 17, Para. 17.2
II:	A117–1979, Art. 17, Para. 17.3
I:	A201–1976, Art. 4, Para. 4.3.1
I:	A201–1976, Art. 4, Para. 4.5.1
I:	A201–1976, Art. 4, Para. 4.3.2
I:	A201–1976, Art. 5, Para. 5.1.1
II:	A201–1976, Art. 5, Para. 5.2.1
II:	A201–1976, Art. 5, Para. 5.2.2
II:	A201–1976, Art. 5, Para. 5.3.1
II:	A201–1976, Art. 6, Para. 6.1.1

II:	A401–1987, Art. 6, Para. 6.4
II:	A401–1987, Art. 6, Para. 6.5
I:	B141–1977, Art. 9, Para. 9.1
I:	B141–1977, Art. 9, Para. 9.2
I:	B141–1977, Art. 9, Para. 9.3
II:	B141–1987, Art. 7, Para. 7.1
II:	B141–1987, Art. 7, Para. 7.2
II:	B141–1987, Art. 7, Para. 7.3
II:	B141–1987, Art. 7, Para. 7.4

Owner appealed an order confirming an arbitration award to architect based on nonpayment for its design work. The trial court confirmed the arbitration award because no application for vacation, modification, or correction was presented by owner within the statutory period. The appellate court affirmed.

The architect, owner (School Board) and County Commission had entered into a contract for design projects including "[a]dditions, renovations and new construction as directed by School Board and County Commission." Specific projects were not listed. The parties used the American Institute of Architects Standard Form of Agreement Between Owner and Architect, Document No. B141, 1977 edition, specifically Paragraphs 9.1, 9.2 and 9.3.

The dispute arose after the architect performed design work for two school renovation projects at the direction of owner, but prior to County Commission's providing funding. Architect demanded arbitration after it was refused payment. School Board and County Commission filed suit seeking a stay of arbitration on the ground that the underlying agreement was invalid, unenforceable and conditioned upon direction by both School Board and County Commission. After the trial court denied the petition for stay, the parties proceeded to arbitration and the architect was awarded payment. The trial court granted architect's motion to confirm the arbitration award.

Owner argued on appeal that the underlying contract was unenforceable due to indefiniteness of the subject matter where specific projects were not listed. The appellate court considered the parties' conduct, including performance by one party and previous dealings under the contract, and also relied on the rule of construction that favors a finding of sufficient definiteness. The court concluded that there was an enforceable agreement and also noted that another basis for affirmance was the owner's failure to contest the award confirmation in the trial court, as required by state statute.

93025   A.W. Wendell & Sons, Inc. v. Qazi, 254 Ill. App. 3d 97, 193 Ill. Dec. 247, 626 N.E.2d 280 (1993)

I:	A107–1978, Art. 10, Para. 10.1
I:	A107–1978, Art. 10, Para. 10.4

Paragraphs 8.1 and 8.2 set forth the parties agreement as to ownership and use of the documents.

The Appellate Court found that it was uncontroverted that at the inception of the project the architect was aware of the owner's intention to convert the apartment complex to condominium ownership at some time in the future. Under the express terms of the contract, the owner was authorized to retain copies of the plans for "information and reference" in connection with the use of the project, and the submission of those plans to meet "official regulatory requirements or for other purposes in connection with the project" did not violate the architect's rights with respect to the plans. Moreover, since a seller of a condominium was required under state statute to furnish prospective buyers with various documents, including a copy of the floor plan of the unit and a copy of the condominium declaration, any use of the plans for that purpose was also authorized under the contract and was not a misappropriation.

The Court also found that the second architect did not misappropriate the first architect's plans. Although the second architect did remove the first architect's seal from the documents, he did not claim the plans to be his own, but instead made it clear that the first architect was the design architect. The second architect did not sell the plans, nor did he build a project from the plans. The second architect's adaptation of the plans was consistent with the owner's use of the plans authorized under the contract.

93024   Anderson County v. Architectural Techniques Corp., 1993 Tenn. App. LEXIS 591 (Tenn. Ct. App. Sept. 9, 1993)

	II:	A107–1978, Art. 13, Para. 13.2
	II:	A107–1987, Art. 10, Para. 10.8
	II:	A117–1979, Art. 17, Para. 17.2
	II:	A117–1987, Art. 15, Para. 15.8
	II:	A201–1976, Art. 7, Para. 7.9.1
	II:	A201–1987, Art. 4, Para. 4.5.1
	II:	A201–1987, Art. 4, Para. 4.5.2
	II:	A201–1987, Art. 4, Para. 4.5.3
	II:	A201–1987, Art. 4, Para. 4.5.4
	II:	A201–1987, Art. 4, Para. 4.5.4.1
	II:	A201–1987, Art. 4, Para. 4.5.4.2
	II:	A201–1987, Art. 4, Para. 4.5.5
	II:	A201–1987, Art. 4, Para. 4.5.6
	II:	A201–1987, Art. 4, Para. 4.5.7
	II:	A401–1978, Art. 13, Para. 13.1
	II:	A401–1987, Art. 6, Para. 6.1
	II:	A401–1987, Art. 6, Para. 6.2
	II:	A401–1987, Art. 6, Para. 6.3

Contractor appealed an adverse decision following a bench trial in an action by owner and its tenant to recover property damage resulting from a construction collapse. Among numerous other issues, the contractor argued on appeal that the claims of owner and tenant were barred by a contractual waiver of subrogation. The Appellate Court affirmed the judgment in favor of tenant, but because the trial court erred in concluding that the contractual waiver of subrogation did not bar owner's claim against contractor, the Court vacated the judgment in favor of owner.

Owner and contractor entered into an owner-contractor agreement that included the American Institute of Architects General Conditions of the Contract for Construction, Document No. A201, 1976 edition, specifically Paragraph 11.3.6. The parties amended Paragraph 11.3.1 to require the contractor to maintain builders' risk insurance. The contractor did not obtain the insurance until after the occurrence of the property damage. The owner and tenant maintained insurance on the lot and the existing building.

Maine's Supreme Judicial Court found that under Paragraph 11.3.6 the parties waived all claims for damages covered by insurance obtained pursuant to Article 11.3, or "any other property insurance applicable to the work." The Court found that the back wall—which had collapsed—was an integral part of the project since the "work" was defined in Paragraph 1.1.3 as comprising the "completed construction required by the contract documents," and since the completed construction involved an addition attached to the existing building at the back wall. Furthermore, the claim of owner's insurer, which sought recovery for damages paid to owner, should have been dismissed where the plain language of Paragraph 11.3.6 barred subrogation recovery between the parties for damage to the extent covered by insurance. As for the tenant, the Court found that, since the tenant was not a party to the owner-contractor agreement, the contractual waiver of subrogation did not apply and did not bar tenant's recovery against contractor.

93023   Wright v. Tidmore, 208 Ga. App. 150, 430 S.E.2d 72 (1993)

	I:	B141–1977, Art. 8, Para. 8.1
	I:	B141–1977, Art. 8, Para. 8.2
	I:	B141–1987, Art. 6, Para. 6.1
	I:	B141–1987, Art. 6, Para. 6.2

Architect brought a breach-of-contract action against owner and a second architect, alleging that the filing of altered plans prepared by the second architect as part of a condominium declaration was a publication in violation of the owner-architect agreement, and that the plans were published a second time when they were included in sales brochures and distributed to the general public as prospective condominium purchasers. The trial court granted owner summary judgment and the architect appealed. The Appellate Court affirmed the judgment of the trial court.

Owner and architect entered into the American Institute of Architects Standard Form of Agreement Between Owner and Architect, Document No. B141, 1977 edition.

the premises or the date on which the [C]ontractor notified the [O]wner in writing of completion of the building, whichever occurs first.

Paragraph 15 governed occupancy under the contract and provided in pertinent part that:

[T]he [o]wner agrees not to interfere with the progress of the work and not to occupy any portion of the building until the construction on that portion is completed, and that portion of the building has been accepted in writing by the [o]wner, and the provisions and conditions of the agreement with respect thereto are fulfilled by both parties. Contractor's "Acknowledgment of Completion And Acceptance Certificate" covering the building of any specified portion thereof shall be executed by the [o]wner and delivered to the [c]ontractor prior to any use or occupancy by the [o]wner. In the event a portion or all of the building is used or occupied by the [o]wner without providing such a certificate, then such use or occupancy shall be conclusive proof of acceptance thereof by the [o]wner.

The Appellate Court concluded that owner's strict and literal interpretation of the term "full performance" in Article 5, after owner occupied the premises, frustrated the intention of the parties where the contract defined delivery and completion as the date upon which the owner began to occupy the premises, and occupancy as proof of completion and acceptance by the owner.

The Court applied the general rule that the contractor is held only to a duty of substantial performance in a workmanlike manner and, in light of the evidence presented at trial, the Court concluded that the trial court had not erred in finding that the contractor substantially performed its duties under the contract, and in offsetting the amount due by the amount necessary to repair or replace the items not completed within the terms of the contract. Furthermore, the Court rejected the owner's argument that interest should not be awarded on money that may be found due if the person withholding payment has done so in good faith. The interest awarded in this case was not statutory but was awarded pursuant to Paragraph 22 of the contract. In addition, the Court found that there was no abuse of discretion in the award of attorney fees.

93022   Willis Realty Assocs. v. Cimino Constr. Co., 623 A.2d 1287 (Me. 1993)

I:	A107–1978, Art. 7, Para. 7.4
I:	A107–1978, Art. 17, Para. 17.3
I:	A107–1978, Art. 17, Para. 17.6
I:	A117–1979, Art. 11, Para. 11.4
I:	A117–1979, Art. 21, Para. 21.3
I:	A117–1979, Art. 21, Para. 21.6
I:	A201–1976, Art. 1, Para. 1.1.3
I:	A201–1976, Art. 11, Para. 11.3.1
I:	A201–1976, Art. 11, Para. 11.3.6

III:	A107–1987, Art. 15, Para. 15.2	
III:	A107–1987, Art. 15, Para. 15.3	
III:	A107–1987, Art. 15, Para. 15.4	
III:	A107–1987, Art. 15, Para. 15.5	
III:	A117–1987, Art. 20, Para. 20.1	
III:	A117–1987, Art. 20, Para. 20.2	
III:	A117–1987, Art. 20, Para. 20.3	
III:	A117–1987, Art. 20, Para. 20.4	
III:	A117–1987, Art. 20, Para. 20.5	
III:	A201–1987, Art. 9, Para. 9.8.1	
III:	A201–1987, Art. 9, Para. 9.8.3	
III:	A201–1987, Art. 9, Para. 9.9.1	
III:	A201–1987, Art. 9, Para. 9.10.1	
III:	A201–1987, Art. 9, Para. 9.10.2	
III:	A201–1987, Art. 9, Para. 9.10.3	
III:	A201–1987, Art. 9, Para. 9.10.4	

Owner appealed an award of prejudgment interest and attorney fees to contractor. Contractor cross-appealed on the grounds that the trial court's award of attorney fees was inadequate and a setoff was improper. Owner argued on appeal that the trial court erred in awarding attorney fees and prejudgment interest to contractor because to do so was contrary to the specific language of the contract. In particular, owner argued that, because the contract was not fully performed, payment never became due and, therefore, attorney fees and prejudgment interest should never have been awarded for the collection of that payment. Contractor argued on appeal that the work was completed and the contract was substantially performed; therefore, payment was due. The Appellate Court affirmed the judgment of the trial court.

The owner-contractor agreement provided in Article 5 that the owner was required to make final payment 30 days after completion of the work, and further provided that the contract was fully performed subject to the provisions of Paragraph 22 of the general conditions. Paragraph 22 of the general conditions provided in pertinent part that "payment is due on the date stated on contractor's invoice in accordance with this agreement. Any amount not paid on date due will bear interest at the rate of 1 [percent] per month or the highest lawful rate allowed, whichever is lower, until paid, plus all costs of collecting said amount due, including all court costs and [attorney] fees."

The Appellate Court interpreted Article 5 in light of the contract was a whole. The Court referred to Paragraph 8 of the general conditions, which provided in pertinent part that:

> [A]s used in this agreement, "[S]ubstantial [C]ompletion" shall mean the date on which the [o]wner begins to occupy the premises or to move his equipment or property onto

extensions, and that this failure resulted in substantial damages. The owner argued on appeal that the contractor's sole remedy for delays under the "no-damages-for-delay" provision was an extension of time. Furthermore, the owner argued that denial of time extensions by the architect may not be considered a delay not contemplated by the parties or active interference by the owner so as to constitute an exception to the no-damages-for-delay clause. The issue on appeal was whether the owner's refusal to grant a time extension was a breach of contract. The Appellate Court reversed the trial court's entry of summary judgment for owner against the prime electrical contractor.

The owner and contractor entered into an agreement which contained provisions identical to Paragraph 8.3.1 of the American Institute of Architects General Conditions of the Contract for Construction, Document No. A201, 1976 edition, and a no-damages-for-delay clause, which provided in pertinent part that "[i]f the Contractor is delayed by the Owner or Architect or any Agent or employee of either, the Contractor's sole and exclusive remedy for the delay shall be the right to a time extension for completion of the Contract and not damages."

The Appellate Court found the contract terms to be ambiguous on their face, and that the intent of the parties was a question of fact for the jury because Paragraph 8.3.1 could be interpreted to give the architect either complete discretion in awarding time extensions or limited discretion to determine the length of the extension once there was a "justifiable" delay under the contract. The Court rejected the owner's argument that, even if the contractor could prove a breach of contract, contractor could not recover damages because the contractor's damages were limited by the no-damages-for-delay clause to time extensions. The Court found that, since the contract did not provide a remedy for an unreasonable denial of a time extension, the question had to be resolved by the jury interpreting the intent of the parties.

The Court rejected the owner's argument that the contractor could not recover since it failed to give timely notice of its claims, which was a condition precedent to recovery under the contract. The owner relied on the contract provision which required that any claims against the owner had to be made in strict accordance with Paragraph 12.3.1. Paragraph 12.3.1 was identical to the same numbered paragraph in the American Institute of Architects General Conditions of the Contract for Construction, Document No. A201, 1976 edition. The court found that the contract was not instructive as to what constituted adequate notice and that there was a disputed issue of material fact regarding sufficiency of the notice given to the architect, which precluded summary judgment.

The Court then interpreted the provisions of Paragraph 12.3.1 in light of the general contractor's argument that it was entitled to delay damages from owner. The Court found that the general contractor failed to satisfy a condition precedent to recovery by not complying with the notice requirements of Paragraph 12.3.1. Here, the general contractor gave notice to the owner or architect more than two years after it was damaged by the delay.

93021   Weidner v. Szostek, 245 Ill. App. 3d 487, 185 Ill. Dec. 438, 614 N.E.2d 879 (1993)

III: A107–1987, Art. 15, Para. 15.1

separate agreement to arbitrate with the owner or contractor. However, subcontractor's motion acted as an offer to arbitrate and consent to arbitration on subcontractor's own behalf. Contractor joined in subcontractor's motion and it was represented that another subcontractor took the same position. Therefore, when contractor sought arbitration against the owner, the contractor in effect consented to arbitration of its dispute with subcontractor. The Court concluded that the parties who joined in the motion to compel arbitration consented to arbitration.

The Court found further that, since the owners were not parties to an arbitration agreement with anyone other than the contractor and did not agree to arbitrate with anyone else, they could not be compelled to arbitrate directly with anyone except the contractor unless they extended the benefits of arbitration under the owner-contractor agreement to others.

The Court then found that, despite the language in Paragraph 7.2, the flow-down language in Paragraph 11.2 contemplated the subcontractor's right to arbitration against the owner. The Court concluded that, although under Paragraph 7.2 no direct contractual relationship was created between the owner and subcontractor, Paragraph 11.2 gave the subcontractor the benefits of the "rights, remedies and redress afforded to" the contractor, and this included the right to institute arbitration.

Furthermore, the subcontractor's claim was not undermined by the provision in the subcontract which stated that "this Agreement constitutes the entire, complete and exclusive statement of the agreement between the Contractor and Subcontractor with respect to the work and materials furnished. . . . No representations, promises or conditions not set forth herein have been relied upon by Subcontractor or shall be binding on either party hereto. . . ." The Court reasoned that this provision had to do with the scope of the work and the subcontract made no mention of integration of the owner-contractor agreement.

The Court then found that the parties had not waived their right to compel arbitration by instituting legal proceedings since the lawsuit had not reached judgment. Furthermore, the contractor did not waive the right to arbitration since he substantially complied with the provisions of Paragraph 10.8.

93020 Watson Elec. Constr. Co. v. City of Winston-Salem, 109 N.C. App. 194, 426 S.E.2d 420, *review denied*, 334 N.C. 167, 432 S.E.2d 369 (1993)

I: A107–1978, Art. 14, Para. 14.3
I: A117–1979, Art. 18, Para. 18.3
I: A201–1976, Art. 8, Para. 8.3.1
I: A201–1976, Art. 12, Para. 12.3.1

Prime electrical contractor appealed the trial court's grant of summary judgment to owner. Among numerous issues raised on appeal by other parties, the contractor argued that the owner, through its architect, breached the contract by failing to grant time

I:	A201–1987, Art. 4, Para. 4.5.1
I:	A201–1987, Art. 4, Para. 4.5.2
I:	A201–1987, Art. 4, Para. 4.5.3
I:	A201–1987, Art. 4, Para. 4.5.4
I:	A201–1987, Art. 4, Para. 4.5.4.1
I:	A201–1987, Art. 4, Para. 4.5.4.2
I:	A201–1987, Art. 4, Para. 4.5.5
I:	A201–1987, Art. 4, Para. 4.5.6
I:	A201–1987, Art. 4, Para. 4.5.7
I:	A201–1976, Art. 5, Para. 5.3.1
I:	A201–1987, Art. 13, Para. 13.1.1
I:	A401–1987, Art. 6, Para. 6.1
I:	A401–1987, Art. 6, Para. 6.2
I:	A401–1987, Art. 6, Para. 6.3
I:	A401–1987, Art. 6, Para. 6.4
I:	A401–1987, Art. 6, Para. 6.5
I:	B141–1987, Art. 7, Para. 7.1
I:	B141–1987, Art. 7, Para. 7.2
I:	B141–1987, Art. 7, Para. 7.3
I:	B141–1987, Art. 7, Para. 7.4

In consolidated cases brought by owners and subcontractors, owners appealed the trial court's grant of subcontractor's motion (in which contractor joined) to compel arbitration. The owners argued on appeal that they could not be compelled to arbitrate any claim in the absence of a contractual agreement with subcontractor, that subcontractor had no direct or derivative right to compel arbitration, and that the parties, including the contractor, had waived any right to compel arbitration by instituting suit, or alternatively, by failing to comply with all conditions precedent to arbitration.

The owners and contractor entered into the American Institute of Architects Abbreviated Form of Agreement Between Owner and Contractor, Document No. A107, 1987 edition, which provided for arbitration of disputes in Paragraph 10.8. Paragraph 7.2 provided in pertinent part that "[t]he contract document shall not be construed to create a contractual relationship of any kind (1) between the Architect, Contractor, (2) between the Owner and a Subcontractor or Sub-Subcontractor or (3) between any persons or entities other than the Owner and Contractor." Paragraph 11.2 provided that each subcontract contain a flow-down provision affording each subcontractor the benefit of all "rights, remedies and redress" afforded the contractor under the owner-contractor agreement.

The Appellate Court found that the owner and contractor had agreed to arbitrate pursuant to Paragraph 10.8. Subcontractor, who brought the motion to compel, had no

indemnify and save harmless [contractor], its officers, agents, servants and employees from and against any and all such claims, and further from and against any and all loss, cost, expense, liability, damage or injury, including legal fees and disbursements, that [contractor], its officers, agents, servants, or employees may directly or indirectly, sustain, suffer or incur as a result thereof and the Subcontractor agrees to and does hereby assume, on behalf of [contractor], its officers, agents, servants, and employees, the defense of any action at law or in equity which may be brought against [contractor], its officers, agents, servants, or employees upon or by reason of such claims and to pay on behalf of [contractor], its officers, agents, servants and employees, upon its demand the amount of any judgment that may be entered against [contractor], its officers, agents, servants or employees in any such action.

The Appellate Court concluded that the language of the indemnity provision was very broad. The fact that the provision obligated the subcontractor to indemnify the contractor for any claims "made or asserted" suggested that the claim need not be successful to trigger indemnification. Furthermore, the use of the word "claim" (as distinguished from the word "liability") in the provision connoted the assertion of a legal right rather than a recognition of that right. Moreover, the provision stated that the subcontractor was to "assume . . . the defense of any action . . . which may be brought against [contractor] . . . upon or by reason of such claims." The Court found that, if this language was to have any meaning, it had to be construed as imposing upon subcontractor the obligation to defend contractor from the assertion of any claims arising out of subcontractor's work.

The Court found further that the purpose of the indemnity provision, when considered in light of the requirement that subcontractor procure insurance to cover the liability assumed, was to shift to subcontractor the insurance burdens covering its area of responsibility. Such insurance was purchased to obligate the insurer to indemnify the insured against liability for judgments suffered because of subcontractor's work and to assume the cost of defending the insured against claims alleging damage or injury arising out of subcontractor's work.

The Court concluded that the contractor was entitled to its reasonable legal fees and costs in defending against the owner's claim.

93019 Wasserstein v. Kovatch, 261 N.J. Super. 277, 618 A.2d 886 (App. Div.), *cert. denied*, 627 A.2d 1145 (N.J. 1993)

I: A107–1987, Art. 7, Para. 7.2
I: A107–1987, Art. 10, Para. 10.8
I: A107–1987, Art. 11, Para. 11.2
I: A117–1987, Art. 12, Para. 12.2
I: A117–1987, Art. 15, Para. 15.8
I: A117–1987, Art. 16, Para. 16.2
I: A201–1987, Art. 1, Para. 1.1.2
I: A201–1987, Art. 4, Para. 4.3.7

of whether the contractor breached that limited duty by failing to provide adequate safeguards.

93018 Urban Inv. & Dev. Co. v. Turner Constr. Co., 35 Mass. App. Ct. 100, 616 N.E.2d 829 (1993)

> II: A107–1978, Art. 10, Para. 10.11
> II: A107–1987, Art. 9, Para. 9.12
> II: A117–1979, Art. 14, Para. 14.11
> II: A117–1987, Art. 14, Para. 14.12
> II: A201–1976, Art. 4, Para. 4.18.1
> II: A201–1987, Art. 3, Para. 3.18.1
> II: A201–1987, Art. 10, Para. 10.1.4
> II: A401–1978, Art. 11, Para. 11.11.1
> II: A401–1987, Art. 4, Para. 4.6.1

Owner brought a negligence and breach of contract action against contractor, subcontractor and engineer for damages resulting from an electrical fire. Contractor filed a cross-claim against subcontractor for contractual indemnity. The trial court entered judgment for contractor, subcontractor and engineer on the owner's claim, and for subcontractor on the cross-claim. The Appellate Court reversed the judgment on the cross-claim and remanded for further hearings to determine the amount to be awarded to contractor for its legal fees and costs in defending the appeal.

Among the numerous issues raised on appeal, contractor argued that the trial judge erred in construing the indemnity agreement to be inapplicable where the contractor and subcontractor prevailed in the action. Contractor argued that the indemnity provision obligated subcontractor to indemnify and to defend contractor against any claim that alleged damage or injury in connection with the subcontractor's work and did not require that such claim be successful. Subcontractor argued that, in the absence of wrongdoing on its part, it had no obligation to indemnify contractor for costs incurred in defending against the claim.

The subcontract provided that:

The Subcontractor hereby assumes entire responsibility and liability for any and all damage or injury of any kind or nature whatever (including death resulting therefrom) to all persons, whether employees of the Subcontractor or otherwise, and to all property caused by, resulting from, arising out of or occurring in connection with the execution of the Work. Except to the extent, if any expressly prohibited by statute, should any claims for such damage or injury (including death resulting therefrom) be made or asserted, whether or not such claims are based upon [contractor's] alleged active or passive negligence or participation in the wrong or upon any alleged breach of any statutory duty or obligation on the part of [contractor], the Subcontractor agrees to

I: B141–1987, Art. 7, Para. 7.3
I: B141–1987, Art. 7, Para. 7.4

The Appellate Court found that where the architect was a third-party beneficiary of the owner-contractor agreement, and where the owner-contractor agreement contained a broad arbitration provision, the architect was not contractually bound to arbitrate if the agreement also contained a limitation of consolidation or joinder provision similar to Paragraph 4.5.5 of the American Institute of Architects General Conditions of the Contract for Construction, Document No. A201, 1987 edition, and if no written consent to arbitration was executed as required by Paragraph 4.5.5.

93017 Unger v. Eichleay Corp., 244 Ill. App. 3d 445, 185 Ill. Dec. 556, 614 N.E.2d 1241 (1993)

III: A107–1987, Art. 16, Para. 16.1
III: A117–1987, Art. 21, Para. 21.1
III: A201–1987, Art. 10, Para. 10.1.1
III: A201–1987, Art. 10, Para. 10.2.1
III: A201–1987, Art. 10, Para. 10.2.2
III: A201–1987, Art. 10, Para. 10.2.3
III: A201–1987, Art. 10, Para. 10.2.5
III: A201–1987, Art. 10, Para. 10.2.6

Subcontractor's injured employee appealed the trial court's grant of summary judgment to contractor. The trial court had held that contractor did not owe a duty to the injured worker. The Appellate Court reversed the judgment of the trial court.

The owner-contractor agreement provided that "[contractor] shall provide and maintain the necessary precautions, supervision, and safeguards for the safety of all persons on the site. [Contractor] shall designate in writing to Owner's Representative a responsible member of his organization at the site of the work whose duty shall be personnel safety and prevention of accidents."

The Appellate Court found that the contractor did owe a contractual duty to the injured worker since contractor maintained mutual control with another contractor over the limited area where the worker was injured. Furthermore, the contractor did not owe a duty to the worker to exercise reasonable care at any other place on the work site. The Court relied on the language in the owner-contractor agreement quoted above. The Court found no indication from the evidence in the record that the language in the contract was in any way limited or that the contractor did not control the particular site where the injury occurred. The Court limited its holding regarding contractor's duty to the worker to the particular site where the worker was injured. The Court remanded the issue

owner and was responsible for continuously inspecting or "supervising" the work of the contractors. The court found that engineer's authority coexisted with owner's, including the right to require that the contractors complied with the safety requirements. The court held that the trial court erred in granting engineer's motion for summary judgment because there were issues of material fact as to whether engineer performed its contractual duty to supervise the workplace, which included a duty to supervise safety at the workplace.

Furthermore, where engineer's employee was acting as construction manager under a separate contract with the owner, the court found that a trial court could determine that the engineer's contractual duties of supervising the work included a duty to ensure that the work was performed safely. Although there was no explicit language in the owner/engineer agreement, the court found that a material fact existed as to whether engineer acted properly as the owner's representative and whether the engineer acted properly in supervising and coordinating the work of the contractors.

In response to injured worker's and owner's arguments that the engineer voluntarily assumed the duty to provide a safe workplace, the court found that the trial court erred in granting engineer's motion for summary judgment where the engineer's employee testified that his duties included an inspection of the site for safety purposes and supervision of the work.

93016 Raffa Assocs. v. Boca Raton Resort & Club, 616 So. 2d 1096 (Fla. Dist. Ct. App. 1993)

I:	A107–1987, Art. 10, Para. 10.8	
I:	A117–1987, Art. 15, Para. 15.8	
I:	A201–1987, Art. 4, Para. 4.5.1	
I:	A201–1987, Art. 4, Para. 4.5.2	
I:	A201–1987, Art. 4, Para. 4.5.3	
I:	A201–1987, Art. 4, Para. 4.5.4	
I:	A201–1987, Art. 4, Para. 4.5.4.1	
I:	A201–1987, Art. 4, Para. 4.5.4.2	
I:	A201–1987, Art. 4, Para. 4.5.5	
I:	A201–1987, Art. 4, Para. 4.5.6	
I:	A201–1987, Art. 4, Para. 4.5.7	
I:	A201–1987, Art. 13, Para. 13.1.1	
I:	A401–1987, Art. 6, Para. 6.1	
I:	A401–1987, Art. 6, Para. 6.2	
I:	A401–1987, Art. 6, Para. 6.3	
I:	A401–1987, Art. 6, Para. 6.4	
I:	A401–1987, Art. 6, Para. 6.5	
I:	B141–1987, Art. 7, Para. 7.1	
I:	B141–1987, Art. 7, Para. 7.2	

III:	A117-1987, Art. 15, Para. 15.3
III:	A117-1987, Art. 21, Para. 21.1
III:	A201-1987, Art. 3, Para. 3.3.1
III:	A201-1987, Art. 3, Para. 3.3.2
III:	A201-1987, Art. 3, Para. 3.4.2
III:	A201-1987, Art. 4, Para. 4.2.2
III:	A201-1987, Art. 4, Para. 4.2.3
III:	A201-1987, Art. 10, Para. 10.1.1
III:	A201-1987, Art. 10, Para. 10.2.1
III:	A201-1987, Art. 10, Para. 10.2.3
III:	A201-1987, Art. 10, Para. 10.2.6
III:	B141-1987, Art. 2, Para. 2.6.4
III:	B141-1987, Art. 2, Para. 2.6.6

A mechanical contractor's injured employee brought a negligence action against the owner and the engineering firm that designed and administered the project. Owner counterclaimed against engineer for contribution. Among numerous other rulings, the trial court entered summary judgment for engineer, reasoning that engineer was not responsible for safety precautions at the job site. Injured worker and owner appealed. On appeal, injured worker argued that the trial court erred by granting summary judgment in favor of engineer because engineer either was negligent in the performance of its contractual duty or was negligent in the performance of its voluntarily assumed duty to ensure that safety measures were taken at the site. The owner argued that the engineer was negligent in the performance of its contractual duties and that those responsibilities included insuring that safety precautions were taken. Alternatively, owner maintained that the engineer was negligent in its performance of a voluntarily assumed duty to supervise safety at the site. The appellate court reversed the judgment of the trial court.

The owner/engineer agreement stated that engineer would provide design engineering services and help select the contractor. Owner entered into a second agreement with engineer for one of engineer's employee's to act as construction manager. Engineer then entered into an agreement with contractor to install the mechanical equipment. The owner/engineer agreement provided in pertinent part that engineer, acting in its capacity as construction site manager, would:

(a) Act as [owner's] representative in the administration of construction contracts.

(b) Supervise and co-ordinate Contractors in the execution of their work. . . .

The owner/contractor agreement provided that:

the contractor shall be responsible for contracting, maintaining and supervising all health and safety precautions and programs in connection with the work.

The appellate court found that, according to paragraphs (a) and (b) of the owner-engineer agreement, the engineer agreed to act as the agent or "representative" of the subcontractor. The Appellate Court reversed the judgment of the trial court granting summary judgment to owner, but affirmed the grant of summary judgment to contractor.

The owner-contractor agreement contained a provision similar to Paragraph 13.2.1 of the American Institute of Architects General Conditions of the Contract for Construction, Document No. A201, 1987 edition, modified to further provide that "[s]uch attempted assignment may, at [owner's] option, terminate this Contract as a material breach on [contractor's] part." The agreement also contained a provision entitled "Extra Work," which stated that:

> Any authorized work necessary or required to carry out the intent of these Contract Documents by changes clearly not indicated in the Contract Documents shall be paid for at the unit price agreed to in the Contract Documents. If this work cannot be classified under any of the items for which unit prices are listed . . . it shall be paid for as extra work at the rate agreed to in writing between the Contractor and [owner] prior to the time of commencing such extra work.

The Appellate Court found that the assignment provision did not prohibit contractor's assignment to subcontractor of claims for damages arising out of the soil compaction tests where the parties contemplated that the contractor would subcontract part of the its obligations to subcontractors and where the only assignment prohibition in the contract was against assignment of the "whole" contract.

The Court also addressed the issue of whether the parties intended the phrase "extra work" to apply to the work performed by the subcontractor. The Court held that the "extra work" provision in the contract was inapplicable to subcontractor's claim. The Court reasoned that the contract provided that "extra work" was work that "cannot be classified under any of the items for which unit prices are listed" and which was "necessary or required to carry out the intent of these Contract Documents by changes clearly not indicated in the Contract Documents . . . ," and that the subcontractor's work was work for which the unit price was listed in the contract.

93015a   Ivanov v. Process Design Assocs., 267 Ill. App. 3d 440, 204 Ill. Dec. 810, 642 N.E.2d 711 (1993), *modified, reh'g denied*, 1993 Ill. App. LEXIS 1572 (1st Dist. Oct. 12, 1993)

	Ill:	A107-1987, Art. 9, Para. 9.1
	Ill:	A107-1987, Art. 9, Para. 9.3
	Ill:	A107-1987, Art. 9, Para. 9.7
	Ill:	A107-1987, Art. 10, Para. 10.2
	Ill:	A107-1987, Art. 10, Para. 10.3
	Ill:	A107-1987, Art. 16, Para. 16.1
	Ill:	A117-1987, Art. 14, Para. 14.1
	Ill:	A117-1987, Art. 14, Para. 14.3
	Ill:	A117-1987, Art. 14, Para. 14.7
	Ill:	A117-1987, Art. 15, Para. 15.2

[subcontractor] is bound, and to the same extent. Where his specific work as set forth in the plans, specifications and addenda, is not described in this order, [sub-subcontractor] shall perform all work normally construed to come within the scope of his activities.

The Court found that the reference to "work performed" in the first sentence and the reference to "his specific work" in the second sentence clearly limited this provision to the "work" performed under the contract and not to indemnity.

Subcontractor then argued that the owner and contractor waived strict compliance with the subcontract provision requiring subcontractor to obtain certain liability insurance naming owner and contractor as additional insureds because they permitted and even encouraged subcontractor to begin work without requiring strict compliance with the contract provision. The subcontract required subcontractor to obtain "comprehensive general and auto liability insurance with limits of $500,000.00 with respect to injury or death of person . . . ." The policies were to name contractor and owner as additional insureds. Although the contract required that certificates of insurance "shall be delivered to [contractor] before the Subcontract Work is commenced," both parties agreed that the certificates were not delivered before the work began. The Court upheld the trial court's finding that this contract provision requiring the subcontractor to obtain insurance naming the owner and contractor as additional insureds was not "knowingly waived" since the parties had dealt with each other on various projects, the contracts on these projects included similar insurance provisions, and this project was a fast-track project, with paperwork completed after agreement was reached.

93015 Humbert Excavating, Inc. v. City of Pendleton, 118 Or. App. 137, 846 P.2d 441, *modified, adhered to, on reconsideration*, 120 Or. App. 431, 852 P.2d 932 (1993)

II:	A107–1987, Art. 13, Para. 13.1
II:	A107–1987, Art. 13, Para. 13.2
II:	A117–1987, Art. 18, Para. 18.1
II:	A117–1987, Art. 18, Para. 18.2
II:	A201–1987, Art. 7, Para. 7.1.4
II:	A201–1987, Art. 13, Para. 13.2.1

Subcontractor appealed the trial court's grant of summary judgment to owner and contractor on subcontractor's claim for additional compensation. Contractor had assigned to subcontractor any claims for damages arising out of the performance of soil compaction tests by the owner. Subcontractor argued on appeal that, because owner's testing was faulty, subcontractor's soil compaction work was erroneously determined to be inadequate resulting in subcontractor's performance of additional unnecessary work. The owner argued on appeal that subcontractor's failure to give timely notice under the principal contact barred its claim, and, in the alternative, that the claim could not be assigned to

required to indemnify the owner and contractor but was not entitled to indemnity from the sub-subcontractor. Subcontractor appealed. The Appellate Court affirmed the judgment of the trial court.

Among numerous points raised on appeal, the subcontractor argued that the trial court erred in finding that the agreement between subcontractor and its sub-subcontractor did not provide for indemnity for another person's negligence. The subcontract provided that:

> [The sub-subcontractor] hereby assumes entire responsibility and liability for any and all damage and injury of any kind or nature whatsoever to all persons, whether employees or otherwise, and to all property, growing out of, or resulting from the labor or material or both used in the performance of this contract or occurring in connection therewith, and agrees to indemnify and save harmless [subcontractor and/or owner] and their agents, servants and employees from and against any and all loss, expense, including legal fees and disbursements, damage or injury growing out of or resulting therefrom, or occurring in connection therewith. . . .

The Appellate Court found that this language lacked the required specificity to obligate the sub-subcontractor to indemnify subcontractor for subcontractor's own negligence. The provision is silent concerning indemnity for injuries caused by subcontractor's negligence and is silent on indemnity for injuries caused by another party for whom subcontractor assumed liability. The Court concluded that the sub-subcontractor neither expressly nor unequivocally agreed to indemnify subcontractor for the negligence of any party other than itself.

In contrast, the Court found that, since the trial court did not specifically find that any party was negligent, the subcontractor had to "indemnify, defend and save the owner and contractor harmless . . . save and except such claims . . . which may result solely and proximately from the negligent willful acts or omissions" of contractor or owner. The Court found that the indemnity clause did not require a finding that another party, in this case the sub-subcontractor, was negligent. Rather, it required subcontractor to provide indemnity for injuries arising out of the execution of the work so long as the injuries were not caused by the sole negligence of owner or contractor. The Court concluded that the evidence supported the trial court's finding that neither owner nor contractor was solely negligent. Consequently, the indemnity provisions were triggered and subcontractor was required to provide indemnity.

Subcontractor then argued that the trial court erred in finding that the subcontract incorporated by reference only the plans and specifications existing on the project. The subcontractor maintained that the plain language of the provision and industry practice incorporated the administrative provisions of all other project documents between subcontractor, owner and contractor, into its subcontract with sub-subcontractor. Subcontractor alleged this included its specific obligation to indemnify and insure for liability imposed on owner and contractor. The agreement between subcontractor and its sub-subcontractor provided that:

> Work performed by [sub-subcontractor] shall be in strict accordance with all applicable plans, general conditions, specifications, and addenda thereto, and [sub-subcontractor] is bound by all provisions of these documents, and also all other documents to which

The roofing consultant appealed the trial court's denial of its motion for summary judgment. In reversing the trial court's denial of summary judgment, the Appellate Court reasoned that the roofing consultant did not owe subcontractor's employee a duty.

The owner-roofing consultant agreement identified the roofing consultant as the "architect" and contained provisions similar to Paragraphs 2.2.3, 2.2.4, 4.3.1, 10.1.1 and 10.2.1 of the American Institute of Architects General Conditions of the Contract for Construction, Document No. A201, 1976 edition. The roofing subcontract contained a provision identical to Paragraph 11.1.1 of the American Institute of Architects Standard Form of Agreement Between Contractor and Subcontractor, Document No. A401, 1978 edition.

The Appellate Court found that the court's decision in *Yow v. Hussey, Gay, Bell & DeYoung Int'l, Inc.*, 201 Ga. App. 857, 412 S.E.2d 565 (1991), *cert. denied*, 1992 Ga. LEXIS 116 (Ga. 1992) (see case digest number 91040), was controlling authority in this case. In *Yow* the court held that a party who "did not expressly or impliedly have control over or assume any responsibility for construction site supervision or safety . . . could not be held liable in tort for claims of common law simple negligence regarding site safety." Moreover, the contract provisions in *Yow* were identical to the language used in this case, and in both cases, the architect's contract with the owner provided that "[t]he Architect will not be responsible for . . . construction means, methods, techniques, sequences or procedures, or for safety precautions and programs in connection with the work . . . ." The Court concluded that the subcontractor had the contractual responsibility for site supervision and safety. The subcontractor, who, as the injured worker's employer, was in a better position to protect the worker from dangerous conditions on the site than the roofing consultant who only periodically visited the site and, in fact, was not present at the site on the day the worker was injured.

93014   Howe v. Lever Bros. Co., 851 S.W.2d 769 (Mo. Ct. App. 1993)

II:	A107–1987, Art. 9, Para. 9.12
II:	A117–1987, Art. 14, Para. 14.12
II:	A201–1987, Art. 10, Para. 10.1.4
II:	A201–1987, Art. 3, Para. 3.18.1
II:	A401–1987, Art. 1, Para. 1.1
II:	A401–1987, Art. 2, Para. 2.1
II:	A401–1987, Art. 2, Para. 2.2
II:	A401–1987, Art. 4, Para. 4.5.1
II:	A401–1987, Art. 4, Para. 4.6.1
II:	A401–1987, Art. 13, Para. 13.1
II:	A401–1987, Art. 13, Para. 13.3

Injured worker brought an action against owner, contractor, subcontractor, and sub-subcontractor, which was settled. The trial court then found that the subcontractor was

The Court, applying the above reasoning to the remaining Paragraphs 4.5.3 through 4.5.7, found that these provisions merely provided details regarding how to initiate and conduct an arbitration proceeding if a right to arbitration existed.

The contractor then argued that Paragraph 4.4.4 (which provided that "the Architect's decision will be made within seven days, which decision shall be final and binding on the parties but subject to arbitration"), together with Paragraph 4.3.2 (which discussed when the architect's decision concerning a dispute was required as a condition precedent to arbitration or litigation), demonstrated that there was an agreement to arbitrate. The Court found that the clauses were meaningless standing alone without the force and effect given them by Paragraph 4.5.1, since Paragraph 4.5.2 made it clear that the disputes referred to in Paragraph 4.4.4 were only arbitrable when Paragraph 4.5.1 declared that they were arbitrable.

93013 Henry Roy Portwood, Inc. v. Smith, 207 Ga. App. 748, 429 S.E.2d 143 (1993)

II:	A107–1978, Art. 8, Para. 8.1	
II:	A107–1978, Art. 8, Para. 8.2	
II:	A107–1978, Art. 10, Para. 10.1	
II:	A107–1978, Art. 10, Para. 10.7	
II:	A107–1978, Art. 17, Para. 16.1	
II:	A117–1979, Art. 12, Para. 12.1	
II:	A117–1979, Art. 12, Para. 12.3	
II:	A117–1979, Art. 14, Para. 14.1	
II:	A117–1979, Art. 14, Para. 14.7	
II:	A117–1979, Art. 20, Para. 20.1	
I:	A201–1976, Art. 2, Para. 2.2.2	
I:	A201–1976, Art. 2, Para. 2.2.4	
I:	A201–1976, Art. 4, Para. 4.3.1	
I:	A201–1976, Art. 4, Para. 4.3.2	
I:	A201–1976, Art. 10, Para. 10.1.1	
I:	A201–1976, Art. 10, Para. 10.2.1	
I:	A201–1976, Art. 10, Para. 10.2.2	
I:	A401–1978, Art. 11, Para. 11.1.1	
I:	B141–1977, Art. 1, Para. 1.5.2	
I:	B141–1977, Art. 1, Para. 1.5.3	
I:	B141–1977, Art. 1, Para. 1.5.5	

Subcontractor's employee brought a personal injury action against numerous parties. All of the defendants, except for the roofing consultant, were dismissed from the action.

I:	A201–1987, Art. 4, Para. 4.5.5
I:	A201–1987, Art. 4, Para. 4.5.6
I:	A201–1987, Art. 4, Para. 4.5.7
I:	A201–1987, Art. 13, Para. 13.1.1
I:	A401–1987, Art. 6, Para. 6.1
I:	A401–1987, Art. 6, Para. 6.2
I:	A401–1987, Art. 6, Para. 6.3
I:	A401–1987, Art. 6, Para. 6.4
I:	A401–1987, Art. 6, Para. 6.5
I:	B141–1987, Art. 7, Para. 7.1
I:	B141–1987, Art. 7, Para. 7.2
I:	B141–1987, Art. 7, Para. 7.3
I:	B141–1987, Art. 7, Para. 7.4

Contractor appealed from a order of the trial court denying its motion to compel arbitration against the owner. The trial court had reasoned that the parties had evidenced their intent not to arbitrate disputes when they deleted the arbitration clause from their contract. The Appellate Court affirmed the judgment of the trial court.

The owner and contractor entered into an agreement which included the American Institute of Architects General Conditions of the Contract for Construction, Document No. A201, 1987 edition, specifically Paragraphs 4.4.4, 4.5.1, and 4.5.2 through 4.5.7. The supplemental general conditions deleted Paragraph 4.5.1 but did not delete Paragraphs 4.5.2 through 4.5.7, which related to and governed the arbitration procedures. Paragraph 4.4.4 provided in pertinent part that the "Architect will notify the parties in writing that the Architect's decision will be made within seven days, which decision shall be final and binding on the parties but subject to arbitration."

The Appellate Court upheld the trial court's finding that Paragraph 4.5.1 was the key provision creating the right to arbitration and, accordingly, that its deletion established the parties' lack of intent to arbitrate disputes. The Court found further that the remaining clauses pertaining to arbitration derived their force from Paragraph 4.5.1. Thus, in the absence of the operative arbitration language, these clauses were without effect.

The Court rejected the contractor's argument that, in the absence of Paragraph 4.5.1, Paragraph 4.5.2 authorized the American Arbitration Association to administer arbitration of the parties' disputes. Paragraph 4.5.2 stated that "[c]laims between the Owner and Contractor not resolved under Paragraph 4.4 shall, if subject to arbitration under Subparagraph 4.5.1, be decided by arbitration in accordance with the Construction Industry Arbitration Rules of the American Arbitration Association currently in effect . . . ." The Court construed this language as providing that the American Arbitration Association only had jurisdiction of the parties disputes if those disputes were subject to arbitration under Paragraph 4.5.1.

Contractor brought an action against owner for denial of extra compensation. Owner had relied on the architect's interpretation of the plans and specifications. Contractor argued that the architect had exceeded his authority. The trial court entered judgment for contractor and owner appealed. At issue on appeal was whether the architect's interpretation of the specifications was final and binding. The Appellate Court reversed and ordered that judgment be entered for the owner on its motion for a directed verdict.

The owner-contractor agreement included the American Institute of Architects General Conditions of the Contract for Construction, Document No. A201, 1987 edition, with all references to "arbitrators" and "arbitration" deleted from Paragraphs 4.1.1, 4.3.2, 4.4.4, 8.3.1, 10.1.2, 11.3.9 and 11.3.10. Article 11 provided that "[t]he work shall be done under the general direction of the Architect and his decision as to the true construction and meaning of the drawings and specifications shall be final." Furthermore, Paragraph 4.4.4 provided that the architect's decision concerning a disputed claim "shall be final and binding on the parties but subject to arbitration."

The Appellate Court found that, although the words "final" and "binding" had a terminal and unconditional quality, the power of the architect was not without limit. However, the Court concluded that the architect's decision was final and binding because the contractor offered no proof that the architect had acted fraudulently or arbitrarily, and because interpretation of the meaning of drawings and specifications was precisely the subject matter remitted to the architect's power of decision.

The contractor then argued that the architect could not, by his power of decision, change the contract. The Court found that contract terms were not changed where the architect decided in the course of construction what a specification meant or whether one specification superseded another.

Finally, the contractor argued that the venue clause was included in the owner-contractor agreement because claims under the agreement were ultimately subject to judicial review. The Court found that the venue clause was wholly compatible with the proposition that, under the contract language, certain questions of contract interpretation generated by the plans and specifications were exclusively for the architect while other decisions would be reviewed by a court.

93012   Glenn H. Johnson Constr. Co. v. Board of Educ., Community Consol. Sch. Dist. No. 15, 245 Ill. App. 3d 18, 185 Ill. Dec. 74, 614 N.E.2d 208 (1993)

I:	A107–1987, Art. 10, Para. 10.8
I:	A117–1987, Art. 15, Para. 15.8
I:	A201–1987, Art. 4, Para. 4.5.1
I:	A201–1987, Art. 4, Para. 4.5.2
I:	A201–1987, Art. 4, Para. 4.5.3
I:	A201–1987, Art. 4, Para. 4.5.4
I:	A201–1987, Art. 4, Para. 4.5.4.1
I:	A201–1987, Art. 4, Para. 4.5.4.2

This case involved the issue of whether the owner's waiver under Paragraph 11.3.6 of the American Institute of Architects General Conditions of the Contract for Construction, Document No. A201, 1976 edition, barred the subrogation claim of its insurer for damages caused by the contractor in areas of the building outside the limits of the Work. Relying on the decision in *S.S.D.W. Co. v. Brisk Waterproofing Co.*, 76 N.Y.2d 228, 557 N.Y.S.2d 290, 556 N.E.2d 1097 (1990) (see case digest number 90043), the District Court concluded that the waiver provision precluded any affirmative defense against the claim of owner's insurer for damages to the building and its contents, other than the Work itself.

93011 Fontaine Bros., Inc. v. City of Springfield, 35 Mass. App. Ct. 155, 617 N.E.2d 1002, *later proceeding*, 1993 Mass. App. LEXIS 948 (Mass. App. Ct. Sept. 27, 1993), *and review denied*, 416 Mass. 1105, 621 N.E.2d 685 (Mass. 1993)

> I: A107–1987, Art. 10, Para. 10.8
> I: A107–1987, Art. 19, Para. 19.1
> I: A117–1987, Art. 15, Para. 15.8
> I: A117–1987, Art. 24, Para. 24.1
> I: A201–1987, Art. 4, Para. 4.5.1
> I: A201–1987, Art. 4, Para. 4.5.2
> I: A201–1987, Art. 4, Para. 4.5.3
> I: A201–1987, Art. 4, Para. 4.5.4
> I: A201–1987, Art. 4, Para. 4.5.4.1
> I: A201–1987, Art. 4, Para. 4.5.4.2
> I: A201–1987, Art. 4, Para. 4.5.5
> I: A201–1987, Art. 4, Para. 4.5.6
> I: A201–1987, Art. 4, Para. 4.5.7
> I: A201–1987, Art. 13, Para. 13.1.1
> I: A401–1987, Art. 6, Para. 6.1
> I: A401–1987, Art. 6, Para. 6.2
> I: A401–1987, Art. 6, Para. 6.3
> I: A401–1987, Art. 6, Para. 6.4
> I: A401–1987, Art. 6, Para. 6.5
> I: B141–1987, Art. 7, Para. 7.1
> I: B141–1987, Art. 7, Para. 7.2
> I: B141–1987, Art. 7, Para. 7.3
> I: B141–1987, Art. 7, Para. 7.4
> I: B141–1987, Art. 9, Para. 9.1

III:	A107–1987, Art. 15, Para. 15.4	
III:	A117–1987, Art. 14, Para. 14.12	
III:	A117–1987, Art. 20, Para. 20.4	
III:	A201–1987, Art. 3, Para. 3.18.1	
III:	A201–1987, Art. 9, Para. 9.10.2	
III:	A201–1987, Art. 10, Para. 10.1.4	

Contractor appealed the order of the trial court denying its request for an award of attorneys' fees. Contractor was the prevailing party in its breach of contract action against owner for improperly terminating contractor's services and for refusing to pay the balance due under the contract. The Appellate Court reversed the judgment of the trial court.

The owner-contractor agreement provided that "[i]n the event of default hereunder and in the event said default is not cured within Ten Days then and in that event the prevailing party shall be entitled to recover in addition to damages, his reasonable attorney's fees irrespective of whether litigation commenced."

The Appellate Court concluded that the trial court erred, as a matter of law, when it interpreted the provision of the parties' contract as requiring that "[a] party must both prevail in the action and not be in breach of the contract in order to be entitled to attorneys' fees." The Court found that the attorney fee provision was unambiguous. The clear intent of the provision was that the prevailing party in a dispute over whether the contract had been breached would be entitled to recover attorney fees in addition to damages. Furthermore, the Court found that the provision could not be read as requiring the prevailing party not to have breached the contract in any way.

93010 Fireman's Fund Ins. Co. v. Krohn, 1993 U.S. Dist. LEXIS 10772 (S.D.N.Y. Aug. 3, 1993)

I:	A107–1978, Art. 7, Para. 7.4	
I:	A107–1978, Art. 17, Para. 17.1	
I:	A107–1978, Art. 17, Para. 17.3	
I:	A107–1978, Art. 17, Para. 17.6	
I:	A117–1979, Art. 11, Para. 11.4	
I:	A117–1979, Art. 21, Para. 21.1	
I:	A117–1979, Art. 21, Para. 21.3	
I:	A117–1979, Art. 21, Para. 21.4	
I:	A201–1976, Art. 1, Para. 1.1.3	
I:	A201–1976, Art. 11, Para. 11.1.1	
I:	A201–1976, Art. 11, Para. 11.3.1	
II:	A201–1976, Art. 11, Para. 11.3.6	

II: B141–1987, Art. 7, Para. 7.2
II: B141–1987, Art. 7, Para. 7.3
II: B141–1987, Art. 7, Para. 7.4

Subcontractor filed a mechanic's lien and filed a petition to foreclose the lien against the contractor. Contractor then filed a mechanic's lien, answered subcontractor's petition and cross-claimed against the owner. Contractor then served owner with a copy of the petition to foreclose. Owner's answer contained an affirmative defense alleging that the owner-contractor dispute was subject to arbitration. The owner moved to compel arbitration. The subcontractor filed a "resistance" and contractor filed a motion for extension of time, which was granted by the trial court. Contractor then filed a "resistance" to owner's motion to compel. After a hearing, the trial court denied owner's motion to compel on the ground that it was untimely. Owner appealed. Contractor and subcontractor argued that the dispute arose when owner failed to make full payment for certain work. They argued that their contracts required that a demand for arbitration be made within a "reasonable time after the claim, dispute or other matter in question has arisen." They claimed that owner's filing of the motion to compel seven months later was untimely. They also claimed that owner's motion failed to demand or initiate arbitration in the manner required by the contract. The Supreme Court of Iowa reversed the order denying owner's motion to compel and remanded with instructions.

The owner-contractor agreement provided that all claims and disputes between the parties relating to the contract or the breach thereof would be subject to arbitration. It also provided that the demand for arbitration be made within a reasonable time after the claim, dispute, or other matter in question arose. The subcontract stated that "any controversy or claim" would be subject to arbitration. The subcontract also stated that arbitration would be conducted in the manner provided for in the owner-contractor agreement.

The Supreme Court found that, because no grounds existed for the revocation of the arbitration clauses under state statute, they were valid and enforceable. Furthermore, the record indicated that slightly over two months had elapsed between the time the owner was served with notice of the foreclosure action and the time owner filed its motion to compel. The Court found that, as a matter of law, once the owner was served with notice of the petition to foreclose, owner acted in a timely manner. Also, the record indicated that owner's answer contained an affirmative defense that alleged that the dispute between the parties was subject to an irrevocable arbitration clause. The Court found that the trial court abused its discretion in denying owner's motion to compel arbitration since the court had set a trial date for the foreclosure action before it had ruled on owner's previously filed motion to compel and after it gave contractor an extension of time to respond to the motion.

93009 Entropic Landscapes, Inc. v. Brown, 615 So. 2d 799 (Fla. Dist. Ct. App. 1993)

III: A107–1987, Art 9, Para. 9.12

of the presence and operations of other contractors working within the limits of the same project.

The Appellate Court held that the grading prime contractor could not recover from owner for losses that it incurred as a result of the bridge contractor's delays. Moreover, the Court found that, if owner was not liable to the grading contractor, then the bridge construction contractor would not be liable to owner. The Court interpreted Paragraph 105.07 as a clear and unambiguous expression of mutual intent that owner would not assume vicarious contractual liability for any losses and expenses incurred by grading contractor resulting from delays in bridge construction work. Under the contract the grading contractor's remedy for delay attributable to bridge construction work was to seek an extension of time to excuse its untimely performance of the grading work and to avoid liability to the owner for liquidated damages.

93008   Des Moines Asphalt & Paving Co. v. Colcon Indus. Corp., 500 N.W.2d 70 (Iowa 1993)

II:	A107–1978, Art. 13, Para. 13.2	
II:	A107–1987, Art. 10, Para. 10.8	
II:	A117–1979, Art. 17, Para. 17.2	
II:	A117–1987, Art. 15, Para. 15.8	
II:	A201–1976, Art. 7, Para. 7.9.1	
II:	A201–1987, Art. 4, Para. 4.5.1	
II:	A201–1987, Art. 4, Para. 4.5.2	
II:	A201–1987, Art. 4, Para. 4.5.3	
II:	A201–1987, Art. 4, Para. 4.5.4	
II:	A201–1987, Art. 4, Para. 4.5.4.1	
II:	A201–1987, Art. 4, Para. 4.5.4.2	
II:	A201–1987, Art. 4, Para. 4.5.5	
II:	A201–1987, Art. 4, Para. 4.5.6	
II:	A201–1987, Art. 4, Para. 4.5.7	
II:	A401–1978, Art. 13, Para. 13.1	
II:	A401–1987, Art. 6, Para. 6.1	
II:	A401–1987, Art. 6, Para. 6.2	
II:	A401–1987, Art. 6, Para. 6.3	
II:	A401–1987, Art. 6, Para. 6.4	
II:	A401–1987, Art. 6, Para. 6.5	
II:	B141–1977, Art. 9, Para. 9.1	
II:	B141–1977, Art. 9, Para. 9.2	
II:	B141–1977, Art. 9, Para. 9.3	
II:	B141–1987, Art. 7, Para. 7.1	

Furthermore, because the language of the arbitration provision contained no qualifying language, the agreement was unrestricted. Therefore, the award arose out of an unrestricted submission. The Court found that the trial court properly reviewed the integrity of the arbitration process and award by considering the relevant statutory criteria and properly confirmed the arbitration award. The Court reasoned that the contractor's allegations focused on the weight of the evidence presented to the arbitrator, which was not, under state statute, a proper subject of review in the case of an unrestricted submission.

93007   Department of Transp. v. Fru-Con Constr. Corp., 207 Ga. App. 180, 427 S.E.2d 513 (1993)

II:	A107–1987, Art. 12, Para. 12.1	
I:	A107–1987, Art. 12, Para. 12.2	
II:	A107–1987, Art. 12, Para. 12.3	
II:	A117–1987, Art. 17, Para. 17.1	
I:	A117–1987, Art. 17, Para. 17.2	
II:	A117–1987, Art. 17, Para. 17.3	
II:	A201–1976, Art. 6, Para. 6.2.1	
III:	A201–1976, Art. 6, Para. 6.2.3	
III:	A201–1976, Art. 6, Para. 6.2.4	
III:	A201–1976, Art. 6, Para. 6.2.5	
I:	A201–1987, Art. 6, Para. 6.2.1	
III:	A201–1987, Art. 6, Para. 6.2.2	
III:	A201–1987, Art. 6, Para. 6.2.3	
III:	A201–1987, Art. 6, Para. 6.2.4	

Owner filed a third-party action against bridge construction prime contractor in an action brought against owner by the grading prime contractor. The grading prime contractor sought to recover liquidated delay damages withheld from its final payment and to recover damages for owner's breach of contract. The trial court granted summary judgment for bridge prime contractor. The owner appealed. The Appellate Court affirmed the judgment of the trial court.

Paragraph 105.07 of the owner-grading contractor agreement provided:

When separate contracts are let within the limits of any one project, each contractor shall conduct his work so as not to interfere with or hinder the progress or completion of the work being performed by other contractors. Contractors working on the same projects shall assume all liability, financial or otherwise, in connection with his [sic] contract and shall protect and save harmless [DOT] from any and all damages or claims that may arise because of inconvenience, delay, or loss experienced by him because

I:	A201–1987, Art. 4, Para. 4.5.3
I:	A201–1987, Art. 4, Para. 4.5.4
I:	A201–1987, Art. 4, Para. 4.5.4.1
I:	A201–1987, Art. 4, Para. 4.5.4.2
I:	A201–1987, Art. 4, Para. 4.5.5
I:	A201–1987, Art. 4, Para. 4.5.6
I:	A201–1987, Art. 4, Para. 4.5.7
I:	A401–1978, Art. 13, Para. 13.1
I:	A401–1987, Art. 6, Para. 6.1
I:	A401–1987, Art. 6, Para. 6.2
I:	A401–1987, Art. 6, Para. 6.3
I:	A401–1987, Art. 6, Para. 6.4
I:	A401–1987, Art. 6, Para. 6.5
I:	B141–1977, Art. 9, Para. 9.1
I:	B141–1977, Art. 9, Para. 9.2
I:	B141–1977, Art. 9, Para. 9.3
I:	B141–1987, Art. 7, Para. 7.1
I:	B141–1987, Art. 7, Para. 7.2
I:	B141–1987, Art. 7, Para. 7.3
I:	B141–1987, Art. 7, Para. 7.4

Contractor appealed the confirmation of an arbitration award in favor of subcontractor. The Appellate Court affirmed the decision of the trial court.

Article 13 of the subcontract, entitled "Arbitration," stated in pertinent part that "[a]ll claims, disputes, and other matters in question arising out of, or relating to, this Subcontract, or the breach thereof, shall be decided by arbitration . . . ." The contract further provided that:

[A]ny dispute arising under this agreement shall be submitted (by an action of either or both parties) to arbitration under the rules of the American Arbitration Association. If the parties fail to agree upon the selection of a single arbitrator, then the selection of a single arbitrator will be made as promptly as possible by the American Arbitration Association in accordance with its procedures for such selection. The arbitration proceeding shall take place in Meriden, Ct. The determination by the arbitrator shall be [final] and binding on the parties and may be enforced by any court of competent jurisdiction. The arbitration proceeding shall be in accordance with Connecticut Law.

The Appellate Court found that the language of the subcontract was clear and unambiguous. The words "the arbitration proceeding shall be in accordance with Connecticut law" left no doubt that the parties intended that the applicable sections of the state statute would govern the arbitration proceedings.

Contractor's employee brought a personal injury action against architect, owner, subcontractor and others. The trial court granted summary judgment for the architect, subcontractor and the materials testing service company. The injured worker appealed. Among other issues on appeal, the injured worker argued that the architect had specified the means and methods for the protection of workers on the project. The Appellate Court affirmed the trial court's grant of summary judgment to the architect.

Paragraph 2.6.6 of the American Institute of Architects Standard Form of Agreement Between Owner and Architect, Document No. B141, 1987 edition, was modified to read as follows: "unless such means or methods have been specified by Architect for the performance of the Work . . . ." The Court also referred to Paragraphs 3.3.1, 10.1.1 and 10.2.1 of the American Institute of Architects General Conditions of the Contract for Construction, Document No. A201, 1987 edition, which set forth the contractor's responsibilities under the contract.

The Appellate Court interpreted the contract provisions and the conditions contained in the Project Manual prepared by the architect as general conditions instructing the contractor to provide shoring, bracing, etc., where needed and not as specific means and methods. Furthermore, the uncontroverted testimony established that the specifications prepared by the architect did not specify means and methods of excavating or protecting the area in which the worker was injured. The plans and specifications did, however, call for certain safety measures where necessary. The Court interpreted that language in the plans and specifications as requiring that safety precautions be taken to assure the safety of the employees working on the project. The Court concluded that the contract provisions, read as a whole, made it the duty of the contractor to take all necessary safety precautions.

The Court rejected the worker's argument that, had the architect inspected the work, he could have taken precautions to protect the trenches from collapse. The Court adopted the majority view that an architect does not, by reason of his inspection or supervisory authority over the construction, assume responsibility for the day-to-day methods utilized by the contractor to complete the construction. The Court reasoned that the architect's basic duty was to see that the owner got a finished product that was structurally sound and that conformed to the plans.

93006 Carabetta Builders, Inc. v. Hotz Corp., 30 Conn. App. 157, 619 A.2d 13, *appeal denied*, 225 Conn. 913, 623 A.2d 1022, *and remanded*, 226 Conn. 812, 629 A.2d 377 (Conn. 1993)

I: A107–1978, Art. 13, Para. 13.2
I: A107–1987, Art. 10, Para. 10.8
I: A117–1979, Art. 17, Para. 17.2
I: A117–1987, Art. 15, Para. 15.8
I: A201–1976, Art. 7, Para. 7.9.1
I: A201–1987, Art. 4, Para. 4.5.1
I: A201–1987, Art. 4, Para. 4.5.2

guarantee period after final payment. Contractor appealed. The Supreme Court of Alabama affirmed the finding of the trial court.

The owner-contractor agreement included provisions similar to the American Institute of Architects General Conditions of the Contract for Construction, Document No. A201, 1976 edition, specifically Paragraphs 7.9.1, 7.9.2, 7.9.3 and 12.3.1.

The Court construed the above-referenced contract language together and found that the contract was narrowly drawn so that only certain types of disputes were arbitrable and that those disputes were required to be submitted to arbitration only for a limited time. The contract did not expressly require arbitration of all "disputes arising under or related to the contract." Rather, the clause limited the arbitrable claims to those specifically listed in the contract. Furthermore, the contract made it clear that those arbitrable claims were subject to arbitration only during construction or before final payment. The arbitration provisions set out the procedure for arbitration but they did not state which claims were to be arbitrated. The Court found that only the damages provision (which stated that claims were limited to "any wrongful act or neglect of the other party or of anyone employed by him") set out the claims to be submitted to arbitration. The Court concluded that a fair reading of the provisions required the Court to find that the primary purpose for requiring arbitration was to ensure that the completion of the work would not be interrupted. The provisions could not be read to apply after the contract was completed. Therefore, the contract did not require that the owner's claim be submitted to arbitration and the trial court had correctly denied contractor's motion to stay.

93005 Burns v. Black & Veatch Architects, Inc., 854 S.W.2d 450 (Mo. Ct. App. 1993)

I:	A107–1987, Art. 9, Para. 9.1
I:	A107–1987, Art. 10, Para. 10.2
I:	A107–1987, Art. 10, Para. 10.3
I:	A107–1987, Art. 16, Para. 16.1
I:	A117–1987, Art. 14, Para. 14.1
I:	A117–1987, Art. 15, Para. 15.2
I:	A117–1987, Art. 15, Para. 15.3
I:	A117–1987, Art. 21, Para. 21.1
I:	A201–1987, Art. 3, Para. 3.3.1
I:	A201–1987, Art. 4, Para. 4.2.2
I:	A201–1987, Art. 4, Para. 4.2.3
I:	A201–1987, Art. 10, Para. 10.1.1
I:	A201–1987, Art. 10, Para. 10.2.1
I:	B141–1987, Art. 2, Para. 2.6.6

Owner filed a demand for arbitration against architect and construction manager and brought an action seeking an order enjoining architect and construction manager to participate in a consolidated arbitration or to participate separately in arbitration. Architect defended the consolidation action by asserting the affirmative defense of the expiration of the limitations period. The trial court denied architect's motion to declare the owner's demand untimely and to stay the arbitration. The architect appealed. The owner cross-appealed from the trial court's denial of consolidation. Because the construction manager was not a party to these appeals the Appellate Court dismissed the cross-appeal. The only remaining issue was whether the timeliness of a demand for arbitration was an issue for the court or for the arbitrator to decide.

The arbitration provisions contained in the owner-architect agreement were identical to Paragraphs 9.1, 9.2, and 9.3 of the American Institute of Architects Standard Form of Agreement Between Owner and Architect, Document No. B141, 1977 edition.

Adopting what is the majority rule, the Appellate Court held that procedural matters were to be decided by the arbitrators. The Court based its decision in part on its finding that the broad and all encompassing contract language evidenced the parties' intent to have their disputes resolved by arbitration.

93004   Blout Int'l, Ltd. v. James River-Pennington, Inc., 618 So. 2d 1344 (Ala. 1993)

III:	A107–1978,	Art. 10, Para. 10.4
III:	A107–1978,	Art. 13, Para. 13.2
III:	A107–1978,	Art. 18, Para. 18.2
III:	A107–1978,	Art. 19, Para. 19.1
III:	A117–1979,	Art. 10, Para. 14.4
III:	A117–1979,	Art. 17, Para. 17.2
III:	A117–1979,	Art. 22, Para. 22.2
III:	A117–1979,	Art. 23, Para. 23.1
III:	A201–1976,	Art. 4, Para. 4.5.1
III:	A201–1976,	Art. 7, Para. 7.9.1
III:	A201–1976,	Art. 7, Para. 7.9.2
III:	A201–1976,	Art. 7, Para. 7.9.3
III:	A201–1976,	Art. 12, Para. 12.3.1
III:	A201–1976,	Art. 13, Para. 13.2.1
III:	A201–1976,	Art. 13, Para. 13.2.2

Owner brought a negligence and breach of contract action against contractor. Contractor moved to stay the action and to compel arbitration pursuant to the owner-contractor agreement. The trial court denied contractor's motion on the ground that the arbitration clause was effective only during construction and during the one-year

to the claim once a third person who was not contractually required to arbitrate filed an action. The Court found that to so interpret the contract would be to ignore the entire second phrase of Paragraph 16.6. The Court found that the language of the arbitration clause clearly provided that, to the extent a claim for contribution or indemnity arose in an action filed by a third party, the claim could be severed and heard in a different forum with the remainder of the claim subject to arbitration. The Court concluded that the trial court properly affirmed the jurisdiction of the arbitration panel.

93003 Beyt, Rish, Robbins Group, Architects, Inc. v. Appalachian Regional Healthcare, Inc., 854 S.W.2d 784 (Ky. Ct. App. 1993)

I: A107–1978, Art. 13, Para. 13.2
I: A107–1987, Art. 10, Para. 10.8
I: A117–1979, Art. 17, Para. 17.2
I: A117–1987, Art. 15, Para. 15.8
I: A201–1976, Art. 7, Para. 7.9.1
I: A201–1987, Art. 4, Para. 4.5.1
I: A201–1987, Art. 4, Para. 4.5.2
I: A201–1987, Art. 4, Para. 4.5.3
I: A201–1987, Art. 4, Para. 4.5.4
I: A201–1987, Art. 4, Para. 4.5.4.1
I: A201–1987, Art. 4, Para. 4.5.4.2
I: A201–1987, Art. 4, Para. 4.5.5
I: A201–1987, Art. 4, Para. 4.5.6
I: A201–1987, Art. 4, Para. 4.5.7
I: A401–1978, Art. 13, Para. 13.1
I: A401–1987, Art. 6, Para. 6.1
I: A401–1987, Art. 6, Para. 6.2
I: A401–1987, Art. 6, Para. 6.3
I: A401–1987, Art. 6, Para. 6.4
I: A401–1987, Art. 6, Para. 6.5
I: B141–1977, Art. 9, Para. 9.1
I: B141–1977, Art. 9, Para. 9.2
I: B141–1977, Art. 9, Para. 9.3
I: B141–1987, Art. 7, Para. 7.1
I: B141–1987, Art. 7, Para. 7.2
I: B141–1987, Art. 7, Para. 7.3
I: B141–1987, Art. 7, Para. 7.4

of South Dakota reversed the trial court on the waiver issue, but affirmed on all other issues.

The owner and contractor had entered into a contract for the design and construction of a hotel-convention center and a connected recreation center. The owner then contracted with the City to act as general contractor for the building of a recreation center that was the same facility that the contractor was in the process of erecting under its contract with the owner. During the course of construction disputes arose between the owner and contractor and were settled, and the parties agreed not to sue one another or seek arbitration proceedings against one another for the claims settled in the agreement. The contractor then filed a demand for arbitration seeking breach of contract damages from the owner. The arbitration panel responded to owner's objection by ruling that claims included in the settlement agreement would not be arbitrated. It deferred ruling on which claims were arbitrable until the hearing and concluded that it would rule on owner's motion after it ruled on arbitrability. The City then filed an action against owner and contractor for breach of contract and construction deficiencies in the recreation center. The arbitrators determined that they did not have jurisdiction over the claims made by the City or over owner's cross-claim against contractor seeking indemnity and contribution. The panel awarded damages and the contractor filed a motion for affirmation of the award. The owner moved the court to vacate the award. The trial court affirmed the arbitration award and owner appealed. Among numerous issues on appeal was whether the arbitration panel had exceeded its jurisdiction in considering claims related to the recreation center.

The owner-contractor agreement provided in Paragraph 16.1 as follows:

All claims, disputes and other matters in question arising out of, or relating to, this Agreement or the breach thereof, except with respect to the Architect/Engineer's decision on matters relating to artistic effect, and except for claims which have been waived by the making or acceptance of Final Payment shall be decided by arbitration in accordance with the Construction Industry Arbitration Rules of the American Arbitration Association then obtaining unless the parties mutually agree otherwise. This Agreement to arbitrate shall be specifically enforceable under the prevailing arbitration law.

Paragraph 16.6 provided that:

These provisions relating to mandatory arbitration shall not be applicable to a claim asserted in an action in a state or federal court by a person who is under no obligation to arbitrate such claim with either of the parties to this Agreement insofar as the parties to this Agreement may desire to assert any rights of indemnity or contribution with respect to the subject matter of such action.

The Appellate Court interpreted Paragraph 16.1 as providing that all claims that arose were to be submitted to arbitration unless a claim was specifically exempted or the parties mutually agreed not to arbitrate the claim. Paragraph 16.6 exempted any claim filed in a state or federal court by a third party who was under no obligation to arbitrate "insofar as" it gave owner or contractor a ground for contribution or indemnity. The owner argued that Paragraph 16.6 should have been interpreted to require severance of any issue relating

undercut work, the contract addressed undercut work, the contractor and subcontractor did not fully inspect the available information, and the quantities stated in the contract were merely estimates. Absent justifiable reliance, the contractor and subcontractor could not assert their claim of negligent misrepresentation.

93002   Azcon Constr. Co. v. Golden Hills Resort, Inc., 498 N.W.2d 630 (S.D. 1993)

I:	A107–1978, Art. 13, Para. 13.2
I:	A107–1987, Art. 10, Para. 10.8
I:	A117–1979, Art. 17, Para. 17.2
I:	A117–1987, Art. 15, Para. 15.8
I:	A201–1976, Art. 7, Para. 7.9.1
I:	A201–1987, Art. 4, Para. 4.5.1
I:	A201–1987, Art. 4, Para. 4.5.2
I:	A201–1987, Art. 4, Para. 4.5.3
I:	A201–1987, Art. 4, Para. 4.5.4
I:	A201–1987, Art. 4, Para. 4.5.4.1
I:	A201–1987, Art. 4, Para. 4.5.4.2
I:	A201–1987, Art. 4, Para. 4.5.5
I:	A201–1987, Art. 4, Para. 4.5.6
I:	A201–1987, Art. 4, Para. 4.5.7
I:	A401–1978, Art. 13, Para. 13.1
I:	A401–1987, Art. 6, Para. 6.1
I:	A401–1987, Art. 6, Para. 6.2
I:	A401–1987, Art. 6, Para. 6.3
I:	A401–1987, Art. 6, Para. 6.4
I:	A401–1987, Art. 6, Para. 6.5
I:	B141–1977, Art. 9, Para. 9.1
I:	B141–1977, Art. 9, Para. 9.2
I:	B141–1977, Art. 9, Para. 9.3
I:	B141–1987, Art. 7, Para. 7.1
I:	B141–1987, Art. 7, Para. 7.2
I:	B141–1987, Art. 7, Para. 7.3
I:	B141–1987, Art. 7, Para. 7.4

Owner appealed denial of its motion to vacate an arbitration award. The trial court had affirmed an arbitration panel's award. The trial court also held that the owner had waived its objection to arbitration by participating in the arbitration. The Supreme Court

93001 APAC-Carolina, Inc. v. Greensboro-High Point Airport Auth., 110 N.C. App. 719, 431 S.E.2d 508 (1993)

    III: A107–1987, Art. 7, Para. 7.1
    III: A107–1987, Art. 7, Para. 7.3
    III: A117–1987, Art. 12, Para. 12.1
    III: A117–1987, Art. 12, Para. 12.3
    III: A201–1987, Art. 3, Para. 3.2.1
    III: A201–1987, Art. 3, Para. 3.2.2

Contractor and subcontractor brought an action against owner and engineer for nonpayment for undercut work, extra erosion control work arising from defective specifications, and increased costs caused by delays resulting from the extras. Among other judgments entered, the trial court granted engineer summary judgment on action by contractor and subcontractor for negligent misrepresentation. Contractor and subcontractor appealed on the grounds that engineer failed to properly prepare plans, misrepresented the amount of necessary undercut work, and misled contractor and subcontractor into believing that such work would not be significant. The Appellate Court upheld the trial court's grant of summary judgment on the ground that contractor and subcontractor failed to adequately inspect available information since the contract clearly stated that any quantities mentioned in the contract were merely estimates.

The contract provided that:

[T]he bidder is expected to carefully examine the site of the proposed work, the proposal, plans, specifications, and contract forms. He shall satisfy himself as to the character, quality, and quantities of work to be performed, materials to be furnished, and as to the requirements of the proposed contract. The submission of a proposal shall be prima facie evidence that the bidder has made such examination and is satisfied as to the conditions to be encountered in performing the work and as to the requirements of the proposed contract, plans, and specifications.

The contract also provided that "[t]he owner does not expressly or by implication agree that the actual quantities involved will correspond exactly therewith; nor shall the bidder plead misunderstanding or deception because of such estimates of quantities, or of the character, location, or other conditions pertaining to the work."

The Appellate Court found that the contract placed upon the contractor and subcontractor the burden of fully inspecting all of the available information, and the evidence indicated that this information would have revealed the necessity of undercut work. The Court did not reach the issue of contributory negligence because the evidence, which showed a lack of justifiable reliance, defeated the claim of negligent misrepresentation. Moreover, relying on case law, the Court found that estimated quantities may not form the basis for a claim of negligent representation.

The Court concluded that any reliance by the contractor and subcontractor was not justifiable in light of evidence that the plans and specifications discussed the potential

The Appellate Court held that the owner properly terminated the contract under the provision that allowed it to do so when a condition beyond its control prevented owner from continuing with the contract. The owner had terminated the contract because of cost overruns, the limited availability of additional funding, and the percentage of unfinished work. The contractor argued that the termination clause was analogous to the common law doctrine of impossibility of performance. The Court found that the contract provision used the word "prevent" as opposed to "impossibility," and that a condition that merely "hindered" or "forestalled" continuation of the contract could "prevent" its continuation. According to the Court, such a condition need not make it impossible to perform the contract. In this case, the Court concluded that the condition beyond the control of the owner was not the availability of funds, but rather the contractor's overruns.

respondent, and acquiesced to the dates of the hearings. Finally, the contractor knew the arbitration would be joint because the caption on the demand for arbitration read "joint."

92021a   Vega v. Griffiths Constr., Inc., 172 Ariz. 46, 833 P.2d 717 (Ct. App. 1992)

        I: A107-1978, Art. 16, Para. 16.1
        I: A117-1979, Art. 20, Para. 20.1
        I: A201-1976, Art. 10, Para. 10.1.1
        I: A201-1976, Art. 10, Para. 10.2.1
        I: A201-1976, Art. 10, Para. 10.2.6

In a suit by sub-subcontractor's injured employee, the trial court granted summary judgment to contractor on the ground that contractor did not owe a duty to sub-subcontractor's employee to provide a safe workplace. On appeal, the Appellate Court reversed the judgment of the trial court on this issue.

The Appellate Court, relying on the Arizona Supreme Court's decision in *Lewis v. N.J. Riebe Enters., Inc.* (see case digest number 92011), held that contractor assumed a duty to provide a reasonably safe workplace to sub-subcontractor's employees. The owner-contractor agreement, which provided in pertinent part that contractor was solely " 'responsible for initiating, maintaining and supervising all safety precautions and programs in connection with the Work . . .' and obligated [contractor] to 'take all reasonable precautions for the safety of . . . all employees' and 'designate a responsible member of his organization at the site whose duty shall be the prevention of accidents,' " was identical to the contract in *Lewis*.

92021b   W.C. English, Inc. v. Commonwealth, Dept. of Transp.,14 Va. App. 951, 420 S.E.2d 252 (1992)

        III: A107-1987, Art. 20, Para. 20.2
        III: A117-1987, Art. 25, Para. 25.2
        III: A201-1987, Art. 14, Para. 14.2

Contractor appealed the judgment of the trial court upholding the owner's right to terminate the owner-contractor agreement, based on unit pricing, when, without fault of either party the amount of work and time required to complete the project greatly exceeded that for which the parties contracted.

The owner-contractor agreement provided that:

    (a) By written notice, the Department [owner], in its discretion, may terminate the Contract or any portion thereof due to any of the following conditions: . . .

        4. Conditions Beyond the Control of the Department—In the event conditions arise which would prevent the Contractor from proceeding with or completing the work contracted for, or any other conditions which would prevent the Department from continuing with the Contract.

Any dispute arising at any time under this Subcontract which is not disposed of by agreement . . . or by submission of a joint claim by [Contractor] and Subcontractor to Owner under Disputes Procedures set out in the Prime Contract, shall be decided in the first instance by [Contractor] who shall reduce its decision to writing without unreasonable delay and mail or deliver three (3) copies thereof to the Subcontractor. The decision of [Contractor] shall be final and conclusive unless, within thirty (30) days from the date of receipt hereof, the Subcontractor mails or delivers to [Contractor] a written notice of rejection, in which event the decision of [Contractor] shall not have further effect . . . and either party may have the dispute, and the subject matter thereof finally settled by arbitration, per section 7.9 of the General Conditions . . . .

The Appellate Court found that the parties' intent to have the question of arbitrability decided by an arbitrator was not reflected in the express terms of the contract but in the broad language of the arbitration clause. Furthermore, the subcontract contained no exclusionary language removing the question of arbitrability from the scope of the arbitrator's authority. The Court concluded that the trial court's finding that this language revealed the parties' intent to have the arbitrator decide whether the preconditions to arbitration were satisfied was not clearly erroneous.

92021   Ure v. Wangler Constr. Co., 232 Ill. App. 3d 492, 173 Ill. Dec. 785, 597 N.E.2d 759 (1992)

II:	A107-1978, Art. 13, Para. 13.2	
II:	A117-1979, Art. 17, Para. 17.2	
I:	A201-1976, Art. 7, Para. 7.9.1	
II:	A401-1978, Art. 13, Para. 13.2	
I:	B141-1977, Art. 9, Para. 9.1	

In contractor's action to reverse a judgment on the pleadings, confirming an arbitration award in favor of the owner, the Appellate Court held that the arbitrator was required to recognize the contract provisions prohibiting consolidation of the owner's action against the contractor with the owner's action against the architect. The arbitration clauses in both the architect's contract and the contractor's contract contained almost identical prohibitions against joinder or consolidation of claims without consent. Contractor's arbitration clause provided in pertinent part that "No arbitration arising out of or relating to the Contract Documents shall include, by consolidation, joinder or in any other manner, the Architect, his employees or consultants except by written consent containing a specific reference to the Owner-Contractor Agreement and signed by the Architect, the Owner, the Contractor and any other person sought to be joined."

The Court held that the contractor had waived its contractual right to preclude consolidation by waiting until the day of arbitration to first raise the issue of consolidation; the contractor did not object to consolidation during the period of time from the filing of the demand to the hearing date; the contractor participated in choosing the arbitrator, rejected an arbitrator, accepted another arbitrator, agreed to the addition of another

contractor or subcontractor from being negligent in causing the fire, but it deprived owner of the ability to seek damages against them.

92020 Touchet Valley Grain Growers, Inc. v. Opp & Seibold Gen. Constr., Inc., 119 Wash. 2d 334, 831 P.2d 724 (1992)

> I: A107-1978, Art. 17, Para. 17.6
> I: A117-1979, Art. 21, Para. 21.6
> I: A201-1976, Art. 11, Para. 11.3.6

The Appellate Court rejected the subcontractor's argument that the subrogation waiver contained in the owner-contractor agreement, which provided that "Subrogation rights, if any, are expressly waived by each party to the extent of insurance coverage afforded on any claim, loss or casualty arising from or in connection with the Project," barred all claims against the subcontractor; it was the intent of the owner and contractor to include a waiver similar to the waiver contained in the American Institute of Architects General Conditions of the Contract for Construction, Document No. A201, 1976 edition, which clause protected subcontractors. The Court found that however expansive the language of the waiver the subcontractor was seeking to benefit by a contract to which it was not a party. The contention that the parties drafted a standard waiver, therefore one that extended to the subcontractor, failed because the parties negotiated the subrogation waiver clause. The Court concluded that the negotiated clause, unlike the AIA General Conditions, did not include subcontractors.

92020a Turner Constr. Co. v. Eppoliti, Inc., 28 Conn. App. 139, 609 A.2d 1064 (1992)

> III: A107-1978, Art. 8, Para. 8.5
> III: A107-1978, Art. 13, Para. 13.2
> III: A117-1979, Art. 12, Para. 12.5
> III: A117-1979, Art. 17, Para. 17.2
> III: A201-1976, Art. 2, Para. 2.2.9
> III: A201-1976, Art. 7, Para. 7.9.1

Contractor appealed from the trial court's judgment compelling arbitration of contractor's dispute with subcontractor. Contractor argued on appeal that where the dispute clause in the subcontract did not expressly authorize the arbitrator to decide the threshold question of arbitrability, the issue of arbitrability had to be decided by the court. Contractor further argued that where the clause was not triggered until there had been a timely demand for payment, a decision by contractor on the demand for payment, and a rejection of contractor's decision, the preconditions to arbitration were not satisfied. The Appellate Court upheld the judgment of the trial court.

The subcontract provided in pertinent part as follows:

breaching Paragraph 11.3.1 by failing to notify them that it was not maintaining insurance on the property to its full insurable value. Subcontractor also argued that it was a third-party beneficiary of the construction contract and was, therefore, entitled to benefit from the contract's provisions. The owner argued on appeal that the owner-contractor agreement was not a blanket waiver of liability and that subcontractor was not entitled to benefit from its provisions. Owner further claimed that even if the waiver clause applied to subcontractor, it applied only to the extent covered by insurance and, therefore, subcontractor was not exonerated from all liability.

The owner-contractor agreement included the American Institute of Architects General Conditions of the Contract for Construction, Document No. A201, 1976 edition, specifically Paragraphs 11.3.1 and 11.3.6.

The Court found that the inclusion of the word "sub-subcontractor" in the waiver clause indicated that a considerable depth of parties was contemplated and that the waiver was not meant to be limited only to those who contracted directly with the contractor. The language, "[t]he Owner and Contractor waive all rights against . . . each other and the Subcontractors, Sub-subcontractors, agents and employees each of the other . . ." in Paragraph 11.3.6 of the contract, revealed owner and contractor's intent that the waiver provision extend to subcontractors. Therefore, the Court concluded, subcontractor was entitled to benefit from the waiver provision as a third-party beneficiary.

The Court ruled that the interpretation of the American Institute of Architects insurance provisions was a matter of first impression in Texas. The Court found that Paragraph 11.3.6 operated as a waiver as to all rights of the owner and contractor against the subcontractors for damages caused by fire or other perils to the extent that such damages were covered by insurance obtained pursuant to Paragraph 11.3.1. Paragraph 11.3.1 placed an affirmative duty on the owner to procure property insurance that covered the interests of the owner, the contractor, and the subcontractors. In the event the owner failed to purchase adequate insurance and failed to notify the contractor that the project was underinsured, the owner bore the risk of loss to the extent that the damages were not covered by insurance. The Court stated that the policy underlying the insurance provisions was to avoid disruption and disputes among the parties. Under Paragraph 11.3.6, owner and contractor waived all rights against each other, the subcontractors, sub-subcontractors, agents, and employees of each other for damages caused by fire or other perils to the extent that the damages were covered by insurance. Paragraph 11.3.1 mandated that owner procure fire insurance for the project and notify the contractor if owner did not intend to purchase such insurance for the full insurable value. The Court held that because owner did not notify contractor of its intention not to maintain adequate property insurance, owner became the insurer liable for damages to the extent that an insurance carrier would have been liable had adequate insurance been obtained, and, furthermore, owner assumed the risk of loss for the damages in excess of the insurance coverage.

The Court found further that Paragraph 11.3.6 operated as a release and settlement of all claims that owner had against contractor and subcontractor where, in executing the waiver, owner agreed not to sue contractor or subcontractor in the event that either negligently caused owner to incur damages from fire. The waiver did not prevent

in question provided that "CONTRACTOR shall carry on the work and adhere to the progress scheduled during all disputes or disagreements with owner. No work shall be delayed or postponed pending resolution of any disputes or disagreements, except as permitted by paragraph 15.5 [termination] or as CONTRACTOR and OWNER may otherwise agree in writing." The Court found that the purpose of this language was to inform the contractor that he was expected to continue his work even though there might be disputes or disagreements with the owner. The Court concluded that the language did not mandate specific performance where the contractor would still be free to breach the contract and then be liable for money damages by reason of that breach.

92019 Tayco Constr. Co. v. LaCuisine Restaurant, Inc., 593 So. 2d 954 (La. Ct. App. 1992)

> I: A107-1987, Art. 10, Para. 10.8
> I: A117-1987, Art. 15, Para. 15.8
> I: A201-1987, Art. 4, Para. 4.5.1

The Appellate Court reversed the arbitrator's award of attorneys' fees to the contractor in its action against the owner for failure to make final payment, on the ground that the owner-contractor agreement did not provide for attorney fees. The parties entered into a cost-plus American Institute of Architects Standard Form of Agreement Between Owner and Contractor, Document No. A111, 1987 edition, which incorporated by reference the American Institute of Architects General Conditions of the Contract for Construction, Document No. A201, 1987 edition.

92019a Temple Eastex, Inc. v. Old Orchard Creek Partners, Ltd., 848 S.W.2d 724 (Tex. Ct. App. 1992)

> II: A107-1978, Art. 17, Para. 17.3
> II: A107-1978, Art. 17, Para. 17.6
> II: A117-1979, Art. 21, Para. 21.3
> II: A117-1979, Art. 21, Para. 21.6
> I: A201-1976, Art. 11, Para. 11.3.1
> I: A201-1976, Art. 11, Para. 11.3.6

Contractor appealed the trial court's grant of summary judgment to subcontractor allowing subcontractor contribution against contractor. The Appellate Court reversed the judgment of the trial court. Among numerous points of error, the contractor and subcontractor contended that the trial court erred in not giving effect to either the waiver or the property insurance provisions of the owner-contractor agreement. The contractor and subcontractor argued that owner waived any claims against them for damages to the extent that owner's fire damage losses were covered by insurance under Paragraph 11.3.6 of the owner-contractor agreement. To the extent that owner's losses exceeded insurance coverage, contractor and subcontractor argued that owner assumed the risk of loss by

II:	A107-1978, Art. 8, Para. 8.4
II:	A107-1978, Art. 8, Para. 8.6
II:	A107-1978, Art. 8, Para. 8.7
II:	A117-1979, Art. 12, Para. 12.1
II:	A117-1979, Art. 12, Para. 12.4
II:	A117-1979, Art. 12, Para. 12.6
II:	A117-1979, Art. 12, Para. 12.7
II:	A201-1976, Art. 2, Para. 2.2.2
II:	A201-1976, Art. 2, Para. 2.2.6
II:	A201-1976, Art. 2, Para. 2.2.13
II:	A201-1976, Art. 2, Para. 2.2.14

The Appellate Court affirmed the ruling of the trial court that the services rendered by the Sagamore Group were not construction manager duties as contemplated by the state statute. In reaching this conclusion the Court relied in part on the definition of construction manager duties contained in the American Institute of Architects General Conditions of the Contract for Construction, Construction Management Edition, Document No. A201/CM, 1980 edition. The definition specified that the duties would include acting as the owner's representative during construction and until the issuance of final payment, reviewing and processing all applications for payment by the contractors, rejecting work that does not conform to the contract (subject to the architects' review), and reviewing shop drawings and samples. Of particular significance to specialty contractors was the construction manager's obligation to schedule and coordinate the work. Under the contract between the parties the Sagamore Group was to provide consulting and supportive services to disadvantaged business enterprises and women's business enterprises doing work on Connecticut Department of Transportation projects. The Sagamore Group was to be paid on an hourly basis for services rendered with a maximum project cost. The Court found that the Sagamore Group provided services which included assisting the enterprises in obtaining certification and recertification for contracts with the DOT, reviewing all DOT contracts for contracting opportunities for the enterprises, making on site visits to monitor the enterprises' job progress and various other details relating to their job performance, and serving several functions related to the enterprises in their dealings and relationships with the DOT. These services, the Court found, were not services rendered by construction managers.

92018a State *ex rel.* Park County v. Montana Sixth Judicial Dist. Ct., 253 Mont. 331, 833 P.2d 210 (1992)

III:	A201-1987, Art. 4, Para. 4.3.4

On appeal in contractor's action for injunctive relief, the Supreme Court of Montana rejected the contractor's argument that the language of the owner-contractor agreement created an obligation of specific performance on the part of the contractor. The language

to the owner on the ground that neither a mistake of law nor sufficiency of the evidence was a statutory ground for vacating the award.

The construction manager argued that the award of damages to owner for lost profits was a prejudicial mistake of law where the award was not contemplated by the parties at the date of contract because the parties specified in their contract the remedies available in the event of a breach. Specifically, in Paragraph 12.1.1 the construction manager agreed to indemnify the owner; in Paragraph 12.4 the owner was required to purchase property insurance; in Paragraph 13.2.1 the owner was required to make good on obligations the construction manager failed to perform; and in Paragraph 13.2.2 the owner could terminate the construction manager if the construction manager failed to perform its duties under the contract. There was no provision for lost profit damages.

The Supreme Court held that the arbitrators had more than enough evidence to conclude that the construction manager was aware that its failure to complete the project in a timely fashion would lead to a significant loss of income and that the owner's damages were reasonably foreseeable.

The construction manager argued further that the award of lost profits should not have been awarded after the date that the project was substantially completed, but before the construction manager was terminated. In determining the meaning of substantial completion, the Court referred to the contract, whose definition was modeled on the American Institute of Architect's definition: "The date of substantial completion of the project or a designated portion thereof is the date when construction is significantly complete in accordance with the drawings and specifications so the owner can occupy or utilize the project or designed portion thereof for the use for which it is intended." The Supreme Court held that the construction manager's argument that delay damages could not be awarded after substantial completion of the contract was amply supported by the case law and construction-industry practice. However, the Court upheld the arbitrator's award because it did not depart from any clear holding that consequential damages could be awarded if the residual effects of nonperformance of the contract were carried over into a period when the building was operational.

The construction manager also argued that the arbitrators erred in failing to decide the issue of wrongful termination which had been submitted to them. The arbitrators were to interpret the contract provision that stated "If after substantial completion of the work final completion thereof is materially delayed, the owner shall, upon certification by the architect and without termination [of] the contract, make payment of the balance due for that portion of the work fully completed and accepted." The Supreme Court found that the arbitrators had awarded lost profit damages to owner, and in doing so, could not have found that the construction manager had satisfactorily performed the contract; a finding that owner had wrongfully discharged the construction manager would have contradicted the award. The Court held that the arbitrators had impliedly determined that owner had properly discharged the construction manager.

92018   Sagamore Group, Inc. v. Commissioner of Transp., 29 Conn. App. 292, 614 A.2d 1255 (1992)

    II: A107-1978, Art. 8, Para. 8.1

I:	A107-1987, Art. 16, Para. 16.2	
I:	A117-1979, Art. 20, Para. 20.1	
I:	A117-1987, Art. 21, Para. 21.1	
I:	A117-1987, Art. 21, Para. 21.2	
I:	A201-1976, Art. 10, Para. 10.1	
I:	A201-1976, Art. 10, Para. 10.2.2	
I:	A201-1987, Art. 10, Para. 10.1	
I:	A201-1987, Art. 10, Para. 10.2	

In a personal injury action brought by the employee of a subcontractor, the trial court granted contractor's motion for summary judgment holding that where there was no provision in the owner-contractor agreement expressly requiring contractor to initiate, maintain, or supervise safety programs, a nondelegable duty, based on the contract, had not been created. On appeal by the employee's estate, the Appellate Court reversed the decision of the trial court.

The owner-contractor agreement provided in pertinent part that:

The contractor shall provide all safeguards, safety devices and protective equipment and take any other needed actions, on his own responsibility, or as the State highway department contracting officer may determine, reasonably necessary to protect the life and health of employees on the job and the safety of the public and to protect property in connection with the performance of the work covered by the contract.

The Appellate Court found that the duty imposed on contractor was nondelegable and contractor could not avoid liability by attempting to shift the responsibility to the subcontractor. Regardless of the obligations of the subcontractor or others, contractor retained the responsibility to provide the deceased worker with a safe place to work.

92017 Perini Corp. v. Greate Bay Hotel & Casino, Inc., 129 N.J. 479, 610 A.2d 364 (1992)

I:	A107-1978, Art. 14, Para. 14.2	
I:	A117-1979, Art. 18, Para. 18.2	
I:	A201-1976, Art. 8, Para. 8.1.3	
I:	A201-1976, Art. 9, Para. 9.9.3	

Construction manager brought an action against owner seeking a declaratory judgment that owner could not terminate the contract after the project was substantially completed. The trial court ordered that the termination issue, as well as any other disputes, were to be arbitrated under the terms of the contract. The arbitrators awarded the owner damages and the construction manager sought to vacate the award. The New Jersey Supreme Court limited its grant of certification to whether the asserted mistake of law was reviewable by the courts, the continued validity of the principle that mistakes of law are the equivalent of undue means, and the disproportionality of the arbitration award. The Supreme Court affirmed the judgment of the Appellate Court in upholding the award provision. The Court also found that even if the default provision had no applicability after the expiration of the one-year warranty period, there was evidence that the defects were apparent before the one-year period expired.

The Court held further that the trial court erred in not instructing the jury that "[The provision of the subcontract requiring the subcontractor to correct defects within one year of acceptance of the project] . . . is an added guarantee, inserted in the contract to extend rather than limit [subcontractor's] liability for faulty construction. As such, it [is] not [contractor's] exclusive remedy, and it in no way impairs [subcontractor's] general obligation to perform his contract in a proper, workmanlike manner." The Court held that it was also error to refuse to give contractor's charge on the law of indemnification where subcontractor was required under the subcontract to indemnify contractor against any claim asserted by owner involving sufficiency of subcontractor's work. The issue of surety's obligation to indemnify should also have been presented to the jury. The Court held that these errors were substantial and harmful as a matter of law.

92016 Miller Bldg. Corp. v. Coastline Assocs. Ltd. Partnership, 105 N.C. App. 58, 411 S.E.2d 420 (1992)

> I: A107-1987, Art. 10, Para. 10.8
> I: A117-1987, Art. 15, Para. 15.8
> I: A201-1987, Art. 4, Para. 4.5.1
> I: A201-1987, Art. 4, Para. 4.5.4.2
> I: A401-1987, Art. 6, Para. 6.1
> I: B141-1987, Art. 7, Para. 7.1
> I: B141-1987, Art. 7, Para. 7.2

Contractor brought an action against owner for interest on late payments. The trial court denied owner's motion to compel arbitration on the ground that the owner had delayed unreasonably in demanding arbitration and had waived any right to arbitration. The Appellate Court reversed.

The owner-contractor agreement incorporated the American Institute of Architects General Conditions of the Contract for Construction, Document No. A201, 1987 edition, which provided for arbitration in Paragraph 4.5.1 and required in Paragraph 4.5.4.2 that a demand for arbitration be made within a reasonable time.

The owner filed its demand approximately two months after the contractor breached the contract by filing suit. The Court therefore found that the owner promptly demanded arbitration and that the contractor was not prejudiced since there was no trial, no evidence was lost, and no discovery was conducted.

92016a Nave v. Harlan Jones Drilling, 252 Mont. 199, 827 P.2d 1239 (1992)

> I: A107-1978, Art. 16, Para. 16.1
> I: A107-1987, Art. 16, Para. 16.1

III: A401-1978, Art. 11, Para. 11.11.1
III: A401-1978, Art. 14, Para. 14.2.1

Contractor brought an action against subcontractor and its surety to recover damages for defective work after employing another subcontractor to perform the repair. Following a jury trial the court entered judgment for the subcontractor and surety. The Appellate Court reversed the judgment of the trial court.

The parties entered into a subcontract providing that "the work shall be performed by subcontractor in a good and workmanlike manner strictly in accordance with the Contract Documents . . . ." It further contained a guarantee whereby "Subcontractor warrants and guarantees the Work to the full extent provided for in the Contract Documents. Without limiting the foregoing or any other liability or obligation with respect to the Work, Subcontractor shall, at its expense and by reason of its express warranty, make good any faulty, defective, or improper part of the Work discovered within one year from the date of acceptance of the project by the Architect and Owner or within such longer period as may be provided in the Contract Documents." The subcontract also required the subcontractor to furnish a performance bond to remain in effect until the subcontractor fully performed under the agreement. Specified as a "Contract Document" and specifically incorporated into the agreement was the American Institute of Architects General Conditions of the Contract for Construction, Document No. A201, 1976 edition as amended by Supplementary Conditions, specifically Paragraphs 4.5.1, 5.3.1 and 13.2.2.

The Court held that the trial court had erred in excluding from the trial any evidence of the default provision in the subcontract, which stated that "Should Subcontractor at any time: fail to supply the labor, materials, equipment, supervision and other things required . . . of sufficient quality to perform the Work with the skill [and] conformity . . . required hereunder . . . fail in the performance or observance of any of the covenants, conditions, or other terms of this subcontract, . . . each of which shall constitute a default hereunder by Subcontractor, Contractor shall, after giving Subcontractor notice of default and 48 hours within which to cure, have right to exercise any one or more of [four specified] remedies." These remedies included correcting the work through others and recovering from subcontractor all losses, damages and reasonable attorney fees incurred by reason of the default. In interpreting the provision, the Court concluded that the express warranty was not an exclusive remedy and that correction of the work was required within the first year "or such longer period of time as may be prescribed by law." Subcontractor was contractually obligated to provide the labor, material and equipment necessary to perform good quality work, free from faults and defects, and an event of default was deemed to have occurred should the subcontractor "at any time" fail to do so. Furthermore, under the indemnification provision of the subcontract, subcontractor was required to "indemnify and save harmless Contractor . . . from and against any liability, loss, damage, or expense arising out of any claim asserted by owner against contractor involving the sufficiency of the performance of the Work." The Court concluded that refusal by the subcontractor and its surety to indemnify contractor for the claim asserted by owner was evidence of failure to perform under the indemnification

92014a McBro, Inc. v. M & M Glass Co., 611 So. 2d 283 (Ala. 1992)

III:	A107-1978, Art. 7, Para. 7.4
III:	A107-1978, Art. 10, Para. 10.11
III:	A107-1978, Art. 17, Para. 17.1
III:	A117-1979, Art. 11, Para. 11.4
III:	A117-1979, Art. 14, Para. 14.11
III:	A117-1979, Art. 21, Para. 21.1
III:	A201-1976, Art. 1, Para. 1.1.3
III:	A201-1976, Art. 4, Para. 4.18.1
III:	A201-1976, Art. 11, Para. 11.1.1
III:	A201-1976, Art. 11, Para. 11.1.3
III:	A401-1978, Art. 2, Para. 2.1
III:	A401-1978, Art. 11, Para. 11.11.1

Construction manager appealed the trial court's grant of summary judgment to contractor. Construction manager argued on appeal that the indemnity clause in the contract between the construction manager and contractor was enforceable because the language was unambiguous and the contract clearly indicated an intention to indemnify.

The parties' contract included provisions identical to Paragraphs 4.18.1, 11.1.1 and 11.1.3 of the American Institute of Architects General Conditions of the Contract for Construction, Document No. A201, 1976 edition.

The Appellate Court, relying on its decision in *McDevitt & Street Co. v. Mosher Steel Co.* (see case digest number 91019), concluded that the indemnity agreement was enforceable.

92015 McDevitt & St. Co. v. K-C Air Conditioning Serv., Inc., 203 Ga. App. 640, 418 S.E.2d 87 (1992), *cert. denied sub nom.* Employers Ins. of Wausau v. McDevitt & St. Co., 1992 Ga. LEXIS 486 (Ga. 1992)

I:	A107-1978, Art. 10, Para. 10.4
I:	A107-1978, Art. 11, Para. 11.2
I:	A107-1978, Art. 19, Para. 19.1
I:	A117-1979, Art. 14, Para. 14.4
I:	A117-1979, Art. 15, Para. 15.2
I:	A117-1979, Art. 23, Para. 23.1
I:	A201-1976, Art. 4, Para. 4.5.1
I:	A201-1976, Art. 5, Para. 5.3.1
I:	A201-1976, Art. 13, Para. 13.2.2
III:	A401-1978, Art. 7
III:	A401-1978, Art. 11, Para. 11.7.1

I: B141-1977, Art. 9, Para. 9.1

Subcontractor brought an action against contractor and its surety for damages resulting from contractor's alleged breach of contract. Contractor moved to stay the action pending arbitration. The trial court denied contractor's motion and contractor appealed. The Appellate Court reversed the judgment of the trial court.

The owner-contractor agreement included the American Institute of Architects General Conditions of the Contract for Construction, Document No. A201, 1976 edition, which provided for arbitration in Paragraph 7.9.1. The subcontract provided that the subcontractor "agrees to be bound to the Contractor by the terms of the hereinbefore described plans; specifications (including all general conditions stated therein) . . ., and to assume to the Contractor all the obligations and responsibilities that the Contractor by those documents assumes to the (Awarding Authority) hereinafter called the 'Awarding Authority,' except to the extent that provisions contained therein are by their terms or by law applicable only to the Contractor. . . ."

The Appellate Court held that since the subcontract incorporated the owner-contractor agreement, the subcontractor and its surety were bound by the arbitration clause in the owner-contractor agreement.

92014 Maxus, Inc. v. Sciacca, 598 So. 2d 1376 (Ala. 1992)

I: A107-1987, Art. 10, Para. 10.8
I: A117-1987, Art. 15, Para. 15.8
I: A201-1987, Art. 4, Para. 4.5.1
I: A401-1987, Art. 6, Para. 6.1
I: B141-1987, Art. 7, Para. 7.1

Contractor brought an action to vacate an arbitration award entered in its billing dispute with owner. The trial court affirmed the award and contractor appealed. At issue before the Supreme Court of Alabama was whether the Court should apply state or federal law in reviewing the arbitration award. Ruling that federal law applied, the Court reversed the judgment of the lower court.

After deciding that federal law applied, the Court addressed the contractor's argument that the scope of the arbitration hearing should have been limited solely to the resolution of the parties' billing disputes. The owner argued that the dispute that was submitted to arbitration required a determination of whether contractor had any warranty obligations, whether certain items had been improperly billed, and whether the contractor's fee was properly calculated before there could be a finding of any amount due contractor. The owner argued further that the arbitration clause was sufficiently broad to cover these claims. The Appellate Court held that in view of the broad language used in the arbitration agreement, coupled with the federal policy favoring liberal construction of arbitration agreements, the disputes were well within the scope of the arbitration agreement.

The rationale upon which the Court ruled that federal law applied was subsequently overruled in *Terminix Int'l Co. v. Jackson*, 628 So. 2d 357 (Ala. 1993), an unrelated case.

under the contract when the owner filed its order to show cause against it. The Court concluded that it had no power to address the dispute between the owner and the architect before an arbitrator decided the matter; it could not compel the architect to permit the contractor to join in that arbitration where the owner-architect agreement clearly provided that "no arbitration, arising out of or relating to this Agreement, shall include, by consolidation, joinder or in any other manner, any additional party not a party to this Agreement except by written consent . . . [of the] parties hereto."

As to the substance of the dispute between the contractor and the owner, the contractor claimed it was entitled to terminate its contract with the owner under Paragraph 14.1.3. The contractor argued that its work had been stopped for a period exceeding sixty days when the owner had failed to provide the contractor with full and complete plans and specifications so that the contractor could properly carry out its work; that the owner failed to provide the contractor with timely access to work areas; and that the owner failed to timely resolve the problems arising out of deficient design. The owner responded that it could not be found to have persistently failed to perform its obligations under the contract where it endeavored with all available resources to provide a resolution to a very complex and difficult problem not of its own making. The Court found that the owner breached its obligation under the contract by submitting plans that were extensively imprecise or incorrect. The Court rejected the owner's argument that it was not liable for the delay because the owner had not prepared the plans. The Court found that the architect had no contractual obligations or agreement with the contractor and could not be held liable to contractor for any breach of contract since there was no privity of contract between the contractor and the architect. As a result, the owner was responsible to the contractor for the design deficiencies. Furthermore, in the Court's opinion, the initial work stoppage was caused by the owner's failure to provide the contractor with sufficient plans. The Court also found that the owner was responsible for the continuation of the stoppage. However, even though the issue of whether the contractor was entitled to delay damages was not properly before the Court, the Court found that during the course of the project the owner's representative told the contractor not to perform any work outside the scope of the contract unless the owner issued a change order, and, because the owner failed to sign the change order issued by the architect, the contractor was under no obligation to do additional work. It was the Court's opinion that it was the owner's failure to issue the change order, rather than the contractor's failure to perform the work, that caused the work stoppage to continue. The Court held that pursuant to Paragraph 14.1.3 of the owner-contractor agreement the contractor was entitled to terminate the contract.

92013 Massachusetts Elec. Sys., Inc. v. R.W. Granger & Sons, Inc., 32 Mass. App. Ct. 982, 594 N.E.2d 545 (1992)

> I: A107-1978, Art. 13, Para. 13.2
> III: A107-1978, Art. 11, Para. 11.1.1
> I: A117-1979, Art. 17, Para. 17.2
> I: A201-1976, Art. 7, Para. 7.9.1
> I: A401-1978, Art. 13, Para. 13.1

I:	A201–1987, Art. 13, Para. 13.1.1
I:	A201–1987, Art. 14, Para. 14.1.1
I:	A201–1987, Art. 14, Para. 14.1.2
I:	A201–1987, Art. 14, Para. 14.1.3
I:	B141–1987, Art. 7, Para. 7.1
I:	B141–1987, Art. 7, Para. 7.3

Prime general contractor brought an action against owner seeking a declaratory judgment that the owner-contractor agreement was terminated due to an extended work stoppage, and that contractor was not obligated to perform any further work on the project. The owner argued that contractor's work had not been suspended but, rather, that contractor had refused to resume work on the project until the owner agreed to pay its delay damages, which the owner asserted were prohibited under the contract. Furthermore, the owner asserted that contractor's complaint should have been dismissed because the contract provided that arbitration was the sole forum for dispute resolution available to contractor. Also before the Court was owner's third-party action against the architect for design deficiencies. The architect filed a motion to stay the owner's third-party complaint pending arbitration.

The parties entered into an owner-contractor agreement which included the American Institute of Architects General Conditions of the Contract for Construction, Document No. A201, 1987 edition, specifically Paragraphs 4.5.1, 7.2.1, 7.3.1, 13.1.1, 14.1.1, 14.1.2, and 14.1.3.

The District Court found that the owner had waived its right to arbitration because the owner declined to arbitrate in response to contractor's demand for arbitration, leading the contractor to conclude that since it could not compel the owner to arbitrate pursuant to Paragraph 4.5.1 it must seek a declaratory judgment. Furthermore, the contractor was placed in the position of waiting indefinitely until the owner consented to arbitration where the architect refused, under the terms of its contract with the owner, to consolidate its dispute with that of the contractor. Under these circumstances, in exercising its contractual right not to arbitrate the matter with contractor, the owner waived its right to compel contractor to arbitrate.

The Court then stayed claims the owner had asserted against the architect pending arbitration, because the contract between the owner and the architect gave the architect the right to compel the owner to arbitrate disputes between the parties. The Court found that the language of the arbitration clause was extremely broad in providing that "all claims, disputes and other matters in question between the parties to this Agreement, arising out of, or relating to this Agreement or the breach thereof, shall be decided by arbitration in accordance with the Construction Industry Arbitration rules of the American Arbitration Association then obtaining unless the parties mutually agree otherwise." The Court rejected the owner's argument that the architect had waited an unreasonable period of time before demanding arbitration, because although the dispute regarding the design defects had been ongoing for several months, the architect promptly asserted its rights

property insurance upon the entire project. Furthermore, the Court found that Article 10 covered another aspect of liability, namely contractor's duty to protect owner from liability for claims by third parties.

92011   Lewis v. N.J. Riebe Enters., Inc., 170 Ariz. 384, 825 P.2d 5 (1992)

        I: A107–1978, Art. 16, Para. 16.1
        I: A117–1979, Art. 20, Para. 20.1
        I: A201–1976, Art. 10, Para. 10.1.1
        I: A201–1976, Art. 10, Para. 10.2.1
        I: A201–1976, Art. 10, Para. 10.2.6

Affirming the judgment of the trial court, the Supreme Court of Arizona held that a contractor had a duty to subcontractor's employees to provide a reasonably safe workplace. This duty was set forth in the American Institute of Architects Standard Form of Agreement Between Owner and Contractor, Document No. A101, 1977 edition, which incorporated the American Institute of Architects General Conditions of the Contract for Construction, Document No. A201, 1976 edition, specifically Paragraphs 10.1.1, 10.2.1 and 10.2.6. The Court further found that under state law the contractor had a general duty to provide employees of subcontractors with a reasonably safe place to work; the scope of the duty extended only as far as the amount of control the contractor retained over the work of the subcontractor. The Court thus concluded that under Paragraphs 10.1.1, 10.2.1 and 10.2.6 of the General Conditions, the contractor had assumed an affirmative duty to maintain safety at the site, and that this safety responsibility constituted a sufficient retention of control over the subcontractors work to subject contractor to liability under the state statute.

92012   Lott Constructors, Inc. v. Jackson Township Bd. of Educ., 1992 U.S. Dist. LEXIS 12891 (D.N.J. Aug. 12, 1992)

        I: A107–1987, Art. 10, Para. 10.8
        I: A107–1987, Art. 13, Para. 13.1
        I: A107–1987, Art. 19, Para. 19.1
        I: A107–1987, Art. 20, Para. 20.1
        I: A117–1987, Art. 15, Para. 15.8
        I: A117–1987, Art. 18, Para. 18.1
        I: A117–1987, Art. 24, Para. 24.1
        I: A117–1987, Art. 25, Para. 25.1
        I: A201–1987, Art. 4, Para. 4.5.1
        I: A201–1987, Art. 7, Para. 7.2.1
        I: A201–1987, Art. 7, Para. 7.3.1

92010b   Len Immke Buick, Inc. v. Architectural Alliance, 81 Ohio App. 3d 459, 611 N.E.2d 399 (1992)

       I: A107–1978, Art. 10, Para. 10.11
       I: A107–1978, Art. 17, Para. 17.1
       I: A107–1978, Art. 17, Para. 17.3
       I: A107–1978, Art. 17, Para. 17.4
       I: A107–1978, Art. 17, Para. 17.6
       I: A117–1979, Art. 14, Para. 14.11
       I: A117–1979, Art. 21, Para. 21.1
       I: A117–1979, Art. 21, Para. 21.3
       I: A117–1979, Art. 21, Para. 21.4
       I: A117–1979, Art. 21, Para. 21.6
       I: A201–1976, Art. 4, Para. 4.18.1
       I: A201–1976, Art. 11, Para. 11.1.1
       I: A201–1976, Art. 11, Para. 11.3.1
       I: A201–1976, Art. 11, Para. 11.3.3
       I: A201–1976, Art. 11, Para. 11.3.6

Owner appealed the trial court's grant of summary judgment to contractor. Owner argued on appeal that the trial court misinterpreted the insurance provisions of the owner-contractor agreement. The Appellate Court upheld the judgment of the trial court, affirming its finding that the insurance provision required owner to procure "all risk" insurance that would cover the entire project to its full insurable value and provide recovery for any property loss or damage.

The owner and contractor had entered into the American Institute of Architects Abbreviated Form of Agreement Between Owner and Contractor, Document No. A107, 1978 edition, specifically Paragraphs 17.3, 17.4 and 17.6. The Appellate Court found that Paragraphs 17.3 and 17.6 clearly required the owner to purchase "all risk" insurance and to waive all claims against contractor for physical loss or damage to the project. The Court based its finding on cases from other jurisdictions in which the courts upheld similar provisions where the parties agreed to waive claims of personal liability in the event of a loss or peril, with the understanding that the loss would be covered by insurance.

Furthermore, the Court ruled that the contract provisions precluded owner's insurer from recovering against contractor on its subrogation claim where the liability and indemnification provisions of Article 10 were consistent with the expressed waiver of claims in Article 17. The Appellate Court agreed with the trial court that Paragraph 17.1, which required the contractor to carry liability insurance for claims other than the project itself, was logically consistent with Paragraph 17.3, which required owner to purchase all risk

The Supreme Court concluded that there was no irreconcilable conflict between Paragraph 7.9.1 of the General Conditions and Paragraph 7.1.1 of the supplementary general conditions. Under Paragraph 7.9.1 of the General Conditions, the parties agreed that they would submit disputes to arbitration, according to the Construction Industry Arbitration Rules of the American Arbitration Association. Paragraph 7.1.1 of the supplementary general conditions merely provided that the contractor consented to the jurisdiction of the courts of North Carolina for any action brought to enforce the arbitration agreement or an award resulting from arbitration. The Court found that where the parties agreed to arbitrate their disputes and the owner failed to show that the agreement was waived, the parties were required to submit the dispute to arbitration.

92010a   King v. Midas Realty Corp., 204 Ga. App. 590, 420 S.E.2d 62 (1992)

I: A107–1978, Art. 16, Para. 16.1
I: A117–1979, Art. 20, Para. 20.1
I: A201–1976, Art. 10, Para. 10.1
I: A201–1976, Art. 10, Para. 10.2.2

Following the collapse of a wall under construction, injured worker and the estate of deceased worker sued owner and contractor for damages. The trial court granted summary judgment to owner on the grounds that no genuine issues of material fact remained that owner had relinquished possession of the premises to contractor, and that neither under the terms and conditions of the owner-contractor agreement nor in actual practice had the owner retained control over the premises or directed the manner in which contractor executed the work, including performance of site safety functions. Plaintiffs appealed.

The owner-contractor agreement clearly and unambiguously placed on contractor "the responsibility for initiating, maintaining and supervising all safety precautions and programs in connection with the [construction]' and for complying with all applicable law, ordinances . . . of any public authority having jurisdiction for the safety of persons or property or to protect them from damage, injury or loss.' "

The Appellate Court held that the contract clearly and unambiguously placed sole responsibility for site safety on the contractor. The Court rejected the workers' argument that the owner exercised control over the project pursuant to the contract clause which stated that contractor's project superintendent, who was to serve as the project's safety inspector, had to be "satisfactory to [owner]" and could not be replaced without owner's consent.

The Court also rejected the workers' argument that the contract provision reserving to owner certain facets of the construction presented a question of fact whether owner controlled the project, given the uncontroverted testimony by the construction manager that the only facet of the construction reserved by owner involved the installation of the roof, which was contracted separately by owner.

rejected by the owner." The Court construed this provision as encouraging, not discouraging, contractor to file a notice of claim for additional compensation to timely resolve a dispute when other options were available to the parties, rather than later when the work was completed and could not be undone.

The Court then held that contractor could not rely on the language of the notice provision which stated that "[n]othing in this subsection shall be construed as a waiver of the contractor's right to dispute final payment based on differences in measurements or computation [,]" because the dispute was not "based on differences in measurements or computations" but upon whether or not contractor was required to give written notice of an intent to claim additional compensation.

92010   Johnson County v. R.N. Rouse & Co., 331 N.C. 88, 414 S.E.2d 30 (1992)

        I: A107–1978, Art. 13, Para. 13.2
        I: A117–1979, Art. 17, Para. 17.2
        I: A201–1976, Art. 7, Para. 7.9.1
        I: A401–1978, Art. 13, Para. 13.1
        I: B141–1977, Art. 9, Para. 9.1

Contractor filed a demand for arbitration against owner for additional compensation for extra work, delays, inefficiencies, interferences and hindrances caused by the owner. The trial court denied contractor's motion to compel arbitration on the ground that the owner-contractor agreement did not contain an agreement to arbitrate. The Appellate Court upheld the ruling of the trial court on the ground that Paragraph 7.1.1 of the supplementary general conditions conflicted with the arbitration provision contained in Paragraph 7.9.1 of the General Conditions. The Supreme Court of North Carolina reversed the Appellate Court, holding that the contract contained a binding arbitration provision, which was not superseded by the language in Paragraph 7.1.1 of the supplementary general conditions.

The parties had entered into the American Institute of Architects Standard Form of Agreement Between Owner and Contractor, Document No. A101, 1977 edition, which incorporated the American Institute of Architects General Conditions of the Contract for Construction, Document No. A201, 1976 edition, supplementary general conditions, and instructions to bidders. The General Conditions contained an arbitration clause in Paragraph 7.9.1. The supplementary general conditions provided in Paragraph 7.1.1 that by "executing a contract for the Project the Contractor agrees to submit itself to the jurisdiction of the courts of the State of North Carolina for all matters arising or to arise hereunder, including but not limited to performance of said contract and payment of all licenses and taxes of whatever nature applicable thereto." The instructions to bidders provided that "in the event of any conflicting statements or requirements in these General Conditions and the Supplementary General Conditions . . . of these Specifications, the Supplementary General Conditions shall have preference."

92009b Johnson Constr., Inc. v. Rugby Mun. Airport Auth., 492 N.W.2d 61 (N.D. 1992)

III:	A107–1987, Art. 13, Para. 13.1
III:	A107–1987, Art. 13, Para. 13.2
III:	A117–1987, Art. 18, Para. 18.1
III:	A117–1987, Art. 18, Para. 18.2
III:	A201–1987, Art. 4, Para. 4.3.7
III:	A201–1987, Art. 7, Para. 7.1
III:	A201–1987, Art. 7, Para. 7.2
III:	A201–1987, Art. 7, Para. 7.3

Contractor appealed the trial court's grant of summary judgment to owner and the dismissal of contractor's excavation and asphalt claims. Among numerous other issues on appeal, the contractor argued that the trial court erred in awarding owner summary judgment based on a finding that contractor waived its claim by failing to provide notice of its intention to seek additional compensation. The Appellate Court affirmed the judgment of the trial court.

The owner-contractor agreement provided in pertinent part that:

If for any reason the contractor deems that additional compensation is due him for work or materials not clearly provided for in the contract, plans, or specifications or previously authorized as extra work, he shall notify the engineer in writing of his intention to claim such additional compensation before he begins the work on which he bases the claim. If such notification is not given or the engineer is not afforded proper opportunity by the contractor for keeping strict account of actual cost as required, then the contractor hereby agrees to waive any claim for such additional compensation. . . .

Nothing in this subsection shall be construed as a waiver of the contractor's right to dispute final payment based on differences in measurements or computations.

The Appellate Court interpreted the notice provision as clearly requiring the contractor to provide written notice if contractor intended to seek additional compensation. The Court concluded that if the contractor believed it was being requested by owner to perform more work than contractor had anticipated, and for which contractor did not believe it was being compensated under the contract, contractor was required by the contract to notify the engineer in writing of its intent to make a claim for additional compensation. The Court concluded that by failing to provide that written notice, contractor waived all claims for additional compensation for the work performed.

The owner-contractor agreement also contained an extra work provision, which stated in pertinent part that "Extra Work that is within the general scope of the contract shall be covered by written change order. . . . Any claim for payment of extra work that is not covered by written agreement (change order or supplemental agreement) shall be

Standard Form of Agreement Between Owner and Architect, Document No. B141, 1978 edition. Paragraphs 10.1, 10.2, 10.3 and 10.4, applied only if the termination was not the fault of the construction manager. Here, owner terminated the contract because of construction manager's allegedly poor performance. However, the Circuit Court had concluded that construction manager was substantially performing and therefore that owner breached the contract. The District Court of Appeal agreed. Therefore the construction manager was entitled to the total amount due under the contract; however, the Court reversed for a proper determination of damages.

92009a Island on Lake Travis, Ltd. v. Hayman Co. Gen. Contractors, Inc., 834 S.W.2d 529 (Tex. Ct. App. 1992), *remanded*, 848 S.W.2d 84 (Tex. 1993)

> I: A107–1978, Art. 13, Para. 13.2
> I: A117–1979, Art. 17, Para. 17.2
> I: A201–1976, Art. 7, Para. 7.9.1
> I: A401–1978, Art. 13, Para. 13.1
> I: B141–1987, Art. 9, Para. 9.1

Owner appealed the trial court's confirmation of an arbitration award in favor of contractor. Owner argued on appeal that the arbitrators exceeded their authority by arbitrating claims and giving an award to contractor where another contractor, to whom contractor had assigned the contract, was the real party in interest.

The owner-contractor agreement contained an arbitration clause identical to Paragraph 7.9.1 of the American Institute of Architects General Conditions of the Contract for Construction, Document No. A201, 1976 edition.

The Appellate Court noted that the arbitration clause was written in very broad terms, covering "[a]ll claims, disputes and other matters in questions between the Contractor [Hayman Company] and the Owner [The Island] arising out of, or relating to, the Contract Documents or the breach thereof. . .." The issue of whether contractor actually owned any claims against owner arising from the project was disputed in the arbitration proceedings. According to the Court, such a dispute arose out of, or related to the contract, the contract documents or the breach thereof, and that "[u]nder such a broad arbitration clause, a dispute between the parties to the contract concerning the ownership of a claim arising from the contract [was] just as arbitrable as a dispute concerning the merits of the claim itself." Here, the arbitrators heard evidence in considering the contractor's claims under the contract and owner's defense that contractor did not have the right to assert those claims because, having assigned the contract, contractor did not own the claims. The arbitrators decided that the contractor owned the claims in question, and, furthermore, there was evidence in the record that the parties treated the two construction companies as interchangeable and the companies were so closely related that any attempted assignment was ineffective. The Court concluded that the claims were clearly arbitrable under Paragraph 7.9.1 and, therefore, the arbitrators did not exceed their authority in deciding the claims. Judgment of the trial court was affirmed.

III: B141–1977, Art. 1, Para. 1.5.9

III: B141–1977, Art. 1, Para. 1.5.10

On further appeal of *Huntington Woods v. Ajax Paving Indus., Inc.* (see case digest number 89023), the owner argued that the trial court erred in dismissing the owner's misrepresentation claims on the grounds that the claims were not arbitrable. The Appellate Court affirmed the finding of the trial court.

Although the owner's misrepresentation claims were arbitrable under the agreement which provided that all claims and disputes relating to the contract or its breach "will be decided by arbitration," and that the claims directly related to the contract price and all disputes involving price were to be referred initially to the engineer for resolution, the Appellate Court found that the agreement also specifically stated that written notice of a claim or dispute had to be delivered to the engineer within thirty days of its occurrence. The Court concluded that because the owner failed to bring its misrepresentation claims within thirty days, owner waived its right to arbitration.

92009 Indian River Colony Club v. Schopke Constr. & Eng'g, Inc., 592 So. 2d 1185 (Fla. Dist. Ct. App. 1992), *appeal after remand, remanded*, 619 So. 2d 6 (Fla. Dist. Ct. App. 1993)

III: A107–1978, Art. 20, Para. 20.1

III: A107–1978, Art. 20, Para. 20.2

III: A117–1979, Art. 24, Para. 24.1

III: A117–1979, Art. 24, Para. 24.2

III: A201–1976, Art. 14, Para. 14.1.1

III: A201–1976, Art. 14, Para. 14.2.1

III: A201–1976, Art. 14, Para. 14.2.2

III: A401–1978, Art. 14, Para. 14.1.1

III: A401–1978, Art. 14, Para. 14.2.1

I: B141–1977, Art. 10, Para. 10.1

I: B141–1977, Art. 10, Para. 10.2

II: B141–1977, Art. 10, Para. 10.3

II: B141–1977, Art. 10, Para. 10.4

In construction manager's breach of contract action against owner, arising from termination of the contract, the Circuit Court awarded damages to construction manager. The District Court of Appeal reversed as to the amount of damages. Paragraph 10.3 of the termination provisions of the owner-construction manager contract was similar to the termination provisions contained in Article 10 of the American Institute of Architects

III:	A117–1987, Art. 14, Para. 14.12	
III:	A117–1987, Art. 22, Para. 22.1	
III:	A201–1987, Art. 3, Para. 3.18.1	
III:	A201–1987, Art. 10, Para. 10.1.4	
III:	A201–1987, Art. 11, Para. 11.1	
III:	A401–1987, Art. 4, Para. 4.6.1	

Contractor asserted a claim against its subcontractor for indemnity "to the extent of the insurance specified in the subcontract agreement" with respect to a claim by subcontractor's injured employee. The trial court had ruled, on a motion for summary judgment, that the duty to purchase insurance under subcontract provisions relating to the subcontractor's indemnification of the contractor was valid and enforceable. The trial court had held that the subcontract required the subcontractor to maintain insurance for purposes of indemnifying the contractor, but the Appellate Court reversed, characterizing the subcontract with respect to such insurance as an unenforceable indemnification agreement pursuant to Minnesota statute. The Minnesota Supreme Court reversed the holding of the Appellate Court.

The subcontract required the subcontractor to "maintain and pay for such insurance as may be required by the general contract . . . and to obtain, maintain and pay for such general liability insurance coverage and endorsements as will insure the provision of this paragraph." The paragraph referred to contained a provision indemnifying the contractor from the type of claims ordinarily brought by an injured worker.

The Minnesota High Court noted that the statute at issue excepted from its general prohibition agreements requiring a party to provide specific insurance coverage for the benefit of others. Thus, the Court declared, the contractor was entitled to the benefit of the insurance procured by the subcontractor in accordance with the subcontract.

92008d Huntington Woods v. Ajax Paving Indus., Inc., 196 Mich. App. 71, 492 N.W.2d 463 (1992)

III:	A107–1978, Art. 8, Para. 8.5	
III:	A107–1978, Art. 13, Para. 13.2	
III:	A117–1979, Art. 12, Para. 12.5	
III:	A117–1979, Art. 17, Para. 17.2	
III:	A201–1976, Art. 2, Para. 2.2.7	
III:	A201–1976, Art. 2, Para. 2.2.9	
III:	A201–1976, Art. 2, Para. 2.2.10	
III:	A201–1976, Art. 2, Para. 2.2.12	
III:	A201–1976, Art. 7, Para. 7.9.1	
III:	A201–1976, Art. 7, Para. 7.9.2	

The Subcontractor agrees to assume entire responsibility and liability for all damages or injury to all persons, whether employees or otherwise, and to all property, arising out of, resulting from or in any manner connected with, the execution of the work provided for in this Subcontract or occurring or resulting from the use by the Subcontractor, his agents or employees of material, equipment, instrumentalities or other property, whether the same be owned by the Contractor, the Subcontractor or third parties, and the Subcontractor agrees to indemnify and save harmless the Contractor, his agents and employees from all such claims including, without limiting the generality of the foregoing, claims for which the Contractor may be, or may be claimed to be, liable, and legal fees and disbursements paid or incurred to enforce the provisions of this paragraph, and the Subcontractor further agrees to obtain, maintain and pay for such contractual liability insurance coverage as will insure the provisions of this paragraph.

The Court concluded that where the dispute concerned parallel obligations in both subcontracts, apportionment was justified on the grounds that the party seeking contribution had conferred a benefit on the party from whom it sought payment.

The Court then addressed the sheet metal subcontractor's argument that its subcontract had no force or effect because the sheet metal subcontractor had subcontracted its work to the sub-subcontractor. Subcontractor argued that the language referring to injuries "arising out of, resulting from or in any manner connected with, the execution of the work provided for in this Subcontract . . . occurring or resulting from the use by the Subcontractor, his agents or employees of material, equipment, instrumentalities or other property, whether the same be owned by the Contractor, the Subcontractor or third parties . . . ," required the subcontractor to assume liability for the use of equipment by its agents and employees, not its subcontractors. Alleging that no agent or employee of subcontractor was involved in the accident, subcontractor contended that the agreement did not clearly and unequivocally impose an obligation upon subcontractor to indemnify contractor. The Court found that the weakness in subcontractor's argument was that it disregarded the primary factor triggering indemnity, namely an injury connected with the execution of the contract. Subcontractor agreed to perform the sheet metal work and then subcontracted its obligation. The sub-subcontract expressly provided that sub-subcontractor assumed all obligations and responsibilities that subcontractor had assumed in connection with the work. Although the worker's injuries occurred while he was performing work under the electrical subcontract, the Court found that the injuries resulted from negligence by sub-subcontractor's employees in the performance of the sheet metal subcontractor's subcontract. Furthermore, the fact that sub-subcontractor was discharging the subcontractor's obligations defeated subcontractor's argument that the contribution was inequitable given subcontractor's identical obligations under the contract and the fact that its own subcontractor was the negligent party.

92008c Holmes v. Watson-Forsberg Co., 488 N.W.2d 473 (Minn. 1992)

   III: A107–1987, Art. 9, Para. 9.12
   III: A107–1987, Art. 17, Para. 17.1

Conditions of the Contract for Construction, Document No. A201, 1976 edition. The "Work" was defined as "electrical work throughout the plant as required by the engineering departments."

After reviewing the contract provisions, the Court found that contractor did unambiguously contract to indemnify owner for owner's own negligence, and that contractor did clearly waive its immunity to suit by an employee under the Workmen's Compensation Act. The Court concluded that even though the jury found the owner to be negligent in causing the accident, the contract unambiguously provided for indemnification. Furthermore, where the clause identical to Paragraph 4.18.2 clearly constituted a waiver of statutory immunity, owner was entitled to indemnification by contractor.

Turning to the question of whether the parties intended for the indemnification obligation to apply under the facts in this case, the Court pointed to language in the contract requiring contractor to indemnify owner "against all claims, damages, losses and expenses including attorneys' fees *arising out of or resulting from the performance of the Work* . . . ." Noting that "Work" was defined in the contract as the performance of "electrical work throughout the plant . . . ," the Court determined that the worker was not in the process of performing electrical work when the accident occurred.

Finally, the Court found that because the owner-contractor agreement did not use the language of the Workmen's Compensation Act, "in the course of employment," to describe the kinds of injuries that were included within contractor's duty to indemnify, but instead expressly required that the worker's loss "arise out of the performance of the Work," the contract language did not clearly include the worker's conduct within the definition of "performance of the Work" and had to be construed as not entitling owner to indemnification from contractor.

92008b   Herter v. Ringland-Johnson-Crowley Co., 492 N.W.2d 672 (Iowa 1992)

> II: A107–1987, Art. 9, Para. 9.12
> II: A117–1987, Art. 14, Para. 14.12
> II: A201–1987, Art. 3, Para. 3.18.1
> II: A201–1987, Art. 10, Para. 10.1.4
> II: A401–1987, Art. 4, Para. 4.6.1

Sheet metal subcontractor and its sub-subcontractor appealed from the judgment of the trial court ordering them to pay one-half of the sum to indemnify contractor where the other one-half was paid by an electrical subcontractor. Both subcontractors were bound by identical indemnification agreements with the contractor. The Supreme Court of Iowa affirmed the judgment of the trial court.

The Court found that although the claim was for contribution, not indemnity, the claim relied on obligations set forth in the subcontracts, which provided in pertinent part as follows:

to pay the contractor. On its face, the Court concluded, the arbitration clause was complete and unambiguous; it specified how disputes were to be settled and did not provide for any exceptions or envisage any conditions.

Furthermore, the Court found that the agreement contained a merger clause which stated that the parties intended to enter into a single completely integrated agreement regarding the project. Article 6 provided that "the Contract Documents, which constitute the entire agreement between the Owner and the Contractor, are listed in Article 7 and, except for modifications issued after execution of this agreement, are enumerated as follows . . . ." After this clause, nine specific documents were enumerated. Article 7 of the contract further elaborated on the meaning of the term "contract documents" as used in Article 6. The Court concluded that, coupled with the specific enumeration of extrinsic items that were part of the contract documents, the clauses established beyond doubt that the parties intended their written contract to be an expression not only of the final agreement as to the terms in the contract but also of the entire agreement they reached. The Court accordingly held that the contract was completely integrated.

92008a   Hershey Foods Corp. v. General Elec. Serv. Co., 422 Pa. Super. 143, 619 A.2d 285 (1992)

> I: A107–1987, Art. 9, Para. 9.12
> I: A107–1987, Art. 10, Para. 10.11
> I: A117–1979, Art. 14, Para. 14.11
> I: A117–1987, Art. 14, Para. 14.12
> I: A201–1976, Art. 4, Para. 4.18.1
> I: A201–1976, Art. 4, Para. 4.18.2
> I: A201–1976, Art. 4, Para. 4.18.2
> I: A201–1987, Art. 3, Para. 3.18.1
> I: A201–1987, Art. 10, Para. 10.1.4
> I: A401–1978, Art. 11, Para. 11.11.1
> I: A401–1987, Art. 4, Para. 4.6.1

Owner brought suit against electrical contractor [hereinafter contractor] seeking indemnification for the amount of damages it incurred as a result of the accidental death of contractor's employee. Owner appealed after the trial court found that it was not entitled to indemnification and granted summary judgment for contractor. Among numerous other issues on appeal were (1) whether contractor agreed to indemnify owner where owner was negligent; (2) whether the contractor waived its immunity under the Workmen's Compensation Act; and (3) whether the worker's injury resulted from the performance of the work. The Appellate Court affirmed the judgment of the trial court.

The owner-contractor agreement contained indemnification provisions identical to Paragraphs 4.18.1, 4.18.2 and 4.18.3 of the American Institute of Architects General

III: A201–1976, Art. 4, Para. 4.18.1
III: A401–1978, Art. 11, Para. 11.11.1

The Appellate Division held that the following indemnification clause clearly exculpated subcontractor from indemnifying either the owner or the construction manager from their own negligent acts: "nothing herein contained shall require the Contractor to provide indemnification against the proportion of any liability for claims which are proven to have arisen from the negligence of the party asked to be defended, indemnified or held harmless."

92008   Hercules & Co. v. Shama Restaurant Co., 613 A.2d 916 (D.C. 1992)

I: A101–1977, Art. 7, Para. 7.2
I: A107–1978, Art. 6, Para. 6.1
I: A107–1978, Art. 7, Para. 7.1
I: A107–1978, Art. 13, Para. 13.2
I: A111–1978, Art. 16, Para. 16.2
I: A117–1979, Art. 10, Para. 10.2
I: A117–1979, Art. 11, Para. 11.1
I: A117–1979, Art. 17, Para. 17.2
I: A201–1976, Art. 1, Para. 1.1.2
I: A201–1976, Art. 7, Para. 7.9.1

Contractor appealed from the trial court's confirmation of an arbitration award in favor of owner on the ground that the arbitration clause had been fraudulently induced. The Appellate Court affirmed the judgment of the trial court.

The parties entered into the American Institute of Architects Abbreviated Form of Agreement Between Owner and Contractor, Document No. A107, 1978 edition, which contained an arbitration clause stating that the parties agreed to have all disputes arising out of the project resolved by independent arbitrators, and a general integration clause stating that the contract "constitute[s] the entire agreement" between the parties.

At issue before the Appellate Court was whether or not the contract was integrated and, if so, whether it was completely or only partially integrated. The Court examined the contract to ascertain the intent of the parties at the time they entered into the agreement, and held that the agreement to arbitrate which contractor signed was unconditional. The agreement provided that "all claims or disputes between [Hercules] and [Shama] arising out of or relating to the Contract Documents or the breach thereof shall be decided by arbitration. . . ." The Court found that the clause did not say that disputes will be sent to arbitration only if the owner was financially sound, or if the owner deposited money into a certain bank account, or if the owner used its construction loan exclusively

The Court concluded that the contract language taken as a whole indicated the owner's intent to retain control over any work not specifically covered by the owner-contractor agreement. The contract did not provide the contractor with an exclusive right to do all extra work necessitated by the construction but not covered by the contract.

92006   F.O. Bailey Co. v. Ledgewood, Inc., 603 A.2d 466 (Me. 1992)

I:	A107–1978, Art. 8, Para. 8.1	
I:	A107–1978, Art. 8, Para. 8.5	
I:	A107–1978, Art. 8, Para. 8.6	
I:	A107–1978, Art. 13, Para. 13.2	
I:	A117–1979, Art. 12, Para. 12.1	
I:	A117–1979, Art. 12, Para. 12.5	
I:	A117–1979, Art. 12, Para. 12.6	
I:	A117–1979, Art. 17, Para. 17.2	
I:	A201–1976, Art. 2, Para. 2.2.2	
I:	A201–1976, Art. 2, Para. 2.2.9	
I:	A201–1976, Art. 2, Para. 2.2.13	
I:	A201–1976, Art. 7, Para. 7.9.1	

The Supreme Court of Maine held that the language of the American Institute of Architects Standard Forms of Agreement Between Owner and Contractor did not set forth a clear and definite intention to make a tenant, F.O. Bailey, a third-party beneficiary of the owner-contractor agreement where the tenant was not mentioned in the contract and, although the building was referred to as the F.O. Bailey Building, F.O. Bailey itself was mentioned only incidentally, appearing on sketches and plans depicting condominium ownership of the building. The Court found that the only direct reference to the tenant was contractor's promise to schedule and coordinate the work so that the tenant and other commercial enterprises could remain open during their normal operating hours. The Court found that the procedure for resolving disputes specifically limited dispute resolution to parties to the contract, with arbitration expressly designated to resolve disputes between owner and contractor, excluding other parties such as tenants. The architect was designated as owner's representative and was authorized to approve or reject work of the contractor and to resolve disputes between the owner and contractor, again, not including tenant. The Court held that the contract language did not generate a fact issue as to a clear intent to create in the tenant an enforceable right as an intended beneficiary.

92007   Harvey v. Mazal American Partners, 179 A.D.2d 1, 581 N.Y.S.2d 748 (1992)

III:	A107–1978, Art. 10, Para. 10.11	
III:	A117–1979, Art. 14, Para. 14.11	

The Appellate Court held that where the arbitration clause stated that "[a]ny controversy or Claim arising out of or related to the Contract, or the breach thereof, shall be settled by arbitration . . . ," and where the owner filed suit against the contractor for deficiencies in the construction of the building alleging, among other things, breach of contract, the owner could not claim that the dispute was not within the scope of the arbitration provision.

92005b   Earth Movers of Fairbanks, Inc. v. State Dept. of Transp. & Pub. Facilities, 824 P.2d 715 (Alaska 1992)

III:	A107–1987, Art. 12, Para. 12.1	
III:	A107–1987, Art. 13, Para. 13.1	
III:	A107–1987, Art. 13, Para. 13.2	
III:	A107–1987, Art. 13, Para. 13.3	
III:	A117–1987, Art. 17, Para. 17.1	
III:	A117–1987, Art. 18, Para. 18.1	
III:	A117–1987, Art. 18, Para. 18.2	
III:	A117–1987, Art. 18, Para. 18.3	
III:	A201–1987, Art. 6, Para. 6.1	
III:	A201–1987, Art. 7, Para. 7.2	
III:	A201–1987, Art. 7, Para. 7.3	

Contractor appealed the judgment of the trial court that contractor did not have an exclusive right under the owner-contractor agreement to perform and receive compensation for any extra work. The Appellate Court affirmed the judgment of the trial court.

The owner-contractor agreement provided that "[t]he Contractor shall perform work for which there is no price included in the Contract wherever it is deemed necessary or desirable in order to complete fully the project. Such work shall be performed in accordance with the specifications and as directed, and will be paid for as provided . . . ." Based on this provision the Court concluded that it was reasonable for contractor to expect to perform and be compensated for all extra work. However, the contract also provided that the owner "reserves the right at any time to contract for and perform other or additional work on or near the work covered by the contract. . . ." The Court concluded that this provision clearly reserved the owner's right to perform additional work.

Furthermore, the contract provided that "it is distinctly understood and agreed that no claim for additional work or materials, done or furnished by the Contractor and not specifically herein provided for, will be allowed by the Contracting Officer, nor shall the Contractor do any work or furnish any material not covered by this Contract, unless such work is ordered in writing by the Contracting Officer . . . ." The Court concluded that this provision clearly stated that the owner was only liable to compensate the contractor for work performed pursuant to owner's written authorization. In this case the owner did not authorize the contractor to perform the extra work.

The owner/contractor also argued that the trial court erred in awarding the subcontractor quantum meruit delay damages where the subcontract provided a remedy. The Court held that Paragraph 11.9.1 was designed to cover situations where there is "changed or revised work" on written order from the contractor. The subcontractor's claim for labor and equipment inefficiency, according to the Court, did not encompass such items. The claim was for labor and equipment inefficiencies attributable to owner/contractor delays and interruptions. The trial court did award the subcontractor damages for plan changes and other extras which conceivably would fall within the terms of Paragraph 11.9.1 but these claims were exclusive of the labor and equipment inefficiency award. Furthermore, the Court held that since Paragraphs 11.2.2, 11.4.2 and 11.9.1 did not specify remedies they did not foreclose the relief granted by the trial court.

92005a   D. Wilson Constr. Co. v. McAllen Indep. School Dist., 848 S.W.2d 226 (Tex. Ct. App. 1992)

I: A107–1987, Art. 10, Para. 10.8
I: A117–1987, Art. 15, Para. 15.8
I: A201–1987, Art. 4, Para. 4.5.1
I: A201–1987, Art. 4, Para. 4.5.2
I: A201–1987, Art. 4, Para. 4.5.3
I: A201–1987, Art. 4, Para. 4.5.4
I: A201–1987, Art. 4, Para. 4.5.5
I: A201–1987, Art. 4, Para. 4.5.6
I: A201–1987, Art. 4, Para. 4.5.7
I: A401–1987, Art. 6, Para. 6.1
I: A401–1987, Art. 6, Para. 6.2
I: A401–1987, Art. 6, Para. 6.3
I: A401–1987, Art. 6, Para. 6.4
I: A401–1987, Art. 6, Para. 6.5
I: B141–1987, Art. 7, Para. 7.1
I: B141–1987, Art. 7, Para. 7.2
I: B141–1987, Art. 7, Para. 7.3
I: B141–1987, Art. 7, Para. 7.4

Contractor appealed the trial court's refusal to compel arbitration of its dispute with owner. The Appellate Court reversed the judgment of the trial court and ordered the court to compel arbitration.

The owner-contractor agreement included general conditions which authorized arbitration pursuant to a paragraph numbered 4.5, which was identical to the arbitration provision contained in the American Institute of Architects General Conditions of the Contract for Construction, Document No. A201, 1987 edition.

I: A401–1978, Art. 11, Para. 11.3.1
I: A401–1978, Art. 11, Para. 11.4.2
I: A401–1978, Art. 11, Para. 11.9.1
I: A401–1978, Art. 11, Para. 11.10.1

Owner/contractor appealed an adverse decision following a bench trial in an action to set aside subcontractor's lien.

The owner/contractor and subcontractor entered into a grading contract and a utilities contract which were the American Institute of Architects Standard Form of Agreement Between Contractor and Subcontractor, Document No. A401, 1978 edition. The grading subcontract called for a start work date and a completion date as soon as possible, but not later than 80 workdays after the start date. The utilities subcontract called for a start work date and a completion date as soon as possible, but not later than 60 workdays after the start date. Both subcontracts provided in a renumbered Paragraph 11.3.1 that "The Subcontractor shall secure and pay for all permits, fees and licenses necessary for the execution of the Work described in the Contract Documents as applicable to this Subcontract." A renumbered Paragraph 11.10.1 provided that "the Subcontractor shall make all claims promptly to the Contractor for additional work, extensions of time, and damage for delays or otherwise, in accordance with the Contractor Documents." A renumbered Paragraph 11.9.1 provided that "The Subcontractor shall make any and all changes in the Work from the Drawings and Specifications of the Contract documents without invalidating this Subcontract when specifically ordered to do so in writing by the Contractor. The Subcontractor, prior to the commencement of such changed or revised work, shall submit promptly to the Contractor written copies of the cost or credit proposal for such revised Work in a manner consistent with the Contract Documents." The contract required the subcontractor to cooperate with the contractor and others whose work might interfere with the subcontractor, and stated that the subcontractor would cooperate with the contractor in scheduling.

The owner/contractor argued on appeal that the damages for which the subcontractor filed a lien were attributable to delays in acquiring the necessary permits that the subcontractor was contractually obligated to obtain. The Court held that there was substantial evidence that the owner/contractor never relied on the subcontractor to secure the permits and instead undertook such obligations itself. Furthermore, the owner/contractor never mentioned, relied upon or sought to enforce Paragraph 11.3.1 during the course of subcontractor's performance. The Court concluded that where the owner/contractor gave the subcontractor every indication that it would take care of the permits the owner/contractor could not assert breach of Paragraph 11.3.1.

The Court held that because the subcontract did not contain a clause relieving the subcontractor of unanticipated soil conditions but did not require the subcontractor to conduct independent tests, the subcontractor was entitled to rely on the soils report and on the representations of the owner/contractor that the soils were suitable in entering into the subcontracts.

The Appellate Court held that the provision clearly made the subcontractor responsible for its work and the words used made the provision a release coupled with an indemnity. The Court found that typical indemnity language was "indemnify, save, protect, save/hold harmless." Release language was generally "release, discharge, relinquish." Both types of language appeared in the subcontract. Subcontractor argued that all of the words used were general words of indemnity that could be used interchangeably. However, the Court ruled that the use of all of these words, separated by the "and" in the same provision, showed an intent to release as well as indemnify. The Court found that the language in the parenthetical further strengthened its interpretation when the differences between a release and an indemnity provision were considered. The parenthetical language made the provision applicable whether the damage was to a third person or his property or to the parties themselves. The Court recognized that parties often included this language in indemnity provisions; however, when this language was coupled with the release language, it provided further proof that the clause was more than a mere indemnity provision.

The indemnity clause was limited by a clause which provided that:

As a limitation on the foregoing . . . , Subcontractor shall have no duty to indemnify or defend Contractor for claims, demands, or causes of action not involving the negligence of the Subcontractor or those from whom the Subcontractor is responsible. With respect only to such claims, demands, or causes of action covered by this subparagraph (a)(ii), Contractor, provided Contractor or its employees were negligent, will owe the obligation to indemnify and to defend to Subcontractor.

The Court found, however, that this limitation was specifically a limitation of subcontractor's duty to indemnify and not a limitation of subcontractor's duty to release the owner, contractor and construction manager.

The final argument made by subcontractor was that because the subcontract was ambiguous, the trial court erred in granting summary judgment in favor of the owner, contractor and construction manager. Subcontractor contended that the release/indemnity provision was in conflict with certain provisions of the owner-contractor agreement which were incorporated by reference into the subcontract. The owner-contractor agreement stated that contractor was responsible for damages to persons or property caused by its own negligence. The Court found that this provision in the owner-contractor agreement could be harmonized with the subcontract so that meaning could be given to all the provisions. The Court construed the provision in the owner-contractor agreement as making the contractor generally liable for damages, and construed the provision in the subcontract as making the subcontractor responsible for any damages to persons or property resulting from its work, thereby alleviating part of the duty imposed on contractor. The Court concluded that there was no conflict between the two unambiguous contracts.

92005 Douglas Northwest, Inc. v. Bill O'Brien & Sons Constr., Inc., 64 Wash. App. 661, 828 P.2d 565 (1992)

I: A401–1978, Art. 11, Para. 11.2.2

In deciding numerous issues on appeal, the Appellate Court interpreted the agreement as clearly and unambiguously expressing the mutual intent of the parties that owner would not assume vicarious contractual liability for untimely performance by its various contractors and would not be liable to plaintiff-contractor for delay damages. Furthermore, the provision merely precluded contractor from recovering damages from owner based upon delay attributable to untimely performance by the other contractors, but it did not authorize owner to recover liquidated damages from the contractor based upon delay which was not attributable to contractor.

The Court found further that owner's actual knowledge of the delay did not act as a waiver of the contractual requirement that contractor request, in writing, an extension of time, as set forth in the agreement which provided in pertinent part that "[i]f the normal progress of the work is delayed for reasons beyond his control, the contractor shall within fifteen days after the start of such a delay, file a written request to the engineer for an extension of time setting forth therein the reasons for the delay which he believes will justify the granting of his request." The Court reasoned that if the owner's mere knowledge were sufficient, the provision requiring timely written request for an extension of time would be meaningless and superfluous.

92004f   Derr Constr. Co. v. City of Houston, 846 S.W.2d 854 (Tex. Ct. App. 1992)

    II: A107–1987, Art. 9, Para. 9.12
    II: A117–1987, Art. 14, Para. 14.12
    II: A201–1987, Art. 3, Para. 3.18.1
    II: A201–1987, Art. 10, Para. 10.1.4
    II: A401–1987, Art. 4, Para. 4.6.1

Subcontractor appealed from the trial court's grant of summary judgment to owner, contractor and construction manager in subcontractor's action for damages to subcontractor's crane. At issue on appeal was whether the subcontractor released, indemnified, or released and indemnified, the owner, contractor and construction manager. The Appellate Court affirmed the judgment of the trial court.

The subcontract required the subcontractor to "assume [] full responsibility and liability for the work to be performed hereunder and hereby release[], relinquish[] and discharge [] and agree [] to indemnify, protect and save harmless Contractor, the City, . . . Construction Administrator . . . from all claims, demands and causes of action of every kind and character including the cost of defense thereof, for any injury to, including death of, persons (whether they be third persons, contractor, or employees of either of the parties hereto) and any loss of or damage to property (whether the same be that either of the parties hereto or of third parties) caused by or alleged to be caused, arising out of, or in connection with Subcontractor's work to be performed hereunder . . . whether or not said claims, demands, and causes of action in whole or in part are covered by insurance . . . ."

owner was liable for negligent breach of an assumed duty which resulted in the worker's injury.

The owner-contractor agreement also provided that "[Owner] and Contractor shall indemnify, defend, and hold the other harmless from claims, demands, and causes of action asserted against the indemnitee by any person (including, without limitation, Contractor's . . . employees . . .) for personal injury . . . resulting from the indemnitor's negligence. . . . Where personal injury . . . is the result of the joint negligence . . . of [Owner] and Contractor, the indemnitor's duty of indemnification shall be in proportion to its allocable share of joint negligence. . . ." The Court, after reviewing the indemnity provision, found that the trial court erred in dismissing the cross-claim because the contractor was not prohibited from contractually agreeing to hold the owner harmless from damages paid to contractor's employee attributable to the joint negligence of the owner and contractor.

92004e   Department of Transp. v. Fru-Con Constr. Corp., 206 Ga. App. 821, 426 S.E.2d 905 (1992)

> II: A107–1987, Art. 12, Para. 12.1
> II: A107–1987, Art. 12, Para. 12.2
> II: A107–1987, Art. 12, Para. 12.3
> II: A107–1987, Art. 14, Para. 14.3
> II: A117–1987, Art. 17, Para. 17.1
> II: A117–1987, Art. 17, Para. 17.2
> II: A117–1987, Art. 17, Para. 17.3
> II: A117–1987, Art. 19, Para. 19.3
> II: A201–1987, Art. 4, Para. 4.3.8
> II: A201–1987, Art. 6, Para. 6.2

Owner appealed the trial court's entry of judgment in favor of contractor in contractor's action seeking the return of liquidated damages withheld by owner from its final payment and damages resulting from owner's breach of contract. The Appellate Court reversed the judgment of the trial court.

The owner-contractor agreement provided that:

When separate contracts are let within the limits of any one project, each contractor shall conduct his work so as not to interfere with or hinder the progress or completion of the work being performed by other contractors. Contractors working on the same project shall assume all liability, financial or otherwise, in connection with his contract and shall protect and save harmless [Owner] from any and all damages or claims that may arise because of inconvenience, delay, or loss experienced by him because of the presence and operations of other contractors working within the limits of the same project.

III: A107–1987, Art. 9, Para. 9.3
III: A107–1987, Art. 16, Para. 16.1
III: A107–1987, Art. 16, Para. 16.2
III: A117–1987, Art. 14, Para. 14.1
III: A117–1987, Art. 14, Para. 14.2
III: A117–1987, Art. 14, Para. 14.3
III: A117–1987, Art. 21, Para. 21.1
III: A117–1987, Art. 21, Para. 21.2
III: A201–1987, Art. 3, Para. 3.3
III: A201–1987, Art. 3, Para. 3.18.1
III: A201–1987, Art. 10, Para. 10.1
III: A201–1987, Art. 10, Para. 10.1.4
III: A201–1987, Art. 10, Para. 10.2
III: A401–1987, Art. 4, Para. 4.6.1

Owner appealed the trial court's dismissal of its cross-claim against contractor seeking indemnification for personal injury damages paid to contractor's employee and the trial court's failure to recognize owner's independent contractor defense. The Appellate Court amended the judgment of the trial court.

The Appellate Court found that where the owner-contractor agreement provided that "Contractor in performing Services hereunder shall be an independent contractor and not an agent or employee of [Owner]," the owner was insulated from liability for the negligent acts of the contractor by virtue of contractor's status.

The contract also contained the following provision:

Although Contractor shall provide its own representative(s) to supervise and inspect all materials and workmanship in performance of Work hereunder, [Owner] reserves the right at anytime (sic), to inspect any part of the Work, the materials to be used in the Work, and the construction tools and equipment furnished by Contractor and its subcontractors for use in performing the work. Any materials or workmanship which [Owner] considers unsatisfactory shall be removed and replaced at Contractor's expense. Neither inspection, waiving of inspection, nor acceptance by [Owner] shall relieve Contractor of its obligation to furnish all materials and workmanship in accordance with specifications of each Release.

In considering this provision, the court held that the owner's daily inspections of the job site to insure that the work was being performed in accordance with the specifications did not constitute exercise of supervision and control over contractor's work. However, the Court found that where the owner voluntarily assumed the task of monitoring the job site for violations of safety standards, and where the contract provided that the "Contractor shall provide a safe place to work for its employees . . ." and "shall . . . enforce such operating practices as are necessary to provide a safe place to work," the

weather conditions, leaks in an aeration basin caused by deficient design, and sewerage overflows, Article 10 on its face did not confer authority upon the engineer to make binding decisions regarding the requests for time extensions nor did that provision give the engineer the authority to make binding decisions regarding the claims for additional compensation. Furthermore, the record indicated that other contract provisions designated the owner as the exclusive entity to consider and determine the merit of contractor's requests for time extensions and additional compensation. The provisions which specifically pertained to claims submitted for additional time and compensation conclusively established the limited scope of authority conferred by Article 10. After considering the contract as a whole, the Court found that Article 10 did not pertain to questions regarding the contractor's claims.

92004c Centex-Rodgers Constr. Co. v. McCann Steel Co., 206 Ga. App. 827, 426 S.E.2d 596 (1992), *cert. denied*, 1993 Ga. LEXIS 343 (Ga. Apr. 8, 1993)

    II: A201–1987, Art. 13, Para. 13.4.1
    II: A401–1987, Art. 6, Para. 6.5

Contractor brought an action for breach of contract against subcontractor seeking damages for delay in fabricating, delivering and erecting structural steel on a construction project. Granting subcontractor's motion for partial summary judgment, the trial court found that the liquidated damage clause contained in the owner-contractor agreement, which limited subcontractor's liability, was incorporated by reference into the subcontract. On contractor's appeal, the Appellate Court reversed.

The Appellate Court held that where the subcontract contained a provision which stated that "[n]o right or remedy in the subcontract is intended to be exclusive of any other right or remedy, but every right or remedy shall be cumulative and shall be in addition to and not a limitation of any duties, obligations, rights and remedies otherwise imposed or available by law," and where the provisions of the subcontract controlled, contractor was not limited to the liquidated damages stated in the general contract. The Court found that because the liquidated delay damage provision purported to limit contractor's right to actual damages, a right which would otherwise be available by law, it conflicted with the paragraph of the subcontract which provided that any right or remedy provided for in the subcontract would not limit any right or remedy otherwise available by law. The Court concluded that the subcontract controlled and the liquidated delay damages provision was ineffective.

92004d Crane v. Exxon Corp., U.S.A., 613 So. 2d 214 (La. Ct. App. 1992), *cert. denied in part, remanded*, 620 So. 2d 858, 1993 La. LEXIS 2278 (La. 1993)

    III: A107–1987, Art. 9, Para. 9.1
    III: A107–1987, Art. 9, Para. 9.2

II:	A107–1987, Art. 10, Para. 10.5
II:	A107–1987, Art. 10, Para. 10.8
II:	A117–1987, Art. 15, Para. 15.1
II:	A117–1987, Art. 15, Para. 15.2
II:	A117–1987, Art. 15, Para. 15.5
II:	A117–1987, Art. 15, Para. 15.8
II:	A201–1987, Art. 4, Para. 4.2.1
II:	A201–1987, Art. 4, Para. 4.2.11
II:	A201–1987, Art. 4, Para. 4.2.12
II:	A201–1987, Art. 4, Para. 4.2.13
II:	A201–1987, Art. 4, Para. 4.3.2
II:	A201–1987, Art. 4, Para. 4.3.7
II:	A201–1987, Art. 4, Para. 4.3.8
II:	B141–1987, Art. 2, Para. 2.6.4
II:	B141–1987, Art. 2, Para. 2.6.15
II:	B141–1987, Art. 2, Para. 2.6.16
II:	B141–1987, Art. 2, Para. 2.6.17
II:	B141–1987, Art. 2, Para. 2.6.18
II:	B141–1987, Art. 2, Para. 2.6.19

Contractor brought suit against owner after the project engineer denied contractor's requests for time extensions and additional compensation. Granting summary judgement to owner, the trial court held that the engineer's determination of the validity of the contractor's claims fell within the scope of the engineer's authority as set forth in the owner-contractor agreement. Appealing, the contractor argued that the trial court erred in interpreting the general conditions of the owner-contractor agreement as vesting in the engineer the final, conclusive and unappealable authority to determine the validity of contractor's requests for time extensions and additional compensation. The Appellate Court reversed the judgment of the trial court.

The owner-contractor agreement provided in Article 10 that:

Engineer shall act as the Owner's representative during the construction period. He shall decide questions which may arise as to the quality and acceptability of products furnished and work performed. He shall interpret the intent of the Contract Documents in a fair and unbiased manner. The Engineer will make visits to the site and determine if the work is proceeding in accordance with the Contract Documents. He shall judge as to the accuracy of quantities submitted by the contractor in partial payment estimates and the acceptability of the work which these quantities represent. The decision of the Engineer shall be final and conclusive and binding upon all parties to the contract.

The Appellate Court found that where the contractor had submitted requests for extensions of time and additional compensation to the engineer resulting from abnormal

III: B141–1987, Art. 2, Para. 2.6.18
III: B141–1987, Art. 2, Para. 2.6.19

Owner appealed the trial court's grant of summary judgment to contractor which was based on the court's finding that the engineer, acting as the owner's agent, was authorized to approve contractor's cost overruns. The owner argued on appeal that the trial court erred in granting the contractor summary judgment based on a contract provision that was void as against public policy. The Appellate Court reversed the judgment of the trial court.

The owner-contractor agreement provided that:

The Engineer shall in all cases determine the amount, quality, acceptability and fitness of the several kinds of work and materials which are to be paid for under this contract, shall determine all questions in relation to said work and decide every question of the fact which may arise relative to the fulfillment of this contract on the part of the Owner and on the part of the Contractor. His estimate and decisions shall be final and conclusive upon both parties of this contract.

The Appellate Court held in several earlier cases that provisions in contracts which attempt to divest the courts of jurisdiction concerning a dispute arising from a contract or provisions that make the decision of a certain person conclusive as to all disputes arising in connection with an agreement are void as against public policy. The Court found that in this case, however, it was clear from reading the provision in context that it did not attempt to divest the courts of jurisdiction or make the decision of the engineer conclusive as to all disputes arising from the contract. Rather, the purpose of the provision, as the Court interpreted it, was to give the engineer authority to make the decisions that had to be made daily on the site without the need to consult with representatives of the owner and contractor. The Court read the provision as limited because the parties did not contend that the trial court was without authority to resolve the dispute that gave rise to this appeal.

Turning to the issue of whether summary judgment was properly granted to the contractor, the Court held that where (1) the contract stated that "[n]o oral statement of any person whomsoever in any manner or degree shall modify or otherwise affect the terms of this Contract," (2) it was undisputed that a valid change order was not executed for the work, and (3) the owner did not waive the requirement that the engineer's orders be in writing or that written change orders were required by the contract, there remained an issue of material fact precluding the trial court's grant of summary judgment to contractor.

92004b C.B.I. Na-Con, Inc. v. Macon Bibb County Water & Sewerage Auth., 205 Ga. App. 82, 421 S.E.2d 111 (1992).

II: A107–1987, Art. 10, Para. 10.1
II: A107–1987, Art. 10, Para. 10.2

III: A107–1978, Art. 10, Para. 10.1
III: A107–1978, Art. 16, Para. 16.1
III: A117–1979, Art. 12, Para. 12.3
III: A117–1979, Art. 14, Para. 14.1
III: A117–1979, Art. 20, Para. 20.1
III: A201–1976, Art. 2, Para. 2.2.4
III: A201–1976, Art. 4, Para. 4.3.1
III: A201–1976, Art. 10, Para. 10.1.1
III: A201–1976, Art. 10, Para. 10.2.1
III: B141–1977, Art. 1, Para. 1.5.5

The Appellate Court found that the architect did not owe a duty to a worker injured in a slip-and-fall accident while working in an asbestos decontamination unit. The accident was not related to the architect's job functions or area of expertise, and the owner-architect agreement relieved the architect of responsibility for site safety. The architect's obligation under the contract was to determine that the asbestos could be removed without causing a health risk. The architect's project manager was responsible for checking the containment areas and the decontamination units for the narrowly defined purpose of seeing whether or not there was any asbestos release or potential for release. The project manager had the power to stop work if there was a danger of asbestos release, however, he was not empowered to stop work for all other potential safety hazards, such as the one that injured the worker. Furthermore, the architect was not required to control safety on the job site, which, under the owner-contractor agreement, was the responsibility of the contractor. The decontamination unit had been designed, constructed and maintained by the contractor, and the owner-architect agreement clearly provided that the architect was not responsible for the means or methods of construction.

92004a Caribbean Lumber Co. v. Anderson, 205 Ga. App. 415, 422 S.E.2d 267 (1992)

III: A107–1987, Art. 10, Para. 10.8
III: A117–1987, Art. 15, Para. 15.8
III: A201–1987, Art. 4, Para. 4.3.1
III: A201–1987, Art. 4, Para. 4.3.2
III: A201–1987, Art. 4, Para. 4.4.1
III: A201–1987, Art. 4, Para. 4.4.4
III: A201–1987, Art. 4, Para. 4.5.1
III: B141–1987, Art. 2, Para. 2.6.15
III: B141–1987, Art. 2, Para. 2.6.16
III: B141–1987, Art. 2, Para. 2.6.17

indemnification clause less than clear and unequivocal. Moreover, the contractor did not cite any authority involving that clause or similar language.

92003a Burns & McDonnell Eng'g Co. v. Torson Constr. Co., 834 S.W.2d 755 (Mo. Ct. App. 1992)

I:	A107–1978, Art. 10, Para. 10.11	
I:	A107–1987, Art. 9, Para. 9.12	
I:	A117–1979, Art. 14, Para. 14.11	
I:	A117–1987, Art. 14, Para. 14.12	
I:	A201–1976, Art. 4, Para. 4.18.1	
I:	A201–1987, Art. 3, Para. 3.18.1	
I:	A201–1987, Art. 10, Para. 10.1.4	
I:	A401–1978, Art. 11, Para. 11.11.1	
I:	A401–1987, Art. 4, Para. 4.6.1	
I:	A201–1976, Art. 4, Para. 4.18.1	

Engineer filed an indemnity action against contractor for attorney's fees and costs pursuant to the indemnity clause in the owner-contractor agreement, which clause was identical to Paragraph 4.18.1 of the American Institute of Architects General Conditions of the Contract for Construction, Document No. A201, 1976 edition. The trial court granted summary judgment to contractor on the grounds that engineer failed to file its claim for indemnity and breach of contract within the limitations period prescribed by state statute. On engineer's appeal, the Appellate Court reversed the decision of the trial court.

The Appellate Court found that where a contract indemnified for both loss and liability, and where the contract was not limited to a single item of liability or loss but included any amounts which might be recovered, the statute of limitations for bringing a claim on indemnity did not begin to run until all the loss or damage was sustained by the indemnitee. In addition, language in the contract provided that contractor would indemnify and hold engineer harmless against all "damages, losses and expenses, including attorney's fees." The Court held that this language contemplated indemnification for "loss." Furthermore, the contractor also agreed to indemnify and hold engineer harmless against all "claims." The use of the word "claims" indemnified engineer from any liability which it might incur. As used in Paragraph 4.18.1, the term "claim" was interpreted by the Court as referring to indemnity against liability.

92004 Busick v. Streator Township High School Dist. #40, 234 Ill. App. 3d 647, 175 Ill. Dec. 423, 600 N.E.2d 46 (1992)

III:	A107–1978, Art. 8, Para. 8.3	

B181, which provided that the "Architect shall conduct inspections to determine the Dates of substantial completion and final completion, and shall issue a final Certificate for Payment." The agreement also provided that the attached HUD "Amendment to AIA Document B181, Appendix 2, 4460.1 REV. CHG" was a part of the agreement. The HUD amendment provided that the provisions of the amendment would supersede and void all inconsistent provisions of the agreement. Relative to substantial completion, the amendment provided that the "Architect shall issue Certificates of Payment and Certificates of Substantial Completion. These certificates shall be in the form prescribed by HUD/FHA." The amendment also required the owner and architect to perform all services in accordance with applicable HUD/FHA requirements.

The Appellate Court reversed the judgment of the trial court, holding that the owner-contractor agreement provided that the date of substantial completion would be the date the HUD representative signed the HUD Representative's Trip Report. Furthermore, the Court found that neither the owner-architect agreement nor certain other HUD forms were intended to amend the terms of the owner-contractor agreement. The Court found that the owner-architect agreement clearly required the architect to conduct inspections to determine the dates of substantial completion and to issue certificates of payment and substantial completion "in the form prescribed by HUD/FHA." In addition, for limitations purposes the critical agreement was the one between the owner and the contractor, and not the one between the owner and architect.

92003 Burns v. DeWitt & Assocs., Inc., 826 S.W.2d 884 (Mo. Ct. App. 1992)

I: A107–1978, Art. 10, Para. 10.11
I: A117–1979, Art. 14, Para. 14.11
I: A201–1976, Art. 4, Para. 4.18.1
I: A401–1978, Art. 11, Para. 11.11.1

Architect brought an indemnification action against the contractor to recover attorneys' fees incurred in defending a personal injury action brought by subcontractor's employee. The trial court entered summary judgment for the architect and the contractor appealed. Among contractor's arguments on appeal was that there was a genuine issue of material fact as to whether or not the indemnification clause in the general conditions of the contract contained clear and unequivocal language that would have allowed the architect to be indemnified for its own negligence. The Appellate Court found contractor's appeal frivolous and affirmed the judgment of the trial court.

The owner and contractor entered into an American Institute of Architects Standard Form of Agreement Between Owner and Contractor, which included the American Institute of Architects General Conditions of the Contract for Construction, Document No. A201, 1976 edition.

The Appellate Court found that contractor's argument consisted of general abstract statements and did not point to any ambiguity which made the language of the

arbitration on the grounds that it was not a party to the contract and did not sign an agreement to arbitrate.

The trial court had denied owner's ensuing petition to compel arbitration. Recognizing contrary authority in other states, the Appellate Court adopted the federal rule binding a performance bond surety by an arbitration clause in the owner-contractor agreement or subcontract to which surety was not a party but which was incorporated into the bond by reference. The Appellate Court concluded that surety had agreed to be bound by the arbitration provision in Paragraph 7.9.1 where the terms of the owner-contractor agreement were incorporated into the bond.

The Court rejected the surety's alternative arguments. The Court concluded that the owner had not waived its right to compel arbitration by delaying its demand for three years because surety failed to show prejudice resulting from the delay. Finally, the Court deferred to the arbitrator the surety's argument that the bond's statute of limitations provision barred owner's demand for arbitration.

92002 Brookridge Apartments, Ltd. v. Universal Constructors, Inc., 844 S.W.2d 637 (Tenn. Ct. App. 1992)

II:	A107–1987, Art. 10, Para. 10.4	
II:	A117–1987, Art. 15, Para. 15.4	
II:	A201–1987, Art. 4, Para. 4.2.5	
II:	A201–1987, Art. 4, Para. 4.2.9	
II:	B141–1987, Art. 2, Para. 2.6.9	
II:	B141–1987, Art. 2, Para. 2.6.10	
II:	B141–1987, Art. 2, Para. 2.6.14	

Owner brought an action against contractor and architect for negligent design, construction and inspection of an apartment complex. The trial court held that owner's cause of action was barred by the statute of limitations because the parties never established by written agreement a date of substantial completion.

The owner and contractor entered into a HUD form contract which provided that the date of substantial completion "shall be the date the HUD Representative signs the final HUD Representative's Trip Report provided that the trip report is subsequently endorsed by the chief Architect." If the work was not substantially completed by a fixed date the contract provided that the contractor's fee would be reduced by an agreed upon amount as liquidated damages for each day of delay until the date of substantial completion. The contract further provided that changes in any terms of the contract documents required the prior written approval of owner's lender and the Federal Housing Commissioner. The contract designated the architect as the design architect and the architect in charge of administering the construction contract.

The owner and architect entered into the American Institute of Architects Standard Form of Agreement Between Owner and Architect for Housing Services, Document No.

owner for the negligence of the City or the negligence of the asphalt contractor. If the clause required this, the indemnification would arise from the language "resulting in any manner directly or indirectly from or in connection with or in the course of the work." The Court found that this phrase clearly contemplated a loss that resulted from the owner's negligence, because the concluding portion of the clause excluded indemnification where the loss was caused solely by the owner's negligence. There would have been no reason to exclude indemnification for a loss caused by the owner's sole negligence unless the parties intended to include loss caused in whole or in part by the owner's negligence within the phrase "resulting in any manner directly or indirectly from or in connection with or in the course of the work." If the parties intended to include in "the work" loss caused in whole or in part by the owner's negligence, there was no reason to suppose they did not also intend to include within the coverage of this phrase loss caused in whole or in part by others, such as the City and the asphalt contractor. Therefore, the Court concluded that the clause required the installation contractor to indemnify the owner for any liability caused solely through the combined negligence of the owner, contractor, installation and asphalt contractors, and the City.

92001b   Boys Club of San Fernando Valley, Inc. v. Fidelity & Deposit Co. of Maryland, 6 Cal. App. 4th 1266, 8 Cal. Rptr. 2d 587 (1992)

	II:	A107–1978, Art. 13, Para. 13.2
	II:	A117–1979, Art. 17, Para. 17.2
	I:	A201–1976, Art. 7, Para. 7.9.1
	II:	A401–1978, Art. 13, Para. 13.1
	II:	B141–1977, Art. 9, Para. 9.1
	II:	B141–1977, Art. 9, Para. 9.2
	II:	B141–1977, Art. 9, Para. 9.3

Owner appealed the denial of its petition to compel a performance-bond surety to join the owner and contractor in arbitration proceedings. The Appellate Court reversed.

The owner-contractor agreement, which provided for the construction of a recreational facility, contained an arbitration clause identical to Paragraph 7.9.1 of the American Institute of Architects General Conditions of the Contract for Construction, Document No. A201, 1976 edition. Pursuant to the agreement, contractor obtained a performance bond from surety naming owner as obligee. The owner-contractor agreement, including the General Conditions, were incorporated into the bond. The bond provided that, if contractor were declared by owner to be in default under the contract, surety could remedy the default, complete the contract itself, or have the work completed by another contractor.

After the facility was completed, owner complained of defects and withheld final payment on the grounds that contractor failed to perform in a workmanlike manner. Owner filed a demand for arbitration against contractor. About three years later, owner amended its demand, naming surety as an additional party. Surety refused to join the

92001   Allen & O'Hara, Inc. v. Bartlett Wrecking, Inc., 964 F.2d 694 (7th Cir. 1992)

    II: A101–1977, Art. 5
    II: A107–1978, Art. 4, Para. 4.2
    II: A111–1978, Art. 14, Para. 14.3
    II: A117–1979, Art. 9, Para. 9.2
    II: A401–1978, Art. 5, Para. 5.4
    II: B141–1977, Art. 14, Para. 14.6

The Court of Appeals held that because the contract provided for interest on payments due and unpaid under the contract, the party was entitled to prejudgment interest.

92001a   Beitzel v. City of Coeur d'Alene, 121 Idaho 709, 827 P.2d 1160 (1992)

    II: A107–1987, Art. 9, Para. 9.12
    II: A117–1987, Art. 14, Para. 14.12
    II: A201–1987, Art. 3, Para. 3.18.1
    II: A201–1987, Art. 10, Para. 10.1.4
    II: A401–1987, Art. 4, Para. 4.6.1

Owner and City appealed the trial court's judgment denying them indemnity from installation contractor and asphalt contractor. Judgment was based on the court's finding that where the owner was negligent, the indemnity clause in the owner-installation contractor agreement was void and unenforceable under state statute. The Appellate Court reversed the judgment of the trial court.

The owner-installation contractor agreement provided that:

Contractor shall indemnify and save [Owner] free and harmless from and against all loss or exposure by reason of liability imposed by law upon [Owner] for damages because of personal injury, including the death at any time resulting therefrom sustained by any person or persons; or destruction or damage to property belonging to [Owner], as well as to property belonging to third persons, resulting in any manner directly or indirectly from or in connection with or in the course of the work, or by any act of Contractor, his employees or agents; provided, however, that Contractor shall not be responsible for any such injury, destruction or damage caused solely by the negligence of [Owner] in connection with the work.

The Appellate Court found that the clause did not require the installation contractor to indemnify the owner if the worker's injuries were caused solely by the owner's negligence. The clause clearly required the installation contractor to indemnify the owner for any negligence of the installation contractor, its employees or agents. There was no specific provision in the contract requiring the installation contractor to indemnify the

Construing the contract provisions in the context of the agreement as a whole, the Court of Appeals found that the architect did not expressly or impliedly have control over or assume any responsibility for construction site supervision or safety, including alerting construction workers and others affected by the construction of potential hazards at the site. Therefore, the Court held that the total absence of contractual responsibility for site supervision and safety precluded the architect's liability in tort for claims of common law negligence regarding site safety.

91040 Yow v. Hussey, Gay, Bell & DeYoung Int'l, Inc., 201 Ga. App. 857, 412 S.E.2d 565 (1991), *cert. denied,* 1992 Ga. LEXIS 116 (Ga. 1992), *remanded,* Hussey, Gay, Bell & DeYoung Int'l v. Clay-Ric, Inc. 212 Ga. App. 53, 441 S.E.2d 274 (Ga. Ct. App. 1994)

II:	A107-1978, Art. 8, Para. 8.1
II:	A107-1978, Art. 8, Para. 8.3
II:	A107-1978, Art. 10, Para. 10.1
II:	A107-1978, Art. 10, Para. 10.7
II:	A107-1978, Art. 16, Para. 16.1
II:	A117-1979, Art. 12, Para. 12.1
II:	A117-1979, Art. 12, Para. 12.3
II:	A117-1979, Art. 14, Para. 14.1
II:	A117-1979, Art. 14, Para. 14.7
II:	A117-1979, Art. 20, Para. 20.1
I:	A201-1976, Art. 2, Para. 2.2.2
I:	A201-1976, Art. 2, Para. 2.2.4
I:	A201-1976, Art. 4, Para. 4.3.1
I:	A201-1976, Art. 4, Para. 4.3.2
I:	A201-1976, Art. 10, Para. 10.1.1
I:	A201-1976, Art. 10, Para. 10.2.1
I:	A201-1976, Art. 10, Para. 10.2.2
I:	B141-1978, Art. 1, Para. 1.5.2
I:	B141-1978, Art. 1, Para. 1.5.3
I:	B141-1978, Art. 1, Para. 1.5.5

A non-construction worker brought a personal injury action against the architect/consulting engineer. The trial court granted architect summary judgment. The Court of Appeals affirmed.

The owner and architect had entered into an American Institute of Architects Abbreviated Form of Agreement Between Owner and Architect for Construction Projects of Limited Scope. It provided in Paragraph 1.4.4 that "the Architect shall provide administration of the construction contract." It also contained a provision similar to Paragraph 2.2.2 of the General Conditions. The owner and contractor had entered into the American Institute of Architects Standard Form of Agreement Between Owner and Contractor, Document No. 101, 1977 edition, which incorporated the American Institute of Architects General Conditions of the Contract for Construction, Document No. A201, 1976 edition, specifically Paragraph 2.2.2, 2.2.4, 4.3.1, 4.3.2, and the safety requirements of Article 10.

I: A201-1976, Art. 12, Para. 12.1.1
I: A201-1976, Art. 12, Para. 12.1.2

Contractor brought a breach of contract action against owner and claimed quantum meruit damages. After a bench trial the court awarded the contractor breach of contract damages and quantum meruit damages. The owner appealed, and the Appellate Court affirmed.

The owner and contractor entered into the American Institute of Architects Standard Form of Agreement Between Owner and Contractor, Document No. A111, 1978 edition, which included the American Institute of Architects General Conditions of the Contract for Construction, Document No. A201, 1976 edition. The contract required written change orders for extras and provided in pertinent part that "the owner would not be responsible for any changes in excess of the stated cost of work unless it was duly executed by Katie Franks, Inc." The Court also cited Paragraph 2.2.2 of the General Conditions, which provided that the architect would be the owner's representative during construction.

The Appellate Court held that because the owner-contractor agreement required written change orders for extras, and because the architect had accepted extra work done on oral change orders in connection with the contract and the owner had made payment, the owner waived the contract clause providing that no claims for extra work or material would be allowed unless made by written change order.

91039 Woodburn v. Consolidation Coal Co., 404 Pa. Super. 359, 590 A.2d 1273 (1991)

III: A107-1978, Art. 10, Para. 10.11
III: A117-1979, Art. 14, Para. 14.11
III: A201-1976, Art. 4, Para. 4.18.1
III: A401-1978, Art. 11, Para. 11.11.1

Affirming the judgment of the trial court, the Superior Court held that the indemnification clause in the subcontract required the subcontractor to indemnify the contractor for liability caused by contractor's own negligence. The last clause of the provision stated that "such indemnification and hold harmless shall not apply to claims for injury or alleged injury or death to persons, or damage to property (other than loss of, damage to, or loss of use of SUBCONTRACTOR'S property) caused by the sole negligence of Consol. or INDUSTRIAL." The Court found that this clause could be construed to infer negatively that any injuries occurring by less than the sole fault of the contractor fell within the scope of the clause.

The Appellate Court found that within the meaning of the agreement, "occasioned" meant "bring about," and "irrespective of" meant "regardless of." The Court construed the terms of the indemnity provision to mean that contractor would indemnify construction manager from liability "brought about" by contractor's own acts "regardless of" construction manager's own negligence. The Court concluded that the terms of the indemnity provision were clear and unambiguous and evidenced contractor's intent to indemnify construction manager for its own acts of negligence. The construction manager had the right to enforce the indemnification clause in the owner-contractor agreement as a third-party beneficiary of the contract. Finally, under the terms of the clause, contractor was liable to construction manager for all legal expenses incurred in defending injured worker's action.

91037   Wenzel v. Boyles Galvanizing Co., 920 F.2d 778 (11th Cir. 1991)

  III: A107-1978, Art. 8, Para. 8.3
  III: A107-1978, Art. 16, Para. 16.1
  III: A117-1979, Art. 12, Para. 12.3
  III: A117-1979, Art. 20, Para. 20.1
  III: A201-1976, Art. 2, Para. 2.2.4
  III: A201-1976, Art. 10, Para. 10.1.1

The Appellate Court found that an architect, acting as both architect and construction manager, was responsible for job site safety. The architect, in its capacity as construction manager, contractually assumed the responsibility for site safety by specifically agreeing to "provide, implement and administer a site safety and health program." The means, methods and procedures clause exculpating the architect from liability did not apply to the architect acting in its capacity as construction manager and did not satisfy state law. That provision stated only that the architect was not liable for the manner in which the project was constructed; it said nothing about architect's own negligence. In order to satisfy state law the clause would have had to state clearly that architect was released from liability for its own negligence. Accordingly, the Court affirmed the judgment against the architect/construction manager.

91038   Winn-Senter Constr. v. Katie Franks, Inc., 816 S.W.2d 943 (Mo. Ct. App. 1991)

  II: A107-1978, Art. 8, Para. 8.1
  II: A107-1978, Art. 18, Para. 18.1
  II: A117-1979, Art. 12, Para. 12.1
  II: A117-1979, Art. 22, Para. 22.1
  I: A201-1976, Art. 2, Para. 2.2.2

The Appellate Court reversed on the basis that the indemnity provision failed to meet the state's statutory requirements for indemnification of an indemnitee for its own negligent acts. The Arizona Supreme Court disagreed and affirmed the trial court's decision.

Paragraph 4.18.1 required the contractor to indemnify the owner "regardless of whether or not [the injury] is caused in part by a party indemnified hereunder." The Supreme Court determined that these words clearly and unequivocally protected the owner against its own active negligence. The words "caused in part" were broad enough to encompass behavior that included the owner's active negligence. Through the use of such broad language, the parties contemplated coverage for any type of damage caused by the negligent behavior of the indemnitor—even if the damage was also caused in part by the active negligence of the indemnitee. The Court held that where the agreement clearly and unequivocally indicated that one party was to be indemnified, regardless of whether or not the injury was caused in part by that party, indemnification was required notwithstanding the indemnitee's active negligence.

91036a   Waterwiese v. KBA Constr. Managers, Inc., 820 S.W.2d 579 (Mo. Ct. App. 1991)

II:	A107–1978, Art. 10, Para. 10.11
II:	A117–1979, Art. 14, Para. 14.11
II:	A201–1976, Art. 4, Para. 4.18.1
II:	A401–1978, Art. 11, Para. 11.11.1

Construction manager and its general liability insurance carrier brought a third-party indemnification action against contractor to recover the amount of the settlement paid to contractor's injured employee. The trial court entered judgment for construction manager and its insurer in the full amount of the settlement. Contractor appealed. The Appellate Court affirmed the judgment of the trial court.

The owner-contractor agreement required the contractor to provide and maintain during the life of the contract liability insurance "for protection of the Owner, the Construction Manager and the Consultant protecting them against the standard hazards, except liability from operation of trucks and automobiles, and with the amount of coverage provided in the Public Liability and Property Damage Insurance of Contractor. . . ." In addition, the contractor agreed to "indemnify and save harmless Owner and Consultant and Construction Manager, their agents, servants and employees, from and against any and all liability for damage arising from injuries to persons or damage to property occasioned by any acts or omissions of Contractor, any subcontractors, agents, servants or employees, including any and all expense, legal or otherwise, which may be incurred by Owner or Consultant or Construction Manager, its agents, servants or employees, in defense of any claim, action or suit, irrespective of any claims that an act, omission or negligence of Owner or Consultant or Construction Manager, its agents, servants or employees contributed to such injury or damage."

I: A117-1979, Art. 10, Para. 10.2
I: A401-1978, Art. 15, Para. 15.2

Owner brought a breach of contract action against contractor. Contractor moved to dismiss the complaint on the ground that the contract incorporated by reference an agreement to arbitrate. The trial court overruled the motion, and the Court of Appeals affirmed.

The parties had entered into the American Institute of Architects Standard Form of Agreement Between Owner and Contractor, Document No. A101, 1977 edition. The face of the contract read "Use only with the 1976 Edition of AIA Document A201, General Conditions of the Contract for Construction." The American Institute of Architects General Conditions of the Contract for Construction, Document No. A201, 1976 edition, contained an agreement to arbitrate in Paragraph 7.9.1. Article 1 stated that the contract documents consisted of "this agreement, the conditions of the contract, (general, supplementary and other conditions), the drawings, the specifications, all addenda issued prior to and all modifications issued after the execution of this agreement." It was then stated in clear language that these formed the contract and were incorporated as if they were attached to the agreement or repeated therein. Article 1 also stated that an "enumeration of the contract documents appears in Article 7." However, the contract documents were not enumerated in Paragraph 7.2.

The Court of Appeals found that the contract documents were not enumerated in Paragraph 7.2, no description of the general conditions was given, and no directions were given to the owners as to where to find the general conditions. Thus, the contract was ambiguous with respect to the general conditions, which contained the arbitration provision. Because the contract's reference to the arbitration clause was unclear, the contract, viewed in its entirety, created an ambiguity which was litigable as to whether the parties agreed to arbitration. Therefore, the trial court properly overruled contractor's motion to dismiss the owner's complaint.

91036   Washington Elementary School Dist. No. 6 v. Baglino Corp., 169 Ariz. 58, 817 P.2d 3 (1991)

II: A107-1978, Art. 10, Para. 10.11
II: A117-1979, Art. 14, Para. 14.11
I: A201-1976, Art. 4, Para. 4.18.1
II: A401-1978, Art. 11, Para. 11.11.1

Owner brought a third-party indemnification action against contractor. The trial court ruled that the indemnity provision in the American Institute of Architects General Conditions of the Contract for Construction, Document No. A201, 1976 edition, obligated the contractor to indemnify the owner for losses where the owner was actively negligent.

Affirming, the Court of Appeal found that the Paragraph 11.3.6 waiver applied to insurance required by Paragraph 11.3.1 "or any other property insurance applicable to the Work. . . ." The Court concluded that the owner had clearly waived its claims against the contractor, subcontractor and sub-subcontractor, and that if the owner cannot bring an action against the contractors or subcontractors, "neither may the insurer in subrogation, since the rights of the insurer are not superior to those of the owner."

91034   Taylor v. Allegretto, 112 N.M. 410, 816 P.2d 479 (1991)

>   I: A107-1978, Art. 7, Para. 7.1
>   I: A117-1979, Art. 11, Para. 11.1
>   I: A201-1976, Art. 1, Para. 1.1.1
>   I: A201-1976, Art. 1, Para. 1.2.3

Contractor brought an action against owner, seeking recovery for breach of contract and for additional work. Judgment was entered in favor of owner. The Supreme Court reversed. Paragraph 7.1 of the American Institute of Architects Abbreviated Form of Agreement Between Owner and Contractor, Document No. A107, 1978 edition, stated in pertinent part that "[t]he Contract Documents are complementary, and what is required by anyone shall be as binding as if required by all. Work not covered in the Contract Documents will not be required unless it is consistent therewith and reasonably inferable therefrom as being necessary to produce the intended results."

The Court found that the clause making all contract documents complementary could only be reasonably read to require that the documents complemented each other insofar as they were consistent. Where the language of the agreement, particularly typed-in language on a printed form contract, specifically indicated that the parties intended to limit the scope of the work to be performed, it was not consistent to expand the agreement because the plans as originally drawn included additional work.

Furthermore, the Court found that the intent of the clause contemplating performance of necessary work not included in the contract documents was to include within the contract the performance of minor tasks which, although not specifically described in the plans, were nevertheless necessary to fully accomplish the work envisioned by the contract. Moreover, the clause specifically required that additional work be not only "necessary" but also "consistent" with the contract documents. Therefore, the trial court erred in finding that certain work, specifically construction of the entire building shell, was covered by the parties' agreement.

91035   Traynham v. Yeargin Enter., Inc., 304 S.C. 188, 403 S.E.2d 329 (Ct. App. 1991)

>   I: A101-1977, Art. 7, Para. 7.2
>   I: A107-1978, Art. 6, Para. 6.1
>   I: A111-1978, Art. 16, Para. 16.2

Furthermore, the disputes provision had to be read in conjunction with the changes provision in the contract where the contractor's claim was for a change in the contract price. The Court concluded that there was no support for the owner's argument that the contractor had to provide additional information to the engineer before bringing suit where it was not clear how the parties elected to compute the amount due for changes.

91032   S.K. Whitty & Co. v. Laurence L. Lambert & Assocs., 576 So. 2d 599 (La. Ct. App.), *cert. denied,* 580 So. 2d 928 (La. 1991)

> III: A201-1976, Art. 2, Para. 2.2.2
> III: A201-1976, Art. 2, Para. 2.2.18

The Appellate Court found that state law provided a cause of action allowing the subcontractor to recover for engineer's preconstruction negligence where subcontractor alleged that the engineer failed to exercise the standard of care normally exercised by reasonable and prudent engineers in preparing plans and specifications. The subcontract contained a provision stating that "[i]n carrying out any of the contract provisions, or in exercising any power or authority granted to him by this contract, there should be no liability upon the engineer, his authorized representative, or any official of the owner, either personally or as an official of the owner." The Court found that this exculpatory clause did not proscribe recovery since the contract did not exist at the time the plans were prepared. Furthermore, the exculpatory clause referred to liability on the part of the engineer in "carrying out any of the contract provisions," not in preparing the provisions.

91033   State v. United States Fidelity & Guar. Co., 577 So. 2d 1037 (La. Ct. App.), *cert. denied,* 581 So. 2d 684 (La. 1991)

> II: A107-1978, Art. 17, Para. 17.6
> II: A117-1979, Art. 21, Para. 21.6
> I: A201-1976, Art. 11, Para. 11.3.6

Owner's insurer brought a subrogation action against contractor, subcontractor and sub-subcontractor for fire damages resulting from their negligence. The trial court granted partial summary judgment in favor of defendants, finding that the owner-contractor agreement contained an express provision under which owner's insurer waived its subrogation rights. Owner's insurer appealed arguing that the damages were paid under a fire policy which was not obtained pursuant to the contract, therefore, the waiver provision did not apply.

The owner-contractor agreement incorporated by reference the American Institute of Architects General Conditions of the Contract for Construction, Document No. A201, 1976 edition, specifically Paragraph 11.3.6. Paragraph 11.3.1 was amended to require the owner to carry insurance for the project and it defined the type and amount of insurance.

II:	A107-1978, Art. 18, Para. 18.3
II:	A117-1979, Art. 12, Para. 12.1
II:	A117-1979, Art. 12, Para. 12.5
II:	A117-1979, Art. 22, Para. 22.1
II:	A117-1979, Art. 22, Para. 22.3
II:	A201-1976, Art. 2, Para. 2.2.2
II:	A201-1976, Art. 2, Para. 2.2.7
II:	A201-1976, Art. 2, Para. 2.2.8
II:	A201-1976, Art. 2, Para. 2.2.9
II:	A201-1976, Art. 12, Para. 12.1.1
II:	A201-1976, Art. 12, Para. 12.1.3
II:	A201-1976, Art. 12, Para. 12.1.4
II:	A201-1976, Art. 12, Para. 12.4.1
II:	B141-1978, Art. 1, Para. 1.5.3
II:	B141-1978, Art. 1, Para. 1.5.9

In contractor's action for additional compensation, owner moved to dismiss complaint on the ground that contractor failed to exhaust the contractual remedies prior to filing suit. The District Court denied owner's motion to dismiss and ordered the parties to proceed with discovery.

The owner-contractor agreement contained numerous provisions (similar to Paragraphs 2.2.2, 2.2.7. 2.2.8, 2.2.9, 12.1.1, 12.1.3, 12.1.4 and 12.4.1 of the American Institute of Architects General Conditions of the Contract for Construction, Document No. A201, 1976 edition) which authorized the engineer to make initial decisions on disputes between the parties. The parties deleted the clause which provided that "all claims for adjustments in the Contract Price shall be determined by the Engineer if the Owner and the Contractor cannot otherwise agree on the amount involved."

The Court therefore found that the contractor's submission of claims to the engineer was not a condition precedent to bringing suit because the contract contained no express language precluding arbitration or litigation absent initial referral to the engineer or prior to issuance of the engineer's final decision. The contract did not adequately define the procedures to limit the time within which the engineer could retain authority over the claims, and the District Court interpreted the disputes provision as only giving the engineer a mediator's role during the work in progress. The disputes provision was in the article entitled "Engineer's Status During Construction." A reasonable reading, according to the Court, was that the article required the contractor to submit to the engineer individual claims for additional compensation and similar matters at the time claims arose while the project, or any portion thereof, was in progress. The engineer had a "reasonable time" within which to provide a written response to contractor's requests. The contract did not define or limit the "reasonable time" allowed for engineer's decision.

person, or for injury or damage to property (including but not limited to adjoining and adjacent property, buildings, driveways, walks, yards) caused or alleged to have been caused by the CONTRACTOR or any of CONTRACTOR'S subcontractors, or the employees or agents of either or any of them in connection with work performed by reason of this order."

The purpose of the insurance provision was to protect the owner from the consequences of its own negligence. Construing the hold harmless and insurance provisions together, the Court concluded that the owner and contractor clearly intended that owner would be indemnified for its own negligence. The Court found further that the contractor need indemnify the owner only to the minimum amounts stated in the agreement and not to the greater amount set forth in the insurance policy. The Court reversed the trial court's judgment to the extent it provided otherwise.

91030   Shepherd Components, Inc. v. Brice Petrides-Donohue & Assocs., Inc., 473 N.W.2d 612 (Iowa 1991)

   II: A107-1978, Art. 8, Para. 8.3
   II: A117-1979, Art. 12, Para. 12.3
   II: A201-1976, Art. 2, Para. 2.2.3
   II: A201-1976, Art. 2, Para. 2.2.4
   II: B141-1978, Art. 1, Para. 1.5.4
   II: B141-1978, Art. 1, Para. 1.5.5

The Supreme Court of Iowa found that the engineer did not owe a duty under the owner-engineer agreement to an adjacent landowner to prevent damage to property. The owner-engineer agreement contained provisions similar to Paragraphs 1.5.4 and 1.5.5 of the American Institute of Architects Standard Form of Agreement Between Owner and Architect, Document No. B141, 1978 edition. The Court found that under these provisions the engineer was responsible for preventing any apparent defects or deficiencies in contractor's work but had no power to control the work performed. The contract further provided that the purpose of the engineer's on-site review services was not to protect the public from unreasonable work methods and means, but to protect the owner by assuring the quality of work performed. Moreover, the Court found that the owner-contractor agreement placed the entire responsibility for avoiding damage to adjoining property on the contractor. Consequently, the trial court erred in not granting the engineer's motion for a directed verdict.

91031   Shook of West Virginia, Inc. v. York City Sewer Auth., 756 F. Supp. 848 (M.D. Pa. 1991)

   II: A107-1978, Art. 8, Para. 8.1
   II: A107-1978, Art. 8, Para. 8.5
   II: A107-1978, Art. 18, Para. 18.1

but actually delivered and stored at the construction site. The Court concluded that this material, not incorporated in the work, was to be insured by the contractor to protect the owner's interest because only when the owner paid for the material did the owner clearly have an insurable interest.

91028   Riggi v. Wade Lupe Constr. Co., 176 A.D.2d 1177, 575 N.Y.S.2d 613 (1991)

I: A201-1976, Art. 2, Para. 2.2.12

In owner's action to stay arbitration of contractor's mechanic's lien claim, the Appellate Division held that the demand for arbitration was timely. Paragraph 2.2.12 of the American Institute of Architects General Conditions of the Contract for Construction, Document No. A201, 1976 edition, provided for a thirty day period in which to demand arbitration when the written decision of the architect so requires. The Court explained that this thirty day limit did not apply where the architect's decision did not explicitly state that any demand for arbitration had to be made within thirty days. The Court construed the contract language as providing under such circumstances that the demand for arbitration had to be made within a reasonable time, which it was. Accordingly, the Court affirmed the trial court's denial of stay.

91029   Rupp v. American Crystal Sugar Co., 465 N.W.2d 614 (N.D. 1991)

III: A107-1978, Art. 10, Para. 10.11
III: A107-1978, Art. 17, Para. 17.1
III: A117-1979, Art. 14, Para. 14.11
III: A117-1979, Art. 21, Para. 21.1
III: A201-1976, Art. 4, Para. 4.18.1
III: A201-1976, Art. 11, Para. 11.1.1
III: A201-1976, Art. 11, Para. 11.1.2
III: A201-1976, Art. 11, Para. 11.1.3
III: A401-1978, Art. 9, Para. 9.1
III: A401-1978, Art. 11, Para. 11.11.1

Owner brought an indemnification action against contractor. The trial court entered judgment for owner. Contractor argued on appeal that the indemnification clause did not cover damages caused by owner's negligence. The Supreme Court affirmed the judgment regarding the indemnification.

The owner-contractor agreement provided that contractor carry liability insurance with specified minimums naming owner as an additional insured and further provided that "The CONTRACTOR agrees to pay on behalf of and hold harmless American Crystal Sugar Company, OWNER, its directors, officers, and employees from all loss, costs, damage and/or expense arising out of any demand, claim, suit or judgment for damages or injuries to any person, firm or corporation whatsoever . . . or for the death of any

of the defect. The Court upheld the ruling of the trial court that the owner was responsible only for the contractor's time and labor involved in making a determination as to whether or not repair work was required, and, where no actual work was required, the owner was not responsible for the costs of the contractor's crew and equipment since the contractor did not sustain its burden of establishing that it had a contractual right to recover the entire amount claimed.

The Court then found that there was an additional basis not raised by the parties on which to affirm the trial court's judgment. The first sentence of the "Uncovering of Work" provision required the contractor to "promptly furnish all necessary facilities, labor, and material" if, before final acceptance of the entire work, the owner considered it necessary to make an examination of the previously completed work "by uncovering the same." The remaining two sentences of the provision stated the factors controlling the determination of who was responsible for the costs of any such examination. The Court concluded that the portions that allocated responsibility for costs applied only when the owner required the uncovering of a portion of previously completed work. The parties presented no evidence that contractor's employees "uncovered" any of the work or were directed by the owner to uncover the work. The Court concluded that the contractor was not entitled to recover under the contract language and contractor asserted no other grounds for recovery under any other contract provisions.

91027   Rapp Constr. Co. v. Jay Realty Co., 809 S.W.2d 490 (Tenn. Ct. App. 1991)

III:	A107-1978, Art. 7, Para. 7.4	
III:	A107-1978, Art. 17, Para. 17.3	
III:	A117-1979, Art. 11, Para. 11.3	
III:	A117-1979, Art. 21, Para. 21.3	
II:	A201-1976, Art. 1, Para. 1.1.3	
II:	A201-1976, Art. 9, Para. 9.3.2	
II:	A201-1976, Art. 11, Para. 11.3.1	

Contractor sued owner to recover the cost of pipe destroyed by a fire. The trial court held in favor of owner, finding that it had no obligation to insure the pipe. The Court of Appeals affirmed.

The owner-contractor agreement required the owner to purchase and maintain property insurance "upon the Work at the site to the full insurable value thereof," and "Work" was defined as "furnishing labor and furnishing and incorporating materials and equipment into the construction. . . ." Consequently, the owner's liability did not extend to insuring contractor's materials stored on the site but not incorporated into the project. Furthermore, the payment provisions evidenced the parties intent that once the construction materials became a part of the realty the risk of loss shifted to the owner and was to be insured by the owner, for, in addition to making an application for payment covering "the work completed as of the date of the application," the provision allowed the contractor to request payment for materials and equipment not incorporated into the work

the presumption that the parties contracted only for themselves. The subcontracts made no reference to the Association or its members, and did not express an intent to directly benefit either the Association or its members. Specific provisions in the construction contracts regarding guarantees to be provided by the contractor and the subcontractors did not mention the unit owners. The provisions entitled "Additional Construction Warranty for Condominium Unit Purchasers" and "Warranty to Condominium Purchasers" provided that the owner would furnish warranties to each unit owner. The Court found that even though there was no question that the parties were aware that the building was being built for subsequent purchasers, it was not enough that the parties knew, expected or even intended that the owners would benefit where they were not referred to in the contracts. The owner and contractor had entered into an American Institute of Architects Standard Form of Agreement Between Owner and Contractor, which included the American Institute of Architects General Conditions of the Contract for Construction, Document No. A201, 1976 edition, supplementary general conditions, general requirements specifications and architectural, engineering and shop drawings. The subcontract incorporated by reference the terms and conditions of the owner-contractor agreement.

91026 Prairie Land Constr., Inc. v. Modesto, 213 Ill. App. 3d 364, 157 Ill. Dec. 191, 571 N.E.2d 1210 (1991)

  Ill: A201-1976, Art. 13, Para. 13.1.1
  Ill: A201-1976, Art. 13, Para. 13.1.2

The "Uncovering of Work" provision in the owner-contractor agreement provided that "[s]hould it be considered necessary or advisable by the Local Public Agency at any time before final acceptance of the entire work to make an examination of the work already completed by uncovering the same, the Contractor shall on request promptly furnish all necessary facilities, labor, and material. If such work is found to be defective in any important or essential respect, due to fault of the Contractor or his subcontractors the Contractor shall defray all the expenses of such examination and of satisfactory reconstruction. If, however, such work is found to meet the requirements of the Contract, the actual cost of labor and material necessarily involved in the examination and replacement, plus 15 percent of such costs to cover superintendence, general expenses and profit, shall be allowed the Contractor and he shall, in addition, if completion of the work of the entire Contract has been delayed thereby, be granted a suitable extension of time on account of the additional work involved." The Appellate Court found that the provision was ambiguous because the words "necessarily involved in the examination and replacement" were capable of being understood in more than one sense. The Court found that under the facts of the case the words could mean the labor necessarily involved in examining the water system for a suspected defect included having a complete crew and the requisite equipment present when a suspected water leak was investigated so repairs could begin immediately; or the words could have meant that having a complete repair crew and equipment present when the water system was examined for a suspected defect was not labor necessarily involved in examining the system, so long as a repair crew and equipment could be obtained in a reasonable amount of time after discovery

warranty of fitness of the design; breached his implied duty to supervise the project's construction; negligently designed the building; negligently supervised the construction; and fraudulently concealed known or suspected design deficiencies, preventing the owner from discovering the cause of the problems. The architect moved for summary judgment on the ground that owner's claims were barred by the statute of limitations. The trial court denied the architect's motion on the ground that since the owner had consulted with the architect and was assured that there was no problem the architect was equitably estopped from relying on a statute of limitations defense. After presentation of the owner's case the court again denied the architect's statute of limitations defense, reserved ruling on the owner's contract claims and granted the architect a directed verdict on the warranty issue. At the close of the evidence the architect again moved for a directed verdict on the statute of limitations defense and the breach of contract claim. The court denied the motion on the timeliness issue but dismissed the contract claim. The court also refused to allow the fraud claim to go to the jury. The jury found that the architect did not negligently design the project but did negligently breach the contract. The owner was awarded damages. The architect then moved for judgment notwithstanding the verdict, raising the timeliness issue for the fourth time. The owner moved for prejudgment interest. Both motions were denied, and both parties appealed.

The appellate court upheld the numerous rulings of the trial court. The Court found that the trial court did not err in allowing the owner's expert to testify on the architect's standard of care where the architect was obligated under the contract to supervise construction of the building, utilizing the ordinary care exercised by members of his profession. The expert did not testify that the architect was an insurer against defects in the project. The Court held that expert testimony on the custom of the architectural profession constituted rebuttable proof aimed at assisting the trier of fact in determining whether the architect had negligently performed the contract. Furthermore, the testimony aided the jury in establishing whether the architect had fulfilled the contract with care, skill, reasonable expediency, and faithfulness according to the standards of the profession.

91025 155 Harbor Drive Condominium Ass'n v. Harbor Point, 209 Ill. App. 3d 631, 154 Ill. Dec. 365, 568 N.E.2d 365 (1991)

II:	A107-1978, Art. 10, Para. 10.4
II:	A117-1979, Art. 14, Para. 14.4
I:	A201-1976, Art. 4, Para. 4.5.1
I:	A201-1976, Art. 13, Para. 13.2.2
III:	A401-1978, Art. 11, Para. 11.7.1

Condominium association appealed the dismissal of its action against a joint venture developer, contractor, subcontractors, and others. The Appellate Court upheld the ruling of the trial court that the association could not maintain a third-party beneficiary action against the contractor and subcontractors for breach of the warranties contained in the owner-contractor agreement and the subcontracts. The Association failed to identify any language in the subcontract that constituted a virtual express declaration to overcome

applicable to the Work, except such rights as they may have to the proceeds of such insurance held by the Owner as trustee.

Based on these provisions, the Appellate Court found that the parties manifested the intention that the insurance provided by contractor on behalf of owner was to protect against any personal liability to both contractor and owner. When insurance is provided as part of a business bargain, "the agreement must be interpreted as providing mutual exculpation to the bargaining parties. The parties are thus deemed to have agreed to look solely to the insurance in the event of loss, and not impose liability on the other." The Court therefore held that owner could not claim the right of contribution after it had been defended, and the intent of the contract had been fulfilled.

91023 Moore Heating & Plumbing, Inc. v. Huber, Hunt & Nichols, 583 N.E.2d 142 (Ind. Ct. App. 1991)

III: A107-1978, Art. 10, Para. 10.11
III: A117-1979, Art. 14, Para. 14.11
III: A201-1976, Art. 4, Para. 4.18.1
III: A401-1978, Art. 11, Para. 11.11.1

In contractor's third party action against subcontractor for indemnification of personal injury damages awarded to subcontractor's employee, the Court of Appeals found that the indemnification provision was valid under the state statute. It was enforceable because it contained an express reference to indemnification for damages resulting from contractor's own negligence. The clause provided for liability for damages from any cause directly or indirectly relating to any action or failure to act by the subcontractor, whether or not the contractor contributed to the alleged wrongdoing or was liable due to a nondelegable duty. The clause then stated that the parties intended the indemnity to cover liability to the fullest extent permitted by law, except that subcontractor need not indemnify contractor for contractor's sole negligence when such would be contrary to law. The indemnity clause contemplated "liability, damages, actions, omissions, duties, and causation," words which clearly, unequivocally, and expressly provided that the indemnification clause applied to contractor's negligence.

91024 Northern Montana Hosp. v. Knight, 248 Mont. 310, 811 P.2d 1276 (1991)

III: A107-1978, Art. 8, Para. 8.3
III: A117-1979, Art. 12, Para. 12.3
III: A201-1976, Art. 2, Para. 2.2.3
III: A201-1976, Art. 2, Para. 2.2.4
III: B141-1977, Art. 1, Para. 1.5.4
III: B141-1977, Art. 1, Para. 1.5.5

Owner brought an action against the architect alleging that the architect had negligently breached his express and implied contractual duties; breached the contract's implied

91022 Monical v. State Farm Ins. Co., 211 Ill. App. 3d 215, 155 Ill. Dec. 619, 569 N.E.2d 1230 (1991)

II:	A107-1978, Art. 17, Para. 17.1
II:	A107-1978, Art. 17, Para. 17.2
II:	A107-1978, Art. 17, Para. 17.3
II:	A107-1978, Art. 17, Para. 17.4
II:	A107-1978, Art. 17, Para. 17.6
II:	A117-1979, Art. 21, Para. 21.1
II:	A117-1979, Art. 21, Para. 21.2
II:	A117-1979, Art. 21, Para. 21.3
II:	A117-1979, Art. 21, Para. 21.4
II:	A117-1979, Art. 21, Para. 21.6
I:	A201-1976, Art. 11, Para. 11.1.1
I:	A201-1976, Art. 11, Para. 11.1.2
I:	A201-1976, Art. 11, Para. 11.1.3
I:	A201-1976, Art. 11, Para. 11.1.4
I:	A201-1976, Art. 11, Para. 11.3.1
I:	A201-1976, Art. 11, Para. 11.3.6

In owner's third-party action against contractor for contribution, the Circuit Court granted summary judgment in contractor's favor. The Appellate Court affirmed. The insurance provisions contained in Article 11 of the American Institute of Architects General Conditions of the Contract for Construction, Document No. A201, 1976 edition, were amended to provide that contractor was responsible for obtaining insurance for the owner as well as for itself. Paragraphs 11.1.1, 11.1.2, 11.1.3 and 11.1.4 were deleted and the following paragraph 11.1.1 was substituted:

> The Contractor shall purchase and maintain comprehensive general liability insurance as required to protect himself, the Architect and the Owner from claims set forth below which may arise out of or result from operations of the Contractor or any Subcontractor under the Contract. . . . Approval of the insurance by the Owner shall not relieve or decrease the liability of the Contractor. The Owner does not in any way represent that the insurance or the limits of insurance specified in these articles are sufficient or adequate to protect the Contractor's interests of liabilities, but are minimums. . . .

Paragraphs 11.3.1 and 11.3.6 were deleted and the following paragraph 11.3.6 was substituted:

> The Owner and Contractor waive all rights against (1) each other and the Sub-Contractors, Sub-subcontractors, agents and employees each of the other, and (2) the Architect and separate contractors, if any, and their subcontractor, sub-subcontractors, agents and employees, for damages caused by fire or other perils to the extent covered by insurance obtained pursuant to this Paragraph 11.3 or any other property insurance

I: A201-1976, Art. 8, Para. 8.3.2
I: A201-1976, Art. 12, Para. 12.1.1
I: A201-1976, Art. 12, Para. 12.1.2
I: A201-1976, Art. 12, Para. 12.3.1

Contractor brought an action against owner for enforcement of a mechanics lien and for breach of contract on the grounds that owner had terminated the contract before the project was completed and had ceased to make payments to the contractor. The owner counterclaimed that the contractor had breached the contract by failing to substantially complete the first two phases of the project on time, by failing to perform its duties in a "skilled and workmanlike manner," by completing two of four phases at a cost in excess of fifty percent of the total project cost, and by charging the owner for costs there were not to be reimbursed under the contract. The breach of contract claims were tried to a jury, which returned a verdict for contractor. The trial court denied the owner's motion for judgment notwithstanding the verdict or in the alternative for a new trial, and the owner appealed. Among the issues on appeal were whether the contractor had a submissible case on its breach of contract claim and whether the owner was entitled to judgment on its counterclaim as a matter of law.

The owner and contractor entered into the American Institute of Architects Standard Form of Agreement Between Owner and Contractor, Document No. A111, 1978 edition, specifically Article 4: Time of Commencement and Substantial Completion, Article 5: Cost of the Work and Guaranteed Maximum Cost, Article 6: Contractor's Fee, Article 7: Changes in the Work, and Article 8: Costs to be Reimbursed. The agreement included the American Institute of Architects General Conditions of the Contract for Construction, Document No. A201, 1976 edition, specifically Paragraphs 8.3.1, 8.3.2, 12.1.1, 12.1.2 and 12.3.1.

The Appellate Court first addressed the owner's argument that the contractor had not complied with the terms of the contract, specifically Paragraphs 12.3.1, 8.3.1 and 8.3.2 and was therefore precluded from recovery for owner's breach. The Court found that the contractor's obligation under the contract to prepare written change orders was an issue for the jury since the contract was ambiguous in establishing the guaranteed maximum costs that could not be exceeded without a written change order.

The Court then addressed the owner's argument that the contractor breached the contract by failing to follow the provisions in Paragraphs 8.3.1 and 8.3.2 of the General Conditions regarding extensions of time. The owner claimed that Paragraph 8.3 was a "no fault" provision that required contractor to request an extension of time in writing even if the delay was caused "by any act or neglect of the Owner." The Court concluded that on the facts the contractor did not, as a matter of law, breach the contract provisions requiring it to request in writing extensions of time. The matter was properly for the jury. The Court held that because questions about contractor's compliance with the contractual provisions regarding change orders and requests for extensions of time limits were jury questions, the trial court did not err in denying owner's motion for judgment notwithstanding the verdict.

hereunder shall not be limited by the provisions of any workmen's compensation or similar act."

The Appellate Court concluded that since the jury found that the prime subcontractor was not solely at fault, the prime subcontractor was entitled to indemnity from the structural steel subcontractor. Furthermore, the trial court should have found as a matter of law that the injured worker was engaged in "work" as contemplated by the contract where the evidence presented at trial clearly established that the worker was, at the time of the injury, taking down a steel structure at the job site.

91020   McGee Constr. Co. v. Neshobe Dev., Inc., 156 Vt. 550, 594 A.2d 415 (1991)

II:	A107-1978, Art. 8, Para. 8.5
II:	A117-1979, Art. 12, Para. 12.5
II:	A201-1976, Art. 2, Para. 2.2.9

In contractor's action for breach of contract, judgment was entered against owner. Affirming in part, the Supreme Court found that there was sufficient evidence showing that the failure to engage in the contractual claims procedure was not wholly attributable to contractor. The contractual language was similar to Paragraph 2.2.9 of the American Institute of Architects General Conditions of the Contract for Construction, Document No. A201, 1976 edition. It stated that "claims . . . shall be referred initially to the Architect. . . ." but did not specify which party was obligated to refer a claim to the architect. Consequently, the contract could be interpreted as requiring referral by either party.

91021   Midwest Materials Co. v. Village Dev. Co., 806 S.W.2d 477 (Mo. Ct. App. 1991)

III:	A107-1978, Art. 14, Para. 14.3
III:	A107-1978, Art. 18, Para. 18.1
III:	A107-1978, Art. 18, Para. 18.2
III:	A107-1978, Art. 18, Para. 18.3
I:	A111-1978, Art. 4
I:	A111-1978, Art. 5
I:	A111-1978, Art. 6
I:	A111-1978, Art. 7
I:	A111-1978, Art. 8
III:	A117-1979, Art. 18, Para. 18.3
III:	A117-1979, Art. 22, Para. 22.1
III:	A117-1979, Art. 22, Para. 22.2
III:	A117-1979, Art. 22, Para. 22.3
I:	A201-1976, Art. 8, Para. 8.3.1

contractually obligated itself, before proceeding with any part of the work, to give the contractor written notification of "any errors in or inconsistencies between or in any of the Contract Documents." The Court concluded that architect/engineer's and subcontractor's responsibilities to the contractor were separate and distinct. Under the subcontract the subcontractor assumed complete responsibility for its work and had no right to transfer to the architect/engineer the responsibility subcontractor owned to contractor by way of shop drawings reviewed by the architect/engineer.

Furthermore, after reviewing the trial testimony, the Court found that the subcontractor/supplier was entitled to a jury instruction that clearly stated that the subcontractor was estopped by its silence from asserting a claim against the subcontractor/supplier if the jury found that the subcontractor had not informed the contractor that the louvers did not meet the specifications.

91019   McDevitt & Street Co. v. Mosher Steel Co., 574 So. 2d 794 (Ala. 1991)

	III:	A107-1978, Art. 7, Para. 7.4
	III:	A107-1978, Art. 10, Para. 10.11
	III:	A117-1979, Art. 11, Para. 11.4
	III:	A117-1979, Art. 14, Para. 14.11
	III:	A201-1976, Art. 1, Para. 1.1.3
	III:	A201-1976, Art. 4, Para. 4.18.1
	III:	A401-1978, Art. 2, Para. 2.1
	III:	A401-1978, Art. 11, Para. 11.11.1

Prime subcontractor and contractor brought a third-party indemnification action against the structural steel subcontractor. The jury returned a verdict for the structural steel subcontractor on the third-party indemnity action. Prime subcontractor's motions for directed verdict on the issue of whether the injured worker was performing "work," judgment notwithstanding the verdict, or, in the alternative, for a new trial, were denied. Subcontractor appealed. The Appellate Court held that the trial court erred in overruling the prime subcontractor's motions.

The indemnification provision contained in the prime subcontractor-structural steel subcontractor's agreement provided that "To the full extent permitted by law, Subcontractor [Mosher] agrees to defend, indemnify, and save harmless Contractor [McDevitt] and Owner, and their agents, servants and employees, from and against any claim, cost, expense or liability (including attorney's fees) attributable to bodily injury, sickness, disease, or death, or the damage to or destruction of property (including loss of use thereof) caused by, arising out of, resulting from, or occurring in connection with the performance of the Work by Subcontractor, its subcontractors, or their agents, servants or employees, whether or not caused in part by the active or passive negligence or other fault of a party indemnified hereunder provided, however, Subcontractor's duty hereunder shall not arise if such injury, sickness, disease, death, damage, or destruction is caused by the sole negligence of a party indemnified hereunder. Subcontractor's obligation

the louvers, provided by the subcontractor/supplier, failed to perform as required by the specifications. The jury returned a verdict against the architect/engineer for negligence, against the subcontractor for comparative negligence in approving the shop drawings, and against the subcontractor/supplier for defectively manufacturing the louvers. The architect/engineer and subcontractor/supplier appealed. The Appellate Court reversed the judgment against the architect/engineer on the grounds that the architect/engineer was entitled to a directed verdict, vacated the judgment against the subcontractor/supplier, and ordered a new trial.

The subcontract provided that the subcontractor was required to perform all work "in accordance with Project Drawings and Specifications." The work was to be done "to the satisfaction of Perini Project Superintendent." The contractor and the owner were authorized to inspect the subcontractor's work, and if the work failed in any way to meet the specifications, the "Subcontractor at his owner expense shall make good all his Work. . . ." Nothing in the subcontract made the subcontractor's work contingent upon any approval by the architect/engineer. The shop drawing provision stated that the subcontractor "shall prepare at his own expense and furnish promptly whenever requested by the Contractor any number of prints of his shop drawings . . . or any other data that may be necessary in the opinion of the Contractor . . . for the proper prosecution of the Work. The Subcontractor shall lay out his own work and be responsible for the accuracy of same. The Subcontractor shall exercise the utmost diligence to obtain all drawings, details, and information necessary to perform his work. . . . The Subcontractor shall, before proceeding with any affected part of the Work, call to the Contractor's attention in writing any errors in or inconsistencies between or in any of the Contract Documents." The subcontract also provided that the subcontractor "shall guarantee his Work against all defects of materials and/or workmanship as called for in the Original Contract." The agreement between the contractor and the architect/engineer contained several provisions not contained in the subcontract, including an arbitration clause that required arbitration of all claims, disputes, and other matters "arising out of, or relating to, this Agreement or the breach thereof." The contract also provided that the law of Massachusetts would govern the terms contained therein, and any disputes arising out of the project would therefore be resolved by binding arbitration in accordance with Massachusetts law. The contract provided that architect/engineer would review "[s]hop drawings, samples and other submittals of the Contractor . . . only for general conformance to the design concept of the project and for general compliance with the contract documents."

The Appellate Court found that the contractor-architect/engineer agreement, by its terms, did not create or contemplate a duty of care by the architect/engineer to the subcontractor. The contract provided that architect/engineer would review "[s]hop drawings, samples and other submittals of the Contractor . . . only for general conformance to the design concept of the project and for general compliance with the contract documents." In addition, the subcontract provided that subcontractor would be responsible for its own work and would exercise the utmost diligence to obtain all drawings, details, and information necessary to perform its own work, which was interpreted by the Court as meaning that if the subcontractor/supplier products failed to meet the specifications the subcontractor answered to the contractor. The subcontractor

contractor. The subcontractor argued on appeal that the indemnity provision was inapplicable in a situation where subcontractor's "negligence" was merely imputed by its employee's acts and was not based on its own acts or omissions, and, secondly, that the indemnity provision should apply only in a situation in which its employee was exclusively at fault so as to prevent shifting the burden from a negligent party, the contractor, to subcontractor who was not at fault. The Appeals Court disagreed and affirmed.

The indemnity clause contained in the subcontract provided in pertinent part that the "Subcontractor shall indemnify and hold harmless the General Contractor and all of his agents and employees from and against all claims, damages, losses and expenses including attorney's fees arising out of or resulting from the performance of the Subcontractor's Work under this subcontract, provided that any such claim, damage, loss or expense (a) is attributable to bodily injury, sickness, disease, or death, or to injury to or destruction of tangible property (other than the Work itself) including the loss of use resulting therefrom and (b) is caused in whole or in part by any negligent act or omission of the Subcontractor or anyone directly or indirectly employed by him or anyone for whose acts he may be liable, regardless of whether it is caused in part by a party indemnified hereunder."

The Appeals Court found that the express language of the provision required subcontractor to underwrite fully the conduct of its employees. Nothing in the provision conditioned indemnification on a finding that subcontractor was responsible, in whole or in part, for the negligent act or omission. Having agreed to underwrite the conduct of its "employees," subcontractor would "not be allowed to escape what it knowingly bargained for," regardless of the degree of fault attributable to it.

91018 Lutz Eng'g Co. v. Industrial Louvers, Inc., 585 A. 2d 631 (R.I. 1991)

III:	A107-1978, Art. 13, Para. 13.2
III:	A117-1979, Art. 17, Para. 17.2
III:	A201-1976, Art. 7, Para. 7.1.1
III:	A201-1976, Art. 7, Para. 7.9.1
III:	A401-1978, Art. 11, Para. 11.2.3
III:	A401-1978, Art. 11, Para. 11.2.5
III:	A401-1978, Art. 11, Para. 11.7.1
III:	A401-1978, Art. 13, Para. 13.1
III:	B141-1977, Art. 1, Para. 1.5.13
III:	B141-1977, Art. 9, Para. 9.1
III:	B141-1977, Art. 11, Para. 11.1

Subcontractor brought a breach of contract action against subcontractor/supplier and a negligence action against architect/engineer for withheld retainage and for additional costs associated with louver requirements that were not part of the original specification on which the subcontractor had based its bid. The owner withheld the retainage after

II:	A117-1979, Art. 21, Para. 21.3
II:	A117-1979, Art. 21, Para. 21.6
I:	A201-1976, Art. 11, Para. 11.3.1
I:	A201-1976, Art. 11, Para. 11.3.6

Owner's insurer brought a subrogation action against subcontractor and others for fire damages resulting from subcontractor's negligence. The trial court directed a verdict in favor of subcontractor. At issue on appeal was whether the insurer, who had paid to the owner proceeds for damages incurred as a result of a fire that occurred during construction, was subrogated to the rights of the owner, and, if so, whether the insurer could sue a subcontractor that was allegedly negligent on the job and whose negligence allegedly caused the fire.

The subcontract provided that "Before commencing the Work and until completion and final acceptance thereof by Owner, Subcontractor shall obtain and maintain, at its expense, at least the insurance coverage specified in Schedule E attached hereto, all from companies, and in form and substance, acceptable to Contractor. . . ." The subcontractor further agreed to "defend, indemnify and save harmless Contractor and Owner, and their agents, servants and employees, from and against any claim, cost, expense or liability." The subcontract also required the subcontractor to "comply with all statutes, ordinances, rules, regulations and orders" of the governmental body having jurisdiction over the construction and to "defend, indemnify and save harmless Contractor and Owner and their agents, servants and employees from and against any loss, liability or expense arising from any such violations and any citations, assessments, fines or penalties resulting therefrom." The subcontract stated that subcontractor "shall take reasonable precautions to protect the Work from loss or damage prior to acceptance by Owner." The subcontract also incorporated by reference the American Institute of Architects General Conditions of the Contract for Construction, Document No. A201, 1976 edition, specifically Paragraph 11.3.1 and Paragraph 11.3.6, which provided for a waiver of subrogation.

Affirming, the Supreme Court held that under Paragraph 11.3.6 the parties expressly waived all rights against each other for damages caused by perils covered under the builder's risk policy. It was clear that the parties intended to allocate property loss to the insurer and to limit the recourse of owner solely to the insurance proceeds. Therefore, the trial court properly directed a verdict for the subcontractor.

91017   Kelly v. Dimeo, Inc., 31 Mass. App. Ct. 626, 581 N.E.2d 1316 (1991), *review denied,* 412 Mass. 1102, 588 N.E. 2d 691 (1992)

II:	A107-1978, Art. 10, Para. 10.11
II:	A117-1979, Art. 14, Para. 14.11
II:	A201-1976, Art. 4, Para. 4.18.1
II:	A401-1978, Art. 11, Para. 11.11.1

Contractor brought an indemnification action against subcontractor to recover payment of an injury claim by subcontractor's employee. The trial court found in favor of

the subcontract provided in pertinent part that "[i]t shall be an express condition precedent to the obligation of the Contractor to pay the Subcontractor that the Owner make payments to the Contractor covering the Subcontractor's portion of the work. . . . Final payment to the Subcontractor will be made upon receipt of final payment from the Owner. . . ." In addition, the subcontract provided in Section 12 that "the Subcontractor agrees to be bound to the Contractor by the terms of the Contractor's agreement with the Owner, General Conditions of such contract, the Supplementary General Conditions, the Drawings, Specifications and all other contract documents required of Contractor by Owner, and to assume toward the Contractor all obligations, responsibilities and limitations, including the termination provisions that the Contractor, by those documents, assumes toward the Owner."

The District Court of Appeal found that the provisions of the owner-contractor agreement were effectively incorporated into the subcontract agreement by Section 12 of the subcontract. The final payment provisions of the owner-contractor agreement, which required the contractor to pay its subcontractors before it was entitled to payment by the owner, and the provisions of the subcontract agreement, requiring that final payment by owner to contractor was a condition precedent to subcontractor's right to final payment from contractor, created an ambiguity regarding when the subcontractor was entitled to payment by the contractor. The Court resolved the ambiguity against the contractor and interpreted the provisions as establishing a reasonable time for contractor to delay in paying the subcontractor while awaiting payment from the owner. Because the trial court made no determination as to whether a reasonable time had passed, it was necessary to reverse and remand for a determination of that question of fact.

91015   Henderson Inv. Corp. v. International Fidelity Ins. Co., 575 So. 2d 770 (Fla. Dist. Ct. App. 1991)

           I: A107-1978, Art. 13, Para. 13.2
           I: A117-1979, Art. 17, Para. 17.2
           I: A201-1976, Art. 7, Para. 7.9.1
           I: A401-1978, Art. 13, Para. 13.1
           I: A401-1978, Art. 13, Para. 13.2
           I: B141-1977, Art. 9, Para. 9.1

The District Court of Appeal held that a surety could compel arbitration pursuant to the arbitration clause contained in the owner-contractor agreement. The clause was incorporated into its performance bond and expressly acknowledged that "other persons substantially involved" may participate where their "presence is required if complete relief is to be accorded in the arbitration."

91016   Industrial Risk Insurers v. Garlock Equip. Co., 576 So. 2d 652 (Ala. 1991)

           II: A107-1978, Art. 17, Para. 17.3
           II: A107-1978, Art. 17, Para. 17.6

the time for payment from the date the owner's representative approved the payment rather than from the end of the month in which the work was performed. The court concluded that the fact that the contractor's draw payment requests were submitted and approved early did not accelerate the time in which payment could be considered late. The Court entered judgment for owner on the counterclaim, and dismissed the contractor's complaint.

91014 Harris Air Sys., Inc. v. Gentrac, Inc., 578 So. 2d 879 (Fla. Dist. Ct. App. 1991)

I:	A101-1987, Art. 3	
II:	A107-1978, Art. 15, Para. 15.4	
II:	A107-1978, Art. 15, Para. 15.5	
II:	A117-1979, Art. 19, Para. 19.4	
II:	A117-1979, Art. 19, Para. 19.5	
I:	A201-1976, Art. 9, Para. 9.9.2	
III:	A401-1978, Art. 5, Para. 5.1	
III:	A401-1978, Art. 5, Para. 5.2	
III:	A401-1978, Art. 5, Para. 5.3	
III:	A401-1978, Art. 5, Para. 5.4	
III:	A401-1978, Art. 6, Para. 6.1	
III:	A401-1978, Art. 6, Para. 6.2	
III:	A401-1978, Art. 11, Para. 11.1.1	
III:	A401-1978, Art. 12, Para. 12.4.1	
III:	A401-1978, Art. 12, Para. 12.4.3	

Subcontractor brought an action against contractor to recover the balance due under the subcontract with interest, costs and attorney's fees. The trial court found for contractor on the ground that the condition precedent of payment of the contractor by the owner had not been met. The District Court of Appeal reversed.

The owner and contractor had entered into the American Institute of Architects Standard Form of Agreement Between the Owner and Contractor, Document No. A101, 1987 edition, the American Institute of Architects General Conditions of the Contract for Construction, Document No. A201, 1976 edition, including Paragraph 9.9.2, and Supplemental Conditions.

Article 6 of the owner-contractor agreement, as modified, provided in pertinent part that "the owner shall not be obligated to make final payment or pay any retainage and the Work shall not be considered complete unless or until the Owner shall have received: . . . (c) a final release of all liens and claims for labor, materials and other forces used or incorporated into the construction of the Work secured by the Contractor and an Affidavit of the Contractor stating that all bills incurred for the purchase of personal property, appliances, machinery and equipment attached or affixed to the Project or the Work as necessary or efficient to the use thereof, had been paid in full." Section 4 of

II: A201-1976, Art. 7, Para. 7.9.1
II: A401-1978, Art. 13, Para. 13.1
II: B141-1977, Art. 9, Para. 9.1

In confirming an arbitration award in subcontractor's favor, the Circuit Court deleted an amount for interest. The Court of Appeals affirmed that decision, but the Supreme Court reversed. It interpreted the arbitration clause of the owner-contractor agreement, which was incorporated into the subcontract, as authorizing the arbitrators to award interest as an element of damages absent an interest provision in the subcontract. The Court found that the clause gave the arbitrators the authority to ascertain the parties' contractual obligations, determine whether either party has breached the contract, and determine the proper amount of damages including whether to include common-law interest as an element of damages in order to fully compensate subcontractor for the loss of the use of its money.

91013 Haden v. Krupp Asset Management Corp., 776 F. Supp. 1151 (S.D. Miss. 1991)

II: A107-1978, Art. 10, Para. 10.4
II: A107-1978, Art. 20, Para. 20.1
II: A107-1978, Art. 20, Para. 20.2
II: A117-1979, Art. 14, Para. 14.4
II: A117-1979, Art. 24, Para. 24.1
II: A117-1979, Art. 24, Para. 24.2
II: A201-1976, Art. 4, Para. 4.5.1
II: A201-1976, Art. 14, Para. 14.1.1
II: A201-1976, Art. 14, Para. 14.2.1

Contractor brought an action against owner for breach of contract; owner counterclaimed. Contractor had abandoned the site pursuant to the contract's termination provision which was a modified version of Paragraph 20.1 of the American Institute of Architects Abbreviated Form of Agreement Between Owner and Contractor, Document No. A107, 1978 edition.

The contract's payment clause provided that "If the Owner's Representative fails to issue a certificate for payment for a period of thirty (30) days through no fault of the Contractor, or if the Owner fails to make payment thereon for a period of thirty days, the Contractor may upon thirty additional days notice to the Owner and the Owner's Representative, terminate the Contract and recover from the Owner payment for all work executed and for any proven loss sustained upon any materials, equipment, tools, and construction equipment and machinery which is lawfully due the contractor and is not subject of a dispute between the Contractor and Owner or Contractor and Subcontractor or both."

The District Court held that the contractor breached the owner-contractor agreement by abandoning the work site without just cause because the contractor began counting

The owner and contractor had entered into an agreement which contained an indemnity provision identical to Paragraph 4.18.1 of the American Institute of Architects General Conditions of the Contract for Construction, Document No. A201, 1976 edition.

The Court of Appeals construed Paragraph 4.18.1 as requiring the contractor to indemnify two parties—the owner who was having the work performed, and the architect who was preparing the plans for the work to be performed. Paragraph 4.18.1 provided that losses and expenses, including attorney's fees, were recoverable if there was an injury to or destruction of tangible property and if such loss or destruction was caused by contractor's negligence. Based upon the jury's finding of contractor negligence, the Court held that contractor was required to indemnify the architect for its losses and expenses, including attorney's fees.

Paragraph 4.18.3 provided that the obligation of the contractor did not extend to the liability of the architect arising out of the preparation or approval of maps, drawings, opinions, reports, surveys, change orders, designs or specifications or the giving of, or the failure to give, directions or instructions by the architect provided that such act or omission was the primary cause of the injury or damage. The Court concluded that this Paragraph did not apply since the jury found that the architect was not at fault.

91011 Gilbane Bldg. Co. v. Brisk Waterproofing Co., 86 Md. App. 21, 585 A.2d 248 (1991)

III: A201-1976, Art. 9, Para. 9.5.2
II: A401-1978, Art. 12, Para. 12.4.1

In an action arising from payment due under a subcontract, the Circuit Court granted summary judgment in subcontractor's favor. The Court of Special Appeals reversed. It held that where a subcontract contained both a pay-when-paid provision and an unambiguous condition precedent provision, the subcontractor bore the credit risk of non-payment by the owner for any reason, including the insolvency of the owner.

The owner-contractor agreement provided that it was "specifically understood and agreed" that the payment to the subcontractor was dependent, as a condition precedent, upon the contractor receiving contract payment, including the retainer from the Owner. The subcontract provided that "monthly and final payments will be made to the trade contractor within five (5) days after receipt of payment by the construction manager from the owner. The retained percentage will be forwarded as soon as received by the construction manager from the owner. . . . [I]t is specifically understood and agreed that the payment to the trade contractor is dependent, as a condition precedent, upon the construction manager receiving contract payments, including retainer from the owner."

91012 Gordon Sel-Way, Inc. v. Spence Bros., Inc., 438 Mich. 488, 475 N.W.2d 704 (1991)

II: A107-1978, Art. 13, Para. 13.2
II: A117-1979, Art. 17, Para. 17.2

Contractor filed a petition to compel arbitration with owner, alleging delay damages, defective and incomplete design documents, and failure to pay amounts due under the base contract and for extra work. Owner filed an action against contractor for breach of contract, negligence and fraud. The trial court ordered arbitration but owner settled its claims against contractor and the arbitration proceedings were dismissed. The owner's lender then brought a negligence action against the contractor as a third-party beneficiary of the owner-contractor agreement. Contractor filed a petition to compel arbitration.

The owner-contractor agreement incorporated the American Institute of Architects General Conditions of the Contract for Construction, Document A201, 1976 edition, which contained an arbitration provision in Paragraph 7.9.1 requiring the parties to arbitrate "all claims, disputes and other matters in question between the Contractor and the Owner arising out of, or relating to, the Contract Documents or the breach thereof. . . ."

After finding that the lender was compelled to arbitrate its claims against the contractor as a third-party beneficiary of the owner-contractor agreement, the Court addressed the issue of whether the lender's negligence claim fell within the scope of Paragraph 7.9.1. The Court found that since the arbitration clause required arbitration of "all claims, disputes and other matters in question . . . arising out of, or relating to, the Contract Documents or the breach thereof . . . ," it clearly encompassed the lender's negligence claims, which were based on contractor's performance under the owner-contractor agreement, and, to be proved, required an inquiry into contractor's obligations under the contract. The Court held that the lender's claims arose out of, and related to, performance under the owner-contractor agreement, were intimately founded in and intertwined with the underlying contract obligations, and were subject to arbitration. The motion to compel arbitration was therefore granted.

91010 Foster, Henry, Henry & Thorpe, Inc. v. J.T. Constr. Co., 808 S.W.2d 139 (Tex. Ct. App. 1991)

I:	A107-1978, Art. 10, Para. 10.11
I:	A117-1979, Art. 14, Para. 14.11
I:	A201-1976, Art. 4, Para. 4.18.1
I:	A201-1976, Art. 4, Para. 4.18.3
I:	A401-1978, Art. 11, Para. 11.11.1
I:	A401-1978, Art. 11, Para. 11.11.3

Architect brought an indemnification action against contractor for the cost of defending an adjoining property owner's damage claim against the contractor and the architect for negligently failing to protect the construction site. The trial court directed a verdict against the architect after the jury found that the contractor and a third party's negligence caused the damage to the adjoining property owner. On appeal the architect argued that under the owner-contractor agreement the architect was entitled to be reimbursed for its attorney's fees and costs. The Court of Appeals agreed and reversed.

of claims under Paragraph 9.9.4. The owner, on the other hand, argued that the delay damages fell into either the exception contained in subsection.3 as "failure of the Work to comply with the requirements of the Contract Documents" or the special warranties exception contained in subsection.4 of Paragraph 9.9.4.

The District Court found that Paragraph 9.9.4 clearly precluded claims for damages after final payment had been made in any situation other than the four exceptions. Moreover, the Court found that the owner's characterization of the delay as a "failure to comply with the requirements of the contract documents" was inconsistent with the provisions of the contract documents when viewed in their entirety, since "work" was defined in Paragraph 1.1.3 of the General Conditions as comprising "the completed construction required by the Contract Documents and including all labor necessary to produce such construction, and all materials and equipment incorporated or to be incorporated in the construction." Relying on Paragraph 1.1.3 the Court concluded that the reference to work in subsection.3 of Paragraph 9.9.4 referred to materials and workmanship and supported an owner's right to claims for noncompliance with contract documents discovered after final payment was made; however, damages for delay in completing performance were treated separately and specifically under the liquidated damages provisions, with specific reference to the difficulty in ascertaining the costs that would be incurred as a result of delay.

The Court also rejected the owner's argument that the performance bond issued by the surety was a "special warranty" under subsection.4 of Paragraph 9.9.4. The performance bond only obligated the surety to insure that the work was done in accordance with the contract, and when the contractor was released from future claims under the contract the surety was also released from such claims. The Court found that the role of the surety was inconsistent with a construction of the performance bond as a "special warranty" that subjected the surety to claims related to performance of the work for which the principal of the contract could not be held responsible.

The Court therefore held that when the owner made final payment it waived its right to delay damages. Accordingly, it granted the surety's motion for summary judgment.

The Court noted briefly that Paragraph 6.2.3, which provided that "any costs caused by defective or ill-timed work shall be borne by the party responsible therefor" would not nullify any other express contract provisions that set forth a calculation of damages for the contractor's delay.

91009 Dunn Constr. Co. v. Sugar Beach Condominium Ass'n, 760 F. Supp. 1479 (S.D. Ala. 1991)

	I:	A107-1978, Art. 13, Para. 13.2
	I:	A117-1979, Art. 17, Para. 17.2
	I:	A201-1976, Art. 7, Para. 7.9.1
	I:	A401-1978, Art. 13, Para. 13.1
	I:	B141-1979, Art. 9, Para. 9.1

substantially completed. Final completion was to be achieved within 150 days. The contract provided that the work was to begin by August 15, 1986; substantial completion was thus due by December 15, 1986, and final completion by January 15, 1987.

The Appellate Court found that the contract was not ambiguous and that the plain language indicated that the listed items were to be provided by the contractor as specifically included within the scope of the "the Work" in the contract; many of the items listed were reiterated in an addendum which was incorporated into the contract before it was signed by the parties. The Court rejected the contractor's interpretation of the language to mean that the contractor would purchase the items, then be reimbursed at cost plus 10 percent, treating the listed items, in effect, as change orders. The Court concluded that since the contract was unambiguous, the trial court had erred in instructing the jury that it was to determine whether the contractor breached the agreement after previously granting the owner partial summary judgment on the issue.

The owner argued that the trial court erred in not instructing the jury that the owner was entitled to liquidated delay damages. The issue before the Appellate Court was whether the delay provisions were applicable where the contractor abandoned or repudiated the contract instead of continuing to perform and completing it later than the date fixed in the contract. The Court found that the clause was applicable but only to delay-related damages, and that had the jury been properly instructed the amount of owner's damages would have been greater and would have been consistent with the evidence. The Court reversed the judgment in favor of owner and remanded for a new trial on the issue of owner's damages.

91008 County of Dauphin v. Fidelity Deposit Co., 770 F. Supp. 248 (M.D. Pa.), *aff'd*, 937 F.2d 596 (3d Cir. 1991)

II:	A107-1978, Art. 7, Para. 7.4	
II:	A107-1978, Art. 12, Para. 12.3	
II:	A107-1978, Art. 15, Para. 15.5	
II:	A117-1979, Art. 11, Para. 11.4	
II:	A117-1979, Art. 16, Para. 16.3	
II:	A117-1979, Art. 19, Para. 19.5	
I:	A201-1976, Art. 1, Para. 1.1.3	
I:	A201-1976, Art. 6, Para. 6.2.3	
I:	A201-1976, Art. 9, Para. 9.9.4	

In owner's action for delay damages against prime contractor's surety, the issue was whether the liquidated damage provisions were ambiguous. They were contained in the Supplemental General Conditions or the final payment provision contained in the General Conditions, which was identical to Paragraph 9.9.4 of the American Institute of Architects General Conditions of the Contract for Construction, Document No. A201, 1976 edition. The surety argued that the owner had waived its right to damages by making final payment because delay damages did not fit into one of four categories excluded from a waiver

91007 Construction Contracting & Management, Inc. v. McConnell, 112 N.M. 371, 815 P.2d 1161 (1991)

III:	A107-1978, Art. 2, Para. 2.1
III:	A107-1978, Art. 7, Para. 7.4
III:	A107-1978, Art. 10, Para. 10.2
III:	A107-1978, Art. 14, Para. 14.3
III:	A117-1979, Art. 4, Para. 4.1
III:	A117-1979, Art. 11, Para. 11.4
III:	A117-1979, Art. 14, Para. 14.2
III:	A117-1979, Art. 18, Para. 18.3
III:	A201-1976, Art. 1, Para. 1.1.3
III:	A201-1976, Art. 4, Para. 4.4.1
III:	A201-1976, Art. 8, Para. 8.3.1
III:	A201-1976, Art. 8, Para. 8.3.4
III:	A201-1976, Art. 12, Para. 12.3.1

Contractor filed an action against owner to rescind the owner-contractor agreement after determining that the contract was unprofitable and after requesting additional compensation. The owner demanded that the contractor perform under the terms of the written contract. The contractor refused, halted its work, and filed a rescission action. The owner counterclaimed for breach of contract. The trial court granted owner summary judgment on the issue of contractor's liability for breach of contract but then submitted the issue to the jury. The jury returned a verdict in favor of the contractor for site preparation damages and for the owner on its counterclaim for damages. The trial court granted owner's motion to set aside the verdict for contractor, denied owner's motion for a new trial, and entered judgment against the contractor on the counterclaim. The owner appealed on the ground that because the jury was confused by the court's erroneous instructions the damage award was inadequate. The Appellate Court found that the only issue for the jury was the nature and extent of owner's damages since the trial court had granted owner summary judgment on the issue of contractor's liability.

The owner-contractor agreement defined the "Work" as "required by the Contractor Documents for the construction of the Wold [sic] Plum Restaurant, per plans and specifications from Lawrence Garcia and Associates and specifications from J.E. Kuykendal. All equipment and fixtures per plans and specifications on the above referenced project as agreed upon, and specifically included Roof tile and installation, Carpeting as per owner's specification, stained glass, mini-blinds, turning lamps, cabinets, stainless steel hoods, shelves, corners and door guards, Tiffany lamps and Lampost, site lighting, clear hemlock paneling, 2 fire hydrants and all necessary pro-rate charges, water meter, etc. Owner only to pay for those fixtures and furniture not mentioned in specifications." Article 3 of the contract, entitled "Time of Commencement and Substantial Completion" provided for substantial completion of the building within 120 days, with liquidated damages set at $250 per day for every day the project was not

Conditions of the Contract for Construction, Document No. A201, 1976 edition. The owner's decision to retain a certain wall constituted a major change in the scope of the work entitling the subcontractor to a written change order acknowledging the additional cost before it proceeded with the work.

91006   C & M Ventures, Inc. v. Wolf, 587 So. 2d 512 (Fla. Dist. Ct. App. 1991), *review denied,* 599 So. 2d 661 (Fla. 1992)

I:	A107-1978, Art. 7, Para. 7.1
I:	A107-1978, Art. 13, Para. 13.2
I:	A107-1978, Art. 18, Para. 18.1
I:	A107-1978, Art. 18, Para. 18.2
I:	A107-1978, Art. 18, Para. 18.3
I:	A117-1979, Art. 11, Para. 11.1
I:	A117-1979, Art. 17, Para. 17.2
I:	A117-1979, Art. 22, Para. 22.1
I:	A117-1979, Art. 22, Para. 22.2
I:	A117-1979, Art. 22, Para. 22.3
I:	A201-1976, Art. 1, Para. 1.1.1
I:	A201-1976, Art. 7, Para. 7.9.1
II:	A201-1976, Art. 12, Para. 12.1.1
II:	A201-1976, Art. 12, Para. 12.1.2
II:	A201-1976, Art. 12, Para. 12.3.1
II:	A401-1978, Art. 1, Para. 1.1
II:	A401-1978, Art. 11, Para. 11.9.1
II:	A401-1978, Art. 13, Para. 13.1
II:	B141-1977, Art. 9, Para. 9.1

In an action between contractor and owner, the trial court ordered arbitration as to disputes arising under the parties' original contract, but ordered trial to go forward on a dispute arising from changes to the original contract. The District Court of Appeal reversed in part, holding that the arbitration clause applied to both the original contract and to any changes therein.

The arbitration provision in Paragraph 13.2 of the American Institute of Architects Abbreviated Form of Agreement Between Owner and Contractor, Document No. A107, 1978 edition, required arbitration of "all claims, or disputes . . . arising out of, or relating to, the Contract Documents. . . ." This provision clearly controlled as to the contract and any change orders issued pursuant to the provisions of Paragraphs 18.1, 18.2 and 18.3, since Paragraph 7.1 clearly provided that the contract documents included "all Modifications issued by the Architect after execution of the Contract such as Change Orders. . . ."

accurately determine the amount of time, work and materials required to complete the project. The owner argued that any changes in the work and the costs of extras were provided for in the owner-contractor agreement, that the asbestos removal was a latent condition defined in the contract, that the owner compensated the contractor for the removal, and that there was no evidence that the removal caused the contractor to incur delay or disruption losses not already compensated for by the owner pursuant to the contract.

The owner-contractor agreement provided that "any change in the work shall be ordered and the adjustment of the contractor price or time shall be determined by one of the following methods. . . . The Contractor shall keep an accurate current account of such work and present it in such form, and substantiated by such supporting papers as the Architect may require. Upon completion and determination of the cost, a Change Order shall be issued establishing the increase or decrease in the contract price or contract time. . . . The cost shall include all direct and necessary production costs of the work itself. . . . Should the Contractor encounter subsurface or latent conditions at the site materially differing from those provided for in this Contract, or unknown physical conditions differing materially from those inherent in work of the character provided for in this contract, he shall promptly, and before such conditions are disturbed, notify the LHA [HABD] in writing. . . . If, on the basis of available evidence, LHA [HABD] determines that an adjustment of the contract price or time is justifiable, the procedure shall then be as provided herein for"changes in the work.' "

The Appellate Court affirmed, finding that the contract clearly provided for the delay costs resulting from the discovery of the asbestos which was a latent defect as defined by the contract, that there was no evidence that the owner or architect had knowledge of the asbestos or in any way prevented the contractor from finishing its work ahead of schedule, and that the contractor and the subcontractor had been paid for the additional work pursuant to the change orders.

91005 Cleveland Wrecking Co. v. Central Nat'l Bank, 216 Ill. App. 3d 279, 160 Ill. Dec. 101, 576 N.E.2d 1055 (1991)

II:	A107-1978, Art. 18, Para. 18.1	
II:	A107-1978, Art. 18, Para. 18.2	
II:	A117-1979, Art. 22, Para. 22.1	
II:	A117-1979, Art. 22, Para. 22.2	
I:	A201-1976, Art. 12, Para. 12.1.1	
I:	A201-1976, Art. 12, Para. 12.1.2	
I:	A201-1976, Art. 12, Para. 12.3.1	

In subcontractor's breach of contract action against contractor arising from the demolition of a building, the trial court entered a judgment of foreclosure and sale. The Appellate Court upheld the trial court's finding that the changes were not within the general scope of the contract, which included Article 12 of the American Institute of Architects General

owner. Accordingly, the Court granted defendant's motion for partial summary judgment on subcontractor's contractual claim.

The owner-contractor agreement provided that it was "specifically understood and agreed" that the payment to the subcontractor was dependent, as a condition precedent, upon the contractor receiving contract payment, including the retainer from the Owner. The subcontract stated that "monthly and final payments will be made to the trade contractor within five (5) days after receipt of payment by the construction manager from the owner. The retained percentage will be forwarded as soon as received by the construction manager from the owner. . . . [I]t is specifically understood and agreed that the payment to the trade contractor is dependent, as a condition precedent, upon the construction manager receiving contract payments, including retainer from the owner."

91004 Castle Constr. Co./Tuskegee Lumber Co. v. Owens & Woods Partnership, 590 So. 2d 186 (Ala. 1991)

III:	A107-1978, Art. 18, Para. 18.1	
III:	A107-1978, Art. 18, Para. 18.2	
III:	A107-1978, Art. 18, Para. 18.3	
III:	A117-1979, Art. 22, Para. 22.1	
III:	A117-1979, Art. 22, Para. 22.2	
III:	A117-1979, Art. 22, Para. 22.3	
III:	A201-1976, Art. 12, Para. 12.1.1	
III:	A201-1976, Art. 12, Para. 12.1.3	
III:	A201-1976, Art. 12, Para. 12.1.4	
III:	A201-1976, Art. 12, Para. 12.2.1	
III:	A201-1976, Art. 12, Para. 12.3.1	

Contractor brought an action against owner for delay damages suffered by the contractor and the subcontractor associated with the removal of asbestos, and against the architect as a third-party beneficiary of the owner-architect agreement on the grounds that the architect had failed to design the project to conform with the applicable laws and regulations regarding asbestos removal and had breached an implied warranty to provide sufficient and accurate plans and specifications. The contractor was compensated by change order for the direct costs of the removal. The owner and architect moved for partial summary judgment and the owner filed a counterclaim against the contractor alleging fraud. The contractor moved for partial summary judgment on the owner's fraud claim. The trial court denied contractor's motion, and entered summary judgment for owner on the subcontractor's claims for delay damages, and for owner and architect on the contractor's claim for delay damages. Contractor appealed.

The contractor argued on appeal that it was entitled to compensation, delay damages, and related disruption and completion costs since the contractor would have completed the project earlier than the agreed upon completion date if the owner and architect discovered the asbestos prior to bidding, which would have allowed the contractor to

II:	A117-1979, Art. 11, Para. 11.3
II:	A117-1979, Art. 11, Para. 11.4
I:	A201-1976, Art. 1, Para. 1.1.2
I:	A201-1976, Art. 1, Para. 1.1.3
I:	A201-1976, Art. 12, Para. 12.2.1

Contractor brought an action against owner to recover payment of the contract balance and additional costs incurred as a result of unforeseen subsurface conditions. The trial court granted owner's motion for summary judgment. The contractor argued on appeal that the trial court erred in granting summary judgment as to its claims of fraudulent concealment of site conditions and that because of unanticipated subsurface conditions it was required to perform work outside the scope of the contract and was entitled to additional compensation. The Court of Appeals affirmed.

The contract between the parties was an amended American Institute of Architects Standard Form of Agreement Between Owner and Contractor, Document No. A101, 1977 edition, and an addendum of supplementary general conditions. The contract provided that the amount to be paid was a stipulated sum "without extra compensation" and that the "intent of the Contract Documents is to include all of the work for the Stipulated Contract Sum and within the Contract Time. . . . [A]ny work which is obviously necessary to complete the work within the limits established by the Drawings and Specifications, shall be considered as part of the Contract and shall be executed by the Contractor in the same manner and with the same character of material as other portions of the Contract without extra compensation." The parties struck the concealed conditions provision in Paragraph 12.2.1 and, even though no similar clause was substituted, the contract did include a site inspection clause, which required the contractor to visit the site and "examine all conditions affecting the Work," and to be "fully familiar with all of the conditions thereon and affecting the same. . . ." The contract included Paragraphs 1.1.2 and 1.1.3 of the American Institute of Architects General Conditions of the Contract for Construction, Document No. A201, 1976 edition.

The Court found that because the contract contained a merger clause in Paragraph 1.1.2, and the contractor did not rescind the contract, the merger clause barred the changed conditions claim. The Court further found that since the contract imposed the risk of uncertain subsurface conditions on the contractor by not containing a changed conditions clause, by limiting payment to a sum certain and by requiring the contractor to inspect the site, the contractor was precluded from recovering additional compensation.

91003 Architectural Sys., Inc. v. Gilbane Bldg. Co., 760 F. Supp. 79 (D. Md. 1991)

III:	A201-1976, Art. 9, Para. 9.5.2
II:	A401-1978, Art. 12, Para. 12.4.1

The District Court held that where a subcontract contained both a pay-when-paid provision and an unambiguous condition precedent provision, the subcontractor bore the credit risk of non-payment by the owner for any reason, including the insolvency of the

provided that "All work shall be done under the direct inspection of the [City's] Engineering and Utility Departments and [Butler] . . . ." The agreement further provided that the engineer was to act as the City's representative during the construction to decide questions and determine acceptability of materials furnished and work performed. The agreement specifically provided that contractor was responsible for initiating, maintaining, and supervising site safety and provided further that the engineer was not responsible for construction means or for safety at the site. The agreement also provided that the contractor agreed to "indemnify and hold harmless [City] and [Butler] and their agents and employees from and against all claims, damages, losses and expenses including attorney's fees arising out of or resulting from the performance of the Work, provided that any such claims, damage, loss or expense is attributable to bodily injury, sickness, disease or death, or the injury to or destruction of tangible property, including the loss of use resulting therefrom; and is caused in whole or in part by any negligent or willful act or omission of [Coffey] . . . anyone directly or indirectly employed by any of them or any one for whose acts any of them may be liable. . . . In any and all claims against [City] or [Butler], or any of their agents or employees, by any employee of [Coffey], anyone directly or indirectly employed by any of them or anyone for whose acts any of them may be liable, the indemnification obligation shall not be limited in any way by any limitation on the amount or type of damages, compensation or benefits payable by or for [Coffey] . . . under workman's compensation acts, disability benefit acts or other employee benefit acts."

The Appellate Court found that the City and engineer did not have a contractual duty of safety where the City-contractor agreement clearly made the contractor responsible for initiating, maintaining and supervising all safety precautions during construction and provided that contractor would be solely responsible for the means and methods of construction. The Court refused to extend the City's and engineer's contractual duty to supervise to a duty to exercise reasonable care for an employee's safety.

The Appellate Court reversed the trial court's grant of summary judgment to contractor on City's third-party indemnification claim on the grounds that the indemnification clause in the City-contractor agreement contained clear language of contractor's agreement to indemnify the City for contractor's negligence where the City was seeking indemnification for contractor's negligence and not for City's own negligence. The Court upheld the trial court's grant of summary judgment to the engineer on the grounds that there was no written indemnification agreement and the Court did not find that the City had a nondelegable duty.

91002   American Demolition, Inc. v. Hapeville Hotel, Ltd. Partnership, 202 Ga. App. 107, 413 S.E.2d 749 (1991), *cert. denied,* 1992 Ga. LEXIS 62 (Ga. 1992)

	II:	A107-1978, Art. 7, Para. 7.1
	II:	A107-1978, Art. 7, Para. 7.3
	II:	A107-1978, Art. 7, Para. 7.4
	II:	A117-1979, Art. 11, Para. 11.1

91001 Alexander v. City of Shelbyville, 575 N.E.2d 1058 (Ind. Ct. App. 1991)

II:	A107-1978, Art. 8, Para. 8.1
II:	A107-1978, Art. 8, Para. 8.3
II:	A107-1978, Art. 10, Para. 10.1
III:	A107-1978, Art. 10, Para. 10.11
II:	A107-1978, Art. 16, Para. 16.1
II:	A117-1979, Art. 12, Para. 12.1
II:	A117-1979, Art. 12, Para. 12.3
II:	A117-1979, Art. 14, Para. 14.1
III:	A117-1979, Art. 14, Para. 14.11
II:	A117-1979, Art. 20, Para. 20.1
III:	A201-1976, Art. 2, Para. 2.2.2
III:	A201-1976, Art. 2, Para. 2.2.3
II:	A201-1976, Art. 2, Para. 2.2.4
II:	A201-1976, Art. 4, Para. 4.3.1
II:	A201-1976, Art. 4, Para. 4.18.1
II:	A201-1976, Art. 4, Para. 4.18.2
II:	A201-1976, Art. 10, Para. 10.1.1
II:	A401-1978, Art. 11, Para. 11.11.1
II:	A401-1978, Art. 11, Para. 11.11.2
III:	B141-1977, Art. 1, Para. 1.5.3
III:	B141-1977, Art. 1, Para. 1.5.4
II:	B141-1977, Art. 1, Para. 1.5.5
III:	B141-1977, Art. 1, Para. 1.6.2
III:	B141-1977, Art. 1, Para. 1.6.3

Contractor's worker's estate brought a wrongful death action against City and engineer. The City brought a third-party indemnification claim against the engineer and contractor. The trial court granted contractor's motion for summary judgment on the ground that workers' compensation was the estate's sole remedy against the contractor. At the close of the trial the court granted City's and engineer's motions for summary judgment on the grounds that the estate failed to prove violation of a duty. The estate appealed. The City appealed the court's grant of summary judgment to the contractor and the dismissal of City's indemnity claim against contractor and engineer. The Appellate Court affirmed the grant of summary judgment to City and engineer on the grounds that the injured worker failed to prove violation of a duty.

The owner-engineer agreement stated that engineer "provide qualified personnel to observe [Coffey's] work to determine compliance with the plans and Specifications." The engineer also had the power to order the contractor to stop work if the work was not being done in accordance with the specifications. The City-contractor agreement

procedures of construction unless such is specifically called for in the Contract Documents.

Finally, the agreement provided that:

[The resident project representative] shall not advise on or issue direction as to safety precautions and programs in connection with the Work.

The appellate court found that the contract clearly defined and limited the duties of the resident project representative. He "had limited authority and was expressly prohibited form guiding [contractor] or its employees" on their methods. Thus, the court concluded that no legal duty under the contract was breached by the resident project representative.

In injured worker's action against owner, contractor and engineer, the appellate court was presented, in engineer's third-party indemnity action against the contractor, with the issue of whether the injured worker's exclusive remedy against his employer, the contractor, was of any significance in limiting the contractor's indemnity obligation under the owner-contractor agreement.

The owner-contractor agreement provided in pertinent part that:

To the fullest extent permitted by law, CONTRACTOR shall indemnify and hold harmless OWNER and ENGINEER and their agents and employees from and against all claims, damages, losses and expenses including but not limited to attorney's fees arising out of or resulting from the performance of the Work, provided that any such claim, damage, loss or expense (a) is attributable to bodily injury, sickness, disease or death, or to injury to or destruction of tangible property (other than the Work itself) including the loss of use resulting therefrom and (b) is caused in whole or in part by any negligent act or omission of CONTRACTOR, any Subcontractor, anyone directly or indirectly employed by any of them or anyone from whose acts anyone of them may be liable, regardless of whether or not it is caused in part by a party indemnified hereunder. . . . [T]he indemnification obligation . . . shall not be limited in any way by any limitation on the amount or type of damages, compensation or benefits payable by or for CONTRACTOR or any Subcontractor under workers' or worker's compensation acts, disability benefits acts or other employee benefits acts.

The appellate court found that the indemnity provision clearly obligated the contractor to indemnify the engineer against liability under certain circumstances. The contractor undertook this indemnity obligation knowingly and in good faith and without reserving or restricting its liability to injuries caused to its own employees. The court concluded that contractor's contractual obligation was separate and distinct from the liability which would have attached to contractor for negligently injuring its own employee, and, the fact that contractor was protected from liability to its employee under the exclusive remedy provisions of the workers' compensation act, did not abrogate or otherwise limit contractor's contractual liability under the indemnity clause of the contract.

On appeal after remand, the injured worker argued that engineer's employee was negligent in failing to observe, warn of, report, or correct an unsafe condition.

The owner/engineer agreement required the engineer "to provide an engineer to act as resident project representative to 'serve as ENGINEER's liaison with CONTRACTOR, working principally through CONTRACTOR's superintendent and assist him in understanding the intent of the Contract Documents.' "

The agreement also required that the resident project representative "conduct on-site observations of the Work in progress to assure ENGINEER in determining if the Work is proceeding in accordance with the Contract Documents and that completed Work will conform to the Contract Documents." Additionally, the resident project representative was prohibited from:

[undertaking any of the responsibilities of Contractor, subcontractors, or CONTRACTOR's superintendent, or [expediting] the Work, and from [advising on or issuing] directions relative to any aspect of the means, methods, techniques, sequences or

90055 White Budd Van Ness Partnership v. Major-Gladys Drive Joint Venture, 798 S.W.2d 805 (Tex. Ct. App. 1990), *writ dismissed,* 811 S.W.2d 541 (Tex.), *cert. denied,* 112 S. Ct. 180, 116 L. Ed. 2d 142 (1991)

III:	A107-1978, Art. 8, Para. 8.3
III:	A117-1979, Art. 12, Para. 12.3
III:	A201-1976, Art. 2, Para. 2.2.3
III:	B141-1977, Art. 1, Para. 1.5.4

In owner's action against architect to recover damages for the architect's failure to properly investigate and advise the owner concerning the use of a specific type of tile, the owner cross-appealed the award of a credit to the architect, which effectively reduced the judgment awarded to the owner. The Appellate Court interpreted an amended Paragraph 1.5.4 of the American Institute of Architects Standard Form of Agreement Between Owner and Architect, Document No. B141, 1977 edition, which provided that "[t]he architect shall make on-site inspections of the work at appropriate intervals to become familiar with the progress of the work, to evaluate the quality of the work and to determine if the work is proceeding according to the contract documents. And if any work of the contractor is defective, deficient or not in accordance with the plans and specifications, the same shall be reported to the owner. The architect shall endeavor to guard against defects and deficiencies in the work and the architect shall promptly reject any defective or deficient work of the contractor," as more beneficial to the owner because the word "shall" was used four times. The Court concluded that since the architect's breach of contract was a substantial factor in owner's damages no credit should have been given to the architect.

90056 Yocum v. Minden, 566 So. 2d 1082 (La. Ct. App. 1990), *appeal after remand,* 649 So. 2d 129 (La. Ct. App. 1995)

II:	A107-1978, Art. 10, Para. 10.11
II:	A117-1979, Art. 14, Para. 14.11
III:	A201-1976, Art. 2, Para 2.2.2
III:	A201-1976, Art. 2, Para 2.2.3
III:	A201-1976, Art. 2, Para 2.2.4
I:	A201-1976, Art. 4, Para. 4.18.1
I:	A201-1976, Art. 4, Para. 4.18.2
II:	A401-1978, Art. 11, Para. 11.11.1
II:	A401-1978, Art. 11, Para. 11.11.2
III:	B141-1977, Art. 1, Para 1.5.3
III:	B141-1977, Art. 1, Para 1.5.4
III:	B141-1977, Art. 1, Para 1.5.5

III: B141-1977, Art. 9, Para. 9.1

In deciding whether the arbitrability of an owner-contractor dispute was to be determined by the arbitrator or by the trial court, the Appellate Court construed dispute resolution language which provided that "all claims, disputes and other matters in question . . . arising from or relating to this Agreement or breach thereof shall be decided by any court having jurisdiction thereof . . . all claims, disputes and other matters in question not involving more than the sum of One Hundred Thousand Dollars ($100,000) arising out of, or relating to, this Agreement or the breach thereof . . . shall be decided by arbitration . . . unless the parties mutually agree otherwise. . . ."

The Court found that although the arbitration provision was broad it contained qualifying language that limited arbitration to claims "not involving more than One Hundred Thousand Dollars ($100,000)." Furthermore, the Court construed the provision which stated that "all claims, disputes and other matters in question between the parties to this Agreement arising from or relating to this Agreement or the breach thereof shall be decided by any court having jurisdiction thereof" as clearly expressing the intent of the parties that all claims and disputes were to be decided by the court subject only to the limited exception for those matters in dispute that were less than $100,000. The Court held that in this case arbitrability was a factual question to be determined by the trial court, and remanded for a determination of whether the dispute involved separate claims of less than $100,000 divided into smaller parts to meet the arbitration threshold.

90054 Wells & Parker Architects, Inc. v. Monroe-McKeen Plaza Hous. Dev. Corp., 556 So. 2d 191 (La. Ct. App. 1990)

III:	B141-1977, Art. 14, Para. 14.1
III:	B141-1977, Art. 14, Para. 14.2.1
III:	B141-1977, Art. 14, Para. 14.2.2
III:	B141-1977, Art. 14, Para. 14.3
III:	B141-1977, Art. 14, Para. 14.4.1
III:	B141-1977, Art. 14, Para. 14.5
III:	B141-1977, Art. 14, Para. 14.7.1
III:	B141-1977, Art. 14, Para. 14.7.2

The Appellate Court found that although the owner-architect agreement was evidenced by a written contract, the architect's action for the balance of fees due for inspection services was an action on an open account and not in contract. The agreement did not specifically establish the amount that would be paid for architectural services but merely fixed the maximum hourly rate and the maximum total fee for such services. The actual payments to be made were based upon the amount of work performed by the architects as invoiced.

Architect will endeavor to require the Contractor to strictly adhere to the plans and specifications, to guard the Owner against defects and deficiencies in the work of Contractors, and shall promptly notify the Owner in writing of any significant departure in the quality of materials or workmanship from the requirements of the plans and specifications, but he does not guarantee the performance of the contracts. . . . The Architect shall make periodic visits to the site and as hereinafter defined to familiarize himself generally with the progress and quality of the Work and to determine in general if the Work is proceeding in accordance with the Contract Documents. On the basis of his on-site observations as an Architect, he shall endeavor to guard the Owner against defects and deficiencies in the work of the Contractor. The Architect shall not be required to make continuous on-site inspections to check the quality of the Work. Architect shall not be responsible for construction means, methods, techniques, sequences or procedures, or for safety precautions and programs in connection with the Work, unless spelled out in the Contract Documents, and he shall not be liable for results of Contractor's failure to carry out the work in accordance with the Contract Documents. . . . The Architect shall not be responsible for the acts or omissions of the Contractor, or any Subcontractors, or any of the Contractor's or Subcontractor's agents or employees, or any other persons performing any of the Work."

The Court found that although the contract clearly made the architect's inspection duty a limited one, it did not absolve the architect from all possible liability or relieve the architect of the duty to perform reasonably the limited contractual duties that it had agreed to undertake. While the agreement may have absolved the architect of liability for any negligent acts or omissions of the contractor and subcontractor, the Court concluded that it did not absolve the architect of liability arising out of its own failure to inspect reasonably. The architect could be held liable for its failure to inspect and to discover the acts or omissions of the contractor or subcontractors in failing to follow the plans and specifications. Under the terms of the contract, the Court found that the architect had at least a duty to perform reasonable inspections, and the owner had a right to a remedy for any failure to perform that duty. The Court concluded that, although the architect had a duty under the contract to inspect, exhaustive, continuous on-site inspections were not required. Furthermore, the Court found that an architect had a legal duty, under such an agreement, to notify the owner of a known defect. An architect could not close his eyes on the construction site and refuse to engage in any inspection procedure whatsoever and then disclaim liability for construction defects that even the most perfunctory monitoring would have prevented. However, the court held as a matter of law that the owner failed to prove that the architect had breached the agreement.

90053   Welch Group, Inc. v. Creative Drywall, Inc., 215 Conn. 464, 576 A.2d 153 (1990)

> III: A107-1978, Art. 13, Para. 13.2
> III: A117-1979, Art. 17, Para. 17.2
> III: A201-1976, Art. 7, Para. 7.9.1
> III: A401-1978, Art. 13, Para. 13.1

II:	A117-1979, Art. 12, Para. 12.6	
II:	A201-1976, Art. 2, Para. 2.2.1	
II:	A201-1976, Art. 2, Para. 2.2.3	
II:	A201-1976, Art. 2, Para. 2.2.6	
II:	A201-1976, Art. 2, Para. 2.2.7	
II:	A201-1976, Art. 2, Para. 2.2.8	
II:	A201-1976, Art. 2, Para. 2.2.9	
II:	A201-1976, Art. 2, Para. 2.2.12	
II:	A201-1976, Art. 2, Para. 2.2.13	
II:	B141-1977, Art. 1, Para. 1.5.3	
II:	B141-1977, Art. 1, Para. 1.5.4	
II:	B141-1977, Art. 1, Para. 1.5.7	
II:	B141-1977, Art. 1, Para. 1.5.9	
II:	B141-1977, Art. 1, Para. 1.5.12	

The Appellate Court upheld the order of the trial court directing the owner and contractor to arbitrate the contractor's claim for amounts due under the contract on the grounds that contractor was not required to file its claim with the architect pursuant to the provisions of the owner-contractor agreement which contained provisions similar to Paragraph 2.2.1, 2.2.3, 2.2.6, 2.2.7, 2.2.8, 2.2.9, 2.2.12 and 2.2.13 of the American Institute of Architects General Conditions of the Contract for Construction, Document No. A201, 1976 edition. The agreement further provided that "Contractor and Owner waive all claims, disputes and other matters in question, of any kind whatsoever in connection with any provision of this Agreement, the Contract, the Work or the Project not timely submitted to the Architect. . . ." The Court found that submission of the contractor's claim to the architect was not a condition precedent to arbitration where the contract was terminated, thereby extinguishing the architect's responsibility to supervise the contractor's performance and, by extension, initially mediating disputes.

90052 Watson, Watson, Rutland/Architects, Inc. v. Montgomery County Bd. of Educ., 559 So. 2d 168 (Ala. 1990)

II:	A107-1978, Art. 8, Para. 8.3	
II:	A117-1979, Art. 12, Para. 12.3	
II:	A201-1976, Art. 2, Para. 2.2.3	
II:	A201-1976, Art. 2, Para. 2.2.4	
II:	B141-1977, Art. 1, Para. 1.5.4	
II:	B141-1977, Art. 1, Para. 1.5.5	

In owner's action against contractor and architect for damages resulting from a roof leak, the Court construed the following exculpatory language in the owner-architect agreement which was modeled after language found in the American Institute of Architects Agreement Between Owner and Architect, Document No. B141, 1977 edition: "The

the trial court denied its motion because it concluded that there was a fact issue as to whether the contractor was obligated under the contract to determine whether the bricks met certain standards. The Court found that, in fact, the language of the trial court's order clearly stated that owner's motion for summary judgment on warranty liability was denied because owner's knowledge of the defect remained a question of fact and precluded the grant of summary judgment.

The owner also argued that the District Court confused suitability with defect. The owner argued that the bricks spalled because they were "suitable yet defective," meaning that they were a bad batch of underfired bricks that otherwise would have performed. The Court found that the evidence was in conflict as to the cause of the spalling and deterioration and that the jury was properly instructed as to owner's defect theory and the surety's unsuitability theory.

The owner argued further that the jury was improperly instructed as to the law if it found that the owner had picked unsuitable bricks. The surety had invoked the *Spearin* doctrine, which provided that where the contractor was bound to build according to plans and specifications prepared by the owner, the contractor would not be responsible for the consequences of defects in the plans and specifications. The owner argued that the *Spearin* doctrine was inapplicable because the owner selected the bricks solely on the basis of color, texture and appearance, not suitability, that the express warranty contained in Paragraph 4.5.1 could not be trumped by a warranty implied from the owner's selection of the brick; the owner made various other arguments distinguishing the *Spearin* doctrine cases, as well as an extended argument concerning the economically efficient result. The Court concluded that the jury instructions were supported by the record and were fair and accurate summaries of the law.

Finally, the owner argued that the jury was improperly instructed to find waiver of the Paragraph 4.5.1 warranty if it found that before the owner made final payment it had evidence that the bricks were spalling and deteriorating. The Court held that the surety had adduced sufficient evidence at trial that the owner had actual knowledge that the bricks were deteriorating and, nevertheless, made final payment. In addition, the owner-contractor agreement, which provided that the final certificate would evidence owner's acceptance of the work, justified the waiver instruction.

90051 Tsombikos v. Brager, 147 Misc. 2d 995, 559 N.Y.S.2d 460 (Sup. Ct. 1990)

II:	A107-1978, Art. 8, Para. 8.1
II:	A107-1978, Art. 8, Para. 8.3
II:	A107-1978, Art. 8, Para. 8.4
II:	A107-1978, Art. 8, Para. 8.5
II:	A107-1978, Art. 8, Para. 8.6
II:	A117-1979, Art. 12, Para. 12.1
II:	A117-1979, Art. 12, Para. 12.3
II:	A117-1979, Art. 12, Para. 12.4
II:	A117-1979, Art. 12, Para. 12.5

a third-party complaint against owner's in-house architect. The District Court bifurcated the third-party action for separate adjudication. Owner filed a cross motion for summary judgment on the ground that as a matter of law contractor breached its Paragraph 4.5.1 warranty by using latently defective bricks. The surety filed a motion for summary judgment requesting dismissal of the entire action. The trial court denied both motions and the case was tried to a jury, which returned a verdict for surety. Owner appealed and the Appellate Court affirmed.

The owner and contractor entered into two agreements containing essentially the same terms, for the construction of four buildings on the University campus. Paragraph 4.5.1 of the General Conditions was identical to Paragraph 4.5.1 of the American Institute of Architects General Conditions of the Contract for Construction, Document No. A201, 1976 edition. The "Work" was defined in Paragraph 1.1.3. The contract specifications contained instructions to the contractor regarding the masonry work and required the contractor to build sample panels of each of the four types of brick specified from which the owner would choose the brick. The brick types listed in the specifications were chosen by the owner's in-house architects and the owner's consulting architects. The Supplementary General Conditions modified the substantial completion and final payment provisions of the General Conditions to provide that upon receipt from the contractor of an application for final payment, the owner and architect would make a final inspection, after which the parties would execute a "final certificate" which "shall constitute the acceptance of the work by the Owner, except as to work thereafter found to be defective. The date of such certificate shall be regarded as the date of acceptance of the work. . . ." The owner, after rejecting the four specified brick types, instructed the contractor to use a fifth type of brick not listed on the specifications. At the conclusion of the construction, the owner found that the buildings had been substantially completed, final payment was certified by the architect, and the owner executed the certificate of final payment, despite the fact that the brick began to "spall" and deteriorate. After extensive replacement work the owner filed this breach of contract action against the contractor's surety.

The owner argued on appeal that the trial court erred in denying owner's motion for summary judgment. The owner claimed that because the trial court stated in its denial of owner's motion for summary judgment that the brick was defective the Court should have found as a matter of law that contractor had breached its Paragraph 4.5.1 warranty by using defective bricks. Furthermore, the owner argued that the court compounded its error by instructing the jury that it could find for the surety if the owner required the contractor to use unsuitable brick. The Appellate Court rejected the owner's argument because the court's order clearly stated that the court was denying the motion because the owner substantially mischaracterized both the predicate and the grounds for the court's ruling. At the time it ruled, the District Court had before it a motion from owner that argued that, as a matter of law, the Paragraph 4.5.1 warranty was breached by contractor when it used bricks with a latent defect. On appeal the owner suggested that what it had really requested was a limited ruling as to the applicability of the Paragraph 4.5.1 warranty, leaving for the jury the question of waiver of the warranty. The Court found that the owner's mischaracterization of the record was compounded by owner's misstatement of the grounds for the court's denial of its motion. The owner argued that

the owner was responsible for securing the coverage, it was not alleged that the harm affected any part of the contractor's work, and, in any event, neither the policy nor the contract directed that any proceeds be paid to the contractor. Had the policy expressed an intent to cover the contractor's property or to make him a loss payee under its terms, he would be considered a co-insured or a third-party beneficiary. But even in that instance the Court found that the contractor's indemnity interest would shield him from subrogation liability only to the extent that the value of his property or of his completed and unpaid performance was insured from loss.

Furthermore, the waiver clause made the owner responsible for procuring coverage only for "the completed value of the [contractor's work]." The contract did not allocate liability for the owner's water damaged interior but held each party harmless for those losses of the other which were connected with the work performed. The Court concluded that the agreement was clearly ineffective to exonerate the contractor from liability for negligently inflicting harm to the owner's interior property since the contract provided that contractor's liability insurance shall be "purchased and maintained by the Contractor to protect against damage claims arising out of the Contractor's operations under this Contract, whether by the Contractor, any subcontractor or anyone directly or indirectly employed by any of them. . . ."

The Court held that a waiver of liability was not reasonably inferable from the contract and that the owner's policy did not make the contractor either a co-insured or a third party beneficiary for the risk that resulted in the loss for which the insurer's claim was asserted.

90050   Trustees of Indiana Univ. v. Aetna Casualty & Sur. Co., 920 F.2d 429 (7th Cir. 1990)

I:	A107-1978, Art. 7, Para. 7.4	
I:	A107-1978, Art. 10, Para. 10.4	
I:	A107-1978, Art. 15, Para. 15.3	
I:	A107-1978, Art. 15, Para. 15.4	
I:	A107-1979, Art. 15, Para. 15.5	
I:	A117-1979, Art. 11, Para. 11.4	
I:	A117-1979, Art. 14, Para. 14.4	
I:	A117-1979, Art. 19, Para. 19.3	
I:	A117-1979, Art. 19, Para. 19.4	
I:	A117-1979, Art. 19, Para. 19.5	
I:	A201-1976, Art. 1, Para. 1.1.3	
I:	A201-1976, Art. 4, Para. 4.5.1	
III:	A201-1976, Art. 9, Para. 9.9.1	
III:	A201-1976, Art. 9, Para. 9.9.4	

Owner brought a breach of contract action against contractor's surety for damages resulting from the deterioration of exterior facing bricks. The surety answered and filed

II: A201-1976, Art. 11, Para. 11.4.1

The issue on certiorari to the Supreme Court of Oklahoma was whether a contractor, who allegedly negligently caused damage to the owner's property for which the owner's insurer had paid, was considered a co-insured, making the contractor immune from liability to the insurer on its subrogation claim. The insurer argued that the contract placed the responsibility for the acts and omissions of the workers upon the contractor, who was in turn responsible for indemnifying and "hold harmless the Owner . . . from and against all claims, damages, losses or expenses resulting from the performance of the Work." The contractor argued that it was a co-insured and that the subrogation claim was barred by the owner-contractor agreement, which provided that the owner and contractor "waive all rights against each other for damages caused by fire or other perils to the extent covered by insurance."

The owner-contractor agreement required the owner to purchase and maintain property insurance covering the "completed value of the Work. Any loss will be adjusted with the Owner and made payable to the Owner as trustee for the Contractor. The Contractor shall be responsible for payment of the deductible amount in the event of a paid claim. The Owner and Contractor waive all rights against each other for damages caused by fire or other perils to the extent covered by insurance, except for such rights as they may have to the proceeds of such insurance held by the Owner as trustee. The Contractor shall require similar waivers in favor of the Owner and Contractor by subcontractors and sub-subcontractors."

The Supreme Court found that the contract and the insurance policy comprised two distinct agreements and that each gave rise to different and separate relationships. The contract's requirement that the owner purchase insurance did not make the contractor a co-insured under the policy and neither did the insurance policy by its reference to "contractors' interest in property covered." The Court concluded that the coverage afforded the owner indemnity for a loss to property in which the contractor had an interest. In case of damage either to any of the completed work for which the contractor had not been paid or to any of his tools or equipment, the contractor would be protected by the policy's coverage as a third-party beneficiary.

Furthermore, the owner-contractor agreement contained a provision similar to Paragraph 11.1.1 of the American Institute of Architects General Conditions of the Contract for Construction, which required the contractor to secure liability coverage. It also required the contractor to "submit a certificate of insurance showing such policy or policies, with the Owner named as additional insured, to Owner or Owner's agent prior to the start of construction operation." The Court found that while this clause required the contractor to include the owner as a co-insured under its liability policy, there was no reciprocal obligation that the contractor be made a co-insured on the owner's policy. Rather, the contract expressly charged the owner with the duty to act as trustee for the contractor in the event of a paid loss for any funds that were due to the contractor. The Court concluded that there was no intent to confer indemnity rights on the contractor. Under the contract the owner was protected from liability for loss to property situated on the covered premises in which the contractor may have had an interest. Although

II:	A201-1976, Art. 2, Para. 2.2.10
II:	A201-1976, Art. 7, Para. 7.6.2
III:	A201-1976, Art. 8, Para. 8.3.1
III:	A201-1976, Art. 12, Para. 12.2.1
III:	A201-1976, Art. 12, Para. 12.3.1

Transmission line contractor brought a breach of contract action against the owner and a negligence action against the construction manager/design professional, alleging entitlement to damages arising from construction manager/design professional's recommendation, implemented by owner, that contractor be denied compensation for acceleration necessary due to events beyond contractor's control. Contractor obtained a jury verdict, from which owner and the construction manager/design professional appealed.

On appeal owner argued that a contract provision that arguably allocated the risks of site conditions to contractor precluded recovery by contractor. Owner also claimed that contractor waived its rights to damages by failing to provide timely notice of its claims. The construction manager/design professional contended that its decisions were contractually immune from suit unless made in bad faith.

The Appellate Court affirmed. The site conditions clause, in the view of the Court, simply provided for allocation of property loss risk. The contractor's claim was supported by a clause which required an extension of time if unforeseen conditions were encountered. The Court held further that despite a clause specifically precluding conduct of the owner from constituting a waiver, owner had waived the provision requiring notice of claims in a short time frame. Finally, a contract provision specifically protecting the construction manager/design professional from negligence suits based on its decisions, limiting such actions to those premised on the construction manager/design professional's bad faith, was insufficient under Oklahoma law to indemnify it against its own negligence.

90049 Travelers Ins. Co. v. Dickey, 799 P.2d 625 (Okla. 1990)

II:	A107-1978, Art. 17, Para. 17.1
II:	A107-1978, Art. 17, Para. 17.2
II:	A107-1978, Art. 17, Para. 17.3
II:	A107-1978, Art. 17, Para. 17.6
II:	A117-1979, Art. 21, Para. 21.1
II:	A117-1979, Art. 21, Para. 21.2
II:	A117-1979, Art. 21, Para. 21.3
II:	A117-1979, Art. 21, Para. 21.6
II:	A201-1976, Art. 11, Para. 11.1.1
II:	A201-1976, Art. 11, Para. 11.1.4
II:	A201-1976, Art. 11, Para. 11.2.1
II:	A201-1976, Art. 11, Para. 11.3.1
II:	A201-1976, Art. 11, Para. 11.3.6

90047 Tonn & Blank, Inc. v. Board of Comm'rs, 554 N.E.2d 827 (Ind. Ct. App. 1990)

II:	A107-1978, Art. 12, Para. 12.1
II:	A107-1978, Art. 12, Para. 12.3
II:	A117-1979, Art. 16, Para. 16.1
II:	A117-1979, Art. 16, Para. 16.3
I:	A201-1976, Art. 6, Para. 6.1.1
I:	A201-1976, Art. 6, Para. 6.1.2
I:	A201-1976, Art. 6, Para. 6.2.1

Prime contractor brought an action against owner and a second prime contractor for delay damages. The trial court entered summary judgment for owner and the second prime contractor. Contractor appealed, arguing that the second prime contractor owed contractor a duty as a third-party beneficiary.

The owner and each prime contractor entered into an agreement which included the American Institute of Architects General Conditions of the Contract for Construction, Document No. A201, 1976 edition, specifically the award of separate contract and mutual responsibility provisions contained in Paragraphs 6.1.1, 6.1.2 and 6.2.1.

The Appellate Court found that the contract expressed the parties' intention to benefit other contractors with properly coordinated work. The contract imposed a duty on a contractor to properly coordinate its work with other contractors. A properly coordinated construction sequence provided a direct benefit to other contractors. Based on this finding the Court held that a third-party beneficiary contract exited and the trial court had erred in granting summary judgment for the second prime contractor.

90048 Transpower Constructors, Div. of Harrison Int'l Corp. v. Grand River Dam Auth., 905 F.2d 1413 (10th Cir. 1990)

III:	A107-1978, Art. 7, Para. 7.3
III:	A107-1978, Art. 8, Para. 8.5
III:	A107-1978, Art. 14, Para. 14.3
III:	A107-1978, Art. 18, Para. 18.1
III:	A117-1979, Art. 11, Para. 11.3
III:	A117-1979, Art. 12, Para. 12.5
III:	A117-1979, Art. 18, Para. 18.3
III:	A117-1979, Art. 22, Para. 22.1
III:	A201-1976, Art. 1, Para. 1.2.2
III:	A201-1976, Art. 2, Para. 2.2.7
III:	A201-1976, Art. 2, Para. 2.2.8
III:	A201-1976, Art. 2, Para. 2.2.9

III: A401-1978, Art. 13, Para. 13.1
III: B141-1977, Art. 9, Para. 9.1

In deciding contractor's appeal of an order denying its motion to compel arbitration, the Appellate Court found that the arbitration provision, which was included in an addendum to the owner-contractor agreement, lacked mutuality and was void for lack of consideration under state statute. In addition to the addendum, the owner-contractor agreement also incorporated by reference the American Institute of Architects General Conditions of the Contract for Construction, Document No. A201, 1976 edition, which contained an arbitration clause in Paragraph 7.9.1. The arbitration clause in the addendum provided the owner with the unilateral option of selecting either arbitration or litigation as the means of dispute resolution if "a claim or dispute arises between the parties to this Contract, or between the Owner and any other person or entity related to or connected with the project, or between any other parties when the resolution of the dispute would substantially affect the interests of the Owner, and if any of the parties do not accept the decision of the Architect rendered pursuant to the General Conditions, the Owner shall have the option of (i) submitting the dispute to arbitration in accordance with the Construction Industry Arbitration Rules of the American Arbitration Association then obtaining, or (ii) foregoing arbitration and filing a lawsuit or filing a claim in an existing lawsuit before any court of competent jurisdiction, submitting the dispute for decision by the court." The addendum also granted owner the right to reconsider its choice of dispute resolution even after having exercised its option and provided further that "the election made by the Owner shall be binding upon all other parties to the dispute. Any one election made by the Owner shall not be a waiver of the right to make further elections in connection with the same dispute; and the Owner shall not relinquish the option, but shall reserve and retain the option throughout any proceedings which may be instituted, for further election at any time, prior to a final judgment in the ongoing proceeding." The arbitration option, being unilateral, was not supportive of the public policy favoring arbitration, and was in fact so inequitable as to violate and undermine the purpose of arbitration. Furthermore, the addendum modified and superseded the standardized arbitration provision contained in the contract, thus becoming the only viable arbitration provision between the parties. Since the addendum was held to be void, the contractor's motion to compel arbitration was properly denied.

90046 Thompson v. Jespersen, 222 Cal. App. 3d 964, 272 Cal. Rptr. 132 (1990), *review denied,* 1990 Cal. LEXIS 4758 (Cal. 1990)

II: A107-1978, Art. 13, Para. 13.2
II: A117-1979, Art. 17, Para. 17.2
II: A201-1976, Art. 7, Para. 7.9.1
II: A401-1978, Art. 13, Para. 13.1
II: B141-1977, Art. 9, Para. 9.1

The Appellate Court found that arbitrators do not have the authority to award attorney's fees in the absence of a provision for attorney's fees in either the arbitration agreement or the submission to arbitration.

contract. Under Paragraph 17.1, the contractor was required to obtain liability insurance protecting it from "claims for damages . . . to property . . . other than to the Work itself." The Court found that in the event of a claim for non-Work property damage, the insurer under the contractor's liability policy would be responsible. The Court concluded that Paragraph 17.6 provided that the contractor was to be responsible for negligently caused damage outside the Work and had to carry a policy insuring its liability.

The Court held that the trial court properly dismissed the owner's claim to the extent it sought recovery for damages to the Work itself. To the extent owner's insurer sought recovery for damage to property other than the Work, the claim was not barred by the waiver in Paragraph 17.6.

90044   State Highway Admin. v. Greiner Eng'g Sciences, Inc., 83 Md. App. 621, 577 A.2d 363, *cert. denied*, 321 Md. 163, 582 A.2d 499 (1990)

   III: A107-1978, Art. 8, Para. 8.2
   III: A107-1978, Art. 14, Para. 14.3
   III: A107-1978, Art. 18, Para. 18.1
   III: A117-1979, Art. 18, Para. 18.3
   III: A117-1979, Art. 22, Para. 22.1
   III: A117-1979, Art. 22, Para. 22.2
   III: A201-1976, Art. 8, Para. 8.3.1
   III: A201-1976, Art. 8, Para. 8.3.4
   III: A201-1976, Art. 12, Para. 12.1.2
   III: A201-1976, Art. 12, Para. 12.3.1

The Appellate Court found that the engineer's claim for delay damages incurred during preparation of construction contract documents for a highway project was precluded. The no-damage-for delay clause in the contract provided that the engineer agreed to "prosecute the work continuously and diligently and no charges or claims for damages shall be made by him for any delays or hindrances from any cause whatsoever during the progress of any portion of the services specified in this Agreement. Such delays or hindrances, if any, may be compensated for by an extension of time for such reasonable period as the Department may decide. Time extensions will be granted only for excusable delays such as delays beyond the control and without the fault or negligence of the Consultant." The clause was clear and unambiguous and there was no finding of intentional wrongdoing or gross negligence.

90045   Stevens/Leinweber/Sullens, Inc. v. Holm Dev. & Management, Inc., 165 Ariz. 25, 795 P.2d 1308 (1990)

   III: A107-1978, Art. 13, Para. 13.2
   III: A117-1979, Art. 17, Para. 17.2
   III: A201-1976, Art. 7, Para. 7.9.1

90043   S.S.D.W. Co. v. Brisk Waterproofing Co., 76 N.Y.2d 228, 557 N.Y.S.2d 290, 556 N.E.2d 1097 (1990)

I:	A107-1978, Art. 7, Para. 7.4
I:	A107-1978, Art. 17, Para. 17.1
I:	A107-1978, Art. 17, Para. 17.3
I:	A107-1978, Art. 17, Para. 17.6
I:	A117-1979, Art. 11, Para. 11.4
I:	A117-1979, Art. 21, Para. 21.1
I:	A117-1979, Art. 21, Para. 21.3
I:	A117-1979, Art. 21, Para. 21.4
I:	A201-1976, Art. 1, Para. 1.1.3
II:	A201-1976, Art. 11, Para. 11.1.1
II:	A201-1976, Art. 11, Para. 11.3.1
II:	A201-1976, Art. 11, Para. 11.3.6

Owner's insurer brought a subrogation action against contractor for reimbursement of costs paid to owner resulting from fire damage. At issue on appeal was whether the subrogation waiver clause in the owner-contractor agreement barred the subrogation claim for damage to the portions of the building not included in the Work.

The owner and contractor entered into the American Institute of Architects Abbreviated Form of Agreement Between Owner and Contractor, Document No. A107-1978, specifically the definition of the Work in Paragraph 7.4 and the insurance provisions contained in Paragraphs 17.1, 17.3 and 17.6.

The Court found that the owner and contractor had agreed upon an allocation of their respective responsibilities, risks and insurance obligations pertaining to the possibility of property damage occurring during the contract and to the contractor's potential liability stemming from its operations. The Court construed the waiver provision in Paragraph 17.6 as barring the claim of the owner's subrogee to the extent that the damages sought were covered either by: (1) "insurance obtained pursuant to [art. 17]" or (2) "any other property insurance applicable to the Work." The first alternative referred to insurance which the owner had procured under Paragraph 17.3 in which owner was obligated to provide insurance "upon the entire Work at the site" and to include therein the interests of the contractor and subcontractors "in the Work." The second alternative referred only to other insurance "applicable to the Work" and it made no difference whether the policy under which subrogation was sought was one which the owner purchased specifically to insure the Work pursuant to Paragraph 17.3 or some other policy covering the owner's property in which the owner had also provided coverage for the Work. The Court concluded that the waiver clause, if given its plain meaning, barred subrogation only for those damages covered by insurance which the owner had provided to meet the requirement of protecting the contractor's limited interest in the building.

Furthermore, the Court found that its construction of Paragraph 17.6 gave full effect to the bargain concerning the parties' respective insurance responsibilities under the

to indemnity, and (3) whether the owner waived indemnification by making final payment.

The parties entered into the American Institute of Architects Standard Form of Agreement Between Owner and Contractor, Document No. A111, 1978 edition. The agreement provided, on its face, "Use only with the 1976 Edition of AIA Document A201, General Conditions of the Contract for Construction."

The Appellate Court reversed and ordered entry of summary judgment in favor of owner. It found that Document A201 was not stapled to Document A111, nor was it physically present when the parties executed the agreement. The only document actually signed by the parties was Document A111, which provided in Paragraph 1.1 that the "Contract Documents consist of this Agreement, the Conditions of the Contract (General, Supplementary and other Conditions), the Drawings, the Specifications, all Addenda issued prior to and all Modifications issued after execution of this Agreement. These form the Contract, and all are as fully a part of the Contract as if attached to this Agreement or repeated herein. An enumeration of the Contract Documents appears in Article 16. If anything in the Contract Documents is inconsistent with this Agreement, this Agreement shall govern." Furthermore, Paragraph 16.2, which was referred to in Paragraph 1.1, read as follows: "The Contract Documents, which constitute the entire agreement between the Owner and Contractor, are listed in Article 1 and, except for Modifications issued after execution of this Agreement, are enumerated as follows: (List below the Agreement, the Conditions of the Contract [General, Supplementary, and other Conditions], the Drawings, the Specifications, and any Addenda and accepted alternates, showing page or sheet numbers in all cases and dates where applicable.)" The Court concluded that to hold that Document A201 was not incorporated by reference would not be a reasonable interpretation of the agreement of the parties. It was clear to the Court that Document A111 was not drafted with the intent that it composed the entire agreement of the parties where it clearly stated that it was to be used in connection with Document A201. The Court therefore held that Document A201 was incorporated by reference into the agreement of the parties.

Furthermore, in holding that the owner was entitled to summary judgment on the issue of whether contractor was required to indemnify the owner under Paragraph 4.18.1, the Court construed Paragraph 4.18.1 as providing that contractor indemnify the owner where the claim, damage, or loss arose out of the performance of the work, was attributable to bodily injury and was caused in whole or in part by the negligence of the contractor.

In deciding whether the owner waived its right to indemnification by making final payment to the contractor, the Court was unsure whether Paragraph 9.9.4 applied to a claim for indemnification under Paragraph 4.18.1. The Court reasoned that Paragraph 4.18.1 applied to claims for personal injuries sustained as a result of the performance of the "work." This provision contemplated a long-term situation in which a third party could have been injured by a defective part of the project long after the final payment had been made. The Court construed Paragraph 9.9.4 as not barring claims for indemnification, but held that it could bar other, more direct contractual disputes between owner and contractor over the quality of the work where the issue was not raised until after payment and issuance of a certificate of completion.

in the prime electrical contractor's arbitration so that their presence was necessary to accord complete relief in that proceeding. The Court reasoned that the factual allegations underlying the electrical contractor's demand for arbitration arose from delays and problems of coordination and scheduling in the construction project. Similarly, the mechanical contractor alleged in its demand for arbitration that it was damaged by delays, scheduling deficiencies and failure of coordination between the prime contractors. The general contractor was responsible for the overall coordination of the construction project. In addition, each prime contractor was responsible for coordination with the other prime contractors. Accordingly, the Court concluded that complete relief on the coordination issue could not be accorded without the presence of all of the responsible parties. Furthermore, where there was evidence that the mechanical contractor was a possible cause of the delay its presence in the electrical contractor's arbitration was necessary to resolve the delay issues, and where the general contractor was responsible for maintaining proper scheduling, complete relief on the electrical contractors claim for damages due to improper scheduling could not be afforded without the general contractor's presence in the arbitration.

90042 Southwest Nat'l Bank v. Simpson & Son, Inc., 14 Kan. App. 763, 799 P.2d 512 (1990)

I:	A101-1977, Art. 1	
I:	A101-1977, Art. 7, Para. 7.2	
II:	A107-1978, Art. 6, Para. 6.1	
II:	A107-1978, Art. 7, Para. 7.1	
II:	A107-1978, Art. 10, Para. 10.11	
II:	A107-1978, Art. 15, Para. 15.5	
I:	A111-1978, Art. 1, Para. 1.1	
I:	A111-1978, Art. 16, Para. 16.2	
II:	A117-1979, Art. 10, Para. 10.2	
II:	A117-1979, Art. 11, Para. 11.1	
II:	A117-1979, Art. 14, Para. 14.11	
II:	A117-1979, Art. 19, Para. 19.5	
II:	A201-1976, Art. 1, Para. 1.1.1	
II:	A201-1976, Art. 4, Para. 4.18.1	
II:	A201-1976, Art. 9, Para. 9.9.4	
II:	A401-1978, Art. 11, Para. 11.11.1	

Owner brought an indemnification action against contractor for damages paid to supplier's injured worker. The trial court granted summary judgment for contractor and owner appealed. Among numerous issues on appeal was (1) whether A201 was incorporated by reference into the owner-contractor agreement where Paragraph 16.2 failed to list the document, and, if so incorporated, (2) whether the owner was entitled

In contractor's appeal of the trial court's entry of summary judgment in favor of the owner, the Appellate Court upheld the trial court's ruling on the grounds that the contractor was responsible for the defective work under an American Institute of Architects Standard Form of Agreement Between Owner and Contractor which incorporated by reference the American Institute of Architects General Conditions of the Contract for Construction, Document No. A201, 1976 edition, where the contractor failed to demand arbitration of the architect's decision pursuant to Paragraph 2.2.10. The Court reviewed Paragraphs 2.2.1, 2.2.4, 2.2.7, 2.2.9, 2.2.10, 2.2.12, 2.2.13, 4.5.1, 7.4.1, 7.7.1, 7.7.2, 9.9.4, 13.2.1, 13.2.2 and 13.2.4 of the General Conditions and held that the failure of the contractor to demand arbitration after receipt of the architect's final decision rendered the decision binding upon the parties under the contract. The contract clearly stated that the contractor warranted that all work was to be of good quality and free from faults and defects, that the contractor was to bear the costs of special testing after the commencement of the work if the architect determined that it was required, and that the contractor was to correct defective work.

90041   Slutsky-Peltz Plumbing & Heating Co. v. Vincennes Community School Corp., 556 N.E.2d 344 (Ind. Ct. App. 1990)

I: A107-1978, Art. 13, Para. 13.2
I: A117-1979, Art. 17, Para. 17.2
I: A201-1976, Art. 7, Para. 7.9.1
I: A401-1978, Art. 13, Para. 13.1
I: A401-1978, Art. 13, Para. 13.2
I: B141-1977, Art. 9, Para. 9.1

Prime electrical contractor filed a demand for arbitration against the owner for delay damages and damages resulting from failure of coordination. The owner filed a motion requesting joinder of the prime mechanical contractor and the general contractor. The prime mechanical contractor then filed a separate demand for arbitration against the owner for delay damages, failure of coordination and scheduling problems. A pre-arbitration hearing was held on the prime electrical contractor's demand and the owner was requested to obtain a court order compelling the joinder of the mechanical and general contractors. The trial court entered summary judgment for owner granting the joinder and ordered a stay of the prime mechanical contractor arbitration. The prime mechanical contractor and the general contractor appealed the order of the trial court, arguing that the consolidation and joinder of all of the prime contractors into one arbitration proceeding was improper under the terms of the prime contracts and under state law.

The prime contracts incorporated the American Institute of Architects General Conditions of the Contract for Construction, Document No. A201, 1976 edition, specifically the arbitration provision contained in Paragraph 7.9.1.

The Appellate Court upheld the trial court's ruling on the grounds that the arbitration provisions in the prime contracts were unambiguous and the prime mechanical and general contractors were substantially involved in the legal and factual questions raised

90040 Sarnoff v. De Graf Bros., Inc., 196 Ill. App. 3d 535, 143 Ill. Dec. 400, 554 N.E.2d 335 (1990), *appeal denied,* 133 Ill. 2d 573, 149 Ill. Dec. 337, 561 N.E.2d 707 (1990)

II:	A107-1978, Art. 8, Para. 8.1
II:	A107-1978, Art. 8, Para. 8.3
II:	A107-1978, Art. 8, Para. 8.5
II:	A107-1978, Art. 8, Para. 8.6
II:	A107-1978, Art. 10, Para. 10.4
II:	A107-1978, Art. 15, Para. 15.5
II:	A107-1978, Art. 19, Para. 19.1
II:	A117-1979, Art. 12, Para. 12.1
II:	A117-1979, Art. 12, Para. 12.3
II:	A117-1979, Art. 12, Para. 12.5
II:	A117-1979, Art. 12, Para. 12.6
II:	A117-1979, Art. 14, Para. 14.4
II:	A117-1979, Art. 19, Para. 19.5
II:	A117-1979, Art. 23, Para. 23.1
I:	A201-1976, Art. 2, Para. 2.2.1
I:	A201-1976, Art. 2, Para. 2.2.4
I:	A201-1976, Art. 2, Para. 2.2.7
I:	A201-1976, Art. 2, Para. 2.2.9
I:	A201-1976, Art. 2, Para. 2.2.10
I:	A201-1976, Art. 2, Para. 2.2.12
I:	A201-1976, Art. 2, Para. 2.2.13
I:	A201-1976, Art. 4, Para. 4.5.1
I:	A201-1976, Art. 7, Para. 7.4.1
I:	A201-1976, Art. 7, Para. 7.7.1
I:	A201-1976, Art. 7, Para. 7.2.1
I:	A201-1976, Art. 9, Para. 9.9.4
I:	A201-1976, Art. 13, Para. 13.2.1
I:	A201-1976, Art. 13, Para. 13.2.2
I:	A201-1976, Art. 13, Para. 13.2.4
II:	B141-1977, Art. 1, Para. 1.5.3
II:	B141-1977, Art. 1, Para. 1.5.5
II:	B141-1977, Art. 1, Para. 1.5.9
II:	B141-1977, Art. 1, Para. 1.5.10
II:	B141-1977, Art. 1, Para. 1.5.12

of the contract. However, the expert witness services rendered pursuant to Paragraph 17.20 were not lienable where they were related to the protection of ownership interests and not to the improvement of the property.

90038 Roscoe v. Jones, 571 So. 2d 1043 (Ala. 1990)

> II: A107-1978, Art. 13, Para. 13.2
> II: A117-1979, Art. 17, Para. 17.2
> II: A201-1976, Art. 7, Para. 7.9.1
> II: A401-1978, Art. 13, Para. 13.1
> I: B141-1977, Art. 9, Para. 9.1
> I: B141-1977, Art. 9, Para. 9.2
> I: B141-1977, Art. 9, Para. 9.3

The Supreme Court of Alabama found that the owner had waived any right to dispute the validity of the arbitration provisions contained in the American Institute of Architects Standard Form of Agreement Between the Owner and Architect, Document No. B141, 1977 edition, where the owner filed a demand for arbitration, did nothing to indicate any objection to the provision, and participated in the arbitration proceeding.

90039 Ruby-Collins, Inc. v. City of Charlotte, 740 F. Supp. 1159 (W.D.N.C. 1990), *aff'd without opinion,* 930 F.2d 23 (4th Cir. 1991)

> III: A107-1978, Art. 7, Para. 7.1
> III: A107-1978, Art. 7, Para. 7.3
> III: A107-1978, Art. 10, Para. 10.2
> III: A117-1979, Art. 11, Para. 11.1
> III: A117-1979, Art. 11, Para. 11.3
> III: A117-1979, Art. 14, Para. 14.2
> III: A201-1976, Art. 1, Para. 1.1.1
> II: A201-1976, Art. 1, Para. 1.2.2
> II: A201-1976, Art. 4, Para. 4.2.1
> II: A201-1976, Art. 4, Para. 4.4.1
> II: A201-1976, Art. 12, Para. 12.2.1

The District Court granted owner's motion for summary judgment on the grounds that where there were concealed conditions affecting the work, where there was no equitable adjustment clause, and where the contract documents did not include the soils report, the contractor bore the risk of concealed conditions pursuant to contract provisions similar to Paragraphs 1.2.2, 4.2.1 and 4.4.1 of the American Institute of Architects General Conditions of the Contract for Construction, Document No. A201, 1976 edition.

90036 Procter & Gamble Paper Prod. Co. v. Yeargin Constr. Co., 196 Ga. App. 216, 396 S.E.2d 38 (1990)

  III: A107-1978, Art. 10, Para. 10.11
  III: A107-1978, Art. 16, Para. 16.1
  III: A117-1979, Art. 14, Para. 14.11
  III: A117-1979, Art. 20, Para. 20.1
  III: A201-1976, Art. 4, Para. 4.18.1
  III: A201-1976, Art. 10, Para. 10.1.1
  III: A401-1978, Art. 11, Para. 11.1.1
  III: A401-1978, Art. 11, Para. 11.5.1

Owner brought an indemnification action against contractor for personal injury damages. The trial court granted contractor summary judgment and owner appealed. The Appellate Court upheld the award of summary judgment on the grounds that the owner did not produce any evidence that the condition giving rise to the injury was due to any action or inaction by contractor.

The agreement provided that "Seller [Yeargin] agrees to protect, defend, indemnify and save Buyer [P&G] harmless from any and all judgments, . . . settlements and claims on account of . . . personal injury . . . which may be sustained by . . . its employees . . . arising out of or in connection with work done whether such loss, damage, injury or liability is contributed to by the negligence of Buyer [P&G] or its employees (except that this indemnity shall not apply to damages, injuries, or the costs incident thereto found to be caused by the sole negligence of Buyer [P&G]. . . ." The agreement further provided that "construction safety is solely the responsibility of the construction contractor. This will include the establishment and execution of an effective safety program incorporating the best safety practices known to the industry and/or required by applicable regulatory or advisory agencies."

90037 Robert M. Swedroe, Architects/Planners, A.I.A., P.A. v. First American Inv. Corp., 565 So. 2d 349 (Fla. Dist. Ct. App. 1990)

  I: B141-1977, Art. 1, Para. 1.7.10
  I: B141-1977, Art. 1, Para. 1.7.16
  I: B141-1977, Art. 1, Para. 1.7.20

Architect appealed the trial court's dismissal of its lien claim for the amount of "additional" services rendered pursuant to Paragraph 1.7.10, 1.7.16 and 1.7.20 of the American Institute of Architects Standard Form of Agreement Between Owner and Architect, Document No. B141, 1977 edition. The Appellate Court reversed the trial court's dismissal of architect's claim for lien on the grounds that the additional services were lienable pursuant to statute where the architect had a direct contract with the owner and the services rendered were provided pursuant to the "Additional Services" portion

The Supreme Court found that the subcontract provision relating to time and condition of payment, when considered in light of the owner-contractor agreement and the general conditions, did not clearly indicate the parties intent to shift the risk of the owner's nonpayment from the contractor to the subcontractor. The Court found that the owner-contractor agreement was a "cost plus" or reimbursement type contract which required contractor to pay its subcontractors before the owner reimbursed the contractor. The general conditions required the contractor to submit an affidavit certifying that its subcontractors had been paid before final payment from the owner became due. In contrast, the subcontract clearly required payment from the owner to contractor as a condition precedent to final payment becoming due the subcontractor. The Court concluded that this conflict between the subcontract and the owner-contractor agreement and general conditions created ambiguity as to who should bear the risk of the owner's nonpayment.

The Court concluded that when the subcontract provision was read in conjunction with the owner-contractor agreement and the general conditions, ambiguity existed which prevented the provision from effectively shifting the risk of the owner's nonpayment from the contractor to the subcontractor, leaving the contractor liable for the final payment owed to the subcontractor.

90035 Parent v. Stone & Webster Eng'g Corp., 408 Mass. 108, 556 N.E.2d 1009 (1990)

	III:	A107-1978, Art. 8, Para. 8.3
	III:	A107-1978, Art. 16, Para. 16.1
	III:	A117-1979, Art. 12, Para. 12.3
	III:	A117-1979, Art. 20, Para. 20.1
	III:	A201-1976, Art. 2, Para. 2.2.4
	III:	A201-1976, Art. 10, Para. 10.1.1
	III:	B141-1977, Art. 1, Para. 1.5.5

The Supreme Court of Massachusetts found that the architect/engineer failed to demonstrate that its contractual relationship with the owner did not give rise to a duty of reasonable care to owner's injured employee. The broad language of the owner-architect/engineer agreement expressly designated the architect/engineer as the project manager and described its duties as "furnish [ing] the necessary engineering and technical direction, design, estimates, cost control, procurement, scheduling, construction services, labor, materials, and equipment to complete this project, including without limitation, the furnishing of those services, specifically delineated in Appendices A1 and A2 of this Agreement." Appendix A2 required the architect/engineer to provide "participation and assistance as may be required" in several specified areas, including "[s]afety." The Court concluded that this contract language created a duty to third persons not parties to the contract injured as a result of the architect/engineer's negligence.

Finally, the contractor failed to offer any evidence to indicate the significance of the architect's failure to certify.

90034   OBS Co. v. Pace Constr. Corp., 558 So. 2d 404 (Fla. 1990)

III:	A107-1978, Art. 4, Para. 4.1
III:	A107-1978, Art. 5, Para. 5.1
III:	A107-1978, Art. 11, Para. 11.2
III:	A107-1978, Art. 15, Para. 15.4
I:	A111-1978, Art. 5, Para. 5.1
I:	A111-1978, Art. 8, Para. 8.1
I:	A111-1978, Art. 8, Para. 8.1.6
III:	A117-1979, Art. 9, Para. 9.1
III:	A117-1979, Art. 15, Para. 15.2
III:	A117-1979, Art. 19, Para. 19.4
I:	A201-1976, Art. 5, Para. 5.3.1
I:	A201-1976, Art. 9, Para. 9.5.2
I:	A201-1976, Art. 9, Para. 9.9.2
III:	A401-1978, Art. 1, Para. 1.1
III:	A401-1978, Art. 6, Para. 6.1
III:	A401-1978, Art. 11, Para. 11.1.1
III:	A401-1978, Art. 12, Para. 12.4.1

Subcontractor brought an action against contractor for payment due under the subcontract and against the sureties under the payment bond. The trial court entered judgment for subcontractor and contractor appealed. On appeal the Appellate Court held that contractor was not liable because the contract was unambiguous, and further, that because contractor was not liable under the subcontract, the sureties could not be liable under the payment bond. Subcontractor appealed.

The subcontract provided that "In addition to any other any other requirements of this Subcontract and the Contract Documents, Final Payment shall not become due unless and until the following conditions precedent to Final Payment have been satisfied: (a) approval and acceptance of Subcontractor's work by Owner, Architect and Contractor, (b) delivery to Contractor of all manuals, "as-built" drawings, guarantees, and warranties for material and equipment furnished by Subcontractor, or any other documents required by the Contract Documents, (c) receipt of Final Payment for Subcontractor's work by Contractor from Owner, (d) furnishing to Contractor of satisfactory evidence by Subcontractor that all labor and material accounts incurred by Subcontractor in connection with his work have been paid in full, (e) furnishings [sic] to Contractor a complete Affidavit, Release of Lien and Waiver of Claim by Subcontractor in the form attached hereto as Exhibit "D," and as required by the Contract Documents."

II:	A117-1979, Art. 24, Para. 24.2
I:	A201-1976, Art. 3, Para. 3.3.1
II:	A201-1976, Art. 14, Para. 14.2.1

The Appellate Court upheld the trial court's finding that the owner had terminated the owner-contractor agreement where the owner sent a letter to the contractor demanding that the contractor stop work completely. The court cited the contract's termination provision which was similar to Paragraph 14.2.1 of the American Institute of Architects General Conditions of the Contract for Construction, Document No. A201, 1976 edition. The Court found that if the owner wished to order the contractor to cease work while the deficiencies in its performance were remedied, the owner should have done so pursuant to the contract provision which was identical to Paragraph 3.3.1 of the General Conditions. The Court found that the owner's termination of the contractor by letter combined with the contractor's leaving the site rescinded the contract, and entitled the contractor to recovery in quantum meruit for the reasonable value of its services.

90033 Mrozik Constr. Inc. v. Lovering Assoc., Inc., 461 N.W.2d 49 (Minn. Ct. App. 1990)

II:	A201-1976, Art. 9, Para. 9.5.2
II:	A401-1978, Art. 6, Para. 6.1
II:	A401-1978, Art. 12, Para. 12.4.1
II:	A401-1978, Art. 12, Para. 12.4.3

Subcontractor brought an action against contractor to recover the amounts due under the subcontract, plus interest. The trial court granted subcontractor's motion for summary judgment on the grounds that the owner's payment to the contractor was not a condition precedent to contractor's payment to the subcontractor. On appeal the contractor argued that the language in the subcontract established payment by the owner to the contractor as a condition precedent to payment to the subcontractor and the architect's failure to certify the completed work for payment further justified contractor's nonpayment. The Appellate Court affirmed the trial court's grant of summary judgment to the subcontractor.

The subcontract provided that "Final payment including all retention becomes due and payable within 30 days after Architects' certification of final payment. At all times the Subcontractor shall be paid to the extent that the Contractor has been paid on the Subcontractor's account." The owner was insolvent.

The Appellate Court held that a subcontract should not be construed to make payment to the contractor a condition precedent to payment to the subcontractor absent unequivocal, unambiguous language to that effect. The provision relied on by the contractor required that payment be made by the contractor to the subcontractor "to the extent that the contractor has been paid on the subcontractor's account." The Court found that this language did not unequivocally shift the owner's insolvency to the subcontractor. The Court construed the language to mean merely that the timing of payment to the subcontractor was not to be delayed after the contractor received funds from the owner.

The Supreme Court of Mississippi found that an architect's Certificate of Substantial Compliance did not relieve the contractor of his obligations under the owner-contractor agreement where the architect signed an affidavit stating that any certificate of substantial compliance, final application for payment, or year-end inspection prepared by him did not certify, guarantee, or imply that there were no hidden defects in the building or that the contractor constructed the building in full compliance with the plans and specifications. Additionally, the specifications and plans for the building stated that the Certificate of Substantial Compliance did not relieve the contractor of his obligations under the contract.

90031   Moore v. PRC Eng'g, Inc., 565 So. 2d 817 (Fla. Dist. Ct. App. 1990)

> III: A201-1976, Art. 2, Para. 2.2.4
> III: A201-1976, Art. 2, Para. 2.2.17
> III: B141-1977, Art. 1, Para. 1.5.5
> III: B141-1977, Art. 1, Para. 1.6.1
> III: B141-1977, Art. 1, Para. 1.6.2
> III: B141-1977, Art. 1, Para. 1.6.3

The Appellate Court reversed the trial court's entry of summary judgment in favor of the engineer on the grounds that the engineer had a contractual duty to an employee of the contractor injured on the job to institute, maintain and inspect safety procedures at the site. Pursuant to the owner-engineer agreement the engineer had the sole responsibility and obligation to "monitor, surveil, coordinate with, and to guide compliance of all other Consultants with respect to their compliance with the time schedules, work performance quality and level. . . ." The owner-contractor agreement provided that the engineer "appoint such inspectors as are necessary to observe the amount, quality and character of the materials to be supplied or to inspect the execution of the work contemplated under this Contract. When in the judgment of the inspectors, the work or materials are being furnished in an manner considered hazardous to persons or property they shall have the power to stop the work, which shall not be resumed until the ENGINEER has rendered his decision upon the matter. The provision of this clause shall not relieve the CONTRACTOR for the sole responsibility of any injury or damage that may result." The Court held that the engineer was liable for negligence in supervising the construction which resulted in personal injuries notwithstanding the absence of privity between the engineer and the injured worker.

90032   Mor-Wood Contractors, Inc. v. Ottinger, 205 Ill. App. 3d 132, 158 Ill. Dec. 444, 562 N.E.2d 1247 (1990)

> I: A107-1978, Art. 9, Para. 9.4
> II: A107-1978, Art. 20, Para. 20.2
> I: A117-1979, Art. 13, Para. 13.4

III:	A107-1978, Art. 10, Para. 10.1	
III:	A107-1976, Art. 16, Para. 16.1	
III:	A117-1979, Art. 12, Para. 12.3	
III:	A117-1979, Art. 14, Para. 14.1	
III:	A117-1979, Art. 20, Para. 20.1	
III:	A201-1976, Art. 2, Para. 2.2.3	
III:	A201-1976, Art. 2, Para. 2.2.4	
III:	A201-1976, Art. 4, Para. 4.3.1	
III:	A201-1976, Art. 10, Para. 10.1.1	

Contractor's employee sued the owner and the consulting engineer whom owner had retained for injuries incurred on the site. The Supreme Court upheld the Appellate Court's reversal of a jury verdict in favor of owner and engineer on the grounds that the owner was protected by sovereign immunity and the engineer had no contractual duty to discover or correct safety hazards.

The engineer's contract required the engineer to "monitor the construction . . . to assure delivery of the specified systems and facilities in accordance with contract drawings and specifications." The contractor's agreement provided that if the contractor failed to comply with OSHA standards creating a life or property hazard, the engineer "may stop any operation of the Contractor affected by the failure until the failure is remedied." However, the contract also made the contractor "solely responsible for all construction means, methods, techniques, sequences and procedures." The injured worker contended that these provisions were to be monitored by the engineer.

The Supreme Court determined that the engineer's duty to monitor imposed a duty to assure the finished product would comply with the plans and specifications. To extend its duty to be actively involved in safety compliance would be inconsistent with the contractor's duty to supervise and direct the work and be responsible for means, methods and procedures. Further provisions of the contract convinced the Court that the engineer's responsibilities were indirect, in the nature of reviewing the contractor's written safety programs, rather than being an on-site safety inspector.

90030 May v. Ralph L. Dickerson Constr. Co., 560 So. 2d 729 (Miss. 1990)

III:	A107-1978, Art. 15, Para. 15.3	
III:	A107-1978, Art. 15, Para. 15.5	
III:	A117-1979, Art. 19, Para. 19.3	
III:	A117-1979, Art. 19, Para. 19.5	
III:	A201-1976, Art. 2, Para. 2.2.16	
III:	A201-1976, Art. 8, Para. 8.1.3	
III:	A201-1976, Art. 9, Para. 9.8.1	
III:	A201-1976, Art. 9, Para. 9.9.4	
III:	B141-1977, Art. 1, Para. 1.5.15	

be free of faults and defects. The Court concluded that the term "special warranty" referred to those warranties which were specific to the project as opposed to those warranties which were of general application in the construction industry. Furthermore, Paragraph 9.9.4, like Paragraph 13.2.2, contained an exception for special warranties so that owner's final payment did not operate as a waiver of its claims against the contractor.

90027   Hurley v. Fox, 559 So. 2d 887 (La. Ct. App. 1990), *later proceeding,* 587 So. 2d 1 (La. Ct. App. 1991)

        I: A107-1978, Art. 13, Para. 13.2
        I: A117-1979, Art. 17, Para. 17.2
        I: A201-1976, Art. 7, Para. 7.9.1
        I: A401-1978, Art. 13, Para. 13.1
        I: B141-1977, Art. 9, Para. 9.1

In architect's action against owner for the unpaid portion of the fee the Appellate Court found that the record clearly supported the trial court's finding that the American Institute of Architects Standard Form of Agreement Between Owner and Architect, Document No. B141, 1977 edition, absent owner's signature, expressed the terms of the agreement between the owner and architect and that the American Institute of Architects General Conditions of the Contract for Construction, Document No. A201, 1976 edition, was incorporated by reference. Based on the broad arbitration provision contained in Paragraph 9.1, which the Court found was valid under the state statute, the Court affirmed the trial court's confirmation of the award of the arbitrator in favor of the architect.

90028   Kinney v. G.W. Lisk Co., 76 N.Y.2d 215, 557 N.Y.S.2d 283, 556 N.E.2d 1090 (1990)

        III: A401-1978, Art. 9, Para. 9.1

The New York Court of Appeals affirmed summary judgment granted to contractor in contractor's third-party action against subcontractor on the grounds that subcontractor had failed to procure insurance coverage naming the contractor against personal injury claims as clearly required by the subcontract. The subcontract stated that "Subcontractor [Hudson] shall maintain such insurance policies . . . as will protect both the Contractor [Cromwell] and the Subcontractor [Hudson] . . . from claims for damages because of bodily injury . . . which may arise both out of and during its performance under this Agreement or after completion thereof." The Court held that the provision did not violate the state statute, which rendered void any agreement in connection with building construction purporting to indemnify a party against liability for injury caused by the party's own negligence. The statute on its face addressed only agreements to indemnify or hold harmless and made no reference to agreements to purchase or maintain insurance.

90029   Marshall v. Port Auth. of Allegheny County, 524 Pa. 1, 568 A.2d 931 (1990)

        III: A107-1978, Art. 8, Para. 8.3

compensation to architect unless and until all three conditions were satisfied. Both parties agreed that all the conditions were not met nor did the architect present evidence that the conditions were excused. The Court found that since the condition precedent was not satisfied, and was not excused, the trial court did not err when it granted defendant's motion for judgment notwithstanding the verdict.

90025   Henson v. James M. Barker Co., 555 So. 2d 901 (Fla. Dist. Ct. App. 1990), *review denied,* 564 So. 2d 487 (Fla. 1990)

        I: A111-1978, Art. 3, Para. 3.1

The Appellate Court interpreted Paragraph 3.1 of the American Institute of Architects Standard Form of Agreement Between Owner and Contractor, Document No. A111, 1978 edition as requiring a contractor to deal openly and fairly with an owner. The Court interpreted the clause which provides that a contractor furnish "his best skill and judgment" as obligating a contractor to make full disclosure to the owner of all problems encountered that may affect the progress of the work and its value to the owner, including all corrections the contractor deemed necessary and the cost thereof whether to be borne by the contractor or by the owner. The Court concluded that Paragraph 3.1 imposed on the contractor, at the very least, a duty to construct the building free of material defects, and a duty to disclose, and not conceal, any latent defect in the construction that would materially impair the value of the structure.

90026   Hillcrest Country Club v. N.D. Judds Co., 236 Neb. 233, 461 N.W.2d 55 (1990)

        II: A107-1978, Art. 10, Para. 10.4
        II: A107-1978, Art. 15, Para. 15.5
        II: A107-1978, Art. 19, Para. 19.1
        II: A117-1979, Art. 14, Para. 14.4
        II: A117-1979, Art. 19, Para. 19.5
        II: A117-1979, Art. 23, Para. 23.1
        I: A201-1976, Art. 4, Para. 4.5.1
        I: A201-1976, Art. 9, Para. 9.9.4
        I: A201-1976, Art. 13, Para. 13.2.2

In lessor's action against contractor for damages resulting from roof failure, the Appellate Court construed the meaning of "special warranties" found in Paragraphs 9.9.4 and 13.2.2 of the American Institute of Architects General Conditions of the Contract for Construction, Document No. A201, 1976 edition. The Court found that the contract itself did not define "special warranties." The contract contained several warranties of general application to the construction industry, such as the contractor's warranty under Paragraph 4.5.1 that all materials will be new unless otherwise specified, that the work would be of good quality and conform to the contract documents, and that the work would

of the arbitration clause, the Court concluded that the change orders were not so unrelated and separate from the contract as to not be arbitrable under an "all disputes" provision.

90023 Granite Computer Leasing Corp. v. Travelers Indem. Co., 894 F.2d 547 (2d Cir. 1990)

> III: A201-1976, Art. 9, Para. 9.7.1
> III: A401-1978, Art. 11, Para. 11.12.1

The owner's assignee sued the subcontractor's surety to recover the cost of completing performance after the subcontractor ceased performance. The district court directed a verdict in favor of the owner's assignee for liability under the surety's bond. The surety appealed and the court of appeals vacated the judgment and remanded the case. The court of appeals construed a clause in the subcontract which provided that "[subcontractor] may stop work if any progress payment is not made . . . within ten (10) days after the due date . . ." as not limiting the subcontractor's right to terminate the contract for nonpayment by the owner. The Court reasoned that although the provision listed no further ground for which a subcontractor could cease performance, it did not thereby establish nonpayment as the sole ground for stopping the work. Had it been contemplated that no other contractual ground could justify stopping the work, the contract could easily have provided that "[subcontractor] may stop work only if any progress payment is not made." The Court construed the clause as providing one express justification which would warrant subcontractor terminating the subcontract, but as not precluding subcontractor from terminating for other reasons.

90024 Hastings & Chivetta Architects v. Burch, 794 S.W.2d 294 (Mo. Ct. App. 1990)

> III: B141-1977, Art. 10, Para. 10.3

Architect brought a breach of contract action against owner. The jury awarded architect damages resulting from owner's termination of the contract. The trial court sustained owner's motion for judgment notwithstanding the verdict and architect appealed. The Appellate Court affirmed the ruling of the trial court.

The owner-architect agreement contained a provision similar to Paragraph 10.3 of the American Institute of Architects Standard Form of Agreement Between Owner and Architect, Document No. B141, 1977 edition, which was deleted before the contract was executed. A typewritten payment provision was included which provided that "It is understood and agreed that the payment of any compensation and expenses shall be conditional upon Owner obtaining the following," and three conditions were listed. The owner terminated the contract based on one of the conditions.

The Appellate Court found that the payment provision was a typewritten section added to a printed form contract. Conspicuously, the word "any" was underscored. The phase "it is understood and agreed that the payment of any compensation and expenses shall be conditional upon owner obtaining the following" was followed by three conditions. The usual and ordinary meaning of the contract, taken as a whole, required no

of contract, the contractor could not recover economic damages based on the allegedly defective plans and specifications. The Court found that the owner-contractor agreement, which included the American Institute of Architects General Conditions of the Contract for Construction, Document No. A201, 1976 edition, contained several provisions which explicitly served to shield the architect from liability, namely Paragraphs 1.1.2, 2.2.4, 2.2.13 and 4.2.1.

90021   Gilliland v. Elmwood Properties, 301 S.C. 295, 391 S.E.2d 577 (1990)

III:	A201-1976, Art. 1, Para. 1.1.2	
III:	B141-1977, Art. 13, Para. 13.1	

The Supreme Court of South Carolina found that where the owner-architect agreement contained no express provisions requiring the architect to design a project which would qualify for tax exempt bond funding, observe the project's budgetary constraints, design a project feasible for conventional financing, and obtain necessary municipal and governmental agency approvals, parol evidence was not admissible as evidence of contractual undertakings not set forth in the agreement.

90022   Granger Northern, Inc. v. Cianchette, 572 A.2d 136 (Me. 1990)

II:	A107-1978, Art. 13, Para. 13.2
III:	A107-1978, Art. 18, Para. 18.1
II:	A117-1979, Art. 17, Para. 17.2
III:	A117-1979, Art. 22, Para. 22.1
II:	A201-1976, Art. 7, Para. 7.9.1
II:	A201-1976, Art. 12, Para. 12.1.1
II:	A401-1978, Art. 13, Para. 13.1
II:	B141-1977, Art. 9, Para. 9.1

Owner appealed the trial court's affirmation of an arbitration award in favor of the contractor. The Appellate Court construed an arbitration clause which provided that "all claims, disputes and other matters in question arising out of, or relating to, this Agreement or the breach thereof, except with respect to the Architect/Engineer's decision on matters relating to artistic effect, and except for claims which have been waived by the making or acceptance of Final Payment, shall be decided by arbitration in accordance with the Construction Industry Arbitration Rules of the American Arbitration Association then obtaining unless the parties mutually agree otherwise" as giving an arbitrator the authority to decide all contract related disputes between the parties. Furthermore, where the contract defined a change order as "a written order to the Contractor signed by the Owner or his authorized agent and issued after the execution of this Agreement, authorizing a Change in the Project and/or an adjustment in the Guaranteed Maximum Price . . .," and where disputes over change orders were not specifically excluded from the scope

90019   Federated Dept. Stores, Inc. v. J.V.B. Indus., Inc., 894 F.2d 862 (6th Cir. 1990)

        II: A107-1978, Art. 13, Para. 13.2
        II: A117-1979, Art. 17, Para. 17.2
        II: A201-1976, Art. 7, Para. 7.9.1
        II: A401-1978, Art. 13, Para. 13.1
        II: B141-1977, Art. 9, Para. 9.1

On appeal from several orders of the District Court relating to an arbitrators award, the Appellate Court held that a broad form arbitration clause permitted contractor to arbitrate claims for "business destruction." Contractor obtained a drywall and ceiling installation contract from owner for two of its department stores. As to one store the contractor completed its work, but the owner terminated the contractor for delayed performance on the other. Contractor initiated suit for allegedly out-of-scope work it claimed it performed, breach of contract and willful interference with its contract. Owner availed itself of the contract's broad form arbitration clause and counterclaimed for its completion costs. When the arbitration commenced contractor attempted to add a claim for "business destruction" which owner refused to arbitrate on the grounds that the arbitration clause did not encompass such claims. The District Court held, and the Appellate Court affirmed, that such claims were arbitrable.

90020   Floor Craft Floor Covering, Inc. v. Parma Community Gen. Hosp. Ass'n, 54 Ohio St. 3d 1, 560 N.E.2d 206 (1990)

        II: A107-1978, Art. 7, Para. 7.1
        II: A107-1978, Art. 7, Para. 7.4
        II: A107-1978, Art. 8, Para. 8.3
        II: A107-1978, Art. 8, Para. 8.6
        II: A117-1979, Art. 11, Para. 11.1
        II: A117-1979, Art. 11, Para. 11.4
        II: A117-1979, Art. 12, Para. 12.3
        II: A117-1979, Art. 12, Para. 12.6
        II: A201-1976, Art. 1, Para. 1.1.2
        II: A201-1976, Art. 2, Para. 2.2.4
        II: A201-1976, Art. 2, Para. 2.2.13
        II: A201-1976, Art. 4, Para. 4.2.1
        II: B141-1977, Art. 1, Para. 1.5.5
        II: B141-1977, Art. 1, Para. 1.5.12

In contractor's action against architect for economic loss, the Supreme Court of Ohio upheld the Appellate Court's ruling that the trial court properly dismissed the contractor's claim for failure to state a cause of action on the grounds that in the absence of privity

substituted another product which was not significantly different from the product the subcontractor contracted to install, but which was to be installed by another subcontractor. The Appellate Court affirmed the trial court's entry of summary judgment for the contractor.

The subcontract incorporated the terms and conditions of the owner-contractor agreement under which the owner had the right to "abandon, postpone or terminate the work or any part hereof for any . . . reason . . . by giving 10 days' written notice. . . ." Upon such termination by the owner the contractor was obligated at owner's direction to terminate any subcontract referable to the terminated portion of the work.

The Appellate Court found that the termination clause clearly provided for termination at owner's will "for any . . . reason" and referred to the termination of all or any part of the "Work." The term "Work" was defined in the owner-contractor agreement as the "materials, labor, services . . . necessary for the complete performance of the Contract." Based on its interpretation of these provisions the Court found that the cancellation of one flooring "material" specified in the contract literally fell within the termination clause irrespective of whether an equivalent material was substituted.

90017   Dixie Roof Decks, Inc. v. Borggren/Dickson Constr., Inc., 195 Ga. App. 881, 395 S.E.2d 19 (1990)

        III: A401-1978, Art. 6, Para. 6.1
        III: A401-1978, Art. 12, Para. 12.4.1

The Appellate Court held that where the subcontract contained as an express condition precedent to final payment that the subcontractor provide a warranty, the subcontractor could not argue that it should be excused from the duty to produce the warranty by contractor's failure to make final payment and contractor's indication that it would dispute certain sums claimed by the subcontractor.

90018   D.M. Ward Constr. Co. v. Electric Corp. of Kansas City, 15 Kan. App. 2d 114, 803 P.2d 593 (1990)

        I: A107-1978, Art. 13, Para. 13.2
        I: A117-1979, Art. 17, Para. 17.2
        I: A201-1976, Art. 7, Para. 7.9.1
        I: A401-1978, Art. 13, Para. 13.1
        I: B141-1977, Art. 9, Para. 9.1

The Appellate Court found that the contractor waived its right to arbitration under the American Institute of Architects Standard Form of Agreement Between Contractor and Subcontractor, Document No. A401, 1978 edition, Paragraph 13.1, based on the evidence and the Court's finding that the contractor's request for arbitration did prejudice the subcontractor where the subcontractor had conducted a substantial amount of discovery in preparation for trial.

III: A201-1976, Art. 8, Para. 8.3.1
III: A201-1976, Art. 8, Para. 8.3.4
III: A201-1976, Art. 9, Para. 9.7
III: A201-1976, Art. 12, Para. 12.2.1
III: A201-1976, Art. 12, Para. 12.3.1

The Pennsylvania Commonwealth Court reversed the Board of Claims finding that the liquidated damage clause in the owner-contractor agreement constituted a penalty. Under the contract the owner could assess liquidated damages at a fixed rate per day if contractor failed to complete the project within the specified period. The damages could be decreased after a significant amount of the work was completed. The contract did not require the owner to issue a formal complaint before assessing liquidated damages. The Appellate Court found that the Board ignored the plain language of the clause which stated, "Compensable Delays—The Department is responsible for delay damages arising only from delays created by its negligent act or omissions. Unless otherwise specified, assume the risk of damages from all other causes of delay." In addition, unless the parties otherwise agreed, the contractor was presumed to undertake the burden of unanticipated happenings absent an act of God, the law or the action of the other party. The Court held further that the text and subject matter of the contract, and the case law on who bears the burden of unforeseen events, also supported the enforceability of the liquidated damages clause.

90016 Desco Vitro Glaze, Inc. v. Mechanical Constr. Corp., 159 A.D.2d 760, 552 N.Y.S.2d 185 (1990)

III: A107-1978, Art. 7, Para. 7.4
III: A107-1978, Art. 11, Para. 11.2
III: A107-1978, Art. 20, Para. 20.2
III: A117-1979, Art. 11, Para. 11.4
III: A117-1979, Art. 15, Para. 15.2
III: A117-1979, Art. 24, Para. 24.2
III: A201-1976, Art. 1, Para. 1.1.3
III: A201-1976, Art. 5, Para. 5.3.1
III: A201-1976, Art. 14, Para. 14.2.1
III: A401-1978, Art. 2, Para. 2.1
III: A401-1978, Art. 11, Para. 11.1.1
III: A401-1978, Art. 14, Para. 14.2.1

Subcontractor brought a breach of contract action against contractor seeking damages resulting from contractor's termination of the subcontract after the specifications had been revised eliminating the work under the subcontract. The trial court granted contractor's motion for summary judgment and subcontractor appealed on the grounds that contemporaneous with the cancellation of the subcontract the owner and contractor merely

owner and its successor partnership from pursuing arbitration of any claim against contractor. The owner and its successor partnership appealed to the Appellate Court which affirmed the decision of the trial court. The Appellate Court granted the owner's petition for certiorari to answer the question of whether, under a construction contract signed, as owner, by a corporation controlled by two individuals developing the property, the contractor was obliged to arbitrate claims on behalf of a limited partnership used by the same two individuals to syndicate the project. The Appellate Court reversed the judgment and held that claims against contractor were arbitrable where the broad arbitration clause in the owner-contractor agreement clearly applied to the parties claims and where the partnership was a "successor" to the owner under Paragraph 7.2.1 of the owner-contractor agreement.

The owner and contractor entered into an agreement which included the American Institute of Architects General Conditions of the Contract for Construction, Document No. A201, 1976 edition, specifically Paragraphs 7.2.1 and 7.9.1. The word "successor" as used in Paragraph 7.2.1 was not defined in the contract.

The Appellate Court found that owner had at least equitably assigned its benefits under the construction contract to the partnership based on evidence of the entire transaction and on the express or implied assumption by the partnership of owner's obligations under the construction contract. The ground lease stated that "Lessee is leasing the Land pursuant to this Lease for the purpose of constructing the hotel complex and retail/office complex, that is, for the purpose of building, owning an operating (i) a 170-room Quality Inn Hotel facility. . . . The development of the Project, and its construction, ownership and operation shall be at the sole cost and expense of Lessee; and in connection therewith, Lessee does hereby indemnify and hold the Lessor harmless from any and all claims, causes of action, bills, reckonings, accounts and/or liabilities of any nature . . . arising out of the construction, ownership or operation of the Project."

The Court found that since the partnership was a successor to the owner within the meaning of Paragraph 7.2.1 the contractor had agreed to arbitrate with the partnership. Furthermore, the Court found that since the obligations of the owner under the contract primarily involved the payment of money to the contractor, nothing in the nature of the performance to be rendered by the owner prevented it from transferring its benefits, or delegating its duties to the partnership.

In addition, the clause in Paragraph 7.2.1 which provided that "neither party to the contract shall assign the contract . . . without the written consent of the other" did not prevent the assignment to the partnership without the consent of the contractor where the contractor suffered no detriment. The Court based its interpretation of Paragraph 7.2.1 on the fact that the assets of the owner, as named in the contract, were still available to contractor for any satisfaction of a breach of contract claim.

90015 Department of Transp. v. Interstate Contractors Supply Co., 130 Pa. Commw. 334, 568 A.2d 294 (1990)

  III: A107-1978, Art. 14, Para. 14.3
  III: A117-1979, Art. 18, Para. 18.3

The Appellate Court upheld the finding of the trial court that the owner and contractor had waived the written change order clause where the parties by a course of conduct operated without written change orders.

90013   Craig Constr. Co. v. Hendrix, 568 So. 2d 752 (Ala. 1990)

II:	A107-1978, Art. 10, Para. 10.11
II:	A117-1979, Art. 14, Para. 14.11
II:	A201-1976, Art. 4, Para. 4.18.1
II:	A401-1978, Art. 11, Para. 11.11.1

The Supreme Court of Alabama upheld the finding of the trial court that contractor was not entitled to indemnification. An indemnity clause contained in the subcontract provided that the "Subcontractor covenants to indemnify and save harmless and exonerate the Contractor and the Owner of and from all liability, claims and demands for bodily injury and property damage arising out of the work undertaken by the Subcontractor, its employees' agents or its subcontractors, and arising out of any other operation no matter by whom performed for and on behalf of the Subcontractor, whether or not due in whole or in part to conditions, acts or omissions done or permitted by the Contractor or Owner." The clause clearly stated that the acts or omissions giving rise to the claim must be done "by [or] for and on behalf of the Subcontractor" and there was no evidence of subcontractor's negligence.

90014   Crown Oil & Wax Co. v. Glen Constr. Co., 320 Md. 546, 578 A.2d 1184 (1990)

I:	A107-1978, Art. 13, Para. 13.2
I:	A117-1979, Art. 17, Para. 17.2
I:	A201-1976, Art. 7, Para. 7.2.1
I:	A201-1976, Art. 7, Para. 7.9.1
II:	A401-1978, Art. 11, Para. 11.1.2
II:	A401-1978, Art. 13, Para. 13.1
II:	B141-1977, Art. 9, Para. 9.1
II:	B141-1977, Art. 12, Para. 12.1

Contractor filed a demand for arbitration of its termination by owner. The owner answered the demand for arbitration and counterclaimed for an amount to be determined. The owner then filed an amended answer and counterclaimed on its own behalf and on behalf of the limited partnership to which owner had assigned its benefits under the construction contract. Contractor then filed a complaint to restrain the owner, as named in the contract, and its successor partnership, from pursuing in arbitration any claim on behalf of the partnership. Contractor argued that it agreed to arbitrate with the owner, and not with the partnership, which was not a party to the contract. The trial court enjoined

90010 City of Elmira v. Larry Walter, Inc., 76 N.Y.2d 912, 563 N.Y.S.2d 45, 564 N.E.2d 655 (1990)

>   III: A101-1977, Art. 3
>   III: A107-1978, Art. 2, Para. 2.1
>   III: A111-1978, Art. 4, Para. 4.1
>   III: A117-1979, Art. 3, Para. 3.1

Owner sued contractor to recover costs for completion of project abandoned by contractor. The owner was awarded actual and liquidated damages. The Appellate Court deleted the liquidated damages award. It held that a liquidated damage clause contained in the owner-contractor agreement, which stated that where "actual damages for any delay in completing the work . . . are impossible to determine, the Contractors and their Sureties shall be liable for . . . the sum of One Thousand Dollars . . . as fixed, agreed and liquidated damages for each calendar day of delay from the above stipulated completion . . . until such work is satisfactorily completed and accepted," did not apply to contractor's abandonment of the project, absent express language to the contrary. The Court interpreted the clause as representing an attempt by the parties to anticipate and provide for the specific possibility that contractor's satisfactory completion of the project might have been delayed beyond the agreed upon completion date. The clause did not contain clear language indicating that it applied as well to abandonment of the project; thus it was not available in this action.

90011 City of New York v. Kalish-Jarcho, Inc., 161 A.D.2d 252, 554 N.Y.S.2d 900 (1990)

>   III: A401-1978, Art. 1, Para. 1.1
>   III: A401-1978, Art. 11, Para. 11.7.1
>   III: A401-1978, Art. 11, Para. 11.11.1

In a case in which the subcontract did not contain a clause expressly negating enforcement of the contract by third parties, the owner was held to be a third-party beneficiary of the subcontract. Various provisions of the subcontract incorporated the owner-contractor agreement into the subcontract and gave the owner inspection and testing rights at subcontractor's plant or at the place of delivery, provided warranties against defects, and obligated the subcontractor to hold contractor and owner harmless from loss, damage or expense resulting from any breach of warranty.

90012 Consolidated Fed. Corp. v. Cain, 195 Ga. App. 671, 394 S.E.2d 605 (1990)

>   II: A107-1978, Art. 18, Para. 18.1
>   II: A117-1979, Art. 22, Para. 22.1
>   II: A201-1976, Art. 12, Para. 12.1.1
>   II: A201-1976, Art. 12, Para. 12.1.2

III:	A107-1978, Art. 18, Para. 18.2
III:	A117-1979, Art. 11, Para. 11.3
III:	A117-1979, Art. 22, Para. 22.2
III:	A201-1976, Art. 1, Para. 1.2.2
III:	A201-1976, Art. 12, Para. 12.3.1

After a trial on the merits, the Court of Claims determined that contractor was entitled to recover from the owner additional costs incurred preparing a roof walk subsurface to receive waterproofing. The lump sum contract provided for the replacement of a roof walk, necessitating removal of the existing walk and rewaterproofing of the surface. The contractor was contractually cautioned to carefully examine the site so as to familiarize itself with existing conditions and to compare the drawings and specifications with the result of its site examination. However, the specifications supported an inference that the contractor could expect an in-place waterproofing system which was asphalt based, but was in fact tar. Tar required unanticipated decontamination to apply the specified new waterproofing system. Based on the federal government's equitable adjustment clause, the Court held that the contractor was entitled to additional compensation since the site conditions differed from those represented.

90009 City of College Park v. Batson-Cook Co., 196 Ga. App. 138, 395 S.E.2d 385 (1990)

I:	A107-1978, Art. 13, Para. 13.2
I:	A107-1978, Art. 18, Para. 18.1
III:	A107-1978, Art. 18, Para. 18.2
I:	A117-1979, Art. 17, Para. 17.2
I:	A117-1979, Art. 22, Para. 22.1
III:	A117-1979, Art. 22, Para. 22.2
I:	A201-1976, Art. 7, Para. 7.9.1
I:	A201-1976, Art. 12, Para. 12.1.1
I:	A201-1976, Art. 12, Para. 12.1.2
I:	A201-1976, Art. 12, Para. 12.3.1
I:	A401-1978, Art. 13, Para. 13.1
I:	B141-1977, Art. 9, Para. 9.1

The Appellate Court upheld the finding of the trial court that the arbitrator did not exceed its authority in making an arbitration award that exceeded the contract's guaranteed maximum cost. The contractor failed to give written notice of claims for increase in the contract sum but presented evidence that all changes which increased the project cost were made by authorized officials of the owner, that the owner agreed to wait until the project was completed to resolve any increases, and that owner waived the requirement regarding the submission of change orders.

II:	A107-1978, Art. 8, Para. 8.6
II:	A117-1979, Art. 12, Para. 12.3
II:	A117-1979, Art. 12, Para. 12.6
II:	A201-1976, Art. 2, Para. 2.2.4
II:	A201-1976, Art. 2, Para. 2.2.13
I:	B141-1977, Art. 1, Para. 1.5.5
I:	B141-1977, Art. 1, Para. 1.5.12

In subcontractor's injured workers negligence action against the architect the Appellate Court concluded that under the provisions of the owner-architect agreement which were identical to the American Institute of Architects Standard Form of Agreement Between Owner and Architect, Document No. B141, 1977 edition, Paragraphs 1.5.5 and 1.5.12, the architect owed a duty to the injured worker to maintain safety at the site. The architect failed to warn the owner and others of unsafe conditions and to perform its supervisory activities in a reasonable manner. However, based on the evidence, the Court affirmed the judgment of the trial court granting the architect's motion for a directed verdict, since even if the architect were found to be negligent, the worker did not prove that architect's negligence was the proximate cause of the injury.

90007 Blau Mechanical Corp. v. City of New York, 158 A.D.2d 373, 551 N.Y.S.2d 228 (1990)

III:	A107-1978, Art. 14, Para. 14.3
III:	A107-1978, Art. 18, Para. 18.1
III:	A107-1978, Art. 18, Para. 18.2
III:	A117-1979, Art. 18, Para. 18.3
III:	A117-1979, Art. 22, Para. 22.1
III:	A117-1979, Art. 22, Para. 22.2
III:	A201-1976, Art. 8, Para. 8.3.1
III:	A201-1976, Art. 8, Para. 8.3.4
III:	A201-1976, Art. 12, Para. 12.1.2
III:	A201-1976, Art. 12, Para. 12.3.1

The Appellate Court upheld a no-damage-for-delay clause which provided that the contractor agreed to make "no claim for damages for delay in the performance of this contract occasioned by any act or omission to act of the [owner]," in a case where the parties foresaw the delays and where the possibility of changes was explicitly anticipated in the owner-contractor agreement. The agreement set forth methods of payment for extra work and reserved to the owner the right to modify or change the contract.

90008 CCM Corp. v. United States, 20 Cl. Ct. 649 (1990)

III:	A107-1978, Art. 7, Para. 7.3

90005   Barth Elec. Co. v. Traylor Bros., Inc., 553 N.E.2d 504 (Ind. Ct. App. 1990)

II:	A107-1978, Art. 12, Para. 12.1
II:	A107-1978, Art. 12, Para. 12.2
II:	A107-1978, Art. 12, Para. 12.3
II:	A107-1978, Art. 16, Para. 16.1
II:	A117-1979, Art. 16, Para. 16.1
II:	A117-1979, Art. 16, Para. 16.2
II:	A117-1979, Art. 16, Para. 16.3
II:	A117-1979, Art. 20, Para. 20.1
I:	A201-1976, Art. 6, Para. 6.2.1
I:	A201-1976, Art. 6, Para. 6.2.2
I:	A201-1976, Art. 6, Para. 6.2.3
I:	A201-1976, Art. 6, Para. 6.2.4
I:	A201-1976, Art. 6, Para. 6.2.5
I:	A201-1976, Art. 10, Para. 10.2.5

In one contractor's breach of contract action against another contractor, the Appellate Court interpreted the mutual responsibility multi-prime provisions of the American Institute of Architects General Conditions of the Contract for Construction, Document No. A201, 1976 edition, specifically Paragraphs 6.2.1, 6.2.3, 6.2.4, 6.2.5 and 10.2.5. At issue on appeal was whether separate, primary construction contracts executed by all prime contractors on a construction project imposed third-party rights and obligations in favor of all other prime contractors. The Court noted that the "mutual responsibility" provisions specifically provided that "any costs caused by defective or ill-timed work shall be borne by the party responsible therefor." Given this provision and the other contract clauses, the Court found that the contract contained provisions necessary to support a third-party beneficiary claim where the General Conditions specifically recognized that one contractor's work may be only part of the entire project and that other prime contractors may also be performing work on the same project. Moreover, the General Conditions specifically stated that time was of the essence of the contract, that each contractor's work should be promptly performed and completed, and that all contractors on the projects had the right to perform their work free from interference. Most importantly, Paragraph 10.2.5 required that each party pay for the damages caused other contractors on the project. Given this contract language, the Court concluded that the contracting parties intended that each contractor involved in the project should benefit from the timely, competent work of the other contractors or should be able to seek compensation from those contractors failing to complete their work in an appropriate manner.

90006   Belgum v. Mitsuo Kawamota & Assocs., Inc., 236 Neb. 127, 459 N.W.2d 226 (1990)

II:	A107-1978, Art. 8, Para. 8.3

have intended that this provision only be a limitation on the scope of the contractor's obligation to indemnify the architect. The Court concluded that the contract language was ambiguous as to the parties intent regarding whether the owner waived all claims against the architect, and remanded for further proceedings to determine the parties' intent.

90003 American Builder's Ass'n v. Au-Yang, 226 Cal. App. 3d 170, 276 Cal. Rptr. 262 (1990)

III:	A107-1978, Art. 13, Para. 13.2	
III:	A117-1979, Art. 17, Para. 17.2	
III:	A201-1976, Art. 7, Para. 7.9.1	
III:	A401-1978, Art. 13, Para. 13.1	
III:	B141-1977, Art. 9, Para. 9.1	

The trial court determined that where the arbitration clause in the owner-contractor agreement provided that "all claims or disputes arising out of this contract or the breach thereof shall be decided by arbitration . . .," the language was sufficient to bind the contractor to arbitrate with any willing claimants including the owner's corporation which was a nonsignatory to the contract and was joined by the arbitrator as a co-claimant. The court of appeals reversed, ruling that a nonsignatory could not be made a party to an arbitration absent an initial factual determination by a court regarding the nonsignatory's status.

90004 Atlantic Shores Resort Joint Venture v. Martin, 731 F. Supp. 1279 (D.S.C. 1990)

II:	A107-1978, Art. 13, Para. 13.2	
II:	A117-1979, Art. 17, Para. 17.2	
II:	A201-1976, Art. 7, Para. 7.9.1	
II:	A401-1978, Art. 13, Para. 13.1	
II:	A401-1978, Art. 13, Para. 13.2	
II:	B141-1977, Art. 9, Para. 9.1	
II:	B141-1977, Art. 9, Para. 9.2	
II:	B141-1977, Art. 9, Para. 9.3	

In architect's action to confirm an arbitration award, the District Court upheld the American Arbitration Association's decision not to consolidate the owner's arbitration with the architect and the owner's arbitration with the contractor. The owner-architect agreement contained a broad arbitration clause similar to the American Institute of Architects Standard Form of Agreement Between the Owner and Architect, Document No. B141, 1977 edition, which provided that consolidation could not be required without the consent of all parties.

90002   Aetna Casualty & Sur. Co. v. Canam Steel Corp., 794 P.2d 1077 (Colo. Ct. App. 1990)

I:	A107-1978, Art. 7, Para. 7.4
I:	A107-1978, Art. 10, Para. 10.11
II:	A107-1978, Art. 11, Para. 11.1.1
II:	A107-1978, Art. 17, Para. 17.6
I:	A117-1979, Art. 11, Para. 11.4
I:	A117-1979, Art. 14, Para. 14.11
II:	A117-1979, Art. 15, Para. 15.1.1
II:	A117-1979, Art. 21, Para. 21.6
I:	A201-1976, Art. 1, Para. 1.1.3
I:	A201-1976, Art. 4, Para. 4.18.3
I:	A201-1976, Art. 5, Para. 5.1.1
I:	A201-1976, Art. 11, Para. 11.3.6
III:	A401-1978, Art. 11, Para. 11.11.1

Owner's builder's risk insurer brought a subrogation action against supplier and architect for damages resulting from a roof collapse. The trial court granted architect's and suppliers motions for summary judgment on the ground that the owner had waived any claims it had against the supplier and the architect. Owner's insurer argued on appeal that the supplier was not a "subcontractor" as defined by the contract, and, therefore, the owner's waiver of claims did not apply to the supplier. The Appellate Court agreed.

The owner and contractor entered into an agreement which included the American Institute of Architects General Conditions of the Contract for Construction, Document No. A201, 1976 edition, specifically Paragraphs 1.1.3, 5.1.1, 4.18.3 and 11.3.6. The owner also entered into a contract with the architect under which the architect served as the project engineer.

The Appellate Court construed Paragraphs 1.1.3 and 5.1.1 as providing that contracting to deliver material to a jobsite did not make the supplier a "subcontractor" under the terms of the contract which defined a subcontractor as "a person or entity . . . performing any of the Work at the site." Furthermore, the definition of "Work" in Paragraph 1.1.3 did not include a party who had a contract to supply or deliver materials to the site. Therefore summary judgment for the supplier was granted in error.

The Court then construed Paragraph 11.3.6 as providing for waiver by the owner and contractor of all rights against the architect. The Court reasoned that since the waiver afforded the architect under Paragraph 11.3.6 did not extend to the liability imposed by Paragraph 4.18.3, the parties may have intended some limitation on the Paragraph 11.3.6 waiver as to the liability imposed by Paragraph 4.18.3. In other words, the parties may have intended that the owner did not waive its claims against the architect under the circumstances outlined in Paragraph 4.18.3. However, the Court found that Paragraph 4.18.3 did not expressly "impose" any liability upon the architect. Thus, the parties may

90001   A. Dubreuil & Sons, Inc. v. Lisbon, 215 Conn. 604, 577 A.2d 709 (1990)

II:	A107-1978, Art. 13, Para. 13.2
II:	A117-1979, Art. 17, Para. 17.2
I:	A201-1976, Art. 7, Para. 7.9.1
I:	A201-1976, Art. 7, Para. 7.9.2
I:	A201-1976, Art. 7, Para. 7.9.3
II:	A401-1978, Art. 13, Para. 13.1
II:	A401-1978, Art. 13, Para. 13.2
II:	A401-1978, Art. 13, Para. 13.5
II:	B141-1977, Art. 9, Para. 9.1
II:	B141-1977, Art. 9, Para. 9.2
II:	B141-1977, Art. 9, Para. 9.3

Contractor filed a demand for arbitration against owner for compensation for extra work. The trial court denied contractor's motion and contractor appealed.

The owner and contractor entered into an agreement that included the American Institute of Architects General Conditions of the Contract for Construction, Document No. A201, 1976 edition which contained a modified Paragraph 7.9.1. The modified paragraph provided in pertinent part that "all claims, disputes and other matters in question between the Contractor and the Owner arising out of, or relating to, the Contract Documents or the breach thereof . . . may be decided by arbitration. . . ." At issue on appeal was whether the parties, by altering the printed contract by substituting "may" for "shall," intended to modify the contract to provide for consensual rather than mandatory arbitration.

The Appellate Court found that the printed form contract contained an arbitration provision that originally included a provision that required that disputes arising under the contract "shall be settled by arbitration." The Court interpreted the use of the word "shall" as denoting that arbitration was mandatory. The Court concluded that the deliberate substitution of "may" for "shall" in the arbitration provision of the contract was an indication that the parties expressly intended something other than mandatory arbitration. The Court held that since the word "shall" was deliberately removed from the contract by the parties and replaced by the word "may," and since the form contract words "shall be decided by arbitration" were replaced by the typed words "may be decided by arbitration," the trial court did not err in determining that the parties intended to modify their contract to provide for consensual rather than mandatory arbitration. Finally, the Court rejected the owner's argument that even though the wording of the contract's arbitration provision was changed to read "may" arbitrate, rather than "shall" arbitrate, there remained other wording in the printed portion of the General Conditions, specifically in Paragraphs 7.9.1, 7.9.2 and 7.9.3, which created an ambiguity. The Court rejected this argument by applying the rule that typed matter controls printed matter.

and owner appealed. The Appellate Court affirmed the trial court's ruling on the grounds that by the clear language of the contract both parties agreed to submit their disputes to arbitration and were bound by that decision. The Court held that the contractor could obtain specific enforcement of that agreement despite the attempted revocation by the owner.

with the General Conditions and where the parties did not vary this provision by way of addendum or otherwise.

89050   Wilson Elec. Contractors, Inc. v. Minnotte Contracting Corp., 878 F.2d 167 (6th Cir. 1989)

III:	A107-1978, Art. 13, Para. 13.2
III:	A117-1979, Art. 17, Para. 17.2
III:	A201-1976, Art. 7, Para. 7.9.1
III:	A401-1978, Art. 13, Para. 13.1
III:	B141-1977, Art. 9, Para. 9.1

In subcontractor's action against contractor alleging breach of contract by wrongful termination, the contractor filed a motion to stay the action pending arbitration. The District Court denied the contractor's motion on the grounds that the arbitration clause lacked consideration and was, therefore, invalid and unenforceable. Contractor appealed, and the Appellate Court reversed.

The arbitration clause in the subcontract provided in relevant part that "except as otherwise specifically provided for in this Subcontract, any controversy or claim arising out of or relating to this Subcontract, or the breach thereof which is not disposed of by agreement, shall, at the election of Contractor, be settled by arbitration. . . ."

The Court of Appeals found that subcontractor had freely signed the contract which contained the arbitration clause allowing contractor alone to elect to arbitrate any controversy or claim arising out of or relating to the contract or breach thereof. The Court concluded that the arbitration clause was enforceable where the subcontractor made no claim of fraud, did not claim that it was coerced into signing the contract, and did not claim that the contract was unconscionable.

89051   Wylie Indep. School Dist. v. TMC Found., Inc., 770 S.W.2d 19 (Tex. Ct. App. 1989)

I:	A107-1978, Art. 13, Para. 13.2
I:	A117-1979, Art. 17, Para. 17.2
I:	A201-1976, Art. 7, Para. 7.9.1
I:	A401-1978, Art. 13, Para. 13.1
I:	B141-1977, Art. 9, Para. 9.1

Contractor demanded arbitration of its claim against owner for reimbursement of fees pursuant to Paragraph 7.9.1 of the American Institute of Architects General Conditions of the Contract for Construction, Document No. A201, 1976 edition. Owner attempted to revoke the agreement to arbitrate and sought to avoid arbitration by filing an action seeking declaratory relief and a temporary injunction to stay the arbitration proceedings. The trial court denied owner's application for a temporary injunction to stay arbitration

II: B141-1977, Art. 11, Para. 11.1

The United States Supreme Court upheld a state court decision staying arbitration pending resolution of related litigation involving third parties not bound by an arbitration agreement where the parties had agreed to be bound by state law. By specifying that the contract would be governed by the law of the state where the project was located, California, the parties had efficiently incorporated California's rules of arbitration into their contract. Application of the rule allowing a stay pending resolution of the litigation did not offend the federal policy favoring arbitration, because the essential purpose of that policy and the Federal Arbitration Act was to ensure that private enforcement agreements are enforced. Thus, the parties were presumed to have agreed that arbitration would not go forward in situations covered by California's rule regarding third parties with whom there was no arbitration agreement. This presumption was not a finding that arbitration had been waived, but rather a finding that under the agreement no right to compel arbitration existed in this situation.

89049   Walker v. V & V Constr. Co., 28 Mass. App. Ct. 908, 545 N.E.2d 1192 (1989)

I: A101-1977, Art. 1
I: A101-1977, Art. 7, Para. 7.2
I: A107-1978, Art. 6, Para. 6.1
I: A107-1978, Art. 7, Para. 7.1
I: A111-1978, Art. 1, Para. 1.1
I: A111-1978, Art. 16, Para. 16.2
I: A117-1979, Art. 10, Para. 10.2
I: A117-1979, Art. 11, Para. 11.1
II: A201-1976, Art. 1, Para. 1.1.1
I: A401-1978, Art. 1, Para. 1.1
I: A401-1978, Art. 15, Para. 15.2

The Appellate Court found that the American Institute of Architects Standard From of Agreement Between Owner and Contractor, Document No. A111, 1978 edition, clearly contemplated inclusion by the parties of a separate document for the General Conditions. At the top of the agreement appears "Use only with the 1976 Edition of AIA Document A201, General Conditions of the Contract for Construction." Article 1 defined the contract documents to include the General Conditions and stated that an enumeration of the contract documents appeared in Article 16. Article 16 provided a space for listing the specific documents forming the contract and contains the instruction "List below the Agreement, the Conditions of the Contract, [General Supplementary and other Conditions], the Drawings, the Specifications, and any Addenda and accepted alternates. . . ." The Court found that although the parties neglected to list the General Conditions in Article 16 they were nonetheless part of the contract where it was plainly indicated on the face of the agreement that the owner-contractor agreement was to be read together

II:	B141-1977, Art. 1, Para. 1.5.9
II:	B141-1977, Art. 1, Para. 1.5.12
III:	B141-1977, Art. 1, Para. 1.6.1
III:	B141-1977, Art. 1, Para. 1.6.2
III:	B141-1977, Art. 1, Para. 1.6.3

Owner brought an action against architect, contractor and contractor's surety for breach of contract damages. The contractor's surety filed a cross-claim for indemnity against the architect. The trial court entered judgment for owner against architect and held that contractor's surety was entitled to indemnity from architect on the bond. The architect appealed. The Supreme Court upheld the judgment of the trial court awarding breach of contract damages to owner and its ruling that architect indemnify the contractor's surety. Architect argued on appeal that the owner-architect agreement absolved the architect of liability resulting from contractor's poor workmanship.

The owner-architect agreement provided that architect would provide architectural services, including design, preparing construction documents, assisting in obtaining bids, and administering the construction contract. For additional compensation, the architect was to provide a full-time resident inspector for administration of the construction contract. Specifically, the agreement contained provisions similar to Paragraphs 1.5.3, 1.5.4, 1.5.5, 1.5.7, 1.5.8, 1.5.9, 1.5.12, 1.6.2 and 1.6.3 of the American Institute of Architects Standard Form of Agreement Between Owner and Architect, Document No. B141, 1977 edition. Further, basic services were provided for in the contract, and project representation beyond basic services was included.

The Supreme Court found that architect had a duty to inspect the roof construction and to protect the owner against defects and deficiencies in the work of the contractor. Architect had a duty to fill the position of resident inspector with a person competent to recognize deficient construction. The evidence reflected that, on a number of occasions, the improper construction of the roof was brought to the attention of architect and inspector, that nothing was done to rectify the improper construction, and that the resident inspector admittedly was not competent as an inspector of roof work. The Court concluded that the architect had breached its duties under the contract.

89048 Volt Information Sciences, Inc. v. Board of Trustees, 489 U.S. 468, 109 S. Ct. 1248, 103 L. Ed. 2d 488 (1989)

I:	A107-1978, Art. 13, Para. 13.1
II:	A107-1978, Art. 13, Para. 13.2
I:	A117-1979, Art. 17, Para. 17.1
II:	A117-1979, Art. 17, Para. 17.2
I:	A201-1976, Art. 7, Para. 7.1.1
I:	A201-1976, Art. 7, Para. 7.9.1
II:	A401-1978, Art. 13, Para. 13.1
II:	B141-1977, Art. 9, Para. 9.1

I:	A201-1976, Art. 7, Para. 7.9.1
I:	A201-1976, Art. 7, Para. 7.9.2
II:	A401-1978, Art. 13, Para. 13.1
I:	B141-1977, Art. 9, Para. 9.1
I:	B141-1977, Art. 9, Para. 9.2

In affirming the trial court's determination that the statute of limitations barred owner's claim for arbitration under an owner-contractor agreement which incorporated the American Institute of Architects General Conditions of the Contract for Construction, Document No. A201, 1976 edition, Paragraphs 7.9.1 and 7.9.2, the Appellate Court found that Paragraph 7.9.2 indicated the parties intent that the statute of limitations clause would limit a party's right to demand arbitration. Therefore, the time and expense of an action to compel arbitration and the actual arbitration hearing would be eliminated under the provisions of Paragraph 7.9.2 if a determination were made that the statute of limitations had expired.

89047 U.R.S. Co. v. Gulfport-Biloxi Regional Airport Auth., 544 So. 2d 824 (Miss. 1989)

II:	A107-1978, Art. 8, Para. 8.1
II:	A107-1978, Art. 8, Para. 8.3
II:	A107-1978, Art. 8, Para. 8.4
II:	A107-1978, Art. 8, Para. 8.5
II:	A107-1978, Art. 8, Para. 8.6
II:	A117-1979, Art. 12, Para. 12.1
II:	A117-1979, Art. 12, Para. 12.3
II:	A117-1979, Art. 12, Para. 12.4
II:	A117-1979, Art. 12, Para. 12.5
II:	A117-1979, Art. 12, Para. 12.6
II:	A201-1976, Art. 2, Para. 2.2.2
II:	A201-1976, Art. 2, Para. 2.2.3
II:	A201-1976, Art. 2, Para. 2.2.4
II:	A201-1976, Art. 2, Para. 2.2.6
II:	A201-1976, Art. 2, Para. 2.2.7
II:	A201-1976, Art. 2, Para. 2.2.13
II:	A201-1976, Art. 9, Para. 9.4.2
II:	B141-1977, Art. 1, Para. 1.5.3
II:	B141-1977, Art. 1, Para. 1.5.4
II:	B141-1977, Art. 1, Para. 1.5.5
II:	B141-1977, Art. 1, Para. 1.5.7
II:	B141-1977, Art. 1, Para. 1.5.8

III: B141-1977, Art. 9, Para. 9.1

Contractor filed a petition to stay arbitration after subcontractor filed a demand for arbitration. The trial court denied contractor's petition. The contractor argued on appeal that the arbitration clause contained in the owner-contractor agreement was not incorporated into the subcontract.

The arbitration provision in the owner-contractor agreement provided that all "claims, disputes and other matters in question between the Contractor and the Owner arising out of, or relating to, the Contract Documents or the breach thereof . . . shall be decided by arbitration in accordance with the Construction Industry Arbitration Rules of the American Arbitration Association then obtaining unless the parties mutually agree otherwise. . . . No person other than the Owner or contractor shall be included as an original third party or additional third party to an arbitration whose interest or responsibility is insubstantial. Any consent to arbitration involving an additional person or persons shall not constitute consent to arbitration of any dispute not described therein or with any person not named or described therein." The subcontract contained no arbitration clause, however, it did contain a flow-down provision.

The subcontract provided that contractor "shall have the same rights and remedies as against the subcontractor as the owner under the terms and provisions of the general contract . . . with the same force and effect as though every such duty, obligation, responsibility, right or remedy were set forth herein in full." The Court concluded that one of the "rights and remedies" which contractor had against the owner was arbitration. Furthermore, the Court found that the subcontract was ambiguous because it preceded the "same rights and remedies" language with the phrase "with respect to the work to be performed." The Court concluded that the subcontract as a whole demonstrated the parties' intent to incorporate the owner-contractor agreement by stating that the terms and provisions of the subcontract were "in addition to and not in substitution for any of the terms and provisions of the General Contract and the other Contract Documents." The subcontract defined "Contract Documents" to include the general conditions of the owner-contractor agreement. Furthermore, the Court found that the subcontract also required subcontractor to represent that it "has carefully examined and understands this Agreement and the other Contract Documents." The Court held that where the owner-contractor agreement contained a flow-down provision that was binding on the subcontractor and the subcontractor was required to identify "any terms and conditions of the proposed subcontract which may be at variance" with the owner-contractor agreement, the parties clearly intended the subcontract to incorporate the owner-contractor agreements provision for "rights and remedies" including the right and obligation to arbitrate disputes.

89046   200 Levee Drive Assocs., Ltd. v. Bor-Son Bldg. Corp., 441 N.W.2d 560 (Minn. Ct. App. 1989)

II: A107-1978, Art. 13, Para. 13.2

II: A117-1979, Art. 17, Para. 17.2

In subcontractor's action against owner and contractor claiming delay damages, the District Court, in ruling on owner and contractor's motions in limine, found that the provision in the general conditions which stated that subcontractor "expressly agrees not to make, and hereby waives any claim for damages, including those resulting from increased labor or material costs, on account of any delay, obstruction or hindrance for any cause whatsoever . . . and agrees that the sole right and remedy therefor shall be an extension of time" did not foreclose the use of evidence of delays.

89044   TDE, Ltd. v. Israel, 185 Ill. App. 3d 1059, 133 Ill. Dec. 843, 541 N.E.2d 1281 (1989)

II:	A107-1978, Art. 13, Para. 13.2
II:	A117-1979, Art. 17, Para. 17.2
I:	A201-1976, Art. 7, Para. 7.9.1
I:	A201-1976, Art. 7, Para. 7.9.2
II:	A401-1978, Art. 13, Para. 13.1
II:	B141-1977, Art. 9, Para. 9.1
II:	B141-1977, Art. 9, Para. 9.2

In contractor's action against owner to recover payments due under the contract, the trial court denied the owner's motion to compel arbitration. On appeal, the Appellate Court found that the contractor's claim for payment was plainly anticipated by the comprehensive phrasing of the arbitration clause contained in Paragraph 7.9.1 of the American Institute of Architects General Conditions of the Contract for Construction, Document No. A201, 1976 edition. The contractor argued that the motion to compel arbitration was correctly denied because Paragraph 7.9.2 required written notice of a demand for arbitration. The Court construed the notice provision as merely providing notice of the nature of the dispute which allowed the parties to comply with the arbitration agreement before the commencement of litigation. Since the contractor had resisted attempts to compel arbitration, it had demonstrated its refusal to honor the Agreement; this refusal triggered the obligation to arbitrate. Accordingly, the Appellate Court reversed and ordered submission to arbitration.

89045   Turner Constr. Co. v. Midwest Curtainwalls, Inc., 187 Ill. App. 3d 417, 135 Ill. Dec. 14, 543 N.E.2d 249 (1989)

III:	A107-1978, Art. 13, Para. 13.2
III:	A117-1979, Art. 17, Para. 17.2
I:	A201-1976, Art. 5, Para. 5.3.1
I:	A201-1976, Art. 7, Para. 7.9.1
III:	A401-1978, Art. 11, Para. 11.1.1
III:	A401-1978, Art. 13, Para. 13.1
III:	A401-1978, Art. 13, Para. 13.2

judgment on the ground that contractor was not responsible for supervising payment to the subcontractor. The Court granted contractor's motion for summary judgment on the grounds that the explicit language of the contracts did not allow the Court to impose payment duties on the contractor.

The general conditions of the owner-contractor agreement provided that a contractor who desired work-in-progress payments or payments for materials had to apply to either the owner and its designated representatives, successors and assigns or to the owner's representative. In certain cases the owner's representative could submit payment applications to the architect. Once approved, payments were the responsibility of the owner or owner's representative. The subcontract incorporated the general conditions of the owner-contractor agreement and payments to the subcontractor were to be made directly from the owner or from funds contractor had received from the owner for payment to subcontractor. The subcontract provided further that "payments, less retention, shall be made in accordance with the procedure as set forth in the Owner's General Conditions."

The District Court found that under the general conditions, only the owner, owner's representative and the architect had contractual responsibility for overseeing payments. No clause in the general conditions obligated the contractor to screen or otherwise approve of payments to subcontractors. Under the subcontract the contractor had the duty to forward moneys received from owner for the account of the subcontractor to the subcontractor.

The Court rejected the surety's argument that the flow-down provision of the owner-contractor agreement obligated the contractor to screen the payment applications. The Court found that the contracts were unambiguous on the issue of who bore responsibility for screening payments and, where the general conditions did incorporate the subcontracts, nothing in the general conditions transposed owner's or owners representatives responsibility to make payments to the contractor. The subcontract explicitly stated that payments were to be made in accordance with the procedures set forth in the general conditions.

89043   Rush Presbyterian St. Luke's Medical Center v. Safeco Ins. Co., 722 F. Supp. 485 (N.D. Ill. 1989)

III:	A107-1978, Art. 14, Para. 14.3
III:	A107-1978, Art. 18, Para. 18.2
III:	A117-1979, Art. 18, Para. 18.3
III:	A117-1979, Art. 22, Para. 22.2
III:	A201-1976, Art. 8, Para. 8.3.1
III:	A201-1976, Art. 8, Para. 8.3.4
III:	A201-1976, Art. 12, Para. 12.3.1
III:	A401-1978, Art. 11, Para. 11.10.1
III:	A401-1978, Art. 11, Para. 12.5.1

17.5 was not a condition precedent to the contractor's commencement of work and that the contractor did not, as a matter of law, waive his reliance on the owner's obligation to buy insurance by proceeding with the project.

89041　　Riggle v. Allied Chemical Corp., 378 S.E.2d 282 (W. Va. 1989)

III:	A107-1978, Art. 10, Para. 10.11
III:	A117-1979, Art. 14, Para. 14.11
III:	A201-1976, Art. 4, Para. 4.18.1
III:	A401-1978, Art. 11, Para. 11.11.1

In contractor's employee's personal injury action against the owner and contractor, owner brought a third-party indemnity action against the contractor. The trial court found for the owner and contractor appealed.

The owner-contractor agreement contained an indemnity provision under which the contractor agreed "to protect, defend, indemnify, exonerate and hold [owner] harmless from and against any and all suits, claims, liability, losses, liens and demands, fines, costs, criminal and civil penalties, causes of action or any other obligations arising out of or in any manner connected with, incidents involving bodily injury, death, property damage or any violation or alleged violation of any federal, state, provincial, or local law or regulation, except if any such incident, spill or pollution and associated clean-up results from the sole negligence of [contractor]."

The Court found that this provision was not contrary to public policy where its object was to allocate risks for insurance purposes. The Court reasoned that under an indemnity provision where the contractor could be held responsible for all damages to a worker regardless of fault, the contractor was expected to buy adequate insurance to protect against this risk.

89042　　Rush Presbyterian St. Luke's Medical Center v. Safeco Ins. Co., 712 F. Supp. 1344 (N.D. Ill. 1989)

III:	A107-1978, Art. 4, Para. 4.1
III:	A117-1979, Art. 9, Para. 9.1
III:	A201-1976, Art. 9, Para. 9.3.1
III:	A201-1976, Art. 9, Para. 9.3.2
III:	A201-1976, Art. 9, Para. 9.4.1
III:	A201-1976, Art. 9, Para. 9.5.1
III:	A201-1976, Art. 9, Para. 9.5.4
III:	A401-1978, Art. 12, Para. 12.4.1
III:	A401-1978, Art. 12, Para. 12.4.3

In subcontractor's surety action against contractor alleging that contractor's overpayment to subcontractor prejudiced surety's position, contractor moved for summary

89040 Richmond v. Grabowski, 781 P.2d 192 (Colo. Ct. App. 1989)

I:	A107-1978, Art. 17, Para. 17.2
I:	A107-1978, Art. 17, Para. 17.3
I:	A107-1978, Art. 17, Para. 17.4
I:	A107-1978, Art. 17, Para. 17.5
I:	A107-1978, Art. 17, Para. 17.6
I:	A117-1979, Art. 21, Para. 21.2
I:	A117-1979, Art. 21, Para. 21.3
I:	A117-1979, Art. 21, Para. 21.4
I:	A117-1979, Art. 21, Para. 21.5
I:	A117-1979, Art. 21, Para. 21.6
II:	A201-1976, Art. 11, Para. 11.1.1
II:	A201-1976, Art. 11, Para. 11.1.4
II:	A201-1976, Art. 11, Para. 11.2.1
II:	A201-1976, Art. 11, Para. 11.3.1
II:	A201-1976, Art. 11, Para. 11.3.4

Owner brought an action against contractor and subcontractor for fire damage allegedly caused by contractor's and subcontractor's negligence. The trial court entered summary judgment for contractor and subcontractor holding that owner's breach of his contractual obligation to procure fire insurance on the premises precluded recovery. Owner argued on appeal that because the contractor began work before receiving copies of the policies pursuant to Paragraph 17.5 of the owner-contractor agreement, the contractor waived and/or was estopped from asserting the contractual requirement as a matter of either law or fact by proceeding despite the lack of insurance. The Appellate Court disagreed.

The owner and contractor had entered into the American Institute of Architects Abbreviated Form of Agreement Between Owner and Contractor, Document No. A107, 1978 edition, specifically Paragraphs 17.2, 17.3, 17.4, 17.5 and 17.6.

The Appellate Court held that Paragraph 17.5 did not establish that the contractor was not to begin work until he had received copies of the insurance policy, but rather imposed an obligation upon the owner to provide the requisite insurance before an exposure to loss could occur because of the work progressing under the contract. Furthermore, Paragraphs 17.2 through 17.5 established that Paragraph 17.5 related to the owner's obligation to procure insurance and the resulting rights of the contractor and subcontractor. The contract unequivocally required the owner to procure fire insurance to shift the risk of loss away from the parties and to place it on the insurer. As construed by the Court, Paragraph 17.5 described the owner's duty to file copies of the insurance policies with the contractor before the contractor was exposed to loss. Reading the contract as a whole, the Court concluded that the only rational objective of this filing requirement was to inform the contractor as to the extent of insurance coverage so that the contractor could procure other or additional insurance if necessary. The Court held that Paragraph

The Supreme Court affirmed, holding that under the plain and unambiguous language of the contract, the owner was entitled to use architects' work product in the construction of the work as provided for in the contract and was only prohibited from using the drawings on other projects or extensions to the current project. The Court found that architect's work product was used to complete the original project, not an "other" project or an "extension" to the project.

89039 Regina Constr. Corp. v. Envirmech Contracting Corp., 80 Md. App. 662, 565 A.2d 693 (1989)

    III: A107-1978, Art. 13, Para. 13.2
    III: A117-1979, Art. 17, Para. 17.2
    III: A201-1976, Art. 7, Para. 7.9.1
    III: A401-1978, Art. 13, Para. 13.2
    III: B141-1977, Art. 9, Para. 9.1

Subcontractor brought an action against contractor for payment of its actual costs plus profit and overhead. Contractor moved to dismiss the action based on the arbitration provision contained in the contract. Subcontractor argued that a motion to dismiss was not procedurally or substantively the appropriate vehicle to raise the defense. Contractor then filed a petition to compel arbitration. The trial court denied contractor's motion to dismiss on the ground that the dispute was not covered by the arbitration clause, because only claims made while the subcontractor was on the job were subject to the arbitration agreement. Contractor appealed.

The subcontract required that disputes arising out of acts, omissions, or responsibilities of the owner be resolved in accordance with the procedures set forth in the owner-contractor agreement. With respect to disputes with the contractor the subcontract required that such disputes "be resolved by arbitration in Washington, D.C. in accordance with the rules of the American Arbitration Association. Disputes shall not interfere with the progress of the job. Work shall proceed as ordered, subject to claim."

In addressing the issue of whether the dispute between the contractor and subcontractor was within the scope of the arbitration provision, the Appellate Court found that the agreement to arbitrate was broad and covered "disputes solely with the Contractor," and articulating no exceptions, obviously included all disputes solely with the contractor. The additional provision that disputes should not interfere with the progress of the work was not a limitation on what had to be arbitrated but a requirement that the work continue while a claim is being arbitrated; the last sentence of the paragraph, which provided that the work proceed "subject to claim," made that clear. The Court concluded that to construe the contract language as limiting the arbitration agreement to claims arising prior to completion of the work would be an undue constriction of the language and would significantly impair the value of the arbitration agreement itself. The Court therefore held that subcontractor's claim was within the scope of the arbitration provision.

II: B141-1977, Art. 1, Para. 1.5.10
II: B141-1977, Art. 1, Para. 1.5.11

Contractor brought an action against owner and architect to recover increased costs and lost earnings. The trial court held that the architect was an agent of the owner as a matter of law and that the owner was vicariously liable to the contractor for architect's actions. The trial court denied the owner's motion for a new trial and granted the owner indemnity against the architect. Among numerous issues on appeal was whether the architect was an agent of the owner.

The parties entered into a modified American Institute of Architects Standard Form of Agreement Between Owner and Architect, Document No. B141, 1977 edition, which incorporated the American Institute of Architects General Conditions of the Contract for Construction, Document No. A201, 1976 edition, specifically Paragraph 2.2.7. The owner-architect agreement provided that the "Architect shall be, in the first instance, the interpreter of the requirements of the Contract Documents and the impartial judge of the performance thereunder by both the Owner and the Contractor. The Architect shall make decisions on all claims of the Owner or Contractor relating to the execution and progress of the Work and on all other matters or questions related thereto. The Architect's decisions in matters relating to artistic effect shall be final if consistent with the intent of the Contract Documents."

The Appellate Court construed these provisions as clearly establishing that the architect was not the representative or agent of the owner at all times during the construction phase. The Court found that in his capacity as interpreter of the documents the architect acted independently and in his capacity as judge of performance by both the owner and the contractor, he also acted independently. The Court concluded that under the contracts the owner did not make the final decision, or have the right to control, the architect's actions in his interpretation of contract documents or in his responses to shop drawings. The Court held that the evidence and the contract provisions supported the conclusion that the architect was not acting as the owner's agent, but as an "arbiter or umpire." Therefore, the trial court erred in its judgment on that issue, and the appellate court held that judgment should be entered against the architect alone.

89038 Reeves v. Hill Aero, Inc., 231 Neb. 345, 436 N.W.2d 494 (1989)

I: B141-1977, Art. 8, Para. 8.1

Architect brought a breach of contract action against the owner seeking damages arising from owner's use of plans substantially the same as those developed by the architect after owner terminated the architect. The trial court entered judgment for owner and architect appealed.

The owner and architect had entered into a modified American Institute of Architects Standard Form of Agreement Between Owner and Architect, Document No. B141, 1977 edition. Paragraph 8.1 provided that the drawings and specifications were to remain the property of the architect and were not to be used by the owner on other projects except by written agreement with appropriate compensation to the architect.

I: A117-1979, Art. 14, Para. 14.11
I: A201-1976, Art. 4, Para. 4.18.1
I: A401-1978, Art. 11, Para. 11.11.1

Owner brought a third party indemnity action against contractor and subcontractor for all claims, damages, losses or expenses, including attorney's fees, arising out of subcontractor's injured workers personal injury action. Contractor also filed a third party indemnity action against the subcontractor. The trial court dismissed the injured workers action and found subcontractor was liable to contractor for attorney's fees, including those incurred by owner. Subcontractor's motion for a new trial was granted and the trial court dismissed the judgment awarding attorney's fees. The owner, contractor and surety appealed. The Appellate Court affirmed the trial court's ruling since the agreement did not provide for indemnity without a finding of fault on the part of the indemnitor or a party for whom the indemnitor was responsible.

The owner-contractor agreement, which included the American Institute of Architects General Conditions of the Contract for Construction, Document No. A201, 1976 edition, provided for indemnification in Paragraph 4.18.1. The subcontract provided for full indemnification by subcontractor from and against all claims, damages, losses and expenses, including attorney's fees, which were incurred by contractor, as well as indemnification obligations to owner under a provision identical to Paragraph 11.11.1 of the American Institute of Architects Standard Form of Agreement Between Contractor and Subcontractor, Document A401, 1978 edition.

The Appellate Court found that the subcontract called for indemnification only if the attorney fee claims were those "arising out of or resulting from the performance, or failure of performance, of the subcontractor's work under this subcontract." The Court found that where the subcontractor was not negligent the subcontractor was not liable to contractor or owner for indemnification or attorneys fees. The Court also found that subcontractor was not liable to the owner for attorney fees in defense of the third-party indemnification action. Furthermore, the indemnity agreements which clearly stated that the party was entitled to indemnity, "provided that any such claim . . . (1) is attributable to bodily injury . . . and (2) is caused in whole or in party by any negligent act or omission of the Contractor, any subcontractor, anyone directly or indirectly employed by any of them . . ." did not provide for indemnity without a finding of fault on the part of the indemnitor or a party for whom the indemnitor was responsible.

89037   Prichard Bros. v. Grady Co., 436 N.W.2d 460 (Minn. Ct. App. 1989)

II: A107-1978, Art. 8, Para. 8.5
II: A117-1979, Art. 12, Para. 12.5
I: A201-1976, Art. 2, Para. 2.2.7
II: A201-1976, Art. 2, Para. 2.2.11
II: A201-1976, Art. 2, Para. 2.2.12
II: B141-1977, Art. 1, Para. 1.5.9

II: B141-1977, Art. 1, Para. 1.5.10
II: B141-1977, Art. 1, Para. 1.5.11

Contractor brought a breach of contract action against owner for amounts withheld based on architect's determination that there was an unremedied artistic defect in the brickwork. The trial court denied contractor's claim and determined that the architect had authority under Paragraph 2.2.11 of the General Conditions to reject the brickwork on the grounds of "artistic effect." Contractor appealed. At issue on appeal was whether the architect's decision regarding the amount of money withheld under Paragraph 9.6.1 was subject to the review provision of Paragraphs 2.2.12 and 7.9.1.

The owner and contractor had entered into the American Institute of Architects Standard Form of Agreement Between Owner and Contractor, Document No. A101, 1977 edition, which included the American Institute of Architects General Conditions of the Contract for Construction, Document No. A201, 1976 edition, specifically Paragraphs 2.2.7, 2.2.9, 2.2.11, 2.2.12, 7.9.1, 9.9.5, 9.6.1 and 9.6.2.

The Appellate Court found that the architect's decision to withhold final certification of payment was an economic decision and not purely artistic. Therefore, the dispute which arose out of the architect's decision was reviewable under the broad arbitration provisions of Paragraph 2.2.12 and 7.9.1. The Court reasoned that the specific exclusion for the architect's decisions "relating to artistic effect," which provided for a final decision, was not applicable because it was not consistent with the intent of the contract documents. The Court found that Paragraph 9.6.1 expressly provided that certification of payment could be withheld for "defective work not remedied." However, while the architect's decision to reject the brickwork on the grounds of artistic effect was not subject to arbitration, the Court found that the issues which related to the amount of money properly withheld were clearly reviewable. The Court then construed Paragraph 9.6.1 in conjunction with the other provisions of the contract, specifically the review provisions of Paragraph 7.9.1 and 2.2.12. The Court found that in this case where the architect concluded that the entire brickwork would have to be replaced because the contracted-for brick was no longer in production, and demanded that the contractor replace the brickwork with a new brick of unspecified type and color for which no artistic standard was agreed upon, the architect's decision was not "final" under Paragraph 2.2.11 and was reviewable under Paragraph 7.9.1. The Court held that the trial court erred in concluding that Paragraph 2.2.11 was applicable.

The Court also found that the condition precedent to the owner's obligation to pay was not satisfied as the architect's issuance of the final payment certificate was not performed, however, it was excused under the provisions of Paragraph 9.6.1. Furthermore, the architect's decision as to the amount of final payment was subject to the mandatory review provisions of Paragraph 7.9.1 and 2.2.12. The Court held that the trial court erred in declining to alter the architect's decision as to damages arising out of the defective brickwork, and as to the amount properly withheld under the contract.

89036   Palmer v. General Health, Inc., 552 So. 2d 750 (La. Ct. App. 1989)

I: A107-1978, Art. 10, Para. 10.11

I:	A117-1979, Art. 17, Para. 17.2
I:	A201-1976, Art. 7, Para. 7.9.1
I:	A401-1978, Art. 13, Para. 13.1
I:	A401-1978, Art. 13, Para. 13.3
I:	A401-1978, Art. 13, Para. 13.4
I:	B141-1977, Art. 9, Para. 9.1

The Appellate Court upheld the trial court's finding that the question of arbitrability of subcontractor's claims was to be decided by the arbitrators and that the contractor could proceed to arbitrate claims on behalf of subcontractors pursuant to the broad arbitration provision contained in Paragraph 7.9.1 of the American Institute of Architects General Conditions of the Contract for Construction, Document No. A201, 1976 edition.

89035   NSC Contractors, Inc. v. Borders, 317 Md. 394, 564 A.2d 408 (1989)

II:	A107-1978, Art. 8, Para. 8.4
II:	A107-1978, Art. 8, Para. 8.5
II:	A107-1978, Art. 8, Para. 8.6
II:	A107-1978, Art. 13, Para. 13.2
II:	A107-1978, Art. 15, Para. 15.2
II:	A107-1978, Art. 15, Para. 15.3
II:	A107-1978, Art. 15, Para. 15.4
II:	A107-1978, Art. 15, Para. 15.5
II:	A117-1979, Art. 12, Para. 12.4
II:	A117-1979, Art. 12, Para. 12.5
II:	A117-1979, Art. 12, Para. 12.6
II:	A117-1979, Art. 17, Para. 17.2
II:	A117-1979, Art. 19, Para. 19.2
II:	A117-1979, Art. 19, Para. 19.3
II:	A117-1979, Art. 19, Para. 19.4
II:	A117-1979, Art. 19, Para. 19.5
I:	A201-1976, Art. 2, Para. 2.2.7
I:	A201-1976, Art. 2, Para. 2.2.9
I:	A201-1976, Art. 2, Para. 2.2.11
I:	A201-1976, Art. 2, Para. 2.2.12
I:	A201-1976, Art. 7, Para. 7.9.1
I:	A201-1976, Art. 9, Para. 9.6.1
I:	A201-1976, Art. 9, Para. 9.6.2
I:	A201-1976, Art. 9, Para. 9.9.5
II:	B141-1977, Art. 1, Para. 1.5.9

III:	A201-1976, Art. 4, Para. 4.7.2
III:	A201-1976, Art. 4, Para. 4.7.3
III:	A201-1976, Art. 4, Para. 4.12.4
III:	A201-1976, Art. 4, Para. 4.12.8
III:	A201-1976, Art. 8, Para. 8.3.1
III:	A201-1976, Art. 8, Para. 8.3.2
III:	A201-1976, Art. 8, Para. 8.3.4
III:	A201-1976, Art. 12, Para. 12.2.1
III:	A201-1976, Art. 12, Para. 12.3.1

Contractor brought an action against owner to recover amounts withheld under the contract. Asserting that the construction delay was contractor's fault, the owner counterclaimed for delay damages. The contractor, however, maintained that the delay was the result of poor soil conditions, inclement weather and extra work. The District Court made the following conclusions:

(1) The owner-contractor agreement, through incorporated specifications, made unanticipated soil conditions the responsibility of the contractor and disclaimed the accuracy of the soil information provided by the owner to the contractor; (2) the contract also provided that the contractor bear the risk of unanticipated weather conditions, and in any event, weather data put into evidence did not demonstrate higher levels of precipitation during relevant time periods; (3) the owner-contractor agreement required written notice of and approval for extra work arising from instructions or clarifications to the contract documents contained in shop drawings, and the contractor failed to give such notice of, or obtain owner's approval for, such additional costs; (4) the owner-contractor agreement precluded damages for owner caused delay; (5) although the contractor provided additional work necessary to conform the project's fire safety piping to local codes and provided owner with notice of the need for such work, the contractor was precluded from obtaining compensation because it agreed to design such systems in conformance with the code even if a change to the contract documents were required; (6) the owner-contractor agreement required written notice of claims for excusable delay and the contractor failed to provide such notice; (7) because the owner-contractor agreement made time of the essence and stated that the "Owner may suffer great financial loss if the Work is not completed by the time specified," owner's damages arising out of delayed completion were reasonably foreseeable and included the loss of use of sales proceeds, lost ground lease revenues and certain additional administrative expenses.

Based on these conclusions, the District Court offset the retained portion of the contract price by the costs and losses incurred by the owner, and awarded the contractor the difference.

89034   Morgant, Inc. v. Boehringer Ingelheim Pharmaceuticals, Inc., 20 Conn. App. 67, 563 A.2d 1055 (1989)

I:	A107-1978, Art. 13, Para. 13.2

coordinate its work with other subcontractors in the absence of a contractual provision imposing such a duty on the contractor; that the subcontractor failed to prove a factual basis for time extensions; and that contractor's termination of the subcontract without providing for a period for cure of 48 hours as required by the subcontract was not a breach where the cure period did not apply, as a matter of law, to breaches which were not curable and for which such a notice would have constituted a useless act.

89032   Markway Constr. Co. v. Kirchenbauer, 769 S.W.2d 836 (Mo. Ct. App. 1989)

> II: A107-1978, Art. 18, Para. 18.1
> II: A117-1979, Art. 22, Para. 22.1
> II: A201-1976, Art. 12, Para. 12.1.1
> II: A201-1976, Art. 12, Para. 12.1.2

In contractor's action against homeowners for amount due under the contract and for work performed pursuant to unsigned change orders, the Appellate Court found that there was no formal agreement as to the use of written or signed change order. The contract provided for "changes in the work" and modifications of contract work by agreement of the parties on a cost-plus basis, and the parties did not agree to adopt the American Institute of Architects General Conditions of the Contract for Construction, Document No. A201, 1976 edition. Furthermore, the work performed pursuant to change orders did not constitute a contract modification because the contract unambiguously contemplated "changes" in the scope of the work and provided for payment of "Changes in the Work on the basis of Cost of Work as defined in [the contract]." Moreover, the contract failed to require written, signed change orders as a prerequisite to payment for performing work designated as a change in the scope of the contract.

89033   McDevitt & Street Co. v. Marriott Corp., 713 F. Supp. 906 (E.D. Va. 1989), *aff'd in part without opinion and rev'd in part without opinion,* 911 F.2d 723 (4th Cir. 1990), *on remand,* 754 F. Supp. 513 (E.D. Va. 1991), *aff'd in part and rev'd in part without opinion,* 948 F.2d 1281 (4th Cir. 1991)

> III: A107-1978, Art. 8, Para. 8.7
> III: A107-1978, Art. 10, Para. 10.5
> III: A107-1978, Art. 10, Para. 10.6
> III: A107-1978, Art. 10, Para. 10.8
> III: A107-1978, Art. 14, Para. 14.3
> III: A117-1979, Art. 12, Para. 12.7
> III: A117-1979, Art. 14, Para. 14.5
> III: A117-1979, Art. 14, Para. 14.6
> III: A117-1979, Art. 14, Para. 14.8
> III: A117-1979, Art. 18, Para. 18.3
> III: A201-1976, Art. 2, Para. 2.2.14

III: A401-1978, Art. 13, Para. 13.1
III: B141-1977, Art. 9, Para. 9.1

In vacating an arbitration award in favor of contractor in an action against owner for final payment, the Appellate Court construed Paragraph 5.1 of the American Institute of Architects Abbreviated Form of Agreement Between Owner and Contractor, Document No. A107, 1978 edition as stating unequivocally that final payment was not due from the owner to the contractor until such time as a final certificate for payment had been issued by the architect. Because no certificate was provided the Court concluded that Paragraph 5.1 had not been satisfied, and as a consequence, there was no obligation upon the owner to pay the contractor. The contractor was not entitled to institute arbitration proceedings against the owner pursuant to Paragraph 13.2 before a final certificate of payment was issued by the architect or the condition was waived.

89031   L.K. Comstock & Co. v. United Eng'g & Constructors, Inc., 880 F.2d 219 (9th Cir. 1989)

II: A401-1978, Art. 11, Para. 11.2.1
II: A401-1978, Art. 11, Para. 11.4.2
II: A401-1978, Art. 11, Para. 11.9.1
I: A401-1978, Art. 11, Para. 11.10.1
II: A401-1978, Art. 14, Para. 14.2.1

Subcontractor brought an action against contractor for wrongful termination damages. Contractor counterclaimed for breach of contract damages. After a bench trial on liability, the District Court found that the termination of the subcontract was proper and that subcontractor was liable to contractor for excess costs incurred to finish the work with a replacement subcontractor.

The contractor and subcontractor entered into an agreement which contained provisions similar to the American Institute of Architects Standard Form of Agreement between the Contractor and Subcontractor, Document No. A401, 1978 edition, Paragraphs 11.9.1 and 14.2.1.

The Court of Appeals affirmed. It held that deviations by the contractor from procedures for issuing change orders did not constitute a breach of contract because both parties mutually consented to a waiver of the requirement for formal change orders in conjunction with the fast track project which subcontractor should have known would require design accommodation changes in the project scope.

The Court also upheld the trial court's factual determinations that custom and usage indicated that the subcontractor had broad engineering responsibilities which it failed to meet; that the contractor's scheduling and coordination efforts and alleged failure to provide a CPM schedule were not in violation of the subcontract in light of subcontractor's contractual duty to "plan and schedule all his work within the project schedule"; that the provision requiring "coordination of work activities shall be Subcontractor's responsibility" and other similar provisions imposed on the subcontractor a duty to

III: A401-1978, Art. 11, Para. 11.2.6
III: A401-1978, Art. 11, Para. 11.5.1

Contractor brought a third-party indemnification action against subcontractor. In the subcontract, subcontractor agreed to "indemnify and save the Contractor . . . harmless from and against any and all costs, loss, expense, liability, damages, or claims for damages arising or resulting from any work of the Subcontractor . . . including attorney's fees, expenses and costs of defending any action on account of any injury or damage to property or persons, or on account of any other action against the contractor . . . for any liability . . . arising out of any work performed by or required from the subcontractor and on account of any injury (including death) to any persons or property arising or resulting from the Work provided for or performed by the Subcontractor. . . ." The Appellate Court construed the broad indemnification provision in light of the definition of the scope of the work which expressly called upon the subcontractor to furnish "all things necessary to complete all work . . .," and the provision requiring the subcontractor to comply with the safety requirements in the owner-contractor agreement, and concluded that the clause placed on the subcontractor unqualified responsibility for injuries arising out of its part of the work.

89029 J.W. Creech, Inc. v. Norfolk Air Conditioning Corp., 237 Va. 320, 377 S.E.2d 605 (1989)

III: A201-1976, Art. 12, Para. 12.3.1
III: A401-1978, Art. 11, Para. 11.10.1

Subcontractor brought an action against contractor for extras. The subcontract provided that "If there is disagreement as to whether an item of work is an extra or a part of the contract, the Architects' and Owners' authorized agents decision on the matter will be final and binding for all parties." The architect was the sole judge of satisfactory completion, and the subcontractor was responsible for "work and equipment until finally inspected, tested, and accepted." The Court held that a refusal by the architect to approve subcontractor's charge for repairs or the charge for replacement as an "extra" was binding under the subcontract.

89030 Kilianek v. Kim, 192 Ill. App. 3d 139, 139 Ill. Dec. 213, 548 N.E.2d 598 (1989)

I: A107-1978, Art. 5, Para. 5.1
I: A107-1978, Art. 13, Para. 13.2
II: A117-1979, Art. 9, Para. 9.3
II: A117-1979, Art. 17, Para. 17.2
II: A201-1976, Art. 2, Para. 2.2.6
II: A201-1976, Art. 7, Para. 7.9.1
II: A201-1976, Art. 9, Para. 9.9.1

89027 J.M. Beeson Co. v. Sartori, 553 So. 2d 180 (Fla. Dist. Ct. App. 1989), *appeal after remand,* 584 So. 2d 572 (Fla. Dist. Ct. App. 1991)

I:	A107-1978, Art. 7, Para. 7.4
II:	A107-1978, Art. 8, Para. 8.4
I:	A107-1978, Art. 14, Para. 14.2
II:	A107-1978, Art. 15, Para. 15.3
I:	A117-1979, Art. 11, Para. 11.4
II:	A117-1979, Art. 12, Para. 12.4
I:	A117-1979, Art. 18, Para. 18.2
II:	A117-1979, Art. 19, Para. 19.3
I:	A201-1976, Art. 1, Para. 1.1.3
I:	A201-1976, Art. 8, Para. 8.1.3
I:	A201-1976, Art. 9, Para. 9.8.1
III:	B141-1977, Art. 1, Para. 1.5.7
III:	B141-1977, Art. 1, Para. 1.5.8

Contractor brought an action against owner for nonpayment and owner counterclaimed for breach of contract and for liquidated damages. The trial court found in favor of owner and contractor appealed. Among numerous arguments on appeal the contractor claimed that the trial court erred in finding that contractor did not substantially complete the work.

The owner-contractor agreement provided that substantial completion occurred when "construction is sufficiently complete in accordance with the Contract Documents, so the owner can occupy or utilize the work or designated portion thereof for the use for which it is intended." The "work" under the contract "comprises the complete construction required by the contract documents." The contract also provided that the date of substantial completion was to be certified by the supervising architect. However, the owner's contract with the architect specifically deleted any responsibility on behalf of the architect to supervise payments or to certify the date of substantial completion.

The Appellate Court held that the work had been substantially completed when all phases had been completed sufficiently so as to obtain certificates of occupancy and the owner was capable of having tenants occupy the spaces and pay rent. At that point the contractor was entitled to his full contract price less the cost of completion and damages due to delay. The Appellate Court therefore reversed the judgment for the owner and remanded for determination of the date of completion.

89028 Jones v. Vappi Co., 28 Mass. App. Ct. 77, 546 N.E.2d 379 (1989)

III:	A107-1978, Art. 10, Para. 10.11
III:	A117-1979, Art. 14, Para. 14.11
III:	A201-1976, Art. 4, Para. 4.18.1
II:	A401-1978, Art. 11, Para. 11.11.1

coverage, created an ambiguity as to the true intention of the parties. Furthermore, there was no indication in the contract that one provision was to override or negate the other.

89026   Jim Carlson Constr., Inc. v. Bailey, 769 S.W.2d 480 (Mo. Ct. App. 1989)

I:	A101-1977, Art. 1
I:	A101-1977, Art. 7, Para. 7.2
III:	A107-1978, Art. 6, Para. 6.1
III:	A107-1978, Art. 7, Para. 7.1
I:	A111-1978, Art. 1, Para. 1.1
I:	A111-1978, Art. 16, Para. 16.2
III:	A117-1979, Art. 10, Para. 10.2
III:	A117-1979, Art. 11, Para. 11.1
III:	A201-1976, Art. 1, Para. 1.1.1
II:	A401-1978, Art. 1, Para. 1.1

Contractor brought a breach of contract action against owner. Owner filed an application to compel arbitration which was denied by the trial court. Owner argued on appeal that the owner-contractor agreement incorporated by reference certain general conditions which contained a clause that required arbitration of all disputes relating to the contract documents.

The parties entered into the American Institute of Architects Standard Form of Agreement Between Owner and Contractor, Document No. A101, 1977 edition, which listed the contract documents in Article 1, required that they be enumerated in Paragraph 7.2, and provided in Paragraph 7.2 that the contract documents constituted the entire agreement between the parties. The contract documents were not enumerated in Paragraph 7.2 and there were no other documents attached to the contract. However, on the face of A101 was the notation "use only with the 1976 Edition of AIA Document A201, General Conditions of the Contract for Construction." Paragraph 7.9.1 of the General Conditions required arbitration of all contract disputes.

The Appellate Court found that the lack of enumeration of the contract documents after Paragraph 7.2 did not render that agreement ambiguous. In construing the agreement as a whole, the Court found that Article 1 definitively stated that the General Conditions were made fully a part of the contract as if attached to the agreement. Furthermore, Paragraph 7.2 stated that the contract documents which constituted the entire agreement between the parties were listed in Article 1. The Court concluded that it would not be a reasonable interpretation of the contract to say that merely because the agreement itself, the general conditions, and the drawings and the specifications were not listed following Paragraph 7.2 they were not a part of the contract and were not binding on the parties in spite of definitive contract language to the contrary. The Court reversed the judgment of the trial court and ordered arbitration pursuant to Paragraph 7.9.1.

89025 International Paper Co. v. Corporex Constructors, Inc., 96 N.C. App. 312, 385 S.E.2d 553 (1989)

I: A107-1978, Art. 10, Para. 10.11
I: A117-1979, Art. 14, Para. 14.11
I: A201-1976, Art. 4, Para. 4.18.1
I: A401-1978, Art. 11, Para. 11.11.1

Owner brought a third-party indemnification action against contractor for attorney's fees incurred in defending against subcontractor's injured workers action. The trial court found that subcontractor was negligent and granted contractor's motion for summary judgment. Owner appealed. The Appellate Court reversed the grant of summary judgment to the contractor and remanded to the trial court to resolve the issue of whether the parties intended to extend indemnification to the negligent acts of subcontractors.

The owner-contractor agreement contained two indemnification provisions. The first did not cover the negligent acts of the subcontractor while the second clause did cover the negligent acts of both the contractor and any subcontractors hired to work on the project. The clause provided that "The Builder shall indemnify and hold harmless the Owner and his agents and employees from and against all claims, losses, and expenses, including attorney's fees arising out of or resulting from the performance of the work, provided that such claim, damage, loss or expense (1) is attributable to bodily injury, sickness, disease or death, or to injury to or destruction of tangible property (other than the Work itself) including the loss of use resulting therefrom, and (2) is caused in whole or in part by any negligent act or omission of the Builder, any Subcontractor, anyone directly or indirectly employed by any of them or anyone for whose acts any of them may be liable, regardless of whether or not it is caused in part by a party indemnified hereunder."

The Appellate Court interpreted the last clause of the second indemnity provision as void and unenforceable as against public policy. However, the Court found that the state statute did not apply to a contract to indemnify another "against liability for damages resulting from the sole negligence of the promisor, its agents or employees." Moreover, the offending term in the indemnity provision was not a central feature of the contract or even of the provision. The general meaning of the provision, that the contractor would indemnify owner for injury or damage resulting from the negligent acts of contractor, its subcontractors, and their employees, was not affected. Based on this reasoning the Appellate Court held that the offending language was severable from the contract.

The Court then found that although the indemnity provisions did not have the same meaning they were not necessarily in conflict. The Court found it reasonable to conclude that the second provision extended the indemnity coverage of the first provision to the negligent acts of subcontractors. The Court found that when the contract was read as a whole contractor appeared to have agreed to indemnify owner from claims arising from the negligence of the contractor or of any subcontractors. However, the Court concluded that the existence of two indemnity provisions, each with clearly different scopes of

III: B141-1977, Art. 1, Para. 1.5.9
III: B141-1977, Art. 1, Para. 1.5.10

The trial court dismissed owner's complaint against the contractor seeking damages for misrepresentation and enforcement of the engineer's award because the owner had not filed its claim with the engineer within the time limit set forth in the owner-contractor agreement. The Appellate Court reversed and reinstate the complaint.

The parties entered into an agreement which contained a dispute procedure similar to that set forth in the American Institute of Architects General Conditions of the Contract for Construction, Document No. A201, 1976 edition, Paragraphs 2.2.7, 2.2.9, 2.2.10, 2.2.12, 7.9.1 and 7.9.2. The agreement also provided that the rendering of a decision by the engineer was a condition precedent to any exercise by owner or contractor of such rights or remedies as either may have had under the contract documents or by law.

When the owner realized it had been overcharged for sod, it notified the contractor and the engineer of its claim. The contractor did not respond and the engineer rendered a decision in favor of the owner. The contractor did not pay, and the owner filed its complaint in the trial court. The trial court denied the contractor's motion to compel arbitration as untimely, and dismissed the owner's complaint for failure to file it with the engineer.

The Appellate Court found that the engineer's decision became final and binding when neither the owner nor contractor demanded arbitration within thirty days after receiving the decision. Because the decision was allowed to become final, it was tantamount to an arbitration award and should have been reviewed as such by the trial court.

89024 *In re* Boston Shipyard Corp., 886 F.2d 451 (1st Cir. 1989)

III: A107-1978, Art. 18, Para. 18.1
III: A117-1979, Art. 22, Para. 22.1
III: A201-1976, Art. 7, Para. 7.9.3
III: A201-1976, Art. 12, Para. 12.1.1
III: A201-1976, Art. 12, Para. 12.1.2

Contractor appealed from the District Court's grant of summary judgment in favor of the government. The Court of Appeals found that the contractor had wrongfully abandoned the contract. The contractor was obligated to continue to work until its dispute with the government was resolved pursuant to the contract clause which provided that "the Contractor shall proceed diligently with performance of this contract, pending final resolution of any request for relief, claim, appeal, or action arising under the contract, and comply with any decision of the Contracting Officer." The Court also found that where the contract between the parties contained a change clause providing for an effective and efficient procedure for dealing with changes that would arise in the course of performance, the number of change orders were not of such a magnitude or extent to constitute a cardinal change of the contract justifying contractor's abandonment.

the engineer for indemnity. The District Court found in favor of the owner and granted the contractor's surety indemnity from the engineering firm. Engineer appealed, arguing that the trial court erroneously interpreted the agreement as imposing on the engineer a duty to detect criminal fraud. The Court of Appeals affirmed the findings of the trial court but vacated the award of attorney's fees granted pursuant to state statute.

The engineer was charged with the duty to monitor and inspect the contractor's work by providing on-site project representatives to view the day to day work performed by contractor. As part of its duties, engineer was to regularly inspect the work as it progressed so as to assure conformance to the contract documents and to verify the testing procedures. Engineer's representatives were to certify work logs intended to document both the location of testing and inspection work performed and the quantity of joint sealing operations. The owner-engineer agreement contained a provision identical to Paragraph 1.5.4 of the American Institute of Architects Standard Form of Agreement Between Owner and Architect, Document No. B141, 1977 edition, and provided further that the engineer's approval of a requested payment constituted assurance that the "quality of the Work is in accordance with the Contract Documents."

The Court of Appeals upheld the finding of the District Court that the contract delegated to the engineer the authority and responsibility to reject work not meeting inspection and testing requirements or not accomplished in accordance with the contract documents. The Court concluded that the District Court did not define a duty greater than that specified in the contract and in no way imposed a duty on the engineer to detect criminal fraud.

The Court then found that the engineer breached its contractual duty by certifying inaccurate or deficient records which purported to verify compliance with the contract specifications. This finding of breach of duty extended to the contractor's surety where the Court found that the engineer was liable to those who might suffer reasonable foreseeable and direct injury because of the engineer's breach of duty.

89023   Huntington Woods v. Ajax Paving Indus., Inc., 177 Mich. App. 351, 441 N.W.2d 99 (1989), *clarified on reh'g,* 179 Mich. App. 600, 446 N.W.2d 331 (1989), *appeal denied,* 434 Mich. 892 (1990)

	III:	A107-1978, Art. 8, Para. 8.5
	III:	A107-1978, Art. 13, Para. 13.2
	III:	A117-1979, Art. 12, Para. 12.5
	III:	A117-1979, Art. 17, Para. 17.2
	II:	A201-1976, Art. 2, Para. 2.2.7
	II:	A201-1976, Art. 2, Para. 2.2.9
	II:	A201-1976, Art. 2, Para. 2.2.10
	II:	A201-1976, Art. 2, Para. 2.2.12
	II:	A201-1976, Art. 7, Para. 7.9.1
	II:	A201-1976, Art. 7, Para. 7.9.2

and architect appealed. At issue on appeal was whether the trial court correctly construed the indemnification clause in the owner-contractor agreement.

The owner and contractor had entered into a standard American Institute of Architects short form of agreement between owner and contractor which contained a renumbered indemnification clause identical to Paragraph 10.11 of the American Institute of Architects Abbreviated Form of Agreement Between Owner and Contractor, Document No. A107, 1978 edition.

The Appellate Court found that the language of the indemnification clause was clear and unambiguous. Under the inclusionary portion of the clause, the contractor unequivocally had agreed to indemnify the architect for "all claims, damages, losses and expenses including attorneys' fees" caused by the contractor's negligence that resulted in death or injury. The Court found that the attorneys' fees were incurred by the architect in defending the litigation resulting from the contractor's negligence. The latter portion of the clause excluded indemnification for "the liability of the Architect" resulting from his professional negligence. Because the jury found that the architect was not negligent the exclusionary provision of the clause had not been triggered and the contractor remained bound to indemnify architect for the attorney fees incurred as a result of contractor's negligence. The Court therefore held that the architect was entitled to indemnification from the contractor for attorney fees under the owner-contractor agreement.

89022   Houma, L.A. v. Municipal & Indus. Pipe Serv., Inc., 884 F.2d 886 (5th Cir. 1989), *reh'g denied,* 1989 U.S. App. LEXIS 19334 (5th Cir. 1989), *reh'g denied,* 1989 U.S. App. LEXIS 19561 (5th Cir. 1989)

II:	A107-1978, Art. 8, Para. 8.3
II:	A107-1978, Art. 8, Para. 8.4
II:	A107-1978, Art. 8, Para. 8.6
II:	A117-1979, Art. 12, Para. 12.3
II:	A117-1979, Art. 12, Para. 12.4
II:	A117-1979, Art. 12, Para. 12.6
I:	A201-1976, Art. 2, Para. 2.2.3
II:	A201-1976, Art. 2, Para. 2.2.13
II:	A201-1976, Art. 9, Para. 9.4.2
I:	B141-1977, Art. 1, Para. 1.5.4
II:	B141-1977, Art. 1, Para. 1.5.8
II:	B141-1977, Art. 1, Para. 1.5.12
III:	B141-1977, Art. 1, Para. 1.6.1
III:	B141-1977, Art. 1, Para. 1.6.2
III:	B141-1977, Art. 1, Para. 1.6.3

Owner brought an action against contractor and its surety to recover payments made under the owner-contractor agreement and the surety brought a third-party action against

I:	B141-1977, Art. 1, Para. 1.5.1
I:	B141-1977, Art. 10, Para. 10.1
I:	B141-1977, Art. 10, Para. 10.2

Owner filed an action seeking a declaratory judgment that architect had been fully paid under the contract. The architect counterclaimed for fees due calculated on a percentage basis. The trial court found for architect and owner appealed. The owner argued on appeal that architect's fee should have been calculated on an hourly basis because no "budget" was established within the meaning of the contract. The architect argued that he calculated his fee as a percentage of the construction costs because he had complied with his contract "duties" and "responsibilities" pertaining to services to be rendered in the schematic phase. The term "budget" was not defined in the contract.

The owner-architect agreement consisted of two letter agreements and the American Institute of Architects Standard Form of Agreement Between the Owner and Architect, Document No. B141, 1977 edition, which was referred to only for definition of phases.

The Appellate Court found that the contract, as modified, clearly established that architect was to be compensated on a percentage of the total construction cost when a budget was established. The Court found that the evidence revealed that there was obviously a difference in interpretation between the parties as to what "budget established" meant. The architect's interpretation was a schematic phase budget of probable construction cost as required by the contract, and the owner's interpretation was a total budget of the total cost of the project, some of which costs the architect could not control. The Court concluded that the evidence in the record was sufficient for the jury to have found that a schematic phase budget was established entitling the architect to a percentage payment of probable construction cost.

The Court interpreted the termination provisions of the contract as providing that the owner could terminate the architect if the architect failed to substantially perform through no fault of the owner or in the event that the project was abandoned. The Court found that the owner wrongfully terminated the architect since the jury found that the architect had substantially performed its contract with the owner.

89021 Hillman v. Leland E. Burns, Inc., 209 Cal. App. 3d 860, 257 Cal. Rptr. 535 (1989)

I:	A107-1978, Art. 10, Para. 10.11
I:	A117-1979, Art. 14, Para. 14.11
II:	A201-1976, Art. 4, Para. 4.18.1
II:	A401-1978, Art. 11, Para. 11.11.1

Contractor's employee brought a wrongful death action against the architect and others. The architect brought a third-party indemnification action against the contractor. The trial court entered judgment in favor of the architect and the architect filed a memorandum of costs seeking attorneys fees from the contractor based on the indemnification provision contained in the owner-contractor agreement. The trial court denied architect's motion

89019 Green Constr. Co. v. Kansas Power & Light Co., 717 F. Supp. 738 (D. Kan. 1989), *aff'd,* 1 F.3d 1005 (10th Cir. 1993)

III:	A107-1978, Art. 7, Para. 7.3
III:	A107-1978, Art. 18, Para. 18.2
III:	A117-1979, Art. 11, Para. 11.3
III:	A117-1979, Art. 22, Para. 22.2
III:	A201-1976, Art. 1, Para. 1.2.1
III:	A201-1976, Art. 12, Para. 12.2.1
III:	A201-1976, Art. 12, Para. 12.3.1

Contractor brought an action against owner seeking additional compensation for work performed under the contract resulting from differing site conditions. The owner moved for partial summary judgment on the ground that the contract placed the risk of unforeseen subsurface conditions on the contractor. Contractor argued that it was entitled to additional compensation where there was a constructive change in the contract, and where the owner breached an implied warranty and misrepresented information provided to bidders. The District Court granted owner's motion for summary judgment.

The instructions to bidders, which were incorporated into the contract, required each bidder to visit the site and conduct its own independent research and analysis of the subsurface conditions. The documents expressly stated that "logs of test borings may not be indicative of all subsurface conditions that may be encountered." The bid documents placed the risk of loss resulting from natural causes on the contractor and provided a method by which the contractor could recover increased compensation for "extra work" or changes to the work required under the contract.

The Court found that the contractor was not entitled to additional compensation under the change order clause which provided that the contractor was entitled to additional compensation for extra work or changes in the work to be performed where the provision applied to changes in the work due to changes in the project design and not to difficulties in the performance of the work resulting from unforeseen subsurface conditions. The Court found that the bid documents clearly placed responsibility for unforeseen subsurface conditions on the contractor. Furthermore, the owner did not impliedly warrant the accuracy of the soil reports provided each bidder where the bid documents clearly stated that "logs of test borings may not be indicative of all subsurface conditions that may be encountered."

89020 Gunter Hotel of San Antonio, Inc. v. Buck, 775 S.W.2d 689 (Tex. Ct. App. 1989)

I:	B141-1977, Art. 1, Para. 1.1.4
I:	B141-1977, Art. 1, Para. 1.2.1
I:	B141-1977, Art. 1, Para. 1.3.1
I:	B141-1977, Art. 1, Para. 1.4.1

lower cost of the house. The Court held that the architect was entitled to a fee based on the "lowest bona fide bid" for "all elements of the Project designed" by the architect.

In addition, since the agreement provided that "Payments due the Architect and unpaid under this Agreement shall bear interest from the date payment is due at the rate entered below, or in the absence thereof, at the legal rate prevailing at the principal place of business of the Architect," the interest on the amount due the architect was an explicit item of recovery for the architect.

89018   Godwin v. Stanley Smith & Sons, 300 S.C. 90, 386 S.E.2d 464 (Ct. App. 1989)

III:	A107-1978, Art. 11, Para. 11.2	
II:	A107-1978, Art. 13, Para. 13.2	
III:	A117-1979, Art. 15, Para. 15.2	
II:	A117-1979, Art. 17, Para. 17.2	
III:	A201-1976, Art. 5, Para. 5.3.1	
I:	A201-1976, Art. 7, Para. 7.9.1	
III:	A401-1978, Art. 11, Para. 11.1.1	
III:	A401-1978, Art. 11, Para. 11.2.6	
III:	A401-1978, Art. 13, Para. 13.1	
II:	B141-1977, Art. 9, Para. 9.1	

Subcontractor brought a breach of contract action against contractor and contractor moved to stay the proceedings and compel arbitration. The trial court denied contractor's motion and contractor appealed. The Appellate Court reversed the decision of the trial court on the ground that the arbitration provision of the owner-contractor agreement was incorporated by reference into the subcontract.

The subcontract did not expressly require arbitration but it referred to the owner-contractor agreement which required arbitration. The subcontract provided that the subcontractor "agrees to furnish all materials and perform all work . . . in accordance with the General Conditions of the Contract between the owner and the Contractor . . . which General Conditions . . . hereby become a part of this contract." Included among the Contract Documents which formed the contract between the contractor and the owner was the American Institute of Architects General Conditions of the Contract for Construction, Document No. A201, 1976 edition, which contained an arbitration agreement in Paragraph 7.9.1. In addition, the subcontract contained a flow-down provision which stated that the subcontractor was "bound to the Contractor by the terms of the Contract Documents and this Agreement, and assume[s] toward the Contractor all the obligations and responsibilities that the Contractor, by those documents, assumes toward the Owner as applicable to this Subcontract."

The Appellate Court found that the subcontractor was bound to arbitrate its dispute with the owner and held that the arbitration clause was sufficiently broad to encompass the subcontractor's action for fraud.

agreement included the American Institute of Architects General Conditions of the Contract for Construction, Document No. A201, 1976 edition, specifically Paragraphs 4.3.1, 4.3.2, 4.18.1, and the safety requirements contained in Paragraphs 10.1.1, 10.2.2, 10.2.6, 10.2.7 and 10.3.1.

The Appellate Division found that where the owner did not have the contractual authority to direct, supervise or control the work or the manner in which the work was discharged, and where owner was not negligent but its liability was vicarious based on its nondelegable duty under the state statute, owner was entitled under the statute to indemnification from the contractor.

89017   Getzschman v. Miller Chem. Co., 232 Neb. 885, 443 N.W.2d 260 (1989)

III:	B141-1977, Art. 1, Para. 1.5.4	
III:	B141-1977, Art. 3, Para. 3.2.1	
III:	B141-1977, Art. 3, Para. 3.2.2	
III:	B141-1977, Art. 6, Para. 6.1.4	
I:	B141-1977, Art. 10, Para. 10.1	
II:	B141-1977, Art. 14, Para. 14.2.2	
II:	B141-1977, Art. 14, Para. 14.6	

Architect brought an action against owner for the balance due under the contract and owner counterclaimed that the architect breached the contract by failing to design a house which could have been built for the agreed upon price, by violating a fiduciary duty of good faith, loyalty and full disclosure, and by failing to use due care in preparing the design. The trial court entered judgment for the architect and denied the owner's counterclaim. The Appellate Court upheld the judgment of the trial court.

The parties had entered into an agreement which provided that architect's fee would be a percentage of the construction cost of the house and the owner would provide the cost estimates. The agreement provided that the architect "shall visit the site of the work semi-monthly for the purposes of inspection of progress, as part of the Basic Services of this agreement." The agreement provided that the contract could be "terminated by either party upon seven days' written notice should the other party fail substantially to perform in accordance with its terms through no fault of the party initiating the termination." The contract did not contain a cost limitation or include a budget restriction on construction.

The Supreme Court found that the architect's duties were determined by the contract, and implicit in the contract was the duty of the architect to exercise skill and care. However, the Court found that the architect had no express contractual obligation to design the house within a specified budget or to estimate the construction cost, the concluded that construction at a cost greater than anticipated by or acceptable to the owner was no defense to the architect's action to recover his fee. Furthermore, the contract clearly provided that the architect's fee was not limited to the cost of actual construction where the owner took the final plans to another draftsman for revisions resulting in a

II: A401-1978, Art. 11, Para. 11.11.1

The Appellate Division, in architect's third-party action against contractor for indemnification, construed an indemnity provision contained in the owner-contractor agreement. The trial court had entered judgment against the owner and the contractor for injuries resulting from a building's collapse. The indemnity clause provided that the contractor would indemnify the architect against "all claims, damages, losses and expenses, including but not limited to attorney's fees" which were to arise or be occasioned by the negligence of the contractor, subcontractor or its agents." The Court found that the purpose of the indemnification clause was to indemnify the architect where the architect incurred expenses (attorneys fees) for claims arising out of the performance of the work, provided, however, that the claims were attributable to bodily injury or death caused in whole or part by a negligent act or omission of the contractor. The Court concluded that the purpose of this indemnification provision and the language of the provision was plain and clear, and affirmed the indemnification award of attorney's fees to the architect.

89016 Francavilla v. Nagar Constr. Co., 151 A.D.2d 282, 542 N.Y.S.2d 557 (1989)

II: A107-1978, Art. 9, Para. 9.4
II: A107-1978, Art. 10, Para. 10.1
II: A107-1978, Art. 10, Para. 10.7
II: A107-1978, Art. 10, Para. 10.11
II: A107-1978, Art. 16, Para. 16.1
II: A117-1979, Art. 13, Para. 13.4
II: A117-1979, Art. 14, Para. 14.1
II: A117-1979, Art. 14, Para. 14.7
II: A117-1979, Art. 14, Para. 14.11
II: A117-1979, Art. 20, Para. 20.1
I: A201-1976, Art. 3, Para. 3.3.1
I: A201-1976, Art. 3, Para. 3.4.1
I: A201-1976, Art. 4, Para. 4.3.1
I: A201-1976, Art. 4, Para. 4.3.2
I: A201-1976, Art. 10, Para. 10.1.1
I: A201-1976, Art. 10, Para. 10.2.2
I: A201-1976, Art. 10, Para. 10.2.6
I: A201-1976, Art. 10, Para. 10.2.7
I: A201-1976, Art. 10, Para. 10.3.1

An injured worker brought a successful personal injury action against owner and contractor. At issue on appeal was whether the owner was entitled to indemnification by the contractor in accordance with the contract and common law. The owner-contractor

1.5.8 provided that the issuance of such certificates constituted a representation by the architect that the work had progressed to the point indicated and, to the best of its knowledge, the quality of the work was in accordance with the contract documents. The Court concluded that regardless of whether or not the architect had actual knowledge, questions of fact existed as to whether the architect failed to fulfill its obligation to inspect, making summary judgment inappropriate.

89013 D & O Contractors, Inc. v. Terrebonne Parish School Bd., 545 So. 2d 588 (La. Ct. App.), *cert. denied*, 550 So. 2d 654 (La. 1989)

    I: A201-1976, Art. 7, Para. 7.5.1

In contractor's action against owner for the retainage withheld under the contract, attorneys' fees and legal interest, the trial court interpreted Paragraph 7.5.1 of the American Institute of Architects General Condition of the Contract for Construction, Document No. A201, 1976 edition, which gave the owner the right to require the contractor to furnish a bond to cover its performance under the contract and the payment of all "obligations arising thereunder," as not including the payment of owner's attorney's fees absent an express provision for the payment of such fees.

89014 Eis Group Cornwall Hill Dev. Corp. v. Rinaldi Constr., Inc., 154 A.D.2d 429, 546 N.Y.S.2d 105 (1989)

    I: A201-1987, Art. 4, Para. 4.5.1
    I: A201-1976, Art. 7, Para. 7.9.1

The Appellate Division upheld the trial court's finding that because of conflicting terms in the American Institute of Architects Standard Form of Agreement Between Owner and Contractor, 1987 edition, and a typewritten rider, there was no clear and unequivocal agreement to arbitrate. The first page of the agreement incorporated by reference the American Institute of Architects General Conditions of the Contract for Construction, Document No. A201, 1987 edition, which contained an arbitration provision in Paragraph 4.5.1, but the General Conditions were not physically annexed to the agreement. Instead, annexed to the owner-contractor agreement and rider was the American Institute of Architects General Conditions of the Contract for Construction, Document No. A201, 1976 edition which was modified by deletions and additions, including the striking of the arbitration clause contained in Paragraph 7.9.1.

89015 Estate of Nasser v. Port Auth. of New York, 155 A.D.2d 250, 546 N.Y.S.2d 626 (1989)

    II: A107-1978, Art. 10, Para. 10.11
    II: A117-1979, Art. 14, Para. 14.11
    II: A201-1976, Art. 4, Para. 4.18.1

I: B141-1977, Art. 1, Para. 1.5.4
I: B141-1977, Art. 1, Para. 1.5.5
I: B141-1977, Art. 1, Para. 1.5.7
I: B141-1977, Art. 1, Para. 1.5.8
I: B141-1977, Art. 1, Para. 1.5.12

Owner brought an action against contractor, architect and several subcontractors for fire damages allegedly caused by the faulty installation of insulation. The issue before the trial court in deciding architect's motion for summary judgment was whether an architect, who allegedly failed to make adequate periodic inspections during construction and thereby failed to learn of defects in the work, is immune from liability by virtue of a contract provision stating that he would not be responsible for the contractor's acts or omissions.

The owner and architect entered into the American Institute of Architects Standard Form of Agreement Between Owner and Architect, Document No. B141, 1977 edition, which required the architect to prepare design and construction documents for the renovation project and imposed certain obligations on the architect during the construction phase of the project under Paragraphs 1.5.4, 1.5.7, 1.5.8 and 1.5.12. However, Paragraph 1.5.5 provided that the architect, "shall not have control or charge of and shall not be responsible for construction means, methods, techniques, sequences or procedures, or for safety precautions and programs in connection with the Work, for the acts or omissions of the Contractor, Subcontractors, or any other persons performing any of the Work, or for the failure of any of them to carry out the Work in accordance with the Contract Documents."

The Court found that the architect's contention that its contract did not impose a duty to inspect was contrary to the express language of its agreement. The Court found that although the architect was not obligated to supervise the construction work or to make exhaustive or continuous on-site inspections, architect was required to visit the site periodically in order to be familiar with the progress and quality of the work, to determine generally if the work was proceeding in accordance with the contract documents, to keep owner informed about the progress and quality of the work, and to guard the owner against defects in the work. The architect's obligation to issue certificates of payment required him to be familiar with both the quantity and quality of the work done and imposed on the him the duty to insure to the owner that before final acceptance of the work the building was completed in accordance with the plans and specifications. The Court concluded that the exculpatory provision contained in Paragraph 1.5.5 did not immunize the architect from liability flowing from a breach of its duties to owner where the exculpatory provision was nothing other than an agreement that the architect was not the insurer or guarantor of the contractor's obligation to carry out the work in accordance with the contract documents.

Furthermore, the Court's findings that the architect failed to undertake sufficient on-site observations and failed to keep the owners informed of the progress and quality of the work were supported by the architect's admission that it did not inspect the installation of the insulation but, nevertheless, issued certificates of payment for the work. Paragraph

89011   D.E. Wright Elec., Inc. v. Henry Ross Constr. Co., 182 Ill. App. 3d 46, 131 Ill. Dec. 626, 538 N.E.2d 1182 (1989)

        II: A107-1978, Art. 13, Para. 13.2
        II: A117-1979, Art. 17, Para. 17.2
        II: A201-1976, Art. 7, Para. 7.9.1
        I: A401-1978, Art. 13, Para. 13.1
        I: A401-1976, Art. 13, Para. 13.6
        II: B141-1977, Art. 9, Para. 9.1

A subcontractor initially brought a mechanics lien action against the owner and contractor for the balance due under the subcontract, and later filed a breach of contract action against the contractor. The trial court found that the subcontractor could not invoke the arbitration provision in the subcontract which provided that "all claims, disputes and other matters in question arising out of, or relating to, this Subcontract, or the breach thereof, shall be decided by arbitration . . ." and also provided that the arbitration clause "shall not be deemed a limitation on any rights or remedies which the Subcontractor may have under any Federal or State mechanics' lien laws" because the subcontractor opposed arbitration when its suit was initially filed.

The Appellate Court reversed. It reasoned that at the time the suit was filed it was brought under the mechanics' liens act and was not subject to arbitration under the terms of the parties contract. Therefore, it was subcontractor's right to oppose arbitration until claims against the owner were settled and subcontractor's lien was released.

Furthermore, the contractor did not waive its arbitration rights by filing a counterclaim where the counterclaim was merely responsive and was filed only to protect contractor's rights. Therefore, the trial court should have stayed the proceedings and submitted the case to arbitration in accordance with the contract.

89012   Diocese of Rochester v. R-Monde Contractors, Inc., 148 Misc. 2d 926, 562 N.Y.S.2d 593 (Sup. Ct. 1989)

        II: A107-1978, Art. 8, Para. 8.3
        II: A107-1978, Art. 8, Para. 8.4
        II: A107-1978, Art. 8, Para. 8.6
        II: A117-1979, Art. 12, Para. 12.3
        II: A117-1979, Art. 12, Para. 12.4
        II: A117-1979, Art. 12, Para. 12.6
        I: A201-1976, Art. 2, Para. 2.2.3
        I: A201-1976, Art. 2, Para. 2.2.4
        I: A201-1976, Art. 2, Para. 2.2.6
        I: A201-1976, Art. 2, Para. 2.2.13
        I: A201-1976, Art. 9, Para. 9.4.2

I:	A117-1979, Art. 8, Para. 8.2
I:	A401-1978, Art. 5, Para. 5.4
I:	B141-1977, Art. 14, Para. 14.6

The Appellate Court found that where the contract provided that "Payments due and unpaid under the Contract Documents shall bear interest from the date payment is due at the rate entered below, or in the absence thereof, at the legal rate prevailing at the place of Project," and no rate of interest was entered, the trial court did not err in awarding the amount of interest as provided by state statute.

89010 David Co. v. Jim W. Miller Constr., Inc., 444 N.W.2d 836 (Minn. 1989)

II:	A107-1978, Art. 13, Para. 13.2
II:	A107-1978, Art. 15, Para. 15.5
II:	A117-1979, Art. 17, Para. 17.2
II:	A117-1979, Art. 19, Para. 19.2
I:	A201-1976, Art. 7, Para. 7.9.1
I:	A201-1976, Art. 9, Para. 9.9.4
I:	A201-1976, Art. 9, Para. 9.9.5
II:	A401-1978, Art. 13, Para. 13.1
II:	B141-1977, Art. 9, Para. 9.1

In contractor's appeal of an arbitration award in favor of owner which ordered the contractor to purchase the real estate on which the buildings were constructed, the Supreme Court relied on Paragraphs 7.9.1, 9.9.4 and 9.9.5 of the American Institute of Architects General Conditions of the Contract for Construction, Document No. A201, 1976 edition. It upheld the trial court's finding that the arbitrators had not exceeded their authority, as well as the court's entry of judgment confirming the award which was not limited by the arbitration clause and was made pursuant to state statute. The contractor, after final payment had been made by the owner, refused to correct numerous and serious construction defects, deficiencies and building code violations. The Court reasoned that the scope of the arbitration clause was extremely broad and authorized the arbitrators to decide "all claims, disputes and other matters in question . . . relating to, the Contract . . . or the breach thereof. . . ." Furthermore, no provision in the arbitration clause expressly or implicitly limited the arbitrators to structuring only a remedy calling for the payment of a monetary award nor did any provision expressly authorize, or prohibit, the arbitrators from formulating remedies that were equitable in nature. The Court concluded that by fashioning the award, the arbitrators not only acted within the scope of the broad grant of authority but also placed the obligation on contractor, the party responsible for the gross construction deficiencies, to remedy them and bear the risk of potential future warranty liabilities arising under state statute.

I: A201-1976, Art. 2, Para. 2.2.12
I: A201-1976, Art. 7, Para. 7.6.1
I: B141-1977, Art. 1, Para. 1.5.9
I: B141-1977, Art. 1, Para. 1.5.10

Contractor appealed from the trial court's denial of its motion to confirm an arbitration award for delay damages against owner on the ground that the arbitration provision in the contract was ambiguous with respect to whether the parties intended for arbitration to be binding. The Appellate Court reversed on the ground that the arbitration agreement was enforceable and irrevocable. On appeal to the Supreme Court the owner argued that the contract provided for advisory arbitration and the parties never agreed to be bound by an arbitrator's decision. The Supreme Court of Kansas affirmed the judgment of the Appellate Court and remanded the case.

The provisions of the owner-contractor agreement regarding the role of the engineer in settling disputes and the remedies provision were identical to Paragraphs 2.2.7, 2.2.9, 2.2.12, and 7.6.1 of the American Institute of Architects General Conditions of the Contract for Construction, Document No. A201, 1976 edition.

The Supreme Court found that the clause which provided that "[T]he rights and remedies available to [the parties] shall be in addition to, and shall not be construed in any way as a limitation of, any rights and remedies available to them which are otherwise imposed or available by law, by special guarantee or by other provisions of the Contract Documents," when read together with the plain and unambiguous arbitration clause, preserved to the parties the "rights and remedies available to them" which, when read together with the language "other provisions of the contract documents" obligated the parties to arbitrate.

Furthermore, the Court rejected the owner's argument that the clause which provided that "The failure to demand arbitration within said thirty days' period shall result in ENGINEER'S decision being final and binding upon [the parties]" created an ambiguity as to whether the engineer's decision or an arbitrator's decision was "final and binding." The Court found that the contract did not call for "advisory" or "nonbinding" arbitration but provided that either owner or contractor "may demand arbitration." Given the legal meaning of the word arbitration, and the fact that the state statute did not distinguish between binding and nonbinding arbitration, the Supreme Court upheld the Appellate Court's finding that the plain meaning of all of the terms of the agreement compelled a holding that the parties bound themselves upon demand of either to arbitrate their disputes.

89009 Commerce, Crowdus & Canton, Ltd. v. DSK Constr., Inc., 776 S.W.2d 615 (Tex. Ct. App. 1989)

I: A101-1977, Art. 5
I: A107-1978, Art. 4, Para. 4.2
I: A111-1978, Art. 14, Para. 14.3

89007 Brown v. Two Exch. Plaza Partners, 146 A.D.2d 129, 539 N.Y.S.2d 889 (1989), *appeal dismissed without opinion*, 74 N.Y.2d 793, 545 N.Y.S.2d 109, 543 N.E.2d 752 (1989), *stay granted*, 74 N.Y.2d 915, 549 N.Y.S.2d 958, 549 N.E.2d 149 (1989), *aff'd*, 76 N.Y.2d 172, 556 N.Y.S.2d 991, 556 N.E.2d 430 (1990)

III:	A107-1978,	Art. 10, Para. 10.11
III:	A117-1979,	Art. 14, Para. 14.11
III:	A201-1976,	Art. 4, Para. 4.18.1
II:	A401-1978,	Art. 11, Para. 11.11.1

Injured worker brought an action against contractor and contractor brought a third-party indemnity action against the subcontractor and its sub-subcontractor. The jury found that the subcontractors were not liable to contractor and that the subcontractors had not been negligent and were not liable to the contractor. Contractor appealed.

The subcontract required the subcontractor to indemnify contractor against, among other things, personal injury to any person "arising out of, in connection with or as a consequence of the performance of the [subcontractor's] Work and/or any act or omission of the Subcontractor or any of its subcontractors . . . as it relates to the scope of this Contract."

The Appellate Court found that the intent of the clause was to make the subcontractor responsible for an injury to a worker employed by a sub-subcontractor sustained while doing the work called for in the subcontract. The Court did not construe the language of the clause as conditioning the right to indemnification upon a showing that subcontractor was negligent. The Court reasoned that the major purpose of such a clause would be the elimination of negligence as a prerequisite to indemnification. By including such a clause in the subcontract, the contractor, anticipating an accident in which no negligence by any party can be established, sought to spread his liability to the subcontractors regardless of fault. The Court concluded that the subcontractor was liable to indemnify the contractor, not because the subcontractor was negligent, but because a worker was injured while doing the subcontractor's work. Furthermore, the Court found that the clause was valid under state law because it began with the words "to the extent permitted by law" and it required indemnification in the absence of negligence on the contractor's part. Thus, the Court modified the trial court's judgment to grant indemnification to the contractor against the subcontractor.

89008 City of Lenexa v. C.L. Fairley Constr. Co., 245 Kan. 316, 777 P.2d 851 (1989), *appeal after remand*, 15 Kan. App. 2d 207, 805 P.2d 507 (1991)

II:	A107-1978,	Art. 8, Para. 8.5
II:	A117-1979,	Art. 12, Para. 12.5
I:	A201-1976,	Art. 2, Para. 2.2.7
I:	A201-1976,	Art. 2, Para. 2.2.9

The Court concluded that these provisions made the prime contractors liable one to the other for damages. The contract imposed a duty of cooperation on all contractors, and stated that when one contractor's work depended on the work of another the "Architect shall be the judge as to the quality of work, and shall settle all disputes on the matter between Contractors." Because there was no privity of contract between any subcontractor and the owner, nor between the subcontractors and the other primes, the Court found that any subcontractor had to be viewed under the contract as an employee or agent of a prime contractor. Therefore, the prime contractor could bring a delay claim against the co-prime general contractor for damages incurred by its subcontractor.

89006 Brixen & Christopher, Architects v. Elton, 777 P.2d 1039 (Utah Ct. App. 1989)

II:	B141-1977, Art. 1, Para. 1.1.4	
II:	B141-1977, Art. 1, Para. 1.2.1	
II:	B141-1977, Art. 1, Para. 1.2.2	
II:	B141-1977, Art. 1, Para. 1.3.1	
II:	B141-1977, Art. 1, Para. 1.3.3	
II:	B141-1977, Art. 1, Para. 1.4.1	
II:	B141-1977, Art. 1, Para. 1.5.1	
II:	B141-1977, Art. 1, Para. 1.5.16	
I:	B141-1977, Art. 1, Para. 1.7	
I:	B141-1977, Art. 1, Para. 2.9	

Architect brought an action against owner for payment for architectural services. The trial court entered judgment against owner and owner appealed. On appeal, the owner argued that the owner-architect agreement provided that owner's approval for each phase was a condition precedent to the next phase.

The owner-architect agreement provided that architectural services were to be performed in phases, each phase requiring the owner's approval of the prior phase design documents and allowing the owner to make any adjustments in the design program or the budget. The contract also stated that "if the Owner observes or otherwise becomes aware of any . . . nonconformance with the Contract Documents, prompt written notice thereof shall be given by the Owner to the Architect."

The Appellate Court found that the plain language of these provisions contained no explicit requirement that approval be given in written form, unlike Paragraph 1.7 which stated that "the following services are not included in Basic Services . . . and shall be provided if authorized or confirmed in writing by the Owner, and they shall be paid for by the Owner as provided in this Agreement, in addition to the compensation for Basic Services." After examining the entire contract and all of its parts in relation to each other, the Court concluded that while the contractual language required the architect to obtain owner's approval prior to beginning work on subsequent phases of the contract, it did not require formal, written approval. It therefore affirmed the trial court's judgment in favor of the architect.

The agreement further provided in Article 35 that the "Architect or Engineer is charged with the responsibility of interpretation of the contract documents and general directions of the work. He shall make decisions on all claims of the Contractor or the Owner, or on any matter dealing with the execution of the work. His decisions relating to artistic effect and technical matters shall be final, provided such decisions are within the limitations of the contract terms."

The Appellate Court construed this language as providing that the architect interpreted the contract that governed the relationship of the parties and made decisions on all claims of contractors "on any matter dealing with the execution of the work." Finality was accorded only to decisions relating to artistic effect and technical matters. The Court concluded that each prime contractor's ability to maintain timely progress was made a part of its work. The Court held that judgment of the quality of a prime contractor's ability to perform its jobs and to maintain timely progress was delegated to the architect by the contract.

Furthermore, the contract defined the architect's role as "judge as to division of responsibility between the several Contractors, and shall apportion to the amount of liquidated damages to be paid by each of them, according to delay caused by any or all of them" and provided in Article 18 that "if any Contractor be delayed at any time in the progress of the work by any act or neglect on the part of . . . any other prime contractor on the work, . . . or by reason of which the Architect . . . considers delay justifiable, then the time of completion will be extended such period considered reasonable by the Architect. . . ." The Court concluded that the contract did not give the architect authority to decide delay disputes among the prime contractors. Article 18 was concerned with each prime's responsibility to the owner for delay and it was plain that the architect was the final judge as to apportionment of liquidated damages to the owner because of delay. The Court held that the architect's decision under Article 18 would be relevant to a contractor's claim under Articles 31 and 35.

Article 12 of the contract made each contractor liable for damage to another contractor's property; Article 14 made each contractor "responsible for any damage to other Contractors' work, and each Contractor shall be held financially responsible for undue delay caused by him to other Contractors on the project." The Court construed this language as allocating responsibility for undue delay to the architect.

The Court held that Articles 32, 33 and 12 established the attributes of the relationship between contractors and subcontractors. These Articles provided that the "Contractor is and remains fully responsible for his own acts or omissions as well as those of any subcontractor or any employee of either. The Contractor agrees that no contractual relationship exits between the sub-contractor and the Owner in regard to this contract, and that the sub-contractor acts on this work as a agent or employee of the Contractor. . . . The Contractor agrees that the terms of these contract documents, including all portions thereof, apply equally to a sub-contractor as to the Contractor, and that the subcontractor is bound by those terms as an employee of the Contractor. . . . [Contractors] shall be responsible for any damage to the Owner's property, or of that of others on the job, by them, their men, or their sub-contractors, and shall made good such damages."

III:	A201-1976, Art. 2, Para. 2.2.9
III:	A201-1976, Art. 2, Para. 2.2.10
III:	A201-1976, Art. 2, Para. 2.2.11
III:	A201-1976, Art. 2, Para. 2.2.12
III:	A201-1976, Art. 5, Para. 5.3.1
III:	A201-1976, Art. 6, Para. 6.1.1
III:	A201-1976, Art. 6, Para. 6.1.3
III:	A201-1976, Art. 6, Para. 6.2.1
III:	A201-1976, Art. 6, Para. 6.2.2
III:	A201-1976, Art. 6, Para. 6.2.3
III:	A201-1976, Art. 6, Para. 6.2.4
III:	A201-1976, Art. 6, Para. 6.2.5
III:	A401-1978, Art. 11, Para. 11.11.1
III:	B141-1977, Art. 1, Para. 1.5.9
III:	B141-1977, Art. 1, Para. 1.5.10
III:	B141-1977, Art. 1, Para. 1.5.11

Prime contractor brought an action against the co-prime general contractor, who was acting as the project expeditor, and the architect for delay damages arising under a public multi-prime contract to build a library. In determining the amount of the architect's liability to one prime contractor the Appellate Court interpreted the contract provisions outlining the architect's contractual duties and obligations to coordinate the work of the contractors. The prime contractor argued that he was a third-party beneficiary of the owner-co-prime general contractor's agreement, which was breached by the co-prime general contractor, whose actions caused the prime contractor to be delayed in completing its work under its contract with the owner.

The owner-contractor agreement allocated to the architect the authority to determine responsibility for delay among the prime contractors. The contract provided in Article 31 that "all contractors shall cooperate in the execution of their work, and shall plan their work in such manner as to avoid conflicting schedules or delay of the work. The Engineer or Architect shall coordinate work schedules. If any part of a Contractor's work depends upon the work of another Contractor, defects which may affect that work shall be reported to the Architect or Engineer in order that prompt inspection may be made and the defects corrected. Commencement of work by a Contractor where such condition exists will constitute acceptance of the other Contractor's work as being satisfactory in all respects to receive the work commenced except as to defects which may later develop. The Engineer or Architect shall be the judge as to the quality of work, and shall settle all disputes on the matter between Contractors."

The Appellate Court, reading the provision as a whole, interpreted the last sentence as explaining that when the work of one prime depended on the work of another the "Architect shall be the judge as to the quality of work, and shall settle all disputes on the matter between Contractors."

The owner and architect had entered into the American Institute of Architects Standard Form of Agreement Between Owner and Architect, Document No. B141, 1977 edition. Under a renumbered Paragraph 1.5.4 the architect was obligated to make periodic visits to the work site "to determine in general if the work is proceeding in accordance with the Contract Documents." The architect was also required to "keep [the owner] informed of the progress of the work, will endeavor to guard [owner] against defects and deficiencies . . . and may condemn work as failing to conform to the Contract Documents." The architect was also authorized to issue certificates of payment, thereby representing that the work was properly performed. The agreement provided that the architect was not required to make "exhaustive or continuous on-site inspections to check the quality or quantity of the work and . . . will not be responsible for the Contractors' failure to carry out the construction work in accordance with the Contract Documents." The agreement also required the architect to assemble any written guarantees required of contractors and to make three annual inspections of the building following completion of construction and to advise the owner of any maintenance and remedial measures required.

The Appellate Court found that the provision under which the architect was absolved from responsibility "for the Contractors' failure to carry out the construction work in accordance with the Contract Documents," could not be read as totally exonerating the architect from liability for construction defects. The Court concluded that while Paragraph 1.5.4 had been given exculpatory effect by the courts, none of the cases involved defects known by the architect during the course of construction of which he failed to apprise the owner under the contractual duty to "keep the [owner] informed of the progress of the work." The Court held that the owner's proof regarding the claim of architect's failure to inform owner of the deviations was thus sufficient to withstand the motion for a directed verdict; it therefore reinstated the claim and remanded it for trial.

89005   Bolton Corp. v. T.A. Loving Co., 94 N.C. App. 392, 380 S.E.2d 796 (1989), *review denied*, 325 N.C. 545, 385 S.E.2d 496 (1989), *and review denied*, 385 S.E.2d 496 (N.C. 1989)

III: A107-1978, Art. 8, Para. 8.5
III: A107-1978, Art. 11, Para. 11.2
III: A107-1978, Art. 12, Para. 12.1
III: A107-1978, Art. 12, Para. 12.2
III: A117-1979, Art. 12, Para. 12.3
III: A117-1979, Art. 15, Para. 15.2
III: A117-1979, Art. 16, Para. 16.1
III: A117-1979, Art. 16, Para. 16.2
III: A117-1979, Art. 16, Para. 16.3
III: A201-1976, Art. 2, Para. 2.2.7
III: A201-1976, Art. 2, Para. 2.2.8

The owner and contractor entered into an American Institute of Architects Standard Form of Agreement Between Owner and Contractor which included the American Institute of Architects General Conditions of the Contract for Construction, Document No. A201, 1976 edition. The General Conditions provided in Paragraphs 2.2.9 and 2.2.12 that prior to arbitration the contractor initially should refer any "claim . . . relating to the progress of the work or the interpretation of the Contract Documents to the Architect for decision to be rendered in writing within a reasonable time." Contractor did not submit its claim to the architect.

The Appellate Court found that contractor's claim, which was asserted prior to the substantial completion of the work, was a claim relating to the execution or progress of the work within the meaning of Paragraph 2.2.9. The Court concluded that pursuant to the clear terms of the contract the contractor was required to first submit its claim to the architect as a condition precedent to arbitration. The Court held that the trial court properly stayed arbitration.

89004   Board of Educ. of Hudson City School Dist. v. Sargent, Webster, Crenshaw & Folley, 146 A.D.2d 190, 539 N.Y.S.2d 814 (1989), *appeal dismissed*, 75 N.Y.2d 702, 551 N.Y.S.2d 906, 551 N.E.2d 107 (1989)

II:	A107-1978, Art. 8, Para. 8.3
II:	A107-1978, Art. 8, Para. 8.4
II:	A117-1979, Art. 12, Para. 12.3
II:	A117-1979, Art. 12, Para. 12.4
II:	A201-1976, Art. 2, Para. 2.2.3
II:	A201-1976, Art. 2, Para. 2.2.6
II:	A201-1976, Art. 2, Para. 2.2.16
I:	B141-1977, Art. 1, Para. 1.5.4
I:	B141-1977, Art. 1, Para. 1.5.7
I:	B141-1977, Art. 1, Para. 1.5.8
II:	B141-1977, Art. 1, Para. 1.5.15

Owner brought a breach of contract action against architect and architect brought a third-party action against contractor for indemnification for damages resulting from defective construction of a roof. At the conclusion of all of the evidence the trial court granted architect's motion for a directed verdict dismissing all causes of action but the count alleging architect's failure to obtain roofing guarantees, directed a verdict in favor of owner on architect's failure to obtain the guarantees, and dismissed architect's third-party action against contractor for indemnification. The owner appealed dismissal of the counts alleging the architect's failure to have informed the owner of the deviation from the specifications in the roof installation, architect's failure to have guarded the owner against the contractor's defective performance, and architect's failure to condemn the work as failing to conform to the contract documents.

pertinent part that "If the system is operable but does not meet the power and fuel design requirements, or in the event that the performance tests are not concluded, the full amount of liquidated damages shall be retained unless the tests are not concluded due to failure of the Owner to perform" as limiting liquidated damages to the power and fuel design.

The Appellate Court upheld the award of attorney's fees to the contractor who won full indemnification from the subcontractor where the subcontract provided that "in the event of litigation . . . the prevailing party shall be entitled to recover its legal fees and expenses from the other party."

89002 B & M Constr., Inc. v. Mueller, 164 Ariz. 52, 790 P.2d 750 (1989), *review denied*, 1990 Ariz. LEXIS 84 (Ariz. 1990)

I: A107-1978, Art. 13, Para. 13.2
I: A117-1979, Art. 17, Para. 17.2
I: A201-1976, Art. 7, Para. 7.9.1
I: A401-1978, Art. 13, Para. 13.1
I: A401-1978, Art. 13, Para. 13.6
I: B141-1977, Art. 9, Para. 9.1

In contractor's breach of contract action against owner, the Appellate Court affirmed the judgment of the trial court in favor of the contractor. The contractor's lien claim did not have to be arbitrated where the arbitration clause provided that "all claims, disputes and other matters in question arising out of, or relating to, this Subcontract, or the breach thereof, shall be decided by arbitration . . ." and further stated that "This Article shall not be deemed a limitation of any rights or remedies which the Subcontractor may have under any Federal or State mechanics' lien laws or under any applicable labor and material payment bonds unless such rights or remedies are expressly waived by him." The Court rejected the owner's argument that the clause meant only that the agreement to arbitrate was not a waiver of lien claims, and construed the provision to mean that the validity of the lien, as opposed to its amount, need not be submitted to arbitration.

89003 Board of Educ., Longwood Cent. School Dist. v. Hatzel & Buehler, Inc., 156 A.D.2d 684, 549 N.Y.S.2d 447 (1989), *appeal denied*, 76 N.Y.2d 703, 559 N.Y.S.2d 932, 559 N.E.2d 676 (1990)

III: A107-1978, Art. 8, Para. 8.5
III: A117-1979, Art. 12, Para. 12.5
I: A201-1976, Art. 2, Para. 2.2.9
I: A201-1976, Art. 2, Para. 2.2.12
III: B141-1977, Art. 1, Para. 1.5.10
III: B141-1977, Art. 1, Para. 1.5.11

Contractor submitted a demand for arbitration to the owner for delay damages. The trial court granted owners motion to stay arbitration. The contractor appealed.

89001   Aiken County v. BSP Div. of Envirotech Corp., 866 F.2d 661 (4th Cir. 1989)

III:	A107-1978, Art. 10, Para. 10.4
III:	A107-1978, Art. 10, Para. 10.11
III:	A117-1979, Art. 14, Para. 14.4
III:	A117-1979, Art. 14, Para. 14.11
III:	A201-1976, Art. 4, Para. 4.5.1
III:	A201-1976, Art. 4, Para. 4.18.1
III:	A401-1978, Art. 11, Para. 11.7.1
III:	A401-1978, Art. 11, Para. 11.11.1

In subcontractor's appeal of the District Court's finding of breach of contract against subcontractor and its award of damages to the owner, the Appellate Court affirmed the District Court's judgment that subcontractor had breached the subcontract provision requiring subcontractor to "warranty to Bay [-Con] and the Owner . . . that all of the Work will be of good quality, . . . will be free from faults and defects, will be in conformance with the requirements of this Subcontract and of the Prime Contract, and will function as intended by the designer of the Work . . ." and the specification which provided that "the systems furnished . . . shall be placed in operation ready to operate continuously on a 24 hour per day basis with not more than 15 percent of total time required for maintenance and repairs . . ." and that the heat exchangers "shall be capable of being operated with all automatic and safety features functioning." Subcontractor argued on appeal that the only requirement under the subcontract was that the heat exchangers be "capable" of operating automatically and that the proof that owner did not operate it automatically did not necessarily establish that it was incapable of doing so.

The Appellate Court found that when the parties contracted for an automatic system they intended that the system be automatic and not only be "capable" of being automatic. The Court found it hard to believe that the parties intended to contract for a system only "capable" of being automatic in some abstract sense; therefore, the district court's finding of a breach by subcontractor was supported by substantial evidence. Likewise, the plain language of the subcontract indicated that the parties contemplated that owner would be furnished a system which would not have more than fifteen percent downtime resulting from maintenance and repair.

Furthermore, the Court found that under the specification, which provided that "In the event that the sludge processing system cannot be operated in a practical manner, even with corrective changes, the Owner shall have the option of having the Contractor and equipment supplier remove the entire system at no cost to the Owner or to allow further revisions and/or replacements," the owner was entitled to reimbursement for the cost of replacing the entire heat treatment unit. However, the Court found that the District Court erred in its computation of the cost of a heat treatment unit and remanded the case for a more certain proof of damages.

In response to subcontractor's claim that owner was entitled only to liquidated damages the Appellate Court construed the contract's remedy provision, which provided in

III: A401-1978, Art. 13, Para. 13.1
III: B141-1977, Art. 9, Para. 9.1

Subcontractor brought an action against contractor for payment of amounts due under the subcontract. Contractor counterclaimed, alleging that subcontractor's inadequate performance caused the delays for which contractor was assessed liquidated damages by owner. Contractor then moved the District Court to stay the proceedings pending arbitration. Subcontractor argued that the arbitration clause was unenforceable because it lacked mutuality.

The subcontract contained a broad form arbitration provision which provided in pertinent part that the "CONTRACTOR may, in its discretion, compromise and settle the same with the Principal. . . ."

The District Court concluded that the claims of both the subcontractor and contractor fell within the scope of the broad arbitration provision which covered "any controversy hereunder." The Court rejected the subcontractor's lack of mutuality argument reasoning that where the agreement to arbitrate was integrated into a larger unitary contract, the consideration for the contract as a whole covered the arbitration clause as well. The Court held that the agreement to arbitrate was valid and enforceable.

88043 Whalen v. K-Mart Corp., 166 Ill. App. 3d 339, 116 Ill. Dec. 776, 519 N.E.2d 991 (1988), *appeal denied,* 121 Ill. 2d 587, 122 Ill. Dec. 448, 526 N.E.2d 841 (1988)

    Ill: A401-1978, Art. 9, Para. 9.1
    Ill: A401-1978, Art. 11, Para. 11.11.1

Injured worker brought an action against contractor and owner. Contractor and owner filed a third-party action against certain subcontractors for contribution and indemnity based on the subcontractors' agreements to procure insurance naming contractor and owner as additional insureds. The trial court dismissed the third-party complaint on the ground that the owner and contractor had waived their rights to enforce the insurance provisions by not insisting upon compliance with the provisions and by making final payment to the subcontractors.

The subcontracts provided in pertinent part that the subcontractors "shall not commence work under this Subcontract until he has obtained all insurances required by the General Conditions and as hereinafter set forth and certificates of insurance delivered to the Contractor." Each subcontractor agreed to "procure at his own expense, before the commencement of the work, comprehensive general liability including Contractors protective liability insurance, completed operations and contractual liability insurance . . . for the benefit of the contractor and owner . . . for damages to property arising out of each occurrence, and to keep such insurance in force until the construction of development is fully completed, and to immediately and before commencing work deliver such policy or policies or certificates of insurance to the Contractor." The insurance provision in the subcontracts required that "Evidence of all insurance indicated within this Paragraph 12 shall be furnished to Contractor and/or Owner in writing and shall indicate that Contractor and/or Owner are additional or co-insured parties. No payments will be made until necessary proof of insurance has been made."

The Appellate Court found that the subcontracts unambiguously stated that "the Subcontractor shall not commence work under this subcontract until he has obtained all insurance required . . ." and that "no payments will be made until necessary proof of insurance has been made," making the obtaining of the required insurance a condition precedent to commencement of work and a condition precedent to receiving payment. Based on the record, which showed that contractor never demanded any proof of insurance, that the subcontractors had completed their performance under the contracts, and that the subcontractors were paid in full for their services, the court held that the trial court did not err in determining that contractor and owner waived their claims for breach of contract against the subcontractors.

88044 W.L. Jorden & Co. v. Blythe Indus., Inc., 702 F. Supp. 282 (N.D. Ga. 1988)

    Ill: A107-1978, Art. 13, Para. 13.2
    Ill: A117-1979, Art. 17, Para. 17.2
    Ill: A201-1976, Art. 7, Para. 7.9.1

Injured worker brought a personal injury action against engineer, engineer's insurer and owner. Owner brought a third-party action against engineer, engineer's joint venture partner, and contractor. Engineer brought a third-party action against contractor. The trial court entered judgment for worker on the grounds that the owner and engineer contracted to enforce OSHA regulations and that their breach of this contractual duty was the proximate cause of the worker's injuries. On appeal by the defendants, the worker alternatively asserted that, even if the owner had no enforcement duty, the engineer was independently responsible because they contractually agreed to undertake enforcement of OSHA.

The owner-engineer agreement provided that "The Architect-Engineer Contractor shall develop, prepare and furnish contract plans and specifications to be used for competitive bidding for procurement and construction and for technical supervision of contraction of all the work included. . . ." The owner-contractor agreement provided that "the undertaking of inspections by the engineers or authorized representative thereof shall not be construed as supervision of actual construction nor make the engineers or their authorized representatives responsible for providing a safe place or safe conditions for the performance or work under the contract by contractor, or contractors' employees or those of the suppliers or subcontractors. . . ."

The Appellate Court found that the provisions of the owner-engineer agreement made it clear that engineer's obligation was to assure the owner that the building was constructed in accordance with the plans and specifications. As owner's representative the engineer was not required to direct the contractor on safety procedures or on how he should conduct his operations. The Court could not find a duty to enforce OSHA in the owner-contractor agreement, nor did the Court interpret the agreement to include such a duty. The Court further found that the inspection language of the owner-engineer agreement was consistent with, and supportive of, its interpretation that the engineer had no duty to enforce OSHA. It therefore reversed the judgment and dismissed the worker's claim.

88042   Wehr Constructors, Inc. v. Steel Fabricators, Inc., 769 S.W.2d 51 (Ky. Ct. App. 1988)

II: A107-1978, Art. 10, Para. 10.2
II: A117-1979, Art. 14, Para. 14.2
I: A201-1976, Art. 4, Para. 4.4.1

In suppliers' action against owner, contractor and subcontractor, the suppliers claimed that they were entitled to payment under Paragraph 4.4.1 of the American Institute of Architects General Conditions of the Contract for Construction, Document No. A201, 1976 edition, which provided that "Contractor shall provide and pay for all labor, materials, equipment, tools . . . and services necessary for the proper execution and completion of the Work. . . ." The Appellate Court found that this language in the agreement between the contractor and the subcontractor created a third-party beneficiary relationship under the circumstances, and that therefore the suppliers were entitled to payment.

III: A401-1978, Art. 11, Para. 11.1.1
III: A401-1978, Art. 11, Para. 11.11.1

Subcontractor's employee's widow brought a wrongful death action against owner alleging that owner's negligence was the proximate cause of her husband's death. Owner then brought a third party indemnification action against subcontractor. The trial court granted owner's motion for summary judgment and subcontractor appealed.

The owner-contractor agreement provided that the contractor would indemnify and hold the owner harmless as to all claims arising out of or in connection with the performance of the contract. Furthermore, the contract provided that contractor would obtain from each subcontractor an independent indemnification agreement whereby the subcontractor would agree to indemnify the owner. In addition, the contract stated that a written subcontract had to contain indemnity provisions protecting the owner. The contractor did not procure the indemnification agreement independent of the subcontract.

The Appellate Court found that the subcontract contained a flow-down provision requiring the subcontractor to "perform all work . . . in accordance with" the owner-contractor agreement which "hereby becomes a part" of the subcontract. The Court found that it was the clear intent of the parties that the owner-contractor agreement be incorporated, in its entirety, into the subcontract, including the provisions which required the subcontractor to indemnify the owner. The subcontract contained subcontractor's agreement that "all work" that it was to perform "shall be pursuant to an appropriate written agreement . . . which contains provisions . . . indemnifying [owner] in accordance with [the indemnity provisions of the general contract, which indemnity provisions are themselves incorporated by reference into the subcontract]." However, the Court also found that the subcontract, when construed in its entirety, clearly indicated that neither party intended that owner be the third-party beneficiary of any promise made by subcontractor to contractor under Paragraph 30 which provided that "this subcontract is solely for the benefit of the signatories hereto." The Court concluded that under the express terms of the subcontract the owner could not be considered a third-party beneficiary of any indemnity provision and held that the owner had no standing to bring a direct indemnification action against the subcontractor.

88041   Walters v. Landis Constr. Co., 522 So. 2d 1306 (La. Ct. App.), *cert. denied,* 530 So. 2d 81 & 89 (La. 1988).

III: A107-1978, Art. 8, Para. 8.3
III: A117-1979, Art. 12, Para. 12.3
III: A201-1976, Art. 2, Para. 2.2.3
III: A201-1976, Art. 2, Para. 2.2.4
III: B141-1977, Art. 1, Para. 1.3.1
III: B141-1977, Art. 1, Para. 1.5.4
III: B141-1977, Art. 1, Para. 1.5.5

88039   Village of Westville v. Loitz Bros. Constr. Co., 165 Ill. App. 3d 338, 116 Ill. Dec. 447, 519 N.E.2d 37 (1988), *appeal denied*, 119 Ill. 2d 576, 119 Ill. Dec. 399, 522 N.E.2d 1258 (1988)

II:	A107-1978,	Art. 13, Para. 13.2
II:	A117-1979,	Art. 17, Para. 17.2
III:	A201-1976,	Art. 7, Para. 7.2.1
II:	A201-1976,	Art. 7, Para. 7.9.1
II:	A401-1978,	Art. 13, Para. 13.1
II:	B141-1977,	Art. 9, Para. 9.1

Subcontractor filed a demand for arbitration against owner. Contractor had assigned its rights to pursue claims under the contract to the subcontractor. The owner filed a motion for stay of the arbitration proceeding. Contractor was added as a claimant in the arbitration proceeding. The trial court denied owner's motion to stay and directed the parties to proceed to arbitration. The owner argued on appeal that no valid assignment of the right to arbitrate occurred where the contract contained a nonassignability clause. The Appellate Court affirmed the ruling of the trial court.

The owner-contractor agreement contained a broad form arbitration provision, which stated that "All claims, disputes and other matters in question arising out of, or relating to, the CONTRACT DOCUMENTS or the breach thereof, except for claims which have been waived by the making and acceptance of final payment as provided by Section 20, shall be decided by arbitration in accordance with the Construction Industry Arbitration Rules of the American Arbitration Association. This agreement to arbitrate shall be specifically enforceable under the prevailing arbitration law. The award rendered by the arbitrators shall be final, and judgment may be entered upon it in any court having jurisdiction thereof."

The Appellate Court held that the claims were clearly disputes "arising out of, or relating to" the agreement and, as such, were required to be resolved by arbitration. The Court held further that even if the scope of the clause was in doubt, the claim should be resolved by the arbitrators by virtue of the broad language of the clause. The Court concluded that the assignment of the right to arbitrate from contractor to subcontractor was valid. Furthermore the Court held that owner's contentions that contractor accepted final payment under the contract, and that this acceptance operated as a release of all claims against the owner, were issues arising out of the contract and had to be resolved by arbitration.

88040   Walls, Inc. v. Atlantic Realty Co., 186 Ga. App. 389, 367 S.E.2d 278 (1988)

III:	A107-1978,	Art. 10, Para. 10.11
III:	A117-1979,	Art. 14, Para. 14.11
III:	A201-1976,	Art. 4, Para. 4.18.1
III:	A201-1976,	Art. 5, Para. 5.3.1

evidence that any changes or extras were agreed to in writing, no finding that the written change order requirement had been waived, and no pleading of waiver; therefore, the contractor was precluded from recovery under the contract.

88037   United States Fidelity & Guar. Co. v. Farrar's Plumbing & Heating Co., 158 Ariz. 354, 762 P.2d 641 (1988)

II:	A107-1978, Art. 17, Para. 17.3
II:	A107-1978, Art. 17, Para. 17.6
II:	A117-1979, Art. 21, Para. 21.3
II:	A117-1979, Art. 21, Para. 21.6
I:	A201-1976, Art. 11, Para. 11.3.1
I:	A201-1976, Art. 11, Para. 11.3.6

Owner's insurer brought a subrogation action against subcontractor for damage resulting from a fire. The trial court granted subcontractor summary judgment based on the insurance provisions in the owner-contractor agreement.

The owner and contractor entered into an agreement which included Paragraphs 11.3.1 and 11.3.6 of the American Institute of Architects General Conditions of the Contract for Construction, Document No. A201, 1976 edition.

The Appellate Court found that the language of Paragraphs 11.3.1 and 11.3.6 clearly provided that fire insurance for the project was to be procured by owner and that all parties to the construction were to look only to the insurance to protect themselves against fire loss. The Court found that the waiver of subrogation avoided disputes among the parties by bringing all property damage under builders risk property insurance.

The Court affirmed the trial court's holding based on its finding that Paragraphs 11.3.1 and 11.3.6 divested the owner of any claim against the subcontractor.

88038   United States Fidelity & Guar. Co. v. West Point Constr. Co., 837 F.2d 1507 (11th Cir. 1988)

III:	A401-1978, Art. 11, Para. 11.1.1
III:	A401-1978, Art. 13, Para. 13.1

The Appellate Court affirmed the holding of the District Court that the surety was bound to submit to arbitration because the performance bond that it issued incorporated by reference the underlying subcontract, which contained an arbitration clause. The subcontract contained its own arbitration provision, and in a separate article modified that provision by reference to the arbitration provisions of the owner-contractor agreement. The performance bond incorporated by reference the subcontract. The Court concluded that the incorporation of the subcontract into the bond expressed the intention of the parties, including the surety, to arbitrate disputes.

construction. The Court held that the same analysis applied with regard to the protest work claims, claims for damages for breach of contract involving questions of law, contract construction, and application of the judicially established limitations for seeking recovery of these claims. The Court concluded that the contractor was not barred by the dispute resolution provision from commencing litigation and arguing that the engineer had erroneously construed the contract. In a later opinion the Appellate Court concluded that the dispute resolution clause, considered in the context of the contractual and historical setting of that standard provision, was not an explicit, unequivocal agreement for alternate dispute resolution, especially not for a dispute resolution procedure that vested final authority for all legal determinations in the owner and was binding only on the contractor.

88036   Uhlir v. Golden Triangle Dev. Corp., 763 S.W.2d 512 (Tex. Ct. App. 1988)

III:	A107-1978, Art. 15, Para. 15.3	
III:	A107-1978, Art. 15, Para. 15.4	
III:	A107-1978, Art. 15, Para. 15.5	
III:	A107-1978, Art. 18, Para. 18.1	
III:	A107-1978, Art. 18, Para. 18.2	
III:	A117-1979, Art. 19, Para. 19.3	
III:	A117-1979, Art. 19, Para. 19.4	
III:	A117-1979, Art. 19, Para. 19.5	
III:	A117-1979, Art. 22, Para. 22.1	
III:	A117-1979, Art. 22, Para. 22.2	
III:	A201-1976, Art. 9, Para. 9.9.1	
III:	A201-1976, Art. 9, Para. 9.9.2	
III:	A201-1976, Art. 9, Para. 9.9.3	
III:	A201-1976, Art. 12, Para. 12.1.1	
III:	A201-1976, Art. 12, Para. 12.1.2	

The Appellate Court found that where the contract provided that "Final payment, constituting the entire unpaid balance of the Contract Sum, shall be paid by the Owner to the Contractor when the Work has been completed, the Contract fully performed, and a final Certificate for Payment has been issued by the Architect," the contractor was entitled to recover on a theory of substantial performance an amount less the cost of remedying defects. The contract expressly stated that final payment was contingent on full completion and the issuance of an architect's certificate, and the jury found that the contractor had substantially performed the contract. The Court held that the issuance of the architect's certificate was merely a method of assuring final completion.

Furthermore, the contract required that "any changes to said plans and specifications after the effective date of this contract shall be in writing with charges determined prior to making changes." The Court, after examining the record, found that there was no

III:	A117-1979, Art. 12, Para. 12.5
III:	A117-1979, Art. 17, Para. 17.2
III:	A201-1976, Art. 2, Para. 2.2.9
III:	A201-1976, Art. 2, Para. 2.2.10
III:	A201-1976, Art. 2, Para. 2.2.11
III:	A201-1976, Art. 2, Para. 2.2.12
III:	A201-1976, Art. 7, Para. 7.9.1
III:	B141-1977, Art. 1, Para. 1.5.9
III:	B141-1977, Art. 1, Para. 1.5.10
III:	B141-1977, Art. 1, Para. 1.5.11

Contractor brought an action for extras and for costs resulting from unanticipated subsurface conditions. The owner, in a second amended answer, argued that the engineer's determinations regarding the contractor's claims for extras were final and conclusive. The trial court denied the owner's motion and the owner appealed. The Appellate Court upheld the trial court's ruling.

The owner-contractor agreement contained a dispute resolution clause, which stated that "To prevent disputes and litigations, the Engineer shall in all cases determine the classification, amount, quality, acceptability and fitness of the several kinds of work and materials which are to be paid for under this contract, shall determine every question in relation to the Works and the construction thereof and shall determine every question which may be relevant to the fulfillment of this contract on the part of the Contractor. His determination and estimate shall be final and conclusive upon the Contractor, and in case any question touching this contract shall arise between the parties hereto such determination and estimate shall be a condition precedent to the right of the Contractor to receive any money under this contract."

The Appellate Court held that it would violate public policy to interpret the dispute resolution clause as making the engineer the final arbitrator over questions of contract construction, because by doing so the owner would be made the final and conclusive arbitrator over its own disputes.

Having concluded that the dispute resolution clause did not bar the contractor from commencing an action to challenge the engineer's determination on questions of law and issues of contract construction, the Court proceeded to hold that the contractor's claim for extras under the changed conditions provision involved a question of contract construction, and was therefore outside the scope of the dispute resolution process, whether or not the changed circumstances clause was deemed subject to mandatory or equitable adjustments. Furthermore, the Court held that there was no merit to owner's argument that the dispute resolution clause precluded the contractor from litigating its claims to recover for extra work and protest work; extra work was defined as that work necessarily required in the performance of the contract, and arose from circumstances which could not be anticipated. The primary guide to determining whether or not certain work was extra work and whether the contractor was entitled to be paid for extra work was the contract itself, interpretation of which was clearly a question of contract

III:	A201-1976, Art. 6, Para. 6.2.4	
III:	A201-1976, Art. 6, Para. 6.2.5	
III:	A201-1976, Art. 10, Para. 10.1.1	
III:	A201-1976, Art. 10, Para. 10.2.1	
III:	A201-1976, Art. 10, Para. 10.2.2	
III:	A201-1976, Art. 10, Para. 10.2.3	

At issue before the Appellate Court was whether the owner-contractor agreement imposed on the contractor, one of several prime contractors, a duty to protect the safety of all employees on the jobsite, including the injured employee of another prime contractor.

The owner-contractor agreement incorporated by reference a set of specifications drawn up by the architect. The specifications indicated some general conditions applicable to all of the prime contractors, but also indicated, under a separate section for each prime contractor, that prime contractor's specific duties at the job site. There was no one "general contractor" responsible for overseeing the completion of the project. Specifically the agreement stated that "The Contractor shall take all necessary precautions for the safety of employees on the work, and shall comply with all applicable provisions of Federal, State and Municipal safety laws . . . to prevent accidents or injury to person on, about or adjacent to the premises where the work is being performed. . . . The enforcement of all of the above is the definite responsibility of the Contractor and he shall make every effort and safeguard to ascertain compliance with all of said rules and regulations. . . ."

The Court found that the injured worker failed to show how the safety provisions of the contract imposed upon one prime contractor a duty to an employee of another prime contractor, since the General Conditions made it clear that the word "Contractor," when not further qualified, referred to all contractors on the site. The Court concluded that this provision of the contract did not impose upon each contractor a duty to protect all of the employees on the job site. Therefore, each contractor was responsible for protecting its own employees during the performance of its portion of the contract; to find otherwise would mean that the cost of avoiding or insuring against such potential liability would be entirely out of proportion to anticipated profits for the contractors. The Court found further that the specifications entitled "Carpentry and Millwork," which were unique to contractor's role in the work, did not require the contractor to protect the safety of everyone on the site at all times where the contractor's role under the specifications did not encompass a great part of the project.

88035a   Thomas Crimmins Contracting Co. v. New York, 138 A.D.2d 138, 530 N.Y.S.2d 779 (1988), *aff'd, certified question answered, en banc,* 74 N.Y.2d 166, 544 N.Y.S.2d 580, 542 N.E.2d 1097 (1989)

III:	A107-1978, Art. 8, Para. 8.5	
III:	A107-1978, Art. 13, Para. 13.2	

II: A107-1978, Art. 10, Para. 10.4
I: A107-1978, Art. 10, Para. 10.7
I: A117-1979, Art. 14, Para. 14.1
II: A117-1979, Art. 14, Para. 14.4
I: A117-1979, Art. 14, Para. 14.7
I: A201-1976, Art. 4, Para. 4.3.1
I: A201-1976, Art. 4, Para. 4.3.2
II: A201-1976, Art. 4, Para. 4.5.1

The Appellate Court found that the contractor had agreed to assume responsibility for any work not conforming to the specifications and for all acts or omissions of its subcontractor. The owner-contractor agreement contained provisions identical to the contractor's supervision and construction provisions of the American Institute of Architects General Conditions of the Contract for Construction, Paragraphs 4.3.1, 4.3.2 and 4.5.1. The Court concluded that the roofing subcontractor's failure to provide the owner with a written confirmation of the materials used did not shift the responsibility for the defective roof from the contractor to the owner.

88034   Statesville Roofing & Heating Co. v. Duncan, 702 F. Supp. 118 (W.D.N.C. 1988)

III: A401-1978, Art. 12, Para. 12.4.1
III: A401-1978, Art. 12, Para. 12.4.3

Subcontractor brought an action against contractor for final payment. The issue before the District Court was whether the "pay-when-paid" clause in the subcontract made owner's payment to contractor a condition precedent to contractor's final payment to subcontractor.

The subcontract provided in pertinent part that "Final payment shall be paid to the Subcontractor . . . conditioned upon payment having been received by the Contractor for all of Subcontractor's Work. . . ."

The Court held that, absent some special circumstances, the words "conditioned upon" did not establish a condition precedent to payment but only a reasonable time for payment. It therefore granted summary judgment in favor of subcontractor.

88035   Teitge v. Remy Constr. Co., 526 N.E.2d 1008 (Ind. Ct. App. 1988)

III: A107-1978, Art. 16, Para. 16.1
III: A117-1979, Art. 20, Para. 20.1
III: A201-1976, Art. 6, Para. 6.1.2
III: A201-1976, Art. 6, Para. 6.1.3
III: A201-1976, Art. 6, Para. 6.2.1
III: A201-1976, Art. 6, Para. 6.2.3

agreed to waive its rights against architect and look solely to the builders risk policy for damages.

The owner and architect entered into a modified American Institute of Architects Standard Form of Agreement Between Owner and Architect, Construction Management Edition, Document B141/CM, 1980 edition, which incorporated by reference, in part, the American Institute of Architects General Conditions of the Contract for Construction, Construction Management Edition, Document A201/CM, 1980 edition. The owner-architect agreement contained a waiver provision in Paragraph 11.4 identical to Paragraph 11.4 of the American Institute of Architects Standard Form of Agreement Between Owner and Architect, Document No. B141, 1977 edition. The applicable waiver provision in the General Conditions was identical to Paragraph 11.3.6 of the American Institute of Architects General Conditions of the Contract for Construction, Document A201, 1976 edition. The General Conditions in Paragraph 11.3.1 required the owner to purchase and maintain property insurance on the work. The owner and architect added a provision to their agreement as Paragraph 11.5 requiring the architect to maintain professional liability insurance covering errors and omissions "for the life of the Project and for that period of time following the date of final completion during which an action for professional liability on the part of the Architect for this Project may be brought by the Owner under North Carolina Law."

The Supreme Court of North Carolina found the above insurance provisions to be ambiguous. The provisions of the owner-architect agreement and the General Conditions could be read as revealing an intent by the parties that the architect would bear the risk of loss for any property damage resulting from architect's negligence in rendering professional services to the owner. Paragraph 11.5, which required the architect to obtain professional liability insurance to protect the owner during the project, also provided that the insurance would be maintained for an additional period of time during which owner could bring an action under state law. Paragraph 11.3.1 required the owner to purchase and maintain builders risk insurance but it did not require the owner to name the architect as an additional insured. However, the Court also found that Paragraphs 11.3.1 of the General Conditions and Paragraph 11.4 of the owner-architect agreement could be read as revealing an intent by the parties to shift the risk of loss to the owner's insurer and waive all subrogation rights. However, Paragraph 11.5 of the owner-architect agreement could be read as revealing an intent by the parties to shift the risk of loss to the architect for damages other than to the work itself which resulted from architect's negligence. The Supreme Court concluded that the contract language was conflicting and ambiguous as to the parties' intent regarding whether the owner waived all claims against the architect for property damage resulting from architect's negligence in rendering architectural services. It therefore affirmed the intermediate appellate court's holding that the trial court had erred in dismissing the action.

88033 Shaw v. Bridges-Gallagher, Inc., 174 Ill. App. 3d 680, 124 Ill. Dec. 241, 528 N.E.2d 1349 (1988)

I: A107-1978, Art. 10, Para. 10.1

A107, 1978 edition, which included the American Institute of Architects General Conditions of the Contract for Construction, Document No. A201, 1976 edition. The contract included additional general conditions issued by the United States Department of Commerce Economic Development Administration. The American Institute of Architects General Conditions contained a broad form arbitration provision in Paragraph 7.9.1. The EDA General Conditions contained no arbitration provision but provided in General Condition 35 that the architect's decisions regarding the acceptability of the work performed by the contractor were final and conclusive. The owner-architect agreement provided for arbitration of all claims arising out of the agreement.

Citing Paragraphs 14.3 and 8.5 of A107, and Paragraph 2.2.12 of A201, the court of appeals found that there was a clear conflict between EDA General Condition 35, which provided that the architect's decisions were final and conclusive, and the AIA documents, which provided that most decisions of the architect were subject to arbitration. The court agreed with the contractor that the EDA provision was controlling, since the EDA document contained language indicating that its conditions would have precedence over any other contract documents. However, even in cases where the architect's decisions are given finality, such decisions may be attacked if there is evidence of fraud or a failure by the architect to exercise honest judgment. Since the owner had alleged faulty design and other breaches of contract by the architect, the question was raised whether the architect or the contractor was responsible for defects in the work. The contract contained no provision regarding how to resolve this sort of conflict. In light of the public policy favoring arbitration, and the fact that the contract, taken as a whole, manifested the parties' intent to submit all disputes to arbitration, the court of appeals affirmed, holding that the trial court had not erred either in refusing to stay the arbitration or in confirming the award.

88032   St. Paul Fire & Marine Ins. Co. v. Freeman-White Assocs., Inc., 322 N.C. 77, 366 S.E.2d 480 (1988)

II:	A107-1978, Art. 17, Para. 17.3	
II:	A107-1978, Art. 17, Para. 17.6	
II:	A117-1979, Art. 21, Para. 21.3	
II:	A117-1979, Art. 21, Para. 21.6	
I:	A201-1976, Art. 11, Para. 11.3.1	
I:	A201-1976, Art. 11, Para. 11.3.6	
I:	B141-1977, Art. 11, Para. 11.4	

The owner and its builders risk insurer brought a negligence and breach of contract action against architect for damage resulting from the collapse of the building's south wing. The trial court granted architect's motion to dismiss for failure to state a claim upon which relief could be granted. The owner appealed. The Appellate Court reversed the trial court, holding that the insurance provisions in the owner-architect agreement were ambiguous and remanding the case for trial. The owner appealed to the state supreme court. At issue on appeal was whether the contract clearly established that the owner

III:	A401-1978, Art. 11, Para. 11.9.1
III:	A401-1978, Art. 11, Para. 11.10.1
III:	A401-1978, Art. 12, Para. 12.4.1

The Appellate Court found that where the owner had not paid the contractor the contractor was not required to pay the subcontractor. The subcontract contained a paid-when-paid clause which provided that "When all work has been finally accepted by the Architect and WILSON/WOODCRAFT, final payment is contingent upon payment to the Contractor and shall be made within thirty (30) days after said payment from the Owner, provided the Subcontractor has previously furnished complete releases of lien and evidence of paid material bills." The change order provision stated that "No Change Orders will be issued for additional work of any kind unless so approved by the Architect and Owner prior to its issuance. In the event a controversy occurs between the Owner and the General Contractor concerning the Contract with the Owner or these Change Order(s), then it is expressly agreed that no compensation for these items shall be due the Subcontractor from the Contractor until payment for them is received by the Contractor, regardless of the fact that payment is delayed due to the Contractor negotiating with the Owner, arbitration, administrative actions, litigation, appeals or other similar activities." The Court held that these provisions plainly and unambiguously made payment by the owner to the contractor a condition precedent to payment by the contractor to the subcontractor.

88031 Ruffin Woody & Assocs., Inc. v. Person County, 92 N.C. App. 129, 374 S.E.2d 165 (1988), *review denied,* 324 N.C. 337, 378 S.E.2d 799, *review dismissed,* 324 N.C. 433, 379 S.E.2d 243 (1989)

I:	A107-1978, Art. 8, Para. 8.5
II:	A107-1978, Art. 13, Para. 13.2
I:	A107-1978, Art. 14, Para. 14.3
I:	A117-1979, Art. 12, Para. 12.5
II:	A117-1979, Art. 17, Para. 17.2
I:	A117-1979, Art. 18, Para. 18.3
I:	A201-1976, Art. 2, Para. 2.2.12
I:	A201-1976, Art. 7, Para. 7.9.1
III:	A401-1978, Art. 13, Para. 13.1
III:	B141-1977, Art. 9, Para. 9.1

Owner filed a demand for consolidation, alleging that both the contractor and the architect had breached their contracts. After the contractor failed to persuade the trial court that the claims were not arbitrable, the arbitrator entered awards against the contractor and the architect. The trial court confirmed the awards and entered judgment thereon and the contractor appealed.

The owner and contractor had entered into the American Institute of Architects Abbreviated Form of Agreement Between the Owner and Contractor, Document No.

The owner and construction manager entered into a standard form American Institute of Architect's agreement which provided in pertinent part that "The Construction Manager shall be solely responsible for construction means, methods, techniques, sequences and procedures employed by subcontractors in their performance of their contract, and shall be responsible for the failure of any subcontractor to carry out Work in accordance with the Contract Documents." The agreement further provided that the "Construction Manager is responsible for subcontracting and material purchases and all such contracts will be between him and the various subcontractors and vendors. The Construction Manager is responsible for payment to the various subcontractors and vendors in accordance with his standard form of Subcontract or Agreement for Purchase of Materials." The addendum provided that "Payment to the Construction Manager for work performed by subcontractors pursuant to subcontracts and in accordance with the provisions of Article 9 of the General Conditions are subject to retention as agreed upon between Owner and Construction Manager." Furthermore, the subcontractor sum "is the total amount payable by the Owner to the Construction Manager and the Construction Manager to the subcontractor for the performance of the work of that subcontract." The Court held that the construction management agreement was essentially a service contract with the fees to be paid to the construction manager for services rendered to the owner in connection with the project. Because the contract did not call for a general contractor, the owner, with the assistance of the construction manager, exercised the function of the general contractor. The Court concluded that the owner had delegated this function to the construction manager.

88029   Quinn Assoc., Inc. v. Borkowski, 41 Conn. Supp. 17, 548 A.2d 480 (1988)

II: A107-1978, Art. 13, Para. 13.2
II: A117-1979, Art. 17, Para. 17.2
II: A201-1976, Art. 7, Para. 7.9.1
II: A401-1978, Art. 13, Para. 13.1
II: B141-1977, Art. 9, Para. 9.1

The Appellate Court noted that the owner-contractor agreement contained a broad form arbitration provision, which stated that "All claims, disputes and other matters in questions between the parties to this Agreement, arising out of or relating to this Agreement or the breach thereof, shall be decided by arbitration in accordance with the Construction Industry Arbitration Rules of the American Arbitration Association. . . ." Where the issues submitted to arbitration covered all claims in question under the contract, and where the award was in full and final settlement of all claims, the arbitrator did not exceed its powers in awarding the architect an amount greater than the amount stated in the demand for arbitration.

88030   Robert F. Wilson, Inc. v. Post-Tensioned Structures, Inc., 522 So. 2d 79 (Fla. Dist. Ct. App. 1988)

III: A201-1976, Art. 9, Para. 9.5.2

contractor was never required to pay delay damages to owner, the subcontractor argued that he was not required to pay delay damages to contractor.

The owner-contractor agreement provided that the "It is expressly agreed and understood that time is of the essence in this agreement and if the contractor fails to complete the work on or before the above specified date, or any extension thereof, authorized in writing by the Owner, the actual damages to the Owner due to such delay will be difficult or impossible to determine." The subcontract provided that "Since time is of essence in this project, and since it is difficult to determine the exact damage that the Owner will sustain by a delay in performance, it shall be agreed that in case of failure on the part of the Subcontractor to complete the work within the time fixed in the Contract by milestones or any extension thereof, the Subcontractor shall agree to pay to the General Contractor liquidated damages. . . . It shall be understood and agreed that the General Contractor may, at his sole determination, make a pro-rata assessment of the maximum liquidated damages for each Subcontractor." The issue before the Court was whether the liquidated damages clauses in the contracts had to be read in tandem, with the clause in the subcontract becoming operative only if liquidated damages were recovered by the owner under the owner-contractor agreement.

The Court found that because the owner-contractor agreement provided that "actual damages to the Owner due to . . . delay will be difficult or impossible to determine," and the subcontract did not provide that actual damages to the contractor would be difficult or impossible to determine, but rather that "it is difficult to determine the exact damage that the Owner will sustain by a delay in performance," the provision in the subcontract was not really a true liquidated damage clause. The Court reasoned that the subcontract referred to the difficulty of establishing the damages of a non-party to the subcontract who would not be claiming damages under the subcontract, and it did not establish a fixed amount as liquidated damages, only a maximum amount. The Court concluded that the subcontract's liquidated damages provision was a pass-through obligation which provided that in the event a subcontractor caused delay in completing the project the owner could collect the fixed amount per day from the contractor, who in turn could pass through the obligation to the subcontractor.

88028 Port Liberte Partners v. Strober Bros., Inc., 228 N.J. Super. 155, 549 A.2d 72 (Law Div. 1988)

II: A201-1976, Art. 4, Para. 4.3.1
II: A201-1976, Art. 5, Para. 5.3.1
II: A201-1976, Art. 9, Para. 9.5.4

In determining whether a materialman or subcontractor was precluded by state law from filing a mechanics' notice of intent by reason of the prior filing of a construction manager agreement, the Court found that the terms of the owner-construction manager agreement placed the construction manager in the same relationship to the laborers and materialmen as that of a contractor in all respects, including the obligation of payment.

the court reduced the amount of post-judgment interest. The owner, contractor and surety appealed.

The owner and contractor had entered into an agreement which included the American Institute of Architects General Conditions of the Contract for Construction, specifically Paragraph 1.1.2. The subcontract provided that subcontractor would "furnish all materials and perform all work as described in Section 2 hereof for Phase 5B: A.I. duPont Institute for the Nemours Foundation Hospital building . . . all in accordance with the Drawings and Specifications . . . and subject in every detail to the supervision and satisfaction of [contractor] and of [owner] or his duly authorized representative." The subcontract provided that subcontractor agreed to be bound to the contractor by "the terms and conditions of this Agreement, the Drawings and . . . to assume toward [contractor] all the obligations and responsibilities that [contractor], by these documents, assumes toward [owner]." The General Conditions provided in Paragraph 1.1.2 that nothing contained in the "Contract Documents" created any contractual relationship between the owner and the subcontractor. However, numerous provisions in the subcontract imposed upon the subcontractor specific obligations *vis-à-vis* the owner.

The Appellate Court first addressed the issue of whether the owner was a third-party beneficiary of the subcontract. The Court found that the subcontract did not evidence an intent on the part of the contractor and subcontractor to confer upon the owner a direct right of action against the subcontractor. The subcontract provided that all work would be in accordance with the American Institute of Architects General Conditions of the Contract for Construction, Document No. A201, 1976 edition. Furthermore, the subcontractor agreed to be bound by the General Contract and the General Conditions. The agreement also provided that "the Terms and Provisions herein contained and the General Conditions . . . shall supersede all previous communications, representations, or agreements, either oral or written between the parties hereto with respect the subject matter hereof." The Court found that the repeated incorporation of the General Conditions, specifically in Paragraph 1.1.2 of the General Conditions into the subcontract was a strong indication of an intent to maintain separate owner-contractor and contractor-subcontractor relationships. Furthermore, the Court found that in every subcontract the owner ultimately benefited from the subcontractor's performance; however, this did not mean that the subcontract created a third-party beneficiary relationship. The Court rejected the owner's argument in support of its third-party beneficiary theory that numerous provisions in the subcontract evidenced an intent that the owner benefit from the subcontractor's performance, namely the provision which stated that the subcontractor's work was subject to the supervision and satisfaction of the contractor and owner, the obligation that the subcontractor submit shop drawings, for the owners' approval, and the requirement that subcontractor indemnify and hold harmless the owner from any expense, liability or loss arising from patent, copyright or trademark infringement.

The Court then addressed the subcontractor's and subcontractor's surety's challenge to the liquidated delay damages award on the ground that the provision for liquidated damages created a "pass through" obligation, triggered only if contractor became obligated to owner under a similar provision in the owner-contractor agreement. Since the

construction manager and architect "against all claims, fines, liabilities, losses, damages, and expenses, (including attorney fees) arising out of or resulting from the contractor's failure to comply with said legal requirements, to perform the work free from faults and defects in conformance with the contract documents, and to take any other prudent or reasonable actions." The Court found that Paragraph 10.2.2 did not express any clear intent to allow the construction manager indemnification for its own negligence. However, the Court refused to find that contractor's obligations to indemnify the construction manager were controlled exclusively by Paragraph 10.2.2 because such a finding would nullify Paragraph 4.18.1. The Court concluded that even if Paragraph 10.2.2 was applicable it did not affect contractor's duty to indemnify construction manager for its negligence as expressly provided in Paragraph 4.18.1.

88027 Pierce Assoc., Inc. v. Nemours Found., 865 F.2d 530 (3d Cir. 1988), *cert. denied,* 492 U.S. 907, 109 S. Ct. 3218, 106 L. Ed. 2d 568 (1989)

I:	A107-1978, Art. 2, Para. 2.1	
I:	A107-1978, Art. 7, Para. 7.1	
I:	A107-1978, Art. 7, Para. 7.2	
I:	A117-1979, Art. 3, Para. 3.1	
I:	A117-1979, Art. 11, Para. 11.1	
I:	A117-1979, Art. 11, Para. 11.2	
I:	A201-1976, Art. 1, Para. 1.1.2	
III:	A201-1976, Art. 8, Para. 8.3.1	
III:	A201-1976, Art. 8, Para. 8.3.2	
III:	A201-1976, Art. 12, Para. 12.3.1	
III:	A401-1978, Art. 3, Para. 3.1	
III:	A401-1978, Art. 3, Para. 3.2	
II:	A401-1978, Art. 11, Para. 11.1.1	
II:	A401-1978, Art. 11, Para. 11.2.1	
II:	A401-1978, Art. 11, Para. 11.2.5	
III:	A401-1978, Art. 11, Para. 11.7.1	
III:	A401-1978, Art. 11, Para. 11.11.1	
III:	A401-1978, Art. 12, Para. 12.5.1	

Contractor and various subcontractors brought actions against the owner and architect for delay damages. After the owner and contractor entered into a settlement agreement the District Court realigned the parties. Owner, contractor and contractor's performance bond surety brought a breach of contract action against subcontractor and subcontractor's performance bond surety. Owner brought an indemnification action against subcontractor for the amount owner paid contractor to settle the delay claim actions. After a jury trial the court entered judgment for owner and contractor and against the subcontractor on its counterclaim. Subcontractor and its surety appealed. After numerous post trial motions

may be increased under the following conditions: . . . H. Where unforeseen delay occurs in the construction phase which may occasion additional expenses on the part of the Architect or Engineer, such as the construction contract time being exceeded or extended by more than 20 percent through no fault of the Architect or Engineer." The owner argued that because the evidence showed that architect contributed to the delay architect should not have been permitted to recover additional fees in contravention of this "no damage" clause. The Court accepted architect's interpretation of the clause as merely providing one circumstance under which it was entitled to extra compensation, and that this one circumstance was not preclusive.

Owner then argued that the trial court erred in submitting to the jury the architect's claim for delay damages attributable to a consultant's bill for services rendered during the time extension granted by change order. The owner claimed that architect could only recover delay damages under the remedies provision, and that, while the contract permitted recovery "if, after the employment of an Architect or Engineer for the design of the project, the Owner, Architect or Engineer desires the services of a consultant, which will require compensation by the Owner beyond the fees of the principal Architect or Engineer" the consultant was not approved as required by the contract. The Court concluded that this provision did not govern the architect's claim for consultant fees because by its terms it related only to the schematic-design phase of the project, while architect's claim for fees related to the extension of architect's contract administration duties during the construction phase of the contract. The Court found that the fees were recoverable as extra allowances permitted by the contract in the event of unforeseen delay.

88026   Oster v. Medtronic, Inc., 428 N.W.2d 116 (Minn. Ct. App. 1988)

    II: A107-1978, Art. 10, Para. 10.11
    II: A117-1979, Art. 14, Para. 14.11
    I: A201-1976, Art. 4, Para. 4.18.1
    II: A401-1978, Art. 11, Para. 11.11.1

Contractor's employee brought a personal injury action against owner and construction manager. Owner and construction manager brought a third-party indemnity action against contractor. The trial court ruled that the owner-contractor agreement obligated contractor to indemnify construction manager for the entire judgment, including amounts attributable to construction manager's own negligence.

The owner-contractor agreement contained an indemnity provision similar to Paragraph 4.18.1 of the American Institute of Architects General Conditions of the Contract for Construction, Document No. A201, 1976 edition.

The Appellate Court concluded that the language "regardless of whether or not it is caused in part by a party indemnified hereunder" required contractor to indemnify the construction manager, even for the percentage of the worker's injuries attributable to construction manager's own negligence. The Court rejected the contractor's argument that its indemnification obligations were set forth in Paragraph 10.2.2 of the General Conditions which was modified to include contractor's agreement to indemnify the owner,

duties during the construction phase, the contract provided that "The Architect or Engineer shall check construction schedules; keep the Owner informed of progress of the work; check and approve shop drawings; approve materials and equipments and tests thereof; maintain accounts for the work, including the issuing of change orders at the direction of the Owner; check Contractor's applications for payment, and issue Certificates for Payment in approved amounts and provide on-site observation of the work." The contract also required architect to visit the site at least twice a month "to familiarize [itself] generally with the progress and quality of the work to determine in general if the work is proceeding in accordance with the contract documents." Finally, the contract charged architect with the duty to "make [its] recommendation to the Owner on all change orders to the construction contract."

The Appellate Court first addressed the issue of whether or not the owner offered expert testimony necessary to prove that the architect breached its standard of care set forth in the owner-architect agreement which required the architect to "check and approve shop drawings; approve materials and equipments and test thereof; . . . and provide on-site observation of the work . . . consistent with normal architectural . . . practices." After reviewing the record the Court concluded that owner failed to present expert testimony sufficient to enable a jury to determine what standard of care was required of the architect in the performance of these duties. The Court held that the owner failed to prove that the architect breached its duties in the administration of the contract.

In response to owner's claim that its design defect action was not barred by the statute of limitations, the Court found that since the agreement divided the architect's performance of the contract into consecutive phases, with varying duties detailed for each phase, and with compensation to the architect reflecting an increasing proportion of the construction cost as each phase was completed, a cause of action for improper design accrued when the plans were approved by the owner; at that time the architect had a right to demand and receive payment for its services for that phase of the project. The Court concluded that owner's claims were time-barred.

In response to owner's claim that the architect had waived its fee as consideration for architect's release from liability for delay damages, the Court found that the executed change order granting the time extension included a no-damage-for delay clause which provided in pertinent part that "any and all claims for delays prior to the date of execution of this change order attributable to or caused by the Owner, the Architects, or previous contractors on this project shall be waived by the Contractor by this change order." The Court accepted the architect's interpretation of this language as affecting only the construction contract between the owner and the contractor, and as having no effect on the architect who merely "issues and recommends" such changes as part of its contract administration duties and where the General Conditions contained a provision specifically stating that any change order executed by the parties affected only the owner-contractor agreement.

The owner then argued that the trial court erred in submitting architect's fee claim to the jury because the owner-architect agreement "restricts delay damages to those cases where [Architect] is not in part responsible for delay." The agreement specifically provided that "The charges as fixed under [the provisions for the architects' basic fee]

III:	B141-1977, Art. 1, Para. 1.1.4
III:	B141-1977, Art. 1, Para. 1.2.1
III:	B141-1977, Art. 1, Para. 1.3.1
III:	B141-1977, Art. 1, Para. 1.5.4
III:	B141-1977, Art. 1, Para. 1.5.5
III:	B141-1977, Art. 1, Para. 1.5.7
III:	B141-1977, Art. 1, Para. 1.5.8
III:	B141-1977, Art. 1, Para. 1.5.13
III:	B141-1977, Art. 1, Para. 1.5.14
III:	B141-1977, Art. 1, Para. 1.5.15
III:	B141-1977, Art. 1, Para. 1.7.13
III:	B141-1977, Art. 1, Para. 1.7.16
III:	B141-1977, Art. 1, Para. 1.7.19
III:	B141-1977, Art. 6, Para. 6.1.1
III:	B141-1977, Art. 6, Para. 6.1.2
III:	B141-1977, Art. 6, Para. 6.1.3
III:	B141-1977, Art. 14, Para. 14.2.1
III:	B141-1977, Art. 14, Para. 14.2.2
III:	B141-1977, Art. 14, Para. 14.2.3
III:	B141-1977, Art. 14, Para. 14.4.1
III:	B141-1977, Art. 14, Para. 14.4.2

Architect brought an action against owner for certain fees and owner counterclaimed alleging that architect breached the contract by defectively designing certain portions of the project and by failing to perform its administrative duties under the contract. The jury awarded the owner damages for architect's breach of its administrative duties and awarded architect its fees. Both owner and architect appealed. Architect argued on appeal that the owner failed to establish the standard of care required of the architect in carrying out its contractual administrative duties. Owner argued on appeal that architect had orally waived its fees as consideration for architect's release from liability for delay damages.

The owner-architect agreement incorporated by reference the "Manual for the Planning and Execution of Capital Outlays" (the Blue Book) and its General Conditions, published by the Division of Engineering and Buildings of the Office of the Governor. The contract divided the architects' basic services into four phases, schematic design, preliminary design, working drawings, and construction. During the initial phase, the architect was required to assist the owner in planning the project and in developing additional detail, including schematic plans. In the second phase, the architect agreed to supply preliminary drawings "to fix and describe the size and character of the entire Project." In the working drawings phase the architect was obligated to provide detailed drawings "setting forth the nature and extent of the work to be performed, the materials, equipment, and supplies required, and the methods of installation and construction." With respect to architect's

American Institute of Architects General Conditions of the Contract for Construction, Document No. A201, 1976 edition, gave the owner the right to inspect the construction as it progressed, as well as the right to order the work uncovered, even if it meant ripping out a completed wall. In view of owner's contractual right of inspection, the owner could not argue that that the statute of limitations was tolled. Since the owner could have inspected the wall and discovered the problems, the defects were not inherently undetectable until actually seen, and therefore the claim accrued for limitations purposes at the time of the breach.

88025 Nelson v. Commonwealth of Virginia, 235 Va. 228, 368 S.E.2d 239 (1988)

      III: A107-1978, Art. 8, Para. 8.1
      III: A107-1978, Art. 8, Para. 8.4
      III: A107-1978, Art. 8, Para. 8.7
      III: A107-1978, Art. 8, Para. 8.8
      III: A107-1978, Art. 14, Para. 14.3
      III: A107-1978, Art. 18, Para. 18.1
      III: A117-1979, Art. 12, Para. 12.1
      III: A117-1979, Art. 12, Para. 12.4
      III: A117-1979, Art. 12, Para. 12.7
      III: A117-1979, Art. 12, Para. 12.8
      III: A117-1979, Art. 18, Para. 18.3
      III: A117-1979, Art. 22, Para. 22.1
      III: A201-1976, Art. 2, Para. 2.2.1
      III: A201-1976, Art. 2, Para. 2.2.3
      III: A201-1976, Art. 2, Para. 2.2.4
      III: A201-1976, Art. 2, Para. 2.2.6
      III: A201-1976, Art. 2, Para. 2.2.13
      III: A201-1976, Art. 2, Para. 2.2.14
      III: A201-1976, Art. 2, Para. 2.2.15
      III: A201-1976, Art. 2, Para. 2.2.16
      III: A201-1976, Art. 2, Para. 2.2.17
      III: A201-1976, Art. 7, Para. 7.6.2
      III: A201-1976, Art. 8, Para. 8.3.1
      III: A201-1976, Art. 8, Para. 8.3.2
      III: A201-1976, Art. 8, Para. 8.3.3
      III: A201-1976, Art. 8, Para. 8.3.4
      III: A201-1976, Art. 12, Para. 12.1.1
      III: A201-1976, Art. 12, Para. 12.3.1
      III: B141-1977, Art. 1, Para. 1.1.1

by a specially drafted provision of the General Conditions. The provision stated that "Each application for a progress payment to be valid must be accompanied by a partial lien waiver and release, in form satisfactory to Owner, from the Contractor covering all work performed through the date of the previous months application together with, if requested by Owner, similar lien waivers from all subcontractors performing work under this Contract or otherwise on the job." The Court found that the Contractor's Affidavit form did not contain the words "lien" or "waiver," and did not expressly state that it was a lien waiver. Furthermore, the Court found that the acknowledgement of payment of all sums due when a dispute exists as to that very fact is not the same as an express waiver of a mechanic's lien.

88023 Mears Park Holding Corp. v. Morse/Diesel, Inc., 427 N.W.2d 281 (Minn. Ct. App. 1988)

I: B141-1977, Art. 12, Para. 12.1.1

Owner and lender appealed from judgment dismissing its action against architect for failure to state a claim. Prior to completion of a construction project, the owner defaulted on its loan from lender and transferred title to the project to a subsidiary of the lender. Although owner attempted to assign its rights to the lender, the architect's consent was given only conditionally and the assignment was never completed. The court of appeals affirmed the trial court's ruling that the attempted assignment was invalid. In doing so, the court interpreted an anti-assignment clause similar to Paragraph 12.1.1 of the American Institute of Architects Standard Form of Agreement Between Owner and Architect, Document No. B141, 1977 edition. The Court construed the language prohibiting the assignment or transfer of "interest in the agreement" as prohibiting assignment of any interest in the performance of an executory contract which was personal in nature and which could not be assigned without consent.

88024 Melrose Hous. Auth. v. New Hampshire Ins. Co., 402 Mass. 27, 520 N.E.2d 493 (1988)

II: A107-1978, Art. 8, Para. 8.3
II: A117-1979, Art. 12, Para. 12.3
I: A201-1976, Art. 2, Para. 2.2.16
I: A201-1976, Art. 2, Para. 2.2.17
I: A201-1976, Art. 13, Para. 13.1.1
I: A201-1976, Art. 13, Para. 13.1.2

In owner's action against contractor and its surety for damages resulting from the costs of removing and reconstructing a brick wall after the wall began to buckle and crack, the trial court entered judgment in favor of the owner. On appeal, the Supreme Judicial Court of Massachusetts reversed, holding that the action was time-barred. It concluded that contract provisions similar to Paragraphs 2.2.16, 2.2.17, 13.1.1 and 13.1.2 of the

The parties had entered into owner-contractor agreements which included the American Institute of Architects General Conditions of the Contract for Construction, Document A201, 1976 edition. The delay procedures were contained in Paragraph 8.3.1 and the change order procedures were contained in Paragraph 12.1.1. The owner issued to each contractor a change order extending the contract time.

The Appellate Court found that Paragraph 8.3.1 provided a procedure for the contractor to obtain an extension of the contract time, and further provided that the contract time be extended by a change order as defined in Paragraph 12.1.1. The contractors followed the specified procedure, and the owner issued change orders altering the contract time. The Court concluded that under the unambiguous language of the contract, the contract was modified such that completion of each contractor's performance was required by a date later than the date specified when the contracts were executed. Because each contractor had substantially completed its performance within the extended time, no contractor could be held responsible for delay damages which may have caused the need to extend the contract time. Furthermore, the Court read Paragraph 8.3.4 as not applying to change orders modifying the contract time, but to claims for delay arising under other contract provisions. It therefore affirmed the judgment of the trial court.

88021 Mario & DiBono Plastering Co. v. Rivergate Corp., 140 A.D.2d 164, 527 N.Y.S.2d 417 (1988)

III: A401-1978, Art. 13, Para. 13.1

The Appellate Court held that the subcontractor did not have to submit its dispute with the contractor to arbitration as a condition precedent to filing a mechanic's lien and a court action, because there was no clear indication in the language of the contract that submission to the architect was a necessary prerequisite to the commencement of litigation. The subcontract provided that any "claim, dispute or other matter in question between the Subcontractor and the General Contractor" was to be "first submitted by the claiming party . . . in writing to the Architect." However, the subcontract did not specify how the expertise of the architect was to be utilized in the dispute resolution process. The Court held that submission to the architect was a mediation and not an arbitration process.

88022 McMerit Constr. Co. v. Knightsbridge Dev. Co., 235 Va. 368, 367 S.E.2d 512 (1988)

III: A107-1978, Art. 15, Para. 15.4
III: A117-1979, Art. 19, Para. 19.4
III: A201-1976, Art. 9, Para. 9.3.1
III: A201-1976, Art. 9, Para. 9.3.3

The Appellate Court found that the contractor did not waive its right to file a mechanic's lien against owner's property by executing contractor's affidavits as required

I: A117-1979, Art. 5, Para. 5.2

Contractor brought an action against owner for the balance due under the owner-contractor agreement. The jury awarded the contractor damages, which the judge reduced to adjust for defects in the work. The owner appealed. The Appellate Court upheld the judgment of the trial court. The owner argued on appeal that the contractor was not entitled to damages where the amount the owner had paid the contractor exceeded the guaranteed maximum cost under the contract. The owner further argued that the contract was unambiguous and that the trial judge had therefore erred in admitting parol evidence concerning interpretations of its terms and conditions.

The owner and contractor entered into an American Institute of Architects Standard Form of Agreement Between Owner and Contractor with a Guaranteed Maximum. The contract stated a guaranteed maximum cost subject to written change orders prepared according to the contract provisions. The contract also stated that the work was to be performed according to the owner's plans and specifications and provided for a contractor's fee over all costs of the project, unless the project, in the absence of approved changes, ran over the guaranteed maximum cost, in which case the owner was to pay only the direct costs.

The Appellate Court found that although the contract stated a guaranteed maximum cost, other provisions of the contract indicated that this limit was not inflexible. For example, the contract specifically provided that in the absence of unapproved changes the owner would pay only direct costs exceeding the guaranteed maximum costs. The Court held that this provision indicated that the parties considered the possibility of cost overruns without agreed-upon changes when they executed the contract. The Court concluded that the contract was ambiguous as to price and, therefore, parol evidence was properly admitted to explain the provisions concerning cost.

88020 Lueder Constr. Co. v. Lincoln Elec. Sys., 228 Neb. 707, 424 N.W.2d 126 (1988)

II: A107-1978, Art. 14, Para. 14.2
II: A107-1978, Art. 18, Para. 18.1
II: A117-1979, Art. 18, Para. 18.3
II: A117-1979, Art. 22, Para. 22.1
I: A201-1976, Art. 8, Para. 8.3.1
I: A201-1976, Art. 8, Para. 8.3.4
I: A201-1976, Art. 12, Para. 12.1.1

This appeal arose out of separate suits by three contractors against owner for delay damages. The owner counterclaimed against each contractor asserting that it suffered delay damages which were the fault of each respective contractor. The trial court granted the contractors' motions for summary judgment on the grounds that the owner had granted time extensions. The owner appealed.

the contractor to carry property insurance covering materials and equipment at the site. In addition, claims for damage to property because of any act or omission of the contractor were covered by Paragraph 7.4.1. Finally, the seizure of the contractor's tools, equipment, machinery and materials was governed by Paragraph 14.2.1. The Court held that the trial court erred in denying owner's motion to compel arbitration because contractor's claim was clearly related to "the contract documents or the breach thereof."

88017 J.A. Moore Constr. Co. v. Sussex Assoc. Ltd. Partnership, 688 F. Supp. 982 (D. Del. 1988)

II: A107-1978, Art. 7, Para. 7.1
II: A117-1979, Art. 11, Para. 11.1
II: A201-1976, Art. 1, Para. 1.1.2

In contractor's action against owner, the project promoter, the developer, and others for breach of contract, fraud, RICO violations, and quantum meruit damages, the District Court found that the existence of an integration or merger clause, similar to Paragraph 1.1.2 of the American Institute of Architects General Conditions of the Contract for Construction, Document No. A201, 1976 edition, in a formal written contract between sophisticated parties was, in the absence of unconscionable or other extraordinary circumstances, conclusive evidence that the parties intended the written contract to be their complete agreement.

88018 JGA Constr. Corp. v. Burns Elec. Co., 145 A.D.2d 945, 536 N.Y.S.2d 318 (1988)

I: A401-1978, Art. 11, Para. 11.1.1
I: A401-1978, Art. 13, Para. 13.1

The Appellate Court found that where the American Institute of Architects Standard Form of Agreement Between Contractor and Subcontractor, Document No. A401, 1978 edition, required arbitration in Paragraph 13.1, but the addendum to the owner-contractor agreement which was incorporated by reference did not, the conflict was resolved by Paragraph 11.1.1 which stated that where any provision of the owner-contractor agreement was inconsistent with any provisions of the subcontract, the subcontract governed.

88019 Lazer Constr. Co. v. Long, 296 S.C. 127, 370 S.E.2d 900 (1988)

I: A111-1978, Art. 5, Para. 5.2
I: A111-1978, Art. 6, Para. 6.1
I: A111-1978, Art. 6, Para. 6.2
I: A117-1979, Art. 4, Para. 4.3
I: A117-1979, Art. 5, Para. 5.1

that the contract required both the owner and the contractor to carry builders risk insurance ignored the plain meaning of the language "unless otherwise provided in the Supplementary Conditions. . . ." Furthermore, the waiver clause had no effect because the owner was not required by the contract to obtain builders risk insurance. The Court held that the contract provided, as a matter of law, that contractor was solely responsible for obtaining builders risk insurance.

88016 Independence Bank v. Erin Mechanical, 49 Ohio App. 3d 17, 550 N.E.2d 198 (1988)

II:	A107-1978, Art. 7, Para. 7.1
II:	A107-1978, Art. 13, Para. 13.2
II:	A107-1978, Art. 16, Para. 16.1
II:	A107-1978, Art. 17, Para. 17.1
II:	A107-1978, Art. 20, Para. 20.2
II:	A117-1979, Art. 11, Para. 11.1
II:	A117-1979, Art. 17, Para. 17.2
II:	A117-1979, Art. 20, Para. 20.1
II:	A117-1979, Art. 21, Para. 21.1
II:	A117-1979, Art. 24, Para. 24.2
I:	A201-1976, Art. 1, Para. 1.1.1
I:	A201-1976, Art. 7, Para. 7.4.1
I:	A201-1976, Art. 10, Para. 10.2.1
I:	A201-1976, Art. 11, Para. 11.1.1
I:	A201-1976, Art. 14, Para. 14.2.1
II:	A401-1978, Art. 13, Para. 13.1
II:	B141-1977, Art. 9, Para. 9.1

Judgment was entered in favor of contractor on contractor's third-party complaint for loss of its tools, materials and equipment which were confiscated by the owner after the contractor walked off the job. At issue on appeal was whether the trial court erred in denying owner's motion to compel arbitration.

The owner-contractor agreement included the American Institute of Architects General Conditions of the Contract for Construction, Document No. A201, 1976 edition. The General Conditions provided for arbitration in Paragraph 7.9.1 of all "claims, disputes other matters in question between the Contractor and the Owner arising out of or relating to the Contract Documents or the breach thereof. . . ."

The Appellate Court found that the language of Paragraph 7.9.1 was broad and clearly included all claims involving the contract documents and breaches thereof. The Court noted that Paragraph 1.1.1 clearly provided that the General Conditions were contract documents. Furthermore, the General Conditions, in Paragraph 10.2.1, made contractor responsible for all materials and equipment at the site, and Paragraph 11.11.1 required

The owner and architect entered into the American Institute of Architects Standard Form of Agreement Between Owner and Architect, Document B141, 1977 edition, which set forth the architect's payment and certification responsibilities in Paragraphs 1.5.7 and 1.5.8.

The Appellate Court interpreted Paragraph 1.5.7 and 1.5.8 as imposing on the architect no obligation to verify the accuracy of the lien waivers presented by the contractor. The architect was obligated to determine whether or not the work had progressed to the point indicated by the contractor and whether it had been performed in accordance with the contract specifications. However, once the architect authorized payment to the contractor, Paragraph 1.5.8 relieved the architect of any responsibility to ascertain how the contractor used the moneys.

88015 Farmer's Elevator & Mercantile Co. v. Farm Bldrs., Inc., 432 N.W.2d 864 (N.D. 1988)

II:	A107-1978, Art. 17, Para. 17.3
II:	A107-1978, Art. 17, Para. 17.6
II:	A117-1979, Art. 21, Para. 21.3
II:	A117-1979, Art. 21, Para. 21.6
I:	A201-1976, Art. 11, Para. 11.3.1
I:	A201-1976, Art. 11, Para. 11.3.6

Owner brought a negligence and breach of contract action against contractor for property damage resulting from a storm which collapsed a temporary support installed by contractor. The jury found that contractor was negligent and that contractor's negligence caused owner's damages. In a post-trial hearing the trial court ruled that contractor had breached the contract. The contractor appealed from both the tort and contract judgments. The contractor argued on appeal from the contract judgment that both the owner and the contractor were required to carry builder's risk insurance and that if the owner had obtained the insurance, the owner's action would have been barred by the contract's waiver provisions.

The General Conditions of the owner-contractor agreement contained insurance provisions identical to the American Institute of Architects General Conditions of the Contract for Construction, Document No. A201, 1976 edition, Paragraphs 11.3.1 and 11.3.6, modified by the Supplemental General Conditions which required the contractor to also purchase and maintain property insurance as required of the owner under Paragraph 11.3.1.

The Appellate Court affirmed. It found that the modified Paragraph 11.3.1 unambiguously provided that "unless otherwise provided in the Supplementary Conditions, OWNER shall purchase and maintain property insurance upon the Work at the site. . . ." The Supplementary Conditions provided that contractor "shall purchase and maintain Property Insurance as called for in paragraph 5.6 [Paragraph 11.3.1, as modified] of Article 5 of the General Conditions." The Court concluded that contractor's argument

relating to the Contract Documents or the breach thereof . . . shall be decided by arbitration. . . ." Article 17 of the General Conditions provided that the "duties and obligations imposed by the General Conditions and the rights and remedies available to the parties hereto, . . . and all of the rights and remedies available to Owner and Engineer thereunder, shall be in addition to and shall not be construed in any way as a limitation of, any rights imposed or available by law or contract. . . ." The Supplemental General Conditions provided in Paragraph 1 that the "Owner and Contractor agree that the following supplemental general provisions shall apply to the work to be performed under this contract and that such provisions shall supersede any conflicting provisions of this contract. . . . The rights and remedies of the Owner provided for in these clauses are in addition to any other rights and remedies provided by law under this contract." The arbitration clause, contained in Paragraph 7 of the Supplemental General Conditions, stated that "Except as may be otherwise provided in this Contract, all claims, counterclaims, disputes and other matters in question between Owner and Contractor arising out of or relating to this agreement or the breach thereof will be decided by arbitration if the parties hereto mutually agree, or in a court of competent jurisdiction within the State in which the Owner is located."

The Appellate Court found that the General Conditions contained a broad arbitration provision that clearly stated the parties intent to submit disputes to arbitration. The Court interpreted the phrase in Paragraph 7 of the Supplemental General Conditions, "except as may be otherwise provided in this Contract" as a mechanism by which the parties could elect to either eliminate the possibility of arbitration entirely or provide for a more binding arbitration provision. The Court concluded that the parties clearly and unambiguously chose to provide for a more binding arbitration provision in Article 16.1. Furthermore, when the "mutual agreement" language was read in the context of the entire Paragraph 7, neither the supersession language of Paragraph 1, nor the prohibitions against limiting rights and remedies in Article 17 and Paragraph 1, were invoked. The Court ordered the parties to arbitrate.

88014   Fabe v. WVP Corp., 760 S.W.2d 490 (Mo. Ct. App. 1988)

II:	A107-1978, Art. 8, Para. 8.4
II:	A117-1979, Art. 12, Para. 12.4
II:	A201-1976, Art. 2, Para. 2.2.6
II:	A201-1976, Art. 9, Para. 9.4.1
II:	A201-1976, Art. 9, Para. 9.4.2
I:	B141-1977, Art. 1, Para. 1.5.7
I:	B141-1977, Art. 1, Para. 1.5.8

Owner's insurer brought an action against architect for negligent certification of contractor's fraudulent lien waivers. The trial court granted architect's motion for summary judgment and insurer appealed. Insurer argued on appeal that architect's act of examining the lien waivers gave rise to a duty to determine the authenticity of the documents.

II:	B141-1977, Art. 1, Para. 1.5.6
II:	B141-1977, Art. 1, Para. 1.6.1
II:	B141-1977, Art. 1, Para. 1.6.2
II:	B141-1977, Art. 1, Para. 1.6.3

Steel supplier and other subcontractors brought an action against contractor for payment. Owner joined in the action against contractor seeking to have all liens cancelled and to be released from liability on future claims. Contractor counterclaimed against owner for the balance of the contract price. The trial court entered judgment for supplier and other subcontractors and for contractor, based on its findings that the contractor had substantially completed the project, and that the delays, including the delayed approval of shop drawings, were due to owner's failure to appoint another architect to finish the project when the project architect became incapacitated. The owner appealed. The primary issues on appeal were whether the delays were the fault of the owner and whether the appointment of a non-architect to complete the project was a breach of the owner-contractor agreement.

The parties had entered into an American Institute of Architects Standard Form of Agreement Between Owner and Contractor which included the American Institute of Architects General Conditions of the Contract for Construction, Document No. A201, 1976 edition, specifically Paragraph 2.1.1 which defined architect and Paragraphs 2 2.1, 2.2.17, 2.2.18 and 2.2.19 which defined the role of the architect in the administration of the contract.

The Appellate Court found that the record and the trial court's interpretation of the contract supported the trial court's finding that the owner breached the contract by replacing the architect with a non-architect, and that this replacement was the principal cause of the delay.

88013   Emlenton Area Mun. Auth. v. Miles, 378 Pa. Super. 303, 548 A.2d 623 (1988), *appeal denied,* 522 Pa. 613, 563 A.2d 498 (1989)

III:	A107-1978, Art. 13, Para. 13.2
III:	A117-1979, Art. 17, Para. 17.2
III:	A201-1976, Art. 7, Para. 7.9.1
III:	A401-1978, Art. 13, Para. 13.1
III:	B141-1977, Art. 9, Para. 9.1

Contractor filed a demand for arbitration of its claims against owner. Owner then filed an action at law against contractor for damages. In response to owner's action, contractor filed a motion to compel arbitration. The trial court held that the agreement to arbitrate provided for the submission of any dispute to arbitration only upon the mutual consent of the parties, and in light of owner's opposition to arbitration, owner could not be compelled to submit to arbitration. Contractor appealed.

The relevant portion of the General Conditions provided in Article 16 that "[a]ll claims, disputes and other matters in question between Owner and Contractor arising out of, or

III:	A107-1978, Art. 18, Para. 18.2
III:	A107-1978, Art. 18, Para. 18.3
III:	A117-1979, Art. 22, Para. 22.1
III:	A117-1979, Art. 22, Para. 22.2
III:	A117-1979, Art. 22, Para. 22.3
II:	A201-1976, Art. 12, Para. 12.1.1
II:	A201-1976, Art. 12, Para. 12.1.2
II:	A201-1976, Art. 12, Para. 12.3.1

Contractor brought an action against owner and engineer for extra work performed without written change orders. The chancellor refused to allow testimony concerning extras because the contractor had not complied with the change order provision in the owner-contractor agreement, which required the contractor to obtain written change orders before proceeding with work not specified in the contract. The court granted contractor's motion for an interlocutory appeal to determine the admissibility of the testimony. The Appellate Court reversed and remanded for a full trial on the merits.

The owner-contractor agreement provided that "The owner may at any time, with the approval of the official designated by the Farmers Home Administration (hereinafter called the Representative), make changes in the drawings and specifications, within the general scope thereof. If such changes cause an increase or decrease in the amount due under this contract or in the time required for its performance, an equitable adjustment will be made, and this contract will be modified accordingly by a"Contract Change Order.' No charge for any extra work or material will be allowed unless the same has been ordered on such contract change order by the Owner with the approval of the Representative, and the price therefor stated in the order." The agreement further provided that "Any notice, consent, or other act to be given or done hereunder will be valid only if in writing."

The Appellate Court held that the contractor could overcome the provision requiring a written change order by establishing waiver of the stipulation. The evidence supported the contractor's contention that it had acted in good faith, performing the additional work in reliance on the owner's oral authorization.

88012   E.B. Ludwig Steel Corp. v. C.J. Waddell Contractors, Inc., 534 So. 2d 1364 (La. Ct. App. 1988), *cert. denied,* 536 So. 2d 1239 (La. 1989)

III:	A107-1978, Art. 8, Para. 8.1
III:	A117-1979, Art. 12, Para. 12.1
I:	A201-1976, Art. 2, Para. 2.1.1
I:	A201-1976, Art. 2, Para. 2.2.1
I:	A201-1976, Art. 2, Para. 2.2.17
I:	A201-1976, Art. 2, Para. 2.2.18
I:	A201-1976, Art. 2, Para. 2.2.19
II:	B141-1977, Art. 1, Para. 1.5.2

II: A201-1976, Art. 7, Para. 7.9.1
II: A401-1978, Art. 13, Para. 13.1
II: B141-1977, Art. 9, Para. 9.1

The Appellate Court found that the arbitrators did not exceed their powers by awarding the owner damages in exchange for lien-free title to the property, which the owner was to convey to the contractor. The owner's claim arose out of the contract documents or the breach thereof, and the claim fell within the scope of the broad arbitration agreement, which provided that "All claims, disputes and other matters in question between the Contractor and the Owner arising out of, or relating to, the Contract Documents or the breach thereof, . . . shall be decided by arbitration in accordance with the Construction Industry Arbitration Rules of the American Arbitration Association. . . . The award rendered by the arbitrators shall be final, and judgment may be entered upon it in accordance with applicable law in any court having jurisdiction thereof."

[*Editor's Note:* For affirmance by the Supreme Court of Minnesota, *see* case number 89010 *infra.*]

88010 Denver Ventures, Inc. v. Arlington Lane Corp., 754 P.2d 785 (Colo. Ct. App. 1988)

II: A107-1978, Art. 20, Para. 20.2
II: A117-1979, Art. 24, Para. 24.2
II: A201-1976, Art. 3, Para. 3.4.1
II: A201-1976, Art. 14, Para. 14.2.1
I: A401-1978, Art. 12, Para. 12.6.1
I: A401-1978, Art. 14, Para. 14.2.1

Sub-subcontractor brought a breach of contract action against subcontractor after subcontractor stopped making progress payments to sub-subcontractor and terminated the subcontract. Subcontractor counterclaimed for damages for the cost of completing the sub-subcontractor's work. The trial court denied subcontractor recovery on the grounds that the subcontractor failed to give sub-subcontractor notice before exercising its right to terminate the subcontract.

The agreement between the parties contained termination and remedy provisions identical to Paragraphs 12.6.1 and 14.2.1 of the American Institute of Architects Standard Form of Agreement Between Contractor and Subcontractor, Document No. A401, 1978 edition.

The Appellate Court affirmed, finding that because subcontractor did not give the notices required by Paragraphs 12.6.1 and 14.2.1, sub-subcontractor was denied the opportunity to cure the defects. The Court held that subcontractor breached the agreement and was not entitled to damages.

88011 Eastline Corp. v. Marion Apartments, Ltd., 524 So. 2d 582 (Miss. 1988)

III: A107-1978, Art. 18, Para. 18.1

obtained pursuant to the agreement, or any other property insurance. The Court concluded that the policy underlying Article 11.3.1, the avoidance of disputes among construction project participants, would be best effectuated by interpreting Paragraph 11.3.6 as abrogating any subrogation right of owner's insurer against the subcontractor. The Court then considered whether owner's insurer had a direct right against subcontractor's insurer under state law. It concluded that the owner's insurer was not precluded from bringing such an action, since the contract envisioned the possibility that two insurers could be liable for one loss, and remanded for further proceedings.

88008   Concourse Beauty School, Inc. v. Polakov, 685 F. Supp. 1311 (S.D.N.Y. 1988)

II:	A107-1978, Art. 13, Para. 13.1
II:	A107-1978, Art. 13, Para. 13.2
II:	A107-1978, Art. 18, Para. 18.1
II:	A117-1979, Art. 17, Para. 17.1
II:	A117-1979, Art. 17, Para. 17.2
II:	A117-1979, Art. 22, Para. 22.1
II:	A201-1976, Art. 7, Para. 7.1.1
I:	A201-1976, Art. 7, Para. 7.9.1
II:	A201-1976, Art. 12, Para. 12.1.2
II:	A401-1978, Art. 13, Para. 13.1
II:	B141-1977, Art. 9, Para. 9.1

The District Court found that the arbitrators did not exceed their power in awarding damages for orally agreed-to extras that were within the scope of the arbitration clause in the owner-contractor agreement, which incorporated the American Institute of Architects General Conditions of the Contract for Construction, Document No. A201, 1976 edition, Paragraph 7.9.1. All of the extras were necessary to complete the original contract and clearly constituted modification of the original agreement rather than entirely new agreements. The Court rejected the owner's argument that the arbitrators were compelled to find that the oral agreement was unenforceable pursuant to the contract provision stating that "all additional work shall be set forth in writing signed by the Owner and Contractor with the cost for the same set forth hereon." The Court held that the arbitration award could not be vacated on the ground that the arbitrator failed to correctly interpret the law applicable to the issues in dispute or that the arbitrator misinterpreted the contract, since there was a sufficient basis both in fact and in law for the arbitrators findings that the oral agreement fell within the arbitration clause and was enforceable.

88009   David Co. v. Jim W. Miller Constr., Inc., 428 N.W.2d 590 (Minn. Ct. App. 1988), *aff'd en banc,* 444 N.W.2d 836 (Minn. 1989)

II:	A107-1978, Art. 13, Para. 13.2
II:	A117-1979, Art. 17, Para. 17.2

II: B141-1977, Art. 9, Para. 9.1

Contractor filed a motion to compel subcontractor's surety to arbitrate contractor's breach of contract and negligence claims against subcontractor. The trial court held that the arbitration clause in the subcontract, which was incorporated by reference into the bonds, required the surety to arbitrate.

The arbitration clause provided that "all claims, disputes, and other matters in question arising out of or relating to this [Subcontract] or the breach thereof, if not settled between the parties by agreement, shall be decided by arbitration. . . ."

In deciding the threshold issue of whether the dispute was within the scope of the arbitration provision, the District Court found that because the surety's obligation was triggered only if subcontractor breached the agreement, the dispute between contractor and subcontractor's surety was a matter "arising out of or relating to" the subcontract. The Court, concluding that the bond incorporated the subcontract's terms by express reference, held that the surety was bound to arbitrate.

88007   Commercial Union Ins. Co. v. Bituminous Casualty Corp., 851 F.2d 98 (3d Cir. 1988)

II: A107-1978, Art. 17, Para. 17.3
II: A107-1978, Art. 17, Para. 17.6
II: A117-1979, Art. 21, Para. 21.3
II: A117-1979, Art. 21, Para. 21.6
I: A201-1979, Art. 11, Para. 11.3.1
I: A201-1976, Art. 11, Para. 11.3.6

Owner's insurer filed an action against subcontractor's insurer seeking a declaration that subcontractor's insurer was liable for contribution or indemnity for owner's loss resulting from the collapse of a masonry building, under construction by subcontractor, due to a windstorm. The District Court held that Article 11.3.6 of the General Conditions acted as a waiver of owner's subrogation rights against subcontractor and barred the owner's insurer's action.

The owner and contractor entered into an American Institute of Architects Standard Form of Agreement between Owner and Contractor which included the American Institute of Architects General Conditions of the Contract for Construction, Document A201, 1976 edition.

The Appellate Court found that courts interpreting Paragraph 11.3.6 had concluded that the contract shifted to the owner the ultimate risk of loss which was then transferred to the insurer for valuable consideration, leaving the insurer no right to proceed by subrogation against a subcontractor with respect to property loss. The Court interpreted Paragraph 11.3.1 of the agreement as obligating the owner to procure property insurance for the site, covering the interests of the owner, the contractor and the subcontractors. Under Article 11.3.6 the owner and the contractor waived all rights against the subcontractor for damages caused by fire or other perils to the extent covered by insurance

I: A401-1978, Art. 11, Para. 11.7.1
III: A401-1978, Art. 12, Para. 12.4.1

Subcontractor brought an action against contractor for the remaining balance due under the subcontract. After a bench trial the court entered judgment in favor of the subcontractor on the grounds that the contractor and owner's architect had approved the use of a substituted exterior insulation system, which had been installed by the subcontractor in accordance with the plans and the manufacturer's specifications. The contractor appealed. The Appellate Court affirmed the judgment.

The contractor and subcontractor entered into an agreement which contained provisions similar to Paragraphs 6.1, 11.7.1 and 12.4.1 of the American Institute of Architects Standard Form of Agreement Between Contractor and Subcontractor, Document No. A401, 1978 edition. The subcontract also contained a final payment clause which provided that "Final Payment shall be due when the Work described in this Subcontract is fully completed and performed in accordance with the Contract Documents, is satisfactory to the Owner and Architect and Final Payment has been made by the Owner to the Contractor."

The Appellate Court rejected the contractor's argument that subcontractor expressly warranted in the subcontract that the materials it used would be free from defects and that any defects found, whether obvious or latent, were covered by the warranty and subcontractor would be liable for the required repairs or damages incurred. The architect and the contractor had approved the use of the substituted materials and the subcontractor did not warrant the adequacy of the design or specifications of the system. The Court found that the subcontractor did not breach the express warranty, since the subcontractor had only warranted that the materials would be new and would be installed properly in accordance with the manufacturer's instructions.

The Court also rejected the contractor's argument that the subcontractor had not met the prerequisites for final payment. The contractor argued that it was not required to pay the subcontractor until the work had been approved by the architect and owner, and final payment had been received by the contractor from the owner. The Court found that the final payment language was ambiguous and could be interpreted as setting a condition precedent or as fixing a reasonable time for payment. A contract provision requiring approval and final payment from the owner as a condition to contractor's obligation to pay a subcontractor had to be clear and unambiguous. In light of the ambiguity of the provision, there was no error in the trial court's ruling in favor of the subcontractor.

88006   Cianbro Corp. v. Empresa Nacional De Ingenieria y Technologia, S.A., 697 F. Supp. 15 (D. Me. 1988)

II: A107-1978, Art. 13, Para. 13.2
II: A117-1979, Art. 17, Para. 17.2
II: A201-1976, Art. 7, Para. 7.9.1
II: A401-1978, Art. 13, Para. 13.1

days which have transpired between the Substantial Completion Date and the Actual Completion Date (hereinafter called the"Liquidated Damages Period'). . . ."

The Appellate Court interpreted the language in Article 6 of the owner-contractor agreement, which stated that final payment was due ten days after the architect issued the certificate of substantial completion, as providing that the architect would issue the certificate by the substantial completion date. The Court rejected the trustee's interpretation of the language as providing that trustee had to make final payment and then wait sixty days after actual completion for the contractor to remit any liquidated damages. The Court also noted that Paragraph 9.6.1 of the General Conditions, which provided that the architect may decline to certify requests for payment and may nullify previous certificates to protect the owner from loss where there was reliable evidence that the work would not be completed on time, clearly indicated that the agreement contemplated the owner's withholding payments to the contractor to cover the accrued liquidated damages where the contractor failed to meet the date of substantial completion. In addition, the Court found that the language of Subsection 3 of Paragraph 9.9.4 of the General Conditions referred to defects in material and workmanship, and not to failure to comply with time deadlines. The Court reasoned that any other interpretation would lead to the conclusion that any non-compliance, known or unknown, would be waived by final payment, thus nullifying Paragraph 9.9.4. The Court affirmed, holding that trustee had waived its right to liquidated damages by making final payment.

88004 Charlebois v. J.M. Weller Assocs., Inc., 72 N.Y.2d 587, 535 N.Y.S.2d 356, 531 N.E.2d 1288 (1988)

III: A201-1976, Art. 2, Para. 2.1.1

The Appellate Court found that where the owner-contractor agreement expressly provided for the contractor to engage a specified licensed engineer, who was not a signatory to the contract, to perform the tasks for which the state statute required a license, the contract was not invalid as against the state's public policy which prohibited the unauthorized practice of engineering. The contract provided that the services of an "Architect/Engineer" will be furnished by the Contractor pursuant to an agreement between the Contractor and the Architect/Engineer;" that "all Architectural & Structural Engineering services are provided by James M. Weller P.E.;" and that the contractor would "furnish the architectural, engineering and construction services."

88005 Charles R. Perry Constr., Inc. v. C. Barry Gibson & Assocs., Inc., 523 So. 2d 1221 (Fla. Dist. Ct. App. 1988)

II: A107-1978, Art. 10, Para. 10.4
II: A117-1979, Art. 14, Para. 14.4
I: A201-1976, Art. 4, Para. 4.5.1
III: A201-1976, Art. 9, Para. 9.5.2
III: A401-1978, Art. 6, Para. 6.1

cause or of any concurrent or contributing fault or negligence of Contractor) or any breach of or failure to comply with any of the provisions of this Subcontract or the Contract Documents by Subcontractor."

The Appellate Court reversed. It held that the language "and regardless of any cause or of any fault or negligence of Contractor" expressly stated the parties intent that subcontractor would indemnify contractor for contractor's own negligence. In comparing this provision to the indemnity clause in the American Institute of Architects Standard Form of Agreement Between Contractor and Subcontractor, Document A401, 1978 edition, which provided in Paragraph 11.11.1 that subcontractor indemnify contractor from claims "resulting and arising out of the operations of the subcontractor . . . caused in whole or in part by [a] negligent act or omission of the subcontractor or anyone . . . for whose acts he may be liable, regardless of whether it is caused in part by the party indemnified hereunder . . .," the Court found that Paragraph 11.11.1 did not expressly state that the subcontractor was to indemnify the contractor for the contractor's own negligence.

88003   Centerre Trust Co. v. Continental Ins. Co., 167 Ill. App. 3d 376, 118 Ill. Dec. 151, 521 N.E.2d 219 (1988)

	II:	A107-1978, Art. 15, Para. 15.2
	II:	A107-1978, Art. 15, Para. 15.3
	II:	A107-1978, Art. 15, Para. 15.4
	II:	A107-1978, Art. 15, Para. 15.5
	II:	A117-1979, Art. 19, Para. 19.2
	II:	A117-1979, Art. 19, Para. 19.3
	II:	A117-1979, Art. 19, Para. 19.4
	II:	A117-1979, Art. 19, Para. 19.5
	I:	A201-1976, Art. 7, Para. 7.6.2
	I:	A201-1976, Art. 9, Para. 9.6.1
	I:	A201-1976, Art. 9, Para. 9.9.4

Bondholder's trustee brought an action against contractor's performance bond surety for liquidated damages. The trial court held that trustee had waived its claim to liquidated damages by making final payment under Paragraph 9.9.4 of the General Conditions, and that trustee's conduct waived Paragraph 7.6.2 of the General Conditions. Trustee argued on appeal that its obligation to make final payment arose before the contractor's obligation to remit liquidated damages.

The owner-contractor agreement, which included the American Institute of Architects General Conditions of the Contractor for Construction, Document A201, 1976 edition, provided that contractor pay owner "within sixty (60) days after the actual completion of the Work (the"Actual Completion Date'), as liquidated damages (not a penalty) an amount equal to Three Thousand Dollars ($3,000) multiplied by the number of calendar

88001 Aetna Casualty & Sur. Co. v. Lumberman's Mut. Casualty Co., 136 A D.2d 246, 527 N.Y.S.2d 143, *appeal denied,* 73 N.Y.2d 701, 535 N.Y.S.2d 595 (1988)

    II: A107-1978, Art. 10, Para. 10.11
    II: A117-1979, Art. 14, Para. 14.11
    I: A201-1976, Art. 4, Para. 4.18.1
    II: A401-1978, Art. 11, Para. 11.11.1

Contractor's employee brought an action against owner for personal injury damages. Owner brought a third party indemnity action against contractor. After the action was settled, contractor's contractual indemnity insurer brought an action against contractor's common law indemnity insurer for contribution. The trial court found that contractor was liable to owner on the basis of common law indemnity, however, because the indemnity clause in the contract was more extensive than common law indemnity, the clause superseded common law indemnity. The contractual indemnity insurer appealed.

The owner-contractor agreement indemnity clause was Paragraph 4.18.1 of the American Institute of Architects General Conditions of the Contract for Construction, Document No. A201, 1976 edition.

The Appellate Court found that the clause was not inconsistent with the owner's right to common law indemnity, and that the right to both common law indemnity and contractual indemnity could coexist. The Court held that both policies provided coverage for contractor's liability to owner and both insurance companies had to share the liability equally.

88002 B-F-W Constr. Co. v. Garza, 748 S.W.2d 611 (Tex. Ct. App. 1988)

    III: A107-1978, Art. 10, Para. 10.11
    III: A117-1979, Art. 14, Para. 14.11
    III: A201-1976, Art. 4, Para. 4.18.1
    I: A401-1978, Art. 11, Para. 11.11.1

Subcontractor's injured employee brought a negligence action against contractor. Contractor brought a third party indemnity action against subcontractor. The trial court granted subcontractor's motion for summary judgment on the grounds that the indemnity clause did not meet the "express negligence doctrine test." Contractor argued on appeal that the indemnity clause was sufficient under the express negligence doctrine to require subcontractor to indemnify contractor.

The state's express negligence doctrine provided that an indemnitor must indemnify an indemnitee for its own negligence only if the intent of the parties to do so was expressly stated in the agreement. The subcontract provided that subcontractor indemnify contractor against "any and all claims, demands, liens, damages, arising in any manner, directly or indirectly, out of or in connection with or in the course of or incidental to any of Subcontractor's work or operations hereunder or in connection herewith (regardless of

automatically preclude arbitration. Moreover, to accept the contractor's arguments would require interpretation of the agreement, and the "inexorable presumption" in favor of arbitration applied.

87053   Walton v. Datry, 185 Ga. App. 88, 363 S.E.2d 295 (1987)

> III: A111-1978, Art. 5, Para. 5.2
> III: A111-1978, Art. 16, Para. 16.2

Owner brought a breach of contract action against contractor for cost overruns and lost income due to untimely completion of construction. The trial court granted contractor's motion for partial summary judgment and owner appealed. The owner argued on appeal that where the contract price was for a fixed amount, reduced by a negotiated amount, where the contract was entitled "for cost of work, plus a fee," and where Paragraph 5.2 was left blank, parol evidence should have been admitted to establish the amount due under the contract. The Court of Appeals disagreed and upheld the judgment of the trial court.

The owner and contractor entered into the American Institute of Architects Standard Form of Agreement Between Owner and Contractor, Document No. A111, 1978 edition. Paragraph 5.2 provided that "the maximum cost to the Owner, including the Cost of the Work and the Contractor's Fee, is guaranteed not to exceed the sum of [*blank*] dollars ($); such Guaranteed Maximum Cost shall be increased or decreased for Changes in the Work as provided in Article 7. (Here insert any provision for distribution of any savings. Delete Paragraph 5.2 if there is no Guaranteed Maximum Cost.)." Paragraph 16.2 provided that "The Contract Documents, which constitute the entire agreement between the Owner and the Contractor, are listed in Article 1 and, except for modifications issued after execution of this Agreement, are enumerated as follows: The contract. The drawing."

The Appellate Court found that despite the contract language requiring deletion of Paragraph 5.2 if there was no Guaranteed Maximum Cost, an examination of the contract within its "four corners" led to the conclusion that the failure to fill in the blanks in effect deleted Paragraph 5.2 because there was no other provision setting forth a limit or a maximum amount. The Court found that the trial court properly held that the contract was complete and entire and not subject to extrinsic proof of its terms.

conditions precedent to sub-subcontractor's right to receive payment had not been satisfied. On appeal sub-subcontractor argued that Article 6 of the subcontract should have been interpreted as setting forth events which marked the time at such subcontractor was to make payment and not as setting forth conditions precedent to payment. The Appellate Court agreed and reversed the judgment in favor of the subcontractor.

The subcontract provided in Article 6 that "Final payment shall be due when the work described in this subcontract is fully completed and performed in accordance with the contract documents and is satisfactory to the architect. Such payment shall be made in accordance with Article 5 and with paragraphs 12.3 and 12.6 inclusive of this contract. Subject to the terms and conditions of this contract, final payment will be made to the subcontractor upon final acceptance of the work by the owner, the approval thereof by the architect, and the receipt of payment in full from the general contractor." Section 12.5 provided that "if the Architect fails to issue a Certificate for Payment or the Contractor does not receive payment for any cause which is not the fault of the Subcontractor, the Contractor shall pay the Subcontractor, on demand, a progress payment computed as provided in Paragraph 12.3 or the final payment as provided in Article 6."

The Appellate Court interpreted the first sentence of Article 6 as providing that payment was to be due when the work was fully completed to the architect's satisfaction. The parties agreed that sub-subcontractor fully performed its duties under the contract. The third sentence addressed the time at which payment was to be made—upon architect's approval and the owner and contractor's actual payment. Section 12.5 corroborated this interpretation of Article 6 by providing for sub-subcontractor's final payment in the event that the "conditions" of Article 6 were not met. Furthermore, Section 12.5 evidenced the parties intention that the sub-subcontractor would not bear the risk of loss in the event the conditions of Article 6 were not satisfied where the non-fulfillment of the conditions was not the fault of the sub-subcontractor.

87052 W.A. Botting Plumbing & Heating Co. v. Constructors-Pamco, 47 Wash. App. 681, 736 P.2d 1100 (1987)

III:	A107-1978,	Art. 13, Para. 13.2
III:	A117-1979,	Art. 17, Para. 17.2
III:	A201-1976,	Art. 7, Para. 7.9.1
III:	A401-1978,	Art. 13, Para. 13.1
III:	B141-1977,	Art. 9, Para. 9.1

Contractor appealed from confirmation of arbitration award in subcontractor's favor. The Court of Appeals affirmed, holding that the parties' dispute was subject to arbitration. The arbitration clause provided that "any controversy or claim affecting only CONTRACTOR and SUBCONTRACTOR and arising out of or relating to this CONTRACT, or the breach thereof, shall be settled in accordance with the Construction Industry Arbitration Rules of the American Arbitration Association, and judgment upon the award may be entered in any court having jurisdiction thereof." Thus, the contractor's assertion that the dispute involved more parties than the contractor and subcontractor did not

II: B141-1977, Art. 1, Para. 1.5.3
II: B141-1977, Art. 1, Para. 1.5.5
II: B141-1977, Art. 1, Para. 1.5.9

The Appellate Court found that the following contract language in the owner-contractor agreement created an agency relationship between the owner and the engineer that released the engineer from liability to the contractor when the contractor settled its claims against the owner: "[T]he Engineer acts as engineering representative of the owner. As such he [Kirkwood] has general authority to review, observe and approve or disapprove data, material, equipment and services submitted and/or furnished by the Contractor, and in general, to direct his efforts toward providing assurance for the Owner that the completed project will conform to the requirements of the contract documents. In behalf of the Owner, the Engineer may determine the amount, quality, acceptability, and fitness of the materials, equipments and services rendered under these contract documents. He will interpret the contract documents and decide questions arising as to the intent. Except as herein specified, the Engineer and his representatives will not be responsible for the Contractor's means, methods, techniques, sequences or procedures of construction, or the safety precautions and programs incident hereto, and he will not be responsible for the Contractor's failure to perform the work in accordance with the contract documents. The Engineer will not be responsible for the acts or omissions of the Contractor, or any subcontractors, nor any of his or their agents or employees, nor any other persons at the site or otherwise performing any of the work. Neither does the Engineer assume the authority to obligate the Owner to monetary commitments or fundamental changes to the scope of the contract. Although the Engineer will advise the Owner on such matters, specific commitments to the Contractor or official directives to the Contractor or contractor personnel shall be issued by the Owner's designated project representative. Directives issued directly by the Engineer or his representative are only advisory and are not binding upon the Contractor until acknowledged and supported by the Owner."Furthermore, the only evidence bearing on the subject of the relationship between the engineer and the owner established that the engineer was an independent contractor to the extent it supplied professional engineering services, but was, at the same time, the owner's agent because the acts of the engineer were subject to the direction and control of the owner, especially in matters where the engineer acted as intermediary in assuring that the contractor performed its contract obligations.

87051 United Plate Glass Co., Div. of Chromalloy Am. Corp. v. Metal Trims Indus., Inc., 106 Pa. Commw. 22, 525 A.2d 468 (1987)

II: A401-1978, Art. 6, Para. 6.1
I: A401-1978, Art. 12, Para. 12.4.1
I: A401-1978, Art. 12, Para. 12.4.3

Sub-subcontractor brought an action against subcontractor for the balance due for labor and materials. The trial court entered judgment for subcontractor on the ground that the

The Appellate Court found that the indemnity agreement in the subcontract, which provided that "Subcontractor shall defend at its own cost and indemnify and hold harmless Contractor and Owner, their agents and employees from any and all liability, damages, losses, claims and expenses, however caused resulting directly or indirectly from or connected with the performance of this subcontract," was voided in its entirety by state statute, which expressly voided indemnity contracts attempting to indemnify the indemnitee for any loss arising in whole or in part from the indemnitee's negligence.

87049 South Dakota Bldg. Auth. v. Geiger-Berger Assocs., P.C., 414 N.W.2d 15 (S.D. 1987)

> III: B141-1977, Art. 1, Para. 1.1.4
> III: B141-1977, Art. 1, Para. 1.2.1
> III: B141-1977, Art. 1, Para. 1.3.1

Owner sued architect and engineer, alleging defective design of an air-supported dome. The architect sought contribution and indemnity from engineer. The trial court denied the motion for indemnity, and the Supreme Court affirmed.

The Court found that the architect agreed to prepare design studies and plans and was authorized to "employ specialists, if necessary, to evaluate and study special considerations of the project, if such expertise is not available in his organization." Thus, the architect was not simply an agent through whom the engineer's plans passed. The Court also found that the architect had an obligation to create, prepare and develop architecturally sound plans. It rejected the argument that the architect did not have a duty to review and approve engineer's plans because of lack of expertise; if the architect did not have the expertise, it should have withdrawn as the architect, or obtained the additional expertise from other sources pursuant to the contract, or notified the owner of the fact that it did not have sufficient expertise and obtain waivers. The Court concluded that the architect "had a higher duty to more scrupulously review the plans of the engineer because of its limited expertise."

87050 Tri-City Constr. Co. v. A.C. Kirkwood & Assocs., 738 S.W.2d 925 (Mo. Ct. App. 1987)

> II: A107-1978, Art. 8, Para. 8.1
> II: A107-1978, Art. 8, Para. 8.3
> II: A107-1978, Art. 8, Para. 8.5
> II: A117-1979, Art. 12, Para. 12.1
> II: A117-1979, Art. 12, Para. 12.3
> II: A117-1979, Art. 12, Para. 12.5
> II: A201-1976, Art. 2, Para. 2.2.2
> II: A201-1976, Art. 2, Para. 2.2.4
> II: A201-1976, Art. 2, Para. 2.2.7

contract a typewritten document entitled "Specifications," the opening line of which read "Section I. General Conditions." The "General Conditions" contained in the "Specifications" made no mention of arbitration. The Court found that the references in the owner-contractor agreement, which was an American Institute of Architects Standard Form of Agreement Between Owner and Contractor, to the American Institute of Architects General Conditions of the Contract for Construction, Document No. A201, 1976 edition, which did contain an arbitration clause in Paragraph 7.9.1, could just as easily have referred to the "General Conditions" contained in the typewritten document. The Court concluded that the agreement viewed as a whole, including the attachment of Specifications entitled "General Conditions," created an ambiguity as to whether or not the parties agreed to arbitration as the means of disposing of disputes under the contract.

87047 Sheetz, Aiken & Aiken, Inc. v. Spann, Hall, Ritchie, Inc., 512 So. 2d 99 (Ala. 1987)

II:	A107-1978, Art. 8, Para. 8.3	
II:	A117-1979, Art. 12, Para. 12.3	
II:	A201-1976, Art. 2, Para. 2.2.3	
II:	A201-1976, Art. 2, Para. 2.2.4	
II:	A201-1976, Art. 9, Para. 9.4.2	
II:	B141-1977, Art. 1, Para. 1.5.4	
II:	B141-1977, Art. 1, Para. 1.5.5	
II:	B141-1977, Art. 1, Para. 1.5.8	

Claiming to be a third-party beneficiary, architect/developer brought a third-party action against a second architect, who had agreed to verify monthly payments to the contractor. The trial court granted summary judgment in favor of second architect. The Supreme Court affirmed.

Language similar to Paragraphs 1.5.4, 1.5.5, and 1.5.8 of the American Institute of Architects Standard Form of Agreement Between Owner and Architect, Document No. B141, 1977 edition, did not confer third-party beneficiary status on the architect/developer. The Court found that the language of the agreement entered into between the owner and a second architect did not express an intent to bestow a benefit upon the architect/developer. The second architect's contract expressly stated that the architect was not responsible for the acts or omission of the contractor, subcontractors, agents, or employees performing the work.

87048 Sierra v. Garcia, 106 N.M. 573, 746 P.2d 1105 (1987)

II:	A107-1978, Art. 10, Para. 10.11	
II:	A117-1979, Art. 14, Para. 14.11	
II:	A201-1976, Art. 4, Para. 4.18.1	
II:	A401-1978, Art. 11, Para. 11.11.1	

Finally, the subcontract specifically provided that the subcontractor would comply with all applicable ordinances and regulations. The Court thus concluded that these provisions expressed an intent in clear and unequivocal terms to impose liability on the subcontractor for injuries resulting from the its failure to provide adequate safety measures.

87045 Sanitary Sewer Auth. of Borough of Shickshinny v. Dial Assocs. Constr. Group, Inc., 367 Pa. Super. 207, 532 A.2d 862 (1987)

> III: A107-1978, Art. 13, Para. 13.2
> III: A117-1979, Art. 17, Para. 17.2
> III: A201-1976, Art. 7, Para. 7.9.1
> III: A401-1978, Art. 13, Para. 13.1
> III: B141-1977, Art. 9, Para. 9.1
> III: B141-1977, Art. 9, Para. 9.2
> III: B141-1977, Art. 9, Para. 9.3

Owner sued to collect on contractor's performance bond. Contractor filed a demand for arbitration against owner seeking damages for breach of a sewer construction contract. The trial court, in owner's action, stayed the arbitration proceedings. Contractor argued on appeal that the trial court erred in granting the stay without first determining whether contractor's claim was subject to arbitration under the contract.

Reversing, the Superior Court held that the trial court erred in failing to determine whether the dispute was within the scope of the arbitration provision. It was not sufficient for the trial court to conclude that a stay was appropriate given its jurisdiction and the fact that time and effort had already been consumed by the court action.

As for whether the parties' dispute fell within the arbitration clause, the owner-contractor agreement contained a broad arbitration clause in Article 16 which provided that "all claims, disputes and other matters in question, arising out of, or relating to this Agreement or the breach thereof . . . shall be decided by arbitration. . . ." The contractor's demand for arbitration alleged that the owner violated the contract by refusing to pay estimates, refusing to make unit price adjustments, and by intentionally acting so as to prevent the contractor from completing the job.

A dispute alleging a breach of contract was covered by the broad language of the arbitration provision. The Court therefore held that the matter was properly the subject of arbitration.

87046 Shaw v. East Coast Builders, Inc., 291 S.C. 482, 354 S.E.2d 392 (1987)

> I: A201-1976, Art. 1, Para. 1.1.1
> I: A201-1976, Art. 7, Para. 7.9.1

The Appellate Court upheld the finding of the trial court that the reference in the contract to the arbitration provision was ambiguous. The parties had attached to the signed

the agreement, of which the subsection was a part, obligated contractor to provide insurance necessary to protect owner and enumerated the types of insurance required. Subparagraph (c) specified the policies the insurance was to contain, including subsection (5) which provided that contractor was to secure insurance for contractual liability "equal to" the indemnity provision. The Court held that these provisions expressed the parties' intent that contractor was to secure insurance to provide indemnification for owner; they did not constitute a promise, prohibited by Illinois state statute, to personally indemnify owner for injuries or property damage. The Court also explained that the use of the phrase "equal to" in subsection (5) as denoted an understanding by the parties that the indemnity provision was not the bargained-for thing itself but merely a description of the scope of coverage that contractor was required to obtain in the insurance policy.

87043 (UNASSIGNED)

87044 St. Paul Fire & Marine Ins. Co. v. Gilpatrick Constr. Co., 731 P.2d 1188 (Wyo. 1987)

   III: A401-1978, Art. 11, Para. 11.1.1
   III: A401-1978, Art. 11, Para. 11.3.1
   III: A401-1978, Art. 11, Para. 11.5.
   III: A401-1978, Art. 11, Para. 11.11.1

Contractor brought a third party indemnification action against subcontractor for failure to provide adequate safety measures. After settlement of the claim against the contractor, the trial court denied contractor's insurer's claim for indemnity as a substituted third-party plaintiff. Insurer appealed.

Article V of the subcontract provided that the subcontractor would "save the Owner and Contractor harmless from all loss, cost or expense resulting either directly or indirectly from the failure of the Sub-Contractor faithfully to carry out any provision of this Sub-Contract." Article VII provided that the subcontractor would "adequately and properly protect his work so as to avoid injury or damage to persons or property and to be directly responsible for damages to persons and property occasioned by failure so to do, or by any negligence of the Sub-Contractor or any of his officers, agents or employees in the performance of his work." The subcontract contained a flow-down provision and a provision requiring the subcontractor to "comply with all applicable federal, state and municipal laws and/or ordinances and regulations effective where the work is to be performed. . . ."

The Supreme Court reversed, holding that the insurer was entitled to indemnification against the subcontractor. The broad language of Article V was insufficient to impose the same obligations and responsibilities on the subcontractor as the general contract imposed on the contractor. However, the subcontract expressly required subcontractor to protect against injury on the site and to assume responsibility for damages caused by its failure to do so. In addition, the subcontract specifically provided that subcontractor would be responsible for any loss resulting from its failure to carry out the subcontract.

The contract provided that the provisions of Paragraph 11.10 were "without prejudice to any other remedy he [the Contractor] may have." Furthermore, Paragraph 11.10 did not purport to guarantee subcontractor three days to remedy defects. Paragraph 11.10 did not grant additional rights to the subcontractor, it did not impose any additional obligation on the contractor, nor did it contain a waiver of any remedies or defenses otherwise available for damages arising out of the subcontract's breach. The Court found that because only the subcontractor "agreed" to the provisions of Paragraph 11.10 it was not intended to be a trap for a contractor who failed to clearly word a notice. The Court held that the contract was not ambiguous and should not be given a meaning other than that expressed. The Court reversed and remanded the case for trial on the facts.

87042   St. John v. City of Naperville, 155 Ill. App. 3d 919, 108 Ill. Dec. 551, 508 N.E.2d 1128 (1987)

	Ill:	A107-1978, Art. 10, Para. 10.11
	Ill:	A107-1978, Art. 17, Para. 17.1
	Ill:	A117-1979, Art. 14, Para. 14.11
	Ill:	A117-1979, Art. 21, Para. 21.1
	Ill:	A201-1976, Art. 4, Para. 4.18.1
	Ill:	A201-1976, Art. 11, Para. 11.1.1
	Ill:	A201-1976, Art. 11, Para. 11.1.3

Owner brought a third-party action against construction manager for breach of contract to insure. Trial court granted summary judgment in favor of owner. Contractor brought an interlocutory appeal, arguing that the contract terms requiring insurance were void under Illinois state statute.

The relevant portions of the owner-contractor agreement provided that "2. The Contractor shall provide all insurance necessary to protect and save harmless the property, the Owner and his representatives and the Contractor within the statutes of the State, and including, but not limited to those herein enumerated: . . . c. Insurance shall include the following requirements, clauses and policies; (1) Operations—Premises Liability; (2) Elevator Liability; (3) Contractor's Protective Liability; (4) Products Liability—Completed Operations Liability; (5) Contractual Liability equal to the following hold harmless agreement: The Contractor agrees to indemnify and save harmless the Owner, their agents and employees from and against all loss and expenses (including costs and damages because of bodily injury, including death at any time resulting therefrom sustained by any person or persons on or account of damage to property, including loss of use thereof, arising out of or in consequence of the performance of this work, whether such injuries to persons or damage to property be due to the negligence of the Contractor, his Subcontractors or the Owner."

The Appellate Court affirmed. It concluded that subsection 2(c)(5) obligated contractor to indemnify owner against all losses and expenses, including costs and attorneys' fees, resulting from injuries or property damage arising from the construction. Section 2 of

The owner and contractor entered into an American Institute of Architects Standard Form of Agreement Between Owner and Contractor, which provided in Article 4 that "The Owner shall pay the Contractor in current funds for the performance of the Work, subject to additions and deductions by Change Order as provided in the Contract Documents, the Contract Sum of EIGHTY-FIVE THOUSAND AND NO/100 DOLLARS. The Contract Sum is determined as follows: (State here the base bid or other lump sum amount, accepted alternates, and unit prices, as applicable). [The remainder of the excerpt was handprinted] IT IS MUTUALLY UNDERSTOOD AND AGREED THAT THE STATED ABOVE AMOUNT IS A NOT TO EXCEED AMOUNT. IT IS FURTHER UNDERSTOOD THAT CONTRACTOR WILL BE PAID A WEEKLY SALARY OF $450 PER WEEK FOR TWENTY WEEKS DURING CONSTRUCTION PERIOD, AND AT FINAL COMPLETION AND ACCEPTANCE BY THE OWNER CONTRACTOR WILL BE PAID $3,000. ALL OTHER COST WILL BE ACTUAL COST." The parties did not complete Article 5, which allowed the parties to delineate the allocation of progress payments between "labor, materials and equipment incorporated in the work" and "materials and equipment suitably stored at the site or at some other location agreed upon in writing and to specify a percentage of the contract sum that is to be paid off upon substantial completion of the entire work."

The Appellate Court upheld the trial court's finding that the contract was ambiguous as to contractor's compensation, since the contractor could have been working as an employee of the owner rather than as an independent contractor. As an employee, contractor could reasonably expect compensation directly payable to him to be separate and apart from any sum specifically allocated to construction costs. The Court concluded that if the owner desired to include contractor's salary in the contract sum the owner could have easily drafted the contract to reflect this intention.

87041   Royal Inv. & Dev. Corp. v. Monty's Air Conditioning Serv., Inc., 511 So. 2d 419 (Fla. Dist. Ct. App. 1987)

II: A401-1978, Art. 12, Para. 12.6.1

Subcontractor brought a breach of contract action against contractor, who filed a counterclaim and sought a set-off. The trial court granted subcontractor summary judgment on the ground that Paragraph 11.10 of the subcontract required three days written notice before the contractor could terminate the relationship. Contractor argued on appeal that there was no waiver of its rights under the agreement to a defense, set-off or counterclaim if it was determined as a matter of fact that notice was not adequate. The District Court of Appeal agreed.

Paragraph 11.10 of the subcontract was identical to Paragraph 12.6.1 of the American Institute of Architects Standard Form of Agreement Between Contractor and Subcontractor, Document No. A401, 1978 edition. It provided in pertinent part that "the Contractor, after three working days written notice to the Subcontractor, may, without prejudice to any other remedy he may have, make good such deficiencies and may deduct the cost thereof from the payments then or thereafter due the Subcontractor. . . ."

Document No. A401, 1978 edition, which apparently included the American Institute of Architects General Conditions of the Contract for Construction, Document No. A201, 1976 edition. The subcontract provided in Article 6.1 that the "unpaid balance of the contract sum shall be due when the work described in the subcontract is fully completed and performed in accordance with the contract documents and is satisfactory to the architect. . . . Following inspection and approval of the stated work by the architect and owner, final payment shall be made within seven (7) days after owner pays contractor." Article 12.4.3 provided that "if the architect does not issue a certificate for payment . . . the contractor shall pay the subcontractor upon demand a progress payment . . . or the final payment as provided in Article 6."

The Court of Appeals held that the language of the subcontract could not be interpreted as providing that architect's determination of whether the work was completed according to the contract was final and binding, and, absent such a provision, the opinion of the architect was not a condition precedent to the subcontractor's right to recover the balance due under the contract. Accordingly, the trial court's judgment was affirmed.

87039 Rego Park Garden Assocs., Inc. v. Elite Gen. Contracting Corp., 134 A.D.2d 199, 520 N.Y.S.2d 784 (1987)

II:	A107-1978, Art. 13, Para. 13.2	
II:	A117-1979, Art. 17, Para. 17.2	
II:	A201-1976, Art. 7, Para. 7.9.1	
II:	A401-1978, Art. 13, Para. 13.1	
II:	B141-1977, Art. 9, Para. 9.1	

The Appellate Court found that where the contract provided that "all claims or disputes between the Contractor and the Owner arising out of, or relating to, the Contract Documents or the breach thereof shall be decided by arbitration," the issue of the contract's termination was clearly within the scope of the arbitration clause and the question of whether the clause covered the dispute, as well as the merits of the dispute, were issues for the arbitrator to decide.

87040 Ringer v. Graham, 293 S.C. 238, 359 S.E.2d 523 (1987)

I:	A101-1977, Art. 4	
I:	A107-1978, Art. 3, Para. 3.1	
I:	A107-1978, Art. 3, Para. 3.2	
I:	A107-1978, Art. 4, Para. 4.1	
I:	A107-1978, Art. 4, Para. 4.2	

On remand of owner's action against contractor the trial court determined that the contract sum was $97,000 and awarded the contractor and other suppliers damages on their counterclaims. The Appellate Court affirmed the rulings of the trial court.

the right to require the contractor to increase the number of employees and to increase and change the amount or kind of tools or equipment if at any time the progress of the work was unsatisfactory to the owner, but owner's failure to give such directions did not relieve the contractor of its obligations to complete the work within the time and manner specified in the contract. The owner and the REA administrator reserved the right to inspect all payrolls, invoices of materials, and other data and records of the contractor relating to the construction of the project. The contractor was required at all times to take all reasonable precautions for the safety of its employees on the project and of the public and to comply with all applicable provisions of federal, state, and municipal safety laws and building construction codes, as well as safety rules and regulations of the owner.

The Appellate Court interpreted the contract as providing that if the contractor violated the safety provisions, after written notice by engineer or owner, contractor would be required to immediately correct the violation, and, if contractor failed to correct the violation, the owner could correct it at the contractor's expense. Furthermore, if the owner deemed it necessary the owner could correct a safety violation at the contractor's expense without prior notice to the contractor.

The Court concluded that the contract did not give the owner any right of control over the manner in which the work was done by the contractor. Furthermore, there was no evidence in the record that the owner exercised any control or retained any right of control over the manner in which the contractor performed any of its work on the project.

The Court rejected the estate's argument that the owner was liable for the negligence of the engineer if the engineer violated its contractual responsibilities by failing to be present on the site and if this failure resulted in the worker's death. The Court found that the engineer did not fail to carry out his contractual duties, since the engineer's inspections and other activities on site had nothing to do with the safety of contractor's employee. Engineer's job was to insure compliance with the plans and specifications for the benefit of the owner.

87038   R.C. Small & Assocs., Inc. v. Southern Mechanical Inc., 730 S.W.2d 100 (Tex. Ct. App. 1987)

        I: A401-1978, Art. 6, Para. 6.1
        I: A401-1978, Art. 12, Para. 12.4.3
        I: A401-1978, Art. 13, Para. 13.1

Subcontractor brought an action against contractor and its bonding company to recover the retainage due under the subcontract. The case was tried to the court. At the conclusion of subcontractor's case the contractor and bonding company moved for a directed verdict. The District Court entered judgment for subcontractor. Among numerous procedural issues on appeal was whether the architect's certificate, which was a prerequisite to payment, was a condition precedent relieving contractor of the obligation to make the final payment due under the contract.

The contractor and subcontractor had entered into an agreement similar to the American Institute of Architects Standard Form of Agreement Between Contractor and Subcontract,

11.1.1 established the contractor's obligation to provide insurance on the Work. Furthermore, the owner chose to rely upon its existing insurance coverage to fulfill its obligations under Paragraph 11.3.1. Thus, the issue was whether the damage to the microfiche was to the "Work" under Paragraph 11.3.1 or to "other than the Work itself" under Paragraph 11.1.1. The Court concluded that the only interpretation consistent with the rules of contract interpretation was that the parties intended that contractor maintain insurance covering any damage to non-Work property caused by its construction activities. The owner was to have purchased insurance to cover the Work. The Court accordingly held that absent uncontroverted evidence that the microfiche records were within the Work, summary judgment was inappropriate.

Furthermore, the Court found that Paragraphs 11.3.6 and 11.4.1 did not preclude owner's action against contractor because the waiver in Paragraph 11.3.6 applied only to damage to the Work, and Paragraph 11.4.1 did not apply because the damages sought by the owner were for repair or replacement of the records and not for the loss of their use. Consequently, the waiver provisions did not preclude insurer from exercising its subrogation rights.

87037   Pugh v. Butler Tel. Co., 512 So. 2d 1317 (Ala. 1987)

III:	A107-1978, Art. 8, Para. 8.3	
III:	A107-1978, Art. 9, Para. 9.4	
III:	A107-1978, Art. 10, Para. 10.1	
III:	A107-1978, Art. 16, Para. 16.1	
III:	A117-1979, Art. 12, Para. 12.3	
III:	A117-1979, Art. 13, Para. 13.4	
III:	A117-1979, Art. 14, Para. 14.1	
III:	A117-1979, Art. 20, Para. 20.1	
III:	A201-1976, Art. 2, Para. 2.2.3	
III:	A201-1976, Art. 2, Para. 2.2.4	
III:	A201-1976, Art. 3, Para. 3.3.1	
III:	A201-1976, Art. 3, Para. 3.4.1	
III:	A201-1976, Art. 4, Para. 4.3.1	
III:	A201-1976, Art. 10, Para. 10.1.1	
III:	A201-1976, Art. 10, Para. 10.2.1	
III:	A201-1976, Art. 10, Para. 10.2.2	

Decedent's estate appealed the grant of summary judgment to owner, and others, and engineer, arguing that contractor was an agent of owner entitling the estate to sue the owner for the negligence of the contractor.

The owner-contractor agreement provided that the owner "reserved the right to require the removal from the project of any of Sandidge's employees if in Butler's judgment such removal was necessary to protect Butler's interest." Furthermore, the owner had

Court concluded that the precautions which should have been taken were bargained for and intended by the parties and that denying indemnity would deprive the owner of the benefit of its bargain in violation of the principle that contracts should be read in a manner which renders them reasonable and capable of being executed. The Court held that the indemnity was viable notwithstanding the jury's finding of owner's active negligence. In so holding the Court disagreed with previous California decisions which relied exclusively on the active/passive distinction to determine whether a party was entitled to indemnification.

87036   Public Employees Mutual Ins. Co. v. Sellen Constr. Co., 48 Wash. App. 792, 740 P.2d 913 (1987), *review denied,* 109 Wash. 2d 1016 (1987)

II:	A107-1978, Art. 7, Para. 7.4
II:	A107-1978, Art. 17, Para. 17.1
II:	A107-1978, Art. 17, Para. 17.2
II:	A107-1978, Art. 17, Para. 17.3
II:	A107-1978, Art. 17, Para. 17.6
II:	A117-1979, Art. 11, Para. 11.4
II:	A117-1979, Art. 21, Para. 21.1
II:	A117-1979, Art. 21, Para. 21.2
II:	A117-1979, Art. 21, Para. 21.3
II:	A117-1979, Art. 21, Para. 21.6
I:	A201-1976, Art. 1, Para. 1.1.3
I:	A201-1976, Art. 11, Para. 11.1.1
I:	A201-1976, Art. 11, Para. 11.3.1
I:	A201-1976, Art. 11, Para. 11.3.6
I:	A201-1976, Art. 11, Para. 11.4.1

Owner's insurer brought a subrogation action against contractor to recover the amount it paid to owner for damage done to owner's microfiche records during construction. Contractor moved for summary judgment on the ground that under the contract insurer had waived any cause of action against contractor for property damage and that subrogation was not permitted because contractor was constructively insured under owner's policy. The trial court granted contractor's motion.

The owner-contractor agreement incorporated by reference the American Institute of Architects General Conditions of the Contract for Construction, Document No. A201, 1976 edition.

The Court of Appeals first considered whether the owner-contractor agreement obligated owner to insure the microfiche records against contractor's negligence, making contractor a constructive insured on the policy and relieving contractor of liability to owner for damage. The Court found that the parties respective insurance obligations were covered by Paragraph 11.3.1. The "Work" was defined in Paragraph 1.1.3. Paragraph

Owner brought an action against contractor to recover for breach of contract to replace a roof. The trial court determined that in terminating the contract for contractor's failure to begin work, owner was proceeding under the contractual provision that required a seven-day grace period; because contractor was not afforded that grace period, the trial court determined that contractor was not liable. The Appellate Court reversed. The owner-contractor agreement was terminated by letter pursuant to a provision identical to Paragraph 13.2.4 of the American Institute of Architects General Conditions of the Contract for Construction, Document No. A201, 1976 edition, and a provision which stated: "If the contractor defaults or neglects to carry out the work in accordance with the contract documents or fails to perform any provision of the contract, the owner may, after seven days' written notice to the contractor and without prejudice to any other remedy he may have, make good such deficiencies. In such case an appropriate change order shall be issued deducting from the payments then or thereafter due the contractor the cost of correcting such deficiencies, including the cost of the architect's additional services made necessary by such default, neglect or failure. The architect must approve both such action and the amount charged to the contractor. If the payments then or thereafter due the contractor are not sufficient to cover such amount, the contractor shall pay the difference to the owner." The owner's right to exercise remedies was not conditioned upon seven (7) days notice to the contractor since the contract under Paragraph 7.6.1 made clear that the owner's contractual remedies were not exclusive, but were "in addition to and not a limitation of any duties, obligations, rights and remedies otherwise imposed or available by law." Furthermore, the contractor did not rely to its detriment on the terms of the termination letter where the contractor did not start the work and did not take any affirmative action after receiving the letter.

87035   Morton Thiokol, Inc. v. Metal Bldg. Alteration Co., 193 Cal. App. 3d 1025, 238 Cal. Rptr. 722 (1987)

> III: A107-1978, Art. 10, Para. 10.11
> III: A117-1979, Art. 14, Para. 14.11
> III: A201-1976, Art. 4, Para. 4.18.1
> III: A401-1978, Art. 11, Para. 11.11.1

In an action arising from the injury of subcontractor's employee, the jury found that the owner was actively negligent, and the Superior Court denied owner's claim for contractual indemnification from contractor.

The indemnity clause required the contractor to "indemnify and hold harmless the Owner and its agents and employees from any and all liability, loss, damage, cost and expense (including attorneys' fees) sustained by reason of Contractor's breach of warranty, breach of contract, misrepresentation or false certification, or failure to exercise due care. All indemnifications shall be continuing."

The Court of Appeal reversed. It held that indemnity should be afforded under any circumstances where to do so furthers the intent of the parties to the contract and where the loss sustained would not have occurred without the indemnitor's negligence. The subcontractor, because the contracts at issue conferred rights and imposed obligations on all three parties. The Court thus concluded that the identical arbitration clauses in the agreements gave rise to the duty to arbitrate in one action where common questions of fact or law existed.

87033   McCarthy Bros. Constr. Co. v. Pierce, 832 F.2d 463 (8th Cir. 1987)

        II: A107-1978, Art. 14, Para. 14.2
        II: A117-1979, Art. 18, Para. 18.2
        I: A201-1976, Art. 8, Para. 8.3.1

Contractor brought an action against HUD and owner for its incentive fee. The District Court found that substantial completion occurred too late for contractor to qualify for the incentive fee. Contractor appealed, and the Court of Appeals affirmed.

Owner and contractor entered into FHA Form 2442A cost-plus contract which included the American Institute of Architects General Conditions of the Contract for Construction, Document No. A201, 1976 edition. Under the contract, contractor was entitled to receive the actual cost of construction plus a fee with a stated maximum. In addition to the basic contract fee, contractor was eligible for an incentive fee if its work was completed at a cost savings by the prescribed date. The date of substantial completion was defined in Paragraph 8.1.3 of the General Conditions. The agreement further provided in Article A that "the provisions of [Form 2442A] . . . take precedence over all inconsistent provisions in the said AIA General Conditions." Article 2D of Form 2442A provided that the date of substantial completion was the date HUD signed Form HUD 5379 which had to be endorsed by the architect as the final inspection report. Article 2C of Form 2442A provided for liquidated damages for work not substantially completed in accordance with the specifications, "including any authorized changes, by the date specified above or by such date to which the contract time may be extended. . . ."

The Court, in applying the rules of contract interpretation, concluded that Article 2D determined the date of substantial completion and controlled the award of the incentive fee. The Court also found that Paragraph 8.3.1 did not operate to backdate HUD Form 5379 to the date it was endorsed by the architect without a finding of bad faith on the part of HUD. The Court therefore upheld the District Court's finding that contractor was not eligible to receive the incentive fee.

87034   Monmouth Pub. Schools Dist. 38 v. D.H. Rouse Co., 153 Ill. App. 3d 901, 106 Ill. Dec. 608, 506 N.E.2d 315 (1987)

        III: A107-1978, Art. 19, Para. 19.1
        III: A117-1979, Art. 23, Para. 23.1
        I: A201-1976, Art. 7, Para. 7.6.1
        III: A201-1976, Art. 13, Para. 13.2.1
        I: A201-1976, Art. 13, Para. 13.2.4

The Court also found that economic injury was not within the scope of the clause. However, the clause specifically exempted the engineer from a financial loss from any cause whatsoever, which encompassed all economic damages alleged by the owner.

The Court held that under the plain language of the agreement the engineer was exempt from liability for the economic damages sought by the owner. Owner's remedy for any claims for property damage, whether caused by negligence, malpractice, or otherwise, was limited to the insurance.

In a later proceeding based on the equipment repair or replace warranty in the contract, the District Court held that the above-cited provisions did not affect the owner's warranty claim. Applying the Uniform Commercial Code, the Court found that the owner's costs were "cover," which the owner was precluded from recovering as incidental or consequential damages. The Court held that the owner, upon proof of damages, was entitled only to damages attributable to the engineer.

87032   Maxum Founds., Inc. v. Salus Corp., 817 F.2d 1086 (4th Cir. 1987)

         II: A107-1978, Art. 13, Para. 13.2
         II: A117-1979, Art. 17, Para. 17.2
         I: A201-1976, Art. 7, Para. 7.9.1
         II: A401-1978, Art. 13, Para. 13.1
         II: B141-1977, Art. 9, Para. 9.1
         II: B141-1977, Art. 9, Para. 9.2
         II: B141-1977, Art. 9, Para. 9.3

Subcontractor brought an action against contractor, who filed a third-party claim against the owner. The District Court dismissed contractor's third party action against owner, concluding that it was subject to the arbitration clause contained in the owner-contractor agreement. Subcontractor's action against contractor was tried, and on appeal the Court of Appeals held that the District Court had erred in refusing to order arbitration of the subcontractor's claim under the arbitration clause, which was incorporated by reference into the subcontract. Subcontractor then filed its demand for arbitration, to which contractor counterclaimed, seeking to consolidate its arbitration with the owner and its arbitration with the subcontractor. The District Court consolidated the proceedings and the Court of Appeals affirmed.

The arbitration clause in both contracts were identical to the American Institute of Architects General Conditions of the Contract for Construction, Document No. A201, 1976 edition, Paragraph 7.9.1, and to the American Institute of Architects Standard Form of Agreement Between Contractor and Subcontractor, Document No. A401, 1978 edition, Paragraph 13.1. They provided that "No arbitration shall include by consolidation, joinder or in any other manner, parties other than the Owner, the Contractor and any other persons substantially involved in a common question of fact or law, whose presence is required if complete relief is to be accorded in the arbitration."

Although the arbitration provision did not unambiguously provide for consolidation, it did so when read in the context of the contracts between the owner, contractor and

because the intent of the agreement was to protect the construction manager and to ensure that the construction manager could use its best judgment. If the Court allowed contractor to bring a third party beneficiary claim against the construction manager the construction manager would in turn seek indemnification from the owner which would defeat the intent of the no-damage-for-delay provision.

87031 Long Island Lighting Co. v. IMO Delaval, Inc., 668 F. Supp. 237 (S.D.N.Y. 1987), *dismissed in part,* 1990 U.S. Dist. LEXIS 5351 (S.D.N.Y. 1990)

III: B141-1977, Art. 11, Para. 11.4

Owner brought an action against engineer for breach of contract and negligent performance of services in connection with the construction of a nuclear power station. Engineer moved to dismiss the two counts against it for failure to state a claim upon which relief could be granted, on the ground that the owner contractually agreed to bear the losses. The owner argued that the limiting clauses in the contract referred only to the specific insurance coverage identified in the contract which did not include coverage for malpractice or breach of warranty, so that engineer's liability should not be limited; that the limitation of liability for personal or property damages was inapplicable because the damages at issue were economic; and that state statute prohibited a contractor from exempting himself from liability for injury to persons or property caused by the contractor's negligence. The District Court dismissed the counts as a matter of law.

The owner-engineer agreement provided that the engineer's "liability irrespective of fault or negligence for loss or damage to LILCO's property including the plant, or to any third party for personal injury or death and property damage, occurring during construction or thereafter and arising out of Stone & Webster's performance of its services under the Agreement shall be limited at contract or at law to the proceeds from the insurance placed by Stone & Webster and LILCO pursuant to paragraphs A and B, C and D, above. If LILCO so elects in writing, Stone & Webster will afford LILCO increased insurance liability limits from those specified in paragraph B above, of this Article. . . ." The agreement further provided that neither the engineer "nor vendors, contractors or subcontractors shall be liable to LILCO, either individually or jointly an irrespective of whether caused by negligence, for loss of anticipated profits, interest, loss by reason of shutdown or nonoperation of the Project or other facilities, increased expenses of operation of the Project or other facilities, or special or consequential loss or damage, arising from any cause whatsoever. . . ."

The District Court found that the agreement clearly stated that engineer's liability "shall be limited" to proceeds from insurance. The Court rejected the owner's argument that engineer's liability was limited as to only those items specified in the paragraphs describing the insurance coverage and that malpractice was not included. The Court refused to read additional language into the express terms of the parties agreement. Moreover, the Court found that malpractice was mentioned among the insured risks and the owner was allowed to elect to increase the excess insurance coverage the engineer was required to carry.

changes in the work, the contract sum being increased or decreased accordingly. All orders and adjustments for any extra work of any kind must be in writing and signed by the Contractor. Sub-Contractor shall have no claim for extra work unless an order in writing is secured from the Contractor, signed by their authorized agent prior to commencement to the work for which such extra charge is claimed, setting forth the extra cost or basis of cost to be allowed for extra work.

Reversing, the Court of Appeals held that the subcontractor could not recover in quantum meruit. The Court, reading the contract as a whole, concluded that it was clear that the "work," as defined in Paragraph 1 of the General Conditions, included the fill. Any additional fill provided by the subcontractor was "extra work" governed by Paragraph 5. The Court held that the subcontract made provisions for extra work and the subcontractor had to look to the contract for compensation. Because the subcontractor had waived recovery under a contract theory, the Court ordered that it take nothing.

87030   L.K. Comstock & Co. v. Morse/UBM Joint Venture, 153 Ill. App. 3d 475, 106 Ill. Dec. 462, 505 N.E.2d 1253 (1987)

Ill:	A107-1978, Art. 8, Para. 8.1	
Ill:	A107-1978, Art. 14, Para. 14.3	
Ill:	A117-1979, Art. 12, Para. 12.1	
Ill:	A117-1979, Art. 18, Para. 18.3	
Ill:	A201-1976, Art. 2, Para. 2.2.2	
Ill:	A201-1976, Art. 8, Para. 8.3.1	
Ill:	A201-1976, Art. 8, Para. 8.3.4	

Contractor brought an action against construction manager for delay damages. The trial court granted construction manager's motion for summary judgment on two of the counts. Contractor appealed, arguing that construction manager's failure to coordinate, direct, supervise, organize and expedite the project were a breach of the owner-construction manager agreement of which contractor was an intended third party beneficiary. The Appellate Court rejected this theory and affirmed.

No contract was entered into between the contractor and the construction manager. The construction manager had entered into a contract with the owner. The owner-contractor agreement contained a no-damage-for-delay clause which provided that contractor "shall not be entitled to any claim for damage or compensation from CDB on account of any delays. . . ."

The owner-contractor agreement expressly provided that construction manager was the representative of owner and had the power to act on owner's behalf; the contract also contained an extensive list of the construction manager's responsibilities. The Court concluded from these contract provisions and the no-damage-for-delay clause that owner intended to protect the construction manager from delay claims so that the construction manager's ability to act for the owner would not be impaired. The Court also held that contractor was not a third party beneficiary of the owner-construction manager agreement

III: A201-1976, Art. 6, Para. 6.2.3
III: A201-1976, Art. 12, Para. 12.1.1
III: A201-1976, Art. 12, Para. 12.1.2

In prime contractor's action against another prime contractor for delay damages, the Appellate Court held that prime contractors are not third party beneficiaries of each other's contracts with the owner. The Court reasoned that the contracted change order provisions reinforced the separate contract-awarding procedure and provided a remedy for delays. Furthermore, the mutual responsibility of the multi-prime contractors did not give each contractor third party beneficiary status. The Court, in reading the contract as a whole, found that the parties realized that other contractors would be involved and could cause delays. For this reason the contract contained a mutual cooperation provision and the change order provisions. The primary purpose of the change order provisions was to grant a contractor who was delayed a form of relief, whether money, a time extension, or both.

87029 Kittyhawk Landing Apartments III v. Anglin Constr. Co., 737 S.W.2d 90 (Tex. Ct. App. 1987)

III: A107-1978, Art. 7, Para. 7.4
III: A107-1978, Art. 18, Para. 18.1
III: A107-1978, Art. 18, Para. 18.2
III: A107-1978, Art. 18, Para. 18.3
III: A117-1979, Art. 11, Para. 11.4
III: A117-1979, Art. 22, Para. 22.1
III: A117-1979, Art. 22, Para. 22.2
III: A117-1979, Art. 22, Para. 22.3
I: A201-1976, Art. 1, Para. 1.1.3
II: A201-1976, Art. 12, Para. 12.1.1
II: A201-1976, Art. 12, Para. 12.1.2
III: A401-1978, Art. 11, Para. 11.9.1
III: A401-1978, Art. 11, Para. 11.10.1

Subcontractor brought an action against owner and contractor for payment for additional fill. The trial court entered judgment for subcontractor in quantum meruit and owner and contractor appealed. Owner and contractor argued on appeal that the written contract governed the work to be performed as well as the award of damages, and that therefore quantum meruit was unavailable. Subcontractor argued in response that the contract required a change order for extra work, not extra materials, allowing subcontractor to recover for fill materials in quantum meruit.

The subcontract included the American Institute of Architects General Conditions of the Contract for Construction, Document No. A201, 1976 edition, and other addenda. Paragraph 5 of the other addenda provided in pertinent part that "the contractor may order

87027 Indiana & Michigan Elec. Co. v. Terre Haute Indus., Inc., 507 N.E.2d 588 (Ind. Ct. App. 1987), *later proceeding,* 525 N.E.2d 1247 (Ind. 1988)

    III: A101-1977, Art. 3,
    III: A107-1978, Art. 2, Para. 2.1
    III: A107-1978, Art. 14, Para. 14.3
    III: A111-1978, Art. 4, Para. 4.1
    III: A117-1979, Art. 3, Para. 3.1
    III: A117-1979, Art. 18, Para. 18.3
    III: A201-1976, Art. 8, Para. 8.1.1
    III: A201-1976, Art. 8, Para. 8.1.2
    III: A201-1976, Art. 8, Para. 8.1.3
    III: A201-1976, Art. 8, Para. 8.2.2
    III: A201-1976, Art. 8, Para. 8.3.1

In contractor's breach of contract action against owner for wrongful termination, for owner's failure to pay amount due under the contract, and for seizing contractor's equipment, the owner appealed the trial court's entry of judgment for contractor. The Appellate Court found that the owner-contractor agreement was ambiguous where it contained stated deadlines, and provided that the work would commence on a fixed date but also provided that the work would commence one week after award notification. The Court held that, based on custom in the industry, the completion date should have been shifted by the number of days of the delay in the award of the contract.

87028 J.F., Inc. v. S.M. Wilson & Co., 152 Ill. App. 3d 873, 105 Ill. Dec. 748, 504 N.E.2d 1266 (1987)

    III: A107-1978, Art. 12, Para. 12.1
    III: A107-1978, Art. 12, Para. 12.2
    III: A107-1978, Art. 12, Para. 12.3
    III: A107-1978, Art. 18, Para. 18.1
    III: A107-1978, Art. 18, Para. 18.2
    III: A107-1978, Art. 18, Para. 18.3
    III: A117-1979, Art. 16, Para. 16.1
    III: A117-1979, Art. 16, Para. 16.2
    III: A117-1979, Art. 16, Para. 16.3
    III: A117-1979, Art. 22, Para. 22.1
    III: A117-1979, Art. 22, Para. 22.2
    III: A117-1979, Art. 22, Para. 22.3
    III: A201-1976, Art. 6, Para. 6.2.1
    III: A201-1976, Art. 6, Para. 6.2.2

87026   Hunt v. Ellisor & Tanner, Inc., 739 S.W.2d 933 (Tex. Ct. App. 1987)

II:	A107-1978, Art. 8, Para. 8.3
II:	A107-1978, Art. 10, Para. 10.1
II:	A107-1978, Art. 10, Para. 10.11
II:	A117-1979, Art. 12, Para. 12.3
II:	A117-1979, Art. 14, Para. 14.1
II:	A117-1979, Art. 14, Para. 14.11
I:	A201-1976, Art. 2, Para. 2.2.3
I:	A201-1976, Art. 2, Para. 2.2.4
I:	A201-1976, Art. 4, Para. 4.3.1
I:	A201-1976, Art. 4, Para. 4.18.1
II:	B141-1977, Art. 1, Para. 1.5.4

Owner brought an action against architect for negligently designing the parking deck of a shopping center and office complex. The jury found that the parking deck was not negligently designed but that the architect had breached its contractual obligation to observe the progress of the work and to guard the owner against defects in the work. The trial court accordingly rendered judgment against architect. Owner appealed the damage award.

The architect argued that it was not responsible for the contractor's failure to carry out the work in accordance with the contract documents, relying on the exculpatory language of Paragraph 2.2.4 of the American Institute of Architects General Conditions of the Contract for Construction, Document No. A201, 1976 edition. It provided in pertinent part that the architect "will not be responsible for the contractor's failure to carry out the Work in accordance with the Contract Documents" and would not be responsible for "the acts or omissions of the Contractor, any Subcontractor, or any of their agents or employees, or any other persons performing any of the Work."

Affirming, the Appellate Court concluded that the contract language constituted nothing other than an agreement that the architect is not the insurer or guarantor of the contractor's obligation to carry out the work in accordance with the contract documents. Because the first three sentences of Paragraph 2.2.4 imposed nonconstruction responsibilities upon the architect, the fourth sentence existed to emphasize the architect's nonconstruction responsibility and to make certain that the architect "will not be responsible for the contractor's failure to carry out the work in accordance with the contract documents." Thus Paragraph 2.2.4 did not exculpate the architect from liability for the contractor's failure to carry out the work in accordance with the contract documents.

The architect also argued that the contractor agreed to hold harmless and indemnify the architect under Paragraph 4.18.1 of the General Conditions. The Court found that this Paragraph applied to damages arising from the contractor's construction work and that it failed to indemnify architect from the damages sought by owner resulting from architect's breach of its obligation to observe the progress of the work and to guard owner against defects in the work.

of Construction Cost for such portions of the Project," the language of the contract was clear and unambiguous and the term "negotiated proposal" referred to a negotiated proposal between the owner and contractor, and not between the owner and architect.

87024　　Hilliard & Bartko Joint Venture v. Fedco Sys., Inc., 309 Md. 147, 522 A.2d 961 (1987)

   II: A107-1978, Art. 19, Para. 19.1

   II: A117-1979, Art. 23, Para. 23.1

   I: A201-1976, Art. 13, Para. 13.2.2

The Appellate Court, in determining whether owner's breach of contract claim against contractor was barred by the statute of limitations, found that where the owner-contractor agreement included the American Institute of Architects General Conditions of the Contract for Construction, Paragraph 13.2.2, the statute of limitations began to run on the date of the notice of defect and not on the date the construction was completed. The Court held that the contractor's obligation to perform was subject to the condition precedent of notice and would not even arise until notice had been given.

87025　　Holy Family Catholic Congregation v. Stubenrauch Assoc., Inc., 136 Wis. 2d 515, 402 N.W.2d 382 (1987)

   III: A107-1978, Art. 14, Para. 14.2

   III: A107-1978, Art. 15, Para. 15.3

   III: A117-1979, Art. 18, Para. 18.2

   III: A117-1979, Art. 19, Para. 19.2

   III: A201-1976, Art. 2, Para. 2.2.16

   III: A201-1976, Art. 8, Para. 8.1.3

   III: A201-1976, Art. 9, Para. 9.8.1

Owner appealed the ruling of the trial court that its action against the architect and contractor was barred by the state statute of limitations. The trial court had found that the state statute was ambiguous because it did not define the date of substantial completion. The Appellate Court rejected the architect's argument that because the contract empowered the architect to determine the date of substantial completion that date should be read into the statute as the commencement date. The Court instead turned to legislative intent to construe the statute. Although the Court adopted the architect's definition of substantial completion, it rejected the notion that an architect may unilaterally determine the period's commencement. For purposes of the statutory period, it was the court, not the architect, who determined the date of substantial completion. The Court held that while the date of an architect's certificate of substantial completion may be persuasive in determining the statutory date of substantial completion, the dispositive event was the owner's occupation of the building for its intended purpose.

87022   Gordon-Maizel Constr. Co. v. Leroy Prod., Inc., 658 F. Supp. 528 (D.D.C. 1987)

II:	A107-1978, Art. 13, Para. 13.2
II:	A117-1979, Art. 17, Para. 17.2
I:	A201-1976, Art. 7, Para. 7.9.1
II:	A401-1978, Art. 13, Para. 13.1
II:	A401-1978, Art. 13, Para. 13.2
II:	A401-1978, Art. 13, Para. 13.3
II:	A401-1978, Art. 13, Para. 13.4
II:	A401-1978, Art. 13, Para. 13.5
II:	A401-1978, Art. 13, Para. 13.6
II:	B141-1977, Art. 9, Para. 9.1
II:	B141-1977, Art. 9, Para. 9.2
II:	B141-1977, Art. 9, Para. 9.3

Contractor brought an action against lessee-owner to enforce its mechanics liens. Lessee counterclaimed seeking to vacate the mechanics liens, compel arbitration of the contract dispute over the suspension of construction and the subsequent termination of the contract, and to recover damages for fraudulent filing of lien claims. Contractor argued in response that lessee had waived it right to demand arbitration and that arbitration would constitute a waste of judicial resources.

The parties had entered into an agreement which incorporated the American Institute of Architects General Conditions of the Contract for Construction, Document No. A201, 1976 edition, Paragraph 7.9.1 which provided for arbitration of disputes.

The District Court found that lessee, by answering contractor's complaint, did not actively participate in litigation to the degree necessary to constitute waiver. Indeed, the lessee raised the duty to arbitrate as an affirmative defense in its answer. A finding of wavier would be appropriate only if there had been substantial delay in asserting the right to arbitrate, or if the lessee had engaged in other prejudicial conduct. The Court held that lessee was entitled to a stay of the proceedings pending arbitration pursuant to the terms of the contract.

87023   Hess v. Zoological Soc'y of Buffalo, Inc. 134 A.D.2d 824, 521 N.Y.S.2d 903 (1987)

I:	B141-1977, Art. 6, Para. 6.1.4

The Appellate Court found that where the owner-architect agreement provided that if portions of the project were not completed, the architect's "compensation . . . shall be payable to the extent services are performed on such portions . . . based on (1) the lowest bona fide bid or negotiated proposal or, (2) if no such bid or proposal is received,the most recent Statement of Probable Construction Cost or Detailed Estimate

87020 Fischbach-Natkin Co. v. Power Process Piping, Inc., 157 Mich. App. 448, 403 N.W.2d 569 (1987)

> III: A107-1978, Art. 10, Para. 10.11
> III: A117-1979, Art. 14, Para. 14.11
> III: A201-1976, Art. 4, Para. 4.18.1
> III: A401-1978, Art. 11, Para. 11.11.1

In contractor's indemnification action against subcontractor, arising from the injury of subcontractor's employee, the Circuit Court granted summary judgment in favor of contractor. The Court of Appeals affirmed. It held that Michigan law required that broad, all-inclusive indemnity language be interpreted to protect the indemnitee against its own negligence if such intent can be ascertained from other language in the contract, from surrounding circumstances, or from the purpose sought to be accomplished by the parties. The Court found that the following subcontract language was broad, clear, and encompassed all liability for injuries, including death: "Section 12. The Subcontractor agrees to and shall indemnify, protect, defend and save harmless Company from and against all liability or claimed liability for injuries, including death, to any and all persons whomsoever and for any and all property damage arising out of or resulting from or in any way connected with the work covered by this Subcontract or the operations or acts of commission or omission of the Subcontractor, his subcontractors, agents and employees."

87021 Ford v. Robertson, 739 S.W.2d 3 (Tenn. Ct. App. 1987)

> I: B141-1977, Art. 12, Para. 12.1

Purchaser of an apartment building brought a breach of contract action against architect for issuing a Certificate of Substantial Completion certifying that the work to be performed under the contract was performed in accordance with the contract documents and was completed. The trial court granted architect's motion for summary judgment on the grounds that the owner-architect agreement precluded assignment. The Appellate Court reversed.

The owner and architect had entered into the American Institute of Architects Standard Form of Agreement Between Owner and Architect, Document No. B141, 1977 edition. It provided in Paragraph 12.1 that "Neither the Owner nor the Architect shall assign, sublet or transfer any interest in this Agreement without the written consent of the other."

The Appellate Court found that if the owner was entitled to recover damages from the architect for breach of contract the owner could assign this right to the purchaser. Paragraph 12.1 prohibited the assignment or transfer of any "interest in this Agreement," and the Court construed the "any interest" language as meaning any interest in the performance of the executory contract. The Court therefore held that Paragraph 12.1 did not preclude the assignment of a cause of action for breach of an executed contract.

II: A401-1978, Art. 13, Para. 13.3
II: A401-1978, Art. 13, Para. 13.4
II: A401-1978, Art. 13, Para. 13.5
II: A401-1978, Art. 13, Para. 13.6
II: B141-1977, Art. 9, Para. 9.1
II: B141-1977, Art. 9, Para. 9.2
II: B141-1977, Art. 9, Para. 9.3

In an action arising out of the construction of a package-handling system for Emery Air Freight, owner filed a counterclaim against contractor, who filed a motion to compel arbitration. The trial court denied contractor's motion and contractor appealed. Paragraph 1 of the standard Conditions of the Contract which vested owner with "any and all powers reserved for the architect under the A.I.A. General Conditions as [owner] may, in its sole right, wish to assume." In addition to providing for arbitration of disputes between the contractor and owner, Paragraph 7.9.1 of the General Conditions provided that no arbitration arising out of the contract documents shall include the architect.

The Appellate Court reversed the order denying arbitration. It held that in the definition section of the contract Emery was the owner and only secondarily was granted the powers of the architect. The Court stressed that the owner should not be allowed to shield itself from resolving claims through arbitration simply because it could, at its own discretion, exercise the power of the architect. Furthermore, the Court found that the contractor did not waive its right to arbitration by filing a counterclaim and answer; the contractor did not initiate the litigation, and the filing of the pleadings was merely to protect its rights.

87019   Ethyl Corp. v. Daniel Constr. Co., 725 S.W.2d 705 (Tex. 1987)

II: A107-1978, Art. 10, Para. 10.11
II: A117-1979, Art. 14, Para. 14.11
II: A201-1976, Art. 4, Para. 4.18.1
II: A401-1978, Art. 11, Para. 11.11.1

The Supreme Court of Texas adopted the express negligence doctrine as the test for whether an indemnification clause clearly and unequivocally required the contractor to indemnify the owner for owner's own negligence or for the parties concurrent negligence. The doctrine provides that parties seeking to indemnify the indemnitee from the consequences of its own negligence must express that intent in specific terms. In the action before it the indemnification provision stated that "Contractor shall indemnify and hold Owner harmless against any loss or damage to persons or property as a result of operations growing out of the performance of this contract and caused by the negligence or carelessness of Contractor, Contractor's employees, Subcontractors and agents or licensees." This provision failed to meet the express negligence test.

87017 E.D.S. Constr. v. North End Health Center, Inc., 412 N.W.2d 783 (Minn. Ct. App. 1987)

> I: A107-1978, Art. 13, Para. 13.2
> II: A107-1978, Art. 14, Para. 14.3
> I: A117-1979, Art. 17, Para. 17.2
> II: A117-1979, Art. 18, Para. 18.3
> I: A201-1976, Art. 7, Para. 7.9.1
> I: A401-1978, Art. 13, Para. 13.1
> I: B141-1977, Art. 9, Para. 9.1

Contractor filed a demand for arbitration against the owner for extras, improper imposition of liquidated damages, acceleration and delay damages together with interest, costs and attorney's fees. The arbitrator awarded owner liquidated damages, fees, and other relief. The trial court denied the contractor's motion to vacate the award and contractor appealed. On appeal the contractor argued that the arbitrator exceeded his powers by awarding damages that were punitive in nature and by awarding the other relief. The Appellate Court affirmed the ruling of the trial court.

The owner and contractor entered into an American Institute of Architects Standard Form of Agreement Between Owner and Contractor, which included the American Institute of Architects General Conditions of the Contract for Construction, Document No. A201, 1976 edition, specifically Paragraphs 7.9.1 and 8.3.2, and supplementary conditions which included a liquidated damages clause and a lien waiver clause.

The Appellate Court first addressed the issue of whether the liquidated damage clause was penal and unenforceable. The Court found that the contractor's argument that the liquidated damages were disproportionate to the owner's actual damages related not to the issue of arbitrability but to the merits of the arbitrator's decision. Given the broad scope of the arbitration provision and the submission by the parties of the dispute to the arbitrator, the Court concluded that the arbitrator acted within his authority. The fact that the arbitrator referred to the liquidated damages clause as a "penalty clause" neither controlled, nor permitted an inference that the arbitrator exceeded his powers.

The Court then found that the arbitrator did not exceed his authority in awarding the other relief.

87018 Edward Elec. Co. v. Automation, Inc., 164 Ill. App. 3d 547, 115 Ill. Dec. 647, 518 N.E.2d 172 (1987), *appeal denied,* 121 Ill. 2d 568, 122 Ill. Dec. 436, 526 N.E.2d 829 (1988)

> II: A107-1978, Art. 13, Para. 13.2
> II: A117-1979, Art. 17, Para. 17.2
> II: A201-1976, Art. 7, Para. 7.9.1
> II: A401-1978, Art. 13, Para. 13.1
> II: A401-1978, Art. 13, Para. 13.2

87015 Diersen v. Joe Kleim Bldrs., Inc., 153 Ill. App. 3d 373, 106 Ill. Dec. 534, 505 N.E.2d 1325, *appeal denied,* 113 Ill. Dec. 296, 515 N.E.2d 105 (1987)

II:	A107-1978, Art. 13, Para. 13.2
II:	A117-1979, Art. 17, Para. 17.2
II:	A201-1976, Art. 7, Para. 7.9.1
II:	A401-1978, Art. 13, Para. 13.1
II:	B141-1977, Art. 9, Para. 9.1

Homeowner brought a breach of contract action against contractor. The trial court ordered a stay of the judicial proceedings and ordered arbitration and the owner appealed.

The arbitration clause in the owner-contractor agreement provided that "all claims, disputes and other matters in question relating to this Agreement, or the breach thereof" would be settled by arbitration.

The Appellate Court interpreted the arbitration clause as encompassing all disputes arising out of the contract. Moreover, owner's claim of fraud in the inducement was directed toward the contract as a whole and not solely against the arbitration clause. The Court found that since the owner's claim was within the scope of the clause the trial court was not required to resolve it before ordering the parties to submit to arbitration.

87016 Drzewinski v. Atlantic Scaffold & Ladder Co., 70 N.Y.2d 774, 521 N.Y.S.2d 216, 515 N.E.2d 902 (1987), *reh'g denied,* 70 N.Y.2d 999, 526 N.Y.S.2d 434, 521 N.E.2d 441 (1988)

III:	A107-1978, Art. 10, Para. 10.11
III:	A117-1979, Art. 14, Para. 14.11
III:	A201-1976, Art. 4, Para. 4.18.1
III:	A401-1978, Art. 11, Para. 11.11.1

A worker brought an action to recover damages resulting from his fall from scaffolding. Modifying the order of the Appellate Division, the New York Court of Appeals held that the owner and architect were entitled to full contractual indemnity. The multi-prime contract provided that each contractor was to "indemnify the Bank and the Architects against claims arising from his work, to the fullest extent permitted by law," and also contained a second indemnification provision which required each contractor to "indemnify and save harmless the Owner . . . and their respective employees from and against all losses and all claims, demands, payments, suits, actions, recoveries, and judgments of every nature and description brought or recovered against them by reason of any omission or act of the contractor, his agents or employees, in the execution of the work or in the guarding of it." Although the owner and architect had been found partially negligent, the contractual provisions in this instance clearly implied full contractual indemnity. In addition, as of the time of the accident, such full contractual indemnification was not prohibited by the statute in effect.

87014 Del E. Webb Constr. v. Richardson Hosp. Auth., 823 F.2d 145 (5th Cir. 1987)

II:	A107-1978, Art. 13, Para. 13.2
II:	A117-1979, Art. 17, Para. 17.2
I:	A201-1976, Art. 7, Para. 7.9.1
II:	A401-1978, Art. 13, Para. 13.1
II:	A401-1978, Art. 13, Para. 13.2
II:	A401-1978, Art. 13, Para. 13.3
II:	A401-1978, Art. 13, Para. 13.4
II:	A401-1978, Art. 13, Para. 13.5
II:	A401-1978, Art. 13, Para. 13.6
II:	B141-1977, Art. 9, Para. 9.1
II:	B141-1977, Art. 9, Para. 9.2
II:	B141-1977, Art. 9, Para. 9.3

Contractor brought an action against owner to recover delay damages. The owner counterclaimed and joined the architect and bonding companies as third party defendants. The architect filed a counterclaim against the contractor. The contractor then filed a motion to compel arbitration which was granted by the District Court. Subcontractor brought an action against contractor which was consolidated with the architect's action. The District Court ordered that all third party claims were to be settled in the same arbitration. The owner and architect appealed. The Court of Appeals reversed in part, holding that the consolidation was improper.

The owner and architect had entered into the American Institute of Architects Standard Form of Agreement Between Owner and Architect, Document No. B141, 1977 edition, which provided in Paragraph 9.1 that all disputes arising from the agreement were to be arbitrated. The owner and contractor entered into an American Institute of Architects Standard Form of Agreement Between Owner and Contractor which included the American Institute of Architects General Conditions of the Contract for Construction, Document No. A201, 1976 edition. The agreement provided in Paragraph 7.9.1 for arbitration of disputes arising from the contract documents.

Architect argued on appeal that it was not a party to the arbitration agreement between owner and contractor, that it did not consent to arbitration and could not be compelled to arbitrate pursuant to Paragraph 7.9.1 of the General Conditions. The Appellate Court found that although the architect could not be compelled to arbitrate under Paragraph 7.9.1, the contractor could compel the owner to arbitrate and, in turn, the owner could then compel the architect to arbitrate under Paragraph 9.1 of the owner-architect agreement. However, Paragraph 7.9.1 explicitly excluded the architect from a consolidated arbitration absent consent, by providing that "[n]o arbitration arising out of or relating to the Contract Documents shall include, by consolidation, joinder, or in any other manner, the Architect. . . ." Therefore, consolidation was improper.

or omission of the Contractor . . . regardless of whether or not it is caused in part by a party indemnified hereunder."

Reversing, the Supreme Court held that owner was entitled to recover its attorneys' fees pursuant to Paragraph 4.18.1 of the contract. The provision was not limited to liability for property damage sustained by third parties; the contractor agreed in Paragraph 4.18.1 to pay owner's attorneys' fees in certain situations and the collapse of the building due to contractors failure to conform to the specifications fell within the terms of that agreement.

The Court held further that the trial court properly excluded testimony that went to the issue of waiver. The plain language of Paragraphs 4.3.3 and 7.6.2 of the General Conditions precluded the contractor from asserting the defense of waiver.

87012   CIG Contractors, Inc. v. Mississippi State Bldg. Comm'n, 510 So. 2d 510 (Miss. 1987)

         I: A201-1970, Art. 6, Para. 6.2.1

The Appellate Court found that where each owner-prime contractor agreement contained a provision stating that "all prime contractors and all subcontractors shall coordinate all work, one with the other, so as to facilitate the general progress of the work" the owner had no implied contractual duty to one prime contractor to coordinate the work of other contractors. The parties had entered into the American Institute of Architects Standard Form of Agreement Between Owner and Contractor, Document No. A101, 1974 edition, which included the American Institute of Architects General Conditions of the Contract for Construction, Document No. A201, 1970 edition.

87013   Cuhaci & Peterson Architects, Inc. v. Huber Constr. Co., 516 So. 2d 1096 (Fla. Dist. Ct. App. 1987), *review denied*, 525 So. 2d 878 (Fla. 1988)

         II: A107-1978, Art. 10, Para. 10.11
         II: A117-1979, Art. 14, Para. 14.11
         I: A201-1976, Art. 4, Para. 4.18.1
         II: A401-1978, Art. 11, Para. 11.11.1

Architect brought an indemnification action against contractor for expenditure of attorneys' fees and costs in defending a wrongful death action brought by subcontractor's employee. The trial court entered summary judgment in contractor's favor finding that the indemnity provision of the owner-contractor agreement was void and unenforceable under Florida state statute. The architect argued on appeal that because it was not making a claim for indemnity for its own negligence the Florida statute was not applicable.

The District Court of Appeal reversed. It held that the Florida statute applied only in circumstances where a party, by contract, seeks to obtain indemnification from another party for its own active negligence. Here, where architect sought indemnification for attorneys' fees incurred in successfully defending a third party claim, the statute did not apply.

The owner-engineer agreement provided that owner would pay to the engineer "all losses, damages and expenses, including legal fees (but not including losses, damages and expense due to the negligent or wrongful acts of Engineer's officers, Engineer's Project Manager or Engineer's Resident Construction Manager, and lawsuits, if any, between the parties hereto), and payment of all judgments or settlements (as approved by Owner), which are actually suffered by engineer in the course and directly as a result of performing the services, to the extent that such losses, damages and other expenses are not compensated for by insurance; provided that Engineer shall have maintained in full force and effect the insurance coverage required under Section 7 hereof."

The Appellate Court concluded that this provision did not contain a clear and unequivocal statement that owner would indemnify engineer for damages arising out of engineer's own negligence. In fact, it specifically excluded any indemnification for expenses arising out of negligence on the part of named employees of engineer. The Court rejected engineer's argument that because the provision stated that owner would not indemnify engineer for damage caused by the negligence of its officers, project manager or resident construction manager, the Court should infer that the parties intended that owner would indemnify engineer for damage caused by those employees who were not specifically named. The Court held that such an inference was precluded by the contract language and prevailing law. The Court found that contractor could recover against engineer only if it was able to establish that engineer's negligence contributed to the damage sustained by owner.

87011 Chesapeake & Potomac Telephone Co. of Virginia v. Sisson & Ryan, Inc., 234 Va. 492, 362 S.E.2d 723 (1987)

II:	A107-1978, Art. 10, Para. 10.11	
II:	A117-1979, Art. 14, Para. 14.11	
I:	A201-1976, Art. 4, Para. 4.3.3	
I:	A201-1976, Art. 4, Para. 4.18.1	
I:	A201-1976, Art. 7, Para. 7.6.2	
II:	A401-1978, Art. 11, Para. 11.11.1	

Owner brought a breach of contract action against contractor after the building under construction collapsed following a heavy rain. The jury returned a verdict for owner but the trial court denied owner's claim for attorneys' fees. Owner appealed.

The owner and contractor had entered into an American Institute of Architects Standard Form of Agreement between Owner and Contractor which included the American Institute of Architects General Conditions of the Contract for Construction, Document No. A201, 1976 edition. Paragraph 4.18.1 of the General Conditions provided in pertinent part that contractor "shall indemnify and hold harmless the Owner . . . from and against all claims, damages, losses and expenses, including but not limited to attorneys' fees, arising out of or resulting from the performance of the Work, provided that any such claim, damage, loss or expense (1) is attributable to . . . injury to or destruction of tangible property (other than the Work itself) and (2) is caused in whole or in part by any negligent act

documents." Furthermore, "if required by engineer prior to approval of final payment, contractor shall promptly, without cost to owner and as specified by engineer, either correct any defective work, whether or not fabricated, installed or completed, or, if the work has been rejected by engineer, remove it from the site and replace it with nondefective work. If the contractor does correct such defective work or remove and replace such rejected work within a reasonable time, all as specified in a written notice from engineer, owner may have the deficiency corrected or the reject work removed and replaced." The contract also contained an inspection clause which provided that "All grades and materials furnished for grading operations shall be subject to inspection by the Owner and/or Engineer. After establishment of proper grading, the Engineer, Owner, and/or their representative shall inspect the existing grades as to their proper elevation. Compaction tests for all areas will be made by the Inspector, if the area does not meet the specifications, the Contractor shall make every effort to obtain the required density. The Contractor shall bear the cost of retesting those areas that previously failed compaction testing."

In determining the admissibility of certain evidence the Appellate Court interpreted the "Inspection" provision of the owner-contractor agreement. The contractor argued that the owner was obligated to watch the job more closely to prevent the contractor from using faulty material. The Court found that the contract did not obligate the owner to guard the contractor against his own mistakes. The contract did not state that the "owner shall inspect" but rather it stated that grades and materials were subject to inspection with no time fixed for such inspection except by the words "after establishment of proper grading." The Court interpreted these words to mean when the job was completed. The Court concluded that the provision that work was subject to inspection did not create a duty on the owner to provide such inspections, nor penalize the owner for failure to do so. The contractor had the primary duty to see that the work was performed in accordance with the specifications. The Court concluded that it was no defense that the owner failed to "catch" the contractor and stop further shoddy work where the contract clearly provided that "Contractor shall be responsible to see that the finished work complies accurately with the contract documents." The the duty of constant inspection was upon the contractor.

87010   Burns & Roe, Inc. v. Central Marine Power Co., 659 F. Supp. 141 (D. Me. 1987)

         III: A107-1978, Art. 10, Para. 10.11
         III: A117-1979, Art. 14, Para. 14.11
         III: A201-1976, Art. 4, Para. 4.18.1
         III: A401-1978, Art. 11, Para. 11.11.1

Engineer brought an action for a declaratory judgment that owner was contractually obligated to indemnify the engineer for damages, expenses, legal fees, judgments or approved settlements arising out of a breach of contract action. The contractor cross-claimed for indemnification against the engineer for any responsibility the engineer shared for damages incurred by the owner.

agents or servants, by reason of injury, death or any claim while in pursuit of this contract and that all employees, agents or servants of the CONTRACTOR shall in no manner be construed to be employees of the OWNER." The contractor was required to furnish public liability insurance "indemnifying and saving harmless the OWNER from any and all personal injury claims arising thereunder by reason of the performance of this contract."

Reversing, the Appellate Court found that the provision requiring the contractor to furnish public liability insurance was not void under the Illinois statute. It was not an indemnification agreement; the language requiring that contractor furnish public liability insurance "indemnifying and saving harmless" the owner did not make the provision an unenforceable indemnity or hold harmless agreement. Rather, the contract provision at issue was an agreement to obtain public liability insurance for all personal injury claims arising from the performance of the contract, including insurance for the owner's benefit. The Court held that the insurance provision was therefore enforceable under the Illinois statute.

87009 Burlington v. Arnold Constr. Co., 727 S.W.2d 241 (Tenn. Ct. App. 1987)

III:	A107-1978, Art. 8, Para. 8.3	
III:	A107-1978, Art. 9, Para. 9.4	
III:	A107-1978, Art. 10, Para. 10.1	
III:	A107-1978, Art. 10, Para. 10.4	
III:	A117-1979, Art. 12, Para. 12.3	
III:	A117-1979, Art. 13, Para. 13.4	
III:	A117-1979, Art. 14, Para. 14.1	
III:	A117-1979, Art. 14, Para. 14.4	
III:	A201-1976, Art. 2, Para. 2.2.3	
III:	A201-1976, Art. 3, Para. 3.4.1	
III:	A201-1976, Art. 4, Para. 4.3.1	
III:	A201-1976, Art. 4, Para. 4.5.1	

In owner's action against contractor and contractor's surety for defective performance, contractor and its surety appealed from the lower court's entry of judgment for owner, and the dismissal of contractor's counterclaim against the owner and cross-suit against the engineer.

The owner-contractor agreement provided that contractor "shall be solely responsible for the means, methods, techniques, sequences and procedures of construction" and that contractor "shall be responsible to see that the finished work complies accurately with the contract documents." The contractor guaranteed the work would be of good quality free from faults or defects and would be performed in accordance with the contract documents. The contract also provided that "Neither observations by engineer or inspections, tests, or approvals by persons other than contractors shall relieve contractor from his obligation to perform the work in accordance with requirements of the contract

Paragraph 1.1.3 of the General Conditions. The owner had acquired a policy of property insurance on the building.

The owner maintained that the waiver provision contained in Paragraph 11.4 of the owner-architect agreement applied only during construction and that the insurance and waiver lapsed at substantial completion and occupancy. The owner also argued that the risk of casualty damage was on the contractor until the date of substantial completion when it shifted to the owner, and that the contractor then had no insurable interest in the project; consequently, the only claim contemplated by the waiver was a claim covered by builders' risk insurance.

The Supreme Court found that the contractor and architect had insurable interests subject to the property insurance in effect on the date of the loss. Although the building was substantially completed and occupied, until final payment was made, both the contractor and architect had a substantial economic interest in preserving the building from loss. Furthermore, the Court found that the insurance and waiver provisions were not limited to the time of substantial completion or occupancy. Paragraph 11.3.1 required the owner to "purchase and maintain property insurance upon the entire Work" insuring "the interest of . . . [all parties] in the Work against "all risks." The waiver clause in Paragraph 11.3.6 applied not only to claims "covered by insurance obtained pursuant to this Paragraph" but also to claims covered by "any other property insurance applicable to the Work" as defined in Paragraph 1.1.3. The Court concluded that the loss suffered by the owner occurred while "the Work" was still in progress and reasoned that the insurance and waiver provisions, when read together, proved that the parties agreed to shift the risk of loss from themselves to a commercial insurer. The Court therefore held that the owner had waived its right to recover against contractor and architect.

87008   Bosio v. Branigar Org., Inc., 154 Ill. App. 3d 611, 107 Ill. Dec. 105, 506 N.E.2d 996 (1987)

Ill:	A107-1978, Art. 10, Para. 10.11
Ill:	A107-1978, Art. 17, Para. 17.1
Ill:	A117-1979, Art. 14, Para. 14.11
Ill:	A117-1979, Art. 21, Para. 21.1
Ill:	A201-1976, Art. 4, Para. 4.18.1
Ill:	A201-1976, Art. 11, Para. 11.1.1
Ill:	A401-1978, Art. 11, Para. 11.11.1

Contractor's injured employee brought a personal injury action against owner. Owner brought a third party indemnity action against contractor. The trial court dismissed the third party action and owner appealed. The issue on appeal was whether the contract provision which required contractor to provide public liability insurance for owner's benefit was enforceable under an Illinois statute which made indemnification agreements in construction contracts void and unenforceable.

The owner-contractor agreement provided that contractor "will save and keep harmless the OWNER from any and all claims that may arise on the part of any of its employees,

right to seek damages for hindrances or delays. The Court concluded that the right to recover damages for hindrances or delays was comprehensively provided for in the no-damage-for-delay clause, subject to the limitations contained in the clause and agreed to by the subcontractor when the subcontractor signed the contract. The Court held that the no-damage-for-delay clause was enforceable and binding upon the subcontractor.

87007 Blue Cross of Southwestern Virginia v. McDevitt & Street Co., 234 Va. 191, 360 S.E.2d 825 (1987)

III:	A107-1978, Art. 7, Para. 7.4
III:	A107-1978, Art. 17, Para. 17.1
III:	A107-1978, Art. 17, Para. 17.2
III:	A107-1978, Art. 17, Para. 17.3
III:	A107-1978, Art. 17, Para. 17.6
III:	A117-1979, Art. 11, Para. 11.4
III:	A117-1979, Art. 21, Para. 21.1
III:	A117-1979, Art. 21, Para. 21.2
III:	A117-1979, Art. 21, Para. 21.2
III:	A117-1979, Art. 21, Para. 21.3
III:	A117-1979, Art. 21, Para. 21.6
I:	A201-1976, Art. 1, Para. 1.1.3
I:	A201-1976, Art. 11, Para. 11.3.1
I:	A201-1976, Art. 11, Para. 11.3.6
I:	A201-1976, Art. 11, Para. 11.4

Owner brought a breach of contract action against contractor and architect for damages resulting from freezing and bursting pipes. The trial court held that owner had waived its contractual rights against contractor and architect. The issue on appeal was whether the trial court misconstrued the contract language. The Supreme Court affirmed.

The owner and architect had entered into the American Institute of Architects Standard Form of Agreement Between Owner and Architect, Document No. B141, 1977 edition; the owner and contractor had entered into an American Institute of Architects Standard Form of Agreement Between Owner and Contractor, which incorporated by reference the American Institute of Architects General Conditions of the Contract for Construction, Document No. A201, 1976 edition. Paragraph 11.4 of the owner-architect agreement provided that the owner and architect waived all rights against each other for damages covered by property insurance. Paragraph 11.3.1 of the General Conditions required the owner to purchase and maintain property insurance on the "entire Work at the site to the full insurable value thereof." In Paragraph 11.3.6 the owner and contractor waived all rights against each other and against the architect for "damage caused by fire or other perils to the extent covered by insurance obtained pursuant to this Paragraph 11.3 or any other property insurance applicable to the Work. . . ." The work was defined in the intent of the contract but not disagreements concerning the performance of the contract. The Court found that ordinarily arbitration clauses contained a requirement by which the parties arbitrated "any controversy or claim arising out of or relating to [the] contract or the breach thereof" or, with minor variation, "any controversy concerning the interpretation, performance or application of [the] contract." However, the disputed clause required that the parties arbitrate only disagreements as to the intent of the contract. The Court concluded that the parties' failure to use phrases or terms ordinarily included in an arbitration clause was evidence that they did not agree to arbitrate all the issues arising out of their business relationship.

87006   B.J. Harland Elec. Co. v. Granger Bros., Inc., 24 Mass. App. Ct. 506, 510 N.E.2d 765 (1987), *review denied,* 400 Mass. 1105, 513 N.E.2d 1288 (1987), *review denied,* 401 Mass. 1101, 517 N.E.2d 1289 (1987)

III:	A201-1976, Art. 5, Para. 5.3.1
III:	A201-1976, Art. 8, Para. 8.3.4
III:	A201-1976, Art. 12, Para. 12.3.1
III:	A401-1978, Art. 11, Para. 11.9.1
III:	A401-1978, Art. 11, Para. 11.10.1
III:	A401-1978, Art. 12, Para. 12.1.1

Subcontractor brought an action under the state public works payment bond statute against contractor and contractor's surety, to recover under the bond extras subcontractor claimed were outside of the contract price. The trial court entered judgment for subcontractor. The Appellate Court reversed the judgment on the ground that the damages claimed by the subcontractor were delay damages that were precluded by the no-damage-for-delay clause in the subcontract.

The General Conditions of the owner-contractor agreement, which were incorporated into the subcontract, provided that "Except as otherwise provided by law the contractor shall not be entitled to damages on account of any hindrances or delays, avoidable or unavoidable; but if such delay be occasioned by the awarding authority, the contractor may be entitled to an extension of time only, in which to complete the work, to be determined by the designer."

The Appellate Court rejected the subcontractor's argument that the no-damage-for-delay clause was not applicable to its claim because it was not seeking damages for delay; rather, subcontractor claimed the increased cost of performing the work piecemeal, out of sequence and in winter weather, were the direct result of owner's failure to begin, prosecute and complete its work in an orderly manner and owner's failure to provide winter heat and weather protection. The Court found that any distinction between delay and hindrance damages was one without a difference. The contract spoke to both, "hindrance or delays" bringing subcontractor's claims within the preclusive terms of the no-damage-for-delay clause.

Furthermore, the Court concluded, reading the contract as a whole, that nothing in the provisions incorporating the language of the state statute gave the subcontractor the

for twenty items. The bid gave a unit and total price for each of the twenty items. The bid also gave a total contract price based on the sum of the total price of each item.

The court found that the use of the plural "prices" suggested that payment was to be based on the unit prices stated and not on the total contract price, which was also stated. The Court found further that other provisions of the contract did not remove the ambiguities. For example, the definition of contract price was the "total monies payable to the CONTRACTOR under the terms and conditions of the CONTRACT DOCUMENTS." The General Conditions required a change order to alter the contract price and listed the methods for determining the value of any increase or decrease in the contract price. The Court found, however, that this provision did not provide any guidance for determining the initial value of the contract price. Furthermore, the provision setting out the method for making partial payments to the contractor did not indicate on what basis the contract price was to be determined. After reviewing the contract provisions, the Court, based on the testimony, upheld the trial court's finding that the parties intended the owner-contractor agreement to be a unit price contract with the price based on the actual amount of work performed.

In addressing the issue of whether the contractor substantially completed the work, the Court found that where the contract defined substantial completion as "The date as certified by the ENGINEER when the construction of the PROJECT or a specified part thereof is sufficiently completed, in accordance with the CONTRACT DOCUMENTS, so that the PROJECT or specified part can be utilized for the purposes for which it was intended" the Court determined that the project was substantially completed when the water lines could be used by the owner.

In addressing the issue of whether the contractor was entitled to recover for extras the Court concluded that, based on a review of the record, the claims for extras were not included under the terms of the contract where the work was not authorized by the contract or by change order and the cost could not be determined from the contract. The Court found that because the items of extra work were not specifically alleged as being owed, the trial court erred in receiving evidence on the value of the items over the objection of the owner.

87005 Beckham v. William Bayley Co., 655 F. Supp. 288 (N.D. Tex. 1987)

III:	A107-1978, Art. 13, Para. 13.2
III:	A117-1979, Art. 17, Para. 17.2
III:	A201-1976, Art. 7, Para. 7.9.1
III:	A401-1978, Art. 13, Para. 13.1
III:	B141-1977, Art. 9, Para. 9.1

The Appellate Court found that where the arbitration clause provided that "Any disagreement between the Seller [Bayley] and the Purchaser [Beckham] as to the intent of this contract, at the request of either, shall be presented for arbitration in accordance with the requirements set forth by the American Institute of Architects, or the American Arbitration Association" the parties were required to arbitrate disagreements regarding

87003   Ambrose v. Biggs, 156 Ill. App. 3d 515, 108 Ill. Dec. 918, 509 N.E.2d 614 (1987)

        III: A107-1978, Art. 18, Para. 18.1
        III: A107-1978, Art. 18, Para. 18.2
        III: A107-1978, Art. 18, Para. 18.3
        III: A117-1979, Art. 22, Para. 22.1
        III: A117-1979, Art. 22, Para. 22.2
        III: A117-1979, Art. 22, Para. 22.3
        III: A201-1976, Art. 12, Para. 12.1.1
        III: A201-1976, Art. 12, Para. 12.1.2
        III: A201-1976, Art. 12, Para. 12.1.3
        III: A201-1976, Art. 12, Para. 12.1.4
        III: A201-1976, Art. 12, Para. 12.3.1

Contractor brought an action against owner, seeking damages for breach of contract. The trial court allowed recovery for extras, and the Appellate Court reversed. The contract provided that extras must be evidenced in writing and any adjustment to the contract price resulting from the extras was to be determined by mutual agreement of the parties. Therefore, the trial court erred in awarding the contractor the extra compensation where the contractor failed to make timely demands, there was no proof that the owner agreed to pay for the extras, and the contractor did not provide the owner with the sworn contractor's statement as required by state statute.

87004   American Druggists Ins. Co. v. Henry Contracting, Inc., 505 So. 2d 734 (La. Ct. App. 1987)

        II: A107-1978, Art. 14, Para. 14.2
        II: A117-1978, Art. 18, Para. 18.2
        II: A201-1976, Art. 8, Para. 8.1.3

Creditor brought an action against contractor to garnish funds which owner did not pay to contractor under the contract. The trial court entered judgment for creditor in an amount which was appealed by both the creditor and the owner. The Appellate Court upheld the trial court's admission of parol evidence to determine the intention of the parties as to the contract price where the owner-contractor agreement was ambiguous as to whether the price was fixed or dependent on the quantity of work actually required.

The contract consisted of a number of documents, including the advertisement for bids, information for bidders, the bid, notice of award, the agreement, a statement of general conditions, and a supplemental statement of general conditions. In its bid for the project, contractor stated that it would perform all work for the construction of a water transmission line "in strict accordance with the CONTRACT DOCUMENTS, within the time set forth therein, and at the prices stated below." The prices stated in the bid were

II: A201-1976, Art. 14, Para. 14.2.1
III: B141-1977, Art. 1, Para. 1.5.3
III: B141-1977, Art. 1, Para. 1.5.4

Owner brought an action against contractor for damages resulting from contractor's faulty installation of a water pipeline. The owner appealed from the trial court's award of damages and, on cross-appeal, contractor raised the issue of whether owner's acceptance of the project limited recovery to the one-year warranty period. The Supreme Court held that it was not so limited and affirmed that aspect of the judgment.

The owner-contractor agreement provided in Section 7.5 that inspections by the engineer, which were authorized in Section 7.6, did not relieve the contractor from his obligation to perform the work in accordance with the contract. Section 7.7, which was similar to Paragraph 13.1.1 of the American Institute of Architects General Conditions of the Contract for Construction, Document No. A201, 1976 edition, required the contractor, at the request of the engineer, to uncover the work for observation. Section 12.1, similar to Paragraph 4.3.1 of the General Conditions, authorized the contractor to supervise and direct the work and provided that the contractor was "solely responsible for the means, methods, techniques, sequences and procedures of construction." Section 16.1, similar to Paragraphs 13.2.3 and 13.2.6 of the General Conditions, provided that the contractor replace any work not in accordance with the contract documents. In addition, the owner had the right to terminate the contractor under Section 18.2. Section 20.1 provided that "Any payment, however, final or otherwise, shall not release the CONTRACTOR or his sureties from any obligations under the CONTRACT DOCUMENTS of the Performance Bond and Payment Bonds." Section 27.1 provided that the engineer was acting as the owner's representative with authority to interpret the intent of the contract documents and with the right to visit the site to determine if the work was proceeding in accordance with the contract documents. The agreement also provided that the contractor repair damage or defects for one year.

The Supreme Court found that these contract provisions clearly indicated that the intent of the parties was that, even though the contractor had to allow the owner and its representatives to inspect the work, the contractor was not released from its obligation to perform its work in accordance with the contract documents. The Court held that owner's acceptance did not limit owner's recovery to defects that appeared within the one-year warranty period because the defects were latent and could not have been reasonably detected. Furthermore, the engineer was not required by the contract to constantly watch over the contractor to ensure compliance with the contract.

The Court also held that the one-year warranty did not limit the contractor's responsibility for repairs to one year since the contractor had breached the contract and the defects were latent. The Court reasoned that if the one-year warranty was to be the owner's exclusive remedy, or if actions for breach of contract were to be limited to a one year period, it was necessary for the contract to contain clear and unequivocal language to that effect. The Court remanded on other grounds.

87001   Aetna Casualty & Sur. Co. v. Jelac Corp., 505 So. 2d 37 (Fla. Dist. Ct. App. 1987)

    II: A107-1978, Art. 13, Para. 13.2
    II: A117-1979, Art. 17, Para. 17.2
    II: A201-1976, Art. 7, Para. 7.9.1
    I: A401-1978, Art. 13, Para. 13.2
    II: B141-1977, Art. 9, Para. 9.1

Subcontractor brought an action against contractor's surety to recover for nonpayment by contractor. The circuit court denied surety's motion to dismiss based on the arbitration provision contained in Paragraph 13.2 of the American Institute of Architects Standard Form of Agreement Between Contractor and Subcontractor, Document No. A401, 1978 edition. The District Court of Appeal affirmed. Paragraph 13.2 precluded the surety from asserting such a contractual right of arbitration; in addition, the surety was only an incidental beneficiary to the contract and could not enforce the arbitration provision.

87002   All Seasons Water Users Ass'n, Inc. v. Northern Improvements Co., 399 N.W.2d 278 (N.D. 1987), *appeal on remand*, 417 N.W.2d 831 (N.D. 1988)

    III: A107-1978, Art. 8, Para. 8.3
    III: A107-1978, Art. 10, Para. 10.1
    III: A107-1978, Art. 17, Para. 17.1
    III: A107-1978, Art. 17, Para. 17.2
    III: A107-1978, Art. 17, Para. 17.3
    III: A107-1978, Art. 17, Para. 17.6
    III: A117-1979, Art. 12, Para. 12.3
    III: A117-1979, Art. 14, Para. 14.1
    III: A117-1979, Art. 21, Para. 21.1
    III: A117-1979, Art. 21, Para. 21.2
    III: A117-1979, Art. 21, Para. 21.3
    III: A117-1979, Art. 21, Para. 21.6
    III: A117-1979, Art. 24, Para. 24.2
    II: A201-1976, Art. 2, Para. 2.2.2
    II: A201-1976, Art. 2, Para. 2.2.3
    II: A201-1976, Art. 4, Para. 4.3.1
    II: A201-1976, Art. 4, Para. 4.3.3
    II: A201-1976, Art. 13, Para. 13.1.1
    II: A201-1976, Art. 13, Para. 13.2.2
    II: A201-1976, Art. 13, Para. 13.2.3
    II: A201-1976, Art. 13, Para. 13.2.6

found that the limitation of damage clause in engineer's contract did not limit owner's damages for breach of contract because the engineer had failed to prepare the plans by the date set forth in the contract. The limitation clause provided that "[t]he OWNER agrees to limit the ENGINEER'S liability to the OWNER and to all Construction Contractors and Subcontractors on the Project, due to the ENGINEER'S professional negligent acts, errors or omissions, such that the total aggregate liability of the ENGINEER to those named shall not exceed Fifty Thousand Dollars ($50,000.00) or the ENGINEER'S total fee for services rendered on this project, whichever is greater." This language clearly limited engineer's liability for "negligent acts, errors or omissions" but it did not contain language specifically limiting the engineer's liability for breach of contract.

86075 Yeshiva Univ. v. Fidelity & Deposit Co. of Maryland, 116 A.D.2d 49. 500 N.Y.S.2d 241, *appeal denied,* 68 N.Y.2d 603 (1986)

III:	A401-1978, Art. 6, Para. 6.1	
III:	A401-1978, Art. 6, Para. 6.2	
III:	A401-1978, Art. 11, Para. 11.2.5	
III:	A401-1978, Art. 12, Para. 12.4	
III:	A401-1978, Art. 12, Para. 12.6.1	

In owner's action against subcontractor's performance bond surety, the lower court denied the surety's motion to dismiss the action as time barred. It found that the two-year contractual limitation period had never commenced to run. The Appellate Division reversed, holding that the lower court erroneously relied upon two provisions in the subcontract. The first provision stated that the "balance owing," called "final payment" in large, printed, block letters set off in the margin, was to become due and payable within 60 days after the completion of all work called for in the subcontract and its acceptance by contractor, owner and architect. The second provided that contractor could hold the subcontractor responsible for "unsound work or materials" permitted to remain on the site during construction for up to one year after completion of the entire project, and that any payments made by contractor to the subcontractor during this period were not to be construed as evidence of an acceptance of the subcontractor's work.

The Appellate Division found that the intent of the second clause was to permit the contractor to make full payment to the subcontractor without waiving the subcontractor's liability for patent defects. The clause related to the duration of the subcontractor's liability for patent defects and, though its enforceability would be problematic were it to result in a lengthening of the statutory period, it had nothing to do with the question of when liability of the subcontractor would accrue. The Court also found that the first clause did not support the view that final payment never fell due where the requirement that the work be accepted as well as completed was of doubtful effect. The fact that the facilities were defective did not mean, at least for purposes of the contract provision in question, that their construction had never been completed.

III: B141-1977, Art. 14, Para. 14.2.2

In owner's counterclaim against the engineer for cost overruns, the trial court found that the engineer had breached the agreement. Before the Supreme Court of Louisiana, the issue was whether the engineer breached its contract by failing to notify the owner until after completion of a "cost-plus" project, without a maximum, that the price had more than doubled. The engineer argued that it did not guarantee the cost of the project and could not be held liable for the overruns. The Supreme Court affirmed.

The owner-engineer agreement provided that during the five phases of the design and construction the engineer gave his "Opinion of the Construction Cost" and was required in the Documents Phase to "advise OWNER of adjustments to previous Opinions of the Construction Cost when changes in requirements, general market conditions, or other conditions warrant. . . ." In addition, the agreement provided that "when the Agreement stipulates that the OWNER shall pay WILLIAMS for Basic Services performed under Article 1 pursuant to a percentage of the Net Construction Cost, the fee shall be initially computed on WILLIAMS' Opinion of the Net Construction Cost. . . . WILLIAMS' fee shall be adjusted by similar computations . . . prepared during the various phases, and, finally, at the conclusion of the services, by computations based on the actual Net Construction Cost of the PROJECT to the OWNER." The engineer was to act as the owner's agent and the engineer's "Opinion of the Net Construction Cost . . . is his best opinion of the probable lowest responsible Contractor's bid for the Work and is supplied as a guide only. Since WILLIAMS has no control over the labor and material market or over competitive bidding and contractor market conditions, he cannot and does not guarantee the accuracy of such cost opinions. . . ."

The Supreme Court found that the engineer failed to make complete and reliable disclosures to the owner's of their construction options and breached the contract by failing to reestimate the cost during construction. The Court rejected the engineer's argument that the written contract was abrogated by the cost-plus, fast track construction, and found that the owners were more in need of reliable estimates of construction costs under the contract than they would have been if bids had been received. Had bids been received, the engineer's responsibility for estimating costs would have ended when he completed his design and bids were submitted. The Court concluded that because the design and construction phases were pursued simultaneously, the engineer had an ongoing responsibility to keep the owner advised of the costs. Although the jury did not find that the engineer acted in bad faith, the owner had placed "immense faith" in both the engineer and the contractor and was lulled into a false sense of security by the engineer.

86074 W. William Graham, Inc. v. Cave City, 289 Ark. 105, 709 S.W.2d 94 (1986)

III: B141-1977, Art. 1, Para. 1.5.10
III: B141-1977, Art. 11, Para. 11.4

In owner's breach of contract action against the design engineer, the trial court awarded owner its full amount of consequential delay damages. The Supreme Court affirmed. It

architect's duties would be provided for in the owner-contractor agreement. Testimony established that a higher design fee would have been charged by the architect had the architect contracted to supervise the work of the contractor.

The Court of Appeals affirmed the dismissal. It found that the limited duty of the architect under Paragraph 2.2.4 was clear, and upheld the findings of the trial court that the design was not faulty or defective based on the architect's own testimony.

86072 Williams v. Gervais F. Favrot Co., 499 So. 2d 623 (La. Ct. App. 1986), *writ denied,* 503 So. 2d 19 (La. 1987), *later proceeding,* 573 So. 2d 533 (La. Ct. App.), *cert. denied,* 576 So. 2d 49 (La. 1991)

II:	A107-1978, Art. 10, Para. 10.6	
II:	A107-1978, Art. 11, Para. 11.2	
II:	A117-1979, Art. 14, Para. 14.6	
II:	A117-1979, Art. 15, Para. 15.2	
I:	A201-1976, Art. 4, Para. 4.7.2	
I:	A201-1976, Art. 5, Para. 5.3.1	
I:	A401-1978, Art. 11, Para. 11.3.1	
II:	A401-1978, Art. 12, Para. 12.3.2	

Engineer sued owner to recover professional fee; owner asserted a counterclaim for damages resulting from costs overruns. The trial court awarded the engineer its fee, but also found that it breached the agreement. The Court of Appeal reversed the engineer's award. Before the Supreme Court, the In decedent's estate's wrongful death action against contractor the Appellate Court found that the existence of the subcontract was not determinative of whether workers' compensation benefits would insure to subcontractor's employees but merely served to establish the relationship between contractor and subcontractor. Furthermore, the subcontract did not make subcontractor's employees statutory employees of the contractor. The Court also found that the subcontract language, which provided that "[t]he contractor shall give all notices and comply with all laws, ordinances, rules and regulations bearing on the conduct of the work," did not create a third party beneficiary relationship between decedent and contractor entitling decedent to recover breach of contract damages against contractor.

86073 Williams Eng'g, Inc. v. Goodyear, 496 So. 2d 1012 (La. 1986)

II:	B141-1977, Art. 1, Para. 1.1.5	
II:	B141-1977, Art. 1, Para. 1.2.2	
II:	B141-1977, Art. 1, Para. 1.3.3	
II:	B141-1977, Art. 1, Para. 1.4.1	
II:	B141-1977, Art. 3, Para. 3.2.1	
III:	B141-1977, Art. 14, Para. 14.2.1	

86070 W.E. Erickson Constr., Inc. v. Congress-Kenilworth Corp., 115 Ill. 2d 119, 104 Ill. Dec. 676, 503 N.E.2d 233 (1986)

II:	A101-1977, Art. 5
II:	A107-1978, Art. 4, Para. 4.1
II:	A107-1978, Art. 4, Para. 4.2
II:	A111-1978, Art. 13, Para. 13.1
II:	A111-1978, Art. 14, Para. 14.3
II:	A117-1979, Art. 8, Para. 8.1
II:	A117-1979, Art. 8, Para. 8.2
III:	A201-1976, Art. 9, Para. 9.3.1
III:	A201-1976, Art. 9, Para. 9.5.1

Contractor brought an action against owner to recover amounts due under the contract. The trial court awarded contractor damages under one count of its complaint and dismissed the remaining counts, as well as the owner's counterclaim. Both parties appealed. The Appellate Court upheld the finding of the trial court and both parties appealed to the Illinois Supreme Court. Among numerous issues on appeal was whether contractor was entitled to interest despite contractor's failure to comply with the contract provision requiring the contractor to make written application for monthly progress payments.

The owner-contractor agreement provided that contractor was obligated to apply for payment "at least ten days before each payment falls due . . . showing in complete detail all the moneys paid out or costs incurred by him on account of the Cost of Work during the previous month for which he is to be reimbursed." The owner was then obligated to pay the amount due within 30 days of the application.

The Supreme Court found that the contract specifically predicated payment and interest on the timely submission of payment applications. The Court found that because contractor failed to comply with the terms of the contract no interest was due.

86071 Weill Constr. Co. v. Thibodeaux, 491 So. 2d 166 (La. Ct. App. 1986)

II:	A107-1978, Art. 8, Para. 8.3
II:	A117-1979, Art. 12, Para. 12.3
I:	A201-1976, Art. 2, Para. 2.2.4
I:	B141-1977, Art. 1, Para. 1.5.5

The trial court dismissed owner's third party action against the architect for defective design and inadequate supervision of construction. On appeal, the owner argued that the architect was obligated to supervise the work under the provisions of the owner-contractor agreement which included Paragraph 2.2.4 of the American Institute of Architects General Conditions of the Contract for Construction, Document No. A201, 1976 edition. No written owner-architect agreement was executed because the parties agreed that the

by fire or other perils to the extent covered by insurance obtained pursuant to this Paragraph 11.3. . . ."

The Appellate Court upheld the judgment below. It determined that the indemnity provisions of the contract did not impose a duty on contractor not waived by Subparagraph 11.3.6. The indemnity did not conflict with the waiver because it dealt with the contractors duty to protect owner from liability for third party claims, not from claims by the owner and that further the enforcement of the indemnity under the circumstances of this case would render the waiver totally meaningless. The Court rejected owners contention that the waiver was only for the actual amount of insurance the owner recovered; such a reading would allow the owner to buy little or no insurance and render the waiver illusory. All damages caused by the collapse, not just the work itself, were subject to the waiver, since the damage at the site did not exist independently from the work but arose from it. The Court also held that damages for delay and for business reputation were covered by the waiver since consequential damages were specifically mentioned in the waiver provision. And as a final matter, the Court determined that the waiver extended to claims for breach of warranty, strict liability and implied warranty. The parties had agreed to have the owner's insurance bear all risk of losses that would have been covered by the all risk insurance described in the contract. Because the damages could have been insured, all claims arising from the collapse were waived.

86069 Village of Turtle Lake v. Orvedahl Constr., Inc., 135 Wis. 2d 385, 400 N.W.2d 475 (1986)

> III: A107-1978, Art. 13, Para. 13.2
> III: A117-1979, Art. 17, Para. 17.2
> III: A201-1976, Art. 7, Para. 7.9.1
> III: A401-1978, Art. 13, Para. 13.1
> III: B141-1977, Art. 9, Para. 9.1

Contractor filed a demand for arbitration to correct a bid calculation error. The owner contested arbitrability and sued to enjoin the arbitration. The Circuit Court permanently enjoined arbitration, and the Court of Appeals reversed.

The owner-contractor agreement contained an arbitration clause which stated that "All claims, disputes and other matters in question arising out of, or relating to, the CONTRACT DOCUMENTS or the breach thereof, except for claims which have been waived by the making and acceptance of final payment . . . shall be decided by arbitration. . . ."

The Court held that the owner was bound to arbitrate the bid dispute where the bid was a contract document as defined in the owner-contractor agreement. By contractually binding the contractor after determining that the contractor was the lowest responsible bidder, the owner bound itself to the terms of the contract including the agreement to arbitrate.

Supplementary Conditions drafted by the parties. The contract provided for arbitration "unless the parties mutually agree otherwise." The Supplemental Conditions provided that if the owner consented "all claims, disputes and other matters in question between the Contractor and Owner arising out of, or relating to, the Contract Documents . . . shall be decided by arbitration . . . unless the parties mutually agree otherwise."

The Court of Appeals affirmed. The subcontractor asserted its right to arbitrate with the surety as an assignee of the contractor rather than as surety on the performance bond. In addition, the Supplemental Conditions explicitly amended the arbitration clause to require the consent of the owner before disputes would be arbitrated. The Court concluded that the subcontract extended a duty to arbitrate only insofar as such a duty was provided in the General Contract. Under the subcontract, the contractor, whose obligations the surety assumed by assignment, stood in the same position as the owner in the General Contract. The Court thus held that the surety had no duty to arbitrate unless it consented to submission of the subcontractor's dispute to arbitration.

86068 Village of Rosemont v. Lentin Lumber Co., 144 Ill. App. 3d 651, 98 Ill. Dec. 470, 494 N.E.2d 592 (1986)

II:	A107-1978, Art. 10, Para. 10.11
II:	A107-1978, Art. 17, Para. 17.3
II:	A107-1978, Art. 17, Para. 17.6
II:	A117-1979, Art. 14, Para. 14.11
II:	A117-1979, Art. 21, Para. 21.3
II:	A117-1979, Art. 21, Para. 21.6
I:	A201-1976, Art. 4, Para. 4.18.1
I:	A201-1976, Art. 11, Para. 11.3.1
I:	A201-1976, Art. 11, Para. 11.3.6
I:	A201-1976, Art. 11, Para. 11.4.1

Owner brought an action against contractor, subcontractor and subcontractor's engineer for damages arising from the collapse of an arena roof during construction. The actions were brought both under breach of contract and tort theories. A supplier, whose contract was similar to that of the other defendants was made a party under theories of breach of contract and products liability. The sureties of both the contractor and subcontractor were also joined. The trial court granted summary judgment in favor of all defendants. The issue on appeal was whether a waiver of claims clause common to all the contracts barred owner's claims.

The owner-contractor agreement included the American Institute of Architects General Conditions of the Contract for Construction, Document No. A201, 1976 edition which provided in Paragraph 11.3.1 that the owner was required to purchase builders risk insurance "upon the entire Work at the site to the full insurable interest thereof" and further provided at Paragraph 11.3.6 for a mutual waiver of claims" for damages caused

In an action arising from contractor's failure to complete a waste treatment facility, owner sought recovery of additional expenses incurred thereby as well as damages from the denial of the facility's benefits. The trial court refused to dismiss these claims, and the Appellate Division affirmed. A liquidated delay damage clause in the owner-contractor agreement provided that "[i]nasmuch as the damage and loss of the Owner which will result from a failure by the Contractor to complete the work . . . may include interest on moneys borrowed for construction and loss from the inability of the Owner to use the site for the purposes intended as scheduled, the damages of the Owner for delay in a case of such failure or failures on the part of such Contractor shall be liquidated in the amount stipulated in the Proposal . . . by which such Contractor shall fail to complete all of his work in accordance with said agreement." This provision was not so clear and unambiguous as to limit the owner's recovery to the amount liquidated; the clause could be interpreted as applying only where the contractor fully performed the contract and not where the contractor abandoned the contract. Therefore, dismissal was not yet warranted.

86067 Travelers Indem. Co. v. Hayes Contractors, Inc., 389 N.W.2d 257 (Minn. Ct. App. 1986)

II:	A107-1978, Art. 11, Para. 11.2	
II:	A107-1978, Art. 13, Para. 13.2	
II:	A117-1979, Art. 15, Para. 15.2	
II:	A117-1979, Art. 17, Para. 17.2	
II:	A201-1976, Art. 5, Para. 5.3.1	
II:	A201-1976, Art. 7, Para. 7.9.1	
I:	A401-1978, Art. 11, Para. 11.1.1	
II:	A401-1978, Art. 13, Para. 13.1	
II:	B141-1978, Art. 9, Para. 9.1	

Subcontractor filed a demand for arbitration against the defaulting contractor's surety, seeking delay damages and acceleration. The surety, in turn, brought a statutory action to stay the arbitration proceedings. The trial court stayed arbitration.

The parties had entered into the American Institute of Architects Standard Form of Agreement Between Contractor and Subcontractor, Document No. A401, 1978 edition, which incorporated the arbitration provisions of the owner-contractor agreement. Paragraph 11.1.1 of the subcontract obligated the subcontractor "to be bound to the contractor by the terms of the General Contract . . . and to assume toward the Contractor all the obligations and responsibilities that the contractor assumes in and by the General Contract toward the Owner. . . ." The contractor was bound to arbitrate "if arbitration of disputes is provided for in the General Contract, any dispute arising between the Contractor and the Subcontractor . . . shall be settled by arbitration in the manner provided for in the General Contract." The General Contract consisted of a standard American Institute of Architects owner-contractor agreement which was modified by

Paragraph 8.3.2 required that "any claim for an extension of time shall be made in writing to the Architect not more than twenty days after commencement of the delay; otherwise it shall be waived."

Reversing the grant of partial summary judgment, the Court of Appeals found that Paragraph 8.3.2 could be strictly construed against the contractor only if the contractor did not raise factual issues which would preclude strict enforcement. After review of the evidence submitted at the time of the motion for summary judgment the Court concluded that questions of fact remained which could not be resolved as a matter of law based on the record. In addition, the Court found that the architect occupied a quasi-judicial position under Paragraph 2.2.7 and was contractually bound to be the "interpreter of the requirements of the Contract Documents and the judge of the performance thereunder." In that capacity he was obligated under Paragraph 2.2.10 not to show partiality to either party. The Court found that if it was factually correct that the architect was a co-owner then Paragraph 8.3.2 was null and void because the "impartial judge" had a direct financial interest in the outcome of the project.

86065   Torcon, Inc. v. Alexian Bros. Hosp., 209 N.J. Super. 239, 507 A.2d 289 (App. Div.), *cert. denied,* 104 N.J. 440, 517 A.2d 431 (1986)

II:	A107-1978, Art. 10, Para. 10.4
II:	A107-1978, Art. 19, Para. 19.1
II:	A117-1979, Art. 14, Para. 14.4
II:	A117-1979, Art. 23, Para. 23.1
II:	A201-1976, Art. 4, Para. 4.5
I:	A201-1970, Art. 13, Para. 13.2.2

On appeal of the denial of owner's claim for defective construction against contractor based on the statute of limitations, the Appellate Court, in response to owner's argument that its cause of action did not accrue until one year after the date of substantial completion, held that Paragraph 13.2.2 of the American Institute of Architects General Conditions of the Contract for Construction, Document No. A201, 1976 edition, was intended to enhance the owner's range of remedies for contractor's defaults not to restrict them. [N.B.: Apparently in error, the case's quotation omits important language from Paragraph 13.2.2.]

86066   Town of North Hempstead v. Sea Crest Constr. Co., 119 A.D.2d 744, 501 N.Y.S.2d 156 (1986)

III:	A107-1978, Art. 14, Para. 14.3
III:	A117-1979, Art. 18, Para. 18.3
III:	A201-1976, Art. 8, Para. 8.3.1
III:	A201-1976, Art. 8, Para. 8.3.4

motion for summary judgment on the grounds that owner would be entitled to indemnification under the contract provision even if there was a finding that owner was solely negligent. The Appeals Court affirmed.

The agreement provided that "you [contractor] promise to indemnity and hold H.P. Hood Inc. [owner] harmless at all times from any of the following arising by the negligent or non-negligent act or omission to act in the fulfillment of this contract of yourself or your agents, employees, independent contractors, or others . . . patent infringements, contributions or taxes, and any and all claims, damages, actions, liability, loss, cost or expense. . . . That you are to furnish evidence to H.P. Hood Inc. by delivering certificates that insurance is in effect . . . (Public Liability shall include coverage for Operations, Products, when a product is sold by you to H.P. Hood Inc. and Contractual Liability to cover the above indemnity agreement. . . ."

The indemnification clause clearly provided that contractor was to save owner harmless from all claims, damages, actions, liability or loss arising from the contractor's acts or omissions, whether negligent or not. The indemnification did not stop short of a case where the indemnitee was itself concurrently or solely negligent. The Court therefore held that the acts of the employee were covered by this clause. Further, by virtue of the contractual provisions describing the types of insurance contractor was to obtain and minimum amounts, it was expected that contractor would obtain insurance to meet the risk.

86064   Steinberg v. Fleischer, 706 S.W.2d 901 (Mo. Ct. App. 1986)

II:	A107-1978, Art. 8, Para. 8.5	
II:	A107-1978, Art. 14, Para. 14.3	
II:	A117-1979, Art. 12, Para. 12.5	
II:	A117-1979, Art. 18, Para. 18.3	
I:	A201-1976, Art. 2, Para. 2.2.7	
I:	A201-1976, Art. 2, Para. 2.2.10	
I:	A201-1976, Art. 8, Para. 8.3.2	
II:	B141-1977, Art. 1, Para. 1.5.9	
II:	B141-1977, Art. 1, Para. 1.5.10	

Owner brought a breach of contract action against contractor, and contractor counterclaimed for delay damages. The trial court entered partial summary judgment in favor of owner on the issue of contractor's liability for breach of contract and the jury awarded owner damages. The contractor appealed the trial court's grant of partial summary judgment to owner.

The parties had entered into an American Institute of Architects Standard Form of Agreement Between Owner and Contractor which included the American Institute of Architects General Conditions of the Contract for Construction, Document No. A201, 1976 edition. The General Conditions were modified by deleting Paragraph 8.3.1 entitled "Delays and Extensions of Time" and Paragraph 12.2.1 entitled "Concealed Conditions."

II:	A401-1978, Art. 13, Para. 13.1
II:	A401-1978, Art. 13, Para. 13.2
II:	A401-1978, Art. 13, Para. 13.3
II:	A401-1978, Art. 13, Para. 13.4
II:	A401-1978, Art. 13, Para. 13.5
II:	A401-1978, Art. 13, Para. 13.6
II:	B141-1977, Art. 9, Para. 9.1
II:	B141-1977, Art. 9, Para. 9.2
II:	B141-1977, Art. 9, Para. 9.3

Contractor filed a demand for arbitration against owner for the unpaid balance due for labor and materials supplied to the project. The lower court's stay of arbitration was affirmed by the Appellate Division. The New York Court of Appeals reversed.

The parties had entered into the American Institute of Architects Abbreviated Form of Agreement Between Owner and Contractor, Document No. A107, 1978 edition which provided for the arbitration of "all claims or disputes between the Contractor and the Owner arising out of, or relating to, the Contract Documents or the breach thereof." The arbitration clause provided broadly for arbitration of all disputes "arising out of, or relating to, the Contract Documents." The Contract Documents referred not only to the original agreement and plans but also to later modifications and written changes with the intent to include "all items necessary for the proper execution and completion of the Work." Paragraph 7.4 defined the work as comprising "the completed construction required by the Contract Documents and includes all labor necessary to produce such construction, and all materials and equipment incorporated or to be incorporated in such construction". The Court held that a dispute relating to extra work allegedly authorized and required for completion of the contractor's work arose out of and related to the Contract Documents and fell within the ambit of the arbitration clause.

86063 Speers v. H.P. Hood, Inc., 22 Mass. App. 598, 495 N.E.2d 880, *review denied*, 398 Mass. 1105, 498 N.E.2d 125 (1986)

III:	A107-1978, Art. 10, Para. 10.11
III:	A107-1978, Art. 17, Para. 17.1
III:	A117-1979, Art. 14, Para. 14.1
III:	A117-1979, Art. 21, Para. 21.1
III:	A201-1976, Art. 4, Para. 4.18.1
III:	A201-1976, Art. 11, Para. 11.1.3
III:	A401-1978, Art. 9, Para. 9.1
III:	A401-1978, Art. 9, Para. 9.2
III:	A401-1978, Art. 11, Para. 11.11.1

Owner brought a third party indemnification action against contractor for personal injury damages paid to contractor's injured employee. The trial court granted owner's

86061 School Bd. of Orange County v. Southeast Roofing & Sheet Metal, Inc., 489 So. 2d 886 (Fla. Dist. Ct. App.), *review dismissed,* 496 So. 2d 143 (Fla. 1986)

       I: A101-1977, Art. 7, Para. 7.2
       II: A107-1978, Art. 6, Para. 6.1
       II: A107-1978, Art. 7, Para. 7.1
       II: A107-1978, Art. 13, Para. 13.2
       II: A117-1979, Art. 10, Para. 10.1
       II: A117-1979, Art. 11, Para. 11.1
       II: A117-1979, Art. 17, Para. 17.2
       II: A201-1976, Art. 1, Para. 1.1.1
       I: A201-1976, Art. 7, Para. 7.9.1
       II: A401-1978, Art. 1, Para. 1.1
       II: A401-1978, Art. 13, Para. 13.1
       II: B141-1977, Art. 9, Para. 9.1
       III: B141-1977, Art. 13, Para. 13.1

A contractor commenced an action against the owner, but subsequently moved to compel arbitration. The Circuit Court granted the motion, and the District Court of Appeal reversed. By initiating litigation and participating in discovery, the contractor had waived its right to arbitration under Paragraph 7.9.1 of the American Institute of Architects General Conditions of the Contract for Construction, Document No. A201, 1976 edition. The Court rejected the contractor's argument that it was unaware of its right to arbitrate because the General Conditions were not attached to the owner-contractor agreement and were not made a part of the agreement. The Court found that the American Institute of Architects Standard Form of Agreement Between Owner and Contractor, Document No. A101, 1977 edition, specifically referred to the General Conditions in Paragraph 7.2. The owner referred to the General Conditions in its answers to contractor's interrogatories, and contractor actively participated in discovery by taking depositions, amending its complaint, filing a request for production of documents, demanding a trial by jury, and submitting additional interrogatories.

86062 Sisters of Saint John the Baptist, Providence Rest Convent v. Phillips R. Geraghty Constructor, Inc., 67 N.Y.2d 997, 502 N.Y.S.2d 997, 494 N.E.2d 102 (1986)

       I: A107-1978, Art. 7, Para. 7.1
       I: A107-1978, Art. 7, Para. 7.4
       I: A107-1978, Art. 13, Para. 13.2
       II: A117-1979, Art. 17, Para. 17.2
       II: A201-1976, Art. 7, Para. 7.9.1
       II: A201-1976, Art. 12, Para. 12.3.1

encountered by the contractor. The differing site conditions clause required only that the contractor give notice to the owner of soil conditions that differed materially from those indicated in the contract. The Court found that while the notice had to be prompt, written, and prior to disturbance of the condition, a damage claim based on a differing site condition could be brought at any time prior to final payment. Because the owner had constructive notice of the differing site conditions throughout the job, the contractor was entitled to the extras despite noncompliance with the written notice requirements.

86060   Roy Strom Excavating & Grading Co. v. Miller-Davis Co., 149 Ill. App. 3d 1093, 103 Ill. Dec. 400, 501 N.E.2d 717 (1986)

        Ill: A107-1978, Art. 7, Para. 7.1
        Ill: A107-1978, Art. 11, Para. 11.2
        Ill: A117-1979, Art. 11, Para. 11.1
        Ill: A117-1979, Art. 15, Para. 15.2
        Ill: A201-1976, Art. 5, Para. 5.3.1
        Ill: A201-1976, Art. 12, Para. 12.2.1
        Ill: A401-1978, Art. 11, Para. 11.1.1

Subcontractor brought an action against the owner and contractor to recover extra costs arising from allegedly concealed soil conditions. The trial court granted the claim. Among the issues on appeal was whether the exculpatory clauses in the subcontract, which disclaimed subcontractors right to rely on soil boring logs, took precedence over the changed conditions clause.

The changed conditions clause provided that if the contractor encountered subsurface conditions materially different from those shown on the drawings or indicated in the specifications "he shall immediately give notice to the Architect of such conditions before they are disturbed. The Architect will thereupon promptly investigate the conditions and, if he finds that they materially differ from those shown on the Drawings or indicated in the Specifications, he will at once make such changes in the Drawings and/or Specifications as he may find necessary, any increase or decrease of cost resulting from such changes shall be adjusted in the manner provided in the article "Changes in Work" of the GENERAL CONDITIONS." Furthermore, the contract provided that "the order of precedence of the Contract Documents in the event of conflict shall be in the same order as listed in the Article entitled "Contract Documents" of the SUPPLEMENTAL GENERAL CONDITIONS."

The Appellate Court did not reach the issue of whether the changed conditions clause took precedence over the exculpatory clauses. Rather, the Court concluded that the contract expressly provided that in case of conflict with other parts of the contract, the changed conditions clause should be given precedence over the exculpatory clauses. The Court held that subcontractor, pursuant to the changed conditions clause, could be compensated for extra costs incurred because of soil conditions not indicated by the soil-boring logs furnished by the contractor.

indemnification language and concluded that it was not clear that the subcontractor was to indemnify the contractor except against claims "arising out of or resulting from the performance of the subcontractor's work. . . ." The Court construed this language as setting forth the parties' intent to limit the subcontractor's liability only to negligence in performing work. The Court therefore concluded that the subcontract did not provide for indemnification of contractor for its own negligence in clear and unequivocal language. Moreover, the contractor had failed to establish that the employee's injuries arose out of the performance of the subcontractor's work.

86059   Roger J. Au & Son, Inc. v. Northeast Ohio Regional Sewer Dist., 29 Ohio App. 3d 284, 504 N.E.2d 1209 (1986)

III:	A107-1978, Art. 18, Para. 18.1
III:	A117-1979, Art. 22, Para. 22.1
III:	A201-1976, Art. 12, Para. 12.2.1
III:	A201-1976, Art. 12, Para. 12.3.1
III:	A201-1976, Art. 12, Para. 12.3.2

Contractor brought an action against owner for additional compensation resulting from changed subsurface conditions. The trial court granted owner summary judgment on the ground that contractor failed (1) to properly plead its damage claim, and (2) to comply with the notice provisions of the contract. Contractor argued on appeal that no notice was required because its claim was based on defective specifications.

The changes clause of the owner-contractor agreement provided that "(d) If any change under this clause causes an increase or decrease in the Contractor's cost of, or time required for, the performance of any part of the work under this contract, whether or not changed by order, an equitable adjustment shall be made and the contract modified in writing accordingly; Provided, however, that except for claims based on defective specifications, no claim for any change under (b) above shall be allowed for any costs incurred more than 20 days after the Contractor gives written notice as therein required; And provided further, that in case of defective specifications for which the Owner is responsible, the equitable adjustment shall include any increase of cost reasonably incurred by the Contractor in attempting to comply with such defective specifications. . . . (e) If the Contractor intends to assert a claim for an equitable adjustment under this clause, he must, within 30 days after receipt of a written change order under (a) above, or the furnishing of a written notice under (b) above submit to the Owner a written statement setting forth the general nature and monetary extent of such claim, unless this period is extended by the Owner. The statement of claim hereunder may be included in the notice under (b) above."

The Court of Appeals reversed. Contractor's claims were based on differing site conditions, rather than defective specifications, and the Court held that where no claim for defective specifications was pleaded the changes clause was inapplicable. However, the Court also held that the contractor arguably gave notice, as required by the differing site conditions clause, by the numerous letters sent to the owner detailing the conditions

Contractor's employee brought a negligence action against engineer for personal injury damages. Engineer asserted a third party indemnification claim against contractor. The trial court dismissed engineer's indemnity action. Engineer argued on appeal that under the indemnification provision contractor had waived its industrial insurance immunity and that engineer was a third party beneficiary of this waiver.

The owner-contractor agreement provided that contractor "shall indemnify and save harmless Owner or their representatives from and against any and all liability arising from injury or death to persons or damage to property occasioned by any negligent act or omission of contractor, its agents, servants or employees, irrespective of whether . . . it is alleged or claimed that negligence of Owner or its representatives caused or contributed thereto. . . ."

The Court of Appeals affirmed the dismissal of the indemnity claim. The indemnity provision did not refer to the workers compensation act, nor did contractor specifically assume liability for actions brought by its employees. Thus, the contractor had assumed liability for losses caused by the negligent acts of its employees and did not assume liability for injuries to its employees. Furthermore, engineer was not a third party beneficiary to the indemnification clause because the owner-contractor agreement expressly provided that no provision of the agreement was intended or was to be construed for the benefit of a third party.

86058 Robert H. Smith, Inc. v. Tennessee Tile, Inc., 719 S.W.2d 385 (Tex. Ct. App. 1986)

II:	A107-1978, Art. 10, Para. 10.11	
II:	A117-1979, Art. 14, Para. 14.11	
II:	A201-1976, Art. 4, Para. 4.18.1	
I:	A401-1978, Art. 11, Para. 11.11.1	
I:	A401-1978, Art. 11, Para. 11.11.2	

Subcontractor's employee brought a personal injury action against contractor. Contractor filed a third party action against subcontractor asserting negligence and claiming indemnification under the subcontract. The trial court granted summary judgment for subcontractor. Among the issues on appeal were whether the indemnification agreement provided an exception to the state workers' compensation act and whether the language of the clause was sufficiently clear and unequivocal so as to be enforceable.

The subcontract's indemnification provisions were identical to the American Institute of Architects Standard Form of Agreement Between Contractor and Subcontractor, Document No. A401, 1978 edition. The state workers' compensation statute provided that an action for damages brought by an employee against a third party that resulted in a settlement or judgment could not be the basis for reimbursement from the employer unless a written agreement provided otherwise.

Affirming, the Court of Appeals held that the indemnification provisions constituted an exception to the state workers' compensation act. However, the Court reviewed the

Contractor also argued that Paragraph 4.17 of the subcontract specifically limited the amount the subcontractor could recover to the amount contractor received from the owner. The Court disagreed. Paragraph 4.17 provided that the contractor "shall not, however, be liable for a greater sum than Contractor obtains from the Owner for such additional work. . . . [T]he recovery by Subcontractor for such work shall be conditioned upon a prior recovery therefor by Contractor from the Owner." No condition precedent limiting recovery to a specific amount was created by this provision because there was no proof of intent that payment to subcontractor was to be made exclusively or only from funds paid by or on behalf of the owner to contractor.

86056 Ridge Sheet Metal Co. v. Morrell, 69 Md. App. 364, 517 A.2d 1133 (1986)

> I: A101-1974, Art. 6
> II: A107-1978, Art. 5, Para. 5.1
> II: A107-1978, Art. 15, Para. 15.4
> II: A111-1978, Art. 14, Para. 14.2
> II: A117-1979, Art. 9, Para. 9.1
> II: A117-1979, Art. 19, Para. 19.4
> I: A201-1976, Art. 9, Para. 9.9.2

Subcontractor filed a petition to qualify for a mechanics lien. The trial court denied the petition, finding that the subcontractor failed to establish that the owner was "indebted under the contract," as defined by the state lien statute. The Court of Special Appeals affirmed, relying on the final payment provisions of Article 6 of the American Institute of Architects Standard Form of Agreement Between Owner and Contractor, Document No. A101, 1976 edition, and of Paragraph 9.9.2 of the American Institute of Architects General Conditions of the Contract for Construction, Document No. A201, 1976 edition. The Court concluded that the owner was not indebted under the contract because the owner paid the contractor the progress payments due until the contractor breached the contract, relieving the owner of its obligation to make the final payment and entitling the owner to the retainage. Furthermore, the subcontractor could have protected itself against loss by requesting joint payment of the progress checks under the contract provision stating that "the owner shall have the right to issue joint payee checks to Contractor and such other subcontractors or materialmen as Owner may deem necessary in Owner's sole discretion."

86057 Riggins v. Bechtel Power Corp., 44 Wash. App. 244, 722 P.2d 819, *review denied,* 107 Wash. 2d 1003 (1986)

> III: A107-1978, Art. 10, Para. 10.11
> III: A117-1979, Art. 14, Para. 14.11
> III: A201-1976, Art. 4, Para. 4.18.1
> III: A401-1978, Art. 11, Para. 11.11.1

I: A201-1976, Art. 5, Para. 5.3.1
I: A201-1976, Art. 10, Para. 10.3.1
I: A201-1976, Art. 12, Para. 12.3.1
II: A401-1978, Art. 11, Para. 11.1.1
II: A401-1978, Art. 11, Para. 11.9.1
II: A401-1978, Art. 11, Para. 11.10.1

Subcontractor brought a negligence and breach of contract action against contractor, seeking compensation for extra work performed at contractor's direction. The contractor filed a third party action against architect, subcontractor and owner alleging that the owner and architect were negligent, that the owner was obligated to increase the contract price and that subcontractor was negligent, breached its contract and was liable to the contractor for indemnification. Judgment was entered in favor of the subcontractor on its claim against the contractor, and also in favor of contractor on its claims against the owner and second subcontractor. Among the issues on appeal was whether the contractor was entitled to judgment where it failed to fulfill a contractual condition precedent to the recovery of such damages.

The owner and contractor entered into an American Institute of Architects Standard Form of Agreement Between Owner and Contractor which included the American Institute of Architects General Conditions of the Contract for Construction, Document No. A201, 1976 edition. Paragraph 12.3.1 set forth the procedures contractor was to follow in making a claim for extra work. The contract also provided that a claim for extra work would be recognized only if the work was authorized in advance by a written directive from the architect. Paragraph 4.18 of the subcontract provided that subcontractor agreed to submit all claims for extra work in sufficient time for the contractor to comply with the provisions of the contract documents for like claims of the contractor upon the owner. Furthermore, Paragraph 4.17 required the subcontractor to submit written copies of cost or credit proposals for revised work to the contractor prior to the commencement of such work. Furthermore, all relevant portions of the owner-contractor agreement were "applicable to this Subcontract and shall be binding upon the Subcontractor." Contractor argued that if it failed to submit the subcontractor's claim to the owner in accordance with the terms of the contract it was solely due to subcontractor's failure to make the information available to contractor in a timely fashion.

The Appellate Court found that the notice provisions of Paragraph 12.3.1 did not apply because contractor's extra work was in response to an emergency that endangered property. The Court concluded that if the contractor's action was in response to an emergency Paragraph 10.3.1 was controlling. Based on these provisions and the owner's "go-ahead" actions, the Court upheld the jury verdict in favor of the subcontractor and contractor. The Court upheld the jury verdict awarding summary judgment to subcontractor and contractor. The Court found that there was sufficient evidence from which the jury could have concluded that contractor had waived the writing requirements set forth in Paragraph 4.17. The Court concluded that it was proper for the trial court to give the waiver instructions because the jury could have resolved any conflicts between the waiver evidence and the other evidence presented at trial.

Contractor sought delay damages resulting from the "staging" of construction of hospital isolation rooms. Contractor prevailed at trial, but the Appellate Division reversed. The owner-contractor agreement contained specific language relating to the "staging" of construction of a hospital so that the hospital could continue to operate during the construction. Thus, the contractor was not entitled to such delay damages because the parties contemplated the staging of the work and the attendant delays. In addition, recovery of delay damages was barred by the contractual "no damages for delay" clause, since the trial court did not find that the delay was intentional, malicious, or the result of willful or gross negligence.

86054 Pine Gravel, Inc. v. Cianchette, 128 N.H. 460, 514 A.2d 1282 (1986)

      III: A107-1978, Art. 13, Para. 13.2

      III: A117-1979, Art. 17, Para. 17.2

      III: A201-1976, Art. 7, Para. 7.9.1

      III: A401-1978, Art. 13, Para. 13.1

      III: A401-1978, Art. 13, Para. 13.6

      III: B141-1977, Art. 9, Para. 9.1

Subcontractors brought a breach of contract action against the contractor and another subcontractor. The trial court dismissed the action, and the Supreme Court affirmed. The subcontract provided that all disputes, controversies or claims of any and all kinds arising under the contract were to be arbitrated and further provided that the subcontractor would "not file or caused to be filed any mechanic's lien for materials furnished or to be furnished and/or for labor performed or to be performed unless default shall first have been made by the Contractor in making a payment under this Agreement. The Subcontractor further agrees that if any subcontractor holding a subcontract from him or any material man supplying materials to him or any one claiming by or through such subcontractor or material man shall file or cause to be filed any lien, the Subcontractor will, upon notice from the Contractor, cause such lien to be cancelled and discharged within ten days from such notice." Based on these provisions, the dismissal of the action was proper. The Court also held that the arbitration provision did not result in the waiver of the subcontractors' right to a materialman's lien. A lien generally does not interfere with the arbitration process, and the duty to arbitrate should not interfere with, or cause waiver of, the right to a lien.

86055 Pioneer Roofing Co. v. Mardian Constr. Co., 152 Ariz. 455, 733 P.2d 652 (1986)

      III: A107-1978, Art. 11, Para. 11.2

      III: A107-1978, Art. 18, Para. 18.2

      III: A117-1979, Art. 15, Para. 15.2

      III: A117-1979, Art. 22, Para. 22.2

III: A117-1979, Art. 19, Para. 19.4
III: A201-1976, Art. 9, Para. 9.3.3
III: A201-1976, Art. 9, Para. 9.9.2

In contractor's action to foreclose a mechanics lien, the trial court refused to discharge the lien. The Appellate Court reversed, holding that the contractor voluntarily and absolutely waived its statutory lien rights. The owner-contractor agreement clearly and unambiguously provided that "[t]he CONTRACTOR agrees that no mechanic's claims or liens will be filed or maintained by CONTRACTOR against the dwelling or other improvements to be constructed or against the PROPERTY." Furthermore, the contractor was obligated to indemnify the owner for its failure to secure lien waivers from its subcontractors and suppliers where the agreement clearly provided that "CONTRACTOR further agrees to indemnify and save OWNER harmless from any costs, expenses, attorneys fees, loss or damage incurred by OWNER by the filing of liens by subcontractors or materialmen."

86052 Phillips v. United Eng'r & Constructors, Inc., 500 N.E.2d 1265 (Ind. Ct. App. 1986)

III: A107-1978, Art. 10, Para. 10.4
III: A107-1978, Art. 16, Para. 16.1
III: A117-1979, Art. 14, Para. 14.4
III: A117-1979, Art. 20, Para. 20.1
III: A201-1976, Art. 4, Para. 4.5.1
III: A201-1976, Art. 10, Para. 10.2.2

In an action brought by the estate of subcontractor's employee, the Appellate Court upheld the grant of summary judgment in favor of the owner. The owner did not retain any control as to the means and methods by which the contractors engaged in their work. The contract also required that the materials furnished and the work performed by the contractors meet the plans and specifications and that the contractors' work was conform to federal, state and local safety requirements. The Court refused to extend a specific duty to the owner where the contract prescribed safety rules and required the contractor to observe the rules or any laws relating to safety.

86053 Phoenix Contracting Corp. v. New York Health & Hosp. Corp., 118 A.D.2d 477, 499 N.Y.S.2d 953 (1986)

III: A107-1978, Art. 14, Para. 14.3
III: A117-1979, Art. 18, Para. 18.3
III: A201-1976, Art. 8, Para. 8.3.1
III: A201-1976, Art. 8, Para. 8.3.4
III: A201-1976, Art. 12, Para. 12.3.1

The retainage provision stated that the contract price was payable less a ten percent retainage, except that the last payment "shall be paid by Contractor to the Subcontractor immediately after all materials and labor installed by the Subcontractor have been completed, approved by the Architect, and final payment received by the Contractor and satisfactory evidence furnished to the Contractor by the Subcontractor that all labor and material accounts on this job have been paid in full, and all instructions manuals, as built drawings and guarantees have been submitted and approved."

The Supreme Court reversed. It found that the trial court did not treat the retainage provision as a liquidated damage clause. The order stated that the provision was "essentially a liquidated damage clause forfeited by the breach," but the trial court did not treat the provision as barring the contractor's recovery in excess of the amount retained. Nor did the trial court base its rejection of the counterclaim on this provision. In addition, the trial court erred in rejecting the owner's counterclaim for costs exceeding the value of the subcontract on the ground that the claimed expenses "could have been avoided." The subcontractor should have been permitted to introduce evidence on the issue of whether the contractor's losses were avoidable.

86050   Payne Plumbing & Heating Co. v. Bob McKiness Excavating & Grading, Inc., 382 N.W.2d 156 (Iowa 1986)

> III: A107-1978, Art. 10, Para. 10.11
> III: A117-1979, Art. 14, Para. 14.11
> III: A201-1976, Art. 4, Para. 4.18.1
> II: A401-1978, Art. 11, Para. 11.11.1

At issue in owner's negligence action against its contractors was whether one of the contractors, who was found to be negligent, was nevertheless entitled to indemnity under the subcontract. The trial court court held that that the contractor's own negligence barred its indemnification claim, and the Supreme Court reversed.

The subcontract provided that the subcontractor would indemnify the contractor from any and all loss or damage "occasioned wholly or in part by any negligent act or omission of the subcontractor . . . regardless of whether or not it is caused in part by a party indemnified hereunder."

The Supreme Court found that a party may contract for indemnification of damages to which it contributed if clearly provided for in the agreement. The Court construed the language of the indemnification provision ("any and all loss or damage . . . regardless of whether or not it is caused in whole or in part by a party indemnified hereunder") as clearly providing that subcontractor indemnify contractor for contractor's own damages which arose in part out of contractor's own negligence.

86051   Pero Bldg. Co. v. Smith, 6 Conn. App. 180, 504 A.2d 524 (1986), *appeal after remand*, 16 Conn. App. 71, 547 A.2d 59 (1988)

> III: A107-1978, Art. 15, Para. 15.4

86048 Olympic Constr., Inc. v. Drywall Interiors, Inc., 180 Ga. App. 142, 348 S.E.2d 688 (1986)

        III: A201-1976, Art. 9, Para. 9.5.2
        III: A401-1978, Art. 11, Para. 11.12.1
        III: A401-1978, Art. 12, Para. 12.4.1

Subcontractor brought an action against owner, contractor and contractor's surety to recover payments which contractor failed to make after owner stopped paying the contractor. The trial court granted subcontractor's motion for summary judgment.

The subcontract provided that "In any instance where Contractor remains unpaid by the Owner for Work performed by the Subcontractor, Contractor shall not be obligated to pay the Subcontractor for that work until Contractor may receive payment therefor from the Owner."

The contractor and surety argued on appeal that the word "may" in the payment provision was mandatory and established actual payment by the owner to the contractor as a condition precedent to payment to the subcontractor. The Appellate Court agreed and reversed the grant of summary judgment. It held that the word "may" was ambiguous and that the trial court erred in ruling that the parties' intent under the contract was not a jury question.

86049 Parem Contracting Corp. v. Welch Constr. Co., 128 N.H. 254, 512 A.2d 1104 (1986)

        III: A107-1978, Art. 4, Para. 4.1
        III: A107-1978, Art. 5, Para. 5.1
        III: A107-1978, Art. 15, Para. 15.4
        III: A117-1979, Art. 8, Para. 8.1
        III: A117-1979, Art. 9, Para. 9.1
        III: A117-1979, Art. 19, Para. 19.4
        III: A201-1976, Art. 9, Para. 9.3.1
        III: A201-1976, Art. 9, Para. 9.3.3
        III: A201-1976, Art. 9, Para. 9.5.2
        III: A201-1976, Art. 9, Para. 9.9.2
        III: A401-1978, Art. 6, Para. 6.1
        III: A401-1978, Art. 6, Para. 6.2
        III: A401-1978, Art. 12, Para. 12.4.1

Subcontractor brought an action against contractor for costs and extras incurred prior to contractor's termination of the subcontract. The trial court awarded subcontractor damages in quantum meruit and rejected the contractor's counterclaim for damages. Among the issues on appeal was whether the retainage clause was a liquidated damage provision limiting contractor's recovery.

86047 Naclerio Contracting Co. v. City of New York, 116 A.D.2d 463, 496 N.Y.S.2d 444 (1986), aff'd, 69 N.Y.2d 794, 513 N.Y.S.2d 115, 505 N.E.2d 625 (1987)

III:	A107-1978, Art. 8, Para. 8.5	
III:	A107-1978, Art. 13, Para. 13.2	
III:	A117-1979, Art. 12, Para. 12.5	
III:	A117-1979, Art. 17, Para. 17.2	
III:	A201-1976, Art. 2, Para. 2.2.7	
III:	A201-1976, Art. 2, Para. 2.2.8	
III:	A201-1976, Art. 2, Para. 2.2.9	
III:	A201-1976, Art. 2, Para. 2.2.10	
III:	A201-1976, Art. 2, Para. 2.2.11	
III:	A201-1976, Art. 2, Para. 2.2.12	
III:	A201-1976, Art. 7, Para. 7.9.1	
III:	A401-1978, Art. 9, Para. 9.1	
III:	A401-1978, Art. 9, Para. 9.2	
III:	A401-1978, Art. 9, Para. 9.3	
III:	B141-1977, Art. 1, Para. 1.5.7	
III:	B141-1977, Art. 1, Para. 1.5.8	
III:	B141-1977, Art. 1, Para. 1.5.9	
III:	B141-1977, Art. 1, Para. 1.5.10	
III:	B141-1977, Art. 1, Para. 1.5.11	
III:	B141-1977, Art. 1, Para. 1.5.15	
III:	B141-1977, Art. 9, Para. 9.1	
III:	B141-1977, Art. 9, Para. 9.2	
III:	B141-1977, Art. 9, Para. 9.3	

Contractor brought an action against owner for delay damages. The owner moved to compel arbitration. The trial court granted owner's motion to dismiss the complaint and to compel arbitration on the grounds that under the broad arbitration clause the Dept. of Environmental Protection Commissioner had the power to act as an arbitrator in a delay damage dispute. The Appellate Division reversed.

The owner-contractor agreement provided in pertinent part that the Commissioner "shall have the power: . . . . [t]o review and determine any and all questions in relation to this contract and its performance."

The Appellate Division found that this provision did not contain language which demonstrated any intention by the parties to utilize arbitration or any other alternative dispute resolution methods because neither the word "arbitration" or the word "arbitrator" was mentioned in the provision. Additionally, a party to a contract should not serve as an arbitrator in matters disputed under that same contract. The Court of Appeals affirmed.

III:	A107-1978, Art. 17, Para. 17.5
III:	A117-1979, Art. 21, Para. 21.1
III:	A117-1979, Art. 21, Para. 21.5
III:	A201-1976, Art. 11, Para. 11.1.1
III:	A201-1976, Art. 11, Para. 11.1.4
II:	A401-1978, Art. 9, Para. 9.1
II:	A401-1978, Art. 9, Para. 9.2
II:	A401-1978, Art. 12, Para. 12.1.1

Contractor was successfully sued for the wrongful death of subcontractor's employee. Subsequently, contractor and contractor's insurer brought an action against subcontractor for breach of contract to maintain adequate insurance. The trial court granted subcontractor's motion for summary judgment on the ground that the flow-down provision in the subcontract did not require the subcontractor to obtain comprehensive general liability insurance naming the contractor as an additional insured.

The flow-down provision in the subcontract provided that subcontractor would "assume toward the CONTRACTOR all obligations and responsibilities which the CONTRACTOR has assumed toward the OWNER under the MAIN CONTRACT, and shall be entitled to all privileges and protection granted the CONTRACTOR by the OWNER, under the MAIN CONTRACT. In case of conflict between the terms of the obligation and the responsibilities of the parties of this SUBCONTRACT and the MAIN CONTRACT, this SUBCONTRACT shall control." The agreement also required the subcontractor to "obtain and keep in force during the term of the contract public liability and property damage insurance with coverage equal to, or greater that, the minimum specified in the MAIN CONTRACT. The SUBCONTRACTOR shall furnish to the CONTRACTOR evidence of this insurance as in the same form as described in Paragraph (R). Such insurance shall indicate that it includes contractual liability coverage applicable to the indemnity provisions of this SUBCONTRACT. The SUBCONTRACTOR shall give CONTRACTOR ten days notice of any cancellation." The owner-contractor agreement required the contractor to furnish "evidence (in duplicate copy) of insurance required hereunder" and that the contractor would not allow any subcontractor to commence work "until the same insurance requirements have been complied with by such subcontractor. . . . Evidence of liability insurance shall be furnished on the "Certificate of Insurance" form included at the end of this article."

The Court of Appeals found that the language requiring the subcontractor to obtain insurance coverage "equal to, or greater than, the minimum specified in the MAIN CONTRACT" was ambiguous and could be interpreted as being a reference only to policy dollar amounts and not to perils covered and persons or entities insured. The Court rejected the contractor's argument that this ambiguity was resolved by the flow-down provision in the subcontract because there was no language contained in the provision that would provide notice to subcontractor that it was expected to obtain an insurance policy naming contractor as an insured. Accordingly, the Court affirmed the trial court's determination that the subcontractor met its contractual obligation to obtain insurance and that it was not required to insure the contractor.

attorney's fees, cost and expenses of whatsoever kind of nature whether arising before or after completion of the work hereunder and in any manner directly or indirectly caused, occasioned or contributed to in whole or in part, by reason, direction, control or on its behalf in connection with or incident to the work performed under this subcontract. Subcontractor's aforesaid indemnity and hold harmless agreement shall not be applicable to any liability caused by the sole action negligence of Contractor or Owner."

The Supreme Court found that attorney's fees would not be awarded under the state's reciprocal fee statute in suits based on indemnity contract claims. It also held that the attorney's fees incurred by contractor in its suit against subcontractor were not within the subject matter of the subcontract. The indemnification language protected contractor from claims made by someone other than the contracting parties. The protection was in contractor's "behalf in connection with or incident to the work performed under the subcontract."

86044 (UNASSIGNED)

86045 Midwest Mechanical Contractors, Inc. v. Commonwealth Constr. Co., 801 F.2d 748 (5th Cir. 1986)

II:	A107-1978,	Art. 13, Para. 13.2
II:	A117-1979,	Art. 17, Para. 17.2
II:	A201-1976,	Art. 7, Para. 7.9.1
I:	A401-1978,	Art. 13, Para. 13.1
II:	B141-1977,	Art. 9, Para. 9.1

Subcontractor filed a demand for arbitration, and the contractor filed a breach of contract action. The AAA determined that the dispute was arbitrable, but the district court denied subcontractor's motion to stay the litigation. In reversing, the Fifth Circuit construed the broad arbitration clause found in Paragraph 13.1 of the American Institute of Architects Standard Form of Agreement Between Contractor and Subcontractor, Document No. A401, 1978 edition, which provided in pertinent part that arbitration "be conducted in the same manner and under the same procedure as provided in the Contract Documents with respect to disputes between the Owner and Contractor." This provision was unambiguous. Although the owner-contractor agreement provided for arbitration "if the parties mutually agree," the Court found that the owner-contractor agreement only determined which procedures would govern the arbitration process and that it did not control whether such disputes would be arbitrated. Contractor's breach of contract claim was within reach of the parties' agreement. Therefore, the District Court incorrectly denied the motion to stay.

86046 Mountain States Constr. Co. v. Tyee Elec., Inc., 43 Wash. App. 542, 718 P.2d 823 (1986)

III:	A107-1978, Art. 17, Para. 17.1

86042 Lampson Universal Rigging, Inc. v. Washington Pub. Power Supply Sys., 44 Wash. App. 237, 721 P.2d 996, *review denied,* 107 Wash. 2d 1006 (1986)

    III: A107-1978, Art. 20, Para. 20.2
    III: A117-1979, Art. 24, Para. 24.2
    III: A201-1976, Art. 14, Para. 14.2.1
    III: A201-1976, Art. 14, Para. 14.2.2

Contractor sued owner to recover for costs incurred because of owner's termination of the contract. Both parties filed motions for summary judgment. The trial court granted partial summary judgment in contractor's favor, awarding it damages based on contract price. Owner argued on appeal that the trial court erred in awarding the contractor the contract price rather than its reasonable costs plus profits for the work performed. The Court of Appeals affirmed the grant of summary judgment.

The parties agreement provided that "[o]wner may by written notice terminate this Contract at any time in whole or in part, without cause, and, except where determination is due to Contractor's default, Owner shall pay Contractor that portion of the Contract price corresponding to Work completed to Owner's satisfaction together with costs necessarily incurred by Contractor in terminating the remaining portion of Work, less any payments made before termination. . . . In no event shall Owner pay Contractor amounts aggregating in excess of the Contract Price."

The Court of Appeals interpreted the termination clause as providing that contractor was entitled to the contract price corresponding to the work completed at the time of termination less "unexpended labor, unexpended consumables and miscellaneous equipment standby time." Although contractor was advised that the equipment was released from the project effective November 1, 1981 with monthly charges to cease on October 31, 1981, contractor did not receive formal notice of the termination until after December 31, 1981. The contractor was therefore entitled to the contract price through that date, less the unexpended labor and consumables, as determined by the Court.

86043 Lasar v. Bechtel Power Corp., 223 Mont. 491, 727 P.2d 526 (1986)

    III: A107-1978, Art. 10, Para. 10.11
    III: A117-1979, Art. 14, Para. 14.11
    III: A201-1976, Art. 4, Para. 4.18.1
    III: A401-1978, Art. 11, Para. 11.11.1

Contractor brought a third party indemnity action against subcontractor for personal injury damages paid to subcontractor's employee. The trial court granted the subcontractor's motion to dismiss, but denied its claim for attorney's fees. The Supreme Court of Montana affirmed.

The indemnity clause in the subcontract provided that "[s]ubcontractor shall indemnify, defend and hold harmless Owner and Contractor . . . against any and all suits, actions, legal or administrative proceedings, claims, demands, damages, liabilities, interest,

The Court found that both the contractor and the owner were primary beneficiaries of the architect's contract. An architect owes a third party beneficiary of his contract the duty to "perform it skillfully, carefully, diligently, and in a workmanlike manner." The architect owed a duty to the homeowners to exercise ordinary professional skill and diligence and to conform to accepted architectural standards making the architect liable for failure to exercise reasonable care and professional skill. The Court held that a negligent failure to perform any of these duties was a tort as well as a breach of contract.

86040   Kenko, Inc. v. Lowry Hill Constr. Co., 392 N.W.2d 18 (Minn. Ct. App. 1986)

         III: A401-1978, Art. 4, Para. 4.1

Subcontractor sought to recover money owed by the contractor under the parties' contract. The trial court found as a matter of law that the contract was a "unit price" contract; the jury awarded the subcontractor over $58,000. The Court of Appeals affirmed, agreeing that the standard subcontract agreement, which provided that contractor pay to subcontractor a stated sum, was a unit-price contract, and not a fixed price contract. It emphasized that the reference to the following Rider provision immediately after the stated sum negated any ambiguity: "The undersigned agree that the quantities bid on this improvement are approximate only and are subject to increase or decrease on a need basis. The sum paid to Kenko, Inc. shall be obtained by multiplying each unit price by the quantities thereof actually incorporated in the project." Furthermore, all other references in the contract and the Rider were to unit prices and, as interpreted by the Court, clearly indicated that the contract was a unit price contract.

86041   Lake Plumbing, Inc. v. Seabreeze Constr. Corp., 493 So. 2d 1100 (Fla. Dist. Ct. App. 1986)

         II: A107-1978, Art. 13, Para. 13.2
         II: A117-1979, Art. 17, Para. 17.2
         II: A201-1976, Art. 7, Para. 7.9.1
         I: A401-1978, Art. 13, Para. 13.1
         II: B141-1977, Art. 9, Para. 9.1

Subcontractor brought an action against owner for damages for non-payment and to recover back charges for remedial work performed by another subcontractor. Contractor moved to compel arbitration. The trial court denied contractor's motion to compel arbitration. The District Court of Appeal reversed.

The parties had entered into the American Institute of Architects Standard Form of Agreement Between Contractor and Subcontractor, Document No. A401, 1978 edition, which contained a broad form arbitration clause in Paragraph 13.1. The Court construed the language of Paragraph 13.1 as binding and obligatory and found that it clearly governed the dispute. Therefore, the trial court erred in denying contractor's motion to compel arbitration.

III: A201-1976, Art. 10, Para. 10.2.2
III: A201-1976, Art. 10, Para. 10.2.3
III: A201-1976, Art. 10, Para. 10.2.4
III: A201-1976, Art. 10, Para. 10.2.6
III: A201-1976, Art. 10, Para. 10.2.7
III: A201-1976, Art. 10, Para. 10.3.1

In a personal injury action brought by subcontractor's employee, the trial court granted summary judgment in favor of contractor and owner. The issue before the Supreme Court of Montana was whether the contractor had a non-delegable contractual duty to maintain safety at the site and whether the contractor reserved sufficient control over the subcontractor's work to render the contractor liable to injured worker.

No provision in the owner-contractor agreement addressed safety. The subcontract provided that "the Subcontractor shall at all times conduct all operations under the Subcontract in a manner to avoid the risk of bodily harm . . . [and] inspect all work, materials and equipment. . . ." The contractor was responsible for establishing a "Project Safety Program" while the subcontractor had to submit a written safety program "with detail commensurate with the work to be performed, for Contractor's review." Contractor's review and approval of subcontractor's program "shall not relieve Subcontractor of its responsibility for safety, nor shall such approval be construed as limiting in any manner Subcontractor's obligation to undertake any action which may be necessary or required to establish and maintain safe working conditions at the site."

The Supreme Court found that because there was no safety provision in the owner-contractor agreement the contractor did not have a nondelegable duty to the worker to maintain safety at the site. Furthermore, the Court found that contractor did not maintain control over the subcontractor's work where the subcontract required the contractor to establish a project safety program but no control over the day-to-day implementation of the program was delegated to the contractor. The subcontract placed the responsibility for on-site implementation of the safety program and job safety on the subcontractor. The Court accordingly affirmed the grant of summary judgment.

86039   Keel v. Titan Constr. Corp., 721 P.2d 828 (Okla. Ct. App. 1986)

III: A107-1978, Art. 7, Para. 7.2
III: A117-1979, Art. 11, Para. 11.2
III: A201-1976, Art. 1, Para. 1.1.2
III: B141-1977, Art. 1

Homeowners brought an action against the contractor and architect for improper design of a solar system. They alleged that architect violated the duty he assumed in its agreement with the contractor to complete the plans in "a good and professional manner." The district court twice sustained the architect's demurrer to the homeowners' petition. On the second appeal, the Court of Appeals vacated and remanded.

86037 John F. Harkins Co. v. Waldinger Corp., 796 F.2d 657 (3d Cir. 1986), *cert. denied sub nom.* TWC Holdings, Inc. v. John F. Harkins Co., 479 U.S. 1059, 107 S. Ct. 939, 93 L. Ed. 2d 989 (1987)

II:	A107-1978, Art. 11, Para. 11.2	
II:	A107-1978, Art. 13, Para. 13.2	
II:	A117-1979, Art. 15, Para. 15.2	
II:	A117-1979, Art. 17, Para. 17.2	
II:	A201-1976, Art. 5, Para. 5.3.1	
II:	A201-1976, Art. 7, Para. 7.9.1	
II:	A401-1978, Art. 11, Para. 11.1.1	
II:	A401-1978, Art. 13, Para. 13.1	
II:	B141-1977, Art. 9, Para. 9.1	

Subcontractor filed a demand for arbitration against contractor for costs incurred from changes in the conditions and sequencing of the work. Contractor then brought an action in federal court seeking to enjoin arbitration on the grounds that arbitration was limited to disputes over signed change orders. The District Court held for contractor. The issue on appeal was whether the subcontractor could submit issues for arbitration under the subcontract even though contractor could not seek arbitration of the same issues under the owner-contractor agreement. The Third Circuit affirmed.

The subcontract provided that "all disputes, claims or questions arising hereunder shall be subject to arbitration and shall be submitted to arbitration in accordance with the provisions then obtaining, of the Standard Form of Arbitration Procedure of the A.I.A. A determination thereunder shall be final and binding on the parties thereto. Pending determination, there shall be no work stoppage." Section 2 of the subcontract provided that the subcontractor "shall be bound by all provisions of these documents and also by applicable provisions of the PRINCIPAL CONTRACT to which the CONTRACTOR is bound, and to the same extent. . . ." The owner-contractor agreement limited arbitration to disputes over written change orders.

The Court of Appeals found that Section 2 of the subcontract could be read to limit the scope of the subcontract's broad arbitration provision to the narrower arbitration provision of the owner-contractor agreement. In addition, there was other evidence to support the District Court's finding of the parties intent. Therefore, the District Court's interpretation of the arbitration provisions was not clearly erroneous.

86038 Kemp v. Bechtel Constr. Co., 221 Mont. 519, 720 P.2d 270 (1986)

III:	A107-1978, Art. 16, Para. 16.1
III:	A117-1379, Art. 20, Para. 20.1
III:	A201-1976, Art. 10, Para. 10.1.1
III:	A201-1976, Art. 10, Para. 10.2.1

The Supreme Court of Kansas affirmed. It found that the inspection provisions clearly stated that the "inspector was not authorized to alter or waive any requirements of the plans or specifications or act as foreman for the contractor." The contract clearly placed responsibility for correcting defective work discovered prior to final acceptance on the contractor despite the failure of the inspector to discover it or even with the inspector's knowledge by providing that "this clause shall have full effect regardless of the fact that the defective work may have been done or the defective materials used with the full knowledge of the Inspector. The fact that the Inspector in change may have previously overlooked such defective work shall not constitute an acceptance of any part of it." In addition, the contract clearly placed the responsibility on the contractor for damages resulting from faulty workmanship. Furthermore, the contract clearly stated that the inspections required by the contract were for the benefit of the Department, not the contractor. The Court therefore concluded that the contractor was not entitled to recover the cost of the remedial work.

86036 Joba Constr. Co. v. Monroe County Drain Comm'r, 150 Mich. App. 173, 388 N.W.2d 251, *appeal denied,* 425 Mich. 877 (1986)

II: A107-1978, Art. 13, Para. 13.2
II: A117-1979, Art. 17, Para. 17.2
II: A201-1976, Art. 7, Para. 7.9.1
II: A401-1978, Art. 13, Para. 13.1
II: B141-1977, Art. 9, Para. 9.1

After the owner issued a stop-work order, the contractor filed an arbitration demand and also a complaint for a writ of mandamus. The Circuit Court stayed arbitration. The issue on appeal was whether contractor had waived its right to arbitration by maintaining a court action against the owner.

The owner-contractor agreement provided that "claims, disputes, and other matters in question arising out of, or relating to, the contract documents or the breach thereof . . . shall be decided by arbitration in accordance with the construction industry arbitration rules of the American Arbitration Association." Rule 47 of the Construction Industry Arbitration Rules provides that "No judicial proceeding by a party relating to the subject matter of the arbitration shall be deemed a waiver of the party's right to arbitrate."

The Court of Appeals affirmed. It explained that Rule 47 should be considered a "factor' because, if it were to be interpreted to mean that no court proceeding could ever constitute waiver, it would run afoul of the state's arbitration statute. Yet despite Rule 47, the Court's equitable powers permitted it to determine that the contractor's conduct amounted to waiver. Even though it requested arbitration, the contractor commenced a court action, and in response to the counterclaim in that action, it did not raise arbitration as a defense. In addition, the contractor pursued discovery, which is inconsistent with arbitration.

Among numerous issues on appeal by owner from a judgment for contractor was whether the contractor was entitled to additional compensation for ledge removal. The contractor had submitted a change order seeking additional compensation which the architect denied on the grounds that contractor's calculation was not in accordance with the contract terms which architect claimed called for a less expensive excavation method.

The owner relied on Article V of the contract which provided in relevant part that "The designer [Architect] shall decide all questions which may arise as to the conduct, quantity, quality, equality, acceptability, fitness and rate of progress of the several kinds of work and materials to be performed and furnished under the contract and shall decide all questions which may arise as to the interpretation of the plans, and specifications and as to the fulfillment of this contract on the part of the contractor."

The Supreme Judicial Court affirmed. It found that the parties may be bound by a third party's interpretation of their contract if the contract specifically stated that the interpretation would be final and conclusive. The Court held that since no such specific language appeared in Article V, the architect had the authority to interpret the contract documents "in the first instance only" and that final interpretation was for the trier of fact. Article V did not address the resolution of disputes about contract interpretation arising for the first time after completion of the relevant work. The trial judge interpreted the contract as authorizing the ledge removal process used by the contractor; the architect was silent when the ledge was removed and apparently acquiesced in contractor's method. The architect was without authority to resolve a subsequent controversy concerning work that was not done in defiance of its directions.

86035 J.A. Tobin Constr. Co. v. Kemp, 239 Kan. 240, 718 P.2d 302 (1986)

III:	A107-1978, Art. 8, Para. 8.3	
III:	A107-1978, Art. 10, Para. 10.1	
III:	A107-1978, Art. 10, Para. 10.4	
III:	A117-1979, Art. 12, Para. 12.3	
III:	A117-1979, Art. 14, Para. 14.1	
III:	A117-1979, Art. 14, Para. 14.4	
III:	A201-1976, Art. 2, Para. 2.2.3	
III:	A201-1976, Art. 2, Para. 2.2.4	
III:	A201-1976, Art. 4, Para. 4.3.1	
III:	A201-1976, Art. 4, Para. 4.3.3	
III:	A201-1976, Art. 4, Para. 4.5.1	

In contractor's action to recover the costs of corrective work on a highway construction project from the Kansas Department of Transportation, the trial court found in favor of the Department. On appeal the contractor argued that the Department's inspections as required by the contract were for contractor's benefit and resulting failure of the Department's inspectors to observe the faulty workmanship absolved the contractor from bearing the cost of the remedial work.

damages resulting from a lack of limit stops. There was no evidence that the contractor failed to construct in accordance with the specifications.

86033 Horton Indus., Inc. v. Village of Moweaqua, 142 Ill. App. 3d 730, 97 Ill. Dec. 17, 492 N.E.2d 220 (1986)

> III: A201-1976, Art. 12, Para. 12.2.1

Contractor brought an action for breach of contract against owner after contractor terminated its performance under the contract. The jury found in favor of contractor and owner appealed. Owner argued on appeal that the contract was unambiguous and provided that it was contractor's responsibility, without additional compensation, to repair, maintain or replace all underground utilities encountered during construction, whether or not the utilities were shown in the plans.

The owner-contractor agreement contained two provisions relating to subsurface conditions. The first provision stated that the contractor would bear the entire risk as to any and all subsurface conditions with the exception of the excavation of rock. Furthermore, the responsibility for and expense of restoring the existing underground utilities not shown in the plans was placed on the contractor. However, the second provision was a representation by the owner that "a very large percentage" of the utility lines were shown in the plans and specifications.

The Appellate Court affirmed. The trial court did not err in refusing to instruct the jury as to contractor's responsibilities under the contract simply because the contract unambiguously stated that contractor was to bear the risk of underground structures. The contract did not preclude the contractor from contending that it was not obligated to replace all field tile regardless of any evidence regarding the location and extent of such field tile. Consequently, the issue of breach was properly submitted to the jury, which decided in favor of the contractor.

86034 J.A. Sullivan Corp. v. Commonwealth, 397 Mass. 789, 494 N.E.2d 374 (1986)

> III: A107-1978, Art. 8, Para. 8.5
> III: A107-1978, Art. 18, Para. 18.2
> III: A117-1979, Art. 12, Para. 12.5
> III: A117-1979, Art. 22, Para. 22.5
> III: A201-1976, Art. 2, Para. 2.2.7
> III: A201-1976, Art. 2, Para. 2.2.8
> III: A201-1976, Art. 2, Para. 2.2.9
> III: A201-1976, Art. 2, Para. 2.2.10
> III: A201-1976, Art. 2, Para. 2.2.11
> III: A201-1976, Art. 2, Para. 2.2.12
> III: A201-1976, Art. 12, Para. 12.3.1

termination of the owner-contractor agreement. The claims of two other subcontractors were consolidated with the first subcontractor's claim. Contractor then brought a declaratory judgment action to procure the consolidation of all the arbitration proceedings. The owner and subcontractors filed motions to dismiss on the grounds that the consolidation would create an unwieldly arbitration proceeding and that the agreements would not permit consolidation. The trial court dismissed contractor's complaint.

The owner and contractor entered into an American Institute of Architects Standard Form of Agreement Between Owner and Contractor which included the American Institute of Architects General Conditions of the Contract for Construction, Document No. A201, 1976 edition. The General Conditions contained a broad form arbitration clause in Paragraph 7.9.1 which provided that no arbitration "shall include by consolidation, joinder or in any other manner, parties other than the Owner, Contractor and any other party substantially involved in the common question of fact or law whose presence is required if complete relief is to be accorded in the arbitration." The subcontract incorporated the arbitration provisions contained in the owner-contractor agreement.

The District Court of Appeal reversed the dismissal of contractor's complaint. It construed the parties' agreements as permitting consolidation of multiple arbitration proceedings and concluded that the parties should have been given an opportunity before the trial court to demonstrate whether a single arbitration of the several claims would be unworkable or whether consolidation was the method least likely to result in confusion and prejudice and the most likely to avoid conflicting awards.

86032   Honey v. Barnes Hosp., 708 S.W.2d 686 (Mo. Ct. App. 1986)

II:	A107-1978, Art. 8, Para. 8.5
II:	A117-1979, Art. 12, Para. 12.5
II:	A201-1976, Art. 2, Para. 2.2.7
II:	A201-1976, Art. 2, Para. 2.2.8
II:	A201-1976, Art. 2, Para. 2.2.9
II:	A201-1976, Art. 2, Para. 2.2.10
II:	B141-1977, Art. 1, Para. 1.5.9
II:	B141-1977, Art. 1, Para. 1.5.10

After their son committed suicide by jumping from a hospital window, plaintiffs brought an action against the owner, the general contractor, and the window manufacturer. Among other things, the jury found in favor of the owner on its cross-claim against the contractor for contractual indemnity. However, the trial court granted the contractor's motion for judgment notwithstanding the verdict on this claim.

The Court of Appeals affirmed. It found that the specifications were ambiguous and that the owner-contractor agreement provided that the architect was in the first instance the interpreter of the requirements of the contract documents. Thus, the interpretation of the specifications by the architect as not requiring limit stops justified the trial court's finding that the contractor was not contractually required to indemnify the owner for

I:	A201-1976, Art. 12, Para. 12.3.1
II:	A401-1978, Art. 11, Para. 11.10.1

Subcontractor brought an action against contractor for a unit price adjustment due to increased costs of excavation. The contractor, in turn, asserted a third party claim against the owner. The trial court found that the subcontractor could recover the excess costs from the contractor and that the contractor was entitled to recover from owner any amounts due subcontractor. Owner appealed. Among the issues raised on appeal was whether the contractor could recover even though it did not give the architect timely notice of its claim for extras, as required by the contract. The Court of Appeals affirmed.

The owner-contractor agreement contained the American Institute of Architects General Conditions of the Contract for Construction, Document No. A201, 1976 edition. It provided in Paragraph 12.3.1 that if the contractor wanted to make a claim for an increase in the contract sum the contractor was required to give the architect twenty days notice before proceeding and the claim had to be authorized by a change order as defined in Paragraph 12.1.1.

The Court of Appeals concluded that the contractor's claim did not require a change order because it was not a change in the work nor was it an adjustment in the contract sum. The subcontractor had notified the owner's representative as required by the specifications and was directed to proceed with the drilling work. Because the evidence showed that the architect was aware that the subcontractor would claim additional compensation for the rock removal no written notice to the architect by the contractor was required. The Court held that the subcontractor's work was clearly being done within the terms of the contract.

86031 Higley South, Inc. v. Park Shore Dev. Co., 494 So. 2d 227 (Fla. Dist. Ct. App. 1986)

II:	A107-1978, Art. 13, Para. 13.2
II:	A117-1979, Art. 17, Para. 17.2
I:	A201-1976, Art. 7, Para. 7.9.1
II:	A401-1978, Art. 13, Para. 13.1
II:	A401-1978, Art. 13, Para. 13.2
II:	A401-1978, Art. 13, Para. 13.3
II:	A401-1978, Art. 13, Para. 13.4
II:	A401-1978, Art. 13, Para. 13.5
II:	A401-1978, Art. 13, Para. 13.6
II:	B141-1977, Art. 9, Para. 9.1
II:	B141-1977, Art. 9, Para. 9.2
II:	B141-1977, Art. 9, Para. 9.3

After terminating the contractor, owner filed a demand for arbitration. Subcontractor also sought to arbitrate its claim against contractor for withheld payments after owner's

III:	A401-1978, Art. 9, Para. 9.1
III:	A401-1978, Art. 9, Para. 9.2
III:	A401-1978, Art. 9, Para. 9.3
III:	B141-1977, Art. 1, Para. 1.5.7
III:	B141-1977, Art. 1, Para. 1.5.8
III:	B141-1977, Art. 1, Para. 1.5.9
III:	B141-1977, Art. 1, Para. 1.5.10
III:	B141-1977, Art. 1, Para. 1.5.11
III:	B141-1977, Art. 1, Para. 1.5.15
III:	B141-1977, Art. 9, Para. 9.1
III:	B141-1977, Art. 9, Para. 9.2
III:	B141-1977, Art. 9, Para. 9.3

Contractor brought an action to confirm architect's decisions as arbitration awards. The trial court found that the agreement between the parties was not an agreement for arbitration and that the summary statutory proceedings to confirm arbitration awards was not applicable. It denied the contractor's application. Contractor appealed.

The owner-contractor agreement provided for resolution of certain disputes between the parties by the architect. Section 20.1 provided that, with respect to any unresolved dispute regarding payment "the issue of whether such payment or any part is then due and owing to the Contractor under this Agreement shall be submitted to the Architect, for determination." Section 20.2 provided that with respect to any dispute regarding certain credit to be given to the contractor "said credit shall be determined by the Architect." Section 20.3 provided for the equal division of the architect's fees for his services in making these determinations. The architect was also to determine the price of certain change orders on which the parties could not agree, and certain other disputed additional costs and progress payments.

The Appellate Court upheld the findings of the trial court that the parties intended that the architect's determinations would constitute a condition precedent to the contractor's right to payment, and that they intended these determinations to be enforceable, not as arbitration awards but by plenary actions based on the architect's decisions. The architect's decisions were binding on the contractor if made in good faith. However, because the lower court was without jurisdiction to confirm the architect's decisions as arbitration awards, rather than denying the injunction, it should have dismissed it.

86030 Hayes Drilling, Inc. v. Curtiss-Manes Constr. Co., 715 S.W.2d 295 (Mo. Ct. App. 1986)

II:	A107-1978, Art. 18, Para. 18.1
II:	A117-1979, Art. 22, Para. 22.1
I:	A201-1976, Art. 12, Para. 12.1.1

1.1.3 to include "the completed construction required by the Contract Documents, . . . all labor necessary to produce such construction and all materials and equipment incorporated or to be incorporated in such construction."

The Appeals Court found that the fire damage was not damage to the "Work," and rejected the owner's position that Paragraph 11.3 required only that it maintain insurance on the "Work." Rather, the preexisting insurance policy the owner had was the insurance the owner chose to provide to comply with Paragraph 11.3.1, even though the policy was more extensive than required. The Court held that by the terms of Paragraph 11.3.6 the waiver of rights extended to the proceeds of any insurance provided under Paragraph 11.3.1.

86029   Harry Skolnick & Sons v. Heyman, 7 Conn. App. 175, 508 A.2d 64, *appeal denied*, 200 Conn. 803, 510 A.2d 191 (1986)

III:	A107-1978, Art. 8, Para. 8.5	
III:	A107-1978, Art. 13, Para. 13.2	
III:	A107-1978, Art. 14, Para. 14.3	
III:	A107-1978, Art. 15, Para. 15.3	
III:	A107-1978, Art. 18, Para. 18.1	
III:	A117-1979, Art. 12, Para. 12.5	
III:	A117-1979, Art. 17, Para. 17.2	
III:	A117-1979, Art. 18, Para. 18.3	
III:	A117-1979, Art. 19, Para. 19.3	
III:	A117-1979, Art. 22, Para. 22.1	
III:	A201-1976, Art. 2, Para. 2.2.7	
III:	A201-1976, Art. 2, Para. 2.2.8	
III:	A201-1976, Art. 2, Para. 2.2.9	
III:	A201-1976, Art. 2, Para. 2.2.10	
III:	A201-1976, Art. 2, Para. 2.2.11	
III:	A201-1976, Art. 2, Para. 2.2.12	
III:	A201-1976, Art. 6, Para. 6.3	
III:	A201-1976, Art. 7, Para. 7.7.2	
III:	A201-1976, Art. 7, Para. 7.9.1	
III:	A201-1976, Art. 8, Para. 8.3.1	
III:	A201-1976, Art. 9, Para. 9.2	
III:	A201-1976, Art. 9, Para. 9.4	
III:	A201-1976, Art. 9, Para. 9.6.1	
III:	A201-1976, Art. 9, Para. 9.8.1	
III:	A201-1976, Art. 12, Para. 12.1.4	
III:	A201-1976, Art. 12, Para. 12.3.1	

The Court then denied the contractor's claim for expenses resulting from differing site conditions on the grounds that the owner did not expressly or impliedly warrant the accuracy of the results of the test borings and contractor failed to make its own test borings. Furthermore, the contract specifically established a procedure for relief when "the [c]ontractor encounter [s] subsurface and/or latent conditions at the site materially differing from those shown on the [p]lans or indicated in the [s]pecifications." This provision, when read together with the other extras provisions established the procedure to be followed by the contractor in requesting an equitable adjustment for unexpected soils conditions. Contractor's failure to follow these procedures precluded recovery.

86028 Haemonetics Corp. v. Brophy & Phillips Co., 23 Mass. App. Ct. 254, 501 N.E.2d 524 (1986)

II:	A107-1978, Art. 7, Para. 7.4
II:	A107-1978, Art. 17, Para. 17.3
II:	A107-1978, Art. 17, Para. 17.6
II:	A117-1979, Art. 11, Para. 11.4
II:	A117-1979, Art. 21, Para. 21.3
II:	A117-1979, Art. 21, Para. 21.6
I:	A201-1976, Art. 1, Para. 1.1.3
I:	A201-1976, Art. 11, Para. 11.3.1
I:	A201-1976, Art. 11, Para. 11.3.6

Owner's insurer brought a subrogation action against contractor and subcontractor for property damage resulting from a fire which occurred while the subcontractor was engaged in electric arc welding on the project. The trial court entered summary judgment for contractor. The insurer argued on appeal that owner was required only to maintain insurance on the Work as defined by the contract, and that the waiver clause applied only "to the extent covered by insurance obtained pursuant to . . . Paragraph 11.3." Therefore, owner did not waive its right to sue the contractor and the subcontractor for the loss. The Appeals Court affirmed.

The owner and contractor had entered into the American Institute of Architects Standard Form of Agreement Between Owner and Contractor, Document No. A101, 1977 edition, which incorporated by reference the American Institute of Architects General Conditions of the Contract for Construction, Document No. A201, 1976 edition. Paragraph 11.3.1 of the General Conditions provided that the owner "shall purchase and maintain property insurance upon the entire Work at the site to the full insurable value thereof. This insurance shall include the interests of the Owner, the Contractor, Subcontractors and Sub-subcontractors in the Work and shall insure against the perils of fire and extended coverage and shall include "all risk" insurance for physical loss or damage. Paragraph 11.3.6, was a waiver clause for damages caused by fire or other perils to the extent covered by insurance obtained pursuant to Paragraph 11.3, or any other property insurance applicable to the "Work." "Work" was defined in Paragraph

The Court also rejected the subcontractor's argument that the arbitration clause of the owner-contractor agreement was inconsistent with the reservation of remedies provision. If the reservation of remedies provision were interpreted as granting the subcontractor a right to file an action at law to recover its additional costs, the arbitration provision would be meaningless. Furthermore, the subcontract expressly provided for arbitration of all claims for additional costs.

86027   Glynn v. City of Gloucester, 21 Mass. App. Ct. 390, 487 N.E.2d 230, *review denied,* 396 Mass. 1107, 489 N.E.2d 1263 (1986)

	III:	A107-1978, Art. 18, Para. 18.1
	III:	A107-1978, Art. 18, Para. 18.2
	III:	A107-1978, Art. 18, Para. 18.3
	III:	A117-1979, Art. 22, Para. 22.1
	III:	A117-1979, Art. 22, Para. 22.2
	III:	A117-1979, Art. 22, Para. 22.3
	III:	A201-1976, Art. 12, Para. 12.1.1
	III:	A201-1976, Art. 12, Para. 12.1.2
	III:	A201-1976, Art. 12, Para. 12.1.3
	III:	A201-1976, Art. 12, Para. 12.1.4
	III:	A201-1976, Art. 12, Para. 12.2.1
	III:	A201-1976, Art. 12, Para. 12.3.1

Receiver brought an action against the owner for additional compensation due to contractor. The trial court entered judgment for the owner, and the receiver appealed.

Affirming, the Appeals Court held that the contractor could not recover, in the absence of waiver by the owner, because the contractor failed to comply with the following contract provision: "[A]ll claims of the Contractor for compensation other than as provided for in the contract on account of any act of omission or commission by the [city] or its agent must be made in writing to the Engineer within 1 week after the beginning of any work or the sustaining of any damage on account such work . . . and the Contractor shall, on or before the 15th day of the month succeeding that in which such work is performed or damage sustained, file with the Engineer an itemized statement of the details and amount of such work or damage and unless such statement shall be made as required, his claim for compensation shall be forfeited and invalidated, and he shall not be entitled to payment on account of any such work or damage. . . ."

The contractor also failed to comply with the provisions of the General Conditions which set forth the method by which extra costs and expenses incurred in connection with the contractor's work were to be adjusted, specifically that "no claims for extra work or cost shall be allowed" unless it had been submitted in writing and approved by the engineer and owner, and processed in accordance with the provisions set forth in the General Conditions.

86026 Gibbons-Grable Co. v. Gilbane Bldg. Co., 34 Ohio App. 3d 170, 517 N.E.2d 559 (1986)

II:	A107-1978, Art. 11, Para. 11.2
III:	A107-1978, Art. 13, Para. 13.2
II:	A117-1979, Art. 15, Para. 15.2
III:	A117-1979, Art. 17, Para. 17.2
II:	A201-1976, Art. 5, Para. 5.3.1
II:	A401-1978, Art. 1, Para. 1.1
II:	A401-1978, Art. 11, Para. 11.1.1
III:	A401-1978, Art. 13, Para. 13.1
III:	B141-1977, Art. 9, Para. 9.1

Subcontractor brought an action against contractor for extras and the costs and expenses incurred in accelerating its performance under the contract. Contractor filed a motion to stay or dismiss the court action pending arbitration. The trial court dismissed the action for lack of subject matter jurisdiction and referred subcontractor's claims to arbitration. The Court of Appeals agreed with the trial court that the claims were subject to arbitration but held that the action should have been stayed rather than dismissed.

The owner-contractor agreement contained an arbitration clause which provided that if "the Contractor claims that additional cost is involved [and] . . . If Owner and Contractor are unable to dispose of such claim in a mutually agreeable fashion, such claim shall be decided by arbitration in accordance with the Construction Industry Arbitration Rules of the American Arbitration Association." The subcontract contained a flow-down clause which provided that "To the extent that the provisions of the contract documents between the Owner and Contractor apply to the work of the Subcontractor as defined in this agreement, the Contractor shall assume toward the Subcontractor all the obligations and responsibilities that the Owner, by those documents, assumes toward the Contractor. The Contractor shall have the benefit of all rights, remedies, and redress against the Subcontractor which the Owner, by those documents, has against the Contractor. Where any provision of the Contract documents between the Owner and the Contractor is inconsistent with any provision of this agreement, this agreement shall govern."

The Court of Appeals found that the arbitration clause was expressly incorporated into the subcontract by the provision which stated that "the contract documents consist of this agreement and any exhibits attached hereto, the agreement between the Owner and the Contractor, the conditions of the agreement between the Owner and contractor, general conditions, supplementary, special and other conditions" and by the flow-down provision by which the subcontractor "agrees to be bound to and assume toward the Contractor all of the obligations and responsibilities that the Contractor by those documents, assumes toward the Owner." Also significant was the provision in the owner-contractor agreement stating that the contractor "shall have the benefit of all rights, remedies, and redress against the Subcontractor which the Owner, by those documents has against the Contractor."

The trial court denied contractor's motion and directed the parties to proceed to arbitration. Contractor appealed. On appeal the contractor argued that the arbitration clause was limited in scope to questions regarding performance, and because the prime contract was terminated, the subcontract was cancelled and the right to arbitration was extinguished. The Appellate Division disagreed, and held that the trial court properly referred the dispute to an arbitrator.

The subcontract provided in pertinent part that "all questions that may arise under this contract and in the performance of the work thereunder shall be submitted to arbitration at the choice of either of the parties hereto." The agreement also contained a termination clause which provided that in the event the owner terminated its agreement with contractor the subcontract would likewise be deemed cancelled. The subcontract limited recovery for termination to certain enumerated costs.

The Court found that the acts giving rise to subcontractor's claims occurred well before the subcontract was terminated. Therefore, under the broad arbitration provision in the subcontract all issues regarding contractor's failure to comply with its substantive obligations, including its abandonment or repudiation of the subcontract, were properly referred to the arbitrator.

86025 Frederickson v. Alton M. Johnson Co., 390 N.W.2d 786 (Minn. Ct. App. 1986), *aff'd in part and rev'd in part,* 402 N.W.2d 794 (Minn. 1987)

II: A107-1966, Art. 11, Para. 11.10
I: A201-1970, Art. 4, Para. 4.18.1
II: A401-1967, Art. 11, Para. 11.20

In action by contractor's employees against engineer for personal injuries, the Appellate Court construed the indemnification provision contained in the American Institute of Architects General Conditions of the Contract for Construction, Document No. A201, 1970 edition. The indemnification clause provided that the contractor "shall indemnify . . . the Owner and the Architect . . . against all . . . damages . . . arising out of or resulting from the performance of the work, provided that any such . . . damage . . . (1) is attributable to bodily injury . . . and (2) is caused in whole or in part by any negligent act . . . of the Contractor . . . regardless of whether or not it is caused in part by a party indemnified hereunder."

The Court concluded that while the provision clearly stated that the negligent contractor must indemnify the architect for the architect's contributing negligence, nothing in the actual language of the provision addressed contractor's duty to indemnify the architect after the contractor's work was completed. The contract provided for a "contractual liability" endorsement that required the contractor to maintain insurance to cover the indemnity agreement; however, there was no indication how long the insurance was required to be maintained, if at all, after the contractor completed its work.

the provisions of this subcontract . . . the provisions of this agreement shall prevail any matter between the Contractor Falcon and the Subcontractor Weber."

The Court found that the subcontract did not expressly incorporate by reference the provisions of the owner-contractor agreement, nor was the agreement incorporated by the flow-down provision, nor was the agreement incorporated by the provision listing the contract documents. The Court construed the subcontract provisions as requiring the subcontractor to follow the applicable requirement of the specifications, drawings, and other prime contract documents and not to effect an incorporation of the entire prime contract. Furthermore, the parties intent to incorporate the prime contract's arbitration clause was negated by Paragraph 5.3.1 of the General Conditions which specifically provided that the subcontract "shall allow to the Subcontractor, unless specifically provided otherwise in the Contractor-Subcontractor Agreement, the benefit of all rights, remedies, and redress against the Contractor that the Contractor Falcon, by these Documents has against the Owner Becton."

The Court construed Paragraph 5.3.1 as allowing a subcontractor to bargain and contract for remedies against the contractor different from those afforded by the owner to the contractor. Furthermore, the Court found that the conflicts clause of the subcontract made the arbitration provision of the subcontract applicable to all claims by subcontractor against contractor and that it did not create an exception for claims which required consideration of the actions of the owner for resolution. Finally, the Court concluded that contractor's defense of waiver should be decided by the arbitrators.

86024 Ferran Concrete Co. v. Commerce Elec., Inc., 118 A.D.2d 619, 499 N.Y.S.2d 769 (1986)

	III:	A107-1978, Art. 13, Para. 13.2
	III:	A117-1979, Art. 17, Para. 17.2
	III:	A201-1976, Art. 7, Para. 7.9.1
	III:	A201-1976, Art. 14, Para. 14.2.1
	III:	A201-1976, Art. 14, Para. 14.2.2
	III:	A401-1978, Art. 13, Para. 13.1
	III:	A401-1978, Art. 13, Para. 13.2
	III:	A401-1978, Art. 13, Para. 13.3
	III:	A401-1978, Art. 13, Para. 13.4
	III:	A401-1978, Art. 13, Para. 13.5
	III:	A401-1978, Art. 13, Para. 13.6
	III:	A401-1978, Art. 14, Para. 14.2.1
	III:	B141-1977, Art. 9, Para. 9.1
	III:	B141-1977, Art. 9, Para. 9.2
	III:	B141-1977, Art. 9, Para. 9.3

Subcontractor filed a demand for arbitration against contractor for claims for abandonment and repudiation of the subcontract. The contractor moved to stay the arbitration.

court granted summary judgment in favor of the design firm, finding that the contract obligated the design firm to indemnify the owner only for losses resulting from the firm's own negligence. On appeal, the owner asserted that the indemnity clause applied to any claim brought against the owner resulting from an act or omission of the design firm in its performance under the contract.

The owner-design firm agreement contained an indemnity provision requiring the firm to "save, hold harmless and indemnify the Borough from any liability, claims, suits or demands, including costs, expenses and reasonable attorney's fees, incurred for or on account of injuries or damages to persons or property as a result of any act or omission of the Contractor in the performance pursuant to this contract."

The Supreme Court held that the indemnity provision was not limited to negligence claims, since a non-negligent act or omission could cause injury. However, the Court found that the language "injuries or damages to persons or property" limited indemnification to claims and liabilities based on physical injury or damage to persons or tangible property. The Court concluded that because the phrase "injuries to damage to property" meant physical damage to tangible property the owner's claim was not within the scope of the indemnification provision. Nevertheless, the Court reversed the trial court's judgment on the ground that the owner was entitled to bring a cross claim for common law indemnity.

86023 Falcon Steel Co. v. Weber Eng'g Co., 517 A.2d 281 (Del. Ch. 1986)

II:	A107-1978, Art. 13, Para. 13.2	
II:	A117-1979, Art. 17, Para. 17.2	
I:	A201-1976, Art. 5, Para. 5.3.1	
II:	A201-1976, Art. 7, Para. 7.9.1	
III:	A401-1978, Art. 1, Para. 1.1	
III:	A401-1978, Art. 11, Para. 11.1.1	
III:	A401-1978, Art. 11, Para. 11.2.5	
III:	A401-1978, Art. 13, Para. 13.1	
III:	B141-1979, Art. 9, Para. 9.	

Subcontractor filed a demand for arbitration against contractor claiming additional costs. Contractor moved to enjoin arbitration on the grounds that the claim was not arbitrable under the arbitration clause contained in the owner-contractor agreement which was incorporated by reference into the subcontract.

The subcontract contained a broad form arbitration clause which provided that "all claims, disputes or other matters in question arising out of or relating to this contract or the breach thereof shall be decided by arbitration. . . ." The owner-contractor agreement required arbitration only for claims amounting to $50,000 or less, and all claims above that amount were to be litigated. The conflicts clause of the subcontract provided that "in case of conflict between the provisions of the prime contract . . . and

was not subject to arbitration as required by the subcontract. The parties had entered into the American Institute of Architects Standard Form of Agreement Between Contractor and Subcontractor, Document No. A401, 1978 edition, which provided for arbitration in Article 13.

The District Court of Appeal reversed. It held that resolution of a payment dispute resulting from the oral agreement was not within the scope of the arbitration provision. The oral and written subcontracts were separate agreements, and state law provided that for a dispute to be arbitrable a written contract had to show the parties' intent to submit the dispute to arbitration.

86021   *Ex parte* Costa & Head (Atrium), Ltd., 486 So. 2d 1272 (Ala. 1986)

> II: A107-1978, Art. 13, Para. 13.2
> II: A117-1979, Art. 17, Para. 17.2
> II: A201-1976, Art. 7, Para. 7.9.1
> II: A401-1978, Art. 13, Para. 13.1
> II: A401-1978, Art. 13, Para. 13.2
> II: B141-1977, Art. 9, Para. 9.1

The trial court denied owner's motion to stay pending arbitration of its dispute with contractor. It reasoned that arbitration would lead to inconsistent results due to the absence of other parties involved in the litigation. The owner sought reversal of the order. The owner and contractor had entered into an American Institute of Architects Standard Form of Agreement Between Owner and Contractor. It included the American Institute of Architects General Conditions of the Contract for Construction, Document No. A201, 1976 edition, which provided for arbitration in Paragraph 7.9.1.

Applying the Federal Arbitration Act, the Alabama Supreme Court held that the trial court was without discretion to stay arbitration. A trial court has no discretion to stay arbitration for reasons of judicial economy, possible inconsistent results or the existence of non-arbitrable claims. Accordingly, the Court granted owner's petition for a writ of mandamus.

86022   Fairbanks North Star Borough v. Roen Design Assocs., Inc., 727 P.2d 758 (Alaska 1986), *appeal after remand*, Fairbanks North Star Borough v. Kandik Constr., Inc., 795 P.2d 793 (Alaska 1990), *vacated in part on rehearing and remanded*, 823 P.2d 632 (Alaska 1991)

> III: A107-1978, Art. 10, Para. 10.11
> III: A117-1979, Art. 14, Para. 14.11
> III: A201-1976, Art. 4, Para. 4.18.1
> III: A401-1978, Art. 11, Para. 11.11.1

Alleging design deficiencies, contractor brought an action against owner and the design firm that prepared the initial plans. On owner's cross claim for indemnification, the trial

The agreement further provided that the contractor "shall provide cover and protect all portions of the structure when the work is not in progress, provide and set all temporary roofs . . . and all other materials necessary to protect all the work on the building. . . . Any work damaged through the lack of proper protection or from any other cause, shall be repaired or replaced without extra cost to Owner." The contractor was also required to maintain all protective devices and signs throughout the progress of the work.

The Court of Appeals found that contractor was not liable to owner under the language making the contractor "responsible for any damage to the owner's property, or that of others on the job, by them, their men, or their sub-contractors, and shall make good such damage" because the damage to the temporary roof was caused by some unknown third party. Contractor had met its contractual obligations to "provide cover to protect all portions of the structure when the work is not in progress" by installing the temporary roof before leaving the site. Furthermore, the owner could not withhold damages from the contractor under the provision requiring that "any work damaged through the lack of proper protection or from any other cause shall be repaired or replaced without extra cost to the Owner" because under the terms of the contract only the temporary roof, which the contractor repaired, constituted "work" within the meaning of the contract. The Court also found that the unambiguous language of the contract provided that the signs and barriers were intended for the protection of persons on the job site and not for the protection of the property upon which the work was being performed. Contractor's failure to conform to the contractual requirements to place the barriers to protect people on the work site could not be used by the owner to hold the contractor liable for damage to the structure. Finally, the Court rejected the claim that contractor was liable under the provision making contractor "responsible for the protection of the buildings and grounds on which they are working . . . during the course of the work." Because the term "during the course of the work" was not defined in the contract the Court gave the words their ordinary meaning and held that the term was meant to encompass only the time while contractor was actually engaged in working on the project and not the time after contractor left the site. The Court thus concluded that none of the contract provisions rendered contractor liable to owner.

86019 (UNASSIGNED)

86020 Eugene W. Kelsey & Son, Inc. v. Architectural Openings, Inc., 484 So. 2d 610 (Fla. Dist. Ct. App.), *review denied*, 492 So. 2d 1330 (Fla. 1986)

II: A107-1978, Art. 13, Para. 13.2
II: A117-1979, Art. 17, Para. 17.2
II: A201-1976, Art. 7, Para. 7.9.1
II: A401-1978, Art. 13, Para. 13.1
II: B141-1977, Art. 9, Para. 9.1

Contractor appealed from the trial court's affirmation of an arbitration award in favor of subcontractor. It argued that a later oral agreement to perform a portion of the work

performance. Each contract further specified a time frame within which performance was to occur.

The trial court concluded that delays in the project were caused exclusively by the gross mismanagement of the owner, and therefore found the owner liable to each plaintiff under theories of breach of contract, estoppel, unjust enrichment and negligence. On appeal, the Court held that the owner failed to preserve the challenges to the recovery of delay costs.

86018   E.L. Scott Roofing Co. v. State of North Carolina, 82 N.C. App. 216, 346 S.E.2d 515 (1986)

	III:	A107-1978, Art. 7, Para. 7.4
	III:	A107-1978, Art. 12, Para. 12.3
	III:	A107-1978, Art. 16, Para. 16.1
	III:	A117-1979, Art. 11, Para. 11.4
	III:	A117-1979, Art. 16, Para. 16.3
	III:	A117-1979, Art. 20, Para. 20.1
	III:	A201-1976, Art. 1, Para. 1.1.3
	III:	A201-1976, Art. 4, Para. 4.13.1
	III:	A201-1976, Art. 4, Para. 4.14.2
	III:	A201-1976, Art. 6, Para. 6.2.4
	III:	A201-1976, Art. 10, Para. 10.2.1
	III:	A201-1976, Art. 10, Para. 10.2.2
	III:	A201-1976, Art. 10, Para. 10.2.3
	III:	A201-1976, Art. 10, Para. 10.2.4
	III:	A201-1976, Art. 10, Para. 10.2.5

Contractor brought an action against owner to recover amounts due under a contract for roof repairs. The trial court held for owner on the grounds that contractor had a duty imposed by the contract to protect the building and its contents from damage while the work was in progress and while it was not in progress, and contractor's failure to prevent access to the roof and to warn and prevent others from walking on the roof was a breach of the owner-contractor agreement. The trial court found that the owner had properly withheld from contractor an amount equal to the damage to the building caused by leaking of the temporary roof and denied contractor any recovery. On appeal contractor argued that the trial court erred in concluding that contractor was contractually liable to owner for damages. The Court of Appeals agreed and reversed.

The owner-contractor agreement provided in pertinent part that contractor was responsible "for the entire site and the buildings or construction of the same and provide all necessary protections, as required by the Owner or Engineer or Architect. . . . They shall be responsible for any damage to the owner's property, or that of others on the job. . . . [T]hey shall be responsible for and pay for any claims against the Owner. . . ."

86016 Dudley v. St. Regis Corp., 635 F. Supp. 1468 (E.D. Mo. 1986)

        III: A107-1978, Art. 20, Para. 20.2
        III: A117-1979, Art. 24, Para. 24.2
        III: A201-1976, Art. 14, Para. 14.2.1
        III: A201-1976, Art. 14, Para. 14.2.2

Contractor brought an action against owner to recover lost profits resulting from owner's cancellation of a contract to refurbish a portion of the roof on owner's factory.

The owner-contractor agreement provided that in the event the owner decided not to proceed with the work "the Owner may terminate this agreement at any time upon written notice to the contractor, thereupon the Owner's own liability shall be to pay to the Contractor all costs for labor and materials incorporated in the work prior to termination and all costs . . . and a reasonable overhead and profit. . . ."

The District Court construed the contract as providing that, upon termination of the contract by the owner, the contractor would recover the reasonable overhead and profit that would have been earned had the contract been completed. The Court found that there was nothing in the owner-contractor agreement to indicate that the clause was restricted only to costs already incurred at the time of the cancellation.

86017 E.B. Jones Constr. Co. v. City & County of Denver, 717 P.2d 1009 (Colo. Ct. App. 1986)

        III: A107-1978, Art. 12, Para. 12.2
        III: A117-1979, Art. 16, Para. 16.2
        III: A201-1976, Art. 6, Para. 6.1.3
        III: A201-1976, Art. 6, Para. 6.2.1
        III: A201-1976, Art. 6, Para. 6.2.2
        III: A201-1976, Art. 6, Para. 6.2.3

Contractors sought delay damages arising from the construction of a police and detention facility. The management agreement provisions and the contractor agreements imposed upon the owner the contractual duty to organize, schedule, expedite, supervise and manage the work of all contractors, to allow each contractor to timely and economically perform its work. Under the terms of the management agreement, the project was to be managed as "fast-track" construction and the project manager was to "establish and implement a comprehensive management program, including all direction, procedures, coordination, administration, review, expediting and counseling required to assist the City and its designated consultants and contractors in completing the Project in a timely, economical and acceptable manner". Each contractor's agreement provided for termination by the owner, stated that "all Contractors understand and agree that all work must be performed in an orderly and closely coordinate sequence so that the date of substantial completion may be met. . .," and gave the City options to enforce timely

86014 Creative Builders, Inc. v. Avenue Dev., Inc., 148 Ariz. 452, 715 P.2d 308 (1986)

> I: A101-1977, Art. 5
> I: A107-1978, Art. 4, Para. 4.2
> I: A107-1978, Art. 13, Para. 13.2
> I: A111-1978, Art. 14, Para. 14.3
> I: A117-1979, Art. 9, Para. 9.2
> I: A117-1979, Art. 17, Para. 17.2
> I: A201-1976, Art. 7, Para. 7.9.1
> I: A401-1978, Art. 13, Para. 13.1
> I: B141-1977, Art. 9, Para. 9.1

In confirming an arbitration award for contractor for the balance due under the owner-contractor agreement, the trial court modified the award to include pre-award interest. The owner appealed. The Court of Appeals held that the trial court erred in modifying the award to include pre-award interest, reasoning that any claim contractor had for accrued interest was merged into the arbitration award.

The Court relied on Paragraph 7.9.1 of the American Institute of Architects General Conditions of the Contract for Construction, Document No. A201, 1976 edition and the owner-contractor agreement which provided that "Payments due and unpaid under the Contract Documents shall bear interest from the date payment is due at the rate entered below, or in the absence thereof, at the legal rate prevailing at the place of the Project." The blank for the insertion of the rate of interest was not filled in.

The Court reasoned that the language contained in Paragraph 7.9.1 which provided for the submission to the arbitrators of "all" claims and disputes between the parties arising out of the owner-contractor agreement supported its finding that part of the claim asserted by the contractor included a claim for accrued interest even thought the contractor did not present evidence or argue for interest before the arbitrators.

86015 Delta Elec., Inc. v. Ingram & Greene, Inc., 123 A.D.2d 369, 506 N.Y.S.2d 594 (1986)

> III: A107-1978, Art. 11, Para. 11.2
> III: A117-1979, Art. 15, Para. 15.2
> III: A201-1976, Art. 5, Para. 5.3.1
> II: A401-1978, Art. 11, Para. 11.1.1

The Appellate Division upheld the trial court's ruling that subcontractor did not state a cause of action against the owner for extras pursuant to the subcontract. The subcontract incorporated the owner-contractor agreement, which specifically provided that nothing contained in the agreement "shall create any contractual relation between any subcontractor and the [owner]."

III: A201-1976, Art. 8, Para. 8.3.1

III: A201-1976, Art. 8, Para. 8.3.4

In a consolidated appeal, the New York Court of Appeals held that damages resulting from uncontemplated delays caused by the contractee may be recovered despite the existence of a broad exculpatory clause relieving the contractee from liability. The Court reaffirmed the Kalish-Jarcho rule (see case digest number 83027) that contract clauses barring a contractor from recovering damages for delay in the performance of a contract were valid and would prevent recovery of damages resulting from a broad range of reasonable and unreasonable conduct by the contractee if the conduct was contemplated by the parties when they entered into the agreement, but that such clauses will not excuse or prevent the recovery of damages resulting from the contractees grossly negligent or willful conduct.

86013   Coverdill v. Lurgi Corp., 146 Ill. App. 3d 112, 99 Ill. Dec. 915, 496 N.E.2d 1007 (1986)

II: A107-1978, Art. 10, Para. 10.11

II: A117-1979, Art. 14, Para. 14.11

II: A201-1976, Art. 4, Para. 4.18.1

II: A401-1978, Art. 11, Para. 11.11.1

Subcontractor's injured employee brought an action against contractor for personal injuries, and contractor asserted an third-party claim for indemnification against the subcontractor. The trial court granted subcontractor's motion to strike the contractual indemnity count. The Appellate Court affirmed, holding that the subcontractor was not required to indemnity the contractor from the consequences of its own actions.

The subcontract provided that subcontractor was to indemnify contractor against "any and all loss, cost, damage or expense of every kind and nature arising out of injuries to or death of persons (including without limitation . . . the Sub-contractor's and sub-subcontractor's, employees, agents, licensees and representatives) . . . in any manner caused by, resulting from, incident to, connected with or growing out of performance of the Contract, unless solely caused by the negligent acts or omissions of Lurgi. . . ." The subcontractor was required to maintain insurance satisfactory to contractor to cover liabilities assumed under the indemnity clause.

The Appellate Court construed the indemnification language as not explicitly providing that subcontractor had to obtain insurance to indemnify contractor against contractor's own negligence. Furthermore, the Court found that the clause excluded indemnification for damages or injuries caused solely by contractor's negligence. Because the insurance provision clearly referred to the indemnity provision, the Court found that the insurance provision should be construed as requiring subcontractor to obtain insurance to indemnify contractor for negligence other than contractor's own negligence.

86011 Commonwealth of Pennsylvania, Dept. of Transp. v. Trumbull Corp., 99 Pa. Commw. 557, 513 A.2d 1110 (1986)

III:	A107-1978, Art. 18, Para. 18.1
III:	A107-1978, Art. 18, Para. 18.2
III:	A107-1978, Art. 18, Para. 18.3
III:	A117-1979, Art. 22, Para. 22.1
III:	A117-1979, Art. 22, Para. 22.2
III:	A117-1979, Art. 22, Para. 22.3
III:	A201-1976, Art. 12, Para. 12.1.2
III:	A201-1976, Art. 12, Para. 12.1.3
III:	A201-1976, Art. 12, Para. 12.1.4
III:	A201-1976, Art. 12, Para. 12.1.5
III:	A201-1976, Art. 12, Para. 12.3.1
III:	A201-1976, Art. 12, Para. 12.3.2
III:	A201-1976, Art. 12, Para. 12.4.1

Contractor entered into a highway resurfacing contract. It subsequently filed a claim with the Board of Claims for additional compensation because its unit costs were increased as a result of the reduced quantity of work. The Board awarded contractor additional compensation and the owner appealed.

The owner-contractor agreement provided that the drawings and specifications could be modified or altered by the engineer and any additional work involved would be paid for at the contract price. Furthermore, "if such changes materially increase or decrease the unit cost of the work . . . payment will be made as extra work in accordance with the provisions of Section 109.04(c). Section 109.04(c) provided that the work "would be performed as extra work, at a price to be negotiated between the engineer and contractor, and ordered in writing by the engineer." If a fair price could not be determined by the engineer the contractor was to perform the work on a force-account basis. The force-account provisions set the contractor's compensation at the contractor's cost plus 25 percent for overhead and profit.

The Court upheld the Board's finding that the contractor's costs were increased as a result of the quantity of repair which the owner designated. It was also proper to apply the force-account provisions because the owner did not make an equitable adjustment. Accordingly, the Board's award was supported by substantial evidence.

86012 Corinno Civetta Constr. Corp. v. City of New York, 67 N.Y.2d 297, 493 N.E.2d 905, 502 N.Y.S.2d 681 (1986), *on remand,* Nab-Tern Constructors v. City of New York, 123 A.D.2d 571, 507 N.Y.S.2d 146 (1986)

III:	A107-1978, Art. 14, Para. 14.3
III:	A117-1979, Art. 18, Para. 18.3

III: A201-1976, Art. 2, Para. 2.2.11
III: A201-1976, Art. 2, Para. 2.2.12
III: A201-1976, Art. 4, Para. 4.2.1
III: A201-1976, Art. 7, Para. 7.9.1
III: A201-1976, Art. 8, Para. 8.3.1
III: A201-1976, Art. 8, Para. 8.3.2
III: A201-1976, Art. 8, Para. 8.3.3
III: A201-1976, Art. 8, Para. 8.3.4
III: A201-1976, Art. 12, Para. 12.2.1
III: A201-1976, Art. 12, Para. 12.3.1

Contractor brought an action against owner to recover additional compensation in excess of the contract price set forth in an excavation contract. The trial court entered a compulsory nonsuit against the contractor and the contractor appealed. The Appellate Court affirmed the trial court's determination. On appeal to the Supreme Court, the owner argued that the contractor was precluded from recovery by the exculpatory language contained in the contract; the contractor argued that the exculpatory provisions relied upon by the owner were not a defense to a claim for additional compensation because the owner affirmatively interfered with the contractor's performance under the contract by failing the drain the lake. The Supreme Court agreed with the contractor, and reversed.

The owner-contractor agreement provided that contractor was not entitled to demand or receive payments for any extra work "unless ordered in writing by the Committee to do the same as such, and at a price fixed by them previously to its commencement." Furthermore, the contractor was required to conduct and rely on his own investigation and research of the conditions affecting the work to be done. Contractor further agreed that he would make "no claim against the Municipality because of any of the estimates, tests or representations of any kind affecting the work made by any agent of the municipality may prove to be in any respect erroneous." The agreement contained a no-damage-for-delay clause entitling the contractor only to an extension of time upon written notice of the cause of the delay. All disputes regarding the execution of the work were to be settled by the Committee whose decisions were final and binding. The contractor also agreed to assume the responsibility for any "loss or damage arising out of the nature of the work to be done under the contract, or from any unforeseen obstructions or difficulties which may be encountered in the prosecution of the same. . . ."

The Supreme Court found that the contract specifications obligated the owner to maintain the lake bed in a drained and drawndown condition during the course of the contractor's performance. Therefore, the owner's notification to the contractor to proceed with the excavation work when the owner knew that the lake was filled with water invalidated the exculpatory provisions of the contract. Ordering the contractor to start work without having the lake drained constituted interference on the part of the owner. Consequently, the owner could not raise the exculpatory provisions as a defense.

resulting from the delay were not within the contemplation of the parties at the time of contracting.

The owner-contractor agreement specifically placed the burden of complying with all local laws, ordinances and regulations on the contractor. The contractor also had the responsibility to secure all necessary permits. In addition, Article 30 of the General Conditions was a no-damage-for-delay clause which placed the risk of delay, including delay caused by governmental acts or regulations, on the contractor. In pertinent part, Article 30 provided that the contractor would have no claim against the owner "for an increase in the contract price or a payment or allowance of any kind based on any damage, loss or additional expense the contractor may suffer as a result of any delays in prosecuting or completing the work under the contract. . . . It is understood that the contractor assumes all risks of delays in prosecuting or completing the work under the contract." In addition, the owner provided the contractor with a site investigation report which required that the preliminary plans were to be submitted to the city planning commission for review and approval.

The Supreme Court found that in the documents dispersed prior to bidding and after the contract was awarded, the owner placed the burden of complying with local ordinances on the contractor. Furthermore, the contractor was aware of its burden to comply with the local laws, ordinances and regulations by the clear language of the owner-contractor agreement and had accepted the risk of cost overruns caused by any delay. The no-damage-for-delay clause specifically mentioned that no claim for damages as a result of delay could be made when the delay was caused by "a governmental act or regulation." Accordingly, the Court reversed the judgment of the Court of Appeals and held that summary judgment for the owner was proper.

86010 Coatsville Contractors & Eng'rs, Inc. v. Borough of Ridley Park, 509 Pa. 553, 506 A.2d 862 (1986)

III:	A107-1978, Art. 8, Para. 8.5	
III:	A107-1978, Art. 13, Para. 13.2	
III:	A107-1978, Art. 14, Para. 14.3	
III:	A107-1978, Art. 18, Para. 18.2	
III:	A107-1978, Art. 18, Para. 18.3	
III:	A117-1979, Art. 12, Para. 12.5	
III:	A117-1979, Art. 17, Para. 17.2	
III:	A117-1979, Art. 18, Para. 18.3	
III:	A117-1979, Art. 22, Para. 22.2	
III:	A117-1979, Art. 22, Para. 22.3	
III:	A201-1976, Art. 2, Para. 2.2.7	
III:	A201-1976, Art. 2, Para. 2.2.8	
III:	A201-1976, Art. 2, Para. 2.2.9	
III:	A201-1976, Art. 2, Para. 2.2.10	

receipt of payment from the owner "the Subcontractor may upon seven (7) days written notice to the Contractor stop work without prejudice to any other remedy he may have."

The Court of Appeal found that the subcontract provided that the retainage withheld by the contractor from the monthly progress payments to the subcontractor was withheld from "the value of the work provided and performed." Additionally, the subcontract provided that "final payment shall be due when the work described in this contract is fully completed and performed. . . ." The Court construed these provisions as contemplating an unconditional obligation on the contractor to pay for work provided and performed by the subcontractor. The Court then decided that payment was due to the subcontractor within a reasonable time and concluded that one year from the date of the completion of the work by the subcontractor and its acceptance by the owner was within a reasonable time.

86009   Carrabine Constr. Co. v. Chrysler Realty Corp., 25 Ohio St. 3d 222, 495 N.E.2d 952 (1986)

	III:	A107-1978, Art. 10, Para. 10.5
	III:	A107-1978, Art. 10, Para. 10.6
	III:	A107-1978, Art. 14, Para. 14.3
	III:	A107-1978, Art. 18, Para. 18.3
	III:	A117-1979, Art. 14, Para. 14.5
	III:	A117-1979, Art. 14, Para. 14.6
	III:	A117-1979, Art. 18, Para. 18.3
	III:	A117-1979, Art. 22, Para. 22.3
	III:	A201-1976, Art. 4, Para. 4.7.1
	III:	A201-1976, Art. 4, Para. 4.7.2
	III:	A201-1976, Art. 4, Para. 4.7.4
	III:	A201-1976, Art. 4, Para. 4.7.4
	III:	A201-1976, Art. 8, Para. 8.3.1
	III:	A201-1976, Art. 8, Para. 8.3.2
	III:	A201-1976, Art. 8, Para. 8.3.3
	III:	A201-1976, Art. 8, Para. 8.3.4
	III:	A201-1976, Art. 12, Para. 12.3.1

Contractor brought an action against owner for delay damages resulting from a zoning problem. The trial court granted owner's motion for summary judgment on the grounds that the no-damage-for-delay clause in the contract prevented contractor from recovering damages for the zoning delay. After numerous appeals by both parties, the Court of Appeals reversed the grant of summary judgment. On appeal to the Supreme Court of Ohio, contractor argued that owner was responsible for the proper zoning of the construction site; the delay was not barred by the no-damage-for-delay clause because the damages

III:	A201-1976, Art. 9, Para. 9.5.2
III:	A201-1976, Art. 9, Para. 9.5.3
III:	A201-1976, Art. 9, Para. 9.5.4
III:	A201-1976, Art. 9, Para. 9.5.5
III:	A201-1976, Art. 9, Para. 9.6.1
III:	A201-1976, Art. 9, Para. 9.6.2
III:	A201-1976, Art. 9, Para. 9.7.1
III:	A201-1976, Art. 9, Para. 9.9.1
III:	A201-1976, Art. 9, Para. 9.9.2
III:	A201-1976, Art. 9, Para. 9.9.3
III:	A201-1976, Art. 9, Para. 9.9.4
III:	A201-1976, Art. 9, Para. 9.9.5
II:	A401-1978, Art. 5, Para. 5.1
II:	A401-1978, Art. 5, Para. 5.2
II:	A401-1978, Art. 5, Para. 5.3
II:	A401-1978, Art. 5, Para. 5.4
II:	A401-1978, Art. 6, Para. 6.1
II:	A401-1978, Art. 6, Para. 6.2
II:	A401-1978, Art. 11, Para. 11.8.1
II:	A401-1978, Art. 11, Para. 11.8.2
II:	A401-1978, Art. 11, Para. 11.8.3
II:	A401-1978, Art. 11, Para. 11.12.1
II:	A401-1978, Art. 12, Para. 12.4.1
II:	A401-1978, Art. 12, Para. 12.4.2
II:	A401-1978, Art. 12, Para. 12.4.3

Subcontractor brought an action against contractor for retainage due under the subcontract. The trial court found for contractor holding that final payment was not due under the subcontract until the contractor received final payment from the owner. The Court of Appeal reversed.

The subcontract provided that the contractor pay the subcontractor progress payments in current funds, subject to additions and deductions for changes agreed to in writing and that such "payments shall be made ten (10) days after payment by the Owner in installments of ninety-five (95) percent of the value of the work provided and performed by the Subcontractor." The subcontract also set forth the application for progress payments procedure to be followed by the subcontractor. It stated that final payment "shall be due when the work described in this contract is fully completed and performed in accordance with the Contract Documents. . . ." Final payment to the subcontractor was due "within ten (10) days after the Contractor receives final payment from the Owner." If the contractor failed to pay the subcontractor within seven days from the contractor's

the accuracy and completeness" of the surveys. The owner was required, under Paragraph 2.8, to give prompt written notice to the architect of "any fault or defect in the Project or non-conformance with the contract documents."

The Appellate Court found that the contract clearly provided that the owner had to obtain a plat of survey which had to show any restrictions. The architect was entitled to rely upon the accuracy and completeness of the survey.

86007   Cafferkey v. Turner Constr. Co., 21 Ohio St. 3d 110, 488 N.E.2d 189 (1986)

> III: A401-1978, Art. 12, Para. 12.2.1

Plaintiffs' decedents died as a result of severe injuries sustained on a construction site. Plaintiffs brought actions against the contractor and subcontractor. The trial court granted summary judgment in favor of the contractor, holding that it owed no duty of care to the decedents because both were working for the subcontractor at the time of injury. The Court of Appeals affirmed, as did the Supreme Court of Ohio.

Relying in part on the subcontract which provided that contractor retained the ability to monitor and coordinate the activities of all subcontractors in order to ensure compliance with the architect's specifications, the Court upheld that trial courts ruling that the contractor, who supervised the worksite but did not control the means or matter of subcontractor's performance, owned no duty of care to subcontractor's employees who were engaged in an inherently dangerous activity. No duty of care was created merely by virtue of its supervisory role.

86008   Cahn Elec. Co. v. Robert E. McKee, Inc., 490 So. 2d 647 (La. Ct. App. 1986)

> III: A107-1978, Art. 15, Para. 15.1
> III: A107-1978, Art. 15, Para. 15.2
> III: A107-1978, Art. 15, Para. 15.3
> III: A107-1978, Art. 15, Para. 15.4
> III: A107-1978, Art. 15, Para. 15.5
> III: A117-1979, Art. 19, Para. 19.1
> III: A117-1979, Art. 19, Para. 19.2
> III: A117-1979, Art. 19, Para. 19.3
> III: A117-1979, Art. 19, Para. 19.4
> III: A117-1979, Art. 19, Para. 19.5
> III: A201-1976, Art. 9, Para. 9.3.1
> III: A201-1976, Art. 9, Para. 9.3.2
> III: A201-1976, Art. 9, Para. 9.3.3
> III: A201-1976, Art. 9, Para. 9.4.1
> III: A201-1976, Art. 9, Para. 9.4.2
> III: A201-1976, Art. 9, Para. 9.5.1

Article 13 of the owner-contractor agreement provided that the contractor agreed "to make no claim for damages for delay in the performance of this contract occasioned by any act or omission to act of the City [owner] or any of its representatives, and agrees that any such claim shall be fully compensated for by an extension of time to complete performance of the work as provided herein."

The Appellate Division held that Article 13 created a bar to contractor's claim for delay damages because the delay was within the contemplation of the parties and it was not caused by owner's willful misconduct or abandonment of the project. The Court also denied the contractor compensation for extra and additional work because the contractor failed to comply with the disputed work procedures set forth in the contract. In addition, extra work due to changed subsurface conditions was compensable under the owner-contractor agreement only by means of a contract modification pursuant to Section 4(b) which had not been requested by the contractor.

86006   Cadral Corp. v. Solomon, Cordwell, Buenz & Assocs., 147 Ill. App. 3d 466, 100 Ill. Dec. 923, 497 N.E.2d 1285 (1986)

II:	A107-1978, Art. 9, Para. 9.1	
II:	A107-1978, Art. 9, Para. 9.2	
II:	A117-1979, Art. 13, Para. 13.1	
II:	A117-1979, Art. 13, Para. 13.2	
II:	A201-1976, Art. 3, Para. 3.2.2	
II:	A201-1976, Art. 3, Para. 3.2.3	
I:	B141-1977, Art. 2, Para. 2.1	
I:	B141-1977, Art. 2, Para. 2.3	
I:	B141-1977, Art. 2, Para. 2.7	
I:	B141-1977, Art. 2, Para. 2.8	

Owner brought an action against architect to recover damages which resulted from violation of a building line restriction. The building was redesigned to remedy the building line violation. The jury returned a verdict for architect and owner appealed. In support of its appeal of the denial of its motion for judgment notwithstanding the verdict, owner argued that the architect undertook the responsibility for providing the surveyor with the survey requirements and the architect's failure to mention "restrictions" in the list of requirements was a bar to architect claiming that owner did not furnish it with notice of the building line restriction.

The owner and architect entered into the American Institute of Architects Standard From of Agreement Between Owner and Architect, Document No. B141, 1977 edition. Article 2, entitled "The Owners Responsibilities" provided in Paragraph 2.1 that the "Owner shall provide full information regarding his requirements for the project." Paragraph 2.3 required the owner to "furnish a certified land survey of the site giving, as applicable, . . . restrictions, easements, encroachments, zoning, deed restrictions, boundaries and contours of the site. . . ." Paragraph 2.7 allowed the architect to "rely upon

anticipated by Contractor, a Change Order shall be issued incorporating the necessary revisions." Section 11.2 provided that the contract price could only be changed by a change order and the owner and the engineer had to be notified within fifteen days "of the occurrence of the event giving rise to the claim." Notice of the amount of the claim had to be delivered within forty-five days of the occurrence. Section 6.29 required the contractor to "carry out the Work and maintain the progress schedule during all disputes or disagreements with Owner."

A careful reading of the contract documents revealed that the engineer's utility line drawings were stamped with a warning that contractor was responsible for determining the location of all underground utilities prior to excavation. In addition, the contract placed the responsibility of verifying utility locations on the contractor. The Court found that the contractor did not submit a change order as required by Section 4.3, nor did the contractor meet the conditions set forth in Section 11.2 for notification of an event which justified a price increase. Because the contractor did not meet the conditions precedent under the contract for payment of its additional costs, the Court held that it was unnecessary to decide whether Section 6.29 required contractor to perform regardless of whether the owner fulfilled its contractual obligations. The contractor had elected to proceed, and consequently was under a duty to comply with the provisions of the contract pertaining to work and price changes.

86005 Buckley & Co. v. City of New York, 121 A.D.2d 933, 505 N.Y.S.2d 140 (1986)

III:	A107-1978, Art. 14, Para. 14.3
III:	A107-1978, Art. 18, Para. 18.1
III:	A107-1978, Art. 18, Para. 18.2
III:	A107-1978, Art. 18, Para. 18.3
III:	A117-1979, Art. 18, Para. 18.3
III:	A117-1979, Art. 22, Para. 22.1
III:	A117-1979, Art. 22, Para. 22.2
III:	A117-1979, Art. 22, Para. 22.3
III:	A201-1976, Art. 8, Para. 8.3.1
III:	A201-1976, Art. 8, Para. 8.3.2
III:	A201-1976, Art. 8, Para. 8.3.3
III:	A201-1976, Art. 8, Para. 8.3.4
III:	A201-1976, Art. 12, Para. 12.2.1
III:	A201-1976, Art. 12, Para. 12.3.1

Contractor brought an action against owner. In its third and fourth causes of action, it sought damages from the delay caused by owner's improper design of a cofferdam which resulted in changed subsurface conditions. The trial court granted owner's motion for summary judgment on these claims. The Appellate Division affirmed, but held that the district court erred in sua sponte allowing the contractor to replead.

Contractor filed a demand to arbitrate its claim for extras. The trial court denied the owner's motion to stay and compelled arbitration. Owner appealed. At issue on appeal was the timeliness of contractor's demand to arbitrate under state statute and the timeliness of contractor's notice to the architect for extras as required by the contract.

Section 12.3.1 of the owner-contractor agreement provided that "If the contractor wishes to make a claim for an increase in the contract sum, he shall give the architect written notice thereof within twenty days after the occurrence of the event giving rise to such claim. . . . No such claim shall be valid unless so made."

Subcontractor advised contractor on July 6, 1984 of the need for the extras. On July 11, 1984, the contractor informed the architect of this need. Accordingly, the Court found that the contractor's letter to the architect requesting a change order covering the extras, which was received by the architect within twenty days of the "event giving rise to such claim," satisfied the written notice requirement of Section 12.3.1.

86004   Brady Contracting Co. v. West Manchester Township Sewer Auth., 97 Pa. Commw. 31, 508 A.2d 1287 (1986), *appeal denied,* 514 Pa. 649, 524 A.2d 495 (1987)

II:	A107-1978, Art. 14, Para. 14.1	
III:	A107-1978, Art. 18, Para. 18.1	
III:	A107-1978, Art. 18, Para. 18.2	
III:	A107-1978, Art. 18, Para. 18.3	
III:	A117-1979, Art. 18, Para. 18.1	
III:	A117-1979, Art. 22, Para. 22.1	
III:	A117-1979, Art. 22, Para. 22.2	
III:	A117-1979, Art. 22, Para. 22.3	
III:	A201-1976, Art. 7, Para. 7.9.3	
III:	A201-1976, Art. 8, Para. 8.2.2	
III:	A201-1976, Art. 12, Para. 12.1.1	
III:	A201-1976, Art. 12, Para. 12.2.1	
III:	A201-1976, Art. 12, Para. 12.3.1	

Contractor brought an action against owner for additional costs due to an obstruction caused by a gas line during excavation. The trial court granted owner's motion for summary judgment on the grounds that the contract placed the risk of loss resulting from mislocation of subsurface utility lines on the contractor. The Appellate Court affirmed.

The owner-contractor agreement contained supplementary conditions which required that the contractor comply with the state statute pertaining to excavation work near underground utility lines. Section 4.3 provided that contractor promptly notify owner and engineer in writing of any differing subsurface conditions and if the engineer found that there were "subsurface or latent physical conditions which differ materially from those intended in the Contract Documents, and which could not reasonably have been

Subcontractor brought an action against contractor for funds received by contractor from owner, the state, resulting from a cost increase in bituminous materials. The trial court held that the material provisions of the prime contract were not incorporated into the subcontract; therefore, contractor was not obligated to pay any funds received from the owner as a result of cost increases to the subcontractor. Subcontractor argued on appeal that Article 1 of the subcontract incorporated all provisions dealing in any way with the asphalt paving, including, but not limited to, payment for the material and the services performed under the subcontract. The Appellate Court rejected this argument, agreeing with the trial court's interpretation.

The contractor and subcontractor entered into the American Institute of Architects Standard Form of Agreement Between Contractor and Subcontractor, Document No. A401, 1978 edition, which defined contract documents in Article 1. Article 2 provided that the subcontractor "furnish all materials, supplies, labor, equipment, engineering services and other necessary items to do and perform for Contractor the following items of work on the above mentioned project for the following contract prices. . . ." Article 4 provided that the contractor pay the subcontractor "in current funds for the performance of the Work, subject to additions and deductions by Change Order, in accordance with the unit prices set out in Article 2. It is understood and agreed that the quantities set out in said articles are estimates only and that the Contractor will pay the Subcontractor for all quantities actually produced by the Subcontractor and approved for payment by the State of Tennessee Department of Transportation." Paragraphs 11.1.1 and 12.1.1 contained flow-up and flow-down provisions of the contractor's and subcontractor's rights and responsibilities. The owner-contractor agreement, on the other hand, contained a provision entitled "Special Provision Regarding Price Adjustment for Bituminous Material" which set forth the method for adjusting the price to be paid by the State for the bituminous materials required under the contract.

The Appellate Court emphasized that the pay provisions of the subcontract contained no provision for pay increases due to material price changes, or for any other reason. To the Court, it was "plausible that different payment amounts could be provided for in a prime contract and in a subcontract." The contracts were quite clear in listing the work to be performed and the amount to be paid. Reading the contract documents as a whole, the Court held that the bituminous material price adjustment provision contained in the owner-contractor agreement was not incorporated into the subcontract.

86003   Board of Educ. Salmon River Cent. School Dist. v. Tracy Trombley Constr. Co., 122 A.D.2d 421, 505 N.Y.S.2d 233 (1986)

I:	A107-1978, Art. 18, Para. 18.1
I:	A107-1978, Art. 18, Para. 18.2
I:	A117-1979, Art. 22, Para. 22.1
I:	A117-1979, Art. 22, Para. 22.2
I:	A201-1976, Art. 12, Para. 12.3.1

86001   Alpha Crane Serv., Inc., v. Capitol Crane Co., 6 Conn. App. 60, 504 A.2d 1376, *cert. denied,* 199 Conn. 808, 508 A.2d 769 (1986)

III:	A107-1978, Art. 10, Para. 10.11	
III:	A117-1979, Art. 14, Para. 14.11	
III:	A201-1976, Art. 4, Para. 4.18.1	
III:	A401-1978, Art. 11, Para. 11.11.1	

Owner sought indemnification against contractor for damages resulting from the death of subcontractor's employee, including attorney's fees, costs of defense and damages to owner's property. The trial court granted owner's motion for summary judgment on liability, leaving the issue of damages to be decided by the jury. Contractor appealed, arguing that the court erred in concluding that the agreement covered attorney's fees and costs of defense, as well as damages to the owner's property.

The owner-contractor agreement provided that contractor agreed to indemnify owner from "any liability, claim of liability, expense, causes of action, loss or damage whatsoever for any injury . . . to any person or property in the performance of this Contract, unless such injury is caused by the sole negligence of [Owner], it being the intent of this agreement to protect and indemnify [Owner] from any and all loss arising out of or in connection with the Work performed under this Contract."

The Appellate Court found that the term "any" provided the broadest coverage and required the contractor to indemnify the owner from "any expense, causes of action, loss or damage whatsoever." However, the Court found that the term "expense" encompassed only attorney's fees incurred in defense of an original action and not in an indemnification action. Both issues were litigated in this action. Absent express contractual language entitling the owner to attorney's fees incurred in pursuing its indemnification action, summary judgment was inappropriate. Therefore, the Court remanded the action "for a determination of the amount of fees which were attributable solely to the defense of the claims of liability . . . as opposed to those fees incurred in obtaining immunity from [the contractor]."

86002   APAC-Tennessee, Inc. v. J.M. Humphries Constr. Co., 732 S.W.2d 601 (Tenn. Ct. App. 1986)

II:	A107-1978, Art. 11, Para. 11.2	
II:	A117-1979, Art. 15, Para. 15.2	
II:	A201-1976, Art. 5, Para. 5.3.1	
I:	A401-1978, Art. 1, Para. 1.1	
I:	A401-1978, Art. 1, Para. 1.2	
I:	A401-1978, Art. 2, Para. 2.1	
I:	A401-1978, Art. 4, Para. 4.1	
I:	A401-1978, Art. 11, Para. 11.1.1	
I:	A401-1978, Art. 12, Para. 12.1.1	

decided by arbitration" and further provided that the "agreement to arbitrate shall be specifically enforceable under the prevailing arbitration law."

The Appellate Court, applying basic rules of contract construction, concluded that the parties had unambiguously agreed to arbitrate the dispute.

85044   Zontelli & Sons, Inc. v. City of Nashwauk, 373 N.W.2d 744 (Minn. 1985)

III:	A107-1978, Art. 18, Para. 18.1
III:	A107-1978, Art. 18, Para. 18.2
III:	A107-1978, Art. 18, Para. 18.3
III:	A117-1979, Art. 22, Para. 22.1
III:	A117-1979, Art. 22, Para. 22.2
III:	A117-1979, Art. 22, Para. 22.3
III:	A201-1976, Art. 12, Para. 12.1.2
III:	A201-1976, Art. 12, Para. 12.2.1
III:	A201-1976, Art. 12, Para. 12.3.1

Contractor brought an action against owner and engineer for additional compensation for extra work resulting from inaccuracies in the plans and specifications upon which contractor based its bid. The trial court awarded damages to contractor to be divided between owner and engineer under a comparative fault theory. All parties appealed. The Appellate Court dismissed the owner's appeal as untimely and reversed the apportionment of fault and remanded for a determination of engineer's liability for contribution. Owner appealed. On second appeal the Court found that the owner's appeal was timely, and then addressed the issue of owner's liability to contractor.

The owner-contractor agreement provided for reimbursement of extra work under a "changed conditions" clause which stated that if the contractor should encounter "subsurface and/or latent conditions at the site materially differing from those shown on the Plans . . . he shall immediately give notice to the Engineer. . . . The Engineer will thereupon promptly investigate the conditions . . . make such changes . . . as he may deem necessary, and any increase or decrease of cost resulting from such changes to be adjusted in the manner provided in Paragraph 13 of the General Conditions." Paragraph 13 provided that "[n]o changes in the work covered by the approved contract documents shall be made without having prior written approval of the Owner. Changes or credits for the work covered by the approved change shall be determined by one or more, or a combination of the following methods. . . . It shall be the owner's option to select whichever method . . . that will be used in computing the payment for extra work." The agreement also provided that the owner had the right to increase or decrease the estimated quantities of work to be done and materials to be furnished and "such increase or diminution shall in no way vitiate this contract, nor shall any such increase or diminution give cause for claims or liability for damages."

The Supreme Court of Minnesota found that contractor's claim for extra work that arose because the actual quantity and quality of concrete and unsuitable materials differed from that shown on the plans was clearly compensable under the contract provisions.

The Appellate Court found that the express terms of the arbitration provision left all questions of breach of contract to the arbitrator unless contractor's nonperformance excused owner from its obligation to arbitrate. The Court concluded that contractor's claim that owner failed to make progress payments was within the scope of the broad arbitration provision. The contract language providing that "CONTRACTOR will carry on the WORK and maintain the progress schedule during any arbitration proceeding" described an arbitration in progress and not an arbitration yet to begin. The Court found that contractor had promised only to carry on the work not in dispute while the work in dispute was arbitrated but not to continue all work or risk forfeiture of the arbitration forum. Furthermore, the promise to arbitrate all claims was unconditional and the contractor's promise to continue work during arbitration only assured that the remainder of the contract would be performed. The Court held that contractor's right to arbitrate was unconditional and the refusal by contractor to continue the work was neither a repudiation nor was it inconsistent with access to the arbitration forum.

The arbitration clause of the second owner-contractor agreement provided that "disputes on matters not governed by the contract documents, and which otherwise cannot amicably be decided or settled, shall be arbitrated by three disinterested parties . . . such arbitration being a condition precedent to any right of legal action. . . ."

The Appellate Court found that the second arbitration clause not only declared an intent to arbitrate, but also defined the method of selection of the arbitrators, the time constraints to exercise the right, and the enforceability of the arbitration decision. However, the Court found that the language "disputes on matters not governed by the contract documents" created uncertainty as to the scope of arbitration making the contract ambiguous. The Court resolved the ambiguity against the proponent of the contract, the owner, and in favor of the arbitrability of the dispute because the full context of the transaction showed that once both bids were awarded to contractor the work was undertaken as a unitary performance. The Court remanded for arbitration in accordance with the agreement of the parties.

85043   Village of Jordan v. Memphis Constr. Co., 109 A.D.2d 1055, 487 N.Y.S.2d 196 (1985)

>   III: A107-1978, Art. 13, Para. 13.2
>   III: A117-1979, Art. 17, Para. 17.2
>   III: A201-1976, Art. 7, Para. 7.9.1
>   III: A401-1978, Art. 13, Para. 13.1
>   III   B141-1977, Art. 9, Para. 9.1

Contractor filed a demand for arbitration against owner seeking payment for extra work performed as a result of unforeseen subsurface conditions. The trial court denied owner's application for a stay of arbitration and owner appealed.

The owner-contractor agreement provided for the arbitration of disputes upon mutual agreement of the parties if the contract did not provide otherwise. The general conditions of the contract required that all claims or disputes arising out of the contract "shall be

III: B141-1977, Art. 9, Para. 9.1

Subcontractor brought an action against contractor for damages resulting from contractor's repudiation of the subcontract. Contractor moved to compel arbitration. The trial court denied contractor's motion on the grounds that contractor had repudiated the subcontract in its entirety, thereby precluding its right to arbitration. Contractor appealed.

The arbitration clause in the subcontract provided that any controversy arising with respect to the contract or project would be decided by the contractor and contractor's decision would be binding unless subcontractor commenced arbitration proceedings within 30 days following the decision. Arbitration would be conducted in accordance with the Construction Industry Arbitration Rules of the American Arbitration Association, and the decision of the arbitrators would be final and binding on both parties.

The Appellate Court considered whether the dispute was within the scope of the arbitration provision. Subcontractor argued that the arbitration provision was limited to disputes arising during the course of performance but not to total breach of contract by anticipatory repudiation. The Court found that the arbitration clause contained no limiting language. The clause was applicable to "any controversy" with respect to "any matter or thing involved in the contract or project. . . ." The Court upheld the arbitration clause but not in its entirety, stating that contractor could not enforce the provision requiring subcontractor to request arbitration within 30 days.

85042 Village of Cairo v. Bodine Contracting Co., 685 S.W.2d 253 (Mo. Ct. App. 1985)

III: A107-1978, Art. 13, Para. 13.2
III: A117-1979, Art. 17, Para. 17.2
III: A201-1976, Art. 7, Para. 7.9.1
III: A401-1978, Art. 13, Para. 13.1
III: B141-1977, Art. 9, Para. 9.1

Contractor demanded arbitration of its claim against owner that progress payments due under two separate contracts had not been paid. Owner brought suit to enjoin the arbitration, for a declaratory judgment that contractor's claims were not within the scope of the arbitration provisions of the two contracts, and for damages for breach of contract. The trial court found that there was no agreement to arbitrate and enjoined contractor from demanding arbitration. Contractor appealed.

The arbitration clause of the first owner-contractor agreement provided that "all claims, disputes and other matters in question arising out of, or relating to, the CONTRACT DOCUMENTS or the breach thereof, except for claims which have been waived by the making and acceptance of final payment . . . shall be decided by arbitration. . . ." The agreement also provided that contractor "will carry on the WORK and maintain the progress schedule during any arbitration proceedings, unless otherwise mutually agreed in writing."

III: A401-1978, Art. 11, Para. 11.10.1

Subcontractor brought an action against contractor for work performed in addition to the contract. Contractor moved for summary judgment on the grounds that subcontractor's failure to comply with the damage notification clause barred subcontractor's claim for additional payment.

The subcontract contained a damage notification clause requiring subcontractor to notify contractor in writing within seven days from commencement of the damage or additional cost which stated in pertinent part that "No claims for such damage shall be valid unless the Subcontractor complies with the requirements of this paragraph."

The District Court in a memorandum opinion, found that subcontractor had failed to comply with the notice provision of the subcontract and was therefore precluded from maintaining an action for additional costs.

85040   URS Co.-Kansas City v. Titus County Hosp. Dist., 604 F. Supp. 423 (W.D. Mo. 1985)

II: A107-1978, Art. 13, Para. 13.2
II: A117-1979, Art. 17, Para. 17.2
II: A201-1976, Art. 7, Para. 7.9.1
II: A401-1978, Art. 13, Para. 13.1
II: B141-1977, Art. 9, Para. 9.1

Owner brought an action against architect for design malpractice and breach of contract. Architect moved for an order to compel owner to arbitrate its claims against architect. Owner argued that its design malpractice claim was not arbitrable.

The owner-architect agreement contained a broad form arbitration provision similar to the arbitration provision contained in the American Institute of Architects Standard Form of Agreement Between Owner and Architect, Document No. B141, 1977 edition.

The District Court found that the arbitration clause did not expressly include or exclude tort claims. Furthermore, the scope of the clause was not limited to contract claims. The broad arbitration clause, viewed in the context of the owner-architect agreement and the nature of their relationship, included within its scope malpractice claims, which the Court found were foreseeable and were disputes "arising out of, or relating to" the agreement. The Court ordered the owner and architect to proceed to arbitration in accordance with the terms and conditions of their agreement.

85041   U.S. Insulation, Inc. v. Hilro Constr. Co., 146 Ariz. 250, 705 P.2d 490 (1985)

III: A107-1978, Art. 13, Para. 13.2
III: A117-1979, Art. 17, Para. 17.2
III: A201-1976, Art. 7, Para. 7.9.1
III: A401-1978, Art. 13, Para. 13.1

I:	A201-1976, Art. 11, Para. 11.3.6
II:	A201-1976, Art. 4, Para. 4.18.1

Owner's insurer brought a subrogation action against contractor and subcontractor alleging that the fire that caused extensive damage to part of the project was caused by contractor's and subcontractor's negligence. The trial court denied contractor's and subcontractor's motion for summary judgment on the grounds that the indemnity clause and the waiver of subrogation clause were inconsistent and that the indemnity clause controlled under the agreement's priority provisions. Contractor and subcontractor appealed.

The owner-contractor agreement consisted of a typewritten agreement which incorporated by reference the American Institute of Architects General Conditions of the Contract for Construction, Document No. A201, 1976 edition. The agreement provided that both documents were intended to be "read so as to be consistent with one another as possible," but if anything contained in the General Conditions was inconsistent with the agreement, the agreement governed. The General Conditions contained an insurance provision in Paragraphs 11.1.1 and 11.3.1 and contained a waiver of subrogation provision in Paragraph 11.3.6. The agreement provided that contractor would furnish workers' compensation, public liability, comprehensive auto liability, disability and "[owners'] protective insurance in the name of the owner, which shall provide bodily injury and property damage on an occurrence basis." In addition, contractor was obligated to indemnify and hold the owner harmless "against all liability, claims, loss, costs, damages and expenses . . . on account of injury or death to any person . . . or damage to property" not caused by the sole negligence of the owner.

The Appellate Court found no inconsistency between the contract provisions. The types of insurance which the contractor was required to provide under the agreement evidenced the intent of the parties that owner would be indemnified and held harmless from liability to a third party. The General Conditions required owner to obtain first party coverage for property loss in the event of damage to the building during construction and a waiver of subrogation in favor of contractor and subcontractor. The Court found that because owner had been fully compensated for the loss the indemnity provision was not applicable and the waiver of subrogation clause governed. The Court therefore granted contractor and subcontractor's motion for summary judgment.

85039   United States v. Centex Constr. Co., 638 F. Supp. 411 (W.D. Va. 1985)

III:	A107-1978, Art. 18, Para. 18.1
III:	A107-1978, Art. 18, Para. 18.2
III:	A107-1978, Art. 18, Para. 18.3
III:	A117-1979, Art. 22, Para. 22.1
III:	A117-1979, Art. 22, Para. 22.2
III:	A117-1979, Art. 22, Para. 22.3
III:	A201-1976, Art. 12, Para. 12.3.1

85037   Swartz v. Ford, Bacon & Davis Constr. Corp., 469 So. 2d 232 (Fla. Dist. Ct. App. 1985)

    III: A107-1978, Art. 8, Para. 8.3
    III: A107-1978, Art. 16, Para. 16.1
    III: A117-1979, Art. 12, Para. 12.3
    III: A117-1979, Art. 20, Para. 20.1
    III: A201-1976, Art. 2, Para. 2.2.4
    III: A201-1976, Art. 10, Para. 10.1.1
    III: A201-1976, Art. 10, Para. 10.2.1
    III: A201-1976, Art. 10, Para. 10.2.2
    III: B141-1977, Art. 1, Para. 1.5.5

Contractor's employee brought an action for personal injury damages against architect. The trial court entered summary judgment for architect and injured worker appealed, arguing that Article X of the owner-architect agreement created a duty for architect to supervise contractor and to require that contractor provide any required safety devices.

The owner-contractor agreement provided in Article X that all of architect's services were to "comply with, satisfy, and be subject to all applicable codes, ordinances, rules and regulations of any governmental authority having jurisdiction over the design and/or construction of the project. . . ." The required flooring and safety nets were not used.

The Appellate Court affirmed. It found that architect could only be held liable if the contract imposed a duty upon architect to supervise and/or control the actual method of construction used by contractor. The Court held that architect's contractual duties were clearly stated in Article II, which did not specify or imply a duty to supervise or control contractor's work. Article X only required that architect's services comply with applicable codes.

85038   Trump-Equitable Fifth Ave. Co. v. H.R.H. Constr. Corp., 106 A.D.2d 242, 485 N.Y.S.2d 65, *aff'd*, 66 N.Y.2d 779, 497 N.Y.S.2d 369, 488 N.E.2d 115 (1985)

    II: A107-1978, Art. 10, Para. 10.11
    II: A107-1978, Art. 17, Para. 17.1
    II: A107-1978, Art. 17, Para. 17.3
    II: A107-1978, Art. 17, Para. 17.6
    II: A117-1979, Art. 14, Para. 14.11
    II: A117-1979, Art. 21, Para. 21.1
    II: A117-1979, Art. 21, Para. 21.3
    II: A117-1979, Art. 21, Para. 21.6
    I: A201-1976, Art. 11, Para. 11.1.1
    I: A201-1976, Art. 11, Para. 11.3.1

The Appellate Court found that because contractor had denied that it was negligent and did not seek to interpose the indemnity agreement in the event of a finding of sole negligence, the agreement was not void on its face and subcontractor could be held obligated to indemnify contractor. The Court further held that contractor was entitled to recover attorney fees under the clear language of the indemnity agreement which provided that subcontractor would indemnify contractor "against all claims, liabilities, losses, damages and expenses of every character whatsoever. . . ."

85036   Steamboat Dev. Corp. v. Bacjac Indus., Inc., 701 P.2d 127 (Colo. Ct. App. 1985)

II:	A107-1976, Art. 17, Para. 17.3	
II:	A107-1976, Art. 17, Para. 17.6	
II:	A117-1979, Art. 21, Para. 21.3	
II:	A117-1979, Art. 21, Para. 21.6	
I:	A201-1976, Art. 11, Para. 11.3.1	
I:	A201-1976, Art. 11, Para. 11.3.6	

Owner sued contractor alleging that contractor's negligence caused the fire that destroyed the project. The trial court granted contractor's motion for summary judgment, holding that the owner-contractor agreement barred owner's claim and that owner had breached the contract.

The owner and contractor entered into an agreement for the construction of condominiums, which included the American Institute of Architects General Conditions of the Contract for Construction, Document No. A201, 1976 edition, insurance provisions contained in Paragraphs 11.3.1 and 11.3.6. Paragraph 11.3.1 required the owner to provide all risk insurance for "physical loss or damage" from the "perils of fire" naming both owner and contractor as insureds. The contract also contained a typewritten paragraph providing that the contractor would not carry builder's risk insurance. Owner failed to procure insurance naming contractor as an additional insured pursuant to Paragraph 11.3.1 and owner did not notify contractor of it's failure to procure the insurance.

The Appellate Court found that the purpose of the insurance required by Paragraph 11.3.1 was to shift the risk of loss away from the contractor and the owner and to place it on the insurer. The owner breached the contract by failing to obtain all risk insurance naming contractor. The Court found that the owner-contractor agreement clearly provided that in the event owner failed to obtain the insurance and contractor was damaged the "owner shall bear all reasonable costs properly attributable thereto." The owner thus became the insurer of the contractor to the same extent as any insurance company. Furthermore, pursuant to Paragraph 11.3.6 the owner waived all rights against contractor for damages caused by fire "to the extent covered by insurance," which the Court found included owner as insurer of contractor. The Court held that the contract clearly set forth the parties' intent to provide mutual exculpation from losses caused by fire and their agreement to look to insurance in the event of loss and not to recovery from the other party.

against all liability, loss, damage, expense, costs . . . of every nature arising out of any failure or alleged failure of SUBCONTRACTOR to perform . . . except such loss or damage which was caused solely by the negligence of CONTRACTOR or of OWNER."

The Appellate Court upheld the trial court's findings that the indemnity clause covered all injuries and damages arising from the work except for injuries caused solely by the negligence of contractor. The Court held that because the injuries were caused by the concurrent negligence of subcontractor, sub-subcontractor and contractor, subcontractor was liable to indemnify contractor.

The contract between subcontractor and sub-subcontractor, which was in the form of a letter of intent and purchase order, contained an indemnity clause which stated that sub-subcontractor agreed to indemnify and hold harmless subcontractor against any and all claims which arose from sub-subcontractor's performance of the contract. The indemnity clause contained in the purchase order required sub-subcontractor to indemnify subcontractor against liability resulting from "death or damage received or sustained by any person or persons, including any employee . . ." of sub-subcontractor resulting from sub-subcontractor's negligence. Furthermore, sub-subcontractor's acceptance of the purchase order "supersedes all prior agreements, and constitutes the entire contract. . . ."

The Appellate Court was faced with the issue of the obligation of sub-subcontractor to indemnify subcontractor for its liability to injured worker and the issue of sub-subcontractor's obligation to indemnify subcontractor with respect to subcontractor's contractual liability to indemnify owner. The Court found that sub-subcontractors agreement to indemnify subcontractor covered only loss or liability caused solely by sub-subcontractor's own acts or conduct. The Court held that the indemnity agreement in the purchase order, which superseded the indemnity agreement in the letter of intent, covered neither the subcontractor's tort liability which resulted from the concurrent negligence of contractor, subcontractor, sub-subcontractor and injured worker; nor did it cover subcontractor's contractual indemnity liability to contractor.

85035   Redfern v. R.E. Dailey & Co., 146 Mich. App. 8, 379 N.W.2d 451 (1985)

III:	A107-1978, Art. 10, Para. 10.1
III:	A117-1979, Art. 14, Para. 14.11
III:	A201-1976, Art. 4, Para. 4.18.1
III:	A401-1978, Art. 11, Para. 11.11.1

Contractor brought a third party indemnity action against subcontractor for personal injury damages paid to subcontractor's injured employee. The trial court entered judgment for contractor, holding that subcontractor's employee alone was negligent and that his negligence could be imputed to subcontractor. Subcontractor appealed.

The indemnity agreement between subcontractor and contractor provided that subcontractor indemnify and hold harmless contractor against "all claims, liabilities, losses, damages and expenses, of every character whatsoever, . . . in any way connected with the Work. . ." regardless of whether contractor was negligent.

negligent in preparing the contract documents, the architect had to indemnify the owner for the utility charges. The trial court found that the charges were the obligation of the owner and also held that the architect was not obligated to indemnify the owner. The owner appealed.

The owner-contractor agreement included the American Institute of Architects General Conditions of the Contract for Construction, Document No. A201, 1976 edition, which provided in Paragraph 4.7.1 that the contractor "shall secure and pay for the building permit and for all other permits and governmental fees, licenses and inspections. . . ." Paragraph 4.4.1 provided that the contractor "shall provide and pay for all labor, materials, equipment, tools, construction equipment and machinery, water, heat, utilities, transportation, and other facilities and services necessary for the proper execution and completion of the Work. . . ." Another contract article provided that the contractor "shall obtain and pay for all fees, permits, and licenses (but not assessments) required by his work. . . ."

The Appellate Court found that certain of the utility charges were not fees, permits, or licenses, and, therefore, were not required to be paid by the contractor. However, certain gas service charges, the Court concluded, were costs incurred in making the heating system operative. These charges fell within Paragraph 4.4.1 which provided that contractor was to pay for such "utilities . . . necessary for the proper execution and completion of the work. . . ." The Court also upheld the trial court's finding that architect was not negligent in preparing the contract documents and was not obligated to indemnify the owner.

85034   Ralph M. Parsons Co. v. Combustion Equip. Assoc., Inc., 172 Cal. App. 3d 211, 218 Cal. Rptr. 170 (1985)

III:	A107-1978, Art. 10, Para. 10.1	
III:	A117-1979, Art. 14, Para. 14.11	
III:	A201-1976, Art. 4, Para. 4.18.1	
III:	A401-1978, Art. 11, Para. 11.11.1	

Sub-subcontractor's employee brought an action for personal injury damages against contractor. Contractor brought an action against subcontractor for express and implied indemnity, partial contribution and declaratory relief. Subcontractor brought an indemnification action against sub-subcontractor. The trial court found that sub-subcontractor was not obligated to indemnify subcontractor. Before trial on the personal injury action contractor settled with the injured worker. The jury found that subcontractor and sub-subcontractor, along with the injured worker, were negligent. Contractor's indemnity action against subcontractor was tried to the court and the court entered judgment in favor of contractor for the amount of contractor's settlement with injured worker. Subcontractor appealed from the award of indemnity to contractor and the denial to subcontractor of indemnity from sub-subcontractor.

The subcontract provided that subcontractor would "hold CONTRACTOR and OWNER respectively free and harmless of and from, and defend and indemnify them

I:	A201-1976, Art. 3, Para. 3.2.4
I:	A201-1976, Art. 8, Para. 8.3.1
I:	A201-1976, Art. 8, Para. 8.3.4
I:	A201-1976, Art. 12, Para. 12.3.1

Contractor brought an action against owner for delay damages resulting from owner's failure to obtain the real estate upon which the school was to be constructed. The trial court entered judgment for contractor and owner appealed. At issue on appeal was whether a Paragraph 8.3.4 claim for delay damages is governed by the Paragraph 12.3.1 notice provisions for claims for additional costs.

The owner-contractor agreement incorporated by reference the American Institute of Architects General Conditions of the Contract for Construction, Document No. A201, 1976 edition, which required in Paragraph 3.2.4 that information or services under the owner's control "shall be furnished by the Owner with reasonable promptness to avoid delay in the orderly progress of the Work." Paragraphs 8.3.1 and 8.3.4 dealt with delays and extensions of time while Paragraph 12.3.1 set forth the procedures a contractor had to follow to make a claim for additional costs.

The Appellate Court affirmed. It found that under the express provisions of Paragraph 3.2.4 the owner had a duty to contractor not to delay the orderly progress of the work. Furthermore, while Paragraph 8.3.1 allowed the contractor an extension of time for owner-caused delay, Paragraph 8.3.4 entitled contractor to recover its delay damages. Paragraph 12.3.1 required that contractor must give notice within 20 days after the occurrence of an event giving rise to contractor's claim for additional compensation. However, the contract did not state that contractor's claims for delay damages had to be presented within 20 days of the occurrence giving rise to the claim. The Court concluded that the contract did state a procedure for filing an additional cost claim but was silent as to the procedure for delay claim damages. The Court held that contractor's delay claim did not fall within the additional cost procedures set forth in Paragraph 12.3.1.

85033   Overland Constructors, Inc. v. Millard School Dist., 220 Neb. 220, 369 N.W.2d 69 (1985)

I:	A107-1978, Art. 10, Para. 10.2
II:	A107-1978, Art. 10, Para. 10.5
I:	A117-1979, Art. 14, Para. 14.2
II:	A117-1979, Art. 14, Para. 14.5
I:	A201-1976, Art. 4, Para. 4.4.1
I:	A201-1976, Art. 4, Para. 4.7.1

Contractor brought an action seeking a declaration as to whether contractor or owner was responsible for certain utility charges. The owner argued that the charges were fees which, under the contract, were to be paid by contractor. The owner filed a third party indemnification action against the architect claiming that, because the architect was

III:	A117-1979, Art. 22, Para. 22.3
III:	A201-1976, Art. 12, Para. 12.2.1
III:	A201-1976, Art. 12, Para. 12.3.1

Contractor brought an action against owner for damages for extra work. The trial court denied owner's motion for partial summary judgment and owner appealed. Owner argued on appeal that contractor waived its claim for extras by failing to comply with the contractual procedures for documenting a claim for extras. The contractor argued on appeal that he was seeking compensation for additional work required by the discovery of changed subsurface conditions.

The owner-contractor agreement provided that an order for extra work, which could not exceed 5 percent of the contract price, "shall be valid only if issued in writing and signed by the Commissioner." To justify additional compensation the contractor "must . . . notify the Commissioner in writing that the work is being performed, or that the determination and direction is being complied with, under protest." Furthermore, contractor was required to submit daily records to owner while the work was being performed. If the contractor failed to comply with the notice and reporting procedures the contractor waived any claim for extra compensation or damages. The changed conditions provision required that the contractor immediately notify the Commissioner, who would promptly investigate and modify the contract if the Commissioner found that the subsurface conditions materially differed from the contract and were not reasonably anticipated by the contractor or by the owner.

The Appellate Court found that the contractor had not demonstrated or even alleged that the contract was modified with the Commissioner's written approval. The Court upheld the denial of owner's motion for partial summary judgment because questions of fact remained as to whether the contractor's claims were for work performed as required by the contract; or extra work requiring the contractor to strictly comply with the extra work notice provisions; or for work attributable to changed conditions requiring a contract modification.

85031   (UNASSIGNED)

85032   Osolo School Bldgs., Inc. v. Thorleif Larsen & Son, Inc., 473 N.E.2d 643 (Ind. Ct. App. 1985)

II:	A107-1978, Art. 14, Para. 14.3
II:	A107-1978, Art. 18, Para. 18.1
II:	A107-1978, Art. 18, Para. 18.2
II:	A107-1978, Art. 18, Para. 18.3
II:	A117-1979, Art. 18, Para. 18.3
II:	A117-1979, Art. 22, Para. 22.1
II:	A117-1979, Art. 22, Para. 22.2
II:	A117-1979, Art. 22, Para. 22.3

that one contractor's work may be only part of the entire project and that the other prime contractor may also be performing work on the same project. The General Conditions explicitly stated that time was of the essence, that each contractor's work should be promptly performed and completed, that all contractors on the project had the right to perform their work free from interference, and that a contractor was obligated to pay for the damages it may have caused to the work of other contractors.

The Court determined, based on its review of the contracts, that contractor was the intended third party beneficiary of the other co-prime contractor's agreement with the owner, since the other co-prime contractor agreed to confer a benefit upon any other prime contractor working on the project, by agreeing to do its work so as not to interfere with their work and by agreeing to be responsible for and to remedy any damages caused to work of the others. The co-prime contractor also agreed to undertake the owner's responsibility to the contractor to make sure that the work was coordinated.

The Appellate Court then addressed the issue of whether the contractor could recover delay damages, despite having failed to prepare and submit a written change order as required by Paragraph 12.3.1 of the General Conditions. The record demonstrated that both the owner and co-prime contractor, by their conduct on the job with specific reference to the delays in completion, had waived their right to rely on the written change order provision found in the contract.

As to the relief available to the contractor whose performance was delayed through no fault of its own, the Court found that two types of relief were available under the General Conditions. Contractor first had the right to an extension of time for performance in accordance with Paragraph 8.3.1. The contractor also had the right to compensation for the increased costs it had incurred as a result of delay in accordance with Paragraph 6.2. The Court concluded that the contractor was entitled to both an extension of time and damages, because the owner and co-prime contractor, by their conduct, waived the written notice requirement in the contract. The owner's conduct supported the Court's finding that owner had consciously decided that formal adherence to the written notice requirements with regard to delay was no longer necessary; owner had knowledge throughout the period that contractor was being delayed through no fault of its own, where it could have reasonably be presumed that the owner knew that the delays would prove costly to the contractor, and where the owner had been unable to demonstrate how it had been prejudiced by contractor's failure to provide owner with written notice.

The Court concluded that the contractor was entitled to damages pursuant to Paragraph 12.1.4; however, the contractor had to adequately prove these damages in order to recover.

85030   Naclerio Contracting Co. v. EPA, 113 A.D.2d 707, 493 N.Y.S.2d 159 (1985)

	III:	A107-1978, Art. 18, Para. 18.1
	III:	A107-1978, Art. 18, Para. 18.2
	III:	A107-1978, Art. 18, Para. 18.3
	III:	A117-1979, Art. 22, Para. 22.1
	III:	A117-1979, Art. 22, Para. 22.2

II:	A107-1978, Art. 14, Para. 14.3
II:	A107-1978, Art. 16, Para. 16.1
II:	A107-1978, Art. 18, Para. 18.1
II:	A107-1978, Art. 18, Para. 18.2
II:	A107-1978, Art. 18, Para. 18.3
II:	A117-1979, Art. 11, Para. 11.4
II:	A117-1979, Art. 18, Para. 18.3
II:	A117-1979, Art. 20, Para. 20.1
II:	A117-1979, Art. 22, Para. 22.1
II:	A117-1979, Art. 22, Para. 22.2
II:	A117-1979, Art. 22, Para. 22.3
I:	A201-1976, Art. 1, Para. 1.1.3
I:	A201-1976, Art. 1, Para. 1.1.4
I:	A201-1976, Art. 3, Para. 3.2.4
I:	A201-1976, Art. 4, Para. 4.10.1
I:	A201-1976, Art. 4, Para. 4.13.1
I:	A201-1976, Art. 4, Para. 4.14.2
I:	A201-1976, Art. 6, Para. 6.1.1
I:	A201-1976, Art. 6, Para. 6.1.3
I:	A201-1976, Art. 6, Para. 6.2.2
I:	A201-1976, Art. 6, Para. 6.2.3
I:	A201-1976, Art. 6, Para. 6.2.4
I:	A201-1976, Art. 8, Para. 8.3.1
I:	A201-1976, Art. 9, Para. 9.4.1
I:	A201-1976, Art. 10, Para. 10.2.5
I:	A201-1976, Art. 12, Para. 12.1.4
I:	A201-1976, Art. 12, Para. 12.3.1

Contractor brought an action for delay damages and extras against owner, co-prime contractor, and co-prime contractor's surety after the owner refused to pay the contractor pursuant to change orders approved by the architect. The trial court entered judgment for contractor against owner and dismissed contractor's claims against the co-prime contractor and its surety. Contractor appealed.

The owner and each prime contractor entered into the American Institute of Architects Standard Form of Agreement Between the Owner and Contractor, Document No. A101, 1977 edition, which incorporated the American Institute of Architects General Conditions of the Contract for Construction, Document No. A201, 1976 edition.

The contractor argued on appeal that it was entitled to damages resulting from co-prime contractor's delay, as an intended third party beneficiary of the owner-contractor agreement and bond. The Court found that the General Conditions specifically recognized the parties, and that both contractor and subcontractor would assume obligations beyond those specified in the subcontract. The Court held that the arbitration clause contained in the General Conditions of the owner-contractor agreement was incorporated by reference into the subcontract and created the power in contractor to insist that the dispute be resolved by arbitration. The Court found that subcontractor's claims all arose out of breaches of the subcontract and were within the scope of the agreement to arbitrate. Furthermore, contractor did not waive its right to arbitration by filing a third party action for indemnity. The Court ordered that the dispute be arbitrated.

[*Editor's Note:* For subsequent appeal after remand, *see* case number 87032 *infra.*]

85028   McDowell v. Austin Co., 105 Wash. 2d 48, 710 P.2d 192 (1985)

	III:	A107-1978, Art. 10, Para. 10.11
	III:	A117-1979, Art. 14, Para. 14.11
	III:	A201-1976, Art. 4, Para. 4.18.1
	III:	A401-1978, Art. 11, Para. 11.11.1

Contractor brought an indemnity action against subcontractor for a settlement payment to subcontractor's injured employee. The trial court dismissed contractor's claim on the grounds that the indemnity clause did not clearly obligate subcontractor to indemnify contractor against liability caused by the concurrent negligence of the parties. Contractor appealed. The Appellate Court reversed and remanded, ruling that the language of the indemnity clause included concurrent negligence. Subcontractor appealed to the Supreme Court of Washington, arguing that clause 8(b) of the subcontract was ambiguous on the issue of indemnification for concurrent negligence.

Contractor and subcontractor entered into an agreement for the erection of steel work that provided in Article 8, clause 8(b) entitled "Insurance," that "Subcontractor agrees to indemnify and save harmless Owner and Austin against all liability for personal injury . . . caused or alleged to have been caused . . . by Owner or Austin." In addition, subcontractor agreed in subsection (c) of Article 8 to indemnify the owner and contractor for injuries sustained by "other" persons where such injuries had been caused by subcontractor, regardless of concurrent or other causation by anyone else, including contractor.

The Supreme Court found that clause 8(b) provided that any liability borne by contractor that was caused, or allegedly caused, by contractor's conduct triggered subcontractor's duty to indemnify contractor completely. The trigger operated independently of how contractor's conduct caused the liability. The Court held that it would enforce a contract that clearly provided fair notice to subcontractor that subcontractor had agreed to indemnify contractor against "all liability" for injuries to subcontractor's employees caused by contractor's conduct.

85029   Moore Constr. Co. v. Clarksville Dept. of Elec., 707 S.W.2d 1 (Tenn. Ct. App. 1985)

	II:	A107-1978, Art. 7, Para. 7.4

The Court of Appeals found that the parties had expressly agreed to resolve all of their disputes by arbitration under the clear and unequivocal language of Article 2. The arbitration clause empowered the architect to resolve "all questions of any nature whatsoever" with no specific restriction upon that authority. The Court held that the parties were bound by the decision of the architect, and therefore it reversed the Appellate Division and reinstated the judgment of the lower court.

85027   Maxum Founds., Inc. v. Salus Corp., 779 F.2d 974 (4th Cir. 1985), *appeal after remand,* 817 F.2d 1086 (4th Cir. 1987)

II:	A107-1978, Art. 11, Para. 11.2
II:	A107-1978, Art. 13, Para. 13.2
II:	A117-1979, Art. 15, Para. 15.2
II:	A117-1979, Art. 17, Para. 17.2
I:	A201-1976, Art. 5, Para. 5.3.1
I:	A201-1976, Art. 7, Para. 7.9.1
II:	A401-1978, Art. 11, Para. 11.1.1
II:	A401-1978, Art. 13, Para. 13.1

Subcontractor brought a breach of contract action against contractor. Contractor moved to dismiss subcontractor's complaint on the grounds that the subcontract provided for arbitration. Subcontractor responded that the subcontract did not provide for arbitration and that contractor had waived any right to arbitration by participating in discovery. The District Court denied contractor's motion for a stay pending arbitration and contractor appealed. The District Court subsequently tried the liability issues and ordered the parties to settle the damages issue. Both parties appealed the District Court's order specifying the settlement terms. Contractor argued on appeal that the arbitration clause in the owner-contractor agreement was incorporated by reference into the subcontract.

The subcontract did not contain an arbitration provision. Article I of the subcontract provided in pertinent part that "the drawings, specifications, general conditions, special conditions and other documents set forth hereinafter and any amendments and addenda thereto are hereinafter collectively referred to as the "Contract Documents." . . . This Agreement and the Contract Documents shall constitute the "Contract." Exhibit A to the subcontract indicated that among the additional documents to be considered part of the "Contract Documents" were the American Institute of Architects General Conditions of the Contract for Construction, Document No. A201, 1976 edition. Article II of the subcontract provided that to "the extent applicable to, or arising in connection with, the Work, the Subcontractor shall be bound by, and expressly assumes for the benefit of the Contractor, all obligations and liabilities which the Contract Documents impose upon the Contractor." The General Conditions to the owner-contractor agreement contained a broad form arbitration provision in Paragraph 7.9.1 and a flow-down provision in Paragraph 5.3.1.

The Appellate Court found that the subcontract manifested the intention of the parties that documents other than the subcontract would become part of the agreement between

85026 Maross Constr., Inc. v. Central N.Y. Regional Transp. Auth., 66 N.Y.2d 341, 497 N.Y.S.2d 321, 488 N.E.2d 67 (1985)

III:	A107-1978, Art. 8, Para. 8.5
III:	A107-1978, Art. 13, Para. 13.2
III:	A117-1979, Art. 12, Para. 12.5
III:	A117-1979, Art. 17, Para. 17.2
III:	A201-1976, Art. 2, Para. 2.2.9
III:	A201-1976, Art. 2, Para. 2.2.10
III:	A201-1976, Art. 2, Para. 2.2.12
III:	A201-1976, Art. 7, Para. 7.9.1

Contractor brought an action seeking a declaration that under the owner-contractor agreement it was not responsible for supplying and installing certain tanks for which it had disclaimed responsibility in its bid. The lower court entered judgment for owner holding that contractor knew and understood the terms of the contract and that contractor had no power to alter a substantial term of a public contract subject to competitive bidding. The Appellate Division reversed and awarded summary judgment to contractor, holding that owner had bound itself to the disclaimer provision added by contractor. The Court stated that the architect's arbitration authority extended only to the resolution of factual disputes and, therefore, the architect's contrary construction of the contract was not binding. Owner appealed to the New York Court of Appeals. At issue on appeal was whether a broad arbitration clause which empowered the architect to resolve all contractual disputes submitted by the parties was binding notwithstanding a provision in the contract with which the determination conflicted.

The owner and contractor entered into an agreement which defined the work in Article 2 as "Work required by the contract documents." Contractor, before signing the agreement, added the following provision to Article 2: "The contractor, Maross Construction, Inc. is not responsible for the supplying and installing of fiber-glass tanks V18 and V28 on page H1.4 of the contract drawings, as the drawings specifically place such responsibility with the general contractor." Contractor did not notify the owner of this change nor did contractor modify other provisions of the agreement pertaining to the same matter. Article 7 of the owner-contractor agreement contained an itemization of the "Contract Documents" which "constitute the entire agreement between Owner and Contractor." This itemization included the tanks. When the issue of responsibility for the installation of the tanks arose owner requested that the dispute be submitted to the architect. Paragraph 2.01 of the general conditions provided in pertinent part that "To resolve all disputes and to prevent litigation the parties to this Contract authorize the Architect to decide all questions of any nature whatsoever . . . and his decisions shall be conclusive, final and binding on the parties." Pursuant to this authority the architect had concluded that the specifications clearly imposed the responsibility for the tanks upon the contractor, and directed the contractor to return to work and to provide the tanks without extra cost to owner.

5.1 governed the ownership of the drawings and specifications. The Court found that Paragraph 5.1 clearly granted owner the right to "retain copies, including reproducible copies, of Drawings and Specifications for information and reference in connection with Owner's use and occupancy of the Project." Moreover, the contract gave owner the right to continue using the plans even if architect was in default. However, the contract was unambiguous that the plans remained the property of the architect. Architect's further argument, that owner exceeded its contractual rights by copying and filing the plans in a way that suggested that another architect created the plans, may have raised a violation of the Latham Act. The question of title was to be decided by arbitration. The Court denied summary judgment for owner.

85025   Kaiser Eng'rs, Inc. v. Grinnell Fire Protection Sys. Co., 173 Cal. App. 3d 1050, 219 Cal. Rptr. 626 (1985)

III:	A107-1978, Art. 10, Para. 10.11
III:	A117-1979, Art. 14, Para. 14.11
III:	A201-1976, Art. 4, Para. 4.18.1
III:	A401-1978, Art. 11, Para. 11.11.1

Injured employee of contractor brought an action for damages for personal injury against construction manager. Construction manager cross-complained against contractor seeking indemnity on both equitable indemnity grounds and the express indemnity provision in the owner-contractor agreement. The trial court dismissed the cross-complaint without leave to amend and denied construction manager's motion for a new trial on the grounds that the California Labor Code did not authorize a person who was not a party to a contract to assert a third party beneficiary indemnity claim. Construction manager appealed.

The owner-contractor agreement contained an indemnity provision in Clause 57 which provided that the "Contractor shall indemnify and hold harmless the Government and its agents and employees from and against all liability, claims and suits for injury or death to persons and damage to property . . . based upon or arising from the operations of the Contractor and his subcontractors in the performance of this contract."

The Appellate Court concluded that the California Labor Code did not require a third party beneficiary to be identified by name in an express indemnity agreement in order to enforce that agreement. The Labor Code did not define the scope of an employer's duty to indemnify under an express contract. Therefore, since the contractor had expressly contracted to indemnify, the extent of the duty was determined from the contract. In this case, the owner and contractor had executed an express contract of indemnity wherein contractor promised to indemnify the owner and its agents. The Court held that construction manager's cross-complaint did state a claim against contractor under the California Labor Code if construction manager was found to be an agent of the owner.

because the supplemental conditions provided that claims for extra work had to be asserted before final payment, while Section G.9.07 provided that acceptance of final payment operated as a release. The contract was not ambiguous and Section G.9.07 was not superseded. The Court held that by accepting final payment contractor had released owner from any further liability on the contract.

85023 John W. Cowper Co. v. Buffalo Hotel Dev. Venture, 115 A.D.2d 346, 496 N.Y.S.2d 127 (1985), *aff'd,* 72 N.Y.2d 890, 532 N.Y.S.2d 742, 528 N.E.2d 1214 (1988)

II:	A107-1978, Art. 10, Para. 10.4	
II:	A107-1978, Art. 19, Para. 19.1	
II:	A117-1979, Art. 14, Para. 14.4	
II:	A117-1979, Art. 23, Para. 23.1	
I:	A201-1976, Art. 4, Para. 4.5.1	
I:	A201-1976, Art. 13, Para. 13.2.2	

Contractor brought an action against owner to recover amounts due under the contract. After this action was instituted owner submitted to contractor a punch list and later submitted a list describing numerous construction defects including those already listed on the earlier punch list. The trial court sustained contractor's objection to proof of construction defects on the grounds that Paragraph 13.2.2 of the owner-contractor agreement required notice of defects within one year of substantial completion.

The owner and contractor entered into a standard form American Institute of Architect's contract for the erection of a hotel.

The Appellate Court found that the one year provision in the General Conditions related solely to the contractor's duty to correct defects through supplemental performance, and could not be construed as an exclusive remedy unless so provided in the contract. The Court held that owner's claims were controlled by the statute of limitations. Furthermore, owner was not prohibited from proving additional defects because contractor established no waiver by acceptance of work as performed.

85024 Joseph J. Legat Architects, P.C. v. United States Dev. Corp., 625 F. Supp. 293 (N.D. Ill. 1985)

I:	A201-1976, Art. 1, Para. 1.3.1	
I:	B141-1977, Art. 8, Para. 8.1	

In architect's action for copyright and trademark infringement against owner, the Court, in ruling on owner's motion to dismiss and for summary judgment, addressed owner's argument that there could be no copyright infringement because the owner-architect agreement gave owner the right to copy and reproduce the architectural plans. The owner and architect had entered into the American Institute of Architects Standard Form of Agreement Between Owner and Architect, Document No. B141, 1977 edition. Paragraph

subcontractors . . . for damages caused by fire or other perils to the extent covered by insurance. . . ." The subcontract subjected the subcontractor to the terms and conditions of the owner-contractor agreement and made all general conditions of the owner-contractor agreement part of the subcontract. The subcontract further provided that subcontractor was required to carry only workers' compensation and public liability insurance.

The Appellate Court found that under the language of the contract, the owner clearly waived its claims against contractor and subcontractor regarding property damage and agreed to look solely to the insurance to be procured and maintained by the owner at its own expense. The Court held that under these circumstances, if the owner could not bring an action against the subcontractor, the insurer could not bring a subrogation action against the subcontractor.

85022 John E. Fisher Constr. Co. v. Town of Onondaga, 115 A.D.2d 993, 497 N.Y.S.2d 557 (1985), *appeal denied,* 67 N.Y.2d 609 (1986)

III:	A107-1978, Art. 15, Para. 15.5
III:	A107-1978, Art. 18, Para. 18.1
III:	A117-1979, Art. 19, Para. 19.5
III:	A117-1979, Art. 22, Para. 22.1
III:	A201-1976, Art. 9, Para. 9.9.4
III:	A201-1976, Art. 9, Para. 9.9.5
III:	A201-1976, Art. 12, Para. 12.1.2

Contractor brought an action against owner seeking damages for extra work performed on the construction of a sewer. The lower court dismissed some of owner's affirmative defenses and denied owner's motion to dismiss contractor's complaint. Owner argued on appeal that contractor's acceptance of final payment released owner from any further liability under the contract. Contractor argued on appeal that under the supplemental conditions its claim for extra work survived final payment.

The owner and contractor entered into a standard form contract with an appendix that incorporated supplemental conditions required for federally aided projects. Section G.9.07 of the general conditions provided that the "acceptance by the contractor of the Final Payment shall be and shall operate as a release to the owner of all claims. . . ." The supplemental conditions, which superseded any conflicting contract provisions, allowed the owner to order changes within the general scope of the contract. Section 2(f) provided that "no claim by the contractor for an equitable adjustment hereunder shall be allowed if asserted after final payment. . . ." The delay provision required contractor to submit its claim in writing "but not later than the date of final payment under the contract." Contractor had asserted delay claims against owner before final payment was made.

The Appellate Court gave full force and effect to the release clause in Section G.9.07 and found that the contract clearly provided that the supplemental conditions superseded Section G.9.07 only if they conflicted with that section. The provisions did not conflict

a change order before additional compensation would be allowed. Article 5 of the contract stated that "Payments due and unpaid under the Contract Documents shall bear interest from the date payment is due at the rate entered below, or in the absence thereof, at the legal rate prevailing at the place of the project. . . ."

The Appellate Court found that contractor did not stop work and obtain a change order after he reached the third section of the roof and found that it was not in any better condition than the lower sections. The Court held that absent compliance by the contractor with the change order provision the trial court correctly denied contractor's claim for additional compensation. The Court further found that Article 5 should be enforced and held that contractor was entitled to interest on the final payment.

85021   Island Villa Developers, Inc. v. Bonner Roofing & Sheet Metal Co., 175 Ga. App. 713, 334 S.E.2d 41 (1985)

II:	A107-1978, Art. 11, Para. 11.2	
II:	A107-1978, Art. 17, Para. 17.3	
II:	A107-1978, Art. 17, Para. 17.6	
II:	A117-1979, Art. 15, Para. 15.2	
II:	A117-1979, Art. 21, Para. 21.3	
II:	A117-1979, Art. 21, Para. 21.6	
I:	A201-1976, Art. 5, Para. 5.3.1	
I:	A201-1976, Art. 11, Para. 11.3.1	
I:	A201-1976, Art. 11, Para. 11.3.6	
II:	A401-1978, Art. 9, Para. 9.1	
II:	A401-1978, Art. 9, Para. 9.2	
II:	A401-1978, Art. 11, Para. 11.1.1	

Owner and contractor submitted a property damage claim to insurer and were jointly paid for the loss. Insurer then brought a subrogation action against subcontractor alleging that subcontractor's negligence caused the loss. The trial court granted subcontractor's motion for summary judgment on the grounds that owner had waived a cause of action against subcontractor under the terms of the owner-contractor agreement. Insurer appealed.

The owner and contractor entered into a standard form agreement promulgated by the American Institute of Architects which incorporated by reference the American Institute of Architects General Conditions of the Contract for Construction, Document No. A201, 1976 edition. Paragraph 11.3.1 provided that "the Owner shall purchase and maintain property insurance upon the entire work at the site to the full insurable value thereof. This insurance shall include the interests of the Owner, the Contractor, subcontractors and sub-subcontractors in the work and shall insure against the perils of fire and extended coverage and shall include all risk' insurance for physical loss or damage. . . ." Pursuant to this provision contractor obtained a builder's risk policy. Paragraph 11.3.6 also provided that "Owner and Contractor waive all rights against (1) each other and the

the encountered subsoil conditions. The Court held that the trial judge did not abuse her discretion in interpreting the written contract so as to allow contractor to recover his extra costs.

85019   Hibbler v. Ockerlund Constr. Co., 130 Ill. App. 3d 30, 85 Ill. Dec. 229, 473 N.E.2d 597 (1985)

II:	A107-1978, Art. 10, Para. 10.11
II:	A117-1979, Art. 14, Para. 14.11
II:	A201-1976, Art. 4, Para. 4.18.1
II:	A401-1978, Art. 11, Para. 11.11.1

Contractor filed an action against subcontractor seeking indemnification for damages paid to subcontractor's injured employee based on an active-passive theory, contribution and express contractual indemnification. The trial court dismissed the claim of express indemnification and contractor appealed.

The subcontract provided that subcontractor would indemnify contractor for any claims of injuries for which contractor might be responsible and which "may arise out of or on account of in consequence of the Sub-contractor's performance of his contract."

The Appellate Court found that the terms of the contract were covered by an Illinois statute which provides that in every construction contract any agreement to indemnify a person from his own negligence is void as against public policy. The Court held that the indemnity provision in the subcontract was proscribed by statute.

85020   Ida Grove Roofing & Improvements, Inc. v. City of Storm Lake, 378 N.W.2d 313 (Iowa Ct. App. 1985)

I:	A101-1977, Art. 5
II:	A107-1978, Art. 18, Para. 18.1
II:	A111-1978, Art. 14, Para. 14.3
II:	A117-1979, Art. 22, Para. 22.1
I:	A201-1976, Art. 7, Para. 7.8.1
I:	A201-1976, Art. 12, Para. 12.3.1

Contractor brought an action against owner for final payment. The trial court granted contractor summary judgment but denied interest. Contractor brought a second action against owner demanding additional compensation because the plans and specifications did not correctly inform contractor of the thickness of the roof. The trial court found that contractor had never requested a change order for extra compensation, and that even if the thickness of the roof was a concealed condition a change order should have been requested before the work was completed. Contractor appealed.

The owner and contractor entered into an agreement that contained provisions identical to the American Institute of Architects General Conditions of the Contract for Construction, Document No. A201, 1976 edition. Paragraph 12.3.1 required contractor to obtain

the drawings and specifications, for the construction of one phase of a hospital project. Article 3 of the agreement provided that "The work to be performed under this Contract shall be commenced within ten (10) days and, subject to authorized adjustments, Substantial Completion shall be achieved not later than 20 December 1980. LIQUIDATED DAMAGES SHALL BE AS FOLLOWS: Five hundred dollars ($500) per consecutive calendar day for each day's delay in completing the work under this contract, beyond 20 December 1980." The Special Conditions, in Paragraph 1.25A, also referred to the liquidated damage amount provided for in Article 3. Section 6.2.5 of the General Conditions provided the remedy for contractor's damage to the work of any other contractor. Work was defined in Paragraph 1.1.3 of the General Conditions.

The District Court found that the liquidated damage provisions encompassed any economic loss to owner caused by contractor's failure to substantially complete its work by the agreed upon completion date. The Court held that the provision was broad enough to extend to claims by other contractors based on contractor's delay. The Court read Paragraph 6.2.5 as requiring contractor to indemnify owner with respect to claims based on contractor's wrongful infliction of physical damage to the property of another contractor or to work previously completed by such contractor; but it did not require contractor to indemnify owner for the full amount of any adverse judgments against owner based on other contractors increased costs. However, the Court held that contractor's indemnification liability was not limited to the liquidated damage amount set forth in the contract because the claims of the other contractors were not based solely on contractor's failure to complete its work by the agreed upon date. The Court therefore denied the contractor's motion for partial summary judgment.

85018 Haener v. Ada County Highway Dist., 108 Idaho 170, 697 P.2d 1184 (1985)

III: A201-1976, Art. 12, Para. 12.2.1

Contractor brought an action against owner for extra costs incurred as a result of unexpected subsurface conditions. The trial court entered judgment for contractor and owner appealed. Owner argued on appeal that the trial court erroneously relied on language in the General Conditions that required contractor to remove all material of whatever nature, for compensation at the unit price.

The owner-contractor agreement provided that if "subsoil conditions be found to differ materially from those indicated by logs of test borings and/or records made by other methods of underground exploration, adjustment in cost, either more or less, shall be made as provided in the general conditions of changes in the work." The specifications provided that excavation consisted of "removal of all material of whatever description that may be encountered. . . . Payment for trench excavation will be made at the contract unit price bid per cubic yard. . . ." Contractor requested a written change order, however, owner orally directed contractor to complete the excavation for which he would receive extra compensation.

The Appellate Court found that the terms of the contract, when read together, were ambiguous. Furthermore, the parties had neither contemplated nor bargained regarding

Section 14 of the subcontract provided that subcontractor "agrees to indemnify, defend, save and hold Contractor and Owner harmless from any liability . . . arising out of any act performed, or representation made, by Subcontractor in the performance of any work hereunder." Section 19 provided that subcontractor "shall indemnify and defend and save harmless Owner and Contractor, and each of them, from and against any and all suits . . . of whatsoever kind or nature and whether they may arise before or after completion of Subcontractor's work under this Subcontract . . . through any act, omission, fault or negligence whether active or passive, of Subcontractor . . . in connection with or incident to the work. . . ." Section 17, which dealt with improper or defective work, provided that subcontractor "agrees to pay the Contractor all costs, expenses . . . of Contractor in connection with said replacement or corrections, whether said replacement or corrections are removed, disposed of and replaced by Subcontractor or Contractor."

The Appellate Court reversed. It found that section 14 required "an act performed" in performance of the contract, section 17 required "improper or defective work" by subcontractor and section 19 required an "act, omission, fault or negligence" of subcontractor. The subcontract did not support a finding of liability against subcontractor because subcontractor's work was not "improper or defective" and subcontractor's driving the piling in accordance with the specifications and without fault of any kind did not cause the settlement of the pads. The Court held that subcontractor was not obligated to indemnify the contractor.

85017 Gilbane Bldg. Co. v. Nemours Found., 666 F. Supp. 649 (D. Del. 1985)

I: A101-1977, Art. 3
II: A107-1978, Art. 7, Para. 7.4
II: A111-1978, Art. 4, Para. 4.1
II: A117-1979, Art. 11, Para. 11.4
I: A201-1976, Art. 1, Para. 1.1.3
I: A201-1976, Art. 6, Para. 6.2.5

One of numerous prime contractors brought an action against owner to recover damages resulting from owner's alleged failure to exercise reasonable care with respect to contractor's performance. Owner counterclaimed for liquidated damages for contractor's failure to substantially complete its work by the mandated date and for indemnification against losses that owner incurred as a result of claims made by other contractors. Contractor sought partial summary judgment limiting its liability, if any, to the liquidated damages provided for in the contract. Owner argued that the contract provided for liquidation of some, but not all, of the damages flowing from contractor's breach and negligence. At issue was which types of damages were within the scope of the liquidated damage clause.

Owner and contractor had entered into the American Institute of Architects Standard Form of Agreement Between Owner and Contractor, Document No. A101, 1977 edition, the American Institute of Architects General Conditions of the Contract for Construction, Document No. A201, 1976 edition, with typewritten insertions, Special Conditions, and

III: A117-1979, Art. 14, Para. 14.11
III: A201-1976, Art. 4, Para. 4.18.1
III: A401-1978, Art. 11, Para. 11.11.1

The architect appealed the trial court's dismissal of its indemnity claim against subcontractor and its supplier for failure to state a cause of action. The architect argued that it was a third party beneficiary of the subcontract's indemnity provision. The Appellate Court affirmed the trial court's ruling.

The subcontract stated that subcontractor's work would not be acceptable unless it satisfied the construction manager, the architect and the owner. The indemnification provision stated that "to the extent permitted by applicable law, it is understood and agreed that Subcontractor shall defend, indemnify and save harmless Contractor, its officers, employees, agents and servants, the Owner, and the Architect against all loss, damage and expense, whether incurred or paid, on account of death, injuries, damages or loss to persons (including, without limiting the generality of the foregoing, employees of Subcontractor) or property, caused by or in any way arising directly or indirectly out of or connected with or incidental to the performance of the work by Subcontractor or the use by Subcontractor it its employees, agents or subcontractors of facilities or equipment furnished or owner by contractor, other subcontractors or the Owner, and including, without limiting the generality of the foregoing, all claims arising out of any structural work law, or law imposing liability arising out of the use of scaffolds, hoists, cranes, stays, ladders, supports or other mechanical contrivances. WE CANNOT INDEMNIFY THE ARCHITECT OR ANYONE ELSE FOR THEIR ERRORS OR OMISSIONS."

The Appellate Court held that because the architect was seeking purely economic damages, and the plain language of the indemnification was limited to personal and property damages, the trial court had properly dismissed architect's complaint.

85016   Gall Landau Young Constr. Co. v. Hurlen Constr., 39 Wash. App. 420, 693 P.2d 207, *review denied*, 103 Wash. 2d 1026 (1985).

II: A107-1978, Art. 10, Para. 10.11
II: A117-1979, Art. 14, Para. 14.11
II: A201-1976, Art. 4, Para. 4.18.1
II: A401-1978, Art. 11, Para. 11.7.1
II: A401-1978, Art. 11, Para. 11.11.1

Contractor filed an action against subcontractor to recover costs of defectively constructed HVAC system and sewerage pads. The trial court, relying on section 14 and 19 of the subcontract, found that subcontractor was obligated to indemnify contractor for costs of repairing the pads. Relying on section 17 of the subcontract the court found that subcontractor was obligated to pay contractor's costs, separate and apart from the indemnity provision. Subcontractor appealed.

had a duty to the contractor to afford the contractor an adequate and fair opportunity to comply with the lender's requirements. The Court held that it was error for the trial court to grant the owner summary judgment, since the owner's actions amounted to a repudiation of the contract, which justified the contractor's treating the contract as breached and suing for damages.

85015 Espaniola v. Cawdrey Mars Joint Venture, 68 Haw. 171, 707 P.2d 365 (1985)

> III: A107-1978, Art. 10, Para. 10.11
> III: A117-1979, Art. 14, Para. 14.11
> III: A201-1976, Art. 4, Para. 4.18.1
> III: A401-1978, Art. 9, Para. 9.1
> III: A401-1978, Art. 9, Para. 9.2
> III: A401-1978, Art. 11, Para. 11.11.1

Contractor brought a third party indemnity action against subcontractor following the death of subcontractor's employee. The trial court entered summary judgment for subcontractor on contractor's claim for indemnification under the contract. Contractor appealed. At issue on appeal was whether subcontractor was contractually obligated to indemnify contractor against any loss or damage arising from the negligence of subcontractor.

The subcontract provided that subcontractor "shall protect and indemnify said Contractor against any loss or damage suffered by any one arising through the negligence of the Sub-contractor. . . ." The subcontract required that subcontractor furnish certificates of insurance evidencing that subcontractor had valid Workmen's Compensation insurance and bodily injury and property damage insurance fully protecting contractor. Subcontractor further agreed to "indemnify and hold harmless Contractor and Owner against any claims . . . for personal injury or death . . . arising out of or in any way connected with the performance of this agreement by Sub-contractor."

The Appellate Court found that the language of the indemnity clause was specific enough to compel indemnification of contractor by subcontractor. Subcontractor agreed to "protect and indemnify [contractor] against any loss or damage suffered by any one arising through his negligence. . . ." Furthermore, subcontractor promised to "bear any expense which [contractor] may have by reason thereof, or on account of being charged therewith." The Court concluded that there had been a clear and unequivocal assumption of liability by the subcontractor. The Court held that the state workers' compensation law did not preclude contractor's claim for indemnification and remanded the case for trial of the contractual indemnity claim, vacating the summary judgment.

85015a Friedman, Altschuler & Sincere v. Arlington Structural Steel Co., 140 Ill. App. 3d 556, 95 Ill. Dec. 87, 489 N.E.2d 308 (1985)

> III: A107-1978, Art. 10, Para. 10.11

contractor's performance unless the architect acts with malice or in bad faith. The owner-contractor agreement incorporated by reference the American Institute of Architects General Conditions of the Contract for Construction, Document No. A201, 1976 edition, which described the roles of the owner, the architect and the contractor and set forth the architect's powers and duties. The owner and architect entered into the American Institute of Architects Standard Form of Agreement Between Owner and Architect, Document No. B141, 1977 edition, which, in Paragraphs 1.5.13 and 1.5.14, authorized the architect to approve a contractor's proposals only for conformance with the design concept and contract requirements and to order minor changes in the work. The Court held that sufficient evidence established that architect acted without malice or bad faith in advising owner to terminate the contractor.

85014a   Eke Bldrs., Inc. v. Quail Bluff Assocs., 714 P.2d 604 (Okla. Ct. App. 1985)

III: A107-1978, Art. 20, Para. 20.2
III: A117-1979, Art. 24, Para. 24.2
III: A201-1976, Art. 3, Para. 3.2.1
III: A201-1976, Art. 14, Para. 14.2.1

Contractor brought a breach of contract action against owner for wrongful termination. The contract provided that "if such construction funds are not, for any reason, obtained and recorded for this project from time to time as required by the Owner, Owner may terminate this Agreement . . ." even though the contractor was at all times ready, willing and able to produce a performance bond. The trial court entered judgment for the owner on the ground that the lender's disapproval of the contractor constituted a failure of a condition precedent to acceptance of the agreement, and that therefore there was no breach. The evidence indicated that the owner informed the contractor that the bank would not approve the contractor under any circumstances, and that the owner then terminated the contractor rather than informing the contractor that the bank had approved the contractor on the condition that the contractor obtain a performance bond.

The owner-contractor agreement provided in Paragraph 6 that "The parties hereto acknowledge and agree that the obligations imposed by the provisions of this Agreement are contingent upon the Owner obtaining a loan from the Lender in a sum of not less than Six and one-half million Dollars, ($6,500,000), for the construction of the Improvements on terms satisfactory to Owner. If such construction funds are not, for any reason, obtained and recorded for this project from time to time as required by the Owner, Owner may terminate this Agreement, or at its option, may designate which portions of the work covered by this Contract shall be performed by Contractor. In the event of such termination, in whole or in part, Owner shall incur no obligation to Contractor other than to make payment for work performed and costs incurred prior to such termination."

The Appellate Court found that implicit in the language of Paragraph 6 was the imposition of a duty on the owner to make a good faith effort to satisfy the loan contingency and to deal fairly with the contractor. The Court concluded that the owner

II: A201-1976, Art. 4, Para. 4.18.1
II: A401-1978, Art. 11, Para. 11.11.1

Owner brought an indemnification action against contractor for damages resulting from contractor's negligence, which caused injury to contractor's employee. Contractor filed a motion for summary judgment arguing that under Maryland state law contractor was under no obligation to indemnify owner for its own negligence.

The owner-contractor agreement contained an indemnity clause which provided that contractor "shall hold owner harmless from any and all claims, liabilities and causes of action for injury to or death of any person (including, but not limited to, employees of contractor or of any subcontractor) . . . resulting from any and all acts or omissions of contractor or contractor's employees in connection with the performance of the Work, and shall defend any such claim asserted or brought against owner. . . ."

The District Court found that in cases where a party was seeking indemnification for damages arising from its own negligence the rule in Maryland was that the indemnity agreement would not be construed to reach that result unless an intention to do so was expressed in unequivocal terms. After reviewing the decisions of the Maryland courts the Court concluded that the cases did not provide definitive guidance so the Court looked to federal law. The Court concluded that review of the language of the indemnity provision did not reveal that it was the intent of the parties to shift the responsibility for owner's negligence to contractor. The Court held, therefore, that owner was not entitled to indemnification from contractor for damages incurred due to its own negligence. However, the clause stated that contractor would be liable for any injury to person or property "resulting from any and all acts or omissions of contractor or contractor's employees in connection with the performance of the Work." The Court concluded that this language evinced the intent of the parties that contractor would indemnify owner for any damages resulting from contractor's negligence. The Court denied contractor's motion for summary judgment and held that the indemnity clause was enforceable against contractor to the extent of contractor's relative degree of fault.

85014   Dehnert v. Arrow Sprinklers, Inc., 705 P.2d 846 (Wyo. 1985)

II: A107-1978, Art. 8, Para. 8.7
II: A117-1979, Art. 12, Para. 12.7
I: A201-1976, Art. 2, Para. 2.2.14
I: A201-1976, Art. 2, Para. 2.2.15
I: B141-1977, Art. 1, Para. 1.5.13
I: B141-1977, Art. 1, Para. 1.5.14

Architect appealed a jury verdict for contractor in its action based on intentional interference with contractor's contractual relationship with owner. The Supreme Court of Wyoming found that an architect who acts within the scope of its contractual obligations to the owner will not be liable for advising the owner to terminate a

85012 Davidson & Jones, Inc. v. North Carolina Dept. of Admin., 315 N.C. 144, 337 S.E.2d 463 (1985)

        III: A107-1978, Art. 14, Para. 14.3
        III: A107-1978, Art. 18, Para. 18.1
        III: A107-1978, Art. 18, Para. 18.2
        III: A117-1979, Art. 18, Para. 18.3
        III: A117-1979, Art. 22, Para. 22.1
        III: A117-1979, Art. 22, Para. 22.2
        III: A201-1976, Art. 12, Para. 12.3.1

Contractor brought an action against owner to recover extra costs at the unit price and duration-related expenses due to a massive 400 percent overrun in the amount of rock to be excavated. The trial court found in favor of contractor and owner appealed. The Appellate Court affirmed the denial of home office expenses and reversed the trial court's decision as to duration-related and other expenses. Contractor appealed to the North Carolina Supreme Court contending that the Appellate Court erred in its interpretation of the controlling state statute and the contract between the parties. The Supreme Court agreed.

The owner-contractor agreement set forth in Article 16 the procedure for contractor to follow in submitting claims for extra costs. The only relief specifically provided was reimbursement for "extra costs."

The Supreme Court of North Carolina noted that it had to determine whether contractor's duration related expenses could be included in the term "extra costs." The Court found that Article 16 required instructions from the architect, written notice by the contractor to the architect, cessation of work by contractor until contractor received further instructions from the architect or, if the instructions meant departing from the contract documents, a change order. The Court found that contractor's extra costs were caused by a greater quantity of rock than either party anticipated and not from an instruction from the architect to remove the extra rock. Nevertheless, Article 16 clearly stated that an instruction could be "in any form" and it contained no requirement that the instruction come after the contract was made. Furthermore, the contract contained specifications requiring excavation to dimensions set by the architect. The Court found that based on the trial court's findings of fact, the contractor was entitled to recover its duration-related expenses as extra costs under Article 16. Because contractor's home office expenses were not contemplated in the contract the Court held that contractor was not entitled to recover for these expenses.

85013 Davison Specialty Chem. Co. v. S & H Erectors, Inc., 621 F. Supp. 783 (E.D. Tenn. 1985)

        II: A107-1978, Art. 10, Para. 10.11
        II: A117-1979, Art. 14, Para. 14.11

or hindrance for any cause whatsoever . . . and agrees that its sole right and remedy in the case of any delay, obstruction or hindrance shall be an extension of the time fixed for completion of the Work." The subcontract also contained a provision stating that the waiver of any contract provision could only be made by an express waiver in writing. Paragraph 35 required the subcontractor to perform his work when and as directed by the contractor. Paragraph 10 provided that "certain items of Work may be stopped and completed at a later date with no additional cost charged to Owner, Architect or Contractor."

The Appellate Court found that contractor, through its words and deeds, had waived its right to insist on a waiver in writing. The contractor's oral representations that subcontractor would be paid for the extraordinary delays constituted behavior inconsistent with an intention to insist on its rights and, therefore, supported a finding of waiver. Since Paragraph 35, Paragraph 10 and Article XI, when read together, allocated the risk of delay to subcontractor, the subcontractor would be precluded from collecting damages for delay absent waiver or modification. The Court held that contractor was liable to subcontractor for delay damages.

85010 (UNASSIGNED)

85011 C.J.M. Constr., Inc. v. Chandler Plumbing & Heating, Inc., 708 P.2d 60 (Alaska 1985)

        III: A107-1978, Art. 10, Para. 10.11

        III: A117-1979, Art. 14, Para. 14.11

        III: A201-1976, Art. 4, Para. 4.18.

        III: A401-1978, Art. 11, Para. 11.11.1

Contractor brought an indemnity action against subcontractor after admitting negligence in a personal injury action brought by owner's employee. The trial court granted contractor's motion for summary judgment and subcontractor appealed. At issue on appeal was the scope of the indemnity provision.

The subcontract provided that subcontractor "indemnify and save harmless the CONTRACTOR from and against any and all suits, claims, actions, losses, costs, penalties, and damages, of whatsoever kind or nature, including attorney's fees, arising out of, in connection with, or incident to the SUBCONTRACTOR'S performance of this SUBCONTRACT." Subcontractor argued on appeal that this broad indemnification provision did not require subcontractor to indemnify contractor for its own negligence.

The Supreme Court of Alaska found that the indemnity clause was broad and inclusive and that because subcontractor agreed to indemnify contractor against "any and all suits . . . of whatsoever kind or nature [,] . . ." the clause shifted the risk to subcontractor even if subcontractor was free of fault. The Court held that since the indemnification provision did not contain a limiting clause the trial court properly held that subcontractor was obligated to indemnify contractor.

negligence. The lower court granted contractor's motion for summary judgment holding that subcontractor was obligated to indemnify contractor for all damages under the terms of the indemnity clause irrespective of contractor's contributory negligence. Subcontractor appealed, arguing that the indemnity clause did not entitle contractor to indemnity for contractor's own negligence.

The parties entered into the American Institute of Architects Standard Form of Agreement Between Contractor and Subcontractor, Document No. A401, 1978 edition, which contained an indemnity clause in Paragraph 11.11.1.

The Appellate Court strictly construed the provision against the contractor and found that the clause requiring subcontractor to indemnify and hold harmless contractor from damages "to the extent caused in whole or in part by any negligent act or omission of Subcontractor . . ." suggested a comparative negligence construction under which each party is accountable to the extent that its negligence contributed to the injury. However, the language "regardless of whether it is caused in part by a party indemnified hereunder" made the provision equivocal and caused it to fail under a strict construction analysis. The Court therefore held that the contractor was not entitled to indemnification from the subcontractor to the extent that damages were caused by contractor's own negligence.

85009 Chicago College of Osteopathic Medicine v. George A. Fuller Co., 776 F.2d 198 (7th Cir. 1985), *later proceeding,* 801 F.2d 908 (7th Cir. 1986)

Ill:	A107-1978, Art. 14, Para. 14.3	
Ill:	A117-1979, Art. 18, Para. 18.3	
Ill:	A201-1976, Art. 8, Para. 8.3.1	
Ill:	A201-1976, Art. 8, Para. 8.3.4	
Ill:	A201-1976, Art. 12, Para. 12.3.1	
Ill:	A401-1978, Art. 11, Para. 11.2.2	
Ill:	A401-1978, Art. 11, Para. 11.9.1	
Ill:	A401-1978, Art. 11, Para. 11.10.1	

As part of a larger dispute arising from the construction of an out-patient clinic (see case digest number 83007), subcontractor brought an action against contractor for delay damages. The District Court found that subcontractor was entitled to delay damages and held that the delay waiver clause in the subcontract did not apply to the extraordinary delays in the excavation of the site. The Appellate Court reversed on the grounds that Illinois state law did not permit such a narrow construction of the delay waiver clause. The Court found that contractor was liable to subcontractor, holding that contractor waived its rights under the clause, that subcontractor had met the test for obtaining payment for extra work, and that the parties had orally modified the contract. On remand the District Court held that contractor was liable to subcontractor for delay damages. Contractor appealed.

The subcontract provided in Article XI that the "Subcontractor expressly agrees not to make, and hereby waives, any claim for damages on account of any delay, obstruction

employees of the owner. The contract, in Article 1.02(c) clearly established that the term "agent" included the engineer. Therefore, contractor was precluded from bringing a claim against engineer even absent the no-damage-for-delay provision. The Court further found that subcontractors were precluded from claiming damages because they were bound by a flow-down provision in the subcontracts to the owner-contractor no-damage-for-delay provision.

85007 B.G. Coney Co. v. Radford Petroleum Equip. Co., 287 Ark. 108, 696 S.W.2d 745 (1985), *later proceeding,* River Valley, Inc. v. American States Ins. Co., 287 Ark. 386, 699 S.W.2d 745 (1985)

II:	A401-1978, Art. 5, Para. 5.1
II:	A401-1978, Art. 5, Para. 5.3
II:	A401-1978, Art. 11, Para. 11.2.5
II:	A401-1978, Art. 11, Para. 11.8.1
II:	A401-1978, Art. 11, Para. 11.12.1
II:	A401-1978, Art. 12, Para. 12.4.1

Contractor brought an action against owner for amounts due under the contract. Subcontractors, who were joined as parties to the action, cross-claimed against contractor for amounts due under the subcontracts. The lower court entered summary judgment for the subcontractors, and contractor appealed. The Appellate Court certified the case to the Arkansas Supreme Court on the issues of whether the lower court was correct in rendering summary judgment in favor of subcontractors. Contractor had argued on appeal that subcontractors were not entitled to payment until contractor had been paid by owner.

The subcontracts provided in Article V that contractor make monthly progress payments to subcontractors and in Article VI that final payment of the entire unpaid balance of the contract sum must be paid to subcontractors within thirty days of completion and acceptance by the contractor. There was no dispute over whether the work of the subcontractors had been completed and accepted.

The Supreme Court of Arkansas found that Article VI controlled as to the final payments claimed by the subcontractors and that there was no latent ambiguity in the contract. The Supreme Court held that the lower court did not err in entering summary judgment for all subcontractors whose work had been completed and accepted.

85008 Braegelmann v. Horizon Dev. Co., 371 N.W.2d 644 (Minn. Ct. App. 1985)

II:	A107-1978, Art. 10, Para. 10.11
II:	A117-1979, Art. 14, Para. 14.11
II:	A201-1976, Art. 4, Para. 4.18.1
I:	A401-1978, Art. 11, Para. 11.11.1

Subcontractor's employee brought a personal injury action against contractor. Contractor filed a third-party indemnity action against subcontractor alleging subcontractor's

The Court therefore held that the trial court did not err in denying contractor's petition because supplier did not consent to arbitration.

85006   Bates & Rogers Constr. Corp. v. Greeley & Hansen, 109 Ill. 2d 225, 93 Ill. Dec. 369, 486 N.E.2d 902 (1985)

Ill:	A107-1978, Art. 8, Para. 8.1
Ill:	A107-1978, Art. 8, Para. 8.3
Ill:	A107-1978, Art. 14, Para. 14.3
Ill:	A117-1979, Art. 12, Para. 12.1
Ill:	A117-1979, Art. 12, Para. 12.3
Ill:	A117-1979, Art. 18, Para. 18.3
Ill:	A201-1976, Art. 2, Para. 2.2.2
Ill:	A201-1976, Art. 2, Para. 2.2.3
Ill:	A201-1976, Art. 2, Para. 2.2.4
Ill:	A201-1976, Art. 8, Para. 8.3.1
Ill:	A201-1976, Art. 8, Para. 8.3.4
Ill:	A201-1976, Art. 12, Para. 12.3.1
Ill:	A401-1978, Art. 11, Para. 11.1.1

Contractor and subcontractors brought an action against engineer claiming that engineer's negligence caused them to incur damages, which the trial court and appellate court held were solely economic and could not be recovered in a negligence action. On second appeal engineer argued that contractor had waived its right to delay damages which the contractor was seeking under the owner-contractor agreement.

The owner-contractor agreement provided in Article 3.05 that contractor agreed "to make no claim for damages for delay in the performance of this Contract occasioned by any act or omission to act of the [Owner] or any of its representatives . . . and agrees that any such claim shall be fully compensated for by an extension of time. . . ." Article 7.01 stated that the engineer was a representative of the owner. The contract specified at length the responsibilities of the engineer to observe the work, to determine the amount, kind, quality, sequence and location of the work, and to coordinate the various subcontractors. The agreement stated that "it is the intent of this contract that all of the work shall be subject to his determination, direction, and approval."

The Appellate Court concluded that based on the record the damages sought by contractor were delay damages which were covered by the no-damages-for-delay clause. The clause clearly provided that contractor shall make "no claim" for delay damages. Even in the case of delays by the engineer contractor agreed that such claims "shall be fully compensated for by an extension of time to complete performance of the work." The Court construed the contract language as extending the benefits of the exculpatory clause to the engineer. Furthermore, under Article 11.05 of the contract the contractor agreed not to make any claims against any individuals including officers, agents and

additional expenses. The Court held that because there was no issue as to the making of an agreement to arbitrate it was error for the trial court to deny architect the right to arbitrate its claim against owner.

85005 Baldwin Co. v. Weyland Mach. Shop, Inc., 14 Ark. App. 118, 685 S.W.2d 537 (1985)

II:	A107-1978, Art. 11, Para. 11.1
II:	A107-1978, Art. 11, Para. 11.2
II:	A107-1978, Art. 13, Para. 13.2
II:	A117-1979, Art. 15, Para. 15.1
II:	A117-1979, Art. 15, Para. 15.2
II:	A117-1979, Art. 17, Para. 17.2
I:	A201-1976, Art. 5, Para. 5.3.1
I:	A201-1976, Art. 5, Para. 5.3.1
I:	A201-1976, Art. 7, Para. 7.9.1

Subcontractor made a demand for arbitration against contractor pursuant to the General Conditions in the owner-contractor agreement, which had been incorporated into the subcontract. Contractor brought suit against a supplier seeking damages and indemnification for any amounts contractor might be required to pay subcontractor.

Contractor petitioned the court that all parties be joined in and bound by a single arbitration proceeding. The trial court ordered arbitration between subcontractor and contractor but denied the petition to require supplier to participate in arbitration because it had not consented in writing to submit claims to arbitration. Contractor appealed, arguing that supplier was required to arbitrate under the joinder of parties provision of Paragraph 7.9.1.

The American Institute of Architects General Conditions of the Contract for Construction, Document No. A201, 1976 edition, were incorporated into the subcontract and into the contractor-supplier agreement. Paragraph 7.9.1 contained a broad form arbitration provision that also provided that no party "shall be joined in the arbitration other than the Owner, the Contractor and any other person substantially involved in a common question of fact or law whose presence is required if complete relief is to be accorded in the arbitration." Paragraph 5.1.1 defined a subcontractor as "a person or entity who has a direct contract with the Contractor to perform any work at the site." Paragraph 5.3.1 provided that a subcontractor would have the benefit of all rights, remedies and redress against the contractor that the contractor had against the owner.

The Appellate Court found that the clear language of the contract required arbitration between subcontractor and contractor. Supplier was not a subcontractor as defined in Paragraph 5.1.1 because supplier did not contract to perform work, but merely delivered materials to the site. The Court interpreted the joinder language of Paragraph 7.9.1 as a procedural provision which specified circumstances under which consenting parties who were not owners, contractors or subcontractors, could be joined in a single arbitration.

contractor, and hereby covenants and agrees that it will conduct itself consistent with such status, that it and its employees will neither hold itself out as or claim to be an officer or employee of the Purchaser by reason hereof, and that it will not by reason hereof, make any claim, demand or application to or for any right or privilege applicable to an officer or employee of the Purchaser, including, but not limited to, workmen's compensation coverage, unemployment insurance benefits, social security coverage or retirement credit.

The Court concluded that the references in the contract to contractor as an independent contractor, and the occasional implication that owner would provide only general or overall supervision, did not outweigh the tenor of the contract that owner supervised to any degree it wished. The Court also held that the contract provisions indicated that owner retained the right to control the manner of performance. This finding was supported by evidence of the owner's actual control over the project.

85004   Anderson-Parrish Assoc., Inc. v. City of St. Petersburg Beach, 468 So. 2d 507 (Fla. Dist. Ct. App. 1985)

	II:	A107-1978, Art. 13, Para. 13.2
	II:	A117-1979, Art. 17, Para. 17.2
	II:	A201-1976, Art. 7, Para. 7.9.1
	II:	A401-1978, Art. 13, Para. 13.2
	I:	B141-1977, Art. 9, Para. 9.1

Contractor brought a breach of contract action against owner. The owner counterclaimed and brought a third party action against architect alleging that architect failed to properly design and supervise construction of a fire station. Architect moved to compel arbitration. The trial court denied architect's motion and architect appealed, arguing that the trial court erred in denying its motion because the owner's third party action was based on the contract which included a compulsory arbitration provision, giving architect a statutory right to arbitration. The owner argued that its third party action was an indemnification action and was not based on the owner-architect agreement.

The owner-architect agreement contained an arbitration clause, identical to the American Institute of Architects Standard Form of Agreement Between Owner and Architect, Document No. B141, 1977 edition, Paragraph 9.1, which provided that "all claims, disputes and other matters in question between the parties to this Agreement, arising out of or relating to this Agreement or the breach thereof, shall be decided by arbitration in accordance with the Construction Industry Arbitration Rules of the American Arbitration Association then obtaining unless the parties mutually agree otherwise. . . ." The state arbitration code provided that "if the court is satisfied that no substantial issue exists as to the making of the agreement . . . it shall grant the application. . . ."

The Appellate Court found that owner's third party action was based on the contract, since the owner had made direct allegations that architect failed to properly design and supervise the construction causing the owner to employ another contractor and incur

The Appellate Court held that the following contract provisions of the owner-contractor agreement clearly proved that the owner reserved the right to control details of contractor's performance and the manner in which the work was done:

[T]he Purchaser desires to enter into an agreement with the Contractor, who shall be an Independent Contractor, for the primary purpose of furnishing certain craft labor and supervision. . . .

. . . .

The Contractor shall furnish labor and supervision of various crafts as may be required by the Purchaser from time to time to perform certain civil, mechanical, and architectural work. . . .

Contractor understands and agrees that Purchaser shall determine the actual quantity of work, labor, supervision, materials, equipment, personnel, subcontracting and other items to be supplied hereunder by Contractor in connection with the construction of R.L. Harris Dam. The Purchaser reserves the right to contract with other contractors to perform any part or parts of the work required for said construction.

. . . .

The Contractor shall ascertain the standard practices and procedures of the Purchaser with respect to the scope of the work, schedules and services to be performed.

All work and activities of the labor, foremen and supervisors and other personnel of the Contractor shall be coordinated and scheduled by the Purchaser, acting through its Project Superintendent.

The furnishing of personnel by the Contractor will generally consist of, but not necessarily be limited to the following:

1. The assigning of one or more qualified persons, as necessary, to full time work at the job site, under the overall direction of Purchaser, who will . . . act in all matters pertaining to the procurement of labor, supervision . . . and consult with Purchaser in the planning and scheduling of the manpower requirements for construction. . . .

2. . . . The Contractor shall furnish personnel in numbers and by job classifications as may be requested by the Purchaser in writing from time to time. All of such personnel shall be employees of and paid by the Contractor; however, they shall perform work under the direction and control of the Purchaser, and its engineers, supervisors and others who shall be in charge of the work. . . .

. . . .

All subcontractors entered into under this provision shall provide that scheduling and coordination, and general supervision of the work will be provided by the Purchaser. . . .

All work shall be under the direct supervision of the Purchaser. . . . The Purchaser shall assume full responsibility for the Project work. . . . The Purchaser shall have full responsibility for the proper and workmanlike construction of the project and compliance with all plans and specifications therefor. . . .

The Contractor, in accordance with its status as an independent contractor, shall not act as an agent or employee of the Purchaser, but shall be and act as an independent

and/or that arbitration was time barred. The trial court compelled arbitration and contractor appealed.

The subcontract provided in Article 1 that subcontractor was to perform his work in accordance with the terms of the "Contract Documents." The Contract Documents were identified as the subcontract, the "General Conditions of the Contract for the Construction of Buildings" of the current edition of the American Institute of Architects (AIA)" and designated documents prepared by the architect for the project. It further provided that "The Contract Documents are hereby made part of this Agreement." Paragraph 5.3.1 of the General Conditions covered relations between the contractor and the subcontractors and granted to "the Subcontractor . . . the benefits of all rights, remedies and redress against the Contractor that the Contractor, by these Documents, has against the Owner." A broad form arbitration provision was contained in Paragraph 7.9.1.

The Appellate Court found that the provisions in the subcontract that incorporated by reference the General Conditions of the owner-contractor agreement effectively bound the subcontractor to assume toward the contractor those responsibilities and obligations which the contractor assumed toward the owner. The provisions also gave the subcontractor the benefit of those conditions which required the parties to submit the dispute to arbitration. The Court held that the parties had a valid agreement to arbitrate disputes arising out of the contract. Referring to the Federal Arbitration Act, Section 2, which established that, as a matter of federal law, any doubts concerning the scope of arbitrable issues should be resolved in favor of arbitration, and which provided in pertinent part that "an allegation of waiver, delay, or a like defense to arbitrability" was arbitrable, the Court held that contractor's allegation that subcontractor's claim was time barred was subject to arbitration.

85003a   Alabama Power Co. v. Beam, 472 So. 2d 619 (Ala. 1985), *later proceeding,* 510 So. 2d 185 (Ala. 1987)

	III:	A107-1978, Art. 10, Para. 10.1
	III:	A107-1978, Art. 10, Para. 10.2
	III:	A107-1978, Art. 10, Para. 10.3
	III:	A107-1978, Art. 10, Para. 10.7
	III:	A117-1979, Art. 14, Para. 14.1
	III:	A117-1979, Art. 14, Para. 14.2
	III:	A117-1979, Art. 14, Para. 14.3
	III:	A117-1979, Art. 14, Para. 14.7
	III:	A201-1976, Art. 4, Para. 4.3.1
	III:	A201-1976, Art. 4, Para. 4.3.2
	III:	A201-1976, Art. 4, Para. 4.3.3
	III:	A201-1976, Art. 4, Para. 4.4.1
	III:	A201-1976, Art. 4, Para. 4.4.2

II:	A401-1978, Art. 13, Para. 13.2
I:	B141-1977, Art. 9, Para. 9.1
I:	B141-1977, Art. 9, Para. 9.2

Engineer filed an action against owner seeking damages for breach of contract for professional design services. The trial court dismissed engineer's complaint for failure to state a cause of action. Engineer appealed. The Appellate Court reversed and owner filed a petition for discretionary review. Among numerous issues raised by owner was whether the arbitration clause in the contract denied the court jurisdiction and mandated that the court dismiss engineer's complaint on jurisdictional grounds.

The parties entered into the American Institute of Architects Standard Form of Agreement Between Owner and Architect, Document Number B141, 1977 edition, which contained a broad arbitration provision in Article 8. Article 8 also provided that a demand for arbitration could not be made "after the date when such dispute would be barred by the applicable statute of limitations."

The Supreme Court of North Carolina found that the owner failed to exercise the appropriate contractual remedy by not moving to compel arbitration and stay the litigation. The Court held that owner, in its motion to dismiss for failure to state a cause of action, had not invoked the arbitration provision and, consequently, the court was not denied jurisdiction. Furthermore, under Article 8 of the contract, owner's failure to demand arbitration within the "applicable statute of limitations" barred owner from asserting a right to arbitrate. Therefore the Court affirmed the Appellate Court's decision remanding the case for trial.

85003 ADC Constr. Co. v. McDaniel Grading, Inc., 177 Ga. App. 223, 338 S.E.2d 733 (1985)

II:	A107-1978, Art. 11, Para. 11.2
II:	A107-1978, Art. 13, Para. 13.2
II:	A117-1979, Art. 15, Para. 15.2
II:	A117-1979, Art. 17, Para. 17.2
I:	A201-1976, Art. 5, Para. 5.3.1
I:	A201-1976, Art. 7, Para. 7.9.1
I:	A401-1978, Art. 1, Para. 1.1
I:	A401-1978, Art. 2, Para. 2.1
I:	A401-1978, Art. 11, Para. 11.1.1
I:	A401-1978, Art. 13, Para. 13.1

Subcontractor filed a demand for arbitration against contractor for final payment. Contractor sued to stay arbitration, alleging that subcontractor breached the subcontract by refusing to return to the jobsite within the time permitted and alleging that there was no valid agreement to arbitrate. Contractor further alleged that even if an arbitration agreement did exist, subcontractor did not comply with its provisions resulting in waiver,

85001   A.A. Conte, Inc. v. Campbell-Lowrie-Lautermilch Corp., 132 Ill. App. 3d 325, 87 Ill. Dec. 429, 477 N.E.2d 30 (1985)

II:	A401-1978, Art. 5, Para. 5.1
II:	A401-1978, Art. 5, Para. 5.3
II:	A401-1978, Art. 11, Para. 11.8.1
II:	A401-1978, Art. 11, Para. 11.12.1
II:	A401-1978, Art. 12, Para. 12.4.1

Subcontractor brought an action against contractor to recover the amount due under the subcontract after failing to foreclose on its mechanics lien which had been subordinated to other liens. The trial court granted contractor's motion for summary judgment and subcontractor appealed. At issue on appeal was whether the trial court erred in granting contractor's motion for summary judgment.

The subcontract provided that subcontractor was to perform certain excavating work. Payments were made to the subcontractor on a monthly basis upon subcontractor's submission of bills to contractor. The owners defaulted on payments to the contractor and the project was terminated. Contractor informed subcontractor that the owners had defaulted and advised the subcontractor to cease work immediately. Contractor was not paid by the owners and in turn made no payments to subcontractor. Subcontractor then filed this action. Contractor raised the affirmative defense that Article 18 of the subcontract, which provided that contractor must first receive payment from the owners before contractor was obligated to pay the subcontractor, was a condition precedent to payment. Furthermore, Article 5 of the subcontract, which required timely submission by subcontractor of material invoices which would be paid by contractor, provided that "payment for invoiced material has been received by Campbell-Lowrie-Lautermilch Corporation under its general contract." The subcontractor argued on appeal that these contract provision were a limitation only as to time of payment, giving contractor a reasonable time in which to pay subcontractor. Subcontractor argued that the provisions were ambiguous, therefore, interpretation of the provisions was a question of fact to be determined by the trier of fact.

The Appellate Court found that the contract language was clear and unambiguous and provided that contractor had no obligation to pay subcontractor since contractor had not been paid by the owners. The Court held that the trial court did not err in granting contractor's motion for summary judgment.

85002   Adams v. Nelsen, 313 N.C. 442, 329 S.E.2d 322 (1985)

II:	A107-1978, Art. 13, Para. 13.2
II:	A117-1979, Art. 17, Para. 17.2
II:	A201-1976, Art. 7, Para. 7.9.1
II:	A201-1976, Art. 7, Para. 7.9.2
II:	A401-1978, Art. 13, Para. 13.1

84040 Willoughby Roofing & Supply Co. v. Kajima Int'l, Inc., 598 F. Supp. 353 (N.D. Ala. 1984), *aff'd,* 776 F.2d 269 (11th Cir. 1985)

II:	A107-1978, Art. 13, Para. 13.2
II:	A117-1979, Art. 17, Para. 17.2
II:	A201-1976, Art. 7, Para. 7.9.1
II:	A401-1978, Art. 13, Para. 13.1

Subcontractor brought a breach of contract action against contractor. Contractor demanded arbitration. The arbitrator entered judgment for subcontractor, who then brought an action to confirm the judgment in its favor. Contractor filed a motion to vacate the award of punitive damages arguing that the arbitration panel lacked authority to consider a claim for punitive damages.

After contractor and subcontractor entered into an agreement whereby subcontractor was to construct and install a roof, contractor materially altered the plans and specifications upon which subcontractor based its bid. Subcontractor sought to renegotiate the contract price or to submit a new bid. Contractor responded by cancelling the contract and engaging another subcontractor to do the work. Subcontractor brought a breach of contract action against contractor.

The dispute was submitted to arbitration pursuant to a broad arbitration clause in the subcontract similar to the American Institute of Architect General Conditions of the Contract for Construction, Document A201, 1976 edition, Paragraph 7.9.1.

The Court found that the broad arbitration clause evinced the intention of the parties to vest the arbitrators with authority to decide virtually any claim that could arise in relation to the contract. In addition, the clause incorporated by reference the Construction Industry Arbitration Rules. Rule 43 provides that the "arbitrator may grant any remedy or relief which is just and equitable. . . ." The Court held that when the extremely broad arbitration clause was read in light of the broad grant of remedial power in Rule 43, the parties by their contract had authorized the arbitrators to award punitive damages.

I:	A201-1976, Art. 1, Para. 1.2.3
I:	A201-1976, Art. 12, Para. 12.1.1
I:	A201-1976, Art. 12, Para. 12.3.1
II:	A401-1978, Art. 1, Para. 1.1
II:	B141-1977, Art. 13, Para. 13.1

In contractor's action against owner alleging breach of a later related oral agreement, the Appellate Court cited to the American Institute of Architects Standard Form of Agreement between Owner and Contractor, Document No. A101, 1977 edition, Article 1 and Article 7.2 and the American Institute of Architects General Conditions of the Contract for Construction, Document No. A201, 1976 edition, Paragraph 1.1.2 and the written change order provisions, to support its holding that all prior and contemporaneous oral agreements were merged into the owner-contractor agreement and the oral agreements were inadmissible parol evidence.

84039 Wesleyan Univ. v. Rissil Constr. Assocs., Inc., 1 Conn. App. 373, 472 A.2d 23, *cert. denied,* 193 Conn. 802, 474 A.2d 1259 (1984)

II:	A107-1974, Art. 11, Para. 11.1
II:	A107-1974, Art. 14
I:	A201-1970, Art. 5, Para. 5.1.3
I:	A201-1970, Art. 7, Para. 7.10.1
II:	A401-1978, Art. 11, Para. 11.1.1

Owner brought an action for a declaratory judgment as to whether it was required to arbitrate claims brought against it by subcontractor, and sought an injunction staying arbitration. The trial court entered judgment denying injunctive relief and ordered owner to proceed with arbitration. Owner appealed. The sole question on appeal was whether owner, which had agreed to arbitrate all claims arising out of the owner-contractor agreement, was required to arbitrate claims with subcontractor arising out of a subcontract to which owner was not a party.

The owner-contractor agreement provided that contractor would supervise the construction of a creative arts center, and in furtherance of this obligation contractor entered into an agreement with subcontractor under which subcontractor was to perform certain cast-in-place concrete work. The owner-contractor agreement included the American Institute of Architects General Conditions of the Contract for Construction, Document A201, 1970 edition, Paragraph 7.10.1 which provided for arbitration and Paragraph 5.1.3 which provided that "nothing contained in the Contract Documents shall create any contractual relationship between Owner . . . and any Subcontractor. . . ."

The Appellate Court found that persons could not compel arbitration of a dispute between or among parties who have not contracted to arbitrate the dispute. The Court held that owner, who had agreed to arbitrate disputes with contractor, could not be required to arbitrate claims of subcontractor arising out of the subcontract where owner was not a party to the subcontract.

was bound to have notice of the contract's provisions requiring arbitration for dispute resolution. The Court referred the claim to arbitration in accordance with the contract and stayed the court action.

84037   State v. Omega Painting, Inc., 463 N.E.2d 287 (Ind. Ct. App.), *reh'g denied*, 464 N.E.2d 940 (Ind. Ct. App. 1984)

  III: A107-1978, Art. 18, Para. 18.1
  III: A107-1978, Art. 18, Para. 18.2
  III: A107-1978, Art. 18, Para. 18.3
  III: A117-1979, Art. 22, Para. 22.1
  III: A117-1979, Art. 22, Para. 22.2
  III: A117-1979, Art. 22, Para. 22.3
  III: A201-1976, Art. 12, Para. 12.3.1

Contractor brought an action against owner for additional costs in completing a bridge project. The jury returned a verdict in favor of the contractor and owner appealed.

The owner-contractor agreement provided in section 105.16 that "if contractor deems that additional compensation will be due him for work . . . not covered in the contract or not ordered as extra work . . . he shall notify the Engineer in writing of his intention to make a claim. . . . If such notification is not given . . . the Contractor shall make no claim for such additional compensation."

The Appellate Court reversed. It found that since neither party contended that the additional work was covered by the contract or ordered as extra work, contractor's claim for compensation was covered by section 105.16. The Court held that absent a showing that owner waived section 105.16, the contractor was precluded from raising a claim for additional compensation when contractor failed to properly notify the engineer.

84038   W.E. Koehler Constr. Co. v. Medical Center of Blue Springs, 670 S.W.2d 558 (Mo. Ct. App. 1984)

  I: A101-1977, Art. 1
  I: A101-1977, Art. 7, Para. 7.2
  II: A107-1978, Art. 7, Para. 7.1
  II: A107-1978, Art. 18, Para. 18.1
  II: A107-1978, Art. 18, Para. 18.2
  II: A111-1978, Art. 1
  II: A111-1978, Art. 16, Para. 16.2
  II: A117-1979, Art. 11, Para. 11.1
  II: A117-1979, Art. 22, Para. 22.1
  II: A117-1979, Art. 22, Para. 22.2
  I: A201-1976, Art. 1, Para. 1.1.2

and/or Specifications as he may find necessary, any increase or decrease of cost resulting from such change to be adjusted. . . ." Paragraph 24 of the General Conditions entitled contractor to monthly payments for the work performed in the previous month and authorized the owner to hold back 10 percent of the amount due until final completion of all of the work. Contractor argued on appeal that the work performed under Paragraph 21 was part of the work contractor was required to perform under the contract and the work performed under the contract should be interpreted as all being part of the performance of the contract. If so interpreted, the time for filing suit did not expire until completion of performance of the entire contract, which occurred within the statute of limitations. The owner argued that because the contract required periodic payments to contractor, a statute of limitations began to run on each installment from its due date.

The Appellate Court found that contractor's claim was for work not definitely required by the terms of the contract but for work possibly contemplated by the contract. However, contractor's right to compensation arose from the terms of the contract. Applying Paragraph 24 to the payments which contractor claimed, contractor would not have been entitled to full payment for the work until the completion of the contract. The Court therefore held that contractor's claim was not barred by the statute of limitations.

84036   Smith v. Dugan & Meyers Constr. Co., 18 Ohio Misc. 2d 5, 480 N.E.2d 830 (1984)

	II:	A107-1978, Art. 11, Para. 11.2
	II:	A107-1978, Art. 13, Para. 13.2
	II:	A117-1979, Art. 15, Para. 15.2
	II:	A117-1979, Art. 17, Para. 17.2
	I:	A201-1976, Art. 5, Para. 5.3.1
	I:	A201-1976, Art. 7, Para. 7.9.1
	I:	A401-1978, Art. 11, Para. 11.1.1
	I:	A401-1978, Art. 13, Para. 13.1

Subcontractor brought an action against contractor. Contractor moved to dismiss the action for failure to state a cause of action because the subcontract provided for arbitration of all disputes.

The subcontract contained a broad form arbitration provision that required arbitration of all disputes relating to the subcontract "in the same manner and under the same procedure as provided in the Contract Documents with respect to the Owner and the [Contractor]. . . ." The owner-contractor agreement provided for arbitration "in accordance with the Construction Industry Rules of the American Arbitration Association. . . ." Subcontractor argued on appeal that because it was not a party to the owner-contractor agreement and was never apprised of its provisions, it was not bound by the arbitration provision.

The Appellate Court found that subcontractor was chargeable with knowledge of the contents of the owner-contractor agreement, and by the wording of the subcontract it

84034 Rosos Litho Supply Corp. v. Hansen, 123 Ill. App. 3d 290, 78 Ill. Dec. 477, 462 N.E.2d 566 (1984)

I:	A201-1976, Art. 2, Para. 2.2.3
I:	A201-1976, Art. 2, Para. 2.2.13
I:	A201-1976, Art. 7, Para. 7.7.1
I:	A201-1976, Art. 7, Para. 7.7.2
I:	B141-1977, Art. 1, Para. 1.5.4
I:	B141-1977, Art. 1, Para. 1.5.12

Owner brought an action against architect for breach of contract, breach of warranty and negligence in the construction of a building addition. The jury returned a verdict for owner on the negligence action and architect appealed. Among the numerous issues on appeal was whether the standard of care for an architect was sufficiently established.

The owner and architect entered into the American Institute of Architects Standard Form of Agreement Between Owner and Architect which provided that architect would oversee the quality and quantity of the various contractors' work, accept full authority to require that any work not meeting the project specifications be remedied, receive daily reports of a soil engineer to be hired by the excavator, and hire a soil engineer when architect deemed necessary.

The Appellate Court found that the services of a soil engineer were significant to the success of the project and that the architect was responsible for hiring a soil engineer. The Court held that architect's standard of care was sufficiently established by the contract requirement that architect oversee the quality and quantity of contractor's work. The finding of liability was therefore affirmed, but because the trial court had erred in its jury instructions on damages, the case was remanded.

84035 Santucci Constr. Co. v. City of Danville, 128 Ill. App. 3d 954, 84 Ill. Dec. 234, 471 N.E.2d 1000 (1984)

II:	A101-1977, Art. 5
II:	A107-1978, Art. 4, Para. 4.1
II:	A201-1976, Art. 7, Para. 7.4.1
II:	A201-1976, Art. 9, Para. 9.5.2
II:	A201-1976, Art. 12, Para. 12.2.1

Contractor brought a breach of contract action against owner. Owner filed a motion contending that the suit was barred by the statute of limitations. The trial court entered judgment in favor of owner and in bar of the action, and contractor appealed.

The owner-contractor agreement provided in its General Conditions, Paragraph 21, "Subsurface Conditions Found Different," that should contractor "encounter sub-surface and/or latent conditions at the site materially differing from those shown on the Plans or indicated in the Specifications, he shall immediately give notice to the Architect/Engineer . . ." who shall "investigate the conditions . . . make such changes in the Plans

III:	A107-1978, Art. 18, Para. 18.2
III:	A107-1978, Art. 18, Para. 18.3
III:	A117-1979, Art. 11, Para. 11.1
III:	A117-1979, Art. 22, Para. 22.1
III:	A117-1979, Art. 22, Para. 22.2
III:	A117-1979, Art. 22, Para. 22.3
III:	A201-1976, Art. 1, Para. 1.1.1
III:	A201-1976, Art. 12, Para. 12.1.1
III:	A201-1976, Art. 12, Para. 12.1.2
III:	A201-1976, Art. 12, Para. 12.1.3
III:	A201-1976, Art. 12, Para. 12.1.4
III:	A201-1976, Art. 12, Para. 12.1.5
III:	A201-1976, Art. 12, Para. 12.3.1
III:	A201-1976, Art. 12, Para. 12.3.2

Contractor brought an action against owner for additional compensation for work performed. The trial court entered judgment for contractor and owner appealed. At issue on appeal was whether or not contractor was entitled to extra compensation.

The owner-contractor agreement provided that contractor excavate and build an embankment for which owner was to pay an agreed-upon unit price. Although contractor completed the work in accordance with the plans and specifications the quantities excavated were substantially less than the original proposal. Contractor argued that the under-run constituted an alteration which entitled contractor to be paid a higher unit price. The contract provided that the owner may alter the work and the engineer was authorized to "make such alterations in the work as may increase or decrease the originally awarded contractor quantities. . . ." The contract further provided that should the altered work exceed 25 percent "such excess work shall be covered by supplemental agreement" by which the unit price would be adjusted.

The Appellate Court found that the above-quoted language referred to alterations in the work to be performed under the contract, which the Court interpreted as having broader meaning than merely alterations in the plans and specifications. The owner argued that contractor was entitled to additional compensation only for the portion of the alteration which exceeded 25 percent. The Court found that an under-run exceeding 25 percent of the originally awarded quantities constituted a substantial change in the contract requiring a supplemental agreement to allow the contractor to increase its unit price. The Court held that there was an alteration within the meaning of the contract provisions governing increases in the original contract price requiring a supplemental agreement when alterations in the work exceeded the 25 percent limitation. Contractor's recovery was not limited only to the excess of the actual quantities over 125 percent of the original proposed quantities.

II:	A107-1978, Art. 11, Para. 11.2
II:	A107-1978, Art. 18, Para. 18.1
II:	A117-1979, Art. 14, Para. 14.2
II:	A117-1979, Art. 15, Para. 15.2
II:	A117-1979, Art. 22, Para. 22.1
II:	A201-1976, Art. 4, Para. 4.4.1
II:	A201-1976, Art. 12, Para. 12.3.1
II:	A401-1978, Art. 11, Para. 11.2.6
II:	A401-1978, Art. 11, Para. 11.9.1

Subcontractor brought an action against contractor to recover compensation for extra work which had not been contemplated by the parties under a grading contract. The jury returned a verdict for subcontractor. The trial court denied contractor's motion for judgment notwithstanding the verdict or for a new trial and contractor appealed. Among numerous issues on appeal were whether the trial court erred in submitting the question of the parties' intent under the contract to the jury and whether the evidence supported judgment in favor of subcontractor.

The subcontract provided that subcontractor would "supply all labor, material and equipment to do a complete grading job per quote . . . and the drawings dated 8/3/81 and specifications." The contractor argued on appeal that the drawings and specifications required subcontractor to do a complete grading job and included the work subcontractor claimed was "extra." The subcontractor argued on appeal that the "quote" referred to was for the dock area only and that its claim was for additional work performed other than in the "dock area." The subcontract also required written authorization for extra work.

The Appellate Court found that the contract language was not clear and unambiguous and held that the trial court did not err in submitting the question of the parties' intent to the jury.

Contractor argued on appeal that the provision requiring written authorization for extra work precluded subcontractor's recovery because subcontractor did not submit a written request for extras. The Court found that the legal principle that the contractor could recover without a written change order where an owner orally ordered the extra work knowing that contractor regarded the work as extra and would expect additional compensation, applied to the instant action. In addition, the subcontractor submitted evidence that the additional work was required because of faulty work on the part of the contractor. The Court held that this evidence supported the judgment in favor of subcontractor. It therefore affirmed the judgment of the trial court.

84033 Ronald Adams, Contractor, Inc. v. State, 457 So. 2d 778 (La. Ct. App. 1984), *later proceeding,* 464 So. 2d 1003 (La. Ct. App. 1985)

III:	A107-1978, Art. 7, Para. 7.1
III:	A107-1978, Art. 18, Para. 18.1

It held that this clause did not defeat subcontractor's claim as a matter of law and found that a jury issue existed as to whether the "delay" was of a kind not contemplated by the parties and/or that the delay was caused by the active interference of the owner.

The owner also argued on appeal that subcontractor had waived its right to claim damages by not requesting an extension of time for the performance of its work and did not provide owner with notice of the change in the work before proceeding. The Court held that there was sufficient evidence to allow the jury to find that the subcontract's requirements of request for an extension of time and notice to the owner were waived where the owner had approved a number of change orders after completion of the contract and had authorized changes in the field while considering other change orders. The Court concluded that owner was not entitled to a directed verdict because fact issues were present.

84031   Pioneer Enters., Inc. v. Edens, 216 Neb. 672, 345 N.W.2d 16 (1984)

         III: A107-1978, Art. 10, Para. 10.4
         III: A107-1978, Art. 19, Para. 19.1
         III: A117-1979, Art. 14, Para. 14.4
         III: A117-1979, Art. 23, Para. 23.1
         III: A201-1976, Art. 4, Para. 4.5.1
         III: A201-1976, Art. 8, Para. 8.1.3
         III: A201-1976, Art. 13, Para. 13.2.2

Contractor brought an action against owner for the balance due on a contract to build a grain storage facility. In a bench trial, the trial court entered judgment in favor of owner and contractor appealed. At issue on appeal was whether there was sufficient evidence to sustain the judgment of the trial court.

The owner-contractor agreement contained an express warranty that provided for "All work to be completed in a workmanlike manner according to standard practices." The Appellate Court also found that in the building and construction industry, in the absence of an express agreement to the contrary, it is implied that the building will be constructed in a workmanlike manner and will be fit for its intended purpose.

The Appellate Court, after reviewing the evidence, affirmed. It found that the evidence of leaks causing extensive water and insect damage was sufficient to support a finding that contractor, who was in the business of erecting grain storage facilities, had failed to substantially perform the contract and that the facility was not fit for its intended purpose. The Court held that contractor was not entitled to the balance of the contract price.

84032   Pro Metal Bldg. Sys., Inc. v. T.E. Driskell Grading Co., 170 Ga. App. 127, 316 S.E.2d 574 (1984)

         II: A107-1978, Art. 10, Para. 10.2

performance by the construction manager. Finally, the one-year requirement to correct work did not preclude owner recovery under Paragraph 4.5.1.

84030 Phoenix Contractors, Inc. v. General Motors Corp., 135 Mich. App. 787, 355 N.W.2d 673 (1984)

III:	A107-1978,	Art. 11, Para. 11.2
III:	A107-1978,	Art. 14, Para. 14.3
III:	A107-1978,	Art. 18, Para. 18.1
III:	A107-1978,	Art. 18, Para. 18.2
III:	A107-1978,	Art. 18, Para. 18.3
III:	A117-1979,	Art. 15, Para. 15.2
III:	A117-1979,	Art. 18, Para. 18.3
III:	A117-1979,	Art. 22, Para. 22.1
III:	A117-1979,	Art. 22, Para. 22.2
III:	A117-1979,	Art. 22, Para. 22.3
III:	A201-1976,	Art. 5, Para. 5.3.1
III:	A201-1976,	Art. 8, Para. 8.3.1
III:	A201-1976,	Art. 8, Para. 8.3.2
III:	A201-1976,	Art. 8, Para. 8.3.3
III:	A201-1976,	Art. 8, Para. 8.3.4
III:	A201-1976,	Art. 12, Para. 12.1.1
III:	A201-1976,	Art. 12, Para. 12.3.1
III:	A401-1978,	Art. 11, Para. 11.1.1
III:	A401-1978,	Art. 11, Para. 11.10.1
III:	A401-1978,	Art. 12, Para. 12.5.1

Subcontractor brought an action against owner for additional costs due to owner's interference. The trial court denied owner's motion for directed verdict and subsequently entered judgment on a jury verdict for subcontractor. Owner appealed.

The subcontract incorporated by reference the General Conditions and a no-damage-for-delay clause which provided in Article 7(c) that "if contractor is delayed in the completion of several portions or the whole of the work comprehended in the Contract due to acts of the Owner, acts of the other contractors . . . the time for completion shall be extended. . . . The Contractor will not be entitled to recover the actual damages he sustains by reason of such delays. . . ." The clause stated further that the contingency items in the contractor's bid were assumed to provide for the costs of any delay. Article 25 of the contract provided that all claims for changes in the work had to be submitted promptly in writing and before the work was done.

Owner argued on appeal that the no-damage-for-delay clause relieved it of responsibility for subcontractor's additional costs as a matter of law. The Appellate Court affirmed.

Lessee brought an action against lessor for breach of lease conditions due to a defective air conditioning system. Lessor brought a third party action against construction manager whom lessor hired to supervise the work and to warrant that all air-conditioning work would be of good quality. The trial court entered summary judgment for construction manager and lessor appealed.

The lessor entered into a contract with construction manager for its services to oversee the construction of a mixed-use real estate complex. The contract consisted of excerpts from the American Institute of Architects General Conditions of the Contract for Construction, Document A201, 1976 edition, and from the Associated General Contractors of America Document No. 8, all integrated into the owner-contractor agreement. The contract required in Paragraph 4.3.1 and 4.5.1 that construction manager "supervise and direct the work using his best skill and attention," and be "solely responsible for all construction means, methods, techniques, sequences and procedures and for coordinating all portions of the Work under the contract," and that construction manager warrant that "all work will be of good quality, free from faults and defects and in conformance with the Contract Documents." Paragraph 4.10 and AGC Article 2.1.13 stated that construction manager was responsible to the owner for acts and omissions of all persons performing under the contract and for inspecting all of the air conditioning subcontractor's work to guard the owner against defects. The construction manager and owner's architect certified that the project was substantially completed in accordance with the contract. The certificate provided that the attached list of incomplete or unsatisfactory items did not alter construction manager's responsibility to complete all work in accordance with the contract. Paragraph 9.7.3 required release of all claims and liens prior to final payment. In addition, Paragraph 13.3.1 required a change order and a price adjustment to reflect acceptance by owner of defective or nonconforming work. The construction manager received final payment of the contract price.

Construction manager argued on appeal that owner, by accepting the work and making final payment, waived any defects and that construction manager did not receive timely written notice of faulty or defective work as required by the contract. Owner argued on appeal that the air conditioning defect was latent and was not waived by final payment.

The Appellate Court, after reviewing the record and the above contract provisions, held that construction manager was not entitled to judgment as a matter of law because substantial facts existed as to whether the defect was latent and whether or not owner knew or should have known of the defect. Furthermore, the construction manager remained responsible under Paragraphs 4.10.1, 9.4.4 and AGC Article 13.2.1 for the work of subcontractors until final payment and pursuant to Paragraph 13.2.1 defective work was to be corrected by construction manager whether observed before or after substantial completion. Although final payment was made by owner, construction manager was aware of the air conditioning installation defects before final payment and steps were taken by the construction manager to correct the problems. Therefore, final payment by the owner under these circumstances supported the inference that owner believed construction manager had corrected the problems prior to final payment. Moreover, Paragraph 9.4.4 provided that final payment would not constitute a waiver of any defective

II:	A107-1978, Art. 10, Para. 10.4
II:	A107-1978, Art. 15, Para. 15.1
II:	A107-1978, Art. 15, Para. 15.2
II:	A107-1978, Art. 15, Para. 15.3
II:	A107-1978, Art. 15, Para. 15.4
II:	A107-1978, Art. 15, Para. 15.5
II:	A107-1978, Art. 18, Para. 18.1
II:	A107-1978, Art. 18, Para. 18.2
II:	A107-1978, Art. 18, Para. 18.3
II:	A107-1978, Art. 19, Para. 19.1
II:	A117-1979, Art. 14, Para. 14.1
II:	A117-1979, Art. 14, Para. 14.2
II:	A117-1979, Art. 19, Para. 19.1
II:	A117-1979, Art. 19, Para. 19.2
II:	A117-1979, Art. 19, Para. 19.3
II:	A117-1979, Art. 19, Para. 19.4
II:	A117-1979, Art. 19, Para. 19.5
II:	A117-1979, Art. 22, Para. 22.1
II:	A117-1979, Art. 22, Para. 22.2
II:	A117-1979, Art. 22, Para. 22.3
II:	A117-1979, Art. 23, Para. 23.1
I:	A201-1976, Art. 4, Para. 4.3.1
I:	A201-1976, Art. 4, Para. 4.3.2
I:	A201-1976, Art. 4, Para. 4.5.1
I:	A201-1976, Art. 9, Para. 9.4.1
I:	A201-1976, Art. 9, Para. 9.4.2
I:	A201-1976, Art. 9, Para. 9.5.5
I:	A201-1976, Art. 9, Para. 9.6.1
I:	A201-1976, Art. 9, Para. 9.9.1
I:	A201-1976, Art. 9, Para. 9.9.2
I:	A201-1976, Art. 9, Para. 9.9.3
I:	A101-1976, Art. 9, Para. 9.9.4
I:	A201-1976, Art. 9, Para. 9.9.5
I:	A201-1976, Art. 12 Para. 12.1.1
I:	A201-1976, Art. 13, Para. 13.2.1
I:	A201-1976, Art. 13, Para. 13.2.2
I:	A201-1976, Art. 13, Para. 13.3.1
I:	A201-1976, Art. 13, Para. 13.2.7

Owner also argued on appeal that, pursuant to Paragraphs 2.2.7 and 2.2.8, the architect's decision that the slabs were not a concealed condition was binding. The Appellate Court found that the only decision rendered by the architect that was binding and final was set forth in the contract in Paragraph 2.2.11 and that Paragraph 2.2.12 provided that all other decisions of the architect were subject to arbitration upon the written demand of either party.

The judgment of the trial court was reversed and remanded.

84028   Open Kitchens, Inc. v. Gullo Int'l Dev. Corp., 126 Ill. App. 3d 62, 81 Ill. Dec. 511, 466 N.E.2d 1313 (1984)

II: A107-1978, Art. 10, Para. 10.11
II: A117-1979, Art. 14, Para. 14.11
II: A201-1976, Art. 4, Para. 4.18.1
II: A401-1978, Art. 11, Para. 11.11.1

Owner brought an action against contractor for damages resulting from deficient construction of a freezer room and associated systems. The trial court dismissed certain counts of owner's complaint and owner appealed. Among numerous issues on appeal was whether the trial court erred in dismissing one count on the grounds that it failed to state a cause of action based on the breach of an express contractual indemnity.

The owner-contractor agreement contained, in the "Supplemental General Conditions of the Agreement" at Paragraph 4.18.1, a modified indemnity provision similar to the American Institute of Architects General Conditions of the Contract for Construction, Document A201, 1976 edition, Paragraph 4.18.1. Contractor argued on appeal that Paragraph 4.18.1 did not provide an indemnity or warranty relating to the performance of the construction, but rather was intended to provide indemnification to owner for claims of third parties arising from the performance of the construction work.

The Appellate Court, viewing the contract as a whole, found that the indemnity and hold harmless provisions of the first sentence of Paragraph 4.18.1 had to be interpreted in light of the next sentence, which provided that the "Contractor shall defend at its own expense, any actions based thereon and shall pay all attorneys' fees, costs and other expenses arising therefrom." The Court found that the words "thereon" and "therefrom" referred to the general language of the first sentence of the paragraph relating to "all claims, damages, losses, liabilities and demands. . . ." The Court concluded that while the first sentence read alone could be read as requiring indemnity from acts or omission of the subcontractors, the next sentence indicated that the indemnity was intended to arise only in the context of liability imposed on owner as a result of losses or injuries incurred by third parties. The Court affirmed, holding that the indemnity agreement imposed liability on contractor only for third-party claims.

84029   Phenix-Georgetown, Inc. v. Chas. H. Tompkins Co., 477 A.2d 215 (D.C. App. 1984)

II: A107-1978, Art. 10, Para. 10.1

II:	A107-1978, Art. 18, Para. 18.1
II:	A117-1979, Art. 12, Para. 12.5
II:	A117-1979, Art. 17, Para. 17.2
II:	A117-1979, Art. 22, Para. 22.1
I:	A201-1976, Art. 2, Para. 2.2.7
I:	A201-1976, Art. 2, Para. 2.2.8
I:	A201-1976, Art. 2, Para. 2.2.11
II:	A201-1976, Art. 4, Para. 4.2.1
I:	A201-1976, Art. 7, Para. 7.9.1
I:	A201-1976, Art. 12, Para. 12.2.1
I:	A201-1976, Art. 12, Para. 12.3.1

Owner and contractor entered into a contract for the demolition of a school building and for the removal of the building, foundation, paving and sidewalks. After the removal the site was to be regraded. The owner-contractor agreement contained the American Institute of Architects General Conditions of the Contract for Construction, Document A201, 1976 edition.

During the demolition work contractor discovered three additional slabs that were not shown on the drawings upon which contractor had based its bid. Contractor requested additional compensation for the removal of the slabs. Owner rejected contractor's request and contractor sought arbitration of the dispute. Contractor then filed suit requesting that the trial court compel arbitration, or in the alternative, award contractor damages for breach of contract. The trial court, at the close of contractor's evidence, directed a verdict for owner. Contractor appealed.

Owner argued on appeal that contractor waived its right to arbitration by failing to comply with the contract, which provided in Paragraph 4.2.2 of the Supplemental General Conditions that after reporting to the architect any error in the contract documents, "Contractor shall not proceed with any Work affected without obtaining specific written instructions from Architect." The Appellate Court found that Paragraph 4.2.2 had to be read in conjunction with Paragraph 4.2.1, and when read together they applied to errors and omissions in the contract documents unknown to the contractor, owner and architect. The Court reasoned that it would make no sense for the contractor to give notice to the architect and wait for written instructions if both the owner and architect knew of the conditions in question. The Court held that because the existence of the slabs was known by architect and owner Paragraph 4.2.2 did not preclude contractor's claim.

Owner also argued on appeal that Paragraph 12.3.1 required contractor to give written notice to the architect before doing the extra work if contractor wanted to make a claim for extra compensation. Contractor argued that the controlling contractual provision was Paragraph 12.2.1 which required equitable adjustment by change order if concealed conditions were encountered. The Appellate Court found that under the facts of the case the provision on concealed conditions was controlling and contractor was not required to follow the notice requirements of Paragraph 12.3.1.

Owner then argued that contractor's claims were barred by contractor's failure to comply with the notice of claim provision, which expressly made notice a condition precedent to recovery for extras. The provision also required the contractor to furnish additional data within fifteen days of written demand; compliance with such a demand was likewise a condition precedent to contractor's recovery since under the contract failure to comply was "deemed a waiver by the contractor of all claims for additional compensation or damages." The Court addressed the issue of whether a short period of limitations or notice of claim provision contained in a municipal construction contract barred a claim for extra work or damages instituted against a municipal agency where the contractor alleged gross negligence or willful misconduct. Based on its interpretation of the contract the court held that it could not be determined whether the additional work performed was properly "extra work" excluded by the various exculpatory provisions, or whether it was extra work and thus compensable as part of the original contract price. In addition, if considered "extra work" but not excluded because the exculpatory provisions were inadequate, there was a triable issue as to whether the owner's alleged gross negligence barred enforcement of the notice of claim provision.

Owner also argued that the contractor was barred from claiming delay damages by the no-damage-for-delay clause in the owner-contractor agreement, which disallowed damages for delay "from any cause" and limited the contractor's remedy to an extension of time. The clause provided that "if because of any act or omission of [owner], its inspectors or its officers, agents or employees . . . or of any Contractor of [owner] engaged in operations upon the site . . . or because of any extension of time granted to any Contractor by [owner], whether with proper cause or without proper cause . . . the completion of the Work or any part thereof is necessarily delayed, without fault of the Contractor, beyond the time for completion . . . [owner] shall not be liable or responsible or answerable in any way for any damages caused thereby and no compensation shall be paid to the Contractor because of any suspension of Work or delay in its performance." In a later opinion the Court held that it was the duty of other contractors and not the owner to furnish such services. The owner's conduct did not evidence malice or gross negligence, but the Court found that the contractor had set forth triable issues of fact regarding owner's gross negligence or willful misconduct in its affidavit, sufficient to avoid dismissal, notwithstanding contractor's ability to cure the pleadings. In addition, based on the contractual provision by which the owner retained some supervisory powers, the Court found sufficient issues of fact as to whether the owner was grossly negligent in its supervisory capacity. Although the contract did not impose a duty on the owner to provide security, the contractor argued that the owner was grossly negligent in its supervisory capacity in failing to require additional security by the third party obligated to provide security under the contract.

84027   Olshan Demolishing Co. v. Angleton Indep. School Dist., 684 S.W.2d 179 (Tex. Ct. App. 1984)

       II: A107-1978, Art. 8, Para. 8.5
       II: A107-1978, Art. 13, Para. 13.2

III:	A107-1978, Art. 17, Para. 17.3
III:	A107-1978, Art. 18, Para. 18.1
III:	A117-1979, Art. 21, Para. 21.1
III:	A117-1979, Art. 21, Para. 21.3
III:	A117-1979, Art. 22, Para. 22.1
III:	A201-1976, Art. 11, Para. 11.1.1
III:	A201-1976, Art. 11, Para. 11.3.1
II:	A201-1976, Art. 12, Para. 12.3.1

Contractor brought an action against owner for extra replacement costs for the original temporary plumbing allegedly necessitated by owner's failure to prevent vandalism on the site.

The owner and contractor entered into a prime plumbing contract which included specifications, instructions to bidders, general conditions and special conditions. The contract imposed upon the contractor the duty to insure the work against "any and all risks of destruction, damage, or loss, including but not limited to fire, theft, and any other casualty or happening." The contract imposed upon the contractor the duty to insure against the specific risk of theft. It further transferred the risk to the contractor by making it insure the owner and agree to hold owner harmless regardless of whether the loss was covered by any insurance carried by the contractor. The provisions for security of the work site further attested to the fact that vandalism was foreseen by the parties. The contract exempted "those risks which result solely from active, affirmative, willful acts done by the [owner]."

The Court found that despite the risk-shifting clauses of the contract it was unlikely that the parties had contemplated owner's alleged gross negligence or willful misconduct in failing to take any action to prevent vandalism. The Court concluded that such unforeseen misconduct of owner was qualitatively different from the contemplated vandalism by third parties, and the essence of contractor's cause of action was based on owner's own acts. Since such conduct was not within the contemplation of the parties at the time of contracting, it was not likely to have been within the scope of the original contract.

The Court rejected the owner's argument that the provision stating "The Plumbing Contractor shall furnish and install all necessary temporary water and waste lines for temporary toilets and shall perform all necessary excavation and backfill. . . . The cost of all the above work shall be included in his Base Bid. . . . The Contractor of Plumbing shall provide, install, and maintain a temporary water system, including the necessary temporary water meters, water lines, valves, fittings, pumps, and other appurtenances, all of such size and capacity as adequately to supply the needs . . ." brought the temporary plumbing work within the contract. It was not readily apparent to the Court that the claims for extra plumbing work, done after the initial installation of the temporary plumbing, were intended to be within the scope of the original contract. The Court concluded that all that was contemplated was ordinary and ongoing maintenance, and not the sort of total replacement necessitated by extraordinary circumstances such as vandalism.

III:	A117-1979, Art. 22, Para. 22.1	
III:	A117-1979, Art. 22, Para. 22.1	
III:	A117-1979, Art. 22, Para. 22.3	
III:	A201-1976, Art. 9, Para. 9.9.5	
III:	A201-1976, Art. 12, Para. 12.1.1	
III:	A201-1976, Art. 12, Para. 12.1.2	
III:	A201-1976, Art. 12, Para. 12.1.3	
III:	A201-1976, Art. 12, Para. 12.1.4	
III:	A201-1976, Art. 12, Para. 12.2.1	
III:	A201-1976, Art. 12, Para. 12.3.1	
III:	A201-1976, Art. 8, Para. 8.3.1	
III:	A201-1976, Art. 8, Para. 8.3.2	
III:	A201-1976, Art. 8, Para. 8.3.3	
III:	A201-1976, Art. 8, Para. 8.3.4	

Contractor brought an action against owner for extras. The trial court granted owner's motion for summary judgment and contractor appealed.

The owner-contractor agreement required that all change orders be in writing and required contractor to request in writing equitable adjustment of the contract sum. The contract also contained a differing site conditions clause that required contractor to submit a written claim for an equitable adjustment for changed conditions. The contractor submitted numerous claims by written change order and owner granted equitable adjustments to the contract sum. The contract further provided that "acceptance by the Contractor of the final payment shall operate as and shall constitute a release. . . ."

Contractor argued that he was damaged beyond the equitable adjustment made in the various change orders. The owner argued that contractor's acceptance of final payment released owner from liability, that contractor's failure to give certain notices prior to final payment precluded recovery and that the no-damage-for-delay clause in the contract limited owner's liability.

The Appellate Court, in interpreting the various contract provisions, found that contractor's acceptance and negotiation of the check in final payment released owner from liability for extra expenses, and owner's motion for summary judgment was properly granted. The Court stated that it was unnecessary to discuss the other theories advanced by owner to bar contractor's recovery.

84026   Novak & Co. v. New York City Hous. Auth., 125 Misc. 2d 647, 480 N.Y.S.2d 403 (Sup. Ct. 1984), *later proceeding,* 105 A.D.2d 665, 482 N.Y.S.2d 7 (1984), *modified on other grounds,* 108 A.D.2d 612, 485 N.Y.S.2d 6 (1985), *appeal dismissed,* 67 N.Y.2d 1027, 503 N.Y.S.2d 326, 494 N.E.2d 457 (1986), *and appeal dismissed without opinion,* 73 N.Y.2d 918, 539 N.Y.S.2d 301, 536 N.E.2d 630 (1989).

III: A107-1978, Art. 17, Para. 17.1

III: A201-1976, Art. 12, Para. 12.1.2
III: A201-1976, Art. 12, Para. 12.1.3
III: A201-1976, Art. 12, Para. 12.1.1
III: A201-1976, Art. 12, Para. 12.3.1

Contractor brought an action against owner for additional expenses incurred in performing a public construction contract. The trial court entered judgment for contractor and owner appealed. The Appellate Court affirmed and owner appealed to the Massachusetts Supreme Court. At issue on appeal was whether contractor had failed to follow the contractual provisions for seeking compensation for extras.

The owner-contractor agreement provided in pertinent part that contractor "shall do any and all work required to effect a change in the plans . . . only when and as directed by (1) a written authorization . . . or (2) an approved formal change order executed by the Department." The contract defined a change as "any addition to, deduction from or modification of the plans, specifications or contract. . . ." The contract protected the owner from excessive extra costs by numerous other contract provisions, insuring that the owner was aware of the nature and extent of the additional claims and has an opportunity to monitor the extra work by requiring contractor to notify owner in writing of the nature and cost of the extra work on or before the first or second day following commencement of the work.

The Supreme Court of Massachusetts, based on the contractor's admission that it failed to submit the written statement of the nature and cost of the extra work and its admission that the claim was submitted subsequent to the completion date of the project, held that since it had failed to timely submit the written notice the contractor was not entitled to reimbursement for the cost of its extra work. The Court also held that certain other contract provisions and statutory provisions incorporated into the contract did not apply to contractor's claim for extra compensation.

84025 Mon-Rite Constr. Co. v. Northeast Ohio Regional Sewer Dist., 20 Ohio App. 3d 255, 485 N.E.2d 799 (1984)

III: A107-1978, Art. 14, Para. 14.1
III: A107-1978, Art. 14, Para. 14.2
III: A107-1978, Art. 14, Para. 14.3
III: A107-1978, Art. 15, Para. 15.5
III: A107-1978, Art. 18, Para. 18.1
III: A107-1978, Art. 18, Para. 18.2
III: A107-1978, Art. 18, Para. 18.3
III: A117-1979, Art. 18, Para. 18.1
III: A117-1979, Art. 18, Para. 18.2
III: A117-1979, Art. 18, Para. 18.3
III: A117-1979, Art. 19, Para. 19.5

I:	A117-1979, Art. 2, Para. 2.1
II:	A117-1979, Art. 4, Para. 4.1
II:	A117-1979, Art. 4, Para. 4.2
II:	A117-1979, Art. 4, Para. 4.3
II:	A117-1979, Art. 5, Para. 5.1
II:	A117-1979, Art. 5, Para. 5.2
II:	A117-1979, Art. 5, Para. 5.3
II:	A117-1979, Art. 6
II:	A117-1979, Art. 7

Contractor brought a mechanic's lien action for balance due under a cost-plus contract. The trial court imposed the lien and owner appealed. The issues on appeal were whether contractor had a duty to know of and advise owner that the actual construction costs had substantially exceeded the estimated cost and whether contractor had breached this duty.

At contractor's urging owner entered into a cost-plus contract which provided in pertinent part that contractor "accepts the relationship of trust and confidence established between him and the [Joneses] by this Agreement." Furthermore, the contractor promised to "use his best skill and judgment in furthering [their] interests . . . and he agrees . . . to perform the Work in the best way and in the most expeditious and economical manner consistent with the interest of the [Joneses]." The contract contained a set cost of construction and an additional percentage fee for the contractor. The contract required contractor to keep full and detailed accounts.

The Appellate Court interpreted the contract as providing that contractor accepted a relationship of trust, agreed to perform the work in an economical manner and agreed to keep detailed accounts. The Court found that under the contract owner was entitled to rely on contractor to protect its financial interests. The Court held that contractor had a duty to advise owner that the actual contract costs were substantially exceeding the estimates, that contractor had breached this duty, and that contractor's breach barred the mechanics lien for any sum larger than the contract sum plus the agreed upon fee percentage.

84024 Lawrence-Lynch Corp. v. Department of Environmental Management, 392 Mass. 681, 467 N.E.2d 838 (1984)

III:	A107-1978, Art. 18, Para. 18.1
III:	A107-1978, Art. 18, Para. 18.2
III:	A107-1978, Art. 18, Para. 18.3
III:	A117-1979, Art. 22, Para. 22.1
III:	A117-1979, Art. 22, Para. 22.2
III:	A117-1979, Art. 22, Para. 22.3
III:	A201-1976, Art. 12, Para. 12.1.1

the contract did not require payment to contractor by owner as a condition precedent to subcontractor's payment by contractor.

84022 John E. Green Plumbing & Heating Co. v. Turner Constr. Co., 742 F.2d 965 (6th Cir. 1984), *cert. denied,* 471 U.S. 1102, 105 S. Ct. 2328, 85 L. Ed. 2d 845 (1985)

III:	A107-1978, Art. 14, Para. 14.3
III:	A117-1979, Art. 18, Para. 18.3
III:	A201-1976, Art. 8, Para. 8.3.1
III:	A201-1976, Art. 8, Para. 8.3.4

Contractor brought an action against construction manager for intentional interference with contractor's work and contractual relationship with owner. The trial court granted in part, and denied in part, construction manager's motion for summary judgment. contractor appealed. At issue on appeal were the effect to be given to the no-damage-for-delay clause in the owner-contractor agreement and the adequacy of contractor's proof of damages.

Construction manager's duties included reviewing work schedules for the project to eliminate potential conflicts between the various contractors, and conducting job-site meetings to resolve those conflicts which did arise. The clause which prevented contractor for collecting damages for delay caused by anyone connected with the project, including the construction manager.

The Appellate Court found that the no-damage-for-delay clause forbade damages "should the Contractor be delayed in the commencement, prosecution, or completion" of the project. this phrase, strictly construed, only barred delay damages and not other kinds of damages, such as damages for hindering work on the project. The Court concluded that the work could not be performed because essential supplies had not been delivered or necessary preliminary work had not been performed. The Court held that it was error for the trial judge to grant summary against contractor on this issue. However, the Court did not reverse the decision because the subcontractor failed to adequately prove damages.

84023 Jones v. J.H. Hiser Constr. Co., 50 Md. App. 671, 484 A.2d 302 (1984), *cert. denied,* 303 Md. 114, 492 A.2d 616 (1985)

I:	A111-1978, Art. 3, Para. 3.1
II:	A111-1978, Art. 5, Para. 5.1
II:	A111-1978, Art. 5, Para. 5.2
II:	A111-1978, Art. 6, Para. 6.1
II:	A111-1978, Art. 6, Para. 6.2
II:	A111-1978, Art. 6, Para. 6.3
II:	A111-1978, Art. 8
II:	A111-1978, Art. 9

II: A401-1972, Art. 11, Para. 11.20

Subcontractor brought an action against contractor for final payment due under the subcontract and for retainage. The contractor counterclaimed for delay damages. The trial court entered judgment for contractor and the subcontractor appealed. The issues on appeal were whether the subcontract limited contractor's recovery to the liquidated damages in the owner-contractor agreement and whether subcontractor was obligated to indemnify contractor for amounts contractor paid to various other subcontractors injured by subcontractor's breach of contract.

The subcontract contained a flow-down provision which incorporated into the subcontract the provisions of the owner-contractor agreement relevant to subcontractor's performance. It also contained an indemnity clause stating that "Contractor and Subcontractor agree to indemnity and save harmless each other from and against any and all suits, claims . . . of whatever kind or nature . . . arising out of, in connection with, or incident to, each party's performance of his particular portion of this contract. . . ."

The Appellate Court found that the flow-down provision conferred on subcontractor all of the "privileges and protections" that the owner-contractor agreement conferred on contractor and held that the liquidation of delay damages in the owner-contractor agreement was incorporated into the subcontract. The Court found that the indemnification provision was not inconsistent with this provision. Based on these findings, the Court found it unnecessary to consider the indemnification issues raised on appeal, and remanded for a determination of the correct amount of damages in accordance with its opinion.

84021 Jeremiah Sullivan & Sons v. Kay-Locke, Inc., 17 Mass. App. Ct. 997, 459 N.E.2d 837 (1984)

III: A201-1976, Art. 9, Para. 9.5.2
III: A201-1976, Art. 9, Para. 9.5.4
III: A201-1976, Art. 9, Para. 9.7.1
III: A201-1978, Art. 12, Para. 12.4.1
III: A201-1978, Art. 12, Para. 12.4.3

Subcontractor brought an action against contractor for payment for work preformed in the excavation of a building site. The contractor appealed. At issue on appeal was whether payment to the contractor by the owner was a condition precedent to payment by the contractor to the subcontractor.

The subcontract provided that contractor would pay subcontractor under the subcontract for work performed "for which payment has been made to the Contractor by the Owner . . . and the Contractor has received payment therefor from the Owner."

The Appellate Court affirmed. It found that the language of the contract only set time for payment sufficient to give the contractor an opportunity to obtain funds from the owner and did not clearly establish a condition precedent. The Court therefore held that

II:	A107-1978, Art. 18, Para. 18.1
II:	A107-1978, Art. 20, Para. 20.1
II:	A117-1979, Art. 12, Para. 12.5
II:	A117-1979, Art. 17, Para. 17.2
II:	A117-1979, Art. 22, Para. 22.1
II:	A117-1979, Art. 24, Para. 24.1
I:	A201-1976, Art. 2, Para. 2.2.2
I:	A201-1976, Art. 2, Para. 2.2.9
I:	A201-1976, Art. 2, Para. 2.2.10
I:	A201-1976, Art. 2, Para. 2.2.12
I:	A201-1976, Art. 7, Para. 7.9.1
I:	A201-1976, Art. 12, Para. 12.1.1
I:	A201-1976, Art. 12, Para. 12.1.4
I:	A201-1976, Art. 14, Para. 14.2.1

Contractor filed a demand for arbitration against owner. The trial court denied owner's application for a stay of arbitration. The issue on appeal was whether a contractor, whose services had been terminated by owner for substantial breach of contract, had to submit his claim for "change order adjustments" to the architect as a condition precedent to arbitration under Paragraph 7.9.1 of the American Institute of Architects General Conditions of the Contract for Construction, Document A201, 1976 edition. The intermediate appellate court affirmed that submission to the architect was not required.

The New York Court of Appeals affirmed. It found that under Article 2 of the General Conditions the architect's role as mediator, to whom all disputes "relating to the execution or progress of the Work or the interpretation of the Contract Documents shall be referred initially to the Architect," was but one aspect of the architect's responsibility to supervise the contract. This role terminates once the architect is no longer responsible for supervising the contractor's performance. The obligation imposed on the architect by Paragraph 14.2.1 is the responsibility of certifying the amount, if any, to be paid to the discharged contractor, and it does not require the architect to resolve disputes or assume the role of mediator for discharged contractors in order to expedite the completion of the contract. Under the terms of Paragraph 14.2.1 such a calculation would not be made until the project was completed. Therefore, this calculation was not intended to serve as a condition precedent to arbitration. The Court held that contractor was not required to submit his claim to architect as a condition precedent to arbitration.

84020   Industrial Indem. Co. v. Wick Constr. Co., 680 P.2d 1100 (Alaska 1984)

II:	A107-1978, Art. 15, Para. 15.2
II:	A117-1979, Art. 11, Para. 11.2
II:	A201-1976, Art. 5, Para. 5.3.1
II:	A401-1972, Art. 11, Para. 11.1

is ordered in writing by the Architect with the consent and signature of the Owner. No bills based upon verbal orders will be considered by the Architect nor the Owner. It is understood and agreed that in case of changes, additions, or modifications to these plans and specifications for which the Contractor intends to make extra charge, it is agreed between the parties that unless the Owner agrees to such changes, additions or modifications in writing, signed by him, including the additional charges for deductions thereof, that the agreed price for each of the changes, additions or modifications shall be the net sum of One Dollar, and the Contractor agrees to accept such said sum in full payment thereof. When changes to the plans and specifications are ordered after the contract is let, the cost of said changes shall be presented to the Owner for consideration in itemized form with complete cost breakdown. After costs are approved, the formal Change Order shall be submitted by the Contractor to the Architect using American Institute of Architects Change Order Form G701."

The Appellate Court considered the following clause contained in Article 7 of the specifications: "Drawings for Husar Industries, Southwest corner 16th & Troost Avenue, Kansas City, Missouri, Sheet Nos. 1 through 4 inclusive, S1, S2 and PE, all dated February 1, 1978. The foregoing provision refers to the following contained within the drawings for Husar, which reads,"7. Existing foundations, structures, rock excavation and buried debris not apparent to view and requiring special handling or removal are not included in this contract . . . .'." It concluded that the clause clearly stated that the extra work performed by the contractor was not included in the contract and was not, therefore, subject to a change order. The Court found that the removal of debris and its replacement with proper soil was proper for a claim in quantum meruit under the facts and circumstances, where, as per the drawings and plans, such work was not within the written contract and not subject to the change order provision; contrary to owner's contention, the written contract was introduced by contractor in supports of its claim on account for the unpaid balance under the contract and not in support of its claim in quantum meruit.

The owner argued further that the contractor was not entitled to the balance of the contract sum because the contractor failed to make a submissible case and because owner's evidence demonstrated that the contractor failed to complete substantial items under the contract in a workmanlike manner. The Appellate Court found that based on the contractor's expert witness testimony there was no architect because the architect had been discharged by the owner; there were no deficiencies brought to contractor's attention; and most of the items were "punchlist items." Contractor's evidence revealed that no punchlist was even compiled due to the absence of an architect; thus there was sufficient evidence to submit the contractor's claim to the jury. The Court accordingly upheld the trial court's denial of contractor's motion to amend.

84019 *In re* Arbitration Between Liebhafsky & Comstruct Assocs., Inc., 62 N.Y.2d 439, 478 N.Y.S.2d 252, 466 N.E.2d 844 (1984)

II: A107-1978, Art. 8, Para. 8.5

II: A107-1978, Art. 13, Para. 13.2

The Appellate Court found that the scope of Paragraph 4.18.1 was limited by Paragraph 4.18.3, which provided that the obligation of the "Contractor under this Paragraph 4.18 shall not extend to the liability of the Architect . . . arising out of . . . the preparation or approval of maps, drawings. . . ." The Court held that architect's claim was barred by Paragraph 4.18.3 and by state statute denying indemnity for architect's own negligence.

84018   Husar Indus., Inc. v. A.L. Huber & Sons, Inc., 674 S.W.2d 565 (Mo. Ct. App. 1984)

II:	A107-1978, Art. 18, Para. 18.1
II:	A107-1978, Art. 18, Para. 18.2
II:	A107-1978, Art. 18, Para. 18.3
II:	A117-1979, Art. 22, Para. 22.1
II:	A117-1979, Art. 22, Para. 22.2
II:	A117-1979, Art. 22, Para. 22.3
I:	A101-1977, Art. 5
I:	A101-1977, Art. 6
I:	A201-1976, Art. 12, Para. 12.1.1
I:	A201-1976, Art. 12, Para. 12.1.2

Architect brought a mechanic's lien action against owner and others. Contractor became a party defendant and cross-complained against all other parties for a mechanic's lien. Contractor also sought recovery from owner, in account and quantum meruit, for the amount due under the contract and extras, after contractor left the job it claimed was substantially completed. Owner counterclaimed against architect for design defects, and against contractor for failing to construct the building in a workmanlike manner pursuant to the plans and specifications. Before trial the architect and owner settled their claims. Contractor's mechanic's lien claim against all parties was tried separately; the claims remaining before the trial court were contract claims and the quantum meruit action of contractor against owner. The trial court realigned the parties, making the owner the plaintiff and the contractor the defendant; it awarded judgment to the contractor on its claim of account and quantum meruit. Contractor filed an appeal which was dismissed. The owner then filed an appeal and the contractor filed a motion to reinstate its appeal; contractor also filed a cross-appeal. All appeals were consolidated.

The owner and contractor had entered into the American Institute of Architects Standard Form of Agreement Between Owner and Contractor, Document No. A101, 1977 edition, which included the American Institute of Architects General Conditions of the Contract for Construction, Document No. A201, 1976 edition.

The owner appealed the trial court's denial of its motion for directed verdict, arguing that the contractor should not have recovered in quantum meruit because the contractor did not obtain the written consent of the owner to do extra work pursuant to Paragraphs 12.1.1 and 12.1.2 of the General Conditions. In addition, the General Conditions within the specifications provided: "Extras: Bills for extras will be allowed only when work

Subcontractor brought an action against contractor to recover payments due under a contract to perform concrete work. The trial court entered judgment for subcontractor and contractor appealed.

The subcontract provided that subcontractor would furnish all material, equipment and labor necessary for the complete cast-in-place concrete portion of the work, to be performed in strict accordance with the plans and specifications prepared by architect. The owner-contractor agreement included the American Institute of Architects General Conditions of the Contract for Construction, Document A201, 1976 edition which was modified to provide for arbitration of "all disputes . . . subject to arbitration under this contract." The subcontract also provided for a lengthy payment procedure and stated that "Contractor shall be under no obligation to pay subcontractor for any work done hereunder until Contractor has been paid therefor by Owner."

As a result of slow payment, subcontractor experienced worker shortages and employed other subcontractors without contractor's permission. Subcontractor then discontinued his work, walked off the job, and filed suit against contractor for amounts due under the contract. Prior to answering, contractor filed a demand for arbitration in accordance with the terms of the contract. The trial court denied contractor's motion and entered judgment in favor of the subcontractor on the finding that contractor failed to make timely payment in accordance with prevailing industry practice, which the court found called for payment every 30 days.

The Appellate Court found that in light of the language of the arbitration clause requiring arbitration of disputes "subject to arbitration under this contract," the trial court did not err in holding that the claim did not fall into the narrow class of disputes subject to arbitration. The Court further held that the trial court erred in finding that the contractor breached the agreement by failing to make timely periodic payments to subcontractor, since the contract specifically provided for method and time of payment.

84017   Henningson, Durham & Richardson, Inc. v. Swift Bros. Constr. Co., 739 F.2d 1341 (8th Cir. 1984)

        I: A107-1978, Art. 10, Para. 10.11
        I: A117-1979, Art. 14, Para. 14.11
        I: A201-1976, Art. 14, Para. 4.18.1
        I: A201-1976, Art. 14, Para. 4.18.3

Architect, which had been held liable to workmen for injuries received in a construction project accident (reported in this volume as case number 83023), filed an action against contractor and subcontractor seeking indemnity or contribution. The trial court granted summary judgment for contractor and subcontractor, holding that South Dakota statute precluded contractual indemnity, prior adjudication of architect's negligence precluded common law indemnity, and state workers' compensation law barred contribution. Architect appealed.

Architect argued on appeal that contractor was obligated to indemnify architect pursuant to the American Institute of Architects General Conditions of the Contract for Construction, Document A201, 1976 edition, Article 4, Paragraph 4.18.1.

Subcontractor's injured employee brought an action against contractor and owner for injuries sustained when he fell from roof of staging area on the site. The injured employee alleged that contractor's duty to maintain safety on the jobsite extended to installation of guard rails on the roof. The trial court entered summary judgment for owner and contractor. Injured employee appealed the summary judgment in favor of contractor. At issue on appeal was whether contractor owed a duty to subcontractor's employee to maintain safety on the site by installing guard rails on the roof.

Injured employee argued on appeal that the owner-contractor agreement imposed a nondelegable duty on contractor to provide fall protection for subcontractor's employee. The agreement provided that "Contractor shall take all necessary precautions for the safety of all employees on the Project. . . ." It further provided that "Contractor shall neither delegate his duty of performance nor assign, in whole or in part, his rights or obligations under the Contract without the prior written consent of the Owner. . . ." An Addendum to the agreement entitled "Temporary Facilities and Controls" required contractor to supply guard rails wherever needed to prevent accidents and losses.

The Appellate Court reversed. It held that the safety provisions of the owner-contractor agreement imposed a contractual duty on contractor to make the work site safe for all employees. The Court further held that where material issues of fact existed as to whether the contractor breached its duty and was the proximate cause of the injury, the trial court erred in entering summary judgment for the contractor.

84016 Havens v. Safeway Stores, 235 Kan. 226, 678 P.2d 625 (1984)

II:	A107-1978, Art. 11, Para. 11.2
II:	A107-1978, Art. 13, Para. 13.2
III:	A107-1978, Art. 15, Para. 15.2
III:	A107-1978, Art. 15, Para. 15.3
III:	A107-1978, Art. 15, Para. 15.4
III:	A107-1978, Art. 15, Para. 15.5
II:	A117-1979, Art. 15, Para. 15.2
II:	A117-1979, Art. 17, Para. 17.2
III:	A117-1979, Art. 19, Para. 19.2
III:	A117-1979, Art. 19, Para. 19.3
III:	A117-1979, Art. 19, Para. 19.4
III:	A117-1979, Art. 19, Para. 19.5
II:	A401-1978, Art. 11, Para. 11.1.1
II:	A401-1978, Art. 11, Para. 11.2.5
II:	A401-1978, Art. 11, Para. 11.2.6
II:	A401-1978, Art. 12, Para. 12.4.1
II:	A401-1978, Art. 12, Para. 12.4.3
II:	A401-1978, Art. 13, Para. 13.1

II: A401-1978, Art. 11, Para. 11.1.1

Owner's injured employee filed an action against trustee in bankruptcy of owner. Injured worker and owner entered into a settlement agreement. Owner's trustee filed suit against subcontractor alleging that owner was entitled to express contractual indemnification for the amount of the settlement judgment and related expenses. The District Court entered summary judgment for owner and subcontractor appealed.

The owner-contractor agreement contained an indemnity provision similar to The American Institute of Architects General Conditions of the Contract for Construction, Document A201, 1976 edition, Article 4, Paragraph 4.18.1 which provided that contractor agreed to indemnify owner against "any and all liability . . . for injuries to . . . persons resulting in whole or in part, directly or indirectly, from or in connection with the performance of this Contract. . . ." The provision also specifically indemnified owner for injuries resulting from or in connection with the "presence of contractor . . . subcontractors and employees upon the premises of the railroad in connection with the performance of this Contract." The subcontract provided that "Subcontractor agrees to be bound by all terms and conditions of all provisions of the General Conditions of the Contract (AIA A201 latest edition unless otherwise specified)."

The Appellate Court upheld the finding of the District Court that the subcontract incorporated the terms of the owner-contractor agreement, including the indemnity provision, and held that subcontractor was contractually required to indemnify owner for the owner's employee's injuries where the worker was performing "work" pursuant to the contract "in connection with the presence" of the subcontractor on the premises. The injuries were, therefore, covered under both contract provisions.

84015   Harris v. Kettelhut Constr., Inc., 468 N.E.2d 1069 (Ind. Ct. App. 1984)

II: A107-1978, Art. 10, Para. 10.1
II: A107-1978, Art. 10, Para. 10.3
II: A107-1978, Art. 10, Para. 10.7
II: A107-1978, Art. 16, Para. 16.1
II: A117-1979, Art. 14, Para. 14.1
II: A117-1979, Art. 14, Para. 14.3
II: A117-1979, Art. 14, Para. 14.7
II: A117-1979, Art. 20, Para. 20.1
II: A201-1976, Art. 4, Para. 4.3.1
II: A201-1976, Art. 4, Para. 4.3.2
II: A201-1976, Art. 4, Para. 4.3.3
II: A201-1976, Art. 7, Para. 7.2.1
II: A201-1976, Art. 10, Para. 10.1.1
II: A201-1976, Art. 10, Para. 10.2.1
II: A201-1976, Art. 10, Para. 10.2.3

The subcontractor argued that since the contractor had consented to litigate a prior claim against subcontractor, contractor had waived the right to arbitrate any claim against subcontractor. The subcontract contained a broad form arbitration provision.

The Appellate Court held that contractor had not waived the right to arbitration; the Court was unwilling to infer a waiver from any action of contractor in an independent suit. The Court further held that the right to arbitrate was not waived since additional parties had been brought into the litigation by subcontractor, and since the state arbitration law allowed piecemeal resolution of claims when necessary to give effect to the arbitration agreement. Therefore, the Court granted contractor's application for a stay pending arbitration and granted contractor's motion to compel arbitration.

84013   Gerdmann v. United States Fire Ins. Co., 119 Wis. 2d 367, 350 N.W.2d 730 (1984)

	III:	A107-1978, Art. 10, Para. 10.11
	III:	A117-1979, Art. 14, Para. 14.11
	III:	A201-1976, Art. 4, Para. 4.18.1

Contractor sought contribution from owner for personal injury damages, and owner counterclaimed for costs and attorneys fees it incurred in defending against contractor's action. The trial court entered judgment for owner and contractor appealed.

The owner-contractor agreement contained an indemnity provision which stated in pertinent part that "Contractor shall reimburse Owner for all costs, expenses, and losses incurred by them in consequence of any claims. . . ." Contractor argued that the word "them" referred to both owner and contractor and that the clause only covered actions brought against both owner and contractor.

The Appellate Court found that if "them" referred to both owner and contractor the clause would require contractor to reimburse owner for costs incurred by contractor. The clause further provided for reimbursement of costs and fees owner incurred "in consequence of any claims, demands and causes of action . . . which may be brought against them and arising out of operations covered by the contract." The Court found that the clause did not distinguish between claims brought by third parties and actions for contribution. The Court therefore held that the indemnity clause applied to contractor's action for contribution against owner, and affirmed the judgment of the trial court.

84014   Gibbons v. Graves Constr. Co., 727 F.2d 753 (8th Cir. 1984)

	II:	A107-1978, Art. 10, Para. 10.11
	II:	A107-1978, Art. 11, Para. 11.2
	II:	A117-1979, Art. 14, Para. 14.11
	II:	A117-1979, Art. 15, Para. 15.2
	I:	A201-1976, Art. 4, Para. 4.18.1
	I:	A201-1976, Art. 5, Para. 5.3.1

84011 First Condominium Dev. Co. v. Apex Constr. & Eng'g Corp., 126 Ill. App. 3d 843, 81 Ill. Dec. 810, 467 N.E.2d 932 (1984)

    I: A107-1978, Art. 13, Para. 13.2
    I: A117-1979, Art. 17, Para. 17.2
    I: A201-1976, Art. 7, Para. 7.9.1
    I: A201-1976, Art. 7, Para. 7.9.2

Owner brought an action against contractor, architect, engineer and subcontractors for damages resulting from allegedly willful and wanton misconduct and breach of contract. Contractor filed a demand for arbitration against owner for the balance due under the contract and extras, and a motion to stay proceedings pending arbitration. Owner filed a motion to stay arbitration, denying the existence of a binding arbitration agreement between the parties. The trial court found that the owner-contractor agreement included a valid arbitration clause and stated that the issue was whether the agreement should be enforced despite the pending multiparty litigation and third party claims. The trial court granted owner's motion to stay arbitration and contractor appealed. The issue on appeal was whether the trial court erred in enjoining arbitration once it had determined that an enforceable arbitration agreement existed between the parties.

The owner-contractor agreement incorporated the American Institute of Architects General Conditions of the Contract for Construction, Document A201, 1976 edition, which included a broad form arbitration clause at Paragraph 7.9.1.

The Appellate Court found that owner initiated the litigation creating the multiplicity problem, that the claims were not intertwined since rights would be determined under separate contracts, and that Paragraph 7.9.1 was a valid arbitration clause which included within its scope the issue of the balance due contractor under the contract. The Court therefore held that the trial court had erred in granting owner's motion to stay arbitration.

84012 Forest City Dillon, Inc. v. Superior Court in and for the County of Pima, 138 Ariz. 410, 675 P.2d 297 (1984)

    III: A107-1978, Art. 13, Para. 13.2
    III: A117-1979, Art. 17, Para. 17.2
    III: A201-1976, Art. 7, Para. 7.9.1
    III: A401-1978, Art. 13, Para. 13.1
    III: A401-1978, Art. 13, Para. 13.2
    III: A401-1978, Art. 13, Para. 13.3
    III: A401-1978, Art. 13, Para. 13.4
    III: A401-1978, Art. 13, Para. 13.5
    III: A401-1978, Art. 13, Para. 13.6

Contractor brought an action to stay litigation initiated by subcontractor and for an order compelling arbitration. The trial court denied contractor's motion and contractor appealed, arguing that the trial court abused its discretion in staying the arbitration.

indemnity provision contained in the subcontract. The jury returned a verdict for injured worker. Contractor and subcontractor moved for judgment notwithstanding the verdict. The District Court held that contractor was the injured worker's statutory employer and was entitled to tort immunity. The Court stated, however, that a resolution of the third party claim was necessary because the indemnity clause in the subcontract included attorneys' fees.

The indemnity clause in the subcontract was identical to the clause contained in the American Institute of Architects Standard Form of Agreement Between Contractor and Subcontractor, Document A401, 1978 edition. The clause provided that "subcontractor agrees to defend, indemnify and hold harmless Contractor . . . from and against any claim, cost, expense or liability (including attorneys' fees) attributable to bodily injury. . . ."

The Court upheld the jury's finding that contractor was not solely at fault for the injuries and held that subcontractor was therefore responsible for contractor's attorneys' fees pursuant to the indemnity provision of the subcontract.

84010   Exchange Mut. Ins. Co. v. Haskell Co., 742 F.2d 274 (6th Cir. 1984)

I:	A107-1978, Art. 13, Para. 13.2
I:	A117-1979, Art. 17, Para. 17.2
I:	A201-1976, Art. 7, Para. 7.9.1
II:	A401-1978, Art. 12, Para. 12.1.1

Contractor made a claim under subcontractor's performance bond and initiated arbitration proceedings against subcontractor's surety. Subcontractor's surety filed a motion to stay arbitration. The District Court ordered the action to proceed to arbitration and the surety appealed.

The owner-contractor agreement, which included the American Institute of Architects General Conditions of the Contract for Construction, Document A201, 1976 edition, contained a broad arbitration provision in Article 7, Paragraph 7.9.1. The subcontract contained a provision similar to the American Institute of Architects Standard From of Agreement Between Contractor and Subcontractor, Document A401, 1978 edition, Article 12, Paragraph 12.1.1 which incorporated by reference the owner-contractor agreement. The subcontractor's performance bond provided that the subcontractor had entered into an agreement with the contractor "which subcontract is hereby referred to and made a part hereof."

The Appellate Court found that although the surety was not a signatory to the owner-contractor agreement, the performance bond incorporated by reference the terms of the subcontract. The subcontract, in turn, incorporated by reference the terms of the owner-contractor agreement which imposed an obligation to submit all unresolved disputes to arbitration. The Court held that the performance bond surety was bound to arbitrate.

and Architect, Document B141, 1977 edition. The agreements contained broad arbitration provisions.

The Appellate Court, in a memorandum opinion, found that the owner-architect agreement required the architect to issue a certificate of final completion. A cause of action against the architect by the owner accrued upon issuance of the certificate. The Court found that where the architect did not issue a certificate, the owner's cause of action against the architect accrued upon completion of the contract, which was within the statute of limitations. Furthermore, the owner's cause of action against the contractor also accrued upon completion of construction, making owner's demand for arbitration of its claims timely.

84008 Cosentino v. A.F. Lusi Constr. Co., 485 A.2d 105 (R.I. 1984)

II: A107-1978, Art. 10, Para. 10.11
II: A117-1979, Art. 14, Para. 14.11
II: A201-1976, Art. 4, Para. 4.18.1
I: A401-1978, Art. 11, Para. 11.11.1

Contractor brought a third party action against subcontractor for indemnification following an action brought by subcontractors' employee's estate. The trial court entered summary judgment for subcontractor on the grounds that contractor had no right of contribution from subcontractor as an alleged joint tort-feaser, and that the claim for indemnification was barred by Rhode Island state statute.

The subcontract contained an indemnification provision identical to the American Institute of Architects Standard Form of Agreement Between Contractor and Subcontractor, Document Number A401, 1978 edition, Paragraph 11.11.1, by which subcontractor agreed to indemnify contractor against all claims or demands "arising out of or resulting from the performance of the subcontractor's Work under this subcontract . . . to the extent caused in whole or in part by any negligent act or omission of the Subcontractor or anyone directly or indirectly employed by him or anyone for whose act he may be liable, regardless of whether it is caused in part by a party indemnified hereunder." The state statute invalidated any agreement in which a party sought indemnification for its own negligence.

The Appellate Court held that the state statute barred the enforcement of that portion of the indemnification clause that attempted to indemnify contractor for its own negligence. However, the statute did not bar subcontractor from indemnifying contractor for claims resulting from subcontractor's negligence.

84009 Dozier v. J.A. Jones Constr. Co., 587 F. Supp. 289 (E.D. La. 1984)

I: A401-1978, Art. 11, Para. 11.11.1

Subcontractor's injured employee brought an action against contractor and its insurer, and contractor brought a third party action against subcontractor on the basis of the

as architect argued on appeal. The Court remanded for a determination of the proper amount of damages.

The Appellate Court also upheld the findings of the trial court that subcontractors were also liable in part for the failure of the roof and were liable to owner for its replacement. The contractor relied upon the owner's final payment under the contract as an acceptance of the job and a waiver of its rights. The Court found that contractor knew that the roof was defective and could not be remedied and failed to so inform owner. The Court found that under these circumstances owner's final payment did not constitute a waiver. In addition, under the terms of the contract the contractor guaranteed the performance of the roof after acceptance.

84007   Chase Architectural Assocs. v. Moyers Corners Fire Dept. Inc., 99 A.D.2d 646, 472 N.Y.S.2d 219 (1984), *later proceeding,* J.R. Gallagher Constr. Co. v. Moyers Corners Fire Dept., Inc., 99 A.D.2d 646, 472 N.Y.S.2d 309 (1984)

II:	A107-1978, Art. 8, Para. 8.4
II:	A107-1978, Art. 13, Para. 13.2
II:	A107-1978, Art. 15, Para. 15.3
II:	A107-1978, Art. 15, Para. 15.4
II:	A117-1979, Art. 12, Para. 12.4
II:	A117-1979, Art. 17, Para. 17.2
II:	A117-1979, Art. 19, Para. 19.3
II:	A117-1979, Art. 19, Para. 19.4
I:	A201-1976, Art. 2, Para. 2.2.16
I:	A201-1976, Art. 7, Para. 7.6.1
I:	A201-1976, Art. 7, Para. 7.6.2
I:	A201-1976, Art. 7, Para. 7.9.1
I:	A201-1976, Art. 7, Para. 7.9.2
I:	A201-1976, Art. 9, Para. 9.9.1
I:	B141-1977, Art. 1, Para. 1.5.8
I:	B141-1977, Art. 9, Para. 9.1
I:	B141-1977, Art. 9, Para. 9.2
I:	B141-1977, Art. 11, Para. 11.3

Architect and contractor appealed from orders denying their applications to stay arbitration which was demanded by owner. The issue on appeal was whether the arbitration should be stayed because owner's claims were barred by the statute of limitations.

The owner and contractor entered into an American Institute of Architects Standard Form Agreement Between Owner and Contractor and the owner and architect entered into the American Institute of Architects Standard Form of Agreement Between Owner

Compensation Act, the subcontractor was statutorily protected from a duty to indemnify contractor.

84006   Campbell County Bd. of Educ. v. Brownlee-Kesterson, Inc., 677 S.W.2d 457 (Tenn. Ct. App. 1984)

II:	A107-1974, Art. 10, Para. 10.4
II:	A107-1974, Art. 16, Para. 16.4
II:	A107-1974, Art. 22
II:	A201-1970, Art. 3, Para. 3.2.1
II:	A201-1970, Art. 4, Para. 4.5.1
II:	A201-1970, Art. 9, Para. 9.7.5
II:	A201-1970, Art. 12, Para. 12.1.6
II:	A201-1970, Art. 13, Para. 13.2.2
I:	B141-1974, Art. 1, Para. 1.1.4
I:	B141-1974, Art. 1, Para. 1.1.6
I:	B141-1974, Art. 1, Para. 1.1.10
I:	B141-1974, Art. 1, Para. 1.1.11
I:	B141-1974, Art. 1, Para. 1.1.12
I:	B141-1974, Art. 1, Para. 1.1.14
I:	B141-1974, Art. 1, Para. 1.1.15
I:	B141-1974, Art. 1, Para. 1.1.20
I:	B141-1974, Art. 1, Para. 1.1.21
I:	B141-1974, Art. 2, Para. 2.4

Owner brought an action against architect, contractor, and certain subcontractors, alleging breach of a contract to construct a school building. The trial court entered a joint and several judgment against architect, contractor and subcontractors, all of whom appealed.

Owner and architect had entered into the American Institute of Architects Standard Form of Agreement Between Owner and Architect, Document B141, 1974 edition.

The Appellate Court affirmed. It adopted the findings of the trial court that the plans and specifications prepared by architect for the roof contained major design errors and omissions that seriously and adversely affected the strength, durability and function of the roof; that architect failed to protect owner against defects and deficiencies in contractor's roofing work; and that architect wrongly recommended to owner that final payment be made for the roof. Furthermore, architect and contractor failed to notify owner of unstable subsurface conditions and architect failed to notify owner that contractor was contractually responsible for additional expenses incurred resulting from the subsurface conditions. Based on these findings the Court held that the architect's liability arose from a departure from acceptable architectural standards and not from the failings of others

The owner-contractor agreement contained a broad form arbitration clause similar to the American Institute of Architects General Conditions of the Contract for Construction, Document A201, Article 7, Paragraph 7.9.1. The clause provided that "all claims, disputes and other matters in question between the contractor and the owner arising out of, or relating to, the Contract Documents or [sic] the breach thereof, . . . shall be decided by Arbitration. . . ."

The Appellate Court found that since the contractor made a prima facie case for rescission, the contract was of no force and effect, and where there was no contract, there was no arbitration clause "of the contract." The Court held that the trial court did not err in staying the arbitration where the contractor sought rescission of the contract.

84005 Brown v. Prime Constr. Co., 102 Wash. 2d 235, 684 P.2d 73 (1984)

II:	A107-1978, Art. 10, Para. 10.11
II:	A117-1979, Art. 14, Para. 14.11
II:	A201-1976, Art. 4, Para. 4.18.1
II:	A201-1976, Art. 4, Para. 4.18.2
II:	A201-1976, Art. 5, Para. 5.3.1
II:	A401-1978, Art. 11, Para. 11.1.1
II:	A401-1978, Art. 11, Para. 11.11.1

Subcontractor's injured employee brought an action against contractor. Contractor filed a third party action for indemnity against subcontractor. The trial court granted subcontractor's motion for summary judgment and contractor appealed.

The subcontract contained a flow down provision and an indemnity clause that provided in relevant part that subcontractor agreed to "indemnify and save harmless the CONTRACTOR . . . from and against any and all suits, claims . . . arising out of, in connection with, or incident to, the work of this SUBCONTRACT, except that caused by the sole negligence of the CONTRACTOR." The owner-contractor agreement contained an indemnity clause similar to the subcontract's indemnity provision covering "any such claims, damage, loss or expense attributable to bodily injury . . . which is caused in whole or in part by any negligent or willful act or omission of the CONTRACTOR and SUBCONTRACTOR. . . ." The agreement also provided that the indemnification obligation would not be limited by benefits payable under workmen's compensation acts."

The Appellate Court held that when the subcontract's flow down provision was read in conjunction with the indemnification provision contained in the owner-contractor agreement the proper construction was that subcontractor must indemnify contractor if contractor had to indemnify owner for loss caused by reason of subcontractor's negligence or willful act. However, because the injured employee never sued owner the contract provision was never triggered and contractor was not entitled to indemnification under the provision. The Court held that because the subcontract's indemnity clause did not clearly and specifically contain a waiver of the immunity provided by the Workers'

The Appellate Court affirmed. It held that the jury was properly instructed that this provision placed a duty upon contractor to alert the architect to any design defects and the failure to alert the architect constituted breach of the contract and negligence.

84003 Board of County Comm'rs of Frederick County v. Cam Constr. Co., 300 Md. 643, 480 A.2d 795 (1984)

      II: A107-1978, Art. 13, Para. 13.2
      II: A117-1979, Art. 17, Para. 17.2
      I: A201-1976, Art. 7, Para. 7.9.1

Contractor demanded arbitration of claims against owner for retainage and for damages resulting from owner's failure to allow contractor access to the site. Contractor also sought recovery of losses suffered by subcontractors. Contractor brought an action against owner when owner failed to produce requested discovery. Owner counterclaimed for an injunction to restrain contractor from proceeding with the arbitration on the basis that there was no privity of contract between the owner and the subcontractors. The trial court denied owner injunctive relief and owner appealed. The Appellate Court granted owner's petition for certiorari.

The owner-contractor agreement included the American Institute of Architects General Conditions of the Contract for Construction, Document A201, 1976 edition, which contains a broad arbitration provision in Article 7, Paragraph 7.9.1. By special supplementary conditions to the contract the parties added a provision that "the General Contractor only shall be recognized as a part [*sic*] of this Contract and it shall be his responsibility to turn over to the Owner a project complete in all respects and in accordance with the Contract Documents."

The Appellate Court found that only the contractor had invoked arbitration and that all the claims made were asserted in contractor's name. Based on the language of Paragraph 7.9.1, which provided that if it was unclear as to whether a dispute fell within its scope it was for the arbitrators to decide whether the clause encompassed the claim, and based on state case law holdings that a contractor may bring claims on behalf of a subcontractor where the liability of contractor to subcontractor is fixed by a liquidating agreement, the Court held that contractor had standing to present in its own name arbitration claims for the benefit of subcontractors.

84004 Borck v. Holewinski, 459 So. 2d 405 (Fla. Dist. Ct. App. 1984)

      II: A107-1978, Art. 13, Para. 13.2
      II: A117-1979, Art. 17, Para. 17.2
      II: A201-1976, Art. 7, Para. 7.9.1

Contractor brought an action against owner for rescission of a contract. Owner moved to dismiss the complaint and to compel arbitration. The trial court entered an order staying arbitration and owner appealed.

84001 Babylon Assocs. v. County of Suffolk, 101 A.D.2d 207, 475 N.Y.S.2d 869 (1984)

      II: A107-1978, Art. 10, Para. 10.7
      II: A117-1979, Art. 14, Para. 14.7
      II: A201-1976, Art. 4, Para. 4.3.2

Contractor brought an action against owner seeking to recover for extras. Owner asserted affirmative defenses and counterclaimed for damages for breach of contract on the ground that contractor was liable for subcontractor's illegal activities. The trial court granted contractor's motion to dismiss owner's counterclaim. Owner appealed.

The relevant portions of the owner-contractor agreement which dealt with contractor's responsibility for its subcontractors provided that "Contractor shall be responsible to the owner for the acts and omissions of all of his employees and all subcontractors. . . ." The agreement further provided that "No subcontractor will be recognized as such, and all persons engaged in the work of construction will be considered as employees of the Contractor and he will be held responsible for their work. . . ."

The Appellate Court found that the terms of the contract provided that contractor would be fully and directly responsible to owner for the acts or omissions of its subcontractor. The Court held that there was a triable issue of fact as to whether the parties intended that contractor assume liability for the criminal acts of its subcontractor in the manufacturing, testing and repairing of reinforced concrete piping. It therefore reversed the dismissal of the owner's counterclaim, and affirmed the denial of the owner's motion for summary judgment.

84002 Bethesda Lutheran Church v. Twin City Constr. Co., 356 N.W.2d 344 (Minn. Ct. App. 1984)

      III: A107-1978, Art. 10, Para. 10.1
      III: A117-1979, Art. 14, Para. 14.1
      III: A201-1976, Art. 4, Para. 4.2.1

Owner brought an action against contractor for breach of contract and negligence for roof defects. Contractor brought a third party action against subcontractor for contribution. The trial court entered judgment on a jury verdict in favor of owner and in favor of contractor on the third party claim. Contractor and subcontractor appealed. Among numerous issues on appeal was whether contractor had a contractual duty to call architect's attention to any defects in the design.

The owner-contractor agreement contained a "Detail Drawings and Instructions" provision stating in relevant part that "if the drawings or specifications require work to be done in a manner which in the contractor's opinion makes it impossible to produce first-class work, he is expected to request an interpretation . . . if the contractor fails to make such a request, no excuse will thereafter be entertained for failure to execute work in a satisfactory manner."

require subcontractor to indemnify contractor for its own negligence. The Court held that the broad indemnity provision in the owner-contractor agreement did not flow down to the subcontractor to extend the obligation of the subcontractor to indemnify the contractor.

fire shall arise from the joint or concurring negligence of both parties hereto, it shall be borne by them equally."

On appeal contractor argued that the comparative negligence of subcontractor's employee should be imputed to subcontractor to hold it liable for one-half of the judgment due injured worker.

The Appellate Court held that worker's negligence could not be imputed to subcontractor, making the subcontractor liable to the contractor under the indemnity provision, where the subcontractor had not acted negligently and neither the subcontractor nor the injured worker breached a duty to a third party.

83050   Wyoming Johnson, Inc. v. Stagg Indus., Inc., 662 P.2d 96 (Wyo. 1983)

II:	A107-1978, Art. 10, Para. 10.11	
II:	A107-1978, Art. 11, Para. 11.2	
II:	A117-1979, Art. 14, Para. 14.11	
II:	A117-1979, Art. 15, Para. 15.2	
I:	A201-1976, Art. 4, Para. 4.18.1	
I:	A201-1976, Art. 5, Para. 5.3.1	
II:	A401-1978, Art. 9, Para. 9.1	
II:	A401-1978, Art. 9, Para. 9.2	
II:	A401-1978, Art. 11, Para. 11.1.1	
II:	A401-1978, Art. 11, Para. 11.11.1	
II:	A401-1978, Art. 11, Para. 11.11.2	

Contractor brought an indemnification action against subcontractor for amounts paid to subcontractor's injured employee. The trial court granted subcontractor's motion for summary judgment and contractor appealed. At issue on appeal was whether subcontractor was contractually required to indemnify contractor.

The subcontract contained an indemnity provision requiring subcontractor to indemnify contractor from "any and all claims, suits or liability for injuries to property, injuries to persons . . . on account of any act or omission of Subcontractor, or any of is officers, agents, employees or servants." The subcontract also included a flow-down provision and a provision requiring subcontractor to carry sufficient insurance to protect his workmen and to "fully indemnify the Contractor from any liability or suit arising from the acts or omissions of the Subcontractor. . . ." The subcontract incorporated by reference the owner-contractor agreement including the American Institute of Architects General Conditions of the Contract for Construction, Document A201, 1976 edition, which contained an indemnity provision in paragraph 4.18.1. The indemnity clause in the owner-contractor agreement provided for indemnity for "all claims, damages, losses and expenses" while the subcontract clause was limited to indemnity for "acts or omissions of the Subcontractor."

The Appellate Court construed the indemnity provisions strictly against the indemnitee, finding that the flow-down provision in the subcontract did not clearly and unequivocally

workmanlike manner. With regard to this issue, the trial court denied the archtect's motion for summary judgment.

83048   Welch v. State of California, 139 Cal. App. 3d 546, 188 Cal. Rptr. 726 (1983)

> III: A107-1978, Art. 7, Para. 7.1
> III: A107-1978, Art. 7, Para. 7.3
> III: A117-1979, Art. 11, Para. 11.1
> III: A117-1979, Art. 11, Para. 11.3
> III: A201-1976, Art. 1, Para. 1.1.1
> III: A201-1976, Art. 1, Para. 1.2.2
> III: A201-1976, Art. 3, Para. 3.2.4

Contractor brought an action against owner for additional compensation. The trial court entered judgment for owner, and contractor appealed. The Appellate Court reversed and remanded.

Contractor, as low bidder, was awarded the contract to repair a damaged portion of a bridge. The contract contained a provision requiring on-site inspection by the contractor as well as other general disclaimers of warranty as to site observation by owner. Contractor did not make an independent investigation of the site conditions. After contractor completed the work and it was accepted by the owner, contractor sought damages for the unanticipated costs of construction, for loss of profits and for loss of an advantageous competitive position in the industry because he was delayed by incorrect plans submitted to owner to bidders on the project. As a separate cause of action, contractor claimed that he was misled by the owner's failure to disclose information in its possession regarding a similar repair project.

The Appellate Court held that where the undisclosed information would have assisted contractor in formulating its bid, the owner was liable to contractor for its additional costs and lost profits. The evidence suggested that the contractor would not have entered into the contract had the disclosure been made.

83049   Wicklund v. Gus J. Bouten Constr. Co., 36 Wash. App. 71, 674 P.2d 184 (1983)

> III: A401-1978, Art. 11, Para. 11.1.1

Subcontractor's injured employee brought a negligence action against contractor, which filed a third party indemnification action against subcontractor. The jury found that contractor was negligent, injured worker was comparatively negligent, and subcontractor was not negligent. The trial court denied contractor's indemnification claim against the subcontractor and contractor appealed.

The subcontract contained an indemnification provision by which subcontractor agreed to indemnify and hold harmless the contractor for "loss . . . from acts or omissions of Subcontractor, its employees or agent . . . and if any claim or liability other than from

I:	A117-1979, Art. 12, Para. 12.3
I:	A117-1979, Art. 14, Para. 14.1
I:	A117-1979, Art. 20, Para. 20.1
I:	A201-1976, Art. 2, Para. 2.2.1
I:	A201-1976, Art. 2, Para. 2.2.2
I:	A201-1976, Art. 2, Para. 2.2.3
I:	A201-1976, Art. 2, Para. 2.2.4
I:	A201-1976, Art. 2, Para. 2.2.18
I:	A201-1976, Art. 4, Para. 4.3.1
I:	A201-1976, Art. 10, Para. 10.1.1
I:	A201-1976, Art. 10, Para. 10.2.1
I:	A201-1976, Art. 10, Para. 10.2.3
I:	A201-1976, Art. 10, Para. 10.2.6
I:	B141-1977, Art. 1, Para. 1.5.2
I:	B141-1977, Art. 1, Para. 1.5.3
I:	B141-1977, Art. 1, Para. 1.5.4
I:	B141-1977, Art. 1, Para. 1.5.5
I:	B141-1977, Art. 1, Para. 1.5.16

Estate of subcontractor's employee brought a wrongful death action against owner, contractor and architect. Architect moved for summary judgment. The estate argued that architect failed to supervise the work of contractor and subcontractors and failed to enforce proper safety precautions and detect safety violations. Architect argued that the owner-architect agreement did not impose on him a duty of care to workmen at the jobsite.

The owner and architect had entered into the American Institute of Architects Standard Form of Agreement Between Owner and Architect, Document B141, 1977 edition, which provided that the role of the architect was to ensure design conformity. The relevant provisions of the American Institute of Architects General Conditions of the Contract for Construction, Document A201, 1976 edition cited by the trial court included paragraphs 2.2.2, 2.2.3, 2.2.4, 4.3.1, 10.1.1, 10.2.1 and 10.2.3. The court interpreted these provisions as "stripping" the architect of all supervisory powers and duties. The contract manifested an unmistakeable intention to place exclusive control over the construction work and the responsibility for protecting workmen against injury with the contractor.

The trial court held that without the contractual right to supervise and control the construction work, as well as site safety, the architect could not be held liable for the worker's death. However, paragraph 2.2.3 of the owner-architect agreement provided, in part, that "on the basis of his on-site observations as an architect, he will keep the owner informed of the progress of the work and will endeavor to guard the owner against defects and deficiencies in the Work of the contractor." Based on this site observation clause, the Court held that there was a triable issue of fact as to whether architect, who visited the site on the day of the accident, had knowledge of an unprotected open stairwell and breached his duty to report to owner this work which was not being done in a

subcontractor entered into the standard form Associated General Contractors subcontract, which required subcontractor to obtain general liability insurance and comprehensive automobile liability insurance protecting subcontractor against claims for bodily injury or property damage. The subcontract specifically excluded any requirement that subcontractor obtain builders risk insurance. Furthermore, the subcontract contained an indemnity provision requiring subcontractor to indemnify contractor from all claims and to obtain general liability insurance coverage to cover the indemnity. Subcontractor obtained the general liability insurance coverage as primary insurance.

The Supreme Court of Minnesota found that the subcontractor was an insured of the contractor's insurer only to the extent its own policy did not provide coverage, because the contractor's insurance was "excess." The contractor's insurer had to cover this "excess," but could recover from the subcontractor's insurer the amount of its primary coverage.

83045 United States Steel Corp. v. Turner Constr. Co., 560 F. Supp. 871 (S.D.N.Y. 1983)

> III: A107-1978, Art. 11, Para. 11.2
> III: A117-1979, Art. 15, Para. 15.2
> III: A201-1976, Art. 5, Para. 5.3.1
> III: A401-1978, Art. 1, Para. 1.1
> III: A401-1978, Art. 11, Para. 11.1.1

Subcontractor brought an action against contractor for the balance due under the subcontract and for extras. Contractor moved to dismiss the complaint. At issue was whether the subcontractor was bound by the terms of the owner-contractor agreement, including the General Conditions which were incorporated by reference into the subcontract.

The District Court held that unless the subcontract contained an express reference to a specific clause in the owner-contractor agreement, the incorporation of that agreement did not extend beyond the scope, quality, character, and manner of the subcontracted work. Therefore, the forum selection clause in the owner-contractor agreement, which required claims to be litigated in state court, was not binding on the subcontractor.

83046 (UNASSIGNED)

83047 Welch v. Grant Dev. Co., 120 Misc. 2d 493, 466 N.Y.S.2d 112 (Sup. Ct. 1983)

> I: A107-1978, Art. 8, Para. 8.1
> I: A107-1978, Art. 8, Para. 8.3
> I: A107-1978, Art. 10, Para. 10.1
> I: A107-1978, Art. 16, Para. 16.1
> I: A117-1979, Art. 12, Para. 12.1

Owner brought an action against contractor, which moved to stay the action and compel arbitration pursuant to the arbitration clause in the owner-contractor agreement. The trial court granted contractor's motion to compel and owner appealed.

At issue on appeal was whether the contractor waived his right to compel arbitration by answering the complaint and participating in discovery. The owner and contractor had entered into the American Institute of Architects Standard Form of Agreement Between Owner and Contractor, Document A107, 1974 edition, which contained a broad form arbitration provision.

The Appellate Court held that contractor's involvement in the litigation to the extent of answering and participating in discovery constituted waiver of contractor's right to arbitration.

83044   United States Fire Ins. Co. v. Ammala, 334 N.W.2d 631 (Minn. 1983)

III:	A107-1978, Art. 17, Para. 17.1	
III:	A107-1978, Art. 17, Para. 17.2	
III:	A107-1978, Art. 17, Para. 17.3	
III:	A107-1978, Art. 17, Para. 17.6	
III:	A117-1979, Art. 21, Para. 21.1	
III:	A117-1979, Art. 21, Para. 21.2	
III:	A117-1979, Art. 21, Para. 21.3	
III:	A117-1979, Art. 21, Para. 21.6	
III:	A201-1976, Art. 11, Para. 11.1.1	
III:	A201-1976, Art. 11, Para. 11.3.1	
III:	A201-1976, Art. 11, Para. 11.3.6	
III:	A401-1978, Art. 9, Para. 9.1	
III:	A401-1978, Art. 9, Para. 9.2	
III:	A401-1978, Art. 11, Para. 11.11.1	

Contractor's insurer brought a subrogation action against subcontractor to recover the cost of repairing damage caused by subcontractor's negligence. The jury returned a verdict for insurer, but the trial court granted subcontractor's motion for judgment NOV on the ground that subcontractor was not liable to contractor's insurer because subcontractor was a named insured under the policy. At issue on appeal was whether contractor's builders risk insurer was precluded from maintaining an action against negligent subcontractor for damages insurer paid to contractor where subcontractor was a co-insured.

The owner-contractor agreement required contractor to obtain builders risk insurance and to obtain comprehensive liability coverage. The builders risk coverage was to be maintained for owner, architect and engineer, contractor, subcontractors, and suppliers as joint insureds. Contractor obtained the builders risk policy naming all joint insureds and including a clause stating that the policy was excess insurance. Contractor and

I:	A201-1970, Art. 7, Para. 7.10.1
I:	A201-1970, Art. 7, Para. 7.10.2
I:	A201-1970, Art. 8, Para. 8.3.1
I:	A201-1970, Art. 8, Para. 8.3.2
I:	A201-1970, Art. 12, Para. 12.1.1
I:	A201-1970, Art. 12, Para. 12.1.2
I:	A201-1970, Art. 12, Para. 12.1.3
I:	A201-1970, Art. 12, Para. 12.1.4
I:	A201-1970, Art. 12, Para. 12.2.1

Contractor filed a demand for arbitration against owner for delay damages, and owner responded by bringing a judicial action to stay the arbitration. The trial court stayed the arbitration, ruling that contractor had waived the right to arbitration by failing to timely and properly present claims to the architect. Contractor appealed. At issue on appeal was whether the trial court had the authority to determine the issue of contractor's waiver of the right to arbitration.

The owner-contractor agreement contained American Institute of Architects General Conditions of the Contract for Construction, Document A201, 1970 edition. The relevant provisions were article 2, which described the functions and authority of the architect; article 8, paragraphs 8.3.1 and 8.3.2, which dealt with delays and extensions of time; article 12, concerning changes in the work; and article 7, paragraph 7.10, providing for arbitration of disputes.

In reviewing these provisions the Appellate Court found that no specific penalty is provided for the failure to present a claim to the architect pursuant to paragraph 2.2.7. Failure to make a timely demand for arbitration under paragraph 2.2.11, after an adverse decision by the architect, or in accordance with paragraph 7.10.2, would serve to preclude arbitration of the issues and leave the contractor to pursue judicial remedies. But noncompliance with paragraphs 8.3 or 12.2 operates to invalidate the claim itself and not just the agreement to arbitrate. The trial court, by invoking paragraph 8.3, purported to adjudicate not just the right to arbitration but the validity of the underlying claims, which the Maryland state statute expressly prohibited. Furthermore, by applying paragraph 8.3 to the contractor's claim for increased compensation, as well as to contractor's assertions regarding the balance due under the contract, the trial court misconstrued the contract. The Appellate Court vacated the judgment of the trial court on the ground that the trial court erred in granting the owner's motion to stay the arbitration where the contractor did not first present its delay damage claims to the architect. The Appellate Court remanded for a determination of whether the contractual right to arbitration had been waived; if not the petition to stay arbitration should be denied.

83043   Sullivan v. Kisly, 93 A.D.2d 783, 461 N.Y.S.2d 808 (1983)

I:	A107-1974, Art. 14
II:	A201-1970, Art. 7, Para. 7.10.1

The owner-contractor agreement provided that as work was completed on various stages of the project, the architect would approve progress payments to the general contractor. Eventually, payments totalled 90 percent of the contract price; at this point the project was complete except for minor corrective work. When the contractor certified that all liens (if any) recorded against the project were released, the project would be accepted and the retainage paid to the contractor. If the architect or owner deemed it expedient to make corrections, they could deduct these costs from the contract price. The contract permitted the owner to withhold the entire retainage until the architect determined that "all work" had been completed.

The Appellate Court found that once the project was substantially complete the owner did not have the right to the full retainage; the contractor was then entitled to the full contract price less the cost of any corrective work. The Court was in complete agreement with the trial court's conclusion that the owner had failed to prove the existence of anything but minor deficiencies, and, therefore, acted unreasonably in withholding the entire retainage.

The contractor argued further that it was entitled to attorney's fees and costs from the subcontractors under the subcontracts, which provided that "should contractor employ an attorney to enforce any of the provisions thereof, or to protect its interest in any matter arising under this contract, or to collect damages for the breach of this contract, or to prosecute or defend any suit resulting from this contract, or to recover on the surety bond given by subcontractor under this contract, subcontractor and his surety, jointly and severally, agree to pay contractor all reasonable costs, changes, expenses and attorney's fees expended or incurred therein." The Court rejected this argument since the trial judge had determined that the subcontractors performed their jobs in good faith and in a workmanlike manner. The Court found that a subcontractor need not indemnify the contractor under this type of provision where the subcontractors successfully prosecuted to obtain full payment for work performed pursuant to the contract terms and specifications.

83042   Stauffer Constr. Co. v. Board of Educ. of Montogomery County, 54 Md. App. 658, 460 A.2d 609 (1983)

	II:	A107-1966, Art. 9, Para. 9.5
	II:	A107-1966, Art. 15
	II:	A107-1966, Art. 16, Para. 16.2
	II:	A107-1966, Art. 22, Para. 22.1
	II:	A107-1966, Art. 22, Para. 22.2
	II:	A107-1966, Art. 22, Para. 22.3
	I:	A201-1970, Art. 2, Para. 2.2.6
	I:	A201-1970, Art. 2, Para. 2.2.7
	I:	A201-1970, Art. 2, Para. 2.2.10
	I:	A201-1970, Art. 2, Para. 2.2.11

II:	A107-1978, Art. 17, Para. 17.3
II:	A117-1979, Art. 14, Para. 14.11
II:	A117-1979, Art. 21, Para. 21.1
II:	A117-1979, Art. 21, Para. 21.3
I:	A201-1976, Art. 4, Para. 4.18.1
II:	A201-1976, Art. 11, Para. 11.1.1
II:	A201-1976, Art. 11, Para. 11.1.3
II:	A201-1976, Art. 11, Para. 11.3.1
II:	A401-1978, Art. 11, Para. 11.11.1

Owner brought an action against contractor for property damage. The trial court entered judgment for contractor and owner appealed. The issues on appeal were whether the property damage was due to contractor's negligence, and whether the owner-contractor agreement, as a matter of law, required contractor to fully indemnify owner for all of the damages it sustained with or without a finding of contractor negligence.

The owner-contractor agreement obligated contractor to obtain its own insurance, and further provided that contractor would indemnify owner for property damage "arising out of anything done or omitted to be done under this agreement." The American Institute of Architects General Conditions of the Contract for Construction, Document A201, 1976 edition were incorporated by reference into the owner-contractor agreement. The General Conditions provided that contractor would indemnify owner only if contractor were negligent.

The Appellate Court affirmed. It held that the trial court's finding that contractor did not cause the property damage by any work contractor performed was not clearly erroneous. The Court found further that the contractor was not contractually required by the General Conditions to indemnify the owner because the contractor was not negligent.

83041 State v. Laconco, Inc., 430 So. 2d 1376 (La. Ct. App. 1983)

III:	A107-1978, Art. 5
III:	A107-1978, Art. 15
III:	A117-1979, Art. 9
III:	A117-1979, Art. 19
III:	A201-1976, Art. 9, Para. 9.6
III:	A201-1976, Art. 9, Para. 9.8.2
III:	A201-1976, Art. 9, Para. 9.9
III:	A401-1978, Art. 11, Para. 11.11.1

On appeal from judgment entered in favor of contractor and subcontractors against the owner, the owner argued that it was justified, under the terms of the owner-contractor agreement, in withholding the retainage for over six years. The Appellate Court affirmed the ruling of the trial court.

and held that the minimum insurance provision did not limit subcontractor's duty to indemnify.

83039 Rudy Brown Bldrs., Inc. v. St. Bernard Linen Serv., Inc., 428 So. 2d 534 (La. Ct. App. 1983)

III:	A101-1977, Art. 6
III:	A107-1978, Art. 5, Para. 5.1
III:	A107-1978, Art. 15, Para. 15.2
III:	A107-1978, Art. 15, Para. 15.3
III:	A107-1978, Art. 15, Para. 15.4
III:	A107-1978, Art. 15, Para. 15.5
III:	A117-1979, Art. 9, Para. 9.3
III:	A117-1979, Art. 19, Para. 19.2
III:	A117-1979, Art. 19, Para. 19.3
III:	A117-1979, Art. 19, Para. 19.4
III:	A117-1979, Art. 19, Para. 19.5
III:	A201-1976, Art. 9, Para. 9.5.5
III:	A201-1976, Art. 9, Para. 9.8.1
III:	A201-1976, Art. 9, Para. 9.8.2
III:	A201-1976, Art. 9, Para. 9.9.1
III:	A201-1976, Art. 9, Para. 9.9.2
III:	A201-1976, Art. 9, Para. 9.9.3
III:	A201-1976, Art. 9, Para. 9.9.4

Contractor brought an action against owner for the final installment payment under the contract, extras and attorney fees. Owner counterclaimed for costs to correct defective work. Following a trial on the merits the trial court awarded contractor its extras but denied contractor recovery of the final installment payment. The court awarded owner costs to correct the defective work. Contractor argued on appeal that it was entitled to the full contract price because it had substantially completed the construction.

The Appellate Court found that the contractor's evidence supported a finding of substantial completion because the building served its intended purpose. However, the Court upheld the trial court's judgment for owner because owner was able to show that the building was defective.

83040 Sears, Roebuck & Co. v. Shamrock Constr. Co., 441 So. 2d 379 (La. Ct. App. 1983)

II:	A107-1978, Art. 10, Para. 10.11
II:	A107-1978, Art. 17, Para. 17.1

83038 Poole v. Ocean Drilling & Exploration Co., 439 So. 2d 510 (La. Ct. App. 1983), *cert. denied,* 443 So. 2d 590 (La. 1983)

II:	A107-1978, Art. 10, Para. 10.11
II:	A107-1978, Art. 17, Para. 17.1
II:	A107-1978, Art. 17, Para. 17.3
II:	A107-1978, Art. 17, Para. 17.4
II:	A107-1978, Art. 17, Para. 17.6
II:	A117-1979, Art. 14, Para. 14.11
II:	A117-1979, Art. 21, Para. 21.1
II:	A117-1979, Art. 21, Para. 21.3
II:	A117-1979, Art. 21, Para. 21.4
II:	A117-1979, Art. 21, Para. 21.6
II:	A201-1976, Art. 4, Para. 4.18.1
II:	A201-1976, Art. 4, Para. 4.18.2
II:	A201-1976, Art. 4, Para. 4.18.3
II:	A201-1976, Art. 11, Para. 11.1.1
II:	A201-1976, Art. 11, Para. 11.1.3
II:	A201-1976, Art. 11, Para. 11.3.1
II:	A201-1976, Art. 11, Para. 11.3.3
II:	A201-1976, Art. 11, Pra. 11.3.6
II:	A401-1978, Art. 9, Para. 9.1
II:	A401-1978, Art. 11, Para. 11.11.1

Injured employee of subcontractor brought an action against contractor and its insurer for injuries received in a drilling accident. Contractor made a third party claim against subcontractor for contractual indemnification and defense. The trial court held that subcontractor was liable to contractor for complete indemnity and defense, and subcontractor appealed. At issue on appeal was whether the contractor's claim was covered by the broad language of the indemnification provision and whether the contract provision requiring subcontractor to obtain minimum amounts of insurance limited subcontractor's liability to those limits.

The relevant subcontract provisions stated that subcontractor agreed to indemnify contractor against all claims for damages to persons in connection with the work to be performed. The subcontract further provided that subcontractor was to maintain minimum amounts of comprehensive general liability insurance.

The Appellate Court, construing the contract as a whole, interpreted the indemnity phrase, "in connection with,"as "being related to or associated with, but not the primary or only purpose of," and held that employee's injury, which occurred during the performance of a contractual duty, was "related to or associated with" that duty. Therefore, the injury was covered by the language of the indemnity provision. Furthermore, the Court found no indication of an intention that subcontractor's liability be limited

subcontractor had caused the delay, and accordingly affirmed the summary judgment in favor of the subcontractor.

83036 NRS Constr. Corp. v. Board of Educ., 92 A.D.2d 803, 460 N.Y.S.2d 50 (1983)

> III: A107-1978, Art. 15, Para. 15.5
> III: A117-1979, Art. 19, Para. 19.5
> III: A201-1978, Art. 9, Para. 9.9.5

Contractor brought an action against owner for delay damages. The trial court denied owner's motion for partial summary judgment and owner appealed. At issue on appeal was whether contractor's claim was barred by the contract provision releasing owner from delay damages after contractor accepted final payment.

The Appellate Court found that had contractor received and accepted final payment and held that contractor was not entitled to recover delay damages. Since contractor knew that owner had accepted and fully paid for the work more than a year before bringing suit, the owner's motion to dismiss the claim should have been granted. Therefore, the Court reversed the trial court's denial of the motion.

83037 Pipe Welding Supply Co. v. Haskell, Conner & Frost, 96 A.D.2d 29, 469 N.Y.S.2d 221 (1983), *aff'd,* 61 N.Y.2d 884, 474 N.Y.S.2d 472, 462 N.E.2d 1190 (1984)

> I: B141-1977, Art. 3, Para. 3.1.1
> I: B141-1977, Art. 3, Para. 3.2.1
> I: B141-1977, Art. 3, Para. 3.2.4

Owner brought an action for malpractice against architect, and the architect counterclaimed for its unpaid fee. Owner terminated the project after receiving bids that substantially exceeded architect's estimated cost. At the time owner terminated the project architect had completed a substantial portion of its work. The owner-architect agreement provided that because neither architect nor owner had control over costing or the contractor's method of determining bid prices the architect did not warrant the Statement of Probable Construction Cost. The architect orally assured owner that bids were always within a certain percentage of the estimate. The jury returned a verdict for owner and architect appealed.

The Appellate Court found that the testimony of owner's expert failed to establish malpractice as a matter of law and failed to overcome the cost warranty disclaimer. The Court further held that the architect was entitled to the unpaid fee. Accordingly, the Court reversed the judgment and ordered a directed verdict in favor of the architect. This order was affirmed by the Court of Appeals of New York.

II: A201-1970, Art. 11, Para. 11.1.1
II: A201-1970, Art. 11, Para. 11.3.6

Owner's insurer brought a subrogation action against contractor to recover sums previously paid to it as an additional insured under an all risk insurance policy issued to the owner as the primary insured party. The trial court denied contractor's motion for summary judgment and contractor appealed.

The owner-contractor agreement imposed the risk of loss on the contractor and required it to repair any damage to property during construction. The agreement obligated the owner to obtain builder's risk insurance against physical damage to the property during construction, naming contractor as additional insured.

The Appellate Court found that contractor had an insurable interest, because contractor was obligated to repair any damage during construction without regard to fault. The Court held that the primary insured owner was barred from any right of action against contractor since owner suffered no loss. Because contractor had an insurable interest and was a co-insured, no right to subrogation existed in favor of insurer against contractor.

83035   Nicholas Acoustics & Specialty Co. v. H & M Constr. Co., 695 F.2d 839 (5th Cir. 1983)

III: A107-1978, Art. 15, Para. 15.2
III: A107-1978, Art. 15, Para. 15.4
III: A117-1979, Art. 19, Para. 19.2
III: A117-1979, Art. 19, Para. 19.4
III: A201-1976, Art. 9, Para. 9.5.2
III: A201-1976, Art. 9, Para. 9.9.2
III: A401-1978, Art. 5, Para. 5.3
III: A401-1978, Art. 11, Para. 11.1.1
III: A401-1978, Art. 12, Para. 12.4

Subcontractor brought an action against contractor and its surety for retainage. The District Court granted summary judgment in favor of subcontractor. Contractor and its surety appealed. At issue was whether a paid-when-paid clause was enforceable when the owner-contractor agreement, which was made part of the subcontract, provided that final payment would be made only on receipt of lien waivers.

The Court of Appeals determined that the clause in the owner-contractor agreement conditioning owner's final payment on release of liens and full payment of the subcontractors was the dominant clause. The Court then interpreted the subcontract provision as allowing contractor to delay final payment to subcontractor only for a reasonable time after the subcontractor completed its work. This finding protected the contractor's primary interest of having a reasonable time after completion to determine whether the subcontractor had adequately performed its subcontract. The Court held that the subcontractor was entitled to payment of the retainage absent a showing that

the decision "shall rest strictly with the owner . . . and what is customary or usual in erecting other buildings shall in no wise enter into any consideration or decision." Owner had rejected subcontractor's work and contractor hired another subcontractor to redo the work. Contractor refused to pay the first subcontractor the balance of the contract price.

The Court of Appeals held that the jury was properly instructed that owner, as a reasonable person, should have been satisfied with the materials and workmanship where the artistic effect clause did not cover a mill-finished aluminum factory wall, and where aesthetic considerations were secondary to function and cost. The words "artistic effect" were followed by the qualifying phrase "if within the Contract Documents" which the Court found limited the clause to aspects of the work in which artistic effect was a primary consideration.

83033   Moses H. Cone Memorial Hosp. v. Mercury Constr., 460 U.S. 1, 103 S. Ct. 927, 74 L. Ed. 2d 765 (1983)

> II: A107-1978, Art. 13, Para. 13.2
>
> II: A117-1979, Art. 17, Para. 17.2
>
> II: A201-1976, Art. 7, Para. 7.9.1
>
> II: A201-1970, Art. 7, Para. 7.9.2

After disputes arose between owner and contractor relating to job progress, owner initiated a suit in state court attempting to enjoin any effort by contractor to obtain arbitration and for other relief. Owner, ex parte, obtained such an injunction, which was later dissolved. Contractor then initiated a suit in the United States District Court for an order compelling arbitration. The District Court stayed the motion pending resolution of the state court action. The Court of Appeals reversed and instructed the District Court to enter an order compelling arbitration on remand.

On certiorari, the Supreme Court determined that no exceptional circumstances existed which would permit the District Court to decline jurisdiction because of a parallel state action. As one reason for its holding the Court stated that federal law, namely the Arbitration Act, governed the issue of arbitrability by creating a body of federal substantive law that applied to all questions of the validity and enforceability or arbitration provisions in contracts involving interstate commerce.

83034   New York Bd. of Fire Underwriters v. Trans Urban Constr. Co., 91 A.D.2d 115, 458 N.Y.S.2d 216 (1983), *aff'd,* 60 N.Y.2d 912, 470 N.Y.S.2d 578, 458 N.E.2d 1255 (1983)

> II: A107-1966, Art. 18
>
> II: A107-1966, Art. 19
>
> II: A107-1966, Art. 20
>
> II: A201-1970, Art. 10, Para. 10.2.1
>
> II: A201-1970, Art. 10, Para. 10.2.4

The Appellate Court did not interpret the contract provision that the architect render a written decision as a condition precedent to a demand for arbitration. It found that Paragraph 7.9.1, which set forth the requirement for arbitration, was controlling. The Court held that the owner was entitled to arbitration of the dispute with contractor despite owner's failure to present the dispute to the architect where no architect was involved in the project, the dispute was in fact submitted to an engineer/designer, and Paragraph 7.9.1 did not require the use of an architect.

83031   Martin County v. R.K. Stewart & Son, Inc., 63 N.C. App. 556, 306 S.E.2d 118 (1983)

        II: A401-1967, Art. 1
        I: A401-1967, Art. 11, Para. 11.1

Owner brought an action against contractor, and contractor filed a third party action against subcontractor for failure to perform roofing work in accordance with the specifications. The trial court granted subcontractor's motion for summary judgment and contractor appealed. At issue on appeal was whether a three year statute of limitations barred the contractor from bringing an action against the subcontractor.

The Appellate Court stated that because not all of the contract documents were before the Court, it could not determine what obligations were created by them, how long they extended and which statute of limitations applied to them. The Court held that summary judgment was improper where the subcontract contained a flow-down clause, which provided that subcontractor had expressly assumed and was responsible for all of the contractor's obligations to the owner, when the nature of those obligations was unknown.

83032   Morin Bldg. Prod. Co. v. Baystone Constr., 717 F.2d 413 (7th Cir. 1983)

        II: A107-1978, Art. 8, Para. 8.5
        II: A117-1979, Art. 12, Para. 12.5
        II: A201-1976, Art. 2, Para. 2.2.7
        II: A201-1976, Art. 2, Para. 2.2.8
        II: A201-1976, Art. 2, Para. 2.2.10
        I: A201-1976, Art. 2, Para. 2.2.11
        II: A401-1978, Art. 11, Para. 11.2.5

Subcontractor brought an action against contractor for balance of the contract sum. The trial court entered judgment for subcontractor and contractor appealed. At issue on appeal was whether the jury was properly instructed to use an objective standard in determining whether the owner, as a reasonable person, should have been satisfied with subcontractor's materials and workmanship.

The owner-contractor agreement provided that all work was subject to the architect's final approval, and that the architect's decision relating to artistic effect was final. The agreement further provided that in the event of a dispute as to materials or workmanship

II: A201-1967, Art. 8, Para. 8.1.3

Owner filed a demand for arbitration against contractor for roof defects. By verified complaint contractor sought to enjoin arbitration, arguing that the demand for arbitration was not made within the statute of limitations, was made after the expiration of the roof warranty, and was not made within a reasonable time as required by the owner-contractor agreement. The trial court held that the statute of limitations did not bar owner from filing a demand for arbitration, since the limitations period did not begin to run until the date the certificates of occupancy were delivered and, in the alternative, if the statute did begin to run earlier, it was tolled by contractor's attempts to repair the roof. The trial court also ruled that whether the demand for arbitration was made within a reasonable time under the contract was an issue for the arbitrators. Contractor's complaint was dismissed and arbitration commenced. Contractor appealed.

The contract defined substantial completion as the date when all certificates of occupancy and approval were issued and delivered to owner. The contract further provided that a notice of demand for arbitration should be filed within a reasonable time after the claim arose, but before the claim would be barred by the statute of limitations.

In affirming the trial court's dismissal of the contractor's request, the Appellate Court found that under the terms of the contract the statute of limitations began to run on the date of substantial completion of the structure and not upon completion of the roof. Therefore, since the demand for arbitration was made within six years of substantial completion, it was not barred by the statute of limitations. The Court held further that the timeliness of the owner's demand for arbitration was an issue to be decided by the arbitrators.

83030   Manalili v. Commercial Mowing & Grading, 442 So. 2d 411 (Fla. Dist. Ct. App. 1983)

   I: A107-1978, Art. 8, Para. 8.5
   I: A107-1978, Art. 13, Para. 13.2
   I: A117-1979, Art. 12, Para. 12.5
   I: A117-1979, Art. 17, Para. 17.2
   I: A201-1976, Art. 2, Para. 2..2.9
   I: A201-1976, Art. 2, Para. 2.2.10
   I: A201-1976, Art. 2, Para. 2.2.12
   I: A201-1976, Art. 7, Para. 7.9.1

Contractor brought an action to foreclose a mechanics' lien, and owner moved to stay the proceedings and compel arbitration. At issue on appeal was whether the trial court erred in denying the owner's motion on the ground that there was no written decision by an architect as required by the owner-contractor agreement. The owner-contractor agreement included the American Institute of Architects General Conditions of the Contract for Construction, Document A201, 1976 edition, which provided for arbitration between the parties.

I:	A201-1976, Art. 9, Para. 9.3.1
I:	A201-1976, Art. 9, Para. 9.3.3
I:	A401-1978, Art. 11, Para. 11.8.1
I:	A401-1978, Art. 11, Para. 11.8.2
I:	A401-1978, Art. 11, Para. 11.8.3
I:	A401-1978, Art. 11, Para. 11.11.1
I:	A401-1978, Art. 12, Para. 12.4.1
I:	A401-1978, Art. 12, Para. 12.4.2
I:	A401-1978, Art. 12, Para. 12.4.3
I:	A401-1978, Art. 13, Para. 13.6

Contractor brought an action against owner to foreclose a mechanics' lien after owner terminated the owner-contractor agreement before the completion of construction. Subcontractors counterclaimed for foreclosure of mechanics' liens and for breach of contract. The trial court entered judgment for subcontractors on their counterclaims. The subcontractors appealed from an order limiting the amount of their liens.

The owner-contractor agreement incorporated by reference the American Institute of Architects General Conditions of the Contract for Construction, Document A201, 1976 edition, including paragraphs 5.3.1 and 9.3.3, and was amended to provide that contractor and all subcontractors waived all lien claims. The subcontracts provided that they would "conform to the AIA document," which contained a waiver of lien provision, but a copy of the General Conditions was not attached to the subcontracts. Owner made three of the four required progress payments to contractor pursuant to the payment terms of the contract, but did not receive lien waivers before making the payments. Owner refused to make the last progress payment before receiving lien waivers. Owner then terminated the project before it was completed.

The Appellate Court affirmed. It held that under the plain language of paragraph 9.3.3 subcontractors were entitled to file their lien claims. Paragraph 9.3.3 gave the owner a right of action against the contractor should contractor breach the paragraph 9.3.3 warranty, but was not a waiver of rights of third parties to assert their claims. Paragraph 5.3 required that the subcontractor's work "be performed in accordance with the Contract Documents." The Court found that paragraph 5.3 obligated the subcontractor to concern himself only with those portions of the prime contract directly relating to his work performance. Furthermore, paragraph 5.3 did not provide sufficient notice, as required by the Illinois Mechanics Lien Act, to constitute waiver. For these reasons the Appellate Court held that subcontractors had not waived their rights to mechanics' liens.

83029 Mahony-Troast Constr. Co. v. Supermarkets Gen. Corp., 189 N.J. Super. 325, 460 A.2d 149 (App. Div. 1983)

III:	A107-1966, Art. 15
II:	A201-1967, Art. 7, Para. 7.10.1
II:	A201-1967, Art. 7, Para. 7.10.2

The owner-contractor agreement contained a mandatory arbitration provision, which stated that if one party demanded arbitration of a dispute governed by the clause, the other party had to arbitrate the claim. The contract contained a second voluntary arbitration clause providing that a dispute could be arbitrated only if both parties agreed. At issue on appeal was whether the owner and contractor had entered into a unilaterally enforceable agreement to arbitrate the dispute.

The Appellate Court, in interpreting the contract to give effect to the whole, found that the dispute was subject to the mandatory arbitration clause where the contract stated that it superseded any conflicting provision of the contract, and where the voluntary clause provided that it was available "except where otherwise provided in this contract."

83027 Kalich-Jarcho, Inc. v. City of New York, 58 N.Y.2d 377, 461 N.Y.S.2d 746, 448 N.E.2d 413 (1983)

>   III: A107-1978, Art. 14, Para. 14.3
>   III: A117-1979, Art. 18, Para. 18.3
>   III: A201-1976, Art. 8, Para. 8.3.1
>   III: A201-1976, Art. 8, Para. 8.3.4

Contractor brought an action against owner claiming damages for delay. The trial court entered judgment for contractor and owner appealed.

At issue on appeal was whether it was reversible error, where the owner-contractor agreement contained a no-damage-for-delay clause, for the trial court to refuse to give a requested jury charge that contractor could not recover delay damages caused by owner unless owner acted in bad faith with deliberate intent. The contract provided that contractor agreed to make no claim for delay damages occasioned by an act or omission of owner and that any such claim would be fully compensated for by an extension of time.

The Appellate Court reversed, holding that the provision, not uncommon in construction contracts, was enforceable because it was entered into at arm's length by sophisticated parties; thus, in order to recover, contractor would have to prove that it was owner's conduct that caused the extraordinarily long delays, that owner failed to coordinate the work of the various contractors, and that the immense number of drawing revisions requested by owner amounted to gross negligence.

83028 Luczak Bros., Inc. v. Generes, 116 Ill. App. 3d 286, 71 Ill. Dec. 900, 451 N.E.2d 1267 (1983)

>   II: A107-1978, Art. 11, Para. 11.2
>   II: A107-1978, Art. 15, Para. 15.4
>   II: A117-1979, Art. 15, Para. 15.2
>   II: A117-1979, Art. 19, Para. 19.4
>   I: A201-1976, Art. 5, Para. 5.3.1

owner-architect agreement provided in Paragraph 1.1.4 that architect was not retained to supervise the performance of the work.

The Appellate Court reversed. It found that subcontractor was charged with the task of manufacturing and delivering the materials to the site, and that contractor was obligated to protect the material from the elements on the site. The Court held that neither architect nor subcontractor was liable to owner for water damage occurring on the site.

83025   J & K Cement Constr. v. Montalbano Bldrs., 119 Ill. App. 3d 524, 456 N.E.2d 889 (1983)

        Ill: A107-1978, Art. 13, Para. 13.2
        Ill: A117-1979, Art. 17, Para. 17.2
        Ill: A201-1976, Art. 7, Para. 7.9.1

Subcontractor brought a lien foreclosure action against owner and owner counterclaimed against contractor. Contractor moved to compel owner to arbitrate and for a stay of all proceedings. The trial court denied contractor's motion and contractor appealed.

On appeal contractor relied on Paragraph 22 of the owner-contractor agreement, which provided that "all claims, disputes . . . arising out of or relating to this Agreement . . . shall be decided by arbitration. . . ." The owner argued that the agreement contained an additional arbitration clause that was incorporated by reference into the general conditions. The additional clause only became operative if the parties did not establish an alternative dispute resolution procedure.

The Appellate Court found that the parties had established an alternative procedure by including Paragraph 22. The Court found that Paragraph 22 was a valid agreement to arbitrate which was sufficiently broad to encompass all of the claims, and held that the trial court should have made a finding with respect to the arbitrability of the dispute. The Court further held that contractor was entitled to enforce the agreement to arbitrate and ordered subcontractor's lien foreclosure action stayed pending arbitration.

[*Editor's Note:* Five years after this case was decided, the Illinois Supreme Court held in Donaldson, Lufkin & Jenrette Futures, Inc. v. Barr, 124 Ill. 2d 435, 125 Ill. Dec. 281, 530 N.E.2d 439 (1988), a securities case, that it was the intention of the Uniform Arbitration Act that the arbitrator should determine arbitrability in the first instance, subject to later review by a court.]

83026   Johnson Controls, Inc. v. City of Cedar Rapids, Iowa, 713 F.2d 370 (8th Cir. 1983)

        Ill: A107-1978, Art. 13, Para. 13.2
        Ill: A117-1979, Art. 17, Para. 17.2
        Ill: A201-1976, Art. 7, Para. 7.9.1

Contractor filed a demand for arbitration against owner for cost overruns. Owner rejected the demand and contractor brought an action to compel arbitration. The District Court ordered arbitration and owner appealed.

architect to review and approve shop drawings and other submissions for compliance with the contract documents. The shop drawings at issue were reviewed and approved by architect, who failed to notice a mistake in them.

On appeal the architect argued that the trial court should have granted architect's motion for a directed verdict because the workers failed to present expert testimony to prove architect's negligence. The Court of Appeals drew a distinction between actions against architects for negligence in preparing plans and actions for negligence in supervising plans and found that architect negligently failed to supervise review of the shop drawings pursuant to the contract. Negligence in supervision came within the "common knowledge" exception to the rule requiring expert testimony on the appropriate standard of care. The Court upheld the trial court's finding that architect was liable for negligence.

83024   Jewish Bd. of Guardians v. Grumman Allied Indus., Inc., 96 A.D.2d 465, 464 N.Y.S.2d 778 (1983), *aff'd,* 62 N.Y.2d 684, 476 N.Y.S.2d 535, 465 N.E.2d 42 (1984).

II:	A107-1978, Art. 8, Para. 8.1
II:	A107-1978, Art. 8, Para. 8.3
II:	A107-1978, Art. 10, Para. 10.1
II:	A107-1978, Art. 10, Para. 10.2
II:	A107-1978, Art. 10, Para. 10.4
II:	A117-1979, Art. 12, Para. 12.1
II:	A117-1979, Art. 12, Para. 12.3
II:	A117-1979, Art. 14, Para. 14.1
II:	A117-1979, Art. 14, Para. 14.2
II:	A117-1979, Art. 14, Para. 14.4
II:	A201-1976, Art. 2, Para. 2.2.2
II:	A201-1976, Art. 2, Para. 2.2.3
II:	A201-1976, Art. 2, Para. 2.2.4
II:	A201-1976, Art. 4, Para. 4.3.1
II:	A201-1976, Art. 4, Para. 4.4.1
II:	A201-1976, Art. 4, Para. 4.5.1
II:	B141-1974, Art. 1, Para. 1.1.4
II:	B141-1974, Art. 2, Para. 2.6.5

Owner brought an action against subcontractor and architect for water damage to materials on site. The architect filed a third-party claim against contractor for indemnification. The trial court entered judgment for owner and held that architect was entitled to indemnification from contractor.

Article 22 of the Specifications provided that contractor was obligated to "provide and install all necessary temporary protection to prevent the intrusion of the elements." The

83022 Hercules Constr. Co. v. C.J. Moritz Co., 655 S.W.2d 779 (Mo. Ct. App. 1983)

   I: A201-1967, Art. 4, Para. 4.13.7
   I: A401-1967, Art. 11, Para. 11.1
   I: A401-1967, Art. 11, Para. 11.9

 Contractor brought an action against subcontractor to recover the cost of replacing a fan. The subcontractor impleaded the engineering consultant, the manufacturer of the fan and the installer of the fan as third party defendants. The trial court granted the engineering consultant's motion for a directed verdict and entered judgment for contractor. The subcontractor appealed.

 The subcontract provided that subcontractor was responsible for all of the heating, ventilation and air conditioning work. Article 11, "Subcontractor's Responsibilities" included a paragraph covering warranties, quality of work and defects. The subcontract also contained a flow-down provision. The specifications provided that architect's approval of shop drawings did not relieve contractor of responsibility for any deviation from the contract documents or from responsibility for errors or omissions in the shop drawings.

 The Appellate Court affirmed, finding that contractor had presented sufficient evidence that the fan was installed upside down to demonstrate that subcontractor breached Article 11 of the subcontract which provided that subcontractor warranted that the fan was free from faults and defects and was installed in a workmanlike manner in accordance with the specifications.

83023 Jaeger v. Henningson, Durham & Richardson, Inc., 714 F.2d 773 (8th Cir. 1983)

   II: A107-1978, Art. 8, Para. 8.7
   II: A107-1978, Art. 10, Para. 10.8
   II: A117-1979, Art. 12, Para. 12.7
   II: A117-1979, Art. 14, Para. 14.8
   I: A201-1976, Art. 2, Para. 2.2.14
   I: A201-1976, Art. 4, Para. 4.12.4
   I: A201-1976, Art. 4, Para. 4.12.5
   I: A201-1976, Art. 4, Para. 4.12.6
   I: B141-1977, Art. 1, Para. 1.3.1
   I: B141-1977, Art. 1, Para. 1.5.13

 Sub-subcontractor's employees brought actions against architect for architect's negligence in failing to detect errors in shop drawings which proximately caused their injuries. The District Court entered judgment for workers and architect appealed.

 The owner-architect agreement required architect to prepare drawings and specifications setting forth in detail the requirements for construction. Paragraph 1.1.18 required

contractual duty to administer the construction of the project the accident would not have occurred. Architect argued on appeal that it fulfilled its obligation to owner to make certain that the construction was progressing satisfactorily and was in conformance with the plans and specifications.

The Supreme Court of Kansas found that the trial court misconstrued the term "Work" in Paragraph 1.1.3 to include safety precautions, and had based that decision upon Paragraph 2.2.1, which stated that architect was to provide general administration of the contract. The Court concluded that the architect was contractually obligated to prepare the plans and specifications and to insure that the building conformed to such plans and specifications. Furthermore, the contract expressly provided that contractor was responsible for safety on the jobsite. Based on these findings, the Court held that architect did not have a contractual duty to provide for jobsite safety, and therefore the instruction to the jury was clearly erroneous.

83021 Henry C. Beck Co. v. Ft. Wayne Structural Steel Co., 701 F.2d 1221 (7th Cir. 1983)

   II: A401-1978, Art. 11, Para. 11.11.1
   II: A401-1978, Art. 11, Para. 11.11.2

Contractor filed a third-party indemnity action against first subcontractor, after injured employee of second subcontractor sued contractor for damages for employee's injuries. After settling with injured worker, contractor brought an indemnification action against both first subcontractor and second subcontractor. First subcontractor filed a cross-claim for indemnification against second subcontractor. The District Court dismissed contractor's and first subcontractor's indemnity claims against second subcontractor for failure to state a claim based on the applicability of the statute of frauds and the policy underlying the exclusive remedy provision of the Indiana Workmen's Compensation Act. Contractor and subcontractor appealed. The issue on appeal was whether the claims were barred by either the statute of frauds or the exclusive remedy provisions of the Indiana Workmen's Compensation Act.

The subcontract contained an indemnity provision similar to paragraphs 11.11.1 and 11.11.2 of the American Institute of Architects Standard Form of Agreement Between Contractor and Subcontractor, Document A401, 1978 edition. The second subcontractor orally agreed to be bound by the terms of the subcontract. The second subcontractor furnished contractor with a certificate of insurance that recited the subcontract's indemnification provision including the clause stating that the indemnification was not limited by "compensation or benefits payable by or for the Subcontractor under workmen's compensation acts."

The Court of Appeals found that contractor's and subcontractor's claims for indemnification, based upon second subcontractor's oral agreement and the certificate of insurance, stated a cause of action sufficient to withstand a motion to dismiss for failure to state a claim where neither the statute of frauds nor the workmen's compensation statute precluded enforcement of an oral indemnification agreement.

and for costs incurred in attempting to mitigate damages by seeking substitute contracts. In a later proceeding the Supreme Court of Colorado remanded the case for a determination of the amount of lost profits and for recomputation of the long term equipment lease damages.

83020 Hanna v. Huer, Johns, Neel, Rivers & Webb, 233 Kan. 206, 662 P.2d 243 (1983)

I:	A201-1970, Art. 1, Para. 1.1.3
I:	A201-1970, Art. 2, Para. 2.1.2
I:	A201-1970, Art. 2, Para. 2.2.2
I:	A201-1970, Art. 2, Para. 2.2.4
I:	A201-1970, Art. 2, Para. 2.2.12
I:	A201-1970, Art. 2, Para. 2.2.17
I:	A201-1970, Art. 2, Para. 2.2.18
I:	A201-1970, Art. 3, Para. 3.3.1
I:	A201-1970, Art. 4, Para. 4.3.1
I:	A201-1970, Art. 10, Para. 10.1.1
I:	A201-1970, Art. 10, Para. 10.2.1
I:	A201-1970, Art. 10, Para. 10.2.2
I:	A201-1970, Art. 10, Para. 10.2.5
II:	A107-1966, Art. 8, Para. 8.3
II:	A107-1966, Art. 9, Para. 9.1
II:	A107-1966, Art. 9, Para. 9.3
II:	A107-1966, Art. 11, Para. 11.1
II:	A107-1966, Art. 18

Subcontractor's injured employees brought a negligence action against subcontractor, contractor, steel fabricator, owner and architect. At the time of trial architect was the only viable party remaining in the action for purposes of liability, although the jury was instructed to apportion fault among all parties. Architect appealed from judgments entered for the injured workers. The issue on appeal was whether the trial court erred in instructing the jury that architect was contractually responsible for safety practices on the jobsite.

Architect had entered into an oral contract with owner to design the building, to prepare the contracts and to develop the plans and specifications. The contract documents prepared by architect included the plans, drawings and specifications and the American Institute of Architects General Conditions of the Contract for Construction, Document A201, 1970 edition. Document A201, although not executed by the architect, specified the duties of the architect. There was no serious contention that A201 was not part of the architect's oral agreement with owner.

Injured workers argued on appeal that subcontractor was notorious for its failure to follow safety procedures and that if architect had not been negligent in performing its

Contractor provided that the contractor was to receive the "actual cost to contractor plus fifteen (15) percent" applied to "deletions and/or additions."

The Appellate Court held that the trial court did not err in limiting recovery as provided in the express written contract where the contract clearly established a procedure for the payment of all changes in material and labor costs.

83018   Graham Contracting, Inc. v. Flagler County, 444 So. 2d 971 (Fla. Dist. Ct. App. 1983), *review denied,* 451 So. 2d 848 (Fla. 1984)

      II: A107-1978, Art. 13, Para. 13.2
      II: A117-1979, Art. 17, Para. 17.2
      II: A201-1976, Art. 7, Para. 7.9.1
      II: A201-1976, Art. 7, Para. 7.9.2

Contractor filed a motion to compel arbitration against owner for payment of additional costs. The owner-contractor agreement contained a broad form arbitration provision requiring that any demand for arbitration be made within a reasonable time after the claim arose. The trial court denied contractor's motion to compel arbitration. Contractor then filed a petition for writ of certiorari for review of the trial court's order.

The Appellate Court found that no claim was made and no dispute arose when contractor was told by owner to cease work. Rather, the dispute arose when owner served its complaint on contractor. The Court held that contractor did not waive its right to arbitration either by delaying in filing its demand or by filing a motion to dismiss owner's complaint for failure to state a cause of action. The Court therefore quashed the order denying the contractor's motion to compel arbitration.

83019   Gundersons, Inc. v. Tull, 678 P.2d 1061 (Colo. Ct. App. 1983), *aff'd in part and rev'd in part on other grounds,* 709 P.2d 940 (Colo. 1985)

      III: A201-1976, Art. 3, Para. 3.2.1
      III: A201-1976, Art. 9, Para. 9.3.1
      III: A201-1976, Art. 9, Para. 9.5.1

Contractor brought a breach of contract action against owner. The trial court awarded contractor the retainage due under the contract. The contractor appealed, arguing that it was entitled to lost profits and other expenses resulting from owner's breach.

The owner-contractor agreement provided that contractor would receive monthly payments for the work completed, less retainage. Owner never obtained the financing necessary to complete the project and contractor brought an action for breach of contract seeking the profits it would have realized had it been allowed to complete the project.

The Appellate Court, based on the testimony of contractor's president, who itemized the cost of doing each task, held that contractor had met its burden of showing with reasonable certainty the amount of expected net profits. Further, the Court held that contractor was also entitled to consequential damages for long term leases on equipment

83016 Garden Grove Community Church v. Pittsburgh-Des Moines Steel Co., 140 Cal. App. 3d 251, 191 Cal. Rptr. 15 (1983)

II:	A107-1978, Art. 13, Para. 13.2
II:	A117-1979, Art. 17, Para. 17.2
II:	A201-1976, Art. 7, Para. 7.9.1
II:	B141-1977, Art. 9, Para. 9.1

Contractor filed a demand for arbitration against owner for cost overruns and the balance due under the contract. After the owner-contractor arbitration commenced, the owner asked the construction manager, architect and structural engineer to join as parties so that owner's rights to indemnification could be simultaneously resolved. When architect and structural engineer refused to join, owner moved to stay the arbitration or in the alternative for an injunction requiring them to join as relevant parties. The trial court entered an order staying the arbitration, finding that neither architect nor engineer was contractually bound to join in the arbitration and that the owner had properly exercised its right to avoid separate arbitration with contractor. The contractor appealed.

The owner-contractor agreement contained a broad form arbitration clause which provided that owner could not arbitrate any dispute with contractor that required any other third party who did not agree to participate in the arbitration. The contract between owner and construction manager also contained an arbitration provision. Owner's contract with architect contained an arbitration clause which precluded consolidation or joinder except by written consent of all parties.

The Appellate Court held that the trial court erred in not consolidating the separate arbitrations between owner and the parties with whom owner separately contracted where state law provided for consolidation if the disputes arose from common questions of fact. The Court accordingly reversed the order staying arbitration and directed the trial court to consolidate the two arbitration proceedings.

83017 Gilbert v. Powell, 165 Ga. App. 504, 301 S.E.2d 683 (1983)

I:	A111-1978, Art. 5, Para. 5.2
I:	A111-1978, Art. 6, Para. 6.2
I:	A117-1979, Art. 4, Para. 4.3
I:	A117-1979, Art. 5, Para. 5.2
I:	A201-1976, Art. 9, Para. 9.1

Contractor brought a lien foreclosure action against owner for extra labor and materials ordered by owner. The owner counterclaimed for damages due to construction defects. The trial court denied the claims of both the owner and the contractor and both parties appealed. The issue on appeal was whether the contractor could sue in quantum meruit even though the parties had agreed to a guaranteed maximum price contract. The American Institute of Architects Standard Form of Agreement Between Owner and

II: A201-1967, Art. 12, Para. 12.1.4

II: A201-1967, Art. 12, Para. 12.2.1

Contractor brought an action against owner to recover delay damages. The trial court entered judgment for contractor and owner appealed, arguing that contractor had not complied with the claim procedure set forth in the contract. The agreement between the owner and contractor established a procedure by which contractor could seek an adjustment in the guaranteed maximum price. Contractor had to notify owner in writing of his claim for an increase in the price or for an extension of time. All claims for delay had to be made within a reasonable time after the delay and had to be authorized by change order.

The Supreme Court of Nevada found that sufficient notice of additional costs had been given by contractor since contractor had sent a letter to owner stating that he was "being delayed" and provided owner with a change order detailing the additional costs. The Court held that the trial court did not err in ruling that the letter provided sufficient notice to meet the contract requirements.

83015 Frank Briscoe Co. v. Georgia Sprinkler Co., 713 F.2d 1500 (11th Cir. 1983)

III: A107-1978, Art. 17, Para. 17.1

III: A107-1978, Art. 17, Para. 17.6

III: A117-1979, Art. 21, Para. 21.1

III: A117-1979, Art. 21, Para. 21.6

III: A201-1976, Art. 11, Para. 11.1.1

III: A201-1976, Art. 11, Para. 11.3.6

III: A401-1978, Art. 11, Para. 11.11.1

Contractor's insurer brought a subrogation action against subcontractor for damages caused by subcontractor's faulty installation of a fire protection sprinkler system.

The owner-contractor agreement provided that contractor would procure and maintain general public liability insurance. The policy named contractor and all subcontractors as insureds. Contractor's agreement with subcontractor contained an indemnity provision indemnifying contractor against any loss arising from the performance of the subcontract. After a leak occurred in the sprinkler system contractor filed a claim with its general liability insurer and granted the insurer the right to enforce in contractor's name any claim of indemnity against subcontractor. Insurer brought this action asserting liability under the indemnification agreement.

The District Court granted summary judgment in favor of subcontractor and contractor appealed. At issue on appeal was whether a right of subrogation existed in favor of contractor's insurer. The Court of Appeals affirmed, holding that under Georgia state law no subrogation right existed against a co-insured subcontractor notwithstanding an indemnity agreement between contractor and subcontractor.

At issue on appeal was whether subcontractor was required to indemnify the contractor pursuant to a clause of the subcontract providing that "subcontractor shall hold the General Contractor harmless from all liability . . . whether or not it is contended the General Contractor contributed thereto in whole, or in part. . . ."

The Supreme Court of Rhode Island found that the contract clause expressed the intent of the parties and held that subcontractor was liable to contractor under the indemnity provision whether or not the contractor was negligent.

83013   D. Federico Co. v. New Bedford Redevelopment Auth., 723 F.2d 122 (1st Cir. 1983)

III:	A107-1978, Art. 7, Para. 7.3
III:	A117-1979, Art. 11, Para. 11.3
III:	A201-1976, Art. 1, Para. 1.2.2
III:	A201-1976, Art. 12, Para. 12.2.1

Contractor brought an action against owner for extra costs necessitated by additional site excavation. The Bankruptcy Court entered judgment for contractor.

Owner argued on appeal that bidders had been advised to carefully examine the area. Contractor argued that owner misled contractor by failing to inform contractor of an engineering report that detailed the conditions encountered.

The Court of Appeals upheld the Bankruptcy Court's findings that contractor was less than prudent in his cursory examination of the site, and that owner had information which would have assisted bidders in bid preparation. The Court affirmed the Bankruptcy Court's holding that owner should not receive the benefit of contractor's substantial additional work without compensating contractor merely because contractor was not conscientious in discovering the undisclosed problem.

83014   Eagle's Nest Ltd. Partnership v. Brunzell, 99 Nev. 710, 669 P.2d 714 (1983)

II:	A107-1966, Art. 16, Para. 16.2
II:	A107-1976, Art. 22, Para. 22.1
II:	A107-1976, Art. 22, Para. 22.2
II:	A107-1976, Art. 22, Para. 22.3
II:	A111-1967, Art. 6, Para. 6.2
II:	A201-1967, Art. 8, Para. 8.3.1
II:	A201-1967, Art. 8, Para. 8.3.2
II:	A201-1967, Art. 8, Para. 8.3.3
II:	A201-1967, Art. 9, Para. 9.2.1
II:	A201-1967, Art. 12, Para. 12.1.1
II:	A201-1967, Art. 12, Para. 12.1.2
II:	A201-1967, Art. 12, Para. 12.1.3

Contractor filed a demand for arbitration against owner. Owner filed suit seeking declaratory and injunctive relief. The District Court found that because the dispute arose from a claim for extra compensation for subcontractor's added labor and materials it was not within the scope of the arbitration provision contained in the owner-contractor agreement. The District Court issued a preliminary injunction staying arbitration and contractor and owner appealed.

The owner-contractor agreement contained a broad form arbitration provision. Owner argued on appeal that it should not be forced to arbitrate a dispute between contractor and subcontractor because contractor had neither been held liable for the disputed costs nor admitted liability for the additional sums.

The Appellate Court found that owner had looked to contractor for completion of the entire project, including all of the subcontracted work, and the fact that subcontractor had a claim against contractor under the subcontract would not deprive contractor of the right to arbitrate a claim against owner that was within the scope of the owner-contractor agreement. The Court held that contractor's claim was arbitrable.

83011 Contracting Northwest, Inc. v. City of Fredericksburg, 713 F.2d 382 (8th Cir. 1983)

> III: A107-1978, Art. 13, Para. 13.2
> III: A117-1979, Art. 17, Para. 17.2
> III: A201-1976, Art. 7, Para. 7.9.1

Contractor filed a demand for arbitration against owner for costs of extra work. The District Court issued an order compelling owner to arbitrate and owner appealed.

The owner-contractor agreement contained two separate arbitration clauses. The mandatory arbitration clause provided that if one party demanded arbitration of a dispute governed by the clause the other party must submit to arbitration so long as the dispute was about "matters involving the decision of the Engineer." The second arbitration clause provided that a dispute governed by the clause could be arbitrated only if both parties consented to arbitration.

The Appellate Court found that the dispute "revolved around a decision of the Engineer" since the engineer had refused to issue a change order or accept contractor's equitable adjustment claim, and held that owner and contractor had obligated themselves to submit the dispute to arbitration.

83012 Corrente v. Conforti & Eisele Co., 468 A.2d 920 (R.I. 1983)

> II: A401-1978, Art. 11, Para. 11.11.1

Injured worker filed a negligence action against contractor, which in turn filed a third party claim for indemnification against subcontractor. The trial court entered judgment for contractor and subcontractor appealed.

The California Supreme Court affirmed the trial court's ruling that the owner had waived its right to arbitration by bringing a suit which had the sole purpose of discovering contractor's legal theories and strategies. The Court further held that it was an abuse of the trial court's discretion to deny contractor's claim for attorneys fees where the contract provided that if either party became involved in litigation arising out of the contract, the court would award attorney fees to the prevailing party.

83009 Cincinnati Gas & Elec. Co. v. Benjamin F. Shaw Co., 706 F.2d 155 (6th Cir. 1983)

	III:	A107-1978, Art. 13, Para. 13.2
	III:	A117-1979, Art. 17, Para. 17.2
	III:	A201-1976, Art. 7, Para. 7.9.1

Contractor filed a demand for arbitration against owner for delay damages. Owner filed an action against contractor in the District Court seeking a declaration that contractor's claim was not subject to arbitration. The District Court ordered the parties to submit the dispute to arbitration and owner appealed.

The owner-contractor agreement contained a mandatory arbitration clause, but that clause specifically stated that the right of arbitration would not extend to any claim or defense that "denies, or challenges, or is inconsistent with the validity of any provision of this Agreement." Owner argued that contractor's claim for delay damages was inconsistent with the contract provisions limiting recovery of overhead costs to an agreed upon maximum.

The Appellate Court held that the District Court did not err in concluding that the claim arose out of the owner-contractor agreement and that it was a claim for breach of contract not inconsistent with the validity of any provision of the owner-contractor agreement. The Court held that the District Court's determination that the parties must submit the dispute to arbitration was supported by the contract language and controlling precedent.

83010 City of Meridian v. Algernon Blair, Inc., 721 F.2d 525 (5th Cir. 1983)

	II:	A107-1978, Art. 10, Para. 10.1
	II:	A107-1978, Art. 10, Para. 10.7
	II:	A107-1978, Art. 13, Para. 13.2
	II:	A117-1979, Art. 14, Para. 14.1
	II:	A117-1979, Art. 14, Para. 14.7
	II:	A117-1979, Art. 17, Para. 17.2
	II:	A201-1976, Art. 4, Para. 4.3.1
	II:	A201-1976, Art. 4, Para. 4.3.2
	II:	A201-1976, Art. 7, Para. 7.9.1

Owner brought an action against contractor alleging breach of contract arising from contractor's failure to carry out the work in an expeditious manner, improper supervision of the work and submission of improper payment applications. Contractor counterclaimed against owner and architect alleging they had breached the contract by delaying the project's progress, refusing to make payments due contractor and terminating contractor. Subcontractor filed a claim against contractor for delay damages. The District Court entered judgment for contractor and the parties appealed.

At issue on appeal was whether subcontractor was entitled to delay damages and whether owner or architect had to indemnify contractor for delay damages paid to subcontractor. The subcontract contained a delay claims provision, which the Appellate Court found plainly waived any claim for damages on account of any delay for any cause whatsoever. The Court found that this provision was applicable where the delay was caused by the owner, contractor and architect. The Court found further that the contractor's agreement with owner did not contain an express indemnity provision and held that an implied indemnity action was not available to contractor under state law if contractor was found liable to subcontractor on remand.

With regard to contractor's counterclaim against owner, contractor argued on appeal that the jury was not properly instructed that owner had waived compliance with the contractual provision requiring contractor to submit a list of proposed subcontractors to architect within 45 days of the award of the contract. The Appellate Court found that owner had proceeded with the contract for almost two years after contractor failed to timely list the subcontractors and concluded that the District Court's failure to give the instruction was error. However, the Court held that the error was harmless.

In contractor's action against the architect, the Appellate Court held that the District Court properly refused to give the contractor's proposed jury instruction that architect breached duties owed to contractor under the owner-contractor agreement. Contractor was not a party to the owner-architect agreement and architect was not a party to the owner-contractor agreement and never expressly agreed to be bound by its terms.

[*Editor's Note:* For subsequent appeal after remand, *see* case number 85009 *infra.*]

83008   Christensen v. Dewor Dev., 3 Cal. 3d 778, 191 Cal. Rptr. 8, 661 P.2d 1088 (1983)

II:	A107-1978, Art. 13, Para. 13.2
II:	A117-1979, Art. 17, Para. 17.2
II:	A201-1976, Art. 7, Para. 7.9.1
II:	A201-1976, Art. 7, Para. 7.9.2

Owner brought an action against contractor for breach of contract, but then dismissed the complaint without prejudice after actively pursuing the litigation. Two months later owner filed a petition to compel arbitration. The trial court found that owner acted in bad faith by litigating for the purpose of discovery, which caused lengthly delay resulting in waiver of the right to arbitrate. The trial court denied both parties motions for attorney's fees pursuant to the contract, and both parties appealed.

insurance should have been in force on the date the structure was damaged. Furthermore, the Court found that contractor relied on its surety to place the builders risk policy in force. The Court accordingly held that it was improper to instruct the jury that the contractor's performance bond surety was discharged, because contractor's failure to obtain the builders risk policy was a breach of the owner-contractor agreement that did not materially alter the performance bond. The Court thus ordered that judgment be entered in favor of the owner against the surety, and in favor of the contractor against the owner and the engineer.

83007 Chicago College of Osteopathic Medicine v. George A. Fuller Co., 719 F.2d 1335 (7th Cir. 1983)

        III: A107-1978, Art. 10, Para. 10.1
        III: A107-1978, Art. 10, Para. 10.4
        III: A107-1978, Art. 10, Para. 10.7
        III: A107-1978, Art. 10, Para. 10.11
        III: A107-1978, Art. 14, Para. 14.3
        III: A107-1978, Art. 15, Para. 15.2
        III: A107-1978, Art. 15, Para. 15.4
        III: A107-1978, Art. 20, Para. 20.2
        III: A117-1979, Art. 14, Para. 14.1
        III: A117-1979, Art. 14, Para. 14.4
        III: A117-1979, Art. 14, Para. 14.7
        III: A117-1979, Art. 14, Para. 14.11
        III: A117-1979, Art. 18, Para. 18.3
        III: A117-1979, Art. 19, Para. 19.2
        III: A117-1979, Art. 19, Para. 19.4
        III: A117-1979, Art. 24, Para. 24.2
        III: A201-1976, Art. 4, Para. 4.3.1
        III: A201-1976, Art. 4, Para. 4.3.2
        III: A201-1976, Art. 4, Para. 4.10.1
        III: A201-1976, Art. 4, Para. 4.18.1
        III: A201-1976, Art. 4, Para. 4.18.3
        III: A201-1976, Art. 5, Para. 5.2.1
        III: A201-1976, Art. 8, Para. 8.2.2
        III: A201-1976, Art. 8, Para. 8.3.1
        III: A201-1976, Art. 9, Para. 9.5.1
        III: A201-1976, Art. 9, Para. 9.6.1
        III: A201-1976, Art. 14, Para. 14.2.1

items, contractor was entitled to payment offset for the balance due owner for defective work.

83006   Carroll-Boone Water Dist. v. M & P Equip. Co., 280 Ark. 560, 661 S.W.2d 345 (1983)

III:	A107-1978, Art. 8, Para. 8.1
III:	A107-1978, Art. 17, Para. 17.1
III:	A107-1978, Art. 17, Para. 17.3
III:	A117-1979, Art. 12, Para. 12.1
III:	A117-1979, Art. 21, Para. 21.1
III:	A117-1979, Art. 21, Para. 21.3
III:	A201-1976, Art. 2, Para. 2.2.2
III:	A201-1976, Art. 2, Para. 2.2.18
III:	A201-1976, Art. 7, Para. 7.5.1
III:	A201-1976, Art. 11, Para. 11.1.1
III:	A201-1976, Art. 11, Para. 11.3.1

Owner brought an action against contractor, contractor's surety, engineer and subcontractor for damages arising from breach of contract and negligence. Contractor counterclaimed against owner and and filed a third party complaint seeking contribution from engineer.

Owner and contractor had entered into an agreement that required contractor to obtain a performance bond and a builder's risk policy. Contractor did not obtain the builders' risk policy. After completing the structure in accordance with the plans and specifications, at the request of the engineer, contractor contracted with subcontractor to engage in blasting which damaged the structure. Contractor incurred extra costs attempting to repair the damage. Contractor's surety refused coverage because no builder's risk policy had been procured.

The trial court entered judgment for owner against engineer and for contractor against owner and dismissed the owner's complaints against subcontractor, contractor's surety and contractor. Owner and engineer appealed.

At issue on appeal was whether certain jury instructions were properly given. The instructions stated that the engineer was owner's agent and that the absence of the builder's risk policy constituted a material alteration to contractor's performance bond contract.

The Arkansas Supreme Court found that the engineer's contract did not create an agency relationship where the contract did not contain a clause providing that the engineer would supervise the construction for owner. The Court also found that the owner-contractor agreement provided that work would not commence until all insurance was in force, and that the agreement clearly provided that the builders risk policy was to be in force when owner had insurable property at the site. The Court concluded that the builders risk with the change order provision relating to extra work and delay did not preclude recovery.

83005 Campagna v. Smallwood, 428 So. 2d 1343 (La. Ct. App. 1983)

III:	A107-1978, Art. 2, Para. 2.1	
III:	A107-1978, Art. 4, Para. 4.1	
III:	A107-1978, Art. 10, Para. 10.4	
III:	A107-1978, Art. 13, Para. 13.2	
III:	A107-1978, Art. 14, Para. 14.2	
III:	A107-1978, Art. 15, Para. 15.2	
III:	A117-1979, Art. 9, Para. 9.1	
III:	A117-1979, Art. 14, Para. 14.4	
III:	A117-1979, Art. 17, Para. 17.2	
III:	A117-1979, Art. 18, Para. 18.2	
III:	A117-1979, Art. 19, Para. 19.2	
III:	A201-1976, Art. 4, Para. 4.5.1	
III:	A201-1976, Art. 7, Para. 7.9.1	
III:	A201-1976, Art. 8, Para. 8.1.3	
III:	A201-1976, Art. 9, Para. 9.5.5	
III:	A201-1976, Art. 9, Para. 9.6.1	
III:	A201-1976, Art. 9, Para. 9.8.1	
III:	A201-1976, Art. 9, Para. 9.8.2	

Owner brought an action against contractor for damages resulting from defective construction of a roof and other deficiencies. Contractor moved to stay the proceedings pending arbitration. The trial court denied contractor's motion and contractor filed an answer and a demand for the balance due under the contract plus compensation for extra work. The trial court entered judgment for owner for defective construction damages but did not render judgment on contractor's demand. Contractor appealed.

The owner-contractor agreement provided that the work was to be completed within 110 days of commencement and that contractor was to be paid in five progress payments with final payment due upon occupancy or acceptance, whichever was sooner. The contract contained a contractor's warranty of good workmanship and provided that payment could be withheld for defective work. The contract also contained a broad form arbitration provision.

The Appellate Court found that where the record on appeal was complete and remand would only cause additional delays, no purpose would be served by setting aside the trial court's judgment and remanding for arbitration. Because contractor substantially performed his obligation under the contract and owner used the building for the purpose intended, even though there were defects in material, workmanship and incomplete punchlist

substantial completion earlier than the date of substantial completion in architect's certificate. The trial court confirmed the award of the arbitrator and owner appealed.

The contract was the American Institute of Architects Standard Form of Agreement Between Owner and Contractor, Document No. A111, 1978 edition, which incorporated the American Institute of Architects General Conditions of the Contract for Construction, Document A201, 1976 edition. The contract provided that the work was to be completed by an agreed upon date, and for each additional day the contractor took to complete the contractor agreed to pay owner liquidated damages. Paragraph 8.3.1 of the General Conditions provided that the date of substantial completion would be certified by the architect. The Architect's Certificate of Substantial Completion was prepared by the architect and signed by the architect, contractor and owner.

Affirming, the Appellate Court held that the arbitrator was the final judge of law and fact. The evidence submitted to the arbitrator supported his finding an earlier date of substantial completion than that certified by owner's architect where the date of substantial completion and the amount of liquidated damages were the precise issues submitted to the arbitrator.

83004   Board of Regents of North Texas State Univ. v. Denton Constr. Co., 652 S.W.2d 588 (Tex. Ct. App. 1983)

III:	A107-1978, Art. 14, Para. 14.3
III:	A107-1978, Art. 18, Para. 18.1
III:	A107-1978, Art. 18, Para. 18.2
III:	A107-1978, Art. 18, Para. 18.3
III:	A117-1979, Art. 18, Para. 18.3
III:	A117-1979, Art. 22, Para. 22.1
III:	A117-1979, Art. 22, Para. 22.2
III:	A117-1979, Art. 22, Para. 22.3
III:	A201-1976, Art. 8, Para. 8.3.1
III:	A201-1976, Art. 12, Para. 12.1.1
III:	A201-1976, Art. 12, Para. 12.1.2
III:	A201-1976, Art. 12, Para. 12.1.3
III:	A201-1976, Art. 12, Para. 12.3

Contractor brought an action against owner for costs resulting from extra work. The trial court entered judgment for contractor and owner appealed. The issue on appeal was whether the contractor's failure to comply with contractual provisions precluded contractor from recovery. The owner asserted that the contractor did not request a change order and did not comply with the provisions requiring notice to the architect, thus causing delays resulting in extra work.

The Appellate Court found that because owner had caused the delays, owner waived its right to require written change orders. Therefore, failure of the contractor to comply

in the use of the more expensive material and in favor of contractor on its claim that architect's decision was arbitrary and wrong. The trial court entered judgment for owner and contractor on the counterclaims against subcontractor and ordered damages to be paid for subcontractor's defective workmanship. The parties cross-appealed.

The agreement between owner and contractor provided that contractor would be fully responsible to owner for the acts and omissions of the subcontractors. The specifications required the use of the specified material or an approved equal, subject to architects approval. They further required that a sample of any material proposed had to be approved by the architect for color, texture and thickness. The General Conditions of the contract provided that any material meeting the specifications could be used if, in the opinion of the architect, it was of "equal substance and function." The scope of the architect's authority was set forth in the General Conditions, which provided that "Architect shall determine the amount, acceptability, and fitness of the several kinds of materials . . ." and that the architect's "decisions shall be final and conclusive."

The Appellate Court reversed, construing the specifications as requiring architect's approval as to color, texture and thickness of any substituted material, and finding that architect's decision not to approve use of the subcontractor's proposed material was binding, final and within the scope of his authority under the contract. Subcontractor had to bear the extra costs of using the more expensive material. The Court adopted the findings of the trial court that subcontractor's work was defective and that owner was entitled to damages and contractor was entitled to indemnification from subcontractor.

83003 Allen v. A & W Contractors, Inc., 433 So. 2d 839 (La. Ct. App.), *cert. denied*, 438 So. 2d 578 (La. 1983)

> I: A101-1977, Art. 3
> I: A107-1978, Art. 2, Para. 2.1
> I: A107-1978, Art. 14, Para. 14.2
> I: A107-1978, Art. 15, Para. 15.3
> I: A111-1978, Art. 4, Para. 4.1
> I: A117-1979, Art. 3, Para. 3.1
> I: A117-1979, Art. 18, Para. 18.2
> I: A117-1979, Art. 19, Para. 19.3
> I: A201-1976, Art. 2, Para. 2.2.16
> I: A201-1976, Art. 8, Para. 8.1.3
> I: A201-1976, Art. 9, Para. 9.8.1
> I: B141-1977, Art. 1, Para. 1.5.15

Owner brought an action against contractor for liquidated damages for delay in completion of the work. Contractor filed a demand for arbitration for the balance due under the contract. The arbitrator ordered owner to pay contractor the balance due. Contractor filed a motion to confirm the award and owner filed a motion to vacate the award on the ground that the arbitrator exceeded his authority by fixing a date of

III:	A107-1978, Art. 11, Para. 11.2
III:	A117-1979, Art. 12, Para. 12.1
III:	A117-1979, Art. 12, Para. 12.3
III:	A117-1979, Art. 12, Para. 12.5
III:	A117-1979, Art. 12, Para. 12.6
III:	A117-1979, Art. 12, Para. 12.7
III:	A117-1979, Art. 14, Para. 14.4
III:	A117-1979, Art. 14, Para. 14.7
III:	A117-1979, Art. 15, Para. 15.2
III:	A201-1976, Art. 2, Para. 2.2.1
III:	A201-1976, Art. 2, Para. 2.2.2
III:	A201-1976, Art. 2, Para. 2.2.7
III:	A201-1976, Art. 2, Para. 2.2.8
III:	A201-1976, Art. 2, Para. 2.2.10
III:	A201-1976, Art. 2, Para. 2.2.13
III:	A201-1976, Art. 2, Para. 2.2.17
III:	A201-1976, Art. 4, Para. 4.3.2
III:	A201-1976, Art. 4, Para. 4.3.3
III:	A201-1976, Art. 4, Para. 4.12.6
III:	A201-1976, Art. 4, Para. 4.12.8
III:	A201-1976, Art. 5, Para. 5.3.1
III:	A401-1978, Art. 11, Para. 11.1.1
III:	A401-1978, Art. 11, Para. 11.2.5
III:	A401-1978, Art. 11, Para. 11.11.1
III:	A401-1978, Art. 11, Para. 11.11.2
III:	A401-1978, Art. 11, Para. 11.11.3
III:	B141-1977, Art. 1, Para. 1.5.3
III:	B141-1977, Art. 1, Para. 1.5.4
III:	B141-1977, Art. 1, Para. 1.5.5
III:	B141-1977, Art. 1, Para. 1.5.9
III:	B141-1977, Art. 1, Para. 1.5.10
III:	B141-1977, Art. 1, Para. 1.5.12

Subcontractor brought an action against contractor to recover extra costs incurred as a result of the architect's order to use a more expensive material, which was called for in the specifications, rather than the material subcontractor proposed to use. Contractor filed a third party complaint against owner alleging that the architect's decision was arbitrary and wrong. Owner counterclaimed against contractor for subcontractor's defective workmanship and contractor counterclaimed against subcontractor for indemnification. The trial court entered judgment in favor of subcontractor for the extras incurred

83001 Acchione & Canuso, Inc. v. Commonwealth Dept. of Transp., 501 Pa. 337, 461 A.2d 765 (1983)

        III: A107-1978, Art. 7, Para. 7.3
        III: A107-1978, Art. 7, Para. 7.4
        III: A107-1978, Art. 18, Para. 18.1
        III: A107-1978, Art. 18, Para. 18.3
        III: A117-1979, Art. 11, Para. 11.3
        III: A117-1979, Art. 11, Para. 11.4
        III: A117-1979, Art. 22, Para. 22.1
        III: A117-1979, Art. 22, Para. 22.3
        III: A201-1976, Art. 1, Para. 1.2.2
        III: A201-1976, Art. 12, Para. 12.1.2
        III: A201-1976, Art. 12, Para. 12.1.3
        III: A201-1976, Art. 12, Para. 12.1.5

Contractor brought an action against owner for increased unit costs due to subcontractor's extra work. The Board of Claims awarded the contractor extra compensation. The owner petitioned for review and the trial court reversed. Contractor appealed.

Subcontractor incurred greater than expected costs in laying conduit for a highway improvement project due to engineer's material misrepresentation in the bid specifications as to the percentage of existing conduit that was reusable. Additional linear footage outside the scope of the contract was required and approved. The contract provided for a set unit price for all extra work unless an increase was approved when the additional work was ordered. Contractor submitted a claim for extra compensation to the owner just prior to completion of the project when contractor became aware of the effect the authorized extra work had on the unit price. The owner denied the claim.

The Pennsylvania Supreme Court found that contractor was justified in relying on the owner's representation where a reasonable site inspection would not have revealed the increased unit cost. The court thus held that the contractor was entitled to the increased costs under a constructive fraud theory.

83002 Acmat v. Daniel O'Connell's Sons, Inc., 17 Mass. App. Ct. 44, 455 N.E.2d 652 (1983), *review denied*, 390 Mass. 1106, 459 N.E.2d 824 (1984)

        III: A107-1978, Art. 8, Para. 8.1
        III: A107-1978, Art. 8, Para. 8.3
        III: A107-1978, Art. 8, Para. 8.5
        III: A107-1978, Art. 8, Para. 8.6
        III: A107-1978, Art. 8, Para. 8.7
        III: A107-1978, Art. 10, Para. 10.4
        III: A107-1978, Art. 10, Para. 10.7

the contractor. The contract contained several provisions showing a "material interest" in payment which could be justified by the owners maintaining good relations with subcontractors, the construction industry and the community. Those provisions included approval of choice of subcontractors and termination of the contract by the owners for failure of the contractor to make prompt payment to the subcontractors. Since the contractor was in default, the judgment creditor and assignee had no greater right to the fund which had been interpleaded into court. Since the owners had disclaimed interest by interpleader, the fund belonged to the other subcontractors.

concluded that architect was not negligent in not providing for temporary connections which were related to "field construction."

The Court held that architect could not be held liable for workers' injuries sustained as a result of unsafe construction procedures for which contractor, and not architect, was responsible for under the contract.

82057 Weeks v. Alabama Elec. Coop., Inc., 419 So. 2d 1381 (Ala. 1982)

        III: A107-1978, Art. 8, Para. 8.3
        III: A117-1979, Art. 12, Para. 12.3
        III: B141-1977, Art. 1, Para. 1.5.5
        III: A201-1976, Art. 2, Para. 2.2.4

Independent contractor's injured employee brought an action against owner, engineer and others for injuries received when a scaffold on which he was standing collapsed. Summary judgment was entered for owner and engineer against worker, and worker appealed.

The Supreme Court of Alabama, in interpreting language in the owner-engineer agreement which provided that "Engineer shall not be required to exercise any actual control over employees of Contractor," held that engineer's responsibility to ensure that the plant was built according to plans and specifications did not include control over the employees of the individual contractors.

82058 Willard, Inc. v. Powertherm Corp., 497 Pa. 628, 444 A.2d 93 (1982)

        II: A107-1978, Art. 11
        II: A107-1978, Art. 15
        II: A117-1979, Art. 15
        II: A117-1979, Art. 19
        II: A201-1976, Art. 5, Para. 5.2
        II: A201-1976, Art. 9, Para. 9.9
        II: A201-1976, Art. 14, Para. 14.2

Contractor brought an action against owners seeking balance of the unpaid contract price. The owners interpleaded the funds into the court. The trial court added all known claimants from the project and other projects, including an attaching judgment creditor and an assignee of the contractor, who asserted prior rights to the fund. The trial court granted a motion for summary judgment on behalf of the claimants who held claims as subcontractors on the project, and the Superior Court reversed.

The Supreme Court of Pennsylvania reversed and reinstated the judgment of the trial court. The Court held that although the time period had expired for filing of mechanic's liens by subcontractors, the owners were entitled to rely on a contract provision which required assurance that subcontractors had been paid before making final payment to

II:	A107-1978, Art. 10, Para. 10.8
II:	A107-1978, Art. 16, Para. 16.1
II:	A117-1979, Art. 12, Para. 12.3
II:	A117-1979, Art. 12, Para. 12.7
II:	A117-1979, Art. 14, Para. 14.1
II:	A117-1979, Art. 14, Para. 14.8
II:	A117-1979, Art. 20, Para. 20.1
I:	A201-1976, Art. 2, Para. 2.2.3
I:	A201-1976, Art. 2, Para. 2.2.4
I:	A201-1976, Art. 2, Para. 2.2.14
I:	A201-1976, Art. 4, Para. 4.3.1
I:	A201-1976, Art. 4, Para. 4.12.5
I:	A201-1976, Art. 10, Para. 10.1.1
I:	A201-1976, Art. 10, Para. 10.2.1
I:	A201-1976, Art. 10, Para. 10.2.6

The estates of deceased workers and injured worker brought actions against the architect, owner and fabricator of metal beams which collapsed during assembly. The case was tried to a jury trial with the architect as the sole defendant, the other defendants having been released by dismissals and summary judgments. At issue was the architect's responsibility for insuring that the contractor employ safe methods and procedures in performing his work. The District Court directed a verdict for the architect. The estates and injured worker appealed.

The Appellate Court, in reversing the District Court, held that architect did owe a duty to the workers because architect "undertook to supervise the construction project." The architect appealed. The issue before the Oklahoma Supreme Court was whether the architect who designed the building was responsible for ensuring that contractor employ safe methods and procedures in performing the work.

The Supreme Court held that architect was liable only for failure to exercise reasonable care and professional skill in preparing and executing the plans according to the contract. The owner-contractor agreement included American Institute of Architects General Conditions of the Contract for Construction, Document A201, 1976 edition. Paragraph 4.3.1 provided that contractor was to supervise the work, being "solely responsible for all construction means, methods, techniques, and sequences and procedures." Although the architect was to periodically visit the site, paragraph 2.2.3 provided that he was not required to make "exhaustive or continuous on-site inspections to check the quality or quantity of the work." The provision goes on to exclude from the architects responsibilities those which are outlined in paragraph 4.3.1 as belonging solely to the contractor. Paragraph 10.1 assigns all responsibility for safety precautions and programs to the contractor.

The Court also reviewed the shop drawing provisions, which clearly provided that contractor, not architect, was to determine and verify all field construction criteria, and

arbitration; and (4) the contractor had waived its claim for extra compensation by accepting final payment.

The Court of Appeals reversed summary judgment for the owner and held that (1) notice for extra compensation for delay was timely, even though given more than 20 days after the original completion date because the construction delay did not occur on a certain date; (2) demanding completion of extra work without issuing a change order after a written request had been made for extra compensation waived the requirement for a written change order; (3) arbitration was not required unless demanded by one of the parties; and (4) final payment waived all claims by contractor against the owner except unsettled claims previously set forth in writing.

82055   Union County School Dist. v. Valley Inland Pacific Constructors, Inc., 59 Or. App. 602, 652 P.2d 349 (1982)

II:	A107-1966, Art. 11, Para. 11.10
II:	A107-1966, Art. 15
II:	A107-1966, Art. 17, Para. 17.4
I:	A201-1970, Art. 4, Para. 4.18
I:	A201-1970, Art. 7, Para. 7.10.1
I:	A201-1970, Art. 7, Para. 7.10.2
I:	A201-1970, Art. 9, Para. 9.7.5
I:	A201-1970, Art. 9, Para. 9.7.6

Contractor demanded arbitration against owner claiming delay and repair costs and indemnification for death and personal injury settlements which arose when the structure being erected collapsed. The owner sought a declaratory judgment that it was not required to arbitrate. At issue was whether (1) final payment precluded arbitration; (2) the contract provided for arbitration of a dispute of this type; (3) the arbitration demand was timely; and (4) the claim was "frivolous" because the contractor was required to indemnify the owner for the claims.

The Court of Appeals reversed in part and affirmed in part judgment for the owner holding that (1) the arbitrator must determine what constitutes final payment and whether final payment bars further claims; (2) the arbitration clause in the contract was sufficiently general to cover all disputes between the parties unless expressly excluded by other provisions in the contract; (3) the arbitrator must determine what is a reasonable time for requesting arbitration; and (4) the indemnity clause did not bar arbitration because the two provisions were not directly related.

82056   Waggoner v. W & W Steel Co., 657 P.2d 147 (Okla. 1982)

II:	A107-1978, Art. 8, Para. 8.3
II:	A107-1978, Art. 8, Para. 8.7
II:	A107-1978, Art. 10, Para. 10.1

II:	A107-1978, Art. 7, Para. 7.1
I:	A111-1978, Art. 1, Para. 1.1
I:	A111-1978, Art. 16, Para. 16.2
II:	A117-1979, Art. 10, Para. 10.2
II:	A117-1979, Art. 11. Para. 11.1
I:	A201-1976, Art. 1, Para. 1.1.1
I:	A201-1976, Art. 1, Para. 1.1.2

Contractor brought an action against owner to recover the balance due under the contract, and the owner counterclaimed alleging defective construction. At issue was whether certain roofing specifications were properly admitted as evidence. The parties had considered two sets of roofing specifications before construction began, but had failed to denote which specification was incorporated into the contract.

On appeal from judgment for contractor, the Nevada Supreme Court held that the contract's reference to incorporated "specifications" was vague and that extrinsic evidence was permissible to establish which specifications were included in the contract when none were expressly listed.

82053 (UNASSIGNED)

82054 Triangle Air Conditioning, Inc. v. Caswell County Bd. of Educ., 57 N.C. App. 482, 291 S.E.2d 808, *petition for review denied,* 306 N.C. 564, 294 S.E.2d 376 (1982)

II:	A107-1966, Art. 9, Para. 9.5
II:	A107-1966, Art. 15
II:	A107-1966, Art. 17, Para. 17.4
II:	A107-1966, Art. 22, Para. 22.1
II:	A107-1966, Art. 22, Para. 22.2
I:	A201-1970, Art. 2, Para. 2.2.7
I:	A201-1970, Art. 2, Para. 2.2.10
I:	A201-1970, Art. 2, Para. 2.2.14
I:	A201-1970, Art. 7, Para. 7.10.1
I:	A201-1970, Art. 7, Para. 7.10.2
I:	A201-1970, Art. 9, Para. 9.7.6
I:	A201-1970, Art. 12, Para. 12.1.1
I:	A201-1970, Art. 12, Para. 12.1.2
I:	A201-1970, Art. 12, Para. 12.2.1

Contractor brought an action against owner for delay damages. At issue was whether (1) proper notice had been given by the contractor in requesting additional compensation; (2) a written change order was required for extra work; (3) the contract required

construed in accordance with Tennessee law. Owner made final payment to contractor and executed a release which provided that certain claims of contractor were reserved.

Contractor filed a demand for arbitration against owner for additional expenses in accordance with the arbitration provision. Owner responded that it had elected to revoke the agreement to arbitrate future disputes. Owner obtained a temporary restraining order staying the arbitration proceedings pending judicial determination of its right to revoke the arbitration agreement. Contractor filed a motion to dissolve the temporary restraining order and to stay the judicial proceedings pending arbitration. The Chancellor issued a memorandum opinion granting contractor's motion, and owner appealed. The Appellate Court reversed the Chancellor's decree, and contractor appealed.

At issue on appeal to the Tennessee Supreme Court was whether a contractual provision to arbitrate future disputes was revocable at will. The Court found that the Federal Arbitration Act, which made arbitration agreements in interstate commerce valid and enforceable, governed and ordered that arbitration proceedings pursuant to the contract be commenced.

82051   Tirante v. Gulf State Utils. Co., 412 So. 2d 128 (La. Ct. App.), *cert. denied*, 414 So. 2d 389 (La. 1982)

I: A201-1970, Art. 4, Para. 4.18.1

Subcontractor's injured employee brought a negligence action against owner, contractor, architect and consulting engineer. At the close of the injured worker's case, the trial court granted owner's, contractor's, architect's and consulting engineer's motions for directed verdict and injured worker appealed. Turning to a third party demand for indemnity filed by owner and architect against contractor, the trial court entered judgment for contractor, and owner appealed to enforce the indemnification provision in the agreement between contractor and owner.

At issue on the owner's appeal was whether the indemnification clause in Paragraph 4.18.1 of the American Institute of Architects General Conditions of the Contract for Construction, Document A201, 1970 edition, which was set forth in the Bid, was part of the agreement between the owner and contractor. A second hold harmless clause appeared in the Supplementary General Conditions which were made part of the contract.

The Appellate Court held that the claims of owner and architect were properly dismissed because the indemnification provisions were ambiguous and it was unclear whether the second hold harmless clause was to supplement and amend or replace Paragraph 4.18.1.

82052   Trans Western Leasing Corp. v. Corrao Constr. Co., 98 Nev. 445, 652 P.2d 1181 (1982)

II: A101-1977, Art. 1
II: A101-1977, Art. 7, Para. 7.2
II: A107-1978, Art. 6, Para. 6.1

appeal that when owner took possession of the bins and started using them, owner waived any alleged defects.

The Supreme Court of Nebraska upheld the trial court's finding that contractor failed to perform the contract in a good and workmanlike manner since he did not construct adequate footings beneath the bins. Contractor allegation that local custom and usage did not require installation of footings was not considered by the Court because contractor never pleaded nor alleged this issue. The Court held that owner, by accepting the bins and using them, was not precluded from claiming damages because at the time owner accepted the bins he was not aware that the footings had not been properly constructed.

82049 Stillwater Leased Housing Assocs. v. Kraus-Anderson Constr. Co., 319 N.W.2d 424 (Minn. 1982)

        II: A107-1978, Art. 13, Para. 13.2
        II: A117-1979, Art. 17, Para. 17.2
        II: A201-1976, Art. 7, Para. 7.9.1

After contracting with owner to construct an apartment building, contractor filed a demand for arbitration against owner seeking damages resulting from differing site conditions in accordance with an arbitration provision similar to Paragraph 7.9.1 of the American Institute of Architects General Conditions of the Contract for Construction, Document A201, 1976 edition, but excluding the consolidation/joinder language. Owner's agreement with its architect also contained an arbitration provision, but owner's contract with the engineer did not include such a provision.

In response to the arbitration demand, owner filed a motion in District Court, pursuant to a Minnesota statute, for a stay of arbitration, arguing that the contractor's claim was not within the scope of the agreement and the District Court had discretion to stay arbitration in order to consolidate related claims. The District Court, exercising its discretion, stayed the arbitration and contractor appealed.

The Supreme Court of Minnesota held that arbitration should be compelled in light of the state policy favoring arbitration when the dispute was clearly within the scope of the provision.

82050 Tennessee River Pulp & Paper Co. v. Eichleay Corp., 637 S.W.2d 853 (Tenn. 1982)

        III: A107-1966, Art. 15
        II: A201-1970, Art. 7, Para. 7.1.1
        II: A201-1970, Art. 7, Para. 7.10.1

Owner and contractor entered into an agreement to expand owner's production facilities. The contract contained a broad form arbitration provision similar to Paragraph 7.10.1 of the American Institute of Architects General Conditions of the Contract for Construction, Document A201, 1970 edition, and also provided that the contract would be

82047 S & M Constructors v. City of Columbus, 70 Ohio St. 2d 69, 434 N.E.2d 1349 (1982)

    III: A201-1976, Art. 1, Para. 1.1.1
    III: A201-1976, Art. 12, Para. 12.2

Contractor brought an action against owner seeking damages for additional costs incurred in completing a sewer construction project. Owner impleaded engineer as a third-party defendant to indemnify it against liability arising out of engineer's subsurface report. The trial court entered judgment for owner, and engineer and contractor appealed. The Appellate Court affirmed, and contractor appealed arguing that the differing site conditions amounted to misrepresentation.

At issue was whether owner was liable for the differing subsurface conditions. The owner-contractor agreement provided that, "Said borings, test excavations, and other subsurface investigations, if any, are incomplete, are not a part of the contract documents, and are not warranted to show the actual subsurface conditions." Furthermore, the contractor agreed that he would not make a claim against the owner or engineer if the actual subsurface conditions differed from the borings.

The Supreme Court of Ohio upheld the trial court's finding that there was no evidence of inaccuracies in the soil reports, and held that owner had contractually disclaimed its liability to contractor for additional expenses resulting from differences between the actual conditions and the soil report.

82048 Smith v. Erftmier, 210 Neb. 486, 315 N.W.2d 445 (1982)

    II: A107-1978, Art. 10, Para. 10.4
    II: A107-1978, Art. 15, Para. 15.5
    II: A117-1979, Art. 14, Para. 14.4
    II: A117-1979, Art. 19, Para. 19.5
    I: A201-1976, Art. 4, Para. 4.5.1
    II: A201-1976, Art. 9, Para. 9.9.4

Contractor brought an action against owner for the balance due under a contract for the construction of a grain-drying and storage complex. Owner filed a counterclaim alleging that contractor failed to construct the bins in a good and workmanlike manner and in accordance with the contract. The trial court entered judgment for owner and contractor appealed.

The owner and contractor entered into the American Institute of Architects Standard Form of Agreement Between Owner and Contractor, Document A101, 1977 edition. Attached to the contract was the American Institute of Architects General Conditions of the Contract for Construction, Document A201, 1976 edition, which provided that contractor warranted to owner that "all work will be of good quality, free from faults and defects and in conformance with the Contract Documents." Contractor argued on

II:	A107-1978, Art. 3, Para. 3.1
II:	A107-1978, Art. 3, Para. 3.2
II:	A107-1978, Art. 14, Para. 14.1
II:	A107-1978, Art. 14, Para. 14.2
I:	A201-1976, Art. 8, Para. 8.1.3
I:	A201-1976, Art. 8, Para. 8.2.1

Contractor brought an action against owner to recover increased balance due under the contract resulting from numerous change orders and to recover consequential damages caused by the loss of contractor's line of credit and its ability to obtain bonding. At issue was whether the owner's retention of the funds constituted a breach and, if so, to what damages the contractor was entitled under the contract.

According to the terms of the owner-contractor agreement, contractor was to construct the building for a fixed sum. The contract provided that the building was to be substantially completed by an agreed upon date. The General Conditions also contained a time of essence provision.

Holding that the owner's conduct was improper and constituted a breach of contract because the building could have been occupied for its intended purpose on the date owner originally planned to occupy the building, the Supreme Court of New Hampshire affirmed an award of direct damages for the contractor. Reversing, however, an additional award of consequential damages, the Court held such award improper because consequential damages were not reasonably foreseeable at the time the parties entered into the agreement.

82046 Shamokin Area School Auth. v. Farfield Co., 308 Pa. Super. 271, 454 A.2d 126 (1982)

II:	A107-1966, Art. 15
I:	A201-1970, Art. 7, Para 7.10.1
I:	A201-1970, Art. 7, Para. 7.10.2
I:	A201-1970, Art. 7, Para. 7.10.3

Contractor filed a demand for arbitration against owner in accordance with the arbitration provision in the owner-contractor agreement which incorporated the American Institute of Architects General Conditions of the Contract for Construction, Document A201, 1970 edition, Paragraph 7.10.1. Owner commenced an action in equity seeking to enjoin arbitration, and contractor moved to compel arbitration and stay the equity suit. The trial court denied contractor's motion and contractor appealed.

The Appellate Court held that where the owner-contractor agreement contained a broad form arbitration provision, procedural questions were reserved for the arbitrators. Furthermore, Paragraph 7.10.3 of the General Conditions did not limit owner's obligation to arbitrate to the period of performance.

Court of Appeals held that the architect was not negligent, nor was the architect liable for any misrepresentation.

82042 Reed, Wible & Brown, Inc. v. Mahogany Run Dev. Corp., 550 F. Supp. 1095 (D.V.I. 1982)

       III: A107-1978, Art. 13, Para. 13.2
       III: A107-1978, Art. 15, Para. 15.5
       III: A117-1979, Art. 17, Para. 17.2
       III: A117-1979, Art. 19, Para. 19.5
       III: A201-1976, Art. 7, Para. 7.9.1
       III: A201-1976, Art. 9, Para. 9.9.5

Contractor sued owner for specific performance under a release, and contractor moved for partial summary judgment and an order fixing the scope of arbitration. At issue was whether the release was binding. The District Court found the release valid and held that there was no arbitrable dispute except as to issues specified in the release.

82043 (UNASSIGNED)

82044 R. Zoppo Co. v. City of Manchester, 122 N.H. 1109, 453 A.2d 1311 (1982)

       III: B141-1977, Art. 1, Para. 1.
       III: B141-1977, Art. 1, Para. 1.3

Contractor brought an action against owner to recover for extra work not included in the specifications. Owner sought indemnity from the architect. The trial court entered judgment in favor of contractor and granted owner's claim for indemnification. Owner and architect appealed.

In interpreting the indemnity provision in the owner-architect agreement, the Supreme Court of New Hampshire found that the architect was obligated to provide plans, specifications and contract documents, as well as its expertise, and would hold the owner harmless for all suits and claims arising out of or in consequence of its acts or failure to act. The Court held that contractor's successful claim against owner was attributable to architect's failure in the preparation and contents of the specifications. Therefore, the architect was properly required to indemnify the owner.

82045 Salem Eng'g & Constr. Corp. v. Londonderry School Dist., 122 N.H. 379, 445 A.2d 1091 (1982)

       I: A101-1977, Art. 3
       I: A101-1977, Art. 4
       II: A107-1978, Art. 2, Para. 2.1

(2) the arbitration provision in the contract was so vague that subcontractor could not be held to the method of dispute resolution provided by that paragraph.

The relevant subcontract provisions stated that subcontractor had examined the contract and all plans and specifications, including the General and Special Conditions, and agreed to be bound by the terms. The subcontract also provided that any disputes concerning questions of fact would be decided by the contractor, appealed to the owner, and if owner did not have jurisdiction over the dispute, it would be arbitrated. Further, the General Conditions provided that owner assumed the risk of loss of materials delivered to the site.

The Appellate Court, in construing the various contract provisions, found that arbitration was the appropriate method of dispute resolution with regard to the claim for the cost of replacing materials stolen from the job site where the owner bore the contractual risk and could not determine its own negligence. However, the claim for reimbursement of additional expenses, which was a question of fact, should have been decided by the owner.

82041   Ramey Constr. Co. v. Apache Tribe of Mescalero Reservation, 673 F.2d 315 (10th Cir. 1982)

> III: A107-1978, Art. 8, Para. 8.1
> III: A107-1978, Art. 8, Para. 8.3
> III: A117-1979, Art. 12, Para. 12.1
> III: A117-1979, Art. 12, Para. 12.3
> III: A201-1976, Art. 2, Para. 2.2.2
> III: A201-1976, Art. 2, Para. 2.2.3
> III: A201-1976, Art. 2, Para. 2.2.4
> III: B141-1977, Art. 1, Para. 1.5.4
> III: B141-1977, Art. 1, Para. 1.5.5
> III: B141-1977, Art. 1, Para. 1.5.12

Contractor brought an action against owner to recover retainage, alleging that the architect and owner had made certain negligent misrepresentations and that the architect had negligently performed its project design and management duties. The District Court, on remand, concluded that the architect was not guilty of negligent misrepresentation. The contractor appealed, arguing that the architect was responsible for the overall management and coordination of the project and was liable for all damages caused by its failure to perform these duties.

The Court of Appeals adopted the trial court's findings that (1) the architect's duties of coordination and management under the contract were limited to "surveillance of project construction to assure compliance with plans, specifications and other contract documents"; (2) although architect had the authority to give orders and directions at the worksite, it had no power to ensure the performance of the various contractors; and (3) the architect had fulfilled the limited duties of coordination specified in the contract. The owner paid the balance due on the contract, except for the sales tax, which he claimed the contractor was contractually bound to pay.

The Court of Appeals reversed the lower court's ruling for the owner and held that the contractual provision that required the contractor to pay all taxes meant that the contractor was to collect the tax from the owner and pay it to the state rather than pay the tax out of the contract price.

82039 Post Tensioned Eng'g Corp. v. Fairways Plaza Assocs., 412 So. 2d 871 (Fla. Dist. Ct. App.), *petition for review denied sub nom.* Fairways Plaza Assocs. v. Commercial Constr. Corp., 419 So. 2d 1197 (Fla. 1982), *and appeal after remand,* Post Tensioned Eng'g Corp. v. Fairways Plaza Assocs., 429 So. 2d 1212 (Fla. Dist. Ct. App. 1983)

II:	A107-1978,	Art. 13, Para. 13.2
II:	A117-1979,	Art. 17, Para. 17.2
II:	A201-1976,	Art. 7, Para. 7.9.1

Owner brought an action against contractor, and contractor moved to compel arbitration pursuant to the arbitration provision contained in the owner-contractor agreement. The trial court denied contractor's motion and a writ of certiorari was granted.

The Appellate Court held that (1) the arbitration clause in contract was valid because owner did not challenge the making of the contract or the making of the provision to arbitrate; (2) the contractor did not waive its right to compel arbitration with owner by failing to bind its subcontractors to arbitration, as required by the agreement between owner and contractor, because the failure to bind was a breach of the agreement subject to arbitration; (3) contractor's right to compel arbitration was not made ineffective by the owner's allegation of fraud and request for equitable relief; and (4) the fact that owner had intended to sue others with whom it had no agreement to arbitrate, did not justify denial of contractor's motion to compel arbitration because there was a strong public policy favoring arbitration.

82040 Premier Elec. Constr. Co. v. Ragnar Benson, Inc., 111 Ill. App. 3d 855, 65 Ill. Dec. 490, 444 N.E.2d 726 (1982)

III:	A401-1978,	Art. 1, Para. 1.1
III:	A401-1978,	Art. 1, Para. 1.2
III:	A401-1978,	Art. 11, Para. 11.1.1
III:	A401-1978,	Art. 13, Para. 13.1

Subcontractor brought an action against contractor for extras not included in the subcontract. Contractor moved to dismiss subcontractor's complaint and to compel arbitration. The trial court held that it had no jurisdiction over the matter and dismissed subcontractor's complaint with prejudice. On appeal, the subcontractor argued that (1) the trial court erred in holding that the disputes were to be resolved by arbitration, and

Contractor brought an action against owner for delay damages. Owner filed a motion for partial summary judgment, claiming that the contractor had waived the claims. The Supreme Court, Trial Term, denied the owner's motion.

The Supreme Court, Appellate Division, reversed and held that the waiver provision, which stated that no claims would be made against the owner based on delays to that date, was clear and unambiguous.

[*Editor's Note:* For related proceeding, *see* case number 85030 *infra.*]

82037　　Pennsylvania Dept. of Gen. Servs. v. G. Weinberger Co., 65 Pa. Commw. 201, 441 A.2d 1341 (1982)

　　　　II:　　A107-1966, Art. 11, Para. 11.10
　　　　II:　　A107-1966, Art. 18
　　　　I:　　 A201-1970, Art. 4, Para. 4.1
　　　　I:　　 A201-1970, Art. 10, Para. 10.2.4
　　　　II:　　A401-1967, Art. 11, Para. 11.18
　　　　II:　　A401-1967, Art. 11, Para. 11.20

Contractor brought an action against owner for payments withheld, and subcontractor intervened for payments withheld by contractor. Owner cross-claimed against architect for indemnification based on architect's failure to indicate certain cable on the contract drawings. Owner appealed from a decision by the Board of Claims for contractor, subcontractor and architect.

The subcontract incorporated by reference Paragraphs 10.2.4 and 4.1 of the American Institute of Architects General Conditions of the Contract for Construction, Document A201, 1970 edition, which stated that subcontractor would indemnify architect and owner for subcontractor's negligence, and contractor, at his own expense, would repair, replace and maintain all damaged utilities during the course of construction.

The Appellate Court held that the architect was not liable to contractor or owner because the architect had no duty to depict existing utilities on the plans. Furthermore, the subcontractor was entitled to intervene in the action brought by contractor against owner since the proceeding affected the likelihood of subcontractor receiving money withheld by contractor. Finally, the evidence supported the court's conclusion that the owner was not entitled to be indemnified by the contractor or subcontractor because the owner had not proved that the contractor or subcontractor were negligent.

82038　　Pomeroy v. Anderson, 32 Wash. App. 781, 649 P.2d 855 (1982)

　　　　I:　　 A107-1978, Art. 10, Para. 10.5
　　　　I:　　 A117-1979, Art. 14, Para. 14.5
　　　　II:　　A201-1976, Art. 4, Para. 4.6.1

Contractor brought an action against owner to collect the balance due on a contract for remodeling. At issue was whether the contract price included state sales tax. The

of creating a security interest for a debt. The owner-contractor agreement incorporated the American Institute of Architects General Conditions of the Contract for Construction, Document A201, 1976 edition, Paragraph 7.2.1, which prohibited assignment. The subcontract contained a provision which prohibited assignment by the subcontractor "without prior written approval from the contractor." Subcontractor assigned the contract to assignee and notice was given to contractor who noted thereon "received but not accepted."

The Supreme Court of Mississippi held that "if [the subcontractor] made an assignment . . . of its right to payment for services rendered under [the subcontract] . . . for the purpose of creating a security interest under chapter 9 of the Mississippi Uniform Commercial Code, then any contractual prohibition against such assignment was ineffective."

82035   Mississippi Coast Coliseum Comm'n v. Stuart Constr. Co., 417 So. 2d 541 (Miss. 1982)

>   II: A107-1966, Art. 9, Para. 9.6
>   I: A201-1967, Art. 2, Para. 2.2.9
>   I: A201-1967, Art. 13, Para. 13.3.1
>   II: B131-1967, Art. 1, Para. 1.1.17

Contractor brought an action against owner to recover a portion of the contract price alleged to have been wrongfully withheld from contractor. The jury returned a verdict in favor of owner. Thereafter, the trial court granted contractor's motion for judgment notwithstanding verdict, and owner appealed seeking reinstatement of the jury verdict.

The contract provided that all exposed concrete was to be "architecturally finished" and matching in color. An otherwise structurally sound portion of the concourse did not match in color. The architect recommended that owner accept the section with certain warranties. Instead, owner withheld payment pursuant to the provisions of Paragraph 13.3.1 of the American Institute of Architects General Conditions of the Contract for Construction, Document A201, 1967 edition. In setting aside the jury verdict, the trial judge found that the "discoloration" was a matter of artistic effect pursuant to Paragraph 2.2.9 of the American Institute of Architects Conditions of the Contract for Construction, Document A201, 1967 edition.

The Supreme Court of Mississippi reinstated the jury verdict, holding that whether the architect unequivocally accepted the discolored portion or did so conditionally was a question for the jury in resolving the issue of whether Paragraph 2.2.9 was operative.

82036   Naclerio Contracting Co. v. EPA, 86 A.D.2d 793, 447 N.Y.S.2d 4, *appeal dismissed*, 56 N.Y.2d 712, 451 N.Y.S.2d 736, 436 N.E.2d 1338 (1982)

>   III: A201-1976, Art. 7, Para. 7.6
>   III: A201-1976, Art. 8, Para. 8.3

provided that the AAA would determine the location of arbitration when the location was in dispute, the Court stated that Kansas could be chosen by the AAA as the site of arbitration.

82033   Mathis v. Daines, 196 Mont. 252, 639 P.2d 503 (1982)

        II: A401-1978, Art. 11

Subcontractor brought an action against contractor to recover for extra work done. The trial court found for the contractor, and the subcontractor appealed.

Affirming, the Supreme Court of Montana held that where the contract provided that all extra work be approved by written change order, a procedure which the subcontractor did not follow, the fact that the contractor subsequently paid for a portion of that extra work did not establish a waiver of the written change order provision for all of the extra work. There was no evidence that the contractor had voluntarily relinquished his right to object to extra work done without written approval.

82034   Mississippi Bank v. Nickles & Wells Constr. Co., 421 So. 2d 1056 (Miss. 1982)

        I: A101-1977, Art. 1
        I: A101-1977, Art. 7, Para. 7.2
        II: A107-1978, Art. 6, Para. 6.1
        II: A107-1978, Art. 7, Para. 7.1
        II: A107-1978, Art. 11, Para. 11.2
        I: A111-1978, Art. 1, Para. 1.1
        I: A111-1978, Art. 16, Para. 16.2
        II: A117-1979, Art. 10, Para. 10.2
        II: A117-1979, Art. 11, Para. 11.2
        II: A117-1979, Art. 15, Para. 15.2
        I: A201-1976, Art. 1, Para. 1.1.1
        I: A201-1976, Art. 1, Para. 1.1.2
        I: A201-1976, Art. 5, Para. 5.3.1
        I: A201-1976, Art. 7, Para. 7.2.1
        I: A401-1978, Art. 1, Para. 1.1
        I: A401-1978, Art. 11, Para. 11.1.2

Assignee brought an action against contractor and its surety for progress payments due subcontractor in the amount of the assignment. Assignee appealed from a dismissal of its complaint. At issue on appeal was whether the prohibition against assignment in the American Institute of Architects standard form construction contracts was effective under the state's Uniform Commercial Code to prevent an assignment for the purpose

I:	A117-1979, Art. 4, Para. 4.3
I:	A117-1979, Art. 6, Para. 6.1.10
I:	A117-1979, Art. 9, Para. 9.2
I:	A201-1976, Art. 7, Para. 7.8.1

Owner brought an action against contractor for failure to complete performance, and the contractor counterclaimed for final payment. The trial court found that the contract was not the complete agreement of the parties, and that the parties had intended a cost-plus-profit contract without a guaranteed maximum cost. At issue on appeal by the owner was the sufficiency of the evidence to support the trial court's findings.

The Nevada Supreme Court found that there was substantial evidence to support the trial court's finding that the parties intended a cost-plus-profit contract without a guaranteed maximum cost. In addition, the Court found that attorneys' fees were properly included in damages for the contractor because they were expressly provided for in the contract. An award of prejudgment interest at the statutory interest rate was also upheld.

82032 L.R. Foy Constr. Co. v. Dean L. Dauley & Waldrof Assocs., 547 F. Supp. 166 (D. Kan. 1982)

I:	A101-1977, Art. 1
I:	A101-1977, Art. 7, Para. 7.2
II:	A107-1978, Art. 6, Para. 6.1
II:	A107-1978, Art. 7, Para. 7.1
II:	A107-1978, Art. 13, Para. 13.2
II:	A117-1979, Art. 17, Para. 17.2
I:	A201-1976, Art. 1, Para. 1.2.1
I:	A201-1976, Art. 4, Para. 4.2.1
I:	A201-1976, Art. 7, Para. 7.9.1

Contractor brought an action against owner to compel arbitration of disputes concerning three construction contracts. The contracts, for stores to be built in various states, were the American Institute of Architects Standard Form of Agreement Between Owner and Contractor, Document A101, 1977 edition, which incorporated the provisions of the American Institute of Architects General Conditions of the Contract for Construction, Document 201, 1976 edition. The District Court found that two of the contracts contained valid arbitration provisions which provided for arbitration in accordance with the Construction Industry Arbitration Rules of the American Arbitration Association (AAA). The third contract contained no provision for arbitration because the clause was deleted from the contract prior to execution.

In construing the arbitration clauses in the two contracts containing such provisions, the Court held that while each respective "contract [did] not state specifically that arbitration [was] to be held in Kansas, it [did] provide that arbitration [was] to be in accordance with the Construction Industry Arbitration Rules of the AAA." Noting that these rules

Subcontractor brought an action against contractor and owner for amounts due under the contract. Owner counterclaimed against subcontractor and cross-claimed against contractor. Contractor and owner subsequently entered into arbitration pursuant to a contract provision and damages were awarded to the contractor. Confirmation of the arbitration award was consolidated with the other actions, and the trial court entered judgment on the award before decision of the other claims. The owner appealed and the Court of Appeals reversed, holding that all claims had to be resolved before entry of a final judgment. Contractor appealed.

The Supreme Court of Colorado reversed. The Court held that the Uniform Arbitration Act required entry of judgment on the award of an arbitrator unless proper grounds for modification, correction, or vacation of award were presented. Furthermore, the existence of cross-claim and the consolidation of the cases did not change or limit the mandate of the Uniform Arbitration Act. Because the Act "authorize [d] a summary procedure to effectuate the public policy in favor of arbitration," the Court held that the entry of judgment prior to the settlement of other claims was valid.

82030   Kelso-Burnett Co. v. Zeus Dev. Corp., 107 Ill. App. 3d 34, 62 Ill. Dec. 789, 437 N.E.2d 26 (1982)

   II: A107-1966, Art. 15
   II: A201-1970, Art. 7, Para. 7.10
   II: A401-1967, Art. 13

Subcontractor brought an action against contractor to foreclose mechanics' lien. The trial court denied contractor's motion to stay proceedings and compel arbitration, and contractor appealed.

The subcontract between the parties included an arbitration provision which provided that "all claims, disputes, and other matters in question arising out of, or relating to, this sub-contract agreement or a default hereunder shall be arbitrated in mode and manner as set forth in Paragraph 7.10 of the latest edition of General Conditions of Contracts for Construction, AIA document A-201.11."

Reversing and remanding, the Appellate Court found that once a valid arbitration agreement was established, the Court had no discretion and had to order arbitration. The Court held that there was insufficient evidence to sustain the trial court's order denying contractor's motion to stay foreclosure pending arbitration.

82031   Laughlin Recreational Enters., Inc. v. Zab Dev. Co., 98 Nev. 285, 646 P.2d 555 (1982)

   I: A111-1978, Art. 5, Para. 5.1
   I: A111-1978, Art. 5, Para. 5.2
   I: A111-1978, Art. 8, Para. 8.1.16
   I: A111-1978, Art. 14, Para. 14.3

limitations period had expired. Since the trial court had proceeded upon the erroneous conclusion that the contract between contractor and owner was a cost plus contract without a guaranteed maximum price, the Court reversed and remanded for a new trial.

82028 Jones v. City of Logansport, 436 N.E.2d 1138 (Ind. Ct. App.), *reh'g denied*, 439 N.E.2d 666 (Ind. Ct. App. 1982)

III:	A107-1978, Art. 8, Para. 8.3	
III:	A107-1978, Art. 10, Para. 10.1	
III:	A107-1978, Art. 16, Para. 16.1	
III:	A117-1979, Art. 12, Para. 12.3	
III:	A117-1979, Art. 14, Para. 14.1	
III:	A117-1979, Art. 20, Para. 20.1	
III:	A201-1976, Art. 2, Para. 2.2.3	
III:	A201-1976, Art. 2, Para. 2.2.4	
III:	A201-1976, Art. 4, Para. 4.3.1	
III:	A201-1976, Art. 10, Para. 10.1.1	
III:	A201-1976, Art. 10, Para. 10.2.1	
III:	A201-1976, Art. 10, Para. 10.2.5	
III:	B141-1977, Art. 1, Para. 1.5.4	
III:	B141-1977, Art. 1, Para. 1.5.5	

Subcontractor's employee brought an action against owner and contractor for damages resulting from injuries he suffered as a result of their negligence. At issue was whether, pursuant to the provisions of the agreement between owner and its authorized representative, the authorized representative was responsible for the safety of subcontractor's employees.

Reading the contract as a whole, the Appellate Court held that the owner's representative was obligated to reduce incidences of defective construction, but was not required to make the premises safe and did not have responsibility for the means and methods of contraction.

The Court further held that the trial court erroneously rejected injured worker's jury instruction, which was supported by the evidence, that contractor had a nondelegable duty to injured worker under its contract with owner to provide subcontractor's employees with a safe place to work.

82029 Judd Constr. Co. v. Evans Joint Venture, 642 P.2d 922 (Colo. 1982)

I:	A107-1978, Art. 13	
I:	A117-1979, Art. 17	
I:	A201-1976, Art. 7, Para. 7.9	

82026   *In re* King Enters., 678 F.2d 73 (8th Cir. 1982)

      III: A107-1978, Art. 18, Para. 18.1
      III: A117-1979, Art. 22, Para. 22.1
      III: A201-1976, Art. 12, Para. 12.1.1
      III: A201-1976, Art. 12, Para. 12.4.1

A bankrupt construction company brought an action against owner for costs not evidenced by written change orders. The Bankruptcy Court entered judgment for contractor and owner appealed. The District Court affirmed and owner appealed.

The contract provided that any changes in the work to be performed would be by written change order. During the course of construction, numerous changes were made on oral directives and only two written change orders were executed.

The Court of Appeals held that owner, by its course of conduct in issuing oral change orders which were never reduced to writing, waived the contract provision requiring written change orders.

82027   John Goffredo & Sons, Inc. v. S.M.G. Corp., 300 Pa. Super. 112, 446 A.2d 255 (1982)

      I: A111-1978, Art. 5, Para. 5.1
      I: A111-1967, Art. 6, Para. 6.1
      I: A111-1967, Art. 6, Para. 6.2
      I: A111-1967, Art. 8, Para. 8.1
      I: A111-1967, Art. 8, Para. 8.2
      I: A111-1978, Art. 9, Para. 9.1.8
      II: A201-1967, Art. 12, Para. 12.1.1
      II: A201-1967, Art. 12, Para. 12.1.2
      II: A201-1967, Art. 12, Para. 12.2.1

Contractor brought an action against owner for costs in excess of the guaranteed maximum provided for in the owner-contractor agreement. The trial court entered judgment in favor of contractor and owner appealed. At issue on appeal was whether the trial judge erred in allowing contractor, after the statute of limitations had run, to amend the complaint to assert the existence of a subsequent oral agreement.

Article 6 of the contract provided that the guaranteed maximum price could be increased or decreased as provided in Article 8, which stated that owner could make changes in accordance with Article 12 of the General Conditions. Article 12 provided that owner's changes had to be made by change order and that such changes would not constitute waiver of the guaranteed maximum price provision.

The Appellate Court held that the trial court erred in allowing contractor to amend its complaint to assert that the written contract was modified by a subsequent oral agreement that waived the contract's guaranteed maximum price provision after the

and injunctive relief and for a stay of arbitration claiming that (1) the contract did not require arbitration; (2) the contract violated state law in requiring disputes to be submitted to the architect as an arbitrator; and (3) the contractor waived his right to arbitrate by filing a material lien.

The owner-contractor agreement incorporated the American Institute of Architects General Conditions of the Contract for Construction, Document No. A201, 1976 edition, specifically Paragraph 7.9.1.

On appeal from the trial court's decision to set aside the temporary restraining order, the Appellate Court held that (1) the contract clearly provided for binding arbitration; (2) the contract did not violate state arbitration law because the architect was acting as owner's agent, not an arbitrator, and his decisions were subject to arbitration; and (3) the contractor did not waive its right to arbitration by simultaneously pursuing both a lien claim and arbitration.

82025 Illinois *ex rel.* Skinner v. Lombard Co., 106 Ill. App. 3d 307, 62 Ill. Dec. 520, 436 N.E.2d 566 (1982)

II:	A107-1966, Art. 15
I:	A201-1970, Art. 7, Para. 7.6.1
I:	A201-1970, Art. 7, Para. 7.10.1
I:	A201-1970, Art. 7, Para. 7.10.3

Owner brought an action against contractor for breach of contract and negligence arising out of defective construction of community college. Contractor moved to dismiss the action or, in the alternative, to compel arbitration as provided for in the contract. The trial court denied contractor's motion and certified the arbitration issue for appeal.

The owner-contractor agreement incorporated the American Institute of Architects General Conditions of the Contract for Construction, Document No. A201, 1976 edition, and supplemental general conditions prepared by the parties. The relevant arbitration provisions in the General Conditions were contained in Paragraphs 7.6 and 7.10.1. The trial court found that it was the clear intention of the parties, as expressed in Paragraphs 7.6.1 and 7.10.1, that arbitration be used for disputes arising during construction; however, once the building was completed, all remedies available by law as provided in Paragraph 7.6.1 were to be used.

The Appellate Court held that Paragraph 7.10.1 clearly and unequivocally provided that all claims arising out of the contract "shall" be decided by arbitration. The Court rejected the owner's argument that the arbitration provision was modified to pertain only to disputes during construction by Paragraph 7.10.3, which provided for construction to continue during arbitration. Furthermore, the Court held that the reservation of remedies provision in Paragraph 7.6.1 did not make the arbitration requirement optional, because if it did, the requirement of mandatory arbitration in Paragraph 7.10.1 would be meaningless.

The Appellate Court held that "tap-in-fees" were not in the nature of a permit, fee or license that the contractor was obligated by contract to pay.

82022 (UNASSIGNED)

82023 Hortman v. Otis Erecting Co., 108 Wis. 2d 456, 322 N.W.2d 482 (1982)

> III: A107-1978, Art. 10, Para. 10.11
> III: A117-1979, Art. 14, Para. 14.11
> III: A201-1976, Art. 4, Para. 4.18.
> III: A401-1978, Art. 11, Para. 11.11.1

Contractor's worker's compensation insurer brought a subrogation action against subcontractor for payments made to injured employee.

The Supreme Court of Wisconsin, in construing the indemnification provision in the subcontract which provided that subcontractor agreed to assume direct responsibility and liability for any and all negligence and/or improper workmanship from or in the performance of its work and to hold harmless the contractor from and against any and all losses arising from any source, determined that the clause clearly limited subcontractor's exposure to claims which arose out of its own negligence or improper workmanship. Noting that the trial court had found subcontractor was not negligent, the Court held that contractor's insurer had no right to recover worker's compensation payments.

82024 H.R.H. Prince Ltc. Faisal M. Saud v. Batson-Cook Co., 161 Ga. App. 219, 291 S.E.2d 249 (1982)

> II: A107-1978, Art. 8, Para. 8.1
> II: A107-1978, Art. 8, Para. 8.5
> II: A107-1978, Art. 13, Para. 13.2
> II: A117-1979, Art. 12, Para. 12.1
> II: A117-1979, Art. 12, Para. 12.5
> II: A117-1979, Art. 17, Para. 17.2
> I: A201-1976, Art. 2, Para. 2.2.2
> I: A201-1976, Art. 2, Para. 2.2.12
> I: A201-1976, Art. 7, Para. 7.9.1
> II: B141-1977, Art. 1, Para. 1.5.3
> II: B141-1977, Art. 1, Para. 1.5.9
> II: B141-1977, Art. 1, Para. 1.5.10
> II: B141-1977, Art. 1, Para. 1.5.11
> II: B141-1977, Art. 9, Para. 9.1

Contractor demanded arbitration against owner for damages associated with changes to the work ordered and approved by the owner. The owner filed a petition for declaratory

I:	A117-1979, Art. 19
I:	A117-1979, Art. 23
I:	A201-1976, Art. 2, Para. 2.2
I:	A201-1976, Art. 4, Para. 4.3
I:	A201-1976, Art. 4, Para. 4.5
I:	A201-1976, Art. 4, Para. 4.12
I:	A201-1976, Art. 9, Para. 9.4
I:	A201-1976, Art. 9, Para. 9.9
I:	A201-1976, Art. 13 Para. 13.2
I:	B141-1977, Art. 1

Owner brought an action against construction manager for the cost of repairing defectively installed granite panels. The District Court entered judgment for the owner on the grounds that the construction manager failed to install the caulking properly, failed to supervise the project, and breached an express warranty that the work would be in accordance with the plans. The construction manager appealed. The Appellate Court affirmed.

On appeal, the construction manager argued that the owner's claims were barred because the owner failed to timely notify the construction manager of the defects and failed to give the construction manager written notice of its claim for the costs of repairing the defectively installed panels.

The Appellate Court held the owner had promptly notified the construction manager of the defects, which notice provided the construction manager with an opportunity to cure, and provided notice of owner's intent to seek redress. The Court further held that the contract's notice provision related exclusively to defects discovered within one year of completion and did not limit the owner's remedy or ability to sue at a later date.

82021 Frank A. Scibetta Plumbing & Heating Corp. v. M & W Ltd. Partnership, 90 A.D.2d 956, 456 N.Y.S.2d 544 (1982), *aff'd*, 58 N.Y.2d 1092, 462 N.Y.S.2d 848, 449 N.E.2d 742 (1983)

II:	A107-1978, Art. 10, Para. 10.2
II:	A107-1978, Art. 10, Para. 10.5
II:	A117-1979, Art. 14, Para. 14.2
II:	A117-1979, Art. 14, Para. 14.5
II:	A201-1976, Art. 4, Para 4.4.1
II:	A201-1976, Art. 4, Para. 4.7.1

Contractor brought an action against owner to foreclose a mechanic's lien. The owner argued that the contractor was liable for payment of "tap-in-fees" required by the water authority. At issue on appeal was whether the "tap-in-fees" fell within contractor's responsibilities under the contract. The contractor argued the fees were essentially taxes or assessments and, therefore, were not his responsibility.

The General Conditions provided that "[t]he Contractor shall give all notices, comply with all laws, ordinances, rules and regulations bearing on the Work. The Contractor agrees to indemnify and hold Owner harmless from any loss, liability or penalty. . . ." At issue was whether the contractor was bound under the contract to pay for smoke and heat vents and an annunciator panel required by the building code regulations.

The Appellate Court interpreted the contract as specifically obligating the contractor to construct the building in accordance with the building code regulations, and held that contractor was liable to owner for the vents and annunciator panel required by the regulations.

82019   Fidelity & Casualty Co. of N.Y. v. Central Bank of Birmingham, 409 So. 2d 788 (Ala. 1982)

III:	A401-1978, Art. 11
III:	A401-1978, Art. 12

Subcontractor brought an action against contractor. A secured creditor of the subcontractor, a bank, and subcontractor's surety as subrogee each claimed priority to the money paid in settlement of subcontractor's action against contractor. The Circuit Court held that the bank had the superior claim and the surety appealed.

The Supreme Court of Alabama reversed and remanded. The Court held that the subcontractor had breached the subcontract by failing to pay a materials supplier, and that pursuant to a subcontract provision, contractor had properly withheld payment to the subcontractor until all materialmen had been paid. Once the surety, pursuant to the payment bond, had discharged all of the subcontractor's obligations, it was entitled to payment from the contractor under the terms of the subcontract. Thus, since the contract funds belonged to the surety and not the subcontractor, the bank as a secured creditor was not entitled to anything, since the subcontractor had not received any funds to pass onto its creditor.

82020   First National Bank of Akron v. Cann, 669 F.2d 415 (6th Cir. 1982)

I:	A107-1978, Art. 8
I:	A107-1978, Art. 10
III:	A107-1978, Art. 15
I:	A107-1978, Art. 19
I:	A111-1978, Art. 3
III:	A111-1978, Art. 9
I:	A111-1978, Art. 14
I:	A117-1979, Art. 2
III:	A117-1979, Art. 7
I:	A117-1979, Art. 12
I:	A117-1979, Art. 14

III:	A201-1976, Art. 4, Para. 4.3.2
III:	A201-1976, Art. 5, Para. 5.3.1
III:	A201-1976, Art. 13, Para. 13.2.1
III:	A401-1978, Art. 11, Para. 11.1.1
III:	A401-1978, Art. 11, Para. 11.7.1
III:	A401-1978, Art. 12, Para. 12.2.1

Owner brought an action against contractor for breach of contract, alleging that contractor had failed to comply with the specifications. The lower court entered judgment for the owner and contractor appealed, arguing that he relied on his subcontractor and that the owner's expert testimony as to what the specifications required was speculative because the expert's investigation took place three years after the actual construction. The contractor also challenged the award of damages.

The Appellate Court held that the contractor was liable for the subcontractor's breach because under the owner-contractor agreement, the contractor was responsible to the owner for all work performed by the subcontractors.

82018 Ethyl Corp. v. Forcum-Lannom Assocs., Inc., 433 N.E.2d 1214 (Ind. Ct. App. 1982)

II:	A107-1978, Art. 10, Para. 10.1
II:	A107-1978, Art. 10, Para. 10.5
II:	A107-1978, Art. 10, Para. 10.6
II:	A107-1978, Art. 10, Para. 10.11
II:	A117-1979, Art. 14, Para. 14.1
II:	A117-1979, Art. 14, Para. 14.5
II:	A117-1979, Art. 14, Para. 14.6
II:	A117-1979, Art. 14, Para. 14.11
II:	A201-1976, Art. 4, Para. 4.3.1
II:	A201-1976, Art. 4, Para. 4.7.1
II:	A201-1976, Art. 4, Para. 4.7.2
II:	A201-1976, Art. 4, Para. 4.7.3
II:	A201-1976, Art. 4, Para. 4.7.4
II:	A201-1976, Art. 4, Para. 4.18.1

Contractor brought an action against owner to enforce a mechanic's lien. Owner appealed from judgment in favor of contractor claiming that the trial court erred in not finding that the contract required the contractor to construct the building in compliance with the state building code regulations. The Appellate Court reversed and remanded.

The contract provided that "CONTRACTOR . . . shall be responsible for all work which is implicit or necessary to this Scope of Work. . . . All work shall be in conformance with all current and applicable codes, rules, regulations, and standards."

contractor was not liable for defective work done at the direction of and under the supervision of the architect/engineer.

The Court found that the contract unambiguously limited the architect/engineer's duty to supervise the construction to an obligation to observe the general progress of the work, and not to make continuous and exhaustive inspections. The Court held that the architect/engineer performed this contractual duty by generally overseeing construction and by conducting soil tests with reasonable care. Furthermore, the Court held that the architect/engineer owed no duty of supervision to contractor other than to exercise reasonable care when it provided instructions and test results at the job site. Having found that the architect/engineer was not negligent, the Court concluded that the contractor was responsible for the unacceptable soil material and was liable to the owner for the resulting damages.

82015 Demers Nursing Home Inc. v. R.C. Foss & Sons, Inc., 122 N.H. 757, 449 A.2d 1231 (1982)

    III: A107-1978, Art. 13, Para. 13.2
    III: A117-1979, Art. 17, Para. 17.2
    III: A201-1976, Art. 2, Para. 2.2.12
    III: A201-1976, Art. 7. Para. 7.9.1

After expiration of their contract, owner brought an action against contractor claiming that contractor failed to perform in accordance with the contract terms. Contractor moved to dismiss the action and compel arbitration. The trial court granted the motion, and owner appealed.

The Appellate Court affirmed holding that the contract language, which required arbitration of all matters relating to a breach of the agreement, revealed the parties' intent to arbitrate after full performance of the contract.

82016 (UNASSIGNED)

82017 Estate of H.C. Jessee v. White, 633 S.W.2d 767 (Tenn. Ct. App. 1982)

    III: A107-1978, Art. 10, Para. 10.1
    III: A107-1978, Art. 10, Para. 10.7
    III: A107-1978, Art. 11, Para. 11.2
    III: A107-1978, Art. 19, Para. 19.1
    III: A117-1979, Art. 14, Para. 14.1
    III: A117-1979, Art. 14, Para. 14.7
    III: A117-1979, Art. 15, Para. 15.2
    III: A117-1979, Art. 23, Para. 23.1
    III: A201-1976, Art. 4, Para. 4.3.1

required the architect/engineer to determine whether the contractor's work was performed in accordance with the specifications, and conferred upon the architect/engineer the power to reject contractor's nonconforming work.

The District Court made the following findings of fact: (1) expert testimony established that the architect/engineer's deficient design led to the failure of the levee and the failure of the access bridge; (2) expert testimony established that the contractor's workmanship did not proximately cause or contribute to the failure of the levee; (3) the evidence clearly established that the architect/engineer contemplated an otherwise adequate design that was not communicated to the contractor in the plans, specifications, or by field instruction, which led to a further finding that the architect/engineer's defective design and its failure to adequately supervise the construction proximately caused damage which made necessary restoration work on the levee; (4) the contractor was entitled to rely on the soil tests performed by the architect/engineer, but remained liable for the materials meeting the requirements of the plans and specifications.

The Court concluded that the architect/engineer's design did not meet professional engineering standards. Furthermore, the architect/engineer's contractual obligation to the owner to provide an adequate design gave rise to a duty to the contractor who relied on the design to its economic detriment.

The Court then found that since the owner-contractor agreement provided that

[t]he contractor shall provide and furnish all the necessary labor, supervision, materials, tools, expendable and permanent equipment, and all utility and transportation services required to perform, and shall perform and complete in a workmanlike manner, all of the work. . . . All work shall be performed in strict accordance with the drawings and specifications prepared by Clark-Dietz and Associates Engineers, Inc., acting as and in these contract documents referred to as the engineer/architect, which drawings and specifications are made a part of this contract, and in strict compliance with the contractor's proposal as accepted, including any amendments agreed upon at the time of the execution of this agreement, and with the other contract documents herein mentioned which are a part of this contract . . . [,]

and further provided that all materials and workmanship were guaranteed by the contractor for a period of one year from the date of final acceptance, the contractor was not liable to the owner where the architect/engineer's defective design was the primary cause of the owner's damages.

The Court next found that because the owner impliedly warranted the plans and specifications, the owner was liable to the contractor for expenses resulting from the defective plans and specifications.

The Court then examined the contract provision which set forth the authority and responsibility of the engineer/architect, the provision regarding the inspection of the work by the engineer/architect and other contract provisions dealing with the approval of compaction equipment, testing soil in the borrow pits, and the owner's right to perform soil density tests to determine the extent of the architect/engineer's duty to supervise construction. The Court found that where these provisions gave the architect/engineer considerable authority to evaluate contractor's work, even so far as to halt the work, the

III: A201-1976, Art. 7, Para. 7.9.1

Owner brought an action against contractor and architect for negligence and breach of contract in the construction and design of a city golf course. The contractor moved to compel arbitration. The trial court denied contractor's motion because the architect could not be compelled to arbitrate, thus creating a likelihood of multiple suits if contractor prevailed on its motion. Contractor appealed. The Supreme Court of South Dakota reversed and remanded, holding that the risk of multiple suits in different forums arising out of same facts and circumstances did not outweigh the rights of the parties to arbitration.

82013 (UNASSIGNED)

82014 Columbus v. Clark-Dietz & Assocs.-Eng'rs, Inc., 550 F. Supp. 610 (N.D. Miss. 1982), *appeal denied,* 702 F.2d 67 (5th Cir. 1983)

III: A107-1978, Art. 8, Para. 8.3
III: A107-1978, Art. 10, Para. 10.1
III: A107-1978, Art. 10, Para. 10.4
III: A107-1978, Art. 19, Para. 19.1
III: A117-1979, Art. 12, Para. 12.3
III: A117-1979, Art. 14, Para. 14.1
III: A117-1979, Art. 14, Para. 14.4
III: A117-1979, Art. 23, Para. 23.1
III: A201-1976, Art. 2, Para. 2.2.3
III: A201-1976, Art. 2, Para. 2.2.4
III: A201-1976, Art. 4, Para. 4.3.3
III: A201-1976, Art. 4, Para. 4.5.1
III: A201-1976, Art. 13, Para. 13.2.2
III: B141-1977, Art. 1, Para. 1.5.4
III: B141-1977, Art. 1, Para. 1.5.5
III: B141-1977, Art. 1, Para. 1.5.8

Owner brought an action against architect and contractor for damages resulting from the failure of a protective levee surrounding the construction site. The issues of liability and damages were bifurcated. Architect/engineer and contractor filed a counterclaim against owner, and contractor filed a cross-claim against the architect. Architect/engineer asserted that it properly designed the structure and supervised the construction, and contractor asserted that it constructed the project in accordance with the design specifications prepared by the architect.

The owner and contractor had entered into an agreement prepared by the architect/engineer which provided that the architect/engineer had general control over the work,

Appellate Court held that because the contracts warranted the work of the contractor and provided for a period of one year for corrections of defects, the trial court did not err in finding that owner's acceptance did not bar the claim for damages.

82010   Charles J. Frank, Inc. v. Associated Jewish Charities Inc., 294 Md. 443, 450 A.2d 1304 (1982)

III:	A107-1978, Art. 13, Para. 13.2
III:	A117-1979, Art. 17, Para. 17.2
III:	A201-1976, Art. 2, Para. 2.2.12
III:	A201-1976, Art. 7, Para. 7.9

Contractor moved to compel arbitration. Owner argued that contractor waived his right to arbitration by litigating a third party claim against the owner in an earlier unrelated case. The Appellate Court found that the contractor's conduct did not constitute a waiver of the right to arbitrate unrelated issues arising under its contract with owner.

82011   City of Dearborn v. Freeman-Darling, Inc., 119 Mich. App. 439, 326 N.W.2d 831 (1982)

I:	A107-1978, Art. 13, Para. 13.2
I:	A117-1979, Art. 17, Para. 17.2
I:	A201-1976, Art. 7, Para. 7.9.1

Contractor filed a demand for arbitration of delay damages pursuant to the arbitration provision in the owner-contractor agreement. Owner moved to stay arbitration and to compel discovery. The trial court denied the owner's motion and owner appealed.

The owner-contractor agreement incorporated the American Institute of Architects General Conditions of the Contract for Construction, Document No. A201, 1976 edition. The agreement provided that all claims were first to be referred to the architect, and, after the architect rendered its decision, the aggrieved party could demand arbitration pursuant to Paragraph 7.9.1.

In interpreting the arbitration provision, the Appellate Court found that the parties had agreed to follow the procedures set forth by the American Arbitration Association (AAA). The Court found that the contractor's demand for arbitration, prepared in accordance with Rule 7 of the AAA, reasonably informed the owner of the nature of the claim. Furthermore, relying on Paragraph 7.9.1, the Court found that discovery had to be in accordance with the AAA Rules. Finally, the Court upheld the trial court's ruling that the timeliness of the arbitration demand was a question for the arbitrator.

82012   City of Hot Springs v. Gunderson's Inc., 322 N.W.2d 8 (S.D. 1982)

III:	A107-1978, Art. 13, Para. 13.2
III:	A117-1979, Art. 17, Para. 17.2

quality of construction and conformity of construction plans to specifications did not constitute retention of the authority to schedule and coordinate. Therefore, the owner was not liable to the contractors for delay damages.

82008   Brookhaven Landscape & Grading Co. v. J.F. Barton Contracting Co., 676 F.2d 516 (11th Cir. 1982)

	III:	A107-1978, Art. 11, Para. 11.2
	III:	A107-1978, Art. 18, Para. 18.2
	III:	A117-1979, Art. 15, Para. 15.2
	III:	A117-1979, Art. 22, Para. 22.2
	III:	A201-1976, Art. 5, Para. 5.3.1
	III:	A201-1976, Art. 12, Para. 12.3.1
	III:	A401-1978, Art. 11, Para. 11.1.1
	III:	A401-1978, Art. 11, Para. 11.9.1
	III:	A401-1978, Art. 11, Para. 11.10.1

Contractor appealed from a jury verdict awarding subcontractor damages for orally agreed upon extra work.

Affirming the judgment of the District Court but reducing the award, the Court of Appeals held the evidence was sufficient for the jury to find that the contractor had actual notice of the extra work, the contractor agreed to pay for the extra work, and the written notice requirements of the subcontract were either not incorporated into the oral agreement or were waived by the contractor.

82009   Brouillette v. Consolidated Constr. Co., 422 So. 2d 176 (La. Ct. App. 1982)

	II:	A107-1978, Art. 10, Para. 10.4
	II:	A107-1978, Art. 15, Para. 15.5
	II:	A107-1978, Art. 19, Para. 19.1
	II:	A117-1979, Art. 14, Para. 14.4
	II:	A117-1979, Art. 19, Para. 19.5
	II:	A117-1979, Art. 23, Para. 23.1
	I:	A201-1976, Art. 4, Para. 4.5.1
	I:	A201-1976, Art. 9, Para. 9.9.4
	I:	A201-1976, Art. 13, Para. 13.2.2

Contractor and its surety appealed from a judgment holding them liable to owner for damages incurred as a result of breaches of three construction contracts. Contractor argued that because owner unqualifiedly accepted all work performed by contractor, owner waived the right to recover for defective work.

Relying on Subparagraphs 4.5.1 and 13.2.2 of the American Institute of Architects General Conditions of the Contract for Construction, Document A201, 1976 edition, the

III:	A107-1978, Art. 10, Para. 10.1
III:	A107-1978, Art. 12, Para. 12.1
III:	A107-1978, Art. 12, Para. 12.3
III:	A107-1978, Art. 14, Para. 14.2
III:	A107-1978, Art. 14, Para. 14.3
III:	A107-1978, Art. 18, Para. 18.2
III:	A117-1979, Art. 12, Para. 12.3
III:	A117-1979, Art. 14, Para. 14.1
III:	A117-1979, Art. 16, Para. 16.1
III:	A117-1979, Art. 16, Para. 16.3
III:	A117-1979, Art. 18, Para. 18.2
III:	A117-1979, Art. 18, Para. 18.3
III:	A117-1979, Art. 22, Para. 22.2
III:	A201-1976, Art. 2, Para. 2.2.3
III:	A201-1976, Art. 2, Para. 2.2.4
III:	A201-1976, Art. 4, Para. 4.3.1
III:	A201-1976, Art. 6, Para. 6.1.1
III:	A201-1976, Art. 6, Para. 6.1.3
III:	A201-1976, Art. 6, Para. 6.2.1
III:	A201-1976, Art. 6, Para. 6.2.3
III:	A201-1976, Art. 8, Para. 8.1.3
III:	A201-1976, Art. 8, Para. 8.3
III:	A201-1976, Art. 12, Para. 12.3
III:	B141-1977, Art. 1, Para. 1.5.4
III:	B141-1977, Art. 1, Para. 1.5.5

After completing their work beyond the contract time, two prime contractors filed complaints against owner for delay damages caused by owner's failure to coordinate the work and to compel timely performance by a third prime contractor. Owner then filed a third party complaint against the prime general contractor alleging that he had agreed to supervise and coordinate the work.

At issue on appeal was whether the prime contractors were intended beneficiaries of the contract between owner and general contractor, and if so, whether owner retained any duty to coordinate the work.

The New Jersey Supreme Court found that the record supported the finding of the trial court that the prime contractors were intended beneficiaries of contracts with other contractors where the parties agreed that all contractors would have valid causes of action against each other for unjustified delay. The Court further determined that the owner's contracts with the contractors provided that overall responsibility for supervision was delegated to the general contractor and held that owner's use of an architect to verify altered contractually established material requirements; and (4) the contractor could recover for unforeseen difficulties encountered under the fixed-sum contract if the owner or architect made a material misrepresentation that the contractor was not reasonably able to uncover and the owner was notified once the mistake was discovered.

82005   Austin v. Parker, 672 F.2d 508 (5th Cir. 1982)

      III: A401-1978, Art. 11, Para. 11.2.6

      III: A401-1978, Art. 12, Para. 12.6.1

Contractor brought an action against subcontractor and surety, and subcontractor counterclaimed for damages for constructive termination of contract. Judgment below was entered for contractor and the counterclaim was dismissed.

On appeal, the District Court's findings were challenged as clearly erroneous. Among numerous issues was whether subcontractor abandoned and defaulted or whether contractor's failure to provide materials and electricity constituted a prior material breach.

The subcontract provided that should subcontractor at any time fail to adequately man the job, contractor was entitled to terminate subcontractor with two days written notice. The contractor exercised this right.

The Court of Appeals found that although the record contained support for subcontractor's complaints, the District Court's factual findings that subcontractor was poorly organized, did shoddy work, and ran behind schedule even with materials on hand, were not "clearly erroneous." The Court held that subcontractor breached the contract when it abandoned the jobsite; therefore, contractor could recover reasonable expenses incurred in completing the job.

82006   Aztec Servs., Inc. v. Quintana-Howell Joint Venture, 632 S.W.2d 160 (Tex. Civ. App. 1982)

      III: B141-1977, Art. 10, Para. 10.1

      III: B141-1977, Art. 10, Para. 10.2

Engineer brought an action against owner for wrongful termination of the contract. The trial court entered summary judgment for owner, and engineer appealed.

The contract provided that the engineer would provide services "as required" by the owner. The owner paid the engineer in full and informed the engineer that his services were no longer required.

The Appellate Court held that the contract was unambiguous and terminable at will upon notice by either party, since the contract was for an indefinite duration and required the engineer to provide services "as required."

82007   Broadway Maintenance Corp. v. Rutgers State Univ., 90 N.J. 253, 447 A.2d 906 (1982)

      III: A107-1978, Art. 8, Para. 8.3

II:	A107-1978, Art. 14, Para. 14.2
II:	A117-1979, Art. 1
II:	A117-1979, Art. 3
II:	A117-1979, Art. 9, Para. 9.3
II:	A117-1979, Art. 11, Para. 11.3
II:	A117-1979, Art. 11, Para. 11.4
II:	A117-1979, Art. 12, Para. 12.1
II:	A117-1979, Art. 12, Para. 12.3
II:	A117-1979, Art. 14, Para. 14.1
II:	A117-1979, Art. 18, Para. 18.2
I:	A201-1976, Art. 1, Para. 1.2.2
I:	A201-1976, Art. 1, Para. 1.2.3
I:	A201-1976, Art. 2, Para. 2.2.2
I:	A201-1976, Art. 2, Para. 2.2.3
I:	A201-1976, Art. 2, Para. 2.2.17
I:	A201-1976, Art. 4, Para. 4.2.1
I:	A201-1976, Art. 4, Para. 4.3.1
I:	A201-1976, Art. 8, Para. 8.1.3
I:	A201-1976, Art. 8, Para. 8.2.2
I:	A201-1976, Art. 12, Para. 12.3.1
II:	B141-1977, Art. 1, Para. 1.5.3
II:	B141-1977, Art. 1, Para. 1.5.4
II:	B141-1977, Art. 1, Para. 1.6

Contractor entered into a fixed-sum contract with owner for excavation and grading based on architectural maps which later proved to be inaccurate in some respects. Weather and the owner's failure to appoint a project representative caused unforeseen expense and delays. The owner subsequently terminated the contractor.

Contractor filed a materialmen's lien against the property, and subsequently brought an action against owner for payment due, reimbursement for extra material expenses, remuneration in quantum meruit and attorney fees. Owner counterclaimed for delay damages, the cost of correcting or completing the work, expenses, and slander of title.

The issues before the court were (1) which parties could seek enforcement of the contract, and (2) whether the contract allowed for recovery of unforeseen expenses and delays.

The District Court held that (1) while the owner-architect agreement required a project representative to be appointed, the owner was entitled to enforce the owner-contractor agreement which provided that the appointment of a project representative was optional; (2) the contractor was entitled to sue for payment without a certificate of final completion from the architect since the owner prevented completion; (3) contractual notice requirements had to be met for additional expenses even after the course of performance had

After entry of judgment for the contractor, the Court of Appeals, relying on Restatement (Second) of Contracts §228, comment a (1981), held that the use of the term "opinion" in the contract did not imply that the reasonable person standard should be used in interpreting the termination clause; rather the clause should be interpreted as implying that termination was within owner's contractual rights if the owner's decision was made in good faith. Therefore, the District Court should have applied the "good faith" standard to the owner's conduct rather than the "reasonableness" standard. Vacating the judgment, the Court of Appeals remanded the case so the District Court could determine whether the owner terminated the contract in good faith.

82003 Allegheny Home Improvement Corp. v. Franklin, 308 Pa. Super. 225, 454 A.2d 103 (1982)

I: A107-1974, Art. 14
II: A201-1970, Art. 7, Para. 7.10.1

Contractor filed a demand for arbitration against owner. The trial court confirmed the award for contractor, and owner appealed. Owner and contractor had entered into the Standard Form of Agreement Between Owner and Contractor—Short Form Agreement for Small Construction Contracts, which provided for arbitration of disputes arising out of the contract. On appeal, owner argued that because the arbitration clause did not contain a provision governing entry of judgment, the contractor could not obtain judgment on the award without bringing an action in assumpsit.

Affirming, the Appellate Court relied on the arbitration clause which provided that disputes submitted to arbitration "are to be decided according to the Construction Industry Rules of the American Arbitration Association." Applying Rule 47, which stated that judgment could be entered in any federal or state court having jurisdiction, the Court held that contractor's contract rights could be enforced without bringing an action in assumpsit.

82004 Anderson v. Golden, 569 F. Supp. 122 (S.D. Ga. 1982)

II: A101-1977, Art. 2
II: A101-1977, Art. 3
II: A101-1977, Art. 6
II: A107-1978, Art. 1
II: A107-1978, Art. 2
II: A107-1978, Art. 5
II: A107-1978, Art. 7, Para. 7.3
II: A107-1978, Art. 7, Para. 7.4
II: A107-1978, Art. 8, Para. 8.1
II: A107-1978, Art. 8, Para. 8.3
II: A107-1978, Art. 10, Para. 10.1

82001 Able Elec. Co. v. Vacanti & Randazzo Constr. Co., 212 Neb. 619, 324 N.W.2d 667 (1982)

II:	A107-1978, Art. 10, Para. 10.1
II:	A117-1979, Art. 14, Para. 14.1
II:	A201-1976, Art. 4, Para. 4.3.1
II:	A401-1978, Art. 3
II:	A401-1978, Art. 11, Para. 11.1.1

Subcontractor brought an action against contractor for the retainage and other amounts due under the subcontract. The trial court entered judgment for subcontractor. At issue on contractor's appeal was whether the trial court erred in instructing the jury.

The contractor's agreement with owner contained a clause requiring the project to be completed within 450 days from the issuance of a notice to proceed. Contractor entered into an agreement with subcontractor which provided, in pertinent part, that subcontractor would "complete all work under the job schedule time period set up by contractor and owner." The subcontract also contained a flow down clause identical to Paragraph 11.1.1 of the American Institute of Architects Standard Form of Agreement Between Contractor and Subcontractor, Document A401, 1978 edition. The subcontract did not contain a time of the essence clause.

The Supreme Court of Nebraska stated that time is not considered the essence of a contract unless it is expressly provided or can be implied from the intention of the parties, and, in interpreting the contract, held that the question of whether the 450-day time limit was the essence of the contract was a question of fact which was properly submitted to the jury. Furthermore, the Court read Paragraph 4.3.1 of the General Conditions, which provided that contractor would schedule and coordinate the work, together with the subcontract, which provided that subcontractor would complete all work in the time period set by contractor and owner, and held that the trial court properly instructed the jury that contractor was solely responsible for coordinating time schedules and that his failure to do so could be considered a sufficient breach so as to entitle subcontractor to sue to recover damages. Judgment was affirmed.

82002 Action Eng'g v. Martin Marietta Aluminum, 670 F.2d 456 (3d Cir. 1982)

III:	A107-1978, Art. 20, Para. 20.1
III:	A117-1979, Art. 24, Para. 24.1
III:	A201-1976, Art. 14, Para. 14.2.1

Contractor brought an action against owner for wrongful termination of contract. The General Conditions required the contractor to submit a progress schedule to owner and stated that time was of the essence. The contract further provided that if in "[o]wner's opinion, contractor fails to carry on the work diligently and on schedule . . . [o]wner shall have the right . . . to terminate this contract forthwith."

Two employees of subcontractor filed suit against contractor for damages for injuries. The contractor filed a third party complaint against the subcontractor for indemnity based on a provision requiring purchase of insurance by the subcontractor. The trial court held the insurance provision void and unenforceable pursuant to an Illinois statute and granted the subcontractor's motion to dismiss.

The Appellate Court reversed. The Court held that the subcontractor was bound to compensate the contractor for all monies it would have to pay to the injured parties and all costs of defense. The Court reasoned that the Illinois statute only prohibited agreements whereby one party agreed to indemnify another party from that party's own negligence. Here the subcontractor did not agree to indemnify, but rather agreed to obtain insurance. Thus, the Court concluded, the agreement to obtain insurance was not contrary to the Illinois statute, and the subcontractor was liable for all damages resulting from its breach.

The owner cross-claimed against the contractor for breach of contract and sought damages for construction defects and delays. During the litigation the owner and contractor were participating in an arbitration proceeding instituted by the contractor, which included a counterclaim by the owner identical to its cross-claim in the litigation. The contractor's motion to either compel arbitration of the cross-claim in the suit or to stay the cross-claim pending completion of arbitration was denied by the trial court, and the contractor filed an interlocutory appeal.

The Court of Appeal reversed and ordered a stay of the owner's cross claim pending arbitration. The Court held that the trial court erred in refusing to compel arbitration in view of an arbitration provision stating that *"all claims, disputes and other matters in question* arising out of . . . this Contractor or the breach thereof . . . *shall be decided by arbitration.* The Court also held that under Florida law, "any action or proceeding involving an issue subject to arbitration should be stayed if an order for arbitration or an application thereof has been made."

The completion of arbitration proceedings resulted in a favorable judgment for the contractor and the denial for the owner's counterclaim. The Court of Appeal held that the "arbitration award determined all issues between the parties and conclusively established that [the owner] proved no construction defects against [the contractor]." Thus, the trial court was correct in subsequently dismissing the owner's cross claim.

81174 Windowmaster Corp. v. B. G. Danis Co., 511 F. Supp. 157 (S.D. Ohio 1981)

> I: A201-1976, Art. 7, Para. 7.9
> I: A311-1970, Performance Bond
> I: A401-1978, Art. 13

A suit was instituted for declaratory and injunctive relief concerning the institution of arbitration proceedings by the contractor against the subcontractor and its surety. Both parties moved for summary judgment. The District Court granted the motions of the surety and subcontractor. The Court stated that the surety could not be held to the arbitration provisions in the contract and the bond to which it was not a signator since under Ohio law "Arbitration is a matter of contract and a party cannot be required to submit to arbitration any dispute which he has not agreed so to submit." The bond's incorporation by reference of the subcontract did not amount to agreement to arbitrate since that only fixed the extent of the surety's obligation. The Court noted that the surety had been sued because it allegedly stated it would not be bound by the results of the arbitration, and the Court further noted that it would be better for the surety to voluntarily submit to arbitration; however, the surety could not be forced into arbitration.

81075 Zettel v. Paschen Contractors, Inc., 100 Ill. App. 3d 614, 427 N.E.2d 189 (1981)

> III: A401-1978, Art. 11

certain portions of the building. These changes as well as others which were discovered during construction required change orders. The State processed the change orders very slowly, causing further delays. Once construction began, the contractor and subcontractors proceeded with the construction for nearly six months and spent nearly $2 million without receiving progress payments.

The Superior Court, Judicial District of Hartford, held that the contractor established that the State failed to make progress payments for contract and change work when such payments were due. The contractor was entitled to bring the action on its own behalf and also on behalf of subcontractors that had not waived claims against the contractor.

81072 Whittle v. Pagani Brothers Construction Co., 422 N.E.2d 779 (Mass. 1981)

I: A107-1978, Art. 10
I: A107-1978, Art. 17
I: A117-1978, Art. 14
I: A117-1978, Art. 21
I: A201-1976, Art. 4, Para. 4.18
I: A201-1976, Art. 11, Para. 11.1
I: A401-1978, Art. 9
I: A401-1978, Art. 11
I: A401-1978, Art. 12

Subcontractor's employee sued the contractor for negligence after the employee was injured on the job. The contractor filed a third party complaint against the subcontractor and its insurers. The third party complaint was dismissed in the trial court.

The Supreme Court reversed the dismissal of the third party complaint. "The natural reading of the subcontract language is to impose the same obligations on the subcontractor to indemnify the contractor against claims arising out of the performance of the subcontract as the main contract imposes on the contractor to indemnify the [owner] against claims arising out of the performance of the main contract." Thus, the subcontractor must "indemnify the contractor against a claim for personal injuries to an employee of the subcontractor caused by the concurrent negligence of the subcontractor and the contractor." The subcontractor's indemnity contract was also held enforceable under Massachusetts law.

81073 William Passalacqua Builders, Inc. v. Mayfair House Association, Inc., 395 So. 2d 1171 (Fla. Dist. Ct. App. 1981)

I: A107-1978, Art. 13
I: A117-1979, Art. 17
I: A201-1976, Art. 7, Para. 7.9

Condominium housing association brought suit against the owner-developer for construction defects, and contractor and its surety for negligence and breach of contract.

Subcontractor brought declaratory action against contractor for damages on the basis of *quantum meruit* and rescinded the contract. Both parties motioned for summary judgment. The District Court granted the contractor's motion.

The District Court affirmed and held that the fact that the subcontractor's performance was delayed by the owner did not amount to a material breach so as to allow rescission. The subcontractor's argument that the "time is of the essence" clause gave it a right to rescind its performance was faulty, since other provisions within the contract required the subcontractor to submit claims for delays, indicating that timeliness was the subcontractor's obligation—rather than its right.

81070 Vey v. Port Auth. of New York & New Jersey, 54 N.Y.2d 221, 429 N.E.2d 762, 445 N.Y.S.2d 84 (1981), *modifying* 434 N.Y.S.2d 412 (App. Div. 1981)

III:	A107-1978, Art. 10	
III:	A117-1979, Art. 14	
III:	A201-1976, Art. 4, Para. 4.18	
III:	A401-1978, Art. 11	

The contractor sought indemnification from subcontractor for the amount the contractor had to indemnify owner. The general contractor's claim was based on tort law and on a contractual indemnification clause. The Supreme Court granted the contractor's claim on both theories. The Appellate Division disallowed recovery on the indemnity clause.

The Court of Appeals modified the Appellate Division's decision and allowed recovery on both theories. The Court held that "the clear language of the indemnification provision, strengthened by the surrounding facts and circumstances demonstrated that the parties intended the [contractor] to be indemnified by the [subcontractor] against all liability arising out of the [subcontractor's] work . . . at the construction site." The indemnification was required even when the contractor was held liable to the owner under an indemnification clause in a separate contract.

81071 Walter Kidde Constructors, Inc. v. State, 37 Conn. Supp. 50, 434 A.2d 962 (1981)

III:	A201-1976, Art. 8, Para. 8.3	
III:	A201-1976, Art. 9, Par. 9.5	
III:	A201-1976, Art. 12, Para. 12.3	
III:	A401-1978, Art. 11	
III:	A401-1978, Art. 12	

Contractor brought action against State for breach of contract. State failed to deliver the construction site and failed to give the contractor access to the site for an unreasonably long period of time after the date required in the contract for commencement of work. The State issued "hold-orders" to the contractor which were in effect for inordinately long periods of time. While the "hold-orders" were in effect, the State was redesigning

encompassed attorney fees. However, attorney fees were awarded only as to the dispute of the owners with the contractor and not the dispute with the surety.

81068   Stepanek v. Kober Construction, 625 P.2d 51 (Mont. 1981)

        II: A107-1978, Art. 16
        II: A117-1979, Art. 20
        II: A201-1976, Art. 10, Para. 10.1

Employee of subcontractor sued contractor and owner for injuries sustained from falling off of a scaffold. The trial court entered summary judgment for the contractor and the owner. The injured employee appealed.

The Supreme Court reversed and remanded. The Court held that the contractor owed a duty of care to the subcontractor under several theories. Under the general contract, the contractor was required to "initat [e], maintain and supervis [e] all safety precautions and programs" on the worksite. This contractual obligation created a non-delegable duty in favor of the subcontractor's employee, leaving the contractor in direct control and thus liable to the subcontractor's employee.

The contractor was also liable under two state statutes. The contractor's liability under the Scaffolding Act was based on its having "direct and immediate control of the work involving the scaffold." The Safe Place statute requiring all employers to furnish safe working conditions for all employees was construed to cover a general contractor's duty to a subcontractor's employee if, as in this case, there was a nondelegable duty arising out of contract.

81068a   Travelers Indem. Co. v. National Gypsum Co., 394 So. 2d 481 (Fla. Dist. Ct. App. 1981), *aff'd,* 417 So. 2d 254 (Fla. 1982)

        I: A311-1970, Labor and Material Payment Bond

Materialman brought an action against subcontractor and its surety on a labor and material payment bond. The trial court denied the surety's motion to dismiss for failure to give notice pursuant to the bond and entered summary judgment for the materialman.

The Court of Appeal reversed and remanded with directions to enter summary judgment for the surety. The Court held that the notice provision in the bond, which required as a condition precedent for filing suit that written notice be given within ninety days after the materialman had furnished the materials for which the claim was made, was "plain and unambiguous" and thus binding upon the parties.

81069   Vermont Marble Co. v. Baltimore Contractors, Inc., 520 F. Supp. 922 (D.D.C. 1981)

        II: A401-1978, Art. 3
        II: A401-1978, Art. 11

I: A111-1978, Art. 4
I: A117-1979, Art. 3
I: A117-1979, Art. 13
I: A117-1979, Art. 18
I: A201-1976, Art. 3, Para. 3.4
I: A201-1976, Art. 8, Para. 8.2
I: A201-1976, Art. 8, Para. 8.3
I: A201-1976, Art. 9, Para. 9.6
I: A311-1970, Labor & Material Payment Bond

Subcontractor sued owners, contractor and its surety to recover payment for work performed and to foreclose upon a materialman's lien. The owners filed a crossclaim against the contractor and its surety for delay damages and expenses incurred for completing the project, and attorney fees. The trial court entered judgment for the subcontractor on its foreclosure, entered partial judgment for the owners on their claim for delay damages, and denied the owners' claim for attorney fees. The owners and the surety appealed.

The Supreme Court affirmed the subcontractor's award, and affirmed in part and reversed in part judgment on the owner's crossclaim. As to the owner's claim for delay damages, the Court held that the trial court erred in basing judgment on the sole fact that the owners allegedly requested the delay in completion. The dispositive factor in the Court's reversal was the contractor's obligation under the contract to obtain a written extension of time "[i]f the Contractor is delayed at any time in the progress of the Work *by any act . . . of the owner. . .*" (emphasis added). Since the contractor failed to request any extensions of time, the Court held that the contractor had waived this right. Since the contract also provided that "time is of the essence," the contractor was liable to the owners for delay damages for lost rent.

On the issue of expenses incurred by the owners in hiring another contractor to complete the site and landscape work, the Court affirmed the trial court's partial award of judgment in the owners' favor. The Court held that the owners' recovery was limited to the contract price, despite the substantially higher cost of completion. This was attributed to the owners' failure to give written notice to the contractor to commence and continue correction of default, followed by a change order compensating the owners for any extra costs, as required by the contract.

The Court also held that the owners were entitled to attorney fees from the contractor and its surety from the ensuing litigation, notwithstanding the owners' failure to pay an application for a progress payment. The refusal to pay was justified because under the contract provision the architect could refuse to certify payment if there is "reasonable evidence that the Work will not be completed within the Contract Time." The contractor and surety's liability was predicated on both a Wyoming statute and the labor and material payment bond, which stated that "the Owner shall not be liable for the payment of any costs or expenses of any such suit." The Court determined that "costs and expenses"

III: A111-1978, Art. 4

III: A117-1979, Art. 3

Contractor filed suit for extra work and owner counterclaimed for liquidated delay damages. The trail court entered partial judgment for the contractor and awarded the owner delay damages. The contractor appealed.

The Court of Appeals affirmed. The Court held that the owner did not waive its right to liquidated delay damages merely by its acceptance of substantial completion of the project since "mere acceptance . . . does not as a matter of law create a waiver of a claim not based upon the quality of the work but upon the delay in performing." In this case, the project was substantially completed a year later than originally contracted for, during which negotiations had taken place and the contractor had been put on notice about the delay damages.

The Court also held that the owner was not estopped from claiming delay damages. The owner had the right to deduct any delay damages from the contract price, but there was no evidence to demonstrate that the owner had misled the contractor into believing that the delay damages would be excused.

81066   Southern Maryland Hospital Center v. Edward M. Crough, Inc., 48 Md. App. 401, 427 A.2d 1051 (1981)

I: A201-1976, Art. 7, Para. 7.9

I: A201-1976, Art. 12, Para. 12.1

I: A201-1976, Art. 12, Para. 12.3

Owner appealed arbitration board's decision to award construction manager additional costs for extras arising from construction changes necessitated by soil conditions, where said changes were not instituted according to procedures set out in contract and where extras pushed project costs above the contract's guaranteed maximum price provision.

The Court of Special Appeals affirmed, noting that judicial intervention in an arbitration proceeding was "severely limited," and that the "interpretation of arbitrators must not be disturbed as long as they are not in"manifest disregard' of the law." The board's interpretation was supported by sufficient rationality, precluding court intervention, where evidence was presented indicating parties had waived change order procedures, despite the fact that owner knowingly allowed noncompliance with the strict terms of the contract on the condition that the guaranteed maximum price was not exceeded.

81067   State Sur. Co. v. Lamb Construction Co., 625 P.2d 184 (Wyo. 1981)

I: A101-1977, Art. 3

I: A107-1978, Art. 2

I: A107-1978, Art. 9

I: A107-1978, Art. 14

a mechanic's lien, the owner was not now allowed to raise these issues. Thus, the architect was entitled to damages in accordance with the contractual provision for termination.

81063 Rio Rancho Estates v. Beyerlein, 662 F.2d 700 (10th Cir. 1981)

> II: A401-1978, Art. 12

Owner and contractor sued subcontractor and the District Court awarded "back charges" to the owner and contractor for amounts paid to others for correction of work not of good quality.

The Court of Appeals affirmed. Pursuant to the contract provision concerning correction of work, "the [subcontractor] had actual notice of the deficiencies and ample time within which to correct them before the framing contract was terminated."

81064 San Ore-Gardner v. Missouri Pacific Railroad Co., 496 F. Supp. 1337 (E.D. Ark. 1980), *aff'd*, 658 F.2d 562 (8th Cir. 1981)

> III: A101-1977, Art. 3
> III: A107-1978, Art. 2
> II: A107-1978, Art. 15
> III: A111-1978, Art. 4
> III: A117-1979, Art. 3
> II: A117-1979, Art. 19
> II: A201-1978, Art. 9, Para. 9.6

Contractor filed a suit against owner to recover balance owed on a construction contract. Owner claimed the balance was justifiably withheld based on both a contractual provision for liquidated damages caused by delay and upon defective work. The District Court held for the contractor.

The District Court held that where the liquidated damages clause had not been the subject of negotiations and the $600 a day damages had no rational basis ". . . the clause was in the nature of a penalty instead of liquidated damages, and not enforceable." Moreover, the Court held that where the party who sought to enforce the liquidated damages provision contributed in part to failure to perform the contract, the liquidated damages provision would not be enforceable.

The District Court also held that the contractor was entitled to payment for allegedly defective work, since the defective work had been corrected.

81065 Southbend Contractors, Inc. v. Parrish of Jefferson, 408 So. 2d 1158 (La. Ct. App. 1981)

> III: A101-1977, Art. 3
> III: A107-1978, Art. 3

. . ." provided indemnity for the contractor only while the work was in progress. The provision was unenforceable once the subcontract work was completed.

81060   Ramada Development Co. v. Rauch, 644 F.2d 1097 (5th Cir. 1981)

        III: A107-1978, Art. 19
        III: A117-1979, Art. 23
        III: A201-1976, Art. 8, Para. 8.1
        III: A201-1976, Art. 13, Para. 13.2

Owner sued contractor for breach of contract. The District Court found for the contractor, and the owner appealed.

The Court of Appeals affirmed, holding that a contract provision obligating the contractor to correct work prior to substantial completion, which required notice by the owner of defects, did not render the jury instruction invalid, since another instruction stated there should be damages for improper performance. The instruction also contained a definition of substantial performance nearly identical to the contract definition.

81061   Redevelopment Authority v. Fidelity & Deposit Co., 665 F.2d 470 (3d Cir. 1981)

        I: A201-1976, Art. 2, Para. 2.2
        I: A201-1976, Art. 9, Para. 9.9
        III: A311-1970, Labor & Material Payment Bond

Subcontractor sued surety under a payment bond for amounts owed by contractor after complete performance of construction contract. The payment bond required that suit be brought within one year of "completion and final settlement." The District Court held for the subcontractor, finding that suit had been timely brought.

The Court of Appeals upheld the District Court's interpretation of "final settlement," which was the date upon which the architect issued a final certificate of payment. The contract provisions established the architect as the owner's representative to render the final certificate, which was a "definite time, fixed by public record and readily ascertainable."

81062   Reeves v. Watkins, 208 Neb. 804, 305 N.W.2d 815 (1981)

        I: B141-1977, Art. 10

Architect filed petition seeking to recover damages pursuant to a contract provision setting forth a formula in the event of termination of the architect's services. The Municipal Court granted summary judgment for the architect. The District Court affirmed.

The Supreme Court affirmed. The Court held that since the validity and performance of the contract had not been raised as a defense in a previous action for foreclosure of

I: A201-1976, Art. 13, Para. 13.2

Owner served a demand for arbitration upon the contractor and architect, each of which sought a stay of arbitration. The owner moved to compel arbitration, which was granted, and the contractor appealed.

The Supreme Court, Appellate Division, affirmed. The dispute was arbitrable even though the owner did not first refer the claim to the architect for decision pursuant to a provision in the owner-contractor agreement. That provision was construed to mean that claims need not be referred to the architect if they arose after substantial completion of the work. The Court also held that the demand for arbitration was timely since the agreement stated that it could not be made later than any statute of limitations, which under the state statute was six years. The cause of action began when the contractor completed correction of work rejected by the architect pursuant to a provision of the agreement.

81058   Plantation Pipe Line Co. v. 3-D Excavators, Inc., 160 Ga. App. 756, 287 S.E.2d 102 (1981)

III: A107-1978, Art. 16
III: A117-1979, Art. 20
III: A201-1976, Art. 10, Para. 10.2.

Pipeline company sued contractor for damages occurring during construction of sewer improvements. The DeKalb Superior Court entered judgment for the contractor.

The Court of Appeals reversed. The Court held that the pipeline company could recover damages as a third party beneficiary on the basis of a contract provision stating that "any damage to existing structures or utilities shall be repaired or made good by the contractor at no expense to the owner." The Court held that the pipeline company was "a member of a small group of intended beneficiaries . . . whose . . . utilities were in such proximity to the construction work . . . as to be reasonably afforded the contractual protection incorporated in the contract."

81059   R.E.M. IV, Inc. v. Robert F. Ackermann & Associates, Inc., 313 N.W.2d 431 (Minn. 1981)

III: A401-1978, Art. 11

Owner sued the architect, the general contractor, and the subcontractor for property damage and lost profits caused by the freezing and bursting of pipes in the owner's building. The District Court granted the general contractor's motion for partial summary judgment against the subcontractor.

The Supreme Court reversed, holding that the terms of the indemnity provision requiring the subcontractor to "assume entire responsibility and liability for all damages or injury . . . resulting from or in any manner connected with, the execution of the work

The indemnitor of performance bond of subcontractor sued contractor for payment under subcontract. The indemnitor claimed the subcontract included a three-page addendum which was attached to it. The Circuit Court entered judgment in favor of indemnitor.

The Supreme Court affirmed on this issue, holding that, where the contract stated that "The Contract Documents for this Subcontract consist of this Agreement and any exhibits attached hereto. . .," the three-page addendum which was affixed to the subcontract at the time of its execution was part of the subcontract. In addition, the addendum had been attached to the subcontract when it was filed with the owner.

81056   Paul Mullins Construction Co. v. Alspaugh, 628 P.2d 113 (Colo. Ct. App. 1981)

        I: A107-1978, Art. 13
        I: A117-1979, Art. 17
        I: A201-1976, Art. 7, Para. 7.9

Owners filed a demand for arbitration pursuant to the contact between owners and contractor. Contractor submitted to arbitration; however, in doing so, the contractor reserved the right to arbitrate "only as a condition precedent to a possible court action." In response to this reservation the owners filed suit claiming the contractor was wrongfully attempting to avoid the finality of arbitration. The contractor then initiated a mechanic's lien foreclosure action, and the owners filed a motion to quash the summons. The trial court conducted a hearing on all the motions and concluded the contractor could not be compelled to arbitrate since all parties waived such rights.

The Court of Appeals reversed and remanded and ordered the trial court to grant arbitration and stay the litigation. The Court stated that although the contractor did not waive its right to a mechanic's lien by executing a contract which contained an arbitration clause, arbitration is a condition precedent to the pursuit of legal action. The Court also stated that the owners did not waive arbitration by initiating litigation since the purpose of that litigation was to preserve to right to arbitrate.

81057   Pignott Construction International, Ltd. v. Rochester Institute of Technology, 84 A.D.2d 679, 446 N.Y.S.2d 632 (1981)

        I: A107-1978, Art. 8
        I: A107-1978, Art. 13
        I: A107-1978, Art. 19
        I: A117-1979, Art. 12
        I: A117-1979, Art. 17
        I: A117-1979, Art. 23
        I: A201-1976, Art. 2, Para. 2.2
        I: A201-1976, Art. 7, Para. 7.9

The District Court held that the contract should be construed as a whole. It also held that where provisions in a contract conflict, the specific provisions control the more general provisions and the typewritten parts take priority over the boiler plate provisions. Using these rules of construction as a guideline, and a prime contract provision which bound the subcontractor to that prime contract only to the extent of its own work, the Court found the language in the contract to be "clearly indicative that the bid reflected a base price, not lump-sum price."

81053   Medical Clinic Board v. Smelley, 408 So. 2d 1203 (Ala. 1981)

         III: A401-1978, Art. 11

Subcontractor sued contractor and owner for payment for work performed, and contractor filed a counterclaim for breach by the subcontractor. The Circuit Court entered judgment for the subcontractor, and the owner appealed.

The Supreme Court affirmed. The Court held that the subcontractor was entitled to be reimbursed for extra work which he performed, according to the contractor's instructions. On the facts of this case, the contract provision requiring that all extra work be approved in writing was not a bar to the subcontractor's recovery.

81054   Miller Construction Co. v. First Baptist Church, 396 So. 2d 281 (Fla. Dist. Ct. App. 1981)

         II: A107-1978, Art. 13
         II: A117-1979, Art. 17
         II: A201-1976, Art. 7, Para. 7.9

Owner brought suit against contractor alleging default because of substantial defects. The contractor filed a motion to dismiss and to compel arbitration, which the trial court denied.

The Court of Appeal reversed and remanded to the trial court to issue an order compelling arbitration. The Court held that the trial court erred in its decision that the contractor had implicitly waived arbitration by its attempt to first settle the dispute amicably without any formal proceedings. The Court also held that the owner had waived arbitration by filing suit because the arbitration clause provided for arbitration of all disputes "unless the parties mutually agree otherwise." Since there was no mutual agreement to suspend arbitration, the contractor's motion to dismiss should have been granted.

81055   Northwestern Engineering Co. v. Thunderbolt Enterprises, Inc., 301 N.W.2d 421 (S.D. 1981)

         I: A401-1978, Art. 1

III: A201-1976, Art. 13, Para. 13.2

Contractor built firewall which was designed by owner. Firewall was adequately suited to its original intended use as interior curtain firewall. After completion of the firewall, contractor was informed that construction of one of the buildings which was to be erected abutting the firewall was to be held in abeyance indefinitely. After examining the firewall in the presence of owner, contractor informed owner that the firewall might not be stable in the absence of the abutting building. Seven months later during a storm, the firewall collapsed. Owner sued contractor for negligence and breach of warranty. The Superior Court held in favor of contractor.

The Supreme Judicial Court affirmed, holding that where firewall designed by owner and built by contractor, in a workmanlike manner and in compliance with owner's specifications, was adequately suited to its original intended use, and the fact that the firewall would be put to an inappropriate use did not become apparent until contractor had completed the job, that contractor told owner that contractor did not approve of an unsupported firewall, and owner did not take any precautions to avert known risk of firewall collapse, owner could not seek to hold contractor responsible for collapse of firewall.

81051 McClane v. Sun Oil Co., 634 F.2d 855 (5th Cir. 1981)

III: A201-1976, Art. 4, Para. 4.18

Subcontractor sued owner for negligence. Owner filed a third party action against the contractor for contractual indemnity. The District Court held that the contractor was required to indemnify the owner pursuant to an indemnity provision in the contract.

The Court of Appeals reversed and held that the contractor was not liable for negligent acts of the owner which were unconnected with the subject of the contract. The contract provision provided for indemnity for claims "arising out of, incident to or in connection with this agreement or performance of work or services hereunder or breach of the terms hereof."

81052 McKinney Drilling Co. v. Collins Co., 517 F. Supp. 320 (N.D. Ala. 1981)

III: A201-1976, Art. 1, Para. 1.1
III: A201-1976, Art. 5, Para. 5.3
III: A201-1976, Art. 9, Para. 9.1
III: A401-1978, Art. 1
III: A401-1978, Art. 4

Subcontractor filed suit against contractor and its surety for breach of contract and to recover under a labor and material payment bond for adjustments to the base price. The contractor claimed the subcontractor was bound to a lump-sum price. The District Court rendered judgment for the subcontractor.

The Supreme Court affirmed. Specific contract clauses provided for interest on overdue payments and for release of the owner from liability upon acceptance by the contractor of final payment. The Court held that a claim for the interest agreed upon followed by a denial and the question whether final payment had been made under the contract, when the payment did not contain the interest, were disputes under the wording of the contract provisions, and were therefore arbitrable. The Court further held that where both parties had contracted for the arbitration process, the owner's suit for declaratory judgment, filed before arbitration had taken place, was premature.

81048   Linton Co. v. Robert Reid Engineers, Inc., 504 F. Supp. 1169 (N.D. Ala. 1981)

> III: A401-1978, Art. 11
> III: A401-1978, Art. 12

Subcontractor brought action against contractor claiming it was entitled to payment for work performed. Contractor claimed that the money it owed to the subcontractor should be reduced due to the fact that certain expenses and fees incurred were disallowed in arriving at a settlement with the owner. The District Court rendered judgment for the subcontractor.

The District Court held that, since the settlement occurred after the contract was terminated due to the contractor's failure to satisfy the terms of the contract and not due to any fault of the subcontractor, "any fees of the [contractor] that were disallowed and expenses that the [contractor] incurred in settling its claim with the [owner] should be borne by the [contractor] and not by the [subcontractor]." The Court also held that an additional amount should have been paid to the subcontractor for its consultants, even though the consultants had not qualified with the State as required by the contract between the State and the contractor, since the parties had waived this requirement by their conduct.

81049   Litton Bionetics, Inc. v. Glen Constr. Co., 292 Md. 34, 437 A.2d 208 (1981)

> I: A201-1976, Art. 7, Para. 7.9
> I: B141-1977, Art. 9

Contractor filed demand for arbitration against owner pursuant to a contract provision for arbitration. Owner counterclaimed against contractor and filed demand for arbitration against architect. Owner brought suit to have the claim consolidated after the contractor objected to consolidation. The Circuit Court denied the request for consolidation.

The Court of Appeals reversed and remanded, holding that absent a contract provision providing for separate arbitration of claims, the court has jurisdiction to consolidate such claims under the Maryland Uniform Arbitration Act or the Federal Arbitration Act if that act applied.

81050   Marine Colloids, Inc. v. M.D. Hardy, Inc., 433 A.2d 402 (Me. 1981)

> III: A201-1976, Art. 4, Para. 4.5

The Supreme Court of Appeals affirmed. The Court held that the contract was entire rather than severable, and the contractor bore the risk of loss until final completion. Although the contract had a provision for partial payments at "intervals of construction," the failure of the parties to follow this provision was evidence of the entirety of the contract. The fact that the contract was for construction of a modular home further convinced the Supreme Court that the parties intended construction of the home for a fixed sum which was to be held in escrow until final completion of the home. Although the owner had obtained property insurance, it was for the benefit of the lender and was not related to the contractor's claim.

81046   Lagerstrom v. Beers Construction Co., 157 Ga. App. 396, 277 S.E.2d 765 (1981)

I: A201-1976, Art. 4, Para. 4.18

Structural engineer brought suit against general contractor for attorney's fees under indemnification provision in owner-contractor agreement. The lower court entered summary judgment for the contractor.

The Court of Appeals affirmed and determined that the structural engineer, an independent contractor retained by the architect as a consultant, was not an agent of the architect. The engineer's occasional representation of the architect for explaining structural designs to the general contract did not qualify him as an agent of the architect since the subject matter of the discussions was always limited to "structural designs in which [the engineer] acted on his own behalf." Thus, the Court held that the indemnification clause in the contract, in which the contractor agreed to indemnify the "architect and their *agents* and employees from . . . expenses including attorney's fees," was not applicable to the structural engineer.

81047   Lindon City v. Engineers Construction Co., 636 P.2d 1070 (Utah 1981)

II: A101-1977, Art. 5
II: A107-1978, Art. 4
II: A107-1978, Art. 13
II: A107-1978, Art. 15
II: A111-1978, Art. 4
II: A117-1979, Art. 9
II: A117-1979, Art. 17
II: A117-1979, Art. 19
II: A201-1976, Art. 7, Para. 7.8
II: A201-1976, Art. 7, Para. 7.9
II: A201-1976, Art. 9, Para. 9.9

Owner filed suit for declaratory judgment after engineer requested arbitration under the contract. The trial court entered judgment for the engineer, and the owner appealed.

Subcontractor brought suit against contractor's surety to recover under payment bond. The Supreme Court granted a motion by the subcontractor to strike the contractor's defense.

The Supreme Court, Appellate Division, reversed. The Court held that the subcontractor was bound by the limitation of filing suit within one year following the date on which the contractor ceased work. "[The subcontractor] as a third party beneficiary is bound by the terms of the bond. . . ." The fact that the payment bond was written on a form which misidentified the principal as subcontractor, rather than general contractor, and the obligee as a general contractor rather than owner, was irrelevant, since the subcontractor claimed not to know of the existence of the bond.

81044 Kleeman v. Fragman Construction Co., 91 Ill. App. 3d 455, 414 N.E.2d 1064 (1981)

        I: A107-1978, Art. 10
        I: A117-1979, Art. 14
        I: A201-1976, Art. 4, Para. 4.3

After a settlement with an injured employee of a subcontractor, the contractor and owner brought a third party claim against the subcontractor. The trial court held for the contractor and the owner, and the subcontractor appealed.

The Court of Appeals affirmed. The Court upheld the determination of the trial court that the introduction of a contract provision stating that "[t]he Contractor shall be responsible to the Owner for the acts and omissions of all his employees and all Subcontractors, their agents and employees, and all other persons performing any of the Work under a contract with the Contractor" was irrelevant for the purposes of determining the authority of the owner and contractor over the work performed by the worker. "[T]his provision only relates to how the owner and general contractor would apportion possible technical liability under the [Illinois] Structural Work Act for the transgressions of the subcontractors, and not to the actual authority of the parties to control any portions of the work on the construction project."

81045 L.D.A., Inc. v. Cross, 279 S.E.2d 409 (W. Va. 1981)

        III: A101-1977, Art. 4
        III: A101-1977, Art. 5
        III: A107-1978, Art. 4
        III: A107-1978, Art. 5
        III: A201-1976, Art. 11, Para. 11.3

Contractor sued owner to recover damages for work performed on modular home which was completely destroyed by fire during construction. The Circuit Court entered a verdict for the owner.

I: A201-1976, Art. 7, Para. 7.9

Contractor and owner were in dispute over bills presented for changes in work. While the dispute was being negotiated, four subcontractors and materialmen brought suit to foreclose their respective mechanic's liens against the contractor and owner. The contractor then demanded arbitration of its dispute with the owner pursuant to the contract. In response to the foreclosure suits and request for arbitration, the owner moved to consolidate the foreclosure suits and enjoin the arbitration. The trial court granted the owner's motion; however, it reversed its decision after a request for reconsideration by the owner.

The Appellate Court reversed and granted the owner's motion. The Court stated "where an arbitration agreement involves some, but not all, of the parties to a multiparty litigation, the policy favoring arbitration must be weighed against the polices favoring joinder of claims. Where arbitration would increase rather than decrease delay, complexity and costs [as it does the case at bar], it should not receive favored treatment. However, it is not sufficient to show merely that litigation would be the speedier and more economical means of resolving controversy. It also must be shown that the issues and the relationships among the parties to the multiparty litigation are closely intermingled."

81042 John D. Ahern Co. v. Trustees of Boston University, 421 N.E.2d 477 (Mass. App. Ct.), *cert. denied,* 440 N.E.2d 1172 (Mass. 1981)

III: A107-1978, Art. 7
III: A117-1979, Art. 11
III: A201-1976, Art. 7, Para. 7.5
III: A311-1970, Labor and Material Payment Bond
III: A401-1978, Art. 7

Subcontractor sued owner, claiming that the owner's failure to advise them that the payment bond had been waived constituted negligent misrepresentation rendering the owner liable for unpaid sums due them. The trial court held for the owner.

The Court of Appeals affirmed, holding that "a requirement by an owner, who invites bids from a contractor, that the contractor furnish a payment bond for the benefit of subcontractors, does not, in the absence of special circumstances, create either a contractual undertaking to the subcontractors or a representation to them that a payment bond will in fact be furnished. . . . Subcontractors should be on their guard to protect their rights . . . by checking with the owner for the actual existence of a bond before entering their subcontracts."

81043 John Johnson Concrete Gutter Co. v. American Empire Insurance Co., 81 A.D.2d 1004, 440 N.Y.S.2d 107 (1981)

III: A311-1970, Labor and Material Payment Bond

81039   *In re* F & T Contractors, Inc., 649 F.2d 1229 (6th Cir. 1981)

       I: A201-1976, Art. 7, Para. 7.9

Contractor sued owner in bankruptcy court and the owner sought to compel arbitration. The Court refused the request for arbitration and the District Court affirmed.

The Court of Appeals affirmed, holding that the decision to deny or compel arbitration was discretionary with the bankruptcy court judge. The judge did not abuse his discretion in denying a request for arbitration where there were third parties involved in the bankruptcy proceedings whose interests would not be represented in an arbitration hearing.

81040   J.C. Penney Co. v. Davis & Davis, Inc., 158 Ga. App. 169, 279 S.E.2d 461 (1981)

       III: A107-1978, Art. 8
       III: A117-1979, Art. 12
       III: A201-1976, Art. 2, Para. 2.2
       III: A401-1978, Art. 1
       III: A401-1978, Art. 2
       III: A401-1978, Art. 11

Subcontractor sued owner and contractor seeking recovery for work performed and rejected by the owner. The Fulton Superior Court entered a verdict in favor of the subcontractor, and the owner and contractor appealed.

The Court of Appeals reversed the lower court's decision. The Court held that under the owner-contractor contract, the owner had an absolute right to reject any work that did not conform to the contract specifications, even if the contracted work was allegedly impossible to perform due to faulty design specifications. The subcontractor could not recover from the owner for tortious interference with a contractual relationship since, under the contract, the owner had an absolute right to interfere. Likewise the claim against the contractor for conspiracy failed because of the same reason.

The Court also held that the contractor did not breach the subcontract by its refusal to renegotiate that part of the agreement which allegedly was impossible to perform, since the subcontractor had the obligation to examine the specifications prior to binding himself to the contract, pursuant to a contract provision. The court stated that "where the [subcontractor] contract [s] to perform covenants that are impossible, *not because of an act of God or the conduct of the [contractor]*, the failure to perform . . . is as fatal to the [subcontractor's] right to recover as a breach . . . for any other reason."

81041   J.F. Inc. v. Vicik, 99 Ill. App. 3d 815, 426 N.E.2d 257 (1981)

       I: A107-1978, Art. 13
       I: A117-1979, Art. 17

III: A201-1976, Art. 10, Para. 10.1
III: A201-1976, Art. 10, Para. 10.2

Employee of subcontractor brought a personal injury suit against owner. The injury occurred while the employee was working on a highway improvement contract. The Court of Claims granted judgment for the employee of the subcontractor on the basis that the State owed a nondelegable duty to safely maintain highways.

The Supreme Court, Appellate Division, reversed and dismissed the employee's claim. The Court stated that "the State owed no duty to [subcontractor's employee] to maintain the Expressway in a safe condition, and the general contractor's failure to install warning devices called for under the contract cannot cast the State in liability."

81037 Hughes Masonry Co. v. Greater Clark County School Building Corp., 659 F.2d 836 (7th Cir. 1981)

I: A201-1976, Art. 2, Para. 2.2
I: A201-1976, Art. 7, Para. 7.9
I: A401-1978, Art. 13, Para. 13.2

Contractor terminated contract with subcontractor and demanded arbitration proceedings. Subcontractor filed a separate action in District Court against the contractor and the construction manager. The contractor's subsequent order for arbitration was denied.

The Court of Appeals reversed, and allowed the order for arbitration. The subcontractor cannot hold the construction manager liable for its failure to perform contractual duties described in the subcontract while denying that the construction manager is a party to the agreement in order to avoid arbitration claims.

81038 I.D.C., Inc. v. McCain-Winkler Partnership, 396 So. 2d 590 (La. Ct. App. 1981)

I: A107-1978, Art. 13
I: A117-1979, Art. 17
I: A201-1976, Art. 7, Para. 7.9

Contractor sued owner to recover money due. Owner counterclaimed for damages, alleging construction defects. On the day of the trial, the owner sought a stay of proceedings and an order compelling arbitration. The trial court granted the motion, and the contractor appealed.

The Court of Appeals reversed and remanded. The Court held that the owner had waived its right to arbitration by failing to make a prior demand, failing to raise the issue in the pleadings and pre-trial conferences, and by acquiescing to litigation, demonstrated by filing a counterclaim. The Court further ruled that the trial court's characterization of the issue as "procedural arbitrability" was erroneous, since prior to the present action neither party expressed a desire to arbitrate.

After obtaining an arbitration award, contractor sought foreclosure of lien in total amount of award, together with interest, court costs and reasonable attorney's fees. Owner tendered payment of award plus interest, which contractor rejected, whereupon the Circuit Court dismissed the foreclosure suit. The Court of Appeals reversed, but denied recovery of attorney's fees incurred in arbitration, and remanded to the Circuit Court to determine the proper amount of the judgment.

On review, the Supreme Court concluded that the contract reserved to the prevailing party in a lien foreclosure suit the full reasonable attorney's fees available under Oregon lien statute, including fees for arbitration proceedings. The Court held that where the agreement provided that rights and remedies available under the contract were "in addition to and not a limitation of any duties, obligations, rights and remedies otherwise imposed or available by law," and the Oregon lien statute provided for recovery of attorney's fees, the remedy of arbitration was not a limitation on collection of attorney's fees, where such fees would have been collectible had the dispute been litigated in court. The Court limited collection of such fees to what would have been reasonable had the issues been litigated in the foreclosure proceeding.

The Court rejected the contention that recovery of attorney's fees could be had under the arbitration clause of the contract, which provided that "the award rendered by the arbitrators shall be final, and judgment may be entered upon it in accordance with applicable law in any court having jurisdiction thereof." The Court ruled that, even if "applicable law" were to be construed to include the lien statute, the clause provided only for entry of judgment upon the award, and said nothing concerning attorney's fees.

81035 Henrico Doctor's Hospital and Diagnostic Clinic, Inc. v. Doyle & Russell, Inc., 221 Va. 710, 273 S.E.2d 547 (1981)

    I: A201-1976, Art. 9, Para. 9.9

Contractor brought suit against owner seeking interest on contract retainage. The trial court entered judgment for the contractor.

The Supreme Court affirmed the trial court's decision. The contractor's delay in providing releases and waiver of liens as required by the contract did not preclude recovery of interest retainage on amounts where there were no mechanic's liens filed prior to submission of the releases and waivers since "the hospital [owner] enjoyed the [use and benefit] of the retainage fund while occupying and using the hospital building constructed by the contractor." The Court also affirmed the trial court's deduction of interest on an amount of an unenforced mechanic's lien from the date it was filed until the date it expired.

81036 Himbele v. New York, 68 A.D.2d 458, 417 N.Y.S.2d 789 (1979), *aff'd,* 427 N.Y.S.2d 931 (N.Y. 1981)

    III: A107-1978, Art. 16
    III: A117-1979, Art. 20

to be performed. The Court held that "the job quotation was not the contract between the parties but was only a preliminary step in arriving at an agreement."

81032 H & H Sewer Systems, Inc. v. Insurance Guaranty Assoc., 392 So. 2d 430 (La. 1981), *aff'g* 350 So. 2d 1211 (La. Ct. App. 1977)

I: A311-1970, Performance Bond

Contractor who was hired by surety as subrogee under defaulting contractor's performance bond brought suit against Insurance Guaranty Association for money due after the surety declared bankruptcy. The Court of Appeal entered judgment for the contractor.

The Supreme Court affirmed. Pursuant to Louisiana law, the Insurance Guaranty Association was bound to provide "the payment of covered claims under certain insurance policies where the insurer becomes insolvent." The Court held that the contractor was a "claimant" under the performance bond because the surety exercised its option to "[c]omplete the Contract in accordance with its terms and conditions," and thereby became responsible for "making payments for all labor and material used in performance of the contract."

81033 Hall v. Andow, 634 P.2d 1052 (Haw. Ct. App. 1981)

III: A401-1978, Art. 11

Subcontractor sued contractor and the trial court granted a directed verdict for the contractor and awarded him attorney's fees. The subcontractor appealed.

The Intermediate Court of Appeals affirmed the directed verdict, but reversed the award of attorney's fees. The subcontract contained a provision that the subcontractor agreed to be bound by the terms of the prime contract. The Court held that where the subcontractor knew that the prime contract required the governor's signature and that the signature had not been obtained when the subcontract was signed, the subcontractor knew that his contract was contingent upon the execution of the prime contract. The prime contract was never executed, through no fault of the contractor and thus the directed verdict was properly granted. The Court ruled, however, that the agreement of the subcontractor to be bound by the terms of the contract did not incorporate the prime contract provision awarding attorney's fees. The provision for attorney's fees was effective only where a suit was instituted on the prime contract, not on the subcontract as was the case here.

81034 Harris v. Dyer, 292 Or. 233, 637 P.2d 918 (1981)

I: A201-1976, Art. 7, Para. 7.6
I: A201-1976, Art. 7, Para. 7.9

to be "inconsistent with an intent to relinquish statutory rights." The agreement for a "reasonable time" was also held not to enlarge the statutory period.

81029 Genstar Southern Development Corp. v. Troup Brothers, Inc., 396 So. 2d 211 (Fla. Dist. Ct. App. 1981)

      II: A201-1976, Art. 2, Para. 2.2

Subcontractor filed mechanic's lien, and the developer filed a complaint to discharge lien. The subcontractor counterclaimed to foreclose the lien, while the engineer's decision over a dispute between the subcontractor and developer was pending. The trial court ruled that the developer could not assert as a defense that the filing of the lien resulted in waiver of an arbitration provision in the contract.

The Court of Appeals affirmed. The Court ruled that the subcontractor's actions were taken to secure all of the developer's debt which the engineer might find due. Thus, the Court held that the arbitration provision was not waived and the developer's failure to "demand arbitration from the engineer's decision within thirty days," pursuant to this provision, rendered the engineer's decision final and binding.

81030 Gurtler. Hebert & Co. v. Weyland Mach. Shop, Inc., 405 So. 2d 660 (La. Ct. App. 1981)

      III: A201-1976, Art. 1, Para. 1.1

Contractor sued subcontractor for breach of contract, and subcontractor impleaded architect as a third party defendant. The trial court dismissed the subcontractor's action, relying on a provision in the prime contract excepting the architect from privity of contract between the subcontractor or the owner.

The Court of Appeal reversed and remanded. The Court agreed that no contract action existed, but held that the subcontractor could assert a tort action, absent of privity of contract. Since the subcontractor alleged tortious conduct by the architect, resulting in construction delays, the Court remanded for trial on that cause of action.

81031 H.E. Wiese, Inc. v. Western Stress, Inc., 407 So. 2d 464 (La. Ct. App. 1981)

      III: A201-1976, Art. 1, Para. 1.1
      III: A401-1978, Art. 1

Contractor and owner sued subcontractor and its surety, seeking damages for improper performance of stress relief work during overhaul of owner's boiler. The trial court entered judgment against the subcontractor and its surety and the subcontractor appealed.

The Court of Appeals affirmed. The Court found that the subcontractor improperly performed its required work. The Court also held that the subcontractor was bound by the work contract provision, which required him to do all necessary work to relieve the stress on the boiler, and not to the bid quotation, which required a lesser amount of work

its express terms, has no application to the subcontractor . . . . We note that the 1976 revision . . . does expressly provide for such a waiver between the owner and the subcontractor."

81027   Freeman v. Town of Many, 394 So. 2d 693 (La. Ct. App.), *cert. denied,* 399 So. 2d 598 (La. 1981)

        III: A201-1976, Art. 10, Para. 10.2

Property owner sued town and contractor for damages to his property as a result of the construction of a sewer line. The trial court rendered judgment for the property owner, and the contractor appealed.

The Court of Appeal affirmed. The town had obtained a servitude from the property owner allowing it to go onto his land to lay sewer lines but obligating the town to repair any damages. The Court held that the resulting damage to the property owner's trees rendered the contractor liable under a provision in the contract between the town and the contractor stating that the contractor was required "to take all necessary precautions to prevent damage to property adjacent to the construction site, such as trees, shrubs, and utilities." The contract also stated that in the event of damage "he was obligated to immediately repair it or have it repaired at his own cost."

81028   Geneseo Central School v. Perfetto & Whalen Construction Corp., 53 N.Y.2d 306, 441 N.Y.S.2d 229, 423 N.E.2d 1058 (1981), *rev'g* 434 N.Y.S.2d 502 (App. Div. 1980)

        I: A107-1978, Art. 13
        I: A117-1979, Art. 17
        I: A201-1976, Art. 7, Para. 7.4
        I: A201-1976, Art. 7, Para. 7.6
        I: A201-1976, Art. 7, Para. 7.9

Contractor demanded arbitration to resolve a dispute over contractor's request for additional compensation. The owner obtained a stay of arbitration in a proceeding before the trial court. The trial court held that the contractor's claim was barred for lack of timeliness under a statute requiring claims to be served within thirty days after their presentment.

The Appellate Division reversed, holding that the contractual provision "within a reasonable time after first observance" superseded the temporal restriction of the state statute, and that reasonableness of time was to be determined by the arbitrator.

The Court of Appeals reversed the Appellate Division, holding that in the absence of an express agreement to the contrary, "the provisions of the statute are deemed to be part and parcel of any contract entered into by the [owner]." A contract provision declaring that "rights and remedies available thereunder shall not be a limitation of any duties, obligations, rights and remedies otherwise imposed or available by law" was held

81024 Fairchild v. W. O. Taylor Commercial Refrigeration & Electric Co., 403 So. 2d 1119 (Fla. Dist. Ct. App. 1981)

      III: A107-1978, Art. 17
      III: A117-1979, Art. 21
      III: A201-1976, Art. 11, Para. 11.3

Owner's insurance company sought subrogation against contractor and its insurance company, when fire caused by negligent installation of air conditioning system caused damage to owner's home. The trial court entered summary judgment for the contractor and its insurance company.

The Court of Appeals reversed and remanded. The Court held that a provision in the contract requiring the owner to carry fire insurance was not applicable five years after the work had been completed. The intention behind the insurance provision was to cover the period during which both parties had an insurable interest. Once the work had been completed and the owner's debt discharged, the owner's obligation to insure against property damage during construction terminated.

81025 Financial Indemnity Co. v. Steele & Sons, Inc., 403 So. 2d 600 (Fla. Dist. Ct. App. 1981)

      II: A311-1970, Labor and Material Payment Bond

Contractor's surety sued subcontractor's surety for indemnification. The trial court entered judgment for the contractor's surety, an subcontractor's surety appealed.

The Court of Appeals affirmed the trial court's decision. The Court construed a provision of the subcontractor's bond in favor of the contractor's surety, which stated that the bond "is one of indemnity only and does not inure to the benefit of or confer any right of action, upon any person other than the [contractor]." The Court held that the contractor's surety became subrogated to the rights of the contractor under the subcontractor's labor and material payment bond, and thus was entitled to indemnification.

81026 Fortin v. Nebel Heating Corp., 429 N.E.2d 363 (Mass. App. Ct. 1981)

      I: A201-1976, Art. 11, Para. 11.3
      I: A401-1978, Art. 9

Owner's insurer sued subcontractor in a subrogation action for negligence. The subcontractor filed a motion for summary judgment which was denied.

The Court of Appeals affirmed the denial. The Court held that the language in the property insurance provisions of previous editions of the AIA General Conditions and AIA Subcontract did not constitute a waiver of the owner's right to recover from the subcontractor for fire damage. In those versions of the contacts "the waiver of damages . . . specifically applies only between the owner and the general [contractor], and, by

Subcontractor sued contractor to recover for extras. The Circuit Court entered judgment in favor of the subcontractor and awarded attorney's fees. The contractor appealed.

The Court of Appeals affirmed judgment for the subcontractor but reversed on the award of attorney's fees. The Court held that the existence of an indemnification provision in the subcontract, in which the subcontractor agreed to indemnify the contractor for "any damage, cost loss or expense, including counsel fees" did not allow the subcontractor to recover attorney's fees in a suit brought by the subcontractor. The Court stated that although it may have been fair to allow the award of attorney's fees to work both ways, it had to deal with the contract fashioned by the parties for themselves.

81022a   Elec-trol, Inc. v. C.J. Kern Contractors, Inc., 54 N.C. App. 626, 284 S.E.2d 119 (1981), *appeal denied,* 305 N.C. 298, 290 S.E.2d 701 (1982)

         I: A201-1976, Art. 12, Para. 12.3

         I: A401-1978, Art. 1

Subcontractor sued general contractor for additional costs for change order work. The Superior Court entered summary judgment for general contractor.

The Court of Appeals of North Carolina affirmed the lower court's decision. The subcontract expressly incorporated all the conditions of the general contract covering claims for additional costs, one section of which provided that "if the Owner and the Contractor cannot agree on the amount of the adjustment in the Contract Sum, it shall be determined by the Architect." The Court held that pursuant to this provision the architect's decision was final and binding.

81023   Evans Electrical Construction Co. v. University of Kansas Medical Center, 230 Kan. 298, 634 P.2d 1079 (1981)

         II: A107-1978, Art. 13

         II: A107-1978, Art. 18

         II: A117-1979, Art. 17

         II: A117-1979, Art. 22

         II: A201-1976, Art. 7, Para. 7.9

         II: A201-1976, Art. 12, Para. 12.1

A contractor sought to have an arbitration award in favor of the State agency set aside. The trial court upheld the award and the contractor appealed.

The Supreme Court affirmed. The Court interpreted various Kansas statutes, including the Kansas version of the Uniform Arbitration Act, and determined that it was lawful for the State agency to abide by the compulsory arbitration process contained in its contract with the contractor. The Court also stated that the evidence showed that there was no agreement or novation to depart from the contract requirement for written change orders.

disregarded the provisions of the contract. Thus, the subcontractor was justified in abandoning the work site and is to be compensated for work performed.

81018   Dan Cowling & Associates, Inc. v. Board of Educ. of Clinton School Dist., 273 Ark. 214, 618 S.W.2d 158 (1981)

        I: A107-1978, Art. 8
        I: A117-1979, Art. 12
        I: A201-1976, Art. 2, Para. 2.2

Owner brought suit against the architect for breach of contract. The owner claimed the architect approved obviously defective work. The Circuit Court entered judgment in favor of the owner.

The Supreme Court affirmed. The Court held that by approving obviously defective work, the architect "breached his contractual duty to guard the owner against defects and deficiencies in the work of the contractor based upon his on-site observations."

81019   Dravo Corp. v. Robert Kerris, Inc., 655 F.2d 503 (3d Cir. 1981)

        I: A311-1970, Labor and Material Payment Bond

Supplier sued contractor and surety under a payment bond. The District Court awarded damages to the supplier.

The Court of Appeals reversed the award. The notice provision in the payment bond was interpreted to require notice after the last labor or delivery of materials, and notice prior to that time was not proper notice within the plain meaning of the bond.

81020   (UNASSIGNED)

81021   E.C. Ernst, Inc. v. Tallahassee, 527 F. Supp. 1141 (N.D. Fla. 1981)

        III: A401-1978, Art. 13

Subcontractor moved for a stay in the proceedings and an order compelling arbitration. Subsequently, the subcontractor attempted to waive its right to arbitration. The District Court denied the subcontractor's attempt to waive arbitration.

The District Court held that where the arbitration proceedings were one-third complete the subcontractor was not entitled to waive its contractual right to arbitration. The Court also held that the contractor's decision to arbitrate was timely since notice was given as soon as it had reason to believe the announcement of arbitration should be made.

81022   Edward L. Nezelek, Inc. v. G. E. Drywall, Inc., 406 So. 2d 1220 (Fla. Dist. Ct. App. 1981)

        III: A401-1978, Art. 11

Owner sued contractors for breach of contract due to failure to complete project by a specified date. The trial court entered judgment for the owner, and the contractors appealed.

The Supreme Court affirmed on this issue. The Court held that although the contract was partly written and partly oral, a Montana statute was applicable, which provided that time is not of the essence unless expressly contained in the contract terms. The owner's oral acceptance of the contractor's bid was expressly conditioned upon completion by the specified date, prior to the approach of cold weather. Thus, the contractors breached by failing to timely complete their work.

81016 Clearwater Constructors, Inc. v. Guiterrez, 626 S.W.2d 789 (Tex. Civ. App. 1981)

III:	A107-1978, Art. 16
III:	A117-1979, Art. 20
III:	A201-1976, Art. 10, Para. 10.2

Decedent's wife, allegedly a third-party beneficiary under the owner-contractor agreement, brought an action against contractor for loss of consortium due to her husband's death resulting from an on-the-job injury. The trial court entered judgment for the wife, and the contractor appealed.

The Court of Appeals reversed. The Court found that the wife was too remote a party to qualify as a third-party beneficiary of the contract provision which stated that the contractor "bound itself to take proper safety and health precautions"to protect the work, the workers, the public and the property of others.'" The language manifested no intent of the parties to the agreement to extend benefits to spouses of employees.

81017 D.M. Holden v. Contractor's Crane Service, 121 N.H. 831, 435 A.2d 529 (1981)

II:	A401-1978, Art. 5
II:	A401-1978, Art. 11
II:	A401-1978, Art. 12

Subcontractor and contractor entered into contract in which subcontractor was to receive periodic payments after its requests were approved by the architect. Subcontractor, after repeated demands for payment, left the job and brought suit for breach of contract. The Superior Court entered judgment for subcontractor.

The Supreme Court affirmed. The Court held the "subcontractor was entitled to be paid even though architect had not approved requisition [because] architect's failure to approve was fault of contractor." The Court also stated that the "subcontractor was entitled to compensation for extras performed on project, even though . . . general contract provided that no payment for extras would be made unless work was approved in advance and in writing," because it was found that during the progress of the project both parties

A workman sued the contractor for injuries sustained at the construction site. The contractor filed a cross-claim against the subcontractor for indemnification of the subcontractor's negligence. The contractor also sought a stay of judicial proceedings and the enforcement of the appointment clause in the contract. The trial court denied the contractor's request for arbitration.

The Court of Appeals affirmed, holding that while the contractor is entitled to indemnification, the issue of the contractor's negligence was "independent of any agreement to arbitrate between the contractor and the subcontractor. The agreement cannot . . . abridge the worker's right to a jury trial. Nor can the voluntary filing of a cross-claim by the contractor . . . serve as a means for staying the entire judicial proceeding or as a means of enlarging the scope of arbitration."

81014   Carpentersville v. Mayfair Construction Co., 100 Ill. App. 3d 128, 426 N.E.2d 558 (1981)

II:	A107-1978, Art. 13	
III:	A107-1978, Art. 18	
II:	A117-1979, Art. 17	
III:	A117-1979, Art. 22	
II:	A201-1976, Art. 2, Para. 2.2	
II:	A201-1976, Art. 7, Para. 7.9	
III:	A201-1976, Art. 12, Para. 12.1	
III:	A201-1976, Art. 12, Para. 12.3	

Owner sought a declaratory judgment that certain claims brought against it by a contractor were not arbitrable. The trial court ordered the parties to proceed to arbitration.

The Appellate Court affirmed. The Court held that the owner did not waive its right to challenge the arbitration award after participating in the arbitration proceedings, since it had preserved its right to challenge the arbitrators' decision by objecting to the proceedings prior to a hearing on the merits. The Court, however, rejected the owner's contention that the contractor's claims were not arbitrable because there were conditions precedent to arbitrability. The Court stated that the contract provisions relating to change orders and extra compensation did not speak to arbitrability and that the claims brought under the provisions concerning timeliness and waiver and other procedural matters should be decided by the arbitrator. The Court did state that had the preconditions been statutory, the claims would have had to have been decided by a court.

81015   Carriger v. Ballenger, 628 P.2d 1106 (Mont. 1981)

III:	A107-1978, Art. 14	
III:	A117-1979, Art. 18	
III:	A201-1976, Art. 8, Para. 8.2	

to within one year, the subcontractor's suit was untimely since it was filed two years after the work was abandoned.

81012   Campbell v. Southern Roof Deck Applicators, Inc., 406 So. 2d 910 (Ala. 1981)

        I: A107-1978, Art. 10
        I: A107-1978, Art. 16
        I: A117-1979, Art. 14
        I: A117-1979, Art. 20
        I: A201-1976, Art. 4, Para. 4.18
        I: A201-1976, Art. 10, Para. 10.2

Owner sued contractor and architect for damages, including indemnification for attorney fees. The architect filed a cross claim against the contractor to also indemnify him for attorney's fees incurred in defending the suit. The Circuit Court entered summary judgment for the contractor, and denied summary judgment for the architect and the owner on this issue.

The Supreme Court affirmed. The indemnification provision defined a claim for which indemnity may be made as one "against the Owner or the Architect or any of their agents or employees by an employee of the Contractor, any Subcontractor, anyone directly or indirectly employed by any of them or anyone for whose acts any of them is liable. . . ." The Court held that this provision referred only to claims of third parties and would not be construed to permit indemnification of the owner and the architect for attorney's fees incurred in a suit which either of them brought against the contractor.

The Court also held that a separate indemnification provision contained in the section "Protection of Persons and Property," in which the contractor agreed to remedy "all damage or loss to any property caused in whole or in part by the Contractor," was not inconsistent with the indemnification provision upon which the claim was based. It was unnecessary to consider this provision since it did not refer to attorney's fees and could not be the grounds for this cause of action.

81013   Caron v. Barkan Construction Co., 420 N.E.2d 18 (Mass. App. Ct. 1981)

        II: A107-1978, Art. 10
        II: A107-1978, Art. 13
        II: A117-1979, Art. 14
        II: A117-1979, Art. 17
        II: A201-1976, Art. 4, Para. 4.18
        II: A201-1976, Art. 7, Para. 7.9
        II: A401-1978, Art. 11
        II: A401-1978, Art. 13

that he has abandoned his right to arbitrate," this was not the case here. Since an objection to venue must be asserted in the earliest defensive pleading, such an objection does not indicate an abandonment of a party's contractual right to arbitrate. Also, the owners' assertion of their right to arbitrate nine months after legal proceedings commenced was held to be timely.

81010 Burke County Public Schools Board of Education v. Juno Construction Corp., 50 N.C. App. 238, 273 S.E.2d 504, *aff'd,* 282 S.E.2d 778 (N.C. 1981)

I: A107-1978, Art. 15
II: A107-1978, Art. 13
I: A117-1979, Art. 19
II: A117-1979, Art. 17
I: A201-1976, Art. 9, Para. 9.9
II: A201-1976, Art. 7, Para. 7.9

Owner sued contractor and subcontractor for damages caused by faulty installation of roof. Based on the jury's determination that the damage caused to the roof resulted solely from design deficiencies, the Superior Court denied the owner recovery. The Court also denied the contractor's motion for a directed verdict. The owner and contractor appealed.

The Court of Appeals affirmed. On the issue of the denial of the contractor's motion for directed verdict, the Court held that the owner's claim was not barred by the issuance of the architect's final certificate of completion and acceptance of final payment by the contractor. The contract did not indicate that the architect's final certificate would be "conclusive as to the completion of the work in accordance with the contract," and an arbitration provision for settlement of disputes between the owner and the contractor had been included in the contract. The owner was also not barred from claims since there was a provision stating that "the making of final payment constitutes a waiver of all claims by the owner except those claims from . . . failure of work to comply with the contract documents."

81011 Camelot Excavating Co. v. St. Paul Fire & Marine Ins. Co., 410 Mich. 118, 301 N.W.2d 275 (1981), *aff'g,* 89 Mich. App. 219, 280 N.W.2d 491 (1979)

III: A311-1970, Labor and Material Payment Bond

Subcontractor sued surety to recover payment on a labor and material bond. The Circuit Court granted subcontractor's motion for summary judgment. The Court of Appeals reversed.

The Supreme Court affirmed, holding that, "neither public policy nor existing authority prohibit private contracting parties from including in a labor and materials bond a provision which reasonably limits claimants to a period within which to bring suit that is shorter than the applicable state statute of limitations." Thus, where the contract limited claims

contract. Therefore the Court determined that the motion to dismiss was not inconsistent with the surety's right to have the dispute submitted to arbitration, and the Court remanded to consider the motion to dismiss and to compel arbitration.

81007 Ben Trovato Properties, Inc. v. Strauss, 159 Ga. App. 510, 284 S.E.2d 632 (1981)

> III: A107-1978, Art. 10
> III: A117-1978, Art. 14
> III: A201-1976, Art. 4, Para. 4.5

Owner sued contractor on breach of warranty. The Fulton State Court entered a verdict for the owner, and the contractor appealed.

The Court of Appeals affirmed. The owner was entitled to damages from the defective waterproofing of his home. The court held that the waterproofing was subject to the construction warranty since waterproofing was required in the construction drawings.

81008 Blount Brothers Corp. v. M. K. Steel, Inc., 524 F. Supp. 1037 (N.D. Ala. 1981)

> III: A401-1978, Art. 13

Contractor filed a petition to enforce the arbitration clause in the construction contract with subcontractor and to stay the state court proceedings. The subcontractor argued that its claim for breach of contract was not subject to the arbitration clause, and that the state court should have decided this matter. The District Court ordered the state proceeding to be stayed.

The District Court held that "[t]here is a strong federal policy in favor of arbitration, and numerous decisions indicate that arbitration clauses are to be construed liberally." The Court held that the dispute was arbitrable, including the question of arbitrability, since the arbitration clause stated "[i]f any question of fact shall arise under this contract. . . ."

81009 Brennan v. Kenwick, 97 Ill. App. 3d 1040, 425 N.E.2d 439 (1981)

> I: A107-1978, Art. 13
> I: A117-1979, Art. 17
> I: A201-1976, Art. 7, Para. 7.9

Contractor sued owners for amount due under a construction contract. The owners filed a motion to transfer venue. After the motion was contested, the owners filed a demand for arbitration pursuant to the contract. The trial court stayed the arbitration proceeding. The owners moved the court to vacate its order to stay the arbitration proceedings, and this motion was denied.

The Appellate Court reversed. The Court held that although "waiver will be found when a party's conduct has been inconsistent with the arbitration clause so as to indicate

for plumbing installations, but was also charged with furnishing materials therefor and unloading and distributing them."

The Court of Appeals affirmed the Appellate Court's ruling, holding that the contractor was entitled to indemnification from the subcontractor where the contract clause provided that the subcontractor was responsible for any injury to its employees "caused by or resulting from or arising out of any act or omission in connection with this Subcontract or the prosecution of the work hereunder." The employee's injury occurred while he was delivering material and the subcontractor was responsible under the subcontract not only for plumbing installations, but also delivery of material.

81004   (UNASSIGNED)

81005   Ardsley Construction Co. v. Port Auth., 75 A.D.2d 760, 427 N.Y.S.2d 814 (1980), aff'd, 444 N.Y.S.2d 907 (N.Y. 1981)

III:	A107-1978, Art. 13
III:	A117-1979, Art. 17
III:	A201-1976, Art. 2, Para. 2.
III:	A201-1976, Art. 7, Para. 7.9

Contractor sued owner for extra expenses incurred on roadway repairs contract after the engineer disallowed the claim. The Supreme Court entered judgment in favor of the contractor.

The Supreme Court, Appellate Division, reversed. The Court held that where there is a contract provision which makes the engineer the arbiter of all claims arising under the contract, the engineer's decision, in the absence of fraud, bad faith or palpable mistake, is final and binding as a matter of law.

81006   Balboa Insurance Co. v. W.G. Mills, Inc., 403 So. 2d 1149 (Fla. Dist. Ct. App. 1981)

I:	A107-1978, Art. 13
I:	A117-1979, Art. 17
I:	A201-1976, Art. 7, Para. 7.9
I:	A401-1978, Art. 13

Contractor filed suit against subcontractor and its surety for failure to complete project, who in turn filed a motion to dismiss for lack of jurisdiction over the subject matter. The trial court denied the motion, and the surety appealed.

The Court of Appeal reversed and remanded. The Court held that the surety did not waive its right to arbitration when it filed the motion to dismiss. Although the surety failed to include in the caption of the motion the words "and to compel arbitration," the material allegations in the motion were based on an arbitration provision in the subcontract, which incorporated by reference the provision for arbitration in the primary

81001 A. Amorello & Sons v. Beacon Construction Co., 422 N.E.2d 467 (Mass. App. Ct. 1981)

> I: A107-1978, Art. 12
> I: A117-1979, Art. 22
> I: A201-1976, Art. 12, Para. 12.2
> I: A401-1978, Art. 4

Subcontractor filed a lawsuit against the contractor claiming payment for extra work not included in the lump sum contract price. The master's report was submitted to the trial court judge who held for the subcontractor.

The Court of Appeals affirmed, holding that the contract provision dealing with concealed conditions "had the effect of casting on [the contractor] the responsibility of adjusting the contract price to reflect the increased cost of removal of ledge in excess of that shown in the borings report." The appropriate measure of adjustment was determined to be the unit prices fixed in the contract.

81002 American Drilling Service Co. v. City of Springfield, 614 S.W.2d 266 (Mo. Ct. App. 1981)

> II: A401-1978, Art. 12

Subcontractor sued owner and contractor for extra work done on project. The trial court dismissed the action against the contractor and the subcontractor appealed.

The Court of Appeals reversed and remanded. As to a clause in the contract providing for final payment by the contractor to the subcontractor within 30 days after the contractor has received payment for such work from the owner, the Court held that the clause "merely fixes the time when payment is due and does not establish a condition precedent to payment."

81003 April v. Sovereign Construction Co., 55 N.Y.2d 627, 446 N.Y.S.2d 252, 430 N.E.2d 1305 (1981), *aff'g* 79 A.D.2d 693, 434 N.Y.S.2d 279 (1980)

> III: A401-1978, Art. 11

Subcontractor's employee sued owner and contractor to recover damages resulting from an injury. Owner and contractor filed a third party claim seeking indemnity from the subcontractor. The Supreme Court rendered judgment for the subcontractor.

The Supreme Court, Appellate Division, reversed. The court held that the subcontractor was required to indemnify the owner and the contractor for damages paid to the subcontractor's employee who was injured while distributing material in connection with the subcontract, since the subcontract stated "the subcontractor would assume responsibility and liability for . . . any damages"caused by or resulting from or arising out' of any act or omission in connection with the subcontract *or the prosecution of the work hereunder* (emphasis added). Under the subcontract, [subcontractor] was not only responsible

80076 City of Lawrence v. Flazarano, 402 N.E.2d 1017 (Mass. 1980), *rev'g* 389 N.E.2d 435 (Mass. App. Ct. 1979)

> II: A107-1978, Art. 13
> II: A117-1979, Art. 17
> II: A201-1976, Art. 7, Para. 7.9

Contractor filed a demand for arbitration pursuant to an arbitration provision in the contract after the city canceled the construction project pursuant to a statute which required a certificate of need. The arbitrator awarded damages for delay and breach of contract, and the City filed an application to vacate the decision. The trial court allowed the application and the Appeals Court affirmed.

The Supreme Court reversed the application to vacate and reinstated the arbitrator's decision. The Court held that delay damages and loss of anticipated profits "are aspects of the potential liability to which any contracting party is commonly subject," and that recovery on either ground in the circumstances of the case was not contrary to public policy. The court also held that "such an extension of the authority of a court to declare . . . that arbitrators have 'exceed their powers' would tend to undermine the predictability and effectiveness of arbitration as a method of dispute resolution."

80074 Waterworks District No. 1 v. Babin, 393 So. 2d 282 (La. Ct. App. 1980)

      III: A107-1978, Art. 8
      III: A107-1978, Art. 13
      III: A117-1979, Art. 12
      III: A117-1979, Art. 17
      III: A201-1976, Art. 2, Para. 2.2
      III: A201-1976, Art. 7, Para. 7.9

Owner sued contractor for damages due to faulty paving work. Contractor was granted a stay of proceeding since the contract provided that all disputes would be referred to arbitration. However since neither party proceeded to arbitration, the trial court granted the owner's motion to rescind the stay order and proceed with trial. The contractor appealed.

The Court of Appeal reversed the trial court and held that under Louisiana law "[i]f any suit or proceeding be brought upon any issue referable to arbitration under an agreement in writing for arbitration, the court in which the suit is pending . . . shall on application of one of the parties stay the trial of the action," until arbitration has been successfully completed. The court also held that under Louisiana law, if both parties fail to abide by an arbitration provision, the trial court can only order the parties to arbitration. Thus, the trial court erred in lifting the stay order.

80075 Western Casualty & Sur. Co. v. Honeywell, Inc., 380 So. 2d 1385 (Miss. 1980)

      I: A311-1970, Labor & Material Payment Bond

Subcontractor's supplier brought suit against surety on general contractor's payment bond. The lower court entered judgment for the supplier and the surety appealed.

The Court of Appeals reversed and remanded. The lower court erred in its determination that a provision in the payment bond requiring a supplier to give notice of a claim "within ninety (90) days after such a claimant did or performed the last of the work or labor, or furnished the last of the materials" was against public policy in view of the Mississippi law requiring a supplier to give notice of a claim within one year after the completion of the work and final settlement.

In construing Mississippi law, the Court of Appeals stated that although it did not include a notice provision, "neither [did] the statute prohibit [the general contractor and the surety] from requiring suppliers of subcontractors to give reasonable notice of their claim." The Court held that the 90-day notice provision in the payment bond did not limit the time in which a supplier could bring suit under Mississippi law, "but relates only to things to be done [by the supplier] before liability thereon becomes fixed," and did not violate Mississippi law.

80072 V.L. Nicholson Co. v. Transcon Investment & Financial Ltd., 595 S.W.2d 474 (Tenn. 1980)

  I: A101-1977, Art. 3
  I: A107-1978, Art. 2
  I: A111-1978, Art. 4
  I: A117-1979, Art. 3

 In suit by contractor against owner and developer for recovery of retainage and for extra work, owner counterclaimed against contractor and surety for liquidated damages due to delay in completion. The trial court found for the contractor against the developer, but dismissed the claim against the owner and the owner's counterclaim against the contractor and surety. The Court of Appeals reversed the award against the developer for extra work, and granted the owner's counterclaim for liquidated damages against the contractor.

 The Tennessee Supreme Court, after finding for the contractor against the owner and developer for extra work on a theory of quasi-contract, reversed the Court of Appeals' award of liquidated damages for that portion of the delay attributable to the contractor. The Court held that where the delays in construction were caused mutually by the developer as agent of the owner and by the contractor, the liquidated damages clause could not be enforced.

80073 Vandygriff v. Commonwealth Edison Co., 87 Ill. App. 3d, 408 N.E.2d 1129 (1980)

  III: A107-1978, Art. 10
  III: A107-1978, Art. 17
  III: A117-1979, Art. 14
  III: A117-1979, Art. 21
  III: A201-1976, Art. 4, Para. 4.18
  III: A201-1976, Art. 11, Para. 11.1

 Owner sued contractor in a third party claim for common law indemnity after contractor's employees sued the owner for injuries sustained at the job site. The trial court granted summary judgment for the contractor.

 The Appellate Court affirmed. Liability insurance was intended to take the place of a void indemnification agreement of the contract. The Court held that "the parties manifested the intention that insurance provided by [the contractor] on behalf of [the owner] was to protect against any personal liability to [the contractor]. . . . [The owner] was indemnified by contract and can not now seek recovery under common law indemnity." The Court also held that the insurer, upon defending the owner, was precluded from bringing an indemnity suit against the contractor, because the liability policy sold to the contractor in the name of the owner, on which the contractor paid premiums, protected the contractor as well as the owner.

III: A117-1979, Art. 22
III: A201-1976, Art. 12, Para. 12.1
I: A401-1978, Art. 9
I: A401-1978, Art. 11

Insurance company, as subrogee of contractor, sued subcontractor for negligent workmanship and breach of contract after a fire, allegedly caused by the subcontractor's unauthorized deviation from the architect's plans, destroyed athletic building. The subcontractor's motion for summary judgment was granted.

The Court of Appeal reversed and remanded. Pursuant to a contract provision both the contractor and subcontractor obtained fire insurance and were indemnified thereunder. The lower court erred in finding that the parties were bound by a contract provision which required that "[t]he contractor and subcontractor waive all rights against each other . . . for damages caused by fire . . . to the extent covered by property insurance." The Court of Appeal held that since the subcontractor installed a used heating system, contrary to the Architect's plans and specifications, but with its and the owner's consent, there existed a genuine issue of fact as to whether the work performed was pursuant to the subcontract and thus covered by the above contract provision.

The Court also held that a question of fact existed regarding the subcontractor's breach of warranty that the materials would be new "unless otherwise specified" and "free from faults and defects and in conformance with the Contract Documents." In addition, it was unsettled whether the owner's agreement with the subcontractor to install the alternate heating system was within the framework of the contract provision permitting the owner to "order extra work or make changes by altering, adding to, or deducting from the work."

80071 Urbinati v. Simplex Wire & Cable Co., 409 N.E.2d 243 (Mass. App. Ct. 1980)

I: A107-1978, Art. 10
I: A117-1979, Art. 14
I: A201-1976, Art. 4, Para 4.18

Owner filed a third party claim for indemnification against the contractor after a worker sued the owner for injuries sustained during the installation of doors on the project. The trial court held for the contractor.

The Court of Appeals affirmed, holding that the evidence presented was insufficient to warrant a jury determination that the owner was entitled to indemnification from the contractor. Where door work was taken from the contractor and assigned to another company by the owner, "[a]s a matter of law, [the contractor] could not be charged with any act or omission on the part of [the other company]. . . . [O]ne could not find that [the worker] was injured by reason of any act or omission of anyone"directly or indirectly' employed by [the contractor]."

expressly indemnify the contractor for the costs of establishing the applicability of that provision in the instant suit, those costs were not allowed.

80068   United States Fidelity & Guar. Co. v. Blankenship Plumbing Co., 153 Ga. App. 335, 265 S.E.2d 66 (1980)

> III: A311-1970, Labor & Material Payment Bond
> III: A311-1970, Performance Bond

Subcontractor sued surety for labor and materials after surety completed construction project. Surety counterclaimed for breach and filed a third party claim against part owner of contracting company under an agreement to indemnify surety for any loss on its payment and performance bond. The Muscogee State Court entered a verdict for the subcontractor and the part owner and the surety appealed.

The Court of Appeals affirmed the lower court's decision. The Court held that the surety contract was unenforceable since it was not supported by any consideration. At the time the surety contract was signed, the performance bond was already in existence and "no benefit was received from the [surety] . . . nor was any obligation created on . . . [its] part."

80069   United States Fidelity & Guar. Co. v. Eastern Hills Methodist Church, 609 S.W.2d 298 (Tex. Civ. App. 1980)

> I: A311-1970, Performance Bond

Owner sued contractor and contractor's surety for damages for defective performance. The trial court found for the owner against both the contractor and the surety, and the surety appealed.

The Court of Civil Appeals affirmed, finding a performance bond provision that "Any suit under this bond must be instituted before the expiration of two (2) years from the date on which final payment under the contract falls due" restricted the time of suit to less than two years and was, therefore, invalid, where a Texas statute provided that parties could not contract to limit the time to sue to a shorter period than two years.

The Court also found that a supplemental agreement entered into between owner and contractor in which the owner agreed not toe terminate the original contract upon the consideration of the contractor agreeing to perform fully the original contract under its plans and specifications was not a material alteration of the original contract which would act to release surety from its performance bond. According to the Court there was no material alteration of the contract, as "Contractor's agreeing for a second time to complete the original contract as required could not place USF&G in a different position."

80070   United States Fidelity & Guar. Co. v. Escambia Electric & Appliance Co., 384 So. 2d 1073 (Ala. 1980)

> III: A107-1978, Art. 18

of labor rates beyond the parties' control, and that "to be negotiated" referred to these negotiations, not to future negotiations between owner and contractor for a possible rise in labor charges.

The Court denied the owner's claim for damages due to delay in performance. Where the contract provision stated that "if the Contractor is delayed . . . by labor disputes . . . then the contract time shall be extended by Change Order for such reasonable time as the Architect may determine," and the delay was due to labor strikes at the supplier's plant, such delay was excused although a change order to extend the time was never issued.

80066 Timberline Electric Supply Corp. v. Insurance Co. of N. Am., 72 A.D.2d 905, 421 N.Y.S.2d 987 (1979), *aff'd*, 52 N.Y.2d 793, 436 N.Y.S.2d 707, 417 N.E.2d 1248 (1980)

I: A311-1970, Labor & Material Payment Bond

Materialman sued surety of bankrupt contractor. The surety motioned for a summary judgment and the Supreme Court denied the surety's motion.

The Supreme Court, Appellate Division, reversed. Although the period of limitation was established by a New York statute, the parties could contract for the shorter period of one year contained within the bond. "Absent proof that the contract is one of adhesion or the product of overreaching or that altered period is unreasonable short, the abbreviated period of limitation will be enforced."

80067 Tri-M. Erectors, Inc. v. Donald M. Drake Co., 27 Wash. App. 2d 529, 618 P.2d 1341 (1980)

II: A401-1978, Art. 11

A subcontractor sued the contractor for damages to equipment, which occurred during an accident in which an employee of the subcontractor was injured. The contractor counterclaimed for indemnification of costs incurred in defending a suit by the injured employee, which was ultimately settled through arbitration. The trial court dismissed the subcontractor's claim and entered judgment for the contractor on its counterclaim. The subcontractor appealed on the issue of indemnification.

The Court of Appeals affirmed. The indemnification provision of the subcontract stated that the contractor would be indemnified for damages including attorney fees arising from acts or omissions of the subcontractor that were connected with the performance of the subcontract. Since the employee was injured when the subcontractor moved equipment at the contractor's request, under the provision the contractor was entitled to indemnification for the costs of defending the action by the injured employee. The Court also held that the suit was not barred because the employee received damages in an arbitration award. The arbitration agreement did not incorporate the subcontract; therefore the indemnity provision controlled. However, since the indemnification provision did not

Subcontractors sued owner for unpaid balances owed them by the contractor. The owner, who was also the lender, had waived the contract requirement that the contractor obtain a performance bond (the AIA standard form document had been amended). The subcontractors were not notified of the waiver, and in reliance upon the bond provision the subcontractors believed that payment for their work was covered by a bond. The District Court held for the subcontractors.

The Court of Appeals affirmed, holding that the owner, because of its unique position as both owner and lender to the contractor, had a fiduciary duty to the subcontractors not to abuse that relationship.

80064 Swindell Dressler Co. v. Commonwealth Department of Transportation, 400 Pa. Commw. 34, 401 A.2d 600 (1979), *aff'd as modified,* 413 A.2d 38 (Pa. 1980)

> III: B141-1977, Art. 3
> III: B141-1977, Art. 15

Engineer entered into a contract with the Department which provided that the engineer's fee would be based on the contractor's bid if the plans and designs were advertised within 90 days of their approval. If the plans and designs were not advertised within 90 days of their approval, the fee was to be based on the estimated construction cost. The project was not advertised until 17 months later. The engineer field for arbitration claiming that its fee should nevertheless be based upon the contractor's bid because the Department had requested the engineer to make substantial modifications on the project, thereby rendering the formerly complete project incomplete pending acceptance of the modifications. The Board found for the Department and the District Court affirmed the Board's determination, holding that the supplemental agreement was "not intended to alter the amount payable to [the engineer] for service already rendered."

80065 The Foley Co. v. Walnut Associates, 597 S.W.2d 685 (Mo. Ct. App. 1980)

> III: A101-1977, Art. 4
> III: A107-1978, Art. 3
> I: A107-1978, Art. 14
> III: A111-1978, Art. 8
> III: A117-1979, Art. 6
> I: A201-1976, Art. 8, Para. 8.3

Contractor sued owner for payment under labor negotiations clause of contract and owner claimed damages for delay in performance by contractor. The trial court found for the contractor and the owner appealed.

The Court of Appeals affirmed the lower court's ruling. The Court held that in the contract provision which stated "labor escalation after April 1, 1974 to be negotiated," the term "labor escalation" was a word of art, referring to industry-wide renegotiations

80061   South Burlington School District v. Calcagni-Frazier-Zajchowski Architects, Inc., 138 Vt. 33, 410 A.2d 1359 (1980)

I:	A107-1978, Art. 8
I:	A107-1978, Art. 10
I:	A117-1979, Art. 12
I:	A117-1979, Art. 14
I:	A201-1976, Art. 2, Para. 2.2
I:	A201-1976, Art. 4, Para. 4.3
I:	A401-1978, Art. 3
I:	B141-1977, Art. 1

School district brought suit against architect, contractor, subcontractor and manufacturer for a defective roof. The Superior Court entered directed verdicts for all defendants and the school district appealed.

The Supreme Court affirmed as to the architect and manufacturer and reversed and remanded as to the contractor and subcontractor. The architect did not breach his contract with the school district as to supervision of construction since the contract stated that the architect was not responsible for means and methods and was not required to make exhaustive or continuous on-site inspections. The contract between the school district and the contractor made the contractor responsible for supervision. The directed verdict was sustained against the contractor because the contract made the contractor responsible for construction means and coordination. The evidence showed a contract breach by the contractor since the subcontractor commenced construction late so as to expose the unfinished roof to precipitation. A directed verdict was also sustained against the subcontractor because of commencement of its work beyond the contract date.

80062   Spencer v. Hoffman, 392 So. 2d 190 (La. Ct. App. 1980)

III:	A201-1976, Art. 7, Para. 7.9

Owner filed a suit against the contractor for reduction of the contract price. The trial court entered judgment for the contractor.

The Court of Appeals affirmed. The Court held that the decision by the arbitrator was binding upon the parties pursuant to an arbitration provision in their contract. The owner's only recourse was to file a motion under a state statute to vacate, modify or correct the award within three months, which she had failed to do.

80063   Superior Glass Co. v. First Bristol County National Bank, 8 Mass. App. Ct. 356, 394 N.E.2d 972 (1979), *aff'd,* 406 N.E.2d 672 (Mass. 1980)

I:	A201-1976, Art. 7, Para. 7.5
I:	A311-1970, Performance Bond

The Court of Civil Appeals reversed and remanded. Despite a provision in the subcontractor's bond limiting suits to the county in which the construction project was located, the pendency of a suit in New York against the project in Texas had no effect on the surety's authority under the indemnity provision to settle the pending claim. According to the Court, the surety "did not act as a volunteer in settling the New York suit, and neither was the settlement made in bad faith, because the settlement discharged the claim, which otherwise would have been enforceable in Texas, regardless of the pendency of the New York suit." Neither did the settlement constitute a novation of the claim as it was not a substitution of one obligation for another. The settlement, therefore, was within the terms of the indemnity agreement, and the lower court should have allowed its admission into evidence.

80059   Salem Building Supply Co. v. J.B.L. Construction Co., 407 N.E.2d 1302 (Mass. App. Ct. 1980)

III: A311-1970, Labor & Material Payment Bond

Materials supplier sued contractor and its surety for payments owed to the supplier by the subcontractor. The trial court granted the supplier's motion for summary judgment and awarded damages and attorney's fees.

The Court of Appeals reversed. The Court held that "because [statutory bond requirements and procedures] did not apply, the [supplier's] rights under the bond are to be determined by the terms of the bond itself. Under those terms, the [supplier] was required to give notice to two of the three named parties: the principal, the owner and the surety." The Court then found that the supplier had given notice to the principal-contractor and to the construction manager. The Court held that "the facts alleged in the affidavit may warrant a finding [that the construction manager was the agent of the owner] but do not require such a finding as a matter of law."

80060   Sehlbert Mechanical Corp. v. Kessel/Duff Construction Corp., 79 A.D.2d 680, 433 N.Y.S.2d 866 (1980)

III: A201-1976, Art. 7, Para. 7.5
III: A311-1970, Performance Bond

Contractor brought an action to foreclose a mechanic's lien. Owner counterclaimed against contractor for breach of contract. The Supreme court held for the contractor.

The Supreme Court, Appellate Division, reversed. The Court held that "[the owner] waived the requirement that [the subcontractor] post a performance bond. since [the owner] was assured that [the contractor] had not posted the bond, but still urged [the contractor] to commence performance, [the owner] was equitably estopped from refusing to pay [the contractor]. . . ." However, since the owner directly paid a portion owning to the subcontractor, the lien was reduced by the amount of these payments.

80056   Rome v. Commonwealth Edison Co., 81 Ill. App. 3d 776, 401 N.E.2d 1032 (1980)

        II: A107-1978, Art. 10
        II: A117-1979, Art. 14
        II: A201-1976, Art. 4, Para. 4.18
        II: A201-1976, Art. 11, Para. 11.1

Contractor's employee sued owner for injuries sustained on the construction site. The owner filed a third party claim for indemnity against the contractor. The trial court dismissed the third party claim.

The Appellate Court reversed. The insurance provision followed a clause regarding the indemnification of the owner, which clause was subsequently declared void, but there was not evidence that the insurance provision was a substitute for the void clause. The contractor's "obligation to obtain insurance was contractual and there was nothing in the contract to indicate that the parties intended the mere obtaining of insurance to relieve [the contractor] of all liability to indemnify [the owner]."

80057   Rutter v. McLaughlin, 101 Idaho 292, 612 P.2d 135 (1980)

        I: A107-1978, Art. 13
        I: A117-1979, Art. 17
        I: A201-1976, Art. 7, Para. 7.9

Contractor sought to foreclose a labor and materialmen's lien on owners' property. The owners filed a counterclaim for breach of contract and sought to have the dispute submitted to arbitration pursuant to an arbitration provision of the General Conditions. The District Court ordered the submission of the dispute to arbitration. An award was made and an amended award was confirmed by the District court.

The Supreme Court affirmed. The Court held that although the General Conditions were never specifically incorporated by reference into the agreement between the owners an the contractor, "provisions of the General Conditions are referred to in several important articles of the written agreement as if the General Conditions were part of the parties' agreement." Thus, the agreement to arbitrate disputes was incorporated into the contract between the owners and the contractor even though neither the General Conditions nor the arbitration provision was specifically included.

80058   Safeco Ins. Co. of Am. v. J. L. Henson, Inc., 601 S.W.2d 183 (Tex. Civ. App. 1980)

        II: A311-1970, Labor & Material Payment Bond

Surety brought suit against subcontractor under its indemnity agreement with the subcontractor. The trial court excluded evidence of payment by surety and found for the subcontractor. The surety appealed.

a suit under a payment on performance bond was not binding upon the parties. The statute was superseded by an indemnification provision obligating the contractor and its surety to pay "reasonable attorney fees." The Court "construed the contractual obligation to be one for the payment of reasonable attorney fees . . . rather than statutory attorney fees."

80054   Robinson v. A.Z. Shmina & Sons Co., 96 Mich. App. 644, 293 N.W.2d 661 (1980)

    I: A107-1978, Art. 10
    I: A117-1979, Art. 14
    I: A201-1976, Art. 4, Para. 4.18
    III: A401-1978, Art. 11

Administrator of estate of deceased employee of subcontractor sued contractor, who filed a third party complaint for indemnification by the subcontractor. The Circuit Court granted the subcontractor's motion for summary judgment and the contractor appealed.

The Court of Appeals reversed and remanded. The subcontract contained a provision binding the subcontractor to the provisions of the owner-contractor agreement, which in turn contained an indemnity provision. The Court stated that the trial court upon remand should decide whether the contracts violated a Michigan statute which prohibited an indemnitee from recovering for its own negligence, and should interpret the clauses as to severability of the valid and invalid promises.

80055   Rockland v. Primiano Construction Co., 51 N.Y.2d 1, 431 N.Y.S.2d 478, 409 N.E.2d 951 (1980), *rev'g* 421 N.Y.S.2d 260 (App. Div. 1979)

    I: A107-1978, Art. 8
    I: A107-1978, Art. 13
    I: A117-1979, Art. 12
    I: A117-1979, Art. 17
    I: A201-1976, Art. 2, Para. 2.2
    I: A201-1976, Art. 7, Para. 7.9

Owner moved to stay arbitration of contractor's claim for damages and contractor cross-motioned to compel arbitration. The Supreme Court granted the contractor's motion to compel arbitration and the Supreme Court, Appellate Division, reversed.

The Court of Appeals reversed and reinstated the Supreme Court's ruling. The court held that the claim did not need to be referred to the architect before it was submitted for arbitration since under the contract the authority of the architect was centered on the operational phase of construction and not claims asserted after substantial completion of the work. The question of whether the demand for arbitration was untimely was to be decided by the arbitrator, since the court stated that the contract provision for arbitration was procedural with respect to the conduct of arbitration proceeding, and it was not a condition precedent to arbitration.

80051 Prince v. R.C. Tolman Construction Co., 610 P.2d 1267 (Utah 1980)

> II: A401-1978, Art. 1
> II: A401-1978, Art. 11
> II: A401-1978, Art. 12

Subcontractor sued contractor for compensation for portions of the work under the subcontract which the contractor took over after the subcontractor was unable to finish it. The trial court awarded to the subcontractor the amount the contractor would otherwise have paid the subcontractor less the cost to the contractor for his completion of these items.

The Supreme Court affirmed. Although the contract required modifications to be in writing, the Court held that "notwithstanding recitals in a prior contract restricting changes or modification in its terms, the parties are as free in appropriate circumstances to renegotiate new terms or to make separate supplemental agreements as they were to make the contract in the first place." The subcontractor was thus allowed to give the unfinished work back to the contractor for the price agreed upon.

80052 Progress Glass Co. v. American Insurance Co., 100 Cal. App. 3d 720, 161 Cal. Rptr. 243 (1980)

> II: A311-1970, Labor & Material Payment Bond

Subcontractor sued surety on labor and materials payment bond given by original contractor as principal in attempt to recover balance due from original contractor. The Superior Court granted surety's motion for summary judgment, and subcontractor appealed.

The Court of Appeal reversed. It held that a California statute in validated a contract provision which limited suits to one year after the contractor ceased work on the contract. The Court construed the payment bond as a "statutory bond" and not as a "common law bond," since that was the intent of the owner in requiring the payment bond.

80053 R. W. King Construction Co. v. City of Melbourne, 384 So. 2d 654 (Fla. Dist. Ct. App. 1980)

> III: A107-1978, Art. 10
> III: A117-1979, Art. 14
> III: A201-1976, Art. 4, Para. 4.18
> III: A201-1976, Art. 7, Para. 7.5

Owner sued contractor and its surety for breach of contract. The trial court awarded the owner damages and attorney's fees.

The Court of Appeal affirmed. On the issue of attorney's fees the Court held that a Florida statute which placed a maximum limitation on the amount of attorney's fees in

of the guarantee." The Court also held that the prime contract provision obligating payment of suppliers did not run to the benefit of the lender as a third party beneficiary since it was not a supplier.

80049   Orto v. Jackson, 413 N.E.2d 273 (Ind. Ct. App. 1980)

III:	A107-1978, Art. 2	
III:	A107-1978, Art. 14	
III:	A117-1979, Art. 3	
III:	A117-1979, Art. 18	
III:	A201-1976, Art. 8, Para. 8.1	
III:	A201-1976, Art. 13, Para. 13.2	

Contractors sued owners to foreclose a mechanic's lien and the owners counterclaimed for damages. The trial court ordered the foreclosure, but also awarded damages to the owners. The contractors were held liable for breach of express warranty, implied warranty of habitability and negligent construction.

The Court of Appeals affirmed. The Court found that a 90-day time limit in the contract clearly made time of the essence, and upheld the award of damages for the rent the owners were required to pay prior to completion. The Court also held that the owners were not required to give notice of defects prior to the filing of the suit where the contractors had been given notice of other defects and had left them unremedied. Because the contractor showed no intention of correcting defects, giving notice would have served no purpose.

80050   Phillips v. Ben M. Hogan Co., 594 S.W.2d 39 (Ark. Ct. App. 1980)

II:	A101-1977, Art. 3	
II:	A107-1978, Art. 2	
II:	A111-1978, Art. 4	
II:	A117-1979, Art. 3	

Owner sued contractor for breach of the contract provisions as to the completion date and liquidated damages. The lower court awarded the liquidated damages to the owner, less the amount still owed the contractor. The owner appealed and the contractor cross-appealed.

The Court of Appeals affirmed. The liquidated damages clause of $100 per day until completion or acceptance was valid where both parties recognized that a substantial loss would ensue if the project were not completed on time and where the impact of inflation on construction costs was such that the amount bore a reasonable relationship to the overall cost of the project. The Court further found that the date of substantial completion was the date upon which accumulation of damages would cease, rejecting the owner's contention that when a breach of contract triggers a liquidated damages clause, the date of substantial performance is irrelevant to the accumulation of those damages.

Contractor brought action against owner, Town of Vernon, for unpaid balance and against town's building committee for tortious interference with the contract. Owner and building committee members brought a motion to dismiss on ground that contractor failed to comply with arbitration provision of contract. The Superior Court granted the motion to dismiss.

The Supreme Court reversed, holding that "[t]he mere agreement to arbitrate, standing alone, does not give rise to the necessary implication that arbitration is a condition precedent to an action in court. For arbitration to be a condition precedent, the agreement to arbitrate must expressly so stipulate, or it must necessarily be implied from the language used." The owner did not bring an action to compel arbitration. Moreover, the building committee members could not have been joined in the arbitration since they were not parties to the contract.

80047 N.B. Harty General Contractors, Inc. v. West Plains Bridge and Grading Co., 498 S.W.2d 194 (Mo. Ct. App. 1980)

III: A401-1978, Art. 2

Subcontractor sued contractor for payment under the contract. The trial court found that certain work done by the contractor was not allocated to the subcontract under the subcontract and that the subcontractor could not, therefore, recover payment it would have received had it done the work. The subcontractor appealed.

The Court of Appeals affirmed. Where the agreement called for the subcontractor to do the drilling and blasting on that portion of the project designated "Class C excavation," the subcontractor could not recover for the bulldozing by the contractor of percentage rock, a mixture of rock and dirt. Despite the fact that this percentage rock *could have been* removed by drilling and blasting and the contractor was paid by the owner for the removal of the rock portion of this mixture under "Class C excavation" rates, the Court held that under the subcontract the subcontractor could only recover for that portion of rock which was actually removed by drilling and blasting, and not for all "Class C excavation" under the primary contract between owner and contractor.

80048 New England Concrete Pipe Corp. v. D/C Systems of New England, 495 F. Supp. 1334 (D. Mass. 1980)

I: A107-1978, Art. 10
I: A201-1976, Art. 4, Para. 4.4

Sub-subcontractor sued owner, vendor, general contractor, subcontractor and guarantor to recover for materials and labor supplied to housing project. The lender cross-claimed against guarantor of contractor's obligations and the contractor based on the materials and labor provision in the contract between the owner and the contractor. The District Court dismissed the cross claims.

The District Court held that where the sub-subcontractor neither dealt directly with the contractor nor filed a lien against the project "the claims did not fall within the letter

all . . . materials used or reasonably required for use in the performance of the contract" to include equipment and "materials necessary for maintaining the structural integrity of a construction project left uncompleted by a defaulting contractor."

The Court held that the jury verdict was supported by sufficient evidence concerning the need for the supplier's equipment to prevent a collapse of the half-completed structure. The trial court erred in granting a new trial.

80044   Modern Builders, Inc. of Tacoma v. Manke, 27 Wash. App. 86, 615 P.2d 1332 (1980)

       III: A101-1977, Art. 4
       III: A107-1978, Art. 3

Contractor sued owners to foreclose a labor and materialmen's lien after the owners refused to make payments in excess of the original contract sum. The trial court found that a fixed price contract had existed, but that the owners abandoned that contract by requesting many changes from the original estimate. In absence of a cost-plus contract, the court found for the contractor on the basis of *quantum meruit*.

The Court of Appeals reversed. The Court found that the "action of [the owners] in ordering extra work and making changes in the original plans should not be deemed an abandonment of the original contract. Costs incurred by [the contractor] for such extra work agreed to by [the owners] may be recovered, if proven in addition to the contract price." The Court also held that recovery under quantum meruit for the entire job was inappropriate where an express contract existed and where the additional work necessary to complete the contract should have been foreseen by the parties prior to contract formation. The Court did, however, allow recovery under quantum meruit for extra work arising outside and independent of the contract.

80045   Mularz v. Greater Park City Co., 623 F.2d 139 (10th Cir. 1980)

       I: B141-1977, Art. 14

Architect sued owner for unpaid balance of architect's fees. Architect had completed three of five phases of the project before the owner abandoned the project. The District Court held for the owner.

The Court of Appeals reversed, holding that because performance of the contract was primarily under the control of the owner, completion of the project was to be interpreted as a promise to pay establishing the time of payment rather than as a condition precedent to payment. Because the project was never completed, payment to the architect was to take place within a "reasonable time" after termination of the contract.

80046   Multi-Service Contractors, Inc. v. Town of Vernon, 181 Conn. 445, 435 A.2d 983 (1980)

       I: A201-1976, Art. 7, Para. 7.9

Subcontractor sued contractor for breach of contract, defamation and tortious breach of contract after the contractor terminated the contract and took over the job. Communications by the contractor to the subcontractor's surety had allegedly caused the surety to deny the subcontractor further bonding. The trial court granted summary judgment for the contractor on the defamation and tort claims, but held in favor of the subcontractor on the contract claim at trial.

The Supreme Court affirmed the grant of summary judgment to the contractor, holding that communications between the contractor and the surety about the subcontractor fell within the privilege of common business interest and were therefore not defamatory. The Court affirmed the refusal to consider the tort claims because the subcontractor failed to tie any evidence of malicious intent by the contractor to its conduct in breaching the contract with the subcontractor. Without this element of malicious intent, a suit in tort for breach of the construction contract could not lie.

80042 Mason v. Callas Contractors, Inc., 494 F. Supp. 782 (D. Md. 1980)

> II: A107-1978, Art. 10
> II: A117-1979, Art. 14
> II: A201-1976, Art. 4, Para. 4.18
> II: A401-1978, Art. 11

Subcontractor's employee brought suit against the owner seeking damages for personal injury he sustained. The owner filed a third-party complaint against the contractor and subcontractor based on an indemnification provision. Contractor and subcontractor sought to vacate the order permitting the owner to file third-party complaints against them. The District Court denied the motion to vacate.

The District Court held that the "Workmen's Compensation Act would not bar recovery against the contractor and subcontractor by virtue of an indemnity agreement, since that statute prohibited indemnity against liability caused by the sole negligence of the indemnitee." The Court also held that the fact that the subcontract was signed after the incident made no difference because "once parties enter into a written contract, into that written contract will merge all prior negotiations, and the written contract will be viewed as the exclusive medium for determining the rights and liabilities of the parties."

80043 Middle-West Concrete Forming and Equipment Co. v. General Insurance Co. of America, 267 S.E.2d 742 (W. Va. 1980)

> I: A311-1970, Labor & Material Payment Bond

Supplier brought suit against surety on labor and material payment bond for leased equipment used at the project after the general contractor defaulted. The trial court reversed the jury's verdict in favor of the supplier and ordered a new trial.

The Supreme Court of Appeals reversed the lower court's decision and reinstated the original jury verdict. The Court construed terms of the bond guaranteeing payment "for

80039   Keith v. Burzynski, 621 P.2d 247 (Wyo. 1980)

> III: A101-1977, Art. 3
> III: A107-1978, Art. 2
> III: A107-1978, Art. 14
> III: A111-1978, Art. 4
> III: A117-1979, Art. 3
> III: A117-1979, Art. 18
> III: A201-1976, Art. 8, Para. 8.3

Owner-developer sued contractor for liquidated delay damages. The trial court apportioned the fault for delay and awarded delay damages to the owner-developer.

The Supreme Court affirmed. The liquidated delay damages provision included an exception to damages, "subject to any extension of time granted [by the owner-developer] under provisions in the General Conditions. . . ." The Court construed this provision to mean that "the contractor contemplates that where both the owner-developer and the contractor cause delays, the contractor shall not be liable for liquidated damages for the delay he caused." Since the contractor did not request an extension of time, as he was entitled to under the General Conditions, the Court held that the trial court's ruling was correct in apportioning the liquidated delay damages.

80040   King Brothers Building Contractors, Inc. v. McCullen, 393 So. 2d 413 (La. Ct. App. 1980)

> III: A107-1978, Art. 15
> III: A117-1979, Art. 19
> III: A201-1976, Art. 9, Para. 9.9

Contractor sued owner for the balance due. The trial court entered judgment in favor of the contractor, and the owner appealed.

The Court of Appeals affirmed. The court held that the trial court was correct in not sustaining the owner's claim that the suit was filed prematurely and should be dismissed. Under the terms of the contract final payment was not due until receipt of the contractor's statement concerning liens. Although there were two existing liens against he property when the suit was filed, intervention by the first lienholder resulting in favorable judgment and the contractor bringing the present action as the second lienholder rendered the issue of prematurity moot.

80041   Lull v. Wick Constr. Co., 614 P.2d 321 (Alaska 1980)

> III: A201-1976, Art. 7, Para. 7.6
> III: A401-1978, Art. 11
> III: A401-1978, Art. 12

III: A201-1976, Art. 12, Para. 12.1

Contractor sued owners to foreclose upon labor and materialmen's liens on owners' house after the owners refused to pay for extra work performed. The trial court held for the contractor.

The Supreme Court affirmed. The court held that the contract requirement that all change orders be in writing was waived by the parties' words and conduct during construction. The contractor's failure to require written change orders was therefore not an acknowledgement that the requested modifications were part of the contractor's original undertaking.

80037   Jetty, Inc. v. Hall-McGuff Architects, 595 S.W.2d 918 (Tex. Civ. App. 1980)

II: B141-1977, Art. 1
II: B141-1977, Art. 14

Architectural firm sued owner to recover for services rendered and for interest. The trail court entered judgment for the architect, and the owner appealed.

The Court of Civil Appeals affirmed, modifying the interest award. The Court held that the plans submitted by the architect under the design development phase did not deviate from what the contract called for. The additions of approximately 3,000 square feet to the office building for common areas such as restrooms, lobbies, and stairways of 21,000 square feet of external area such as parking lots and walkways were additions of "necessary facilities incident to a modern office building," and did not contravene the contract, which called for 10,000 square feet of leasable office space. Furthermore, these areas had been approved by the owner when, after reviewing the plans, he told the architect to proceed to the next phase of the project.

The Court modified the award of nine percent interest to the architects. Where the contract provided that payments due the architect should bear interest at the legal rate, this did not refer to the maximum rate allowed by law, but to a statutory provision setting the interest rate at six percent when the parties had not agreed to a specific rate.

80038   Johnson v. E.V. Cox Construction Co., 620 P.2d 917 (Okla. Ct. App. 1980)

III: A201-1976, Art. 11

Subcontractor sued contractor to recover for extra work performed. The trial court entered judgment for the subcontractor, and the contractor appealed.

The Court of Appeals affirmed. The court held that the contract provision requiring authorization of written change orders to be made solely by the "prime contractor" was not binding upon the parties. The contractor's project superintendent authorized all of the change orders, and by accepting the benefits implicitly waived the contractual circumscription and ratified the project superintendent's authorization.

Owners sued surety to recover on two performance bonds. The Supreme Court entered judgment for the owners and surety appealed.

The Supreme Court, Appellate Division, modified the lower court's ruling. The Court held that "the amount recoverable from a surety shall not exceed the amount specified in the undertaking." The Court also held that since the surety failed to complete construction it was liable for "all damages which flowed reasonably and naturally from the contractor's breach and its own." Therefore, the surety was liable for the losses sustained by the owners due to reductions in the sales prices of the buildings, since these were less than the losses of rent to which the owners would also have been entitled as damages.

80035 Hyatt Cheek Builders-Engineers Co. v. Board of Regents of University of Texas, 607 S.W.2d 288 (Tex. Civ. App. 1980)

    II: A107-1978, Art. 10
    II: A117-1979, Art. 14
    II: A201-1976, Art. 4, Para. 4.3

Owner brought suit against contractor and subcontractor for failure to perform the contract in a good and workmanlike manner and for the negligent installation of water pipes. The trial court found for the owner and the contractor and subcontractor appealed.

The Court of Civil Appeals affirmed and reformed the judgment on other grounds. The Court held that "the fact that another is subsequently obligated to supervise work does not necessarily relieve one who has previously contracted to supervise it, unless the subsequently assumed obligation is incompatible with the former." Where the contract provided that the contractor was responsible for the acts or omissions of the subcontractor, the contractor was not relieved of his duty to supervise the work by a subsequent contract between the owner, subcontractor, and city government which provided that the city would inspect the work to insure proper installation. While the contractor's duty was to insure that the work was performed in a good and workmanlike manner, the city's duty was to insure observance of city ordinances and building codes. The two contracts were therefore not incompatible. Neither did the subsequent contract constitute a novation, as such requires a new agreement between the original parties, which was not the case.

In denying the contractor indemnity against the subcontractor, the Court stated that "in every contract between a contractor and his subcontractor, the law implies an obligation on the part of the contractor to so perform his part of the work that the subcontractor's ability to perform his work is not prevented or impaired." The Court then noted the trial court findings which held the contractor's failure to perform in a good and workmanlike manner contributed to the loss and held that indemnity was not proper.

80036 Javernick v. Smith, 101 Idaho 104, 609 P.2d 171 (1980)

    III: A107-1978, Art. 18
    III: A117-1979, Art. 22

80032 Hartford Accident & Indemnity Co. v. Boise Cascade Corp., 489 F. Supp. 855 (N.D. Ill. 1980)

      I: A101-1977, Art. 3
      I: A107-1978, Art. 2
      I: A111-1978, Art. 4
      I: A117-1979, Art. 3

Surety brought action against owner seeking recovery of sum due under contract with owner with respect to completion of the project by the surety. Owner counterclaimed for losses suffered as a result of surety's failure to complete project by scheduled completion date. The District Court granted summary judgment for the surety.

The District Court held that the contract provision as to the completion date did not specify that the completion of the project by the established date was a condition precedent to payment. That clause also was not completed as to a provision for liquidated damages which would have established the appropriate damages for delay.

80033 Howard P. Foley Co. v. J.L. Williams & Co., 622 F.2d 402 (8th Cir. 1980)

      II: A201-1976, Art. 8, Para. 8.3
      II: A201-1976, Art. 12, Para. 12.1
      II: A201-1976, Art. 12, Para. 12.3
      II: A401-1978, Art. 3
      II: A401-1978, Art. 11

Subcontractor brought action against owner and contractor for delay damages. The District Court entered judgment for the owner and contractor, and the subcontractor appealed.

The Court of Appeals affirmed in part and reversed in part. The Court held that the subcontract provision which incorporated by reference the prime contract did not mean that the delay damage provision in favor of the owner also extended to the subcontractor. The Court also dealt with an extension of time clause, which stated that "[t]his Article does not exclude the recovery of damages for delay by either party under other provisions in the Contract Document." This clause in conjunction with a "changes and extra work" clause and a "claims for extra cost and damages" clause did not mean that the parties contemplated delay damages for the subcontractor. In addition, a "time-is-of-the-essence" clause in the subcontract did not implicitly give rise to delay damages.

80034 Hunt v. Bankers & Shippers Insurance Co. of New York, 73 A.D.2d 797, 423 N.Y.S.2d 718 (1979), *aff'd,* 431 N.Y.S.2d 454 (N.Y. 1980)

      III: A311-1970, Performance Bond

III: A201-1976, Art. 10, Para. 10.2

Store owner sued highway contractor for damages sustained during construction project. The trial court found for the store owner and the contractor appealed.

The Court of Appeals affirmed. Although a contractor for a public agency normally shares that body's sovereign immunity from liability for incidental damages necessarily involved in the performance of the contract, where damage results from the contractor's negligent performance of the work, it will have no such immunity. When the contractor chose a method of reconstructing a portion of the highway which was not the common method employed in such instances, it was liable for the foreseeable damages resulting therefrom.

80030   Hammond v. Bechtel, Inc., 606 P.2d 1269 (Alaska 1980)

III: A201-1976, Art. 10, Para. 10.2

Employee of a separate contractor sued construction management contractor and owner for injuries sustained at the construction project. The trial court granted summary judgment to the contractor and the owner.

The Supreme Court reversed the entry of summary judgment and remanded the case for trial. The Court held that in this case "the safety responsibility provisions of the . . . contract are more than mere boilerplate and, particularly in light of [the contractor's] alleged safety activities and powers, leave ample room for the implication that [the contractor] had affirmative contractual safety duties." thus, "whether voluntary or contractual, a question of fact was presented as to the extent of the duty assumed by [the contractor]." Summary judgment had therefore been erroneously granted.

80031   Harsco Corp. v. Cisne & Associates, Inc., 45 N.C. App. 538, 263 S.E.2d 43 (1980)

I: A311-1970, Labor & Material Payment Bond

Supplier filed suit against the owner and a surety on the general contractor's labor and material payment bond for a breach occurring in South Carolina. The Superior Court of Mecklenburg County entered summary judgment for the surety, and the supplier appealed.

The Court of Appeals affirmed. The Court, applying conflict of laws principles, held that South Carolina law would confer jurisdiction upon a court in accordance with a provision in the bond limiting jurisdiction to a "state . . . or United States District Court of the district in which the Project or any part thereof, is situated." Summary judgment was properly entered because under South Carolina law such a provision limiting the right to be sued was not void.

stating that "title to all . . . materials . . . whether incorporated in the Project or not, will pass . . . upon receipt of such payment . . . *free and clear of all . . . security interests"* (emphasis added). since the contractor had received payment for the electrical supplies, the Court held that it had title to the goods and the bank's security interest was terminated.

80028 Griffin Wellpoint Corp. v. Englehardt, Inc., 92 Ill. App. 3d 252, 414 N.E.2d 941 (1980)

III: A311-1970, Labor & Material Payment Bond

Subcontractor sought a mechanic's lien against public funds on a public construction project. Subcontractor also sued the contractor and the contractor's surety on a payment bond. The contractor and the surety filed a counterclaim against the subcontractor and any other parties with a potential claim on the contractor's bond. One such party, a materials supplier, filed a mechanic's lien for sums owed to it by the subcontractor's predecessor in interest, and filed a counterclaim against the contractor and the surety on the contract bond. The trial court granted the materials supplier's motion for summary judgment and awarded damages and prejudgment interest. The contractor and the surety appealed.

The Appellate Court affirmed the grant of summary judgment. The Court held first that "the principal and surety are not discharged from further liability upon the bond merely because the principal made payments in the course of construction which exceeded the penal sum of the bond. . . . The bond in this case provided . . . that the obligation thereunder would remain in full force and effect unless the principal shall"promptly pay all debts incurred by the contractor or any subcontractor . . .' and shall"pay any and all valid claims for labor and materials furnished.' . . . The performance of the principal which was guaranteed by the bond is measured by the foregoing provisions, not by the bond's penal amount."

The Court also held that because the materials supplier explicitly reserved its rights against the surety when it lent credit to the subcontractor's predecessor in interest by extending the time for payment, the contractor and surety were not discharged from any obligation under the bond. Furthermore, "no notice or consent to the surety is required before a"reservation of rights' clause will be held effective."

Finally, the Appellate Court reversed the amount of prejudgment interest awarded to the materials supplier. Although the trial court was correct that the award of interest was not dependent on a due date for payment in the bond, interest should have been allowed only from the date the suit was commended and not from the date that the materials supplier first demanded payment from the surety.

80029 Guerin Contractors, Inc. v. Reaves, 606 S.W.2d 143 (Ark. Ct. App. 1980)

III: A107-1978, Art. 16
III: A117-1979, Art. 20

construction in 200 days, $50 per day would be deducted from the contract price for a period not to exceed 60 days—a maximum of $3,000. The Court held this to be a valid provision for liquidated damages, where it was carefully negotiated by the parties to insulate the owner from increased interest rates which would result from a delay in completion, where it bore a reasonable relationship to the owner's actual damages as determined by the jury's award and where the damages were difficult to estimate at the time of the execution of the contract. As such the provision was enforceable and the trial court erred in awarding the owner damages in excess of the $3,000 provided in the contract.

80026   Fowler v. Insurance Co. of N. Am., 155 Ga. App. 439, 270 S.E.2d 845 (1980)

    III: A101-1977, Art. 6
    III: A107-1978, Art. 5
    III: A107-1978, Art. 11
    III: A117-1979, Art. 21
    III: A201-1976, Art. 11, Para. 11.3

Contractor and his insurance company sued owner and owner's insurance company seeking recovery for materials and labor supplied for repair of home, which was later totally destroyed by fire. The Superior Court entered judgment for the owner and the contractor appealed.

The Court of Appeals reversed. Under Georgia law the risk of loss in a repair contract, as opposed to a contract to erect a building, falls on the owner, not on the contractor, where neither party is at fault. Thus, the Court held that the fire "excused [the contractor's] duty of performance and entitled him to recover the reasonable value of repairs . . . prior to the destruction of the premises."

The Court also held that a contract provision stating that final payment would be due upon completion was subordinate to Georgia law and did not contractually shift the risk of loss in a repair contract. The existence of a contract provision requiring the owner to carry fire insurance, and the fact that the owner had been totally reimbursed by his insurance company, further supported judgment in favor of the contractor.

80027   Graves Constr. Co. v. Rockingham National Bank, 220 Va. 834, 263 S.E.2d 408 (1980)

    I: A201-1976, Art. 9, Para. 9.3

Creditor bank of electrical subcontractor brought suit against owner and general contractor for the value of electrical supplies which the subcontractor furnished and installed in construction project. The Circuit Court entered judgment for the bank.

The Supreme Court reversed. The Circuit Court erred in its determination that the interest of the owner and general contractor was subordinate to the security interest of the bank. The Supreme Court held that the parties were bound by the terms of the contract

80024 F.D. Borkholder Co. v. Sandock, 413 N.E.2d 567 (Ind. 1980), *aff'g* 396 N.E.2d 955 (Ind. Ct. App. 1979)

III: A201-1976, Art. 4, Para. 4.5

Owner sued contractor for breach of contract for the construction of an addition to a pre-existing structure. The trial court awarded compensatory and punitive damages to the owner.

The Court of Appeals affirmed the award of compensatory damages but reversed the award of punitive damages.

The Supreme Court affirmed the decision of the trial court. The Court found that the terms of the construction contract provided that "all labor and material would be furnished in accordance with specifications" and that there was "cogent and convincing proof that the [contractor] engaged in intentional wrongful acts constituting fraud, misrepresentation, deceit and gross negligence. . . ." Accordingly the Court held that "[U]nder these circumstances certainly the imposition of punitive damages furthers the public interest."

80025 Fidelity & Deposit Co. of Maryland v. Stool, 607 S.W.2d 17 (Tex. Civ. App. 1980)

II: A101-1977, Art. 3
II: A107-1978, Art. 2
II: A107-1978, Art. 13
II: A117-1979, Art. 17
II: A201-1976, Art. 14, Para. 14.2

Contractor filed suit against owner and its surety for the balance due, and owner counterclaimed against contractor and surety for failure to substantially perform the contract, failure to construct in a good and workmanlike manner, and failure to meet the timeliness provision of the contract. The trial court rendered judgment for the owner and the contractor and surety appealed.

The Court of Civil Appeals affirmed cost-of-repair as the correct measure of damages and modified the award to the owner for the contractor's failure to complete construction in a timely manner. The Court held that where a contract clause allowing the owner to complete work upon the failure of the contractor to perform any provision of the contract state that "if the unpaid balance of the contract sum exceeds the expense of finishing the work, such shall be paid to the contractor, but if such expense *exceeds such unpaid balance, the contractor shall pay the difference to the owner*" (emphasis added by the court), the parties had contracted for a cost-of-repair measure of damages in the event the contractor failed to conform to the plans and specifications of the contract, and that the parties were bound to that measure.

In modifying the trial court's award of $3,794.96 to the owner for breach of the timeliness provision of the contract by the contractor, the Court noted that the parties had added a provision to the agreement which stated that if the contractor did not complete

Contractor sued owners to foreclose upon a construction lien for the balance owed on a remodeling contract. The owners counterclaimed for damages for delay. The trial court held for the contractor, and the owners appealed.

The Court of Appeals affirmed. The Court held that where the delay was caused by the owners, who requested a change in the materials used, the contractor need not give notice of the delay. "[A]ctual notice can, in some circumstances, dispense with formal notice."

80022a   E.C. Ernst, Inc. v. Koppers Co., 626 F.2d 324 (3d Cir. 1980), *aff'g in part* 476 F. Supp. 729 (W.D. Pa. 1979)

III: A401-1978, Art. 11

A subcontractor brought action against the contractor for delay damages and compensation for extra work. The District Court entered judgment for the subcontractor, and both parties appealed.

The Court of Appeals affirmed in part and reversed and remanded in part. Among other issues the Court held that the contractor was estopped from asserting as a defense the subcontractor's failure to comply with a contract provision requiring submission of written claims within thirty days of receipt of a drawing revision. The huge number of drawing revisions drastically changed the scope of the work, the contractor continually pressed the subcontractor to complete its work and the subcontractor notified the contractor that the contract provision should be dispensed with.

80023   E & F Construction Co. v. Rissil Constr. Assocs., Inc., 181 Conn. 317, 435 A.2d 343 (1980)

I: A201-1976, Art. 5, Para. 5.3
I: A201-1976, Art. 7, Para. 7.9
I: A401-1978, Art. 1
I: A401-1978, Art. 13
I: A401-1978, Art. 15

Subcontractor filed demand for arbitration against contractor, and contractor brought action for declaratory judgment and for an injunction against arbitration. The Superior Court held in favor of the subcontractor.

The Supreme Court affirmed, holding that the contract and the subcontractor intended to make the terms of the contract between the contractor and owner a part of their contract. The contract between subcontractor and contractor provided that the subcontractor was bound to contractor in the same manner as contractor was bound to owner. Furthermore, the contractor supplied subcontractor with copies of the owner/contractor agreement.

Employee of a subcontractor sued architect and eight other parties for personal injuries. The trial court granted the architect's motion for summary judgment.

The Court of appeals affirmed, holding that "we do not see how the right to"reject' work which fails to conform to contract documents [given to the architect in the construction contract] can be interpreted as the right to stop work when hazardous conditions, manner or means of construction existed." Therefore, after examining the "totality of the circumstances" and finding that the architect had no more than a general requirement to oversee the work performed in order to insure the completion of the work, the Court found that the architect was not "in charge of" the project under the Illinois Structural Work Act.

80021   Dondlinger & Sons' Construction Co. v. Emcco, Inc., 237 Kan. 301, 606 P.2d 1026 (1980)

    III: A107-1978, Art. 11
    III: A107-1978, Art. 17
    III: A117-1979, Art. 15
    III: A117-1979, Art. 21
    III: A201-1976, Art. 5, Para. 5.3
    III: A201-1976, Art. 11, Para. 11.1

Contractor sued corporation, which had completed bankrupt subcontractor's work, for negligence resulting in destruction of the contractor's property. The trial court held for the contractor, but denied recovery for additional sums spent by the contractor to mitigate damages.

The Supreme Court affirmed the judgment, but reversed the denial of recovery for extra damages. The Court held that because the corporation responsible for the damage had not been selected or hired by the contractor, but was appointed by the surety, the corporation was not a subcontractor of the contractor, and was therefore not a coinsured under the contractor's policy. "Consequently [the insurer] must bear the loss, even though . . . the loss resulted from the negligence of [the corporation's] employees." The Court also held that the contractor "having proved the negligence and liability of [the corporation] was entitled to judgment for the full amount of the stipulated damages."

80022   E. Carl Schiewe, Inc. v. Brady, 46 Or. App. 441, 611 P.2d 1184 (1980)

    III: A107-1978, Art. 14
    III: A107-1978, Art. 18
    III: A117-1979, Art. 18
    III: A117-1979, Art. 22
    III: A201-1976, Art. 8, Para. 8.3
    III: A201-1976, Art. 12, Para. 12.1

with another contractor to supervise the project was more persuasive but there was still was not evidence of a new contract with the owner or the previous contractor under which the supplier was made a third party beneficiary. There was also evidence that the supplier continued to deal only with the previous contractor.

80018 D.K. Meyer Corp. v. Bevco, Inc., 206 Neb. 318, 292 N.W.2d 773 (1980)

      III: A201-1976, Art. 12, Para. 12.1
      III: A401-1978, Art. 11
      III: A401-1978, Art. 12

Subcontractor sued contractor for additional costs incurred by the subcontractor as a result of modifications performed by it. The District Court held for the subcontractor.

The Supreme Court affirmed the decision. The subcontractor's failure to obtain a written change order prior to modification of the project did not bar recovery where the conduct of both parties clearly demonstrated a modification of the contract and a recognition that payment was due. "Where the parties ignore such a provision in the contract it will not furnish a defense to a claim for compensation for the additional work performed."

The Court also held that a contract provision barring payment by the contractor to the subcontractor in excess of the amount paid by the owner to the contractor for the subcontractor's work simply allowed the contractor "a reasonable time within which to obtain payment from the owner before he is contractually bound to the subcontractors for immediate payment." The provision was not intended to delay indefinitely payment to the subcontractor because of disputes between the owner and the contractor to which the subcontractor is not a party.

80019 Denta Rama, Inc. v. Lavastone Industries of Central Texas, Inc., 597 S.W.2d 507 (Tex. Civ. App. 1980)

      II: A401-1978, Art. 5

Subcontractor sued contractor to recover payment and sought interest on the amount from the date payment was due, as provided in the contract. The District Court found for the subcontractor, and the contractor appealed.

The Court of Civil Appeals affirmed. Where the subcontractor submitted a final bill for an amount which exceeded that due, the contractor was not excused from tendering the correct amount so as to avoid prejudgment interest. The evidence failed to show that the demand for an excessive amount by the subcontractor was sought in bad faith.

80020 Diomar v. Landmark Associates, 81 Ill. App. 3d 1135, 401 N.E.2d 1287 (1980)

      I: A201-1976, Art. 2, Para. 2.2

or the Surety. . . ." By not specifically requiring that notice be given to the surety, the surety did not make such notice to it a condition precedent to recovery under the bond.

80015 (UNASSIGNED)

80016 Construction Materials, Inc. v. American Fidelity Fire Insurance Co., 388 So. 2d 365 (La. 1980)

  III: A311-1970, Labor & Material Payment Bond

Highway contractor and surety on payment bond were sued by seller of signs, barricades, and component parts in an action to recover for materials sold to contractor for use during construction of drainage structures under contract with the state. The District Court entered judgment for the supplier, and the surety appealed.

The Court of Appeal reversed, holding that the state Act governing public contracts prohibited a surety from obligating itself on a contractor's performance and payment bond to pay claims not covered under the Act. Even though the bond language was broad enough to allow payment of the supplier, payment was not allowed because the supplier's claim for materials not incorporated into the project was not protected by the Act.

Reversing and reinstating the trial court's judgment, the Supreme Court observed that the Act contained a savings clause which assured each person protected by the contractor's bond of his right of action. Finding that this provision specifically benefited those whose rights depended solely on the bond, the Court held that the Act did "not prohibit a contractor's surety from voluntarily contracting to pay claims to unpaid workmen or suppliers who [were] unprotected by the [A]ct. . . ."

80017 Copeland Sand & Gravel, Inc. v. Insurance Co. of N. Am., 288 Or. 325, 607 P.2d 718 (1980)

  II: A311-1970, Labor & Material Payment Bond
  II: A311-1970, Performance Bond

Supplier brought action against contractor's surety and its insurance agent on a performance and payment bond for services, materials, and equipment provided following the contractor's financial difficulties. The Circuit Court entered judgment for the surety and its agent, and the Court of Appeals reversed on the issue of the surety's liability.

The Supreme Court reversed and reinstated the Circuit Court's decision. The Court held that the evidence did not conclusively prove, as a matter of law, that the surety, by assuming the contractor's role in performance of the contract, had also assumed all of the contractor's legal obligations in excess of the limit of liability of the bond.

The fact that the contractor assigned to the surety its right to receive progress payments, that the surety did receive payment from the owner, and that it authorized payments to subcontractors and suppliers was no evidence that the surety had made itself the contractor since any surety would do so for a project in trouble. The fact that the surety contracted

80012 Cocke v. Odom, 385 So. 2d 1321 (Ala. Civ. App. 1980)

      III: A107-1978, Art. 10
      III: A107-1978, Art. 19
      III: A117-1979, Art. 14
      III: A117-1979, Art. 23
      III: A201-1976, Art. 4, Para. 4.5
      III: A201-1976, Art. 13, Para. 13.2

Owner sued contractor on warranty in contract to repair pool leakage. The Circuit Court entered judgment for the contractor.

The Court of Appeals affirmed. The Court held that to recover for a breach of warranty, the owner had the burden of proving that damage to the pool was directly caused by contractor's defective work. Evidence of leakage after the pool was repaired was not sufficient to prove a breach of warranty, absent a showing that "the loss was from leaks repaired by [the contractor], and that the leaks were the result of [the contractor's] failure to use adequate materials or make the repairs in a workmanlike manner."

80013 Community Consolidated School District v. Meneley Construction Co., 86 Ill. App. 3d 1101, 409 N.E.2d 66 (1980)

      III: A311-1970, Performance Bond

Owner sued contractor and its surety under a performance bond, after contractor refused to perform due to a mistake in its bid. The contractor counterclaimed for rescission of the contract. The trial court granted the owner's claim for breach of contract and awarded the difference between the contract price and a subsequent contract price. It did not allow recovery on the full amount of the bond. The contractor and surety appealed.

The Appellate Court affirmed. The court held that the bond was a contract which was breached by the surety. However, the owner could not recover the full amount of the bond as actual damages because the owner was not damaged in that amount. The owner also could not recover the amount of the bond as punitive damages since there was no evidence to support an independent action of intentional tort.

80014 Conesco Industries, Ltd. v. Conforti & Eisele, Inc., 627 F.2d 312 (D.C. Cir. 1980)

      I: A311-1970, Labor & Material Payment Bond

Subcontractor sued contractor and its surety under a payment bond for compensation for the use of materials in a construction project. The District Court dismissed the action against the surety because the subcontractor failed to comply with the notice provision in the bond.

The Court of Appeals reversed, holding that under the bond the subcontractor was required to give "[w]ritten notice to any two of the following: the Principal, the Owner,

III: A117-1979, Art. 14
III: A201-1976, Art. 4, Para. 4.5

Owners sued contractor for negligence in the faulty construction of their home. The contractor counterclaimed for payment for extra work. The trial court held for the owners and dismissed the contractor's counterclaim. The contractor appealed, and the owners cross-appealed for suit costs.

The Supreme Court affirmed the judgment in favor of the owners and the dismissal of the contractor's counterclaim. The Court also reversed the order denying the owners' costs. The Court held that the contractor could not recover for supplemental work because the contractor had a pre-existing duty to build a home in a workmanlike manner and thus consideration was lacking in the claimed supplemental agreement. The contractor was not allowed to rely on an estoppel theory because estoppel may not be used "Where the omissions of the party claiming the estoppel brought about the problem."

80011 City of Whitehall v. Southern Mechanical Contracting, Inc., 599 S.W.2d 430 (Ark. Ct. App. 1980)

II: A101-1977, Art. 3
II: A107-1978, Art. 2
II: A107-1978, Art. 20
II: A117-1979, Art. 3
II: A117-1979, Art. 24
II: A201-1976, Art. 8, Para. 8.3
II: A201-1976, Art. 14, Para. 14.2
II: A311-1970, Performance Bond

Contractor brought suit against City for unpaid balance of contract price and damages. City counterclaimed against contractor for liquidated damages for failure of contractor to complete construction within the time provisions of the contract and for expenses incurred in completing the contract. City also sought judgment against surety on performance bond. The trial court held for contractor and surety, and City appealed.

The Court of Appeals affirmed. The Court held that, although the contractor did not complete construction by the time called for in the contract, he had been prevented from doing so by numerous delays on the part of the City. When the City did not provide the contractor with the site for construction of one portion of the project until well after the expiration of the allotted time for completion of the contract, the City had effectively waived the time limitation and liquidated damages provisions of the contract. The Court also ruled that, even if the City's claims against the contractor had been upheld, judgment against the surety would not have been obtained. The City failed to give notice of cancellation to the surety as expressly required by the contract between the contractor and the City, and thereby failed to afford the surety the opportunity to complete the work under the contract.

III: A117-1979, Art. 17
III: A201-1976, Art. 7, Para. 7.9

After the owners notified the contractor that they were terminating the contract, the contractor filed a demand for arbitration pursuant to the contract provisions for arbitration and the United States Arbitration Act. The owners sought a temporary injunction prohibiting the contractor from pursuing arbitration, and the trial court refused to issue the injunction.

The Court of Civil Appeals of Texas affirmed the lower court's ruling, stating that the construction contract "evidenced a transaction"involving commerce' in view of the interstate flow of materials, supplies, services and personnel in connection with the construction of the project," and was thereby brought within the purview of the Arbitration Act, which provides that a written agreement to arbitrate in a "contract evidencing a transaction involving commerce shall be valid, irrevocable, and enforceable. . . ." The fact that no diversity of citizenship existed between the parties was not determinative.

80009 Brezina Construction Co. v. South Dakota Dept. of Transportation. 297 N.W.2d 454 (S.D. 1980)

III: A101-1977, Art. 3
III: A107-1978, Art. 2
III: A107-1978, Art. 14
III: A111-1978, Art. 4
III: A117-1979, Art. 3
III: A117-1979, Art. 18
III: A201-1976, Art. 2, Para. 2.2
III: A201-1976, Art. 8, Para. 8.3

Contractor sued owner for money owed for extra work performed. The owner claimed that such a determination should be made solely by the owner's engineer and that damages should be calculated in accordance with the liquidated damages provision. The Circuit Court held for the contractor.

The Supreme Court reversed in part and affirmed in part, holding that 1) a contract clause which provides that an engineer shall be the final arbiter is binding, unless, as is the case at bar, it is found that the engineer's decision is manifestly arbitrary or rendered in bad faith, and 2) the lower court erred in not apply the liquidated damages provision of the contract since the contract provisions concerning delays and extensions of time indicated that the parties recognized the possibility that the extra work would be necessary to complete the contract.

80010 Carroccia v. Todd, 615 P.2d 225 (Mont. 1980)

III: A107-1978, Art. 10

Surety as subrogee under contractor's performance bond sued owner for money due. The trial court granted the owner's motion to dismiss on grounds that a two year limitation in the performance bond barred the suit.

The Court of Appeal reversed and remanded. The Court held that the trial court erred because the surety alleged in the complaint that the suit was brought under an assignment and indemnification agreement and not under the performance bond. The time limitation in the bond was not applicable to the present suit, and the Court noted that it need not decide whether the two year limitation was valid under Florida law.

80006   Barbera v. Sokol, 101 Cal. App. 3d 725, 161 Cal. Rptr. 843 (1980)

   III: A401-1978, Art. 3

Subcontractor sued owner and contractor for breach of contract. Owner and contractor cross-claimed against subcontractor to recover damages based on a $400-a-day liquidated-damage provision. The Superior court entered judgment in favor of the subcontractor.

The Court of Appeals affirmed. The Court held that the liquidated damages provision acted as a rebuttable presumption pursuant to a California statute. The party who utilizes the presumption has the burden of introducing evidence and proving the existence of the foundational facts of the presumption. The failure to do so relieves a party of the benefit of the presumed fact. Since the owner and contractor failed to establish the foundational fact of the agreement and any damages attributable to the delay, they were precluded from using the liquidated damages provision as a basis to obtain recovery.

80007   Bartak v. Bell-Gallyardt & Wells, Inc., 473 F. Supp. 737 (D.S.D. 1979), *rev'd on other grounds,* 629 F.2d 523 (8th Cir. 1980)

   I: A107-1978, Art. 10
   I: A117-1979, Art. 14
   I: A201-1976, Art. 4, Para. 4.18

Architects filed a claim of indemnity against contractor for the losses assessed against them by the jury. The District Court entered judgment for the contractor.

The District Court held that "[s]pecific language must be used in an indemnity contract if one is to be held liable for losses attributable to another's negligent acts." The contract provisions prevented indemnification in circumstances where the liability was due to "the preparation or approval of maps, drawings, opinions, reports, surveys, change orders, designs, or specifications." Thus, an architect was not entitled to indemnification where the contract prohibited such for losses due to his own negligent preparation of drawings, designs and specifications.

80008   Blanks v. Midstate Constructors, Inc., 610 S.W.2d 220 (Tex. Civ. App. 1980)

   III: A107-1978, Art. 13

certificate of final payment. "[T]he final certificate for payment is not 'procedural chaff.' It is a major substantive right, which "serves a vital interest, in that it induces the contractor to render a performance that conforms in fact to plans and specifications . . . and, upon completion, furnishes the incentive to make conforming corrections.'

80003 Argonaut Insurance Co. v. Commercial Standard Insurance Co., 380 So. 2d 1066 (Fla. Dist. Ct. App. 1980)

I: A311-1970, Performance Bond

Surety for defaulting general contractor brought suit against surety for defaulting subcontractor. The Circuit Court entered summary judgment for the subcontractor's surety.

The Court of Appeal reversed and remanded. The lower court erred in holding that a limiting clause in the subcontractor's performance bond stating that "No right of action shall accrue on this bond to or for the use of any person or corporation other than the Obligee named herein or the heirs, executors, administrators or successors of the Obligee" precluded the general contractor's surety from having standing to sue. The court held that the general contractor's surety "became subrogated to the rights of both its principal [general contractor] and it's obligee [owner]," and had the right to assert a claim that the subcontractor breached its contract with the general contractor.

The Court also held that under Florida law, the general contractor's surety occupied the status of a "successor to the [owner], because it stepped into the shoes left by [the general contractor] . . . and assumed [its] rights and obligations" under the performance bond. Under this interpretation, the general contractor's surety had standing to sue the subcontractor's surety.

80004 Aronson v. Keating, 386 So. 2d 822 (Fla. Dist. Ct. App. 1980)

I: A111-1978, Art. 1
I: A111-1978, Art. 11
I: A201-1976, Art. 13, Para. 13.2

Contractor filed lien against owner for the remainder of the contract price. The trial court entered summary judgment for the contractor and the owner appealed.

The Court of Appeal reversed and remanded. The Court held that the timeliness of the filing of the lien pursuant to a Florida Statute was a disputed issue. The Court also held that the owner's reliance on a warranty provision in the general contract, which obligated the contractor to correct defective work after completion, left unresolved the issue whether the warranty provision was in fact incorporated into the "cost plus basis" contract which the parties executed.

80005 Balboa Insurance Co. v. W. C. B. Assoc., 390 So. 2d 172 (Fla. Dist. Ct. App. 1980)

I: A311-1970, Performance Bond

80001 Aetna Casualty & Sur. Co. v. Crabtree, 383 So. 2d 657 (Fla. Dist. Ct. App.), *appeal denied,* 392 So. 2d 1371, 1373 (Fla. 1980)

    III: A311-1970, Performance Bond
    III: A311-1970, Labor & Material Payment Bond

Lessors brought suit on a third party beneficiary theory against surety on payment and performance bond issued to contractor. Circuit Court entered judgment for lessors and surety appealed.

The District Court of Appeal reversed. As to the issue of whether the lessors were entitled to recover as third party beneficiaries of the surety bond, the Court found that "[t]he intent of the parties to the payment and performance bond determined whether appellees were entitled to maintain an action as third party creditor beneficiaries of the bond, based on its terms and evidence of related transactions between the parties."

80002 American Continental Life Insurance Co. v. Ranier Construction Co., 125 Ariz. 53, 607 P.2d 372 (1980)

    I: A101-1977, Art. 6
    I: A107-1978, Art. 5
    I: A107-1978, Art. 14
    I: A107-1978, Art. 15
    I: A107-1978, Art. 18
    I: A111-1978, Art. 14
    I: A117-1979, Art. 9
    I: A117-1979, Art. 18
    I: A117-1979, Art. 19
    I: A117-1979, Art. 22
    I: A201-1976, Art. 8, Para. 8.3
    I: A201-1976, Art. 9, Para. 9.8
    I: A201-1976, Art. 9, Para. 9.9
    I: A201-1976, Art. 12, Para. 12.1

Contractor sued owner for breach of contract to recover funds retained under the contract and damages for delays and lost profits. The owner counterclaimed to recover damages for faulty construction and delays. The trial court awarded damages to both the contractor and the owner.

The Supreme Court reversed. As to the lack of strict compliance with the formal contract requirements, the Court held that even though "[the owner] did waive other rights under the contract relating to change orders or extensions of time, that conduct does not manifest an intent to waive any right relating to payment for work."

The Court also held that although the owner had refused to sign the certificate of substantial completion, the contractor was not excused from its duty of acquiring a

entitled to compensation for their services under the contract. Where the initial project had called for the construction of two schools, however, and only one of those was ultimately funded, the architects were entitled to compensation only in relation to that one school and not for services rendered on the entire initial project.

of the job site, including a utility designated as "Telegraph Company," was sufficient to show that the parties to the contract intended the telegraph company to be a third party beneficiary under the contract, entitling it to sue to enforce the contract's provisions. By finding the action to be grounded in contract, the date for the tolling of the statute of limitations was extended to the date on which the contractor repudiated liability.

79072   Yamnitz v. Polytech, Inc., 586 S.W.2d 76 (Mo. Ct. App. 1979)

    III: A107-1978, Art. 10
    III: A117-1979, Art. 14
    III: A201-1976, Art. 4, Para. 4.5

Contractor sued owner for failure to pay balance due under the contract and sought the imposition of a mechanic's lien for the unpaid balance and for extra work performed. Owner counterclaimed, seeking damages for failure to conform to contract specifications and for damage to property caused by contractor's employees. The jury found in favor of the contractor for the unpaid balance and extras. The trial court dismissed that portion of the complaint seeking imposition of a mechanic's lien. Both the contractor and the owner appealed.

The Court of Appeals reversed and remanded. The Court held that a warranty provision of the contract which stated that "the Work shall be free from defects due to faulty materials, equipment or workmanship *until the expiration of one year from the date of final payment under the Contract. . .*" (emphasis added by the Court) did not mean that the warranty would become effective only upon the date of final payment, but merely operated to fix a "final, outside time limitation beyond which defendant cannot claim that any unsatisfactory conditions . . . were the result of faulty workmanship or material." To interpret the warranty provision otherwise would negate a preceding article giving the owner the right to withhold payment to the contractor to protect himself from loss due to the contractor's breach.

79073   Yearwood and Johnson Architects, Inc. v. Langford, 589 S.W.2d 378 (Tenn. Ct. App. 1979)

    I: B141-1977, Art. 10
    I: B141-1977, Art. 14

Architects filed suit against Board of Education for contract sum. The lower court found for the architects and the Board appealed.

The Court of Appeals modified the award to the architects and remanded for entry of judgment. The contract stated that, if the architects were not retained through completion of the project, they would be compensated for work done to the point of termination of their services, but only if funds for the project were appropriated by the county. Although the initial project was not funded, the record showed that the project funded six years later was a continuation of that initial project, and thus the architects were

The Superior Court entered summary judgment for the subcontractor and contractor appealed.

The Court of Appeals affirmed as to the liability issue and remanded as to the amount of damages. The subcontract provision, which stated that the subcontractor would be paid to the extent that the contractor was paid by the owner, was not a condition precedent to payment but rather provided a convenient or normal time for payment.

79070 Westerfield v. Arjack, Co. 78 Ill. App. 3d 137, 397 N.E.2d 451 (1979)

   III: A107-1978, Art. 10
   III: A107-1978, Art. 16
   III: A117-1979, Art. 14
   III: A117-1979, Art. 20
   III: A201-1976, Art. 4, Para. 4.3
   III: A201-1976, Art. 10, Para. 10.2

Subcontractor's employees sued contractor for injuries sustained at the construction site. The contractor brought a third party claim for indemnity against the subcontractor. The trial court found in favor of the employees and the subcontractor in the third party action.

The Court of Appeals affirmed, holding that the contractor was "in charge" of the work within the meaning of the Illinois Structural Work Act, and that in order to impose liability, "it is not necessary that a party be in direct charge of the particular operation from which the injury arose if it is in charge of the overall work for the project under construction." The Court found that the contractor supervised the progress of the construction. Under the contract it was to have a superintendent on the job at all times, it had the right to stop the work, it had the responsibility for safety precautions, and it was responsible for the work of the subcontractors.

79071 Western Union Telegraph Company v. Massman Construction Co., 402 A.2d 1275 (D.C. 1979)

   III: A107-1978, Art. 16
   III: A117-1979, Art. 20
   III: A201-1976, Art. 10, Para. 10.2

Telegraph company sued contractor for damages to its underground equipment caused by work done under a contract between contractor and local transit authority. In holding the complaint to be grounded in tort and dismissing it as untimely filed, the Superior Court held that the telegraph company was not a third party beneficiary to the contract.

The Court of Appeals reversed and remanded. Although the telegraph company was not mentioned by name in the contract, the provision that the contractor would maintain, protect, and restore those utilities whose equipment ran through the underground area

II:	A107-1978, Art. 10
II:	A111-1978, Art. 2
II:	A117-1979, Art. 1
II:	A117-1979, Art. 2
II:	A117-1979, Art. 14
II:	A201-1976, Art. 4, Para. 4.5
II:	A201-1976, Art. 4, Para. 4.7
II:	A201-1976, Art. 4, Para. 4.15

Purchaser sued seller for damages owed due to numerous breaches of a sales contract, which incorporated plans and specifications for the moving and remodeling of a house. The Supreme Court rendered judgment for the purchaser.

The Supreme Court, Appellate Division, affirmed with respect to the various breaches. The Court cited contract provisions entitled Contract Documents, Permits and Regulations, Materials, Workmanship and Employees, Guarantee and Cleaning Up. The Court held that where the work was defective and did not follow plans and specifications, the seller was liable for damages. The Court also held that the claims were not waived by the purchaser's occupancy of the house, since the waiver necessitated knowledge and one cannot easily learn of defects until occupancy. The claims were not time-barred by a guarantee clause, since the seller cited no authority for this proposition, nor was it ever pled as a defense.

79068 Tony and Leo, Inc. v. United States Fidelity & Guar. Co., 281 N.W.2d 862 (Minn. 1979)

      I: A311-1970, Performance Bond

Subcontractor sued contractor and subcontractor's surety on a performance bond for money the subcontractor had paid to another subcontractor to complete performance. The District Court permitted the subcontractor to recover from the surety.

The Supreme Court reversed. The court held that where the performance bond expressly stated that "no right of action shall accrue on this bond to or for the use of any person or corporation other than the owner named herein or the heirs, executors, administrators or successors of the owner," the subcontractor was precluded from bringing an action on the bond.

79069 Watson Construction Co. v. Reppel Steel & Supply Co., 123 Ariz. 138, 598 P.2d 116 (1979)

      III: A401-1978, Art. 12

Mortgagee filed foreclosure action involving numerous parties and claims, including a crossclaim of a subcontractor against the contractor for unpaid labor and materials.

79064 Stouffer Construction Co. v. Tate Engineering, Inc., 44 Md. App. 240, 407 A.2d 1191 (1979)

    III: A311-1970, Labor & Material Payment Bond

Subcontractor of a subcontractor filed suit against the contractor and its surety on a payment bond. The trial court entered judgment for the subcontractor.

The Court of Special Appeals affirmed. Notice under the "Little Miller Act" of Maryland (which is similar to the notice provision of A311) was timely. Although the notice was given more than 90 days after the date of the invoice for the full contract sum, the contract was indivisible. The work was substantially performed before the notice was given and any later notice would have been identical.

79065 Stucki-Miller, Inc. v. Santa Fe Engineers, Inc., 593 P.2d 133 (Utah 1979)

    II: A401-1978, Art. 1
    II: A401-1978, Art. 15

Subcontractor brought action against contractor for work and materials claimed to be extra work not included under the subcontract. The District Court entered judgment for the contractor, and the subcontractor appealed.

The Supreme Court affirmed, holding that the work was sufficiently detailed in the plans, which were incorporated by reference as part of the subcontract. Prior to execution of the subcontract there was opportunity to fully examine those plans.

79066 Sullins v. Third and Catalina Construction Partnership, 124 Ariz. 114, 602 P.2d 495 (1979)

    III: A201-1976, Art. 12, Para. 12.1

Employee of subcontractor brought suit for personal injuries against, among others, the owner. The Superior Court entered summary judgment for the owner, and the employee appealed.

The Court of Appeals affirmed. The power of the owner to initiate changes did not constitute sufficient retention of control to establish a basis for liability under the "retained control" exception to the rule that the owner of property is not liable for the negligence of an independent contractor, absent the owner's reservation of the right to exercise daily control over the manner and means of the work. In this instance the power of the owner to initiate changes was said to arise from the repairs made after the accident at the request of the owner, and no mention is made in the decision of a contractual right of the owner.

79067 Ting-Wan Liang v. Malawista, 70 A.D.2d 415, 421 N.Y.S.2d 594 (1979)

    II: A101-1977, Art. 2
    II: A107-1978, Art. 1

III: A107-1978, Art. 2
III: A111-1978, Art. 4
III: A117-1979, Art. 3

Contractor sued city for balance of payment after the city withheld part of the final payment as liquidated damages for the contractor's failure to complete a construction project on time. The District Court held for the city.

The Court of Appeals affirmed, stating:

[t]he right to stipulate for liquidated damages for delay . . . is generally recognized, and the stipulated amount may be recovered, if reasonable. Provisions for fixed per diem payments for delay . . . are usually construed as stipulations for liquidated damages, and not as penalties, where the actual damages are uncertain or difficult of ascertainment. . . .

No proof of actual damages was necessary to recover liquidated damages.

In addition, the Court of Appeals held that enforcement of the liquidated damages provision would not work an absurdity or oppression upon the contractor because of adverse weather conditions, where the record indicates that the contractor had ample opportunity to complete the project under favorable weather conditions.

79063 South Tippecanoe School Building Corp. v. Shambaugh & Son, 395 N.E.2d 320 (Ind. Ct. App. 1979)

I: A107-1978, Art. 10
I: A107-1978, Art. 17
I: A117-1979, Art. 14
I: A117-1979, Art. 21
I: A201-1976, Art. 4, Para. 4.18
II: A201-1976, Art. 5, Para. 5.3
I: A201-1976, Art. 11, Para. 11.3

Insurance company in the name of the owner, after paying under a builder's risk policy, sued architect, contractor, subcontractor and materialman for negligence, strict liability, breach of implied warranty and breach of contractual warranty. The Circuit Court granted summary judgment for the architect, contractor, subcontractor and materialman and the insurance company appealed.

The Court of Appeals affirmed, holding that the insurance provisions in the contract applied to the architect and the contractor, and by reference to the subcontractor and the materialman or sub-subcontractor. The insurer, therefore, was precluded from suing its own insureds. Since it construed the purpose of the insurance provision as allocating the construction risks to the insurance company without the right of subrogation, the Court also noted that the indemnification provision conspicuously did not include injury or destruction to the work.

Subcontractor brought action against contractor to obtain payment for additional work allegedly performed. Contractor moved to stay the proceeding pending arbitration of the claim in accordance with the contract provision. Subcontractor claimed arbitration was not appropriate because the dispute was not within the ambit of the arbitration provision or its assent to that provision was fraudulently induced. The District Court granted the motion to stay.

The District Court held that absent any provision requiring that a demand for arbitration be made prior to final payment, no such requirement would be implied. It also held that, "except where the parties express a different intention, where no claim is made that fraud was directed to the arbitration clause itself, a broad arbitration clause will be held to encompass arbitration of the claim that the contract itself was induced by fraud."

79060 Seaman Unified School District v. Casson Construction Co., 3 Kan. App. 2d 289, 594 P.2d 241 (1979)

I: A201-1976, Art. 10, Para. 10.2

School District brought suit against contractor, contractor's insurer, engineer and architects for water damage to building. The District Court held for the school district and all defendants appealed.

The Court of Appeals affirmed in part and reversed in part. The judgment against the engineer was reversed since a contract provision in the owner-contractor agreement placed the responsibility for protection of the property upon the contractor. Since the engineer had completed its work, it was not reasonable to hold that the engineer had a continuing duty of protection of the property.

79061 Shoffner Industries, Inc. v. W.B. Lloyd Construction Co., 42 N.C. App. 259, 257 S.E.2d 50, *appeal denied,* 259 S.E.2d 301 (N.C. 1979)

III: A201-1976, Art. 1, Para. 1.1

Supplier brought a debt action against contractor. Contractor counterclaimed against supervising architect for damages for the negligent erection of trusses. The Superior Court dismissed the counterclaim, holding that the architect was absolved from liability to contractor since they were not in privity of contract.

The Court of Appeals reversed and remanded. The Court held that under general principles of tort law, privity of contract is not a prerequisite for the incurrence of tort liability upon a negligent party. The lower court erred in not holding the architect liable for the contractor's damages caused by the architect's negligent approval of defective materials and workmanship.

79062 Sides Construction Co. v. City of Scott City, 581 S.W.2d 443 (Mo. Ct. App. 1979)

III: A101-1977, Art. 3

in the owner-contractor agreement concerning termination by the owner and its completion of the project, which provision did not mention recovery of attorney's fees. The owner was not allowed to recover charges for correction of non-conforming work where that amount was already recovered as damages for breach of contract. In addition, the owner was not allowed to recover the estimated value of a one year warranty since more than a year had elapsed since completion of the project and no claim that would have been cognizable under the agreed warranty, if given, had arisen.

The Court of Appeals affirmed the District Court's calculation of liquidated damages. The contract provision established liquidated damages as a certain amount per day multiplied by the number of days for the entire period of delay. The court did not allow the owner's theory of damages which was liquidated damages up to the date the contract was terminated, plus legal interest on all sums paid to the contractor prior to termination, all sums spent completing the project after termination, and all other amounts expended in connection with the project.

79058   Sacramento v. Trans Pacific Industries, Inc., 98 Cal. App. 3d 389, 159 Cal. Rptr. 514 (1979)

II: A107-1978, Art. 14
II: A117-1979, Art. 18
II: A201-1976, Art. 8, Para. 8.3
II: A311-1970, Performance Bond

City sued the developer and its surety on a contract for failure to perform its obligations under a subdivision agreement with the city. The Superior Court entered judgment in favor of city, and developer and its surety appealed.

The Court of Appeals affirmed. In reaching a decision it looked at both the terms of the written agreement between the city and the general contractor and the performance bond. It held that: (1) the surety was not exonerated under its bond for alterations of developer's performance since (a) the developer had not performed its work in a workmanlike manner ("[a]ny additional costs incurred as a result were precisely what . . . surety . . . had obligated itself to pay when it promised to pay City if said Principal [should] fail to improve and complete in a good and workmanlike manner, the construction of the public improvements . . ."), and (b) the contract specifically provided for extensions of time such as occurred; and (2) although it was not a party to the engineering services agreement between city and developer, surety was nevertheless liable under both the bond terms and the subdivision agreement by which it agreed to be bound, since "[T]he builder's incurring of expenses for engineering services was within the foreseeable scope of the City-[developer] subdivision agreement."

79059   Schneider, Inc. v. Research-Cottrell, Inc., 474 F. Supp. 1179 (W.D. Pa. 1979)

II: A401-1978, Art. 13, Para. 13.1

I:	A101-1977, Art. 3
I:	A101-1977, Art. 7
I:	A201-1976, Art. 7, Para. 7.6
I:	A201-1976, Art. 8, Para. 8.3
I:	A201-1976, Art. 9, Para. 9.6
I:	A311-1970, Labor and Material Payment Bond

Owner brought suit against contractor and its surety on a performance bond, seeking damages for negligence and delay. The District Court entered judgment for the owner, and all parties appealed.

The Supreme Court affirmed in part, reversed in part, and remanded. The court reviewed various provisions in the owner-contractor agreement and the general conditions and determined that the commencement date for completion of the work was not the date in the agreement, but rather the date upon which it was executed. The contractor was not allowed any extensions of time by the Court in its computation of the time for performance, since the contract required all requests for extensions to be in writing. An escrow agreement did not resolve the issue of damages for negligence since final payment did not constitute a waiver of the claims pursuant to a contract provision concerning the effect of final payment and a provision allowing other remedies than imposed by the contract documents. finally, the suit against the surety was not timely brought under the terms of the performance bond, since, although the suit was commenced within the two year period, there was no service upon the surety until two and one-half years later.

79057 Ranger Construction Co. v. Prince William County School Board, 605 F.2d 1298 (4th Cir. 1979)

I:	A101-1977, Art. 3
I:	A107-1978, Art. 2
I:	A111-1978, Art. 4
I:	A117-1979, Art. 3
I:	A201-1976, Art. 4, Para. 4.5
I:	A201-1976, Art. 13, Para. 13.2
I:	A201-1976, Art. 14, Para. 14.2
I:	A311-1970, Performance Bond

Contractor sued owner after the owner terminated the contract. The owner counterclaimed against the contractor and brought in the surety as a defendant on its performance bond. The District court held for the owner and awarded damages, and all three parties appealed.

The Court of Appeals reversed part of the award, holding that the bond provision referring to "costs" did not include attorney's fees. In addition, that provision dealt with the surety's completion of the project, which it never under took since it never agreed that the contractor had breached the contract. The owner instead had relied on a provision

this in no way affected the surety's obligations under the bond, but rather it served to reduce the amount for which bonds were required. The Court also held that the lower court erred in granting judgment for the full face amount of the bond where the town made no showing that the amounts fixed in the bond reflected a reasonable measure of the anticipated harm resulting from the discontinued construction.

79054   Powell's General Contracting Co. v. Marshfield Housing Auth., 7 Mass. App. Ct. 763, 390 N.E.2d 267 (1979)

        III: A107-1978, Art. 13

        III: A117-1979, Art. 17

        III: A201-1976, Art. 7, Para 7.9

A dispute between the owner and contractor for extra costs was submitted with the owner's consent for arbitration before a master pursuant to an arbitration provision in the contract. Prior to the master's decision a dispute decision and addenda based on the master's report was rendered by the trial court. Both the master's decision and the trial court held for the contractor. The owner appealed the court decision.

The Court of Appeals affirmed with modifications and held that "by relitigating the underlying dispute without seeking a ruling as to the propriety of the master's hearings, and by not objecting until after his final report [the owner] waived its right to a binding . . . decision."

79055   Puritan Mills, Inc. v. Pickering Construction Co., 152 Ga. App. 309, 262 S.E.2d 586 (1979)

        III: A107-1978, Art. 18

        III: A117-1979, Art. 22

        III: A201-1976, Art. 12, Para. 12.1

Contractor sued owner for compensation due under change order. The trial court held for the contractor, and the owner appealed.

The Court of Appeals affirmed. The Court granted the contractor the reasonable value of his work for removal of hidden rock which was not anticipated when the contract was made. The Court held that even though removal of the rock was not an express contract condition, the owner's acceptance of the removal, which was necessary to achieve the contractual objective, implied a promise to pay for the reasonable value of the work performed. The Court also held that the lower court was correct in permitting testimony that local custom and usage of trade indicated that the "removal of rock was extra work, if not contemplated by the contract."

79056   Quin Blair Enterprises, Inc. v. Julien Construction Co., 597 P.2d 945 (Wyo. 1979)

        I: A101-1977, Art. 1

day after the architect's refusal to act. Since the contractor had not filed the demand for arbitration, the motion to compel arbitration was premature.

79052   Planning Systems Corp. v. Murrell, 374 So. 2d 719 (La. Ct. App.), *cert. denied*, 376 So. 2d 319 (La. 1979)

III:	A101-1977, Art. 4
III:	A107-1978, Art. 3
III:	A111-1978, Art. 6
III:	A111-1978, Art. 8
III:	A111-1978, Art. 12
III:	A111-1978, Art. 13
III:	A117-1979, Art. 4
III:	A117-1979, Art. 5
III:	A117-1979, Art. 6
III:	A117-1979, Art. 8

Contractor sued owner for payment due under a repair contract. The owner counterclaimed for breach. The jury awarded damages to the owner and dismissed the contractor's claim.

The Court of Appeals affirmed. The Court construed the contract as a "cost plus construction contract" because although it contained an estimated contract price, it also provided that the contractor furnish to the owner monthly statements showing amounts of material and labor for reimbursement.

The Court held that the dismissal of the contractor's claim was proper since at the time the contractor discontinued work the owner had paid 90 percent of the estimated contract price, and the "premises were nowhere near completion." The Court also found merit in the owner's claim that he discontinued payment because work had not progressed proportionately with the amount of payments made, and awarded damages to the owner for the contractor's breach.

79053   Poughkeepsie v. Holden Construction Co., 71 A.D.2d 886, 419 N.Y.S.2d 531 (1979)

   II: A311-1970, Performance Bond

Town sued surety for the full face amount of the performance bond. The Supreme Court granted summary judgment against the surety. The surety appealed, claiming it should not have been required to make a cash deposit in addition to the performance bond and that judgment should not have been entered without a trial to assess damages.

The Supreme Court, Appellate Division, reversed and remitted the action to the Supreme Court for an assessment of damages. The Court held that the town was not allowed to require a cash deposit in addition to a "full cost" performance bond. However,

The Supreme Court vacated and held that a letter from the subcontractor to the contractor which requested a joint check was sufficient notice as required under the statute (which is substantially the same as the A311 notice provision). In addition, it was not necessary that the letter be sent by registered or certified mail and ordinary mail was sufficient under the statute.

79050   PPG Industries, Inc. v. Continental Heller Corp., 124 Ariz. 216, 613 P.2d 108 (1979)

        III: A401-1978, Art. 9
        III: A401-1978, Art. 11

Employee of subcontractor brought an action against contractor for negligence in failure to properly maintain a stairwell. Contractor filed a third party claim against the subcontractor on the basis that the subcontractor required insurance which would have protected the contractor from the claim. The Superior Court entered judgment for the employee in the main action and in favor of the contractor on the third party claim. The subcontractor appealed.

The Court of Appeals affirmed. The subcontract placed responsibility for safety upon the subcontractor for its work, and therefore the employee's accident would have been covered by the insurance required but not obtained under the subcontract. The subcontract also required the subcontractor to comply with all laws, and an OSHA standard as adopted by Arizona was violated by the subcontractor.

79051   Pettinaro Construction Co. v. Harry Partridge, Jr., & Sons, 408 A.2d 957 (Del. Ch. 1979)

        I: A201-1976, Art. 2, Para. 2.2
        I: A201-1976, Art. 7, Para. 7.9
        II: A401-1978, Art. 1
        II: A401-1978, Art. 11
        II: A401-1978, Art. 12
        II: A401-1978, Art. 13

The contractor filed a lawsuit to compel its subcontractor to submit to arbitration proceedings pursuant to an arbitration provision in the contract and the subcontractor moved for summary judgment. The Chancery Court granted the summary judgment and held that: "The question of what procedure must be followed to initiate the arbitration process is obviously a matter of construing the contract and thus within the scope of the arbitration agreement. The proper method of initiating arbitration . . . is a matter for the decision of the arbitrator." In accordance with the arbitration agreement since the architect had advised the contractor that he would not make a decision on the dispute, the contractor had a right to, and should have, filed a demand to arbitrate on the tenth

III: A311-1970, Labor & Material Payment Bond

Subcontractors sued stockholders of general contractor on guaranty given to owners and were awarded judgment from which stockholders appealed.

The District Court of Appeal reversed. In reaching its conclusion, the Court looked at the document the stockholders had executed, a "Guaranty of Completion," and considered whether it was more in the nature of a performance than a payment bond. The Court held "that the guarantee in question has the effect of a performance bond to indemnify the owners of the real property against liens and thus does not benefit [subcontractor] for breach of contract by [general contractor]." The Court stated that the guaranty lent itself to a "performance" interpretation "because of 1) the repeated use of the word "performance,' 2) the absence of any mention of duties to subcontractors or materialmen, and 3) the strict statutory requirements for payment bonds."

79048   Misener Marine Construction Co. v. Southport Marine, Inc., 377 So. 2d 757 (Fla. Dist. Ct. App. 1979)

II: A401-1978, Art. 11

Employee of contractor who was injured while operating equipment leased by contractor to subcontractor sued both of them for damages. The contractor and subcontractor filed cross claims for indemnification. Although a settlement was reached with the employee, a trial commenced on the cross claims. The trail court denied either party recovery, and they both appealed.

The Court of Appeal affirmed. In determining the contractor's claim for indemnification pursuant to a contract provision the Court stated that "[s]ince the [injured employee] was furnished by the [contractor] to perform services which were [the contractor's] duty under the lease agreement, the services did not arise under the subcontract duties of [the subcontractor]." The court held that the intention of the indemnity clause which indemnified the contractor against "all claims . . . of damages or injury to persons . . . sustained in connection with the performance of this subcontract . . . was to have [the subcontractor] reimburse [the contractor] for any loss sustained by [the contractor] where injury to person or property arose out of duties to be performed by [the subcontractor]" (emphasis added). Under this interpretation, the injured employee was not performing work under the subcontract. Therefore the contractor was not entitled to indemnification.

79049   Norman S. Wright & Co., S.W. v. Slaysman, 124 Ariz. 321, 604 P.2d 252, *vacating* 604 P.2d 361 (Ariz. Ct. App. 1970)

III: A311-1970, Labor & Material Payment Bond

Subcontractor brought action under "Little Miller Act" against contractor for payment for materials supplied. The trial court granted summary judgment for the contractor, and the Court of Appeals affirmed.

The Supreme Court affirmed. The Court held that under a Wisconsin safe place statute the architect would only be held liable if he had the right of supervision and control. Where the architect was only required to make periodic visits to the construction site, and he was not responsible for construction means, or safety precautions in connection with the work, the requisite control was not present.

79045 J'Aire Corp. v. Gregory, 24 Cal. App. 3d 799, 598 P.2d 60 (1979)

> III: A101-1977, Art. 3
> III: A107-1978, Art. 2
> III: A111-1978, Art. 4
> III: A117-1979, Art. 3

Lessee brought suit against contractor to recover business losses arising from delay in completion of work under contract between lessor and the contractor. The Superior Court dismissed the suit, and the lessee appealed.

The Supreme Court reversed. Although the contract contained no completion date, the contractor breached a duty to complete construction so as to avoid unnecessary injury to the lessee's business since that risk of harm was reasonably foreseeable.

79046 Jasper Construction, Inc. v. Foothill Junior College, 91 Cal. App. 3d 1, 153 Cal. Rptr. 767 (1979)

> III: A101-1977, Art. 3
> III: A107-1978, Art. 2
> III: A111-1978, Art. 4
> III: A117-1979, Art. 3

Contractor sued owner and architect to recover for delays and additional costs. The Superior Court held for contractor, and the owner appealed.

The Court of Appeals reversed. The Court held that the trial court erred in giving jury instructions stating that if the owner was found to have caused any part of the delay, damages could not be apportioned between the parties, and the owner was liable to the contractor for all liquidated delay damages.

Under the provision relating to time extensions, the contract stated that "the Contractor shall not be charged with the liquidated damages . . . when the delay in completion of the work is due . . . to unforeseeable cause beyond the control and without the fault or negligence of the Contractor, including . . . *acts of the Owner.*" The Court construed this clause to contain an explicit provision allowing apportionment of liquidated delay damages.

79047 Jones v. W. L. Cobb Construction Co., 371 So. 2d 550 (Fla. Dist. Ct. App. 1979)

> III: A311-1970, Performance Bond

The Court of Appeals affirmed. The contract bound the contractor to "indemnify . . . the owner . . . against all . . . damages . . . resulting from the performance of the work." The Court also held that the contract provision which required the contractor to carry liability insurance did not remove his liability under the indemnification clause of the contract. Under the terms of the performance bond, the surety was liable to the owner for consequential damages caused by the contractor's negligence.

79043 Hemenway Co. v. Bartex, Inc. of Texas, 373 So. 2d 1356 (La. Ct. App.), *cert. denied,* 376 So. 2d 1272 (La. 1979)

        I: A101-1977, Art. 3
        I: A107-1978, Art. 2
        I: A107-1978, Art. 10
        I: A107-1978, Art. 15
        I: A111-1978, Art. 3
        I: A117-1979, Art. 3
        I: A117-1979, Art. 4
        I: A117-1979, Art. 19
        I: A201-1976, Art. 4, Para. 4.5
        I: A201-1976, Art. 9, Para. 9.7
        I: A201-1976, Art. 9, Para. 9.8

Owner sued contractor and its surety for defects and damages due to delay of construction. The trial court entered judgment for the owner and the contractor appealed.

The Court of Appeal affirmed. The Court held that the owner was entitled to actual damages for delay despite a provision for liquidated delay damages. Under this provision the parties were required to reach a separate agreement concerning the amount of liquidated damages for each day of delay. The parties' failure to make this agreement permitted the trial court to award actual damages for delay.

The Court also held that the owner's acceptance of the "substantial completion" of the project did not act as a waiver of a claim for defective work. Under Louisiana law, substantial completion "indicates only that the facility may be used for the purpose intended even though certain defects or omissions exist." In addition, the Court held that the absence of a clear and express waiver bound the parties to a warranty provision stating that "all Work will be of good quality and free from faults and defects."

79044 Hortman v. Becker Construction Co., 92 Wis. 2d 210, 284 N.W.2d 621 (1979)

        II: B141-1977, Art. 1

General contractor's employee sued general contractor, architect and owner to recover damages for injuries sustained on the job site. Architect motioned for summary judgment. The Circuit Court granted the architect's motion for summary judgment.

Employee of contractor brought suit against owner for injuries sustained during construction project. Owner sought indemnification from contractor as provided in the contract. The trial court found for the owner and the contractor appealed.

The Court of Civil Appeals affirmed. The Court held that where it was customary for employees of the contractor, in the regular course of their work, to assist other employees of the contractor, injuries resulting to the contractor's employee in such an instance were incident to, or the result of, the contractor's work. The injuries, therefore, fell within the indemnity provision of the contract.

79041 Hartline-Thomas, Inc. v. Arthur Pew Construction Co., 151 Ga. App. 598, 260 S.E.2d 744 (1979)

	III:	A107-1978, Art. 10
	III:	A117-1979, Art. 14
	III:	A201-1976, Art. 4, Para. 4.18
	III:	A401-1978, Art. 1
	III:	A401-1978, Art. 11
	III:	A401-1978, Art. 15

Contractor sued the subcontractor under an indemnification provision in the subcontract for attorney fees arising from the successful defense of a personal injury suit. The DeKalb State Court entered summary judgment for the contractor.

The Court of Appeals affirmed. The indemnification agreement of the general contract incorporated into the subcontract had two separate provisions: (1) indemnification of the contractor for damages on claims caused by the work performed by the subcontractor, his agents, and employees, and (2) indemnification of the contractor against his own negligence. The Court stated the two provisions were severable, and "dealt with separate, distinct and cumulative obligations. Thus the first [provision] would not be nullified by any public policy failures of the second [provision]." The trial court correctly entered summary judgment for the contractor because under the first provision the contractor was to be indemnified "for attorney fees arising on account of personal injury *claimed to have been caused by* . . . [subcontractor's] work. . . ."

79042 Haywood County Consolidated School System v. United States Fidelity & Guar. Co., 43 N.C. App. 71, 257 S.E.2d 670 (1979)

	I:	A201-1976, Art. 4, Para. 4.18
	I:	A201-1976, Art. 11, Para. 11.1
	III:	A201-1976, Art. 7, Para. 7.5
	II:	A311-1970, Performance Bond

Owner sued the surety on a contractor's performance bond for damages to the project when plumbing pipes burst after the completion of the contract. The Superior Court held for owner and surety appealed.

79038 Floors, Inc. v. B.G. Danis of New England, Inc., 7 Mass. App. Ct. 356, 387 N.E.2d 1166, aff'd, 401 N.E.2d 839 (Mass. 1979)

III: A201-1976, Art. 7, Para. 7.9
III: A401-1978, Art. 13

Subcontractor brought a claim against contractor pursuant to an arbitration provision of the contract. The arbitrator held for the subcontractor, who then moved to confirm the award before the trial court. The trial court entered a judgment in the amount of the arbitration award, the costs of arbitration and legal fees for the court action.

The Court of Appeals reversed, holding that under the state arbitration statute, where arbitration was the primary remedy, legal fees "should be limited to lawyers' work directly related to the preservation and prosecution of the [state arbitration statute] rights. . . . The legal fees which the [subcontractor] may recover are those connected with . . . the drafting and filing of the complaint and the preparation and presentation of the motion to stay the . . . action pending arbitration."

79039 Gateway Drywall & Decorating, Inc. v. Village Construction Co., 76 Ill. App. 3d 812, 395 N.E.2d 613 (1979)

III: A107-1978, Art. 13
III: A117-1979, Art. 17
III: A201-1976, Art. 7, Para. 7.9
I: A401-1978, Art. 13

Subcontractors brought suit against the owner, general contractor and a bank and sought foreclosure on mechanic's liens. The defendants sought on several occasions to delay the trial, and when this was no longer possible, the defendants filed for arbitration. The trial court denied the petition for arbitration, and the owner, general contractor and bank appealed.

The Court of Appeals affirmed, holding that "a contractual right to arbitration can be waived . . . and that waiver must be deemed to have occurred when a party's conduct has been inconsistent with the arbitration clause so as to indicate that he has abandoned his right to avail himself of such right." By filing answers in the litigation and participating in discovery for two years, "the defendants' assertion of their right to arbitrate came too late. . . ."

79040 Gulf Offshore Co. v. Mobil Oil Corp., 594 S.W.2d 233 (Tex. Civ. App. 1979)

II: A107-1978, Art. 10
II: A117-1979, Art. 14
II: A201-1976, Art. 4, Para. 4.18

III: A401-1978, Art. 11

Adjoining property owner brought suit against contractor, subcontractor and others for property damage. The District Court entered judgment against the defendants, and the contractor appealed.

The Supreme Court affirmed. The contractor was partially negligent. Neither the subcontract, not the prime contract that was incorporated by reference into the subcontract, provided for the indemnity of the contractor by the subcontractor when the contractor was negligent. Indemnity was provided for only where the contractor had been liable for the subcontractor's negligence. In addition, the failure of the subcontractor to purchase insurance in the amount required by the subcontract was not relevant. The insurance would not have provided coverage to the contractor for its own negligence.

79036 Fauntleroy v. Walker, 220 Va. 168, 257 S.E.2d 766 (1979)

III: A101-1977, Art. 3
III: A107-1978, Art. 2
III: A111-1978, Art. 4
III: A117-1979, Art. 3

Owner sued the contractor for failure to commence construction by the agreed time and for an increase in the construction cost resulting form the delay. The Circuit Court found the damages too speculative since the evidence had consisted of construction estimates remote from the date of contract breach. The court entered summary judgment for the contractor.

The Supreme Court reversed and remanded. The Court held that the availability of other evidence, the increased cost of construction demanded by the contractor, should have been used as a measure for determining damages.

79037 Fidelity & Deposit Co. of Maryland v. Parsons & Whittemore Contractors Corp., 48 N.Y.2d 127, 421 N.Y.S.2d 869, 397 N.E.2d 380 (1979)

III: A311-1970, Performance Bond
III: A401-1978, Art. 13

Contractor served a demand for arbitration against the subcontractor and the surety of subcontractor under a performance bond, and the surety filed an application to stay the arbitration. The Supreme Court granted the surety's application and the Supreme Court, Appellate Division, affirmed.

The Court of Appeals modified the lower court's ruling and held that the surety was not entitled to stay arbitration of disputes arising from an arbitration provision of the subcontract, since the subcontract was incorporated in the performance bond. Whether the surety could be compelled to participate in arbitration or whether it could force its way into arbitration over the objection of one of the parties were issues that the Court stated it was not required to determine.

I:	A201-1976, Art. 10, Para. 10.3
I:	A201-1976, Art. 12, Para. 12.2

Contractor filed a complaint against the owner with the Board of Arbitration to recover expenses incurred from the removal of soil and debris deposited at the construction site from a hurricane. The Board of Arbitration found for the owner, and the contractor appealed.

The Commonwealth Court affirmed, citing a provision in the contract which clearly placed the risk of loss on the contractor. The contractor was not allowed to recover under a provision allowing additional payment for removal of concealed or subsurface conditions because this provision was held to pertain to flooding or the deposit of soil. The Court also held that a provision allowing payment to the contractor for expenses incurred during emergencies applied to the prevention of loss, and not to repairs for damages already suffered. In addition, the Court held that the architect, in processing the contractor's claim for payment, interpreted the contract only in the first instance, leaving the final decision in such matters up to the owner.

79034   Fairway Builders, Inc. v. Malouf Towers Rental Co., 124 Ariz. 242, 603 P.2d 513 (1979)

I:	A101-1977, Art. 1
I:	A101-1977, Art. 3
I:	A101-1977, Art. 7
I:	A107-1978, Art. 2
I:	A107-1978, Art. 7
I:	A201-1976, Art. 1, Para. 1.2

Contractor brought action against lessee of real property for amount due under construction contract. The Superior Court entered judgment for contractor and cross appeals were filed.

The Court of Appeals affirmed in part and reversed in part. A letter was not required to be executed in accordance with a contract provision requiring execution in duplicate by both parties, since the letter related to oral requests for extra work outside of the contract. In addition, it was possible that it was a "contract document" even though never signed. By analogy, signatures on the "general conditions" were not required since there was an incorporation by reference of the general conditions. The contract also mentioned an agreement with the same date as the letter. A contract provision which required tenant floor layouts to be provided by a certain date was construed by the Court to refer to the date of completion, rather than work within the sum certain contract price. The plans only contained a sample layout and no specific layouts had been drawn.

79035   Farmington Plumbing & Heating Co. v. Fischer Sand & Aggregate, Inc., 281 N.W.2d 838 (Minn. 1979)

III:	A401-1978, Art. 9

all material has been paid for, will be construed to benefit the materialman so as to avoid injustice.

79032   E.V. Cox Construction Co. v. Brookline Associates, 604 P.2d 867 (Okla. Ct. App. 1979)

        I: A101-1977, Art. 3
        I: A101-1977, Art. 5
        I: A107-1978, Art. 4
        I: A107-1978, Art. 14
        I: A111-1978, Art. 4
        I: A111-1978, Art. 14
        I: A117-1979, Art. 9
        I: A117-1979, Art. 18
        I: A201-1976, Art. 8, Para. 8.3
        I: A201-1976, Art. 9, Para. 9.5
        I: A201-1976, Art. 9, Para. 9.9
        I: A201-1976, Art. 14, Para. 14.2

Contractor sued owner to recover unpaid progress payments, retainage, and lost profits due to owner's breach. Owner counterclaimed for breach of the timeliness provision of the contract. The trial court found for the contractor on the issue of unpaid progress payments and denied owner's counterclaim. Both the contractor and owner appealed.

The Court of Appeals affirmed the trial court's ruling, modified to include recovery of the retainage. The Court held that although the contractor breached the time limit provision of the contract and did not submit a written request for extension of the time period as required in the contract, the fact that the owner continued to make progress payments to the contractor as segments of construction were completed constituted an implicit waiver of the time limitation. As such, the contractor became subject to a statutory duty of completion within a reasonable time. As there was no evidence that the contractor's delay in completion was unreasonable, the owner's termination of the contract amounted to a breach thereof. By breaching the contract, the provision which required substantial completion of construction as a prerequisite to recovery by the contractor of retainage was rendered inoperative; therefore, the contractor was allowed to recover retainage.

79033   F.J. Busse, Inc. v. Department of General Services, 47 Pa. Commw. 539, 408 A.2d 578 (1979)

        III: A107-1978, Art. 8
        III: A117-1979, Art. 12
        III: A201-1976, Art. 2, Para. 2.2

Subcontractor's employee sued several defendants including the architect pursuant to the Illinois Structural Work Act for personal injuries suffered at the construction site. The trial court granted the architect's motion for summary judgment, and the employee appealed.

The Court of Appeals affirmed. The Act allowed a right of action against "[a]ny owner, contractor, subcontractor . . . having charge of . . . the construction. . . ." The Court held that according to the construction contracts, the architect "had no authority to stop the work, had no control of construction methods or techniques, was not responsible for safety precautions and programs, had not continuous supervision duties." The architect's rights and duties "were simply to see that contractual specifications were met." Thus, the architect was held not to be in charge of the construction as required by the Illinois Structural Work Act.

79030   County of Jefferson v. Barton-Douglas Contractors, Inc., 282 N.W.2d 155 (Iowa 1979)

> III: A107-1978, Art. 13
> III: A117-1979, Art. 17
> III: A201-1976, Art. 7, Para. 7.9

County brought suit against architect, engineer, contractors and sureties for alleged unsatisfactory performance. One of the contractors sought to have its claim arbitrated as provided in its contract. The District Court entered an order dissolving a temporary injunction which restrained the contractor from submitting the claim to arbitration.

The Supreme Court reversed. The Court held that "[t]he prospect of multiple proceedings carrying a potential for inconsistent findings provides a basis for overriding the freedom to contract for arbitration." Thus, the Court stayed arbitration and chose to resolve all related claims in one legal action in order to decrease the risk of complexity, delay, and expense.

79031   Duluth Lumber and Plywood Co. v. Delta Development, Inc., 281 N.W.2d 377 (Minn. 1979)

> II: A107-1978, Art. 15
> II: A117-1979, Art. 19
> II: A201-1976, Art. 9, Para. 9.9

Materialman brought suit against owner for money owed on lumber supplied to the contractor. Owner claimed it was not liable for payment due on materials obtained by contractors. The District Court ruled in the materialman's favor.

The Supreme Court affirmed. The Court held that where there is a construction contract to perform work on public property that is exempt from a mechanic's lien, a provision in the contract, which states the owner will withhold final payment to the contractor until

filed within thirty days after a notice of completion had been recorded. Had the subcontractor waited until payment was due it under the terms of the contract, the remedy of stop notice would have been barred. Thus, the Court held that under the terms of the contract the subcontractor was entitled to the judgment which it originally sought.

79027   Central Louisiana Electric Co. v. Giant Enterprises, Inc., 371 So. 2d 641 (La. Ct. App.), *cert. denied,* 375 So. 2d 646 (La. 1979)

>   III: A107-1978, Art. 18
>   III: A117-1979, Art. 22
>   III: A201-1976, Art. 12, Para. 12.1

Owner sued contractor and its surety for various breaches of a land clearing contract. The surety claimed it was not liable to the contractor, since the contract was altered without its consent, and was not notified of the contractor's alleged breaches. The trial court entered judgment for the contractor and its surety.

The Court of Appeals reversed and remanded. The Court held that all of the alleged changes were unsubstantiated, in light of its determination that the owner did not substantially breach the contract. Therefore, the surety was liable to the contractor, since the contractor did not breach its agreement with the surety.

79028   City School District v. Jacques, 73 A.D.2d 707, 422 N.Y.S.2d 527 (1979)

>   I: B141-1977, Art. 9

Architect initiated arbitration proceedings against the owner after its refusal to pay for work performed. The owner sought to stay the arbitration, and the trial court denied the owner's petition.

The Supreme Court, Appellate Division, reversed. The Court held that the contract provision which stated "in no event shall the demand for arbitration be made after the date when institution of legal or equitable proceedings . . . would be barred by the applicable statute of limitations," did not act as a waiver of the requirement of the Education Law that all claims must be presented to the owner within three months after the accrual of such claim. The Court then remanded the case to determine if the Education Law had been complied with or waived by some other means such as the owner's conduct.

79029   Fruzyna v. Walter C. Carlson Associates, 78 Ill. App. 3d 1050, 398 N.E.2d 60 (1979)

>   I: A107-1978, Art. 8
>   I: A117-1979, Art. 12
>   I: A201-1976, Art. 2, Para. 2.2
>   I: B141-1977, Art. 1

The Court of Appeals reversed with directions to enter an order directing the arbitration, and staying the Municipal Court action. The order denying arbitration was in error because the owner's presence in the Municipal Court action did not prevent arbitration. If the owner required protection, the Municipal Court action should have been stayed. Since the subcontractor had not participated in the arbitration proceeding, a new hearing was required.

79025   Carolina Builders Corp. v. AAA Dry Wall, Inc., 43 N.C. App. 444, 259 S.E.2d 364 (1979)

         II: A201-1976, Art. 7, Para. 7.5
         II: A401-1976, Art. 11

Supplier sued general contractor and owner for subcontractor's failure to pay for materials. The Superior Court held for the general contractor and owner, and supplier appealed.

The Court of Appeals affirmed. The Court held that the supplier could not bring suit as a third party beneficiary to the contract between the owner and the general contractor. The general contractor failed to obtain a labor and material payment bond from the subcontractor, as required by the contract. The Court, however, stated that the owner's failure to enforce this provision demonstrated that there was no intention, expressly or impliedly, to confer a benefit upon the third party supplier. Since the supplier was "a mere incidental beneficiary of the contract," it could not recover for a breach.

79026   Central Industrial Engineering Co. v. Strauss Construction Co., 98 Cal. App. 3d 460, 159 Cal. Rptr. 564 (1979)

         III: A401-1978, Art. 6

Subcontractor sued contractor to recover final payment, plus interest and attorney fees on the work which had been accepted by the owner. The subcontractor filed a stop notice with the owner prior to the contractor receiving final payment from the owner. Contractor cross-complained for breach of contract, and sought a set-off for attorneys' fees and costs from final payment which it admitted was due to the subcontractor. The Superior Court granted the contractor's set-off, and the subcontractor appealed.

The Court of Appeals reversed. The trial court erred in holding that the formal documents, which provided that final payment was due "to the said Subcontractor within 30 days after the Subcontractor shall have completed his work to the full satisfaction of the . . . Owner, all provided that the Contractor has received payment from the Owner," constituted the "contract," when a rider attached to the documents and signed by both parties specifically deleted the requirement that payment was conditioned upon the contractor receiving payment from the owner.

The Court held that the subcontractor's "premature" filing of the stop notice was not a breach of contract since under California law a stop notice would be ineffective if not

and subcontractor made motions for summary judgment, which the Supreme Court granted.

The Court of Appeals affirmed. The Court stated that a clause which read "[T]he Owner, Contractor, and all subcontractors waive all rights, each against the others, for damages caused by fire or other perils covered by insurance provided for under the terms of the Contract Documents, except such rights as they may have to the proceeds of insurance," precluded the owner from recovering any damage. The provision did not seek to exempt a party from liability but rather it required one of the parties to provide insurance for all parties, thus not violating a New York statute concerning exemption from liability.

79023   Brick Township Municipal Utilities Authority v. Diversified R. B. & T. Construction Co., 171 N.J. Super. 397, 409 A.2d 806 (App. Div. 1979)

   III: A107-1978, Art. 13

   III: A117-1979, Art. 17

   III: A201-1976, Art. 7, Para. 7.9

Contractor filed a claim against the owner pursuant to an arbitration provision in their contract which required a demand within thirty days of the engineer's decision. The trial court held for the owner.

The Court of Appeals affirmed. It held that a letter from the engineer rejecting the contractor's claims was not vague and ambiguous and that it did trigger the thirty day period. If the contractor had regarded the letter as merely a stage in the negotiation and not a rejection, it should have responded in kind. It further held that the demand for arbitration demonstrated the letter's finality. The Court also found no proof that the owner intentionally lulled the contractor into letting the limitation period expire by suggesting a continuance of negotiations. Therefore the owner was not estopped from asserting the thirty day limit.

79024   CBCO, Inc. v. Grani Installation, Inc., 95 Cal. App. 3d 290, 157 Cal. Rptr. 28 (1979)

   III: A201-1976, Art. 7, Para. 7.9

   III: A401-1978, Art. 13

Subcontractor brought suit in Municipal Court against contractor and owner, and contractor moved for an order staying the action and directing arbitration. The Municipal Court then allowed the contractor to apply for that relief in the Superior Court, which entered an order denying arbitration. The contractor appealed. At the insistence of the contractor an arbitration was held over the objection of the subcontractor and without appearance by it, resulting in an award for the contractor. The subcontractor moved for an order vacating that award on the ground that the previous order had denied arbitration. That petition was denied and the subcontractor appealed.

79020 Armand v. Territorial Construction Inc., 90 Mich. App. 491, 282 N.W.2d 365 (1979)

    I: A311-1970, Labor and Material Payment Bond

Subcontractor brought suit on payment bond against contractor and its surety. Surety was granted an accelerated judgment by the Circuit Court based on the one-year limitation of action clause contained in the bond.

The Court of Appeals reversed. The Court stated that where the bond provided that a claim could not be filed until ninety days after the date on which the last of such claimant's work or labor was done or performed, the one-year limitation of action period would commence from the point in which the claimant may first file suit. This would best effectuate the "literal language of the limitations provision."

79021 Atlas Assurance Co. v. General Builders, Inc., 93 N.M. 398, 600 P.2d 850 (1979)

    II: A201-1976, Art. 4, Para. 4.5
    II: A201-1976, Art. 4, Para. 4.18
    II: A201-1976, Art. 11, Para. 11.1
    II: A201-1976, Art. 11, Para. 11.3
    II: A201-1976, Art. 13, Para. 13.2

Insurer brought subrogation action against contractor and subcontractor for losses it paid owner for wind damage to shopping center. The District Court granted summary judgment for the contractor and subcontractor and insurer appealed.

The Court of Appeals reversed and remanded. Summary judgment was inappropriate since a genuine issue of material fact existed as to whether the contractor and subcontractor were intended to be co-insureds with the owner. Contract provisions concerning "performance and guaranty of work" and "repairs and replacements" did not concern themselves with insurance. Contract provisions concerning liability insurance and indemnification were concerned with third party claims and not builder's risk insurance.

79022 Board of Educ., Union Free School District No. 3, Town of Brookhaven v. Valden Associates, 46 N.Y.2d 653, 416 N.Y.S.2d 202, 389 N.E.2d 798 (1979), *aff'g* 400 N.Y.S.2d 152 (N.Y. App. Div. 1977)

    II: A107-1978, Art. 17
    II: A117-1979, Art. 21
    II: A201-1976, Art. 11, Para. 11.3
    II: A201-1976, Art. 11, Para. 11.4

Owner sued contractor and subcontractor for property damage which resulted from a fire caused by either the contractor's or the subcontractor's negligence. The contractor

Contractor sued the owner to recover for the balance due under the contract and for extras which had been orally agreed upon. The District Court held for the contractor.

The Court of Civil Appeals reversed and remanded. The contract required written approval of all extras or change orders. Since there was an express contract, there could not be a recovery based on the reasonable value of the work, and exceptions to this rule did not apply to the facts of that lawsuit.

79018   Weeshoff Construction Co. v. Los Angeles County Flood Control District, 88 Cal. App. 3d 579, 152 Cal. Rptr. 19 (1979)

III: A201-1976, Art. 12, Para. 12.1

Contractor sued the city-owner to recover for extra work. The Superior Court held for the contractor.

The Court of Appeals affirmed. The city's conduct in urging the use of temporary paving not included in the original specifications waived the contract requirement for a written change order. The city also waived the contract requirement for daily submission of expenditures, since that was dependent upon the issuance of a written change order, which had been waived by the city.

79019   Argonaut Insurance Co. v. ABC Steel Products Co., 582 S.W.2d 883 (Tex. Civ. App. 1979)

II: A311-1970, Labor and Material Payment Bond

Subcontractor sued contractor and surety to recover payment for material sold and work done under the subcontract. The District Court found for the subcontractor, awarding the contract price plus interest and attorney's fees, and the surety appealed.

The Court of Civil Appeals affirmed the award of the contract price and interest, but lowered the amount of attorney's fees. The Court held that under the payment bond the surety was obligated to pay the amount owed by the contractor if the contractor failed to make payment itself. Where the contractor did not take advantage of a contract provision which allowed a 25 percent discount if payments were made before the fifteenth of the month following installation, the contractor, and hence the surety, became liable for the full contract price. The language of the bond making the surety's liability contingent upon the failure of the contractor to promptly pay the materialmen was not to be interpreted as restricting the surety's liability for the full payment price. Tender by the surety to the subcontractor of the discounted price was therefore ineffectual, and the subcontractor was under no obligation to accept such tender.

The Court further held that "a seller of products may lawfully exact one price for his goods if . . . payment is made promptly and he may demand a larger price if . . . the payment is delayed," and that the difference in price did not constitute interest. The award of interest by the lower court, therefore, was not a double recovery.

contractor's directions, "as to the manner in which the payments were to be disbursed." It was not binding on the county and therefore interpleader was not proper.

79015   Richmond Shopping Center, Inc. v. Wiley N. Jackson Co., 220 Va. 135, 255 S.E.2d 518 (1979)

        III: A107-1978, Art. 16
        III: A201-1976, Art. 10, Para. 10.2
        III: A311-1970, Performance Bond

Adjacent landowner to a highway construction project sued the contractor and surety seeking to recover as a third-party beneficiary on the construction contract and the performance bond. The Circuit Court awarded damages for the adjacent landowner.

The Supreme Court reversed. A construction contract provision stated that it was not intended to create a right upon a member of the public as a third-party beneficiary. Letters from representatives of the highway department stating that the landowner should look for reimbursement to the parties causing the damage did not involve any recognition that the owner was a third-party beneficiary. In addition, the landowner's position was unlike a previous case in which a subcontractor recovered under a performance bond as a third-party beneficiary, since one purpose of the bond in that case was to establish credit for the contractor. The landowner was a mere incidental beneficiary that had no right to sue on the bond.

79016   Rodriguez v. McDonnell Douglas Corp., 87 Cal. App. 3d 626, 151 Cal. Rptr. 399 (1979)

        III: A201-1976, Art. 4, Para. 4.18
        III: A401-1978, Art. 11

Injured employee of fire protection subcontractor sued the contractor and steel subcontractor, who sought indemnity from the fire protection subcontractor. The Superior Court held for the worker and ordered indemnity.

The Court of Appeals affirmed in part and reversed in part. The contractor and steel subcontractor had been "passively" negligent and thus, were entitled to indemnity from the "actively" negligent fire protection subcontractor. The contract clauses at issue were for "general" indemnity and did not prohibit indemnity merely because the indemnitee had been passively negligent. The adoption of a "comparative fault" standard in tort indemnity cases did not require its use in contractual indemnity cases.

79017   Union Building Corp. v. J. & J. Building & Maintenance Contractors, Inc., 578 S.W.2d 519 (Tex. Civ. App. 1979)

        II: A201-1976, Art. 12, Para. 12.1

paid, the subcontractor should have sued him and not the owners. The fact that the owners made some payments directly to other subcontractors because of the contractor's financial problems did not change the contractor from an "independent contractor" into an agent of the owner. There also was no evidence that the owners had controlled the work so as to make the contractor an agent of the owner.

79012   Lyons v. Krathen, 368 So. 2d 906 (Fla. Dist. Ct. App. 1979)

      I: A201-1976, Art. 2, Para. 2.2
      I: A201-1976, Art. 7, Para. 7.9

The owners filed suit against the contractors, their surety, the architects and engineers. The contractors filed a motion against the owners seeking to compel arbitration. The Circuit Court denied the motion, and the District Court of Appeals affirmed. The contractors' demand for arbitration was not filed in a reasonable period of time, as required by the contract since they had known of the defects for nine months and the architect's decision for four months. The demand for arbitration also should have been made within thirty days of the architect's decision. Additionally, the contractors never filed a written notice of demand for arbitration with the American Arbitration Association and the architect, as required by the contract.

79013   Macchia v. Liggett, 67 A.D.2d 905, 413 N.Y.S.2d 174 (1979)

      III: A201-1976, Art. 7, Para. 7.7
      III: A201-1976, Art. 9, Para. 9.9

Contractor sued the owners for the balance due. The Supreme Court granted summary judgment for the contractor. The Appellate Division reversed. The contractor was not entitled to the final payment until the issuance of a "Plumbing Completion Certificate." This acceptance was a condition precedent to the owner's obligation to pay.

The owner who signed the contract was bound by it. The nonsignatory owner could be found liable under a theory of *quantum meruit.*

79014   Newkirk Construction Corp. v. Gulf County, 366 So. 2d 813 (Fla. Dist. Ct. App. 1979)

      III: A201-1976, Art. 9, Para. 9.5

County interpleaded the contractor and its surety as to whether the contract provision, as to progress payments, had been modified by the contractor's letter which purported to create an irrevocable assignment of progress payments to the surety and contractor as joint payees. The Circuit Court permitted the interpleader, having found the letter to be a modification of the contract.

The District Court reversed. The contractor's letter made the surety a co-payee along with the contractor, but did not modify the contract. At most the letter was simply the

was against the architect and not the contractor who followed the plans exactly. The owner also failed to provide evidence that the contractor was negligent in failing to discover the error.

79009   Joseph F. Trionfo & Sons, Inc. v. Board of Educ., 41 Md. App. 103, 395 A.2d 1207 (1979)

      III: A201-1976, Art. 3, Para. 3.2

      III: A201-1976, Art. 12, Para. 12.2

The contractor brought suit against the county for additional expenses on the basis of unexpected subsurface conditions. The Circuit Court granted summary judgment for the owners.

The Court of Special Appeals affirmed. The contractor had not been entitled to rely on the subsurface soil data, and thus, there was no misrepresentation. Although referred to in the contract, the subsurface data was not made a part of the contract. An exculpatory clause of the contract disclaimed responsibility by the owner and was specifically directed at the subsurface soil conditions. There was no evidence that the contractor could not have made its own test borings before the bids were closed. The contractor could have adjusted its bid to reflect the risk of not relying on the data. The contractor had also executed a release of the owner in return for obtaining its soil data.

79010   Kleb v. Wendling, 67 Ill. App. 3d 1016, 385 N.E.2d 346 (1979)

      III: A201-1976, Art. 2, Para. 2.2

      III: B141-1977, Art. 1

Architects sued the owner for their fees, and the owner counterclaimed for failure to supervise construction and for defective design. The Circuit Court held for the architects.

The Appellate Court reversed in part. The architects had never requested borings or other subsurface information and so designed an eleven foot excavation which was in fact eight feet from bedrock. The court remanded to determine if this constituted negligence of the architects. Since the contract called for the architect's supervision, they had the duty to prevent gross carelessness or imperfect construction.

79011   Kosmerl v. Barbor, 180 Mont. 208, 589 P.2d 1017 (1979)

      III: A201-1976, Art. 1, Para. 1.1

      III: A201-1976, Art. 9, Para. 9.5

      III: A401-1978, Art. 12

Subcontractor sued the owners for the balance due on a subcontract. The District Court held for the owners.

The Supreme Court affirmed, holding that the owners had fully paid the contractor, who was then responsible for paying the subcontractors. Since the contractor had been

contractor was a co-insured of the policy, the insurer could not sue a co-insured by subrogation or by the indirect method of requiring the owner to file the suit.

79006 Episcopal Housing Corp. v. Federal Insurance Co., 273 S.C. 181, 255 S.E.2d 451 (1979)

    III: A201-1976, Art. 7, Para. 7.9
    III: B141-1977, Art. 9

Contractor appealed from an order consolidating owner-contractor and the owner-architect arbitrations.

The Supreme Court affirmed the consolidation order. There was no convincing evidence that prejudice would result. Consolidation would not be the denial of the contracted for right to arbitration; rather, the consolidation was a "logical, expeditious method by which to enforce that right."

79007 Fireman's Insurance Co. of Newark, New Jersey v. State of New York, 65 A.D.2d 241, 412 N.Y.S.2d 206 (1979)

    II: A311-1970, Performance Bond
    II: A311-1970, Labor and Material Payment Bond

Surety who had completed the defaulted contractor's performance pursuant to its bond sued the state-owner for the balance due. The Court of Claims held for the surety.

The Supreme Court, Appellate Division, affirmed. The surety had completed the entire obligation of its defaulted contractor-principal. The state had not exercised its rights under the labor and material payment bond for unpaid employer's unemployment insurance contributions, but withheld that amount from payment to the surety from funds retained from the contract price. The surety was subrogated upon completion of the work to the right of its principal to the retainage, and since the retainage occurred prior to the default in the insurance contributions, the owner could not offset that amount from the retainage.

79008 Homeco, Inc. v. Belford, 38 Or. App. 299, 589 P.2d 1202 (1979)

    III: A201-1976, Art. 2, Para. 2.2
    III: A201-1976, Art. 4, Para. 4.2
    III: A201-1976, Art. 12, Para. 12.1

Contractor sued the homeowner for extras. The owner counterclaimed for defects. The Circuit Court held for the contractor.

The Court of Appeals affirmed. The requirement in the form contract that all extras be authorized in writing did not prevail over a typed provision which merely required a discussion and concurrence.

The architect had marked an incorrect measurement on the plans that resulted in a defective bathroom. Since the architect was the agent of the owner, the owner's recourse

The Circuit Court of Appeals affirmed, holding that the sums were liquidated damages and not a penalty. The contractor had waived its right to dispute the propriety of the sums withheld when it accepted progress payments diminished by the liquidated damages.

79004   Davidson & Jones, Inc. v. County of New Hanover, 41 N.C. App. 661, 255 S.E.2d 580 (1979)

> I: A201-1976, Art. 1, Para. 1.1
> I: A201-1976, Art. 3, Para. 3.2
> I: A401-1978, Art. 11

Contractor sued owner for balance owed on the contract, and owner counterclaimed for reimbursement of owner-made repairs based upon contractor's negligent performance. Numerous cross-claims and counterclaims followed involving the contractor, the architect, subcontractors, and soil engineers. The Superior Court granted the architect's motion to dismiss all claims against it for "failure to state a claim upon which relief can be granted."

The Supreme Court reversed, holding that despite a lack of contractual privity, parties in an economic relationship to the architect could sue the architect in negligence based upon the architect's "breach of its common law duty of care." This common law duty arose from the working relationship of the parties and a binding contract between the parties was not a prerequisite to suit by the contractor or subcontractors against the architect.

The court also held that a lack of contractual privity was not a bar to the contractor's or subcontractors' claim of negligent misrepresentation against the soil engineer. Although the owner-contractor agreement stated that the contractor was not to rely on the soil report supplied by the owner and would conduct its own soil test, the soil engineers were not immune from a negligence action by the contractor or subcontractors.

79005   E.C. Long, Inc. v. Brennan's of Atlanta, 148 Ga. App. 796, 252 S.E.2d 642 (1979)

> I: A201-1976, Art. 1, Para. 1.1
> I: A201-1976, Art. 11, Para. 11.3

Owner brought suit against the contractor and subcontractor to recover for damages caused by a gas explosion that destroyed the work site. The owner had been directed to file suit by the insurer after it paid for loss under the owner's policy, and the owner was further directed to remit the proceeds to the insurer. The Superior Court granted partial summary judgment for the owner.

The Court of Appeals reversed, holding that under the contract provision relating to property insurance there had been a waiver of claims to the extent covered by insurance. Although the contract required that the "work" be insured, it did not matter that the "mansion" was insured, since the waiver applied to any insurance proceeds. Since the

79001   Acme Builders, Inc. v. Facilities Development Corp., 69 A.D.2d 937, 415 N.Y.S.2d 291 (1979)

      III: A201-1976, Art. 1, Para. 1.1
      III: A201-1976, Art. 4, Para. 4.2

Owner and contractor were in dispute as to whether the contractor should paint the entire work site (as per incorporated drawing) or the areas disturbed by alterations (as per the specifications) or nothing at all (as per the alternative bids and proposals). The contractor sued the owner for damages sustained for painting an entire room where the plans, specifications and an alternate proposal contradicted one another. The Supreme Court entered judgment for the owner.

The Appellate Divisions affirmed. The contractor should have submitted any questions it had on the scope of the work to the architect before making its bid proposals.

79002   Alexander v. Gerald E. Morrisey, Inc., 137 Vt. 20, 399 A.2d 503 (1979)

      III: A201-1976, Art. 4, Para. 4.3
      III: A201-1976, Art. 12, Para. 12.1
      III: B141-1977, Art. 11

Owner brought suit against the architect and contractor over the installation of nonconforming insulation. The Superior Court dismissed, holding the architect protected by the statute of limitations and the contractor shielded by his compliance with the architect's instructions.

The Supreme Court reversed, holding that the architect's actual knowledge and representations amounted to a fraudulent concealment which tolled the statute of limitations. The architect lacked the contractual authority to unilaterally agree to the contractor's proposal to use insulation that did not meet specifications. The contractor was not shielded from liability because he did not faithfully follow the plans. His suggested changes on the insulation to be installed removed the protection he would have had if he had conformed with the architect's plans.

79003   Dahlstrom Corp. v. State Highway Comm'n of the State of Mississippi, 590 F.2d 614 (5th Cir. 1979)

      III: A101-1977, Art. 3
      III: A107-1978, Art. 2
      III: A111-1978, Art. 4

General contractor sued the highway commission-owner to recover for amounts withheld from the progress payments as liquidated damages. The District Court granted summary judgment for the state.

The Supreme Court, Appellate Division, affirmed but modified the judgment. The contract had been sufficiently detailed as to the disputed item, but changes occurred in a disorderly fashion so as to cause severe disruption in the subcontractor's work schedule. Since the owner was apprised of the claims for extra work, so as to constitute proper notice, the extra work was compensable by the contractor on behalf of the subcontractor.

78078   Woodward Heating & Air Conditioning Co. v. American Arbitration Ass'n, 259 Pa. Super. 460, 393 A.2d 917 (1978)

    I: A201-1976, Art. 7, Para. 7.9

Contractor sought to enjoin an arbitration proceeding initiated by owners. The Court of Common Pleas refused the stop the arbitration.

The Superior Court affirmed, holding that while the Court had jurisdiction to decide upon arbitrability, the factual disputes present made arbitration the proper method of resolving those disputes. In addition, whether the statute of limitations had barred arbitration should have been determined by the arbitrators, and other claims of the contractors were frivolous. Having agreed to arbitration of all claims and disputes, the contractors would be held to their agreement.

78079   Wrecking Corp. of America v. Memorial Hospital for Cancer and Allied Diseases, 63 A.D.2d 615, 405 N.Y.S.2d 83 (1978)

    III: A201-1976, Art. 3, Para. 3.2
    III: A201-1976, Art. 12, Para. 12.2

Excavation subcontractor sued the owner for increased costs and for its delay resulting from unexpected subsurface conditions. The Supreme Court denied a motion by the owner for summary judgment.

The Appellate Division reversed. The Supreme Court should have granted summary judgment for the owner. The owner could not be held liable for the subcontractor's unanticipated difficulties in constructing the foundation. The owner's failure to supply "as built" plans for a previous building on the site was not a material withholding. Since there was no showing that such plans had ever existed or that the plans were relevant, since the foundation loads would have been different, the subcontractor had clearly assumed the risk of subsurface conditions.

subcontractor merely gave the owner a cause of action against both the contractor and subcontractor.

78075 Valley Force Industries, Inc. v. Armand Corporation, Inc., 38 Pa. Commw. 603, 394 A.2d 677 (1978)

        III: A311-1970, Labor and Material Payment Bond

Subcontractor sued the contractor and its surety to recover on the labor and material payment bond. The Court of Common Pleas dismissed the case due to the expiration of the period of the statute of limitations.

The Commonwealth Court reversed holding that the period had not expired. The language "the day on which the last of the labor was performed or materials were supplied" as used in the Public Works Contractors' Bond Law to determine when the one year statute of limitations begins to run includes work performed on demand of the contracting body for the purpose of correcting defects in the work as originally completed.

78076 Wheeler & Lewis v. Slifer, 195 Colo. 291, 577 P.2d 1092 (1978)

        I: A201-1976, Art. 2, Para. 2.2
        I: A201-1976, Art. 10, Para. 10.1
        I: A201-1976, Art. 10, Para. 10.2
        III: B141-1977, Art. 1

Injured employee of subcontractor sued the architect for negligent supervision. The District Court entered a decision for the architect despite a jury verdict for the worker. The Court of Appeals reversed and held for the worker.

The Supreme Court reversed the Court of Appeals and held for the architect. The terms of the owner-architect and owner-contractor agreements did not impose a legal duty on the architect to supervise the method and manner of construction to insure that the work be performed safely. The Court rejected the reasoning of courts in other jurisdictions and stated that the architect's right to stop the work did not create a duty to stop the work for safety violations.

78077 Whitmyer Bros., Inc. v. State of New York, 63 A.D.2d 103, 406 N.Y.S.2d 617 (1978)

        III: A107-1978, Art. 18
        III: A111-1978, Art. 7
        III: A201-1976, Art. 8, Para. 8.3
        III: A201-1976, Art. 12, Para. 12.1

The contractor, on behalf of the subcontractor, sued the state-owner claiming that the state's numerous revisions of the original contract constituted "active interference with the performance of the contract." The Court of Claims held for the contractor.

78072   Twin Village Construction Corp. v. State of New York, 64 A.D.2d 866, 407 N.Y.S.2d 366 (1978)

    III: A201-1976, Art. 12, Para. 12.1
    III: A201-1976, Art. 12, Para. 12.2

A highway contractor brought suit against the State of New York for extras. The Court of Claims held for the state.

The Supreme Court, Appellate Division, modified the judgment and affirmed. The state had been at fault in that it provided "inadequate" information concerning the need for filler material, and the incomplete records of the contractor did not defeat its right to recover for the inadequacy. The state had notice of the discrepancy between the bid specifications and the final contract specifications, and by contract should have ordered that work be performed. Since the work was outside the scope of the contract, the appropriate basis for recovery was *quantum meruit*. The state was also not responsible for the cost of excavation of unsuitable soil, since the contractor had only visually inspected the soil, and the state was not responsible for the delays occasioned by that excavation.

78073   United Nations Development Corp. v. Norkin Plumbing Co., 45 N.Y.2d 358, 408 N.Y.S.2d 424, 380 N.E.2d 253 (1978)

    I: A201-1976, Art. 7, Para. 7.9

Contractor served a demand for arbitration against the subcontractor, who sought a court ordered stay of arbitration. The Supreme Court, Appellate Division, denied the stay.

The Court of Appeals affirmed. The court interpreted the contract provision for arbitration as not containing an express condition precedent that the demand for arbitration be served within 60 days after the claim had arisen. Consequently, the question of compliance with the condition was to be determined by the arbitrator and not by the court.

78074   United States Fidelity & Guar. Co. v. Jacksonville State University, 357 So. 2d 952 (Ala. 1978)

    I: A201-1976, Art. 4, Para. 4.3

The owner brought suit against the architect, the contractor and its surety for breach of contract and breach of implied warranties. The Circuit Court awarded damages to the owner.

The Supreme Court affirmed. Under the contract the contractor was responsible for the acts and omissions of the subcontractors, and therefore, was liable for defective workmanship of a subcontractor. The contractor was liable even though the architect had specified the material that proved to be defective. The giving of a bond by the

78070   Sweetman v. Strescon Industries, Inc., 389 A.2d 1319 (Del. Super. Ct. 1978)

      I: A401-1978, Art. 11

Injured workers sued in tort the general contractor and two subcontractors. The first subcontractor moved against the second subcontractor for summary judgment based on an indemnity clause. The general contractor moved for summary judgment against the first subcontractor on indemnity grounds.

The trial judge held that the motions between the contractor and subcontractor would be denied as contrary to public policy. The indemnity clause was not "crystal clear or sufficiently unequivocal" to give adequate notice to focus the attention of the subcontractor on the fact that it was bound to indemnify the contractor for the contractor's own liability.

78071   Texas Bank & Trust Co. v. Campbell Bros., Inc., 569 S.W.2d 35 (Tex. Civ. App. 1978)

      I: A111-1974, Art. 13
      I: A111-1974, Art. 14
      I: A111-1974, Art. 15
      I: A201-1976, Art. 9, Para. 9.3
      I: A201-1976, Art. 9, Para. 9.4
      I: A201-1976, Art. 9, Para. 9.5
      I: A201-1976, Art. 9, Para. 9.7
      III: A311-1970, Performance Bond

When the owner stopped making progress payments, the contractor brought suit against the owner and lender for the balance due on the contract, and for damages for breach of contract. The owner counterclaimed against the contractor and its surety on the performance bond for the contractor's breach of contract. The District Court held for the contractor and its surety.

The Court of Civil Appeals affirmed. Although the lack of an architect on the entire job prevented an architect's approval of the progress payments, the owner was not relieved of its duty to make progress payments. The owner also could not avoid its duty to make progress payments because earlier progress payments had included extras. The earlier "overstatement" of completed work had been designed to pay for extras and was done with the owner's consent. The contractor was justified in stopping its work because of failure to issue progress payments. The lender as co-obligee on the contractor's performance bond had "no independent right to demand performance without payment of the amount due." The owner's default on the progress payments was imputed to the bank and prevented it from enforcing the performance bond.

78068   Sturdy Concrete Corp. v. NAB Construction Corp., 65 A.D.2d 262, 411 N.Y.S.2d 637 (1978)

      III: A401-1978, Art. 1
      III: A401-1978, Art. 5
      III: A401-1978, Art. 11
      III: A401-1978, Art. 13
      III: A401-1978, Art. 14

Subcontractor sued the contractor for the balance due and extras. The contractor counterclaimed for unsatisfactory performance of the subcontractor's work. The Supreme Court held for the contractor.

The Appellate Division modified the judgment and remanded the case. Since the owner's engineer had not yet arbitrated the dispute involving a progress payment from the owner to the contractor for the value of those extras, the contractor was not required to pay "immediately, in full" to the subcontractor. Final payment to the subcontractor was not due until the contractor received final payment.

None of the extra work was authorized in writing as the contract required. The subcontractor received payment only for work for which a waiver by conduct could be found. Where the authorized and performed extra had to be totally redone by a second contractor, no payment was due to the original subcontractor for his attempted performance unless the original subcontractor could show that the failure was not its fault.

Since there was a contract provision giving the subcontractor three days after notice to cure defective work, the contractor's counterclaims were reduced by those items for which no notice or opportunity to cure had been given the subcontractor. Only complaints of defective performance actually listed on the "punchlist" given the subcontractor, or claims for which the contractor could show the subcontractor's actual knowledge, would be compensated.

78069   Sukut-Coulson, Inc. v. Allied Canon Co., 83 Cal. App. 3d 501, 147 Cal. Rptr. 909 (1978), *aff'd on rehearing,* 85 Cal. App. 3d 648, 149 Cal Rptr. 711 (1978)

      III: A311-1970, Labor and Material Payment Bond

Contractor brought suit against sureties on payment bonds, provided by the owner and for foreclosure of its mechanic's lien against the owner. The owner sought a declaratory judgment that the surety bonds, not the mechanic's liens, were the contractor's primary source of recovery. The Superior Court entered an order which foreclosed the liens and held the sureties liable for any deficiency after foreclosure.

The Court of Appeals reversed in part. The contractor should have been given its choice on whether to foreclose its mechanic's lien or seek payment from the sureties, since the sureties had not made a formal demand upon the contractor to pursue the foreclosure of its mechanic's lien as required by state statute.

The Supreme Court affirmed. Since the AIA standard form contract was amended to require approval of preliminary studies before further compensation, the owner's approval of the preliminary studies was a condition precedent to further compensation; he was not obligated to pay for later work performed by the architect. The owner was allowed to use cost consideration as a major element in its decision to approve or reject the preliminary plans, despite the absence of any maximum cost-to-complete clause. By contracting for a preliminary study before any further architectural work, the owner had the option to refuse to accept the preliminary plans because of "unsatisfactory design, dissatisfaction with the presentation, disagreement over space usage or materials or any reason whatsoever, including too high costs."

78065 Sibille v. Meyer, 355 So. 2d 1003 (La. Ct. App. 1978)

III: A401-1978, Art. 11

Subcontractor sued the contractor for payment for the work. The Civil District Court dismissed the suit.

The Court of Appeals affirmed the dismissal. A subcontract provision stated that the contract or any part thereof could not be assigned without written consent of the contractor. Since from the beginning the subcontractor had no employees but subcontracted the work to others, it had breached the contract and was not entitled to further payment from the contractor.

78066 (UNASSIGNED)

78067 Standard Co. of New Orleans, Inc. v. Elliott Construction Co., 363 So. 2d 671 (La. 1978)

I: A201-1976, Art. 7, Para. 7.
I: A201-1976, Art. 7, Para. 7.9

The subcontractor sued the contractor who filed a third-party claim against the state-owner. A demand for arbitration was then filed by the contractor. The District Court ordered arbitration, but the Court of Appeals reversed holding that the third-party claim had waived the arbitration provision.

The Supreme Court reversed and reinstated the original decision of the District Court holding that there had been no waiver. The arbitrators are preferred to the judicial system on the issue of waiver, but for practical reasons the Court decided that issue. The Court held that there was no waiver of the contractor's right of arbitration since the issues in the lawsuit and arbitration were separate and distinct, since the contractor had not voluntarily and intentionally relinquished the right, and since the state-owner was not misled to its detriment by the contractor's actions. The Court also held that the Federal Arbitration Act did not apply to the contract. The contractor had argued that the act applied since there was interstate commerce, and the court held that the contract specifically provided that the law of the project site governed.

The Appellate Court affirmed. The indemnity was based on a clear and unambiguous contract provision. There was no evidence that the owner-indemnitee was in any way being indemnified for its own negligence, and the Illinois statute which voided such contract provisions postdated the date of the contract. The contractor was contractually bound to supply all the goods and equipment not supplied by the owner and was liable for not providing safety devices required under state law.

78062   Rovnak v. Union Carbide Corp., 64 A.D.2d 839, 407 N.Y.S.2d 323 (1978)

>   III: A201-1976, Art. 1, Para. 1.1
>   III: A201-1976, Art. 4, Para. 4.18

Personal representative of estate of an employee of the contractor sued the owner, who in turn sought indemnity from the contractor. The Supreme Court upheld the validity of the indemnity clause between the owner and the contractor.

The Appellate Division affirmed the validity of the indemnity clause. The language of the clause clearly showed the intent to have indemnity even for the indemnitee's own negligence. The clause was not violative of public policy, since a statute made such clauses unenforceable only if the agreement was made after August 7, 1975. The work the decedent was doing at the time of the accident was pursuant to a valid modification of the contract. The entire terms of the original contract, including the indemnity provisions, applied to the modifications.

78063   Schwarz-Jordan, Inc. of Houston v. Delisle Construction Co., 569 S.W.2d 878 (Tex. 1978)

>   III: A401-1978, Art. 1
>   III: A401-1978, Art. 11

A subcontractor sued the contractor for the balance due on the subcontract. The District Court held for the subcontractor but was reversed by the Court of Appeals.

The Supreme Court reversed the Court of Appeals, thus holding for the subcontractor. The subcontract had incorporated the prime contract by reference. The prime contract required a model to be built and approved by the owner's engineer. The engineer did not approve the model, and this approval was interpreted to be a condition precedent to further construction but not a condition precedent for payment for building the model.

78064   Shanahan v. Universal Tavern Corp., 585 P.2d 1314 (Mont. 1978)

>   I: B141-1977, Art. 1
>   I: B141-1977, Art. 3
>   I: B141-1977, Art. 14

Architect sued the owner to foreclose on a mechanic's lien for his fee. The District Court held for the owner.

78058 Ozdeger v. Altay, 64 Ill. App. 3d 1036, 382 N.E.2d 268 (1978)

      I: B141-1977, Art. 9
      I: B141-1977, Art. 13
      I: B141-1977, Art. 15

Owners sued the architects, who requested a stay pending arbitration. The trial court ordered a stay.

The Appellate Court affirmed. In a printed contract the parties had by "clear language" agreed to arbitration and a typed addendum was part of that contract.

78059 Ozdeger v. Altay, 66 Ill. App. 3d 629, 384 N.E.2d. 82 (1978)

      I: A201-1976, Art. 7, Para. 7.9

The owners filed suit against the contractors, who had orally agreed to act as carpentry managers subsequent to the execution of the written contract. The contractors filed a motion to compel arbitration pursuant to the arbitration clause in the written contract. The Circuit Court held for the owners on the basis that the clause was not applicable to the oral agreement as to carpentry management.

The Appellate Court reversed and remanded. The dispute concerning the oral contract was "arising out of, or relating to" the written contract, and arbitration was proper as to that dispute.

78060 Palmer Steel Structures v. Westech, Inc., 178 Mont. 347, 584 P.2d 152 (1978)

      II: A107-1978, Art. 13
      II: A201-1976, Art. 7, Para. 7.9

Contractor sought to restrain arbitration with the owner, and the District Court refused to reinstate a temporary restraining order against arbitration. The Supreme Court remanded with instructions to the District Court to enjoin the parties from arbitration. Under state law an agreement for arbitration was void as to the arbitration of future questions of law. Accordingly, the owner could not compel arbitration of the mixed questions of law and fact.

78061 Quilico v. Union Oil Co. of California, 58 Ill. App. 3d 87, 374 N.E.2d 219 (1978)

      III: A201-1976, Art. 4, Para. 4.4
      III: A201-1976, Art. 4, Para. 4.18

Injured worker of contractor sued the owner, who sought indemnity from the contractor. The Circuit Court ordered the contractor to indemnify the owner for the amount of the worker's judgment against the owner.

The Appellate Court affirmed. The owner was contractually given the power to terminate after written notice to the contractor for persistent and uncorrected safety ordinance violations. The owner also had frequently inspected the job site and had the right to make work order changes and to remedy any deficiency in the contractor's performance.

78056   Norair Engineering Corp. v. Saint Joseph's Hospital, Inc., 147 Ga. App. 595, 249 S.E.2d 642 (1978)

II:	A107-1978, Art. 8	
II:	A107-1978, Art. 10	
II:	A107-1978, Art. 19	
II:	A201-1976, Art. 2, Para. 2.2	
II:	A201-1976, Art. 4, Para. 4.3	
II:	A201-1976, Art. 4, Para. 4.4	
II:	A201-1976, Art. 13, Para. 13.2	

Owner sued the completion contractor over defects in the construction of a hospital. The Superior Court awarded judgment for the owner.

The Court of Appeals affirmed. The negligent supervision by the architect's project supervisor could not reduce even in part the liability of the completion contractor for its use of inferior materials, equipment or workmanship contrary to its contract guarantee. The contractor's guarantee of work until "one year from the date of final completion" did not preclude the owner from asserting claims on defects that did not appear until after the one-year period. The contractor was liable for damages for work of the subcontractor, since its negligence was not attributable to the subcontractor.

78057   O'Dell v. Custom Builders Corp., 560 S.W.2d 862 (Mo. 1978)

III:	A201-1976, Art. 4, Para. 4.4	
III:	B141-1977, Art. 1	

Homeowners sued the firm which had custom designed a home for them and constructed the shell of the home. The Circuit Court held for the owners.

The Supreme Court affirmed, holding that the failure to design piers to support footings for the foundations was a breach of the implied warranty of fitness for use.

The contract provided that the owners would act as general contractors and arrange for subcontractors while the design firm would merely erect the shell of the house. The owners were justified in relying on the plans provided by the designer-contractor. There was an implied warranty of fitness for use when the design firm-contractor sold the plans, even if it was not acting as the "general" contractor. Since the designer held itself out as an expert and provided the design, it was responsible for making any modifications to the plans required by the terrain at the worksite.

and specifications caused the damage. This burden was not met, and the contractor was liable for the cost of hiring another contractor to complete the work.

78053 Meathe v. State University Construction Fund, 65 A.D.2d 49, 410 N.Y.S.2d 702 (1978)

> III: B141-1977, Art. 3
> III: B141-1977, Art. 6
> III: B141-1977, Art. 14

The architects under a "fast track" scheme signed a contract to design the building (for a percentage of the construction cost) and to act as general contractors (for a "cost plus" fee). There was a "total compensation" clause, the effect of which the parties disputed. The owner stopped progress payments during construction, contending that payments to that point had met the limit of the "total compensation" clause. The architect-contractor completed the project and sued the owner. The Supreme Court held for the architect-contractor and dismissed the owner's counterclaims.

The Appellate Division upheld the trial court. The contract as a whole was ambiguous and parol evidence of the signer's intentions was admissible. The total compensation provision limited only compensation for the contracted for services. It did not limit compensation for the various extra services agreed to during the course of the project's completion.

78054 Miller v. Racine Trust, 65 Ill. App. 3d 207, 382 N.E.2d 41 (1978)

> III: A201-1976, Art. 13. Para. 13.2

Contractor sued owners for balance due on a contract to repair a leaking roof. The Circuit Court held for the owners.

The Appellate Court reversed and remanded. Since the sole purpose of the contract was to repair the leaky roof, the express warranty of the contractor was effective even though the owners had not made full payment. The contractor could not recover the contract price and could only recover for the value of his labor and material.

78055 Moore v. Clearing Industrial District, Inc., 64 Ill. App. 3d 391, 380 N.E.2d 1063 (1978)

> III: A201-1976, Art. 3, Para. 3.3
> III: A201-1976, Art. 3, Para. 3.4
> III: A201-1976, Art. 4, Para. 4.18
> III: A201-1976, Art. 14, Para. 14.2

Contractor's injured worker sued the owner, who sought noncontractual indemnity from the contractor. The Circuit Court refused to enter a directed verdict for the owner, and eventually found for the worker against the owner and the owner against the contractor.

78050   Lehigh Electric Products Co. v. Pennsylvania National Mutual Casualty Insurance Co., 257 Pa. Super. 198, 390 A.2d 781 (1978)

        III: A311-1970, Labor and Material Payment Bond

Subcontractor sought to recover for labor and material from the contractor's surety on the payment bond, and the surety added the contractor as a defendant. The Court of Common Pleas granted summary judgment for the surety on the grounds that the labor and materials were furnished more than one year from the commencement of the suit, and therefore, the statute of limitations in the state statute barred the suit.

The Superior Court reversed and remanded for retrial. The running of the statute of limitations could have been started by certain work which could have been an adjustment during the breaking-in period rather than a repair during the warranty period.

78051   Lester N. Johnson Co. v. City of Spokane, 22 Wash. App. 265, 588 P.2d 1214 (1978)

        III: A201-1976, Art. 7, Para. 7.6

Contractor sued the city-owner for breach of a sewer construction contract, and the Superior Court held for the contractor.

The Court of Appeals affirmed. There was an implied duty of the owner not to interfere with or hinder or delay the contractor's performance. The owner's pumping of raw sewage into the area created a morass that was an unallowable interference with the contractor.

78052   Mayville-Portland School District No. 10 v. C. L. Linfoot Co., 261 N.W.2d 906 (N.D. 1978)

        I: A201-1976, Art. 2, Para. 2.2
        I: A201-1976, Art. 3, Para. 3.4
        I: A201-1976, Art. 4, Para. 4.3
        I: A201-1976, Art. 4, Para. 4.5
        I: A201-1976, Art. 7, Para. 7.4
        I: A201-1976, Art. 9, Para. 9.8
        I: A201-1976, Art. 13, Para. 13.2

School district-owner sued the contractor for breach of contract and costs of hiring another contractor after it refused to replace a tank rejected by the architect. The District Court held for the owner.

The Supreme Court affirmed. After quoting various provisions of the contract, the Court held that the intent of the contract was to place the risk of loss on the contractor until a certificate of substantial completion was issued by the architect. Since the risk of loss was on the contractor, it had the burden of proof to prove that defective plans

The Supreme Court reversed. Although the contract between the owner and the contractor required that the contractor obtain insurance which also named the sub-subcontractor as an insured, the contractor failed to include it as an insured. The sub-subcontractor alleged that it was an intended third party beneficiary as to insurance coverage required by the owner-contractor contract. The Supreme Court stated that summary judgment was inappropriate because of the issues of material fact.

78047 Krieger v. J. E. Greiner Co., 282 Md. 50, 382 A.2d 1069 (1978)

> III: A201-1976, Art. 2, Para. 2.2
> III: A201-1976, Art. 4, Para. 4.3
> III: B141-1977, Art. 1
> III: C141-1979, Art. 1

Subcontractor's employee brought an action alleging that the contracts signed by the supervising engineers made them responsible for injuries received as a result of the negligence of its subcontractor. The Superior Court granted the engineers' demurrer.

The Court of Appeals reversed. The engineers owed no duty to the employee to ensure safe working conditions. There was no duty to supervise the methods of construction, and they were only responsible for the end result. The engineers were not responsible for supervision of work for compliance with safety laws and regulations.

Even if not under a contractual duty, the fact that the engineers did halt construction previously might legally have constituted a gratuitous assumption of duty, thus creating liability.

78048 (UNASSIGNED)

78049 Landis Construction Co. v. Health Education Authority, 359 So. 2d 1045 (La. Ct. App. 1978)

> I: A201-1976, Art. 7, Para. 7.9

The contractor was awarded a Civil District Court order which forced the city agency-owner to comply with the arbitration provision of the contract.

The Court of Appeals reversed. The Louisiana Civil Code required express authority to stipulate to arbitration. Neither the contractor's corporate resolution, nor the city agency's resolution, included express authority to arbitrate. A resolution which specifically granted to an officer the authority to sign a particularly described or attached contract would bind the signator to every clause of that contract, including a stipulation for arbitration. However, a resolution granting general power to sign contracts did not constitute the necessary special authority required by the Civil Code.

contractor-subcontractor agreement. That clause did not require a formal arbitration and award, but allowed for an initial determination by the architect. The language used was not intended to give the architect a role as arbitrator in a payment dispute after the construction was completed.

78044   K.L. House Construction Co. v. City of Albuquerque, 91 N.M. 492, 576 P.2d 752 (1978)

      I: A201-1976, Art. 7, Para. 7.9

Contractor, its surety and a subcontractor sought a declaratory judgment as to whether there had been full performance. The District Court ordered arbitration, and the arbitrators granted the city-owner an award.

The Supreme Court affirmed. Although the job had been accepted and the warranties of the contractor and subcontractor had expired, the dispute was "arising out of, or relating to, this Contract," and thus should be arbitrated. The court should decide only the threshold question of whether there was an agreement to arbitrate, and if there is such an agreement, the court should order arbitration.

78045   Kelly v. Northwest Community Hospital, 66 Ill. App. 3d 679, 384 N.E.2d 102 (1978)

      I: A201-1976, Art. 2, Para. 2.2
      I: A201-1976, Art. 10, Para. 10.2
      I: B141-1977, Art. 1

The personal representative of the estate of a hospital visitor sued the hospital-owner, architect, contractor and subcontractor for wrongful death as a result of a fall from incomplete construction. The Circuit Court granted summary judgment against the personal representative.

The Appellate Court affirmed. The owner, architect, contractor and subcontractor had complied with all needed safety precautions and were not responsible for a hospital visitor who voluntarily entered the construction site. The architect was not liable as a matter of law since the architect's contract with the owner did not require him to administer the construction contract, control methods or techniques of construction used, or stop the work when necessary.

78046   Klinger-Holtz v. Sulzbach Construction Co., 262 N.W.2d 290 (Iowa 1978)

      III: A201-1976, Art. 11, Para. 11.1

The contractor and subcontractor sued the sub-subcontractor and its supplier for damages for a defective pipe and consequent flooding. The District Court granted summary judgment to the sub-subcontractor.

Contractor sued on a promissory note owners had given for the balance due on the contract. The owners counterclaimed for delay and alleged loss of their financing. The District Court granted a directed verdict for the contractor.

The Supreme Court affirmed. The owner's attempt to preserve their claims for delays, by inserting a reservation of rights clause in a change order was not effective, since a later change order did not contain such a clause. The owners also waived their delay claims by making a final payment, since the contract stated that such a payment waived all claims of the owners.

78041 John v. Bovee, 40 Colo. App. 317, 574 P.2d 513 (1978)

        III: A201-1976, Art. 14, Para. 14.1

The contractor sought to foreclose on a mechanic's lien, and homeowners counterclaimed for defective performance. The District Court held for the contractor.

The Court of Appeals affirmed. The homeowners had breached the contract by not making progress payments, and therefore, the contractor properly stopped work. However the contractor could not recover damages on a restitution basis for more than the contract amount.

78042 Joray Mason Contractors, Inc. v. Four J's Construction Corp., 61 Ill. App. 3d 410, 378 N.E.2d 328 (1978)

        III: A201-1976, Art. 12, Para. 12.1

Subcontractor sued the contractor to recover for extras. The Circuit Court held for the subcontractor.

The Appellate Court affirmed. Although the contractor contended that no award should be made for any extras, the contract requirement for written authorization of extras had been waived by the contractor's conduct. The contractor had admitted that some extra work had been allowed without an agreement in writing.

78043 Joseph F. Trionfo & Sons, Inc. v. Ernest B. LaRosa & Sons, Inc., 38 Md. App. 598, 381 A.2d 727 (1978)

        I: A107-1978, Art. 8
        I: A107-1978, Art. 13
        II: A201-1976, Art. 7, Para. 7.9
        II: A401-1978, Art. 1
        II: A401-1978, Art. 11

Subcontractor sued contractor seeking to compel arbitration. The Circuit Court denied the motion to order arbitration.

The Court of Special Appeals affirmed the holding that the provision of the general conditions for architect's interpretation was incorporated by reference into the charges for services in that locale. The District Court was justified in using the estimated construction cost as the basis for the architect's fee. The court also stated that the District Court could have concluded from the evidence that the homeowners gave their approval to the preliminary design plans of the work, and by their conduct authorized the architect to continue his work on the construction documents.

78038　　Housing Auth. of the City of Texarkana v. E. W. Johnson Construction Co., 264 Ark. 523, 573 S.W.2d 316 (1978)

        III:　　A201-1976, Art. 4, Para. 4.2

        III:　　A201-1976, Art. 12, Para. 12.1

Contractor sued the owner for supplying defective plans which resulted in major delays of the project. The Circuit Court held for the contractor, and the Supreme Court affirmed.

The owner had breached the contract by its failure to make timely decisions on change orders. The owner's implied warranty of fitness and suitability of its plans and specifications was not nullified by a contract provision which required the contractor to examine and check these plans and specifications. The contractor may be held liable if it was aware, or should have been aware, of defects in the plans. The owner's breach was not remedied by merely extending the time of performance.

78039　　Jacksonville Port Authority v. Parkhill-Goodloe Co., 362 So. 2d 1009 (Fla. Dist. Ct. App. 1978)

        III:　　A201-1976, Art. 3, Para. 3.2

        III:　　A201-1976, Art. 12, Para. 12.2

Dredging contractor sued the city-owner for damaged equipment and for the delay in completing the contract caused by concealed subsurface conditions and the owner's concealing of information relating to those conditions during the bidding phase. The Circuit Court entered judgment for the contractor.

The District Court affirmed. The owner knew that concealed rock had been encountered by another dredger in a contiguous area. The owner had a duty to furnish information which would not mislead bidders and not to withhold relevant, adverse data. The contractor could properly rely on the owner's borings, since boring tests were prohibitively expensive and would have discouraged bidding if the tests had to be rerun by the bidders.

78040　　John Price Associates v. Davis, 588 P.2d 713 (Utah 1978)

        I:　　A201-1976, Art. 8, Para. 8.3

        I:　　A201-1976, Art. 9, Para. 9.9

        I:　　A201-1976, Art. 12, Para. 12.1

arbitration to the extent that it might encompass disputes involved in the owner's suit. The Supreme Court, Appellate Division, modified the decree.

The Court of Appeals affirmed. The arbitration clause in the owner-contractor contract, which was incorporated by reference into the subcontract, was held to be irrelevant and the court interpreted the arbitration clause in the subcontract. That clause was held to mean that "all disputes are to be submitted to arbitration in the normal manner except that as to disputes which are also raised in proceedings between the owner and general contractor, the results in the latter shall also determine the outcome in arbitration between the general contractor and the subcontractor."

78036 Hartford Fire Insurance Co. v. Riefolo Construction Co., 161 N.J. Super. 99, 390 A.2d 1210 (App. Div. 1978)

> III: A107-1977, Art. 17
> III: A201-1976, Art. 9, Para. 9.8
> III: A201-1976, Art. 11, Para. 11.3
> III: A311-1970, Performance Bond

Insurer as the subrogee of the owner sued five prime contractors and their sureties to force them to pay for repair costs for a building that had been partially destroyed by fire. The Superior Court, Chancery Division, held that since the structure had been substantially completed and partially occupied prior to the fire loss, the contractors were not responsible for lapse of their builder's risk insurance required under the contract. The Superior Court held that under these conditions such insurance could not be maintained.

The Superior Court, Appellate Division, reversed, holding the contractors responsible for the cost of repair. The Superior Court, Appellate Division, assuming *arguendo* that the Chancery Division was correct concerning the ability of the building contractors to maintain builder's risk insurance, held that this did not override the common law which placed the risk of loss on the builder until entire completion of the work. The sureties also were obligated to pay the insurer since the performance bond included a default of the obligation to repair for fire loss.

78037 Holmquest v. Priesmeyer, 574 S.W.2d 173 (Tex. Civ. App. 1978)

> II: B141-1977, Art. 1
> II: B141-1977, Art. 6
> II: B141-1977, Art. 14

Architect sued homeowners to recover his fee, and the District Court held for the architect. The Court of Appeals affirmed. Under a contract provision the architect was entitled to compensation for services performed to the date of termination, when this was not attributable to fault of the architect. Since the architect was not at fault, the court upheld the method of computing compensation on the basis of reasonable and customary

Owner sued the contractor and subcontractor concerning a leaking roof. The Superior Court dismissed the complaint as being barred by the statute of limitations.

The Court of Appeals reversed. As to a count of negligence the owner knew almost immediately that the roof leaked, and therefore, the leak was a patent defect on which the statute of limitations began to run upon discovery. However, the contractor's three year long series of attempts to fix the leaks may have constituted an "inducement not to sue" so that the suit was timely and within the statute of limitations. The court remanded for trial on the interpretation of an ambiguous contract clause on responsibility for correction of work. The owner was a third-party beneficiary of the subcontract and could properly sue on the breach of the subcontractor's implied warranty of fitness. The Court stated that it was, therefore, unnecessary to decide the issue of privity of contract between the owner and the subcontractor.

78033   Gonzales v. R.J. Novick Construction Co., 144 Cal. Rptr. 408, 575 P.2d 1190 (Cal. 1978)

> III: A401-1978, Art. 11

Subcontractor's injured employee sued the contractor who sought indemnity from the subcontractor. The Superior Court held for the worker and ordered indemnity by the subcontractor.

The Supreme Court affirmed. The indemnity provision did not address itself to the issue of the indemnitee's negligence, and it was construed to allow indemnity where the indemnitee was only passively negligent. A statute which voided contract provisions that indemnified a party for his own negligence did not preclude recovery where that party was passively negligent. Nonfeasance by the contractor was passive negligence.

78034   (UNASSIGNED)

78035   HRH Construction Corp. v. Bethlehem Steel Corp., 45 N.Y.2d 675, 412 N.Y.S.2d 366, 384 N.E.2d 1289 (1978)

> I: A201-1976, Art. 4, Para. 4.3
> I: A201-1976, Art. 7, Para. 7.9
> III: A401-1978, Art. 1
> III: A401-1978, Art. 1
> III: A401-1978, Art. 15

A subcontractor filed a demand for arbitration against the contractor. The owner then filed suit against the contractor for damages for delays allegedly caused by the subcontractor, on the basis that the contract made the contractor responsible for the acts or omissions of its subcontractors. The contractor impleaded the subcontractor in the owner's suit. The contractor filed a motion to stay the arbitration, and the subcontractor filed a motion to compel arbitration. The Supreme Court, Special Term, stayed the

III: A201-1976, Art. 4, Para. 4.12
III: A201-1976, Art. 8, Para. 8.3

Contractor sued the state-owner on a public work contract over the state's inactions in providing access and easements to the worksite. The Court of Claims held for the contractor.

The Supreme Court, Appellate Division, affirmed. The state had breached the contractual duty of providing a reasonable opportunity for the contractor to perform its work by an excessive number of design changes, failing to grant access to parts of the worksite and failing to remove or relocate power lines. The state also materially delayed the processing of revised shop drawings caused by the changes in the contract drawings.

78030   Fred McGilvray, Inc. v. International Builders of Florida, Inc., 354 So. 2d. 103 (Fla. Dist. Ct. App. 1978)

III: A107-1978, Art. 17
III: A201-1976, Art. 11, Para. 11.3
III: A401-1978, Art. 9

Subcontractor sued the contractor seeking payment for the cost of repairing vandalized work. The Circuit Court granted judgment for the contractor.

The District Court of Appeals reversed. Since the owner-contractor agreement required the contractor to maintain vandalism insurance and since the subcontract was silent on the assumption of risk for vandalism and vandalism insurance, the contractor bore the risk of vandalism.

78031   Garver v. Ferguson, 63 Ill. App. 3d 453, 380 N.E.2d 401, (1978)

I: A201-1976, Art. 7, Para. 7.9
I: A201-1976, Art. 14, Para. 14.2

Contractors demanded arbitration with the owner for payment, and the owner counterclaimed for the cost of completion in excess of the contract price. The award for the contractors was conformed by the Circuit Court.

The Appellate Court reversed and remanded. The owner had properly rejected substandard work and terminated the contract. The arbitrators' award was vacated because the arbitrators never considered the owner's right to terminate the contract.

78032   Gilbert Financial Corp. v. Steelform Contracting Co., 82 Cal. App. 3d 65, 145 Cal. Rptr. 448 (1978)

III: A201-1976, Art. 1, Para. 1.1
III: A201-1976, Art. 13, Para. 13.2
III: A401-1978, Art. 11

78026 Delta Construction, Inc. v. Dressler, 64 Ill. App. 3d 867, 381 N.E.2d 1023 (1978)

      III: A201-1976, Art. 12, Para. 12.1

Subcontractor sued the contractor of the balance due under the contract. The Superior Court held for the contractor.

The Appellate Court reversed. The subcontractor had substantially performed its contract, and so was entitled to payment. The requirement of the contract for written modifications had been waived by the contractor's action in partially paying for the extras and through the uncontradicted testimony that the contractor requested the extras and agreed to them without a requirement of a writing.

78027 E. E. Dean Snavely, Inc. v. Sullivan, 360 So. 2d 451 (Fla. Dist. Ct. App. 1978)

      III: A311-1970, Labor and Material Payment Bond
      III: A311-1970, Performance Bond

A subcontractor and its laborer brought suit on the contractor's performance and payment bond and the Circuit Court denied partial summary judgment.

The District Court reversed in part. The bond, which incorporated the owner-contractor contract, was in the face amount of the original contract. After the contractor-principal had defaulted and left the job, the amount of the bond could not be extended to provide additional compensation beyond the original face amount to other persons, and it made no difference that the subcontractor performed the additional work as a different business entity.

78028 E. L. White, Inc. v. City of Huntington Beach, 146 Cal. Rptr. 614, 579 P.2d 505 (Cal. 1978)

      III: A201-1976, Art. 4, Para. 4.18

Contractor sued the city seeking indemnity from a judgment in favor of two injured employees of a subcontractor. The Superior Court dismissed the action.

The Supreme Court reversed. The fact that the contract set out the positive duties of indemnity by the contractor, did not preclude noncontractual, or equitable indemnity. A contractual provision on indemnity preempts any "implied rights which might otherwise arise within the scope of its operations." However, the contractual provision was inappropriate to the factual setting and the case was remanded for retrial under the principles of equitable indemnity.

78029 Fehlhaber Corp. v. State of New York, 65 A.D.2d 119, 410 N.Y.S.2d 920 (1978)

      III: A201-1976, Art. 3, Para. 3.2

architect could not compel the subcontractor to join into an arbitration proceeding based on the owner-architect contract. Even though the general contract between the owner and contractor had been incorporated by reference into the contractor-subcontractor agreement, the architect could not stand in the owner's shoes to enforce it against the subcontractor.

78024 DeKalb County v. PMS Construction Co., 148 Ga. App. 413, 251 S.E.2d 334 (1978)

> I: A107-1978, Art. 7
> I: A107-1978, Art. 8
> I: A201-1976, Art. 2, Para. 2.1
> I: A201-1976, Art. 2, Para. 2.2
> I: B141-1977, Art. 1, Para. 1.5

Owner-county entered into a contract with the architect which, the court stated, did not incorporate the General Conditions. The owner-county then entered into a contract with the contractor that incorporated the general conditions. The county then contracted with an engineering firm to undertake some of the duties ascribed in the general conditions to the architect, leading the contractor to believe that it could rely on decisions to be made by an architect which were in fact delegated to a nonarchitectural firm. The owner terminated the contract before ground was broken. The contractor's surety built the building, and the contractor sued the owner, the engineer, the architect and others based on the contract, *quantum meruit,* interference with a contractual relationship, and the "unauthorized delegation of architectural responsibilities." The Superior Court granted summary judgment for all the defendants against the contractor.

The Court of Appeals reversed. The architect had no duty to the contractor since the general conditions had not been incorporated into the owner-architect contract. The architectural duties, which in the owner-contractor agreement were placed on the architect, could not be delegated. By corresponding and working with the engineers, the contractor may have waived his claims for the improper delegation of architectural duties. Since the question of waiver was a fact in dispute, summary judgment was inappropriate.

78025 DeKalb County v. Scruggs, 147 Ga. App. 711, 250 S.E.2d 159 (1978)

> I: A101-1977, Art. 6

A subcontractor sued the contractor, who cross-claimed against the county-owner on express and implied contract theories. The DeKalb State Court entered judgment against the county-owner, although the jury verdict did not specify the theory of recovery.

The Court of Appeals reversed. Under state law there could be no recovery from a county on an implied contract, since the county was liable only for authorized written contracts entered in the county minutes. For the same reason, the subcontractor could not recover as a third-party beneficiary of that contract.

Subcontractor sued the contractor to recover damages for breach of contract. The Circuit Court held for the subcontractor, but the Court of Appeals reversed.

The Supreme Court reversed, ruling for the subcontractor. The contractor had insisted that the subcontractor give a rebate as a result of an architect's decision concerning the plans and specifications. The subcontractor had offered to begin performance and simultaneously arbitrate the rebate issue. The contractor canceled the subcontract and engaged another subcontractor to do the work and consequently breached its contract with the first subcontractor.

78022 Culligan Corp. v. Transamerica Insurance Co., 580 F.2d 251 (7th Cir. 1978)

    II: A201-1976, Art. 9, Para. 9.9
    II: A311-1970, Labor and Material Payment Bond
    II: A401-1978, Art. 6

Subcontractor brought suit against the contractor's surety on its labor and material payment bond for retainages for work performed. The District Court entered judgment for the subcontractor.

The Seventh Circuit Court of Appeals affirmed. Under the terms of the bond, the architect's acceptance was not needed for payment. The bond did incorporate by reference the owner-contractor contract but not the subcontract. The reference to the owner-contractor contract serves merely as a "reference to identify the construction project covered by the bond and does not thereby change or modify the terms of the bond." The court also ruled that there had been an implied acceptance of the work in issue as a result of a letter from the owner and architect to the contractor which cataloged other defects but did not mention any defects in the work of this subcontractor. The contractor also expressed its satisfaction both orally and in writing over the subcontractor's work.

The dispute between the owner-obligee and the contractor-principal was not a defense for the surety against the materialmen or subcontractors. Court opinions involving statutory bonds were applicable to private bonds as far as this principal was concerned.

78023 Cumberland-Perry Area Vocational-Technical School Authority v. Bogar & Bink, 261 Pa. Super. 350, 396 A.2d 433 (1978)

    I: A201-1976, Art. 7, Para. 7.9
    I: A401-1978, Art. 1
    I: A401-1978, Art. 13
    I: B141-1977, Art. 9

Architect sought to compel arbitration between itself and the owner, contractor and subcontractor. The Court of Common Pleas ordered arbitration between all of those parties regardless of the lack of contractual privity between some of them.

The Superior Court reversed, holding that the arbitration provision in the contractor-subcontractor agreement required arbitration only between the contracting parties. The

The Court of Civil Appeals affirmed. Mere variation between the architect's estimate of costs and the actual cost was not negligence as a matter of law since the owners were in part responsible. The evidence showed that the architect had only estimated the "probable" cost of construction, not promised a maximum cost. The architect did not have a duty to advise the owners of the true completion date unless he had possessed actual knowledge of the fact. The owner-contractor agreement was on a "cost-plus" basis, and did not contain a maximum cost clause.

78019 Corbetta Construction Co. of Illinois v. Lake County Public Building Commission, 64 Ill. App. 3d 313, 381 N.E.2d 758 (1978)

        III: A201-1976, Art. 2, Para. 2.2
        III: A201-1976, Art. 4, Para. 4.3
        III: B141-1977, Art. 1

Contractor sought a declaratory judgment that the architect's faulty plans and not the contractor's construction had caused the defects. The owner filed a counterclaim against the contractor and a third-party complaint against the architect. The Circuit Court held for the owner.

The Appellate Court reversed in part. Since the contractor had not complied with the plans and specifications, the owner was not obligated to pay the contractor for extra work to correct the omissions and defects. The failure of the contractor to comply with the architect's faulty design did not exculpate the architect. The architect's contractual duty to supervise could not be delegated or fulfilled by a "clerk of the works" appointed by the owner and architect.

78020 Corrao Constr. Co. v. Curtis, 94 Nev. 569, 584 P.2d 1303 (1978)

        II: A201-1976, Art. 4, Para. 4.18

Injured contractor's employee sued the owners who sought indemnity from the contractor. The District Court found for the employee and ordered indemnity.

The Supreme Court affirmed. The indemnity agreement was not contrary to a statute for workmen's compensation, since the agreement did not enlarge, change or modify the liability of the contractor to its employees. The reason given by the court was that this was not a case where a third party (the owner) was responsible for the injuries of the employee so as to change the liability of the contractor. The indemnitor-contractor, however, was responsible under the indemnity agreement for the owner's reasonable defense costs and attorney's fees.

78021 Crabtree Masonry Co. v. C & R Construction, Inc., 575 S.W.2d 4 (Tenn. 1978)

        I: A201-1976, Art. 14, Para. 14.2
        I: A401-1978, Art. 14

The Supreme Court, Appellate Division, affirmed with modifications. The reason for the excavation claims was that the contractor had not thoroughly read the plans and related documents, and it was not proper for the contractor to assume that the excavation figures provided by the state meant after topsoil was stripped. There was also no showing that the state was reckless or withheld material information.

78016   City of Mounds View v. Walijarvi, 263 N.W.2d 420 (Minn. 1978)

        I: B141-1977, Art. 13

The city-owner sued the architect for negligence and breach of warranties in relation to water seepage. The District Court granted summary judgment for the architect.

The Supreme Court affirmed. Since the contract provided that the agreement could be modified only by a writing signed by both parties, an exchange of letters which were not signed by both parties could not amend the contract so as to provide an express warranty of watertightness. Since one of the letters was not in evidence, the court did not decide whether the letters were "fused" into one modification because each was signed by the other party. There was no implied warranty of fitness for the purpose for which it was designed, since the indeterminate nature of the architectural profession made it impossible to legally imply any warranty beyond negligence standards.

78017   City Stores Co. v. Gervais F. Favrot Co., 359 So. 2d 1031 (La. Ct. App. 1978)

        III: A201-1976, Art. 7, Para. 7.9

The owner and contractor had entered into three separate cost-plus contracts over a period of time, which related to different aspects of the same project. The contractor demanded arbitration on only the first contract, but later presented a "Claim for an Equitable Adjustment" which covered all three contract areas, to which the owner responded and added claims of its own. The arbitrators made their award based on all three contracts. The owner then sought a declaratory judgment but was denied relief in the Judicial District Court.

The Court of Appeals affirmed. The fact that the demand for arbitration was on only the first contract did not preclude the arbitrators from considering all three contracts since they were interrelated and all dealt with the same project.

78018   Cobb v. Thomas, 565 S.W.2d 281 (Tex. Civ. App. 1978)

        I: B141-1978, Art. 1
        I: B141-1978, Art. 3
        III: A111-1978, Art. 5

Homeowners sued the architect and the contractor for breach of contract, breach of fiduciary duties and negligence over the unexpected cost and lateness of completion of the house. The District Court held for the architect and contractor.

School board sued the architect both in negligence and on a breach of contract. The Circuit Court held for the school board.

The duties of the architect included those expressly set out in the contract as to the phases of its work. Other duties were imposed by law out of the relationship created by the contract. The architect had implied duties to specify the "use of reasonably good materials," to perform its architectural duties "in a reasonably workmanlike manner, and in such a way as reasonably to satisfy such requirements as it had notice the work was required to meet."

78013   Burdette v. Lascola, 40 Md. App. 720, 395 A.2d 169 (1978)

    III: A201-1976, Art. 12, Para. 12.1
    III: A311-1970, Performance Bond

Owner sued the contractor and surety for specific performance of the contract. The Circuit Court held the surety liable for the contractor's failure to complete the house.

The Court of Special Appeals affirmed. The surety was not released by the verbal modification of the owner-contractor agreement. Whether oral or written, the change order to the principal agreement will discharge the surety only if it constitutes a material alteration of the owner-contractor contract. A verbal modification of $700 involving the length, height and direction of a wall contemplated in the $89,863 contract was not material.

The lack of a written change order as required by both the contract and the bond did not release the surety.

78014   Butler v. Metz, Train, Olson & Youngren, 62 Ill. App. 3d 424, 379 N.E.2d 1255 (1978)

    III: B141-1977, Art. 3

Owner sued for declaratory judgment on the fees owing to the architect who counterclaimed for its fees and requested foreclosure on a security interest in one of the lots of the project. The Circuit Court held for the owner.

The Appellate Court reversed and remanded. Although a second building was never constructed though fully designed, the architect was entitled to its fee based on estimated construction costs, since the term "construction costs" could be so interpreted.

78015   Chemical Bank v. State of New York, 64 A.D.2d 755, 406 N.Y.S.2d 633 (1978)

    III: A201-1976, Art. 4, Para. 4.2
    III: A201-1976, Art. 12, Para. 12.2

Contractor sued the state-owner for alleged misrepresentation of the amount of excavation. The Court of Claims held for the contractor.

Architect sued the owner to recover fees for architectural services. The District Court held for the architect.

The Court of Civil Appeals affirmed. The architect had performed part of his fee for the required services when the owner terminated the contract. Recovery was allowed on the basis of *quantum meruit* and not on the schedule of payments stated in the contract. The fact that the structure he designed was never built did not defeat the architect's right to recover the reasonable value of his services.

78010 Benning Construction Co. v. Lakeshore Plaza Enterprises, Inc., 240 Ga. 426, 241 S.E.2d 184 (1977), *later proceeding,* 144 Ga. App. 518, 241 S.E.2d 627 (1978)

      III: A201-1976, Art. 13, Para. 13.2

Owner sued the contractor for breach of contract for a leaking roof. The State Court, Fulton County, granted the contractor's motion for a judgment on the pleadings, and the Court of Appeals reversed.

The Supreme Court reversed the Court of Appeals and remanded to the State Court. The date from which the statute of limitations ran for breach of the one year warranty was from the time the owner discovered and notified the contractor of the defect and not from the final acceptance of the building as stated in the written guarantee. The State Court on remand was to hear evidence as to the date when the owner discovered and notified the contractor of the defect.

78011 Bleck v. Stephanich, 64 Ill. App. 3d 436, 381 N.E.2d 363 (1978)

      II: B141-1977, Art. 3
      II: B141-1977, Art. 13

The architects sued the owners for payment of their fees for the design of a building that was never built. The contract had called for payment of a percentage of the building cost as the architects' fee. The trial court held that the contract was incomplete and allowed outside evidence as to the intent of the parties on the cost issue.

The Appellate Court affirmed. Whether the contract was intended to be complete and final should be determined from the language of the contract and its circumstances. The contract did not provide for the total cost or any upper limit on cost and "in the face of the absence of such an essential part of the contract, the trial court was correct in finding that the contract was incomplete and in allowing parol evidence to supply the missing cost figure."

78012 Board of Educ. of Community Consolidated School District No. 54 v. Del Bianco & Associates, Inc., 57 Ill. App. 3d 302, 372 N.E.2d 953 (1978)

      I: B141-1977, Art. 1

The contractor filed suit to foreclose on its mechanic's lien in a dispute over the proper measure of liquidated damages for delay. The District Court held for the owner.

The Supreme Court affirmed. The owner had given the contractor sufficient extensions of time in which to complete construction despite flood, cold weather, wind conditions, alleged fuel shortage and delay of the owner in approving a subcontractor, some of which delays were found to be overlapping and concurrent.

78007   Atlantic National Bank of Jacksonville v. Modular Age, Inc., 363 So. 2d 1152 (Fla. Dist. Ct. App. 1978)

      I: A201-1976, Art. 4, Para. 4.7
      I: A201-1976, Art. 13, Para. 13.2

Mortgagee bank sued on the performance bond seeking to recover for walls which did not meet the building code. The contractor's defense was that the defect was the responsibility of the architect. The Circuit Court granted summary judgment for the contractor.

The District Court of Appeals affirmed. Since the architect's duty to ensure that the plans and drawings met the building code was a nondelegable duty, he could not avoid it by not personally designing the walls. The contract also stated that the contractor was not liable for the plans' failure to comply with the building code. The failure of the walls was a design failure for which the architect was responsible and not a material failure for which the contractor would be responsible. The contract provisions concerning the warranty of the contractor for its work did not apply since the work was defective as a result of design error.

78008   Batson-Cook Co. v. Poteat, 147 Ga. App. 506, 249 S.E.2d 319 (1978)

      II: A401-1978, Art. 11

A husband brought suit against the contractor and subcontractor for injuries, and his wife brought a consortium suit against them. The contractor filed a cross-claim against the subcontractor for indemnity. Summary judgment was granted for the subcontractor by the Superior court.

The Court of Appeals affirmed. The printed form clause allowed indemnity, but it conflicted with an added typed clause. Under general rules of contract construction the typed clause prevailed over the printed clause.

78009   Beller v. DeLara, 565 S.W.2d 319 (Tex. Civ. App. 1978)

      I: B141-1977, Art. 1
      I: B141-1977, Art. 10
      I: B141-1977, Art. 14

to the subcontractor. The subcontractor interpreted this cessation of voluntary advances as a breach and ceased work under the contract. The contractor was justified in stopping the advances, since it had already paid for all of the completed work. The subcontractor was not liable for the contractor's attorney's fees on a claim against the subcontractor for breach of contract, since the contract provision specifying attorney's fees was only applicable to those incurred under an indemnity clause.

78004 Alvord & Swift v. Stewart M. Muller Construction Co., 46 N.Y.2d 276. 413 N.Y.S.2d 309, 385 N.E.2d 1238 (1978)

        I: A201-1976, Art. 1, Para. 1.1
        I: A401-1976, Art. 11

The subcontractor brought suit against the owner and architects for damages due to delays in the performance of its subcontract. The Supreme Court entered summary judgment for the owner and architects.

The Court of Appeals affirmed. The contractor was insolvent, and the claims were asserted against the owner and the architects despite explicit language in the prime contract and the subcontract which asserted that there was no contractual relationship. The subcontractor also could not assert a claim for the tort of intentional interference with contractual relationships, since there was no tort liability to incidental beneficiaries not in privity.

78005 Alwinseal, Inc. v. Travelers Indem. Co., 61 A.D.2d 803, 402 N.Y.S.2d 33 (1978)

        III: A201-1976, Art. 7, Para. 7.1
        III: A311-1970, Labor & Material Payment Bond
        III: A401-1978, Art. 11

Subcontractor sued the contractor's surety. The Supreme Court held for the surety.

The Appellate Division affirmed. The bond contained a forum selection clause which required that any suit be brought in the state where the project was located (i.e, New Jersey). The bond was incorporated by reference into the subcontract. The subcontract contained a clause specifying that it was to be governed by the laws of New Jersey. The fact that the subcontractor was a New York corporation did not control, since the parties themselves by agreement obviated considerations of inconvenience to a party or a witness.

78006 Arrowhead, Inc. v. Safeway Stores, Inc., 179 Mont. 510, 587 P.2d 411 (1978)

        III: A101-1977, Art. 3
        III: A107-1978, Art. 2
        III: A111-1978, Art. 4
        III: A201-1976, Art. 8, Para. 8.3

78001 A. E. Finley & Associates, Inc. v. Hendrix, 271 S.C. 312, 247 S.E.2d 328 (1978)

    III: A201-1976, Art. 7, Para. 7.2
    III: A201-1976, Art. 14, Para. 14.2

Contractor made an assignment of the contract proceeds to its equipment supplier in exchange for the supplier dropping repossession proceedings. The owner acknowledged the assignment in writing, and did not terminate the contract. Work delays reduced the progress payments, and the supplier later repossessed the equipment. Since the contractor was unable to complete the contract, it hired a subcontractor. The supplier sued the owner to recover the money allegedly due under the assignment. The Common Pleas Court granted summary judgment for the supplier.

The Supreme Court affirmed, holding that since the owner had expressly consented to the assignment and had received consideration, it was bound by the assignment. The owner was obligated to disburse further progress payments in accordance with the assignment. The fact that the contractor completed his work through the use of a subcontractor did not excuse the owner from having to pay.

78002 Aetna Casualty & Sur. Co. v. Warren Brothers Co., 355 So. 2d 785 (Fla. 1978)

    III: A311-1970, Performance Bond
    III: A401-1978, Art. 6
    III: A401-1978, Art. 11

Subcontractor sued the contractor and its surety for payment for completed work. Summary judgment was granted against the surety by the Circuit Court. The District Court of Appeals affirmed.

The Supreme Court affirmed that the surety was liable to the same extent as its contractor. Payment from the owner to the contractor was not a condition precedent to the contractor's payment to the subcontractor.

78003 Al Smith's Plumbing & Heating Service, Inc. v. River Crest, Inc., 365 So. 2d 1122 (La. Ct. App. 1978)

    I: A401-1978, Art. 5
    I: A401-1978, Art. 11

The subcontractor sued the contractor for the balance due under two subcontracts. The owner counterclaimed for breach of contract and joined the surety as a defendant under its performance bond. The District Court held for the contractor.

The Court of Appeals affirmed in part. When the subcontractor had financial difficulties, the contractor had assisted with "generous payments" until it concluded that the percent of completion lagged seriously behind the percent of total payments given

contract provisions only if "fraudulent, arbitrary, capricious or so grossly erroneous as to necessarily imply bad faith." The state had refused to allow the contractor to see files which the engineer apparently relied on in making his decision. The Court of Appeals held that there was an implied covenant requiring the engineer to reach his decision without violating the due process rights of either party. Due process was violated when the engineer failed to advise the contractor in advance of the factual material upon which he intended to rely, and thus, failed to give the contractor a reasonable opportunity to refute any such material. The court remanded with instructions to the Superior Court to order the engineer to reconsider its decision after satisfying the contractor's due process rights.

III: A201-1976, Art. 8, Para. 8.3
III: A201-1976, Art. 12, Para. 12.1

Contractor sought to stay the owner's demand for arbitration, which was served in response to the contractor's demand. The Supreme Court granted the stay, and the Appellate Division reversed.

The Court of Appeals affirmed. The stay of arbitration should not have been granted, since an agreement to refer to arbitration "any dispute or disagreement in connection with the performance of the work" embraced both a determination of the liability of the contractor and the computation of damages, particularly in light of the contract provisions relating to delays and extension of time and to changes in work.

77085 Westminster Construction Corp. v. PPG Industries, Inc., 119 R.I. 205, 376 A.2d 708 (1977)

I: A201-1976, Art. 7, Para. 7.8
I: A201-1976, Art. 7, Para. 7.9
I: A201-1976, Art. 9, Para. 9.4
I: A401-1978, Art. 13

General contractor sought to "vacate, modify or correct" an arbitration award which had ordered payment to the subcontractor, despite the lack of an architect's certificate for payment required under a contract provision.

The Supreme Court affirmed the Superior Court's confirmation of the award. The arbitrators "are under no obligation to set out the reasons for their award or the findings of law." There are exceptions requiring itemized findings if the "applicable statute, arbitration agreement or the submissions so requires." The award was not in "manifest disregard of the law" merely because the architect never certified the work.

The arbitrators had the authority to award interest, even though the arbitration agreement was silent on the subject. The arbitrator's authority to award interest arose from the contract provision allowing interest. Moreover, the construction industry arbitration rules, referred to in the arbitration clause of the contract, gave them the right to award interest according to the contract of the parties.

77086 Zurn Engineers v. State, 69 Cal. App. 3d 798, 138 Cal. Rptr. 478 (1977)

III: A201-1976, Art. 2, Para. 2.2

Contractor sued the state-owner for breach of contract after the state engineer, who was empowered to resolve disputes under the contract, decided against the contractor. The Superior Court held for the contractor.

The Court of Appeals affirmed in part and reversed in part. To the extent that there had been substantial evidence put before the engineer, the Superior Court was incorrect in trying the case *de novo*. The engineer's decision was reversible according to the

bought for the bonded project but directed to a nonbonded project would be covered by the bonds. Otherwise, the burden would be on the innocent materialman to trace fungible goods to their ultimate use.

77083   V. Petrillo & Son, Inc. v. American Construction Co., 148 N.J. Super. 1, 371 A.2d 799 (App. Div. 1977)

      I: A201-1976, Art. 2, Para. 2.2
      I: A201-1976, Art. 9, Para. 9.9
      II: A311-1970, Labor and Material Payment Bond

Subcontractor sued surety on labor and material payment bond after the contractor was declared bankrupt. The Superior Court denied the surety's motion to dismiss on the basis of the statute of limitations and lack of required notice.

The Superior Court, Appellate Division, reversed, holding that the suit was barred by the statute of limitations. The subcontractor was required by the bond to file suit within one year of when the contractor "ceased work."

The nonissuance of a certificate of final compliance cannot be construed to mean that the contractor has not ceased work. "The nonissuance of a certificate of final acceptance by the owner is at best evidence that the general contractor has not completed its work under the contract."

The contract required written notice to be sent by registered mail. The notice was received but had not been sent by registered mail. The court did not decide this issue since it was not necessary in view of its reversal on the statute of limitations issue.

77083a   Vespe Contracting Co. v. Anvan Corp. 433 F. Supp. 1226 (E.D. Pa. 1977), *rehearing* of 399 F. Supp. 516 (E. D. Pa. 1975)

      I: A201-1976, Art. 7, Para. 7.9

The subcontractor sued the contractor for breach of contract, and the contractor moved to stay the suit pending arbitration. The District Court ruled that arbitration of the issue was proper. The subcontractor then amended this complaint so as to seek monetary damages. The District Court again ruled in favor of the contractor and held that the substitution of a request for monetary damages rather than an injunction did not alter the previously adjudicated issue that arbitration of the dispute was proper. The addition of new parties and new claims by the subcontractor did not abrogate the propriety of arbitration. However, because the new claims, among them conspiracy to defraud the subcontractor, were factually and legally separate and distinct and because of the length of time involved in the litigation, justice would be served by the judicial determination of these claims.

77084   Walter A. Stanley & Son, Inc. v. Trustees of Hackley School, 42 N.Y.2d 436, 397 N.Y.S.2d 985, 366 N.E.2d 1339 (1977)

      III: A201-1976, Art. 7, Para. 7.9

Materialman sued the subcontractor, its surety and the contractor and its surety for the amount still due on materials supplied. The District Court granted summary judgment against the subcontractor's surety.

The Supreme Court reversed. The materialman to the subcontractor could not rely on the subcontractor's performance bond, nor on the incorporated-by-reference subcontract. The fact that the subcontract required the subcontractor to pay the materialman did not bind the surety to the same duty since the bond did not contain a provision for payment of a materialman. The two documents were construed together so that the materialman was not a third-party beneficiary.

77081   Ukrainian National Urban Renewal Corp. v. Joseph L. Muscarelle, Inc., 151 N.J. Super. 386, 376 A.2d 1299 (App. Div. 1977)

I: A201-1976, Art. 5, Para. 5.3
I: A201-1976, Art. 7, Para. 7.9
I: A201-1976, Art. 12, Para. 12.3
III: A401-1978, Art. 11
III: A401-1978, Art. 13

Owner challenged the arbitration award on the grounds that the subcontractors' claims for damages were nonarbitrable and should not have been presented on the subcontractor's behalf by the contractor. The Superior Court held that while the subcontractors were not parties to the master agreement of the owner-contractor, and thus lacked standing, the owner had waived this lack of standing.

The Superior Court, Appellate Division, modified the decree of the Superior Court, but affirmed the award. Under the broad language of the contract, the claims of nonparty subcontractors were arbitrable as "claims, disputes and other matters in question arising out of, or related to, this Contract. . . ." The lack of contractual privity between the owner and the subcontractor did not prevent arbitration.

> The subcontractors became beneficiaries of the promises to arbitrate and to pay delay expenses between . . . [owner and contractor] with at least the right to have their claims arbitrated in a proceeding between [owner and contractor].

77082   United States Fidelity & Guar. Co. v. Miller, 549 S.W.2d 316 (Ky. 1977)

III: A311-1970, Labor and Material Payment Bond

Materialman sued the surety to recover for cost of unpaid lumber. The Circuit Court held for the materialman.

The Court of Appeals reversed in part. Some of the lumber at issue had been supplied for an earlier, unbonded project. The fact that the lumber had been salvaged and reused did not make it "furnished for use" for the bonded project within the meaning of the bonds. The contracts and payment bonds did not require that material purchased for the bonded job be actually used on the job to be covered by the payment bonds. Thus, lumber

responsible for paying the contractors. The fact that one of the owners thought the changes to be relatively minor and inexpensive, did not excuse liability. Other testimony established that numerous and extensive changes were required by another of the owners.

77078   Texas Construction Associates, Inc. v. Balli, 558 S.W.2d 513 (Tex. Civ. App. 1977)

        III: A311-1970, Labor and Material Payment Bond
        III: A401-1978, Art. 11

Subcontractor sued the contractor and its surety. The subcontractor's materialman intervened against the subcontractor, contractor and its surety. The District Court held for the subcontractor against the contractor and surety and for the materialman against the subcontractor.

The Court of Civil Appeals reformed the judgment but affirmed. The materialman's legal argument was that since he was entitled to a direct claim and judgment against the subcontractor, he should also be entitled to a claim and judgment against the contractor and its surety for the funds which they would eventually pay the subcontractor. The Court of Civil Appeals rejected this premise since it was not based on any authority and ignored possible competing claims of creditors.

The requirement for a written agreement for extras was impliedly waived by the owner's conduct, since the subcontractor had been led by that conduct into an "honest belief that the writing requirement had been waived."

77079   Town & Country Bank of Springfield v. James M. Canfield Contracting Co., 55 Ill. App. 3d 91, 370 N.E.2d 630 (1977)

        III: A401-1978, Art. 11

The subcontractor assigned the contract to a bank in exchange for cash advances, and the contractor paid the progress payments to the bank. The bank took a judgment by confession against the subcontractor and garnished the amount owed by the contractor. The Circuit Court did not allow claims of sub-subcontractors and held for the bank in the garnishment action.

The Appellate Court reversed and remanded. The contractor was not obligated to pay the bank since the subcontractor had not supplied any lien waivers or affidavits of payments to sub-subcontractors as required by the contract. The rights of the bank could rise no higher than that of the subcontractor.

The sub-subcontractors were entitled to assert the provisions of the contractor-subcontractor agreement as third-party beneficiaries, and they had vested rights against the contractors for payment once the contract was signed, which had priority over those of the bank.

77080   Treasure State Industries, Inc. v. Welch, 173 Mont. 403, 567 P.2d 947 (1977)

        III: A311-1970, Performance Bond

77075 Ralph Korte Construction Co. v. Springfield Mechanical Co., 54 Ill. App. 3d 445, 369 N.E.2d 561 (1977)

        III: A201-1976, Art. 11, Para. 11.3
        III: A401-1978, Art. 9

Subcontractor's employee caused fire damage at part of the work site, and the contractor sued the subcontractor. The Circuit Court held for the subcontractor.

The Appellate Court affirmed. The contract provisions by which the parties waived all rights against each other to the extent covered by insurance was not void as against public policy under a statute making void any agreement the effect of which indemnifies one against his own negligence in construction contracts. The legislature had not intended to prohibit agreements affecting only negligence between the parties to the contract, since the public was not involved.

77076 Schuler-Haas Electric Corp. v. Wager Construction Corp., 57 A.D.2d 707, 395 N.Y.S.2d 272 (1977)

        III: A201-1976, Art. 1, Para. 1.1
        III: A401-1978, Art. 1
        III: A401-1978, Art. 11

Subcontractor sued the owner, contractor and its sureties for damages due to delays, change orders and interference with performance of the contract. The Supreme Court dismissed the complaint against the owner.

The Appellate Division affirmed. Since the terms of the general contract, which had been incorporated into the subcontract, "expressly negated any contractual liability between the owner and the subcontractor," the subcontractor was not a third-party beneficiary of the owner-contractor contract. Nor could the subcontractor claim a "presumed assent" of the owner to be responsible for payment as creating liability or a contractual or quasi-contractual relationship, because of the express negation of the general contract. The owner's extensive revision of the plans and specifications did not create liability to the subcontractor on a theory of quasi-contract or a contract implied in law because of the express negation.

77077 Smith v. Scott, 345 So. 2d 981 (La. Ct. App. 1977)

        III: A201-1976, Art. 12, Para. 12.1

Subcontractors sought to impose a lien and recover the balance due on the contract. The owners filed a third-party claim against the contractors who counterclaimed against the owners for the payment of extras. The Judicial District Court awarded judgment for the subcontractors and the contractors.

The Court of Appeals modified, but affirmed the judgment. Since the contractors added the extras with either the knowledge of the owner or his authorization, the owners were

Although the subcontractor purported to have accepted the contract in Ohio, the subcontractor submitted the proposal in Arkansas, the contractor signed it in Arkansas and it was performed in Arkansas. Since the subcontractor drafted the contract, any ambiguity should be resolved against the subcontractor.

77073 R & R Construction Co. v. Junior College District No. 529, 55 Ill. App. 3d 115, 370 N.E.2d 599 (1977)

        III: A201-1976, Art. 1, Para. 1.1
        III: A201-1976, Art. 4, Para. 4.3
        III: A201-1976, Art. 12, Para. 12.1
        III: A201-1976, Art. 12, Para. 12.2
        III: A201-1976, Art. 12, Para. 12.3

Contractor sued the owner to recover for cost of extras. The Circuit Court held for the owner.

The Appellate Court affirmed. The means used were merely one method of performing the contracted for job. The fact that the contractor had hoped to use a cheaper method to reach the same end, but could not, did not make the method used an extra. The definition of "work" in the contract also included this method. There had also been no waiver of the requirement that extra work be ordered in writing since the owner's agents told the contractor that the method was not an extra and refused to issue a written change order for additional compensation.

Since the bidding information showed a moisture content of 23-25 percent in the subsurface, the presence of 28-30 percent was not an unforseen subsurface condition materially differing from the drawings. Therefore, the contract provision for subsurface conditions also did not allow for additional compensation.

77074 Ralph Allen, Inc. v. Lumpkin, 279 Or. 71, 566 P.2d 872 (1977)

        I: A111-1978, Art. 3
        I: A111-1978, Art. 8
        I: A111-1978, Art. 11

Contractor sued to foreclose a mechanic's lien on the owner's property. The Circuit Court held for the contractor.

The Supreme Court affirmed. The contractor did not breach its fiduciary duty under the contract since the job was difficult and in fact was commended by the architect. The contractor also had not breached its contract duty to deliver subcontract bids to the architect, since it was difficult to obtain definite bids for the job. The "cost" in the "cost plus" contract included a charge for procuring and supervising subcontractors.

77069 (UNASSIGNED)

77070 Post Bros. Construction Co. v. Yoder, 20 Cal. 3d 1, 141 Cal. Rptr. 28, 569 P.2d 133 (1977), *rev'g* 66 Cal. App. 3d 44, 135 Cal. Rptr. 730 (1977)

    II: A201-1976, Art. 9, Para. 9.
    II: A311-1970, Labor and Material Payment Bond

Materialman brought suit to recover from owner and surety on a labor and material payment bond for rental charges. The owner had "paid" with checks made jointly payable to the contractor and several materialmen. The Superior Court held for the owner and surety, and the Court of Appeals reversed.

The Supreme Court reversed the Court of Appeals and reinstated the Superior Court's holding for the owner and surety. This specific materialman had failed to protect its interest by taking its share of each check, as it endorsed the check. Since the subcontractor and materialman were joint payees and no agreement existed with the owner or the general contractor as to allocation of proceeds, the materialman's endorsement represented that he had received the money due him. The joint check rule also applied where there were more than two joint payees.

77071 Prater v. Luhr Bros. 51 Ill. App. 3d 685, 366 N.E.2d 399 (1977)

    III: A201-1976, Art. 4, Para. 4.18
    III: A401-1978, Art. 11

Subcontractor's injured employee sued the contractor who sought indemnity from the subcontractor. The Circuit Court held for the employee and ordered indemnity.

The Appellate Court reversed and remanded. The existence of a contract for indemnity precluded recovery under implied indemnity. However, since the contract provision was not specific and clear as to whether it required indemnity when the indemnitee was also negligent, the court remanded for retrial under the common law principles of implied indemnity.

77072 Prepakt Concrete Co. v. Whitehurst Bros., Inc., 261 Ark. 814, 552 S.W.2d 212 (1977)

    III: A201-1976, Art. 7, Para. 7.1
    III: A201-1976, Art. 7, Para. 7.9
    III: A401-1978, Art. 13

Contractor obtained an order from a Circuit Court in Arkansas preventing subcontractor from instituting an arbitration proceeding in Ohio. The Supreme Court affirmed. The architect's plans had provided for arbitration under Arkansas state law, but the contract specifically employed the rules and procedure of the American Arbitration Association.

77066 Pacific County v. Sherwood Pacific, Inc., 17 Wash. App. 790, 567 P.2d 642 (1977)

        III: A311-1970, Performance Bond

The county sued the developer and its surety to either force completion of a road system or payment of the face amount of two performance bonds. The District Court awarded the county the full amount of the bonds.

The Court of Appeals affirmed, holding that the surety was responsible. Contrary to the surety's claim that the county had no legal interest as an owner, the county as obligee of the bonds was a "trustee" which was required to attempt to recover the funds from the surety and use them to complete the roads and sewers for the property owners and members of the general public.

77067 Peacock Construction Co. v. Modern Air Conditioning, Inc., 353 So. 2d 840 (Fla. 1977)

        III: A401-1978, Art. 6
        III: A401-1978, Art. 12

Subcontractors sued the contractor for the final payment on the completed subcontract work. The Circuit Court entered summary judgment in favor of the subcontractors, and the District Court of Appeals affirmed.

The Supreme Court affirmed. Payment by the owners to the contractor was not a condition precedent to payments by the contractor to the subcontractors, and payment by the owner merely started the time period within which payment should be reasonably due. The intent was to not shift the risk of nonpayment of the owner to the subcontractors, since small subcontractors must have payment for their work in order to remain in business.

77068 Perkins & Will Partnership v. Syska & Hennessy, 41 N.Y.2d 1045, 396 N.Y.S.2d 167, 364 N.E.2d 832 (1977)

        III: C141-1979, Art. 9

Consulting engineers sought to stay an arbitration proceeding demanded by the architect. The Supreme Court vacated the architect's demand for an arbitration.

The Court of Appeals affirmed. Under the contract between the architect and engineers, arbitration between the owner and the architect would bind the engineers only if they had been vouched into the arbitration. The proper course for the architect was to vouch the engineers into the owner-architect arbitration rather than to start a second arbitration between the architect and the engineers.

I: A401-1978, Art. 11

Contractor and subcontractors brought suit against the owner upon a *quantum meruit* theory of recovery for semitortious interference. The Superior Court held for the contractors.

The Court of Appeals reversed. The contract clauses were controlling and recovery under *quantum meruit* was not appropriate. The contract documents were AIA standard forms but were greatly amended as to the areas of dispute. The contract clause that allowed time extensions for causes "beyond the contractor's control" meant that extensions of time were the sole remedy for owner-caused delay. Delays caused by change orders, architect's interpretations and stop orders were covered by the contract scheme for determining the price of such changes. The delay caused by the lack of a permit was also covered by the contract which made permits the contractor's responsibility. Errors in the initial specifications were also contractually controlled, since the contractor had the duty to carefully study the contract and specifications and report any errors, omissions or inconsistencies to the architects.

The subcontracts incorporated the prime contract by reference, and therefore the subcontractors were also denied recovery under *quantum meruit*.

77064 New York Telephone Co. v. Schumacher & Forelle, Inc., 60 A.D.2d 151, 400 N.Y.S.2d 332 (1977)

I: A201-1976, Art. 2, Para. 2.2
I: A201-1976, Art. 7, Para. 7.9
I: A401-1978, Art. 13

The contractor served a demand for arbitration on the owner and the subcontractor. The owner sought to stay the arbitration proceeding, and the Supreme Court denied the stay.

The Appellate Division reversed. The condition precedent of the architect's decision prior to a demand for arbitration had not been fulfilled.

77065 Obray v. Mitchell, 98 Idaho 533, 567 P.2d 1284 (1977)

III: A201-1976, Art. 12, Para. 12.1

A subcontractor sued the contractor to recover for extras. The District Court held for the contractor.

The Supreme Court affirmed in part and remanded. The requirement of written approval for extras had been waived by the contractor's regular course of conduct in ignoring the requirement and making oral contracts. Even though the owners had also approved the changes, the contractor was responsible for paying the subcontractor. The work involved was "extra work" not required in the course of performance of the contract rather than "additional work" necessarily required in the performance of the contract.

77061 Moundsview Independent School District No. 621 v. Buetow & Associates, Inc., 253 N.W.2d 836 (Minn. 1977)

    I: B141-1977, Art. 1
    II: A201-1976, Art. 2, Para. 2.2

Owner sued the architect, contractor and subcontractor over wind damage to the improperly anchored roof on the completed project. The architect's motion for summary judgment was granted.

The Supreme Court affirmed. The architect's contract required only general supervision and did not require the detailed supervision that would have been needed to determine that the contractor had ignored the plans and omitted the bolts anchoring the roof to the wall on one side of the building. The architect was merely required to use the reasonable care and competence of a professional and, under a contract provision, was not responsible for the acts and omissions of the contractor.

77062 N.E. Finch Co. v. R.C. Mahon Co., 54 Ill. App. 3d 573, 370 N.E.2d 160 (1977)

    III: A201-1976, Art. 4, Para. 4.18
    III: A401-1978, Art. 11

Equipment lessor's employee was injured while acting under the direction of the contractor. The worker sued the contractor who requested the lessor to assume the defense and to indemnify the contractor, which the lessor refused to do. The contractor negotiated a settlement with the employee and sued the lessor to recover the amount paid in settlement. The Circuit Court granted judgment for the contractor.

The Appellate Court affirmed. The contractor was not merely a volunteer when it settled with the employee. It was not necessary for the party seeking indemnity to obtain a judicial determination that it is liable to another in order to preserve its rights to indemnity. "[O]nce defense of the principal action has been tendered to the prospective indemnitor and refused by him, the indemnitor cannot thereafter assert that the indemnitee was a legal volunteer who gratuitously settled the initial matter." The proper time for the indemnitor to deny the liability of the indemnitee was in the original action by the injured party against the indemnitee.

77063 Nelse Mortensen & Co. v. Group Health Cooperative of Puget Sound, 17 Wash. App. 703, 566 P.2d 560 (1977)

    I: A201-1976, Art. 4, Para. 4.2
    I: A201-1976, Art. 4, Para. 4.7
    I: A201-1976, Art. 8, Para. 8.2
    I: A201-1976, Art. 8, Para. 8.3
    I: A201-1976, Art. 12, Para. 12.1
    I: A201-1976, Art. 12, Para. 12.3

77058   Meek v. Spinney, Coady and Parker Architects, Inc., 50 Ill. App. 3d 919, 365 N.E.2d 1378 (1977)

        III: A201-1976, Art. 2, Para. 2.2
        III: B141-1977, Art. 1

Injured contractor's employee sued the architect and building inspector alleging that, within the meaning of the state statute, they had been in control of the worksite and, hence, liable. The Circuit Court dismissed the complaint, finding as a matter of law that the architect and inspector were not liable.

The Appellate Court affirmed. While more than one entity may be "in charge" of a worksite, the architect merely had the duty to ensure the compliance with the building specifications. The architect did not have the right to stop the work, nor did it have any duty of continuous supervision. The independent building inspector hired by the owner had extremely limited powers and he could only inspect and not control the work in any respect.

77059   Meyers v. Lakeridge Development Co., 173 Conn. 133, 376 A.2d 1105 (1977)

        I: B141-1977, Art. 9
        I: B141-1977, Art. 11

Architect sought to confirm an arbitration award over the owner's objections, and the Superior Court confirmed.

The Supreme Court affirmed the confirmation. The contract provision establishing the law of the architect's state as the governing law did not allow the court to review the arbitration award. Merely to declare which state's law would control in a conflict of law case does not curtail the power of the arbitrator to make final decisions of law and fact.

77060   Miller v. Melany, 172 Mont. 81, 560 P.2d 902 (1977)

        III: A201-1976, Art. 1, Para. 1.1
        III: A401-1978, Art. 11

Subcontractor brought suit to foreclose a mechanic's lien against the owners and contractor. The owners counterclaimed for defective workmanship as a breach of contract. The District Court held for the owners.

The Supreme Court reversed in part. The owners were entitled to a "breach of contract" action against the subcontractor even though there was no contract directly between them, since the mechanic's lien laws were enacted for the protection of owners as well as lien claimants. The District Court erred when it held that the contractor could not be liable for indemnity to the subcontractor for the inadequate design and specifications it had supplied the subcontractor.

The District Court of Appeals affirmed in part and reversed in part. There was no negligence in the architect's assistance in selecting the contractor, approval of when and to whom progress payments should be made, or failing to post a required notice of commencement under the mechanic's lien statute, since such duties were not imposed by the contract nor by custom and practice.

The AIA standard form contractor contract was altered to provide for payment by "probable construction costs." The Circuit Court erred in applying the percentage to increased costs of construction. The court also stated that the altered version would take precedence over the printed version.

77056 Marathon Steel Co. v. Tilley Steel, Inc., 66 Cal. App. 3d 413, 136 Cal. Rptr. 73 (1977)

III: A201-1976, Art. 4, Para. 4.18
III: A401-1978, Art. 11

Sub-subcontractor's injured worker sued the contractor, who sought indemnity from its subcontractors, who in turn sought indemnity from its sub-subcontractor. The Superior Court granted summary judgment for the sub-subcontractor.

The Court of Appeals reversed, holding that summary judgment was inappropriate since the cause of the injury was not determined.

The subcontractor would not have been liable to the contractor unless it had been, at least in part, negligent. Any such negligence by the subcontractor would have negated its contractual right to indemnity from the sub-subcontractor. The subcontractor may, however, have been vicariously liable to the contractor for the acts of the sub-subcontractor principally for nondelegable duties and inherently dangerous work. In such circumstances the subcontractor would be required to indemnify the contractor and could in turn be indemnified from the sub-subcontractor.

77057 Mayer Paving and Asphalt Co. v. Carl A. Morse, Inc., 48 Ill. App. 3d 73, 365 N.E.2d 360 (1977)

II: A201-1976, Art. 12, Para. 12.1
II: A401-1978, Art. 11

A subcontractor sued the contractor and owner for the balance due on various extras. The owner and contractor counterclaimed for the defective work by the subcontractor. The Circuit Court held for the subcontractor on its claim and for the contractor on its counterclaim.

The Appellate Court affirmed. The contractor had waived the contract requirement that changes to the contract be in writing, since there was evidence: that the extras had the contractor's approval; that the extras were made on its instructions and that it allowed the work to proceed on oral agreements.

CASES

77053 Leatherby Insurance Co. v. City of Tustin, 76 Cal. App. 3d 678, 143 C Rptr. 153 (1977)

        III: A201-1976, Art. 7, Para. 7.4
        III: A311-1970, Labor and Material Payment Bond

Surety sued the city-owner seeking payments stopped by the actions filed by unpaid subcontractors and suppliers. The city counterclaimed for the expenses of investigating and defending against the stop-notice claimants. The Superior Court held for the surety on its claim but allowed a setoff for the city based on its counterclaim.

The Court of Appeals modified the judgment. The insurance company was a surety and not an indemnitor. Since the surety had paid off the stop-notice claimants under the payment bond, it was subrogated to the sums withheld by the city to the contractor.

The owner-contractor agreement had been incorporated into the bonds. However, the "responsibility for damages" clause did not cover actions such as those filed by the stop-notice claimants, but referred to suits for wrongful death, personal injury and property damage.

77054 Lewis-Brady Builders Supply, Inc. v. Bedros, 32 N.C. App. 209, 231 S.E.2d 199 (1977)

        I: A201-1976, Art. 9, Para. 9.5
        I: A201-1976, Art. 9, Para. 9.6

Subcontractor sued contractor and owner on mechanic's lien. The Superior Court held for the subcontractor against the contractor but not against the owner.

The Court of Appeals affirmed. The architect's initial approval of a progress payment, which was later withheld by the architect pursuant to a contract provision, did not constitute "irrebuttable evidence" of the amount that the owner owed to the contractor. Since the architect was entitled to withhold the progress payment, the contractor had no right to halt his performance. The damages of the owner exceeded the amount due the contractor and under the mechanic's lien law, the subcontractor could not recover against the owner, if the owner was not liable to the contractor when the notice of lien was given by the subcontractor.

77055 MacIntyre v. Green's Pool Service, Inc., 347 So. 2d 1081 (Fla. Dist. Ct. App. 1977)

        I: A111-1978, Art. 1
        III: A111-1978, Art. 14

A contractor brought suit against the owner to foreclose on its mechanic's lien, and the owner filed a third-party complaint against the architect for negligence. The architect counterclaimed to recover the remainder of his fee. The Circuit Court found for the architect on both the third-party claim and the counterclaim.

subcontractor filed suit against the town and the architect for damages based on a claim of tortious interference with a contract.

The Supreme Court affirmed the Superior Court's finding the no tortious acts had been proved. Since the architect was giving "honest advice" pursuant to his contract obligation, he had a qualified privilege. It would have been tortious interference if the architect had exceeded this privilege through fraud, misrepresentation, intimidation, molestation or maliciousness.

77050   L.H. Lacy Co. v. City of Lubbock, 559 S.W.2d 348 (Tex. 1977)

      III: A201-1976, Art. 7, Para. 7.9

Contractor sued the City of Lubbock to enforce an arbitration award. The District Court affirmed the award, but the Court of Civil Appeals reversed.

The Supreme Court reversed, thereby affirming the trial court. The arbitration clause in the contract was not valid under a Texas arbitration statute. It was valid under Texas common law because once the city had participated in the arbitration proceedings, it was bound by the award. The city failed to make an effective withdrawal from the arbitration by its participation.

77051   Lange v. Blake, 58 A.D.2d 1034, 397 N.Y.S.2d 290 (1977)

      III: A201-1976, Art. 4, Para. 4.5

The homeowner sued the contractor for installing a septic system that did not work properly. The Supreme Court held for the owner.

The Appellate Division affirmed. There was an implied warranty that the septic system would work. Furthermore, the price charged was slightly above the contractor's ordinary price, which indicated that it understood both the risk of nonperformance and the need to provide for extra precautions.

77052   Laura Roofing & Renovating Co. v. Board of Educ. of the City of New York, 57 A.D.2d 586, 393 N.Y.S.2d 593 (1977)

      III: A201-1976, Art. 12, Para. 12.2

Contractor sued the owner to recover for extra costs due to concealed conditions. The Supreme Court granted summary judgement for the owner.

The Appellate Division reversed. Although the contractor was obligated by the contract to remove entirely and replace the old roof, the owner had refused to allow a test cut to determine how many layers of roofing were to be removed. There were in fact eight layers of roofing material, rather than the four layers mentioned in the specifications. Summary judgment was inappropriate because of the material issue of whether the owner knew of the roof condition prior to the signing of the contract.

CASES

The Supreme Court, Appellate Division, reversed and remanded. The owner-contr. contract provided that all questions relating to execution or progress of the work the contractor's performance should be determined by the architect and other disputes should be submitted to arbitration. The court remanded for a hearing as to whether the contractor had worded its extra work claims so as to disqualify the role of the architect as the arbitrator through a claim of self-interest. The architect was also not disqualified to act as the sole arbitrator even though he had been retained by the owner.

77048   J.A. Jones Constr. Co. v. City of Dover, 372 A.2d 540 (Del. Super. Ct.), *aff'd on other grounds,* 377 A.2d 1 (1977)

   III: A107-1978, Art. 12
   III: A201-1976, Art. 6, Para. 6.1
   III: A201-1976, Art. 7, Para. 7.6
   III: A201-1976, Art. 8, Para. 8.3

Contractor sued city-owner to recover additional expenses caused by delays beyond the contractor's control, and the city-owner filed a third-party complaint against other contractors seeking delay damages. The contractor filed a motion for summary judgment against the city-owner, and the city-owner, relying on a "no damages for delay" contract clause, filed a motion for summary judgment against the first contractor. The Superior Court denied all motions and noted that the contract clause protected the owner only against damages for "reasonable delays," and since the contractor was alleging that these delays were unreasonable because they were caused by the acts of the city-owner in the coordination of the separate contractors, that issue of material fact made summary judgment inappropriate.

Concerning the denial of the other contractor's motion of summary judgment against the city-owner's complaint, the court found that there existed factual issues concerning the validity of the contractors' disclaimers of liability for the nonconformity of equipment they had supplied. These owner-contractor contracts involved the sale of goods and were, therefore, subject to the provisions of the Uniform Commercial Code. Under the applicable U.C.C. provisions, contractual limitations on warranty and remedy were allowable subject to the condition that they did not produce an unconscionable result. Although the conscionability of a clause was held to be a matter of law and not one of fact, summary judgment was not appropriate since the court had yet to determine the relationship between, and the bargaining power of, the parties.

77049   Kecko Piping Co. v. Town of Monroe, 172 Conn. 197, 374 A.2d 179 (1977)

   I: A107-1978, Art. 11
   I: A201-1976, Art. 5, Para. 5.2

Pursuant to a contract provision the subcontractor had been listed by the contractor for approval by the Town of Monroe and the architect, but had been rejected. The

III: A201-1976, Art. 9, Para. 9.7
III: A311-1970, Performance Bond

Owners sued the surety to recover on the contractor's performance bonds and were granted summary judgment on the issue of liability by the Supreme Court, Special Term.

The Supreme Court, Appellate Division, reversed and remanded. Summary judgment was inappropriate since there were triable issues of fact. The surety's liability was conditioned upon the owners having substantially performed their obligations under the contract, and the owners may have failed to make progress payments to the contractor. When the surety took over for the defaulting contractor and executed an owner-surety agreement, it waived its claim that there was no architect named to assist in the performance of the work. The surety had a duty to make a reasonable inquiry before agreeing to complete the work.

[*Editor's Note:* For subsequent appeal after remand, *see* case number 80034 *infra.*]

77046   Illinois Valley Asphalt, Inc. v. La Salle National Bank, 54 Ill. App. 3d 317, 369 N.E.2d 525 (1977)

III: A201-1976, Art. 6, Para. 6.2
III: A201-1976, Art. 13, Para. 13.2
III: A401-1978, Art. 11
III: A401-1978, Art. 12

Asphalt subcontractor sued the contractor for the balance due under the contract, and the contractor counterclaimed for the subcontractor's refusal to make warranty repairs. The Circuit Court held for the subcontractor.

The Appellate Court reversed and remanded. The asphalt subcontractor was required to make the repairs even though the stone base for the asphalt was improperly provided by the contract, since the contract gave the subcontractor the option of rejecting base material or performing warranty repairs if not rejected. However, a handwritten addendum to the warranty prevailed over the typed or printed forms, and thus the addendum was effective to relieve the asphalt subcontractor's burden in those areas where the base was higher than five inches. The court remanded for the trial court to determine the damages on this basis.

77047   In the Matter of Dutchess Community College, 57 A.D.2d 555, 393 N.Y.S.2d 77 (1977)

II: A201-1976, Art. 2, Para. 2.2
II: A201-1976, Art. 7, Para. 7.9

Contractor demanded arbitration for claims for extra work. The Supreme Court, Dutchess County, denied the owner's and architect's motion to stay arbitration.

Code which the local municipality had decided to adopt. Architects are liable for a b̶̶̶
of the local code as they represent themselves to be competent in the preparation of p̶̶
and specifications for suitable structures. Disregarding issues on the propriety and legality
of adopting the Chicago Code and its enforceability, the Court held that the architect
and subcontractor had notice of the purported code. Having had notice, they were liable
for not complying with the code.

77043   Hobbs v. Scorse, 59 A.D.2d 1037, 399 N.Y.S.2d 783 (1977)

   III: A201-1976, Art. 4, Para. 4.18
   III: A401-1978, Art. 11

Injured worker sued the subcontractor and its worker, who in turn filed a third-party complaint seeking apportionment and contribution from the contractor. The Supreme Court dismissed a motion to dismiss filed by the contractor on the basis of the indemnity clause.

The Appellate Division affirmed. The indemnity clause did not require dismissing the subcontractor's complaint against the contractor. Indemnity was said to be not appropriate until there was a determination of the underlying obligation. Until the injured worker collected, there was no reason to utilize the indemnity provision. "The indemnity clause provides for recovery after liability is established; it does not shield an indemnitee from the fixing of liability."

77044   Huber, Hunt & Nichols, Inc. v. Moore, 67 Cal. App. 3d 278, 136 Cal. Rptr. 603 (1977)

   III: A201-1976, Art. 1, Para. 1.1
   III: A201-1976, Art. 2, Para. 2.2

Contractor sued the owner and architects for increased costs, which was followed by various cross-claims. The Superior Court entered a judgment for the architects against the contractor, and against the architects in favor of engineering consultants on architects' claims for indemnity.

The Court of Appeals affirmed. The architects were liable to the contractor in negligence, and it did not matter that there was no privity of contract between them for that cause of action. However, the contractor, in attempting to prove a case of negligence against the architects, was required to distinguish: those acts of negligence by the architects as independent contractors, as to which they were liable to the contractor; those acts as supervisors of the work, as to which they were agents of the owner and not liable to the contractor; and finally, those acts as arbiters of disputes, as to which an architect has a certain immunity as a quasi-judicial officer.

77045   Hunt v. Bankers & Shippers Insurance Co. of New York, 60 A.D.2d 781, 400 N.Y.S.2d 645 (1977)

   III: A201-1976, Art. 7, Para. 7.2

Owner stopped making progress payments. Contractor stopped work and sued the owner and owner's parent corporation on an "alter ego" theory. The District Court held for the contractor against both defendants.

The Court of Civil Appeals reversed. The parent corporation could not be held liable for the acts of the subsidiary because of "identity of ownership, directors and officers unless the purpose of the relationship is to defeat public convenience, protect fraud, defend crime or justify wrongs, such as violation of antitrust laws."

As to the owner, the owner's obtaining a construction loan was not a condition precedent to payments to the contractor, since the contract as a whole was interpreted as referring only to the source of funds for the payments and responsibilities of the contractor to the lender. The owner's approval of the contractor's choice of subcontractors was not a condition precedent, since the contract only allowed the owner to recommend substitutes. However, because the award against the owner was based on hearsay, the claim was remanded for a new trial.

77041 Hayle Floor Covering, Inc. v. First Minnesota Construction Co., 253 N.W.2d 809 (Minn. 1977)

        III: A201-1976, Art. 12, Para. 12.1
        III: A311-1970, Labor and Material Payment Bond
        III: A401-1978, Art. 11

Subcontractor brought suit to foreclose on its mechanic's lien against the owner, who filed a third-party claim against the contractor and surety. The District Court ordered foreclosure.

The Supreme Court reversed in part. A suit against the owner by a sub-subcontractor working under an oral sub-subcontract was barred, since the subcontract stated that there would be no such contracts without the written consent of the contractor. Liens by other subcontractors in whole or in part were disallowed because there were no change orders in writing as required by the contract, or there was no clear and convincing evidence of an oral waiver. The owner-obligee was a proper party for the suit on the labor and material payment bond, even if it was not a "claimant" as defined in the bond. The owner-obligee would have no other recourse, where as here, the lien claimants chose not to sue on the bond. The surety was also liable for the extras since there was no material deviation from the contract.

77042 Himmel Corp. v. Stade, 52 Ill. App. 3d 294, 367 N.E.2d 411 (1977)

        III: B141-1977, Art. 1

Owner sued the architect and its subcontractor over the completed electrical system's violation of local building codes. The Circuit Court held for the architect and its subcontractor.

The Appellate Court reversed and remanded. The use of open trays rather than airtight conduits conformed to the National Electric Code but did not meet the Chicago Electrical

for the arbitrators under a "broad arbitration clause," and the arbitrators could decide whether the owner's payment to the contractor was an accord and satisfaction in view of the contract provision that unsettled claims made in writing are not deemed to be waived by acceptance of final payment.

77038 General State Authority v. Kline, 29 Pa. Commw. 567, 370 A.2d 402 (1977)

        III: A201-1976, Art. 4, Para. 4.5

        III: A201-1976, Art. 13, Para. 13.2

State-owner sued architect, contractor and its surety alleging that negligent design and construction produced leaking roofs and resulting damages. The Commonwealth Court stated that because the owner was a state agency, sovereign immunity excluded it from the statute of limitations. The contract provision for a one-year period in which the owner seek actual repairs was an additional guarantee and not a contractual shortening of the statute of limitations.

77039 Grow Construction Co. v. State of New York, 56 A.D.2d 95, 391 N.Y.S.2d 726 (1977)

        III: A201-1976, Art. 3, Para. 3.2

        III: A201-1976, Art. 8, Para. 8.3

        III: A201-1976, Art. 12, Para. 12.2

Highway contractor sued the state for increased costs of performance. The Supreme Court held for the contractor.

The Appellate Division modified the Supreme Court's judgment by making the state responsible for 75 percent of the increased costs, since the contractor was responsible for certain mistakes in performance. The state had supplied a negligent design, had supplied misleading information on subsurface conditions and had delayed the contractor by slow redesign and decisions.

Various exculpatory clauses did not relieve the state of its responsibility, since the true conditions were not discoverable by inspection, and since it appeared that the state had withheld information. Despite the fact that the work was completed before the contract completion date, the state was liable for damages for the delays it had caused.

77040 Hanson Southwest Corp. v. Dal-Mac Construction Co., 554 S.W.2d 712 (Tex. Civ. App. 1977)

        III: A201-1976, Art. 3, Para. 3.2

        III: A201-1976, Art. 5, Para. 5.2

        III: A201-1976, Art. 9, Para. 9.3

        III: A201-1976, Art. 14, Para. 14.1

The Supreme Court affirmed. The United States Arbitration Act of 1925 was applicable since the performance of the contract involved interstate commerce. The law upheld the validity, enforceability and irrevocability of the contract clause for arbitration of disputes.

77035 530 East 89 Corp. v. Unger, 43 N.Y.2d 776, 402 N.Y.S.2d 382, 373 N.E.2d 276 (1977)

III: B141-1977, Art. 1

The owner sued the architect for both breach of contract and negligence after the city department of building rejected the proposed plans.

The Supreme Court entered judgment dismissing the complaint.

The Appellate Division and the Court of Appeals affirmed. The contract stated that the architects would "make every effort" to prepare acceptable plans but also stated that they did not guarantee approval of any set of plans. "The mere failure to produce acceptable plans is not evidence of negligence." The expert testimony of an architect also did not support a claim of negligence in this instance.

77036 Gay v. Stratton, 559 S.W.2d 131 (Tex. Civ. App. 1977)

III: A111-1978, Art. 5

Contractor sued homeowner to collect balance due on a cost plus fixed fee contract. The District Court held for the contractor. The Court of Civil Appeals affirmed. The contract was plain and unambiguous. While there was a maximum set for the contractor's profit, there was no corresponding limitation on the costs of construction.

77037 George A. Fuller Co. v. Albin Gustafson Co., 55 A.D.2d 872, 390 N.Y.S.2d 416 (1977)

II: A201-1976, Art. 2, Para. 2.2
II: A201-1976, Art. 7, Para. 7.9
II: A201-1976, Art. 9, Para. 9.9

Subcontractor demanded arbitration against the contractor, and the contractor responded that any delays were caused by the owner. The contractor then demanded arbitration against the owner for delays and alleged fault by the architect. The owner filed a motion in the Supreme Court seeking a stay and claimed that the contractor had not first allowed the architect 10 days to render his decision in accordance with the owner-contractor contract. The contractor sought consolidation of the two arbitrations. The Supreme court declined to stay the arbitration and ordered both arbitrations to proceed consecutively before the same arbitrators.

The Appellate Division affirmed. The contractor had not violated a condition precedent as to the architect's decision, since the contractor's allegation of fault by the architect would have made his decision futile. Interpretation of the owner-contractor contract was

CASES

77032 Fauss Construction, Inc. v. City of Hooper, 197 Neb. 398, 249 N.W.2d (1977)

    I: A201-1976, Art. 2, Para. 2.2
    I: A201-1976, Art. 4, Para. 4.12
    I: A201-1976, Art. 12, Para. 12.1
    I: A201-1976, Art. 12, Para. 12.2

Contractor sued the city-owner for extras. The county court held for the contractor, but the District Court vacated the judgment and dismissed the claim.

The Supreme Court affirmed the District Court. Although the contract contained provisions for change orders and claims for extras, no change orders or claims were made by the contractor. The architect had initially approved the shop drawings showing the substitution of particleboard core doors for the specified solid wood core doors. The state inspector required the replacement of the non-conforming doors. The contractor could not recover for the extra work in replacing the doors, since he was merely meeting the contract specifications. The architect lacked authority to approve the substitutions, and therefore, could not modify the contract or bind the owner.

77033 Firmin v. Garber, 353 So. 2d 975 (La. 1977)

    II: B141-1977, Art. 9
    II: B141-1977, Art. 14

Architect sought to confirm the arbitrator's award against the owner. The District Court affirmed the award of the architect's fees.

The Court of Appeals reversed and held that since the fee award was based on a cost to complete the project of $110,270 and since the owner contended that the cost limit on the entire project was only $60,000, the award was so "grossly irrational as to be tantamount to undue means and evident partiality."

The Supreme Court reversed the Court of Appeals and reinstated the District Court's confirmation of the award based on the $110,270 construction cost. The arbitration award was proper since the owner had presented no evidence to support his allegation that the cost maximum was $60,000 and since the contract itself contained no such limitation.

77034 Fite and Warmath Construction Co. v. MYS Corp., 559 S.W.2d 729 (Ky. 1977)

    I: A201-1976, Art. 7, Para. 7.9

The owner and contractor terminated the contract by mutual agreement, although they agreed that disputes should be decided by reference to the original contract and that interpretation of the contract shall be by the laws of Kentucky. The owner sought to confirm the award that had resulted from its demand for arbitration. The Circuit Court entered the arbitration award as the court's judgment.

Injured worker sued the owner and architect who filed a third party claim against the contractor. The Circuit Court held that under a state statute the owner and architect were liable for the injuries at the work site.

The Appellate Court reversed. The owner and architect could be liable only if they had some direct connection with the construction operations. The right to stop or reject the work, to make inspections and issue change orders did not establish the control required under the state statute. The architect's duties were related to insuring compliance with the contract specifications.

77030 Episcopal Housing Corp. v. Federal Insurance Co., 269 S.C. 631, 239 S.E.2d 647 (1977)

> I: A201-1976, Art. 1, Para. 1.1
> I: A201-1976, Art. 1, Para. 1.2
> I: A201-1976, Art. 7, Para. 7.1
> I: A201-1976, Art. 7, Para. 7.9

Owner sought to enjoin arbitration proceedings begun by the contractors and architects, because the surety refused to participate. The Common Pleas Court denied the injunction.

The Supreme Court affirmed with modification. Although the contract provided that it should be governed by the law of the place where the project was located, the Federal Arbitration Act applied, since upon examination of the contract provisions relating to the contract documents, the work and the intention of the parties with reference to the contract documents, interstate commerce was involved. The court particularly noted that the specifications named out-of-state suppliers and another contract document named out-of-state subcontractors. Under the Federal Arbitration Act, arbitration could proceed without the surety, who was not a party to the arbitration agreement.

[*Editor's Note:* For related proceeding, *see* case number 79006 *infra.*]

77031 F.J. Siller & Co. v. City of Hart, 400 Mich. 578, 255 N.W.2d 347 (1977)

> III: A201-1976, Art. 7, Para. 7.9

Contractor sued owner for payment. The Circuit Court granted judgment for the owner on the grounds that arbitration was a condition precedent to filing suit. The Court of Appeals reversed.

The Supreme Court reversed, upholding the Circuit Court's decision that arbitration was a condition precedent. Since arbitration was a condition precedent, it necessarily implied that the arbitrators' decision would be final. The final decision of the arbitration could be challenged only as to the validity of the award, and the parties could not relitigate from the start what the arbitrators had decided once they had agreed to make arbitration a condition precedent to court actions.

The contractor brought suit against a homeowner for foreclosure of a mechanic's lien. The Circuit Court granted the foreclosure.

The Appellate Court affirmed. The homeowner had waived the requirement that all change orders be in writing, since she testified that she had disagreed with two minor extra changes and had orally agreed to change the style of the building and change the basement layout.

77027   Dickerson Construction Co. v. Process Engineering Co., 341 So. 2d 646 (Miss. 1977)

         I: A201-1976, Art. 2, Para. 2.2
         I: A201-1976, Art. 9, Para. 9.4
         II: B141-1977, Art. 1

The owner of a leaky, cracked building sued the architect for improper design and failure to properly supervise and sued the contractor for failing to build according to the plans and specifications. The court entered judgment for the owner.

The Supreme Court affirmed. Under the terms of the owner-architect and owner-contractor agreements, the architect's duties were properly described in jury instructions as supervision, although inspection would have been a better term. The instruction did not imply continuous on-site inspection or supervision.

77028   E.V. Love v. Double "AA" Constructors, Inc., 117 Ariz. 41, 570 P.2d 812 (1977)

         II: A201-1976, Art. 1, Para. 1.1
         II: A201-1976, Art. 2, Para. 2.2
         II: B141-1977, Art. 1
         II: B141-1977, Art. 13

Contractor sued a prospective lessee, who had contracted for some remodeling work, for the balance due on the contract. The Superior Court held for the contractor.

The Court of Appeals affirmed. The contract did not include a maximum cost limitation, and the contractor dealt almost exclusively with the architect. The court held that the architect had the authority to orally waive and modify the contract provisions as to the lessee, the contract provisions on changes, cost estimates, approval of plans and waiver of bid requirements for subcontractors and materialmen.

77029   Emberton v. State Farm Mutual Automobile Insurance Co., 44 Ill. App. 3d 839, 358 N.E.2d 1254 (1977)

         I: A201-1976, Art. 2, Para. 2.2
         I: B141-1977, Art. 1